Earle Birney, b. 1904
Richard Eberhart, b. 1904
C. Day Lewis, 1904–1972
W. H. Auden, 1907–1973
A. D. Hope, b. 1907
Theodore Roethke, 1907–1963
Walter Van Tilburg Clark, 1909–1971
Stephen Spender, b. 1909
Eudora Welty, b. 1909
Fray Angelico Chavez, b. 1910
Elizabeth Bishop, 1911–1979
J. V. Cunningham, b. 1911
Josephine Miles, b. 1911
Tennessee Williams, 1911–1983
John Cheever, 1912–1982
Irving Layton, b. 1912
Robert Hayden, b. 1913
Tillie Olsen, b. 1913
Muriel Rukeyser, b. 1913
Delmore Schwartz, 1913–1966
Karl Shapiro, b. 1913
Irwin Shaw, 1913–1984
Ralph Ellison, b. 1914
Barbara Howes, b. 1914
Randall Jarrell, 1914–1965
Dudley Randall, b. 1914
Henry Reed, b. 1914
William Stafford, b. 1914
Dylan Thomas, 1914–1953
Isabella Gardner, 1915–1981
Arthur Miller, b. 1915
Americo Parédes, b. 1915
Margaret Walker, b. 1915
Gwendolyn Brooks, b. 1917
Robert Lowell, 1917–1977
Margaret Avison, b. 1918
Tom Whitecloud, ca. 1918–?
Shirley Jackson, 1919–1965
Doris Lessing, b. 1919
May Swenson, b. 1919
Edwin Morgan, b. 1920
Howard Nemerov, b. 1920
James Emanuel, b. 1921
Mona Van Duyn, b. 1921
Richard Wilbur, b. 1921
Philip Larkin, b. 1922
Grace Paley, b. 1922
James Dickey, b. 1923
Alan Dugan, b. 1923
Anthony Hecht, b. 1923
Richard Hugo, 1923–1982
Louis Simpson, b. 1923
Edward Field, b. 1924
Vassar Miller, b. 1924
John Fandel, b. 1925
Donald Justice, b. 1925
Carolyn Kizer, b. 1925
Maxine Kumin, b. 1925
Flannery O'Connor, 1925–1964
Gerald Stern, b. 1925
A. R. Ammons, b. 1926
Robert Bly, b. 1926

Allen Ginsberg, b. 1926
James Merrill, b. 1926
Frank O'Hara, 1926–1966
W. D. Snodgrass, b. 1926
David Wagoner, b. 1926
John Ashbury, b. 1927
Galway Kinnell, b. 1927
W. S. Merwin, b. 1927
James Wright, 1927–1980
Edward Albee, b. 1928
Maya Angelou, b. 1928
Philip Levine, b. 1928
Anne Sexton, 1928–1974
John Hollander, b. 1929
Adrienne Rich, b. 1929
Jon Silkin, b. 1930
John Engels, b. 1931
Alice Munro, b. 1931
Linda Pastan, b. 1932
Sylvia Plath, 1932–1963
John Updike, b. 1932
Etheridge Knight, b. 1933
Imamu Amiri Baraka (LeRoi Jones),
   b. 1934
Leonard Cohen, b. 1934
Marge Piercy, b. 1934
Sonia Sanchez, b. 1934
Mark Strand, b. 1934
Paul Zimmer, b. 1934
Lucille Clifton, b. 1936
Marvin Bell, b. 1937
Judith Minty, b. 1937
Luis Omar Salinas, b. 1937
Diane Wakowski, b. 1937
Michael S. Harper, b. 1938
Virginia Scott, b. 1938
Charles Simic, b. 1938
Margaret Atwood, b. 1939
Seamus Heaney, b. 1939
Ben Luna, b. 1941
Tino Villanueva, b. 1941
Don L. Lee, b. 1942
Sharon Olds, b. 1942
Dave Smith, b. 1942
Nikki Giovanni, b. 1943
Thomas Rabbitt, b. 1943
James Tate, b. 1943
Alice Walker, b. 1944
Carol Muske, b. 1945
Maura Stanton, b. 1946
Leonard Adamé, b. 1947
Roberta Hill, b. 1947
Leslie Ullman, b. 1947
Heather McHugh, b. 1948
Leslie Marmon Silko, b. 1948
Olga Broumas, b. 1949
Carolyn Forche, b. 1950
Mari Evans, 20th century
Cynthia MacDonald, 20th century
Arthur W. Monks, 20th century
Mary Ellen Solt, 20th century
Cathy Song, 20th century

LITERATURE

An Introduction to Reading and Writing

LITERATURE

An Introduction
to Reading and Writing

EDGAR V. ROBERTS

Lehman College,
The City University of New York

HENRY E. JACOBS

University of Alabama

PRENTICE-HALL, ENGLEWOOD CLIFFS, NEW JERSEY 07632

Library of Congress Cataloging in Publication Data

Roberts, Edgar V.
  Literature: an introduction to reading and writing.

  Includes index.
    1. Literature.   2. Literature—Collections.
3. Rhetoric.   I. Jacobs, Henry E.   II. Title.
PN45.R575 1986   808'.0668   85-25569
ISBN   0-13-537572-X

Editorial/production supervision and interior design: **Marjorie Borden**
Cover design: **Bruce D. Kenselaar**
Manufacturing buyer: **Harry P. Baisley**
Developmental editor: **Raymond Mullaney**

© 1986 by Prentice-Hall
A Division of Simon & Schuster, Inc.
Englewood Cliffs, New Jersey 07632

Printed in the United States of America

10 9 8 7 6 5 4 3 2 1

0-13-537572-X

Prentice-Hall International (UK) Limited, *London*
Prentice-Hall of Australia Pty. Limited, *Sydney*
Prentice-Hall Canada Inc., *Toronto*
Prentice-Hall Hispanoamericana, S.A., *Mexico*
Prentice-Hall of India Private Limited, *New Delhi*
Prentice-Hall of Japan, Inc., *Tokyo*
Prentice-Hall of Southeast Asia Pte. Ltd., *Singapore*
Editora Prentice-Hall do Brasil, Ltda., *Rio de Janeiro*
Whitehall Books Limited, *Wellington, New Zealand*

Brief Contents

1   INTRODUCTION: WHAT IS LITERATURE?   *1*

Fiction

2   FICTION   *73*

3   PLOT AND STRUCTURE   *102*

4   CHARACTERS: THE PEOPLE IN FICTION   *134*

5   POINT OF VIEW   *177*

6   SETTING: PLACE AND OBJECTS IN FICTION   *205*

7   STYLE: THE WORDS THAT TELL THE STORY   *236*

8   TONE: ATTITUDE AND CONTROL IN FICTION   *266*

9   SYMBOLISM AND ALLEGORY: KEYS TO EXTENDED
     MEANING   *294*

10   IDEA OR THEME: THE MEANING AND THE MESSAGE
     IN FICTION   *333*

     ADDITIONAL STORIES   *375*

Poetry

11   MEETING POETRY: SIMPLE THEME AND FORM   *459*

12   CHARACTER: THE PEOPLE IN POERTY   *480*

13   WHEN, WHERE, AND WHAT: SETTING AND SITUATION   *509*

14   THE WORDS IN POETRY   *539*

15   IMAGERY   *569*

16   RHETORICAL FIGURES: METAPHOR AND SIMILE   *590*

17   OTHER RHETORICAL FIGURES   *620*

18   TONE: THE CREATION OF ATTITUDE IN POETRY   *641*

19   THE RHYTHM OF POETRY: BEAT, METER, AND SCANSION   *666*

20   SOUNDS AND SEGMENTS   *693*

21   RHYME: THE ECHOING SOUND OF POETRY   *713*

22   FORM: THE SHAPE OF THE POEM   *739*

23   SYMBOLISM AND ALLUSION: WINDOWS TO A WIDE EXPANSE OF MEANING   *784*

24   MYTH: SYSTEMS OF SYMBOLIC ALLUSION IN POETRY   *814*

25   THEME: THE IDEAS AND THE MEANING IN POETRY   *839*

26   POETIC CAREERS: THE WORK OF THREE POETS   *872*

ADDITIONAL POEMS   *919*

Drama

27   THE ELEMENTS OF DRAMA   *1033*

28   TRAGEDY   *1122*

29   COMEDY   *1378*

30   REALISTIC AND NONREALISTIC DRAMA   *1502*

APPENDIX A: EVALUATING LITERATURE   *1627*

APPENDIX B: COMPARISON-CONTRAST AND EXTENDED COMPARISON-CONTRAST   *1634*

APPENDIX C: WRITING AND DOCUMENTING THE RESEARCH ESSAY   *1643*

APPENDIX D: TAKING EXAMINATIONS ON LITERATURE   *1670*

GLOSSARY   *1679*

INDEX OF AUTHORS, TITLES, AND FIRST LINES   *1705*

Detailed Contents

PREFACE   *xxiii*

1   **INTRODUCTION: WHAT IS LITERATURE?**   *1*

Types of Literature: The Genres, 3   •   *Reading and Studying
Literature, 3*   •   *Writing Essays about Literature, 5*   •   *What
Is an Essay?, 6*   •   *The Process of Writing an Essay, 7*   •   *The
Sample Essay, 15*   •   *Some Common Problems in Writing Essays,
17*

GAIUS PETRONIUS   *The Widow of Ephesus, 28*
✓ SIR ARTHUR CONAN DOYLE   *The Adventure of the Speckled Band,
31*
ANTON CHEKHOV   *The Bear: A Joke in One Act, 49*
E. E. CUMMINGS   *Nobody Loses All the Time, 59*

Writing about Your Likes and Dislikes, 66   •   *Sample Essays, 16,
67*

Fiction

2   **FICTION**   *73*

Modern Fiction, 74   •   *The Short Story, 75*   •   *Elements of
Fiction, 76*   •   *Character, Plot, and Structure, 78*   •   *The
Writer's Tools, 80*

JOHN UPDIKE   *A & P, 86*
GUY DE MAUPASSANT   *The Necklace, 90*

How to Write a Précis, 97   •   *Sample Essay, 100*

3   PLOT AND STRUCTURE   *102*

What Is Plot?, 102   •   The Structure of Fiction, 104

STEPHEN CRANE   The Bride Comes to Yellow Sky, 107
EUDORA WELTY   A Worn Path, 116
TOM WHITECLOUD   Blue Winds Dancing, 122

Writing about the Plot of a Story, 127   •   Writing about Structure
in a Story, 130   •   Sample Essays, 129, 132

4   CHARACTERS: THE PEOPLE IN FICTION   *134*

Choice and Character, 134   •   Major Character Traits,
135   •   Appearance, Action, and Character, 135   •   Types of
Characters: Round and Flat, 135   •   How Is Character Disclosed
in Fiction?, 137   •   Reality and Probability: Verisimilitude, 139

KATHERINE ANNE PORTER   María Concepción, 140
JAMES THURBER   The Catbird Seat, 153
✓ WILLIAM FAULKNER   Barn Burning, 160

Writing about Character, 173   •   Sample Essay, 175

5   POINT OF VIEW   *177*

Point of View and "Throwing the Voice," 178   •   Point of View
as a Physical Position, 179   •   Kinds of Points of View,
179   •   Mingling Points of View, 182   •   Point of View and
"Evidence," 183

KATHERINE MANSFIELD   Miss Brill, 184
FRANK O'CONNOR   First Confession, 187
SHIRLEY JACKSON   The Lottery, 194   Topic: Irony in "The Lottery"

Writing about Point of View in a Story, 200   •   Sample Essay,
203

6   SETTING: PLACE AND OBJECTS IN FICTION   *205*

Types of Settings, 205   •   Studying the Uses of Setting, 206

EDGAR ALLAN POE   The Masque of the Red Death, 209
WALTER VAN TILBURG CLARK   The Portable Phonograph, 214
IRWIN SHAW   Act of Faith, 219

Writing about Setting, 231   •   Sample Essay, 234

7   STYLE: THE WORDS THAT TELL THE STORY   *236*

Diction: Choice of Words, 236   •   Rhetoric, 241   •   Style in
General, 244

SAMUEL CLEMENS   *Luck, 245*
ERNEST HEMINGWAY   *A Clean, Well-Lighted Place, 249*
ALICE MUNRO   *The Found Boat, 253*

Writing about Style, 260   •   *Sample Essay*, 262

8   TONE: ATTITUDE AND CONTROL IN FICTION   *266*

Literary Tone and Speaking Tone of Voice, 266   •   *Tone of
Characters within the Story*, 266   •   *Tone and the Author's Attitude
toward Readers*, 267   •   *Literary Artistry as an Aspect of Tone*,
268   •   *Laughter, Comedy, and Farce*, 269   •   *Reading for
Tone*, 272

AMERICO PARÉDES   *The Hammon and the Beans, 274*
JOHN COLLIER   *The Chaser, 278*
SHIRLEY JACKSON   *About Two Nice People, 281*

Writing about Tone in Fiction, 289   •   *Sample Essay*, 291

**9   SYMBOLISM AND ALLEGORY: KEYS TO EXTENDED
MEANING** Transition to poetry.   *294*

Symbolism, 294   •   *Allegory*, 296   •   *Allusion in Symbolism and
Allegory*, 298   •   *Reading for Symbolism and Allegory*, 299

AESOP   *The Fox and the Grapes, 300*
THE GOSPEL OF ST. LUKE 15:11–32   *The Parable of the Prodigal
Son, 300*
NATHANIEL HAWTHORNE   *Young Goodman Brown, 302*
MARJORIE PICKTHALL   *The Worker in Sandalwood, 312*
JOHN STEINBECK   *The Chrysanthemums, 318*

Writing about Symbolism and Allegory, 326   •   *Sample Essay*, 330

**10   IDEA OR THEME: THE MEANING AND THE MESSAGE
IN FICTION**   *333*

Ideas, Topics, Assertions, and Meaning, 333   •   *Formulating the
Ideas in Fiction*, 334   •   *Distinguishing Ideas from Summaries*,
335   •   *Ideas and Values*, 335   •   *Finding the Ideas in Fiction*,
336

JAMES JOYCE   *Araby, 339*
D. H. LAWRENCE   *The Horse Dealer's Daughter, 343*
RALPH ELLISON   *Flying Home, 356*

Writing about Meaning in Fiction, 370   •   *Sample Essay*, 372

ADDITIONAL STORIES   375

JOHN CHEEVER   *The Season of Divorce, 375*
ANTON CHEKHOV   *Lady with Lapdog, 382*
JOSEPH CONRAD   *Youth, 394*
LANGSTON HUGHES   *Slave on the Block, 414*
FRANZ KAFKA   *A Hunger Artist, 419*
DORIS LESSING   *The Old Chief Mshlanga, 425*
FLANNERY O'CONNOR   *A Good Man Is Hard to Find, 433*
GRACE PALEY   *Goodbye and Good Luck, 449*

Poetry

11   MEETING POETRY: SIMPLE THEME AND FORM   *459*

*What Poetry Is, 459   •   Why Study Poetry, 460   •   How Poetry
Works, 460   •   How to Read a Poem, 462   •   Studying Poetry,
465*

RANDALL JARRELL   *The Death of the Ball Turret Gunner, 461*
ANONYMOUS   *Sir Patrick Spens, 465*
WILLIAM SHAKESPEARE   *Sonnet 55: Not Marble, Nor the Gilded
Monuments, 468*
A. E. HOUSMAN   *Loveliest of Trees, the Cherry Now, 470*
EMILY DICKINSON   *Because I Could Not Stop for Death, 473*
THOMAS HARDY   *The Man He Killed, 474*
ROBERT FROST   *Stopping by Woods on a Snowy Evening, 475*
JAMES WRIGHT   *Two Hangovers, 476*

Paraphrasing Poetry, 477   •   Sample Essay, 478

12   CHARACTER: THE PEOPLE IN POETRY   *480*

*The Speaker or Persona, 480   •   The Listener, 483   •   Other
Characters in Poetry, 484   •   Studying Character in Poetry, 484*

BEN JONSON   *To the Reader, 481*
ROBERT HERRICK   *His Prayer to Ben Jonson, 481*
CHRISTOPHER MARLOWE   *The Passionate Shepherd to His Love,
484*
SIR WALTER RALEIGH   *The Nymph's Reply to the Shepherd, 486*
ROBERT BROWNING   *My Last Duchess, 488*
THOMAS HARDY   *Channel Firing, 492*
ANONYMOUS   *Bonny George Campbell, 495*
GEORGE HERBERT   *Love, 496*

ALFRED, LORD TENNYSON   *Tithonus*, 497
C. DAY LEWIS   *Song*, 499
JAMES MERRILL   *Laboratory Poem*, 500
RANDALL JARRELL   *The Woman at the Washington Zoo*, 501
MAURA STANTON   *The Conjurer*, 502

Writing about Characters in Poetry, 503   •   *Sample Essay*, 506

13   WHEN, WHERE, AND WHAT: SETTING AND SITUATION   *509*

JAMES DICKEY   *Cherrylog Road*, 510
ROBERT BROWNING   *Soliloquy of the Spanish Cloister*, 514
CHRISTINA ROSSETTI   *A Christmas Carol*, 517
ANDREW MARVELL   *Bermudas*, 519
THOMAS GRAY   *Elegy Written in a Country Churchyard*, 520
WILLIAM BLAKE   *London*, 524
WILLIAM WORDSWORTH   *Lines Composed a Few Miles Above Tintern Abbey*, 525
MATTHEW ARNOLD   *Dover Beach*, 529
THOMAS HARDY   *The Walk*, 530
RICHARD HUGO   *Degrees of Gray in Philipsburg*, 531
JAMES WRIGHT   *A Blessing*

Writing about Setting in a Poem, 533   •   *Sample Essay*, 536

14   THE WORDS IN POETRY   *539*

Words and Meaning, 540   •   *Denotation and Connotation*,
540   •   *Diction*, 546   •   *Diction and Poetry*,
549   •   *Syntax*, 553

✓ ROBERT GRAVES   *The Naked and the Nude*, 542
HEATHER MCHUGH   *Language Lesson, 1976*, 549
BEN JONSON   *On My First Son*, 555
JOHN DONNE   *Holy Sonnet 14: Batter My Heart, Three-Personed God*, 556
WILLIAM BLAKE   *The Lamb*, 556
LEWIS CARROLL   *Jabberwocky*, 557
✓ EDWARD ARLINGTON ROBINSON   *Richard Cory*, 559
WALLACE STEVENS   *Disillusionment of Ten O'Clock*, 559
THEODORE ROETHKE   *Dolor*, 560
HENRY REED   *Naming of Parts*, 561
RICHARD EBERHART   *The Fury of Aerial Bombardment*, 562

Writing about Diction and Syntax in Poetry, 563   •   *Sample Essay*,
566

15   IMAGERY   *569*

Imagery in Poetry, 570 • *Our Responses and the Poet's Use of Detail*, 570 • *Images of Sight*, 571 • *Images of Sound*, 572 • *Images of Smell, Taste, and Touch*, 573 • *Other Frames of Reference of Imagery*, 574 • *Imagery Derived Purely from Lore and Imagination*, 578 • *Imagery, Completeness, and Truth*, 578

JOHN MASEFIELD   *Cargoes*, 571
WILFRED OWEN   *Anthem for Doomed Youth*, 572
ELIZABETH BISHOP   *The Fish*, 574
GEORGE HERBERT   *The Pulley*, 577
WILLIAM SHAKESPEARE   *Sonnet 130: My Mistress' Eyes Are Nothing Like the Sun*, 579
RICHARD CRASHAW   *On Our Crucified Lord, Naked and Bloody*, 580
WILLIAM BLAKE   *The Tyger*, 581
SAMUEL TAYLOR COLERIDGE   *Kubla Khan*, 582
GERARD MANLEY HOPKINS   *Spring*, 584
EZRA POUND   *In a Station of the Metro*, 585
H. D. (HILDA DOOLITTLE)   *Heat*, 585

Writing about Imagery, 586 • *Sample Essay*, 587

16   RHETORICAL FIGURES: METAPHOR AND SIMILE   *590*

Imagery, Metaphor, and Simile, 591 • *Vehicle and Tenor*, 594 • *Characteristics of Metaphorical Language*, 594 • *Individual Understanding and Metaphorical Language*, 597 • *Degrees of Development*, 598 • *Reading, Thinking, and Using a Dictionary*, 602

JOHN KEATS   *On First Looking into Chapman's Homer*, 592
ROBERT BURNS   *O My Luve's Like a Red, Red Rose*, 594
WILLIAM SHAKESPEARE   *Sonnet 30: When to the Sessions of Sweet Silent Thought*, 595
JOHN DONNE   *A Valediction: Forbidding Mourning*, 599
WILLIAM SHAKESPEARE   *Sonnet 18: Shall I Compare Thee to a Summer's Day?*, 602
THOMAS CAMPION   *Cherry Ripe*, 603
HENRY KING   *Sic Vita*, 604
EDMUND WALLER   *Go, Lovely Rose*, 605
GEORGE GORDON, LORD BYRON   *The Destruction of Sennacherib*, 606
OGDEN NASH   *Very Like a Whale*, 607
LANGSTON HUGHES   *Lenox Avenue Mural: Harlem*, 609
FRAY ANGELICO CHAVEZ   *Rattlesnake*, 610
SYLVIA PLATH   *Metaphors*, 610

LINDA PASTAN   *Marks*, 611
MARGE PIERCY   *A Work of Artifice*, 612
JUDITH MINTY   *Cojoined*, 613
SEAMUS HEANEY   *Valediction*, 614

Writing about Metaphors and Similes in Poetry, 615 • *Sample Essay*, 618

17   OTHER RHETORICAL FIGURES   620

Paradox, 620 • *Apostrophe*, 622 • *Personification*, 622 • *Synecdoche and Metonymy*, 623 • *Synesthesia*, 624 • *The Pun*, 625 • *Overstatement and Understatement*, 625 • *Reading for Other Rhetorical Figures*, 626

SIR THOMAS WYATT   *I Find No Peace*, 620
WILLIAM WORDSWORTH   *London, 1802*, 627
JOHN KEATS   *To Autumn*, 628
ALFRED, LORD TENNYSON   *Break, Break, Break*, 629
T. S. ELIOT   *Eyes That Last I Saw in Tears*, 630
OGDEN NASH   *Exit, Pursued by a Bear*, 631
ELIZABETH BISHOP   *Rain Towards Morning*, 632
JOHN FANDEL   *Indians*, 633
MARK STRAND   *The Remains*, 634
DIANE WAKOWSKI   *Inside Out*, 634

Writing about Rhetorical Figures other than Simile and Metaphor, 636 • *Sample Paragraph*, 637 • *Sample Essay*, 638

18   TONE: THE CREATION OF ATTITUDE IN POETRY   641

The Elements of Tone, 641 • *Tone, Choice, and Reader Response*, 642 • *Tone and the Need for Control*, 644 • *Common Grounds of Assent*, 646 • *Tone and Irony*, 647 • *Satire*, 650 • *Reading for Tone in Poetry*, 651

CORNELIUS WHUR   *The First-Rate Wife*, 643
WILFRED OWEN   *Dulce et Decorum Est*, 644
THOMAS HARDY   *The Workbox*, 647
ALEXANDER POPE   *Epigram from the French*, 650
ALEXANDER POPE   *Epigram Engraved on the Collar of a Dog*, 650
ANNE BRADSTREET   *The Author to Her Book*, 652
ANNE FINCH   *To the Nightingale*, 653
ARTHUR O'SHAUGHNESSY   *A Love Symphony*, 654
E. E. CUMMINGS   *She being Brand / -new*, 655
LANGSTON HUGHES   *Theme for English B*, 656
THEODORE ROETHKE   *My Papa's Waltz*, 658

Writing about Tone in Poetry, 659 • *Sample Essay*, 662

19   **THE RHYTHM OF POETRY: BEAT, METER, AND
SCANSION**   *666*

Things to Consider in Studying Rhythm, 667   •   *Cadence Groups*,
667   •   *Syllables*, 668   •   *Stress*, *Meter*, *Feet*, *Beat*, *and
Metrical Scansion*, 669   •   *Metrical Feet*, 670   •   *The Caesura*,
or Pause, 677   •   *Emphasis by Formal Substitution*,
678   •   *Emphasis by Rhetorical Variation*, 678

WILLIAM SHAKESPEARE   *Sonnet 29: When in Disgrace with Fortune
and Men's Eyes*, 679
WILLIAM SHAKESPEARE   *Sonnet 73: That Time of Year Thou Mayest
in Me Behold*, 680
JOHN KEATS   *Bright Star*, 681
ROBERT BROWNING   *My Star*, 682
FRANCIS THOMPSON   *To a Snowflake*, 683
T. S. ELIOT   *Macavity: The Mystery Cat*, 684
GWENDOLYN BROOKS   *We Real Cool*, 685
JAMES EMANUEL   *The Negro*, 686

Writing about Rhythm in Poetry, 687   •   *Sample Essay*, 690

20   **SOUNDS AND SEGMENTS**   *693*

Vowel Sounds, 693   •   *Consonant Sounds*,
694   •   *Distinguishing Sounds from Spelling*, 694   •   *Segmental
Poetic Devices*, 694   •   *Euphony and Cacophony*,
696   •   *Studying for Sound*, 697

ROBERT HERRICK   *Upon Julia's Voice*, 697
JONATHAN SWIFT   *A Description of the Morning*, 698
ALFRED, LORD TENNYSON   *Idylls of the King: The Passing of
Arthur*, 699
EDGAR ALLAN POE   *The Bells*, 700
GERARD MANLEY HOPKINS   *God's Grandeur*, 705
A. E. HOUSMAN   *Eight O'Clock*, 704
DYLAN THOMAS   *The Force that Through the Green Fuse Drives
the Flower*, 704
DAVID WAGONER   *March for a One-Man Band*, 705

Writing about Sounds and Segments in Poetry, 706   •   *Sample
Essay*, 708

21   **RHYME: THE ECHOING SOUND OF POETRY**   *713*

The Functions of Rhyme, 713   •   *Types of Rhymes*,
715   •   *Variants in Rhyme*, 717   •   *Describing Rhyme Schemes*,
717   •   *Meter*, *Sound*, *and Rhyme*, 718

ALEXANDER POPE   *From An Essay on Criticism*, 718
ANONYMOUS   *Barbara Allan*, 722
MICHAEL DRAYTON   *Since there's No Help*, 723
JOHN DONNE   *Death, Be Not Proud*, 724
CHRISTINA ROSSETTI   *Echo*, 725
EMILY DICKINSON   *To Hear an Oriole Sing*, 726
A. E. HOUSMAN   *To an Athlete Dying Young*, 727
EDWIN ARLINGTON ROBINSON   *Miniver Cheevy*, 728
OGDEN NASH   *The Turtle*, 729
BARBARA HOWES   *Death of a Vermont Farm Woman*, 730
ISABELLA GARDNER   *At a Summer Hotel*, 731

Writing about Rhyme in Poetry, 731   •   *Sample Essay*, 735

22   FORM: THE SHAPE OF THE POEM   739

Major Poetic Forms, 739   •   *The Building Blocks of Closed-Form Poetry*, 740   •   *Closed-Form Poetry*, 743   •   *Closed Form and Meaning*, 748   •   *Open-Form Poetry*, 751   •   *Open Form and Meaning*, 751   •   *Visual Poetry and Concrete Poetry*, 753   •   *Form and Meaning in Visual Poetry*, 754

ALFRED, LORD TENNYSON   *The Eagle*, 742
ALEXANDER POPE   *Epitaph on the Stanton-Harcourt Lovers*, 745
SAMUEL TAYLOR COLERIDGE   *What Is an Epigram*, 746
E. E. CUMMINGS   *A Politician*, 746
J. V. CUNNINGHAM   *Epitaph for Someone or Other*, 746
ANTHONY HECHT   *Nominalism*, 748
ARTHUR W. MONKS   *Twilight's Last Gleaming*, 748
WILLIAM SHAKESPEARE   *Sonnet 116: Let Me Not to the Marriage of True Minds*, 749
WALT WHITMAN   *Reconciliation*, 752
GEORGE HERBERT   *Easter Wings*, 755
JOHN MILTON   *When I Consider How My Light Is Spent*, 756
PERCY BYSSHE SHELLEY   *Ozymandias*, 756
CLAUDE MCKAY   *In Bondage*, 757
JOHN DRYDEN   *To the Memory of Mr. Oldham*, 758
JEAN TOOMER   *Reapers*, 759
GEORGE HERBERT   *Virtue*, 760
ROBERT FROST   *Desert Places*, 761
JOHN KEATS   *Ode to a Nightingale*, 761
PERCY BYSSHE SHELLEY   *Ode to the West Wind*, 764
DYLAN THOMAS   *Do Not Go Gentle into That Good Night*, 766
DUDLEY RANDALL   *Ballad of Birmingham*, 767
WALT WHITMAN   *When I Heard the Learn'd Astronomer*, 769
E. E. CUMMINGS   *Buffalo Bill's Defunct*, 769
WILLIAM CARLOS WILLIAMS   *The Dance*, 770
ALLEN GINSBERG   *A Supermarket in California*, 771

NIKKI GIOVANNI   *Nikki-Rosa*, 773
MAY SWENSON   *Women*, 774
MARY ELLEN SOLT   *Forsythia*, 775
EDWIN MORGAN   *The Computer's First Christmas Card*, 776
JOHN HOLLANDER   *Swan and Shadow*, 777

Writing about Form in Poetry, 778   •   *Sample Essay*, 781

23   SYMBOLISM AND ALLUSION: WINDOWS TO A WIDE EXPANSE OF MEANING   784

Symbolism as a Window to Greater Meaning, 784   •   *How Does Symbolism Operate?*, 785   •   *The Introduction of Symbols*, 788   •   *Qualities of Symbols*, 789   •   *Allusion in Poetry*, 789   •   *Studying for Symbol and Allusion*, 791

VIRGINIA SCOTT   *Snow*, 786
GEORGE HERBERT   *The Collar*, 793
ANNE FINCH   *To Mr. Finch, now Earl of Winchelsea*, 794
JOHN KEATS   *La Belle Dame Sans Merci: A Ballad*, 797
THOMAS HARDY   *In Time of "The Breaking of Nations,"* 799
WILLIAM BUTLER YEATS   *The Second Coming*, 800
ROBINSON JEFFERS   *The Purse-Seine*, 802
T. S. ELIOT   *Sweeney Among the Nightingales*, 803
E. E. CUMMINGS   *In Just-*, 805
ISABELLA GARDNER   *Collage of Echoes*, 807
CAROL MUSKE   *Real Estate*, 807

Writing about Symbolism and Allusion in Poetry, 809   •   *Sample Essay*, 811

24   MYTH: SYSTEMS OF SYMBOLIC ALLUSION IN POETRY   814

The Nature of Mythology, 814   •   *Mythology and Literature*, 816   •   *Strategies for Dealing with Mythology in Poetry*, 817   •   *Studying Mythology in Poetry*, 818   •   *The "Icarus" Poems*, 819

WILLIAM BUTLER YEATS   *Leda and the Swan*, 819
ALFRED, LORD TENNYSON   *Ulysses*, 821
DOROTHY PARKER   *Penelope*, 823
W. S. MERWIN   *Odysseus*, 824
MARGARET ATWOOD   *Siren Song*, 825
OLGA BROUMAS   *Circe*, 826
MURIEL RUKEYSER   *Myth*, 827
STEPHEN SPENDER   *Icarus*, 829
W. H. AUDEN   *Musée des Beaux Arts*, 829
ANNE SEXTON   *To a Friend Whose Work Has Come to Triumph*, 831

WILLIAM CARLOS WILLIAMS   *Landscape with the Fall of Icarus,
831*
EDWARD FIELD   *Icarus, 832*

Writing about Myth in Poetry, 833   •   *Sample Essay*, 836

25   THEME: THE IDEAS AND THE MEANING IN POETRY   *839*

Must a Poem Have a Theme?, 840   •   *Strategies for Dealing with
Theme*, 841   •   *Studying Message and Meaning in Poetry*, 844

ARCHIBALD MACLEISH   *Ars Poetica, 844*
BEN JONSON   *To Celia, 848*
ANDREW MARVELL   *To His Coy Mistress, 849*
ROBERT HERRICK   *To the Virgins, to Make Much of Time, 850*
EDMUND SPENSER   *Amoretti 75: One Day I Wrote Her Name upon
the Strand, 851*
MARIANNE MOORE   *Poetry, 852*
WILLIAM WORDSWORTH   *Ode: Intimations of Immortality, 853*
JOHN KEATS   *Ode on a Grecian Urn, 859*
PHILIP LARKIN   *Next, Please, 860*
DONALD JUSTICE   *On the Death of Friends in Childhood, 861*
LINDA PASTAN   *Ethics, 861*
SHARON OLDS   *35/10, 863*

Writing about Theme and Meaning in Poetry, 864   •   *Sample Essay*,
868

26   POETIC CAREERS: THE WORK OF THREE POETS   *872*

JOHN DONNE   872

The Good Morrow, 875
Song, 876
The Sun Rising, 876
The Canonization, 877
A Fever, 879
The Flea, 879
The Bait, 880
The Relic, 881
Holy Sonnet 6: This Is My Play's Last Scene, 882
Holy Sonnet 7: At the Round Earth's Imagined Corners, 883
Good Friday, 1613, Riding Westward, 883
A Hymn to God the Father, 884
Hymn to God My God, in My Sickness, 885

EMILY DICKINSON   886

The Gentian Weaves Her Fringes, 889
I Never Lost as Much but Twice, 889
Success Is Counted Sweetest, 890

Just Lost, When I Was Saved!, 890
"Faith" is a Fine Invention, 891
I Taste a Liquor Never Brewed, 891
Safe in Their Alabaster Chambers, 891
Wild Nights—Wild Nights!, 892
There's a Certain Slant of Light, 892
The Soul Selects Her Own Society, 892
Some Keep the Sabbath Going to Church, 893
After Great Pain, a Formal Feeling Comes, 893
Much Madness is Divinest Sense, 894
I Heard a Fly Buzz—When I Died, 894
I Like to See It Lap the Miles, 894
I Cannot Live with You, 895
Pain—Has an Element of Blank, 896
One Need Not Be a Chamber—to Be Haunted, 896
The Bustle in a House, 897
My Triumph Lasted Till the Drums, 897
The Heart Is the Capital of the Mind, 898
"Heavenly Father"—Take to Thee, 898
My Life Closed Twice Before Its Close, 898

ROBERT FROST   899

The Tuft of Flowers, 901
Mending Wall, 902
After Apple-Picking, 903
Birches, 904
The Road Not Taken, 906
'Out, Out—', 906
Fire and Ice, 907
Nothing Gold Can Stay, 907
Misgiving, 908
Acquainted with the Night, 908
Design, 909
The Gift Outright, 909
A Considerable Speck, 909
Choose Something Like a Star, 910
U. S. 1946 King's X, 911

Writing about a Poet's Work, 911   •   *Sample Essay*, 914

ADDITIONAL POEMS   *919*

LEONARD ADAMÉ   *My Grandmother Would Rock Quietly and Hum*,
919
A. R. AMMONS   *Dunes*, 920
MAYA ANGELOU   *My Arkansas*, 921

ANONYMOUS   *Edward*, 922

ANONYMOUS   *Lord Randal*, 923

ANONYMOUS   *The Three Ravens*, 924

JOHN ASHBURY   *Illustration*, 925

W. H. AUDEN   *The Unknown Citizen*, 926

MARGARET AVISON   *Tennis*, 927

IMAMU AMIRI BARAKA   *Ka 'Ba*, 928

APHRA BEHN   *Love Armed*, 928

MARVIN BELL   *Things We Dreamt We Died For*, 929

EARLE BIRNEY   *Can. Lit*, 929

WILLIAM BLAKE   *The Sick Rose*, 930

WILLIAM BLAKE   *Ah Sun-Flower*, 930

ROBERT BLY   *Snowfall in the Afternoon*, 931

LOUISE BOGAN   *Women*, 931

ARNA BONTEMPS   *A Black Man Talks of Reaping*, 932

ANNE BRADSTREET   *To My Dear And Loving Husband*, 932

ROBERT BRIDGES   *Nightingales*, 932

GWENDOLYN BROOKS   *Primer for Blacks*, 933

ELIZABETH BARRETT BROWNING   *Number 43: Sonnets from the Portuguese*, 934

ROBERT BURNS   *To a Mouse*, 935

LUCILLE CLIFTON   *My Mama Moved Among the Days*, 936

LEONARD COHEN   *Suzanne Takes You Down*, 936

STEPHEN CRANE   *Do Not Weep, Maiden, for War Is Kind*, 938

STEPHEN CRANE   *The Impact of a Dollar upon the Heart*, 938

ISABELLA VALANCY CRAWFORD   *Gisli the Chieftain: The Song of the Arrow*, 939

COUNTEE CULLEN   *Yet Do I Marvel*, 940

E. E. CUMMINGS   *Next to of course god america i*, 940

E. E. CUMMINGS   *If there are any heavens*, 941

JAMES DICKEY   *The Lifeguard*, 941

H. D. (HILDA DOOLITTLE)   *Pear Tree*, 943

ALAN DUGAN   *Love Song: I and Thou*, 943

PAUL LAWRENCE DUNBAR   *Sympathy*, 944

SIR EDWARD DYER   *My Mind to Me a Kingdom Is*, 944

RICHARD EBERHARDT   *The Groundhog*, 946

T. S. ELIOT   *The Love Song of J. Alfred Prufrock*, 947

JOHN ENGELS   *Naming the Animals*, 950

MARI EVANS   *I Am a Black Woman*, 951

CAROLYN FORCHE   *The Visitor*, 952

NIKKI GIOVANNI   *Woman*, 952

FRANCES E. W. HARPER   *She's Free!*, 953

MICHAEL HARPER   *Called*, 953

ROBERT HAYDEN   *Those Winter Sundays*, 954

ROBERT HERRICK   *Corinna's Going A-Maying*, 955

ROBERTA HILL   *Dream of Rebirth*, 956

A. D. HOPE   *Coup de Grâce*, 957

GERARD MANLEY HOPKINS   *The Windhover*, 957

GERARD MANLEY HOPKINS   *Pied Beauty*, 958
A. E. HOUSMAN   *Terence, This Is Stupid Stuff*, 958
LANGSTON HUGHES   *Negro*, 960
RANDALL JARRELL   *Next Day*, 961
ROBINSON JEFFERS   *The Answer*, 962
GALWAY KINNELL   *The Fly*, 963
CAROLYN KIZER   *Night Sounds*, 964
ETHERIDGE KNIGHT   *Haiku*, 964
MAXINE KUMIN   *Woodchucks*, 965
PHILIP LARKIN   *Church Going*, 966
IRVING LAYTON   *Rhine Boat Trip*, 968
DON L. LEE   *Change Is Not Always Progress*, 968
PHILIP LEVINE   *They Feed They Lion*, 969
RICHARD LOVELACE   *To Lucasta, Going to the Wars*, 970
AMY LOWELL   *Patterns*, 970
ROBERT LOWELL   *For the Union Dead*, 973
BEN LUNA   *In Days of Wine*, 975
CYNTHIA MACDONALD   *The Lobster*, 975
CLAUDE MCKAY   *The White City*, 976
JOSEPHINE MILES   *Belief*, 976
EDNA ST. VINCENT MILLAY   *What My Lips Have Kissed, and Where, and Why*, 977
VASSAR MILLER   *Loneliness*, 977
JOHN MILTON   *How Soon Hath Time*, 978
JOHN MILTON   *O Nightingale!*, 978
OGDEN NASH   *The Camel*, 978
OGDEN NASH   *The Lama*, 979
THOMAS NASHE   *A Litany in Time of Plague*, 979
HOWARD NEMEROV   *The Goose Fish*, 980
FRANK O'HARA   *Poem*, 981
AMERICO PAREDES   *Guitarreros*, 982
DOROTHY PARKER   *Resume*, 982
KATHERINE PHILLIPS   *To My Excellent Lucasia, on Our Friendship*, 982
MARGE PIERCY   *The Secretary Chant*, 983
SYLVIA PLATH   *Last Words*, 984
SYLVIA PLATH   *Mirror*, 984
EZRA POUND   *The River-Merchant's Wife: A Letter*, 985
E. J. PRATT   *The Shark*, 986
THOMAS RABBITT   *Gargoyle*, 987
JOHN CROWE RANSOM   *Bells for John Whiteside's Daughter*, 987
ADRIENNE RICH   *Diving into the Wreck*, 988
EDWARD ARLINGTON ROBINSON   *Mr. Flood's Party*, 990
THEODORE ROETHKE   *I Knew a Woman*, 991
THEODORE ROETHKE   *The Waking*, 992
DANTE GABRIEL ROSSETTI   *The Blessed Damozel*, 993
LUIS OMAR SALINAS   *In a Farmhouse*, 996
SONIA SANCHEZ   *Right on: white america*, 997

CARL SANDBURG   *Chicago*, 997

SIEGFRIED SASSOON   *Dreamers*, 998

DELMORE SCHWARTZ   *The Heavy Bear Who Goes with Me*, 999

ALAN SEEGER   *I Have a Rendezvous with Death*, 999

ANNE SEXTON   *Three Green Windows*, 1000

WILLIAM SHAKESPEARE   *Fear No More the Heat o' the Sun*, 1001

WILLIAM SHAKESPEARE   *Sonnet 146: Poor Soul, The Center of My Sinful Earth*, 1002

KARL SHAPIRO   *Auto Wreck*, 1002

SIR PHILIP SIDNEY   *Astrophil and Stella, Number 71*, 1003

JON SILKIN   *Worm*, 1004

LESLIE MARMON SILKO   *Where Mountain Lion Lay Down with Deer*, 1004

CHARLES SIMIC   *Fork*, 1005

LOUIS SIMPSON   *The Pawnshop*, 1005

DAVE SMITH   *Bluejays*, 1006

STEVIE SMITH   *Not Waving but Drowning*, 1006

W. D. SNODGRASS   *Lobsters in the Window*, 1006

CATHY SONG   *Lost Sister*, 1007

ANNE SPENCER   *At the Carnival*, 1009

EDMUND SPENSER   *Amoretti 54: Of This World's Theater in Which We Stay*, 1010

WILLIAM STAFFORD   *Traveling Through the Dark*, 1011

GERALD STERN   *Burying an Animal on the Way to New York*, 1011

WALLACE STEVENS   *The Emperor of Ice-Cream*, 1012

JONATHAN SWIFT   *A Description of a City Shower*, 1012

JAMES TATE   *The Blue Booby*, 1014

EDWARD TAYLOR   *Upon a Spider Catching a Fly*, 1015

DYLAN THOMAS   *Fern Hill*, 1016

DYLAN THOMAS   *A Refusal to Mourn the Death, by Fire, of a Child in London*, 1017

LESLIE ULLMAN   *Why There are Children*, 1018

MONA VAN DUYN   *Advice to a God*, 1019

TINO VILLANUEVA   *Day-Long Day*, 1020

DIANE WAKOWSKI   *The Ring*, 1021

ALICE WALKER   *Revolutionary Petunias*, 1021

MARGARET WALKER   *Iowa Farmer*, 1022

PHYLLIS WHEATLEY   *On Being Brought from Africa to America*, 1023

RICHARD WILBUR   *In a Bird Sanctuary*, 1023

WILLIAM CARLOS WILLIAMS   *The Red Wheelbarrow*, 1024

WILLIAM CARLOS WILLIAMS   *The Yachts*, 1024

WILLIAM WORDSWORTH   *Lines Written in Early Spring*, 1025

WILLIAM WORDSWORTH   *The Solitary Reaper*, 1026

ELEANOR WYLIE   *The Eagle and the Mole*, 1027

WILLIAM BUTLER YEATS   *Sailing to Byzantium*, 1027

WILLIAM BUTLER YEATS   *Byzantium*, 1028

PAUL ZIMMER   *The Day Zimmer Lost Religion*, 1030

Drama

27   THE ELEMENTS OF DRAMA   *1033*

The Nature and History of Drama, 1033   •   *Play Texts and
Production*, 1034   •   *Types of Drama*, 1035   •   *The Basic
Elements of Dramatic Literature*, 1037   •   *How to Read a Play*,
1046

THORNTON WILDER   *The Happy Journey to Trenton and Camden*,
1049
EUGENE O'NEILL   *Before Breakfast*, 1061
EDWARD ALBEE   *The Sandbox*, 1068
ANONYMOUS   *Everyman*, 1075
SUSAN GLASPELL   *Trifles*, 1101

Writing about the Elements of Drama, 1112   •   *Sample Essays*,
1116, 1118

28   TRAGEDY   *1122*

The Nature and Origin of Tragedy, 1122   •   *Language and Tone
in Tragedy*, 1126   •   *The Theater of Shakespeare*, 1173   •   *The
Theater of Arthur Miller*, 1288

SOPHOCLES   *Oedipus the King*, 1132
WILLIAM SHAKESPEARE   *The Tragedy of Hamlet, Prince of
Denmark*, 1180
ARTHUR MILLER   *Death of a Salesman*, 1294

Writing about Tragedy, 1365   •   *Sample Essays*, 1370, 1375

29   COMEDY   *1378*

Old and New Comedy, 1379   •   *Comic and Funny: The Pattern
of Comedy*, 1379   •   *Characters in Comedy*, 1381   •   *Language
in Comedy*, 1381   •   *Types of Comedy*, 1381   •   *The Theater
of Molière*, 1443

WILLIAM SHAKESPEARE   *A Midsummer Night's Dream*, 1387
MOLIÈRE   *The Misanthrope*, 1448

Writing about Comedy, 1495   •   *Sample Essay*, 1499

30   REALISTIC AND NONREALISTIC DRAMA   *1502*

The Rebellion against Realism, 1504   •   *Elements of Realistic and
Nonrealistic Drama*, 1505   •   *The Spectrum of Realism*, 1507

HENRIK IBSEN   *A Doll's House*, 1509
TENNESSEE WILLIAMS   *The Glass Menagerie*, 1565

Writing about Realistic and Nonrealistic Drama, 1619   •   *Sample Essay*, 1623

APPENDIX A: EVALUATING LITERATURE   *1627*

Standards for Evaluation, 1627   •   *Writing an Evaluation Essay*, 1630   •   *Sample Essay*, 1631

APPENDIX B: COMPARISON-CONTRAST AND EXTENDED COMPARISON-CONTRAST   *1634*

Clarify Your Intention, 1634   •   *Find Common Grounds for Comparison*, 1634   •   *Methods of Comparison*, 1635   •   *The Extended Comparison-Contrast*, 1636   •   *Documentation and the Extended Comparison-Contrast Essay*, 1637   •   *Writing Comparison-Contrast Essays*, 1637   •   *Sample Essay (Extended Comparison-Contrast)*, 1638

APPENDIX C: WRITING AND DOCUMENTING THE RESEARCH ESSAY   *1643*

Selecting a Topic, 1644   •   *Setting Up a Bibliography*, 1646   •   *Taking Notes and Paraphrasing Material*, 1647   •   *Documentation: Notes and Parenthetical References*, 1657   •   *Organizing Your Essay*, 1661   •   *Sample Research Essay*, 1663   •   *A List of Works Cited*, 1668

APPENDIX D: TAKING EXAMINATIONS ON LITERATURE   *1670*

Preparation, 1672   •   *Two Basic Types of Questions about Literature*, 1674

GLOSSARY   *1679*

INDEX OF AUTHORS, TITLES, AND FIRST LINES   *1705*

Preface

Literature: An Introduction to Reading and Writing is a unique book. It is not only an excellent anthology, but it is also a comprehensive guide to writing essays about literature. It therefore has a broader sense of mission than do most anthologies. Indeed, it was with the aim of combining literary selections with a comprehensive guide to writing that we began. As we planned and wrote this book, we thus had two related goals: to teach students how to read literature with understanding and how to write about literature with skill and conviction.

In order to fulfill the first goal, we offer an anthology of great literature and a guide to reading it. The text introduces the three major genres (or groups) of literature: prose fiction, poetry, and drama. This arrangement reflects our conviction that fiction, while not "easier" than other genres, is more familiar to most students. The skills and habits acquired in reading fiction will, in turn, make poetry more open and enjoyable. Drama, which can be written in either prose or verse, will become most accessible after the other two genres have been explored.

The selections are drawn from diverse periods and cultures ranging from ancient Greece and Palestine to contemporary England, America, and Canada. Along the way, and in no particular chronological order, we offer literature from the English Renaissance, seventeenth-century France, eighteenth-century America, nineteenth-century Russia, and a host of other cultures and periods.

We have also sought to provide a broad range of authors from a variety of cultural and ethnic groups. Thus, there are works by men and women, blacks and whites, Hispanics and American Indians, conservatives and liberals, people with strong religious convictions, and others who have no apparent concern for spiritual matters. We have included works by well-known writers who have secure places in the history of literature as well as works by writers who are much less well known.

In order to place each writer and work in historical context, we have included the author's date of birth (and death) where possible. In addition, we have attempted to provide a date of composition, publication, or both for each work in the text. In most cases, a date of publication is provided, and when possible, it is followed by a date of composition in parentheses.

Within the fiction and poetry sections of this book, each chapter covers a particular element of literature such as style, character, or theme. In the drama section, each chapter deals with a major category of drama. We chose this approach rather than, for example, a historical approach because we feel that it permits the reader to analyze particular aspects of literature one at a time and in depth. Most chapters begin with a general discussion of the topic or technique under consideration. Within this discussion, key terms and concepts are highlighted in bold type. The discussions often include some analysis or explanation of a work of literature included in the chapter. Such analysis highlights the significant features of individual works. We do not mean to suggest, however, that our ideas about a story, poem, or play are the only right ones. To the contrary, a work of literature can be understood and experienced in many different ways, all of which can be considered absolutely "correct" so long as they are supported by the work itself. This is one of the features that separates literature from mathematics or chemistry; a math problem has one right answer, but a literary work can have many different and valid interpretations, all supported by the text.

The introductory material in each chapter is followed by selections of literature to be read, studied, enjoyed, and thought about. To aid intelligent reading, we have included both marginal definitions and some longer explanatory notes. Words that are defined or explained in notes are highlighted by small degree signs (°) in the text. Following each selection are study questions meant to awaken the reader's feelings and ideas. Some of these questions are easily answered; others may provoke extended thought.

Our second (but not secondary) goal in this book is to teach students how to write about literature with skill and conviction. For us, writing about literature is not a minor topic that can be addressed in twenty pages at the back of the book. It is a coequal concern that deserves and receives consideration in every chapter. The approaches to writing, developed from tested principles of studying literature together with our own experience in the classroom, have been presented for more than twenty years in *Writing Themes About Literature* by Edgar V. Roberts.

The skills needed for writing effective essays about literature do not represent a completely separate or distinct body of knowledge. Rather, careful reading and effective writing are integrated: Both ask that the student make important decisions and discoveries about the story, poem, or play under consideration, and both require that the student be able to point to specific features in the literary work at hand to justify his or her conclusions.

To this end, we have attempted to supply road maps that can show the way to move from reading to responding and thinking, and then to planning and writing. Each chapter of the text ends with an extensive discussion on writing about literature. These focus on the topic or element of literature being studied in the chapter. For example, the chapter on setting in prose fiction deals with strategies for planning, organizing, developing, and writing an essay about the relationship between setting and meaning.

These discussions of the prewriting and writing processes are carefully designed to help the student proceed confidently to the task of writing. Each writing section contains suggestions and questions for planning an essay, developing a central idea, selecting supporting details from the literary work, organizing thoughts most effectively, and beginning the writing process and bringing it to a conclusion.

In these sections we do not simply *say* what can be done with a topic of literary study, we also *show* one way in which it might be done. Each chapter includes a sample essay (sometimes more than one) to exemplify the methods and strategies discussed. Thus, the general guidelines are combined with specific examples to make the writing process as open and clear as possible. Following each essay is a brief commentary that explains the focus and strategies employed in the essay.

Reading and writing skills are not useful only with literature; effective and careful reading and writing techniques will help students in virtually every college course and in any profession. Students may never read another Shakespearean sonnet or play by Edward Albee, but they will certainly read—newspapers, legal documents, magazine articles, technical reports, business proposals, and much more. Similarly, students may never write about character or plot in a short story or play again, but they will certainly find future situations requiring that they write. The more effectively a person can write about literature, the better he or she will be able to write about anything.

This book is designed both to teach and to delight. Sometimes students and teachers forget that these form a natural pair of processes. We hope that the literature in this text will teach students about humanity, about their own life and feelings, and about timeless patterns of human existence. We hope that they will take delight in such discoveries. We also hope that the commentary and discussions in the text will contribute to their learning about literature and their enjoyment of it. We present this book in the hope that it will be thought of not as an end, but as the beginning of lifelong understanding and joy in great literature.

ACKNOWLEDGMENTS

This book has been a long time in the making, and many people have offered helpful advice and suggestions along the way. At the University of Alabama, we wish to express our gratitude to Professors Robert Halli, Claudia Johnson, Matthew Marino, and Matthew Winston, and to Christel Bell, Linda Bridgers, Catherine Davis, Edward Hoeppner, Anna F. Jacobs, and Eleanor Tubbs. At Lehman College, we thank Professors Billy Collins, Alice Griffin, Gerhard Joseph, Francis Kearns, Ruth Milberg-Kaye, and Michael Paull, and to David Brady, Nanette Roberts, Virginia Scott, and Eve Zarin. We also want to thank Professors Anne S. Agee, Anne Arundel Community College; Vivian Brown, Laredo Junior College; Sara Burroughs, Northwestern State University; Iain Crawford, Berry College; Peter B. DeBlois, Syracuse University; C. R. Embry, Truckee Meadows Community College; Delryn R. Fleming, Brookhaven College; Patricia H. Graves, Georgia State University; George F. Hayhoe, formerly Virginia Tech; Ronald Janssen, Hofstra University; Alexander J. Kucsma, County College of Morris; Dallas Lacy, University of Texas at Arlington; Marylou Lewandowski, San Jose State University; Joanne H. McCarthy, Tacoma Community College; Ellis Marie Melder, Northwestern State University; Louis E. Murphy, Bucks County Community College; Georgia A. Newman, Polk Community College; Ghita P. Orth, University of Vermont; Richard M. Sippel, Community College of Allegheny County; Louie Skipper, Shelton State College; Ken M. Symes, Western Washington University; William B. Thesing, University of South Carolina; Charles Workman, Samford University. A word of special thanks goes to Bill Oliver, formerly of Prentice-Hall, and to Phil Miller, of Prentice-Hall, for their imagination, foresight, support, and patience in the development of this project. We are also grateful to Ray Mullaney, of Prentice-Hall's Product Development Department, for his wide knowledge, extra energy, tolerance, and special organizing skill. His efforts on our behalf have been invaluable and immeasurable. Additional thanks go to our production editor, Marjorie Borden, and to our copyeditor, Ilene McGrath.

Edgar V. Roberts
Henry E. Jacobs

1

Introduction: What Is Literature?

The question "What is literature?" is not easily answered; whole books have been devoted to the topic. No single definition can satisfy everyone; furthermore, once a definition has been made, the limits that it imposes often make it inadequate for at least some writing that some people may want to call *literature*. Nevertheless, we can say many things about literature that will help us begin to understand what it might be.

Technically, anything spoken or written may be called literature. By this definition, both a grocery list and a Shakespearean sonnet would qualify. It is clear, however, that a grocery list does not do those things that we expect from a literary work. It does not interest, entertain, stimulate, broaden, or ennoble us. Even though it may be structured according to the areas in a supermarket (dairy, frozen foods, produce, and so on), just as a Shakespearean sonnet is structured by three four-line stanzas and a concluding set of two lines, it is not designed to engage our emotions or imagination. A grocery list, in short, is simply useful; it is not literature. Rather, we will confine our definition to works that, like Shakespeare's sonnets, invite our emotional and intellectual involvement and response.

The literature that we are concerned about here is in written form, even though it may be performed on stage, in film, or on radio or television. The first advantage of written literature is flexibility. You can choose to read a work at any time according to your mood, and you may read and reread for your own comprehension and appreciation. You can stop at a word, should you wish, and you can go back to look at an earlier sentence. All you need to do is turn a page and fix your eyes on the desired spot. But can't we do much the same thing with a video cassette recorder? It is of course possible to backtrack with a VCR, but to go back to a previous part of a show, you need to operate machinery, and you can never stop at a particular point and still get motion or sound; all you will have is a still picture. On the other hand, with a book you can see a number of words at a glance and can comprehend them all at the same time.

When you read, you depend only on your own effort and imagination. There are no actors, no settings, no photographic or musical techniques to supersede your own reconstruction of the author's ideas. Some might consider this aspect a weakness of reading, but remember that the spectacle of performance, while graphic and stimulating, is also limiting. Even though reading is more demanding than passively watching images on a screen, it allows you to do your own thinking; you can achieve independence more readily by savoring the written word. With reading you may take the time to reflect and digest. You can stop reading and think for a while about what you have just read. You can leave a text and then return to it hours or days later and continue it just where you stopped. The book will always wait for you and will not change during the time you are gone. You can carry it around with you, and you may browse in it during private moments or when riding public transportation.

This is not to belittle the "warmer" media of television and film, but only to contrast them with written forms of literature. All literature, no matter what the form, has many things to offer, and the final word on the value of literary study has not been written. Quite often, in fact, people read literature without explaining, even to themselves, why they enjoy it, because goals and ideals are not easily defined. There are, however, areas of general agreement about some of the things that reading great works of literature can do.

Literature helps us grow, both personally and intellectually; it provides an objective base for our knowledge and understanding; it helps us to connect ourselves to the cultural context of which we are a part; it enables us to recognize human dreams and struggles in different societies that we would never otherwise get to know; it helps us to develop mature sensibility and compassion for the condition of *all* living things—human, animal, and vegetable; it gives us the knowledge and perception needed to appreciate the beauty of order and arrangement, just as a well-structured song or a beautifully done painting can; it provides the comparative basis from which we can see worthiness in the aims of all people, and it therefore helps us see beauty in the world around us; it exercises our emotions through the arousal of interest, concern, tension, excitement, hope, fear, regret, laughter, and sympathy. Through a process of cumulative experience, great literature can shape our goals and values by helping us clarify our own identities, both positively, through identification with the admirable in human life, and negatively, through rejection of the sinister. It can help us to shape our judgments through the constant comparison of the good against the bad. It enables us, both in our everyday activities and in the decisions we are responsible for making as citizens, to develop a perspective on the events that are occurring in the world. It encourages us to assist creative, talented people who are in need. It is one of the things that shape our lives. It helps to make us human.

TYPES OF LITERATURE: THE GENRES

We usually classify imaginative literature into (1) prose fiction, (2) poetry, and (3) drama. These three forms have many common characteristics. While none of the genres is designed primarily to convey information, for example, all do to some degree. All are art forms, each with its own requirements of structure and style. In varying degrees, all the genres are dramatic and imaginative; they have at least some degree of action or are based in part on a dramatic situation.

Imaginative literature differs from textbooks, historical and biographical works, and news articles, all of which are based on fact or recount facts. Imaginative literature, while related to the truths of human life, may be based upon situations that never have and never may occur. This is not to say that literature is not truthful, but rather that the truth of literature is truth to life and human nature, not necessarily to the world of historical and scientific facts.

Although the three main genres have much in common, they also differ in many ways. **Prose fiction,** or **narrative fiction,** is in prose form and includes *novels*, *short stories*, *myths*, *parables*, *romances*, and *epics*. These works generally focus on one or a few major characters who undergo some kind of change as they meet other characters or deal with problems or difficulties in their lives. **Poetry,** in contrast to prose fiction, is much more economical in the use of words and relies heavily on *imagery*, *figurative language*, *rhythm*, and *sound*. **Drama,** or **plays,** are meant to be performed on stage by actors. Like fiction, drama may focus on a single character or a small number of characters, and it presents fictional events as if they were happening in the present. Some dramas employ much of the imagery, rhythm, and sound of poetry. A complete introduction to each of the major genres is contained in the first chapter of the major section of this book that deals with that genre.

READING AND STUDYING LITERATURE

There is obviously a difference between just reading literature and studying it. We read many things in the course of daily life, but we do not read everything the same way. For example, reading a menu, reading a comic page, reading a news article, and reading an editorial require different attention and involvement and also evoke different responses. The menu requires a decision about what food to order; the comic page requires a coordination of picture and the ballon-enclosed speeches. The article requires that we assimilate details and also that we begin to form a response. The editorial requires that we understand the subject under discussion together with the political views of the writer so that we can decide to agree or disagree with the position. All these reading tasks require different amounts of time and thought.

By the same token, the *study* of a literary work requries a larger investment of thought than a simple *reading*, yet many people assume that reading alone is a sufficient form of study. One can read a work casually, without being able to say much about the lives of the characters, the events, the form, or the ideas. Although such an offhand process might be called "reading the material," there is no way to support a claim that a job of studying has been done.

Studying is something else. It is a process of reading, reading again while taking notes, going back over material, practicing writing about it, and reading it again until it is fairly well fixed in the mind. We have presumed that the reader of this book is going to *study* in preparation for classroom discussion and either in-class or out-of-class writing. Many educators believe that you should spend two hours of study for every period you spend in class. We have therefore provided study questions for many of the pieces contained here. We assume that you will be developing your own systematic way of recording and testing your responses to literature so that you can become a *disciplined* rather than a casual reader.

The tasks that make up the process of study are not difficult. Your objective should be to develop as complete an understanding as possible. If a particular study method has worked for you in the past, keep using it. Most study methods, however, will follow similar patterns: first, a general reading to get an overview of the work, and then as many subsequent readings as you need to develop fuller understanding. As you read, mark off interesting or noteworthy passages, and later give these crucial passages the time and thought they require. From that point on, you should try to follow this set of general procedures:

1. Use a dictionary for words that are new or unfamiliar. When you find a passage that you do not readily understand, determine whether the problem arises from words that you cannot define easily. Once you have used your dictionary, be sure to compare the definitions with the passage where the word occurs, so that your understanding of the words in context is clear.

2. Consider your thoughts and responses as you read. Did you laugh, smile, worry, get scared, feel a thrill, learn a great deal, feel proud, find a lot to think about? Try to describe how the various parts of the work caused your reactions.

3. Make notes on interesting characterizations, events, techniques, and ideas. If you like a character, try to describe what you like. If you dislike an idea, try to put your reasons for dislike into your own words.

4. Try to see patterns developing. Make an outline or scheme for the plot or the main ideas. What are the conflicts in the work? How does the author resolve them? Is one force, idea, or side the winner? Why? How do you respond to the winner, or the loser?

5. Is there anything you do not understand? Make a note of the difficulty so that you may ask your instructor about it.

6. For further study, think further about any passages you have underlined or marked out in the margins.

7. Make a practice of writing one or more paragraphs describing your thoughts and responses after reading and considering the work. If you are reading the work in preparation for writing a specific type of essay, your paragraphs may be useful later. Even if you are making only a general preparation, however, try to continue the practice of committing your thoughts to paper.

WRITING ESSAYS ABOUT LITERATURE

Writing is the sharpened, focused expression of thought and study. As you develop your writing skills, you will also improve your perceptions and increase your critical abilities. Although no one can ever reach a point of being a perfect master of the art of writing, the attempt to achieve such a state is worthwhile, and everyone can improve writing to the best of his or her ability.

The subject of this book is literature: you will study it, ask questions about it, and write about it. The development of your ability to think and to write about literature will also prepare you to write about any other topic. Literature contains the subject material of philosophy, religion, psychology, sociology, and politics. As you learn to analyze and write about literature, you will also be improving your perception of these other disciplines. You can bring your capacity for analysis to bear on future problems as well.

Writing ultimately boils down to the development of an idea. Some ideas are better than others. Getting good ideas is an acquired skill that grows out of your development as a thinker and writer. You will discover that your thinking will improve the longer you engage in the analysis of literature. In the same way, the quality of your ideas will improve as you go through the process of originating ideas, seeing the flaws in some of your thinking, proposing new avenues of development, securing new data to support ideas, and creating new aspects of an idea. Your objective always will be to convince a person reading your essays that your considerations are based on facts and that your conclusions are valid.

Unlike ordinary conversation and classroom discussion, writing must stick with great determination to a specific point of development. Ordinary conversation is usually random and disorganized; it shifts frequently from topic to topic—sometimes without clear cause—and it is sometimes repetitive. Classroom discussion is more organized, but there may be digressions and irrelevancies. Thus classroom discussion, while formal, is free and spontaneous. Writing, by contrast, is the most concise and highly organized form of expression that will ever be required of you.

WHAT IS AN ESSAY?

It needs to be emphasized again and again that writing demands tight organization and control. The first requirement of the finished essay—although it is *not* the first requirement in the writing *process*—is that it have a **central idea.** Thus, an **essay** can be defined as a fully developed set of interconnected paragraphs that grow systematically out of a central idea. Everything in the essay should be directly related to the idea or should contribute to the reader's understanding of the idea.

Let us consider this definition in relation to essays about literature. Such an essay should be a brief examination rather than an exhaustive treatment of a particular subject. It might be a character study or an analysis of the point of view of a story or poem. Unity in the essay is achieved through the consistent reference to the central idea throughout the essay. Typical central ideas might be (1) that a character is strong and tenacious, as in Guy De Maupassant's "The Necklace," p. 90, or (2) that the point of view makes the action seem "up close" and personal, as in Frank O'Connor's "First Confession" (p. 187). Everything in the essay is to be related to the central idea. Thus, it is a fact that Mathilde Loisel in "The Necklace" spends ten years working almost like a slave to repay a debt. This fact is not relevant to an essay on character unless you show that the hard work reveals Mathilde's strength and tenacity. Similarly, in an essay about point of view in "First Confession" it is not important to say that Jackie and Nora speak to each other unless you relate their conversations to the personal quality of the story resulting from the first-person point of view. By the same token, any attempt to show that "First Confession" reveals more about character than "The Necklace" must be introduced as part of an argument that O'Connor's story is different from or superior to De Maupassant's in regard to the development of character.

All these principles should be your goal when you are planning and writing your essay, and they should all hold in your finished essay. Here they are again:

1. The essay should cover the assigned topic such as those described in the various chapters of this book (e.g., character or point of view).

2. The essay should have a central idea that governs its development.
3. The essay should be organized so that every part contributes something to the reader's understanding of the central idea.

THE PROCESS OF WRITING AN ESSAY

There are a number of things you can do to make systematic the process of writing an essay about literature. Two are **invention** and **prewriting.** Invention is the process of discovering or creating the things you want to say. Prewriting is the process of studying, thinking, raising and answering questions, planning, developing tentative ideas and first drafts, crossing out, erasing, changing, rearranging, and adding. In a way, prewriting and invention are merely different words for planning and thinking. They both acknowledge the sometimes uncertain way in which the mind works and also the fact that ideas are often not known until they get written down. Writing, at any stage, should always be thought of as a process of discovery and creation. There is always something more to develop.

The following description of the planning and writing process is presented as an approximation of what you should be doing in planning and writing an essay. You may change the order or omit some steps. In the overall process, however, you will probably not vary the steps widely.

Not every single step in the various stages of composition can be detailed here. There is not enough space to illustrate the development of various drafts before the final draft. If you compare the original notes with early drafts of observations and paragraphs, however, you can see that many changes take place and that one step really merges with another.

1. *Read the work through at least once for general understanding.* It is important that you have a general knowledge of the work before you try to start developing materials for your theme. Be sure, in this reading, to follow all the general principles outlined earlier (pp. 4–5).

2. *Take notes with your specific assignment in mind.* If you are to write about a character, for example, take notes on things done, said, and thought about by that character. The same applies if your assignment is on imagery, ideas, and so on. By concentrating your notes in this way, and by excluding other elements of the work, you are already focusing on the subject at hand.

3. *Use a pen, pencil, typewriter, or word processor as an extension of your thought.* Writing, together with actually *seeing* the things written, is for most people a vital part of thinking. Therefore, you must get your thoughts into a visible form so that you may develop them further. For many people, the hand is a psychological necessity in this process. For others, thought may proceed through the fingers into a typewriter or a word processor. The important thing is that unwritten thought is still incomplete thought. Get it out onto something you can see and work with.

In addition, at some advanced step in your composing process, prepare a complete draft of what you have written thus far. Even with a word processor, you cannot lay everything out in front of you at once but can see only a small part on your screen. A clean, readable draft gives you the chance to see everything together and to make even more improvements. Sight is vital.

4. *Use the questions in the chapter on which the assignment is based.* Your answers to these questions, together with your notes and ideas, can often serve as the basis for parts of an essay.

5. *For all your preliminary materials, use cards or only one side of the paper.* In this way, you may spread out everything and get an overview as you plan and write your essay. Do not write on both sides of the paper, for ideas that are out of sight are often out of mind.

6. *Once you have put everything together in this way, try to develop a central idea.* This will serve as the focus of your planning and writing.

Finding a Central Idea or a Thesis

You cannot find a central idea in a hat. It comes about as a result of the steps just described. In a way, you might think of discovering a central idea as a major goal in the prewriting process. Once you have the idea, you have a guide for accepting some of your materials, rejecting others, rearranging, changing, and rewording. It is therefore necessary to see how the central idea may be developed and how it may be used.

MAKING NOTES.   Let us assume that your assignment is a theme about the character Jackie in O'Connor's story "First Confession." (To read the complete story, see p. 187.) The following is a collection of notes and observations that you might write when reading the story. Notice that page numbers are noted so that you can easily go back to the story at any time to refresh your memory on any details.

> Jackie blames others, mainly his grandmother, for his troubles. He hates her bare feet and her eating and drinking habits. He dislikes his sister, Nora for "sucking up" to the grandmother. Also, Nora tells on him. He is ashamed to bring a friend home to play because of grandmother. (p. 188)
>
> He likes money rather than Mrs. Ryan's talk of hell.
> He is shocked by the story about the "fellow" who "made a bad confession." (pp. 188–89)
> After learning to examine his conscience, he believes that he has broken all ten commandments because of the grandmother.
> He lies about a toothache to avoid confession. A kid's lie. (p. 189)
>
> He believes his sister is a "raging malicious devil." He remembers her "throwing" him through the church door. (p. 190)
> Very imaginative. Believes that he will make a "bad confession and then die in the night and be continually coming back and burning people's furniture."

This is funny, and also childish. He thinks women are hypocrites. (p. 190)
He is frightened by the dark confessional. (p. 190)

Curious and adventurous. He gets up on the shelf and kneels.
He is also frightened by the tone of the priest's voice. He falls out on the
church floor and gets whacked by his sister. (p. 191)

Note: All the things about Jackie as a child are told by Jackie as an older
person. The man is sort of telling a joke on himself.

Jackie is smart, can think about himself as a sinner once the priest gives
him a clue. He likes the kind words of the priest, is impressed with him.
He begins reacting against the words of Mrs. Ryan and Nora, calling them
"cackling." (p. 191)

He has sympathy for his mother. Calls her "poor soul." Seems to fear his
father, who has given him the "flaking." (p. 192)

Note: Jackie is a child, and easily swayed. He says some things that are particularly childish and cute, such as coming back to burn furniture. His fears
show that he is childish and naive. He is gullible. His memory of his anger
against his sister shows a typical attitude of brother and sister.

WRITING OBSERVATIONS FROM YOUR NOTES: "BRAINSTORMING." Once you
have a set of notes like these, your job is to make something out of them.
The notes do not make up an essay; they are disorganized and unfocused.
However, they represent a starting point from which ideas may be organized
and developed. Since the imaginary assignment we are discussing concerns
character (rather than plot, imagery, symbolism, or the like), you should
go back over your notes and extract single-sentence observations that relate
specifically to character traits and development. Care must be taken to
ensure that these sentences focus on the subject at hand—character—and
do not offer plot summary or digressions. Such a reformulated list of sentences about Jackie's character might look like this:

Jackie likes thinking about money (the half crown) rather than hell. Is he
irreligious, or does this show his childish nature?

He seems to be older when he is telling the story.

He has a dislike for his sister that seems to be normal brother-and-sister
rivalry.

He tells a fib about the toothache, but he tells everything else to the priest.
He is not a liar.

He blames his gran for his troubles. Is he irresponsible? No, he is just behaving
like a child.

He is curious and adventurous, as much as a seven-year-old can be.

He is easily scared and impressed (see his response to the bad confession
story, and his first response to the priest).

He says cute things, the sort of things a child would say (the old man in the pew, coming back to burn the furniture). He seems real as a child.

These are all observations that might or might not turn out to be worth much in your essay. It is not possible to tell until you do some further thinking about them. These basic ideas, however, are worth working up further, along with additional substantiating details.

DEVELOPING YOUR OBSERVATIONS AS PARAGRAPHS.   As you develop these basic ideas, you should be consulting the original set of notes and also looking at the text to make sure that all your facts are correct. As you write, you should bring in any new details that seem relevant. Here are some paragraphs that expand upon some of the observations presented above. You might consider this paragraph-writing phase a "second step" in the brainstroming needed for the essay:

1. Jackie comes to life. He seems real. His experiences are those that a child might have, and his reactions are lifelike. All brothers and sisters fight. All kids are "heart scalded" when they get a "flaking."

2. Jackie shows a great amount of anger. He kicks his grandmother on the shin and won't eat her cooking. He is mad at Nora for the penny that she gets from grandmother, and he "lashes out" at Nora with the bread knife. He blames his troubles on his grandmother. He talks about the "hypocrisy of women." He thinks that the stories of Mrs. Ryan and the religion of his sister are the "cackle of old women and girls." (p. 191)

3. Everything about Jackie as a child that we get in the story is told by Jackie when he is older, probably a grown man. The story is comic, and part of the comedy comes because the man is telling a jokelike story about himself.

4. Jackie's main characteristic is that he is a child and does many childish things. He remembers his anger with his sister. He also remembers being shocked by Mrs. Ryan's stories about hell. He crawls onto the ledge in the confessional. He is so impressed with the bad confession story that he says twice that he fears burning furniture. Some of these things are charming and cute, such as the observation about the old man having a grandmother and his thinking about the money when Mrs. Ryan offers the coin to the first boy who holds his finger in the candle flame.

DETERMINING YOUR CENTRAL IDEA.   Once you have reached this stage in your thinking, you are ready to pull the materials together and form a central idea or a thesis for the essay. To do this, look for a common thread or term that runs through many of your observations. In the notes, sentences, and paragraphs developed in the hypothetical assignment on character in "First Confession," one common thread is the term "childish." The anger, the sibling rivalry, the attraction to the coin, the fear of burning someone's furniture, the fib about the toothache—all these can be seen

Don't settle for superficial
ideas.

← Note

XXX

as signs of childishness. Once you have found this <u>common thread</u> (and it could easily have been some other point, such as Jackie's anger, or his attitude toward the females around him), it can be used as the central idea in an evolving essay.

Because the central idea is so vital in shaping an essay, it should be formed as carefully as possible in a complete sentence. Just the word "child-ishness" would not give us as much as any of the following sentences:

1. The main trait of Jackie is his childishness.
2. Jackie is bright and sensitive, but above all childlike.
3. Jackie is no more than a typical child.
4. Jackie is above all a child, with all the beauties of childhood.

Sample thesis statements

Each one of these ideas would make a different kind of essay. The first would promote an essay showing that Jackie's actions and thoughts are childish. The third would do much the same thing but would also stress Jackie's limitations as a child. The second would try to show Jackie's better qualities and would show how they are limited by his age. The fourth might try to emphasize the charm and "cuteness" that were pointed out in some of the notes and observations.

You might try phrasing the thesis several different ways before you choose the one that will yield the most focused essay. Once you have a central idea (let us use the first one), you will be able to use it to bring your observations and conclusions into focus.

Let's take paragraph two in the brainstorming phase, the one about Jackie. With childishness as our central idea, we can use the topic of anger as a way of illustrating Jackie's childish character. Is his <u>anger</u> adult or childish? Is it \normal or psychotic?\ Is it sudden or deliberate? In the light of these questions, we may conclude that all the examples of angry action and thought can be seen as the normal responses or reflections of a child. With the material thus "arranged" in this way, we can reshape the second paragraph as follows:

Note
↓

ORIGINAL PARAGRAPH

Jackie shows a great amount of anger. He kicks his grandmother on the shin and won't eat her cooking. He is mad at Nora for the penny that she gets from grandmother, and he "lashes out" at Nora with the bread knife. He blames his troubles on his grandmother. He talks about the "hypocrisy of women." He thinks the stories of Mrs. Ryan and the religion of his sister are the "cackle of old women and girls." (p. 191)

RESHAPED PARAGRAPH *Ideas are connected*

Jackie's great amount of anger is child-ish. Kicking his grandmother, refusing to eat her cooking, and lashing out at Nora with the bread knife are instances of childish anger. His jealousy of Nora and his distrust of women (as hypocrites) are the results of immature and childish thought. His religious anger evident in his claim that the fears of Mrs. Ryan and Nora are the "cackle of old women and girls" (p. 191) is <u>also childish</u>.

Examples ←

Notice here that the materials in each paragraph are substantially the same but that the central idea has shaped the right-hand paragraph. The left-hand column describes Jackie's anger, while the one on the right makes the claim that all the examples of angry action and thought are childish and immature. Once our paragraph has been shaped in this way, it is almost ready for placement into the emerging essay.

The Thesis Sentence

Using the central idea as a guide, we can now go back to the earlier materials for arrangement. The goal is to establish a number of points to be developed as paragraphs in support of the central idea. The paragraphs written as the second step of brainstorming will serve us well. Paragraph 2, the one we have just "shaped," discusses childish anger. Paragraph 3 has material that could be used in an introduction (since it does not directly discuss any precise characteristics but instead describes how the reader gets the information about Jackie). Paragraph 1 has material that might be good in a conclusion. Paragraph 4 has two topics (it is not a unified paragraph), which may be labeled "responses" and "outlook." We may put these points into a list:

1. Responses
2. Outlook
3. Anger

Once we have established this list, we may use it as the basic order for the development of our essay.

For the benefit of the reader, however, we should also use this ordering for the writing of our **thesis sentence.** This sentence is the operative sentence in the first part of the following general plan for most essays:

Tell what you are going to say.
Say it.
Tell what you've said.

The thesis sentence tells your reader what to expect. It is a plan for your essay: it connects the central idea and the list of topics in the order in which you plan to present them. Thus, if we put the central idea at the left and our list of topics at the right, we have the shape of a thesis sentence:

CENTRAL IDEA   TOPICS

The main trait of Jackie is his childishness.   1. Responses
                                                 2. Outlook
                                                 3. Anger

From this arrangement we can write the following thesis sentence, which should usually be the concluding sentence before the body of the essay (that section in which you "say it," that is, in which you develop your central idea):

The childishness is emphasized in his responses, outlook, and anger.

With any changes made necessary by the context of your final essay, this thesis sentence and your central idea can go directly into your introduction. The central idea, as we have seen, is the glue of the essay. The thesis sentence shows the parts that are to be fastened together, that is, the topics in which the central idea will be demonstrated.

The Body of the Essay: Topic Sentences

The term regularly used in this book for the development of the central idea is **body.** The body is the section where you present the materials you have been working up in your planning. You may rearrange or even reject some of what you have developed, as you wish, as long as you change your thesis sentence to account for the changes. Since the thesis sentence we have generated contains three topics, we will use these to form the essay.

Just as the organization of the entire essay is based on the thesis sentence, the organization of each paragraph is based on its **topic sentence.** The topic sentence is made up of one of the topics listed in the thesis sentence, combined with some assertion about how the topic will support the central idea. The first topic in our example is Jackie's responses, and the topic sentence should show how these responses illustrate a phase of Jackie's childishness. Suppose we choose the phase of the child's gullibility or impressionability. We can put together the topic and the phase, to get the following topic sentence:

Jackie's responses show childish impressionability.

The details that will be used to develop the paragraph will then show how Jackie's responses illustrate the impressionability and gullibility associated with children.

You should follow the same process in forming the other topic sentences, so that when you finish them you can use them in writing your essay.

The Outline

All along we have actually been developing an **outline** to shape and organize the essay. Some writers never use a formal outline at all, whereas others find one to be quite helpful to them as they write. Still other writers insist that they cannot produce an outline until they have finished their essay. All of these views can be reconciled if you realize that finished essays should have a tight structure. At some point, therefore, you should create an outline as a guide. It may be early in your prewriting, or it may be late. What is important is that your final essay follow an outline form.

The kind of outline we have been developing here is the "analytical sentence outline." This type is easier to create than it sounds, for it is nothing more than a graphic form, a skeleton, of your essay. It consists of the following:

1. Title
2. Introduction
    a. Central idea
    b. Thesis sentence
3. Body
    a. ⎫
    b.   ⎬ points predicted in the thesis sentence
    c. etc. ⎭
4. Conclusion

The conclusion is optional in this scheme. Because the topic of the conclusion is a separate item, it is technically independent of the body, but it is part of the thematic organization and hence should be closely tied to the central idea. It may be a summary of the main points in the essay ("tell what you've said"). It may also be an evaluation of the ideas, or it may suggest further points of analysis that you did not write about in the body. Each of the following chapters offers suggestions to help you develop materials for your conclusions.

Remember that your outline should be a guide for organizing many thoughts and already completed paragraphs. Throughout our discussion of the process of writing the essay, we have seen that writing is discovery. At the right point, your outline can help you in this discovery. That is, the need to make your essay conform to the plan of the outline may help you to reshape, reposition, and reword some of your ideas.

When completed, the outline should have the following appearance (using the character study of Jackie in "First Confession"):

1. Title: "Jackie's Childish Character in O'Connor's 'First Confession' "
2. Introduction. Paragraph 1
    a. Central idea: The main trait of Jackie is his childishness.
    → b. Thesis sentence: This childishness is emphasized in his responses, out-
       look, and anger.
3. Body: Topic sentences for paragraphs 2–4
    a. Jackie's responses show childish impressionability.
    b. His outlook reflects the simplicity of a child.
    c. His anger is also that of a child.
4. Conclusion. Paragraph 5
    Topic sentence: Jackie seems real as a child.

By the time you have created an outline like this one, you will have been planning and drafting your essay for quite some time. The outline will thus be a guide for *finishing* and *polishing* your essay, not for actually developing it. Usually you will have already completed the main parts of the body and will use the outline for the introduction and conclusion.

Briefly, here is the way to use the outline:

1. Include both the central idea and the thesis sentence in your introduction. (Some instructors require a fusion of the two in the final draft of the essay. Therefore, make sure you know what your instructor expects.) Use the suggestions in the chapter assignment to determine what else might be included in the introduction.

2. Include the various topic sentences at the beginning of your paragraphs, changing them as necessary to provide transitions or qualifications. Throughout this book the various topics are confined to separate paragraphs. However, it is also acceptable to divide the topic into two or more paragraphs, particularly if the topic is difficult or highly detailed. Should you make this division, your topic then is really a *section*, and your second and third paragraphs should each have their own topic sentences.

In paragraphs designed to demonstrate the validity of an assertion, the topic sentence usually begins the paragraph. The details then illustrate the truth of the assertion in the topic sentence. (Details about the use of evidence will follow below, pp. 19–21.) It is also acceptable to have the topic sentence elsewhere in the paragraph, particularly if your paragraph is a "thought paragraph," in which you use details to lead up to your topic idea.

Throughout this book, for illustrative purposes, all the central ideas, thesis sentences, and topic sentences are underlined so that you may distinguish them clearly as guides for your own writing.

THE SAMPLE ESSAY

The following essay is a sample of the finished product of the process we have been illustrating. You will recognize the various organizing sentences because they are underlined. These are the sentences from the outline, with changes made to incorporate them into the essay and to provide transitions from paragraph to paragraph. You will also see that some of the paragraphs and thoughts have been taken from the prewriting stages, with necessary changes to bring them into tune with the central idea. (See the illustration of this change on p. 11.)

In each of the chapters in this book there are similar sample essays. It would be impossible to show the complete writing process for each of these, but you may assume that each one was completed more or less like the one that has been illustrated here. There were many good starts, and many false ones. Much was changed and rearranged, and much was redone once the outline for the essay was established. The materials for each essay were developed in the light of the issues introduced and exemplified in the first parts of each of the chapters. The plan for each essay corresponds to an outline, and its length is within the limits of many of the essays you will be assigned to write.

SAMPLE ESSAY

Jackie's Childish Character in O'Connor's "First Confession"

[1]   Jackie, the main character in O'Connor's "First Confession," is a child at the time of the action. All the things we learn about him, however, are told by him as an older person. The story is funny, and part of the humor is produced because the narrator is telling what amounts to a joke on himself. For this reason he brings out his own childhood childishness. That is, if Jackie were mature, the joke would not work because so much depends on his being young, powerless, and gullible. The main thing about Jackie, then, is his childishness.° This quality is emphasized in his responses, outlook, and anger.□

[2]   Jackie's responses show the ease with which a child may be impressed. His grandmother embarasses him with her drinking, eating, and unpleasant habits. He is so "shocked" by the story about the bad confession that twice he states his fear of saying a bad confession and coming back to burn furniture. He is quickly impressed by the priest and is able to change his mind, about his sins (to his own favor) after no more than a few words with this man.

[3]   His outlook above all reflects the limitations and the simplicity of a child. He is not old enough to know anything about the outside world, and therefore he supposes that the old man next to him at confession has also had problems with a grandmother. This same limited view causes him to think only about the half crown when Mrs. Ryan talks about punishment. It is just like a child to see everything in personal terms, without the detached, broad views of an experienced adult.

[4]   His anger is also that of a child, although an intelligent one. Kicking his grandmother and lashing out against Nora with the bread knife are the reflexive actions of childish anger. He also has anger that he thinks about. His jealousy of Nora and his claim that women are hypocrites are the results of thought, even though this thought is immature and childish. His thinking about religion after first speaking to the priest makes him claim that the fears of Mrs. Ryan

For the text of this story, see p. 187.
° Central idea
□ Thesis sentence

and Nora are the "cackle of old women and girls" (p. 191). He is intelligent, but he is also childish.

[5]

    <u>Jackie therefore seems real as a child.</u> His reactions are the right ones for a child to have. All brothers and sisters fight, and all children are "heart scalded" when they get a "flaking." The end of life and eternal punishment are remote for a child, whose first concern is the pleasure that money can buy. Therefore, Jackie's thoughts about the half crown are truly those of a child, as are all his thoughts and actions. The strength of "First Confession" is the reality and consistency of Jackie as a child.

Essay Commentaries

Throughout this book, short commentaries follow each sample essay. Each discussion points out how the assignment is handled and how the instruction provided in the first part of the chapter is incorporated into the essay. For essays in which several approaches are suggested, the commentary points out which one is employed. When a sample essay uses two or more approaches, the commentary makes this fact clear. It is hoped that the commentaries will help you develop the insight necessary to use the sample essays as aids in your own study and writing.

SOME COMMON PROBLEMS IN WRITING ESSAYS

The fact that you understand the early stages of the composition process and can apply the principles of developing a central idea and organizing with an outline and thesis sentence does not mean that you will have no problems in writing well. It is not hard to recognize good writing when you see it, but it can be difficult to explain why it is superior.

    The most difficult and perplexing questions you will ask as you write are: (1) "How can I improve my writing?" (2) "If I got a *C* on my last essay, why wasn't the grade a *B* or an *A*? How can I get higher grades?" These are really the same question, but each has a different emphasis. Another way to ask this question is: "When I first read a work, I have a hard time following it. Yet when my instructor explains it, my understaning is greatly increased. How can I develop the ability to understand the work and write about it well without my instructor's help? How can I become an independent, confident reader and writer?"

    The chapter discussions accompanying the readings in this book are designed to help you do just that. One of the major flaws in many essays about literature is that, despite the writer's best intentions and plans, they do no more than retell a story or describe an idea. Retelling the story shows only that you have read the work, not that you have thought about it. Writing a good essay, however, shows that you have digested the material and have been able to put it into an analytical pattern of thought.

Establishing an Order in Making References

There are a number of ways in which you may set up patterns of development to show your understanding. One is to refer to events or passages in an order that you yourself establish. You do not have to present them in the order in which they occurred but can change them around to make them fit into your own thematic plans. Rarely, if ever, should you begin your essay by describing the opening of the work; it is better to talk about the conclusion or the middle of the work first. Beginning the body of your essay by referring to later parts of the work will almost force you to discuss your own central idea rather than to retell a story or summarize a poem. If you look back at paragraph 3 of the sample essay on "First Confession," you will see that this technique has been used. The two references there are presented in reverse order from the story. This reversal shows the essay writer's own organization, not the organization of the work being analyzed.

Your Mythical Reader: A Student Who Has Read but Not Thought

Consider the "mythical reader" for whom you are writing your essay. Imagine that you are writing to other students. They have read the assigned work, just as you have, but they have not thought about it. It is easy to imagine how to write for such mythical readers. They know the events or have followed the thread of the argument. They know who says what and when it is said. As a result, you do not need to tell these readers about everything in the work but should think of your role as that of an *explainer* or *interpreter*. Tell them what things mean in relationship to your central idea. *Do not, however, tell them the things that happen.*

To look at the situation in still another way, let us draw a comparison from Sir Arthur Conan Doyle's Sherlock Holmes story "The Adventure of the Speckled Band." Both Dr. Watson and Holmes are together when they examine the room of the potential murder victim, and both are able to see the same things. As the two men discuss their observations, Watson says, "You have evidently seen more in these rooms than was visible to me." To this, Holmes makes a telling and famous response: "No, but I fancy that I may have deduced a little more. I imagine that you saw all that I did." You should consider your role as a writer to be like that of Holmes as a detective. Thus, you explain and interpret facts and draw conclusions that your mythical readers, like Watson, are unable to draw for themselves even though they can see the same things that you do. If you look back at the sample essay on "First Confession," you will notice that everywhere *the assumption has been made that the reader has read the story already*. References to the story are thus made primarily to remind the reader of something he or she already knows, but *the principal emphasis of the essay is to draw conclusions and develop arguments*.

Using Literary Material as Evidence

The comparison with Sherlock Holmes should remind you that whenever you write on any topic, your position is much like that of a detective using clues as evidence for building a case, or of a lawyer using evidence as support for arguments. If you argued in favor of securing a greater voice for students in college government, for example, you would introduce such evidence as past successes with student government, increased maturity of modern-day students, the constitutional amendment granting 18-year-olds the right to vote, and so on.

Writing about literature requires evidence as well. *For practical purposes only*, when you are writing an essay, you may conveniently regard the work assigned as evidence for your arguments. You should make references to the work only as a part of the logical development of your discourse. Your objective is to convince your reader of your own knowledge and reasonableness, just as lawyers attempt to convince a jury of the reasonableness of their arguments.

The proper use of evidence in literary studies, as in law, psychology, or physics, is important and complex. Would it be accurate, for example, to deduce from the "evidence" of Doyle's "The Adventure of the Speckled Band" that Dr. Roylott is a good and kind man? The story gives us four pieces of evidence: (1) Roylott murdered a servant in India; (2) he is continually in a violent rage; (3) he probably murdered Helen Stoner's sister; (4) he is trying to murder Helen. The evidence, ladies and gentlemen of the literary jury, is clear: Roylott is not a pleasant individual. Instead, the only logical conclusion we can reach from Doyle's presentation of Roylott is that the man is dangerous and evil. We can see a similar use of literary "evidence" in the sample essay on "First Confession." The fourth paragraph, which focuses on Jackie's anger as an aspect of his childishness, introduces four pieces of "evidence" from the story as support. These details are not introduced to summarize plot or retell the story; they explicitly relate to the topic of Jackie's anger and childishness.

The correct and effective use of such literary evidence is vital to good writing. Look, for example, at these two paragraphs; both are from essays about the plot structure in "The Adventure of the Speckled Band":

1

Midway in this conversation, Dr. Grimesby Roylott, Helen Stoner's stepfather, bursts into the room. Before this point we had learned that he was an unpleasant, violent man. He had beaten a servant to death in India, and back in England had become known as a brawler and a man to avoid. The impression he gives in the scene with Holmes and Dr. Watson confirms all these stories of menace and anger that Helen had told Holmes earlier in the day. Roylott is a giant of a man, big enough to throw even a blacksmith into a stream, as Helen had related about him. His evil nature is shown in his face, also a fact which confirms Helen's story about his many angry quarrels with people who lived in his neighborhood. His appearance is not only evil, but it is also threatening. Dr. Watson says he resembles a bird of prey. Roylott, after stating his name, immediately demands to know what Helen had been saying to Holmes. When the great detective refuses to tell him, Roylott makes a number of insults, calling Holmes a meddler, a busy body, and a "Scotland Yard Jack-in-office." Then he threatens Holmes and anyone else who meddles in his affairs, and, to show his strength, he seizes a poker and bends it. After throwing the bent poker in the fireplace, he angrily leaves. Holmes then straightens the poker itself, while asserting that he, too, has strength.

2

Doyle uses the entry of Dr. Grimesby Roylott as a pivot point in the story. Roylott is the villain and will soon try to murder Helen Stoner, but at his first appearance the readers do not know that. Instead, he has been no more than a stormy, angry figure in Helen's narration. With his entry, however, Doyle makes him real. His rudeness, threats, and demonstration of brute strength with the poker confirm what Helen had said about him, even though at first his mad behavior could easily be explained as that of an angry stepfather and guardian rather than of a guilty murderer. In light of the ending of the story, however, in which Doyle, for the sake of the mystery, has Roylott work out his scheme of murder in darkness and concealment, the confrontation with Holmes is the only first-hand view we get of Roylott's evil character. By dramatizing this potential for violence in this way, Doyle makes it believable that Roylott could indeed be a murderer. Thus, this brief interruption and encounter are pivotal to Doyle's plot, for they confirm the earlier part of the story and establish the credibility of the latter part.

Although the first example has more words than the second (240 in passage 1, 196 in 2), it is not adequate, for the writer is just restating things that the reader already should know. The paragraph is cluttered with details, and its conclusions and observations are minimal. If you judge it for what you might learn about Conan Doyle's actual *use* of the episode from "The Speckled Band," you cannot avoid concluding that it does not give you a single piece of new information and that it is no help at all in understanding the story. The writer did not have to think much in order to write the paragraph.

On the other hand, the second passage is responsive to the reader's needs, and it required a good deal of thought to write. Phrases like "Doyle uses" and "Doyle makes it believable" show that the writer of passage 2 has assumed the reader knows the story and now wants help in interpretation. Passage 2 therefore leads readers into a new and informative pattern of thought and analysis. It uses details from the story only to furnish evidence for a topic idea (the "pivotal" role of the episode) but excludes irrelevant details. Passage 1 includes nothing but raw, undirected actions. Passage 2 has a point; passage 1 does not. The answer to the difficult question at how to turn *C*-grade writing into *A*-grade writing is to be found in the comparison of the two passages. Besides using English correctly, superior writers always allow their minds to play upon the materials. They try to give readers the results of their thoughts. They dare to trust their responses and are not afraid to make judgments about the literary work they are considering. Their principal aim in referring to events in a work is to develop their own thematic pattern. Observe this quality again by comparing two sentences that deal with the same details from the story:

1	2
Midway in this conversation, Dr. Grimesby Roylott, Helen Stoner's stepfather, bursts into the room.	Doyle uses the entry of Dr. Grimesby Roylott as a pivot point in the story.

Sentence 1 is detailed and accurate but no more. Sentence 2 is admittedly less detailed, but it links the essential detail of the entry to a major idea about the plot of the story. The words "Doyle uses" and "as a pivot point" indicate the writer's thoughtful use of detail as a part of an argument or observation, not just as an undigested passing on of detail. There are many things that make good writing good, but perhaps the most important is the way in which a writer uses known and accepted facts as evidence in an original pattern of thought. Always try to achieve this quality in your writing.

Keeping to Your Point

Whenever you write an essay about literature, then, you must pay great attention to the proper organization and to the proper use of references to the work assigned. As you write, you should try constantly to keep your material unified, for should you go off on a tangent, you are following the material rather than leading it. It is all too easy to start with your point but then wander off into a retelling of events or ideas. Once again, resist the tendency to be a narrator rather than an interpreter.

Let us look at another example. The following paragraph is taken from an essay on "The value of methodical intelligence in Doyle's 'The

Adventure of the Speckled Band.' " In this paragraph the writer attempts to demonstrate the importance to this idea of the section of the story where Holmes and Watson investigate the house in which Helen Stoner feels threatened.

Not

It is in the direct examination of the Roylott building, Stoke Moran, that the power of active intelligence is seen to be most practical and effective. Holmes and Watson first examine the outside of the right wing, where Helen Stoner is temporarily sleeping next to the room of Dr. Roylott. Then they go inside, where Holmes examines Helen's room, even using a magnifying glass to see things closely. He discovers that the bell rope is a dummy and that the ventilator opens not to the outside but to Dr. Roylott's room next door. Then they examine Roylott's room and discover a number of seemingly strange and unexplainable things, such as the large iron safe, the saucer of milk, the wooden chair, and a strange dog leash. It is then that Holmes truly realizes the danger and forms a plan of protection, action, and discovery.

This paragraph shows how easily writers may be diverted from their objective. The first sentence is an effective topic sentence that suggests that the writer began with a good plan. The remainder of the paragraph, however, does not follow through. It is simply an accurate account of what happens in the story but does not get tied in to the topic set forth in the opening sentence. The material is relevant to the topic, but the writer does not point out its relevance. Writers should not rely on detail alone to make meanings clear. They must make the connections between details and conclusions explicit.

Let us see how the problem shown in the paragraph may be corrected through revision. If the ideal paragraph could be schematized with line drawings, we might say that the paragraph's topic should be a straight line, moving directly toward a specific goal (explicit meaning), with an exemplifying line moving away from the straight line briefly in order to bring in evidence but returning to the line after each new fact in order to demonstrate the relevance of this fact. Thus, the ideal scheme would look like this:

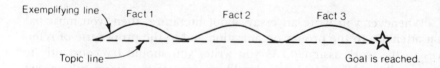

Exemplifying line   Fact 1   Fact 2   Fact 3

Topic line   Goal is reached.

Notice that the exemplifying line always returns to the topic line. A scheme for the above paragraph on "The Adventure of the Speckled Band," however, would look like this:

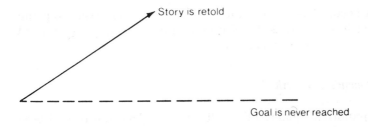

How might this paragraph be revised and improved? The best way is to reintroduce the topic again and again throughout the paragraph to keep reminding the reader of the relevance of the exemplifying material. Each time you mention the topic you are bringing yourself back to the line, and this practice should prevail no matter what the topic. If you are analyzing point of view, for example, you should keep pointing out the relevance of your material to the point of view of the work, and the same applies to *character* or whatever aspect of literature you are studying. According to this principle, we might revise the paragraph on "The Adventure of the Speckled Band" as follows, keeping as much of the original wording as we can. (Parts of sentences stressing the relationship of the examples to the topic of the paragraph are underlined.)

The revision! Better developed.

    It is in the direct examination of the Roylott building, Stoke Moran, that the power of active intelligence is seen to be most practical and effective. In examining the outside of the right wing, where Helen Stoner is temporarily sleeping next to the room of Dr. Roylott, Holmes rules out the threat of forceful entry by the Gypsies. It is clear then, but only in the retrospect of the entire story, that Holmes concludes that the threat is internal, from Roylott himself. The inside examination of Helen's room and then Roylott's room is a discovery of the nature and method of Roylott's threat, or attack. It is clear that the physical details of both rooms—such as the dummy bell rope, the misdirected ventilator, the large iron safe, the saucer of milk, the wooden chair, and the strange dog leash—form the basis of Holmes's intelligent deductions. Once he has formulated his analysis of the danger, he almost instantly devotes his mind to form a plan of protection, action, and discovery. The idea that intelligence can be practically and effectively applied could hardly be more strongly illustrated.

The paragraph has been lengthened and improved. You might object that if all your paragraphs were lengthened in this way your essay would grow too long. The answer to this objection is that *it is better to develop a few topics fully than many scantily*. Such revision might require you to throw away some of your topics or else to incorporate them as subpoints in the topics you keep. This process can only improve your essay. But the result of greater length here is that the exemplifying detail points toward the topic, and the paragraph reaches its goal.

Insight, Newness, Growth

Another important quality of excellence is making the central idea expand and grow. The word *growth* is a metaphor for development, the creation of new insights, the disclosure of ideas that were not at first noticeable, the expression of new, fresh, and original interpretations.

You might suppose that it is difficult to be original when you are writing about someone else's work. "The author has said everything," you might argue, "and therefore I can do little more than follow the story (poem, or play)." This claim assumes that there is no choice whatever in the selection of material for an essay, and no opportunity for individual thoughts and orignal contributions. However, there is. The author has presented the work to you, and you can, if you look hard, find layer upon layer of meaning. One obvious area where you can exert your power of originality is the development and formulation of the central idea for your essay. For example, a first thought about Chekhov's comedy *The Bear* is that is it about love. Just this topic does not go very far, however, and an additional idea might be developed from the observation that the love is "sudden." This idea is regrettably not very original either. However, a more original insight can be provided if the topic is related directly to the anger of the major characters. Then an idea might be that "love is so strong a force that it emerges even against the apparently conscious wills of those falling in love." With this idea, it is possible to create a fresher, more original essay analyzing the improbable events and dialogue of the play than one might create with the simple topic "love."

You can also develop your ability to treat your subject freshly and originally if you plan the body of the essay to build up to what you think is your most important, most incisive, and best-conceived idea. The following arrangement of topics illustrates how a central idea may be built up. Let us assume the central idea is "The power of intelligence in Doyle's 'The Adventure of the Speckled Band.'" The following paragraphs are presented not as finished essay but rather as a set of thoughts in an ascending order of importance to show how the exemplification of a central idea may also allow for originality and growth:

1.   Holmes as a mental power

 Holmes's methods show his great power of observation and deduction. When he first meets Helen Stoner he deduces much about her from her appearance.

His questions to her show that his mind is working, searching for possible answers to the questions raised by her fears. When he goes to her home for an on-the-spot inspection, his investigation is thorough and intelligent. Always his mind is applied to the problem, and he solves the crime early, well before he and Watson begin their evening's vigil.

2. Holmes as a power for helping individuals

To Helen Stoner, Holmes is a natural source of help. She acknowledges that she is unable to get out of danger by herself, for she cannot identify the forces against her. Holmes therefore represents the possible power of systematic knowledge that can be applied to the solution of difficult and dangerous problems. He is an agent of investigative action and therefore of improvement on the side of right and justice. For all these reasons, Holmes is a force for optimism and the belief that problems should not crush human beings.

3. Holmes as a force of security and stability in civilization

Just as Holmes represents the power of applied knowledge, so he represents the hope to achieve civilized security and stability. At the end of the story, Holmes has made all his deductions, has made a plan of action, has defeated Dr. Roylott, and has explained his procedure. All danger is overcome and security is restored. Thus, Holmes is the means by which the world may be improved. All his mental effort is designed to ease fear and to restore security. The character of Sherlock Holmes therefore appeals to basic human desires. He is not simply a clever detective; his character is rooted in the same earth which causes people to pray, to dream, and to work toward a better future.

These examples suggest a thread of development from personal, to social, to cosmic. An essay along this line would attempt to show that Doyle's apparently straightforward detective story is actually an embodiment of universal human needs. The topic has definitely grown. Details from the story are included as a part of this developing pattern of growth, and in no way are they introduced simply to retell the story. The pattern shows how two primary standards of excellence in essays—organization and growth—can be met. Without these qualities, there is no totally successful writing, just as there is no successful thinking.

It should be clear that whenever you write, an important goal should be the development of your central idea. You should try to go somewhere with your idea, to give your readers insights about the literary materials that they did not have before they started reading. To the degree that you can learn to develop your ideas, you will receive recognition for increasingly superior writing achievements.

Admittedly, in a short essay you will be able to move only a short distance with an idea, but you should never be satisfied to leave the idea exactly where you found it. Constantly adhere to your topic and constantly develop it. Nurture it and make it grow.

Using Accurate and Forceful Language

The best writing has a quality of accuracy and force. Quite often the first products of our minds are rather weak, and they need to be re-thought, recast, and reworded. Sometimes this process cannot be carried out immediately, for it may take days or even weeks for us to gain objectivity about what we say. As a student you usually do not have that kind of time, and thus you must acquire the habit of challenging your own statements almost as soon as you write them. Ask yourself whether they really mean what you want, or if you can make a stronger statement than you have.

As an example, consider the following statement, put forward as a central idea about Doyle's "The Adventure of the Speckled Band":

> The central idea in this story is about how Sherlock Holmes solves the mystery of the story.

This statement could not carry anyone very far in the development of an essay, because it promises nothing more than a retelling of the story. It needs further thought. Here are two possible central ideas developed from this sentence that might be more productive bases for an essay:

1. In the story Doyle embodies the idea that careful observation is a necessary step in the solution of problems.
2. Doyle makes Holmes's solution of the mystery a tribute to orderly methodology.

Although both these sentences might produce similar essays, the first would probably emphasize the investigative part of the story: the listening, the checking, the close observing. The direction the essay would likely take would be toward the need for getting details right before any accurate conclusions can be drawn. The second sentence points toward an essay that would likely cover Holmes's entire procedure, not just the observing and concluding, but the planning to thwart Dr. Roylott. The second essay, since it includes the word *tribute*, would probably also emphasize all the powers of Holmes as exhibited in the story. In any event, either of the two sentences would be more helpful as a statement of a central idea than the original sentence.

Sometimes, in seeking to say something, we wind up saying nothing. For example, consider these two sentences from essays about Robert Frost's poem "Stopping by Woods on a Snowy Evening" (p. 475):

1. It seems as though the author's anticipation of meeting with death causes him to respond as he does in the poem.
2. This incident, although it may seem trivial or unimportant, has substantial significance in the creation of his poem; by this I mean the incident which occurred is essentially what the poem is all about.

The vagueness of sentences like these must be resisted. A sentence should not end up in limbo the way these do. The first sentence is satisfactory enough up to the verb "causes," but then it falls apart. If Frost has created a response for the speaker in the poem, it is best to describe *what* that response is rather than to state simply that there *is* a response. A more forceful restatement of the first sentence may thus be, "It seems as though the author's anticipation of meeting with death causes him to think about the need to meet his present responsibilities." With this revision, the writer could go on to a consideration of the meaning of Frost's final stanza and could relate the ideas there to the events and ideas described in the first part of the poem. Without the revision, it is not clear where the writer would go.

The second sentence is so vague that it confuses rather than informs. Essentially, such sentences hint at an idea and claim importance for it, but they never directly define what the idea is. If we adopt the principle that it is always better to name the specific things we are talking about, perhaps the second sentence could be revised as follows:

> Although stopping by the woods to watch the snow fall may seem trivial or insignificant, the incident causes the poet to meditate on beauty and responsibility; the important thoughts in the poem thus grow from the simplest of events.

When you write your own sentences, you might test them in a similar way. Are you referring to an idea? State the idea directly. Are you mentioning a response or impression? Do not say simply, "The poem left me with a definite impression," but describe the impression: "The poem left me with an impression of sympathy," or "of understanding the hard lot of the migrant farmer." Similarly, do not rest with a statement such as "I found this story interesting," but try to describe what was interesting and why it was interesting. If you always confront your impressions and responses by trying to name them and to pin them down, your sentences should take on exactness and force. Your instructor will probably also tell you whatever you have accomplished or failed to accomplish. Good writing habits that you develop from these criticisms of your work, and from discussions with your instructor, will help you to write more forcefully and accurately.

Whenever you write an essay, then, keep these ideas in mind. Keep returning to the point you wish to make; regard the material of the work you have read as evidence to substantiate your arguments, not as material to be described. Keep demonstrating that all exemplifying detail is relevant to your main point. Keep trying to develop your topic; make it bigger than it was when you began writing. Constantly try to make your statements accurate and forceful. If you observe these precepts, you should be well on the way toward the successful handling of any assignments derived from the chapter discussions and study questions included in this book.

GAIUS PETRONIUS (d. 66 A.D.)

The Widow of Ephesus   *(1st Century A.D.)*

From *The Satyricon*, Chs. 108–112
An English version by Edgar V. Roberts

We shook hands and congratulated ourselves, while the entire ship we were riding on rang with our songs and choruses. Seagulls landed on the yard-arms, and the poet Eumolpus, slightly drunk with wine, began cracking some bawdy jokes. He was determined that our cheerfulness should be buoyed up by a few of his stories, so he started attacking the character of women. He told about their lack of resistance in falling in love, and about their negligence, while having an affair, even of their own children. Moreover, he claimed that absolutely no woman he had ever known possessed a high enough moral character to save her from getting involved with a handsome man. He assured us that he was not relying for his claims upon old-fashioned melodramas or the typical women described by historians. He himself had seen what he was talking about, and he offered to tell us a true story if we were willing to hear. All of us on board were eager, and we watched and listened to him attentively. This is how Eumolpus began his tale:

"Once upon a time there lived in the city of Ephesus, on the Coast of Asia Minor, a certain woman whose virtue and faithfulness to her husband were so widely recognized that women from nearby and even distant towns and villages flocked to Ephesus just to get a glimpse of her. Unfortunately, her husband got sick and died, and this lady herself arranged for his funeral and burial. After the service she was not satisfied just with following the cortège in the usual way, with her hair torn and frizzed while she beat her naked breast for all to see. She actually accompanied the dead body right into the mausoleum, and when the coffin had been placed in the vault in the custom of the Greeks, she began a vigil beside it, weeping and wailing constantly both day and night. In fact she was starving herself to death and making herself weaker by the hour, but neither her parents nor her closest relatives could persuade her to come back home. Even the local politicians and judges could not win out against her; she snubbed them, and so, with their dignity ruffled, they gave up trying.

"By this time this most amazing woman was already in the fifth day of her fasting, to the sorrow of everyone in town, who believed that her death would come at any moment. At her side was her faithful handmaiden, who shed as many tears as the mournful Widow did. This maiden took care of the torch in the tomb; she refueled and relit it whenever it showed signs of going out. Through all the city of Ephesus, from one end to another, no one talked about anything else. All the people from the richest to the poorest claimed that the Widow had shown herself to be a supreme, shining example of wifely love and fidelity. They had never seen or heard of anyone like her.

"At this time the provincial governor commanded that a gang of local hoodlums should be executed by being crucified near the mausoleum in which the Widow was standing vigil. On the night of the crucifixion a soldier was stationed there to guard the crosses; his duty was to keep away all friends or relatives who wanted to take down the bodies in order to give them a proper burial. As he stood, he happened to notice a bright light shining from inside one of the tombs, and at the same time he heard the moans of someone in great sorrow.

"Curiosity is a weakness of humankind, and this soldier was typically human. 5 So he went down the stairs into the vault of the Widow and her husband to take a look. Imagine his shock at seeing this pretty woman; at first he was as frightened as if he had seen a ghost, or an apparition out of hell. But he soon saw the corpse of the husband, and when he saw the Widow's tears and her nail-scarred face, he correctly concluded that this woman was in the grips of an insupportable sorrow. Therefore he ran up to his station to get his supper, which he brought down into the sepulchre. He then pleaded with the mourning woman to give up her fruitless sorrow and to stop tearing herself apart with ineffective sobs. 'The same inescapable fate stands waiting for all human beings,' he said, 'the final trip of everyone to the home of the dead.' He racked his brain for the usual words of condolence and consolation which are intended to knit together the broken hearts of those who are bereaved. But the lady, who was upset rather than consoled by these words of this strange man, only tore at her bosom more violently and ripped out some of her hair and threw it on the corpse. The soldier kept making his point with her, however, and repeated his soothing words, while at the same time he tried to tempt her with tasty bits of food. At last the handmaiden, her resistance broken by the aromatic bouquet of the wine, held out her hand and accepted the soldier's generous offer.

"Brought back to life by the wine and the food, she also joined the soldier in his siege against the fortress of her mistress's resolve. She cried out, 'What good can it do anyone if you let yourself starve to death, if you bury yourself alive, or if you speed up the day of your last breath before your time has truly come?

Do you believe that ashes or buried ghosts can feel?°

My Lady, come back to life, please! Give up this misguided idea of wifely faithfulness and, as long as you are able, enjoy the light of the sun once more. Even the

Virgil, *Aeneid*, IV. 34.

body of your dead husband, if it could speak, would advise you to get on with living.'

"Nobody is deaf when told to eat or continue living, and so the Widow, starving after her long days of fast, allowed her resolution to be overcome. She refreshed herself with the food just as greedily as the handmaiden who had surrendered first.

"But everybody knows that one appetite follows another. The soldier soon began wooing the Widow with the same tempting words he had used to bring her back from the brink of starvation. He was a strapping young man, and she was not unaware of his handsome good looks, even though she was as modest as they come. He was also persuasive, and her handmaiden aided him in his suit. This little maiden finally quoted the lines,

Would you hold out against a pleasure-giving passion?°

"Why make the story last longer? This Widow quickly gave up all resistance,   10
and the young soldier brought her to bed just as he had brought her to eat. So they spent the night together—and not just this first night, but the next night, and the next. Naturally they kept the door of the tomb barred and bolted so that if any people passing by, either strangers or friends, should come near the sepulchre, they would conclude that the ever-faithful wife had died and fallen upon the body of her dead husband. The soldier was enchanted both by the beauty of his new sweetheart and by their secret affair, and out of his small wage he bought a few little nothings for her. As soon as night came he took his presents to the tomb.

"The result of his absence from his post was that the parents of one of the crucified thieves assumed that the close guard had been withdrawn. They saw their chance, took down the body of their son from the cross, and had the final ceremony for the dead performed over it. The soldier was thus tricked because of his own dereliction of duty while enjoying his night of love. The next morning he saw that one corpse was gone, and he fell into a cold sweat at the thought of the punishment he knew would come to him. He told the story to the Widow. He swore that he could not wait for a court-martial and a sentence, but that he would punish himself for his folly by committing suicide on his own sword. He then asked her to set aside a place for his corpse and permit the sepulchre to be the final resting place not only for her husband, but also for him, her lover. The Widow, however, was just as sympathetic as she was virtuous.

" 'No,' she cried, 'heaven forbid that I should be forced by nothing but bad luck to stand vigil at the same time beside the bodies of the only two men in the world that I ever loved. I would rather hang up a dead man on the cross than permit a living man to die.'

"After these words she told him to take her husband's corpse from the vault, carry it to the empty cross, and nail it up. The next day everyone in town was asking how on earth the dead man had been able to climb onto the cross."

Virgil, *Aeneid*, IV. 38.

QUESTIONS

1. Who tells the story of the widow of Ephesus? What is his attitude toward women? How is his attitude brought out in the story? How is he introduced as the narrator?

2. What virtue is the widow known for? How does she demonstrate this virtue upon her husband's death? How much do you learn about her as a person? What does her abandonment of her intention of self-sacrifice show about her?

3. What kind of person is the soldier? Why do you think he wanted to offer food to the widow and her servant? In what ways does he show both earnestness and fidelity?

4. Consider the widow's plan to substitute the body of her dead husband for that of the dead thief. Does her explanation defending her plan seem acceptable as a genuine expression of her feelings and needs?

5. Should the story be taken as a joke, as it apparently was intended, at the expense of the female protagonist? What values might make it still seem a joke? What values might make it seem more serious than it was originally intended?

6. In light of the misogynistic theme, to what degree are you able to like the story?

7. Consider the locations of the story. How well are they described? Does the location in the tomb help to make the story seem more realistic than it otherwise might seem? How normal does it seem that the crucifixions of the thieves were carried out in public and that the dead thieves were left on open exhibition so that the soldier would need to be posted as a guard?

SIR ARTHUR CONAN DOYLE (1859–1930)

The Adventure of the Speckled Band   *1883*

On glancing over my notes of the seventy odd cases in which I have during the last eight years studied the methods of my friend Sherlock Holmes, I find many tragic, some comic, a large number merely strange, but none commonplace; for, working as he did rather for the love of his art than for the acquirement of wealth, he refused to associate himself with any investigation which did not tend towards the unusual, and even the fantastic. Of all these varied cases, however, I cannot recall any which presented more singular features than that which was associated with the well-known Surrey family of the Roylotts of Stoke Moran. The events in question occurred in the early days of my association with Holmes, when we were sharing rooms as bachelors in Baker Street. It is possible that I might have placed them upon record before, but a promise of secrecy was made at the time, from which I have only been freed during the last month by the untimely death of the lady to whom the pledge was given. It is perhaps as well that the facts should now come to light, for I have reasons to know that there are widespread rumours as to the death of Dr. Grimesby Roylott which tend to make the matter even more terrible than the truth.

It was early in April in the year '83 that I woke one morning to find Sherlock Holmes standing, fully dressed, by the side of my bed. He was a late riser, as a rule, and as the clock on the mantelpiece showed me that it was only a quarter-past seven, I blinked up at him in some surprise, and perhaps just a little resentment, for I was myself regular in my habits.

"Very sorry to knock you up,° Watson," said he, "but it's the common lot this morning. Mrs. Hudson has been knocked up, she retorted upon me, and I on you."

"What is it, then—a fire?"

"No; a client. It seems that <u>a young lady has arrived</u> in a considerable state   5
of excitement, who insists upon seeing me. She is waiting now in the sitting-room. Now, when young ladies wander about the metropolis at this hour of the morning, and knock sleepy people up out of their beds, I presume that it is something very pressing which they have to communicate. Should it prove to be an interesting case, you would, I am sure, wish to follow it from the outset. I thought, at any rate, that I should call you and give you the chance."

"My dear fellow, I would not miss it for anything."

⌈I had no keener pleasure than in following Holmes in his professional investigations, and in admiring the rapid deductions, as swift as intuitions, and yet always founded on a logical basis, with which he unravelled the problems which were submitted to him⌉ I rapidly threw on my clothes and was ready in a few minutes to accompany my friend down to the sitting-room. A lady dressed in black and heavily veiled, who had been sitting in the window, rose as we entered.

"Good-morning, madam," said Holmes cheerily. "My name is Sherlock Holmes. This is my intimate friend and associate, Dr. Watson, before whom you can speak as freely as before myself. Ha! I am glad to see that Mrs. Hudson has had the good sense to light the fire. Pray draw up to it, and I shall order you a cup of hot coffee, for I observe that you are shivering."

"It is not cold which makes me shiver," said the woman in a low voice, changing her seat as requested.

"What, then?"   10

"It is fear, Mr. Holmes. It is terror." She raised her veil as she spoke, and we could see that she was indeed in a pitiable state of agitation, her face all drawn and gray, with restless, frightened eyes, like those of some hunted animal. Her features and figure were those of a woman of thirty, but her hair was shot with premature gray, and her expression was weary and haggard. Sherlock Holmes ran her over with one of his quick, all-comprehensive glances.

"You must not fear," said he soothingly, bending forward and patting her forearm. "We shall soon set matters right, I have no doubt. You have come in by train this morning, I see."

"You know me, then?"

"No, but I observe the second half of a return ticket in the palm of your left glove. You must have started early, and yet you had a good drive in a dog-cart,° along heavy roads, before you reached the station."

knock you up: to wake up, a custom whereby a person was designated to make the rounds of a neighborhood and wake people up by knocking at their doors.
dog-cart: an open, horse-drawn cart with back-to-back seats.

The lady gave a violent start and stared in bewilderment at my companion.   15

"There is no mystery, my dear madam," said he, smiling. "The left arm of your jacket is spattered with mud in no less than seven places. The marks are perfectly fresh. There is no vehicle save a dog-cart which throws up mud in that way, and then only when you sit on the left-hand side of the driver."

"Whatever your reasons may be, you are perfectly correct," said she. "I started from home before six, reached Leatherhead at twenty past, and came in by the first train to Waterloo.° Sir, I can stand this strain no longer; I shall go mad if it continues. I have no one to turn to—none, save only one, who cares for me, and he, poor fellow, can be of little aid. I have heard of you, Mr. Holmes; I have heard of you from Mrs. Farintosh, whom you helped in the hour of her sore need. It was from her that I had your address. Oh, sir, do you not think that you could help me, too, and at least throw a little light through the dense darkness which surrounds me? At present it is out of my power to reward you for your services, but in a month or six weeks I shall be married, with the control of my own income, and then at least you shall not find me ungrateful."

Holmes turned to his desk and, unlocking it, drew out a small casebook, which he consulted.

"Farintosh," said he. "Ah yes, I recall the case; it was concerned with an opal tiara. I think it was before your time, Watson. I can only say, madam, that I shall be happy to devote the same care to your case as I did to that of your friend. As to reward, my profession is its own reward; but you are at liberty to defray whatever expenses I may be put to, at the time which suits you best. And now I beg that you will lay before us everything that may help us in forming an opinion upon the matter."

"Alas!" replied our visitor, "the very horror of my situation lies in the fact   20
that my fears are so vague, and my suspicions depend so entirely upon small points, which might seem trivial to another, that even he to whom of all others I have a right to look for help and advice looks upon all that I tell him about it as the fancies of a nervous woman. He does not say so, but I can read it from his soothing answers and averted eyes. But I have heard, Mr. Holmes, that you can see deeply into the manifold wickedness of the human heart. You may advise me how to walk amid the dangers which encompass me."

"I am all attention, madam."

"My name is Helen Stoner, and I am living with my stepfather, who is the last survivor of one of the oldest Saxon families in England, the Roylotts of Stoke Moran, on the western border of Surrey."

Holmes nodded his head. "The name is familiar to me," said he.

"The family was at one time among the richest in England, and the estates extended over the borders into Berkshire in the north, and Hampshire in the west. In the last century, however, four successive heirs were of a dissolute and wasteful disposition, and the family ruin was eventually completed by a gambler in the days of the Regency.° Nothing was left save a few acres of ground, and the two-hundred-year-old house, which is itself crushed under a heavy mortgage.

Waterloo: Waterloo Station in west London, the station for trains going to western England.

The Regency: the period from 1811 to 1820, when George III was declared incompetent and the Prince of Wales, later George IV (1820–1830), ruled as regent.

The last squire dragged out his existence there, living the horrible life of an aristo-cratic pauper; but his only son, my stepfather, seeing that he must adapt himself to the new conditions, obtained an advance from a relative, which enabled him to take a medical degree and went out to Calcutta, where, by his professional skill and his force of character, he established a large practice. In a fit of anger, however, caused by some robberies which had been perpetrated in the house, he beat his native butler to death and narrowly escaped a capital sentence. As it was, he suffered a long term of imprisonment and afterwards returned to England a morose and disappointed man.

"When Dr. Roylott was in India he married my mother, Mrs. Stoner, the   25
young widow of Major-General Stoner, of the Bengal Artillery. My sister Julia and I were twins, and we were only two years old at the time of my mother's re-marriage. She had a considerable sum of money—not less than £1000 a year°— and this she bequeathed to Dr. Roylott entirely while we resided with him, with a provision that a certain annual sum should be allowed to each of us in the event of our marriage. Shortly after our return to England my mother died—she was killed eight years ago in a railway accident near Crewe. Dr. Roylott then abandoned his attempts to establish himself in practice in London and took us to live with him in the old ancestral house at Stoke Moran. The money which my mother had left was enough for all our wants, and there seemed to be no obstacle to our happiness.

"But a terrible change came over our stepfather about this time. Instead of making friends and exchanging visits with our neighbours, who had at first been overjoyed to see a Roylott of Stoke Moran back in the old family seat, he shut himself up in his house and seldom came out save to indulge in ferocious quarrels with whoever might cross his path. Violence of temper approaching to mania has been hereditary in the men of the family, and in my stepfather's case it had, I believe, been intensified by his long residence in the tropics. A series of disgraceful brawls took place, two of which ended in the police-court, until at last he became the terror of the village, and the folks would fly at his approach, for he is a man of immense strength, and absolutely uncontrollable in his anger.

"Last week he hurled the local blacksmith over a parapet into a stream, and it was only by paying over all the money which I could gather together that I was able to avert another public exposure. He had no friends at all save the wandering gypsies, and he would give these vagabonds leave to encamp upon the few acres of bramble-covered land which represent the family estate, and would accept in return the hospitality of their tents, wandering away with them sometimes for weeks on end. He has a passion also for Indian animals, which are sent over to him by a correspondent, and he has at this moment a cheetah and a baboon, which wander freely over his grounds and are feared by the villagers almost as much as their master.

"You can imagine from what I say that my poor sister Julia and I had no great pleasure in our lives. No servant would stay with us, and for a long time we did all the work of the house. She was but thirty at the time of her death, and yet her hair had already begun to whiten, even as mine has."

"Your sister is dead, then?"

"She died just two years ago, and it is of her death that I wish to speak to   30

£1000: worth perhaps $100,000.00 or more today.

you. You can understand that, living the life which I have described, we were little likely to see anyone of our own age and position. We had, however, an aunt, my mother's maiden sister, Miss Honoria Westphail, who lives near Harrow, and we were occasionally allowed to pay short visits at this lady's house. Julia went there at Christmas two years ago, and met there a half-pay major of marines, to whom she became engaged. My stepfather learned of the engagement when my sister returned and offered no objection to the marriage; but within a fortnight of the day which had been fixed for the wedding, the terrible event occurred which has deprived me of my only companion."

Sherlock Holmes had been leaning back in his chair with his eyes closed and his head sunk in a cushion, but he half opened his lids now and glanced across at his visitor.

"Pray be precise as to details," he said.

"It is easy for me to be so, for every event of that dreadful time is seared into my memory. The manor-house is, as I have already said, very old, and only one wing is now inhabited. The bedrooms in this wing are on the ground floor, the sitting-rooms being in the central block of the buildings. Of these bedrooms the first is Dr. Roylott's, the second my sister's, and the third my own. There is no communication between them, but they all open out into the same corridor. Do I make myself plain?"

"Perfectly so."

"The windows of the three rooms open out upon the lawn. That fatal night Dr. Roylott had gone to his room early, though we knew that he had not retired to rest, for my sister was troubled by the smell of the strong Indian cigars which it was his custom to smoke. She left her room, therefore, and came into mine, where she sat for some time, chatting about her approaching wedding. At eleven o'clock she rose to leave me, but she paused at the door and looked back.

" 'Tell me, Helen,' said she, 'have you ever heard anyone whistle in the dead of the night?'

" 'Never,' said I.

" 'I suppose that you could not possibly whistle, yourself, in your sleep?'

" 'Certainly not. But why?'

" 'Because during the last few nights I have always, about three in the morning, heard a low, clear whistle. I am a light sleeper, and it has awakened me. I cannot tell where it came from—perhaps from the next room, perhaps from the lawn. I thought that I would just ask you whether you had heard it.'

" 'No, I have not. It must be those wretched gypsies in the plantation.'

" 'Very likely. And yet if it were on the lawn, I wonder that you did not hear it also.'

" 'Ah, but I sleep more heavily than you.'

" 'Well, it is of no great consequence, at any rate.' She smiled back at me, closed my door, and a few moments later I heard her key turn in the lock."

"Indeed," said Holmes. "Was it your custom always to lock yourselves in at night?"

"Always."

"And why?"

"I think that I mentioned to you that the doctor kept a cheetah and a baboon. We had no feeling of security unless our doors were locked."

"Quite so. Pray proceed with your statement."

Setting (handwritten, left margin)

"I could not sleep that night. A vague feeling of impending misfortune impressed me. My sister and I, you will recollect, were twins, and you know how subtle are the links which bind two souls which are so closely allied. It was a wild night. The wind was howling outside, and the rain was beating and splashing against the windows. Suddenly, amid all the hubbub of the gale, there burst forth the wild scream of a terrified woman. I knew that it was my sister's voice. I sprang from my bed, wrapped a shawl round me, and rushed into the corridor. As I opened my door I seemed to hear a low whistle, such as my sister described, and a few moments later a clanging sound, as if a mass of metal had fallen. As I ran down the passage, my sister's door was unlocked, and revolved slowly upon its hinges. I stared at it horror-stricken, not knowing what was about to issue from it. By the light of the corridor-lamp I saw my sister appear at the opening, her face blanched with terror, her hands groping for help, her whole figure swaying to and fro like that of a drunkard. I ran to her and threw my arms round her, but at that moment her knees seemed to give way and she fell to the ground. She writhed as one who is in terrible pain, and her limbs were dreadfully convulsed. At first I thought that she had not recognized me, but as I bent over her she suddenly shrieked out in a voice which I shall never forget, 'Oh, my God! Helen! It was the band! The speckled band!' There was something else which she would fain have said, and she stabbed with her finger into the air in the direction of the doctor's room, but a fresh convulsion seized her and choked her words. I rushed out, calling loudly for my stepfather, and I met him hastening from his room in his dressing-gown. When he reached my sister's side she was unconscious, and though he poured brandy down her throat and sent for medical aid from the village, all efforts were in vain, for she slowly sank and died without having recovered her consciousness. Such was the dreadful end of my beloved sister."

"One moment," said Holmes; "are you sure about this whistle and metallic sound? Could you swear to it?"

"That was what the county coroner asked me at the inquiry. It is my strong impression that I heard it, and yet, among the crash of the gale and the creaking of an old house, I may possibly have been deceived."

"Was your sister dressed?"

"No, she was in her night-dress. In her right hand was found the charred stump of a match, and in her left a match-box."

"Showing that she had struck a light and looked about her when the alarm took place. That is important. And what conclusions did the coroner come to?"

"He investigated the case with great care, for Dr. Roylott's conduct had long been notorious in the county, but he was unable to find any satisfactory cause of death. My evidence showed that the door had been fastened upon the inner side, and the windows were blocked by old-fashioned shutters with broad iron bars, which were secured every night. The walls were carefully sounded and were shown to be quite solid all round, and the flooring was also thoroughly examined, with the same result. The chimney is wide, but is barred up by four large staples. It is certain, therefore, that my sister was quite alone when she met her end. Besides, there were no marks of any violence upon her."

"How about poison?"

"The doctors examined her for it, but without success."

50

55

"What do you think that this unfortunate lady died of, then?"

"It is my belief that she died of pure fear and nervous shock, though what   60
it was that frightened her I cannot imagine."

"Were there gypsies in the plantation at the time?"

"Yes, there are nearly always some there."

"Ah, and what did you gather from this allusion to a band—a speckled band?"

"Sometimes I have thought that it was merely the wild talk of delirium, sometimes that it may have referred to some band of people, perhaps to these very
gypsies in the plantation. I do not know whether the spotted handkerchiefs which
so many of them wear over their heads might have suggested the strange adjective
which she used."

Holmes shook his head like a man who is far from being satisfied.   *Note. He   65
doesn't show
"These are very deep waters," said he; "pray go on with your narrative."   his
feeling

"Two years have passed since then, and my life has been until lately lonelier
than ever. A month ago, however, a dear friend, whom I have known for many
years, has done me the honour to ask my hand in marriage. His name is Armitage—
Percy Armitage—the second son of Mr. Armitage, of Crane Water, near Reading.
My stepfather has offered no opposition to the match, and we are to be married
in the course of the spring. Two days ago some repairs were started in the west
wing of the building, and my bedroom wall has been pierced, so that I have had
to move into the chamber in which my sister died, and to sleep in the very bed
in which she slept. Imagine, then, my thrill of terror when last night, as I lay
awake, thinking over her terrible fate, I suddenly heard in the silence of the night
the low whistle which had been the herald of her own death. I sprang up and lit
the lamp, but nothing was to be seen in the room. I was too shaken to go to
bed again, however, so I dressed, and as soon as it was daylight I slipped down,
got a dog-cart at the Crown Inn, which is opposite, and drove to Leatherhead,
from whence I have come on this morning with the one object of seeing you
and asking your advice."

"You have done wisely," said my friend. "But have you told me all?"

"Yes, all."

"Miss Roylott, you have not. You are screening your stepfather."   70

"Why, what do you mean?"

For answer Holmes pushed back the frill of black lace which fringed the
hand that lay upon our visitor's knee. Five little livid spots, the marks of four
fingers and a thumb, were printed upon the white wrist.

"You have been cruelly used," said Holmes.

The lady coloured deeply and covered over her injured wrist. "He is a hard
man," she said, "and perhaps he hardly knows his own strength."

There was a long silence, during which Holmes leaned his chin upon his   75
hands and stared into the crackling fire.

"This is a very deep business," he said at last. "There are a thousand details
which I should desire to know before I decide upon our course of action. Yet we
have not a moment to lose. If we were to come to Stoke Moran to-day, would it
be possible for us to see over these rooms without the knowledge of your stepfather?"

"As it happens, he spoke of coming into town to-day upon some most important business. It is probable that he will be away all day, and that there would be

nothing to disturb you. We have a housekeeper now, but she is old and foolish, and I could easily get her out of the way."

"Excellent. You are not averse to this trip, Watson?"

"By no means."

"Then we shall both come. What are you going to do yourself?"   80

"I have one or two things which I would wish to do now that I am in town. But I shall return by the twelve o'clock train, so as to be there in time for your coming."

"And you may expect us early in the afternoon. I have myself some small business matters to attend to. Will you not wait and breakfast?"

"No, I must go. My heart is lightened already since I have confided my trouble to you. I shall look forward to seeing you again this afternoon." She dropped her thick black veil over her face and glided from the room.

"And what do you think of it all, Watson?" asked Sherlock Holmes, leaning back in his chair.

"It seems to me to be a most dark and sinister business."   85

"Dark enough and sinister enough."

"Yet if the lady is correct in saying that the flooring and walls are sound, and that the door, window, and chimney are impassable, then her sister must have been undoubtedly alone when she met her mysterious end."

"What becomes, then, of these nocturnal whistles, and what of the very peculiar words of the dying woman?"

"I cannot think."

"When you combine the ideas of whistles at night, the presence of a band   90
of gypsies who are on intimate terms with this old doctor, the fact that we have every reason to believe that the doctor has an interest in preventing his stepdaughter's marriage, the dying allusion to a band, and, finally, the fact that Miss Helen Stoner heard a metallic clang, which might have been caused by one of those metal bars that secured the shutters falling back into its place, I think that there is good ground to think that the mystery may be cleared along those lines."

"But what, then, did the gypsies do?"

"I cannot imagine."

"I see many objections to any such theory."

"And so do I. It is precisely for that reason that we are going to Stoke Moran this day. I want to see whether the objections are fatal, or if they may be explained away. But what in the name of the devil!"

The ejaculation had been drawn from my companion by the fact that our   95
door had been suddenly dashed open, and that a huge man had framed himself in the aperture. His costume was a peculiar mixture of the professional and of the agricultural, having a black tophat, a long frock-coat, and a pair of high gaiters,° with a hunting-crop swinging in his hand. So tall was he that his hat actually brushed the cross bar of the doorway, and his breadth seemed to span it across from side to side. A large face, seared with a thousand wrinkles, burned yellow with the sun, and marked with every evil passion, was turned from one to the other of us, while his deep-set, bile-shot eyes, and his high, thin, fleshless nose, gave him somewhat the resemblance to a fierce old bird of prey. Comparison.

gaiters: leggings.

"Which of you is Holmes?" asked this apparition.

"My name, sir; but you have the advantage of me," said my companion quietly.

"I am Dr. Grimesby Roylott, of Stoke Moran."

"Indeed, Doctor," said Holmes blandly. "Pray take a seat."

"I will do nothing of the kind. My stepdaughter has been here. I have traced   100
her. What has she been saying to you?" *He's rude,*

"It is a little cold for the time of the year," said Holmes.

"What has she been saying to you?" screamed the old man furiously. *He can't*

"But I have heard that the crocuses promise well," continued my companion *control*
imperturbably.   *himself.*

"Ha! You put me off, do you?" said our new visitor, taking a step forward
and shaking his hunting-crop. "I know you, you scoundrel! I have heard of you
before. You are Holmes, the meddler." *Note the contrast*

My friend smiled.   *of the 2 characters,*   105

"Holmes, the busybody!"

His smile broadened.

"Holmes, the Scotland Yard Jack-in-office!"

Holmes chuckled heartily. "Your conversation is most entertaining," said
he. "When you go out close the door, for there is a decided draught." *Polite but*
                                                                        clear.
"I will go when I have said my say. Don't you dare to meddle with my affairs.   110
I know that Miss Stoner has been here. I traced her! I am a dangerous man to
fall foul of! See here." He stepped swiftly forward, seized the poker, and bent it
into a curve with his huge brown hands.

"See that you keep yourself out of my grip," he snarled, and hurling the
twisted poker into the fireplace he strode out of the room.

"He seems a very amiable person," said Holmes, laughing. "I am not quite
so bulky, but if he had remained I might have shown him that my grip was not
much more feeble than his own." As he spoke he picked up the steel poker and,
with a sudden effort, straightened it out again. *They're matched adversaries*

"Fancy his having the insolence to confound me with the official detective
force! This incident gives zest to our investigation, however, and I only trust that
our little friend will not suffer from her imprudence in allowing this brute to trace
her. And now, Watson, we shall order breakfast, and afterwards I shall walk down
to Doctors' Commons,° where I hope to get some data which may help us in
this matter."

It was nearly one o'clock when Sherlock Holmes returned from his excursion.
He held in his hand a sheet of blue paper, scrawled over with notes and figures.

"I have seen the will of the deceased wife," said he. "To determine its exact   115
meaning I have been obliged to work out the present prices of the investments
with which it is concerned. The total income, which at the time of the wife's death
was little short of £1100, is now, through the fall in agricultural prices, not more
than £750. Each daughter can claim an income of £250, in case of marriage. It is
evident, therefore, that if both girls had married, this beauty would have had a
mere pittance, while even one of them would cripple him to a very serious extent.

Doctors' Commons: the place in London where records of wills and other deeds were
kept in official storage.

My morning's work has not been wasted, since it has proved that he has the very strongest motives for standing in the way of anything of the sort. And now, Watson, this is too serious for dawdling, especially as the old man is aware that we are interesting ourselves in his affairs; so if you are ready, we shall call a cab and drive to Waterloo. I should be very much obliged if you would slip your revolver into your pocket. An Eley's No. 2° is an excellent argument with gentlemen who can twist steel pokers into knots. That and a tooth-brush are, I think, all that we need."

At Waterloo we were fortunate in catching a train for Leatherhead, where we hired a trap° at the station inn and drove for four or five miles through the lovely Surrey lanes. It was a perfect day, with a bright sun and a few fleecy clouds in the heavens. The trees and wayside hedges were just throwing out their first green shoots, and the air was full of the pleasant smell of the moist earth. To me at least there was a strange contrast between the sweet promise of the spring and this sinister quest upon which we were engaged. My companion sat in the front of the trap, his arms folded, his hat pulled down over his eyes, and his chin sunk upon his breast, buried in the deepest thought. Suddenly, however, he started, tapped me on the shoulder, and pointed over the meadows.

"Look there!" said he.

A heavily timbered park stretched up in a gentle slope, thickening into a grove at the highest point. From amid the branches there jutted out the gray gables and high roof-tree of a very old mansion.

"Stoke Moran?" said he.

"Yes, sir, that be the house of Dr. Grimesby Roylott," remarked the driver.   120

"There is some building going on there," said Holmes; "that is where we are going."

"There's the village," said the driver, pointing to a cluster of roofs some distance to the left; "but if you want to get to the house, you'll find it shorter to get over this stile, and so by the foot-path over the fields. There it is, where the lady is walking."

"And the lady, I fancy, is Miss Stoner," observed Holmes, shading his eyes. "Yes, I think we had better do as you suggest."

We got off, paid our fare, and the trap rattled back on its way to Leatherhead.

"I thought it as well," said Holmes as we climbed the stile, "that this fellow   125 should think we had come here as architects, or on some definite business. It may stop his gossip. Good-afternoon, Miss Stoner. You see that we have been as good as our word."

Our client of the morning had hurried forward to meet us with a face which spoke her joy. "I have been waiting so eagerly for you," she cried, shaking hands with us warmly. "All has turned out splendidly. Dr. Roylott has gone to town, and it is unlikely that he will be back before evening."

"We have had the pleasure of making the doctor's acquaintance," said Holmes, and in a few words he sketched out what had occurred. Miss Stoner turned white to the lips as she listened.

"Good heavens!" she cried, "he has followed me, then."

Eley's No. 2: a handgun.
trap: a small horse-drawn coach.

"So it appears."

"He is so cunning that I never know when I am safe from him. What will   130
he say when he returns?"

"He must guard himself, for he may find that there is someone more cunning
than himself upon his track. You must lock yourself up from him to-night. If he
is violent, we shall take you away to your aunt's at Harrow. Now, we must make
the best use of our time, so kindly take us at once to the rooms which we are to
examine."

The building was of gray, lichen-blotched stone, with a high central portion
and two curving wings, like the claws of a crab, thrown out on each side. In one
of these wings the windows were broken and blocked with wooden boards, while
the roof was partly caved in, a picture of ruin. The central portion was in little
better repair, but the right-hand block was comparatively modern, and the blinds
in the windows, with the blue smoke curling up from the chimneys, showed that
this was where the family resided. Some scaffolding had been erected against the
end wall, and the stone-work had been broken into, but there were no signs of
any workmen at the moment of our visit. Holmes walked slowly up and down
the ill-trimmed lawn and examined with deep attention the outsides of the windows.

"This, I take it, belongs to the room in which you used to sleep, the centre
one to your sister's, and the one next to the main building to Dr. Roylott's chamber?"

"Exactly so. But I am now sleeping in the middle one."

"Pending the alterations, as I understand. By the way, there does not seem   135
to be any very pressing need for repairs at that end wall."

"There were none. I believe that it was an excuse to move me from my
room."

"Ah! that is suggestive. Now, on the other side of this narrow wing runs
the corridor from which these three rooms open. There are windows in it, of
course?"

"Yes, but very small ones. Too narrow for anyone to pass through."

"As you both locked your doors at night, your rooms were unapproachable
from that side. Now, would you have the kindness to go into your room and bar
your shutters?"

Miss Stoner did so, and Holmes, after a careful examination through the   140
open window, endeavoured in every way to force the shutter open, but without
success. There was no slit through which a knife could be passed to raise the
bar. Then with his lens he tested the hinges, but they were of solid iron, built
firmly into the massive masonry. "Hum!" said he, scratching his chin in some
perplexity, "my theory certainly presents some difficulties. No one could pass these
shutters if they were bolted. Well, we shall see if the inside throws any light upon
the matter."

A small side door led into the whitewashed corridor from which the three
bedrooms opened. Holmes refused to examine the third chamber, so we passed
at once to the second, that in which Miss Stoner was now sleeping, and in which
her sister had met with her fate. It was a homely little room, with a low ceiling
and a gaping fireplace, after the fashion of old country-houses. A brown chest of
drawers stood in one corner, a narrow white-counterpaned bed in another, and a
dressing-table on the left-hand side of the window. These articles, with two small

wicker-work chairs, made up all the furniture in the room save for a square of Wilton carpet in the centre. The boards round and the panelling of the walls were of brown, worm-eaten oak, so old and discoloured that it may have dated from the original building of the house. Holmes drew one of the chairs into a corner and sat silent, while his eyes travelled round and round and up and down, taking in every detail of the apartment.

"Where does that bell communicate with?" he asked at last, pointing to a thick bell-rope° which hung down beside the bed, the tassel actually lying upon the pillow.

"It goes to the housekeeper's room."

"It looks newer than the other things?"

"Yes, it was only put there a couple of years ago."   145

"Your sister asked for it, I suppose?"

"No, I never heard of her using it. We used always to get what we wanted for ourselves."

"Indeed, it seemed unnecessary to put so nice a bell-pull there. You will excuse me for a few minutes while I satisfy myself as to this floor." He threw himself down upon his face with his lens in his hand and crawled swiftly backward and forward, examining minutely the cracks between the boards. Then he did the same with the wood-work with which the chamber was panelled. Finally he walked over to the bed and spent some time in staring at it and in running his eye up and down the wall. Finally he took the bell-rope in his hand and gave it a brisk tug.

"Why, it's a dummy," said he.

"Won't it ring?"   150

"No, it is not even attached to a wire. This is very interesting. You can see now that it is fastened to a hook just above where the little opening for the ventilator is."

"How very absurd! I never noticed that before."

"Very strange!" muttered Holmes, pulling at the rope. "There are one or two very singular points about this room. For example, what a fool a builder must be to open a ventilator into another room, when, with the same trouble, he might have communicated with the outside air!"

"That is also quite modern," said the lady.

"Done about the same time as the bell-rope?" remarked Holmes.   155

"Yes, there were several little changes carried out about that time."

"They seem to have been of a most interesting character—dummy bell-ropes, and ventilators which do not ventilate. With your permission, Miss Stoner, we shall now carry our researches into the inner apartment."

Dr. Grimesby Roylott's chamber was larger than that of his stepdaughter, but was as plainly furnished. A camp-bed, a small wooden shelf full of books, mostly of a technical character, an armchair beside the bed, a plain wooden chair against the wall, a round table, and a large iron safe were the principal things which met the eye. Holmes walked slowly round and examined each and all of them with the keenest interest.

"What's in here?" he asked, tapping the safe.

bell rope: a rope attached to a bell in the quarters of a servant so that the master or mistress could use it as an instant demand for service.

"My stepfather's business papers." 160

"Oh! you have seen inside, then?"

"Only once, some years ago. I remember that it was full of papers."

"There isn't a cat in it, for example?" *What is in it?*

"No. What a strange idea!"

"Well, look at this!" He took up a small saucer of milk which stood on the 165
top of it.

"No; we don't keep a cat. But there is a cheetah and a baboon."

"Ah, yes, of course! Well, a cheetah is just a big cat, and yet a saucer of
milk does not go very far in satisfying its wants, I daresay. There is one point
which I should wish to determine." He squatted down in front of the wooden
chair and examined the seat of it with the greatest attention.

"Thank you. That is quite settled," said he, rising and putting his lens in
his pocket. "Hello! Here is something interesting!"

The object which had caught his eye was a small dog lash° hung on one
corner of the bed. The lash, however, was curled upon itself and tied so as to
make a loop of whipcord.

"What do you make of that, Watson?" 170

"It's a common enough lash. But I don't know why it should be tied."

"That is not quite so common, is it? Ah, me! it's a wicked world, and when
a clever man turns his brains to crime it is the worst of all. I think that I have
seen enough now, Miss Stoner, and with your permission we shall walk out upon
the lawn." *He has solved the crime already.*

I had never seen my friend's face so grim or his brow so dark as it was
when we turned from the scene of this investigation. We had walked several times
up and down the lawn, neither Miss Stoner nor myself liking to break in upon
his thoughts before he roused himself from his reverie.

"It is very essential, Miss Stoner," said he, "that you should absolutely follow
my advice in every respect."

"I shall most certainly do so." 175

"The matter is too serious for any hesitation. Your life may depend upon
your compliance."

"I assure you that I am in your hands."

"In the first place, both my friend and I must spend the night in your room."

Both Miss Stoner and I gazed at him in astonishment.

"Yes, it must be so. Let me explain. I believe that that is the village inn 180
over there?"

"Yes, that is the Crown."

"Very good. Your windows would be visible from there?"

"Certainly."

"You must confine yourself to your room, on pretence of a headache, when
your stepfather comes back. Then when you hear him retire for the night, you
must open the shutters of your window, undo the hasp, put your lamp there as a
signal to us, and then withdraw quietly with everything which you are likely to
want into the room which you used to occupy. I have no doubt that, in spite of
the repairs, you could manage there for one night."

"Oh, yes, easily." 185

lash: leash

"The rest you will leave in our hands."

"But what will you do?"

"We shall spend the night in your room, and we shall investigate the cause of this noise which has disturbed you."

"I believe, Mr. Holmes, that you have already made up your mind," said Miss Stoner, laying her hand upon my companion's sleeve.

"Perhaps I have."   190

"Then, for pity's sake, tell me what was the cause of my sister's death."

"I should prefer to have clearer proofs before I speak."

"You can at least tell me whether my own thought is correct, and if she died from some sudden fright."

"No, I do not think so. I think that there was probably some more tangible cause. And now, Miss Stoner, we must leave you, for if Dr. Roylott returned and saw us our journey would be in vain. Good-bye, and be brave, for if you will do what I have told you you may rest assured that we shall soon drive away the dangers that threaten you."

Sherlock Holmes and I had no difficulty in engaging a bedroom and sitting-   195
room at the Crown Inn. They were on the upper floor, and from our window we could command a view of the avenue gate, and of the inhabited wing of Stoke Moran Manor House. At dusk we saw Dr. Grimesby Roylott drive past, his huge form looming up beside the little figure of the lad who drove him. The boy had some slight difficulty in undoing the heavy iron gates, and we heard the hoarse roar of the doctor's voice and saw the fury with which he shook his clinched fists at him. The trap drove on, and a few minutes later we saw a sudden light spring up among the trees as the lamp was lit in one of the sitting-rooms.

"Do you know, Watson," said Holmes as we sat together in the gathering darkness, "I have really some scruples as to taking you to-night. There is a distinct element of danger."

"Can I be of assistance?"

"Your presence might be invaluable."

"Then I shall certainly come."

"It is very kind of you."   200

"You speak of danger. You have evidently seen more in these rooms than was visible to me."

"No, but I fancy that I may have deduced a little more. I imagine that you saw all that I did."

"I saw nothing remarkable save the bell-rope, and what purpose that could answer I confess is more than I imagine."

"You saw the ventilator, too?"

"Yes, but I do not think that it is such a very unusual thing to have a small   205
opening between two rooms. It was so small that a rat could hardly pass through."

"I knew that we should find a ventilator before ever we came to Stoke Moran."

"My dear Holmes!"

"Oh, yes, I did. You remember in her statement she said that her sister could smell Dr. Roylott's cigar. Now, of course that suggested at once that there must be a communication between the two rooms. It could only be a small one, or it would have been remarked upon at the coroner's inquiry. I deduced a ventilator."

"But what harm can there be in that?"

"Well, there is at least a curious coincidence of dates. A ventilator is made, 210 a cord is hung, and a lady who sleeps in the bed dies. Does not that strike you?"

"I cannot as yet see any connection."

"Did you observe anything very peculiar about that bed?"

"No."

"It was clamped to the floor. Did you ever see a bed fastened like that before?"

"I cannot say that I have." 215

"The lady could not move her bed. It must always be in the same relative position to the ventilator and to the rope—or so we may call it, since it was clearly never meant for a bell-pull."

"Holmes," I cried, "I seem to see dimly what you are hinting at. We are only just in time to prevent some subtle and horrible crime."

"Subtle enough and horrible enough. When a doctor does go wrong he is the first of criminals. He has nerve and he has knowledge. Palmer and Pritchard were among the heads of their profession. This man strikes even deeper, but I think, Watson, that we shall be able to strike deeper still. But we shall have horrors enough before the night is over; for goodness' sake let us have a quiet pipe and turn our minds for a few hours to something more cheerful."

About nine o'clock the light among the trees was extinguished, and all was dark in the direction of the Manor House. Two hours passed slowly away, and then, suddenly, just at the stroke of eleven, a single bright light shone out right in front of us.

"That is our signal," said Holmes, springing to his feet; "it comes from 220 the middle window."

As we passed out he exchanged a few words with the landlord, explaining that we were going on a late visit to an acquaintance, and that it was possible that we might spend the night there. A moment later we were out on the dark road, a chill wind blowing in our faces, and one yellow light twinkling in front of us through the gloom to guide us on our sombre errand.

There was little difficulty in entering the grounds, for unrepaired breaches gaped in the old park wall. Making our way among the trees, we reached the lawn, crossed it, and were about to enter through the window when out from a clump of laurel bushes there darted what seemed to be a hideous and distorted child, who threw itself upon the grass with writhing limbs and then ran swiftly across the lawn into the darkness.

"My God!" I whispered; "did you see it?"

Holmes was for the moment as startled as I. His hand closed like a vise upon my wrist in his agitation. Then he broke into a low laugh and put his lips to my ear.

"It is a nice household," he murmured. "That is the baboon." 225

I had forgotten the strange pets which the doctor affected. There was a cheetah, too; perhaps we might find it upon our shoulders at any moment. I confess that I felt easier in my mind when, after following Holmes's example and slipping off my shoes, I found myself inside the bedroom. My companion noiselessly closed the shutters, moved the lamp onto the table, and cast his eyes round the room. All was as we had seen it in the daytime. Then creeping up to me and making a trumpet of his hand, he whispered into my ear again so gently that it was all that I could do to distinguish the words:

"The least sound would be fatal to our plans."

I nodded to show that I had heard.

"We must sit without light. He would see it through the ventilator."

I nodded again.   230

"Do not go asleep; your very life may depend upon it. Have your pistol ready in case we should need it. I will sit on the side of the bed, and you in that chair."

I took out my revolver and laid it on the corner of the table.

Holmes had brought up a long thin cane, and this he placed upon the bed beside him. By it he laid the box of matches and the stump of a candle. Then he turned down the lamp, and we were left in darkness.

How shall I ever forget that dreadful vigil? I could not hear a sound, not even the drawing of a breath, and yet I knew that my companion sat open-eyed, within a few feet of me, in the same state of nervous tension in which I was myself. The shutters cut off the least ray of light, and we waited in absolute darkness. From outside came the occasional cry of a night-bird, and once at our very window a long drawn catlike whine, which told us that the cheetah was indeed at liberty. Far away we could hear the deep tones of the parish clock, which boomed out every quarter of an hour. How long they seemed, those quarters! Twelve struck, and one and two and three, and still we sat waiting silently for whatever might befall.

Suddenly there was the momentary gleam of a light up in the direction of   235
the ventilator, which vanished immediately, but was succeeded by a strong smell of burning oil and heated metal. Someone in the next room had lit a dark-lantern. I heard a gentle sound of movement, and then all was silent once more, though the smell grew stronger. For half an hour I sat with straining ears. Then suddenly another sound became audible—a very gentle, soothing sound, like that of a small jet of steam escaping continually from a kettle. The instant that we heard it, Holmes sprang from the bed, struck a match, and lashed furiously with his cane at the bell-pull.

"You see it, Watson?" he yelled. "You see it?"

But I saw nothing. At the moment when Holmes struck the light I heard a low, clear whistle, but the sudden glare flashing into my weary eyes made it impossible for me to tell what it was at which my friend lashed so savagely. I could, however, see that his face was deadly pale and filled with horror and loathing.

He had ceased to strike and was gazing up at the ventilator when suddenly there broke from the silence of the night the most horrible cry to which I have ever listened. It swelled up louder and louder, a hoarse yell of pain and fear and anger all mingled in the one dreadful shriek. They say that away down in the village, and even in the distant parsonage, that cry raised the sleepers from their beds. It struck cold to our hearts, and I stood gazing at Holmes, and he at me, until the last echoes of it had died away into the silence from which it rose.

"What can it mean?" I gasped.

"It means that it is all over," Holmes answered. "And perhaps, after all, it   240
is for the best. Take your pistol, and we will enter Dr. Roylott's room."

With a grave face he lit the lamp and led the way down the corridor. Twice he struck at the chamber door without any reply from within. Then he turned the handle and entered, I at his heels, with the cocked pistol in my hand.

It was a singular sight which met our eyes. On the table stood a dark-lantern with the shutter half open, throwing a brilliant beam of light upon the iron safe, the door of which was ajar. Beside this table, on the wooden chair, sat Dr. Grimesby Roylott, clad in a long gray dressing-gown, his bare ankles protruding beneath, and his feet thrust into red heelless Turkish slippers. Across his lap lay the short stock with the long lash which we had noticed during the day. His chin was cocked upward and his eyes were fixed in a dreadful, rigid stare at the corner of the ceiling. Round his brow he had a peculiar yellow band, with brownish speckles, which seemed to be bound tightly round his head. As we entered he made neither sound nor motion.

"The band! the speckled band!" whispered Holmes.

I took a step forward. In an instant his strange headgear began to move, and there reared itself from among his hair the squat diamond-shaped head and puffed neck of a loathsome serpent.

"It is a swamp adder!" cried Holmes; "the deadliest snake in India. He has   245
died within ten seconds of being bitten. Violence does, in truth, recoil upon the violent, and the schemer falls into the pit which he digs for another. Let us thrust this creature back into its den, and we can then remove Miss Stoner to some place of shelter and let the county police know what has happened."

As he spoke he drew the dog-whip swiftly from the dead man's lap, and throwing the noose round the reptile's neck he drew it from its horrid perch and, carrying it at arm's length, threw it into the iron safe, which he closed upon it.

Such are the true facts of the death of Dr. Grimesby Roylott, of Stoke Moran. It is not necessary that I should prolong a narrative which has already run to too great a length by telling how we broke the sad news to the terrified girl, how we conveyed her by the morning train to the care of her good aunt at Harrow, of how the slow process of official inquiry came to the conclusion that the doctor met his fate while discreetly playing with a dangerous pet. The little which I had yet to learn of the case was told me by Sherlock Holmes as we travelled back next day.

"I had," said he, "come to an entirely erroneous conclusion which shows, my dear Watson, how dangerous it always is to reason from insufficient data. The presence of the gypsies, and the use of the word 'band,' which was used by the poor girl, no doubt to explain the appearance which she had caught a hurried glimpse of by the light of her match, were sufficient to put me upon an entirely wrong scent. I can only claim the merit that I instantly reconsidered my position when, however, it became clear to me that whatever danger threatened an occupant of the room could not come either from the window or the door. My attention was speedily drawn, as I have already remarked to you, to this ventilator, and to the bell-rope which hung down to the bed. The discovery that this was a dummy, and that the bed was clamped to the floor, instantly gave rise to the suspicion that the rope was there as bridge for something passing through the hole and coming to the bed. The idea of a snake instantly occurred to me, and when I coupled it with my knowledge that the doctor was furnished with a supply of creatures from India, I felt that I was probably on the right track. The idea of using a form of poison which could not possibly be discovered by any chemical test was just such a one as would occur to a clever and ruthless man who had had an Eastern training. The rapidity with which such a poison would take effect would also, from his point of view, be an advantage. It would be a sharp-eyed coroner, indeed, who could distinguish <u>the two little dark punctures</u> which would show where the poison fangs had done their work. Then I thought of the <u>whistle.</u> Of course he must recall the snake before the morning light revealed it to the victim. He had trained it, probably by the use of the <u>milk</u> which we saw, to return to him when summoned. He would put it through this ventilator at the hour that he thought best, with the certainty that it would crawl down the rope and land on the bed. It might or might not bite the occupant, perhaps she might escape every night for a week, but sooner or later she must fall a victim.

"I had come to these conclusions before ever I had entered his room. An inspection of his chair showed me this: he had been in the habit of standing on it, which of course would be necessary in order that he should reach the ventilator. The sight of the safe, the saucer of milk, and the loop of whipcord were enough to finally dispel any doubts which may have remained. The metallic clang heard by Miss Stoner was obviously caused by her stepfather hastily closing the door of his safe upon its terrible occupant. Having once made up my mind, you know the steps which I took in order to put the matter to the proof. I heard the creature <u>hiss</u> as I have no doubt that you did also, and <u>I instantly lit the light and attacked it.</u>"

"With the result of driving it through the ventilator."

250

"And also with the result of causing it to turn upon its master at the other side. Some of the blows of my cane came home and <u>roused its snakish temper,</u> so that it flew upon the first person it saw. In this way I am no doubt indirectly responsible for Dr. Grimesby Roylott's death, and <u>I cannot say that it is likely to weigh very heavily upon my conscience.</u>" Tone

QUESTIONS

1. Who tells us the story of "The Adventure of the Speckled Band"? Doyle? Doctor Watson? Sherlock Holmes? Who is the "I" in the first sentence?

2. What do the first four or five paragraphs of the story tell us about the relationship between Watson and Holmes? How well do they know each other? What sort of regard do they have for each other? Why does Watson admire Holmes?

3. How does Watson get drawn into the case? What qualities does he have as a storyteller? Could the story be effectively told if, for example, Sherlock Holmes himself had been the teller? What can Watson say that Holmes could not say?

4. What does the discussion about the ticket and the mud indicate about Holmes's ability as an observer? Why do you think that Doyle includes the discussion as early in the story as he does?

5. According to Helen Stoner, what sort of person is Dr. Roylott? What sort of reputation does he have locally? How does he impress Holmes when he comes in? Has he been kind or cruel to Helen?

6. Why is the detail important about the impending marriages of, first, Julia and, second, Helen?

7. Why are the references to the nearby gypsies introduced?

8. Describe Holmes's method as an investigator. At what point do you think he concludes that Roylott is the murderer?

9. Describe Holmes's plan to foil Roylott. How do you learn about it?

10. Is the story more about the mystery or about Holmes? Is Holmes only a one-dimensional person, or do you learn more about his character as the story progresses?

11. Do you like this story? Try to explain reasons for either liking or disliking it.

ANTON CHEKHOV (1860–1904)

The Bear: A Joke in One Act   *1900*

CAST OF CHARACTERS

> Mrs. Popov. *A widow of seven months, Mrs. Popov is small and pretty, with dimples. She is a landowner. At the start of the play, she is pining away in memory of her dead husband.*
> Grigory Stepanovich Smirnov. *Easily angered and loud, Smirnov is older. He is a landowner, too, and a gentleman farmer of some substance.*
> Luka. *Luka is Mrs. Popov's footman (a servant whose main tasks were to wait table and attend the carriages, in addition to general duties). He is old enough to feel secure in telling Mrs. Popov what he thinks.*
> Gardener, Coachman, Workmen, *who enter at the end.*

The drawing room of MRS. POPOV'S country home.

[*MRS. POPOV, in deep mourning, does not remove her eyes from a photograph.*]

Luka.   It isn't right, madam . . . you're only destroying yourself. . . . The chambermaid and the cook have gone off berry picking; every living being is rejoicing; even the cat knows how to be content, walking around the yard catching birds, and you sit in your room all day as if it were a convent, and you don't take pleasure in anything. Yes, really! Almost a year has passed since you've gone out of the house!

Mrs. Popov.   And I shall never go out. . . . What for? My life is already ended. *He* lies in his grave; I have buried myself in these four walls . . . we are both dead.

Luka.   There you go again! Your husband is dead, that's as it was meant to be, it's the will of God, may he rest in peace. . . . You've done your mourning and that will do. You can't go on weeping and mourning forever. My wife died when her time came, too. . . . Well? I grieved, I wept for a month, and that was enough for her; the old lady wasn't worth a second more. [*Sighs*.] You've forgotten all your neighbors. You don't go anywhere or accept any calls. We live, so to speak, like spiders. We never see the light. The mice have eaten my uniform. It isn't as if there weren't any nice neighbors—the district is full of them . . . there's a regiment stationed at Riblov, such officers—they're like candy—you'll never get your fill of them! And in the barracks, never a Friday goes by without a dance; and, if you please, the military band plays music every day. . . . Yes, madam, my dear lady: you're young, beautiful, in the full bloom of youth—if only you took a little pleasure in life . . . beauty doesn't last forever, you know! In ten years' time, you'll be wanting to wave your fanny in front of the officers—and it will be too late.

MRS. POPOV [*determined*].   I must ask you never to talk to me like that! You know that when Mr. Popov died, life lost all its salt for me. It may seem to you that I am alive, but that's only conjecture! I vowed to wear mourning to my grave and not to see the light of day. . . . Do you hear me? May his departed spirit see how much I love him. . . . Yes, I know, it's no mystery to you that he was often mean to me, cruel . . . and even unfaithful, but I shall remain true to the grave and show him I know how to love. There, beyond the grave, he will see me as I was before his death. . . .

LUKA.   Instead of talking like that, you should be taking a walk in the garden or have Toby or Giant harnessed and go visit some of the neighbors . . .

MRS. POPOV.   Ai! [*She weeps*.]

LUKA.   Madam! Dear lady! What's the matter with you! Christ be with you!

MRS. POPOV.   Oh, how he loved Toby! He always used to ride on him to visit the Korchagins or the Vlasovs. How wonderfully he rode! How graceful he was when he pulled at the reins with all his strength! Do you remember? Toby, Toby! Tell them to give him an extra bag of oats today.

LUKA.   Yes, madam.

[*Sound of loud ringing*.]

MRS. POPOV [*shudders*].   Who's that? Tell them I'm not at home!

LUKA.   Of course, madam. [*He exits*.]

MRS. POPOV [*alone. Looks at the photograph*].   You will see, Nicholas, how much I can love and forgive . . . my love will die only when I do, when my poor heart stops beating. [*Laughing through her tears*.] Have you no shame? I'm a good girl, a virtuous little wife. I've locked myself in and I'll be true to you to the grave, and you . . . aren't you ashamed, you chubby cheeks? You deceived me, you made scenes, for weeks on end you left me alone . . .

LUKA [*enters, alarmed*].   Madam, somebody is asking for you. He wants to see you. . . .

MRS. POPOV.   But didn't you tell them that since the death of my husband, I don't see anybody?

LUKA.   I did, but he didn't want to listen; he spoke about some very important business.

MRS. POPOV.   I am *not at home*!

LUKA. That's what I told him . . . but . . . the devil . . . he cursed and pushed past me right into the room . . . he's in the dining room right now.

MRS. POPOV [*losing her temper*]. Very well, let him come in . . . such manners! [*LUKA goes out.*] How difficult these people are! What does he want from me? Why should he disturb my peace? [*Sighs.*] But it's obvious I'll have to go live in a convent. . . . [*Thoughtfully.*] Yes, a convent. . . .

SMIRNOV [*to LUKA*]. You idiot, you talk too much. . . . Ass! [*Sees MRS. POPOV and changes to dignified speech.*] Madam, may I introduce myself: retired lieutenant of the artillery and landowner, Grigory Stepanovich Smirnov! I feel the necessity of troubling you about a highly important matter. . . .

MRS. POPOV [*refusing her hand*]. What do you want?

SMIRNOV. Your late husband, who I had the pleasure of knowing, has remained in my debt for two twelve-hundred-ruble notes. Since I must pay the interest at the agricultural bank tomorrow, I have come to ask you, madam, to pay me the money today.

MRS. POPOV. One thousand two hundred. . . . And why was my husband in debt to you?

SMIRNOV. He used to buy oats from me.

MRS. POPOV [*sighing, to LUKA*]. So, Luka, don't you forget to tell them to give Toby an extra bag of oats.

[*LUKA goes out.*]

[*To SMIRNOV.*] If Nikolai, my husband, was in debt to you, then it goes without saying that I'll pay; but please excuse me today. I haven't any spare cash. The day after tomorrow, my steward will be back from town and I will give him instructions to pay you what is owed; until then I cannot comply with your wishes. . . . Besides, today is the anniversary—exactly seven months ago my husband died, and I'm in such a mood that I'm not quite disposed to occupy myself with money matters.

SMIRNOV. And I'm in such a mood that if I don't pay the interest tomorrow, I'll be owing so much that my troubles will drown me. They'll take away my estate!

MRS. POPOV. You'll receive your money the day after tomorrow.

SMIRNOV. I don't want the money the day after tomorrow. I want it today.

MRS. POPOV. You must excuse me. I can't pay you today.

SMIRNOV. And I can't wait until after tomorrow.

MRS. POPOV. What can I do, if I don't have it now?

SMIRNOV. You mean to say you can't pay?

MRS. POPOV. I can't pay. . . .

SMIRNOV. Hm! Is that your last word?

MRS. POPOV. That is my last word.

SMIRNOV. Positively the last?

MRS. POPOV. Positively.

SMIRNOV. Thank you very much. We'll make a note of that. [*Shrugs his shoulders.*] And people want me to be calm and collected! Just now, on the way here, I met a tax officer and he asked me: why are you always so angry, Grigory Stepanovich? Goodness' sake, how can I be anything but angry? I need money desperately . . . I rode out yesterday early in the morning, at daybreak, and went to see all my debtors; and if only one of them had paid his debt . . . I was dog-tired, spent the night God knows where—a Jewish tavern beside a barrel of vodka. . . . Finally I got here, fifty miles from home, hoping to be paid, and you treat me to a "mood." How can I help being angry?

MRS. POPOV.   It seems to me that I clearly said: My steward will return from the country and then you will be paid.

SMIRNOV.   I didn't come to your steward, but to you! What the hell, if you'll pardon the expression, would I do with your steward?

MRS. POPOV.   Excuse me, my dear sir, I am not accustomed to such unusual expressions nor to such a tone. I'm not listening to you any more. [*Goes out quickly.*]

SMIRNOV [*alone*].   Well, how do you like that? "A mood." . . . "Husband died seven months ago"! Must I pay the interest or mustn't I? I ask you: Must I pay, or must I not? So, your husband's dead, and you're in a mood and all that finicky stuff . . . and your steward's away somewhere; may he drop dead. What do you want me to do? Do you think I can fly away from my creditors in a balloon or something? Or should I run and bash my head against the wall? I go to Gruzdev—and he's not at home; Yaroshevich is hiding, with Kuritsin it's a quarrel to the death and I almost throw him out the window; Mazutov has diarrhea, and this one is in a "mood." Not one of these swine wants to pay me! And all because I'm too nice to them. I'm a sniveling idiot, I'm spineless, I'm an old lady! I'm too delicate with them! So, just you wait! You'll find out what I'm like! I won't let you play around with me, you devils! I'll stay and stick it out until she pays. Rrr! . . . How furious I am today, how furious! I'm shaking inside from rage and I can hardly catch my breath. . . . Damn it! My God, I even feel sick! [*He shouts.*] Hey, you!

LUKA [*enters*].   What do you want?

SMIRNOV.   Give me some beer or some water! [*LUKA exits.*] What logic is there in this! A man needs money desperately, it's like a noose around his neck—and she won't pay because, you see, she's not disposed to occupy herself with money matters! . . . That's the logic of a woman! That's why I never did like and do not like to talk to women. I'd rather sit on a keg of gunpowder than talk to a woman. Brr! . . . I even have goose pimples, this broad has put me in such a rage! All I have to do is see one of those spoiled bitches from a distance, and I get so angry it gives me a cramp in the leg. I just want to shout for help.

LUKA [*entering with water*].   Madam is sick and won't see anyone.

SMIRNOV.   Get out! [*LUKA goes.*] Sick and won't see anyone! No need to see me . . . I'll stay and sit here until you give me the money. You can stay sick for a week, and I'll stay for a week . . . if you're sick for a year, I'll stay a year. . . . I'll get my own back, dear lady! You can't impress me with your widow's weeds and your dimpled cheeks . . . we know all about those dimples! [*Shouts through the window.*] Semyon, unharness the horses! We're not going away quite yet! I'm staying here! Tell them in the stable to give the horses some oats! You brute, you let the horse on the left side get all tangled up in the reins again! [*Teasing.*] "Never mind" . . . I'll give you a never mind! [*Goes away from the window.*] Shit! The heat is unbearable and nobody pays up. I slept badly last night and on top of everything else this broad in mourning is "in a mood" . . . my head aches

. . . [*Drinks, and grimaces.*] Shit! This is water! What I need is a drink! [*Shouts.*] Hey, you!

LUKA [*enters*]. What is it?

SMIRNOV. Give me a glass of vodka. [*LUKA goes out.*] Oof! [*Sits down and examines himself.*] Nobody would say I was looking well! Dusty all over, boots dirty, unwashed, unkept, straw on my waistcoat. . . . The dear lady probably took me for a robber. [*Yawns.*] It's not very polite to present myself in a drawing room looking like this; oh well, who cares? . . . I'm not here as a visitor but as a creditor, and there's no official costume for creditors. . . .

LUKA [*enters with vodka*]. You're taking liberties, my good man. . . .

SMIRNOV [*angrily*]. What?

LUKA. I . . . nothing . . . I only . . .

SMIRNOV. Who are you talking to? Shut up!

LUKA [*aside*]. The devil sent this leech. An ill wind brought him. . . . [*LUKA goes out.*]

SMIRNOV. Oh how furious I am! I'm so mad I could crush the whole world into a powder! I even feel faint! [*Shouts.*] Hey, you!

MRS. POPOV [*enters, eyes downcast*]. My dear sir, in my solitude, I have long ago grown unaccustomed to the masculine voice and I cannot bear shouting. I must request you not to disturb my peace and quiet!

SMIRNOV. Pay me my money and I'll go.

MRS. POPOV. I told you in plain language: I haven't any spare cash now; wait until the day after tomorrow.

SMIRNOV. And I also told you respectfully, in plain language: I don't need the money the day after tomorrow, but today. If you don't pay me today, then tomorrow I'll have to hang myself.

MRS. POPOV. But what can I do if I don't have the money? You're so strange!

SMIRNOV. Then you won't pay me now? No?

MRS. POPOV. I can't. . . .

SMIRNOV. In that case, I can stay here and wait until you pay. . . . [*Sits down.*] You'll pay the day after tomorrow? Excellent! In that case I'll stay here until the day after tomorrow. I'll sit here all that time . . . [*Jumps up.*] I ask you: Have I got to pay the interest tomorrow, or not? Or do you think I'm joking?

MRS. POPOV. My dear sir, I ask you not to shout! This isn't a stable!

SMIRNOV. I wasn't asking you about a stable but about this: Do I have to pay the interest tomorrow or not?

MRS. POPOV. You don't know how to behave in the company of a lady!

SMIRNOV. No, I don't know how to behave in the company of a lady!

MRS. POPOV. No, you don't! You are an ill-bred, rude man! Respectable people don't talk to a woman like that!

SMIRNOV. Ach, it's astonishing! How would you like me to talk to you? In French, perhaps? [*Lisps in anger.*] Madam, je vous prie° . . . how happy I am that you're not paying me the money. . . . Ah, pardon, I've made you uneasy! Such lovely weather we're having today! And you look so becoming in your mourning dress. [*Bows and scrapes.*]

188 *Madame, je vous prie*: Madam, I beg you.

MRS. POPOV. That's rude and not very clever!

SMIRNOV [teasing]. Rude and not very clever! I don't know how to behave in the company of ladies. Madam, in my time I've seen far more women than you've seen sparrows. Three times I've fought duels over women; I've jilted twelve women, nine have jilted me! Yes! There was a time when I played the fool; I became sentimental over women, used honeyed words, fawned on them, bowed and scraped. . . . I loved, suffered, sighed at the moon; I became limp, melted, shivered . . . I loved passionately, madly, every which way, devil take me, I chattered away like a magpie about the emancipation of women, ran through half my fortune as a result of my tender feelings; but now, if you will excuse me, I'm on to your ways! I've had enough! Dark eyes, passionate eyes, ruby lips, dimpled cheeks; the moon, whispers, bated breath—for all that I wouldn't give a good goddamn. Present company excepted, of course, but all women, young and old alike, are affected clowns, gossips, hateful, consummate liars to the marrow of their bones, vain, trivial, ruthless, outrageously illogical, and as far as this is concerned [taps on his forehead], well, excuse my frankness, any sparrow could give pointers to a philosopher in petticoats! Look at one of those romantic creatures: muslin, ethereal demigoddess, a thousand raptures, and you look into her soul—a common crocodile! [Grips the back of a chair; the chair cracks and breaks.] But the most revolting part of it all is that this crocodile imagines that she has, above everything, her own privilege, a monopoly on tender feelings. The hell with it—you can hang me upside down by that nail if a woman is capable of loving anything besides a lapdog. All she can do when she's in love is slobber! While the man suffers and sacrifices, all her love is expressed in playing with her skirt and trying to lead him around firmly by the nose. You have the misfortune of being a woman, you know yourself what the nature of a woman is like. Tell me honestly; Have you ever in your life seen a woman who is sincere, faithful, and constant? You never have! Only old and ugly ladies are faithful and constant! You're more liable to meet a horned cat or a white woodcock than a faithful woman!

MRS. POPOV. Pardon me, but in your opinion, who is faithful and constant in love? The man?

SMIRNOV. Yes, the man!

MRS. POPOV. The man! [Malicious laugh.] Men are faithful and constant in love! That's news! [Heatedly] What right have you to say that? Men are faithful and constant! For that matter, as far as I know, of all the men I have known and now know, my late husband was the best. . . . I loved him passionately, with all my being, as only a young intellectual woman can love; I gave him my youth, my happiness, my life, my fortune; he was my life's breath; I worshipped him as if I were a heathen, and . . . and, what good did it do—this best of men himself deceived me shamelessly at every step of the way. After his death, I found his desk full of love letters; and when he was alive—it's terrible to remember—he used to leave me alone for weeks at a time, and before my eyes he paid court to other women and deceived me. He squandered my money, made a mockery of my feelings . . . and, in spite of all that, I loved him and was true to him . . . and besides, now that he is dead, I am still faithful and constant. I have shut myself up in these four walls forever and I won't remove these widow's weeds until my dying day. . . .

SMIRNOV [*laughs contemptuously*].   Widow's weeds! . . . I don't know what you take me for! As if I didn't know why you wear that black outfit and bury yourself in these four walls! Well, well! It's no secret, so romantic! When some fool of a poet passes by this country house, he'll look up at your window and think: "Here lives the mysterious Tamara, who, for the love of her husband, buried herself in these four walls." We know these tricks!

MRS. POPOV [*flaring*].   What? How dare you say that to me?

SMIRNOV.   You may have buried yourself alive, but you haven't forgotten to powder yourself!

MRS. POPOV.   How dare you use such expressions with me?

SMIRNOV.   Please don't shout. I'm not your steward! You must allow me to call a spade a spade. I'm not a woman and I'm used to saying what's on my mind! Don't you shout at me!

MRS. POPOV.   I'm not shouting, you are! Please leave me in peace!

SMIRNOV.   Pay me my money and I'll go.

MRS. POPOV.   I won't give you any money!

SMIRNOV.   Yes, you will.

MRS. POPOV.   To spite you, I won't pay you anything. You can leave me in peace!

SMIRNOV.   I don't have the pleasure of being either your husband or your fiancé, so please don't make scenes! [*Sits down.*] I don't like it.

MRS. POPOV [*choking with rage*].   You're sitting down?

SMIRNOV.   Yes, I am.

MRS. POPOV.   I ask you to get out!

SMIRNOV.   Give me my money . . . [*Aside.*] Oh, I'm so furious! Furious!

MRS. POPOV.   I don't want to talk to impudent people! Get out of here! [*Pause.*] You're not going? No?

SMIRNOV.   No.

MRS. POPOV.   No?

SMIRNOV.   No!

MRS. POPOV.   We'll see about that. [*Rings.*].

[*LUKA enters.*]

Luka, show the gentleman out!

LUKA [*goes up to SMIRNOV*].   Sir, will you please leave, as you have been asked. You mustn't . . .

SMIRNOV [*jumping up*].   Shut up! Who do you think you're talking to? I'll make mincemeat out of you!

LUKA [*his hand to his heart*].   Oh my God! Saints above! [*Falls into chair.*] Oh, I feel ill! I feel ill! I can't catch my breath!

MRS. POPOV.   Where's Dasha? Dasha! [*She shouts.*] Dasha! Pelagea! Dasha! [*She rings.*]

LUKA.   Oh! They've all gone berry picking . . . there's nobody at home . . . I'm ill! Water!

MRS. POPOV.   Will you please get out!

SMIRNOV.   Will you please be more polite?

MRS. POPOV [*clenches her fist and stamps her feet*].   You're nothing but a crude bear! A brute! A monster!

SMIRNOV.   What? What did you say?

MRS. POPOV.   I said that you were a bear, a monster!

SMIRNOV [*advancing toward her*].   Excuse me, but what right do you have to insult me?

MRS. POPOV.   Yes, I am insulting you . . . so what? Do you think I'm afraid of you?

SMIRNOV.   And do you think just because you're one of those romantic creations, that you have the right to insult me with impunity? Yes? I challenge you!

LUKA.   Lord in Heaven! Saints above! . . . Water!

SMIRNOV.   Pistols!

MRS. POPOV.   Do you think just because you have big fists and you can bellow like a bull, that I'm afraid of you? You're such a bully!

SMIRNOV.   I challenge you! I'm not going to let anybody insult me, and I don't care if you are a woman, a delicate creature!

MRS. POPOV [*trying to get a word in edgewise*].   Bear! Bear! Bear!

SMIRNOV.   It's about time we got rid of the prejudice that only men must pay for their insults! Devil take it, if women want to be equal, they should behave as equals! Let's fight!

MRS. POPOV.   You want to fight! By all means!

SMIRNOV.   This minute!

MRS. POPOV.   This minute! My husband had some pistols . . . I'll go and get them right away. [*Goes out hurriedly and then returns.*] What pleasure I'll have putting a bullet through that thick head of yours! The hell with you! [*She goes out.*]

SMIRNOV.   I'll shoot her down like a chicken! I'm not a little boy or a sentimental puppy. I don't care if she is delicate and fragile.

LUKA.   Kind sir! Holy father! [*Kneels.*] Have pity on a poor old man and go away from here! You've frightened her to death and now you're going to shoot her?

SMIRNOV [*not listening to him*].   If she fights, then it means she believes in equality of rights and emancipation of women. Here the sexes are equal! I'll shoot her like a chicken! But what a woman! [*Imitates her.*] "The hell with you! . . . I'll put a bullet through that thick head of yours! . . ." What a woman! How she blushed, her eyes shone . . . she accepted my challenge! To tell the truth, it was the first time in my life I've seen a woman like that. . . .

LUKA.   Dear sir, please go away! I'll pray to God on your behalf as long as I live!

SMIRNOV.   That's a woman for you! A woman like that I can understand! A real woman! Not a sour-faced nincompoop but fiery, gunpowder! Fireworks! I'm even sorry to have to kill her!

LUKA [*weeps*].   Dear sir . . . go away!

SMIRNOV.   I positively like her! Positively! Even though she has dimpled cheeks, I like her! I'm almost ready to forget about the debt. . . . My fury has diminished. Wonderful woman!

MRS. POPOV [*enters with pistols*].   Here they are, the pistols. Before we fight, you must show me how to fire. . . . I've never had a pistol in my hands before . . .

LUKA. Oh dear Lord, for pity's sake. . . . I'll go and find the gardener and the coachman. . . . What did we do to deserve such trouble? [*Exit.*]

SMIRNOV [*examining the pistols*]. You see, there are several sorts of pistols . . . there are special dueling pistols, the Mortimer with primers. Then there are Smith and Wesson revolvers, triple action with extractors . . . excellent pistols! . . . they cost a minimum of ninety rubles a pair. . . . You must hold the revolver like this . . . [*Aside.*] What eyes, what eyes! A woman to set you on fire!

MRS. POPOV. Like this?

SMIRNOV. Yes, like this . . . then you cock the pistol . . . take aim . . . put your head back a little . . . stretch your arm out all the way . . . that's right . . . then with this finger press on this little piece of goods . . . and that's all there is to do . . . but the most important thing is not to get excited and aim without hurrying . . . try to keep your arm from shaking.

MRS. POPOV. Good . . . it's not comfortable to shoot indoors. Let's go into the garden.

SMIRNOV. Let's go. But I'm giving you advance notice that I'm going to fire into the air.

MRS. POPOV. That's the last straw! Why?

SMIRNOV. Why? . . . Why . . . because it's my business, that's why.

MRS. POPOV. Are you afraid? Yes? Aahhh! No, sir. You're not going to get out of it that easily! Be so good as to follow me! I will not rest until I've put a hole through your forehead . . . that forehead I hate so much! Are you afraid?

SMIRNOV. Yes, I'm afraid.

MRS. POPOV. You're lying! Why don't you want to fight?

SMIRNOV. Because . . . because you . . . because I like you.

MRS. POPOV [*laughs angrily*]. He likes me! He dares say that he likes me! [*Points to the door.*] Out!

SMIRNOV [*loads the revolver in silence, takes cap and goes; at the door, stops for half a minute while they look at each other in silence; then he approaches* MRS. POPOV *hesitantly*]. Listen. . . . Are you still angry? I'm extremely irritated, but, do you understand me, how can I express it . . . the fact is, that, you see, strictly speaking . . . [*He shouts.*] Is it my fault, really, for liking you? [*Grabs the back of a chair, which cracks and breaks.*] Why the hell do you have such fragile furniture! I like you! Do you understand? I . . . I'm almost in love with you!

MRS. POPOV. Get away from me—I hate you!

SMIRNOV. God, what a woman! I've never in my life seen anything like her! I'm lost! I'm done for! I'm caught like a mouse in a trap!

MRS. POPOV. Stand back or I'll shoot!

SMIRNOV. Shoot! You could never understand what happiness it would be to die under the gaze of those wonderful eyes, to be shot by a revolver which was held by those little velvet hands. . . . I've gone out of my mind! Think about it and decide right away, because if I leave here, then we'll never see each other again! Decide . . . I'm a nobleman, a respectable gentleman, of good family. I have an income of ten thousand a year. . . . I can put a bullet through a coin tossed in the air . . . I have some fine horses. . . . Will you be my wife?

MRS. POPOV [*indignantly brandishes her revolver*].   Let's fight! I challenge you!

SMIRNOV.   I'm out of my mind . . . I don't understand anything . . . [*Shouts.*] Hey, you, water!

MRS. POPOV [*shouts*].   Let's fight!

SMIRNOV.   I've gone out of my mind. I'm in love like a boy, like an idiot! [*He grabs her hand, she screams with pain.*] I love you! [*Kneels.*] I love you as I've never loved before! I've jilted twelve women, nine women have jilted me, but I've never loved one of them as I love you. . . . I'm weak, I'm a limp rag. . . . I'm on my knees like a fool, offering you my hand. . . . Shame, shame! I haven't been in love for five years, I vowed I wouldn't; and suddenly I'm in love, like a fish out of water. I'm offering my hand in marriage. Yes or no? You don't want to? You don't need to! [*Gets up and quickly goes to the door.*]

MRS. POPOV.   Wait!

SMIRNOV [*stops*].   Well?

MRS. POPOV.   Nothing . . . you can go . . . go away . . . wait. . . . No, get out, get out! I hate you! But—don't go! Oh, if you only knew how furious I am, how angry! [*Throws revolver on table.*] My fingers are swollen from that nasty thing. . . . [*Tears her handkerchief furiously.*] What are you waiting for? Get out!

SMIRNOV.   Farewell!

MRS. POPOV.   Yes, yes, go away! [*Shouts.*] Where are you going? Stop. . . . Oh, go away! Oh, how furious I am! Don't come near me! Don't come near me!

SMIRNOV [*approaching her*].   How angry I am with myself! I'm in love like a student. I've been on my knees. . . . It gives me the shivers. [*Rudely.*] I love you! A lot of good it will do me to fall in love with you! Tomorrow I've got to pay the interest, begin the mowing of the hay. [*Puts his arm around her waist.*] I'll never forgive myself for this. . . .

MRS. POPOV.   Get away from me! Get your hands away! I . . . hate you! I . . . challenge you!

[*Prolonged kiss. LUKA enters with an ax, the GARDENER with a rake, the COACHMAN with a pitchfork, and WORKMEN with cudgels.*]

LUKA [*catches sight of the pair kissing*].   Lord in heaven! [*Pause.*]

MRS. POPOV [*lowering her eyes*].   Luka, tell them in the stable not to give Toby any oats today.

CURTAIN

QUESTIONS

1. What is the situation when the play opens? How long has Mrs. Popov been in mourning? What advice does Luka give her? How do Luka's presence and commentary affect your perception of the seriousness of Mrs. Popov's situation?

2. What is the significance of Toby?

3. Why has Smirnov come to the house? What sort of person is he? What do you learn about his past experiences with women? Can Mrs. Popov immediately grant his request? What does he say about women?

4. What effect might be created on stage by the breaking chairs? Is this kind of activity more appropriate to serious or slapstick action?

5. What did Mrs. Popov learn about her husband after his death? How has this knowledge affected her? Has it affected her declared fidelity to his memory? Do you think that she is telling everything that she might be feeling?

6. What leads Mrs. Popov to call Smirnov a bear, a brute, a monster? What is his immediate response?

7. When he is alone on stage as Mrs. Popov goes to get the duelling pistols, what does Smirnov say has happened to him? Why is his confession funny?

8. Do you think the conclusion is too sudden, too surprising? What is your response to it?

9. Can you determine any causes in the characters of Mrs. Popov and Smirnov for the suddenness of their falling in love? On consideration, is the action as surprising as it might at first seem?

10. Where were the spots, if any, at which you laughed? Try to determine the causes for your response.

11. *The Bear* has been one of Chekhov's most popular plays. Can you explain why people have liked it? What are your responses to it?

12. Compare the play with "The Widow of Ephesus" by Petronius. In what ways are character and situation similar? How does Chekhov arrange things to focus more attention on the unlikelihood of the onset of love than does Petronius? What is the focus of the play as opposed to the focus of the story?

E. E. CUMMINGS [1894–1962]

nobody loses all the time   *1926*

nobody loses all the time

i had an uncle named
Sol who was a born failure and
nearly everybody said he should have gone
into vaudeville perhaps because my Uncle Sol could   5
sing McCann He Was A Diver on Xmas Eve like Hell Itself which
may or may not account for the fact that my Uncle

Sol indulged in that possibly most inexcusable
of all to use a highfalootin phrase
luxuries that is or to   10
wit farming and be

it needlessly
added

my Uncle Sol's farm
failed because the chickens   15
ate the vegetables so
my Uncle Sol had a
chicken farm till the
skunks ate the chickens when

my Uncle Sol   20
had a skunk farm but
the skunks caught cold and
died and so
my Uncle Sol imitated the
skunks in a subtle manner   25

or by drowning himself in the watertank
but somebody who'd given my Uncle Sol a Victor
Victrola and records while he lived presented to
him upon the auspicious occasion of his decease a
scrumptious not to mention splendiferous funeral with   30
tall boys in black gloves and flowers and everything and

i remember we all cried like the Missouri
when my Uncle Sol's coffin lurched because
somebody pressed a button
(and down went   35
my Uncle
Sol

and started a worm farm)

QUESTIONS

1. Briefly describe the events in Uncle Sol's life. How did he die?
2. What is the relationship between the speaker of the poem and Uncle Sol?
    How close was the speaker with his uncle?
3. What attitudes does the speaker express or imply about Sol's various enter-
    prises as a farmer?
4. What lesson does the speaker draw from the example of the failures in Uncle
    Sol's life? Does he offer this lesson seriously? How much consolation might
    it offer to those who are left behind?
5. Those present at Uncle Sol's funeral cried "like the Missouri" when his coffin
    was lowered into the grave. Does this comparison suggest deep grief, does
    it mask deep grief, or does it indicate a lack of concern?

6. Consider words and phrases like "imitated the skunks in a subtle manner," "splendiferous," and "auspicious occasion." Would these words be appropriate if the speaker were serious? As they appear in the poem, what is their effect?

7. How else might the topic of suicide be treated? Is the treatment here what you might normally expect? Is it possible to prevent yourself from laughing as you read the poem?

8. What is the effect of the spatial arrangement of the words and lines of the poem? Is the poem designed to be read aloud or silently?

9. Do you like or dislike this poem? Explain the reasons for your response.

RESPONDING TO LITERATURE: LIKES AND DISLIKES

As we read works of literature, we respond to them emotionally as well as intellectually, and we should be able to describe our responses. Reduced to their simplest form, these emotional responses take the form of pleasure or pain: we like or we dislike a specific piece of literature. There are, of course, many different levels and expressions of approval or disapproval; we might like one work very much indeed, be unmoved by another, and be thoroughly repulsed by a third. These are first reactions; they do not really convey much information about the literary work itself. In expressing likes or dislikes, we should seek to present responses that are *informed* and *informative* rather than *uninformed* and *unexplained*.

Sometimes the first response that readers express about a work of literature is that it is "boring." This reaction is often simply a mask to cover an incomplete and superficial first reading of a work; it is neither informative nor informed. As you study most works, however, you will discover that you will invariably get drawn into them. One word that describes this process is *interest*—literally, to be in it, inside it, that is, to be taken right into the work emotionally. Another word is *involvement*, referring to having one's emotions become almost rolled into the work, to get taken up by the characters, problems, and outcomes. Sometimes both of these words are used defensively, just like the word *boring*; it is easy to say that something you read was "interesting" or that you got "involved" in it, and you might say these things with a hope that no one will ask you what you mean. Both interest and involvement do describe genuine responses to reading, however. Once you become interested, your reading becomes less of a task than a pleasure, and, although you may undertake some assignments rather grudgingly because of the time and effort they may take, your deepening study will start to become its own reward.

Often you can equate your interest in a work with liking it. You can carry the specifics of liking further, however, by considering some of the following as reasons for your favorable responses:

You like and admire the characters and approve of what they do and stand for.

You learn more about topics that are important to you.

You learn something you had never known or thought before.

You gain new insights into things you had already known.

You learn about characters from different ways of life.

You are involved and interested in the outcome of the action or ideas and do not want to put the work down until you have finished it.

You feel happy because of reading the work.

You are amused and laugh often as you read.

You like the presentation.

You find that some of the ideas and expressions are beautiful and worth remembering.

Obviously, if you find none of these things in the work, or find something that is distasteful, you will not like the work.

Keeping a Notebook for First Responses

Of course no one can tell you what you should or should not like; liking is your own concern. In any consideration of your responses, therefore, you should begin by keeping a notebook record of your thoughts immediately after finishing a work, or even while you are reading it. Be absolutely frank in your opinion. Write down your likes and dislikes, and try to explain the reasons for your response, even if these are not completely thought through. If later you change or modify your first impressions with more thought and fuller understanding, record these changes too. Here is such a notebook entry about Doyle's "The Adventure of the Speckled Band."

> I liked "The Speckled Band" because of the way Sherlock Holmes took charge to solve the mystery. He began by knowing nothing about what was happening to Helen Stoner, but he used the record office (the Doctors' Commons) and also the observations of the house, inside and outside, to learn. And learn he does. It was this example of his going from zero to a hundred that impressed me. By knowing what to do, he mastered the situation.

This paragraph could easily be expanded with further study and discussion. The virtue of it is that it is a clear statement of the student's liking, followed by the major reasons for this response. This pattern, which might best be phrased as "I like [dislike] this work because . . . ," can be quite helpful in your notebook entries.

The challenge in considering positive or negative reactions to literature is that you must eventually consider some of the "because" areas more fully. For this reason it is important to pinpoint some of the specific things you liked or disliked while your informed first impressions are still fresh. If you cannot come up with full sentences detailing the causes of your responses, at least make a brief list of those things that you liked or disliked. If you write nothing, you will likely forget your responses, and recovering them later, when you will need them for discussion or writing, will be difficult.

What Do You Do with Dislikes?

Although so far we have dismissed *boring* and stressed *interest, involvement*, and *liking*, it is important to know that disliking an entire work, or something in it, is normal and acceptable. You do not need to hide this response. Here, for example, are three short notebook responses expressing dislike for the tale by Petronius, "The Widow of Ephesus" (p. 28).

1. I didn't like "The Widow of Ephesus" because the widow seemed hypocritical and too quickly accepted the first man, the soldier, who came along.
2. "The Widow of Ephesus" is not exciting like Doyle's "The Adventure of the Speckled Band," and I like reading only exciting mystery or adventure stories.
3. I found "The Widow of Ephesus" distasteful because it is sexist and prejudiced. It began with a false generalization about women and then went on to "prove" it with a single example.

These are all legitimate responses because they are based on a clearly expressed standard of judgment. The first stems from a distaste for an unlikable trait shown by the main character; the second, from a preference for mystery or adventure stories, which contain rapid action to evoke interest in the dangers faced and overcome by main characters; the third, from the offense taken to the sexist tone of the work and from a criticism of its faulty logic.

Here is a notebook-type entry that might be developed from the first response. What is important is that the reasons for dislike are explained. They would need only slightly more development to be expressed later in classroom discussion or in an essay form.

I did not like "The Widow of Ephesus" because the widow seemed hypocritical. She too quickly accepted the first man, the soldier, who came along. Even though she is shown as faithful to her husband, she is faithful only to a point. She seems concerned with nothing but outward show to impress the townspeople around her, and therefore she goes right into the tomb with her dead husband because that is the showy thing to do. Once she is there, and no one can see what is going on, she becomes the mistress of the soldier. Some fidelity. She is so hypocritical that she even suggests putting her husband's body on the cross to cover up the soldier's neglect of his guard duty. I don't like this sudden shift in loyalty and don't like the story because of it.

Thus, if you list your reasons for dislike right away, you can later study and consider them further. You might even change your mind. However, it is better to record your honest responses of dislike than to force yourself into a position of liking which you do not hold.

Putting Dislikes into a Larger Context

Even though one can honestly dislike a given work, one should try to expand one's taste. For example, the dislike for "The Widow of Ephesus" based on a preference for mystery or adventure stories could cause a person to dislike most works of literature.

If a person can put negative responses into a larger context, it is possible to expand his or her likes in line with very personal responses. A woman might be deeply involved in personal concerns and therefore be uninterested in seemingly remote literary figures. However, if by reading about literary characters she can gain insight into general problems of life, and therefore her own concerns, she might find something to like in just about any work of literature. A man might like sports events and therefore not care for reading anything but sports magazines. But what interests him in sports might be the competition. If he can find competition, or conflict, in a work of literature, he might come to appreciate that work. The principle here is that already established reasons for liking something may be stimulated by works that at first did not seem to bring them out.

As an example, let us consider again the dislike based on a preference for mystery stories and see if this preference can be analyzed. Here are some reasons for liking mysteries:

1. Mysteries get your attention by creating a puzzle. To get the solution, you need to keep reading to the end.
2. Mysteries involve danger.
3. Mysteries have characters who are active.
4. Mysteries have characters who are also clever, resourceful, and daring.
5. Mysteries present difficult obstacles that the characters must work hard to overcome.

No one could claim that "The Widow of Ephesus" can be completely described by any of these points, but the fourth point is promising. If we consider the widow as a character, she is indeed clever and resourceful, for she thinks of the plan to use her husband's body to cover up the soldier's neglect of duty. If a student likes mystery stories because the characters are clever in finding solutions to difficult problems, perhaps this student can also like "The Widow of Ephesus" because of this same quality in the Widow. A comparison like this one can become the basis for a thoughtful favorable response.

The following paragraph shows how the thought processes of the comparison might work:

> I usually like only mystery stories, and at first I disliked "The Widow of Ephesus" because it is not a mystery. But one of the reasons for which I like mysteries is that the characters in them are clever, resourceful, and daring. The widow has these qualities, because she is quick-witted and resourceful enough to suggest the use of her husband's body to substitute for the one of the thief that was taken away. In this way she uses one loved one, who is dead, to rescue another loved one, who is living. She is also daring, because the misuse of the dead in this way was probably a risky thing to do. Although she does not seem likable for much of the story, at the end these qualities come out, almost as a surprise, and therefore I came to like the story.

Thus an accepted principle of liking can be applied to a different work. A person who adapts principles in this open-minded way can, no matter how slowly, redefine dislikes and expand the ability to like and appreciate many kinds of literature.

An equally open-minded way to develop understanding and widen taste is to try to put dislikes in the following light: An author's creation of an unlikable character, situation, attitude, or expression may be deliberate. Your dislike might then result from the author's *intentions*. A first task of study therefore becomes the attempt to understand and explain the intention or plan. As you put the plan into your own words, you may find that you can like a work with unlikable things in it. Here is a paragraph that traces this pattern of thinking, based on Cummings's poem "nobody loses all the time" (p. 59).

> Cummings apparently thought the reader might dislike the speaker's rather insensitive and amused attitude toward the failures and death of Uncle Sol. I do. This speaker hides any seriousness Uncle Sol might have had, and instead treats as a joke all of Sol's attempts at various kinds of farming. Even when Sol committed suicide, the speaker says he did it in a "subtle" manner. But I can see another way of looking at this speaker's attitude. Sol is dead, and there is nothing to be done. If people can't shrug their shoulders and smile, then there would be nothing but sorrow, and people could never get back to living at all. This point almost demands that the speaker present a rather insensitive, uncaring attitude about Sol. So, because I can see the validity of this other way, I can smile at the story, and I do not feel a need to spend too much time thinking about the disasters of Uncle Sol's working life. Therefore my final response is that I like the poem. In fact, I find myself laughing about it despite all the miseries of Uncle Sol.

Neither of these two methods of broadening the contexts of dislike is dishonest to the original negative reactions. In the first paragraph, the thinker applies one of his principles of liking to include "The Widow of Ephesus." In the second, the thinker considers her initial dislike in relationship to the issues brought up in the poem and discovers a rationale for liking the poem as a whole while still not approving of the speaker's manner. The main concern in both responses is to keep an open mind despite initial dislike and then to see if the unfavorable response can be more fully and broadly considered.

However, if, after consideration, you decide that your dislike outweighs any reasons you can find for liking, then you should be prepared to detail and defend your dislike of the work. As long as you are able to relate your response accurately to details in the work, and to measure it against a clearly stated standard of judgment, your dislike of even a commonly liked work will be acceptable.

WRITING ABOUT YOUR LIKES AND DISLIKES

In planning an essay about why you like or dislike a work, you should rely on your initial informed reactions. Because it is not easy to reconstruct responses after a lapse of time, be sure to use your notes as your guide in the prewriting stage. Develop your essay in terms of what made you get interested, or not interested, in the work.

In your essay, be sure to relate the details of the work to the point you are making about your ongoing negative or positive responses. If you begin by indicating that you like the work and then you describe what it is that you like, it is easy to forget your basic response as you enumerate details. It is therefore necessary to keep stressing your involvement in the work as you draw in evidence and details. You can show your attitudes by indicating approval (or disapproval), by commenting favorably (or unfavorably) on the details, by indicating things that seem new (or shopworn) and particularly instructive (or wrong), and by giving assent to (or dissent from) ideas or expressions of feeling.

Organizing Your Essay

INTRODUCTION. You should open by describing briefly the conditions that influenced your response. Your central idea should be whether you like or dislike the work. The thesis sentence should list the major causes of your response, to be developed in the body of your essay.

BODY. The most common approach is to consider the thing or things about the work that you like or dislike (for a list of possible reasons for liking a work, see p. 62). You may like a particular character, or maybe you got so interested in the story that you could not put it down. Also, it may be that a major idea, a fresh insight, or a particular outcome is the major point that you wish to develop. A sample notebook paragraph earlier (p. 62) shows how the positive example of the use of intelligence can be the source of a favorable response to Doyle's "The Adventure of the Speckled Band." The sample essay (p. 67) expands upon the thoughts in this paragraph.

Another approach is to give details about how your responses occurred or changed in your reading of the work. This method of development requires that you pinpoint, in order, the various good (or bad) parts of the work, and how you responded to them. Your aim here should be not to retell the story, but to discuss those details that caused you to like or dislike the story. The greatest pitfall to avoid here is a mere retelling of a story or summary of an argument. If you emphasize how the details brought out your responses, however, and if you stress these responses, your essay should rise above the level of a summary.

Two other approaches bring out a shift or development of response, either from negative to positive (most common) or vice versa. The first approach allows the writer to show that a principle for liking one kind of literature may be applied to the work being discussed. The second suggests that a writer may have first responded unfavorably to something about the work, but that on further consideration she or he has been able to establish a larger context which permitted a favorable response. (These responses were discussed earlier, pp. 63–66.)

Conclusion. Here you might briefly summarize the reasons for your major response. You might also try to face any issues brought up by a change in your responses, if there is one. That is, if you have always held certain assumptions about your taste but like the work despite these assumptions, you may wish to talk about your own change or development. This topic is personal, but in an essay about likes or dislikes, discovery about yourself is something toward which you should aim.

SAMPLE ESSAY

Some Reasons for Liking A. Conan Doyle's "The Adventure of the Speckled Band"*

Mystery stories are good reading because the solution to a baffling problem is not known until the end. It might be hard for a reader to get into the mystery, however, because many of the characters are totally enmeshed in

* See p. 31 for this story.

[1] circumstances and therefore do not become fully interesting people. For this reason it seems necessary that a mystery focus first on a mastermind of some sort—a kind of friend of the reader—who creates immediate interest in himself or herself before the mystery plot thickens. "The Adventure of the Speckled Band," by A. Conan Doyle, is exactly this kind of mystery. I like the story because I like its master detective, Sherlock Holmes, and like to follow him.° From beginning to end, Holmes is presented as an admirable model of skill, resourcefulness, and bravery.▫

[2] Holmes's skill is an admirable demonstration of his intelligence. At the beginning of the story, he knows nothing about what is happening to Helen Stoner. But he knows what to do once he starts listening to her. So, for example, he immediately goes to the records office in Doctors' Commons to determine something about her estate. In this way, he learns about any possible financial motive that someone might have to kill her. Similar is his exacting method of examining the Roylott house, both inside and out, to narrow suspicion on Roylott himself as the murderer. By this exertion of his skill and the application of his method, Holmes earns the reader's confidence and approval.

[3] Holmes's excellence is shown not only in his skill, but in his resourcefulness. Once his examination of the premises is complete, it is clear that he knows exactly how Roylott's plot is designed to work. His plan, although we as readers do not learn it until he carries it out in practice, shows his ability to improvise with what is available to him. His warning to Watson about the danger, and his caution about the need for stealth, secrecy, darkness, and silence, all show that he has planned and is able to coordinate all the events of the night in order to save Helen and beat Roylott at his own game. Such resourcefulness is admirable.

[4] The most admirable quality of Holmes is his bravery. When Roylott enters the London apartment and tries to browbeat him, Holmes speaks coolly and bravely. Even when Roylott turns to threats, Holmes faces the angry opponent down by asking him to leave. This same bravery enables Holmes to devise the plan to beat back the snake once Roylott has pushed the creature into Helen's room. The bite of the "speckled band" could be almost instantly fatal, but Holmes takes the risk, and his success is an example for all.

[5] Holmes has just about everything that can arouse the reader's liking. Through all the mystery and the danger, he is center stage, and he performs his role well. He is the trusted one, who notices things that others pass over in ignorance. Because of his superiority, he controls and manages everything. With Holmes out in front as he is, it is impossible not to like "The Adventure of the Speckled Band." I certainly like it, and I recommend it highly.

Commentary on the Essay

This essay demonstrates the first approach described on p. 67, and it is drawn from the first reason for liking a work as listed on p. 62. The opening paragraph explains why a mystery story needs a central figure

° Central idea.
▫ Thesis sentence.

as a focal point of interest and concern. Then the paragraph asserts that Holmes, the master detective in "The Adventure of the Speckled Band," is this central figure and therefore that he is the major cause for which the writer likes the story. The thesis sentence ends the paragraph.

Paragraph 2 points out that Holmes's method as a detective is the first reason for liking the story. The reason brought out in the third paragraph is Holmes's resourcefulness—that is, his development of a plan to stop the murderer and his foresight and control in making sure that his plan works. The fourth paragraph refers to Holmes's bravery. Because this quality is "most admirable," the essay brings it out as the climax of the three traits for which Holmes is likable.

The conclusion pulls everything together, once again stressing the idea brought out in the opening paragraph that Holmes is the major focus of interest and admiration in the story.

Throughout the essay, the central idea that the story is liked is brought out in words and expressions like "admirable," "knows what to do," "shows his ability," "is able to coordinate," and "success," among others. These expressions, mixed as they are with references to many details from the story, create thematic continuity that shapes and develops the essay. It is the thematic development, together with the use of the details from the story as supporting evidence, that distinguishes the sample essay from a summary.

Fiction

Fiction

2

Fiction

Fiction originally meant anything made up, crafted, or shaped. As we understand the word today, it means a prose story based in the imagination of the author, not in literal facts. In English the first recorded use of the word in this sense was in the year 1599. The original meaning of the word in reference to things made up or crafted is helpful to us in focusing on the fact that fiction is to be distinguished from works that it has often imitated, such as reports, historical accounts, biographies, autobiographies, collections of letters, and personal memoirs and meditations. While writers of fiction may deliberately design their works to resemble these forms, fiction has a separate identity because of its origin in the creative, shaping powers of the writers. It is a fact that writers of fiction may include true and historically accurate details in their works, but they create their main stories not because of a wish to be faithful to history but rather because of a hope to say something significant about human life.

The essence of fiction, as opposed to drama, is **narration,** the relating or recounting of a sequence of events or actions. The earliest works of fiction relied almost exclusively on narration, with speeches and dialogue being reported rather than quoted directly. Many recent works of fiction include extended passages of dialogue, thereby rendering the works more dramatic even though narration is still the primary mode.

Fiction had its roots in ancient myths and folk tales. In primitive civilizations, stories were circulated by word of mouth, and often traveling storytellers would appear in a court or village to entertain eager listeners with tales based on the exploits of heroes and gods. Although many of these were heavily fictionalized accounts of events and people who may or may not ever have existed, they were largely accepted by the people as fact or history. An especially long tale, an **epic,** was recited over a period of days, and to aid their memories the storytellers delivered these works in poetic lines, perhaps also impressing and entertaining their listeners by playing stringed instruments.

Although the retelling of myths and legends was meant in part to be entertainment, these stories made a point or taught a lesson considered important either for the local religion or the dominant power structure. Myths of gods like Zeus and Athena (Greece), or Jupiter and Minerva (Rome) abounded, together with stories of famous men and women like Jason, Helen of Troy, Agamemnon, Hercules, Andromeda, Achilles, Odysseus, and Penelope. The ancient Macedonian king and conqueror Alexander the Great (356–323 B.C.) developed many of his ideas about nobility and valor from his boyhood learning of Homer's epic *The Iliad*, which told of the Trojan War. Perhaps nowhere is the moralistic-argumentative aspect of storytelling better illustrated than in the **fables** of Aesop, a Greek who wrote in the sixth century, B.C., and in the **parables** of Jesus as told in the Gospels of the New Testament. In these works, a short narrative is clearly directed to a religious, philosophic, or psychological conclusion. "The Widow of Ephesus" by Petronius illustrates this type of persuasive intention. Whether you agree with the author's conclusion or not, the subordination of the narrative events to a rhetorical and moralizing purpose is made clear right at the beginning of the story.

Beginning about 800 years ago, storytelling was developed to a fine art by writers such as Marie de France, a Frenchwoman who wrote in England near the end of the twelfth century, Giovanni Boccaccio (Italian, 1313–1375), and Geoffrey Chaucer (English, c. 1340–1400). William Shakespeare (1564–1616) drew heavily on history and legend for the stories and characters in his plays.

MODERN FICTION

Fiction in the modern sense of the word did not begin to flourish until the late seventeenth and eighteenth centuries, when human beings of all social stations and ways of life became important literary topics. As one writer put it in 1709, human nature could not be explained simply, but only with reference to many complex motives like "passion, humor, caprice, zeal, faction, and a thousand other springs."[1] Thus fiction moved toward the characteristic concerns that it has today—the psychological and the highly individual. Indeed, fiction gains its strength from being grounded in the concrete and individual. Most characters have both first and last names; the cities and villages in which they live and move are modeled on real places; and the events and responses recounted are like those that readers themselves have experienced, could experience, or could easily imagine themselves experiencing.

[1] Anthony Ashley Cooper, Third Earl of Shaftesbury, *Sensus Communis*, pt. III, sec. iii.

The first true works of fiction as we know it were the lengthy Spanish and French **romances** written in the sixteenth and seventeenth centuries. (The French word for "novel" is still *roman*.) In English the word **novel** was borrowed from French and Italian to describe these works and to distinguish them from medieval and classical romances as something that was *new* (the meaning of *novel*). In England the word *story* was used along with *novel* in reference to this new literary form.

It was natural that increased levels of general education and literacy in the eighteenth century would make possible the further development of fiction. In Shakespeare's time the only way a writer could make money out of writing was to write a play and then receive either a percentage of the admissions or the proceeds from an "author's benefit" performance. The audiences, however, were limited to people who lived within a short distance of the theater (or who could afford the cost of travel to a performance) and who had the leisure time to attend a play. Once great numbers of people could read, the paying audience for literature expanded. A writer could write a novel and have it printed by a publisher, who could then sell it widely to many people, giving a portion of the proceeds to the writer. Readers could pick up the book at their leisure and finish it as they chose. Reading a novel could even be a social event: people read to each other as a means of sharing the experience. With this wider audience, authors could make a career out of writing. Fiction had arrived as a major genre of literature. For a more literate public. Lit. began w. the group, then became a subject of an individual's scrutiny.

THE SHORT STORY

Most novels were long, and reading them required many hours. It took an American writer, Edgar Allan Poe (1809–1849), to develop a theory of the **short story**, which he described in a review of Nathaniel Hawthorne's *Twice-Told Tales*. Poe was convinced that "worldly interests" prevented most readers from concentrating on their reading, and that as a result they lost the "totality" of comprehension and emotional reaction that careful reading should permit. He added to this practical consideration the belief that a short, concentrated story (which he called "a brief prose tale") could create a powerful, single impression on the reader. Thus he concluded that the best work of fiction was the short story that could be read at a single sitting of not more than an hour." Philosophy of Composition"

Once Poe had expressed his theory, the convenience if not the correctness of his recommendation prompted many later writers to work extensively in the short story form. Today, innumerable short stories are printed in weekly and monthly periodicals and in collections. Many writers who publish stories over a long period of time collect their works for inclusion in single volumes. Writers like William Faulkner, F. Scott Fitzgerald, Ernest

Hemingway, Shirley Jackson, Guy de Maupassant, Flannery O'Connor, Frank O'Connor, and Eudora Welty, to name only a small number, have had their works collected in this way.

ELEMENTS OF FICTION

Modern fiction is in a sense similar to myth and epic in that it may teach a lesson or make a point that the writer views as important. Even works purportedly written with a goal of simply entertaining are based in an idea or position. Thus, writers of comic works are usually committed to the belief that human difficulties can be ironed out by discussion and humor. More serious works may instruct by involving characters in difficult moral choices, with the underlying assumption that in losing situations the only winner is the one who can maintain honor and self-respect. Works designed to create mystery and suspense are based in the belief that problems have solutions, even if they may not at first seem apparent. In the creation of stories, writers may deal with the triumphs and defeats of life, the admirable and the despicable, the humorous and the pathetic, but whatever their goal, they always have something to say about the human experience. If they are successful as writers, they will communicate their vision directly to us through their stories.

As a first aspect of this vision, fiction, along with drama, has a basis in **realism** or **verisimilitude.** That is, the situations or characters, though they are the **invention** of writers, are similar to those that many human beings know or experience in their lives. Even **fantasy,** the creation of events that are dreamlike or fantastic (and in this sense a counter to realism), is derived from a perception of life and action that is ultimately real. This similarity of art to life has led some critics to label fiction, and also drama, as an art of **imitation.** Shakespeare's Hamlet states that an actor attempts to portray real human beings in realistic situations (to "hold a mirror up to Nature"). That might also be said of the writer of fiction.

In accord with the idea of verisimilitude or imitation, therefore, everything in fiction is related in one way or another to the reality of everyday life. Some stories are told as though they actually occurred in life, not unlike reports of actual news events in a newspaper. Eudora Welty's "A Worn Path" is such a story. It recounts a woman's walking journey through a wooded area, to the streets of a town, and then to the interior of a building. The events of the story are on the level of the real: They could actually happen in life just as Welty tells about them.

Other levels of reality may also be offered in fiction. Shirley Jackson's "The Lottery," for example, seems at first to be happening on a plane of absolute, small-town reality. By the story's end, however, it is apparent that something else is happening, that the realistic level has changed into a more symbolic one. Such a story suggests that fiction may have many kinds of connections with reality. This link with reality in "The Lottery" may be regarded as a **postulate,** a given **premise,** what Henry James called a *donné* (something given). Here the premise is this: "What would happen if a small, ordinary town held a lottery in which the 'winner' would be ritually stoned to death?" Everything follows from this given idea. The connection with reality can become remote, or fanciful, as in Poe's "The Masque of the Red Death," in which the given idea is, "What would happen if Death could actually attend a party in person and claim all the party-goers?" The connection can become symbolic or even miraculous, as in Marjorie Pickthall's "The Worker in Sandalwood," in which Jesus, who in life had worked as a carpenter, returns to earth and builds masterly furniture. In Shirley Jackson's "About Two Nice People" the given situation is farcical but romantic, and disputes lead not to hatred but to love. In Walter Clark's "A Portable Phonograph" the events occur in a possible future after much of the world's civilization has been destroyed in an atomic war. As you read works such as these, in which the actions and scenes do not seem realistic in our ordinary sense of the word, you should not dismiss the works as unreal. Instead, you should seek meaning in the actions as caused by the given situation. Always, you may judge a work by the standard of whether it is true if one grants the premises, or the *donnés*, created by the writer.

Indeed, you may accurately say that in fiction there is always some element of control that shapes the actions the author depicts. Even an apparently everyday level of reality disguises the craft and selectivity of the author. This control may be an occasion (such as the social worker calling the mother and expressing concern about the daughter in Tillie Olsen's "I Stand Here Ironing"). It may be a level of behavior (the boy's reactions to the people around him in O'Connor's "First Confession"). It may be an environment and a social situation, as in Crane's "The Bride Comes to Yellow Sky." Some controls apply to particular types of fiction. There are, for example, "love stories." In the simplest love story two people meet and overcome an obstacle of some sort (usually not a really serious one) on the way to falling in love. Interesting variations on this type may be seen in D. H. Lawrence's "The Horse Dealer's Daughter" and Anton Chekhov's "Lady with Lapdog." In James Joyce's "Araby" only one of the major characters is in love; this is the narrator, who is telling about his boyhood crush on the sister of a friend. In another type of story, the "detective story" like Doyle's "The Adventure of the Speckled Band," a mysterious event is posited, and then the detective (Sherlock Holmes, in this case) draws conclusions based on the available evidence. Most stories, however, resist easy classification into types like these. They are simply stories about characters like those you find in real life, characters who undergo experiences that are sometimes difficult and painful, other times happy and successful, sometimes a mixture of many emotions. In short, stories represent the full range of human experience.

CHARACTER, PLOT, AND STRUCTURE

All works of fiction share a number of common elements which will be discussed in detail in the various chapters. The more apparent ones, for reference here, are *character*, *plot*, and *structure*.

Character

Stories, like drama, are about characters—characters who, though not real people, are drawn from life. A character (see Chapter 4, p. 134) is a reasonable facsimile of a human being, with all the good and bad traits of being human.[2] A story is usually concerned with a major problem that a character must face. This may involve interaction with another character, with a difficult situation, or with an idea or general circumstances that force action. The character may win, lose, or tie. He or she may learn and be the better for the experience or may miss the point and be unchanged despite what has happened.

Earlier we mentioned that modern fiction rose coincidentally with the development of a psychological interest in human beings. Psychology itself has grown out of the philosophical and religious idea that people are not necessarily evil, but rather that they have an inborn capacity for goodness. They are not free of problems, and they make many mistakes in their lives, but they nevertheless are of independent interest and they are therefore worth writing about in literature, whether they are male or female; white, black, tan, or yellow; rich or poor; worker or industrialist; farmer, secretary, shepherd, clerk, or salesperson.

It would therefore seem that there is virtually nothing in the modern world that is beyond the scope of fiction. The plight of a married couple struggling under an enormous debt, the meditation of a woman about the growth of her daughter, the experience of a boy learning about sin and forgiveness, the solution to a personality clash in a business, the pathos of a woman surrounded by insensitive and self-seeking men, the development of power and the grounds for domination in a marriage of Mexican

[2] Even the beings from other worlds and the lifelike robots and computers that we meet in science fiction, along with animals who populate beast fables and modern comics and films, interest us only as they exhibit human characteristics. Thus, Yogi Bear prefers honey to berries; a supremely intelligent computer with a conflicting program turns destructive; and an alien of superhuman strength riding on a spaceship tries to destroy all the human passengers. But we all know human beings with a sweet tooth; we all know that internal conflicts can produce unpredictable and sometimes destructive results; and who would say that the desire for power is not human?

peasants—all of these are important because human beings are important. In fiction, you may expect characters from every area of life, and, because we all share the same human capacities for concern, involvement, sympathy, happiness, sorrow, exhilaration, and disappointment, you should be able to become interested in the plights of characters and in how they try to handle the world around them.

Plot

Fictional characters, imitated from life, must go through a series of lifelike **actions,** or **incidents,** which in total make up the story. The interrelationship of incidents and character within a total design is the **plot** of the story. Plot has been compared to a map, scheme, or blueprint. In a carefully worked plot, all the actions, speeches, thoughts, and observations are inextricably linked to make up an entirety, sometimes called an **organic unity.** The essence of this unity of plot is the development and resolution of a **conflict,** in which a **protagonist,** or central character, is engaged in a struggle of some sort. Often this struggle is directed against another character, an **antagonist,** or group of antagonists. Just as often, however, the struggle may occur between opposing forces, ideas, and choices. The conflict may be carried out wherever human beings spend their lives, such as in open nature, communities, houses, courts of law, or mountain resorts. The conflict may also take place internally, within the mind of the protagonist.

Plot in its simplest stage is worked out in a pattern of **cause and effect** that can be traced in a **sequence** or **chronology.** That is, the incidents happen over a period of time, but chronology alone is not the cause of the sequence of actions. Instead, time enters into the cause-and-effect pattern to give the opportunity for effects to follow causes.

Structure

Whereas a plot is related to chronology, the **structure** of a story may be different because authors often choose to present their stories in something other than direct chronological order. If a story is told in straightforward narrative from beginning to end, then plot and structure are virtually identical, but if the story gets pieced together through out-of-sequence events, speeches, remembrances, fragments of letters, descriptions of actions, overheard conversations, and the like, then the actual arrangement or structure of the story may diverge from the plot. Also, whereas the plot refers to the entire pattern of conflict as evidenced through cause and effect in the story, the study of structure may be directed toward a smaller aspect of arrangement. Structure, in other words, refers to the way in which the plot is assembled, either in whole or in part.

Theme

We have said that writers write because they have things to say about life. One of the elements unifying a story is the existence of an underlying **theme** or **central idea,** which is present throughout the work. The theme is somewhat comparable to a scaffold that is used by workers in the construction of a large building; once the building is complete, it is removed, but the effect of the scaffold is still apparent.

The comparison is not totally valid, however, because authors may sometimes leave some of the "scaffolding" in their stories in the form of a direct statement. Thus de Maupassant, in "The Necklace," indicates that people may be destroyed or made fortunate by the most insignificant of events. The accidental loss of the necklace is just such an event; this misfortune ruins the lives of both Mathilde and her husband for the following ten years. Here the author has presented us with a direct statement of an idea, as it were, a part of his scaffold. There are many other ideas, however, that we might also locate in the story, such as that adversity may bring out worth, or that good fortune is never recognized until it is lost. With each of these alternatives, the story can be seen as being a consistent embodiment of an idea.

The process of determining and describing ideas in stories is probably never complete; there is always another idea that is equally valid and applicable. Such wide opportunity for discussion and interpretation is one of the things that makes fiction interesting and valuable.

THE WRITER'S TOOLS

Narration

Writers have a number of modes of presentation, or "tools," with which they may create their stories. The principal of these tools (and the heart of fiction) is **narration,** the reporting of actions in chronological sequence. The object of narration is, as much as possible, to *render* the story, to make it clear and to bring it alive to the reader's imagination.

Style

The medium of fiction and of all literature is language, and the manipulation of language—the **style**—is a primary skill of the writer of fiction. A mark of a good writer's style is the use of *active verbs*, and the use of nouns that are *specific* and *concrete*. Even with the most active and graphic diction possible, writers can never make an exact rendering of their incidents and scenes, but they can indeed be judged on the extent to which they make their narration vivid.

Point of View

One of the most important ways in which writers knit their stories together, and also an important way in which they try to interest and engage readers, is the careful control of **point of view** (see Chapter 5). Point of view is the voice of the story, the speaker who is doing the narration. It is the means by which the reality and truthfulness of a story are made to seem authentic. It may be regarded as the *focus* of the story, the *angle of vision* from which things are not only seen and reported but also judged.

A story may be told by a fictitious "observer" who tells us what he or she saw, heard, concluded, and thought. This **speaker** or observer may sometimes seem to be the author speaking directly using an authorial voice, but just as often the speaker is a **persona** with characteristics that separate him or her from the author. Sometimes the speaker is a fictitious actor or participant in the story. Stories told in either of these ways have **first-person** points of view, for the speaker usually uses the "I" personal pronoun in referring to his or her position as an observer or commentator.

The other point of view is the **third person**.[3] The third-person point of view may be (1) **limited,** with the focus being on one particular character and what he or she does, says, hears, thinks, and otherwise experiences, (2) **omniscient,** with the thoughts and behaviors of all the characters being open and fully known by the speaker, and (3) **dramatic,** or **objective,** with the story being confined *only* to essential reporting of actions and speeches, with no commentary and no revelation of the thoughts of any of the characters.

Point of view is often quite subtle—indeed, it may be one of the most difficult of all concepts in the study of literature. In fuller perspective, therefore, it may be considered as the position from which things are viewed, understood, and then communicated. It is point of view that makes fiction lifelike, although the author arranges the point of view so that the reader may be properly guided to learn of actions and dialogue. But point of view raises some of the same questions that are found in life. For example, we cannot always be sure of the reliability of what people tell us; we often need to know what their position is. In life, all people have their own limitations, attitudes, and opinions, so that their description of any event, and their attributions or conclusions about such events, will invariably be colored by these attitudes. For example, would the testimony of a near-sighted person who witnessed a distant incident while not wearing glasses be accurate? Would someone's report be reliable if the person were inter-

---

[3] Note Chapter 5, pp. 180–81, where the possibilities of a second-person point of view are discussed.

preting an activity of someone he or she did not like? The same applies to the speakers that we encounter in fiction. For readers, the perception of a fictional point of view can be as complex as life itself, and it may be as difficult to find and rely upon proper sources of information.

Description

Together with narration, an important aspect of fiction is the use of **description,** which brings scenes and feelings to the imagination of readers. Description can be both physical (places and persons) and psychological (an emotion or set of emotions). As an end in itself, description can interrupt action, so that many writers include only as much as is necessary for the highlighting of important actions. In Olsen's "I Stand Here Ironing," for example, there is a minimum of physical description, although all of us can imagine where a woman doing the week's ironing might be and what she might look like. Other writers may make lavish descriptions in their works. Joseph Conrad, for example, provided extensive descriptions in his novels and stories. His scenes are not only places in which the characters act, but are so evocative that they provide a backdrop designed to give philosophical and even a semireligious perspective to the actions. Edgar Allan Poe used descriptions extensively. In "The Fall of the House of Usher" he attempted to evoke an impression of decay and doom; in "The Masque of the Red Death" his descriptions suggest a mood of macabre festivity.

Mood and **atmosphere** are important adjuncts of descriptive writing, and to the degree that descriptions evoke ideas and actions beyond those they stand for on the surface, they may reach the level of **metaphor** and **symbolism.** These characteristics of fiction are a property of all literature, and you will also encounter them in your considerations of poetry and drama.

Dialogue

Another major tool of the writer of fiction is the creation of **dialogue.** At its simplest, dialogue is the conversation of two people, but more characters may participate, depending on their importance, the number present, and also the circumstances of the scene and action. The major medium of the dramatist, dialogue is just one of the means by which the fiction writer makes a story vivid and dramatic. Straight narration and description can do no more than say that a character's thoughts and responses exist, but dialogue makes eveything real and firsthand. Dialogue is hence a means of *rendering* rather than presenting. If characters feel pain or declare love, their speeches can be the exact expressions (or inexact, depending on the degree of their articulateness) of what is on their minds, in their own words. Some dialogue may be terse and minimal, like that found in Hemingway. Other dialogue may be expanded, depending on the situation, the personalities of the characters, and the author's intent. Dialogue may be about virtually anything, including future plans and goals, reactions, indications of emotion, and political, social, philosophical, or religious ideas.

The language of dialogue indicates the intelligence, articulateness, educational levels, or emotional states of the speakers. Hence the author might use *grammatical mistakes*, *faulty pronunciation*, or *slang* to show a character of limited or disadvantaged background or a character who is trying to be seen in that light. *Dialect* clearly shows the regional location from which the speaker came, just as an accent indicates the place of national origin. *Jargon* and *cliché* suggest a person who is pretentious—usually an infallible directive for the reader's laughter. The use of *private, intimate expressions* might show people who are close to each other emotionally. Speech that is interrupted with *voiced pauses* ("er," "ah," "um," "you know," and so on) and speech that is characterized by *inappropriate words* might show a character who is unsure or is not in control. There are many possibilities in dialogue, but no matter what specific qualities you observe, writers include dialogue in order to enable you better to know the characters peopling the scenes and the experiences they face.

Commentary

Writers may also include **commentary, analysis,** or **interpretation** in the expectation that readers need at least some insight or illumination about the characters and actions. We have already spoken of "scaffolding" in relation to the ideas in fiction. Commentary is the use of scaffolding as a means of showing how things are put together. When fiction was new, authors often expressed such commentary. Henry Fielding (1707–1754), for example, divided his novels into "books" and included a chapter of philosophical or artistic commentary at the beginning of each book. In the next century George Eliot (1819–1880) included many extensive passages of commentary in her novels.

Later writers have kept commentary at a minimum, preferring instead to concentrate on direct action and dialogue. They have left it to readers to draw their own conclusions about meaning—to erect their own scaffolding, as it were. One is likely, however, to encounter something like interpretive observations in first-person narrations, particularly where the speaker not only is a storyteller but also has been a participant. Joseph Conrad's "Youth" is such a work, as is Olsen's "I Stand Here Ironing." Observations made by dramatic speakers in works like these may be accepted at face value, but you should recognize that anything the speakers say is also a mode of character disclosure. Such commentary is therefore just as much a part of the story as the narrative incidents.

Tone and Irony

In every story one may consider **tone,** that is, an attitude or attitudes that the author conveys about the material in the story and also toward the readers of the story. In "The Necklace," for example, De Maupassant presents the bitter plight of Mathilde and her husband. Pity is thus an appropriate way of describing the attitude that the author conveys in this section of the story, and pity is indeed an appropriate response for the reader. But De Maupassant also shows that to a great degree Mathilde has brought her misfortune directly on herself, so the attitude is one of at least partial satisfaction that justice has been done. But Mathilde works hard and unselfishly; hence admiration tempers any inclination that the reader might have had to condemn her. But then the story's conclusion shows that Mathilde's virtual enslavement was unnecessary. Hence regret enters into the response. In a discussion of the tone of the story, it would be necessary to describe this mixture or complexity of attitudes. Usually, tone is complex in this way.

Because Mathilde's sacrifice for a period of ten years is unnecessary, her situation is ironic. **Irony** is the use of language and situations that are widely inappropriate or opposite from what might be ordinarily expected. **Situational irony** is a means by which authors create a strong emotional impact by presenting circumstances in which punishments do not fit crimes, or in which rewards are not earned. Forces, in other words, are beyond human control or comprehension. The characteristic of **dramatic irony** is that a character may perceive his or her situation in a limited way while the reader sees things more broadly and comprehensively. In John Collier's "The Chaser," for example, the main character believes that he is about to embark upon lifelong ecstasy and romance, but Collier makes the reader aware that the character's life will be sinister and not ecstatic. In **verbal irony,** which applies to language, what is *meant* is different from, or opposite to, what is *said*. Thus, De Maupassant in "The Necklace" does not directly say that Mathilde's husband is a crashing bore during the big party, but by asserting ironically that he had been sleeping "in a little empty room with three other men whose wives had also been enjoying themselves," De Maupassant conveys this idea with amusing force.

Symbolism and Allegory

Because fiction impresses itself upon the human imagination, it is almost a necessary consequence that the incidents, speeches, and characters acquire an underlying idea or value. To this degree, even an apparently ordinary thing may be construed as a **symbol;** that is, the thing may be understood to mean something beyond itself, something bigger than itself. Because Sammy in Updike's "A & P" walks out on his job in protest against the way the girls in swimsuits are treated, he might easily serve as a symbol standing for freedom of personal behavior. To consider Sammy as a symbol, however, depends on the reader's willingness to make the necessary connection and justification. Many other symbols do not need such explanation, for sometimes writers deliberately create symbols. The cane in Hawthorne's "Young Goodman Brown" is such an example, for Hawthorne describes it as resembling the serpent associated with Satan. The cane therefore is a symbol showing that Brown's woodland companion is actually the Devil himself.

When a story, in addition to maintaining its own narrative integrity, may be clearly applied to another, parallel, set of situations, it is an **allegory.** "Young Goodman Brown" may be considered as an allegory of the development of hatred, distrust, and paranoia. Stories are usually not like "Young Goodman Brown," however, even though they may contain sections that have allegorical parallels. Thus, the narrative of Mathilde's long servitude in De Maupassant's "The Necklace" is similar to the lives and activities of many people who carry out tasks for reasons that are incorrect or even meaningless. For this reason, "The Necklace" may be considered allegorically, even though it is not a complete allegory.

These, then, are the major tools of writers of fiction. For analytical purposes, one or another of them may be discussed so that the artistic achievement of a particular author may be recognized. It is important to realize, however, that in a story everything is happening at once. The story may be told by a character who is a witness, and thus there is a *first-person point of view*. The major *character*, the *protagonist*, goes through a series of *actions* as a result of a carefully arranged *plot*. Because of this plot, together with the author's chosen method of narration, the story will exhibit an organization, or *structure*. One of the things that the actions may demonstrate will be the *theme* or *central idea* of the story. The writer's *style* may be manifested in *ironic* expressions. The description of the character's activity may reveal *irony of situation*, while at the same time this situation is made vivid through *dialogue* in which the character is a participant. Because the plight of the character is like the plight of many persons in the world, it may be considered as an *allegory*, and the character herself or himself may be a *symbol*.

Throughout the story, no matter what characteristics one is considering at the moment, it is most important to realize that a work of fiction is an entirety, a unity. Any reading of a story should be undertaken not to break things down into parts, but to understand and assimilate the work as a whole. The separate analysis of various topics, to which this book is committed, is thus the means to that end, not the end itself. Finally, the study of fiction, like the study of all literature, is designed to foster growth and understanding and to encourage the ultimate improvement of life.

JOHN UPDIKE (b. 1932)

A & P   1961

In walks these three girls in nothing but bathing suits. I'm in the third checkout slot, with my back to the door, so I don't see them until they're over by the bread. The one that caught my eye first was the one in the plaid green two-piece. She was a chunky kid, with a good tan and a sweet broad soft-looking can with those two crescents of white just under it, where the sun never seems to hit, at the top of the backs of her legs. I stood there with my hand on a box of HiHo crackers trying to remember if I rang it up or not. I ring it up again and the customer starts giving me hell. She's one of these cash-register-watchers, a witch about fifty with rouge on her cheekbones and no eyebrows, and I know it made her day to trip me up. She'd been watching cash registers for fifty years and probably never seen a mistake before.

By the time I got her feathers smoothed and her goodies into a bag—she gives me a little snort in passing, if she'd been born at the right time they would have burned her over in Salem—by the time I get her on her way the girls had circled around the bread and were coming back, without a pushcart, back my way along the counters, in the aisle between the checkouts and the Special bins. They didn't even have shoes on. There was this chunky one, with the two-piece—it was bright green and the seams on the bra were still sharp and her belly was still pretty pale so I guessed she just got it (the suit)—there was this one, with one of those chubby berry-faces, the lips all bunched together under her nose, this one, and a tall one, with black hair that hadn't quite frizzed right, and one of these sunburns right across under the eyes, and a chin that was too long—you know, the kind of girl other girls think is very "striking" and "attractive" but never quite makes it, as they very well know, which is why they like her so much—and then the third one, that wasn't quite so tall. She was the queen. She kind of led them, the other two peeking around and making their shoulders round. She didn't look around, not this queen, she just walked straight on slowly, on these long white prima-donna legs. She came down a little hard on her heels, as if she didn't walk in her bare feet that much, putting down her heels and then letting the weight move along to her toes as if she was testing the floor with every step, putting a little deliberate extra action into it. You never know for sure how girls' minds work (do you really think it's a mind in there or just a little buzz like a bee in a glass jar?) but you got the idea she had talked the other two into coming in here with her, and now she was showing them how to do it, walk slow and hold yourself straight.

She had on a kind of dirty-pink—beige maybe, I don't know—bathing suit with a little nubble all over it and, what got me, the straps were down. They were off her shoulders looped loose around the cool tops of her arms, and I guess as a result the suit had slipped a little on her, so all around the top of the cloth there was this shining rim. If it hadn't been there you wouldn't have known there could have been anything whiter than those shoulders. With the straps pushed off, there was nothing between the top of the suit and the top of her head except just *her*, this clean bare plane of the top of her chest down from the shoulder bones like a dented sheet of metal tilted in the light. I mean, it was more than pretty.

She had sort of oaky hair that the sun and salt had bleached, done up in a bun that was unraveling, and a kind of prim face. Walking into the A & P with your straps down, I suppose it's the only kind of face you *can* have. She held her head so high her neck, coming up out of those white shoulders, looked kind of stretched, but I didn't mind. The longer her neck was, the more of her there was.

She must have felt in the corner of her eye me and over my shoulder Stokesie in the second slot watching, but she didn't tip. Not this queen. She kept her eyes moving across the racks, and stopped, and turned so slow it made my stomach rub the inside of my apron, and buzzed to the other two, who kind of huddled against her for relief, and then they all three of them went up the cat-and-dog-food-breakfast-cereal-macaroni-rice-raisins-seasonings-spreads-spaghetti-soft-drinks-crackers-and-cookies aisle. From the third slot I look straight up this aisle to the meat counter, and I watched them all the way. The fat one with the tan sort of fumbled with the cookies, but on second thought she put the package back. The sheep pushing their carts down the aisle—the girls were walking against the usual traffic (not that we have one-way signs or anything)—were pretty hilarious. You could see them, when Queenie's white shoulders dawned on them, kind of jerk, or hop, or hiccup, but their eyes snapped back to their own baskets and on they pushed. I bet you could set off dynamite in an A & P and the people would by and large keep reaching and checking oatmeal off their lists and muttering "Let me see, there was a third thing, began with A, asparagus, no ah, yes, apple-sauce!" or whatever it is they do mutter. But there was no doubt, this jiggled them. A few houseslaves in pin curlers even looked around after pushing their carts past to make sure what they had seen was correct.

You know, it's one thing to have a girl in a bathing suit down on the beach, where what with the glare nobody can look at each other much anyway, and another thing in the cool of the A & P, under the fluorescent lights, against all those stacked packages, with her feet paddling along naked over our checkerboard green-and-cream rubber-tile floor.

"Oh Daddy," Stokesie said beside me. "I feel so faint."

"Darling," I said. "Hold me tight." Stokesie's married, with two babies chalked up on his fuselage already, but as far as I can tell that's the only difference. He's twenty-two, and I was nineteen this April.

"Is it done?" he asks, the responsible married man finding his voice. I forgot to say he thinks he's going to be manager some sunny day, maybe in 1990 when it's called the Great Alexandrov and Petrooshki Tea Company or something.

What he meant was, our town is five miles from a beach, with a big summer colony out on the Point, but we're right in the middle of town, and the women generally put on a shirt or shorts or something before they get out of the car into the street. And anyway these are usually women with six children and varicose veins mapping their legs and nobody, including them, could care less. As I say, we're right in the middle of town, and if you stand at our front doors you can see two banks and the Congregational church and the newspaper store and three real-estate offices and about twenty-seven old freeloaders tearing up Central Street because the sewer broke again. It's not as if we're on the Cape; we're north of Boston and there's people in this town haven't seen the ocean for twenty years.

The girls had reached the meat counter and were asking McMahon something. He pointed, they pointed, and they shuffled out of sight behind a pyramid of Diet Delight peaches. All that was left for us to see was old McMahon patting his mouth and looking after them sizing up their joints. Poor kids, I began to feel sorry for them, they couldn't help it.

Now here comes the sad part of the story, at least my family says it's sad, but I don't think it's so sad myself. The store's pretty empty, it being Thursday afternoon, so there was nothing much to do except lean on the register and wait for the girls to show up again. The whole store was like a pinball machine and I didn't know which tunnel they'd come out of. After a while they come around out of the far aisle, around the light bulbs, records at discount of the Caribbean Six or Tony Martin Sings or some such gunk you wonder they waste the wax on, sixpacks of candy bars, and plastic toys done up in cellophane that fall apart when a kid looks at them anyway. Around they come, Queenie still leading the way, and holding a little gray jar in her hand. Slots Three through Seven are unmanned and I could see her wondering between Stokes and me, but Stokesie with his usual luck draws an old party in baggy gray pants who stumbles up with four giant cans of pineapple juice (what do these bums *do* with all that pineapple juice? I've often asked myself) so the girls come to me. Queenie puts down the jar and I take it into my fingers icy cold. Kingfish Fancy Herring Snacks in Pure Sour Cream: 49¢. Now her hands are empty, not a ring or a bracelet, bare as God made them, and I wonder where the money's coming from. Still with that prim look she lifts a folded dollar bill out of the hollow at the center of her nubbled pink top. The jar went heavy in my hand. Really, I thought that was so cute.

Then everybody's luck begins to run out. Lengel comes in from haggling with a truck full of cabbages on the lot and is about to scuttle into that door marked MANAGER behind which he hides all day when the girls touch his eye. Lengel's pretty dreary, teaches Sunday school and the rest, but he doesn't miss that much. He comes over and says, "Girls, this isn't the beach."

Queenie blushes, though maybe it's just a brush of sunburn I was noticing for the first time, now that she was so close. "My mother asked me to pick up a jar of herring snacks." Her voice kind of startled me, the way voices do when you see the people first, coming out so flat and dumb yet kind of tony, too, the way it ticked over "pick up" and "snacks." All of a sudden I slid right down her voice into her living room. Her father and the other men were standing around in ice-cream coats and bow ties and the women were in sandals picking up herring snacks on toothpicks off a big glass plate and they were all holding drinks the color of water with olives and sprigs of mint in them. When my parents have somebody over they get lemonade and if it's a real racy affair Schlitz in tall glasses with "They'll Do It Every Time" cartoons stenciled on.

"That's all right," Lengel said. "But this isn't the beach." His repeating this struck me as funny, as if it had just occurred to him, and he had been thinking all these years the A & P was a great big dune and he was the head lifeguard. He didn't like my smiling—as I say he doesn't miss much—but he concentrates on giving the girls that sad Sunday-school-superintendent stare.

Queenie's blush is no sunburn now, and the plump one in plaid, that I liked better from the back—a really sweet can—pipes up, "We weren't doing any shopping. We just came in for the one thing."

15

"That makes no difference," Lengel tells her, and I could see from the way his eyes went that he hadn't noticed she was wearing a two-piece before. "We want you decently dressed when you come in here."

"We *are* decent," Queenie says suddenly, her lower lip pushing, getting sore now that she remembers her place, a place from which the crowd that runs the A & P must look pretty crummy. Fancy Herring Snacks flashed in her very blue eyes.

"Girls, I don't want to argue with you. After this come in here with your shoulders covered. It's our policy." He turns his back. That's policy for you. Policy is what the kingpins want. What the others want is juvenile delinquency.

All this while, the customers had been showing up with their carts but, you know, sheep, seeing a scene, they had all bunched up on Stokesie, who shook open a paper bag as gently as peeling a peach, not wanting to miss a word. I could feel in the silence everybody getting nervous, most of all Lengel, who asks me, "Sammy, have you rung up their purchase?"

I thought and said "No" but it wasn't about that I was thinking. I go through the punches, 4, 9, GROC, TOT—it's more complicated than you think, and after you do it often enough, it begins to make a little song, that you hear words to, in my case "Hello (*bing*) there, you (*gung*) hap-py *pee*-pul (*splat*)!"—the *splat* being the drawer flying out. I uncrease the bill, tenderly as you may imagine, it just having come from between the two smoothest scoops of vanilla I had ever known were there, and pass a half and a penny into her narrow pink palm, and nestle the herrings in a bag and twist its neck and hand it over, all the time thinking.

The girls, and who'd blame them, are in a hurry to get out, so I say "I quit" to Lengel quick enough for them to hear, hoping they'll stop and watch me, their unsuspected hero. They keep right on going, into the electric eye; the door flies open and they flicker across the lot to their car, Queenie and Plaid and Big Tall Goony-Goony (not that as raw material she was so bad), leaving me with Lengel and a kink in his eyebrow.

"Did you say something, Sammy?"

"I said I quit."

"I thought you did."

"You didn't have to embarrass them."

"It was they who were embarrassing us."

I started to say something that came out "Fiddle-de-doo." It's a saying of my grandmother's, and I know she would have been pleased.

"I don't think you know what you're saying," Lengel said.

"I know you don't," I said. "But I do." I pull the bow at the back of my apron and start shrugging it off my shoulders. A couple customers that had been heading for my slot begin to knock against each other, like scared pigs in a chute.

Lengel sighs and begins to look very patient and old and gray. He's been a friend of my parents for years. "Sammy, you don't want to do this to your Mom and Dad," he tells me. It's true, I don't. But it seems to me that once you begin a gesture it's fatal not to go through with it. I fold the apron, "Sammy" stitched in red on the pocket, and put it on the counter, and drop the bow tie on top of it. The bow tie is theirs, if you've ever wondered. "You'll feel this for the rest of your life," Lengel says, and I know that's true, too, but remembering how he made that pretty girl blush makes me so scrunchy inside I punch the No Sale tab and the machine whirs "pee-pul" and the drawer splats out. One advantage to this scene taking place in summer, I can follow this up with a clean exit, there's no fumbling around getting your coat and galoshes, I just saunter into the electric eye in my white shirt that my mother ironed the night before, and the door heaves itself open, and outside the sunshine is skating around on the asphalt.

I look around for my girls, but they're gone, of course. There wasn't anybody but some young married screaming with her children about some candy they didn't get by the door of a powder-blue Falcon station wagon. Looking back in the big windows, over the bags of peat moss and aluminum lawn furniture stacked on the pavement, I could see Lengel in my place in the slot, checking the sheep through. His face was dark gray and his back stiff, as if he'd just had an injection of iron, and my stomach kind of fell as I felt how hard the world was going to be to me hereafter.

QUESTIONS

1. Describe Updike's exposition in this story. That is, how does he introduce Sammy, let you know something about his character, and lead up to the major conflict?
2. From Sammy's language what do you learn about his view of himself? About his educational and class level? The first sentence, for example, is grammatically incorrect in Standard English but not uncommon in colloquial English. Point out similar passages. Do they suggest that he violates Standard English deliberately or unwittingly?
3. Indicate evidence in the narration that Sammy is an experienced "girl watcher." What is his estimation of the intelligence of most girls? Is this judgment consistent with what he finally does?
4. Describe the community in which the A & P is located.
5. What is the role of Lengel in the development of the conflict of the story? What values does he represent? What values does Sammy attach, in conflict, to his perception of the rights of the girls?
6. Why does Sammy say "I quit" so abruptly? Does it seem to him at the time that his gesture is meaningful? What do you think he means at the end by saying that the world is going to be hard to him afterwards?
7. Why does Sammy think about the fact that the summer season will permit him to make a "clean exit"? Does this thought in any way affect the value of his gesture?

GUY DE MAUPASSANT (1850–1893)

The Necklace°   1884

Translated by Edgar V. Roberts

She was one of those pretty and charming women, born, as if by an error of destiny, into a family of clerks and copyists. She had no dowry, no prospects, no way of getting known, courted, loved, married by a rich and distinguished man.

She finally settled for a marriage with a minor clerk in the Ministry of Education.

She was a simple person, without the money to dress well, but she was as unhappy as if she had gone through bankruptcy, for women have neither rank nor race. In place of high birth or important family connections, they can rely only on their beauty, their grace, and their charm. Their inborn finesse, their elegant taste, their engaging personalities, which are their only power, make working-class women the equals of the grandest duchesses.

She suffered constantly, feeling herself destined for all delicacies and luxuries. She suffered because of her grim apartment with its drab walls, threadbare furniture, ugly curtains. All such things, which most other women in her situation would not even have noticed, tortured her and filled her with despair. The sight of the young country girl who did her simple housework awakened in her only a sense of desolation and lost hopes. She daydreamed of large, silent anterooms, decorated with oriental tapestries and lighted by high bronze floor lamps, with two elegant valets in short culottes dozing in large armchairs under the effects of forced-air heaters. She visualized large drawing rooms draped in the most expensive silks, with fine end tables on which were placed knickknacks of inestimable value. She dreamed of the perfume of dainty private rooms, which were designed only for intimate tête-à-têtes with the closest friends, who because of their achievements and fame would make her the envy of all other women.

When she sat down to dinner at her round little table covered with a cloth that had not been washed for three days, in front of her husband who opened the kettle while declaring ecstatically, "Oh boy, beef stew, my favorite," she dreamed of expensive banquets with shining placesettings, and wall hangings depicting ancient heroes and exotic birds in an enchanted forest. She imagined a gourmet-prepared main course carried on the most exquisite trays and served on the most beautiful dishes, with whispered gallantries which she would hear with a sphinxlike smile as she dined on the pink meat of a trout or the delicate wing of a quail.

She had no decent dresses, no jewels, nothing. And she loved nothing but these; she believed herself born only for these. She burned with the desire to please, to be envied, to be attractive and sought after.   5

She had a rich friend, a comrade from convent days, whom she did not want to see anymore because she suffered so much when she returned home. She would weep for the entire day afterward with sorrow, regret, despair, and misery.

Well, one evening, her husband came home glowing and carrying a large envelope.

"Here," he said, "this is something for you."

She quickly tore open the envelope and took out a card engraved with these words:

The Chancellor of Education and Mrs. George Ramponneau request that Mr. and Mrs. Loisel do them the honor of coming to dinner at the Ministry of Education on the evening of January 8.

Instead of being delighted, as her husband had hoped, she threw the invitation   10 spitefully on the table while muttering:

"What do you expect me to do with this?"

"But Honey, I thought you'd be glad. You never get to go out, and this is a special occasion! I had a lot of trouble getting the invitation. Everyone wants one; the demand is high and not many clerks get invited. Everyone important will be there."

She looked at him angrily and stated impatiently:

"What do you want me to wear to go there?"

He had not thought of that. He stammered: 15

"But your theatre dress. That seems nice to me . . ."

He stopped, amazed and bewildered, as his wife began to cry. Large tears fell slowly from the corners of her eyes to her mouth. He said falteringly:

"What's wrong? What's wrong?"

But with a strong effort she had recovered, and she answered calmly as she wiped her damp cheeks:

"Nothing, except that I have nothing to wear and therefore can't go to the   20
party. Give your invitation to someone else at the office whose wife will have nicer clothes than mine."

Distressed, he responded:

"Well, okay, Mathilde. How much would a new dress cost, something you could use at other times, but not anything fancy?"

She thought for a few moments, adding things up and thinking also of an amount that she could ask without getting an immediate refusal and a frightened outcry from the frugal clerk.

Finally she responded tentatively:

"I don't know exactly, but it seems to me that I could get by on four hundred   25
francs."

He blanched slightly at this, because he had set aside just that amount to buy a shotgun and go with a few friends to Nanterre on Sundays the next summer to shoot larks.

However, he said:

"Okay, you've got four hundred francs, but make it a pretty dress."

As the day of the party drew near, Mrs. Loisel seemed sad, uneasy, anxious, even though her dress was all ready. One evening her husband said to her:

"What's up? You've been acting strangely for several days."   30

She answered:

"It's awful, but I don't have any jewels, not a single stone, nothing for match- ing jewelry. I'm going to look impoverished. I'd almost rather not go to the party."

He responded:

"You can wear a corsage of cut flowers. This year that's really the in thing. For no more than ten francs you can get two or three gorgeous roses."

She was not convinced.   35

"No . . . there's nothing more humiliating than to look ragged in the middle of rich women."

But her husband exclaimed:

"God, but you're silly! Go to your friend Mrs. Forrestier, and ask her to lend you some jewelry. You know her well enough to do that."

She uttered a cry of joy:

"That's right. I hadn't thought of that."   40

The next day she went to her friend's house and described her problem.

Mrs. Forrestier went to her glass-plated wardrobe, took out a large jewel box, opened it, and said to Mrs. Loisel:

"Choose, my dear."

She saw bracelets, then a pearl necklace, then a Venetian cross of finely worked gold and gems. She tried on the jewelry in front of a mirror, and hesitated, unable to make up her mind about which ones to give back. She kept asking:

"Do you have anything else?"

"Certainly. Look to your heart's content. I don't know what will please you most."

Suddenly she found, in a black satin box, a superb diamond necklace, and her heart throbbed with desire for it. Her hands shook as she took it up. She fastened it around her neck, watched it gleam at her throat, and looked at herself ecstatically.

Then she asked, haltingly and anxiously:

"Could you lend me this, nothing but this?"

"Why yes, certainly."

She jumped up, hugged her friend joyfully, then hurried away with her treasure.

The day of the party came. Mrs. Loisel was a success. She was prettier than anyone else, stylish, graceful, smiling, and wild with joy. All the men saw her, asked her name, and sought to be introduced. All the important administrators stood in line to waltz with her. The Chancellor himself eyed her.

She danced joyfully, passionately, intoxicated with pleasure, thinking of nothing but the moment, in the triumph of her beauty, in the glory of her success, in a cloud-nine of happiness made up of all the admiration, of all the aroused desire, of this victory so complete and so sweet to the heart of any woman.

She did not leave until four o'clock in the morning. Her husband, since midnight, had been sleeping in a little empty room with three other men whose wives had also been enjoying themselves.

He threw over her shoulders the shawl that he had brought for the trip home, modest clothing from everyday life, the poverty of which contrasted sharply with the elegance of the party dress. She felt it and hurried away to avoid being noticed by the other women who luxuriated in rich furs.

Liosel tried to hold her back:

"Wait a while. You'll catch cold outdoors. I'll call a cab."

But she paid no attention and hurried down the stairs. When they reached the street they found no carriages. They began to look for one, shouting at cabmen passing by at a distance.

They walked toward the Seine, desperate, shivering. Finally, on a quay, they found one of those old night-going buggies that are seen in Paris only after dark, as if they were ashamed of their wretched appearance in daylight.

It took them to their door, on the Street of Martyrs, and they sadly climbed the stairs to their flat. For her, it was finished. As for him, he could think only that he had to begin work at the Ministry of Education at ten o'clock.

She took the shawl off her shoulders, in front of the mirror, to see herself once more in her glory. But suddenly she cried out. The necklace was no longer around her neck!

Her husband, already half undressed, asked:

"What's wrong with you?"

She turned toward him frantically:

"I . . . I . . . I no longer have Mrs. Forrestier's necklace."   65

He stood up, bewildered:

"What! . . . How! . . . It's not possible!"

And they looked in the folds of the dress, in the creases of the shawl, in the pockets, everywhere. They found nothing.

He asked:

"You're sure you still had it when you left the party?"   70

"Yes. I checked it in the vestibule of the Ministry."

"But if you had lost it in the street, we would have heard it fall. It must be in the cab."

"Yes, probably. Did you notice the number?"

"No. Did you see it?"

"No."   75

Overwhelmed, they looked at each other. Finally, Loisel got dressed again:

"I'm going out to retrace all our steps," he said, "to see if I can find the necklace that way."

And he went out. She stayed in her evening dress, without the energy to get ready for bed, prostrated in a chair, drained of strength and thought.

Her husband came back at about seven o'clock. He had found nothing.

He went to Police Headquarters and to the newspapers to announce a reward.   80
He went to the samll cab companies, and finally he followed up even the slightest hopeful lead.

She waited the entire day, in the same enervated state, in the face of this frightful disaster.

Loisel came back in the evening, his face pale and haggard. He had found nothing.

"You'll have to write to your friend," he said, "that you broke a fastening on her necklace and that you will have it fixed. That will give us time to look around."

She wrote as he dictated.

At the end of a week they had lost all hope.   85

And Loisel, seemingly five years older, declared:

"We'll have to see about replacing the jewels."

The next day, they took the case which had contained the necklace, and went to the jeweler whose name was inside. He looked at his books:

"I wasn't the one, Madam, who sold the necklace. I only made the case."

Then they went from jeweler to jeweler, searching for a necklace like the   90
other one, racking their memories, both of them sick with worry and anguish.

In a shop in the Palais-Royal, they found a string of diamonds that seemed to them exactly like the one they were seeking. It was priced at forty thousand francs. They could buy it for thirty-six thousand.

They got the jeweler to promise not to sell it for three days. And they made an agreement that he would buy it back for thirty-four thousand frances if the original was recovered before the end of February.

Loisel had saved eighteen thousand francs that his father had left him. He would have to borrow the rest.

He borrowed, asking a thousand francs from one, five hundred from another, five louis° here, three louis here. He made promissory notes, undertook ruinous obligations, did business with loan sharks and the whole tribe of finance companies. He compromised himself for the remainder of his days, risked his signature without knowing whether he would be able to honor it, and, terrified by anguish over the future, by the black misery that was about to descend on him, by the prospect of all kinds of physical deprivations and moral tortures, he went to get the new necklace, and put down thirty-six thousand francs on the jeweler's counter.

Mrs. Loisel took the necklace back to Mrs. Forrestier, who said with an offended tone: 95

"You should have brought it back sooner, because I might have needed it."

She did not open the case, as her friend feared she might. If she had noticed the substitution, what would she have thought? What would she have said? Would she not have taken her for a thief?

Mrs. Loisel soon discovered the horrible life of the needy. She did her share, however, completely, heroically. That horrifying debt had to be paid. She would pay. They dismissed the maid; they changed their address; they rented an attic flat.

She learned to do heavy housework, dirty kitchen jobs. She washed the dishes, wearing away her manicured fingernails on greasy pots and encrusted baking dishes. She handwashed dirty linen, shirts, and dish towels that she hung out on the line to dry. Each morning, she took the garbage down to the street, and she carried up water, stopping at each floor to catch her breath. And, dressed in cheap house dresses, she went to the fruit dealer, the grocer, the butchers, with her basket under her arms, haggling, insulting, defending her measly cash penny by penny.

They had to make installment payments every month, and, to buy more time, to refinance loans.   100

The husband worked evenings to make fair copies of tradesmen's accounts, and late into the night he made copies at five cents a page.

And this life lasted ten years.

At the end of ten years, they had paid back everything—everything—including the extra charges imposed by loan sharks and the accumulation of compound interest.

Mrs. Loisel seemed old now. She had become the strong, hard, and rude woman of poor households. He hair unkempt, with uneven skirts and rough, red hands, she spoke loudly, washed floors with large buckets of water. But sometimes, when her husband was at work, she sat down near the window, and she dreamed of that evening so long ago, of that party, where she had been so beautiful and so admired.

What would life have been like if she had not lost that necklace? Who knows?   105 Who knows? Life is so peculiar, so uncertain. How little a thing it takes to destroy you or to save you!

---

louis: a twenty-franc coin.

Well, one Sunday, as she had gone on a stroll along the Champs-Elysées to relax from the cares of the week, she suddenly noticed a woman walking with a child. It was Mrs. Forrestier, always youthful, always beautiful, always attractive.

Mrs. Loisel felt moved. Would she speak to her? Yes, certainly. And now that she had paid, she could tell all. Why not?

She walked closer.

"Hello, Jeanne."

The other did not recognize her at all, being astonished to be addressed 11◖ so intimately by this working woman. She stammered:

"But . . . Madam! . . . I don't know. . . . You must have made a mistake."

"No. I'm Mathilde Loisel."

Her friend cried out:

"Oh! . . . My poor Mathilde, you've changed so much."

"Yes. I've had some hard times since I saw you last; in fact, miseries . . . 11⸃ and all this because of you! . . ."

"Of me . . . how so?"

"You remember the diamond necklace that you lent me to go to the party at the Ministry of Education?"

"Yes. What then?"

"Well, I lost it."

"How, since you gave it back to me?" 12◖

"I brought back another exactly like it. And for ten years we've been paying for it. You understand that this wasn't easy for us, who have nothing. . . . Finally it's over, and I'm mighty damned glad."

Mrs. Forrestier stopped her.

"You say that you bought a diamond necklace to replace mine?"

"Yes, You didn't notice it, eh? They were exactly like yours."

And she smiled with proud and childish joy. 12⸃

Mrs. Forrestier, deeply moved, took both her hands.

"Oh, my poor Mathilde! But mine was false. At the most, it was worth five hundred francs! . . ."

QUESTIONS

1. Describe the character of Mathilde. On balance, is she as negative as she might seem at first? Why does De Maupassant describe her efforts to cooperate in paying the debt as "heroic"? How does her character as first described create the situation that causes the financial penance the Loisels must undergo?

2. Are Mathilde's daydreams unusual for a woman in her station? Do you think that De Maupassant fashioned the ironic conclusion to demonstrate that Mathilde somehow deserved her misfortune?

3. What sort of person is Loisel? How does his character contribute to the financial disaster?

4. Describe the relationship between Mathilde and Loisel as shown in their

conversations. Does their relationship seem to be intimate or is it less personal?

5. De Maupassant's speaker states that small things save or destroy people. Do you think that "The Necklace" bears out this idea? Does there seem to be any role for a concept of fate in such a view of existence, or is chance the governing influence?

6. Can an argument be made that De Maupassant is presenting a view in the story that might be described as econmic determinism? That is, to what degree does he relate economic status, either positively or negatively, to happiness and character fulfillment?

HOW TO WRITE A PRÉCIS

The words *précis* and *precise* are closely related, and this connection is helpful in enabling an understanding of the nature of a précis—namely, a cutting down of a long story into its *precise,* essential parts. The object is to make a very short encapsulation of a story. Other words describing the précis are *abridgment, paraphrase, abstract, condensation*, and *epitome*. Epitome is particularly helpful as a description for a précis, for an epitome is a cutting away of inessentials so that only the important, most vital parts remain.

The technique of writing a précis of a story can be significant not only in reading fiction, but in undertaking many other areas of study. Précis writing can be used for taking notes, preparing for exams, establishing and clarifying facts for any body of discourse, studying for classroom discussion, and reinforcing things learned in the past. The object of a précis should be not to tell *everything*, but only to give the highlights, so that any reader would be able to know the main points of the story.

Some guidelines to follow in the development of a précis are discussed in the following sections.

Selection

Only essential details belong in a précis. For example, at the opening of the story "The Necklace," De Maupassant describes the pleasing daydreams of Mathilde Loisel. She is preoccupied with visions of what wealth could bring, such as large anterooms, tapestries, lamps, valets, silks, end tables, expensive bric-a-brac, private rooms, and elegant and exotic meals. Including references to all these would needlessly lengthen a précis of "The Necklace." Instead, it is sufficient to say something like "Mathilde daydreams of wealth," which gets at the vital facts about her dissatisfaction with her life and her dreams for a wealthier one.

This concentration on only essentials allows a précis to be shortened. A 5,000-word story might be epitomized in 100, 200, or 400 words. It is clear that more details might be selected for inclusion in the longer précis than in the shorter ones. Whatever the length of the final précis, however, selection of detail is to be based on the importance of the material in the story being described.

Accuracy

There should be no mistakes in a précis, so all details should be correctly recorded. Because the essay is an abbreviation of a lengthy story, there is a risk not just of factual misstatement, but also of using words that might give a misleading impression of the original. Thus, in "The Necklace," Mathilde Loisel cooperates with her husband for ten long years to repay their 36,000-franc debt. It would be easy just to say that she "works" during this time, but this word might mislead, for some readers might assume that it refers to outside employment. What De Maupassant actually tells us is that Mathilde does heavy housework as a part of her general economizing in her *own* household, not in the houses of others.

The need to condense long sections of a story necessarily produces the need for comprehensive words that accurately account for sections of the story. Thus, in "The Necklace" Loisel needs to borrow money to pay for half of the 36,000 francs the replacement will cost. Just to say "he borrows money," however, does not convey the usurious rates of interest he must accept to get the loans from various lenders and loansharks. An accurate précis description of this borrowing must include some account of these desperate promises to pay. Thus, a clause like "he almost literally mortgages his future to get the needed loans" would cover not only the borrowing but also the high rates of interest. For any précis, the choice of proper wording should be made with comprehensive accuracy in mind.

Diction

The précis is to be an original work, and therefore it should be written in words that are not taken directly from the story. The best way to ensure original wording is to read the story, record the major things that happen, and then put the story out of sight during the writing process. That way the temptation to borrow words directly can be avoided.

However, if some of the story's words find their way into the précis even after a careful try to be totally original, it is important to put these words into quotation marks. As long as direct quotations are kept at a minimum, they are satisfactory. Too many quoted words, however, indicate that the précis is not really original writing.

Objectivity

A précis should be scrupulously factual. It must avoid explanatory or introductory material unless that is actually a part of the story. As much effort should be made to *avoid* conclusions in a précis as is exerted to *include* them in other kinds of writing about fiction. Here is a comparative example of what to do and what to avoid:

WHAT TO DO

Mathilde Loisel, a French housewife married to a minor clerk, is unhappy with her poor household possessions. She daydreams about wealth and is even more dissatisfied after visiting Jeane Forrestier, a rich woman who is a former schoolmate. One day Loisel, Mathilde's husband, brings home an invitation to an exclusive dinner dance. Mathilde angrily claims that she has nothing to wear, but Loisel gives her all his money to buy a party dress.

WHAT TO AVOID

De Maupassant opens the story by introducing the dissatisfaction that ultimately will propel Mathilde Loisel and her husband to their ten-year disaster. Mathilde's unhappiness with her own household possessions, and her dreams about wealth, lead her naturally to reproach her husband when he brings home the invitation to the dinner at the Ministry of Education. It is clear that her unhappiness leads her to spend beyond their means for a special party dress.

The right-hand column contains a guiding topic sentence, to which the following sentences adhere. Such writing is commendable everywhere else, but not in a précis. The left-hand column is better writing *as a précis*, for it presents a selection of details only as they appear in the story, without introductory sentences, because in the story there are no such introductions.

Paragraphs

The normal principle of devoting a paragraph to only one topic may also be applied to a précis. If each major division, episode, scene, action, or section of the story is considered a topic, then the précis may be divided into paragraphs devoted to each of the divisions. Thus the first paragraph of the sample précis of "The Necklace" includes the material leading up to the dinner dance, while the last is devoted to the meeting near the Champs-Elysées. In most stories similar divisions into scenes and episodes may serve as natural topics which limit the extent of paragraphs.

Arrangement and Sequence

In a précis the arrangement and sequence are to remain as in the order of the original story. Thus, if the story has a surprise ending, like that in "The Necklace," the conclusion is also withheld until the end of the précis. By contrast, in an analysis of an idea, say, or in the study of a character, the surprise ending might be included whenever it becomes important. It is proper, however, to introduce names, places, and other essential details of circumstance at the beginning of the précis, even though these details are not brought out immediately in the story. For example, De Maupassant does not name Mathilde right away, and he never says that she is French, but a précis of "The Necklace" would be obscure if these details were withheld.

Sentences

Because of the precise, factual nature of the précis, it is tempting to write choppy sentences, comparable to short bursts of machine gun fire. Here is an example of choppy sentences:

> Mathilde gives up her nice apartment. She works hard for ten years. She climbs stairs. She cleans the floors. She uses big buckets of water. She gets coarse and loud. She haggles with shopkeepers. She is no longer young and beautiful.

An entire essay consisting of sentences like these might make readers feel as though they actually have been machine gunned. The problem is to include detail but also to remember to shape and organize sentences. Here is a more acceptable set of sentences revised to contain the same information:

> She gives up her nice apartment and devotes herself to hard work for the entire ten years. At home she climbs many stairs and throws buckets of water to clean the floors. When marketing, she haggles with shopkeepers for bargains. At the end of the time this hard work has made her loud and coarse, and her youthful beauty is gone.

This revision blends the shorter sentences together and makes a contrast between the second and third sentences. Even though sentences in a précis are to be almost rigidly factual, there should be an effort to make them as graceful as possible.

SAMPLE ESSAY

A Précis of De Maupassant's "The Necklace"*

[1]
Mathilde Loisel, a French housewife married to a minor clerk, is unhappy with her poor household possessions. She daydreams about wealth and is even more dissatisfied after visiting Jeanne Forrestier. a rich woman who is a former schoolmate. One day Loisel, Mathilde's husband, brings home an invitation to an exclusive dinner dance. Mathilde angrily claims that she has nothing to wear, but Loisel gives her all his money to buy a party dress. With no jewelry to match, she is ready to give up the affair, but at Loisel's suggestion she borrows a beautiful necklace from Jeanne.

* See p. 90 for this story.

[2] At the party Mathilde is a huge success, but afterward she and Loisel hurry away because she is ashamed to be seen in her everyday shawl. Upon arriving home she is horrified to discover that she has lost the necklace.

[3] In desperation, Loisel and she spend a week looking for the necklace. Unable to find it, Loisel buys another for 36,000 francs. He uses his entire inheritance for half of this sum and borrows the rest wherever he can, almost literally mortgaging his future to get the needed loans.

[4] For the next ten years Mathilde and Loisel make sacrifices to pay back all the loans. She gives up her nice apartment and devotes herself to hard work for the entire ten years. At home she climbs many stairs and throws buckets of water to clean the floors. When marketing, she haggles with shopkeepers for bargains. At the end of the time this hard work has made her loud and coarse, and her youthful beauty is gone.

[5] One Sunday she takes a walk and sees Jeanne, who does not recognize her at first because of her changed appearance. Mathilde tells Jeanne of her ten years of sacrifice. Sympathetically, Jeanne responds by explaining that the original necklace had been false, and worth no more than 500 francs.

Commentary on the Essay

This précis, about 300 words long, illustrates the selection of major actions and the omission of interesting but inessential detail. Thus, the clause "she daydreams about wealth" contains four words, and it condenses more than 150 words of detailed description in the story. The next clause about the rich friend, Jeanne Forrestier, is longer, and it condenses a relatively short passage in the story. The clause is important, however, because it related Mathilde's increased dissatisfaction upon seeing Jeanne, and Jeanne is doubly important, for she is the owner of the false necklace which is the cause of the Loisel family's downfall. The principle here is this: The selection of what to include in a précis depends not so much upon the length as upon the significance of parts in the original.

Each of the five paragraphs in the précis is devoted to a comparable episode of "The Necklace." Paragraph 1 describes the story up to the party; paragraph 2, the events of the party leading up to the discovery of the loss. The third and fourth paragraphs deal with the borrowing of money to restore the necklace and with the ten-year sacrifice to pay back the loans. The last paragraph describes the scene in which Mathilde learns that the sacrifice was unnecessary.

The basis for determining the appropriateness of episode for paragraph is not time but unity. Thus, paragraph 2 describes an episode that takes place within a few hours, but the unifying element is the party and the discovery of the loss immediately after it. The events of paragraph 4, on the other hand, take ten years, and the unifying principle is the coarsening of Mathilde's character under the effects of her difficult labor.

3

Plot and Structure

Just as the people or characters in fiction are derived from life, so are the **actions.** The actions, as we have observed, occur in sequence, or in chronological order. Once we have established the narrative or sequential order, we consider **plot,** or the plan of development of the actions.

WHAT IS PLOT?

Without a plot, we do not have a story. A plot is a plan or groundwork for a story, based in conflicting human motivations, with the actions resulting from believable and realistic human response. In a well-plotted story, nothing is irrelevant; everything is related. The British novelist E. M. Forster, in *Aspects of the Novel*, presented a memorable illustration of plot. As a bare minimum narration of actions in contrast to a story with a plot, he used the following: "The king died, and then the queen died." This sentence describes a sequence, a chronological order, but it is no more. To have a plot, a sequence must be integrated with human motivation. Thus the following sentence qualifies as fiction with a plot: "The king died, and then the queen died of grief." Once the narrative introduces the operative element "of grief," which shows that one thing (grief over the king's death) produces or overcomes another (the death of the queen), there is a plot. Thus, in a story, time is important not simply because one thing happens *after* another but because one thing happens *because* of another. It is response, interaction, opposition, and causation that make a plot out of a simple series of actions.

Conflict

Fictional human responses are brought out to their highest degree in the development of a **conflict.** In its most elemental form, a conflict is the opposition of two people. They may fight, argue, enlist help against each other, and otherwise carry on their opposition. Conflicts may also exist between larger groups of people, although in fiction conflicts between individuals are more identifiable and therefore more interesting. Conflict may also exist between an individual and larger forces, such as natural objects, ideas, modes of behavior, public opinion, and the like. The existence of difficult *choices* within an individual's mind may also be presented as conflict, or **dilemma**. In addition, the conflict may be presented not as direct opposition, but rather as a set of comparative or contrastive ideas or values. In short, there are many ways to bring out a conflict in fiction.

CONFLICT, DOUBT, TENSION, AND INTEREST. The reason that conflict is the major ingredient in plot is that once two forces are in opposition, there may be doubt about the outcome. The doubt, if the reader becomes interested and engaged with the characters, produces curiosity and tension. The same concern furnishes the lifeblood of athletic competition. For just a moment, consider which kind of football game is more interesting: (1) one in which the score goes back and forth and there is doubt about the outcome right up to the last second, or (2) one in which one of the teams gets so far ahead in the first quarter that there is no more doubt about who will win. The interest that a highly contested game provides is also generated by a conflict in a story. The conflict should be a genuine contest, an engagement between characters or forces of approximately equal strength. It should never be a "walkaway," "mismatch," "rout," or "laugher," to use terminology from the sports world. Unless there is doubt, there is no tension, and unless there is tension, there is no interest.

CONFLICT IN PLOT. To see a plot in operation, let us build on Forster's description. Here is a bare plot for a story: "John and Jane meet, fall in love, and get married." This plot would probably not get many readers, for it lacks any conflict. Now, using this same essential narrative of "boy meets girl," let us introduce some elements of conflict:

> John and Jane meet at school and fall in love. They go together for two years, and they plan to marry, but a problem arises. Jane wants to develop a career first, and after marriage she wants to be an equal contributor to the family. John understands Jane's desire for a career, but he wants to marry first and let her continue her studies afterward in preparation for her goal. Jane believes that this solution will not work, insisting instead that it is a trap from which she will never escape. This conflict interrupts their plans, and they part in regret and anger. Going their separate ways even though they still love each other, both marry other people and build their lives and careers. Neither is completely happy even though they like and respect their spouses. Many years later, after they have children and grandchildren of their own, they meet again. John is now a widower and Jane has divorced. Their earlier conflict no longer being a barrier, they marry and live successfully together. Druing their marriage, however, even their new happiness is

tinged with reproach and regret because of their earlier conflict, their increasing age, and the lost years that they might have spent with each other.

Here we have a plot, with a conflict that takes a number of shapes. The (1) initial conflict is resolved by a (2) separation leading each of the characters to a new life that is (3) satisfactory but not totally happy. The final marriage produces (4) not unqualified happiness, but a note of regret and (5) a sense of time lost that cannot be restored. It is the establishment of these contrasting or conflicting situations and responses that produces the interest the short-short story contains. The situation is lifelike; the conflict stems out of realistic values; the outcome is true to life. The imposition of the various conflicts and contrasts has made an interesting plot out of what could have been a common "boy meets girl" sequence.

THE STRUCTURE OF FICTION

Thus the plot of a story is the establishment of a conflict and the consequences, variations, and developments that stem from it. To the degree that the plot requires a set of events that may be laid out in a chronological order, which may have a clearly formed shape, it may be termed a major *structure* of the story.

Structure describes the arrangement and placement of the story's materials. The word *structure* belongs to a whole family of words that are concerned with spreading and ordering, including *instruct, construct, street, streusel (a layering of dough in a pastry)*, and *stratagem*. The study of structure in fiction is a study of the causes and reasons (*stratagem* here is a helpful related word) behind matters such as placement, balance, recurring themes, juxtapositions, true and misleading conclusions, suspense, and the imitation of models or forms (like letters, conversations, confessions, and the like). Thus a story may be divided into parts, or it might be arranged according to principal actions that occur outdoors or indoors, or it might be laid out according to the pattern of movement of a vehicle such as a train. Structure relates to these arrangements and the purposes for which they are made.

Formal Categories of Structure

Many aspects of structure are common to all genres of literature, and often the structure of fiction is parallel to that of drama. In any story, however, there will be the following aspects that form the backbone, skeleton, or pattern of development.

EXPOSITION.   **Exposition** is the *laying out*, the putting forth, of the materials in the story: the main characters, their backgrounds, their characteristics, goals, limitations, and potentials. It presents everything that is going to be important in the story. It is not necessarily limited to the beginning of a story, but it may be found anywhere. Thus, there may be intricacies, twists, turns, false leads, blind alleys, surprises, and other quirks introduced in order to perplex, intrigue, please, and otherwise interest readers. Whenever something new arises, to the degree that it is new it is a part of exposition. At a certain point, however, the introduction of new materials must cease and the story must proceed to a conclusion with only those elements that have already been included.

COMPLICATION.   The **complication** marks the onset of the major conflict in the story. The participants are the protagonist and the antagonist, together with whatever ideas and values they represent, such as good and evil, individualism and collectivization, childhood and age, love and hate, intelligence and stupidity, knowledge and ignorance, freedom and slavery, desire and resistance, and the like.

CRISIS.   The **crisis** is the turning point, the separation between what has gone before and what will come after. In practice, the crisis is usually a decision or action undertaken in an effort to *resolve* the conflict. It is important to stress, however, that the crisis, though a result of operating forces and decisions, may not produce the intended results. That situation is the next part of the formal structure, the climax.

CLIMAX.   The **climax** (from the Greek for *ladder*) is the *high point* in the action, in which the conflict and the consequent tension are brought out to the fullest extent. Another way to think of climax is to define it as that point in a story in which all the rest of the action becomes inevitable. This inevitability does not, of course, occur in an instant but happens as a result of the fact that once the high point is reached, there must be an action or development that brings the climax to a conclusion. For example, in Stephen Crane's "The Bride Comes to Yellow Sky" the climax is the confrontation of Potter and Scratchy Wilson. Since Scratchy is alcoholic and therefore unpredictable, there is at least some doubt about the outcome. Once Potter declares that he is not carrying his gun, however, Scratchy's primitive sense of honor demands that he back down from his wanted shootout. Thus the declaration is the end of the climax and the point which marks the beginning of the end of the story.

RESOLUTION OR DENOUEMENT.   The **resolution** (a releasing or untying) or **denouement** (untying) is the set of actions bringing the story to its conclusion. Scratchy Wilson's brief queries into the truth of Potter's declaration, for example, and his learning about Potter's marriage, are the resolution of the conflict of "The Bride Comes to Yellow Sky." Once the "untying" has been done, the author usually concludes the story as quickly as possible. Both "The Bride Comes to Yellow Sky" and Eudora Welty's

"A Worn Path," for example, end with characters walking away. The major actions are completed and the final action, the walking, underscores the note of finality.

Formal and Actual Structure

The formal structure just described is an ideal one, a pattern that is almost identical to the plot and that takes place in straightforward, chronological order. In practice, however, the structure of a story will usually vary the ideal pattern, even though all the elements will be present. Mystery stories, for example, postpone climaxes until the last possible moment and also necessarily delay crucial exposition, inasmuch as the goal is to mystify. In a story where the exposition allows readers to know who a wrongdoer is, by contrast, the goal of the story is often to create suspense about whether the protagonist can maintain life while seeking the wrong-doer out. More realistic, less "artificial" stories might also embody structural variations. In Welty's "A Worn Path," for example, a memorable variation is produced by the information introduced at the very end. During most of the story the complication seems to be that Phoenix Jackson's major conflict is with (1) her age and (2) the natural environment. At the end, however, we learn the additional detail that she is the sole guardian and caretaker of an invalid grandson. Thus, even at the end we get exposition and complication, so much so that our previous understanding of the conflict is augmented. The anguish of our reponse is made more acute, for Phoenix's antagonist is not just age and environment but also hopeless illness. The *structure* of the story is designed to withhold an essential detail to maximize impact. The resolution of the story, coming at the same moment as this crucial complication, points toward the final, inevitable defeat of Phoenix while it also demonstrates her determined character.

Variants in structure are almost as numerous as the stories you will encounter. There might be a "flashback" method, for example: The moment at which the flashback is taking place might actually be during the resolution of the plot, and the flashback might lead you into a moment of climax but then go on to develop the details that are more properly part of the exposition. Let us again consider our brief plot about John and Jane, and develop a possible flashback way of structuring the story.

> Jane is now old, and a noise outside causes her to think of the argument that forced her to part with John many years before. Then she thinks of the years she and John spent happily together after they married. She then contrasts her happiness with her earlier, less happy marriage, and from there she reflects on her years of courtship with John before their conflict over career plans developed. Then she looks over at John, reading in a chair, and smiles. John smiles back, and the story ends.

This structure suggests one way of telling the story, but there might be others. Let us suppose that John is in a sickbed at the time Jane thinks about their past, or he might be dead in his coffin. These variables would produce different stories. Or, let us suppose that Jane is a widow of many years, either thinking about her past or giving advice to a son or daughter. Then, too, she might be looking back as a divorcee from her first marriage, having just met John again, with the final action being their wedding. The years of happiness might then be introduced as anticipation, or as a resolution described by a narrator, who might have heard about things later from a friend. In short, the possibilities of structuring our story are great. Using the flashback method such as the one demonstrated here, we would necessarily bring out all the formal elements of plot, but the actual arrangement—the real structure—would be unique.

There are, of course, many other ways to structure a story. A plot might be developed by a group of persons, each one with a part of the details; by the time all finish making their contribution, all the necessary complications and resolutions would be clear. If a story is structured as though it is a dream, elements of exposition and complication might naturally be introduced out of the sequence that the ideal structure might require. Parts of a story might also be arranged in fragments of overheard conversation, or portions of letters. Another story might develop with partial narration and partial dialogue, and still another might be total dialogue.

Questions for the Study of Structure

In the determination of the structure of any story, there are a number of questions that one might ask. What does the reader need to know in order to understand the story? Are all these things actually included? How are these things ordered? Do they come at a point when they might be expected, in the light of the story's plot? What comes first, and why? What comes afterward, and why? If the second and following things preceded the first thing, how would the story be different? How does the present ordering of actions, scenes, speeches, and narration contribute to the completion of the story? How are these placements influential in the effect produced by the story?

STEPHEN CRANE (1871–1900)

The Bride Comes to Yellow Sky   *1898*

I

The great pullman was whirling onward with such dignity of motion that a glance from the window seemed simply to prove that the plains of Texas were pouring eastward. Vast flats of green grass, dull-hued spaces of mesquit and cactus, little groups of frame houses, woods of light and tender trees, all were sweeping into the east, sweeping over the horizon, a precipice.

A newly married pair had boarded this coach at San Antonio. The man's face was reddened from many days in the wind and sun, and a direct result of his new black clothes was that his brick-coloured hands were constantly performing in a most conscious fashion. From time to time he looked down respectfully at his attire. He sat with a hand on each knee, like a man waiting in a barber's shop. The glances he devoted to other passengers were furtive and shy.

The bride was not pretty nor was she very young. She wore a dress of blue cashmere, with small reservations of velvet here and there, and with steel buttons abounding. She continually twisted her head to regard her puff sleeves, very stiff, straight, and high. They embarrassed her. It was quite apparent that she had cooked, and that she expected to cook, dutifully. The blushes caused by the careless scrutiny of some passengers as she had entered the car were strange to see upon this plain, under-class countenance, which was drawn in placid, almost emotionless lines.

They were evidently very happy. "Ever been in a parlour-car before?" he asked, smiling with delight.

"No," she answered; "I never was. It's fine, ain't it?"

"Great! And then after a while we'll go forward to the diner, and get a big lay-out. Finest meal in the world. Charge a dollar."

"Oh, do they?" cried the bride. "Charge a dollar? Why, that's too much—for us—ain't it, Jack?"

"Not this trip, anyhow," he answered bravely. "We're going to go the whole thing."

Later he explained to her about the trains. "You see, it's a thousand miles from one end of Texas to the other; and this train runs right across it, and never stops but four times." He had the pride of an owner. He pointed out to her the dazzling fittings of the coach; and in truth her eyes opened wider as she contemplated the sea-green figured velvet, the shining brass, silver, and glass, the wood that gleamed as darkly brilliant as the surface of a pool of oil. At one end a bronze figure sturdily held a support for a separated chamber, and at convenient places on the ceiling were frescos in olive and silver.

To the minds of the pair, their surroundings reflected the glory of their marriage that morning in San Antonio; this was the environment of their new estate; and the man's face in particular beamed with an elation that made him appear ridiculous to the negro porter. This individual at times surveyed them from afar with an amused and superior grin. On other occasions he bullied them with skill in ways that did not make it exactly plain to them that they were being bullied. He subtly used all the manners of the most unconquerable kind of snobbery. He oppressed them; but of this oppression they had small knowledge, and they speedily forgot that infrequently a number of travellers covered them with stares of derisive enjoyment. Historically there was supposed to be something infinitely humorous in their situation.

"We are due in Yellow Sky at 3:42," he said, looking tenderly into her eyes.

"Oh, are we?" she said, as if she had not been aware of it. To evince surprise at her husband's statement was part of her wifely amiability. She took from a pocket a little silver watch; and as she held it before her, and stared at it with a frown of attention, the new husband's face shone.

"I bought it in San Anton' from a friend of mine," he told her gleefully.

"It's seventeen minutes past twelve," she said, looking up at him with a kind of shy and clumsy coquetry. A passenger, noting this play, grew excessively sardonic, and winked at himself in one of the numerous mirrors.

At last they went to the dining-car. Two rows of negro waiters, in glowing white suits, surveyed their entrance with the interest, and also the equanimity, of men who had been forewarned. The pair fell to the lot of a waiter who happened to feel pleasure in steering them through their meal. He viewed them with the manner of a fatherly pilot, his countenance radiant with benevolence. The patronage, entwined with the ordinary deference, was not plain to them. And yet, as they returned to their coach, they showed in their faces a sense of escape. 15

To the left, miles down a long purple slope, was a little ribbon of mist where moved the keening Rio Grande. The train was approaching it at an angle, and the apex was Yellow Sky. Presently it was apparent that, as the distance from Yellow Sky grew shorter, the husband became commensurately restless. His brick-red hands were more insistent in their prominence. Occasionally he was even rather absent-minded and far-away when the bride leaned forward and addressed him.

As a matter of truth, Jack Potter was beginning to find a shadow of a deed weigh upon him like a leaden slab. He, the town marshal of Yellow Sky, a man known, liked, and feared in his corner, a prominent person, had gone to San Antonio to meet a girl he believed he loved, and there, after the usual prayers, had actually induced her to marry him, without consulting Yellow Sky for any part of the transaction. He was now bringing his bride before an innocent and unsuspecting community.

Of course people in Yellow Sky married as it pleased them, in accordance with a general custom; but such was Potter's thought of his duty to his friends, or of their idea of his duty, or of an unspoken form which does not control men in these matters, that he felt he was heinous. He had committed an extraordinary crime. Face to face with this girl in San Antonio, and spurred by his sharp impulse, he had gone headlong over all the social hedges. At San Antonio he was like a man hidden in the dark. A knife to sever any friendly duty, any form, was easy to his hand in that remote city. But the hour of Yellow Sky—the hour of daylight— was approaching.

He knew full well that his marriage was an important thing to his town. It could only be exceeded by the burning of the new hotel. His friends could not forgive him. Frequently he had reflected on the advisability of telling them by telegraph, but a new cowardice had been upon him. He feared to do it. And now the train was hurrying him toward a scene of amazement, glee, and reproach. He glanced out of the window at the line of haze swinging slowly in toward the train.

Yellow Sky had a kind of brass band, which played painfully, to the delight 20 of the populace. He laughed without heart as he thought of it. If the citizens could dream of his prospective arrival with his bride, they would parade the band at the station and escort them, amid cheers and laughing congratulations, to his adobe home.

He resolved that he would use all the devices of speed and plainscraft in making the journey from the station to his house. Once within that safe citadel, he could issue some sort of vocal bulletin, and then not go among the citizens until they had time to wear off a little of their enthusiasm.

The bride looked anxiously at him. "What's worrying you, Jack?"

He laughed again. "I'm not worrying, girl; I'm only thinking of Yellow Sky."

She flushed in comprehension.

A sense of mutual guilt invaded their mind and developed a finer tenderness. They looked at each other with eyes softly aglow. But Potter often laughed the same nervous laugh; the flush upon the bride's face seemed quite permanent.

The traitor to the feelings of Yellow Sky narrowly watched the speeding landscape. "We're nearly there," he said.

Presently the porter came and announced the proximity of Potter's home. He held a brush in his hand, and, with all his airy superiority gone, he brushed Potter's new clothes as the latter slowly turned this way and that way. Potter fumbled out a coin and gave it to the porter, as he had seen others do. It was a heavy and muscle-bound business, as that of a man showing his first horse.

The porter took their bag, and as the train began to slow they moved forward to the hooded platform of the car. Presently the two engines and their long string of coaches rushed into the station of Yellow Sky.

"They have to take water here," said Potter, from a constricted throat and in mournful cadence, as one announcing death. Before the train stopped his eye had swept the length of the platform, and he was glad and astonished to see there was none upon it but the station-agent, who, with a slightly hurried and anxious air, was walking toward the water-tanks. When the train had halted, the porter alighted first, and placed in position a little temporary step.

"Come on, girl," said Potter, hoarsely. As he helped her down they each laughed on a false note. He took the bag from the negro, and bade his wife cling to his arm. As they slunk rapidly away, his hang-dog glance perceived that they were unloading the two trunks, and also that the station-agent, far ahead near the baggage-car, had turned and was running toward him, making gestures. He laughed, and groaned as he laughed, when he noted the first effect of his marital bliss upon Yellow Sky. He gripped his wife's arm firmly to his side, and they fled. Behind them the porter stood, chuckling fatuously.

II

The California express on the Southern Railway was due at Yellow Sky in twenty-one minutes. There were six men at the bar of the Weary Gentleman saloon. One was a drummer who talked a great deal and rapidly; three were Texans who did not care to talk at that time; and two were Mexican sheep-herders, who did not talk as a general practice in the Weary Gentleman saloon. The barkeeper's dog lay on the board walk that crossed in front of the door. His head was on his paws, and he glanced drowsily here and there with the constant vigilance of a dog that is kicked on occasion. Across the sandy street were some vivid green grassplots, so wonderful in appearance, amid the sands that burned near them in a blazing sun, that they caused a doubt in the mind. They exactly resembled the grass mats used to represent lawns on the stage. At the cooler end of the railway station, a man without a coat sat in a tilted chair and smoked his pipe. The fresh-cut bank of the Rio Grande circled near the town, and there could be seen beyond it a great plum-coloured plain of mesquit.

Save for the busy drummer and his companions in the saloon, Yellow Sky was dozing. The new-comer leaned gracefully upon the bar, and recited many tales with the confidence of a bard who has come upon a new field.

"—and at the moment that the old man fell downstairs with the bureau in his arms, the old woman was coming up with two scuttles of coal, and of course—"

The drummer's tale was interrupted by a young man who suddenly appeared in the open door. He cried: "Scratchy Wilson's drunk, and has turned loose with both hands." The two Mexicans at once set down their glasses and faded out of the rear entrance of the saloon.

The drummer, innocent and jocular, answered: "All right, old man. S'pose he has? Come in and have a drink, anyhow."   35

But the information had made such an obvious cleft in every skull in the room that the drummer was obliged to see its importance. All had become instantly solemn. "Say," said he, mystified, "what is this?" His three companions made the introductory gesture of eloquent speech; but the young man at the door forestalled them.

"It means, my friend," he answered, as he came into the saloon, "that for the next two hours this town won't be a health resort."

The barkeeper went to the door, and locked and barred it; reaching out of the window, he pulled in heavy wooden shutters, and barred them. Immediately a solemn, chapel-like gloom was upon the place. The drummer was looking from one to another.

"But say," he cried, "what is this, anyhow? You don't mean there is going to be a gun-fight?"

"Don't know whether there'll be a fight or not," answered one man, grimly;   40
"but there'll be some shootin'—some good shootin'."

The young man who had warned them waved his hand. "Oh, there'll be a fight fast enough, if any one wants it. Anybody can get a fight out there in the street. There's a fight just waiting."

The drummer seemed to be swayed between the interest of a foreigner and a perception of personal danger.

"What did you say his name was?" he asked.

"Scratchy Wilson," they answered in chorus.

"And will he kill anybody? What are you going to do? Does this happen   45
often? Does he rampage around like this once a week or so? Can he break in that door?"

"No; he can't break down the door," replied the barkeeper. "He's tried it three times. But when he comes you'd better lay down on the floor, stranger. He's dead sure to shoot at it, and a bullet may come through."

Therafter the drummer kept a strict eye upon the door. The time had not yet been called for him to hug the floor, but, as a minor precaution, he sidled near to the wall. "Will he kill anybody?" he said again.

The men laughed low and scornfully at the question.

"He's out to shoot, and he's out for trouble. Don't see any good in experimentin' with him."

"But what do you do in a case like this? What do you do?"   5●

A man responded: "Why, he and Jack Potter—"

"But," in chorus the other men interrupted, "Jack Potter's in San Anton'."

"Well, who is he? What's he got to do with it?"

"Oh, he's the town marshal. He goes out and fights Scratchy when he gets on one of these tears."

"Wow!" said the drummer, mopping his brow. "Nice job he's got."   5●

The voices had toned away to mere whisperings. The drummer wished to ask further questions, which were born of an increasing anxiety and bewilderment; but when he attempted them, the men merely looked at him in irritation and motioned him to remain silent. A tense waiting hush was upon them. In the deep shadows of the room their eyes shone as they listened for sounds from the street. One man made three gestures at the barkeeper; and the latter, moving like a ghost, handed him a glass and a bottle. The man poured a full glass of whisky, and set down the bottle noiselessly. He gulped the whisky in a swallow, and turned again toward the door in immovable silence. The drummer saw that the barkeeper, without a sound, had taken a Winchester from beneath the bar. Later he saw this individual beckoning to him, so he tiptoed across the room.

"You better come with me back of the bar."

"No, thanks," said the drummer, perspiring; "I'd rather be where I can make a break for the back door."

Whereupon the man of bottles made a kindly but peremptory gesture. The drummer obeyed it, and, finding himself seated on a box with his head below the level of the bar, balm was laid upon his soul at sight of various zinc and copper fittings that bore a resemblance to armour-plate. The barkeeper took a seat comfortably upon an adjacent box.

"You see," he whispered, "this here Scratchy Wilson is a wonder with a   6●
gun—a perfect wonder; and when he goes on the war-trail, we hunt our holes—naturally. He's about the last one of the old gang that used to hang out along the river here. He's a terror when he's drunk. When he's sober he's all right—kind of simple—wouldn't hurt a fly—nicest fellow in town. But when he's drunk—whoo!"

There were periods of stillness. "I wish Jack Potter was back from San Anton'," said the barkeeper. "He shot Wilson up once—in the leg—and he would sail in and pull out the kinks in this thing."

Presently they heard from a distance the sound of a shot, followed by three wild yowls. It instantly removed a bond from the men in the darkened saloon. There was a shuffling of feet. They looked at each other. "Here he comes," they said.

III

A man in a maroon-coloured flannel shirt, which had been purchased for purposes of decoration, and made principally by some Jewish women on the East Side of New York, rounded a corner and walked into the middle of the main street of Yellow Sky. In either hand the man held a long, heavy, blue-black revolver. Often he yelled, and these cries rang through a semblance of a deserted village, shrilly flying over the roofs in a volume that seemed to have no relation to the ordinary vocal strength of a man. It was as if the surrounding stillness formed the arch of a tomb over him. These cries of ferocious challenge rang against walls of silence. And his boots had red tops with gilded imprints, of the kind beloved of winter by little sledding boys on the hillsides of New England.

The man's face flamed in a rage begot of whisky. His eyes, rolling, and yet keen for ambush, hunted the still doorways and windows. He walked with the creeping movement of the midnight cat. As it occurred to him, he roared menacing information. The long revolvers in his hands were as easy as straws; they were moved with an electric swiftness. The little fingers of each hand played sometimes in a musician's way. Plain from the low collar of the shirt, the cords of his neck straightened and sank, straightened and sank, as passion moved him. The only sounds were his terrible invitations. The calm adobes preserved their demeanour at the passing of this small thing in the middle of the street.

There was no offer of fight—no offer of fight. The man called to the sky. 65 There were no attractions. He bellowed and fumed and swayed his revolvers here and everywhere.

The dog of the barkeeper of the Weary Gentleman saloon had not appreciated the advance of events. He yet lay dozing in front of his master's door. At sight of the dog, the man paused and raised his revolver humorously. At sight of the man, the dog sprang up and walked diagonally away, with a sullen head, and growling. The man yelled, and the dog broke into a gallop. As it was about to enter an alley, there was a loud noise, a whistling, and something spat the ground directly before it. The dog screamed, and, wheeling in terror, galloped headlong in a new direction. Again there was a noise, a whistling, and sand was kicked viciously before it. Fear-stricken, the dog turned and flurried like an animal in a pen. The man stood laughing, his weapons at his hips.

Ultimately the man was attracted by the closed door of the Weary Gentleman saloon. He went to it and, hammering with a revolver, demanded drink.

The door remaining imperturbable, he picked a bit of paper from the walk, and nailed it to the framework with a knife. He then turned his back contemptuously upon this popular resort and, walking to the opposite side of the street and spinning there on his heel quickly and lithely, fired at the bit of paper. He missed it by a half-inch. He swore at himself, and went away. Later he comfortably fusilladed the windows of his most intimate friend. The man was playing with this town; it was a toy for him.

But still there was no offer of fight. The name of Jack Potter, his ancient antagonist, entered his mind, and he concluded that it would be a glad thing if he should go to Potter's house, and by bombardment induce him to come out and fight. He moved in the direction of his desire, chanting Apache scalp-music.

When he arrived at it, Potter's house presented the same still front as had 70 the other adobes. Taking up a strategic position, the man howled a challenge. But this house regarded him as might a great stone god. It gave no sign. After a decent wait, the man howled further challenges, mingling with them wonderful epithets.

Presently there came the spectacle of a man churning himself into deepest rage over the immobility of a house. He fumed at it as the winter wind attacks a prairie cabin in the North. To the distance there should have gone the sound of a tumult like the fighting of two hundred Mexicans. As necessity bade him, he paused for breath or to reload his revolvers.

IV

Potter and his bride walked sheepishly and with speed. Sometimes they laughed together shamefacedly and low.

"Next corner, dear," he said finally.

They put forth the efforts of a pair walking bowed against a strong wind. Potter was about to raise a finger to point the first appearance of the new home when, as they circled the corner, they came face to face with a man in a maroon-coloured shirt, who was feverishly pushing cartridges into a large revolver. Upon the instant the man dropped his revolver to the ground and, like lightning, whipped another from its holster. The second weapon was aimed at the bridegroom's chest.

There was a silence. Potter's mouth seemed to be merely a grave for his tongue. He exhibited an instinct to at once loosen his arm from the women's grip, and he dropped the bag to the sand. As for the bride, her face had gone as yellow as old cloth. She was a slave to hideous rites, gazing at the apparitional snake.

The two men faced each other at a distance of three paces. He of the revolver smiled with a new and quiet ferocity.

"Tried to sneak up on me," he said. "Tried to sneak up on me!" His eyes grew more baleful. As Potter made a slight movement, the man thrust his revolver venomously forward. "No; don't you do it, Jack Potter. Don't you move a finger toward a gun just yet. Don't you move an eyelash. The time has come for me to settle with you, and I'm goin' to do it my own way, and loaf along with no interferin'. So if you don't want a gun bent on you, just mind what I tell you."

Potter looked at his enemy. "I ain't got a gun on me Scratchy," he said. "Honest, I ain't." He was stiffening and steadying, but yet somewhere at the back of his mind a vision of the Pullman floated: the sea-green figured velvet, the shining brass, silver, and glass, the wood that gleamed as darkly brilliant as the surface of a pool of oil—all the glory of the marriage, the environment of the new estate. "You know I fight when it comes to fighting, Scratchy Wilson; but I ain't got a gun on me. You'll have to do all the shootin' yourself."

His enemy's face went livid. He stepped forward, and lashed his weapon to and fro before Potter's chest. "Don't you tell me you ain't got no gun on you, you whelp. Don't tell me no lie like that. There ain't a man in Texas ever seen you without no gun. Don't take me for no kid." His eyes blazed with light, and his throat worked like a pump.

"I ain't takin' you for no kid," answered Potter. His heels had not moved an inch backward. "I'm takin' you for a damn fool. I tell you I ain't got a gun, and I ain't. If you're goin' to shoot me up, you better begin now; you'll never get a chance like this again."

So much enforced reasoning had told on Wilson's rage; he was calmer. "If you ain't got a gun, why ain't you got a gun?" he sneered. "Been to Sunday-school?"

"I ain't got a gun because I've just come from San Anton' with my wife. I'm married," said Potter. "And if I'd thought there was going to be any galoots like you prowling around when I brought my wife home, I'd had a gun, and don't you forget it."

"Married!" said Scratchy, not at all comprehending.

"Yes, married. I'm married," said Potter, distinctly.

"Married?" said Scratchy. Seemingly for the first time, he saw the drooping, drowning woman at the other man's side. "No!" he said. He was like a creature allowed a glimpse of another world. He moved a pace backward, and his arm, with the revolver, dropped to his side. "Is this the lady?" he asked. 85

"Yes; this is the lady," answered Potter.

There was another period of silence.

"Well," said Wilson at last, slowly, "I s'pose it's all off now."

"It's all off if you say so, Scratchy. You know I didn't make the trouble." Potter lifted his valise.

"Well, I 'low it's off, Jack," said Wilson. He was looking at the ground. 90 "Married!" He was not a student of chivalry; it was merely that in the presence of this foreign condition he was a simple child of the earlier plains. He picked up his starboard revolver, and, placing both weapons in their holsters, he went away. His feet made funnel-shaped tracks in the heavy sand.

QUESTIONS

1. What is a Pullman? Why are Jack Potter and his new bride on it? What is the attitude of the other people in the car to the newly married couple? Why? Is it possible for you to be amused, too?

2. Describe the plot in terms of the principal conflict between Potter and Scratchy, and also of the various related conflicts.

3. Where is the crisis of the story? How extended is it? At what point does it become clear that there will be a peaceful resolution?

4. Describe the structural relationship of each of the four sections of the story to the development of the plot.

5. Why is Potter apprehensive about returning to Yellow Sky? What is the relationship between his concern and his later showdown with Scratchy Wilson? Describe the "code" that previously governed the gunslinging conduct of Jack and Scratchy. How does the presence of Potter's wife affect Scratchy's perception of his new role with regard to Potter?

6. What is the scene in the Weary Gentleman saloon? Is there any expository purpose for which Crane has included a drummer (a traveling salesman who is unfamiliar with life in Yellow Sky) in the group of men?

7. The story is designed to be comic. Because of this intention, how seriously is Scratchy Wilson, with his gun, to be taken? How do the speeches of the men in the bar contribute to your understanding of the danger Scratchy poses?

EUDORA WELTY (b. 1909)

A Worn Path   1941

It was December—a bright frozen day in the early morning. Far out in the country there was an old Negro woman with her head tied in a red rag, coming along a path through the pinewoods. Her name was Phoenix Jackson. She was very old and small and she walked slowly in the dark pine shadows, moving a little from side to side in her steps, with the balanced heaviness and lightness of a pendulum in a grandfather clock. She carried a thin, small cane made from an umbrella, and with this she kept tapping the frozen earth in front of her. This made a grave and persistent noise in the still air, that seemed meditative like the chirping of a solitary little bird.

She wore a dark striped dress reaching down to her shoe tops, and an equally long apron of bleached sugar sacks, with a full pocket: all neat and tidy, but every time she took a step she might have fallen over her shoelaces, which dragged from her unlaced shoes. She looked straight ahead. Her eyes were blue with age. Her skin had a pattern all its own of numberless branching wrinkles and as though a whole little tree stood in the middle of her forehead, but a golden color ran underneath, and the two knobs of her cheeks were illumined by a yellow burning under the dark. Under the rag her hair came down on her neck in the frailest of ringlets, still black, and with an odor like copper.

Now and then there was a quivering in the thicket. Old Phoenix said, "Out of my way, all you foxes, owls, beetles, jack rabbits, coons and wild animals! . . . Keep out from under these feet, little bob-whites. . . . Keep the big wild hogs out of my path. Don't let none of those come running my direction. I got a long way." Under her small black-freckled hand her cane, limber as a buggy whip, would switch at the brush as if to rouse up any hiding things.

On she went. The woods were deep and still. The sun made the pine needles almost too bright to look at, up where the wind rocked. The cones dropped as light as feathers. Down in the hollow was the mourning dove—it was not too late for him.

The path ran up a hill. "Seem like there is chains about my feet, time I get this far," she said, in the voice of argument old people keep to use with themselves. "Something always take a hold of me on this hill—pleads I should stay."

After she got to the top she turned and gave a full, severe look behind her where she had come. "Up through pines," she said at length. "Now down through oaks."

Her eyes opened their widest, and she started down gently. But before she got to the bottom of the hill a bush caught her dress.

Her fingers were busy and intent, but her skirts were full and long, so that before she could pull them free in one place they were caught in another. It was not possible to allow the dress to tear. "I in the thorny bush," she said. "Thorns, you doing your appointed work. Never want to let folks pass, no sir. Old eyes thought you was a pretty little *green* bush."

Finally, trembling all over, she stood free, and after a moment dared to stoop for her cane.

"Sun so high!" she cried, leaning back and looking, while the thick tears   10
went over her eyes. "The time getting all gone here."

At the foot of this hill was a place where a log was laid across the creek.

"Now comes the trial," said Phoenix.

Putting her right foot out, she mounted the log and shut her eyes. Lifting
her skirt, leveling her cane fiercely before her, like a festival figure in some parade,
she began to march across. Then she opened her eyes and she was safe on the
other side.

"I wasn't as old as I thought," she said.

But she sat down to rest. She spread her skirts on the bank around her   15
and folded her hands over her knees. Up above her was a tree in a pearly cloud
of mistletoe. She did not dare to close her eyes, and when a little boy brought
her a plate with a slice of marble-cake on it she spoke to him. "That would be
acceptable," she said. But when she went to take it there was just her own hand
in the air.

So she left that tree, and had to go through a barbed-wire fence. There
she had to creep and crawl, speading her knees and stretching her fingers like a
baby trying to climb the steps. But she talked loudly to herself: she could not let
her dress be torn now, so late in the day, and she could not pay for having her
arm or her leg sawed off if she got caught fast where she was.

At last she was safe through the fence and risen up out in the clearing. Big
dead trees, like black men with one arm, were standing in the purple stalks of
the withered cotton field. There sat a buzzard.

"Who you watching?"

In the furrow she made her way along.

"Glad this not the season for bulls," she said, looking sideways, "and the   20
good Lord made his snakes to curl up and sleep in the winter. A pleasure I don't
see no two-headed snake coming around that tree, where it come once. It took a
while to get by him, back in the summer.

She passed through the old cotton and went into a field of dead corn. It
whispered and shook and was taller than her head. "Through the maze now,"
she said, for there was no path.

Then there was something tall, black, and skinny there, moving before her.

At first she took it for a man. It could have been a man dancing in the
field. But she stood still and listened, and it did not make a sound. It was as
silent as a ghost.

"Ghost," she said sharply, "who be you the ghost of? For I have heard of
nary death close by."

But there was no answer—only the ragged dancing in the wind.   25

She shut her eyes, reached out her hand, and touched a sleeve. She found
a coat and inside that an emptiness, cold as ice.

"You scarecrow," she said. Her face lighted. "I ought to be shut up for
good," she said with laughter. "My senses is gone. I too old. I the oldest people
I ever know. Dance, old scarecrow," she said, "while I dancing with you."

She kicked her foot over the furrow, and with mouth drawn down, shook
her head once or twice in a little strutting way. Some husks blew down and whirled
in streamers about her skirts.

Then she went on, parting her way from side to side with the cane, through

the whispering field. At last she came to the end, to a wagon track where the
silver grass blew between the red ruts. The quail were walking around like pullets,
seeming all dainty and unseen.

"Walk pretty," she said. "This is the easy place. This the easy going."

She followed the track, swaying through the quiet bare fields, through the
little strings of trees silver in their dead leaves, past cabins silver from weather,
with the doors and windows boarded shut, all like old women under a spell sitting
there. "I walking in their sleep," she said, nodding her head vigorously.

In a ravine she went where a spring was silently flowing through a hollow
log. Old Phoenix bent and drank. "Sweet-gum makes the water sweet," she said,
and drank more. "Nobody know who made this well, for it was here when I was
born."

The track crossed a swampy part where the moss hung as white as lace
from every limb. "Sleep on, aligators, and blow your bubbles." Then the track
went into the road.

Deep, deep the road went down between the high green-colored banks. Overhead the live-oaks met, and it was as dark as a cave.

A black dog with a lolling tongue came up out of the weeds by the ditch.
She was meditating, and not ready, and when he came at her she only hit him a
little with her cane. Over she went in the ditch, like a little puff of milkweed.

Down there, her senses drifted away. A dream visited her, and she reached
her hand up, but nothing reached down and gave her a pull. So she lay there
and presently went to talking. "Old woman," she said to herself, "that black dog
come up out of the weeds to stall you off, and now there he sitting on his fine
tail smiling at you."

A white man finally came along and found her—a hunter, a young man,
with his dog on a chain.

"Well, Granny!" he laughed. "What are you doing there?"

"Lying on my back like a June-bug waiting to be turned over, mister," she
said, reaching up her hand.

He lifted her up, gave her a swing in the air, and set her down. "Anything
broken, Granny?"

"No sir, them old dead weeds is springy enough," said Phoenix, when she
had got her breath. "I thank you for your trouble."

"Where do you live, Granny?" he asked, while the two dogs were growling
at each other.

"Away back yonder, sir, behind the ridge. You can't even see it from here."

"On your way home?"

"No sir, I going to town."

"Why, that's too far! That's as far as I walk when I come out myself, and I
get something for my trouble." He patted the stuffed bag he carried, and there
hung down a little closed claw. It was one of the bob-whites, with its beak hooked
bitterly to show it was dead. "Now you go on home, Granny!"

"I bound to go to town, mister," said Phoenix. "The time come around."

He gave another laugh, filling the whole landscape. "I know you old colored
people! Wouldn't miss going to town to see Santa Claus!"

But something held old Phoenix very still. The deep lines in her face went
into a fierce and different radiation. Without warning, she had seen with her own
eyes a flashing nickel fall out of the man's pocket onto the ground.

"How old are you, Granny?" he was saying. 50

"There is no telling, mister," she said, "no telling."

Then she gave a little cry and clapped her hands and said, "Git on away from here, dog! Look! Look at that dog!" She laughed as if in admiration. "He ain't scared of nobody. He a big black dog." She whispered, "Sic him!"

"Watch me get rid of that cur," said the man. "Sic him, Pete! Sic him!"

Phoenix heard the dogs fighting, and heard the man running and throwing sticks. She even heard a gunshot. But she was slowly bending forward by that time, further and further forward, the lids stretched down over her eyes, as if she were doing this in her sleep. Her chin was lowered almost to her knees. The yellow palm of her hand came out from the fold of her apron. Her fingers slid down and along the ground under the piece of money with the grace and care they would have in lifting an egg from under a setting hen. Then she slowly straightened up, she stood erect, and the nickel was in her apron pocket. A bird flew by. Her lips moved. "God watching me the whole time. I come to stealing."

The man came back, and his own dog panted about them. "Well, I scared 55 him off that time," he said, and then he laughed and lifted his gun and pointed it at Phoenix.

She stood straight and faced him.

"Doesn't the gun scare you?" he said, still pointing it.

"No, sir, I seen plenty go off closer by, in my day, and for less than what I done," she said, holding utterly still.

He smiled, and shouldered the gun. "Well, Granny," he said, "you must be a hundred years old, and scared of nothing. I'd give you a dime if I had any money with me. But you take my advice and stay home, and nothing will happen to you."

"I bound to go on my way, mister," said Phoenix. She inclined her head in 60 the red rag. Then they went in different directions, but she could hear the gun shooting again and again over the hill.

She walked on. The shadows hung from the oak trees to the road like curtains. Then she smelled wood-smoke, and smelled the river, and she saw a steeple and the cabins on their steep steps. Dozens of litle black children whirled around her. There ahead was Natchez shining. Bells were ringing. She walked on.

In the paved city it was Christmas time. There were red and green electric lights strung and crisscrossed everywhere, and all turned on in the daytime. Old Phoenix would have been lost if she had not distrusted her eyesight and depended on her feet to know where to take her.

She paused quietly on the sidewalk where people were passing by. A lady came along in the crowd, carrying an armful of red-, green- and silver-wrapped presents; she gave off perfume like the red roses in hot summer, and Phoenix stopped her.

"Please, missy, will you lace up my shoe?" She held up her foot.

"What do you want, Grandma?" 65

"See my shoe," said Phoenix. "Do all right for out in the country, but wouldn't look right to go in a big building."

"Stand still then, Grandma," said the lady. She put her packages down on the sidewalk beside her and laced and tied both shoes tightly.

"Can't lace 'em with a cane," said Phoenix. "Thank you, missy. I doesn't mind asking a nice lady to tie up my shoe, when I gets out on the street."

Moving slowly and from side to side, she went into the big building, and into a tower of steps, where she walked up and around and around until her feet knew to stop.

She entered a door, and there she saw nailed up on the wall the document that had been stamped with the gold seal and framed in the gold frame, which matched the dream that was hung up in her head.

"Here I be," she said. There was a fixed and ceremonial stiffness over her body.

"A charity case, I suppose," said an attendant who sat at the desk before her.

But Phoenix only looked above her head. There was sweat on her face, the wrinkles in her skin shone like a bright net.

"Speak up, Grandma," the woman said. "What's your name? We must have your history, you know. Have you been here before? What seems to be the trouble with you?"

Old Phoenix only gave a twitch to her face as if a fly were bothering her.

"Are you deaf?" cried the attendant.

But then the nurse came in.

"Oh, that's just old Aunt Phoenix," she said. "She doesn't come for herself—she has a little grandson. She makes these trips just as regular as clockwork. She lives away back off the Old Natchez Trace." She bent down. "Well, Aunt Phoenix, why don't you just take a seat? We won't keep you standing after your long trip." She pointed.

The old woman sat down, bolt upright in the chair.

"Now, how is the boy?" asked the nurse.

Old Phoenix did not speak.

"I said, how is the boy?"

But Phoenix only waited and stared straight ahead, her face very solemn and withdrawn into rigidity.

"Is his throat any better?" asked the nurse. "Aunt Phoenix, don't you hear me? Is your grandson's throat any better since the last time you came for the medicine?"

With her hands on her knees, the old woman waited, silent, erect and motionless, just as if she were in armor.

"You mustn't take up our time this way, Aunt Phoenix," the nurse said. "Tell us quickly about your grandson, and get it over. He isn't dead, is he?"

At last there came a flicker and then a flame of comprehension across her face, and she spoke.

"My grandson. It was my memory had left me. There I sat and forgot why I made my long trip."

"Forgot?" the nurse frowned. "After you came so far?"

Then Phoenix was like an old woman begging a dignified forgiveness for waking up frightened in the night. "I never did go to school, I was too old at the Surrender," she said in a soft voice. "I'm an old woman without an education. It was my memory fail me. My little grandson, he is just the same, and I forgot it in the coming."

"Throat never heals, does it?" said the nurse, speaking in a loud, sure voice to old Phoenix. By now she had a card with something written on it, a little list. "Yes. Swallowed lye. When was it—January—two, three years ago—"

Phoenix spoke unasked now. "No, missy, he not dead, he just the same. Every little while his throat begin to close up again, and he not able to swallow. He not get his breath. He not able to help himself. So the time come around, and I go on another trip for the soothing medicine."

"All right. The doctor said as long as you came to get it, you could have it," said the nurse. "But it's an obstinate case."

"My little grandson, he sit up there in the house all wrapped up, waiting by himself," Phoenix went on. "We is the only two left in the world. He suffer and it don't seem to put him back at all. He got a sweet look. He going to last. He wear a little patch quilt and peep out holding his mouth open like a little bird. I remembers so plain now. I not going to forget him again, no, the whole enduring time. I could tell him from all the others in creation."

"All right." The nurse was trying to hush her now. She brought her a bottle of medicine. "Charity," she said, making a check mark in a book.   95

Old Phoenix held the bottle close to her eyes, and then carefully put it into her pocket.

"I thank you," she said.

"It's Christmas time, Grandma," said the attendant. "Could I give you a few pennies out of my purse?"

"Five pennies is a nickel," said Phoenix stiffly.

"Here's a nickel," said the attendant.   100

Phoenix rose carefully and held out her hand. She received the nickel and then fished the other nickel out of her pocket and laid it beside the new one. She stared at her palm closely, with her head on one side.

Then she gave a tap with her cane on the floor.

"This is what come to me to do," she said. "I going to the store and buy my child a little windmill they sells, made out of paper. He going to find it hard to believe there such a thing in the world. I'll march myself back where he waiting, holding it straight up in this hand."

She lifted her free hand, gave a little nod, turned around, and walked out of the doctor's office. Then her slow step began on the stairs, going down.

QUESTIONS

1. From the fact that Phoenix wears an apron of "bleached sugar sacks" and ties her hair with a red rag, what do you conclude about her economic condition? Has she taken the path through the woods before? How do you know? Is she accustomed to being alone? What do you make of her speaking to animals, and of her imagining a boy offering her a piece of cake? What does her speech show about her education and general background?

2. Describe the plot of the story. With Phoenix as the protagonist, what are the antagonisms ranged against her? Are they malevolent to any degree? How might Phoenix be considered to be in the grip of large and indifferent social and political forces?

3. Describe the structure of the story according to the classes of exposition, complication, crisis, climax, and resolution. Does the actual structure correspond to this orderly arrangement? Wherein does it depart? Why?

4. Comment on the meaning of this dialogue between Phoenix and the hunter:

> "Doesn't the gun scare you?" he said, still pointing it.
> "No, sir, I seen plenty go off closer by, in my day, and for less than what I done," she said, holding utterly still.

5. A number of responses might be made to this story, among them admiration for Phoenix, pity for her and her grandson and for the downtrodden generally, anger at her impoverished condition, and apprehension about her approaching senility. Do you share in any of these responses? Do you have any others?

TOM WHITECLOUD (b. ca. 1918)

Blue Winds Dancing   (1938)

There is a moon out tonight. Moon and stars and clouds tipped with moonlight. And there is a fall wind blowing in my heart. Ever since this evening, when against a fading sky I saw geese wedge southward. They were going home. . . . Now I try to study, but against the pages I see them again, driving southward. Going home.

Across the valley there are heavy mountains holding up the night sky, and beyond the mountains there is home. Home, and peace, and the beat of drums, and blue winds dancing over snow fields. The Indian lodge will fill with my people, and our gods will come and sit among them. I should be there then. I should be at home.

But home is beyond the mountains, and I am here. Here where fall hides in the valleys, and winter never comes down from the mountains. Here where all the trees grow in rows; the palms stand stiffly by the roadsides, and in the groves' the orange trees line in military rows, and endlessly bear fruit. Beautiful, yes; there is always beauty in order, in rows of growing things! But it is the beauty of captivity. A pine fighting for existence on a windy knoll is much more beautiful.

In my Wisconsin, the leaves change before the snows come. In the air there is the smell of wild rice and venison cooking; and when the winds come whispering through the forests, they carry the smell of rotting leaves. In the evenings, the loon calls, lonely; and birds sing their last songs before leaving. Bears dig roots and eat late fall berries, fattening for their long winter sleep. Later, when the first snows fall, one awakens in the morning to find the world white and beautiful and clean. Then one can look back over his trail and see the tracks following. In the woods there are tracks of deer and snowshoe rabbits, and long streaks where partridges slide to alight. Chipmunks make tiny footprints on the limbs; and one can hear squirrels busy in hollow trees, sorting acorns. Soft lake waves wash the shores, and sunsets burst each evening over the lakes, and make them look as if they were afire.

That land which is my home! Beautiful, calm—where there is no hurry to get anywhere, no driving to keep up in a race that knows no ending and no goal. No classes where men talk and talk, and then stop now and then to hear their own words come back to them from the students. No constant peering into the maelstrom of one's mind; no worries about grades and honors; no hysterical preparing for life until that life is half over; no anxiety about one's place in the thing they call Society.

I hear again the ring of axes in deep woods, the crunch of snow beneath my feet. I feel again the smooth velvet of ghost-birch bark. I hear the rhythm of the drums. . . . I am tired. I am weary of trying to keep up this bluff of being civilized. Being civilized means trying to do everything you don't want to, never doing anything you want to. It means dancing to the strings of custom and tradition; it means living in houses and never knowing or caring who is next door. These civilized white men want us to be like them—always dissatisfied—getting a hill and wanting a mountain.

Then again, maybe I am not tired. Maybe I'm licked. Maybe I am just not smart enough to grasp these things that go to make up civilization. Maybe I am just too lazy to think hard enough to keep up.

Still, I know my people have many things that civilization has taken from the whites. They know how to give; how to tear one's piece of meat in two and share it with one's brother. They know how to sing—how to make each man his own songs and sing them; for their music they do not have to listen to other men singing over a radio. They know how to make things with their hands, how to shape beads into design and make a thing of beauty from a piece of birch bark.

But we are inferior. It is terrible to have to feel inferior; to have to read reports of intelligence tests, and learn that one's race is behind. It is terrible to sit in classes and hear men tell you that your people worship sticks of wood—that your gods are all false, that the Manitou forgot your people and did not write them a book.

I am tired. I want to walk again among the ghost-birches. I want to see the leaves turn in autumn, the smoke rise from the lodgehouses, and to feel the blue winds. I want to hear the drums; I want to hear the drums and feel the blue whispering winds. 10

There is a train wailing into the night. The trains go across the mountains. It would be easy to catch a freight. They will say he has gone back to the blanket; I don't care. The dance at Christmas. . . .

A bunch of bums warming at a tiny fire talk politics and women and joke about the Relief and the WPA and smoke cigarettes. These men in caps and overcoats and dirty overalls living on the outskirts of civilization are free, but they pay the price of being free in civilization. They are outcasts. I remember a sociology professor lecturing on adjustment to society; hobos and prostitutes and criminals are individuals who never adjusted, he said. He could learn a lot if he came and listened to a bunch of bums talk. He would learn that work and a woman and a place to hang his hat are all the ordinary man wants. These are all he wants, but other men are not content to let him want only these. He must be taught to want radios and automobiles and a new suit every spring. Progress would stop if he did not want these things. I listen to hear if there is any talk of communism or socialism in the hobo jungles. There is none. At best there is a sort of disgusted philosophy about life. They seem to think there should be a better distribution of wealth, or more work, or something. But they are not rabid about it. The radicals live in the cities.

I find a fellow headed for Albuquerque, and talk road-talk with him. "It is hard to ride fruit cars. Bums break in. Better to wait for a cattle car going back to the Middle West, and ride that." We catch the next east-bound and walk the tops until we find a cattle car. Inside, we crouch near the forward wall, huddle, and try to sleep. I feel peaceful and content at last. I am going home. The cattle car rocks. I sleep.

Morning and the desert. Noon and the Salton Sea, lying more lifeless than a mirage under a somber sun in a pale sky. Skeleton mountains rearing on the skyline, thrusting out of the desert floor, all rock and shadow and edges. Desert. Good country for an Indian reservation. . . .

Yuma and the muddy Colorado. Night again, and I wait shivering for the dawn.

Phoenix. Pima country. Mountains that look like cardboard sets on a forgotten stage. Tucson. Papago country. Giant cacti that look like petrified hitchhikers along the highways. Apache country. At El Paso my road-buddy decides to go on to Houston. I leave him, and head north to the mesa country. Las Cruces and the terrible Organ Mountains, jagged peaks that instill fear and wondering. Albuquerque. Pueblos along the Rio Grande. On the boardwalk there are some Indian women in colored sashes selling bits of pottery. The stone age offering its art to the twentieth century. They hold up a piece and fix the tourists with black eyes until, embarrassed, he buys or turns away. I feel suddenly angry that my people should have to do such things for a living. . . .

Santa Fe trains are fast, and they keep them pretty clean of bums. I decide to hurry and ride passenger coaltenders. Hide in the dark, judge the speed of the train as it leaves, and then dash out, and catch it. I hug the cold steel wall of the tender and think of the roaring fire in the engine ahead, and of the passengers back in the dining car reading their papers over hot coffee. Beneath me there is a blur of rails. Death would come quick if my hands should freeze and I fall. Up over the Sangre De Cristo range, around cliffs and through canyons to Denver. Bitter cold here, and I must watch out for Denver Bob. He is a railroad bull who has thrown bums from fast freights. I miss him. It is too cold, I suppose. On north to the Sioux country.

Small towns lit for the coming Christmas. On the streets of one I see a beam-shouldered young farmer gazing into a window filled with shining silver toasters. He is tall and wears a blue shirt buttoned, with no tie. His young wife by his side looks at him hopefully. He wants decorations for his place to hang his hat to please his woman. . . .

Northward again. Minnesota, and great white fields of snow; frozen lakes, and dawn running into dusk without noon. Long forests wearing white. Bitter cold, and one night the northern lights. I am nearing home.

I reach Woodruff at midnight. Suddenly I am afraid, now that I am but twenty miles from home. Afraid of what my father will say, afraid of being looked on as a stranger by my own people. I sit by a fire and think about myself and all other young Indians. We just don't seem to fit in anywhere—certainly not among the whites, and not among the older people. I think again about the learned sociology professor and his professing. So many things seem to be clear now that I am away from school and do not have to worry about some man's opinion of my ideas. It is easy to think while looking at dancing flames.

Morning. I spend the day cleaning up, and buying some presents for my family with what is left of my money. Nothing much, but a gift is a gift, if a man buys it with his last quarter. I wait until evening, then start up the track toward home.

Christmas Eve comes in on a north wind. Snow clouds hang over the pines, and the night comes early. Walking along the railroad bed, I feel the calm peace of snowbound forests on either side of me. I take my time; I am back in a world where time does not mean so much now. I am alone; alone but not nearly so lonely as I was back on the campus at school. Those are never lonely who love the snow and the pines; never lonely when the pines are wearing white shawls and snow crunches coldly underfoot. In the woods I know there are the tracks of deer and rabbit; I know that if I leave the rails and go into the woods I shall find them. I walk along feeling glad because my legs are light and my feet seem to know that they are home. A deer comes out of the woods just ahead of me, and stands silhouetted on the rails. The North, I feel, has welcomed me home. I watch him and am glad that I do not wish for a gun. He goes into the woods quietly, leaving only the design of his tracks in the snow. I walk on. Now and then I pass a field, white under the night sky, with houses at the far end. Smoke comes from the chimneys of the houses, and I try to tell what sort of wood each is burning by the smoke; some burn pine, others aspen, others tamarack. There is one from which comes black coal smoke that rises lazily and drifts out over the tops of the trees. I like to watch houses and try to imagine what might be happening in them.

Just as a light snow begins to fall I cross the reservation boundary; somehow it seems as though I have stepped into another world. Deep woods in a white-and-black winter night. A faint trail leading to the village.

The railroad on which I stand comes from a city sprawled by a lake—a city with a million people who walk around without seeing one another; a city sucking the life from all the country around; a city with stores and police and intellectuals and criminals and movies and apartment houses; a city with its politics and libraries and zoos.

Laughing, I go into the woods. As I cross a frozen lake I begin to hear the drums. Soft in the night the drums beat. It is like the pulse beat of the world. The white line of the lake ends at a black forest, and above the trees the blue winds are dancing.

25

I come to the outlying houses of the village. Simple box houses, etched black in the night. From one or two windows soft lamplight falls on the snow. Christmas here, too, but it does not mean much; not much in the way of parties and presents. Joe Sky will get drunk. Alex Bodidash will buy his children red mittens and a new sled. Alex is a Carlisle man, and tries to keep his home up to white standards. White standards. Funny that my people should be ever falling farther behind. The more they try to imitate whites the more tragic the result. Yet they want us to be imitation white men. About all we imitate well are their vices.

The village is not a sight to instill pride, yet I am not ashamed; one can never be ashamed of his own people when he knows they have dreams as beautiful as white snow on a tall pine.

Father and my brother and sister are seated around the table as I walk in. Father stares at me for a moment, then I am in his arms, crying on his shoulder.

I give them the presents I have brought, and my throat tightens as I watch my sister save carefully bits of red string from the packages. I hide my feelings by wrestling with my brother when he strikes my shoulder in token of affection. Father looks at me, and I know he has many questions, but he seems to know why I have come. He tells me to go on alone to the lodge, and he will follow.

I walk along the trail to the lodge, watching the northern lights forming in the heavens. White waving ribbons that seem to pulsate with the rhythm of the drums. Clean snow creaks beneath my feet, and a soft wind sighs through the trees, singing to me. Everything seems to say "Be happy! You are home now— you are free. You are among friends—we are your friends; we, the trees, and the snow, and the lights." I follow the trail to the lodge. My feet are light, my heart seems to sing to the music, and I hold my head high. Across white snow fields blue winds are dancing.

Before the lodge door I stop, afraid. I wonder if my people will remember   30
me. I wonder—"Am I Indian, or am I white?" I stand before the door a long time. I hear the ice groan on the lake, and remember the story of the old woman who is under the ice, trying to get out, so she can punish some runaway lovers. I think to myself, "If I am white I will not believe that story; if I am Indian, I will know that there is an old woman under the ice." I listen for a while, and I know that there is an old women under the ice. I look again at the lights, and go in.

Inside the lodge there are many Indians. Some sit on benches around the walls, others dance in the center of the floor around a drum. Nobody seems to notice me. It seems as though I were among a people I have never seen before. Heavy women with long black hair. Women with children on their knees—small children that watch with intent black eyes the movements of the dancers, whose small faces are solemn and serene. The faces of the old people are serene, too, and their eyes are merry and bright. I look at the old men. Straight, dressed in dark trousers and beaded velvet vests, wearing soft moccasins. Dark, lined faces intent on the music. I wonder if I am at all like them. They dance on, lifting their feet to the rhythm of the drums, swaying lightly, looking upward. I look at their eyes, and am startled at the rapt attention to the rhythm of the music.

The dance stops. The men walk back to the walls, and talk in low tones or with their hands. There is little conversation, yet everyone seems to be sharing some secret. A woman looks at a small boy wandering away, and he comes back to her.

Strange, I think, and then remember. These people are not sharing words— they are sharing a mood. Everyone is happy. I am so used to white people that it seems strange so many people could be together without someone talking. These Indians are happy because they are together, and because the night is beautiful outside, and the music is beautiful. I try hard to forget school and white people, and be one of these—my people. I try to forget everything but the night, and it is a part of me; that I am one with my people and we are all a part of something universal. I watch eyes, and see now that the old people are speaking to me. They nod slightly, imperceptibly, and their eyes laugh into mine. I look around the room. All the eyes are friendly; they all laugh. No one questions my being here. The drums begin to beat again, and I catch the invitation in the eyes of the old men. My feet begin to lift to the rhythm, and I look out beyond the walls into the night and see the lights. I am happy. It is beautiful. I am home.

QUESTIONS

1. Describe the first section of the story in terms of the plot. How much is exposition? How much complication? Could a case be made that this first section contains its own crisis and climax and that the rest of the story is really a resolution?
2. What do you learn in the first section about the conflict in the attitudes of the young Indian narrator? What is his attitude about "civilization"? What values derived from his home make him think this way? If he is the protagonist, who or what is the antagonist?
3. What does it mean to "catch a freight"? What is the narrator's judgment about the value of acquiring things and property? Is there any contradiction in the fact that he later buys Christmas presents for his family?
4. What does the narrator mean by saying, "I am alone; alone but not nearly so lonely as I was back on the campus at school"?
5. Do you believe that the author, Tom Whitecloud, wants you to think that the choice made by the narrator to return home is wise or foolish? Why?
6. What is meant by the dancing of the blue winds? What kind of wisdom is represented by this perception? What is the place for such wisdom in a computerized, industrialized society?
7. The narrator claims that the only things that Indians can imitate well from whites are their vices. In light of this assertion, and considering the rest of the story, what sorts of roles can Indians take in society so that they might be successful while preserving their identity and integrity?
8. Is it absolutely necessary for civilized people to forsake their love of nature and family as they become "modern," as the narrator asserts?

WRITING ABOUT THE PLOT OF A STORY

In planning an essay about a story's plot you will need to analyze the conflict and the developments and routes it takes. The goal is not just a straightforward chronological listing, as with the précis essay (see Chapter 2). The organization of an essay about plot is not based on parts of the story or principal events, because these would invite a chronological summary. Instead, plan on organization that is grounded in the various important elements of the conflict or conflicts.

Organizing Your Essay

INTRODUCTION. The introduction contains brief references to the principal characters, circumstances, and issues of the plot. It also states the central idea for the essay in a sentence formulating the plot or the principal conflict. The thesis sentence concludes the introduction.

BODY.   The body focuses on the major elements of the plot, emphasizing the plan of conflict in the story. Who is the main character? What are the qualities of this character that are important in the conflict? What strengths and weaknesses does the character have? What is the conflict? How is it embodied in the story? What person or persons are the antagonists? Is the conflict one of ideas or values? What are these? Does the character face a difficult decision of any sort? Are the effects of any decision the intended ones? In terms of success by personal, occupational, or political standards, does the conflict make the principal character rise or fall? In terms of personal integrity, does the character emerge from the conflict in triumph, defeat, or somewhere in the middle? Answers to questions like these form the basis of the body of the essay.

Because a description of elements in a plot can easily become long, it is necessary to be selective and also to decide on a particular aspect to emphasize. One kind of development might treat the aspects of the conflict equally. Such an essay on "The Bride Comes to Yellow Sky," for example, might contrast Potter's new values as a married man with his older values as a single man frequently involved with juvenile but dangerous showdowns like the one Scratchy Wilson wishes to have.

Another kind of development might emphasize the protagonist and his or her qualities and values. In "Blue Winds Dancing," for example, such an essay would stress the narrator's resentment, homesickness, and desire for an Indian identity. It might be possible, too, to emphasize more broadly the values of the Indian culture to which the narrator is returning, as a contrast to the values of the predominant "civilized" culture which he is leaving. It would be possible, of course, to make the same treatment for the antagonistic side of the plot.

It is thus important to realize that there are choices in the development of the body of the essay. The plot may be analyzed simply in terms of the persons involved in the conflict, or more broadly in terms of factors such as impulses, goals, ideas, values, issues, and historical perspectives.

CONCLUSION.   The conclusion might contain a brief summary of the points in the body. Also, quite often a study of plot necessarily leaves out one of the most important reasons for reading, and that is the impact of the plot. Thus the conclusion is a fitting location for a brief consideration of effect. Additional comments might concentrate on an evaluation of the plot, such as whether the author has contrived it in any way to tip the balance toward one side or the other, or whether it is realistic, true to life, fair, and impartial.

SAMPLE ESSAY

The Plot of Eudora Welty's "A Worn Path"*

[1]   At first, the plot complexity of Eudora Welty's "A Worn Path" is not clear. The main character is Phoenix Jackson, an old, poor, and frail black woman; the story seems to be no more than a record of her walk to Natchez through the woods from her rural home. By the story's end, however, the plot is clear: It presents the brave attempts of a courageous, valiant woman to carry on normally despite overwhelming negative forces.° It is the gap between her determination and the odds against her that gives the story its impact. The powers she opposes in the story are environment, poverty, and old age.□

[2]   Environment is shown, during that portion of the story when Phoenix walks to town, as almost an active opponent. Thus she must contend against and overcome a long hill, a thornbush, a log across a creek that poses a threat of falling, and a barbed-wire fence. Also a part of the force is the dog which attacks her. Against these obstacles, Phoenix attempts to assert her determination by carrying on a cheerful monologue. She prevails, for the moment at least, because she finally reaches her destination, the city of Natchez.

[3]   The poverty against which Phoenix must contend is not evident in any one spot, but is shown throughout. She cannot take her trip to town by car, for example, but must walk alone on the long "worn path" wearing only tennis shoes. She has no money and keeps the nickel dropped by the hunter; at the medical office she asks for and gets another nickel. She is the recipient of charity and is given the "soothing syrup" for her grandson as a free service. Despite the boy's obvious need for advanced medical care, she does not have the means to provide it, and thus her guardianship is doomed to be failure.

[4]   Old age as an opponent is shown in signs of Phoenix's increasing senility. It is not her mind but her feet, for example, that tell her where to find the medical office in Natchez. Despite her quiet inner strength, she is unable to state her purpose to the nursing attendant, instead sitting dumbly and unknowingly for a time. Against the power of advancing age, Phoenix is slowly losing. The implication is that she soon will lose entirely.

[5]   This brief description of the plot can only hint at the final power of the story. Phoenix emerges as strong and admirable, but with everything against her nothing can enable her ever to win. The story itself is layered to bring out the full range of the conditions against her. Welty saves the most hopeless fact, the condition of the invalid grandson, to the very end. It is this delayed final revelation of the plot that creates an almost overwhelming sympathy for Phoenix. The plot is powerful because it is so real, and Phoenix is a memorable protagonist struggling against overwhelming odds.

---

* See p. 116 for this story.
° Central idea.
□ Thesis sentence.

Commentary on the Essay

In this essay on plot, emphasis is given to the major aspects of the conflict in "A Worn Path." The plot involves the protagonist, Phoenix, who is opposed not by any person, for the other persons in the story are nice to her, but by the forces of environment, poverty, and old age. The introduction points out how these forces cumulatively account for the story's impact. Paragraph 2 details the environmental obstacles of the conflict. Paragraph 3 examines Phoenix's poverty, and the fourth paragraph considers her old age. The concluding paragraph introduces one other major conflict—the invalid condition of the grandson—as another of the forces aginst which Phoenix contends. This paragraph also points out that in this set of conflicts the protagonist cannot win, except as she lives out her duty and her devotion to help her grandson. Continuing the theme of the introduction, the last paragraph also accounts for the power of the plot: By building up to Phoenix's personal affirmation against unbeatable forces, the story evokes both strong sympathy and great admiration.

WRITING ABOUT STRUCTURE IN A STORY

An essay about the structure of a story is concerned with arrangement and shape. In form, the essay does not need to follow the pattern of the story part by part. Rather it explains why things are where they are. "Why is this here and not there?" is the fundamental question you should aim to answer in your prewriting and planning. Thus you may begin with the crisis of the story, and in explaining its position to consider how the author's manipulation of the exposition and complication have built up to it. Some vital piece of information, for example, might have been withheld in the earlier exposition and delayed until the crisis; thus the crisis might be heightened because there might have been less suspense if the detail had been introduced earlier. An essay might also consider the effect or impact of the story and then analyze how the structuring produced this effect.

Organizing Your Essay

INTRODUCTION.   The introduction first presents a general overview of the story and then centers on the aspect or aspects of structure to be emphasized in the body of the essay. The central idea is a succinct statement about the structure. The thesis sentence points out the various main headings of the body.

Body. The body is best developed in the light of what the story contains. For example, suppose a story contains a number of separate scenes or settings, such as the countryside, city, and building in "A Worn Path." An essay based on the structural importance of these locations would try to explain the relationship of each to the development of the plot. Similarly, both "Blue Winds Dancing" and "The Bride Comes to Yellow Sky" involve characters riding trains and then arriving at their destinations. A structural study of these stories might stem out of these locations and their relationship to the resolution of the plot.
and Structure
    Other noteworthy characteristics of the story can be used to develop an essay on structure. For example, in "A Worn Path" a vital piece of exposition is withheld until the conclusion. An essay on structure might consider what effects this delay produces in the story, and therefore the benefit (or detriment) of this kind of mystery or suspense structure.

It is also possible to devote the body of the essay not to the entire structure of the story, but to a major part, character, or action. Thus the climax of a story might be the principal subject. Some questions to be explored might be these: Where does the climax begin? What events are included in it? Is any new piece of information introduced in the climax? Why then and not earlier? What is the apparent way in which the climax is going to be resolved? How and how soon does the reader learn what the resolution is going to be? Similar questions might be posed and answered if the topic of the essay were to be some other aspect of the structure. With such a concentration on only one aspect of the story's structure, naturally, the introduction would need to make clear that a part rather than the whole will be explored.

In writing about the author's structuring of particular characters, it would be important to establish how the characters are introduced, how information is brought out about them, how they figure in the plot, and how they are treated in the resolution. With an action, it might be that one seemingly minor event is introduced to show the importance of fate, chance, or casual happenings in life. Or it might be that the action is not the one intended by the character or by a group. Thus the event could be seen as it influences the structuring and arrangement of the story's outcome.

Conclusion. Here any necessary summarizing is made. Also, the conclusion might deal briefly with the relationship of structure to the plot. Much can be learned from a brief statement about any departures the structure makes from the strict chronological sequence that elements of plot might ordinarily be expected to require.

SAMPLE ESSAY

The Structure of Eudora Welty's "A Worn Path"*

[1] On the surface, Eudora Welty's "A Worn Path" is structured simply. The narrative is not difficult to follow, and things go forward in straight chronology. The main character is Phoenix Jackson, an old, poor black woman. She walks from her rural home in Mississippi through the woods to Natchez to get a free bottle of medicine for her grandson, who is a hopeless invalid; everything takes place in just a few hours. This action is only the frame, however, for a more skillfully structured plot making for a story of great power.° The masterly control of structure is shown in the story's locations, delayed revelation, and complicated climax.°

[2] The locations in the story are arranged to coincide with the increasing difficulties set out against Phoenix. The first and most obvious "worn path," for example, is the rural woods with all its difficulties. For most people the obstacles would be natural and not especially difficult, but for an old woman they are formidable. In Natchez, the location of the next part of the story, Phoenix's inability to bend over to tie her shoe demonstrates the lack of flexibility of old age. In the medical office, where the final scene takes place, two major difficulties of the plot are brought out. One is Phoenix's increasing senility, and the other is the disclosure that her grandson is an incurable invalid. This set of oppositions, the major conflicts in the plot, thus coincide with the places or locations in the story to demonstrate the increasing insurmountability of the conditions against which Phoenix must contend.

[3] It is the delay of the important revelation about the grandson that makes the story something like a mystery. Because this detail is not known until the end, the reader is left wondering during most of the story what might happen next to Phoenix. In fact, some of the details that are presented to show the conflicting forces against Phoenix are really false leads in terms of the major reason for which she is walking to town. For example, the episode with the dog is threatening, but it leads nowhere; Phoenix, with the aid of the hunter, is unharmed by the animal. Her theft of the nickel might be cause for punishment, but the young hunter is ignorant of the missing coin, and he makes no accusations against her. Right up to the moment of her entering the medical building, therefore, there is no apparent pending resolution. The reader is still wondering what might happen.

[4] Hence the details about the grandson, carefully concealed as they are right until the end, heighten and intensify the climax of the story. The effect is that this information forces a reconsideration of the entire story—a double take. In view of the grandson's condition, Phoenix's walk into town and all her efforts have really been a mission of mercy, but also a totally hopeless one. The delayed final detail also causes a reevaluation of Phoenix's character. She is not just a funny old woman who speaks to the objects and animals around

---

* See p. 116 for this story.
° Central idea.
□ Thesis sentence.

her, but she is an amazingly brave although pathetic woman trying to carry on normally against crushing odds. These conclusions are not apparent for most of the story, and when the carefully concealed details are brought out, the story takes on added force and pathos.

[5] Thus the parts of "A Worn Path," while seemingly simple, are skillfully arranged. The key to the double take and reevaluation is Welty's withholding of the crucial detail of exposition right until the very end. As it were, parts of the exposition and complication merge with the climax at just about the same point near the end of the story. And in some respects, the detail makes it seem as though Phoenix's entire existence is actually a crisis, although she is not aware of this condition as she leaves the office to buy the little paper windmill. It is this complex buildup and emotional peak that make the structure of "A Worn Path" the creation of a master writer.

Commentary on the Essay

To highlight the differences between essays on plot and structure, the topic of this sample essay is Welty's "A Worn Path," the same story analyzed in the sample essay on plot. While both essays are concerned with the conflicts of the story, the essay on plot concentrates on the forces involved, while the essay on structure focuses on the placement and arrangement of the plot elements.

The introduction of this essay points out that the masterly structure accounts for the story's power. The second paragraph develops the topic that the geographical locations are arranged climactically to demonstrate the forces against the major character. Paragraph 3 deals with the delayed revelation about the invalid grandson, pointing out that the suspended detail leaves the reader concerned but baffled about the ultimate climax and resolution of the plot. The fourth paragraph deals with the complexity brought about by the delayed information: The necessary reevaluation of Phoenix's character and her mission to town. The concluding paragraph deals further with this complexity, accounting for the story's power by pointing out the virtual merging of a number of plot elements near the very end to bring things out swiftly and powerfully.

4

Characters:
The People in Fiction

Character in literature generally, and in fiction specifically, is an extended verbal representation of a human being, the inner self that determines thought, speech, and behavior. Through dialogue, action, and commentary, authors capture some of the interactions of character and circumstance. Fiction makes these interactions interesting by portraying characters who are worth caring about, rooting for, and even loving, although there are also characters at whom you may laugh or whom you may dislike or even hate.

CHOICE AND CHARACTER

The choices that people make indicate their characters, if we assume that they have freedom of choice. We always make silent comparisons with the choices made or rejected. Thus, if you know that John works twelve hours a day, while Tom puts in five, and Jim sleeps under a tree, you have a number of separate facts, but you do not conclude anything about their characters unless you have a basis for comparison. This basis is easy: The usual, average number of working hours is eight. With no more than this knowledge for comparison, you might conclude that John is a workaholic, Tom lazy, and Jim either unwell or a dropout. To be fair, you would need to know much more about the lives and financial circumstances of each character before your conclusions would be final.

In fiction you may expect such completeness of context. You may think of each action or speech, no matter how small or seemingly unusual, as an accumulating part of a total portrait. Whereas in life things may "just happen," in fiction the actions, interactions, speeches, and observations are all arranged to give you the details you need for conclusions about character. Thus you read about important events like a plan to discredit a disliked fellow worker (James Thurber's "The Catbird Seat"), an action of jealousy and revenge (Katherine Anne Porter's "María Concepción"), or an act of defiance (William Faulkner's "Barn Burning"). From these events in their contexts you draw conclusions about the characters involved.

MAJOR CHARACTER TRAITS

In studying a literary character, you should try to determine the character's major trait or traits. As in life, characters may be lazy or ambitious, anxious or serene, aggressive or fearful, assertive or bashful, confident or self-doubting, adventurous or timid, noisy or quiet, visionary or practical, reasonable or hotheaded, careful or careless, fair or partial, straightforward or underhanded, "winners" or "losers," and so on.

With this sort of list, to which you may add at will, you can analyze and develop your own conclusions about character. For example, in studying Erwin Martin, the main character in Thurber's "The Catbird Seat" (and the subject of the sample essay at the end of this chapter), you would note that on the surface he is a quiet, unassuming man, one who is normally as unnoticeable as the furniture in the office where he works. Once Mrs. Barrows enters the business and upsets his normal placidity, however, his disturbance causes him to develop a dangerous scheme to eliminate her. It is out of conflicts and reactions such as this that you can get a "handle" on characters.

APPEARANCE, ACTION, AND CHARACTER

When you study character, be sure to consider physical descriptions, but also be sure to relate the physical to the mental. Suppose your author stresses the neatness of one character and the sloppiness of another. Most likely, these descriptions can be related to your character study. The same also applies to your examination of what a character *does*. Go beyond the actions themselves and try to determine what they show *about* the character. Always try to get from the outside to the inside, for it is on the inside that character resides.

TYPES OF CHARACTERS: ROUND AND FLAT

In fiction you will encounter two types of characters, which E. M. Forster (in *Aspects of the Novel*) called "round" and "flat." **Round chracters** are usually the major figures in a story. They have many realistic traits and are relatively fully developed by the author. For this reason they are often given the names **hero** or **heroine.** Because many major characters are anything but heroic, however, it is probably best to use the more descriptive term, which we have introduced before, **protagonist.** The protagonist is central to the action, moves against an **antagonist,** and usually exhibits the human attributes we expect of rounded characters.

To the degree that round characters possess many individual and unpredictable human traits they may be considered as **dynamic;** that is, they demonstrate their capacity to change or to grow. In Porter's "María Concepción," for example, María is a dynamic character. She begins the story as an apparently dutiful and devoted woman who attends faithfully to her chores and religious obligations. But events bring out some of her jealousy, coldness, and rage so that she commits a violent act of revenge. By the story's end, she is not a subservient but a dominant woman.

In considering a round character, you may decide for yourself whether such alterations are really *change* or whether they are *growth*. Is human character capable of change, or is change more accurately described as growth or development? If María is apparently dutiful and quiet, for example, but commits an act of vengeance, does this act show that she has changed, or does it show that firmness, resoluteness, personal honor, and ruthlessness are qualities of her character that were latent but that could be brought out by strong provocation? With round or full characters, a question of this type is appropriate, for round characters are just as complex and as difficult to understand as individual living people. A round character therefore stands out, totally identifiable within the class, occupation, or circumstances of which she or he is a part. Obviously, in a brief story we cannot learn everything there is to know about a major character, but if the author is skillful, there will be enough in the story to enable us to get the significant details that add up to a memorable character. Indeed, an author is to be judged by how fully he or she can bring round characters to life as memorable individuals.

As contrasted with round characters, **flat characters** are essentially undistinguishable from their group or class. Therefore they are not individual, but representative. They are usually minor characters, although not all minor characters are flat. They are mostly useful and structural in the stories. Usually they stay the same; they are **static,** and not dynamic like round characters. Thus, they make announcements, drive major characters to airports, describe duties or services they performed, serve meals, provide essential information, and perform the innumerable other tasks that are important in the development of a story. We learn little if anything about their traits and their lives. They are not developed, and because they are not central to the plot they do not change or grow.

Sometimes flat characters are prominent in certain types of fiction, such as cowboy, police, and detective stories, where the main characters need to be strong, tough, steadfast, and clever so that they may overcome the obstacles before them or solve the crime. These and other types of stories feature recurring situations and require characters to perform similar roles. The term **stock character** is used to refer to characters that perform in these repeating situations. Obviously, names, ages, and sexes are often changed, and places and offices are slightly different, but stock characters have many common traits. Some of the many stock characters are the clown, the revenger, the foolish boss, the bewildered parent, the macho male, the unfaithful husband or wife, the long-suffering wife, the angry police captain, the lovable drunk, the kid sister or brother, and the nice hotel keeper.

These characters are not necessarily flat, but they stay flat as long as they perform only their functions, exhibit conventional and unindividual characteristics, and then disappear from the story and from your memory. When stock characters possess no attitudes except those to be expected from their class, they are often given the label **stereotype,** because they all seem to be cast in the same mold. Often in highly conventionalized stories like the cowboy and police stories mentioned above, and in romances, even the major characters are flat and stereotypical even though they occupy center stage throughout.

Complications occur when round characters are in stock situations and might be expected to behave stereotypically. Thus Juan Villegas in "María Concepción" exhibits characteristics of the macho male and unfaithful husband. The plot of the story develops, however, because María Concepción does not accept the role of the stereotypical long-suffering wife, but takes on some of the qualities of a revenger. Because of this complication, and also because of her very human responses to the murder, she is dynamic, a fully realized and round individual. Had she simply looked the other way at Juan's philanderings, she would have been flat, representative, and stereotypical, and there would have been no story. Erwin Martin of "The Catbird Seat" is another character who emerges from a stock role as an office wallflower to assume status as a round character. The other people in the story have always taken him as quiet and unassuming, but by the story's end he has become individual, round, human, and therefore memorable.

HOW IS CHARACTER DISCLOSED IN FICTION?

Authors use four different ways to convey information about characters in fiction. As you read, remember that you must use your own knowledge and experience with human beings to make judgments about the qualities—the flatness or roundness—of the characters being revealed.

1. *What the characters themselves say* (*and think*, *if the author expresses their thoughts*). On the whole, speeches may be accepted at face value to indicate the character of the speaker. Sometimes, however, a speech may be made offhand, or it may reflect a momentary emotional or intellectual state. Thus, if characters in deep despair say that life is worthless, you must balance this speech with what the same characters say when they are happy. You must also consider the situation or total context of a statement. Macbeth's despair at the end of Shakespeare's play *Macbeth* is voiced after he has been guilty of ruthless political suppression and assassination. His speech therefore reflects his own guilt and self-hatred. You should also consider whether speeches show change or development. A despairing character might say depressing things at the start but happy things at the end. Your analysis of such speeches should indicate how they show change in your character.

2. *What the characters do*. You have heard that "actions speak louder than words," and you should interpret actions as signs of character. Thus you might consider Phoenix's trip through the woods (Welty's "A Worn Path") as a sign of a loving, responsible character, even though Phoenix nowhere says that she is loving and responsible. The difficulty and hardship she goes through on the walk, however, justify such a conclusion about this character.

Sometimes you may find that action is inconsistent with words. Here you might have hypocrisy, weakness, or an approaching change. Smirnov, in Chekhov's play *The Bear*, would be crazy to teach Mrs. Popov how to use the dueling pistol properly, because she has threatened to kill him with it. But he is about ready to declare love for her, and this cooperative if potentially self-destructive act shows that his loving nature is even stronger than his sense of self-preservation.

3. *What other characters say about them*. In stories and plays, as in life, people often talk about other people. If the speakers are shown as honest, you may usually accept their opinions as accurate descriptions of character. However, sometimes a person's prejudices and interests distort what that person says. You know, for example, that the word of a person's enemy is usually slanted, unfair, or even untrue. Therefore an author may give you a good impression of characters by having a bad character say bad things about them. Similarly, the word of a close friend may be biased in favor of a particular character. You must always consider the context and source of all remarks before you use them in your evaluation.

4. *What the author says about them, speaking as storyteller or observer*. What the author says about a character is usually to be accepted as truth. Naturally, authors must be accepted on matters of fact. However, when they *interpret* the actions and characteristics of their characters, they themselves assume the critic's role, and their opinions may be either right or wrong. For this reason authors frequently avoid interpretations and devote their

skill instead to arranging events and speeches so that the conclusions may be drawn by the reader.

REALITY AND PROBABILITY: VERISIMILITUDE

You are entitled to expect that characters in literature will be true to life. That is, their actions, statements, and thoughts must all be what human beings are *likely* to do, say, and think under given conditions. This expectation is often called the standard of **probability, verisimilitude** ("similar to truth"), or **plausibility.** That is, there are often unusual persons in life who do exceptional things. Such characters in a work of fiction would not be true to life, however, because they are not within our judgment of *normal* human behavior. They are not probable or believable.

One should therefore distinguish between what can *possibly* happen and what would frequently or most usually happen. Some reactions do not belong in a story involving full, round characters. Thus, for example, in De Maupassant's "The Necklace," it is possible that Mathilde could have told Jeanne Forrestier that she had lost the necklace. In light of the sense of pride, honor, shame, and respectability of Mathilde and her husband, however, it is more normal for her to hide the fact, buy a replacement necklace, and endure the ten-year hardship needlessly. The probable here has overshadowed the possible.

Nevertheless, probability does not rule out surprise or even exaggeration. Thus in Thurber's "The Catbird Seat" the main character, Erwin Martin, improvises an outrageously clever and effective scheme to discredit Ulgine Barrows. This action is farcical and sudden, but it is not improbable given the energetic but secret private life of Martin and also the extremity of his original plot to murder her. Martin's later imperturbability is actually less probable than his enactment of his "confession" with Mrs. Barrows.

There are, of course, many ways of rendering the probable in literature. Fiction that attempts to mirror life—the realistic, naturalistic, or "slice of life" types of fiction—sets up conditions and raises expectations about the characters that are different from those of fiction that attempts to portray a romantic, fanciful world. A character's behavior and speech in the "realistic" setting would be out of place in the romantic setting.

But the situation is more complex than this, for within the romantic setting a character might reasonably be *expected* to behave and speak in a fanciful, dreamlike way. Speech and action under both conditions are therefore *probable* as we understand the word, although different aspects of human character are presented in these two different types of works.

It is also possible that within the same work you might find some characters who are realistic and others who are not. In such works you have contrasting systems of reality. Mathilde in "The Necklace" exhibits such a contrast. Her dream world at the beginning is so powerful that she makes unrealistic demands on her husband. When the borrowed necklace is lost, her character as a dreamer has effectively destroyed her life in the real world. You might also encounter works where there are *mythical* or *supernatural* figures who contrast with the reality of the other characters. Such a contrast may be found in Marjorie Pickthall's "The Worker in Sandalwood," where there is a young boy who is real and who is visited on Christmas Eve by the boy Jesus. The magic of the story results from the mingling of the real and the miraculous.

You may reasonably wonder about how you should judge the characters of gods, like the boy Jesus in Pickthall's story, or devils, like the woodland guide in Nathaniel Hawthorne's "Young Goodman Brown." Usually gods embody the qualities of the best human beings, whereas devils take on the attributes of the worst. However, one should also remember that the devil is often imagined as a character with many engaging traits, the easier to deceive poor sinners and lead them into hell. In judging characters of this or any type, the best guide is that of probability, consistency, and believability.

As you read, then, look carefully at the development of character. When comments are made about a figure, determine whether these are true. When characters go into action, consider what these actions tell about their natures. If there are unusual traits, determine what they show. Above all, try to conclude whether the characters come to life as round, individual, and dynamic, or whether they stay on the page as flat, static, and only representative.

KATHERINE ANNE PORTER (1890–1980)

María Concepción   1930

María Concepción walked carefully, keeping to the middle of the white dusty road, where the maguey thorns and the treacherous curved spines of organ cactus had not gathered so profusely. She would have enjoyed resting for a moment in the dark shade by the roadside, but she had no time to waste drawing cactus needles from her feet. Juan and his chief would be waiting for their food in the damp trenches of the buried city.

She carried about a dozen living fowls slung over her right shoulder, their feet fastened together. Half of them fell upon the flat of her back, the balance dangled uneasily over her breast. They wriggled their benumbed and swollen legs against her neck, they twisted their stupefied eyes and peered into her face inquiringly. She did not see them or think of them. Her left arm was tired with the weight of the food basket, and she was hungry after her long morning's work.

Her straight back outlined itself strongly under her clean bright blue cotton rebozo.° Instinctive serenity softened her black eyes, shaped like almonds, set far

rebozo: a long scarf or shawl.

apart, and tilted a bit endwise. She walked with the free, natural, guarded ease of the primitive woman carrying an unborn child. The shape of her body was easy, the swelling life was not a distortion, but the right inevitable proportions of a woman. She was entirely contented. Her husband was at work and she was on her way to market to sell her fowls.

Her small house sat half-way up a shallow hill, under a clump of pepper-trees, a wall of organ cactus enclosing it on the side nearest to the road. Now she came down into the valley, divided by the narrow spring, and crossed a bridge of loose stones near the hut where María Rosa the beekeeper lived with her old godmother, Lupe the medicine woman. María Concepción had no faith in the charred owl bones, the singed rabbit fur, the cat entrails, the messes and ointments sold by Lupe to the ailing of the village. She was a good Christian, and drank simple herb teas for headache and stomachache, or bought her remedies bottled, with printed directions that she could not read, at the drugstore near the city market, where she went almost daily. But she often bought a jar of honey from young María Rosa, a pretty, shy child only fifteen years old.

María Concepción and her husband, Juan Villegas, were each a little past   5
their eighteenth year. She had a good reputation with the neighbors as an energetic religious woman who could drive a bargain to the end. It was commonly known that if she wished to buy a new rebozo for herself or a shirt for Juan, she could bring out a sack of hard silver coins for the purpose.

She had paid for the license, nearly a year ago, the potent bit of stamped paper which permits people to be married in the church. She had given money to the priest before she and Juan walked together up to the altar the Monday after Holy Week. It had been the adventure of the villagers to go, three Sundays one after another, to hear the banns called by the priest for Juan de Dios Villegas and María Concepción Manríquez, who were actually getting married in the church, instead of behind it, which was the usual custom, less expensive, and as binding as any other ceremony. But María Concepción was always as proud as if she owned a hacienda.

She paused on the bridge and dabbled her feet in the water, her eyes resting themselves from the sun-rays in a fixed gaze to the far-off mountains, deeply blue under their hanging drift of clouds. It came to her that she would like a fresh crust of honey. The delicious aroma of bees, their slow thrilling hum, awakened a pleasant desire for a flake of sweetness in her mouth.

"If I do not eat it now, I shall mark my child," she thought, peering through the crevices in the thick hedge of cactus that sheered up nakedly, like bared knife blades set protectingly around the small clearing. The place was so silent she doubted if María Rosa and Lupe were at home.

The leaning jacal° of dried rush-withes and corn sheaves, bound to tall saplings thrust into the earth, roofed with yellowed maguey leaves flattened and overlapping like shingles, hunched drowsy and fragrant in the warmth of noonday. The hives, similarly made, were scattered towards the back of the clearing, like small mounds of clean vegetable refuse. Over each mound there hung a dusty golden shimmer of bees.

A light gay scream of laughter rose from behind the hut; a man's short laugh   10
joined in. "Ah, hahahaha!" went the voices together high and low, like a song.

jacal: a small, thatched-roof hut.

"So María Rosa has a man!" María Concepción stopped short, smiling, shifted her burden slightly, and bent forward shading her eyes to see more clearly through the spaces of the hedge.

María Rosa ran, dodging between beehives, parting two stunted jasmine bushes as she came, lifting her knees in swift leaps, looking over her shoulder and laughing in a quivering, excited way. A heavy jar, swung to her wrist by the handle, knocked against her thighs as she ran. Her toes pushed up sudden spurts of dust, her half-raveled braids showered around her shoulders in long crinkled wisps.

Juan Villegas ran after her, also laughing strangely, his teeth set, both rows gleaming behind the small soft black beard growing sparsely on his lips, his chin, leaving his brown cheeks girl-smooth. When he seized her, he clenched so hard her chemise gave way and ripped from her shoulder. She stopped laughing at this, pushed him away and stood silent, trying to pull up the torn sleeve with one hand. Her pointed chin and dark red mouth moved in an uncertain way, as if she wished to laugh again; her long black lashes flickered with the quick-moving lights in her hidden eyes.

María Concepción did not stir nor breathe for some seconds. Her forehead was cold, and yet boiling water seemed to be pouring slowly along her spine. An unaccountable pain was in her knees, as if they were broken. She was afraid Juan and María Rosa would feel her eyes fixed upon them and would find her there, unable to move, spying upon them. But they did not pass beyond the enclosure, nor even glance towards the gap in the wall opening upon the road.

Juan lifted one of María Rosa's loosened braids and slapped her neck with it playfully. She smiled softly, consentingly. Together they moved back through the hives of honey-comb. María Rosa balanced her jar on one hip and swung her long full petticoats with every step. Juan flourished his wide hat back and forth, walking proudly as a game-cock.

María Concepción came out of the heavy cloud which enwrapped her head and bound her throat, and found herself walking onward, keeping the road without knowing it, feeling her way delicately, her ears strumming as if all María Rosa's bees had hived in them. Her careful sense of duty kept her moving toward the buried city where Juan's chief, the American archeologist, was taking his midday rest, waiting for his food.

Juan and María Rosa! She burned all over now, as if a layer of tiny fig-cactus bristles, as cruel as spun glass, had crawled under her skin. She wished to sit down quietly and wait for her death, but not until she had cut the throats of her man and that girl who were laughing and kissing under the cornstalks. Once when she was a young girl she had come back from market to find her jacal burned to a pile of ash and her few silver coins gone. A dark empty feeling had filled her; she kept moving about the place, not believing her eyes, expecting it all to take shape again before her. But it was gone, and though she knew an enemy had done it, she could not find out who it was, and could only curse and threaten the air. Now here was a worse thing, but she knew her enemy. María Rosa, that sinful girl, shameless! She heard herself saying a harsh, true word about María Rosa, saying it aloud as if she expected someone to agree with her: "Yes, she is a whore! She has no right to live."

At this moment the gray untidy head of Givens appeared over the edges of the newest trench he had caused to be dug in his field of excavations. The long deep crevasses, in which a man might stand without being seen, lay crisscrossed like orderly gashes of a giant scalpel. Nearly all of the men of the community worked for Givens, helping him to uncover the lost city of their ancestors. They worked all the year through and prospered, digging every day for those small clay heads and bits of pottery and fragments of painted walls for which there was no good use on earth, being all broken and encrusted with clay. They themselves could make better ones, perfectly stout and new, which they took to town and peddled to foreigners for real money. But the unearthly delight of the chief in finding these worn-out things was an endless puzzle. He would fairly roar for joy at times, waving a shattered pot or a human skull above his head, shouting for his photographer to come and make a picture of this!

Now he emerged, and his young enthusiast's eyes welcomed María Concepción from his old-man face, covered with hard wrinkles and burned to the color of red earth. "I hope you've brought me a nice fat one." He selected a fowl from the bunch dangling nearest him as María Concepción, wordless, leaned over the trench. "Dress it for me, there's a good girl, I'll broil it."

María Concepción took the fowl by the head, and silently, swiftly drew her   20
knife across its throat, twisting the head off with the casual firmness she might use with the top of a beet.

"Good God, woman, you do have nerve," said Givens, watching her. "I can't do that. It gives me the creeps."

"My home country is Guadalajara," explained María Concepción, without bravado, as she picked and gutted the fowl.

She stood and regarded Givens condescendingly, that diverting white man who had no woman of his own to cook for him, and moreover appeared not to feel any loss of dignity in preparing his own food. He squatted now, eyes squinted, nose wrinkled to avoid the smoke, turning the roasting fowl busily on a stick. A mysterious man, undoubtedly rich, and Juan's chief, therefore to be respected, to be placated.

"The tortillas are fresh and hot, señor," she murmured gently. "With your permission I will now go to market."

"Yes, yes, run along; bring me another of these tomorrow." Givens turned   25
his head to look at her again. Her grand manner sometimes reminded him of royalty in exile. He noticed her unnatural paleness. "The sun is too hot, eh?" he asked.

"Yes, sir. Pardon me, but Juan will be here soon?"

"He ought to be here now. Leave his food. The others will eat it."

She moved away; the blue of her rebozo became a dancing spot in the heat waves that rose from the gray-red soil. Givens liked his Indians best when he could feel a fatherly indulgence for their primitive childish ways. He told comic stories of Juan's escapades, of how often he had saved him, in the past five years, from going to jail, and even from being shot, for his varied and always unexpected misdeeds.

"I am never a minute too soon to get him out of one pickle or another," he would say. "Well, he's a good worker, and I know how to manage him."

After Juan was married, he used to twit him, with exactly the right shade   30
of condescension, on his many infidelities to María Concepción. "She'll catch you

yet, and God help you!" he was fond of saying, and Juan would laugh with immense pleasure.

It did not occur to María Concepción to tell Juan she had found him out. During the day her anger against him died, and her anger against María Rosa grew. She kept saying to herself, "When I was a young girl like María Rosa, if a man had caught hold of me so, I would have broken my jar over his head." She forgot completely that she had not resisted even so much as María Rosa, on the day that Juan had first taken hold of her. Besides she had married him afterwards in the church, and that was a very different thing.

Juan did not come home that night, but went away to war and María Rosa went with him. Juan had a rifle at his shoulder and two pistols at his belt. María Rosa wore a rifle also, slung on her back along with the blankets and the cooking pots. They joined the nearest detachment of troops in the field, and María Rosa marched ahead with the battalion of experienced women of war, which went over the crops like locusts, gathering provisions for the army. She cooked with them, and ate with them what was left after the men had eaten. After battles she went out on the field with the others to salvage clothing and ammunition and guns from the slain before they should begin to swell in the heat. Sometimes they would encounter the women from the other army, and a second battle as grim as the first would take place.

There was no particular scandal in the village. People shrugged, grinned. It was far better that they were gone. The neighbors went around saying that María Rosa was safer in the army than she would be in the same village with María Concepción.

María Concepción did not weep when Juan left her; and when the baby was born, and died within four days, she did not weep. "She is mere stone," said old Lupe, who went over and offered charms to preserve the baby.

"May you rot in hell with your charms," said María Concepción.

If she had not gone so regularly to church, lighting candles before the saints, kneeling with her arms spread in the form of a cross for hours at a time, and receiving holy communion every month, there might have been talk of her being devil-possessed, her face was so changed and blind-looking. But this was impossible when, after all, she had been married by the priest. It must be, they reasoned, that she was being punished for her pride. They decided that this was the true cause for everything: she was altogether too proud. So they pitied her.

During the year that Juan and María Rosa were gone María Concepción sold her fowls and looked after her garden and her sack of hard coins grew. Lupe had no talent for bees, and the hives did not prosper. She began to blame María Rosa for running away, and to praise María Concepción for her behavior. She used to see María Concepción at the market or at church, and she always said that no one could tell by looking at her now that she was a woman who had such a heavy grief.

"I pray God everything goes well with María Concepción from this out," she would say, "for she has had her share of trouble."

When some idle person repeated this to the deserted woman, she went down to Lupe's house and stood within the clearing and called to the medicine woman, who sat in her doorway stirring a mess of her infallible cure for sores: "Keep your prayers to yourself, Lupe, or offer them for others who need them. I will ask God for what I want in this world."

"And will you get it, you think, María Concepción?" asked Lupe, tittering 40 cruelly and smelling the wooden mixing spoon. "Did you pray for what you have now?"

Afterward everyone noticed that María Concepción went oftener to church, and even seldomer to the village to talk with the other women as they sat along the curb, nursing their babies and eating fruit, at the end of the market-day.

"She is wrong to take us for enemies," said old Soledad, who was a thinker and a peace-maker. "All women have these troubles. Well, we should suffer together."

But María Concepción lived alone. She was gaunt, as if something were gnawing her away inside, her eyes were sunken, and she would not speak a word if she could help it. She worked harder than ever, and her butchering knife was scarcely ever out of her hand.

Juan and María Rosa, disgusted with military life, came home one day without asking permission of anyone. The field of war had unrolled itself, a long scroll of vexations, until the end had frayed out within twenty miles of Juan's village. So he and María Rosa, now lean as a wolf, burdened with a child daily expected, set out with no farewells to the regiment and walked home.

They arrived one morning about daybreak. Juan was picked up on sight by 45 a group of military police from the small barracks on the edge of town, and taken to prison, where the officer in charge told him with impersonal cheerfulness that he would add one to a catch of ten waiting to be shot as deserters the next morning.

María Rosa, screaming and falling on her face in the road, was taken under the armpits by two guards and helped briskly to her jacal, now sadly run down. She was received with professional importance by Lupe, who helped the baby to be born at once.

Limping with foot soreness, a layer of dust concealing his fine new clothes got mysteriously from somewhere, Juan appeared before the captain at the barracks. The captain recognized him as head digger for his good friend Givens, and dispatched a note to Givens saying: "I am holding the person of Juan Villegas awaiting your further disposition."

When Givens showed up Juan was delivered to him with the urgent request that nothing be made public about so humane and sensible an operation on the part of military authority.

Juan walked out of the rather stifling atmosphere of the drumhead court, a definite air of swagger about him. His hat, of unreasonable dimensions and embroidered with silver thread, hung over one eyebrow, secured at the back by a cord of silver dripping with bright blue tassels. His shirt was of a checkerboard pattern in green and black, his white cotton trousers were bound by a belt of yellow leather tooled in red. His feet were bare, full of stone bruises, and sadly ragged as to toenails. He removed his cigarette from the corner of his full-lipped wide mouth. He removed the splendid hat. His black dusty hair, pressed moistly to his forehead, sprang up suddenly in a cloudy thatch on his crown. He bowed to the officer, who appeared to be gazing at a vacuum. He swung his arm wide in a free circle upsoaring towards the prison window, where forlorn heads poked over the window sill, hot eyes following after the lucky departing one. Two or three of the heads nodded, and a half dozen hands were flipped at him in an effort to imitate his own casual and heady manner.

Juan kept up this insufferable pantomine until they rounded the first clump   50
of fig-cactus. Then he seized Givens' hand and burst into oratory. "Blessed be the day your servant Juan Villegas first came under your eyes. From this day my life is yours without condition, ten thousand thanks with all my heart!"

"For God's sake stop playing the fool," said Givens irritably. "Some day I'm going to be five minutes too late."

"Well, it is nothing much to be shot, my chief—certainly you know I was not afraid—but to be shot in a drove of deserters, against a cold wall, just in the moment of my home-coming, by order of that. . . ."

Glittering epithets tumbled over one another like explosions of a rocket. All the scandalous analogies from the animal and vegetable worlds were applied in a vivid, unique and personal way to the life, loves, and family history of the officer who had just set him free. When he had quite cursed himself dry, and his nerves were soothed, he added: "With your permission, my chief!"

"What will María Concepción say to all this?" asked Givens. "You are very informal, Juan, for a man who was married in the church."

Juan put on his hat.   55

"Oh, María Concepción! That's nothing. Look, my chief, to be married in the church is a great misfortune for a man. After that he is not himself any more. How can that woman complain when I do not drink even at fiestas enough to be really drunk? I do not beat her; never, never. We were always at peace. I say to her, Come here, and she comes straight. I say, Go there, and she goes quickly. Yet sometimes I looked at her and thought, Now I am married to that woman in the church, and I felt a sinking inside, as if something were lying heavy on my stomach. With María Rosa it is all different. She is not silent; she talks. When she talks too much, I slap her and say, Silence, thou simpleton! and she weeps. She is just a girl with whom I do as I please. You know how she used to keep those clean little bees in their hives? She is like their honey to me. I swear it. I would not harm María Concepción because I am married to her in the church; but also, my chief, I will not leave María Rosa, because she pleases me more than any other woman."

"Let me tell you, Juan, things haven't been going as well as you think. You be careful. Some day María Concepción will just take your head off with that carving knife of hers. You keep that in mind."

Juan's expression was the proper blend of masculine triumph and sentimental melancholy. It was pleasant to see himself in the role of hero to two such desirable women. He had just escaped from the threat of a disagreeable end. His clothes were new and handsome, and they had cost him just nothing. María Rosa had collected them for him here and there after battles. He was walking in the early sunshine, smelling the good smells of ripening cactus-figs, peaches, and melons, of pungent berries dangling from the pepper-trees, and the smoke of his cigarette under his nose. He was on his way to civilian life with his patient chief. His situation was ineffably perfect, and he swallowed it whole.

"My chief," he addressed Givens handsomely, as one man of the world to another, "women are good things, but not at this moment. With your permission,

I will now go to the village and eat. My God, *how* I shall eat! Tomorrow morning very early I will come to the buried city and work like seven men. Let us forget María Concepción and María Rosa. Each one in her place. I will manage them when the time comes."

News of Juan's adventure soon got abroad, and Juan found many friends   60
about him during the morning. They frankly commended his way of leaving the army. It was in itself the act of a hero. The new hero ate a great deal and drank somewhat, the occasion being better than a feast-day. It was almost noon before he returned to visit María Rosa.

He found her sitting on a clean straw mat, rubbing fat on her three-hour-old son. Before this felicitous vision Juan's emotions so twisted him that he returned to the village and invited every man in the "Death and Resurrection" pulque° shop to drink with him.

Having thus taken leave of his balance, he started back to María Rosa, and found himself unaccountably in his own house, attempting to beat María Concepción by way of reestablishing himself in his legal household.

María Concepción, knowing all the events of that unhappy day, was not in a yielding mood, and refused to be beaten. She did not scream nor implore; she stood her ground and resisted; she even struck at him. Juan, amazed, hardly knowing what he did, stepped back and gazed at her inquiringly through a leisurely whirling film which seemed to have lodged behind his eyes. Certainly he had not even thought of touching her. Oh, well, no harm done. He gave up, turned away, half-asleep on his feet. He dropped amiably in a shadowed corner and began to snore.

María Concepción, seeing that he was quiet, began to bind the legs of her fowls. It was market-day and she was late. She fumbled and tangled the bits of cord in her haste, and set off across the plowed fields instead of taking the accustomed road. She ran with a crazy panic in her head, her stumbling legs. Now and then she would stop and look about her, trying to place herself, then go on a few steps, until she realized that she was not going towards the market.

At once she came to her senses completely, recognized the thing that troubled   65
her so terribly, was certain of what she wanted. She sat down quietly under a sheltering thorny bush and gave herself over to her long devouring sorrow. The thing which had for so long squeezed her whole body into a tight dumb knot of suffering suddenly broke with shocking violence. She jerked with the involuntary recoil of one who receives a blow, and the sweat poured from her skin as if the wounds of her whole life were shedding their salt ichor. Drawing her rebozo over her head, she bowed her forehead on her updrawn knees, and sat there in deadly silence and immobility. From time to time she lifted her head where the sweat formed steadily and poured down her face, drenching the front of her chemise, and her mouth had the shape of crying, but there were no tears and no sound. All her being was a dark confused memory of grief burning in her at night, of deadly baffled anger eating at her by day, until her very tongue tasted bitter, and her feet were as heavy as if she were mired in the muddy roads during the time of rains.

After a great while she stood up and threw the rebozo off her face, and set out walking again.

pulque: a milky alcoholic drink.

Juan awakened slowly, with long yawns and grumblings, alternated with short relapses into sleep full of visions and clamors. A blur of orange light seared his eyeballs when he tried to unseal his lids. There came from somewhere a low voice weeping without tears, saying meaningless phrases over and over. He began to listen. He tugged at the leash of his stupor, he strained to grasp those words which terrified him even though he could not quite hear them. Then he came awake with frightening suddenness, sitting up and staring at the long sharpened streak of light piercing the corn-husk walls from the level disappearing sun.

María Concepción stood in the doorway, looming colossally tall to his betrayed eyes. She was talking quickly, and calling his name. Then he saw her clearly.

"God's name!" said Juan, frozen to the marrow, "here I am facing my death!" for the long knife she wore habitually at her belt was in her hand. But instead, she threw it away, clear from her, and got down on her knees, crawling toward him as he had seen her crawl many times toward the shrine at Guadalupe Villa. He watched her approach with such horror that the hair of his head seemed to be lifting itself away from him. Falling forward upon her face, she huddled over him, lips moving in a ghostly whisper. Her words became clear, and Juan understood them all.

For a second he could not move nor speak. Then he took her head between both his hands, and supported her in this way, saying swiftly, anxiously reassuring, almost in a babble:

"Oh, thou poor creature! Oh, madwoman! Oh, my María Concepción, unfortunate! Listen. . . . Don't be afraid. Listen to me! I will hide thee away, I thy own man will protect thee! Quiet! Not a sound!"

Trying to collect himself, he held her and cursed under his breath for a few moments in the gathering darkness. María Concepción bent over, face almost on the ground, her feet folded under her, as if she would hide behind him. For the first time in his life Juan was aware of danger. This was danger. María Concepción would be dragged away between two gendarmes, with him following helpless and unarmed, to spend the rest of her days in Belén Prison, maybe. Danger! The night swarmed with threats. He stood up and dragged her up with him. She was silent and perfectly rigid, holding to him with resistless strength, her hands stiffened on his arms.

"Get me the knife," he told her in a whisper. She obeyed, her feet slipping along the hard earth floor, her shoulders straight, her arms close to her side. He lighted a candle. María Concepción held the knife out to him. It was stained and dark even to the handle with drying blood.

He frowned at her harshly, noting the same stains on her chemise and hands. "Take off thy clothes and wash thy hands," he ordered. He washed the knife carefully, and threw the water wide of the doorway. She watched him and did likewise with the bowl in which she had bathed.

"Light the brasero and cook food for me," he told her in the same peremptory tone. He took her garments and went out. When he returned, she was wearing an old soiled dress, and was fanning the fire in the charcoal burner. Seating himself cross-legged near her, he stared at her as at a creature unknown to him, who bewildered him utterly, for whom there was no possible explanation. She did not turn her head, but kept silent and still, except for the movements of her strong hands fanning the blaze which cast sparks and small jets of white smoke, flaring and dying rhythmically with the motion of the fan, lighting her face and darkening it by turns.

Juan's voice barely disturbed the silence: "Listen to me carefully, and tell me the truth, and when the gendarmes come here for us, thou shalt have nothing to fear. But there will be something for us to settle between us afterward."

The light from the charcoal burner shone in her eyes; a yellow phosphorescence glimmered behind the dark iris.

"For me everything is settled now," she answered, in a tone so tender, so grave, so heavy with suffering, that Juan felt his vitals contract. He wished to repent openly, not as a man, but as a very small child. He could not fathom her, nor himself, nor the mysterious fortunes of life grown so instantly confused where all had seemed so gay and simple. He felt too that she had become invaluable, a woman without equal among a million women, and he could not tell why. He drew an enormous sigh that rattled in his chest.

"Yes, yes, it is all settled. I shall not go away again. We must stay here together." 80

Whispering, he questioned her and she answered whispering, and he instructed her over and over until she had her lesson by heart. The hostile darkness of the night encroached upon them, flowing over the narrow threshold, invading their hearts. It brought with it sighs and murmurs, the pad of secretive feet in the near-by road, the sharp staccato whimper of wind through the cactus leaves. All these familiar, once friendly cadences were now invested with sinister terrors; a dread, formless and uncontrollable, took hold of them both.

"Light another candle," said Juan, loudly, in too resolute, too sharp a tone. "Let us eat now."

They sat facing each other and ate from the same dish, after their old habit. Neither tasted what they ate. With food half-way to his mouth, Juan listened. The sound of voices rose, spread, widened at the turn of the road along the cactus wall. A spray of lantern light shot through the hedge, a single voice slashed the blackness, ripped the fragile layer of silence suspended above the hut.

"Juan Villegas!"

"Pass, friends!" Juan roared back cheerfully. 85

They stood in the doorway, simple cautious gendarmes from the village, mixed-bloods themselves with Indian sympathies, well known to all the community. They flashed their lanterns almost apologetically upon the pleasant, harmless scene of a man eating supper with his wife.

"Pardon, brother," said the leader. "Someone has killed the woman María Rosa, and we must question her neighbors and friends." He paused, and added with an attempt at severity, "Naturally!"

"Naturally," agreed Juan. "You know that I was a good friend of María Rosa. This is bad news."

They all went away together, the men walking in a group, María Concepción following a few steps in the rear, near Juan. No one spoke.

The two points of candlelight at María Rosa's head fluttered uneasily; the shadows shifted and dodged on the stained darkened walls. To María Concepción everything in the smothering enclosing room shared an evil restlessness. The watchful faces of those called as witnesses, the faces of old friends, were made alien by the look 90 of speculation in their eyes. The ridges of the rose-colored rebozo thrown over the body varied continually, as though the thing it covered was not perfectly in repose. Her eyes swerved over the body in the open painted coffin, from the candle tips at the head to the feet, jutting up thinly, the small scarred soles protruding, freshly washed, a mass of crooked, half-healed wounds, thornpricks and cuts of sharp stones. Her gaze went back to the candle flame, to Juan's eyes warning her, to the gendarmes talking among themselves. Her eyes would not be controlled.

With a leap that shook her her gaze settled upon the face of María Rosa. Instantly her blood ran smoothly again: there was nothing to fear. Even the restless light could not give a look of life to that fixed countenance. She was dead. María Concepción felt her muscles give way softly; her heart began beating steadily without effort. She knew no more rancor against the pitiable thing, lying indifferently in its blue coffin under the fine silk rebozo. The mouth drooped sharply at the corners in a grimace of weeping arrested half-way. The brows were distressed; the dead flesh could not cast off the shape of its last terror. It was all finished. María Rosa had eaten too much honey and had had too much love. Now she must sit in hell, crying over her sins and her hard death forever and ever.

Old Lupe's cackling voice arose. She had spent the morning helping María Rosa, and it had been hard work. The child had spat blood the moment it was born, a bad sign. She thought then that bad luck would come to the house. Well, about sunset she was in the yard at the back of the house grinding tomatoes and peppers. She had left mother and babe asleep. She heard a strange noise in the house, a choking and smothered calling, like someone wailing in sleep. Well, such a thing is only natural. But there followed a light, quick, thudding sound—

"Like the blows of a fist?" interrrupted an officer.

"No, not at all like such a thing."

"How do you know?"

"I am well acquainted with that sound, friends," retorted Lupe. "This was something else."

She was at a loss to describe it exactly. A moment later, there came the sound of pebbles rolling and slipping under feet; then she knew someone had been there and was running away.

"Why did you wait so long before going to see?"

"I am old and hard in the joints," said Lupe. "I cannot run after people. I walked as fast as I could to the cactus hedge, for it is only by this way that anyone can enter. There was no one in the road, sir, no one. Three cows, with a dog driving them; nothing else. When I got to María Rosa, she was lying all tangled up, and from her neck to her middle she was full of knife-holes. It was a sight to move the Blessed Image Himself! Her eyes were—"

"Never mind. Who came oftenest to her house before she went away? Did you know her enemies?"

Lupe's face congealed, closed. Her spongy skin drew into a network of secretive wrinkles. She turned withdrawn and expressionless eyes upon the gendarmes.

"I am an old woman. I do not see well. I cannot hurry on my feet. I know no enemy of María Rosa. I did not see anyone leave the clearing."

"You did not hear splashing in the spring near the bridge?"

"No, sir."

"Why, then, do our dogs follow a scent there and lose it?"

"God only knows, my friend. I am an old wo—"

"Yes. How did the footfalls sound?"

"Like the tread of an evil spirit!" Lupe broke forth in a swelling oracular tone that startled them. The Indians stirred uneasily, glanced at the dead, then at Lupe. They half expected her to produce the evil spirit among them at once.

The gendarme began to lose his temper.

"No, poor unfortunate; I mean, were they heavy or light? The footsteps of a man or of a woman? Was the person shod or barefoot?"   110

A glance at the listening circle assured Lupe of their thrilled attention. She enjoyed the dangerous importance of her situation. She could have ruined that María Concepción with a word, but it was even sweeter to make fools of these gendarmes who went about spying on honest people. She raised her voice again. What she had not seen she could not describe, thank God! No one could harm her because her knees were stiff and she could not run even to seize a murderer. As for knowing the difference between footfalls, shod or bare, man or woman, nay, between devil and human, who ever heard of such madness?

"My eyes are not ears, gentlemen," she ended grandly, "but upon my heart I swear those footsteps fell as the tread of the spirit of evil!"

"Imbecile!" yapped the leader in a shrill voice. "Take her away, one of you! Now, Juan Villegas, tell me—"

Juan told his story patiently, several times over. He had returned to his wife that day. She had gone to market as usual. He had helped her prepare her fowls. She had returned about mid-afternoon, they had talked, she had cooked, they had eaten, nothing was amiss. Then the gendarmes came with the news about María Rosa. That was all. Yes, María Rosa had run away with him, but there had been no bad blood between him and his wife on this account, nor between his wife and María Rosa. Everybody knew that his wife was a quiet woman.

María Concepción heard her own voice answering without a break. It was   115
true at first she was troubled when her husband went away, but after that she had not worried about him. It was the way of men, she believed. She was a church-married woman and knew her place. Well, he had come home at last. She had gone to market but had come back early, because now she had her man to cook for. That was all.

Other voices broke in. A toothless old man said: "She is a woman of good reputation among us, and María Rosa was not." A smiling young mother, Anita, baby at breast, said: "If no one thinks so, how can you accuse her? It was the loss of her child and not of her husband that changed her so." Another: "María Rosa had a strange life, apart from us. How do we know who might have come from another place to do her evil?" And old Soledad spoke up boldly: "When I saw María Concepción in the market today, I said, 'Good luck to you, María Concepción, this is a happy day for you!' " and she gave María Concepción a long easy stare, and the smile of a born wise-woman.

María Concepción suddenly felt herself guarded, surrounded, upborne by her faithful friends. They were around her, speaking for her, defending her, the forces of life were ranged invincibly with her against the beaten dead. María Rosa had thrown away her share of strength in them, she lay forfeited among them. María Concepción looked from one to the other of the circling, intent faces. Their eyes gave back reassurance, understanding, a secret and mighty sympathy.

The gendarmes were at a loss. They, too, felt that sheltering wall cast impenetrably around her. They were certain she had done it, and yet they could not accuse her. Nobody could be accused; there was not a shred of true evidence. They shrugged their shoulders and snapped their fingers and shuffled their feet. Well, then, good night to everybody. Many pardons for having intruded. Good health!

A small bundle lying against the wall at the head of the coffin squirmed like an eel. A wail, a mere sliver of sound, issued. María Concepción took the son of María Rosa in her arms.

"He is mine," she said clearly, "I will take him with me."   120

No one assented in words, but an approving nod, a bare breath of complete agreement, stirred among them as they made way for her.

María Concepción, carrying the child, followed Juan from the clearing. The hut was left with its lighted candles and a crowd of old women who would sit up all night, drinking coffee and smoking and telling ghost stories.

Juan's exaltation had burned out. There was not an ember of excitement left in him. He was tired. The perilous adventure was over. María Rosa had vanished, to come no more forever. Their days of marching, of eating, of quarreling and making love between battles, were all over. Tomorrow he would go back to dull and endless labor, he must descend into the trenches of the buried city as María Rosa must go into her grave. He felt his veins fill up with bitterness, with black unendurable melancholy. Oh, Jesus! what bad luck overtakes a man!

Well, there was no way out of it now. For the moment he craved only to sleep. He was so drowsy he could scarcely guide his feet. The occasional light touch of the woman at his elbow was as unreal, as ghostly as the brushing of a leaf against his face. He did not know why he had fought to save her, and now he forgot her. There was nothing in him except a vast blind hurt like a covered wound.

He entered the jacal, and without waiting to light a candle, threw off his   125
clothing, sitting just within the door. He moved with lagging, half-awake hands, to strip his body of its heavy finery. With a long groaning sigh of relief he fell straight back on the floor, almost instantly asleep, his arms flung up and outward.

María Concepción, a small clay jar in her hand, approached the gentle little mother goat tethered to a sapling, which gave and yielded as she pulled at the rope's end after the farthest reaches of grass about her. The kid, tied up a few feet away, rose bleating, its feathery fleece shivering in the fresh wind. Sitting on her heels, holding his tether, she allowed him to suckle a few moments. Afterward—all her movements very deliberate and even—she drew a supply of milk for the child.

She sat against the wall of her house, near the doorway. The child, fed and asleep, was cradled in the hollow of her crossed legs. The silence overfilled the world, the skies flowed down evenly to the rim of the valley, the stealthy moon crept slantwise to the shelter of the mountains. She felt soft and warm all over; she dreamed that the newly born child was her own, and she was resting deliciously.

María Concepción could hear Juan's breathing. The sound vapored from the low doorway, calmly; the house seemed to be resting after a burdensome day. She breathed, too, very slowly and quietly, each inspiration saturating her with repose. The child's light, faint breath was a mere shadowy moth of sound in the silver air. The night, the earth under her, seemed to swell and recede together with a limitless, unhurried, benign breathing. She drooped and closed her eyes, feeling the slow rise and fall within her own body. She did not know what it was, but it eased her all through. Even as she was falling asleep, head bowed over the child, she was still aware of a strange, wakeful happiness.

QUESTIONS

1. Characterize the society of which María Concepción and Juan Villegas are a part. To what ethnic group do the people belong? What is their economic status? How do the people form their attitudes, and what role do these play in the resolution of the story?

2. Describe María Concepción's character. What does her behavior show about her during the absence of Juan and María Rosa? What are her strengths, her weaknesses? What does her church affiliation signify? What values cause her to kill María Rosa yet permit her to feel happy at the end of the story? To what extent does her use of her knife seem representative of her character? In what ways does she grow or change in the course of the story?

3. Describe Juan Villegas. Would you characterize him as responsible or irresponsible, caring or uncaring? Are any elements of his character more properly considered flat rather than round? What facet of his character is brought out in his behavior during the investigation about María Rosa's death? What do we learn about Juan during the encounter with María Concepción after she appears with the bloody knife?

4. Discuss your attitude toward María Concepción's murder of María Rosa. What do you think about the killer's going free? How do the circumstances of the story influence your responses?

5. What is the central conflict or conflicts in the story? Who is the protagonist? Is there only one antagonist, or are there more? Describe the crisis of the story, the climax. Whom does the resolution satisfy more, María Concepción or her husband?

6. Consider the characters of Givens and Lupe. They are lesser characters, but are they therefore flat? What static elements do they exhibit? Are there any elements of growth or dynamism evident in them?

7. What techniques does Porter use to reveal the character of María Concepción? How important is the voice of the narrator? The use of dialogue? The use of action? Reports of the opinions of others?

JAMES THURBER (1894–1961)

The Catbird Seat 1945

Mr. Martin bought the pack of Camels on Monday night in the most crowded cigar store on Broadway. It was theater time and seven or eight men were buying cigarettes. The clerk didn't even glance at Mr. Martin, who put the pack in his overcoat pocket and went out. If any of the staff at F & S had seen him buy the cigarettes, they would have been astonished, for it was generally known that Mr. Martin did not smoke, and never had. No one saw him.

It was just a week to the day since Mr. Martin had decided to rub out Mrs. Ulgine Barrows.° The term "rub out" pleased him because it suggested nothing more than the correction of an error—in this case an error of Mr. Fitweiler. Mr. Martin had spent each night of the past week working out his plan and examining it. As he walked home now he went over it again. For the hundredth time he resented the element of imprecision, the margin of guesswork that entered into the business. The project as he had worked it out was casual and bold, the risks were considerable. Something might go wrong anywhere along the line. And therein lay the cunning of his scheme. No one would ever see in it the cautious, painstaking hand of Erwin Martin, head of the filing department at F & S, of whom Mr. Fitweiler had once said, "Man is fallible but Martin isn't." No one would see his hand, that is, unless it were caught in the act.

Sitting in his apartment, drinking a glass of milk, Mr. Martin reviewed his case against Mrs. Ulgine Barrows, as he had every night for seven nights. He began at the beginning. Her quacking voice and braying laugh had first profaned the halls of F & S on March 7, 1941 (Mr. Martin had a head for dates). Old Roberts, the personnel chief, had introduced her as the newly appointed special adviser to the president of the firm, Mr. Fitweiler. The woman had appalled Mr. Martin instantly, but he hadn't shown it. He had given her his dry hand, a look of studious concentration, and a faint smile. "Well," she had said, looking at the papers on his desk, "are you lifting the oxcart out of the ditch?" As Mr. Martin recalled that moment, over his milk, he squirmed slightly. He must keep his mind on her crimes as a special adviser, not on her peccadillos as a personality. This he found difficult to do, in spite of entering an objection and sustaining it. The faults of the woman as a woman kept chattering on in his mind like an unruly witness. She had, for almost two years now, baited him. In the halls, in the elevator, even in his own office, into which she romped now and then like a circus horse, she was constantly shouting these silly questions at him. "Are you lifting the oxcart out of the ditch? Are you tearing up the pea patch? Are you hollering down the rain barrel? Are you scraping around the bottom of the pickle barrel? Are you sitting in the catbird seat?"

It was Joey Hart, one of Mr. Martin's two assistants, who had explained what the gibberish meant. "She must be a Dodger fan," he had said. "Red Barber° announces the Dodger games over the radio and he uses those expressions—picked 'em up down South." Joey had gone on to explain one or two. "Tearing up the pea patch" meant going on a rampage; "sitting in the catbird seat" meant sitting pretty, like a batter with three balls and no strikes on him. Mr. Martin dismissed all this with an effort. It had been annoying, it had driven him near to distraction, but he was too solid a man to be moved to murder by anything so childish. It was fortunate, he reflected as he passed on to the important charges against Mrs. Barrows, that he had stood up under it so well. He had maintained always an outward appearance of polite tolerance. "Why, I even believe you like the woman," Miss Paird, his other assistant, had once said to him. He had simply smiled.

barrow: Among other things, it means a castrated pig.
Red Barber: Harold ("Red") Barber later announced Yankee games.

A gavel rapped in Mr. Martin's mind and the case proper was resumed. 5
Mrs. Ulgine Barrows stood charged with willful, blatant, and persistent attempts
to destroy the efficiency and system of F & S. It was competent, material, and
relevant to review her advent and rise to power. Mr. Martin had got the story
from Miss Paird, who seemed always able to find things out. According to her,
Mrs. Barrows had met Mr. Fitweiler at a party, where she had rescued him from
the embraces of a powerfully built drunken man who had mistaken the president
of F & S for a famous retired Middle Western football coach. She had led him to
a sofa and somehow worked upon him a monstrous magic. The aging gentleman
had jumped to the conclusion there and then that this was a woman of singular
attainments, equipped to bring out the best in him and in the firm. A week later
he had introduced her into F & S as his special adviser. On that day confusion
got its foot in the door. After Miss Tyson, Mr. Brundage, and Mr. Bartlett had
been fired and Mr. Munson had taken his hat and stalked out, mailing in his resignation later, old Roberts had been emboldened to speak to Mr. Fitweiler. He mentioned that Mr. Munson's department had been "a little disrupted" and hadn't
they perhaps better resume the old system there? Mr. Fitweiler had said certainly
not. He had the greatest faith in Mrs. Barrow's ideas. "They require a little seasoning, a little seasoning, is all," he had added. Mr. Roberts had given it up. Mr.
Martin reviewed in detail all the changes wrought by Mrs. Barrows. She had begun
chipping at the cornices of the firm's edifice and now she was swinging at the
foundation stones with a pickaxe. *Sudden, needless change.*

Mr. Martin came now, in his summing up, to the afternoon of Monday, November 2, 1942—just one week ago. On that day, at 3 P.M., Mrs. Barrows had bounced
into his office. "Boo!" she had yelled. "Are you scraping around the bottom of
the pickle barrel?" Mr. Martin had looked at her from under his green eyeshade,
saying nothing. She had begun to wander about the office, taking it in with her
great, popping eyes. "Do you really need *all* these filing cabinets?" she had demanded suddenly. Mr. Martin's heart had jumped. "Each of these files," he had
said, keeping his voice even, "plays an indispensable part in the system of F &
S." She had brayed at him, "Well, don't tear up the pea patch!" and gone to the
door. From there she had bawled, "But you sure have got a lot of fine scrap° in
here!" Mr. Martin could no longer doubt that the finger was on his beloved department. Her pickaxe was on the upswing, poised for the first blow. It had not come
yet; he had received no blue memo from the enchanted Mr. Fitweiler bearing
nonsensical instructions deriving from the obscene woman. But there was no doubt
in Mr. Martin's mind that one would be forthcoming. He must act quickly. Already
a precious week had gone by. Mr. Martin stood up in his living room, still holding
his milk glass. "Gentlemen of the jury," he said to himself, "I demand the death
penalty for this horrible person."

The next day Mr. Martin followed his routine, as usual. He polished his
glasses more often and once sharpened an already sharp pencil, but not even
Miss Paird noticed. Only once did he catch sight of his victim; she swept past

scrap: During World War II (1941–1945) the government constantly collected scrap
metal to be used in wartime manufacture. Saving scrap was considered patriotic.

him in the hall with a patronizing "Hi!" At five-thirty he walked home, as usual, and had a glass of milk, as usual. He had never drunk anything stronger in his life—unless you could count ginger ale. The late Sam Schlosser, the S of F & S, had praised Mr. Martin at a staff meeting several years before for his temperate habits. "Our most efficient worker neither drinks nor smokes," he had said. "The results speak for themselves." Mr. Fitweiler had sat by, nodding approval.

Mr. Martin was still thinking about that red-letter day as he walked over to the Schrafft's on Fifth Avenue near Forty-sixth Street. He got there, as he always did, at eight o'clock. He finished his dinner and the financial page of the *Sun* at a quarter to nine, as he always did. It was his custom after dinner to take a walk. This time he walked down Fifth Avenue at a casual pace. His gloved hands felt moist and warm, his forehead cold. He transferred the Camels from his overcoat to a jacket pocket. He wondered, as he did so, if they did not represent an unnecessary note of strain. Mrs. Barrows smoked only Luckies. It was his idea to puff a few puffs on a Camel (after the rubbing-out), stub it out in the ashtray holding her lipstick-stained Luckies, and thus drag a small red herring across the trail. Perhaps it was not a good idea. It would take time. He might even choke, too loudly.

Mr. Martin had never seen the house on West Twelfth Street where Mrs. Barrows lived, but he had a clear enough picture of it. Fortunately, she had bragged to everybody about her ducky first-floor apartment in the perfectly darling three-story red-brick. There would be no doorman or other attendants; just the tenants of the second and third floors. As he walked along, Mr. Martin realized that he would get there before nine-thirty. He had considered walking north on Fifth Avenue from Schrafft's to a point from which it would take him until ten o'clock to reach the house. At that hour people were less likely to be coming in or going out. But the procedure would have made an awkward loop in the straight thread of his casualness, and he had abandoned it. It was impossible to figure when people would be entering or leaving the house, anyway. There was a great risk at any hour. If he ran into anybody, he would simply have to place the rubbing-out of Ulgine Barrows in the inactive file forever. The same thing would hold true if there were someone in her apartment. In that case he would just say that he had been passing by, recognized her charming house and thought to drop in.

It was eighteen minutes after nine when Mr. Martin turned into Twelfth Street. A man passed him, and a man and a woman talking. There was no one within fifty paces when he came to the house, halfway down the block. He was up the steps in the small vestibule in no time, pressing the bell under the card that said "Mrs. Ulgine Barrows." When the clicking in the lock started, he jumped forward against the door. He got inside fast, closing the door behind him. A bulb in a lantern hung from the hall ceiling on a chain seemed to give a monstrously bright light. There was nobody on the stair, which went up ahead of him along the left wall. A door opened down the hall in the wall on the right. He went toward it swiftly, on tiptoe.

"Well, for God's sake, look who's here!" bawled Mrs. Barrows, and her braying laugh rang out like the report of a shotgun. He rushed past her like a football tackle, bumping her. "Hey, quit shoving!" she said, closing the door behind them. They were in her living room, which seemed to Mr. Martin to be lighted by a hundred lamps. "What's after you?" she said. "You're as jumpy as a goat." He found he was unable to speak. His heart was wheezing in his throat. "I—yes," he finally brought out. She was jabbering and laughing as she started to help him off with his coat. "No, no," he said. "I'll put it here." He took it off and put it on a chair near the door. "Your hat and gloves, too," she said. "You're in a lady's house." He put his hat on top of the coat. Mrs. Barrows seemed larger than he had thought. He kept his gloves on. "I was passing by," he said. "I recognized— is there anyone here?" She laughed louder than ever. "No," she said, "we're all alone. You're as white as a sheet, you funny man. Whatever *has* come over you? I'll mix you a toddy." She started toward a door across the room. "Scotch-and-soda be all right? But say, you don't drink, do you?" She turned and gave him her amused look. Mr. Martin pulled himself together. "Scotch-and-soda will be all right," he heard himself say. He could hear her laughing in the kitchen.

Mr. Martin looked quickly around the living room for the weapon. He had counted on finding one there. There were andirons and a poker and something in a corner that looked like an Indian club. None of them would do. It couldn't be that way. He began to pace around. He came to a desk. On it lay a metal paper knife with an ornate handle. Would it be sharp enough? He reached for it and knocked over a small brass jar. Stamps spilled out of it and it fell to the floor with a clatter. "Hey," Mrs. Barrows yelled from the kitchen, "are you tearing up the pea patch?" Mr. Martin gave a strange laugh. Picking up the knife, he tried its point against his left wrist. It was blunt. It wouldn't do.

When Mrs. Barrows reappeared, carrying two highballs, Mr. Martin, standing there with his gloves on, became acutely conscious of the fantasy he had wrought. Cigarettes in his pocket, a drink prepared for him—it was all too grossly improbable. It was more than that; it was impossible. Somewhere in the back of his mind a vague idea stirred, sprouted. "For heaven's sake, take off those gloves," said Mrs. Barrows. "I always wear them in the house," said Mr. Martin. The idea began to bloom, strange and wonderful. She put the glasses on a coffee table in front of a sofa and sat on the sofa. "Come over here, you odd little man," she said. Mr. Martin went over and sat beside her. It was difficult getting a cigarette out of the pack of Camels, but he managed it. She held a match for him, laughing. "Well," she said, handing him his drink, "this is perfectly marvelous. You with a drink and a cigarette."

Mr. Martin puffed, not too awkwardly, and took a gulp of the highball. "I drink and smoke all the time," he said. He clinked his glass against hers. "Here's nuts to that old windbag, Fitweiler," he said, and gulped again. The stuff tasted awful, but he made no grimace. "Really, Mr. Martin," she said, her voice and posture changing, "you are insulting our employer." Mrs. Barrows was now all special adviser to the president. "I am preparing a bomb," said Mr. Martin, "which will blow the old goat higher than hell." He had only had a little of the drink, which was not strong. It couldn't be that. "Do you take dope or something?" Mrs. Barrows asked coldly. "Heroin," said Mr. Martin. "I'll be coked to the gills when I bump that old buzzard off." "Mr. Martin!" she shouted, getting to her feet. "That will be all of that. You must go at once." Mr. Martin took another swallow of his drink. He tapped his cigarette out in the ashtray and put the pack of Camels on the coffee table. Then he got up. She stood glaring at him. He walked over and put on his hat and coat. "Not a word about this," he said, and laid an index finger against his lips. All Mrs. Barrows could bring out was "Really!" Mr. Martin put his hand on the doorknob. "I'm sitting in the catbird seat," he said. He stuck his tongue out at her and left. Nobody saw him go.

Mr. Martin got to his apartment, walking, well before eleven. No one saw him go in. He had two glasses of milk after brushing his teeth, and he felt elated. It wasn't tipsiness, because he hadn't been tipsy. Anyway, the walk had worn off all effects of the whisky. He got in bed and read a magazine for a while. He was asleep before midnight.

Mr. Martin got to the office at eight-thirty the next morning, as usual. At a quarter to nine, Ulgine Barrows, who had never before arrived at work before ten, swept into his office. "I'm reporting to Mr. Fitweiler now!" she shouted. "If he turns you over to the police, it's no more than you deserve!" Mr. Martin gave her a look of shocked surprise. "I beg your pardon?" he said. Mrs. Barrows snorted and bounced out of the room, leaving Miss Paird and Joey Hart staring after her. "What's the matter with that old devil now?" asked Miss Paird. "I have no idea," said Mr. Martin, resuming his work. The other two looked at him and then at each other. Miss Paird got up and went out. She walked slowly past the closed door of Mr. Fitweiler's office. Mrs. Barrows was yelling inside, but she was not braying. Miss Paird could not hear what the woman was saying. She went back to her desk.

Forty-five minutes later, Mrs. Barrows left the president's office and went into her own, shutting the door. It wasn't until half an hour later that Mr. Fitweiler sent for Mr. Martin. The head of the filing department, neat, quiet, attentive, stood in front of the old man's desk. Mr. Fitweiler was pale and nervous. He took his glasses off and twiddled them. He made a small, bruffing sound in his throat. "Martin," he said, "you have been with us more than twenty years." "Twenty-two, sir," said Mr. Martin. "In that time," pursued the president, "your work and your—uh—manner have been exemplary." "I trust so, sir," said Mr. Martin. "I have understood, Martin," said Mr. Fitweiler, "that you have never taken a drink or smoked." "That is correct, sir," said Mr. Martin. "Ah, yes." Mr. Fitweiler polished his glasses. "You may describe what you did after leaving the office yesterday, Martin," he said. Mr. Martin allowed less than a second for his bewildered pause. "Certainly, sir," he said. "I walked home. Then I went to Schrafft's for dinner. Afterward I walked home again. I went to bed early, sir, and read a magazine for a while. I was asleep before eleven." "Ah, yes," said Mr. Fitweiler again. He was silent for a moment, searching for the proper words to say to the head of the filing department. "Mrs. Barrows," he said finally, "Mrs. Barrows has worked hard, Martin, very hard. It grieves me to report that she has suffered a severe breakdown. It has taken the form of a persecution complex accompanied by distressing hallucinations." "I am very sorry, sir," said Mr. Martin. "Mrs. Barrows is under the delusion," continued Mr. Fitweiler, "that you visited her last evening and behaved yourself in an—uh—unseemly manner." He raised his hand to silence Mr. Martin's little pained outcry. "It is the nature of these psychological diseases," Mr. Fitweiler said, "to fix upon the least likely and most innocent party as the—uh—source of persecution. These matters are not for the lay mind to grasp, Martin. I've just had my psychiatrist, Dr. Fitch, on the phone. He would not, of course, commit himself, but he made enough generalizations to substantiate my suspicions. I suggested to Mrs. Barrows when she had completed her—uh—story to me this morning, that she visit Dr. Fitch, for I suspected a condition at once. She flew, I regret to say, into a rage, and demanded—uh—requested that I call you on the carpet. You may not know, Martin, but Mrs. Barrows had planned a reorganization of your department—subject to my approval, of course, subject to my approval. This brought you, rather than anyone else, to her mind—but again that is a phenomenon for Dr. Fitch and not for us. So, Martin, I am afraid Mrs. Barrows' usefulness here is at an end." "I am dreadfully sorry, sir," said Mr. Martin.

It was at this point that the door to the office blew open with the suddenness of a gas-main explosion and Mrs. Barrows catapulted through it. "Is the little rat denying it?" she screamed. "He can't get away with that!" Mr. Martin got up and moved discreetly to a point beside Mr. Fitweiler's chair. "You drank and smoked at my apartment," she bawled at Mr. Martin, "and you know it! You called Mr. Fitweiler an old windbag and said you were going to blow him up when you got coked to the gills on your heroin!" She stopped yelling to catch her breath and a new glint came into her popping eyes. "If you weren't such a drab, ordinary little man," she said, "I'd think you'd planned it all. Sticking your tongue out at me, saying you were sitting in the catbird seat, because you thought no one would believe me when I told it! My God, it's really too perfect!" She brayed loudly and hysterically, and the fury was on her again. She glared at Mr. Fitweiler. "Can't you see how he has tricked us, you old fool? Can't you see his little game?" But Mr. Fitweiler had been surreptitiously pressing all the buttons under the top of his desk and employees of F & S began pouring into the room. "Stockton," said Mr. Fitweiler, "You and Fishbein will take Mrs. Barrows to her home. Mrs. Powell, you will go with them." Stockton, who had played a little football in high school, blocked Mrs. Barrows as she made for Mr. Martin. It took him and Fishbein together to force her out of the door into the hall, crowded with stenographers and office boys. She was still screaming imprecations at Mr. Martin, tangled and contradictory imprecations. The hubbub finally died out down the corridor.

"I regret that this has happened," said Mr. Fitweiler. "I shall ask you to dismiss it from your mind, Martin." "Yes, sir," said Mr. Martin, anticipating his chief's "That will be all" by moving to the door. "I will dismiss it." He went out and shut the door, and his step was light and quick in the hall. When he entered his department he had slowed down to his customary gait, and he walked quietly across the room to the W20 file, wearing a look of studious concentration.

QUESTIONS

1. Why does Erwin Martin change his plan? When do you learn completely what the full plan really is? What role does Martin's twenty-two–year employment with F & S play in Fitweiler's reaction? Why is the plan successful?

2. Describe Martin's character. Is he round or flat? Do you learn enough about him to determine if he is dynamic? Does his character suggest that he is capable of going through with his original plan of murder? What does his use of the following terms indicate about some of the ways he has spent his time: "rub out," "old goat," "coked to the gills," and "buzzard"? What

do you learn about his inner life? What do his habits of milk drinking, regular
dinner times, and general efficiency contribute to your understanding of his
character? What is the catbird seat, and is Martin one of its occupants at
the end of the story?

3.   What is the effect upon Martin's plan of Fitweiler's experience with psychiatry?
When Martin is in Mrs. Barrows's apartment and develops his plan, do you
think he is predicting what Fitweiler's response will be to her report of his
"confession"?

4.   Summarize Mrs. Barrows's career at F & S. Does it seem to you that the
"death penalty" is justifiable for her? What do phrases like "quacking voice
and braying laugh" and "she romped now and then like a circus horse"
contribute to your attitude toward her? How are you affected by her behavior
in her home when Martin visits her? Is there any discrepancy in your responses? Do you think that Thurber is fair to her?

5.   Is the story serious, farcical, or a little bit of both? What parts are funny
(i.e., characters, the language of Mrs. Barrows, the plot, the climax, the resolution)? Even though there is much that is comic, what values embodied in
the conflict between Martin and Mrs. Barrows might have a more serious
implication?

WILLIAM FAULKNER (1897–1962)

Barn Burning   *1939*

The store in which the Justice of the Peace's court was sitting smelled of cheese.
The boy, crouched on his nail keg at the back of the crowded room, knew he
smelled cheese, and more: from where he sat he could see the ranked shelves
close-packed with the solid, squat, dynamic shapes of tin cans whose labels his
stomach read, not from the lettering which meant nothing to his mind but from
the scarlet devils and the silver curve of fish—this, the cheese which he knew he
smelled and the hermetic meat which his intestines believes he smelled coming
in intermittent gusts momentary and brief between the other constant one, the
smell and sense just a little of fear because mostly of despair and grief, the old
fierce pull of blood. He could not see the table where the Justice sat and before
which his father and his father's enemy (*our enemy* he thought in that despair;
ourn! mine and hisn both! He's my father!) stood, but he could hear them, the two
of them that is, because his father had said no word yet:

"But what proof have you, Mr. Harris?"

"I told you. The hog got into my corn. I caught it up and sent it back to
him. He had no fence that would hold it. I told him so, warned him. The next
time I put the hog in my pen. When he came to get it I gave him enough wire
to patch up his pen. The next time I put the hog up and kept it. I rode down to
his house and saw the wire I gave him still rolled on to the spool in his yard. I
told him he could have the hog when he paid me a dollar pound fee. That evening
a nigger came with the dollar and got the hog. He was a strange nigger. He said,
'He say to tell you wood and hay kin burn.' I said, 'What?' 'That whut he say to

tell you,' the nigger said. 'Wood and hay kin burn.' That night my barn burned. I got the stock out but I lost the barn."

"Where is the nigger? Have you got him?"

"He was a strange nigger, I tell you. I don't know what became of him."   5

"But that's not proof. Don't you see that's not proof?"

"Get that boy up here. He knows." For a moment the boy thought too that the man meant his older brother until Harris said, "Not him. The little one. The boy," and, crouching, small for his age, small and wiry like his father, in patched and faded jeans even too small for him, with straight, uncombed, brown hair and eyes gray and wild as storm scud, he saw the men between himself and the table part and become a lane of grim faces, at the end of which he saw the Justice, a shabby, collarless, graying man in spectacles, beckoning him. He felt no floor under his bare feet; he seemed to walk beneath the palpable weight of the grim turning faces. His father, stiff in his black Sunday coat donned not for the trial but for the moving, did not even look at him. *He aims for me to lie,* he thought, again with that frantic grief and despair. *And I will have to do hit.* He doesn't want to, tho.

"What's your name, boy?" the Justice said.

"Colonel Sartoris Snopes," the boy whispered.

"Hey?" the Justice said. "Talk louder. Colonel Sartoris? I reckon anybody   10 named for Colonel Sartoris in this country can't help but tell the truth, can they?" The boy said nothing. *Enemy! Enemy!* he thought; for a moment he could not even see, could not see that the Justice's face was kindly nor discern that his voice was troubled when he spoke to the man named Harris: "Do you want me to question this boy?" (But he could hear, and during those subsequent long seconds while there was absolutely no sound in the crowded little room save that of quiet and intent breathing it was as if he had swung outward at the end of a grape vine, over a ravine, and at the top of the swing had been caught in a prolonged instant of mesmerized gravity, weightless in time.) Analogy

"No!" Harris said violently, explosively. "Damnation! Send him out of here!" Now time, the fluid world, rushed beneath him again, the voices coming to him again through the smell of cheese and sealed meat, the fear and despair and the old grief of blood:

"This case is closed. I can't find against you, Snopes, but I can give you advice. Leave this country and don't come back to it."

His father spoke for the first time, his voice cold and harsh, level, without emphasis: "I aim to. I don't figure to stay in a country among people who . . ." he said something unprintable and vile, addressed to no one.

"That'll do," the Justice said, "Take your wagon and get out of this country before dark. Case dismissed."

His father turned, and he followed the stiff black coat, the wiry figure walking   15 a little stiffly from where a Confederate provost's man's musket ball had taken him in the heel on a stolen horse thirty years ago, followed the two backs now, since his older brother had appeared from somewhere in the crowd, no taller than the father but thicker, chewing tobacco steadily, between the two lines of grim-faced men and out of the store and across the worn gallery and down the sagging steps and among the dogs and half-grown boys in the mild May dust, where as he passed a voice hissed:

"Barn burner!"

his defending
his father

Again he could not see, whirling; there was a face in a red haze, moonlike, bigger than the full moon, the owner of it half again his size, he leaping in the red haze toward the face, feeling no blow, feeling no shock when his head struck the earth, scrabbling up and leaping again, feeling no blow this time either and tasting no blood, scrabbling up to see the other boy in full flight and himself already leaping into pursuit as his father's hand jerked him back, the harsh, cold voice speaking above him: "Go get in the wagon."

It stood in a grove of locusts and mulberries across the road. His two hulking sisters in their Sunday dresses and his mother and her sister in calico and sunbonnets were already in it, sitting on and among the sorry residue of the dozen and more movings which even the boy could remember—the battered stove, the broken beds and chairs, the clock inlaid with mother-of-pearl, which would not run, stopped at some fourteen minutes past two o'clock of a dead and forgotten day and time, which had been his mother's dowry. She was crying, though when she saw him she drew her sleeve across her face and began to descend from the wagon. "Get back," the father said.

"He's hurt. I got to get some water and wash his . . . ."

"Get back in the wagon," his father said. He got in too, over the tail-gate. 2
His father mounted to the seat where the older brother already sat and struck the gaunt mules two savage blows with the peeled willow, but without heat. It was not even sadistic; it was exactly that same quality which in later years would cause his descendants to over-run the engine before putting a motor car into motion, striking and reining back in the same movement. The wagon went on, the store with its quiet crowd of grimly watching men dropped behind; a curve in the road hid it. *Forever* he thought. *Maybe he's done satisfied now, now that he has . . .* stopping himself, not to say it aloud even to himself. His mother's hand touched his shoulder.

"Does hit hurt?" she said.

"Naw," he said. "Hit don't hurt. Lemme be."

"Can't you wipe some of the blood off before hit dries?"

"I'll wash tonight," he said. "Lemme be, I tell you."

The wagon went on. He did not know where they were going. None of 2
them ever did or ever asked, because it was always somewhere, always a house of sorts waiting for them a day or two days or even three days away. Likely his father had already arranged to make a crop on another farm before he . . . Again he had to stop himself. He (the father) always did. There was something about his wolflike independence and even courage when the advantage was at least neutral which impressed strangers, as if they got from his latent ravening ferocity not so much a sense of dependability as a feeling that his ferocious conviction in the rightness of his own actions would be of advantage to all whose interest lay with his.

That night they camped, in a grove of oaks and beeches where a spring ran. The nights were still cool and they had a fire against it, of a rail lifted from a nearby fence and cut into lengths—a small fire, neat, niggard almost, a shrewd fire; such fires were his father's habit and custom always, even in freezing weather. Older, the boy might have remarked this and wondered why not a big one; why should not a man who had not only seen the waste and extravagance of war, but who had in his blood an inherent voracious prodigality with material not his own, have burned everything in sight? Then he might have gone a step farther and thought that that was the reason: that niggard blaze was the living fruit of nights passed during those four years in the woods hiding from all men, blue or gray, with his strings of horses (captured horses, he called them). And older still, he might have divined the true reason: that the element of fire spoke to some deep mainspring of his father's being, as the element of steel or of powder spoke to other men, as the one weapon for the preservation of integrity, else breath were not worth the breathing, and hence to be regarded with respect and used with discretion.

But he did not think this now and he had seen those same niggard blazes all his life. He merely ate his supper beside it and was already half asleep over his iron plate when his father called him, and once more he followed the stiff back, the stiff and ruthless limp, up the slope and on to the starlit road where, turning, he could see his father against the stars but without face or depth—a shape black, flat, and bloodless as though cut from tin in the iron folds of the frockcoat which had not been made for him, the voice harsh like tin and without heat like tin:

"You were fixing to tell them. You would have told him." He didn't answer. His father struck him with the flat of his hand on the side of the head, hard but without heat, exactly as he had struck the two mules at the store, exactly as he would strike either of them with any stick in order to kill a horse fly, his voice still without heat or anger: "You're getting to be a man. You got to learn. You got to learn to stick to your own blood or you ain't going to have any blood to stick to you. Do you think either of them, any man there this morning, would? Don't you know all they wanted was a chance to get at me because they knew I had them beat? Eh?" Later, twenty years later, he was to tell himself, "If I had said they wanted only truth, justice, he would have hit me again." But now he said nothing. He was not crying. He just stood there. "Answer me," his father said.

"Yes," he whispered. His father turned.

"Get on to bed. We'll be there tomorrow."

Tomorrow they were there. In the early afternoon the wagon stopped before a paintless two-room house identical almost with the dozen others it had stopped before even in the boy's ten years, and again, as on the other dozen occasions, his mother and aunt got down and began to unload the wagon, although his two sisters and his father and brother had not moved.

"Likely hit ain't fitten for hawgs," one of the sisters said.

"Nevertheless, fit it will and you'll hog it and like it," his father said. "Get out of them chairs and help your Ma unload."

The two sisters got down, big, bovine, in a flutter of cheap ribbons; one of them drew from the jumbled wagon bed a battered lantern, the other a worn broom. His father handed the reins to the older son and began to climb stiffly over the wheel. "When they get unloaded, take the team to the barn and feed them." Then he said, and at first the boy thought he was still speaking to his brother: "Come with me."

"Me?" he said.

"Yes," his father said. "You."

"Abner," his mother said. His father paused and looked back—the harsh level stare beneath the shaggy, graying, irascible brows.

30

35

"I reckon I'll have a word with the man that aims to begin tomorrow owning me body and soul for the next eight months." *Major de Spain.*

They went back up the road. A week ago—or before last night, that is—he would have asked where they were going, but not now. His father had struck him before last night but never before had he paused afterward to explain why; it was as if the blow and the following calm, outrageous voice still rang, repercussed, divulging nothing to him save the terrible handicap of being young, the light weight of his few years, just heavy enough to prevent his soaring free of the world as it seemed to be ordered but not heavy enough to keep him footed solid in it, to resist it and try to change the course of its events.

Presently he could see the grove of oaks and cedars and the other flowering trees and shrubs where the house would be, though not the house yet. They walked beside a fence massed with honeysuckle and Cherokee roses and came to a gate swinging open between two brick pillars, and now, beyond a sweep of drive, he saw the house for the first time and at that instant he forgot his father and the terror and despair both, and even when he remembered his father again (who had not stopped) the terror and despair did not return. Because, for all the twelve movings, they had sojourned until now in a poor country, a land of small farms and fields and houses, and he had never seen a house like this before. *Hit's big as a courthouse* he thought quietly, with a surge of peace and joy whose reason he could not have thought into words, being too young for that: [*They are safe from him. People whose lives are a part of this peace and dignity are beyond his touch, he no more to them than a buzzing (wasp) capable of stinging for a little moment but that's all; the spell of this peace and dignity rendering even the barns and stable and cribs which belong to it impervious to the puny flames he might contrive*] . . . this, the peace and joy, ebbing for an instant as he looked again at the stiff black back, the stiff and implacable limp of the figure which was not dwarfed by the house, for the reason that it had never looked big anywhere and which now, against the serene columned backdrop, had more than ever that impervious quality of something cut ruthlessly from tin, depthless, as though, sidewise to the sun, it would cast no shadow. Watching him, the boy remarked the absolutely undeviating course which his father held and saw the stiff foot come squarely down in a pile of fresh droppings where a horse had stood in the drive and which his father could have avoided by a simple change of stride. But it ebbed only for a moment, though he could not have thought this into words either, walking on in the spell of the house, which he could even want but without envy, without sorrow, certainly never with that ravening and jealous rage which unknown to him walked in the ironlike black coat before him: [*Maybe he will feel it too. Maybe it will even change him now from what maybe he couldn't help but be.*]

They crossed the portico. Now he could hear his father's stiff foot as it came down on the boards with clocklike finality, a sound out of all proportion to the displacement of the body it bore and which was not dwarfed either by the white door before it, as though it had attained to a sort of vicious and ravening minimum not to be dwarfed by anything—the flat, wide, black hat, the formal coat of broadcloth which had once been black but which had now that friction-glazed greenish cast of the bodies of old house (flies,) the lifted sleeve which was too large, the lifted hand like a curled claw. The door opened so promptly that the boy knew the Negro must have been watching them all the time, an old man with neat grizzled hair, in a linen jacket, who stood barring the door with his body, saying "Wipe yo foots, white man, fo you come in here. Major ain't home nohow."

"Get out of my way, nigger," his father said, without heat too, flinging the door back and the Negro also and entering, his hat still on his head. And now the boy saw the prints of the stiff foot on the doorsill and saw them appear on the pale rug behind the machinelike deliberation of the foot which seemed to bear (or transmit) twice the weight which the body compassed. The Negro was shouting "Miss Lula! Miss Lula!" somewhere behind them, then the boy, deluged as though by a warm wave by a suave turn of carpeted stair and a pendant glitter of chandeliers and a mute gleam of gold frames, heard the swift feet and saw her too, a lady—perhaps he had never seen her like before either—in a gray, smooth gown with lace at the throat and an apron tied at the waist and the sleeves turned back, wiping cake or biscuit dough from her hands with a towel as she came up the hall, looking not at his father at all but at the tracks on the blond rug with an expression of incredulous amazement. *Why does Snopes do this?*

"I tried," the Negro cried. "I tole him to . . ."

"Will you please go away?" she said in a shaking voice. "Major de Spain is not at home. Will you please go away?"

His father had not spoken again. He did not speak again. He did not even look at her. He just stood stiff in the center of the rug, in his hat, the shaggy iron-gray brows twitching slightly above the pebble-colored eyes as he appeared to examine the house with brief deliberation. Then with the same deliberation he turned; the boy watched him pivot on the good leg and saw the stiff foot drag round the arc of the turning, leaving a final long and fading smear. His father never looked at it, he never once looked down at the rug. The Negro held the door. It closed behind them, upon the hysteric and indistinguishable woman-wail. His father stopped at the top of the steps and scraped his boot clean on the edge of it. At the gate he stopped again. [He stood for a moment, planted stiffly on the stiff foot, looking back at the house. "Pretty and white, ain't it?" he said. "That's sweat. Nigger sweat. Maybe it ain't white enough yet to suit him. Maybe he wants to mix some white sweat with it."] *Jealous rage.*

Two hours later the boy was chopping wood behind the house within which his mother and aunt and the two sisters (the mother and aunt, not the two girls, he knew that; even at this distance and muffled by walls the flat loud voices of the two girls emanated an incorrigible idle inertia) were setting up the stove to prepare a meal, when he heard the hooves and saw the linen-clad man on a fine sorrel mare, whom he recognized even before he saw the rolled rug in front of the Negro youth following on a fat bay carriage horse—a suffused, angry face vanishing, still at full gallop, beyond the corner of the house where his father and brother were sitting in the two tilted chairs; and a moment later, almost before he could have put the axe down, he heard the hooves again and watched the sorrel mare go back out of the yard, already galloping again. Then his father began to shout one of the sisters' names, who presently emerged backward from the kitchen door dragging the rolled rug along the ground by one end while the other sister walked behind it. *Lazy*

"If you ain't going to tote, go on and set up the wash pot," the first said.

"You, Sarty!" the second shouted. "Set up the wash pot!" His father appeared at the door, framed against that shabbiness, as he had been against that other

45

bland perfection, impervious to either, the mother's anxious face at his shoulder.

"Go on," the father said. "Pick it up." The two sisters stooped, broad, lethargic; stooping, they presented an incredible expanse of pale cloth and a flutter of tawdry ribbons.

"If I thought enough of a rug to have to git hit all the way from France I   50
wouldn't keep hit where folks coming in would have to tromp on hit," the first said. They raised the rug.

"Abner," the mother said. "Let me do it."

"You go back and git dinner," his father said. "I'll tend to this."

From the woodpile through the rest of the afternoon the boy watched them, the rug spread flat in the dust beside the bubbling wash pot, the two sisters stooping over it with that profound and lethargic reluctance, while the father stood over them in turn, implacable and grim, driving them though never raising his voice again. He could smell the harsh homemade lye they were using; he saw his mother come to the door once and look toward them with an expression not anxious now but very like despair; he saw his father turn, and he fell to with the axe and saw from the corner of his eye his father raise from the ground a flattish fragment of field stone and examine it and return to the pot, and this time his mother actually spoke: "Abner. Abner. Please don't. Please, Abner."

Then he was done too. It was dusk; the whippoorwills had already begun. He could smell coffee from the room where they would presently eat the cold food remaining from the mid-afternoon meal, though when he entered the house he realized they were having coffee again probably because there was a fire on the hearth, before which the rug now lay spread over the backs of the two chairs. The tracks of his father's foot were gone. Where they had been were now long, water-cloudy scoriations resembling the sporadic course of a Lilliputian mowing machine.

It still hung there while they ate the cold food and then went to bed, scattered   55
without order or claim up and down the two rooms, his mother in one bed, where his father would later lie, the older brother in the other, himself, the aunt, and the two sisters on pallets on the floor. But his father was not in bed yet. The last thing the boy remembered was the depthless, harsh silhouette of the hat and coat bending over the rug and it seemed to him that he had not even closed his eyes when the silhouette was standing over him, the fire almost dead behind it, the stiff foot prodding him awake. "Catch up the mule," his father said.

When he returned with the mule his father was standing in the black door, the rolled rug over his shoulder. "Ain't you going to ride?" he said.

"No. Give me your foot."

He bent his knee into his father's hand, the wiry, surprising power flowed smoothly, rising, he rising with it, on to the mule's bare back (they had owned a saddle once; the boy could remember it though not when or where) and with the same effortlessness his father swung the rug up in front of him. Now in the starlight they retraced the afternoon's path, up the dusty road rife with honeysuckle, through the gate and up the black tunnel of the drive to the lightless house, where he sat on the mule and felt the rough warp of the rug drag across his thighs and vanish.

"Don't you want me to help?" he whispered. His father did not answer and now he heard again that stiff foot striking the hollow portico with that wooden and clocklike deliberation, that outrageous overstatement of the weight it carried. The rug, hunched, not flung (the boy could tell that even in the darkness) from his father's shoulder, struck the angle of wall and floor with a sound unbelievably loud, thunderous, then the foot again, unhurried and enormous; a light came on in the house and the boy sat, tense, breathing steadily and quietly and just a little fast, though the foot itself did not increase its beat at all, descending the steps now; now the boy could see him.

"Don't you want to ride now?" he whispered. "We kin both ride now," the   60 light within the house altering now, flaring up and sinking. *He's coming down the stairs now*, he thought. He had already ridden the mule up beside the horse block; presently his father was up behind him and he doubled the reins over and slashed the mule across the neck, but before the animal could begin to trot the hard, thin arm came round him, the hard, knotted hand jerking the mule back to a walk.

In the first red rays of the sun they were in the lot, putting plow gear on the mules. This time the sorrel mare was in the lot before he heard it at all, the rider collarless and even bareheaded, trembling, speaking in a shaking voice as the woman in the house had done, his father merely looking up once before stooping again to the hame he was buckling, so that the man on the mare spoke to his stooping back:

"You must realize you have ruined that rug. Wasn't there anybody here, any of your women . . ." He ceased, shaking, the boy watching him, the older brother leaning now in the stable door, chewing, blinking slowly and steadily at nothing apparently. "It cost a hundred dollars. But you never had a hundred dollars. You never will. So I'm going to charge you twenty bushels of corn against your crop. I'll add it in your contract and when you come to the commissary you can sign it. That won't keep Mrs. de Spain quiet but maybe it will teach you to wipe your feet off before you enter her house again."

Then he was gone. The boy looked at his father, who still had not spoken or even looked up again, who was now adjusting the logger-head in the hame.

"Pap," he said. His father looked at him—the inscrutable face, the shaggy brows beneath which the gray eyes glinted coldly. Suddenly the boy went toward him, fast, stopping as suddenly. "You done the best you could!" he cried. "If he wanted hit done different why didn't he wait and tell you how? He won't git no twenty bushels! He won't git none! We'll get hit and hide hit! I kin watch . . ."

"Did you put the cutter back in that straight stock like I told you?"   65

"No, sir," he said.

"Then go do it."

That was Wednesday. During the rest of that week he worked steadily, at what was within his scope and some which was beyond it, with an industry that did not need to be driven nor even commanded twice; he had this from his mother, with the difference that some at least of what he did he liked to do, such as splitting wood with the half-size axe which his mother and aunt had earned, or saved money somehow, to present him with at Christmas. In company with the two older women (and on one afternoon even one of the sisters), he built pens for the shoat and the cow which were a part of his father's contract with the landlord, and one afternoon, his father being absent, gone somewhere on one of the mules, he went to the field.

They were running a middle buster now, his brother holding the plow straight while he handled the reins, and walking beside the straining mule, the rich black soil shearing cool and damp against his bare ankles, he thought *Maybe this is the end of it. Maybe even that twenty bushels that seems hard to have to pay for just a rug will be a cheap price for him to stop forever and always from being what he used to be*; thinking, dreaming now, so that his brother had to speak sharply to him to mind the mule: *Maybe he even won't collect the twenty bushels. Maybe it will all add up and balance and vanish—corn, rug, fire; the terror and grief, the being pulled two ways like between two teams of horses—gone, done with forever and ever.*

Then it was Saturday; he looked up from beneath the mule he was harnessing   70
and saw his father in the black coat and hat. "Not that," his father said. "The wagon gear." And then, two hours later, sitting in the wagon bed behind his father and brother on the seat, the wagon accomplished a final curve, and he saw the weathered paintless store with its tattered tabocco- and patent-medicine posters and the tethered wagons and saddle animals below the gallery. He mounted the gnawed steps behind his father and brother, and there again was the lane of quiet, watching faces for the three of them to walk through. He saw the man in spectacles sitting at the plank table and he did not need to be told this was a Justice of the Peace; he sent one glare of fierce, exultant, partisan defiance at the man in collar and cravat now, whom he had seen but twice before in his life, and that on a galloping horse, who now wore on his face an expression not of rage but of amazed unbelief which the boy could not have known was at the incredible circumstance of being sued by one of his own tenants, and came and stood against his father and cried at the Justice: "He ain't done it! He ain't burnt . . ."

"Go back to the wagon," his father said.

"Burnt?" the Justice said. "Do I understand this rug was burned too?"

"Does anybody here claim it was?" his father said. "Go back to the wagon." But he did not, he merely retreated to the rear of the room, crowded as that other had been, but not to sit down this time, instead, to stand pressing among the motionless bodies, listening to the voices:

"And you claim twenty bushels of corn is too high for the damage you did to the rug?"

"He brought the rug to me and said he wanted the tracks washed out of it.   75
I washed the tracks out and took the rug back to him."

"But you didn't carry the rug back to him in the same condition it was in before you made the tracks on it."

His father did not answer, and now for perhaps half a minute there was no sound at all save that of breathing, the faint, steady suspiration of complete and intent listening.

"You decline to answer that, Mr. Snopes?" Again his father did not answer. "I'm going to find against you, Mr. Snopes. I'm going to find that you were responsible for the injury to Major de Spain's rug and hold you liable for it. But twenty bushels of corn seems a little high for a man in your circumstances to have to pay. Major de Spain claims it cost a hundred dollars. October corn will be worth about fifty cents. I figure that if Major de Spain can stand a ninety-five-dollar loss on something he paid cash for, you can stand a five-dollar loss you haven't earned yet. I hold you in damages to Major de Spain to the amount of ten bushels of corn over and above your contract with him, to be paid to him out of your crop at gathering time. Court adjourned."

It had taken no time hardly, the morning was but half begun. He thought they would return home and perhaps back to the field, since they were late, far behind all other farmers. But instead his father passed on behind the wagon, merely indicating with his hand for the older brother to follow with it, and crossed the road toward the blacksmith shop opposite, pressing on after his father, overtaking him, speaking, whispering up at the harsh, calm face beneath the weathered hat: "He won't git no ten bushels neither. He won't git one. We'll . . ." until his father glanced for an instant down at him, the face absolutely calm, the grizzled eyebrows tangled above the cold eyes, the voice almost pleasant, almost gentle: "You think so? Well, we'll wait till October anyway."

80

The matter of the wagon—the setting of a spoke or two and the tightening of the tires—did not take long either, the business of the tires accomplished by driving the wagon into the spring branch behind the shop and letting it stand there, the mules nuzzling into the water from time to time, and the boy on the seat with the idle reins, looking up the slope and through the sooty tunnel of the shed where the slow hammer rang and where his father sat on an upended cypress bolt, easily, either talking or listening, still sitting there when the boy brought the dripping wagon up out of the branch and halted it before the door.

"Take them on to the shade and hitch," his father said. He did so and returned. His father and the smith and a third man squatting on his heels inside the door were talking, about crops and animals; the boy, squatting too in the ammoniac dust and hoof-parings and scales of rust, heard his father tell a long and unhurried story out of the time before the birth of the older brother even when he had been a professional horsetrader. And then his father came up beside him where he stood before a tattered last year's circus poster on the other side of the store, gazing rapt and quiet at the scarlet horses, the incredible poisings and convolutions of tulle and tights and the painted leers of comedians, and said, "It's time to eat."

But not at home. Squatting beside his brother against the front wall, he watched his father emerge from the store and produce from a paper sack a segment of cheese and divided it carefully and deliberately into three with his pocket knife and produce crackers from the same sack. They all three squatted on the gallery and ate slowly, without talking; then in the store again, they drank from a tin dipper tepid water smelling of the cedar bucket and of living beech trees. And still they did not go home. It was a horse lot this time, a tall rail fence upon and along which men stood and sat and out of which one by one horses were led, to be walked and trotted and then cantered back and forth along the road while the slow swapping and buying went on and the sun began to slant westward, they— the three of them—watching and listening, the older brother with his muddy eyes and his steady, inevitable tobacco, the father commenting now and then on certain of the animals, to no one in particular.

It was after sundown when they reached home. They ate supper by lamplight, then, sitting on the doorstep, the boy watched the night fully accomplish, listening to the whippoorwills and the frogs, when he heard his mother's voice: "Abner! No! No! Oh, God. Oh, God. Abner!" and he rose, whirled, and saw the altered light through the door where a candle stub now burned in a bottle neck on the table and his father, still in the hat and coat, at once formal and burlesque as though dressed carefully for some shabby and ceremonial violence, emptying the reservoir of the lamp back into the five-gallon kerosene can from which it had been filled, while the mother tugged at his arm until he shifted the lamp to the other hand and flung her back, not savagely or viciously, just hard, into the wall, her hands flung out against the wall for balance, her mouth open and in her face the same quality of hopeless despair as had been in her voice. Then his father saw him standing in the door.

"Go to the barn and get that can of oil we were oiling the wagon with," he said. The boy did not move. Then he could speak.

"What . . ." he cried. "What are you . . ."

"Go get that oil," his father said. "Go."

Then he was moving, running, outside the house, toward the stable: this the old habit, the old blood which he had not been permitted to choose for himself, which had been bequeathed him willy nilly and which had run for so long (and who knew where, battening on what of outrage and savagery and lust) before it came to him. *I could keep on,* he thought. *I could run on and on and never look back, never need to see his face again. Only I can't. I can't,* the rusted can in his hand now, the liquid sploshing in it as he ran back to the house and into it, into the sound of his mother's weeping in the next room, and handed the can to his father.

"Ain't you going to even send a nigger?" he cried. "At least you sent a nigger before!" To warn de Spain

This time his father didn't strike him. The hand came even faster than the blow had, the same hand which had set the can on the table with almost excruciating care flashing from the can toward him too quick for him to follow it, gripping him by the back of his shirt and on to tiptoe before he had seen it quit the can, the face stooping at him in breathless and frozen ferocity, the cold, dead voice speaking over him to the older brother who leaned against the table, chewing with that steady, curious, sidewise motion of cows:

"Empty the can into the big one and go on. I'll catch up with you."

"Better tie him up to the bedpost," the brother said.

"Do like I told you," the father said. Then the boy was moving, his bunched shirt and the hard, bony hand between his shoulder-blades, his toes just touching the floor, across the room and into the other one, past the sisters sitting with spread heavy thighs in the two chairs over the cold hearth, and to where his mother and aunt sat side by side on the bed, the aunt's arms about his mother's shoulders.

"Hold him," the father said. The aunt made a startled movement. "Not you," the father said. "Lennie. Take hold of him. I want to see you do it." His mother took him by the wrist. "You'll hold him better than that. If he gets loose don't you know what he is going to do? He will go up yonder." He jerked his head toward the road. "Maybe I'd better tie him."

"I'll hold him," his mother whispered.

"See you do then." Then his father was gone, the stiff foot heavy and measured upon the boards, ceasing at last.

Then he began to struggle. His mother caught him in both arms, he jerking and wrenching at them. He would be stronger in the end, he knew that. But he had no time to wait for it. "Lemme go!" he cried. "I don't want to have to hit you!"

"Let him go!" the aunt said. "If he don't go, before God, I am going up there myself!"

"Don't you see I can't?" his mother cried. "Sarty! Sarty! No! No! Help me, Lizzie!"

Then he was free. His aunt grasped at him but it was too late. He whirled, 100
running, his mother stumbled forward on to her knees behind him, crying to the
nearer sister: "Catch him, Net! Catch him!" But that was too late too, the sister
(the sisters were twins, born at the same time, yet either of them now gave the
impression of being, encompassing as much living meat and volume and weight
as any other two of the family) not yet having begun to rise from the chair, her
head, face, alone merely turned, presenting to him in the flying instant an astonishing expanse of young female features untroubled by any surprise even, wearing
only an expression of bovine interest. Then he was out of the room, out of the
house, in the mild dust of the starlit road and the heavy rifeness of honeysuckle,
the pale ribbon unspooling with terrific slowness under his running feet, reaching
the gate at last and turning in, running, his heart and lungs drumming, on
up the drive toward the lighted house, the lighted door. He did not knock, he
burst in, sobbing for breath, incapable for the moment of speech; he saw the astonished face of the Negro in the linen jacket without knowing when the Negro had
appeared.

"De Spain!" he cried, panted. "Where's . . ." then he saw the white man
too emerging from a white door down the hall. "Barn!" he cried. "Barn!"

"What?" the white man said. "Barn?"

"Yes!" the boy cried. "Barn!"

"Catch him!" the white man shouted.

But it was too late this time too. The Negro grasped his shirt, but the entire 105
sleeve, rotten with washing, carried away, and he was out that door too and in
the drive again, and had actually never ceased to run even while he was screaming
into the white man's face.

Behind him the white man was shouting, "My horse! Fetch my horse!" and
he thought for an instant of cutting across the park and climbing the fence into
the road, but he did not know the park nor how high the vine-massed fence might
be and he dared not risk it. So he ran on down the drive, blood and breath roaring;
presently he was in the road again though he could not see it. He could not hear
either: the galloping mare was almost upon him before he heard her, and even
then he held his course, as if the very urgency of his wild grief and need must in
a moment more find him wings, waiting until the ultimate instant to hurl himself
aside and into the weed-choked roadside ditch as the horse thundered past and
on, for an instant in furious silhouette against the stars, the tranquil early summer
night sky which, even before the shape of the horse and rider vanished, strained
abruptly and violently upward: a long, swirling roar incredible and soundless, blot-
ting the stars, and he springing up and into the road again, running again, knowing
it was too late yet still running even after he heard the shot and, an instant later,
two shots, pausing now without knowing he had ceased to run, crying "Pap! Pap!,"
running again before he knew he had begun to run, stumbling, tripping over something and scrabbling up again without ceasing to run, looking backward over his
shoulder at the glare as he got up, running on among the invisible trees, panting,
sobbing, "Father! Father!"

At midnight he was sitting on the crest of a hill. He did not know it was
midnight and he did not know how far he had come. But there was no glare
behind him now and he sat now, his back toward what he had called home for
four days anyhow, his face toward the dark woods which he would enter when

breath was strong again, small, shaking steadily in the chill darkness, hugging himself into the remainder of his thin, rotten shirt, the grief and despair now no
longer terror and fear but just grief and despair. *Father. My father*, he thought.
"He was brave!" he cried suddenly, aloud but not loud, no more than a whisper:
"He was! He was in the war! He was in Colonel Sartoris' cav'ry!" not knowing
that his father had gone to that war a private in the fine old European sense,
wearing no uniform, admitting the authority of and giving fidelity to no man or
army or flag, going to war as Malbrouck himself did: for booty—it meant nothing
and less than nothing to him if it were enemy booty or his own.

   The slow constellations wheeled on. It would be dawn and then sun-up after
a while and he would be hungry. But that would be tomorrow and now he was
only cold, and walking would cure that. His breathing was easier now and he
decided to get up and go on, and then he found that he had been asleep because
he knew it was almost dawn, the night almost over. He could tell that from the
whippoorwills. They were everywhere now among the dark trees below him, constant and inflectioned and ceaseless, so that, as the instant for giving over to the
day birds drew nearer and nearer, there was no interval at all between them. He
got up. He was a little stiff, but walking would cure that too as it would the cold,
and soon there would be the sun. He went on down the hill, toward the dark
woods within which the liquid silver voices of the birds called unceasing—the rapid
and urgent beating of the urgent and quiring heart of the late spring night. He
did not look back.

QUESTIONS

1. What is the story's setting (time and place)? How does Faulkner convey this
    information to the reader?

2. Who is telling the story? Why are the boy and his father in court?

3. Describe the Snopes family. How does Faulkner let us know that they have
    moved often from place to place? What does this tell us about the family?
    Are the mother and sisters round or flat? Explain.

4. What is Abner Snopes like as a character? How does his behavior in court
    help define his character? To what extent does his Civil War experience
    contribute to this definition? What is his attitude toward the de Spain family?
    To what extent does his behavior with the rug illustrate his attitude and
    help define his character?

5. What does Major de Spain expect Abner Snopes to do in order to pay for
    the rug? What does the court decide? How does Abner react to the court's
    decision? What does he plan to do to the de Spains? What does this sequence
    of events tell us about Abner Snopes?

6. What is Sarty (Colonel Sartoris Snopes) like? What is his attitude toward
    his father? Toward his father's decision to act against the de Spains? Why
    does Sarty leave and "not look back" at the end of the story?

7. Whose story is this: Abner's or Sarty's? In other words, which is the protago-
    nist? Explain.

8. What sorts of different conflicts are developed in the story? What is the central conflict? To what extent is this conflict resolved in the climax? To what extent does this resolution help us identify the protagonist of the story?

9. For what reasons might we argue that Sarty is a round (rather than flat) character and a dynamic (rather than static) character? In what ways does Sarty change and grow in the story? What does he learn?

10. In the old Testament book of 2 Samuel (Chapters 2 and 3), Abner, the cousin of King Saul, was a powerful commander, warrior, and king maker. He was loyal to the son of Saul and fought against the supporters of King David. When Abner died, it became possible for David to become uncontested king over the ancient holy land. Do you see any significance in Faulkner's selection of the name *Abner* as the father of the Snopes family? Why do you think that Faulkner, at the end of "Barn Burning," points out that Abner Snopes entered the Civil War purely "for booty"? Could you think of Abner as a hero without scruple, a hero in reverse, an antihero, a symbol of degeneration?

11. At the climax, who is the rider of the horse? Who fires the three shots? Why does Faulkner not tell us the result of the shooting? (In Book I of *The Hamlet*, we learn that Abner and his other son, Flem, escape.)

WRITING ABOUT CHARACTER

Most likely your assignment for study in your essay will be a major character, although it is possible that it might be a minor character or characters. Either way, your prewriting procedures will be much the same. After your customary overview, begin taking notes. In light of the discussion about character beginning this chapter, try to determine as many traits as you can, and also determine how the story presents information about the character.

To assemble materials for writing, try to answer questions like these: Does the character come to life? Is he or she "round" or "flat," lifelike or wooden? Are there admirable qualities, or are there many shortcomings? What are they? Is the character central to the action and therefore the hero or protagonist of the story? What traits make the character genuinely major? Do you like him or her? Why? Who or what is the antagonist? How does reaction to the antagonist bring out qualities in your character? What are they? Does the character exhibit any stock or stereotypical qualities? If so, does he or she rise above them, and how? What is the relationship of the character to the other characters? What do the others say or think about him or her? How accurate are their observations?

Once you have gathered materials in response to these and other questions, it will be possible to go ahead to do the necessary classifying and sorting necessary for the composition of the essay.

Organizing Your Essay

INTRODUCTION.   The introduction may begin with a brief identification of the character to be analyzed, which may be followed by reference to any noteworthy problems in defining the character's qualities. The central idea is a statement about the major trait or quality of the character. The thesis sentence is a brief sentence linking the central idea to the main sections to be covered in the body of the essay.

BODY.   The organization is designed to illustrate the central idea to make it convincing. There is much freedom in the approach you can take, such as the following:

1. *Organization around central traits or major habits and characteristics*, such as "kindness, gentleness, generosity, firmness," or "resoluteness of will frustrated by inopportune moments for action, resulting in despondency, doubt, and melancholy." A body containing this sort of structure would demonstrate how the story brings out each of these qualities. For example, there might be a particular speech in which one of the traits is studied, or an action in which the character himself or herself dramatizes the trait. With such specific topics of treatment, the task of speaking about character can be greatly facilitated.

2. *Organization around the growth of change of a character.* The beginning of such a body would establish the traits that the character possesses at the start of the story and then would describe the changes or developments that occur. It is important here to be careful to avoid a summary, and to stress the actual alterations as they emerge from the circumstances of the story. It is also important to determine whether the growth or change is genuine; do the traits belong clearly to the character, and are they logically produced, or are they manufactured as needed by the events of the story?

3. *Organizations around central incidents that reveal, even if they do not cause, primary characteristics.* Certain key incidents may stand out in a work, and the body of the essay might effectively be structured according to these as signposts for the discussion. As with the second organization just described, it is important to stress in the topic sentences that the purpose is to illuminate the character, not just develop a discussion of the incidents themselves. With this arrangement, the emphasis should be on the causal relationship of incident to trait, if there is one, or on the relationship of incident to the development of character.

4. *Organization around qualities of a flat character or characters.* If the assigned essay is on a character who is not round but flat, the body might treat topics like the plot function of the character, the group of which the character is representative, the relationship of the flat character to the round ones and the importance of this relationship, and any additional qualities or traits that are delineated by the writer.

CONCLUSION. The conclusion is the place for statements about how the discussed characteristics are related to the story as a whole. If the person was good but came to a bad end, does this discrepancy elevate him or her to tragic stature? If the person was a nobody and came to a bad end, does this fact suggest any authorial attitudes about the class or type of which he or she is a part? Or does it seem to illustrate the author's general view of human life? Or both? Do the characteristics explain why the person helps or hinders other characters? Does the essay help in the clearing up of any misunderstandings that might have been present on a first reading? Questions like these may be raised and answered in the conclusion.

SAMPLE ESSAY

The Character of Erwin Martin in Thurber's "The Catbird Seat"*

[1] Erwin Martin is the major character in "The Catbird Seat" by James Thurber. The action is reported as though it is seen over his shoulder if not through his eyes, and he is the constant subject, or focus, of the story. Although the action might be considered whimsical or farcical, Martin is nevertheless well realized and developed. As a character, he is fully round.° He is real because of his image in the eyes of others, his active inner life, and his clever plan of action."

[2] Externally, as others see him, Martin has established himself as a model of withdrawn colorlessness. For plot purposes, in fact, this image is essential, but it seems that from Martin's viewpoint it is intentional. Thus Martin in the past has done nothing daring, for his purchase of cigarettes is unlike what people had ever seen him do. His present boss, Fitweiler, praises him for his "exemplary" work and manner. Fitweiler also says, "Man is fallible but Martin isn't." The earlier boss, Sam Schlosser, had praised Martin's teetotaling habits, and even Mrs. Barrows recognizes him as a "drab, ordinary little man." In every respect, Martin has developed a reputation for cooperation and reliability, even though he has also created a self-image of overstability and dullness. To achieve such recognition is perhaps by itself worthy of note.

[3] It is his apparently vigorous inner life that makes him especially distinctive. It is clear from his conversation with Mrs. Barrows that there is more to him than appears on the surface. His use of terms like "bump off," "old goat," "coked to the gills," and "old buzzard" suggest that he has been responsive to the colorful world of popular culture around him. His own inner trial of Mrs. Barrows, with his concluding verdict of "the death penalty for this horrible per-

---

* See p. 153 for this story.
° Central idea.
" Thesis Sentence.

son," demonstrates not a withdrawn, flat, colorless person, but one with a vigorous imagination.

[4]   The greatest mark of his character, of course, is his impromptu development of his "strange and wonderful" idea about discrediting Mrs. Barrows. This scheme, which Thurber does not describe beforehand, but which is dramatized in the last 40 percent of the story, suggests not just imagination but also cleverness, nerve, control, effrontery, and bravery. To make the scheme work, Martin must be clever enough to predict how others—particularly Fitweiler with his reliance on psychoanalysis—will respond to the true story Mrs. Barrows will tell, and he must therefore be able to predict his own victory. It is this element of control that makes him round and memorable, a doer and not just a responder.

[5]   The story of course is not a fully realistic one, but it does rely on elements of reality. Thus Martin's triumph as a character is also a triumph of individuality over mere efficiency. His annoyance at the unpleasant expressions of Mrs. Barrows is like the annoyance of subordinate people everywhere who must listen to the unpleasant and even stupid words of superiors. To this degree, Martin is representative. But because of his outrageous scheme he becomes an individual, a major character who asserts himself against the pressures to cast him out of the niche which he has made for himself. He is not a hero, but he does have his moment of victory, and he is certainly a round, well-developed character.

Commentary on the Essay

The essay demonstrates the study of a major character, based on a quality, habit, and idea. In this respect it illustrates the first approach described above. The introductory paragraph establishes the status of Martin as a round character despite the problem that the story itself is not completely realistic. Paragraph 2 deals with the apparent drabness of Martin's character. The topic is that even an apparently withdrawn individual can be seen as round if the details about him or her are believably presented. The third paragraph deals with Martin's vigorous inner life, a second major aspect of the character. Paragraph 4 considers the traits manifested in Martin's impromptu scheme. The conclusion treats the relationship of Martin to the large class of those who are annoyed and downtrodden. The central idea is again stressed, however, that Martin is round and well realized and not just a representative of that class.

5

Point of View

Point of view is the position from which details in a work of fiction are perceived and related to the reader. It is a method of rendering, a means by which authors create a centralizing intelligence, a narrative personality, an intellectual filter through which you receive the narration or argument. Other terms describing point of view are *viewpoint*, *unifying voice*, *perspective*, *angle of vision*, *persona*, *mask*, *center of attention*, and *focus*. Another helpful term is *coign of vantage*, which implies a high spot or corner—a vantage point—from which things below may be seen.

In practice, you can think of point of view as the character or speaker who does the talking.

You might respond that our definition means that authors do not use their own "voices" when they write but somehow change themselves into another character, who may be a totally separate creation. This response is right. It is true that authors, as writers of their own works, are always in control of what gets written, but it does not follow that they always use their own voices. It is not easy to determine exactly what one's "own voice" is. Test yourself: When you speak to your instructor, to your friend, to a child, to a person you love, or to a distant relative, your voice always sounds the same, but the personality—or persona—that you employ changes according to the person you are talking to.

In examining point of view, therefore, you should try to determine the nature of the speaker. It is not helpful to deal vaguely with "the author's point of view," as though you were talking about opinions. What you need is to analyze the character and circumstances of the speaker who is relating the events of the story.

POINT OF VIEW AND "THROWING THE VOICE"

A helpful way to consider point of view is to think of the speaker as a ventriloquist's dummy and the author not as the speaker but the ventriloquist. The author "throws" the voice into the dummy, whose written words you actually read. Although the dummy or speaker is the one who is talking, the author is the one who has made the speaker believable and consistent.

Often this speaker, or **voice,** is separate and totally independent, a character who is completely imagined and consistently maintained by the author. A problem of identifying the voice occurs when the speaker seems to be the author in person. To claim that authors are also speakers, however, assumes that we have *absolute* biographical and psychological knowledge about them. Authors, like all people, change. They may have been changing even as they were writing the works you are reading. In addition, they may have been creating a separate personality, or aspect of themselves, as the voice they used when they wrote. Beyond all that, there is the general problem that human personality is elusive. For all these reasons, in works where the author seems to be talking directly, it is more proper to refer to the author's **authorial** voice as the speaker rather than the author himself or herself.

In short, the author creates not only stories and ideas, but also the speakers or voices of their works. To study and discuss point of view is to consider these speakers, even the authorial voices.

It is most important to understand this fact. As an exercise, suppose for a moment that you are an author and are planning a set of stories. Try to imagine the speakers you would create for the following situations:

> A happy niece who has just inherited $25 million from an uncle recalls a childhood experience with the uncle years ago.
>
> A disappointed nephew who was cut off without a cent describes a childhood experience with the same uncle.
>
> A ship's captain who is filled with ideas of personal honor, integrity, and responsibility describes the life of a sailor who has committed a cowardly act.
>
> A person who has survived a youth of poverty and degradation describes a brother who has succumbed to drugs and crime.
>
> An economist looks at problems of unemployment.
>
> A person who has just lost a job looks at problems of unemployment.

In trying to create voices and stories for the various situations, you will recognize the importance of your *imagination* in the selection of point of view. You are always yourself, but your imagination can enable you to speak like someone else totally distinct from yourself. Point of view is hence an imaginative creation, just as much a part of the author's work as the events narrated or the ideas discussed.

POINT OF VIEW AS A PHYSICAL POSITION

Thus far we have considered point of view as an interaction of personality and circumstance. There are also purely physical aspects, specifically (1) the actual place or position from which speakers or narrators see and hear the action, and (2) the capacities of the speakers as receivers of information from others. If narrators have been at the "scene" of an action, this position gives them credibility because they are reporting events they actually saw or heard. Some speakers may have been direct participants in the action; others may have been bystanders. It is possible that a speaker may have overheard a conversation, or may have witnessed a scene through a keyhole. If the speakers were not "on the spot," they must have gained their "facts" in a believable way. They could get them from someone else who was a witness or participant. They could receive letters, read newspaper articles, go through old papers in an attic or library, or hear things on a radio or television program. Sometimes the unidentified voice of the author comes from a person who seems to be hovering somehow right above the characters as they move and speak. Such a speaker, being present everywhere without being noticed, is a reliable source of all information presented in the narrative.

KINDS OF POINTS OF VIEW

The kinds of points of view may be classified fairly easily. You may detect the point of view in any work by determining the grammatical voice of the speaker. Then, of course, you should go on to all the other considerations thus far discussed.

First Person

If the story is told by an "I," the author is using the **first-person** point of view—the voice of a fictional narrator and not the author's own voice. First-person speakers report significant things that they see, hear, and think and, as they do so, they convey not only the action of the work, but also some of their own background, thinking, attitudes, and prejudices. The speaker's particular type of speech will have a great effect on the language of the work itself. Thus a sailor uses many seagoing terms, and a young boy may use much slang.

There are a number of possible first-person storytellers, depending on their involvement in the events being narrated. One kind of speaker has acquired information because he or she was a direct participant in the action as a major character (or "mover"). Marlow in Joseph Conrad's "Youth," for example, is such a narrator (even though his tale is reported verbatim by an unnamed recorder who introduces the story). Sammy, in Updike's "A & P," and Jackie, in O'Connor's "First Confession," are also narrators in this mold. One type of major participant deserves special mention. This is a speaker like Dr. Watson, who in "The Adventure of the Speckled Band" is involved in all the action but actually is an observer. Even though he is and must be a major participant, he is not a major mover, for that role is assigned to the brilliant master detective Sherlock Holmes. Watson's first-person narration, however, is essential to the authenticity of the story.

Both the age and the understanding of the narrators are significant in what they say and therefore in our perception of the stories they tell. A mature adult, like Marlow in "Youth," presents his or her recollection and also provides adult commentary on the nature of the experience. A less aware, naive narrator, like the narrator of Americo Paredes's "The Hammon and the Beans," actually presents a more dramatic account, because such a narrator is to be accepted as accurate on actions and conversations even though he or she does not make adult observations about them. Also, the narrator may have reached adulthood, but may not indicate an adult's understanding. Such speakers are Jackie in "First Confession" and the unnamed narrator in James Joyce's "Araby." With first-person points of view like these the reader must sort out details and also must judge the observations included by the narrator as commentary on the action.

One thing seems clear in regard to stories containing the first-person point of view. Whenever the speaker uses the "I" and comments on the action, that speaker is also an important part of the story. Everything we read is reported by the speaker. Therefore, his or her abilities, position as an observer, character, attitudes, and possible prejudices or self-interests are to be considered along with everything that is said. The first-person speaker of Tillie Olsen's "I Stand Here Ironing," for example, is the mother of the girl, and as she speaks we can follow her own attempts at self-explanation and justification. She, like virtually all first-person narrators, is as much a focus of interest as the events themselves.

Second Person

Although a *second person* narration (in which the narrator tells a listener what he or she has done, using the "you" personal pronoun) is possible, it is rare because in effect the second-person actually requires a first-person voice. The viewpoint requires also that the listener be the character who lived through the narration. Thus a parent might be telling a child what the child did during infancy, for which the child has no memory. Or a doctor might tell a patient with amnesia about what occurred during the time when the memory was gone, or a lawyer might present a story of a crime directly to the accused criminal by way of accusation. In practice, the second-person point of view is of only passing use in most fiction, and it is so rarely used that it is almost negligible. A. A. Milne uses it for a time at the beginning of the children's story *Winnie the Pooh*, but drops it as soon as the events of Pooh Bear and the rest of the animals get under way.

Third Person

If the narrator is not introduced as a character, and if everything in the work is described in the third person (that is, *he*, *she*, *it*, *they*), the author is using the **third-person** point of view. There are three variants: omniscient, limited omniscient, and dramatic or objective.

OMNISCIENT. The third-person point of view is called **omniscient** (all-knowing) when the speaker not only describes the action and dialogue of the work, but also seems to know everything that goes on in the minds of the characters. In the third-person omniscient point of view authors take great responsibility: By delving into the minds of their characters, they assume a stance that exceeds our ordinary experience with other persons. The result is that an omniscient story is not realistic, according to our present way of seeing things. This viewpoint was much used when prose fiction was a relatively new genre. Because it is not probable that any narrator can truly know the inner workings of others' minds, however, there are few if any writers today who employ it.

LIMITED OMNISCIENT. Most common is the **limited omniscient** point of view, in which the author uses the third person but confines the story to what one single character does, says, sees, and sometimes thinks. Often this viewpoint will use expressions that the point-of-view character might use, as in Katherine Mansfield's "Miss Brill." While the omniscient point of view can include thoughts of almost all the characters, the limited focuses on only one. Sarty of "Barn Burning," Erwin Martin of "The Catbird Seat" and Mathilde Loisel of "The Necklace" are such limited-point-of-view characters. Everything in these stories is there because these characters, like Miss Brill, experienced it, heard about it, and thought about it. Obviously there are variations in how deeply the limited omniscience may extend. Thus, we learn more about Miss Brill and Erwin Martin, for example, than about Mathilde, because Mansfield and Thurber present more of the inner thoughts of these characters than does De Maupassant.

DRAMATIC OR OBJECTIVE.   Writers using the dramatic point of view (also called **third-person objective**) confine the work mainly to quotations and descriptions of actions. They avoid telling that certain characters thought this or felt that but instead allow the characters themselves to state what is on their minds. Shirley Jackson's "The Lottery" is a prime example of the dramatic point of view in a story, as is John Collier's "The Chaser" and the "Prodigal Son" from the Gospel according to St. Luke. The narrator of the dramatic point of view perceives things and reports them in a way that is roughly analogous to a hovering or tracking motion-picture camera. Thus, characters in the out of doors may be seen at a distance or up close, and when they move indoors or into a conveyance of some sort, the speaker continues to observe and report their activities.

Though actions and dialogue are the main substance of the dramatic point of view, authors may allow certain characters to express their own attitudes and feelings, which then also become a part of the story. Old Man Warner in "The Lottery" is an example of the commentator who represents a conservative voice in favor of the institution of the lottery even as he notes that there are persons in other communities in favor of giving it up.

The key to the dramatic point of view is that the writer presents actions and dialogue and leaves any conclusions and interpretations up to the readers. Naturally, however, the author does not relinquish his or her shaping spirit with the choice of the dramatic viewpoint. Hence the reader's conclusions are shaped by the author's ordering of the materials of the story.

MINGLING POINTS OF VIEW

In most stories there is a mingling of viewpoints. Hence a point of view may be limited omniscient when focused on the thoughts of a major character, but dramatic when focused on the actions and dialogue. The writer may tell most of the story in one type of point of view but then shift at an important point for the purpose of sustaining interest or creating suspense. For example, Thurber in "The Catbird Seat" ends his limited omniscient disclosure of the thoughts of Erwin Martin when Martin develops his plan in the apartment of Mrs. Barrows. After this point Thurber uses the dramatic point of view so that the reader will not know the plan until it has been fully enacted. As you analyze point of view in a story, you will find the following summary helpful.

POINTS OF VIEW

1. First Person ("I") All these first-person narrators may have (1) complete understanding, (2) partial or incorrect understanding, or (3) no understanding at all.
   a. Major participant
      i. telling his or her own story as a major mover
      ii. telling a story about others and also about herself or himself as one of the major inter-actors
      iii. telling a story mainly about others; this narrator is on the spot and completely involved but is not a major mover.
   b. Minor participant, telling a story about events experienced and/or witnessed.
   c. Uninvolved character, telling a story not witnessed but reported to the narrator by other means.
2. Second person ("you") Occurs only when speaker has more authority on a character's actions than the character himself or herself; for example, parent, psychologist, lawyer. Occurs only in brief passages when necessary.
3. Third person ("she," "he," "it," "they")
   a. Omniscient. Omniscient speaker sees all, reports all, knows inner workings of minds of characters.
   b. Limited omniscient. Action is focused on one major character.
   c. Dramatic or third-person objective. Speaker reports only actions and speeches. Thoughts of characters can be expressed only as dialogue.

POINT OF VIEW AND "EVIDENCE"

In considering point of view, you should try to analyze all aspects that bear on the presentation of the material in the work. You may imagine yourself somewhat like a member of a jury. Jury members cannot accept testimony uncritically, for some witnesses may have much to gain by misstatements, distortions, or outright lies. Before rendering a verdict, jury members must consider all these possibilities. Speakers in literary works are usually to be accepted as reliable witnesses, but it is true that their characters, interests, capacities, personal involvements, and positions to view action may have a bearing on the material they present. A classic example is the Japanese film *Rashomon* (1950), directed by Akira Kurosawa, in which four different people tell a story as evidence in a court, and each presents a version that makes that person seem more honorable than he or she actually was. While most stories are not as complex as this, you should always consider the character of the speaker before you render your verdict on what the story is about.

KATHERINE MANSFIELD (1888–1923)

Miss Brill   1920

Although it was so brilliantly fine—the blue sky powdered with gold and great spots of light like white wine splashed over the Jardins Publiques° —Miss Brill was glad that she had decided on her fur. The air was motionless, but when you opened your mouth there was just a faint chill, like a chill from a glass of iced water before you sip, and now and again a leaf came drifting—from nowhere, from the sky. Miss Brill put up her hand and touched her fur. Dear little thing! It was nice to feel it again. She had taken it out of its box that afternoon, shaken out the moth-powder, given it a good brush, and rubbed the life back into the dim little eyes. "What has been happening to me?" said the sad little eyes. Oh, how sweet it was to see them snap at her again from the red eiderdown! . . . But the nose, which was of some black composition, wasn't at all firm. It must have had a knock, somehow. Never mind—a little dab of black sealing-wax when the time came—when it was absolutely necessary. . . . Little rogue! Yes, she really felt like that about it. Little rogue biting its tail just by her left ear. She could have taken it off and laid it on her lap and stroked it. She felt a tingling in her hands and arms, but that came from walking, she supposed. And when she breathed, something light and sad—no, not sad, exactly—something gentle seemed to move in her bosom.

There were a number of people out this afternoon, far more than last Sunday. And the band sounded louder and gayer. That was because the Season had begun. For although the band played all the year round on Sundays, out of season it was never the same. It was like some one playing with only the family to listen; it didn't care how it played if there weren't any strangers present. Wasn't the conductor wearing a new coat, too? She was sure it was new. He scraped with his foot and flapped his arms like a rooster about to crow, and the bandsmen sitting in the green rotunda blew out their cheeks and glared at the music. Now there came a little "flutey" bit—very pretty!—a little chain of bright drops. She was sure it would be repeated. It was; she lifted her head and smiled.

Only two people shared her "special" seat: a fine old man in a velvet coat, his hands clasped over a huge carved walking-stick, and a big old woman, sitting upright, with a roll of knitting on her embroidered apron. They did not speak. This was disappointing, for Miss Brill always looked forward to the conversation. She had become really quite expert, she thought, at listening as though she didn't listen, at sitting in other people's lives just for a minute while they talked round her.

She glanced, sideways, at the old couple. Perhaps they would go soon. Last Sunday, too, hadn't been as interesting as usual. An Englishman and his wife, he wearing a dreadful Panama hat and she button boots. And she'd gone on the whole time about how she ought to wear spectacles; she knew she needed them; but that it was no good getting any; they'd be sure to break and they'd never

Jardins Publiques: public gardens, or public park.

keep on. And he'd been so patient. He'd suggested everything—gold rims, the kind that curved round your ears, little pads inside the bridge. No, nothing would please her. "They'll always be sliding down my nose!" Miss Brill had wanted to shake her.

The old people sat on the bench, still as statues. Never mind, there was always the crowd to watch. To and fro, in front of the flower-beds and the band rotunda, the couples and groups paraded, stopped to talk, to greet, to buy a handful of flowers from the old beggar who had his tray fixed to the railings. Little children ran among them, swooping and laughing; little boys with big white silk bows under their chins, little girls, little French dolls, dressed up in velvet and lace. And sometimes a tiny staggerer came suddenly rocking into the open from under the trees, stopped, stared, as suddenly sat down "flop," until its small high-stepping mother, like a young hen, rushed scolding to its rescue. Other people sat on the benches and green chairs, but they were nearly always the same, Sunday after Sunday, and—Miss Brill had often noticed—there was something funny about nearly all of them. They were odd, silent, nearly all old, and from the way they stared they looked as though they'd just come from dark little rooms or even—even cupboards!

Behind the rotunda the slender trees with yellow leaves down drooping, and through them just a line of sea, and beyond the blue sky with gold-veined clouds.

Tum-tum-tum tiddle-um! tiddle-um! tum tiddley-um tum ta! blew the band.

Two young girls in red came by and two young soldiers in blue met them, and they laughed and paired and went off arm-in-arm. Two peasant women with funny straw hats passed, gravely, leading beautiful smoke-coloured donkeys. A cold, pale nun hurried by. A beautiful woman came along and dropped her bunch of violets, and a little boy ran after to hand them to her, and she took them and threw them away as if they'd been poisoned. Dear me! Miss Brill didn't know whether to admire that or not! And now an ermine toque° and a gentleman in grey met just in front of her. He was tall, stiff, dignified, and she was wearing the ermine toque she'd bought when her hair was yellow. Now everything, her hair, her face, even her eyes, was the same colour as the shabby ermine, and her hand, in its cleaned glove, lifted to dab her lips, was a tiny yellowish paw. Oh, she was so pleased to see him—delighted! She rather thought they were going to meet that afternoon. She described where she'd been—everywhere, here, there, along by the sea. The day was so charming—didn't he agree? And wouldn't he, perhaps? . . . But he shook his head, lighted a cigarette, slowly breathed a great deep puff into her face, and, even while she was still talking and laughing, flicked the match away and walked on. The ermine toque was alone; she smiled more brightly than ever. But even the band seemed to know what she was feeling and played more softly, played tenderly, and the drum beat, "The Brute! The Brute!" over and over. What would she do? What was going to happen now? But as Miss Brill wondered, the ermine toque turned, raised her hand as though she'd seen some one else, much nicer, just over there, and pattered away. And the band changed again and played more quickly, more gaily than ever, and the old couple on Miss Brill's seat got up and marched away, and such a funny old man with

5

toque: a hat. An "ermine toque" is therefore here a woman wearing a hat made of the fur of a weasel.

long whiskers hobbled along in time to the music and was nearly knocked over by four girls walking abreast.

Oh, how fascinating it was! How she enjoyed it! How she loved sitting here, watching it all! It was like a play. It was exactly like a play. Who could believe the sky at the back wasn't painted? But it wasn't till a little brown dog trotted on solemn and then slowly trotted off, like a little "theatre" dog, a little dog that had been drugged, that Miss Brill discovered what it was that made it so exciting. They were all on the stage. They weren't only the audience, not only looking on; they were acting. Even she had a part and came every Sunday. No doubt somebody would have noticed if she hadn't been there; she was part of the performance after all. How strange she'd never thought of it like that before! And yet it explained why she made such a point of starting from home at just the same time each week—so as not to be late for the performance—and it also explained why she had quite a queer, shy feeling at telling her English pupils how she spent her Sunday afternoons. No wonder! Miss Brill nearly laughed out loud. She was on the stage. She thought of the old invalid gentleman to whom she read the newspaper four afternoons a week while he slept in the garden. She had got quite used to the frail head on the cotton pillow, the hollowed eyes, the open mouth and the high pinched nose. If he'd been dead she mightn't have noticed for weeks; she wouldn't have minded. But suddenly he knew he was having the paper read to him by an actress! "An actress!" The old head lifted; two points of light quivered in the old eyes. "An actress—are ye?" And Miss Brill smoothed the newspaper as though it were the manuscript of her part and said gently: "Yes, I have been an actress for a long time."

The band had been having a rest. Now they started again. And what they played was warm, sunny, yet there was just a faint chill—a something, what was it?—not sadness—no, not sadness—a something that made you want to sing. The tune lifted, lifted, the light shone; and it seemed to Miss Brill that in another moment all of them, all the whole company, would begin singing. The young ones, the laughing ones who were moving together, they would begin, and the men's voices, very resolute and brave, would join them. And then she too, she too, and the others on the benches—they would come in with a kind of accompaniment—something low, that scarcely rose or fell, something so beautiful—moving. . . . And Miss Brill's eyes filled with tears and she looked smiling at all the other members of the company. Yes, we understand, we understand, she thought—though what they understood she didn't know.

Just at that moment a boy and a girl came and sat down where the old couple had been. They were beautifully dressed; they were in love. The hero and heroine, of course, just arrived from his father's yacht. And still soundlessly singing, still with that trembling smile, Miss Brill prepared to listen.

"No, not now," said the girl. "Not here, I can't."

"But why? Because of that stupid old thing at the end there?" asked the boy. "Why does she come here at all—who wants her? Why doesn't she keep her silly old mug at home?"

"It's her fu-fur which is so funny," giggled the girl. "It's exactly like a fried whiting."

"Ah, be off with you!" said the boy in an angry whisper. Then: "Tell me, ma petite chérie—"

"No, not here," said the girl. "Not *yet*."

On her way home she usually bought a slice of honeycake at the baker's. It was her Sunday treat. Sometimes there was an almond in her slice, sometimes not. It made a great difference. If there was an almond it was like carrying home a tiny present—a surprise—something that might very well not have been there. She hurried on the almond Sundays and struck the match for the kettle in quite a dashing way.

But to-day she passed the baker's by, climbed the stairs, went into the little dark room—her room like a cupboard—and sat down on the red eiderdown. She sat there for a long time. The box that the fur came out of was on the bed. She unclasped the necklet quickly; quickly, without looking, laid it inside. But when she put the lid on she thought she heard something crying.

QUESTIONS

1. Describe the point of view of "Miss Brill." Is it in the third person limited, omniscient, or dramatic? Who says, in paragraph 1, "Dear little thing!" about the fur? How do you justify your conclusion about the source of this and similar insights that appear throughout the story?

2. Would this story be possible if told in the first person by Miss Brill herself? What might it have been like if told by a walker in the park who observed Miss Brill and overheard the conversation about her by the boy and girl?

3. A shift in the point of view occurs when the boy and girl sit down and Miss Brill overhears them. Describe the nature of this shift. Why do you think that Mansfield made the change at this point?

4. In relation to the point of view, explain the last sentence of the story: "But when she put the lid on she thought she heard something crying." Is this sentence consistent with the point of view of the previous seven paragraphs, or with the great bulk of the story before that?

5. Briefly describe the things that happen in the story. Are there many genuine actions? On the basis of your answers to these questions, would you say that "Miss Brill" is mainly active, or mainly reflective and psychological?

6. In what ways does Miss Brill think of her presence in the park as her being on the stage? Describe her sense of *camaraderie* with the other people in the park.

7. What is illustrated in the description of the woman wearing the ermine toque? Is there any parallel with the life of Miss Brill herself?

8. Do you like Miss Brill? Do you feel sorry for her? How do you think Mansfield wanted you to feel about her?

FRANK O'CONNOR (1903–1966)

First Confession   1951

All the trouble began when my grandfather died and my grandmother—my father's mother—came to live with us. Relations in the one house are a strain at the best of times, but, to make matters worse, my grandmother was a real old countrywoman and quite unsuited to the life in town. She had a fat, wrinkled old face, and, to Mother's great indignation, went round the house in bare feet—the boots had her crippled, she said. For dinner she had a jug of porter° and a pot of potatoes with—sometimes—a bit of salt fish, and she poured out the potatoes on the table and ate them slowly, with great relish, using her fingers by way of a fork.

Now, girls are supposed to be fastidious, but I was the one who suffered most from this. Nora, my sister, just sucked up to the old woman for the penny she got every Friday out of the old-age pension, a thing I could not do. I was too honest, that was my trouble; and when I was playing with Bill Connell, the sergeant-major's son, and saw my grandmother steering up the path with the jug of porter sticking out from beneath her shawl I was mortified. I made excuses not to let him come into the house, because I could never be sure what she would be up to when we went in.

When Mother was at work and my grandmother made the dinner I wouldn't touch it. Nora once tried to make me, but I hid under the table from her and took the bread-knife with me for protection. Nora let on to be very indignant (she wasn't, of course, but she knew Mother saw through her, so she sided with Gran) and came after me. I lashed out at her with the bread-knife, and after that she left me alone. I stayed there till Mother came in from work and made my dinner, but when Father came in later Nora said in a shocked voice: "Oh, Dadda, do you know what Jackie did at dinnertime?" Then, of course, it all came out; Father gave me a flaking; Mother interfered, and for days after that he didn't speak to me and Mother barely spoke to Nora. And all because of that old woman! God knows, I was heart-scalded.

Then, to crown my misfortune, I had to make my first confession and communion. It was an old woman called Ryan who prepared us for these. She was about the one age with Gran; she was well-to-do, lived in a big house on Montenotte, wore a black cloak and bonnet, and came every day to school at three o'clock when we should have been going home, and talked to us of hell. She may have mentioned the other place as well, but that could only have been by accident, for hell had the first place in her heart.

She lit a candle, took out a new half-crown, and offered it to the first boy who would hold one finger—only one finger!—in the flame for five minutes by the school clock. Being always very ambitious I was tempted to volunteer, but I thought it might look greedy. Then she asked were we afraid of holding one finger— only one finger!—in a little candle flame for five minutes and not afraid of burning all over in roasting hot furnaces for all eternity. "All eternity! Just think of that! A whole lifetime goes by and it's nothing, not even a drop in the ocean of your sufferings." The woman was really interesting about hell, but my attention was all fixed on the half-crown. At the end of the lesson she put it back in her purse. It was a great disappointment; a religious woman like that, you wouldn't think she'd bother about a thing like a half-crown.

Another day she said she knew a priest who woke one night to find a fellow he didn't recognize leaning over the end of his bed. The priest was a bit frightened— naturally enough—but he asked the fellow what he wanted, and the fellow said in a deep, husky voice that he wanted to go to confession. The priest said it was

5

---

porter: beer.

an awkward time and wouldn't it do in the morning, but the fellow said that last time he went to confession, there was one sin he kept back, being ashamed to mention it, and now it was always on his mind. Then the priest knew it was a bad case, because the fellow was after making a bad confession and committing a mortal sin. He got up to dress, and just then the cock crew in the yard outside, and—lo and behold!—when the priest looked round there was no sign of the fellow, only a smell of burning timber, and when the priest looked at his bed didn't he see the print of two hands burned in it? That was because the fellow had made a bad confession. This story made a shocking impression on me.

But the worst of all was when she showed us how to examine our conscience. Did we take the name of the Lord, our God, in vain? Did we honour our father and our mother? (I asked her did this include grandmothers and she said it did.) Did we love our neighbours as ourselves? Did we covet our neighbour's goods? (I thought of the way I felt about the penny that Nora got every Friday.) I decided that, between one thing and another, I must have broken the whole ten commandments, all on account of that old woman, and so far as I could see, so long as she remained in the house I had no hope of ever doing anything else.

I was scared to death of confession. The day the whole class went I let on to have a toothache, hoping my absence wouldn't be noticed; but at three o'clock, just as I was feeling safe, along comes a chap with a message from Mrs. Ryan that I was to go to confession myself on Saturday and be at the chapel for communion with the rest. To make it worse, Mother couldn't come with me and sent Nora instead.

Now, that girl had ways of tormenting me that Mother never knew of. She held my hand as we went down the hill, smiling sadly and saying how sorry she was for me, as if she were bringing me to the hospital for an operation.

"Oh, God help us!" she moaned. "Isn't it a terrible pity you weren't a good boy? Oh, Jackie, my heart bleeds for you! How will you ever think of all your sins? Don't forget you have to tell him about the time you kicked Gran on the shin."   10

"Lemme go!" I said, trying to drag myself free of her. "I don't want to go to confession at all."

"But sure, you'll have to go to confession, Jackie," she replied in the same regretful tone. "Sure, if you didn't, the parish priest would be up to the house, looking for you. 'Tisn't, God knows, that I'm not sorry for you. Do you remember the time you tried to kill me with the bread-knife under the table? And the language you used to me? I don't know what he'll do with you at all, Jackie. He might have to send you up to the bishop."

I remember thinking bitterly that she didn't know the half of what I had to tell—if I told it. I knew I couldn't tell it, and understood perfectly why the fellow in Mrs. Ryan's story made a bad confession; it seemed to me a great shame that people wouldn't stop criticizing him. I remember that steep hill down to the church, and the sunlit hillsides beyond the valley of the river, which I saw in the gaps between the houses like Adam's last glimpse of Paradise.

Then, when she had manœuvered me down the long flight of steps to the chapel yard, Nora suddenly changed her tone. She became the raging malicious devil she really was.

"There you are!" she said with a yelp of triumph, hurling me through the   1!
church door. "And I hope he'll give you the penitential psalms, you dirty little
caffler."

I knew then I was lost, given up to eternal justice. The door with the coloured-
glass panels swung shut behind me, the sunlight went out and gave place to deep
shadow, and the wind whistled outside so that the silence within seemed to crackle
like ice under my feet. Nora sat in front of me by the confession box. There
were a couple of old woman ahead of her, and then a miserable-looking poor
devil came and wedged me in at the other side, so that I couldn't escape even if
I had the courage. He joined his hands and rolled his eyes in the direction of
the roof, muttering aspirations in an anguished tone, and I wondered had he a
grandmother too. Only a grandmother could account for a fellow behaving in
that heartbroken way, but he was better off than I, for he at least could go and
confess his sins; while I would make a bad confession and then die in the night
and be continually coming back and burning people's furniture.

Nora's turn came, and I heard the sound of something slamming, and then
her voice as if butter wouldn't melt in her mouth, and then another slam, and
out she came. God, the hypocrisy of women! Her eyes were lowered, her head
was bowed, and her hands were joined very low down on her stomach, and she
walked up the aisle to the side altar looking like a saint. You never saw such an
exhibition of devotion, and I remembered the devilish malice with which she had
tormented me all the way from our door, and wondered were all religious people
like that, really. It was my turn now. With the fear of damnation in my soul I
went in, and the confessional door closed of itself behind me.

It was pitch-dark and I couldn't see priest or anything else. Then I really
began to be frightened. In the darkness it was a matter between God and me,
and He had all the odds. He knew what my intentions were before I even started;
I had no chance. All I had ever been told about confession got mixed up in my
mind, and I knelt to one wall and said: "Bless me, father, for I have sinned; this
is my first confession." I waited for a few minutes, but nothing happened, so I
tried it on the other wall. Nothing happened there either. He had me spotted all
right.

It must have been then that I noticed the shelf at about one height with
my head. It was really a place for grown-up people to rest their elbows, but in
my distracted state I thought it was probably the place you were supposed to
kneel. Of course, it was on the high side and not very deep, but I was always
good at climbing and managed to get up all right. Staying up was the trouble.
There was room only for my knees, and nothing you could get a grip on but a
sort of wooden moulding, a bit above it. I held on to the moulding and repeated
the words a little louder, and this time something happened all right. A slide
was slammed back; a little light entered the box, and a man's voice said: "Who's
there?"

" 'Tis me, father," I said for fear he mightn't see me and go away again. I   2(
couldn't see him at all. The place the voice came from was under the moulding,
about level with my knees, so I took a good grip of the moulding and swung
myself down till I saw the astonished face of a young priest looking up at me.
He had to put his head on one side to see me, and I had to put mine on one
side to see him, so we were more or less talking to one another upside-down. It

struck me as a queer way of hearing confessions, but I didn't feel it my place to criticize.

"Bless me, father, for I have sinned; this is my first confession," I rattled off all in one breath, and swung myself down the least shade more to make it easier for him.

"What are you doing up there?" he shouted in an angry voice, and the strain the politeness was putting on my hold of the moulding, and the shock of being addressed in such an uncivil tone, were too much for me. I lost my grip, tumbled, and hit the door an unmerciful wallop before I found myself flat on my back in the middle of the aisle. The people who had been waiting stood up with their mouths open. The priest opened the door of the middle box and came out, pushing his biretta back from his forehead; he looked something terrible. Then Nora came scampering down the aisle.

"Oh, you dirty little caffler!" she said. "I might have known you'd do it. I might have known you'd disgrace me. I can't leave you out of my sight for one minute."

Before I could even get to my feet to defend myself she bent down and gave me a clip across the ear. This reminded me that I was so stunned I had even forgotten to cry, so that people might think I wasn't hurt at all, when in fact I was probably maimed for life. I gave a roar out of me.

"What's all this about?" the priest hissed, getting angrier than ever and 25 pushing Nora off me. "How dare you hit the child like that, you little vixen?"

"But I can't do my penance with him, father," Nora cried, cocking an outraged eye up to him.

"Well, go and do it, or I'll give you some more to do," he said, giving me a hand up. "Was it coming to confession you were, my poor man?" he asked me.

" 'Twas, father," said I with a sob.

"Oh," he said respectfully, "a big hefty fellow like you must have terrible sins. Is this your first?"

" 'Tis, father," said I.

"Worse and worse," he said gloomily. "The crimes of a lifetime. I don't 30 know will I get rid of you at all today. You'd better wait now till I'm finished with these old ones. You can see by the looks of them they haven't much to tell."

"I will, father," I said with something approaching joy.

The relief of it was really enormous. Nora stuck out her tongue at me from behind his back, but I couldn't even be bothered retorting. I knew from the very moment that man opened his mouth that he was intelligent above the ordinary. When I had time to think, I saw how right I was. It only stood to reason that a fellow confessing after seven years would have more to tell than people that went every week. The crimes of a lifetime, exactly as he said. It was only what he expected, and the rest was the cackle of old women and girls with their talk of hell, the bishop, and the penitential psalms. That was all they knew. I started to make my examination of conscience, and barring the one bad business of my grandmother it didn't seem so bad.

The next time, the priest steered me into the confession box himself and left the shutter back the way I could see him get in and sit down at the further side of the grille from me.

"Well, now," he said, "what do they call you?"

"Jackie, father," said I.

"And what's a-trouble to you, Jackie?"

"Father," I said, feeling I might as well get it over while I had him in good humour, "I had it all arranged to kill my grandmother."

He seemed a bit shaken by that, all right, because he said nothing for quite a while.

"My goodness," he said at last, "that'd be a shocking thing to do. What put that into your head?"

"Father," I said, feeling very sorry for myself, "she's an awful woman."

"Is she?" he asked. "What way is she awful?"

"She takes porter, father," I said, knowing well from the way Mother talked of it that this was a mortal sin, and hoping it would make the priest take a more favourable view of my case.

"Oh, my!" he said, and I could see he was impressed.

"And snuff, father," said I.

"That's a bad case, sure enough, Jackie," he said.

"And she goes round in her bare feet, father," I went on in a rush of self-pity, "and she knows I don't like her, and she gives pennies to Nora and none to me, and my da sides with her and flakes me, and one night I was so heart-scalded I made up my mind I'd have to kill her."

"And what would you do with the body?" he asked with great interest.

"I was thinking I could chop that up and carry it away in a barrow I have," I said.

"Begor, Jackie," he said, "do you know you're a terrible child?"

"I know, father," I said, for I was just thinking the same thing myself. "I tried to kill Nora too with a bread-knife under the table, only I missed her."

"Is that the little girl that was beating you just now?" he asked.

" 'Tis, father."

"Someone will go for her with a bread-knife one day, and he won't miss her," he said rather cryptically. "You must have great courage. Between ourselves, there's a lot of people I'd like to do the same to but I'd never have the nerve. Hanging is an awful death."

"Is it, father?" I asked with the deepest interest—I was always very keen on hanging. "Did you ever see a fellow hanged?"

"Dozens of them," he said solemnly. "And they all died roaring."

"Jay!" I said.

"Oh, a horrible death!" he said with great satisfaction. "Lots of the fellows I saw killed their grandmothers too, but they all said 'twas never worth it."

He had me there for a full ten minutes talking, and then walked out the chapel yard with me. I was genuinely sorry to part with him, because he was the most entertaining character I'd ever met in the religious line. Outside, after the shadow of the church, the sunlight was like the roaring of waves on a beach; it dazzled me; and when the frozen silence melted and I heard the screech of trams on the road my heart soared. I knew now I wouldn't die in the night and come back, leaving marks on my mother's furniture. It would be a great worry to her, and the poor soul had enough.

Nora was sitting on the railing, waiting for me, and she put on a very sour puss when she saw the priest with me. She was made jealous because a priest had never come out of the church with her.

"Well," she asked coldly, after he left me, "what did he give you?"

"Three Hail Marys," I said.

"Three Hail Marys," she repeated incredulously. "You mustn't have told him anything."

"I told him everything," I said confidently.

"About Gran and all?"   65

"About Gran and all."

(All she wanted was to be able to go home and say I'd made a bad confession.)

"Did you tell him you went for me with the bread-knife?" she asked with a frown.

"I did to be sure."

"And he only gave you three Hail Marys?"   70

"That's all."

She slowly got down from the railing with a baffled air. Clearly, this was beyond her. As we mounted the steps back to the main road she looked at me suspiciously.

"What are you sucking?" she asked.

"Bullseyes."

"Was it the priest gave them to you?"   75

" 'Twas."

"Lord God," she wailed bitterly, "some people have all the luck! 'Tis no advantage to anybody trying to be good. I might just as well be a sinner like you."

QUESTIONS

1. Could this story be effective if it had been told in the third-person point of view limited to the character of Jackie? How might it have been different, or better or worse?

2. Read the sample essay on the point of view in the story (p. 203). Do you agree or disagree with the assertion there that Jackie, from an adult perspective, lacks maturity? Might he be more easily explained if you judged him as an adolescent rather than as an adult?

3. Describe the character of Jackie as a storyteller. What vestiges of childhood perception can you find in his narration? That is, what sorts of perceptiveness does he show with regard to Mrs. Ryan? His sister? The approaching confession? The nature of women? His ability to learn from experience?

4. Is Jackie's confession a "good" one? What sort of religiosity is more appealing and effective, the sort represented by Mrs. Ryan or by the priest?

5. Do you think that the relationships among members of Jackie's family seem unusual or potentially damaging? Does the sister, Nora, seem out of the ordinary at all in light of her treatment of her younger brother? Does the narrator's judgment of her, and of women generally, seem justified, coming from an adult? Why or why not?

6. "First Confession" is a funny story. What makes it funny, and why?

SHIRLEY JACKSON (1919–1965)

The Lottery   1948

The morning of June 27th was clear and sunny, with the fresh warmth of a full-summer day; the flowers were blossoming profusely and the grass was richly green. The people of the village began to gather in the square, between the post office and the bank, around ten o'clock; in some towns there were so many people that the lottery took two days and had to be started on June 26th, but in this village, where there were only about three hundred people, the whole lottery took less than two hours, so it could begin at ten o'clock in the morning and still be through in time to allow the villagers to get home for noon dinner.

The children assembled first, of course. School was recently over for the summer, and the feeling of liberty sat uneasily on most of them; they tended to gather together quietly for a while before they broke into boisterous play, and their talk was still of the classroom and the teacher, of books and reprimands. Bobby Martin had already stuffed his pockets full of stones, and the other boys soon followed his example, selecting the smoothest and roundest stones; Bobby and Harry Jones and Dickie Delacroix—the villagers pronounced this name "Della-croy"—eventually made a great pile of stones in one corner of the square and guarded it against the raids of the other boys. The girls stood aside, talking among themselves, looking over their shoulders at the boys, and the very small children rolled in the dust or clung to the hands of their older brothers or sisters.

Soon the men began to gather, surveying their own children, speaking of planting and rain, tractors and taxes. They stood together, away from the pile of stones in the corner, and their jokes were quiet and they smiled rather than laughed. The women, wearing faded house dresses and sweaters, came shortly after their menfolk. They greeted one another and exchanged bits of gossip as they went to join their husbands. Soon the women, standing by their husbands, began to call to their children, and the children came reluctantly, having to be called four or five times. Bobby Martin ducked under his mother's grasping hand and ran, laughing, back to the pile of stones. His father spoke up sharply, and Bobby came quickly and took his place between his father and his oldest brother.

The lottery was conducted—as were the square dances, the teen-age club, the Halloween program—by Mr. Summers, who had time and energy to devote to civic activities. He was a round-faced, jovial man and he ran the coal business, and people were sorry for him, because he had no children and his wife was a scold. When he arrived in the square, carrying the black wooden box, there was a murmur of conversation among the villagers, and he waved and called, "Little late today, folks." The postmaster, Mr. Graves, followed him, carrying a three-legged stool, and the stool was put in the center of the square and Mr. Summers set the black box down on it. The villagers kept their distance, leaving a space between themselves and the stool, and when Mr. Summers said, "Some of you fellows want to give me a hand?" there was a hesitation before two men, Mr. Martin and his oldest son, Baxter, came forward to hold the box steady on the stool while Mr. Summers stirred up the papers inside it.

The original paraphernalia for the lottery had been lost long ago, and the black box now resting on the stool had been put into use even before Old Man Warner, the oldest man in town, was born. Mr. Summers spoke frequently to the villagers about making a new box, but no one liked to upset even as much tradition as was represented by the black box. There was a story that the present box had been made with some pieces of the box that had preceded it, the one that had been constructed when the first people settled down to make a village here. Every year, after the lottery, Mr. Summers began talking again about a new box, but every year the subject was allowed to fade off without anything's being done. The black box grew shabbier each year; by now it was no longer completely black but splintered badly along one side to show the original wood color, and in some places faded or stained.

Mr. Martin and his oldest son, Baxter, held the black box securely on the stool until Mr. Summers had stirred the papers thoroughly with his hand. Because so much of the ritual had been forgotten or discarded, Mr. Summers had been successful in having slips of paper substituted for the chips of wood that had been used for generations. Chips of wood, Mr. Summers had argued, had been all very well when the village was tiny, but now that the population was more than three hundred and likely to keep on growing, it was necessary to use something that would fit more easily into the black box. The night before the lottery, Mr. Summers and Mr. Graves made up the slips of paper and put them in the box, and it was then taken to the safe of Mr. Summers' coal company and locked up until Mr. Summers was ready to take it to the square next morning. The rest of the year, the box was put away, sometimes one place, sometimes another; it had spent one year in Mr. Graves's barn and another year underfoot in the post office, and sometimes it was set on a shelf in the Martin grocery and left there.

There was a great deal of fussing to be done before Mr. Summers declared the lottery open. There were the lists to make up—of heads of families, heads of households in each family, members of each household in each family. There was the proper swearing-in of Mr. Summers by the postmaster, as the official of the lottery; at one time, some people remembered, there had been a recital of some sort, performed by the official of the lottery, a perfunctory, tuneless chant that had been rattled off duly each year; some people believed that the official of the lottery used to stand just so when he said or sang it, others believed that he was supposed to walk among the people, but years and years ago this part of the ritual had been allowed to lapse. There had been, also, a ritual salute, which the official of the lottery had had to use in addressing each person who came up to draw from the box, but this also had changed with time, until now it was felt necessary only for the official to speak to each person approaching. Mr. Summers was very good at all this; in his clean white shirt and blue jeans, with one hand resting carelessly on the black box, he seemed very proper and important as he talked interminably to Mr. Graves and the Martins.

Just as Mr. Summers finally left off talking and turned to the assembled villagers, Mrs. Hutchinson came hurriedly along the path to the square, her sweater thrown over her shoulders, and slid into place in the back of the crowd. "Clean forgot what day it was," she said to Mrs. Delacroix, who stood next to her, and they both laughed softly. "Thought my old man was out back stacking wood," Mrs. Hutchinson went on, "and then I looked out the window and the kids was gone, and then I remembered it was the twenty-seventh and came a-running."

She dried her hands on her apron, and Mrs. Delacroix said, "You're in time, though. They're still talking away up there."

Mrs. Hutchinson craned her neck to see through the crowd and found her husband and children standing near the front. She tapped Mrs. Delacroix on the arm as a farewell and began to make her way through the crowd. The people separated good-humoredly to let her through; two or three people said, in voices just loud enough to be heard across the crowd, "Here comes your Missus, Hutchinson," and "Bill, she made it after all." Mrs. Hutchinson reached her husband, and Mr. Summers, who had been waiting, said cheerfully, "Thought we were going to have to get on without you, Tessie." Mrs. Hutchinson said, grinning, "Wouldn't have me leave m'dishes in the sink, now, would you, Joe?," and soft laughter ran through the crowd as the people stirred back into position after Mrs. Hutchinson's arrival.

"Well, now," Mr. Summers said soberly, "guess we better get started, get   10
this over with, so's we can go back to work. Anybody ain't here?"

"Dunbar," several people said. "Dunbar, Dunbar."

Mr. Summers consulted his list. "Clyde Dunbar," he said. "That's right. He's broke his leg, hasn't he? Who's drawing for him?"

"Me, I guess," a woman said, and Mr. Summers turned to look at her. "Wife draws for her husband," Mr. Summers said. "Don't you have a grown boy to do it for you, Janey?" Although Mr. Summers and everyone else in the village knew the answer perfectly well, it was the business of the official of the lottery to ask such questions formally. Mr. Summers waited with an expression of polite interest while Mrs. Dunbar answered.

"Horace's not but sixteen yet," Mrs. Dunbar said regretfully. "Guess I gotta fill in for the old man this year."

"Right," Mr. Summers said. He made a note on the list he was holding.   15
Then he asked, "Watson boy drawing this year?"

A tall boy in the crowd raised his hand. "Here," he said. "I'm drawing for m'mother and me." He blinked his eyes nervously and ducked his head as several voices in the crowd said things like "Good fellow, Jack," and "Glad to see your mother's got a man to do it."

"Well," Mr. Summers said, "guess that's everyone. Old Man Warner make it?"

"Here," a voice said, and Mr. Summers nodded.

A sudden hush fell on the crowd as Mr. Summers cleared his throat and looked at the list. "All ready?" he called. "Now, I'll read the names—heads of families first—and the men come up and take a paper out of the box. Keep the paper folded in your hand without looking at it until everyone has had a turn. Everything clear?"

The people had done it so many times that they only half listened to the   20
directions; most of them were quiet, wetting their lips, not looking around. Then Mr. Summers raised one hand high and said, "Adams." A man disengaged himself from the crowd and came forward. "Hi, Steve," Mr. Summers said, and Mr. Adams said, "Hi, Joe." They grinned at one another humorlessly and nervously. Then Mr. Adams reached into the black box and took out a folded paper. He held it firmly by one corner as he turned and went hastily back to his place in the crowd, where he stood a little apart from his family, not looking down at his hand.

"Allen," Mr. Summers said. "Anderson. . . . Bentham."

"Seems like there's no time at all between lotteries any more," Mrs. Delacroix said to Mrs. Graves in the back row. "Seems like we got through with the last one only last week."

"Time sure goes fast," Mrs. Graves said.

"Clark. . . . Delacroix."

"There goes my old man," Mrs. Delacroix said. She held her breath while   25
her husband went forward.

"Dunbar," Mr. Summers said, and Mrs. Dunbar went steadily to the box while one of the women said, "Go on, Janey," and another said, "There she goes."

"We're next," Mrs. Graves said. She watched while Mr. Graves came around from the side of the box, greeted Mr. Summers gravely, and selected a slip of paper from the box. By now, all through the crowd there were men holding the small folded papers in their large hands, turning them over and over nervously. Mrs. Dunbar and her two sons stood together, Mrs. Dunbar holding the slip of paper.

"Harburt. . . . Hutchinson."

"Get up there, Bill," Mrs. Hutchinson said, and the people near her laughed.

"Jones."   30

"They do say," Mr. Adams said to Old Man Warner, who stood next to him, "that over in the north village they're talking of giving up the lottery."

Old Man Warner snorted. "Pack of crazy fools," he said. "Listening to the young folks, nothing's good enough for *them*. Next thing you know, they'll be wanting to go back to living in caves, nobody work any more, live *that* way for a while. Used to be a saying about 'Lottery in June, corn be heavy soon.' First thing you know, we'd all be eating stewed chickweed and acorns. There's *always* been a lottery," he added petulantly. "Bad enough to see young Joe Summers up there joking with everybody."

"Some places have already quit lotteries," Mrs. Adams said.

"Nothing but trouble in *that*," Old Man Warner said stoutly. "Pack of young fools."

"Martin." And Bobby Martin watched his father go forward. "Overdyke. . . .   35
Percy."

"I wish they'd hurry," Mrs. Dunbar said to her older son. "I wish they'd hurry."

"They're almost through," her son said.

"You get ready to run tell Dad," Mrs. Dunbar said.

Mr. Summers called his own name and then stepped forward precisely and selected a slip from the box. Then he called, "Warner."

"Seventy-seventh year I been in the lottery," Old Man Warner said as he   40
went through the crowd. "Seventy-seventh time."

"Watson." The tall boy came awkwardly through the crowd. Someone said, "Don't be nervous, Jack," and Mr. Summers said, "Take your time, son."

"Zanini."

After that, there was a long pause, a breathless pause, until Mr. Summers, holding his slip of paper in the air, said, "All right, fellows." For a minute, no one moved, and then all the slips of paper were opened. Suddenly, all the women began to speak at once, saying, "Who is it?" "Who's got it?" "Is it the Dunbars?" "Is it the Watsons?" Then the voices began to say, "It's Hutchinson. It's Bill," "Bill Hutchinson's got it."

"Go tell your father," Mrs. Dunbar said to her older son.

People began to look around to see the Hutchinsons. Bill Hutchinson was standing quiet, staring down at the paper in his hand. Suddenly, Tessie Hutchinson shouted to Mr. Summers, "You didn't give him time enough to take any paper he wanted. I saw you. It wasn't fair!"

"Be a good sport, Tessie," Mrs. Delacroix called, and Mrs. Graves said, "All of us took the same chance."

"Shut up, Tessie," Bill Hutchinson said.

"Well, everyone," Mr. Summers said, "that was done pretty fast, and now we've got to be hurrying a little more to get done in time." He consulted his next list. "Bill," he said, "you draw for the Hutchinson family. You got any other households in the Hutchinsons?"

"There's Don and Eva," Mrs. Hutchinson yelled. "Make *them* take their chance!"

"Daughters draw with their husbands' families, Tessie," Mr. Summers said gently. "You know that as well as anyone else."

"It wasn't *fair*," Tessie said.

"I guess not, Joe," Bill Hutchinson said regretfully. "My daughter draws with her husband's family, that's only fair. And I've got no other family except the kids."

"Then, as far as drawing for families is concerned, it's you," Mr. Summers said in explanation, "and as far as drawing for households is concerned, that's you, too. Right?"

"Right," Bill Hutchinson said.

"How many kids, Bill?" Mr. Summers asked formally.

"Three," Bill Hutchinson said. "There's Bill, Jr., and Nancy, and little Dave. And Tessie and me."

"All right, then," Mr. Summers said. "Harry, you got their tickets back?"

Mr. Graves nodded and held up the slips of paper. "Put them in the box, then," Mr. Summers directed. "Take Bill's and put it in."

"I think we ought to start over," Mrs. Hutchinson said, as quietly as she could. "I tell you it wasn't *fair*. You didn't give him time enough to choose. *Every-*body saw that."

Mr. Graves had selected the five slips and put them in the box, and he dropped all the papers but those onto the ground, where the breeze caught them and lifted them off.

"Listen, everybody," Mrs. Hutchinson was saying to the people around her.

"Ready, Bill?" Mr. Summers asked, and Bill Hutchinson, with one quick glance around at his wife and children, nodded.

"Remember," Mr. Summers said, "take the slips and keep them folded until each person has taken one. Harry, you help little Dave." Mr. Graves took the hand of the little boy, who came willingly with him up to the box. "Take a paper out of the box, Davy," Mr. Summers said. Davy put his hand into the box and laughed. "Take just *one* paper," Mr. Summers said. "Harry, you hold it for him." Mr. Graves took the child's hand and removed the folded paper from the tight fist and held it while little Dave stood next to him and looked up at him wonderingly.

"Nancy next," Mr. Summers said. Nancy was twelve, and her school friends breathed heavily as she went forward, switching her skirt, and took a slip daintily from the box. "Bill, Jr.," Mr. Summers said, and Billy, his face red and his feet over-large, nearly knocked the box over as he got a paper out. "Tessie," Mr. Summers said. She hesitated for a minute, looking around defiantly, and then set her lips and went up to the box. She snatched a paper out and held it behind her.

"Bill," Mr. Summers said, and Bill Hutchinson reached into the box and felt around, bringing his hand out at last with the slip of paper in it.

The crowd was quiet. A girl whispered, "I hope it's not Nancy," and the   65
sound of the whisper reached the edges of the crowd.

"It's not the way it used to be," Old Man Warner said clearly. "People ain't the way they used to be."

"All right," Mr. Summers said. "Open the papers. Harry, you open little Dave's."

Mr. Graves opened the slip of paper and there was a general sigh through the crowd as he held it up and everyone could see that it was blank. Nancy and Bill, Jr., opened theirs at the same time, and both beamed and laughed, turning around to the crowd and holding their slips of paper above their heads.

"Tessie," Mr. Summers said. There was a pause, and then Mr. Summers looked at Bill Hutchinson, and Bill unfolded his paper and showed it. It was blank.

"It's Tessie," Mr. Summers said, and his voice was hushed. "Show us her   70
paper, Bill."

Bill Hutchinson went over to his wife and forced the slip of paper out of her hand. It had a black spot on it, the black spot Mr. Summers had made the night before with the heavy pencil in the coal-company office. Bill Hutchinson held it up, and there was a stir in the crowd.

"All right, folks," Mr. Summers said. "Let's finish quickly."

Although the villagers had forgotten the ritual and lost the original black box, they still remembered to use stones. The pile of stones the boys had made earlier was ready; there were stones on the ground with the blowing scraps of paper that had come out of the box. Mrs. Delacroix selected a stone so large she had to pick it up with both hands and turned to Mrs. Dunbar. "Come on," she said. "Hurry up."

Mrs. Dunbar had small stones in both hands, and she said, gasping for breath, "I can't run at all. You'll have to go ahead and I'll catch up with you."

The children had stones already, and someone gave little Davy Hutchinson   75
a few pebbles.

Tessie Hutchinson was in the center of a cleared space by now, and she held her hands out desperately as the villagers moved in on her. "It isn't fair," she said. A stone hit her on the side of the head.

Old Man Warner was saying, "Come on, come on, everyone." Steve Adams was in the front of the crowd of villagers with Mrs. Graves beside him.

"It isn't fair, it isn't right," Mrs. Hutchinson screamed, and then they were upon her.

QUESTIONS

1. Describe the point of view of the story. Is it best described as third-person limited, omniscient, or dramatic? What seems to be the position from which the narrator sees and describes the events? How much extra information does the narrator provide? Does the narrator anywhere express any opinion about the events connected with the lottery?

2. What would the story be like if it were attempted with an omniscient point of view? What if the first person? Could the story be as suspenseful as it is? Would it be necessary to provide more information than is now present about the lottery? Why so? In what other ways might the story be different with a different point of view?

3. Does the conclusion of "The Lottery" seem to come as a surprise? In retrospect, are there hints earlier in the story about what is to come? Discuss how you perceived these hints before and after you read the conclusion.

4. A scapegoat, in the ritual of purification described in the Old Testament (Leviticus 16), was an actual goat that was released into the wilderness after having been ceremonially heaped with the "iniquities" of the people (Leviticus 16:22). What traces of such a ritual are suggested in "The Lottery" by references to things like the abandoned salute and the recital, and also the jingle "Lottery in June, corn be heavy soon"? Can you think of any other kinds of rituals that are retained today even though their basis in belief is now remote or even nonexistent?

5. Is the story a horror story or a surprise story, or neither or both?

6. What idea or ideas do you think Jackson is asserting by making the characters in "The Lottery" seem to be just plain, ordinary folks? What would the story have been like if the people had been criminals? If they had all been devil worshippers?

WRITING ABOUT POINT OF VIEW

In prewriting activity for an essay on point of view, you must consider things like language, authority and opportunity for observation, selection of detail, characterization, interpretive commentaries, and narrative development. You might plan an analysis of one, a few, or all of these elements. Generally the essay should explain how the point of view has contributed to making the story uniquely as it is. One of the major purposes in an essay on point of view is to establish the nature and adherence to verisimilitude of the narration, the similarity to truth achieved by the way the events are presented. The basic question is whether the story's actions and speeches are reported authentically so that the telling of the story is just as "true" as the story itself.

Organizing Your Essay

INTRODUCTION.   In your introduction you should get at the matters
that you plan to develop. Which point of view is used in the work? What
is the major influence of this point of view on the work? (For example,
"The omniscient point of view causes full, leisurely insights into many
shades of character," or "The first-person point of view enables the work
to resemble an exposé of back-room political deals.") To what extent does
the selection of point of view make the work particularly interesting and
effective, or uninteresting and ineffective? What particular aspects of the
work (action, dialogue, characters, description, narration, analysis) do you
wish to analyze in support of your central idea?

BODY.   The questions you raise here will of course depend on the
work you have studied. It would be impossible to answer all of the following
questions in your analysis, but going through them should make you aware
of the sorts of things you can include in the body of your theme.

If you have read a work with the first-person point of view, your
analysis will necessarily involve the speaker. Who is she (supposing, for
the moment, a woman)? Is she a major or a minor character? What is
her background? What is her relationship to the person listening to her
(if there is a listener)? Does she speak directly to you, the reader, in such
a way that you are a listener or an eavesdropper? How does the speaker
describe the various situations? Is her method uniquely a function of her
character? Or (supposing a man), how reliable is he as an observer? How
did he acquire the information he is presenting? How much does he disclose? How much does he hide? Does he ever rely on the information of
others for his material? How reliable are these other witnesses? Does the
speaker undergo any changes in the course of the work that have any
bearing on the ways he presents the material? Does he notice one kind
of thing (for example, discussion) but miss others (for example, natural
scenery)? What might have escaped him, if anything? Does the author
put the speaker into situations that he can describe but not understand?
Why? Is the speaker ever confused? Is he close to the action, or distant
from it? Does he show emotional involvement in any situations? Are you
sympathetic to his concerns or are you put off by them? If the speaker
makes any commentary, are his thoughts valid? To what extent, if any, is
the speaker of as much interest as the material he presents?

If you encounter any of the third-person points of view, try to determine the characteristics of the voice employed by the author. Does it seem
that the author is speaking in an authorial voice, or that the narrator has
a special voice? You can approach this problem by answering many of
the questions that are relevant to the first-person point of view. Also try

to determine the distance of the narrator to the action. How is the action described? How is the dialogue recorded? Is there any background information given? Do the descriptions reveal any bias toward any of the characters? Are the descriptions full or bare? Does the author include descriptions or analyses of a character's thoughts? What are these like? Do you see evidence of the author's own philosophy? Does the choice of words direct you toward any particular interpretations? What limitations or freedoms devolve upon the story as a result of the point of view?

CONCLUSION. In your conclusion you should evaluate the success of the story's point of view: Was it consistent, effective, truthful? What did the writer gain (if anything) by the selection of point of view? What was lost (if anything)? How might a less skillful writer have handled similar material? After answering questions like these, you may end your theme.

Problems

1. In considering point of view, you will encounter the problem of whether to discuss the author or the speaker as the originator of attitudes and ideas. If the author is employing the first-person point of view, there is no problem. Use the speaker's name, if he or she is given one (for example, Sammy from "A & P," Jackie from "First Confession"), or else talk about the "speaker" or "persona" if there is no name (for example, the speaker of Whitecloud's "Blue Winds Dancing" is unnamed). You face a greater problem with the third-person points of view, but even here it is safe for you to discuss the "speaker" rather than the "author," remembering always that the author is manipulating the narrative voice. Sometimes authors emphasize a certain phase of their own personalities in their authorial voices. Many ideas are therefore common to both the author and the speaker, but your statements about these must be inferential, not absolute.

2. You may have a tendency to wander away from point of view into retelling the story or discussing the ideas. Emphasize the presentation of the events and ideas, and the causes for this presentation. Do not emphasize the subject material itself, but use it only as it bears on your consideration of point of view. Your object is not just to interpret the work, but also to show how the point of view enables you to interpret the work.

Obviously you must talk about the material in the work, but use it only to illustrate your assertions about point of view. Avoid the following pattern of statement, which will always lead you astray: "The speaker says this, which means this." Instead, adhere to the following pattern, which will keep your emphasis always on your central idea: "The speaker says this, which shows this about her and her attitudes." If a particular idea is difficult, you might need to explain it, but do not do so unless it illustrates your central idea.

3. Remember that you are dealing with point of view in the *entire* work and not simply in single narrations and conversations. For example, an individual character has her own way of seeing things when she states something, but in relation to the entire work her speech is a function of the dramatic point of view. Thus, you should not talk about Character A's point of view, and Character B's, but instead should state that "Using the dramatic point of view, Author Z allows the various characters to argue their cases, in their own words and with their own limitations."

4. Be particularly careful to distinguish between point of view and opinions or beliefs. Point of view refers to the total position from which things are seen, heard, and reported, whereas an opinion is a thought about something. In this essay, you are to describe not the ideas, but the method of narration of an author.

SAMPLE ESSAY

Frank O'Connor's First-Person Point of View in "First Confession"*

[1]   In Frank O'Connor's "First Confession," a story based in early twentieth-century Ireland, the point of view is first person. The speaker is an adult named Jackie, who recalls the events leading up to and including his first confession as a boy of seven. Jackie has good recall and organizing ability, but has limited adult perspective.° These qualities make the story detailed, dramatic, and objective.▫

[2]   The detail of the story seems vivid and real because O'Connor presents Jackie as a person with strong recall. Events such as the knife scene, the drinking and eating by the barefoot grandmother, and the stories of Mrs. Ryan are colorful. They seem like high points of childhood that an adult would truly remember. The entire confession is presented as if it just happened, not as if it were an almost forgotten event of the past. Such vivid details, which give the story great interest, depend on their being still alive in the narrator's memory.

[3]   Beyond simple recall, O'Connor's drama rests on the organizing skills of the narrator. The story is made up of scenes that are unified and connected. Thus the first part of the confession, ending with Jackie's falling out of the confessional and being whacked by Nora, is a short but complete farce. The burning handprints of the man of the bad confession become a theme in Jackie's mind as he waits for the priest. In the confession itself Jackie mentions even the dramatic pause before the priest responds to the confessed plan to kill the grandmother. The drama in all these scenes results from a good storytelling narrator.

* See p. 187 for this story.
° Central idea
▫ Thesis sentence

[4]   The objective quality of "First Confession," accounting for O'Connor's humor, is related to a flaw in the narrator. Jackie makes remarks about the action, but these are childish and not adult. A more mature narrator might comment about the fear the boy gains through his religious instruction, the difficulties of his family life, or the beauty of his first confession. But from the adult Jackie's point of view we get no such comments. O'Connor makes Jackie stick to the events, and therefore he keeps the story objective, simple, and funny.

[5]   Thus O'Connor's selection of the first-person point of view gives the story strength and humor. Jackie the adult is faithful to his childhood feelings. We get everything from his side, and only his side. He never gives his father or his sister any credit. It is the consistent point of view that makes "First Confession" both comic and excellent. If Jackie showed more adult understanding, O'Connor's humor would be gone, and the story would not be such good entertainment.

Commentary on the Essay

This essay emphasizes both the abilities and the flaw of the narrator and attempts to relate these qualities to the nature of "First Confession." The introduction provides a brief background of the story but gets right to the point of view. The qualification of Jackie as a first-person observer is mentioned, followed by the central idea and thesis sentence. The second paragraph states that the vivid detail of the story results from Jackie's powerful recall. The third paragraph connects the dramatic quality of the various scenes with his skill as a storyteller. In the fourth paragraph a flaw in Jackie's adult character—a lack of adult perceptiveness—is shown as the cause of the objectivity and humor in the story. The conclusion states that the point of view is consistent, even if it is immature. The last sentence goes back to paragraph 4: The humor depends on the narrator's having a lack of sympathy for, and understanding of, childhood antagonists. Throughout the essay, therefore, certain qualities of the story are connected directly to the character, ability, and limited perspective of the point of view or centralizing mind.

6

Setting: Place and Objects in Fiction

Setting refers to the natural and artificial scenery or environment in which characters in literature live and move. Things such as the time of day and the amount of light, the trees and animals, the sounds described, the smells, and the weather are part of the setting. Paint brushes, apples, pitchforks, rafts, six-shooters, watches, automobiles, horses and buggies, and many other items belong to the setting. References to clothing, descriptions of physical appearance, and spatial relationships among the characters are also part of setting. In short, the setting of a work is the sum total of references to physical and temporal objects and artifacts.

The setting of a story or novel is much like the sets and properties of the stage or the location for a motion picture. The dramatist writing for the stage is physically limited by what can be constructed and moved or carried onto the stage. Writers of nondramatic works, however, are limited only by their imaginations. It is possible for them to include details of many places without the slightest external restraint. For our purposes, the references will be to stories that establish a setting either in nature or in manufactured things.

The action of a story may occur in more than one place. In a novel, the locale may shift constantly. There may be several settings in a work, and the term *setting* refers to all the places mentioned. If a story is short, all the scenes may be in one city or countryside.

TYPES OF SETTINGS

Natural

The setting for a great number of stories is the out-of-doors, and, naturally enough, Nature herself is seen as a force that shapes action and therefore directs and redirects lives. A deep woods may make walking difficult or dangerous, or may be a place for a sinister meeting of devil worshippers. The open road may be a place where one person seeks flight, others face a showdown, and still others may meet their fate. A lake may be the location where one person literally rescues another and also silently and unconsciously makes a direct commitment to the saved person. Bushes may furnish places of concealment, while a mountain top is a spot protecting occupants from the outside world. The ocean may be the location of a test of youth but also may provide the environment for the memory of vanished dreams. Nature, in short, is one of the major forces governing the circumstances of characters who go about facing the conflicts on which the plots of stories depend.

Manufactured

Manufactured things always reflect the people who made them. A building or a room tells about the people who built it and live in it, and ultimately about the social and political orders that maintain the conditions. A richly decorated house shows the expensive tastes and resources of the characters owning it. A few cracks in the plaster and some chips in the paint may show the same persons declining in fortune and power. Ugly and impoverished surroundings may contribute to the weariness, insensitivity, negligence, or even hostility of the characters living in them.

STUDYING THE USES OF SETTING

In studying the setting of a story, your first concern should be to discover all the details that conceivably form a part of setting, and then to determine how the author has used these details. For example, as writers stress character, plot, or action, they may emphasize or minimize setting. At times a setting will be no more than a roughly sketched place where events occur. In other stories, the setting may be so prominent that it may almost be considered as a participant in the action. An instance of such "participation" is Welty's "A Worn Path," where the woods and roadway provide obstacles that are almost active antagonists against Phoenix as she pushes her way to Natchez.

Setting and Credibility

One of the major purposes of setting is to lend realism or verisimilitude; to set a story in a particular place or time makes the action credible. Irwin Shaw's "Act of Faith" presents the realistic conditions of France as a genuine background in which authentic soldiers plan an actual trip to Paris so that they may have a truly great weekend. The more detailed the description of setting, the more believable the events of the story become. Because the details of the woodworking shop are well delineated in Marjorie Pickthall's "The Worker in Sandalwood" (p. 312), for example, they lend authenticity to the miraculous event that occurs there. Even futuristic, unrealistic, symbolic, and fantastic stories, as well as ghost stories, take on authenticity if the details of setting are presented as though the world of these stories is the one we normally see and experience. Walter Van Tilburg Clark's "The Portable Phonograph," Franz Kafka's "The Hunger Artist," Nathaniel Hawthorne's "Young Goodman Brown," and Edgar Allan Poe's "The Masque of the Red Death" are such stories. Without a basis in detailed settings, these works would lose some of their credibility even though they make no pretenses at actual realism.

Setting and Statement

Setting may be a kind of pictorial language, a means by which the author makes statements much as a painter uses certain images as ideas in a painting. Thus the dwelling place of Dr. Jenkins in Clark's "The Portable Phonograph" is compared to "the mouth of a mine tunnel." In this respect it is also somewhat like a cave. Because the scene of the story is the dark, bleak, cold world after a catastrophic war, the visual effect is that the war has sent human beings back to the caves in which they presumably lived during the Stone Age, before our modern civilization.

Setting and Character

In the same vein, setting may intersect with character as one of the means by which character is to be underscored and therefore understood. To refer again to Dr. Jenkins of "The Portable Phonograph," we must realize that he has come to his present circumstances as a mature, sophisticated person. Amid the hostile surroundings, his character as a strong, tenacious person emerges, so that he clings to the past joys of life as represented by his meager record collection. But he is also adaptable, and hence he arranges things in his cave so that he can continue to exist even though the conditions are so grim. Here the setting is clearly designed to help shape our ideas of his character. A similar blending of the setting and the major character of Guy De Maupassant's "The Necklace" (p. 90) is explored in the sample essay. In virtually every story that you encounter, a comparable relationship may be found and studied.

Setting and Organization

Authors might also use setting as a means of organizing their works. It is often comic, for example, to move a character from one setting to another (provided that no harm is done in the process). Thus, Stephen

Crane provokes smiles in the first part of "The Bride Comes to Yellow Sky" (p. 107) by shifting a backwoods town marshal into the plush setting of a Pullman railroad car. Crane's descriptions of the awkwardness of the marshal and the patronizing airs of the other characters are humorous. Poe achieves a grimly opposite effect in "The Masque of the Red Death" by transposing the specter of death, usually the inhabitant of cemeteries and mausoleums, into a large group of nobles at a masquerade party or revel.

Another organizational use of setting may be thought of as a **framing** or **enclosing method.** An author frames a story by opening with a description of a setting, and then returns to the description at the end. Like a picture frame, the setting constantly affects the reader's thoughts about the story. An example of this method is Irwin Shaw's "Act of Faith," which is set in France immediately after the victory against Germany in World War II but which also refers to many other locations. The story begins with two soldiers slogging through the mud with the hope of getting enough money to go on a weekend pass to Paris. At the end the same two soldiers, together with a third, are walking in "damp, dead grass"—the same activity over similar ground. The intention to go to town has not changed, but the stakes have changed dramatically, from a simple intention of having a good time to a major commitment in regard to the entire future of a Jew living in postwar America. Shaw's setting of muddy and slippery ground over which soldiers walk, in short, frames a story of remarkably serious importance.

Setting and Atmosphere

Setting also affects the **atmosphere** or **mood** of stories. You might note that the description of an action requires no more than a functional description of setting. Thus, an action in a forest needs just the statement that the forest is there. However, if you read descriptions of the trees, the shapes, the light and shadows, the animals, the wind, and the sounds, you may be sure that the author is working to create an atmosphere or mood for the action. There are many ways of creating moods. Descriptions of "warm" colors (red, orange, yellow) may contribute to a mood of happiness. "Cooler" colors may suggest gloom. References to smells and sounds bring the setting even more to life by asking additional sensory responses from the reader. The setting of a story on a farm or in a city apartment may evoke a response to these habitats that may contribute to a story's atmosphere.

Setting and Irony

Just as setting is present as an element of concurrence, agreement, reinforcement, and strengthening of character and theme, so it may work as an element of irony. The setting, in other words, may create an environment that is the opposite of what actually occurs in the story. Thus the setting of Shirley Jackson's "The Lottery" (p. 194) builds up the background of a small town in which a prize of value rather than death is to be won. This normal, rural America atmosphere makes the conclusion grimly ironic, for it is just real folks who cast the stones of ritual execution. Poe uses a similar ironic twist in "The Masque of the Red Death," where Prince Prospero seals off his palace from the outside world of pestilence and infection, but at the same moment he actually seals in Death himself and thereby ensures the end of all the revelers. The irony is that closed doors may just as easily prevent exit as entry. Mark Twain creates the same sort of irony of setting in the story "Luck" p. 245, where the Russian army reinforcements are befuddled by the witless charge of the forces headed by the main character. Here, unlike the case in the stories of Poe and Jackson, the irony is used in a mode of comedy rather than grimness.

EDGAR ALLAN POE (1809–1849)

The Masque of the Red Death   1842

The "Red Death" had long devastated the country. No pestilence had ever been so fatal, or so hideous. Blood was its Avatar° and its seal—the redness and the horror of blood. There were sharp pains, and sudden dizziness, and then profuse bleeding at the pores, with dissolution. The scarlet stains upon the body and especially upon the face of the victim, were the pest ban which shut him out from the aid and from the sympathy of his fellow-men. And the whole seizure, progress, and termination of the disease, were the incidents of half an hour.

But the Prince Prospero° was happy and dauntless and sagacious. When his dominions were half depopulated, he summoned to his presence a thousand hale and light-hearted friends from among the knights and dames of his court, and with these retired to the deep seclusion of one of his castellated abbeys. This was an extensive and magnificent structure, the creation of the prince's own eccentric yet august taste. A strong and lofty wall girdled it in. This wall had gates of iron. The courtiers, having entered, brought furnaces and massy hammers and welded the bolts. They resolved to leave means neither of ingress nor egress to the sudden impulses of despair or of frenzy from within. The abbey was amply provisioned. With such precautions the courtiers might bid defiance to contagion. The external world could take care of itself. In the meantime it was folly to grieve, or to think. The prince had provided all the appliances of pleasure. There were buffoons, there were improvisatori, there were ballet-dancers, there were musicians, there was Beauty, there was wine. All these and security were within. Without was the "Red Death."

It was toward the close of the fifth or sixth month of his seclusion, and

---

Avatar: model, incarnation, manifestation.

Prospero: that is, "prosperous." See Shakespeare's *The Tempest*, where the principal character is Prospero.

while the pestilence raged most furiously abroad, that the Prince Prospero entertained his thousand friends at a masked ball of the most unusual magnificence.

It was a voluptuous scene, that masquerade. But first let me tell of the rooms
in which it was held. There were seven—an imperial suite. In many palaces, however,
such suites form a long and straight vista, while the folding doors slide back nearly
to the walls on either hand, so that the view of the whole extent is scarcely impeded.
Here the case was very different; as might have been expected from the duke's
love of the *bizarre*. The apartments were so irregularly disposed that the vision
embraced but little more than one at a time. There was a sharp turn at every
twenty or thirty yards, and at each turn a novel effect. To the right and left, in
the middle of each wall, a tall and narrow Gothic window looked out upon a closed
corridor which pursued the windings of the suite. These windows were of stained
glass whose color varied in accordance with the prevailing hue of the decorations
of the chamber into which it opened. That at the eastern extremity was hung,
for example, in blue—and vividly blue were its windows. The second chamber
was purple in its ornaments and tapestries, and here the panes were purple. The
third was green throughout, and so were the casements. The fourth was furnished
and lighted with orange—the fifth with white—the sixth with violet. The seventh
apartment was closely shrouded in black velvet tapestries that hung all over the
ceiling and down the walls, falling in heavy folds upon a carpet of the same material
and hue. But in this chamber only, the color of the windows failed to correspond
with the decorations. The panes here were scarlet—a deep blood color. Now in
no one of the seven apartments was there any lamp or candelabrum, amid the
profusion of golden ornaments that lay scattered to and fro or depended from
the roof. There was no light of any kind emanating from lamp or candle within
the suite of chambers. But in the corridors that followed the suite, there stood,
opposite to each window, a heavy tripod, bearing a brazier of fire, that projected
its rays through the tinted glass and so glaringly illumined the room. And thus
were produced a multitude of gaudy and fantastic appearances. But in the western
or black chamber the effect of the fire-light that streamed upon the dark hangings
through the blood-tinted panes was ghastly in the extreme, and produced so wild
a look upon the countenances of those who entered, that there were few of the
company bold enough to set foot within its precincts at all.

It was in this apartment, also, that there stood against the western wall, a
gigantic clock of ebony. Its pendulum swung to and fro with a dull, heavy, monotonous clang; and when the minute-hand made the circuit of the face, and the hour
was to be stricken, there came from the brazen lungs of the clock a sound which
was clear and loud and deep and exceedingly musical, but of so peculiar a note
and emphasis that, at each lapse of an hour, the musicians of the orchestra were
constrained to pause, momentarily, in their performance, to hearken to the sound;
and thus the waltzers perforce ceased their evolutions; and there was a brief disconcert of the whole gay company; and, while the chimes of the clock yet rang, it
was observed that the giddiest grew pale, and the more aged and sedate passed
their hands over their brows as if in confused revery or meditation. But when
the echoes had fully ceased, a light laughter at once pervaded the assembly; the
musicians looked at each other and smiled as if at their own nervousness and
folly, and made whispering vows, each to the other, that the next chiming of the
clock should produce in them no similar emotion; and then, after the lapse of

sixty minutes (which embrace three thousand and six hundred seconds of the Time that flies), there came yet another chiming of the clock, and then were the same disconcert and tremulousness and meditation as before.

But, in spite of these things, it was a gay and magnificent revel. The tastes of the duke were peculiar. He had a fine eye for colors and effects. He disregarded the *decora*° of mere fashion. His plans were bold and fiery, and his conceptions glowed with barbaric lustre. There are some who would have thought him mad. His followers felt that he was not. It was necessary to hear and see and touch him to be *sure* that he was not.

He had directed, in great part, the movable embellishments of the seven chambers, upon occasion of this great fête,° and it was his own guiding taste which had given character to the masqueraders. Be sure they were grotesque. There were much glare and glitter and piquancy and phantasm—much of what has been since seen in "Hernani."° There were arabesque figures with unsuited limbs and appointments. There were delirious fancies such as the madman fashions. There were much of the beautiful, much of the wanton, much of the *bizarre*, something of the terrible, and not a little of that which might have excited disgust. To and fro in the seven chambers there stalked, in fact, a multitude of dreams. And these— the dreams—writhed in and about, taking hue from the rooms, and causing the wild music of the orchestra to seem as the echo of their steps. And, anon, there strikes the ebony clock which stands in the hall of the velvet. And then, for a moment, all is still, and all is silent save the voice of the clock. The dreams are stiff-frozen as they stand. But the echoes of the chime die away—they have endured but an instant—and a light, half-subdued laughter floats after them as they depart. And now again the music swells, and the dreams live, and writhe to and fro more merrily than ever, taking hue from the many-tinted windows through which stream the rays from the tripods. But to the chamber which lies most westwardly of the seven there are now none of the maskers who venture; for the night is waning away; and there flows a ruddier light through the blood-colored panes; and the blackness of the sable drapery appals; and to him whose foot falls upon the sable carpet, there comes from the near clock of ebony a muffled peal more solemnly emphatic than any which reaches *their* ears who indulge in the more remote gaieties of the other apartments.

But these other apartments were densely crowded, and in them beat feverishly the heart of life. And the revel went whirlingly on, until at length there commenced the sounding of midnight upon the clock. And then the music ceased, as I have told; and the evolutions of the waltzers were quieted; and there was an uneasy cessation of all things as before. But now there were twelve strokes to be sounded by the bell of the clock; and thus it happened, perhaps that more of thought crept, with more of time, into the meditations of the thoughtful among those who revelled. And thus too, it happened, perhaps, that before the last echoes of the last chime had utterly sunk into silence, there were many individuals in the crowd who had found leisure to become aware of the presence of a masked figure which had arrested the attention of no single individual before. And the rumor of this new

decora: schemes, patterns.
fête: party, revel.
Hernani: a tragedy by Victor Hugo (1802–1885), a play with elaborate scenes and costumes.

presence having spread itself whisperingly around, there arose at length from the whole company a buzz, or murmur, expressive of disapprobation and surprise—then, finally, of terror, of horror, and of disgust.

In an assembly of phantasms such as I have painted, it may well be supposed that no ordinary appearance could have excited such sensation. In truth the masquerade license of the night was nearly unlimited; but the figure in question had out-Heroded Herod,° and gone beyond the bounds of even the prince's indefinite decorum. There are chords in the hearts of the most reckless which cannot be touched without emotion. Even with the utterly lost, to whom life and death are equally jests, there are matters of which no jest can be made. The whole company, indeed, seemed now deeply to feel that in the costume and bearing of the stranger neither wit nor propriety existed. The figure was tall and gaunt, and shrouded from head to foot in the habiliments of the grave. The mask which concealed the visage was made so nearly to resemble the countenance of a stiffened corpse that the closest scrutiny must have had difficulty in detecting the cheat. And yet all this might have been endured, if not approved, by the mad revellers around. But the mummer had gone so far as to assume the type of the Red Death. His vesture was dabbled in *blood*—and his broad brow, with all the features of the face, was besprinkled with the scarlet horror.

When the eyes of Prince Prospero fell upon this spectral image (which, with   10
a slow and solemn movement, as if more fully to sustain its *rôle*, stalked to and fro among the waltzers) he was seen to be convulsed, in the first moment with a strong shudder either of terror or distaste; but, in the next, his brow reddened with rage.

"Who dares"—he demanded hoarsely of the courtiers who stood near him—"who dares insult us with this blasphemous mockery? Seize him and unmask him—that we may know whom we have to hang, at sunrise, from the battlements!"

It was in the eastern or blue chamber in which stood the Prince Prospero as he uttered these words. They rang throughout the seven rooms loudly and clearly, for the prince was a bold and robust man, and the music had become hushed at the waving of his hand.

It was in the blue room where stood the prince, with a group of pale courtiers by his side. At first, as he spoke, there was a slight rushing movement of this group in the direction of the intruder, who, at the moment was also near at hand, and now, with deliberate and stately step, made closer approach to the speaker. But from a certain nameless awe with which the mad assumptions of the mummer had inspired the whole party, there were found none who put forth hand to seize him; so that, unimpeded, he passed within a yard of the prince's person; and, while the vast assembly, as if with one impulse, shrank from the centres of the rooms to the walls, he made his way uninterruptedly, but with the same solemn and measured step which had distinguished him from the first, through the blue chamber to the purple—through the purple to the green—through the green to the orange—through this again to the white—and even thence to the violet, ere a decided movement had been made to arrest him. It was then, however, that the Prince Prospero, maddening with rage and the shame of his own momentary

out-Heroded Herod: quoted from Shakespeare's *Hamlet*, act 3, scene 2, in reference to extreme overacting.

cowardice, rushed hurriedly through the six chambers, while none followed him on account of a deadly terror that had seized upon all. He bore aloft a drawn dagger, and had approached, in rapid impetuosity, to within three or four feet of the retreating figure, when the latter, having attained the extremity of the velvet apartment, turned suddenly and confronted his pursuer. There was a sharp cry— and the dagger dropped gleaming upon the sable carpet, upon which, instantly afterward, fell prostrate in death the Prince Prospero. Then, summoning the wild courage of despair, a throng of the revellers at once threw themselves into the black apartment, and, seizing the mummer, whose tall figure stood erect and motionless within the shadow of the ebony clock, gasped in unutterable horror at finding the grave cerements and corpse-like mask, which they handled with so violent a rudeness, untenanted by any tangible form.

And now was acknowledged the presence of the Red Death. He had come like a thief in the night.° And one by one dropped the revellers in the blood-bedewed halls of their revel, and died each in the despairing posture of his fall. And the life of the ebony clock went out with that of the last of the gay. And the flames of the tripods expired. And Darkness and Decay and the Red Death held illimitable dominion over all.

QUESTIONS

1. What is happening throughout the country in Poe's "Masque of the Red Death"? How does Prince Prospero react to these events? What does the Prince's reaction tell us about him?

2. How is the building in which Prince Prospero and his thousand nobles take shelter described? To what extent does the description of this "abbey" help us form an opinion of Prince Prospero?

3. How many rooms are used in the masquerade ball or revel in the story? In what ways might this number be significant? What is the dominant color of each room? How are the rooms lighted? How do these details help create the atmosphere and mood of the story?

4. What color is the last room? What color is its window? Why does this room make the revellers nervous? To what extent does this last room reflect the plot and ideas of the story?

5. What single object is located in this last room? How is this object described? What effect does it have on the revellers when it sounds? How might you explain this effect? What do you think Poe is suggesting symbolically with this object and its effects?

6. How are the nobles dressed for the masquerade? Why does the "masked figure" introduced near the end of the story stand out as remarkable? How does Prospero react to this masked figure? Can you explain Prospero's reaction? What does this figure represent?

7. What is the central conflict in this story? Who is the protagonist? The antagonist? Where is the climax of the story? How is the central conflict resolved at the climax?

thief in the night: 2 Peter 3:10.

8. What point of view is employed in the story? Explain why Poe chose to use this point of view.

WALTER VAN TILBURG CLARK (1909–1971)

The Portable Phonograph   *1942*

The red sunset, with narrow, black cloud strips like threats across it, lay on the curved horizon of the prairie. The air was still and cold, and in it settled the mute darkness and greater cold of night. High in the air there was wind, for through the veil of the dusk the clouds could be seen gliding rapidly south and changing shapes. A sensation of torment, of two-sided, unpredictable nature, arose from the stillness of the earth air beneath the violence of the upper air. Out of the sunset, through the dead, matted grass and isolated weed stalks of the prairie, crept the narrow and deeply rutted remains of a road. In the road, in places, there were crusts of shallow, brittle ice. There were little islands of an old oiled pavement in the road too, but most of it was mud, now frozen rigid. The frozen mud still bore the toothed impress of great tanks, and a wanderer on the neighboring undulations might have stumbled, in this light, into large, partially filled-in and weed-grown cavities, their banks channeled and beginning to spread into badlands. These pits were such as might have been made by falling meteors, but they were not. They were the scars of gigantic bombs, their rawness already made a little natural by rain, seed and time. Along the road there were rakish remnants of fence. There was also, just visible, one portion of tangled and multiple barbed wire still erect, behind which was a shelving ditch with small caves, now very quiet and empty, at intervals in its back wall. Otherwise there was no structure or remnant of a structure visible over the dome of the darkling earth, but only, in sheltered hollows, the darker shadows of young trees trying again.

Under the wuthering arch of the high wind a V of wild geese fled south. The rush of their pinions sounded briefly, and the faint, plaintive notes of their expeditionary talk. Then they left a still greater vacancy. There was the smell and expectation of snow, as there is likely to be when the wild geese fly south. From the remote distance, toward the red sky, came faintly the protracted howl and quick yap-yap of a prairie wolf.

North of the road, perhaps a hundred yards, lay the parallel and deeply intrenched course of a small creek, lined with leafless alders and willows. The creek was already silent under ice. Into the bank above it was dug a sort of cell, with a single opening, like the mouth of a mine tunnel. Within the cell there was a little red of fire, which showed dully through the opening, like a reflection or a deception of the imagination. The light came from the chary burning of four blocks of poorly aged peat, which gave off a petty warmth and much acrid smoke. But the precious remnants of wood, old fence posts and timbers from the long-deserted dugouts, had to be saved for the real cold, for the time when a man's breath blew white, the moisture in his nostrils stiffened at once when he stepped out, and the expansive blizzards paraded for days over the vast open, swirling and settling and thickening, till the dawn of the cleared day when the sky was a thin blue-green and the terrible cold, in which a man could not live for three hours unwarmed, lay over the uniformly drifted swell of the plain.

Around the smoldering peat four men were seated cross-legged. Behind them, traversed by their shadows, was the earth bench, with two old and dirty army blankets, where the owner of the cell slept. In a niche in the opposite wall were a few tin utensils which caught the glint of the coals. The host was rewrapping in a piece of daubed burlap, four fine, leather-bound books. He worked slowly and very carefully, and at last tied the bundle securely with a piece of grass-woven cord. The other three looked intently upon the process, as if a great significance lay in it. As the host tied the cord, he spoke. He was an old man, his long, matted beard and hair gray to nearly white. The shadows made his brows and cheekbones appear gnarled, his eyes and cheeks deeply sunken. His big hands, rough with frost and swollen by rheumatism, were awkward but gentle at their task. He was like a prehistoric priest performing a fateful ceremonial rite. Also his voice had in it a suitable quality of deep, reverent despair, yet perhaps, at the moment, a sharpness of selfish satisfaction.

"When I perceived what was happening," he said, "I told myself, 'It is the   5
end. I cannot take much; I will take these.'

"Perhaps I was impractical," he continued. "But for myself, I do not regret, and what do we know of those who will come after us? We are the doddering remnant of a race of mechanical fools. I have saved what I love; the soul of what was good in us here; perhaps the new ones will make a strong enough beginning not to fall behind when they become clever."

He rose with slow pain and placed the wrapped volumes in the niche with his utensils. The others watched him with the same ritualistic gaze.

"Shakespeare, the Bible, *Moby Dick*,° *The Divine Comedy*,"° one of them said softly. "You might have done worse; much worse."

"You will have a little soul left until you die," said another harshly. "That is more than is true of us. My brain becomes thick, like my hands." He held the big, battered hands, with their black nails, in the glow to be seen.

"I want paper to write on," he said. "And there is none."   10

The fourth man said nothing. He sat in the shadow farthest from the fire, and sometimes his body jerked in its rags from the cold. Although he was still young, he was sick, and coughed often. Writing implied a greater future than he now felt able to consider.

The old man seated himself laboriously, and reached out, groaning at the movement, to put another block of peat on the fire. With bowed heads and averted eyes, his three guests acknowledged his magnanimity.

"We thank you, Doctor Jenkins, for the reading," said the man who had named the books.

They seemed then to be waiting for something. Doctor Jenkins understood, but was loath to comply. In an ordinary moment he would have said nothing. But the words of *The Tempest*,° which he had been reading, and the religious attention of the three, made this an unusual occasion.

Moby Dick: By Herman Melville (1819–1891), a classic American novel published in 1851.

The Divine Comedy: By Dante (1265–1321), regarded as the supreme poem of the Italian Renaissance, circulated about 1300.

The Tempest: By Shakespeare, first performed about 1611–1612.

"You wish to hear the phonograph,"° he said grudgingly.   15

The two middle-aged men stared into the fire, unable to formulate and expose the enormity of their desire.

The young man, however, said anxiously, between suppressed coughs, "Oh, please," like an excited child.

The old man rose again in his difficult way, and went to the back of the cell. He returned and placed tenderly upon the packed floor, where the firelight might fall upon it, an old, portable phonograph in a black case. He smoothed the top with his hand, then opened it. The lovely green-felt-covered disk became visible.

"I have been using thorns as needles," he said. "But tonight, because we have a musician among us"—he bent his head to the young man, almost invisible in the shadow—"I will use a steel needle. There are only three left."

The two middle-aged men stared at him in speechless adoration. The one   20
with the big hands, who wanted to write, moved his lips, but the whisper was not audible.

"Oh, don't," cried the young man, as if he were hurt. "The thorns will do beautifully."

"No," the old man said. "I have become accustomed to the thorns—but they are not really good. For you, my young friend, we will have good music tonight.

"After all," he added generously, and beginning to wind the phonograph, which creaked, "they can't last forever."

"No, nor we," the man who needed to write said harshly. "The needle, by all means."

"Oh, thanks," said the young man. "Thanks," he said again, in a low, excited   25
voice, and then stifled his coughing with a bowed head.

"The records, though," said the old man when he had finished winding, "are a different matter. Already they are very worn. I do not play them more than once a week. One, once a week, that is what I allow myself.

"More than a week I cannot stand it; not to hear them," he apologized.

"No, how could you?" cried the young man. "And with them here like this."

"A man can stand anything," said the man who wanted to write, in his harsh, antagonistic voice.

"Please, the music," said the young man.   30

"Only the one," said the old man. "In the long run we will remember more that way."

He had a dozen records with luxuriant gold and red seals. Even in that light the others could see that the threads of the records were becoming worn. Slowly he read out the titles, and the tremendous, dead names of the composers and the artists and the orchestras. The three worked upon the names in their minds, carefully. It was difficult to select from such a wealth what they would at

---

phonograph: a wind-up type in use before electrically driven record players. It played records at a speed of 78 revolutions per minute, and steel needles had to be changed after each side was played. The phonograph is especially valuable to the characters in the story because there is no electricity.

once most like to remember. Finally the man who wanted to write named Gershwin's "New York."°

"Oh, no," cried the sick young man, and then could say nothing more because he had to cough. The others understood him, and the harsh man withdrew his selection and waited for the musician to choose.

The musician begged Doctor Jenkins to read the titles again, very slowly, so that he could remember the sounds. While they were read, he lay back against the wall, his eyes closed, his thin, horny hand pulling at his light beard, and listened to the voices and the orchestras and the single instruments in his mind.

When the reading was done he spoke despairingly. "I have forgotten," he   35
complained. "I cannot hear them clearly."

"There are things missing," he explained.

"I know," said Doctor Jenkins. "I thought that I knew all of Shelley° by heart. I should have brought Shelley."

"That's more soul than we can use," said the harsh man. "*Moby Dick* is better.

"By God, we can understand that," he emphasized.

The doctor nodded.   40

"Still," said the man who had admired the books, "we need the absolute if we are to keep a grasp on anything."

"Anything but these sticks and peat clods and rabbit snares," he said bitterly.

"Shelley desired an ultimate absolute," said the harsh man. "It's too much," he said. "It's no good; no earthly good."

The musician selected a Debussy° nocturne. The others considered and approved. They rose to their knees to watch the doctor prepare for the playing, so that they appeared to be actually in an attitude of worship. The peat glow showed the thinness of their bearded faces, and the deep lines in them, and revealed the condition of their garments. The other two continued to kneel as the old man carefully lowered the needle onto the spinning disk, but the musician suddenly drew back against the wall again, with his knees up, and buried his face in his hands.

At the first notes of the piano the listeners were startled. They stared at   45
each other. Even the musician lifted his head in amazement, but then quickly bowed it again, strainingly, as if he were suffering from a pain he might not be able to endure. They were all listening deeply, without movement. The wet, blue-green notes tinkled forth from the old machine, and were individual, delectable presences in the cell. The individual, delectable presences swept into a sudden tide of unbearably beautiful dissonance, and then continued fully the swelling and ebbing of that tide, the dissonant inpourings, and the resolutions, and the diminishments, and the little, quiet wavelets of interlude lapping between. Every sound was piercing and singularly sweet. In all the men except the musician, there occurred rapid

George Gershwin (1898–1937): an American composer who wrote in the idiom of jazz, not in the classical manner.
Percy Bysshe Shelley (1792–1822): English poet who wrote poems about the soul, intellectual beauty, and mutability.
Claude Debussy (1862–1918): French composer. A "nocturne" is a "night piece" of music.

sequences of tragically heightened recollection. He heard nothing but what was there. At the final, whispering disappearance, but moving quietly, so that the others would not hear him and look at him, he let his head fall back in agony, as if it were drawn there by the hair, and clenched the fingers of one hand over his teeth. He sat that way while the others were silent, and until they began to breathe again normally. His drawn-up legs were trembling violently.

Quickly Doctor Jenkins lifted the needle off, to save it, and not to spoil the recollection with scraping. When he had stopped the whirling of the sacred disk, he courteously left the phonograph open and by the fire, in sight.

The others, however, understood. The musician rose last, but then abruptly, and went quickly out at the door without saying anything. The others stopped at the door and gave their thanks in low voices. The doctor nodded magnificently.

"Come again," he invited, "in a week. We will have the 'New York.' "

When the two had gone together, out toward the rimmed road, he stood in the entrance, peering and listening. At first there was only the resonant boom of the wind overhead, and then, far over the dome of the dead, dark plain, the wolf cry lamenting. In the rifts of clouds the doctor saw four stars flying. It impressed the doctor that one of them had just been obscured by the beginning of a flying cloud at the very moment he heard what he had been listening for, a sound of suppressed coughing. It was not near by, however. He believed that down against the pale alders he could see the moving shadow.

With nervous hands he lowered the piece of canvas which served as his door,   50 and pegged it at the bottom. Then quickly and quietly, looking at the piece of canvas frequently, he slipped the records into the case, snapped the lid shut, and carried the phonograph to his couch. There, pausing often to stare at the canvas and listen, he dug earth from the wall and disclosed a piece of board. Behind this there was a deep hole in the wall, into which he put the phonograph. After a moment's consideration, he went over and reached down his bundle of books and inserted it also. Then, guardedly, he once more sealed up the hole with the board and the earth. He also changed his blankets, and the grass-stuffed sack which served as a pillow, so that he could lie facing the entrance. After carefully placing two more blocks of peat on the fire, he stood for a long time watching the stretched canvas, but it seemed to billow naturally with the first gusts of a lowering wind. At last he prayed, and got in under his blankets, and closed his smoke-smarting eyes. On the inside of the bed, next the wall, he could feel with his hand, the comfortable piece of lead pipe.

QUESTIONS

1. Clark devotes the first three paragraphs of this story completely to description, thus establishing the general setting. What kind of environment is described? How would you characterize the scene? What has obviously happened before the story opens? To what extent do these paragraphs establish the tone and atmosphere of the entire story?

2. The first three descriptive paragraphs are loaded with adjectives. In the first, for example, we find *narrow*, *black*, *still*, *cold*, *mute*, *dead*, *isolated*, *shallow*, *brittle*,

old, *frozen*, *tangled*, *quiet*, and *empty*. What do most of these adjectives have in common? How do they contribute to the establishment of setting and, in turn, mood?

3. How is "the host's" home described? What adjectives and comparisons are employed? What objects and utensils are described? What do these specific details tell us about humanity and existence in the world of the story?

4. Who is "the host"? What was his profession? What things does he seem to value most highly? What do his valued possessions tell us about him?

5. What record do the men choose to hear? How do the listeners react to it? What do the phonograph and the music represent to these men?

6. What does Dr. Jenkins do with the books, the phonograph, and records after the men leave? How does he readjust his bed? Why does he do these things? What do these actions imply?

7. Who is the protagonist in this story? Who or what is the antagonist? What are the conflicts here? Which is the central conflict? To what extent is it resolved in the story?

IRWIN SHAW (1913–1984)

Act of Faith

1946

"Present it in a pitiful light," Olson was saying, as they picked their way through the mud toward the orderly room° tent. "Three combat-scarred veterans, who fought their way from Omaha Beach to—what was the name of the town we fought our way to?"

"Konigstein," Seeger said.

"Konigstein." Olson lifted his right foot heavily out of a puddle and stared admiringly at the three pounds of mud clinging to his overshoe. "The backbone of the army. The noncommissioned officer. We deserve better of our country. Mention our decorations in passing."

"What decorations should I mention?" Seeger asked. "The marksman's medal?"

"Never quite made it," Olson said. "I had a cross-eyed scorer at the butts.°   5
Mention the Bronze Star, the Silver Star, the Croix de Guerre, with palms, the unit citation, the Congressional Medal of Honor."

"I'll mention them all." Seeger grinned. "You don't think the CO° 'll notice that we haven't won most of them, do you?"

"Gad, sir," Olson said with dignity, "do you think that one southern military gentleman will dare doubt the word of another southern military gentleman in the hour of victory?"

"I come from Ohio," Seeger said.

"Welch comes from Kansas," Olson said, coolly staring down a second lieu-

orderly room: administrative headquarters of an army unit.
butts: mound of dirt used as a backstop on a target range.
CO: abbreviation for "Commanding Officer."

tenant who was passing. The lieutenant made a nervous little jerk with his hand as though he expected a salute, then kept it rigid, as a slight superior smile of scorn twisted at the corner of Olson's mouth. The lieutenant dropped his eyes and splashed on through the mud. "You've heard of Kansas," Olson said. "Magnolia-scented Kansas."

"Of course," said Seeger. "I'm no fool."

"Do your duty by your men, Sergeant." Olson stopped to wipe the rain off his face and lectured him. "Highest ranking noncom° present took the initiative and saved his comrades, at great personal risk, above and beyond the call of you-know-what, in the best traditions of the American army."

"I will throw myself in the breach," Seeger said.

"Welch and I can't ask more," said Olson, approvingly.

They walked heavily through the mud on the streets between the rows of tents. The camp stretched drearily over the Rheims plain, with the rain beating on the sagging tents. The division had been there over three weeks by now, waiting to be shipped home, and all the meager diversions of the neighborhood had been sampled and exhausted, and there was an air of watchful suspicion and impatience with the military life hanging over the camp now, and there was even reputed to be a staff sergeant in C Company who was laying odds they would not get back to America before July Fourth.

"I'm redeployable," Olson sang. "It's so enjoyable . . ." It was a jingle he had composed to no recognizable melody in the early days after the victory in Europe, when he had added up his points and found they only came to 63. "Tokyo, wait for me . . ."

They were going to be discharged as soon as they got back to the States, but Olson persisted in singing the song, occasionally adding a mournful stanza about dengue fever° and brown girls with venereal disease. He was a short, round boy who had been flunked out of air cadets' school and transferred to the infantry, but whose spirits had not been damaged in the process. He had a high, childish voice and a pretty baby face. He was very good-natured, and had a girl waiting for him at the University of California, where he intended to finish his course at government expense when he got out of the army, and he was just the type who is killed off early and predictably and sadly in motion pictures about the war, but he had gone through four campaigns and six major battles without a scratch.

Seeger was a large lanky boy, with a big nose, who had been wounded at Saint Lô, but had come back to his outfit in the Siegfried Line,° quite unchanged. He was cheerful and dependable, and he knew his business and had broken in five or six second lieutenants who had been killed or wounded and the CO had tried to get him commissioned in the field, but the war had ended while the paperwork was being fumbled over at headquarters.

They reached the door of the orderly tent and stopped. "Be brave, Sergeant," Olson said. "Welch and I are depending on you."

"O.K." Seeger said, and went in.

The tent had the dank, army-canvas smell that had been so much a part of Seeger's life in the past three years. The company clerk was reading a July, 1945,

noncom: a noncommissioned officer (corporal and above), distinguished from a commissioned officer (second lieutenant and above).
dengue fever: a tropical disease.
Siegfried Line: a German line of fortifications.

issue of the *Buffalo Courier-Express*, which had just reached him, and Captain Taney, the company CO, was seated at a sawbuck table he used as a desk, writing a letter to his wife, his lips pursed with effort. He was a small, fussy man, with sandy hair that was falling out. While the fighting had been going on, he had been lean and tense and his small voice had been cold and full of authority. But now he had relaxed, and a little pot belly was creeping up under his belt and he kept the top button of his trousers open when he could do it without too public loss of dignity. During the war Seeger had thought of him as a natural soldier, tireless, fanatic about detail, aggressive, severely anxious to kill Germans. But in the past few months Seeger had seen him relapsing gradually and pleasantly into a small-town wholesale hardware merchant, which he had been before the war, sedentary and a little shy, and, as he had once told Seeger, worried, here in the bleak champagne fields of France, about his daughter, who had just turned twelve and had a tendency to go after the boys and had been caught by her mother kissing a fifteen-year-old neighbor in the hammock after school.

"Hello, Seeger," he said, returning the salute in a mild, offhand gesture. "What's on your mind?"

"Am I disturbing you, sir?"

"Oh, no. Just writing a letter to my wife. You married, Seeger?" He peered at the tall boy standing before him.

"No, sir."

"It's very difficult," Taney sighed, pushing dissatisfiedly at the letter before   25
him. "My wife complains I don't tell her I love her often enough. Been married fifteen years. You'd think she'd know by now." He smiled at Seeger. "I thought you were going to Paris," he said. "I signed the passes yesterday."

"That's what I came to see you about, sir."

"I suppose something's wrong with the passes." Taney spoke resignedly, like a man who has never quite got the hang of army regulations and has had requisitions, furloughs, requests for court-martial returned for correction in a baffling flood.

"No, sir," Seeger said. "The passes're fine. They start tomorrow. Well, it's just . . ." He looked around at the company clerk, who was on the sports page.

"This confidential?" Taney asked.

"If you don't mind, sir."   30

"Johnny," Taney said to the clerk, "go stand in the rain some place."

"Yes, sir," the clerk said, and slowly got up and walked out.

Taney looked shrewdly at Seeger, spoke in a secret whisper. "You pick up anything?" he asked.

Seeger grinned. "No, sir, haven't had my hands on a girl since Strasbourg."

"Ah, that's good." Taney leaned back, relieved, happy he didn't have to   35
cope with the disapproval of the Medical Corps.

"It's—well," said Seeger, embarrassed, "it's hard to say—but it's money."

Taney shook his head sadly. "I know."

"We haven't been paid for three months, sir, and . . ."

"Damn it!" Taney stood up and shouted furiously. "I would like to take every bloody chair-warming old lady in the Finance Department and wring their necks."

The clerk stuck his head into the tent. "Anything wrong? You call for me,   40
sir?"

"No," Taney shouted. "Get out of here."

The clerk ducked out.

Taney sat down again. "I suppose," he said, in a more normal voice, "they have their problems. Outfits being broken up, being moved all over the place. But it is rugged."

"It wouldn't be so bad," Seeger said. "But we're going to Paris tomorrow, Olson, Welch and myself. And you need money in Paris."

"Don't I know it." Taney wagged his head. "Do you know what I paid for a bottle of champagne on the Place Pigalle° in September . . . ?" He paused significantly. "I won't tell you. You won't have any respect for me the rest of your life."

Seeger laughed. "Hanging," he said, "is too good for the guy who thought up the rate of exchange."

"I don't care if I never see another franc as long as I live." Taney waved his letter in the air, although it had been dry for a long time.

There was silence in the tent and Seeger swallowed a little embarrassedly, watching the CO wave the flimsy sheet of paper in regular sweeping movements. "Sir," he said, "the truth is, I've come to borrow some money for Welch, Olson and myself. We'll pay it back out of the first pay we get, and that can't be too long from now. If you don't want to give it to us, just tell me and I'll understand and get the hell out of here. We don't like to ask, but you might just as well be dead as be in Paris broke."

Taney stopped waving his letter and put it down thoughtfully. He peered at it, wrinkling his brow, looking like an aged bookkeeper in the single gloomy light that hung in the middle of the tent.

"Just say the word, Captain," Seeger said, "and I'll blow . . . ."

"Stay where you are, son," said Taney. He dug in his shirt pocket and took out a worn, sweat-stained wallet. He looked at it for a moment. "Alligator," he said, with automatic, absent pride. "My wife sent it to me when we were in England. Pounds don't fit in it. However . . . ." He opened it and took out all the contents. There was a small pile of francs on the table in front of him. He counted them. "Four hundred francs," he said. "Eight bucks."

"Excuse me," Seeger said humbly. "I shouldn't have asked."

"Delighted," Taney said vigorously. "Absolutely delighted." He started dividing the francs into two piles. "Truth is, Seeger, most of my money goes home in allotments. And the truth is, I lost eleven hundred francs in a poker game three nights ago, and I ought to be ashamed of myself. Here . . . ." he shoved one pile toward Seeger. "Two hundred francs."

Seeger looked down at the frayed, meretricious paper, which always seemed to him like stage money, anyway. "No, sir," he said, "I can't take it."

"Take it," Taney said. "That's a direct order."

Seeger slowly picked up the money, not looking at Taney. "Some time, sir," he said, "after we get out, you have to come over to my house and you and my father and my brother and I'll go on a real drunk."

"I'll regard that," Taney said, gravely, "as a solemn commitment."

Place Pigalle: A notorious district in Paris. Mispronounced as "pig alley" by American soldiers, whiskey and prostitutes were plentiful there.

They smiled at each other and Seeger started out.

"Have a drink for me," said Taney, "at the Café de la Paix. A small drink."
He was sitting down to write his wife he loved her when Seeger went out of the
tent.

Olson fell into step with Seeger and they walked silently through the mud   60
between the tents.

"Well, *mon vieux*?"° Olson said finally.

"Two hundred francs," said Seeger.

Olson groaned. "Two hundred francs! We won't be able to pinch a whore's
behind on the Boulevard des Capucines° for two hundred francs. That miserable,
penny-loving Yankee!"

"He only had four hundred," Seeger said.

"I revise my opinion," said Olson.   65

They walked disconsolately and heavily back toward their tent.

Olson spoke only once before they got there. "These raincoats," he said,
patting his. "Most ingenious invention of the war. Highest saturation point of
any modern fabric. Collect more water per square inch, and hold it, than any
material known to man. All hail the quartermaster!"

Welch was waiting at the entrance of their tent. He was standing there peering
excitedly and short-sightedly out at the rain through his glasses, looking angry
and tough, like a big-city hack driver, individual and incorruptible even in the
ten-million colored uniform. Every time Seeger came upon Welch unexpectedly,
he couldn't help smiling at the belligerent stance, the harsh stare through the
steel-rimmed GI glasses, which had nothing at all to do with the way Welch really
was. "It's a family inheritance," Welch had once explained. "My whole family stands
as though we were getting ready to rap a drunk with a beer glass. Even my old
lady." Welch had six brothers, all devout, according to Welch, and Seeger from
time to time idly pictured them standing in a row, on Sunday mornings in church,
seemingly on the verge of general violence, amid the hushed Latin and Sabbath
millinery.

"How much?" Welch asked loudly.

"Don't make us laugh," Olson said, pushing past him into the tent.   70

"What do you think I could get from the French for my combat jacket?"
Seeger said. He went into the tent and lay down on his cot.

Welch followed them in and stood between the two of them, a superior
smile on his face. "Boys," he said, "on a man's errand."

"I can just see us now," Olson murmured, lying on his cot with his hands
clasped behind his head, "painting Montmartre red. Please bring on the naked
dancing girls. Four bucks worth."

"I am not worried," Welch announced.

"Get out of here." Olson turned over on his stomach.   75

"I know where we can put our hands on sixty-five bucks." Welch looked
triumphantly first at Olson, then at Seeger.

Olson turned over slowly and sat up. "I'll kill you," he said, "if you're kidding."

---

mon vieux: French for "my old"; i.e., "old boy," "old friend," "old fellow."
Boulevard des Capucines: a street where prostitutes were cheap.

"While you guys are wasting your time," Welch said, "fooling around with the infantry, I used my head. I went into Reems° and used my head."

"Rance," Olson said automatically. He had had two years of French in college and he felt, now that the war was over, that he had to introduce his friends to some of his culture.

"I got to talking to a captain in the air force," Welch said eagerly. "A little   80
fat old paddle-footed captain that never got higher off the ground than the second floor of the Com Z headquarters, and he told me that what he would admire to do more than anything else is to take home a nice shiny German Luger pistol with him to show to the boys back in Pacific Grove, California."

Silence fell on the tent and Welch and Olson looked tentatively at Seeger.

"Sixty-five bucks for a Luger, these days," Olson said, "is a very good figure."

"They've been sellin' for as low as thirty-five," said Welch hesitantly. "I'll bet," he said to Seeger, "you could sell yours now and buy another one back when you get some dough and make a clear twenty-five on the deal."

Seeger didn't say anything. He had killed the owner of the Luger, an enormous SS major, in Coblenz, behind some paper bales in a warehouse, and the major had fired at Seeger three times with it, once knicking his helmet, before Seeger hit him in the face at twenty feet. Seeger had kept the Luger, a long, heavy, well-balanced gun, very carefully since then, lugging it with him, hiding it at the bottom of his bedroll, oiling it three times a week, avoiding all opportunities of selling it, although he had been offered as much as a hundred dollars for it and several times eighty and ninety, while the war was still on, before German weapons became a glut on the market.

"Well," said Welch, "there's no hurry. I told the captain I'd see him tonight   85
around 8 o'clock in front of the Lion d'Or Hotel. You got five hours to make up your mind. Plenty of time."

"Me," said Olson, after a pause. "I won't say anything."

Seeger looked reflectively at his feet and the other two men avoided looking at him. Welch dug in his pocket. "I forgot," he said. "I picked up a letter for you." He handed it to Seeger.

"Thanks," Seeger said. He opened it absently, thinking about the Luger.

"Me," said Olson, "I won't say a bloody word. I'm just going to lie here and think about that nice fat air force captain."

Seeger grinned a little at him and went to the tent opening to read the   90
letter in the light. The letter was from his father, and even from one glance at the handwriting, scrawly and hurried and spotted, so different from his father's usual steady, handsome, professorial script, he knew that something was wrong.

"Dear Norman," it read, "sometime in the future, you must forgive me for writing this letter. But I have been holding this in so long, and there is no one here I can talk to, and because of your brother's condition I must pretend to be cheerful and optimistic all the time at home, both with him and your mother, who has never been the same since Leonard was killed. You're the oldest now, and although I know we've never talked very seriously about anything before, you have been through a great deal by now, and I imagine you must have matured considerably, and you've seen so many different places and people. . . . Norman,

---

Reems: Welch mispronounces *Reims*; Olson corrects him.

I need help. While the war was on and you were fighting, I kept this to myself. It wouldn't have been fair to burden you with this. But now the war is over, and I no longer feel I can stand up under this alone. And you will have to face it some time when you get home, if you haven't faced it already, and perhaps we can help each other by facing it together. . . ."

"I'm redeployable," Olson was singing softly, on his cot. "It's so enjoyable, In the Pelilu° mud, With the tropical crud . . ." He fell silent after his burst of song.

Seeger blinked his eyes, at the entrance of the tent, in the wan rainy light, and went on reading his father's letter, on the stiff white stationery with the University letterhead in polite engraving at the top of each page.

"I've been feeling this coming on for a long time," the letter continued, "but it wasn't until last Sunday morning that something happened to make me feel it in its full force. I don't know how much you've guessed about the reason for Jacob's discharge from the army. It's true he was pretty badly wounded in the leg at Metz, but I've asked around, and I know that men with worse wounds were returned to duty after hospitalization. Jacob got a medical discharge, but I don't think it was for the shrapnel wound in his thigh. He is suffering now from what I suppose you call combat fatigue, and he is subject to fits of depression and hallucinations. Your mother and I thought that as time went by and the war and the army receded, he would grow better. Instead, he is growing worse. Last Sunday morning when I came down into the living room from upstairs he was crouched in his old uniform, next to the window, peering out . . ."

"What the hell," Olson was saying, "if we don't get the sixty-five bucks we can always go to the Louvre. I understand the Mona Lisa is back."

"I asked Jacob what he was doing," the letter went on. "He didn't turn around. 'I'm observing,' he said. 'V-1's and V-2's. Buzz-bombs and rockets. They're coming in by the hundreds.' I tried to reason with him and he told me to crouch and save myself from flying glass. To humor him I got down on the floor beside him and tried to tell him the war was over, that we were in Ohio, 4,000 miles away from the nearest spot where bombs had fallen, that America had never been touched. He wouldn't listen. 'These're the new rocket bombs,' he said, 'for the Jews.' "

"Did you ever hear of the Pantheon?" Olson asked loudly.

"No," said Welch.

"It's free."

"I'll go," said Welch.

Seeger shook his head a little and blinked his eyes before he went back to the letter.

"After that," his father went on, "Jacob seemed to forget about the bombs from time to time, but he kept saying that the mobs were coming up the street armed with bazookas and Browning automatic rifles. He mumbled incoherently a good deal of the time and kept walking back and forth saying, 'What's the situation? Do you know what the situation is?' And he told me he wasn't worried about himself, he was a soldier and he expected to be killed, but he was worried about Mother and myself and Leonard and you. He seemed to forget that Leonard was

95

100

Pelilu: in the South Pacific.

dead. I tried to calm him and get him back to bed before your mother came down, but he refused and wanted to set out immediately to rejoin his division. It was all terribly disjointed and at one time he took the ribbon he got for winning the Bronze Star and threw it in the fireplace, then he got down on his hands and knees and picked it out of the ashes and made me pin it on him again, and he kept repeating, 'This is when they are coming for the Jews.' "

"The next war I'm in," said Olson, "they don't get me under the rank of colonel."

It had stopped raining by now and Seeger folded the unfinished letter and went outside. He walked slowly down to the end of the company street, and facing out across the empty, soaked French fields, scarred and neglected by various armies, he stopped and opened the letter again.

"I don't know what Jacob went through in the army," his father wrote, "that   105
has done this to him. He never talks to me about the war and he refuses to go to a psychoanalyst, and from time to time he is his own bouncing, cheerful self, playing in tennis tournaments, and going around with a large group of girls. But he has devoured all the concentration camp reports, and I have found him weeping when the newspapers reported that a hundred Jews were killed in Tripoli some time ago.

"The terrible thing is, Norman, that I find myself coming to believe that it is not neurotic for a Jew to behave like this today. Perhaps Jacob is the normal one, and I, going about my business, teaching economics in a quiet classroom, pretending to understand that the world is comprehensible and orderly, am really the mad one. I ask you once more to forgive me for writing you a letter like this, so different from any letter or any conversation I've ever had with you. But it is crowding me, too. I do not see rockets and bombs, but I see other things.

"Wherever you go these days—restaurants, hotels, clubs, trains—you seem to hear talk about the Jews, mean, hateful, murderous talk. Whatever page you turn to in the newspapers you seem to find an article about Jews being killed somewhere on the face of the globe. And there are large, influential newspapers and well-known columnists who each day are growing more and more outspoken and more popular. The day that Roosevelt died I heard a drunken man yelling outside a bar, 'Finally, they got the Jew out of the White House.' And some of the people who heard him merely laughed and nobody stopped him. And on V-E Day,° in celebration, hoodlums in Los Angeles savagely beat a Jewish writer. It's difficult to know what to do, whom to fight, where to look for allies.

"Three months ago, for example, I stopped my Thursday night poker game, after playing with the same men for over ten years. John Reilly happened to say that the Jews were getting rich out of this war, and when I demanded an apology, he refused, and when I looked around at the faces of the men who had been my friends for so long, I could see they were not with me. And when I left the house no one said good night to me. I know the poison was spreading from Germany before the war and during it, but I had not realized it had come so close.

"And in my economics class, I find myself idiotically hedging in my lectures. I discover that I am loath to praise any liberal writer or any liberal act and find

V-E Day: May 8, 1945, the day of Victory in Europe.

myself somehow annoyed and frightened to see an article of criticism of existing abuses signed by a Jewish name. And I hate to see Jewish names on important committees, and hate to read of Jews fighting for the poor, the oppressed, the cheated and hungry. Somehow, even in a country where my family has lived a hundred years, the enemy has won this subtle victory over me—he has made me disfranchise myself from honest causes by calling them foreign, Communist, using Jewish names connected with them as ammunition against them.

"And, most hateful of all, I find myself looking for Jewish names in the   110
casualty lists and secretly being glad when I discover them there, to prove that there at least, among the dead and wounded, we belong. Three times, thanks to you and your brothers, I have found our name there, and, may God forgive me, at the expense of your blood and your brother's life, through my tears, I have felt that same twitch of satisfaction. . . .

"When I read the newspapers and see another story that Jews are still being killed in Poland, or Jews are requesting that they be given back their homes in France, or that they be allowed to enter some country where they will not be murdered, I am annoyed with them, I feel they are boring the rest of the world with their problems, they are making demands upon the rest of the world by being killed, they are disturbing everyone by being hungry and asking for the return of their property. If we could all fall through the crust of the earth and vanish in one hour, with our heroes and poets and prophets and martyrs, perhaps we would be doing the memory of the Jewish race a service. . . .

"This is how I feel today, son. I need some help. You've been to the war, you've fought and killed men, you've seen the people of other countries. Maybe you understand things that I don't understand. Maybe you see some hope somewhere. Help me. Your loving father."

Seeger folded the letter slowly, not seeing what he was doing because the tears were burning his eyes. He walked slowly and aimlessly across the dead autumn grass of the empty field, away from the camp.

He tried to wipe away his tears, because with his eyes full and dark, he kept seeing his father and brother crouched in the old-fashioned living room in Ohio and hearing his brother, dressed in the old, discarded uniform, saying, "These're the new rocket bombs. For the Jews."

He sighed, looking out over the bleak, wasted land. Now, he thought, now   115
I have to think about it. He felt a slight, unreasonable twinge of anger at his father for presenting him with the necessity of thinking about it. The army was good about serious problems. While you were fighting, you were too busy and frightened and weary to think about anything, and at other times you were relaxing, putting your brain on a shelf, postponing everything to that impossible time of clarity and beauty after the war. Well, now, here was the impossible, clear, beautiful time, and here was his father, demanding that he think. There are all sorts of Jews, he thought, there are the sort whose every waking moment is ridden by the knowledge of Jewishness, who see signs against the Jew in every smile on a streetcar, every whisper, who see pogroms° in every newspaper article, threats in every change of the weather, scorn in every handshake, death behind each closed door. He had not been like that. He was young, he was big and healthy and easy-

---

pogrom: an organized massacre of a minority, specifically Jews.

going and people of all kinds had seemed to like him all his life, in the army and out. In America, especially, what was going on in Europe had seemed remote, unreal, unrelated to him. The chanting, bearded old men burning in the Nazi furnaces, and the dark-eyed women screaming prayers in Polish and Russian and German as they were pushed naked into the gas chambers had seemed as shadowy and almost as unrelated to him as he trotted out onto the Stadium field for a football game, as they must have been to the men named O'Dwyer and Wickersham and Poole who played in the line beside him.

They had seemed more related in Europe. Again and again in the towns that had been taken from the Germans, gaunt, gray-faced men had stopped him humbly, looking searchingly at him, and had asked, peering at his long, lined, grimy face, under the anonymous helmet, "Are you a Jew?" Sometimes they asked it in English, sometimes French, or Yiddish. He didn't know French or Yiddish, but he learned to recognize the phrase. He had never understood exactly why they had asked the question, since they never demanded anything from him, rarely even could speak to him, until, one day in Strasbourg, a little bent old man and a small, shapeless woman had stopped him, and asked, in English, if he was Jewish.

"Yes," he said, smiling at them.

The two old people had smiled widely, like children. "Look," the old man had said to his wife. "A young American soldier. A Jew. And so large and strong." He had touched Seeger's arm reverently with the tips of his fingers, then had touched the Garand° he was carrying. "And such a beautiful rifle . . ."

And there, for a moment, although he was not particularly sensitive, Seeger got an inkling of why he had been stopped and questioned by so many before. Here, to these bent, exhausted old people, ravaged of their families, familiar with flight and death for so many years, was a symbol of continuing life. A large young man in the uniform of the liberator, blood, as they thought, of their blood, but not in hiding, not quivering in fear and helplessness, but striding secure and victorious down the street, armed and capable of inflicting terrible destruction on his enemies.

Seeger had kissed the old lady on the cheek and she had wept and the old man had scolded her for it, while shaking Seeger's hand fervently and thankfully before saying good-bye.

And, thinking back on it, it was silly to pretend that, even before his father's letter, he had been like any other American soldier going through the war. When he had stood over the huge dead SS major with the face blown in by his bullets in the warehouse in Coblenz, and taken the pistol from the dead hand, he had tasted a strange little extra flavor of triumph. How many Jews, he'd thought, has this man killed, how fitting it is that I've killed him. Neither Olson nor Welch, who were like his brothers, would have felt that in picking up the Luger, its barrel still hot from the last shots its owner had fired before dying. And he had resolved that he was going to make sure to take this gun back with him to America, and plug it and keep it on his desk at home, as a kind of vague, half-understood sign to himself that justice had once been done and he had been its instrument.

Maybe, he thought, maybe I'd better take it back with me, but not as a memento. Not plugged, but loaded. America by now was a strange country for him.

Garand: an American standard infantry rifle.

He had been away a long time and he wasn't sure what was waiting for him when he got home. If the mobs were coming down the street toward his house, he was not going to die singing and praying.

When he was taking basic training he'd heard a scrawny, clerklike-looking soldier from Boston talking at the other end of the PX° bar, over the watered beer. "The boys at the office," the scratchy voice was saying, "gave me a party before I left. And they told me one thing. 'Charlie,' they said, 'hold onto your bayonet. We're going to be able to use it when you get back. On the Yids.' "°

He hadn't said anything then, because he'd felt it was neither possible nor desirable to fight against every random overheard voice raised against the Jews from one end of the world to another. But again and again, at odd moments, lying on a barracks cot, or stretched out trying to sleep on the floor of a ruined French farmhouse, he had heard that voice, harsh, satisfied, heavy with hate and ignorance, saying above the beery grumble of apprentice soldiers at the bar, "Hold onto your bayonet. . . ."

And the other stories—Jews collected stories of hatred and injustice and inklings of doom like a special, lunatic kind of miser. The story of the naval officer, commander of a small vessel off the Aleutians, who, in the officers' wardroom, had complained that he hated the Jews because it was the Jews who had demanded that the Germans be beaten first and the forces in the Pacific had been starved in consequence. And when one of his junior officers, who had just come aboard, had objected and told the commander that he was a Jew, the commander had risen from the table and said, "Mister, the Constitution of the United States says I have to serve in the same navy with Jews, but it doesn't say I have to eat at the same table with them." In the fogs and the cold, swelling Arctic seas off the Aleutians, in a small boat, subject to sudden, mortal attack at any moment . . . 125

And the two young combat engineers in an attached company on D Day,° when they were lying off the coast right before climbing down into the landing barges. "There's France," one of them had said.

"What's it like?" the second one had asked, peering out across the miles of water toward the smoking coast.

"Like every place else," the first one had answered. "The Jews've made all the dough during the war."

"Shut up!" Seeger had said, helplessly thinking of the dead, destroyed, wandering, starving Jews of France. The engineers had shut up, and they'd climbed down together into the heaving boat, and gone into the beach together.

And the million other stories. Jews, even the most normal and best adjusted of them, became living treasuries of them, scraps of malice and bloodthirstiness, clever and confusing and cunningly twisted so that every act by every Jew became suspect and blameworthy and hateful. Seeger had heard the stories, and had made an almost conscious effort to forget them. Now, holding his father's letter in his hand, he remembered them all. 130

He stared unseeingly out in front of him. Maybe, he thought, maybe it would've been better to have been killed in the war, like Leonard. Simpler. Leonard

PX: Post Exchange, where military persons may buy at cost.
Yids: Jews.
D Day: June 6, 1944, the day on which the allied forces invaded France from the sea.

would never have to face a crowd coming for his mother and father. Leonard would not have to listen and collect these hideous, fascinating little stories that made of every Jew a stranger in any town, on any field, on the face of the earth. He had come so close to being killed so many times, it would have been so easy, so neat and final.

Seeger shook his head. It was ridiculous to feel like that, and he was ashamed of himself for the weak moment. At the age of twenty-one, death was not an answer.

"Seeger!" It was Olson's voice. He and Welch had sloshed silently up behind Seeger, standing in the open field. "Seeger, *mon vieux*, what're you doing—grazing?"

Seeger turned slowly to them. "I wanted to read my letter," he said.

Olson looked closely at him. They had been together so long, through so many things, that flickers and hints of expression on each other's faces were recognized and acted upon. "Anything wrong?" Olson asked.

"No," said Seeger. "Nothing much."

"Norman," Welch said, his voice young and solemn. "Norman, we've been talking. Olson and me. We decided—you're pretty attached to that Luger, and maybe—if you— well . . ."

"What he's trying to say," said Olson, "is we withdraw the request. If you want to sell it, O.K. If you don't, don't do it for our sake. Honest."

Seeger looked at them, standing there, disreputable and tough and familiar. "I haven't made up my mind yet," he said.

"Anything you decide," Welch said oratorically, "is perfectly all right with us. Perfectly."

They walked aimlessly and silently across the field, away from camp. As they walked, their shoes making a wet, sliding sound in the damp, dead grass, Seeger thought of the time Olson had covered him in the little town outside Cherbourg, when Seeger had been caught going down the side of a street by four Germans with a machine gun on the second story of a house on the corner and Olson had had to stand out in the middle of the street with no cover at all for more than a minute, firing continuously, so that Seeger could get away alive. And he thought of the time outside Saint Lô when he had been wounded and had lain in a mine field for three hours and Welch and Captain Taney had come looking for him in the darkness and found him and picked him up and run for it, all of them expecting to get blown up any second.

And he thought of all the drinks they'd had together and the long marches and the cold winter together, and all the girls they'd gone out with together, and he thought of his father and brother crouching behind the window in Ohio waiting for the rockets and the crowds armed with Browning automatic rifles.

"Say," he stopped and stood facing them. "Say, what do you guys think of the Jews?"

Welch and Olson looked at each other, and Olson glanced down at the letter in Seeger's hand.

"Jews?" Olson said finally. "What're they? Welch, you ever hear of the Jews?"

Welch looked thoughtfully at the gray sky. "No," he said. "But remember, I'm an uneducated fellow."

"Sorry, Bud," Olson said, turning to Seeger. "We can't help you. Ask us another question. Maybe we'll do better."

Seeger peered at the faces of his friends. He would have to rely upon them, later on, out of uniform, on their native streets, more than he had ever relied on them on the bullet-swept street and in the dark mine field in France. Welch and Olson stared back at him, troubled, their faces candid and tough and dependable.

"What time," Seeger asked, "did you tell that captain you'd meet him?"

"Eight o'clock," Welch said. "But we don't have to go. If you have any feeling about that gun . . ." 150

"We'll meet him," Seeger said. "We can use that sixty-five bucks."

"Listen," Olson said, "I know how much you like that gun and I'll feel like a heel if you sell it."

"Forget it," Seeger said, starting to walk again. "What could I use it for in America?"

QUESTIONS

1. Why is it important to the story to include at the beginning the details about the states from which the various characters come? Even though the immediate setting is just after World War II, can a case be made that the setting is the entire United States?

2. How many separate scenes are introduced as places for action in the story? What function and importance might these have as bases of organization?

3. Why is the mud of the streets mentioned early in the story, and why is the wet grass mentioned at the end? Can you perceive any contrast between this drab setting and the ideas in the minds of the soldiers about the streets of Paris?

4. Describe the significance of the German Luger in the story. How is it a source of possible conflict among the soldiers? In what way is it the cause of the story's resolution?

5. What is the immediate central conflict in the story? How does the larger fear that Seeger has about the future figure into this conflict? How is the immediate conflict resolved?

6. Describe the point of view of the story. How does it begin? At what point does it shift to become limited to Seeger? What issue becomes prominent with this shift?

7. What stories does Seeger recall about prejudice toward Jews? What does he recall about his associations with Welch, Taney, and Olson? What is his act of faith? Does his question at the end, "What could I use it [the Luger] for in America?" seem to be an accurate assessment on which to base his decision?

8. In what ways do Welch, Taney, and Olson all make acts of faith?

WRITING ABOUT SETTING

In preparing to write about setting, you should take notes directed toward the locations and artifacts that figure prominently in the story. Generally you should determine if there is one location of action or more. Raise questions about how much detail is included: Are things described visually so that you can make a sketch or draw a plan (such a sketch might help you organize your essay), or are the locations left vague? Why? What influence do the locations have upon the characters in the story, if any? Do the locations bring characters together, push them apart, make it easy for them to be private, make intimacy and conversation difficult? What artifacts are important in the action, and how important are they? Are they well described? Are they vital to the action? Are things like shapes, colors, times of day, locations of the sun, conditions of light, seasons of the year, and conditions of vegetation described? Do characters respect or mistreat the environment around them?

With answers to questions like these, you can then formulate ideas for your essay. Remember to work toward a central idea so you avoid writing no more than a description of scenes and objects (such an essay would be analogous to doing no more than retelling the story). Emphasize the connection between setting and whatever aspect or aspects you choose about the story. A possible central idea might thus be, "The palatial setting not only is gaudily shown, but is also a force preventing the revelers from escaping their fate," or "The drab, cold, bleak setting underscores the elemental, barbaric conditions of life in this destroyed world." Emphasis on such central ideas would force you to use description only as illustration and evidence and not as an end in itself.

Organizing Your Essay

INTRODUCTION.   The introduction should give a brief description of the setting or scenes of the story, with a characterization of the degree of detail presented by the author (that is, a little, a lot; visual, aural; colorful, monochromatic, and so on). The central idea explains the relationship to be explored in the essay, and the thesis sentence determines the major topics in which the central idea will be traced.

BODY.   Following are five possible approaches to essays about setting. Which one you choose is your decision, but you may find that some works almost invite you to pick one approach over the others. Although each approach outlines a major emphasis in your essay, you may wish to bring in details from one of the others if they seem important at any point.

1. *Setting and action.*   Here you explore the use of setting in the various actions of the work. Among the questions to be answered are these: How detailed and extensive are the descriptions of the setting? Are the scenes related to the action? (Are they essential or incidental?) Does the setting serve as part of the action (places of flight or concealment; public places where people meet openly or out-of-the-way places where they meet

privately; natural or environmental obstacles; sociological obstacles; seasonal conditions such as searing heat or numbing cold, and so on)? Do details of setting get used regularly, or are they mentioned only when they become necessary to an action? Do any physical objects figure into the story as causes of aspiration or conflict (for example, a diamond necklace, a boat, a phonograph, a pistol, a bag of groceries, a sail, a dog, a blanket)?

2. *Setting and organization.* A closely related way of writing about setting is to connect it to the organization of the work. Some questions to help you get started with this approach are these: Is the setting a frame, an enclosure? Is it mentioned at various parts, or at shifts in the action? Does the setting undergo any expected or unexpected changes as the action changes? Do any parts of the setting have greater involvement in the action than other parts? Do any objects, such as money or property, figure into the developing or changing motivation of the characters? Do descriptions made at the start become important in the action later on? If so, in what order?

3. *Setting and character.* Your aim here is to pick those details that seem to have a bearing on character and to write about their effects. The major question is the degree to which the setting seems to interact with or influence character. You might get at this topic through additional questions: Are the characters happy or unhappy where they live? Do they express their feelings, or get into discussions or arguments about them? Do they seem adjusted? Do they want to stay or leave? Does the economic, cultural, or ethnic level of the setting make the characters think in any unique ways? What jobs do the characters perform because of their ways of life? What freedoms or restraints do these jobs cause? How does the setting influence their decisions, transportation, speech habits, eating habits, attitudes about love and honor, and general folkways?

4. *Setting and atmosphere.* Here you should write about those aspects of setting that seem designed to evoke a mood. Some questions are: Does the detail of setting go beyond the minimum needed for action or character? Do clear details help make clear the conflicts in the story, or do vague and amorphous details help to make these conflicts problematic? Are descriptive words used mainly to paint verbal pictures, to evoke a mood through references to colors, shapes, sounds, smells, or tastes? Does the setting establish a mood, say, of joy or hopelessness, lushness or spareness? Do things happen in daylight or night? Are the movements of the characters permanent, or do the locations emphasize impermanence (like footsteps in the sand, or movement through water)? If temperatures are mentioned, are things warm and pleasant, or cold and harsh? Does the mood established seem to suggest that life, too, is this way?

5. *Other aspects.* In an earlier section of this chapter, "Setting and Statement" and "Setting and Irony" were listed as important uses of setting.

Not all stories lend themselves to either treatment, but for stories that do, you could create an interesting essay. If the author has used setting as a means of underscoring the circumstances and ideas of the story, you might use the section on statement as a guide for the body of your essay. If you perceive a contrast between setting and content, that too could be the basis of an essay such as those described in the paragraph on "Setting and Irony."

CONCLUSION.   You always have the option of summarizing your major points as your conclusion, but you might also want to write about anything you neglected in the body of your essay. Thus, you might have been treating the relationship of the setting to the action and may wish to mention something about any ties the setting has with character or atmosphere. You might also wish to point out whether your central idea about the setting also applies to other major aspects of the work.

SAMPLE ESSAY

De Maupassant's Use of Setting in "The Necklace"* to Show the Character of Mathilde

[1]   In "The Necklace" De Maupassant does not give much detail about the setting. He does not describe even the necklace, which is the central object in the plot, but he says only that it is "superb." Rather he uses setting to reflect the character of the major figure, Mathilde Loisel.° He gives no more detail than is needed to explain her feelings. This carefully directed setting may be considered as the first apartment, the dream-life mansion rooms, and the attic flat.°

[2]   Details about the first walkup apartment on the Street of Martyrs are presented to explain Mathilde's unhappiness. The walls are "drab," the furniture "threadbare," and the curtains "ugly." There is only a country girl to do housework. The tablecloth is not cleaned, and the best dinner dish is beef stew boiled in a kettle. Mathilde has no pretty dresses, but only a theater dress which she does not like. These details show her dissatisfaction about life with her low-salaried husband.

[3]   The dream-life, mansionlike setting is like the apartment, because it too makes her unhappy. In Mathilde's daydreams, the rooms are large, filled with expensive furniture and bric-a-brac, and draped in silk. She imagines private rooms for intimate talks, and big dinners with delicacies like trout and quail. With dreams of such a rich home, she feels even more despair about her modest apartment.

* See p. 90 for this story.
° Central idea.
° Thesis sentence.

[4]   Finally, the attic flat indicates the coarsening of her character. There is little detail about this flat except that it is cheap and that Mathilde must carry water up many stairs to reach it. De Maupassant emphasizes the drudgery that she must bear to keep up the flat, such as washing the floor using large pails of water. He indicates her loss of refinement by writing that she gives up caring for her hair and hands, wears cheap dresses, speaks loudly, and swears. In this setting, she no longer has her dreams of the mansionlike rooms. Thus the flat in the attic goes along with the loss of her youth and beauty.

[5]   In summary, De Maupassant focuses everything, including the setting, on Mathilde. Anything extra is not needed, and he does not include it. Thus he says little about the big party scene, but emphasizes the necessary detail that Mathilde was a great "success." In "The Necklace," De Maupassant uses setting as a means to his end—the story of Mathilde and her needless misfortune.

Commentary on the Essay

This essay illustrates the approach of relating setting to character. The introduction makes the point that De Maupassant uses only as much detail as he needs, and no more. There is nothing to excess. The central idea is that the details of setting may be directly related to Mathilde's character and feelings. The thesis sentence does not indicate a plan to deal with all the aspects of setting in the story, but only two real ones and one imaginary one.

Paragraphs 2 and 3 show how Mathilde's real-life apartment and dream-life mansion fill her with despair about her life. The fourth paragraph relates her flat in the attic in a cheaper neighborhood to the dulling and coarsening of her character. The idea here is that while better surroundings at the start fill her with despair, the ugly attic flat does not seem to affect her at all. At least, De Maupassant says nothing about her unhappiness with the poorer conditions.

The conclusion makes the assertion that, in the light of the general concentration in the story on the character of Mathilde, the setting is typical of De Maupassant's technique in "The Necklace."

7

Style: The Words That Tell the Story

The word **style,** derived from the Latin word *stilus* (a writing instrument), is understood to mean the way in which writers assemble words to tell the story, develop the argument, dramatize the play, or compose the poem. Often the definition is extended to distinguish style from content. It is probably wiser, however, not to make this separation but to consider style as the placement of words in the *service* of content. The way a thing is said, in other words, cannot be separated from the thing itself.

Style is also highly individualistic. It is a matter of the way in which specific authors put words together under specific conditions in specific works. It is therefore possible to speak of the style of Ernest Hemingway, for example, and of Samuel Clemens, even though both writers at any time are adapting their words to the situations imagined in their works. Thus authors may actually have a separate style for narrative and descriptive passages, and their style in dialogue is likely different from either of these. Indeed, it would be a mark of an inferior style if a writer were to use the same manner for all the varying purposes that must exist in a story. It must therefore be emphasized that style is to be judged on the degree of its adaptability. The better the writer, the more that writer's words will fit the precise situation called for in the story. Jonathan Swift defined style as the right words in the right places. We may add to this definition that style is also the right words at the right time and in the right circumstances.

DICTION: CHOICE OF WORDS

The study of style begins with words, and **diction** refers to a writer's selection of specific words. The selection should be accurate and explicit, so that all actions and ideas are clear. It is perhaps difficult to judge accuracy and completeness, inasmuch as often we do not have any basis of comparison. Nevertheless, if a passage comes across as effective, if it conveys an idea well or gets at the essence of an action vividly and powerfully, we may confidently say that the words have been the right ones. In a passage describing action, for example, there should be active verbs, whereas in a description of a place there should be nouns and adjectives that provide locations, relationships, colors, and shapes. An explanatory or reflective passage should probably include a number of words that convey thoughts, states of mind and emotion, and various conditions of human relationships.

Formal, Neutral, and Informal Diction

Words fall naturally into three basic groups, or classes, that may be called **formal** or *high*, **neutral** or *middle*, and **informal** or *low*. Formal or high diction consists of standard and often elegant words (frequently polysyllabic), the retention of correct word order, and the absence of contractions. The sentence "It is I," for example, is formal. The following sentences from Poe's "The Masque of the Red Death" use formal language:

> They resolved to leave means neither of ingress nor egress to the sudden impulses of despair or of frenzy from within. The abbey was amply provisioned. With such precautions the courtiers might bid defiance to contagion.

Note here words like *ingress*, *egress*, *provisioned*, *bid defiance*, and *contagion*. These words are not in ordinary, everyday vocabulary and have what we may call elegance. Though they are used accurately and aptly, and though the sentences are brief and simple, the diction is high.

Neutral or middle diction is ordinary, everyday but still standard vocabulary, with a shunning of longer words but with the use of contractions when necessary. The sentence "It's me," for example, is neutral, the sort of thing many people say in preference to "It is I" when identifying themselves on the telephone. The following passage from Alice Munro's "The Found Boat" illustrates middle, neutral diction:

> What surprised them in the second place was that when the boys did actually see what boat was meant, this old flood-smashed wreck held up in the branches, they did not understand that they had been fooled, that a joke had been played on them. They did not show a moment's disappointment, but seemed as pleased at the discovery as if the boat had been whole and new. They were already barefoot, because they had been wading in the water to get lumber, and they waded in here without a stop, surrounding the boat and appraising it and paying no attention even of an insulting kind to Eva and Carol who bobbed up and down on their log. Eva and Carol had to call to them.

In this passage the words are ordinary and easy. Even the longer words, like *surprised*, *disappointment*, *surrounding*, *appraising*, and *insulting*, are not beyond the level of conversation, although *appraising* and *surrounding* would not be out of place in a more formal passage. Essentially, however, the words do not draw attention to themselves but are centered on the topic. In a way, such words in the neutral style are designed to be like clear windows, while words of the high style are more like stained glass.

Informal or low diction may range from colloquial—the language used by people in relaxed, common activities—to the level of substandard or slang expressions. A person speaking to a very close friend is likely to use diction and idiom that would not be appropriate in public and formal situations, and even in some social situations. Low language is thus appropriate for dialogue in stories, depending on the characters speaking, and for stories told in the first-person point of view as though the speaker is talking directly to a group of sympathetic and relaxed close friends. For example, Sammy's opening sentence in John Updike's "A & P" illustrates the informal, low style:

> In walks these three girls in nothing but bathing suits.

Note the idiomatic "In walks," a singular verb, followed by a plural subject. Note also the use of "these" girls, an idiom used indefinitely to refer to specific people. In Grace Paley's story "Good Bye, and Good Luck" the diction is informal; the uniqueness is caused by the omission of certain key words and the unusual positioning of phrases, as in this passage:

> Nowadays you could find me any time in a hotel, uptown or downtown. Who needs an apartment to live like a maid with a dustrag in the hand, sneezing?

Note here the misuse of *could* for *can*, the omission of *at* which more formally would begin the phrase *any time*. The second sentence is almost impossible to analyze except to note that it has been arranged with masterly skill to duplicate exactly the idiomatic speech of the Jewish woman who is the speaker.

Specific–General and Concrete–Abstract Language

Specific refers to a real thing or things that may be readily perceived or imagined; "my pet dog" is specific. **General** statements refer to broad classes of persons or things. "Dogs make good pets" is a generalization. **Concrete** refers to words that describe qualities or conditions; in the phrase "a cold day" the word *cold* is concrete. You cannot see cold, but you know the exact difference between cold and hot, and therefore you understand the word readily in reference to the external temperature. **Abstract** refers to qualities that are more removed from the concrete, and abstract words can therefore refer to many classes of separate things. On a continuum of qualities, ice cream may be noted as being cold, sweet, and creamy.

If we go on to say that it is *good*, however, this word is so widely applicable that it is abstract and therefore difficult to apply. Anything may be good, including other food, scenes, actions, words, and ideas. If we say that something is *good*, we indicate approval but not much else.

Usually, good narrative and descriptive writing feature specific and concrete words in preference to those that are general and abstract. If a narrative passage contains much general and abstract diction, it is difficult to understand because it is not easy to apply the words to any imaginable reality. Let us look at two examples of prose, the first from Hemingway's novel *A Farewell to Arms*, the second from Theodore Dreiser's *The Titan*:

> In the late summer of that year we lived in a house in a village that looked across the river and the plain to the mountains. In the bed of the river there were pebbles and boulders, dry and white in the sun, and the water was clear and swiftly moving and blue in the channels. Troops went by the house and down the road and the dust they raised powdered the leaves of the trees. The trunks of the trees too were dusty and the leaves fell early that year and we saw the troops marching along the road and the dust rising and leaves, stirred by the breeze, falling and the soldiers marching and afterward the road bare and white except for the leaves.

> From New York, Vermont, New Hampshire, Maine had come a strange company, earnest, patient, determined, unschooled in even the primer of refinement, hungry for something the significance of which, when they had it, they could not even guess, anxious to be called great, determined so to be without ever knowing how.

Hemingway's diction is specific; that is, many of the words, such as *house*, *river*, *plain*, *mountains*, *dust*, *leaves*, and *trees*, describe something that can be seen or felt. In describing aspects of the scene, Hemingway uses concrete words, like *dry*, *clear*, *swiftly moving*, *dusty*, *stirred*, *falling*, *marching*, and *bare*. These words indicate clearly perceivable actions or states. Dreiser's words are in marked contrast. The names of states are specific, but *company* is a general word for a group of any sort, unlike Hemingway's *troops*. Dreiser's key descriptive words are *strange*, *earnest*, *patient*, *determined*, *hungry*, and *anxious*. Because none of these words describes anything that can be perceived, unlike *dry* and *dusty*, they are called *abstract*. Obviously the two passages are on different topics, and both are successful in their ways, but Hemingway's diction indicates an attempt to present a specific, concrete perception of things while Dreiser's indicates an attempt at psychological penetration.

Denotation and Connotation

Another way of getting at style is to be alert for the author's management of *denotation* and *connotation*. **Denotation** refers to what a word means, and **connotation** to what the word suggests. It is one thing to call a person skinny, for example, another to use the word thin, and still something else to say svelte or shapely. Similarly, both cat and kitten are accurate words denotatively, but kitten connotes more playfulness and cuteness than one might associate with a cat. If a person in a social situation behaves in ways that are described as friendly, warm, polite, or correct, these words all suggest slight differences in behavior, not because the words are not approximately synonymous, but because the words have different connotations.

It is through the careful choice of words not only for denotation but also for connotation that authors create unique effects even though they might be describing similar or even identical situations. Let us look, for example, at the concluding paragraph of Joseph Conrad's novel Nostromo (1904). The hero of the novel, Nostromo, has just died, and the woman who loves him has cried out in grief:

> In that true cry of love and grief that seemed to ring aloud from Punta Mala to Azuera and away to the bright line of the horizon, overhung by a big white cloud shining like a mass of solid silver, the genius of the magnificent capataz de cargadores dominated the dark gulf containing his conquests of treasure and love.

This circumstance is not uncommon, for people die every day, and their loved ones grieve for them. But through connotative words like bright line, shining, solid silver, genius, magnificent, and dominated, Conrad suggests that Nostromo was more than ordinary, a person of great worth and power, a virtual demigod.

In contrast, here is the concluding paragraph of Hemingway's A Farewell to Arms:

> But after I had got them out and shut the door and turned off the light it wasn't any good. It was like saying good-by to a statue. After a while I went out and left the hospital and walked back to the hotel in the rain.

Hemingway's situation is similar to Conrad's. The heroine, Catherine Barclay, has died, and the hero, Frederick Henry, expresses his grief. He had loved her deeply, but their dreams for a happy future have been destroyed. Hemingway is interested in emphasizing the finality of the moment and he does so through phrases like shut the door, turned off the light, went out, and walked back. These expressions are all so common that you might at first be surprised to find them at so emotional a point in the book. But these flat, bare words serve a purpose; they suggest that death is as much a part of life as shutting a door and turning off a light. Both passages show clearly the ways in which control over connotation may create different effects.

RHETORIC

Broadly, **rhetoric** refers to the art of persuasive writing and, even more broadly, to the general art of writing. Any passage can be studied for its rhetorical qualities. For this reason it is necessary to develop both the methods and the descriptive vocabulary with which to carry out an analysis. Some things that may easily be done involve counting various elements in a passage and analyzing the types of sentences the author uses.

Counting

Doing a count of the number of words in a sentence; or the number of verbs, adjectives, prepositions, and adverbs; or the number of syllables in relation to the total number of words can often lead to valuable conclusions about style, especially if the count is related to other aspects of the passage. The virtue of counting is that it is easy to do and therefore it provides a "quick opening" into at least one aspect of style. Always remember that conclusions based on a count will provide *tendencies* of a particular author rather than absolutes. For illustration, let us say that Author *A* uses words mainly of 1 or 2 syllables, while Author *B* includes many words of 3, 4, and 5 syllables. Going further, let us say that *A* uses an average of 12 words per sentence while *B* uses 35. It would be fair to conclude that Author *A* is brief while Author *B* is more expansive. This is not to say that Author *A*'s passage would be easier or superior, however, for a long string of short sentences with short words might become choppy and tiresome and might cause your mind to wander.

Sentence Types

You can often learn much about a passage by determining the sorts of sentences it contains. Though you have probably learned the basic sentence types at one time or another, let's review them here:

1. **Simple sentences** contain one subject and one verb, together with modifiers and complements. They are often short and are most appropriate for actions and declarations. Often they are idiomatic, particularly in dialogue.
2. **Compound sentences** contain two simple sentences joined by a conjunction (*and, but, for, or, nor*, and so on) and a comma, or by a semicolon without a conjunction. Frequently, compound sentences are strung together as a series of three or four or more simple sentences.
3. **Complex sentences** contain a main clause and a subordinate clause. Because of the subordinate clause, the complex sentence is often suitable for describing cause-and-effect relationships in narrative, and also for analysis and reflection.

4. **Compound-complex sentences** contain two main clauses and a dependent clause. In practice, many authors produce sentences that may contain a number of subordinate clauses together with many more than two main clauses. Usually the more clauses, the more difficult the sentence.

Loose and Periodic Sentences

A major way to describe sentences in terms of the development of their content is to use the terms *loose* and *periodic*. A **loose sentence** unfolds easily, with no surprises. Because it is fairly predictable, it is the most commonly used sentence in stories. Here is an example:

> In America, the idea of equality was first applied only to white males.

Periodic sentences are arranged as much as possible in an order of climax, with the concluding information or thought being withheld to make the sentence especially interesting or surprising. Usually the periodic sentence begins with a dependent clause so that the content may be built up to the final detail, as in this sentence:

> Although in America the idea of equality was first applied only to males of European ancestry, in this century, despite the reluctance and even the opposition of many men who have regarded equality as a mark of their own status and not as a right for everyone, it has been extended to women and to persons of all races.

In narrative prose, sentences of this type are usually carefully placed in spots of crucial importance. Often the sentence alone might be said to contain the crisis and resolution at the same moment, as in this sentence from Edgar Allan Poe's "The Fall of the House of Usher":

> For a moment she remained trembling and reeling to and fro upon the threshold, then, with a low moaning cry, fell heavily inward upon the person of her brother, and in her violent and now final death-agonies, bore him to the floor a corpse, and a victim to the terrors he had anticipated.

Parallelism

To create interest, authors often rely on the rhetorical device called **parallelism,** which is common and easily recognized. Parallelism is the repetition of the same grammatical form (nouns, verbs, phrases, clauses) to balance expressions, conserve words, and build up to climaxes. Here, for example, is another sentence from Poe, which occurs in the story "The Black Cat":

I grew, day by day, more moody, more irritable, more regardless of the feelings of others.

Arrangements like this are called *parallel* because they may actually be laid out graphically, according to parts of speech, in parallel lines, as in the following (with the phrase "day by day" left out):

more moody

I grew more irritable

more regardless of the feelings of others

Poe's sentence achieves an order of increasing severity of psychological depression developing from the personal to the social. Such an ascending order marks a deliberate attempt at climax, unlike the parallelism in the following sentence from the concluding paragraph of Clark's "The Portable Phonograph":

```
            1                2                                     1
Then quickly and quietly, looking at the piece of canvas frequently, he slipped
                      2                        3
the records into the case, snapped the lid shut, and carried the phonograph
to his couch.
```

Here there are two parallel adverbs at the beginning, both ending in -*ly*, and three past tense verbs ending in -*ed*, all of which have direct objects. The order here is time; in a short sentence, Clark conveys a great deal of information.

The same parallel arrangements may be seen also in individual sentences within a paragraph or longer unit. In the following passage from Alice Munro's "The Found Boat," for example, there are a number of sentences of identical structure which sum up the exhilaration of young people dashing naked to swim in a river. Parallel sentences begin "They felt," "They felt," "They thought," "They went running," and finally "They dipped and floated and separated":

Nobody said a word this time, they all bent and stripped themselves. Eva, naked first, started running across the field, and then all the others ran, all five of them running bare through the knee-high hot grass, running towards the river. Not caring now about being caught but in fact leaping and yelling to call attention to themselves, if there was anybody to hear or see. They felt as if they were going to jump off a cliff and fly. They felt that something was happening to them different from anything that had happened before, and it had to do with the boat, the water, the sunlight, the dark ruined station, and each other. They thought of each other now hardly as names or people, but as echoing shrieks, reflections, all bold and white and loud and scandalous, and as fast as arrows. They went running without a break into the cold water and when it came almost to the tops of their legs they fell on it and swam. It stopped their noise. Silence, amazement, came over them in a rush. They dipped and floated and separated, sleek as mink.

CUMULATIO OR ACCUMULATION.   The paragraph from "The Found Boat" also illustrates another rhetorical device much used by writers, namely **cumulatio** or **accumulation.** While parallelism refers to grammatical constructions, cumulatio refers to the building up of details, such as the materials in the "they" sentences in Munro's paragraph.[1] The device is therefore a brief way of introducing much information, for once the parallel rhythm of the buildup begins, readers will readily accept new material directly into the pattern. The device thus acts as a series of quick glimpses, or vignettes, and vividness is established through the parallel repetition.

CHIASMUS OR ANTIMETABOLE.   Also fitting into the pattern of parallelism is a favorite device called **chiasmus** or **antimetabole.** This pattern is designed to create vividness through memorable repetition. The pattern is *A B B A*, which can be arranged graphically at the ends of an X (which is the same as the Greek letter *chi*):

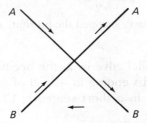

Samuel Clemens, in the story "Luck," creates a sentence that shows the pattern:

    A   *B*   *B*   *A*

I drilled him and crammed him, and crammed him and drilled him.

You may not always encounter such easily observed patterns, but you should always be alert to positions and arrangements that you think are particularly noticeable or effective. Even though you may not be able to use a technically correct name, your analysis should go well as long as you focus your attention on important aspects of effective writing in the stories that you read.

STYLE IN GENERAL

If the work is successful, you probably will not think of the style as you read, for clear expressions and easy reading are marks of a writer's success. On consideration, however, you can begin to understand the author's

---

[1] For another example of cumulatio, by Jonathan Swift, see p. 273.

achievement through a study of style. The action described in a particular passage, the relationship of the passage to the entire work, the level of the diction, the vividness of the descriptions—all these can enter into an assessment of the passage.

In the paragraph quoted above from Munro's "The Found Boat," for example, great stylistic mastery can be perceived beyond the parallelism that we noted. The passage could readily be considered the climax of the story, which is, among other things, about emerging sexuality. In an almost ritualistic way, the paragraph describes young people running impetuously toward a river and diving in—an action that may be construed as having symbolic sexual overtones. Note that after the first two sentences describing action, Munro's narrator shifts the focus with four sentences of omniscient analysis describing the feelings of the young people. If her intention had been to create searching psychological scrutiny here, she might have selected words from the language of psychology (*libido*, *urge*, *sublimation*, and so on). Instead, Munro uses words that could genuinely have been in the vocabularies of the characters. Hence the young people feel "as if they were going to jump off a cliff and fly" and feel "that something was happening to them different from anything that had happened before." With these neutral words, the passage focuses on the excitement of the situation rather than upon any hidden psychological significance. In light of all these considerations, the style of the paragraph seems just right. Munro describes the actions adequately but not extensively, she objectivizes the feelings of the characters, and she avoids the sort of psychological analysis that here would interrupt rather than instruct.

Observations of this kind may not occur on first reading, but on reflection you will find that the style of just about any passage will yield relatively full material for study. As long as the focus is on the content and also on the relationship of words to content, fruitful analysis of style will result.

SAMUEL LANGHORNE CLEMENS (1835–1910) [MARK TWAIN]

Luck[1]   *1891*

It was at a banquet in London in honor of one of the two or three conspicuously illustrious English military names of this generation. For reasons which will presently appear, I will withhold his real name and titles and call him Lieutenant-General Lord Arthur Scoresby, Y.C., K.C.B., etc., etc., etc. What a fascination there is in a renowned name! There sat the man, in actual flesh, whom I had heard of so many thousands of times since that day, thirty years before, when his name shot

---

[1] This is not a fancy sketch. I got it from a clergyman who was an instructor at Woolwich forty years ago, and who vouched for its truth. [Clemens' note.]

suddenly to the zenith from a Crimean battlefield, to remain forever celebrated. It was food and drink to me to look, and look, and look at that demi-god; scanning, searching, noting: the quietness, the reserve, the noble gravity of his countenance; the simple honesty that expressed itself all over him; the sweet unconsciousness of his greatness—unconsciousness of the hundreds of admiring eyes fastened upon him, unconsciousness of the deep, loving, sincere worship welling out of the breasts of those people and flowing toward him.

The clergyman at my left was an old acquaintance of mine—clergyman now, but had spent the first half of his life in the camp and field and as an instructor in the military school at Woolwich. Just at the moment I have been talking about a veiled and singular light glimmered in his eyes and he leaned down and muttered confidentially to me—indicating the hero of the banquet with a gesture:

"Privately—he's an absolute fool."

This verdict was a great surprise to me. If its subject had been Napoleon, or Socrates, or Solomon, my astonishment could not have been greater. Two things I was well aware of: that the Reverend was a man of strict veracity and that his judgment of men was good. Therefore I knew, beyond doubt or question, that the world was mistaken about this hero: he *was* a fool. So I meant to find out, at a convenient moment, how the Reverend, all solitary and alone, had discovered the secret.

Some days later the opportunity came, and this is what the Reverend told me: 5

About forty years ago I was an instructor in the military academy at Woolwich. I was present in one of the sections when young Scoresby underwent his preliminary examination. I was touched to the quick with pity, for the rest of the class answered up brightly and handsomely, while he—why, dear me, he didn't know *anything*, so to speak. He was evidently good, and sweet, and lovable, and guileless; and so it was exceedingly painful to see him stand there, as serene as a graven image, and deliver himself of answers which were veritably miraculous for stupidity and ignorance. All the compassion in me was aroused in his behalf. I said to myself, when he comes to be examined again he will be flung over, of course; so it will be simply a harmless act of charity to ease his fall as much as I can. I took him aside and found that he knew a little of Caesar's history; and as he didn't know anything else, I went to work and drilled him like a galley-slave on a certain line of stock questions concerning Caesar which I knew would be used. If you'll believe me, he went through with flying colors on examination day! He went through on that purely superficial "cram," and got compliments too, while others, who knew a thousand times more than he, got plucked. By some strangely lucky accident—an accident not likely to happen twice in a century—he was asked no question outside of the narrow limits of his drill.

It was stupefying. Well, all through his course I stood by him, with something of the sentiment which a mother feels for a crippled child; and he always saved himself—just by miracle, apparently.

Now, of course, the thing that would expose him and kill him at last was mathematics. I resolved to make his death as easy as I could; so I drilled him and crammed him, and crammed him and drilled him, just on the line of questions which the examiners would be most likely to use, and then launched him on his fate. Well, sir, try to conceive of the result: to my consternation, he took the first prize! And with it he got a perfect ovation in the way of compliments.

Sleep? There was no more sleep for me for a week. My conscience tortured me day and night. What I had done I had done purely through charity, and only to ease the poor youth's fall. I never had dreamed of any such preposterous results as the thing that had happened. I felt as guilty and miserable as Frankenstein. Here was a wooden-head whom I had put in the way of glittering promotions and prodigious responsibilities, and but one thing could happen: he and his responsibilities would all go to ruin together at the first opportunity.

The Crimean War had just broken out. Of course there had to be a war, I said to myself. We couldn't have peace and give this donkey a chance to die before he is found out. I waited for the earthquake. It came. And it made me reel when it did come. He was actually gazetted to a captaincy in a marching regiment! Better men grow old and gray in the service before they climb to a sublimity like that. And who could ever have foreseen that they would go and put such a load of responsibility on such green and inadequate shoulders? I could just barely have stood it if they had made him a cornet; but a captain—think of it! I thought my hair would turn white.

Consider what I did—I who so loved repose and inaction. I said to myself, I am responsible to the country for this, and I must go along with him and protect the country against him as far as I can. So I took my poor little capital that I had saved up through years of work and grinding economy, and went with a sigh and bought a cornetcy in his regiment, and away we went to the field.

And there—oh, dear, it was awful. Blunders?—why he never did anything *but* blunder. But, you see, nobody was in the fellow's secret. Everybody had him focused wrong, and necessarily misinterpreted his performance every time. Consequently they took his idiotic blunders for inspirations of genius. They did, honestly! His mildest blunders were enough to make a man in his right mind cry; and they did make me cry—and rage and rave, too, privately. And the thing that kept me always in a sweat of apprehension was the fact that every fresh blunder he made increased the luster of his reputation! I kept saying to myself, he'll get so high that when discovery does finally come it will be like the sun falling out of the sky.

He went right along, up from grade to grade, over the dead bodies of his superiors, until at last, in the hottest moment of the battle of —— down went our colonel, and my heart jumped into my mouth, for Scoresby was next in rank! Now for it, said I; we'll all land in Sheol in ten minutes, sure.

The battle was awfully hot; the allies were steadily giving way all over the field. Our regiment occupied a position that was vital; a blunder now must be destruction. At this crucial moment, what does this immortal fool do but detach the regiment from its place and order a charge over a neighboring hill where there wasn't a suggestion of an enemy! "There you go!" I said to myself; "this *is* the end at last."

And away we did go, and were over the shoulder of the hill before the insane movement could be discovered and stopped. And what did we find? An entire and unsuspected Russian army in reserve! And what happened? We were eaten up? That is necessarily what would have happened in ninety-nine cases out of a hundred. But no; those Russians argued that no single regiment would come brows-

ing around there at such a time. It must be the entire English army, and that the
sly Russian game was detected and blocked; so they turned tail, and away they
went, pell-mell, over the hill and down into the field, in wild confusion, and we
after them; they themselves broke the solid Russian center in the field, and tore
through, and in no time there was the most tremendous rout you ever saw, and
the defeat of the allies was turned into a sweeping and splendid victory! Marshal
Canrobert looked on, dizzy with astonishment, admiration, and delight; and sent
right off for Scoresby, and hugged him, and decorated him on the field in presence
of all the armies!

And what was Scoresby's blunder that time? Merely the mistaking his right
hand for his left—that was all. An order had come to him to fall back and support
our right; and, instead, he fell *forward* and went over the hill to the left. But the
name he won that day as a marvelous military genius filled the world with his
glory, and that glory will never fade while history books last.

He is just as good and sweet and lovable and unpretending as a man can
be, but he doesn't know enough to come in when it rains. Now that is absolutely
true. He is the supremest ass in the universe; and until half an hour ago nobody
knew it but himself and me. He has been pursued, day by day and year by year,
by a most phenomenal astonishing luckiness. He has been a shining soldier in all
our wars for a generation; he has littered his whole military life with blunders,
and yet has never committed one that didn't make him a knight or a baronet or
a lord or something. Look at his breast; why, he is just clothed in domestic and
foreign decorations. Well, sir, every one of them is the record of some shouting
stupidity or other; and, taken together, they are proof that the very best thing in
all this world that can befall a man is to be born lucky. I say again, as I said at
the banquet, Scoresby's an absolute fool.

QUESTIONS

1. Describe Clemens's style as a writer of narrative prose. What kinds of detail
    does he present? Does he give you enough detail about the battle during
    the Crimean War (1854–1856), for example, to justify an assertion that he
    describes action vividly? Or does he confine his detail to illuminate the life
    of Scoresby?

2. What elements in the story are amusing? Does Clemens's style have any
    influence on laughter? If so, how does the development of humor depend
    on the arrangement of words?

3. Study the first paragraph for rhetorical effect. What does it seem that Clemens
    intended after the "look, and look, and look" phrase? Why do you think
    that he begins the story with such a description that might even be called
    heroic? Contrast this paragraph with the rhetoric of paragraph 12, where
    the word "blunder" is repeated.

4. Who begins telling the story? Who finally tells the story? What is the effect
    of this change of point of view upon the debunking of Scoresby that is the
    main subject? How does the clergyman narrator learn about all that Scoresby
    does? How does he summarize Scoresby's career?

5. How does Clemens explain things so as to make it believable that Scoresby

could have passed his exams? Why is it necessary to include this cramming as a first step in the great career?

6. Describe the organization of the story. What is the climax? Where does it occur? What is the relationship of the story's title to the resolution of the plot?

7. Describe the character of Scoresby. Aside from his luck, what things do you learn about him? Is there enough to justify the claim of the narrator that Scoresby is "an absolute fool"?

ERNEST HEMINGWAY (1899–1961)

A Clean, Well-Lighted Place 1933

It was late and every one had left the café except an old man who sat in the shadow the leaves of the tree made against the electric light. In the day time the street was dusty, but at night the dew settled the dust and the old man liked to sit late because he was deaf and now at night it was quiet and he felt the difference. The two waiters inside the café knew that the old man was a little drunk, and while he was a good client they knew that if he became too drunk he would leave without paying, so they kept watch on him.

"Last week he tried to commit suicide," one waiter said.

"Why?"

"He was in despair."

"What about?"

"Nothing."   5

"How do you know it was nothing?"

"He has plenty of money."

They sat together at a table that was close against the wall near the door of the café and looked at the terrace where the tables were all empty except where the old man sat in the shadow of the leaves of the tree that moved slightly in the wind. A girl and a soldier went by in the street. The street light shone on the brass number on his collar. The girl wore no head covering and hurried beside him.

"The guard will pick him up," one waiter said.   10

"What does it matter if he gets what he's after?"

"He had better get off the street now. The guard will get him. They went by five minutes ago."

The old man sitting in the shadow rapped on his saucer with his glass. The younger waiter went over to him.

"What do you want?"

The old man looked at him. "Another brandy," he said.   15

"You'll be drunk," the waiter said. The old man looked at him. The waiter went away.

"He'll stay all night," he said to his colleague. "I'm sleepy now. I never get into bed before three o'clock. He should have killed himself last week."

The waiter took the brandy bottle and another saucer from the counter inside the café and marched out to the old man's table. He put down the saucer and poured the glass full of brandy.

"You should have killed yourself last week," he said to the deaf man. The old man motioned with his finger. "A little more," he said. The waiter poured on into the glass so that the brandy slopped over and ran down the stem into the top saucer of the pile. "Thank you," the old man said. The waiter took the bottle back inside the café. He sat down at the table with his colleague again.

"He's drunk now," he said.   20

"He's drunk every night."

"What did he want to kill himself for?"

"How should I know."

"How did he do it?"

"He hung himself with a rope."   25

"Who cut him down?"

"His niece."

"Why did they do it?"

"Fear for his soul."

"How much money has he got?"   30

"He's got plenty."

"He must be eighty years old."

"Anyway I should say he was eighty."

"I wish he would go home. I never get to bed before three o'clock. What kind of hour is that to go to bed?"

"He stays up because he likes it."   35

"He's lonely. I'm not lonely. I have a wife waiting in bed for me."

"He had a wife once too."

"A wife would be no good to him now."

"You can't tell. He might be better with a wife."

"His niece looks after him. You said she cut him down."   40

"I know."

"I wouldn't want to be that old. An old man is a nasty thing."

"Not always. This old man is clean. He drinks without spilling. Even now, drunk. Look at him."

"I don't want to look at him. I wish he would go home. He has no regard for those who must work."

The old man looked from his glass across the square, then over at the waiters.   45

"Another brandy," he said, pointing to his glass. The waiter who was in a hurry came over.

"Finished," he said, speaking with that omission of syntax stupid people employ when talking to drunken people or foreigners. "No more tonight. Close now."

"Another," said the old man.

"No. Finished." The waiter wiped the edge of the table with a towel and shook his head.

The old man stood up, slowly counted the saucers, took a leather coin purse   50
from his pocket and paid for the drinks, leaving half a peseta tip.

The waiter watched him go down the street, a very old man walking unsteadily but with dignity.

"Why didn't you let him stay and drink?" the unhurried waiter asked. They were putting up the shutters. "It is not half-past two."

"I want to go home to bed."

"What is an hour?"

"More to me than to him."   55

"An hour is the same."

"You talk like an old man yourself. He can buy a bottle and drink at home."

"It's not the same."

"No, it is not," agreed the waiter with a wife. He did not wish to be unjust. He was only in a hurry.

"And you? You have no fear of going home before your usual hour?"   60

"Are you trying to insult me?"

"No, hombre, only to make a joke."

"No," the waiter who was in a hurry said, rising from pulling down the metal shutters. "I have confidence. I am all confidence."

"You have youth, confidence, and a job," the older waiter said. "You have everything."

"And what do you lack?"   65

"Everything but work."

"You have everything I have."

"No. I have never had confidence and I am not young."

"Come on. Stop talking nonsense and lock up."

"I am of those who like to stay late at the café," the older waiter said. "With   70
all those who do not want to go to bed. With all those who need a light for the night."

"I want to go home and into bed."

"We are of two different kinds," the older waiter said. He was now dressed to go home. "It is not only a question of youth and confidence although those things are very beautiful. Each night I am reluctant to close up because there may be some one who needs the café."

"Hombre, there are bodegas° open all night long."

"You do not understand. This is a clean and pleasant café. It is well lighted. The light is very good and also, now, there are shadows of the leaves."

"Good night," said the younger waiter.   75

"Good night," the other said. Turning off the electric light he continued the conversation with himself. It is the light of course but it is necessary that the place be clean and pleasant. You do not want music. Certainly you do not want music. Nor can you stand before a bar with dignity although that is all that is provided for these hours. What did he fear? It was not fear or dread. It was a nothing that he knew too well. It was all a nothing and a man was nothing too. It was only that and light was all it needed and a certain cleanness and order. Some lived in it and never felt it but he knew it all was nada y pues nada° y nada y pues nada. Our nada who art in nada, nada be thy name thy kingdom nada thy will be nada in nada as it is in nada. Give us this nada our daily nada and nada us our nada as we nada our nadas and nada us not into nada but deliver us from nada; pues nada. Hail nothing full of nothing, nothing is with thee.

bodega: a store.
nada y pues nada: "nothing and then nothing."

He smiled and stood before a bar with a shining steam pressure coffee machine.

"What's yours?" asked the barman.

"Nada."

"Otro loco mas,"° said the barman and turned away.

"A little cup," said the waiter.   80

The barman poured it for him.

"The light is very bright and pleasant but the bar is unpolished," the waiter said.

The barman looked at him but did not answer. It was too late at night for conversation.

"You want another copita?"° the barman asked.

"No, thank you," said the waiter and went out. He disliked bars and bodegas.   85
A clean, well-lighted café was a very different thing. Now, without thinking further, he would go home to his room. He would lie in the bed and finally, with daylight, he would go to sleep. After all, he said to himself, it is probably only insomnia. Many must have it.

> otro loco mas: "another [even] more crazy."
> copita: "little cup."

QUESTIONS

1. Describe the diction of the story. Can it be called high, middle, or low? Are there any unusual words? What is the effect of the Spanish words used in the story?

2. Briefly characterize the two waiters and the circumstances of their lives that Hemingway includes. From their conversations, can you identify which one is speaking even though Hemingway does not introduce many of their speeches? Do you think that the speeches sufficiently identify the waiters, or should Hemingway have included introductions?

3. Analyze paragraph 9 as an example of descriptive prose. How is each sentence used? Can you visualize the scene as a result of the description? Of the four sentences, why do you think the first is longer than the other three combined?

4. What is the point of view of the story? Can you see any shift as the story follows the older waiter after he leaves the café?

5. What is the conflict or conflicts of the story? Are there any antagonists? What problem is the old man facing? What problem does the older waiter face? What is the resolution of their conflicts?

6. Describe the older waiter's parody of the first part of the Lord's Prayer and the opening of the Ave Maria. Why does the waiter substitute "nada" (nothing) for key words in the prayers? In view of this negativism, what is the meaning of the older waiter's sympathies for the old man and also of his assessment of human needs? What is the meaning of the title? Why are cleanliness and light stressed? Are the assertions about life made in the story accurate or overly negative?

7. Describe the setting of the story. How much detail do you find? What things in the story are important, as things or artifacts? How does Hemingway tell you, for example, that there is a nearby streetlight? Are the settings best described as vivid or impressionistic?

ALICE MUNRO (b. 1931)

The Found Boat   1974

At the end of Bell Street, McKay Street, Mayo Street, there was the Flood. It was the Wawanash River, which every spring overflowed its banks. Some springs, say one in every five, it covered the roads on that side of town and washed over the fields, creating a shallow choppy lake. Light reflected off the water made every-thing bright and cold, as it is in a lakeside town, and woke or revived in people certain vague hopes of disaster. Mostly during the late afternoon and early evening, there were people straggling out to look at it, and discuss whether it was still rising, and whether this time it might invade the town. In general, those under fifteen and over sixty-five were most certain that it would.

Eva and Carol rode out on their bicycles. They left the road—it was the end of Mayo Street, past any houses—and rode right into a field, over a wire fence entirely flattened by the weight of the winter's snow. They coasted a little way before the long grass stopped them, then left their bicycles lying down and went to the water.

"We have to find a log and ride on it," Eva said.

"Jesus, we'll freeze our legs off."

"Jesus, we'll freeze our legs off!" said one of the boys who were there too   5
at the water's edge. He spoke in a sour whine, the way boys imitated girls although it was nothing like the way girls talked. These boys—there were three of them—were all in the same class as Eva and Carol at school and were known to them by name (their names being Frank, Bud and Clayton), but Eva and Carol, who had seen and recognized them from the road, had not spoken to them or looked at them or, even yet, given any sign of knowing they were there. The boys seemed to be trying to make a raft, from lumber they had salvaged from the water.

Eva and Carol took off their shoes and socks and waded in. The water was so cold it sent pain up their legs, like blue electric sparks shooting through their veins, but they went on, pulling their skirts high, tight behind and bunched so they could hold them in front.

"Look at the fat-assed ducks in wading."

"Fat-assed fucks."

Eva and Carol, of course, gave no sign of hearing this. They laid hold of a log and climbed on, taking a couple of boards floating in the water for paddles. There were always things floating around in the Flood—branches, fence-rails, logs, road signs, old lumber; sometimes boilers, washtubs, pots and pans, or even a car seat or stuffed chair, as if somewhere the Flood had got into a dump.

They paddled away from shore, heading out into the cold lake. The water   10
was perfectly clear, they could see the brown grass swimming along the bottom. Suppose it was the sea, thought Eva. She thought of drowned cities and countries. Atlantis. Suppose they were riding in a Viking boat—Viking boats on the Atlantic

were more frail and narrow than this log on the Flood—and they had miles of clear sea beneath them, then a spired city, intact as a jewel irretrievable on the ocean floor.

"This is a Viking boat," she said. "I am the carving on the front." She stuck her chest out and stretched her neck, trying to make a curve, and she made a face, putting out her tongue. Then she turned and for the first time took notice of the boys.

"Hey, you sucks!" she yelled at them. "You'd be scared to come out here, this water is ten feet deep!"

"Liar," they answered without interest, and she was.

They steered the log around a row of trees, avoiding floating barbed wire, and got into a little bay created by a natural hollow of the land. Where the bay was now, there would be a pond full of frogs later in the spring, and by the middle of summer there would be no water visible at all, just a low tangle of reeds and bushes, green, to show that mud was still wet around their roots. Larger bushes, willows, grew around the steep bank of this pond and were still partly out of the water. Eva and Carol let the log ride in. They saw a place where something was caught.

It was a boat, or part of one. An old rowboat with most of one side ripped   15 out, the board that had been the seat just dangling. It was pushed up among the branches, lying on what would have been its side, if it had a side, the prow caught high.

Their idea came to them without consultation, at the same time:

"You guys! Hey, you guys!"

"We found you a boat!"

"Stop building your stupid raft and come and look at the boat!"

What surprised them in the first place was that the boys really did come,   20 scrambling overland, half running, half sliding down the bank, wanting to see.

"Hey, where?"

"Where is it, I don't see no boat."

What surprised them in the second place was that when the boys did actually see what boat was meant, this old flood-smashed wreck held up in the branches, they did not understand that they had been fooled, that a joke had been played on them. They did not show a moment's disappointment, but seemed as pleased at the discovery as if the boat had been whole and new. They were already barefoot, because they had been wading in the water to get lumber, and they waded in here without a stop, surrounding the boat and appraising it and paying no attention even of an insulting kind to Eva and Carol who bobbed up and down on their log. Eva and Carol had to call to them.

"How do you think you're going to get it off?"

"It won't float anyway."   25

"What makes you think it will float?"

"It'll sink. Glub-blub-blub, you'll all be drownded."

The boys did not answer, because they were too busy walking around the boat, pulling at it in a testing way to see how it could be got off with the least possible damage. Frank, who was the most literate, talkative and inept of the three, began referring to the boat as *she*, an affectation which Eva and Carol acknowledged with fish-mouths of contempt.

"She's caught two places. You got to be careful not to tear a hole in her bottom. She's heavier than you'd think."

It was Clayton who climbed up and freed the boat, and Bud, a tall fat boy, who got the weight of it on his back to turn it into the water so that they could half float, half carry it to shore. All this took some time. Eva and Carol abandoned their log and waded out of the water. They walked overland to get their shoes and socks and bicycles. They did not need to come back this way but they came. They stood at the top of the hill, leaning on their bicycles. They did not go on home, but they did not sit down and frankly watch, either. They stood more or less facing each other, but glancing down at the water and at the boys struggling with the boat, as if they had just halted for a moment out of curiosity, and staying longer than they intended, to see what came of this unpromising project.

About nine o'clock, or when it was nearly dark—dark to people inside the houses, but not quite dark outside—they all returned to town, going along Mayo Street in a sort of procession. Frank and Bud and Clayton came carrying the boat, upside-down, and Eva and Carol walked behind, wheeling their bicycles. The boys' heads were almost hidden in the darkness of the overturned boat, with its smell of soaked wood, cold swampy water. The girls could look ahead and see the street lights in their tin reflectors, a necklace of lights climbing Mayo Street, reaching all the way up to the standpipe. They turned onto Burns Street heading for Clayton's house, the nearest house belonging to any of them. This was not the way home for Eva or for Carol either, but they followed along. The boys were perhaps too busy carrying the boat to tell them to go away. Some younger children were still out playing, playing hopscotch on the sidewalk though they could hardly see. At this time of year the bare sidewalk was still such a novelty and delight. These children cleared out of the way and watched the boat go by with unwilling respect; they shouted questions after it, wanting to know where it came from and what was going to be done with it. No one answered them. Eva and Carol as well as the boys refused to answer or even look at them.

The five of them entered Clayton's yard. The boys shifted weight, as if they were going to put the boat down.

"You better take it round to the back where nobody can see it," Carol said. That was the first thing any of them had said since they came into town.

The boys said nothing but went on, following a mud path between Clayton's house and a leaning board fence. They let the boat down in the back yard.

"It's a stolen boat, you know," said Eva, mainly for the effect. "It must've belonged to somebody. You stole it."

"You was the ones who stole it then," Bud said, short of breath. "It was you seen it first."

"It was you took it."

"It was all of us then. If one of us gets in trouble then all of us does."

"Are you going to tell anybody on them?" said Carol as she and Eva rode home, along the streets which were dark between the lights now and potholed from winter.

"It's up to you. I won't if you won't."

"I won't if you won't."

They rode in silence, relinquishing something, but not discontented.

The board fence in Clayton's back yard had every so often a post which

supported it, or tried to, and it was on these posts that Eva and Carol spent several
evenings sitting, jauntily but not very comfortably. Or else they just leaned against
the fence while the boys worked on the boat. During the first couple of evenings
neighborhood children attracted by the sound of hammering tried to get into the
yard to see what was going on, but Eva and Carol blocked their way.

"Who said you could come in here?"

"Just us can come in this yard."   45

These evenings were getting longer, the air milder. Skipping was starting
on the sidewalks. Further along the street there was a row of hard maples that
had been tapped. Children drank the sap as fast as it could drip into the buckets.
The old man and woman who owned the trees, and who hoped to make syrup,
came running out of the house making noises as if they were trying to scare away
crows. Finally, every spring, the old man would come out on his porch and fire
his shotgun into the air, and then the thieving would stop.

None of those working on the boat bothered about stealing sap, though all
had done so last year.

The lumber to repair the boat was picked up here and there, along back
lanes. At this time of year things were lying around—old boards and branches,
sodden mitts, spoons flung out with the dishwater, lids of pudding pots that had
been set in the snow to cool, all the debris that can sift through and survive winter.
The tools came from Clayton's cellar—left over, presumably, from the time when
his father was alive—and though they had nobody to advise them the boys seemed
to figure out more or less the manner in which boats are built, or rebuilt. Frank
was the one who showed up with diagrams from books and *Popular Mechanics* magazines. Clayton looked at these diagrams and listened to Frank read the instructions
and then went ahead and decided in his own way what was to be done. Bud was
best at sawing. Eva and Carol watched everything from the fence and offered criticism and thought up names. The names for the boat that they thought of were:
Water Lily, Sea Horse, Flood Queen, and Caro-Eve, after them because they had
found it. The boys did not say which, if any, of these names they found satisfactory.

The boat had to be tarred. Clayton heated up a pot of tar on the kitchen
stove and brought it out and painted slowly, his thorough way, sitting astride the
overturned boat. The other boys were sawing a board to make a new seat. As
Clayton worked, the tar cooled and thickened so that finally he could not move
the brush any more. He turned to Eva and held out the pot and said, "You can
go in and heat this on the stove."

Eva took the pot and went up the back steps. The kitchen seemed black   5•
after outside, but it must be light enough to see in, because there was Clayton's
mother standing at the ironing board, ironing. She did that for a living, took in
wash and ironing.

"Please may I put the tar pot on the stove?" said Eva, who had been brought
up to talk politely to parents, even wash-and-iron ladies, and who for some reason
especially wanted to make a good impression on Clayton's mother.

"You'll have to poke up the fire then," said Clayton's mother, as if she doubted
whether Eva would know how to do that. But Eva could see now, and she picked
up the lid with the stove-lifter, and took the poker and poked up a flame. She
stirred the tar as it softened. She felt privileged. Then and later. Before she went
to sleep a picture of Clayton came to her mind; she saw him sitting astride the

boat, tar-painting, with such concentration, delicacy, absorption. She thought of him speaking to her, out of his isolation, in such an ordinary peaceful taking-for-granted voice.

On the twenty-fourth of May, a school holiday in the middle of the week, the boat was carried out of town, a long way now, off the road over fields and fences that had been repaired, to where the river flowed between its normal banks. Eva and Carol, as well as the boys, took turns carrying it. It was launched in the water from a cow-trampled spot between willow bushes that were fresh out in leaf. The boys went first. They yelled with triumph when the boat did float, when it rode amazingly down the river current. The boat was painted black, and green inside, with yellow seats, and a strip of yellow all the way around the outside. There was no name on it, after all. The boys could not imagine that it needed any name to keep it separate from the other boats in the world.

Eva and Carol ran along the bank, carrying bags full of peanut butter-and-jam sandwiches, pickles, bananas, chocolate cake, potato chips, graham crackers stuck together with corn syrup and five bottles of pop to be cooled in the river water. The bottles bumped against their legs. They yelled for a turn.

"If they don't let us they're bastards," Carol said, and they yelled together, 55 "We found it! We found it!"

The boys did not answer, but after a while they brought the boat in, and Carol and Eva came crashing, panting down the bank.

"Does it leak?"

"It don't leak yet."

"We forgot a bailing can," wailed Carol, but nevertheless she got in, with Eva, and Frank pushed them off, crying, "Here's to a Watery Grave!"

And the thing about being in a boat was that it was not solidly bobbing, 60 like a log, but was cupped in the water, so that riding in it was not like being on something in the water, but like being in the water itself. Soon they were all going out in the boat in mixed-up turns, two boys and a girl, two girls and a boy, a girl and a boy, until things were so confused it was impossible to tell whose turn came next, and nobody cared anyway. They went down the river—those who weren't riding, running along the bank to keep up. They passed under two bridges, one iron, one cement. Once they saw a big carp just resting, it seemed to smile at them, in the bridge-shaded water. They did not know how far they had gone on the river, but things had changed—the water had got shallower, and the land flatter. Across an open field they saw a building that looked like a house, abandoned. They dragged the boat up on the bank and tied it and set out across the field.

"That's the old station," Frank said. "That's Pedder Station." The others had heard this name but he was the one who knew, because his father was the station agent in town. He said that this was a station on a branch line that had been torn up, and that there had been a sawmill here, but a long time ago.

Inside the station it was dark, cool. All the windows were broken. Glass lay in shards and in fairly big pieces on the floor. They walked around finding the larger pieces of glass and tramping on them, smashing them, it was like cracking ice on puddles. Some partitions were still in place, you could see where the ticket window had been. There was a bench lying on its side. People had been here, it looked as if people came here all the time, though it was so far from anywhere. Beer bottles and pop bottles were lying around, also cigarette packages, gum and

candy wrappers, the paper from a loaf of bread. The walls were covered with
dim and fresh pencil and chalk writings and carved with knives.

I LOVE RONNIE COLES

I WANT TO FUCK

KILROY WAS HERE

RONNIE COLES IS AN ASS-HOLE

WHAT ARE YOU DOING HERE?

WAITING FOR A TRAIN

DAWNA   MARY-LOU   BARBARA   JOANNE

It was exciting to be inside this large, dark, empty place, with the loud noise
of breaking glass and their voices ringing back from the underside of the roof.
They tipped the old beer bottles against their mouths. That reminded them that
they were hungry and thirsty and they cleared a place in the middle of the floor
and sat down and ate the lunch. They drank the pop just as it was, lukewarm.
They ate everything there was and licked the smears of peanut butter and jam
off the bread-paper in which the sandwiches had been wrapped.

They played Truth or Dare.

"I dare you to write on the wall, I am a Stupid Ass, and sign your name."   65

"Tell the truth—what is the worst lie you ever told?"

"Did you ever wet the bed?"

"Did you ever dream you were walking down the street without any clothes
on?"

"I dare you to go outside and pee on the railway sign."

It was Frank who had to do that. They could not see him, even his back,   70
but they knew he did it, they heard the hissing sound of his pee. They all sat
still, amazed, unable to think of what the next dare would be.

"I dare everybody," said Frank from the doorway, "I dare—Everybody."

"What?"

"Take off all our clothes."

Eva and Carol screamed.

"Anybody who won't do it has to walk—has to *crawl*—around this floor on   75
their hands and knees."

They were all quiet, till Eva said, almost complacently, "What first?"

"Shoes and socks."

"Then we have to go outside, there's too much glass here."

They pulled off their shoes and socks in the doorway, in the sudden blinding
sun. The field before them was bright as water. They ran across where the tracks
used to go.

That's enough, that's enough," said Carol. "Watch out for thistles!"   80

"Tops! Everybody take off their tops!"

"I won't! We won't, will we, Eva?"

But Eva was whirling round and round in the sun where the track used to
be. "I don't care, I don't care! Truth or Dare! Truth or Dare!"

She unbuttoned her blouse as she whirled, as if she didn't know what her
hand was doing, she flung it off.

Carol took off hers. "I wouldn't have done it, if you hadn't!"   8.

"Bottoms!"

Nobody said a word this time, they all bent and stripped themselves. Eva, naked first, started running across the field, and then all the others ran, all five of them running bare through the knee-high hot grass, running towards the river. Not caring now about being caught but in fact leaping and yelling to call attention to themselves, if there was anybody to hear or see. They felt as if they were going to jump off a cliff and fly. They felt that something was happening to them different from anything that had happened before, and it had to do with the boat, the water, the sunlight, the dark ruined station, and each other. They thought of each other now hardly as names or people, but as echoing shrieks, reflections, all bold and white and loud and scandalous, and as fast as arrows. They went running without a break into the cold water and when it came almost to the tops of their legs they fell on it and swam. It stopped their noise. Silence, amazement, came over them in a rush. They dipped and floated and separated, sleek as mink.

Eva stood up in the water her hair dripping, water running down her face. She was waist deep. She stood on smooth stones, her feet fairly wide apart, water flowing between her legs. About a yard away from her Clayton also stood up, and they were blinking the water out of their eyes, looking at each other. Eva did not turn or try to hide; she was quivering from the cold of the water, but also with pride, shame, boldness, and exhilaration.

Clayton shook his head violently, as if he wanted to bang something out of it, then bent over and took a mouthful of river water. He stood up with his cheeks full and made a tight hole of his mouth and shot the water at her as if it was coming out of a hose, hitting her exactly, first one breast and then the other. Water from his mouth ran down her body. He hooted to see it, a loud self-conscious sound that nobody would have expected, from him. The others looked up from wherever they were in the water and closed in to see.

Eva crouched down and slid into the water, letting her head go right under.   90
She swam, and when she let her head out, downstream, Carol was coming after her and the boys were already on the bank, already running into the grass, showing their skinny backs, their white, flat buttocks. They were laughing and saying things to each other but she couldn't hear, for the water in her ears.

"What did he do?" said Carol.

"Nothing."

They crept in to shore. "Let's stay in the bushes till they go," said Eva. "I hate them anyway. I really do. Don't you hate them?"

"Sure," said Carol, and they waited, not very long, until they heard the boys still noisy and excited coming down to the place a bit upriver where they had left the boat. They heard them jump in and start rowing.

"They've got all the hard part, going back," said Eva, hugging herself and   95
shivering violently. "Who cares? Anyway. It never was our boat."

"What if they tell?" said Carol.

"We'll say it's all a lie."

Eva hadn't thought of this solution until she said it, but as soon as she did she felt almost light-hearted again. The ease and scornfulness of it did make them both giggle, and slapping themselves and splashing out of the water they set about developing one of those fits of laughter in which, as soon as one showed signs of exhaustion, the other would snort and start up again, and they would make helpless—soon genuinely helpless—faces at each other and bend over and grab themselves as if they had the worst pain.

QUESTIONS

1. Consider the details used in passages of description in the story. What kinds of details are included? In the first paragraph, for example, what is the focus of interest, the flood or people's reactions to it?

2. What is the level of diction in the dialogue of the story? Do you see contractions? Slang? Grammatical mistakes? Profanity? From the dialogue what do you learn about the various speakers?

3. Study paragraph 10 as an example of the relationship of style to the character Eva as a limited-point-of-view center of interest. What does the paragraph tell you about her? How does it do so?

4. Consider the last paragraph in the story as an example of writing about action. How much action is selected for description? What verbs are used and how well do they help you visualize and imagine the sounds of the scene? What is the effect of the verb "snort"? How does the paragraph cause you to respond at the story's end?

5. What is "Truth or Dare"? What is the dare that concludes the game? To what degree is the game a guise under which boys and girls may develop their emotions toward each other?

6. Characterize the relationship between Eva and Clayton. How does this relationship help you focus on the main topic matter of the story?

7. What is the plot of the story? Who or what is in conflict? What elements are introduced as complication? What are the climax and resolution of the story?

8. How many details of setting are included? From the lifestyle and artifacts mentioned, what do you learn about the approximate time of the events in the story? About the economic level of the town? How well realized is the town? What is the effect of the facts that it is early springtime, that the water is still cold, but that in May the water is swimmable? Are there any implications for summer?

9. From the descriptions of the boys, try to characterize them. Which seems to be a planner but not a doer? Which seems competent and practical? Of Eva and Carol, which seems the leader and which the follower?

WRITING ABOUT STYLE

In prewriting, you should consider the selected passage in the context of the entire story. What sort of passage is it? Narrative? Descriptive? Does it contain any dialogue? Is there a speaker with clearly established characteristics? How does the passage reflect his or her personality? Try to determine the level of the diction: Did you need to use a dictionary to discover the meaning of any of the words? Are there any unusual words? Any especially difficult or uncommon words? Do any of the words distract you as you read? Is there any slang? Are any words used only in particular occupations or ways of life (such as words used about drink, or automobiles, or horses, words from other languages, and so on)? Are there any contractions? Do they indicate a conversational, intimate level of speech? Are the words the most common ones that might be used? Can you think of more difficult ones? Easier ones? More accurate ones? Are there many short words? Long words?

Can you easily imagine the situations described by the words? If you have difficulty, can you find any reasons that stem out of the level of diction?

Are the sentences long, or short? Is there any variation in length? Can you observe any relationship between length and topic material? Are the sentences simple, compound, or complex? Does one type predominate? Why? Can you describe any noteworthy rhetorical devices? Are there any sentences that may be clearly established to be periodic as opposed to loose? What sort of effect is gained by this sentence or sentences? Are there any other noticeable devices? What are they? How are they used? What is their effect?

With answers to questions like these, you will readily assemble materials for your essay on the style of a passage from a story.

Organizing Your Essay

INTRODUCTION. In your introduction you should establish the particulars about the passage you are studying and should present a central idea that relates the style to these particulars. You should mention the place of the passage in the work, the general subject matter, any special ideas, the speaker, the apparent audience (if any except the general reader), and the basic method of presentation (that is, monologue, dialogue, or narration, all of which might be interspersed with argument, description, or comparison).

BODY. In the body of your essay you should describe and evaluate the style of the passage. Always remember to consider the style in relationship to the circumstances of the work. For example, suppose the speaker is in a plane crashing to the ground, or in a racing car just approaching the finish line, or hurrying to meet a sweetheart; or suppose the speaker is recalling the past or considering the future. Such conditions must be kept foremost throughout your analysis.

To focus your essay, you might wish to single out one aspect of style, or to discuss everything, depending on the length of the assignment. Be sure to treat things like levels of diction, categories like specific–general and concrete–abstract, the degree of simplicity or complexity, length, numbers of words (an approach that is relatively easy for a beginning), and denotation–connotation. In discussing rhetorical aspects, go as far as you can with the nomenclature at your command. Consider things like sentence types and any specific rhetorical devices you notice and are able to describe. If you can draw attention to the elements in a parallel structure by using grammatical terms, do so. If you are able to detect the ways in which the sentences are kept simple or made complex, describe these ways. Be sure to use examples from the passage to illustrate your point; indent them and leave spaces between them and your own material.

The sort of essay envisaged here is designed to sharpen your levels of awareness at your own stage of development as a reader. Later, to the degree that you will have gained sharper perceptions and a wider descriptive vocabulary, you will be able to enhance the sophistication of your analyses.

CONCLUSION.   Whereas the body is the place for detailed descriptions and examples, your conclusion is the place where you can make evaluations of the author's style. To what extent have your discoveries in your analysis increased or reinforced your appreciation of the author's technique? Does the passage take on any added importance as a result of your study? Is there anything elsewhere in the work comparable to the content, words, or ideas that you have discussed in the passage?

Numbers for Easy Reference

Include a copy of your passage at the beginning of your essay, as in the example. For your reader's convenience, number the sentences in the passage, and use these numbers as they become relevant in your essay.

SAMPLE ESSAY

O'Connor's Economy of Style in "First Confession"*

[1] Nora's turn came, and I heard the sound of something slamming, and then her voice as if butter wouldn't melt in her mouth, and then another slam, and out she came. [2] God, the hypocrisy of women. [3] Her eyes were lowered, her head was bowed, and her hands were joined very low down on her stomach, and she walked up the aisle to the side altar looking like a saint. [4] You never saw such an exhibition of devotion, and I remembered the devilish malice with which she had tormented me all the way from our door, and wondered were all religious people like that, really. [5] It was my turn now. [6] With the fear of damnation in my soul I went in, and the confessional door closed of itself behind me.

This paragraph from "First Confession" appears midway in the story. It is transitional, coming between the recollections by Jackie, the narrator, of

* See p. 187 for this story.

[1] his childhood troubles at home and his happier memory of his first confession. Though mainly narrative, the passage is punctuated by Jackie's personal reactions. While Jackie is an accurate observer, his reactions do not show much subtlety or understanding. O'Connor's economic but well-controlled style in the passage reflects both this accuracy and simplicity.° In all respects—accuracy, word level, brevity, concreteness, and grammatical control—the passage is typical of the directness and conciseness of the entire story.°

[2] The actions and responses in the paragraph are treated fully but also with great economy. The first four sentences are devoted to Nora's confession and Jackie's reactions to it. Sentence 1 refers to the sounds of Nora's confession, while the third sentence describes her show of devotion as she leaves the confessional. Each of these descriptive sentences is followed by Jackie's angry reactions. This depth of feeling is transformed to "fear of damnation" at the beginning of sentence 6, which describes Jackie's own entry into the confessional. In other words, the paragraph succinctly presents the sounds, reactions, sights, confusion, and fear inherent in the scene. O'Connor moves all these things along so swiftly and economically that the reader is hardly aware that so much is going on in so short a passage.

[3] Just as the passage is accurately observed, the level of diction is middle or neutral, enabling a full concentration on the subject. None of the words are unusual or difficult. What could be more ordinary, for example, than words like *butter*, *slam*, *hands*, *joined*, *low*, *people*, and *closed*? One may grant that *hypocrisy*, *exhibition*, *devilish malice*, *tormented*, and *damnation* are not in the speech of everyday life, but in this context they accurately describe Jackie's reactions against the religious forces which he believes are gaining control over him. Because of their aptness and because they are not excessive granted the situation, they enable the reader to focus entirely on Jackie's responses and in this respect are appropriate to the middle level of diction of the passage.

[4] In keeping with Jackie's powers of direct observation and narrative swiftness, most of the words are short. Over 78 percent have only one syllable. If one adds the nineteen two-syllable words to this total, the fraction of short words goes to 93 percent. The highest percentage of one-syllable words is in the narrative sentences (81 percent for number 1, 85 percent for 3, 100 percent for 5, and 80 percent for 6), while in the two responsive sentences, 2 and 4, the percentage of one-syllable words is lower (60 percent and 69 percent). The second sentence contains only five words, and therefore the percentage is on a small base. The percentage in the fourth sentence, however, is significant, because any expression of reactions, including Jackie's, are naturally expressed in longer, more abstract words.

Not only are the words accurate, common, and short, but most of them are specific and concrete. Nora's "turn" came, for example, and "something slammed," and Nora's "voice" was heard, and "another slam" happened and then "out she came." Equally specific is Nora's appearance while walking to the altar. Her eyes, her head, and her hands are all easily visualized. More

° Central idea.
□ Thesis sentence.

[5] abstract are sentences 2 and 4, which detail Jackie's angry responses. Jackie's word *hypocrisy*, however (sentence 2), though an abstraction, has a clear meaning even if Jackie's attribution of the fault to women generally is not warranted by all his experiences with women in the story. Sentence 4 contains more abstractions which are highly connotative—first the "exhibition of devotion," and second the "devilish malice with which she had tormented me." But these are conclusions about the sister alone, and in context they are understandable. More problematic is Jackie's general doubt about "religious people." The observation is expressed as a child's question, and therefore, in the context, it lends itself to that aspect of the story's humor that Jackie brings directly on himself. In the last sentence, "fear of damnation" is abstract, but again it is meaningful in the light of the specific punishments described earlier in the communicants class taught by Mrs. Ryan. Despite these abstract and general words, however, most words in the paragraph are specific and concrete.

[6] Grammatically, as well, there is great economy. Thus in the first sentence, the verb *heard* is used with three parallel direct objects (*sound*, *voice*, and *slam*), in this way cutting down on words while still detailing the major sounds of Nora's confession. Only three nouns in the paragraph are preceded by descriptive adjectives (*devilish* malice, *religious* people, and *confessional* door), and of these, only *devilish* is nonessential even though it is also colorful. Even here, however, *devilish* helps to characterize the narrator, Jackie, and therefore its presence can be justified as necessary. The third sentence best illustrates the swiftness and spareness of O'Connor's narrative style. Each of the first three clauses contains four words ("her eyes were lowered," "her head was bowed," and "her hands were joined"), with only the third being given a modifying phrase ("very low down on her stomach"). There could be no way to express these actions with fewer words, and this brevity is typical of the entire paragraph. While Jackie is an accurate observer, the skill here, of course, belongs to O'Connor.

[7] In all respects, the passage seems to be a model of the right use of words in the right places. It is hard to imagine any other way to say what O'Connor says here. The speaker, Jackie, still retains a vivid memory of the incident as he is telling the story, and the words skillfully revive that. He also remembers his anger, and that, too, is accurately expressed. The words are direct and well chosen, and the sentences are brief and to the point, being shorter or longer as the need arises. In all respects the economic style is a means of rendering and displaying the content and is in no way a detraction of any sort. The paragraph is an example of accurate, concise narrative prose.

Commentary on the Essay

The opening of the introductory paragraph demonstrates the way in which a passage being studied may be related to the entire work of which it is a part. Because the central idea is connected to a brief characterization of O'Connor's narrator, Jackie, the point is made that style and substance are integrated. The thesis sentence indicates five aspects of style to be considered in the essay. Any one of these, if necessary, could be more fully developed as a separate, complete essay.

Paragraph 2 treats that aspect of the style by which O'Connor covers much action and response with great economy. Paragraph 3 deals with the level of O'Connor's (or Jackie's) diction. In paragraph 4, which is closely tied to the idea in paragraph 3, the topic is the comparative shortness of most of the words. The paragraph shows how simple calculations may be used to support conclusions about diction. In paragraph 5 the topic is that the words are mostly concrete and specific, making for easy visualizing of the details. This paragraph also deals with the problem of why a slightly increased number of abstract and general words appear in those sentences in which Jackie is expressing his reactions.

Paragraph 6 treats some easily perceived aspects of grammar, always relating the discussion to the central idea. Noted in this paragraph are parallelism (and therefore the cutting down of words), the absence of descriptive adjectives, and the use of only essential words in the first three clauses of O'Connor's sentence 3. The concluding paragraph, 7, is a tribute to O'Connor's style, emphasizing again the connection of the speaker's character to the choice of words.

8

Tone: Attitude and Control in Fiction

Tone refers to the methods by which writers convey attitudes, although the discussion of tone sometimes becomes focused on the attitudes themselves. For this reason, *tone* and *attitude* are often confused. You should remember, however, that tone refers not to attitudes but to those techniques and modes of presentation that *reveal* or *create* these attitudes.

LITERARY TONE AND SPEAKING TONE OF VOICE

In literary study the word *tone* has been borrowed from the phrase *tone of voice*. Tone of voice in speech is a reflection of your control over your attitude toward whomever you are addressing and toward your subject matter. It is made up of many elements in addition to what you actually say: the speed with which you speak, the amount of enthusiasm that you project into your thoughts, the pitch and loudness of your speech, your facial expressions, the way you hold your body, and your distance from the person to whom you are speaking.

TONE OF CHARACTERS WITHIN THE STORY

The idea underlying a study of tone is that all authors, like all real-life speakers, have a *choice* about what to say and how to say it, and that they make their choices in full consideration of their readers. One obvious judgment that authors make about their audience is that readers are intelligent human beings who can perceive the intricacies involved in both real and fictional human interchanges. As a specific example, John Collier, at the beginning of the grimly fanciful story "The Chaser" (the topic of the sample essay in this chapter), creates an extremely difficult situation: A young man, Alan Austen, comes to a chemist's shop seeking a love potion. The chemist, an old man, wants to tell Austen about a deadly and untraceable poison. Here the proper tone is absolutely essential. Collier must heed the integrity of his characters, which requires that not all things can be directly stated if the aims and goals of each are to be fulfilled. Therefore he has the old man speak indirectly about the poison, as follows:

> "I look at it like this," said the old man. "Please a customer with one article, and he will come back when he needs another. Even if it *is* more costly. He will save up for it, if necessary."

The indirect, veiled style of this speech shows the old chemist's assessment of the young man, Austen. If he were to say outright that Austen will eventually come back for the poison to kill the woman whom he now wants so desperately, Austen would flee immediately. So the old man uses the phrase "come back when he needs another" to suggest that in the future Austen may indeed remember these words and find himself in the category of men who want the poison. The tone of the speech, therefore, is right for the circumstances. The example shows how an author may judge and control the tone of speaking characters within a story.

TONE AND THE AUTHOR'S ATTITUDE
TOWARD READERS

The author is always aware that readers are virtual participants in the creative act and that therefore all elements of a story must be created with the audience in mind.

By controlling the style of the speech of the old man in "The Chaser," Collier also demonstrates a tone of confidence in the perceptiveness of his readers, who are able to judge whether the dialogue in the story is realistic. Suppose that Collier had written an interchange in which the old man does indeed tell Austen that someday he will return for the poison. Could one then expect sophisticated and intelligent readers to believe that Austen would still buy the love potion for which he came? Obviously Collier's answer is no. The point is that Austen, *at the moment of the story*, is young, romantic, and idealistic, but that *at a future time* he will become so cynical and so weary of his sweetheart that he will want to kill her, and that he will then remember that the old man can sell him the necessary poison. The story therefore goes forward as it does, with the old man speaking ambiguously and ominously, and with Austen hearing but not understanding the implications of what is said. Collier clearly wrote the story not only with due regard for the probability of the characters and situation, but also with a clear vision of the intelligence and perceptiveness of readers.

This example illustrates that aspect of tone involving the author's attitude toward his or her audience. Readers would instantly know that any departures from normally expected behavior—from verisimilitude— would strain credibility, as would any inappropriate language, settings, motivation, chronology, and so on.

LITERARY ARTISTRY AS AN ASPECT OF TONE

It is possible for writers to deviate from what is ordinary—they can, should, and do—but they should never deviate from what is *human*. The task is enormous: to be sufficiently skilled to cause readers continuously to accept the story as plausible, no matter how initially implausible the outcome might seem, or how special or particular the ideas. Writers, like all speakers, may feel deeply about a subject, and they may wish to get their feelings across. If they simply express their feelings but neglect getting readers on their side, however, they are likely to create no more than an emotional display rather than a literary work. Writers must always control sentiment by tying it to objective, realistic details, because their appeal must be not only to their readers' sympathies, but also to their understandings.

With this idea in mind, let us consider the story "The Hammon and the Beans," by Américo Parédes. Underlying the story is a sense of outrage against the miseries of poverty among Mexican peasants, but the story is not an indignant diatribe; instead, the principal action is the death of a little Mexican peasant girl named Chonita. The problem is determining the control with which Parédes treats this event. The death of a poor, helpless child, serious as it is, could easily become an occasion for sentimentality. It could also be received indifferently unless the death can be related to other things about which we care. In view of these problems, Parédes controls his material skillfully in order to put the death in perspective and at the same time to cause deep concern in the reader. He uses a doctor to report Chonita's death. This doctor, conversing with the narrator's father, then discusses disease, the callous behavior of Chonita's stepfather, the wretched life of the local Mexican peasants, and other topics that are both political and historical. Their commentary, which includes the doctor's angry outburst, followed by the narrator's personal response of tears, provides a context for Chonita's death. She becomes not only an object of pathos, but a case study of the effects of injustice and political neglect. By thus providing a larger context of human, personal, medical, social, military, and political matters, Parédes has exhibited great artistic control over tone in "The Hammon and the Beans." His social and political ideas are clear, and the underlying note of indignation is also clear, but above all the story is effective, well controlled, and beautiful.

LAUGHTER, COMEDY, AND FARCE

A major aspect of tone is laughter and the methods of comedy and farce. No two critics agree on what exactly makes people laugh, but all agree that laughter is essential in a person's psychological well-being. Laughter is an unpredictable action; what a person finds amusing today will not move him or her tomorrow. The causes of laughter are complicated and difficult to analyze and isolate. However, the major elements in laughter seem to be these:

1. *An object of laughter*. There must be something to laugh at, whether a person, thing, situation, custom, habit of speech or dialect, or arrangement of words.

2. *Incongruity*. Human beings have a sense of what to expect under given conditions, and anything that violates these expectations may be a cause of laughter. On a day when the temperature is 100°F., for example, you would reasonably expect people to dress lightly. But if you saw a person dressed in a heavy overcoat, a warm hat, a muffler, and large gloves, who was shivering, waving his arms, and stamping his feet as though to keep them warm, you would likely laugh because this person would have violated your expectation of what a sane person would do under the conditions. His response to the weather is inappropriate or *incongruous*, an incongruity of *situation*. The standup comedian's story that, "Yesterday afternoon I was walking down the street and turned into a drugstore," is funny because "turned into" can have two incompatible meanings. Here the language itself has furnished its own incongruity. A student once wrote that in high school he had enjoyed singing in the "archipelago choir." This is an inadvertent verbal mistake called a *malapropism*, after Mrs. Malaprop, a character in Richard Brinsley Sheridan's play *The Rivals*. In the student's report about the choir, you expect to see *a capella*—or at least a recognizable misspelling of the word—and when you see *archipelago*, a word that makes sense elsewhere and sounds something like *a capella*, you laugh, or at least smile. Incongruity is the quality common to all these instances of laughter. In the literary creation of such verbal slips, the tone is directed against the speaker, and the author and reader both share the enjoyment.

3. *Safety and/or goodwill*. Seeing a person who has just slipped on a banana peel hurtling through the air and about to crack his or her skull may cause laughter as long as we ourselves are not that person, for our laughter depends on our being insulated from danger and pain. In farce,

where a great deal of physical abuse takes place, such as falling through trapdoors or being hit in the face by cream pies, the abuse never harms the participants. The incongruity of such situations causes laughter, and one's safety from personal consequences—together with the insulation from pain of the participants—prevents the interference of more grave or even horrified responses. The element of goodwill enters into laughter in romantic comedy or in works where you are drawn into general sympathy with the major figures, such as Walter and Ellen in Shirley Jackson's "About Two Nice People." Here the infectiousness of laughter and happiness influences your responses. As the author leads the characters toward success, your involvement with them will produce a general sense of happiness which may cause you to smile and also may cause you to laugh sympathetically.

4. *Unfamiliarity, newness, uniqueness, spontaneity.*   Laughter depends on seeing something new or unique, or on experiencing a known thing freshly. Laughter usually occurs in a flash of insight or revelation, and the situation producing laughter must always possess spontaneity. This is not to say that ordinary situations are excluded as topics of humor. Indeed, the task of the comic writer is to develop ordinary materials to the point of instant recognition, when spontaneity enables laughter to proceed. For example, Jackson's "About Two Nice People" is, among other things, about the friction that develops between people living in adjoining apartments. There is nothing unusual here, but Jackson's artistry creates humor out of the ordinary. As a crisis of the situation between the young man, Walter, and the young woman, Ellen, Walter calls in his wealthy aunt, Mrs. Nesmith, to scare Ellen. However, this lady, who owns the apartment building, stops short in her badgering by refraining from threatening Ellen with eviction, because, she says, "Apartments are too hard to get these days. . . . That would have been too unkind." Here the author has developed a joke out of the housing shortage and in this way has created the spontaneity necessary for laughter.

Irony

One of the most human traits is the capacity to have two or more attitudes toward something. You might love someone but on occasion express your affection by insults rather than praise. A large number of contemporary greeting cards feature witty insults, because many people cannot stand the sentimentality of the "straight" cards and send the insulting card in the expectation that the person receiving it will be amused and will recognize genuine fondness on the sender's part. Expressions in which one attitude is conveyed by its opposite are *ironic*. **Irony** is a mode of ambiguous or indirect expression; it is natural to human beings who are aware of the possibilities and complexities in life. Irony is a function of the realization that life does not always measure up to promise, that friends and loved ones may sometimes be angry and bitter toward each other, that the universe offers mysteries that human beings cannot comprehend, that doubt exists even in the face of certainty, and that character is built through chagrin, regret, and pain as much as through emulation and praise. In expressing an idea ironically, writers pay the greatest compliment to their readers, for they assume sufficient skill and understanding to see through the surface statement into the seriousness or levity beneath.

The major types of irony are *verbal*, *situational*, and *dramatic*. **Verbal irony** is a statement in which one thing is said and another is meant. For example, one of the American astronauts was once asked how he would feel if all his reentry safety equipment failed as he was coming back to earth. He answered, "A thing like that could ruin your whole day." His words would have been appropriate for day-to-day minor mishaps, but since failed safety equipment would cause his death, his answer was ironic. This form of verbal irony is **understatement.** By contrast, **overstatement** or **hyperbole** is exaggeration for effect, as in "I'll love you till the oceans go dry." Often verbal irony is ambiguous, having double meaning or **double-entendre.** At the end of Collier's "The Chaser," for example, the old man responds to Austen's "Good-bye" with the French farewell salutation "Au revoir." This phrase, meaning "Until I see you again," is not especially unusual, and on the surface it seems fairly innocent, but the context makes clear that the old man's final words are a dire prediction that Austen will return one day for the untraceable poison. In other words, the old man's statement has two meanings, one innocent and the other sinister. Ambiguity of course may be used in relation to any topic. Quite often *double-entendre* is used in statements about sexuality and love, usually for the amusement of listeners or readers.

The term **situational irony,** or **irony of situation,** refers to conditions that are measured against forces that transcend and overpower human capacities. These forces may be psychological, social, political, or environmental. The sample essay on Collier's "The Chaser" develops the idea that Collier's story is based on the irony of the situation in which an unrealistic desire for romantic possession leads people inevitably toward destructiveness rather than everlasting love. Situational irony that is connected with a pessimistic or fatalistic view of life is sometimes called **irony of fate** or **cosmic irony.** It is such an irony of fate that we find in "The Hammon and the Beans" by Parédes. In the setting of Mexican-American families living in poverty in Texas, the dead little girl, Chonita, is no more than a minor statistic; her life is only an insignificant part of a gigantic pattern of social and political neglect. If we consider that she had been a human being with a great potential for growth, however, we could justifiably conclude that she might have matured to be an engaging, bright adult who could lead a productive, happy life. She could have been important. However, under the circumstances of poverty, ill education, and poor nutrition and care she never has a chance. Her situation, and that of those like her, is ironically fatal, for the implication of "The Hammon and the Beans" is that human beings are caught in a web of circumstances from which they cannot escape.

Situational irony could of course work in a more optimistic context. For example, an average, or even blockheaded person could go through a set of difficult circumstances and be on the verge of losing everything in life, but, through someone's perversity or through luck, might emerge successfully, as does Scoresby in Samuel Clemens's story "Luck." Such a situation could reflect an author's conception of a benevolent universe, or, as in the case of Scoresby, a more arbitrarily comic one. Most often, however, situational irony is like that in the story by Parédes.

Dramatic irony is a special kind of situational irony; it applies when a character perceives a situation in a limited way while the audience, including other characters, may see it in greater perspective. The character therefore is able to understand things in only one way while the larger audience can perceive two. The character Austen in "The Chaser" is locked into such irony; he believes that the only potion he will ever need is the one that will win him love, while the old man and the readers know that he will one day return for the poison. The classic example of dramatic irony is found in the play *Oedipus Rex* by Sophocles (p. 1132). All his life Oedipus has been enclosed by fate, which he can never escape. As the play draws to its climax and Oedipus believes that he is about to discover the murderer of his father, the audience knows that he is drawing closer to the point of his own self-destruction: As he condemns the murderer, he is also condemning himself.

READING FOR TONE

Because so many parts of a story—situation, character, style, audience— are relevant to a consideration of tone, it is important to read with alertness to the potential full impact of any particular passage. To see how everything can work at once, let us consider Jonathan Swift's novelistic satire *Gulliver's Travels* (1726), a work known for its control of tone. The following passage from the fourth voyage is readily approachable for modern readers, for it contains a list of weaponry and the horrors of warfare (alas). Swift's speaker is the protagonist Gulliver, who is describing eighteenth-century English military exploits with a certain degree of naive pride:

. . . being no stranger to the art of war, I gave . . . a description of cannons, culverins, muskets, carabines, pistols, bullets, powder, swords, bayonets, battles, sieges, retreats, attacks, undermines, countermines, bombardments, sea-fights; ships sunk with a thousand men, twenty thousand killed on each side; dying groans, limbs flying in the air, smoke, noise, confusion, trampling to death under horses' feet; flight, pursuit, victory; fields strewed with carcasses left for food to dogs, and wolves, and birds of prey; plundering, stripping, ravishing, burning and destroying. And to set forth the valour of my own dear countrymen, I assured him, that I had seen them blow up a hundred enemies at once in a siege, and as many in a ship, and beheld the dead bodies drop down in pieces from the clouds, to the great diversion of all the spectators.

The tone is that of condemnation, angry but cold. Swift is in control. He achieves his tone in a number of ways. First, Gulliver thinks he is praising war while the sensitive reader receives entirely different signals. The reader and Swift provide a humane political and moral context against which Gulliver's words are to be measured. Thus we have an example of situational irony. Second, the texture of the passage is one of accumulation. Swift has Gulliver list all the death-dealing weapons and all the horrible consequences of warfare. The condemnation of war is achieved by the multiplication of examples alone, virtually overcoming all possible opposing views. Third, there is verbal irony in phrases like "the valour of my own dear countrymen" and "to the great diversion of all the spectators." This is hyperbole that cuttingly exposes the callousness to suffering that usually accompanies war. Fourth, the passage is capable of producing laughter— not happy laughter, but laughter of amazement and repulsion at the incongruity caused by the common moral pretensions of many people and their dereliction of these pretensions during warfare. When you read the passage, you respond to everything at once, yet analysis reveals a passage of high complexity. Swift's control of tone is the cause of your responses.

As you read, then, remember that studying tone requires an awareness of everything in a work that contributes to more than denotative statement. To perceive tone you should be constantly aware of the general impressions that various passages leave you with and you should be analytical enough to study the ways the writers achieve these effects. It is necessary first to understand all the words and all the situations. Read the work carefully, and then study passages selected for discussion to determine matters such as the situations that prompt dialogue, the appropriateness of style (e.g., speech to character, descriptions to setting and action), the comparative freedom the characters may exert to control their fates, the presence of humor, and apparent attitudes toward readers. Because so much in the story may affect the tone, it is important not to overlook anything that can be relevant.

AMÉRICO PARÉDES (b. 1915)

The Hammon and the Beans   *1963*

Once we lived in one of my grandfather's houses near Fort Jones.° It was just a
block from the parade grounds, a big frame house painted a dirty yellow. My
mother hated it, especially because of the pigeons that cooed all day about the
eaves. They had fleas, she said. But it was a quiet neighborhood at least, too far
from the center of town for automobiles and too near for musical, night-roaming
drunks.

At this time Jonesville-on-the Grande was not the thriving little city that it
is today. We told off our days by the routine on the post. At six sharp the flag
was raised on the parade grounds to the cackling of the bugles, and a field piece
thundered out a salute. The sound of the shot bounced away through the morning
mist until its echoes worked their way into every corner of town. Jonesville-on-
the-Grande woke to the cannon's roar, as if to battle, and the day began.

At eight the whistle from the post laundry sent us children off to school.
The whole town stopped for lunch with the noon whistle, and after lunch everybody
went back to work when the post laundry said that it was one o'clock, except for
those who could afford to be old-fashioned and took the siesta. The post was
the town's clock, you might have said, or like some insistent elder person who
was always there to tell you it was time.

At six the flag came down, and we went to watch through the high wire fence
that divided the post from the town. Sometimes we joined in the ceremony,
standing at salute until the sound of the cannon made us jump. That must have
been when we had just studied about George Washington in school, or recited
"The Song of Marion's Men"° about Marion the Fox and the British cavalry that
chased him up and down the broad Santee. But at other times we stuck out our
tongues and jeered at the soldiers. Perhaps the night before we had hung at the
edges of a group of old men and listened to tales about Aniceto Pizaña and the
"border troubles,"° as the local paper still called them when it referred to them
gingerly in passing.

It was because of the border troubles, ten years or so before, that the soldiers
had come back to old Fort Jones. But we did not hate them for that; we admired
them even, at least sometimes. But when we were thinking about the border troubles
instead of Marion the Fox we hooted them and the flag they were lowering, which
for the moment was theirs alone, just as we would have jeered an opposing ball

Fort Jones: The setting of Fort Jones and Jonesville-on-the-Grande in Texas is fictional.
The story takes place in the mid-1920s, one of the most turbulent periods of Mexican history
and only a few years after the deaths of two of the greatest heroes of the Mexican revolution—
Pancho Villa (1877–1923) and Emiliano Zapata (ca. 1879–1919).

    "Song of Marion's Men": a poem by William Cullen Bryant (1794–1878) about Colonel
Francis Marion (ca. 1732–1795), who was a leader of irregular guerilla forces in South Carolina
during the Revolutionary War. Because of his hit-and-run tactics, involving his hiding in
the swamps near the "broad Santee" river in South Carolina, Marion was given the name
of the "Swamp Fox."

    border troubles: The most serious border incidents occurred in 1916, when Pancho Villa
was responsible for deaths of Americans on both sides of the border. He made repeated
raids into New Mexico and Texas.

team, in a friendly sort of way. On these occasions even Chonita would join in the mockery, though she usually ran home at the stroke of six. But whether we taunted or saluted, the distant men in khaki uniforms went about their motions without noticing us at all.

The last word from the post came in the night when a distant bugle blew. At nine it was all right because all the lights were on. But sometimes I heard it at eleven when everything was dark and still, and it made me feel that I was all alone in the world. I would even doubt that I was me, and that put me in such a fright that I felt like yelling out just to make sure I was really there. But next morning the sun shone and life began all over again. With its whistles and cannon shots and bugles blowing. And so we lived, we and the post, side by side with the wire fence in between.

The wandering soldiers whom the bugle called home at night did not wander in our neighborhood, and none of us ever went into Fort Jones. None except Chonita. Every evening when the flag came down she would leave off playing and go down towards what was known as the "lower" gate of the post, the one that opened not on Main Street but against the poorest part of town. She went into the grounds and to the mess halls and pressed her nose against the screens and watched the soldiers eat. They sat at long tables calling to each other through food-stuffed mouths.

"Hey bud, pass the coffee!"

"Give me the ham!"

"Yeah, give me the beans!"   10

After the soldiers were through the cooks came out and scolded Chonita, and then they gave her packages with things to eat.

Chonita's mother did our washing, in gratefulness—as my mother put it— for the use of a vacant lot of my grandfather's which was a couple of blocks down the street. On the lot was an old one-room shack which had been a shed long ago, and this Chonita's father had patched up with flattened-out pieces of tin. He was a laborer. Ever since the end of the border troubles there had been a development boom in the Valley, and Chonita's father was getting his share of the good times. Clearing brush and building irrigation ditches he sometimes pulled down as much as six dollars a week. He drank a good deal of it up, it was true. But corn was just a few cents a bushel in those days. He was the breadwinner, you might say, while Chonita furnished the luxuries.

Chonita was a poet too. I had just moved into the neighborhood when a boy came up to me and said, "Come on! Let's go hear Chonita make a speech."

She was already on top of the alley fence when we got there, a scrawny little girl of about nine, her bare dirty feet clinging to the fence almost like hands. A dozen other kids were there below her, waiting. Some were boys I knew at school; five or six were her younger brothers and sisters.

"Speech! Speech!" they all cried. "Let Chonita make a speech! Talk in En-   15
glish, Chonita!"

They were grinning and nudging each other except for her brothers and sisters, who looked up at her with proud serious faces. She gazed out beyond us all with a grand, distant air and then she spoke.

"Give me the hammon and the beans!" she yelled. "Give me the hammon and the beans!"

She leaped off the fence and everybody cheered and told her how good it was and how she could talk English better than the teachers at the grammar school.

I thought it was a pretty poor joke. Every evening almost, they would make her get up on the fence and yell, "Give me the hammon and the beans!" And everybody would cheer and make her think she was talking English. As for me, I would wait there until she got it over with so we could play at something else. I wondered how long it would be before they got tired of it all. I never did find out because just about that time I got the chills and fever, and when I got up and around Chonita wasn't there anymore.

In later years I thought of her a lot, especially during the thirties when I was growing up. Those years would have been just made for her. Many's the time I have seen her in my mind's eyes, in the picket lines demanding not bread, not cake, but the hammon and the beans. But it didn't work out that way.   20

One night Doctor Zapata came into our kitchen through the back door. He set his bag on the table and said to my father, who had opened the door for him, "Well, she is dead."

My father flinched. "What was it?" he asked.

The doctor had gone to the window and he stood with his back to us, looking out toward the light of Fort Jones. "Pneumonia, flu, malnutrition, worms, the evil eye," he said without turning around. "What the hell difference does it make?"

"I wish I had known how sick she was," my father said in a very mild tone. "Not that it's really my affair, but I wish I had."

The doctor snorted and shook his head.   25

My mother came in and I asked her who was dead. She told me. It made me feel strange but I did not cry. My mother put her arm around my shoulders. "She is in Heaven now," she said. "She is happy."

I shrugged her arm away and sat down in one of the kitchen chairs.

"They're like animals," the doctor was saying. He turned round suddenly and his eyes glistened in the light. "Do you know what that brute of a father was doing when I left? He was laughing! Drinking and laughing with his friends."

"There's no telling what the poor man feels," my mother said.

My father made a deprecatory gesture. "It wasn't his daughter anyway."   30

"No?" the doctor said. He sounded interested.

"This is the woman's second husband," my father explained. "First one died before the girl was born, shot and hanged from a mesquite limb. He was working too close to the tracks the day the Olmito train was derailed."

"You know what?" the doctor said. "In classical times they did things better. Take Troy, for instance. After they stormed the city they grabbed the babies by the heels and dashed them against the wall. That was more humane."

My father smiled. "You sound very radical. You sound just like your relative down there in Morelos."°

"No relative of mine," the doctor said. "I'm a conservative, the son of a conservative, and you know that I wouldn't be here except for that little detail."   35

"Habit," my father said. "Pure habit, pure tradition. You're a radical at heart."

"It depends on how you define radicalism," the doctor answered. "People tend to use words too loosely. A dentist could be called a radical, I suppose. He pulls up things by the roots."

Morelos: the home state of Zapata.

My father chuckled.

"Any bandit in Mexico nowadays can give himself a political label," the doctor went on, "and that makes him respectable. He's a leader of the people."

"Take Villa, now—" my father began.   40

"Villa was a different type of man," the doctor broke in.

"I don't see any difference."

The doctor came over to the table and sat down. "Now look at it this way," he began, his finger in front of my father's face. My father threw back his head and laughed.

"You'd better go to bed and rest," my mother told me. "You're not completely well, you know."

So I went to bed, but I didn't go to sleep, not right away. I lay there for a   45
long time while behind my darkened eyelids Emiliano Zapata's cavalry charged down to the broad Santee, where there were grave men with hoary hairs.° I was still awake at eleven when the cold voice of the bugle went gliding in and out of the dark like something that couldn't find its way back to wherever it had been. I thought of Chonita in Heaven, and I saw her in her torn and dirty dress, with a pair of bright wings attached, flying round and round like a butterfly shouting, "Give me the hammon and the beans!"

Then I cried. And whether it was the bugle, or whether it was Chonita or what, to this day I do not know. But cry I did, and I felt much better after that.

Grave men with hoary hairs: Cf. lines 49–52 of Bryant's "Song of Marion's Men:"

> Grave Men there are by broad Santee,
> Grave men with hoary hairs;
> Their hearts are all with Marion,
> For Marion are their prayers.

QUESTIONS

1. How does Parédes establish the setting of the story? What is the significance of the fort? Of the "dirty yellow" paint? Of the vacant lot and the shack?

2. What is the point of view in the story? Who is the narrator? About how old was the narrator when the events related in the story occurred? About how old is the narrator as he or she tells the story? What effect is produced by this difference in age?

3. What effect does "Fort Jones" have on "Jonesville-on-the-Grande"? What two opposing attitudes do the children have toward the fort and the soldiers? How might you account for these two attitudes?

4. Who is the protagonist in the story? Who (or what) is the antagonist?

5. How is Chonita described? What is her family like? How do her actions at the mess hall and her "speeches" help characterize her and her family?

6. Is Chonita a round or flat character? Dynamic or static? Individual or representative? To what extent do the author's choices about this character allow her to work as a symbol or representative of a whole ethnic group?

7. What is the central conflict in the story? Where is the climax? To what extent is the central conflict resolved?

8. What is the tone of the story (some possibilities: joyful, sorrowful, ironic, cynical, resigned, bitter, resentful)? What techniques does Parédes use to control the tone?

9. To what extent does the characterization of Doctor Zapata (interesting name) help to control the tone? How does the doctor's own attitude toward Chonita's death and the words he uses to announce it help to control the tone?

10. Describe the concern in the story with political, social, and broadly human problems. How does the tale of Chonita's brief life and her death figure into the larger sociopolitical framework of the story?

11. Describe the irony of the situation in which the Mexican-American children learn in school about Washington, the American Revolutionary War, and the guerilla tactics of Marion but seem to be taught nothing about the political movements represented by Villa and Zapata?

12. Near the conclusion of Bryant's "Song of Marion's Men" the following four lines appear:

> And lovely ladies greet our band [i.e., of soldiers]
> With kindliest welcoming,
> And smiles like those of summer,
> And tears like those of spring.
> —lines 53–56

Contrast the women of these lines with the narrator's vision of Chonita in heaven. How might this vision affect the narrator's thoughts about the meaning of Chonita's life in subsequent years (he says that he thought about her many times in the 1930's)?

JOHN COLLIER (b. 1901)

The Chaser   1940

Alan Austen, as nervous as a kitten, went up certain dark and creaky stairs in the neighborhood of Pell Street, and peered about for a long time on the dim landing before he found the name he wanted written obscurely on one of the doors.

He pushed open this door, as he had been told to do, and found himself in a tiny room, which contained no furniture but a plain kitchen table, a rocking-chair, and an ordinary chair. On one of the dirty buff-coloured walls were a couple of shelves, containing in all perhaps a dozen bottles and jars.

An old man sat in the rocking-chair, reading a newspaper. Alan, without a word, handed him the card he had been given. "Sit down, Mr. Austen," said the old man very politely. "I am glad to make your acquaintance."

"Is it true," asked Alan, "that you have a certain mixture that has—er—quite extraordinary effects?"

"My dear sir," replied the old man, "my stock in trade is not very large—I don't deal in laxatives and teething mixtures—but such as it is, it is varied. I think nothing I sell has effects which could be precisely described as ordinary."

"Well, the fact is . . ." began Alan.

"Here, for example," interrupted the old man, reaching for a bottle from

the shelf. "Here is a liquid as colourless as water, almost tasteless, quite imprecepti-
ble in coffee, wine, or any other beverage. It is also quite imperceptible to any
known method of autopsy."

"Do you mean it is a poison?" cried Alan, very much horrified.

"Call it a glove-cleaner if you like," said the old man indifferently. "Maybe
it will clean gloves. I have never tried. One might call it a life-cleaner. Lives need
cleaning sometimes.

"I want nothing of that sort," said Alan. 10

"Probably it is just as well," said the old man. "Do you know the price of
this? For one teaspoonful, which is sufficient, I ask five thousand dollars. Never
less. Not a penny less."

"I hope all your mixtures are not as expensive," said Alan apprehensively.

"Oh dear, no," said the old man. "It would be no good charging that sort
of price for a love potion, for example. Young people who need a love potion
very seldom have five thousand dollars. Otherwise they would not need a love
potion."

"I am glad to hear that," said Alan.

"I look at it like this," said the old man. "Please a customer with one article, 15
and he will come back when he needs another. Even if it *is* more costly. He will
save up for it, if necessary."

"So," said Alan, "you really do sell love potions?"

"If I did not sell love potions," said the old man, reaching for another bottle,
"I should not have mentioned the other matter to you. It is only when one is in
a position to oblige that one can afford to be so confidential."

"And these potions," said Alan. "They are not just—just—er—"

"Oh, no," said the old man. "Their effects are permanent, and extend far
beyond the mere casual impulse. But they include it. Oh, yes, they include it.
Bountifully, insistently. Everlastingly."

"Dear me!" said Alan, attempting a look of scientific detachment. "How 20
very interesting!"

"But consider the spiritual side," said the old man.

"I do, indeed," said Alan.

"For indifference," said the old man, "they substitute devotion. For scorn,
adoration. Give one tiny measure of this to the young lady—its flavour is imperceptible in orange juice, soup, or cocktails—and however gay and giddy she is, she
will change altogether. She will want nothing but solitude and you."

"I can hardly believe it," said Alan. "She is so fond of parties."

"She will not like them any more," said the old man. "She will be afraid of 25
the pretty girls you may meet."

"She will actually be jealous?" cried Alan in a rapture. "Of me?"

"Yes, she will want to be everything to you."

"She is, already. Only she doesn't care about it."

"She will, when she has taken this. She will care intensely. You will be her
sole interest in life."

"Wonderful!" cried Alan. 30

"She will want to know all you do," said the old man. "All that has happened
to you during the day. Every word of it. She will want to know what you are
thinking about, why you smile suddenly, why you are looking sad."

"That is love!" cried Alan.

"Yes," said the old man. "How carefully she will look after you! She will never allow you to be tired, to sit in a draught, to neglect your food. If you are an hour late, she will be terrified. She will think you are killed, or that some siren has caught you."

"I can hardly imagine Diana like that!" cried Alan, overwhelmed with joy.

"You will not have to use your imagination," said the old man. "And, by   35
the way, since there are always sirens, if by any chance you *should*, later on, slip a little, you need not worry. She will forgive you, in the end. She will be terribly hurt, of course, but she will forgive you—in the end."

"That will not happen," said Alan fervently.

"Of course not," said the old man. "But, if it did, you need not worry. She would never divorce you. Oh, no! And, of course, she will never give you the least, the very least, grounds for—uneasiness."

"And how much," said Alan, "is this wonderful mixture?"

"It is not as dear," said the old man, "as the glove-cleaner, or life-cleaner, as I sometimes call it. No. That is five thousand dollars, never a penny less. One has to be older than you are, to indulge in that sort of thing. One has to save up for it."

"But the love potion?" said Alan.   40

"Oh, that," said the old man, opening the drawer in the kitchen table, and taking out a tiny, rather dirty-looking phial. "That is just a dollar."

"I can't tell you how grateful I am," said Alan, watching him fill it.

"I like to oblige," said the old man. "Then customers come back, later in life, when they are better off, and want more expensive things. Here you are. You will find it very effective."

"Thank you again," said Alan. "Good-bye."

"Au revoir," said the old man.   45

QUESTIONS

1. Summarize the plot of this story. What are the qualities of the poison that the old man tells Austen about? What are the powers of the love potion? What is the connection between the love potion and the "spot remover"?

2. Who is the protagonist in the story? What is his problem? What is the solution to his problem?

3. What is the central conflict in the story? How is this conflict resolved? To what extent is this resolution complete? What new problem or conflict is introduced at the end of the story?

4. Are the two characters in this story static or dynamic? Round or flat? Representative or individual? To what extent do these choices help focus the story and control the tone?

5. What type of person is Alan Austen? What does he think love should be? What is the old man's attitude toward love?

6. What is Diana like? What does Alan want her to be like? What does the old man say she will be like after drinking the love potion?

7. How is the setting of the story described? What is the old man's apartment like? How does this description contribute to the mood of the story and the characterization of the old man?

8. What point of view is used in the story? What is the effect of using this point of view? What does it force us to do?

9. To what extent do the words of the story control the tone and attitude? What specific words help us form an attitude toward Alan Austen? Toward the old man?

10. To what extent is the story ironic? What do we and the old man know that Alan Austen doesn't?

11. How is the title of the story ironic? What is a "chaser"? How are the old man's last words in the story ironic?

12. What point does this story make about love? About youth? About human desire? How can the story be taken as a commentary about the need for developing love relationships that preserve individuality as well as romantic commitment?

SHIRLEY JACKSON (1919–1965)

About Two Nice People   *1951*

A problem of some importance, certainly, these days, is that of anger. When one half of the world is angry at the other half, or one half of a nation is angry at the rest, or one side of town feuds with the other side, it is hardly surprising, when you stop to think about it, that so many people lose their tempers with so many other people. Even if, as in this case, they are two people not usually angry, two people whose lives are obscure and whose emotions are gentle, whose smiles are amiable and whose voices are more apt to be cheerful than raised in fury. Two people, in other words, who would much rather be friends than not and who yet, for some reason, perhaps chemical or sociological or environmental, enter upon a mutual feeling of dislike so intense that only a very drastic means can bring them out of it.

Take two such people:

Ellen Webster was what is referred to among her friends as a "sweet" girl. She had pretty, soft hair and dark, soft eyes, and she dressed in soft colors and wore frequently a lovely old-fashioned brooch which had belonged to her grandmother. Ellen thought of herself as a very happy and very lucky person, because she had a good job, was able to buy herself a fair number of soft-colored dresses and skirts and sweaters and coats and hats; she had, by working hard at it evenings, transformed her one-room apartment from a bare, neat place into a charming little refuge with her sewing basket on the table and a canary at the window; she had a reasonable conviction that someday, perhaps soon, she would fall in love with a nice young man and they would be married and Ellen would devote herself wholeheartedly to children and baking cakes and mending socks. This not-very-unusual situation, with its perfectly ordinary state of mind, was a source of great happiness to Ellen. She was, in a word, not one of those who rail against their fate, who live in sullen hatred of the world. She was—her friends were right—a sweet girl.

On the other hand, even if you would not have called Walter Nesmith sweet, you would very readily have thought of him as a "nice" fellow, or an "agreeable" person, or even—if you happened to be a little old white-haired lady—a "dear boy." There was a subtle resemblance between Ellen Webster and Walter Nesmith. Both of them were the first resort of their friends in trouble, for instance. Walter's ambitions, which included the rest of his life, were refreshingly similar to Ellen's: Walter thought that someday he might meet some sweet girl, and would then devote himself wholeheartedly to coming home of an evening to read his paper and perhaps work in the garden on Sundays.

Walter thought that he would like to have two children, a boy and a girl.   5 Ellen thought that she would like to have three children, a boy and two girls. Walter was very fond of cherry pie, Ellen preferred Boston cream. Ellen enjoyed romantic movies, Walter preferred Westerns. They read almost exactly the same books.

In the ordinary course of events, the friction between Ellen and Walter would have been very slight. But—and what could cause a thing like this?—the ordinary course of events was shattered by a trifle like a telephone call.

Ellen's telephone number was 3—4126. Walter's telephone number was 3—4216. Ellen lived in apartment 3-A and Walter lived in apartment 3-B; these apartments were across the hall from each other and very often Ellen, opening her door at precisely quarter of nine in the morning and going toward the elevator, met Walter, who opened *his* door at precisely quarter of nine in the morning and went toward the elevator. On these occasions Ellen customarily said "Good morning" and looked steadfastly the other way. Walter usually answered "Good morning," and avoided looking in her direction. Ellen thought that a girl who allowed herself to be informal with strangers created a bad impression, and Walter thought that a man who took advantage of living in the same building to strike up an acquaintance with a girl was a man of little principle. One particularly fine morning, he said to Ellen in the elevator, "Lovely day," and she replied, "Yes, isn't it?" and both of them felt scarcely that they had been bold. How this mutual respect for each other's dignity could have degenerated into fury is a mystery not easily understood.

It happened that one evening—and, to do her strict justice, Ellen had had a hard day, she was coming down with a cold, it had rained steadily for a week, her stockings were unwashed, and she had broken a fingernail—the phone which had the number 3—4126 rang. Ellen had been opening a can of chicken soup in the kitchenette, and she had her hands full; she said "Darn," and managed to drop and break a cup in her hurry to answer the phone.

"Hello?" she said, thinking, *This is going to be something cheerful*.

"Hello, is Walter there?"   10

"Walter?"

"Walter Nesmith. I want to speak to Walter, please."

"This is the wrong number," Ellen said thinking with the self-pity that comes with the first stages of a head cold that no one ever called *her*.

"Is this three—four two one six?"

"This is three four one two six," Ellen said, and hung up.   15

At that time, although she knew that the person in the apartment across the hall was named Walter Nesmith, she could not have told the color of his hair or even of the outside of his apartment door. She went back to her soup and had a match in her hand to light the stove when the phone rang again.

"Hello?" Ellen said without enthusiasm; this *could* be someone cheerful, she was thinking.

"Hello, is Walter there?"

"This is the wrong number again," Ellen said; if she had not been such a very sweet girl she might have let more irritation show in her voice.

"I *want* to *speak* to Walter Nesmith, *please*." 20

"This is three—four one two six again," Ellen said patiently. "You want three—four two one six."

"What?" said the voice.

"This," said Ellen, "is number three—four one two six. The number you want is three—four two one six." Like anyone who has tried to say a series of numbers several times, she found her anger growing. Surely anyone of *normal* intelligence, she was thinking, surely anyone *ought* to be able to dial a phone, anyone who can't dial a phone shouldn't be allowed to have a nickel.

She got all the way back into the kitchenette and was reaching out for the can of soup before the phone rang again. This time when she answered she said "Hello?" rather sharply for Ellen, and with no illusions about who it was going to be.

"Hello, may I please speak to Walter?" 25

At that point it started. Ellen had a headache and it was raining and she was tired and she was apparently not going to get any chicken soup until this annoyance was stopped.

"Just a minute," she said into the phone.

She put the phone down with an understandable bang on the table, and marched, without taking time to think, out of her apartment and up to the door across the hall. "Walter Nesmith" said a small card at the doorbell. Ellen rang the doorbell with what was, for her, a vicious poke. When the door opened she said immediately, without looking at him:

"Are you Walter Nesmith?"

Now Walter had had a hard day, too, and *he* was coming down with a cold, 30 and *he* had been trying ineffectually to make himself a cup of hot tea in which he intended to put a spoonful of honey to ease his throat, that being a remedy his aunt had always recommended for the first onslaught of a cold. If there had been one fraction less irritation in Ellen's voice, or if Walter had not taken off his shoes when he came home that night, it might very probably have turned out to be a pleasant introduction, with Walter and Ellen dining together on chicken soup and hot tea, and perhaps even sharing a bottle of cough medicine. But when Walter opened the door and heard Ellen's voice, he was unable to answer her cordially, and so he said briefly:

"I am. Why?"

"Will you please come and answer my phone?" said Ellen, too annoyed to realize that this request might perhaps bewilder Walter.

"Answer your phone?" said Walter stupidly.

"Answer my phone," said Ellen firmly. She turned and went back across the hall, and Walter stood in his doorway in his stocking feet and watched her numbly. "Come on," she said sharply, as she went into her own apartment, and Walter, wondering briefly if they allowed harmless lunatics to live alone as though they were just like other people, hesitated for an instant and then followed her, on the theory that it would be wiser to do what she said when she seemed so cross, and reassuring himself that he could leave the door open and yell for help if necessary. Ellen stamped into her apartment and pointed at the phone where it lay on the table. "There. Answer it."

Eying her sideways, Walter edged over to the phone and picked it up. "Hello," 35 he said nervously. Then, "Hello? Hello?" Looking at her over the top of the phone, he said, "What do you want me to do now?"

"Do you mean to say," said Ellen ominously, "that that terrible terrible person has hung up?"

"I guess so," said Walter, and fled back to his apartment.

The door had only just closed behind him when the phone rang again, and Ellen, answering it, heard, "May I speak to Walter, please?"

Not a very serious mischance, surely. But the next morning Walter pointedly avoided going down in the elevator with Ellen, and sometime during that day the deliveryman left a package addressed to Ellen at Walter's door.

When Walter found the package he took it manfully under his arm and went 40 boldly across the hall, and rang Ellen's doorbell. When Ellen opened her door she thought at first—and she may have been justified—that Walter had come to apologize for the phone call the evening before, and she even thought that the package under his arm might contain something delightfully unexpected, like a box of candy. They lost another chance then; if Walter had not held out the package and said "Here," Ellen would not have gone on thinking that he was trying to apologize in his own shy way, and she would certainly not have smiled warmly, and said, "You *shouldn't* have bothered."

Walter, who regarded transporting a misdelivered parcel across the hall as relatively little bother, said blankly, "No bother at all," and Ellen, still deceived, said, "But it really wasn't *that* important."

Walter went back into his own apartment convinced that this was a very odd girl indeed, and Ellen, finding that the package had been mailed to her and contained a wool scarf knitted by a cousin, was as much angry as embarrassed because, once having imagined that an apology is forthcoming, it is very annoying not to have one after all, and particularly to have a wool scarf instead of a box of candy.

How this situation disintegrated into the white-hot fury which rose between these two is a puzzle, except for the basic fact that when once a series of misadventures has begun between two people, everything tends to contribute further to a state of misunderstanding. Thus, Ellen opened a letter of Walter's by mistake, and Walter dropped a bottle of milk—he was still trying to cure his cold, and thought that perhaps milk toast was the thing—directly outside Ellen's door, so that even after his nervous attempts to clear it up, the floor was still littered with fragments of glass, and puddled with milk.

Then Ellen—who believed by now that Walter had thrown the bottle of milk against her door—allowed herself to become so far confused by this succession of small annoyances that she actually wrote and mailed a letter to Walter, asking politely that he try to turn down his radio a little in the evenings. Walter replied with a frigid letter to the effect that certainly if he had known that she was bothered by his radio, he should surely never have dreamed—

That evening, perhaps by accident, his radio was so loud that Ellen's canary woke up and chirped hysterically, and Ellen, pacing her floor in incoherent fury, might have been heard—if there had been anyone to hear her, and if Walter's radio had not been so loud—to say, "I'll get even with him!" A phrase, it must be said, which Ellen had never used before in her life.

Ellen made her preparations with a sort of loving care that might well have been lavished on some more worthy object. When the alarm went off she turned in her sleep and smiled before quite waking up, and, once awake and the alarm turned off, she almost laughed out loud. In her slippers and gown, the clock in her hand, she went across her small apartment to the phone; the number was one she was not soon apt to forget. The dial tone sounded amazingly loud, and for a minute she was almost frightened out of her resolution. Then, setting her teeth, she dialed the number, her hand steady. After a second's interminable wait, the ringing began. The phone at the other end rang three times, four times, with what seemed interminable waits between, as though even the mechanical phone system hesitated at this act. Then, at last, there was an irritable crash at the other end of the line, and a voice said, "Wah?"

"Good morning," said Ellen brightly. "I'm so terribly sorry to disturb you at this hour."

"Wah?"

"This is Ellen Webster," said Ellen still brightly. "I called to tell you that my clock has stopped—"

"Wah?"

"—and I wonder if you could tell me what time it is?"

There was a short pause at the other end of the line. Then after a minute, his voice came back: "Tenny minna fah."

"I beg your pardon?"

There was another short pause at the other end of the line, as of someone opening his eyes with a shock. "Twenty minutes after four," he said. "*Twenty minutes after four.*"

"The reason I thought of asking you," Ellen said sweetly, "was that you were so *very* obliging before. About the radio, I mean."

"—calling a person at—"

"Thanks so much," said Ellen. "Good-by."

She felt fairly certain that he would not call her back, but she sat on her bed and giggled a little before she went back to sleep.

Walter's response to this was miserably weak: he contacted a neighboring delicatessen a day or so later, and had an assortment of evil-smelling cheese left in Ellen's apartment while she was out. This, which required persuading the superintendent to open Ellen's apartment so that the package might be left inside, was a poor revenge but a monstrous exercise of imagination upon Walter's part, so that, in one sense, Ellen was already bringing out in him qualities he never knew he had. The cheese, it turned out, more than evened the score: the apartment was small, the day was warm, and Ellen did not get home until late, and long after most of the other tenants on the floor had gone to the superintendent with their complaints about something dead in the woodwork.

Since breaking and entering had thus become one of the rules of their game,

45

50

55

60

Ellen felt privileged to retaliate in kind upon Walter. It was with great joy, some evenings later, that Ellen, sitting in her odorous apartment, heard Walter's scream of pure terror when he put his feet into his slippers and found a raw egg in each.

Walter had another weapon, however, which he had been so far reluctant to use; it was a howitzer of such proportions that Walter felt its use would end warfare utterly. After the raw eggs he felt no compunction whatever in bringing out his heavy artillery.

It seemed to Ellen, at first, as though peace had been declared. For almost a week things went along smoothly; Walter kept his radio turned down almost to inaudibility, so that Ellen got plenty of sleep. She was over her cold, the sun had come out, and on Saturday morning she spent three hours shopping, and found exactly the dress she wanted at less than she expected to pay.

About Saturday noon she stepped out of the elevator, her packages under her arm, and walked briskly down the hall to her apartment, making, as usual, a wide half circle to avoid coming into contact with the area around Walter's door.

Her apartment door, to her surprise, was open, but before she had time to phrase a question in her own mind, she had stepped inside and come face to face with a lady who—not to make any more mysteries—was Walter Nesmith's aunt, and a wicked old lady in her own way, possessing none of Walter's timidity and none of his tact.

"Who?" said Ellen weakly, standing in the doorway.   65

"Come in and close the door," said the old lady darkly. "I don't think you'll want your neighbors to near what I have to say. I," she continued as Ellen obeyed mechanically, "am Mrs. Harold Vongarten Nesmith. Walter Nesmith, young woman, is my nephew."

"Then you are in the wrong apartment," said Ellen, quite politely considering the reaction which Walter Nesmith's name was beginning by now to arouse in her. "You want Apartment Three-B, across the hall."

"I do *not*," said the old lady firmly. "I came here to see the designing young woman who has been shamelessly pursuing my nephew, and to warn her"—the old lady shook her gloves menacingly—"to warn her that *not one cent* shall she have from me if she marries Walter Nesmith."

"Marries?" said Ellen, thoughts too great for words in her heart.

"It has long been my opinion that some young woman would be after Walter   70
Nesmith for his money," said Walter's aunt with satisfaction.

"Believe me," said Ellen wholeheartedly, "there is not that much money in the world."

"You deny it?" The old lady leaned back and smiled triumphantly. "I expected something of the sort. Walter," she called suddenly, and then, putting her head back and howling, "Wal-l-l-l-ter."

"Sh-h-h," said Ellen fearfully. "They'll hear you all over."

"I expect them to," said the old lady. "Wal-l-l-l—Oh, there you are."

Ellen turned, and saw Walter Nesmith, with triumph in his eyes, peering   75
around the edge of the door. "Did it work?" he asked.

"She denies everything," said his aunt.

"About the eggs?" Walter said, confused. "You mean, she denies about the eggs and the phone call and—"

"Look," Ellen said to Walter, stamping across the floor to look him straight in the eye, "of all the insufferable, conceited, rude, self-satisfied—"

"What?" said Walter.

"I wouldn't want to marry you," said Ellen, "if—if—" She stopped for a word, helpless. 80

"If he were the last man on earth," Walter's aunt supplied obligingly. "I think she's really after your *money*, Walter."

Walter stared at his aunt. "I didn't tell you to tell her—" he began. He gasped, and tried again. "I mean," he said, "I never thought—" He appealed to Ellen. "I don't want to marry you, either," he said, and he gasped again, and said, "I mean, I told my aunt to come and tell you—"

"If this is a proposal," Ellen said coldly, "I decline."

"All I wanted her to do was scare you," Walter said finally.

"It's a good way," his aunt said complacently. "Turned out to be the only 85 way with your Uncle Charles and a Hungarian adventuress."

"I mean," Walter said desperately to Ellen, "she owns this building. I mean, I wanted her to tell you that if you didn't stop—I mean, I wanted her to scare you—"

"Apartments are too hard to get these days," his aunt said. "That would have been *too* unkind."

"That's how I got my apartment at all, you see," Walter said to Ellen, still under the impression he was explaining something Ellen wanted to understand.

"Since you have an apartment," Ellen said with restraint, "may I suggest that you take your aunt and the both of you—"

The phone rang. 90

"Excuse me," said Ellen mechanically, moving to answer it. "Hello?" she said.

"Hello, may I speak to Walter, please?"

Ellen smiled rather in the manner that Lady Macbeth might have smiled if she found a run in her stocking.

"It's for you," she said, holding the phone out to Walter.

"For me?" he said, surprised. "Who is it?" 95

"I really could not say," said Ellen sweetly. "Since you have so many friends that one phone is not adequate to answer all their calls—"

Since Walter made no move to take the phone, she put it gently back on the hook.

"They'll call again," she assured him, still smiling in that terrible fashion.

"I ought to turn you both out," said Walter's aunt. She turned to Ellen. "Young woman," she said, "do you deny that all this nonsense with eggs and telephone calls is an attempt to entangle my nephew into matrimony?"

"Certainly not," Ellen said. "I mean, I *do* deny it." 100

"Walter Nesmith," said his aunt, "do you admit that all your finagling with cheeses and radios is an attempt to strike up an acquaintance with this young woman?"

"Certainly," said Walter. "I mean, I do *not* admit it."

"Good," said Walter's aunt. "You are precisely the pair of silly fools I would have picked out for each other." She rose with great dignity, motioned Walter away from her, and started for the door. "Remember," she said, shaking her gloves again at Ellen, "not one cent."

She opened the door and started down the hall, her handkerchief over her eyes, and—a sorry thing in such an old lady—laughing until she had to stop and lean against the wall near the elevator.

"I'm sorry," Walter was saying to Ellen, almost babbling, "I'm *really* sorry   105
this time—please believe me, I had *no* idea—I wouldn't for the world—nothing but the most profound respect—a joke, you know—hope you didn't really think—"

"I understand perfectly," Ellen said icily. "It is all perfectly clear. It only goes to show what I have always believed about young men who think that all they have to do is—"

The phone rang.

Ellen waited a minute before she spoke. Then she said, "You might as well answer it."

"I'm *terribly* sorry," Walter said, not moving toward the phone. "I mean, I'm *terribly* sorry." He waved his hands in the air. "About what she said about what she thought about what you wanted me to do—" His voice trailed off miserably.

Suddenly Ellen began to giggle.   110

Anger is certainly a problem that will bear much analysis. It is hardly surprising that one person may be angry at another, particularly if these are two people who are gentle, usually, and rarely angry, whose emotions tend to be mild and who would rather be friends with everyone than be enemies with anyone. Such an anger argues a situation so acute that only the most drastic readjustment can remedy it.

Either Walter Nesmith or Ellen Webster could have moved, of course. But, as Walter's aunt had pointed out, apartments are not that easy to come by, and their motives and their telephone numbers were by now so inextricably mixed that on the whole it seemed more reasonable not to bother.

Moreover, Walter's aunt, who still snickers when her nephew's name is mentioned, did not keep them long in suspense, after all. She was not lavish, certainly, but she wrote them a letter which both of them found completely confusing and which enclosed a check adequate for a down payment on the extremely modest house in the country they decided upon without disagreement. They even compromised and had four children—two boys and two girls.

QUESTIONS

1. Describe Walter and Ellen as characters. How individually are they presented? Are they round or flat? Are there any stereotypical qualities about them? Does their marriage seem sterotypical?

2. Develop a plan or structure for the story. What relationship do the various farcical incidents have upon Jackson's development of the structure?

3. What is the setting of the story? Can it be easily visualized? What way of life do the two principal characters follow, and how does this way make their eventual union possible? What does the fact that all the action takes place on the third floor of the apartment building contribute to the happy mood of the story?

4. What is the central conflict of the story? Who and/or what are the protagonists and antagonists? How is the complication developed? Where is the crisis of the story, and how is it resolved?

5. Mrs. Nesmith has a small but vital role in the story. Is she flat or round? How much do you learn about her?

6. What is the point of view of the story? To which character does it become limited? How completely does the point of view inform us about this character? At the end, does the point of view continue as being limited, or does it become more properly described as dramatic?

7. In the light of the fact that during most of the story the principal characters are "feuding," describe the irony of the story's resolution. Discuss Jackson's use of the various farcical incidents as one of the means by which she shapes your responses to the story. In terms of tone, how does she keep the little war from being taken too seriously?

8. What sinister turns might the story have taken (such as getting lawyers, dragging each other into court, suing for damages, and so on)? How does Jackson avoid making Mrs. Nesmith one of these more sinister forces, and how does she keep the story comic?

WRITING ABOUT TONE

In preparing to write about tone in a story you will, as always, need to begin with a careful reading. As you study, it is important to note those elements of the story that touch particularly on attitudes or authorial consideration. Thus, for example, as you read Collier's "The Chaser," it would be necessary to consider whether the story asks too much of the reader: Is the prediction of the old man really the horror at the end of the road for all romantic loves? In this respect, the story may cause a certain mental squirming. But is this right? Did Collier want this squirming to occur? Perhaps if the question is phrased another way, the tone might be more adequately understood. If "overly possessive love" is substituted for "romantic love," the story may become more satisfactory, less disturbing. In seeking answers like this one, you will find that the author has been directing you and guiding your responses; that is, that the author's control over tone has been firmly, clearly established.

Similarly, the farcical happenings in "About Two Nice People" might more likely produce anger than love. Does the story ask too much of the reader in the way of belief? Perhaps it does, if we were to accept it as realism, but in the farcical story that it is, the tone might be considered as being right. The story is not real, nor was it intended that way.

The same sorts of questions can apply when you study internal qualities such as style and characterization. Do all the speeches seem right for the speakers and the situations? Are all the descriptions appropriate? Are all the actions believable? In other words, does the author seem to be faithful to the established integrity of the characters? For example, this question might be asked about Mathilde and her husband Loisel in De Maupassant's "The Necklace" (p. 90). Is it plausible that they would not have told Jeanne Forrestier about the loss? In the same way, in Tom Whitecloud's "Blue Winds Dancing" (p. 122), is the young Indian narrator's return home to be accepted as a permanent sacrifice of his educational future, or just a manifestation of homesickness? In studying questions of this sort, you are in fact dealing with issues about the attitudes of the author toward the subject and also toward the audience—the substance of a discussion on tone.

ORGANIZING YOUR ESSAY

INTRODUCTION.   The introduction should begin with a brief description of the situation in the story that prompts the discussion about tone. The central idea should be a brief statement about the tone—such as that the story is one leading to cynicism, as in "The Chaser," or one leading to delight, as in "About Two Nice People." If there are any particular obstacles to the proper determination of the tone, either in the work or in your personal attitudes, these should also be mentioned in the introduction.

BODY.   In the body of your theme you should examine all aspects that in your judgment have a bearing on the tone of the work. Some of the things to cover are these:

1. *The audience, situation,* and *characters.* Is any person or group being directly addressed by the author? What attitude toward the audience seems to be expressed (love, respect, condescension, confidentiality, etc.)? What is the basic situation in the work? Is there any irony in it? If so, what type is it? What does the irony show about the author's attitudes (optimism or pessimism, for example)? How does the author use the situation to shape your responses? That is, can any action, situation, or character be seen as an expression of attitude, or as a means of controlling attitude (see, for example, the old man in "The Chaser")? What is the nature of the author's voice or persona? Does the author seem to manipulate this voice to any degree to convey attitudes? How? Does the author seem to respect, admire, dislike, or evidence other feeling about any characters or situations? Through what techniques are these feelings made clear?

2. *Descriptions, diction.* Analysis of these is stylistic, but your concern here is to relate stylistic technique to attitude. Are there any systematic references, such as to colors, sounds, noises, natural scenes, and so on, that collectively show or seem to reflect an attitude? Does the author manipulate connotation to control your responses? Is any special speech or dialect pattern used to indicate an attitude about speakers or their condition of

life? Do the speech patterns conform to normal or standard usage? What can you make of this? Are there any unusual or noteworthy kinds of expression? What is their effect on the apparent attitude of the author? Does the author use verbal irony? To what effect?

3. *Humor*. Is there humor in the work? What is its intensity? Does the humor develop out of incongruous situations or out of language? Is there an underlying basis of attack in the humor, or are the objects of laughter still respected or even loved despite having humor directed against them?

4. *Ideas*. Ideas may be advocated, defended mildly, or attacked. Which do you seem to have in the work you have been studying? How does the author make his or her attitude clear—directly, by statement, or indirectly, through understatement, overstatement, or the language of a character?

5. *Unique characteristics of the work*. Each work has unique properties that may contribute to the tone. Collier's "The Chaser," for example, is developed almost entirely through the dialogue between the old man and Austen. The tone of the story is therefore to be perceived by an awareness of the attitudes of each of the participants. In other works there might be some recurring word or theme that seems special. Samuel Clemens in "Luck," for example, develops a passage centering on the word *blunder* and thereby makes his attitude clear about the boob hero, Scoresby. When you study any assigned story, be alert for anything unusual or individual that you may use in your essay about tone.

CONCLUSION. The conclusion may summarize the main points of the essay and from there go on to any concluding thoughts about the tone of the story. Redefinitions, explanations, or afterthoughts might belong here, together with reinforcing ideas in support of earlier points. If there are any personal thoughts, any changes of mind, any awakening awarenesses, a brief account of these would also be appropriate here, as long as you demonstrate that they rose out of your analysis of the story's tone.

SAMPLE ESSAY

The Situational and Verbal Irony of Collier's "The Chaser"*

[1] John Collier's "The Chaser" is based on the situational irony of the unreal hope of youth as opposed to the extreme disillusion of age and experience. Collier builds the brief story almost entirely in dialogue between a young man, Alan Austen, who is deeply in love and wants to possess his sweetheart entirely, and an unnamed old man who believes in a life free of romantic involvement. The situation reflects disillusionment so completely that the story may in fact

* See p. 278 for this story.

be called cynical.° This attitude is made plain by the situation, the old man, and the use of double meaning.°

[2] The situation between the two men establishes the story's dominant tone of cynicism. Austen, the young man full of illusions and unreal expectations about love, has come to the old man to buy a love potion so that his sweetheart, Diana, will love him with slavelike adoration. Collier makes it clear that the old man has seen many young men like Austen in the grips of romantic desire before, and he therefore knows that their possessive love will eventually bore and anger them. He knows, because he has already seen these disillusioned customers return to buy the "chaser," which is a deadly, untraceable poison, so that they could kill the women for whom they previously bought the love potion. Thus Collier creates the ironic situation of the story—the beginning of an inevitable process in which Austen, like other young men before him, are made to appear so unrealistic and self-defeating that their enthusiastic passion will someday change into hate and murderousness.

[3] The sales method used by the old man reveals his cynical understanding of men like Austen. Collier makes clear, right at the start, that the old man knows why Austen has come: Before showing his love potion, the old man describes the untraceable poison, which he calls a "glove-cleaner" or "life-cleaner." His aim is actually to sell the expensive poison by using the love potion as inexpensive bait. Thus we see the old man's art of manipulation, for even though Austen is at the moment horrified by the poison, the seed has been planted in his mind. He will always know, when his love for Diana changes, that he will have the choice of "cleaning" his life. This unscrupulous sales method effectively corrupts Austen in advance. Such a calculation on the old man's part is grimly cynical.

[4] Supporting the tone of cynicism in the old man's sales technique is his use of double meaning. His concluding words, "Au revoir" (i.e., "until I see you again"), for example, carry an ironic double meaning. On the one hand, the words conventionally mean "good bye." On the other hand, however, they suggest that the old man expects a future meeting when Austen will return to buy the poison to kill Diana. The old man's acknowledgement of Austen's gratitude shows the same ironic double edge. He says,

> I like to oblige. . . . Then customers come back, later in life, when they are better off, and want more expensive things.

Clearly the "expensive" thing is "the chaser," the undetectable poison. Through such ironic speeches, the old man is politely but cynically telling Austen that his love will not last and that it will eventually bore, irritate, and then torment him to the point where he will want to murder Diana rather than to continue living with her potion-induced possessiveness.

Before "The Chaser" is dismissed as being hopelessly cynical, however, we should note that Austen's ideas about love must inevitably produce just

---

° Central idea.
° Thesis sentence.

[5] such cynicism. The old man's descriptions of the total enslavement that Austen has dreamed about would leave no breathing room for either Austen or Diana. This sort of love excludes everything else in life and becomes suffocating rather than pleasing. It is normal to wish freedom from such psychological imprisonment, even if the prison is of one's own making. Under these conditions, the cynical tone of "The Chaser" suggests that the desire to be totally possessing and possessed—to "want nothing but solitude" and the loved one—can lead only to disaster for both man and woman. The old man's cynicism and the young man's desire suggest the need for an ideal of love that permits interchange, individuality, and understanding. Even though this better ideal is not described anywhere in the story, it is compatible with Collier's situational irony. Thus, cynical as the story unquestionably is, it does not exclude an idealism of tolerant and more human love.

Commentary on the Essay

This essay presents a way in which you can write about a story of dominating pessimism and cynicism without giving in to the underlying negative situational irony. Therefore the essay illustrates how a consideration of tone can aid the development of objective literary judgment.

The introductory paragraph indicates that the aspect of tone to be discussed will be an ironic situation—youthful but unrealistic hope in the context of aged cynicism. The thesis sentence indicates that the body of the essay will deal with (1) this situation and how it is related to (2) the sales method of a major character—the old man—and (3) his speeches containing double meaning.

The second paragraph establishes the situational irony by describing the desires of Austen and the cynical attitude of the old man. In the third paragraph the topic is the sinister manipulation of Austen as a result of the old man's skillful and subtle salesmanship. By stressing that the old man plants the seeds of corruption in Austen, this paragraph continues the topic of the tone of cynicism which is the thematic basis of the essay. The subject of the fourth paragraph, the last in the body of the essay, is Collier's use of double meaning in the speeches of the old man to emphasize the idea that Austen will someday want to kill his wife.

The concluding paragraph is a reflective one. In view of the cynical tone of the story, this paragraph suggests that a more realistic and optimistic attitude about love is possible—a view that while not perceivable in the story is also not incompatible with it.

9

Symbolism and Allegory: Keys to Extended Meaning

SYMBOLISM

Symbolism and *allegory* are modes of literary expression that are designed to extend meaning. **Symbolism** is derived from a Greek word meaning "to throw together" (*syn*, together, and *ballein*, to throw). In literature, a symbol pulls or draws together (1) a specific thing with (2) ideas, values, persons, or ways of life, in a direct relationship that otherwise would not be apparent. A symbol might also be regarded as a substitute for the elements being signified, much as the flag stands for the ideals of the nation.

In short stories and other types of literature, a symbol is usually a person, thing, place, action, situation, or even thought. It possesses its own reality and meaning and may function at the normal level of reality within a story. There is often a topical or integral relationship between the symbol and things it stands for, but a symbol may also have no apparent connection and therefore may be considered arbitrary. What is important, however, is that the symbol points beyond itself to greater and more complex meaning. When a symbol is introduced, like a key opening a lock, it signifies a specific combination of attitudes, a sustained constancy of meaning, and the potential for wide-ranging application. A symbol might appear over and over again in the same story, yet it always maintains the same meaning. Thus you might think of a symbol as a constant against a background of variables, like a theme with variations.

To determine whether something in a story is symbolic, we must decide if it consistently refers beyond itself to a significant idea, emotion, or quality. For example, the ancient mythological character Sisyphus may be considered as a symbol because he is consistently linked with specific ideas. According to legend, he is doomed in the underworld to roll a large boulder up a high hill forever. Just as he gets it to the top, it rolls down, and he is fated to roll it up again, and again, and again, because the rock always rolls back as he gets it to the top. His plight may be seen as a symbol of the human condition: A person rarely if ever completes anything. Work must always be done over and over in every generation, and the same problems confront humanity in each age without any final solution. In the light of such infinitely fruitless effort, life seems to have little meaning. Nevertheless there is hope. People who meet frustration like that experienced by Sisyphus are involved and active in their work even if they are never more than temporarily successful, and in this way they may find meaning in their lives. A writer using Sisyphus as a symbol would want us to understand these ideas as a result of the reference. Symbolism, as you can see, can be a conventionalized shorthand form of communication.

There are other symbols like Sisyphus that are generally or universally recognized, and authors referring to them rely on this common understanding. These types of symbols are sometimes called **cultural** or **universal** symbols. They embody ideas or emotions that the writer and the reader share in common as a result of their social and cultural heritage. When using these symbols, a writer does not have to take the time to invest objects or people with symbolic resonance within the story; she or he can simply assume that the reader knows what the symbol represents. Thus, water, which is the substance in the sacrament of baptism, is acknowledged to be a symbol of life. When water spouts up in a fountain, it may symbolize optimism (as upwelling, bubbling life). A stagnant pool may symbolize life being polluted or diminished. In terms of psychology, water is often understood as a reference to sexuality. Thus, lovers may meet by a quiet lake, a cascading waterfall, a murmuring stream, a wide river, or a stormy sea. The condition of the water in each instance may be interpreted as a symbol of the lovers' romantic relationship. Another generally recognized universal symbol is the serpent, which is often used to represent the Devil, or simply evil. (It was in the form of a serpent, you remember from Genesis 3: 1–7, that Satan tempted Eve in the Garden of Eden.) In "Young Goodman Brown," Nathaniel Hawthorne describes a walking stick that "bore the likeness of a great black snake," in this way instantly evoking the idea of Satanic evil. However, because the stick "might almost be seen to twist and wriggle itself like a living serpent," it may also symbolize human tendencies to see evil where it does not exist.

Objects and descriptions that are not universally recognized as symbols can be developed as symbols only within an individual work. These types of symbols may be termed **private, authorial,** or **contextual** symbols. Unlike universal symbols, these are not derived from common historical, cultural, or religious ground but gain their symbolic meaning within the *context* of the specific work of fiction. For example, the jug of beer carried by Jackie's grandmother in O'Connor's "First Confession" (p. 187) is one of the things that symbolize the grandmother's peasantlike and boorish habits. Similarly, the chrysanthemums tended by Elisa in Steinbeck's "The Chrysanthemums" (p. 318) seem at first nothing more than deeply prized flowers. As the story progresses, however, the flowers gain symbolic significance. The traveling tinsmith's apparent interest in them is the wedge he uses to get a small mending job from Elisa. Her description of the care needed in planting and tending the flowers suggests that they signify her qualities of kindness, love, orderliness, femininity, and, ultimately, her maternal instincts. When, at the end of the story, the flowers are seen dumped at the side of the road, we may conclude that her values have also been dumped and that she has been used and deceived. In short, the chrysanthemums are a major symbol in the story. If you were to encounter references to porter or chrysanthemums in a context other than "First Confession" and "The Chrysanthemums," however, they would not necessarily be symbolic.

In determining whether a particular object or person in a story is a symbol, you need to make decisions based on your judgment of its total significance. If it appears to be of major importance, you can claim it has symbolic value as long as you can show its scope and sustained reference beyond itself. Thus, at the end of Welty's "A Worn Path" (p. 121), Phoenix plans to buy a toy windmill for her sick grandson. The windmill is a small thing, and she will spend all her money for it. It will break soon under constant use, like her life and that of her grandson, but buying it is her attempt to give the boy a little pleasure despite her poverty and the hopelessness of her life. For all these reasons it is justifiable to interpret the windmill as a symbol of her strong character, generous nature, and pathetic existence.

ALLEGORY

Allegory is like symbolism in that both use one thing to refer to something else. The term is derived from the Greek word *allégorein*, which means "to speak so as to imply other than what is said." Allegory, however, tends to be more complex and sustained than symbolism. An allegory is to a symbol as a motion picture is to a still picture; allegory puts symbols into consistent and sustained action. In form, an allegory is a complete and self-sufficient narrative, but it also signifies another series or level of events or conditions of life as expressed in a habit of thought, a philosophy, or a religion. While some works are allegories from beginning to end, many works that are not allegories contain sections or episodes that may be considered allegories.

Allegories and the allegorical method do not exist simply to enable authors to engage in mysterious literary exercises. Rather it was understood at some point in the past that people might more willingly listen to stories instead of moral lessons. Thus, the allegorical method evolved to entertain and instruct at the same time. In addition, the threat of reprisal or censorship sometimes caused authors to express their views indirectly in the form of allegory rather than to write directly. The double meaning that you will find in allegory is hence quite real.

As you study a work for allegory, you should try to determine how an entire story, or a self-contained episode, may be construed as having an extended, allegorical meaning that points consistently to a system of ideas or events beyond the actual occurrences in the text. The popularity of the film *Star Wars* and its sequels, for example, is attributable at least partly to the fact that it may be taken as an allegory of the conflict between good and evil. Obi Wan Kenobi (intelligence) enlists the aid of Luke Skywalker (heroism, boldness) and instructs him in "the force" (religious faith). Thus armed and guided, Skywalker opposes the strength of Darth Vader (evil) to rescue the Princess Leia (purity and goodness) with the aid of the latest spaceships and weaponry (technology). The story is accompanied by ingenious special effects and almost tactile sound effects and music, and hence as an adventure film it stands by itself. With the clear allegorical overtones, however, it stands for any person's quest for self-fulfillment.

To see how it applies, let us consider that Vader is so strong that he imprisons Skywalker for a time, and Skywalker must exert all his skill and strength to get free and to overcome the evil Vader. In the allegorical application of the episode to people generally, it would not be improper to take the temporary imprisonment to refer to those moments of doubt, discouragement, and depression that often beset people seeking an education, a work goal, the good life, a satisfactory marriage, or whatever.

In one form or another, this allegory has been told over and over again. At one time the substance was the hero who went to far lands to gain the prize of the golden fleece; at another, the knight who braved dangers to overcome the dragon. The allegory, in short, is as old as the capacity of human beings to tell stories. As long as the parallel interpretation is kept close and consistent, as in the *Star Wars* films, an extended allegorical interpretation will have validity.

Fable, Parable, and Myth

There are three narrative forms that are special types of allegory: *fable*, *parable*, and *myth*.

FABLE. A **fable** is a short story, often featuring animals with human traits, to which writers and editors attach "morals" or explanations. Such stories are often called **beast fables.** Fables are a very old literary form and have found a place in the literature of most societies. Aesop (sixth century B.C.) was supposedly a slave who composed beast fables in ancient Greece. His fable of "The Fox and the Grapes," for example, signifies the tendency to belittle those things we cannot have. Joel Chandler Harris (1848–1908) was a black American writer whose "Uncle Remus" stories are also beast fables. Walt Disney's "Mickey Mouse" and Walt Kelly's "Pogo" are part of the tradition.

PARABLE.   A **parable** is really a short, simple allegory. Parables are often associated with Jesus, who used them in his teaching to embody religious insights and truth. Parables like those of the Good Samaritan and the Prodigal Son are interpreted to show God's active love, concern, understanding, and forgiveness for human beings.

MYTH (see also Chapter 24).   A **myth** is a story, that myth of Sisyphus, that is associated with the religion, philosophy, and collective psychology of various groups of cultures. Myths sometimes embody scientific truths for prescientific societies; they codify the social and cultural values of the civilization in which they were composed. Sometimes, unfortunately, the term *mythical* is used to suggest that something is untrue. This minimizing of the word reflects a limited appreciation of the psychological and social truths embedded in myths. The truths in mythology are not found literally in the stories themselves, but rather in our symbolic or allegorical interpretation of them.

ALLUSION IN SYMBOLISM AND ALLEGORY

Universal or cultural symbols and allegories often allude to other works from our cultural heritage, such as the Bible, Greco-Roman mythology, or classical literature. Sometimes understanding a story may require knowledge of politics and history. Thus, for example, a major character in Hawthorne's "Young Goodman Brown" is Brown's wife, Faith, who stays at home when he leaves to go on his journey. Later, in the forest, when Brown is seeing his vision of sinful human beings, he exclaims, "My Faith is gone." On the primary level of reading, this statement makes perfect sense, because Brown has concluded that his wife has been lost. However, the symbol of his being married to Faith takes on additional meaning when one notes that it is also an allusion to the Biblical book of Ephesians (2:8) and to the Protestant-Calvinist tradition that the virtue faith is a key to salvation:

> For by grace you have been saved through faith; and this is not your own doing, it is the gift of God—

This Biblical passage might easily take a volume of explanation, but in brief the allusion makes clear that Brown's loss of faith also indicates his perception that he has been abandoned by God. Here is an instance where a symbol gains its resonance and impact through allusion.

This example brings up the issue of how much background you need for detecting allusions in symbolism and allegory. You can often rely on your own knowledge. Sometimes, however, an allusion may escape you if you do not pursue the point in a dictionary or other reference work. The scope of your college dictionary will surprise you. If you cannot find an entry in your dictionary, however, try one of the major encyclopedias, or ask your reference librarian about standard guides like *The Oxford Companion to English Literature*, *The Oxford Companion to Classical Literature*, and William Rose Benet's *The Reader's Encyclopaedia*. A useful aid in finding Biblical references is *Cruden's Complete Concordance*, which in various editions has been used by scholars and readers for more than two centuries (since 1737). This work lists all words used in the King James translation of the Bible, so that you may easily locate the chapter and verse of any Biblical quotation. If you still have trouble after using sources like these, see your instructor for more help.

READING FOR SYMBOLISM AND ALLEGORY

To the extent that literature is true and probable, much of it may be considered symbolic or allegorical. A story is about *one* or *two* persons and those closely associated with them, but if these persons were unlike everyone else in the world, a reading would not promote any extended understanding. Because of similarity to life, a good story therefore lends itself to the kind of reading you will be doing here. Despite this fact, you may be tempted to find symbolism and allegorical meaning where none might exist. Some minor details may be no more significant than being necessary to carry on the story. There will be other significant details, however, that readily bear consideration as symbolism and allegory. In the Parable of the Prodigal Son, for example, the party given by the father might seem like nothing more than a party unless it is taken in conjunction with verse 32 about the rejoicing for the recovery of the son. With this explanation, it is clear that the party is a symbol for the New Testament assertion that God knows human beings, loves them like a parent, sorrows when they lose faith, and rejoices when their faith is restored.

For an allegorical reading the same reservation and care are needed. Thus the story "The Chrysanthemums" operates with total effectiveness as a narrative about an isolated woman on a farm. Her relationship with her husband is relatively inarticulate, and the episode with the traveling tinsmith is a brief awakening of her self-esteem about her own attractiveness and sexuality. To determine whether an allegorical reading is possible, it would be necessary to establish whether her isolation is common to many other married women, whether Henry's seeing her talent with flowers as potentially commercial rather than esthetic is typical of the way husbands see wives, and whether her disappointment is like that experienced by many women. Without a statistical study of many such relationships, perhaps, it would be difficult to claim that the story is broadly allegorical, but it would indeed be possible to claim without such a study that the story of Elisa has many allegorical overtones.

As you read, then, be alert for the ways in which actions, things, and characters may be considered symbolically or allegorically. If something seems special, if there is an allusion, if the author has pointed up something in an unusual or special way, the chances are good that a case for the presence of symbolism or allegory may be made. There is no need to make extravagant claims; following the more obvious leads of the author is enough.

AESOP

The Fox and the Grapes   (ca. 6th C. B.C.)

A hungry Fox coming into a vineyard where there hung delicious clusters of ripe Grapes, his mouth watered to be at them; but they were nailed up to a trellis so high, that with all his springing and leaping he could not reach a single bunch. At last, growing tired and disappointed, "Let who will take them!" says he, "they are but green and sour; so I'll e'en let them alone."

QUESTIONS

1. How much do you learn about the characteristics of the fox? How are these characteristics related to the moral or message of the fable?
2. What is the plot of the fable, the principal conflict? What is the resolution of the conflict?
3. In your own words, explain the meaning of the fable. Is the "sour grape" explanation a satisfactory excuse, or is it a rationalization for failure?
4. From your reading of "The Fox and the Grapes," explain the characteristics of the fable as a type of literature.

THE GOSPEL OF ST. LUKE 15:11–32

The Parable of the Prodigal Son   (ca. 80 A.D.)

11 ¶ And he said, A certain man had two sons:
12 And the younger of them said to *his* father, Father, give me the portion of goods that falleth *to me*. And he divided unto them *his* living.°

───────────────

divided . . . his living: one-third of the father's estate; the son had to renounce all further claim.

13 And not many days after the younger son gathered all together, and took his journey into a far country,° and there wasted his substance with riotous living.

14 And when he had spent all, there arose a mighty famine in that land; and he began to be in want.

15 And he went and joined himself to a citizen of that country; and he sent him into his fields to feed swine.°

16 And he would fain have filled his belly with the husks° that the swine did eat: and no man gave unto him.

17 And when he came to himself, he said, How many hired servants of my father's have bread enough and to spare, and I perish with hunger!

18 I will arise and go to my father, and will say unto him, Father, I have sinned against heaven, and before thee,

19 And am no more worthy to be called thy son: make me as one of thy hired servants.

20 And he arose, and came to his father. But when he was yet a great way off, his father saw him, and had compassion, and ran, and fell on his neck, and kissed him.

21 And the son said unto him, Father, I have sinned against heaven, and in thy sight, and am no more worthy to be called thy son.

22 But the father said to his servants, Bring forth the best robe, and put *it* on him; and put a ring on his hand, and shoes on *his* feet:

23 And bring hither the fatted calf,° and kill *it*; and let us eat, and be merry:

24 For this my son was dead, and is alive again; he was lost, and is found. And they began to be merry.

25 Now his elder son was in the field: and as he came and drew nigh to the house, he heard musick and dancing.

26 And he called one of the servants, and asked what these things meant.

27 And he said unto him, Thy brother is come; and thy father hath killed the fatted calf, because he hath received him safe and sound.

28 And he was angry, and would not go in: therefore came his father out, and intreated him.

29 And he answering said to *his* father, Lo, these many years do I serve thee, neither transgressed I at any time thy commandment: and yet thou never gavest me a kid, that I might make merry with my friends:

30 But as soon as this thy son was come, which hath devoured thy living with harlots, thou hast killed for him the fatted calf.

31 And he said unto him, Son, thou art ever with me, and all that I have is thine.

far country: countries of the Jewish dispersal, or *diaspora,* in the areas bordering the Mediterranean Sea.

feed swine: In Jewish custom, pigs were unclean.

husks: pods of the carob tree, the eating of which was thought to be penitential.

fatted calf: grain-fed calf.

32 It was meet° that we should make merry, and be glad: for this thy brother was dead, and is alive again; and was lost, and is found.

QUESTIONS

1. Describe the character of the Prodigal Son. If one considers the parable a story, is this character flat or round, representative or individual? Why is it necessary that the character be considered representatively, even though he has individual characteristics?
2. What is the plot of the parable? What is the force of the antagonism against which the Prodigal Son must contend? Considering the moral and religious point of the parable, why is it necessary that the brother be resentful of the brother's return?
3. What is the resolution of the parable? Why is there no "they lived happily ever after" ending?
4. Using verse numbers, analyze the structure of the parable. What determines your division of the parts? Do these parts coincide with the development of the plot? On the basis of your answer, describe the relationship of plot to structure in the parable.
5. What is the point of view of the parable? Is it consistently applied? How does the emphasis shift with verse 22?
6. On the basis of the fact that there are many characteristics here of many of the stories you have read, write a description of the parable as a type of literature.

NATHANIEL HAWTHORNE (1804–1864)

Young Goodman Brown   1835

Young Goodman Brown came forth at sunset, into the street of Salem village,° but put his head back, after crossing the threshold, to exchange a parting kiss with his young wife. And Faith, as the wife was aptly named, thrust her own pretty head into the street, letting the wind play with the pink ribbons of her cap, while she called to Goodman Brown.

"Dearest heart," whispered she, softly and rather sadly, when her lips were close to his ear, "prithee, put off your journey until sunrise, and sleep in your own bed to-night. A lone woman is troubled with such dreams and such thoughts, that she's afeard of herself, sometimes. Pray, tarry with me this night, dear husband, of all nights in the year!"

"My love and my Faith," replied young Goodman Brown, "of all nights in

---

meet: appropriate.
Salem village: in Massachusetts.

the year, this one night must I tarry away from thee. My journey, as thou callest it, forth and back again, must needs be done 'twixt now and sunrise. What, my sweet, pretty wife, dost thou doubt me already, and we but three months married!"

"Then God bless you!" said Faith with the pink ribbons, "and may you find all well, when you come back."

"Amen!" cried Goodman Brown. "Say thy prayers, dear Faith, and go to   5
bed at dusk, and no harm will come to thee."

So they parted; and the young man pursued his way, until, being about to turn the corner by the meeting-house, he looked back and saw the head of Faith still peeping after him, with a melancholy air, in spite of her pink ribbons.

"Poor little Faith!" thought he, for his heart smote him. "What a wretch am I, to leave her on such an errand! She talks of dreams, too. Methought, as she spoke, there was trouble in her face, as if a dream had warned her what work is to be done to-night. But no, no! 't would kill her to think it. Well; she's a blessed angel on earth; and after this one night, I'll cling to her skirts and follow her to Heaven."

With this excellent resolve for the future, Goodman Brown felt himself justified in making more haste on his present evil purpose. He had taken a dreary road, darkened by all the gloomiest trees of the forest, which barely stood aside to let the narrow path creep through, and closed immediately behind. It was all as lonely as could be; and there is this peculiarity in such a solitude, that the traveller knows not who may be concealed by the innumerable trunks and the thick boughs overhead; so that, with lonely footsteps, he may yet be passing through an unseen multitude.

"There may be a devilish Indian behind every tree," said Goodman Brown to himself; and he glanced fearfully behind him, as he added, "What if the devil himself should be at my very elbow!"

His head being turned back, he passed a crook of the road, and looking   10
forward again, beheld the figure of a man, in grave and decent attire, seated at the foot of an old tree. He arose at Goodman Brown's approach, and walked onward, side by side with him.

"You are late, Goodman Brown," said he. "The clock of the Old South° was striking, as I came through Boston; and that is full fifteen minutes agone."

"Faith kept me back awhile," replied the young man, with a tremor in his voice, caused by the sudden appearance of his companion, though not wholly unexpected.

It was now deep dusk in the forest, and deepest in that part of it where these two were journeying. As nearly as could be discerned, the second traveller was about fifty years old, apparently in the same rank of life as Goodman Brown, and bearing a considerable resemblance to him, though perhaps more in expression than features. Still, they might have been taken for father and son. And yet, though the elder person was as simply clad as the younger, and as simple in manner too, he had an indescribable air of one who knew the world, and would not have felt abashed at the governor's dinner-table, or in King William's° court, were it possible that his affairs should call him thither. But the only thing about him that

Old South: The Old South Church, in Boston, is still there.
King William: William IV, King of England from 1830 to 1837.

could be fixed upon as remarkable, was his staff, which bore the likeness of a great black snake, so curiously wrought, that it might almost be seen to twist and wriggle itself like a living serpent. This, of course, must have been an ocular deception, assisted by the uncertain light.

"Come, Goodman Brown!" cried his fellow-traveller, "this is a dull pace for the beginning of a journey. Take my staff, if you are so soon weary."

"Friend," said the other, exchanging his slow pace for a full stop, "having kept covenant by meeting thee here, it is my purpose now to return whence I came. I have scruples, touching the matter thou wot'st of."   15

"Sayest thou so?" replied he of the serpent, smiling apart. 'Let us walk on, nevertheless, reasoning as we go, and if I convince thee not, thou shalt turn back. We are but a little way in the forest, yet."

"Too far, too far!" exclaimed the goodman, unconsciously resuming his walk. "My father never went into the woods on such an errand, nor his father before him. We have been a race of honest men and good Christians, since the days of the martyrs.° And shall I be the first of the name of Brown that ever took this path and kept—"

"Such company, thou wouldst say," observed the elder person, interrupting his pause. "Well said, Goodman Brown! I have been as well acquainted with your family as with ever a one among the Puritans; and that's no trifle to say. I helped your grandfather, the constable, when he lashed the Quaker woman so smartly through the streets of Salem. And it was I that brought your father a pitch-pine knot, kindled at my own hearth, to set fire to an Indian village, in King Philip's war.° They were my good friends, both; and many a pleasant walk have we had along this path, and returned merrily after midnight. I would fain be friends with you, for their sake."

"If it be as thou sayest," replied Goodman Brown, "I marvel they never spoke of these matters. Or, verily, I marvel not, seeing that the least rumor of the sort would have driven them from New England. We are a people of prayer, and good works to boot, and abide no such wickedness."

"Wickedness or not," said the traveller with twisted staff, "I have a very   20
general acquaintance here in New England. The deacons of many a church have drunk the communion wine with me; the selectmen, of divers towns, make me their chairman; and a majority of the Great and General Court are firm supporters of my interest. The governor and I, too—but these are state secrets."

"Can this be so!" cried Goodman Brown, with a stare of amazement at his undisturbed companion. "Howbeit, I have nothing to do with the governor and council; they have their own ways, and are no rule for a simple husbandman like me. But, were I to go on with thee, how should I meet the eye of that good old man, our minister, at Salem village? Oh, his voice would make me tremble, both Sabbath-day and lecture-day!"

   days of the martyrs: The martyrdoms of Protestants in England during the reign of Queen Mary (1553–1558).
   King Philip's War (1675–1676): It resulted in the suppression of Indian tribal life in New England and prepared the way for unlimited settlement of the area by European immigrants. "Philip" was the English name of Chief Metacomet of the Wampanoag Indian Tribe.

Thus far, the elder traveller had listened with due gravity, but now burst into a fit of irrepressible mirth, shaking himself so violently, that his snakelike staff actually seemed to wriggle in sympathy.

"Ha! ha! ha!" shouted he, again and again; then composing himself, "Well, go on, Goodman Brown, go on; but, prithee, don't kill me with laughing!"

"Well, then, to end the matter at once," said Goodman Brown, considerably nettled, "there is my wife, Faith. It would break her dear little heart; and I'd rather break my own!"

"Nay, if that be the case," answered the other, "e'en go thy ways, Goodman Brown. I would not, for twenty old women like the one hobbling before us, that Faith should come to any harm."

As he spoke, he pointed his staff at a female figure on the path, in whom Goodman Brown recognized a very pious and exemplary dame, who had taught him his catechism in youth, and was still his moral and spiritual adviser, jointly with the minister and Deacon Gookin.

"A marvel, truly, that Goody° Cloyse should be so far in the wilderness, at nightfall!" said he. "But, with your leave, friend, I shall take a cut through the woods, until we have left this Christian woman behind. Being a stranger to you, she might ask whom I was consorting with, and whither I was going."

"Be it so," said his fellow-traveller. "Betake you to the woods, and let me keep the path."

Accordingly, the young man turned aside, but took care to watch his companion, who advanced softly along the road, until he had come within a staff's length of the old dame. She, meanwhile, was making the best of her way, with singular speed for so aged a woman, and mumbling some indistinct words, a prayer, doubtless, as she went. The traveller put forth his staff, and touched her withered neck with what seemed the serpent's tail.

"The devil!" screamed the pious old lady.

"Then Goody Cloyse knows her old friend?" observed the traveller, confronting her, and leaning on his writhing stick.

"Ah, forsooth, and is it your worship, indeed?" cried the good dame. "Yea, truly is it, and in the very image of my old gossip,° Goodman Brown, the grandfather of the silly fellow that now is. But, would your worship believe it? My broomstick hath strangely disappeared, stolen, as I suspect, by that unhanged witch, Goody Cory,° and that, too, when I was all anointed with the juice of smallage and cinquefoil and wolf's-bane—"

"Mingled with fine wheat and the fat of a new-born babe," said the shape of old Goodman Brown.

"Ah, your worship knows the recipe," cried the old lady, cackling aloud. "So, as I was saying, being all ready for the meeting, and no horse to ride on, I made up my mind to foot it; for they tell me there is a nice young man to be

Goody: a shortened form of "goodwife," a respectful name for a married woman of low rank. A "Goody Cloyse" was one of the women sentenced to execution by Hawthorne's great grandfather, Judge John Hathorne.
gossip: from "good sib" or "good relative."
Goody Cory: the name of a woman who was also sent to execution by Judge Hathorne.

taken into communion to-night. But now your good worship will lend me your arm, and we shall be there in a twinkling."

"That can hardly be," answered her friend. "I will not spare you my arm,   35
Goody Cloyse, but here is my staff, if you will."

So saying, he threw it down at her feet, where, perhaps, it assumed life, being one of the rods which its owner had formerly lent to the Egyptian Magi.° Of this fact, however, Goodman Brown could not take cognizance. He had cast up his eyes in astonishment, and looking down again, beheld neither Goody Cloyse nor the serpentine staff, but his fellow-traveller alone, who waited for him as calmly as if nothing had happened.

"That old woman taught me my catechism!" said the young man; and there was a world of meaning in this simple comment.

They continued to walk onward, while the elder traveller exhorted his companion to make good speed and persevere in the path, discoursing so aptly, that his arguments seemed rather to spring up in the bosom of his auditor, than to be suggested by himself. As they went he plucked a branch of maple, to serve for a walking-stick, and began to strip it of the twigs and little boughs, which were wet with evening dew. The moment his fingers touched them, they became strangely withered and dried up, as with a week's sunshine. Thus the pair proceeded, at a good free pace, until suddenly, in a gloomy hollow of the road, Goodman Brown sat himself down on the stump of a tree, and refused to go any farther.

"Friend," said he, stubbornly, "my mind is made up. Not another step will I budge on this errand. What if a wretched old woman do choose to go to the devil, when I thought she was going to Heaven! Is that any reason why I should quit my dear Faith, and go after her?"

"You will think better of this by and by," said his acquaintance, composedly.   40
"Sit here and rest yourself a while; and when you feel like moving again, there is my staff to help you along."

Without more words, he threw his companion the maple stick, and was as speedily out of sight as if he had vanished into the deepening gloom. The young man sat a few moments by the roadside, applauding himself greatly, and thinking with how clear a conscience he should meet the minister, in his morning walk, nor shrink from the eye of good old Deacon Gookin. And what calm sleep would be his, that very night, which was to have been spent so wickedly, but purely and sweetly now, in the arms of Faith! Amidst these pleasant and praiseworthy meditations, Goodman Brown heard the tramp of horses along the road, and deemed it advisable to conceal himself within the verge of the forest, conscious of the guilty purpose that had brought him thither, though now so happily turned from it.

On came the hoof-tramps and the voices of the riders, two grave old voices, conversing soberly as they drew near. These mingled sounds appeared to pass along the road, within a few yards of the young man's hiding-place; but owing, doubtless, to the depth of the gloom, at that particular spot, neither the travellers nor their steeds were visible. Though their figures brushed the small boughs by the wayside, it could not be seen that they intercepted, even for a moment, the

lent to the Egyptian Magi: See Exodus 7:10–12.

faint gleam from the strip of bright sky, athwart which they must have passed. Goodman Brown alternately crouched and stood on tiptoe, pulling aside the branches, and thrusting forth his head as far as he durst, without discerning so much as a shadow. It vexed him the more, because he could have sworn, were such a thing possible, that he recognized the voices of the minister and Deacon Gookin, jogging° along quietly, as they were wont to do, when bound to some ordination or ecclesiastical council. While yet within hearing, one of the riders stopped to pluck a switch.

"Of the two, reverend Sir," said the voice like the deacon's, "I had rather miss an ordination dinner than to-night's meeting. They tell me that some of our community are to be here from Falmouth and beyond, and others from Connecticut and Rhode Island; besides several of the Indian powwows,° who, after their fashion, know almost as much deviltry as the best of us. Moreover, there is a goodly young woman to be taken into communion."

"Mighty well, Deacon Gookin!" replied the solemn old tones of the minister. "Spur up, or we shall be late. Nothing can be done, you know, until I get on the ground."

The hoofs clattered again, and the voices, talking so strangely in the empty air, passed on through the forest, where no church had ever been gathered, nor solitary Christian prayed. Whither, then, could these holy men be journeying, so deep into the heathen wilderness? Young Goodman Brown caught hold of a tree, for support, being ready to sink down on the ground, faint and over-burthened with the heavy sickness of his heart. He looked up to the sky, doubting whether there really was a Heaven above him. Yet, there was the blue arch, and the stars brightening in it. Note

"With Heaven above, and Faith below, I will yet stand firm against the devil!" cried Goodman Brown. The Christian stance,

While he still gazed upward, into the deep arch of the firmament, and had lifted his hands to pray, a cloud, though no wind was stirring, hurried across the zenith, and hid the brightening stars. The blue sky was still visible, except directly overhead, where this black mass of cloud was sweeping swiftly northward. Aloft in the air, as if from the depths of the cloud, came a confused and doubtful sound of voices. Once, the listener fancied that he could distinguish the accents of town's-people of his own, men and women, both pious and ungodly, many of whom he had met at the communion-table, and had seen others rioting at the tavern. The next moment, so indistinct were the sounds, he doubted whether he had heard aught but the murmur of the old forest, whispering without a wind. Then came a stronger swell of those familiar tones, heard daily in the sunshine, at Salem village, but never, until now, from a cloud at night. There was one voice, of a young woman, uttering lamentations, yet with an uncertain sorrow, and entreating for some favor, which, perhaps, it would grieve her to obtain. And all the unseen multitude, both saints and sinners, seemed to encourage her onward.

jogging: riding a horse at a slow trot.
powwow: a Narragansett Indian word describing a ritual ceremony of dancing, incantation, and magic.

"Faith!" shouted Goodman Brown, in a voice of agony and desperation; and the echoes of the forest mocked him, crying—"Faith! Faith!" as if bewildered wretches were seeking her, all through the wilderness.

The cry of grief, rage, and terror was yet piercing the night, when the unhappy husband held his breath for a response. There was a scream, drowned immediately in a louder murmur of voices fading into far-off laughter, as the dark cloud swept away, leaving the clear and silent sky above Goodman Brown. But something fluttered lightly down through the air, and caught on the branch of a tree. The young man seized it and beheld a pink ribbon.

"My Faith is gone!" cried he, after one stupefied moment. "There is no good on earth, and sin is but a name. Come, devil! for to thee is this world given." 50

And maddened with despair, so that he laughed loud and long, did Goodman Brown grasp his staff and set forth again, at such a rate, that he seemed to fly along the forest path, rather than to walk or run. The road grew wilder and drearier, and more faintly traced, and vanished at length, leaving him in the heart of the dark wilderness, still rushing onward, with the instinct that guides mortal man to evil. The whole forest was peopled with frightful sounds; the creaking of the trees, the howling of wild beasts, and the yell of Indians; while, sometimes, the wind tolled like a distant church bell, and sometimes gave a broad roar around the traveller, as if all Nature were laughing him to scorn. But he was himself the chief horror of the scene, and shrank not from its other horrors.

"Ha! ha! ha!" roared Goodman Brown, when the wind laughed at him. "Let us hear which will laugh loudest! Think not to frighten me with your deviltry! Come witch, come wizard, come Indian powwow, come devil himself! and here comes Goodman Brown. You may as well fear him as he fear you!"

In truth, all through the haunted forest, there could be nothing more frightful than the figure of Goodman Brown. On he flew, among the black pines, brandishing his staff with frenzied gestures, now giving vent to an inspiration of horrid blasphemy, and now shouting forth such laughter, as set all the echoes of the forest laughing like demons around him. The fiend in his own shape is less hideous, than when he rages in the breast of man. Thus sped the demoniac on his course, until, quivering among the trees, he saw a red light before him, as when the felled trunks and branches of a clearing have been set on fire, and throw up their lurid blaze against the sky, at the hour of midnight. He paused, in a lull of the tempest that had driven him onward, and heard the swell of what seemed a hymn, rolling solemnly from a distance, with the weight of many voices. He knew the tune. It was a familiar one in the choir of the village meeting-house. The verse died heavily away, and was lengthened by a chorus, not of human voices, but of all the sounds of the benighted wilderness, pealing in awful harmony together. Goodman Brown cried out; and his cry was lost to his own ear, by its unison with the cry of the desert.

In the interval of silence, he stole forward, until the light glared full upon his eyes. At one extremity of an open space, hemmed in by the dark wall of the forest, arose a rock, bearing some rude, natural resemblance either to an altar or a pulpit, and surrounded by four blazing pines, their tops aflame, their stems untouched, like candles at an evening meeting. The mass of foliage, that had overgrown the summit of the rock, was all on fire, blazing high into the night, and fitfully illuminating the whole field. Each pendent twig and leafy festoon was in a blaze.

As the red light arose and fell, a numerous congregation alternately shone forth, then disappeared in shadow, and again grew, as it were, out of the darkness, peopling the heart of the solitary woods at once.

"A grave and dark-clad company!" quoth Goodman Brown.   55

In truth, they were such. Among them, quivering to-and-fro, between gloom and splendor, appeared faces that would be seen, next day, at the council-board of the province, and others which, Sabbath after Sabbath, looked devoutly heavenward, and benignantly over the crowded pews, from the holiest pulpits in the land. Some affirm that the lady of the governor was there. At least, there were high dames well known to her, and wives of honored husbands, and widows a great multitude, and ancient maidens, all of excellent repute, and fair young girls, who trembled lest their mothers should espy them. Either the sudden gleams of light, flashing over the obscure field, bedazzled Goodman Brown, or he recognized a score of the church members of Salem village, famous for their especial sanctity. Good old Deacon Gookin had arrived, and waited at the skirts of that venerable saint, his reverend pastor. But, irreverently consorting with these grave, reputable, and pious people, these elders of the church, these chaste dames and dewy virgins, there were men of dissolute lives and women of spotted fame, wretches given over to all mean and filthy vice, and suspected even of horrid crimes. It was strange to see, that the good shrank not from the wicked, nor were the sinners abashed by the saints. Scattered, also, among their pale-faced enemies, were the Indian priests, or powwows, who had often scared their native forest with more hideous incantations than any known to English witchcraft.

"But, where is Faith?" thought Goodman Brown; and, as hope came into his heart, he trembled.

Another verse of the hymn arose, a slow and mournful strain, such as the pious love, but joined to words which expressed all that our nature can conceive of sin, and darkly hinted at far more. Unfathomable to mere mortals is the lore of fiends. Verse after verse was sung, and still the chorus of the desert swelled between, like the deepest tone of a mighty organ. And, with the final peal of that dreadful anthem, there came a sound, as if the roaring wind, the rushing streams, the howling beasts, and every other voice of the unconverted wilderness were mingling and according with the voice of guilty man, in homage to the prince of all. The four blazing pines threw up a loftier flame, and obscurely discovered shapes and visages of horror on the smoke-wreaths, above the impious assembly. At the same moment, the fire on the rock shot redly forth, and formed a glowing arch above its base, where now appeared a figure. With reverence be it spoken, the apparition bore no slight similitude, both in garb and manner, to some grave divine of the New England churches. The devil resembles us.

"Bring forth the converts!" cried a voice, that echoed through the field and rolled into the forest.

At the word, Goodman Brown stepped forth from the shadow of the trees,   60
and approached the congregation, with whom he felt a loathful brotherhood, by the sympathy of all that was wicked in his heart. He could have well-nigh sworn, that the shape of his own dead father beckoned him to advance, looking downward from a smoke-wreath, while a woman, with dim features of despair, threw out her hand to warn him back. Was it his mother? But he had no power to retreat one step, nor to resist, even in thought, when the minister and good old Deacon

Gookin seized his arms, and led him to the blazing rock. Thither came also the slender form of a veiled female, led between Goody Cloyse, that pious teacher of the catechism, and Martha Carrier, who had received the devil's promise to be queen of hell. A rampant hag was she! And there stood the proselytes, beneath the canopy of fire.

"Welcome, my children," said the dark figure, "to the communion of your race! Ye have found, thus young, your nature and your destiny. My children, look behind you!"

They turned; and flashing forth, as it were, in a sheet of flame, the fiend-worshippers were seen; the smile of welcome gleamed darkly on every visage.

"There," resumed the sable form, "are all whom ye have reverenced from youth. Ye deemed them holier than yourselves, and shrank from your own sin, contrasting it with their lives of righteousness and prayerful aspirations heavenward. Yet, here are they all, in my worshipping assembly! This night it shall be granted you to know their secret deeds; how hoary-bearded elders of the church have whispered wanton words to the young maids of their households; how many a woman, eager for widow's weeds, has given her husband a drink at bedtime, and let him sleep his last sleep in her bosom; how beardless youths have made haste to inherit their father's wealth; and how fair damsels—blush not, sweet ones!—have dug little graves in the garden, and bidden me, the sole guest, to an infant's funeral. By the sympathy of your human hearts for sin, ye shall scent out all the places—whether in church, bed-chamber, street, field, or forest—where crime has been committed, and shall exult to behold the whole earth one stain of guilt, one mighty blood-spot. Far more than this! It shall be yours to penetrate, in every bosom, the deep mystery of sin, the fountain of all wicked arts, and which inexhausti-bly supplies more evil impulses than human power—than my power, at its utmost!—can make manifest in deeds. And now, my children, look upon each other."

They did so; and, by the blaze of the hell-kindled torches, the wretched man beheld his Faith, and the wife her husband, trembling before that unhallowed altar.

"Lo! there ye stand, my children," said the figure, in a deep and solemn   65
tone, almost sad, with its despairing awfulness, as if his once angelic nature could yet mourn for our miserable race. "Depending upon one another's hearts, ye had still hoped that virtue were not all a dream! Now are ye undeceived!—Evil is the nature of mankind. Evil must be your only happiness. Welcome, again, my children, to the communion of your race!"

"Welcome!" repeated the fiend-worshippers, in one cry of despair and tri-umph.

And there they stood, the only pair, as it seemed, who were yet hesitating on the verge of wickedness, in this dark world. A basin was hollowed, naturally, in the rock. Did it contain water, reddened by the lurid light? or was it blood? or, perchance, a liquid flame? Herein did the Shape of Evil dip his hand, and prepare to lay the mark of baptism upon their foreheads, that they might be partak-ers of the mystery of sin, more conscious of the secret guilt of others, both in deed and thought, than they could now be of their own. The husband cast one look at his pale wife, and Faith at him. What polluted wretches would the next glance show them to each other, shuddering alike at what they disclosed and what they saw!

"Faith! Faith! cried the husband. "Look up to Heaven, and resist the Wicked One!"

Whether Faith obeyed, he knew not. Hardly had he spoken, when he found himself amid calm night and solitude, listening to a roar of the wind, which died heavily away through the forest. He staggered against the rock, and felt it chill and damp, while a hanging twig, that had been all on fire, besprinkled his cheek with the coldest dew.

The next morning, young Goodman Brown came slowly into the street of   70
Salem village staring around him like a bewildered man. The good old minister was taking a walk along the grave-yard, to get an appetite for breakfast and meditate his sermon, and bestowed a blessing, as he passed, on Goodman Brown. He shrank from the venerable saint, as if to avoid an anathema. Old Deacon Gookin was at domestic worship, and the holy words of his prayer were heard through the open window. "What God doth the wizard pray to?" quoth Goodman Brown. Goody Cloyse, that excellent old Christian, stood in the early sunshine, at her own lattice, catechising a little girl, who had brought her a pint of morning's milk. Goodman Brown snatched away the child, as from the grasp of the fiend himself. Turning the corner by the meetinghouse, he spied the head of Faith, with the pink ribbons, gazing anxiously forth, and bursting into such joy at sight of him that she skipt along the street, and almost kissed her husband before the whole village. But Goodman Brown looked sternly and sadly into her face, and passed on without a greeting.

Had Goodman Brown fallen asleep in the forest, and only dreamed a wild dream of a witch-meeting? *Were the ribbons real?*

Be it so, if you will. But, alas! it was a dream of evil omen for young Goodman Brown. A stern, a sad, a darkly meditative, a distrustful, if not a desperate man did he become, from the night of that fearful dream. On the Sabbath day, when the congregation were singing a holy psalm, he could not listen, because an anthem of sin rushed loudly upon his ear, and drowned all the blessed strain. When the minister spoke from the pulpit, with power and fervid eloquence, and with his hand on the open Bible, of the sacred truths of our religion, and of saint-like lives and triumphant deaths, and of future bliss or misery unutterable, then did Goodman Brown turn pale, dreading lest the roof should thunder down upon the gray blasphemer and his hearers. Often, awaking suddenly at midnight, he shrank from the bosom of Faith, and at morning or eventide, when the family knelt down at prayer, he scowled, and muttered to himself, and gazed sternly at his wife, and turned away. And when he had lived long, and was borne to his grave, a hoary corpse, followed by Faith, an aged woman, and children and grand-children, a goodly procession, besides neighbors not a few, they carved no hopeful verse upon his tombstone; for his dying hour was gloom. *He's both cruel + He's lost his faith; he has been self-righteous. corrupted.*

QUESTIONS

1. Who is the protagonist in the story? Who *seems* to be the antagonist? What, if anything, do you think the antagonist really is?

2. What *seems* to be the central conflict in the story? How is this apparent conflict

* He who looks under the bed has been there himself.

resolved? How is Goodman Brown's life changed by this resolution? To what extent does this change in Goodman Brown point to another conflict that remains unresolved?

3. Near the end of the story the narrator intrudes to ask the following: "Had Goodman Brown fallen asleep in the forest, and only dreamed a wild dream of a witch-meeting?" What do you think the answer to this question is? If Goodman Brown's visions come out of his own dreams (mind, subconscious), what do they tell us about him?

4. Is Goodman Brown a round or flat character? Individual or representative? To what extent is he designed to serve as a symbolic "everyman" or representative of humankind?

5. What point of view is employed in the story? What are the advantages of using this point of view in this kind of story?

6. Consider Hawthorne's use of symbolism in the story, such as the symbolism of sunset and night, the walking stick, the witches' sabbath, the marriage to Faith, and the vague shadows amid the darkness, together with other symbols that you may find.

7. What details go into the establishment of the two distinct settings in this story? What characterizes Salem? The woods? Why might we be justified in seeing the forest as a symbolic setting?

8. What sort of sin does Goodman Brown discover in most of his friends and neighbors during the night in the woods? What common thread runs through most of this sin?

9. To what extent are the people, objects, and events in Goodman Brown's adventure invested with enough *consistent* symbolic resonance to justify calling his episode in the woods an allegory? Consider Brown's wife, Faith, as an allegorical figure. What do you make of Brown's statements that "I'll cling to her skirts and follow her to Heaven" (paragraph 7) and "Faith kept me back awhile" (paragraph 12). In this same light, consider the other characters Brown meets in the forest, the sunset, the walk into the forest, and the staff "which bore the likeness of a great black snake."

MARJORIE PICKTHALL (1883–1922)

The Worker in Sandalwood   1923

I like to think of this as a true story, but you who read may please yourselves, siding either with the curé,° who says Hyacinthe dreamed it all, and did the carving himself in his sleep, or with Madame. I am sure that Hyacinthe thinks it true, and so does Madame, but then she has the cabinet, with the little birds and the lilies carved at the corners. Monsieur le curé shrugs his patient shoulders; but then he is tainted with the infidelities of cities, good man, having been three times to Montreal, and once, in an electric car, to Saint Anne. He and Madame still talk it over whenever they meet, though it happened so many years ago, and each leaves the other forever unconvinced. Meanwhile the dust gathers in the infinite

curé: a parish priest.

fine lines of the little birds' feathers, and softens the lily stamens where Madame's duster may not go; and the wood, ageing, takes on a golden gleam as of immemorial sunsets: that pale red wood, heavy with the scent of the ancient East; the wood that Hyacinthe loved.

It was the only wood of that kind which had ever been seen in Terminaison.° Pierre L'Oreillard brought it into the workshop one morning; a small heavy bundle wrapped in sacking, and then in burlap, and then in fine soft cloths. He laid it on a pile of shavings, and unwrapped it carefully and a dim sweetness filled the dark shed and hung heavily in the thin winter sunbeams.

Pierre L'Oreillard rubbed the wood respectfully with his knobby fingers. "It is sandalwood," he explained to Hyacinthe, pride of knowledge making him expansive; "a most precious wood° that grows in warm countries, thou great goblin. Smell it, *imbécile*. It is sweeter than cedar. It is to make a cabinet for the old Madame at the big house. Thy great hands shall smooth the wood, *nigaud*,° and I—I, Pierre the cabinet-maker, shall render it beautiful." Then he went out, locking the door behind him.

When he was gone, Hyacinthe laid down his plane, blew on his stiff fingers, and shambled slowly over to the wood. He was a great clumsy boy of fourteen, dark-faced, very slow of speech, dull-eyed and uncared for. He was clumsy because it is impossible to move gracefully when you are growing very big and fast on quite insufficient food. He was dull-eyed because all eyes met his unlovingly; uncared for, because none knew the beauty of his soul. But his heavy young hands could carve simple things, like flowers and birds and beasts, to perfection, as the curé pointed out. Simon has a tobacco-jar, carved with pine-cones and squirrels, and the curé has a pipe whose bowl is the bloom of a moccasin-flower, that I have seen. But it is all very long ago. And facts, in these lonely villages, easily become transfigured, touched upon their gray with a golden gleam.

"Thy hands shall smooth the wood, *nigaud*, and I shall render it beautiful,"   5 said Pierre L'Oreillard, and went off to drink brandy at the Cinq Chateaux.

Hyacinthe knew that the making of the cabinet would fall to him, as most of the other work did. He also touched the strange sweet wood, and at last laid his cheek against it, while the fragrance caught his breath. "How it is beautiful," said Hyacinthe, and for a moment his eyes glowed and he was happy. Then the light passed, and with bent head he shuffled back to his bench through a foam of white shavings curling almost to his knees.

"Madame perhaps will want the cabinet next week, for that is Christmas," said Hyacinthe, and fell to work harder than ever, though it was so cold in the shed that his breath hung like a little silver cloud and the steel stung his hands. There was a tiny window to his right, through which, when it was clear of frost, one looked on Terminaison, and that was cheerful and made one whistle. But to the left, through the chink of the ill-fitting door, there was nothing but the forest and the road dying away in it, and the trees moving heavily under the snow. Yet, from there came all Hyacinthe's dumb dreams and slow reluctant fancies, which he sometimes found himself able to tell—in wood, not in words.

Terminaison: a town imagined as a part of French Canada.
   a most precious wood: Sandalwood is still rare and precious; it is grown mainly in India and yields to exquisite detail in carving and decoration.
   nigaud: simpleton.

Brandy was good at the Cinq Chateaux, and Pierre L'Oreillard gave Hyacinthe plenty of directions, but no further help with the cabinet.

"That is to be finished for Madame on the festival, *gros escargot*!"° said he, cuffing Hyacinthe's ears furiously, "finished, and with a prettiness about the corners, hearest thou, *ourson*?° I suffer from a delicacy of the constitution and a little feebleness in the legs on these days, so that I cannot handle the tools. I must leave this work to thee, *gacheur*.° See it is done properly, and stand up and touch a hand to thy cap when I address thee, *orvet*,° great slow-worm."

"Yes, monsieur," said Hyacinthe, wearily.   10

It is hard, when you do all the work, to be cuffed into the bargain, and fourteen is not very old. He went to work on the cabinet with slow, exquisite skill, but on the eve of Noel, he was still at work, and the cabinet unfinished. It meant a thrashing from Pierre if the morrow came and found it still unfinished, and Pierre's thrashings were cruel. But it was growing into a thing of perfection under his slow hands, and Hyacinthe would not hurry over it.

"Then work on it all night, and show it to me all completed in the morning, or thy bones shall mourn thy idleness," said Pierre with a flicker of his little eyes. And he shut Hyacinthe into the workshop with a smoky lamp, his tools, and the sandalwood cabinet.

It was nothing unusual. The boy had often been left before to finish a piece of work overnight while Pierre went off to his brandies. But this was Christmas Eve, and he was very tired. The cold crept into the shed until the scent of the sandalwood could not make him dream himself warm, and the roof cracked sullenly in the forest. There came upon Hyacinthe one of those awful, hopeless despairs that children know. It seemed to be a living presence that caught up his soul and crushed it in black hands. "In all the world, nothing!" said he, staring at the dull flame; "no place, no heart, no love! O kind God, is there a place, a love for me in another world?"

I cannot endure to think of Hyacinthe, poor lad, shut up despairing in the workshop with his loneliness, his cold, and his hunger, on the eve of Christmas. He was but an overgrown, unhappy child, and for unhappy children no aid, at this season, seems too divine for faith. So Madame says, and she is very old and very wise. Hyacinthe even looked at the chisel in his hand, and thought that by a touch of that he might lose it all, all, and be at peace, somewhere not far from God; only it was forbidden. Then came the tears, and great sobs that sickened and deafened him, so that he scarcely heard the gentle rattling of the latch.

At least, I suppose it came then, but it may have been later. The story is   1[
all so vague here, so confused with fancies that have spoiled the first simplicity. I think that Hyacinthe must have gone to the door, opening it upon the still woods and the frosty stars, and the lad who stood outside must have said: "I see you are working late, comrade. May I come in?" or something like it.

Hyacinthe brushed his ragged sleeve across his eyes, and opened the door wider with a little nod to the other to enter. Those little lonely villages strung

gros escargot: big snail.
ourson: bear cub.
gacheur: bungler, spoiler.
orvet: blind worm, slow worm.

along the great river see strange wayfarers adrift inland from the sea. Hyacinthe said to himself that surely here was such a one.

Afterwards he told the curé that for a moment he had been bewildered. Dully blinking into the stranger's eyes, he lost for a flash the first impression of youth and received one of some incredible age or sadness. But this also passed and he knew that the wanderer's eyes were only quiet, very quiet, like the little pools in the wood where the wild does went to drink. As he turned within the door, smiling at Hyacinthe and shaking some snow from his fur cap, he did not seem more than sixteen or so.

"It is very cold outside," he said. "There is a big oak tree on the edge of the fields that has split in the frost and frightened all the little squirrels asleep there. Next year it will make an even better home for them. And see what I found close by!" He opened his fingers, and showed Hyacinthe a little sparrow lying unruffled in his palm.

"*Pauvrette!*"° said the dull Hyacinthe. "*Pauvrette!* Is it then dead?" He touched it with a gentle forefinger.

"No," answered the strange boy, "it is not dead. We'll put it here among the shavings, not far from the lamp, and it will be well by morning."°

20

He smiled at Hyacinthe again, and the shambling lad felt dimly as if the scent of sandalwood had deepened, and the lamp-flame burned clearer. But the stranger's eyes were only quiet, quiet.

"Have you come far?" asked Hyacinthe. "It is a bad season for travelling, and the wolves are out in the woods."

"A long way," said the other; "a long, long way. I heard a child cry. . . ."

"There is no child here," answered Hyacinthe, shaking his head. "Monsieur L'Oreillard is not fond of children, he says they cost too much money. But if you have come far, you must be cold and hungry, and I have no food or fire. At the Cinq Chateaux you will find both!"

The stranger looked at him again with those quiet eyes, and Hyacinthe fancied his face was familiar. "I will stay here," he said, "you are very late at work and you are unhappy."

25

"Why, as to that," answered Hyacinthe, rubbing again at his cheeks and ashamed of his tears, "most of us are sad at one time or another, the good God knows. Stay here and welcome if it pleases you, and you may take a share of my bed, though it is no more than a pile of balsam boughs and an old blanket, in the loft. But I must work at this cabinet, for the drawer must be finished and the handles put on and these corners carved, all by the holy morning; or my wages will be paid with a stick."

"You have a hard master," put in the other boy, "if he would pay you with blows upon the feast of Noel."

"He is hard enough," said Hyacinthe; "but once he gave me a dinner of sausages and white wine, and once, in the summer, melons. If my eyes will stay open, I will finish this by morning, but indeed I am sleepy. Stay with me an hour or so, comrade, and talk to me of your wanderings, so that the time may pass more quickly."

Pauvrette: poor little thing.
See Psalms 84:4.

"I will tell you of the country where I was a child," answered the stranger.

And while Hyacinthe worked, he told—of sunshine and dust; of the shadows   30
of vine-leaves on the flat white walls of a house; of rosy doves on the flat roof;
of the flowers that come in the spring, crimson and blue, and the white cyclamen
in the shadow of the rocks; of the olive, the myrtle and almond; until Hyacinthe's
slow fingers ceased working, and his sleepy eyes blinked wonderingly.

"See what you have done, comrade," he said at last; "you have told of such
pretty things that I have done no work for an hour. And now the cabinet will
never be finished, and I shall be beaten."

"Let me help you," smiled the other; "I also was bred a carpenter."°

At first Hyacinthe would not, fearing to trust the sweet wood out of his
own hands, but at length he allowed the stranger to fit in one of the little drawers,
and so deftly was the work done, that Hyacinthe pounded his fists on the bench
in admiration. "You have a pretty knack," he cried; "it seemed as if you did but
hold the drawer in your hands a moment, and hey! ho! it jumped into its place!"

"Let me fit in the other little drawers, while you go and rest a while," said
the wanderer. So Hyacinthe curled up among the shavings, and the stranger fell
to work upon the little cabinet of sandalwood.

Here begins what the curé will have it is a dream within a dream. Sweetest   35
of dreams was ever dreamed, if that is so. Sometimes I am forced to think with
him, but again I see as clearly as with old Madame's eyes, that have not seen the
earthly light for twenty years, and with her and Hyacinthe, I say "Credo."°

Hyacinthe said that he lay upon the shavings in the sweetness of the sandalwood, and was very tired. He thought of the country where the stranger had been
a boy; of the flowers on the hills; of the laughing leaves of aspen, and poplar; of
the golden flowering anise and the golden sun upon the dusty roads, until he
was warm. All the time through these pictures, as through a painted veil, he was
aware of that other boy with the quiet eyes, at work upon the cabinet, smoothing,
fitting, polishing. "He does better work than I," thought Hyacinthe, but he was
not jealous. And again he thought, "It is growing towards morning. In a little
while I will get up and help him." But he did not, for the dream of warmth and
the smell of the sandalwood held him in a sweet drowse. Also he said that he
thought the stranger was singing as he worked, for there seemed to be a sense
of some music in the shed, though he could not tell whether it came from the
other boy's lips, or from the shabby old tools as he used them, or from the stars.
"The stars are much paler," thought Hyacinthe, "and soon it will be morning,
and the corners are not carved yet. I must get up and help this kind one in a
little moment. Only I am so tired, and the music and the sweetness seem to wrap
me and fold me close, so that I may not move."

He lay without moving, and behind the forest there shone a pale glow of
some indescribable colour that was neither green nor blue, while in Terminaison
the church bells began to ring. "Day will soon be here!" thought Hyacinthe, immovable in that deep dream of his, "and with day will come Monsieur L'Oreillard and
his stick. I must get up and help, for even yet the corners are not carved."

. . . *bred a carpenter*: See Matthew 13:55.
Credo: "I believe," the opening words of the *Credo* section of the Catholic Mass ("Credo
in unum Deum . . ." ["I believe in one God . . ."].

But he did not get up. Instead, he saw the stranger look at him again, smiling as if he loved him, and lay his brown finger lightly upon the four empty corners of the cabinet. And Hyacinthe saw the little squares of reddish wood ripple and heave and break, as little clouds when the wind goes through the sky. And out of them thrust forth little birds, and after them the lilies, for a moment living, but even while Hyacinthe looked, growing hard and reddish-brown and settling back into the sweet wood. Then the stranger smiled again, and laid all the tools neatly in order, and, opening the door quietly, went away into the woods.

Hyacinthe lay still among the shavings for a long time, and then he crept slowly to the door. The sun, not yet risen, set its first beams upon the delicate mist of frost afloat beneath the trees, and so all the world was aflame with splendid gold. Far away down the road a dim figure seemed to move amid the glory, but the glow and the splendour were such that Hyacinthe was blinded. His breath came sharply as the glow beat in great waves on the wretched shed; on the foam of shavings; on the cabinet with the little birds and the lilies carved at the corners.

He was too pure of heart to feel afraid. But, "Blessed be the Lord," whispered   40
Hyacinthe, clasping his slow hands, "for He hath visited and redeemed His people.°
But who will believe?"

Then the sun of Christ's day rose gloriously, and the little sparrow came from his nest among the shavings and shook his wings to the light.°

. . . *His people*: See Luke 1:68.
. . . *wings to the light*: See Malachi 4:2.

QUESTIONS

1. What point of view is employed in the story? Who or what is the narrator? To what extent does the narrator know a great deal more than we might expect? Why does the narrator repeat several times that the events in the story happened "very long ago"?

2. What sort of person is Hyacinthe? How does he deal with his life? How does he react to Pierre L'Oreillard's treatment? Why does the "strange child" with "quiet eyes" appear to him?

3. What is the narrator's attitude toward Hyacinthe? In what ways does this shape your attitude?

4. How does Pickthall control the tone of the story? Why does the narrator stress the quality of Hyacinthe's work in the first and third paragraphs? Why does the narrator stress the possibility that Hyacinthe dreamed the events of the story? To what extent do these points of emphasis keep the story from becoming too fantastic or sentimentalized?

5. What kind of person is Pierre L'Oreillard? How does he treat Hyacinthe? How much work does he do?

6. Are the characters in this story round or flat? Static or dynamic? Individual

or representative? In what way do these choices contribute to the total effect of the story?

7. To what extent does the setting work symbolically to establish mood and tone? Consider the time of year, the specific night, the description of the shed in which Hyacinthe works, the forest, and the animals noted throughout.

8. Consider the symbolism associated with the "quiet" stranger: his homeland, his training as a carpenter, the sparrow he revives, the heightening of the lamp-flame, and the warming of the workshop. What do these details suggest? How consistent is this symbolism?

9. Would you consider this story an allegory, a myth, a fable, a parable, or simply symbolic? Explain your answer.

JOHN STEINBECK (1902–1968)

The Chrysanthemums   *1937*

The high grey-flannel fog of <u>winter</u> <u>closed off</u> the Salinas Valley° from the sky and from all the rest of the world. On every side it sat like a lid on the mountains and made of the great valley <u>a closed pot.</u> On the broad, level land floor the gang plows bit deep and left the black earth shining like metal where the shares had cut. On the foothill ranches across the Salinas River, the yellow stubble fields seemed to be bathed in pale cold sunshine, but there was no sunshine in the valley now in December. The thick willow scrub along the river flamed with sharp and positive yellow leaves.

It was a time of quiet and of waiting. The air was cold and tender. A light wind blew up from the southwest so that the farmers were mildly hopeful of a good rain before long; but fog and rain do not go together.

Across the river, on Henry Allen's foothill ranch there was little work to be done, for the hay was cut and stored and the orchards were plowed up to receive the <u>rain</u> deeply <u>when it should come.</u> The cattle on the higher slopes were becoming shaggy and rough-coated.

<u>Elisa Allen,</u> working in her flower garden, looked down across the yard and saw Henry, her husband, talking to two men in business suits. The three of them stood by the tractor shed, each man with one foot on the side of the little Fordson.° They smoked cigarettes and studied the machines as they talked.

Elisa watched them for a moment and then went back to her work. She was <u>thirty-five.</u> Her face was lean and strong and her eyes were as clear as water. <u>Her figure looked blocked and heavy</u> in her gardening costume, a <u>man's black hat pulled low down over her eyes,</u> clodhopper shoes, a figured print <u>dress almost completely covered</u> by a big corduroy apron with four big pockets to hold the snips, the trowel and scratcher, the seeds and the knife she worked with. She wore <u>heavy leather gloves</u> to protect her hands while she worked.

5

the Salinas Valley: in Monterey County, California, about 50 miles south of San José. Steinbeck was born in Salinas, and his home there is open to the public.
Fordson: a tractor manufactured by the Ford Motor Company, with large rear steel lugged wheels.

She was cutting down the old year's chrysanthemum stalks with a pair of short and powerful scissors. She looked down toward the men by the tractor shed now and then. Her face was eager and mature and handsome; even her work with the scissors was over-eager, over-powerful. The chrysanthemum stems seemed too small and easy for her energy.

She brushed a cloud of hair out of her eyes with the back of her glove, and left a smudge of earth on the cheek in doing it. Behind her stood the neat white farm house with red geraniums close-banked around it as high as the windows. It was a hard-swept looking little house, with hard-polished windows, and a clean mud-mat on the front steps. And she's isolated.

Elisa cast another glance toward the tractor shed. The strangers were getting into their Ford coupe. She took off a glove and put her strong fingers down into the forest of new green chrysanthemum sprouts that were growing around the old roots. She spread the leaves and looked down among the close-growing stems. No aphids were there, no sowbugs or snails or cutworms. Her terrier fingers destroyed such pests before they could get started.

Elisa started at the sound of her husband's voice. He had come near quietly, and he leaned over the wire fence that protected her flower garden from cattle and dogs and chickens.

"At it again," he said. "You've got a strong new crop coming." 10

Elisa straightened her back and pulled on the gardening glove again. "Yes. They'll be strong this coming year." In her tone and on her face there was a little smugness.

"You've got a gift with things," Henry observed. "Some of those yellow chrysanthemums you had this year were ten inches across. I wish you'd work out in the orchard and raise some apples that big."

Her eyes sharpened. "Maybe I could do it, too. I've a gift with things, all right. My mother had it. She could stick anything in the ground and make it grow. She said it was having planters' hands that knew how to do it."

"Well, it sure works with flowers," he said.

"Henry, who were those men you were talking to?" 15

"Why, sure, that's what I came to tell you. They were from the Western Meat Company. I sold those thirty head of three-year-old steers. Got nearly my own price, too."

"Good," she said. "Good for you."

"And I thought," he continued, "I thought how it's Saturday afternoon, and we might go to Salinas for dinner at a restaurant, and then to a picture show—to celebrate, you see."

"Good," she repeated. "Oh, yes. That will be good."

Henry put on his joking tone. "There's fights tonight. How'd you like to 20 go to the fights?"

"Oh, no," she said breathlessly. "No, I wouldn't like fights."

"Just fooling, Elisa. We'll go to a movie. Let's see. It's two now. I'm going to take Scotty and bring down those steers from the hill. It'll take us maybe two hours. We'll go in town about five and have dinner at the Cominos Hotel. Like that?"

"Of course I'll like it. It's good to eat away from home."

"All right, then. I'll go get up a couple of horses."

She said, "I'll have plenty of time to transplant some of these sets, I guess."
She heard her husband calling Scotty down by the barn. And a little later she saw the two men ride up the pale yellow hillside in search of the steers.

There was a little square sandy bed kept for rooting the chrysanthemums. With her trowel she turned the soil over and over, and smoothed it and patted it firm. Then she dug ten parallel trenches to receive the sets. Back at the chrysanthemum bed she pulled out the little crisp shoots, trimmed off the leaves of each one with her scissors and laid it on a small orderly pile.

A squeak of wheels and plod of hoofs came from the road. Elisa looked up. The country road ran along the dense bank of willows and cottonwoods that bordered the river, and up this road came a curious vehicle, curiously drawn. It was an old spring-wagon, with a round canvas top on it like the cover of a prairie schooner. It was drawn by an old bay horse and a little grey-and-white burro. A big stubble-bearded man sat between the cover flaps and drove the crawling team. Underneath the wagon, between the hind wheels, a lean and rangy mongrel dog walked sedately. Words were painted on the canvas in clumsy, crooked letters. "Pots, pans, knives, sisors, lawn mores. Fixed." Two rows of articles and the triumphantly definitive "Fixed" below. The black paint had run down in little sharp points beneath each letter.

Elisa, squatting on the ground, watched to see the crazy, loose-jointed wagon pass by. But it didn't pass. It turned into the farm road in front of her house, crooked old wheels skirling and squeaking. The rangy dog darted from between the wheels and ran ahead. Instantly the two ranch shepherds flew out at him. Then all three stopped, and with stiff and quivering tails, with taut straight legs, with ambassadorial dignity, they slowly circled, sniffing daintily. The caravan pulled up to Elisa's wire fence and stopped. Now the newcomer dog, feeling outnumbered, lowered his tail and retired under the wagon with raised hackles and bared teeth.

The man on the wagon seat called out. "That's a bad dog in a fight when he gets started."

Elisa laughed. "I see he is. How soon does he generally get started?"

The man caught up her laughter and echoed it heartily. "Sometimes not for weeks and weeks," he said. He climbed stiffly down, over the wheel. The horse and the donkey drooped like unwatered flowers.

Elisa saw that he was a very big man. Although his hair and beard were greying, he did not look old. His worn black suit was wrinkled and spotted with grease. The laughter had disappeared from his face and eyes the moment his laughing voice ceased. His eyes were dark and they were full of the brooding that gets in the eyes of teamsters and of sailors. The calloused hands he rested on the wire fence were cracked, and every crack was a black line. He took off his battered hat.

"I'm off my general road, ma'am," he said. "Does this dirt road cut over across the river to the Los Angeles highway?"

Elisa stood up and shoved the thick scissors in her apron pocket. "Well, yes, it does, but it winds around and then fords the river. I don't think your team could pull through the sand."

He replied with some asperity, "It might surprise you what them beasts can pull through."

"When they get started?" she asked.

He smiled for a second. "Yes. When they get started."

"Well," said Elisa, "I think you'll save time if you go back to the Salinas road and pick up the highway there."

He drew a big finger down the chicken wire and made it sing. "I ain't in   40
any hurry, ma'am. I go from Seattle to San Diego and back every year. Takes all my time. About six months each way. I aim to follow nice weather." Mythic cycle.

Elisa took off her gloves and stuffed them in the apron pocket with the scissors. She touched the under edge of her man's hat, searching for fugitive hairs. ("That sounds like a nice kind of a way to live," she said.) ✓

He leaned confidentially over the fence. "Maybe you noticed the writing on my wagon. I mend pots and sharpen knives and scissors. You got any of them things to do?"

"Oh, no," she said quickly. "Nothing like that." Her eyes hardened with resistance.

"Scissors is the worst thing," he explained. "Most people just ruin scissors trying to sharpen 'em, but I know how. I got a special tool. It's a little bobbit kind of thing, and patented. But it sure does the trick."

"No. My scissors are all sharp."   45

"All right, then. Take a pot," he continued earnestly, "a bent pot, or a pot with a hole. I can make it like new so you don't have to buy no new ones. That's a saving for you."

"No," she said shortly. "I tell you I have nothing like that for you to do."

His face fell to an exaggerated sadness. His voice took on a whining undertone. "I ain't had a thing to do today. Maybe I won't have no supper tonight. You see I'm off my regular road. I know folks on the highway clear from Seattle to San Diego. They save their things for me to sharpen up because they know I do it so good and save them money."

"I'm sorry," Elisa said irritably. "I haven't anything for you to do."

His eyes left her face and fell to searching the ground. They roamed about   50
until they came to the chrysanthemum bed where she had been working. "What's them plants, ma'am?"

The irritation and resistance melted from Elisa's face. "Oh, those are chrysanthemums, giant whites and yellows. I raise them every year, bigger than anybody around here."

"Kind of a long-stemmed flower? Looks like a quick puff of colored smoke?" he asked.

"That's it. What a nice way to describe them."

"They smell kind of nasty till you get used to them," he said.

"It's a good bitter smell," she retorted, "not nasty at all."   55

He changed his tone quickly. "I like the smell myself."

"I had ten-inch blooms this year," she said.

The man leaned farther over the fence. "Look. I know a lady down the road a piece, has got the nicest garden you ever seen. Got nearly every kind of flower but no chrysanthemums. Last time I was mending a copper-bottom washtub for her (that's a hard job but I do it good), she said to me, 'If you ever run acrost some nice chrysanthemums I wish you'd try to get me a few seeds.' That's what she told me."

Elisa's eyes grew alert and eager. "She couldn't have known much about chrysanthemums. You can raise them from seed, but it's much easier to root the little sprouts you see there."

"Oh," he said. "I s'pose I can't take none to her, then."

"Why yes you can," Elisa cried. "I can put some in damp sand, and you can carry them right along with you. They'll take root in the pot if you keep them damp. And then she can transplant them."

"She'd sure like to have some, ma'am. You say they're nice ones?"

"Beautiful," she said. "Oh, beautiful." Her eyes shone. She tore off the battered hat and shook out her dark pretty hair. "I'll put them in a flower pot, and you can take them right with you. Come into the yard."

While the man came through the picket gate Elisa ran excitedly along the geranium-bordered path to the back of the house. And she returned carrying a big red flower pot. The gloves were forgotten now. She kneeled on the ground by the starting bed and dug up the sandy soil with her fingers and scooped it into the bright new flower pot. Then she picked up the little pile of shoots she had prepared. With her strong fingers she pressed them into the sand and tamped around them with her knuckles. The man stood over her. "I'll tell you what to do," she said. "You remember so you can tell the lady."

"Yes, I'll try to remember."

"Well, look. These will take root in about a month. Then she must set them out, about a foot apart in good rich earth like this, see?" She lifted a handful of dark soil for him to look at. "They'll grow fast and tall. Now remember this. In July tell her to cut them down, about eight inches from the ground."

"Before they bloom?" he asked.

"Yes, before they bloom." Her face was tight with eagerness. "They'll grow right up again. About the last of September the buds will start."

She stopped and seemed perplexed. "It's the budding that takes the most care," she said hesitantly. "I don't know how to tell you." She looked deep into his eyes, searchingly. Her mouth opened a little, and she seemed to be listening. "I'll try to tell you," she said. "Did you ever hear of planting hands?"

"Can't say I have, ma'am."

"Well, I can only tell you what it feels like. It's when you're picking off the buds you don't want. Everything goes right down into your fingertips. You watch your fingers work. They do it themselves. You can feel how it is. They pick and pick the buds. They never make a mistake. They're with the plant. Do you see? Your fingers and the plant. You can feel that, right up your arm. They know. They never make a mistake. You can feel it. When you're like that you can't do anything wrong. Do you see that? Can you understand that?"

She was kneeling on the ground looking up at him. Her breast swelled passionately.

The man's eyes narrowed. He looked away self-consciously. "Maybe I know," he said. "Sometimes in the night in the wagon there—"

Elisa's voice grew husky. She broke in on him. "I've never lived as you do, but I know what you mean. When the night is dark—why, the stars are sharp-pointed, and there's quiet. Why, you rise up and up! Every pointed star gets driven into your body. It's like that. Hot and sharp and—lovely."

Kneeling there, her hand went out toward his legs in the greasy black trousers. Her hesitant fingers almost touched the cloth. Then her hand dropped to the ground. She crouched low like a fawning dog.

He said, "It's nice, just like you say. Only when you don't have no dinner, it ain't."

She stood up then, very straight, and her face was ashamed. She held the flower pot out to him and placed it gently in his arms. "Here. Put it in your wagon, on the seat, where you can watch it. Maybe I can find something for you to do."

At the back of the house she dug in the can pile and found two old and battered aluminum saucepans. She carried them back and gave them to him. "Here, maybe you can fix these."

His manner changed. He became professional. "Good as new I can fix them." At the back of his wagon he set a little anvil, and out of an oily tool box dug a small machine hammer. Elisa came through the gate to watch him while he pounded out the dents in the kettles. His mouth grew sure and knowing. At a difficult part of the work he sucked his under-lip.

"You sleep right in the wagon?" Elisa asked. 80

"Right in the wagon, ma'am. Rain or shine. I'm dry as a cow in there."

"It must be nice," she said. "It must be very nice. I wish women could do such things."

"It ain't the right kind of a life for a woman."

Her upper lip raised a little, showing her teeth. "How do you know? How can you tell?" she said.

"I don't know ma'am," he protested. "Of course I don't know. Now here's 85 your kettles, done. You don't have to buy no new ones."

"How much?"

"Oh, fifty cents'll do. I keep my prices down and my work good. That's why I have all them satisfied customers up and down the highway."

Elisa brought him a fifty-cent piece from the house and dropped it in his hand. "You might be surprised to have a rival some time. I can sharpen scissors, too. And I can beat the dents out of little pots. I could show you what a woman might do."

He put his hammer back in the oily box and shoved the little anvil out of sight. "It would be a lonely life for a woman, ma'am, and a scarey life, too, with animals creeping under the wagon all night." He climbed over the single-tree, steadying himself with a hand on the burro's white rump. He settled himself in the seat, picked up the lines. "Thank you kindly, ma'am," he said. "I'll do like you told me; I'll go back and catch the Salinas road."

"Mind," she called, "if you're long in getting there, keep the sand damp." 90

"Sand, ma'am? . . . Sand? Oh, sure. You mean round the chrysanthemums. Sure I will." He clucked his tongue. The beasts leaned luxuriously into their collars. The mongrel dog took his place between the back wheels. The wagon turned and crawled out the entrance road and back the way it had come, along the river.

Elisa stood in front of her wire fence watching the slow progress of the caravan. Her shoulders were straight, her head thrown back, her eyes half-closed, so that the scene came vaguely into them. Her lips moved silently, forming the words "Good-bye—good-bye." Then she whispered, "That's a bright direction. There's a glowing there." The sound of her whisper startled her. She shook herself free and looked about to see whether anyone had been listening. Only the dogs had heard. They lifted their heads toward her from their sleeping in the dust, and then stretched out their chins and settled asleep again. Elisa turned and ran hurriedly into the house.

In the kitchen she reached behind the stove and felt the water tank. It was full of hot water from the noonday cooking. In the bathroom she tore off her soiled clothes and flung them into the corner. And then she scrubbed herself with a little block of pumice, legs and thighs, loins and chest and arms, until her skin was scratched and red. When she had dried herself she stood in front of a mirror in her bedroom and looked at her body. She tightened her stomach and threw out her chest. She turned and looked over her shoulder at her back.

After a while she began to dress, slowly. She put on her newest under-clothing and her nicest stockings and the dress which was the symbol of her prettiness. She worked carefully on her hair, pencilled her eyebrows and rouged her lips.

Before she was finished she heard the little thunder of hoofs and the shouts   95
of Henry and his helper as they drove the red steers into the corral. She heard the gate bang shut and set herself for Henry's arrival.

His step sounded on the porch. He entered the house calling "Elisa, where are you?"

"In my room, dressing. I'm not ready. There's hot water for your bath. Hurry up. It's getting late."

When she heard him splashing in the tub, Elisa laid his dark suit on the bed, and shirt and socks and tie beside it. She stood his polished shoes on the floor beside the bed. Then she went to the porch and sat primly and stiffly down. She looked toward the river road where the willow-line was still yellow with frosted leaves so that under the high grey fog they seemed a thin band of sunshine. This was the only color in the grey afternoon. She sat unmoving for a long time. Her eyes blinked rarely.

Henry came banging out of the door, shoving his tie inside his vest as he came. Elisa stiffened and her face grew tight. Henry stopped short and looked at her. "Why—why, Elisa. You look so nice!"

"Nice? You think I look nice? What do you mean by 'nice'?"   100

Henry blundered on. "I don't know. I mean you look different, strong and happy."

"I am strong? Yes, strong. What do you mean 'strong'?"

He looked bewildered. "You're playing some kind of a game," he said helplessly. "It's a kind of a play. You look strong enough to break a calf over your knee, happy enough to eat it like watermelon."

For a second she lost her rigidity. "Henry! Don't talk like that. You didn't know what you said." She grew complete again. "I'm strong," she boasted. "I never knew before how strong."

Henry looked down toward the tractor shed, and when he brought his eyes   105
back to her, they were his own again. "I'll get out the car. You can put on your coat while I'm starting."

Elisa went into the house. She heard him drive to the gate and idle down his motor, and then she took a long time to put on her hat. She pulled it here and pressed it there. When Henry turned the motor off she slipped into her coat and went out.

The little roadster bounced along on the dirt road by the river, raising the birds and driving the rabbits into the brush. Two cranes flapped heavily over the willow-line and dropped into the river-bed.

Far ahead on the road Elisa saw a dark speck. She knew.

She tried not to look as they passed it, but her eyes would not obey. She whispered to herself sadly. "He might have thrown them off the road. That wouldn't have been much trouble, not very much. But he kept the pot," she explained. "He had to keep the pot. That's why he couldn't get them off the road."

The roadster turned a bend and she saw the caravan ahead. She swung full 110 around toward her husband so she could not see the little covered wagon and the mismatched team as the car passed them.

In a moment it was over. The thing was done. She did not look back. She said loudly, to be heard above the motor, "It will be good, tonight, a good dinner."

"Now you're changed again," Henry complained. He took one hand from the wheel and patted her knee. "I ought to take you in to dinner oftener. It would be good for both of us. We get so heavy out on the ranch."

"Henry," she asked, "could we have wine at dinner?"

"Sure we could. Say! That will be fine."

She was silent for a little while; then she said, "Henry, at those prize fights, 115 do the men hurt each other very much?"

"Sometimes a little, not often. Why?"

"Well, I've read how they break noses, and blood runs down their chests. I've read how the fighting gloves get heavy and soggy with blood." *Anger.*

He looked around at her. "What's the matter, Elisa? I didn't know you read things like that." He brought the car to a stop, then turned to the right over the Salinas River bridge.

"Do any women ever go to the fights?" she asked.

"Oh, sure, some. What's the matter, Elisa? Do you want to go? I don't think 120 you'd like it, but I'll take you if you really want to go."

She relaxed limply in the seat. "Oh, no. No. I don't want to go. I'm sure I don't." Her face was turned away from him. "It will be enough if we can have wine. It will be plenty." She turned up her coat collar so he could not see that she was crying weakly—like an old woman. *She's lost her dreams & hopes of personal fulfillment, of self-expression. What she values is meaningless now. She gives up.*

QUESTIONS

1. What point of view is used in the story? What are the advantages of using this point of view? What does Steinbeck force us to do by using this point of view?

2. Summarize the plot of the story. What are the conflicts? Which is the central conflict? Where is the climax of the story? To what extent does it resolve the central conflict?

3. How fully is Henry Allen described? Is he a round or flat character? Static or dynamic? How well does he understand his wife?

4. Consider the symbolism of the setting in this story with respect to the Salinas Valley, the time of year, and the description of the Allen house. What do these things tell us about Elisa Allen and her world?

5. To what extent is Steinbeck's description of Elisa in paragraphs 5 and 6 also symbolic? What is she wearing? What do her clothes hide or suppress? What does this description tell us about Elisa?

6. What is the central symbol in the story?

7. What do the chrysanthemums symbolize for Elisa? What do they symbolize about Elisa? What role do these flowers play in her life?

8. What is Elisa's first reaction to giving the tinker work? How does the tinker change Elisa's attitude? How does Elisa change as she speaks with the tinker? How would you explain this change?

9. How does Elisa's character or sense of self change during the episode in which she washes and dresses for dinner? To what extent is this washing-dressing episode symbolic? How would you explain the symbolism here?

10. Consider the symbolic impact of Elisa's seeing the chrysanthemum sprouts on the side of the road. How does this vision affect Elisa? What does it tell us about Elisa's life and values?

WRITING ABOUT SYMBOLISM AND ALLEGORY

In preparing to write about symbolism or allegory, you will need to be alert and to employ all facilities that can aid your understanding. In the light of the introductory discussion in this chapter, test the material to determine parallels that may genuinely establish the presence of symbolism or allegory. It is particularly helpful to make a list showing how qualities of symbols may be lined up with qualities of a character or action. Such a list can help you think more deeply about the effectiveness of symbols. Here is such a list for the symbol of the toy windmill in Welty's "A Worn Path":

QUALITIES IN THE WINDMILL	COMPARABLE QUALITIES IN PHOENIX AND HER LIFE
1. Cheap	1. Poor, but she gives all she has for the windmill
2. Breakable	2. Old, and not far from death
3. A gift	3. Generous
4. Not practical	4. Needs some relief from reality and practicality
5. Colorful	5. Same as 4

An aid for figuring out an allegory or allegorical passage can work well with a diagram of parallel lines. You can place corresponding characters, actions, things, or ideas along these lines as follows (using the film *Star Wars* as the specimen work):

STAR WARS	Luke Skywalker	Obi Wan Kenobi	Darth Vader	Princess Leia	Capture	Escape, and defeat of Vader
ALLEGORICAL APPLICATION TO MORALITY AND FAITH	Forces of good	Education and faith	Forces of evil	Object to be saved, ideals to be rescued and restored	Doubt, spiritual negligence	Restoration of faith
ALLEGORICAL APPLICATION TO PERSONAL AND GENERAL CONCERNS	Individual in pursuit of goals	The means by which goals may be reached	Obstacles to be overcome	Occupation, happiness, goals	Temporary failure, depression, discouragement, disappointment	Success

Lists and schemes like this may have the drawback of being too limiting or reductive. If you were to limit your responses only to the material on such visual aids, you might miss much of the impact and resonance of the story. Nevertheless, the knowledge and understanding you have to use in developing aids of this kind can be quite helpful to you when you are formulating the ways in which symbolism and allegory work, and therefore they can help you in getting together materials for your essay. As you make progress with such a method, you might wish to revise and focus things by crossing out some elements and adding others. As long as you transfer your materials directly to your own writing, you will stay on the right track and even improve the accuracy and forcefulness of your final essay.

In developing a thesis for your essay, it is important to begin by establishing significant general ideas about the story. "Young Goodman Brown," for example, is a work about the darkening of the soul of the major character, Brown. As he goes into the woods, he resolves to "stand firm against the devil," and he then looks up to "heaven above." As he looks, a "black mass of cloud" suddenly appears to hide the "brightening stars." Clearly this symbol is a direct visual representation of what is happening to Brown's character. Out of this relationship you could build a thesis about the relationship of Hawthorne's symbolism to his character development.

Similarly, "The Worker in Sandalwood" describes a miraculous rescue from misery and depression. The concluding sentence describes how the swallow "shook her wings to the light." Because this bird comes to the story with Biblical resonance, and arrives the night before the miracle, it is to be taken as one of the story's symbols of regeneration. A central idea to be developed from this relationship might ultimately depend on the latter part of the story, to be contrasted with the less optimistic symbols of the earlier part.

As you develop your central idea and plan what materials to use in the body of the essay, it is important to be able to justify the claims that you make about symbolism or allegory. In the Parable of the Prodigal Son, for example, the aim is to demonstrate the extreme lowness to which the Son sinks. His job feeding swine, and his sharing food with them, symbolize this depth of his degradation, for a reference to Jewish religion and custom will establish that pigs and pork are unclean and therefore that the Son has reached the nadir of life both spiritually and economically. A discussion of the swine as a symbol should include reference to this cultural and religious attitude. In the same way, the allegorical aspects of "Young Goodman Brown" would need to be established in the observation that people in life lose their ideals and forsake their principles not because they are evil but because they misperceive and misunderstand the events and people around them.

Organizing Your Essay

INTRODUCTION.   The introduction should establish the grounds for the discussion of symbolism and allegory in the story. There may be a recurring symbol, for example, or a regular pattern of symbolism. Or there may be actions that have clear allegorical applications. The central idea will refer to the nature of the symbols or allegory, like the benighting symbols in "Young Goodman Brown" or the regenerative symbols in "The Worker in Sandalwood." The thesis sentence will determine the topics to be developed in the body. These topics may refer to specific things, like the "walking stick," or to classes, like "regenerative symbols."

BODY.   There are a number of ways in which you might approach the topic of symbolism and allegory. You might wish to use one exclusively, or a combination. The choice is yours. If your choice is symbols and symbolism, you might consider the following:

1. *The meaning of a major symbol.* Here you interpret the symbol and try to show what it stands for both inside and outside the work. A few of the questions you might pursue are these: How do you determine that the symbol is really a symbol? How do you derive from the work a reasonable interpretation of the meaning of the symbol? What is the extent of the meaning? Does the symbol undergo any modification if it reappears in the work? By the same token, does the symbol affect your understanding of other parts of the work? How? Does the author create any ironies by using the symbol? Does the symbol give any special strength to the work?

2. *The meaning and relationship of a number of symbols.* What are the symbols? Do they have any specific connection or common bond? Do they suggest a unified reading or a contradictory one? Do the symbols seem to have general significance, or do they operate only in the context of the work? Do the symbols control the form of the work? How? For example, in "The Worker in Sandalwood" the concluding episode begins in doubt during the night of Christmas Eve and ends in success on the morning of Christmas Day. By contrast, the conclusion of Joyce's "Araby" (see p. 339) begins in anticipation during the day and ends in disillusionment at night. May these contrasting times be viewed symbolically in relationship to the development of the two stories? Other questions you may consider are whether the symbols fit naturally into the context of the story, or whether they seem to be drawn in artificially. Still another question is whether the writer's use of symbols makes for any unique qualities or excellences.

If you choose to write about allegory, you might address the following:

1. *The application of the allegory.* Does the allegory (fable, parable, myth) refer to anything or anyone specific? Does it refer to an action or particular period of history? Or does the allegory refer to human tendencies or ideas?

Does it illustrate, point by point, particular philosophies or religions? If so, what are these? If the original meaning of the allegory seems outdated, how much can be salvaged for people living today?

2. *The consistency of the allegory*. Is the allegory maintained consistently throughout the work, or is it intermittently used and dropped? Explain and detail this use. Would it be correct to call your work *allegorical* rather than *an allegory*? Can you determine how elements in the story have been especially introduced because of the requirements of the allegory (such as, perhaps, the complaints of the brother in "The Prodigal Son," which prompt the speech of the joyful father)? Positively, does the element seem natural, or, negatively, does it in any way seem unnatural or arbitrary?

CONCLUSION.   In your conclusion you might summarize your main points, describe your general impressions, try to describe the impact of the images or symbolic methods, indicate your personal responses, or show what might further be done along the lines you have been developing in the body. You might also try to assess the quality of the symbolism or allegory and to make a statement about the appropriateness of the specific details to the applied ideas.

SAMPLE ESSAY

Allegory and Symbolism in Hawthorne's "Young Goodman Brown"*

[1]
It is hard to read beyond the third paragraph of "Young Goodman Brown" without finding allegory and symbolism. The opening seems realistic—Goodman Brown, a young Puritan, leaves his home in colonial Salem to take an overnight trip—but his wife's name, "Faith," immediately suggests a symbolic reading. Before long, Brown's walk into the forest becomes an allegorical trip into evil. The idea that Hawthorne shows by this trip is that rigid belief destroys the best human qualities, such as understanding and love.° He develops this thought in the allegory and in many symbols, particularly the sunset, the walking-stick, and the path.▫

[2]
The allegory is about how people develop destructive ideas. Most of the story is dreamlike and unreal, and therefore the ideas that Brown gains are unreal. After the weird night he thinks of his wife and neighbors not with love, but with hatred for their sins during the "witch meeting" deep in the

* See p. 302 for this story.
° Central idea.
▫ Thesis sentence.

dream forest. Because of his own dream vision, he condemns everyone around him, and he lives out his life in unforgiving harshness. The story thus allegorizes the pursuit of any ideal or system beyond human love and forgiveness.

[3]
The attack on such dehumanizing belief is found not just in the allegory, but also in Hawthorne's many symbols. The seventh word in the story, *sunset*, may be seen as a symbol. Sunset indicates the end of the day. Coming at the beginning of the story, however, it suggests that Goodman Brown is beginning the long night of his hatred, his spiritual death. For him the night will never end because his final days are shrouded in "gloom" (p. 311). The story suggests that Brown, like anyone else who gives up on human beings, is cut off from humanity, and is locked in an inner prison of bitterness.

[4]
The next symbol, the walking-stick, suggests the ambiguous and arbitrary standard by which Brown judges his neighbors. The stick is carried by the guide who looks like Brown's father. It "might almost be seen to twist and wriggle itself like a living serpent" (p. 304). The serpent is a clear symbol for Satan, who tempted Adam and Eve (Genesis 3:1–7). The staff is also still a walking-stick, however, and in this respect it is innocent. Given this double vision, it symbolizes human tendencies to see evil where evil does not really exist. This double meaning squares with the statement about "the instinct that guides mortal man to evil" (p. 308). This instinct is not just the temptation to do bad things, but also the invention of wrongs for arbitrary reasons, and, more dangerously, the condemnation of those who have "done" these wrongs even though they have done nothing more than lead their own quiet lives.

[5]
In the same vein, the path through the forest is a major symbol of the destructive mental confusion that overcomes Brown. As he walks, the path before him grows "wilder and drearier, and more faintly traced," and "at length" it vanishes (p. 308). This is like the description of the "broad" Biblical way that leads "to Destruction" (Matthew 7:13). As a symbol, the path shows that most human acts are bad, while a small number, like the "narrow" way to life (Matthew 7:14), are good. Goodman Brown's path is at first clear, as though sin is at first unique and unusual. Soon, however, it is so indistinct that he can see only sin wherever he turns. The symbol suggests that, as people follow evil, their moral vision becomes blurred and they cannot choose the right way even if it is in front of them. With such vision, they can hardly be anything other than destructive of their best instincts.

[6]
Through Hawthorne's allegory and symbols, then, the story presents the paradoxes of how a seemingly good system can lead to bad results and also of how noble beliefs can backfire destructively. Goodman Brown dies in gloom because he believes strongly that his wrong vision is real. This form of evil is the hardest to stop, no matter what outward set of beliefs it takes, because wrongdoers who are convinced of their own goodness are beyond reach. Such a blend of evil and self-righteousness causes Hawthorne to write that "the fiend in his own shape is less hideous than when he rages in the breast of man" (p. 308). Young Goodman Brown thus becomes the central symbol of the story. He is one of those who walk in darkness and have forever barred themselves from the light.

Commentary on the Essay

The introduction justifies the treatment of allegory and symbolism because of the way in which Hawthorne early in the story invites a symbolic reading. The central idea relates Hawthorne's method to the idea that rigid belief destroys the best human qualities. The thesis sentence outlines two major areas of discussion: (1) allegory, and (2) symbolism.

Paragraph 2 considers the allegory as a criticism of rigid Puritan morality. Paragraphs 3, 4, and 5 deal with three major symbols: the sunset, the walking-stick, and the path. The aim of this discussion is to show the meaning and application of these symbols for Hawthorne's attack on rigidity of belief. Throughout these three paragraphs the central idea—the relationship of rigidity to destructiveness—is stressed. Hawthorne's allusions to both the Old and New Testaments are pointed out in paragraphs 4 and 5. The concluding paragraph raises questions that lead to the idea that Brown himself is a symbol of Hawthorne's idea that the primary cause of evil is the inability to separate reality from unreality.

10

Idea or Theme: The Meaning and the Message in Fiction

The term **idea** is connected to the actions of seeing and knowing; indeed, the words *view* and *wit* (in the sense of knowledge) are close relatives of *idea*. Originally, the term was applied to mental images that, once seen, could be remembered and therefore known. Because of this mental activity, an idea was considered as a conceptual **form** as opposed to external reality. The word is now commonly understood to refer to a concept, thought, opinion, or belief. Some typical ideas as delimited by philosophers and historians of ideas are these: *infinity, justice, right and good, necessity, the problem of evil, causation*, and, not unsurprisingly, *idea* itself. A full consideration of ideas like these requires a good deal of knowledge, understanding, and thought. In this respect, therefore, ideas involve the interrelation of thinking and knowing.

In stories, ideas are likely to be concerned not so much with abstract and speculative definitions as with the human side of things. The ancient Greek philosopher Plato, in his *Republic*, attempted a lengthy definition of the idea of justice. By contrast, in "Flying Home" the black American writer Ralph Ellison created a *story* about justice by showing how a young black Air Force pilot is subject to injustice. When an idea is developed throughout a story in this way, it is often given the name **theme**. This word refers to something laid down, a postulate, a central or unifying idea. Loosely, the *theme* of a work and its *central idea* may be considered as synonymous.

IDEAS, TOPICS, ASSERTIONS, AND MEANING

Writers often (but not always) work with ideas or themes as they shape literary works. The general **subject** or **topic** of a story indicates the idea or group of ideas that the writer is concerned about. These may be broad topics or classes, like those just mentioned, that may be given titles of single words, such as *love, sacrifice, justice, persecution, power, honor, growth, maturity*, and so on. Just the topic alone is not enough, however, for the specific idea or theme must embody an **assertion** that the story makes about the subject. Thus, we might find stories with assertions that love is necessary but also irrational, hatred is built on misunderstanding, slavery is worse than death, power destroys youthful dreams, or growth is difficult but exciting.

In other words, the central idea or theme in a story embodies the work's **meaning.** In answering the question, "What does this, or that, *mean*, the response will usually be in the form of a principle about human nature, conduct, or motivation—in other words, in the form of an idea. In Eudora Welty's "A Worn Path" we might formulate an idea about the character of Phoenix Jackson as follows: "Phoenix illustrates the idea that human beings who are committed to caring for others may actually suffer for this commitment." Similarly, it might be argued that Mabel Pervin in D. H. Lawrence's "The Horse Dealer's Daughter" embodies the idea that "even if a commitment to the dead is strong, the commitment to life is stronger."

In considering a story for ideas, keep in mind that an idea pervades a work just as a key signature dominates a musical composition and therefore governs the notes as part of a clearly established scale. In a story, most things happen only as they have a bearing on the idea. Thus, actions, characters, statements, symbols, and dialogue may be judged in terms of how closely they relate to the idea or theme. In this sense, a theme runs throughout a story and ties things together much like a continuous thread. As readers, we can attempt to trace such threads, with all the patterns or variations that writers may work upon them. In Ellison's "Flying Home," for example, all the events may be seen in relationship to the idea that it is only with difficulty and against opposition that minority blacks can accomplish their goals in a majority white society.

FORMULATING THE IDEAS IN FICTION

Although an idea may be expressed in a phrase or single word, gaining a full understanding of ideas in a work will be difficult unless they can be formulated in complete sentences. Thus, "love for human beings" may be an idea, but it is not an assertion about anything, and therefore it is not specific enough significantly to help someone studying a work in which love of any sort is illustrated. In dealing with Lawrence's "The Horse Dealer's Daughter," for example, little is accomplished with the statement that the story is about the love between a man and a woman. This topic does little more than identify the area of concern. The process must go a step further and ask what the story *says* about love, because the formulation of ideas in literature, like the development of a thesis in an essay, must move beyond subject to assertion. Thus, it is much more helpful to see Lawrence's story as expressing the idea that the love of a man and a woman is so positive that it can literally rescue people from death. In this story Mabel, one of the two major characters, tries to drown herself. She is close to death but is rescued by Dr. Fergusson. When she recovers consciousness, she and the doctor both realize that they have fallen suddenly in love. The events, in other words, illustrate the idea that we have just formulated about the story. Similarly, the thought that selfless love may lead to bravery against hopeless odds can be shown to be a major idea in Welty's "A Worn Path."

DISTINGUISHING IDEAS FROM SUMMARIES

It is vitally important to make a distinction between ideas and short descriptions of events, or story summaries. Unfortunately, it is easy to go astray. After reading Frank O'Connor's "First Confession," for example, a reader might want to express the central idea in the story as follows: " 'First Confession' is a story about a young boy's family troubles before going to his first confession." This sentence accounts for many of the actions in the story quite well, but it does not state an idea. For this reason it is not helpful in study or analysis. In fact, the sentence might even get in the way of understanding, since it would direct further thought only toward what happens in the story. It does not provide any guidance for seeing the characters and events as they relate to an idea. A better way of approaching the theme in this story might be to assert that "O'Connor's 'First Confession' shows the limitation of trying to instill religion through fear and punishment." This sentence focuses attention on the behavior and advice of the sister, father, and Mrs. Ryan, and also on how their making Jackie confused illustrates the weakness of their threats of punishment. The end result of the clearer formulation is that thinking may be directed toward the idea and away from the sequential events of the story.

IDEAS AND VALUES

The idea or ideas that an author expresses are closely tied to his or her values, or "value system." Unless an idea is completely abstract, like the idea of a geometric form, it usually carries with it some value judgment. In "Flying Home," for example, one of Ellison's dominant ideas is the very basic one that all human beings are equal regardless of race. His values are made clearly apparent as he directs disapproval against those who are so locked into their own prejudicial habits that they do not help but actually harass an injured fellow human being. It would be almost impossible to analyze Ellison's ideas in the story without considering his value system at the same time. As a general rule, then, we should assume that the ideas of authors grow out of their values, and that values are embodied in their stories along with the ideas.

FINDING THE IDEAS IN FICTION

To find ideas in fiction, one must read the work carefully, considering the main characters and actions and evaluating such variables as tone, setting, and symbolism. Often, several readings of the story are helpful. At some point in the process, you should be able to begin formulating the story's meaning or message in terms of an idea. There are, of course, many different ways of stating the same general idea, but the result should always assert a specific point about the story's general subject. In dealing with James Joyce's story "Araby," for example, an initial expression of the story's idea might take any of the following forms: (1) The force of sexual attraction is strong and begins early in life. (2) The attraction can lead some individuals to strong idealization, or "pedestalization" of the loved one. (3) Sexual feelings are private and may therefore be a source of embarrassment and shame. (4) The sense of shame may produce ambiguous feelings even among those who are otherwise loyal to what produces the shame (in this case, the Church). Although any one of these choices could be an idea around which to build a study of "Araby," together with others that might be developed, they all have in common the idealization by the narrator of his friend's sister. If, in studying for ideas, you attempt to follow this sort of process, fully stating the idea of a story and then revising it in the light of further analysis, you should be able to deal skillfully with ideas in stories.

Authors may express ideas in many different ways. Although we cannot explain every possible method, we can introduce you to some of the most common. You should remember, however, that the following classifications are neither exhaustive nor restrictive; rather, they are for convenience and reference. In actual practice, all these methods (and more) may be employed at the same time.

Direct Statements by the Author's Unnamed Speaker

Often the unnamed speaker, who may or may not represent the author's exact views, states ideas directly, by way of **commentary,** to guide us or deepen understanding. These ideas, while helping our reading, might also disrupt our understanding of the story. In the second paragraph of "The Necklace," for example, De Maupassant's authorial voice states the idea that women without strong family connections must rely on their charm and beauty to get on in the world. This idea might seem sexist or patronizing today, but it is nevertheless an accurate restatement of what De Maupassant's speaker says. In considering it as an idea, just as you might consider other ideas expressed directly by any other author's authorial voice, you might want to adapt it somewhat in line with your own understanding of the story. Thus, an adequate restatement of the De Maupassant idea might be this: " 'The Necklace' shows the idea that women, with no power except their charm and beauty, are helpless against chance or bad luck."

Direct Statements by the Persona

Often the first-person narrators or speakers state their own ideas. (See also Chapter 5, on Point of View.) It is possible that the narrator's ideas may be identical with ideas held by the author or the authorial speaker, for the author may use the speaker as a direct mouthpiece for ideas. There is a danger in making a direct equation, however, for any ideas expressed by a persona speaking within a story may belong only to himself or herself, and the author may genuinely not be underwriting the ideas, but only examining them. Careful consideration is therefore necessary to determine the extent to which the narrator's ideas correspond with or diverge from the author's ideas. Sometimes the narrators speak views that are directly opposed to what the author might stand for. Usually these instances are clear. Jonathan Swift, for example, makes his speaker, Gulliver of *Gulliver's Travels*, say many things that Swift himself would have rejected. In addition, the author may cause the persona to make statements indicating a limited understanding of the situation he or she is telling about. Thus the adult Jackie, in O'Connor's "First Confession," says things that show some of his ideas to be immature.

Dramatic Statements Made by Characters

In many works, different characters state ideas that are in conflict. The English story writer and novelist Aldous Huxley, for example, frequently introduced "mouthpiece" characters specifically to state ideas related to the fictional story being developed. Authors may thus present thirteen ways of looking at a blackbird and leave the choice up to you. They may provide you with guides for your interpretations, however. For instance, they may create an admirable character whose ideas may be the ones they admire. The reverse would be true for a bad character.

Figurative Language

Authors often use figurative language to express or reinforce their ideas. As an example, here is a comparison from Joyce's "Araby," where the narrator describes the effect that his youthful admiration for his friend's sister had upon him: "But my body was like a harp and her words and gestures were like fingers running upon the wires." This comparison is based on the thought that young, first love is a powerful, irresistible force that may possess a person not only deeply but overwhelmingly. Joyce's entire story bears out this idea.

Characters Who Stand for Ideas

Although characters are busy in the action of their respective works, they may also be employed symbolically to stand for ideas or values. Mathilde Loisel in "The Necklace" may be thought of as an embodiment of the idea that women of the nineteenth-century middle class, without the possibility of a career, are hurt by unrealizable dreams of wealth. With two diverse or opposed characters, the ideas they represent may be compared or contrasted. Mrs. Ryan and the priest in O'Connor's "First Confession," for instance, represent opposing ideas about the way in which religion is to be instilled in the young.

In effect, characters who stand for ideas may be considered as symbols. Thus, in Ellison's "Flying Home," the character Todd is symbolic of the black who is trying to gain success but who, like most average human beings, experiences a reversal—his plane crashes. Todd's wish to move ahead is hard for him to fulfill because he is denied the assistance that others are granted by right. Seen in this way, characters like Todd and actions they go through achieve a symbolic status that can be analyzed in the more abstract, less narrative language of ideas.

The Work Itself as it Represents Ideas

One of the most important ways in which authors express ideas is to render them as an inseparable part of the total impression of the work. All the events and characters may add up to an idea that is made forceful by the impact of the story itself. Thus, although an idea may not be directly stated in so many words, it will be clear after you have finished reading. For example, in "Flying Home," Ellison makes objective the idea that racial barriers separate human beings and make them cruel when it would be to everyone's interest to unite and to be helpful. Although he never states this concept directly, the idea is clearly embodied in the story. Similarly, Shakespeare's *Hamlet* (see p. 1180) dramatizes the idea that a person doing evil sets strong forces in motion that cannot be stopped until everything in the person's path is destroyed. Even "escape literature," which is ostensibly designed to help readers forget about problems, will develop plots that stem out of conflicts between forces of good and evil, love and hate, good spies and bad, the earthlings versus the aliens, and so on.

Such stories in fact *do* embody ideas and themes, even though they admittedly do not set out to strike readers with the boldness or originality of their ideas.

JAMES JOYCE (1882–1941)

Araby   *1914*

North Richmond Street, being blind,° was a quiet street except at the hour when the Christian Brothers' School set the boys free. An uninhabited house of two storeys stood at the blind end, detached from its neighbours in a square ground. The other houses of the street, conscious of decent lives within them, gazed at one another with brown imperturbable faces.

The former tenant of our house, a priest, had died in the back drawing room. Air, musty from having long been enclosed, hung in all the rooms, and the waste room behind the kitchen was littered with old useless papers. Among these I found a few paper-covered books, the pages of which were curled and damp: *The Abbott*, by Walter Scott, *The Devout Communicant* and *The Memoirs of Vidocq*. I liked the last best because its leaves were yellow. The wild garden behind the house contained a central apple-tree and a few straggling bushes under one of which I found the late tenant's rusty bicycle-pump. He had been a very charitable priest; in his will he had left all his money to institutions and the furniture of his house to his sister.

When the short days of winter came dusk fell before we had well eaten our dinners. When we met in the street the houses had grown sombre. The space of sky above us was the colour of ever-changing violet and towards it the lamps of the street lifted their feeble lanterns. The cold air stung us and we played till our bodies glowed. Our shouts echoed in the silent street. The career of our play brought us through the dark muddy lanes behind the houses where we ran the gantlet of the rough tribes from the cottages, to the back doors of the dark dripping gardens where odours arose from the ashpits, to the dark odorous stables where a coachman smoothed and combed the horse or shook music from the buckled harness. When we returned to the street light from the kitchen windows had filled the areas. If my uncle was seen turning the corner we hid in the shadow until we had seen him safely housed. Or if Mangan's sister came out on the doorstep to call her brother in to his tea we watched her from our shadow peer up and down the street. We waited to see whether she would remain or go in and, if she remained, we left our shadow and walked up to Mangan's steps resignedly. She was waiting for us, her figure defined by the light from the half-opened door. Her brother always teased her before he obeyed and I stood by the railings looking at her. Her dress swung as she moved her body and the soft rope of her hair tossed from side to side.

Every morning I lay on the floor in the front parlor watching her door. The blind was pulled down within an inch of the sash so that I could not be seen. When she came out on the doorstep my heart leaped. I ran to the hall,

°*blind*: a dead-end street in Dublin.

seized my books and followed her. I kept her brown figure always in my eye and, when we came near the point at which our ways diverged, I quickened my pace and passed her. This happened morning after morning. I had never spoken to her, except for a few casual words, and yet her name was like a summons to all my foolish blood.

Her image accompanied me even in places the most hostile to romance. On Saturday evenings when my aunt went marketing I had to go to carry some of the parcels. We walked through the flaring street, jostled by drunken men and bargaining women, amid the curses of labourers, the shrill litanies of shop-boys who stood on guard by the barrels of pigs' cheeks, the nasal chanting of street singers, who sang a *come-all-you* about O'Donovan Rossa, or a ballad about the troubles in our native land. These noises converged in a single sensation of life for me: I imagined that I bore my chalice safely through the throng of foes. Her name sprang to my lips at moments in strange prayers and praises which I myself did not understand. My eyes were often full of tears (I could not tell why) and at times a flood from my heart seemed to pour itself out into my bosom. I thought little of the future. I did not know whether I would ever speak to her or not or, if I spoke to her, how I could tell her of my confused adoration. But my body was like a harp and her words and gestures were like fingers running upon the wires.

One evening I went into the back drawing-room in which the priest had died. It was a dark rainy evening and there was no sound in the house. Through one of the broken panes I heard the rain impinge upon the earth, the fine incessant needles of water playing in the sodden beds. Some distant lamp or lighted window gleamed below me. I was thankful that I could see so little. All my senses seemed to desire to veil themselves and, feeling that I was about to slip from them, I pressed the palms of my hands together until they trembled, murmuring: *O love! O love!* many times.

At last she spoke to me. When she addressed the first words to me I was so confused that I did not know what to answer. She asked me was I going to *Araby*. I forget whether I answered yes or no. It would be a splendid bazaar, she said; she would love to go.

—And why can't you? I asked.

While she spoke she turned a silver bracelet round and round her wrist. She could not go, she said, because there would be a retreat° that week in her convent. Her brother and two other boys were fighting for their caps and I was alone at the railings. She held one of the spikes, bowing her head towards me. The light from the lamp opposite our door caught the white curve of her neck, lit up her hair that rested there and, falling, lit up the hand upon the railing. It fell over one side of her dress and caught the white border of a petticoat, just visible as she stood at ease.

—It's well for you, she said.

—If I go, I said, I will bring you something.

What innumerable follies laid waste my waking and sleeping thoughts after that evening! I wished to annihilate the tedious intervening days. I chafed against

retreat: a special time of two or more days set aside for concentrated religious instruction, discussion, and prayer.

the work of school. At night in my bedroom and by day in the classroom her image came between me and the page I strove to read. The syllables of the word *Araby* were called to me through the silence in which my soul luxuriated and cast an Eastern enchantment over me. I asked for leave to go to the bazaar on Saturday night. My aunt was surprised and hoped it was not some Freemason° affair. I answered few questions in class. I watched my master's face pass from amiability to sternness; he hoped I was not beginning to idle. I could not call my wandering thoughts together. I had hardly any patience with the serious work of life which, now that it stood between me and my desire, seemed to me child's play, ugly monotonous child's play.

On Saturday morning I reminded my uncle that I wished to go to the bazaar in the evening. He was fussing at the hall-stand, looking for the hatbrush, and answered me curtly:

—Yes, boy, I know.

As he was in the hall I could not go into the front parlour and lie at the   15
window. I left the house in bad humour and walked slowly towards the school. The air was pitilessly raw and already my heart misgave me.

When I came home to dinner my uncle had not yet been home. Still it was early. I sat staring at the clock for some time and, when its ticking began to irritate me, I left the room. I mounted the staircase and gained the upper part of the house. The high cold empty gloomy rooms liberated me and I went from room to room singing. From the front window I saw my companions playing below in the street. Their cries reached me weakened and indistinct and, leaning my forehead against the cool glass, I looked over at the dark house where she lived. I may have stood there for an hour, seeing nothing but the brown-clad figure cast by my imagination, touched discreetly by the lamplight at the curved neck, at the hand upon the railing and at the border below the dress.

When I came downstairs again I found Mrs Mercer sitting at the fire. She was an old garrulous woman, a pawnbroker's widow, who collected used stamps for some pious purpose. I had to endure the gossip of the tea-table. The meal was pro-longed beyond an hour and still my uncle did not come. Mrs Mercer stood up to go: she was sorry she couldn't wait any longer, but it was after eight o'clock and she did not like to be out late, as the night air was bad for her. When she had gone I began to walk up and down the room, clenching my fists. My aunt said:

—I'm afraid you may put off your bazaar for this night of Our Lord.

At nine o'clock I heard my uncle's latchkey in the halldoor. I heard him talking to himself and heard the hall-stand rocking when it had received the weight of his overcoat. I could interpret these signs. When he was midway through his dinner I asked him to give me the money to go to the bazaar. He had forgotten.

—The people are in bed and after their first sleep now, he said.   20

I did not smile. My aunt said to him energetically:

—Can't you give him the money and let him go? You've kept him late enough as it is.

My uncle said he was very sorry he had forgotten. He said he believed in the old saying: *All work and no play makes Jack a dull boy*. He asked me where I was going and, when I had told him a second time he asked me did I know *The Arab's*

Freemason: and therefore Protestant.

Farewell to his Steed. When I left the kitchen he was about to recite the opening lines of the piece to my aunt.

I held a florin° tightly in my hand as I strode down Buckingham Street towards the station. The sight of the streets thronged with buyers and glaring with gas recalled to me the purpose of my journey. I took my seat in a third-class carriage of a deserted train. After an intolerable delay the train moved out of the station slowly. It crept onward among ruinous houses and over the twinkling river. At Westland Row Station a crowd of people pressed to the carriage doors; but the porters moved them back, saying that it was a special train for the bazaar. I remained alone in the bare carriage. In a few minutes the train drew up beside an improvised wooden platform. I passed out on to the road and saw by the lighted dial of a clock that it was ten minutes to ten. In front of me was a large building which displayed the magical name.

I could not find any sixpenny entrance and, fearing that the bazaar would   25
be closed, I passed in quickly through a turnstile, handing a shilling to a weary-looking man. I found myself in a big hall girdled at half its height by a gallery. Nearly all the stalls were closed and the greater part of the hall was in darkness. I recognized a silence like that which pervades a church after a service. I walked into the centre of the bazaar timidly. A few people were gathered about the stalls which were still open. Before a curtain, over which the words *Café Chantant* were written in coloured lamps, two men were counting money on a salver. I listened to the fall of the coins.

Remembering with difficulty why I had come I went over to one of the stalls and examined porcelain vases and flowered tea-sets. At the door of the stall a young lady was talking and laughing with two young gentlemen. I remarked their English accents and listened vaguely to their conversation.

—O, I never said such a thing!

—O, but you did!

—O, but I didn't!

—Didn't she say that?   30

—Yes I heard her

—O, there's a . . . fib!

Observing me the young lady came over and asked me did I wish to buy anything. The tone in her voice was not encouraging; she seemed to have spoken to me out of a sense of duty. I looked humbly at the great jars that stood like eastern guards at either side of the dark entrance to the stall and murmured:

—No, thank you.

The young lady changed the position of one of the vases and went back to   35
the two young men. They began to talk of the same subject. Once or twice the young lady glanced at me over her shoulder.

I lingered before her stall, though I knew my stay was useless, to make my interest in her wares seem the more real. Then I turned away slowly and walked down the middle of the bazaar. I allowed the two pennies to fall against the sixpence in my pocket. I heard a voice call from one end of the gallery that the light was out. The upper part of the hall was now completely dark.

Gazing up into the darkness I saw myself as a creature driven and derided by vanity; and my eyes burned with anguish and anger.

florin: a two-shilling coin; in the 1890s (when the story takes place), worth perhaps ten dollars in today's money.

QUESTIONS

1. What is the point of view in the story? Why is this point of view especially effective, given the story's nature?

2. Who is the narrator? About how old is he at the time of the events related in the story? About how old when he tells the story? What effect is produced by this difference in age between narrator-as-character and narrator-as-story-teller?

3. Three specific places are described in detail: the street, the house, and the market. In addition, the weather is frequently noted. How would you characterize these elements of setting? How effectively do the adjectives help to create an atmosphere? To what extent does the setting work against the protagonist's emotions but with the climax and resolution of the story?

4. How might the bazaar, "Araby," be considered symbolically in the story? What does Araby symbolize for the protagonist before he gets there? What does it come to symbolize at the close of the story? To what extent does this symbol embody the story's central idea?

5. How would you characterize the speaker's boyhood feelings about Mangan's sister? Are these feelings unusual in any way, or are they normal? Does the speaker's disappointment at being unable to buy a gift for the girl seem to be sufficient cause for his concluding shame and self-criticism, or is there some other cause or causes that are described or hinted at earlier in the story?

6. Consider the attitude of the speaker toward his home as indicated in the first paragraph. What does he think of the school, and of the houses as they represent the people living in them? Why do you think the speaker chose the word *blind* to describe the dead-end street? Can you relate the speaker's disappointment and humiliation at the end of the story to his attitude as it emerges in the first paragraph?

7. Describe what you consider to be the story's major idea about youthful admiration and love (if you wish, you might consider the speaker to be describing a childhood "crush"). Should such admiration be respected and cherished as a memory? How does the speaker think of himself because of his admiration?

D. H. LAWRENCE (1885–1930)

The Horse Dealer's Daughter   *1922*

"Well, Mabel, and what are you going to do with yourself?" asked Joe, with foolish flippancy. He felt quite safe himself. Without listening for an answer, he turned aside, worked a grain of tobacco to the tip of his tongue, and spat it out. He did not care about anything, since he felt safe himself.

The three brothers and the sister sat round the desolate breakfast table, attempting some sort of desultory consultation. The morning's post had given the final tap to the family fortunes, and all was over. The dreary dining-room itself, with its heavy mahogany furniture, looked as if it were waiting to be done away with.

But the consultation amounted to nothing. There was a strange air of ineffectuality about the three men, as they sprawled at table, smoking and reflecting vaguely on their own condition. The girl was alone, a rather short, sullen-looking young woman of twenty-seven. She did not share the same life as her brothers. She would have been good-looking, save for the impassive fixity of her face, "bulldog," as her brothers called it.

There was a confused tramping of horses' feet outside. The three men all sprawled round in their chairs to watch. Beyond the dark holly-bushes that separated the strip of lawn from the high-road, they could see a cavalcade of shire horses swinging out of their own yard, being taken for exercise. This was the last time. These were the last horses that would go through their hands. The young men watched with critical, callous look. They were all frightened at the collapse of their lives, and the sense of disaster in which they were involved left them no inner freedom.

Yet they were three fine, well-set fellows enough. Joe, the eldest, was a man   5
of thirty-three, broad and handsome in a hot, flushed way. His face was red, he twisted his black moustache over a thick finger, his eyes were shallow and restless. He had a sensual way of uncovering his teeth when he laughed, and his bearing was stupid. Now he watched the horses with a glazed look of helplessness in his eyes, a certain stupor of downfall.

The great draught-horses swung past. They were tied head to tail, four of them, and they heaved along to where a lane branched off from the highroad, planting their great hoofs floutingly in the fine black mud, swinging their great rounded haunches sumptuously, and trotting a few sudden steps as they were led into the lane, round the corner. Every movement showed a massive, slumbrous strength, and a stupidity which held them in subjection. The groom at the head looked back, jerking the leading rope. And the cavalcade moved out of sight up the lane, the tail of the last horse, bobbed up tight and stiff, held out taut from the swinging great haunches as they rocked behind the hedges in a motionlike sleep.

Joe watched with glazed hopeless eyes. The horses were almost like his own body to him. He felt he was done for now. Luckily, he was engaged to a woman as old as himself, and therefore her father, who was steward of a neighbouring estate, would provide him with a job. He would marry and go into harness. His life was over, he would be a subject animal now.

He turned uneasily aside, the retreating steps of the horses echoing in his ears. Then, with foolish restlessness, he reached for the scraps of bacon-rind from the plates, and making a faint whistling sound, flung them to the terrier that lay against the fender. He watched the dog swallow them, and waited till the creature looked into his eyes. Then a faint grin came on his face, and in a high, foolish voice he said:

"You won't get much more bacon, shall you, you little b———?"

The dog faintly and dismally wagged its tail, then lowered its haunches,   10
circled round, and lay down again.

There was another helpless silence at the table. Joe sprawled uneasily in his seat, not willing to go till the family conclave was dissolved. Fred Henry, the second brother, was erect, clean-limbed, alert. He had watched the passing of the horses with more *sang-froid*.° If he was an animal, like Joe, he was an animal which controls, not one which is controlled. He was master of any horse, and he carried himself with a well-tempered air of mastery. But he was not master of the situations of life. He pushed his coarse brown moustache upwards, off his lip, and glanced irritably at his sister, who sat impassive and inscrutable.

"You'll go and stop with Lucy for a bit, shan't you?" he asked. The girl did not answer.

"I don't see what else you can do," persisted Fred Henry.

"Go as a skivvy,"° Joe interpolated laconically.

The girl did not move a muscle.   15

"If I was her, I should go in for training for a nurse," said Malcolm, the youngest of them all. He was the baby of the family, a young man of twenty-two, with a fresh, jaunty *museau*.°

But Mabel did not take any notice of him. The had talked at her and round her for so many years, that she hardly heard them at all.

The marble clock on the mantel-piece softly chimed the half-hour, the dog rose uneasily from the hearthrug and looked at the party at the breakfast table. But still they sat on in ineffectual conclave.

"Oh, all right," said Joe suddenly, *à propos* of nothing. "I'll get a move on."

He pushed back his chair, straddled his knees with a downward jerk, to get   20
them free, in horsey fashion, and went to the fire. Still he did not go out of the room; he was curious to know what the others would do or say. He began to charge his pipe, looking down at the dog and saying, in a high, affected voice:

"Going wi' me? Going wi' me are ter? Tha'rt goin' further than tha counts on just now, dost hear?"

The dog faintly wagged its tail, the man stuck out his jaw and covered his pipe with his hands, and puffed intently, losing himself in the tobacco, looking down all the while at the dog, with an absent brown eye. The dog looked up at him in mournful distrust. Joe stood with his knees stuck out, in real horsey fashion.

"Have you had a letter from Lucy?" Fred Henry asked of his sister.

"Last week," came the neutral reply.

"And what does she say?"   25

There was no answer.

"Does she *ask* you to go and stop there?" persisted Fred Henry.

"She says I can if I like."

"Well, then, you'd better. Tell her you'll come on Monday."

This was received in silence.   30

"That's what you'll do then, is it?" said Fred Henry, in some exasperation.

But she made no answer. There was a silence of futility and irritation in the room. Malcolm grinned fatuously.

"You'll have to make up your mind between now and next Wednesday," said Joe loudly, "or else find yourself lodgings on the kerbstone."

The face of the young woman darkened, but she sat on immutable.

sang-froid: cold blood; i.e., unconcern.
skivvy: British slang for housemaid.
museau: muzzle, or snout (as of an animal), a French word.

"Here's Jack Fergusson!" exclaimed Malcolm, who was looking aimlessly out   35
of the window.

"Where?" exclaimed Joe, loudly.

"Just gone past."

"Coming in?"

Malcolm craned his neck to see the gate.

"Yes," he said.   40

There was a silence. Mabel sat on like one condemned, at the head of the
table. Then a whistle was heard from the kitchen. The dog got up and barked
sharply. Joe opened the door and shouted:

"Come on."

After a moment, a young man entered. He was muffled up in overcoat and
a purple woollen scarf, and his tweed cap, which he did not remove, was pulled
down on his head. He was of medium height, his face was rather long and pale,
his eyes looked tired.

"Hello Jack! Well, Jack!" exclaimed Malcolm and Joe. Fred Henry merely
said "Jack!"

"What's doing?" asked the newcomer, evidently addressing Fred Henry.   45

"Same. We've got to be out by Wednesday.—Got a cold?"

"I have—got it bad, too."

"Why don't you stop in?"

"*Me* stop in? When I can't stand on my legs, perhaps I shall have a chance."
The young man spoke huskily. He had a slight Scotch accent.

"It's a knock-out, isn't it," said Joe boisterously, "if a doctor goes round   50
croaking with a cold. Looks bad for the patients, doesn't it?"

The young doctor looked at him slowly.

"Anything the matter with *you*, then?" he asked, sarcastically.

"Not as I know of. Damn your eyes, I hope not. Why?"

"I thought you were very concerned about the patients, wondered if you
might be one yourself."

"Damn it, no, I've never been patient to no flaming doctor, and hope I   55
never shall be," returned Joe.

At this point Mabel rose from the table, and they all seemed to become
aware of her existence. She began putting the dishes together. The young doctor
looked at her, but did not address her. He had not greeted her. She went out of
the room with the tray, her face impassive and unchanged.

"When are you off then, all of you?" asked the doctor.

"I'm catching the eleven-forty," replied Malcolm. "Are you goin' down wi'
th' trap,° Joe?"

"Yes, I've told you I'm going down wi' th' trap, haven't I?"

"We'd better be getting her in then. —So long, Jack, if I don't see you   60
before I go," said Malcolm, shaking hands.

He went out, followed by Joe, who seemed to have his tail between his legs.

"Well, this is the devil's own," exclaimed the doctor, when he was left alone
with Fred Henry. "Going before Wednesday, are you?"

"That's the orders," replied the other.

trap: a small wagon.

"Where, to Northampton?"

"That's it."

"The devil!" exclaimed Fergusson, with quiet chagrin.

And there was silence between the two.

"All settled up, are you?" asked Fergusson.

"About."

There was another pause.

"Well, I shall miss yer, Freddy boy," said the young doctor.

"And I shall miss thee, Jack," returned the other.

"Miss you like hell," mused the doctor.

Fred Henry turned aside. There was nothing to say. Mabel came in again, to finish clearing the table.

"What are *you* going to do then, Miss Pervin?" asked Fergusson. "Going to your sister's, are you?"

Mabel looked at him with her steady, dangerous eyes, that always made him uncomfortable, unsettling his superficial ease.

"No," she said.

"Well, what in the name of fortune *are* you going to do? Say what you *mean* to do," cried Fred Henry, with futile intensity.

But she only averted her head, and continued her work. She folded the white table-cloth, and put on the chenille cloth.

"The sulkiest bitch that ever trod!" muttered her brother.

But she finished her task with perfectly impassive face, the young doctor watching her interestedly all the while. Then she went out.

Fred Henry stared after her, clenching his lips, his blue eyes fixing in sharp antagonism, as he made a grimace of sour exasperation.

"You could bray her into bits, and that's all you'd get out of her," he said, in a small, narrowed tone.

The doctor smiled faintly.

"What's she *going* to do then?" he asked.

"Strike me if *I* know!" returned the other.

There was a pause. Then the doctor stirred.

"I'll be seeing you to-night, shall I?" he said to his friend.

"Ay—where's it to be? Are we going over to Jessdale?"

"I don't know. I've got such a cold on me. I'll come round to the Moon and Stars, anyway."

"Let Lizzie and May miss their night for once, eh?"

"That's it—if I feel as I do now."

"All's one—"

The two young men went through the passage and down to the back door together. The house was large, but it was servantless now, and desolate. At the back was a small bricked house-yard, and beyond that a big square, gravelled fine and red, and having stables on two sides. Sloping, dank, winter-dark fields stretched away on the open sides.

But the stables were empty. Joseph Pervin, the father of the family, had been a man of no education, who had become a fairly large horse dealer. The stables had been full of horses, there was a great turmoil and come-and-go of horses and of dealers and grooms. Then the kitchen was full of servants. But of late things had declined. The old man had married a second time, to retrieve his fortunes. Now he was dead and everything was gone to the dogs, there was nothing but debt and threatening.

For months, Mabel had been servantless in the big house, keeping the home together in penury for her ineffectual brothers. She had kept house for ten years. But previously, it was with unstinted means. Then, however brutal and coarse everything was, the sense of money had kept her proud, confident. The men might be foul-mouthed, the women in the kitchen might have bad reputations, her brothers might have illegitimate children. But so long as there was money, the girl felt herself established, and brutally proud, reserved.

No company came to the house, save dealers and coarse men. Mabel had no associates of her own sex, after her sister went away. But she did not mind. She went regularly to church, she attended to her father. And she lived in the memory of her mother, who had died when she was fourteen, and whom she had loved. She had loved her father, too, in a different way, depending upon him, and feeling secure in him, until at the age of fifty-four he married again. And then she had set hard against him. Now he had died and left them all hopelessly in debt.

She had suffered badly during the period of poverty. Nothing, however, could shake the curious sullen, animal pride that dominated each member of the family. Now, for Mabel, the end had come. Still she would not cast about her. She would follow her own way just the same. She would always hold the keys of her own situation. Mindless and persistent, she endured from day to day. Why should she think? Why should she answer anybody? It was enough that this was the end, and there was no way out. She need not pass any more darkly along the main street of the small town, avoiding every eye. She need not demean herself any more, going into the shops and buying the cheapest food. This was at an end. She thought of nobody, not even of herself. Mindless and persistent, she seemed in a sort of ecstasy to be coming nearer to her fulfilment, her own glorification, approaching her dead mother, who was glorified.°

In the afternoon she took a little bag, with shears and sponge and a small scrubbing brush, and went out. It was a grey, wintry day, with saddened, dark-green fields and an atmosphere blackened by the smoke of foundries not far off. She went quickly, darkly along the causeway, heeding nobody, through the town to the churchyard.

There she always felt secure, as if no one could see her, although as a matter   100
of fact she was exposed to the stare of everyone who passed along under the churchyard wall. Nevertheless, once under the shadow of the great looming church, among the graves, she felt immune from the world, reserved within the thick church-yard wall as in another country.

Carefully she clipped the grass from the grave, and arranged the pinky-white, small chrysanthemums in the tin cross. When this was done, she took an empty jar from a neighbouring grave, brought water, and carefully, most scrupulously sponged the marble headstone and the coping-stone.

It gave her sincere satisfaction to do this. She felt in immediate contact with the world of her mother. She took minute pains, went through the park in a state bordering on pure happiness, as if in performing this task she came into a subtle,

who was glorified: see Romans 8:17,30.

intimate connection with her mother. For the life she followed here in the world was far less real than the world of death she inherited from her mother.

The doctor's house was just by the church. Fergusson, being a mere hired assistant, was slave to the countryside. As he hurried now to attend to the outpatients in the surgery, glancing across the graveyard with his quick eye, he saw the girl at her task at the grave. She seemed so intent and remote, it was like looking into another world. Some mystical element was touched in him. He slowed down as he walked, watching her as if spell-bound.

She lifted her eyes, feeling him looking. Their eyes met. And each looked again at once, each feeling, in some way, found out by the other. He lifted his cap and passed on down the road. There remained distinct in his consciousness, like a vision, the memory of her face, lifted from the tombstone in the churchyard, and looking at him with slow, large, portentous eyes. It *was* portentous, her face. It seemed to mesmerise him. There was a heavy power in her eyes which laid hold of his whole being, as if he had drunk some powerful drug. He had been feeling weak and done before. Now the life came back into him, he felt delivered from his own fretted, daily self.

He finished his duties at the surgery as quickly as might be, hastily filling up the bottles of the waiting people with cheap drugs. Then, in perpetual haste, he set off again to visit several cases in another part of his round, before teatime. At all times he preferred to walk, if he could, but particularly when he was not well. He fancied the motion restored him.

The afternoon was falling. It was grey, deadened, and wintry, with a slow, moist, heavy coldness sinking in and deadening all the faculties. But why should he think or notice? He hastily climbed the hill and turned across the dark-green fields, following the black cinder-track. In the distance, across a shallow dip in the country, the small town was clustered like smouldering ash, a tower, a spire, a heap of low, raw, extinct houses. And on the nearest fringe of the town, sloping into the dip, was Oldmeadow, the Pervins' house. He could see the stables and the outbuildings distinctly, as they lay towards him on the slope. Well, he would not go there many more times! Another resource would be lost to him, another place gone: the only company he cared for in the alien, ugly little town he was losing. Nothing but work, drudgery, constant hastening from dwelling to dwelling among the colliers and the iron-workers. It wore him out, but at the same time he had a craving for it. It was a stimulant to him to be in the homes of the working people, moving as it were through the innermost body of their life. His nerves were excited and gratified. He could come so near, into the very lives of the rough, inarticulate, powerfully emotional men and women. He grumbled, he said he hated the hellish hole. But as a matter of fact it excited him, the contact with the rough, strongly-feeling people was a stimulant applied direct to his nerves.

Below Oldmeadow, in the green, shallow, soddened hollow of fields, lay a square, deep pond. Roving across the landscape, the doctor's quick eye detected a figure in black passing through the gate of the field, down towards the pond. He looked again. It would be Mabel Pervin. His mind suddenly became alive and attentive.

Why was she going down there? He pulled up on the path on the slope above, and stood staring. He could just make sure of the small black figure moving in the hollow of the failing day. He seemed to see her in the midst of such obscurity,

105

that he was like a clairvoyant, seeing rather with the mind's eye than with ordinary sight. Yet he could see her positively enough, whilst he kept his eye attentive. He felt, if he looked away from her, in the thick, ugly falling dusk, he would lose her altogether.

He followed her minutely as she moved, direct and intent, like something transmitted rather than stirring in voluntary activity, straight down the field towards the pond. There she stood on the bank for a moment. She never raised her head. Then she waded slowly into the water.

He stood motionless as the small black figure walked slowly and deliberately   110 towards the centre of the pond, very slowly, gradually moving deeper into the motionless water, and still moving forward as the water got up to her breast. Then he could see her no more in the dusk of the dead afternoon.

"There!" he exclaimed. "Would you believe it?"

And he hastened straight down, running over the wet, soddened fields, pushing through the hedges, down into the depression of callous wintry obscurity. It took him several minutes to come to the pond. He stood on the bank, breathing heavily. He could see nothing. His eyes seemed to penetrate the dead water. Yes, perhaps that was the dark shadow of her black clothing beneath the surface of the water.

He slowly ventured into the pond. The bottom was deep, soft clay, he sank in, and the water clasped dead cold round his legs. As he stirred he could smell the cold, rotten clay that fouled up into the water. It was objectionable in his lungs. Still, repelled and yet not heeding, he moved deeper into the pond. The cold water rose over his thighs, over his loins, upon his abdomen. The lower part of his body was all sunk in the hideous cold element. And the bottom was so deeply soft and uncertain, he was afraid of pitching with his mouth underneath. He could not swim, and was afraid.

He crouched a little, spreading his hands under the water and moving them round, trying to feel for her. The dead cold pond swayed upon his chest. He moved again, a little deeper, and again, with his hands underneath, he felt all around under the water. And he touched her clothing. But it evaded his fingers. He made a desperate effort to grasp it.

And so doing he lost his balance and went under, horribly, suffocating in   115 the foul earthy water, struggling madly for a few moments. At last, after what seemed an eternity, he got his footing, rose again into the air and looked around. He gasped, and knew he was in the world. Then he looked at the water. She had risen near him. He grasped her clothing, and drawing her nearer, turned to take his way to land again.

He went very slowly, carefully, absorbed in the slow progress. He rose higher, climbing out of the pond. The water was now only about his legs; he was thankful, full of relief to be out of the clutches of the pond. He lifted her and staggered on to the bank, out of the horror of wet, grey clay.

He laid her down on the bank. She was quite unconscious and running with water. He made the water come from her mouth, he worked to restore her. He did not have to work very long before he could feel the breathing begin again in her; she was breathing naturally. He worked a little longer. He could feel her live beneath his hands; she was coming back. He wiped her face, wrapped her in his overcoat, looked round into the dim, dark-grey world, then lifted her and staggered down the bank and across the fields.

It seemed an unthinkably long way, and his burden so heavy he felt he would never get to the house. But at last he was in the stable-yard, and then in the house-yard. He opened the door and went into the house. In the kitchen he laid her down on the hearthrug, and called. The house was empty. But the fire was burning in the grate.

Then again he knelt to attend to her. She was breathing regularly, her eyes were wide open and as if conscious, but there seemed something missing in her look. She was conscious in herself, but unconscious of her surroundings.

He ran upstairs, took blankets from a bed, and put them before the fire to warm. Then he removed her saturated, earthy-smelling clothing, rubbed her dry with a towel, and wrapped her naked in the blankets. Then he went into the dining-room, to look for spirits. There was a little whiskey. He drank a gulp himself, and put some into her mouth. 120

The effect was instantaneous. She looked full into his face, as if she had been seeing him for some time, and yet had only just become conscious of him.

"Dr. Fergusson?" she said.

"What?" he answered.

He was divesting himself of his coat, intending to find some dry clothing upstairs. He could not bear the smell of the dead, clayey water, and he was mortally afraid for his own health.

"What did I do?" she asked. 125

"Walked into the pond," he replied. He had begun to shudder like one sick, and could hardly attend to her. Her eyes remained full on him, he seemed to be going dark in his mind, looking back at her helplessly. The shuddering became quieter in him, his life came back in him, dark and unknowing, but strong again.

"Was I out of my mind?" she asked, while her eyes were fixed on him all the time.

"Maybe, for the moment," he replied. He felt quiet, because his strength had come back. The strange fretful strain had left him.

"Am I out of my mind now?" she asked.

"Are you?" he reflected a moment. "No," he answered truthfully, "I don't 130 see that you are." He turned his face aside. He was afraid, now, because he felt dazed, and felt dimly that her power was stronger than his, in this issue. And she continued to look at him fixedly all the time. "Can you tell me where I shall find some dry things to put on?" he asked.

"Did you dive into the pond for me?" she asked.

"No," he answered. "I walked in. But I went in overhead as well."

There was silence for a moment. He hesitated. He very much wanted to go upstairs to get into dry clothing. But there was another desire in him. And she seemed to hold him. His will seemed to have gone to sleep, and left him, standing there slack before her. But he felt warm inside himself. He did not shudder at all, though his clothes were sodden on him.

"Why did you?" she asked.

"Because I didn't want you to do such a foolish thing," he said. 135

"It wasn't foolish," she said, still gazing at him as she lay on the floor, with a sofa cushion under her head. "It was the right thing to do. *I* knew best, then."

"I'll go and shift these wet things," he said. But still he had not the power to move out of her presence, until she sent him. It was as if she had the life of his body in her hands, and he could not extricate himself. Or perhaps he did not want to.

Suddenly she sat up. Then she became aware of her own immediate condition. She felt the blankets about her, she knew her own limbs. For a moment it seemed as if her reason were going. She looked round, with wild eye, as if seeking something. He stood still with fear. She saw her clothing lying scattered.

"Who undressed me?" she asked, her eyes resting full and inevitable on his face.

"I did," he replied, "to bring you round."   140

For some moments she sat and gazed at him awfully, her lips parted.

"Do you love me then?" she asked.

He only stood and stared at her, fascinated. His soul seemed to melt.

She shuffled forward on her knees, and put her arms round him, round his legs, as he stood there, pressing her breasts against his knees and thighs, clutching him with strange, convulsive certainty, pressing his thighs against her, drawing him to her face, her throat, as she looked up at him with flaring, humble eyes of transfiguration, triumphant in first possession.

"You love me," she murmured, in strange transport, yearning and triumphant   145
and confident. "You love me. I know you love me, I know."

And she was passionately kissing his knees, through the wet clothing, passionately and indiscriminately kissing his knees, his legs, as if unaware of everything.

He looked down at the tangled wet hair, the wild, bare, animal shoulders. He was amazed, bewildered, and afraid. He had never thought of loving her. He had never wanted to love her. When he rescued her and restored her, he was a doctor, and she was a patient. He had had no single personal thought of her. Nay, this introduction of the personal element was very distasteful to him, a violation of his professional honour. It was horrible to have her there embracing his knees. It was horrible. He revolted from it, violently. And yet—and yet—he had not the power to break away.

She looked at him again, with the same supplication of powerful love, and that same transcendent, frightening light of triumph. In view of the delicate flame which seemed to come from her face like a light, he was powerless. And yet he had never intended to love her. He had never intended. And something stubborn in him could not give way.

"You love me," she repeated, in a murmur of deep, rhapsodic assurance. "You love me."

Her hands were drawing him, drawing him down to her. He was afraid,   150
even a little horrified. For he had, really, no intention of loving her. Yet her hands were drawing him towards her. He put out his hand quickly to steady himself, and grasped her bare shoulder. A flame seemed to burn the hand that grasped her soft shoulder. He had no intention of loving her: his whole will was against his yielding. It was horrible— And yet wonderful was the touch of her shoulder, beautiful the shining of her face. Was she perhaps mad? He had a horror of yielding to her. Yet something in him ached also.

He had been staring away at the door, away from her. But his hand remained on her shoulder. She had gone suddenly very still. He looked down at her. Her eyes were now wide with fear, with doubt, the light was dying from her face, a shadow of terrible greyness was returning. He could not bear the touch of her eyes' question upon him, and the look of death behind the question.

With an inward groan he gave way, and let his heart yield towards her. A sudden gentle smile came on his face. And her eyes, which never left his face, slowly, slowly filled with tears. He watched the strange water rise in her eyes, like some slow fountain coming up. And his heart seemed to burn and melt away in his breast.

He could not bear to look at her any more. He dropped on his knees and caught her head with his arms and pressed her face against his throat. She was very still. His heart, which seemed to have broken, was burning with a kind of agony in his breast. And he felt her slow, hot tears wetting his throat. But he could not move.

He felt the hot tears wet his neck and the hollows of his neck, and he remained motionless, suspended through one of man's eternities. Only now it had become indispensable to him to have her face pressed close to him; he could never let her go again. He could never let her head go away from the close clutch of his arm. He wanted to remain like that for ever, with his heart hurting him in a pain that was also life to him. Without knowing, he was looking down on her damp, soft brown hair.

Then, as it were suddenly, he smelt the horrid stagnant smell of that water.   155
And at the same moment she drew away from him and looked at him. Her eyes were wistful and unfathomable. He was afraid of them, and he fell to kissing her, not knowing what he was doing. He wanted her eyes not to have that terrible, wistful, unfathomable look.

When she turned her face to him again, a faint delicate flush was glowing, and there was again dawning that terrible shining of joy in her eyes, which really terrified him, and yet which he now wanted to see, because he feared the look of doubt still more.

"You love me?" she said, rather faltering.

"Yes." The word cost him a painful effort. Not because it wasn't true. But because it was too newly true, the *saying* seemed to tear open again his newly-torn heart. And he hardly wanted it to be true, even now.

She lifted her face to him, and he bent forward and kissed her on the mouth gently, with the one kiss that is an eternal pledge. And as he kissed her his heart strained again in his breast. He never intended to love her. But now it was over. He had crossed over the gulf to her, and all that he had left behind had shrivelled and become void.

After the kiss, her eyes again slowly filled with tears. She sat still, away from   160
him, with her face drooped aside, and her hands folded in her lap. The tears fell very slowly. There was complete silence. He too sat there motionless and silent on the hearthrug. The strange pain of his heart that was broken seemed to consume him. That he should love her? That this was love! That he should be ripped open in this way!—Him, a doctor!—How they would all jeer if they knew!—It was agony to him to think they might know.

In the curious naked pain of the thought he looked again to her. She was sitting there drooped into a muse. He saw a tear fall, and his heart flared hot. He saw for the first time that one of her shoulders was quite uncovered, one arm bare, he could see one of her small breasts; dimly, because it had become almost dark in the room.

"Why are you crying?" he asked, in an altered voice.

She looked up at him, and behind her tears the consciousness of her situation for the first time brought a dark look of shame to her eyes.

"I'm not crying, really," she said, watching him half frightened.

He reached his hand, and softly closed it on her bare arm.   165

"I love you! I love you!" he said in a soft, low vibrating voice, unlike himself.

She shrank, and dropped her head. The soft, penetrating grip of his hand on her arm distressed her. She looked up at him.

"I want to go," she said. "I want to go and get you some dry things."

"Why?" he said. "I'm all right."

"But I want to go," she said. "And I want you to change your things."   170

He released her arm, and she wrapped herself in the blanket, looking at him rather frightened. And still she did not rise.

"Kiss me," she said wistfully.

He kissed her, but briefly, half in anger.

Then, after a second, she rose nervously, all mixed up in the blanket. He watched her in her confusion, as she tried to extricate herself and wrap herself up so that she could walk. He watched her relentlessly, as she knew.

And as she went, the blanket trailing, and as he saw a glimpse of her feet   175
and her white leg, he tried to remember her as she was when he had wrapped her in the blanket. But then he didn't want to remember, because she had been nothing to him then, and his nature revolted from remembering her as she was when she was nothing to him.

A tumbling muffled noise from within the dark house startled him. Then he heard her voice:—"There are clothes." He rose and went to the foot of the stairs, and gathered up the garments she had thrown down. Then he came back to the fire, to rub himself down and dress. He grinned at his own appearance, when he had finished.

The fire was sinking, so he put on coal. The house was now quite dark, save for the light of a street-lamp that shone in faintly from beyond the holly trees. He lit the gas with matches he found on the mantel-piece. Then he emptied the pockets of his own clothes, and threw all his wet things in a heap into the scullery. After which he gathered up her sodden clothes, gently, and put them in a separate heap on the copper-top in the scullery.

It was six o'clock on the clock. His own watch had stopped. He ought to be back to the surgery. He waited, and still she did not come down. So he went to the foot of the stairs and called:

"I shall have to go."

Almost immediately he heard her coming down. She had on her best dress   180
of black voile, and her hair was tidy, but still damp. She looked at him—and in spite of herself, smiled.

"I don't like you in those clothes," she said.

"Do I look a sight?" he answered.

They were shy of one another.

"I'll make you some tea," she said.

"No, I must go."   185

"Must you?" And she looked at him again with the wide, strained, doubtful eyes. And again, from the pain of his breast, he knew how he loved her. He went and bent to kiss her, gently, passionately, with his heart's painful kiss.

"And my hair smells so horrible," she murmured in distraction. "And I'm so awful, I'm so awful! Oh, no, I'm too awful." And she broke into bitter, heartbroken sobbing. "You can't want to love me, I'm horrible."

"Don't be silly, don't be silly," he said, trying to comfort her, kissing her, holding her in his arms. "I want you, I want to marry you, we're going to be married, quickly, quickly—to-morrow if I can."

But she only sobbed terribly, and cried.

"I feel awful. I feel awful. I feel I'm horrible to you."   190

"No, I want you, I want you," was all he answered, blindly, with that terrible intonation which frightened her almost more than her horror lest he should *not* want her.

QUESTIONS

1. What has happened to the Pervin family as the story begins? How does the initial description of the setting (especially the adjectives) reinforce the mood associated with these events?

2. How is Joe Pervin described? In what ways is he like the horses that he is watching? What is Fred Henry Pervin like? To what extent is he also compared to horses?

3. What kind of person is Mabel Pervin? How old is she? How do her brothers treat her? What is her attitude toward her brothers? What dilemma does she face as the story begins?

4. To what extent does Mabel seem committed to the past rather than the present and to death rather than life?

5. What is Dr. Fergusson like? What does his initial attitude toward Mabel seem to be like?

6. Fergusson watches Mabel in the churchyard and at the pond. How does she affect him in both instances? What does this effect suggest about Fergusson?

7. What does Mabel try to do at the pond? What does Fergusson do? How does the setting here reinforce both the actions and the mood at this point in the story?

8. What do Mabel and Fergusson realize about themselves and each other in the Pervin home as he tries to warm her? What is Mabel's attitude toward this realization? Fergusson's attitude?

9. Why does the narrator keep telling us at the end of the story that Fergusson "had no intention of loving" Mabel? What idea about love does this repeated assertion convey?

10. Often in stories, when authors describe how people fall in love, there is

little further detail beyond the declarations and a concluding "they lived happily ever after." In "The Horse Dealer's Daughter," however, there is a relatively extensive portrayal of the ambiguous feelings of both Dr. Fergusson and Mabel Pervin. Explain what you think are the reasons for which Lawrence explores these feelings so extensively.

11.   Consider the narrator's comparison of Joe Pervin and the draft horses. In light of the fact that the horses have great strength but no individuality, being guided and controlled by those with the reins, can this comparison be extended to other characters in the story? To what degree is the love that emerges between Mabel and Dr. Fergusson within their control? Do you think Lawrence believes that love is generally within the control of people falling in love?

RALPH ELLISON (b. 1914)

Flying Home °   1944

When Todd came to,° he saw two faces suspended above him in a sun so hot and blinding that he could not tell if they were black or white. He stirred, feeling a pain that burned as though his whole body had been laid open to the sun which glared into his eyes. For a moment an old fear of being touched by white hands seized him. Then the very sharpness of the pain began slowly to clear his head. Sounds came to him dimly. He done come to. Who are they? he thought. Naw he ain't, I coulda sworn he was white. Then he heard clearly:

"You hurt bad?"

Something within him uncoiled. It was a Negro sound.

"He's still out," he heard.

"Give 'im time. . . . Say, son, you hurt bad?"   5

Was he? There was that awful pain. He lay rigid, hearing their breathing and trying to weave a meaning between them and his being stretched painfully upon the ground. He watched them warily, his mind traveling back over a painful distance. Jagged scenes, swiftly unfolding as in a movie trailer, reeled through his mind, and he saw himself piloting a tailspinning plane and landing and falling from the cockpit and trying to stand. Then, as in a great silence, he remembered the sound of crunching bone, and now, looking up into the anxious faces of an old Negro man and a boy from where he lay in the same field, the memory sickened him and he wanted to remember no more.

"How you feel, son?"

Todd hesitated, as though to answer would be to admit an inacceptable weakness. Then, "It's my ankle," he said.

"Which one?"

"Flying Home" is the title of a song made popular by Glenn Miller in the early 1940s.

When Todd came to: Todd is a military pilot in training during World War II (1941–1945). He is black and has just crashed in the south in a field owned by a white man.

"The left."   10

With a sense of remoteness he watched the old man bend and remove his boot, feeling the pressure ease.

"That any better?"

"A lot. Thank you."

He had the sensation of discussing someone else, that his concern was with some far more important thing, which for some reason escaped him.

"You done broke it bad," the old man said. "We have to get you to a doctor."   15

He felt that he had been thrown into a tailspin. He looked at his watch; how long had he been here? He knew there was but one important thing in the world, to get the plane back to the field before his officers were displeased.

"Help me up," he said. "Into the ship."

"But it's broke too bad. . . ."

"Give me your arm!"

"But, son . . ."   20

Clutching the old man's arm he pulled himself up, keeping his left leg clear, thinking, "I'd never make him understand," as the leather-smooth face came parallel with his own.

"Now, let's see."

He pushed the old man back, hearing a bird's insistent shrill. He swayed giddily. Blackness washed over him, like infinity.

"You best sit down."

"No, I'm OK."   25

"But, son. You jus' gonna make it worse. . . ."

It was a fact that everything in him cried out to deny, even against the flaming pain in his ankle. He would have to try again.

"You mess with that ankle they have to cut your foot off," he heard.

Holding his breath, he started up again. It pained so badly that he had to bite his lips to keep from crying out and he allowed them to help him down with a pang of despair.

"It's best you take it easy. We gon' git you a doctor."   30

Of all the luck, he thought. Of all the rotten luck, now I have done it. The fumes of high-octane gasoline clung in the heat, taunting him.

"We kin ride him into town on old Ned," the boy said.

Ned? He turned, seeing the boy point toward an ox team browsing where the buried blade of a plow marked the end of a furrow. Thoughts of himself riding an ox through the town, past streets full of white faces, down the concrete runways of the airfield made swift images of humiliation in his mind. With a pang he remembered his girl's last letter. "Todd," she had written, "I don't need the papers to tell me you had the intelligence to fly. And I have always known you to be as brave as anyone else. The papers annoy me. Don't you be contented to prove over and over again that you're brave or skillful just because you're black, Todd. I think they keep beating that dead horse because they don't want to say why you boys are not yet fighting. I'm really disappointed, Todd. Anyone with brains can learn to fly, but then what? What about using it, and who will you use it for? I wish, dear, you'd write about this. I sometimes think they're playing a trick on us. It's very humiliating. . . ." He wiped cold sweat from his face, thinking, What does she know of humiliation? She's never been down South. Now the humiliation

would come. When you must have them judge you, knowing that they never accept
your mistakes as your own, but hold it against your whole race—that was humiliation.
Yes, and humiliation was when you could never be simply yourself, when you
were always a part of this old black ignorant man. Sure, he's all right. Nice and
kind and helpful. But he's not you. Well, there's one humiliation I can spare myself.

"No," he said, "I have orders not to leave the ship. . . ."

"Aw," the old man said. Then turning to the boy, "Teddy, then you better   35
hustle down to Mister Graves and get him to come. . . ."

"No, wait!" he protested before he was fully aware. Graves might be white.
"Just have him get word to the field, please. They'll take care of the rest."

He saw the boy leave, running.

"How far does he have to go?"

"Might' nigh a mile."

He rested back, looking at the dusty face of his watch. But now they know   40
something has happened, he thought. In the ship there was a perfectly good radio,
but it was useless. The old fellow would never operate it. That buzzard knocked
me back a hundred years, he thought. Irony danced with him like the gnats circling
the old man's head. With all I've learned I'm dependent upon this "peasant's"
sense of time and space. His leg throbbed. In the plane, instead of time being
measured by the rhythms of pain and a kid's legs, the instruments would have
told him at a glance. Twisting upon his elbows he saw where dust had powdered
the plane's fuselage, feeling the lump form in his throat that was always there
when he thought of flight. It's crouched there, he thought, like the abandoned
shell of a locust. I'm naked without it. Not a machine, a suit of clothes you wear.
And with a sudden embarrassment and wonder he whispered, "It's the only dignity
I have. . . ."

He saw the old man watching, his torn overalls clinging limply to him in
the heat. He felt a sharp need to tell the old man what he felt. But that would
be meaningless. If I tried to explain why I need to fly back, he'd think I was
simply afraid of white officers. But it's more than fear . . . a sense of anguish
clung to him like the veil of sweat that hugged his face. He watched the old man,
hearing him humming snatches of a tune as he admired the plane. He felt a furtive
sense of resentment. Such old men often came to the field to watch the pilots
with childish eyes. At first it had made him proud; they had been a meaningful
part of a new experience. But soon he realized they did not understand his accomplishments and they came to shame and embarrass him, like the distasteful praise
of an idiot. A part of the meaning of flying had gone then, and he had not been
able to regain it. If I were a prizefighter I would be more human, he thought.
Not a monkey doing tricks, but a man. They were pleased simply that he was a
Negro who could fly, and that was not enough. He felt cut off from them by age,
by understanding, by sensibility, by technology and by his need to measure himself
against the mirror of other men's appreciation. Somehow he felt betrayed, as he
had when as a child he grew to discover that his father was dead. Now for him
any real appreciation lay with his white officers; and with them he could never
be sure. Between ignorant black men and condescending whites, his course of
flight seemed mapped by the nature of things away from all needed and natural
landmarks. Under some sealed orders, couched in ever more technical and mysterious terms, his path curved swiftly away from both the shame the old man symbolized
and the cloudy terrain of white men's regard. Flying blind, he knew but one point

of landing and there he would receive his wings. After that the enemy would appreciate his skill and he would assume his deepest meaning, he thought sadly, neither from those who condescended nor from those who praised without understanding, but from the enemy who would recognize his manhood and skill in terms of hate. . . .

He sighed, seeing the oxen making queer, prehistoric shadows against the dry brown earth.

"You just take it easy, son," the old man soothed. "That boy won't take long. Crazy as he is about airplanes."

"I can wait," he said.

"What kinda airplane you call this here'n?"   45

"An Advanced Trainer," he said, seeing the old man smile. His fingers were like gnarled dark wood against the metal as he touched the low-slung wing.

"'Bout how fast can she fly?"

"Over two hundred an hour."

"Lawd! That's so fast I bet it don't seem like you moving!"

Holding himself rigid, Todd opened his flying suit. The shade had gone   50
and he lay in a ball of fire.

"You mind if I take a look inside? I was always curious to see. . . ."

"Help yourself. Just don't touch anything."

He heard him climb upon the metal wing, grunting. Now the questions would start. Well, so you don't have to think to answer. . . .

He saw the old man looking over into the cockpit, his eyes bright as a child's.

"You must have to know a lot to work all these here things."   55

He was silent, seeing him step down and kneel beside him.

"Son, how come you want to fly way up there in the air?"

Because it's the most meaningful act in the world . . . because it makes me less like you, he thought.

But he said: "Because I like it, I guess. It's as good a way to fight and die as I know."

"Yeah? I guess you right," the old man said. "But how long you think before   60
they gonna let you all fight?"

He tensed. This was the question all Negroes asked, put with the same timid hopefulness and longing that always opened a greater void within him than that he had felt beneath the plane the first time he had flown. He felt light-headed. It came to him suddenly that there was something sinister about the conversation, that he was flying unwillingly into unsafe and uncharted regions. If he could only be insulting and tell this old man who was trying to help him to shut up!

"I bet you one thing. . . ."

"Yes?"

"That you was plenty scared coming down."

He did not answer. Like a dog on a trail the old man seemed to smell out   65
his fears, and he felt anger bubble within him.

"You sho' scared me. When I seen you coming down in that thing with it a-rolling' and a-jumpin' like a pitchin' hoss, I thought sho' you was a goner. I almost had me a stroke!"

He saw the old man grinning. "Ever'thin's been happening round here this morning, come to think of it."

"Like what?" he asked.

"Well, first thing I know, here come two white fellers looking for Mister Rudolph, that's Mister Graves's cousin. That got me worked up right away. . . ."

"Why?"   70

"Why? 'Cause he done broke outta the crazy house, that's why. He liable to kill somebody," he said. "They oughta have him by now though. Then here you come. First I think it's one of them white boys. Then doggone if you don't fall outta there. Lawd, I'd done heard about you boys but I haven't never seen one o' you-all. Cain't tell you how it felt to see somebody what look like me in a airplane!"

The old man talked on, the sound streaming around Todd's thoughts like air flowing over the fuselage of a flying plane. You were a fool, he thought, remembering how before the spin the sun had blazed bright against the billboard signs beyond the town, and how a boy's blue kite had bloomed beneath him, tugging gently in the wind like a strange, odd-shaped flower. He had once flown such kites himself and tried to find the boy at the end of the invisible cord. But he had been flying too high and too fast. He had climbed steeply away in exultation. Too steeply, he thought. And one of the first rules you learn is that if the angle of thrust is too steep the plane goes into a spin. And then, instead of pulling out of it and going into a dive you let a buzzard panic you. A lousy buzzard!

"Son, what made all that blood on the glass?"

"A buzzard," he said, remembering how the blood and feathers had sprayed back against the hatch. It had been as though he had flown into a storm of blood and blackness.

"Well, I declare! They's lots of 'em around here. They after dead things.   75
Don't eat nothing what's alive."

"A little bit more and he would have made a meal out of me," Todd said grimly.

"They bad luck all right. Teddy's got a name for 'em, calls 'em jimcrows,"° the old man laughed.

"It's a damned good name."

"They the damnedest birds. Once I seen a hoss all stretched out like he was sick, you know. So I hollers, 'Gid up from there, suh!' Just to make sho! An' doggone, son, if I don't see two ole jimcrows come flying right up outa that hoss's insides! yessuh! The sun was shinin' on 'em and they couldn't a been no greasier if they'd been eating barbecue."

Todd thought he would vomit, his stomach quivered.   80

"You made that up," he said.

"Nawsuh! Saw him just like I see you."

"Well, I'm glad it was you."

"You see lots a funny things down here, son."

"No, I'll let you see them," he said.   85

"By the way, the white folks round here don't like to see you boys up there in the sky. They ever bother you?"

"No."

"Well, they'd like to."

---

jimcrows: an insulting slang term for blacks and for the customs and laws segregating blacks.

"Someone always wants to bother someone else," Todd said. "How do you know?"

"I just know." 90

"Well," he said defensively, "no one has bothered us."

Blood pounded in his ears as he looked away into space. He tensed, seeing a black spot in the sky, and strained to confirm what he could not clearly see.

"What does that look like to you?" he asked excitedly.

"Just another bad luck, son."

Then he saw the movement of wings with disappointment. It was gliding 95 smoothly down, wings outspread, tail feathers gripping the air, down swiftly—gone behind the green screen of trees. It was like a bird he had imagined there, only the sloping branches of the pines remained, sharp against the pale stretch of sky. He lay barely breathing and stared at the point where it had disappeared, caught in a spell of loathing and admiration. Why did they make them so disgusting and yet teach them to fly so well? It's like when I was up in heaven, he heard, starting.

The old man was chuckling, rubbing his stubbled chin.

"What did you say?"

"Sho', I died and went to heaven . . . maybe by time I tell you about it they be done come after you."

"I hope so," he said wearily.

"You boys ever sit around and swap lies?" 100

"Not often. Is this going to be one?"

"Well, I ain't so sho', on account of it took place when I was dead."

The old man paused, "That wasn't no lie 'bout the buzzards, though."

"All right," he said.

"Sho' you want to hear 'bout heaven?" 105

"Please," he answered, resting his head upon his arm.

"Well, I went to heaven and right away started to sproutin' me some wings. Six good ones, they was. Just like them the white angels had. I couldn't hardly believe it. I was so glad that I went off on some clouds by myself and tried 'em out. You know, 'cause I didn't want to make a fool outta myself the first thing. . . ."

It's an old tale, Todd thought. Told me years ago. Had forgotten. But at least it will keep him from talking about buzzards.

He closed his eyes, listening.

". . . First thing I done was to git up on a low cloud and jump off. And 110 doggone, boy, if them wings didn't work! First I tried the right; then I tried the left; then I tried 'em both together. Then Lawd, I started to move on out among the folks. I let 'em see me. . . ."

He saw the old man gesturing flight with his arms, his face full of mock pride as he indicated an imaginary crowd, thinking, It'll be in the newspapers, as he heard, ". . . so I went and found me some colored angels—somehow I didn't believe I was an angel till I seen a real black one, ha, yes! Then I was sho'—but they tole me I better come down 'cause us colored folks had to wear a special kin' a harness when we flew. That was how come they wasn't flyin'. Oh yes, an' you had to be extra strong for a black man even, to fly with one of them harnesses. . . ."

This is a new turn, Todd thought, what's he driving at?

"So I said to myself, I ain't gonna be bothered with no harness! Oh naw! 'Cause if God let you sprout wings you oughta have sense enough not to let nobody make you wear something what gits in the way of flyin'. So I starts to flyin'. Heck, son," he chuckled, his eyes twinkling, "you know I had to let eve'ybody know that old Jefferson could fly good as anybody else. And I could too, fly smooth as a bird! I could even loop-the-loop—only I had to make sho' to keep my long white robe down roun' my ankles. . . ."

Todd felt uneasy. He wanted to laugh at the joke, but his body refused, as of an independent will. He felt as he had as a child when after he had chewed a sugar-coated pill which his mother had given him, she had laughed at his efforts to remove the terrible taste.

". . . Well," he heard, "I was doing all right 'til I got to speeding. Found out I could fan up a right strong breeze, I could fly so fast. I could do all kin'sa stunts too. I started flying up to the stars and divin' down and zooming roun' the moon. Man, I like to scare the devil outa some ole white angels. I was raisin' hell. Not that I meant any harm, son. But I was just feeling good. It was so good to know I was free at last. I accidentally knocked the tips offa some stars and they tell me I caused a storm and a coupla lynchings down here in Macon County—though I swear I believe them boys what said that was making up lies on me. . . ."   115

He's mocking me, Todd thought angrily. He thinks it's a joke. Grinning down at me. . . . His throat was dry. He looked at his watch; why the hell didn't they come? Since they had to, why? One day I was flying down one of them heavenly streets. You got yourself into it, Todd thought. Like Jonah in the whale.

"Justa throwin' feathers in everybody's face. An' ole Saint Peter called me in. Said, 'Jefferson, tell me two things, what you doin' flyin' without a harness; an' how come you flyin' so fast?' So I tole him I was flyin' without a harness 'cause it got in my way, but I couldn'ta been flyin' so fast, 'cause I wasn't usin' but one wing. Saint Peter said, 'You wasn't flyin' with but one wing?' 'Yessuh,' I says, scared-like. So he says, 'Well, since you got sucha extra fine pair of wings you can leave off yo' harness awhile. But from now on none of that there one-wing flyin', 'cause you gittin' up too damn much speed!'"

And with one mouth full of bad teeth you're making too damned much talk, thought Todd. Why don't I send him after the boy? His body ached from the hard ground and seeking to shift his position he twisted his ankle and hated himself for crying out.

"It gittin' worse?"

"I. . . . I twisted it," he groaned.   120

"Try not to think about it, son. That's what I do."

He bit his lip, fighting pain with counter-pain as the voice resumed its rhythmical droning. Jefferson seemed caught in his own creation.

". . . After all that trouble I just floated roun' heaven in slow motion. But I forgot, like colored folks will do, and got to flyin' with one wing again. This time I was restin' my old broken arm and got to flyin' fast enough to shame the devil. I was comin' so fast, Lawd, I got myself called befo' ole Saint Peter again. He said, 'Jeff, didn't I warn you 'bout that speedin'?' 'Yessuh,' I says, 'but it was an accident.' He looked at me sadlike and shook his head and I knowed I was gone. He said, 'Jeff, you and that speedin' is a danger to the heavenly community. If I was to let you keep on flyin', heaven wouldn't be nothin' but uproar. Jeff, you got to go!' Son, I argued and pleaded with that old white man, but it didn't do a bit of good. They rushed me straight to them pearly gates and gimme a parachute and a map of the state of Alabama. . . ."

Todd heard him laughing so that he could hardly speak, making a screen between them upon which his humiliation glowed like fire.

"Maybe you'd better stop awhile," he said, his voice unreal.   125

"Ain't much more," Jefferson laughed. "When they gimme the parachute ole Saint Peter ask me if I wanted to say a few words before I went. I felt so bad I couldn't hardly look at him, specially with all them white angels standin' around. Then somebody laughed and made me mad. So I tole him, 'Well, you done took my wings. And you puttin' me out. You got charge of things so's I can't do nothin' about it. But you got to admit just this: While I was up here I was the flyinest sonofabitch what ever hit heaven!' "

At the burst of laughter Todd felt such an intense humiliation that only great violence would wash it away. The laughter which shook the old man like a boiling purge set up vibrations of guilt within him which not even the intricate machinery of the plane would have been adequate to transform and he heard himself screaming, "Why do you laugh at me this way?"

He hated himself at that moment, but he had lost control. He saw Jefferson's mouth fall open, "What—?"

"Answer me!"

His blood pounded as though it would surely burst his temples and he tried   130
to reach the old man and fell, screaming, "Can I help it because they won't let us actually fly? Maybe we are a bunch of buzzards feeding on a dead horse, but we can hope to be eagles, can't we? Can't we?"

He fell back, exhausted, his ankle pounding. The saliva was like straw in his mouth. If he had the strength he would strangle this old man. This grinning, gray-headed clown who made him feel as he felt when watched by the white officers at the field. And yet this old man had neither power, prestige, rank nor technique. Nothing that could rid him of this terrible feeling. He watched him, seeing his face struggle to express a turmoil of feeling.

"What you mean, son? What you talking 'bout . . . ?"

"Go away. Go tell your tales to the white folks."

"But I didn't mean nothing like that . . . I . . . I wasn't tryin' to hurt your feelings. . . ."

"Please. Get the hell away from me!"   135

"But I didn't, son. I didn't mean all them things a-tall."

Todd shook as with a chill, searching Jefferson's face for a trace of the mockery he had seen there. But now the face was somber and tired and old. He was confused. He could not be sure that there had ever been laughter there, that Jefferson had ever really laughed in his whole life. He saw Jefferson reach out to touch him and shrank away, wondering if anything except the pain, now causing his vision to waver, was real. Perhaps he had imagined it all.

"Don't let it get you down, son," the voice said pensively.

He heard Jefferson sigh wearily, as though he felt more than he could say. His anger ebbed, leaving only the pain.

"I'm sorry," he mumbled.   140

"You just wore out with pain, was all. . . ."

He saw him through a blur, smiling. And for a second he felt the embarrassed silence of understanding flutter between them.

"What you was doin' flyin' over this section, son? Wasn't you scared they might shoot you for a cow?"

Todd tensed. Was he being laughed at again? But before he could decide, the pain shook him and a part of him was lying calmly behind the screen of pain that had fallen between them, recalling the first time he had ever seen a plane. It was as though an endless series of hangars had been shaken ajar in the air base of his memory and from each, like a young wasp emerging from its cell, arose the memory of a plane.

The first time I ever saw a plane I was very small and planes were new in   145
the world. I was four-and-a-half and the only plane that I had ever seen was a model suspended from the ceiling of the automobile exhibit at the State Fair. But I did not know that it was only a model. I did not know how large a real plane was, nor how expensive. To me it was a fascinating toy, complete in itself, which my mother said could only be owned by rich little white boys. I stood rigid with admiration, my head straining backwards as I watched the gray little plane describing arcs above the gleaming tops of the automobiles. And I vowed that, rich or poor, someday I would own such a toy. My mother had to drag me out of the exhibit and not even the merry-go-round, the Ferris wheel, or the racing horse could hold my attention for the rest of the Fair. I was too busy imitating the tiny drone of the plane with my lips, and imitating with my hands the motion, swift and circling, that it made in flight.

After that I no longer used the pieces of lumber that lay about our back yard to construct wagons and autos . . . now it was used for airplanes. I built biplanes, using pieces of board for wings, a small box for the fuselage, another piece of wood for the rudder. The trip to the Fair had brought something new into my small world. I asked my mother repeatedly when the Fair would come back again. I'd lie in the grass and watch the sky, and each fighting bird became a soaring plane. I would have been good a year just to have seen a plane again. I became a nuisance to everyone with my questions about airplanes. But planes were new to the old folks, too, and there was little that they could tell me. Only my uncle knew some of the answers. And better still, he could carve propellers from pieces of wood that would whirl rapidly in the wind, wobbling noisily upon oiled nails.

I wanted a plane more than I'd wanted anything; more than I wanted the red wagon with rubber tires, more than the train that ran on a track with its train of cars. I asked my mother over and over again:

"Mamma?"

"What do you want, boy?" she'd say.

"Mamma, will you get mad if I ask you?" I'd say.   150

"What do you want now? I ain't got time to be answering a lot of fool questions. What you want?"

"Mamma, when you gonna get me one . . ?" I'd ask.

"Get you one what?" she'd say.

"You know, Mamma; what I been asking you. . . ."

"Boy," she'd say, "if you don't want a spanking you better come on an'   155
tell me what you talking about so I can get on with my work."

"Aw, Mamma, you know. . . ."

"What I just tell you?" she'd say.

"I mean when you gonna buy me a airplane."

"AIRPLANE! Boy, is you crazy? How many times I have to tell you to stop that foolishness. I done told you them things cost too much. I bet I'm gon' wham the living daylight out of you if you don't quit worrying me 'bout them things!"

But this did not stop me, and a few days later I'd try all over again.   160

Then one day a strange thing happened. It was spring and for some reason I had been hot and irritable all morning. It was a beautiful spring. I could feel it as I played barefoot in the backyard. Blossoms hung from the thorny black locust trees like clusters of fragrant white grapes. Butterflies flickered in the sunlight above the short new dew-wet grass. I had gone in the house for bread and butter and coming out I heard a steady unfamiliar drone. It was unlike anything I had ever heard before. I tried to place the sound. It was no use. It was a sensation like that I had when searching for my father's watch, heard ticking unseen in a room. It made me feel as though I had forgotten to perform some task that my mother had ordered. . . . then I located it, overhead. In the sky, flying quite low and about a hundred yards off was a plane! It came so slowly that it seemed barely to move. My mouth hung wide; my bread and butter fell into the dirt. I wanted to jump up and down and cheer. And when the idea struck I trembled with excitement: "Some little white boy's plane's done flew away and all I got to do is stretch out my hands and it'll be mine!" It was a little plane like that at the Fair, flying no higher than the eaves of our roof. Seeing it come steadily forward I felt the world grow warm with promise. I opened the screen and climbed over it and clung there, waiting. I would catch the plane as it came over and swing down fast and run into the house before anyone could see me. Then no one could come to claim the plane. It droned nearer. Then when it hung like a silver cross in the blue directly above me I stretched out my hand and grabbed. It was like sticking my finger through a soap bubble. The plane flew on, as though I had simply blown my breath after it. I grabbed again, frantically, trying to catch the tail. My fingers clutched the air and disappointment surged tight and hard in my throat. Giving one last desperate grasp, I strained forward. My fingers ripped from the screen. I was falling. The ground burst hard against me. I drummed the earth with my heels and when my breath returned, I lay there bawling.

My mother rushed through the door.

"What's the matter, chile! What on earth is wrong with you?"

"It's gone! It's gone!"

"What gone?"   165

"The airplane. . . ."

"Airplane?"

"Yessum, jus' like the one at the Fair. . . . I . . . I tried to stop it an' it kep' right on going. . . ."

"When, boy?"

"Just now," I cried, through my tears.   170

"Where it go, boy, what way?"

"Yonder, there . . ."

She scanned the sky, her arms akimbo and her checkered apron flapping in the wind as I pointed to the fading plane. Finally she looked down at me, slowly shaking her head.

"It's gone! It's gone!" I cried.

"Boy, is you a fool?" she said. "Don't you see that there's a real airplane   175
'stead of one of them toy ones?"

"Real. . . ?" I forgot to cry. "Real?"

"Yass, real. Don't you know that thing you reaching for is bigger'n a auto?
You here trying to reach for it and I bet it's flying 'bout two hundred miles higher'n
this roof." She was disgusted with me. "You come on in this house before somebody
else sees what a fool you done turned out to be. You must think these here lil
ole arms of you'n is mighty long. . . ."

I was carried into the house and undressed for bed and the doctor was called.
I cried bitterly, as much from the disappointment of finding the plane so far beyond
my reach as from the pain.

When the doctor came I heard my mother telling him about the plane and
asking if anything was wrong with my mind. He explained that I had had a fever
for several hours. But I was kept in bed for a week and I constantly saw the plane
in my sleep, flying just beyond my fingertips, sailing so slowly that it seemed barely
to move. And each time I'd reach out to grab it I'd miss and through each dream
I'd hear my grandma warning:

> Young man, young man,
> Yo' arms too short
> To box with God. . . .

"Hey, son!"   180

At first he did not know where he was and looked at the old man pointing,
with blurred eyes.

"Ain't that one of you-all's airplanes coming after you?"

As his vision cleared he saw a small black shape above a distant field, soaring
through waves of heat. But he could not be sure and with the pain he feared
that somehow a horrible recurring fantasy of being split in twain by the whirling
blades of a propeller had come true.

"You think he sees us?" he heard.

"See? I hope so."   185

"He's coming like a bat outa hell!"

Straining, he heard the faint sound of a motor and hoped it would soon be
over.

"How you feeling?"

"Like a nightmare," he said.

"Hey, he's done curved back the other way!"   190

"Maybe he saw us," he said. "Maybe he's gone to send out the ambulance
and ground crew." And, he thought with despair, maybe he didn't even see us.

"Where did you send the boy?"

"Down to Mister Graves," Jefferson said. "Man what owns this land."

"Do you think he phoned?"

Jefferson looked at him quickly.   195

"Aw sho'. Dabney Graves is got a bad name on accounta them killings but
he'll call though. . . ."

"What killings?"

"Them five fellers . . . ain't you heard?" he asked with surprise.

"No."

"Everybody knows 'bout Dabney Graves, especially the colored. He done   200
killed enough of us."

Todd had the sensation of being caught in a white neighborhood after dark.

"What did they do?" he asked.

"Thought they was men," Jefferson said, "An' some he owed money, like
he do me. . . ."

"But why do you stay here?"

"You black, son."   205

"I know, but . . ."

"You have to come by the white folks, too."

He turned away from Jefferson's eyes, at once consoled and accused. And
I'll have to come by them soon, he thought with despair. Closing his eyes, he
heard Jefferson's voice as the sun burned blood-red upon his lips.

"I got nowhere to go," Jefferson said, "an' they'd come after me if I did.
But Dabney Graves is a funny fellow. He's all the time making jokes. He can be
mean as hell, then he's liable to turn right around and back the colored against
the white folks. I seen him do it. But me, I hates him for that more'n anything
else. 'Cause just as soon as he gits tired helping a man he don't care what happens
to him. He just leaves him stone cold. And then the other white folks is double
hard on anybody he done helped. For him it's just a joke. He don't give a hilla
beans for nobody—but hisself. . . ."

Todd listened to the thread of detachment in the old man's voice. It was   210
as though he held his words arm's length before him to avoid their destructive
meaning.

"He'd just as soon do you a favor and then turn right around and have
you
strung up. Me, I stays outa his way 'cause down here that's what you gotta do."

If my ankle would only ease for a while, he thought. The closer I spin toward
the earth the blacker I become, flashed through his mind. Sweat ran into his eyes
and he was sure that he would never see the plane if his head continued whirling.
He tried to see Jefferson, what it was that Jefferson held in his hand. It was a
little black man, another Jefferson! A little black Jefferson that shook with fits of
belly-laughter while the other Jefferson looked on with detachment. Then Jefferson
looked up from the thing in his hand and turned to speak, but Todd was far
away, searching the sky for a plane in a hot dry land on a day and age he had
long forgotten. He was going mysteriously with his mother through empty streets
where black faces peered from behind drawn shades and someone was rapping
at a window and he was looking back to see a hand and a frightened face frantically
beckoning from a cracked door and his mother was looking down the empty perspective of the street and shaking her head and hurrying him along and at first it was
only a flash he saw and a motor was droning as through the sun-glare he saw it
gleaming silver as it circled and he was seeing a burst like a puff of white smoke
and hearing his mother yell, Come along, boy, I got no time for them fool airplanes,
I got no time, and he saw it a second time, the plane flying high, and the burst
appeared suddenly and fell slowly, billowing out and sparkling like fireworks and
he was watching and being hurried along as the air filled with a flurry of white
pinwheeling cards that caught in the wind and scattered over the rooftops and
into the gutters and a woman was running and snatching a card and reading it
and screaming and he darted into the shower, grabbing as in winter he grabbed

for snowflakes and bounding away at his mother's, Come on here, boy! Come on, I say! and he was watching as she took the card away, seeing her face grow puzzled and turning taut as her voice quavered, "Niggers Stay From the Polls," and died to a moan of terror as he saw the eyeless sockets of a white hood staring at him from the card and above he saw the plane spiraling gracefully, agleam in the sun like a fiery sword. And seeing it soar he was caught, transfixed between a terrible horror and a horrible fascination.

The sun was not so high now, and Jefferson was calling and gradually he saw three figures moving across the curving roll of the field.

"Look like some doctors, all dressed in white," said Jefferson.

They're coming at last, Todd thought. And he felt such a release of tension   215
within him that he thought he would faint. But no sooner did he close his eyes than he was seized and he was struggling with three white men who were forcing his arms into some kind of coat. It was too much for him, his arms were pinned to his sides and as the pain blazed in his eyes, he realized that it was a straitjacket. What filthy joke was this?

"That oughta hold him, Mister Graves," he heard.

His total energies seemed focused in his eyes as he searched their faces. That was Graves: the other two wore hospital uniforms. He was poised between two poles of fear and hate as he heard the one called Graves saying, "He looks kinda purty in that there suit, boys. I'm glad you dropped by."

"This boy ain't crazy, Mister Graves," one of the others said. "He needs a doctor, not us. Don't see how you led us way out here anyway. It might be a joke to you, but your cousin Rudolph liable to kill somebody. White folks or niggers, don't make no difference. . . ."

Todd saw the man turn red with anger. Graves looked down upon him, chuckling.

"This nigguh belongs in a straitjacket, too, boys. I knowed that the minit   220
Jeff's kid said something 'bout a nigguh flyer. You all know you cain't let the nigguh git up that high without his going crazy. The nigguh brain ain't built right for high altitudes. . . ."

Todd watched the drawling red face, feeling that all the unnamed horror and obscenities that he had ever imagined stood materialized before him.

"Let's git outta here," one of the attendants said.

Todd saw the other reach toward him, realizing for the first time that he lay upon a stretcher as he yelled.

"Don't put your hands on me!"

They drew back, surprised.   225

"What's that you say, nigguh?" asked Graves.

He did not answer and thought that Graves's foot was aimed at his head. It landed on his chest and he could hardly breathe. He coughed helplessly, seeing Graves's lips stretch taut over his yellow teeth, and tried to shift his head. It was as though a half-dead fly was dragging slowly across his face and a bomb seemed to burst within him. Blasts of hot, hysterical laughter tore from his chest, causing his eyes to pop and he felt that the veins in his neck would surely burst. And then a part of him stood behind it all, watching the surprise in Graves's red face and his own hysteria. He thought he would never stop, he would laugh himself to death. It rang in his ears like Jefferson's laughter and he looked for him, centering his eyes desperately upon his face, as though somehow he had become his sole salvation in an insane world of outrage and humiliation. It brought a certain relief. He was suddenly aware that although his body was still contorted it was an echo that no longer rang in his ears. He heard Jefferson's voice with gratitude.

"Mister Graves, the Army done tole him not to leave his airplane."

"Nigguh, Army or no, you gittin' off my land! That airplane can stay 'cause it was paid for by taxpayers' money. But you gittin' off. An' dead or alive, it don't make no difference to me."

Todd was beyond it now, lost in a world of anguish.   230

"Jeff," Graves said, "you and Teddy come and grab holt. I want you to take this here black eagle over to that nigguh airfield and leave him."

Jefferson and the boy approached him silently. He looked away, realizing and doubting at once that only they could release him from his overpowering sense of isolation.

They bent for the stretcher. One of the attendants moved toward Teddy.

"Think you can manage it, boy?"

"I think I can, suh," Teddy said.   235

"Well, you better go behind then, and let yo' pa go ahead so's to keep that leg elevated."

He saw the white men walking ahead as Jefferson and the boy carried him along in silence. Then they were pausing and he felt a hand wiping his face; then he was moving again. And it was as though he had been lifted out of his isolation, back into the world of men. A new current of communication flowed between the man and boy and himself. They moved him gently. Far away he heard a mockingbird liquidly calling. He raised his eyes, seeing a buzzard poised unmoving in space. For a moment the whole afternoon seemed suspended and he waited for the horror to seize him again. Then like a song within his head he heard the boy's soft humming and saw the dark bird glide into the sun and glow like a bird of flaming gold.

QUESTIONS

1. What is the point of view in "Flying Home"? What advantages does this point of view give the author? Whose thoughts are accessible to us?

2. Who is the protagonist in the story? Who or what is the antagonist? What is the central conflict?

3. What is the climax of the story? To what extent is the central conflict resolved? Do you think the protagonist is completely victorious, completely defeated, or something in between? What sorts of ideas does the climax suggest?

4. What do flying and airplanes symbolize for Todd? How is this symbolism developed in the long digression in which Todd remembers his childhood feelings about airplanes (paragraphs 146 through 179)? What ideas do these symbols embody?

5. To what extent are animals and setting used symbolically to express ideas? Consider especially the dust, the sun, mule, oxen, and the buzzard. Why does Ellison (through Jefferson) carefully point out that buzzards are called "jimcrows"?

6. How would you describe Jefferson and the black boy? Are they round or flat characters? Static or dynamic? Individual or representative? How do they help establish the ideas of the story?

7. To what extent can Jefferson's story about his experiences in heaven be considered an allegory of the plight of blacks in twentieth-century America? What ideas about life can be derived from this episode?

8. The story contains two long digressions—Jefferson's story about heaven and Todd's childhood memories. How effectively are these worked into the story? How do they advance the story's message or meaning?

9. What is Todd's attitude toward white officers? What is Jefferson's attitude toward white landowners? How are these attitudes similar? How might you account for these attitudes?

10. How is the symbolism of flying associated with Todd modified and even undercut by the crash, the image of the soaring buzzard, and Jefferson's story about heaven? What ideas emerge from the interaction of all these symbols and episodes?

11. What do we learn about Dabney Graves? What type of character is he (round or flat, static or dynamic, individual or representative)? How do his presence and behavior clarify the story's message?

12. To what extent is the straitjacket put on Todd at the end of the story symbolic? What ideas are expressed with this object?

WRITING ABOUT MEANING IN FICTION

When you prepare to write an essay about ideas in fiction, you should explore all the methods of expressing ideas described earlier and use as many as you think will best provide you with useful information. You may rely most heavily on the direct statements of the authorial voice or on a combination of these and your interpretation of characters and actions. Or you might focus exclusively on a persona or speaker and use his or her ideas as a means of determining those of the author, as nearly as they can be determined.

In your prewriting and early drafts, as in your final essay, make a point of stating the sources of facts. Thus, your sentences might be like these:

> In "The Horse Dealer's Daughter," Lawrence's anonymous narrator describes the reservations that Mabel and Dr. Fergusson have about their new-found love. This description illustrates his idea that love not only creates the excitement of anticipated joy, but also brings out resistance to the possibility of being as controlled as a draught animal in harness. [Here the first sentence refers to a statement by the author's unnamed persona. The second sentence interprets this statement.]

> In one of the last speeches in "The Chaser," the old man implies that his clients will someday return for his expensive poison so that they may eliminate

the wives for whom they had felt such youthful infatuation. It is clear that Collier introduces this speech to demonstrate the idea that life sometimes leads to unconquerable cynicism and evil. [Here the source of the detail in the first sentence is a dramatic statement by a character in the story. The second sentence is interpretive.]

The speaker in "Araby" states that the boys from the Christian Brothers School are like inmates just released from prison when school lets out for the day. This comparison, coming as it does right at the beginning, establishes a slightly comic tone that emphasizes the childish, rather embarrassed confession that the speaker goes on to make in the story. [Here the first sentence locates the source as the first-person narrator, while the second is interpretive.]

In "First Confession," the priest's thoughtful, good-humored treatment of Jackie, as contrasted with the harsh, punishing treatment by the others, shows the idea that religious incentive is best implanted by kindness and understanding, not by fear. [Here the idea, expressed as a single sentence, is derived from a consideration of the work as a whole].

Recognizing sources in this way keeps the lines of your conclusions clear. Thereby you will help your reader in verifying and following your arguments.

In developing and writing your essay, you can help yourself by answering questions like these: What is the best wording of the idea that you can make? What has the author done with the idea? How can the actions be related to the idea as you have stated it? Might any characters be measured according to whether they do or do not live up to the idea? What values does the idea seem to suggest? Does the author seem to be proposing a particular cause? Is this cause personal, social, economic, political, scientific, ethical, esthetic, or religious? Can the idea be shown to affect the organization of the work? How? Does imagery or symbolism develop or illustrate the idea?

Organizing Your Essay

INTRODUCTION.   In your introduction you might state any special circumstances in the work that affect ideas generally or your idea specifically. Your statement of the idea will serve as the central idea for your essay. Your thesis sentence should indicate the particular parts or aspects of the story that you will examine.

BODY.   The exact form of your essay will be controlled by your goals, which are (1) to define the idea, and (2) to show its importance in the work. Each story will invite its own approach, but here are a number of areas and strategies that might be helpful in the development of the body of your essay:

1. *The form of the work as a plan, scheme, or logical format.* Example: "The idea makes for a two-part work, the first showing religion as punishment and the second showing religion as kindness and reward."

2. *A speech or speeches.* Example: "The priest's conversation and responses to Jackie show in operation the idea that kindness and understanding are the best means to encourage religious commitment."

3. *A character or characters.* Example: "Todd is an embodiment of the idea that black Americans can achieve success and recognition only through their own efforts, and then only against many obstacles."

4. *An action or actions.* Example: "Dr. Ferguson's saving Mabel from drowning indicates the story's idea that love is an outgoing, physical force that almost literally rescues human lives."

5. *Shades or variations of the idea.* Example: "The idea of punishment as a corrective is brought out through the simplicity of the father's 'flaking' of Jackie, the spitefulness of Nora, and the sadistic threats of pain and cosmic intimidation by Mrs. Ryan."

6. *A combination of these together with any other aspect relevant to the work.* Example: "The idea in 'Araby' that devotion is complex and contradictory is shown in the narrator's romantic mission as a carrier of parcels, his outcries to love in the backroom of his house, and his self-reproach and shame at the story's end. [Here the idea is to be traced as action, speech, and character in the story would reflect upon it.]

CONCLUSION.   You might wish to begin your conclusion with a summary of ideas as appropriate to what you have written in the body of the essay. You might also add your own thoughts, such as your evaluation of the validity or force of the idea. If you are convinced, you might wish to say that the author has expressed the idea forcefully and convincingly, or else to show possible application of the idea to current conditions. If you are not convinced, it is never enough just to say that you disagree; you should try to show the reasons for your disagreement, or to demonstrate the shortcomings or limitations of the idea. If you wish to mention an idea related to the one you have discussed, you might introduce that here, being sure to stress the connections.

SAMPLE ESSAY

The Idea in D. H. Lawrence's "The Horse Dealer's Daughter"*
That Human Destiny Is to Love

There are many ideas in "The Horse Dealer's Daughter" about the love between men and women. The story suggests that love is a part of the uncontrollable and emotional side of human life, and that love cannot exist without a

* See p. 343 for this story.

[1] physical basis. It also suggests that love transforms life into something new, that love gives security, that only love gives meaning to life, and that love is not only something to live for but something to be feared. The one idea that takes in all these is that loving is an essential part of human nature and that it is human destiny to love.° This idea controls the form of Lawrence's story, and the characters are judged on the standard of how they live up to it. The idea is embodied negatively in characters who are without love, and positively in characters who find love.□

[2] In the first part of the story, loveless characters are negative and incomplete. Their lack of love causes them to be frustrated, sullen, argumentative, and even cruel. Their lives are similar to those of the draught horses on the Pervin farm, who move with "a massive, slumbrous strength, and a stupidity which [holds] . . . them in subjection" (p. 344). The idea is brought across with great force, for the story implies that time is running out on people in this condition, and unless they find love they are doomed to misery. And the love they find must be real, for the underlying theme is that anything short of that is an evasion and will hasten their doom. Joe, the eldest of the Pervin brothers, is the major example of what can happen without love, for even though he is planning to marry, he is doing so without love. His motives are destroying him; as the narrator says, Joe's "life was over, he would be a subject animal" like the horses (p. 344).

[3] The thought that life is impossible without love is exemplified most fully in Mabel Pervin. She is alone among the males in the Pervin family and the character for whom the story is named. Just as the death of the father is breaking up the family, so is it forcing her to drastic action. She clearly assumes that the loss of first her mother and now her father has deprived her of all love. Therefore, her attempted suicide symbolically demonstrates the futility of the loveless, purposeless life.

[4] Rather than ending Mabel's life, however, the pond really begins it, for it is the occasion of her finding love. Dr. Fergusson, who rescues her, is in fact her destiny. He has been introduced previously as a person leading a life of quiet desperation. His common cold, which is pointedly mentioned when he first appears in the Pervin home, may be seen as an indication of the sickness of the soul without love. When he leaves the house his route is aimless and without any eagerly sought goal, and his seeing Mabel go into the water is clearly not deliberate but accidental. When he acts heroically, therefore, he saves not only Mabel, but himself too. The rescue thus suggests the idea that once love is attained, it restores life.

[5] But love is also complex, and it creates new problems once it has been found. It brings out new and strange emotions, and it upsets the habits and attitudes of a lifetime. Indeed, there is a strong element of fear in love; it changes life so completely that no one can ever be the same after experiencing it. We see this kind of fearful change in Doctor Fergusson. The narrator tells us that the doctor "had no intention of loving" Mabel, but that destiny drives him into this state. The final paragraph of the story indicates the mixture of desire and terror that love and change can produce:

° Central idea.
□ Thesis sentence.

"No, I want you, I want you," was all he answered, blindly, with that terrible intonation which frightened her almost more than the horror lest he should *not* want her (p. 355).

Thus, the story suggests that the human destiny that drives people toward love is both joyful and fearful at the same time.

[6]   This realistic presentation of human emotions raises Lawrence's treatment of his idea above the level of the popular or romantic conception of love. Love itself creates problems as great as those it solves, but it also builds a platform of emotional strength from which these new problems can be attacked. This strength can be achieved only when men and women know love, because only then are they living life as it was designed. The problems facing them then are the real ones that men and women should face, since such problems are a natural result of destiny. By contrast, men and women without love, like those at the beginning of the story, have never reached fulfillment. Consequently, they face problems that, though certainly severe and immediate, are really irrelevant to life as it should be lived. The entire story of Mabel and Jack is an illustration of the idea that it is the destiny of men and women to love.

Commentary on the Essay

The introductory paragraph first illustrates the many formulations of the ideas about love that the story suggests and then produces a comprehensive statement of the theme which is made the central idea of the essay. This assertion is developed as it applies (1) to characters without love and (2) to those who find it. In the body of the essay, paragraphs 2 and 3 emphasize the emptiness of the lives of characters without love. The relationship of these two paragraphs to the main idea is that if the characters are not living in accord with human destiny, they are cut off from life. Thus Joe is dismissed in the story as a "subject animal," and Mabel, his sister, attempts suicide. These details are brought out in support of the essay's central idea. Paragraphs 4 and 5 treat the positive aspects of the main idea, focusing on the renewing effect of love on both Mabel and Dr. Fergusson, but also on the complexity of their emotional response to their new love. The last paragraph evaluates the idea or theme of the story and concludes that it is realistic and well balanced.

Additional Stories

JOHN CHEEVER (1912–1982)

The Season of Divorce 1973

My wife has brown hair, dark eyes, and a gentle disposition. Because of her gentle disposition, I sometimes think that she spoils the children. She can't refuse them anything. They always get around her. Ethel and I have been married for ten years. We both come from Morristown, New Jersey, and I can't even remember when I first met her. Our marriage has always seemed happy and resourceful to me. We live in a walk-up in the East Fifties. Our son, Carl, who is six, goes to a good private school, and our daughter, who is four, won't go to school until next year. We often find fault with the way we were educated, but we seem to be struggling to raise our children along the same lines, and when the time comes, I suppose they'll go to the same school and colleges that we went to. The pattern

Ethel graduated from a women's college in the East, and then went for a year to the University of Grenoble. She worked for a year in New York after returning from France, and then we were married. She once hung her diploma above the kitchen sink, but it was a short-lived joke and I don't know where the diploma is now. Ethel is cheerful and adaptable, as well as gentle, and we both come from that enormous stratum of the middle class that is distinguished by its ability to recall better times. Lost money is so much a part of our lives that I am sometimes reminded of expatriates, of a group who have adapted themselves energetically to some alien soil but who are reminded, now and then, of the escarpments of their native coast. Because our lives are confined by my modest salary, the surface what of Ethel's life is easy to describe. about the inner life?

She gets up at seven and turns the radio on. After she is dressed, she rouses the children and cooks the breakfast. Our son has to be walked to the school bus at eight o'clock. When Ethel returns from this trip, Carol's hair has to be braided. I leave the house at eight-thirty, but I know that every move that Ethel makes for the rest of the day will be determined by the housework, the cooking,

375

the shopping, and the demands of the children. I know that on Tuesdays and Thursdays she will be at the A & P between eleven and noon, that on every clear afternoon she will be on a certain bench in a playground from three until five, that she cleans the house on Mondays, Wednesdays, and Fridays, and polishes the silver when it rains. When I return at six, she is usually cleaning the vegetables or making some other preparation for dinner. Then when the children have been fed and bathed, when the dinner is ready, when the table in the living room is set with food and china, she stands in the middle of the room as if she has lost or forgotten something, and this moment of reflection is so deep that she will not hear me if I speak to her, or the children if they call. Then it is over. She lights the four white candles in their silver sticks, and we sit down to a supper of corned-beef hash or some other modest fare.

We go out once or twice a week and entertain about once a month. Because of practical considerations, most of the people we see live in our neighborhood. We often go around the corner to the parties given by a generous couple named Newsome. The Newsomes' parties are large and confusing, and the arbitrary impulses of friendship are given a free play.

We became attached at the Newsomes' one evening, for reasons that I've never understood, to a couple named Dr. and Mrs. Trencher. I think that Mrs. Trencher was the aggressor in this friendship, and after our first meeting she telephoned Ethel three or four times. We went to their house for dinner, and they came to our house, and sometimes in the evening when Dr. Trencher was walking their old dachshund, he would come up for a short visit. He seemed like a pleasant man to have around. I've heard other doctors say that he's a good physician. The Trenchers are about thirty; at least he is. She is older.

I'd say that Mrs. Trencher is a plain woman, but her plainness is difficult to specify. She is small, she has a good figure and regular features, and I suppose that the impression of plainness arises from some inner modesty, some needlessly narrow view of her chances. Dr. Trencher doesn't smoke or drink, and I don't know whether there's any connection or not, but the coloring in his slender face is fresh—his cheeks are pink, and his blue eyes are clear and strong. He has the singular optimism of a well-adjusted physician—the feeling that death is a chance misfortune and that the physical world is merely a field for conquest. In the same way that his wife seems plain, he seems young.

The Trenchers live in a comfortable and unpretentious private house in our neighborhood. The house is old-fashioned; its living rooms are large, its halls are gloomy, and the Trenchers don't seem to generate enough human warmth to animate the place, so that you sometimes take away from them, at the end of an evening, an impression of many empty rooms. Mrs. Trencher is noticeably attached to her possessions—her clothes, her jewels, and the ornaments she's bought for the house—and to Fräulein, the old dachshund. She feeds Fräulein scraps from the table, furtively, as if she has been forbidden to do this, and after dinner Fräulein lies beside her on the sofa. With the play of green light from a television set on her drawn features and her thin hands stroking Fräulein, Mrs. Trencher looked to me one evening like a good-hearted and miserable soul.

Mrs. Trencher began to call Ethel in the mornings for a talk or to ask her for lunch or a matinee. Ethel can't go out in the day and she claims to dislike long telephone conversations. She complained that Mrs. Trencher was a tireless

5

and aggressive gossip. Then late one afternoon Dr. Trencher appeared at the playground where Ethel takes our two children. He was walking by, and he saw her and sat with her until it was time to take the children home. He came again a few days later, and then his visits with Ethel in the playground, she told me, became a regular thing. Ethel thought that perhaps he didn't have many patients and that with nothing to do he was happy to talk with anyone. Then, when we were washing dishes one night, Ethel said thoughtfully that Trencher's attitude toward her seemed strange. "He stares at me," she said. "He sighs and stares at me," I know what my wife looks like in the playground. She wears an old tweed coat, overshoes, and Army gloves, and a scarf is tied under her chin. The playground is a fenced and paved lot between a slum and the river. The picture of the well-dressed, pink-cheeked doctor losing his heart to Ethel in this environment was hard to take seriously. She didn't mention him then for several days, and I guessed that he had stopped his visits. Ethel's birthday came at the end of the month, and I forgot about it, but when I came home that evening, there were a lot of roses in the living room. They were a birthday present from Trencher, she told me. I was cross at myself for having forgotten her birthday, and Trencher's roses made me angry. I asked her if she'd seen him recently.

"Oh, yes," she said, "he still comes to the playground nearly every afternoon. I haven't told you, have I? He's made his declaration. He loves me. He can't live without me. He'd walk through fire to hear the notes of my voice." She laughed. "That's what he said."

"When did he say this?"

"At the playground. And walking home. Yesterday."

"How long has he known?"

"That's the funny part about it," she said. "He knew before he met me at the Newsomes' that night. He saw me waiting for a crosstown bus about three weeks before that. He just saw me and he said that he knew then, the minute he saw me. Of course, he's crazy."

I was tired that night and worried about taxes and bills, and I could think of Trencher's declaration only as a comical mistake. I felt that he was a captive of financial and sentimental commitments, like every other man I know, and that he was no more free to fall in love with a strange woman he saw on a street corner than he was to take a walking trip through French Guiana or to recommence his life in Chicago under an assumed name. His declaration, the scene in the playground, seemed to me to be like those chance meetings that are a part of the life of any large city. A blind man asks you to help him across the street, and as you are about to leave him, he seizes your arm and regales you with a passionate account of his cruel and ungrateful children; or the elevator man who is taking you up to a party turns to you suddenly and says that his grandson has infantile paralysis. The city is full of accidental revelation, half-heard cries for help, and strangers who will tell you everything at the first suspicion of sympathy, and Trencher seemed to me like the blind man or the elevator operator. His declaration had no more bearing on the business of our lives than these interruptions.

Mrs. Trencher's telephone conversations had stopped, and we had stopped visiting the Trenchers, but sometimes I would see him in the morning on the crosstown bus when I was late going to work. He seemed understandably embarrassed whenever he saw me, but the bus was always crowded at that time of day,

10

15

and it was no effort to avoid one another. Also, at about that time I made a mistake in business and lost several thousand dollars for the firm I work for. There was not much chance of my losing my job, but the possibility was always at the back of my mind, and under this and under the continuous urgency of making more money the memory of the eccentric doctor was buried. Three weeks passed without Ethel's mentioning him, and then one evening, when I was reading, I noticed Ethel standing at the window looking down into the street.

"He's really there," she said.

"Who?"

"Trencher. Come here and see."

I went to the window. There were only three people on the sidewalk across the street. It was dark and it would have been difficult to recognize anyone, but because one of them, walking toward the corner, had a dachshund on a leash, it could have been Trencher.

"Well, what about it?" I said. "He's just walking the dog."   20

"But he wasn't walking the dog when I first looked out of the window. He was just standing there, staring up at this building. That's what he says he does. He says that he comes over here and stares up at our lighted windows."

"When did he say this?"

"At the playground."

"I thought you went to another playground."

"Oh, I do, I do, but he followed me. He's crazy, darling. I know he's crazy,   25 but I feel so sorry for him. He says that he spends night after night looking up at our windows. He says that he sees me everywhere—the back of my head, my eyebrows—that he hears my voice. He says that he's never compromised in his life and that he isn't going to compromise about this. I feel so sorry for him, darling. I can't help but feel sorry for him."

For the first time then, the situation seemed serious to me, for in his helplessness I knew that he might have touched an inestimable and wayward passion that Ethel shares with some other women—an inability to refuse any cry for help, to refuse any voice that sounds pitiable. It is not a reasonable passion, and I would almost rather have had her desire him than pity him. When we were getting ready for bed that night, the telephone rang, and when I picked it up and said hello, no one answered. Fifteen minutes later, the telephone rang again, and when there was no answer this time, I began to shout and swear at Trencher, but he didn't reply—there wasn't even the click of a closed circuit—and I felt like a fool. Because I felt like a fool, I accused Ethel of having led him on, of having encouraged him, but these accusations didn't affect her, and when I finished them, I felt worse, because I knew that she was innocent, and that she had to go out on the street to buy groceries and air the children, and that there was no force of law that could keep Trencher from waiting for her there, or from staring up at our lights.

We went to the Newsomes' one night the next week, and while we were taking off our coats, I heard Trencher's voice. He left a few minutes after we arrived, but his manner—the sad glance he have Ethel, the way he sidestepped me, the sorrowful way that he refused the Newsomes when they asked him to stay longer, and the gallant attentions he showed his miserable wife—made me angry. Then I happened to notice Ethel and saw that her color was high, that her eyes were bright, and that while she was praising Mrs. Newsome's new shoes, her mind was not on what she was saying. When we came home that night, the baby-sitter told us crossly that neither of the children had slept. Ethel took their temperatures. Carol was all right, but the boy had a fever of a hundred and four. Neither of us got much sleep that night, and in the morning Ethel called me at the office to say that Carl had bronchitis. Three days later, his sister came down with it.

For the next two weeks, the sick children took up most of our time. They had to be given medicine at eleven in the evening and again at three in the morning, and we lost a lot of sleep. It was impossible to ventilate or clean the house, and when I came in, after walking through the cold from the bus stop, it stank of cough syrups and tobacco, fruit cores and sickbeds. There were blankets and pillows, ashtrays, and medicine glasses everywhere. We divided the work of sickness reasonably and took turns at getting up in the night, but I often fell asleep at my desk during the day, and after dinner Ethel would fall asleep in a chair in the living room. Fatigue seems to differ for adults and children only in that adults recognize it and so are not overwhelmed by something they can't name; but even with a name for it they are overwhelmed, and when we were tired, we were unreasonable, cross, and the victims of transcendent depressions. One evening after the worst of the sickness was over, I came home and found some roses in the living room. Ethel said that Trencher had brought them. She hadn't let him in. She had closed the door in his face. I took the roses and threw them out. We didn't quarrel. The children went to sleep at nine, and a few minutes after nine I went to bed. Sometime later, something woke me.

A light was burning in the hall. I got up. The children's room and the living room were dark. I found Ethel in the kitchen sitting at the table, drinking coffee.

"I've made some fresh coffee," she said. "Carol felt croupy again, so I steamed 30
her. They're both asleep now."

"How long have you been up?"

"Since half past twelve," she said. "What time is it?"

"Two."

I poured myself a cup of coffee and sat down. She got up from the table and rinsed her cup and looked at herself in a mirror that hangs over the sink. It was a windy night. A dog was wailing somewhere in an apartment below ours, and a loose radio antenna was brushing against the kitchen window.

"It sounds like a branch," she said.   35

In the bare kitchen light, meant for peeling potatoes and washing dishes, she looked very tired.

"Will the children be able to go out tomorrow?"

"Oh, I hope so," she said. "Do you realize that I haven't been out of this apartment in over two weeks?" She spoke bitterly and this startled me.

"It hasn't been quite two weeks."

"It's been over two weeks," she said.   40

"Well, let's figure it out," I said. "The children were taken sick on a Saturday night. That was the fourth. Today is the—"

"Stop it, stop it," she said. "I know how long it's been. I haven't had my shoes on in two weeks."

"You make it sound pretty bad."

"It is. I haven't had on a decent dress or fixed my hair."

"It could be worse."   45
"My mother's cooks had a better life."
"I doubt that."
"My mother's cooks had a better life," she said loudly.
"You'll wake the children."
"My mother's cooks had a better life. They had pleasant rooms. No one   50
could come into the kitchen without their permission." She knocked the coffee
grounds into the garbage and began to wash the pot.
"How long was Trencher here this afternoon?"
"A minute. I've told you."
"I don't believe it. He was in here."
"He was not. I didn't let him in. I didn't let him in because I looked so
badly. I didn't want to discourage him."
"Why not?"   55
"I don't know. He may be a fool. He may be insane but the things he's
told me have made me feel marvelously, he's made me feel marvelously."
"Do you want to go?"
"Go? Where would I go?" She reached for the purse that is kept in the
kitchen to pay for groceries and counted out of it two dollars and thirty-five cents.
"Ossining? Montclair?"
"I mean with Trencher."
"I don't know, I don't know," she said, "but who can say that I shouldn't?   60
What harm would it do? What good would it do? Who knows. I love the children
but that isn't enough, that isn't nearly enough. I wouldn't hurt them, but would
I hurt them so much if I left you? Is divorce so dreadful and of all the things
that hold a marriage together how many of them are good?" She sat down at
the table.
"In Grenoble," she said, "I wrote a long paper on Charles Stuart in French.
A professor at the University of Chicago wrote me a letter. I couldn't read a French
newspaper without a dictionary today, I don't have the time to follow any newspaper,
and I am ashamed of my incompetence, ashamed of the way I look. Oh, I guess
I love you, I do love the children, but I love myself, I love my life, it has some
value and some promise for me and Trencher's roses make me feel that I'm losing
this, that I'm losing my self-respect. Do you know what I mean, do you understand
what I mean?"
"He's crazy," I said.
"Do you know what I mean? Do you understand what I mean?"
"No," I said. "No."
Carl woke up then and called for his mother. I told Ethel to go to bed. I   65
turned out the kitchen light and went into the children's room.

The children felt better the next day, and since it was Sunday, I took them
for a walk. The afternoon sun was clement and pure, and only the colored shadows
made me remember that it was midwinter, that the cruise ships were returning,
and that in another week jonquils would be twenty-five cents a bunch. Walking
down Lexington Avenue, we heard the drone bass of a church organ sound from
the sky, and we and the others on the sidewalk looked up in piety and bewilderment,
like a devout and stupid congregation, and saw a formation of heavy bombers
heading for the sea. As it got late, it got cold and clear and still, and on the

stillness the waste from the smokestacks along the East River seemed to articulate, as legibly as the Pepsi-Cola plane, whole words and sentences. Halcyon. Disaster. They were hard to make out. It seemed the ebb of the year—an evil day for gastritis, sinus, and respiratory disease—and remembering other winters, the markings of the light convinced me that it was the season of divorce. It was a long afternoon, and I brought the children in before dark.

I think that the seriousness of the day affected the children, and when they returned to the house, they were quiet. The seriousness of it kept coming to me with the feeling that this change, like a phenomenon of speed, was affecting our watches as well as our hearts. I tried to remember the willingness with which Ethel had followed my regiment during the war, from West Virginia to the Carolinas and Oklahoma, and the day coaches and rooms she had lived in, and the street in San Francisco where I said goodbye to her before I left the country, but I could not put any of this into words, and neither of us found anything to say. Sometime after dark, the children were bathed and put to bed, and we sat down to our supper. At about nine o'clock, the doorbell rang, and when I answered it and recognized Trencher's voice on the speaking tube, I asked him to come up.

He seemed distraught and exhilarated when he appeared. He stumbled on the edge of the carpet. "I know that I'm not welcome here," he said in a hard voice, as if I were deaf. "I know that you don't like me here. I respect your feelings. This is your home. I respect a man's feelings about his home. I don't usually go to a man's home unless he asks me. I respect your home. I respect your marriage. I respect your children. I think everything ought to be aboveboard. I've come here to tell you that I love your wife."

"Get out," I said.

"You've got to listen to me," he said. "I love your wife. I can't live without her. I've tried and I can't. I've even thought of going away—of moving to the West Coast—but I know that it wouldn't make any difference. I want to marry her. I'm not romantic. I'm matter-of-fact. I'm very matter-of-fact. I know that you have two children and that you don't have much money. I know that there are problems of custody and property and things like that to be settled. I'm not romantic. I'm hardheaded. I've talked this all over with Mrs. Trencher, and she's agreed to give me a divorce. I'm not underhanded. Your wife can tell you that. I realize all the practical aspects that have to be considered—custody, property, and so forth. I have plenty of money. I can give Ethel everything she needs, but there are the children. You'll have to decide about them between yourselves. I have a check here. It's made out to Ethel. I want her to take it and go to Nevada. I'm a practical man and I realize that nothing can be decided until she gets her divorce."

"Get out of here!" I said. "Get the hell out of here!"

He started for the door. There was a potted geranium on the mantelpiece, and I threw this across the room at him. It got him in the small of the back and nearly knocked him down. The pot broke on the floor. Ethel screamed. Trencher was still on his way out. Following him, I picked up a candlestick and aimed it at his head, but it missed and bounced off the wall. "Get the hell out of here!" I yelled, and he slammed the door. I went back into the living room. Ethel was pale but she wasn't crying. There was a loud rapping on the radiator, a signal from the people upstairs for decorum and silence—urgent and expressive, like the communications that prisoners send to one another through the plumbing in a penitentiary. Then everything was still.

70

We went to bed, and I woke sometime during the night. I couldn't see the clock on the dresser, so I don't know what time it was. There was no sound from the children's room. The neighborhood was perfectly still. There were no lighted windows anywhere. Then I knew that Ethel had wakened me. She was lying on her side of the bed. She was crying.

"Why are you crying?" I asked.

"Why am I crying?" she said. "Why am I crying?" And to hear my voice   75
and to speak set her off again, and she began to sob cruelly. She sat up and slipped her arms into the sleeves of a wrapper and felt along the table for a package of cigarettes. I saw her wet face when she lighted a cigarette. I heard her moving around in the dark.

"Why do you cry?"

"Why do I cry? Why do I cry?" she asked impatiently. "I cry because I saw an old woman cuffing a little boy on Third Avenue. She was drunk. I can't get it out of my mind." She pulled the quilt off the foot of our bed and wandered with it toward the door. "I cry because my father died when I was twelve and because my mother married a man I detested or thought that I detested. I cry because I had to wear an ugly dress—a hand-me-down dress—to a party twenty years ago, and I didn't have a good time. I cry because of some unkindness that I can't remember. I cry because I'm tired—because I'm tired and I can't sleep." I heard her arrange herself on the sofa and then everything was quiet.

I like to think that the Trenchers have gone away, but I still see Trencher now and then on a crosstown bus when I'm late going to work. I've also seen his wife, going into the neighborhood lending library with Fräulein. She looks old. I'm not good at judging ages, but I wouldn't be surprised to find that Mrs. Trencher is fifteen years older than her husband. Now when I come home in the evenings, Ethel is still sitting on the stool by the sink cleaning vegetables. I go with her into the children's room. The light there is bright. The children have built something out of an orange crate, something preposterous and ascendant, and their sweetness, their compulsion to build, the brightness of the light are reflected perfectly and increased in Ethel's face. Then she feeds them, bathes them, and sets the table, and stands for a moment in the middle of the room, trying to make some connection between the evening and the day. Then it is over. She lights the four candles, and we sit down to our supper.

ANTON CHEKHOV (1860–1904)

Lady with Lapdog   1899

Translated by David Magarshack.

I

The appearance on the front of a new arrival—a lady with a lapdog—became the topic of general conversation. Dmitry Dmitrich Gurov, who had been a fortnight in Yalta and got used to its ways, was also interested in new arrivals. One day, sitting on the terrace of Vernet's restaurant, he saw a young woman walking along the promenade; she was fair, not very tall, and wore a toque; behind her trotted a white pomeranian.

Later he came across her in the park and in the square several times a day. She was always alone, always wearing the same toque, followed by the white pomeranian. No one knew who she was, and she became known simply as the lady with the lapdog.

"If she's here without her husband and without any friends," thought Gurov, "it wouldn't be a bad idea to strike up an acquaintance with her."

He was not yet forty, but he had a twelve-year-old daughter and two schoolboy sons. He had been married off when he was still in his second year at the university, and his wife seemed to him now to be almost twice his age. She was a tall, black-browed woman, erect, dignified, austere, and, as she liked to describe herself, a "thinking person." She was a great reader, preferred the new "advanced" spelling, called her husband by the more formal "Dimitry" and not the familiar "Dmitry"; and though he secretly considered her not particularly intelligent, narrow-minded, and inelegant, he was afraid of her and disliked being at home. He had been unfaithful to her for a long time, he was often unfaithful to her, and that was why, perhaps, he almost always spoke ill of women, and when men discussed women in his presence, he described them as *the lower breed*.

He could not help feeling that he had had enough bitter experience to have the right to call them as he pleased, but all the same without *the lower breed* he could not have existed a couple of days. He was bored and ill at ease among men, with whom he was reticent and cold, but when he was among women he felt at ease, he knew what to talk about with them and how to behave, even when he was silent in their company he experienced no feeling of constraint. There was something attractive, something elusive in his appearance, in his character and his whole person that women found interesting and irresistible; he was aware of it, and was himself drawn to them by some irresistible force.

5

Long and indeed bitter experience had taught him that every new affair, which at first relieved the monotony of life so pleasantly and appeared to be such a charming and light adventure, among decent people and especially among Muscovites, who are so irresolute and so hard to rouse, inevitably developed into an extremely complicated problem and finally the whole situation became rather cumbersome. But at every new meeting with an attractive woman he forgot all about this experience, he wanted to enjoy life so badly and it all seemed so simple and amusing.

And so one afternoon, while he was having dinner at a restaurant in the park, the woman in the toque walked in unhurriedly and took a seat at the table next to him. The way she looked, walked and dressed, wore her hair, told him that she was of good social standing, that she was married, that she was in Yalta for the first time, that she was alone and bored. . . . There was a great deal of exaggeration in the stories about the laxity of morals among the Yalta visitors, and he dismissed them with contempt, for he knew that such stories were mostly made up by people who would gladly have sinned themselves if they had had any idea how to go about it; but when the woman sat down at the table three yards away from him he remembered these stories of easy conquests and excursions to the mountains and the tempting thought of a quiet and fleeting affair, an affair with a strange woman whose very name he did not know, suddenly took possession of him.

He tried to attract the attention of the dog by calling softly to it, and when the pomeranian came up to him he shook a finger at it. The pomeranian growled. Gurov again shook a finger at it.

The woman looked up at him and immediately lowered her eyes.

"He doesn't bite," she said and blushed.   10

"May I give him a bone?" he asked, and when she nodded, he said amiably: "Have you been long in Yalta?"

"About five days."

"And I am just finishing my second week here."

They said nothing for the next few minutes.

"Time flies," she said without looking at him, "and yet it's so boring here."   15

"That's what one usually hears people saying here. A man may be living in Belev and Zhizdra or some other God-forsaken hole and he isn't bored, but the moment he comes here all you hear from him is "Oh, it's so boring! Oh, the dust!" You'd think he'd come from Granada!"

She laughed. Then both went on eating in silence, like complete strangers; but after dinner they strolled off together, and they embarked on the light playful conversation of free and contented people who do not care where they go or what they talk about. They walked, and talked about the strange light that fell on the sea; the water was of such a soft and warm lilac, and the moon threw a shaft of gold across it. They talked about how close it was after a hot day. Gurov told her that he lived in Moscow, that he was a graduate in philology but worked in a bank, that he had at one time thought of singing in a private opera company but had given up the idea, that he owned two houses in Moscow. . . . From her he learnt that she had grown up in Petersburg, but had got married in the town of S——, where she had been living for the past two years, that she would stay another month in Yalta, and that her husband, who also needed a rest, might join her. She was quite unable to tell him what her husband's job was, whether he served in the offices of the provincial governor or the rural council, and she found this rather amusing herself. Gurov also found out that her name and patronymic were Anna Sergeyevna.

Later, in his hotel room, he thought about her and felt sure that he would meet her again the next day. It had to be. As he went to bed he remembered that she had only recently left her boarding school, that she had been a schoolgirl like his own daughter; he recalled how much diffidence and angularity there was in her laughter and her conversation with a stranger—it was probably the first time in her life she had found herself alone, in a situation when men followed her, looked at her, and spoke to her with only one secret intention, an intention she could hardly fail to guess. He remembered her slender, weak neck, her beautiful grey eyes.

"There's something pathetic about her, all the same," he thought as he fell asleep.

II

A week had passed since their first meeting. It was a holiday. It was close indoors,   20
while in the streets a strong wind raised clouds of dust and tore off people's hats. All day long one felt thirsty, and Gurov kept going to the terrace of the restaurant, offering Anna Sergeyevna fruit drinks and ices. There was nowhere to go.

In the evening, when the wind had dropped a little, they went to the pier to watch the arrival of the steamer. There were a great many people taking a walk on the landing pier; some were meeting friends, they had bunches of flowers in their hands. It was there that two peculiarities of the Yalta smart set at once arrested attention: the middle-aged women dressed as if they were still young girls and there was a great number of generals.

Because of the rough sea the steamer arrived late, after the sun had set, and she had to swing backwards and forwards several times before getting alongside the pier. Anna Sergeyevna looked at the steamer and the passengers through her lorgnette, as though trying to make out some friends, and when she turned to Gurov her eyes were sparkling. She talked a lot, asked many abrupt questions, and immediately forgot what it was she had wanted to know; then she lost her lorgnette in the crowd of people.

The smartly dressed crowd dispersed; soon they were all gone, the wind had dropped completely, but Gurov and Anna were still standing there as though waiting to see if someone else would come off the boat. Anna Sergeyevna was no longer talking. She was smelling her flowers without looking at Gurov.

"It's a nice evening," he said. "Where shall we go now? Shall we go for a drive?"

She made no answer.

Then he looked keenly at her and suddenly put his arms round her and kissed her on the mouth. He felt the fragrance and dampness of the flowers and immediately looked round him fearfully: had anyone seen them?

"Let's go to your room," he said softly.

And both walked off quickly.

It was very close in her hotel room, which was full of the smell of the scents she had bought in a Japanese shop. Looking at her now, Gurov thought: "Life is full of strange encounters!" From his past he preserved the memory of carefree, good-natured women, whom love had made gay and who were grateful to him for the happiness he gave them, however short-lived; and of women like his wife, who made love without sincerity, with unnecessary talk, affectedly, hysterically, with such an expression, as though it were not love or passion, but something much more significant; and of two or three very beautiful, frigid women, whose faces suddenly lit up with a predatory expression, an obstinate desire to take, to snatch from life more than it could give; these were women no longer in their first youth, capricious, unreasoning, despotic, unintelligent women, and when Gurov lost interest in them, their beauty merely aroused hatred in him and the lace trimmings on their négligés looked to him then like the scales of a snake.

But here there was still the same diffidence and angularity of inexperienced youth—an awkward feeling; and there was also the impression of embarrassment, as if someone had just knocked at the door. Anna Sergeyevna, this lady with the lapdog, apparently regarded what had happened in a peculiar sort of way, very seriously, as though she had become a fallen woman—so it seemed to him, and he found it odd and disconcerting. Her features lengthened and drooped, and her long hair hung mournfully on either side of her face; she sank into thought in a despondent pose, like a woman taken in adultery in an old painting.

"It's wrong," she said. "You'll be the first not to respect me now."

There was a water-melon on the table. Gurov cut himself a slice and began to eat it slowly. At least half an hour passed in silence.

Anna Sergeyevna was very touching; there was an air of a pure, decent, naïve woman about her, a woman who had very little experience of life; the solitary candle burning on the table scarcely lighted up her face, but it was obvious that she was unhappy.

"But, darling, why should I stop respecting you?" Gurov asked. 'You don't know yourself what you're saying."

"May God forgive me," she said, and her eyes filled with tears. "It's terrible." 35

"You seem to wish to justify yourself."

"How can I justify myself? I am a bad, despicable creature. I despise myself and have no thought of justifying myself. I haven't deceived my husband, I've deceived myself. And not only now. I've been deceiving myself for a long time. My husband is, I'm sure, a good and honest man, but, you see, he is a flunkey. I don't know what he does at his office, all I know is that he is a flunkey. I was only twenty when I married him, I was eaten up by curiosity, I wanted something better. There surely must be a different kind of life, I said to myself. I wanted to live. To live, to live! I was burning with curiosity. I don't think you know what I am talking about, but I swear I could no longer control myself, something was happening to me, I could not be held back, I told my husband I was ill, and I came here. . . . Here too I was going about as though in a daze, as though I was mad, and now I've become a vulgar worthless woman whom everyone has a right to despise."

Gurov could not help feeling bored as he listened to her; he was irritated by her naïve tone of voice and her repentance, which was so unexpected and so out of place; but for the tears in her eyes, he might have thought that she was joking or play-acting.

"I don't understand," he said gently, "what it is you want."

She buried her face on his chest and clung close to him. 40

"Please, please believe me," she said. "I love a pure, honest life. I hate immorality. I don't know myself what I am doing. The common people say "the devil led her astray," I too can now say about myself that the devil has led me astray."

"There, there . . ." he murmured.

He gazed into her staring, frightened eyes, kissed her, spoke gently and affectionately to her, and gradually she calmed down and her cheerfulness returned; both of them were soon laughing.

Later, when they went out, there was not a soul on the promenade, the town with its cypresses looked quite dead, but the sea was still roaring and dashing itself against the shore; a single launch tossed on the waves, its lamp flickering sleepily.

They hailed a cab and drove to Oreanda. 45

"I've just found out your surname, downstairs in the lobby," said Gurov. "Von Diederitz. Is your husband a German?"

"No. I believe his grandfather was German. He is of the Orthodox faith himself."

In Oreanda they sat on a bench not far from the church, looked down on the sea, and were silent. Yalta could scarcely be seen through the morning mist. White clouds lay motionless on the mountain tops. Not a leaf stirred on the trees, the cicadas chirped, and the monotonous, hollow roar of the sea, coming up from below, spoke of rest, of eternal sleep awaiting us all. The sea had roared like that down below when there was no Yalta or Oreanda, it was roaring now, and it would go on roaring as indifferently and hollowly when we were here no more. And in this constancy, in this complete indifference to the life and death of each one of us, there is perhaps hidden the guarantee of our eternal salvation, the never-ceasing movement of life on earth, the never-ceasing movement towards perfection. Sitting beside a young woman who looked so beautiful at the break of day, soothed and enchanted by the sight of all that fairy-land scenery—the sea, the mountains, the clouds, the wide sky—Gurov reflected that, when you came to think of it, everything in the world was really beautiful, everything but our own thoughts and actions when we lose sight of the higher aims of existence and our dignity as human beings.

Someone walked up to them, a watchman probably, looked at them, and went away. And there seemed to be something mysterious and also beautiful in this fact, too. They could see the Theodosia boat coming towards the pier, lit up by the sunrise, and with no lights.

"There's dew on the grass," said Anna Sergeyevna, breaking the silence.   50

"Yes. Time to go home."

They went back to the town.

After that they met on the front every day at twelve o'clock, had lunch and dinner together, went for walks, admired the sea. She complained of sleeping badly and of her heart beating uneasily, asked the same questions, alternately worried by feelings of jealousy and by fear that he did not respect her sufficiently. And again and again in the park or in the square, when there was no one in sight, he would draw her to him and kiss her passionately. The complete idleness, these kisses in broad daylight, always having to look round for fear of someone watching them, the heat, the smell of the sea, and the constant looming into sight of idle, well-dressed, and well-fed people seemed to have made a new man of him; he told Anna Sergeyevna that she was beautiful, that she was desirable, made passionate love to her, never left her side, while she was often lost in thought and kept asking him to admit that he did not really respect her, that he was not in the least in love with her and only saw in her a vulgar woman. Almost every night they drove out of town, to Oreanda or to the waterfall; the excursion was always a success, and every time their impressions were invariably grand and beautiful.

They kept expecting her husband to arrive. But a letter came from him in which he wrote that he was having trouble with his eyes and implored his wife to return home as soon as possible. Anna Sergeyevna lost no time in getting ready for her journey home.

"It's a good thing I'm going," she said to Gurov. "It's fate."   55

She took a carriage to the railway station, and he saw her off. The drive took a whole day. When she got into the express train, after the second bell, she said:

"Let me have another look at you. . . . One last look. So."

She did not cry, but looked sad, just as if she were ill, and her face quivered.

"I'll be thinking of you, remembering you," she said. "Good-bye. You're staying, aren't you? Don't think badly of me. We are parting for ever. Yes, it must be so, for we should never have met. Well, good-bye. . . ."

The train moved rapidly out of the station; its lights soon disappeared, and   60 a minute later it could not even be heard, just as though everything had conspired to put a quick end to this sweet trance, this madness. And standing alone on the platform gazing into the dark distance, Gurov listened to the churring of the grass-hoppers and the humming of the telegraph wires with a feeling as though he had just woken up. He told himself that this had been just one more affair in his life, just one more adventure, and that it too was over, leaving nothing but a memory. He was moved and sad, and felt a little penitent that the young woman, whom he would never see again, had not been happy with him; he had been amiable and affectionate with her, but all the same in his behaviour to her, in the tone of his voice and in his caresses, there was a suspicion of light irony, the somewhat coarse arrogance of the successful male, who was, moreover, almost twice her age. All the time she called him good, wonderful, high-minded; evidently she must have taken him to be quite different from what he really was, which meant that he had involuntarily deceived her.

At the railway station there was already a whiff of autumn in the air; the evening was chilly.

"Time I went north, too," thought Gurov, as he walked off the platform. "High time!"

III

At home in Moscow everything was already like winter: the stoves were heated, and it was still dark in the morning when the children were getting ready to go to school and having breakfast, so that the nurse had to light the lamp for a short time. The frosts had set in. When the first snow falls and the first day one goes out for a ride in a sleigh, one is glad to see the white ground, the white roofs, the air is so soft and wonderful to breathe, and one remembers the days of one's youth. The old lime trees and birches, white with rime, have such a benignant look, they are nearer to one's heart than cypresses and palms, and beside them one no longer wants to think of mountains and the sea.

Gurov had been born and bred in Moscow, and he returned to Moscow on a fine frosty day; and when he put on his fur coat and warm gloves and took a walk down Petrovka Street, and when on Saturday evening he heard the church bells ringing, his recent holiday trip and the places he had visited lost their charm for him. Gradually he became immersed in Moscow life, eagerly reading three newspapers a day and declaring that he never read Moscow papers on principle. Once more, he could not resist the attraction of restaurants, clubs, banquets, and anniversary celebrations, and once more he felt flattered that well-known lawyers and actors came to see him and that in the Medical Club he played cards with a professor as his partner. Once again he was capable of eating a whole portion of the Moscow speciality of sour cabbage and meat served in a frying-pan. . . .

Another month and, he thought, nothing but a memory would remain of Anna Sergeyevna; he would remember her as through a haze and only occasionally dream of her with a wistful smile, as he did of the others before her. But over a month passed, winter was at its height, and he remembered her as clearly as though he had only parted from her the day before. His memories haunted him more and more persistently. Every time the voices of his children doing their homework

65

1. Awk intro's to quotations.

2. Slashes, line #s, blocked quotes.

3. Quoting frags. (Work the quote grammatically into the sentence.

4. Stop & develop connotation, & the figures — if imp. Don't spend time on the unnecessary mes.

5. Make sure the lead ins aren't ~~frags~~ main clauses.

6. Revisions

7.

reached him in his study in the stillness of the evening, every time he heard a popular song or some music in a restaurant, every time the wind howled in the chimney—it all came back to him: their walks on the pier, early morning with the mist on the mountains, the Theodosia boat, and the kisses. He kept pacing the room for hours remembering it all and smiling, and then his memories turned into daydreams and the past mingled in his imagination with what was going to happen. He did not dream of Anna Sergeyevna, she accompanied him everywhere like his shadow and followed him wherever he went. Closing his eyes, he saw her as clearly as if she were before him, and she seemed to him lovelier, younger, and tenderer than she had been; and he thought that he too was much better than he had been in Yalta. In the evenings she gazed at him from the bookcase, from the fireplace, from the corner—he heard her breathing, the sweet rustle of her dress. In the street he followed women with his eyes, looking for anyone who resembled her. . . .

He was beginning to be overcome by an overwhelming desire to share his memories with someone. But at home it was impossible to talk of his love, and outside his home there was no one he could talk to. Not the tenants who lived in his house, and certainly not his colleagues in the bank. And what was he to tell them? Had he been in love then? Had there been anything beautiful, poetic, edifying, or even anything interesting about his relations with Anna Sergeyevna? So he had to talk in general terms about love and women, and no one guessed what he was driving at, and his wife merely raised her black eyebrows and said:

"Really, Dimitry, the role of a coxcomb doesn't suit you at all!"

One evening, as he left the Medical Club with his partner, a civil servant, he could not restrain himself, and said:

"If you knew what a fascinating woman I met in Yalta!"

The civil servant got into his sleigh and was about to be driven off, but   70
suddenly he turned round and called out:

"I say!"

"Yes?"

"You were quite right: the sturgeon *was* a bit off."

These words, so ordinary in themselves, for some reason hurt Gurov's feelings: they seemed to him humiliating and indecent. What savage manners! What faces! What stupid nights! What uninteresting, wasted days! Crazy gambling at cards, gluttony, drunkenness, endless talk about one and the same thing. Business that was of no use to anyone and talk about one and the same thing absorbed the greater part of one's time and energy, and what was left in the end was a sort of dock-tailed, barren life, a sort of nonsensical existence, and it was impossible to escape from it, just as though you were in a lunatic asylum or a convict chain-gang!

Gurov lay awake all night, fretting and fuming, and had a splitting headache   75
the whole of the next day. The following nights too he slept badly, sitting up in bed thinking, or walking up and down his room. He was tired of his children, tired of the bank, he did not feel like going out anywhere or talking about anything.

In December, during the Christmas holidays, he packed his things, told his wife that he was going to Petersburg to get a job for a young man he knew, and set off for the town of S——. Why? He had no very clear idea himself. He wanted to see Anna Sergeyevna, to talk to her, to arrange a meeting, if possible.

He arrived in S—— in the morning and took the best room in a hotel, with a fitted carpet of military grey cloth and an inkstand grey with dust on the table, surmounted by a horseman with raised hand and no head. The hall porter supplied him with all the necessary information: Von Diederitz lived in a house of his own in Old Potter's Street, not far from the hotel. He lived well, was rich, kept his own carriage horses, the whole town knew him. The hall-porter pronounced the name: Dridiritz.

Gurov took a leisurely walk down Old Potter's Street and found the house. In front of it was a long grey fence studded with upturned nails.

"A fence like that would make anyone wish to run away," thought Gurov, scanning the windows and the fence.

As it was a holiday, he thought, her husband was probably at home. It did not matter either way, though, for he could not very well embarrass her by calling at the house. If he were to send in a note it might fall into the hands of the husband and ruin everything. The best thing was to rely on chance. And he kept walking up and down the street and along the fence, waiting for his chance. He watched a beggar enter the gate and the dogs attack him; then, an hour later, he heard the faint indistinct sounds of a piano. That must have been Anna Sergeyevna playing. Suddenly the front door opened and an old woman came out, followed by the familiar white pomeranian. Gurov was about to call to the dog, but his heart began to beat violently and in his excitement he could not remember its name. 80

He went on walking up and down the street, hating the grey fence more and more, and he was already saying to himself that Anna Sergeyevna had forgotten him and had perhaps been having a good time with someone else, which was indeed quite natural for a young woman who had to look at that damned fence from morning till night. He went back to his hotel room and sat on the sofa for a long time, not knowing what to do, then he had dinner and after dinner a long sleep.

"How stupid and disturbing it all is," he thought, waking up and staring at the dark windows: it was already evening. "Well, I've had a good sleep, so what now? What am I going to do tonight?"

He sat on a bed covered by a cheap grey blanket looking exactly like a hospital blanket, and taunted himself in vexation:

"A *lady* with a lapdog! Some adventure, I must say! Serves you right!"

At the railway station that morning he had noticed a poster announcing in 85 huge letters the first performance of *The Geisha Girl* at the local theatre. He recalled it now, and decided to go to the theatre.

"Quite possibly she goes to first nights," he thought.

The theatre was full. As in all provincial theatres, there was a mist over the chandeliers and the people in the gallery kept up a noisy and excited conversation; in the first row of the stalls stood the local dandies with their hands crossed behind their backs; here, too, in the front seat of the Governor's box, sat the Governor's daughter, wearing a feather boa, while the Governor himself hid modestly behind the portière so that only his hands were visible; the curtain stirred, the orchestra took a long time tuning up. Gurov scanned the audience eagerly as they filed in and occupied their seats.

Anna Sergeyevna came in too. She took her seat in the third row, and when

Gurov glanced at her his heart missed a beat and he realized clearly that there was no one in the world nearer and dearer or more important to him than that little woman with the stupid lorgnette in her hand, who was in no way remarkable. That woman lost in a provincial crowd now filled his whole life, was his misfortune, his joy, and the only happiness that he wished for himself. Listening to the bad orchestra and the wretched violins played by second-rate musicians, he thought how beautiful she was. He thought and dreamed.

A very tall, round-shouldered young man with small whiskers had come in with Anna Sergeyevna and sat down beside her; he nodded at every step he took and seemed to be continually bowing to someone. This was probably her husband, whom in a fit of bitterness at Yalta she had called a flunkey. And indeed there was something of a lackey's obsequiousness in his lank figure, his whiskers, and the little bald spot on the top of his head. He smiled sweetly, and the gleaming insignia of some scientific society which he wore in his buttonhole looked like the number on a waiter's coat.

In the first interval the husband went out to smoke and she was left in her 90
seat. Gurov, who also had a seat in the stalls, went up to her and said in a trembling voice and with a forced smile:

"Good evening!"

She looked up at him and turned pale, then looked at him again in panic, unable to believe her eyes, clenching her fan and lorgnette in her hand and apparently trying hard not to fall into a dead faint. Both were silent. She sat and he stood, frightened by her embarrassment and not daring to sit down beside her. The violinists and the flautist began tuning their instruments, and they suddenly felt terrified, as though they were being watched from all the boxes. But a moment later she got up and walked rapidly towards one of the exits; he followed her, and both of them walked aimlessly along corridors and up and down stairs. Figures in all sorts of uniforms—lawyers, teachers, civil servants, all wearing badges— flashed by them; ladies, fur coats hanging on pegs, the cold draught bringing with it the odour of cigarette-ends. Gurov, whose heart was beating violently, thought:

"Oh, Lord, what are all these people, that orchestra, doing here?"

At that moment, he suddenly remembered how after seeing Anna Sergeyevna off he had told himself that evening at the station that all was over and that they would never meet again. But how far they still were from the end!

She stopped on a dark, narrow staircase with a notice over it: "To the Upper 95
Circle."

"How you frightened me!" she said, breathing heavily, still looking pale and stunned. "Oh, dear, how you frightened me! I'm scarcely alive. Why did you come? Why?"

"But, please, try to understand, Anna," he murmured hurriedly. "I beg you, please, try to understand. . . ."

She looked at him with fear, entreaty, love, looked at him intently, so as to fix his features firmly in her mind.

"I've suffered so much," she went on, without listening to him. "I've been thinking of you all the time. The thought of you kept me alive. And yet I tried so hard to forget you—why, oh, why did you come?"

On the landing above two schoolboys were smoking and looking down, but 100

Gurov did not care. He drew Anna Sergeyevna towards him and began kissing her face, her lips, her hands.

"What are you doing? What are you doing?" she said in horror, pushing him away. "We've both gone mad. You must go back tonight, this minute. I implore you, by all that's sacred . . . Somebody's coming!"

Somebody was coming up the stairs.

"You must go back," continued Anna Sergeyevna in a whisper. "Do you hear? I'll come to you in Moscow. I've never been happy, I'm unhappy now, and I shall never be happy, never! So please don't make me suffer still more. I swear I'll come to you in Moscow. But now we must part. Oh, my sweet, my darling, we must part!"

She pressed his hand and went quickly down the stairs, looking back at him all the time, and he could see from the expression in her eyes that she really was unhappy. Gurov stood listening for a short time, and when all was quiet he went to look for his coat and left the theatre.

IV

Anna Sergeyevna began going to Moscow to see him. Every two or three months she left the town of S——, telling her husband that she was going to consult a Moscow gynaecologist, and her husband believed and did not believe her. In Moscow she stayed at the Slav Bazaar and immediately sent a porter in a red cap to inform Gurov of her arrival. Gurov went to her hotel, and no one in Moscow knew about it.

One winter morning he went to her hotel as usual (the porter had called with his message at his house the evening before, but he had not been in). He had his daughter with him, and he was glad of the opportunity of taking her to school, which was on the way to the hotel. Snow was falling in thick wet flakes.

"It's three degrees above zero," Gurov was saying to his daughter, "and yet it's snowing. But then, you see, it's only warm on the earth's surface, in the upper layers of the atmosphere the temperature's quite different."

"Why isn't there any thunder in winter, Daddy?"

He explained that, too. As he was speaking, he kept thinking that he was going to meet his mistress and not a living soul knew about it. He led a double life: one for all who were interested to see, full of conventional truth and conventional deception, exactly like the lives of his friends and acquaintances; and another which went on in secret. And by a kind of strange concatenation of circumstances, possibly quite by accident, everything that was important, interesting, essential, everything about which he was sincere and did not deceive himself, everything that made up the quintessence of his life, went on in secret, while everything that was a lie, everything that was merely the husk in which he hid himself to conceal the truth, like his work at the bank, for instance, his discussions at the club, his ideas of the lower breed, his going to anniversary functions with his wife—all that happened in the sight of all. He judged others by himself, did not believe what he saw, and was always of the opinion that every man's real and most interesting life went on in secret, under cover of night. The personal, private life of an individual was kept a secret, and perhaps that was partly the reason why civilized man was so anxious that his personal secrets should be respected.

Having seen his daughter off to her school, Gurov went to the Slav Bazaar. 110
He took off his fur coat in the cloakroom, went upstairs, and knocked softly on
the door. Anna Sergeyevna, wearing the grey dress he liked most, tired out by
her journey and by the suspense of waiting for him, had been expecting him since
the evening before; she was pale, looked at him without smiling, but was in his
arms the moment he went into the room. Their kiss was long and lingering, as if
they had not seen each other for two years.

"Well," he asked, "how are you getting on there? Anything new?"

"Wait, I'll tell you in a moment. . . . I can't . . ."

She could not speak because she was crying. She turned away from him
and pressed her handkerchief to her eyes.

"Well, let her have her cry," he thought, sitting down in an armchair. "I'll
wait."

Then he rang the bell and ordered tea; while he was having his tea, she 115
was still standing there with her face to the window. She wept because she could
not control her emotions, because she was bitterly conscious of the fact that their
life was so sad: they could only meet in secret, they had to hide from people,
like thieves! Was not their life ruined?

"Please stop crying!" he said.

It was quite clear to him that their love would not come to an end for a
long time, if ever. Anna Sergeyevna was getting attached to him more and more
strongly, she worshipped him, and it would have been absurd to tell her that all
this would have to come to an end one day. She would not have believed it, anyway.

He went up to her and took her by the shoulders, wishing to be nice to
her, to make her smile; and at that moment he caught sight of himself in the
looking glass.

His hair was already beginning to turn grey. It struck him as strange that
he should have aged so much, that he should have lost his good looks in the last
few years. The shoulders on which his hands lay were warm and quivering. He
felt so sorry for this life, still so warm and beautiful, but probably soon to fade
and wilt like his own. Why did she love him so? To women he always seemed
different from what he was, and they loved in him not himself, but the man their
imagination conjured up and whom they had eagerly been looking for all their
lives; and when they discovered their mistake they still loved him. And not one
of them had ever been happy with him. Time had passed, he had met women,
made love to them, parted from them, but not once had he been in love; there
had been everything between them, but no love.

It was only now, when his hair was beginning to turn grey, that he had 120
fallen in love properly, in good earnest—for the first time in his life.

He and Anna Sergeyevna loved each other as people do who are very dear
and near, as man and wife or close friends love each other; they could not help
feeling that fate itself had intended them for one another, and they were unable
to understand why he should have a wife and she a husband; they were like two
migrating birds, male and female, who had been caught and forced to live in separate
cages. They had forgiven each other what they had been ashamed of in the past,
and forgave each other everything in their present, and felt that this love of theirs
had changed them both.

Before, when he felt depressed, he had comforted himself by all sorts of arguments that happened to occur to him on the spur of the moment, but now he had more serious things to think of, he felt profound compassion, he longed to be sincere, tender. . . .

"Don't cry, my sweet," he said. "That'll do, you've had your cry. . . . Let's talk now, let's think of something."

Then they had a long talk. They tried to think how they could get rid of the necessity of hiding, telling lies, living in different towns, not seeing one another for so long. How were they to free themselves from their intolerable chains?

"How? How?" he asked himself, clutching at his head. "How?"   125

And it seemed to them that in only a few more minutes a solution would be found and a new, beautiful life would begin; but both of them knew very well that the end was still a long, long way away and that the most complicated and difficult part was only just beginning.

JOSEPH CONRAD (1857–1924)
Youth   *1902*

This could have occurred nowhere but in England, where men and sea interpenetrate, so to speak—the sea entering into the life of most men, and the men knowing something or everything about the sea, in the way of amusement, of travel, or of breadwinning.

We were sitting round a mahogany table that reflected the bottle, the claret glasses, and our faces as we leaned on our elbows. There was a director of companies, an accountant, a lawyer, Marlow, and myself. The director had been a *Conway* boy, the accountant had served four years at sea, the lawyer—a fine crusted Tory, High Churchman, the best of old fellows, the soul of honor—had been chief officer in the P. & O. service in the good old days when mailboats were square-rigged at least on two masts, and used to come down the China Sea before a fair monsoon with stun'sails set alow and aloft. We all began life in the merchant service. Between the five of us there was the strong bond of the sea, and also the fellowship of the craft, which no amount of enthusiasm for yachting, cruising, and so on can give, since one is only the amusement of life and the other is life itself.

Marlow (at least I think that is how he spelt his name) told the story, or rather the chronicle, of a voyage:

"Yes, I have seen a little of the Eastern seas; but what I remember best is my first voyage there. You fellows know there are those voyages that seem ordered for the illustration of life, that might stand for a symbol of existence. You fight, work, sweat, nearly kill yourself, sometimes do kill yourself, trying to accomplish something—and you can't. Not from any fault of yours. You simply can do nothing, neither great nor little—not a thing in the world—not even marry an old maid, or get a wretched 600-ton cargo of coal to its port of destination.

"It was altogether a memorable affair. It was my first voyage to the East,   5
and my first voyage as second mate; it was also my skipper's first command. You'll admit it was time. He was sixty if a day; a little man, with a broad, not very straight back, with bowed shoulders and one leg more bandy than the other, he had that

queer twisted-about appearance you see so often in men who work in the fields. He had a nutcracker face—chin and nose trying to come together over a sunken mouth—and it was framed in iron-gray fluffy hair, that looked like a chinstrap of cotton-wool sprinkled with coaldust. And he had blue eyes in that old face of his, which were amazingly like a boy's, with that candid expression some quite common men preserve to the end of their days by a rare internal gift of simplicity of heart and rectitude of soul. What induced him to accept me was a wonder. I had come out of a crack Australian clipper, where I had been third officer, and he seemed to have a prejudice against crack clippers as aristocratic and high-toned. He said to me, 'You know, in this ship you will have to work.' I said I had to work in every ship I had ever been in. 'Ah, but this is different, and you gentlemen out of them big ships; . . . but there! I dare say you will do. Join tomorrow.'

"I joined tomorrow. It was twenty-two years ago; and I was just twenty. How time passes! It was one of the happiest days of my life. Fancy! Second mate for the first time—a really responsible officer! I wouldn't have thrown up my new billet for a fortune. The mate looked me over carefully. He was also an old chap, but of another stamp. He had a Roman nose, a snow-white, long beard, and his name was Mahon, but he insisted that it should be pronounced Mann. He was well connected; yet there was something wrong with his luck, and he had never got on.

"As to the captain, he had been for years in coasters, then in the Mediterranean, and last in the West Indian trade. He had never been round the Capes. He could just write a kind of sketchy hand, and didn't care for writing at all. Both were thorough good seamen of course, and between those two old chaps I felt like a small boy between two grandfathers.

"The ship also was old. Her name was the *Judea*. Queer name, isn't it? She belonged to a man Wilmer, Wilcox—some name like that; but he has been bankrupt and dead these twenty years or more, and his name don't matter. She had been laid up in Shadwell basin for ever so long. You may imagine her state. She was all rust, dust, grime—soot aloft, dirt on deck. To me it was like coming out of a palace into a ruined cottage. She was about 400 tons, had a primitive windlass, wooden latches to the doors, not a bit of brass about her, and a big square stern. There was on it, below her name in big letters, a lot of scrollwork, with the gilt off, and some sort of coat of arms, with the motto 'Do or Die' underneath. I remember it took my fancy immensely. There was a touch of romance in it, something that made me love the old thing—something that appealed to my youth!

"We left London in ballast—sand ballast—to load a cargo of coal in a northern port for Bangkok. Bangkok! I thrilled. I had been six years at sea, but had only seen Melbourne and Sydney, very good places, charming places in their way—but Bangkok!

"We worked out of the Thames under canvas, with a North Sea pilot on 10 board. His name was Jermyn, and he dodged all day long about the galley drying his handkerchief before the stove. Apparently he never slept. He was a dismal man, with a perpetual tear sparkling at the end of his nose, who either had been in trouble, or was in trouble, or expected to be in trouble—couldn't be happy unless something went wrong. He mistrusted my youth, my common sense, and my seamanship, and made a point of showing it in a hundred little ways. I dare say he was right. It seems to me I knew very little then, and I know not much more now; but I cherish a hate for that Jermyn to this day.

"We were a week working up as far as Yarmouth Roads, and then we got into a gale—the famous October gale of twenty-two years ago. It was wind, lightning, sleet, snow, and a terrific sea. We were flying light, and you may imagine how bad it was when I tell you we had smashed bulwarks and a flooded deck. On the second night she shifted her ballast into the lee bow, and by that time we had been blown off somewhere on the Dogger Bank. There was nothing for it but go below with shovels and try to right her, and there we were in that vast hold, gloomy like a cavern, the tallow dips stuck and flickering on the beams, the gale howling above, the ship tossing about like mad on her side; there we all were, Jermyn, the captain, everyone, hardly able to keep our feet, engaged on that grave-digger's work, and trying to toss shovelfuls of wet sand up to windward. At every tumble of the ship you could see vaguely in the dim light men falling down with a great flourish of shovels. One of the ship's boys (we had two), impressed by the weirdness of the scene, wept as if his heart would break. We could hear him blubbering somewhere in the shadows.

"On the third day the gale died out, and by and by a north-country tug picked us up. We took sixteen days in all to get from London to the Tyne! When we got into dock we had lost our turn for loading, and they hauled us off to a pier where we remained for a month. Mrs. Beard (the captain's name was Beard) came from Colchester to see the old man. She lived on board. The crew of runners had left, and there remained only the officers, one boy and the steward, a mulatto who answered to the name of Abraham. Mrs. Beard was an old woman, with a face all wrinkled and ruddy like a winter apple, and the figure of a young girl. She caught sight of me once, sewing on a button, and insisted on having my shirts to repair. This was something different from the captains' wives I had known on board crack clippers. When I brought her the shirts, she said: 'And the socks? They want mending, I am sure, and John's—Captain Beard's—things are all in order now. I would be glad of something to do.' Bless the old woman. She over-hauled my outfit for me, and meantime I read for the first time *Sartor Resartus* and Burnaby's *Ride to Khiva*. I didn't understand much of the first then; but I remembered I preferred the soldier to the philosopher at the time; a preference which life has only confirmed. One was a man, and the other was either more— or less. However, they are both dead and Mrs. Beard is dead, and youth, strength, genius, thoughts, achievements, simple hearts—all dies. . . . No matter.

"They loaded us at last. We shipped a crew. Eight able seamen and two boys. We hauled off one evening to the buoys at the dock gates, ready to go out, and with a fair prospect of beginning the voyage next day. Mrs. Beard was to start for home by a late train. When the ship was fast we went to tea. We sat rather silent through the meal—Mahon, the old couple, and I. I finished first, and slipped away for a smoke, my cabin being in a deckhouse just against the poop. It was high water, blowing fresh with a drizzle; the double dock gates were opened, and the steam colliers were going in and out in the darkness with their lights burning bright, a great plashing of propellers, rattling of winches, and a lot of hailing on the pierheads. I watched the procession of headlights gliding high and of green lights gliding low in the night, when suddenly a red gleam flashed at me, vanished, came into view again, and remained. The fore end of a steamer loomed up close. I shouted down the cabin, 'Come up, quick!' and then heard a startled voice saying afar in the dark, 'Stop her, sir.' A bell jingled. Another voice cried warningly, 'We are going right into that bark, sir.' The answer to this was a gruff 'All right,' and the next thing was a heavy crash as the steamer struck a glancing blow with the bluff of her bow about our forerigging. There was a moment of confusion, yelling, and running about. Steam roared. Then somebody was heard saying, 'All clear, sir.' . . . 'Are you all right?' asked the gruff voice. I had jumped forward to see the damage, and hailed back, 'I think so.' 'Easy astern,' said the gruff voice. A bell jingled. 'What steamer is that?' screamed Mahon. By that time she was no more to us than a bulky shadow maneuvering a little way off. They shouted at us some name—a woman's name, Miranda or Melissa—or some such thing. 'This means another month in this beastly hole,' said Mahon to me, as we peered with lamps about the splintered bulwarks and broken braces. 'But where's the captain?'

'We had not heard or seen anything of him all that time. We went aft to look. A doleful voice arose hailing somewhere in the middle of the dock, *'Judea* ahoy!' . . . How the devil did he get there? . . . 'Hallo!' we shouted. 'I am adrift in our boat without oars,' he cried. A belated water-man offered his services, and Mahon struck a bargain with him for a half crown to tow our skipper alongside; but it was Mrs. Beard that came up the ladder first. They had been floating about the dock in that mizzly cold rain for nearly an hour. I was never so surprised in my life.

"It appears that when he heard my shout 'Come up' he understood at once what was the matter, caught up his wife, ran on deck, and across, and down into our boat, which was fast to the ladder. Not bad for a sixty-year-old. Just imagine that old fellow saving heroically in his arms that old woman—the woman of his life. He set her down on a thwart, and was ready to climb back on board when the painter came adrift somehow, and away they went together. Of course in the confusion we did not hear him shouting. He looked abashed. She said cheerfully, 'I suppose it does not matter my losing the train now?' 'No, Jenny—you go below and get warm,' he growled. Then to us: 'A sailor has no business with a wife—I say. There I was, out of the ship. Well, no harm done this time. Let's go and look at what that fool of a steamer smashed.'

"It wasn't much, but it delayed us three weeks. At the end of that time, the captain being engaged with his agents, I carried Mrs. Beard's bag to the railway station and put her all comfy into a third-class carriage. She lowered the window to say, 'You are a good young man. If you see John—Captain Beard—without his muffler at night, just remind him from me to keep his throat well wrapped up.' 'Certainly, Mrs. Beard,' I said. 'You are a good young man; I noticed how attentive you are to John—to Captain——' The train pulled out suddenly; I took my cap off to the old woman: I never saw her again. . . . Pass the bottle.

"We went to sea next day. When we made that start for Bangkok we had been already three months out of London. We had expected to be a fortnight or so—at the outside.

"It was January, and the weather was beautiful—the beautiful sunny winter weather that has more charm than in the summertime, because it is unexpected, and crisp, and you know it won't, it can't, last long. It's like a windfall, like a godsend, like an unexpected piece of luck.

"It lasted all down the North Sea, all down Channel; and it lasted till we were three hundred miles or so to the westward of the Lizards; then the wind

15

went round to the sou'west and began to pipe up. In two days it blew a gale. The *Judea*, hove to, wallowed on the Atlantic like an old candle-box. It blew day after day: it blew with spite, without interval, without mercy, without rest. The world was nothing but an immensity of great foaming waves rushing at us, under a sky low enough to touch with the hand and dirty like a smoked ceiling. In the stormy space surrounding us there was as much flying spray as air. Day after day and night after night there was nothing round the ship but the howl of the wind, the tumult of the sea, the noise of water pouring over her deck. There was no rest for her and no rest for us. She tossed, she pitched, she stood on her head, she sat on her tail, she rolled, she groaned, and we had to hold on while on deck and cling to our bunks when below, in a constant effort of body and worry of mind.

"One night Mahon spoke through the small window of my berth. It opened right into my very bed, and I was lying there sleepless, in my boots, feeling as though I had not slept for years, and could not if I tried. He said excitedly: 20

" 'You got the sounding rod in here, Marlow? I can't get the pumps to suck. By God! It's no child's play.'

"I gave him the sounding rod and lay down again, trying to think of various things—but I thought only of the pumps. When I came on deck they were still at it, and my watch relieved at the pumps. By the light of the lantern brought on deck to examine the sounding rod I caught a glimpse of their weary, serious faces. We pumped all the four hours. We pumped all night, all day, all the week—watch and watch. She was working herself loose, and leaked badly—not enough to drown us at once, but enough to kill us with the work at the pumps. And while we pumped the ship was going from us piecemeal: the bulwarks went, the stanchions were torn out, the ventilators smashed, the cabin door burst in. There was not a dry spot in the ship. She was being gutted bit by bit. The longboat changed, as if by magic, into matchwood where she stood in her gripes. I had lashed her myself, and was rather proud of my handiwork, which had withstood so long the malice of the sea. And we pumped. And there was no break in the weather. The sea was white like a sheet of foam, like a caldron of boiling milk; there was not a break in the clouds, no—not the size of a man's hand—no, not for so much as ten seconds. There was for us no sky, there were for us no stars, no sun, no universe—nothing but angry clouds and an infuriated sea. We pumped watch and watch, for dear life; and it seemed to last for months, for years, for all eternity, as though we had been dead and gone to a hell for sailors. We forgot the day of the week, the name of the month, what year it was, and whether we had ever been ashore. The sails blew away, she lay broadside on under a weather cloth, the ocean poured over her, and we did not care. We turned those handles, and had the eyes of idiots. As soon as we had crawled on deck I used to take a round turn with a rope about the men, the pumps, and the mainmast, and we turned, we turned incessantly, with the water to our waists, to our necks, over our heads. It was all one. We had forgotten how it felt to be dry.

"And there was somewhere in me the thought: By Jove! This is the deuce of an adventure—something you read about; and it is my first voyage as second mate—and I am only twenty—and here I am lasting it out as well as any of these men, and keeping my chaps up to the mark. I was pleased. I would not have given up the experience for worlds. I had moments of exultation. Whenever the old dismantled craft pitched heavily with her counter high in the air, she seemed to me to throw up, like an appeal, like a defiance, like a cry to the clouds without mercy, the words written on her stern: *'Judea*, London. Do or Die.'

"O youth! The strength of it, the faith of it, the imagination of it! To me she was not an old rattletrap carting about the world a lot of coal for a freight— to me she was the endeavor, the test, the trial of life. I think of her with pleasure, with affection, with regret—as you would think of someone dead you have loved. I shall never forget her. . . . Pass the bottle.

"One night when tied to the mast, as I explained, we were pumping on, deafened with the wind, and without spirit enough in us to wish ourselves dead, a heavy sea crashed aboard and swept clean over us. As soon as I got my breath I shouted, as in duty bound, 'Keep on, boys!' when suddenly I felt something hard floating on deck strike the calf of my leg. I made a grab at it and missed. It was so dark we could not see each other's faces within a foot—you understand.

"After that thump the ship kept quiet for a while, and the thing, whatever it was, struck my leg again. This time I caught it—and it was a saucepan. At first, being stupid with fatigue and thinking of nothing but the pumps, I did not understand what I had in my hand. Suddenly it dawned upon me, and I shouted, 'Boys, the house on deck is gone. Leave this, and let's look for the cook.'

"There was a deckhouse forward, which contained the galley, the cook's berth, and the quarters of the crew. As we had expected for days to see it swept away, the hands had been ordered to sleep in the cabin—the only safe place in the ship. The steward, Abraham, however, persisted in clinging to his berth, stupidly, like a mule—from sheer fright I believe, like an animal that won't leave a stable falling in an earthquake. So we went to look for him. It was chancing death, since once out of our lashings we were as exposed as if on a raft. But we went. The house was shattered as if a shell had exploded inside. Most of it had gone overboard—stove, men's quarters, and their property, all was gone; but two posts, holding a portion of the bulkhead to which Abraham's bunk was attached, remained as if by a miracle. We groped in the ruins and came upon this, and there he was, sitting in his bunk, surrounded by foam and wreckage, jabbering cheerfully to himself. He was out of his mind; completely and forever mad, with this sudden shock coming upon the fag-end of his endurance. We snatched him up, lugged him aft, and pitched him headfirst down the cabin companion. You understand there was no time to carry him down with infinite precautions and wait to see how he got on. Those below would pick him up at the bottom of the stairs all right. We were in a hurry to go back to the pumps. That business could not wait. A bad leak is an inhuman thing.

"One would think that the sole purpose of that fiendish gale had been to make a lunatic of that poor devil of a mulatto. It eased before morning, and next day the sky cleared, and as the sea went down the leak took up. When it came to bending a fresh set of sails the crew demanded to put back—and really there was nothing else to do. Boats gone, decks swept clean, cabin gutted, men without a stitch but what they stood in, stores spoiled, ship strained. We put her head for home, and—would you believe it? The wind came east right in our teeth. It blew fresh, it blew continuously. We had to beat up every inch of the way, but she did not leak so badly, the water keeping comparatively smooth. Two hours' pumping in every four is no joke—but it kept her afloat as far as Falmouth.

"The good people there live on casualties of the sea, and no doubt were glad to see us. A hungry crowd of shipwrights sharpened their chisels at the sight of that carcass of a ship. And, by Jove! they had pretty pickings off us before they were done. I fancy the owner was already in a tight place. There were delays. Then it was decided to take part of the cargo out and calk her topsides. This was done, the repairs finished, cargo reshipped; a new crew came on board, and we went out—for Bangkok. At the end of a week we were back again. The crew said they weren't going to Bangkok—a hundred and fifty days' passage—in a something hooker that wanted pumping eight hours out of the twenty-four; and the nautical papers inserted again the little paragraph: '*Judea*. Bark. Tyne to Bangkok; coals; put back to Falmouth leaky and with crew refusing duty.'

"There were more delays—more tinkering. The owner came down for a   30
day, and said she was as right as a little fiddle. Poor old Captain Beard looked like the ghost of a Geordie skipper—through the worry and humiliation of it. Remember he was sixty, and it was his first command. Mahon said it was a foolish business, and would end badly. I loved the ship more than ever, and wanted awfully to get to Bangkok. To Bangkok! Magic name, blessed name. Mesopotamia wasn't a patch on it. Remember I was twenty, and it was my first second-mate's billet, and the East was waiting for me.

"We went out and anchored in the outer roads with a fresh crew—the third. She leaked worse than ever. It was as if those confounded shipwrights had actually made a hole in her: This time we did not even go outside. The crew simply refused to man the windlass.

"They towed us back to the inner harbor, and we became a fixture, a feature, an institution of the place. People pointed us out to visitors as 'That 'ere bark that's going to Bangkok—has been here six months—put back three times.' On holidays the small boys pulling about in boats would hail, '*Judea*, ahoy!' and if a head showed above the rail shouted, 'Where you bound to?—Bangkok?' and jeered. We were only three on board. The poor old skipper mooned in the cabin. Mahon undertook the cooking, and unexpectedly developed all a Frenchman's genius for preparing nice little messes. I looked languidly after the rigging. We became citizens of Falmouth. Every shopkeeper knew us. At the barber's or tobacconist's they asked familiarly, 'Do you think you will ever get to Bangkok?' Meantime the owner, the underwriters, and the charters squabbled amongst themselves in London, and our pay went on. . . Pass the bottle.

"It was horrid. Morally it was worse than pumping for life. It seemed as though we had been forgotten by the world, belonged to nobody, would get nowhere, it seemed that, as if bewitched, we would have to live for ever and ever in that inner harbor, a derision and a byword to generations of longshore loafers and dishonest boatmen. I obtained three months' pay and a five days' leave, and made a rush for London. It took me a day to get there and pretty well another to come back—but three months' pay went all the same. I don't know what I did with it. I went to a music hall, I believe, lunched, dined, and supped in a swell place in Regent Street, and was back on time, with nothing but a complete set of Byron's works and a new railway rug to show for three months' work. The boatman who pulled me off to the ship said: 'Hallo! I thought you had left the old thing. *She* will never get to Bangkok.' 'That's all *you* know about it,' I said, scornfully—but I didn't like that prophecy at all.

"Suddenly a man, some kind of agent to somebody, appeared with full powers. He had grog-blossoms all over his face, an indomitable energy, and was a jolly soul. We leaped into life again. A hulk came alongside, took our cargo, and then we went into dry dock to get our copper stripped. No wonder she leaked. The poor thing, strained beyond endurance by the gale, had, as if in disgust, spat out all the oakum of her lower seams. She was recalked, new-coppered, and made as tight as a bottle. We went back to the hulk and reshipped our cargo.

"Then, on a fine moonlight night, all the rats left the ship. 35

"We had been infested with them. They had destroyed our sails, consumed more stores than the crew, affably shared our beds and our dangers, and now, when the ship was made seaworthy, concluded to clear out. I called Mahon to enjoy the spectacle. Rat after rat appeared on our rail, took a last look over his shoulder, and leaped with a hollow thud into the empty hulk. We tried to count them, but soon lost the tale. Mahon said: 'Well, well! don't talk to me about the intelligence of rats. They ought to have left before, when we had that narrow squeak from foundering. There you have the proof how silly is the superstition about them. They leave a good ship for an old rotten hulk, where there is nothing to eat, too, the fools! . . . I don't believe they know what is safe or what is good for them, any more than you or I.'

"And after some more talk we agreed that the wisdom of rats had been grossly overrated, being in fact no greater than that of men.

The story of the ship was known, by this, all up the Channel from Land's End to the Forelands, and we could get no crew on the south coast. They sent us one all complete from Liverpool, and we left once more—for Bangkok.

"We had fair breezes, smooth water right into the tropics, and the old *Judea* lumbered along in the sunshine. When she went eight knots everything cracked aloft, and we tied our caps to our heads; but mostly she strolled on at the rate of three miles an hour. What could you expect? She was tired—that old ship. Her youth was where mine is—where yours is—you fellows who listen to this yarn; and what friend would throw your years and your weariness in your face? We didn't grumble at her. To us aft, at least, it seemed as though we had been born in her, reared in her, had lived in her for ages, had never known any other ship. I would just as soon have abused the old village church at home for not being a cathedral.

"And for me there was also my youth to make me patient. There was all 40 the East before me, and all life, and the thought that I had been tried in that ship and had come out pretty well. And I thought of men of old who, centuries ago, went that road in ships that sailed no better, to the land of palms, and spices, and yellow sands, and of brown nations ruled by kings more cruel than Nero the Roman, and more splendid than Solomon the Jew. The old bark lumbered on, heavy with her age and the burden of her cargo, while I lived the life of youth in ignorance and hope. She lumbered on through an interminable procession of days; and the fresh gilding flashed back at the setting sun, seemed to cry out over the darkening sea the words painted on her stern, '*Judea*, London, Do or Die.'

"Then we entered the Indian Ocean and steered northerly for Java Head. The winds were light. Weeks slipped by. She crawled on, do or die, and people at home began to think of posting us as overdue.

"One Saturday evening, I being off duty, the men asked me to give them an extra bucket of water or so—for washing clothes. As I did not wish to screw on the fresh-water pump so late, I went forward whistling, and with a key in my hand to unlock the forepeak scuttle, intending to serve the water out of a spare tank we kept there.

"The smell down below was as unexpected as it was frightful. One would have thought hundreds of paraffin lamps had been flaring and smoking in that hole for days. I was glad to get out. The man with me coughed and said, 'Funny smell, sir.' I answered negligently, 'It's good for the health, they say,' and walked aft.

"The first thing I did was to put my head down the square of the midship ventilator. As I lifted the lid a visible breath, something like a thin fog, a puff of faint haze, rose from the opening. The ascending air was hot, and had a heavy, sooty, paraffiny smell. I gave one sniff, and put down the lid gently. It was no use choking myself. The cargo was on fire.

"Next day she began to smoke in earnest. You see it was to be expected, for though the coal was of a safe kind, that cargo had been so handled, so broken up with handling, that it looked more like smithy coal than anything else. Then it had been wetted—more than once. It rained all the time we were taking it back from the hulk, and now with this long passage it got heated, and there was another case of spontaneous combustion.

"The captain called us into the cabin. He had a chart spread on the table, and looked unhappy. He said, "The coast of West Australia is near, but I mean to proceed to our destination. It is the hurricane month, too; but we will just keep her head for Bangkok, and fight the fire. No more putting back anywhere, if we all get roasted. We will try first to stifle this 'ere damned combustion by want of air.'

"We tried. We battened down everything, and still she smoked. The smoke kept coming out through imperceptible crevices; it forced itself through bulkheads and covers; it oozed here and there and everywhere in slender threads, in an invisible film, in an incomprehensible manner. It made its way into the cabin, into the forecastle; it poisoned the sheltered places on the deck; it could be sniffed as high as the mainyard. It was clear that if the smoke came out the air came in. This was disheartening. This combustion refused to be stifled.

"We resolved to try water, and took the hatches off. Enormous volumes of smoke, whitish, yellowish, thick, greasy, misty, choking, ascended as high as the trucks. All hands cleared out aft. Then the poisonous cloud blew away, and we went back to work in a smoke that was no thicker now than that of an ordinary factory chimney.

"We rigged the force pump, got the hose along, and by and by it burst. Well, it was as old as the ship—a prehistoric hose, and past repair. Then we pumped with the feeble head pump, drew water with buckets, and in this way managed in time to pour lots of Indian Ocean into the main hatch. The bright stream flashed in sunshine, fell into a layer of white crawling smoke, and vanished on the black surface of coal. Steam ascended mingling with the smoke. We poured salt water as into a barrel without a bottom. It was our fate to pump in that ship, to pump out of her, to pump into her; and after keeping water out of her to save ourselves from being drowned, we frantically poured water into her to save ourselves from being burnt.

"And she crawled on, do or die, in the serene weather. The sky was a miracle   50
of purity, a miracle of azure. The sea was polished, was blue, was pellucid, was
sparkling like a precious stone, extending on all sides, all round to the horizon—
as if the whole terrestrial globe had been one jewel, one colossal sapphire, a single
gem fashioned into a planet. And on the luster of the great calm waters the *Judea*
glided imperceptibly, enveloped in languid and unclean vapors, in a lazy cloud
that drifted to leeward, light and slow; a pestiferous cloud defiling the splendor
of sea and sky.

"All this time of course we saw no fire. The cargo smoldered at the bottom
somewhere. Once Mahon, as we were working side by side, said to me with a
queer smile: 'Now, if she only would spring a tidy leak—like that time when we
first left the Channel—it would put a stopper on this fire. Wouldn't it?' I remarked
irrelevantly, 'Do you remember the rats?'

"We fought the fire and sailed the ship too as carefully as though nothing
had been the matter. The steward cooked and attended on us. Of the other twelve
men, eight worked while four rested. Everyone took his turn, captain included.
There was equality, and if not exactly fraternity, then a deal of good feeling. Sometimes a man, as he dashed a bucketful of water down the hatchway, would yell
out, 'Hurrah for Bangkok!' and the rest laughed. But generally we were taciturn
and serious—and thirsty. Oh! how thirsty! And we had to be careful with the
water. Strict allowance. The ship smoked, the sun blazed. . . . Pass the bottle.

"We tried everything. We even made an attempt to dig down to the fire.
No good, of course. No man could remain more than a minute below. Mahon,
who went first, fainted there, and the man who went to fetch him out did likewise.
We lugged them out on deck. Then I leaped down to show how easily it could
be done. They had learned wisdom by that time, and contented themselves by
fishing for me with a chainhook tied to a broom handle, I believe. I did not offer
to go and fetch up my shovel, which was left down below.

"Things began to look bad. We put the longboat into the water. The second
boat was ready to swing out. We had also another, a fourteen-foot thing, on davits
aft, where it was quite safe.

"Then, behold, the smoke suddenly decreased. We redoubled our efforts   55
to flood the bottom of the ship. In two days there was no smoke at all. Everybody
was on the broad grin. This was on a Friday. On Saturday no work, but sailing
the ship of course, was done. The men washed their clothes and their faces for
the first time in a fortnight, and had a special dinner given them. They spoke of
spontaneous combustion with contempt, and implied *they* were the boys to put
out combustions. Somehow we all felt as though we each had inherited a large
fortune. But a beastly smell of burning hung about the ship. Captain Beard had
hollow eyes and sunken cheeks. I had never noticed so much before how twisted
and bowed he was. He and Mahon prowled soberly about hatches and ventilators,
sniffing. It struck me suddenly poor Mahon was a very, very old chap. As to me,
I was pleased and proud as though I had helped to win a great naval battle. O
youth!

"The night was fine. In the morning a homewardbound ship passed us hull
down—the first we had seen for months; but we were nearing the land at last,
Java Head being about 190 miles off, and nearly due north.

"Next day it was my watch on deck from eight to twelve. At breakfast the captain observed, 'It's wonderful how that smell hangs about the cabin.' About ten, the mate being on the poop, I stepped down on the main deck for a moment. The carpenter's bench stood abaft the mainmast: I leaned against it sucking at my pipe, and the carpenter, a young chap, came to talk to me. He remarked, 'I think we have done very well, haven't we?' and then I perceived with annoyance the fool was trying to tilt the bench. I said curtly, 'Don't, Chips,' and immediately became aware of a queer sensation, of an absurd delusion—I seemed somehow to be in the air. I heard all round me like a pent-up breath released—as if a thousand giants simultaneously had said Phoo!—and felt a dull concussion which made my ribs ache suddenly. No doubt about it—I was in the air, and my body was describing a short parabola. But short as it was, I had the time to think several thoughts in, as far as I can remember, the following order: 'This can't be the carpenter—What is it?—Some accident—Submarine volcano?—Coals, gas!—By Jove! We are being blown up—Everybody's dead—I am falling into the afterhatch—I see fire in it.'

"The coaldust suspended in the air of the hold had glowed dull-red at the moment of the explosion. In the twinkling of an eye, in an infinitesimal fraction of a second since the first tilt of the bench, I was sprawling full length on the cargo. I picked myself up and scrambled out. It was quick like a rebound. The deck was a wilderness of smashed timber, lying crosswise like trees in a wood after a hurricane; an immense curtain of solid rags waved gently before me—it was the mainsail blown to strips. I thought: the masts will be toppling over directly; and to get out of the way bolted on all fours towards the poop ladder. The first person I saw was Mahon, with eyes like saucers, his mouth open, and the long white hair standing straight on end round his head like a silver halo. He was just about to go down when the sight of the main deck stirring, heaving up, and changing into splinters before his eyes, petrified him on the top step. I stared at him in unbelief, and he stared at me with a queer kind of shocked curiosity. I did not know that I had no hair, no eyebrows, no eyelashes, that my young mustache was burnt off, that my face was black, one cheek laid open, my nose cut, and my chin bleeding. I had lost my cap, one of my slippers, and my shirt was torn to rags. Of all this I was not aware. I was amazed to see the ship still afloat, the poop deck whole—and, most of all, to see anybody alive. Also the peace of the sky and the serenity of the sea were distinctly surprising. I suppose I expected to see them convulsed with horror. . . . Pass the bottle.

"There was a voice hailing the ship from somewhere—in the air, in the sky— I couldn't tell. Presently, I saw the captain—and he was mad. He asked me eagerly, 'Where's the cabin table?' and to hear such a question was a frightful shock. I had just been blown up, you understand, and vibrated with that experience—I wasn't quite sure whether I was alive. Mahon began to stamp with both feet and yelled at him, 'Good God! don't you see the deck's blown out of her?' I found my voice, and stammered out as if conscious of some gross neglect of duty, 'I don't know where the cabin table is.' It was like an absurd dream.

"Do you know what he wanted next? Well, he wanted to trim the yards. Very placidly, and as if lost in thought, he insisted on having the foreyard squared. 'I don't know if there's anybody alive,' said Mahon, almost tearfully. 'Surely,' he said, gently, 'there will be enough left to square the foreyard.'

"The old chap, it seems, was in his own berth winding up the chronometers when the shock sent him spinning. Immediately it occurred to him—as he said afterwards—that the ship had struck something, and ran out into the cabin. There, he saw, the cabin table had vanished somewhere. The deck being blown up, it had fallen down into the lazarette of course. Where we had our breakfast that morning he saw only a great hole in the floor. This appeared to him so awfully mysterious, and impressed him so immensely, that what he saw and heard after he got on deck were mere trifles in comparison. And, mark, he noticed directly the wheel deserted and his bark off her course—and his only thought was to get that miserable, stripped, undecked, smoldering shell of a ship back again with her head pointing at her port of destination. Bangkok! That's what he was after. I tell you this quiet, bowed, bandy-legged, almost deformed little man was immense in the singleness of his idea and in his placid ignorance of our agitation. He motioned us forward with a commanding gesture, and went to take the wheel himself.

"Yes; that was the first thing we did—trim the yards of that wreck! No one was killed, or even disabled, but everyone was more or less hurt. You should have seen them! Some were in rags, with black faces, like coal heavers, like sweeps, and had bullet heads that seemed closely cropped, but were in fact singed to the skin. Others, of the watch below, awakened by being shot out from their collapsing bunks, shivered incessantly, and kept on groaning even as we went about our work. But they all worked. That crew of Liverpool hard cases had in them the right stuff. It's my experience they always have. It is the sea that gives it—the vastness, the loneliness surrounding their dark stolid souls. Ah! Well! We stumbled, we crept, we fell, we barked our shins on the wreckage, we hauled. The masts stood, but we did not know how much they might be charred down below. It was nearly calm, but a long swell ran from the west and made her roll. They might go at any moment. We looked at them with apprehension. One could not foresee which way they would fall.

"Then we retreated aft and looked about us. The deck was a tangle of planks on edge, of planks on end, of splinters, of ruined woodwork. The masts rose from that chaos like big trees above a matted undergrowth. The interstices of that mass of wreckage were full of something whitish, sluggish, stirring—of something that was like a greasy fog. The smoke of the invisible fire was coming up again, was trailing, like a poisonous thick mist in some valley choked with dead wood. Already lazy wisps were beginning to curl upwards amongst the mass of splinters. Here and there a piece of timber stuck upright, resembled a post. Half of a fife rail had been shot through the foresail, and the sky made a patch of glorious blue in the ignobly soiled canvas. A portion of several boards holding together had fallen across the rail, and one end protruded overboard, like a gangway leading upon nothing, like a gangway leading over the deep sea, leading to death—as if inviting us to walk the plank at once and be done with our ridiculous troubles. And still the air, the sky—a ghost, something invisible was hailing the ship.

"Someone had the sense to look over, and there was the helmsman, who had impulsively jumped overboard, anxious to come back. He yelled and swam lustily like a merman, keeping up with the ship. We threw him a rope, and presently he stood amongst us streaming with water and very crestfallen. The captain had surrendered the wheel, and apart, elbow on rail and chin in hand, gazed at the sea wistfully. We asked ourselves, What next? I thought, Now, this is something like. This is great. I wonder what will happen. O youth!

"Suddenly Mahon sighted a steamer far astern. Captain Beard said, 'We   65 may do something with her yet.' We hoisted two flags, which said in the international language of the sea, 'On fire. Want immediate assistance.' The streamer grew bigger rapidly, and by and by spoke with two flags on her foremast, 'I am coming to your assistance.'

"In half an hour she was abreast, to windward, within hail, and rolling slightly, with her engines stopped. We lost our composure, and yelled all together with excitement, 'We've been blown up.' A man in a white helmet, on the bridge, cried, 'Yes! All right! all right!' and he nodded his head, and smiled, and made soothing motions with his hand as though at a lot of frightened children. One of the boats dropped in the water, and walked towards us upon the sea with her long oars. Four Calashes pulled a swinging stroke. This was my first sight of Malay seamen. I've known them since, but what struck me then was their unconcern: they came alongside, and even the bowman standing up and holding to our main chains with the boathook did not deign to lift his head for a glance. I thought people who had been blown up deserved more attention.

"A little man, dry like a chip and agile like a monkey, clambered up. It was the mate of the steamer. He gave one look, and cried, 'O boys—you had better quit!'

"We were silent. He talked apart with the captain for a time—seemed to argue with him. Then they went away together to the steamer.

"When our skiper came back we learned that the steamer was the *Somerville*, Captain Nash, from West Australia to Singapore via Batavia with mails, and that the agreement was she should tow us to Anjer or Batavia, if possible, where we could extinguish the fire by scuttling, and then proceed on our voyage—to Bangkok! The old man seemed excited. 'We will do it yet,' he said to Mahon, fiercely. He shook his fist at the sky. Nobody else said a word.

"At noon the steamer began to tow. She went ahead slim and high, and what was left of the *Judea* followed at the end of seventy fathom of towrope— followed her swiftly like a cloud of smoke with mastheads protruding above. We went aloft to furl the sails. We coughed on the yards, and were careful about the bunts. Do you see the lot of us there, putting a neat furl on the sails of that ship doomed to arrive nowhere? There was not a man who didn't think that at any moment the masts would topple over. From aloft we could not see the ship for smoke, and they worked carefully, passing the gaskets with even turns. 'Harbor furl—aloft there!' cried Mahon from below.

"You understand this? I don't think one of those chaps expected to get down in the usual way. When we did I heard them saying to each other, 'Well, I thought we would come down overboard, in a lump—sticks and all—blame me if I didn't.' 'That's what I was thinking to myself,' would answer wearily another battered and bandaged scarecrow. And, mind, these were men without the drilled-in habit of obedience. To an onlooker they would be a lot of profane scallywags without a redeeming point. What made them do it—what made them obey me when I, thinking consciously how fine it was, made them drop the bunt of the foresail twice to try and do it better? What? They had no professional reputation— no examples, no praise. It wasn't a sense of duty; they all knew well enough how to shirk, and laze, and dodge—when they had a mind to it—and mostly they had. Was it the two pounds ten a month that sent them there? They didn't think their pay half good enough. No; it was something in them, something inborn and subtle

70

and everlasting. I don't say positively that the crew of a French or German merchant-man wouldn't have done it, but I doubt whether it would have been done in the same way. There was a completeness in it, something solid like a principle, and masterful like an instinct—a disclosure of something secret—of that hidden some-thing, that gift of good or evil that makes racial difference, that shapes the fate of nations.

"It was that night at ten that, for the first time since we had been fighting it, we saw the fire. The speed of the towing had fanned the smoldering destruction. A blue gleam appeared forward, shining below the wreck of the deck. It wavered in patches, it seemed to stir and creep like the light of a glowworm. I saw it first, and told Mahon. 'Then the game's up,' he said. 'We had better stop this towing, or she will burst out suddenly fore and aft before we can clear out.' We set up a yell; rang bells to attract their attention; they towed on. At last Mahon and I had to crawl forward and cut the rope with an axe. There was no time to cast off the lashings. Red tongues could be seen licking the wilderness of splinters under our feet as we made our way back to the poop.

"Of course they very soon found out in the steamer that the rope was gone. She gave a loud blast of her whistle, her lights were seen sweeping in a wide circle, she came up ranging close alongside, and stopped. We were all in a tight group on the poop looking at her. Every man had saved a little bundle or a bag. Suddenly a conical flame with a twisted top shot up forward and threw upon the black sea a circle of light, with the two vessels side by side and heaving gently in its center. Captain Beard had been sitting on the gratings still and mute for hours, but now he rose slowly and advanced in front of us, to the mizzen-shrouds. Captain Nash hailed: 'Come along! Look sharp. I have mailbags on board. I will take you and your boats to Singapore.'

" 'Thank you! No! said our skipper. 'We must see the last of the ship.'

" 'I can't stand by any longer,' shouted the other. 'Mails—you know.'

" 'Ay! ay! We are all right.'

" 'Very well! I'll report you in Singapore. . . . Good-by!'

"He waved his hand. Our men dropped their bundles quietly. The steamer moved ahead, and passing out of the circle of light, vanished at once from our sight, dazzled by the fire which burned fiercely. And then I knew that I would see the East first as commander of a small boat. I thought it fine; and the fidelity to the old ship was fine. We should see the last of her. Oh, the glamor of youth! Oh, the fire of it, more dazzling than the flames of the burning ship, throwing a magic light on the wide earth, leaping audaciously to the sky, presently to be quenched by time, more cruel, more pitiless, more bitter than the sea—and like the flames of the burning ship surrounded by an impenetrable night.

"The old man warmed us in his gentle and inflexible way that it was part of our duty to save for the underwriters as much as we could of the ship's gear. Accordingly we went to work aft, while she blazed forward to give us plenty of light. We lugged out a lot of rubbish. What didn't we save? An old barometer fixed with an absurd quantity of screws nearly cost me my life: a sudden rush of smoke came upon me, and I just got away in time. There were various stores, bolts of canvas, coils of rope; the poop looked like a marine bazaar, and the boats were lumbered to the gunwales. One would have thought the old man wanted to take as much as he could of his first command with him. He was very, very quiet, but off his balance evidently. Would you believe it? He wanted to take a length of old stream-cable and a kedge anchor with him in the longboat. We said, 'Ay, ay, sir,' deferentially, and on the quiet let the things slip overboard. The heavy medicine chest went that way, two bags of green coffee, tins of paint—fancy, paint!—a whole lot of things. Then I was ordered with two hands into the boats to make a stowage and get them ready against the time it would be proper for us to leave the ship.

"We put everything straight, stepped the longboat's mast for our skipper, 80 who was to take charge of her, and I was not sorry to sit down for a moment. My face felt raw, every limb ached as if broken, I was aware of all my ribs, and would have sworn to a twist in the backbone. The boats, fast astern, lay in a deep shadow, and all around I could see the circle of the sea lighted by the fire. A gigantic flame arose forward straight and clear. It flared fierce, with noises like the whirr of wings, with rumbles as of thunder. There were cracks, detonations, and from the cone of flame the sparks flew upwards, as man is born to trouble, to leaky ships, and to ships that burn.

"What bothered me was that the ship, lying broadside to the swell and to such wind as there was—a mere breath—the boats would not keep astern where they were safe, but persisted, in a pigheaded way boats have, in getting under the counter and then swinging alongside. They were knocking about dangerously and coming near the flame, while the ship rolled on them, and, of course, there was always the danger of the masts going over the side at any moment. I and my two boatkeepers kept them off as best we could, with oars and boathooks; but to be constantly at it became exasperating, since there was no reason why we should not leave at once. We could not see those on board, nor could we imagine what caused the delay. The boatkeepers were swearing feebly, and I had not only my share of the work but also had to keep at it two men who showed a constant inclination to lay themselves down and let things slide.

"At last I hailed, 'On deck there,' and somone looked over. 'We're ready here,' I said. The head disappeared, and very soon popped up again. 'The captain says, All right, sir, and to keep the boats well clear of the ship.'

"Half an hour passed. Suddenly there was a frightful racket, rattle, clanking of chain, hiss of water, and millions of sparks flew up into the shivering column of smoke that stood leaning slightly above the ship. The catheads had burned away, and the two red-hot anchors had gone to the bottom, tearing out after them two hundred fathom of red-hot chain. The ship trembled, the mass of flame swayed as if ready to collapse, and the fore-topgallant mast fell. It darted down like an arrow of fire, shot under, and instantly leaping up within an oar's length of the boats, floated quietly, very black on the luminous sea. I hailed the deck again. After some time a man in an unexpectedly cheerful but also muffled tone, as though he had been trying to speak with his mouth shut, informed me, 'Coming directly, sir,' and vanished. For a long time I heard nothing but the whirr and roar of the fire. There were also whistling sounds. The boats jumped, tugged at the painters, ran at each other playfully, knocked their sides together, or, do what we would, swung in a bunch against the ship's side. I couldn't stand it any longer, and swarming up a rope, clambered aboard over the stern.

"It was as bright as day. Coming up like this, the sheet of fire facing me was a terrifying sight, and the heat seemed hardly bearable at first. On a settee cushion dragged out of the cabin Captain Beard, his legs drawn up and one arm under his head, slept with the light playing on him. Do you know what the rest were busy about? They were sitting on deck right aft, round an open case, eating bread and cheese and drinking bottled stout.

"On the background of flames twisting in fierce tongues above their heads   85 they seemed at home like salamanders, and looked like a band of desperate pirates. The fire sparkled in the whites of their eyes, gleamed on patches of white skin seen through the torn shirts. Each had the marks as of a battle about him—bandaged heads, tied-up arms, a strip of dirty rag round a knee—and each man had a bottle between his legs and a chunk of cheese in his hand. Mahon got up. With his handsome and disreputable head, his hooked profile, his long white beard, and with an uncorked bottle in his hand, he resembled one of those reckless sea robbers of old making merry amidst violence and disaster. 'The last meal on board,' he explained solemnly. 'We had nothing to eat all day, and it was no use leaving all this.' He flourished the bottle and indicated the sleeping skipper. 'He said he couldn't swallow anything, so I got him to lie down,' he went on; and as I stared, 'I don't know whether your are aware, young fellow, the man had no sleep to speak of for days—and there will be dam' little sleep in the boats.' 'There will be no boats by and by if you fool about much longer,' I said, indignantly. I walked up to the skipper and shook him by the shoulder. At last he opened his eyes, but did not move. 'Time to leave her, sir,' I said quietly.

"He got up painfully, looked at the flames, at the sea sparkling round the ship, and black, black as ink farther away; he looked at the stars shining dim through a thin veil of smoke in a sky black, black as Erebus.

"'Youngest first,' he said.

"And the ordinary seaman, wiping his mouth with the back of his hand, got up, clambered over the taffrail, and vanished. Others followed. One, on the point of going over, stopped short to drain his bottle, and with a great swing of his arm flung it at the fire. 'Take this!' he cried.

"The skipper lingered disconsolately, and we left him to commune alone for a while with his first command. Then I went up again and brought him away at last. It was time. The ironwork on the poop was hot to the touch.

"Then the painter of the longboat was cut, and the three boats, tied together,   90 drifted clear of the ship. It was just sixteen hours after the explosion when we abandoned her. Mahon had charge of the second boat, and I had the smallest— the fourteen-foot thing. The longboat would have taken the lot of us; but the skipper said we must save as much property as we could—for the underwriters— and so I got my first command. I had two men with me, a bag of biscuits, a few tins of meat, and a breaker of water. I was ordered to keep close to the longboat, that in case of bad weather we might be taken into her.

"And do you know what I thought? I thought I would part company as soon as I could. I wanted to have my first command all to myself. I wasn't going to sail in a squadron if there were a chance for independent cruising. I would make land by myself. I would beat the other boats. Youth! All youth! The silly, charming, beautiful youth.

"But we did not make a start at once. We must see the last of the ship. And so the boats drifted about that night, heaving and setting on the swell. The men dozed, waked, sighed, groaned. I looked at the burning ship.

"Between the darkness of earth and heaven she was burning fiercely upon a disc of purple sea shot by the blood-red play of gleams; upon a disc of water glittering and sinister. A high, clear flame, an immense and lonely flame, ascended from the ocean, and from its summit the black smoke poured continuously at the sky. She burned furiously; mournful and imposing like a funeral pile kindled in the night, surrounded by the sea, watched over by the stars. A magnificent death had come like a grace, like a gift, like a reward to that old ship at the end of her laborious days. The surrender of her weary ghost to the keeping of stars and sea was stirring like the sight of a glorious triumph. The masts fell just before daybreak, and for a moment there was a burst and turmoil of sparks that seemed to fill with flying fire the night patient and watchful, the vast night lying silent upon the sea. At daylight she was only a charred shell, floating still under a cloud of smoke and bearing a glowing mass of coal within.

"Then the oars were got out, and the boats forming in a line moved round her remains as if in procession—the longboat leading. As we pulled across her stern a slim dart of fire shot out viciously at us, and suddenly she went down, head first, in a great hiss of steam. The unconsumed stern was the last to sink; but the paint had gone, had cracked, had peeled off, and there were no letters, there was no word, no stubborn device that was like her soul, to flash at the rising sun her creed and her name.

"We made our way north. A breeze sprang up, and about noon all the boats came together for the last time. I had no mast or sail in mine, but I made a mast out of a spare oar and hoisted a boat-awning for a sail, with a boathook for a yard. She was certainly over-masted, but I had the satisfaction of knowing that with the wind aft I could beat the other two. I had to wait for them. Then we all had a look at the captain's chart, and, after a sociable meal of hard bread and water, got our last instructions. These were simple: steer north, and keep together as much as possible. 'Be careful with that jury-rig, Marlow,' said the captain: and Mahon, as I sailed proudly past his boat, wrinkled his curved nose and hailed, 'You will sail that ship of yours under water, if you don't look out, young fellow.' He was a malicious old man—and may the deep sea where he sleeps now rock him gently, rock him tenderly to the end of time!

"Before sunset a thick rain-squall passed over the two boats, which were far astern, and that was the last I saw of them for a time. Next day I sat steering my cockleshell—my first command—with nothing but water and sky round me. I did sight in the afternoon the upper sails of a ship far away, but said nothing, and my men did not notice her. You see I was afraid she might be homeward bound, and I had no mind to turn back from the portals of the East. I was steering for Java—another blessed name—like Bangkok, you know. I steered many days.

"I need not tell you what it is to be knocking about in an open boat. I remember nights and days of calm, when we pulled, we pulled, and the boat seemed to stand still, as if bewitched within the circle of the sea horizon. I remember the heat, the deluge of rain-squalls that kept us baling for dear life (but filled our water cask), and I remember sixteen hours on end with a mouth dry as a cinder and a steering oar over the stern to keep my first command head on to a breaking sea. I did not know how good a man I was till then. I remember the drawn faces, the dejected figures of my two men, and I remember my youth and the feeling that will never come back any more—the feeling that I could last forever, outlast the sea, the earth, and all men; the deceitful feeling that lures us on to joys, to perils, to love, to vain effort—to death; the triumphant conviction of strength, the heat of life in the handful of dust, the glow in the heart that with every year grows dim, grows cold, grows small, and expires—and expires, too soon, too soon—before life itself.

"And this is how I see the East. I have seen its secret places and have looked into its very soul; but now I see it always from a small boat, a high outline of mountains, blue and afar in the morning; like faint mist at noon; a jagged wall of purple at sunset. I have the feel of the oar in my hand, the vision of a scorching blue sea in my eyes. And I see a bay, a wide bay, smooth as glass and polished like ice, shimmering in the dark. A red light burns far off upon the gloom of the land, and the night is soft and warm. We drag at the oars with aching arms, and suddenly a puff of wind, a puff faint and tepid and laden with strange odors of blossoms, of aromatic wood, comes out of the still night—the first sigh of the East on my face. That I can never forget. It was impalpable and enslaving, like a charm, like a whispered promise of mysterious delight.

"We had been pulling this finishing spell for eleven hours. Two pulled, and he whose turn it was to rest sat at the tiller. We had made out the red light in that bay and steered for it, guessing it must mark some small coasting port. We passed two vessels, outlandish and high-sterned, sleeping at anchor, and, approaching the light, now very dim, ran the boat's nose against the end of a jutting wharf. We were blind with fatigue. My men dropped the oars and fell off the thwarts as if dead. I made fast to a pile. A current rippled softly. The scented obscurity of the shore was grouped into vast masses, a density of colossal clumps of vegetation, probably—mute and fantastic shapes. And at their foot the semicircle of a beach gleamed faintly, like an illusion. There was not a light, not a stir, not a sound. The mysterious East faced me, perfumed like a flower, silent like death, dark like a grave.

"And I sat weary beyond expression, exulting like a conqueror, sleepless   100
and entranced as if before a profound, a fateful enigma.

"A splashing of oars, a measured dip reverberating on the level of water, intensified by the silence of the shore into loud claps, made me jump up. A boat, a European boat, was coming in. I invoked the name of the dead; I hailed: '*Judea* ahoy!' A thin shout answered.

"It was the captain. I had beaten the flagship by three hours, and I was glad to hear the old man's voice again, tremulous and tired. 'Is it you, Marlow?' 'Mind the end of that jetty, sir,' I cried.

"He approached cautiously, and brought up with the deep-sea lead line which we had saved—for the underwriters. I eased my painter and fell alongside. He sat, a broken figure at the stern, wet with dew, his hands clasped in his lap. His men were asleep already. 'I had a terrible time of it,' he murmured. 'Mahon is behind—not very far.' We conversed in whispers, in low whispers, as if afraid to wake up the land. Guns, thunder, earthquakes would not have awakened the men just then.

"Looking round as we talked, I saw away at sea a bright light traveling in the night. 'There's a steamer passing the bay,' I said. She was not passing, she was entering, and she even came close and anchored. 'I wish,' said the old man, 'you would find out whether she is English. Perhaps they could give us a passage somewhere.' He seemed nervously anxious. So by dint of punching and kicking I started one of my men into a state of somnambulism, and giving him an oar, took another and pulled towards the lights of the steamer.

"There was a murmur of voices in her, metallic hollow clangs of the engine   105
room, footsteps on the deck. Her ports shone, round like dilated eyes. Shapes moved about, and there was a shadowy man high up on the bridge. He heard my oars.

"And then, before I could open my lips, the East spoke to me, but it was in a Western voice. A torrent of words was poured into the enigmatical, the fateful silence; outlandish, angry words, mixed with words and even whole sentences of good English, less strange but even more surprising. The voice swore and cursed violently; it riddled the solemn peace of the bay by a volley of abuse. It began by calling me Pig, and from that went crescendo into unmentionable adjectives— in English. The man up there raged aloud in two languages, and with a sincerity in his fury that almost convinced me I had, in some way, sinned against the harmony of the universe. I could hardly see him, but began to think he would work himself into a fit.

"Suddenly he ceased, and I could hear him snorting and blowing like a porpoise. I said:

" 'What steamer is this, pray?'

" 'Eh? What's this? And who are you?'

" 'Castaway crew of an English bark burnt at sea. We came here tonight. I   110
am the second mate. The captain is in the longboat, and wishes to know if you would give us a passage somewhere.'

" 'Oh, my goodness! I say. . . . This is the *Celestial* from Singapore on her return trip. I'll arrange with your captain in the morning, . . . and, . . . I say, . . . did you hear me just now?'

" 'I should think the whole bay heard you.'

" 'I thought you were a shoreboat. Now, look here—this infernal lazy scoundrel of a caretaker has gone to sleep again—curse him. The light is out, and I nearly ran foul of the end of this damned jetty. This is the third time he plays me this trick. Now, I ask you, can anybody stand this kind of thing? It's enough to drive a man out of his mind. I'll report him. . . . I'll get the Assistant Resident to give him the sack, by—! See—there's no light. It's out, isn't it? I take you to witness the light's out. There should be a light, you know. A red light on the—'

" 'There was a light,' I said, mildly.

" 'But it's out, man! What's the use of talking like this? You can see for   115
yourself it's out—don't you? If you had to take a valuable steamer along this Godforsaken coast you would want a light, too. I'll kick him from end to end of his miserable wharf. You'll see if I don't. I will—'

" 'So I may tell my captain you'll take us?' I broke in.

" 'Yes, I'll take you. Good night,' he said, brusquely.

"I pulled back, made fast again to the jetty, and then went to sleep at last. I had faced the silence of the East. I had heard some of its language. But when I opened my eyes again the silence was as complete as though it had never been broken. I was lying in a flood of light, and the sky had never looked so far, so high, before. I opened my eyes and lay without moving.

"And then I saw the men of the East—they were looking at me. The whole length of the jetty was full of people. I saw brown, bronze, yellow faces, the black eyes, the glitter, the color of an Eastern crowd. And all these beings stared without a murmur, without a sigh, without a movement. They stared down at the boats, at the sleeping men who at night had come to them from the sea. Nothing moved. The fronds of palms stood still against the sky. Not a branch stirred along the shore, and the brown roofs of hidden houses peeped through the green foliage, through the big leaves that hung shining and still like leaves forged of heavy metal. This was the East of the ancient navigators, so old, so mysterious, resplendent and somber, living and unchanged, full of danger and promise. And these were the men. I sat up suddenly. A wave of movement passed through the crowd from end to end, passed along the heads, swayed the bodies, ran along the jetty like a ripple on the water, like a breath of wind on a field—and all was still again. I see it now—the wide sweep of the bay, the glittering sands, the wealth of green infinite and varied, the sea blue like the sea of a dream, the crowd of attentive faces, the blaze of vivid color—the water reflecting it all, the curve of the shore, the jetty, the high-sterned outlandish craft floating still, and the three boats with the tired men from the West sleeping, unconscious of the land and the people and of the violence of sunshine. They slept thrown across the thwarts, curled on bottomboards, in the careless attitudes of death. The head of the old skipper, leaning back in the stern of the longboat, had fallen on his breast, and he looked as though he would never wake. Farther out old Mahon's face was upturned to the sky, with the long white beard spread out on his breast, as though he had been shot where he sat at the tiller; and a man, all in a heap in the bows of the boat, slept with both arms embracing the stemhead and with his cheek laid on the gunwale. The East looked at them without a sound.

"I have known its fascination since; I have seen the mysterious shores, the   120
still water, the lands of brown nations, where a stealthy Nemesis lies in wait, pursues, overtakes so many of the conquering race, who are proud of their wisdom, of their knowledge, of their strength. But for me all the East is contained in that vision of my youth. It is all in that moment when I opened my young eyes on it. I came upon it from a tussle with the sea—and I was young—and I saw it looking at me. And this is all that is left of it! Only a moment; a moment of strength, of romance, of glamor—of youth! . . . A flick of sunshine upon a strange shore, the time to remember, the time for a sigh, and—good-by!—Night—Good-by . . . !"

He drank.

"Ah! The good old time—the good old time. Youth and the sea. Glamor and the sea! The good, strong sea, the salt, bitter sea, that could whisper to you and roar at you and knock your breath out of you."

He drank again.

"By all that's wonderful it is the sea, I believe, the sea itself—or is it youth alone? Who can tell? But you here—you all had something out of life: money, love—whatever one gets on shore—and, tell me, wasn't that the best time, that time when we were young at sea, young and had nothing, on the sea that gives nothing except hard knocks—and sometimes a chance to feel your strength—that only—that you all regret?"

And we all nodded at him: the man of finance, the man of accounts, the   125
man of law, we all nodded at him over the polished table that like a still sheet of brown water reflected our faces, lined, wrinkled; our faces marked by toil, by decep-

tions, by success, by love; our weary eyes looking still, looking always, looking anxiously for something out of life, that while it is expected is already gone—has passed unseen, in a sigh, in a flash—together with the youth, with the strength, with the romance of illusions.

LANGSTON HUGHES (1902–1967)

Slave on the Block   (*1938*)

They were people who went in for Negroes—Michael and Anne—the Carraways. But not in the social-service, philanthropic sort of way, no. They saw no use in helping a race that was already too charming and naive and lovely for words. Leave them unspoiled and just enjoy them, Michael and Anne felt. So they went in for the Art of Negroes—the dancing that had such jungle life about it, the songs that were so simple and fervent, the poetry that was so direct, so real. They never tried to influence that art, they only bought it and raved over it, and copied it. For they were artists, too.

In their collection they owned some Covarrubias originals. Of course Covarrubias wasn't a Negro, but how he caught the darky spirit! They owned all the Robeson records and all the Bessie Smith. And they had a manuscript of Countee Cullen's. They saw all the plays with or about Negroes, read all the books, and adored the Hall Johnson Singers. They had met Doctor DuBois, and longed to meet Carl Van Vechten. Of course they knew Harlem like their own backyard, that is, all the speakeasies and night clubs and dance halls, from the Cotton Club and the ritzy joints where Negroes couldn't go themselves, down to places like the Hot Dime, where white folks couldn't get in—unless they knew the man. (And tipped heavily.)

They were acquainted with lots of Negroes, too—but somehow the Negroes didn't seem to like them very much. Maybe the Carraways gushed over them too soon. Or maybe they looked a little like poor white folks, although they were really quite well off. Or maybe they tried too hard to make friends, dark friends, and the dark friends suspected something. Or perhaps their house in the Village was too far from Harlem, or too hard to find, being back in one of those queer and expensive little side streets that had once been alleys before the art invasion came. Anyway, occasionally, a furtive Negro might accept their invitation for tea, or cocktails; and sometimes a lesser Harlem celebrity or two would decorate their rather slow parties; but one seldom came back for more. As much as they loved Negroes, Negroes didn't seem to love Michael and Anne.

But they were blessed with a wonderful colored cook and maid—until she took sick and died in her room in their basement. And then the most marvellous ebony boy walked into their life, a boy as black as all the Negroes they'd ever known put together.

"He *is* the jungle," said Anne when she saw him.

"He's 'I Couldn't Hear Nobody Pray,' " said Michael.

For Anne thought in terms of pictures: she was a painter. And Michael thought in terms of music: he was a composer for the piano. And they had a most wonderful idea of painting pictures and composing music that went together, and then having a joint "concert-exhibition" as they would call it. Her pictures and his music. The Carraways, a sonata and a picture, a fugue and a picture. It would be lovely, and such a novelty, people would have to like it. And many of their things would be Negro. Anne had painted their maid six times. And Michael had composed several themes based on the spirituals, and on Louis Armstrong's jazz. Now here was this ebony boy. The essence in the flesh.

They had nearly missed the boy. He had come, when they were out, to gather up the things the cook had left, and take them to her sister in Jersey. It seems that he was the late cook's nephew. The new colored maid had let him in and given him the two suitcases of poor dear Emma's belongings, and he was on his way to the Subway. That is, he was in the hall, going out just as the Carraways, Michael and Anne, stepped in. They could hardly see the boy, it being dark in the hall, and he being dark, too.

"Hello," they said. "Is this Emma's nephew?"

"Yes'm," said the maid. "Yes'm."   10

"Well, come in," said Anne, "and let us see you. We loved your aunt so much. She was the best cook we ever had."

"You don't know where I could get a job, do you?" said the boy. This took Michael and Anne back a bit, but they rallied at once. So charming and naive to ask right away for what he wanted.

Anne burst out, "You know, I think I'd like to paint you."

Michael said, "Oh, I say now, that would be lovely! He's so utterly Negro."

The boy grinned.   15

Anne said, "Could you come back tomorrow?"

And the boy said, "Yes, indeed. I sure could."

The upshot of it was that they hired him. They hired him to look after the garden, which was just about as big as Michael's grand piano—only a little square behind the house. You know those Village gardens. Anne sometimes painted it. And occasionally they set the table there for four on a spring evening. Nothing grew in the garden really, practically nothing. But the boy said he could plant things. And they had to have some excuse to hire him.

The boy's name was Luther. He had come from the South to his relatives in Jersey, and had had only one job since he got there, shining shoes for a Greek in Elizabeth. But the Greek fired him because the boy wouldn't give half his tips over to the proprietor.

"I never heard of a job where I had to pay the boss, instead of the boss   20
paying me," said Luther. "Not till I got here."

"And then what did you do?" said Anne.

"Nothing. Been looking for a job for the last four months."

"Poor boy," said Michael; "poor, dear boy."

"Yes," said Anne. "You must be hungry." And they called the cook to give him something to eat.

Luther dug around in the garden a little bit that first day, went out and   25
bought some seeds, came back and ate some more. They made a place for him to sleep in the basement by the furnace. And the next day Anne started to paint him, after she'd bought the right colors.

"He'll be good company for Mattie," they said. "She claims she's afraid to stay alone at night when we're out, so she leaves." They suspected, though, that Mattie just liked to get up to Harlem. And they thought right. Mattie was not as settled as she looked. Once out, with the Savoy open until three in the morning, why come home? That was the way Mattie felt.

In fact, what happened was that Mattie showed Luther where the best and cheapest hot spots in Harlem were located. Luther hadn't even set foot in Harlem before, living twenty-eight miles away, as he did, in Jersey, and being a kind of quiet boy. But the second night he was there Mattie said, "Come on, let's go. Working for white folks all day, I'm tired. They needn't think I was made to answer telephones all night." So out they went.

Anne noticed that most mornings Luther would doze almost as soon as she sat him down to pose, so she eventually decided to paint Luther asleep. "The Sleeping Negro," she would call it. Dear, natural childlike people, they would sleep anywhere they wanted to. Anyway, asleep, he kept still and held the pose.

And he *was* an adorable Negro. Not tall, but with a splendid body. And a slow and lively smile that lighted up his black, black face, for his teeth were very white, and his eyes, too. Most effective in oil and canvas. Better even than Emma had been. Anne could stare at him at leisure when he was asleep. One day she decided to paint him nude, or at least half nude. A slave picture, that's what she would do. The market at New Orleans for a background. And call it "The Boy on the Block."

So one morning when Luther settled down in his sleeping pose, Anne said, "No," she had finished that picture. She wanted to paint him now representing to the full the soul and sorrow of his people. She wanted to paint him as a slave about to be sold. And since slaves in warm climates had no clothes, would he please take off his shirt.

Luther smiled a sort of embarrassed smile and took off his shirt.

"Your undershirt, too," said Anne. But it turned out that he had on a union suit, so he had to go out and change altogether. He came back and mounted the box that Anne said would serve just then for a slave block, and she began to sketch. Before luncheon Michael came in, and went into rhapsodies over Luther on the box without a shirt, about to be sold into slavery. He said he must put him into music right now. And he went to the piano and began to play something that sounded like Deep River in the jaws of a dog, but Michael said it was a modern slave plaint, 1850 in terms of 1933. Vieux Carré° remembered on 135th Street, Slavery in the Cotton Club.

Anne said, "It's too marvellous!" And they painted and played till dark, with rest periods in between for Luther. Then they all knocked off for dinner. Anne and Michael went out later to one of Lew Leslie's new shows. And Luther and Mattie said, "Thank God!" and got dressed up for Harlem.

Funny, they didn't like the Carraways. They treated them nice and paid them well. "But they're too strange," said Mattie, "they makes me nervous."

"They is mighty funny," Luther agreed.

They didn't understand the vagaries of white folks, neither Luther nor Mattie, and they didn't want to be bothered trying.

Vieux Carré: the old quarter of New Orleans.

"I does my work," said Mattie. "After that I don't want to be painted, or asked to sing songs, nor nothing like that."

The Carraways often asked Luther to sing, and he sang. He knew a lot of southern worksongs and reels, and spirituals and ballads.

> *"Dear Ma, I'm in hard luck:*
> *Three days since I et,*
> *And the stamp on this letter's*
> *Gwine to put me in debt."*

The Carraways allowed him to neglect the garden altogether. About all Luther did was pose and sing. And he got tired of that.

Indeed, both Luther and Mattie became a bit difficult to handle as time went on. The Carraways blamed it on Mattie. She had got hold of Luther. She was just simply spoiling a nice simple young boy. She was old enough to know better. Mattie was in love with Luther.   40

As least, he slept with her. The Carraways discovered this one night about one o'clock when they went to wake Luther up (the first time they'd ever done such a thing) and ask him if he wouldn't sing his own marvellous version of John Henry for a man who had just come from Saint Louis and was sailing for Paris tomorrow. But Luther wasn't in his own bed by the furnace. There was a light in Mattie's room, so Michael knocked softly. Mattie said, "Who's that?" And Michael poked his head in, and here were Luther and Mattie in bed together!

Of course, Anne condoned them. "It's so simple and natural for Negroes to make love." But Mattie, after all, was forty if she was a day. And Luther was only a kid. Besides Anne thought that Luther had been ever so much nicer when he first came than he was now. But from so many nights at the Savoy, he had become a marvellous dancer, and he was teaching Anne the Lindy Hop to Cab Calloway's records. Besides, her picture of "The Boy on the Block" wasn't anywhere near done. And he did take pretty good care of the furnace. So they kept him. At least, Anne kept him, although Michael said he was getting a little bored with the same Negro always in the way.

For Luther had grown a bit familiar lately. He smoked up all their cigarettes, drank their wine, told jokes on them to their friends, and sometimes even came upstairs singing and walking about the house when the Carraways had guests in who didn't share their enthusiasm for Negroes, natural or otherwise.

Luther and Mattie together were a pair. They quite frankly lived with one another now. Well, let that go. Anne and Michael prided themselves on being different; artists, you know, and liberal-minded people—maybe a little scatter-brained, but then (secretly, they felt) that came from genius. They were not ordinary people, bothering about the liberties of others. Certainly, the last thing they would do would be to interfere with the delightful simplicity of Negroes.

But Mattie must be giving Luther money and buying him clothes. He was really dressing awfully well. And on her Thursday afternoons off she would come back loaded down with packages. As far as the Carraways could tell, they were all for Luther.   45

And sometimes there were quarrels drifting up from the basement. And often, all too often, Mattie had moods. Then Luther would have moods. And it was pretty awful having two dark and glowering people around the house. Anne couldn't paint and Michael couldn't play.

One day, when she hadn't seen Luther for three days, Anne called downstairs and asked him if he wouldn't please come up and take off his shirt and get on the box. The picture was almost done. Luther came dragging his feet upstairs and humming:

> *"Before I'd be a slave*
> *I'd be buried in ma grave*
> *And go home to my Jesus*
> *And be free."*

And that afternoon he let the furnace go almost out.

That was the state of things when Michael's mother (whom Anne had never liked) arrived from Kansas City to pay them a visit. At once neither Mattie nor Luther liked her either. She was a mannish old lady, big and tall, and inclined to be bossy. Mattie, however, did spruce up her service, cooked delicious things, and treated Mrs. Carraway with a great deal more respect than she did Anne.

"I never play with servants," Mrs. Carraway had said to Michael, and Mattie must have heard her.

But Luther, he was worse than ever. Not that he did anything wrong, Anne   50
thought, but the way he did things! For instance, he didn't need to sing now all the time, especially since Mrs. Carraway had said she didn't like singing. And certainly not songs like "You Rascal, You."

But all things end! With the Carraways and Luther it happened like this: One forenoon, quite without a shirt (for he expected to pose) Luther came sauntering through the library to change the flowers in the vase. He carried red roses. Mrs. Carraway was reading her morning scripture from the Health and Life.

"Oh, good morning," said Luther. "How long are you gonna stay in this house?"

"I never liked familiar Negroes," said Mrs. Carraway, over her nose glasses.

"Huh!" said Luther. "That's too bad! I never liked poor white folks."

Mrs. Carraway screamed, a short, loud, dignified scream. Michael came run-   55
ning in bathrobe and pyjamas. Mrs. Carraway grew tall. There was a scene. Luther talked. Michael talked. Anne appeared.

"Never, never, never," said Mrs. Carraway, "have I suffered such impudence from servants—and a nigger servant—in my own son's house."

"Mother, Mother, Mother," said Michael. "Be calm. I'll discharge him." He turned on the nonchalant Luther. "Go!" he said, pointing toward the door. "Go, go!"

"Michael," Anne cried, "I haven't finished 'The Slave on the Block.' " Her husband looked nonplussed. For a moment he breathed deeply.

"Either he goes or I go," said Mrs. Carraway, firm as a rock.

"He goes," said Michael with strength from his mother.   6

"Oh!" cried Anne. She looked at Luther. His black arms were full of roses he had brought to put in the vases. He had on no shirt. "Oh!" His body was ebony.

"Don't worry 'bout me!" said Luther. "I'll go."

"Yes, we'll go," boomed Mattie from the doorway, who had come up from below, fat and belligerent. "We've stood enough foolery from you white folks! Yes, we'll go. Come on, Luther."

What could she mean, "stood enough"? What had they done to them, Anne and Michael wondered. They had tried to be kind. "Oh!"

"Sneaking around knocking on our door at night," Mattie went on. "Yes, we'll go. Pay us! Pay us! Pay us!" So she remembered the time they had come for Luther at night. That was it.   65

"I'll pay you," said Michael. He followed Mattie out.

Anne looked at her black boy.

"Good-bye," Luther said. "You fix the vases."

He handed her his armful of roses, glanced impudently at old Mrs. Carraway and grinned—grinned that wide, beautiful, white-toothed grin that made Anne say when she first saw him, "He looks like the jungle." Grinned, and disappeared in the dark hall, with no shirt on his back.

"Oh," Anne moaned distressfully, "my 'Boy on the Block'!"   70

"Huh!" snorted Mrs. Carraway.

FRANZ KAFKA (1883–1924)

A Hunger Artist   (1922)

Translated by Willa and Edwin Muir.

During these last decades the interest in professional fasting has markedly diminished. It used to pay very well to stage such great performances under one's own management, but today that is quite impossible. We live in a different world now. At one time the whole town took a lively interest in the hunger artist; from day to day of his fast the excitement mounted; everybody wanted to see him at least once a day; there were people who bought season tickets for the last few days and sat from morning till night in front of his small barred cage; even in the nighttime there were visiting hours, when the whole effect was heightened by torch flares; on fine days the cage was set out in the open air, and then it was the children's special treat to see the hunger artist; for their elders he was often just a joke that happened to be in fashion, but the children stood openmouthed, holding each other's hands for greater security, marveling at him as he sat there pallid in black tights, with his ribs sticking out so prominently, not even on a seat but down among straw on the ground, sometimes giving a courteous nod, answering questions with a constrained smile, or perhaps stretching an arm through the bars so that one might feel how thin it was, and then again withdrawing deep into himself, paying no attention to anyone or anything, not even to the all-important striking of the clock that was the only piece of furniture in his cage, but merely staring into vacancy with half-shut eyes, now and then taking a sip from a tiny glass of water to moisten his lips.

Besides casual onlookers there were also relays of permanent watchers selected by the public, usually butchers, strangely enough, and it was their task to watch the hunger artist day and night, three of them at a time, in case he should

have some secret recourse to nourishment. This was nothing but a formality, insti-
tuted to reassure the masses, for the initiates knew well enough that during his
fast the artist would never in any circumstances, not even under forcible compulsion,
swallow the smallest morsel of food; the honor of his profession forbade it. Not
every watcher, of course, was capable of understanding this, there were often groups
of night watchers who were very lax in carrying out their duties and deliberately
huddled together in a retired corner to play cards with great absorption, obviously
intending to give the hunger artist the chance of a little refreshment, which they
supposed he could draw from some private hoard. Nothing annoyed the artist
more than such watchers; they made him miserable; they made his fast seem unendurable; sometimes he mastered his feebleness sufficiently to sing during their
watch for as long as he could keep going, to show them how unjust their suspicions
were. But that was of little use; they only wondered at his cleverness in being
able to fill his mouth even while singing. Much more to his taste were the watchers
who sat close up to the bars, who were not content with the dim night lighting
of the hall but focused him in the full glare of the electric pocket torch given
them by the impresario. The harsh light did not trouble him at all, in any case
he could never sleep properly, and he could always drowse a little, whatever the
light, at any hour, even when the hall was thronged with noisy onlookers. He
was quite happy at the prospect of spending a sleepless night with such watchers;
he was ready to exchange jokes with them, to tell them stories out of his nomadic
life, anything at all to keep them awake and demonstrate to them again that he
had no eatables in his cage and that he was fasting as not one of them could
fast. But his happiest moment was when the morning came and an enormous
breakfast was brought them, at his expense, on which they flung themselves with
the keen appetite of healthy men after a weary night of wakefulness. Of course
there were people who argued that this breakfast was an unfair attempt to bribe
the watchers, but that was going rather too far, and when they were invited to
take on a night's vigil without a breakfast, merely for the sake of the cause, they
made themselves scarce, although they stuck stubbornly to their suspicions.

   Such suspicions, anyhow, were a necessary accompaniment to the profession
of fasting. No one could possibly watch the hunger artist continuously, day and
night, and so no one could produce first-hand evidence that the fast had really
been rigorous and continuous; only the artist himself could know that, he was
therefore bound to be the sole completely satisfied spectator of his own fast. Yet
for other reasons he was never satisfied; it was not perhaps mere fasting that had
brought him to such skeleton thinness that many people had regretfully to keep
away from his exhibitions, because the sight of him was too much for them, perhaps
it was dissatisfaction with himself that had worn him down. For he alone knew,
what no other initiate knew, how easy it was to fast. It was the easiest thing in
the world. He made no secret of this, yet people did not believe him, at the best
they set him down as modest; most of them, however, thought he was out for
publicity or else was some kind of cheat who found it easy to fast because he
had discovered a way of making it easy, and then had the impudence to admit
the fact, more or less. He had to put up with all that, and in the course of time
had got used to it, but his inner dissatisfaction always rankled, and never yet,
after any term of fasting—this must be granted to his credit—had he left the cage
of his own free will. The longest period of fasting was fixed by his impresario at

forty days, beyond that term he was not allowed to go, not even in great cities, and there was good reason for it, too. Experience had proved that for about forty days the interest of the public could be stimulated by a steadily increasing pressure of advertisement, but after that the town began to lose interest, sympathetic support began notably to fall off; there were of course local variations as between one town and another or one country and another, but as a general rule forty days marked the limit. So on the fortieth day the flower-bedecked cage was opened, enthusiastic spectators filled the hall, a military band played, two doctors entered the cage to measure the results of the fast, which were announced through a megaphone, and finally two young ladies appeared, blissful at having been selected for the honor, to help the hunger artist down the few steps leading to a small table on which was spread a carefully chosen invalid repast. And at this very moment the artist always turned stubborn. True, he would entrust his bony arms to the outstretched helping hands of the ladies bending over him, but stand up he would not. Why stop fasting at this particular moment, after forty days of it? He had held out for a long time, an illimitably long time; why stop now, when he was in his best fasting form, or rather, not yet quite in his best fasting form? Why should he be cheated of the fame he would get for fasting longer, for being not only the record hunger artist of all time, which presumably he was already, but for beating his own record by a performance beyond human imagination, since he felt that there were no limits to his capacity for fasting? His public pretended to admire him so much, why should it have so little patience with him; if he could endure fasting longer, why shouldn't the public endure it? Besides, he was tired, he was comfortable sitting in the straw, and now he was supposed to lift himself to his full height and go down to a meal the very thought of which gave him a nausea that only the presence of the ladies kept him from betraying, and even that with an effort. And he looked up into the eyes of the ladies who were apparently so friendly and in reality so cruel, and shook his head, which felt too heavy on its strengthless neck. But then there happened yet again what always happened. The impresario came forward, without a word—for the band made speech impossible—lifted his arms in the air above the artist, as if inviting Heaven to look down upon its creature here in the straw, this suffering martyr, which indeed he was, although in quite another sense; grasped him around the emaciated waist, with exaggerated caution, so that the frail condition he was in might be appreciated; and committed him to the care of the blenching ladies, not without secretly giving him a shaking so that his legs and body tottered and swayed. The artist now submitted completely; his head lolled on his breast as if it had landed there by chance; his body was hollowed out; his legs in a spasm of self-preservation clung close to each other at the knees, yet scraped on the ground as if it were not really solid ground, as if they were only trying to find solid ground; and the whole weight of his body, a featherweight after all, relapsed onto one of the ladies, who, looking around for help and panting a little—this post of honor was not at all what she had expected it to be—first stretched her neck as far as she could to keep her face at least free from contact with the artist, then finding this impossible, and her more fortunate companion not coming to her aid but merely holding extended in her own trembling hand the little bunch of knucklebones that was the artist's, to the great delight of the spectators burst into tears and had to be replaced by an attendant who had long been stationed in readiness. Then came the food, a little of which the impresario managed to get between the artist's lips, while he sat in a kind of half-fainting trance, to the accompaniment of cheerful patter designed to distract the public's attention from the artist's condition; after that, a toast was drunk to the public, supposedly prompted by a whisper from the artist in the impresario's ear; the band confirmed it with a mighty flourish, the spectators melted away, and no one had any cause to be dissatisfied with the proceedings, no one except the hunger artist himself, he only, as always.

So he lived for many years, with small regular intervals of recuperation, in visible glory, honored by the world, yet in spite of that troubled in spirit, and all the more troubled because no one would take his trouble seriously. What comfort could he possibly need? What more could he possibly wish for? And if some good-natured person, feeling sorry for him, tried to console him by pointing out that his melancholy was probably caused by fasting, it could happen, especially when he had been fasting for some time, that he reacted with an outburst of fury and to the general alarm began to shake the bars of his cage like a wild animal. Yet the impresario had a way of punishing these outbreaks which he rather enjoyed putting into operation. He would apologize publicly for the artist's behavior, which was only to be excused, he admitted, because of the irritability caused by fasting; a condition hardly to be understood by well-fed people; then by natural transition he went on to mention the artist's equally incomprehensible boast that he could fast for much longer than he was doing; he praised the high ambition, the good will, the great self-denial undoubtedly implicit in such a statement; and then quite simply countered it by bringing out photographs, which were also on sale to the public, showing the artist on the fortieth day of a fast lying in bed almost dead from exhaustion. This perversion of the truth, familiar to the artist though it was, always unnerved him afresh and proved too much for him. What was a consequence of the premature ending of his fast was here presented as the cause of it! To fight against this lack of understanding, against a whole world of nonunderstanding, was impossible. Time and again in good faith he stood by the bars listening to the impresario, but as soon as the photographs appeared he always let go and sank with a groan back onto his straw, and the reassured public could once more come close and gaze at him.

A few years later when the witnesses of such scenes called them to mind, they often failed to understand themselves at all. For meanwhile the aforementioned change in public interest had set in; it seemed to happen almost overnight; there may have been profound causes for it, but who was going to bother about that; at any rate the pampered hunger artist suddenly found himself deserted one fine day by the amusement-seekers, who went streaming past him to other more-favored attractions. For the last time the impresario hurried him over half Europe to discover whether the old interest might still survive here and there; all in vain; everywhere, as if by secret agreement, a positive revulsion from professional fasting was in evidence. Of course it could not really have sprung up so suddenly as all that, and many premonitory symptoms which had not been sufficiently remarked or suppressed during the rush and glitter of success now came retrospectively to mind, but it was now too late to take any countermeasures. Fasting would surely come into fashion again at some future date, yet that was no comfort for those living in the present. What, then, was the hunger artist to do? He had been applauded by thousands in his time and could hardly come down to showing himself

5

in a street booth at village fairs, and as for adopting another profession, he was not only too old for that but too fanatically devoted to fasting. So he took leave of the impresario, his partner in an unparalleled career, and hired himself to a large circus; in order to spare his own feelings he avoided reading the conditions of his contract.

A large circus with its enormous traffic in replacing and recruiting men, animals, and apparatus can always find a use for people at any time, even for a hunger artist, provided of course that he does not ask too much, and in this particular case anyhow it was not only the artist who was taken on but his famous and long-known name as well; indeed considering the peculiar nature of his performance, which was not impaired by advancing age, it could not be objected that here was an artist past his prime, no longer at the height of his professional skill, seeking a refuge in some quiet corner of a circus; on the contrary, the hunger artist averred that he could fast as well as ever, which was entirely credible, he even alleged that if he were allowed to fast as he liked, and this was at once promised him without more ado, he could astound the world by establishing a record never yet achieved, a statement that certainly provoked a smile among the other professionals, since it left out of account the change in public opinion, which the hunger artist in his zeal conveniently forgot.

He had not, however, actually lost his sense of the real situation and took it as a matter of course that he and his cage should be stationed, not in the middle of the ring as a main attraction, but outside, near the animal cages, on a site that was after all easily accessible. Large and gaily painted placards made a frame for the cage and announced what was to be seen inside it. When the public came thronging out in the intervals to see the animals, they could hardly avoid passing the hunger artist's cage and stopping there for a moment, perhaps they might even have stayed longer had not those pressing behind them in the narrow gangway, who did not understand why they should be held up on their way toward the excitements of the menagerie, made it impossible for anyone to stand gazing quietly for any length of time. And that was the reason why the hunger artist, who had of course been looking forward to these visiting hours as the main achievement of his life, began instead to shrink from them. At first he could hardly wait for the intervals; it was exhilarating to watch the crowds come streaming his way, until only too soon—not even the most obstinate self-deception, clung to almost consciously, could hold out against the fact—the conviction was borne in upon him that these people, most of them, to judge from their actions, again and again, without exception, were all on their way to the menagerie. And the first sight of them from the distance remained the best. For when they reached his cage he was at once deafened by the storm of shouting and abuse that arose from the two contending factions, which renewed themselves continuously, of those who wanted to stop and stare at him—he soon began to dislike them more than the others—not out of real interest but only out of obstinate self-assertiveness, and those who wanted to go straight on to the animals. When the first great rush was past, the stragglers came along, and these, whom nothing could have prevented from stopping to look at him as long as they had breath, raced past with long strides, hardly even glancing at him, in their haste to get to the menagerie in time. And all too rarely did it happen that he had a stroke of luck, when some father of a family fetched up before him with his children, pointed a finger at the hunger artist, and explained at length what the phenomenon meant, telling stories of earlier years when he himself had watched similar but much more thrilling performances, and the children, still rather uncomprehending, since neither inside nor outside school had they been sufficiently prepared for this lesson—what did they care about fasting?—yet showed by the brightness of their intent eyes that new and better times might be coming. Perhaps, said the hunger artist to himself many a time, things would be a little better if his cage were set not quite so near the menagerie. That made it too easy for people to make their choice, to say nothing of what he suffered from the stench of the menagerie, the animals' restlessness by night, the carrying past of raw lumps of flesh for the beasts of prey, the roaring at feeding times, which depressed him continually. But he did not dare to lodge a complaint with the management; after all, he had the animals to thank for the troops of people who passed his cage, among whom there might always be one here and there to take an interest in him, and who could tell where they might seclude him if he called attention to his existence and thereby to the fact that, strictly speaking, he was only an impediment on the way to the menagerie.

A small impediment, to be sure, one that grew steadily less. People grew familiar with the strange idea that they could be expected, in times like these, to take an interest in a hunger artist, and with this familiarity the verdict went out against him. He might fast as much as he could, and he did so; but nothing could save him now, people passed him by. Just try to explain to anyone the art of fasting! Anyone who has no feeling for it cannot be made to understand it. The fine placards grew dirty and illegible, they were torn down; the little notice board telling the number of fast days achieved, which at first was changed carefully every day, had long stayed at the same figure, for after the first few weeks even this small task seemed pointless to the staff; and so the artist simply fasted on and on, as he had once dreamed of doing, and it was no trouble to him, just as he had always foretold, but no one counted the days, no one, not even the artist himself, knew what records he was already breaking, and his heart grew heavy. And when once in a while some leisurely passer-by stopped, made merry over the old figure on the board, and spoke of swindling, that was in its way the stupidest lie ever invented by indifference and inborn malice, since it was not the hunger artist who was cheating, he was working honestly, but the world was cheating him of his reward.

Many more days went by, however, and that too came to an end. An overseer's eye fell on the cage one day and he asked the attendants why this perfectly good cage should be left standing there unused with dirty straw inside it; nobody knew, until one man, helped out by the notice board, remembered about the hunger artist. They poked into the straw with sticks and found him in it. "Are you still fasting?" asked the overseer, "when on earth do you mean to stop?" "Forgive me, everybody," whispered the hunger artist; only the overseer, who had his ear to the bars, understood him. "Of course," said the overseer, and tapped his forehead with a finger to let the attendants know what state the man was in, "we forgive you." "I always wanted you to admire my fasting," said the hunger artist. "We do admire it," said the overseer, affably. "But you shouldn't admire it," said the hunger artist. "Well then we don't admire it," said the overseer, "but why shouldn't we admire it?" "Because I have to fast, I can't help it," said the hunger artist. "What a fellow you are," said the overseer, "and why can't you help it?" "Because," said the hunger artist, lifting his head a little and speaking, with his lips pursed, as if for a kiss, right into the overseer's ear, so that no syllable might be lost, "because I couldn't find the food I liked. If I had found it, believe me, I should have made no fuss and stuffed myself like you or anyone else." These were his last words, but in his dimming eyes remained the firm though no longer proud persuasion that he was still continuing to fast.

"Well, clear this out now!" said the overseer, and they buried the hunger artist, straw and all. Into the cage they put a young panther. Even the most insensitive felt it refreshing to see this wild creature leaping around the cage that had so long been dreary. The panther was all right. The food he liked was brought him without hesitation by the attendants; he seemed not even to miss his freedom; his noble body, furnished almost to the bursting point with all that it needed, seemed to carry freedom around with it too; somewhere in his jaws it seemed to lurk; and the joy of life streamed with such ardent passion from his throat that for the onlookers it was not easy to stand the shock of it. But they braced themselves, crowded around the cage, and did not want ever to move away.

DORIS LESSING (b. 1919)

The Old Chief Mshlanga

1951

They were good, the years of ranging the bush over her father's farm which, like every white farm, was largely unused, broken only occasionally by small patches of cultivation. In between, nothing but trees, the long sparse grass, thorn and cactus and gully, grass and outcrop and thorn. And a jutting piece of rock which had been thrust up from the warm soil of Africa unimaginable eras of time ago, washed into hollows and whorls by sun and wind that had travelled so many thousands of miles of space and bush, would hold the weight of a small girl whose eyes were sightless for anything but a pale willowed river, a pale gleaming castle— a small girl singing: "Out flew the web and floated wide, the mirror cracked from side to side . . ."

Pushing her way through the green aisles of the mealie stalks, the leaves arching like cathedrals veined with sunlight far overhead, with the packed red earth underfoot, a fine lace of red starred witchweed would summon up a black bent figure croaking premonitions: the Northern witch, bred of cold Northern forests, would stand before her among the mealie fields, and it was the mealie fields that faded and fled, leaving her among the gnarled roots of an oak, snow falling thick and soft and white, the woodcutter's fire glowing red welcome through crowding tree trunks.

A white child, opening its eyes curiously on a sun-suffused landscape, a gaunt and violent landscape, might be supposed to accept it as her own, to take the msasa trees and the thorn trees as familiars, to feel her blood running free and responsive to the swing of the seasons.

This child could not see a msasa tree, or the thorn, for what they were. Her books held tales of alien fairies, her rivers ran slow and peaceful, and she knew the shape of the leaves of an ash or an oak, the names of the little creatures that lived in English streams, when the words "the veld" meant strangeness, though she could remember nothing else.

Because of this, for many years, it was the veld that seemed unreal; the sun was a foreign sun, and the wind spoke a strange language.

The black people on the farm were as remote as the trees and the rocks. They were an amorphous black mass, mingling and thinning and massing like tadpoles, faceless, who existed merely to serve, to say "Yes, Baas," take their money and go. They changed season by season, moving from one farm to the next, according to their outlandish needs, which one did not have to understand, coming from perhaps hundreds of miles North or East, passing on after a few months—where? Perhaps even as far away as the fabled gold mines of Johannesburg, where the pay was so much better than the few shillings a month and the double handful of mealie meal twice a day which they earned in that part of Africa.

The child was taught to take them for granted: the servants in the house would come running a hundred yards to pick up a book if she dropped it. She was called "Nkosikaas"—Chieftainess, even by the black children her own age.

Later, when the farm grew too small to hold her curiosity, she carried a gun in the crook of her arm and wandered miles a day, from vlei to vlei, from *kopje* to *kopje*, accompanied by two dogs: the dogs and the gun were an armour against fear. Because of them she never felt fear.

If a native came into sight along the kaffir paths half a mile away, the dogs would flush him up a tree as if he were a bird. If he expostulated (in his uncouth language which was by itself ridiculous) that was cheek. If one was in a good mood, it could be a matter for laughter. Otherwise one passed on, hardly glancing at the angry man in the tree.

On the rare occasions when white children met together they could amuse themselves by hailing a passing native in order to make a buffoon of him; they could set the dogs on him and watch him run; they could tease a small black child as if he were a puppy—save that they would not throw stones and sticks at a dog without a sense of guilt.

Later still, certain questions presented themselves in the child's mind; and because the answers were not easy to accept, they were silenced by an even greater arrogance of manner.

It was even impossible to think of the black people who worked about the house as friends, for if she talked to one of them, her mother would come running anxiously: "Come away; you mustn't talk to natives."

It was this instilled consciousness of danger, of something unpleasant, that made it easy to laugh out loud, crudely, if a servant made a mistake in his English of if he failed to understand an order—there is a certain kind of laughter that is fear, afraid of itself.

One evening, when I was about fourteen, I was walking down the side of a mealie field that had been newly ploughed, so that the great red clods showed fresh and tumbling to the vlie beyond, like a choppy red sea; it was that hushed and listening hour, when the birds send long sad calls from tree to tree, and all the colours of earth and sky and leaf are deep and golden. I had my rifle in the curve of my arm, and the dogs were at my heels.

In front of me, perhaps a couple of hundred yards away, a group of three Africans came into sight around the side of a big antheap. I whistled the dogs close in to my skirts and let the gun swing in my hand, and advanced, waiting for them to move aside, off the path, in respect for my passing. But they came on steadily, and the dogs looked up at me for the command to chase. I was angry. It was "cheek" for a native not to stand off a path, the moment he caught sight of you.

In front walked an old man, stooping his weight on to a stick, his hair grizzled white, a dark red blanket slung over his shoulders like a cloak. Behind him came two young men, carrying bundles of pots, assegais, hatchets.

The group was not a usual one. They were not natives seeking work. These had an air of dignity, of quietly following their own purpose. It was the dignity that checked my tongue. I walked quietly on, talking softly to the growling dogs, till I was ten paces away. Then the old man stopped, drawing his blanket close.

"Morning, Nkosikaas," he said, using the customary greeting for any time of the day.

"Good morning," I said. "Where are you going?" My voice was a little truculent.

The old man spoke in his own language, then one of the young men stepped forward politely and said in careful English: "My Chief travels to see his brothers beyond the river." 20

A Chief! I thought, understanding the pride that made the old man stand before me like an equal—more than an equal, for he showed courtesy, and I showed none.

The old man spoke again, wearing dignity like an inherited garment, still standing ten paces off, flanked by his entourage, not looking at me (that would have been rude) but directing his eyes somewhere over my head at the trees.

"You are the little Nkosikaas from the farm of Baas Jordan?"

"That's right," I said.

"Perhaps your father does not remember," said the interpreter for the old man, "but there was an affair with some goats. I remember seeing you when you were . . ." The young man held his hand at knee level and smiled. 25

We all smiled.

"What is your name?" I asked.

"This is Chief Mshlanga," said the young man.

"I will tell my father that I met you," I said.

The old man said: "My greetings to your father, little Nkosikaas." 30

"Good morning," I said politely, finding the politeness difficult, from lack of use.

"Morning, little Nkosikaas," said the old man, and stood aside to let me pass.

I went by, my gun hanging awkwardly, the dogs sniffing and growling, cheated of their favorite game of chasing natives like animals.

Not long afterwards I read in an old explorer's book the phrase: "Chief Mshlanga's country." It went like this: "Our destination was Chief Mshlanga's country, to the north of the river; and it was our desire to ask his permission to prospect for gold in his territory."

The phrase "ask his permission" was so extraordinary to a white child, brought up to consider all natives as things to use, that it revived those questions, which could not be suppressed: they fermented slowly in my mind. 35

On another occasion one of those old prospectors who still move over Africa looking for neglected reefs, with their hammers and tents, and pans for sifting gold from crushed rock, came to the farm and, in talking of the old days, used that phrase again: "This was the Old Chief's country," he said. "It stretched from those mountains over there way back to the river, hundreds of miles of country." That was his name for our district: "The Old Chief's Country"; he did not use our name for it—a new phrase which held no implication of usurped ownership.

As I read more books about the time when this part of Africa was opened up, not much more than fifty years before, I found Old Chief Mshlanga had been a famous man, known to all the explorers and prospectors. But then he had been young; or maybe it was his father or uncle they spoke of—I never found out.

During that year I met him several times in the part of the farm that was traversed by natives moving over the country. I learned that the path up the side of the big red field where the birds sang was the recognized highway for migrants. Perhaps I even haunted it in the hope of meeting him: being greeted by him, the exchange of courtesies, seemed to answer the questions that troubled me.

Soon I carried a gun in a different spirit; I used it for shooting food and not to give me confidence. And now the dogs learned better manners. When I saw a native approaching, we offered and took greetings; and slowly that other landscape in my mind faded, and my feet struck directly on the African soil, and I saw the shapes of tree and hill clearly, and the black people moved back, as it were, out of my life: it was as if I stood aside to watch a slow intimate dance of landscape and men, a very old dance, whose steps I could not learn.

But I thought: this is my heritage, too; I was bred here; it is my country as   40
well as the black man's country; and there is plenty of room for all of us, without elbowing each other off the pavements and roads.

It seemed it was only necessary to let free that respect I felt when I was talking with old Chief Mshlanga, to let both black and white people meet gently, with tolerance for each other's differences: it seemed quite easy.

Then, one day, something new happened. Working in our house as servants were always three natives: cook, houseboy, garden boy. They used to change as the farm natives changed: staying for a few months, then moving on to a new job, or back home to their kraals. They were thought of as "good" or "bad" natives; which meant: how did they behave as servants? Were they lazy, efficient, obedient, or disrespectful? If the family felt good-humoured, the phrase was: "What can you expect from raw black savages?" If we were angry, we said: "These damned niggers, we would be much better off without them."

One day, a white policeman was on his rounds of the district, and he said laughingly: "Did you know you have an important man in your kitchen?"

"What!" exclaimed my mother sharply. "What do you mean?"

"A Chief's son." The policeman seemed amused. "He'll boss the tribe when   45
the old man dies."

"He'd better not put on a Chief's son act with me," said my mother.

When the policeman left, we looked with different eyes at our cook: he was a good worker, but he drank too much at week-ends—that was how we knew him.

He was a tall youth, with very black skin, like black polished metal, his tightly-growing black hair parted white man's fashion at one side, with a metal comb from the store stuck into it; very polite, very distant, very quick to obey an order. Now that it had been pointed out, we said: "Of course, you can see. Blood always tells."

My mother became strict with him now she knew about his birth and prospects. Sometimes, when she lost her temper, she would say: "You aren't the Chief yet, you know." And he would answer her very quietly, his eyes on the ground: "Yes, Nkosikaas."

One afternoon he asked for a whole day off, instead of the customary half- 50
day, to go home next Sunday.

"How can you go home in one day?"

"It will take me half an hour on my bicycle," he explained.

I watched the direction he took; and the next day I went off to look for
this kraal; I understood he must be Chief Mshlanga's successor: there was no other
kraal near enough our farm.

Beyond our boundaries on that side the country was new to me. I followed
unfamiliar paths past *kopjes* that till now had been part of the jagged horizon,
hazed with distance. This was Government land, which had never been cultivated
by white men; at first I could not understand why it was that it appeared, in merely
crossing the boundary, I had entered a completely fresh type of landscape. It was
a wide green valley, where a small river sparkled, and vivid water-birds darted
over the rushes. The grass was thick and soft to my calves, the trees stood tall
and shapely.

I was used to our farm, whose hundreds of acres of harsh eroded soil bore 55
trees that had been cut for the mine furnaces and had grown thin and twisted,
where the cattle had dragged the grass flat, leaving innumerable criss-crossing
trails that deepened each season into gullies, under the force of the rains.

This country had been left untouched, save for prospectors whose picks had
struck a few sparks from the surface of the rocks as they wandered by; and for
migrant natives whose passing had left, perhaps, a charred patch on the trunk of
a tree where their evening fire had nestled.

It was very silent: a hot morning with pigeons cooing throatily, the midday
shadows lying dense and thick with clear yellow spaces of sunlight between and
in all that wide green park-like valley, not a human soul but myself.

I was listening to the quick regular tapping of a woodpecker when slowly a
chill feeling seemed to grow up from the small of my back to my shoulders, in a
constricting spasm like a shudder, and at the roots of my hair a tingling sensation
began and ran down over the surface of my flesh, leaving me goosefleshed and
cold, though I was damp with sweat. Fever? I thought; then uneasily, turned to
look over my shoulder; and realized suddenly that this was fear. It was extraordinary,
even humiliating. It was a new fear. For all the years I had walked by myself over
this country I had never known a moment's uneasiness; in the beginning because
I had been supported by a gun and the dogs, then because I had learnt an easy
friendliness for the Africans I might encounter.

I had read of this feeling, how the bigness and silence of Africa, under the
ancient sun, grows dense and takes shape in the mind, till even the birds seem
to call menacingly, and a deadly spirit comes out of the trees and the rocks. You
move warily, as if your very passing disturbs something old and evil, something
dark and big and angry that might suddenly rear and strike from behind. You
look at groves of entwined trees, and picture the animals that might be lurking
there; you look at the river running slowly, dropping from level to level through
the vlei, spreading into pools where at night the bucks come to drink, and the
crocodiles rise and drag them by their soft noses into underwater caves. Fear possessed me. I found I was turning round and round, because of that shapeless
menace behind me that might reach out and take me; I kept glancing at the files
of *kopjes* which, seen from a different angle, seemed to change with every step so

that even known landmarks, like a big mountain that had sentinelled my world since I first became conscious of it, showed an unfamiliar sunlit valley among its foothills. I did not know where I was. I was lost. Panic seized me. I found I was spinning round and round, staring anxiously at this tree and that, peering up at the sun which appeared to have moved into an eastern slant, shedding the sad yellow light of sunset. Hours must have passed! I looked at my watch and found that this state of meaningless terror had lasted perhaps ten minutes.

The point was that it was meaningless. I was not ten miles from home: I had only to take my way back along the valley to find myself at the fence; away among the foothills of the *kopjes* gleamed the roof of a neighbor's house, and a couple of hours' walking would reach it. This was the sort of fear that contracts the flesh of a dog at night and sets him howling at the full moon. It had nothing to do with what I thought or felt; and I was more disturbed by the fact that I could become its victim than of the physical sensation itself: I walked steadily on, quietened, in a divided mind, watching my own pricking nerves and apprehensive glances from side to side with a disgusted amusement. Deliberately I set myself to think of this village I was seeking, and what I should do when I entered it—if I could find it, which was doubtful, since I was walking aimlessly and it might be anywhere in the hundreds of thousands of acres of bush that stretched about me. With my mind on that village, I realized that a new sensation was added to the fear: loneliness. Now such a terror of isolation invaded me that I could hardly walk; and if it were not that I came over the crest of a small rise and saw a village below me, I should have turned and gone home. It was a cluster of thatched huts in a clearing among trees. There were neat patches of mealies and pumpkins and millet, and cattle grazed under some trees at a distance. Fowls scratched among the huts, dogs lay sleeping on the grass, and goats friezed a *kopje* that jutted up beyond a tributary of the river lying like an enclosing arm round the village.

As I came close I saw the huts were lovingly decorated with patterns of yellow and red and ochre mud on the walls; and the thatch was tied in place with plaits of straw.

This was not at all like our farm compound, a dirty and neglected place, a temporary home for migrants who had no roots in it.

And now I did not know what to do next. I called a small black boy, who was sitting on a lot playing a stringed gourd, quite naked except for the strings of blue beads round his neck, and said: "Tell the Chief I am here." The child stuck his thumb in his mouth and stared shyly back at me.

For minutes I shifted my feet on the edge of what seemed a deserted village, till at last the child scuttled off, and then some women came. They were draped in bright cloths, with brass glinting in their ears and on their arms. They also stared, silently; then turned to chatter among themselves.

I said again: "Can I see Chief Mshlanga?" I saw they caught the name; they did not understand what I wanted. I did not understand myself.

At last I walked through them and came past the huts and saw a clearing under a big shady tree, where a dozen old men sat cross-legged on the ground, talking. Chief Mshlanga was leaning back against the tree, holding a gourd in his hand, from which he had been drinking. When he saw me, not a muscle of his face moved, and I could see he was not pleased: perhaps he was afflicted with my own shyness, due to being unable to find the right forms of courtesy for the occasion. To meet me, on our own farm, was one thing; but I should not have come here. What had I expected? I could not join them socially: the thing was unheard of. Bad enough that I, a white girl, should be walking the veld alone as a white man might: and in this part of the bush where only Government officials had the right to move.

Again I stood, smiling foolishly, while behind me stood the groups of brightly clad, chattering women, their faces alert with curiosity and interest, and in front of me sat the old men, with old lined faces, their eyes guarded, aloof. It was a village of ancients and children and women. Even the two young men who kneeled beside the Chief were not those I had seen with him previously: the young men were all away working on the white men's farms and mines, and the Chief must depend on relatives who were temporarily on holiday for his attendants.

"The small white Nkosikaas is far from home," remarked the old man at last.

"Yes," I agreed, "it is far." I wanted to say: "I have come to pay you a friendly visit, Chief Mshlanga." I could not say it. I might now be feeling an urgent helpless desire to get to know these men and women as people, to be accepted by them as a friend, but the truth was I had set out in a spirit of curiosity: I had wanted to see the village that one day our cook, the reserved and obedient young man who got drunk on Sundays, would one day rule over.

"The child of Nkosi Jordan is welcome," said Chief Mshlanga. 70

"Thank you," I said, and could think of nothing more to say. There was a silence, while the flies rose and began to buzz around my head; and the wind shook a little in the thick green tree that spread its branches over the old men.

"Good morning," I said at last. "I have to return now to my home."

"Morning, little Nkosikaas," said Chief Mshlanga.

I walked away from the indifferent village, over the rise past the staring amber-eyed goats, down through the tall stately trees into the great rich green valley where the river meandered and the pigeons cooed tales of plenty and the woodpecker tapped softly.

The fear was gone; the loneliness had set into stiff-necked stoicism; there 75 was now a queer hostility in the landscape, a cold, hard, sullen indomitability that walked with me, as strong as a wall, as intangible as smoke; it seemed to say to me: you walk here as a destroyer. I went slowly homewards, with an empty heart: I had learned that if one cannot call a country to heel like a dog, neither can one dismiss the past with a smile in an easy gush of feeling, saying: I could not help it, I am also a victim.

I only saw Chief Mshlanga once again.

One night my father's big red land was trampled down by small sharp hooves, and it was discovered that the culprits were goats from Chief Mshlanga's kraal. This had happened once before, years ago.

My father confiscated all the goats. Then he sent a message to the old Chief that if he wanted them he would have to pay for the damage.

He arrived at our house at the time of sunset one evening, looking very old and bent now, walking stiffly under his regally draped blanket, leaning on a big stick. My father sat himself down in his big chair below the steps of the house; the old man squatted carefully on the ground before him, flanked by his two young men.

The palaver was long and painful, because of the bad English of the young 80 man who interpreted, and because my father could not speak dialect, but only kitchen kaffir.

From my father's point of view, at least two hundred pounds' worth of damage had been done to the crop. He knew he could not get the money from the old man. He felt he was entitled to keep the goats. As for the old Chief, he kept repeating angrily: "Twenty goats! My people cannot lose twenty goats! We are not rich, like the Nkosi Jordan, to lose twenty goats at once."

My father did not think of himself as rich, but rather as very poor. He spoke quickly and angrily in return, saying that the damage done meant a great deal to him, and that he was entitled to the goats.

At last it grew so heated that the cook, the Chief's son, was called from the kitchen to be interpreter, and now my father spoke fluently in English, and our cook translated rapidly so that the old man could understand how very angry my father was. The young man spoke without emotion, in a mechanical way, his eyes lowered, but showing how he felt his position by a hostile uncomfortable set of the shoulders.

It was now in the late sunset, the sky a welter of colours, the birds singing their last songs, and the cattle, lowing peacefully, moving past us towards their sheds for the night. It was the hour when Africa is most beautiful; and here was this pathetic, ugly scene, doing no one any good.

At last my father stated finally: "I'm not going to argue about it. I am keeping   85
the goats."

The old Chief flashed back in his own language: "That means that my people will go hungry when the dry season comes."

"Go to the police, then," said my father, and looked triumphant.

There was, of course, no more to be said.

The old man sat silent, his head bent, his hands dangling helplessly over his withered knees. Then he rose, the young men helping him, and he stood facing my father. He spoke once again, very stiffly; and turned away and went home to his village.

"What did he say?" asked my father of the young man, who laughed uncom-   90
fortably and would not meet his eyes.

"What did he say?" insisted my father.

Our cook stood straight and silent, his brows knotted together. Then he spoke. "My father says: All this land, this land you call yours, is his land, and belongs to our people."

Having made this statement, he walked off into the bush after his father, and we did not see him again.

Our next cook was a migrant from Nyasaland, with no expectations of great-ness.

Next time the policeman came on his rounds he was told this story. He   95
remarked: "That kraal has no right to be there; it should have been moved long ago. I don't know why no one has done anything about it. I'll have a chat with the Native Commissioner next week. I'm going over for tennis on Sunday, anyway."

Some time later we heard that Chief Mshlanga and his people had been moved two hundred miles east, to a proper Native Reserve; the Government land was going to be opened up for white settlement soon.

I went to see the village again, about a year afterwards. There was nothing there. Mounds of red mud, where the huts had been, had long swathes of rotting thatch over them, veined with the red galleries of the white ants. The pumpkin vines rioted everywhere, over the bushes, up the lower branches of trees so that the great golden balls rolled underfoot and dangled overhead: it was a festival of pumpkins. The bushes were crowding up, the new grass sprang vivid green.

The settler lucky enough to be allotted the lush warm valley (if he chose to cultivate this particular section) would find, suddenly, in the middle of a mealie field, the plants were growing fifteen feet tall, the weight of the cobs dragging at the stalks, and wonder what unsuspected vein of richness he had struck.

FLANNERY O'CONNOR (1925–1964)

A Good Man Is Hard to Find 1953

The grandmother didn't want to go to Florida. She wanted to visit some of her connections in east Tennessee and she was seizing at every chance to change Bailey's mind. Bailey was the son she lived with, her only son. He was sitting on the edge of his chair at the table, bent over the orange sports section of the *Journal*. "Now look here, Bailey," she said, "see here, read this," and she stood with one hand on her thin hip and the other rattling the newspaper at his bald head. "Here this fellow that calls himself The Misfit is aloose from the Federal Pen and headed toward Florida and you read here what it says he did to these people. Just you read it. I wouldn't take my children in any direction with a criminal like that aloose in it. I couldn't answer to my conscience if I did."

Bailey didn't look up from his reading so she wheeled around then and faced the children's mother, a young woman in slacks, whose face was as broad and innocent as a cabbage and was tied round with a green head-kerchief that had two points on the top like rabbit's ears. She was sitting on the sofa, feeding the baby his apricots out of a jar. "The children have been to Florida before," the old lady said. "You all ought to take them somewhere else for a change so they would see different parts of the world and be broad. They never have been to east Tennessee."

The children's mother didn't seem to hear her but the eight-year-old boy, John Wesley, a stocky child with glasses, said, "If you don't want to go to Florida, why dontcha stay at home?" He and the little girl, June Star, were reading the funny papers on the floor.

"She wouldn't stay at home to be queen for a day," June Star said without raising her yellow head.

"Yes and what would you do if this fellow, The Misfit, caught you?" the grandmother asked.

"I'd smack his face," John Wesley said.

"She wouldn't stay at home for a million bucks," June Star said. "Afraid she'd miss something. She has to go everywhere we go."

"All right, Miss," the grandmother said. "Just remember that the next time you want me to curl your hair."

5

June Star said her hair was naturally curly.

The next morning the grandmother was the first one in the car, ready to   10
go. She had her big black valise that looked like the head of a hippopotamus in
one corner, and underneath it she was hiding a basket with Pitty Sing, the cat, in
it. She didn't intend for the cat to be left alone in the house for three days because
he would miss her too much and she was afraid he might brush against one of
the gas burners and accidentally asphyxiate himself. Her son, Bailey, didn't like
to arrive at a motel with a cat.

She sat in the middle of the back seat with John Wesley and June Star on
either side of her. Bailey and the children's mother and the baby sat in the front
and they left Atlanta at eight forty-five with the mileage on the car at 55890. The
grandmother wrote this down because she thought it would be interesting to say
how many miles they had been when they got back. It took them twenty minutes
to reach the outskirts of the city.

The old lady settled herself comfortably, removing her white cotton gloves
and putting them up with her purse on the shelf in front of the back window.
The children's mother still had on slacks and still had her head tied up in a green
kerchief, but the grandmother had on a navy blue straw sailor hat with a bunch
of white violets on the brim and a navy blue dress with a small white dot in the
print. Her collar and cuffs were white organdy trimmed with lace and at her neckline
she had pinned a purple spray of cloth violets containing a sachet. In case of an
accident, anyone seeing her dead on the highway would know at once that she
was a lady.

She said she thought it was going to be a good day for driving, neither too
hot nor too cold, and she cautioned Bailey that the speed limit was fifty-five miles
an hour and that the patrolmen hid themselves behind billboards and small clumps
of trees and sped out after you before you had a chance to slow down. She pointed
out interesting details of the scenery: Stone Mountain; the blue granite that in
some places came up to both sides of the highway; the brilliant red clay banks
slightly streaked with purple; and the various crops that made rows of green lace-
work on the ground. The trees were full of silver-white sunlight and the meanest
of them sparkled. The children were reading comic magazines and their mother
had gone back to sleep.

"Let's go through Georgia fast so we won't have to look at it much," John
Wesley said.

"If I were a little boy," said the grandmother, "I wouldn't talk about my   15
native state that way. Tennessee has the mountains and Georgia has the hills."

"Tennessee is just a hillbilly dumping ground," John Wesley said, "and Georgia is a lousy state too."

"You said it," June Star said.

"In my time," said the grandmother, folding her thin veined fingers, "children
were more respectful of their native states and their parents and everything else.
People did right then. Oh look at the cute little pickaninny!" she said and pointed
to a Negro child standing in the door of a shack. "Wouldn't that make a picture,
now?" she asked and they all turned and looked at the little Negro out of the
back window. He waved.

"He didn't have any britches on," June said.

"He probably didn't have any," the grandmother explained. "Little niggers   20 in the country don't have things like we do. If I could paint, I'd paint that picture," she said.

The children exchanged comic books.

The grandmother offered to hold the baby and the children's mother passed him over the front seat to her. She set him on her knee and bounced him and told him about the things they were passing. She rolled her eyes and screwed up her mouth and stuck her leathery thin face into his smooth bland one. Occasionally he gave her a faraway smile. They passed a large cotton field with five or six graves fenced in the middle of it, like a small island. "Look at the graveyard!" the grandmother said, pointing it out. "That was the old family burying ground. That belonged to the plantation."

"Where's the plantation?" John Wesley asked.

"Gone With the Wind," said the grandmother. "Ha. Ha."

When the children finished all the comic books they had brought, they opened the lunch and ate it. The grandmother ate a peanut butter sandwich and an olive and would not let the children throw the box and the paper napkins out the window. When there was nothing else to do they played a game by choosing a cloud and making the other two guess what shape it suggested. John Wesley took one the shape of a cow and June Star guessed a cow and John Wesley said, no, an automobile, and June Star said he didn't play fair, and they began to slap each other over the grandmother.   25

The grandmother said she would tell them a story if they would keep quiet. When she told a story, she rolled her eyes and waved her head and was very dramatic. She said once when she was a maiden lady she had been courted by a Mr. Edgar Atkins Teagarden from Jasper, Georgia. She said he was a very good-looking man and a gentleman and that he brought her a watermelon every Saturday afternoon with his initials cut in it, E. A. T. Well, one Saturday, she said, Mr. Teagarden brought the watermelon and there was nobody at home and he left it on the front porch and returned in his buggy to Jasper, but she never got the watermelon, she said, because a nigger boy ate it when he saw the initials, E. A. T.! This story tickled John Wesley's funny bone and he giggled and giggled but June Star didn't think it was any good. She said she wouldn't marry a man that just brought her a watermelon on Saturday. The grandmother said she would have done well to marry Mr. Teagarden because he was a gentleman and had bought Coca-Cola stock when it first came out and that he had died only a few years ago, a very wealthy man.

They stopped at The Tower for barbecued sandwiches. The Tower was a part stucco and part wood filling station and dance hall set in a clearing outside of Timothy. A fat man named Red Sammy Butts ran it and there were signs stuck here and there on the building and for miles up and down the highway saying, TRY RED SAMMY'S FAMOUS BARBECUE. NONE LIKE FAMOUS RED SAMMY'S! RED SAM! THE FAT BOY WITH THE HAPPY LAUGH. A VETERAN! SAMMY'S YOUR MAN!

Red Sammy was lying on the bare ground outside The Tower with his head under a truck while a gray monkey about a foot high, chained to a small chinaberry tree, chattered nearby. The monkey sprang back into the tree and got on the highest limb as soon as he saw the children jump out of the car and run toward him.

Inside, The Tower was a long dark room with a counter at one end and tables at the other and dancing space in the middle. They all sat down at a broad table next to the nickelodeon and Red Sam's wife, a tall burnt-brown woman with hair and eyes lighter than her skin, came and took their order. The children's mother put a dime in the machine and played "The Tennessee Waltz," and the grandmother said that tune always made her want to dance. She asked Bailey if he would like to dance but he only glared at her. He didn't have a naturally sunny disposition like she did and trips made him nervous. The grandmother's brown eyes were very bright. She swayed her head from side to side and pretended she was dancing in her chair. June Star said play something she could tap to so the children's mother put in another dime and played a fast number and June Star stepped out onto the dance floor and did her tap routine.

"Ain't she cute?" Red Sam's wife said, leaning over the counter. "Would   30
you like to come be my little girl?"

"No I certainly wouldn't," June Star said. "I wouldn't live in a broken-down place like this for a million bucks!" and she ran back to the table.

"Ain't she cute?" the woman repeated, stretching her mouth politely.

"Aren't you ashamed?" hissed the grandmother.

Red Sam came in and told his wife to quit lounging on the counter and hurry with these people's order. His khaki trousers reached just to his hip bones and his stomach hung over them like a sack of meal swaying under his shirt. He came over and sat down at a table nearby and let out a combination sigh and yodel. "You can't win," he said. "You can't win," and he wiped his sweating red face off with a gray handkerchief. "These days you don't know who to trust," he said. "Ain't that the truth?"

"People are certainly not nice like they used to be," said the grandmother.   35

"Two fellers come in here last week," Red Sammy said, "driving a Chrysler. It was a old beat-up car but it was a good one and these boys looked all right to me. Said they worked at the mill and you know I let them fellers charge the gas they bought? Now why did I do that?"

"Because you're a good man!" the grandmother said at once.

"Yes'm, I suppose so," Red Sam said as if he were struck with the answer.

His wife brought the orders, carrying the five plates all at once without a tray, two in each hand and one balanced on her arm. "It isn't a soul in this green world of God's that you can trust," she said. "And I don't count anybody out of that, not nobody," she repeated, looking at Red Sammy.

"Did you read about that criminal, The Misfit, that's escaped?" asked the   40
grandmother.

"I wouldn't be a bit surprised if he didn't attact this place right here," said the woman. "If he hears about it being here, I wouldn't be none surprised to see him. If he hears it's two cent in the cash register, I wouldn't be a tall surprised if he . . ."

"That'll do," Red Sam said. "Go bring these people their Co'Colas," and the woman went off to get the rest of the order.

"A good man is hard to find," Red Sammy said. "Everything is getting terrible. I remember the day you could go off and leave your screen door unlatched. Not no more."

He and the grandmother discussed better times. The old lady said that in her opinion Europe was entirely to blame for the way things were now. She said

And I awoke and found me here
    On the cold hill's side.

12

And this is why I sojourn here,
    Alone and palely loitering,
Though the sedge is wither'd from the lake,
    And no birds sing.

5

10

45

The meaning of this encounter is never made explicit. But the knight longs for what he can't have. A richly suggestive poem of haunting beauty & mystery.

Which is proper. And the knight doesn't have any power.

the way Europe acted you would think we were made of money and Red Sam said it was no use talking about it, she was exactly right. The children ran outside into the white sunlight and looked at the monkey in the lacy chinaberry tree. He was busy catching fleas on himself and biting each one carefully between his teeth as if it were a delicacy.

They drove off again into the hot afternoon. The grandmother took cat naps and woke up every few minutes with her own snoring. Outside of Toombsboro she woke up and recalled an old plantation that she had visited in this neighborhood once when she was a young lady. She said the house had six white columns across the front and that there was an avenue of oaks leading up to it and two little wooden trellis arbors on either side in front where you sat down with your suitor after a stroll in the garden. She recalled exactly which road to turn off to get to it. She knew that Bailey would not be willing to lose any time looking at an old house, but the more she talked about it, the more she wanted to see it once again and find out if the little twin arbors were still standing. "There was a secret panel in this house," she said craftily, not telling the truth but wishing that she were, "and the story went that all the family silver was hidden in it when Sherman° came through but it was never found . . ." 45

"Hey!" John Wesley said, "Let's go see it! We'll find it! We'll poke all the woodwork and find it! Who lives there? Where do you turn off at? Hey Pop, can't we turn off there?"

"We never have seen a house with a secret panel!" June Star shrieked. "Let's go to the house with the secret panel! Hey, Pop, can't we go see the house with the secret panel!"

"It's not far from here, I know," the grandmother said. "It wouldn't take over twenty minutes."

Bailey was looking straight ahead. His jaw was as rigid as a horseshoe. "No," he said.

The children began to yell and scream that they wanted to see the house with the secret panel. John Wesley kicked the back of the front seat and June Star hung over her mother's shoulder and whined desperately into her ear that they never had any fun even on their vacation, and that they could never do what THEY wanted to do. The baby began to scream and John Wesley kicked the back of the seat so hard that his father could feel the blows in his kidney. 50

"All right!" he shouted, and drew the car to a stop at the side of the road. "Will you all shut up? Will you all just shut up for one second? If you don't shut up, we won't go anywhere."

"It would be very educational for them," the grandmother murmured.

"All right," Bailey said, "but get this: this is the only time we're going to stop for anything like this. This is the one and only time."

"The dirt road that you have to turn down is about a mile back," the grandmother directed. "I marked it when we passed."

"A dirt road," Bailey groaned. 55

After they had turned around and were headed toward the dirt road, the grandmother recalled other points about the house, the beautiful glass over the

---

Sherman: William Tecumseh Sherman (1820–1891), Union general during the Civil War.

front doorway and the candle-lamp in the hall. John Wesley said that the secret panel was probably in the fireplace.

"You can't go inside this house," Bailey said. "You don't know who lives there."

"While you all talk to the people in front, I'll run around behind and get in a window," John Wesley suggested.

"We'll all stay in the car," his mother said.

They turned onto the dirt road and the car raced roughly along in a swirl   60
of pink dust. The grandmother recalled the times when there were no paved roads and thirty miles was a day's journey. The dirt road was hilly and there were sudden washes in it and sharp curves on dangerous embankments. All at once they would be on a hill, looking down over the blue tops of trees for miles around, then the next minute, they would be in a red depression with the dust-coated trees looking down on them.

"This place had better turn up in a minute," Bailey said, "or I'm going to turn around."

The road looked as if no one had traveled on it in months.

"It's not much farther," the grandmother said and just as she said it, a horrible thought came to her. The thought was so embarrassing that she turned red in the face and her eyes dilated and her feet jumped up, upsetting her valise in the corner. The instant the valise moved, the newspaper top she had over the basket under it rose with a snarl and Pitty Sing, the cat, sprang onto Bailey's shoulder.

The children were thrown to the floor and their mother, clutching the baby, was thrown out the door onto the ground, the old lady was thrown into the front seat. The car turned over once and landed right-side-up in a gulch on the side of the road. Bailey remained in the driver's seat with the cat—gray-striped with a broad white face and an orange nose—clinging to his neck like a caterpillar.

As soon as the children saw they could move their arms and legs, they scram-   65
bled out of the car, shouting, "We've had an ACCIDENT!" The grandmother was curled up under the dashboard, hoping she was injured so that Bailey's wrath would not come down on her all at once. The horrible thought she had had before the accident was that the house she had remembered so vividly was not in Georgia but in Tennessee.

Bailey removed the cat from his neck with both hands and flung it out the window against the side of a pine tree. Then he got out of the car and started looking for the children's mother. She was sitting against the side of the red gutted ditch, holding the screaming baby, but she only had a cut down her face and a broken shoulder. "We've had an ACCIDENT!" the children screamed in a frenzy of delight.

"But nobody's killed," June Star said with disappointment as the grandmother limped out of the car, her hat still pinned to her head but the broken front brim standing up at a jaunty angle and the violet spray hanging off the side. They all sat down in the ditch, except the children, to recover from the shock. They were all shaking.

"Maybe a car will come along," said the children's mother hoarsely.

"I believe I have injured an organ," said the grandmother, pressing her side, but no one answered her. Bailey's teeth were clattering. He had on a yellow sport shirt with bright blue parrots designed in it and his face was as yellow as the shirt. The grandmother decided that she would not mention that the house was in Tennessee.

The road was about ten feet above and they could see only the tops of the trees on the other side of it. Behind the ditch they were sitting in there were more woods, tall and dark and deep. In a few minutes they saw a car some distance away on top of a hill, coming slowly as if the occupants were watching them. The grandmother stood up and waved both arms dramatically to attract their attention. The car continued to come on slowly, disappeared around a bend and appeared again, moving even slower, on top of the hill they had gone over. It was a big black battered hearse-like automobile. There were three men in it.

It came to a stop just over them and for some minutes, the driver looked down with a steady expressionless gaze to where they were sitting, and didn't speak. Then he turned his head and muttered something to the other two and they got out. One was a fat boy in black trousers and a red sweat shirt with a silver stallion embossed on the front of it. He moved around on the right side of them and stood staring, his mouth partly open in a kind of loose grin. The other had on khaki pants and a blue striped coat and a gray hat pulled down very low, hiding most of his face. He came around slowly on the left side. Neither spoke.

The driver got out of the car and stood by the side of it, looking down at them. He was an older man than the other two. His hair was just beginning to gray and he wore silver-rimmed spectacles that gave him a scholarly look. He had a long creased face and didn't have on any shirt or undershirt. He had on blue jeans that were too tight for him and was holding a black hat and a gun. The two boys also had guns.

"We've had an ACCIDENT!" the children screamed.

The grandmother had the peculiar feeling that the bespectacled man was someone she knew. His face was as familiar to her as if she had known him all her life but she could not recall who he was. He moved away from the car and began to come down the embankment, placing his feet carefully so that he wouldn't slip. He had on tan and white shoes and no socks, and his ankles were red and thin. "Good afternoon," he said. "I see you all had a little spill."

"We turned over twice!" said the grandmother.

"Oncet," he corrected. "We seen it happen. Try their car and see will it run, Hiram," he said quietly to the boy with the gray hat.

"What you got that gun for?" John Wesley asked, "Whatcha gonna do with that gun?"

"Lady," the man said to the children's mother, "would you mind calling them children to sit down by you? Children make me nervous. I want all you all to sit down right together there where you're at."

"What are you telling us what to do for?" June Star asked.

Behind them the line of woods gaped like a dark open mouth. "Come here," said their mother.

"Look here now," Bailey began suddenly, "we're in a predicament! We're in . . ."

The grandmother shrieked. She scrambled to her feet and stood staring. "You're The Misfit!" she said. "I recognized you at once."

"Yes'm," the man said, smiling slightly as if he were pleased in spite of himself to be known, "but it would have been better for all of you, lady, if you hadn't of reckernized me."

Bailey turned his head sharply and said something to his mother that shocked even the children. The old lady began to cry and The Misfit reddened.

"Lady," he said, "don't you get upset: Sometimes a man says things he don't   85
mean. I don't reckon he meant to talk to you thataway."

"You wouldn't shoot a lady, would you?" the grandmother said and removed a clean handkerchief from her cuff and began to slap at her eyes with it.

The Misfit pointed the toe of his shoe into the ground and made a little hole and then covered it up again. "I would hate to have to," he said.

"Listen," the grandmother almost screamed, "I know you're a good man. You don't look a bit like you have common blood. I know you must come from nice people!"

"Yes mam," he said, "finest people in the world." When he smiled he showed a row of strong white teeth. "God never made a finer woman than my mother and my daddy's heart was pure gold," he said. The boy with the red sweat shirt had come around behind them and was standing with his gun at his hip. The Misfit squatted down on the ground. "Watch them children, Bobby Lee," he said. "You know they make me nervous." He looked at the six of them huddled together in front of him and he seemed to be embarrassed as if he couldn't think of anything to say. "Ain't a cloud in the sky," he remarked, looking up at it. "Don't see no sun but don't see no cloud neither."

"Yes, it's a beautiful day," said the grandmother. "Listen," she said, "you   90
shouldn't call yourself The Misfit because I know you're a good man at heart. I can just look at you and tell."

"Hush!" Bailey yelled. "Hush! Everybody shut up and let me handle this!" He was squatting in the position of a runner about to sprint forward but he didn't move.

"I pre-chate that, lady," The Misfit said and drew a little circle in the ground with the butt of his gun.

"It'll take a half a hour to fix this here car," Hiram called, looking over the raised hood of it.

"Well, first you and Bobby Lee get him and that little boy to step over yonder with you," The Misfit said, pointing to Bailey and John Wesley. "The boys want to ask you something," he said to Bailey. "Would you mind stepping back in them woods there with them?"

"Listen," Bailey began, "we're in a terrible predicament. Nobody realizes   95
what this is," and his voice cracked. His eyes were as blue and intense as the parrots in his shirt and he remained perfectly still.

The grandmother reached up to adjust her hat brim as if she were going to the woods with him but it came off in her hand. She stood staring at it and after a second she let it fall on the ground. Hiram pulled Bailey up by the arm as if he were assisting an old man. John Wesley caught hold of his father's hand and Bobby Lee followed. They went off toward the woods and just as they reached the dark edge, Bailey turned and supporting himself against a gray naked pine trunk, he shouted, "I'll be back in a minute, Mamma, wait on me!"

"Come back this instant!" his mother shrilled but they all disappeared into the woods.

"Bailey Boy!" the grandmother called in a tragic voice but she found she was looking at The Misfit squatting on the ground in front of her. "I just know you're a good man," she said desperately. "You're not a bit common!"

"Nome, I ain't a good man," The Misfit said after a second as if he had considered her statement carefully, "but I ain't the worst in the world neither. My daddy said I was different breed of dog from my brothers and sisters. 'You know,' Daddy said, 'it's some that can live their whole life out without asking about it and it's others has to know why it is, and this boy is one of the latters. He's going to be into everything!' " He put on his black hat and looked up suddenly and then away deep into the woods as if he were embarrassed again. "I'm sorry I don't have on a shirt before you ladies," he said, hunching his shoulders slightly. "We buried our clothes that we had on when we escaped and we're just making do until we can get better. We borrowed these from some folks we met," he explained.

"That's perfectly all right," the grandmother said. "Maybe Bailey has an extra shirt in his suitcase." 100

"I'll look and see terrectly," the Misfit said.

"Where are they taking him?" the children's mother screamed.

"Daddy was a card himself," the Misfit said. "You couldn't put anything over on him. He never got in trouble with the Authorities though. Just had the knack of handling them."

"You could be honest too if you'd only try," said the grandmother. "Think how wonderful it would be to settle down and live a comfortable life and not have to think about somebody chasing you all the time."

The Misfit kept scratching in the ground with the butt of his gun as if he were thinking about it. "Yes'm, somebody is always after you," he murmured. 105

The grandmother noticed how thin his shoulder blades were just behind his hat because she was standing up looking down on him. "Do you ever pray?" she asked.

He shook his head. All she saw was the black hat wiggle between his shoulder blades. "Nome," he said.

There was a pistol shot from the woods, followed closely by another. Then silence. The old lady's head jerked around. She could hear the wind move through the tree tops like a long satisfied insuck of breath. "Bailey Boy!" she called.

"I was a gospel singer for a while," The Misfit said. "I been most everything. Been in the arm service, both land and sea, at home and abroad, been twict married, been an undertaker, been with the railroads, plowed Mother Earth, been in a tornado, seen a man burnt alive oncet," and he looked up at the children's mother and the little girl who were sitting close together, their faces white and their eyes glassy; "I even seen a woman flogged," he said.

"Pray, pray," the grandmother began, "pray, pray . . ." 110

"I never was a bad boy that I remember of," The Misfit said in an almost dreamy voice, "but somewheres along the line I done something wrong and got sent to the penitentiary. I was buried alive," and he looked up and held her attention to him by a steady stare.

"That's when you should have started to pray," she said. "What did you do to get sent to the penitentiary that first time?"

"Turn to the right, it was a wall," The Misfit said, looking up again at the cloudless sky. "Turn to the left, it was a wall. Look up it was a ceiling, look down it was a floor. I forgot what I done, lady. I set there and set there, trying to remember what it was I done and I ain't recalled it to this day. Oncet in a while, I would think it was coming to me, but it never come."

"Maybe they put you in by mistake," the old lady said vaguely.

"Nome," he said. "It wasn't no mistake. They had the papers on me."   115

"You must have stolen something," she said.

The Misfit sneered slightly. "Nobody had nothing I wanted," he said. "It was a head-doctor at the penitentiary said what I had done was kill my daddy but I know that for a lie. My daddy died in nineteen ought nineteen of the epidemic flu and I never had a thing to do with it. He was buried in the Mount Hopewell Baptist churchyard and you can go there and see for yourself."

"If you would pray," the old lady said, "Jesus would help you."

"That's right," The Misfit said.

"Well then, why don't you pray?" she asked trembling with delight suddenly.   120

"I don't want no hep," he said. "I'm doing all right by myself."

Bobby Lee and Hiram came ambling back from the woods. Bobby Lee was dragging a yellow shirt with bright blue parrots in it.

"Throw me that shirt, Bobby Lee," The Misfit said. The shirt came flying at him and landed on his shoulder and he put it on. The grandmother couldn't name what the shirt reminded her of. "No, lady," The Misfit said while he was buttoning it up. "I found out the crime don't matter. You can do one thing or you can do another, kill a man or take a tire off his car, because sooner or later you're going to forget what it was you done and just be punished for it."

The children's mother had begun to make heaving noises as if she couldn't get her breath. "Lady," he asked, "would you and that little girl like to step off yonder with Bobby Lee and Hiram and join your husband?"

"Yes, thank you," the mother said faintly. Her left arm dangled helplessly   125
and she was holding the baby, who had gone to sleep, in the other. "Hep that lady up, Hiram," The Misfit said as she struggled to climb out of the ditch, "and Bobby Lee, you hold onto that little girl's hand."

"I don't want to hold hands with him," June Star said. "He reminds me of a pig."

The fat boy blushed and laughed and caught her by the arm and pulled her off into the woods after Hiram and her mother.

Alone with The Misfit, the grandmother found that she had lost her voice. There was not a cloud in the sky nor any sun. There was nothing around her but woods. She wanted to tell him that he must pray. She opened and closed her mouth several times before anything came out. Finally she found herself saying, "Jesus, Jesus," meaning Jesus will help you, but the way she was saying it, it sounded as if she might be cursing.

"Yes'm," The Misfit said as if he agreed. "Jesus thown everything off balance. It was the same case with Him as with me except He hadn't committed any crime and they could prove I had committed one because they had the papers on me. Of course," he said, "they never shown me any papers. That's why I sign myself now. I said long ago, you get you a signature and sign everything you do and keep a copy of it. Then you'll know what you done and you can hold up the crime to the punishment and see do they match and in the end you'll have something to prove you ain't been treated right. I call myself The Misfit," he said, "because I can't make what all I done wrong fit what all I gone through in punishment."

There was a piercing scream from the woods, followed closely by a pistol 130 report. "Does it seem right to you, lady, that one is punished a heap and another ain't punished at all?"

"Jesus!" the old lady cried. "You've got good blood! I know you wouldn't shoot a lady! I know you come from nice people! Pray! Jesus, you ought not to shoot a lady: I'll give you all the money I've got!"

"Lady," The Misfit said, looking beyond her far into the woods, "there never was a body that give the undertaker a tip."

There were two more pistol reports and the grandmother raised her head like a parched old turkey hen crying for water and called, "Bailey Boy, Bailey Boy!" as if her heart would break.

"Jesus was the only One that ever raised the dead," The Misfit continued, "and He shouldn't have done it. He thrown everything off balance. If He did what He said, then it's nothing for you to do but thow away everything and follow Him, and if He didn't, then it's nothing for you to do but enjoy the few minutes you got left the best way you can—by killing somebody or burning down his house or doing some other meanness to him. No pleasure but meanness," he said and his voice had become almost a snarl.

"Maybe He didn't raise the dead," the old lady mumbled, not knowing what 135 she was saying and feeling so dizzy that she sank down in the ditch with her legs twisted under her.

"I wasn't there so I can't say He didn't," The Misfit said, "I wisht I had of been there," he said, hitting the ground with his fist. "It ain't right I wasn't there because if I had of been there I would of known. Listen lady," he said in a high voice, "if I had of been there I would of known and I wouldn't be like I am now." His voice seemed about to crack and the grandmother's head cleared for an instant. She saw the man's face twisted close to her own as if he were going to cry and she murmured, "Why you're one of my babies. You're one of my own children!" She reached out and touched him on the shoulder. The Misfit sprang back as if a snake had bitten him and shot her three times through the chest. Then he put his gun down on the ground and took off his glasses and began to clean them.

Hiram and Bobby Lee returned from the woods and stood over the ditch, looking down at the grandmother who half-sat and half lay in a puddle of blood with her legs crossed under her like a child's and her face smiling up at the cloudless sky.

Without his glasses, The Misfit's eyes were red-rimmed and pale and defenseless-looking. "Take her off and thow her where you thown the others," he said, picking up the cat that was rubbing itself against his leg.

"She was a talker, wasn't she?" Bobby Lee said, sliding down the ditch with a yodel.

"She would of been a good woman," The Misfit said, "if it had been somebody 140 there to shoot her every minute of her life."

"Some fun!" Bobby Lee said.

"Shut up, Bobby Lee," The Misfit said. "It's no real pleasure in life."

TILLIE OLSEN (b. 1913)

I Stand Here Ironing   1953–1954

I stand here ironing, and what you asked me moves tormented back and forth with the iron.

"I wish you would manage the time to come in and talk with me about your daughter. I'm sure you can help me understand her. She's a youngster who needs help and whom I'm deeply interested in helping."

"Who needs help.". . . Even if I came, what good would it do? You think because I am her mother I have a key, or that in some way you could use me as a key? She has lived for nineteen years. There is all that life that has happened outside of me, beyond me.

And when is there time to remember, to sift, to weigh, to estimate, to total? I will start and there will be an interruption and I will have to gather it all together again. Or I will become engulfed with all I did or did not do, with what should have been and what cannot be helped.

She was a beautiful baby. The first and only one of our five that was beautiful   5
at birth. You do not guess how new and uneasy her tenancy in her now-loveliness. You did not know her all those years she was thought homely, or see her poring over her baby pictures, making me tell her over and over how beautiful she had been—and would be, I would tell her—and was now, to the seeing eye. But the seeing eyes were few or nonexistent. Including mine.

I nursed her. They feel that's important nowadays. I nursed all the children, but with her, with all the fierce rigidity of first motherhood, I did like the books then said. Though her cries battered me to trembling and my breasts ached with swollenness, I waited till the clock decreed.

Why do I put that first? I do not even know if it matters, or if it explains anything.

She was a beautiful baby. She blew shining bubbles of sound. She loved motion, loved light, loved color and music and textures. She would lie on the floor in her blue overalls patting the surface so hard in ecstasy her hands and feet would blur. She was a miracle to me, but when she was eight months old I had to leave her daytimes with the woman downstairs to whom she was no miracle at all, for I worked or looked for work and for Emily's father, who "could no longer endure" (he wrote in his good-bye note) "sharing want with us."

I was nineteen. It was the pre-relief, pre-WPA world of the depression. I would start running as soon as I got off the streetcar, running up the stairs, the place smelling sour, and awake or asleep to startle awake, when she saw me she would break into a clogged weeping that could not be comforted, a weeping I can hear yet.

After a while I found a job hashing at night so I could be with her days,   10
and it was better. But it came to where I had to bring her to his family and leave her.

It took a long time to raise the money for her fare back. Then she got chicken pox and I had to wait longer. When she finally came, I hardly knew her, walking quick and nervous like her father, looking like her father, thin, and dressed in a shoddy red that yellowed her skin and glared at the pockmarks. All the baby loveliness gone.

She was two. Old enough for nursery school they said, and I did not know then what I know now—the fatigue of the long day, and the lacerations of group life in the kinds of nurseries that are only parking places for children.

Except that it would have made no difference if I had known. It was the only place there was. It was the only way we could be together, the only way I could hold a job.

And even without knowing, I knew. I knew the teacher that was evil because all these years it has curdled into my memory, the little boy hunched in the corner, her rasp, "why aren't you outside, because Alvin hits you? that's no reason, go out, scaredy." I knew Emily hated it even if she did not clutch and implore "don't go Mommy" like the other children, mornings.

She always had a reason why we should stay home. Momma, you look sick.   15
Momma, I feel sick. Momma, the teachers aren't there today, they're sick. Momma, we can't go, there was a fire there last night. Momma, it's a holiday today, no school, they told me.

But never a direct protest, never rebellion. I think of our others in their three-, four-year-oldness—the explosions, the tempers, the denunciations, the demands—and I feel suddenly ill. I put the iron down. What in me demanded that goodness in her? And what was the cost, the cost to her of such goodness?

The old man living in the back once said in his gentle way: "You should smile at Emily more when you look at her." What *was* in my face when I looked at her? I loved her. There were all the acts of love.

It was only with the others I remembered what he said, and it was the face of joy, and not of care or tightness or worry I turned to them—too late for Emily. She does not smile easily, let alone almost always as her brothers and sisters do. Her face is closed and sombre, but when she wants, how fluid. You must have seen it in her pantomimes, you spoke of her rare gift for comedy on the stage that rouses a laughter out of the audience so dear they applaud and applaud and do not want to let her go.

Where does it come from, that comedy? There was none of it in her when she came back to me that second time, after I had had to send her away again. She had a new daddy now to learn to love, and I think perhaps it was a better time.

Except when we left her alone nights, telling ourselves she was old enough.   20
"Can't you go some other time, Mommy, like tomorrow?" she would ask. "Will it be just a little while you'll be gone? Do you promise?"

The time we came back, the front door open, the clock on the floor in the hall. She rigid awake. "It wasn't just a little while. I didn't cry. Three times I called you, just three times, and then I ran downstairs to open the door so you could come faster. The clock talked loud. I threw it away, it scared me what it talked."

She said the clock talked loud again that night I went to the hospital to have Susan. She was delirious with the fever that comes before red measles, but she was fully conscious all the week I was gone and the week after we were home when she could not come near the new baby or me.

She did not get well. She stayed skeleton thin, not wanting to eat, and night after night she had nightmares. She would call for me, and I would rouse from exhaustion to sleepily call back: "You're all right, darling, go to sleep, it's just a dream," and if she still called, in a sterner voice, "now go to sleep, Emily, there's nothing to hurt you." Twice, only twice, when I had to get up for Susan anyhow, I went in to sit with her.

Now when it is too late (as if she would let me hold and comfort her like I   25
do the others) I get up and go to her at once at her moan or restless stirring. "Are you awake, Emily? Can I get you something?" And the answer is always the same: "No, I'm all right, go back to sleep, Mother."

They persuaded me at the clinic to send her away to a convalescent home in the country where "she can have the kind of food and care you can't manage for her, and you'll be free to concentrate on the new baby." They still send children to that place. I see pictures on the society page of sleek young women planning affairs to raise money for it, or dancing at the affairs, or decorating Easter eggs or filling Christmas stockings for the children.

They never have a picture of the children so I do not know if the girls still wear those gigantic red bows and the ravaged looks on the every other Sunday when parents can come to visit "unless otherwise notified"—as we were notified the first six weeks.

Oh it is a handsome place, green lawns and tall trees and fluted flower beds. High up on the balconies of each cottage the children stand, the girls in their red bows and white dresses, the boys in white suits and giant red ties. The parents stand below shrieking up to be heard and the children shriek down to be heard, and between them the invisible wall "Not To Be Contaminated by Parental Germs or Physical Affection."

There was a tiny girl who always stood hand in hand with Emily. Her parents never came. One visit she was gone. "They moved her to Rose Cottage" Emily shouted in explanation. "They don't like you to love anybody here."

She wrote once a week, the labored writing of a seven-year-old. "I am fine.   30
How is the baby. If I write my leter nicly I will have a star. Love." There never was a star. We wrote every other day, letters she could never hold or keep but only hear read—once. "We simply do not have room for children to keep any personal possessions," they patiently explained when we pieced one Sunday's shrieking together to plead how much it would mean to Emily, who loved so to keep things, to be allowed to keep her letters and cards.

Each visit she looked frailer. "She isn't eating." they told us.

(They had runny eggs for breakfast or mush with lumps, Emily said later, I'd hold it in my mouth and not swallow. Nothing ever tasted good, just when they had chicken.)

It took us eight months to get her released home, and only the fact that she gained back so little of her seven lost pounds convinced the social worker.

I used to try to hold and love her after she came back, but her body would stay stiff, and after a while she'd push away. She ate little. Food sickened her, and I think much of life too. Oh she had physical lightness and brightness, twinkling by on skates, bouncing like a ball up and down up and down over the jump rope, skimming over the hill; but these were momentary.

She fretted about her appearance, thin and dark and foreign-looking at a   35
time when every little girl was supposed to look or thought she should look a chubby blonde replica of Shirley Temple. The doorbell sometimes rang for her, but no one seemed to come and play in the house or be a best friend. Maybe because we moved so much.

There was a boy she loved painfully through two school semesters. Months later she told me how she had taken pennies from my purse to buy him candy. "Licorice was his favorite and I brought him some every day, but he still liked Jennifer better'n me. Why, Mommy?" The kind of question for which there is no answer.

School was a worry to her. She was not glib or quick in a world where glibness and quickness were easily confused with ability to learn. To her overworked and exasperated teachers she was an overconscientious "slow learner" who kept trying to catch up and was absent entirely too often.

I let her be absent, though sometimes the illness was imaginary. How different from my now-strictness about attendance with the others. I wasn't working. We had a new baby, I was home anyhow. Sometimes, after Susan grew old enough, I would keep her home from school, too, to have them all together.

Mostly Emily had asthma, and her breathing, harsh and labored, would fill the house with a curiously tranquil sound. I would bring the two old dresser mirrors and her boxes of collections to her bed. She would select beads and single earrings, bottle tops and shells, dried flowers and pebbles, old postcards and scraps, all sorts of oddments; then she and Susan would play Kingdom, setting up landscapes and furniture, peopling them with action.

Those were the only times of peaceful companionship between her and Susan. I have edged away from it, that poisonous feeling between them, that terrible balancing of hurts and needs I had to do between the two, and did so badly, those earlier years.

Oh there are conflicts between the others too, each one human, needing, demanding, hurting, taking—but only between Emily and Susan, no, Emily toward Susan that corroding resentment. It seems so obvious on the surface, yet it is not obvious. Susan, the second child, Susan, golden- and curly-haired and chubby, quick and articulate and assured, everything in appearance and manner Emily was not; Susan, not able to resist Emily's precious things, losing or sometimes clumsily breaking them; Susan telling jokes and riddles to company for applause while Emily sat silent (to say to me later: that was *my* riddle, Mother, I told it to Susan); Susan, who for all the five years' difference in age was just a year behind Emily in developing physically.

I am glad for that slow physical development that widened the difference between her and her contemporaries, though she suffered over it. She was too vulnerable for that terrible world of youthful competition, of preening and parading, of constant measuring of yourself against every other, of envy, "If I had that copper hair," "If I had that skin. . . ." She tormented herself enough about not looking like the others, there was enough of the unsureness, the having to be conscious of words before you speak, the constant caring—what are they thinking of me? without having it all magnified by the merciless physical drives.

Ronnie is calling. He is wet and I change him. It is rare there is such a cry now. That time of motherhood is almost behind me when the ear is not one's own but must always be racked and listening for the child cry, the child call. We sit for a while and I hold him, looking out over the city spread in charcoal with its soft aisles of light. "*Shoogily*," he breathes and curls closer. I carry him back to bed, asleep. *Shoogily*. A funny word, a family word, inherited from Emily, invented by her to say: *comfort*.

40

In this and other ways she leaves her seal, I say aloud. And startle at my saying it. What do I mean? What did I start to gather together, to try and make coherent? I was at the terrible, growing years. War years. I do not remember them well. I was working, there were four smaller ones now, there was not time for her. She had to help be a mother, and housekeeper, and shopper. She had to set her seal. Mornings of crisis and near hysteria trying to get lunches packed, hair combed, coats and shoes found, everyone to school or Child Care on time, the baby ready for transportation. And always the paper scribbled on by a smaller one, the book looked at by Susan then mislaid, the homework not done. Running out to that huge school where she was one, she was lost, she was a drop; suffering over the unpreparedness, stammering and unsure in her classes.

There was so little time left at night after the kids were bedded down. She   45
would struggle over books, always eating (it was in those years she developed her enormous appetite that is legendary in our family) and I would be ironing, or preparing food for the next day, or writing V-mail to Bill, or tending the baby. Sometimes, to make me laugh, or out of her despair, she would imitate happenings or types at school.

I think I said once: "Why don't you do something like this in the school amateur show?" One morning she phoned me at work, hardly understandable through the weeping: "Mother, I did it. I won, I won; they gave me first prize; they clapped and clapped and wouldn't let me go."

Now suddenly she was Somebody, and as imprisoned in her difference as she had been in anonymity.

She began to be asked to perform at other high schools, even in colleges, then at city and statewide affairs. The first one we went to, I only recognized her that first moment when thin, shy, she almost drowned herself into the curtains. Then: Was this Emily? The control, the command, the convulsing and deadly clowning, the spell, then the roaring, stamping audience, unwilling to let this rare and precious laughter out of their lives.

Afterwards: You ought to do something about her with a gift like that—but without money or knowing how, what does one do? We have left it all to her, and the gift has as often eddied inside, clogged and clotted, as been used and growing.

She is coming. She runs up the stairs two at a time with her light graceful   50
step, and I know she is happy tonight. Whatever it was that occasioned your call did not happen today.

"Aren't you ever going to finish the ironing, Mother? Whistler painted his mother in a rocker. I'd have to paint mine standing over an ironing board." This is one of her communicative nights and she tells me everything and nothing as she fixes herself a plate of food out of the icebox.

She is so lovely. Why did you want me to come in at all? Why were you concerned? She will find her way.

She starts up the stairs to bed. "Don't get me up with the rest in the morning." "But I thought you were having midterms." "Oh, those," she comes back in, kisses me, and says quite lightly, "in a couple of years when we'll all be atom-dead they won't matter a bit."

She has said it before. She *believes* it. But because I have been dredging the past, and all that compounds a human being is so heavy and meaningful in me, I cannot endure it tonight.

I will never total it all. I will never come in to say: She was a child seldom   55
smiled at. Her father left me before she was a year old. I had to work her first
six years when there was work, or I sent her home and to his relatives. There
were years she had care she hated. She was dark and thin and foreign-looking in
a world where the prestige went to blondeness and curly hair and dimples, she
was slow where glibness was prized. She was a child of anxious, not proud, love.
We were poor and could not afford for her the soil of easy growth. I was a young
mother, I was a distracted mother. There were the other children pushing up,
demanding. Her younger sister seemed all that she was not. There were years
she did not want me to touch her. She kept too much in herself, her life was
such she had to keep too much in herself. My wisdom came too late. She has
much to her and probably little will come of it. She is a child of her age, of depression, of war, of fear.

Let her be. So all that is in her will not bloom—but in how many does it?
There is still enough left to live by. Only help her to know—help make it so
there is cause for her to know—that she is more than this dress on the ironing
board, helpless before the iron.

GRACE PALEY (b. 1922)

Goodbye and Good Luck   *(1959)*

I was popular in certain circles, says Aunt Rose. I wasn't no thinner then, only
more stationary in the flesh. In time to come, Lillie, don't be surprised—change
is a fact of God. From this no one is excused. Only a person like your mama
stands on one foot, she don't notice how big her behind is getting and sings in
the canary's ear for thirty years. Who's listening? Papa's in the shop. You and
Seymour, thinking about yourself. So she waits in a spotless kitchen for a kind
word and thinks—poor Rosie. . . .

Poor Rosie! If there was more life in my little sister, she would know my
heart is a regular college of feelings and there is such information between my
corset and me that her whole married life is a kindergarten.

Nowadays you could find me any time in a hotel, uptown or downtown.
Who needs an apartment to live like a maid with a dustrag in the hand, sneezing?
I'm in very good with the bus boys, it's more interesting than home, all kinds of
people, everybody with a reason. . . .

And my reason, Lillie, is a long time ago I said to the forelady, "Missus, if
I can't sit by the window, I can't sit." "If you can't sit, girlie," she says politely,
"go stand on the street corner." And that's how I got unemployed in novelty
wear.

For my next job I answered an ad which said: "Refined young lady, medium   5
salary, cultural organization." I went by trolley to the address, the Russian Art
Theater of Second Avenue where they played only the best Yiddish plays. They
needed a ticket seller, someone like me, who likes the public but is very sharp
on crooks. The man who interviewed me was the manager, a certain type.

Immediately he said: "Rosie Lieber, you surely got a build on you!"

"It takes all kinds, Mr. Krimberg."

"Don't misunderstand me, little girl," he said. "I appreciate, I appreciate.

A young lady lacking fore and aft, her blood is so busy warming the toes and the finger tips, it don't have time to circulate where it's most required."

Everybody likes kindness. I said to him: "Only don't be fresh, Mr. Krimberg, and we'll make a good bargain."

We did: Nine dollars a week, a glass of tea every night, a free ticket once a week for Mama, and I could go watch rehearsals any time I want.   10

My first nine dollars was in the grocer's hands ready to move on already, when Krimberg said to me, "Rosie, here's a great gentleman, a member of this remarkable theater, wants to meet you, impressed no doubt by your big brown eyes."

And who was it, Lillie? Listen to me, before my very eyes was Volodya Vlashkin, called by the people of those days the Valentino of Second Avenue. I took one look, and I said to myself: Where did a Jewish boy grow up so big? "Just outside Kiev," he told me.

How? "My mama nursed me till I was six. I was the only boy in the village to have such health."

"My goodness, Vlashkin, six years old! She must have had shredded wheat there, not breasts, poor woman."

"My mother was beautiful," he said. "She had eyes like stars."   15

He had such a way of expressing himself, it brought tears.

To Krimberg, Vlashkin said after this introduction: "Who is responsible for hiding this wonderful young person in a cage?"

"That is where the ticket seller sells."

"So, David, go in there and sell tickets for a half hour. I have something in mind in regards to the future of this girl and this company. Go, David, be a good boy. And you, Miss Lieber, please, I suggest Feinberg's for a glass of tea. The rehearsals are long. I enjoy a quiet interlude with a friendly person."

So he took me there, Feinberg's, then around the corner, a place so full of Hungarians, it was deafening. In the back room was a table of honor for him. On the tablecloth embroidered by the lady of the house was "Here Vlashkin Eats." We finished one glass of tea in quietness, out of thirst, when I finally made up my mind what to say.   20

"Mr. Vlashkin, I saw you a couple weeks ago, even before I started working here, in *The Sea Gull*. Believe me, if I was that girl, I wouldn't look even for a minute on the young bourgeois fellow. He could fall out of the play altogether. How Chekhov could put him in the same play as you, I can't understand."

"You liked me?" he asked, taking my hand and kindly patting it. "Well, well, young people still like me . . . so, and you like the theater too? Good. And you, Rose, you know you have such a nice hand, so warm to the touch, such a fine skin, tell me, why do you wear a scarf around your neck? You only hide your young, young throat. These are not olden times, my child, to live in shame."

"Who's ashamed?" I said, taking off the kerchief, but my hand right away went to the kerchief's place, because the truth is, it really was olden times, and I was still of a nature to melt with shame.

"Have some more tea, my dear."

"No, thank you, I am a samovar already."   25

"Dorfmann!" he hollered like a king. "Bring this child a seltzer with fresh ice!"

In weeks to follow I had the privilege to know him better and better as a person—also the opportunity to see him in his profession. The time was autumn; the theater full of coming and going. Rehearsing without end. After *The Sea Gull* flopped *The Salesman from Istanbul* played, a great success.

Here the ladies went crazy. On the opening night, in the middle of the first scene, one missus—a widow or her husband worked too long hours—began to clap and sing out, "Oi, oi, Vlashkin." Soon there was such a tumult, the actors had to stop acting. Vlashkin stepped forward. Only not Vlashkin to the eyes . . . a younger man with pitch-black hair, lively on restless feet, his mouth clever. A half a century later at the end of the play he came out again, a gray philosopher, a student of life from only reading books, his hands as smooth as silk. . . . I cried to think who I was—nothing—and such a man could look at me with interest.

Then I got a small raise, due to he kindly put in a good word for me, and also for fifty cents a night I was given the pleasure together with cousins, in-laws, and plain stage-struck kids to be part of a crowd scene and to see like he saw every single night the hundreds of pale faces waiting for his feelings to make them laugh or bend down their heads in sorrow.

The sad day came, I kissed my mama goodbye. Vlashkin helped me to get a reasonable room near the theater to be more free. Also my outstanding friend would have a place to recline away from the noise of the dressing rooms. She cried and she cried. "This is a different way of living, Mama," I said. "Besides, I am driven by love." ⟶ 30

"You! You, a nothing, a rotten hole in a piece of cheese, are you telling me what is life?" she screamed.

Very insulted, I went away from her. But I am good-natured—you know fat people are like that—kind, and I thought to myself, poor Mama . . . it is true she got more of an idea of life than me. She married who she didn't like, a sick man, his spirit already swallowed up by God. He never washed. He had an unhappy smell. His teeth fell out, his hair disappeared, he got smaller, shriveled up little by little, till goodbye and good luck he was gone and only came to Mama's mind when she went to the mailbox under the stairs to get the electric bill. In memory of him and out of respect for mankind, I decided to live for love.

Don't laugh, you ignorant girl.

Do you think it was easy for me? I had to give Mama a little something. Ruthie was saving up together with your papa for linens, a couple knives and forks. In the morning I had to do piecework if I wanted to keep by myself. So I made flowers. Before lunch time every day a whole garden grew on my table.

This was my independence, Lillie dear, blooming, but it didn't have no roots and its face was paper. ⟶ 35

Meanwhile Krimberg went after me too. No doubt observing the success of Vlashkin, he thought, "Aha, open sesame . . ." Others in the company similar. After me in those years were the following: Krimberg I mentioned. Carl Zimmer, played innocent young fellows with a wig. Charlie Peel, a Christian who fell in the soup by accident, a creator of beautiful sets. "Color is his middle name," says Vlashkin, always to the point.

I put this in to show you your fat old aunt was not crazy out of loneliness. In those noisy years I had friends among interesting people who admired me for reasons of youth and that I was a first-class listener.

The actresses—Raisele, Marya, Esther Leopold—were only interested in tomorrow. After them was the rich men, producers, the whole garment center; their
past is a pincushion, future the eye of a needle.

Finally the day came, I no longer could keep my tact in my mouth. I said:
"Vlashkin, I hear by carrier pigeon you have a wife, children, the whole combination."

"True, I don't tell stories. I make no pretense."   40

"That isn't the question. What is this lady like? It hurts me to ask, but tell
me, Vlashkin . . . a man's life is something I don't clearly see."

"Little girl, I have told you a hundred times, this small room is the convent
of my troubled spirit. Here I come to your innocent shelter to refresh myself in
the midst of an agonized life."

"Ach, Vlashkin, serious, serious, who is this lady?"

"Rosie, she is a fine woman of the middle classes, a good mother to my
children, three in number, girls all, a good cook, in her youth handsome, now
no longer young. You see, could I be more frank? I entrust you, dear, with my
soul."

It was some few months later at the New Year's ball of the Russian Artists   45
Club, I met Mrs. Vlashkin, a woman with black hair in a low bun, straight and
too proud. She sat at a small table speaking in a deep voice to whoever stopped
a moment to converse. Her Yiddish was perfect, each word cut like a special jewel.
I looked at her. She noticed me like she noticed everybody, cold like Christmas
morning. Then she got tired. Vlashkin called a taxi and I never saw her again.
Poor woman, she did not know I was on the same stage with her. The poison I
was to her role, she did not know.

Later on that night in front of my door I said to Vlashkin, "No more. This
isn't for me. I am sick from it all. I am no home breaker."

"Girlie," he said, "don't be foolish."

"No, no, goodbye, good luck," I said. "I am sincere."

So I went and stayed with Mama for a week's vacation and cleaned up all
the closets and scrubbed the walls till the paint came off. She was very grateful,
all the same her hard life made her say, "Now we see the end. If you live like a
bum, you are finally a lunatic."

After this few days I came back to my life. When we met, me and Vlashkin,   50
we said only hello and goodbye, and then for a few sad years, with the head we
nodded as if to say, "Yes, yes, I know who you are."

Meanwhile in the field was a whole new strategy. Your mama and your grand-
mama brought around—boys. Your own father had a brother, you never even
seen him. Ruben. A serious fellow, his idealism was his hat and his coat, "Rosie,
I offer you a big new free happy unusual life." How? "With me, we will raise up
the sands of Palestine to make a nation. That is the land of tomorrow for us
Jews." "Ha-ha, Ruben, I'll go tomorrow then." "Rosie!" says Ruben. "We need
strong women like you, mothers and farmers." "You don't fool me, Ruben, what
you need is dray horses. But for that you need more money." "I don't like your
attitude, Rose." "In that case, go and multiply. Goodbye."

Another fellow: Yonkel Gurstein, a regular sport, dressed to kill, with such
an excitable nature. In those days—it looks to me like yesterday—the youngest
girls wore undergarments like Battle Creek, Michigan. To him it was a matter of

seconds. Where did he practice, a Jewish boy? Nowadays I suppose it is easier, Lillie? My goodness, I ain't asking you nothing—touchy, touchy. . . .

Well, by now you must know yourself, honey, whatever you do, life don't stop. It only sits a minute and dreams a dream.

While I was saying to all these silly youngsters "no, no, no," Vlashkin went to Europe and toured a few seasons . . . Moscow, Prague, London, even Berlin— already a pessimistic place. When he came back he wrote a book, you could get from the library even today, *The Jewish Actor Abroad.* If someday you're interested enough in my lonesome years, you could read it. You could absorb a flavor of the man from the book. No, no, I am not mentioned. After all, who am I?

When the book came out I stopped him in the street to say congratulations. But I am not a liar, so I pointed out, too, the egotism of many parts—even the critics said something along such lines.

"Talk is cheap," Vlashkin answered me. "But who are the critics? Tell me, do they create? Not to mention," he continues, "there is a line in Shakespeare in one of the plays from the great history of England. It says, 'Self-loving is not so vile a sin, my liege, as self-neglecting.' This idea also appears in modern times in the moralistic followers of Freud. . . . Rosie, are you listening? You asked a question. By the way, you look very well. How come no wedding ring?"

I walked away from this conversation in tears. But this talking in the street opened the happy road up for more discussions. In regard to many things. . . . For instance, the management—very narrow-minded—wouldn't give him any more certain young men's parts. Fools. What youngest man knew enough about life to be as young as him?

"Rosie, Rosie," he said to me one day, "I see by the clock on your rosy, rosy face you must be thirty."

"The hands are slow, Vlashkin. On a week before Thursday I was thirty-four."

"Is that so? Rosie, I worry about you. It has been on my mind to talk to you. You are losing your time. Do you understand it? A woman should not lose her time."

"Oi, Vlashkin, if you are my friend, what is time?"

For this he had no answer, only looked at me surprised. We went instead, full of interest but not with our former speed, up to my new place on Ninety-fourth Street. The same pictures on the wall, all of Vlashkin, only now everything painted red and black, which was stylish, and new upholstery.

A few years ago there was a book by another member of that fine company, an actress, the one that learned English very good and went uptown—Marya Kavkaz, in which she says certain things regarding Vlashkin. Such as, he was her lover for eleven years, she's not ashamed to write this down. Without respect for him, his wife and children, or even others who also may have feelings in the matter.

Now, Lillie, don't be surprised. This is called a fact of life. An actor's soul must be like a diamond. The more faces it got the more shining is his name. Honey, you will no doubt love and marry one man and have a couple kids and be happy forever till you die tired. More than that, a person like us don't have to know. But a great artist like Volodya Vlashkin . . . in order to make a job on the stage, he's got to practice. I understand it now, to him life is like a rehearsal.

Myself, when I saw him in *The Father-in-law*—an older man in love with a

55

60

65

darling young girl, his son's wife, played by Raisele Maisel—I cried. What he said to this girl, how he whispered such sweetness, how all his hot feelings were on his face . . . Lillie, all this experience he had with me. The very words were the same. You can imagine how proud I was.

So the story creeps to an end.

I noticed it first on my mother's face, the rotten handwriting of time, scribbled up and down her cheeks, across her forehead back and forth—a child could read—it said, old, old, old. But it troubled my heart most to see these realities scratched on Vlashkin's wonderful expression.

First the company fell apart. The theater ended. Esther Leopold died from being very aged. Krimberg had a heart attack. Marya went to Broadway. Also Raisele changed her name to Roslyn and was a big comical hit in the movies. Vlashkin himself, no place to go, retired. It said in the paper, "an actor without peer, he will write his memoirs and spend his last years in the bosom of his family among his thriving grandchildren, the apple of his wife's doting eye."

This is journalism.

We made for him a great dinner of honor. At this dinner I said to him, for 70
the last time, I thought, "Goodbye, dear friend, topic of my life, now we part."
And to myself I said further: Finished. This is your lonesome bed. A lady what they call fat and fifty. You made it personally. From this lonesome bed you will finally fall to a bed not so lonesome, only crowded with a million bones.

And now comes? Lillie, guess.

Last week, washing my underwear in the basin, I get a buzz on the phone. "Excuse me, is this the Rose Lieber formerly connected with the Russian Art Theater?"

"It is."

"Well, well, how do you do, Rose? This is Vlashkin."

"Vlashkin! Volodya Vlashkin?"

"In fact. How are you, Rose?" 75

"Living, Vlashkin, thank you."

"You are all right? Really, Rose? Your health is good? You are working?"

"My health, considering the weight it must carry, is first-class. I am back for some years now where I started, in novelty wear."

"Very interesting." 80

"Listen, Vlashkin, tell me the truth, what's on your mind?"

"My mind? Rosie, I am looking up an old friend, an old warmhearted companion of more joyful days. My circumstances, by the way, are changed. I am retired, as you know. Also I am a free man."

"What? What do you mean?"

"Mrs. Vlashkin is divorcing me."

"What come over her? Did you start drinking or something from melancholy?" 85

"She is divorcing me for adultery."

"But, Vlashkin, you should excuse me, don't be insulted, but you got maybe seventeen, eighteen years on me, and even me, all this nonsense—this daydreams and nightmares—is mostly for the pleasure of conversation alone."

"I pointed all this out to her. My dear, I said, my time is past, my blood is as dry as my bones. The truth is, Rose, she isn't accustomed to have a man around all day, reading out loud from the papers the interesting events of our time, waiting for breakfast, waiting for lunch. So all day she gets madder and madder. By nighttime a furious old lady gives me my supper. She has information from the last fifty years to pepper my soup. Surely there was a Judas in that theater, saying every day, 'Vlashkin, Vlashkin, Vlashkin . . .' and while my heart was circulating with his smiles he was on the wire passing the dope to my wife."

"Such a foolish end, Volodya, to such a lively story. What is your plans?"

"First, could I ask you for dinner and the theater—uptown, of course? After this . . . we are old friends. I have money to burn. What your heart desires. Others are like grass, the north wind of time has cut out their heart. Of you, Rosie, I recreate only kindness. What a woman should be to a man, you were to me. Do you think, Rosie, a couple of old pals like us could have a few good times among the material things of this world?" 90

My answer, Lillie, in a minute was altogether. "Yes, yes, come up," I said. "Ask the room by the switchboard, let us talk."

So he came that night and every night in the week, we talked of his long life. Even at the end of time, a fascinating man. And like men are, too, till time's end, trying to get away in one piece.

"Listen, Rosie," he explains the other day. "I was married to my wife, do you realize, nearly half a century. What good was it? Look at the bitterness. The more I think of it, the more I think we would be fools to marry."

"Volodya Vlashkin," I told him straight, "when I was young I warmed your cold back many a night, no questions asked. You admit it, I didn't make no demands. I was softhearted. I didn't want to be called Rosie Lieber, a breaker up of homes. But now, Vlashkin, you are a free man. How could you ask me to go with you on trains to stay in strange hotels, among Americans, not your wife? Be ashamed."

So now, darling Lillie, tell this story to your mama from your young mouth. 95 She don't listen to a word from me. She only screams, "I'll faint, I'll faint." Tell her after all I'll have a husband, which, as everybody knows, a woman should have at least one before the end of the story.

My goodness, I am already late. Give me a kiss. After all, I watched you grow from a plain seed. So give me a couple wishes on my wedding day. A long and happy life. Many years of love. Hug Mama, tell her from Aunt Rose, goodbye and good luck.

Poetry

11

Meeting Poetry:
Simple Theme and Form

WHAT POETRY IS

There is no neat and simple definition of poetry. Any definition would inevitably be too limited. Poetry embraces too many different forms, styles, subjects, motives, and emotions to be captured in a single descriptive statement. In addition, such an attempt at definition would prevent you from developing your own ideas about poetry. It is our hope that you will learn what poetry is by studying and enjoying a great number of poems and then forming some general ideas about the genre.

We cannot even tell what poetry is from the way it looks. People often assume that anything written in short lines with white space on each side and a certain amount of rhythm and rhyme (words at the ends of lines that sound alike) is poetry. We might call this the "I can't define it, but I know it when I see it" school of thought. Experience teaches us, however, that even this method of identification is inadequate. There are many things that look like poetry and even sound like poetry but clearly are not poetry. Consider, for example, the memory device that many of us use to remember how to spell words containing the letters *i* and *e* together:

> I before E
> Except after C
> Or when sounded like A
> As in "neighbor" and "weigh."

This jingle has rhyme, rhythm, short lines, and plenty of white space, but few of us would call it a poem. By the same token, some poetry in this text is not written in short lines, has no rhythm or rhyme, is not arranged in neat stanzas, and has very little white space. You will see poetry that

459

looks just like prose, whose lines form a picture of a specific object, or whose words are scattered all over the page. Poetry simply cannot be defined by the way it looks.

Since we cannot define poetry or say what it looks like, what can we know about it as we begin this exploration? To begin with, we can assert that poetry is an imaginative statement expressed in words that are used with the utmost economy and resonance. It offers us a compressed moment of thought, feeling, and experience. Poetry may tell a story, express an idea, delineate a character, convey an emotion, describe a setting, examine a situation, do all these at once, or do almost anything else the poet desires. It is designed to surprise, delight, move, and broaden the reader. Ideally, it evokes both an emotional and a thoughtful response from us. Poetry often asks us to reexamine our lives, world, ideas, or feelings from a new perspective.

WHY STUDY POETRY?

It is often asserted that poetry should not be studied at all. Some people take this position partly out of fear and partly out of disinterest; they have conditioned themselves to ignore poetry because they consider it an unnecessarily difficult way of saying things. But poetry does a great deal more than say things in a complicated way. It enriches us, moves us, makes us think in new ways, and sharpens our analytical skills. As our oldest literary genre, poetry has been an important part of human society since primitive tribes first chanted poetic rites of death, fertility, and rebirth at the dawn of civilization. In its earliest forms, it was closely linked with magic, religion, and divine inspiration; it expressed the spiritual side of human consciousness. Thus, we study poetry because it represents an important part of what it means to be human. It is a central part of our heritage as a species.

Some people may object to the study of poetry because they consider reading poetry an ecstatic or religious experience that should not be diminished by analysis or discussion. To these objections, we answer that informed appreciation, and even informed ecstasy, is more valuable than simple swooning. The study of poetry inevitably leads to greater enjoyment and appreciation through greater understanding. Moreover, poems are hearty and resilient creatures that survive whatever analytical operations we perform on them. Indeed, we might argue that poetry thrives under the scalpel and microscope of close analysis; the poems we know best and like most are usually the ones we have studied most carefully.

HOW POETRY WORKS

Poetry has a great deal in common with prose fiction: it creates an imaginative statement through language, and it shares such elements as speaker (or narrator), point of view, tone, style, and theme. Still, there are many significant differences between poetry and prose fiction. Four of these are **economy, imagery, rhythm,** and **sound.** By **economy,** we mean that poetry is far more condensed and compressed than prose, and consequently each word must effectively carry part of the burden of the poem's total impact and meaning. Thus, careful attention must be given to every word. Poetry also relies much more heavily on imagery than does prose. **Imagery,** in general, refers to forms of compressed representation that work through comparison, allusion, or suggestion. Also, because poetry is so compact and economical, the **rhythms** of poetic speech become as important as the words, images, and ideas. Finally, the **sound** of a poem when it is read aloud (or sounded in the mind) often contributes to the impact of the work.

As we begin our examination of poetry, we should keep a number of general considerations in mind. People often assume that poetry must be beautiful and must convey a clearly stated message or moral. Neither of these assumptions is true. Consider the following poem by the American poet Randall Jarrell:

The Death of the Ball Turret Gunner   *1945*

From my mother's sleep I fell into the State
And I hunched in its belly till my wet fur froze.
Six miles from earth, loosed from its dream of life,
I woke to black flak and the nightmare fighters.
When I died they washed me out of the turret with a hose.

The poem describes the death of a gunner on a World War II bomber. After it was first published, Jarrell added a note in which he explained that "a ball turret was a Plexiglas sphere set into the belly of a B-17 or B-24 and inhabited by two .50-calibre machine guns and one man, a short small man. When this gunner tracked with his machine guns a fighter attacking his bomber from below, he revolved with the turret; hunched upside-down in his little sphere, he looked like a fetus in the womb. The fighters which attacked him were armed with cannon firing exploding shells. The hose was a steam hose."

The central comparison in this poem is between the image of the fetus in the womb and the ball turret gunner in his little sphere. In the first two lines, the gunner (who speaks the poem) moves from his mother's womb ("sleep") into the world, the war, the bomber, and the gun turret (all subsumed in the word *State*). The speaker "hunched" in the cramped ball turret just as a fetus sleeps in the womb. The frozen "wet fur" combines the two situations, referring to both the wet fur of a newly born animal and the fur collars on the jackets worn by World War II fliers. The transition from "sleep" to "State" removes the gunner from the earth and life—"its dream of life"—to a world of death "six miles" in the air, defined by "black flak and the nightmare fighters." Finally, the gory insignificance of the gunner's death is captured in the image of washing his scattered remains "out of the turret with a hose."

The last line is grimly ironic, since "washing out" in army jargon usually referred to being dismissed from a training program because of incompetence. This gunner was "washed out" in an entirely different manner. This last line also reconnects the images of the dead gunner and the sleeping fetus through an indirect reference to abortion. Aborted fetuses are "washed out" of the womb just as this gunner is "washed out" of the ball turret. There is nothing beautiful or sweet about this poem; it conveys the grisly reality of aerial warfare in World War II. Similarly, there is no explicit message or moral here; the poet does not tell us what to think about the gunner, his death, or war in general. Instead, he presents a vivid image of an event and lets us draw our own conclusions.

Jarrell's poem illustrates the kind of real experience that poetry can embody. Poetry is not limited to considerations of love, flowers, or spring. Rather, it comes to grips with all of life: the beautiful and the ugly, the common and the extraordinary. The topic material of poetry can be just about anything. Love, hatred, personal meditations, psychological studies, attacks on government, religious worship, friendship, death, taxes, the details of day-to-day life—these are just a few of its subjects.

Before you begin to read poems, we offer a word of encouragement and advice. Do not be afraid of poetry. There is nothing inherently difficult or mysterious about it. Fear simply gets in your way and blocks your ability to think and feel. Dismiss your fears and forge on ahead into the poems. Most important, do not be misled by the "Deep Hidden Meaning" (or the DHM) theory of poetry. Poetry is not some sort of secret code with a specific number of DHMs that must be deciphered and decoded by the cryptographer-instructor. Rather, poems mean what they say, and they say what they mean. Understanding what poems say is partly a function of reading carefully and partly a function of what information you bring to the poem. In Jarrell's "Death of the Ball Turret Gunner," for example, we would have a great deal of difficulty if we did not know what a "ball turret" was or that "black flak" refers to anti-aircraft fire. These are not "Deep Hidden Meanings." Rather, they are pieces of information that we must bring to the poem in order to understand it.

HOW TO READ A POEM

Carefully. That single word sums up the best approach to reading poetry. A fast once-over might yield some enjoyment and understanding, but much would be lost. The economy and compression that characterize poetry mean that every part of the poem must carry some of the impact and meaning and thus every part is worth careful attention. There should be an interaction between the poem and the reader. This relationship should not be one-sided; you cannot sit back and ask the poem (or the poet) to do all the work. The poem contributes its language, imagery, rhythms, ideas, and all the other aspects that make it poetry. The reader must bring a willingness to open his or her mind to the poem's impact and a commitment to understand the words and hear the music. The reader also brings to the experience everything he or she knows about literature, poetry, life, history, religion, language, and the like. Some poems demand a great deal of prior knowledge, others very little.

No single technique for reading poetry can guarantee an enjoyable and valuable experience in understanding a poem, but we can suggest a general pattern that will help you begin to deal with poetry. You should consider reading the poem four times (they are, after all, usually short). The first time, you might read the poem straight through, without dwelling on difficult passages or obscure words. This reading will give you a general sense of the poem's geography. In the second reading, you should exercise more care and energy and should deal with all the obscurities that arise. Doing this requires working out the syntax of confusing sentences or passages and looking up the meanings of unfamiliar words. It may also mean figuring out implications of any references to history, mythology, science, or the like. Take as much time as you need with this second reading. When you are finished, you should have a fairly clear grasp of what the poem is saying.

In these first two readings you should make a special effort to read the poem *sentence by sentence* instead of line by line. A reading that focuses on the line endings and ignores the syntax will inevitably yield confusion. The third time through, read the poem aloud, or at least sound each word clearly in your mind. Doing this will give you a chance to hear the music of the poem and to assess the contributions that rhythm, rhyme, and sound make to the total effect. This kind of information will often change or clarify your understanding of the poem. If you read "Death of the Ball Turret Gunner" aloud, for example, you will notice the added impact of rhyming *froze* with *hose* and the suggestion of cannon fire in the repeated *k* sounds of *black flak*. Finally, you should move through the poem one last time and try to **paraphrase** it. A paraphrase is a rewriting of the poem in your own words (for more on paraphrasing, see Chapter 2, pp. 97–101, and pp. 477–79 in this chapter). This process will help you crystallize your understanding of the poem.

As you encounter a new poem for the first time, you should try to answer five important questions that can aid your understanding significantly:

1. *What does the title tell about the poem?* Sometimes poets use titles that make no sense until the poem has been read. In addition, poets often

leave poems untitled, and the poems "inherit" their first lines as titles. In other cases, however, titles are often effective summaries of poems and may provide a great deal of information and a way into the poem. The title of "Death of the Ball Turret Gunner," for example, supplies information on both the subject and the circumstances of the poem. Similarly, the title of Robert Frost's "Stopping by Woods on a Snowy Evening" tells us the setting and the situation that the poem present. The title of Christopher Marlowe's "The Passionate Shepherd to His Love" identifies both the speaker and the person to whom the poem is addressed. Such information may seem obvious, but it should never be overlooked.

2. *What do the individual words in the poem mean, and what do they suggest?* This question is especially important for words that are unfamiliar or that are used in an unfamiliar way. You should always use a dictionary to look up words that you don't know or that seem odd in the specific context. In addition, you should consider the implications and overtones of familiar words that are used in an unfamiliar way. In Jarrell's poem, for example, the speaker refers to the "belly" of the state. Why *belly* instead of *arms*, *grasp*, or some other term? In other words, consider how *belly* contributes to the imagery and the impact of the poem.

3. *Who (or what) is speaking the poem?* This is a very important question. Too often, readers assume that the speaker and the poet are one and the same. This is rarely the case. Indeed, it might be helpful at the outset if you assume that the speaker is someone other than the poet. In answering this question, first determine whether the speaker is "inside" or "outside" the poem—in other words, if the perspective is first person or third person. An important clue in this regard is the presence of the word *I* in the poem. Jarrell's "Death of the Ball Turret Gunner" begins, "From my mother's sleep I fell into the State." Similarly, Robert Frost's "Stopping by Woods on a Snowy Evening" begins, "Whose woods these are I think I know." In both cases, the first-person pronoun tells us that the speaker is inside the poem. We find a different situation in "Sir Patrick Spens," which begins, "The king sits in Dumferline town/Drinking the blood-red wine." In this instance, the speaker is outside the poem and the perspective is parallel to the third-person point of view in prose fiction. Next, you should seek to discover exactly who or what the speaker is. In Jarrell's poem, for example, we quickly figure out that the speaker is the (dead) ball turret gunner. In Frost's poem the speaker is the person who is stopping by woods on a snowy evening. We know a great deal less about the speaker in "Sir Patrick Spens," since he or she is not involved in the poem but is simply narrating events.

4. *What are the setting and situation in the poem?* Some poems establish their settings and circumstances with vivid clarity. "Stopping by Woods on a Snowy Evening," for example, announces both its setting and situation in the title. Both are even more clearly established in the first stanza:

Whose woods these are I think I know.
His house is in the village though;
He will not see me stopping here
To watch his woods fill up with snow.

We acquire a great deal of information very quickly. We know that the speaker is in or near woods, in the evening, during a snowfall. We also know that the speaker has stopped "to watch [the] woods fill up with snow." Although many poems do not establish setting and situation so clearly or so quickly, you should always try to figure out as much as you can about the *where* and *when* of a given poem.

   5. *What is the subject of the poem and what is the theme?* These two considerations, of course, are quite different (see Chapter 10, pp. 333–34). **Subject** indicates the general or specific topic of the poem, while **theme** refers to the specific idea or ideas that the poem explores. Jarrell's poem announces its subject in the title: "The Death of the Ball Turret Gunner." The theme, however, concerns the destructiveness of war and the brutality of death in battle. The preceding sentence, of course, is a statement *about* theme rather than a clear formulation of Jarrell's ideas. Go back to Jarrell's poem and try to come up with a sharper statement of the theme.

   These five questions are not always easy to answer. Sometimes you will have to do a fair amount of work with the poem to answer them. The work, however, will always pay off. Once you can answer these five questions, you will be well on the way to an effective and fruitful reading of any poem.

STUDYING POETRY

Let us now look at several poems in some detail. A complete and detailed analysis of a poem is called an **explication.** When a reader explicates a poem, he or she is expected to deal with every significant element in it. We are not yet ready for full-fledged explications, so at this point we will be looking at poems with an eye to beginning the processes of explication and understanding.

   We have already noted that poems can tell stories. The following poem was composed orally as a song sometime during the Middle Ages and passed on from person to person for a long time before it was written down. It tells a story which is probably true, or is at least based on actual events.

Sir Patrick Spens

The king sits in Dumferline town,
   Drinking the blood-red wine:
"O where will I get a good sailor
   To sail this ship of mine?"

Up and spoke an eldern° knight,   *old, elderly*   5
  Sat at the king's right knee:
"Sir Patrick Spens is the best sailor
  That sails upon the sea."

The king has written a braid° letter   ~~Transition~~   *large*
  And signed it wi'° his hand,   *with*   10
And sent it to Sir Patrick Spens,
  Was walking on the sand.

The first line that Sir Patrick read,
  A loud laugh laughed he;
The next line that Sir Patrick read,   15
  A tear blinded his eye.

"O who is this has done this deed,
  This ill deed done to me,
To send me out this time o' the year,
  To sail upon the sea?"   20

"Make haste, make haste, my merry men all,
  Our good ship sails the morn."
"O say not so, my master dear,
  For I fear a deadly storm.

Late late yestere'en° I saw the new moon   *last evening* 25
  Wi' the old moon in her arm,   *Personification*
And I fear, I fear, my dear master,
  That we will come to harm."

O our Scots nobles were right loath
  To wet their cork-heeled shoon,°   *understatement*   *shoes*   30
But long ere a'° the play were played   *all*
  Their hats they swam aboon.°   *above*

O long, long may their ladies sit,
  Wi'° their fans into their hand,   *with*
Or e'er they see Sir Patrick Spens   35
  Come sailing to the land.

O long, long may the ladies stand,
  Wi' their gold combs in their hair,
Waiting for their own dear lords,
  For they'll see them no more.   40

Half o'er, half o'er to Aberdour
  It's fifty fathom deep,
And there lies good Sir Patrick Spens,
  Wi' the Scots lords at his feet.

This kind of poem is called a **narrative ballad.** A narrative tells a story,
and the term *ballad* defines the poem's shape or form. The first two stanzas
set up the general situation: the king needs a sailor to go somewhere

and an old knight—one of the king's advisors—suggests Sir Patrick Spens. We know that this knight is an advisor since he sits "at the king's right knee."

The rest of the poem focuses on the feelings and eventual deaths of Sir Patrick and his men. The third stanza provides a transition from the king to Sir Patrick; the king writes a letter ordering Sir Patrick to sea, and Sir Patrick reads the letter. When he reads the first line, Sir Patrick laughs—probably because the letter flatteringly calls him "the best sailor/ That sails upon the sea." But he clearly sees the orders as a personal disaster; he cries when he reads them and he wonders who is responsible for sending him to sea at "this time o' the year." Our sense of impending disaster is increased when we see that Sir Patrick's men are also frightened by these orders (lines 23–28).

The actual disaster, which occurs in stanza 8, is related with ironic understatement. We are told that the nobles in Sir Patrick's crew did not want to get their shoes wet. We do not see the storm, the panic among the crew, the masts splitting, or the ship sinking under the waves. Instead, we next view the hats of the sailors floating on the waves. The disaster has been omitted, but the floating hats are grim evidence of the shipwreck. The remainder of the poem continues in this vein of ironic understatement. In stanzas 9 and 10 the focus shifts back to the land and the ladies who will wait a "long, long" time (forever) for Sir Patrick Spens and his men to return. The poem ends with a vision of Sir Patrick and the "Scots lords" lying "fifty fathom deep" at the bottom of the sea.

There is nothing hard to understand about this poem; it tells a sad story in a fairly straightforward way. We do find a bit of irony in the poem's understatement—the floating hats and the waiting ladies—but even this technique is reasonably clear. The subject of the poem is the drowning of Sir Patrick and his crew of Scots nobles. The poem might not have a theme. However, you might consider what the poem suggests about the *Theme* conflict between individual judgment and loyalty to authority. Sir Patrick knows the risks when he sets to sea, yet he obeys the king's command. There are clearly two contradictory forces at work here. The poem (and the story it tells) gives us a vicarious experience of how power operates, of how someone responds to an intolerable dilemma, and of the consequences of that response.

We will look at two additional poems, one by William Shakespeare and another by A. E. Housman. Neither tells a story in quite the same way as "Sir Patrick Spens," and both require more effort to understand clearly. Before you read our comments about the poems, try to understand them on your own, following the suggestions we have outlined for reading poetry. In addition, try to answer the questions on each poem before you move along in the text.

WILLIAM SHAKESPEARE (1564–1616)

Sonnet 55:
Not Marble, nor the Gilded Monuments   1609

Not marble, nor the gilded monuments
Of princes, shall outlive this powerful rhyme;
But you shall shine more bright in these contents
Than unswept stone, besmeared with sluttish time.
When wasteful war shall statues overturn,   5
And broils root out the work of masonry,
Nor Mars his° sword nor war's quick fire shall burn   *Mars's*
The living record of your memory.
'Gainst death and all-oblivious enmity
Shall you pace forth; your praise shall still find room
Even in the eyes of all posterity   10
That wear this world out to the ending doom.°   *Judgment day*
So, till the judgment that yourself arise,
You live in this, and dwell in lovers' eyes.

QUESTIONS

1. Who (or what) is the speaker of this poem?
2. To whom is the poem spoken?
3. What powers of destruction are mentioned in the poem?
4. What does the speaker claim will survive all these forces of destruction?
5. What exactly is "the living record of your memory" mentioned in line 8?
6. What is the subject of the poem? What is the theme?

This poem, written by William Shakespeare in the 1590s and published in 1609, expresses love and simultaneously makes a point about poetry. Because of its form, this poem is called a **sonnet**. We will discuss the sonnet form in detail later in the text. For a moment, note that the poem is made up of three groups of four lines each (called **quatrains**) and two final lines that rhyme (called a **couplet**). The speaker of the sonnet—not identical with William Shakespeare—is a lover and a poet; indeed, the speaker has written the sonnet that we are reading. We can tell that the sonnet is addressed to a particular person because of the repetition of *you* and *your* six times in the poem. While we do not learn very much about this "you," the Renaissance tradition of sonnets allows us to assume that it refers to an idealized friend or beloved of the speaker. This is one of the items of information that we must bring to this poem.

The key to understanding this sonnet is the first two lines, where the speaker makes his point. He says that "this powerful rhyme" (this sonnet) will outlast the marble buildings and decorated monuments constructed to honor princes and rulers. These lines embody the thesis statement of the sonnet: poetry is more powerful and more enduring than buildings. The speaker goes on to say that his loved one (the "you" in line 3) will be remembered longer and more vividly than anyone commemorated by neglected monuments that decay over time. The agent of destruction in this first quatrain is time; the term "sluttish time" is especially interesting since it suggests that time is indiscriminate and wanton in its destruction.

The second quatrain makes the same point in slightly different terms. Here, the agent of destruction is "wasteful war," referred to in line 7 as "Mars his sword" and "war's quick fire." In this quatrain the speaker asserts that the memory of his beloved will endure even though war destroys monuments ("statues") and buildings ("work of masonry"). The linchpin of this quatrain is the realization that "the living record of your memory" (line 8) refers to "this powerful rhyme" (line 2) and "these contents" (line 3). Thus, the "living record of your memory" is poetry, specifically the sonnet that we are reading.

The third quatrain repeats the sonnet's central argument again but shifts the focus from war to death and "all-oblivious enmity." Death is the ultimate destroyer; "all-oblivious enmity" is an odd combination of forgetfulness and ill will. Thus, the sonnet systematically deals with four agents of destruction: time, war, death, and malevolent forgetfulness. In this quatrain, the speaker asserts that the memory of his loved one—"your praise"—will live on in all succeeding generations until the end of time. "The ending doom" (line 12) refers to the apocalypse described in the Bible. Again, the key to understanding is the realization that "your praise" is another reference to "this powerful rhyme" and thus to the sonnet itself. Finally, in the concluding couplet, the speaker argues that his beloved will live on in this sonnet and in lovers' eyes (who read the sonnet) until she herself rises again on Judgment Day.

There are no secret codes or "Deep Hidden Meanings" here; Shakespeare's sonnet means exactly what it says. This is not to suggest that the poem is easy to understand or that it does not require work on your part. This poem expects more from the reader than does "Sir Patrick Spens." It helps, for example, if you bring to this poem the knowledge that Elizabethan sonnets were usually addressed to an imaginary or idealized loved one. Similarly, the poem becomes clearer once you recognize that Mars is the Roman god of war, "ending doom" is an allusion to the apocalypse, and "judgment" refers to Judgment Day. Ultimately, however, the central discovery in this sonnet is that 'this powerful rhyme" (line 2), "these contents" (line 3), "the living record of your memory" (line 8), and "this" (line 14) all refer to the sonnet that you are reading. Once this connection is established, the subject and the theme become fairly clear. The subject is the memory of the speaker's beloved; the sonnet asserts that her memory will live on because she has been immortalized in poetry. It is the sonnet, not the person, that is immortal. The theme is simply an abstraction and a universal application of the subject. Thematically, the sonnet argues that poetry (and by extension, any good work of art) has the power to endure regardless of time, war, death, envy, and humanity's tendency to forget. Thus, the sonnet asserts that art is immortal, and this assertion is still valid as we read the poem almost four hundred years after it was written.

A. E. HOUSMAN (1859–1936)

Loveliest of Trees, the Cherry Now   1896

Loveliest of trees, the cherry now
Is hung with bloom along the bough,
And stands about the woodland ride°   *path*
Wearing white for Eastertide.

Now, of my threescore years and ten,   5
Twenty will not come again,
And take from seventy springs a score,
It only leaves me fifty more.

And since to look at things in bloom
Fifty springs are little room,   10
About the woodland I will go
To see the cherry hung with snow.

QUESTIONS

1. In what season or time of year is the poem set?
2. How old is the speaker? How can you tell? Why does he assume he will live seventy years ("threescore years and ten")?
3. How would you describe the speaker's perception or sense of time? What is the effect of the words *only* (line 8) and *little* (line 10)?
4. What ideas about time, beauty, and life does this poem explore? What does it suggest about the way we should live?

This poem certainly looks simpler than Shakespeare's sonnet; the words are more familiar and the three-stanza structure is immediately clear. Nevertheless, the ideas expressed in Housman's poem are as complex as those in the sonnet. This poem is a **lyric,** a short poem that expresses the thoughts and feelings of the speaker. One of the oldest forms of poetry, lyrics were popular in ancient Greece, where they were sung to accompaniment on a lyre (notice the connection between the words *lyre* and *lyric*). This poem, like most lyrics, is written in the first person; we know that the speaker is "inside" the poem because of the first-person pronouns used in lines 5, 8, and 11.

Reaching a tentative understanding of "Loveliest of Trees" should not present serious problems. Most of the words are straightforward, and even the slightly unfamiliar ones—like *ride*, *Eastertide*, and *threescore*—can be understood in context. If you go to a dictionary, you will discover that a *ride* is a pathway or road made especially for horseback riding and that *Eastertide* means Easter time, or the week following Easter, or even the fifty days after Easter Sunday. *Threescore* is a bit more difficult until you remember that a score is twenty; thus, "threescore years and ten" is a way of saying seventy years.

Once you have control of the words, you will be able to paraphrase the poem. You might end up with this sort of rewritten version: "It's Easter time and the cherry trees, the prettiest of all trees, are now blooming on each side of the riding paths in the woods. I'm twenty years old, so I've already used up twenty of my seventy years and I have only fifty more. Since fifty years really isn't very much time to look at beautiful things, I will go out right now and look at the white blossoms on the cherry trees." The paraphrase obviously loses all the beauty, elegance, economy, music, and impact of the poem. It does, however, make the speaker's logic and argument fairly clear.

We can now examine the speaker, the language, and the structure of the poem in more detail. We never do learn very much about the speaker. We know from the first three words that he or she thinks that the cherry in bloom is more beautiful than any other tree. We also know that the speaker is twenty years old; the speaker tells us in the second stanza that twenty of his or her seventy allotted years are gone ("will not come again"). The speaker's assumption that he or she will live seventy years is derived from Psalm 90, verse 10: "The days of our years are threescore years and ten." This quotation from the Bible, along with the word *Eastertide* in line 4, gives the poem religious overtones.

If we look at the poem stanza by stanza, the logical progression of the speaker's thoughts becomes still more evident. In the first stanza the speaker praises the beauty of the cherry trees in bloom. The stanza also establishes the seasonal setting of the poem. The assertion that the trees are *"wearing* white for Eastertide" implies that the cherry has put on white clothing in celebration of the Resurrection. The verb *wearing* has the effect of making the trees seem like people. This white clothing, in turn, suggests both beauty and purity.

The second stanza shifts to a consideration of time. The speaker tells us how old he is, how long he expects to live, and how little time he has left. Fifty years probably does not strike you as a short period of time. By using the word *only* in line 8, however, the speaker strongly implies that fifty years is not very much time at all. In the final stanza, the speaker connects the focus on beauty in the first stanza with the focus on time in the second. The speaker asserts that fifty "springs" are "little" time "to look at things in bloom." The word *little* reemphasizes the speaker's sense that life is short and time is flying by.

Finally, the speaker concludes that he had better go into the woods now to "see the cherry hung with snow." The snow in the last line presents us with a bit of a problem. Is it really snow? Has it suddenly become winter? Or is the snow another reference to the white blossoms of the cherry tree? These are the kinds of questions that a single word in a poem can provoke. Such questions often cannot be answered with a "correct" statement that you can jot down in your notes and reproduce on an exam. The snow may be a metaphor referring to the blossoms, or it may suggest a complete shift in time to winter. A more sophisticated reading combines both possibilities, seeing the snow as a metaphor for the blossoms that carry spring into winter, and thus implies that all living things carry the seeds of their own mortality. In any event, we should sense the speaker's eagerness (almost desperation) to go out into the world and look at beautiful things.

Each step in our analysis of "Loveliest of Trees" has brought us closer to a thoughtful understanding of the poem. It remains to consider the difference between the poem's subject and its theme. The subject is clearly the "loveliest of trees, the cherry." The title of the poem announces the subject, and the speaker focuses on the beauty of the cherry in the first stanza. In determining the theme, however, we must take into account not only the beauty of the cherry tree but also the speaker's constant awareness of time and his eagerness to look at beauty. The second and third stanzas show that the speaker is concerned with his or her own relationship to beautiful things and with the brevity of life.

Ultimately, the poem argues that we do not really have much time. Therefore, we should experience all the beauty we can at every opportunity. Once we recognize the theme of Housman's poem, we can place it in its poetical context. There is a long tradition of poetry that addresses itself to the brevity of life and the need to act immediately in order to experience as much as possible. Poems that make this argument are called *carpe diem* poetry. *Carpe diem* is a Latin phrase that means literally "seize the day." Thus, Housman's poem, like *carpe diem* poetry in general, asserts that life is fleeting and that we should therefore take full advantage of the present.

POEMS FOR STUDY

EMILY DICKINSON (1830–1886)

Because I Could Not Stop for Death   *1890 (c. 1863)*

Because I could not stop for Death—
He kindly stopped for me—
The Carriage held but just Ourselves—
And Immortality.

We slowly drove—He knew no haste   5
And I had put away
My labor and my leisure too,
For His Civility—

We passed the School, where Children strove
At Recess—in the Ring—   10
We passed the Fields of Gazing Grain—
We passed the Setting Sun—

Or rather—He passed Us—
The Dews drew quivering and chill—
For only Gossamer,° my Gown—   *thin fabric*   15
My Tippet°—only Tulle°—   *cape, scarf; thin silk*

We paused before a House that seemed
A Swelling of the Ground—
The Roof was scarcely visible—
The Cornice—in the Ground—   20

Since then—'tis Centuries—and yet
Feels shorter than the Day
I first surmised the Horses' Heads
Were toward Eternity—

QUESTIONS

1. How is the speaker characterized? Why couldn't she stop for death?
2. How is death characterized in the poem? How is this characterization unconventional?
3. What do the passengers in the carriage pass on their journey? What do these things suggest?

4. What event is suggested by the fact that the sun passes the speaker in line 13?

5. What is the carriage (line 3)? What is the house (line 17)?

6. Where is the speaker in the present time? From what perspective is the poem spoken?

THOMAS HARDY (1840–1928)

The Man He Killed   1902

> "Had he and I but met
> By some old ancient inn,   *[handwritten: Redundant. Speaker isn't educated, A working man.]*
> We should have sat us down to wet
> Right many a nipperkin!°   *half-pint cup*
>
> "But ranged as infantry,   5
> And staring face to face,
> I shot at him as he at me,
> And killed him in his place.
>
> "I shot him dead because—   *[handwritten: He's not a deep thinker,]*
> Because he was my foe.   10
> Just so: my foe of course he was;
> That's clear enough; although
>
> "He thought he'd 'list,° perhaps,   *enlist*
> Off-hand like—just as I—
> Was out of work—had sold his traps°—   *possessions*   15   *[handwritten left margin: Kills to live.]*
> No other reason why.
>
> "Yes; quaint and curious war is!   *[handwritten: Central Purpose: To make us see the irrationality of war, esp. when men could be friends ordinarily.]*
> You shoot a fellow down
> You'd treat if met where any bar is,
> Or help to half-a-crown."°   *about 60 cents*   20

QUESTIONS

[handwritten: A soldier, but not a career soldier.]

1. Who and what is the speaker? What do you learn about him?

2. What situation and event is the speaker recalling and relating?

3. What can you deduce about the speaker from his language and choice of words?

4. What is the effect produced by repeating the word *because* in lines 9 and 10 and using the word *although* in line 12?

5. What is the speaker's attitude toward his "foe" and toward what he has done?

6. What point, if any, does this poem make about war? What are the similarities between this poem and Jarrell's "Death of the Ball Turret Gunner"? The differences?

ROBERT FROST (1874–1963)

Stopping By Woods on a Snowy Evening   *1923*

Whose woods these are I think I know.
His house is in the village though;
He will not see me stopping here
To watch his woods fill up with snow.

My little horse must think it queer   5
To stop without a farmhouse near
Between the woods and frozen lake
The darkest evening of the year.

He gives his harness bells a shake
To ask if there is some mistake.   10
The only other sound's the sweep
Of easy wind and downy flake.

The woods are lovely, dark and deep,
But I have promises to keep,
And miles to go before I sleep,   15
And miles to go before I sleep.

QUESTIONS

1. What do we learn about the speaker of this poem? Where is he? What is he doing?

2. What is the setting of this poem? What is the weather like? What time is it?

3. Why do you suppose that the speaker wants to watch the "woods fill up with snow"?

4. What evidence do we find in the poem to conclude that the speaker is embarrassed or self-conscious about stopping? Consider the words *though* in line 2 and *must* in line 5.

5. The last stanza offers two alternative attitudes and courses of action. What are they? Which does the speaker choose?

6. To what extent does the sound of this poem contribute to its impact? Note especially the *s* words in line 11 and the *w* sounds in line 12.

7. How does Frost use the sound of his rhyme words to hold the poem together and link one stanza to the next? How and why is the pattern of rhyme sounds different in the last stanza?

JAMES WRIGHT (1927–1980)

Two Hangovers   1963

NUMBER ONE
I slouch in bed.
Beyond the streaked trees of my window,
All groves are bare.
Locusts and poplars change to unmarried women   5
Sorting slate from anthracite
Between railroad ties:
The yellow-bearded winter of the depression
Is still alive somewhere, an old man
Counting his collection of bottle caps   10
In a tarpaper shack under the cold trees
Of my grave.

I still feel half drunk,
And all those old women beyond my window
Are hunching toward the graveyard.   15

Drunk, mumbling Hungarian,
The sun staggers in,
And his big stupid face pitches
Into the stove.
For two hours I have been dreaming   20
Of green butterflies searching for diamonds
In coal seams;
And children chasing each other for a game
Through the hills of fresh graves.
But the sun has come home drunk from the sea,   25
And a sparrow outside
Sings of the Hanna Coal Co. and the dead moon.
The filaments of cold light bulbs tremble
In music like delicate birds.
Ah, turn it off.   30

NUMBER TWO: I TRY TO WAKEN AND GREET THE WORLD ONCE AGAIN
In a pine tree,
A few yards away from my window sill,
A brilliant blue jay is springing up and down, up and down,
On a branch.   35
I laugh, as I see him abandon himself
To entire delight, for he knows as well as I do
That the branch will not break.

QUESTIONS

1. What do we learn about the speaker in hangover "Number One"? What is his physical condition? Where is he? What is he trying to do?
2. How does the speaker's condition affect the way he views the trees outside his window? The world? His own life?
3. Who or what is drunk and "mumbling Hungarian" in line 16?
4. Do you think the sun really "staggers in" and falls "into the stove"? What does the sun stand for in "Number One"?
5. Find all the images of death and desolation that you can in "Number One." Why do you suppose these images are so dominant?
6. Why is hangover "Number Two" so much shorter than "Number One"?
7. How does the speaker's mood, attitude, perspective, or tone of voice change from hangover "Number One" to hangover "Number Two"? How do you account for this shift?

PARAPHRASING POETRY

A paraphrase of a poem is basically a rewriting of the poem in your own words. The length of a paraphrase is determined partly by the length of the original work and partly by the amount of detail you choose to include. When you are dealing with lyrics, sonnets, and other short poems, it is often common for the paraphrase to include every detail and thus to be as long as or longer than the original. Paraphrases of long poems, however, are usually much shorter than the original.

Paraphrasing is especially useful in the study of poetry. It often produces clearer understanding. In order to write an effective paraphrase, you should deal with each part of the poem. This process often leads to the discovery of new aspects or information that you had overlooked previously. In addition, paraphrasing can fix both the general shape and the details of a specific poem in your mind, thus giving you a strong advantage both in classroom discussion and in examinations. Paraphrasing can also reveal exactly what sorts of poetic devices are at work in a given poem. By its very nature, a paraphrase tends to exclude the poetic diction and rhetorical structures that characterize poetry. In essence, a paraphrase turns economical and figurative verse into expanded and literal prose. As a result, a comparison of the original poem with the paraphrase will often highlight the poetic devices that make the poem a moving experience.

In writing a paraphrase, you should strive for accuracy. Make sure that you rewrite an accurate version of the poem's actions, statements, and ideas. In other words, remain faithful to the poem and avoid introducing extraneous material. You should try to use your own words and avoid quoting the poem. Doing this can be very difficult, especially because poets try to use just the right word to express an image or idea. One way to avoid quoting the poet's words is to write a paraphrase from what you remember about the poem after several readings. Once you have done that, you can go back to the poem and check for both accuracy and quotation. Paraphrasing well also requires that you pay careful attention to the details that you choose to include. In paraphrasing a short poem, you will probably want to include almost every detail. With longer poems, however, you will have to decide exactly which details are important enough to include and which can be handled with a generalization. Finally, guard against putting your own conclusions or interpretations in the paraphrase. It would be wrong, for example, to begin a paraphrase of Randall Jarrell's "Death of the Ball Turret Gunner" by asserting that "this poem makes a forceful argument against the brutal and wasteful deaths caused by war." While such an assertion might be a fair summary of the poem's theme, it does not reflect the *actual content* of the poem.

Organizing Your Paraphrase

Your task, in paraphrasing a poem, is to rewrite the work in your own words with as little distortion as possible. The organization of your paraphrase should reflect the structure of the poem, and so you should paraphrase material in the order in which it occurs. When dealing with short poems, organize your paraphrase to reflect the poem's development line by line or stanza by stanza. In rewriting Shakespeare's "Not Marble, nor the Gilded Monuments," for example, you would want to follow the natural subdivisions of the sonnet and deal in sequence with each quatrain and then the couplet. In working with longer poems, look for natural divisions like groups of related stanzas, verse paragraphs, or other units suggested by the work. In every situation, the shape of the poem should determine the structure of your paraphrase.

SAMPLE ESSAY

A Paraphrase of Emily Dickinson's "Because I Could Not Stop for Death"*

[1]   I was too preoccupied with life to die, so Death, out of kindness and courtesy, paused to pick me up. The three of us (Death, Immortality, and I) made our journey in a horse-drawn coach. We traveled slowly (Death was

* See p. 473 for this poem.

not in a hurry), and Death's courtesy led me to abandon both work and play. On our journey we went by a school where children were playing, a field of ripe wheat, and the Setting Sun.

[2]   At the end of the journey we stopped, and the sun went by us. The dew made me quite chilly because I was wearing a light, gauze dress and a thin scarf made of silk. Our trip ended at a building that was no more than a mound in the earth. I could scarcely see the roof, and the top edge of the building was flush with the ground.

[3]   All these events happened hundreds of years ago. Nevertheless, the intervening years seem shorter to me than that one moment when I first recognized that I was dying.

Commentary on the Essay

Because Dickinson's poem is relatively short, the paraphrase attempts to deal with every detail. The organization of the paraphrase closely follows the structure of the poem. The first paragraph restates the contents of the first three stanzas, which focus on the speaker's journey. The second paragraph deals with the fourth and fifth stanzas, the end of the journey. Finally, the last paragraph paraphrases the last stanza. This stanza is given its own paragraph because it embodies a shift in perspective—from past to present—and it defines the present moment of the poem. Notice that the sample paraphrase carefully avoids drawing conclusions or interpreting the poem. It does not, for example, call the "Carriage" a hearse or the "House" a grave, even though hearse and grave are *implied* by the context. Similarly, the paraphrase does not point out that the speaker's journey took her symbolically through three stages of life: youth in the children at play, maturity in the "Gazing Grain," and death in the "Setting Sun." Although these observations may be completely valid in dealing with Dickinson's poem, they do not belong in a paraphrase.

12

Character:
The People in Poetry

Poets, like other writers, populate their work with fictional characters whose pain or pleasure, love or hatred, we experience. As in fiction, characters in poetry are created and defined by how they are described, what they say, what they do, and what other characters say about them. In reading poetry, however, we are no longer concerned primarily with protagonists and antagonists or with round and flat characters. Instead, we are concerned with three specific types of character: the speaker, the listener, and characters who are described or take an active role in the poem.

THE SPEAKER OR PERSONA

Of these three possible types of character in poetry, the most important and most difficult to understand is the speaker. In prose fiction, we call this character the **narrator** (See Chapter 5, p. 177). In poetry, however, the commonly used terms are **speaker** or **persona** (plural: *personae*), a term that comes from the Latin word meaning "mask." We can think of the speaker in a poem as the mask that the poet puts over his or her own face to voice the poem. Alternatively, we might think of the speaker as the pose or role that the poet adopts within the poem. In "Because I Could Not Stop for Death," Emily Dickinson assumes the mask or pose of a woman who died hundreds of years earlier and is looking back from eternity on the moment of her death.

One of the first things to decide in reading a poem is whether the speaker is *inside* or *outside* the poem. What this really means is determining the **point of view** used by the poet (see Chapter 5, p. 179). The speaker is *inside* the poem if the point of view is first person. This point of view is often indicated by the presence of first-person pronouns like *I* or *me*. Randall Jarrell's "The Woman at the Washington Zoo" begins, "The saris go by me from the embassies." The *me* indicates that the speaker is inside the poem speaking in the first person. The speaker is *outside* the poem, however, if the poem is spoken in the third person. In such cases, the speaker is usually not involved with the action of the poem; he or she simply narrates. Such is the case in both the anonymous "Bonny George Campbell" (p. 495) and James Merrill's "Laboratory Poem" (p. 500).

It is usually quite easy to determine a poem's point of view. We run into a more difficult problem when we seek to determine who or what the speaker is. Our natural tendency to identify the poet with the speaker is justified only in rare instances. In some poems there is *almost* no distinction between the poet and the speaker. Here, the mask that the poet wears when speaking the poem is a fictional version of his or her own face. Look, for example, at the poem Ben Jonson used to begin his book of epigrams published in 1616:

To the Reader   *1616*

Pray thee, take care, that tak'st my book in hand,
To read it well: that is, to understand.

This **epigram** (short and witty poem) is spoken by a poetic re-creation of the poet (Ben Jonson) within the poem. The speaker warns us to make the necessary effort to read the poems carefully so that we can "understand" them. We find a similar poem in Robert Herrick's *The Hesperides*, published in 1648. Herrick was part of a group of poets called "the Sons of Ben" that admired and imitated Ben Jonson:

His Prayer to Ben Jonson   *1648*

When I a verse shall make,
Know I have prayed thee,
For old religion's sake,
Saint Ben to aid me.

Make the way smooth for me   5
When I, thy Herrick,
Honoring thee, on my knee,
Offer my lyric.

Candles I'll give to thee
And a new altar;   10
And thou Saint Ben shalt be
Writ in my psalter.

This poem is spoken in the first person—the speaker is inside the poem—and again the speaker is a fictionalized version of the poet himself. The first line tells us that the speaker is a poet since he makes "verse." Indeed, the speaker identifies himself as "I, thy Herrick" in line 6. The poem thus acknowledges Herrick's debt to Jonson in an amusing way. The speaker becomes a suppliant and Jonson is turned into a saint to whom Herrick prays for help in writing. The speaker carries the joke as far as he can, offering to give "Saint Ben" candles and "a new altar" if Ben will "make the way smooth for me" (line 5).

This sort of poem, in which the poet and the speaker are almost identical, is the exception rather than the rule. In almost all poetry there is a distinction between the poet and the speaker. Indeed, you should *assume* that the poet and the speaker are different unless there is clear evidence to the contrary. Sometimes this distinction is so slight or hard to make that we are tempted to see the poet as the speaker. In Shakespeare's "Not Marble, nor the Gilded Monuments" (p. 468), for example, we recognize that the speaker is a poet talking about the immortality of poetry and we are tempted to identify him as Shakespeare. We must resist this temptation; the sonnet offers no evidence that will support such a conclusion. In many other poems, however, the distinction between the poet and the speaker is quite obvious once you stop to think about it. In both Jarrell's "Death of the Ball Turret Gunner" and Dickinson's "Because I Could Not Stop for Death," the speakers are dead. Since the poets were obviously alive when they wrote the poems, we quickly recognize the difference between the poets and the speakers.

Poets have used all sorts of speakers to voice their poems. This text contains poems spoken by kings and dukes, husbands and wives, lovers and killers, shepherds, secretaries, civil servants, children, beggars, and almost every other kind of person you can imagine. In addition, you will meet speakers who are gods, historical figures, mythological heroes and heroines, corpses, and ghosts. The speaker does not even have to be human; poems can be spoken by animals, clouds, buildings, whirlwinds, or almost anything else the imagination can encompass.

Identifying the speaker and finding out about him or her are related but different tasks. Once we know who or what the speaker is, we must find out all we can about him, her, or it. Sometimes the title gives us relevant information. The title of Marlowe's "The Passionate Shepherd to His Love" informs us that the speaker is a "passionate shepherd" and in love. Often, the speaker tells us something about himself or herself in the poem. Such is the case in Housman's "Loveliest of Trees" (p. 470), where the speaker reveals that he is twenty years old and thinks that cherry trees in bloom are the "loveliest of trees." Similarly, in the first two lines of Browning's "My Last Duchess," the speaker tells us that he is a duke and a widower. The focus of a poem tells us something about the speaker's concerns; the speaker's ideas contribute to our understanding of his or her nature. Word choice and language will often define a speaker's social class or level of education. Similarly, a speaker's attitude toward the subject and his or her tone of voice often indicate the speaker's emotional state.

THE LISTENER

The second type of character we encounter in poetry is the listener—the person to whom a poem is addressed. Ultimately, of course, all poems are spoken to *us*, the readers, but poets can use a number of different strategies to do this. In some cases, poets speak directly to us; their poems are public in tone and addressed to the world at large. Ben Jonson's "To The Reader" clearly employs this strategy. The *thee* (you) in the first line refers directly to us. Here, we are the listeners and are clearly outside the poem. In other situations the speaker seems to be voicing private thoughts or meditations. Here, we are to imagine that we "overhear" the poem; it is not addressed to anyone or anything in particular. Such is the case in Housman's "Loveliest of Trees," in which we overhear a meditation on time, death, and beauty. Again, there is no listener within the poem.

In still other instances, the poet chooses to include a listener inside and addresses the poem to a specific character, object, or abstraction. Sometimes the presence of an inside listener is announced in the title, as in Marlowe's "The Passionate Shepherd to His Love" or in Andrew Marvell's "To His Coy Mistress" (p. 849). Often, the presence of a listener inside the poem is indicated by the word *you*. In Browning's "My Last Duchess" the speaker invites a listener to look at a painting of his dead wife: "Will't please *you* sit and look at her?" Here, the *you* signifies the presence of an internal listener. Since poets can use *you* or *thee* to refer either to us as readers or to an internal listener, you must be careful to determine if this second person is inside or outside the poem.

Such a determination may be complicated in modern poetry, where the speaker can use *you* to mean *one* or even refer to himself or herself. Richard Hugo's "Degrees of Gray in Philipsburg" (p. 531) begins "You might come here Sunday on a whim." The *you* in this poem is neither the reader nor an internal listener. Rather, it is an oblique or indirect way for the speaker to talk about himself.

Although poets rarely tell us as much about listeners as they do about speakers, we should look for information that will help us define this second character. Such information can often be found in adjectives that describe the listener or in the speaker's attitude toward the listener. Indeed, everything the speaker says to the listener should help us to understand the listener's character.

OTHER CHARACTERS IN POETRY

Poets also create characters who are neither speakers nor listeners. The speaker may describe other characters, tell what they have done, or even repeat what they have said. In these instances, just as in prose fiction, we cannot always accept the speaker's presentation of another character at face value. Sometimes the speaker reports information about other characters without distortion; in other cases, however, we must be aware of the speaker's attitudes and prejudices as we evaluate what he or she says about others. In "Sir Patrick Spens" (p. 465), for example, the speaker is detached and objective as he describes the actions of the king, the king's advisor, Sir Patrick, a member of the crew, and the ladies who await Sir Patrick's return. Although we learn varying amounts of information about each of these characters, what we learn is objective and straightforward. In "My Last Duchess" the speaker describes his dead wife extensively; she becomes one of the three central characters even though she is not "on stage" in the present moment of the poem. In this instance, however, we must be careful to distinguish the wife's actual character from the speaker's distorted perceptions of her.

STUDYING CHARACTER IN POETRY

We are now ready to look at some poems and pay special attention to the characters who are created by the poet. As you read these poems, try to answer the five questions we presented in Chapter 11 (pp. 463–465). In addition, try to figure out as much as you can about the characters in the poems: the speaker, the listener, and the other "actors."

CHRISTOPHER MARLOWE (1564–1593)

The Passionate Shepherd to His Love   *1599*

Come live with me and be my love,
And we will all the pleasures prove°   *test*
That valleys, groves, hills, and fields,
Woods, or steepy mountain yields.

And we will sit upon the rocks,   5
Seeing the shepherds feed their flocks,
By shallow rivers to whose falls
Melodious birds sing madrigals.

And I will make thee beds of roses
And a thousand fragrant posies, 10
A cap of flowers, and a kirtle°   *long dress*
Embroidered all with leaves of myrtle;

A gown made of the finest wool
Which from our pretty lambs we pull;
Fair lined slippers for the cold, 15
With buckles of the purest gold;

A belt of straw and ivy buds,
With coral clasps and amber studs:
And if these pleasures may thee move,
Come live with me, and be my love. 20

The shepherds' swains° shall dance and sing   *lovers*
For thy delight each May morning:
If these delights thy mind may move,
Then live with me and be my love.

QUESTIONS

1. Who is the speaker? What do you learn about him?
2. Who or what is the listener?
3. What does the speaker want the listener to do?
4. What specific gifts does the speaker offer the listener?
5. What sort of world does the speaker offer the listener?
6. What is unrealistic about the life that the speaker offers his love? Does the speaker know that his offer is unrealistic? How can you tell?

   This poem, written by Christopher Marlowe and published in 1599, is an "invitation to love." The title identifies the speaker as the "passionate shepherd" and the listener as "his love." The poem is an argument (a process of reasoning) in which the shepherd tries to persuade the lady to join him in love. Since the speaker is trying to persuade, we may assume that the listener has resisted his advances up to this point. In his attempt to convince his beloved, the shepherd offers her a world of "valleys, groves, hills, and fields" where they can watch "shepherds feed their flocks" and listen to "melodious birds sing madrigals." The world is further described in the last stanza when the speaker says that his love will be able to watch the young shepherds and shepherdesses "dance and sing" each "May morning." The shepherd thus offers his beloved a world of "delights."

   The speaker's desire to persuade the lady leads him to present an idealized image of the world eternally fixed in spring, specifically in May. He never mentions the discomforts of winter; his argument ignores the passing of time, the changing of the seasons, and the aging of lovers. The shepherd suppresses these realities in his effort to convince his love. Nevertheless, he is aware of these things as we see in the long list of clothing and gifts that he offers his love. In stanzas 3 through 5 he promises the lady a bed of roses, thousands of flowers, a cap, an embroidered gown, slippers, and a belt. The gifts continue the illusion of an ideal world since each is derived from nature's bounty. The speaker slips, however, when he mentions the "cold" in line 15. This is his only acknowledgment that spring and May are not eternal. Thus, the shepherd offers his lover a world of gifts, love, and nature that is eternally young and true. His argument assumes that love and the world will never change.

SIR WALTER RALEIGH (1552–1618)

The Nymph's Reply to the Shepherd   *1600*

If all the world and love were young,
And truth in every shepherd's tongue,
These pretty pleasures might me move
To live with thee and be thy love.

Time drives the flocks from field to fold°   *fenced field*   5
When rivers rage and rocks grow cold,
And Philomel° becometh dumb;   *the nightingale*
The rest complains of cares to come.

The flowers do fade, and wanton fields
To wayward winter reckoning yields;   10
A honey tongue, a heart of gall,
Is fancy's spring, but sorrow's fall.

Thy gowns, thy shoes, thy beds of roses,
Thy cap, thy kirtle,° and thy posies°   *long dress; flowers and poems*
Soon break, soon wither, soon forgotten—   15
In folly ripe, in reason rotten.

Thy belt of straw and ivy buds,
Thy coral clasps and amber studs,
All these in me no means can move
To come to thee and be thy love.   20

But could youth last and love still° breed,   *always*
Had joys no date nor age no need,
Then these delights my mind might move
To live with thee and be thy love.

QUESTIONS

1. Who is the speaker? What do we learn about the speaker? Who is the listener?
2. How does the form of this poem (rhythm, rhyme pattern, stanza form) relate to Marlowe's poem?
3. How are the ideas of love and the world in this poem different from those in Marlowe's poem?
4. To what extent is this poem a parody (an imitation that makes fun) of Marlowe's poem? To what extent is it a refutation of Marlowe's poem?
5. Determine the steps of the speaker's logical argument in this poem.

Raleigh's poem, published in 1600, is a logical refutation of the argument put forward in Marlowe's poem. Again, the speaker and the listener are identified in the title: the speaker is the "nymph" whom the shepherd loves; the listener is the shepherd-lover who advocated love in Marlowe's poem. The connection between the two poems is evident in both form and content. Raleigh's poem imitates the rhythm, rhyming words, and stanza form of Marlowe's poem. Both offer six four-line stanzas and rhyme on the word "love" at the beginning and end. In addition, the speaker in Raleigh's poem mentions most of the natural settings and the gifts that the shepherd offers his love in the earlier poem.

This poem is a lyric in which the nymph rejects the "invitation to love" advanced by Marlowe's shepherd. The speaker's rejection of love is based on her awareness of what the world and love are really like. In addition, her refutation is almost a logical proof represented by the following pattern: (1) *if A then B*; (2) *not A*; (3)*therefore not B*. The major premise—*if A then B*—is expressed in the first and last stanzas. Here, the speaker argues that *if* the world and love were eternally young and *if* shepherds always spoke the truth, *then* she might be convinced "To live with thee and be thy love." The next three stanzas express the minor premise: *not A*. Here, the nymph argues that the world and love are *not* eternally young and that shepherds do *not* always tell the truth about love. In the second stanza, the speaker points out that time and winter force the flocks out of the fields, drive the birds away, and lead people to complain about their troubles. In the next stanza, she similarly points out that these forces destroy the beauty of flowers and fields. She also suggests (in lines 11–12) that the sweet words of love (the "honey tongue") that characterize spring give way to bitterness and rancor ("gall") as summer changes to fall.

Finally, in the fourth stanza, the nymph points out that time and change will destroy all the gifts that the shepherd can offer. The speaker's reference to "posies" that will "soon break, soon wither" and soon be "forgotten" is a double-edged attack on the "passionate" shepherd, because the term encompasses both flowers and his poetry. The nymph's argument is based on her awareness that time has the power to destroy spring, youth, and love. She understands that love, beauty, and truth are all subject to the ravages of time and change. The final step of the nymph's argument is stated in the fifth stanza, where she concludes that she will *therefore not* be moved "To come to thee and be thy love" (line 20). Her rejection of the shepherd and his offered love is the logical result of her own reasoning and her demonstration that the world is not eternally young or pleasant.

ROBERT BROWNING (1812–1889)

My Last Duchess°   *1842*

FERRARA

That's my last Duchess painted on the wall,
Looking as if she were alive. I call
That piece a wonder, now: Frà Pandolf's° hands
Worked busily a day, and there she stands.
Will't please you sit and look at her? I said   5
"Frà Pandolf" by design, for never read
Strangers like you that pictured countenance,
The depth and passion of its earnest glance,
But to myself they turned (since none puts by
The curtain I have drawn for you, but I)   10
And seemed as they would ask me, if they durst,°   *dared*
How such a glance came there; so, not the first
Are you to turn and ask thus. Sir, 'twas not
Her husband's presence only, called that spot
Of joy into the Duchess' cheek: perhaps   15
Frà Pandolf chanced to say "Her mantle laps
Over my lady's wrist too much," or "Paint
Must never hope to reproduce the faint
Half-flush that dies along her throat": such stuff
Was courtesy, she thought, and cause enough   20
For calling up that spot of joy. She had
A heart—how shall I say?—too soon made glad,
Too easily impressed; she liked whate'er
She looked on, and her looks went everywhere.
Sir, 'twas all one! My favor at her breast,   25
The dropping of the daylight in the West,
The bough of cherries some officious fool

MY LAST DUCHESS. The poem is based on incidents in the life of Alfonso II, Duke of Ferrara, whose first wife died in 1561. The Duke negotiated his second marriage to the daughter of the Count of Tyrol through an agent.   3 *Frà Pandolf*: an imaginary painter who is also a monk.

Broke in the orchard for her, the white mule
She rode with round the terrace—all and each
Would draw from her alike the approving speech,   30
Or blush, at least. She thanked men—good! but thanked
Somehow—I know not how—as if she ranked
My gift of a nine-hundred-years-old name
With anybody's gift. Who'd stoop to blame
This sort of trifling? Even had you skill   35
In speech—(which I have not)—to make your will
Quite clear to such an one, and say, "Just this
Or that in you disgusts me; here you miss,
Or there exceed the mark"—and if she let
Herself be lessoned so, nor plainly set   40
Her wits to yours, forsooth, and made excuse
—E'en then would be some stooping; and I choose
Never to stoop. Oh sir, she smiled, no doubt,
Whene'er I passed her; but who passed without
Much the same smile? This grew; I gave commands;   45
Then all smiles stopped together. There she stands
As if alive. Will't please you rise? We'll meet
The company below, then. I repeat,
The Count your master's known munificence
Is ample warrant that no just pretense   50
Of mine for dowry will be disallowed;
Though his fair daughter's self, as I avowed
At starting, is my object. Nay, we'll go
Together down, sir. Notice Neptune,° though,
Taming a sea horse, thought a rarity,   55
Which Claus of Innsbruck° cast in bronze for me!

54 *Neptune*: the Roman god of the sea.   56 *Claus of Innsbruck*: an imaginary sculptor.

QUESTIONS

1. Who is the speaker of the poem? The listener?
2. What are the setting and situation? Where are the characters? What are they looking at?
3. What third character is described? Who describes her? What was she like?
4. How is your final opinion of this third character different from the speaker's? How can you account for the difference?
5. What kind of person do you finally decide the speaker is? Why?

This poem by Robert Browning is a **dramatic monologue.** As the term suggests, dramatic monologues derive from the theater and are voiced by a single speaker to either a silent listener or the reader. As this poem begins, we see the speaker showing off a painting of his last duchess. Lines 1–2 tell us that the speaker is a duke (since his wife was a duchess) and a widower; the phrase "as if she were alive" implies that his last duchess is dead. The lines also tell us that the speaker is with someone and that they are looking at a painting of the dead Duchess.

In lines 3–10, the speaker talks about the painting. At the same time, he unwittingly begins to reveal aspects of his own personality. He points out that the painting was done in a single day ("busily a day") by a monk named Frà (Brother) Pandolf. As he invites the listener to admire the painting, he notes that "strangers like you" never get to see ("read") the painting unless invited. Indeed, the Duke makes it clear that he keeps the painting for himself because only he is permitted to draw back the curtain that usually hides it. These accumulated details begin to suggest things about the speaker. The fact that the Duke chose a monk-painter and gave him only one day to finish the portrait suggests that he is both jealous and possessive. Both characteristics are further implied by the Duke's hoarding of the painting for himself and his absolute control of the curtain.

At this point in the poem we must imagine that the listener asks a question about the Duchess's appearance. The Duke says that "you" are "not the first" to ask about the lady, and he goes on, in lines 13–20, to discuss the "spot of joy" on the Duchess's cheek that Frà Pandolf captured in the portrait. At the same time, the speaker continues to reveal information about himself and he begins to describe his dead wife—the third character in the poem. He points out that other things beside his "presence" could produce that "spot of joy" on the Duchess's cheek, and he gives two examples—polite comments by the painter about the lady's mantle and about the color of her throat. The Duke calls these remarks "such stuff" (line 19) and notes that the Duchess reacted to it with courtesy and happiness. He clearly resents the fact that his "presence" and "such stuff" could produce the same reaction. At the same time, however, the spot of joy suggests that the Duchess was a joyful person who delighted in simple courtesy.

Beginning at line 21, the speaker shifts from the painting to the Duchess herself, and he begins to discuss her attitude toward life. He asserts that "She had / A heart" that was "too soon made glad" and "too easily impressed." He also claims that she liked everything she saw and that "her looks went everywhere" (line 24). Again, we sense that the Duchess took delight from all of life and that the Duke resented this indiscriminant but innocent happiness. He goes on to mention four specific things that gave the Duchess pleasure: "My favor at her breast" (line 25), the sunset (line 26), a "bough of cherries" (line 27), and riding a white mule "around the terrace" (line 29). The Duchess was grateful for each of these pleasures. The key to understanding the Duke's attitude toward this joy is in his assertion that the Duchess treated everything "as if she ranked / My gift of a nine-hundred-years-old name / With anybody's gift" (lines 32–34).

This specific detail suggests that the Duke resented her joy since it made no proud distinction between his noble name and all other pleasures. Here, we begin to feel the full weight of the speaker's arrogance and egotism.

In the next thirteen lines (34–46) the speaker discusses his own reaction to the Duchess's abundant sense of life. He calls her behavior "this sort of trifling" and he makes it clear that he never bothered to correct the Duchess or explain what disgusted him about her. More to the point, he observes that any sort of correction would have been "some stooping" or demeaning of himself, and he proudly claims that "I choose / Never to stoop" (lines 42–43). This assertion conveys the speaker's arrogance and disdain for anything he considers common. His resentment of his wife's attitude is indicated again when he notes that she smiled at him but gave the same smile to everyone else. Finally, he became so disgusted and enraged that he took action: "I gave commands; / Then all smiles stopped together" (lines 45–46). These lines hint that the Duke had the Duchess killed or imprisoned; in any event, he disposed of her. The lines are especially ominous because the reference is indirect and ambiguous.

At this point in the poem the speaker returns his attention to the portrait ("There she stands / As if alive") and then invites the listener to join "the company below." Here, we learn more about the listener and the immediate situation. The Duke mentions the business that brought the listener to his palace (lines 49–51):

The Count your master's known munificence
Is ample warrant that no just pretense
Of mine for dowry will be disallowed.

Thus, we learn that the listener is an agent from "The Count" who has come to arrange the marriage of the Duke to the Count's daughter. The Duke asserts that he is sure the dowry will be sufficient, although it is the Count's "fair daughter's self" that is his "object" (lines 52–53). The word *object* is used by the poet with an ironic double meaning here. The Duke says that the daughter is the real focus of his attention rather than the dowry. However, the word suggests that his next duchess will become his object or possession, just as his last duchess is now an object hanging on the wall rather than a living woman; she was not enough of an object while she was alive.

As the Duke and the agent prepare to go downstairs, one final piece of art halts their progress: "Notice Neptune, though, / Taming a sea horse, thought a rarity, / Which Claus of Innsbruck cast in bronze for me" (lines 54–56). These lines sum up in a single image all that the Duke has revealed about himself and his last Duchess. The statue, like a painting or a wife, is a rare object that the Duke holds with obsessive possessiveness. Moreover, the statue symbolizes the Duke's need to possess and dominate his wife completely. The last Duchess, like the sea horse, was a rare and wonderful creature. The Duke is like Neptune in his need to tame and control such a creature.

There is no clear engagement with ideas or theme in this poem; it is primarily designed to reveal two characters. One of these, the Duke-speaker, shows us that he is an arrogant, egotistical, and vicious man who kills what he cannot control and possess completely. The other character, the last Duchess, is revealed to have been an innocent and unaffected woman who found joy in everything. She was clearly guilty of a failure to discriminate between her proud husband and the rest of the world. She was not guilty of anything else, although the Duke may have imagined much more serious crimes. The poem does not come right out and tell us these things about either character. The Duke never says that he is proud, possessive, jealous, or cruel, nor does he describe his dead wife as innocent or joyful. Instead, Browning lets the speaker present himself in his own words. As readers, we are left to make our own evaluation of the Duke and his last duchess. But Browning loads the dice; he has the speaker give us just the right details so that we cannot help reacting with revulsion to this monster of egotism and arrogance.

THOMAS HARDY (1840–1928)

Channel Firing 1914

That night your great guns, unawares,
Shook all our coffins° as we lay,
And broke the chancel window-squares,
We thought it was the Judgment Day

And sat upright. While drearisome 5
Arose the howl of wakened hounds:
The mouse let fall the altar-crumb,
The worms drew back into the mounds,

The glebe° cow drooled. Till God called, "No;
It's gunnery practice out at sea 10
Just as before you went below;
The world is as it used to be:

"All nations striving strong to make
Red war yet redder. Mad as hatters
They do no more for Christés sake 15
Than you who are helpless in such matters.

CHANNEL FIRING.   2 *coffins*: it has been common practice in England for hundreds of years to bury people in the floors or basements of churches.   9 *glebe*: a parcel of land adjoining and belonging to a church.

"That this is not the judgment hour
For some of them's a blessed thing,
For if it were they'd have to scour
Hell's floor for so much threatening. . . .   20

"Ha, ha. It will be warmer when
I blow the trumpet (if indeed
I ever do; for you are men,
And rest eternal sorely need)."

So down we lay again. "I wonder,   25
Will the world ever saner be,"
Said one, "than when He sent us under
In our indifferent century!"

And many a skeleton shook his head.
"Instead of preaching forty year,"   30
My neighbor Parson Thirdly said,
"I wish I had stuck to pipes and beer."

Again the guns disturbed the hour,
Roaring their readiness to avenge,
As far inland as Stourton Tower,°   35
And Camelot,° and starlit Stonehenge.°

35 *Stourton Tower:* tower commemorating King Alfred the Great's defeat of the Danes in
879 A.D.   36 *Camelot:* legendary seat of King Arthur's court.   *Stonehenge:* group of
standing stones on Salisbury Plain, probably built as a place of worship before 1000 B.C.

QUESTIONS

1. Who or what is the speaker in this poem? What is the setting? The situation?
2. To whom does the *your* in line 1 refer? The *our* in line 2?
3. What has awakened the speaker and his companions? What mistake have
   they made?
4. Beyond the primary speaker, what three other voices are heard in the poem?
5. What is the effect of the references to Stourton Tower, Camelot, and Stonehenge in the last two lines?
6. What ideas about war and the nature of humanity does this poem explore?

We might expect a poem about warfare written immediately before
the outbreak of World War I and spoken by a corpse to be thoroughly
depressing. Surprisingly, Hardy's "Channel Firing" is rather amusing until
we stop and think about its implications; then it becomes depressing indeed.
The poem is fairly easy to read and understand; the language is straightforward, and the poem requires little in the way of previous knowledge. On

the other hand, it does present an interesting problem in dealing with the characters. In addition to the central speaker, Hardy includes three secondary speakers in the poem. Our task here is to keep these four voices distinct and to find out what we can about each.

The first ten lines of the poem establish the situation, the setting, the primary speaker, and the listener. The immediate situation is "gunnery practice out at sea" (line 10). The "great guns" belong to the living. Thus, the *your* in line 1 identifies us as the listeners. The booming of the guns has disturbed a church and the graves in its floor. The gunnery has shaken the coffins, broken the windows near the altar, awakened the hounds, and frightened the church-mouse, worms, and glebe cow. Most important, it has awakened the corpses buried in the church. The speaker is one of these corpses; he tells us that "We thought it was the Judgment Day" (line 4). The speaker and his fellow corpses have mistakenly confused gunnery with the last judgment. At least part of the poem's humor is derived from the reinvigoration of a cliché that hides behind the text; the gunnery practice was loud enough to wake the dead.

The second speaker is introduced in the third stanza where God informs the corpses that it is not Judgment Day, just "gunnery practice." God claims that the world has not changed since the years when each of the corpses lived and died ("went below"). He condemns humanity for "striving" to make war even more destructive ("Red war yet redder"), and He asserts that the living do "no more" for Christ's sake than the dead. God goes on, in the fifth stanza, to state that some of humanity would end up in Hell "for so much threatening" if it were Judgment Day. Finally, God looks ahead to a Judgment Day that may never come— "when / I blow the Trumpet (if indeed / I ever do . . .)"—and notes that even then many will be damned ("it will be warmer"). He closes on a more compassionate note, observing that humanity badly needs "rest eternal." The God in this poem is not loving and forgiving. Instead, He has a rather cynical and negative view of humanity; He has no faith that people will ever be any better than they are.

In the seventh stanza the speaker tells us that he and his fellow corpses returned to their coffins. At this point, a conversation among the corpses and skeletons begins, and we hear a series of speakers. The first is an unidentified corpse ("one") who wonders if the world will ever be any saner "than when He sent us under / In our indifferent century!" The question implies its own answer; the world will always be the same. The word *indifferent* has a double meaning here; it implies that all centuries have been the same (indifferent) since all have been uncaring (indifferent) about God's law and salvation. The next speaker is Parson Thirdly, whose name suggests both the Holy Trinity and the rhetorical practice of sermonizing by the numbers ("Firstly . . . Secondly . . . Thirdly"). Thirdly shares God's negative view of humanity, but he expresses it in a more personal and humorous tone. He wishes that he had "stuck to pipes and beer" "instead of preaching forty year" (lines 30–32). Thirdly thus suggests that his preaching did no good whatsoever.

The last stanza changes both the sense and the scope of the poem. Up to this point, the various speakers have been both funny and bitter at the same time. Here, however, the speaker's voice becomes more detached as he observes that the guns have started again and roared "As far inland as Stourton Tower, / And Camelot, and starlit Stonehenge" (lines 35–36). The reference to these three places has a profound effect on the poem; it expands the poem's time frame from the immediate present (the twentieth century) back through history (Stourton Tower) and legend (Camelot) to the dim past of prehistoric Britain (Stonehenge). The reference has two parallel effects. On the one hand, each place symbolizes a civilization that has disappeared from the earth. The implication is that our world could easily join these remnants in destruction. On the other hand, this movement back through time also suggests that humanity has been the same for thousands of centuries. "Channel Firing" thus makes a statement about war and about humanity. The subject of the poem is the gunnery practice and the immediate reaction of the corpses. Thematically, however, the poem suggests that war is a damnable act that violates God's law and Christ's teachings. The implications for humanity are even more disturbing; the poem asserts that humanity has always pursued war and will continue on this course forever.

POEMS FOR STUDY

ANONYMOUS

Bonny George Campbell   *Medieval*

High upon Highlands
  And low upon Tay,
Bonny George Campbell
  Rode out on a day.

Saddled and bridled   5
  And gallant rode he;
Home came his good horse,
  But never came he.

Out came his old mother,
  Greeting full sair°   *weeping full sore*   10
And out came his bonny bride,
  Riving° her hair.   *tearing*

Saddled and bridled
  And booted rode he;
Toom° home came the saddle,   *empty*   15
  But never came he.

"My meadow lies green,
  And my corn° is unshorn,   *wheat*
My barn is to build°   *not built*
  And my babe is unborn."   20

Saddled and bridled
  And booted rode he;
Toom home came the saddle,
  But never came he.

QUESTIONS

1. What can you determine about the speaker of this poem? Is he *inside* or *outside* the poem? Engaged in the action or detached?
2. Who are the three characters in the poem? How fully are they described? What can you deduce about their social status, way of life, and feelings?
3. Why are there quotation marks around the fifth stanza? Who or what is the speaker here?
4. What events does this poem describe?
5. What is the effect of repetition in this poem? How does it shape your response?

GEORGE HERBERT (1593–1633)

Love (*III*)   *1633*

Love bade me welcome: yet my soul drew back,
    Guilty of dust and sin.
But quick-eyed Love, observing me grow slack
    From my first entrance in,
Drew nearer to me, sweetly questioning   5
    If I lacked° anything.

"A guest," I answered, "worthy to be here":
    Love said, "You shall be he."
"I, the unkind, ungrateful? Ah, my dear,
    I cannot look on thee."   10
Love took my hand, and smiling did reply,
    "Who made the eyes but I?"

LOVE (III).   6 *lacked*: wanted; the phrase is a standard question asked by innkeepers.

"Truth, Lord; but I have marred them; let my shame
    Go where it doth deserve."
"And know you not," says Love, "who bore the blame?"   15
    "My dear, then I will serve."
"You must sit down," says Love, "and taste my meat."
    So I did sit and eat.

QUESTIONS

1. Who are the two characters in this poem? Which is the primary speaker?
2. What does the primary speaker think of himself? Of his own spiritual state?
3. Who or what is "Love"? What does Love tell us about himself when he asks "who made the eyes but I?" (line 12) and "who bore the blame" (line 15)?
4. What sort of meal does the speaker finally "sit and eat"?
5. What relationship is this poem finally about?

ALFRED, LORD TENNYSON (1809–1892)

Tithonus   *Expresses his isolation + loneliness + alienation from the gods + humanity.*   *1860*

  The woods decay, the woods decay and fall,   *The cycles of Nature.*
The vapors weep their burthen to the ground,
Man comes and tills the field and lies beneath,
And after many a summer dies the swan.
Me only cruel immortality *He's separate.*   5
Consumes; I wither slowly in thine arms, *Eos, goddess of the Dawn. He*
Here at the quiet limit of the world,   *speaks to her.*
A white-haired shadow roaming like a dream
The ever-silent spaces of the East,
Far-folded mists, and gleaming halls of morn.   10
  Alas! for this gray shadow, once a man—
So glorious in his beauty and thy choice,
Who madest him thy chosen, that he seemed
To his great heart none other than a God!
I asked thee, "Give me immortality."   15
Then didst thou grant mine asking with a smile,
Like wealthy men who care not how they give.
But thy strong Hours indignant worked their wills,
And beat me down and marred and wasted me,
And though they could not end me, left me maimed *Aged.*   20
To dwell in presence of immortal youth,
Immortal age beside immortal youth,

And all I was in ashes. Can thy love,
Thy beauty, make amends, though even now,
Close over us, the silver star, thy guide,
Shines in those tremulous eyes that fill with tears   25
To hear me? Let me go; take back thy gift.
Why should a man desire in any way
To vary from the kindly race of men,
Or pass beyond the goal of ordinance   30
Where all should pause, as is most meet for all?
    A soft air fans the cloud apart; there comes
A glimpse of that dark world where I was born.
Once more the old mysterious glimmer steals
From thy pure brows, and from thy shoulders pure,   35
And bosom beating with a heart renewed.
Thy cheek begins to redden through the gloom,
Thy sweet eyes brighten slowly close to mine,
Ere yet they blind the stars, and the wild team
Which love thee, yearning for thy yoke, arise,   40
And shake the darkness from their loosened manes,
And beat the twilight into flakes of fire.
    Lo! ever thus thou growest beautiful
In silence, then before thine answer given
Departest, and thy tears are on my cheek.   45
    Why wilt thou ever scare me with thy tears,
And make me tremble lest a saying learnt,
In days far-off, on that dark earth, be true?
"The Gods themselves cannot recall their gifts."
    Ay me! ay me! with what another heart   50
In days far-off, and with what other eyes
I used to watch—if I be he that watched—
The lucid outline forming round thee; saw
The dim curls kindle into sunny rings;
Changed with thy mystic change, and felt my blood   55
Glow with the glow that slowly crimsoned all
Thy presence and thy portals, while I lay,
Mouth, forehead, eyelids, growing dewy-warm
With kisses balmier than half-opening buds
Of April, and could hear the lips that kissed   60
Whispering I knew not what of wild and sweet,
Like that strange song I heard Apollo sing,
While Ilion like a mist rose into towers.
    Yet hold me not forever in thine East;
How can my nature longer mix with thine?   65
Coldly thy rosy shadows bathe me, cold
Are all thy lights, and cold my wrinkled feet
Upon thy glimmering thresholds, when the steam
Floats up from those dim fields about the homes
Of happy men that have the power to die,   70

mounds

And grassy <u>barrows</u> of the <u>happier dead.</u>
<u>Release me</u>, and <u>restore me to the ground.</u>
Thou seest all things, thou wilt see my grave;
Thou wilt renew thy beauty morn by morn,
I earth in earth <u>forget</u> these <u>empty courts,</u>
And thee returning on thy silver wheels.   75

*The poem explores the con-
trasting states of being:*
* *Youth — Age*
* *Mortality — Immortality*
* *Natural — Supernatural*
* *Community — Isolation*

QUESTIONS

1. Look up Tithonus in an encyclopedia or a dictionary of mythology. Who was he? Whom did he marry? What error occurred?

2. Who is the speaker of the poem? What is the speaker's physical condition? To whom is the poem spoken? What is this listener like?

3. How does the speaker indicate that he is different from all mortal beings? How is he different? How does he indicate that he is different and isolated from the gods?

4. The poem contains two "flashbacks" (lines 11–17 and 50–63). What past events do these flashbacks present?

5. Why does the listener begin to cry at line 45?

6. What does the speaker of this poem want?

C. DAY LEWIS (1904–1972)

Song   *1935*

Come, live with me and be my love,
And we will all the pleasures prove
Of peace and plenty, bed and board,
That chance employment may afford.

I'll handle dainties on the docks   5
And thou shalt read of summer frocks:
At evening by the sour canals
We'll hope to hear some madrigals.

Care on thy maiden brow shall put
A wreath of wrinkles, and thy foot   10
Be shod with pain: not silken dress
But toil shall tire thy loveliness.

Hunger shall make thy modest zone
And cheat fond death of all but bone—
If these delights thy mind may move,   15
Then live with me and be my love.

QUESTIONS

1. What is the connection or relationship between this poem and Marlowe's "Passionate Shepherd to His Love"?
2. To what other poem in this chapter is this poem related? How?
3. Who is the speaker in this poem? The listener?
4. What sort of life does the speaker offer the listener?
5. What is the effect of words like *chance employment* (line 4), *read* (line 6), and *hope* (line 8)?
6. How is the world of this poem different from the world in Marlowe's poem?

JAMES MERRILL (b. 1926)

Laboratory Poem   *1958*

Charles used to watch Naomi, taking heart
And a steel saw, open up turtles, live.
While she swore they felt nothing, he would gag
At blood, at the blind twitching, even after
The murky dawn of entrails cleared, revealing   5
Contours he knew, egg-yellows like lamps paling.

Well then. She carried off the beating heart
To the kymograph° and rigged it there, a rag
In fitful wind, now made to strain, now stopped
By her solutions tonic or malign°   10
Alternately in which it would be steeped.
What the heart bore, she noted on a chart,

For work did not stop only with the heart.
He thought of certain human hearts, their climb
Through violence into exquisite disciplines   15
Of which, as it now appeared, they all expired.
Soon she would fetch another and start over,
Easy in the presence of her lover.

LABORATORY POEM.   8 *kymograph*: an instrument that measures pulsations or variations
of pressure and records them on a revolving scroll of paper.   10 *tonic or malign*: healthful
or poisonous, virtuous or evil.

QUESTIONS

1. What can you determine about the speaker here? Is he *inside* or *outside* the poem? Engaged in the action or detached?
2. Who are the two characters in the poem? What are they like? What is their relationship? What are they doing?

3. Which character's thoughts does the speaker relate? What are they? What conclusions does this character come to about science? Love? Human endeavor?

4. What is the setting of the poem? The situation? The event described? What aspects of human existence does the poem explore?

RANDALL JARRELL (1914–1965)

The Woman at the Washington Zoo   *1960*

The saris go by me from the embassies.

Cloth from the moon. Cloth from another planet.
They look back at the leopard like the leopard.

And I. . . .
     this print of mine, that has kept its color
Alive through so many cleanings; this dull null   5
Navy I wear to work, and wear from work, and so
To my bed, so to my grave, with no
Complaints, no comment: neither from my chief,
The Deputy Chief Assistant, nor his chief—
Only I complain. . . . this serviceable   10
Body that no sunlight dyes, no hand suffuses
But, dome-shadowed, withering among columns,
Wavy beneath fountains—small, far-off, shining
In the eyes of animals, these beings trapped
As I am trapped but not, themselves, the trap,   15
Aging, but without knowledge of their age,
Kept safe here, knowing not of death, for death—
Oh, bars of my own body, open, open!

The world goes by my cage and never sees me.
And there come not to me, as come to these   20
The wild beasts, sparrows pecking the llamas' grain,
Pigeons settling on the bears' bread, buzzards
Tearing the meat the flies have clouded. . . .
        Vulture,
When you come for the white rat that the foxes left,
Take off the red helmet of your head, the black   25
Wings that have shadowed me, and step to me as man:
The wild brother at whose feet the white wolves fawn,
To whose hand of power the great lioness
Stalks, purring. . . .
     You know what I was,
You see what I am: change me, change me!   30

QUESTIONS

1. Who is the speaker? Where is the speaker?
2. How does the speaker contrast herself to the women wearing saris?
3. What is the speaker's attitude toward her work?
4. How is the speaker like the animals in the zoo? How is the speaker different from the animals?
5. What is the speaker's attitude toward her clothing? Body? Life?
6. What does the speaker want?

MAURA STANTON (b. 1946)

The Conjurer   1975

In a mayonnaise jar I keep the tiny
people I shrank with my magic; I didn't
know they'd hold each other's hands & cry
so sharply when I said, no, the spell's
irreversible, do you eat grass or breadcrumbs?   5
Two are lovers who claim the air's bad
down there, & bite my fingers when I offer
a ride. They don't understand me.
I keep the jar by a window, washing
soot off the glass walls periodically . . .   10
When I gave them a flower, some ants
in the stamen attacked viciously,
gnawing the man-in-the-fur-cap's leg
completely off, while the others squealed
at the punched lid for his rescue: 15
I thumbed the ant dead, but were they grateful?
Lately they've begun to irritate me,
refusing raw meat, demanding more privacy
as if they were parrots who need cage covers
for daytime sleep. The awkward lovers   20
break apart at my shadow, nonchalant . . .
They're weaving something out of grass,
a blanket maybe, growing thin to save
their stalks, eating only breadcrumbs.
Don't they see? I could dump them   25
out into a real garden, let them tunnel
through the weeds to an anthill.
One night I dreamed those lovers crawled
inside my left ear with candles,
trying to find my brain in a fog.   30
They moved deep among the stalactites

searching for the magic spell they thought
I'd lost in sleep. I knew better.
Still, I woke with something resurrected
in my memory, maybe only a trick,   35
yes, a trick, I'll tell them to close
their eyes I've something for them.

QUESTIONS

1. Who is the speaker?
2. What is the speaker's attitude toward the other characters in the poem?
3. Who are the other characters in the poem? What is their attitude toward the speaker?
4. How does the speaker treat these other characters? What does he treat them as?
5. What "trick" do you think the speaker has in mind for these other characters?
6. What is your final assessment of the speaker?

WRITING ABOUT CHARACTERS IN POETRY

See p. 174 on essay organization.

Writing about character involves many of the same considerations whether you are dealing with prose fiction or poetry. Therefore, you might review the material on writing about character presented in Chapter 4 (pp. 173–75). There are, however, some important differences between the two tasks. One of these is the way you find out about characters. In prose fiction, you can usually judge a character on the basis of what the narrator tells you about his or her actions, words, thoughts, appearance, opinions, and the like. In poetry, however, the speaker is less likely to give you a great deal of information about character. Consequently, many of the conclusions you make about characters in poems will be based on implication and interpretation rather than on clear statements of fact.

Another difference between writing about character in fiction and in poetry concerns the types of character on which you will focus your attention. In fiction, there is a broad range of options; you may choose to write about the protagonist, the antagonist, the narrator, or any one of the incidental characters. In poetry, however, your options are usually limited to the speaker, the listener, or one of the characters described by the speaker. You usually learn the most about the speaker and described characters. In writing an essay on Browning's "My Last Duchess," for example, you could focus on either the Duke or the Duchess; you learn enough from the poem to write about either.

Before you begin to write the essay, you should find out and note
down as much as you can about the characters and their relationships to
the action, emotion, and ideas in the poem under consideration. These
notes will help you decide which character or characters to write about.
They will also help you to develop a central idea for the essay and to
organize your observations about character.

In examining the speaker of a poem, you may want to consider the
following: Where is the speaker? What is he or she doing? What has already
occurred? What does the speaker say about himself or herself? About others? What opinions or ideas does the speaker express? What kinds of words
and references does he or she use? What tone of voice is employed? What
is the speaker's relationship to the action or thought of the poem and to
the other characters?

When you are looking at characters other than the speaker, the process
of study and planning is slightly different. Again, you must rely on the
speaker's description of this other character's action, appearance, emotions,
and ideas. You might consider how this character is described, what he
or she does and says, what he or she thinks and feels. In this case, however,
you should ask yourself if your opinion of the described character diverges
from the speaker's. When this happens, as it does in "My Last Duchess,"
be careful to take the speaker's prejudices and personality into account.

As you answer these questions and others that come to mind, you
will be creating a set of notes that will serve as the basis of your essay.
Be sure to include in these notes specific references to parts of the poem
that support your conclusions about the characters. The conclusions will
become the central idea of the essay; the supporting references will become
paragraphs in the body. By the time you complete this process of study
and note taking, you should be able to select a specific character or group
of characters to write about. Similarly, you will have reached some tentative
conclusions about character that may be shaped into an initial central idea
for the paper.

A final principle to keep in mind when planning an essay about character in poetry is selectivity. Poems provide a vast amount of material that
can be related to character. This may include everything from straightforward description to rhyme, words, rhythm, sound, and the arrangement
of lines on the page. You cannot bring all of these details into a single
essay. Rather, make selective use of details and quotation from the poem;
choose those items of information and evidence that most clearly illustrate
your point and most effectively advance your argument.

Organizing the Essay

You should not begin to write the essay until you have a fairly clear
idea about what you are going to assert about the character and how you
are going to support this assertion with evidence from the poem. Once

you move from prewriting to writing, we suggest a three-part organization that includes an introduction, a body, and a conclusion.

INTRODUCTION.   The introduction should state the central idea of the essay. This is usually a general and accurate statement about the character or characters you are discussing. [If you are writing about the Duke in "My Last Duchess," for example, your thesis might claim that the Duke is an arrogant and jealous man who has an obsessive need to possess and control the people in his life.] Similarly, in writing about the central character in "Sir Patrick Spens" (p. 465), you might assert that Sir Patrick faces a conflict between personal judgment and the demands of authority which he resolves by sacrificing his life.

When you write about a single character, <u>the central idea</u> will usually provide <u>a focused conclusion about his or her personality or status</u>. When you deal with a series of characters, the central idea can express some relationship or commonality among them. Thus, in writing about "Bonny George Campbell," you might argue that all the characters are designed to convey the grief of sudden and unexpected death. Whatever the central idea is, the introduction should also briefly outline the ways in which you plan to support it in the body of the essay. Do not list your intentions here; simply note the major points of your argument in your thesis statement.

BODY.   The body of the paper will produce the evidence necessary to support your central idea in a logical and orderly way. There are various methods of organizing this material, depending on the focus of your essay. [If you are writing about a single character, for instance, you might choose to deal with different elements of the poem as they help define him or her in separate paragraphs. Thus, you can deal with <u>words</u>, syntax, sound, rhyme, and <u>ideas</u> in a series of discrete paragraphs. Alternatively, you can discuss the various aspects of the character <u>in the order in which they are revealed in the poem</u>. In this case, <u>the structure of your paper</u> would <u>follow</u> the <u>structure of the poem</u> fairly closely. In such an essay on the Duke in "My Last Duchess," you might devote separate paragraphs to the Duke's treatment of the painting, his reaction to the "spot of joy," his thoughts on the Duchess's smile, and his use of the word *object*.]

When you opt to write about more than one character, other organizational strategies are available. You might decide to treat the characters in the order in which you meet them in the poem. Thus, in writing about "Bonny George Campbell," you would deal with Campbell's mother, his wife, and finally the dead man himself. As an alternative, you can focus on several of the most important characters in the poem and explore the relationship between them. Such an essay on "Sir Patrick Spens" might treat the relationship between the sailor and the king in discrete stages.

Whatever strategy you choose, keep in mind that the organization of the essay is finally determined by the poem under consideration. Each poem will suggest its own avenues of exploration and organization. The goal here is to present the support for your central idea in logical and coherent units of writing.

As you write the first draft of the body, you may discover that specific aspects of character or even specific characters are less or more important than you had originally thought. When this happens, and the paper begins to go off in a new direction, follow your inclination and explore. You will eventually have to revise the introduction to account for these changes. Such revision should be an ongoing process as you write the various drafts of the essay.

CONCLUSION. The conclusion of the essay should be as firm and assertive as the introduction. Here you can summarize what you have discovered about the character or characters under consideration. You can also tie this information back into an assessment of the poem as a whole. Thus, you might briefly discuss the connection between character and the ideas or emotions that the poem explores.

SAMPLE ESSAY

The Nature of the Speaker in Randall Jarrell's "The Woman at the Washington Zoo"*

[1] *Thesis* Randall Jarrell's "The Woman at the Washington Zoo" is a dramatic monologue spoken by an aging woman who feels trapped and who despairs over her dull and drab life.° This despair is expressed in two central contrasts and a final plea for change. The speaker contrasts herself to the other women visiting the zoo and to the zoo animals; she seeks a change in her life, but she knows that change cannot come from within.°

[2] We sense the speaker's despair and desperation in the initial contrast she establishes between herself and the other visitors to the zoo. The first line of the poem places the speaker and these other women in the same place: "the saris go by me from the embassies." The saris—colorful, draped dresses worn by Hindu women—indicate the exotic otherness of these visitors. The speaker calls these saris "Cloth from the moon. Cloth from another planet" (line 2). In this way, she suggests that the distance between herself and these strange women is astronomical. The exotic quality of the saris is also indicated when the speaker notes that "They look back at the leopard like the leopard" (line 3). This compact line opens out into two related ideas; both the saris and the leopards are surprising and both are colorfully alien or different.

---

* See p. 501 for this poem.
° Central idea.
□ Thesis sentence.

Note the use of topic sentences.

[3]   The speaker moves directly from this observation of kinship between the saris and the leopards to the overwhelming contrast that she represents. This distinction is signaled in the arrangement of lines, which literally separates the speaker—"And I"—from the rest of the poem. Unlike the "Cloth from the moon," the speaker's "print" is "dull null / Navy" (lines 5–6). She wears this uniform "to work" and "from work, and so / To my bed, so to my grave" (lines 6–7). Like her uniform, her life is "dull null" and uninteresting; she sees an inevitable progression from work to bed and then to "the grave." And like her uniform and her life, her body is "dull null" and only "serviceable." It is untouched and colorless; it is a "Body that no sunlight dyes, no hand suffuses" (lines 11). Since the words "dye" and "suffuse" both refer to color, this line relates to the exotic and colorful nature of the saris and the leopards; it reinforces the speaker's sense of distance and difference. It also suggests that she is untouched by nature ("sunlight") or humanity ("hand").

[4]   The speaker goes on to establish a clear contrast between herself and the animals at the zoo. *transition* At first, she seems to feel a kinship with the animals, since both are trapped: "these beings trapped / As I am trapped" (lines 14–15). *quotes in support* But the speaker moves immediately to the central distinction between the two traps. The animals are trapped in cages; the speaker is trapped within her own aging body. She says that the animals are "not, themselves, the trap / Aging, but without knowledge of their age" (lines 15–16). Here, she admits that *she* is her own trap. She also points up other significant differences between herself and the animals. The animals have no awareness of aging or mortality; they know "not of death" (line 17). Moreover, the zoo animals are visited (touched, noticed, affected) by the outside world of people and uncaged "wild" animals alike.

[5]   The speaker's cage is very different from the trap that holds the zoo animals. In her case, she is her own trap; her body is her cage. She cries out, "Oh, bars of my own body, open, open!" (line 18). The speaker, unlike the animals, knows that she is aging and that she will die. Even worse, the world ignores her: "The world goes by my cage and never sees me" (line 19). She is even ignored (untouched) by the "wild beasts" who visit and mingle with the animals at the zoo. Her life is devoid of attention, change, or touch. She does not interact at all with the world or with nature. (Her body and her life are thus shown to be isolated, sterile, and sexless.) *Sums up her analysis.*

[6]   The woman's despair and desire for change reach a peak in the last eight lines of the poem. She tells us that she wants to be changed from without. *Note* She calls on the Vulture—Death—to remake himself: "Take off the red helmet of your head, the black / Wings that have shadowed me, and step to me as man" (lines 25–26). And she calls on this Vulture-Death-Man to touch and change her; she wants to be reshaped by an external force that is "wild" and powerful. *quote* The poem closes with the speaker's desperate call for change: "You know what I was, / You see what I am: change me, change me!" (lines 29–30). This is a call for death, life, human contact, natural power, and sexuality all rolled into one. The figure of the (Vulture-Death-Man) becomes the external force that must impose change on the speaker. She realizes that change is absolutely essential, but she also knows that it will never come from within herself. *Any would transform her from her present state.*

We thus see that the speaker in Jarrell's poem is alienated and distanced from her own dull life, from other people, from the zoo animals, and from nature itself. She feels trapped in the "dull null" untouched cage of her own body. The speaker's awareness of her desperate situation suggests that she [7]   has the potential for change and redemption. She realizes, however, that such redemption must be imposed by external forces. Finally, the poem offers little hope for the speaker or for the rest of us trapped in the cages of our routine lives and dull bodies.

Commentary on the Essay

This essay focuses on a single character, the speaker in Randall Jarrell's "The Woman at the Washington Zoo." The structure follows the second method described above: it deals with aspects of the character in the order in which they are revealed in the poem. The introduction presents the central idea—a general conclusion about the speaker in Jarrell's poem—and it outlines the specific points that are raised in the body of the essay to support this assertion.

The body takes up these subjects in exactly the same order in which they are noted in the introduction. Paragraphs 2 and 3 deal with the contrast between the speaker and the women in saris who visit the zoo. Paragraphs 4 and 5 focus on the distinction between the speaker and the zoo animals. The sixth paragraph discusses the speaker's desire for change. Each of these begins with a sentence that restates part of the central idea and provides transition from the previous paragraph. Note also that almost all the evidence used in the paper to support the argument is direct quotation from the poem. The essay does occasionally deal with individual words or line arrangements, but for the most part it sticks to a single type of evidence.

The conclusion summarizes the points about the speaker made in the essay. Moreover, it relates these observations to the poem's general thematic focus. Thus, the conclusion briefly considers the larger implications of character in Jarrell's poem.

13

When, Where, and What: Setting and Situation

As we have seen in Chapter 12, every poem begins with the establishment of a situation that indicates some human relationship, perhaps between the speaker and another person or between the speaker and a group, the speaker and the reader, or even between the speaker and an inner self, as an interior monologue. In determining this human situation, you need to assume that something has been happening before the poem opens. You may not know exactly what that something was, but you need to infer from the poem as many details as possible about the activity that prompted the speaker to begin speaking.

Something similar applies to the establishment of the setting and situation of poetry. Setting in poetry is like setting in prose fiction (see Chapter 6, pp. 205–35). You may find descriptions of the outdoors or indoors; there may be references to the conditions that the speaker is observing or has observed; a number of important things may be said about natural scenery or about the conditions within a building or city; there may be a discussion of the states of various artifacts such as boats, automobiles, teaspoons, paintings, windowpanes, subway stations, and the like. Quite often a poem may be totally locked into the setting, much the way Eudora Welty's "A Worn Path" is connected to the scenes in the countryside around Natchez and within Natchez itself (p. 116).

A poem that is connected equally firmly to its setting is "Cherrylog Road" by James Dickey, a brief narrative that describes a meeting of lovers in a wrecked car in the middle of an automobile junkyard.

JAMES DICKEY (b. 1923)

Cherrylog Road   1963

Off Highway 106
At Cherrylog Road I entered
The '34 Ford without wheels,
Smothered in kudzu,
With a seat pulled out to run   5
Corn whiskey down from the hills,

And then from the other side
Crept into an Essex
With a rumble seat of red leather
And then out again, aboard   10
A blue Chevrolet, releasing
The rust from its other color,

Reared up on three building blocks.
None had the same body heat;
I changed with them inward, toward   15
The weedy heart of the junkyard,
For I knew that Doris Holbrook
Would escape from her father at noon

And would come from the farm
To seek parts owned by the sun   20
Among the abandoned chassis,
Sitting in each in turn
As I did, leaning forward
As in a wild stock-car race

In the parking lot of the dead.   25
Time after time, I climbed in
And out the other side, like
An envoy or movie star
Met at the station by crickets.
A radiator cap raised its head,   30

Become a real toad or a kingsnake
As I neared the hub of the yard,
Passing through many states,
Many lives, to reach
Some grandmother's long Pierce-Arrow   35
Sending platters of blindness forth

From its nickel hubcaps
And spilling its tender upholstery
On sleepy roaches,

The glass panel in between
Lady and colored driver
Not all the way broken out,   40

The back-seat phone
Still on its hook.
I got in as though to exclaim,   45
"Let us go to the orphan asylum,
John; I have some old toys
For children who say their prayers."

I popped with sweat as I thought
I heard Doris Holbrook scrape   50
Like a mouse in the southern-state sun
That was eating the paint in blisters
From a hundred car tops and hoods.
She was tapping like code,

Loosening the screws,   55
Carrying off headlights,
Sparkplugs, bumpers,
Cracked mirrors and gear-knobs,
Getting ready, already,
To go back with something to show   60

Other than her lips' new trembling
I would hold to me soon, soon,
Where I sat in the ripped back seat
Talking over the interphone,
Praying for Doris Holbrook   65
To come from her father's farm

And to get back there
With no trace of me on her face
To be seen by her red-haired father
Who would change, in the squalling barn,   70
Her back's pale skin with a strop,
Then lay for me

In a bootlegger's roasting car
With a string-triggered 12-gauge shotgun
To blast the breath from the air.   75
Not cut by the jagged windshields,
Through the acres of wrecks she came
With a wrench in her hand,

Through dust where the blacksnake dies
Of boredom, and the beetle knows   80
The compost has no more life.

Someone outside would have seen
The oldest car's door inexplicably
Close from within:

I held her and held her and held her,   85
Convoyed at terrific speed
By the stalled, dreaming traffic around us,
So the blacksnake, stiff
With inaction, curved back
Into life, and hunted the mouse   90

With deadly overexcitement,
The beetles reclaimed their field
As we clung, glued together,
With the hooks of the seat springs
Working through to catch us red-handed   95
Amidst the gray breathless batting

That burst from the seat at our backs.
We left by separate doors
Into the changed, other bodies
Of cars, she down Cherrylog Road   100
And I to my motorcycle
Parked like the soul of the junkyard

Restored, a bicycle fleshed
With power, and tore off
Up Highway 106, continually   105
Drunk on the wind in my mouth,
Wringing the handlebar for speed,
Wild to be wreckage forever.

QUESTIONS

1. Describe the scene of the action of the poem. Is it specific or general?
2. Why has the speaker come to the auto junkyard? Who has come there to
   be with him? For what purpose?
3. What sorts of things does the speaker imagine about the old cars?
4. How do the speaker and Doris get to the "long Pierce-Arrow" in the middle
   of the junkyard? What can you conclude about the nature of the setting in
   the poem in the light of the answer to this question?
5. Why is the speaker apprehensive about Doris's father?
6. How do the speaker and Doris leave? How is Doris to justify her having
   gone to the junkyard?
7. As developed in the poem, how strong or how fully explained are the emotional ties between the speaker and Doris?

8. Why is the speaker "Wild to be wreckage forever"? How does this line pull together the setting, action, and emotional impact of the poem?

In this poem, artifacts are inseparable from the action: The speaker has come to the scene on his motorcycle, and his woman friend, Doris Holbrook, has come on the pretext of carrying away things such as head-lights, bumpers, and gear-knobs for use on her father's farm. The speaker is concerned about secrecy because he fears that Doris's father might go after him with a shotgun if he found out that his daughter was sneaking off to make love in the junkyard. In order to get to the middle of the junkyard for maximum privacy, both the speaker and Doris must make a path through a number of the cars in the yard, and many of these cars suggest the lives of their former owners. Because of this close integration of setting and action, this poem is particularly locked into the *where* and *what* of its present form. Before you can begin determining anything about the ideas in the poem, such as the conclusions that young love is precarious and that young lovers must often resort to deception and ingenuity to be with each other, you must first understand the details of setting.

A poem similarly integrated with setting is Thomas Gray's "Elegy Written in a Country Churchyard" (p. 520), although Gray's scene is not quite as specific as Dickey's. The poem is imagined as taking place in a country churchyard, but it might be any churchyard among the thousands that still exist in England where people of the local area have been buried for centuries. Because the observations and speculations that Gray draws from the scene are designed to be general in nature, the reader's imaginative task of reconstruction is to visualize the general scene of a nearby pasture, a graveyard with a large number of modest-sized tombstones, and, in the center of the graveyard, a small church. The time of the poem is clearly established as late afternoon or early evening, just before dark, when local farmers drive their cows home for evening milking. The time of day in which a poem is set is often insignificant and even unspecified. In "Elegy Written in a Country Churchyard," however, the time is extremely important, because meditations on the relationship of death to life are naturally and traditionally associated with dusk and nightfall. Ultimately Gray's poem explores the sadness, solemnity, and certainty of death, the untimely loss of many people, and the need for living a life of quiet piety. These ideas would not be as effective and moving, however, if the poet had not merged them with the reality of life as represented by the scene of the ordinary country churchyard at the end of the day.

Degrees and details of setting vary with individual poems. In "Soliloquy of the Spanish Cloister," for example, Browning uses the title to locate the setting. The poem is an interior monologue—the inner revelation of a disgruntled, disaffected, spiteful monk who is not named and who is venting all his anger and frustration in solitude on his eating companion and fellow monk, Brother Lawrence.

ROBERT BROWNING (1812–1889)

Soliloquy of the Spanish Cloister   1842

1

Gr-r-r—there go, my heart's abhorrence!
    Water your damned flowerpots, do!
If hate killed men, Brother Lawrence,
    God's blood, would not mine kill you!
What? your myrtle bush wants trimming?   5
    Oh, that rose has prior claims—
Needs its leaden vase filled brimming?
    Hell dry you up with its flames!

2

At the meal we sit together:
    Salve tibi!° I must hear   *Hail to thee!*   10
Wise talk of the kind of weather,
    Sort of season, time of year:
Not a plenteous cork crop: scarcely
    Dare we hope oak-galls, I doubt:
What's the Latin name for "parsley"?   15
    What's the Greek name for Swine's Snout?

3

Whew! We'll have our platter burnished,
    Laid with care on our own shelf!
With a fire-new spoon we're furnished,
    And a goblet for ourself,   20
Rinsed like something sacrificial
    Ere 'tis fit to touch our chaps°   *jaws*
Marked with L. for our initial!
    (He-he! There his lily snaps!)

4

Saint, forsooth! While brown Dolores   25
    Squats outside the Convent bank
With Sanchicha, telling stories,
    Steeping tresses in the tank,
Blue-black, lustrous, thick like horsehairs,
    —Can't I see his dead eye glow,   30
Bright as 'twere a Barbary corsair's?°   *pirate's*
    (That is, if he'd let it show!)

5

When he finishes refection,°   *dinner*
    Knife and fork he never lays
Cross-wise, to my recollection,   35
    As do I, in Jesu's praise.
I the Trinity illustrate,
    Drinking watered orange-pulp—

In three sips the Arian° frustrate: *Anti-Trinitarian*
    While he drains his at one gulp.   40
             6
Oh, those melons? If he's able
    We're to have a feast! so nice!
One goes to the Abbot's table,
    All of us get each a slice.
How go on your flowers? None double?   45
    Not one fruit-sort can you spy?
Strange!—And I, too, at such trouble,
Keep them close-nipped on the sly!
             7
There's a great text in Galatians,°   *perhaps 5:19–21 or 3:10*
    Once you trip on it, entails   50
Twenty-nine distinct damnations,
    One sure, if another fails:
If I trip him just a-dying,
    Sure of heaven as sure can be,
Spin him round and send him flying   55
    Off to hell, a Manichee?°   *heretic*
             8
Or, my scrofulous° French novel   *pornographic*
    On gray paper with blunt type!
Simply glance at it, you grovel
    Hand and foot in Belial's° gripe: *the Devil*   60
If I double down its pages
    At the woeful sixteenth print,
When he gathers his greengages,
    Ope a sieve and slip it in't?
             9
Or, there's Satan!—one might venture   65
    Pledge one's soul to him, yet leave
Such a flaw in the indenture°   *contract*
    As he'd miss till, past retrieve,
Blasted lay that rose-acacia
    We're so proud of! *Hy, Zy, Hine* . . .   70
'St, there's Vespers! *Plena gratiâ*°   *full of grace*
    Ave, Virgo!° Gr-r-r—you swine!   *Hail Virgin!*

QUESTIONS

1. Who is the speaker of the poem? What does he think of Brother Lawrence?
2. Where is the speaker as the poem unfolds? Who is he watching? What is this other person doing as the speaker watches? What is the connection between this activity and the speaker's thoughts?

3. Which monk is more observant of refectory regulations? Do these really matter?
4. What sorts of plans is the speaker devising to force Brother Lawrence to damn himself? Does it sound as though these plans could ever be successful? What does the speaker's knowledge of the text in Galatians and the "scrofulous French novel" indicate about the state of his own soul?
5. In what ways is the poem comic? In which way might it be considered as the self-revelation of a seriously disturbed personality?

Here, as the speaker curses his associate, he is due to go to one of the regular religious services that he is obliged to attend daily. The setting of the poem thus figures into his mentality as a part of his total way of life. Natural and manufactured objects become significant as they enter his mind as the means by which he may cause Brother Lawrence, who seems to be totally saintly, to damn himself. In addition, two young women living near the cloister become a part of the setting. These are "Brown Dolores" and "Sanchicha," two attractive women whom the speaker has desired. Rather than recognize his own feelings, however, he attributes sexual interest, which he considers damnatory, to Brother Lawrence. Thus, in "Soliloquy of a Spanish Cloister," Browning develops a satiric and comic situation by bringing to life the inner thoughts of an unmonklike person in a monk's role, who reveals his all too human failings and hypocrisies. The setting in the Spanish cloister is significant not only for itself but also because it is an integral part of the speaker's mentality.

Quite often you will encounter poems in which, as in "Soliloquy in a Spanish Cloister," the setting shifts between (1) the scene of action and (2) a part of the speaker's observations and reflections. Such a poem is Hardy's "The Walk" (p. 530), in which the location of "the hilltop tree / By the gated ways" is meaningful in the speaker's mind as a place of treasured companionship and love. The loved one is now old and infirm and can no longer share the walk. Ultimately the poem is about the speaker's realization that all future walks will be solitary and that as people get old they lose first their youth and vitality and then their freedom of movement. Here, the setting is almost totally the subject of reflection rather than action.

Often the setting is rarely mentioned in detail but instead is implied, being almost totally transformed into responses in the mind of a speaker. A poem with such a psychological tie to setting is T. S. Eliot's "The Love Song of J. Alfred Prufrock" (p. 947). The poem gradually reveals to us that the speaker, Prufrock, is at a party and is contemplating asking some woman to leave with him when the party is over. However, we read no details about the party except that people are talking about art ("Michelangelo"), and we find no descriptions of any woman to whom he is speaking. Indeed, everything about the setting after the opening descriptions indicates that the speaker is responding to things rather than attempting to describe or define them. Beyond these responses, he is also being reminded of other places he has visited or has read about (such as the "floors of silent seas"). The poem, in other words, is reflective of a particular location in place and time, but it is more importantly connected to the total pattern of Prufrock's complex and troubled consciousness.

These poems are all visualized as bearing a direct, indirect, or remote relationship to real places that the speaker has seen and which you as the reader may readily imagine. Sometimes, however, the poet may include fabled and mythical places as a part of the setting, as in the following devotional poem.

CHRISTINA ROSSETTI (1830–1894)

A Christmas Carol   *1872*

In the bleak mid-winter
  Frosty wind made moan,
Earth stood hard as iron,
  Water like a stone;
Snow had fallen, snow on snow,   5
  Snow on snow,
In the bleak mid-winter
  Long ago.

Our God, Heaven cannot hold Him
  Nor earth sustain;   10
Heaven and earth shall flee away
  When He comes to reign:
In the bleak mid-winter
  A stable-place sufficed°   *see Luke 2:7*
The Lord God Almighty   15
  Jesus Christ.

Enough for Him whom cherubim
  Worship night and day,
A breastful of milk
  And a mangerful of hay;   20
Enough for Him whom angels
  Fall down before,
The ox and ass and camel
  Which adore.

Angels and archangels   25
  May have gathered there,
Cherubim and seraphim
  Throng'd the air,

But only His mother
  In her maiden bliss   30
Worshipped the Beloved
  With a kiss.

What can I give Him,
  Poor as I am?
If I were a shepherd°   *see Luke 2:8–20*   35
  I would bring a lamb,
If I were a wise man°   *see Matthew 2:1–12*
  I would do my part,—
Yet what I can I give Him,
  Give my heart.   40

QUESTIONS

1. What is the place and time visualized by the speaker for the events of the poem? Why do you think that the poet stressed the bitterness and bleakness of the winter setting?

2. What is the location where the "Lord God almighty" "comes to reign"? Why does the speaker stress the simplicity of the birthplace? From what sources is the setting derived?

3. How does the fourth stanza, with its stress both on the angelic scene and the presence of the mother, prepare you for the speaker's description of her own condition in stanza 5?

4. What gifts does the speaker consider giving? How are these objects part of the setting traditionally associated with the appearance of Jesus? Which is the only gift the speaker can choose? How does the poem make plain that this gift is really the most valuable of all?

In this poem the setting described in the first stanza is one that may readily be imagined by anyone who has ever experienced a cold day in a part of the world that has cold, snowy winters. Rossetti transfers the scene, however, from our northern climate to the Middle-Eastern location of the stable in Bethlehem where the baby Jesus was born. In the last stanza, by referring to the Wise Men and to the shepherds, she introduces settings respectively from the Biblical books of Matthew and Luke. This use of setting, which has been frequently dramatized and pictured, is of less significance as a graphic scene, however, than as the occasion that prompts the speaker to present her gift of her heart, that is, the warmth of her love and allegiance.

As you read in order to determine the setting or settings of poems, prepare to see a wide variety of references to place and time. Sometimes you may find a close tie of place and content, but other times you will find that there is not much action as such and that a poem is only loosely located in real places. As long as you are ready to adjust to encountering many variations, you should be able to deal effectively with the *when, where, and what* of poetry.

POEMS FOR STUDY

ANDREW MARVELL (1621–1678)

Bermudas   *1681*

Where the remote Bermudas ride,
In the ocean's bosom unespied,
From a small boat, that rowed along,
The listening winds received this song:
  "What should we do but sing His praise,   5
That led us through the watery maze,
Unto an isle so long unknown,
And yet far kinder than our own?
Where He the huge sea-monsters wracks,°   *injures, destroys*
That lift the deep upon their backs;   10
He lands us on a grassy stage,
Safe from the storms and prelates' rage.
He gave us this eternal spring,
Which here enamels° every thing,   *embellishes with bright colors*
And sends the fowls to us in care,   15
On daily visits through the air;
He hangs in shades the orange bright,
Like golden lamps in a green night,
And does in the pomegranates close
Jewels more rich than Ormus° shows;   20
He makes the figs our mouths to meet,
And throws the melons at our feet;
But apples° plants of such a price,   *causes to bear fruit*
No tree could ever bear them twice;
With cedars chosen by His hand,   25
From Lebanon,° He stores the land,
And makes the hollow seas, that roar,
Proclaim the ambergris° on shore;
He cast (of which we rather boast)
The Gospel's pearl upon our coast,   30
And in these rocks for us did frame
A temple where to sound His name.

BERMUDAS.   20 *Ormus*: town in ancient Persia.   26 *Lebanon*: Cedars from Lebanon
were used in Solomon's temple (2 Chronicles 2:8).   28 *ambergris*: a substance, secreted
by sperm whales, used in perfume.

Oh! let our voice His praise exalt,
Till it arrive at Heaven's vault,
Which thence perhaps, rebounding, may   35
Echo beyond the Mexique Bay."
    Thus sung they in the English boat,
An holy and a cheerful note;
And all the way, to guide their chime,
With falling oars they kept the time.   40

QUESTIONS

1. To English people living in the seventeenth century, why would it have seemed
   accurate to call the Bermudas (which are about 600 miles east of North Carolina) "remote?"

2. What is happening as described in lines 1–4 and 37–40, during the time
   the "song" is being expressed from lines 5–36?

3. Where are the speaker and his or her companions during this poem? Have
   they ever been to the Bermudas? If not, what do you make of the detailed
   description of setting in lines 5 through 36?

4. To what extent is the speaker's description of the Bermudas an indirect reference to the Garden of Eden? What do the Bermudas and Eden seem to
   have in common?

5. As explained in the "holy and cheerful note" of lines 5–36, what are the
   reasons for which the praise is given? How many separate things are listed
   to justify the praise?

THOMAS GRAY (1716–1771)

Elegy Written in a Country Churchyard   *1751*

The curfew tolls the knell of parting day,
    The lowing herd wind slowly o'er the lea,
The ploughman homeward plods his weary way,
    And leaves the world to darkness and to me.

Now fades the glimm'ring landscape on the sight,   5
    And all the air a solemn stillness holds,
Save where the beetle wheels his droning flight,
    And drowsy tinklings lull the distant folds;

Save that from yonder ivy-mantled tower
    The moping owl does to the moon complain   10
Of such as wand'ring near her secret bower
    Molest her ancient solitary reign.

Beneath those rugged elms, that yew-tree's shade,
  Where heaves the turf in many a mold'ring heap,
Each in his narrow cell forever laid,   15
  The rude forefathers of the hamlet sleep.

The breezy call of incense-breathing morn,
  The swallow twitt'ring from the straw-built shed,
The cock's shrill clarion, or the echoing horn,°   *hunting horn*
  No more shall rouse them from their lowly bed.   20

For them no more the blazing hearth shall burn,
  Or busy housewife ply her evening care;
No children run to lisp their sire's return,
  Or climb his knees the envied kiss to share.

Oft did the harvest to their sickle yield,   25
  Their furrow oft the stubborn glebe° has broke;   *turf*
How jocund did they drive their team afield!
  How bowed the woods beneath their sturdy stroke!

Let not Ambition mock their useful toil
  Their homely joys, and destiny obscure;
Nor Grandeur hear with a disdainful smile   30
  The short and simple annals of the poor.

The boast of heraldry, the pomp of power,
  And all that beauty, all that wealth e'er gave,
Awaits alike th'inevitable hour.   35
  The paths of glory lead but to the grave.

Nor you, ye proud, impute to these the fault,
  If mem'ry o'er their tomb no trophies raise,
Where through the long-drawn aisle and fretted vault
  The pealing anthem swells the note of praise.   40

Can storied urn or animated bust
  Back to its mansion call the fleeting breath?
Can Honor's voice provoke the silent dust,
  Or Flatt'ry soothe the dull cold ear of death?

Perhaps in this neglected spot is laid   45
  Some heart once pregnant with celestial fire;
Hands that the rod of empire might have swayed,
  Or waked to ecstasy the living lyre.

But Knowledge to their eyes her ample page
  Rich with the spoils of time did ne'er unroll;   50
Chill Penury repressed their noble rage,
  And froze the genial current of the soul.

Full many a gem of purest ray serene,
  The dark unfathomed caves of ocean bear;
Full many a flower is born to blush unseen,   55
  And waste its sweetness on the desert air.

Some village Hampden,° that with dauntless breast
  The little tyrant of his fields withstood;
Some mute inglorious Milton here may rest,
  Some Cromwell guiltless of his country's blood.   60

Th'applause of list'ning senates to command,
  The threats of pain and ruin to despise,
To scatter plenty o'er a smiling land,
  And read their hist'ry in a nation's eyes

Their lot forbade: nor circumscribed alone   65
  Their growing virtues, but their crimes confined;
Forbade to wade through slaughter to a throne,
  And shut the gates of mercy on mankind,

The struggling pangs of conscious truth to hide,
  To quench the blushes of ingenuous shame,   70
Or heap the shrine of luxury and pride
  With incense kindled at the Muse's flame.

Far from the madding° crowd's ignoble strife,   *raving*
  Their sober wishes never learned to stray;
Along the cool sequestered vale of life   75
  They kept the noiseless tenor of their way.

Yet ev'n these bones from insult to protect
  Some frail memorial still erected nigh,
With uncouth rhymes and shapeless sculpture decked,
  Implores the passing tribute of a sigh.   80

Their names, their years, spelt by th'unlettered Muse,
  The place of fame and elegy supply;
And many a holy text around she strews,
  That teach the rustic moralist to die.

For who to dumb forgetfulness a prey,   85
  This pleasing anxious being e'er resigned,
Left the warm precincts of the cheerful day,
  Nor cast one longing ling'ring look behind?

On some fond breast the parting soul relies,
  Some pious drops the closing eye requires;   90
Ev'n from the tomb the voice of Nature cries,
  Ev'n in our ashes live their wonted fires.

For thee, who mindful of th'unhonored dead
  Dost in these lines their artless tale relate;
If chance, by lonely contemplation led,   95
  Some kindred spirit shall inquire thy fate,

ELEGY WRITTEN IN A COUNTRY CHURCHYARD.   57 *Hampden* John Hampden
(1594–1643), English statesman who defended the rights of the people against King Charles
I and who died in the English Civil War of 1642–1646.

Haply some hoary-headed swain may say,
  "Oft have we seen him at the peep of dawn
Brushing with hasty steps the dews away
  To meet the sun upon the upland lawn.   100

"There, at the foot of yonder nodding beech
  That wreathes its old fantastic roots so high,
His listless length at noontide would he stretch
  And pore upon the brook that babbles by.

"Hard by yon wood, now smiling as in scorn,   105
  Mutt'ring his wayward fancies he would rove,
Now drooping, woeful wan, like one forlorn,
  Or crazed with care, or crossed in hopeless love.

"One morn I missed him on the 'customed hill,
  Along the heath and near his fav'rite tree;   110
Another came; nor yet beside the rill,
  Nor up the lawn, nor at the wood was he;

"The next with dirges due in sad array
  Slow through the church-way path we saw him borne.
Approach and read (for thou canst read) the lay,   115
  Graved on the stone beneath yon aged thorn."

The Epitaph

Here rests his head upon the lap of earth
  A youth to fortune and to fame unknown;
Fair Science frowned not on his humble birth,
  And Melancholy marked him for her own.   120

Large was his bounty, and his soul sincere,
  Heav'n did a recompense as largely send:
He gave to mis'ry all he had, a tear:
  He gain'd from Heav'n ('twas all he wished) a friend.

No farther seek his merits to disclose,   125
  Or draw his frailties from their dread abode,
(There they alike in trembling hope repose)
  The bosom of his Father and his God.

QUESTIONS

1. What time of day is described as the time of the speaker's meditation? What is happening in nature and the world as the poem opens?

2. Why does it seem natural to shift from the close of day to the "forefathers of the hamlet" sleeping in their graves?

3. What kinds of people are buried in the church graveyard? What different talents might they have realized and fulfilled if they had not died? On balance, has the world been a loser because of these premature deaths?

4. Who is the "thee" of line 93? What sort of life does he lead? What happens to him?

5. Describe Gray's use of sights and sounds in the poem. How do these descriptions complement the sober mood that Gray evokes?

WILLIAM BLAKE (1757–1827)

London   *1794*

I wander thro' each charter'd° street,
Near where the charter'd Thames does flow,
And mark in every face I meet
Marks of weakness, marks of woe.

In every cry of every Man,   5
In every Infant's cry of fear,
In every voice, in every ban,°   *public pronouncement*
The mind-forg'd manacles I hear.

How the Chimney-sweeper's cry
Every blackning Church appalls;°   10
And the hapless Soldier's sigh
Runs in blood down Palace walls.

But most thro' midnight streets I hear
How the youthful Harlot's curse
Blasts the new-born Infant's tear,   15
And blights with plagues the Marriage hearse.

LONDON.   1 *charter'd*: privileged, licensed, authorized (also hired).   10 *appalls*: (1) weakens, makes pale, (2) shocks.

QUESTIONS

1. What does London represent to the speaker? How does the speaker's observation of the persons who live there contribute to the poem's ideas about the oppressed state of humanity?

2. What sounds does the speaker mention specifically as a part of the London scene? What would these sounds be like? Characterize the meaning of these sounds in relation to the poem's main idea.

3. Why are the words *charter'd* and *mark* repeated in the first stanza? Explain the speaker's choice of the words *blast* and *blights* in stanza 4.

4. Because of the tension in the poem between civilized, ordered, regulated activity (as represented in the chartering of the street and the river) and free human impulses, explain how the poem might be considered revolutionary.

5. The poem is part of a collection entitled *Songs of Experience*, which Blake published in 1794. Explain the appropriateness of his including the poem in a collection so named.

WILLIAM WORDSWORTH (1770–1850)

Lines Composed a Few Miles Above Tintern Abbey on Revisiting the Banks of the Wye During a Tour, July 13, 1798   *1798*

Five years have past; five summers, with the length
Of five long winters! and again I hear
These waters, rolling from their mountain-springs
With a soft inland murmur.—Once again
Do I behold these steep and lofty cliffs,   5
That on a wild secluded scene impress
Thoughts of more deep seclusion, and connect
The landscape with the quiet of the sky.
The day is come when I again repose
Here, under this dark sycamore, and view   10
These plots of cottage-ground, these orchard-tufts,
Which at this season, with their unripe fruits,
Are clad in one green hue, and lose themselves
'Mid groves and copses. Once again I see
These hedge-rows, hardly hedge-rows, little lines   15
Of sportive wood run wild; these pastoral farms,
Green to the very door; and wreaths of smoke
Sent up, in silence, from among the trees!
With some uncertain notice, as might seem
Of vagrant dwellers in the houseless woods,   20
Or of some Hermit's cave, where by his fire
The Hermit sits alone.
                       These beauteous forms,
Through a long absence, have not been to me
As is a landscape to a blind man's eye:
But oft, in lonely rooms, and 'mid the din   25
Of towns and cities, I have owed to them
In hours of weariness, sensations sweet,
Felt in the blood, and felt along the heart;

LINES.   Wordsworth first visited the valley of the Wye in southwest England in August 1793 at age 23. On this second visit he was accompanied by his sister Dorothy (the "friend" in line 115).

And passing even into my purer mind,
With tranquil restoration:—feelings too   30
Of unremembered pleasure: such, perhaps,
As have no slight or trivial influence
On that best portion of a good man's life,
His little, nameless, unremembered acts
Of kindness and of love. Nor less, I trust,   35
To them I may have owed another gift,
Of aspect more sublime; that blessed mood,
In which the burden of the mystery,
In which the heavy and the weary weight
Of all this unintelligible world,   40
Is lightened:—that serene and blessed mood,
In which the affections gently lead us on,—
Until, the breath of this corporeal frame
And even the motion of our human blood
Almost suspended, we are laid asleep   45
In body, and become a living soul:
While with an eye made quiet by the power
Of harmony, and the deep power of joy,
We see into the life of things.
                              If this
Be but a vain belief, yet, oh!—how oft—   50
In darkness and amid the many shapes
Of joyless daylight; when the fretful stir
Unprofitable, and the fever of the world,
Have hung upon the beatings of my heart—
How oft, in spirit, have I turned to thee,   55
O sylvan Wye! thou wanderer thro' the woods,
How often has my spirit turned to thee!
   And now, with gleams of half extinguished thought,
With many recognitions dim and faint,
And somewhat of a sad perplexity,   60
The picture of the mind revives again:
While here I stand, not only with the sense
Of present pleasure, but with pleasing thoughts
That in this moment there is life and food
For future years. And so I dare to hope,   65
Though changed, no doubt, from what I was when first
I came among these hills; when like a roe
I bounded o'er the mountains, by the sides
Of the deep rivers, and the lonely streams,
Wherever nature led: more like a man   70
Flying from something that he dreads, than one
Who sought the thing he loved. For nature then
(The coarser pleasures of my boyish days,
And their glad animal movements all gone by)
To me was all in all.—I cannot paint   75

What then I was. The sounding cataract
Haunted me like a passion: the tall rock,
The mountain, and the deep and gloomy wood,
Their colours and their forms, were then to me
An appetite; a feeling and a love,   80
That had no need of a remoter charm,
By thought supplied, nor any interest
Unborrowed from the eye.—That time is past,
And all its aching joys are now no more,
And all its dizzy raptures. Not for this   85
Faint I, nor mourn nor murmur; other gifts
Have followed; for such loss, I would believe,
Abundant recompense. For I have learned
To look on nature, not as in the hour
Of thoughtless youth; but hearing oftentimes   90
The still, sad music of humanity,
Nor harsh nor grating, though of ample power
To chasten and subdue. And I have felt
A presence that disturbs me with the joy
Of elevated thoughts; a sense sublime   95
Of something far more deeply interfused,
Whose dwelling is the light of setting suns,
And the round ocean, and the living air,
And the blue sky, and in the mind of man;
A motion and a spirit, that impels   100
All thinking things, all objects of all thought,
And rolls through all things. Therefore am I still
A lover of the meadows and the woods,
And mountains; and of all that we behold
From this green earth; of all the mighty world   105
Of eye, and ear,—both what they half create,
And what perceive; well pleased to recognize
In nature and the language of the sense,
The anchor of my purest thoughts, the nurse,
The guide, the guardian of my heart, and soul   110
Of all my moral being.
                Nor perchance,
If I were not thus taught, should I the more
Suffer my genial spirits to decay:
For thou art with me here upon the banks
Of this fair river; thou my dearest Friend,   115
My dear, dear Friend; and in thy voice I catch
The language of my former heart, and read
My former pleasures in the shooting lights
Of thy wild eyes. Oh! yet a little while
May I behold in thee what I was once,   120
My dear, dear Sister! and this prayer I make,
Knowing that Nature never did betray

The heart that loved her; 'tis her privilege,
Through all the years of this our life, to lead
From joy to joy: for she can so inform   125
The mind that is within us, so impress
With quietness and beauty, and so feed
With lofty thoughts, that neither evil tongues,
Rash judgments, nor the sneers of selfish men,
Nor greetings where no kindness is, nor all   130
The dreary intercourse of daily life,
Shall e'er prevail against us, or disturb
Our cheerful faith that all which we behold
Is full of blessings. Therefore let the moon
Shine on thee in thy solitary walk;   135
And let the misty mountain-winds be free
To blow against thee: and, in after years,
When these wild ecstasies shall be matured
Into a sober pleasure; when thy mind
Shall be a mansion for all lovely forms,   140
Thy memory be as a dwelling-place
For all sweet sounds and harmonies; oh! then,
If solitude, or fear, or pain, or grief,
Should be thy portion, with what healing thoughts
Of tender joy wilt thou remember me,   145
And these my exhortations! Nor, perchance—
If I should be where I no more can hear
Thy voice, nor catch from thy wild eyes these gleams
Of past existence—wilt thou then forget
That on the banks of this delightful stream   150
We stood together; and that I, so long
A worshipper of Nature, hither came
Unwearied in that service: rather say
With warmer love—oh! with far deeper zeal
Of holier love. Nor wilt thou then forget,   155
That after many wanderings, many years
Of absence, these steep woods and lofty cliffs,
And this green pastoral landscape, were to me
More dear, both for themselves and for thy sake!

QUESTIONS

1. What is the scene at the beginning of the poem? How much time has elapsed
   since the speaker viewed the scene he is revisiting?
2. Is the scene specific or general? What has it meant to the speaker during
   the previous five years? Where was he when he remembered the scenes?
3. To the speaker, what is the relationship between remembered scenes and
   the development of moral behavior?

4. What effect does the speaker consider that this present experience will have on him in future years?

5. Study lines 93–111. How successful is the speaker in making concrete his ideas about the moral forces he perceives along with his vision of the natural scenes?

6. Whom does the speaker address beginning with line 111?

7. What is the power that the speaker attributes to Nature? Characterize the "cheerful faith" described in lines 133–134.

8. Is the setting in this poem purely descriptive, or is it more clearly the basis of the speaker's philosophic discourse?

MATTHEW ARNOLD (1822–1888)

Dover Beach   *1867 (1849)*

The sea is calm tonight.
The tide is full, the moon lies fair
Upon the straits—on the French coast the light
Gleams and is gone; the cliffs of England stand,
Glimmering and vast, out in the tranquil bay.   5
Come to the window, sweet is the night air!
Only, from the long line of spray
Where the sea meets the moon-blanched land,
Listen! you hear the grating roar
Of pebbles which the waves draw back, and fling,   10
At their return, up the high strand,
Begin, and cease, and then again begin,
With tremulous cadence slow, and bring
The eternal note of sadness in.

Sophocles long ago   15
Heard it on the Aegean, and it brought
Into his mind the turbid ebb and flow
Of human misery; we
Find also in the sound a thought,
Hearing it by this distant northern sea.   20

The Sea of Faith
Was once, too, at the full, and round earth's shore
Lay like the folds of a bright girdle furled.
But now I only hear
Its melancholy, long, withdrawing roar,   25
Retreating, to the breath
Of the night wind, down the vast edges drear
And naked shingles° of the world.   *large pebbles*

Ah, love, let us be true
To one another! for the world, which seems   30
To lie before us like a land of dreams,
So various, so beautiful, so new,
Hath really neither joy, nor love, nor light,
Nor certitude, nor peace, nor help for pain;
And we are here as on a darkling plain   35
Swept with confused alarms of struggle and flight,
Where ignorant armies clash by night.

QUESTIONS

1. Who is the speaker? To whom is the poem spoken?
2. What is the setting (place, time, location)? What specific words, details, and phrases in the first fourteen lines establish the setting?
3. Where are the speaker and listener? What can they see? Hear?
4. What sort of movement may be topographically traced in the first six lines of the poem, so that the scene finally focuses on the speaker and the listener?
5. What do the sounds of lines 9–14 evoke in the speaker's mind?
6. What is the effect of the speaker's comparison of the English Channel with the Aegean Sea, and of the effect of the Aegean surf on the thought of Sophocles?
7. To what extent does the setting—specifically the "ebb and flow" of the sea (line 17)—become symbolic? What does it symbolize?
8. What kind of faith remains in light of the loss of absolute religious faith? Defend the assertion that the faith is personal fidelity rather than love.
9. What new image of the grimness of the world is introduced in the last three lines? What does this image say about human beings and governments? How does this reference further isolate the speaker and the listener?

THOMAS HARDY (1840–1928)

The Walk   1913

You did not walk with me
Of late to the hilltop tree
    By the gated ways,
    As in earlier days;
    You were weak and lame,   5
    So you never came,
And I went alone, and I did not mind,
Not thinking of you as left behind.

I walked up there today
Just in the former way;   10
   Surveyed around
   The familiar ground
   By myself again:
   What difference, then?
Only that underlying sense   15
Of the look of a room on returning thence.

QUESTIONS

1. What relationship does the speaker have to the person being addressed?
2. Why did the speaker's companion not walk to the hilltop tree? Does the speaker admit to being in solitude even though the most recent walk was done alone?
3. What does the poem seem to be saying about the effects of age upon companionship?
4. Consider the final two lines. What impression do they convey about the location where the couple used to walk?

RICHARD HUGO (1923–1982)

Degrees of Gray in Philipsburg   *1973*

You might come here Sunday on a whim.
Say your life broke down. The last good kiss
you had was years ago. You walk these streets
laid out by the insane, past hotels
that didn't last, bars that did, the tortured try   5
of local drivers to accelerate their lives.
Only churches are kept up. The jail
turned 70 this year. The only prisoner
is always in, not knowing what he's done.

The principal supporting business now   10
is rage. Hatred of the various grays
the mountain sends, hatred of the mill,
The Silver Bill repeal, the best liked girls
who leave each year for Butte. One good
restaurant and bars can't wipe the boredom out.   15
The 1907 boom, eight going silver mines,
a dance floor built on springs—
all memory resolves itself in gaze,
in panoramic green you know the cattle eat
or two stacks high above the town,   20
two dead kilns, the huge mill in collapse
for fifty years that won't fall finally down.

Isn't this your life? That ancient kiss
still burning out your eyes? Isn't this defeat
so accurate, the church bell simply seems   25
a pure announcement: ring and no one comes?
Don't empty houses ring? Are magnesium
and scorn sufficient to support a town,
not just Philipsburg, but towns
of towering blondes, good jazz and booze   30
the world will never let you have
until the town you came from dies inside?

Say no to yourself. The old man, twenty
when the jail was built, still laughs
although his lips collapse. Someday soon,   35
he says, I'll go to sleep and not wake up.
You tell him no. You're talking to yourself.
The car that brought you here still runs.
The money you buy lunch with,
no matter where it's mined, is silver   40
and the girl who serves your food
is slender and her red hair lights the wall.

QUESTIONS

1. How does the speaker characterize Philipsburg? What was the past like there?
    Why has so much changed in the town? Who is the "you" addressed in
    line 1?
2. What is life like in the town now? What is the principal supporting business?
3. What does the speaker think should characterize a living, as opposed to a
    dead, town?
4. How does the fading of life in Philipsburg suggest that life generally is going
    to fade along with it?
5. How can this poem be seen as a philosophic reflection on the ability of
    human beings to endure and adjust even though new circumstances change
    previous ways of life?
6. What is implied by "gray" in the title? What relationship does the color
    have to age, silver, boredom, magnesium, the kilns? How does the color
    symbolize the condition of a city that has outlived its economic base?

JAMES WRIGHT (1927–1980)

A Blessing   *1963*

Just off the highway to Rochester, Minnesota,
Twilight bounds softly forth on the grass.
And the eyes of those two Indian ponies

Darken with kindness.
They have come gladly out of the willows   5
To welcome my friend and me.
We step over the barbed wire into the pasture
Where they have been grazing all day, alone.
They ripple tensely, they can hardly contain their happiness
That we have come.   10
They bow shyly as wet swans. They love each other.
There is no loneliness like theirs.
At home once more,
They begin munching the young tufts of spring in the darkness.
I would like to hold the slenderer one in my arms,   15
For she has walked over to me
And nuzzled my left hand.
She is black and white,
Her mane falls wild on her forehead,
And the light breeze moves me to caress her long ear   20
That is delicate as the skin over a girl's wrist.
Suddenly I realize
That if I stepped out of my body I would break
Into blossom.

QUESTIONS

1. What has happened just before the poem opens? Account for the poet's use of the present tense in his descriptions.

2. Is the setting here portrayed as specific or general? What happens as the poem progresses?

3. What realization overtakes the speaker? How does this realization constitute a "blessing"?

4. To what degree is it necessary for the poet to include all the detail of the first 21 lines before the realization of the last three?

WRITING ABOUT SETTING IN A POEM

It is important to try to describe the details about the setting in the poem you have been analyzing, but it is equally important to gauge how the details actually are used in relationship to the poet's ideas and images. You might find that you can develop ideas for your essay by trying to answer a number of questions like the following (bear in mind, however, that each poem will provide its own clues for additional questions): (1) If the poem contains an action or actions, to what degree, if any, is the setting important in the action? (2) Is the setting a location in which a speaker carries on any kind of reverie or organized thought? Does the location seem to be related to the thought in any way? (3) How is the detail of setting presented? That is, how specific are the details? Do you find descriptions of shapes, sizes, and proportions, or are the details represented vaguely or impressionistically? Is the detail clearly outlined and distinguished? (4) What sorts of things does the poet choose to include and exclude—for example, colors, contrasts, shadows; references to noises; specific or generalized animals or objects; natural or manufactured scenes? (5) Is the time of day or the time of year important to the action or to the ideas of the poet? (6) Does the setting seem to be complementary to the social or psychological state of any persons who are being described or who are doing important things in the poem? (7) Does the setting seem to be symbolic in any way? (8) To what degree, if any, is the outcome of the poem dependent on the poet's manipulation of the setting?

Organizing Your Essay

INTRODUCTION.   In the introduction to your essay you should be guided by what you have discovered from questions like those above. Your central idea should promise an approach that you plan to develop in the body of the essay. For example, is the setting a frame, the scene of something remembered, that is integral to the action of a narrative poem (like the ballad of Sir Patrick Spens, p. 465)? Or is the setting merely the source of a memory of past experience and therefore the occasion of present thought (as in Hardy's "The Walk")? Your thesis sentence, as always, should direct your reader to the main topics to be developed in the body.

BODY.   In the body you should bring out detailed references to support the ideas you introduced in your first paragraph. Your aim should be not merely to list the details of setting, but to show how they are being used in the poem. Some of the following approaches might prove effective.

1. *Setting and action, description, and character.* If your poem is a narrative, or if there are narrative portions, you may relate the setting to the action. You should try to determine the degree to which setting and action are interrelated, just as you would do in writing about the setting of a story. You should also try to describe the amount of detail in descriptive passages. Does the description seem to be an end in itself, or is it apparently designed to be functional? If characters are introduced, how do they respond to their surroundings, or to their duties as they must be carried out in the surroundings? How strongly do the surroundings seem to be influencing decisions and modes of action? Do you learn anything in particular about the characters because of their relationship to the setting? How is the relationship made clear?

2. *Setting and organization.* To what degree does the setting figure into the apparent plan or organization of the poem? Is there a shift of any sort as the poem moves from stanza to stanza or from section to

section? Does the setting change in any way along with these shifts? Is there an intensive introductory passage describing setting, followed by a set of reflections that can be fairly well derived from this description? Has the setting changed in any way, and do the changes relate to the development of the thought in the poem? Do references to the season of the year (if any) bear any connection to the development of thought in the poem? Describe that connection. Do references to the time of day or the condition of light figure into the development of the poem? Describe this relationship.

3. *Setting as an aspect of the speaker's consciousness.* Quite often in poetry, as we have noted, you will not encounter the fully described and realized settings characteristic of fiction, but instead will find that most references to place, time, season, and artifacts have become a part of the consciousness of the speaker. In writing about setting in such poems, you must be prepared to determine how it is important in the interactions of characters with the speaker, in the speaker's memories of conversations, in his or her recollections of ideas, and in the blending of the memory of place and action with current thought. In developing an essay along these lines, you are in effect analyzing the development of a speaker's consciousness.

4. *Setting and mood and atmosphere.* In poetry the setting or settings, being often less realistic than in fiction, may be considered as they figure into mood and atmosphere. Thus, in Hardy's "The Walk," the speaker remembers the scene of a previous place of visit as being like the "look of a room on returning thence." If you were writing about this passage, you would clearly not be able to analyze Hardy's treatment of the setting of a room, for he supplies none. Instead you would need to consider the scene as Hardy presents it—as a place associated with cherished past experience. In writing about the mood of the poem you would need to consider the effect of the realization that the past is past and continues to live only through the memory of persons whose hold on life is growing more and more precarious. When stated in these terms, you would likely conclude that the mood is one of seriousness and sobriety. Although the setting of Dickey's "Cherrylog Road" is much more fully realized than Hardy's room, there is much to be made of the mood Dickey creates by his contrasting the age and abandonment of the junked automobiles with the furtiveness and closeness yet newness of the couple loving each other within the shelter of so much of the past. Would it be correct to cite a mood of defiance and self-assertion about these circumstances? Is there any irony in the situation? Might the rusting and rotting cars be considered as a commentary on the eventual outcome of the current love relationship, new as it is, of the speaker and his sweetheart? What should the reader's thoughts therefore be about this relationship? It is questions like these that you would consider in a discussion of a poem's mood and atmosphere. They are of course difficult to answer with precision, yet an attempt to

treat the relationship of setting to mood and atmosphere would be of great value for you as a writer and thinker about poetry.

CONCLUSION. In your <u>conclusion</u> you might <u>reinforce some of your major points</u> by briefly <u>summarizing them.</u> You might also wish to touch on some other aspects of the setting that you did not develop in the body of your essay. Thus, for example, if you have been discussing the setting in Andrew Marvell's "Bermudas," in your conclusion you might wish to refer briefly to the symbolic (or allusive) nature of some of these references, such as the cedars in the newly discovered islands being like the Biblical cedars of Lebanon. In addition, there might be a need to consider any ambiguous or difficult references in the poem that you are considering. Thus, in "Bermudas" the Lord is portrayed as injuring "huge sea-monsters." Since this reference describes a destructive attribute of the Creator rather than the constructive one praised elsewhere in the poem, you would be helping your reader by trying to confront and explain the apparent contradiction.

SAMPLE ESSAY

The Setting of Marvell's "Bermudas"*

[1]   The setting of Andrew Marvell's "Bermudas" supports the poem's dominant mood of reverent cheer. The islands had been discovered in the sixteenth century, not long after Columbus found America. To at least some of the people living in the seventeenth century the descriptions made by returning travelers must have seemed to be outright proof of God's kindness to humanity. Marvell's setting of the poem is thus integrated with his worshipful thoughts.° <u>He makes the connection as a frame, as a set of references for the religious song by the people in the boat, and as supporting evidence for the praise of the guiding, saving, and nurturing attributes of God.</u>°

[2]   As a frame described both at the beginning and ending, the setting is a small boat being rowed on the Bermuda waters by a visiting group of people. Marvell gives the islands almost living attributes. He says that the Bermudas are "remote" (line 1), as though they almost choose to exist a long distance away from England, and he describes the winds as "listening," as though they are an audience for the song of praise while the boat continues moving throughout the poem. At the end of the poem, Marvell notes that the "falling oars" have kept time to the song. Thus the setting is the frame both for the space and time of the poem, and it is also an almost active witness.

* See p. 519 for this poem.
° Central idea.
° Thesis sentence.

[3] In the song of praise framed by the moving boat, the bulk of details about the setting of the islands are introduced as evidence for holy kindness. First, in lines 5–12, the setting is shown to consist of natural difficulties and obstacles that God has allowed the visitors to conquer. Thus, with divine guidance the sailors have overcome a "watery maze" (line 6) to find the Bermudas as a refuge that is far kinder (that is, with a more pleasant climate) than England. The Bermudas have a safe harbor and are also so far away from European religious influence that the "rage" of prelates cannot reach them. The setting, therefore, is a shelter from both natural storms and human stresses.

[4] In support of the idea that God is a guide, protector, and nurturer, Marvell introduces a series of things for which human beings may offer thanks. These are the "eternal spring" (line 13), abundant flying game (15), oranges (17), pomegranates (19), figs (21), melons (22), and many other fruits that are virtually priceless (23–24). In addition, cedarwood (25), ambergris (28), and pearls (30) are present in abundance, as though in a new garden of Eden, to supply the stuff of trade and therefore of wealth. All these details are carefully selected to demonstrate the power and benevolence of God, and also to justify the use of the term "holy and cheerful" (38) in the concluding references to the song of praise.

[5] An additional element supporting the assertion about the benevolence of God is included by Marvell in lines 31–36. This is the idea that the Bermudas form a vast natural rocky temple in which to sing God's praises, just as the people in the boat are actually doing. This observation serves as a climax of the poem, for it underscores the relationship of God to human beings. In this relationship, God furnishes the material world and enables human endeavors to be successful, while the human role is to accept the blessing and also to sing hymns of thankful praise.

As is shown, in "Bermudas" the setting is the main set of references for the poem, the reason for the structure, the frame of dutiful and grateful people singing a hymn of praise, and a basis for determining divine power and kindness. Setting is here part and parcel of the poem, the cause for worship, adoration, and optimism. Even though God is described as being hurtful to the "huge sea-monsters" of line 9, this hostility should not be construed as unkindness to the natural world so much as divine protection over human beings.

[6] In addition, the thought of God's bounty is brought out in lines 25–26 in the reference to the Biblical cedars of Lebanon. It is as though Marvell is suggesting that the Bermudas represent a restoration of the prosperity of King Solomon, whose pact with God was exemplified in his building the Temple at Jerusalem with timber cut from these ancient cedars. All the details of Marvell's setting confirm the mood of reverent happiness caused by the new revelation of so exciting and fruitful a place as the Bermudas.

Commentary on the Essay

The first paragraph introduces relevant historical detail and supposition. More important, it conveys the central idea that Marvell uses the setting not simply as background but makes it totally integral and inseparable within the poem. The thesis sentence indicates three ways in which the integration is brought about.

Paragraph 2 deals with the physical and temporal aspect of the setting. Here the point is made that Marvell endows the setting with qualities that almost literally bring it to life. The third paragraph brings out how the Bermudas are integrated into Marvell's song of praise inasmuch as they are presented in the poem as evidence for divine protection over human beings. Paragraphs 4 and 5 reinforce the causes for which human beings should render praise. Paragraph 4 deals with material goods while paragraph 5 emphasizes the idea that the natural world of the Bermudas is a divinely created temple in which people can live and give thanks.

The last paragraph summarizes the foregoing details and also introduces two special matters that are mentioned above in the guide for writing the conclusion of this type of essay. While the opening sentence treats the connection of the physical setting and the subject references in the poem, the last emphasizes the setting as an integral aspect of Marvell's ideas.

14

The Words in Poetry

Poems are constructed of words. Words create the rhythm, rhyme, meter, and stanza form. They define the speaker, the other characters, the setting, and the situation. They also carry the ideas and the emotions of the poem. For this reason, each poet seeks the perfect and indispensable word, the word that looks right, sounds right, and conveys all the compressed meanings, overtones, and emotions that the poem requires.

We can see evidence of this quest for the perfect word in the numerous revisions that poems go through as poets shape them. When a poet's manuscripts survive, we can actually look at some of the various stages of specific poems. William Butler Yeats's notebooks contain six complete or fragmentary revisions of "Leda and the Swan" (p. 819), all different from the version finally published in 1924. Here is the first line of each version:

(1st)	Now can the swooping Godhead have his will
(2nd)	The trembl godhead is half hovering still
(3rd)	The swooping godhead is half hovering still
(4th)	A rush upon great wings and hovering still
(5th)	A swoop upon great wings and hovering still
(6th)	A rush, a sudden wheel and hovering still
(1924)	A sudden blow: the great wings beating still

As we move through this sequence of revisions, we can almost feel the poet striving to find the absolutely right combination of words. Note, for example, the way "have his will" becomes "hovering still" and finally "beating still." Each revision is more active, more immediate, and more violent.

WORDS AND MEANING

All systems of communication are based on signs that have acquired conventional and accepted meanings. In any natural language, words are the signifiers for thoughts, things, or actions. Life, and poetry, would be a great deal simpler (and less interesting) if there were an exact one-to-one correspondence between words and the ideas they are supposed to signify. We find an approximation of this close correspondence in artificial language systems such as chemical equations and computer languages that convey exact meanings. Such correspondence, however, is not characteristic of English or any other natural language. Instead, words have the unfortunate (and wonderful) habit of moving around and acquiring a vast array of different meanings.

Most of us recognize the slippery nature of words at some level, even if we have not devoted much time to thinking about language. Much of our humor is built on the ambiguities of words and phrases. When the comedian says, "Take my wife, please," the joke works because *take* has two entirely different meanings, both of which come into play. In reading poetry, we must recognize this ambiguity and understand that poets exploit the shifty nature of words and language; they rejoice in the movement of words.

DENOTATION AND CONNOTATION

You are probably already familiar with this famous pair, which was discussed in Chapter 7 (pp. 239–40). Because individual words are much more important in poetry than in any other form of literature, we will consider denotation and connotation in more detail here. **Denotation** refers to the standard dictionary meaning of a word; it indicates conventional correspondences between a sign (the word) and an idea. We might expect that denotation would be fairly straightforward. Even here, however, language is not cooperative. Most English words have multiple denotations. The word *house*, for example, can refer to a home, a chamber of congress, a theater, an audience, a fraternity, and a brothel. Although context often makes the denotation of *house* more specific, the six different meanings give this simple word some built-in ambiguity. The situation becomes far more complicated with a word like *fall*, which has over fifty different definitions or denotations. As a verb, *fall* means descend, hang down, succumb to temptation, be overthrown, killed, and chopped down. As a noun, the word denotes a descent, a season of the year, a slope, the state of sin, a capture, and even a hairpiece, among other things. In prose, a writer will usually try to limit the denotative value of *fall* to one of these meanings. Poets, however, frequently try to hold on to as many useful and appropriate denotations as possible.

We can see an example of the poet's use of multiple denotation in the couplet that ends Shakespeare's Sonnet 115:

No want of conscience hold it that I call
Her "love" for whose dear love I rise and fall.

The two lines are full of slippery words, and in the last, the speaker uses "rise and fall" as a sly reference to the physical aspects of lovemaking. Shakespeare employs the multiple denotations of such words as *want* (lack), *hold*, *love*, and *rise* here. For the sake of our example, let us focus on *dear* and *fall*. *Dear* means beloved, but it also means costly or expensive. *Fall* means to drop, droop, die, succumb to sin or temptation, and be overthrown. The context does not exclude *any* of these denotations. As a result, the couplet says a great deal with very few words. *Dear* means that the speaker cherishes both his beloved and his emotions, but it also means that both are costly (or even exhausting) in terms of effort, emotion, and cash. A paraphrase of the couplet, though much less elegant than the original, gives us a chance to display the full range of *dear* and *fall*: "I don't consider it a failure or lack of conscience that I call that woman my "love" for whose beloved, expensive, and exhausting love I rise and am overthrown, drop, droop, descend, succumb to temptation, sink into sin, and die.

Denotation can also present us with problems because of the way words gain new meanings and lose old ones over long periods of time. Language changes slowly, but the shift can be quite dramatic over several centuries. In reading poems written before the nineteenth century, we occasionally encounter words that have changed meaning so completely that a modern dictionary is not much help. In these cases, it is useful to refer to *The Oxford English Dictionary* (*OED*). Consider, for example, the word *vegetable* in Andrew Marvell's "To His Coy Mistress" (p. 849). The speaker asserts that "My vegetable love should grow / Vaster than empires and more slow." Our first impulse may be to imagine a giant and passionate cabbage. When we turn to a modern dictionary, we discover that "vegetable" is an adjective that means "plantlike," but "plantlike love" does not get us much beyond "vegetable love." The *OED*, however, tells us that "vegetable" was used as an adjective in the seventeenth century to mean "living or growing like a plant." Thus, we find out that "vegetable love" can be an emotion that grows slowly and steadily larger.

Thus far we have been discussing denotation, the easy part of the message that words convey. Words really get slippery when we consider connotations. **Connotation** refers to the emotional, psychological, or social overtones that words carry in addition to their denotations. We can see connotation at work in the synonyms *childish* and *childlike*. According to the dictionary, these two adjectives both denote the state of being like a child. Nevertheless, the two words connote or imply very different sets of characteristics. *Childish* suggests a person who is bratty, stubborn, immature, silly, and petulant; we can imagine a "childish" person throwing a tantrum or threatening to hold his breath until he turns blue. *Childlike*, on the other hand, describes a person who is innocent, charming, and unaffected. These very different descriptions are based entirely on the connotations of the two words; the denotations make little distinction.

We encounter the manipulation of connotation all the time, even though we may be unaware of it. Advertising depends to a large extent on the skillful management of connotation. This manipulation may be as simple as calling a "used" car "previously owned" to avoid the **negative connotations** of the word *used*. On the other hand, it may be as sophisticated as the current use of the words *lite* or *light* to describe specific foods and drinks. In all these products, the word *lite* means dietetic, low-calorie, or even weak. The distinction—and the selling point—is found in connotation. Imagine how difficult it would be to sell a drink called "dietetic beer" or "weak beer." *Light* and *lite*, however, carry none of the negative connotations of *weak* or *dietetic*. Instead, *lite* suggests a product that is pleasant, sparkling, bright, and healthy. "Weak beer" would grow dusty on the shelves; "lite beer" sells very well indeed.

Denotation and connotation are important factors in any consideration of language and literature, but they become especially significant in poetry. Prose writers and dramatists often seek to confine words to a single meaning; they do not always exploit the denotative and connotative values of words. Poets, however, often work a single word as hard as they can; they strive to make the word carry as many appropriate and effective denotations and connotations as possible. To put it another way, poets often try to use *packed* or *loaded* words that will carry a broad range of meaning and association. In reading poems, one of our jobs is to "unpack" these loaded words and to enjoy the play of language. With this in mind, take a look at the following poem by Robert Graves.

ROBERT GRAVES (b. 1895)

The Naked and the Nude   1957

For me, the naked and the nude
(By lexicographers° construed
As synonyms that should express
The same deficiency of dress

THE NAKED AND THE NUDE.   2 *lexicographers*: people who write dictionaries.

Or shelter) stand as wide apart   5
As love from lies, or truth from art.

Lovers without reproach will gaze
On bodies naked and ablaze;
The Hippocratic° eye will see
In nakedness, anatomy;   10
And naked shines the Goddess when
She mounts her lion among men.

The nude are bold, the nude are sly
To hold each treasonable eye.
While draping by a showman's trick   15
Their dishabille° in rhetoric,
They grin a mock-religious grin
Of scorn at those of naked skin.

The naked, therefore, who compete
Against the nude may know defeat;   20
Yet when they both together tread
The briary pastures of the dead,
By Gorgons° with long whips pursued,
How naked go the sometime nude!

9 *Hippocratic*: medical; the adjective derives from Hippocrates, an ancient Greek considered the father of medicine.   16 *dishabille*: being carelessly or partly dressed.   23 *Gorgons*: hideous mythological female monsters who had snakes for hair.

QUESTIONS

1. What does the speaker tell us about the denotations of *naked* and *nude* in the first stanza? About the connotations?
2. What examples of "the naked" does the second stanza provide? What do the examples have in common?
3. How are "the nude" described in the third stanza? What are the connotations of words like *sly, draping, dishabille, rhetoric,* and *grin*?
4. What attitude do "the nude" have toward "the naked"? What does the speaker suggest about this attitude?
5. Where will both "the naked" and "the nude" go after death? Which will be punished more severely? How is *naked* used in a new way in the last line?
6. What is suggested by the fact that *naked* is derived from the Old English word *nacod* while *nude* is derived from the Latin *nudus*?

"The Naked and the Nude" explores the connotative distinctions between two words that share a common denotation. The title tells us that the poem will consider "the naked and the nude" and that we are dealing with both words and people. If the speaker were simply considering the words, she or he would say "naked" and "nude" instead of "*the* naked and *the* nude." The speaker's use of *the* signifies a double focus on human conditions and values as well as language.

The denotations of *naked* and *nude* are identical. The dictionary defines *naked* as nude or without clothing, and *nude* as without clothing or naked. Lines 1–5 of the poem express this commonality. The speaker observes that "lexicographers" consider naked and nude to be "synonyms" that "should express / The same deficiency of dress" (lines 2–4). Although these lines establish the common denotation of *naked* and *nude*, they also question this commonality through the utilization of elevated and complex words. By using terms like *lexicographers*, *construed*, *express*, and *deficiency* instead of simpler and more common words, the poem implies that the connection between "the naked" and "the nude" is artificial.

The first stanza also explores the connotative distinction between "the naked" and "the nude." The speaker asserts that "for me" the words and the people "stand as wide apart / As love from lies, or truth from art" (lines 5–6). Thus, the speaker announces the poem's thesis: There is a vast difference between the naked and the nude. The sentence structure of this assertion also begins the process of attaching connotations to the words and people under consideration. The syntax offers three parallel compound phrases:

The naked	and	the nude
As love	from	lies
or truth	from	art

As this arrangement suggests, the effect of this sentence structure is to link the naked with "love" and "truth," and the nude with "lies" and "art." The first stanza thus begins to clarify the connotative distinction between the naked and the nude. The naked are linked with passion (love) and honesty (truth), but the nude are associated with dishonesty (lies) and faking (art).

In the second stanza the speaker focuses on "the naked" and provides three examples that expand the web of connotations: lovers (lines 7–8), physicians (9–10), and the Goddess (11–12). The lovers are naked and "gaze" on "bodies naked and ablaze" without shame or "reproach." Graves continues to exploit connotative overtones here; he uses *gaze* instead of *look* because the word implies intensity and rapture. The physician ("The Hippocratic eye"), like the lovers, looks on nakedness and the naked without shame; she or he is consumed with the passion of the quest for knowledge and the truth of "anatomy." Finally, the Goddess is naked when "She mounts her lion among men." Like lovers and physicians, she exists beyond shame or guilt; the word *shines* suggests both passion and truth. In all three examples, nakedness and the naked are without shame, trickery, temptation, or deceit; they are linked with honesty, passion, truth, and love.

The connotative flavor of the poem changes in the third stanza, when the speaker begins to consider "the nude." They are described as "bold" and "sly," words with negative connotations that suggest dishonesty. *Bold* implies a pushy and defiant attitude while *sly* hints at animal cunning and shiftiness. This sense of dishonesty is amplified by the speaker's reference to "each treasonable eye" (line 14). The word *treasonable* suggests that the nude are associated with treachery and shame; it condemns both the nude and those who look at nudity. In addition, the phrase reminds us of "the Hippocratic eye" and might, through the association of sound, imply "hypocritical eye."

The dishonest trickery of the nude is conveyed in their ability to drape "by a showman's trick / Their dishabille in rhetoric" (lines 15–16). These lines imply that the nude can be dressed and undressed at the same time. By using loaded words like *draping*, *showman's trick*, *dishabille*, and *rhetoric*, the speaker asserts that this ambiguity is intentional. *Draping* (instead of dressing or clothing) connotes contrived carelessness and fakery. When it is combined with *showman's trick*, we get a sense of a now-you-see-it-now-you-don't staginess. *Dishabille* means being partly or carelessly dressed; it thus reinforces the connotations of *draping*. It also implies dressing in a suggestive or pornographic manner, hinting at intentional temptation. *Rhetoric* denotatively refers to the study of the effective use of language. It thus returns our attention to the key words under consideration in the poem. But *rhetoric* has come to connote the dishonest or deceptive use of language to prove a dubious case or to defend a questionable position with dazzling verbal trickery. The term thus points in two directions— toward the lexical meanings of words and toward contrived deceptions.

In lines 17–18 the speaker considers the attitude that the nude have toward the naked. The nude "grin a mock-religious grin / Of scorn at those of naked skin." Again, the words are loaded with negative connotations. *Grin* (instead of *smile*) implies viciousness and sarcasm; *scorn* (instead of *rage*) suggests condescension as well as disapproval. The speaker argues here that the nude take a condescending attitude toward the naked. The claim to superiority, however, is undercut by the term *mock-religious*. Like everything else about the nude, this attitude is a fraud and a trick.

In the last stanza the speaker admits that "the nude" will almost always triumph over "the naked" in this world, but goes on to point out that the nude will be punished after death. Both the naked and the nude will "tread the briary pastures of the dead" and be pursued by "Gorgons with long whips" (lines 21–23). Here, the speaker imagines a Greco-Roman afterlife; the "briary pastures of the dead" are the thorny fields of Hades, the underworld of classical mythology. In Hades, the naked and the nude will be "together" just as the words are "together" for "lexicographers."

In the last line, however, Graves skillfully inverts the terms *naked* and *nude*. The speaker claims that "the sometime nude" will be "naked" in the underworld. In this context, *naked* takes on another meaning; it implies that the nude will be completely unprotected and at the mercy of the pursuing Gorgons. The nude will thus be punished for their seductive and deceptive trickery by becoming unprotected. The nakedness of "the nude" in this last line may also suggest that trickery and artifice disappear in the underworld and the nude are finally confronted with the reality of their existence.

DICTION

English is one of the richest languages in the world; we can usually find half a dozen words that mean pretty much the same thing. Given this wealth of vocabulary, poets are inevitably blessed with choices among words. **Diction** refers to the specific words and types of words selected by a writer to produce a desired effect. We discuss diction at some length in Chapter 7 (p. 236); you might review this material. Again, however, word choice is so important in poetry that the subject deserves reexamination.

Types of Words: Specific or General and Concrete or Abstract

The distinctions among these types of words are centrally important to poetry because the choices can determine the impact and immediacy in a poem. **Specific** words refer to objects or conditions that can easily be seen or imagined, while **general** words signify broad classes of persons or things. Similarly, **concrete** words describe conditions or qualities that are exact and vivid, while **abstract** words refer to circumstances that are difficult to envision. These distinctions become clear when we consider the difference between Housman's "three score years and ten" or "Cherry . . . hung with bloom" and Richard Eberhart's "infinite spaces" or "eternal truth." The terms and images that Housman uses in "Loveliest of Trees" (p. 470) are specific and concrete; they evoke an exact and focused sense of time and object. Eberhart's terms, in "The Fury of Aerial Bombardment" (p. 562), are general and abstract; it is hard to envision "infinite spaces" or "eternal truth" with any vivid clarity or exactness.

As these examples indicate, poets can employ all four types of words to good effect. The choice is often determined by the subject and the emotional response the poet wants to evoke in the reader. Poems written in predominantly general and abstract terms tend to be detached and cerebral; they often deal in an impersonal manner with universal questions or emotions. Poems written in concrete and specific terms, on the other hand, are usually more immediate, familiar, and compelling. For the most part, poets employ a mixture of these types of diction. Theodore Roethke's "Dolor" (p. 560), for example, uses a large number of specific and concrete words to define a series of more abstract emotional states.

Levels of Diction

Like other writers, poets have recourse to three levels of diction: high or formal, middle or neutral, and low or informal. **Formal diction** is elevated and elaborate; it requires the proper words in the proper order and avoids idioms, colloquialisms, contractions, or slang. Beyond such correctness, formal language is often characterized by complex words and a lofty tone. Robert Graves uses formal diction in "The Naked and the Nude" when the speaker asserts that the terms are "By lexicographers construed / As synonyms that should express / The same deficiency of dress." These Latinate words heighten the diction and tone. We find "lexicographers" instead of *writers of dictionaries*, "construed" (from the Latin *construere*) instead of *thought*, "express" (from the Latin *expressus*) instead of *say* or *show*, and deficiency (from the Latin *deficientia*) instead of *lack*.

Middle or **neutral diction** maintains the correct language and word order of formal diction but avoids the elaborate words and elevated tone. Emily Dickinson's "Because I Could Not Stop for Death" (p. 473) is written almost entirely in neutral diction. The correct neutrality of this level of language makes it difficult to form judgments based on diction alone.

Informal or **low diction** is the kind of language that we use when we are talking with friends; it is relaxed, colloquial, and conversational. Poems written in informal diction often include fairly common and simple words, slang, idiomatic expressions, and contractions. We can see an example of informal diction in Thomas Hardy's "The Man He Killed" (p. 474), where the poet uses words and phrases like "many a nipperkin," "He thought he'd 'list," and "off-hand like." In general, formal diction tends to use words derived from Latin or Greek whereas informal diction utilizes words derived from Old English.

For the last few centuries, poets have had the option of writing in formal, middle, or informal language, or even employing a mixture of levels. This was not always the case. In the eighteenth century, writers felt that only formal diction was appropriate to poetry. These writers developed rules about the subjects and styles that were suitable for poetry; common life and colloquial language were almost always excluded. These rules of **poetic decorum** (appropriateness, suitability) made it necessary for poets to use elevated language rather than common words and phrases. Instead of writing about fish, for example, an eighteenth-century poet might refer to "the finny multitude" or "the piscatorian denizens of the deep." Alexander Pope, one of the greatest English poets of that century, maintained these rules of decorum and made fun of them at the same time in *The Rape of the Lock*. In this mock epic poem about a lock of hair, Pope describes the pouring of coffee from silver pots into china cups as follows:

From silver spouts the grateful liquors glide,
While China's earth receives the smoking tide.

Pope avoids the simple term *coffee* and substitutes the more complex "grateful liquors" and "smoking tide"; he employs "china's earth" instead of saying *cups*.

Special Types of Diction

In addition to the three levels of diction already noted, poets and writers have access to four special types of informal diction: dialect, idiom, slang, and jargon. **Dialect** refers to the language of a particular social class, region, or group. We can recognize certain common dialects such as Brooklynese, American Black English, Yiddish English, Texan, Southern, and Scottish English. Dialect is often a key technique of characterization and setting in modern literature.

Idiom, like dialect, indicates a style of speaking and writing that is characteristic of a particular group, class, region, or nation. The term *idiom* comes from the Greek word meaning private citizen or something personal. It thus suggests an individual or particular way of speaking. Unlike dialect, however, idiom is usually a term or expression whose meanings cannot be derived, by someone who is not familiar with the phrase, from an analysis of its constituent parts. Ideal examples of idioms in English are the phrases we have developed to describe dying. Americans rarely die; instead, they "buy the farm," "kick the bucket," "go west," "pass away," "cash in their chips," "meet their maker," or "get wasted." A non-native speaker of English would have a difficult time figuring out that a person who "kicked the bucket" or was "wasted" had actually died.

Slang is related to both dialect and idiom in that it is often particular to a specific group of speakers. In general, slang is a very informal and often metaphorical use of vocabulary and idiom; it often moves into the mainstream of English and then passes out of usage or becomes standard. Like idiom, slang is often difficult to understand through lexical analysis. In the last decade, for example, a large number of slang terms that combine a standard word with *out* have come in and out of fashion. These include phrases like "drop out," "cop out," "luck out," "gross out," and "pig out." It takes "insider" information to understand that "luck out" means to succeed by fortunate happenstance.

Jargon, like idiom and slang, denotes words that are characteristic of a particular group and often incomprehensible to the world at large.

The difference, however, is that the group is usually defined by a specific profession or trade rather than by class, race, or region. For example, lawyers, plumbers, astronauts, doctors, and football players all have terms and phrases that are particular to their trades. Jargon becomes interesting and problematic when it moves into the mainstream of English or is used in literature to create specific effects. Two poems in this chapter that illustrate the poet's use of jargon for effect are Henry Reed's "Naming of Parts" (p. 561) and Richard Eberhart's "The Fury of Aerial Bombardment" (p. 562). In both cases, the poets use the military jargon to create tone, setting, and contrast.

DICTION AND POETRY

Word choice and levels of diction, like denotation and connotation, have a profound effect on poetry. Poets try to maintain careful control of diction to shape impact and focus. Diction is often crucial in defining the speaker, setting, and situation in a given poem. Moreover, the diction often reveals the poet's or the speaker's attitude toward the poem's subject. Finally, diction may control the mood or atmosphere and the remoteness or immediacy of a poem. Given this range of possibilities, we will now turn to a poem that examines and uses the variables associated with diction, jargon, idiom, denotation, and connotation.

HEATHER McHUGH (b. 1948)

Language Lesson, 1976   *1981 (1976)*

When Americans say a man
takes liberties, they mean
he's gone too far. In Philadelphia

today a kid on a leash ordered
bicentennial burger,   5
hold the relish. Hold

is forget, in American.
On the courts of Philadelphia
the rich prepare

to serve, to fault.   10
The language is a game in which
love means nothing, doubletalk

means lie. I'm saying doubletalk
with me. I'm saying go so far
the customs are untold,   15

make nothing without words
and let me be
the one you never hold.

QUESTIONS

1. Why does the poet refer to 1976 and Philadelphia? What associations are evoked?
2. What are the multiple denotations, connotations, and idiomatic values of the words *liberties* (line 2) and *hold* (6)? What happens to the concept of a "bicentennial" in the phrase *bicentennial burger*?
3. What special kind of diction or jargon is evident in the words *courts* (line 8), *serve* (10), *fault* (10), and *love* (12)?
4. What pun hides behind the speaker's request that the listener "doubletalk / with me" (lines 13–14)?
5. How is the apparent paradox or contradiction of the last two lines resolved by reference to idiom?
6. What does the poem suggest about language? About love?

Like "The Naked and the Nude," Heather McHugh's "Language Lesson, 1976" is partly about language and partly about people. The poet uses diction, denotation, connotation, jargon, and idiom to create a rich and complicated verbal fabric of double meanings and implications. The poem is also an invitation to love, and it explores the relationship between language and love.

The general context of the poem is established in the title and the first stanza. "Language Lesson" indicates a concern with diction and suggests that the poem will teach us something about language. The year "1976" is more loaded because it refers to the bicentennial of the United States. This web of meaning and suggestion is expanded in lines 1–3 through references to "Americans," "liberties," and "Philadelphia." Philadelphia, of course, is the city in which the Declaration of Independence was signed in 1776. All these references produce an awareness of the particularly American concepts of liberty, justice, public service, and freedom. The ideals thus evoked become, in turn, the standards by which language is examined and judged in the poem.

The first four stanzas play with idiom, jargon, denotation, and connotation. The level of diction here is consistently colloquial and the poem has a familiar and informal tone. The first sentence offers an example of idiom: "When Americans say a man / takes liberties, they mean / he's gone too far." To "take liberties" means idiomatically to go too far, but "liberties" also relates back to "1776," "Philadelphia," and the Declaration of Independence. Thus, the idiom represents a degeneration of language and of the concept of liberty.

This process of debasement through idiom and language is repeated in the central image of lines 4–6, the "kid on a leash" who orders "bicentennial burger, / hold the relish." These lines overflow with packed words, double meanings, and slippery idioms. The slang term *kid* connotes unruly scruffiness. Because *kid* can also refer to a baby goat, the word connotes animal behavior. This combination of child and animal is reinforced by putting the "kid on a leash." The leash keeps the kid from going too far; it restricts his "liberties."

"Bicentennial burger" also demonstrates the human tendency to trivialize and degrade through language. *Bicentennial* calls to mind all the ideals associated with "1776" and the Declaration of Independence. It is fascinating, however, to see what happens to the word when it is used to describe a hamburger. The combination makes *bicentennial* almost silly. The third part of the image—"hold the relish—is equally loaded. *Hold* means keep or possess. In this instance, however, "hold / is forget." The idiom reverses the normal meaning of the word. *Relish* also has a double meaning; it signifies both a condiment and pleasure. "Hold the relish" thus becomes both "forget the pickles" and "possess the pleasure." The distance between these two concepts again illustrates our tendency to corrupt language and meaning.

Lines 8–12 shift from idiom to jargon. The central image here is a tennis game, and the jargon terms that the speaker employs—*courts, serve, fault,* and *love*—all relate to tennis. Like the diction and idiom of earlier stanzas, jargon here debases and trivializes both language and the concepts signified through language. The "courts of Philadelphia" again evoke the halls of justice and the building in which the Declaration of Independence was signed. Here, however, the phrase is reduced to the tennis courts at country clubs frequented by the rich. *Serve* can mean to wait upon or even to hold public office, but here the jargon debases the word to mean the beginning of a point in tennis. *Fault,* which normally denotes error or criticism, is reduced to a missed serve in tennis. The speaker also introduces a final idiomatic term here: "doubletalk / means lie" (lines 12–13). The word *doubletalk* is linked with the tennis jargon because it reminds us of doubles and double faults. The most shocking use of jargon in these lines is the speaker's assertion that "love means nothing" (line 12). The entire emotional range of *love* is trivialized to "nothing" in the jargon of tennis, where *love* means "no score."

The impact of all these jargon terms is summed up in the claim that "language is a game in which / love means nothing" (lines 11–12). The speaker is talking about language, tennis, people, and love at the same time. The jargon suggests that language is a game like tennis, a constant give-and-take in which people in "courts" can "serve" and "fault" with "love." It also suggests that language itself is a game in which words like *love* often mean "nothing." The implication is that language can be so trivializing that it is frequently impossible to talk about concepts like "love" without reducing them to "nothing." The speaker thus puts forward the idea that language and love may be mutually exclusive and antagonistic.

This antagonism between language and love is explored in the last two stanzas, where the subject of the poem shifts from language to love. We are suddenly aware of both a speaker and a listener, and we discover that the poem is a monologue spoken by a lover to his or her beloved. The informal diction contributes to a sense of intimacy between speaker and listener. The speaker begins to apply the slippery idioms and jargon terms of the first four stanzas to his or her relationship with the listener. We see this shift of focus in the speaker's request that the listener "double-talk / with me" (lines 13–14). We already know that "doubletalk means lie," so the phrase becomes "lie with me" through substitution. Even this request is ambiguous because of the double denotation of *lie*; the word means "to speak falsely" and "to recline" or "to go to bed." The speaker thus captures the vast distinction between language and love in a single ambiguous phrase. In the world of language, to *doubletalk* is to "speak falsely" about love. In the world of love, however, the phrase suggests action without words.

The key to this poem is found in the next two phrases: "go so far / the customs are untold" and "make nothing without words" (lines 14–16). The first of these is the central play on words in the poem. "Go so far" refers to "take liberties" and encourages the listener to act. *Customs* denotes habits, usage, or conventions; it can refer to either love or language. *Untold* can mean "unspoken," but also "uncounted" or "boundless." The speaker is thus asking the listener to act in such a way that the "customs" or habits of love are boundless *and* unspoken. Language is banished from the world of love. The second phrase makes much the same point. At first reading, "make nothing without words" seems to assert that language is essential and that "nothing" can be made "without words." But the poem has already established that "love means nothing." Through another substitution, we see that the speaker is asking the listener to make love without language. Again we see that love can often exist only in silence and action.

The final two lines of the poem present a paradox that focuses our sense of the wide gap between language and love. The speaker's request that she or he be "the one you never hold" seems to be a rejection of love. We recall, however, that idiomatically "Hold / is forget." The paradox resolves when we recognize that the last lines actually mean "let me be the one you never forget." The opposed meanings of these lines illustrates the difficulty of fusing language and love. The poem thus deals with the basic impossibility of loving through language. By exploring the ambiguities of words, idiom, jargon, and diction, the poem reveals that language becomes a game in which significant concepts and emotions are trivialized and debased. And since we must use language to speak about love, the poem advocates love without any words at all.

SYNTAX

Syntax is a general term that refers to word order and sentence structure. The normal word order in English sentences is firmly fixed in a subject–verb–object sequence. At the simplest level, we tend to say "John (subject) threw (verb) the ball (object)." This rigid order is necessary to convey meaning; when we change English word order, we usually change the meaning as well. "Dog bites man," for instance, is obviously very different from "Man bites dog."

Word order in English is so rigidly established that any shift or adjustment is likely to have a significant impact on the meaning of a sentence. When poets employ irregular word order, they usually do so to achieve a specific effect. Sometimes normal word order is altered in poetry to meet the demands of meter or the rhyme scheme. In other instances, however, the word order may be shifted out of the ordinary to create emphasis, to heighten the connection between two words, or to pick up on specific implications or traditions.

Clear examples of the alteration of word order for effect are the first sentences of John Milton's *Paradise Lost* and Alexander Pope's *The Rape of the Lock*. Both poems are in the epic tradition and both imitate many aspects of Vergil's *Aeneid*; Milton's is an epic, while Pope's is a mock epic (an **epic** is usually a long narrative poem that features heroic characters and highly elevated diction). Vergil (70–19 B.C.) was a Roman poet who modeled his national epic on Homer's *Iliad* and *Odyssey*. The *Aeneid* begins, "*Arma virumque cano*," which translates literally as "Of arms and the man I sing." The word order here is typical of Latin, in which the verb is usually placed at the end of a phrase or sentence. In normal English word order, we would translate this opening as "I sing of arms and the man." Milton's *Paradise Lost* begins as follows:

Of man's first disobedience, and the fruit
Of that forbidden tree whose mortal taste
Brought death into the world, and all our woe,
With loss of Eden, till one greater Man
Restore us, and regain the blissful seat,
Sing, Heavenly Muse . . .

Pope begins *The Rape of the Lock* in a similar manner:

What dire offense from amorous causes springs,
What mighty contests rise from trivial things,
I sing.

In both cases the word order is shifted so that the sentence reflects Latin syntax; as in the beginning of the *Aeneid*, the verb is moved from its normal position in English to the end of the phrase. Both Milton and Pope employ this readjustment of normal word order to emphasize the epic quality of their poems and the affinity of their work to the *Aeneid*. Similarly, both use the verb *sing* to echo Vergil's *cano* (I sing).

Many other adjustments to word order create specific effects. One of these is the placement of adjectives. Normally, adjectives are placed immediately before the nouns they modify; we speak, for example, of sunny days and bloody war. If we were to reverse the sequence, and refer to days sunny or war bloody, the word order would strike us as peculiar. Nevertheless, this sort of reversal is employed frequently in poetry to good advantage. Early in *Paradise Lost*, for example, Milton speaks of the time when Satan rebelled against God and "Raised impious war in Heaven and battle proud." The word order is unusual in two respects. In the first place, we would normally find both "impious war" and "battle proud" before the modifying prepositional phrase "in Heaven." Second, we expect the adjective *proud* to be before *battle*. Instead of writing, "Raised impious war and proud battle in Heaven," Milton readjusted the normal word order twice in order to place the word *proud* at the end of the line. The altered word order partly serves metrical demands, but it also stresses the word *proud*. This emphasis is consistent with the overall focus of *Paradise Lost* on human and Satanic pride.

These examples of the ways in which poets can readjust word order for emphasis or effect illustrate a general technique. There are hundreds, perhaps thousands, of ways that word order can be shifted for impact. It is impossible to describe or illustrate all of them here. As a general rule, however, you should pay careful attention to any variation in normal word order. Most variations have a purpose; your task is to figure out the effect that is produced by such adjustments.

One major area of syntax that becomes important in understanding poetry is sentence structure. We discuss this subject in Chapter 7 (p. 241), but two specific aspects merit a closer look in connection with poetry. One of these is **repetition.** Repeating the same phrase or structure several times in a poem usually adds emphasis and sharpens focus. In William Blake's "The Lamb," for example, the same question is repeated four times with slight variation in the first stanza:

Little Lamb, who made thee?
Dost thou know who made thee?
   . . .
Little Lamb who made thee?
Dost thou know who made thee?

This repetition has two primary effects. Initially, it tends to make the poem sound simple and childlike. At the same time, however, the repetitive structure focuses our attention on the central concern of the poem: the nature of the creator.

Another aspect of sentence structure that has a significant effect on poetry is **parallelism,** a rhetorical figure in which the same grammatical forms are repeated in the same order. This technique is closely related to repetition; indeed, repetition may be called parallelism carried to an extreme. The effect of parallelism on poetry is twofold. It produces balanced lines that mirror each other form for form, and it allows the poet to link dissimilar concepts in parallel grammatical constructs. We have already examined an interesting example of parallelism in our discussion of the first stanza of Robert Graves' "The Naked and the Nude." Graves uses three parallel phrases—"the naked and the nude," "As love from lies," and "or truth from art"—that repeat the same pattern of noun–conjunction/preposition–noun. The parallel syntax thus associates "the naked" with "love" and "truth" and "the nude" with "lies" and "art."

POEMS FOR STUDY

BEN JONSON (1572–1632)

On My First Son °   *1616 (1603?)*

Farewell, thou child of my right hand,° and joy;
My sin was too much hope of thee, loved boy;
Seven years thou wert lent to me, and I thee pay,
Exacted by thy fate, on the just day.
Oh, could I lose all father, now! For why   5
Will man lament the state he should envy?
To have so soon scaped° world's, and flesh's rage,   *escaped*
And, if no other misery, yet age?
Rest in soft peace, and, asked, say here doth lie
Ben Jonson his° best piece of poetry,   *Jonson's*   10
For whose sake, henceforth, all his vows be such,
As what he loves may never like too much.

ON MY FIRST SON. Jonson's eldest son, also named Benjamin, died on his seventh birthday in 1603.   1 *child of my right hand*: a literal translation of the Hebrew name Benjamin (*ben* means "son of" and *jamin* means "right hand").

QUESTIONS

1. What special language is evoked by the phrase "child of my right hand"?
2. What metaphor is developed in lines 3–4? How do words like *lent, pay, exacted,* and *just* advance this comparison? Explain the irregular word order in line 3.
3. What does the speaker mean by "all father" (line 5)? What point does he make about his sadness and his son's present state in lines 5–8?
4. What kind of special diction is reflected in "Rest in soft peace" and "here doth lie" (line 9)? Where are such phrases normally found? Why are they here?

5. To whom does "Ben Jonson" (line 10) refer? How is the name used two
   ways?
6. The speaker calls his son "his best piece of poetry" (line 10). Look up the
   derivation of the word *poet* and explain this assertion.

JOHN DONNE (1572–1631)

Holy Sonnet 14: Batter My Heart, Three-Personed God   1633

Batter my heart, three-personed God; for You
As yet but knock, breathe, shine, and seek to mend;
That I may rise and stand, o'erthrow me, and bend
Your force to break, blow, burn and make me new.
I, like an usurped° town, to another due,   *stolen*   5
Labor to admit You, but Oh, to no end;
Reason, Your viceroy in me, me should defend,
But is captived, and proves weak or untrue.
Yet dearly I love You, and would be loved fain,°   *gladly*
But am betrothed unto Your enemy.   10
Divorce me, untie or break that knot again;
Take me to You, imprison me, for I,
Except You enthrall me, never shall be free,
Nor ever° chaste, except you ravish me.   *never*

QUESTIONS

1. What kind of God is suggested by the words *batter*, *knock*, *overthrow*, and
   break? What does "three-personed God" mean?
2. With which person of God might the verbs *knock* and *break* be associated?
   The verbs *breathe* and *blow*? The verbs *shine* and *burn*? What pun lurks behind
   this last pair of verbs?
3. To what does the speaker compare himself in lines 5–8? To what does he
   compare his "Reason"? Who is the usurper?
4. What is the effect of the altered word order at the ends of lines 7 and 9?
5. To what does the speaker compare himself in lines 9–14? Who is "your
   enemy"? What is the metaphorical relationship between the speaker and
   this enemy?
6. Unpack and explain the words *enthrall* (line 13) and *ravish* (line 14) to resolve
   the apparent paradox or contradiction in the last two lines.

WILLIAM BLAKE (1757–1827)

The Lamb   1789

Little Lamb, who made thee?
  Dost thou know who made thee?
Gave thee life & bid thee feed,

By the stream & o'er the mead;
Gave thee clothing of delight,   5
Softest clothing wooly bright;
Gave thee such a tender voice,
Making all the vales rejoice!
   Little Lamb who made thee?
   Dost thou know who made thee?   10

   Little Lamb I'll tell thee,
   Little Lamb I'll tell thee!
He is callèd by thy name,
For he calls himself a Lamb:
He is meek & he is mild,   15
He became a little child:
I a child & thou a lamb,
We are callèd by his name.
   Little Lamb God bless thee.
   Little Lamb God bless thee.   20

QUESTIONS

1. Who or what is the speaker in this poem? The listener? How are they related?
2. What central question does the poem ask and then answer?
3. What is the effect of repetition in the poem?
4. How would you characterize the diction in this poem? High, middle, or low? Abstract or concrete? How is it consistent with the speaker?
5. What are the connotations of *softest*, *bright*, *tender*, *meek*, and *mild*? What do these words imply about the Creator?
6. Describe the characteristics of the Creator imagined in this poem. Compare the image presented here with the image of God in Donne's "Batter My Heart, Three-Personed God." What differences do you find?

LEWIS CARROLL (1832–1898)

Jabberwocky°   *1871*

'Twas brillig, and the slithy toves
  Did gyre and gimble in the wabe;
All mimsy were the borogoves,
  And the mome raths outgrabe.

JABBERWOCKY. The poem, which appears in the first chapter of *Through the Looking Glass*, is full of nonsense words that Carroll made up with the sound (rather than the sense) in mind. Alice admits that the poem makes some sense even though she does not know the words: "It seems very pretty . . . but it's rather hard to understand! . . . Somehow it seems to fill my head with ideas—only I don't exactly know what they are!"

"Beware the Jabberwock, my son!   5
    The jaws that bite, the claws that catch!
Beware the Jubjub bird, and shun
    The frumious Bandersnatch!"

He took his vorpal sword in hand;
    Long time the manxome foe he sought—   10
So rested he by the Tumtum tree,
    And stood awhile in thought.

And, as in uffish thought he stood,
    The Jabberwock, with eyes of flame,
Came whiffling through the tulgey wood,   15
    And burbled as it came!

One, two! One, two! And through and through
    The vorpal blade went snicker-snack!
He left it dead, and with its head
    He went galumphing back.   20

"And hast thou slain the Jabberwock?
    Come to my arms, my beamish boy!
O frabjous day! Callooh! Callay!"
    He chortled in his joy.

'Twas brillig, and the slithy toves   25
    Did gyre and gimble in the wabe;
All mimsy were the borogoves,
    And the mome raths outgrabe.

QUESTIONS

1. Summarize in your own words the story that this poem tells.
2. Humpty Dumpty begins to explain or explicate this poem for Alice in Chapter
   6 of *Through the Looking Glass*. He explains that " 'brillig' means four o'clock
   in the afternoon—the time when you begin *broiling* things for dinner." He
   also explains that " 'slithy' means 'lithe' and 'slimy.' 'Lithe' is the same as
   'active.' You see it's like a portmanteau—there are two meanings packed
   into one word." Go through the poem and list all the portmanteau words
   you can find. Then unpack the words; try to determine what combinations
   of words are packed into these portmanteau words. *Brillig*, for example, might
   be seen as a combination of *broiling*, *brilliant*, and *light*.

EDWIN ARLINGTON ROBINSON (1869–1935)

Richard Cory   *1897*

Whenever Richard Cory went down town,
We people on the pavement looked at him:
He was a gentleman from sole to crown,
Clean favored, and imperially slim.

And he was always quietly arrayed,   5
And he was always human when he talked;
But still he fluttered pulses when he said,
'Good-morning,' and he glittered when he walked.

And he was rich—yes, richer than a king—
And admirably schooled in every grace: 10
In fine, we thought that he was everything
To make us wish that we were in his place.

So on we worked, and waited for the light,
And went without the meat, and cursed the bread;
And Richard Cory, one calm summer night,   15
Went home and put a bullet through his head.

QUESTIONS

1. What can you surmise about the speaker of this poem? What is his or her status?
2. What is the effect of using *down town*, *pavement*, *meat*, and *bread* in connection with the people who admire Richard Cory?
3. What are the connotations and implications of the name *Richard Cory*? Of the word *gentleman*?
4. Why does the poet use "sole to crown" instead of "head to toe" and "imperially slim" instead of "very thin" to describe Cory?
5. What effect does repetition produce in this poem? Consider especially the six lines that begin with "And."
6. What positive characteristics does Richard Cory possess (at least from the perspective of the speaker) besides wealth?
7. What ideas about the human condition does this poem explore?

WALLACE STEVENS (1879–1955)

Disillusionment of Ten O'Clock   *1923*

The houses are haunted
By white night-gowns.
None are green,

Or purple with green rings,
Or green with yellow rings,   5
Or yellow with blue rings.
None of them are strange,
With socks of lace
And beaded ceintures.°   *belts*
People are not going   10
To dream of baboons and periwinkles.
Only, here and there, an old sailor,
Drunk and asleep in his boots,
Catches tigers
In red weather.   15

QUESTIONS

1. Is the "Ten O'Clock" here morning or night? How can you tell?
2. What do "haunted" and "white night-gowns" suggest about the people who
    live in the houses? What do the negative images in lines 3–9 suggest?
3. To whom are these people contrasted in lines 12–15?
4. What are the connotations of "socks with lace" and "beaded ceintures"?
    With which character in the poem would you associate these things?
5. What is the effect of using words and images like *baboons*, *periwinkles*, *tigers*,
    and *red weather* in lines 11–15? Who will dream of these things?
6. What do the people in "white night-gowns" lack that the "old sailor" has?
7. Unpack the term *disillusionment* and explore its relation to the point that this
    poem makes about dreams, images, and imagination.

THEODORE ROETHKE (1907–1963)

Dolor   1943

I have known the inexorable sadness of pencils,
Neat in their boxes, dolor of pad and paper-weight,
All the misery of manila folders and mucilage,
Desolation in immaculate public places,
Lonely reception room, lavatory, switchboard,   5
The unalterable pathos of basin and pitcher,
Ritual of multigraph, paper-clip, comma,
Endless duplication of lives and objects.
And I have seen dust from the walls of institutions,
Finer than flour, alive, more dangerous than silica,   10
Sift, almost invisible, through long afternoons of tedium,
Dropping a fine film on nails and delicate eyebrows,
Glazing the pale hair, the duplicate grey standard faces.

QUESTIONS

1. What does *dolor* mean? Locate all the words in the poem related to "dolor." What do they have in common? Are they concrete or abstract? Specific or general? Latinate or common?
2. How are specific and concrete words used in this poem to define concepts and conditions that are presented in general and abstract terms?
3. What are the institutions, conditions, and places that the speaker associates with "dolor"? What do these institutions and places have in common?
4. What point does this poem make about the public world and about the details of day-to-day existence?

HENRY REED (b. 1914)

Naming of Parts   *1946*

To-day we have naming of parts. Yesterday,
We had daily cleaning. And to-morrow morning,
We shall have what to do after firing. But to-day,
To-day we have naming of parts. Japonica
Glistens like coral in all of the neighboring gardens,   5
    And to-day we have naming of parts.

This is the lower sling swivel. And this
Is the upper sling swivel, whose use you will see,
When you are given your slings. And this is the piling swivel,
Which in your case you have not got. The branches   10
Hold in the gardens their silent, eloquent gestures,
    Which in our case we have not got.

This is the safety-catch, which is always released
With an easy flick of the thumb. And please do not let me
See anyone using his finger. You can do it quite easy   15
If you have any strength in your thumb. The blossoms
Are fragile and motionless, never letting anyone see
    Any of them using their finger.

And this you can see is the bolt. The purpose of this
Is to open the breech, as you see. We can slide it   20
Rapidly backwards and forwards: we call this
Easing the spring. And rapidly backwards and forwards
The early bees are assaulting and fumbling the flowers:
    They call it easing the Spring.

They call it easing the Spring: it is perfectly easy   25
If you have any strength in your thumb: like the bolt,
And the breech, and the cocking-piece, and the point of balance,
Which in our case we have not got; and the almond-blossom

Silent in all of the gardens and the bees going backwards and forwards,
    For to-day we have naming of parts.   30

QUESTIONS

1. There may be two speakers in this poem, or one speaker repeating the words of another and adding his own thoughts. In any event, what two voices do you hear?
2. What is the setting? The situation? How do these affect the speaker?
3. What two completely different sets of "parts" are named in this poem? How are the two sets related to each other?
4. How and why is jargon used in the poem? With what set of "parts" is the jargon initially associated? How does this change?
5. How are phrases like "easing the spring" (lines 22, 24, 25) and "point of balance" (27) used with more than one meaning? What is the effect of repetition?
6. What ideas about war, the military, and nature does this poem explore?

RICHARD EBERHART (b. 1904)

The Fury of Aerial Bombardment   1947

You would think the fury of aerial bombardment
Would rouse God to relent; the infinite spaces
Are still silent. He looks on shock-pried faces.
History, even, does not know what is meant.

You would feel that after so many centuries   5
God would give man to repent; yet he can kill
As Cain could, but with multitudinous will,
No farther advanced than in his ancient furies.

Was man made stupid to see his own stupidity?
Is God by definition indifferent, beyond us all?   10
Is the eternal truth man's fighting soul
Wherein the Beast ravens in its own avidity?

Of Van Wettering I speak, and Averill,
Names on a list, whose faces I do not recall
But they are gone to early death, who late in school   15
Distinguished the belt feed lever from the belt holding pawl.

QUESTIONS

1. Who or what is the speaker in this poem? What does the last stanza tell you about him (Eberhart was a gunnery instructor during World War II)?
2. To whom does the "you" in lines 1 and 5 refer?

3. What type and level of diction predominate in lines 1–12? What observations about God are made in these lines? Compare the image of God presented here with the one found in Donne's "Batter My Heart, Three-Personed God," and Blake's "The Lamb." What similarities or differences do you find?

4. How does the level and type of diction change in the last stanza? What is the effect of these changes? How is jargon used here?

5. What ideas about humanity and war does this poem explore? Compare this poem with Thomas Hardy's "Channel Firing" (p. 492). How are the ideas in the poems similar?

WRITING ABOUT DICTION AND SYNTAX IN POETRY

In setting out to write an essay on a poem's diction or syntax, you will usually be looking for a connection between one of these elements and another element of poetry, such as character, setting, or ideas. Consequently, you cannot begin to develop your own ideas about the impact of language until you have a clear general understanding of the poem you have chosen to consider.

First note down as much as you can about the speaker, the listener, the other characters, the setting and situation, the subject, and the ideas of the poem. You may ultimately use little of this material in your essay, but it will help shape your response to questions of diction and syntax. Moreover, you will find that the diction and syntax contribute to the development and impact of these other elements. Thus, you are likely to end up writing about word choice or language in connection with some other crucial element of poetry.

Once you understand the general meaning and impact, you can move back through the poem and examine it word by word and sentence by sentence. Look for any consistent patterns of diction or syntax that relate to the elements you have already considered. If you were planning to write about diction in Frost's "Stopping by Woods on a Snowy Evening" (p. 475), for example, you might isolate the following words and phrases connected with setting and situation: "woods," "fill up with snow," "without a farmhouse," "between the woods and frozen lake," "sound's the sweep," "easy wind," "downy flake," "lovely," "dark," and "deep." Some of these are quite straightforward, but others lend themselves to further investigation and explanation. You might consider the implications of "fill up," "without a farmhouse near," and "between the woods and frozen lake"; these phrases all suggest more than they say. In addition, you might deal with the connotative values of words like *woods*, *darkest*, *sweep*, *easy*, *downy*, and *deep*. A careful analysis of the diction employed here will lead you to a series of connected discoveries about Frost's language. These discoveries, in turn, can produce the raw materials for an essay about the link between diction and setting in "Stopping by Woods."

As you develop your ideas, you should look for any effective and consistent patterns of word choice, connotation, repetition, idiom, or the like that help create and reinforce the conclusions you have already reached about the poem. You might ask yourself the following questions:

1. Does the poem contain a preponderance of loaded or connotative words in connection with any single element like setting, speaker, or theme?

2. Does the poem contain a large number of general and abstract or specific and concrete words? What is the effect of these choices?

3. Is the level of diction in the poem elevated, neutral, or informal, and how does this level affect your perception of the speaker, subject, and the like?

4. Does the poem contain examples of special diction such as idiom or jargon? If so, how do these help shape your response to the poem as a whole?

5. Can you find instances of abnormal English word order in the poem, and if so, what is the effect of these alterations?

6. Has the poet used any striking patterns of sentence structure such as parallelism or repetition? If so, what is the effect?

These questions isolate places to begin an exploration of diction or syntax with an eye to writing an effective essay. Eventually, you should focus your efforts on a single aspect of word choice or language. Once you deal with these six questions, however, the most fruitful area of investigation should be clear.

When you have narrowed your examination down to one or two specific areas of diction or syntax, list the words, phrases, and sentences that are relevant and unpack them—that is, investigate the full range of meaning and effect produced by the examples. At this point, begin to look for examples that work in similar ways or produce similar effects. Doing this will allow you to group related examples together as you organize your notes. Eventually, you will want to reorganize your initial list of instances and explanations so that related examples are grouped together in logical units that will become paragraphs when you write the essay.

Finally, you will be ready to formulate a tentative central idea and arrange your examples in the most effective way to support this thesis. The central idea will naturally emerge from your investigation of the specific group or groups of examples of diction or syntax that prove to be most fruitful and interesting. Since diction and syntax contribute to the general impact and meaning of the poem, your thesis and examples will almost always relate to conclusions you have reached about the poem through other avenues of exploration.

Organizing Your Essay

INTRODUCTION.   The introduction should begin by making a general observation about theme, character, speaker, or other key element in the poem under consideration. The central idea of the essay—a focused statement about the effects of word choice or language—should relate to this general point. If you are writing an essay about "The Naked and the Nude," for example, your central idea might assert that Graves employs words with multiple denotations and connotations to emphasize the moral and lexical distinctions between "the naked" and "the nude." Such a formulation makes a clear connection between diction and meaning. The introduction should also suggest the ways in which the central idea will be supported in the body of the essay.

BODY.   The body of the essay normally provides evidence, in an orderly and convincing manner, to support the assertion about diction or syntax made in the introduction. There are many different ways that such material can be organized. If you choose to deal with only one aspect of diction, such as connotative words or jargon, you might treat these in the order in which they appear in the poem. When you deal with two or three different aspects of diction and syntax, however, you can group related examples together regardless of where they occur in the poem. Thus, you might treat examples of multiple denotation, then connotation, and finally jargon in a series of paragraphs. In this instance, the organization of the essay is controlled by the types of material under consideration rather than by the order in which the words occur in the poem.

Alternatively, you might deal with the impact of diction or syntax on a series of other elements, such as character, setting, *and* situation. In such a paper you would focus on a single type of lexical or syntactic device as it relates to these different elements in sequence. Thus, you might discuss the link between connotation and character, then setting, and finally situation in sequential paragraphs. Whatever organization you select initially, keep in mind that each poem will finally suggest its own avenues of exploration and strategies of organization.

CONCLUSION.   The conclusion should bring the essay to a strong and assertive close. Here, you can summarize the conclusions you have reached about the impact of diction or syntax in the poem. You can also consider the larger implications of your ideas in connection with the thoughts and emotions conveyed by the poem and evoked in your reading.

SAMPLE ESSAY

Diction and Character in Edwin Arlington Robinson's "Richard Cory"*

[1]   In "Richard Cory," Edwin Arlington Robinson makes a general observation about the human condition; the poem ultimately suggests that nothing can ensure happiness. Robinson explores this idea by focusing on a central character— Richard Cory—who seems to have everything: wealth, status, dignity, taste, respect, and humanity. Cory's suicide at the end of the poem, however, reveals that these things cannot be equated with happiness. Robinson sets us up for the surprising reversal in the last two lines—the suicide—by creating a vast gulf between Cory and the people of the town who admire and envy him. This distinction is produced, at least in part, through Robinson's use of loaded words that demean the general populace and elevate the central character.° The speaker and his or her fellow workers have words associated with them that connote their common lot, while Richard Cory is described in terms that imply nobility and privilege.□

[2]   For the most part, the poem focuses on Richard Cory. This character is seen, however, from the perspective of the townspeople, who wished "that we were in his place" (line 12). Robinson skillfully employs words in connection with these common folk to suggest their low status and impoverished way of life. In the first line of the poem, for example, the speaker places himself or herself and these other people "down town." The phrase denotes the central business district of a city. Nevertheless, it also carries all the denotations and connotations of the word down. The term thus implies that Cory's journey to town is a descent or a lowering "down" and that the people exist continually in this "down" condition. We find a similar instance of loaded diction in the term pavement (line 2). Robinson employs pavement instead of sidewalk to create a stronger sense of inferiority for the speaker and the common people. Pavement can mean sidewalk, but it can also mean street or roadbed. The net effect of the term pavement here is to place "we people" even lower than Richard Cory—literally on the street.

[3]   In contrast to these few examples of diction that suggest the negative status of the people, the poem overflows with terms that connote Richard Cory's elevated status. Many of these words and phrases also carry the suggestion of nobility or royalty. These implications begin with the title of the poem and the name "Richard Cory." Richard contains the word rich, thus implying wealth and privileged status through sound. It is also the name of a number of English kings, including Richard the Lion Hearted (Coeur de Lion). The central character's first name thus links him with a series of royal figures. The name Cory is equally connotative. On first reading, it reminds us of the word core, the central or innermost part of anything. The name thus points toward Cory's singular position and significance in the town and in the poem. Through sound,

---

* See p. 559 for this poem.
° Central idea.
□ Thesis sentence.

Cory also suggests both the French word cour (court) and the English word court. In addition, it points to the French word coeur (heart) and thus to "Richard Coeur de Lion." The name "Richard Cory" thus begins a process of association through sound and implication that links the central character of this poem with images of kingship and the court.

[4]

We find similarly loaded words throughout the first stanza of the poem. The speaker describes Richard Cory as "a gentleman from sole to crown" (line 3). Gentleman is a packed word here; it denotes a civilized and well-mannered individual, but it also means "highborn" or "noble" in older usage. The phrase "from sole to crown" means "from head to toe," but it connotes a great deal more than that. Sole means both "the bottom of a shoe or foot" and "alone" or "singular"; thus, the word suggests Cory's isolation and separation from the common folk. The word is also a pun and a homonym on soul, implying that Cory's gentility is inward as well as external. The final touch is the word crown. In context, the term denotes the top of the head, but its aristocratic and royal connotations are self-evident.

[5]

The speaker also describes Cory as "clean favored" and "imperially slim" (line 4). Both phrases advance the connotative connection between the central character and the privileges of nobility. "Clean favored," instead of the more common good looking, connotes crisp and untouched features; it again suggests that Cory is set apart and isolated. More to the point, the term favored also means "preferred," "elevated," "honored," and "privileged." "Imperially slim," instead of thin, is equally connotative of wealth and status. While both terms denote the same physical condition, slim connotes elegance, wealth, and choice, while thin suggests poverty, disease, and necessity. The adverb imperially, like crown, makes an explicit connection between Cory and emperors.

[6]

Although instances of this type of diction taper off after the first stanza, Robinson employs enough similar terms in the rest of the poem to sustain the connotative link between Richard Cory and royalty. In the second stanza, for example, we find "quietly arrayed" and "glittered." Both carry elevated and imperial connotations. Arrayed means "dressed," but it is not a verb we associate with commonplace clothing. Rather, it implies elegant finery. "Quietly arrayed" means dressed with taste and modesty, but quietly also suggests solitude and introversion. Glittered works against quietly; it connotes richness of dress and manner, suggesting that the man himself is golden. In the third stanza, the deliberate cliché "richer than a king" again clearly links Richard Cory to royalty. The speaker also notes that Cory was "schooled in every grace" (line 10). The phrase means that Cory was trained in manners and social niceties, but grace also connotes privilege and nobility, because it is the formal title used when addressing a monarch or member of the nobility (as in "Your Grace").

[7]

In conclusion, we can see that Robinson uses loaded words and connotation to lower the common folk and elevate the central character in "Richard Cory." The words linked with the speaker and the other townspeople have demeaning and negative implications. At the same time, the poet uses a series of words and phrases that connote royalty and privilege in connection with Cory. This careful manipulation of diction widens the gulf between Richard

Cory and the speaker. It also heightens our sense that Cory is possessed of aristocratic looks, manners, taste, and breeding. The network of associations between Cory and royalty built through this skillful diction shapes our image of the central figure and thus makes the ending of the poem that much more shocking. The diction reinforces the poem's message that wealth, looks, breeding, and status cannot ensure happiness.

Commentary on the Essay

This essay deals with the ways in which E. A. Robinson uses loaded and connotative words to define and differentiate the townspeople and the central character in "Richard Cory." The opening paragraph makes a general assertion about the theme of the poem, connects character to this assertion, and argues that Robinson manipulates diction to achieve specific effects in connection with character. The central idea and the thesis sentence both assert that the poet employs diction to demean the common people (and the speaker of the poem) and to elevate Richard Cory.

The body of the essay deals with eleven instances of word choice and diction in five paragraphs. The organization illustrates a modified version of the first strategy discussed above. The examples of connotative words are arranged to reflect partly the characters they define and partly the order in which they appear in the poem. Thus, the second paragraph discusses the common people and the speaker in connection with two loaded words: *down town* and *pavement*.

The next four paragraphs (3–6) focus on Richard Cory and words or phrases that suggest royalty and privilege. The nine examples of diction examined here are taken up in the order in which they appear in the poem. Thus, the third paragraph unpacks Cory's name, and the fourth explores the connotative effects of *gentleman* and "sole to crown." The fifth and sixth paragraphs continue this process, examining six instances of diction that sustain the association between Richard Cory and nobility. Taken together, the four paragraphs devoted to this central character illustrate Robinson's consistent manipulation of diction to enoble and isolate Cory.

The conclusion of the essay summarizes the observations about word choice and connotation made in the body. It also ties these observations back into a general consideration of character and theme. The conclusion asserts that Robinson's management of diction contributes to the isolation of Richard Cory from the other characters in the poem and that it adds to the impact of Cory's suicide in the last two lines. In this way, the words and phrases examined in the essay are linked to the poem's exploration of ideas about the human condition.

15

Imagery

As the word _imagery_ is understood apart from literary and artistic analysis, it refers to <u>sensory impressions stored in the memory.</u> Whenever you remember things you have seen, smelled, heard, tasted, or felt, you are recollecting these things as _images_. If you bring to mind a recent activity, your memory of that activity is an image. In fact, everything that you have ever experienced is part of your memory as a collection of innumerable and separate impressions, which you may describe as images. Even in recalling abstract ideas, you may link them to an image of the circumstances in which you learned about them. Thus, the image you have retained of a particular day in a classroom might become suddenly and unexpectedly fresh in your mind as you think about an idea that you learned there during a lecture or discussion.

Images and memory, then, are tied closely together because <u>the memory is composed of many images.</u> At one time, in fact, the exercise of memory was regarded synonymously with the use of imagination, because both referred to that faculty of the human mind that records and stores experiences and makes them available for people when they are speaking, writing, and engaging in other activities of expression. Even today, when we think about using our imaginations, we mean the attempt to bring out of our minds new ideas or new applications in relation to a particular problem.

Within our minds, images may be clear or cloudy, strong or weak. If you consider your own memory, you know that some images are quite vivid, perhaps because you experienced them recently. Others are indistinct and vague, maybe because they happened in the distant past. Sometimes, however, you may be able to recall memories of long ago quite vividly. The key to the vividness of an image in the memory seems to be not its immediacy or remoteness in time, but its <u>importance.</u>

IMAGERY IN POETRY

Imagery in poetry, as in all literature, refers to <u>sensory experiences transmitted through the literary form</u>. The medium is words, which render what William Wordsworth called "this mighty world of eye and ear." A single image is a single experience that may appeal to one or more senses. For example, a reference to falling leaves is an image that describes the dropping of the leaves (<u>sight</u>), the sound of wind <u>rustling</u> them as they hit the ground (<u>hearing</u>), and their <u>dry and shriveled</u> texture (<u>feeling, touch</u>). The reference to a song may refer to the sound and also to the visual image of the person singing it. The imagery of a single poem is the collective set of recorded references to things and experiences in the poem. Imagery in a broader sense refers to the sets of referents and descriptions in a group of poems, or in the entire body of a poet's work. Thus, we might speak of (1) the imagery of line 5 or of stanza 6 in a poem, (2) the imagery of, say, Coleridge's "Kubla Khan," (3) the imagery of Shakespeare's sonnets (as a group), or (4) the development of Shakespeare's imagery.

OUR RESPONSES AND THE POET'S USE OF DETAIL

In studying imagery, we want to determine how the poet brings the world alive so that we may reconstruct something like the set of pictures and impressions presented in the poem. This almost magical act cannot happen successfully unless <u>we as readers</u> are willing to <u>make an imaginative leap over our everyday experience</u> so that we are receptive and responsive to the language of the poem. We must read the poet's words but then let them percolate in our minds to develop what the poet intended. To make such an imaginative reconstruction, we do not need full-scale, measured details (although they might be helpful), such as Wordsworth used to describe a pool of water in an early version of his poem "The Thorn":

. . . to the left, three yards beyond,
You see a little muddy pond
Of water—never dry;
I've measured it from side to side;
'Tis three feet long, and two feet wide.

Instead, only the essential words are usually enough to permit us to get our imaginations stirring. Thus, we might follow Coleridge in this description from "Kubla Khan":

A damsel with a dulcimer
In a vision once I saw:
It was an Abyssinian maid,

And on her dulcimer she played,
Singing of Mount Abora.

We do not read about the color of the damsel's clothing or anything else about her appearance; we are told only that she was playing on a stringed instrument and that she was singing a song about a mountain in a foreign, remote land. But Coleridge's reference is enough. From it we can imagine a distant, exotic, vivid picture of a woman singing. The image lives.

IMAGES OF SIGHT

Most often the language of imagery is sensuous inasmuch as "the language of the sense" stimulates our imaginations directly. The most frequent references are to things we can visualize either exactly or approximately, for human beings' principal sense is vision. Thus, John Masefield, in his poem "Cargoes," asks us to share his vision of ocean-going merchant vessels from three separate periods of human history.

JOHN MASEFIELD (1878–1967)

Cargoes   *1902*

Quinquereme° of Nineveh° from distant Ophir,°
Rowing home to haven in sunny Palestine,
With a cargo of ivory,
And apes and peacocks,
Sandalwood, cedarwood, and sweet white wine.   5

Stately Spanish galleon coming from the Isthmus,°
Dipping through the Tropics by the palm-green shores,
With a cargo of diamonds,
Emeralds, amethysts,
Topazes, and cinnamon, and gold moidores.°   10

Dirty British coaster with a salt-caked smoke-stack,
Butting through the Channel in the mad March days,
With a cargo of Tyne coal,°
Road-rails, pig-lead,
Firewood, iron-ware, and cheap tin trays.   15

CARGOES.   1 *quinquereme*: one of the largest types of ancient ships, having five tiers of oars.   *Nineveh*: capital of ancient Assyria, an "exceeding great city" (Jonah 3:3).   *Ophir*: a seaport, probably in Africa, from which cargoes like those described by Masefield were brought to King Solomon. See I Kings 9:11, 10:11, 10:22, and 2 Chronicles 9:2. Masefield echoes some of these verses in his first stanza.   6 *Isthmus*: of Panama.   10 *moidores*: former coin of Brazil and Portugal.   13 *Tyne coal*: Newcastle-upon-Tyne, in northern England, famous for its coal.

QUESTIONS

1. Consider the images that you find in each of the stanzas as they picture life during three periods of history: Ancient Israel at the time of Solomon, sixteenth-century Spain, and modern England. What do these images tell you about Masefield's interpretation of modern commercial life?

2. Consider the nature and type of the images in the poem. That is, do they refer mainly to things that you might see, or hear? What is the range of the imagery?

3. There are no complete sentences in this poem. Why do you think that Masefield included only the verbals (*rowing, dipping, butting*) beginning the second line of each of the stanzas rather than finite verbs?

4. Describe the effect of the verbals on the differing impressions that are given in the stanzas.

5. Let us suppose that the rowing of the Quinquereme of Nineveh was done by slaves and that the cargo of the Spanish galleons was seized by force from natives of Central America. Might these unpleasant suppositions disturb the romanticized impressions that Masefield intends for stanzas 1 and 2?

Masefield's images are vivid as they stand and they need no more detailed amplification. In order to reconstruct them imaginatively, for example, we do not need ever to have seen "distant Ophir" (scholars are uncertain about where it was anyway), or to have seen or handled "pig-lead." We have seen enough in our lives both firsthand and in pictures to *imagine* places and objects like these, and hence Masefield is successful in implanting his images into our minds.

IMAGES OF SOUND

Screeching brakes.
Fingernails on a blackboard

Poets also create images derived from the sense of sound. These *auditory* images are frequent. For auditory images in a poem, let us consider Wilfred Owen's "Anthem for Doomed Youth."

WILFRED OWEN (1893–1918)

Anthem for Doomed Youth   1920

What passing-bells for these who die as cattle?
Only the monstrous anger of the guns.
Only the stuttering rifles' rapid rattle
Can patter out their hasty orisons.°   *prayers*
No mockeries for them from prayers or bells,
Nor any voice of mourning save the choirs—

The shrill, demented choirs of wailing shells;
And bugles calling for them from sad shires.

What candles may be held to speed them all?
Not in the hands of boys, but in their eyes   10
Shall shine the holy glimmers of good-byes.
The pallor of girls' brows shall be their pall;
Their flowers the tenderness of patient minds,
And each slow dusk a drawing-down of blinds.

QUESTIONS

1. What is the predominant type of imagery in the first eight lines? How does the imagery change in the last six lines?

2. Describe the contrast throughout the poem of the sorts of images usually associated with death as observed in religious funerals and death as experienced on the battlefield. What is the effect of this contrast on your ability to experience and understand this poem?

3. Consider the following phrases as images: "holy glimmers of good-byes"; "pallor of girls' brows"; "patient minds"; "drawing-down of blinds." Who are the people who are being considered in these images? What is their relationship to the doomed youth?

4. Would this sonnet be more effective as an anti-war poem if it were more strident in its condemnation of war? Why or why not? Does the poem focus your attention upon the brutality or the pathos of war?

Here, in asking what "passing-bells" may be tolled for "those who die as cattle," Owen's speaker is referring to the traditional ringing of a parish church bell immediately after a person's death to announce the death to the parishioners. Such a ceremonial tolling usually suggests a period of peace and order, with time for appropriate observation and respect for the dead. But the speaker in Owen's poem goes on to point out that the only sound for the dead in battle is the "rapid rattle" of "stuttering" rifles—in other words, not the solemn, dignified sounds of peace, but the angry, percussive, intimidating noises of war. These auditory images evoke corresponding sounds in our imaginations and help us to experience the poem as completely as possible.

IMAGES OF SMELL, TASTE, AND TOUCH

gyms
bacon
sour milk
a penny

You will find references in poems to the senses of smell (*olfactory*), taste (*gustatory*), and touch (*tactile*) as well. A great deal of love poetry, for example, includes observations about the fragrances of flowers. In Sonnet 130 (p. 579) Shakespeare creates a speaker who considers the beauty of the

sticky
clammy
dusty

scent of roses, but then he develops a surprising and amusing twist on this olfactory image by contrasting it with "the breath that from my mistress reeks."

Images derived from and referring to taste are also common, though less frequent than those referring to sight and sound. In line 5 of Masefield's "Cargoes," for example, there are references in line 5 to "sweet white wine" and in line 10 to "cinnamon." Although these gustatory images refer to these things as cargoes aboard ships, the words themselves inevitably register in our minds because of their appeal to our sense of taste.

Images of touch and texture are perhaps the least common in poetry because these are often more personal and subjective than sights and sounds. It is also obvious that references to touching in love poetry, for example, would be sensual as well as sensuous.

OTHER FRAMES OF REFERENCE OF IMAGERY

The frames of reference of imagery may also take in virtually every sort of activity in which human beings may engage. Motion and action, for example, are common in poetry. Imagery referring to activities is termed *kinetic* if general motion is described, or *kinesthetic* if the imagery refers to human or animal activity. Both types may be seen at the conclusion of "The Fish" by Elizabeth Bishop.

[handwritten margin: swaying bobbing]

[handwritten: galloping, swinging, ↓ "swinging both ways"]

ELIZABETH BISHOP (1911–1979)

The Fish — *[handwritten: Imagery is both ordinary + unusual. Kinesthetic images; images of endurance and indomitability.]*   1946

I caught a tremendous fish
and held him beside the boat
half out of water, with my hook
fast in a corner of his mouth.
He didn't fight.
He hadn't fought at all.   5
He hung a grunting weight,
battered and venerable
and homely. Here and there   *[handwritten: He's described in such detail*
his brown skin hung in strips   *to give us a sense of his identity*
like ancient wallpaper,   *+ value.]*   10
and its pattern of darker brown
was like wallpaper: *[handwritten: Simile]*
shapes like full-blown roses
stained and lost through age.
He was speckled with barnacles,   15

fine rosettes of lime,
and infested
with <u>tiny white sea-lice,</u>
and underneath two or three   20
<u>rags of green weed hung down.</u>
While his gills were breathing in
<u>the terrible oxygen</u>   *ironic because it'll kill him,*
—the frightening <u>gills,</u>
fresh and crisp with blood,   25
that can cut so badly—
I thought of the coarse white flesh
<u>packed in like feathers,</u>   *Simile*
the big bones and the little bones,
the dramatic reds and blacks   30
of his shiny entrails,
and the pink swim-bladder
<u>like a big peony.</u>
I looked into his eyes
which were far larger than mine   *Hyperbole*   35
but shallower, and yellowed,
the irises backed and packed
with <u>tarnished tinfoil</u>   *Realistic comparison*
seen through the lenses
of old scratched isinglass.   40
They shifted a little, <u>but not</u>
<u>to return my stare.</u>   *The fish is proud!*
—It was more like the tipping
of an object toward the light.
<u>I admired his sullen face,</u>   45
the mechanism of his jaw,
and then I saw
that from his lower lip
—if you could call it a lip—
grim, wet, and weaponlike,   50
hung <u>five old pieces of fish-line,</u>
or four and a wire leader
with the swivel still attached,
with all their five big hooks
grown firmly in his mouth.   55
A green line, frayed at the end
where he broke it, two heavier lines,
and a fine black thread
still crimped from the stain and snap
when it broke and he got away.   60
<u>Like medals with their ribbons</u>   *A soldier*
frayed and wavering,
a five-haired <u>beard of wisdom</u>   *Aged*
trailing from his aching jaw.

I stared and stared   65
and victory filled up

[handwritten annotation: The growing sense of victory pulls the reader into the poem.]

the little rented boat,
from the pool of bilge
where oil had spread a rainbow
around the rusted engine   70
to the bailer rusted orange,
the sun-cracked thwarts,
the oarlocks on their strings,
the gunnels—until everything
[handwritten: Kinesthetic] was rainbow, rainbow, rainbow! *[handwritten: Victory! Success!]*   75
And I let the fish go.

[handwritten annotation: He respected the old fighter. Just catching him is success enough — a triumph for the speaker.]

QUESTIONS

1. What are the images of actions in the poem? Are they especially ordinary, or are they unusual?
2. What sort of impression does the fish make upon the speaker? Is the fish beautiful? Ugly? Why is the fish described in such detail?
3. What do the "five old pieces of fish-line" indicate about the previous existence of the fish?
4. How is the rainbow being formed around the engine of the boat? What does this rainbow suggest to the speaker?
5. Does the letting go of the fish seem abrupt, or is there a connection between the previous images of the fish and the release?
6. To what degree does it seem to be a matter of right for the fish to be free? Does the speaker seem to have a right to keep the fish? Why does the speaker finally let the fish go?

The kinetic images at the end are those of victory filling the boat (difficult to visualize) and the oil spreading the rainbow (easier to imagine). The kinesthetic images are readily imagined—the speaker's staring, observing, and letting the fish go—yet they are vivid and real. The final gesture is the necessary outcome of the observed contrast between the deteriorating artifacts of human beings and the natural world of the fish, and it is a vivid expression of the right of the natural world to exist without the intervention and pollution of human civilization. Bishop's kinetic and kinesthetic imagery, in short, is designed to objectivize the need for freedom not only for human beings but for all creatures.

The range of objects or activities that poets employ as imagery is both vast and unpredictable. Indeed, an important quality about imagery is its very unpredictability. At a first reading of "The Pulley," by George Herbert, for example, you might be hard put to explain the connection between the title and the poem itself. Here is the poem:

GEORGE HERBERT (1593–1633)

The Pulley   *1633*

When God at first made man,
Having a glass of blessings standing by,
  "Let us," said he, "pour on him all we can.
Let the world's riches, which dispersed lie,
    Contract into a span."°   5

  So strength first made a way;
Then beauty flowed, then wisdom, honor, pleasure.
  When almost all was out, God made a stay,
Perceiving that, alone of all his treasure,
    Rest° in the bottom lay.   10

  "For if I should," said he,
"Bestow this jewel also on my creature.
He would adore my gifts instead of me.
And rest in Nature, not the God of Nature;
    So both should losers be.   15

  "Yet let him keep the rest,
But keep them with repining restlessness.
  Let him be rich and weary, that at least,
If goodness lead him not, yet weariness
    May toss him to my breast."   20

THE PULLEY.   5 *span*: that is, within the control of human beings.   10 *rest*: (1) repose, security; (2) all that remains.

QUESTIONS

1. Describe the dramatic scene of the poem. Who is doing what?
2. What are the particular "blessings" that God confers on humanity, according to the speaker? Why should these be considered as blessings?
3. What remaining blessing does God withhold from all the treasures that have been bestowed on human beings? What is God's rationale, according to Herbert, for withholding it?
4. How might restlessness be manifested in human behavior? How adequate are the following words as synonyms for what Herbert seems to mean by restlessness: *dissatisfaction, anxiety, aimlessness, uncertainty, unhappiness, rootlessness, alienation*?
5. To what extent is it true or possible, as Herbert suggests, that "repining restlessness" might be the means that leads human beings to become religious?
6. Consider the image of the pulley as the means, or device, by which God has arranged that people will become worshipful.

The connection between title and poem becomes clear if only we recall that pulleys, because they increase mechanical advantage, may enable large and heavily resistant objects to be moved easily by only a small force. Herbert's image of the pulley makes the human race such a resistant object. People, according to Herbert's speaker, have been blessed with so much that they can easily neglect God. But God nevertheless has mechanical advantage because human beings are never satisfied with all their blessings. God's hold is human restlessness and dissatisfaction, and these are the power that God uses as an attraction to pull human beings away ultimately from their worldly preoccupations toward faith and adoration. Thus, through this image from the area of physics, Herbert makes the unpredictable relevant. Indeed, once we have finished "The Pulley," the image somehow seems no longer unusual or unpredictable at all, because it so aptly illustrates the connection between human behavior and divine power. Herbert, in other words, has chosen and developed his image in a masterly way.

Imagery may be derived from many other areas, almost too many to enumerate. Occupations, trades, professions, businesses, recreational activities—all these might become the subjects of the poet's imagery. Shakespeare, for example, was fond in his sonnets of developing images from the worlds of lawyers and bankers. The freshness and constant newness of his sonnets is a result of the aptness and thoroughness of his imagery.

IMAGERY DERIVED PURELY FROM LORE AND IMAGINATION

Because there are few restrictions upon the human imagination, the references of imagery may be real or totally imagined. Coleridge in "Kubla Khan," for example, gives us both in a single line:

By woman [real] wailing for her demon lover [unreal].

Herbert in "The Pulley" asks us to imagine a time during the creation of the universe when God distributed the various attributes that characterize human nature.

IMAGERY, COMPLETENESS, AND TRUTH

Poets do not create imagery within individual poems just to present a series of pictures or other sensory impressions. There would be little point to lists of images if the poets did not utilize these images to render experiences, ideas, and attitudes. Their aim is to help you see the world in a new way, to widen your understanding, to transfer their own ideas by the *authenticating* effects of the vision and perceptions underlying those ideas. Strong, vivid images are thus a means by which poetry renders truth. It would be difficult to share Masefield's views about modern commercial life if the description of his "Dirty British coaster with a salt-caked smokestack" did not ring true. A weakness in the poem, in fact, is that the vessels that he contrasts with the coaster were probably not as glamorous as he expects us to assume. The "Quinquereme of Nineveh" was likely rowed by slaves, not free men, and the cargo of the "Stately Spanish galleon" was likely gained from the Caribbean world (the "Isthmus" of Panama) by plunder. Comparable imagery used for a totally different purpose may be seen in Shakespeare's Sonnet 130. Here the speaker expressly denies the overly romantic compliments that men give women but stresses instead the everyday reality of the mistress. The concluding lines are these:

And yet, by heaven, I think my love as rare
As any She belied with false compare.

By emphasizing the image of the mistress as a real woman, Shakespeare gains assent to the view that everyday life is superior to dream life because it provides a basis for a relationship between people. Shakespeare's image of the real-life mistress is objective, and its objectivity makes his conclusions possible and acceptable. Masefield's images, by contrast, may be questioned, and as a result, the conclusions that seem to be invited in the poem may also be questioned. As you read poems and find images in them, try to determine their aptness, consistency, and reliability, for the poetry is only as durable as the authenticity of the imagery.

POEMS FOR STUDY

WILLIAM SHAKESPEARE (1564–1616)

Sonnet 130: My Mistress' Eyes Are Nothing Like the Sun   *1609*

My mistress'° eyes are nothing like the sun;   *woman friend*
Coral is far more red than her lips' red;
If snow be white, why then her breasts are dun;
If hairs be wires, black wires grow on her head.
I have seen roses damasked,° red and white,   *set in an elaborate bouquet*   5
But no such roses see I in her cheeks;
And in some perfumes is there more delight
Than in the breath that from my mistress reeks.

I love to hear her speak, yet well I know
That music hath a far more pleasing sound;   10
I grant I never saw a goddess go;
My mistress, when she walks, treads on the ground.
And yet, by heaven, I think my love as rare
As any she belied with false compare.

QUESTIONS

1. To what does the speaker negatively compare his mistress's eyes? Lips? Breasts? Hair? Cheeks? Breath? Voice? Walk? What kinds of images are created in these negative comparisons?

2. What conventional images and comparisons does this poem ridicule? What sort of poem is Shakespeare mocking by using the negative images in lines 1–12?

3. Do the images seem insulting? In the light of the last two lines, do you think the speaker intends the images as insults? If not as insults, how should they be taken?

4. Are most of the images in the poem auditory, olfactory, visual, or kinesthetic? Explain your answer.

5. What point does this poem make about love poetry? About human relationships? How does the imagery contribute to the development of both points?

RICHARD CRASHAW (1613–1649)

On Our Crucified Lord, Naked and Bloody   1646

Th' have° left Thee naked, Lord, O that they had;   *they have*
This garment too I would they had denied.
Thee with Thyself they have too richly clad,
Opening the purple° wardrobe of Thy side.
  O never could be found garments too good   5
  For Thee to wear, but these, of Thine own blood.

ON OUR CRUCIFIED LORD, NAKED AND BLOODY: 4 *purple*: Royal purple, but also here referring to blood.

QUESTIONS

1. Describe the two aspects of the imagery of clothing in this poem. How might the blood of Christ be considered as a garment?

2. Explain the contradiction and irony in the poem. Why does clothing made by human beings seem unworthy of being draped upon the crucified Lord?

3. What is meant by "this garment" in line 2? What is the relationship between this phrase and "Thee with Thyself" in line 3?

4. Does the emphasis on the blood of Christ in this poem seem appropriate or inappropriate for a devotional poem?

WILLIAM BLAKE (1757–1827)

The Tyger°   *1794*

Tyger! Tyger! burning bright
In the forests of the night,
What immortal hand or eye
Could frame thy fearful symmetry?

In what distant deeps or skies   5
Burnt the fire of thine eyes?
On what wings dare he aspire?
What the hand, dare seize the fire?

And what shoulder, & what art,
Could twist the sinews of thy heart?   10
And when thy heart began to beat,
What dread hand? & what dread feet?

What the hammer? what the chain?
In what furnace was thy brain?
What the anvil? what dread grasp   15
Dare its deadly terrors clasp?

When the stars threw down their spears,
And water'd heaven with their tears,
Did he smile his work to see?
Did he who made the Lamb make thee?   20

Tyger! Tyger! burning bright
In the forests of the night,
What immortal hand or eye
Dare frame thy fearful symmetry?

THE TYGER. The title refers not only to a tiger, but to any large, wild, ferocious cat.

QUESTIONS

1. What do the associations of the image of "burning" suggest? Why is the burning being done in the forests of the night rather than the day? What does the image of night suggest?

2. What is meant by "immortal hand or eye"?

3. Describe the kinesthetic images of lines 4–20. What ideas is Blake's speaker representing by these images? What sorts of actions are mentioned? What possible attributes does the speaker suggest may belong to the blacksmith-type initiator of these actions?

4. Line 20 is a question about the kinesthetic image of a creator. What is implied in the question concerning the mixture of good and evil in the world? What answer do you think the poem is suggesting? Why does Blake phrase this line as one of the many questions in the poem, rather than as an assertion?

5. Stanza 6 repeats stanza 1 with only one change of imagery of action. Contrast these stanzas, stressing the difference between *could* in 4 and *dare* in 24.

SAMUEL TAYLOR COLERIDGE (1772–1834)

Kubla Khan   *1816*

In Xanadu did Kubla Khan
A stately pleasure dome decree:
Where Alph,° the sacred river, ran
Through caverns measureless to man
  Down to a sunless sea.   5
So twice five miles of fertile ground
With walls and towers were girdled round:
And there were gardens bright with sinuous rills,
Where blossomed many an incense-bearing tree;
And here were forests ancient as the hills,   10
Enfolding sunny spots of greenery.

But oh! that deep romantic chasm which slanted
Down the green hill athwart a cedarn cover!
A savage place! as holy and enchanted
As e'er beneath a waning moon was haunted   15
By woman wailing for her demon lover!
And from this chasm, with ceaseless turmoil seething,
As if this earth in fast thick pants were breathing,
A mighty fountain momently was forced:
Amid whose swift half-intermitted burst   20
Huge fragments vaulted like rebounding hail,
Or chaffy grain beneath the thresher's flail:
And 'mid these dancing rocks at once and ever
It flung up momently the sacred river.
Five miles meandering with a mazy motion   25
Through wood and dale the sacred river ran,
Then reached the caverns measureless to man,
And sank in tumult to a lifeless ocean:

KUBLA KHAN.   3 *Alph*: possibly a reference to the river Alpheus in Greece, as described by the ancient writers Virgil and Pausanias.

And 'mid this tumult Kubla heard from far
Ancestral voices prophesying war!   30
   The shadow of the dome of pleasure
   Floated midway on the waves;
   Where was heard the mingled measure
   From the fountain and the caves.
It was a miracle of rare device,   35
A sunny pleasure dome with caves of ice!

   A damsel with a dulcimer
   In a vision once I saw:
   It was an Abyssinian maid,
   And on her dulcimer she played   40
   Singing of Mount Abora.°
Could I revive within me
Her symphony and song,
To such a deep delight 'twould win me,
That with music loud and long,   45
I would build that dome in air,
That sunny dome! those caves of ice!
And all who heard should see them there,
And all should cry, Beware! Beware!
His flashing eyes, his floating hair!   50
Weave a circle round him thrice,
And close your eyes with holy dread,
For he on honeydew hath fed,
And drunk the milk of Paradise.

41 *Mount Abora*: a mountain of Coleridge's imagination. But see Milton, *Paradise Lost*, IV,
pp. 268–84.

QUESTIONS

1. What is imagined as the poem's locale?

2. Study the poem's images closely. How many of them might be sketched or visualized? Which ones would be panoramic landscapes? Which might be closeups?

3. Discuss the extent of auditory imagery in the poem. What is the effect of images such as "wailing," "fast thick pants," "tumult," "ancestral voices prophecying war," and "mingled measure"?

4. When Coleridge was writing this poem, he was recalling it from a dream. At line 54 he was interrupted, and when he returned he could write no more. Does it seem that the poem is unfinished? How might an argument be made that the poem is finished?

5. How do lines 35–36 establish the pleasure dome as a place of mysterious oddity? What is the effect of the words *miracle* and *rare*? The effect of combining the images "sunny" with "caves of ice"?

6. Why does the speaker yearn for the power of the singing Abyssinian maid? What kinesthetic images end the poem? What importance do these images possess as part of the speaker's desire to reconstruct the vision of the pleasure dome?

GERARD MANLEY HOPKINS (1844–1889)

Spring   1877

Nothing is so beautiful as Spring—
　When weeds, in wheels, shoot long and lovely and lush;
　Thrush's eggs look little low heavens, and thrush
Through the echoing timber does so rinse and wring
The ear, it strikes like lightnings to hear him sing;   5
　The glassy peartree leaves and blooms, they brush
　The descending blue; that blue is all in a rush
With richness; the racing lambs too have fair their fling.

What is all this juice and all this joy?
　A strain of the earth's sweet being in the beginning   10
In Eden garden.—Have, get, before it cloy,

　Before it cloud, Christ, lord, and sour with sinning,
·Innocent mind and Mayday in girl and boy,
　Most, O maid's child, thy choice and worthy the winning.

QUESTIONS

1. What images does the speaker mention as support for his first line, "Nothing is so beautiful as Spring"? Are these images those that you would normally expect? To what degree do they seem to be new or unusual?

2. What images of motion and movement do you find in the poem? Are these mainly static or dynamic? What do these suggest about the speaker's view of spring?

3. What is the relationship between "Eden garden" in line 11 and the scene described in lines 1–8? To what extent can spring and "innocent mind and Mayday" be considered a glimpse of what life might have been like in the Garden of Eden?

4. Christ is mentioned in line 12 and again in line 14 (as "maid's child"). Do these references seal the poem off from readers who are not Christian? Why or why not?

5. Compare the images in this poem with the images in Marvell's "The Bermudas" (p. 519). Which of the two sets of images seems more vivid and lively? Which offers the more conventional Edenic imagery? Why?

EZRA POUND (1885–1972)

In a Station of the Metro°   Note   1916

ghost
The apparition of these faces in the crowd;
Petals on a wet, black bough.   Metaphor

IN A STATION OF THE METRO.   *Metro*: the Paris subway.

QUESTIONS

1. Does the image of the petals on the wet, black bough evoke cheer or sadness?
   If the petals were "blooming" on a tree in the sunlight in spring, would
   the image be more pleasant? Explain.

2. What is the meaning of the image suggested by *apparition*? Does it suggest
   a positive or negative view of human life?

3. This poem contains only two lines. Is it proper to consider it as a poem
   nevertheless? If it is not to be considered as a poem, how should it be considered?

H. D. (HILDA DOOLITTLE) (1886–1961)

Heat   1916

O wind, rend open the heat,
cut apart the heat,
rend it to tatters.

Fruit cannot drop
through this thick air—
fruit cannot fall into heat   5
that presses up and blunts
the points of pears
and rounds the grapes.

Cut the heat—   10
plough through it,
turning it on either side
of your path.

QUESTIONS

1. What is the meaning of the images of rending and cutting in the first three
   lines?

2. In lines 4–9, is it literally true that fruit cannot fall? If it is not, what is the

meaning of the image that heat may blunt the points of pears and make grapes round?

3. Discuss the image of a plough as a cutter and separater of heat.

4. In the light of the various images in the poem, what impression of heat does the poet succeed in expressing?

WRITING ABOUT IMAGERY

In preparing to write about imagery, you should work with a thoughtfully developed set of notes. With imagery it will be particularly important to be ready to classify references to the various senses to which they belong, such as sight and sound. In determining other classifications, you may be able to find a consistent pattern of references to a particular activity or related set of activities. If accurate classification is not possible, you may be able to make much of your poet's diversity of images.

Organizing Your Essay

INTRODUCTION.   Here you will set out the main points that you plan for the body of your essay; for example, you might assert that the poet refers heavily to images of sight or sound or action, and so on. Your central idea should clearly delineate your objective, and your thesis sentence should contain brief references to the topics of the following paragraphs or groups of paragraphs, depending on the length of your essay.

BODY.   There are a number of aspects of imagery that may be developed in the body of your essay. You might choose one of these exclusively, but quite likely your essay may bring in two or more of the following approaches:

1. *The type of images.* Is there a predominance of a particular type of imagery, such as references to sight, or is there a blending? Is there a bunching of types at particular points in the poem? What might be a reason for this bunching? Is there any shifting from type to type as the poem develops? How do the images relate to the content, to the ideas, of the poem? Are they appropriate? Do they assist in making the ideas seem convincing? If there seems to be any inappropriateness, what is the effect upon the total impact of the poem?

2. *The level of images.* Do the images lend themselves to the establishment of any particular mood in the poem? Do they seem cheerful? Melancholy? Exciting? Vivid? Do they seem to be conducive to humor? Or surprise? How does the poet manipulate the images to achieve these effects? Are the images what they at first seem, or may they be taken in a different way as the poem progresses? (For example, Shakespeare's references in

Sonnet 130 might initially be construed as insults. However, in a total consideration of the sonnet, are they insults or compliments?)

3. *The development of any systems of images.* In effect this is another way of considering the appropriateness of the imagery in a poem. Do all the images adhere consistently to a particular frame of reference, such as the life of a big fish (see Bishop's "The Fish"), or the building of a vast forest and garden (Coleridge's "Kubla Khan"), or the sailing of merchant vessels (Masefield's "Cargoes")? Is there anything unusual or unique about the set of images? Do they provide you with any unexpected or new responses to the situation and ideas of the poem?

4. *The creation of a characteristic mode of images.* Does the poet rely on a particular type of image? If you find such a characteristic line of images, this line may be considered a mode for that poem if not for that poet. It may be hard to determine a modal type on the basis of only one poem, but there are questions to help you determine if there is a mode in the poem you have studied. Does the imagery seem to rely upon shapes, colors, sounds, actions? Is it especially vivid, and if so, how does the poet achieve this vividness? Does the poet present the images completely or sketchily? Is one type of image used rather than another—for example, as images of natural scenery rather than interiors, or loud sounds rather than silence? What kinds of conclusions can you draw about the poem and the author as a result of your answers?

CONCLUSION. Whereas in the body of the essay you will have developed a fairly detailed analysis of the types and appropriateness of the poet's images, in your conclusion you might wish to stress any insights you have gained from your study. It would not be proper to introduce entirely new directions here, but you might briefly take up one or more of the conclusions you had reached but did not develop in the body. In short, what have you learned from your study of imagery in the poem about which you have written?

SAMPLE ESSAY

The Images of John Masefield's Poem "Cargoes"*

[1]   In the three-stanza poem "Cargoes," John Masefield develops imagery to create a negative impression of modern commercial life.° There is a contrast between the first two stanzas and the third, with the first two evoking the romantic, distant past and the third demonstrating the modern, gritty, grimy present. Mase-

_____

* See p. 571 for the poem.
° Central idea.

field's images are thus both positive and lush, on the one hand, and negative and stark, on the other.[□]

The most evocative and pleasant images in the poem are included in the first stanza. The speaker asks that we imagine a "Quinquereme of Nineveh from distant Ophir," an ocean-going, many-oared vessel loaded with treasure for the Biblical King Solomon. The visual impression is colorful, rich, and romantic. The imagery of richness is established with ivory (line 3) and is continued with the exoticism of "apes and peacocks" in all their strangeness and colorfulness. The speaker suggests the fullness of this scene by referring to the senses of smell (sandalwood and cedarwood) and taste (sweet white wine). The "sunny" light of ancient Palestine not only illuminates Masefield's scene, but invites readers to imagine the sun's touch of warmth. Thus, in this lush first stanza, images derived from all the senses are introduced to create the impression and experience of the gloriousness of this first cargo.

Almost equally lush are the images of the second stanza, which completes the first part of the poem. Here the visual imagery evokes the royal splendor of a tall-masted, full-sailed ship of Spain at the height of its commercial power in the sixteenth century. The cargo of the galleon suggests vast wealth, with diamonds and amethysts sparkling to the eye, and "gold moidores" of Portugal gleaming in colorful chests. With cinnamon in the second stanza's bill of lading, Masefield includes a reference to a pleasant-tasting spice.

The negative imagery of the third stanza is a stark contrast to the first two stanzas. Here the poem draws the visual image of a modern "Dirty British coaster" to focus on the griminess and suffocation of modern civilization. This spray-swept ship is loaded with materials that will eventually pollute the earth with noise and smoke. The smoke-stack of the coaster (line 11) and the firewood it is carrying suggest the creation of choking smog. The Tyne coal (line 13) and road-rails (line 14) suggest the noise and smoke of puffing railroad engines. As if this were not enough, the "pig-lead" (line 14) to be used in various industrial processes indicates not just more unpleasantness, but also something more poisonous and deadly. In contrast to the lush and stately imagery of the first two stanzas, the images in the third stanza invite the conclusion that people now, when the "Dirty British coaster" butts through the English Channel, are surrounded and threatened by visual, olfactory, and auditory pollution.

The poem thus establishes its negative view of the present through images of sight, smell, and sound. The images of motion are in agreement with the negative impression of modern commercial life, for in stanzas 1 and 2 the quinquereme is "rowing" and the galleon is "dipping." These participles describing motion suggest dignity and lightness. The British coaster, however, is "butting," an image of motion indicating bull-like hostility and blind force. These, together with all the other images, focus the poem's negative views of today's consumer-oriented life. The facts that life for both the ancient Palestinians and the renaissance Spaniards included slavery (of those men rowing the quinquereme) and piracy (by those Spanish "explorers" who exploited the natives of the Isthmus) should probably not be emphasized as a protest against Masefield's otherwise valid contrasts in images. His final commentary may

[□] Thesis sentence.

hence be thought of as the banging of his "cheap tin trays" as a percussive climax for the oppressive images crowding too large a portion of modern lives.

Commentary on the Essay

The introductory paragraph presents the central idea that Masefield uses his images climactically to lead to his negative view of modern commercialism. The thesis sentence indicates that the topics to be developed are those of (1) lushness, and (2) starkness. Another possible way of developing such an essay, not shown, might have been to classify according to types, such as those of sight and sound. The method illustrated here, however, is to use a category that includes references to imagery of any type.

Paragraphs 2 and 3 form a unit in which the lushness and exoticism of the images in stanzas 1 and 2 of the poem are stressed. All the examples, derived directly from the poem, emphasize the qualities of Masefield's images. The discussion presented in paragraphs 2 and 3 illustrates no more than the minimal use of imagination needed to make adequate sense of the images. Thus, in the real world the peacocks of stanza 1 would have had feathers containing a number of bright, arresting colors, but these colors are not stressed in the sample essay beyond a reference to the general colorfulness of these birds. Ivory would unquestionably have been sculpted into various statues and ornaments, but because no mention is made by Masefield to any such shapes, the sample essay does not try to go beyond Masefield's general reference to "ivory." His images, in short, are considered only as they evoke an impression of lushness and richness, not as they might be further imaginatively amplified. *Not specific pictures.*

The fourth paragraph stresses the contrast of Masefield's images in stanza 3 with those of stanzas 1 and 2. To this end the paragraph illustrates the need for a high enough degree of imaginative reconstruction to develop an understanding of this contrast. The unpleasantness, annoyance, and even the danger of the cargoes mentioned in stanza 3 are therefore emphasized as the qualities evoked by the images. *Suggested*

The last paragraph demonstrates that the imagery of motion—not much stressed in the poem—is in agreement with the rest of Masefield's imagery. As a demonstration of the need for fair, impartial judgment, the conclusion introduces the possible objection that Masefield's imagistic portraits may be slanted because they include not a full but a partial view of their respective historical periods. This demurrer, however, is not emphasized. Thus the concluding paragraph adds balance to the analysis illustrated in paragraphs 2, 3, and 4.

16

Rhetorical Figures: Metaphor and Simile

The word *figure* is derived from a word that originally signified the shaping of clay. Today the word still retains this sense of form or shape throughout all its meanings. We use the word to refer to pictures or illustrations, calculations, numbers, estimates, body shapes, noted persons, and patterns of thought. The term **figurative language** is used to describe expressions that conform to a particular pattern or form, and these patterns, each of which has a special name, have become the tools of rhetoric and poetry. Briefly, they are intended to create force in a poem, to make the poem effective and persuasive.

There are many rhetorical figures, also called *devices*, but the two most important ones are **metaphor** and **simile**. Both of these are ways of making comparisons. The word *metaphor* is derived from the Greek *meta*, signifying "change," and *pherein*, "to bear or carry." A metaphor therefore is a change or transformation of some sort, in effect the equation of one thing with another. The sentence "All the arts are sisters," for example, contains a metaphor that emphasizes the close family relationship between the major arts—writing, music, sculpture, painting, architecture, and acting. Notice that the metaphor is not that the arts are *like* sisters, but rather that the arts *are* sisters. The phrase thus *transforms* the arts into a family. If it asserted that "the arts are *like* sisters," it would be a simile rather than a metaphor. In general, however, the terms *metaphor* and *metaphorical language* refer to all types of rhetorical comparisons, whether metaphors or similes.

The word *simile* is derived from the Latin *similis*, meaning "of the same kind." The key element in the word is the root *sim*, meaning "one." A simile is hence a comparison designed to indicate the sameness or oneness of two things that at first might appear totally dissimilar. You can remember the meaning of *simile* quite easily if you think of the closely related words *resemblance* and *similarity*. Remember that a simile is an expression that emphasizes *comparison* and *similarity*, whereas metaphor is an *equation*. The characteristic of simile is the use of words such as *like*, *as*, *as if*, or *as when* to introduce the comparison. Thus the sentence, "I'm like a ship on the oceans tossed" (a line from John Gay's *The Beggar's Opera*) asks the reader or listener to see that the speaker feels out of personal control. He or she is compelled by external forces that seem to be overwhelming, just as a ship on the high seas may be thrown about uncontrollably and threatened with destruction during rough weather. Because the simile is introduced by *like*, the emphasis is on the *similarity* of the person and the ship, not the *identification* of the two or the *transformation* of one into another.

IMAGERY, METAPHOR, AND SIMILE

To see the relationship of metaphor and simile to imagery (see Chapter 15, on imagery), you should realize that the purpose of poetry is to extend, broaden, deepen, enrich, and expand the consciousnesses and souls of the many readers who will experience many poems over many years. The use of imagery is a direct way to this goal, for imagery refers to vivid and readily imagined descriptions of actions, places, and objects. Through the use of imagery, poets make their poems accurate, vivid, and memorable.

By extension, metaphors and similes enable poets to reach out into images and human experience that go beyond the imagery that would normally be expected within the confines of the announced topic of a given poem. In effect, these figures of speech are a means by which the poets may connect something to be communicated—an observation, attitude, idea, feeling, or action—with a new insight that is made plain through the comparison of simile or the equation of metaphor. In this way, poets may reach directly into the experiences and imaginations of their readers to shed a new light on something that has not been seen in quite this way in the past. These figures are therefore a major means by which poets use language as an extension into ideas and emotions that otherwise might remain difficult and perhaps even unknown. They are a mode of expression, but more fundamentally they are an inseparable part of the way of seeing the world anew that is the special contribution of genuinely fine poets. Note

For example, to communicate a character's joy and excitement, the sentence "She was happy" is accurate but not interesting or effective. A more vivid way of saying the same thing might be to use an image of an action, such as, "She jumped for joy." This image gives us a concrete picture of an action—a kinesthetic image—that a person might perform as a demonstration of happiness. An even better way of communicating happiness, however, would be to introduce a comparison, such as this simile: "She felt as if she had just inherited five million tax-free dollars." Because readers can quickly grasp the combination of excitement, disbelief, exhilaration, and joy that such an event would bring, they can also sense the true depth of the happiness the user of the simile is expressing.

As a poetic parallel, let us use John Keats's poem "On First Looking into Chapman's Homer." Keats wrote the poem after he first read John Chapman's translations of *The Iliad* and *The Odyssey*, epic poems attributed to the ancient Greek epic poet Homer. His main idea is that Chapman not only translated Homer's words but also transmitted his greatness. A brief paraphrase of the poem is this:

> I have enjoyed much art and read much European literature, and have been told that Homer is the best writer of all, but not knowing Greek, I could not genuinely appreciate his works until I discovered them in Chapman's translation. To me, this experience was exciting and awe-inspiring.

But this paraphrase in no way conveys Keats's true sense of wonder. Contrast the paraphrase with the sonnet as Keats wrote it:

JOHN KEATS (1795–1821)

On First Looking into Chapman's Homer   *1816*

Much have I travell'd in the realms of gold,
   And many goodly states and kingdoms seen;
   Round many western islands have I been
Which bards in fealty to Apollo° hold.
Oft of one wide expanse had I been told   5
   That deep-brow'd Homer ruled as his demesne;°
   Yet did I never breathe its pure serene°
Till I heard Chapman speak out loud and bold:
Then felt I like some watcher of the skies
   When a new planet swims into his ken;°   10
Or like stout Cortez° when with eagle eyes
   He star'd at the Pacific—and all his men
Look'd at each other with a wild surmise—
   Silent, upon a peak in Darien.

ON FIRST LOOKING INTO CHAPMAN'S HOMER. George Chapman (c. 1560–1634) published his powerful Elizabethan translations of Homer's *Iliad* in 1612 and *Odyssey* in 1614–1615.   4 *bards in fealty to Apollo*: writers who are sworn subjects of Apollo, the Greek god of light, music, poetry, and prophecy.   6 *demesne*: realm, estate.   7 *serene*: a clear expanse of air; also grandeur, clarity.   10 *ken*: field of sight.   11 *Cortez*: Hernando Cortez (1485–1547), a Spanish general and the conquerer of Mexico. Keats has confused him with Vasco de Balboa (c. 1475–1519), the first European to see the Pacific Ocean (in 1510) from Darien, an old name for the Isthmus of Panama.

QUESTIONS

1. Explain the metaphor of land and travel that Keats develops in lines 1–6. Be careful to consider the words *realms*, *states*, *kingdoms*, *islands*, *expanse*, and *demesne*.

2. In what sense is Chapman as a "loud and bold" speaker to be considered metaphorical?

3. It was customary during the days of absolute monarchs to use the word *serene* in reference to a ruler, as in "her serene majesty." In what way does Keats use the word in line 7? How is it possible, except in a metaphorical sense, to "breathe" serene? What do you think Keats intended by this phraseology?

4. What is the effect of the similes in lines 9–10 and 11–14? Is Keats successful in these figures at communicating a sense of excitement upon a new discovery? Create a simile of your own to express a feeling about discovery; how does yours compare with Keats's?

5. Describe Keats's metaphorical use of *swims* in line 10. What might have been the impact if he had used words like *drifts*, *floats*, *flows*, or *wanders*?

6. Keats here confuses Cortez with Balboa. How does this confusion affect the meaning or impact of the poem? Must a poet be an accurate historian to write effective verse?

7. What is being discovered in this poem? To what extent is this process of discovery a universal experience?

Look at the metaphors and similes in this poem, and use your imagination to experience them fully. Let the similes of discovery, for example, take you as far as they can, for your understanding can be deepened and enriched only by fully opening your imagination, unlocked by Keats's comparisons. You can see that if all Keats had written were our paraphrase, we would probably pay little attention to it. In the paraphrase we can find no justification for either the value of reading poetry or the excitement of reading Homer in Chapman's translation. In considering the poem, however, we find references to objects and events that can interest and stimulate us. Thus the metaphor "realms of gold" suggests that the study of literature and art is to be valued highly. Similarly, the similes of lines 9–14 help us to *imagine* the exhilaration, wonder, and joy we would have felt if we had suddenly discovered a new planet, or if we had been the first European explorers to see the Pacific along with Balboa (not Cortez). By presenting these similes, Keats has extended the simple act of reading an ancient author in translation into an area of thought that draws upon our capacities to dream and to feel. He has enlarged us.

VEHICLE AND TENOR

To describe the relationship between a writer's ideas and the metaphors
and similes chosen to objectify them, two useful terms have been coined
by I. A. Richards (in *The Philosophy of Rhetoric*). First is the **tenor,** which
is the totality of ideas and attitudes not only of the literary speaker but
also of the author. Second is the **vehicle,** or the details that carry the
tenor. For example, the tenor of the similes in the last six lines of Keats's
sonnet is awe and wonder; the vehicle is the reference to astronomical
and geographical discovery.

CHARACTERISTICS OF METAPHORICAL LANGUAGE

Almost all good writing uses some metaphorical language. Such language
is most vital, however, in imaginative writing—particularly poetry, where
it promotes understanding and shapes the reader's responses.

As we saw in Chapter 15, images refer to sensory experience that
may lead to many associations. A single word naming a flower, say *rose*,
usually evokes a positive response. A person might think of the color of
a rose, recall its smell, associate it with the summer sun and pleasant days,
and recall the love and respect that a bouquet of roses means as a gift.
However, the word *rose* is not a metaphor or simile until its associations
are used in a comparative or analogical way, as in the opening lines of
the following poem:

ROBERT BURNS (1759–1796)

O My Luve's Like a Red, Red Rose   1796

O my Luve's like a red, red rose,
  That's newly sprung in June:
O my Luve's like the melodie
  That's sweetly play'd in tune.

As fair art thou, my bonnie lass,   5
  So deep in luve am I;
And I will luve thee still, my Dear,
  Till a'° the seas gang° dry.   *all; go*

Till a' the seas gang dry, my Dear,
  And the rocks melt wi'° the sun: *with*   10
And I will luve thee still, my Dear,
  While the sands o' life shall run.

And fare thee weel, my only Luve!
  And fare thee weel, awhile!
And I will come again, my Luve,   15
  Tho' it were ten thousand mile!

QUESTIONS

1. What is the situation of the poem? What sort of person is the speaker? How is the situation here similar to that of Donne's "A Valediction: Forbidding Mourning" (p. 598)?

2. Is there a shift in the person being addressed from stanza 1 to the remaining stanzas? If so, what is the shift; how does the listener change? How are the last three stanzas related to the first?

3. In light of the character and background of the speaker, do the two similes that open the poem seem common or unusual? If they are what you might expect, does that fact diminish their value in any way?

4. Consider the speaker's metaphors in lines 9–16 of the passage of time and the traveling of great distance. How does the speaker use these metaphors as a means of assurance? How do the metaphors assist in the comprehension of the speaker's character?

Here, in understanding the feelings the speaker is expressing about his sweetheart, we are entitled to bring to our minds all the possible associations that we might have with roses. Compared with winter's drabness and leaflessness, late spring and early summer are lush with new growth. Perhaps one of the loveliest of the flowers of this period is the red rose, whose bright color contrasts most highly with the monochrome of winter. When roses appear, then, they signal the development of summer and consequent growth. When we consider that the rose possesses lovely form and odor in addition to color, we have expanded the simile fully enough to enable us to understand the poet's enthusiasm about his sweetheart.

    To see how metaphors similarly compress the thought of poets, let us look at a poem by Shakespeare.

WILLIAM SHAKESPEARE (1564–1616)

Sonnet 30: When to the Sessions of Sweet Silent Thought   *1609*

When to the sessions° of sweet silent thought,	*holding of court, legal hearing*
I summon up remembrance of things past,	
I sigh the lack of many a thing I sought,	
And with old woes new wail° my dear time's waste:	*lament anew*
Then can I drown an eye (un-used to flow)	5

For precious friends hid in death's dateless° night,   *endless*
And weep afresh love's long since cancelled° woe,   *paid in full*
And moan th'expense° of many a vanished sight.   *cost, loss*
Then can I grieve at grievances foregone,
And heavily° from woe to woe tell° o'er   *sadly; count*   10
The sad account of fore-bemoanèd moan,
Which I new pay, as if not paid before.
    But if the while I think on thee (dear friend)
    All losses are restored, and sorrows end.

QUESTIONS

1. Explain the metaphor embodied in the words *sessions* and *summon* in lines 1–2. Where are the *sessions* being held? What is a *summons* for remembrance?

2. Does it seem that *sigh* (line 3), *wail* (line 4), and *drown an eye* (line 5) are excessive as expressions of regret about failed opportunity and misapplied time? If so, what conclusion are you expected to draw? Is the speaker being comic? Serious? Is he trying to put his introspection into an acceptable perspective? Explain.

3. What is the metaphor brought out by *cancelled* in line 7? In what sense might a *woe* of love be cancelled? What is the reference of the metaphor brought out by *expense* in line 8? Consider the meaning of the expense of vanished sights.

4. What sort of transactions does Shakespeare ask you to imagine in the metaphor of lines 9–12? Does the metaphor cast any new light on the sadness and regret that a person might feel about past mistakes and sorrows?

5. What role does the speaker assign to the "dear friend" of line 13 in relation to the metaphors of the poem?

6. Consider the entire poem as a tribute to the friend being addressed and to friendship in general. Does it seem that the friend can genuinely restore the speaker's spirits which are depressed over past losses and regrets, or does it seem that the claims of the speaker are made as a rather fully developed compliment?

    The word *sessions* in "when to the sessions of sweet silent thought" is the legal name for that period of time in which judges, juries, lawyers, and witnesses carry out the court's business ("the court is now in *session*"; think also of "school is now in *session*"). A "summons" (see *summon* in line 2) is an official command that a person appear before a court, usually to stand as a defendant for some alleged wrongdoing or as a witness in a case. Through the use of these metaphors, the speaker in Shakespeare's sonnet is saying that in his retrospective and reflective moments he sends a summons into his memory to compel his recollections to appear in his consciousness so that they may be newly considered and judged. In a way,

Shakespeare's speaker asks us to think of his "sweet silent thought" as a period when he somehow sits in judgment over his memories, which have been summoned into the present. The implication of this metaphor is that the total experience of a person is constantly alive and present; that the memory is like an entire society with wrongs, shortcomings, and transgressions; that judgment and reassessment are constant living processes; and that the consciousness of individuals is not an unchanging, solid state but is instead a series of conflicting or contrasting impulses.

This development of Shakespeare's metaphor may seem at first like a great deal more than Shakespeare intended; indeed, we have used more words in prose than he used in verse. Once we have understood his language, however, our minds are unlocked, and we may then allow ourselves this kind of expansion as we consider the full ramifications of the comparison or equation.

INDIVIDUAL UNDERSTANDING
AND METAPHORICAL LANGUAGE

Personal and particular responses may also become a part of the reader's comprehension and consideration of metaphorical language. Some readers may have special knowledge that might give them further ideas about the figurative language of any poet. If these ideas are consistent with the poet's metaphors—that is, if they do not contain details that are not a logical extension of the poet's frames of reference and do not involve anything especially unusual or idiosyncratic—they are relevant.

For example, suppose that you are considering Shakespeare's metaphors in "When to the sessions" more fully than we have done, and that you have had some experience with courtroom procedures. Suppose further that you have thought about the necessity of preserving the rules of evidence, such as the swearing in of witnesses and the consequent assurance of true testimony on penalty of perjury. Even though Shakespeare does not mention such courtroom procedures, you could relate these procedures to the general need that all of us have to be totally honest with ourselves in considering the past facts of our lives. Certainly this observation would belong in the development of parallels between personal introspection and the activities of a court of law. Shakespeare has invited his readers to develop as many such parallels as they can.

It is by this kind of development that metaphorical language creates insights into the experiences and ideas the poet is presenting; also, as a necessary by-product of the productive thought needed to appreciate poetry, the process may create additional insights into the metaphor or simile itself.

DEGREES OF DEVELOPMENT

As you look at poetry for metaphor and simile, you will find that these devices are developed to varying degrees. Often you will encounter no more than a single word. Shakespeare's use of the word *tell* in line 10 of "when to the sessions," for example, indicates a way of counting out past sorrows in the same way that a bank teller counts ("tells") money. Similarly, Fray Angelico Chavez uses a single-word metaphor in the last line of "Rattlesnake" (p. 610): "coil of cloisonné!" The poet here refers to the danger of a rattlesnake coiled and ready to strike, but in using the word *cloisonné* he introduces an equation of the snake and a beautiful artwork characterized by segments of colored enamel separated by edges of metal. At the same time, then, the poet acknowledges the danger offered by the coiled snake and recognizes its dramatic beauty.

Sometimes a single word will reach out into the area of nearby words and thereby incorporate them into the metaphorical system required by the word. Thus, in line 4 of Keats's "On First Looking into Chapman's Homer," Keats introduces the word *fealty*. Here he refers to the medieval feudal system of holding land. A person who was granted the right to manage an estate would hold that land in *fealty* to his lord. That is, his control would be at the lord's pleasure and with the lord's permission; the landholder would then owe loyalty and knightly service to the lord. In a real sense, any benefits that the person enjoyed from the land came about as a direct result of the lord's generosity and favor. This metaphorical equation of holding land and exercising one's ability as a poet enables us to understand lines 3 and 4 of the poem in the following way: "I have read many of the best works of European literature in the various genres ("western islands"), such as fiction, tragedy, comedy, and farce, and lyric, epic, and discursive poetry, all of which show that their authors ("bards") had received the supreme effects of divine inspiration ("in fealty to Apollo hold")." Without an awareness of the metaphor, Keats's lines would be difficult to understand.

In some instances, you may find metaphor or simile embodied in a pun, that is, in a word that is used in two different senses at the same time. A notable example may be seen in a famous line from Alexander Pope's mock epic poem *The Rape of the Lock* (1712, 1717), where Pope uses the word *stain* with two separate meanings, one metaphorical, the other normal: "Or stain her honor, or her new brocade." By employing the metaphorical meaning of *stain* in the first half of the line, with the sense of damaging a reputation or sense of self-esteem as a person of virtue, Pope establishes a high degree of importance regarding the potential danger that might befall the heroine of the poem, Belinda. By switching the meaning in the second half of the line, however, so that the word *stain* is understood in its usual sense of soiling or spotting, he trivializes the apparent danger. The contrast between the metaphorical and literal meaning creates surprise and humor, and in addition adds satiric disapproval of the values that would cause a person (in this line a mythical character whom Pope called a "sylph") to regard both dangers as equally important.

Most often, poets use metaphors and similes and then leave the interpretation to the reader, who may develop, linger over, and expand the figures. Occasionally, however, a poet will carry out the expansion, using the poem itself as the explication of the equation or comparison. Perhaps the most celebrated internal metaphorical development is in John Donne's "Valediction: Forbidding Mourning."

JOHN DONNE (1572–1631)

A Valediction: Forbidding Mourning   *1633*

As virtuous men pass mildly away,
  And whisper to their souls to go,
Whilst some of their sad friends do say
  The breath goes now, and some say, No;

So let us melt, and make no noise,   5
  No tear-floods, nor sigh-tempests move,
'Twere profanation of our joys
  To tell the laiety our love.

Moving of th'earth° brings harms and fears,   *earthquakes*
  Men reckon what it did and meant;   10
But trepidation of the spheres,°
  Though greater far, is innocent.°   *harmless*

Dull sublunary° lovers' love
  (Whose soul is sense°) cannot admit
Absence, because it doth remove   15
  Those things which elemented° it.

But we by a love so much refined
  That our selves know not what it is,
Inter-assured of the mind,
  Care less, eyes, lips, and hands to miss.   20

Our two souls therefore, which are one,
  Though I must go, endure not yet

A VALEDICTION: FORBIDDING MOURNING.   11 *trepidation of the spheres*: In Ptolemaic astronomy, before telescopes were used in astronomical study, all planets were assumed to have orbits that were perfectly circular. Apparent irregularities that were actually caused by elliptical orbits were explained by the concept of trepidation, or a quivering of the bodies during orbit.   13 *sublunary*: living beneath the moon; earthly.   14 *sense*: the body as opposed to the mind or spirit.   16 *elemented*: composed, made [it] up.

A breach, but an expansion,
  Like gold to airy thinness beat.

If they be two, they are two so   25
  As stiff twin compasses are two;
Thy soul, the fixt foot, makes no show
  To move, but doth, if th'other do.

And though it in the center sit,
  Yet when the other far doth roam,   30
It leans and harkens after it,
  And grows erect, as that comes home.

Such wilt thou be to me, who must
  Like th'other foot, obliquely run;
Thy firmness draws my circle just,   35
  And makes me end where I begun.

QUESTIONS

1. What is the situation envisioned as the occasion for the poem? Who is talking to whom? What is their relationship?

2. What is the intention of the first two stanzas? Do you think the phrases "tear-floods" and "sigh-tempests" might be sufficiently comic to cause a stopping of tears?

3. Describe the effect of the opening simile about men on their death beds.

4. What is the metaphor of stanza 3 (lines 9–12)? In what sense might the "trepidation of the spheres" be less harmful than the parting of the lovers?

5. In lines 13–20 there is a comparison making the love of the speaker and his sweetheart superior to the love of average lovers. What is the basis for the speaker's claim?

6. What is the comparison begun by the word *refined* in line 17 and continued by the simile in line 24?

7. How seriously do you take the discussion of souls in lines 21–24? What perspective on love is developed here? Does this idea about love seem a climax of the claims made in lines 13–16?

8. The simile in lines 25–36 is one of the most famous in English poetry. Why should it be so? Is the comparison one you would ordinarily expect about lovers? Does the development by Donne seem consistent and appropriate? To what degree does the simile shed any new light on the relationship between people in love?

In the last three stanzas of this poem, Donne develops an extended simile comparing a man and woman in love with a compass used to draw circles. As you read Donne's development of the simile, you might consider it in relationship to the following drawings of a compass in use.

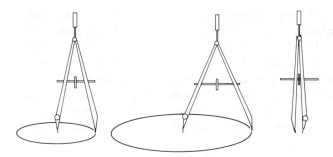

Bear in mind that the key feature of the comparison is that the central point of the circle is occupied by the leg of the compass representing the woman and that the moving circle is traced out by the moving leg representing the speaker, who is about to travel. You might also note that the handle of the compass joins both legs (so that even if the circle is large, the two legs of the compass are always joined together at the top), and that the circle represents the perfection of love between two people (often symbolized by the wedding ring). If you keep all these relationships in mind, you will see with what detail Donne has worked out the development of his simile.

In studying poems for metaphors and similes, you should be aware of what are called "dead" metaphors, words that were originally metaphorical but that have lost their original force. For example, the word *lady* refers now mainly to an adult woman. Originally, however, the Anglo-Saxon word that has given us *lady* meant "the kneader of the loaf" (*hlæf dige*); the creation of this word was apparently based on the fact that the principal woman of the household was responsible for the management of all the domestic affairs. Similarly, the word *lord*, which is retained often in reference to the deity, meant "the guardian of the loaf" (*hlæf weard*); in other words, the principal man of the household was responsible for the safety and security of the house and its occupants. Thus, the Anglo-Saxon terms *lady* and *lord* were originally metaphors that equated or transposed the *person* into the *function* he or she enacted in the household. In addition, as was noted earlier, the word *figure* has retained its original sense of form or shape throughout the many meanings that we attach to the word today. These are only a few of an almost endless list of "dead" metaphors.

Whereas in common speech we employ such words without much consideration of their original force, in poetry the case is somewhat different. Quite often poets draw on the original sense of words in their use of language. Thus, for example, in the opening line of Donne's "Valediction: Forbidding Mourning"—"As virtuous men pass mildly away"—the word *virtuous* refers to high moral character, but it also retains some of its original meaning derived from the Latin word *vir*, "man." Thus it has the sense of "men of exemplary manly qualities," that is, typical excellence appropriate to the highest, most distinguished men. Similarly, *mildly* here at first suggests "not harmfully," but the word originally referred to something soft. Thus an additional meaning of the word is "easefully," "gently," "quietly," or "softly." By looking carefully at each word in this way to determine any origins in metaphor, you can add layers of meaning and association that may not have seemed apparent at first reading. Indeed, one of the glories of poetry is the way in which such ordinary and common words take on new life and richness because of their metaphorical beginnings.

READING, THINKING, AND USING A DICTIONARY

Despite what we have just said, you will likely discover that an early and exhaustive interpretation of metaphors and similes will prove difficult. However, the process will be easier if you dwell on the poem a bit, use your ingenuity, and consult a dictionary to uncover meanings that may not be apparent at first. In Shakespeare's line "And heavily from woe to woe tell o'er," for example, you may miss the metaphorical meaning of *tell* entirely unless you are aware that the word does not mean just "talk" but also means to keep records by counting, in the way a bank *teller* counts and keeps a record of money. Thus Shakespeare equates the recalling of past occasions of unhappiness with the commercial process of record keeping and accounting. You can easily miss a metaphor like this one because the word is a common one that makes sense itself without further consideration as a metaphor. Be alert, therefore. Use your dictionary often. Allow the similes and metaphors to resonate in your mind. Try some possibilities, and if they do not seem probable, be willing to reject them. But keep working on applying new potential meanings that occur to you. Above all, never let the similes and metaphors escape from your thought.

POEMS FOR STUDY

WILLIAM SHAKESPEARE (1564–1616)

Sonnet 18: Shall I Compare Thee to a Summer's Day?   1609

Shall I compare thee to a summer's day?
Thou art more lovely and more temperate:
Rough winds do shake the darling buds of May,
And summer's lease hath all too short a date:
Sometime too hot the eye of heaven° shines,   *the sun*   5
And often is his gold complexion dimmed;

And every fair from fair sometime declines,
By chance, or nature's changing course, untrimmed;
But thy eternal summer shall not fade,   10
Nor lose possession of that fair thou owest°;   *ownest*
Nor shall Death brag thou wander'st in his shade,
When in eternal lines to time thou growest:
  So long as men can breathe, or eyes can see,
  So long lives this, and this gives life to thee.   15

QUESTIONS

1. What is a possible dramatic situation out of which this poem springs?
2. Is the comparison offered in the first line a common or uncommon one?
3. What are the metaphors in lines 1–8 designed to assert? Why is the speaker emphasizing the brevity of life?
4. What is meant by *temperate* (line 2)? What sense of fragility is brought out by the metaphor of "darling buds of May"?
5. What is the metaphorical meaning of *lease* and *date* in line 4?
6. In lines 5 and 6, what happens to the sun, and why is the comparison appropriate to the person being addressed?
7. How does the topic shift in line 9? What new metaphor is introduced in line 11?
8. What is the relationship of the last two lines to the rest of the sonnet? What is the *this* that gives the life that will last beyond a day in summer? What sort of immortality is it that Shakespeare's speaker is exalting in the sonnet?

THOMAS CAMPION (1567–1620)

Cherry Ripe   *1617*

There is a garden in her face,
Where roses and white lilies grow;
A heavenly paradise is that place,
Wherein all pleasant fruits do flow.
There cherries grow, which none may buy   5
Till "Cherry ripe" themselves do cry.

Those cherries fairly do enclose
Of orient pearl a double row;
Which when her lovely laughter shows,
They look like rosebuds filled with snow.   10
Yet them nor peer nor prince can buy
Till "Cherry ripe" themselves do cry.

Her eyes like angels watch them still;
Her brows like bended bows do stand,
Threatening with piercing frowns to kill   15
All that attempt, with eye or hand,
Those sacred cherries to come nigh
Till "Cherry ripe" themselves do cry.

QUESTIONS

1. What does the metaphor of the garden signify? What is the meaning of "roses and white lilies"?
2. *Paradise* originally referred to a walled-in garden. How is this metaphor appropriate to the lady's mouth? What are the "pleasant fruits" of line 4?
3. What is the metaphor of "orient pearl"? How is the simile comparing the lady's smile to "rosebuds filled with snow" appropriate?
4. What is the compliment intended by the comparison of the lady's eyes to guardian angels, and her brows being "like bended bows"? Do these figures suggest anger, or protectiveness, or both?
5. What does the metaphor of cherries suggest? Why may no one buy them until they cry "cherry ripe"? Does ripeness refer to age? Maturity? Love? Anything else? In stanza 2, does the "Cherry ripe" refer to nobility or to trustworthiness, or to both? In stanza 3, does "Cherry ripe" refer to honesty or spiritual worthiness, or both?
6. Does the progression of ideas about "Cherry ripe" through the three stanzas signify only desire, only admiration, only worship, or a combination of these? Explain.

HENRY KING (1592–1669)

Sic Vita   *1657*

Like to the falling of a star,
Or as the flights of eagles are,
Or like the fresh spring's gaudy hue,
Or silver drops of morning dew,
Or like a wind that chafes the flood,   5
Or bubbles which on water stood:
Even such is man, whose borrowed light
Is straight called in, and paid to night.
   The wind blows out, the bubble dies;
   The spring entombed in autumn lies;   10
   The dew dries up, the star is shot;
   The flight is past, and man forgot.

QUESTIONS

1. Consider the following groups of lines as distinct sections of this poem: 1–6; 7–8; 9–12. Explain causes for these divisions.
2. How many similes do you find in lines 1–6? Describe the range of references; that is, from what sources are the similes derived? What do all these similes (and references) have in common?
3. Explain the two metaphors in lines 7–8. (One is brought out by the words *borrowed*, *called in*, and *paid*; the other by *light* and *night*.)
4. Explain the continuation in lines 9–12 of the similes in 1–6. Do you think that these last four lines are essential, or might the poem have been successfully concluded with line 8? Explain.
5. What point does this poem make about humanity? In what ways do the similes in the poem help explore these ideas and bring them to life?

EDMUND WALLER (1606–1687)

Go, Lovely Rose   *1645*

Go, lovely rose!
Tell her that wastes her time and me
  That now she knows,
When I resemble° her to thee,   *compare*
How sweet and fair she seems to be.   5

  Tell her that's young,
And shuns to have her graces spied,
  That hadst thou sprung
In deserts, where no men abide,
Thou must have uncommended died.   10

  Small is the worth
Of beauty from the light retired;
  Bid her come forth,
Suffer herself to be desired,
And not blush so to be admired.   15

  Then die! that she
The common fate of all things rare
  May read in thee;
How small a part of time they share
That are so wondrous sweet and fair.   20

QUESTIONS

1. What is the situation in this poem? Who or what is being addressed? To whom is the speaker sending the rose? Why does he think that the rose is the proper object with which to embody his ideas?

2. In stanza 1, what qualities does the speaker attach to the rose?

3. What negative attitude is the speaker responding to in stanza 2? Is the message logical that the rose is to deliver to the sweetheart?

4. In what way may the reference to darkness in lines 11–12 be considered metaphorical? Does the imperative in lines 13–15 follow from this comparison? Is the speaker asking for an abandonment of all modesty?

5. Consider the cut flower metaphor of lines 16–20. In what way is this metaphor parallel to the life of the sweetheart and to human life generally? In what way or ways is the comparison not apt?

6. "Go, Lovely Rose" is in the so-called *carpe diem* tradition, that is, a tradition of living to the hilt today because tomorrow we may die. What do the ideas in this poem contribute to this tradition? Is the poem to be considered as one of earthly vitality or as one of philosophical reflection?

GEORGE GORDON, LORD BYRON (1788–1824)

The Destruction of Sennacherib° [*Senakerrib*]   1815

[*Cruel*]   [*, Innocent*]
The Assyrian came down like the wolf on the fold, [*simile*]
And his cohorts were gleaming in purple and gold;
[*Human power is mighty*] And the sheen of their spears was like stars on the sea,
When the blue wave rolls nightly on deep Galilee.

Like the leaves of the forest when summer is green,   5
That host with their banners at sunset were seen:
Like the leaves of the forest when autumn hath blown,
That host on the morrow lay withered and strown. [*like leaves*]

[*Divine Power – as natural as the seasons*] For the Angel of Death spread his wings on the blast, [*No excessive detail about their deaths.*]
And breathed in the face of the foe as he passed;   10
And the eyes of the sleepers waxed deadly and chill,
And their hearts but once heaved—and for ever grew still!

And there lay the steed with his nostril all wide,
But through it there rolled not the breath of his pride;
And the foam of his gasping lay white on the turf,   15
And cold as the spray of the rock-beating surf.

And there lay the rider distorted and pale, [*Focuses upon the one man —*]
With the dew on his brow, and the rust on his mail;
And the tents were all silent, the banners alone,
The lances unlifted, the trumpet unblown.   20

THE DESTRUCTION OF SENNACHERIB. Sennacherib was king of the ancient Near Eastern empire of Assyria from 705 to 681 B.C. He laid siege to Jerusalem in about 702 B.C., even though King Hezekiah had already rendered tribute to Assyria. According to 2 Kings 19:35–36, a miracle occurred to save the besieged Hebrews: "the angel of the Lord went out and smote . . . [185,000 Assyrian soldiers]; and when they [the Hebrews] arose early in the morning, behold, they [the Assyrians] were all dead corpses."

And the widows of Ashur° are loud in their wail, *Mentions this only, focuses*
And the idols are broke in the temple of Baal;° *instead upon the theme:*
And the might of the Gentile, unsmote by the sword, *God's protection of the*
Hath <u>melted like snow</u> in the glance of the Lord! *Hebrews against injustice*

21 *Ashur*: the land of the Assyrians.   22 *Baal*: a god who supposedly controlled weather and storms.

QUESTIONS

1. What is the effect of the opening simile? Is the comparison between the Assyrian armies and a wolf menacing a sheepfold appropriate?

2. The similes of lines 3–6 are designed to emphasize the size and power of the Assyrian army; the simile in 7–8 is designed to emphasize the death of the army. What are the relationship and effect of these similes on the comparative power of human beings and God?

3. In lines 9–20 Byron emphasizes the details of the death of the Assyrian army and their horses. Do these details seem excessive, or justifiable? Why?

4. Compare the last stanza of this poem with the conclusion of "Sir Patrick Spens" (p. 465). How are the conclusions similar? To what extent do they evoke similar feelings? In what way does the reference to Baal, a pagan idol, undercut these feelings in Byron's poem?

OGDEN NASH (1902–1971) *A humorous look at the appropriateness of metaphors & similes.*

Very Like a Whale – *Polonius agrees (ingratiatingly) with* 1934
Hamlet that the cloud looks like a whale.

One thing that literature would be greatly the better for
Would be a more restricted employment by authors of <u>simile and metaphor.</u>
Authors of all races, be they Greeks, Romans, Teutons or Celts,
Can't seem just to say that anything is the thing it is but have to go out of their
    way to say that it is like something else.
What does it mean when we are told   5
That the Assyrian came down like a wolf on the fold?
In the first place, George Gordon Byron had had enough experience
To know that it probably wasn't just one Assyrian, it was a lot of Assyrians.
However, as too many arguments are apt to induce <u>apoplexy</u> and thus hinder
    longevity,
We'll let it pass as one Assyrian for the sake of brevity.   10
Now then, this particular Assyrian, the one whose cohorts were gleaming in purple
    and gold,
Just what does the poet mean when he says he came down like a wolf on the
    fold?
In heaven and earth more than is dreamed of in our philosophy there are a great
    many things,

But I don't imagine that among them there is a wolf with purple and gold cohorts
  or purple and gold anythings.
No, no, Lord Byron, before I'll believe that this Assyrian was actually like a wolf   15
  I must have some kind of proof;
Did he run on all fours and did he have a hairy tail and a big red mouth and big
  white teeth and did he say Woof woof woof? *Looks at it literally.*
Frankly I think it very unlikely, and all you were entitled to say, at the very most,
Was that the Assyrian cohorts came down like a lot of Assyrian cohorts about to
  destroy the Hebrew host.
But that wasn't fancy enough for Lord Byron, oh dear me no, he had to invent a
  lot of figures of speech and then interpolate them,
With the result that whenever you mention Old Testament soldiers to people they   20
  say Oh yes, they're the ones that a lot of wolves dressed up in gold and purple
  ate them.
That's the kind of thing that's being done all the time by poets, from Homer to
  Tennyson;
They're always comparing ladies to lilies and veal to venison.
How about the man who wrote,
* Her little feet stole in and out like mice beneath her petticoat?
Wouldn't anybody but a poet think twice   25
Before stating that his girl's feet were mice?
Then they always say things like that after a winter storm
The snow is a white blanket. Oh it is, is it, all right then, you sleep under a six-
  inch blanket of snow and I'll sleep under a half-inch blanket of unpoetical blanket
  material and we'll see which one keeps warm.
And after that maybe you'll begin to comprehend dimly
What I mean by too much metaphor and simile.   30

Suggests that we use reality as opposed to metaphor to

* *"Belle for John Whitside's Daughter"*

QUESTIONS

1. For the title of this poem, see *Hamlet*, Act 3, Scene 2, where Polonius agrees
   with Hamlet, who disdainfully compares a cloud to a whale. Does this original
   location shed any light on the ideas of Nash's poem?

2. Explain the structure of the poem, using as parts the following divisions:
   lines 1–4; 5–22; 23–26; 27–30.

3. Do you think that Nash is objecting to all metaphors and similes, or simply
   to overelaborate and unnatural ones?

4. A speaker may assume one of many different stances, or personas, when
   speaking, such as that of an oracle, a confidential friend, an ardent lover, a
   leader, or a naive but shrewd homespun philosopher. What is the persona
   assumed by Nash's speaker here? Would the poem be possible as it now
   stands if the persona had been, say, a teacher of literature?

Down to earth, no-nonsense kind of person

5. In line 22 Nash criticizes the comparison of ladies to lilies. See Campion's
   "Cherry Ripe" (p. 603), stanza 1, where the metaphor of white lilies is used,

and also Burns's "O My Luve's Like a Red, Red Rose" (p. 594). In the light of these poems, how strongly should Nash's objections be taken?

6. Sir John Suckling (1609–1642), in an earthy poem "A Ballad upon a Wedding" (1641), is the source of the lines Nash quotes in line 24: "Her feet beneath her petticoat / Like little mice stole in and out." Justify Nash's criticism of this metaphor. By the same token, what might be said in criticism of Robert Herrick's brief poem complimenting the feet of Susanna Southwell (1648), where he wrote, "Her pretty feet / Like snails did creep."

7. What is the method by which Nash criticizes the metaphor of snow being a blanket? By such a literal method of interpretation, could any metaphor or simile be maintained? Why or why not?

8. This poem is comic. How does Nash achieve his goal of amusing the reader?

LANGSTON HUGHES (1902–1967)

From Lenox Avenue Mural
Harlem   *1951*

What happens to a dream deferred?

Does it dry up
like a raisin in the sun?
Or fester like a sore—
And then run?   5
Does it stink like rotten meat?
Or crust and sugar over—
like a syrupy sweet?

Maybe it just sags
like a heavy load.   10

Or does it explode?

QUESTIONS

1. In the light of the black experience with the "American Dream," what do you think is meant by the phrase "dream deferred"?

2. Explain the structure of the poem in terms of the speaker's questions and answers. How is the structure here similar to the one in Shakespeare's sonnet, "Shall I Compare Thee to a Summer's Day" (p. 602)?

3. Explain the similes in lines 3, 4, 6, 8, and 10. Why are these apt comparisons? What sorts of human actions are implied in these figures?

4. What is the meaning of the metaphor in line 11? Why do you think Hughes shifted from similes to a metaphor in this line?

FRAY ANGELICO CHAVEZ (b. 1910)

Rattlesnake   1945

Line of beauty scrawled alive
by God's finger on the sand,
diamond-patterned inlaid band
scrolling inward like a hive—

Stay away,   5
crawl-created,
articulated
coil of cloisonné!

QUESTIONS

1. Consider the metaphors and similes embodied in the following expressions
   in the poem: "line of beauty"; "inlaid band"; "like a hive"; "coil of cloisonné."
   Which of these figures seems favorable? Which unfavorable? Which ominous
   or threatening?
2. Do the two stanzas of the poem seem related or entirely separate? In what
   ways does the conclusion of the first stanza anticipate the responses expressed
   in the second?
3. Consider the metaphor in the first stanza. What is suggested by the word
   scrawled? How is the metaphor appropriate? To what extent is it demeaning
   to our conventional image of God as the creator? How is the metaphor expressed in *scrolling* related to that of *scrawled*?
4. Would you describe this poem as descriptive, impressionistic, or both?
   In what ways is the poem effective? How does metaphor contribute to its impact?

SYLVIA PLATH (1932–1963)

Metaphors   [Speaker is a pregnant woman]   1960

I'm a riddle in nine syllables,
An elephant, a ponderous house,
A melon strolling on two tendrils.
O red fruit, ivory, fine timbers!   [skin] [bones]   [Child]
This loaf's big with its yeasty rising.
Money's new-minted in this fat purse.   5
I'm a means, a stage, a cow in calf.
I've eaten a bag of green apples,   [And swollen up]
Boarded the train there's no getting off.
[pregnancy]

QUESTIONS

1. What evidence can you find in the poem that the speaker here is a woman?
2. The speaker calls herself a "riddle in nine syllables." What is the answer to the riddle? Why nine syllables (as opposed to eight or ten)? In what sense is the poem also a riddle? How are the answers to both riddles related?
3. What do all the metaphors in the poem have in common? How effectively does each one convey part of the feelings and experience of pregnancy? Do they strike you as commonplace or unusual? Why?
4. Which of the metaphors do you find amusing, shocking, or demeaning? What do these suggest about the speaker's attitude toward herself?
5. What aspect of early pregnancy is captured in the "bag of green apples" metaphor (line 8)? What two meanings are suggested by the *stage* metaphor (line 7)? Why is the *train* metaphor (line 9) appropriate to creating life and becoming a parent?

LINDA PASTAN (b. 1932)

Marks   *1978*

My husband gives me an A
for last night's supper,
an incomplete for my ironing,
a B plus in bed.
My son says I am average,   5
an average mother, but if
I put my mind to it
I could improve.
My daughter believes
in Pass/Fail and tells me   10
I pass. Wait 'til they learn
I'm dropping out.

QUESTIONS

1. What metaphor is extended throughout this poem? To what situation does the speaker metaphorically equate housework? What sort of marks does the speaker get?
2. On the basis of the metaphorical "marks," what are the sorts of "courses" on which she is being rated? By whom is she being graded?
3. Consider the son's comments in lines 5–8. Where might such remarks normally be expected?

4. Why is the speaker "dropping out"? What attitude is conveyed at the end of the extended metaphor? To what extent is this conclusion a determined resolution? A concluding joke? Both?

5. What points does this poem explore about the role of wife and mother? In what ways does the extended metaphor make these considerations vivid and palpable?

MARGE PIERCY (b. 1934)

A Work of Artifice   1973

The bonsai tree
in the attractive pot
could have grown eighty feet tall
on the side of a mountain
till split by lightning.   5
But a gardener
carefully pruned it.
It is nine inches high.
Every day as he
whittles back the branches   10
the gardener croons,
It is your nature
to be small and cozy,
domestic and weak;
how lucky, little tree,   15
to have a pot to grow in.
With living creatures
one must begin very early
to dwarf their growth:
the bound feet,   20
the crippled brain,
the hair in curlers,
the hands you
love to touch.

QUESTIONS

1. In what sense may this poem be divided into a second part beginning with line 17? What is a bonsai tree? In what ways is it an apt metaphor for women? The tree "could have grown eighty feet tall." What would be the comparable growth and development of a woman?

2. What do you make of the gardener's song (lines 12–16)? If the bonsai tree were able to respond, would it accept the gardener's consolation for its trun-

cated life? What conclusions about women's lives are implied by the metaphor of the tree?

3. How does the poem shift in method and focus at line 17? To what extent do the four images that follow (lines 20–24) embody the lives of women? What attitude do these images convey?

JUDITH MINTY (b. 1937)

Conjoined   *1981*

> *a marriage poem*

The onion in my cupboard, a monster, actually
two joined under one transparent skin:
each half-round, then flat and deformed
where it pressed and grew against the other.

An accident, like the two-headed calf rooted   5
in one body, fighting to suck at its mother's teats;
or like those other freaks, Chang and Eng,° twins
joined at the chest by skin and muscle, doomed
to live, even make love, together for sixty years.

Do you feel the skin that binds us   10
together as we move, heavy in this house?
To sever the muscle could free one,
but might kill the other. Ah, but men
don't slice onions in the kitchen, seldom see
what is invisible. We cannot escape each other.   15

CONJOINED.   7 *Chang and Eng:* The original and most famous Siamese twins, who were born in 1811. They were never separated but nevertheless fathered twenty-two children. They died in 1874.

QUESTIONS

1. What are the two things—the "us" and "we" of lines 10 and 11—that are conjoined? Since this is "a marriage poem," might they be the man and the woman? Why might they also be considered as the body and soul of the speaker; or the desire to be married and subordinated, on the one hand, and the desire to be free and in control of destiny, on the other?

2. Explore the metaphor of the onion and the similes of the two-headed calf and the Siamese twins. Why do you think the poet introduces the words *monster*, *accident*, and *freaks* into these figures in lines 1, 5, and 7? In what sense do you believe that these words are applicable to the nature and plight of women?

3. Explain what is meant by lines 12 and 13. Does the idea here, together with the last sentence in line 15, represent a reconciliation, a decision to adjust, a reluctant concession, or an angry admission of defeat?

4. Is it true that *all* "men / don't slice onions in the kitchen, seldom see / what is invisible"? Explain.

SEAMUS HEANEY (b. 1939)

Valediction   1966

Lady with the frilled blouse
And simple tartan skirt,
Since you have left the house
Its emptiness has hurt
All thought. In your presence   5
Time rode easy, anchored
On a smile; but absence
Rocked love's balance, unmoored
The days. They buck and bound
Across the calendar   10
Pitched from the quiet sound
Of your flower-tender
Voice. Need breaks on my strand;
You've gone, I am at sea.
Until you resume command   15
Self is in mutiny.

QUESTIONS

1. What is the effect of the opening word, *Lady*? What would the effect have been if the speaker had chosen *Woman*, *Dear*, *My Sweet*, or some other similar noun of address?

2. In what way is the verb phrase *has hurt* metaphorical? How has thought been hurt? Can thought be hurt in any but a metaphorical sense?

3. Lines 5–16 contain an expanded metaphor. Explain all the various aspects of this metaphor explored by the speaker. Does the metaphor make the speaker's position more clear than sentences like "I miss you," "My days are aimless," and "I need you" might do?

4. Compare this poem with Donne's "A Valediction: Forbidding Mourning," and Burns's "O My Luve's Like a Red, Red Rose." In what ways are the speakers and the situations the same or different? In what other ways are the three poems related?

WRITING ABOUT METAPHORS AND SIMILES
IN POETRY

When you begin your essay on metaphors or similes in poetry, you will not know what direction your essay will finally take. Thus you will need to write down your discoveries about similes and metaphors as you study the poem. Determine the existence, line by line, of metaphors or similes. Obviously, similes are much easier to recognize than metaphors, because of the *like* or *as* with which they begin. Metaphors may be recognizable because of the transference you will be able to note from the topic of discussion to another topic—the metaphor.

Once you have listed all the figures that you can identify, determine their characteristics. How many have you found? How extensive are they? Are they brought out in only a word, like *cloisonné* in Chavez's "Rattlesnake," or are they more extensively detailed, as in the Shakespeare sonnet "When to the sessions of sweet silent thought"? Next, attempt to describe the thoughts that are embodied in the figures: What ideas can you locate and delineate there? What impressions of experience, what attitudes? How extensively do the figures bear the burden of thought and development in the poem? Are the figures the major means of development, or are they no more than an embellishment to a more discursive or conversational development? If you have discovered a number of metaphors or similes, what relationships can you find among them (such as the judicial and financial relationships in the Shakespeare sonnet just mentioned)? How are the similes or metaphors related to the structure of the poem? Do you find that one type of figure is used in a particular section while another predominates in another?

Once you have these things clearly determined and sketched out in a set of notes, you are ready to begin developing the initial stages of your essay.

Organizing Your Essay

INTRODUCTION. In determining your central idea you should attempt to relate the quality of the figures to the general nature of the poem. If there is any discrepancy between the metaphorical language and the topic material, that contrast may be a possible central idea, for then the poet would clearly be developing an ironic perspective on his or her material. Suppose the topic of the poem is love but the metaphors are those of darkness and cold: What would the poet be saying about the quality of love?

You should also try to justify any claims that you make about similes or metaphors. For example, as we have noted, at the end of Fray Angelico Chavez's poem "Rattlesnake," the poet introduces a metaphor equating the coiled rattlesnake with cloisonné. How is this metaphor to be taken in light of the fact that a rattlesnake is usually regarded as a threat to the person approaching it? Your introduction is the place to establish ideas and justifications of this sort. Once you have determined your central idea, develop your thesis sentence to guide your reader for the remainder of your essay.

BODY.   There are a number of approaches for discussing simile and metaphor. They are not mutually exclusive, and you may combine them as you wish. Most likely, in fact, your essay will bring in most of the following classifications.

1. *The meaning and effect of the figures.* Here you explain your interpretation of the various similes or metaphors. In lines 7–8 of "A Valediction: Forbidding Mourning," for example, Donne introduces a metaphor equating the condition of love with the organization and hierarchy of the church:

'Twere profanation of our joys
    To tell the laity our love.

Here Donne emphasizes the private, mystical relationship of two lovers and links it to the view that the clergy should not share the more esoteric mysteries of religion with the mass of the people, lest the mysteries be thereby profaned. The idea that Donne dramatizes is that love is rare, heaven-sent, private, privileged, and so fragile that its sacredness would be diminished if the lovers announced their feelings to the public ("the laity"). With this approach you will be expanding upon the meaning of the metaphors or similes and introducing references and allusions to make your expansion fully meaningful.

2. *The sources of the figures and their appropriateness to the subject matter.* Here you would try to locate and classify the sources and types of the images and to determine the appropriateness of this range of references to the subject matter of the poem. Questions you might ask are similar to those you might bring out in a study of straightforward imagery: Does the poet favor figures from nature, science, warfare, politics, business, reading? Thus, at the beginning of "The Destruction of Sennacherib" Lord Byron introduces a simile comparing the Assyrian hordes to a wolf attacking a fold of sheep. This simile likens Sennacherib's forces besieging the camp of the Hebrews to a wolf stalking a sheepfold with the intention of carrying off and eating a sheep. Here Byron has given us a simile drawn from the life of shepherds, who often must drive their sheep into wild, unknown regions. In considering any similes and metaphors in the poem, you would need to classify according to sources, and try to determine the appropriateness of this body of figures to the poem's ideas.

3. *The interests and sensibilities of the poet.* In a way this approach is like the second one, but your emphasis here should be on what the poet's selection of metaphors and similes might show about his or her vision and interests. You might begin by listing the figures in the poem and then determining the sources, just as you would do in discussing the sources of images generally. But then you should ask questions like the following: Does the poet use figures derived from one sense rather than another (sight, hearing, taste, smell, taste, touch)? Does he or she record color, brightness, shadow, shape, depth, height, number, size, slowness, speed, emptiness, fullness, richness, drabness? Has the poet relied on the associations of figures of sense? Do metaphors and similes referring to green plants and trees, to red roses, or to rich fabrics, for example, suggest that life is full and beautiful, or do references to touch suggest amorous warmth? This approach is designed to enable you to draw whatever conclusions you can about the author's—or the speaker's—taste or sensibility.

4. *The effect of one figure on the other figures and ideas of the poem.* The assumption underlying this approach is that each poem is a unified whole, so that each part is closely related to and inseparable from everything else. Usually it is best to pick a simile or metaphor that occurs at the beginning of the poem and then see how this figure influences your perception of the rest of the work. To refer again to Byron's "The Destruction of Sennacherib," for example, the opening simile comparing the Assyrian host to a predatory wolf is designed to make the subsequent destruction of the Assyrians seem justified. As a comparison, suppose the reference in the simile were to a peaceful shepherd defending his herd; what would be your reaction to the visitation of the Angel of Death and to the consequent destruction? Similarly, the beginning of Donne's "A Valediction: Forbidding Mourning" contains a simile comparing the parting of the lovers to the quiet dying of "virtuous men." How does this figure affect your understanding of the rest of the poem? In an analysis of this sort, your aim should be to consider the relationship of part to parts, and part to whole.

CONCLUSION. In your conclusion you might summarize your main points, describe your general impressions, try to describe the impact of the figures, indicate your personal responses, or show what might further be done along the lines you have been developing in the body of your essay. If you know other poems by the same poet, or poems by other poets with comparable or contrasting figures, you might briefly consider this other work and the light it might shed on the poem you have been analyzing.

SAMPLE ESSAY

A Study of Shakespeare's Metaphors in "When to the Sessions of Sweet Silent Thought"*

[1]   In this sonnet Shakespeare's speaker stresses the sadness and regret of remembered experience, but he states that a person with these feelings may be cheered by the thought of a friend. His metaphors, cleverly used, create new and fresh ways of seeing personal life in this perspective.° He presents metaphors drawn from the public and business world of the courtroom, money, and banking or money-handling.□

[2]   The courtroom metaphor of the first four lines is used to summon the past into the present. Like a justice or judge at a hearing, the speaker "summon[s]" his memory of "things" to appear on trial before him. This figure suggests that people are their own judges and that their ideals and morals are like laws by which they measure themselves. The speaker finds himself guilty of wasting his time in the past. Removing himself, however, from the strict punishment that the metaphor would require, he does not condemn himself for his "dear time's waste," but instead laments it (line 4).

[3]   With the closely related reference of money in the next group of four lines, Shakespeare shows that living is a lifelong investment and is valuable for this reason. It is not money that is spent, according to his metaphor, but emotions and commitment. Thus, his dead friends are "precious" because he invested time and love in them, and the "sights" that have "vanished" from his eyes make him "moan" because he went to great "expense" for them (line 8).

[4]   Like the money metaphor, the references to banking or money-handling in the next four lines emphasize the fact that life's experiences are on deposit in the mind. They are recorded there, and may be withdrawn in moments of "sweet silent thought" just as money may be withdrawn. Thus the speaker states that he counts out his woes just as a teller counts money ("And heavily from woe to woe tell o'er"). He pays with new woe the accounts that he had already paid with old woe in the past. The metaphor suggests that the past is so much a part of the present that a person never finishes paying both the principal and interest of past emotional investments. Because of this combination of banking and legal figures, the speaker indicates that his memory puts him in double jeopardy, for the thoughts of his losses overwhelm him in the present just as much as they did in the past.

[5]   The legal, financial, and money-handling metaphors combine in the last two lines to suggest that a healthy present life may overcome past regrets. The "dear friend" being addressed in these lines has the resources (financial) to settle all the emotional judgments that the speaker as a self-judge has made against himself (legal). It is as though the friend is a rich patron who rescues him from emotional bankruptcy (legal and financial) and the possible doom

---

* See p. 595 for this poem.
° Central idea.
□ Thesis sentence.

resulting from the potential sentence of emotional misery and depression (legal).

[6] In these metaphors Shakespeare's references are drawn from everyday public and business actions, but his use of them is creative, unusual, and excellent. In particular, the idea of line 8 ("And moan th'expense of many a vanished sight") stresses that people spend much emotional energy on others. Without emotional commitment, one cannot have precious friends and loved ones. In keeping with this metaphor of money and investment, one could measure life not in months or years, but in the spending of emotion and involvement in personal relationships. Shakespeare, by inviting readers to explore the values brought out by his metaphors, gives a new sense of the value of life itself.

Commentary on the Essay

This essay treats the three kinds of metaphors that Shakespeare introduces in "When to the Sessions of Sweet Silent Thought" (Sonnet 30). It thus illustrates the second approach (p. 616). The aim of the discussion, however, is not to explore the extent and nature of the comparison between the metaphors and the personal situations spoken about in the sonnet, but rather to explain how the metaphors develop Shakespeare's meaning. This method therefore also illustrates the first approach (p. 616).

The introduction provides a brief description of the sonnet, the central idea, and the thesis sentence. Paragraph 2 deals with the meaning of Shakespeare's courtroom metaphor. His money metaphor is explained in paragraph 3. Paragraph 4 considers the banking, or money-handling figure. The fifth paragraph shows how Shakespeare's last two lines bring together the three separate strands, or classes, of metaphor. Note how the transitions from one separate topic to the next are brought about by linking words in the topic sentences. In paragraph 3, for example, the words "closely related" and "next group" move the reader from paragraph 2 to the new content. In paragraph 4, the words effecting the transition are "like the money metaphor" and "the next four lines." The opening sentence of paragraph 5 refers collectively to the subjects of paragraphs 2, 3, and 4, thereby focusing them together on the new topic of paragraph 5.

The conclusion comments generally on the creativity of Shakespeare's metaphors in the sonnet. It also amplifies the way in which the money metaphor leads toward an increased understanding and valuation of life.

17

Other Rhetorical
Figures

In addition to metaphor and simile, poets use many other related rhetorical figures to strengthen and reinforce their ideas. Indeed, poetry abounds with figures, some of them readily recognizable and some disguised. For the most part, the reading of poetry can go forward without the detailed study of each and every figure that poets use. They are, however, a major part of the poet's craft, and the disciplined reader should be aware of the possibilities that exist for every poet who sets ideas to paper. It is not that a poet determines to use this or that figure just for the sake of using it, but rather that a particular situation or idea may fit naturally into a pattern that is also a rhetorical figure.

PARADOX

The speaker of Sir Thomas Wyatt's "I Find No Peace" describes his romantic desires not as a constant, steady flame, but rather as a conflicting mixture of wishes and fears. On the one hand, he desires to be totally in love, but on the other he also fears the commitment of love and he therefore wishes to be free. These conflicting states of feeling cause Wyatt to build the sonnet around the rhetorical figure called **paradox** (from *para*, beyond, and *dokein*, to think), a device in which a seeming contradiction may reveal an unexpected truth.

SIR THOMAS WYATT (1503–1542)

I Find No Peace   1557

I find no peace, and all my war is done,
  I fear and hope; I burn and freeze like ice;
  I fly above the wind yet can I not arise;

620

And naught I have and all the world I season.
That looseth nor locketh holdeth me in prison,°   5
  And holdeth me not, yet can I scape° nowise;   *escape*
  Nor letteth me live nor die at my devise,°   *choice*
  And yet of death it giveth none occasion.
Without eyen° I see, and without tongue I plain;°   *eyes*
  I desire to perish, and yet I ask health;   10
  I love another, and thus I hate myself;
I feed me in sorrow, and laugh in all my pain.
  Likewise displeaseth me both death and life°
  And my delight is causer of this strife.

I FIND NO PEACE.   5 *that . . . prison*: that is, "that which neither lets go nor contains holds me in prison." At the time of Wyatt, *-eth* was used for the third person singular present tense.   9 *plain*: express desires about love.   13 *likewise . . . life*: literally, "it is displeasing to me, in the same way, both death and life." That is, "both death and life are equally distasteful to me."

QUESTIONS

1. What situation is the speaker reflecting upon? How does he feel about it? Do the feelings strike you as artificial or genuine? Why?

2. How many separate paradoxes are in the poem? What is the cumulative effect of so many? What is the general topic of the paradoxes in lines 1–4? In lines 5–8? Why does the speaker in line 11 declare that hating himself is a consequence of loving another? Why is it ironic that his "delight" is the "causer of this strife"?

3. To what extent do you think the paradoxes are an accurate expression of the feelings of a person in love, particularly in light of the fact that in the sixteenth century the completely free and unchaperoned meetings of lovers were not easily arranged?

4. To what extent do the paradoxes help you feel and experience the agonies of the speaker? How do they bring alive the implications about love in the poem?

The second line of the sonnet—"I fear and hope; I burn and freeze like ice"—illustrates the creation of two paradoxes; it expresses simultaneously contradictory states of fear and hope and of fire and ice. The paradoxes, in turn, reflect the contradictory feelings created by love in the speaker. The situation of the speaker is real and it is true; it came first. The figure of paradox, on which the poem is based, came second as an embodiment of the situation and as the means through which to express it to the reader.

Thus the use of rhetorical figures is a means of building upon natural, normal ideas in order to make them especially vivid and memorable. It is difficult to forget Wyatt's opening line, "I find no peace, and all my war is done," because it expresses so vividly the state of a lover who, having made a romantic commitment, is nevertheless unsure that his loved one is returning love with equal intensity. The paradox, though expressive of a contradiction, thus vivifies the uncertainty that has plagued many people who wage the "war" of love and personal commitment.

APOSTROPHE

Another important rhetorical figure that strengthens and undergirds poetic statement is **apostrophe** (originally a "turning away," that is, a redirection of attention to some new object), which is not only a common mark of punctuation but also the addressing of discourse to a real or imagined listener.

The poetic apostrophe is not the same as an intimate speech to a person assumed to be present at the time the poem is taking place; rather, it is a speech to a person or an abstraction who is not present. Thus, a poem that includes the figure of apostrophe may be addressed to a famous person or to an abstraction such as duty, loyalty, or nature. The apostrophe is consequently similar to an open public speech. In a poem the advantage of the apostrophic pattern is that the poet can make assumptions and develop ideas and attitudes that arise naturally out of such an address. The readers of the poem are not the ones being spoken to; they are rather in the position of an audience of listeners or witnesses.

A good example of apostrophe can be seen in William Wordsworth's "London, 1802" (p. 627), which is addressed to the English poet John Milton. Wordsworth considered Milton to have been an advanced thinker and a champion of liberty and social reform. In creating an apostrophe to Milton in this poem, Wordsworth acknowledges his indebtedness to the dead poet and at the same time expresses critical views about society. Those who read the poem are not intimate listeners but are more like onlookers. Similarly, John Keats addresses "To Autumn" directly to the season itself as a song of praise for the benefits and beauties that autumn brings to human beings. Readers of this poem are like an audience at a play, verifying through their own imaginations the many examples Keats introduces from the world of autumnal nature and human activity. Therefore the situations leading to the poetic use of apostrophe are real; the device itself provides a structural basis for the development of ideas.

PERSONIFICATION

Apostrophe often works hand-in-hand with another rhetorical figure called **personification,** the attribution of human characteristics to nonhuman things or abstractions. Indeed, the previous sentence is an instance of personification in that we have rhetorically given two rhetorical figures hands and the ability to work. Keats's apostrophe to autumn is an example of personification because the poem grants the season human characteristics such as hair and human abilities to conspire, sit, and sleep.

To personify things and qualities is a normal human habit. At an earlier period of human history, people believed that spirits inhabited things such as trees, mountains, lakes, and even roadways. For example, the ancient Greek god of travel was Hermes, who originally was thought to personify each road marker (or "herm") which measured distances along a road. People getting ready to travel would ask this god to guard them and keep them safe on their journeys. Even today, people often give names and human attributes to inanimate things, such as automobiles.

Personification is useful in poetry because poets often explore the relationships between people and their environments, their ideals, or their inner lives. Keats's personification of autumn deals ultimately with the idea that nature has benefited human beings by making autumn a time of fruition and harvest. Shakespeare's speaker in Sonnet 146, "Poor Soul, the Center of My Sinful Earth" (p. 1002), personifies his own soul so that he can deal with issues of earthly versus heavenly expenditures of his own personal and emotional resources. In the sonnet "Bright Star" (p. 681) Keats personifies a star, probably the North Star, to establish the star's constancy as a model for his speaker's desire to be forever and unchangeably united with his sweetheart.

SYNECDOCHE AND METONYMY

Two rhetorical figures that are close in purpose and effect are *synecdoche* and *metonymy*. **Synecdoche** (i.e., taking one thing out of another) is a device in which a part stands for the whole, or a whole for a part, like the expression "all hands aboard" to signify that all the people who make up the crew of a ship should get on board. **Metonymy** (a transfer of name) is a figure whereby one thing is used as a substitute for another with which it is closely identified, like "the White House" referring to policies and activities of the President. The objective of both devices is to create new insights and attitudes, to provide a perspective that might otherwise not occur. Because synecdoche and metonymy extend meaning in this way, they are both similar to metaphor, simile, and symbolism.

An example of snyecdoche may be seen in Keats's ode "To Autumn," where the gourd and the hazel shells in lines 7–8, which are single examples of ripening produce, stand for the entire harvest of the autumnal season. In Wordsworth's "London, 1802" (p. 627) the phrase "thy heart" (line 13) is a synecdoche referring to the entire person and mind of Milton.

As a synecdoche in which the whole stands for a part, Shakespeare frequently used the names of entire countries or regions as a means of representing individuals. Thus, in *Antony and Cleopatra*, "Egypt" is used to mean Cleopatra, the Queen of Egypt. In *King Lear*, "Albany" is used for the Duke of Albany, and so on.

Metonymy appears in Keats's "To Autumn," when the speaker mentions a "granary floor" to suggest the harvest of grain of autumn. In this example, the place where the grain is stored is used with the transferred meaning of what is stored there. John Fandel in the poem "Indians" illustrates the process of metonymic thinking. In lines 11–13 he writes "*Indians*, starts me. I / think of their wigwams. I / Think of canoes. . . ." The wigwam may be interpreted as a metonym for the territories formerly controlled by Indians, and the canoe as a metonym for their freedom of access through these territories. The key here is the transfer of meaning through the use of a closely related word.

Indeed, the habit of metonymic thinking is so common that we often overlook the fact that our thoughts take this rhetorical pattern. In using brand names, for example, we accept the brand for the product, such as *Kleenex* for hand tissues, *Kodak* for film, and *Xerox* for copiers. In "Exit, Pursued by a Bear" Ogden Nash metonymically uses brand names, the names of artists, and the names of cities to replace objects, artworks, and places. Thus "Chippendale" is a metonym for a valuable piece of ornate antique furniture, and "Picasso" is a metonym substituting the name of the artist for the work of art. Nash's entire poem is built up with such metonyms, which cumulatively symbolize the civilization of art and culture that may so easily be destroyed by global war.

SYNESTHESIA

Another figure transferring one thing to another, and therefore closely related to synecdoche and metonymy, is **synesthesia,** which means a union or fusion of separate sensations or feelings. With this device, a poet describes one type of perception or thought with words that are appropriate to another. Andrew Marvell, for example, in his poem "The Garden," speaks of a "green thought in a green shade" in reference to thinking conducive to life and the preservation and nurturing of living things. A thought obviously cannot be green—who has ever *seen* any thought, let alone a *colored* one?—nevertheless, "green thought" makes vivid sense. Keats uses synesthesia extensively, as, for example, in the "Ode to a Nightingale" (p. 628), where a plot of ground is "melodious," a draught of wine tastes of "Dance, and Provençal song, and sunburnt mirth," and beaded bubbles of wine "wink" at the brim of a glass.

THE PUN

Another rhetorical figure that involves a transfer of meaning is the **pun** (which probably originally meant a *point* or *puncture*). A pun is a word play in which the writer surprisingly reveals that words with totally different meanings have similar or even identical sounds. For example John Donne, in his "Hymn to God the Father" (p. 884), creates a pun out of the fact that the past participle of the verb *do*—*done*—sounds just like his name. It is this identical sound that permits a line like the following to make sense: "And, having done that, thou hast done." Here the last word clearly means both "finished" and "Donne"; it is a pun.

Because puns can be outrageous and require a little bit of thinking, people often groan when they hear them (even while they probably are enjoying them). Also, because puns often play with sounds rather than ideas, they have not always enjoyed great favor with critics, let alone poets. A good pun, however, may always be relished, for it works both with sound and with thought, as in the example by John Donne. John Gay (1685–1732), in his play *The Beggar's Opera* (1728), utilizes clever and complex puns in the song for chorus, "Let Us Take the Road."

Let us take the road.
  Hark! I hear the sound of coaches!
  The hour of attack approaches,
To your arms, brave boys, and load.
    See the ball I hold! [*holding up bullet*]   5
  Let the chymists° toil like asses,   *alchemists*
  Our fire their fire surpasses,
    And turns all our lead to gold.

Here *fire*, *lead*, and *gold* are puns. *Lead* was the "base" or low metal that the medieval alchemists ("chymists") tried to transform into *gold*, using the heat from their *fires*. This much is clear. Gay's puns develop because the gang of thieves singing the song is about to go out to hold up people riding in horse-drawn coaches. Hence their *lead* is in the form of bullets, which through their robberies will be transformed into the money of *gold* coins. Their *fire* is not the alchemists' fire, but rather the firing of guns. In the context of the play, and the song, the villains in the gang thus charm us by their wit, even though the threatening situation they describe would be distressing in real life.

OVERSTATEMENT AND UNDERSTATEMENT

Two additional figures often used both by poets and by people in everyday life are *overstatement* and *understatement*, which are both devices of emphasis. **Overstatement,** or **hyperbole** ("excess, the throwing in of too much"), or *the overreacher*, is a device of exaggeration. In "London, 1802," for example (p. 627), Wordsworth declares that England is a "fen of stagnant waters." That is, the country and its people make up collectively a stinking, smelly, polluted marsh, a dump. Without question, this claim overstates the case. What Wordsworth establishes by the overstatement, however, is his judgment that the nation in 1802 needed a writer to unite the people around noble moral and political ideas, just as Milton had once done.

Sometimes the device of overstatement may reach fanciful extremes of thought. In Diane Wakoski's "Inside Out" (p. 634), for example, the opening line is "I walk the purple carpet into your eye." Because purple carpets are commonly used for royalty, the speaker is elevating herself to the status of a queen. Hence the overstatement becomes both a clever and beautiful way of saying "You look at me and think well of me" (just think how much better Wakoski's line is). In overstating the situation so fancifully, the line illuminates some of the magic in the mutual evaluations of people in love.

On the other side of the scale, **understatement** is the deliberate underplaying or undervaluing of a thing for purposes of emphasis. To say that something is "not uncommon," for example, is a way of emphasizing its commonness. After Mark Twain learned that a news service had announced that he had died, he sent the company a cable from London, claiming, "The reports of my death are greatly exaggerated." This clever understatement has amused people ever since. One of the most famous poetic understatements is in Andrew Marvell's "To His Coy Mistress":

The grave's a fine and private place,
But none, I think, do there embrace.

Here the understatement grimly emphasizes the eternity of death by contrasting the permanent privacy of the grave with the temporary privacy sought by lovers. Another ironic use of understatement is in lines 17–20 of Ogden Nash's "Exit, Pursued by a Bear," where the speaker indicates that the "lion and the lizard" cannot hear "heavenly harmonies." In this way Nash emphasizes the idea that the people who once inhabited the rooms, and who regularly heard and appreciated such melodies, are unable to hear them now because they have been killed during a war.

READING FOR OTHER RHETORICAL FIGURES

When dealing with figures like those just described, it is important to begin by reading the poems for their total effect, not just for the rhetorical devices. Indeed, the better your command of an entire poem, the better you will be able to find any figures that are present. In studying Eliot's "Eyes That Last I Saw in Tears" (p. 630), for example, you would note that the first stanza describes the speaker's emotional state after an argument ("division") of some sort that left another person crying. The speaker states that he still cannot reconcile himself with the causes over which the tears were shed, and, he claims, "This is my affliction" (line 6). Once this situation is understood, it is possible to find a *paradox*, inasmuch as the speaker claims to value the other person but not to understand her. In addition, this other person is identified not by name, but by "eyes." That is, the identification is made through a *synecdoche* which emphasizes those aspects of vision and the evaluation that characterizes sight and perception. The relationship of the speaker to the other person is hence established as suffering one of those irreconcilable breaches that unfortunately sometimes develop between human beings.

In short, as with any study of literature, the task is first to do the best that you can with the entire text and then to begin to pinpoint the specific study task at hand. The goal should then be to determine the role of the specific figure or figures in the entire fabric of the poem. Once the situation is established, it becomes easier to "spot" a figure than it would be if you read just for the figures.

POEMS FOR STUDY

WILLIAM WORDSWORTH (1770–1850)

London, 1802   *1807 (1802)*

Milton! thou should'st be living at this hour:	
England hath need of thee: she is a fen°	*bog, marsh*
Of stagnant waters: altar, sword, and pen,	
Fireside, the heroic wealth of hall and bower,	
Have forfeited their ancient English dower°	*widow's inheritance* 5
Of inward happiness. We are selfish men;	
Oh! raise us up, return to us again;	
And give us manners,° virtue, freedom, power.	
Thy soul was like a star, and dwelt apart:	
Thou hadst a voice whose sound was like the sea:	10
Pure as the naked heavens, majestic, free,	
So didst thou travel on life's common way,	
In cheerful godliness; and yet thy heart	
The lowliest duties on herself did lay.	

LONDON, 1802.   8 *manners*: customs, moral modes of social and political conduct.

QUESTIONS

1. What is the effect of Wordsworth's apostrophe to Milton? What elements of Milton's career as a writer does Wordsworth emphasize?
2. In lines 3 and 4, the device of metonymy is used. What do these details represent, and how does Wordsworth judge the respective institutions represented by the details?
3. Consider the use of overstatement, or hyperbole, from lines 2–6. What effect does Wordsworth achieve by using the device as extensively as he does here?
4. What effect does Wordsworth make through his use of overstatement in his praise of Milton in lines 9–14? What does he mean by the metonymic references to *soul* (line 9) and *heart* (line 13)?

JOHN KEATS (1795–1821)

To Autumn   *1820 (1819)*

Season of mists and mellow fruitfulness!
  Close bosom-friend of the maturing sun;
Conspiring with him how to load and bless
  With fruit the vines that round the thatch-eaves run;
To bend with apples the mossed cottage-trees,   5
  And fill all fruit with ripeness to the core;
    To swell the gourd, and plump the hazel shells
With a sweet kernel; to set budding more,
  And still more, later flowers for the bees,
  Until they think warm days will never cease,   10
    For Summer has o'erbrimmed their clammy cells.

Who hath not seen thee oft amid thy store?
  Sometimes whoever seeks abroad may find
Thee sitting careless on a granary floor,
  Thy hair soft-lifted by the winnowing wind,   15
Or on a half-reaped furrow sound asleep,
Drowsed with the fume of poppies, while thy hook
  Spares the next swath and all its twinèd flowers;
And sometimes like a gleaner thou dost keep
  Steady thy laden head across a brook;   20
  Or by a cider-press, with patient look,
    Thou watchest the last oozings hours by hours.

Where are the songs of Spring? Ay, where are they?
  Think not of them, thou hast thy music too,—
While barrèd clouds bloom the soft-dying day,   25
  And touch the stubble-plains with rosy hue;

Then in a wailful choir the small gnats mourn
  Among the river sallows, borne aloft
    Or sinking as the light wind lives or dies;
And full-grown lambs loud bleat from hilly bourn;   30
  Hedge-crickets sing; and now with treble soft
  The redbreast whistles from a garden-croft;
    And gathering swallows twitter in the skies.

QUESTIONS

1. How is personification used in the first stanza? How does it change in the second? What is the effect of such personification?

2. How does Keats structure the poem to accord with his apostrophe to autumn? That is, in what ways may the stanzas be distinguished by the type of discourse addressed to the season?

3. Analyze Keats's use of metonymy in stanza 1 and synecdoche in stanza 2. What effects does he achieve with these devices for the transference of meaning?

4. How, through the use of images, does Keats develop his idea that autumn is a season of "mellow fruitfulness"?

ALFRED, LORD TENNYSON (1809–1892)

Break, Break, Break   *1842*

Break, break, break,
  On thy cold gray stones, O Sea!
And I would that my tongue could utter
  The thoughts that arise in me.

O, well for the fisherman's boy,   5
  That he shouts with his sister at play!
O, well for the sailor lad,
  That he sings in his boat on the bay!

And the stately ships go on
  To their haven under the hill;   10
But O for the touch of a vanish'd hand,
  And the sound of a voice that is still!

Break, break, break,
  At the foot of thy crags, O Sea!
But the tender grace of a day that is dead   15
  Will never come back to me.

QUESTIONS

1. Why does Tennyson begin and end the poem with an apostrophe to the Sea? How may this apostrophe be related to the structure of the poem?
2. What is the meaning and effect of the use of synecdoche in lines 5–10? How do these examples contrast with the synecdoche intended by *hand* (line 11), *voice* (line 12), and *day* (line 15)? What effect is achieved by this contrast?
3. What symbolic relationship is there between the breaking of the waves and the feelings of the poet? What human organ is thought to break, and how does this organ apply metonymically to human emotions?
4. Rhetorical considerations aside, why is "Break, Break, Break" a beautiful poem?

T. S. ELIOT (1888–1965)

Eyes That Last I Saw in Tears   *1924*

Eyes that last I saw in tears
Through division
Here in death's dream kingdom
The golden vision reappears
I see the eyes but not the tears   5
This is my affliction

This is my affliction
Eyes I shall not see again
Eyes of decision
Eyes I shall not see unless   10
At the door of death's other kingdom
Where, as in this,
The eyes outlast a little while
A little while outlast the tears
And hold us in derision.   15

QUESTIONS

1. What do *eyes* and *tears* signify as a synecdoche and as a metonymy?
2. What is the cause of the tears (line 2)? What is meant by the eyes outlasting the tears (lines 13, 14)? Why should the eyes "hold us in derision"? In line 9 the eyes are "of decision." What does this synecdoche mean?
3. Explain the paradox of the speaker's declaration in line 5 that he sees the eyes but not the tears. Why does he say that this is his "affliction"?

4. Why might the entire poem be considered a paradox? What happened in life? What does the speaker look forward to in death?

5. What is the distinction in the poem between "death's dream kingdom" and "death's other kingdom."

6. What effect is achieved in the poem by the use of repeated words and phrases?

OGDEN NASH (1902–1970)

Exit, Pursued by a Bear   *1954*

Chipmunk chewing the Chippendale,°
Mice on the Meissen° shelf,
Pigeon stains on the Aubusson,°
Spider lace on the delf.°

Squirrel climbing the Sheraton,°   5
Skunk on the Duncan Phyfe,°
Silverfish in the Gobelins°
And the calfbound volumes of *Life*.

Pocks on the pink Picasso,
Dust on the four Cézannes,   10
Kit on the keys of the Steinway,
Cat on the Louis Quinze.°

Rings on the Adam° mantel
From a thousand bygone thirsts,
Mold on the Henry Millers°   15
And the Ronald Firbank° firsts.

The lion and the lizard°
No heavenly harmonies hear
From the high-fidelity speaker
Concealed behind the Vermeer.   20

EXIT, PURSUED BY A BEAR. The title is a stage direction in Shakespeare's *The Winter's Tale* (act 3. scene 2, 58). The character is torn apart by the bear. When this poem was first published, the atomic bomb had existed for nine years, and the hydrogen bomb for two. In late 1953, Russia, which is sometimes symbolized by a bear, announced that it possessed the hydrogen bomb.   1 *Chippendale*: ornate furniture made by Thomas Chippendale (1718–1779).   2 *Meissen*: expensive chinaware made in Meissen, Germany. Also called "Dresden China."   3 *Aubusson*: carpet imported from France.   4 *delf*: expensive pottery made in Delft, The Netherlands.   5 *Sheraton*: furniture made by Thomas Sheraton (1751–1806).   6 *Duncan Phyfe*: furniture made by Duncan Phyfe (1768–1854), a Scotsman who came to America in 1783.   7 *Gobelins*: rare and exquisitely crafted tapestries made by Gobelin of Paris.   12 *Louis Quinze*: furniture made in France during the reign of Louis XV (1710–1774).   13 *Adam*: Robert Adam (1728–1792) was one of the most famous English architects.   15 *Henry Miller*: American author (1891–1980).   16 *Ronald Firbank*: Arthur Ainsley Ronald Firbank (1886–1926), British author.   17 *The lion and the lizard*: see Edward Fitzgerald's (1809–1883) version of *The Rubáiyát of Omar Khayyam*, stanza 18, particularly in reference to Nash's last stanza.

Jamshid° squats in a cavern
Screened by a waterfall,
Catered by Heinz and Campbell,
And awaits the fireball.

21 *Jamshid*: a reference to the legendary Persian hero Jamshid, who lived for 700 years and found a cup containing the elixir of life. At one point in the story Jamshid remained hidden for a hundred years. Note also the reference to Fitzgerald's *Rubáiyát*, stanza 18.

QUESTIONS

1. In relationship to the serious subject matter of the poem, what is the effect of the title? What is the possible pun on the word *bear*?
2. What location is the speaker describing? How is metonymy used to suggest the wealth of the collections of household items and art? What sort of lifestyle is suggested by the metonymy?
3. What has hypothetically occurred so that the animals rather than people are living with the expensive artifacts? Judging from the evidence of line 15, how long has this situation existed?
4. How might the situation presented in the poem be considered as a paradox?
5. What fireball is expected (line 24)? In the light of this expectation, what ideas is the poet expressing about war? Compare this poem to Yeats's "The Second Coming" (p. 802) and Robinson Jeffers's "The Purse-Seine" (p. 800). What similarities and differences do you find among these works?

ELIZABETH BISHOP (1911–1979)

Rain Towards Morning   1947

The great light cage has broken up in the air,
freeing, I think, about a million birds
whose wild ascending shadows will not be back,
and all the wires come falling down.
No cage, no frightening birds; the rain   5
is brightening now. The face is pale
that tried the puzzle of their prison
and solved it with an unexpected kiss,
whose freckled unsuspected hands alit.

QUESTIONS

1. What sort of personal situation is being described in the poem? How much does the poet allow you to learn about the situation? Do you discover enough to determine the general pattern of what is happening?

2. Describe the poet's use of overstatement in lines 1–4. What effect is achieved? In light of the "kiss" mentioned in line 8, which is more powerful: understatement or overstatement?

3. What is the meaning of the "great light cage" in lines 1–4? What is the "puzzle" of the birds' prison in line 7?

4. How can the "face" of line 6 and the "kiss" in line 8 be explained, through the figure of synecdoche, to have "hands" in line 9? What do these figures suggest about the nature of the experience being described?

5. Explain the paradox of how rain can be brightening (line 6).

JOHN FANDEL (b. 1925)

Indians   *1959*

Margaret mentioned Indians,
And I began to think about Indians—

Indians once living
Where now we are living—

About Indians. Oh, I know   5
About Indians. Oh, I know

What I have heard. Not much,
When I think how much

I wonder about them,
When a mere mention of them,   10

Indians, starts me. I
Think of their wigwams. I

Think of canoes. I think
Of quick arrows. I think

Of things Indian. And still   15
I think of their bright, still

Summers, when these hills
And meadows on these hills

Shone in the morning
Suns before this morning.   20

QUESTIONS

1. What kind of person is the speaker? Why does he think about Indians? How does he feel about time past and the civilization of the Indians? What lines or words suggest that he feels regret?

2. Describe the poem's use of synecdoche in lines 12–20. What meaning and effect does the poet achieve through these figures?

3. Describe the structure of the poem. How does the poem begin? What leads the speaker into his meditation? Explain the structural purpose of the seeming hesitations and the repetitions in lines 5–11.

MARK STRAND (b. 1934)

The Remains   1969

I empty myself of the names of others.
I empty my pockets, I empty my shoes and leave them beside
the road. At night I turn back the clocks; I open the family
album and look at myself as a boy.

What good does it do? The hours have done their job.   5
I say my own name. I say goodbye.
The words follow each other downwind.
I love my wife but send her away.

My parents rise out of their thrones
into the milky rooms of clouds. How can I sing?   10
Time tells me what I am. I change and I am the same.
I empty myself of my life and my life remains.

QUESTIONS

1. Explain the paradoxical nature of the personal situation described by the speaker. How do lines 11 and 12 make sense in terms of paradox?

2. Describe the poet's use of synecdoche in words such as *names*, *pockets*, *shoes*, *road*, and *hours*. What do these signify?

3. What is the major idea of the poem? In what sense does the poet indicate that life is a perpetual state of saying goodbye? How does time tell the speaker what he is? Where does his past experience go? Is the influence of this experience constant as a part of his present consciousness?

DIANE WAKOSKI (b. 1937)

Inside Out   1965

I walk the purple carpet into your eye,
carrying the silver butter server,
but a truck rumbles by,
          leaving its black tire prints on my foot,

and old images—   5
      the sound of banging screen doors on hot afternoons
      and a fly buzzing over Kool-Aid spilled on the sink—
flicker, as reflections on the metal surface.

Come in, you said,
inside your paintings, inside the blood factory, inside the   10
old songs that line your hands, inside
eyes that change like a snowflake every second,

inside spinach leaves holding that one piece of gravel,

inside the whiskers of a cat,

inside your old hat, and most of all inside your mouth where you   15
grind the pigments with your teeth, painting
with a broken bottle on the floor, and painting
with an ostrich feather on the moon that rolls out of my mouth.

You cannot let me walk inside you too long
inside the veins where my small feet touch   20
bottom.
You must reach inside and pull me
like a silver bullet°
from your arm.

INSIDE OUT.   23 *silver bullet*: According to legend, silver bullets were used to kill vampires.
The Lone Ranger, of the radio and television series popular in the 1940s and 1950s, always
used silver bullets as a trademark of his pursuit of justice.

QUESTIONS

1. Who is the speaker? Who is the person being addressed? From what the
   speaker says in lines 15–19, what is the profession of the addressee? What
   sort of relationship does the speaker have with him? How close, how intimate,
   are they? What knowledge of domestic details do they have in common?
   How may this knowledge be used in the drawing of conclusions about their
   relationship?
2. What "inside out" details of the listener's anatomy does the speaker mention?
   What do you think is meant by the poem's title?
3. Consider details of the eye and the veins as synecdoche, and the paintings
   and the old hat as metonymy. In the determination of the poem's characterization of the "you" inside the poem, what do these details stand for?
4. Consider the truck's black tire prints on the speaker's foot (lines 3–4) as
   an instance of synesthesia, that is, the application of one set of sensuous
   references to another sense. What might this figure mean? Do the same
   for the mouth with the ground pigments (lines 15–16), the ostrich feather
   and the rolling moon (line 18), and the walk inside the veins (lines 19–20).

5. What is meant by lines 19–24? Why, after the establishment of so personal and intimate a relationship, might the speaker express the reservations that are contained here? How might these lines be interpreted as a reflection upon the paradoxical nature of the love relationship generally?
6. Describe the paradox implicit in the speaker's mentioning the red carpet in line 1 and the silver butter server in line 2.

WRITING ABOUT RHETORICAL FIGURES OTHER THAN SIMILE AND METAPHOR

As you prepare to write about rhetorical figures, your first task is to write a brief overview of the poem. From this basis you can determine the presence of figures. Some of these, such as personification, puns, apostrophes, and overstatements, are easily recognized. Others, like synecdoche and metonymy, may take more examination and testing.

Once you have established that certain figures are present in the poem, you should make notes describing such things as the type of the figure, its extensiveness, its importance in the development of the poem, its appropriateness, and its influence upon your comprehension and appreciation. With a set of materials focused on these elements, you are well on your way to an effective composition on your topic.

For this essay, two types of compositions are possible. One is a full-scale essay. The other, because some rhetorical figures may occupy only a small part of the poem, is a single paragraph. Let us consider the single paragraph first.

1. *A paragraph*. Here there will be only one topic, such as the opening paradox in Eliot's "Eyes That Last I Saw in Tears," or the opening metonym in the same poem. The goal in such a paragraph should be to deal with an individual figure and its relationship to the main idea of the poem. Thus the figure should be described, and its meaning and implications should be discussed. It is important to begin the paragraph with a comprehensive topic sentence, such as one that explains the cleverness of the puns in John Gay's "Let Us Take the Road" (p. 625), or the use of hyperbole or overstatement in Elizabeth Bishop's "Rain Towards Morning" (p. 634) to signify the sense of freedom and release of tension that love can bring.

2. *A full-length essay*. Two possibilities exist for full-length essays on rhetorical figures. One type of essay examines just one figure, presupposing that the figure is pervasive enough in the poem to justify a full treatment. The second explores the effect, impact, or meaning of two or more figures, with the various parts of the body of the essay being taken up with each of the figures. The unity in this type of essay is achieved by the linking of a series of two or three different rhetorical devices to a single idea or emotion conveyed in the poem.

Organizing Your Essay

INTRODUCTION. The introduction should begin with a brief description of the type of figure or figures and also of their extent and importance in the poem. The central idea is to be concerned with the figure or figures as they define or are controlled by the major ideas in the poem. The thesis sentence thus becomes the bridge between the central idea and the major points to be discussed in the body.

BODY. The body should be organized to deal with questions like the following: Where do the figures occur in the poem? Are they of major or relatively minor importance? Structurally, how are they developed, if any development occurs? How naturally do the figures rise out of the situation or major ideas? How do any figures relate to other aspects of the poem? How do they broaden, deepen, or otherwise assist in making the ideas in the poem forceful? How vivid are the figures? How obvious? How unusual? How much effort is needed to understand the figures in their context? Are any figures concerned with ideas and situations, or are they primarily used as devices depending on words alone? In short, how appropriate are any figures in the poem, and how well do they assist you in your perception and appreciation of the poem?

CONCLUSION. You might conclude with a brief summary, together with a brief examination of any additional but less important figures that you noted as you studied the poem. If you have been puzzled, amused, perplexed, or otherwise affected by any figures, you might wish to describe this effect as a part of your general commentary on the poem. If the poet's use of figures helped you to see things that you might not have seen otherwise, you should make this sort of observation a part of your concluding remarks.

SAMPLE PARAGRAPH

Wordsworth's Use of Overstatement in "London, 1802"*

Through overstatement, Wordsworth emphasizes his tribute to Milton as a master of idealistic thought. The speaker's claim that England is "a fen / Of stagnant waters" (lines 2–3) is overstated, just as is the implication that people ("we") in England have no "manners, virtue, freedom, [or] power" (line 8). With the overstatement, however, Wordsworth makes the case that the nation's well-being depends on the constant flow of creative thoughts by persons of great ideas. Because Milton was clearly the greatest of these, in the view of

* See p. 627 for this poem.

Wordsworth's speaker, the overstatement stresses the importance of voices of leadership. Milton is the model, and the overstated need lays the foundation in the real political and moral world for a revival of Milton's ideas. Thus, through overstatement, Wordsworth emphasizes the importance of Milton, and in this way pays tribute to him.

Commentary on the Paragraph

This paragraph shows how a rhetorical figure that is not necessarily prominent in a poem (although this one actually is prominent) may nevertheless become the basis of a short written exercise. The topic is Wordsworth's use of overstatement in "London, 1802." The detail of overstatement selected from the poem is Wordsworth's assertion about the immoral state of his country in 1802. The goal of the paragraph is not to describe the details of the figure, however, but to show how the figure affects Wordsworth's poetic tribute to Milton. The paragraph therefore illustrates the need, even in a short assignment, of writing to illustrate a point.

SAMPLE ESSAY

Paradox in Sir Thomas Wyatt's "I Find No Peace"*

[1] Wyatt's "I Find No Peace" is a sonnet built on paradox. The first-person speaker is describing the effects his love has upon him, and he indicates forcefully that he is caught between commitment, on the one hand, and the desire to be free, on the other. Because of his conflict, he describes his own conditions of amazement, dismay, and also amusement, but he states also that he is reconciled to his contrary states. His situation blends naturally with the rhetorical pattern of paradox.° *In the poem, the paradox is extended to the speaker's personal reactions, his attitude toward his beloved, and his general public situation.*°

[2] The speaker's personal reactions are most vividly described within the contrary states defined by paradox. Thus the speaker at the beginning declares his satisfaction at having won his "war" because he has apparently convinced his sweetheart to love him. But at the same time he can never really be sure of her. Hence he also states the paradox that he can "find no peace." Throughout the sonnet the speaker develops these contradictory emotional states. He is at the height of desire, but he cannot find consummation. He therefore speaks ambiguously of his sexual frustration (line 7, where he cannot "live or die at . . . [his] devise," with die being a sexual pun), and the frustration in turn

* See p. 620 for this poem.
° Central idea.
□ Thesis sentence.

continues his uncertainty. Throughout, in almost every line, the speaker stresses other paradoxes that point out his inner anguish.

[3] In the speaker's descriptions of his attitude toward his beloved, *the same paradoxes are apparent.* He calls her his "delight," for example (line 14), and yet he confesses that he is blind to whatever human faults she might possess ("Without eyen I see," line 9). He would like to pursue his quest further but does not want to offend, and thus he states, "without tongue I plain" (line 9). In short, his sweetheart is also a human being to whom he must grant individuality and freedom. Because of the gap between this recognition and his desire, he paradoxically experiences the joy of love and the pain of uncertainty.

[4] Finally, the speaker claims that his attempts to carry on normally in life are also afflicted with his paradoxical personal condition. In line 12 the speaker explains that he continues to eat and also to laugh; that is, his life has not stopped, and he goes about his affairs. But all the time he is at meals, which should be a joyful time, he is in sorrow, and even when he is laughing, he is also in pain. In this way, the poet develops the paradox in which a person functioning well publicly is personally torn and uncertain.

[5] The poem thus stresses the paradoxical effects of intense love in all major phases of the speaker's life. The human basis of the paradoxes is the difficulty that people have in truly knowing each other, even the ones they love most dearly. In the poem, this inability to know the true mind of the beloved, even though she is "all the world" to the speaker (line 4), creates the uncertainty out of which the paradoxes arise. This state is convincingly real, particularly because of the speaker's intensity of feeling. Wyatt's complete incorporation of paradox into the sonnet therefore dramatizes the conflicting feelings of a person in love. Paradox here is precisely fitted to the subject of the poem.

Commentary on the Essay

This sample illustrates how a pervasive rhetorical figure may be divided for consideration in a full-length essay. The figure chosen is *paradox* because it is so prominent in "I Find No Peace." For any other poem in which any particular figure is important, the same method might be followed. If the essay were to be based on two or more figures, each one of these might form a separate part or paragraph in the body.

In the introduction to this particular essay, attention is focused on the figure of paradox and its importance in the situation described in the poem. The central idea proposes the argument that idea and figure are blended. The thesis sentence lists three areas of the poem to be explored in the body. Paragraph 2 describes the paradox as developed in the speaker's perception of his own condition as a lover. Because the sonnet is primarily about the speaker rather than about his love, this paragraph is the longest in the body of the essay. Paragraph 3 is concerned with the paradox as it affects the speaker's descriptions of his beloved. His difficulty results from the fact that she is an individual, and hence he cannot control her as much as his love would dictate that he would like to do. The fourth paragraph, the shortest of the body, is concerned with the sparse information that the speaker discloses about his public life as it is affected by the paradox of his private turmoil. The conclusion briefly summarizes the main topics of the body, and then it attempts to explain the paradoxes in terms of the difficulty people have in knowing each other. The last sentence is a restatement of the central idea.

18

Tone: The Creation of Attitude in Poetry

Read "Love"

Tone, also discussed in Chapter 8, is the means by which poets reveal attitudes and feelings. You may remember that the term is borrowed from the phrase *tone of voice* as applied to speech. Let us suppose that Mike is speaking to two acquaintances about a recent movie he liked. Let us also suppose that Bill responds, "Now that I know that *you* liked the picture, I *know* that I will like it too when I see it." The *tone* of this comment indicates friendliness and respect—recognition that Mike's judgment counts. But let us additionally suppose that Sam responds, "Now that I know that *you* liked the picture, I know that I will *not* like it at all." Beyond the changed words here, the tone is markedly different. Although Sam does not say that Mike's opinion is worthless and that he holds him in contempt, this attitude is nevertheless expressed by the *tone* of his remark.

THE ELEMENTS OF TONE

In the study of tone in poetry, the object is to consider the ways in which poets, like Bill and Sam above, express and control attitudes. Literally *everything* in the poem helps convey the tone. The poet's stance toward the material and toward possible readers is one of the most important aspects. In establishing a speaker or an authorial voice, the poet must develop a character to do the speaking in relation to the purpose of the poem: How much self-awareness, how many traits, what kind of background, what kind of relationship to establish between the speaker and the readers? How much knowledge to assume for both the speaker and the readers, what kind of interests and assumptions to attribute to the readers? All these enter into the writing of the poem and therefore influence its tone.

In addition, things like irony, understatement, overstatement, the creation of humor or seriousness, the use of diction and the control of connotation, the images, similes, and metaphors, are a part of tone. The sentences must be just long enough, no shorter and no longer, for the intended effect of the material. If a conversational style is established, overly formal words must be avoided; similarly, slang would not suit a formal style. In a serious poem, the use of jingling or bouncing rhythms might seem frivolous and therefore inappropriate. Any ambiguities should be deliberate and not unintentional. In all these aspects that collectively make up the tone of a poem, the poet's consistency is of primary importance. If anything falls short, the poem sinks and the poet will have failed.

TONE, CHOICE, AND READER RESPONSE

Remember that a major rhetorical objective of poets is to secure total reader acceptance, no matter what their topic matter. They may wish to shape, enrich, stimulate, inform, and generally affect readers. Thus, poets may begin their poems with not much more than a brief idea, a vague feeling, or a fleeting impression. Then, in the light of their developing design, their own attitudes, and their judgment of possible reader responses, they *choose* what to say, what form in which to present the material, and what words and phrases to use. The poem "Theme for English B" by Langston Hughes (the topic of the sample essay) illustrates almost in outline form the process by which a poet structures reader response in order to gain reader acceptance. Hughes's speaker lays out those areas of his life in which he and his intended reader, the English teacher, share a common bond of interests. In this way Hughes establishes grounds for acceptance of his ideas of human equality, regardless of color.

The poet's need to balance poetic intention with all possible reader responses requires the greatest skill. For this reason, an effective control over tone is essential, for the reader's total acceptance must not only be that of *recognition* and *understanding*, but also of *emotion*. It may be that in the long run a reader might not agree with all the ideas in the poem, but, with a successful poem, the reader's assent will exist at least during the time of reading because the sum total of choices marking the poet's control over tone will have been right.

Each poem, in short, attempts to evoke *total* responses, which any interfering lapse of tone might destroy. Such lapses may take the form of an objectionable assumption about the qualities of a person or idea in the poem, a misinterpretation of how readers will take an idea, an uncertain expression, or some ambiguity that will create a misimpression. Let us look at a poem that misses, and misses badly, in its control of tone.

CORNELIUS WHUR (1782–1853)

The First-Rate Wife   *1837*

This brief effusion I indite,
  And my vast wishes send,
That thou mayst be directed right,
And have ere long within thy sight
  A most *enchanting* friend!   5

The *maiden* should have *lovely face*,
  And be of *genteel mien*;
If not, within thy dwelling place,
There may be vestige of disgrace,
  Not much admired—when seen.   10

Nor will thy dearest be complete
  Without *domestic* care;
If otherwise, howe'er discreet,
Thine eyes will very often meet
  What none desire to share!   15

And further still—thy future *dear*,
  Should have some *mental* ray;
If not, thou mayest drop a tear,
Because no *real sense* is there
  To charm life's dreary day!   20

QUESTIONS

1. What is the situation of the poem? What sort of person is the speaker? Who is the listener? Why does the speaker address the listener? How does the speaker's tone reveal his character? In the light of the tone of line 3, what relationship does the speaker establish between himself and the listener?

2. What requirements does the speaker create for the "first-rate wife"? In what ways might the advice be considered helpful? From the tone of the speaker's requirements, what attitude toward women does the speaker expect his listener to share?

3. Consider the tone of these phrases: "vestige of disgrace" (line 9), "what none desire to share" (line 15), and "to charm life's dreary day" (line 20). What does this tone show about the assumptions and attitudes toward marriage held by the speaker?

4. What sorts of requirements does the speaker *not* include about a "first-rate wife"? What do these omissions demonstrate about him?

The dramatic situation of this poem is that the speaker is giving advice to a male listener about the traits that he should look for in a woman so that she might become his "first-rate wife." In stanza 1 the speaker sets himself up as an advice-giver, and in stanzas 2, 3, and 4 he asserts the need for three basic qualities in a woman: beauty, responsibility for household care, and intelligence. From the tone of the speaker's remarks it is clear that he regards the decision to marry as being roughly comparable to the hiring of a housekeeper or the buying of a diverting book. Note the tone of the phrase "some *mental* ray," for example. The word *some* does not mean "a great deal," but in this instance is more like "*at least* some," as though it would be unreasonable to expect anything more of a woman. From the tone of the final three lines, it is clear that the speaker's requirement for intelligence is not that the woman be intellectually or emotionally on a par with the listener, but rather that she should be charming enough to rescue him from dreariness and boredom. Even granted the fact that the poem was written in the nineteenth century and that it represents a traditionally masculine view of marriage, it is shortsighted, and as a result verges on being offensive. Do you wonder why you probably never heard of Cornelius Whur before?

TONE AND THE NEED FOR CONTROL

"The First-Rate Wife" emphasizes the need for the poet to be in control over the entire situation of the poem. The speaker must be aware of his or her situation and should not, like the speaker of "The First-Rate Wife," demonstrate any smugness or insensitivity, unless the poet is deliberately revealing the shortcomings of the speaker by dramatizing them for the reader's amusement, as e. e. Cummings does in the poem "Next to of course God" (p. 940). In a poem characterized by well-controlled tone, values should be clear, details should be introduced correctly, and the climax of the poem should come at the right spot. The following poem exhibits such total control over tone:

WILFRED OWEN (1893–1918) — Owen died in WW I, one week before the Armistice.

Vivid imagery

Dulce et Decorum Est   1920

Bent double, like old beggars under sacks,
Knock-kneed, coughing like hags, we cursed through sludge,
Till on the haunting flares we turned our backs
And towards our distant rest began to trudge.
Men marched asleep. Many had lost their boots

5

But limped on, <u>blood-shod.</u> All went lame; all blind;
Drunk with fatigue; deaf even to the hoots
Of tired, outstripped Five-Nines° that dropped behind.

Gas!° GAS! Quick, boys!—An ecstasy of fumbling,
Fitting the clumsy helmets° just in time;   10
But someone still was yelling out and stumbling
And flound'ring like a man in fire or lime . . .
Dim, through <u>the misty panes</u> and thick green° light,   *Panes of the mask.*
As under a green sea, I saw him drowning.   *A nightmarish quality here.*

In all my dreams, before my helpless sight,   15
He plunges at me, guttering, choking, drowning.

If in some smothering dreams you too could pace
Behind the wagon that we flung him in.
And watch <u>the white eyes writhing in his face,</u>   *Dying in battle is*
His hanging face, like a devil's sick of sin;   *hideous.*   20
If you could hear, at every jolt, the blood
Come gargling from the froth-corrupted lungs,
Obscene as cancer, bitter as the cud
Of vile, incurable sores on innocent tongues.—
<u>My friend</u>, you would not tell with such <u>high zest</u>   *The tone is bitter,* 25
To children ardent for some desperate glory,   *full of disgust toward*
<u>The old Lie</u>: Dulce et decorum est   *those who would glorif*
Pro patria mori.° *Propaganda*   *war.*

DULCE ET DECORUM EST.   8 *Five-Nines*: Artillery shells that made such a sound just
before landing.   9 *Gas*: Poisonous gas was first used as an anti-personnel weapon in 1915
by the Germans.   10 *helmets*: Soldiers carried gas masks as a part of normal battle
equipment.   13 *thick green*. The chlorine gas used in gas attacks has a greenish-yellow
color.   27–28 *Dulce . . . mori*: From Horace, *Odes*, Book 3, line 13: "It is sweet and
honorable to die [while fighting] for [one's] country."

QUESTIONS

1. What is the scene described in lines 1–8? What expressions does the speaker use to indicate his attitude toward the conditions?
2. What does the title of the poem mean? What attitude or conviction does it embody?
3. What is the tonal relationship between the patriotic fervor of the Latin phrase and the images of the poem? How does this tonal difference create the dominant tone of the poem? What is the dominant tone?
4. Does the speaker really mean "my friend" in line 25? In what tone of voice might this phrase be spoken?
5. What ideas does this poem explore about war and about dying in battle? About patriotism? To what extent does the tone of the poem help establish these ideas?

In this poem the poet is in total command over the tone. The speaker is addressing a listener, whom he identifies as "you" and "my friend," who before the poem begins has presumably been talking about the need for young men to die in the service of their country. The reader is hence not being addressed, but instead is a witness to the scene. The speaker is recounting an incident in which he, as a soldier in World War I, witnessed the painful, agonized death of a comrade in a chlorine gas attack. Once he finishes his narrative, the speaker testifies to the grisly horror by claiming that it has dominated his dreams. Then he addresses the listener directly, claiming that if the friend could witness the real horror of warfare, he would never again claim that dying, even for one's country, is sweet or appropriate.

The tone never once lapses in the poem. The poet intends the description to evoke a response of horror, for he contrasts the *strategic* goals of warfare with the *up-close* grimness and pain of death in battle. The language skillfully emphasizes first the dreariness and fatigue of warfare (with words like *sludge*, *trudge*, *lame*, and *blind*) and second the agony of violent death from chlorine (embodied in the participles *guttering*, *choking*, *drowning*, *smothering*, and *writhing*). With these details carefully established, the concluding attack against the "glory" of war is difficult to refute, even if warfare is undertaken in preservation of one's country. Although the details about the agonized death clearly create distress or discomfort for a sensitive reader, they are not designed to do that alone but instead are integral to the poem's argument. Ultimately, it is the contrast between the high ideals of the Latin phrase and the realities of death during a gas attack that creates the dominant tone of the poem. The Latin phrase treats war and death in the abstract; the poem brings images of battle and death vividly alive. The resultant tone is both bitter and ironic.

COMMON GROUNDS OF ASSENT

This is not to say that all those reading "Dulce et Decorum Est" will immediately deny that war is ever necessary. The issues of politics and warfare are far too complex for that. But the poem does show another important aspect of tone, namely, the degree to which the poet judges and tries to control the possible responses of readers through the establishment of a **common ground of assent.** An appeal to a bond of commonly held interests, concerns, and assumptions is essential if a poet is to maintain an effective tone. Wilfred Owen, for example, does not create arguments against the necessity of a just war. Instead, he bases the poem upon realistic details about the writhing, spastic death suffered by the speaker's comrade, and he makes the poem appeal to emotions that everyone, pacifist and militarist alike, would agree upon—a sense of horror at the contemplation of violent death. Even assuming a widely divergent audience, in other words, the *tone* of the poem is successful because it is based on commonly acknowledged facts and commonly felt emotions. Faced with a poem like this one, even advocates of warfare would need to defend their ideas on the grounds of *prevention* of just such needless, ugly deaths. Owen has wisely and carefully considered the responses of his readers and has controlled speaker, situation, detail, and argument in order to make the poem acceptable for the broadest possible spectrum of opinion.

TONE AND IRONY

Irony is a mode of indirection, a means of establishing an assertion by the emphasis upon a discrepancy or opposite (see also pp. 270–72). Thus Owen uses the title "Dulce et Decorum Est" to emphasize that death in warfare is not fitting and noble, but rather horrible and painful. The title ironically reminds us of eloquent speeches on the Fourth of July at the tombs of unknown soldiers, but as we have seen, it also reminds us of the reality of the agonized death of Owen's soldier. As an aspect of tone, therefore, irony is a powerful way of conveying attitudes, for it draws your attention to at least two ways of seeing the situation being presented, and through such a perspective it enables you not only to understand, but also to feel.

    Situational Irony. Poetry shares with fiction and drama the various kinds of ironies that poets believe may afflict human life. "The Workbox," by Thomas Hardy, illustrates a skillful manipulation of irony.

THOMAS HARDY (1840–1928)

The Workbox   *1914*

"See, here's the workbox, little wife,
   That I made of polished oak."
He was a joiner°, of village life;   *cabinetmaker*
   She came of borough folk.

He holds the present up to her   5
   As with a smile she nears
And answers to the profferer,
   " 'Twill last all my sewing years!"

THE WORKBOX.   4.5 *village, borough*: A village was small and rustic; a borough was larger and more sophisticated.

"I warrant it will. And longer too.
   'Tis a scantling that I got   10
Off poor John Wayward's coffin, who
   Died of they knew not what.

"The shingled pattern that seems to cease
   Against your box's rim
Continues right on in the piece   15
   That's underground with him.

"And while I worked it made me think
   Of timber's varied doom:
One inch where people eat and drink,
   The next inch in a tomb.   20

"But why do you look so white, my dear,
   And turn aside your face?
You knew not that good lad, I fear,
   Though he came from your native place?"

"How could I know that good young man,   25
   Though he came from my native town,
When he must have left far earlier than
   I was a woman grown?"

"Ah, no. I should have understood!
   It shocked you that I gave   30
To you one end of a piece of wood
   Whose other is in a grave?"

"Don't, dear, despise my intellect,
   Mere accidental things
Of that sort never have effect   35
   On my imaginings."

Yet still her lips were limp and wan,
   Her face still held aside,
As if she had known not only John,
   But known of what he died.   40

10 *scantling*: a small, leftover piece of wood.

QUESTIONS

1. Who does most of the speaking in this poem? What does the tone of the
   speeches show about the characters of the man and the wife? What does
   the tone indicate about the poet's attitude toward them?

2. In lines 21–40, what does the dialogue indicate about the wife's knowledge
   of John and about her possible earlier relationship with him? Why does the
   wife deny such knowledge? What does stanza 10 suggest about her? What

is the possible insinuation about her in these lines? Why is a mystery preserved about the cause of John's death?

3. In lines 17–20, the man describes the "varied doom" of timber. What sort of irony is suggested by the symbolism of the wood made into the workbox?

4. In what way is the irony described by the man more complex than he realizes?

5. The narrator, or speaker, of the poem speaks only in lines 3–7 and 37–40. How much of the explanation he gives is essential? How much indicates his attitude? How might the poem have been more effectively concluded?

This poem is a little domestic drama of deception and sadness. The extremely complex details are evidence of situational irony; that is, an awareness that human beings do not control themselves but are rather controlled by powerful, overwhelming forces—in this case, both death and earlier feelings and commitments. Beyond this irony evolving out of the domestic scene, Hardy also emphasizes symbolically the direct connection that death has with the living. As a result of the husband's gift made of the same wood with which he has also made a coffin for the dead man, the wife shall live all the rest of her days with the constant reminder of this man. Her future will be characterized by regret and also by the apparently endless need to deny her true emotions.

Dramatic Irony. In addition, the deception practiced by the wife reveals that the husband is in a situation of dramatic irony, that is, a situation in which a character understands one set of circumstances while the readers understand, in greater perspective, something completely different. In this poem, the husband does not know what the readers and the wife know, namely, that the wife is not being truthful or open about her earlier relationship with the dead man. The tone of "The Workbox" suggests that the husband may be suspicious, however, and by his emphasis on the piece of wood he may be trying to draw her out and make her reveal something. But he does not actually *know* the true circumstances, and hence he is unsure of his wife's attitude toward him. The wife's denials do not resolve the situation. Because of this mixture of dramatic and situational irony, Hardy has created a poem of great complexity.

Verbal Irony. In addition, poetry may be filled with verbal irony, that is, the use of language of ambiguity. "She being Brand / -new" by e. e. cummings (p. 655) is such a poem, filled with *double-entendre*, or double meaning. The speaker of the poem describes a sexual encounter in terms of breaking in a new car, and as a result the entire poem is a virtuoso piece of double meaning. Another example of verbal irony may be seen in Theodore Roethke's "My Papa's Waltz" (p. 658), in which the speaker uses the name of this orderly, stately dance to describe his childhood memory of his father's whirling him around the kitchen in wild, boisterous drunkenness.

SATIRE

Of major importance as an aspect of tone is satire. **Satire** is designed, negatively, to dispraise or blame human follies or vices, as measured positively against a normative moral or social standard. The emphasis in satire is on the negative, with the positive usually being assumed. In method, a satiric poem may be bitter and vituperative in its attack, but quite often it employs humor and irony, on the grounds that anger turns readers away while a comic tone more easily gains agreement. The speaker of a satiric poem either may attack folly or vice *directly*, or may dramatically *embody* the folly or vice, and hence be an illustration of the subject of satire. An example of the first type is the following short poem by Alexander Pope, in which the speaker directly attacks a listener who has claimed identity as a poet, but whom the speaker considers as nothing more than a fool. The speaker cleverly uses insult as the tone of attack:

ALEXANDER POPE (1688–1744)

Epigram from the French   1732

Sir, I admit your general rule
That every poet is a fool:
But you yourself may serve to show it,
That every fool is not a poet.

An example of the second type is the following short epigram by the same poet, in which the speaker is an actual embodiment of the subject of attack:

ALEXANDER POPE (1688–1744)

*Epigram. Engraved on the Collar of a Dog which I gave
to his Royal Highness.*   1738 (1737)

I am his Highness' dog at Kew:°   *near London, a place of one of the royal residences*
Pray tell me sir, whose dog are you?

Here the speaker is the King's dog at the palace at Kew, and the listener an unknown dog. Pope's satire is directed not against canine habits, however, but against human class pretentiousness. The tone of the first line ridicules derived, not earned, status, while the tone of the second line implies an unwillingness to recognize the listener until the question of rank is resolved. Pope, by using the dog as a speaker, reduces such snobbishness to an absurdity. Another satiric poem attacking pretentiousness is "Next to of Course God" by E. E. Cummings (p. 940), where the speaker voices a set of patriotic platitudes, and in doing so illustrates Cummings's satiric point that such claims are often void of understanding and thought. Satiric tone may thus range widely, sometimes being objective, comic, and distant; sometimes deeply concerned and scornful; and sometimes dramatic, ingenuous, and revelatory. Always, however, the satiric mode confronts and exposes various degrees of human follies and vices.

READING FOR TONE IN POETRY

In order to understand and describe the tone of any poem, you need to determine the situation, the speaker, the listener, and the assumptions that are expected of you as a reader. What apparent common grounds does the poet establish with you so that the material of the poem may effectively develop? You need to determine whether these grounds are genuinely shared, or whether any special concession may be necessary on your part so that the poem may proceed. Any such dispensations should be reasonable and realistic, such as those for accepting the verbal irony of Cummings's "she being Brand / -new," or for accepting the description of the horrible death in "Dulce et Decorum Est." By contrast, as we have seen, the dispensation for reading and accepting "The First-Rate Wife"— that the reader must accept the qualification of the pompous speaker to offer marital guidance to his listener—is difficult to make.

Once you determine the basic situation and assumptions, you'll need to examine content and style. Are the details introduced in an order of reasonable expectation, so that your responses are properly considered? Does the poem in any way let you down and therefore reflect a breakdown of tone? (For example, the concluding stanza of "The Workbox" may be offensive to those readers who might consider the possible insinuation of infidelity as the imposition of an unfair burden upon the wife.)

With regard to expressions and language, it is necessary to determine that denotations and connotations are appropriate. Many words or expressions may at first seem unusual, even though they are obviously the ones intended by the poet. Assuming that the poet controlled word choice carefully, any unusual phrases will require detailed consideration, such as the references in "she being Brand / -new" by Cummings, or the descriptions of the boy dancing with the father in "My Papa's Waltz." The goal in this consideration should be to determine that the diction either is or is not an appropriate aspect of the entire situation, and therefore of the tone, of the poem.

POEMS FOR STUDY

ANNE BRADSTREET (1612–1672)

The Author to Her Book   1678

Thou ill-formed offspring of my feeble brain,
Who after birth did'st by my side remain,
Till snatched from thence by friends, less wise than true,
Who thee abroad exposed to public view;
Made thee in rags, halting, to the press to trudge,
Where errors were not lessened, all may judge.
At thy return my blushing was not small,
My rambling brat° (in print) should mother call;
I cast thee by as one unfit for light,
Thy visage was so irksome in my sight;
Yet being mine own, at length affection would
Thy blemishes amend, if so I could:
I washed thy face, but more defects I saw,
And rubbing off a spot, still made a flaw.
I stretched thy joints to make thee even feet,°   *regular poetic meter*
Yet still thou run'st more hobbling than is meet;
In better dress to trim thee was my mind,
But nought save homespun cloth, in the house I find.
In this array, 'mongst vulgars may'st thou roam;
In criticks hands beware thou dost not come;
And take thy way where yet thou are not known.
If for thy Father asked, say thou had'st none;
And for thy Mother, she alas is poor,
Which caused her thus to send thee out of door.

THE AUTHOR TO HER BOOK.   8 *brat*: The word here emphasizes the insignificance
rather than the unpleasant aspects of a child.

QUESTIONS

1. What attitude toward "Her Book" (that is, a collection of poems) does the
    speaker express in line 1? What metaphor does she use that would be appro-
    priate for a woman but not necessarily for a man? How extensively does
    she develop this metaphor in the rest of the poem, and how does the tone
    of this metaphor express her attitudes about her book?

2. What is the tone of the speaker's references to those friends who "exposed"
    her book to "public view" (that is, circulated it without her consent)? How
    does this tone indicate her ambiguous feelings about them?

3. How does the speaker excuse the fact that she is now issuing her book of poetry on her own initiative? How does the tone produce humor? How does the tone of the concluding metaphor encourage you to smile, or even to laugh?

4. What attitude toward herself does the speaker express? How do you react to this attitude? How do you think you are expected by the poet to react?

5. What is the tone of the extended metaphor of the child in lines 11–18?

ANNE FINCH, COUNTESS OF WINCHELSEA (1661–1720)

To the Nightingale   *1713*

Exert thy voice, sweet harbinger° of spring!	*forerunner, herald*
This moment is thy time to sing,	
This moment I attend to praise,	
And set my numbers to thy lays.°	*ballads*
Free as thine shall be my song	5
As thy music, short or long.	
Poets, wild as thee, were born,	
Pleasing best when unconfined,	
When to please is least designed,	
Soothing but their cares to rest;	10
Cares do still their thoughts molest,	
And still the unhappy poet's breast,	
Like thine, when best he sings, is placed against a thorn.°	
She begins. Let all be still!	
Muse, thy promise now fulfil!	15
Sweet, oh sweet! still sweeter yet!	
Can thy words such accents fit,	
Canst thou syllables refine,	
Melt a sense that shall retain	
Still some spirit of the brain,	20
Till with sounds like these it join?	
'Twill not be! then change thy note,	
Let division shake thy throat.	
Hark! division now she tries,	
Yet as far the Muse outflies.	25
Cease then, prithee, cease thy tune!	
Trifler, wilt thou sing till June?	
Till thy business all lies waste,	
And the time of building's past?	
Thus we poets that have speech,	30

TO THE NIGHTINGALE.   13 *thorn*: a reference to the (untrue) legend that nightingales sing most sweetly only when they are in pain because of thorns.   23 *division*: a feature of the nightingale's song is the apparent sustaining of two harmonious notes (hence "division") at one time.

Unlike what thy forests teach,
  If a fluent vein be shown
  That's transcendent to our own,
Criticize, reform, or preach,
Or censure what we cannot reach.   35

QUESTIONS

1. What is the tone of the speaker's description of the nightingale? Is the tone
    consistent or mixed? How do you know?

2. For what reasons does the speaker admire the song of the bird? Describe
    the tone of the speaker's description of the bird's song as noted from lines
    14–25. Why does the speaker censure the bird in lines 26–29? What attitude
    toward the speaker does the poet intend by the tone of these lines?

3. What is the tone of the connection the speaker makes between the song of
    the nightingale and the works of poets? What ideas does the speaker derive
    from this connection about the nature of poetic creativity?

4. In lines 11–13 what is the tone of the speaker's metaphor of the thorn?
    How does the tone reveal the speaker's attitude toward herself?

5. What is the purpose of lines 30–35? What does the tone of these lines show
    about the speaker's attitude toward herself? What is the purpose for which
    the speaker mentions "we poets"?

ARTHUR O'SHAUGHNESSY (1844–1881)

A Love Symphony   *1881*

Along the garden° ways just now   *a green area*
  I heard the flowers speak;
The white rose told me of your brow,
  The red rose of your cheek;
The lily of your bended head,   5
  The bindweed of your hair;
Each looked its loveliest and said
  You were more fair.

I went into the wood anon,°   *later, soon after*
  And heard the wild birds sing   10
How sweet you were; they warbled on,
  Piped, trilled the self-same thing,
Thrush, blackbird, linnet, without pause
  The burden did repeat,
And still began again because   15
  You were more sweet.

And then I went down to the sea,
  And heard it murmuring too,
Part of an ancient mystery,
  All made of me and you.   20
How many a thousand years ago
  I loved, and you were sweet—
Longer I could not stay, and so
  I fled back to your feet.

QUESTIONS

1. What is the "symphony" of love? What is the tone of the speaker's descriptions
    of the symphony as coming from flowers, birds, and the sea?
2. What is the tone of the phrase "ancient mystery / All made of me and you"
    (lines 19–20)? Compare this use of the idea of religious mysteriousness and
    love with the use in John Donne's "The Canonization" (p. 877) and Anne
    Finch's "To Mr. Finch Now Earl of Winchelsea" (p. 794). What common
    attitudes about love do these three poems contain? What differences?
3. What tone is expressed about the loved one in lines 23–24? In the light of
    his tone in describing her qualities, what sort of relationship is he celebrating?

E. E. CUMMINGS (1894–1962)

she being Brand / -new   *1926*

she being Brand

_-new;and you
know consequently a
little stiff i was
careful of her and(having   5

thoroughly oiled the universal
joint tested my gas felt of
her radiator made sure her springs were O.

K.)i went right to it flooded-the-carburetor cranked her

up,slipped the   10
clutch(and then somehow got into reverse she
kicked what
the hell)next
minute i was back in neutral tried and

again slo-wly;bare,ly nudg. ing(my   15

lev-er Right-
oh and her gears being in

A 1 shape passed
from low through
second-in-to-high like
greasedlightning) just as we turned the corner of Divinity

avenue i touched the accelerator and give

her the juice,good

                    (it

was the first ride and believe i we was
happy to see how nice she acted right up to
the last minute coming back down by the Public
Gardens i slammed on

the
internalexpanding
&
externalcontracting
brakes Bothatonce and

brought allofher tremB
-ling
to a:dead.

stand-
;Still)

QUESTIONS

1. Consider the verbal irony, the double-entendre, of this poem. How extensive
    is it? How does it make the poem comic (if you indeed agree that the poem
    is comic)?

2. How do the spacing and alignment affect your reading of the poem? How
    does the unexpected and sometimes absent punctuation—such as line 15,
    "again slo-wly;bare,ly nudg. ing(my"—contribute to the humor?

3. Can this poem in any respect be said to be "off color" or "bawdy"? How
    might the charge be refuted in the light of the tone of the speaker's equation
    of an initial sexual experience with the "breaking in" of a new car?

LANGSTON HUGHES (1902–1967)

Theme for English B   *1959*

The instructor said,

    Go home and write
    a page tonight.

And let that page come out of you—
Then, it will be true.   5

I wonder if it's that simple?

I am twenty-two, colored, born in Winston-Salem.
I went to school there, then Durham, then here
to this college on the hill above Harlem.°
I am the only colored student in my class.   10
The steps from the hill lead down to Harlem,
through a park, then I cross St. Nicholas,
Eighth Avenue, Seventh, and I come to the Y,
the Harlem Branch Y, where I take the elevator
up to my room, sit down, and write this page: 15

It's not easy to know what is true for you or me
at twenty-two, my age. But I guess I'm what
I feel and see and hear. Harlem, I hear you:
hear you, hear me—we two—you, me talk on this page.
(I hear New York, too.) Me—who?   20

Well, I like to eat, sleep, drink, and be in love.
I like to work, read, learn, and understand life.
I like a pipe for a Christmas present,
or records—Bessie,° bop,° or Bach.°

I guess being colored doesn't make me not like   25
the same things other folks like who are other races.
So will my page be colored that I write?
Being me, it will not be white.
But it will be
a part of you, instructor.   30
You are white—
yet a part of me, as I am a part of you.
That's American.
Sometimes perhaps you don't want to be a part of me.
Nor do I often want to be a part of you.   35
But we are, that's true!
As I learn from you,
I guess you learn from me—
although you're older—and white—
and somewhat more free.   40

This is my page for English B.

THEME FOR ENGLISH B.   9 *Harlem*: A reference to Columbia University in New York
City. The other streets and buildings (lines 9–14) similarly refer to specific places in New
York near Columbia.   24 *Bessie*: Bessie Smith (c. 1898–1937), American jazz singer, famed
as the "Empress of the Blues."   *bop*: a type of popular music which was in vogue in the
1940s through the 1960s.   *Bach*: Johann Sebastian Bach (1685–1750), German composer,
considered the master of the Baroque style of music.

QUESTIONS

1. What is the tone of the speaker's assessment of himself? What does the tone indicate about his feelings toward the situation in the class and at the Y?
2. What is the tone implicit in the fact that the speaker, in response to a theme assignment, has composed a poem rather than a prose essay?
3. What is the tone of lines 21–24, where the speaker indicates a number of his likes? Why does the poet have him include these details? In what way may the characteristics brought out in these lines serve as an argument for social and political equality?
4. How does the tone in lines 27–40, particularly lines 34–36, prevent the assertions of the speaker from becoming overly assertive or strident?

THEODORE ROETHKE (1907–1963)

My Papa's Waltz   1942

The whiskey on your breath
Could make a small boy dizzy;
But I hung on like death:
Such waltzing was not easy.

We romped until the pans   5
Slid from the kitchen shelf;
My mother's countenance
Could not unfrown itself.

The hand that held my wrist
Was battered on one knuckle;   10
At every step you missed
My right ear scraped a buckle.

You beat time on my head
With a palm caked hard by dirt,
Then waltzed me off to bed   15
Still clinging to your shirt.

QUESTIONS

1. What is the tone of the speaker's opening description of his father? What is the tone of the phrases "like death" and "such waltzing"?
2. What is the "waltz" the speaker describes? What is the tone of his words describing it in lines 5–15?

3. What does the reference to his "mother's countenance" contribute to the tone of the poem? What sort of situation is suggested by the selection of the word "unfrown"?

4. What does the tone of the physical descriptions of the father contribute to your understanding of the speaker's attitude toward his childhood experiences as his father's dancing partner?

WRITING ABOUT TONE IN POETRY

In writing an essay about tone in a poem, a first task is to determine what kinds of attitudes the poem presents. For example, the poet may seem closely involved with the material or relatively distant from it. You may determine that the poet seems amused by the material, but even then it is important to make conclusions about how to take the amusement. Does the poet seem to be involved with the things, characters, situations, language, or objects at which she or he laughs? Does it seem that he or she shares delight with the reader? In more serious situations, the poem may give evidence of a degree of pity, or the poet may seem to be lamenting the human condition. Whatever the attitudes you determine are present, the problem will be to determine what you think produces these attitudes. Your task will be essentially inferential; that is, if you discover that you have a certain emotional response, you may reasonably conclude that it is the one the poet intended you to have, and then you will need to determine what specific aspects of the poem caused you to have this response.

In taking notes about what to include in your essay, therefore, you should concentrate on those features of the poem that most saliently produce or emphasize the attitudes. Thus, one avenue of exploration may be about the apparent assumptions that the poet shares with the reader: What are these assumptions? How do you learn, from the poem, what is expected of you as a reader? Are these assumptions valid, or do they require any kind of special effort or concession?

Another approach might be to concentrate on the apparent attitude of the poet toward the speaker of the poem: What sort of person is he or she? Does this person seem to be intelligent or stupid, cowardly or heroic, exceptional or ordinary, idealistic or realistic? What attitudes does the poet intend as a result of these characterizations?

Another avenue of study might be the diction of the poem. In selecting details for study, you'll need to write down both the normal words and any special words, such as dialect, difficult words, foreign words or phrases, or loaded or connotative words, as well as the effect of these. No matter what the topic or topics you finally treat in your essay, it will be necessary throughout your preparation to keep pinpointing the ways in which the poet brings out the attitudes you find in the poem.

Organizing Your Essay

INTRODUCTION.   The introduction describes the general situation of the poem and the mood or impression that the poem gives. The central idea should be about the aspect or aspects that you plan to develop in the body, such as that the diction is designed to portray the life of ordinary people, or to convey the idea that the speaker is pretentious, or to call upon the reader's ability to visualize experience, or to produce happiness, or revulsion. The thesis sentence contains the major aspects to be explored in the body.

BODY.   There are a number of ways to approach a discussion of tone. Depending on the degree to which you can develop any of these, you may wish to select one, combine several, or develop an entirely new plan. Keep in mind that the poem at hand will ultimately determine the approach necessary for an effective essay.

1. *The situation of the poem*. Here the goal is to discuss the situation in the poem and to determine how the poet has controlled the attitudes. Who is talking to whom? What situation has prompted the speech? Is there any interchange (assuming that there are two characters in the poem)? What do the speakers say, and what do they withhold (and how do you know what they are withholding)? Why do they speak as they do? To what degree do their speeches seem controlled specifically by the situation in which they find themselves? What do their speeches show about the poet's attitudes toward them? How do the speeches indicate how the poet has attempted to structure reader response toward the characters and toward the situation?

2. *"Common ground" of poet, listeners, and readers*. Here the goal is to establish the attitudes that the poet assumes in common with the readers or with persons being addressed. What are the common attitudes? How sincerely are they expressed in the poem? To what degree are they special, unusual, or conventional? What kind of relationship do they suggest between the speaker and the listener, or person being addressed? How do you know what these common attitudes are? Are the attitudes easily accepted, or do they demand a concession? What might the concession be? For example, a religious poem like George Herbert's "The Pulley" (p. 577) might ask the reader to assume an overwhelming need for religious devotion. Not everyone can grant such a need, but even an irreligious reader might find common ground on the basis of psychological or historical interest, or interest based simply on learning the maximum amount possible about human beings. With such a concession of commonality,

the tone of a religious poem may be approached just like that of any other poem.

3. *Diction and references*. Here the idea is to analyze the language of the poem to determine how word choice is evidence of the poet's attitude toward the subject matter. Are the words and references in normal use, or does the level indicate that the poet assumes special knowledge by the reader? In Ogden Nash's "Exit, Pursued by a Bear," for example (p. 631), the references to art and furniture, together with the title, indicate that Nash assumes that his readers will be highly literate and knowledgeable. In William Butler Yeats's "The Second Coming" (p. 800), the poet introduces special, personal references, such as the gyre, and he assumes that the interested reader will follow these to derive the poet's attitudes of concern and apprehension about the ominous future of human civilization. References such as these indicate the special pact, or bond, that poets make with their intended readers.

4. *Direct appeals to emotion*. In a comic poem the poet's goal may be to evoke laughter or at least to entertain. In a serious poem the goal may be to produce sorrow or elevation. Whatever the emotion, an avenue of analysis is to determine how the poet achieves the desired effect. In "she being Brand / -new," for example, E. E. Cummings relies for the poem's humor on the reader's ability to understand the sexual ambiguity of a description of breaking in a new car. In "Theme for English B," Langston Hughes relies on the reader's sense of involvement in causes of justice so that the poem may effectively make its assertions about human equality. The same capacity for involvement is assumed by Wilfred Owen in "Dulce et Decorum Est," where it is almost impossible not to be deeply moved.

5. *Special characteristics*. Poems, like stories, are individual, separate works of art, each with its own characteristics. Because there is so much that is specific to each poem, any consideration of tone would need to take these specifics into consideration. Anne Bradstreet, for example, in "The Author to Her Book" introduces the metaphor of her work being like an unwanted child—literally a bastard that she is sending out into the world. Her apology for the work hence introduces a tone of amused but sincere self-effacement that the reader must consider. Theodore Roethke's "My Papa's Waltz" is a brief narrative in which the speaker's feelings about memories of his childhood participation in his father's boisterous behavior must be inferred from understatement like "waltz." Each poem may thus offer something unique for consideration under the topic of tone.

CONCLUSION.   Just as with any conclusion, you might wish to summarize your main points about the tone of the poem, perhaps emphasizing one of the points as you go over them. In addition, you might feel that you have missed stressing some special aspect that makes the poem forceful, or there might be some particularly weak part of the poem that you wish to emphasize again. If the study of tone has enabled you to draw any conclusions about the way of life mentioned in the poem, or has changed your own perceptions about life or people around you, a brief discussion of these conclusions would be appropriate here. Finally, you might wish to discuss some other major aspect of the tone of the poem that you did not include in the body of your essay. Any or all of these details would be fitting here, so long as you emphasize aspects of the poet's technique as a poet.

SAMPLE ESSAY

The Tone of Confidence in "Theme for English B"* by Langston Hughes

[1]   "Theme for English B" is based on the situational irony of racial differences. The situation is the long-standing one of unequal opportunity, seen from the perspective of a college student whose race has been oppressed. This situation might easily produce bitterness, anger, outrage, or vengefulness. However, the poem contains none of these. It is not angry or indignant; it is not an appeal for revenge or revolution. It is rather a declaration of personal independence and individuality. The tone is one of objectivity, daring, occasional playfulness, but above all, confidence.° These attitudes are made plain in Hughes's description of the speaker's situation, the ideas, the use of the poetic form itself, the diction, and the expressions.□

[2]   Hughes's treatment of the situation is objective, factual, and personal, not emotional or political. The poem contains a number of factual details presented clearly, like these: The speaker is a black in an otherwise all-white English class. He has been displaced from his home in North Carolina and is now living alone in a room at the Harlem YMCA, away from his family and roots. He is also, at 22, an older student. The class is a freshman class (English B), yet he is the age of many seniors. There is clear evidence here of disadvantage, yet Hughes does no more than present the facts objectively, without comment. He is in control, presenting the details straightforwardly, in a tone of total objectivity.

[3]   Hughes's thoughts about equality—the idea underlying the poem—are presented in the same objective, cool manner. The speaker is writing to his instructor, and he does so as an equal, not as an inferior. In describing his identity (for the assignment was to "let that page come out of" him), he does not deal in abstractions, but rather in reality. Thus he defines himself in language descriptive of everyday abilities, needs, activities, and likes. He is cool and

* See p. 656 for this poem.
° Central idea.
□ Thesis sentence.

direct here, for his presentation takes the form of a set of inclusive principles, which may be abbreviated in the following way: "All the traits I describe about myself are normal. I have them; you have them; everyone has them. Therefore, I am like you, and you are like me. By extension, everyone is the same." The clear idea is that people should follow their ideals and put away their prejudices. Yet Hughes, by causing his speaker to avoid emotionalism and controversy, makes counterarguments difficult if not impossible. He is so much in control that the facts themselves carry his argument for equality.

[4] The selection of the poetic form itself demonstrates bravery and confidence. One would normally expect a short prose essay in response to the instructor's assignment to write a page. But a poem is unexpected and therefore is daring and original. It is as though Hughes's speaker is showing his mettle and imagination, and thereby he is personally justifying the idea that he is on an equal footing with the instructor. The wit behind the use of the form itself is a basis for equality.

[5] Hughes's diction is in keeping with the tone of confidence and daring. The words are studiously simple, showing the confidence of the speaker in the directness and truth of his ideas. Almost all the words in the poem are of one or two syllables; this high proportion reflects a conscious attempt to control the diction for the sake of simplicity and directness. A result is that Hughes avoids any possible ambiguity, as the following section of the poem shows:

Well, I like to eat, sleep, drink, and be in love.
I like to work, read, learn, and understand life.
I like a pipe for a Christmas present,
or records—Bessie, bop, or Bach.

With the exception of what it means to "understand life," these words are direct, simple, descriptive, and free of emotional overtones. They reflect the speaker's confidence that the time for recognizing human equality has replaced the time for allowing inequality and prejudice to continue.

[6] A number of the speaker's phrases and expressions also show this same confidence. Although most of the material is expressed straightforwardly, one can perceive playfulness and irony, too. Thus, in lines 18–20 there seems to be a deliberate use of confusing language to bring about a verbal merging of the identities of the speaker, the instructor, Harlem, and the greater New York area:

Harlem, I hear you:
hear you, hear me—we two—you, me talk on this page.
(I hear New York, too.) Me—who?

The speaker's confidence is strong enough to allow him to write and keep in the poem an expression that seems almost childish. This expression is in line 26, the second line of the following excerpt:

I guess being colored doesn't make me not like
the same things other folks like who are other races.

There is also whimsicality in line 27, in which the speaker is treating the irony
of the black–white situation:

So will my page be colored that I write?

Underlying this last expression is an awareness that, despite the claim that
people are equal and are tied to each other by their common humanity, there
are also strong differences among individuals. The speaker is confidently asserting grounds for independence as well as for equality.

[7]   Thus, an examination of "Theme for English B" reveals vitality and confidence. The poem is a statement of trust and an almost open challenge on
the personal level to the American ideal of equality. Hughes is saying that
since it is American to have such ideals, there is nothing to do but to live up
to them. He makes this point through the almost conscious naiveté of the speaker's simple words and descriptions. Yet the poem is not without its irony, particularly at the end, where the speaker mentions that the instructor is "somewhat
more free" than he is. "Theme for English B" is complex and engaging; it
shows the speaker's confidence as it is evidenced in objectivity, daring, and
playfulness.

Commentary on the Essay

The central idea in this essay is that the dominant attitude in "Theme
for English B" is the speaker's confidence and that this confidence is shown
in the similar but separable attitudes of objectivity, daring, and playfulness.
The purpose of the essay is to discuss how Hughes makes plain these
and other related attitudes. The tone is studied as it is shown in five separate
aspects of the poem.

Paragraph 2 deals with the situational irony of the speaker in relation
to a larger set of social and political circumstances, in this case racial dis-
crimination. Paragraph 3 considers the idea of equality as Hughes presents
it through the eyes of the speaker. The aim of the paragraph, however,
is not to consider equality as an idea, but to show how the speaker expresses
his attitude toward it. Paragraph 4 contains a discussion of how the selection
of the poetic form is a mark of the speaker's assurance. This quality is
unique to the circumstances of this poem; hence, to consider the form
as a mark of tone illustrates approach 5 in the discussion of the body,
above, that "special characteristics" may be considered as an aspect of
tone in poetry. Paragraphs 5 and 6 consider the stylistic matters of word
choice and expression. The attention given to monosyllabic words is justified by the high percentage of such words in the poem.

The concluding paragraph stresses again the attitude of confidence in the poem and also notes additional attitudes of vigor, trust, challenge, ingenuousness, irony, objectivity, daring, playfulness, and enjoyment.

Because this essay deals with a number of approaches by which tone may be studied in any work (situation, common ground, diction, special characteristics), it is typical of many essays that use a combined, eclectic approach to the study of tone. The fourth paragraph is particularly instructive inasmuch as it shows how a topic that might ordinarily be taken for granted, such as the basic form of expression, can be seen as a feature of tone unique to the work being studied.

19

The Rhythm of Poetry: Beat, Meter, and Scansion

Rhythm in poetry—also called *beat, metrics, versification, mechanics of verse,* and *numbers*—refers to the comparative speed and loudness in the flow of words spoken in poetic lines. Poets, being especially attuned to sounds, build certain rhythms into their language. They select words not just for content but also for sound, and they arrange words so that important ideas and climaxes of sound coincide. Sensitive readers, when reading poetry aloud, interpret the lines to develop an appropriate speed and expressiveness of delivery—a proper rhythm. Indeed, some persons think of rhythm as the *music* of poetry, since it refers to measured sounds much like rhythms and tempos in music. Like music, poetry requires some regularity of beat, although the tempo and loudness of poetry may be freer and less regular. To achieve emphasis during the reading of many parts of a poem—often within individual lines—the speaking voice may be accelerated or retarded, intensified or softened.

It is important to emphasize that rhythm is never to be separated from the content of a poem. It is important only as it supports and underscores content. Alexander Pope wrote that "the sound [of poetry] must seem an echo to the sense." This idea is important, for in poetry each word must count. Everything—not just the meanings of the words but their sounds and their positions in lines and in the entire poem—should work to convey ideas and attitudes. Words must be placed in the most effective location so that they may furnish emphasis through the comparative speed and loudness of their pronunciation as well as through their meaning and position within a train of thought, description, or narrative. The poet uses every linguistic skill to strike your mind and spirit, to fix the poem in your memory. Thus, the study of rhythm and beat is an attempt to determine how poets have arranged the words of their poems to make sound complement content.

THINGS TO CONSIDER IN STUDYING RHYTHM

It is difficult to undertake a study of rhythm without a grasp of a few basic linguistic facts. Fortunately, you have the essential details readily at hand as a result of your own experience as a speaker and reader. Let us say once again that rhythm refers to the relative loudness and tempo of words as pronounced in groups. Large units of words, poetry aside, make up sentences and paragraphs. Smaller units make up phrases, or *cadence groups* and, in poetry, *metrical feet*. Principally we will be concerned here with cadence groups and metrical feet, for these form the basic blocks of rhythmical analysis.

CADENCE GROUPS

Words do not function alone but are meaningful only when they are related to other words, as a part of sentences. This interdependence of words is a fact of any language, and one should never ignore it in studying the rhythm of a poem. Sentences do not stretch out forever, but rather they are composed of separate phrases and clauses that relate to each other through definite principles of coherence. The term used to describe the coinciding of speaking units with grammatical units, separated by slight pauses (or *junctures*), is **cadence group.** The words *on* and *to*, for example, are, grammatically, prepositions, but they are not very meaningful alone. In phrases like *on this continent* and *to the proposition*, however, they become part of a unit of meaning—prepositional phrases—that when spoken are also cadence groups. As another example, the word *nation* conveys a certain amount of meaning, but the phrase *a new nation* forms a syntactic and rhythmical unit, a cadence group. We do not utter words separately, but rather put them together into such cadence groups that coincide both grammatically and rhythmically. Let us for the moment consider the beginning of Abraham Lincoln's Gettysburg Address. If we use separate lines and spaces to indicate both the noticeable and slight vocal pauses that separate the various cadence groups, we can see that it is made up of these units of both rhythm and meaning:

> Fourscore and seven years ago
> our fathers brought forth   on this continent
> a new nation
> conceived in liberty
> and dedicated to the proposition
> that all men   are created equal.

This sentence is, of course, famous prose, and you can see that a sympathetic reading of it would be difficult without a grouping of the words

approximately as they are laid out here. The following lines by Walt Whitman are spaced according to such cadence groups:

> When lilacs last   in the dooryard bloom'd,
> And the great star   early droop'd
> in the western sky   in the night.

Such groups may or may not correspond to regular rhythmical configura-
tions in poetry. Here is an example of poetry (from Alexander Pope's
Essay on Man) in which the cadence groups are patterned upon a rhythmical
norm:

> O happiness!   our being's end and aim!
> Good,   pleasure,   ease,   content!   whate'er thy name:
> That something still   which prompts th'eternal sigh,
> For which we bear to live,   or dare to die.

You may observe that *O happiness, that something still,* and *or dare to die* are
rhythmically similar: the second and fourth syllables in each of these groups
are pronounced more emphatically than the first and third. You may also
perceive the same rhythmical similarity of the groups *our being's end and
aim, which prompts th'eternal sigh,* and *for which we bear to live.* This kind of
poetry, in which cadence groups create a recurring pattern, is called **traditional poetry,** or poetry having a **closed form** (see Chapter 22, on poetic
forms). Poetry like Whitman's, however, in which cadence groups are arranged more or less as in prose according to meaning and the poet's
apparent wishes rather than according to rhythmical regularity, is called
free verse, or poetry having an **open form.** Whether they use the open
or closed form, all poets desire to create effective, moving ideas through
the manipulation of cadence groups. However, the open-form poet relies
almost exclusively on the arrangements of cadence groups, whereas the
poet of closed form merges cadence groups and regular rhythmical patterns. Thus, open verse takes no apparently regular shape; lines may be
long or short as the poet wishes to expand or concentrate the ideas. Traditional, closed verse takes on a more formal appearance, and its rhythms
can be systematically measured.

SYLLABLES

The words that compose cadence groups are made up of **syllables,** the
individual units of meaning and rhythm. A syllable is a separately pronounced part of a word or, in some cases, a complete word. Thus, *nation*
is a complete word of two syllables, while *word,* also complete, has only

one syllable. A syllable may be made up of (1) a vowel alone, as in the indefinite article *a* ("*a* star"), or (2) a vowel with a consonant, as in *to* in the word *together*, or (3) two consonant sounds enclosing a vowel, as in *geth* in *together*. There are other combinations. For example, in the word *abide* the portion *bide* is a single syllable because the final *e* is not pronounced (sometimes this type of *e* is called a "silent *e*"or "diacritic *e*"). In the word *through* there are two consonant sounds (*th* and *r*) preceding the *oo* sound of *ough*, but they do not create a separate syllable. Because the *gh* combination is not pronounced at all, *through* is a word of only *one* syllable. In words ending in *tion*, consonants enclose two vowels. However, the *ti* combines to form the *sh* sound (one consonant), and the letters hence make up only one syllable (as in *na-tion*). A concluding *es* or *ed* may make up a new syllable in words such as *musses* and *suited*, but quite often there is no new syllable at all, as in *mussed* and *fashioned*. Thus, in Francis Thompson's line "fashioned so purely," the syllables may be determined as follows:

Fash - ioned   so   pure - ly.

This line thus has five distinctly pronounced syllables. Sometimes people experience difficulty in distinguishing the syllables in words. Hence, as a first step in perceiving rhythm, it is important to make an effort to recognize syllables. The word *merrier*, for example, is a three-syllable, not a two-syllable, word (*merr - i - er*), as is *solitude* (*sol - i - tude*). If you have difficulty in recognizing syllables, a good idea is to read each word aloud separately, pronouncing every syllable, before reading the words in poetic context. If you are still not sure, consult a dictionary. The practice of reading poetry aloud is good in any event. If you have been encouraged to read for speed, you will be better off abandoning this approach when you judge the rhythms of poetry.

STRESS, METER, FEET, BEAT, AND METRICAL SCANSION

When you speak, and especially when you read poetry, you naturally give more force, intensity, or loudness to some syllables than to others. Those syllables that receive more force are *heavily stressed* or *heavily accented*, and those receiving less force are *lightly stressed* or *lightly accented*. In Browning's line "All that I know," for example, *all* and *know* are more heavily accented than *that* and *I*. In Pope's line "For fools rush in where angels fear to tread," the syllables receiving major stress are *fools*, *rush*, *an-*, *fear*, and *tread*. The syllables with less emphasis are *for*, *in*, *where*, *-gels*, and *to*.

Beat and the Metrical Foot. The beat or accent of the lines just cited, and of all lines of poetry, is determined by the syllables receiving major stress, and the rhythm of any line is determined by the relationship of heavily and lightly stressed syllables. The basic building block of a line of poetry is a metrical foot, which usually consists of one heavily stressed syllable and one or more lightly stressed syllables. There are various types of feet, each with a characteristic pattern. Poets writing in traditional or closed forms usually fill their lines with a specific number of the same feet, and that number determines the regular **meter,** or measure, of that line. Thus five feet in a line are **pentameter,** four are **tetrameter,** three are **trimeter,** and two are **dimeter.** (To these may be added the less common line lengths **hexameter,** a six-foot line, **heptameter,** or **septenary,** seven feet, and **octameter,** eight feet.) In terms of accent or beat, a trimeter line has three beats (or stressed syllables), a pentameter line five beats, and so on.

Frequently, rhetorical needs cause poets to substitute other feet for the regular foot established in the poem. Whether there is substitution or not, however, the number and kind of feet in each line constitute the metrical description of that line. In order to discover the prevailing metrical system in any poem, you *scan* the poem. The act of scanning is called **scansion.**

A Notational System to Indicate Rhythms. In scansion, it is important to use an agreed-upon notational system to record **stress** or **accent.** A heavy or primary accent is commonly indicated by a prime mark or acute accent (´), and a light accent may be indicated by a short accent (˘). (A circle or degree symbol may also be used for a light accent.) To separate one foot from another, a virgule (/) or slash is used. Thus, the following line, from Coleridge's "The Rime of the Ancient Mariner," may be schematized formally in this way:

Wa - tĕr, / wá - tĕr, / ev́ - erȳ whére,

Here the virgules show that the line may be divided into two two-syllable feet and one three-syllable foot.

METRICAL FEET

Equipped with this degree of knowledge, you are ready to scan a poem in order to determine the rhythmical pattern of feet. The most important ones, the specific names of which are derived from Greek poetry, may be generally classed as the two-syllable foot, the three-syllable foot, and the imperfect (or one-syllable) foot.

The Two-Syllable Foot

1. IAMB.   A light stress followed by a heavy stress:

the wínds

The iamb is the most common foot in English-language poetry because it most nearly reflects the natural rhythmic cadences of the language. It is among the most versatile of poetic feet, capable of great variation. Even within the same line, iambic feet may vary in intensity, so that they may support or undergird the shades of meaning designed by the poet. For example, in this line from Wordsworth, each foot is unique:

The wínds / that wíll / be hówl - / ing át / all hoúrs.

Even though *will* and *at* are stressed syllables, they are not as heavily stressed as *winds, howl-,* and *hours* (indeed, they are also less strong than *all,* which is in an unstressed position). Such variability, approximating the stresses and rhythms of actual speech, makes the iambic foot suitable for just about any purpose, serious or light. The iamb therefore assists poets in focusing attention on their ideas and emotions. If they use it with skill, and vary it, it never becomes monotonous, for it does not distract the reader by drawing attention to its own rhythm.

2. TROCHEE.   A heavy accent followed by a light:

flów-er

The iamb and the trochee deserve special attention. Most English words of two syllables or more are trochaic; for example:

région, wáter, snówfall, aúthor, willow, mórning, eárly
assúrance, cónsider, retúrning, depénded

Words of two syllables having an iambic pattern are usually words with prefixes, or else they have been borrowed from a foreign language, such as French:

Words with prefixes: contról, becaúse, despaír, sublíme
French words: machíne, garáge, technique, chemíse

Trochaic rhythm is often called *falling, dying, light,* or *anticlimactic,* and iambic rhythm is usually called *rising, elevating, serious,* and *climactic.* A major problem encountered by many English poets has been to fit trochaic words into iambic patterns. A common way to deal with the problem—and a way consistent with the natural word order of English—is to place a definite or indefinite article, a possessive pronoun, or some other single-syllable word, before a trochaic word. For example:

the cúrfĕw;   ă présĕnce;   whăt máttĕr;   hăs ópenĕd;   whĕn yéllŏw

Such additions produce an iamb followed by the light stress needed for the next iamb. For example, Thomas Gray, when developing the third line of the "Elegy Written in a Country Churchyard," an iambic poem (p. 520), introduced the definite article *the* before the trochaic word *plough-man*. Next he wrote a two-syllable adverb, *homeward*, which is also trochaic. After this he placed *plods*, a one-syllable verb, and completed the line with a three-word phrase, *his weary way*. Notice his use of a single-syllable pronoun before the trochaic word *weary* in order to fit this word into the iambic pattern. The complete line is a perfectly regular iambic line of five feet (*iambic pentameter*).

Thĕ plóugh - / măn hóme - / wărd plóds / hĭs wéar - / ў wáy. /

Shakespeare does virtually the same thing in this line from his sonnet "Let Me Not to the Marriage of True Minds":

Wĭth - ín / hĭs bénd - / ĭng síck - / lĕ's cóm - / păss cóme. /

Here Shakespeare begins the second foot with the possessive pronoun *his*, a one-syllable word that enables him to include three successive trochaic words within the iambic pattern. The inclusion of the single-syllable word *come* at the end of the line completes the pattern and makes the line an example of regular, but very skillfully composed, iambic pentameter.

Another obvious means of using trochaic words is to substitute them for iambs, a device often used at the beginning of a line, as Yeats does here:

Túrn - ĭng / ănd túrn - / ĭng ín / ă wíd - / ĕn - ĭng gýre.

Often poets avoid the problem entirely by reducing the number of polysyllabic words in their lines and relying heavily on one-syllable words, as Shakespeare does in this line:

Tŏ lóve / thăt wéll / whĭch thóu / mŭst léave / ĕre lóng.

In scanning a poem, you might wish to consider the number of polysyllabic words and observe the methods by which the poet arranges them to fit or to conflict with the basic metrical pattern.

    3. SPONDEE. Two successive, equally heavy accents, as in *men's eyes* in Shakespeare's line:

When, ĭn / dĭs - gráce / wĭth fór - / tŭne aňd / men's eyes.

The spondee—sometimes called a **hovering accent**—is primarily a substitute foot in English because at a certain point successive spondees would more properly develop the rhythms of iambs or trochees. For this reason it is virtually impossible within traditional metrical patterns for an entire poem to be written in spondees (but see the section on strong-stressed verse, p. 676). As a substitute, however, as in the case of "men's eyes," the spondee emphasizes the image or idea being expressed by the poet. The usual way to indicate the spondee in metrical scansion is to link the two syllables together with chevronlike marks (⋀).

    4. PYRRHIC. Two unstressed syllables (even though one of them may be in a position normally receiving stress), as in *on their* in Pope's line:

Nŏw sleep - / ĭng flócks / oň thĕir / soft fleec - / ĕs líe.

The pyrrhic foot consists of weakly accented words like prepositions and articles. Like the spondee, it is usually substituted for an iamb or trochee, and therefore a complete poem cannot be written in pyrrhics. As a substitute foot, however, the pyrrhic acts as a kind of rhythmic catapult to move the reader swiftly to the next strongly accented syllable, and therefore it undergirds the ideas connected to the words that are accented.

The Three-Syllable Foot

    1. ANAPEST. Two light stresses followed by a heavy:

Bў the dáwn's / ear - lў líght

    2. DACTYL. A heavy stress followed by two lights:

mígh - ĭ - est

Both of these meters are relatively rare in English and American poetry, but both have been employed with some success. We can see an example of anapestic tetrameter in Clement Moore's "A Visit from St. Nicholas" (1822):

'Twas thĕ níght / befŏre Chríst / măs ănd all / thrŏugh thĕ hoúse

Dactylic verse can be seen in the form called double dactyls (p. 747). The first lines of these poems are usually two dactylic nonsense words:

Híggledy / Píggledy

The Imperfect Foot

The imperfect foot consists of a single syllable: (˘) by itself, or (´) by itself. This foot is a variant or substitute occurring in a poem in which one of the major feet forms the metrical pattern. The second line of "The Star-Spangled Banner," for example, is anapestic, but it contains an imperfect foot at the end:

Whăt sŏ proúd - / lў wĕ haíled / ăt thĕ twí - / light's lăst gleám - / ing.

Most scansion of English verse can be carried out with reference to the metrical feet described above. The following lines illustrate all the feet listed.

trochee	*iamb*	*iamb*	*anapest*	*spondee*

Hów ĭn / mў thóughts / thŏse háp - / pĭ - est daýs / shíne fórth—

trochee	*dactyl*	*iamb*	*pyrrhic*	*spondee*

Daýs ŏf / mél - ŏ - dў / ănd lóve / ănd ă / greát dréam.

Uncommon Meters

In many poems you might encounter variants other than those described above. Poets like Browning, Tennyson, Poe, and Swinburne experimented with uncommon meters. Other poets manipulated pauses or *caesurae* (discussed below) to create the effects of uncommon meters. For these reasons, you might need to refer to other metrical feet, such as the following.

1. AMPHIBRACH.   A light, heavy, and light, as in the following line from Swinburne's "Dolores":

Ăh, feéd me / and fíll me / wĭth pléa - sŭre.

The amphibrach is the major foot in Browning's "How They Brought the Good News from Ghent to Aix"; for instance:

Ănd ín - tŏ / the míd - nĭght / wĕ gál - lopĕd / ă - bréast.

2. AMPHIMACER OR CRETIC.   A heavy, light, and heavy, as in Browning's lines: "Lóve ĭs bést" and "práise ănd práy."

The amphimacer occurs mainly in short lines or refrains, and also may be seen as a substitute foot, as in the last foot of this line from Tennyson's "Locksley Hall":

Ĭn thĕ / spríng ă / yŏúng măn's / fán - cy / líght - lў / tŭrns tŏ / thoŭghts ŏf lóve.

3. BACCHIUS OR BACCHIC.   A light followed by two heavy stresses, as in "Some late lark" in W. E. Henley's line:

Sŏme láte lárk / sĭng - ĭng.

The bacchius often occurs as a substitute for an anapest, as in the last foot of this line from Browning's "Saul":

Whĕre thĕ lóng / grăss - ĕs stí - / flĕ thĕ wá - / tĕr wĭth - ín / thĕ stréam's bĕd.

4. DIPODIC.   Dipodic measure (literally, "two feet" combining to make one) develops in longer lines when a poet submerges two normal feet, usually iambs or trochees, under a stronger beat, so that a "galloping" or "rollicking" rhythm results. The following line from Browning's "A Toccata of Galuppi's," for example, may be scanned as trochaic heptameter (seven feet), with the concluding foot being an amphimacer or cretic:

Dĭd yŏung / péople / táke thĕir / pléas - uĕre / whĕn thĕ / séa wăs / wárm ĭn Máy?

In reading, however, a stronger beat is superimposed, which creates dipodic feet:

Dĭd yŏung péoplĕ / tăke thĕir pléasŭre / whĕn thĕ séa / wăs wărm ĭn Máy?

The dipodic foot can be used for a homespun, naive effect, as in James Whitcomb Riley's "When the Frost Is on the Punkin," where the foot overpowers the trochees:

Ŏh ĭt séts / my hĕart ă clícklĭn' / lĭke thĕ tíckĭn' / ŏf ă clóck,

Whĕn the frost / ĭs on thĕ púnkĭn / and the fódder's / ĭn the shóck.

T. S. Eliot, in the burlesque poem "Macavity: The Mystery Cat," superimposes dipodic measure over iambs for comic effect:

Măcávĭty̆, / Măcávĭty̆, / there's nó one lĭke / Măcávĭty̆,

He's brókĕn / evĕry húmăn lăw, / he bréaks thĕ lăw / of grávĭty̆.

5. ACCENTUAL, STRONG-STRESS, AND "SPRUNG" RHYTHMS. A number of modern poets do not use traditional meters in their poems but instead build their lines out of numbers of major stresses, regardless of the number of lightly stressed words and syllables. These accentual, or strong-stress lines are historically derived from the type of poetry composed a thousand years ago during the age of Anglo-Saxon English. At that time, each line was divided in two, with two major stresses occurring in each half. In the nineteenth century Gerard Manley Hopkins (1844–1889) developed "sprung" rhythm, or a rhythm in which the major stresses would be released or "sprung" from the poetic line. The method is complex, but one characteristic is the juxtaposing of one-syllable stressed words, as in this line from "Pied Beauty":

Wĭth swift, slów; swéet, sóur; ădázzle, dím;

Here a number of elements combine to create six major stresses in the line, which contains only nine syllables. Many of Hopkins's lines combine alliteration and strong stresses in this way to create the same effect of heavy emphasis.

A parallel instance of strongly stressed lines may be seen in "We Real Cool" by Gwendolyn Brooks (p. 685). In this poem the effect is achieved by the exclusive use of monosyllabic stressed words combined with internal rhyme, repetition, and alliteration.

Note: In scanning a poem to determine its formal meter, always try to explain the lines simply, by reference to the more common feet, before turning to the less common ones. If a line can be analyzed as iambic, for example, do not attempt to fit the bacchius or the amphibrach to it unless these feet are unmistakably indicated. The following line is iambic pentameter with a substitute spondee as the third foot.

The file / ŏf mén / rŏde forth / ă- móng / thĕ hílls. /

It would be a mistake to scan it thus:

The / file ŏf mén / róde / forth ă- mong / thĕ hílls. /

This incorrect analysis correctly accents "file of men" and "forth among," but by describing these phrases as two amphimacers, it must resort to the explanation that "The" and "rode" are imperfect feet. Such an analysis creates unnecessary complications.

THE CAESURA, OR PAUSE

In rhythmic study the pause separating cadence groups, however brief, is called a **caesura** (the plural is **caesurae**). For noting scansion, the caesura is indicated by two diagonal lines or virgules (/ /) to distinguish it from the single virgule separating feet. The following line by Ben Jonson contains two caesurae:

> Thou art / not, / / Pens- / hurst, / / built / to en- / vious show. /

If a caesura follows an accented syllable, it may be called a *stressed* or *rising* caesura; if it follows an unaccented syllable, *unstressed* or *falling*. In the following line from William Blake, a stressed caesura follows the word *divine*:

> With hands / divine / / he mov'd / the gen- / tle Sod. /

The following line from the same poem ("To Mrs. Anna Flaxman") contains a falling caesura after the word *lovely*:

> Its form / was love- / ly / / but / its col- / ours pale. /

The word *caesura* is usually reserved for references to pauses within lines, but when a pause ends a line—usually marked by a comma, semicolon, or period—such a line is **end-stopped**. If you are writing about a poet's use of pauses, you should treat not only the caesurae but also the end-stopping; you might use the double virgules to show the concluding pause, as in the following line from Keats's "Endymion" (1818):

> A thing / of beau- / ty / / is / a joy / forever. / /

If a line has no punctuation at the end and runs over to the next line, it is called **run-on**. A term also used to indicate run-on lines is **enjambement**. The following passage, a continuation of the line from Keats, contains three run-on lines that are enjambed.

> Its loveliness increases; / / it will never
> Pass into nothingness; / / but still will keep
> A bower quiet for us, / / and a sleep
> Full of sweet dreams, / / . . .

EMPHASIS BY FORMAL SUBSTITUTION

Most poems are written in a pattern that can readily be perceived. Thus Shakespeare's plays usually follow the pattern of **blank verse** (unrhymed iambic pentameter) and Milton's *Paradise Lost* follows this same pattern. Such a pattern is no more than a rhythmical norm, however. For interest and emphasis (and perhaps because of the very nature of the English language) the norm is varied by *substituting* other feet for the normal feet.

The following line is from the "January" eclogue of Spenser's *Shepherd's Calendar*. Although the abstract pattern of the line is iambic pentameter, it is varied by the substitution of two other feet:

Áll iñ / ă sún - / shine day, / / ăs díd / ğe - fáll.

All in is a trochee, and *shine day* is a spondee. This line shows formal substitution; that is, a separate, formally structured foot is substituted for one of the original feet. The effect of these substitutions is to enable one's voice to emphasize *all* as a strong syllable, almost a separate imperfect foot. Then the phrase *in a sun* rolls off the tongue as an anapest, and the spondee on *shine day* enables the voice to emphasize the words. In the context, Spenser has just been stressing the miseries of winter, and this line with its substitutions encourages the reader to think of spring as the voice lingers on the words:

A shepherd's boy (no better do him call)
When winter's wasteful spite was almost spent,
All in a sunshine day, as did befall,
Led forth his flock, that had been long ypent [enclosed].

When you study rhythm, try in this way to relate the substitutions to the ideas and attitudes of the poet.

EMPHASIS BY RHETORICAL VARIATION

The effect of formal substitution is to create opposing or contrasting internal rhythms. The same effect is also achieved by the manipulation of the caesura. Placing the caesura in a perfectly regular line has the same effect, in a spoken line, as if formal substitution had occurred. This variation may be called **rhetorical substitution.** A noteworthy example in an iambic pentameter line is this one by Pope:

Hĭs ác - / tĭons', / / pás - / sĭons', / / bé - / ing's, / / use / ănd énd;

Ordinarily there is one caesura in a line of this type, but in this one there are three, each producing a strong pause. The line is regularly iambic and should be scanned as regular. But in reading, the effect is different. Because of the pauses in the middle of the second, third, and fourth feet, the line is actually read as an amphibrach, a trochee, a trochee, and an amphimacer, thus:

His ác - tioñs', / / pas - sioñs', / / bé - ing's, / / use and end;

Although the line is regular, the practical effect—the rhetorical effect—is of variation and tension. In the following well-known line from Shakespeare's *Twelfth Night*, rhetorical substitution may also be seen:

If music / / be the food of love, / / play on!

This line is regularly iambic except, perhaps, for a spondee in *play on*, but the reading of the line conflicts with the formal pattern. Thus, *If music* may be read as an amphibrach and *be the food* is in practice an anapest because of the short pause after *music* and the light stress on the word *be* following the caesura. The words stressed in the line are *music, food, love*, and the command *play on*. The line reads like normal speech even though it is in a formal rhythmical structure, and Shakespeare has provided us with the best of both worlds.

In whatever poetry you study, your main concern in noting substitutions is to determine the formal metrical pattern and then to analyze the formal and rhetorical variations on the pattern and the principal causes and effects of these variations. Always show how these variations have assisted the poet in achieving emphasis.

POEMS FOR STUDY

WILLIAM SHAKESPEARE (1564–1616)

Sonnet 29: When in Disgrace with Fortune and Men's Eyes   *1609*

When, in disgrace with fortune and men's eyes,
I all alone beweep my outcast state,
And trouble deaf heaven with my bootless° cries,   *futile, useless*
And look upon myself, and curse my fate,
Wishing me like to one more rich in hope,   5
Featured like him, like him with friends possessed,
Desiring this man's art and that man's scope,

With what I most enjoy contented least;
Yet in these thoughts myself almost despising,
Haply I think on thee—and then my state,   10
Like to the lark at break of day arising
From sullen earth, sings hymns at heaven's gate;
For thy sweet love remembered such wealth brings
That then I scorn to change my state with kings.

QUESTIONS

1. Describe the situation of the speaker as expressed in lines 1–12. If the speaker were more specific about the causes of his depression, what would this knowledge add to your understanding of these lines?

2. What idea does the speaker explore in lines 9–14? If you consider that lines 1–8 do not form a complete sentence (note that lines 5–8 are all participial phrases), whereas the speaker constructs complete sentences to form lines 9–14, what conclusions can you draw about the relationship of style to subject matter?

3. Consider the sonnet as a structure of iambic pentameter. What use does Shakespeare make of formal substitutions (for example, in the first and last feet of line 1)?

4. How does Shakespeare use caesurae in the sonnet? In light of the fact that all the lines are end-stopped, how does he nevertheless move the content along smoothly and logically from one line to the next?

WILLIAM SHAKESPEARE (1564–1616)

Sonnet 73: That Time of Year Thou Mayest in Me Behold   1609

That time of year thou mayst in me behold
When yellow leaves, or none, or few, do hang
Upon those boughs which shake against the cold,
Bare ruined choirs,° where late the sweet birds sang.
In me thou see'st the twilight of such day
As after sunset fadeth in the west;
Which by and by black night doth take away,
Death's second self,° that seals up all in rest.
In me thou see'st the glowing of such fire,
That on the ashes of his° youth doth lie,   *its*   10
As the death-bed whereon it must expire,

SONNET 73.   4 *choirs*: the part of a church just in front of the altar.   8 *Death's . . .
self*: that is, Night is a mirror image of death inasmuch as it brings the sleep of rest just as
death brings the sleep of actual death.

Consumed with that which it was nourished by,°
This thou perceivest, which makes thy love more strong,
To love that well which thou must leave ere long.   15

12 *Consumed . . . by:* that is, the ashes of the fuel burned at the fire's height now prevent the fire from continuing, and in fact extinguish it.

QUESTIONS

1. Describe the content of lines 1–4, 5–8, and 9–12. What common link connects these three sections of the poem? How does the concluding couplet relate to the first twelve lines?

2. Analyze the iambic pentameter of the poem. Consider the spondees in lines 2 (*do hang*), 4 (*bare ru-* and *birds sang*), 5 (*such day*), 7 (*black night*), 8 (*death's sec-*), 9 (*such fire*), 10 (*doth lie*), 11 (*death-bed*), 13 (*more strong*), and 14 (*ere long*). What effect do these substitutions have upon the development and flow of the ideas of the poem?

3. Consider Shakespeare's use of enjambement in lines 1–3 and 5–6. How do these lines seem to conclude as lines even though grammatically they carry over to form sentences?

4. In lines 2, 5, 6, and 9, where does Shakespeare place the caesurae? What relationship is there between the rhythms produced by these caesurae and the content of lines 1–12? In lines 13 and 14, how do the rising stressed caesurae relate to the content?

JOHN KEATS (1795–1821)

Bright Star   *1838 (1819)*

Bright star! would I were steadfast as thou art—
   Not in lone splendor hung aloft the night,
And watching, with eternal lids apart,
   Like Nature's patient, sleepless eremite,°   *hermit*
The moving waters at their priestlike task   5
   Of pure ablution round earth's human shores,
Or gazing on the new soft-fallen mask
   Of snow upon the mountains and the moors;
No—yet still steadfast, still unchangeable,
   Pillowed upon my fair love's ripening breast,   10
To feel forever its soft fall and swell,
   Awake forever in a sweet unrest,
Still, still to hear her tender-taken breath,
And so live ever—or else swoon to death.

QUESTIONS

1. With what topic is the speaker concerned in this sonnet? What tasks does he attribute to the star in lines 1–8? Why, in lines 9–14, does he contrast his desires and his wishes to be steadfast, on the one hand, with the constancy of the star, on the other?

2. How regular is Keats's use of iambic pentameter in this sonnet? What formal substitutions do you find in the lines? What effect do you associate with these substitutions?

3. Describe the recurring cadence groups or rhythmical patterns in the sonnet (such as line 3, *And watching*, and line 7, *Or gazing*). How do these patterns help to unify the poem, even though the entire poem is difficult grammatically?

4. Describe the use of caesurae in the sonnet. What effects do these caesurae have upon the poem's content and rhythms?

ROBERT BROWNING (1812–1889)

My Star   1855

        All that I know
            Of a certain star
        Is, it can throw
            (Like the angled spar)°
        Now a dart of red,
            Now a dart of blue;   5
        Till my friends have said
            They would fain see, too,
    My star that dartles the red and the blue!
    Then it stops like a bird; like a flower, hangs furled: 10
        They must solace themselves with the Saturn° above it.
    What matter to me if their star is a world?
        Mine has opened its soul to me; therefore
            I love it.

MY STAR.   4 *angled spar*: Iceland spar, a transparent calcite used in lenses. Prismlike, it refracts light into the colors of the rainbow.   11 *Saturn*: the planet, but here representative of planets generally.

QUESTIONS

1. This poem, a favorite of Browning's, is considered a tribute by the poet to his wife, Elizabeth Barrett Browning. If the "star" refers to her, in what way are the images appropriate as attributes of a woman?

2. Why is it difficult to establish a metrical norm for the poem? What foot is

used most frequently? What other feet can you discover? Why do you think Browning introduced such variety into the metrical pattern?

3. Analyze the placement of caesurae in the poem. How do they help achieve a conversational rhythm, despite the numerous anapests in the lines?

FRANCIS THOMPSON (1859–1907)

To a Snowflake   *1897*

What heart could have thought you?
Past our devisal
(O filigree petal!)
Fashioned so purely,
Fragilely, surely,   5
From what Paradisal
Imagineless metal,
Too costly for cost?
Who hammered you, wrought you
From argentine vapour?—   10
"God was my shaper.
Passing surmisal,
He hammered, He wrought me.
From curled silver vapour,
To lust of His mind:—   15
Thou could'st not have thought me!
So purely, so palely,
Tinily, surely,
Mightily, frailly,
Insculped and embossed,   20
With His hammer of wind,
And His graver of frost."

QUESTIONS

1. This poem takes the shape of questions and answers. Who is speaking, and who responds? What metaphor of creation dominates the poem? How might the poem be considered a religious tribute?

2. The poem is in dimeter (lines consisting of two feet). Why is this short line appropriate to the subject?

3. What is the prevailing metrical pattern? How is this meter appropriate for the subject of a snowflake? Would iambs have been more or less appropriate? What variations on the predominant foot can you find in the poem? Why do you think the poet made the last three lines conclude with stressed syllables?

4. Compare this poem with Blake's "The Lamb" (p. 556) and "The Tyger" (p. 581). To which of the two Blake poems is "To a Snowflake" more similar? Why? In what ways is Thompson's poem different from those of Blake?

T. S. ELIOT (1888–1965)

Macavity: The Mystery Cat   1939

Macavity's a Mystery Cat: he's called the Hidden Paw—
For he's the master criminal who can defy the Law.
He's the bafflement of Scotland Yard, the Flying Squad's despair:
For when they reach the scene of the crime—*Macavity's not there*!

Macavity, Macavity, there's no one like Macavity,   5
He's broken every human law, he breaks the law of gravity.
His powers of levitation would make a fakir stare,
And when you reach the scene of crime—*Macavity's not there*!
You may seek him in the basement, you may look up in the air—
But I tell you once and once again, *Macavity's not there*!   10

Macavity's a ginger cat, he's very tall and thin;
You would know him if you saw him, for his eyes are sunken in.
His brow is deeply lined with thought, his head is highly domed;
His coat is dusty from neglect, his whiskers are uncombed.
He sways his head from side to side, with movements like a snake;   15
And when you think he's half asleep, he's always wide awake.

Macavity, Macavity, there's no one like Macavity,
For he's a fiend in feline shape, a monster of depravity.
You may meet him in a by-street, you may see him in the square—
But when a crime's discovered, then *Macavity's not there*!   20

He's outwardly respectable. (They say he cheats at cards.)
And his footprints are not found in any file of Scotland Yard's.
And when the larder's looted, or the jewel-case is rifled,
Or when the milk is missing, or another Peke's been stifled,°
Or the greenhouse glass is broken, and the trellis past repair—   25
Ay, there's the wonder of the thing! *Macavity's not there*!

And when the Foreign Office find a Treaty's gone astray,
Or the Admiralty lose some plans and drawings by the way,
There may be a scrap of paper in the hall or on the stair—
But it's useless to investigate—*Macavity's not there*!   30
And when the loss has been disclosed, the Secret Service say:

MACAVITY: THE MYSTERY CAT.   24 *Peke's been stifled*: a Pekingese dog (a small animal, with silky hair) has been found dead.

"It *must* have been Macavity!"—but he's a mile away.
You'll be sure to find him resting, or a-licking of his thumbs,
Or engaging in doing complicated long division sums.

Macavity, Macavity, there's no one like Macavity,   35
There never was a Cat of such deceitfulness and suavity.
He always has an alibi, and one or two to spare:
At whatever time the deed took place—MACAVITY WASN'T THERE!
And they say that all the Cats whose wicked deeds are widely known
(I might mention Mungojerrie, I might mention Griddlebone)   40
Are nothing more than agents for the Cat who all the time
Just controls their operations: the Napoleon of Crime!

QUESTIONS

1. What are some of Macavity's major "crimes" as a master criminal and "mystery cat"? What attitude does the speaker express toward Macavity? How, if the "crimes" had been attributed to a human being, would they be grievous wrongs? Since they are attributed to a cat, how do they add to the comic qualities of the poem?

2. What is the basic metrical foot of the poem? How many feet are contained in each of the lines? What is the norm?

3. Once you begin reading and "getting into" the lines, what new kind of pattern emerges? How many major stresses appear in each line? In light of the nature of the poem, how is the dipodic rhythm appropriate?

4. In his essay on "The Music of Poetry" (1942), Eliot wrote, in reference to the "nonsense verse" of another poet, "We enjoy the music, which is of a higher order, and we enjoy the feeling of irresponsibility toward the sense." Explain how Eliot's own comment may be applied to "Macavity: The Mystery Cat."

GWENDOLYN BROOKS (b. 1917)

We Real Cool   *1959*

The Pool Players.
Seven at the Golden Shovel.

We real cool. We
Left school. We

Lurk late. We
Strike straight. We

Sing sin. We
Thin gin. We
Jazz June. We   5
Die soon.

QUESTIONS

1. What is the major idea of the poem? Who is the speaker? How is the last
    sentence a climax? How is this sentence consistent with the declarations in
    lines 1–7? How is the poet's attitude made clear?
2. Describe the patterning of stresses in the poem. Explain the absence of light
    stresses in view of the shortness of the lines. What method is employed to
    achieve the constant strong stresses?
3. What is the effect of the repetition of the pronoun *We* ending lines 1–7?
    Compare this usage with that of E. E. Cummings in the poem "In just" (p.
    805).

JAMES EMANUEL (b. 1921)

The Negro   1968

Never saw him.
Never can.
Hypothetical,
Haunting man:

Eyes a-saucer,
Yessir bossir,   5
Dice a-clicking,
Razor flicking.

The-ness froze him
In a dance.   10
A-ness never
Had a chance.

QUESTIONS

1. What attributes of the black are described in lines 1–4, lines 5 and 6, and
    lines 7 and 8? Are these attributes new or conventional? What attitude does
    the poem convey about the plight of the black?
2. What is the meaning of *The-ness* and *A-ness* in the third stanza?
3. What metrical foot is dominant in the poem? Why do you think the poet
    chose this foot in preference to a foot having a rising rhythm, such as the
    iamb?

4. Inasmuch as stanzas 1 and 3 establish a pattern of line lengths, what is the effect of the variation in lines 6 and 8 in stanza 2?

WRITING ABOUT RHYTHM IN POETRY

Because studying for poetic scansion requires a good deal of specific detail and, ultimately, much specific description, it is best to limit your choice of poem to a short passage or a complete short poem. A sonnet, a stanza of a lyric poem, or fragment from a long poem will usually be of sufficient length for your study. If you choose a fragment, it should be a self-contained one, such as an entire speech or short episode or scene (as in the example from Tennyson chosen for the sample essay in Chapter 20).

The analysis of even a short poem, however, can become quite long because of the need to describe the positions of words and stresses and the need to determine the various effects. For this reason you do not have to exhaust all aspects of your topic. Try to make your reading selective and representative of the rhythms of the passage you have chosen.

Your first reading in preparation for your essay might be a reading for comprehension. On second and third readings, however, try to make yourself aware of sound and accent by reading the poem aloud. One student helped herself to a comprehension of rhythm by reading aloud in an exaggerated fashion in front of a mirror. If you have privacy, or are not especially self-conscious, you might do the same. Let yourself go a bit. As you dramatize your reading, you might find that certain heightened levels of reading also accompany the poet's expression of important ideas. Mark out these spots for later study, so that you eventually can make good points about the relationship of the poem's rhythm to its content.

In planning an essay on scansion, it is important to prepare materials that will later be helpful, and to make sure that you make your observations exactly and correctly, for your conclusions may go astray if some of your factual analysis is wrong. Furthermore, the job of writing can be facilitated by a careful preparation of materials. Therefore the first task in developing your essay is to make a triple-spaced copy of the poem or passage you have chosen for rhythmic analysis. Leave spaces between syllables and words for the marking out of the various feet of the poem. Ultimately, this duplication of the passage, with your markings, should be included as a first page, as in the sample essay.

Carry out your study of the passage in the following way:

1. Number each line of the passage, regardless of length, beginning with 1, so that you may use these numbers as location references in your essay.
2. Determine the formal pattern of feet, using the short acute accent for heavily stressed syllables (´), and the short symbol for lightly stressed syllables (˘). Use chevrons to mark spondees (⋀).

3. Indicate the separate feet by a diagonal line or virgule (/). Indicate caesurae and the pauses at end-stopped lines by double virgules (/ /).

4. Underline, or mark with various colored pencils, any formal and rhetorical substitutions, and provide a numbered key at the bottom of the page. Colored pencils have proved particularly useful in the distinguishing of the various effects, and often they prevent mistakes that result from confusion about monochromatic markings.

5. When sketching out and preparing drafts of your essay, use your worksheet as a reference for your reader. In the final writing of your essay, however, it will not be sufficient just to point out line numbers as your supporting data. Instead, you will need to make your examples specific and illustrative at the spot where they are relevant (using, for example, words, phrases, and entire lines, with proper marks and accents), just as they should be for essays on other topics.

Once you have fully analyzed the effects of meter in the poem under consideration and you have recorded these on your worksheet and in your notes, you will be ready to formulate a tentative central idea and organization for the essay. The focus for the essay should reflect what you have found to be the most significant feature of metrics as it applies to some other element of the poem, such as speaker, tone, or ideas. Keep in mind that the essay will normally assert some connection between metrical effects and content. Thus, in planning an essay about Eliot's "Macavity," you might decide to argue that the employment of dipodic rhythm gives the poem an amused tone and makes the portrait of the feline "Napoleon of Crime" comic.

After forming a tentative idea for the essay, you can begin to gather examples of metrical evidence that will support your central assertion. These examples can be grouped into units of related or similar effects that will eventually become paragraphs in the body of the essay. Make sure that all your examples are relevant to your central idea. If you find the metrical evidence leading you in new directions, rethink the essay and revise the central idea accordingly.

Organizing Your Essay

INTRODUCTION. The introduction should lead as quickly as possible to the central idea. After a brief description of the poem (such as that it is a sonnet, a two-stanza lyric, a short satirical piece in tetrameter couplets, an iambic pentameter description of a character, a dipodic burlesque poem, and so on), try to establish the scope of your essay. You might wish to discuss all aspects of rhythm, or perhaps just one, such as the poet's use of (1) regular meter, (2) a particular substitution, such as the anapest or the trochee, and (3) the caesura and its effects. (For comprehensiveness, the sample essay treats all these topics, but an essay might deal with just one or two of them.) Your central idea will outline the thought you wish to carry out in your metrical analysis, such as that regularity of meter is consistent with the desire to be constant (as in the sample essay), or that the meter undergirds particular aspects of description, or that the poet builds up particular ideas so that they are rhythmically as well as logically stressed. Your thesis sentence should outline the aspects you plan to treat in the body of the essay.

BODY. In writing about meter, you should first establish the formal metrical pattern. What is the dominant metrical foot used for the poem? Are the lines of any consistent length, or do they vary? If the poem demonstrates any variable lengths, what relationship do these variations have with the subject matter? If the poem is a lyric, or a sonnet, you should try to determine if the poet is successful in placing important words and syllables in stressed positions as a means of achieving emphasis. Try to relate line lengths to whatever exposition and development of ideas and whatever rising and falling of emotion you find. It is also important to look for either repeating or varying metrical patterns as the subject matter reaches peaks or climaxes. Generally, deal with the relationship between the formal rhythmical pattern and the poet's ideas and attitudes.

In writing about substitutions, you might analyze the formal variations and the principal effects of these, as nearly as you can determine what the effects are. The aim is to relate substitutions to ideas and emotions emphasized by the poet. If you decide to concentrate on one particular metrical substitution, try to describe any apparent pattern in its use, that is, its locations, recurrences, and effects on meaning.

In the analysis of caesurae, treat the effectiveness of the poet's control. Can you see any pattern of use? Are the pauses regular, or do they seem randomly placed? What conclusions can you draw as a result of your answer? Describe any noticeable principles of placement, such as (1) the creation of rhythmical similarities in various parts of the poem, (2) the development of particular rhetorical effects, or (3) the creation of interest through rhythmical variety. Do the caesurae lead to important ideas and attitudes? Are the lines all end-stopped, or do you discover enjambement? How do these rhythmical characteristics aid in the poet's expression of subject matter?

CONCLUSION. Beyond summarizing your main idea in the essay, you might try to develop a short evaluation of the poet's metrical performance. Without going into excessive detail (and in effect writing another body for the essay), can you say here any more than you have in the body? What has been the value of your study to your understanding and appreciating this particular poem? If you think your analysis has helped you to develop new awareness of the craft of poetry generally, it would be appropriate in your conclusion to describe what you have learned.

SAMPLE ESSAY

The Rhythms of Keats's Sonnet "Bright Star"

Bright star! // would I / were stead- / fast // as / thou art/ — // — 1

Not in / lone splen- / dor // hung / a-loft / the night, // 2

And watch- / ing, // with / e- ter- / nal lids / a- part, // 3

Like Na- / ture's pa- / tient // sleep-/ less E- / re- mite, // 4

The mov- / ing wa- / ters // at / their priest- / like task 5

Of pure / ab-lu- / tion // round / earth's hu- / man shores, // 6

Or gaz- / ing // on / the new / soft- fall- / en mask 7

Of snow / up- on / the moun- / tains // and / the moors— // 8

No— // yet / still stead- / fast, // still / un-change- / a-ble, // 9

Pill-owed / up- on / my fair / love's ripe- / ning breast, // 10

To feel / forev - / er //its / soft fall / and swell, // 11

A- wake / forev- / er // in / a sweet / un- rest, // 12

Still, // still // to hear / her ten- / der-ta- / ken breath, // 13

And so / live ev- / er— // or / else swoon / to death. // 14

1 = spondee   5 = effect of amphibrach
2 = effect of bacchius   6 = effect of anapest
3 = effect of imperfect foot   7 = trochee
4 = effect of amphimacer   8 = effect of trochee

[1] This personal poem, in which Keats's speaker describes the wish to be a "steadfast" lover like the "bright star" which is a witness to the earth's waters and snows, is a fourteen-line sonnet in form. Keats emphasizes steadiness and regularity, and his meter, too, is constant, even in its variations.° The regularity is apparent in the formal iambic pattern, the substitutions, and the caesurae.°

[2] Because the sonnet, being made up of only one long sentence, is difficult to follow, Keats relies on metrical regularity to help the reader. Twelve of the fourteen lines are end-stopped, ending on stressed syllables in iambic feet, to climax particular ideas and descriptions. The two lines that are enjambed are 5 and 7. Even these create an identical pattern, however, because they are first and third in the second quatrain, and the carry-over words are alike both grammatically and metrically (*tásk / Ŏf púre*, and *másk / Ŏf snów*). Keats uses parallel patterns in 3 and 7 (*Ănd wátch- / iñg*, and *Ŏr gáz- / iñg*). The iambic-infinitives *tŏ féel* and *tŏ héar* appear in 11 and 13, and the accented single-syllable verbs *líve* and *swóon* are balanced together in the last line. The iambic preposition *ŭpón* is repeated in the second foot of 8 and 10, and the adverb *fŏr-é / vĕr* recurs in 11 and 12.

[3] The same pattern of regularity can be seen in Keats's substitutions, mainly spondees. He frames his first line with opening and closing spondees (*Bright star* and *thou art*). For balance, he uses spondees again in the second and fourth feet of the concluding line, an effective inner frame. He uses a total of fourteen spondees. The spondee appears in the fourth foot of five separate lines (6, 7, 10, 11, and 14), enough to undergird his idea of steadfastness. Keats uses two successive spondees in the first line (*Bright star, / would I /*) and uses this rhythm again at the start of line 9, as his thought shifts from the star to himself (*No—yet / still stead- /*). He also uses a spondee at the opening of the last couplet (*Still, still*), thus employing this substitution at the beginning of each major grouping of the sonnet (lines 1–8 as group one; 9–12 as two; and 13 and 14 as three). He uses one spondee in 11 (*soft fall*) to echo another one he uses in 7 (*soft fall- / ĕn*). All these strategically placed spondees help to unify Keats's thought. The trochees in lines 1, 2, and 10 are not by themselves enough to be seen as part of any trochaic pattern of substitution.

[4] More to the effect of trochaic patterning is Keats's regularity in his use of caesurae. In eight lines, the caesura is in the middle, after the fifth syllable, thereby causing a trochaic or falling rhythm in the previous two syllables. This pattern is exemplified in line 4:

° Central idea.
° Thesis sentence.

falling rhythm

Like Nát- / uře's pa- / tiĕnt / / slĕep- / lĕss É- / rĕ- míte,

The caesura in such a position creates not just apparent trochees, as in *pá-tiĕnt* and *wá-tĕrs* in 4 and 5, but also the effects of amphibrachs, as in *ăb-lú-tion* and *fŏré-vĕr* in 6 and 11. Keats also puts caesurae after uneven-numbered syllables in four of the other lines (1, 2, 5, and 13). Only two internal caesurae are rising ones after even-numbered syllables (1 and 13). Thus, the characteristic mode of caesurae for this poem is a falling one. In a real sense, the falling rhythm, balanced by the rising rhythm at the ends of the end-stopped lines, may be compared to the "fair love's" breathing described in lines 10 and 11.

[5]   It would be possible to add still more descriptions of other recurring rhythmical effects by which Keats unites the poem (for example, the effect of the bacchius repeated twice in the opening and closing lines: *wĕre stéad-fast* and *ăs thóu árt*, and *ănd só líve* and *ŏr élse swóon*). It is enough here, however, to restate that his metrics are used and varied with regularity. They reinforce his speaker's main theme—the wish to be as eternally steadfast as the bright star.

Commentary on the Essay

Detailed as it is, this essay is a selective discussion of the rhythms of Keats's poem. It would be possible, for example, to extend the essay with a more searching study of the tension caused by the rhetorical variations which result from the placement of the caesurae.

The introductory paragraph relates the metrics to the constant, steadfast star. Paragraph 2 stresses the way in which the regularly placed accents help the reader to comprehend the poem, which consists of a single sentence. Note is made of the repeated words and grammatical forms which are also repeated rhythmical units.

The third paragraph treats the spondee as a regular substitution throughout the poem. Paragraph 4 deals with the caesurae and relates these to the central idea by submitting that the falling rhythms before the caesurae, balanced by the rising rhythms of the end-stopped lines, can be likened to the regular breathing of the speaker's "fair love."

The final paragraph suggests, as has been already mentioned, that there might be other aspects of the rhythm that could be examined. The essay, however, concludes here, on the principle that the writer has demonstrated a satisfactory understanding of rhythm.

20

Sounds and Segments

Just as poetry stresses rhythm, it also emphasizes the sounds of individual words. These sounds have been classified by linguists as **segments**. Each segment is a sound essential to the meaningful understanding of words. Thus, in the word *top* there are three segments: *t*, *o*, and *p*. It takes three letters—*t*, *o*, and *p*—to spell (**graph**) the word, because each letter is identical with a segment. Sometimes it takes more than one letter to spell a segment. In *enough*, for example, there are four segments but *six* letters: *e*, *n*, *ou*, and *gh*. The last two segments (*ŭ* and *f*) require two letters each (two letters forming one segment are called a **digraph**). In the word *through* there are three segments but *seven* letters. To be correctly spelled in this word, the $\overline{oo}$ segment must have four letters, *ough*. Note, however, that in the word *flute* the $\overline{oo}$ segment requires only one letter, the *u*.

Segments may be treated as **vowel sounds** and **consonant sounds** (including **semivowels**). It is important to emphasize the word *sound* as distinguished from the letters of the alphabet, for, as you will see, the same letters often represent different sounds.

To study the effects of sounds and segments in poetry, we need an acceptable notational system for indicating sounds. The most readily available systems of pronunciation are those in the collegiate dictionaries; they take into account regional differences in pronunciation. If questions arise about syllabication and the position of stresses, you should use your dictionary as your authority.

VOWEL SOUNDS

Vowel sounds are vibrations resonating in the space between the tongue and the top of the mouth. Some are relatively straight and "short," such as *ĭ* (fĭt), *ŭ* (fŭn), and *ĕ* (sĕt). Some are long, such as *ō* (snow), *ā* (stay),

693

ē (fl*ee*), and $\overline{oo}$ (f*oo*d). There are three **diphthongs**—that is, sounds that begin with one vowel sound and move to another—namely *ī* (fl*y*), *ou* (h*ou*se), and *oi* (f*oi*l). A great number of vowel sounds in English are pronounced as a *schwa* (the *e* in "th*e* boy"), despite their spellings. Thus "*a*bout," "stag*e*s," "rap*i*d," "nati*o*n," and "circ*u*s" are spelled with the vowels *a*, *e*, *i*, *o*, and *u*, but all these different vowels make the same *schwa* sound.

CONSONANT SOUNDS

There are various classifications of consonant sounds, but basically they are of three types: (1) **Stop sounds** are made by the momentary stoppage and release of breath either when the lips touch each other or when the tongue touches the teeth or palate. The stop sounds are *p*, *b*, *t*, *d*, *k*, and *g*. (2) **Continuant sounds** are produced by the steady release of the breath in conjunction with various positions of the tongue in relation to the teeth and palate, as in *n*, *ng*, *l*, *r*, *th* (*th*orn), *th* (*th*e), *s*, *z*, *sh* (*sh*arp), and *zh* (plea*s*ure); or with the touching of the lower lip and upper teeth for the sounds *f* and *v*; or with the touching of both lips for the sound *m*. Two sounds, called **affricates,** begin with the stops *t* (*ch*ew) and *d* (*j*aw) and then become the continuants *sh* and *zh*. (3) **Semivowel sounds** are midway between vowels and consonants. These are *w* (*w*agon), *y* (*y*es, *u*nion), and *h* (*h*ope).

Another way of classifying consonant sounds is according to whether they are **voiced,** that is, produced with vibration of the vocal chords (*b*, *d*, *v*, *z*), or **voiceless,** produced by the breath alone (*p*, *t*, *f*, *s*).

DISTINGUISHING SOUNDS FROM SPELLING

When discussing segments, it is important to distinguish between spelling, or **graphics,** and pronunciation, or **phonetics.** Thus the letter *s* has three very different sounds in the words *sweet*, *sugar*, and *flows*: *s*, *sh*, and *z*. On the other hand, the words *shape*, *ocean*, *nation*, *sure*, and *machine* use different letters or combinations of letters to spell the same *sh* sound.

Vowel sounds may also be spelled in different ways. The *ē* sound, for example, can be spelled with *i* in *machine*, *ee* in *speed*, *ea* in *eat*, *e* in *even*, and *y* in *funny*, yet the vowel sounds in *eat*, *break*, and *bear* are not the same even though they are spelled the same. Remember this: With both consonants and vowels, do not confuse spellings with actual sounds.

SEGMENTAL POETIC DEVICES

Poets use segments in various patterns to link sound with sense. A poet may use words containing the same segments and thereby impress your memory by merging sound and idea. In descriptive poetry, the segments may actually combine, with rhythm, to imitate some of the things being described. The segmental devices most common to poetry are *assonance*, *alliteration*, and *onomatopoeia*.

ASSONANCE.   The repetition of identical *vowel* sounds in different words —for example, short ĭ in "swi̇ft Cami̇lla ski̇ms," is called **assonance.** It is a strong means of emphasis, as in the following line, where the ŭ sound connects the two words *lull* and *slumber*, and the short ĭ connects *him*, *in*, and *his*:

And more, to lu̇ll hi̇m i̇n hi̇s slu̇mber soft

In some cases, poets use assonance quite elaborately, as in this line from Pope:

'Ti̇s hȧrd to say, i̇f greȧter wȧnt of ski̇ll

Here the line is framed and balanced with the short ĭ in *'Tis*, *if*, and *skill*. The ä in *hard* and *want* forms another, internal frame, and the *a* in *say* and *greater* creates still another. Such a balanced use of vowels is unusual, however, for in most lines assonance is a means by which the poet emphasizes certain words by making them stand out phonetically.

In studying assonance, a reader must avoid selecting isolated instances of a particular sound. If, for example, a line in a poem includes three words that contain a long *a* sound, these form a pattern of assonance. A word containing the same long *a* sound that occurs six lines later, however, is not part of this pattern because it is too far removed from the original instances of the sound.

ALLITERATION.   Like assonance, **alliteration** is a means of highlighting ideas by the selection of words containing the same *consonant* sound—for example, the repeated *m* in "*m*ixed with a *m*urmuring wind," or the *s* sound in "Your never-failing *s*word made war to *c*ease," which emphasizes the connection between the words *sword* and *cease*.

There are two kinds of alliteration. (1) Most commonly, alliteration is regarded as the repetition of identical consonant sounds that begin syllables in relatively close patterns—for example, "*Lab*orious, heavy, *b*usy, *b*old, and *b*lind," and "While *p*ensive *p*oets *p*ainful vigils keep." Used sparingly, alliteration gives strength to a poem by emphasizing key words, but too much *c*an *c*ause *c*omic *c*onsequences. (2) Another form of alliteration occurs when a poet repeats identical or similar consonant sounds that do not begin syllables but nevertheless create a pattern—for example, the *z* segment in the line "In the*s*e places free*z*ing bree*z*es ea*s*ily cau*s*e snee*z*es," or the *b*, *m*, and *p* segments (all of which are made *bilabially*, that is, with both lips) in "The *m*um*b*ling and *m*urm*u*ring *b*eggar throws *p*egs and *p*e*bb*les in the *b*u*bb*ling *p*ool." Such patterns, apparently deliberately organized, are hard to overlook.

ONOMATOPOEIA.   **Onomatopoeia** is a blending of consonant and vowel sounds designed to imitate or suggest a sense or action. It is thus one of the most vivid and colorful aspects of poetry. Onomatopoeia depends on the fact that many words in English are **echoic;** that is, they are verbal echoes of the action they describe, such as *buzz*, *bump*, *slap*, and so on. In the following passage from John Donne's sonnet "Batter My Heart" (p. 556) we may see onomatopoeia in action:

> Batter my heart, three-personed God; for you
> As yet but knock, breathe, shine, and seek to mend,
> That I may rise, and stand, o'erthrow me, and bend
> Your force, to break, blow, burn, and make me new.

Notice here the words *batter*, *knock*, *seek*, *bend*, *break*, *blow*, and *burn*. These sounds, like the abrupt sounds of blows, provide a tactile illustration of the spiritual "violence" described in the lines.

Poe created a memorable use of onomatopoeia in his poem "The Bells," where through the combined use of assonance and alliteration he attempts to imitate the kinds of bells he celebrates. Thus wedding bells sound softly with "molten golden notes" (*o*), while alarm bells "clang and clash and roar" (*kl*). David Wagoner includes imitative words like *tweedledy*, *thump*, and *wheeze* to suggest the sounds of his "March for a One-Man Band."

EUPHONY AND CACOPHONY

Words describing either positive or negative qualities of sound, particularly resulting from the placement of consonants, are *euphony* and *cacophony*. **Euphony** ("good sound") refers to words containing consonants that permit an easy and pleasant flow of spoken sound. Although there is no rule that some consonants are inherently more pleasant than others, students of poetry often cite continuant sounds like *m*, *n*, *ng*, *l*, *v*, and *z*, together with *w* and *y*, as offering especially easy pronunciation. The conclusion of Keats's line, "Thy hair soft-lifted by the winnowing wind," for example, is euphonious. The opposite of euphony is **cacophony** ("bad sound"), in which the words do not flow smoothly but rather bump against each other harshly and jarringly. As with euphony, there are no particularly "bad" sounds, for it is the combination that makes for harshness, as in tongue-twisters like "black bug's blood" and "selfish shellfish." Obviously, unintentional cacophony is a mark of imperfect control. When a poet deliberately creates cacophony for effect, however, as in Tennyson's "The bare black cliff clang'd round him," Pope's "The hoarse, rough verse should like the torrent roar," and Donne's lines from "Batter My Heart" quoted above, cacophony is a mark of poetic skill. Although poets generally aim to provide easily flowing, euphonious lines, cacophony does have a place, always depending on the poet's intention and subject matter.

STUDYING FOR SOUND

Because we usually read silently, even when we are reading poetry, we rarely become fully aware of the *sounds* of the words on the page. Therefore, in studying a poem for recurring segmental patterns, it is essential to consider both the words *and* the sounds carefully. If you have ignored sounds in the past, you might begin by observing recurrences of specific letters of the alphabet. Thus, in Swift's "A Description of the Morning" (p. 698), the letter *s* occurs in lines 11–13 as part of the words *small, was, shriller, notes, sweep, Duns*, and *lordship's*. Once these instances of the alphabetical letter are noted, however, the actual *sounds* must be checked by a spoken reading. Such a check reveals that the *s* sound is not common to *all* these words. Thus the *s* sound does indeed register in the words *small, notes, sweep,* and *lordship's* (as ship's), but in *was* and *duns* it is a *z* sound, while in *shriller* and *lordship's* it is locked into a digraph giving the *sh* sound (in *sh*rill and *sh*ip).

By the same token, the *s* sound appears in the word *cadence* in these lines, even though it is spelled with a *c* (as "en*ce*"). This same *c*, of course, will give other sounds in other words. Thus, in *calm* it is *k*; in *check* it is part of a digraph giving *ch*; and in *machine* it is in another digraph giving *sh*. Many other letters, particularly vowels, may present similar variants in sound. Therefore, before you begin to exemplify a pattern of assonance, alliteration, onomatopoeia, euphony, or cacophony, be sure that the segments in your pattern are truly spoken and not "paper" sounds.

POEMS FOR STUDY

ROBERT HERRICK (1591–1674)

Upon Julia's Voice   *1648*

So smooth, so sweet, so silv'ry is thy voice,
As, could they hear, the damned would make no noise,
But listen to thee (walking in thy chamber)
Melting melodious words, to lutes of amber.

QUESTIONS

1. Does the poet praise Julia's speaking or singing voice? What effect do the words *silv'ry* and *amber* contribute to the praise? How powerful does the speaker claim that Julia's voice is?

2. What is the "joke" of the poem; that is, why should the damned make no noise if they could hear her? How can the praise of Julia's voice be interpreted as general praise for Julia herself?

3. How and where is alliteration used in the poem? Which of the alliterative sounds, if any, best complement the words praising the sweetness of Julia's voice?

JONATHAN SWIFT (1667–1745)

A Description of the Morning   *1709*

Now hardly here and there a hackney-coach
Appearing, showed the ruddy morn's approach.
Now Betty from her master's bed had flown,
And softly stole to discompose her own.
The slip-shod 'prentice from his master's door
Had pared the dirt, and sprinkled round the floor.
Now Moll had whirled her mop with dextrous airs,
Prepared to scrub the entry and the stairs.
The youth with broomy stumps began to trace
The kennel's edge,° where wheels had worn the place.
The small-coal man° was heard with cadence deep,   *charcoal seller*
Till drowned in shriller notes of chimney-sweep.
Duns° at his lordship's gate began to meet;   *bill collectors*
And brickdust Moll had screamed through half the street.
The turnkey° now his flock returning sees,
Duly let out a-nights to steal for fees.
The watchful bailiffs take their silent stands,
And schoolboys lag° with satchels in their hands.

A DESCRIPTION OF THE MORNING.   10 *kennel's edge*: i.e., the edge of the gutter.
Swift annotated this line "To find old Nails."   15 *turnkey*: an entrepreneur, operating a
jail for profit, who allowed prisoners to go free at night so that they might bring him a
night's booty to pay for the necessities provided them in jail.   18 *schoolboys lag*: cf.
Shakespeare's *As You Like It*, Act 2, Scene 7, lines 145–147.

QUESTIONS

1. What anti-heroic images of life in London in 1709 are presented in this poem? What level of life is described? What attitude does the speaker show toward "his lordship," a member of the nobility who nevertheless is clearly in debt?

2. Analyze the poem for alliterative patterns. What is their effect in the poem?

3. Make the same kind of analysis for assonance. How many different assonantal patterns are there? What is their effect?

ALFRED, LORD TENNYSON (1809–1892)

From Idylls of the King: The Passing of Arthur   *1869 (1842)*

But, as he walked, King Arthur panted hard,
Like one that feels a nightmare on his bed   345
When all the house is mute. So sighed the King,
Muttering and murmuring at his ear, "Quick, quick!
I fear it is too late, and I shall die."
But the other swiftly strode from ridge to ridge,
Clothed with his breath, and looking, as he walked,   350
Larger than human on the frozen hills.
He heard the deep behind him, and a cry
Before. His own thought drove him like a goad.
Dry clashed his harness in the icy caves
And barren chasms, and all to left and right   355
The bare black cliff clanged round him, as he based
His feet on juts of slippery crag that rang
Sharp-smitten with the dint of armed heels—
And on a sudden, lo! the level lake,
And the long glories of the winter moon.   360

Then saw they how there hove a dusky barge,
Dark as a funeral scarf from stem to stern,
Beneath them; and descending they were ware°   *aware*
That all the decks were dense with stately forms,
Black-stoled, black-hooded, like a dream—by these   365
Three Queens with crowns of gold: and from them rose
A cry that shivered to the tingling stars,
And, as it were one voice, an agony
Of lamentation, like a wind that shrills
All night in a waste land, where no one comes,   370
Or hath come, since the making of the world.

Then murmured Arthur, "Place me in the barge."
So to the barge they came. There those three Queens
Put forth their hands, and took the King, and wept.
But she, that rose the tallest of them all   375
And fairest, laid his head upon her lap,
And loosed the shattered casque,° and chafed his hands,   *helmet*
And called him by his name, complaining loud,
And dropping bitter tears against a brow
Striped with dark blood: for all his face was white   380
And colorless, and like the withered moon
Smote by the fresh beam of the springing east;
And all his greaves and cuisses° dashed with drops   *pieces of armor*
Of onset;° and the light and lustrous curls—   *blood*
That made his forehead like a rising sun   385
High from the dais-throne—were parched with dust:

Or, clotted into points and hanging loose,
Mixed with the knightly growth that fringed his lips.
So like a shattered column lay the King:
Not like that Arthur who, with lance in rest,   3
From spur to plume a star of tournament,
Shot through the lists at Camelot, and charged
Before the eyes of ladies and of kings.

QUESTIONS

1. What events occur in this passage? How does Tennyson develop the mood
    of depression and loss associated with the dying of Arthur? What is the
    effect of the concluding simile?

2. Analyze the patterns of assonance and alliteration in the passage. What pat-
    terns are developed most extensively? What effects are thus achieved?

3. Describe Tennyson's use of onomatopoeia in lines 349–360, 369–371, and
    380–383. What segments does he use for the onomatopoeic effect, and how
    do these segments contribute to this effect?

EDGAR ALLAN POE (1809–1849)

The Bells   1849

I

Hear the sledges with the bells—
        Silver bells!
What a world of merriment their melody foretells!
How they tinkle, tinkle, tinkle,
    In the icy air of night!
While the stars that oversprinkle
All the heavens, seem to twinkle
    With a crystalline delight;
        Keeping time, time, time,
        In a sort of Runic rhyme,
To the tintinnabulation that so musically wells
        From the bells, bells, bells, bells,
            Bells, bells, bells—
From the jingling and the tinkling of the bells.
                    II
    Hear the mellow wedding bells—
        Golden bells!
What a world of happiness their harmony foretells!
    Through the balmy air of night
    How they ring out their delight!—
        From the molten-golden notes,

And all in tune,
What a liquid ditty floats
To the turtle-dove that listens, while she gloats
On the moon!
Oh, from out the sounding cells,   25
What a gush of euphony voluminously wells!
How it swells!
How it dwells
On the Future!—how it tells
Of the rapture that impels   30
To the swinging and the ringing
Of the bells, bells, bells—
Of the bells, bells, bells, bells,
Bells, bells, bells—
To the rhyming and the chiming of the bells!   35

                        III
Hear the loud alarum bells—
Brazen bells!
What a tale of terror, now, their turbulency tells!
In the startled ear of night
How they scream out their affright!   40
Too much horrified to speak,
They can only shriek, shriek,
Out of tune,
In a clamorous appealing to the mercy of the fire,
In a mad expostulation with the deaf and frantic fire,   45
Leaping higher, higher, higher,
With a desperate desire,
And a resolute endeavor
Now—now to sit, or never,
By the side of the pale-faced moon.   50
Oh, the bells, bells, bells!
What a tale their terror tells
Of Despair!
How they clang, and clash, and roar!
What a horror they outpour   55
On the bosom of the palpitating air!
Yet the ear, it fully knows,
By the twanging
And the clanging,
How the danger ebbs and flows;   60
Yet the ear distinctly tells,
In the jangling
And the wrangling,
How the danger sinks and swells,
By the sinking or the swelling in the anger of the bells—   65
Of the bells,—
Of the bells, bells, bells, bells,

Bells, bells, bells—
In the clamor and the clangor of the bells!
IV
Hear the tolling of the bells—
    Iron bells!
What a world of solemn thought their monody compels!   70
    In the silence of the night,
    How we shiver with affright
At the melancholy menace of their tone!   75
    For every sound that floats
    From the rust within their throats
        Is a groan.
        And the people—ah, the people—
        They that dwell up in the steeple,
            All alone,   80
And who tolling, tolling, tolling,
    In that muffled monotone,
Feel a glory in so rolling
        On the human heart a stone—   85
They are neither man nor woman—
They are neither brute nor human—
        They are Ghouls:—
    And their king it is who tolls:—
    And he rolls, rolls, rolls,
        Rolls   90
        A paean from the bells!
    And his merry bosom swells
        With the paean of the bells!
    And he dances, and he yells;
Keeping time, time, time,   95
In a sort of Runic rhyme,
        To the paean of the bells—
        Of the bells:
Keeping time, time, time,
In a sort of Runic rhyme,   100
        To the throbbing of the bells—
    Of the bells, bells, bells—
        To the sobbing of the bells;
Keeping time, time, time,
    As he knells, knells, knells.   105
In a happy Runic rhyme,
        To the rolling of the bells—
    Of the bells, bells, bells:—
        To the tolling of the bells—
    Of the bells, bells, bells, bells,   110
        Bells, bells, bells—
To the moaning and the groaning of the bells.

QUESTIONS

1. What kinds of bells does Poe extol in each of the stanzas? What metals, and images, does he associate with each type of bell? How appropriate are these? Why do you think the stanzas become progressively longer?
2. What segmental sounds does Poe utilize as imitative of the various bells? What differences in vowels are observable between the silver sledge bells, for example, and the brass ("brazen") alarum bells? Between the vowels describing the iron bells and the golden bells?
3. What is the effect of the repetition of the word *bells* throughout? What onomatopoeic effect is created by these repetitions?

GERARD MANLEY HOPKINS (1844–1889)

God's Grandeur   *1877*

The world is charged with the grandeur of God.
  It will flame out, like shining from shook foil;
  It gathers to a greatness, like the ooze of oil
Crushed. Why do men then now not reck his rod?
Generations have trod, have trod, have trod;   5
  And all is seared with trade; bleared, smeared with toil;
  And wears man's smudge and shares man's smell: the soil
Is bare now, nor can foot feel, being shod.

And for all this, nature is never spent;
  There lives the dearest freshness deep down things;   10
And though the last lights off the black West went
  Oh, morning, at the brown brink eastward, springs—
Because the Holy Ghost over the bent
  World broods with warm breast and with ah! bright wings.

QUESTIONS

1. What is the contrast between the assertions in lines 1–4 and 5–8? How do lines 9–14 develop out of this contrast?
2. What manifestations of God does Hopkins describe in the poem? What metaphors does he employ to embody his praise and adoration?
3. Analyze Hopkins's use of alliteration. What alliterative patterns occur? How do these affect meter and emphasis?
4. What instances of assonance, repetitions, and internal rhyme do you find?
5. In light of the various patterns of the poem, how might you describe Hopkins's use of segmental textures?

A. E. HOUSMAN (1859–1936)

Eight O'Clock°   *1896*

He stood, and heard the steeple
  Sprinkle the quarters on the morning town.
One, two, three, four, to market-place and people
  It tossed them down.

Strapped, noosed, nighing his hour,   5
  He stood and counted them and cursed his luck;
And then the clock collected in the tower
  Its strength, and struck.

EIGHT O'CLOCK. The title refers to the hour of the morning at which hangings traditionally
took place in England.

QUESTIONS

1. Who is the "he" on whom the poem focuses. What is he listening to? Why
   is the clock significant in his life? What will happen to him when the clock
   strikes 8? How does the poet make this man representative of the plight of
   many who have bad "luck"?
2. How are the *st* and *k* consonant sounds in the second stanza, together with
   the monosyllables *stood, tossed, strapped, noosed, cursed, clock, strength*, and *struck*
   related to the content of the poem?
3. In light of the fact that village clocks worked by springs, what is the effect
   of the phrase "in the tower" being included between "collected" and "Its
   strength" rather than following "clock"?

DYLAN THOMAS (1914–1953)

The Force That Through the Green Fuse Drives the Flower   *1939*

The force that through the green fuse° drives the flower
Drives my green age; that blasts the roots of trees
Is my destroyer.
And I am dumb to tell the crooked rose
My youth is bent by the same wintry fever.

The force that drives the water through the rocks
Drives my red blood; that dries the mouthing streams
Turns mine to wax.

THE FORCE THAT THROUGH THE GREEN FUSE.   1 *fuse*: The stem of a flower is
here compared to a fuse for explosives.

And I am dumb to mouth unto my veins
How at the mountain spring the same mouth sucks. 10

The hand that whirls the water in the pool
Stirs the quicksand; that ropes the blowing wind
Hauls my shroud sail.
And I am dumb to tell the hanging man
How of my clay is made the hangman's lime.° 15

The lips of time leech to the fountain head;
Love drips and gathers, but the fallen blood
Shall calm her sores.
And I am dumb to tell a weather's wind
How time has ticked a heaven round the stars. 20

And I am dumb to tell the lover's tomb
How at my sheet goes the same crooked worm.

15 *hangman's lime*: To hasten decomposition, lime was shoveled onto the bodies of executed persons at burial.

QUESTIONS

1. What is the speaker saying about himself? What does *drive* mean in the poem? What power is driving his "green age"? What images of decay and death does the speaker introduce?

2. Compare this poem with Shakespeare's sonnet "That Time of Year" (p. 680). What similarities do you observe in the conditions described by the speakers? In what ways do the poems reach different conclusions?

3. How many different patterns of alliteration and assonance do you discover in the poem? What use of these patterns does Thomas make?

4. To what extent are the alliterating *l* in lines 16–18, and *t* and *w* in lines 19–20 a means of creating aural emphasis for the speaker's descriptions of conditions that are not easily understood?

DAVID WAGONER (b. 1926)

March for a One-Man Band *1983*

He's *a boom a blat* in the uniform
Of an army *tweedledy* band *a toot*
Complete with medals *a honk* cornet
Against *a thump* one side of his lips
And the other stuck with *a sloop a tweet* 5
A whistle *a crash* on top of *a crash*

A helmet *a crash* a cymbal a drum
At his *bumbledy* knee and a *rimshot* flag
A click he stands at attention *a wheeze*
And plays the Irrational Anthem *bang*.

QUESTIONS

1. What attitude does the speaker convey about the one-man band? Why is the Anthem "Irrational" rather than "National"?

2. Describe the onomatopoeic effect of the italicized percussive words. What kinds of rhythm are caused by these interjected words? What is the purpose of this rhythm?

3. What possible ambiguity is suggested by the "bang" concluding the last line? How does this ambiguity make the poem seem more than simply an entertaining display of sounds?

4. Compare this poem with Poe's "The Bells" as instances in which the sounds of words are used to focus your attention on real sounds. To what extent does this device work similarly in both poems?

WRITING ABOUT SOUNDS AND SEGMENTS IN POETRY

In writing an essay on sound in poetry, you should assume that all the words in a poem or passage are there because the poet chose them not only for meaning, but also for sound. There is thus nothing accidental; all the effects are intended. Readers sometimes claim that the relationship of sound to sense is subjective and murky. While there will always be an element of subjectivity, it is possible to show the objective basis for all conclusions. Thus, if a number of words with identical segments appear close together in a poem, this closeness justifies your study of them as a pattern.

Perhaps the greatest subjectivity occurs when you make observations about onomatopoeia. Should a poet be describing a strong wind, however, and if the description contains many words with h, th, f, and s segments (all of which require a continuous, breathy aspirated release of air), you would be justified in a claim that the sounds echo the description—an instance of onomatopoeia. If you are thus able to objectify your interpretation of sounds, your claims will stand most challenges.

As with essays on meter or rhyme, the aim in an essay on segments is to demonstrate the connection between a poem's sounds and its content. You cannot write about sound in isolation; segmental effects are normally linked to another aspect of the poem, such as speaker, tone, or meaning. Thus, the first step in planning your essay is to choose an appropriate poem or passage and discover as much as you can about its speaker, setting and situation, imagery, ideas, and so on.

When you are ready to move from these general considerations to a specific examination of sound, you should prepare a worksheet on which you can note the segmental patterns that you discover. This worksheet should provide a triple-spaced copy of the poem or passage, with each line numbered. A carefully prepared worksheet will simplify the planning and writing of the essay and, if handed in with the essay, will help your reader significantly.

Scrutinize the poem or passage carefully for patterns of assonance and alliteration and for instances of onomatopoeia, and indicate these on your worksheet with different colored pencils or markers. Use one color for each segment, and draw lines to indicate connections. If you use only one pencil or marker (as we do in the sample essay below), you might employ a system of dotted, dashed, and unbroken lines to signify connections. At the bottom of the worksheet make an explanatory key to your circles and lines. Use a standard pronunciation guide from a dictionary to describe sounds, and indicate in a footnote which dictionary you are using.

After you have identified all the segmental patterns and your worksheet is covered with interconnected sounds, you can begin to isolate the most significant and effective instances. At this point in prewriting, selectivity and focus come into play. You will rarely use all your discoveries about sound in a single essay. Instead, look for those segmental patterns that have the most noticeable effect on the way you experience the poem.

The central idea for the essay will normally emerge from this connection between sound and content. If you are exploring Poe's "The Bells," for example, you might determine that onomatopoeia and repetition have the strongest impact on your reading, and a tentative central idea might assert that Poe employs onomatopoeia and repetition to bring the images of the poem alive and to make sound echo sense. Whatever patterns of sound and segment lead you to such conclusions about the poem under consideration will become the supporting evidence in the body of the essay.

Organizing Your Essay

INTRODUCTION. In a sentence or two, make a brief overview of your poem or passage. Is it descriptive, reflective? Does it contain much action? Is it down to earth and "real," or is it romanticized or idealized? Is it about love, friendship, loyalty, selfishness, betrayal, or what? Try to fashion your central idea as a link between the subject matter and the sound. Is there a strong relationship, or does it seem that any segmental effects are unsystematic or unintended? Your thesis sentence should outline the topics you will discuss in the body.

BODY. The body should be the report of your linkage of sound and sense. Be sure to establish that the instances you choose have really occurred systematically enough to be grouped as a pattern. You should illustrate sounds by including the relevant words within parentheses. You might wish to make separate paragraphs on alliteration, assonance, onomatopoeia, and any seemingly important pattern of segments. Also, because space in an essay is always at a premium, you might wish to concentrate on one noteworthy effect, like a certain pattern of assonance, rather than on everything in the poem. Throughout your discussion always keep foremost the relationship between the content and the sounds you are considering.

As a means of making illustrations clear, underline all sounds to which you are calling attention. If you use an entire word to illustrate a sound, underline only the sound and not the entire word, but put the word within quotation marks (for example, The poet uses a *t* ["tip," "top," and "terrific"]). When you refer to entire words containing particular segments, however, underline these words (for example, The poet uses a t in tip, top, and terrific.).

CONCLUSION. Here you might make a brief evaluation of the poet's use of segments. A poem is designed not only to inform, but also to transfer attitudes and to stimulate the reader. To what degree did the use of sound contribute to these goals? Any personal reflections or discoveries that you have made as a result of your study would be appropriate here. If it seems too difficult to write an evaluation, it would be possible here, as in any essay, to conclude with a short summary.

SAMPLE ESSAY

A Study of Tennyson's Use of Segments in "The Passing of Arthur," 349–360*

NOTE: *For illustrative purposes, this essay analyzes a passage from Tennyson's "The Passing of Arthur," which is part of* Idylls of the King. *Containing 469 lines, "The Passing of Arthur" describes the last battle and death of Arthur, legendary king of early Britain. After the fight, in which Arthur has been mortally wounded by the traitor Mordred, only Arthur and his follower Sir Bedivere remain alive. Arthur commands Bedivere to throw the royal sword "Excalibur" into the lake from which it had been originally given to Arthur. After much hesitation, Bedivere does throw the sword into the lake, and a hand rises out of the water to catch it. Bedivere then carries Arthur to the shore of the lake, where the dying king is taken aboard a magical funeral barge. The passage analyzed here is the description of Bedivere carrying Arthur from the chapel at the battlefield down the hills to the shore of the lake.*

* See p. 699 for this poem.

WORKSHEET NO. 1: ALLITERATION

But the other (s) wiftly (s) trode from ridge to ridge, 1

Clothed with his breath, and looking, as (h) e walked, 2

Larger than (h) uman on the frozen (h) ills. 3

(H) e (h) eard the deep be (h) ind (h) im, and a cry 4

Before. (H) is own thought drove him like a goad. 5

Dry (c) lashed (h) is (h) arness in the icy (c) aves 6

And (b) arren (ch) asms, and all to left and right 7

The (b) are (b) (l) ack (c) (l) iff (c) (l) anged round him, as he (b) ased 8

His feet on juts of s (l) ippery (c) rag that rang 9

Sharp-smitten with the dint of armed heels— 10

And on a sudden, (l) o! the (l) evel (l) ake, 11

And the (l) ong g (l) ories of the winter moon. 12

ᴡᴡᴡᴡᴡ = s   ——————= b

---------- = h   ⁓⁓⁓⁓⁓= l as second consonant
                                           sound in words

············ = k

                                 —·—·—· = l

WORKSHEET NO. 2: ASSONANCE

But the other sw (i) ftly str (o) de from r (i) dge to r (i) dge,   1

Cl (o) thed w (i) th h (i) s breath, and looking, as he walked,   2

Larger than human on the fr (o) zen hills.   3

He heard the deep beh (i) nd him, and a cr (y)   4

Before. His (ow) n thought dr (o) ve him l (i) ke a g (oa) d.   5

Dr (y) clashed his harness in the (i) cy caves   6

And barren ch (a) sms, and all to left and r (i) ght   7

The bare bl (a) ck cliff cl (a) nged round him, as he based   8

H (i) s feet on juts of sl (i) ppery cr (a) g that r (a) ng   9

Sh (ar) p-sm (i) tten w (i) th the d (i) nt of (ar) med heels—   10

And on a sudden, lo, the level lake,   11

And the long glories of the winter moon!   12

———————— = ō*   •—•—•—• = ä

------------ = ī   ∿∿∿∿∿ = ĭ

•••••••• = a

* Pronunciation symbols as in *Webster's New World Dictionary,* 2nd ed.

[1] In this passage from "The Passing of Arthur," Tennyson describes Sir Bedivere's effort in carrying the dying King Arthur from the chapel near the battlefield to the shores of the nearby lake. Many of Tennyson's words contain sounds which support and echo his descriptions of setting and action.° This blending of sound and meaning is shown in Tennyson's use of alliteration, assonance, general segmental texture, and onomatopoeia.□

[2] Tennyson's use of alliterative words ties together key ideas and assists in oral interpretation. In line 1, s's begin the words swiftly and strode. In 7 and 8, b's connect barren, bare, black, and based. Aspirated h's appear in 2–6 on human, hills, heard, behind, and harness. There are also h's in he, him, and his in these lines, but these words do not require the same breathy h pronunciation. Hard k sounds are repeated in nouns and active verbs in 6–9 (clashed, caves, chasms, cliff, clanged, crag). Two sets of l's appear. One is made up of the second segments in heavy, ringing words in 8 and 9 (black, cliff, clanged, and slippery). The other is the first segment in words describing the lake in 11 and 12 (lo, level, lake, long; note also glories). In their contexts, these l's assist in producing contrasting effects. They seem heavy and sharp in 8 and 9, but in 11 and 12 they help the voice to relax.

[3] Through assonance, Tennyson gains the same kind of emphasis. To choose a notable example from many, the long o segment appears in six words in the first five lines. The first three words are descriptive and metaphoric (strode, clothed, and frozen), while the next three describes Bedivere's troubled spirit as he struggles on the barren crags (own, drove, and goad). By sound alone, therefore, the long ō ties the physical to the psychological.

[4] Combining assonance with a skillful use of segmental texture, Tennyson creates a remarkable contrast at the end of the passage. In lines 8 through 10 he introduces a number of words containing vowels that are pronounced with the tongue forward and high in the mouth (he, based, feet, heels; and the short i assonance in cliff, him, his, slippery, smitten, with, and dint). These segments are penetrating and sharp, in keeping with Bedivere's exertion as he climbs down the dreary hills. By contrast, in the last two lines Tennyson uses words that invite a lowering of vocal pitch and a relaxed and lingering pronunciation. These are on, sudden, lo, long, glories, of, and moon (particularly long, glories, and moon). In reading, the contrast is both sudden and effective, a memorable and euphonious conclusion.

[5] Also in these last two lines, and elsewhere in the passage, onomatopoeia may be noted. The l sounds in lo, level, lake, long, and glories suggest the gentle lapping of waves on a shore. At the start of the passage, in line 2, Tennyson indicates that the mountainous ridges are so chilly that Bedivere's condensing breath resembles clothing. In the next five lines there are a number of words, already noted, that contain the breathy h. In the context, these sounds are literally identical with the sounds of Bedivere's labored breathing as he carries his royal burden. Similarly, the stop sounds in 6–10 (b and k, which have been noted, and also d [in dry, dint] and t [clashed, left, right, based,

---

° Central idea.
□ Thesis sentence.

feet, juts, smitten, dint]) are cacophonous, like the sounds that Bedivere would have made in struggling to keep his feet on the "juts of slippery crag."

Thus Tennyson's choice of words with identical or similar sounds is designed to undergird his descriptions of Bedivere's heroic efforts. It is right to claim that the sounds, in the context, have their own complementary meaning.

[6] They help Tennyson emphasize the grandeur of both Arthur and his faithful follower. As long as there are readers for the poem, this grandeur, if only for a moment, may be remembered.

Commentary on the Essay

The sample essay demonstrates the clear and significant connection between patterns of sound and descriptions of setting and action in the passage from Tennyson's "The Passing of Arthur." The introductory paragraph briefly describes the topic material of the passage from Tennyson. The central idea connects many of the segments with his descriptions. The thesis sentence indicates that four topics will be developed in the essay.

Paragraph 2 examines all the instances of alliteration discovered in the analysis, with particular attention to the two groups of *l* sounds. Even within a comprehensive treatment, in other words, it is possible and desirable to go into detail on a single subtopic that is especially noteworthy.

The third paragraph considers assonance, not selecting all instances but instead providing detail about only a single pattern (the long *o*) and its effects. Such a treatment helps to keep the essay within a reasonably brief length. The worksheets, which pinpoint all the noted instances of assonance, protect the writer from a potential criticism that the discussion focuses on only one point because all the other points were not discovered.

Paragraph 4 deals with the specific effects of vowel quality in the last two lines. To make this treatment meaningful, the paragraph contrasts vowels in the preceding three lines with the vowels in the last two.

The fifth paragraph considers three separate instances of onomatopoeia, enough to justify the claim in the central idea that there is a close connection between sound and sense.

The concluding paragraph stresses the heroism and grandeur that Tennyson tried to evoke about his subject, and the paragraph also stresses the place of sound in this evocation.

Because confusion might result if both assonance and alliteration were marked together on only one worksheet, a single sheet is devoted to each aspect. The numbering, the circles, the connecting lines, and the key are all designed to assist readers in following the essay and in verifying the conclusions.

21

Rhyme: The Echoing Sound of Poetry

Rhyme is the repetition of identical or similar concluding syllables in different words, most often at the ends of lines. Words with the same concluding vowel sounds rhyme; such rhymes are a special kind of assonance. Thus *day* rhymes with *weigh*, *grey*, *bouquet*, and *matinee*. Rhyme may also combine assonance and identical consonant sounds, as in *ache*, *bake*, *break*, and *opaque*, or *turn*, *yearn*, *fern*, and *adjourn*. As these examples illustrate, rhyme is predominantly a function of *sound* rather than spelling; the words do not have to be spelled the same way or look alike to rhyme.

THE FUNCTIONS OF RHYME

Rhyme is not a universal feature of poetry; thousands of excellent poems have been written without any recourse to rhyming whatsoever. Indeed, many contemporary poets have abandoned rhyme completely in favor of other ways of joining sound and sense because they find rhyme too restrictive or artificial. Nevertheless, rhyme has been an important aspect of poetry for thousands of years, and it remains a valid and useful poetic technique today.

When rhyme is employed to good effect in poetry, it becomes much more than a simple ornament. Rhyme adds to the sensory impact of poetry by providing a pleasing network of related sounds that echo in the mind. Through rhyme, sound may join with sense in a coherent whole. Rhyme can also contribute significantly to the impression that a given poem makes on our memories. In its simplest form, it jingles in the mind, with rhymes like *bells* and *tells*. We have all learned common rhyming jingles like "Thirty days hath September / April, June, and November," and "An apple a day / Keeps the doctor away." To hear such rhymes once is to know them forever, so strongly do they impress themselves on us. People in the advertising business are well aware of the power of rhyme to fix ideas and images in our minds. A whole generation remembers, "You'll wonder where the yellow went, / When you brush your teeth with Pepsodent." Rhyme can also provide emphasis and reinforce ideas. It is a powerful way of clinching a thought by the physical link of related sounds.

Rhyme is also closely connected with the degree to which a given poem moves us or leaves us flat. Wherever rhyme is employed with skill and originality, it leads the mind into fresh, unusual, and even surprising turns of thought. Poets may thus be judged, at least to some extent, on their rhymes. Alexander Pope criticized "easy" rhymers who always paired obvious words like *trees* and *breeze*. The world will always be full of such easy rhymers who use **cliché rhymes** like *love* and *above* or *moon* and *June*. Such versifiers are followers of language rather than leaders who utilize rhyme to achieve freshness and newness. The seventeenth-century poet John Dryden admitted that the need for rhymes led him into turns of thought that he had not anticipated. In such a sense, rhyme had—and still has—a vital role in poetic creativity.

Rhyme may also lead to witty, surprising, and comic effects. The name *Julia* is rhymed with *peculiar* in a turn-of-the-century popular song. Samuel Butler rhymed *ecclesiastic* with *a stick* in his long poem "Hudibras." A part of a word may be employed as a rhyme, with the rest of the word carrying over to the next line, as in the following short stanza:

He would adorn
Himself with orn-
Aments.

Rhymes are often amusing, as in this limerick:

There once was a man from Tarentum
Who gnashed his false teeth till he bent 'em.
    When asked the cost
    Of what he had lost,
He said, "I can't say, for I rent 'em."

In this instance, the rhyming sounds in *Tarentum*, *bent 'em*, and *rent 'em* add to the humorous impact of the poem. Thus, comical sound is joined with amusing content to produce a unified experience.

Rhyme serves several additional significant functions in the shaping of poetry. One of these is the determination of **form** (discussed extensively in Chapter 22). Patterns of rhyming words are one of the central variables in determining the structure or stanza form of a poem. In addition, rhyme can be a valuable device in providing unity. Rhyming sounds may occur in interlocking patterns and sequences that bind any number of lines together into a coherent unit.

TYPES OF RHYMES

As you might expect, rhyme is a bit more complicated than it looks. The effects of rhyme are closely connected with those of rhythm and meter. Rhymes that are produced with one-syllable words—like *moon*, *June*, *tune*, and *soon*—or with multisyllabic words in which the accent falls on the last syllable—like *combine*, *decline*, *refine*, *consign*, and *repine*—have traditionally been called **masculine rhymes.** It is more accurate, however, to refer to this type of rhyme as **heavy stress rhyme, accented rhyme,** or **rising rhyme.** In general, rising rhyme lends itself to serious effects. The accenting of heavy stress rhyme appears in the opening lines of Robert Frost's "Stopping by Woods on a Snowy Evening" (p. 475):

Whose woods / these are / Ĭ thínk / Ĭ *knów*

His house / ĭs ín / the víl - / lăge *though*.

Here, the rhyming sounds are produced by one-syllable words—*know* and *though*—that occur in the final accented positions of the lines (which are basically iambic tetrameter with initial spondees).

Rhymes using words of two or more syllables in which the accent falls on any syllable other than the last have traditionally been called **feminine,** but this term may now seem sexist. Preferable terms are the more accurate **trochaic** or **double rhyme** for rhymes of two syllables and **dactylic** or **triple rhyme** for rhymes of three syllables. Less technically, these types of rhymes are also called **falling** or **dying rhymes;** this is probably because the line seems to fall off from the accented syllable to a whisper in the last syllable or two.

In general, double and triple rhymes lend themselves more readily to amusing or light poetry than they do to serious verse. The rhyming sounds in the first, second, and last lines of the limerick quoted above— *Tarentum*, *bent 'em*, and *rent 'em*—are all double rhymes with the accent on the penultimate (next-to-last) syllable. The accents of falling rhyme may also be seen in lines 2 and 4 of the first stanza of "Miniver Cheevy" by Edwin Arlington Robinson (p. 728):

Miniver Cheevy, child of scorn,
  Grew lean while he assailed the *seasons*;
He wept that he was ever born,
  And he had *reasons*.

In this poem the effect of the double rhyme is humorous and thus helps to make Miniver Cheevy a slightly ridiculous and pathetic figure. Occasionally, however, double rhyme can be used successfully in a serious poem, as in Robert Herrick's "To the Virgins, to Make Much of Time" (p. 850):

Gather ye rosebuds while ye may,
  Old time is still *a-flying*;
And this same flower that smiles today
  Tomorrow will be *dying*.

A-flying and *dying* are both double rhymes; indeed, falling rhymes are uti-
lized in the second and fourth lines of every stanza of this poem. Herrick's
use of falling rhymes throughout this poem lightens the tone a bit, but it
does not modify the seriousness of the poem's ideas at all.

    Dactylic or triple rhyme is extremely rare and almost always humorous
in effect. It may be seen in these lines from Robert Browning's "The Pied
Piper of Hamlin."

Small feet were *pattering*, wooden shoes *clattering*,
Little hands clapping and little tongues *chattering*.
And, like fowls in a farm-yard when barley is *scattering*, . . .

Here, *cláttering*, *cháttering*, and *scáttering* are all instances of triple rhyme.
The first line also offers an example of **internal rhyme,** the presence of
a rhyming word within a line of verse. In this case, *pattering* rhymes with
clattering and also maintains the triple rhyme pattern.

    One of the acknowledged masters of comic triple rhyme in English
was William S. Gilbert (1836–1911), the author of many nineteenth-century
light operas including *The Mikado* and *H. M. S. Pinafore*. His skill is evident
in the following song from *The Pirates of Penzance* (1879).

Here's a first-rate opportunity
To get married with impunity,
And indulge in the felicity
Of unbounded domesticity.
You shall quickly be parsonified,
Conjugally matrimonified,
By a doctor of divinity,
Who resides in this vicinity.

In this instance, a comical situation is made more amusing by a generous
helping of falling, triple rhyme. The pirates have spotted a group of beautiful young women, and their thoughts instantly (and surprisingly) turn toward marriage. The rhyming words are all multisyllabic, and the resultant
end rhymes are all dactylic or triple: *opportúnity*, *impúnity*, *felícity*, *domésticity*,
parsónified, *matrimónified*, *divínity*, and *vicínity*. In each case, the accent falls
on the antepenultimate (next-to-the-next-to-the-last) syllable. In addition,
the rhyme words in the fifth and sixth lines—*parsonified* and *matrimonified*—
illustrate the poetic tendency to make up new words when necessary to
achieve rhyme in comic verse.

VARIANTS IN RHYME

A wide latitude of rhyming forms has traditionally been accepted in English. Perfect rhyming words, where both the vowel and the consonant sounds rhyme, are called **exact rhymes.** Not all rhymes, however, are exact. We often find in poetry words that *almost* rhyme; in most of these instances, the vowel segments are different while the consonants are the same. This type of rhyme is variously called **slant rhyme, near rhyme, half rhyme,** or **off rhyme.** In employing slant rhyme, a poet can pair *bleak* with *broke* or *could* with *solitude.* Emily Dickinson uses slant rhyme extensively in "To Hear an Oriole Sing" (p. 726); in the second stanza of the poem she rhymes *Bird, unheard,* and *Crowd. Bird* and *unheard* make up an exact rhyme, but the vowel and consonant shift in *Crowd* produces a slant rhyme.

Another variant that shows up in poetry written in English is **eye** or **sight rhyme.** In these instances, we find the pairing of words that look alike but do not sound alike. Thus, according to eye rhyme, "I *wind* [a clock]" may be joined to "The North *Wind*" or *bough* may be rhymed with *cough, dough, enough,* and *tough.* Ben Jonson's "To Celia" (p. 848) begins with a typical eye rhyme:

Come, my Celia, let us *prove,*
While we can, the sports of *love*

Prove and *love* look as though they ought to rhyme, but when the lines are read aloud, we realize that they do not. As in all other instances of eye rhyme, the *spelling* is more important than the sound.

DESCRIBING RHYME SCHEMES

A **rhyme scheme** refers to the pattern of rhyming sounds in a given poem. In describing rhyme schemes, alphabetical letters are used to indicate the rhyming sounds. Each repeated letter indicates a rhyme. Therefore, lines ending with *love* and *dove* would be indicated as *a a.* Each new rhyming sound is signified by a new letter. Thus, lines ending with the words *love, moon, dove, june, above,* and *croon* would be schematized as *a b a b a b.* To formulate a rhyme scheme or pattern, you should include the meter and the number of feet in each line as well as the letters indicating rhymes. Here is such a formulation:

Iambic pentameter: *a b a b, c d c d*

This scheme shows that all the lines in the poem are predominantly iambic, with five feet in each. It also indicates that the rhyming lines are 1 and

3, 2 and 4, 5 and 7, 6 and 8. Finally, it signifies that the poem is two stanzas and eight lines in length. Should the number of feet in the lines of a specific poem vary, you can show this fact by using a number in front of each letter:

Iambic: *4a 3b 4a 3b*

This formulation shows that the poem (or stanza) under consideration alternates lines of iambic tetrameter with iambic trimeter; it also signifies that lines 1 and 3 rhyme and 2 and 4 rhyme. The absence of a rhyme sound is indicated by an *x*. Thus, you might find a rhyme scheme formulated like this:

Iambic: *4x 3a 4x 3a*

Again, the stanza under consideration alternates iambic tetrameter with trimeter, and again the stanza is four lines long. This time, however, only lines 2 and 4 rhyme; there is no end rhyme in lines 1 and 3.

METER, SOUND, AND RHYME

A poet may combine meter, sound, and rhyme to good effect in a harmonious fusion of the music of a poem and its meaning. The following twelve lines, extracted from a much longer poem called "An Essay on Criticism," illustrate such a skillful fusion. The entire poem discusses ways of writing and judging good poetry.

ALEXANDER POPE (1688–1744)

From *An Essay on Criticism*   *1711 (1709)*

True ease in writing comes from art, not chance,
As those move easiest who have learned to dance.
'Tis not enough no harshness gives offense,
The sound must seem an echo to the sense.
Soft is the strain when Zephyr° gently blows,   *west wind*   5
And the smooth stream in smoother numbers° flows;   *rhythms*
But when loud surges lash the sounding shore,
The hoarse, rough verse should like the torrent roar.
When Ajax° strives some rock's vast weight to throw,

ESSAY ON CRITICISM.   9 *Ajax*: a Grecian hero of the Trojan war. In Homer's *Iliad*, he throws a huge rock at the Trojan Hector.

The line too labors, and the words move slow;   10
Not so when swift Camilla° scours the plain,
Flies o'er the unbending corn,° and skims along the main.°   *wheat; sea*

11 *Camilla*: a mythological queen and warrior devoted to Diana, the goddess of chastity and hunting. She could supposedly run so fast over land or sea that her tread would not disturb plants or water.

These twelve lines are actually about the fusion of sound and sense in poetry. The heart of Pope's idea—and the thesis statement of the passage—is found in line 4: "The sound must seem an echo of the sense." Pope argues in these lines that sound and meaning must work together rather than against one another; musical devices (including rhyme) must echo and reinforce content.

Pope does not simply assert that sound must echo sense in these lines; he skillfully illustrates the point by using alliteration, assonance, onomatopoeia, dissonance, rhythm, and rhyme to shape this passage into a cohesive unit in which sound and meaning are unified. Since sound and rhyme are closely connected to rhythm and meter, it might be helpful to look at Pope's lines again, this time with the scansion and the rhyme scheme indicated:

1   True ease / in writ - / ing comes / from art, / not chance,   *a*
2   As those / move eas - / iest who / have learned / to dance.   *a*
3   'Tis not / enough / no harsh - / ness gives / offense,   *b*
4   The sound / must seem / an ech - / o to / the sense.   *b*
5   Soft is / the strain / when Zeph - / yr gent - / ly blows,   *c*
6   And the / smooth stream / in smooth - / er num - / bers flows;   *c*
7   But when / loud sur - / ges lash / the sound - / ing shore,   *d*
8   The hoarse, / rough verse / should like / the tor - / rent roar.   *d*
9   When A - / jax strives / some rock's / vast weight / to throw,   *e*
10 The line / too la - / bors, and / the words / move slow;   *e*
11 Not so / when swift / Camil - / la scours / the plain,   *f*
12 Flies o'er / the unbend - / ing corn, / and skims / along / the main.   *6f*

QUESTIONS

1. What is the dominant meter? How does it change in line 12?
2. Where do you find instances of alliteration, assonance, or onomatopoeia? What are the effects of these devices?
3. How and where is meter employed to echo meaning?

4. What type of rhyme (rising or falling, exact or slant) is used? What is the effect?

5. How and where is rhyme used to clinch and emphasize ideas?

The predominant metrical unit here is the iamb. The twelve lines contain 61 feet. Of these, 51 are iambs (˘ ´), six are spondees (⋀), two are trochees (´ ˘), and two are pyrrhics (˘ ˘). In addition, all lines but the last contain five feet; thus, the dominant meter is iambic pentameter. The last line, which contains six rather than five feet, is called an **alexandrine** (a line of 12 syllables) and is an instance of iambic hexameter.

Pope employs alliteration and assonance extensively in these lines to make the music reflect the meaning and to unify individual lines or pairs of rhyming lines (couplets). Line 4 provides an excellent example of alliteration. Here, the *s* sounds in "The *s*ound mus*t s*eem an echo to the *s*ense" unify the line and provide an echoing *s* throughout. In addition, the scansion indicates that the *s* sounds in *sound*, *seem*, and *sense* all occur in the accented or stressed syllables of their respective iambic feet. As a result, the repeated *s* is further emphasized.

Pope combines alliteration, assonance, and onomatopoeia in line 6 to produce a pleasing and effective fusion of music and meaning. Here, both the *s* and the *m* sounds are repeated to form an alliterative network of smooth sounds: "And the *sm*ooth *s*tream in *sm*oother num*b*er*s* flows." Most of the *s* and *m* sounds occur in accented syllables, thus emphasizing the network of reiterated sounds. In addition, the *o* sound is repeated in various forms in *smooth*, *smoother*, and *flows* to create a similar pattern of assonance. Taken together, all these reiterated sounds produce a cohesive pattern of vowels and continuant consonants that must be articulated very smoothly. Thus, the line is an instance of onomatopoeia; the smoothness of articulation echoes and imitates the smoothness of the "stream" and the "numbers."

This sort of analysis of musical effects could be done for almost every line in the passage; Pope uses device after device to make sound echo sense. In line 7, for example, the sharp *l* sounds of *loud* and *lash* create an onomatopoetic effect in which we are reminded of the waves striking the shore. Similarly, a series of harsh and dissonant consonants in line 8—"*Th*e *h*oar*s*e *r*ough *v*er*s*e *sh*ould li*k*e the to*rr*ent *r*oar"—makes the line very difficult to say aloud. The result is a harsh or rough sound that mirrors the content of the line. In addition, the repeated *r* sounds produce an onomatopoetic effect, and we almost find ourselves roaring out the line.

Pope also uses the musical effects of meter to make the sound echo the sense. He employs perfect iambic rhythms when the sense of the line calls for even and regular metrics. In line 6, for example, the phrase "in smoother numbers flows" is written in absolutely smooth and regular iambic "numbers." The strict iambic meter is abandoned, however, when such variation contributes to the union of sound and meaning. This effect occurs in line 10, where metrical variation reflects content. Here, Pope introduces two spondees that produce two sequences of three accented syllables: "*line too la*bors" and "*words move slow*." The result is a line of poetry that actually moves very slowly; the spondees and the resultant triple accents make it impossible to read the line aloud very quickly.

Rhyme also contributes to the overall effect of this passage and the fusion of sound and sense. The words employed to produce end rhymes in these lines are *chance* and *dance*, *offense* and *sense*, *blows* and *flows*, *shore* and *roar*, *throw* and *slow*, *plain* and *main*. Since all the lines but the last are iambic pentameter, we may formulate the rhyme scheme as follows: Iambic pentameter: *a a b b c c d d e e f 6f*. The formulation indicates that the passage is twelve lines long and that the meter is iambic pentameter. The 6 preceding the last *f* rhyme signifies that the final line is an alexandrine. In addition, the formulation shows that the lines rhyme in pairs or couplets.

One of the first things we should notice is that all the rhyme words except *offense* are one syllable and that all are rising or heavy stress rhymes. Such choices in rhyme words avoid the light effect normally produced by double or triple rhymes and give these lines a stately and serious sound that underscores the gravity of Pope's argument. We should also notice that all the rhymes in the passage are exact; Pope avoids both eye and slant rhymes. This precision in the rhymes excludes any discordant or jarring effects; it makes the verse flow evenly and sound harmonious. More important, the dominance of exact rhyme creates a very tight network of rhyming sounds that strongly unifies each pair of lines.

Pope also provides rhyming words that offer a variety of grammatical or syntactic forms. Half of the rhyme words are nouns: *chance*, *offense*, *sense*, *shore*, *plain*, and *main*. Most of the others are verbs—*dance*, *blows*, *flows*, *roar*, and *throw*—with one adverb in line 10. This variety produces another kind of balance in the poetry: it splits the rhyming words fairly evenly between actions and things. In addition, almost all the rhyming words are specific and concrete; they signify actions, places, or things that we can readily imagine. As a result, the rhymes contribute to the sharp focus and the immediacy of the verse.

Rhyme is also employed in this passage to emphasize and clinch ideas. Rhymed words are implicitly associated with one another, and this linkage is strengthened because of the tendency of the last word in a line to linger and receive a fair amount of stress. Pope uses this tendency of association to link key words and concepts through rhyme. In lines 1–4, for example, the rhyming words effectively yoke opposing concepts together and thus underscore the syntax and content of the first two couplets. *Chance* rhymes with and opposes *dance*. *Chance* denotes random events, but there is nothing random or chaotic about dancing (at least not in the way people danced in the eighteenth century). Thus the rhyme, linking the opposed concepts of *chance* and *dance*, reinforces the meaning of the first couplet, which rejects *chance* as a source for art. Similarly, *offense* is rhymed with *sense*. Again, the rhyming words are antithetical, and this linked opposition reinforces the meaning of the lines in which *offense* is set against the idea that "sound must seem an echo to the sense."

Beyond such rhymes that fuse opposite concepts, Pope employs rhyming words that are consistent with the content of specific lines; the rhyming words seem remarkably appropriate to the lines in which they occur. In line 5, for instance, Pope mentions "Zephyr," and the rhyming word— *blows*—accurately reflects the action of the wind. Similarly, *flows* in line 6 neatly captures the actions of both a smooth stream and a smooth line of poetry. In much the same way, the rhyming words *roar* and *slow* in lines 8 and 10 reinforce the meanings of their respective lines. In all these instances, the rhyme is used to emphasize and clinch the ideas expressed in the lines.

POEMS FOR STUDY

ANONYMOUS

Barbara Allan   *Medieval*

It was in and about the Martinmas° time,   *November 11*
   When the green leaves were a-fallin',
That Sir John Graeme in the West Country
   Fell in love with Barbara Allan.

He sent his man down through the town   5
   To the place where she was dwellin':
"O haste and come to my master dear,
   Gin° ye be Barbara Allan."   *if*

O slowly, slowly rose she up,
   To the place where he was lyin',   10
And when she drew the curtain by:
   "Young man, I think you're dyin'."

"O it's I'm sick, and very, very sick,
   And 'tis all for Barbara Allan."
"O the better for me ye shall never be,   15
   Though your heart's blood were a-spillin'."

"O dinna ye mind,° young man," said she,   *don't you recall*
   "When ye the cups were fillin',

That ye made the healths° go round and round,   *toasts*
   And slighted Barbara Allan?"   20

He turned his face unto the wall,
   And death with him was dealin':
"Adieu, adieu,° my dear friends all,   *farewell*
   And be kind to Barbara Allan."

And slowly, slowly, rose she up,   25
   And slowly, slowly left him;
And sighing said she could not stay,
   Since death of life had reft° him.   *taken*

She had not gone a mile but twa,°   *two*
   When she heard the dead-bell knellin',   30
And every jow° that the dead-bell ga'ed°   *stroke; made*
   It cried, "Woe to Barbara Allan!"

"O mother, mother, make my bed,
   O make it soft and narrow:
Since my love died for me today,   35
   I'll die for him tomorrow."

QUESTIONS

1. Who does the speaker quote in lines 15–20 and 33–36? In lines 7–8? In lines 13–14 and 23–24? In line 32?

2. What are the setting and situation? Beyond season, what do the phrases "leaves were a-fallin' " and "in the West Country" imply?

3. Why is Sir John Graeme dying? Why does Barbara Allan reject him? What does this poem suggest about pride and human relationships?

4. Formulate the rhyme scheme of this poem. What repetition of rhyme sounds and words do you find? What is the effect of such repetition? Where is this pattern of repetition varied? What is the effect of such variation?

5. What type of rhyme (rising or falling, exact or slant) predominates and what effects are thus produced?

MICHAEL DRAYTON (1563–1631)

Since There's No Help   *1619*

Since there's no help, come let us kiss and part;
Nay, I have done, you get no more of me,
And I am glad, yea glad with all my heart
That thus so cleanly I myself can free;
Shake hands forever, cancel all our vows,   5

And when we meet at any time again,
Be it not seen in either of our brows
That we one jot of former love retain.
Now at the last gasp of love's latest breath,
When, his pulse failing, passion speechless lies,   1●
When faith is kneeling by his bed of death,
And innocence is closing up his eyes;
Now if thou wouldst, when all have given him over,
From death to life thou mightst him yet recover.

QUESTIONS

1. What can you deduce about the speaker in this poem? The listener? What
   seems to be happening to the relationship between the two in lines 1–8?

2. Lines 9–14 present an allegorical death-bed scene. Who or what is dying?
   Are "love" and "passion" different or a single allegorical figure? What allegorical figures attend this death?

3. Is it the speaker's or the listener's love that is allegorized here? To what
   do the pronouns *his* and *him* in lines 10–14 refer? Who has the power to
   "recover" love–passion "from death to life"? How can you tell that the speaker
   wants such a recovery?

4. Formulate the rhyme scheme of this sonnet. What type of rhyme (rising or
   falling, exact or slant) predominates? How does rhyme affect the poem's
   impact?

5. How does the rhyme scheme help divide this poem into cohesive units of
   thought and unify it at the same time?

6. To what extent do rhyme words help clinch the ideas? Note especially *part–
   heart*, *me–free*, *breath–death*, and *over–recover*.

JOHN DONNE (1572–1631)

Holy Sonnet 10: Death Be Not Proud   1633

Death, be not proud, though some have called thee
Mighty and dreadful, for thou art not so;
For those whom thou think'st thou dost overthrow
Die not, poor Death, nor yet canst thou kill me.
From rest and sleep, which but thy pictures° be,   *images*   5
Much pleasure; then from thee much more must flow,
And soonest our best men with thee do go,
Rest of their bones, and soul's delivery.
Thou art slave to fate, chance, kings, and desperate men,
And dost with poison, war, and sickness dwell,   10
And poppy° or charms can make us sleep as well   *opium*

And better than thy stroke; why swell'st° thou then?   *puff up with pride*
One short sleep past, we wake eternally°   *on Judgment Day*
And death shall be no more; Death, thou shalt die.

QUESTIONS

1. What human characteristics does the speaker attribute to death? What does the speaker tell death about those whom death thinks it has overthrown?
2. To what is death compared in lines 5–6? What men die "soonest"? What powers control death? What do all these facts suggest about death?
3. Explain and resolve the paradox in line 14. Is this poem finally about death or about salvation? Explain.
4. Formulate the rhyme scheme of this sonnet. What similarities and differences do you see between this rhyme scheme and the one in Drayton's "Since There's No Help"?
5. What type of rhyme (rising or falling, exact or slant) predominates? How do these choices affect the sound and sense of the poem?
6. How does rhyme divide this poem into coherent units of thought? To what extent does it echo and emphasize meaning? Consider especially *thee–me–be–delivery*, *dwell–well*, and *eternally–die*.

CHRISTINA ROSSETTI (1830–1894)

Echo   *1862*

Come to me in the silence of the night;
  Come in the speaking silence of a dream;
Come with soft rounded cheeks and eyes as bright
    As sunlight on a stream;
      Come back in tears,   5
O memory, hope, love of finished years.

O dream how sweet, too sweet, too bitter sweet,
  Whose wakening should have been in Paradise,
Where souls brimful of love abide and meet;
    Where thirsty longing eyes   10
      Watch the slow door
That opening, letting in, lets out no more.

Yet come to me in dreams, that I may live
  My very life again though cold in death;
Come back to me in dreams, that I may give   15
    Pulse for pulse, breath for breath:
      Speak low, lean low,
As long ago, my love, how long ago.

QUESTIONS

1. What can we surmise about the speaker of this poem? To whom or what is the poem addressed? What does the speaker want the listener to do?

2. In what ways is present reality contrasted with memory in this poem? In what ways is the real world contrasted with dreams? Which does the speaker prefer?

3. To what extent does repetition contribute to the fusion of sound and sense in this poem? How are alliteration and assonance used?

4. What type of rhyme predominates? To what extent does rhyme advance the meaning and impact of the poem? In this regard, consider especially *night–bright*, *sweet–meet*, and *death–breath*. Also consider that rhyme itself is a kind of echo.

5. Compare this poem to Dante Gabriel Rossetti's "The Blessed Damozel" (p. 993). In what ways do the two poems present similar circumstances and situations? In what ways are the poems opposites or mirror images of each other? (Dante was Christina's brother.)

EMILY DICKINSON (1830–1886)

To Hear an Oriole Sing   1891 (c. 1862)

To hear an Oriole sing
May be a common thing–
Or only a divine.

It is not of the Bird
Who sings the same, unheard,
As unto Crowd–

The Fashion of the Ear
Attireth that it hear
In Dun, or fair–

So whether it be Rune,   1̇
Or whether it be none
Is of within.

The "Tune is in the Tree–"
The Skeptic–showeth me–
"No Sir! In Thee!"   1̇5

QUESTIONS

1. What can you deduce about the speaker? The listener? Who speaks in line 13? To whom is line 15 addressed?

2. What idea about the way people hear things and respond to them does this

poem explore? What connection do you see between this idea and the old saying, "Beauty is in the eye of the beholder"?

3. Formulate the rhyme scheme of this poem. How does it help subdivide the poem into cohesive units of thought? To what extent does it unify the poem?

4. Locate all the slant rhymes in this poem. What effect do these have on your reading and perception of the poem? How is the rhyme here like the oriole's song?

5. To what degree does rhyme reinforce meaning? Note especially the rhyme words in the final stanza.

A. E. HOUSMAN (1859–1936)

To an Athlete Dying Young   *1896*

The time you won your town the race
We chaired you through the market-place;
Man and boy stood cheering by,
And home we brought you shoulder-high.

To-day, the road all runners come,   5
Shoulder-high we bring you home,
And set you at your threshold down,
Townsman of a stiller town.

Smart lad, to slip betimes away
From fields where glory does not stay   10
And early though the laurel grows
It withers quicker than the rose.

Eyes the shady night has shut
Cannot see the record cut,
And silence sounds no worse than cheers   15
After earth has stopped the ears:

Now you will not swell the rout
Of lads that wore their honours out,
Runners whom renown outran
And the name died before the man.   20

So set, before its echoes fade,
The fleet foot on the sill of shade,
And hold to the low lintel up
The still-defended challenge-cup.

And round that early-laurelled head   25
Will flock to gaze the strengthless dead
And find unwithered on its curls
The garland briefer than a girl's.

QUESTIONS

1. What past events are reported in lines 1–4? What present events are reported in lines 5–8? How are they parallel? Different?

2. How do *town* and *home* change meaning from stanza 1 to stanza 2? What is "the road all runners come" (line 5)?

3. What is the speaker's attitude toward the athlete's death? Why does he call him "Smart lad" (line 9)? What ideas about fame and youth are explored here?

4. What is the poem's rhyme scheme? What types of rhyme predominate? How do these choices affect the sound and sense of the poem?

5. To what extent does rhyme advance meaning and impact? Consider especially *down–town* (lines 7–8), *cheers–ears* (lines 15–16), and *fade–shade* (lines 21–22).

6. Compare this poem with Ben Jonson's "On My First Son" (p. 555) and John Dryden's "To the Memory of Mr. Oldham" (p. 758). In what ways do these poems present similar subjects and circumstances? Why is Housman's poem closer in tone and meaning to Dryden's than it is to Jonson's?

EDWIN ARLINGTON ROBINSON (1869–1935)

Miniver Cheevy   *1910*

Miniver Cheevy, child of scorn,
　Grew lean while he assailed the seasons;
He wept that he was ever born,
　And he had reasons.

Miniver loved the days of old   5
　When swords were bright and steeds were prancing;
The vision of a warrior bold
　Would set him dancing.

Miniver sighed for what was not,
　And dreamed, and rested from his labors;   10
He dreamed of Thebes° and Camelot,°
　And Priam's° neighbors.

Miniver mourned the ripe renown
　That made so many a name so fragrant;
He mourned Romance, now on the town,   15
　And Art, a vagrant.

MINIVER CHEEVY.   11 *Thebes*: a city in Greece prominent in Greek legend and mythology in connection with Cadmus and Oedipus.   *Camelot*: legendary seat of the Round Table and capital of Britain during the reign of King Arthur.   12 *Priam's*: Priam was the king of Troy during the Trojan War.

Miniver loved the Medici,°
  Albeit he had never seen one;
He would have sinned incessantly
  Could he have been one.   20

Miniver cursed the commonplace
  And eyed a khaki suit with loathing;
He missed the medieval grace
  Of iron clothing.

Miniver scorned the gold he sought,   25
  But sore annoyed was he without it;
Miniver thought, and thought, and thought,
  And thought about it.

Miniver Cheevy, born too late,
  Scratched his head and kept on thinking;   30
Miniver coughed, and called it fate,
  And kept on drinking.

17 *Medici*: wealthy Italian family that ruled Florence from the fifteenth to the eighteenth century. During the Renaissance, Lorenzo dé Medici was an important patron of the arts.

QUESTIONS

1. Who is the central character in this poem? What is his problem?
2. What is the speaker's attitude toward the central character? How does rhyme help define this attitude?
3. How does diction help shape your poem's image of the central character? Note especially *neighbors* (line 12) and *iron clothing* (line 24).
4. How does repetition reinforce the image of the central character and the speaker's attitude? Consider the beginning of each stanza and lines 27–28.
5. What type of rhyme predominates in lines 2 and 4 of each stanza? How does this reinforce the image of the central character and make sound echo sense?

OGDEN NASH (1902–1970)

The Turtle   *1929*

The turtle lives 'twixt plated decks
Which practically conceal its sex.
I think it clever of the turtle
In such a fix to be so fertile.

QUESTIONS

1. To what extent is this poem unified by alliteration?
2. What type of rhyme is found in lines 1–2? In lines 3–4? How does the change affect the impact of the poem?
3. What is the tone of this poem? To what extent do sound and rhyme contribute to the establishment of tone?

BARBARA HOWES (b. 1914)

Death of a Vermont Farm Woman   *1954*

Is it time now to go away?
July is nearly over; hay
Fattens the barn, the herds are strong,
Our old fields prosper; these long
Green evenings will keep death at bay.   5

Last winter lingered; it was May
Before a flowering lilac spray
Barred cold for ever. I was wrong.
          Is it time now?

Six decades vanished in a day!   10
I bore four sons: one lives; they
Were all good men; three dying young
Was hard on us. I have looked long
For these hills to show me where peace lay.
          Is it time now?   15

QUESTIONS

1. Who and what is the speaker? How old is she? What has happened in her life? What is she looking for? Waiting for?
2. What is the setting? The season? How do these relate to meaning and impact?
3. What does this poem suggest about the life of "A Vermont Farm Woman"? About the lives of all women?
4. How many different rhyme sounds are used in this poem? What is the effect of using so few?
5. To what extent does rhyme divide the poem into coherent units of thought and tie the whole poem together?
6. Normally, repetition of the same rhyming word is judged to be a flaw in poetry. To what extent is this the case in this poem?

ISABELLA GARDNER (1915–1981)

At a Summer Hotel 1979

I am here with my beautiful bountiful womanful child
to be soothed by the sea not roused by these roses roving wild.
My girl is gold in the sun and bold in the dazzling water,
She drowses on the blond sand and in the daisy fields my daughter
dreams. Uneasy in the drafty shade I rock on the veranda   5
reminded of Europa Persephone Miranda.°

AT A SUMMER HOTEL.   6 *Europa Persephone Miranda*: Europa is a princess in Greek
mythology who attracted the attention of Zeus, the king of the gods. He took the form of
a bull and carried her over the sea to Crete. She bore him three sons. Persephone, in Greek
mythology, is the daughter of Zeus and Demeter, the goddess of fertility. She attracted the
attention of Hades, the god of the underworld, who forcibly carried her off and married
her. Miranda is an innocent young woman in Shakespeare's *The Tempest* who was exiled on
an island for twelve years with her father, Prospero. One of his servants—the beastly Caliban—
attempted to rape her.

QUESTIONS

1. What can you surmise about the speaker? Setting? Situation?
2. Who is described in the poem besides the speaker? How is she described?
   What is she doing? What is her relationship to the speaker?
3. Why is the speaker "uneasy" (line 5)? How do the references to Europa,
   Persephone, and Miranda help define this uneasiness?
4. To what extent do alliteration and repetition unify the lines and make the
   sound echo sense? Note especially the *b* and *ful* sounds in line 1, the *s* and
   r sounds in line 2, and the *d* sounds in lines 4–5.
5. What is the effect of internal rhyme in this poem?
6. What kind of rhyme (rising or falling, exact or slant) occurs in lines 1–2?
   To what extent does this rhyme capture a central idea of the poem? What
   kind of rhyme occurs in lines 3–6? How does this rhyme affect the tone
   and impact of the poem? To what extent does it capture a central idea of
   the poem?

WRITING ABOUT RHYME IN POETRY

In writing an essay about rhyme in poetry, your aim should be to demonstrate the relationship between sound and sense. As a result, the essay
requires two parallel and connected processes of analysis and discovery:
one dealing with sense or meaning and the other dealing with rhyme and

sound. The completed essay will almost always connect rhyme to some other aspect of the poem, such as character or theme.

The first problem is to choose an appropriate poem for investigation. If the selection is left up to you, pick either a short, representative passage from a long poem or an entire shorter poem such as a sonnet or a three-stanza lyric. This will allow you to do a thorough analysis of the sound and to deal with most of the important and interesting effects of rhyme.

Once you have selected an appropriate poem or passage, you should work toward a full understanding of the poem's sense. Consider as many of the variables we have discussed thus far in the text as possible: speaker, listener, other characters, setting and situation, language, imagery, rhetorical devices such as metaphor and simile, and tone. All these elements contribute to the impact and sense of the poem, and all can help you find a significant meeting place between sound and meaning.

When you have completed a general consideration of the poem's content and meanings, you will be ready to focus on the contributions of rhyme and sound to sense. At this point in the prewriting process, prepare a detailed worksheet on the poem (a clean copy of this worksheet should be submitted with the essay). It should contain a double-spaced copy of the poem or passage, with each line numbered. It should also indicate the number of feet in each line and any significant variations in the meter of the rhyme words. Each different rhyme sound should be assigned a different letter (*a*, *b*, *c*, *d*, and so on). You can also use the worksheet to identify other important aspects of the analysis of rhyme: repeated words and sounds, the parts of speech of each rhyme word, and pairs of rhyming words that work especially well together. Information of this nature can be recorded on the worksheet and in your notes.

As you set out to investigate the rhymes and sounds of the poem in detail and to make notes on your worksheet, you might consider the following questions:

1. What is the predominant meter? What is the rhyme scheme? Are there significant variations to the dominant rhyme scheme and if so, why?

2. Does the rhyme scheme contribute in any way to the organization or structure of the poem? Does it subdivide the poem into coherent units of thought? Does it unify the poem through interlocking patterns of sound?

3. Are most of the rhymes exact, slant, or eye rhymes? Are most of the rhyming words one syllable, or longer? Are most of the rhymes rising (heavy stress) or falling (trochaic or dactylic)? What effects do these choices have on the sound and sense of the poem?

4. What are the grammatical features of the rhyming words? Are they mostly nouns, verbs, or adjectives, or do the forms vary? Can you determine the syntactic positions of the rhyming words? Are they mostly subjects or objects?

Do they occur mostly in straightforward sentences or in subordinated constructions like prepositional phrases or dependent clauses? Is it possible to relate these discoveries to the content of the poem?

5. What kinds of words are used to create rhyme? Are the words specific? Concrete? Abstract? How do these choices relate to the sense of the poem?

6. Is rhyme used anyplace in the poem to clinch ideas or link together opposing concepts? Are there specific pairs of rhyming words that are especially important, given the general tone and meaning of the poem?

7. Is there significant repetition of words or sounds *within* the lines of the poem or scattered throughout? Since rhyme is concerned with the effects of echoing sounds, other repetitions of sound become valid areas of consideration. Do any of the rhyming sounds (assonance, alliteration, internal rhyme) appear elsewhere in the poem to an appreciable degree?

Most poems will not provide useful answers to all seven of these questions. Nevertheless, you should investigate each of these areas. Indeed, part of the value of such analysis is to discover which questions are worth asking of a particular poem. Your results will determine, to a large extent, the ultimate focus of your essay.

The processes of investigation and analysis outlined in these questions will usually yield enough information for you to form some ideas about the interrelationship of sound and sense in the poem under consideration. Because the essay will ultimately assert that sound echoes or reinforces the content or the structure of the poem in some specific way, you should reevaluate your data with an eye to discovering exactly where sound and sense are most effectively joined. You might discover, for example, that the rhymes shape your response to the speaker, the listener, or some other character. Or rhyme might help to establish the dominant tone of the poem or underscore the central ideas. In any event, you should locate an area of significant and effective interaction between rhyme and content.

At this point, you can begin to formulate a tentative central idea for the essay that connects rhyme to some other aspect of the poem. This idea should be expressed in a statement that is as exact and focused as possible. It is not sufficient simply to assert that rhyme underscores or echoes meaning, character, or structure; the thesis must explain how rhyme does this. The central idea for an essay on rhyme in "Miniver Cheevy," for example, might argue that Robinson employs falling rhyme and repetition throughout the poem to reinforce the sense that Miniver Cheevy is both amusing and pathetic. The body of the essay could then discuss specific instances of these general phenomena.

Once you have formulated a tentative central idea, the rest of the essay will usually fall into place. From your notes, select examples that illustrate the effects asserted in the thesis. Organize these examples into related groups that can be formed into paragraphs; multiple examples of the same effect may be treated in the same paragraph or in sequential paragraphs. Make sure all the examples you discuss are relevant to the central idea and advance the argument of the essay. As you begin to group these examples into units of support, you may find that some rhyming effects are less or more important than you had initially thought. When this happens, you can rethink the direction of the essay and revise the central idea accordingly.

Organizing Your Essay

INTRODUCTION.   In the introduction, you can make any general remarks you wish about the poem, but concentrate on the relationship of the rhyme to the content. That is, does rhyme seem to be only a decorative adjunct to the poem, or is it integrated in some effective way? In stating the central idea, try to define and limit this relationship to a specific aspect of the poem's structure or content. The thesis sentence should introduce the topics covered in the body of the essay.

BODY.   The body should be dedicated to proving the assertions made in the introduction; always keep your central idea in mind as you organize this supporting material. At the same time, your essay should include a fairly detailed description of the major features of rhyme, including the scheme, the number of rhymes employed, the type of rhyme, and any other significant factors. As a general rule, this description occurs early in the essay, usually in the second paragraph.

In subsequent paragraphs, deal with as many different aspects of rhyme and sound as are relevant to the central idea. These include the grammatical features of the rhymes, the qualities of the rhyme words, and any striking effects produced by rhyme. Since you will usually want to group similar or related rhyming effects together in the body of the essay, your organization will normally reflect various types of musical effects rather than the order in which such devices occur in the poem. Hence, the body will shift from one aspect of rhyme or sound to another several times in the course of the essay.

CONCLUSION.   As in other essays, the conclusion should be as strong and assertive as the introduction. It might contain any additional observations about rhyme and sound that strike you as relevant. As always, a short summary of your main points is also appropriate here. Finally, you can reassert the connection between rhyme and any other aspect of the poem, such as speaker or theme, that you have explored.

SAMPLE ESSAY

The Rhymes in Christina Rossetti's "Echo"

		n	
1	Come to me in the silence of the *night*;		5a

		n	
2	Come in the speaking silence of a *dream*;		5b

		adj	
3	Come with soft rounded cheeks and eyes as *bright*		5a

		n	
4	As sunlight on a *stream*;		3b

		n	
5	Come back in *tears*,		2c

		n	
6	O memory, hope, love of finished *years*.		5c

		adj	
7	O *dream* how *sweet*, too *sweet*, too bitter *sweet*,		5d

		n	
8	Whose wakening should have been in *Paradise*,		5e

		v	
9	Where souls brimful of love abide and *meet*;		5d

		n	
10	Where thirsty longing *eyes*		3e

		n	
11	Watch the slow *door*		2f

		adv	
12	That opening, letting in, lets out no *more*.		5f

		v	
13	Yet *come* to me in *dreams*, that I may *live*		5g

		n	
14	My very life again though cold in *death*;		5h

		v	
15	Come back to me in *dreams*, that I may *give*		5g

		n	
16	Pulse for pulse, *breath* for *breath*:		3h

		adv	
17	Speak *low*, lean *low*,		2i

		adj	
18	As *long ago*, my love, how *long ago*.		5i

[1] In the three-stanza poem "Echo," Christina Rossetti creates a high degree of correspondence between sound and sense. Specifically, rhyme and repeated words are employed as a second way of suggesting that one might regain in dreams a love that is lost in reality.° As the dream and memory of love are to the speaker's present reality, so the echoing sounds of the rhymes and repetitions are to the original instances of each sound. This analogy accounts for the title of the poem and shapes the careful employment of rhyme. Aspects of rhyme that help to produce this echo of the poem's content and theme include the rhyme scheme, the grammatical forms and syntactic positions of the rhymes, the qualities of the rhyming words, significant pairs of rhymes, and the special use of repetition.°

[2] The rhyme scheme is simple, and, like rhyme generally, may be considered a pattern of echoes. Each stanza contains four lines of alternating rhymes concluded by a couplet, as follows: Iambic: 5a 5b 5a 3b 2c 5c. There are nine separate rhymes throughout the poem, three in each stanza. Only two words are used for each rhyme and no rhyme is repeated. Of the eighteen rhyming words, sixteen are of one syllable. With such a great number of single-syllable words, the rhymes are all heavy stress or rising; they all occur in the accented halves of the iambic feet. By the same token, the end-of-line emphasis is on relatively simple words. In addition, all the rhyming pairs except Paradise–eyes are exact rather than slant or eye rhymes. This high concentration of rising and exact rhymes adds seriousness and intensity to the poem. We find no falling rhymes that might modify or diminish the poem's wistful and longing tone.

[3] The grammatical forms and positions of the rhyming words lend support to the inward, introspective subject matter. Although there is variety, more than half of the rhyming words are nouns. There are ten nouns in all, and eight are placed within prepositional phrases as the objects of prepositions. Such syntactic enclosure echoes the personal and introspective focus of the poem, where the speaker expresses the desire to relive her love within dreams. In addition, the repeated verb come in stanzas 1 and 3 is in the form of commands to the absent lover. Thus, most of the verbal energy in these stanzas is in the first parts of the, lines, leaving the rhymes to occur in elements modifying the command. We can see this subordinated structure in the first three lines:

Come to me in the silence of the night;
Come in the speaking silence of a dream;
Come with soft rounded cheeks and eyes as bright

In line 1, come is modified by "to me" and "in the silence of the night." The rhyme word is thus subordinated within a prepositional phrase. Lines 2 and 3 repeat this pattern. Most of the other rhymes are also in such internalized positions. The three rhyming verbs in lines 9, 13, and 15 occur in subordinate and relative clauses. The entire ninth line, for example, is a relative clause

---

° Central idea.
° Thesis sentence.

that modifies Paradise (line 8). Similarly, the two nouns that are not the objects of prepositions are the subject (line 10) and object (line 11) of a single relative clause that also modifies Paradise.

[4] The qualities of the rhyming words are also consistent with the poem's emphasis on the speaker's internal life. Most of the rhyming words are abstract and impressionistic. Words like dream and sweet reflect the speaker's inner state; they have no objective or external referent. Even the concrete and specific rhyming words—night, stream, tears, eyes, door, and breath—reflect the speaker's mental condition rather than describing reality. The first three define ways in which the speaker wants her absent lover to return in a dream. Similarly, eyes and door clarify the speaker's internalized image of Paradise, another subjective concept. Finally, breath again defines events that can occur only in the speaker's dreams. Thus, virtually all the rhyme words echo the subjective and internalized experience of a love that exists merely in dreams and memory.

[5] Pairs of rhyming words in this poem reflect and emphasize the contrast between the dream of love and the emptiness of the speaker's present reality. In lines 1 and 3, for example, the rhyme scheme effectively links and opposes night and bright. This pair contrasts the bleakness of the speaker's condition to the vitality of her inner life and dreams. We find another effective contrast in lines 14 and 16, where death and breath are rhymed. This pair again opposes the void of present reality to the vitality of dreams and memory. It also shows that even though the speaker's love is past, it can live again in memory just as an echo continues to sound.

[6] Finally, rhyme and repetition emphasize the way in which memory and dreams echo past experience. The poem contains the skillful repetition of a number of words that act as echoes. The major echoing word is come; it appears six times at the beginnings of lines in stanzas 1 and 3. This reiterated command expresses the speaker's desires and desolation. Rhyming words are also repeated systematically to create an echo. The most notable of these is dream, which appears as the rhyme word in line 2 and is repeated in line 7; the plural form is repeated in lines 13 and 15. This repetition establishes a specific sound that echoes throughout the poem. At the same time, it focuses our attention on the dream state, which is an echo of the past.

We can find other instances of repeated rhyme words throughout the poem. In line 7, for example, the rhyming word sweet appears three times: "how sweet, too sweet, too bitter sweet." The rhyme thus becomes a triple echo within a single line. At the end of the poem, this technique of repetition is employed three times to focus our awareness of the connection between dreams and echoes:

[7] Pulse for pulse, breath for breath:
Speak low, lean low,
As long ago, my love, how long ago.

This special use of repetition justifies the title "Echo," and it stresses the major idea that only in one's memory can past experience exist; dreams are the echoes of this past.

Thus, rhyme is not just ornamental in "Echo"; it helps create an effective

738 21/Rhyme: The Echoing Sound of Poetry

fusion of sound and sense. The rhyme scheme itself is a pattern of echoes. Similarly, repeated words set up networks of echoing sounds throughout the poem. These musical effects recreate the thematic relationship between dreams [8] and past reality. At the same time, rhyme underscores the introspective and subjective focus of the poem, and it crystalizes the contrast between present reality and the past. "Echo" is a poem in which rhyme is inseparable from meaning.

Commentary on the Essay

This essay seeks to establish a connection between rhyme and the thematic content of the poem. The introductory paragraph asserts that rhyme is of great importance in "Echo." The second sentence announces the central idea of the essay, and the thesis sentence indicates the five aspects of rhyme developed in the body.

The body of the essay deals with the five topics in the thesis sentence in the same order in which they are mentioned. It is organized in such a way that related effects of rhyme and sound are considered together in single or sequential paragraphs. The second paragraph provides a general description of the poem's rhyme scheme. In addition, it asserts that the heavy stress and exact rhymes help create and sustain the tone of the poem.

The third paragraph treats the grammar and syntax of the rhymes. A simple analysis and count reveal that there are ten rhyming nouns and three rhyming verbs. The verb of command—*come*—is mentioned to show that most of the rhyming words occur within phrases modifying this word, and three lines from the poem illustrate this fact. The grammatical analysis is also related to the internalized nature of the subject of the poem.

Paragraph 4 emphasizes the impressionistic and subjective nature of the rhyming words, showing that the rhyme underscores the distinction between dream and reality. Similarly, the fifth paragraph considers pairs of rhyming words that produce the same effect: a contrast between external life and the speaker's inner life of dreams and memory.

The sixth and seventh paragraphs focus on the repetition of five words: *come*, *dream*, *breath*, *low*, and *ago*. This repetition is shown to be another pattern of echoes that restates the relationship between past reality and present dreaming. The concluding paragraph reviews the major points of the essay, restates the central argument, and reasserts the connection between Rossetti's use of rhyme and the major concerns of the poem.

22

Form: The Shape
of the Poem

When we speak about poems, we are likely to identify some as *ballads*, *sonnets*, *limericks*, *lyrics*, or the like. These are the names of specific, traditional forms of poetry. **Form** is the shape or the general pattern of a poem; it indicates the poem's *structure* or *design*. Visually, form is the way a poem looks on the printed page. To a large extent, form is a matter of variables that we have already discussed: meter, line length, and rhyme scheme. When these elements work together, they often produce a specific poetic form.

MAJOR POETIC FORMS

The two major subdivisions of poetic form are closed and open. The terms refer to structure and technique rather than to content or ideas. **Closed-form** poetry is written in specific and often traditional patterns of lines produced through rhyme, meter, line length, and line groupings. **Stanzas** are groups of lines, analogous to paragraphs, that are grouped together visually in a poem. Many closed forms have been in use for hundreds of years and have acquired specific names. For example, the *ballad*, *sonnet*, *limerick*, and *lyric* are traditional closed forms that are recognizable because of their structure. (We will say more about these forms shortly.) A poem written in a closed form need not conform strictly to a traditional shape; it may use traditional devices in an original way to produce a new pattern. In any event, closed forms are characterized by a clear structure based on rhyme, meter, line length, and stanzas or units of verse.

Open form, on the other hand, signifies a poem that avoids traditional patterns of organization and does not rely on meter, rhyme, line length, or stanzas to produce order. In open-form poetry we are unlikely to find sustained rhyme schemes, dominant meters, or regular stanzas. Instead, an open-form poem often presents radical variations in line length, no rhyme scheme, and no discrete stanzas at all. Open form poetry is not necessarily disorganized or chaotic, however. The poet has merely sought new ways to arrange words and lines, new ways to express thoughts and feelings, and new ways to order the experience of poetry.

THE BUILDING BLOCKS OF CLOSED-FORM POETRY

Closed-form poetry depends on the poet's use of traditional techniques such as meter, rhyme, and line groupings. The basic building block of closed form, however, is the line of verse. Various numbers of lines may be grouped together through rhyme to form stanzas or sections of poems. These stanzas or sections may, in turn, be assembled to create traditional forms.

The most common and popular one-line pattern in English poetry is **blank verse,** or unrhymed iambic pentameter (see Chapter 19, p. 671). In a poem or play written in blank verse, each line comprises a poetic unit (but not a stanza, which must contain at least two lines). Since rhyme is not employed in blank verse, the form is defined by the meter (iambic) and the line length (five feet per line). Blank verse has been used by poets and playwrights since the sixteenth century. William Shakespeare, for example, wrote most of his plays in blank verse, and John Milton used the form in his epic, *Paradise Lost*. We can see an example of blank verse in these lines from Shakespeare's *Hamlet*, where the prince is telling his mother that his mourning is real rather than simply an outward show:

> Seems, madam? nay it is, I know not "seems."
> 'Tis not alone my inky cloak good mother,
> Nor customary suits of solemn black,
> Nor windy suspiration of forced breath,
> No, nor the fruitful river in the eye,°   *tears*
> Nor the dejected havior° of the visage,°   *appearance; face*
> Together with all forms, moods, shapes of grief,
> That can denote me truly; these indeed seem,
> For they are actions that a man might play,
> But I have that within which passes show,
> These but the trappings and the suits of woe.   *(1.2.76–86)*

While the verse offers no rhyme scheme (except in the final pair of lines), each line is written in iambic pentameter. Blank verse is one of the most flexible closed forms of poetry since its requirements are only metric.

The basic two-line building block of poetic form is called a **couplet.** The two lines can be any length and any meter, but they must rhyme. In addition, they are usually the same length. Couplets may be made up of extremely short lines; in fact, two single words like "Flee/Me" or "Night/ Flight" can comprise a couplet. Most couplets, however, are not this short. The most common meters and line lengths for couplets are iambic tetrameter (four heavy stresses per line) and iambic pentameter. The first two lines of Robert Frost's "Stopping by Woods on a Snowy Evening" form an iambic tetrameter couplet:

Whose woods these are I think I know,
His house is in the village though.

Similarly, the couplet that ends Hamlet's speech on mourning is in iambic pentameter.

Couplets can be used as components of all sorts of poems. Many sonnets end with a couplet, and many four-line stanzas contain couplets. In other words, couplets can be employed to build larger units or forms of poetry. Couplets can also be used throughout a poem. For instance, Alexander Pope wrote both "An Essay on Criticism" and "The Rape of the Lock" entirely in couplets. In such a case, the pairs of lines that make up each couplet (and stanza) are usually printed together without any break or white space between them.

Couplets have been employed in English poetry since the fourteenth century. They came into widest use, however, in the seventeenth and eighteenth centuries during the careers of John Dryden and Alexander Pope, when poets made extensive use of the **closed** or **heroic couplet,** two rhymed lines of iambic pentameter that are *end-stopped* (see p. 677). The heroic couplet usually expresses a complete idea. It also makes rhetorical strategies such as parallelism and antithesis very easy. Look, for example, at these lines from Pope's "The Rape of the Lock," a mock-epic poem that tells the story of a stolen lock of hair:

Here Britain's statesmen oft the fall foredoom
Of foreign tyrants and of nymphs at home;
Here thou, great Anna! whom three realms obey,
Dost sometimes counsel take—and sometimes tea.

These lines describe Hampton Court, a royal palace and residence of Queen Anne (reigned 1702–1714). Notice that the first heroic couplet allows Pope to link "Britain's statesmen" with two entirely dissimilar events: the fall of nations and the seduction of young women. Similarly, the second heroic couplet allows for the outrageous linking of royal meetings of state (*counsel*) and tea time (in the eighteenth century, *tea* was pronounced "tay"). The heroic couplets here facilitate placing antithetical ideas and events in amusing and ironic parallels.

The three-line stanza is called a **tercet** or a **triplet.** Tercets may be written in any line length or meter, but the length of the three lines must be uniform and they often contain a single rhyme sound (*a a a, b b b,* and so on). The following poem is written in iambic tetrameter triplets:

ALFRED, LORD TENNYSON (1809–1892)

The Eagle   *1851*

He clasps the crag with crooked hands;
Close to the sun in lonely lands,
Ring'd with the azure world, he stands.

The wrinkled sea beneath him crawls;
He watches from his mountain walls,
And like a thunderbolt he falls.

The lines are even and the same rhyme sound is repeated three times in each stanza. In the first triplet we are viewing the eagle; he passively "clasps" and "stands" in splendid isolation. In the second, however, our perspective shifts and we both look at the eagle and see through his eyes. Here, the verbs become more active: the sea "crawls" and the eagle "falls." While the two tercets and the shift in perspective seem to divide the poem in half, alliteration pulls it back together. This is especially true of the *"c"* sound in *clasps, crag, crooked, close,* and *crawls,* and the *"w"* sound in *with, world, watches,* and *walls.*

An exception to the triple rhyme of the tercet is **terza rima,** a three-line stanza form in which each stanza interlocks with the next through rhyme. Thus, the rhyme pattern in terza rima is *a b a, b c b, c d c,* and so on. You can see an example of terza rima in Shelley's "Ode to the West Wind" (p. 764). Still another exception to the *a a a* pattern of the tercet is found in a traditional verse form called the **villanelle,** in which every triplet in the poem is rhymed *a b a* (for an example, see Dylan Thomas's "Do Not Go Gentle Into That Good Night," p. 766). As these two forms illustrate, the tercet, like the couplet, is very adaptable. No single definition or illustration can adequately encompass the variability of these traditional stanza patterns.

The most adaptable and popular building block in English and American poetry is the four-line **quatrain.** This stanza has been popular and useful for hundreds of years and has lent itself to a vast number of variations. Like couplets and triplets, quatrains may be written in any line length and meter; even the line lengths *within* a quatrain may vary. The determining factor is always the rhyme scheme, and even that can vary significantly, given the demands of the form and the desires of the poet. Quatrains may be rhymed *a a a a*, but they can also be rhymed *a b a b, a b b a, a a b a*, or even *a b c b*. All these variations are determined, at least in part, by the larger patterns or forms that quatrains are used to build. Quatrains are basic components of many traditional closed forms, including ballads and sonnets.

CLOSED-FORM POETRY

Over the centuries English and American poetry has evolved or appropriated hundreds of traditional closed forms, all of them determined by some combination of meter, rhyme scheme, line length, and stanza form. In addition, most of them involve some combination of the basic building blocks of poetic form: the couplet, tercet, and quatrain. While it is impossible to provide a complete catalog of all the traditional forms here, we will introduce you to the most common ones.

The Italian, or Petrarchan Sonnet

The sonnet has proved to be one of the most durable and popular traditional forms in poetry. All sonnets are fourteen lines long. Initially, they were an Italian poetic form (*sonnetto* means "little song") popularized by Francesco Petrarch (1304–1374), who wrote long collections or *cycles* of sonnets to an idealized mistress named Laura. The form and style of Petrarch's sonnets were adapted to English poetry in the early sixteenth century and have been used ever since. The **Italian** or **Petrarchan sonnet** is written in iambic pentameter and is composed of two quatrains and two tercets. The first eight lines are called the **octave** (indicating an eight-line unit of thought) and the last six are called the **sestet**. The rhyme scheme of the octave is usually fixed in an *a b b a, a b b a* pattern. The sestet offers a number of different rhyming possibilities, including *c d c, c d c* and *c d e, c d e*. An Italian sonnet rarely ends with a couplet. In terms of structure and meaning, the octave of the Italian sonnet usually presents a conflict or dilemma, and the sestet offers some sort of resolution. As a result, there is often a clear shift or turn in thought from the octave to the sestet. John Milton's "When I Consider How My Light Is Spent" (p. 756) is an example of an Italian sonnet.

The English, or Shakespearean Sonnet

The **English,** or **Shakespearean sonnet** named after its most famous practitioner, is written in iambic pentameter and has the following rhyme scheme: *a b a b, c d c d, e f e f, g g*. The development of the English sonnet from the Italian sonnet in sixteenth-century England represents a major shift in shape and a concurrent reorganization of thought. The Shakespearean sonnet, as is indicated by its rhyme scheme, is composed of three quatrains and a couplet. As a result, the pattern of thought shifts from the octave-sestet organization in the Italian sonnet to a four-part argument on a single thought or emotion. Each quatrain usually contains a separate development of the sonnet's central idea, with the couplet providing a conclusion, climax, and resolution. Shakespeare's Sonnet 116, "Let Me Not to the Marriage of True Minds" (p. 749), is an example of the English sonnet.

The Ballad

The **ballad,** which has its origins in folk literature, is one of the oldest traditional closed forms in English poetry; it has been used continuously from the Middle Ages to the present. Ballads are composed of a long series of quatrains in which lines of iambic tetrameter alternate with iambic trimeter. Normally, only the second and fourth lines of each stanza contain rhyming words, and so the rhyme scheme is *a b c b, d e f e,* and so on. Ballads are often narrative in development, telling a complete story, as in the anonymous "Sir Patrick Spens" (p. 465) and "Barbara Allan" (p. 722).

Common Measure or Hymnal Stanza

Common measure is probably derived from the ballad stanza; it shares with the ballad the alternation of four-beat and three-beat iambic lines but adds a second rhyme to each quatrain: *a b a b, c d c d,* and so on. As with the ballad, the basic building block of common measure is the quatrain. The measure is most commonly used in hymns, so it is sometimes called **hymnal stanza.** Many of Emily Dickinson's poems, including "Because I Could Not Stop for Death" (p. 473), are in common measure.

The Song or Lyric

The **lyric** is a free stanzaic form that was originally designed to be sung to a repeated melody. The structure and rhyme scheme of the first stanza are therefore duplicated in all subsequent stanzas. Like the ballad, it is one of the oldest traditional closed forms in poetry. The individual stanzas of a lyric may be built from any combination of single lines, couplets, triplets, and quatrains; the line lengths may shift, and a great deal of metrical variation is common. There is theoretically no limit to the number of stanzas in a lyric, although there are usually no more than five or six. We can find a great deal of variation in the structure. A. E. Housman's "Loveliest of Trees" (p. 470), for example, is a lyric made up of three quatrains containing two couplets each; it is written in iambic tetrameter and rhymes *a a b b*. The second and third stanzas repeat the same pattern. Christina Rossetti's "Echo" (p. 725) is also a lyric, but its structure is very different from that of Housman's poem. Here, the structural formulation of each stanza is iambic: *5a 5b 5a 3b 2c 5c*. Lyrics can have very complex and ingenious stanzaic structures. John Donne's "The Canonization" (p. 877), for instance, contains five stanzas that reflect the following pattern: Iambic: *5a 4b 5b 5a 4c 4c 4c 4a 3a*. The nine-line stanza contains three different rhymes and three different line lengths; nevertheless, the same complicated pattern is repeated in each of the five stanzas.

The Ode

The **ode** is a stanzaic form far more complex than the lyric, with varying line lengths and intricate rhyme schemes. Some odes have repeating patterns that are duplicated in each stanza, while others offer no duplication and introduce a new structure in each stanza. Although some odes were designed to be set to music, most do not fit repeating melodies. There is no set form for the ode; poets have developed their own structures according to their needs. John Keat's great odes were particularly congenial to his ideas, as in the "Ode to a Nightingale" (p. 761), which consists of ten stanzas in iambic pentameter with the repeating form *a b a b c d e 3c d e*. By contrast, each of the ten stanzas in William Wordsworth's "Ode: Intimations of Immortality" (p. 853) introduces a totally new pattern.

Some Other Closed-Form Types

Many other closed forms have enjoyed long popularity. One of these, the **epigram,** is a short and witty poem that usually makes a humorous or satiric point. Epigrams are usually two to four lines long and written in couplets. The form was developed by the Roman poet Martial (A.D. 40–102) and has remained popular to the present. Humorous **epitaphs,** lines composed to mark the death of someone, can also be epigrams. The following epitaph–epigram was written to commemorate John Hewet and Sara Drew, who were killed by lightning on July 31, 1718, while helping bring in the harvest; it is followed by a selection of epigrams:

ALEXANDER POPE (1688–1744)

Epitaph on the Stanton-Harcourt Lovers   *1950 (1718)*

Here lie two poor Lovers, who had the mishap,
Though very chaste people, to die of a Clap.

SAMUEL TAYLOR COLERIDGE (1772-1834)

What is an Epigram   *1802*

What is an epigram? a dwarfish whole,
Its body brevity, and wit its soul.

E. E. CUMMINGS (1894-1962)

A Politician   *1944*

a politician is an arse upon
which everyone has sat except a man.

J. V. CUNNINGHAM (b. 1911)

Epitaph for Someone or Other   *1950*

Naked I came, naked I leave the scene,
And naked was my pastime in between.

QUESTIONS

1. What do these four epigrams have in common? To what extent do they
    share a common tone and form?
2. Consider the relationship between epigrams and the couplets that close En-
    glish sonnets or the heroic couplets of the eighteenth century. Look at the
    concluding couplets of Shakespeare's sonnets in this text (use the index)
    and look at Alexander Pope's couplets in the extract from "An Essay on
    Criticism" (p. 718). To what extent do these couplets have effects similar
    to those produced by epigrams?

Another popular closed-form type is the **limerick.** Like the epigram,
the limerick is usually humorous, the humor often being reinforced by
double or falling rhymes (see Chapter 21, pp. 715–16). In addition, contemporary limericks are often bawdy or worse. We do not know who invented
the limerick as a form, but it was popularized by Edward Lear (1812–
1888), an English artist and humorist. Limericks are always five lines long
and the meter is basically anapestic (˘ ˘ ´). The structure of most limericks
may thus be described as anapestic: *3a 3a 2b 2b 3a.* Here are a few limericks
for your enjoyment.

A diner while dining at Crewe,
Found a rather large mouse in his stew.
   Said the waiter, "Don't shout
   And wave it about,
Or the rest will be wanting one too."

There was a young lady from Trent
Who said that she knew what it meant
   When men asked her to dine:
   Private room, lots of wine.
She knew—O she knew!—but she went.

   Humorous closed forms continue to be devised by enterprising writers. Although none has become as popular as the limerick, they illustrate both the pleasures and the agonies of working within closed forms. The **clerihew,** invented in the late nineteenth century by Edmund Clerihew Bentley (1875–1956), is clearly related to the epigram. Clerihews are usually composed of two couplets and focus on a well-known person, who is named in the first line. Here are two clerihews, both written by Bentley and published in 1937.

George the Third
Ought never to have occurred.
One can only wonder
At so grotesque a blunder.

Alfred, Lord Tennyson
Lived upon venison:
Not cheap, I fear,
Because venison's deer.

QUESTIONS

1. What do these clerihews have in common? To what extent do they share a common tone and structure?
2. Write several clerihews about contemporary figures and share them with your class. Try to maintain the tone and style of Bentley's work.

   As a final illustration of humorous closed form, we offer the **double dactyl,** devised in the 1960s by Anthony Hecht and John Hollander. The form is related to that of the epigram, limerick, and clerihew, and the rules that govern this form are fairly complex; they dictate the meter, line length, and specific content of lines 1, 2, and 6 or 7. Here are two examples.

ANTHONY HECHT (b. 1923)

Nominalism   1967

Higgledy-piggledy
Juliet Capulet
Cherished the tenderest
Thoughts of a rose:

"What's in a name?" said she,
Etymologically,
"Save that all Montagues
Stink in God's nose."

ARTHUR W. MONKS

Twilight's Last Gleaming   1967

Higgled-piggledy
President Jefferson
Gave up the ghost on the
Fourth of July.

So did John Adams, which
Shows that such patriots
Propagandistically
Knew how to die.

QUESTIONS

1. How many lines long is a double dactyl? How many stanzas?
2. What form must line 1 take? What requirement governs line 2? Line 6 or 7?
3. What is the dominant meter? How does it change in lines 4 and 8?
4. What rhyming requirements does the form impose?
5. Try to write a few double dactyls, maintaining the tone and spirit of the examples. You will probably have the most trouble with line 2 and 6 or 7, but keep at it.

CLOSED FORM AND MEANING

Although traditional closed forms are thought by many contemporary poets to be excessively restrictive, these forms provide a general framework within which a poet can work to create feeling and express ideas. Closed forms provide a ready-made structure; the poet's challenge is to take this structure and breathe new life into it by arranging images, emotions, and ideas to create something vital and effective. A skillful poet uses the demands of a closed form to his or her own ends. With this in mind, let us look at the way a specific closed form may be employed to shape thoughts and emotions.

WILLIAM SHAKESPEARE (1564–1616)

Sonnet 116: Let Me Not to the Marriage of True Minds   *1609*

Let me not to the marriage of true minds
Admit impediments.° Love is not love
Which alters when it alteration finds,
Or bends with the remover to remove:
Oh, no! it is an ever-fixed mark,   5
That looks on tempests and is never shaken;
It is the star to every wandering bark,
Whose worth's unknown, although his height° be taken.   *altitude*
Love's not Time's fool,° though rosy lips and cheeks   *slave*
Within his° bending sickle's compass come;   *Time's*   10
Love alters not with his brief hours and weeks,
But bears it out even to the edge of doom.°   *The Last Judgment*
If this be error and upon me proved,
I never writ, nor no man ever loved.

SONNET 116.   2 *impediments*: a reference to the marriage service in the Anglican *Book of Common Prayer*: "If either of you do know any impediments why ye may not be lawfully joined. . . ."

QUESTIONS

1. What is the meter of this poem? The rhyme scheme? The closed form?
2. What point does the speaker make about love in the first quatrain?
3. With what is love metaphorically compared in the second quatrain? What qualities does the speaker assert that love has?
4. What opposes love in the third quatrain? What idea about love is explored here?
5. How does the couplet clinch the ideas and emotions of the poem?
6. To what extent is the argument of this poem organized by its closed form?

We recognize almost immediately that this poem is a Shakespearean sonnet; it is written in iambic pentameter and is composed of three quatrains and a concluding couplet, rhyming *a b a b, c d c d, e f e f, g g*. The general topic is love, specifically the love or "marriage of true minds." The sonnet puts forward the idea that love, when based on the union of true minds or spirits, is unaffected by time and change. The sonnet form provides shape and organization for the poem's argument; each quatrain advances a different restatement of the poem's central thought. The final couplet offers a summation of the argument and clinches the central idea through rhyme.

The first quatrain advances the *thesis* of the sonnet: true and permanent love is based on the "marriage of true minds." This kind of love will not "admit impediments"; nothing will stand in its way. In addition, it will not change even though the lovers might change ("alteration") or be separated ("remove"). The rhetorical strategy here is negation; the speaker tells us what true love is *not*. This strategy is indicated by the phrases "Let me not" and "Love is not." The allusion to the Anglican marriage ceremony in the term *impediments* makes the tone of this quatrain public and ceremonial, as though the lines were being spoken during a wedding or a formal social occasion.

In lines 5–8 the speaker illustrates the permanence of true love by comparing it to "an ever-fixed mark" and "the star." The metaphor here is nautical and navigational; love is compared to an unchanging beacon and to a fixed star guiding sailors. The "ever-fixed mark" is unaffected by changes and turbulence in the world; it "looks on tempests and is never shaken" (line 6). Similarly, the star is fixed and permanent; although its "worth" or inner nature might be unknown, its "height" or altitude is known and always dependable in navigation. This quatrain reverses the rhetorical strategy of the first; it tells us what true love *is* rather than what it is not.

The third quatrain returns to the negative strategy of the first, and the speaker asserts that love is "not Time's fool." Time metaphorically becomes a reaper whose sickle eventually cuts down all living things. The speaker admits that time can destroy the physical beauty of the lovers, the "rosy lips and cheeks." Nevertheless, love itself is not subject to the power ("compass") of time; "Love alters not with his [Time's] brief hours and weeks" (line 11). To the contrary, real love will last until the very brink ("the edge") of the Last Judgment.

In the concluding couplet the speaker returns to the public and formal tone of the first quatrain. He invites rebuttal to his assertions about love in the conditional phrasing of line 13—"If this be error, and upon me proved"—and he offers two proofs that his ideas are valid. One of these is the poem itself; the speaker claims that if I am not correct, then "I never writ." Since the poem proves that the speaker wrote, its presence supports the speaker's assertions about love. For the second proof the speaker claims that if he is wrong then "no man ever loved." Because men have obviously loved, the speaker's argument must be valid. In both proofs we must be willing to accept the speaker's conditions in order to validate his conclusions. The couplet thus brings the sonnet neatly to a close. The final two lines and the two rhyming words—*proved* and *loved*—clinch the central idea introduced in the first quatrain.

OPEN-FORM POETRY

As we noted earlier, poets who write in open rather than closed forms avoid the ready-made patterns of traditional structures such as the ballad or sonnet. Similarly, they do not use such traditional devices as rhyme schemes or regular meters to organize their poems. Instead, they look for other ways of organizing letters, words, lines, and sentences into cohesive and effective poetic statements. In many respects, open forms have come to dominate modern and contemporary poetry. As we shall see, however, writing open-form verse is no easier than writing closed forms; it is a different process and concerns itself with different variables.

Open-form poetry was once termed **free verse** (from the French *vers libre*) to signify its freedom from regular metrical rules and its dependence on the *cadences* of spoken language (see Chapter 19, pp. 667–68). That term is not really appropriate, however. While open-form poetry is indeed liberated from the rigid demands of meter, rhyme, and stanza, there is nothing *free* about the poems; they reflect different types of patterns.

OPEN FORM AND MEANING

Poets who write in open forms must develop a new set of organizing principles for each poem. They give up the shaping power of traditional devices such as meter, rhyme, and stanza; in exchange, they gain the freedom to create a new kind of fusion between form and content based on such devices as rhythm and cadence, line lengths and breaks, pauses, and the groupings of words and phrases. Poets working in open forms can also isolate specific words or phrases in a single line and employ the white spaces within and without a poem for emphasis. They may even write poems that look exactly like prose and are printed in paragraphs instead of stanzas or lines. These **prose poems** rely on the cadences of language and the progression of images to convey the poetic experience. As a general rule, we should remember that most open-form poetry is neither disorganized nor formless. On the contrary, each poem simultaneously seeks and speaks its own principles of structure.

We can see an early instance of open-form poetry in Walt Whitman's "Reconciliation." It was written as part of *Drum Taps*, a collection of fifty-three poems concerned with the poet's reaction to Civil War battles in Virginia.

WALT WHITMAN (1819–1892)

Reconciliation   *1865, 1881*

Word over all, beautiful as the sky,
Beautiful that war and all its deeds of carnage must in time be utterly lost,
That the hands of the sisters Death and Night incessantly softly wash again, and
    ever again, this soil'd world;
For my enemy is dead, a man divine as myself is dead,
I look where he lies white-faced and still in the coffin—I draw near,   5
Bend down and touch lightly with my lips the white face in the coffin.

QUESTIONS

1. How do individual lines, varying line lengths, punctuation, pauses, and cadences create rhythm and organize the images and ideas in this poem?
2. To what extent does alliteration, assonance, and the repetition of words unify
   the poem and reinforce its content?
3. What is the "word" referred to in line 1? What does the speaker find "beautiful" about this "word" and the passage of time?
4. What instances of personification can you find? What do these personified
   figures do? What does the speaker do in lines 5–6? Why does he do this?

Whitman's "Reconciliation" is an example of open-form poetry; the
poem has no dominant meter, rhyme scheme, or stanza pattern. Instead,
the poet uses the individual lines and varying line lengths to organize
and emphasize the ideas, images, and emotions. He also employs repetition
and alliteration to hold each line together, link it to the next, and reinforce
meaning. In addition, the punctuation, caesurae, and cadences create a
strong rhythm when the poem is read aloud.

Line 1 introduces the "word over all" that is "beautiful as the sky."
The word may be "peace," "reconciliation," God's word, or even the words
of the poem. In any event, the "word" leads to peace and reconciliation
in the poem. This image and idea are emphasized by the shortness of
this line and its division, by punctuation, into two coequal cadences.

The idea of the "word" is linked through the repetition of *beautiful*
and *all* with the idea that war and its carnage "must in time be utterly
lost" (line 2). This idea, in turn, is linked through the repetition of *that*
to the image of the two personified figures, Death and Night, who "wash"
war and carnage out of "this soil'd world" (line 3). In this line, unity
and emphasis are created through the repetition of *again* and the alliteration
on the "*ly*" sound of *incessantly* and *softly*, the "*s*" sound in *hands, sisters,
incessantly, softly,* and *soil'd,* and the "*d*" sound in *hands, Death, soil'd,* and

World. The punctuation and pauses of the line break it up into units of sound and thought that create a remarkable internal rhythm: "That the hands // of the sisters // Death // and Night // incessantly softly wash // again, // and ever again, // this soil'd world."

To this point, each line has introduced a new idea and a new image, but repetition provides continuity. In addition, the first three lines are held together by the alliteration on the *"w"* sound in *word, war, wash,* and *world*. These *"w"* sounds, combined with the *"s"* sounds in line 3, create a soft and whispering tone that underscores the pathos and desolation of the scene.

In line 4 we become aware of two characters, a more immediate situation, and a symbol of the carnage of war—the corpse of the speaker's enemy. Again, the line is unified and its ideas emphasized through repetition of the words *is dead* and the *"e"* sound in *enemy, dead,* and *myself*. The second part of the line, which is broken into three cadences by caesurae, establishes the common humanity and divinity of the speaker and his enemy.

This commonality and the central idea of reconciliation are reasserted in lines 5–6, when the speaker approaches the coffin, bends down, and kisses the face of his enemy. Again, the images and actions are contained within separate natural cadences of speech that create a rhythm—"I look where he lies // white-faced and still // in the coffin— // I draw near." Similarly, repetition stresses the key ideas and unifies the lines. Here the pattern of repetition includes the *I, white-faced,* and *coffin,* and alliteration on the sound *"l"* in *look, lies, still, lightly,* and *lips*.

VISUAL POETRY AND CONCRETE POETRY

With **visual poetry,** we are dealing with poems that draw much (and sometimes most) of their power from the appearance of the poem as a shape. Some visual poetry seeks to strike a balance between the pleasures of seeing and those of hearing the poem; other visual poetry, however, abandons sound completely and invests all its impact in our perception of the visual image or picture. In any event, all visual poetry must sacrifice the pleasures of hearing the poem to some extent since the impact of the form depends on *seeing* it.

Visual poetry is not a recent development; the Chinese have been producing it for thousands of years, and there are surviving examples from ancient Greece. Even in the English tradition, visual poetry dates back to the seventeenth century when ingenious writers created poems in the shapes of squares, circles, triangles, stars, and the like. This type of poetry, called **shaped verse,** was usually more ingenious than significant; there was rarely an organic connection between the shape and the sense of the poem. Exceptional poets, however, produced shaped verse in which the visual image and the meaning strikingly echoed each other.

Since the seventeenth century, various poets, including Lewis Carroll and Dylan Thomas, have created picture poems or shaped verse. However, it was only after World War II that visual poetry burst back onto the literary landscape with the birth of a new movement called **concrete poetry.** Poets who work in this tradition focus their attention almost completely on the medium from which the poem is created. In the case of printed work, this means that the writers pay far more attention to the visual arrangement of letters, words, lines, and white spaces than they do to ideas or emotions. Concrete poetry represents a fusion of writing with painting or graphic design, and the emphasis is on the side of the visual arts. The concrete poet is interested in the poem mostly as an object or an image rather than as an expression. For these poets, structure becomes both the means and the end of creation.

FORM AND MEANING IN VISUAL POETRY

In reading visual and concrete poetry, we should seek whatever correspondence may exist between the image and the words. Valid considerations include the shape of the poem, the connotations of this shape, the varying line lengths, the placement of individual words and phrases, and the use of white spaces. We can see a superb example of seventeenth-century visual poetry in George Herbert's "Easter Wings," a poem that offers two different pictures that are both relevant to the content.

This poem is an admission of sin and a prayer for redemption. It compares humanity's fall from grace ("wealth and store") in Eden to the spiritual state of the speaker, who seeks salvation through Christ's sacrifice. When viewed sideways, the poem resembles a pair of angel's wings. This image is thus linked with the title of the poem and connotes Christ's rising, salvation, and divine grace. Viewed straight on, each stanza resembles an hourglass, thus reinforcing the speaker's discussion of the spiritual history of humanity (in lines 1–5) and his or her own personal history of sin (in lines 11–15).

The correspondence between shape and meaning, however, goes far beyond these two images. Herbert employs typography to echo the content of each line. Thus, when the speaker discusses the spiritual history of humanity, the original "wealth and store" of Eden is described in a full and abundant line of verse. As the fall is described, however, the lines get progressively shorter or thinner, until humanity's fallen and "most poor" state is described in the narrowest and "most poor" line. This same typographical pattern is repeated in lines 11–15, where the speaker describes the sinful state that has left him or her spiritually "most thin." Again, the length of the line echoes the content. In the second half of each stanza, this typographical pattern is reversed and the lines get progressively longer or fuller. This expansion is concurrent with the speaker's prayers for grace and salvation. Thus, the fullness of lines 10 and 20 reflects the original states of grace, described in lines 1 and 11, and the glorious wealth of redemption.

GEORGE HERBERT (1593–1633)

Easter Wings   *1633*

Lord, who createdst man in wealth and store,°   *abundance*
  Though foolishly he lost the same,
    Decaying more and more
      Till he became
        Most poor: 5
        With thee
        O let me rise
      As larks, harmoniously,
  And sing this day thy victories:
Then shall the fall further the flight in me.   10

My tender age in sorrow did begin:
  And still with sicknesses and shame
    Thou didst so punish sin,
      That I became
        Most thin.   15
        With thee
        Let me combine,
      And feel this day thy victory;
  For, if I imp° my wing on thine,
Affliction shall advance the flight in me.   20

EASTER WINGS   19 *imp*: to repair a falcon's wing or tail by grafting on a feather.

QUESTIONS

1. What does the poem look like when viewed sideways? When viewed straight on? How do these two images echo and emphasize the poem's content?
2. How does the typographical arrangement of the lines of this poem echo the sense? As a starting point, consider lines 5 and 15. How are typography, shape, and meaning fused in these lines?
3. What do lines 1–5 tell you about humanity's spiritual history? What do lines 11–15 tell you about the speaker's spiritual state? How are these parallel?
4. Who or what is the speaker? The listener? What does the speaker want? What is the connection between this desire and the title of the poem?

POEMS FOR STUDY

JOHN MILTON (1608–1674)

When I Consider How My Light Is Spent°   *1655*

When I consider how my light is spent
  Ere half my days, in this dark world and wide,
  And that one talent° which is death to hide,
  Lodged with me useless, though my soul more bent
To serve therewith my Maker, and present   5
  My true account, lest he returning chide;
  "Doth God exact day-labor, light denied?"
  I fondly° ask; but Patience to prevent°   *foolishly; forestall*
That murmur, soon replies, "God doth not need
  Either man's work or his own gifts; who best   10
  Bear his mild yoke, they serve him best. His state
Is kingly. Thousands at his bidding speed
  And post o'er land and ocean without rest:
  They also serve who only stand and wait."

WHEN I CONSIDER HOW MY LIGHT IS SPENT. Milton began to go blind in the late
1640s and was completely blind by 1651.   *3 talent*: both a skill and a reference to the
talents discussed in the parable in Matthew 25: 14–30.

QUESTIONS

1. What is the meter of this poem? The rhyme scheme? The closed form?
2. To what extent do the two major divisions of this form organize the poem's
   ideas?
3. What problem is raised in the octave? What are the speaker's complaints?
   Who is the speaker in the sestet? How are the conflicts raised in the octave
   resolved?
4. Explore the word *talent* and relate its various meanings to the poem as a
   whole. To understand the term fully, you should refer to the parable in
   Matthew and see what the term represents there.

PERCY BYSSHE SHELLEY (1792–1822)

Ozymandias   *1818*

I met a traveller from an antique land,
Who said—"Two vast and trunkless legs of stone
Stand in the desert. . . . Near them, on the sand,

Half sunk a shattered visage lies, whose frown,
And wrinkled lip, and sneer of cold command,   5
Tell that its sculptor well those passions read
Which yet survive, stamped on these lifeless things,
The hand that mocked them, and the heart that fed;
And on the pedestal, these words appear:
My name is Ozymandias, King of Kings,   10
Look on my Works, ye Mighty, and despair!
Nothing beside remains. Round the decay
Of that colossal Wreck, boundless and bare
The lone and level sands stretch far away."

QUESTIONS

1. What is the meter of this poem? The rhyme scheme? What traditional closed
    form is modified here? How do the modifications affect the poem?

2. To what extent are content and meaning shaped by the closed form? What
    is described in the octave? In the sestet?

3. Characterize Ozymandias (Ramses II, Pharoah of Egypt, who died in 1225
    B.C.) from the way he is portrayed in this poem.

4. Into how many pieces is the statue of Ozymandias shattered? What is the
    effect of distributing these fragments throughout the poem? Whose "hand"
    and "heart" are mentioned in line 8?

5. What point does this poem make about power? Time? Art?

CLAUDE McKAY (1890–1948)

In Bondage   1953

I would be wandering in distant fields
Where man, and bird, and beast, lives leisurely,
And the old earth is kind, and ever yields
Her goodly gifts to all her children free;
Where life is fairer, lighter, less demanding,   5
And boys and girls have time and space for play
Before they come to years of understanding—
Somewhere I would be singing, far away.
For life is greater than the thousand wars
Men wage for it in their insatiate lust,   10
And will remain like the eternal stars,
When all that shines to-day is drift and dust.

But I am bound with you in your mean graves,
O black men, simple slaves of ruthless slaves.

QUESTIONS

1. What is the meter of this poem? The rhyme scheme? The form? To what extent does the form organize the speaker's thoughts?

2. Lines 1–8 present a conditional (rather than actual) situation that the speaker desires. What word signals this conditional nature? What is the speaker's wish?

3. What point does the speaker make about life in lines 9–12?

4. To what extent does the couplet undermine the rest of the poem? What single word conveys this reversal? How effectively do the rhymes in the couplet clinch the poem's meaning? What is the speaker telling us about the lives of black people?

JOHN DRYDEN (1631–1700)

To the Memory of Mr. Oldham   *1684*

Farewell, too little and too lately known,
Whom I began to think and call my own:
For sure our souls were near allied, and thine
Cast in the same poetic mold with mine.
One common note on either lyre did strike,
And knaves and fools we both abhorred alike.
To the same goal did both our studies drive;
The last set out the soonest did arrive.
Thus Nisus° fell upon the slipp'ry place,
While his young friend performed and won the race.   10
O early ripe! to thy abundant store
What could advancing age have added more?
It might (what nature never gives the young)
Have taught the numbers of thy native tongue.
But satire needs not those, and wit will shine   15
Through the harsh cadence of a rugged line;
A noble error, and but seldom made,
When poets are by too much force betrayed.
Thy gen'rous fruits, though gathered ere their prime,
Still showed a quickness; and maturing time   20
But mellows what we write to the dull sweets of rhyme.
Once more, hail and farewell;° farewell, thou young,

TO THE MEMORY OF MR. OLDHAM. John Oldham (1653–1683) was a young poet whom Dryden admired.   9 *Nisus*: a character in Vergil's *Aeneid* who slipped in a pool of blood while running a race, thus allowing his best friend to win.   22 *hail and farewell*: an echo of the Latin phrase "ave atque vale" spoken by gladiators about to fight.

But ah too short, Marcellus° of our tongue;
Thy brows with ivy and with laurels° bound;
But fate and gloomy night encompass thee around.   25

23 *Marcellus*: a Roman general who was adopted by the Emperor Augustus as his successor
but died at the age of twenty.   24 *laurels*: a plant sacred to Apollo, the Greek god of
poetry; the traditional prize given to poets is a wreath of laurel.

QUESTIONS

1. What is the meter of this poem? The rhyme scheme? The closed form? How
    does the form control the poem's pace or tempo? Why is this tempo appropri-
    ate?
2. What does the speaker reveal about himself in lines 1–10? About Oldham?
    About his relationship with Oldham? What did the two have in common?
3. What point does the speaker make about Oldham's death in lines 11–25?
    How might his death have been an advantage?
4. What is the effect of Dryden's frequent classical allusions? Which pairs of
    rhyming words most effectively clinch ideas?
5. Compare this poem with A. E. Housman's "To an Athlete Dying Young"
    (p. 727). How are the ideas in the two poems similar? What other similarities
    can you find?

JEAN TOOMER (1894–1967)

Reapers   *1923*

Black reapers with the sound of steel on stones
Are sharpening scythes. I see them place the hones
In their hip-pockets as a thing that's done,
And start their silent swinging, one by one.
Black horses drive a mower through the weeds,   5
And there, a field rat, startled, squealing bleeds,
His belly close to ground. I see the blade,
Blood-stained, continue cutting weeds and shade.

QUESTIONS

1. What is the meter of this poem? The rhyme scheme? The form? How does
    Toomer use the same form as Dryden (in "Mr. Oldham") in a different way?
2. What are the central images of this poem? How do they relate to each other?

How does the image of the bleeding field rat and the "blood-stained" blade heighten the emotional impact?

3. How does alliteration unify this poem and make sound echo sense? Note especially the "*s*" and "*b*" sounds, and the phrase *silent swinging*.

4. What feeling is created by this poem? What does the poem tell us about the lives of black reapers?

GEORGE HERBERT (1593–1633)

Virtue   *1633*

Sweet day, so cool, so calm, so bright,
The bridal of the earth and sky:
The dew shall weep thy fall tonight;
    For thou must die.

Sweet rose, whose hue, angry° and brave,°   *splendid*   5
Bids the rash gazer wipe his eye:
Thy root is ever in its grave,
    And thou must die.

Sweet spring, full of sweet days and roses,
A box where sweets° compacted lie;   *perfumes*   10
My music shows ye have your closes,°
    And all must die.

Only a sweet and virtuous soul,
Like seasoned timber, never gives;
But though the whole world turn to coal,°   15
    Then chiefly lives.

VIRTUE   5 *angry*: having the color of an angry, red face.   11 *closes*: the musical term for the concluding cadences in songs.   15 *coal*: reduced to ash at the Last Judgment.

QUESTIONS

1. What is the rhyme scheme of this poem? The meter? The form?
2. What point does the speaker make about the "day" in lines 1–4? The "rose" in lines 5–8? The "spring" in lines 9–12? The "soul" in lines 13–16?
3. How does the poet draw the images of the first two stanzas into the third? What do the day, rose, and spring have in common? How is the "virtuous soul" different?
4. To what extent do the rhyme scheme and stanzaic structure of this poem shape and reinforce the poem's theme?

ROBERT FROST (1874–1963)

Desert Places   *1936*

Snow falling and night falling fast, oh, fast
In a field I looked into going past,
And the ground almost covered smooth in snow,
But a few weeds and stubble showing last.

The woods around it have it—it is theirs.   5
All animals are smothered in their lairs.
I am too absent-spirited to count;
The loneliness includes me unawares.

And lonely as it is that loneliness
Will be more lonely ere it will be less—   10
A blanker whiteness of benighted snow
With no expression, nothing to express.

They cannot scare me with their empty spaces
Between stars—on stars where no human race is.
I have it in me so much nearer home   15
To scare myself with my own desert places.

QUESTIONS

1. What is the meter? The rhyme scheme? The form?
2. What setting and situation are established in lines 1–4? What does the snow affect here? What does it affect in lines 5–8? In lines 9–12?
3. What different kinds of "desert places" is this poem about? Which kind is the most important? Most frightening?
4. How does the type of rhyme (rising or falling) change in the last stanza? To what extent does this change affect the tone and impact of the poem?
5. How does the stanzaic pattern of this poem organize the progression of the speaker's thoughts, feelings, and conclusions?

JOHN KEATS (1795–1821)

Ode to a Nightingale   *1819*

1

My heart aches, and a drowsy numbness pains
  My sense, as though of hemlock° I had drunk,   *a poisonous herb*
Or emptied some dull opiate to the drains

One minute past, and Lethe-wards° had sunk:
'Tis not through envy of thy happy lot,   5
But being too happy in thine happiness,—
That thou, light-winged Dryad° of the trees,
In some melodious plot
Of beechen green, and shadows numberless,
Singest of summer in full-throated ease.   10
2
O, for a draught of vintage! that hath been
Cool'd a long age in the deep-delved earth,
Tasting of Flora° and the country green,
Dance, and Provençal song, and sunburnt mirth!
O for a beaker full of the warm South,   15
Full of the true, the blushful Hippocrene,°
With beaded bubbles winking at the brim,
And purple-stained mouth;
That I might drink, and leave the world unseen,
And with thee fade away into the forest dim: 20
3
Fade far away, dissolve, and quite forget
What thou among the leaves hast never known,
The weariness, the fever, and the fret
Here, where men sit and hear each other groan;
Where palsy shakes a few, sad, last gray hairs,   25
Where youth grows pale, and spectre-thin, and dies;
Where but to think is to be full of sorrow
And leaden-eyed despairs,
Where Beauty cannot keep her lustrous eyes,
Or new Love pine at them beyond to-morrow.   30
4
Away! away! for I will fly to thee,
Not charioted by Bacchus° and his pards,°   *leopards*
But on the viewless wings of Poesy,°   *poetry*
Though the dull brain perplexes and retards:
Already with thee! tender is the night,   35
And haply the Queen-Moon is on her throne,
Cluster'd around by all her starry Fays;°   *fairies*
But here there is no light,
Save what from heaven is with the breezes blown
Through verdurous glooms and winding mossy ways.   40

ODE TO A NIGHTINGALE.   4 *Lethe-wards*: toward the river of forgetfulness in Hades,
the underworld of Greek mythology.   7 *Dryad*: in Greek mythology, a semidivine tree
spirit.   13 *Flora*: the Roman goddess of flowers.   16 *Hippocrene*: the fountain of the
Muses on Mt. Helicon in Greek mythology; the phrase thus refers to both the waters of
poetic inspiration and a cup of wine.   32 *Bacchus*: the Greek god of wine.

5

I cannot see what flowers are at my feet,
  Nor what soft incense hangs upon the boughs,
But, in embalmed° darkness, guess each sweet   *fragrant*
  Wherewith the seasonable month endows
The grass, the thicket, and the fruit-tree wild;   45
  White hawthorn, and the pastoral eglantine;°   *honeysuckle*
    Fast fading violets cover'd up in leaves;
      And mid-May's eldest child,
  The coming musk-rose, full of dewy wine,
    The murmurous haunt of flies on summer eves.   50

6

Darkling° I listen; and, for many a time   *in the dark*
  I have been half in love with easeful Death,
Call'd him soft names in many a mused rhyme,
  To take into the air my quiet breath;
Now more than ever seems it rich to die,   55
  To cease upon the midnight with no pain,
    While thou art pouring forth thy soul abroad
      In such an ecstasy!
  Still wouldst thou sing, and I have ears in vain—
    To thy high requiem become a sod.   60

7

Thou wast not born for death, immortal Bird!
  No hungry generations tread thee down;
The voice I hear this passing night was heard
  In ancient days by emperor and clown:
Perhaps the self-same song that found a path   65
  Through the sad heart of Ruth,° when, sick for home,
    She stood in tears amid the alien corn;°   *wheat*
      The same that oft-times hath
  Charm'd magic casements, opening on the foam
    Of perilous seas, in faery lands forlorn.   70

8

Forlorn! the very word is like a bell
  To toll me back from thee to my sole self!
Adieu! the fancy° cannot cheat so well   *imagination*
  As she is fam'd to do, deceiving elf.
Adieu! adieu! thy plaintive anthem fades   75
  Past the near meadows, over the still stream,
    Up the hill-side; and now 'tis buried deep
      In the next valley-glades:
  Was it a vision, or a waking dream?
    Fled is that music:—Do I wake or sleep?   80

66 *Ruth*: the widow of Boaz in the Biblical Book of Ruth.

QUESTIONS

1. Formulate the structure (meter of each line and rhyme scheme) of the first stanza, and then see if it is repeated in the second and third. What traditional form is employed here?

2. What is the speaker's mental and emotional state in stanza 1? What similes are employed to describe this condition?

3. What does the speaker want in stanza 2? Whom does he want to join? Why? From what aspects of the world (stanza 3) does he want to escape?

4. How do the speaker's mood and perspective change in stanza 4? How does he achieve this transition? What characterizes the world that the speaker enters in stanza 5? What senses are employed to describe this world?

5. In the sixth stanza the speaker comes up with another way of achieving a visionary state. What is it? Why will it not work?

6. What does the speaker establish about the nightingale's song in the seventh stanza? What does the song come to symbolize?

PERCY BYSSHE SHELLEY (1792–1822)

Ode to the West Wind   *1820*

I

O wild West Wind, thou breath° of Autumn's being,
Thou, from whose unseen presence the leaves dead
Are driven, like ghosts from an enchanter fleeing,

Yellow, and black, and pale, and hectic° red,
Pestilence-stricken multitudes: O Thou,   5
Who chariotest to their dark wintry bed

The winged seeds, where they lie cold and low,
Each like a corpse within its grave, until
Thine azure sister of the Spring° shall blow

Her clarion o'er the dreaming earth, and fill   10
(Driving sweet buds like flocks to feed in air)
With living hues and odours plain and hill:

Wild Spirit, which art moving everywhere;
Destroyer and Preserver; hear, O hear!

II

Thou on whose stream, 'mid the steep sky's commotion,   15
Loose clouds like Earth's decaying leaves are shed,
Shook from the tangled boughs of Heaven and Ocean,

ODE TO THE WEST WIND.   1 *breath*: in many languages, the words for *wind*, *breath*, *soul*, *spirit*, and *inspiration* are the same (as in the Latin *spiritus*). In English, inspiration literally means to breathe or blow into.   4 *hectic*: a fever that produces flushed cheeks.   9 *Spring*: the wind that will blow in the spring.

Angels of rain and lightning: there are spread
On the blue surface of thine aery surge,
Like the bright hair uplifted from the head   20

Of some fierce Maenad,° even from the dim verge
Of the horizon to the zenith's height,
The locks of the approaching storm. Thou Dirge

Of the dying year, to which this closing night
Will be the dome of a vast sepulchre,   25
Vaulted with all thy congregated might

Of vapours,° from whose solid atmosphere   *clouds*
Black rain and fire and hail will burst: O hear!
                        III
Thou who didst waken from his summer dreams
The blue Mediterranean, where he lay,   30
Lulled by the coil of his crystalline streams,

Beside a pumice isle in Baiae's bay,°
And saw in sleep old palaces and towers
Quivering within the wave's intenser day,

All overgrown with azure moss and flowers   35
So sweet, the sense faints picturing them! Thou
For whose path the Atlantic's level powers

Cleave themselves into chasms, while far below
The sea-blooms and the oozy woods which wear
The sapless foliage of the ocean, know   40

Thy voice, and suddenly grow grey with fear,
And tremble and despoil themselves: O hear!
                        IV
If I were a dead leaf thou mightest bear;
If I were a swift cloud to fly with thee;
A wave to pant beneath thy power, and share   45

The impulse of thy strength, only less free
Than thou, O Uncontrollable! If even
I were as in my boyhood, and could be

The comrade of thy wanderings over Heaven,
As then, when to outstrip thy skiey speed   50
Scarce seemed a vision; I would ne'er have striven

As thus with thee in prayer in my sore need.
Oh! lift me as a wave, a leaf, a cloud!
I fall upon the thorns of life! I bleed!

---

21 *Maenad*: a frenzied female worshipper of Dionysus, the god of wine and fertility in Greek
mythology.   32 *Baiae's bay*: a bay of the Mediterranean Sea west of Naples, famous for
the elaborate villas built on the shore by Roman emperors.

A heavy weight of hours has chained and bowed   55
One too like thee: tameless, and swift, and proud.
                               V
Make me thy lyre,° even as the forest is:
What if my leaves are falling like its own!
The tumult of thy mighty harmonies

Will take from both a deep, autumnal tone,   60
Sweet though in sadness. Be thou, Spirit fierce,
My spirit! Be thou me, impetuous one!

Drive my dead thoughts over the universe
Like withered leaves to quicken a new birth!
And, by the incantation of this verse,   65

Scatter, as from an unextinguished hearth
Ashes and sparks, my words among mankind!
Be through my lips to unawakened Earth

The trumpet of a prophecy! O Wind,
If Winter comes, can Spring be far behind?   70

57 *lyre*: an Aeolian harp, a musical device which is sounded by the wind blowing across
strings.

QUESTIONS

1. Formulate the structure (meter of each line and rhyme scheme) of the first
   stanza, and then see if it is repeated throughout the poem. What two traditional closed forms are combined in this poem?

2. How many times (and where) is the *e* rhyme of the first stanza repeated as
   a rhyme sound throughout the poem? What is the effect of this repetition?

3. What aspect of the natural world does the wind affect in the first section of
   the poem? The second section? The third?

4. What does the speaker assert (in section 4) that time has done to him? What
   does he want from the West Wind? What does he want to become?

5. To what extent are the thoughts and feelings of the speaker organized by
   the five sections of this poem? What is the logical progression from section
   to section?

6. What does the West Wind symbolize? Compare this poem to Keat's "Ode
   to a Nightingale." How are the nightingale's song and the West Wind related
   to each other as symbols?

DYLAN THOMAS (1914–1953)

Do Not Go Gentle into That Good Night   *1951*

Do not go gentle into that good night,
Old age should burn and rave at close of day;
Rage, rage against the dying of the light.

Though wise men at their end know dark is right,
Because their words had forked no lightning they
Do not go gentle into that good night.   5

Good men, the last wave by, crying how bright
Their frail deeds might have danced in a green bay,
Rage, rage against the dying of the light.

Wild men who caught and sang the sun in flight,   10
And learn, too late, they grieved it on its way,
Do not go gentle into that good night.

Grave men, near death, who see with blinding sight
Blind eyes could blaze like meteors and be gay,
Rage, rage against the dying of the light.   15

And you, my father, there on the sad height,
Curse, bless, me now with your fierce tears, I pray.
Do not go gentle into that good night.
Rage, rage against the dying of the light.

QUESTIONS

1. This poem is written in a traditional closed form called the **villanelle,** which was developed in France during the Middle Ages. A villanelle must be 19 lines long. There are additional rules governing the length and structure of stanzas, the rhyme scheme, and the repetition of complete lines. Try to formulate these rules. To look at another example, see Roethke's "The Waking" (p. 992).

2. What can you surmise about the speaker here? The listener? The situation?

3. What four different kinds of men does the speaker discuss in lines 4–15? What do they have in common?

4. What puns and connotative words can you find in this poem? Consider the *good* of "good night" and the word *grave* (line 13).

5. What does the speaker want the listener to do? What is the poem's theme?

DUDLEY RANDALL (b. 1914)

Ballad of Birmingham   *1969*

(*On the bombing of a church in Birmingham, Alabama, 1963*)

"Mother dear, may I go downtown
Instead of out to play,
And march the streets of Birmingham
In a Freedom March today?"

BALLAD OF BIRMINGHAM. Four black children were killed when the 16th Street Baptist Church in Birmingham, Alabama, was bombed in 1963. A man was finally indicted for the murders in 1977 and convicted in 1982.

"No, baby, no, you may not go,
For the dogs are fierce and wild,
And clubs and hoses, guns and jails
Aren't good for a little child."

"But, mother, I won't be alone.
Other children will go with me,
And march the streets of Birmingham
To make our country free."

"No, baby, no, you may not go,
For I fear those guns will fire.
But you may go to church instead
And sing in the children's choir."

She has combed and brushed her night-dark hair,
And bathed rose petal sweet,
And drawn white gloves on her small brown hands,
And white shoes on her feet.

The mother smiled to know her child
Was in the sacred place,
But that smile was the last smile
To come upon her face.

For when she heard the explosion,
Her eyes grew wet and wild.
She raced through the streets of Birmingham
Calling for her child.

She clawed through bits of glass and brick,
Then lifted out a shoe.
"O, here's the shoe my baby wore,
But, baby, where are you?"

QUESTIONS

1. Formulate the structure (meter, rhyme scheme, stanza form) of this poem. What traditional closed form is employed here?

2. Who is the speaker in stanzas 1 and 3? In stanzas 2 and 4? How are quotation and repetition employed to create tension?

3. What ironies do you find in the mother's assumptions? In the poem as a whole? In the society pictured in the poem?

4. Compare this poem to "Sir Patrick Spens" (p. 465) and to "Barbara Allan" (p. 722). How are the structures of all three alike? What devices do you find in all three? To what extent do all three deal with the same type of subject matter?

WALT WHITMAN (1819–1892)

When I Heard the Learn'd Astronomer   *1865*

When I heard the learn'd astronomer,
When the proofs, the figures, were ranged in columns before me,
When I was shown the charts and diagrams, to add, divide, and measure them,
When I sitting heard the astronomer where he lectured with much applause in
  the lecture-room,
How soon unaccountable I became tired and sick,   5
Till rising and gliding out I wander'd off by myself,
In the mystical moist night-air, and from time to time,
Look'd up in perfect silence at the stars.

QUESTIONS

1. Explain why you consider the form of this poem closed or open.
2. How does Whitman use line lengths, cadences, and punctuation to create rhythm?
3. What are the effects produced by lists, repetition, and alliteration here?
4. What two worlds and ways of thinking are contrasted in this poem? Try to list the qualities of each world that are mentioned in the poem.

E. E. CUMMINGS (1894–1962)

Buffalo Bill's Defunct°   *1923*

Buffalo Bill's
defunct
        who used to
        ride a watersmooth-silver
                        stallion   5
and break onetwothreefourfive pigeonsjustlikethat
                        Jesus

he was a handsome man
                and what i want to know is
how do you like your blueeyed boy   10
Mister Death

BUFFALO BILL'S DEFUNCT. The poem has no title; it is usually referred to as "Portrait" or by its first two lines. Buffalo Bill (William F. Cody, 1846–1917) was an American plainsman, hunter, army scout, sharpshooter, and showman whose Wild West show began touring the world in 1883; he became a symbol of the Wild West.

QUESTIONS

1. What is the effect of devoting a whole line to *Buffalo Bill's* (line 1), *defunct* (line 2), *stallion* (line 5), *Jesus* (line 7), and *Mister Death* (line 11)? How does this technique reflect and emphasize the content of the poem?

2. How does the typographical arrangement of line 6 contribute to the fusion of sound and sense? What other examples of this technique are found in the poem?

3. Explain the denotations and connotations of *defunct*. What would be lost (or gained) by using the term *dead* or *deceased* instead?

4. To what extent is this poem a "portrait" of Buffalo Bill? What do we learn about him? Is the portrait respectful, mocking, or something in between?

WILLIAM CARLOS WILLIAMS (1883–1963)

The Dance   *1944*

In Breughel's° great picture, The Kermess,
the dancers go round, they go round and
around, the squeal and the blare and the
tweedle of bagpipes, a bugle and fiddles

THE DANCE.   1 *Breughel's*: Pieter Breughel (c. 1525–1569), a Flemish painter who often portrayed a world of robust and joyful peasants. *The Kermess* shows the dancing of peasants in celebration of a feast day.

tipping their bellies (round as the thick-   5
sided glasses whose wash they impound)
their hips and their bellies off balance
to turn them. Kicking and rolling about
the Fair Grounds, swinging their butts, those
shanks must be sound to bear up under such   10
rollicking measures, prance as they dance
in Breughel's great picture, The Kermess.

QUESTIONS

1. What effect is produced by repeating the first line of the poem as the last
    line?
2. How do repetition, alliteration, assonance, onomatopoeia, and internal rhyme
    affect the tempo, feeling, and meaning of the poem? How do the numerous
    participles (like *tipping*, *kicking*, *rolling*) make sound echo sense?
3. What words are capitalized? What effect is produced by omitting the capital
    letters at the beginning of each line? How does this typographical choice
    reinforce the sound and the sense of the poem?
4. Most of the lines of this poem are run-on rather than end-stopped, and
    many of them end with fairly weak words such as *and*, *the*, *about*, and *such*.
    What effect is produced through these techniques?
5. How successful is Williams in making the words and sentence rhythms of
    his poem echo the visual rhythms in Breughel's painting? Why is this open
    form more appropriate to the images of the poem than any closed form
    could be?

ALLEN GINSBERG (b. 1926)

A Supermarket in California   *1955*

What thoughts I have of you tonight, Walt Whitman,° for
I walked down the sidestreets under the trees with a headache
self-conscious looking at the full moon.
    In my hungry fatigue, and shopping for images, I went
into the neon fruit supermarket, dreaming of your enumera-   5
tions!°
What   peaches   and   what   penumbras!   Whole   families
shopping   at   night!   Aisles   full   of   husbands!   Wives   in   the

A SUPERMARKET IN CALIFORNIA.   1 *Walt Whitman*: American poet (1819–1892) who
experimented with open forms and significantly influenced the development of twentieth-
century poetry in Europe and the Americas.   6 *enumerations*: many of Whitman's poems
contain long lists.

avocados, babies in the tomatoes!—and you, Garcia Lorca,° what
were you doing down by the watermelons?   10

I saw you, Walt Whitman, childless, lonely old grubber,
poking among the meats in the refrigerator and eyeing the
grocery boys.
I heard you asking questions of each: Who killed the pork
chops? What price bananas? Are you my Angel?   15
I wandered in and out of the brilliant stacks of cans
following you, and followed in my imagination by the store
detective.
We strode down the open corridors together in our solitary
fancy tasting artichokes, possessing every frozen delicacy, and   20
never passing the cashier.

Where are we going, Walt Whitman? The doors close in
an hour. Which way does your beard point tonight?
(I touch your book and dream of our odyssey in the supermarket
and feel absurd.)   25
Will we walk all night through solitary streets? The trees
add shade to shade, lights out in the houses, we'll both be
lonely.

Will we stroll dreaming of the lost America of love past blue
automobiles in driveways, home to our silent cottage?   30
Ah, dear father, graybeard, lonely old courage-teacher,
what America did you have when Charon° quit poling his ferry
and you got out on a smoking bank and stood watching the
boat disappear on the black waters of Lethe?°

9 *Garcia Lorca*: Spanish surrealist poet and playwright (1896–1936) whose late poetry became
progressively more like prose.   32 *Charon*: boatman in Greek mythology who ferried the
souls of the dead across the river Styx into Hades, the underworld.   34 *Lethe*: the river
of forgetfulness in Hades. The dead drank from this river and forgot their former lives.

QUESTIONS

1. Where is the speaker? What is he doing? What is his problem? His condi-
    tion?
2. What effect is produced by placing Whitman and Lorca in the market?
3. To what extent do we find Whitman-like enumerations in this work? What
    is the effect of such enumerations?
4. Why is this a poem? What poetic devices are employed here? To what extent
    might it make more sense to consider this prose rather than poetry?

NIKKI GIOVANNI (b. 1943)

Nikki-Rosa   *1968*

childhood remembrances are always a drag
if you're Black
you always remember things like living in Woodlawn°
with no inside toilet
and if you become famous or something   5
they never talk about how happy you were to have your mother
all to yourself and
how good the water felt when you got your bath from one of those
big tubs that folk in chicago barbecue in
and somehow when you talk about home   10
it never gets across how much you
understood their feelings
as the whole family attended meetings about Hollydale
and even though you remember
your biographers never understand   15
your father's pain as he sells his stock
and another dream goes
and though you're poor it isn't poverty that
concerns you
and though they fought a lot   20
it isn't your father's drinking that makes any difference
but only that everybody is together and you
and your sister have happy birthdays and very good christmasses
and I really hope no white person ever has cause to write about me
because they never understand Black love is Black wealth and they'll 25
probably talk about my hard childhood and never understand that
all the while I was quite happy

NIKKI-ROSA.   3 *Woodlawn*: a predominantly black suburb of Cincinnati, Ohio.

QUESTIONS

1. To what extent do individual lines, caesurae, and cadences create a rhythm and reinforce the sense of this poem?
2. What points does the speaker make about childhood in general, the childhoods of blacks, and his or her own childhood? What images of childhood are evoked?
3. What is the speaker's attitude toward himself or herself? What expectations does the speaker seem to have?
4. What ideas about the ways in which whites understand or misunderstand blacks does this poem explore?

MAY SWENSON (b. 1919)

Women   *1968*

Women   Or they
  should be   should be
    pedestals   little horses
     moving   those wooden
    pedestals   sweet
     moving   oldfashioned
    to the   painted
    motions   rocking
    of men   horses

     the gladdest things in the toyroom   10

    The   feelingly
   pegs   and then
  of their   unfeelingly
  ears   To be
 so familiar   joyfully
and dear   ridden
 to the trusting   rockingly
fists   ridden until
To be chafed   the restored

egos dismount and the legs stride away   20

Immobile   willing
 sweetlipped   to be set
  sturdy   into motion
  and smiling   Women
   women   should be
   should always   pedestals
   be waiting   to men

QUESTIONS

1. Is this poem an instance of closed form, open form, or visual poetry? In what different ways or sequences can it be read? How do the different sequences change the meaning?

2. How well does the image of the poem reinforce its meaning? Would the effect be different if the columns of words were straight instead of undulating?

3. How does the typography affect rhythm and emphasize meaning? Note especially isolated words, the arrangements of lines 10 and 20, and capitalization.

4. To what extent do repetition and alliteration help to organize the poem and underscore its sense. Note especially the "*w*," "*m*," "*f*," "*r*," and "*s*" sounds.

5. What does this poem *say* that women should be? Does it mean what it says?

How are men characterized? What is the speaker's attitude toward men? In what ways might this poem be ironic?

MARY ELLEN SOLT

Forsythia

1966

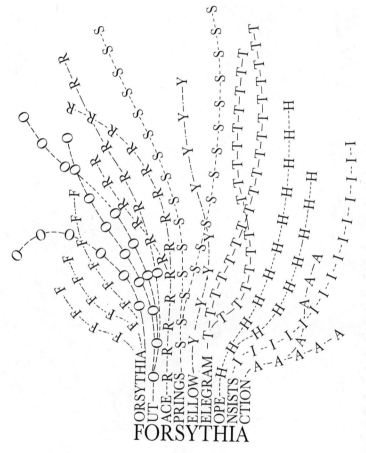

FORSYTHIA

QUESTIONS

1. What does this work tell you about forsythia?
2. When this work was originally published, it was printed over a square of yellow. What additional visual effect might have been produced by this field of yellow?
3. What is the significance of the dots and dashes placed between each letter of "FORSYTHIA"? What is the link between this device and the word "TELE-GRAM"?

4. What meaning or emotion, if any, does this work convey beyond its visual image? Is this a poem, an object of graphic art, or both?

EDWIN MORGAN (b. 1920)

The Computer's First Christmas Card   *1968*

```
jollymerry
hollyberry
jollyberry
merryholly
happyjolly                                                              5
jollyjelly
jellybelly
bellymerry
hollyheppy
jollyMolly                                                              10
marryJerry
merryHarry
hoppyBarry
heppyJarry
boppyheppy                                                              15
berryjorry
jorryjolly
moppyjelly
Mollymerry
Jerryjolly                                                              20
bellyboppy
jorryhoppy
hollymoppy
Barrymerry
Jarryhappy                                                              25
happyboppy
boppyjolly
jollymerry
merrymerry
merrymerry                                                              30
merryChris
ammerryasa
Chrismerry
asMERRYCHR
YSANTHEMUM                                                              35
```

QUESTIONS

1. To what extent is the effect of this work visual? What aspects or devices link it to a computer?
2. The writer (or computer) has generated some interesting word variations

and images. To what extent can you find logic in the movement from line to line?

3. How successful is this work in conveying ideas or images of Christmas? How far away from Christmas does "the computer" wander? What do you make of the fact that the work ends "asMERRYCHR / YSANTHE-MUM"?

4. Why might you consider this a poem?

JOHN HOLLANDER (b. 1929)

Swan and Shadow   *1969*

```
                           Dusk
                         Above the
                      water hang the
                            loud
                             flies                                          5
                            Here
                            O so
                            gray
                            then
             What              A pale signal will appear              10
             When           Soon before its shadow fades
             Where         Here in this pool of opened eye
             In us     No Upon us As at the very edges
                 of where we take shape in the dark air
                    this object bares its image awakening          15
                      ripples of recognition that will
                        brush darkness up into light
    even after this bird this hour both drift by atop the perfect sad instant now
                         already passing out of sight
                      toward yet-untroubled reflection             20
                    this image bears its object darkening
                    into memorial shades Scattered bits of
             light         No of water Or something across
             water        Breaking up No Being regathered
             soon            Yet by then a swan will have          25
             gone              Yes out of mind into what
                           vast
                           pale
                           hush
                           of a                                             30
                          place
                           past
                     sudden dark as
                       if a swan
                          sang                                              35
```

QUESTIONS

1. How effectively and consistently does the image or shape reinforce meaning?
2. What specific words, phrases, and lines are emphasized by the typographical arrangement here? To what extent does this effect give added impact to the poem?
3. What are the verbal images of the poem? How well does the structure echo these?
4. Do you find this experiment with shaped verse as successful as George Herbert's in "Easter Wings" (p. 754)? If so, demonstrate how it succeeds. If not, explain why.

WRITING ABOUT FORM IN POETRY

The aim in writing an essay about form in poetry is to demonstrate a relationship between structure and content. The form or shape of a poem should not be discussed in isolation; such an essay would simply produce a detailed description. Instead, structural analysis should always be tied into an evaluation of some aspect of the poem's content. As with essays about meter, sound, and rhyme, composition follows a double process of discovery in which both the sense and the form of the poem are investigated.

Your first task, of course, is to find an appropriate poem. If the choice is left up to you, you will have to decide at the outset whether you want to work with a closed form or an open form. In either event, you should select a poem that is short enough so that you can deal with the entire form and several structural components.

The next step in the prewriting process is a detailed investigation of the poem's sense. Consider the various elements that contribute to the poem's impact and effectiveness: the speaker, listener, setting, situation, diction, imagery, rhetorical devices, and the like. Once you understand these aspects of the poem, it will be easier to find the connection between form and content.

When you have completed a general consideration of the poem's impact and meaning, you will be ready to focus on the connection between form and content. At this point, it will be helpful if you prepare a worksheet much like the one employed when writing about meter (p. 687), sound (p. 702), or rhyme (p. 732). In this case the worksheet will highlight structural elements. For closed forms, these will include the rhyme scheme, meter, line lengths, and stanzaic pattern. They may also include significant words and phrases that link specific stanzas together. The worksheet for an open-form poem should indicate variables such as the rhythm and cadences, pauses or enjambements, significant words that are isolated or emphasized through typography, and patterns of repeated sounds, words, phrases, or images.

As you begin to consider the relationship between form and content, you will inevitably examine all the components of structure. In dealing with a closed form, you might want to consider the following questions:

1. What is the predominant meter? Line length? Rhyme scheme? To what extent do these establish and/or reinforce the form?
2. What is the form of each stanza or unit of the poem? What basic building blocks make up the stanza or the poem? How many stanzas or divisions does the poem contain? Is the pattern that is established in the first stanza or unit repeated in each subsequent unit?
3. Does the poem exemplify a traditional closed form such as the ballad or sonnet? If so, what is it? Does the poem sustain the form, or does it introduce variations? If there are variations, what is their effect?
4. How effectively does the structure create or reinforce the poem's internal logic? Can you find and explain a logical progression from unit to unit?
5. To what extent does the form organize the images of the poem? Are key images developed *within* single units or stanzas? Do images recur in several units? How does the structure help create a meaningful progression of images?
6. To what extent does the form help to create an organized pattern for the ideas or emotions of the poem? How does the structure emphasize these?

In dealing with open-form poetry, the questions you should ask are slightly different, but the concerns remain the same. With open forms you might explore the following areas:

1. What does the poem look like on the page? How does its general shape reflect its meaning?
2. How does the poet use variable line lengths, white spaces, punctuation, capitalization, and the like to shape the poem? To what extent do these variables contribute to the poem's sense?
3. What rhythms or cadences are built into the poem through language or typography? How are these cadences relevant to the poem's content?
4. Can you find a logical progression of ideas, images, and/or emotions? If so, how is this logic created and how does it contribute to the poem's impact?
5. How extensively are specific words or phrases isolated or grouped and thus emphasized through form or typography? What is the effect of such emphasis? To what extent is this technique one of the organizing principles of the poem?
6. What repeated patterns of words or sounds can you find in the poem? To what degree do these repetitions create order or structure? How do they underscore the sense of the poem?

In dealing with all these questions, you are seeking the most significant areas of interaction between form and content. Not every poem may provide meaningful answers to all the questions, but investigation of these topics will provide a great deal of information and will supply the raw materials for your essay.

At this stage in prewriting, you can begin to organize your information and formulate a tentative central idea for the essay. This idea should be as clearly focused and limited as possible. Since you cannot hope to deal with every aspect of form in a single essay, concentrate on the most important and effective ways that form shapes or reflects content.

In developing a central idea, it is not enough simply to assert that form organizes and underscores meaning; you should try to explain *how* this occurs. If you are planning an essay on Shakespeare's Sonnet 116, "Let Me Not to the Marriage of True Minds," for example, you might want to argue that form controls meaning. Such an assertion, while perhaps true, is not an adequate central idea. A better initial formulation might be stated as follows: "The sonnet form organizes the speaker's thoughts into a four-part argument in which each quatrain examines a different aspect of love's permanence, and the couplet provides closure."

Sometimes the formation of a central idea can involve a two-step connection between form and content. In planning an essay on William Carlos Williams's "The Dance," for instance, you might decide that meaning is most effectively reinforced and echoed through rhythm. Hence, you would focus on the ways in which form creates rhythm and your central idea would link form to rhythm and meaning.

As with many other essays about literature, formulating an adequate thesis is half the battle. Once you have managed this, you can organize your data into logical and cohesive units that will become paragraphs. At the same time, you can begin to select examples and aspects of the poem to support your central idea. Here, as in any other essay, you should make sure that all your evidence is clearly relevant to the original thesis. If you find that your examples are leading you away from your central idea, you should rethink the essay and revise to reflect this new direction.

ORGANIZING YOUR ESSAY

INTRODUCTION.   The introduction may contain some general remarks about the poem, but it should focus on the connection between form and substance. It should include the thesis of the essay—a statement about the ways in which structure and content interact—and a brief survey of the specific topics that will be discussed in the body.

BODY.   The body of the essay is devoted to supporting and proving the assertion made in the introduction. As a general rule, the topics covered in the body should be taken up in subsequent paragraphs in the same order in which they are mentioned in the first paragraph. The organization of these supporting paragraphs will reflect the discoveries about the linkage between form and content that you made while planning the essay. You will also want to provide a paragraph that describes the structure of the poem fairly early in the essay. In dealing with closed forms, this paragraph will detail such standard features as the traditional form, meter, rhyme scheme, stanzaic structure, and number of stanzas. With open-form poetry, the paragraph should focus on the most striking and significant features of the verse.

CONCLUSION. The conclusion of the essay might contain any additional observations about shape or structure that seems relevant. It should also include a summation of your argument. Here, as in all other essays about literature, you should make sure that you reach an actual conclusion rather than simply a stopping point.

SAMPLE ESSAY

Structure and Meaning in George Herbert's "Virtue"*

[1]   George Herbert's poem, "Virtue," considers the difference between those things of the world that will inevitably die and the immortality of the "virtuous soul." Every component of structure works harmoniously in this poem to organize the images in a logical progression and to underscore the difference between things that "must die" and that one thing that "chiefly lives."° The stanzaic organization of the poem creates a structural and visual distinction between the "sweet" soul and the rest of creation through the skillful use of line groupings, rhyme scheme, and repeated words.▫

[2]   "Virtue" is a seventeenth-century lyric of four quatrains containing three lines of iambic tetrameter and a final line of iambic dimeter. This shift from four to two beats gives the concluding line of each quatrain great impact. Each stanza also follows the same basic *a b a b* rhyme scheme. Since some rhyme sounds and words are repeated throughout the first three stanzas, however, the structure of the poem may be formulated as 4a 4b 4a 2b, 4c 4b 4c 2b, 4d 4b 4d 2b, 4e 4f 4e 2f.

The stanzaic structure of this lyric provides a pattern of organization for the images of the poem and simultaneously underscores the logic of the ideas. The first stanza focuses on the image of the "Sweet day"; it compares the day to "The bridal of the earth and sky" (line 2) and asserts that the day inevitably "must die." Similarly, the second stanza focuses exclusively on the

---

* See p. 760 for this poem.
° Central idea.
▫ Thesis sentence.

[3]   image of the "Sweet rose" and asserts that it too "must die." The third stanza shifts to the image of the "Sweet spring." Here the poet collapses the images of the first two stanzas into the third by noting that the "Sweet spring" is "full of sweet days and roses" (line 9). The stanza concludes that "all must die." In this way, the third stanza becomes the climax of both the images employed to this point and the idea of universal mortality. The last stanza introduces a totally new image—"a sweet and virtuous soul"—and an assertion completely opposed to the ideas expressed in the previous three. Although the day, the rose, and the spring "must die," the soul "never gives" and "chiefly lives" even though "the whole world turn to coal" (line 15). The logical conclusion of the argument and the key image of the poem are thus presented in a separate stanza; the organization of the lyric allows for the structural isolation of the "virtuous soul" and for a spatial separation between those things that die and the one thing that lives.

[4]   This structural organization of images and ideas is repeated and reinforced by several other techniques that help establish the poem's overall form. The rhyme scheme, for example, contributes significantly to the linkage among the first three stanzas and the isolation of the fourth. The first three all repeat the b rhyme at the ends of the second and fourth lines, rhyming a b a b, c b c b, and d b d b. In the fourth stanza, however, the b rhyme is replaced by an f rhyme. The rhyme scheme thus produces effects parallel to the grouping of images and the logic of the ideas. The final stanza is separated and isolated from the rest of the poem by the deletion of the b rhyme and the introduction of the f rhyme.

[5]   In a similar manner, the repetition of key words and phrases underscores both the stanzaic structure and the resultant organization of the poem's images and ideas. Each of the first three stanzas begins with sweet and ends with must die. This repetition again links the first three stanzas tightly together. In addition, the triple repetition of must die drives home the idea that death is universal. In the last stanza, however, this pattern of repetition is abandoned. The initial sweet that characterized the first three stanzas is replaced by Only (line 13). Similarly, must die is displaced by chiefly lives. Both substitutions create a striking disjunction between this final stanza and the three previous stanzas. More important, the shift in the verbal pattern emphasizes the conceptual transition from death to the immortality of the "virtuous soul."

[6]   We have seen that the lyric form of Herbert's "Virtue" provides an organizational pattern for the poem's images and ideas. At the same time, the stanzaic pattern and the rhyme scheme make it possible to draw a vivid structural distinction between the corruptible world and the immortal soul. Form in this poem is not arbitrary or incidental; it becomes another way of asserting the singularity of the "sweet and virtuous soul."

Commentary on the Essay

This essay considers the relationship between form and meaning in Herbert's "Virtue." The introductory paragraph begins by stating the focus of the poem itself: the distinction between the "virtuous soul" and everything else. It goes on, in the second sentence, to assert a specific connection between form and meaning. Finally, the third sentence enumerates a series of ways in which form organizes and reinforces the substance of the poem.

The second paragraph is purely descriptive; it identifies the traditional closed form exemplified by "Virtue," notes some of the significant structural features of the poem, and closes with a schematic formulation of the entire lyric. While this paragraph does not advance the argument of the essay, it does provide a summary of information that will be useful later in the paper.

The last sentence of the opening paragraph speaks of line groupings (or stanzas), rhyme scheme, and repeated words and phrases as the structural elements that shape the poem and underscore meaning. The body of the essay (paragraphs 3, 4, and 5) takes up these subjects in exactly the same order. The third paragraph focuses on the organization of both images and ideas from stanza to stanza. Here, the essay demonstrates that the image of the "virtuous soul" and the idea of immortality are isolated and emphasized through the stanzaic pattern.

The fourth paragraph begins with a transitional sentence that repeats part of the essay's central idea and, at the same time, connects it to paragraph 3. In this way, paragraph 4 is closely tied to both paragraphs 1 and 3. The main topic here, the rhyme scheme of "Virtue," is introduced in the second sentence, which asserts that it also reinforces the division between mortality and immortality.

Paragraph 5 takes up the last structural element mentioned in the introduction—the repetition of key words and phrases. This paragraph is linked with the first because its topic is noted there. Transition between the previous paragraph and this one is established with the first phrase of the opening sentence: "In a similar manner." The paragraph goes on to illustrate that repeated words and phrases underscore the central division between the mortality of the world and the immortality of the "virtuous soul."

The conclusion provides an overview and summation of the essay's argument. In addition, it concludes that form in "Virtue" is neither arbitrary nor incidental, but rather an integral part of the poem's meaning.

23

Symbolism and Allusion: Windows to a Wide Expanse of Meaning

Symbolism, also discussed in Chapter 9, refers to the use of symbols in literary works. A symbol, in simple terms, is something that has meaning in and of itself but also stands for something else, like the flag for the country or the school song for the school. Symbols occur in stories as well as in poems, but poetry relies more heavily on symbolism than does fiction, for it is more concise and involves more forms than fiction, which relies on a narrative structure.

While a symbol is indeed something that stands for something else, the word implies a special relationship that extends beyond our ordinary understanding of words, descriptions, and arguments. In a real sense, words themselves are symbols, for they stand for something that they really are not. As a graphic illustration, a painter recently titled a painting of an apple, "This Is Not an Apple." This title is perplexing at first, until one realizes that the work of art is only a *painting* of an apple, *not* an apple itself. Words are analogous to the painting: they are symbols for referents in the real world or in the realm of ideas and feelings. When we say *horse*, for example, or *tree*, these words are not horses or trees, but only *symbols* for these things; they direct our minds to things in the real world that we have seen and can therefore imagine easily when we read or hear the words.

SYMBOLISM AS A WINDOW TO GREATER MEANING

Symbolism goes beyond this close referral of word to thing; it is more like a window through which one can get a glimpse at the extensive world outside. Poetry, remember, is a compact form that may be structured in many more ways than fiction. Even though it may be based in a narrative just like fiction, it may also take such diverse forms as a profession of love, a meditation on the state of the world, an expression of distress or amazement, or an argument appealing to the desire to be free. Symbolism is a shorthand way of referring to extensive ideas or attitudes that otherwise would be impossible in the relatively brief format of poetry. Thus William Butler Yeats, who believed that the city of Constantinople, or Byzantium, represented a high point of human civilization, used the city as a symbol of the highest state of human achievement in peace, politics, and particularly art and literature. His poem "Byzantium" (p. 1027) does not expand upon the full meaning and interpretation of this idea, for it would take a long history and a detailed analysis of Byzantine art and literature to do that. The poem, does, however, take Byzantium and its excellence as a base of meaning from which Yeats develops his own worries about what he thought was the declining state of civilization during the twentieth century. The use of symbols, in other words, becomes a means by which poets may assume a common extensive knowledge and are therefore freed to consider their thoughts and attitudes resulting from this knowledge.

HOW DOES SYMBOLISM OPERATE?

The effect of symbolism is thus to expand meaning beyond the normal connotation of words. For example, at the time of William Blake (1757–1827) the word *tiger*, had the general meaning of a large, wild cat in addition to the specific animal we call tiger. Its obvious connotation linked it with wildness, predation, and fierceness. As a symbol in the poem "The Tyger," however, Blake uses the tiger as a stand-in for the negativism and evil in the world—the sum total of savage, wild forces which prompt human beings to evil actions. Thus the tiger as a symbol is more meaningful than either the denotation or the connotation of the word would indicate.

In poetry, some symbols possess a ready-made, clearly agreed-upon meaning. These are the kinds of symbols described in Chapter 9 as **general, cultural,** or **universal symbols.** Many such symbols, like the tiger, are drawn directly from the world of nature. Springtime and morning are ready-made symbols signifying beginnings, growth, hope, optimism, and love. A reference to spring is normal and appropriate in a love poem. If the topic were death, however, the symbol of spring would still be appropriate as the basis of ironic observations about the untimeliness with which death claims its victims. "Excell bun"

Cultural symbols are drawn from history and custom. Because the Judeo-Christian tradition has been so pervasive a force in Western culture for 3,000 years, many religious symbols have been taken up by poets. References to the lamb, Eden, bondage, shepherds, exile, temple, blood, water, bread, the cross, and wine—all Jewish and/or Christian symbols—

appear over and over again in poetry of the English language. Sometimes these symbols occur in purely devotional poems; at other times they may be contrasted with symbols of warfare and corruption to show how far removed people have become from their moral and religious obligations.

Symbols that are not widely or universally recognized are termed **private, authorial,** or **contextual symbols** (these are also discussed in Chapter 9). Some of these have a natural relationship with the things being symbolized. Snow, for example, is cold and white, and when it falls it covers everything. A poet can thus exploit this particular quality and make snow a symbol. James Joyce, in his story "The Dead" from *The Dubliners*, for example, uses snow in this way. At the beginning of the extensive poem "The Waste Land," T. S. Eliot uses the symbol of snow ironically to symbolize a retreat from life, an intellectual and moral hibernation. Another poem utilizing snow as a symbol linking the living and the dead both literally and figuratively is "Snow," by Virginia Scott:

VIRGINIA SCOTT (b. 1938)

Snow   1977

A doe stands at the roadside,
spirit of those who have lived here
and passed known through our memory.
The doe stands at the edge of the icy road,
then darts back into the woods.

Snow falling,
mother-spirit hovering,
white on the drops in the road and fields,
light from the windows
of the old house
brightening the snow.

Presences: mother,
grandmother,
here in their place
at the foot of *ben lomond,*°
green trees black in the hemlock night.

The doe stands at the edge of the icy road,
then darts back into the woods.

Golden Grove, New Brunswick
Canada
January 5, 1977

SNOW.   15 *ben lomond*: a small mountain in Golden Grove, not far from Saint John, New Brunswick. The Scots name reflects that the area, not far from the Maine border, was settled by Scots immigrants.

QUESTIONS

1. What visual images are described in the poem? What actions? Colors? Textures?
2. How is snow described in the poem? How and where is it seen? As a symbol, what does it signify in relationship to the doe, the memory of persons, the mother-spirit, the old house, the light, the presences, the mountains, and the trees?
3. Explain the structural purpose for which the doe is mentioned three times in the poem, with lines 17 and 18 repeating 4 and 5. As a symbol, what might the doe signify?
4. What are the relationships described in the poem between memory of the past and existence in the present?

This poem describes a real circumstance at a real place at a real time; the poet has even provided an actual location and date, just as we do for a letter. The snow was real snow, falling at a time in the evening when lights had been put on in the nearby house. This detail by itself would be sufficient as a realistic image. But as Scott develops the poem, the snow symbolizes the link between the speaker's memory of the past and perception of the present; the reality of the moment is suffused with the memory of the people—"mother, / grandmother"—who "lived here." The poet is meditating on the idea that individuals, though they may often be alone like the speaker, are never alone as long as the memory of the past is a vivid part of their consciousness. The past and present are in effect connected just as the snow covers the scene. At the conclusion of the poem, the symbolic doe darting into the woods suggests a linking of the present with the future. The poem is dealing with difficult questions of identity, and it is short; the idea of connection and continuity would therefore be difficult to achieve without the suggestive symbols of the snow and the deer. Here the poet has developed ideas out of the actual physical property of the substance being used as a symbol. Both symbols in this poem—the snow and the doe—are private and contextual; they are established and developed within the poem. By this means the poet has converted a very private and meditative moment into a symbolic one.

Similarly, seemingly ordinary materials may become symbolic if the poet emphasizes them or repeats details about them. John Keats in "La Belle Dame Sans Merci" (p. 797), for example, repeats the image of the sedge or grass being withered around the lake. What might seem like an appropriate detail therefore becomes symbolic of the sense of loss and bewilderment felt by people when the persons they love seem to be unreal, faithless, and destructive to them rather than genuine, loyal, and supportive. Symbols evoke feelings.

THE INTRODUCTION OF SYMBOLS

SINGLE WORDS.   Poets may introduce symbols into their poems in many ways. With general or universal symbols, a single word is sufficient, like references to the lamb, shepherd, cross, blood, bread, and wine, or to summer and winter, or to drought and flood, morning and night, heat and shade, or storm and calm. The nightingale may be taken as an example of how a single word may become instantly symbolic. Because the bird has such a beautiful song, it frequently symbolizes natural, unspoiled beauty as contrasted with the contrived attempts by human beings to create beauty. Keats refers to the bird in this way in his "Ode to a Nightingale," where he compares the virtually eternal beauty of this singer with his own mortality.

Anne Finch, in "To the Nightingale" (p. 653), makes a similar comparison of the human poet and the nightingale, drawing attention to the legend that the "unhappy poet's breast, / Like thine, when best he sings, is plac'd against a thorn." Here the symbol emphasizes the claim that poetic expression originates in the deep pain and feeling of poets. By contrast, T. S. Eliot uses the less idealistic aspects of the bird in "Sweeney Among the Nightingales." Here Eliot refers to the bird's song not as a symbol of beauty, but rather as a backdrop for the human horror of the murder of the ancient king Agamemnon. The only contribution the nightingales make as a symbol is their droppings as a staining, dirtying commentary on human affairs. Despite Eliot's usage, however, poets usually emphasize the lovelier aspects of the bird in their symbols.

ACTIONS.   Not only words but also actions may be presented as symbols. In Virginia Scott's "Snow," as we have just observed, the doe darting into the darkening woods symbolizes both the renewal and the mystery of life. In Thomas Hardy's "In Time of 'The Breaking of Nations' " (p. 799), the action of the man plowing a field symbolizes the continued life and vitality of the folk, the people, despite political and military changes that are constantly raging in the world.

SETTING.   Sometimes a setting or natural scene may be symbolic. For example, Randall Jarrell's brief poem "The Death of the Ball Turret Gunner" (p. 461), unites the ball turret of a World War II high-altitude bomber with a mother's womb, symbolically indicating that war and brutal death are the human lot from the very beginning of life. Similarly, the "elfin grot" of the "lady in the meads" in Keats's "La Belle Dame Sans Merci" is an unreal and magical, womblike location symbolizing both the allure and the disappointment that sometimes characterizes sexual attraction.

CHARACTERS.   The many characters or people in poetry may also reach symbolic status if the poet designs them to represent ideas or values. In E. E. Cummings's "In just," for example, the balloon man is such a figure.

Although the balloon man is not extensively visualized, Cummings includes enough detail about him to indicate that he symbolizes the basic and primitive vitality, joy, and sexuality with which children are literally called out of childhood. The faery child of "La Belle Dame Sans Merci" is a symbol of the mystery of love. The figures in Hardy's "In Time of 'The Breaking of Nations' " are symbolic of the poet's faith in the power of unimportant people to endure even though "Dynasties pass."

✱ witch   ✱ wise old person   */ "The Road Not Taken"*

SITUATIONS. In addition, situations, circumstances, or conditions may be symbolic. The condition of Jarrell's ball turret gunner, exposed and helpless six miles in the air, may be understood as a symbol of the condition of all people in the age of fear and anxiety produced by the threat of global wars and technologically expert destructiveness. The speaker of Anne Finch's "To Mr. F., Now Earl of W." symbolizes human confrontation with the emotion of a love so strong that it transcends human capacity for expression and hence must remain unexpressed and private.

QUALITIES OF SYMBOLS

Just as symbols may be expressed in these various ways, the meanings of symbols may be placed on a continuum of qualities from good to bad, high to low, favorable to unfavorable. For example, Cumming's old balloon man of "In just" is on the positive end, symbolizing the irresistible and joyful call of growth and sexuality. The gray leaves of Hardy's "Neutral Tones," on the other hand, are not neutral but negative. As a symbol, the leaves lend their own deadness to the terminated relationship spoken of by the speaker to the person being addressed. Outright horror is suggested by the symbol of the rough beast slouching toward Bethlehem in Yeats's "The Second Coming" (p. 800). This symbol is not like Jesus, who was born in Bethlehem, but ironically is a horrible force of anger, suppression, and brutality that in Yeats's judgment was becoming dominant in twentieth-century politics, even long before the development of nuclear warfare.   *white → Death*

ALLUSION IN POETRY

/ Curiosity - kills the cat

Just as symbolism enriches meaning, so does *allusion*. **Allusion,** which is also discussed in Chapter 9, refers to the inclusion, in a work, of unacknowledged quotations from other works and of references to historical events and any aspect of human culture—art, music, literature, and so on. It is a means of recognizing both the literary tradition and broader cultural environment of which the poet is a part. In addition it assumes a common bond of knowledge between the poet and the reader. On the one hand,

"How Very Like a Whale"

allusion compliments the heritage of the past, and on the other it salutes the reader who is able to recognize it and find meaning in it.

Allusions may be no more than a single word, provided the word is unusual enough or associative enough to bear the weight of the reference. Virginia Scott's "Snow," for example, speaks of "green trees black in the hemlock night." *Hemlock* refers to a type of evergreen tree in the woods observed by the speaker, but hemlock was also the poison drunk by Socrates when he was executed by the ancient Athenians. Just about any literary reference to hemlock calls to mind the death of Socrates and also the idea that death is oblivion and the common end of all life. At the beginning of "Ode to a Nightingale" (p. 761), Keats's speaker describes a numbness that might come "As though of hemlock . . . [he] had drunk." Here the allusion is placed in the context of a wish to be connected and united to the universal spirit not of oblivion but of creative power.

Allusions may also consist of extensive phrases, descriptions, or situations. These allusions add their own interest and power before the poet moves on to other ideas. Line 6 of Scott's "Snow," for example, is simply "Snow falling." This phrase is descriptive and accurate, but it also is a direct quotation from the first line of Robert Frost's poem "Desert Places" (p. 761). The context is of course different. Frost's line introduces the topic of the speaker's fear of bleakness, unconcern, coldness—his "desert places"—whereas in "Snow" Scott is referring to the continuity of the past and the present. There are bleakness and isolation in Scott's scene, but her old house also throws light on the snow, and the dead are fondly remembered because their spirit and memory are as alive as the doe who darts back into the woods. By making the allusion, Scott actually emphasizes the difference between her idea and Frost's.

THE SOURCES OF ALLUSIONS.   Allusions may be drawn from just about any area of life, history, and art. Sometimes symbols are allusions as well as symbols. In "The Second Coming" Yeats's "lion body and the head of a man" is a descriptive allusion to the sphinx figure of ancient Egypt. As Yeats uses the description, he is referring to the monstrous aspects of the figure as a means of focusing on both the horror and mystery, the brutality and coldness that often infest human political institutions. As works become well known and popular, they become a source of allusions. One of Robert Frost's most famous lines, for example, is the conclusion of "Stopping by Woods on a Snowy Evening": "And miles to go before I sleep." It would be difficult to estimate the number of times this line has been quoted by people who have a task to complete before they turn to recreational activities or to rest. Isabella Gardner alludes to the line in her poem "Collage of Echoes," a poem that is deliberately built out of allusions. Interestingly enough, Frost's line itself alludes to a line in Keats's sonnet "Keen Fitful Gusts," where Keats says "The stars are very cold about the sky, / And I have many miles on foot to fare." Any allusion to Frost is therefore also an indirect allusion to Keats's lines.

ALLUSIONS AND THE ORIGINAL CONTEXT. If an allusion is made to a literary work, it carries with it the entire context of the work from which it is drawn. Perhaps the richest storehouses of such ready-made stories and quotations are the King James version of the Bible and the plays of Shakespeare. In "Ode to a Nightingale" Keats alludes to the Biblical story of Ruth, who, he says, was "sick with tears amid the alien corn." This allusion is particularly rich, because Ruth became the mother of Jesse; it was from the line of Jesse that King David was born, and it was from the house of David that Jesus was born. Thus Keats's nightingale is not only a symbol of natural beauty, but through this Biblical allusion it becomes symbolic of regeneration and redemption, much in keeping with Keats's assertion that the bird was not born for death. In Yeats's "The Second Coming" the reference to the "blood-dimmed tide" suggests the soliloquy in the second act of Shakespeare's *Macbeth*, when Macbeth, after murdering Duncan, asks if there is enough water in Neptune's ocean to wash the blood from his hands. His immediate, guilt-ridden response is that Duncan's blood will instead stain the ocean, turning the green of the water to red. This image of crime being so bloody that it can stain the water of the ocean is thus the visual referent, the allusion, of Yeats's "blood-dimmed tide," for Yeats's authorial speaker is just as concerned about the global implications of evil as is Shakespeare's Macbeth.

Allusions are therefore an important means by which poets broaden the context and therefore deepen the meaning of their poems. The issues raised by a poet in a specific poem, in other words, not only are important there, but are linked through allusion to issues raised earlier by other thinkers or brought out by previous events, places, or persons. With connections made through allusions, poets attempt to make the significance and applicability of their own ideas plain. The situations in their works are not isolated but are general problems for many times and places. Allusion is hence not literary "theft," but rather a means of literary enrichment.

STUDYING FOR SYMBOL AND ALLUSION

As you study poetry for its symbols and allusions, it is important to realize that these devices do not come ready marked with special notice and fanfare. A decision to call a feature of a poem symbolic is based on qualities within the poem: Perhaps a major item of importance is introduced at a climactic part of the poem, or a description has something noteworthy or unusual about it, such as the connection between "stony sleep" and the "rough beast" in Yeats's "The Second Coming." When such a connection occurs, the element may no longer be taken just literally, but may be read as a symbol.

Even after you have found a hint such as this, however, the term may not be a symbol unless it has a referent or body of referents that yield to a fairly detailed commentary. Thus the "rough beast" raises questions about what Yeats meant. In the context of the poem it might refer to the person or persons hinted at in traditional interpretations of the New Testament as the "anti-Christ" figure. In a secular frame of reference, the associations of blankness and pitilessness suggest that some aspect of brutality and suppression is being suggested. Still further, however, if the twentieth century were not a period in which millions of people have been persecuted and exterminated in military and secret police operations, even these associations might make the "rough beast" quizzical but not necessarily symbolic. But because of the rightness of the application together with the traditional Biblical associations, the figure clearly should be construed as a symbol.

[As you can see, the interpretation of a symbol requires that you be able to identify and objectivize the person, thing, situation, or action in question. To the degree that the element can be seen as general and representative—characteristic of the condition of a large number of human beings—it assumes the nature of a symbol, for it then stands definitely for something else that is extensive. [As a rule, the more ideas you can associate specifically with the element, the more likely it is to be a symbol.]

With regard to allusions in poetry, there is less possible ambiguity but also greater difficulty, depending on your background and education. There is a vast body of written tradition and history to which a poet may allude at any time. Not all of this tradition is readily available to all readers. Explanatory footnotes, of course, are an obvious help, for they give information about the allusion. However, an allusion, though it refers only briefly to a source, place, person, or event, may ask readers to call to mind the entire situation in the original. Theoretically, the reader might be required to study the original sources of all allusions, and such an extensive task would be too great for most readers of poetry.

In one respect, then, identification of an allusion is quite simple. Either a word, situation, or phrase is an allusion or it is not, and hence the matter is easily settled once an original reference can be located. The problem comes in determining how the allusion affects the context of the poem you are reading. Thus we have determined that Virginia Scott alludes to Robert Frost's "Desert Place" by using the phrase "Snow falling" in the poem "Snow." Once this allusion is identified, its purpose must still be established. Thus the allusion might mean that the situation in "Snow" is the same as in Frost's poem, namely that the authorial speaker is making observations about interior blankness—Frost's "desert places." On the other hand, the poet may be using the allusion in a new sense—for example,

Frost uses the falling snow to symbolize a coldness of spirit whereas Scott uses it, more warmly, to connect the natural scene to the memory of family. In other words, once the presence of an allusion is established, the business of reading and understanding must still continue.

POEMS FOR STUDY

GEORGE HERBERT (1593–1633)

The Collar°   *1633*

I struck the board, and cry'd, "No more;
    I will abroad!
What? shall I ever sigh and pine?
My lines and life are free; free as the road,
    Loose as the wind, as large as store,   5
      Shall I be still in suit?°
Have I no harvest but a thorn°
To let me blood, and not restore
What I have lost with cordial fruit?
      Sure there was wine   10
    Before my sighs did dry it: there was corn
    Before my tears did drown it.
    Is the year only lost to me?
    Have I no bays° to crown it?
No flowers, no garlands gay? all blasted?   15
      All wasted?
    Not so, my heart: but there is fruit,
      And thou hast hands.
    Recover all thy sigh-blown age
On double pleasures: leave thy cold dispute   20
Of what is fit, and not; forsake thy cage,
      Thy rope of sands,
Which petty thoughts have made, and made to thee
    Good cable, to enforce and draw,
      And be thy law,   25
While thou didst wink and wouldst not see.
      Away; take heed:
      I will abroad.
Call in thy death's head there: tie up thy fears.
    He that forbears   30

THE COLLAR.   *collar*: (1) the collar worn by a member of the clergy; (2) the collar of the harness of a draught animal such as a horse; (3) a restraint placed on prisoners; (4) a pun on *choler* (yellow bile), a bodily substance thought to cause quick rages.   6 *in suit*: waiting upon a person of power to gain favor or position.   7 *thorn*: see Mark 15:17.   14 *bays*: laurel crowns to signify victory and honor.

>   To suit° and serve his need,
>   Deserves his load."   *follow*
>   But as I rav'd and grew more fierce and wild
>   At every word,
>   Me thought I heard one calling, "Child:"
>   And I replied, "*My Lord*."

QUESTIONS

1. What situation does the speaker describe at the opening of the poem? Why is he angry or impatient? Who is speaking to whom? Against what role in life is the speaker complaining?

2. In light of the many possible meanings of *collar* (see note), explain the title as a symbol in the poem.

3. Explain the symbolism of the thorn (line 7), blood (line 8), wine (line 10), bays (line 14), flowers and garlands (line 15), cage (line 21), rope of sands (line 22), death's head (line 29), and the dialogue in lines 35 and 36.

4. What arguments does the speaker make against his vocation as a member of the clergy? What argument is proposed in favor of his role? Which argument is more compelling, according to the speaker?

5. Consider the allusions to the thorn (line 7), wine (line 10), and the New Testament concept that God is like a parent to human beings (lines 35 and 36). How do these allusions assist in developing the arguments made by the speaker in the poem?

ANNE FINCH, COUNTESS OF WINCHELSEA (1661–1720)

To Mr. F[inch], now Earl of W[inchelsea]   1689

> Who going abroad, had desired Ardelia° to write some verses upon whatever subject she thought fit, against his return in the evening.

Written in the Year 1689

> No sooner, Flavio,° were you gone,
> But your injunction thought upon,
>   Ardelia took the pen;
> Designing to perform the task
> Her Flavio did so kindly ask,
>   Ere he returned again.

TO MR. F[INCH], NOW EARL OF W[INCHELSEA]. In her personal poems, Anne Finch used the name "Ardelia" in reference to herself, so that she could use the third person to refer to her feelings and attitudes. The name suggests warmth and devotion (ardency).
1 *Flavio*: the name that she assigned to Mr. Finch, her husband. The name *Flavio* was common in ancient Rome, but Cnaeus Flavianus, a Roman of the fourth century B.C., was particularly known for his justice and leadership.

Unto Parnassus° straight she sent,
And bid the messenger, that went
   Unto the Muses' court,°
Assure them she their aid did need,   10
And begg'd they'd use their utmost speed,
   Because the time was short.

The hasty summons was allow'd:
And being well-bred they rose and bow'd,
   And said they'd post away: 15
That well they did Ardelia know,
And that no female's voice below
   They sooner would obey.

That many of that rhyming train°   *poets*
On like occasions sought in vain   20
   Their industry t' excite:
But for Ardelia all they'd leave.
Thus flatt'ring can the Muse deceive
   And wheedle us to write.

Yet since there was such haste requir'd,   25
To know the subject 'twas desired
   On which they must infuse,°   *give judgment*
That they might temper words and rules,
And with their counsel carry tools
   As country doctors use.   30

Wherefore to cut off all delays,
'Twas soon replied, a husband's praise
   (Tho' in these looser times)
Ardelia gladly would rehearse
A husband's who indulged her verse,   35
   And now requir'd her rhymes.

"A husband!" echo'd all around:
And to Parnassus sure that sound
   Had never yet been sent.
Amazement in each face was read,   40
In haste th' affrighted sisters fled,
   And into council went.

Erato° cried, "since Grizel's° days,
Since Troy-town pleas'd, and Chevy Chase,°

7 *Parnassus*: Mount Parnassus was the home of the nine muses and was also sacred to Apollo, the God of Poetry, Music, and Dance.   9 *Muses' court*: the court of the muses, who governed art, music, literature, and the sciences.   43 *Erato*: the muse of lyrical love poetry.   *Grizel's*: refers to Griselda, in Chaucer's "Clerk's Tale," who proverbially was known for her patient and forgiving love for her husband, Walter.   44 *Troy-town, Chevy Chase*: Ancient Troy ("Troy-town") was besieged by the Greeks. Hector, the most famous Trojan hero, was deeply loved by his wife, Andromache. In the late medieval ballad of Chevy Chase, the Douglases and Percies made war against each other and were mourned by their wives (Child A57; B55–56).

No such design was known;"
And 'twas their business to take care
It reach'd not to the public ear,
    Or got about the town,

Nor came where evening beaux° were met,   *dandies*
O'er billet-doux° and chocolate,   *love letters*
    Lest it destroyed the house:
For in that place who could dispense
(That wore his clothes with common sense)
    With mention of a spouse?

'Twas put unto the vote at last,
And in the negative it passed,
    None to her aid should move;
Yet since Ardelia was a friend,
Excuses 'twas agreed to send
    Which plausible might prove:

That Pegasus° of late had been
So often rid thro' thick and thin
    With neither fear nor wit,
In panegyric° been so spurr'd,   *poems of praise*
He could not from the stall be stirr'd,
    Nor would endure a bit.

Melpomene° had given a bond
By the new house° alone to stand
    And write alone of war and strife;
Thalia,° she had taken fees
And stipends from the patentees,
    And durst not for her life.

Urania° only liked the choice;
Yet not to thwart the public voice,
    She whispering did impart:
"They need no foreign aid invoke,
No help to draw a moving stroke,
    Who dictate from the heart."

"Enough!" the pleas'd Ardelia cried:
And slighting ev'ry Muse beside,
    Consulting now her breast.
Perceived that ev'ry tender thought
Which from abroad she vainly sought
    Did there in silence rest:

---

61 *Pegasus*: the famous winged horse of Greek mythology.   67 *Melpomene*: the muse of
tragedy.   68 *new house*: There were two authorized or "patent" theaters in London in
1689. The "new house" was the Drury Lane Theater, built in 1673. "Patentees" (line 71)
were the managers; a dramatist who contracted to write plays for them could not do the
same for someone else without breaking the contract. The allusion may be to the well-
publicized breach of contract by the poet laureate John Dryden in 1682.   70 *Thalia*: the
muse of pastoral poetry and also of comedy.   73 *Urania*: The muse of astronomers; hence
the muse closest to heaven.

And should unmov'd that post maintain,   85
Till in his quick return again,
   Met in some neighb'ring grove,
(Where vice nor vanity appear)
Her Flavio them alone might hear
   In all the sounds of love.   90

For since the world does so despise
Hymen's° endearments and its ties,
   They should mysterious be:
Till we that pleasure too possess
(Which makes their fancied happiness)   95
   Of stolen secrecy.

.92 *Hymen's*: the Greek god of marriage.

QUESTIONS

1. What situation prompts the speaker to write the poem? What imaginary journey does Ardelia make, and for what reason? Whom does she meet, and
   what happens? What traits does Ardelia show? How does she feel about
   Flavio?

2. Describe the structure and development of the narrative of Ardelia's mission
   to the muses. At what point does the narrative change to describe Ardelia's
   self-analysis of her love for Flavio?

3. Why is the response of the muses comic? Upon what usual assessment of
   married love is the muses' response based (see lines 91, 92)? Why do the
   muses think Ardelia's request is unusual?

4. Describe the poet's symbolic use of allusions in lines 43 and 44. What are
   these symbols introduced to represent? What do the beaux symbolize (line
   49)? How may the situation between Ardelia and Flavio be seen as symbolic
   of the privacy of marital love?

JOHN KEATS (1795–1821)

La Belle Dame sans Merci: A Ballad   With a dominant air of melancholy mystery. (Many ballads have unresolved mysteries)   1820 (1819)

1

O what can ail thee, knight at arms,   The speaker questions him.
   Alone and palely loitering?
The sedge has wither'd from the lake,   grasslike plants that grow in wet places
   And no birds sing.

LA BELLE DAME SANS MERCI: A BALLAD. French for "The beautiful lady without pity"
(that is, "The heartless woman"). "La Belle Dame Sans Merci" is the title of a medieval
poem by Alain Chartier; Keats's poem bears no other relationship to the medieval poem,
which was thought at the time to have been by Chaucer.

2

O what can ail thee, knight at arms,   5
  So haggard and so woe-begone?
The squirrel's granary is full,
    And the harvest's done. And winter comes.

3

I see a lily on thy brow   10
  With anguish moist and fever dew,
And on thy cheeks a fading rose
    Fast withereth too.

      4 The knight tells his story

I met a lady in the meads,°   meadows
  Full beautiful, a fairy's child;
Her hair was long, her foot was light,   15
    And her eyes were wild.

5

I made a garland for her head,
  And bracelets too, and fragrant zone;°   belt
She look'd at me as she did love,
    And made sweet moan.   20

6

I set her on my pacing steed,
  And nothing else saw all day long,
For sidelong would she bend, and sing
    A fairy's song.

7

She found me roots of relish° sweet,   magical potion   25
  And honey wild, and manna° dew,   see Exodus 16:14–36
And sure in language strange she said—
    I love thee true.

8

She took me to her elfin grot,
  And there she wept, and sigh'd full sore,   30
And there I shut her wild wild eyes
    With kisses four. And they made love.

9

And there she lullèd me asleep,
  And there I dream'd—Ah! woe betide!
The latest° dream I ever dream'd   last   35
    On the cold hill's side.

10

I saw pale kings, and princes too,   Previous victims.
  Pale warriors, death pale were they all;   They symbolize doubt &
They cried—"La belle dame sans merci   negation.
    Hath thee in thrall!"°   He loves an illusion, tho.   slavery   40

11

I saw their starv'd lips in the gloom
  With horrid warning gaped wide,

And I awoke and found me here
  On the cold hill's side.
      12
And this is why I sojourn here,   45
  Alone and palely loitering,
Though the sedge is wither'd from the lake,
  And no birds sing.

[Handwritten margin note: The meaning of their encounter is never made explicit. But the knight longs for what he can't have. A richly suggestive poem of haunting beauty + mystery.]

[Handwritten note after "And no birds sing.": Which is proper. And the knight doesn't belong here.]

QUESTIONS

1. How is the poem developed? Who is the speaker of stanzas 1–3? Who speaks after that? *[handwritten: / From the 1st meeting]*

2. What is the structure of the story of the poem? What is the source of information on which the knight concludes that he has been put into thrall? *[handwritten: His own dream + imagination.]*

3. In light of the dreamlike content of the poem, how can the knight's experience be viewed as symbolic? What is being symbolized?

4. Consider *relish* (line 25), *honey* (line 26), and *manna* (line 26) as symbols. Are they realistic or mythical? What does the allusion represented by manna *[handwritten: Food from God.]* signify? What is symbolized by the "pale kings, and princes too / [and] Pale warriors"?

5. Consider the aspects of setting as described in the poem as symbols of the knight's state of mind.

THOMAS HARDY (1840–1928)

In Time of "The Breaking of Nations"   1916 (1915)

Only a man harrowing clods
  In a slow silent walk,
With an old horse that stumbles and nods
  Half asleep as they stalk.

Only thin smoke without flame   5
  From the heaps of couch grass:°   *quack grass*
Yet this will go onward the same
  Though Dynasties pass.

Yonder a maid and her wight°   *fellow*
  Come whispering by;   10
War's annals will fade into night
  Ere their story die.

IN TIME OF "THE BREAKING OF NATIONS." See Jeremiah 51:20, "with you I break nations in pieces."

QUESTIONS

1. What does Hardy symbolize by the man and the horse, the smoke, and the couple? How realistic and vivid are these symbols? Are they universal or contextual? As images, to what senses do they refer (for example, sight, sound, and so on)?

2. How does Hardy in stanzas 2 and 3 show that the phrase "breaking of nations" is to be taken symbolically? What meaning is gained by the Biblical allusion of this phrase?

3. Contrast the structure of stanza 1 with that of stanzas 2 and 3. How does the form of stanzas 2 and 3 enable Hardy to emphasize the main idea in the poem?

4. How does the speaker show his evaluation of the importance of the life of the common people as opposed to the business of warfare and international politics? You might wish to consider that at the time (1915), World War I was raging in Europe.

WILLIAM BUTLER YEATS (1865–1939)

The Second Coming   1920 *(1919)*

Turning and turning in the widening gyre°
The falcon cannot hear the falconer;
Things fall apart; the center cannot hold;

THE SECOND COMING. The phrase "second coming" was traditionally used to refer to expectations of the return of Jesus for the salvation of believers, as described in Mark 13, Matthew 24, Luke 21, Revelation, the writings of Paul, and elsewhere in the New Testament. The prophecies claimed that the appearance would be preceded by famine, epidemics, nation warring against nation, and general civil disturbance. Yeats believed that human history could be measured in cycles of approximately 2,000 years (see line 19, "twenty centuries"). In this cycle, the birth of Jesus had ended the Greco-Roman cycle, and in 1919, when Yeats wrote "The Second Coming," it appeared to him that the Christian period was ending and a new era was about to take its place. The New Testament expectation was of course that Jesus would reappear. Yeats, by contrast, states that the disruptions of the twentieth century were preceding a takeover by the forces of evil.   1 *gyre*: a radiating spiral, cone, or vortex. Yeats used the intersecting of two of these shapes as a visual symbol of his cyclic theory. As one gyre spiraled and widened out, to become dissipated, one period of history would end; at the same time a new gyre, closer to the center, would begin and spiral in a reverse direction to the starting point of the old gyre. A drawing of this plan looks like this:

The falcon of line 2 is at the broadest, centripetal point of one gyre, symbolically illustrating the end of a cycle. The "indignant desert birds" of line 17 "reel" in a tighter circle, symbolizing the beginning of the new age in the new gyre.

Mere anarchy is loosed upon the world,
The blood-dimmed tide° is loosed, and everywhere   5
The ceremony of innocence is drowned;
The best lack all conviction, while the worst
Are full of passionate intensity.
Surely some revelation is at hand;
Surely the Second Coming is at hand.   10
The Second Coming! Hardly are those words out
When a vast image out of *Spiritus Mundi*°
Troubles my sight; somewhere in sands of the desert
A shape with lion body and the head of a man,°
A gaze blank and pitiless as the sun,   15
Is moving its slow thighs, while all about it
Reel shadows of the indignant desert birds.
The darkness drops again; but now I know
That twenty centuries of stony sleep
Were vexed to nightmare by a rocking cradle,   20
And what rough beast, its hour come round at last,
Slouches towards Bethlehem to be born?

5 *blood-dimmed tide*: Shakespeare's *Macbeth*, act 2, scene 2, lines 60–63.   12 *Spiritus Mundi*: literally, the spirit of the world, a collective human consciousness that furnished writers and thinkers with a common fund of images and symbols. Yeats referred to this collective repository as "a great memory passing on from generation to generation."   14 *lion body and the head of a man*: i.e., a sphinx, which in ancient Egypt symbolized the pharaoh as a spirit of the sun. Because of this pre-Christian origin, the reincarnation of a sphinx could therefore represent qualities associated in New Testament books like Revelation (11, 13, 17), Mark (13:14–20) and 2 Thessalonians (2:1–12) with a monstrous, superhuman, Satanic figure.

QUESTIONS

1. Consider the following as symbols: the gyre, the falcon, the "blood-dimmed tide," the ceremony of innocence, the "worst" who are "full of passionate intensity." What ideas and values do these symbolize in the poem?

2. Why does Yeats capitalize the phrase "Second Coming"? To what does this phrase refer? Explain the irony of Yeats's use of the phrase in this poem.

3. Consider the structure of the poem. What does the space after line 8 do by way of dividing the poem into parts?

4. Contrast the symbols of the falcon of line 2 and the desert birds of line 17. Considering that these are realistically presented, how does the realism contribute to their identity as symbols?

5. What attributes are symbolized by the sphinx figure being revealed as a "rough beast"? What is the significance of his going "to Bethlehem to be born"?

ROBINSON JEFFERS (1887-1962)

The Purse-Seine   1937

1

Our sardine fishermen work at night in the dark of the moon; daylight or moonlight
They could not tell where to spread the net, unable to see the phosphorescence
    of the shoals of fish.
They work northward from Monterey, coasting Santa Cruz; off New Year's Point
    or off Pigeon Point
The look-out man will see some lakes of milk-color light on the seas's night-purple;
    he points, and the helmsman
Turns the dark prow, the motorboat circles the gleaming shoal and drifts out   5
    her seine-net. They close the circle
And purse the bottom of the net, then with great labor haul it in.

2

                                                                 I cannot tell you
How beautiful the scene is, and a little terrible, then, when the crowded fish
Know they are caught, and wildly beat from one wall to the other of their closing
    destiny the phosphorescent
Water to a pool of flame, each beautiful slender body sheeted with flame, like a   10
    live rocket
A comet's tail wake of clear yellow flame; while outside the narrowing
Floats and cordage of the net great sea-lions come up to watch, sighing in the
    dark; the vast walls of night
Stand erect to the stars.

3

                                                                 Lately I was looking from a night mountain-top
On a wide city, the colored splendor, galaxies of light: how could I help but recall   15
    the seine-net
Gathering the luminous fish? I cannot tell you how beautiful the city appeared,
    and a little terrible.
I thought, We have geared the machines and locked all together into
    interdependence; we have built the great cities; now
There is no escape. We have gathered vast populations incapable of free survival,
    insulated
From the strong earth, each person in himself helpless, on all dependent. The
    circle is closed, and the net
Is being hauled in. They hardly feel the cords drawing, yet they shine already.   20
    The inevitable mass-disasters
Will not come in our time nor in our children's, but we and our children
Must watch the net draw narrower, government take all powers—or revolution,
    and the new government
Take more than all, add to kept bodies kept souls—or anarchy, the mass-disasters.

4

                        These things are Progress;
Do you marvel our verse is troubled or frowning, while it keeps its reason? Or it   25
    lets go, lets the mood flow

In the manner of the recent young men into mere hysteria, splintered gleams,
  crackled laughter. But they are quite wrong.
There is no reason for amazement: surely one always knew that cultures decay,
  and life's end is death.

QUESTIONS

1. Describe how the purse-seine is used to haul in the sardines. What is the
   speaker's reaction to the scene as described in stanza 2?

2. How does the speaker explain in stanza 3 that the purse-seine is to be understood as a symbol? What does it symbolize? What do the sardines symbolize?
   Of what is the poet speaking?

3. Compare the ideas of Jeffers in this poem with those of Yeats in "The Second
   Coming." In contrast with Yeats's cyclical scheme, do the ideas of Jeffers
   seem to be less methodical?

4. Why is the word *Progress* capitalized in line 24? What is usually meant by
   progress? How does Jeffers indicate that he is using the word and the idea
   ironically?

5. Is the statement at the end to be taken as recognition of a fact or as a
   resigned acceptance of that fact? In the light of the poem's major symbol,
   does the poem offer any solution to the problem? What is it that the speaker
   fears?

6. How may the sea lions of line 12, and their sighs, be construed as a symbol?
   Might the "you" of line 25 be responding to the poem in the way the sea
   lions respond to the capture of the sardines?

T. S. ELIOT (1888–1965)

Sweeney Among the Nightingales   *1918*

ὤμοι, πέπληγμαι καιρίαν πληγὴν ἔσω.

Apeneck Sweeney spreads his knees
Letting his arms hang down to laugh,
The zebra stripes along his jaw
Swelling to maculate° giraffe.   *dirty, stained*

SWEENEY AMONG THE NIGHTINGALES. Eliot wrote two othe works featuring Sweeney.
These are "Sweeney Erect" (a poem) and "Sweeney Agonistes" (a drama). The character
represented the grosser aspects of modern human beings; see Sweeney in "Sweeney
Agonistes," saying "Birth, and copulation, and death, / That's all, that's all, that's all." *Sweeney*
is also the name of a hero of Irish legend and folklore.   The Greek below the title may
be translated "Alas I am struck with a mortal blow within." This is from Aeschylus, *Agamemnon*,
line 1348; the scream of Agamemnon off stage when he is being murdered.

The circles of the stormy moon   5
Slide westward toward the River Plate,°
Death and the Raven° drift above
And Sweeney guards the hornéd gate.°

Gloomy Orion° and the Dog°   10
Are veiled; and hushed the shrunken seas;
The person in the Spanish cape
Tries to sit on Sweeney's knees

Slips and pulls the tablecloth
Overturns a coffee-cup,   15
Reorganized upon the floor
She yawns and draws a stocking up;

The silent man in mocha brown°   *Sweeney*
Sprawls at the window sill and gapes;
The waiter brings in oranges
Bananas figs and hothouse grapes;   20

The silent vertebrate in brown°   *Sweeney*
Contracts and concentrates, withdraws;
Rachel *née* Rabinovitch
Tears at the grapes with murderous paws;

She and the lady in the cape   25
Are suspect, thought to be in league;
Therefore the man with heavy eyes
Declines the gambit, shows fatigue,

Leaves the room and reappears   30
Outside the window, leaning in,
Branches of wistaria
Circumscribe a golden grin;

The host with someone indistinct°
Converses at the door apart,
The nightingales are singing near   35
The Convent of the Sacred Heart,

6 *River plate*: The River Plate, or Rio de la Plata, is the large estuary extending from the
Atlantic Ocean to Buenos Aires. It separates Argentina and Uruguay.   7 *Raven*: a bird
of ill omen; also the constellation Corvus.   8 *hornéd gate*: One of the two gates of the
underworld, according to Virgil, *Aeneid*, book 6:1192–1193. The usual guardian of the gates
was the three-headed dog, Cerberus.   9 *Orion*: a mythological Greek giant and hunter.
Because of a misunderstanding, he was killed by Artemis, the Goddess of the Moon and of
the Hunt. Orion is also one of the most prominent winter constellations.   *Dog*: Orion's
dog. The "dog star," Sirius, is in the constellation Canis Major, east of Orion, and it is the
brightest star in the sky.   33 *someone indistinct*: a murderer, corresponding to Aegisthus,
the murderer of Agamemnon.

And sang within the bloody° wood
When Agamemnon cried aloud,
And let their liquid siftings fall
To stain the stiff dishonored shroud.   40

37 *bloody*: A pun: (1) covered in blood, (2) the word *bloody*, profane in British English.

QUESTIONS

1. What does Sweeney represent as a symbol? Why does the poet use as the epigraph the passage from Aeschylus in which Agamemnon cries out in the pain of death? Why do you think the speaker describes Sweeney as "apeneck" (line 1) and as a "vertebrate in brown (line 21)"?

2. Why do you think Eliot included references to the constellations in the first part of the poem? Consider also the geography in the poem (i.e., South America, Greece, the Greek mythological underworld) in addition to the constellations. What is the effect of this broad set of references upon the symbolic meaning of the central incidents involving Agamemnon and Sweeney?

3. In stanza 2, how might the reference to the moon, westward, the raven, and horned gate be considered as symbols? What do these symbols represent?

4. Why does the speaker describe "Rachel *nee* Rabinovitch" as being like an animal (with "murderous paws"). Because of the fact that Sweeney is the name of a hero of Irish folklore, what do you make of Eliot's selection of the name *Sweeney* for his anti-hero?

5. What are the host and the "indistinct" man conferring about? What is going to happen to Sweeney?

6. What do nightingales usually symbolize? What do they represent here? How may this use of the nightingales be considered as ironic?

7. Consider the setting of the poem as a symbol of the circumstances of life in the twentieth century. What comforts and advantages of modern life are included? To what extent does the poem suggest that these improvements in the quality of life have had any effect upon human nature and greed?

E. E. CUMMINGS (1894–1962)

In Just-   *1923*

in Just-
spring   when the world is mud-
luscious the little
lame balloonman

```
whistles      far      and wee

and eddieandbill come
running from marbles and
piracies and it's
spring

when the world is puddle-wonderful                              1(

the queer
old balloonman whistles
far and wee
and bettyandisbel come dancing

from hop-scotch and jump-rope and                               1!

it's
spring
and
        the

                goat-footed°                                    2(

balloonMan      whistles
far
and
wee
```

IN JUST-.   20 goat-footed: The mythological Greek god Pan, a free-spirited and lascivious god who presided over fields, forests, and herds, was portrayed with the body of a man and the legs of a goat.

QUESTIONS

1. Consider and explain the following as symbols: spring, mud-luscious, marbles, puddle-wonderful, hop-scotch. What does the whistle of the balloon man symbolize?

2. In what way is the balloonman symbolic?

3. Beyond the balloon man, there are four characters in the poem. Who are they? Why does Cummings run their names together? What impulses do these characters represent symbolically?

4. Why do you think the poem ends as it does? How is the third wee in line 24 different from the word as it appears in lines 5 and 13?

5. Read the poem aloud, taking into account the spacing and alignment. How does the physical arrangement on the page influence your reading and perception of the lines?

ISABELLA GARDNER (1915–1981)

Collage of Echoes   *1979*

I have no promises to keep
Nor miles to go before I sleep.°
For miles of years I have made promises
and (mostly) kept them.
          It's time I slept.   5
Now I lay me down to sleep°
With no promises to keep.
          My sleeves are ravelled°
          I have travelled.°

COLLAGE OF ECHOES.   2 *miles to go before I sleep*: see Robert Frost, "Stopping by Woods
on a Snowy Evening," lines 13–16 (p. 475).   6 *Now I lay me down to sleep*: see the child's
prayer: Now I lay me down to sleep; / I pray the Lord my soul to keep. / If I should die
before I wake, / I pray the Lord my soul to take.   8 *My sleeves are ravelled*: see Macbeth,
act 2, scene 2, line 37: "Sleep that knits up the ravelled sleeve of care."   9 *I have travelled*:
see Keats, "On First Looking into Chapman's Homer," line 1 (p. 592).

QUESTIONS

1. Given the allusions in the poem, what do you conclude about the speaker's
    judgment of the reader's knowledge of literature?
2. What is the effect of the echoes? Consider the contexts of the sources being
    echoed. How reliant is "Collage of Echoes" upon these contexts? How do
    the echoes assist in enabling enjoyment and appreciation of the poem? Has
    the speaker truly incorporated them into the poem?
3. In relationship to the speaker's character as demonstrated in the poem, con-
    sider the phrases "(mostly) kept them," "With no promises to keep," and
    "My sleeves are ravelled." What do they show about the speaker's assessment
    of self? In what way might these phrases be considered comic?

CAROL MUSKE (b. 1945)

Real Estate   *1981*

You think you earned this space on earth,
but look at the gold face of the teen-age
pharaoh,° smug as a Shriner, in his box

REAL ESTATE.   3 *pharaoh*: Tutankhamen, the "boy king" of the fourteenth century B.C.
of ancient Egypt. The discovery of his tomb in 1922, when hundreds of precious household
objects were found with the sarcophagus, showed the lavishness of Egyptian royal burials.
The mummy of King Tut was covered with a mask of gold and colored metals.

with no diploma, a plot flashy enough
for Manhattan.° Early death, then what.   5
a task dragging a sofa into the grave,
a couple of floor lamps, the alarm set

for another century. Someday we'll heed
the testament of that paid escort watching
himself in all the ballroom mirrors: slide   10

with each slide of the old trombone,
be good to the bald, press up against
the ugly duck-like.° Time is never old,

never lies. What a past you'd have
if you'd only admit to it: the real estate   15
your family dabbled in for generations,
the vacant lots° developed like the clan

overbite—through years of sudden
foreclosure. Who knows what it costs?
First you stand for the national anthem,   20

then you start waltzing around without
strings, reminding yourself of yourself,
expecting to live in that big city
against daddy's admonition: buy land°

get some roots down under those spike   25
heels, let the river bow and scrape as
it enters the big front door of your property.

5 *Manhattan*: In 1981 a large number of treasures from Tutankhamen's tomb were being
displayed at the Metropolitan Museum of Art in Manhattan.   13 *ugly duck-like*: The Ugly
Duckling is a children's story by Hans Christian Andersen.   17 *vacant lots*: see T. S. Eliot,
"Preludes" concluding lines.   24 *buy land*: see Robert Frost's poem "Build Soil" (1932).

QUESTIONS

1. Who is speaking? Who is being addressed? What sort of person is the speaker?
   What does she think of old age? Of sex? What advice does she offer as a
   security against advancing age?

2. What does "the teen-age pharaoh" symbolize? Why does the poet mention
   a modern set of objects that might be found in a comparable tomb of a
   person of the twentieth century? What might these things symbolize? How
   do the things contrast?

3. What does the "paid escort" (line 9) symbolize? What does the "old trombone" symbolize? What does the choice of these symbolize about the traditional role of women with regard to men? What attitude is conveyed by
   this choice?

4. Consider the ambiguity of lines 25–27. What might "roots" and "property" mean as the means of causing the "river" to "bow and scrape"? Why is it difficult to understand these lines without resorting to symbolic explanations?

5. Consider the allusion in line 24 to Robert Frost's "Build Soil" (1932). Frost delivered his poem at Columbia University just before the party conventions of 1932. The nation was in depression, and Frost spoke of agriculture and world politics and spoke about the need of developing the nation's resources. In comparison, what does Muske achieve by the allusion?

WRITING ABOUT SYMBOLISM AND ALLUSION IN POETRY

As you read the poem on which you will be writing, take notes and make all the observations you can about the presence of symbols and/or allusions. Footnotes will help you establish basic information, but you still will need to make your own prose expansion of the meaning of what you are discovering. You might also wish to use a dictionary to build up your understanding of words or phrases that seem to be worthy of further study. For allusions, you might wish to go to the original source to determine the situation referred to. Try to determine the ways in which your poem is similar to, or different from, the original work or source, and then try to determine the purpose served by the allusion.

In the perception of symbols, you might wish to call on whatever personal experience you have had with symbols. Perhaps dinner time has been especially important in your family—a time when everyone gets together and chats over events of the day. If you are currently living away from home, you might miss the symbolic significance of this gathering time. Try to determine if a similar process of association might enable you to conclude that elements in the poem you are considering may be taken as symbols. Look for noteworthy or highlighted things; try to determine whether they are general or universal, particular or contextual. If you think that an element is symbolic, write a brief paragraph describing why you think it is. Determine how many symbols there are in the poem, and try to describe their nature. Consider a question like whether the poem would work in the same way if the element were not symbolic. Once you have set up a pattern of study in this way, you can begin developing and drafting your essay.

ORGANIZING YOUR ESSAY

INTRODUCTION. Your introduction might begin with a brief description of the poem and of the symbols or allusions in it. A symbol might be central to the poem, or an allusion might be made at a particularly important point at the climax. Your central idea should briefly state the theme of the essay, such as that the symbolism is visual and particular, or that it is not particularized and also general; the nature of the symbol may make it applicable to political or personal topic material; allusions may emphasize the differences between the poem and the source or sources of the allusions; symbols or allusions may make the poem seem optimistic, or pessimistic, and so on. The thesis sentence connects the central idea to the various points about symbols or allusions to be explored in the body of the essay.

BODY.   Some possible approaches for the body of the essay, which may be combined as need arises, are described in the following sections.

1. *The meaning of symbols or allusions*. This approach is the most natural one to take. If you have discovered a symbol or allusion, the intent is to explain the meaning as best you can. In effect, you are writing about the ideas of the poem as they are carried primarily by the devices you are exploring. What is the major idea of the poem? How do you know that this interpretation is valid? How far can the symbol or allusion be extended? To what degree do the materials in the rest of the poem serve as evidence for the ideas? If you have determined that there are many symbols or allusions in the poem, which of these, if any, predominate? What do they mean? Do the ideas of one relate to those of another? How?

2. *The importance of symbols or allusions to the form of the poem*. Here the goal should be to determine how symbolism or allusion is related to the poetic structure or form. Where is the symbol introduced? If it is early, how do the following parts relate to the ideas of the symbol? What sort of logical or chronological function does the symbol serve in the development of the poem? Is the symbol repeated? What effect does the repetition produce? If the symbol is introduced later in the poem, is it anticipated earlier? Can it be described in any way as being climactic? What might the structure of the poem have been like if the symbolism had not been used? (Answering this question can give an idea of how the symbol has influenced the structure of the poem.) In addition, for an allusion, it would be important to compare the contexts of both the poem and the source to determine how the poet has used the allusion for an illuminating, reinforcing, or contrasting effect.

3. *The relationship between the literal and the symbolic*. The object here is to describe the literal nature of the symbols and then to determine the appropriateness of the symbol in the context of the poem. If the symbol emerges as a part of a narrative, what is its literal function? If the symbol is a person, object of some sort, or setting, what physical aspects are described? Are colors included? Shapes? Sizes? Sounds? In the light of this actual description, how applicable is the symbol to the ideas it crystallizes? How appropriate is the literal condition to the symbolic? The answers to these and similar questions should lead not so much to a detailed account

of the meaning of the symbols, but rather to an analysis of enough of the meaning to explain the appropriateness of the relationship.

4. *Implications and resonances of symbols and allusions.* We have used the term *resonance* elsewhere in this book to refer to the complex of suggestions and associations that are brought out by a particular aspect of literature. The term is rather vague, but in a major respect it is at the very heart of literary experience. Here, particularly, it could be a fruitful direction to take for an essay. Ideas to explore would be about the chain of thinking that is brought out through symbols or allusions. In a way, you would be following a process of thought similar to the poet's, except that you are free to move in your own direction as long as you base your discussion on the symbols and allusions in the poem under consideration. If the poet is speaking in general terms about the end of an era, for example, as in "The Second Coming" and "The Purse-Seine," then you could include your own thoughts about the observations. It is often difficult to summon the knowledge and authority to contradict the work of a poet, but if you are able to point out shortcomings in the thought of the symbols or allusions, you should go right ahead.

CONCLUSION. Your conclusion might contain a summary of the main points in the body of your essay. If the poem is particularly rich in symbols or allusions, you might also consider briefly some of these elements that you did not consider fully in the body and try to tie these together with those you have already discussed. It would also be appropriate to introduce any personal responses you developed as a result of your study.

SAMPLE ESSAY

Symbol and Allusion in Yeats's "The Second Coming"*

"The Second Coming" is a prophetical poem that lays out reasons for being scared about the future. The poem's symbolism and allusiveness combine traditional materials from ancient history and literature together with Yeats's own visual scheme designed to explain the rise and fall of civilizations. These [1] devices are arranged to explain both the disruption of our present but old culture, and also the installation of a fearsome new one.° To make the explanation clear, Yeats uses the symbols of the gyre and the sphinx-like creature, and he alludes to New Testament prophecy.□

Yeats's first symbol, the gyre, or rather two gyres interconnecting, is pervasive in the poem, for it indicates the cyclical nature of political changes. Rotating

* See p. 800 for this poem.
° Central idea.
□ Thesis sentence.

outward at the visual top of the gyre symbolizing our present era, the falcon is used to introduce the idea that "the center cannot hold." The desert birds, hovering around the "lion body and the head of a man," show a tighter circle in a second gyre symbolizing the new civilization establishing itself. Thus the [2] widening symbolic gyre in line 1 is interpenetrating with the narrowing gyre pointing at the "rough beast." This blending and intersecting show that new things blend into old things, while separating from them at the same time. As the symbol thus illustrates, the order of the past is breaking up, while the future order is about to take the shape of the past not at its best, but rather at its worst.

Embodying this horror-to-be, the second major symbol is the sphinx-like creature moving its slow things in the sands of the desert. The attributes of the creature—a monster, really—are blankness and pitilessness. Yeats describes it as a "rough beast," with "indignant desert birds," perhaps vultures, flying in circles above it. This description of the symbol emphasizes the brutal [3] nature of the new age. Yeats wrote the poem in 1919, right after the conclusion of World War I, which had seen particularly senseless trench warfare. The disruption of life caused by this war was a disturbing indicator that the new period would be one of political repression and continued brutality.

It is this possible emergence of brutality that causes the poem's major allusion, to the "second coming" to be ironic. Yeats makes the allusion in the title, and also in lines 10 and 11 of the poem. The allusion is to the usual understanding of the New Testament prophecies about the return of Christ to rescue and save true believers. In the Bible, war and rumors of war are claimed as being the signs indicating that the return, or "second coming," is near. [4] Thus far, both the Biblical signs and the observations of Yeats coincide. The twist, however, is that Yeats is suggesting in the allusion that after the breakup of the present age, the new age will be marked not by Christ but by the rough beast. Because Yeats describes the beast as a sphinx, his model is the kind of despotism known in ancient Egypt, when power was held absolutely by the pharaoh and when few people were granted any freedom or civil rights.

"The Second Coming" is therefore visual and historical, with symbols both personal and traditional. There are more symbols and allusions than the ones just discussed. The falcon out of control, for example, symbolizes the anarchy that Yeats mentions in line 4 as being "loosed." The "ceremony of innocence" being drowned suggests the loss of the purification that is symbolized by the sacrament of communion. The "Spiritus Mundi" is a rather abstract symbol, but it indicates the complex idea that each individual shares in a common bond of images and perceptions that Yeats thought of as a vast human memory. [5] The description of the "blood-dimmed tide" suggests Shakespeare's Macbeth, who after killing Duncan says that the ocean is not big enough to wash the blood from his guilty hands. Rather, he says, his hands will make the ocean— "the green one"—red. This allusion is not verbal, but the image is the same. The "blood-dimmed tide" is therefore a borrowed symbol to indicate the global importance of any act of evil. Also, the reference to Bethlehem is an allusion to the town where Jesus was born. In the poem, however, the new birth will not lead to attempts to bring peace but will lead instead to repression and brutality. "The Second Coming" thus offers a rich fabric of symbol and allusion.

Commentary on the Essay

This essay combines the topics of symbolism and allusion, and therefore it illustrates how each may be handled. The introduction briefly characterizes the poem and asserts that the arguments are made through the use of symbols and allusions. The central idea is about the replacement of the old by the new, and the thesis sentence lists two major symbols and one allusion to be discussed in the body. Paragraph 2 describes the shape of the symbol, thus illustrating method 2 as described above, and also explains it, illustrating method 1. Paragraph 3 considers the "rough beast" as a symbol of emerging brutality. Paragraph 4 treats the title's allusion to New Testament prophetic tradition, showing how Yeats makes his point by reversing the outcome that tradition had predicted. The last paragraph summarizes and characterizes the body briefly and proceeds to illustrate the richness of "The Second Coming" with brief reference to additional symbols and other allusions.

24

Myth: Systems of Symbolic Allusion in Poetry

THE NATURE OF MYTHOLOGY

When poets employ mythology in their verse, they are actually using a very special kind of symbolism and allusion. We have already defined a **symbol** (in Chapters 9 and 23) as a person, place, action, thing, situation, or thought that possesses its own meaning but also points beyond itself to a greater and more complex meaning. Similarly, we have defined an **allusion** (in Chapter 23) as a direct or indirect reference to any significant moment, event, character, action, or phrase from history or literature. Both these devices produce **resonance,** an emotional and intellectual reverberation and amplification of the ideas or images evoked. Poets who retell myths or employ mythic material combine these two techniques to pull a vast body of meaning and resonance into their poems.

The term *myth* is derived from the Greek word *mythos*, which means story, narrative, or plot. Myths are thus stories that illustrate or define the religion, philosophy, culture, collective psychology, or history of a specific group or civilization. In addition, myths often explain particular features of a people's environment—like an especially high mountain in Greece or the seemingly endless winters in Northern Europe—and they frequently embody explanations of scientific facts for prescientific societies. The stories organize and formalize a civilization's social and cultural values. When these stories combine to form a system of belief and religious or historical doctrine, they become a **mythology** or a *mythos*. Thus, **myth** may briefly be defined as a system of belief sometimes (but not always) based on supernatural figures or "gods" who control the physical universe, who shape (or at least know) the destinies of humans, and who influence the flow of history.

We tend to think of myths as fables that are both fantastic and untrue. This accounts for our tendency to use the word *myth* to label political or social systems as false or invalid, as in "the myth of Communism" or "the myth of the middle class." This conception of myth, while at least partly accurate, limits the term and the concept too severely. Two considerations should modify our assumptions about myths and systems of mythology. On the one hand, myths can reflect truth symbolically even if the stories themselves are blatantly impossible; the truths of mythology are not found in the actual stories but rather in what they suggest about humanity. On the other hand, the term *myth* or *mythos* has come to refer to any organized system of narratives—true or false—that accounts for the origins and beliefs of a specific group. In this sense, the Old Testament embodies the mythos of the Jewish people just as Homer's *Iliad* and *Odyssey* represent the mythic histories of the Trojans and the Greeks. Thus, we can refer to the Islamic mythos, the Christian mythos, or the Jewish mythos without implying any sense of evaluation; the term simply refers to a system of belief.

Almost every culture has generated its own mythic system or absorbed the mythology of another people and adapted it to its own ends. The Romans, for example, swallowed up the whole body of Greek mythology and fused it with their own stories and values; most Roman myths and mythic figures parallel those in Greek mythology. Moreover, mythic systems have been produced in both primitive and sophisticated civilizations.

Why myths exist or why they have been generated by so many civilizations throughout the ages is difficult to tell. In fact, there are too many rather than too few explanations. We may begin by assuming that myths satisfy a basic human need to explain, organize, and humanize events or conditions that would otherwise remain mysterious and frightening. Thus, various cultures have produced myths that account for such natural phenomena as thunder and lightning, summer and winter, the ebb and flow of the sea, earthquakes and volcanoes. Most societies have also created myths that address the basic elements of human existence: birth, death, sexuality, and the existence of the world. In short, humanity seems to rely on myth to explain those aspects of life that are too complex to be easily understood.

Since myths address common human fears and events, it is not surprising to find various cultures separated by vast amounts of time and space producing parallel myths that relate to similar phenomena. Most cultures, for example, have stories that account for the creation of the world. The details of the myths may be quite different, but the patterns are often similar and the aim in every case remains the desire to explain the existence of the universe. Similarly, most civilizations have produced myths that deal with the coming of summer, the return of the earth's fertility, and humanity's redemption from the death and sterility of winter. These myths often involve the sacrifice of a god-hero or goddess-heroine to ensure the coming of spring and renewed vitality. In *The Golden Bough*, a massive collection and analysis of mythic stories, Sir James Frazer (1854–1941) compares a series of myths that account for the end of winter and the renewal of the earth through the death and subsequent rebirth or return of a god or goddess. Among such sacrificed and reborn gods are Thammuz (Babylonia), Attis (Phrygia), Osiris (Egypt), and Adonis, Dionysus, and Persephone (Greece). Again, the specific myths take many different forms, but they reflect the same mysteries, fears, and hopes.

Scholars and anthropologists like Frazer were among the first to notice the interrelationships among myths produced by diverse cultures. The Swiss psychoanalyst Carl Gustav Jung (1875–1961) offered one explanation for this duplication. Jung noticed that specific images, characters, and events drawn from literature, mythology, and religion recurred in the dreams of his patients. He termed these recurrent images *archetypes* (from the Greek word meaning "model" or "first mold") and theorized the existence of a universal or collective unconscious mind shared by all humanity. Not all of Jung's archetypes were related to mythology; for example, he included figures like wicked stepmothers. Nevertheless, the idea of a collective or shared unconscious is one way to account for parallel mythic figures or patterns in diverse cultures. Even if we dismiss Jung's theories completely, the fact remains that specific types of mythic figures and events like dragons, centaurs, sacrifices, and heroic quests recur throughout various mythologies and resonate in our literature and our minds.

MYTHOLOGY AND LITERATURE

Many people believe that literature actually started as mythology; the very first stories and poems probably retold myths. In any event, we are concerned here with the opposite process—the absorption of mythology into poetry. When Greek or Roman poets like Homer or Ovid recounted mythic stories in their verse, the result was a combination of literature and religion that served the double purpose of teaching and entertaining. Their poetry offered both a religious and an esthetic experience to their listeners. This remarkable combination of literature and religious doctrine occurred whether or not the poet believed the myths he was retelling; Homer's belief was probably sincere, but Ovid may have viewed his mythic poetry simply as literature. When an English poet in the sixteenth or seventeenth century includes Greek mythology in his or her verse, however, the effect is quite different. The poem no longer reinforces the dominant mythos of the society. Instead, it draws upon the body of mythology referred to in the work to symbolize universal truths or patterns of thought in a kind of allusive shorthand.

For thousands of years poets and other writers have found mythology to be an attractive and useful source of symbols, images, patterns, and ideas. To this day, mythology remains a significant storehouse of poetic symbol and allusion. In the English language we find poems that work with mythology in virtually every age and generation since the earliest Anglo-Saxon poems and legends. The poet's impulse to retell and rework myth is as alive today as it was in the Renaissance or the Victorian age; indeed, most of the poems in this chapter are from the twentieth century.

Most poets who incorporate mythological material into their verse turn to long-standing and well-established systems of myth, particularly Greco-Roman, Norse-Teutonic, and Judeo-Christian mythology. We might term these systems of mythology **public** or **universal,** since they are part of most people's common knowledge. Like public symbols, they exist outside the mind and the work of specific writers; they make up a common reservoir of material that all writers are free to employ. Thus, John Milton draws extensively on the Judeo-Christian mythos in his epic poem *Paradise Lost*, and T. S. Eliot alludes to the Buddhist mythos and pagan myths of fertility and rebirth in *The Waste Land*.

Some poets—like William Blake (1757–1827) and William Butler Yeats (1865–1939)—go beyond the allusive and symbolic use of public mythologies and invent their own mythic systems. Blake, for example, created a private system of mythology based on various semidivine figures called the Four Zoas. Similarly, Yeats invented a private mythos based on 2,000-year-long cycles or gyres of history and the phases of the moon (see p. 800). Poets who resort to such private mythic systems risk making their poetry almost inaccessible to most readers. Fortunately, much of their work is often meaningful and effective without any knowledge of their private mythologies.

STRATEGIES FOR DEALING WITH MYTHOLOGY IN POETRY

When a poet incorporates a mythic story or figure into a poem, he or she expects the readers to recognize the mythic allusion and the symbolic resonance produced in the work. If a poet mentions Ulysses (the Latin name for Homer's Odysseus), for example, the reader is expected to recall the stories associated with this mythic Greek hero, his role in the Trojan War, and the adventures he endured in his ten-year efforts to return home from Troy. Most of this material is recounted in Homer's *Iliad* and *Odyssey*. Thus, when we read Tennyson's "Ulysses" (p. 821), we are expected to bring to the poem a great deal of information about this mythic figure which should help us understand the dissatisfaction and the desires of this character in Tennyson's poem.

In the past the poet's assumptions about his or her readers were usually accurate; British and American readers in past generations had strong training in classical literature and mythology, and each culture was relatively homogeneous. Today, however, poets can no longer assume that their readers will have such detailed knowledge. Thus, modern poets who employ mythology have two options: they can refer to figures who are so well known that the reader will instantly recognize the allusion, or they can expect us to read with the poem in one hand and an encyclopedia of mythology in the other.

When dealing with a poem that employs mythic material, you should make every effort to identify the mythological allusion and to understand its implications or overtones. In some cases, poets (or editors) help with this process; they provide brief notes that identify the events or figures alluded to in the poem. In *The Waste Land*, for example, T. S. Eliot wrote his own notes to explain some of the more obscure mythic allusions. Even in these cases, however, the notes rarely give enough information to help you understand fully the implications and symbolic power of the mythic allusion.

More often than not, you will be on your own when dealing with mythology in poetry. In these cases, you will have to develop a slightly different strategy for studying the works and coming to an understanding of them. As usual, you should read through the poem several times to develop a general grasp of speaker, setting, situation, form, tone, and meaning. At the same time, make special note of figures or events that seem to allude to mythic systems.

At some point, you should leave the poem and find out as much as you can about the mythic elements in the work. A good place to start is a dictionary or general encyclopedia, which often provide brief identifications of mythic figures and a key to further reading. Eventually you will want access to more detailed information about the mythic allusions. Any appropriate mythology anthology will help in this respect. Thus, if you find allusions to Paul Bunyan and Johnny Appleseed, you would want to look in a collection of American folk tales. References to Odin, Thor, the Valkyries, or Asgard should lead you to a collection of Norse-Teutonic mythology. The most frequent mythic allusions in Western poetry are to Greco-Roman mythology. To learn more about these figures and events, you may turn to any anthology of Greek and Roman mythology. Two well-known books that retell these stories are Thomas Bulfinch's *The Age of Fable* and Edith Hamilton's *Mythology*.

Once this investigation is completed and you understand the mythic allusions, you can return to the poem and carefully reexamine the verse. You will now be able to understand how and why the poet works a specific mythological allusion into his or her poem. More to the point, you will be in a position to understand the symbolic resonances that such an allusion adds to the text.

STUDYING MYTHOLOGY IN POETRY

We are now ready to look at a poem that depends to a great extent on the resonance of its mythic allusions. The poem is by William Butler Yeats (1865–1939), but it does not refer extensively to his private mythic system. Rather, it draws on the well-known body of Greco-Roman mythology.

WILLIAM BUTLER YEATS (1865–1939)

Leda and the Swan   *1924 (1923)*

A sudden blow: the great wings beating still
Above the staggering girl, her thighs caressed
By the dark webs, her nape caught in his bill,
He holds her helpless breast upon his breast.

How can those terrified vague fingers push   5
The feathered glory from her loosening thighs?
And how can body, laid in that white rush,
But feel the strange heart beating where it lies?

A shudder in the loins engenders there
The broken wall, the burning roof and tower   10
And Agamemnon dead.
                          Being so caught up,
So mastered by the brute blood of the air,
Did she put on his knowledge with his power
Before the indifferent beak could let her drop?   15

QUESTIONS

1. What does the title tell you? What mythic event is recounted in the poem?
    Who was Leda? The swan? Who were Leda's children? What mythological/
    historical events are alluded to in lines 10 and 11?

2. What is the meter of the poem? The rhyme scheme? The form? Do you
    find significant irregularities in any of these? If so, what is their effect? To
    what extent are the events recounted in the poem organized by the structure?

3. How is Leda described? What words suggest her helplessness? How is the
    swan described? What phrases suggest his power, mystery, and divinity?

4. What question is raised in the last two lines? To what extent does the poem
    provide an answer to this question?

Yeats's poem focuses on a specific mythic event—the rape of Leda
by Zeus—and the mythological and historical consequences of that event.
The poem is thus very rich in mythic allusion and symbolism. The two
central characters—Leda and the swan—are identified only in the title.
The title consequently becomes an important key to understanding and
experiencing the poem. The poem is an Italian sonnet (see p. 743) and
generally follows an octave-sestet organization. It is composed of two quatrains (*a b a b, c d c d*) and two triplets (*e f g, e f g*).

At a basic level, the sonnet retells the mythological story of Zeus's
rape of Leda, a Spartan queen. In the attack, the king of the gods took
the form of a massive white swan. According to one version of the myth,

the children born from this rape were Helen of Troy and Clytemnestra. Helen ultimately became the central cause of the Trojan War; thus, the "broken wall, the burning roof and tower" (line 10) alludes to the destruction of Troy. Clytemnestra eventually married Agamemnon, the king of Mycenae and leader of the Greek forces at Troy; she and her lover murdered him when he returned home from the Trojan War.

The first quatrain (lines 1–4) details the sudden violence of the initial attack. The first three words—"A sudden blow"—begin both the poem and the rape with violent speed. Leda's helplessness is conveyed in adjectives like *staggering* (line 2) and *helpless* (line 4). Zeus's power and dominance are expressed in such phrases as "great wings" and "dark webs" and in words like *beating*, *caught* and *holds*. At the same time, the intense sexuality of the action is indicated by the single word *caressed* (line 2) and the image of "her helpless breast upon his breast" (line 4).

The second quatrain (lines 5–8) presents the consummation of the rape. Again, Leda's subjugation is expressed in phrases like "terrified vague fingers" (line 5) and "loosening thighs" (line 6). The words themselves produce an intense focus on Leda's body and the physical sexuality of the action. And again, the majesty and power of Zeus are conveyed in "the feathered glory" (line 6) and "that white rush" (line 7). The quatrain asks two rhetorical questions (lines 5–6 and 7–8). Both must clearly be answered in the negative; the "terrified fingers" *cannot* "push / The feathered glory from her loosening thighs" and Leda's "body" *cannot* help "But feel the strange heart beating where it lies."

The first half of the sestet (lines 9–11) presents both the climax of the rape and the historical (or mythical) consequences of Leda's unwilling union with Zeus. In this triplet, "A shudder in the loins engenders" the children of Leda and the god. The children, however, are not named. Instead, they are replaced by the events they will eventually produce: the burning of Troy and the murder of Agamemnon. This replacement of the names of Leda's daughters with the mythic or historical events they will cause suggests the interrelationship of events in history and the consequences that can evolve from violent actions.

The final triplet (actually half of line 11 and lines 12–14) raises the central question of the sonnet. The lines assert that Leda "put on" some of Zeus's divine power during the rape. They ask, however, if she also "put on his knowledge" (line 13). Literally, the question asks if Leda understood the historical consequences of the sexual union while it was occurring; it asks if she took on part of Zeus's foreknowledge of the fall of Troy and murder of Agamemnon. The question can be rephrased in several ways, each of which expands the scope of the problem. Can sexuality (violent or otherwise) encompass both power and knowledge? Can power and knowledge ever exist at the same time in humanity? Can there be effective connections among power, knowledge, and creation? The poem offers no clear answers to these questions; it merely raises them. The sonnet may imply an answer; since the two questions in the second quatrain demand negative answers, perhaps these questions do the same. Finally, however, the logic of the poem does not provide a solution; we must answer its central questions for ourselves.

Yeats employs mythic material in this sonnet to symbolize historical processes and raise central questions about history, power, and sexuality. The historical process is embodied in the rape and the children produced through the rape. The rape itself becomes the single catastrophic event in history that leads to other catastrophic events like the fall of Troy and the murder of Agamemnon. Thus, the myth of Leda and the rape itself become symbols within the poem of historical events that have far-reaching consequences. More to the point, Leda is used as a symbolic figure who may or may not represent the fusion of power and knowledge in creative action. She thus becomes the embodiment of the central question in the sonnet.

POEMS FOR STUDY

ALFRED, LORD TENNYSON (1809–1892)

Ulysses   *1842 (1833)*

It little profits that an idle king,
By this still hearth, among these barren crags,
Matched with an aged wife, I mete and dole
Unequal laws° unto a savage race,   *rewards and punishments*
That hoard, and sleep, and feed, and know not me.   5

I cannot rest from travel; I will drink
Life to the lees.° All times I have enjoyed   *dregs*
Greatly, have suffered greatly, both with those
That loved me, and alone; on shore, and when
Through scudding drifts the rainy Hyades°   10
Vexed the dim sea. I am become a name;
For always roaming with a hungry heart
Much have I seen and known—cities of men
And manners, climates, councils, governments,
Myself not least, but honored of them all—   15
And drunk delight of battle with my peers,
Far on the ringing plains of windy Troy.
I am a part of all that I have met;
Yet all experience is an arch wherethrough
Gleams that untraveled world whose margin fades   20

ULYSSES.   10 *Hyades*: nymphs who were placed among the stars by Zeus, the king of the gods. The name means "rain," and the rising of the stars was thought to precede a storm.

Forever and forever when I move.
How dull it is to pause, to make an end,
To rust unburnished, not to shine in use!
As though to breathe were life! Life piled on life
Were all too little, and of one to me   25
Little remains; but every hour is saved
From that eternal silence, something more,
A bringer of new things; and vile it were
For some three suns to store and hoard myself,
And this gray spirit yearning in desire   30
To follow knowledge like a sinking star,
Beyond the utmost bound of human thought.

   This is my son, mine own Telemachus,
To whom I leave the scepter and the isle—
Well-loved of me, discerning to fulfill   35
This labor, by slow prudence to make mild
A rugged people, and through soft degrees
Subdue them to the useful and the good.
Most blameless is he, centered in the sphere
Of common duties, decent not to fail   40
In offices of tenderness, and pay
Meet adoration to my household gods,
When I am gone. He works his work, I mine.

   There lies the port; the vessel puffs her sail;
There gloom the dark, broad seas. My mariners,   45
Souls that have toiled, and wrought, and thought with me—
That ever with a frolic welcome took
The thunder and the sunshine, and opposed
Free hearts, free foreheads—you and I are old;
Old age hath yet his honor and his toil.   50
Death closes all; but something ere the end,
Some work of noble note, may yet be done,
Not unbecoming men that strove with Gods.
The lights begin to twinkle from the rocks;
The long day wanes; the slow moon climbs; the deep   55
Moans round with many voices. Come, my friends,
'Tis not too late to seek a newer world.
Push off, and sitting well in order smite
The sounding furrows; for my purpose holds
To sail beyond the sunset, and the baths   60
Of all the western stars, until I die.
It may be that the gulfs will wash us down;
It may be we shall touch the Happy Isles,°
And see the great Achilles,° whom we knew.

63 Happy Isles: the Elysian Fields, the dwelling place of mortals who have been made immortal
by the gods.   64 Achilles: Greek hero of the Trojan War who killed Hector and was, in
turn, killed by Paris.

Though much is taken, much abides; and though   65
We are not now that strength which in old days
Moved earth and heaven, that which we are, we are—
One equal temper of heroic hearts,
Made weak by time and fate, but strong in will
To strive, to seek, to find, and not to yield.   70

QUESTIONS

1. What information does the title convey? Who was Ulysses (or Odysseus)? What role did he play in the Trojan War? What happened to him on the way home from Troy? How much time has passed between his return home and the present of the poem?

2. Who is the speaker of the poem? To whom is he speaking? What is his attitude toward his life in Ithaca and his wife? What key phrases and adjectives in lines 1–5 establish this attitude?

3. How have Ulysses's past experiences affected his present character and desires? What is his attitude toward life? What does he want to do?

4. Who is Telemachus? What is the speaker's attitude toward him? How are the speaker and Telemachus different?

5. What aspects of Ulysses are emphasized in this poem? To what extent does he become symbolic? What does he symbolize?

6. What ideas about life does this poem consider? How does the mythic resonance linked to the figure of Ulysses help to clarify these ideas?

DOROTHY PARKER (1893–1967)

Penelope   *1936*

In the pathway of the sun,
  In the footsteps of the breeze,
Where the world and sky are one,
  He shall ride the silver seas,
    He shall cut the glittering wave.   5
I shall sit at home, and rock;
Rise, to heed a neighbor's knock;
Brew my tea, and snip my thread;
Bleach the linen for my bed.
    They will call him brave.   10

QUESTIONS

1. What information does the title of this poem give you? Who was Penelope? Who is the speaker of the poem?

2. Who is the "he" referred to in lines 1–5? How is he described? What things will he do? Who is the "they" referred to in line 10?

3. How does the speaker describe her life? How is her life different from that of the male figure described in lines 1–5?

4. On what aspects of Penelope's life does this poem focus? To what extent does Penelope become a symbol? What does she symbolize? How does our understanding of the myth deepen our response to this symbolism?

5. What ideas about the lives of men and women and about the preconceived notions of society in the 1930s does this poem explore? Are these ideas still valid?

W. S. MERWIN (b. 1927)

Odysseus   1960

Always the setting forth was the same,
Same sea, same dangers waiting for him
As though he had got nowhere but older.
Behind him on the receding shore
The identical reproaches, and somewhere   5
Out before him, the unravelling patience
He was wedded to. There were the islands
Each with its woman and twining welcome
To be navigated, and one to call "home."
The knowledge of all that he betrayed   10
Grew till it was the same whether he stayed
Or went. Therefore he went. And what wonder
If sometimes he could not remember
Which was the one who wished on his departure
Perils that he could never sail through,   15
And which, improbable, remote, and true,
Was the one he kept sailing home to?

QUESTIONS

1. What aspects of the Odysseus myth are evoked in this poem? What point does the poem make about Odysseus's experiences?

2. What mythic figures are alluded to in the phrase "identical reproaches"? The phrase "the one who wished on his departure / Perils that he could never sail through"? The phrases "unravelling patience" and "the one he kept sailing home to"?

3. What ideas about life and experience does this poem explore? To what extent does Odysseus become symbolic of a specific kind of life and attitude toward

life? How does our knowledge of Odysseus contribute to the impact and meaning of the poem?

4. Compare the image of Penelope in this poem with the one in Dorothy Parker's "Penelope." How is the same mythic material used toward different ends in these poems?

5. Compare the image of Odysseus in this poem with the one in Alfred, Lord Tennyson's "Ulysses." What are the similarities and/or differences? Explain how and why the same mythic figure can be used to convey such different ideas.

MARGARET ATWOOD (b. 1939)

In myth, the Siren's song represents the seduction of rest from travel plus ... sexuality.

Siren Song — In the present day.

1974

This is the one song everyone
would like to learn: the song
that is irresistible:

the song that forces men
to leap overboard in squadrons   Colloquial siren.   5
even though they see the beached skulls

the song nobody knows   The hook. She draws us in,
because anyone who has heard it
is dead, and the others can't remember.

Shall I tell you the secret   10
and if I do, will you get me
out of this bird suit?   This + the diction "demyth" her. But this is the duel.

I don't enjoy it here
squatting on this island
looking picturesque and mythical   15

with these two feathery maniacs,
I don't enjoy singing
this trio, fatal and valuable.

I will tell the secret to you,
to you, only to you.   20
Come closer. This song

is a cry for help: Help me!
Only you, only you can,
you are unique   But you're not. The song works every time. She appeals to the male ego & suckers him in. Gullible men.

at last. Alas   25
it is a boring song
but it works every time.

Women find the pattern of seduction boring because it's predictable.

QUESTIONS

1. What does the title tell you? Who were the sirens? What was their song? What effect did their song have on men?

2. Who is the speaker in this poem? What is the effect of her colloquial diction? What does she tell you about her song?

3. Who is the "you" referred to in lines 10–24? What does the speaker offer to tell this person? What is the speaker's "secret"? What does the speaker say about her life? What happens to the "you" at the close of the poem? What "works every time"?

4. To what extent does your knowledge of the sirens help you to understand this poem? What does the siren in the poem symbolize? What does the listener symbolize?

5. What point does this poem make about women? About men? About gullibility, ego, and manipulation?

OLGA BROUMAS (b. 1949)

Circe   1977

The Charm *Her power*
Her desire to use the power

The fire bites, the fire bites. Bites
to the little death. Bites

till she comes to nothing. Bites
on her own sweet tongue. She goes on. Biting.   5

The Anticipation *Sets up the social + sexual context in which*
her power can work.

men,   They tell me a woman waits, motionless
society   till she's wooed. I wait

spiderlike, effortless as they weave
even my web for me, tying the cord in knots   10

Limitations, with their courting hands. Such power *of sexuality*
customs,   over them. And the spell
boundaries

their own. Who could release them? Who
would untie the cord

with a cloven hoof? *A swine*   15

The Bite *The transformation myth. Circe is confident, happy,*
powerful, divine.

What I wear in the morning pleases
me: green shirt, skirt of wine. I am wrapped

in myself as the smell of night *Self-satisfied.*
wraps round my sleep when I sleep   20

outside. By the time
I get to the corner ~~the turning point~~

bar, corner store, corner construction
site, I become divine. I turn

men into swine. Leave   25
them behind me whistling, grunting, wild.

QUESTIONS

1. Who was Circe in mythology? What powers did she have? What could she do to men?

2. Who or what is the speaker in this poem? What is the connection between the speaker and Circe? Why is the poem entitled "Circe"?

3. What do Circe and the speaker symbolize in the poem? What is the source of Circe's power in the myth and the poem? What does this power symbolize?

4. What is the "fire" (lines 1–5)? Who are "they" (lines 6–15)? What is the effect of "spiderlike" (line 9) and "courting hands" (line 11)? What is "the spell" (line 12)? What is the significance of "a cloven hoof" (line 15)?

5. What is the speaker's attitude toward herself in lines 16–26? What happens to her in these lines? What happens to the men she encounters?

6. How does knowledge of Circe help you understand this poem? What symbolic resonances are drawn from the myth into the poem? What does the poem suggest about women? Men? Sexuality?

MURIEL RUKEYSER (b. 1913)

Myth   *1978*

Long afterward, Oedipus, old and blinded, walked the
roads.   He smelled a familiar smell.   It was
the Sphinx.   Oedipus said, "I want to ask one question.
Why didn't I recognize my mother?"   "You gave the
wrong answer," said the Sphinx.   "But that was what   5
made everything possible," said Oedipus.   "No," she said.
"When I asked, What walks on four legs in the morning,
two at noon, and three in the evening, you answered,
Man.   You didn't say anything about woman."
"When you say Man," said Oedipus, "you include women   10
too. Everyone knows that."   She said, "That's what
you think."

QUESTIONS

1. Who was Oedipus? The Sphinx? What was wrong with Oedipus's answer to the Riddle of the Sphinx?
2. What elements and techniques in this work allow you to consider it a poem?
3. What explorations of diction occur in this work? Consider the words *myth* and *man*. What are the two myths and meanings of *myth* embodied in the title?
4. To what extent does the colloquial language in this poem undercut or revitalize the mythic material?
5. What point does this poem make about men? Women? Men's attitudes toward women? How does our knowledge of the Oedipus myth help clarify these aspects of the poem?

THE "ICARUS" POEMS

The following five poems, written between 1933 and 1963, all draw on the same mythic material—the story of the death of Icarus—to create symbolic resonance, meaning, and impact. According to Greek myth, Icarus was the son of Daedalus, an inventor and craftsman who was employed by Minos, the king of Crete, to design and build a labyrinth in which the king wanted to imprison the Minotaur, a monster that was half man and half bull. With Daedalus's help, Theseus killed the Minotaur and freed Athens from its annual tribute of sacrificial youths. As punishment for helping Theseus, Minos imprisoned Daedalus and Icarus in a tower. He also posted guards permanently on all roads and at the seaport to prevent escape. Daedalus realized that he and Icarus could escape only by air, so he fashioned two pairs of wings made of feathers and wax. As father and son were about to fly away from Crete and imprisonment, Daedalus warned Icarus not to fly too near the sun, because the heat would melt the wax and destroy the wings. [In the glory of flight, however, Icarus forgot his father's warnings and began to soar higher and higher toward the sun. Icarus continued to mount upward, despite his father's passionate cries, until the wax melted and the wings fell apart; he plunged into the sea and drowned.

Although all the following poems feature Icarus as the central mythic figure, the focus and the symbolic resonance is different in each. In other words, each poet went to the common storehouse of Greco-Roman mythology, selected the story and the figure of Icarus, and shaped them according to his or her own poetic goals. These goals are different in each poem. Thus, Icarus is variously employed to illustrate and symbolize ideas about pride, daring, suffering, creativity, idealism, society, and the tedium of daily life. Each of the "Icarus" poems offers its own meaning, impact, and poetic experience. Taken together, however, the group of poems illustrates the way myth can be used for very different effects in various poetic contexts. As you study these poems, try to answer the following questions.

1. What is Icarus's symbolic meaning or value in the myth? What qualities or characteristics does Icarus represent in mythology?
2. On what aspects of the Icarus myth does each poet focus? Some possibilities include character, action, motivation, emotion, death, suffering, or the implications of the action.
3. To what extent does the allusion to Icarus contribute symbolic resonance and meaning to each poem? In what ways is the poetic effect of the mythic allusion different in each?
4. How do such poetic elements as diction, meter, rhyme, tone, and form help to reshape the myth and the figure of Icarus in each poem?
5. What themes or ideas are explored in each poem? Explain the connection between the Icarus myth and the meaning in each poem.

STEPHEN SPENDER (b. 1909)

Icarus Proud, arrogant　　　　　　　　Pride, Flight : *1933*

He will watch the hawk with an indifferent eye Indifferent to those beneath
　Or pitifully;　　　　　　　　　　　　　　him.
Nor on those eagles that so feared him, now
　Will strain his brow;
Weapons men use, stone, sling and strong-thewed bow　　　　　5
　He will not know.

This aristocrat, superb of all instinct,
　With death close linked　　　　　　　　Fall :
Had paced the enormous cloud, almost had won
　War on the sun;　　　　　　　　　　　　　　　　　10
Till now, like Icarus mid-ocean-drowned,
　Hands, wings, are found. Shattered image – stresses destruction +
　　　　　　　　　　　　　finality.

W. H. AUDEN (1907–1973)

　　　　　　　　　　Explores ideas about suffering + the world's
Musée des Beaux Arts°　reaction to it.　　　　　　　*1940*

About suffering they were never wrong,
The Old Masters: how well they understood
Its human position; how it takes place　　　moves now from general to
　　　　　　　　　　　　　　　　　　　　specifics.

MUSÉE DES BEAUX ARTS. "Museum of Fine Arts."

While someone else is eating or opening a window or just walking dully along;
How, when the aged are reverently, passionately waiting   5
For the miraculous birth, there always must be
Children who did not specially want it to happen, skating
On a pond at the edge of the wood:
They never forgot
That even the dreadful martyrdom must run its course   10
Anyhow in a corner, some untidy spot
Where the dogs go on with their doggy life and the torturer's horse
Scratches its innocent behind on a tree.
In Brueghel's° *Icarus*, for instance: how everything turns away
Quite leisurely from the disaster; the ploughman may   15
Have heard the splash, the forsaken cry,
But for him it was not an important failure; the sun shone
As it had to on the white legs disappearing into the green
Water; and the expensive delicate ship that must have seen
Something amazing, a boy falling out of the sky,   20
Had somewhere to get to and sailed calmly on.

14 *Brueghel*: Pieter Brueghel or Breughel (ca. 1525–1569) was a Flemish painter whose subjects included the Nativity ("the miraculous birth"), the Crucifixion ("the dreadful martyrdom"), and the fall of Icarus. See pp. 770 and 831 for two other poems based on the work of Brueghel.

Pieter Brueghel's painting, "Fall of Icarus." Scala/Art Resource. *The painting ignores Icarus' heroic aspirations. Deals only with his fall.*

ANNE SEXTON (1928–1974)

To a Friend Whose Work Has Come to Triumph°   *[handwritten: Focuses on the 1962 daring + heroic triumph of his flight.]*

Consider Icarus, pasting those sticky wings on,
testing that strange little tug at his shoulder blade,
and think of that first flawless moment over the lawn
of the labyrinth. Think of the difference it made!   *[handwritten: Icarus is contrasted with]*
There below are the <u>trees</u>, as awkward as camels;   *[handwritten: the creatures of the earth.]*
and here are the shocked <u>starlings</u> pumping past
and think of innocent Icarus who is doing quite well:
larger than a sail, over the fog and the blast
of the plushy ocean, he goes. Admire his wings!
Feel the fire at his neck and see how casually   10
he glances up and is caught, wondrously tunneling
into that <u>hot eye</u>. <u>Who cares that he fell back to the sea?</u>   *[handwritten: The Fall is de-emphasized]*
See him acclaiming the sun and come plunging down   *[handwritten: Contrast]*
while his <u>sensible daddy</u> goes straight into town.

TO A FRIEND WHOSE WORK HAS COME TO TRIUMPH. The title alludes to and reverses
the title of a poem by William Butler Yeats, "To a Friend Whose Work Has Come to Nothing"
(1914).

WILLIAM CARLOS WILLIAMS (1883–1963)

Landscape with the Fall of Icarus   *[handwritten: Like Auden's, Williams' treatment is filtered thro the painting. 1962]*

According to Brueghel°   *[handwritten: •Williams uses verbal images to recreate the painting.]*
when Icarus fell   *[handwritten: Icarus himself seems secondary.]*
it was <u>spring</u>

a <u>farmer</u> was ploughing   *[handwritten: The poem "pans" the landscape from left to right.]*
his field
the whole <u>pageantry</u>   5

<u>of the year</u> was
awake tingling
near

the edge of the sea   10
concerned
with itself

sweating in the sun
that melted
the wings' wax   15

LANDSCAPE WITH THE FALL OF ICARUS.   1 *Brueghel*: See the note for Auden's
"Musée des Beaux Arts" and the accompanying illustration, p. 830.

unsignificantly *[handwritten: To the burgeoning, busy world intent upon itself.]*
off the coast
there was

[handwritten left margin: The sentence runs off / away from the disaster]

a splash quite unnoticed
this was   20
Icarus drowning

[handwritten: I]

[handwritten: Mention Hollywood stars]

EDWARD FIELD (b. 1924)

Icarus *[handwritten: Focus is squarely upon Icarus. Places him into the modern world. Rewrites the myth.]*   1963

Only the feathers floating around the hat
Showed that anything more spectacular had occurred
Than the usual drowning. The police preferred to ignore
The confusing aspects of the case,
And the witnesses ran off to a gang war.   5
So the report filed and forgotten in the archives read simply
"Drowned," but it was wrong: Icarus
Had swum away, coming at last to the city
Where he rented a house and tended the garden. *[handwritten: Ironic descent into the mundane.]*

"That nice Mr. Hicks" the neighbors called him,   *[handwritten: Explores his feelings &]*   10
Never dreaming that the gray, respectable suit   *[handwritten: his place or lack of]*
Concealed arms that had controlled huge wings   *[handwritten: place in this world]*
Nor that those sad, defeated eyes had once
Compelled the sun. And had he told them
They would have answered with a shocked, uncomprehending stare.   15
No, he could not disturb their neat front yards; *[handwritten: Complacent,]*
[handwritten left margin: Suburban, doggy worlds.] Yet all his books insisted that this was a horrible mistake:
What was he doing aging in a suburb? *[handwritten: He embodies alienation &]*
Can the genius of the hero fall   *[handwritten: despair. Poem explores]*
To the middling stature of the merely talented?   *[handwritten: the idea that the]*   20
[handwritten: hero can be reduced to the ordinary, mundane,]
And nightly Icarus probes his wound   *[handwritten: and pathetic in the]*
And daily in his workshop, curtains carefully drawn,   *[handwritten: modern world.]*
Constructs small wings and tries to fly
To the lighting fixture on the ceiling:
Fails every time and hates himself for trying.   25

[He had thought himself a hero, had acted heroically,
And dreamt of his fall, the tragic fall of the hero;]
But now rides commuter trains,
Serves on various committees,
And wishes he had drowned.   30

*[handwritten: * Field illustrates what can happen when a hero goes on living too long past the moment of glory/tragedy.]*

WRITING ABOUT MYTH IN POETRY

As with many other elements of poetry, it is difficult to write about the element of myth in isolation. Instead, an essay on myth in poetry will normally connect the mythic material in a poem to some other consideration, such as speaker, tone, or meaning. This suggests a two-part exploration of the poem, one concerned with its general sense, and the other concerned with the ways in which myth shapes and controls that sense.

When planning an essay on the mythic elements in a poem, you should first go through the process of discovery and investigation described earlier in this chapter. If you can select the poem, choose one that is short enough to be handled well in a brief essay and yet offers a wealth of mythic allusion with which you are at least partly familiar. In any case, read the poem carefully several times, note any possible allusions to myth, and try to find out as much as possible about the mythic content.

Once you have both a general understanding of the poem and specific information about the mythic content, you can work back through the poem to develop the raw materials for your essay; you can begin to think about a central idea and supporting evidence. At this point, you should be considering the mythological content of the poem and its effect on other elements, including speaker, character, action, setting, situation, imagery, form, and meaning.

As you reexamine the poem in the light of its mythological content, you will be dealing with a number of variables. In general, however, you are looking for the ways in which myth enriches the poem and focuses its meaning. Thus, you should seek the most significant area of interaction between myth and poem. The following questions should help in this quest:

1. To what extent does the title help identify the mythic content of the poem and thus provide a key for understanding?

2. Who is the speaker in this poem? The central figure or figures? Is the speaker also the central figure, or is there a distinction?

3. Is either the speaker or the central character drawn from mythology? If so, what qualities and characteristics of the mythic figure are evoked by the speaker or character in the poem? To what extent does our understanding of the relevant myth help us come to grips with the speaker and/or the characters in the poem?

4. If the characters are drawn from mythology, how are they symbolic in the *myth* (apart from the poem)? What aspects of this symbolism are carried into the poem? How does the poem maintain, undercut, increase, or change the symbolism?

5. Does the poem retell a myth? In other words, how much of the poem's action, setting, and situation are borrowed from mythology? What is the

significance of the action in the *myth*? To what extent is this material symbolic? How does the poet reshape the action and its significance to his or her own ends?

6. Beyond character and action, what mythic images occur in the poem? How do these affect the meaning and the impact of the poem?

7. How do the various formal elements of poetry such as diction, rhyme, meter, and form reshape the mythic material and the impact or meaning of the myth? Do specific words and phrases, for instance, undercut or reinforce the ideas and implications that we find in the myth itself? Does the rhyme (if any) lead us to deal with the mythic content seriously or humorously? Does the tone of the poem support or undercut the implications of the myth?

8. How does the mythic content help create and clarify what the poem is about?

Not every poem will provide meaningful answers to all these questions. Nor is this list exhaustive; you will often find other subjects worthy of examination. Nevertheless, the answers to these sorts of questions will yield a great deal of information about the role of myth in the poem. In addition, these data will usually point toward the specific area in which the myth and the poem interact most profoundly. This area will become the subject of the essay.

As with most other essays, developing a tentative focus or central idea is the most difficult part of prewriting. Whatever discoveries you have made about the poem and its mythic elements will be most helpful in this respect. If, for example, you find that the poem retells a myth in order to make a point about history or society, your central idea will reflect that connection. Similarly, if the poem employs a speaker or character from mythology to convey ideas about war or heroism, your essay will focus on the linkage among myth, character, and those ideas.

When you formulate a tentative central idea, draft it as a complete sentence that conveys the full scope of your own ideas about the poem. It is not enough merely to assert that a given poem contains a great deal of mythic material. If you are writing an essay about Yeats's "Leda and the Swan," for example, you might be tempted to form a central idea that argues that "William Butler Yeats's 'Leda and the Swan' retells the myth of Leda's rape by Zeus and the consequences of that event." That sentence does not tell the reader anything about the *way* myth works in the poem. Nor does it provide a basis for moving beyond simple summary and paraphrase. A more effective formulation of a central idea might read as follows: "In Yeats's 'Leda and the Swan,' the myth of Leda's rape by Zeus and the consequences of that rape are employed to illustrate the historical process and to question the connection between knowledge and power." This formulation argues for a specific connection between mythological content and the poem's effect, and it gives a clear direction to the essay.

Once you have formed a tentative focus and central idea, reorganize your data in support of the thesis. At this point, you can begin to shape your insights and conclusions about the poem into tentative paragraphs. You may have to rethink or refocus the central idea of the essay several times. Do not let such revision bother you; it is quite normal and, in fact, helpful. Indeed, rethinking and revision should occur at virtually every stage of both the prewriting and the writing processes.

Organizing Your Essay

INTRODUCTION.   The introduction should name the poet and the poem and make whatever general points you wish about the poem. For instance, you might want to provide relevant information about the poem's form or any special circumstances of composition. More important, the introduction should state the essay's central idea and the way that idea will be supported in the body. Thus, the introduction should identify the important mythic aspect(s) of the poem, link it with other relevant poetic elements, and make an assertion about the effect of this connection.

BODY.   The body of the essay will prove the central idea asserted in the introduction with supporting details drawn from the poem. Because this central idea will normally assert a connection between the mythic material and another poetic element—speaker, character, action, image, meaning, or the like—you will have to deal with both the myth and the poem, continually discussing the relationship between the two. At some point early in the essay, you might want to summarize briefly the relevant parts of the myth under consideration. For the most part, however, the essay should focus on the poem (and the mythic material within the poem) rather than on the myth itself.

Various strategies can be employed to organize the body of the essay. You might decide to echo the organization of the poem, and shape the central paragraphs so as to reflect the line-by-line or stanza-by-stanza logic of the poem (as in the discussion of "Leda and the Swan" above). Alternatively, you might choose an organization based on a series of different mythic elements or figures. If a poem alludes to Odysseus, his wife, Penelope, and his son, Telemachus, for instance, you might devote a paragraph or two to the way each figure shapes the impact and meaning of the poem. As a third option, you might use the relevant elements of poetry as the focal points of organization. Thus, if you argue that diction, rhyme, and tone shape the mythological material in a poem to produce significant effects, you would deal with each element in turn.

CONCLUSION.   The conclusion should bring the essay to a convincing and assertive close rather than a mere stopping point. To do this, you can summarize the major points that were asserted in the introduction and supported in the body. At the same time, you can draw the reader's attention to the significance of your observations and to any further implications that might arise from the unique fusion of myth and poetry under consideration.

SAMPLE ESSAY

Myth and Meaning in Dorothy Parker's "Penelope"*

[1] Dorothy Parker's short lyric poem "Penelope" employs mythic allusion and symbolism to make a point about men and women and the way society perceives them. The mythic figure who speaks the poem and becomes one of its central symbols is Penelope. This speaker, and thus the poem, suggests that women must endure tedium and suffering in silence, and that society consistently misjudges and undervalues women's lives.° Through diction, tone, and mythic resonance, the speaker describes the active and heroic life of Odysseus, her own passive existence, and society's mistaken evaluation of both.▫

[2] The key to the poem's mythic resonance is the title, "Penelope." This is the only place where the mythological speaker of the poem is named. The title alludes to the wife of Odysseus, who waited at home in Ithaca for twenty years while her husband fought in the Trojan War and struggled against Poseidon, the god of the sea, to return home. Penelope's story is found in Homer's *Odyssey*, where we learn that her ten-year wait for Odysseus's return after the end of the Trojan War was anything but peaceful or pleasant. Her palace filled with boorish suitors who assumed that Odysseus was dead and demanded that the queen of Ithaca choose a new husband. Only Penelope and Telemachus, her son, clung to the hope that Odysseus was still alive. Penelope kept the arrogant suitors at bay by promising to marry one of them after she finished weaving a shroud for Odysseus's father. In order to delay this eventuality, she worked at the loom each day and unraveled the work each night. Thus, she lived a domestic but stressful life for ten years in which she bravely resisted both despair and the demands of the suitors.

[3] Although the title refers directly to Penelope, the poem itself draws on mythic material that relates to both Penelope and Odysseus. Lines 1–5 evoke our memory of Odysseus; his wanderings and adventures are alluded to in phrases like "He shall ride the silver seas" (line 4) and "He shall cut the glittering wave" (line 5). Odysseus is never mentioned by name, and none of his specific adventures is cited. Nevertheless, the poem's title naturally leads to the assumption that the "he" in these lines is Odysseus. At the same time, however, the absence of any specific identification allows us to see this male figure as a symbol for all men who leave home and pursue an active life of

* See p. 823 for this poem.
° Central idea.
▫ Thesis sentence.

adventure. The adjectives and verbs used in these lines make this active life seem attractive and exciting. Such phrases as "the pathway of the sun" (line 1) and "the footsteps of the breeze" (line 2) add a sense of romance and mystery to the active life of the male. The adjectives silver and glittering connote splendor and glory. Verbs such as ride and cut reinforce the active and violent nature of the male's existence. We also find, however, a subtle undercutting of this heroic male figure in the same lines. Many of these phrases, like "ride the silver seas," are clichés. The speaker's use of such clichés suggests that this image of the active hero is both trite and, to some extent, inaccurate.

[4]
    Just as "he" in lines 1–5 refers to both Odysseus and a symbolic representative of all men, so the speaker of the poem is both Penelope and an embodiment of all women. This symbolic speaker contrasts her own life to the active life of Odysseus and mankind in lines 6–9. Here we find no adjectives at all; the woman's existence is thus rendered drab and tedious. In addition, the verbs represent passive and domestic activities: sit, rock, rise, brew, snip, and bleach. These last two verbs are especially effective. The phrase "snip my thread" (line 8) is the only allusion to Penelope's unhappy existence in Ithaca; it refers to her daring deception of the suitors through weaving and unraveling the shroud. At the same time, snip is contrasted with the verb cut used earlier in the poem. While the words are synonyms, they carry very different connotations; cut implies grand and violent action while snip suggests careful and delicate activity. Bleach is equally connotative; although it refers directly to "the linen for my bed," it implies that the speaker's life is faded and colorless. The passive and domestic life described here can be seen as a symbolic model for the lives of most women in the 1930s. The speaker suggests through detail and diction that such a life is tedious and passive; the lines only hint at the courage and strength necessary to play out such a role.

[5]
    The final line of the poem crystallizes its message and clarifies the speaker's attitude toward the different roles that men and women play. Here, the speaker asserts that "They will call him brave." They refers to society, to the world at large, and to generations of readers who have admired Odysseus in Homer's *Iliad* and *Odyssey*. The speaker assures us that he—both Odysseus in particular and the active male in general—will be admired by society. The meter of the line places a great deal of stress on the word him, thus emphasizing the speaker's ironic tone and her realization that society will always ignore or dismiss the quiet bravery of women. In myth and in life, the woman's role often demands more courage and conviction than the man's. Certainly Penelope's desperate existence for ten years in Ithaca, besieged in her own home by arrogant suitors who ignored her wishes, testifies to the strength and bravery of women. Nevertheless, Penelope, speaking for all women in all nations and all ages, bitterly observes that "they will call him brave."

[6]
    This poem thus employs mythic figures and events to examine the roles traditionally played by men and women, and society's distorted perception of those roles. Odysseus, as a symbol for all men, is presented as both a heroic and a trite figure; the words that describe his life carry implications of mystery, adventure, and splendor, yet they are often clichés. Penelope, as a symbol for all women, describes her own life as tedious, drab, and passive. She hints,

however, at the courage and desperation that often lurk behind domestic routine. Our knowledge of Penelope's courageous survival in Ithaca during her husband's absence adds significantly to the impact of these implications. Finally, the mythic figures and symbols in this poem illustrate the degree to which society admires the active male and ignores the strength and courage of women.

Commentary on the Essay

The sample essay deals with the connection between mythic characters and meaning in Dorothy Parker's "Penelope." The introduction identifies the poem as a lyric and Penelope as the central mythic figure. Most important, it states the central idea of the essay and enumerates the ways that idea will be supported in the body. Thus, the introduction asserts that two mythic characters, redefined by diction and tone, are employed symbolically in the poem to make a point about the lives of women and men and the way society values those lives.

The body of the essay is organized along the lines of the first strategy mentioned on page 835; it follows the organization of the poem itself. Thus, paragraph 2 focuses on the title, paragraph 3 on lines 1–5, paragraph 4 on lines 6–9, and paragraph 5 on the last line of the poem. Each of the paragraphs also advances a specific aspect of the essay's central idea. In paragraph 2 Penelope is identified and the relevant mythic material is summarized. The title and its mythic resonance are used, in turn, to introduce Odysseus and the symbol of the heroic male in paragraph 3. Here, diction is examined to demonstrate that the active male is simultaneously made to appear attractive and undercut. The paragraph thus asserts that Odysseus is employed in the poem symbolically to represent the ideal *and* the cliché of the active and heroic male.

The first sentence of paragraph 4 provides transition from the discussion of Odysseus and heroic males to that of Penelope and the perceived passiveness of women. Again, the essay explores the way diction and mythic allusion in the poem demonstrate that women's lives can be domestic and desperate at the same time. Paragraph 5 looks at the poem's final line in relation to the contrasted lives of heroic men and passive women. Here, the essay takes up tone and meter to reveal the speaker's attitude toward these contrasting lives and society's misperception of them.

The conclusion basically summarizes the major points of the essay. Thus, the first sentence repeats the subject of the poem. The next three summarize the essay's observations about Odysseus and Penelope. Finally, the last two sentences of the conclusion reconnect the poem to the myth and repeat the poem's central point about society's mistaken evaluation of bravery in women and men.

25

Theme: The Ideas and the Meaning in Poetry

When we speak about the theme of a poem, we are actually talking about the ideas or points that the poem conveys. Poets often (but not always) work with ideas or themes in mind as they shape their poetry. The general **subject** of a poem indicates the idea or group of ideas that the poet addresses. These are usually very general and may include such broad concepts as love, death, war, or art. Thomas Hardy's "Channel Firing" (p. 492) and Wilfred Owen's "Dulce et Decorum Est" (p. 644), for example, are both about war and thus share the same subject. Similarly, Andrew Marvell's "to His Coy Mistress" (p. 849) and Robert Herrick's "To the Virgins, To Make Much of Time" (p. 850) have as their common subjects the connection between time and love.

The **theme** or **central idea** of a poem, however, is different from its subject. It is, in fact, the specific point that the poem makes about its subject. We can find many poems about love, death, war, or poetry, but each one is likely to convey an idea that is slightly different from any other. Thus, Hardy's "Channel Firing" and Owen's "Dulce et Decorum Est" share a common subject but have different themes. Hardy's poem asserts that war is a damnable characteristic of humanity and that humanity is unlikely to change. Owen's poem, in contrast, explores the obscenity of war and the idea that there is nothing fitting or sweet about dying for one's country. By the same token, Marvell's "Coy Mistress" and Herrick's "To the Virgins" assert different points about time and love. While Marvell's poem argues that the pressures of time should lead us to grab every opportunity to enjoy life, Herrick's poem morally asserts that these same pressures should lead us to marriage. Clearly, poems with identical subjects can have very different themes.

The total **meaning** of a poem is different again from either its subject or its theme: it combines the poem's central idea with its emotional impact and the experience it creates for the reader. The experience of this total meaning is the level of engagement we should aim for in our meetings with poetry. It is important to understand a poem's theme; the central idea is crucial to our interaction with the poem. However, we should not reduce the art of reading poetry to a single-minded quest for the poem's message. While theme is an adequate formulation of a specific kind of meaning, it omits the emotional response and the actual experience of the poem by the reader. Meaning must ultimately encompass both halves of the reading experience—both the text and the reader. Thus, the total meaning of a poem consists of the poem's themes or ideas and our response to every element of the poem. Poetry is not primarily a vehicle for expressing ideas or opinions; an essay or even a newspaper article could do that just as well or better. Rather, poetry is one way of creating an imaginative experience in which we travel with and through the poem to a complicated and sometimes ambiguous internalization of ideas, emotions, and sensations. The total meaning of a poem includes not only what the poem says to us, but also how it says it and what it does to our emotions, intellect, and sense of being.

The related concepts of subject and theme in poetry should not be new to you; we introduced them in Chapter 11, and we have been speaking about them to some extent ever since. This chapter, however, deals with the questions of what a poem means and how it conveys that meaning directly. Two important principles should first be kept in mind. The first is that theme is different from summary or paraphrase. A summary of the action in Owen's "Dulce et Decorum Est" or in Spenser's "One Day I Wrote Her Name Upon the Strand" (p. 851) will give us a good idea of what happens in the poem, but it will not tell us anything about the poem's ideas or impact. Similarly, a paraphrase of the argument in Herrick's "To the Virgins" or Marvell's "To His Coy Mistress" will reveal the logic of each poem, but the central ideas and the experience of each will be missing. The second principle to keep in mind is that poems generally say what they mean and mean what they say. This is not to suggest that it is always easy to understand what a poem means. It does suggest, however, that reading poetry is not an exercise in decoding the "secret codes" or "deep hidden meanings" that a cryptographer has hidden in a text. Rather, meaning is created in poetry through all the skills and devices in the poet's repertoire. Thus, any determination of meaning depends on paying attention to what the poet says and the way he or she says it.

MUST A POEM HAVE A THEME?

In recent years people have argued that poems need not and, indeed, should not have a theme or a central idea. Some assert that a poem should "be" rather than "mean." Such an approach to poetry, or any other type of literature, values the esthetic or emotional experience of the work above any rigorous examination or intellectual engagement. Ultimately, however, this approach limits our appreciation of poetry and distorts the facts. First of all, a full appreciation of poetry should combine the emotional and esthetic response to "being" with an intellectual response to "meaning." Neither an emotional nor an intellectual response, isolated from the other, can provide the full experience that poetry offers us. Furthermore, we must face the fact that many poems make a thematic point. It would be less than honest to assert that Herrick's "To the Virgins, to Make Much of Time" should be valued only for its emotional impact and that its central idea is unimportant. To the contrary, the emotional impact of the poem depends, to a large extent, on an understanding of its ideas.

The debate about "being" versus "meaning" raises another important question: Must all poems convey a thematic message or specific idea? The answer, simply put, is no. Poems can describe a scene, tell a story, relate an event, portray a character, or convey an emotion. "Sir Patrick Spens" (p. 465) and "Barbara Allan" (p. 722), for example, simply tell tragic stories. Similarly, Robert Browning's "My Last Duchess" (p. 488) presents us with portraits of two contrasting characters. None of these poems comes to grips directly with ideas, although all of them may *imply* attitudes or conclusions about experience or human nature. In these cases, however, the ideas are not *in* the poems; rather, they are generated by our interaction with the poems. Such poems, in fact, have no immediate theme or message beyond their emotional impact and the singular experience of the poetic moment. This does not mean that they are better or worse than most other poetry; it means that the poets had different goals in mind when they wrote them. The strengths of such poems must be judged on their own terms; such a poem succeeds or fails as an esthetic experience. In general, however, it is safe to assume that most poems have thematic significance or convey an idea. You should not decide that a poem is without a theme until you have exhausted all avenues of exploration and consideration.

STRATEGIES FOR DEALING WITH THEME

As we noted earlier, the theme of a poem is established partly by *what* the poem says and partly by the *way* the poem says it. A tentative and initial understanding of meaning can be gained by looking carefully at a poem's statements, its logic, and its argument. The first step in understanding theme, then, is a sentence-by-sentence or unit-by-unit reading of the poem. Occasionally this is enough; some poems express their central ideas immediately and clearly. In most instances, however, our initial, literal reading of the poem is affected by many of the devices available to poets. In other words, theme is more often implied than stated, and every element of poetry can be employed to shape the message and meaning of a poem. These include speaker, character, setting and situation, action, diction, sound, imagery, metaphor and simile, tone, meter, rhyme, form, symbol, allusion, and others. Thus, in studying poems for meaning, you should consider all the potential methods through which a poem's thematic point and emotional impact may be established or modified.

SPEAKER.   Who or what the speaker is can significantly affect the meaning of a poem. It helps us understand the poems, for example, when we realize that the speaker in Thomas Hardy's "Channel Firing" (p. 492) is a corpse and that the speaker in Sharon Olds's "35/10" (p. 863) is a mother brushing her daughter's hair. It is also important and useful to determine whether the speaker is trustworthy or prejudiced. Thus, in Browning's "My Last Duchess" the speaker says one thing but his views are so distorted that the poem conveys an entirely different portrait.

CHARACTER, SETTING, ACTION.   The characters, settings, and actions in a poem do much to shape the central idea. A poem that is set in a graveyard and describes gunnery practice out at sea conveys a different meaning from one that tells about a walk through the woods in spring or describes a mother brushing her daughter's hair at bedtime. Even if all three poems share a common concern with death, the radically different contexts and actions in each produce a new perspective, a different emotional response, a new experience, and a different meaning.

DICTION.   The words employed in a poem—the denotation, connotation, diction, and syntax—can all reshape a poem's emotional impact and total meaning. In Ben Jonson's "To Celia" (p. 848), for instance, the speaker refers to sexual activity as "the sports of love" and "love's fruits." Both *sports* and *fruits* are loaded words and metaphors; they help determine both the nature of the speaker and the meaning of the poem. In contrast, Robert Herrick speaks of love in "To the Virgins, to Make Much of Time" (p. 850) in terms of marriage. The vast difference between "sports of love" and "go marry" underscores the differences in tone and meaning between these two poems.

IMAGERY AND RHETORICAL FIGURES.   Imagery, metaphor, simile, and other devices of language almost always make an abstract idea or situation concrete and immediate. At the same time, however, a poet may employ imagery or metaphor either to advance or to undercut what appears to be the major thrust of a poem. In Owen's "Dulce et Decorum Est" (p. 644), for example, soldiers are described as "Bent double, like old beggars under sacks." The simile is consistent with the rest of the poem; it helps to define the speaker's attitude toward war and to shape the poem's ultimate point. In contrast, we find clichéd images in Dorothy Parker's "Penelope" (p. 823) that undercut the heroic ideal of the active male and thus make us reconsider our attitudes toward heroism.

TONE.   The tone of a poem can have a significant effect on theme. Most often it reinforces a poem's total meaning. In Herrick's "To the Virgins," for example, the tone is warm and somewhat detached, consistent with the poem's friendly moral advice. Tone becomes a dominant factor in meaning, however, when it works against many of the other elements in a poem. The most common instance of this effect occurs when the dominant tone is ironic. In these cases, the tone can reverse the total meaning. In Dorothy Parker's "Penelope," for instance, the ironic tone of the last line forces us to reconsider the meaning and our experience of the whole poem.

RHYTHM, METER, AND SOUND.   Elements such as rhythm, meter, alliteration, assonance, and onomatopoeia rarely shape meaning independently of other elements. Rather, these tend to reinforce the ideas and emotions created through the other aspects of the poem. Such elements can, however, refine and focus meaning significantly. Rhythm and meter can stress important words and thus shape our sense of a poem. Similarly, meaning can be refined through the skillful use of alliteration, assonance, or the repetition of key sounds. In all these instances, sound and meter echo sense and meaning.

RHYME, STRUCTURE, AND FORM.   Rhyme may be employed to clinch ideas, regulate the tone, and thus shape meaning; the falling or double rhymes in Herrick's "To The Virgins" lighten the tone and thus modify the poem's message. Structure can be equally important in shaping meaning. Marvell's "To His Coy Mistress," for instance, is arranged in a pseudo-logical argument that imitates the order of formal syllogistic logic. Once a reader recognizes that this pseudo-logic creates the poem's structure, the central idea becomes much more accessible. Form too can provide a method for ordering and shaping a poem's theme and meaning. The coherent units or stanzas of a closed form often reflect specific steps in the poem's expression of meaning. Such is the case in Spenser's *Amoretti* 75, "One Day I Wrote Her Name upon the Strand" (p. 851). In this poem the formal divisions of the sonnet reflect a logical pattern that moves from an action to a reaction and finally to an explanation.

SYMBOL AND ALLUSION.   Poets employ symbol and allusion as a kind of shorthand to convey very complex ideas and a great deal of information as quickly and economically as possible. In "To the Virgins," for example, two symbols—rosebuds and flowers—point beyond themselves to human sexuality, marriage and families, and full engagement with life. The symbols thus carry much of the poem's impact and message. Allusion can be equally important. In "To His Coy Mistress" we find geographic and Biblical allusions that are crucial in shaping the meaning of the first part of the poem's argument.

These eight areas may seem like a large number of variables to consider in working toward an understanding of a poem's central idea and total meaning; at first, the process may seem quite difficult. Keep in mind, however, that all eight are seldom equally relevant to a given poem. As you study more poetry, you will learn how to focus your attention on two or three significant aspects of a poem and to give others only secondary consideration. Eventually, you will be able to evaluate the impact of most of these elements on meaning rather quickly. Indeed, experienced readers of poetry do much of this step-by-step analysis almost unconsciously and simultaneously as they study a poem.

STUDYING MESSAGE AND MEANING IN POETRY

Let us now turn to a specific poem and see how we might arrive at an understanding of its theme and meaning. The poem, "Ars Poetica," which means "the art of poetry," should help us understand the nature of meaning in poetry, since it is "about" that very thing.

ARCHIBALD MacLEISH (1892–1982)

Ars Poetica   *1926*

A poem should be palpable and mute
As a globed fruit,

Dumb
As old medallions to the thumb,

Silent as the sleeve-worn stone
Of casement ledges where the moss has grown—

A poem should be wordless
As the flight of birds.

*

A poem should be motionless in time
As the moon climbs,

Leaving, as the moon releases
Twig by twig the night-entangled trees,

Leaving, as the moon behind the winter leaves,
Memory by memory the mind—

A poem should be motionless in time   15
As the moon climbs.

*

A poem should be equal to:
Not true.

For all the history of grief
An empty doorway and a maple leaf.   20

For love
The leaning grasses and two lights above the sea—

A poem should not mean
But be.

QUESTIONS

1. What is the subject of this poem? To what extent does the title help define the subject? Why did the poet call it "Ars Poetica" instead of "The Art of Poetry"?

2. What does the first section (lines 1–8) assert that a poem should be? How are similes employed to make this assertion clearer and more concrete?

3. How can a poem be "mute" (line 1), "dumb" (line 3), "silent" (line 5), and "wordless" (line 7)? Since a poem (and this poem) must be made of words, how can this paradox be resolved?

4. What does the second section (lines 9–16) assert about a poem? How are symbolism and simile used to clarify this assertion? How can something be "motionless" and "climb" at the same time? What is the effect of repetition in this section?

5. What does the third section (lines 17–24) assert about a poem? What symbolizes "all the history of grief" here? What symbolizes "love"? Why are these two examples of symbolism included in the poem?

6. What does this poem finally assert about poetry? To what extent does "Ars Poetica" embody and illustrate its own ideas and total meaning?

The subject of "Ars Poetica" is the art of poetry and the nature of poems; it is announced in the title and taken up in every section. The elevated diction of the Latin title connotes philosophical seriousness and great scholarship. Indeed, the title is borrowed from a treatise on poetry written by the Roman poet Horace (65–8 B.C.). In a sense, the title is partly ironic. The poem treats the nature of poetry quite seriously, but it is certainly not a scholarly essay.

"Ars Poetica" represents an attempt to define and describe poetry;

to that extent, it presents a philosophy of poetry. The poem does this in two ways; it *tells* us and it *shows* us what a poem should be. The poem's central idea is found in the third section, where the speaker asserts that "A poem should be equal to: / Not true" and that "A poem should not mean / But be." In other words, a poem should embody an experience that is parallel to reality rather than simply convey a specific idea or truth. Does this mean that a poem should have no theme? Not really, although this may appear to be the point of "Ars Poetica" at first. If this were the case, the poem would cancel its own assertion and create a paradox simply by making this point. Rather, the poem asserts that the total experience of a poem is more important and valuable than any single stated idea it might relate.

The first section of "Ars Poetica" tells us that a poem should be "mute" (line 1), "dumb" (line 3), "silent" (line 5), and "wordless" (line 7). This appears to be an impossible requirement and a paradox; poems are obviously made of words. The poem goes on, however, in each two-line stanza of this section to show us exactly what "wordless" means. It suggests through example that a poem must communicate its experience to us in images that come alive and that we can feel as well as understand. Thus, each two-line stanza contains a simile that makes both the meaning and the experience of wordless or silent existence clear. The four comparisons—to "globed fruit," "old medallions," "sleeve-worn stone," and "the flights of birds"—present images of silence that we can recreate and experience in our minds.

We might pause and look at how one of these similes works in the poem and in the reader's mind to evoke the state of "wordless" silence with words. In lines 5 and 6 the poem asserts that a poem should be "Silent as the sleeve-worn stone / Of casement ledges where the moss has grown." The image begins as a cliché: "as quiet or as still as a stone." This is familiar ground; we can easily summon this image up in our imagination. But the poet is not satisfied with the cliché; he breathes new life into it by particularizing the stone. The stone is "sleeve-worn"; it has been worn down by the friction of many people's arms over hundreds of years. In addition, it is the stone of a "casement ledge" or windowsill "where the moss has grown." In focusing the image of the stone, the poem expands our sense of silence by adding overtones of elapsed time, slow erosion, and quiet natural growth. The image becomes particular but still familiar; it embodies not only the feeling and the idea of silence, but also a state of being that we can experience. This brings us back to perhaps the most important word in the first section of the poem: *palpable* (line 1). Literally it means easily seen, heard, perceived, or felt. If we take all the meanings together, this section of the poem suggests that a poem cannot simply be words; it must be a process that unites reader and text in an emotional, sensual, and intellectual experience.

The second section of the poem (lines 9–16), like the first, defines an aspect of poetry and begins with what appears to be a paradox: "A poem should be motionless in time / As the moon climbs." How can something be "motionless" and "climb" (or move) at the same time? The answer lies in the way we experience the moon and poetry. The moon becomes both the central image and symbol here. As an image, it illustrates the way we experience poetry; as a symbol, it is "equal to" this experience. Each time we look at the moon at night, it appears to be motionless; yet over the course of an entire night it does move, rising in the east, crossing the heavens, and setting in the west. We perceive its movement as an infinite series of moments of stillness. "Motionless," like "wordless," has more to do with the way we perceive and experience things than it does with actuality. The image thus emphasizes the parallel between poetry and our experience of time, motion, and the moon.

Here, as in the first section, the poem offers two similes that clarify the way we experience motionless movement in time and in poetry. The two middle stanzas compare the effect of moonlight on the landscape to the effect of poetry on the reader; just as moonlight "releases" the shadows of the trees "twig by twig," so the poem should leave the mind "memory by memory," evoking timeless responses and experiences in us. This process of timeless and motionless experience in poetry is also illustrated in the structure of this middle section. The lines that open the section also close it. Thus, the beginning and the end are identical; we end up where we started. We have moved and the poem has moved; we have traveled through four lines and two similes. Yet we haven't moved; we end up exactly where we began. Thus, MacLeish employs repetition to make concrete the experience of motionless and timeless processes in poetry.

By the time we reach the third section of "Ars Poetica," we are in a much better position to understand what the poem *means* when it says that "A poem should not mean / But be." This does not indicate that poetry should be without themes, but that a poem should represent truth and offer a "palpable" experience. The poem offers two more sets of symbols as examples of the way poetry creates experience. The first example suggests that "all the history of grief" may be symbolized by "An empty doorway and a maple leaf" (lines 19–20). The second symbolizes "love" by "The leaning grasses and two lights above the sea" (line 22). The symbols themselves are private (rather than public) but accessible. The "empty doorway" suggests that someone is gone, missing, dead; "doorway" presupposes presence and movement, but "empty" conveys absence. In a like manner, the "maple leaf" implies seasonal change and death. [The symbols create experiences parallel to grief and love.] More important, however, they illustrate the importance of symbolism as a vehicle for meaning.

These symbols embody a key concept for poetry: provide the concrete detail to evoke the experience of the abstract whole. This is one of the processes of poetry; this is the way imagery, simile, and symbol work in the poem and in the reader. "Ars Poetica" is finally not "mute"; it does have a theme. It asserts that poems should create a "palpable" experience that parallels (but is not the same as) life. And as this poem illustrates, that experience is created through imagery, comparison, and symbolism. The poem also makes it clear that the experience is more important than either the words that create it or the words evoked in the reader by it. In that sense, a poem is "mute" and "wordless"; its existence and value derive from the experience it offers us.

POEMS FOR STUDY

BEN JONSON (1572–1632)

To Celia   1606

Come my Celia, let us prove,°   *try*
While we may, the sports of love;
Time will not be ours forever;
He at length our good will sever.
Spend not then his gifts in vain.   5
Suns that set may rise again;
But if once we lose this light,
'Tis with us perpetual night.
Why should we defer our joys?
Fame° and rumor are but toys.   *reputation*   10
Cannot we delude the eyes
Of a few poor household spies,
Or his° easier ears beguile,   *Celia's husband*
So removed by our wile?
'Tis no sin love's fruit to steal,   15
But the sweet theft to reveal,
To be taken, to be seen,
These have crimes accounted been.

TO CELIA. The poem is from Jonson's play *Volpone*; it is spoken by Volpone (the name means "the fox") to Celia, a married woman whom he is trying to seduce.

QUESTIONS

1. What is the speaker like? What is his attitude toward time? Love? Celia?
2. What is personified in lines 3–5? What power does this force have?
3. This type of poem (and the specific argument in lines 1–8) is called *carpe diem* (Latin for "seize the day"). How is the idea of "seizing the day" relevant to the first eight lines of this poem?

4. How does the speaker's argument change in the last ten lines (9–18)? What does he claim that he and Celia can do? What assertions does he (and the poem) make about time, love, reputation, and crime?

5. How consistent is the speaker's argument? How convincing? How moral?

6. What is the tone of the poem? How is it created? How does it affect the total meaning of the poem?

ANDREW MARVELL (1621–1678)

To His Coy Mistress *1681*

Had we but world enough, and time,
This coyness, lady, were no crime.
We would sit down, and think which way
To walk, and pass our long love's day.
Thou by the Indian Ganges'° side   5
Shouldst rubies find; I by the tide
Of Humber° would complain. I would
Love you ten years before the flood°,   *Noah's flood*
And you should, if you please, refuse
Till the conversion of the Jews.°   10
My vegetable love should grow
Vaster than empires and more slow;
An hundred years should go to praise
Thine eyes, and on thy forehead gaze;
Two hundred to adore each breast,   15
But thirty thousand to the rest;
An age at least to every part,
And the last age should show your heart.
For, lady, you deserve this state,
Nor would I love at lower rate.   20
  But at my back I always hear
Time's wingéd chariot hurrying near;
And yonder all before us lie
Deserts of vast eternity.
Thy beauty shall no more be found,   25
Nor, in thy marble vault, shall sound
My echoing song; then worms shall try
That long-preserved virginity,
And your quaint honor turn to dust,
And into ashes all my lust: 30
The grave's a fine and private place,

TO HIS COY MISTRESS.   5 *Ganges*: a large river that runs across most of
India.   7 *Humber*: small river that runs through the north of England to the North
Sea.   10 *Jews*: traditionally, this conversion is supposed to occur just before the Last
Judgment.

But none, I think, do there embrace.
  Now therefore, while the youthful hue
Sits on thy skin like morning dew,
And while thy willing soul transpires   35
At every pore with instant fires,
Now let us sport us while we may,
And now, like amorous birds of prey,
Rather at once our time devour
Than languish in his slow-chapped° power.   *slow-jawed*   40
Let us roll all our strength and all
Our sweetness up into one ball,
And tear our pleasures with rough strife
Thorough° the iron gates of life: *through*
Thus, though we cannot make our sun   45
Stand still, yet we will make him run.

QUESTIONS

1. What can we deduce about the speaker in this poem? The listener? What
   does the title tell us? What does the speaker want?

2. In lines 1 through 20 the speaker sets up a hypothetical situation and the
   first part of a pseudo-logical proof: If *A* then *B*. What specific words indicate
   the logic of this section? What hypothetical situation is established?

3. How do geographic and Biblical allusions affect our sense of time and place?

4. In lines 21 through 32 the speaker presents the second step of his argument;
   he refutes the hypothetical condition set up in the first twenty lines. What
   specific word indicates that this is a refutation? How does the speaker refute
   the first part of his argument? How does imagery help create and reinforce
   meaning here?

5. The last part of the poem (lines 33–46) presents the speaker's "logical"
   conclusion. What words indicate that this is a conclusion? What is the conclusion?

6. This poem, like Jonson's "To Celia," is in the *carpe diem* tradition. How is
   the idea of "seizing the day" relevant to this poem? To what extent do Marvell's poem and Jonson's poem make similar points? How are their central
   ideas different? To what extent do differences in tone account for differences
   in meaning?

ROBERT HERRICK (1591–1674)

To the Virgins, to Make Much of Time   *1648*

Gather ye rosebuds while ye may,
  Old time is still a-flying;
And this same flower that smiles today
  Tomorrow will be dying.

The glorious lamp of heaven, the sun,   5
  The higher he's a-getting,
The sooner will his race be run,
  And nearer he's to setting.

That age is best which is the first,
  When youth and blood are warmer;   10
But being spent, the worse, and worst
  Times still succeed the former.

Then be not coy, but use your time,
  And, while ye may, go marry;
For, having lost but once your prime,   15
  You may forever tarry.

QUESTIONS

1. What does the title of this poem tell us? What can we deduce about the
   speaker? To whom is the poem addressed?
2. What point does this poem make about time? Life? Love?
3. How does symbolism help shape the message and meaning of the poem?
   Consider especially "rosebuds," "flower," and "the sun."
4. How do rhyme and tone help create and focus the meaning of this poem?
5. Compare this poem to Jonson's "To Celia" and Marvell's "To His Coy Mistress." How well does this poem express the central idea of the *carpe diem*
   tradition? How are the tone and message of this poem similar to and different
   from those in the poems by Jonson and Marvell?

EDMUND SPENSER (1552–1599)

Amoretti 75: One Day I Wrote Her Name upon the Strand   *1595*

One day I wrote her name upon the strand,°   *beach*
But came the waves and washed it away:
Again I wrote it with a second hand,
But came the tide and made my pains his prey.
"Vain man," said she, "that doest in vain assay,   5
A mortal thing so to immortalize,
For I myself shall like to this decay,
And eek° my name be wiped out likewise."   *also, indeed*
"Not so," quod° I, "let baser things devise,   *said*
To die in dust, but you shall live by fame: 10
My verse your virtues rare shall eternize,
And in the heavens write your glorious name.
Where whenas death shall all the world subdue,
Our love shall live, and later life renew."

QUESTIONS

1. What action is described in the first quatrain of this sonnet? What point does the speaker's mistress make about this action in the second quatrain?
2. How does the speaker deal with his mistress's objections in the third quatrain and the couplet? What point does he make about her "fame" or reputation?
3. What is the subject of this poem? What is its theme?
4. To what extent do rhyme, meter, and form contribute to the formation of this poem's meaning?
5. Compare this poem with Shakespeare's "Not Marble, Nor the Gilded Monuments" (p. 468). How are the two poems similar in form, tone, and meaning? Which is more convincing? More dramatic?

MARIANNE MOORE (1887–1982)

Poetry   *1921*

I, too, dislike it: there are things that are important beyond all this fiddle.
  Reading it, however, with a perfect contempt for it, one discovers in
  it after all, a place for the genuine.
    Hands that can grasp, eyes
    that can dilate, hair that can rise   5
      if it must, these things are important not because a

high-sounding interpretation can be put upon them but because they are
  useful. When they become so derivative as to become unintelligible,
  the same thing may be said for all of us, that we
    do not admire what   10
    we cannot understand: the bat
      holding on upside down or in quest of something to

eat, elephants pushing, a wild horse taking a roll, a tireless wolf under
  a tree, the immovable critic twitching his skin like a horse that feels a
    flea, the base-
  ball fan, the statistician—   15
    nor is it valid
      to discriminate against 'business documents and

school-books';° all these phenomena are important. One must make a distinction
  however: when dragged into prominence by half poets, the result is not poetry,
  nor till the poets among us can be   20

POETRY. In the last edition of her *Collected Poems*, Moore deleted everything in this poem following "genuine" in line 3.   17–18 *"business . . . school-books"*: the phrase is quoted from the Russian novelist, Leo Tolstoy (1828–1910). Moore's original note cites a passage in Tolstoy's *Diaries* (1917) in which he discusses the difference between prose and poetry: "Where the boundary between prose and poetry lies, I shall never be able to understand. . . . Poetry is verse: prose is not verse. Or else poetry is everything with the exception of business documents and school books" (p. 96).

'literalists of
the imagination'°—above
    insolence and triviality and can present
for inspection, 'imaginary gardens with real toads in them', shall we have
    it. In the meantime, if you demand on the one hand,   25
    the raw material of poetry in
        all its rawness and
        that which is on the other hand
            genuine, you are interested in poetry.

21–22 *literalists of the imagination*: Moore's original note refers to W. B. Yeats's discussion
of William Blake in *Ideas of Good and Evil* (1903), where Yeats observes that Blake was "a
too literal realist of imagination" (p. 182).

QUESTIONS

1. What can we surmise about the speaker in this poem? To whom is the poem
   addressed? What does the speaker assume about the listener?
2. What is the tone of this poem? How do words like *fiddle* (line 1) and *perfect
   contempt* (line 2) affect the tone? How does tone affect the meaning?
3. What is the subject of this poem? The theme?
4. How does the speaker modify his or her initial assertion about poetry? What
   can poetry provide? What is its value? How should we experience it?
5. What does the speaker say about poems "we cannot understand" (line 11)?
   How does imagery clarify the speaker's assertion about incomprehensible
   things?
6. What does the speaker assert that poets must be and must do before we
   shall have "it" (line 25)? What is "it"?
7. To what extent does this poem provide the experience it asserts is necessary
   to have poetry?

WILLIAM WORDSWORTH (1770–1850)

Ode   *1807 (1802–1804)*

*Intimations of Immortality from Recollections
        of Early Childhood* °

The Child is father of the Man;
And I could wish my days to be
Bound each to each by natural piety.

ODE: INTIMATIONS OF IMMORTALITY FROM RECOLLECTIONS OF EARLY
CHILDHOOD. The ideas in this poem are based, in part, on the Platonic theory of the
preexistence of the soul before birth and the Neoplatonic theory that the glory of the unborn
soul is gradually lost as it is immersed in the physical matter of the body and the world.

1

There was a time when meadow, grove, and stream,
The earth, and every common sight,
            To me did seem
            Apparelled in celestial light,
The glory and the freshness of a dream.   5
It is not now as it hath been of yore—
            Turn whereso'er I may,
                By night or day,
The things which I have seen I now can see no more.

2

            The Rainbow comes and goes,   10
            And lovely is the Rose,
            The Moon doth with delight
Look round her when the heavens are bare,
            Waters on a starry night
            Are beautiful and fair;   15
    The sunshine is a glorious birth;
    But yet I know, where'er I go,
That there hath passed away a glory from the earth.

3

Now while the birds thus sing a joyous song,
    And while the young lambs bound   20
        As to the tabor's° sound,   *small drum*
To me alone there came a thought of grief:
A timely utterance gave that thought relief,
        And I again am strong:
The cataracts blow their trumpets from the steep;   25
No more shall grief of mine the season wrong;
I hear the Echoes through the mountains throng,
The Winds come to me from the fields of sleep,
        And all the earth is gay;
            Land and sea   30
    Give themselves up to jollity,
        And with the heart of May
    Doth every Beast keep holiday—
        Thou Child of Joy,
Shout round me, let me hear thy shouts, thou happy   35
        Shepherd-boy!

4

Ye blessed Creatures, I have heard the call
    Ye to each other make; I see
The heavens laugh with you in your jubilee;
    My heart is at your festival,   40
    My head hath its coronal,°   *wreath of flowers*
The fullness of your bliss, I feel—I feel it all.
        Oh, evil day! if I were sullen
        While Earth herself is adorning,

This sweet May morning,   45
And the Children are culling
    On every side,
In a thousand valleys far and wide,
Fresh flowers; while the sun shines warm,
And the Babe leaps up on his Mother's arm—   50
    I hear, I hear, with joy I hear!
    —But there's a Tree, of many, one,
A single Field which I have looked upon,
Both of them speak of something that is gone:
    The Pansy at my feet   55
    Doth the same tale repeat:
Whither is fled the visionary gleam?
Where is it now, the glory and the dream?

                              5

Our birth is but a sleep and a forgetting:
The Soul that rises with us, our life's Star,°   sun   60
    Hath had elsewhere its setting,
    And cometh from afar:
    Not in entire forgetfulness,
    And not in utter nakedness,
But trailing clouds of glory do we come   65
    From God, who is our home:
Heaven lies about us in our infancy!
Shades of the prison-house° begin to close   the world
    Upon the growing Boy
    But he   70
Beholds the light, and whence it flows,
    He sees it in his joy;
The Youth, who daily farther from the east°   from birth and God
    Must travel, still is Nature's Priest,
    And by the vision splendid   75
    Is on his way attended;
At length the Man perceives it die away,
And fade into the light of common day.

                              6

Earth fills her lap with pleasures of her own;
Yearnings she hath in her own natural kind,   80
And, even with something of a Mother's mind,
    And no unworthy aim,
    The homely° Nurse doth all she can   simple, friendly
To make her foster child, her Inmate Man,
    Forget the glories he hath known,   85
And that imperial palace whence he came.

                              7

Behold the Child among his newborn blisses,
A six-years' Darling of a pygmy size!
See, where 'mid work of his own hand he lies,

Fretted by sallies of his mother's kisses,   90
With light upon him from his father's eyes!
See, at his feet, some little plan or chart,
Some fragment from his dream of human life,
Shaped by himself with newly-learned art;
       A wedding or a festival,   95
       A mourning or a funeral;
         And this hath now his heart,
        And unto this he frames his song;
         Then will he fit his tongue
To dialogues of business, love, or strife;   100
       But it will not be long
        Ere this be thrown aside,
        And with new joy and pride
The little Actor cons another part;
Filling from time to time his "humorous° stage"   *moody, changing*   105
With all the Persons, down to palsied Age,
That Life brings with her in her equipage;
       As if his whole vocation
       Were endless imitation.
              8
Thou, whose exterior semblance doth belie   110
       Thy Soul's immensity;
Thou best Philosopher, who yet dost keep
Thy heritage, thou Eye among the blind,
That, deaf and silent, read'st the eternal deep,
Haunted forever by the eternal mind—   115
       Mighty Prophet! Seer blest!
       On whom those truths do rest,
Which we are toiling all our lives to find,
In darkness lost, the darkness of the grave;
Thou, over whom thy Immortality   120
Broods like the Day, a Master o'er a Slave,
A Presence which is not to be put by;
Thou little Child, yet glorious in the might
Of heaven-born freedom on thy being's height,
Why with such earnest pains dost thou provoke   125
The years to bring the inevitable yoke,
Thus blindly with thy blessedness at strife?
Full soon thy Soul shall have her earthly freight,
And custom lie upon thee with a weight,
Heavy as frost, and deep almost as life!   130
              9
       O joy! that in our embers
       Is something that doth live,
       That nature yet remembers
       What was so fugitive!
The thought of our past years in me doth breed   135

Perpetual benediction: not indeed
For that which is most worthy to be blest;
Delight and liberty, the simple creed
Of Childhood, whether busy or at rest,
With new-fledged hope still fluttering in his breast—   140
    Not for these I raise
    The song of thanks and praise;
  But for those obstinate questionings
  Of sense and outward things,
  Fallings from us, vanishings;   145
  Blank misgivings of a Creature
Moving about in worlds not realized,°   *seeming real*
High instincts before which our mortal Nature
Did tremble like a guilty Thing surprised;
  But for those first affections,   150
  Those shadowy recollections,
  Which, be they what they may,
Are yet the fountain light of all our day,
Are yet a master light of all our seeing;
  Uphold us, cherish, and have power to make   155
Our noisy years seem moments in the being
Of the eternal Silence: truths that wake,
    To perish never;
Which neither listlessness, nor mad endeavor,
  Nor Man nor Boy,   160
Nor all that is at enmity with joy,
Can utterly abolish or destroy!
  Hence in a season of calm weather
  Though inland far we be,
Our Souls have sight of that immortal sea   165
  Which brought us hither,
  Can in a moment travel thither,
And see the Children sport upon the shore,
And hear the mighty waters rolling evermore.
     10
Then sing, ye Birds, sing, sing a joyous song!   170
  And let the young Lambs bound
  As to the tabor's sound!
We in thought will join your throng,
  Ye that pipe and ye that play,
  Ye that through your hearts today   175
  Feel the gladness of the May!
What though the radiance which was once so bright
Be now forever taken from my sight,
  Though nothing can bring back the hour
Of splendor in the grass, of glory in the flower;   180
  We will grieve not, rather find
  Strength in what remains behind;

In the primal sympathy
Which having been must ever be;
In the soothing thoughts that spring   185
Out of human suffering;
In the faith that looks through death,
In years that bring the philosophic mind.
                            11
And O, ye Fountains, Meadows, Hills, and Groves,
Forebode not any severing of our loves!   190
Yet in my heart of hearts I feel your might;
I only have relinquished one delight
To live beneath your more habitual sway.
I love the Brooks which down their channels fret,
Even more than when I tripped lightly as they;   195
The innocent brightness of a newborn Day
       Is lovely yet;
The clouds that gather round the setting sun
Do take a sober coloring from an eye
That hath kept watch o'er man's mortality;   200
Another race hath been, and other palms are won.
Thanks to the human heart by which we live,
Thanks to its tenderness, its joys, and fears,
To me the meanest flower that blows can give
Thoughts that do often lie too deep for tears.   205

QUESTIONS

1. In the first four stanzas of the ode the speaker realizes he has lost something. What did he once have? What has he lost? How do images drawn from nature show the speaker and us that he (rather than the world) has changed?

2. This first section (stanzas 1 through 4) ends with two questions. What are they? How do they relate to the speaker's changed perception of nature? How does the loss noted here relate to poetry and to the imagination?

3. In stanzas 5 and 6 the speaker provides one answer to his own questions by discussing the soul. What does he assert about the soul? What does the soul bring with it from its source? What happens to the soul as a person grows older?

4. How are stanzas 7 and 8 related to 5 and 6? What does the child in stanzas 7 and 8 exemplify? What warning does the speaker give the child?

5. In the last three stanzas the speaker offers an alternative answer to the problem of maturity and the loss of the "visionary gleam." What is this answer? What replaces the "gleam"?

6. To what extent can we experience the speaker's initial grief and ultimate consolation through the images and structure of the ode?

JOHN KEATS (1795–1821)

Ode on a Grecian Urn   *1820 (1819)*

1

Thou still unravish'd bride of quietness,
  Thou foster-child of silence and slow time,
Sylvan historian, who canst thus express
A flowery tale more sweetly than our rhyme:
What leaf-fring'd legend° haunts about thy shape   *border and tale*   5
  Of deities or mortals, or of both,
    In Tempe or the dales of Arcady?°
  What men or gods are these? What maidens loth?
What mad pursuit? What struggle to escape?
    What pipes and timbrels? What wild ecstasy?   10

2

Heard melodies are sweet, but those unheard
  Are sweeter; therefore, ye soft pipes, play on;
Not to the sensual ear, but, more endear'd,
  Pipe to the spirit ditties of no tone:
Fair youth, beneath the trees, thou canst not leave   15
  Thy song, nor ever can those trees be bare;
    Bold lover, never, never canst thou kiss,
Though winning near the goal—yet, do not grieve;
    She cannot fade, though thou hast not thy bliss,
  For ever wilt thou love, and she be fair!   20

3

Ah, happy, happy boughs! that cannot shed
  Your leaves, nor ever bid the spring adieu;
And, happy melodist, unwearied,
  For ever piping songs for ever new;
More happy love! more happy, happy love!   25
  For ever warm and still to be enjoy'd,
    For ever panting, and for ever young;
All breathing human passion far above,
  That leaves a heart high-sorrowful and cloy'd,
    A burning forehead, and a parching tongue.   30

4

Who are these coming to the sacrifice?
  To what green altar, O mysterious priest,
Lead'st thou that heifer lowing at the skies,

ODE ON A GRECIAN URN. The imaginary Grecian urn to which the poem is addressed combines design motifs from many different existing urns. This imaginary one is decorated with a border of leaves and trees, men (or gods) chasing women, a young musician sitting under a tree, lovers, and a priest and congregation leading a heifer to sacrifice.   7 *Tempe*: a beautiful rustic valley in Greece.   *Arcady*: refers to the valleys of Arcadia, a state in ancient Greece.

And all her silken flanks with garlands drest?
What little town by river or sea shore,   35
  Or mountain-built with peaceful citadel,
    Is emptied of this folk, this pious morn?
And, little town, thy streets for evermore
  Will silent be; and not a soul to tell
    Why thou art desolate, can e'er return.   40

                                5

O Attic shape! Fair attitude! with brede°   braid, pattern
  Of marble men and maidens overwrought,°   ornamented
With forest branches and the trodden weed;
  Thou, silent form, dost tease us out of thought
    As doth eternity: Cold Pastoral!   45
When old age shall this generation waste,
  Thou shalt remain, in midst of other woe
    Than ours, a friend to man, to whom thou say'st,
"Beauty is truth, truth beauty," —that is all
    Ye know on earth, and all ye need to know.   50

QUESTIONS

1. What is the dramatic situation of the poem? What is the speaker doing as
   he speaks the poem? What does the speaker see?

2. What does the speaker call the urn in the first stanza? What is suggested
   in these lines about the urn's relationship to time and change? To poetry?

3. What are "unheard melodies" (line 11) and "ditties of no tone" (line 14)?
   Why are these "sweeter" than songs heard by "the sensual ear" (line 13)?
   What central contrast is created through this comparison?

4. What do the trees on the urn, the musician "beneath the trees," and the
   lovers have in common? How are all three like "ditties of no tone"? How
   are all these things related to the real world of time and change?

5. What new image does the speaker see on the urn in the fourth stanza? What
   does he observe about the town? Where does this town exist?

6. What does this ode assert about the relationship of art (the urn, the poem)
   to time and change? To an absolute and unchanging ideal? To truth?

7. To what extent are the experience and meaning of this poem for us parallel
   to the experience and meaning of the urn for the speaker?

PHILIP LARKIN (b. 1922)

Next, Please   1955

Always too eager for the future, we
Pick up bad habits of expectancy.
Something is always approaching; every day
Till then we say,

hill

Watching from a bluff the tiny, clear,   5
Sparkling armada of promises draw near.   Metaphor
How slow they are! And how much time they waste,
Refusing to make haste!

Yet still they leave us holding wretched stalks   decapitated flowers
Of disappointment, for, though nothing balks   stops   10
Each big approach, leaning with brasswork prinked,   primped
Each rope distinct,

Flagged, and the figurehead with golden tits
Arching our way, it never anchors; it's
No sooner present than it turns to past.   Like time. It's never "then";   15
Right to the last   it's only an eternal now.

We think each one will heave to and unload   Optimistic to the end
All good into our lives, all we are owed   Life owes us happiness.
For waiting so devoutly and so long.
But we are wrong: 20

Only one ship is seeking us, a black-   Death
Sailed unfamiliar, towing at her back
A huge and birdless silence. In her wake
No waters breed or break.   Sterile, motionless.

QUESTIONS

1. What is the subject of the poem? The theme? What point does it make
    about time, expectation, human nature, and the way we live our lives?

2. Why does the speaker use the pronouns *we* and *us* throughout the poem;
    what do the speaker and listener(s) have in common?

3. What cliché does the extended metaphor that begins in the second stanza
    ironically revitalize and reverse? How does this metaphor make the total
    meaning of the poem clearer and more palpable?

4. How do elements such as meter, rhyme, and diction help create meaning?
    Consider, for example, the metrical variation in the fourth line of each stanza,
    rhyming pairs such as *waste–haste* and *wake–break*, or words such as *bluff* and
    armada.

5. Compare this poem to the three *carpe diem* poems in this chapter. To what
    extent is "Next, Please" a *carpe diem* poem?

DONALD JUSTICE (b. 1925)

On the Death of Friends in Childhood   *1960*

We shall not ever meet them bearded in heaven,
Nor sunning themselves among the bald of hell;
If anywhere, in the deserted schoolyard at twilight,

Forming a ring, perhaps, or joining hands
In games whose very names we have forgotten.   5
Come, memory, let us seek them there in the shadows.

QUESTIONS

1. What is the subject of this poem: the living, or the dead? How accurate is
   the title as a guide to subject and theme?
2. What point (if any) does this poem make about death? Time? Memory? The
   living?
3. How do imagery, diction, rhetoric and tone contribute to the total meaning
   of this poem? Consider phrases like "bearded in heaven" and "sunning themselves among the bald of hell." What is personified in the last line?
4. To what extent do you think the age of the reader controls her or his (your)
   response to this poem?

LINDA PASTAN (b. 1932)

Ethics   1980

In ethics class so many years ago
our teacher asked this question every fall:
if there were a fire in a museum
which would you save, a Rembrandt painting
or an old woman who hadn't many   5
years left anyhow? Restless on hard chairs
caring little for pictures or old age
we'd opt one year for life, the next for art
and always half-heartedly. Sometimes
the woman borrowed my grandmother's face   10
leaving her usual kitchen to wander
some drafty, half-imagined museum.
One year, feeling clever, I replied
why not let the woman decide herself?
Linda, the teacher would report, eschews   15
the burdens of responsibility.
This fall in a real museum I stand
before a real Rembrandt, old woman,
or nearly so, myself. The colors
within this frame are darker than autumn,   20
darker even than winter—the browns of earth,
though earth's most radiant elements burn
through the canvas. I know now that woman

and painting and season are almost one
and all beyond saving by children.   25

QUESTIONS

1. What can we surmise about the speaker in this poem? How does this knowledge contribute to our understanding of theme?

2. What are the two settings, situations, and actions presented here? How are they related? How much time has passed between them? How does the contrast between them help create meaning?

3. What question was asked "every fall" in the ethics class? What were the speaker's and her classmates' attitudes toward "pictures" and "old age" (line 7) in the past?

4. How has the passage of time changed the speaker's attitudes? What does she now realize about "woman / and painting and season" (lines 23–24)? About children?

5. What is the subject of this poem? The theme? What point does it make about art, life, time, and values?

6. How do you experience this poem? Do you identify more fully with the speaker as student or as adult? To what extent do you think the age of the reader controls his or her (your) experience of this poem?

SHARON OLDS (b. 1942)

35/10   *1984*

Brushing out my daughter's dark
silken hair before the mirror
I see the grey gleaming on my head,
the silver-haired servant behind her. Why is it
just as we begin to go   5
they begin to arrive, the fold in my neck
clarifying as the fine bones of her
hips sharpen? As my skin shows
its dry pitting, she opens like a small
pale flower on the tip of a cactus;   10
as my last chances to bear a child
are falling through my body, the duds among them,
her full purse of eggs, round and
firm as hard-boiled yolks, is about
to snap its clasp. I brush her tangled   15
fragrant hair at bedtime. It's an old
story—the oldest we have on our planet—
the story of replacement.

QUESTIONS

1. What is the speaker in this poem? What is she doing? What is the setting?
2. How does the speaker contrast her own state of being to her daughter's stage of life? How are images, metaphors, and similes used to clarify this contrast? How does this contrast help convey the poem's meaning?
3. What point does this poem make about life and nature? To what extent does the last sentence clarify (or overclarify) the poem's theme?
4. Does this poem create a palpable experience? Do you identify more fully with the speaker or the daughter? To what extent does the age of the reader control his or her (your) experience of this poem?

WRITING ABOUT THEME AND MEANING IN POETRY

When you set out to write an essay about the meaning of a poem, you will be dealing with three related topics: (1) what the poem says, (2) the way the poem says it, and (3) the experience the poem creates. The prewriting process for such an essay includes a period of reading and studying, developing your initial ideas about the poem, testing those ideas against the poem itself, formulating a tentative thesis for the essay, and organizing your observations about the poem into coherent units. The first step is to choose a poem. Sometimes the poem will be assigned. If the choice is left up to you, however, select a poem that you like and that has meaning for you. Planning and writing this kind of essay will be considerably more rewarding if you work with a poem to which you have a strong positive reaction.

Once the poem is chosen or assigned, you should move through the process of study and discovery about theme and meaning outlined earlier in this chapter (pp. 841–44). At the beginning of your study, you should deal with three basic questions: (1) What is the poem's subject? (2) What is the poem's theme? (3) What aspects of the poem contribute most significantly to the creation of meaning? In other words, you will deal with *what* the theme is and *how* it is created. The answers to these questions will almost always become parts of the finished essay. More important, they will help you considerably in the planning stage to formulate a tentative central idea and to organize your support for this idea.

The *what* and *how* of a poem are finally inseparable; the way a poem tells us and shows us what it means are parts of its total meaning. In planning an essay, you can temporarily separate the poem's theme from the way that theme is conveyed. In writing, however, you will have to bring them back together. Thus, the essay will ultimately connect the poem's theme and meaning to some other poetic elements, such as speaker, imagery, metaphor, symbol, or tone. In the prewriting stage it is essential to consider the relationship between meaning and all the other elements of poetry. The following questions may be helpful in planning the focus and finding the information necessary for such an essay: N̲o̲t̲e̲ ;

1. What does the title of the poem tell you about subject and meaning?
2. What can you discover about the speaker? How does the speaker shape and communicate theme?
3. How do the other characters in the poem (if any) affect theme and meaning?
4. What impact do setting, situation, and action have on theme?
5. How does diction affect theme? How are multiple denotations and connotations employed? To what extent are special types of diction or word order used?
6. How do imagery, metaphor, simile, and other rhetorical devices help determine the impact and theme of the poem? To what extent do they particularize the ideas and events of the poem to create a palpable experience?
7. What is the poem's tone? What effect does tone have on theme?
8. What role do rhythm, meter, sound, and rhyme play (if any) in shaping and emphasizing the theme and total meaning of the poem?
9. How does the form of the poem help shape its theme and your response?
10. How are symbol, allusion, or myth used to create the poem's theme and impact?

You will find poems for which all these questions are relevant; some poets employ every element and device in the poetic repertoire to create meaning and impact. Other poems will offer useful information in only a few of these areas. Whatever you discover about the poem at hand, you cannot deal with all these variables in one paper; the resultant essay would be too unwieldy and fragmented. Instead, you should look for those few elements that have the most profound impact on the poem's theme and on your ability to experience the poetic moment. These will become the secondary focuses of the essay.

Once you have substantial information about the poem in your notes, you can formulate a tentative central idea and a thesis statement. In most instances, this "working" idea will restate what you consider to be the theme of the poem. Be careful at this stage, however, to distinguish between subject and theme. In planning an essay about "Ars Poetica," for example, one might come up with the following idea: "Archibald MacLeish's 'Ars Poetica' makes a clear assertion about the nature and meaning of poetry." This statement announces the *subject* of the poem; it might, in fact, be a good sentence to begin an essay. It is not, however, an adequate formulation of a central idea for an essay since it tells the reader nothing about the poem's theme or meaning. A better central idea for such an essay might be, "Archibald MacLeish's 'Ars Poetica' asserts that the value and meaning of a poem are found in the 'wordless' and 'timeless' experience it creates."

for the reader." This sentence summarizes the theme of the poem and makes a strong assertion on which to build an effective paper.

Forming a tentative central idea for your essay is half the battle; now you can focus on the relationship between this idea and the ways in which the poem creates meaning for you. At this stage you can utilize the information gained from asking the ten questions listed above. You can begin to forge the link between the meaning and the methods of the poem, and you can begin to plan the organization of the entire essay. Thus, if you find that the theme of a poem is established through symbol and allusion, your initial plan for the essay and the thesis statement should express this connection by relating meaning to these elements. Similarly, a general sense of organization begins to emerge that divides the essay into three areas of concern: (1) theme, (2) theme and symbol, (3) theme and allusion. In MacLeish's poem, for example, some readers might conclude that meaning is most effectively articulated through direct statement, simile, and symbolism. Thus, an initial plan for the essay's scope and direction might combine these conclusions with the central idea as follows: "Archibald MacLeish's 'Ars Poetica' conveys these ideas about the nature of poetry through direct statement and illustrates them through simile and symbolism."

The scope and focus of the essay are now taking shape. Your notes contain three tentative formulations: one on subject, one on theme, and one linking theme to other poetic elements. These three sentences comprise not only a plan for the whole essay but also the raw materials for the first draft of the introductory paragraph. As illustrations, here are three statements about Archibald MacLeish's "Ars Poetica."

1. "Archibald MacLeish's 'Ars Poetica' makes a clear assertion about the nature and meaning of poetry."

2. "Archibald MacLeish's 'Ars Poetica' asserts that the value and meaning of a poem are found in the 'wordless' and 'timeless' experience that it creates for the reader."

3. "Archibald MacLeish's 'Ars Poetica' conveys these ideas about the nature of poetry through direct statement and illustrates them through simile and symbolism."

Each of these sentences does a specific job that is useful in planning and writing an essay. The first establishes the poem's subject. The second states what the reader/writer has determined to be the poem's theme; this is the central idea of the essay. The third makes the crucial connection between the poem's theme and the ways that the reader/writer feels it is created in the poem; this sentence thus becomes both a thesis statement and an initial plan for the body of the essay. The three statements cannot serve as an opening paragraph without a great deal of revision because there is too much repetition and too little connection. Nevertheless, they represent the major goals of the prewriting process; they provide a focus and direction for planning the essay.

The remainder of your planning can be given over to organizing your observations about the poem into coherent units that support the central idea and that will eventually become paragraphs in the essay. At this stage, however, you can reexamine the poem and your data to make sure your central idea and the supporting evidence hang together and are consistently relevant to the poem's meaning. As with other essays, this final stage of prewriting affords another opportunity to revise and fine-tune your central idea and tentative organization. Such revision, as we have noted frequently, is a crucial and valuable part of both the prewriting and writing processes.

Organizing Your Essay [Note carefully]

INTRODUCTION. As with most other essays discussed in this text, we recommend a traditional three-part organization that includes an introduction, a supporting body, and a conclusion. In the introduction, make any general points about the poem that seem relevant to the essay. If the poem under consideration was written by a British soldier in 1917, for example, you might want to establish its context in World War I. In any event, the introduction should make four specific statements: (1) announce [Note] the author and title of the poem, (2) state what you consider to be the poem's subject, (3) establish the central idea of the essay and what you feel to be the theme of the poem, and (4) briefly enumerate the ways in which the body of the essay will support the assertion made in the introduction. In other words, the first paragraph should tell your reader what the essay is going to prove about the poem and how it is going to do it. The introduction thus becomes a plan for *writing* and *reading* the whole essay.

BODY. The basic function of the body is to support the assertion, made in the introduction, concerning the ways in which the poem creates meaning for you. The body is thus crafted out of the coherent units of information gained during the prewriting process. The most significant of these units are formed into supporting paragraphs that show how the poem articulates its theme and creates an effective poetic experience for the reader.

Various methods of organization can be employed. In general, the organization is determined by your own observations about the most significant and effective ways in which the poem creates meaning for you. You may have discovered, for example, that the poem conveys meaning mostly through direct statement. Under such circumstances, the organization of the essay might reflect the line-by-line or sentence-by-sentence structure of the poem itself. In other cases, you might find that the logic (or pseudo-logic) of the speaker's argument most effectively creates meaning; such might be the case if you were writing about Marvell's "To His Coy Mistress." Such an essay may be organized to reflect the speaker's apparent logic. In some cases, you might decide that the meaning and impact hinge on the poet's extended use of a single element or device. In this situation, the organization might reflect the ways this element works and develops throughout the poem. Frequently, you will find that three or four different poetic elements work together to shape a poem's theme and impact. In these instances, the structure of the essay can be based on a sequential discussion of each element's contribution to meaning. Each poem offers its own particular methods and moments of experience that will control the shape of the essay. The four structural patterns noted above can be modified and combined. You should always be prepared to adjust whatever plan you choose to accommodate the specific poem under consideration.

Since the thesis statement in the introduction provides a brief outline for the body of the essay, you will usually have settled on a general structure before you actually begin to write. As you draft the body of the essay, however, you may find that particular subjects or elements are less or more important than you had originally thought. When this happens, you can re-think the shape of the whole essay and revise the introduction accordingly.

CONCLUSION.   In the conclusion, you have the opportunity to pull all the strands of the essay back together and to reaffirm the connection between the poem's method and meaning. This can often be done through a summary of the major points in the essay. The conclusion is also the place where you can consider additional aspects of the poem's theme and impact. The ideas and experiences created when you read a poem often point beyond themselves to other ideas or implications. Similarly, you might want to consider the extent to which your own circumstances (such as age, sex, race, or religion) help determine the meaning and impact that the poem has for you. However you conclude the essay, make sure that the end is as strong and assertive as the beginning.

SAMPLE ESSAY

Metaphor and Meaning in Philip Larkin's "Next, Please"*

[1]   Philip Larkin's "Next, Please" deals with the human tendency to live for the future rather than the present. The lyric poem establishes its subject through the title and the direct statements of the first stanza. Ultimately, the poem asserts that our habits of passive anticipation and expectation always lead to disappointment and death.° This theme is conveyed through the single extended metaphor

---

* See p. 860 for this poem.
° Central idea.

of an "armada of promises" that begins in the second stanza and runs throughout the rest of the poem; within the metaphor, diction and meter reinforce
the meaning of the poem and the moment of human experience that it creates.[°] ⟧ Thesis

[2] The poem announces its subject and begins to develop its theme through
the title and the direct statements of the first stanza. The title refers to the human desire to move on, look ahead, and get on to the next item; it suggests
a continual movement from person to person or moment to moment. These
implications are brought into focus in the first stanza, where the speaker notes
that we are "Always too eager for the future" and that "we / Pick up bad [Note]
habits of expectancy" (lines 1–2). For most of us, life's goodness is in the
future rather than the present: "Something is always approaching" (line 3).
Our habitual focus on the promise of the future is captured in the speaker's
observation that "every day / Till then we say" (lines 3–4). By using the pronouns
we and us here and throughout, the speaker implies that all of us, including
himself, habitually indulge in such wishful thinking.

[3] To this point, the speaker has isolated a specific human characteristic—
our habitual anticipation that wonderful things are "just around the corner."
Beginning in the second stanza, however, the poem asserts that these "bad
habits of expectancy" will always leave us disappointed. The poem makes
this point through an extended metaphor that is based on a hidden cliché
which embodies our habits of wishful thinking: "someday my ship will come
in." The cliché expresses the common belief that we will get everything we
want or deserve "someday" in the future. Larkin's metaphor, however, shows
us that the cliché is wrong; it draws out the cliché into a dramatic experience
to suggest that our hopes for the future inevitably lead to failure and death.

[4] The extended metaphor creates meaning by placing us in a dramatic ⟧ Quoting
situation that we can experience. We are "Watching from a bluff" as the "tiny,
clear, / Sparkling armada of promises draw near" (lines 5–6). Our ship has
become an entire fleet. Even at this early point in the development of the conceit,
however, the diction begins to undercut the cliché and our habit of expectation.
We are watching from a bluff rather than a cliff; a bluff is a hill, but it is also
an attempt to mislead or deceive through false confidence. The word thus
suggests that our hopes for the future stand on self-deception and false confidence. Armada is similarly loaded. For British and American readers, the term
evokes the memory of a specific Spanish fleet that sailed against England in
1588 and was destroyed by sea battles and storms. Overtones of failure and [Analyzes]
destruction are thus built into the metaphor from its very beginning. makes the
connection

[5] The metaphor makes the poem's meaning vivid and immediate through
a wealth of detail. We notice that the "armada of promises" moves very slowly:
"How slow they are! And how much time they waste, / Refusing to make
haste" (lines 7–8). As the metaphor is extended, more and more details are
brought to our attention; we see progressively more of each ship as the speaker
mentions the shining "brasswork," "Each rope distinct," the flag, and "the
figurehead with golden tits / Arching our way" (lines 11–14). Through such
details, the metaphor suggests that the fleet draws ever closer. Even as we
experience this approach, however, the failure of such promise is also established: "Yet still they leave us holding wretched stalks / Of disappointment"

[°] Thesis sentence.

(lines 9–10). This image—within the metaphor—leaves us standing on the "bluff" holding decapitated flowers and hopes; disappointment is again implied even in the approach of the armada.

[6] This disappointment is brought into explicit focus as the "armada" conceit continues in the fourth stanza. We see that the fleet "never anchors"; "it's / No sooner present than it turns to past" (lines 14–15). Most of these words carry double meanings. It, for example, refers to both the ships and time. Turns to indicates both a change of course and the inevitable transformation of the present into the past. Similarly, present and past signify both the physical status of the ships and the movement of time. The metaphor thus conveys the experience of disappointment both in terms of the "armada of promises" and the time we waste passively waiting for the future to reward us.

[7] The last two stanzas of "Next, Please" conclude the armada metaphor and expand on the theme of inevitable disappointment. The fifth stanza summarizes the development of the metaphor and so the entire poem; the speaker observes that we always expect one of these ships to "heave to" and to deliver "All good into our lives" (line 18). The last line of the stanza, however, completely undercuts all hope. Here, we sense the full impact of a metrical technique that Larkin has employed throughout. The poem is predominantly in iambic pentameter, but the fourth line of each stanza is cut short to two or three feet. This metrical falling-off creates a sound parallel to the feeling of disappointment; like the "armada" and the future, each stanza fails to deliver what we expect. The force of this device strikes us at the close of the fifth stanza, when the final two-beat line bleakly tells us, "But we are wrong" (line 20). The metaphor and the falling meter make it clear that our ship will never "heave to" and deliver. There is, however, "one ship" that "is seeking us" (line 21). It is not a ship full of good things; instead, it is a "black- / Sailed unfamiliar" ship "towing at her back / A huge and birdless silence" (lines 22–23). This is the only ship that will come in for us if we passively await the future—the ship of death.

[8] "Next, Please" thus tells us that a life spent in passive expectation and hope for the future will offer only disappointment and death. The poem lets us experience this meaning through an extended metaphor in which an "armada of promises" approaches and then leaves without yielding anything but disappointment. The meaning of the poem becomes our movement through the metaphor, and our experience of the metaphor is ultimately disappointment and a vision of inevitable death. At the same time, the poem implies that we should stop living lives of false expectation dedicated to the future. Instead, we should live in and for the present, making the most of what we have. To this extent, "Next, Please" may be considered a *carpe diem* poem; it suggests that we should "seize" today rather than hope for tomorrow.

Commentary on the Essay

The essay illustrates the need to combine and adjust abstract strategies of organization when you are dealing with a specific poem; it combines a focus on a specific poetic element (metaphor) with secondary interest in two other elements (diction and meter). The essay thus represents a modification and combination of the third and fourth organizational plans noted earlier (pp. 867–68). Basically, however, it traces the development of theme and meaning through the progressive stages of a dominant and central metaphor.

The introduction conveys a great deal of information and lays out a plan for the entire essay. The first sentence announces author, title, and subject. The second briefly explains how the poem establishes its subject; this material is expanded in the second paragraph. The third sentence contains both the central idea of the essay and a summary of the poem's theme. The fourth sentence makes the connection between *what* the poem says and *how* it says it. The paragraph thus promises that the essay will deal with the way metaphor, diction, and meter combine to create meaning.

Paragraph 2 deals primarily with the subject of the poem; it grows directly out of the first two sentences of the introduction. This discussion is essential because it provides the foundation for the essay's subsequent treatment of theme and meaning.

Paragraphs 3 through 7 develop out of the last two sentences of the introduction; they treat the connection between metaphor and meaning, and they take up the secondary subjects of diction and meter. Paragraph 3 provides transition from subject to theme, introduces the dominant metaphor, and explains the hidden cliché on which the metaphor is based. Paragraph 4 examines the way that the "armada" metaphor begins to create a palpable experience and how diction immediately begins to undercut the promise of the future. The first sentence of this paragraph links it both to the introduction and to the previous paragraph through its reference to metaphor and meaning.

Paragraph 5 sustains the focus on the link between metaphor and meaning through attention to the details that the speaker mentions in the second, third, and fourth stanzas of the poem. Again, the first sentence connects this paragraph to both the introduction and the previous paragraph. Similarly, the concluding sentence leads into paragraph 6, which takes up the next stage of the extended metaphor and the articulation of disappointment. This focus on the end of the conceit and on the experience of disappointment is continued in paragraph 7, which explores the poem's assertion that if we wait passively, only death will arrive. Here, the essay also deals with the impact of meter on meaning.

The concluding paragraph begins by repeating the poem's theme; it thus links the end of the essay to the introduction. The next two sentences similarly reiterate the connection between this theme and the extended metaphor that makes it palpable; they summarize the material in paragraphs 3 through 7. Finally, the conclusion considers the implications of the poem's meaning, offers a second and implied theme for the poem, and connects "Next, Please" to a longstanding poetic tradition.

26

Poetic Careers: The Work of Three Poets

We have now looked at poetry in terms of its elements and effects; at this point it is useful for us to consider a collection of poems by a single author. Three popular poets have been chosen: John Donne (1572–1631), Emily Dickinson (1830–1886), and Robert Frost (1874–1963). Donne, one of the most important English poets of the seventeenth century, developed what we call the *metaphysical* (or philosophical) style. Emily Dickinson and Robert Frost are both American poets and New Englanders; Dickinson is considered a significant formative influence on American poetry, and Frost represents one of the dominant poetic voices of twentieth-century America. While the poems included here cannot present full pictures of poetic careers, they do provide an opportunity to read and consider extended collections of verse by individual poets. We have chosen poems that illustrate the central concerns and major characteristics of each poet's work. Thus, the material provides an opportunity to look for common themes and techniques or for sudden shifts of concern within a poet's career.

JOHN DONNE

Traditionally, scholars have argued that John Donne had two poetic careers, one as a love poet and satirist in his youth and another as a religious poet after he became an Anglican priest in 1615. Such a clear division cannot be maintained, however, since Donne wrote a great deal of religious verse before 1615, and very little poetry at all after that year. Donne's poetry does fall into two broad categories, love poetry and religious verse, but his style remains constant.

Donne was born to a Roman Catholic family in a newly Protestant land; religion thus had a significant impact on his life even before he took holy orders. Although he attended both Oxford and Cambridge universities between 1584 and 1590, his Catholicism barred him from receiving degrees. In 1591 Donne moved to London and enrolled at the law school at Lincoln's Inn, where he studied science, philosophy, law, languages, and literature. All these subjects (and more) were worked into his poetry. During these years Donne had a reputation as a wit and a ladies' man; he wrote many of the love poems and satires and circulated them among his friends (very little of his poetry was published until 1633).

In 1593 Donne converted to Anglicanism (the official state religion in England) and began to rise in aristocratic circles. He became private secretary to Sir Thomas Egerton (an important court official) in 1598 and was on the verge of a brilliant career when he eloped (in 1601) with Egerton's sixteen-year-old niece, Anne More. This destroyed his chances for advancement; the girl's father had Donne dismissed from court, had him jailed, and barred his further employment. Donne spent the next fourteen years writing poetry, eking out a meager living at various jobs, and desperately seeking royal employment. King James I (reigned 1603–1625) was sympathetic, but he refused to help Donne, believing that Donne's proper place was as a priest in the Anglican Church.

Donne finally gave in to this inevitability; in 1615 he took holy orders and began a meteoric rise in the church. In 1621 he was appointed dean of St. Paul's Cathedral in London, the most fashionable church in seventeenth-century England. He became a famous preacher—over 130 of his sermons were published—and the noble and wealthy flocked to his services. Donne remained a powerful speaker and poet up to his death in May 1631; he previewed his own funeral sermon before the king on February 25, 1631, and supposedly wrote his last poem eight days before his death.

Donne's poetry is commonly termed *metaphysical*, a word used to describe poetry that is highly intellectual and characterized by complexity, subtlety and elaborate imagery. The label was first used scornfully by John Dryden (1631–1700), who asserted in *A Discourse Concerning the Original and Progress of Satire* (1693) that Donne's love poetry "affects the metaphysics" and "perplexes the minds of the fair sex with nice [careful] speculations of philosophy." Although Dryden originally employed the term to condemn Donne's work, it has come to signify both the style of his verse and a "school" of poetry.

In *poetic style*, Donne's poetry represents a radical departure from earlier Elizabethan verse. He rebelled against the smooth rhythms, flowery language, and conventional imagery of the sixteenth century. His poems are characterized by abrupt beginnings, dramatic shifts in tone, irregular rhythms, puns, paradoxes, and rigorous logic. Their major characteristic, however, is the *metaphysical conceit*. A **conceit** is an elaborate metaphor, and a **metaphysical conceit** is an extended comparison that links two unrelated fields or subjects in a surprising or shocking conjunction of ideas. In "A Valediction: Forbidding Mourning" (p. 599), for example, Donne compares two lovers to the two legs of a drawing compass. Above all else, Donne's poems illustrate *wit*, the ability to advance a complex or even outrageous argument through subtle logic, bizarre analogy, and diverse allusion.

In terms of *diction and language*, Donne's verse is equally unconventional. The poems include a great deal of harsh language and numerous terms borrowed from various fields of learning, including alchemy, law, theology, philosophy, and geography. The characteristic *poetic forms* for both the love poetry and the religious verse include the lyric and the sonnet (see pp. 743–45). The stanzaic structure of Donne's lyrics tends to be highly inventive, with varying line lengths and complex rhyme schemes.

Donne's love poetry, written mostly between 1590 and 1615, established the metaphysical style. These poems are ingenious, often outrageous, and overflowing with images and allusions. Taken as a group, they suggest that passion is both wonderful and dangerous and that love is a mystery much like religion. They also imply that lovers can and should be self-sufficient and separate from the public world.

The religious verse maintains the characteristics of the love poetry but shifts the ground from human passion to divine love. In the Holy Sonnets, for instance, Donne uses a traditional poetic form normally associated with love poetry and considers human sin and divine grace. In these poems Donne often employs the techniques of religious meditation, focusing at first on a specific time or event and then considering the meaning of that event in connection with his own spiritual state. In "At the Round Earth's Imagined Corners" (p. 883), for example, Donne begins with a vivid meditation on the moment of the Last Judgment. The Hymns, like the Holy Sonnets, maintain the metaphysical style and deal with spiritual matters. The "Hymn to God the Father" (p. 884), for instance, plays repeatedly with a pun on Donne's name. Similarly, the "Hymn to God My God, In My Sickness," supposedly written eight days before Donne died in May 1631, is full of puns, paradoxes, convoluted logic, and metaphysical conceits.

John Donne's poetry received little attention from the seventeenth century until the beginning of the twentieth. Although an awareness of Donne's work was growing in the late 1800s, two events in the twentieth century dramatically rekindled interest in his poetry. One was the publication of Sir Herbert Grierson's complete edition of *The Poems of John Donne* (1912) and the other was T. S. Eliot's spirited defense of Donne and metaphysical poetry (see, for example, Eliot's essay, "The Metaphysical Poets," published in 1921 and reprinted in 1960 in his *Selected Essays*). Although Donne's verse may have seemed unpoetic and overly complex to earlier generations, it appeals with great strength to the sensibilities of the contemporary world. More recent editions of Donne's work include Helen Gardner's edition of *The Divine Poems* (1952) and of *The Elegies and the Songs and Sonnets* (1965). Significant critical discussions of Donne's work may be found in Cleanth Brooks, *The Well-Wrought Urn* (1932), Helen White, *The Metaphysical Poets* (1936), J. B. Leishman, *The Monarch of Wit* (1951), Louis L. Martz, *The Poetry of Meditation* (1954), Richard E. Hughes, *The Progress of the Soul* (1968), and John Carey, *John Donne: Life, Mind and Art* (1981). Additional poems by John Donne may be found in this text on pp. 556, 599, and 724.

The Good Morrow   1633

I wonder, by my troth, what thou and I
Did, till we loved! Were we not weaned till then,
But sucked on country pleasures, childishly?
Or snorted we in the seven sleepers' den?°
T'was so; But this, all pleasures fancies be.   5
If ever any beauty I did see,
Which I desired, and got, t'was but a dream of thee.

And now good morrow to our waking souls,
Which watch not one another out of fear;
For love all love of other sights controls,   10
And makes one little room an everywhere.
Let sea-discoverers to new worlds have gone,
Let maps to other,° worlds on worlds have shown,
Let us possess one world; each hath one, and is one.

My face in thine eye, thine in mine appears,°   15
And true plain hearts do in the faces rest;
Where can we find two better hemispheres
Without sharp North, without declining West?
Whatever dies was not mixed equally;°
If our two loves be one, or thou and I   20
Love so alike that none do slacken, none can die.

THE GOOD MORROW.   4 *seven sleepers' den*: a reference to the miracle of the seven Christian youths who took shelter in a cave to avoid religious persecution by the Emperor Decius (ca. A.D. 250) and were sealed inside. The young men supposedly slept for about 185 years and emerged in perfect health during the reign of Theodosius II (ca. A.D. 435).   13 *other*: others, that is, other discoverers.   15 *My face . . . appears*: each face is reflected in the pupils of the other lover's eyes.   19 *Whatever . . . equally*: Scholastic philosophy argues that elements that are either perfectly balanced or united will never change or decay; hence, such a mixture cannot die.

Song
1633

Go and catch a falling star,
  Get with child a mandrake root,°
Tell me where all past years are,
  Or who cleft the Devil's foot,
Teach me to hear mermaids singing,   5
  Or to keep off envy's stinging,
        And find
        What wind
Serves to advance an honest mind.

If thou beest born to strange sights,   10
  Things invisible to see,
Ride ten thousand days and nights,
  Till age snow white hairs on thee,
Thou, when thou return'st, wilt tell me
All strange wonders that befell thee,   15
        And swear
        Nowhere
Lives a woman true, and fair.

If thou findst one, let me know,
  Such a pilgrimage were sweet;   20
Yet do not, I would not go,
  Though at next door we might meet;
Though she were true when you met her,
And last till you write your letter,
        Yet she   25
        Will be
False, ere I come, to two, or three.

SONG.   2 *mandrake root*: the mandrake, or mandragora, is a European narcotic herb once considered an aphrodisiac. The fleshy, forked root was thought to resemble the human form. To impregnate such a root, of course, is impossible.

The Sun Rising
1633

    Busy old fool, unruly sun,
      Why dost thou thus,
Through windows and through curtains call on us?
Must to thy motions lovers' seasons run?
    Saucy pedantic wretch, go chide   5
    Late school boys and sour prentices,°   *apprentices*
  To tell court huntsmen that the King will ride,
Call country ants to harvest offices; °   *duties*

Love, all alike, no season knows nor clime,
Nor hours, days, months, which are the rags of time.   10

    Thy beams, so reverend and strong
    Why shouldst thou think?
I could eclipse and cloud them with a wink,
But that I would not lose her sight so long;
    If her eyes have not blinded thine,   15
    Look, and tomorrow late, tell me,
Whether both the Indias of spice and mine°
Be where thou leftst them, or lie here with me.
Ask for those kings whom thou saw'st yesterday,
And thou shalt hear, All here in one bed lay.   20

    She is all states, and all princes, I,
    Nothing else is.
Princes do but play us; compared to this,
All honor's mimic, all wealth alchemy.°   *counterfeit*
    Thou, sun, art half as happy as we,   25
    In that the world's contracted thus;
    Thine age asks ease, and since thy duties be
To warm the world, that's done in warming us.
Shine here to us, and thou art everywhere;
This bed thy center° is, these walls, thy sphere.   30

THE SUN RISING.　　17 *Indias of spice and mine*: the India of "spice" is East India or the
East Indies; the India of "mine" or gold is the West Indies.　　30 *center*: the central point
of the sun's orbit.

The Canonization   *1633*

For God's sake hold your tongue,° and let me love,
    Or chide my palsy, or my gout,
My five gray hairs, or ruined fortune, flout,
    With wealth your state, your mind with arts improve,
      Take you a course,° get you a place,°   5
      Observe His Honor, or His Grace,
Or the King's real, or his stamped face°
      Contemplate,—what you will, approve,°   *test, try*
      So you will let me love.

Alas, alas, who's injured by my love?   10
    What merchant's ships have my sighs drowned?
Who says my tears have overflowed his ground?

THE CANONIZATION.　　1 *your tongue*: "your" refers to either the public world in general
or a specific but unheard critic who attacks the speaker's love.　　5 *course*: a course of
action.　　*place*: office or position, probably at court.　　7 *stamped face*: the king's portrait
on coins.

When did my colds a forward spring remove?
   When did the heats which my veins fill
   Add one more to the plaguy bill?°   15
Soldiers find wars, and lawyers find out still
   Litigious men, which quarrels move,
   Though she and I do love.

Call us what you will, we are made such by love;
   Call her one, me another fly,   20
We're tapers too, and at our own cost die,°
   And we in us find the eagle and the dove.°
     The phoenix riddle° hath more wit
     By us,—we two being one, are it.
So, to one neutral thing both sexes fit.   25
   We die and rise the same, and prove
   Mysterious by this love.

We can die by it, if not live by love,
   And if unfit for tombs and hearse
Our legend be, it will be fit for verse;   30
   And if no piece of chronicle we prove,
     We'll build in sonnets pretty rooms;
     As well a well-wrought urn becomes°   *befits, suits*
The greatest ashes, as half-acre tombs,
   And by these hymns, all shall approve°   35
   Us canonized for love:

And thus invoke us: "You whom reverend love
   Made one another's hermitage;
You, to whom love was peace, that now is rage;
   Who did the whole world's soul contract, and drove   40
     Into the glasses of your eyes
     (So made such mirrors, and such spies,
That they did all to you epitomize)
   Countries, towns, courts: Beg from above
   A pattern of your love!"°   45

---

15 *plaguy bill*: a weekly list of people who have died from the plague.   20–21 *fly . . . die*: both flies and candles are symbols of the brevity of life. Since the word *die* was a common euphemism in the seventeenth century for sexual orgasm, the line suggests that each sex act shortens the lovers' lives.   22 *eagle and the dove*: proverbial symbols of male strength and female mildness.   23 *phoenix riddle*: the riddle of the phoenix's perpetuation; the phoenix is a mythological Arabian bird—only one exists at a time—that lives for a thousand years and then burns itself to ashes on a funeral pyre. The new phoenix then miraculously rises from the ashes of the old. The phoenix thus symbolizes immortality, death and resurrection, and the rekindling of sexual desire.   35 *hymns . . . approve*: the hymns refer to the speaker's poetry and this poem in particular. The idea is that succeeding generations will confirm ("approve") the sainthood of the lovers in a new religion of love because of this poem.   37–45 "*You . . . love*": these lines are spoken by lovers in succeeding generations who are praying to the lover-saints that the speaker and his beloved have become. Hence, the *You* (line 37) refers to the speaker and his mistress.

A Fever   *1633*

Oh do not die, for I shall hate
    All women so, when thou art gone,
That thee I shall not celebrate,°   *mourn*
    When I remember, thou wast one.

But yet thou canst not die, I know;   5
    To leave this world behind, is death;
But when thou from this world wilt go,
    The whole world vapours° with thy breath.   *evaporates*

Or if, when thou, the world's soul, goest,
    It stay, 'tis but thy carcase then;   10
The fairest woman, but thy ghost,
    But corrupt worms, the worthiest men.

O wrangling schools,° that search what fire
    Shall burn this world, had none the wit
Unto this knowledge to aspire,   15
    That this her fever might be it?

And yet she cannot waste by this,
    Nor long bear this torturing wrong,
For much corruption needful is,
    To fuel such a fever long.°   *for long*   20

These burning fits but meteors be,
    Whose matter in thee is soon spent:
Thy beauty, and all parts which are thee,
    Are unchangeable firmament.°

Yet 'twas of my mind, seizing thee,   25
    Though it in thee cannot persever:°   *persist*
For I had rather owner be
    Of thee one hour, than all else ever.

A FEVER.   13 *wrangling schools*: competing sects of pagan and Christian philosophy that
debated what sort of fire would ultimately destroy the world.   24 *firmament*: the vault of
heaven and the stars.

The Flea   *1633*

Mark° but this flea, and mark in this,   *note, look at*
How little that which thou deniest me is;
It sucked me first, and now sucks thee,
And in this flea our two bloods mingled be;
Thou know'st that this cannot be said°   *called*   5
A sin, nor shame, nor loss of maidenhead,
    Yet this enjoys before it woo,°   *marry*

And pampered swells with one blood made of two,°
And this, alas, is more than we would do.

Oh stay, three lives in one flea spare,   1◐
Where we almost, yea more than married, are.
This flea is you and I, and this
Our marriage bed and marriage temple is;
Though parents grudge, and you,° w'are met,
And cloister'd in these living walls of jet,   1▮
  Though use° make you apt to kill me   *custom*
  Let not to that, self-murder added be,
  And sacrilege, three sins in killing three.

Cruel and sudden, hast thou since
Purpled thy nail, in blood of innocence?°
Wherein could this flea guilty be,   2◐
Except in that drop which it sucked from thee?
Yet thou triumph'st, and say'st that thou
Find'st not thy self nor me the weaker now;
  'Tis true, then learn how false fears be;   25
  Just so much honor, when thou yield'st to me,
  Will waste, as this flea's death took life from thee.

THE FLEA.   8 *two*: the flea has bitten both the speaker and the lady and thus mingles
their blood; the image also suggests pregnancy.   14 *you*: you [the lady] also "grudge" or
resent the idea of premarital sex.   20 *innocence*: a possible allusion to Herod's slaughter
of the innocents (Matthew 2:16).

The Bait   *1633*

Come live with me, and be my love,
And we will some new pleasures prove,
Of golden sands, and crystal brooks,
With silken lines, and silver hooks.

There will the river whispering run,   5▮
Warmed by thy eyes, more than the sun.
And there the enamored fish will stay,
Begging° themselves they may betray.   *begging that*

When thou wilt swim in that live bath,°   *with fish*
Each fish, which every channel hath,   10▮
Will amorously to thee swim,
Gladder to catch thee, than thou him.

THE BAIT. The poem is a reply to Marlowe's "The Passionate Shepherd to His Love" (p.
484).

If thou, to be so seen,° be'st loath   *naked*
By sun, or moon, thou dark'nest both,
And if myself have leave to see,   15
I need not their light, having thee.

Let others freeze with angling reeds,°   *rods*
And cut their legs with shells and weeds,
Or treacherously poor fish beset,
With strangling snare or windowy net: 20

Let coarse bold hands, from slimy nest
The bedded fish in banks out-wrest,
Or curious traitors, sleave-silk flies,°
Bewitch poor fishes' wand'ring eyes.

For thee, thou need'st no such deceit,   25
For thou thyself art thine own bait;
That fish that is not catched thereby,
Alas, is wiser far than I.

23 *sleave-silk flies*: fishing flies made out of unraveled silk threads.

The Relic   *1633*

    When my grave is broke up again
    Some second guest to entertain,°
    (For graves have learned that woman-head°
    To be to more than one a bed),
        And he that digs it, spies   5
A bracelet of bright hair° about the bone,
        Will he not let us alone,
And think that there a loving couple lies,
Who thought that this device might be some way
To make their souls, at the last busy day,°   *Judgment Day*   10
Meet at this grave, and make a little stay?

    If this fall° in a time, or land,   *occur*
    Where mis-devotion° doth command,
    Then he that digs us up, will bring
    Us to the Bishop and the King,   15
        So make us relics; then

THE RELIC.   1-2 *grave . . . entertain*: in the seventeenth century, old graves were
commonly dug up and the bones removed to provide new burial places.   3 *woman-head*:
female characteristic, with a pun on "maidenhead."   6 *hair*: bracelets woven of one's
mistress's hair were common gifts of love.   13 *mis-devotion*: superstition or idolatry, with
a possible allusion to the Roman Catholic Church.

Thou shalt be a Mary Magdalen,° and I
    A something else° thereby;
All women shall adore us, and some men;
And since at such time, miracles are sought,   2*
I would have that age by this paper° taught   *this poem*
What miracles we harmless lovers wrought.

    First, we lov'd well and faithfully,
    Yet knew not what we lov'd, nor why,
    Difference of sex no more we knew,   2
    Than our guardian angels do;
        Coming and going, we
Perchance might kiss,° but not between those meals;°   *kisses*
        Our hands ne'r touched the seals,
Which nature, injured by late law, sets free:°   3*
These miracles we did; but now, alas,
All measure and all language I should pass,
Should I tell what a miracle she was.

17   *Mary Magdalen*: traditionally considered a reformed prostitute, Magdalen waited at the
cross and was among the first to see the risen Christ (Matthew 27 and 28).   18 *something
else*: the allusion to Magdalen and the rhythm of the line suggest that Donne means to
imply "A Jesus Christ thereby," and complete the blasphemous parallel.   27–28
Coming . . . kiss: kisses of salutation and parting were considered characteristically English
in the seventeenth century.   29–30 *Our hands . . . free*: we never attempted those
physical intimacies that natural law permits but that more recent ("late") human law
forbids.

Holy Sonnet 6: This Is My Play's Last Scene   1633

This is my play's last scene; here heavens appoint
My pilgrimage's last mile; and my race
Idly, yet quickly run, hath this last pace,
My span's last inch, my minute's last point,
And gluttonous Death will instantly unjoint
My body, and soul, and I shall sleep a space,
But my ever-waking part° shall see that face,   *the soul*
Whose fear already shakes my every joint.
Then, as my soul, t'heaven her first seat, takes flight,
And earth-borne body, in the earth shall dwell,   1*
So, fall my sins, that all may have their right,
To where they are bred, and would press me, to hell.
Impute me righteous, thus purged of evil,
For thus I leave the world, the flesh, and devil.

Holy Sonnet 7: At the Round Earth's Imagined Corners   *1633*

At the round earth's imagined corners, blow
Your trumpets, angels,° and arise, arise
From death, you numberless infinities
Of souls, and to your scattered bodies go,
All whom the flood did, and fire shall o'erthrow,   5
All whom war, dearth, age, agues, tyrannies,
Despair, law, chance, hath slain, and you whose eyes
Shall behold God, and never taste death's woe.°
But let them sleep, Lord, and me mourn a space,
For, if above all these, my sins abound,   10
'Tis late to ask abundance of Thy grace,
When we are there. Here on this lowly ground,
Teach me how to repent; for that's as good
As if Thou hadst sealed my pardon with Thy blood.

AT THE ROUND EARTH'S IMAGINED CORNERS.   1–2 *At . . . . angels:* the lines combine
the image of the angels or winds drawn at the four corners of old maps with an allusion to
the four angels mentioned in Revelations 7:1.   7–8 *you whose eyes . . . woe:* a reference to
those people who are still living on the day of the Last Judgment and thus move directly
from life to judgment without experiencing death.

Good Friday, 1613. Riding Westward   *1633 (1613)*

Let man's soul be a sphere, and then, in this,
The intelligence that moves, devotion is,°
And as the other spheres, by being grown
Subject to foreign motions, lose their own,
And being by others hurried every day,   5
Scarce in a year their natural form obey;
Pleasure or business, so, our souls admit
For their first mover, and are whirled by it.°
Hence is't, that I am carried towards the west
This day, when my soul's form bends towards the east.   10
There I should see a sun, by rising, set,
And by that setting endless day beget:°
But that Christ on this cross did rise and fall,
Sin had eternally benighted all.

GOOD FRIDAY, 1613. RIDING WESTWARD.   1–2 *Let . . . devotion is:* that is, just as
intelligence or principles guide the movement of planets, so should devotion be the principle
that guides the soul.   3–8 *And as . . . whirled by it:* that is, just as planets are deflected
from their natural orbits by "foreign" objects, so our souls are "whirled" from their true
motion by "pleasure or business."   11–12 *sun . . . beget:* the sun-son pun is traditional;
Jesus, the son of God, "set" by rising on the cross, and gave rise to eternal life by dying
("setting") and rising.

Yet dare I almost be glad I do not see   15
That spectacle, of too much weight for me.
Who sees God's face, that is self-life, must die;
What a death were it then to see God die?
It made his own lieutenant, Nature, shrink;
It made his footstool crack, and the sun wink.°   20
Could I behold those hands which span the poles,
And tune all spheres at once, pierced with those holes?
Could I behold that endless height which is
Zenith to us, and to our antipodes,
Humbled below us? Or that blood which is   25
The seat of all our souls, if not of His,
Make dirt of dust, or that flesh which was worn
By God, for his apparel, ragg'd and torn?
If on these things I durst not look, durst I
Upon his miserable mother cast mine eye,   30
Who was God's partner here, and furnished thus
Half of that sacrifice which ransomed us?
Though these things, as I ride, be from mine eye,
They are present yet upon my memory,
For that looks towards them; and Thou look'st towards me,   35
O Saviour, as Thou hang'st upon the tree.
I turn my back to Thee but to receive
Corrections, till Thy mercies bid Thee leave.
O think me worth Thine anger; punish me;
Burn off my rusts and my deformity;   40
Restore Thine image so much, by Thy grace,
That Thou may'st know me, and I'll turn my face.

20 *footstool . . . wink*: an earthquake and a solar eclipse supposedly occurred during the
Crucifixion.

A Hymn to God the Father   *1633 (1623?)*

Wilt Thou forgive that sin where I begun,
    Which is my sin, though it were done before?
Wilt Thou forgive those sins through which I run,
    And do them still, though still I do deplore?
        When Thou hast done, Thou hast not done,   5
            For I have more.

Wilt Thou forgive that sin by which I won
    Others to sin and made my sin their door?
Wilt Thou forgive that sin which I did shun
    A year or two, but wallowed in a score?   10
        When Thou hast done, Thou hast not done,
            For I have more.

I have a sin of fear, that when I have spun
 My last thread, I shall perish on the shore;
Swear by Thy self, that at my death Thy sun   15
 Shall shine as it shines now and heretofore;
  And, having done that, Thou hast done,
   I have no more.

Hymn to God My God, in My Sickness   *1635 (1631?)*

Since I am coming to that holy room
 Where, with Thy choir of saints forevermore,
I shall be made Thy music; as I come
 I tune the instrument° here at the door,   *the soul*
 And what I must do then, think now before.   5

Whilst my physicians by their love are grown
 Cosmographers,° and I their map, who lie   *map-makers*
Flat on this bed, that by them may be shown
 That this is my southwest discovery°
 Per fretum febris,° by these straits to die,   10

I joy, that in these straits, I see my West;°   *sunset, death*
 For, though their currents yield return to none,
What shall my West hurt me? As West and East
 In all flat maps (and I am one) are one,°
 So death doth touch the resurrection.   15

Is the Pacific Sea my home? Or are
 The eastern riches? Is Jerusalem?
Anyan,° and Magellan, and Gibraltar,   *the Bering Straits*
 All straits, and none but straits,° are ways to them,
 Whether where Japhet dwelt, or Cham, or Shem.°   20

HYMN TO GOD MY GOD, IN MY SICKNESS. 9 *southwest discovery*: both the Straits of
Magellan and the spiritual straits through which the soul must pass to salvation. South connotes
the heat of the speaker's fever and west implies death, since it is where the sun sets.
10 *Per fretum febris*: through the straits (*fretum*) and the heat or disturbance (*fretum*) of
fever; the two meanings of the Latin word *fretum* create a pun in this phrase.   13–14
As West . . . are one: the image plays on the relation between a flat map and a globe. In
a flat map, east is at the extreme right and west at the extreme left; if, however, the map
is wrapped about a sphere to approximate a globe, extreme right and left (or east and
west) become the same point.   19 *All straits, and none but straits*: here and throughout,
Donne may be playing with the word, combining geographic straits with the "strait gate"
and "narrow way" that leads to salvation (Matthew 7:14).   20 *Japhet, Cham, Shem*: the
sons of Noah (Genesis 9 and 10) who repopulated the earth after the Flood. Church fathers
supposed Japhet's descendants inhabited Europe, Cham's (Ham's) Africa, and Shem's
Asia.

We think that Paradise and Calvary,
  Christ's cross, and Adam's tree, stood in one place;°
Look Lord, and find both Adams met in me;
  As the first Adam's sweat surrounds my face,
  May the last Adam's blood my soul embrace.

So, in his purple wrapped,° receive me, Lord;
  By these his thorns give me his other crown;
And, as to others' souls I preached Thy word,
  By this my text, my sermon to mine own;
  Therefore that he may raise the Lord throws down.

21-22 *Paradise . . . one place*: Donne suggests that the cross on Calvary stood in the same place as the Tree of Knowledge in the Garden of Eden.   26 *purple wrapped*: both a royal garment and Christ's blood.

EMILY DICKINSON

Emily Dickinson never met Walt Whitman or read his poetry—in a letter she observes that she "was told he was disgraceful"—but together they establish the real beginnings of modern American poetry. Whitman's experiments with form and Dickinson's with language and imagery go far toward creating the American poetic idiom.

Emily Dickinson lived in the small, religious, and tradition-bound community of Amherst, Massachusetts. Her family was dominated by her father, Edward Dickinson, who was a prosperous lawyer, a trustee of Amherst College, and eventually a member of Congress; he ruled his home with unquestioned authority. Emily Dickinson's life was shaped by a combination of public submission and poetic rebellion against this authority. Although she spent three years at school—two at Amherst Academy and one at South Hadley Seminary for Women (now Mount Holyoke College)—she was largely self-taught and her life was restricted to Amherst and her family home; after 1862 she became progressively more reclusive and shut off from the world at large.

Emily Dickinson never married and may never have had what we would call a love affair. Nevertheless, her poetry is very much concerned with love, marriage, and the psychology of human relationships. This choice of subject may have resulted from suppression and sublimation; Dickinson becomes in her poetry what she did not choose to become in life. It also results, at least in part, from her relationships with three men around whom she built an emotional life in her poetry. The first of these was Benjamin Newton, a young law student in Edward Dickinson's offices. Newton was an educated and literate freethinker; he met Emily Dickinson in 1848 and began to direct and encourage her reading. This guidance was cut short, however, when Newton married and moved away from Amherst;

he died of tuberculosis in 1856. Scholars have always assumed that Newton is one of the two persons referred to in Dickinson's "I Never Lost as Much But Twice" (p. 891), written about 1858.

The second man who influenced Emily Dickinson's life and poetic career was the Reverend Charles Wadsworth, a minister whom she met on a visit to Philadelphia in 1855. Because Wadsworth was married, a romantic involvement never actually occurred. In her poetry, however, Dickinson focuses directly on love, marriage, and relationships during this period of her life. "I Cannot Live with You" (p. 895), for example, seems to deal with Dickinson's internalized and psychological relationship with Wadsworth; the dating of the poem (ca. 1862) and the religious imagery suggest that the "you" is Wadsworth. Like Newton, Wadsworth was predominantly a mentor, an educator, and a friend to Dickinson. He may have visited Amherst once or twice, but their conversations were conducted mostly by correspondence. Wadsworth's guidance ended in 1862, when he accepted a ministry in San Francisco.

We can never know the exact connection between these events and Dickinson's life as a poet. Emily Dickinson probably began writing poetry in her early twenties; her earliest efforts were occasional poems and valentines. She did not begin writing in earnest until 1857 or 1858, and between 1858 and 1861 she wrote about 300 poems. At this point she seems to have experienced a burst of creative energy; she wrote 366 poems in 1862, 141 in 1863, 174 in 1864, and about 80 in 1865. After 1865 she wrote about 20 poems per year until her death in 1886; in all she wrote 1,775 poems. Thus, Dickinson produced about one-third of her total poetic work in the three years between 1862 and 1864. We can only surmise that this prodigious output was connected in some way with the loss of Reverend Wadsworth as a guiding influence and with Dickinson's feelings for the man. It was, no doubt, also connected with her growth as a poet and her increasing skepticism about the values of her family and community.

After Wadsworth left for California, Dickinson became even more reclusive and began to dress completely in white. One more person, however, seems to have had some influence on her poetry. In 1862 she began to correspond with Thomas Wentworth Higginson, a literary critic who had written an article encouraging young writers. Dickinson wrote to Higginson, enclosing some of her poetry and asking if her verses were "alive" and ready for publication. She may have viewed Higginson initially as another mentor, but she quickly discovered that his literary judgments were conventional and traditional; he suggested that she regularize her rhymes and rhythms. Ironically, Higginson became one of the first editors of Dickinson's work after her death in 1886.

Dickinson's *poetic style* might best be described as metaphysical. Her poetry is simple and passionate and at the same time highly economical and concentrated. We see in her verse, as in John Donne's, a highly elliptical style that produces both concentration of language and the rapid movement of thoughts and images. Her poetry is also characterized by sharp and often bizarre images, rapid turns of thought, sudden and witty conjunctions or comparisons, questions, and riddles. In terms of *language and diction*, Dickinson's verse is full of grammatical irregularities and eccentricities of punctuation. The most obvious of these is her frequent abandonment of conventional punctuation in favor of the dash. She even developed a special length of dash that helps to control the rhythm and pauses in her poetry.

The *poetic forms* that Emily Dickinson most frequently used are common measure and ballad stanza (see p. 744). She may have gained her interest in these forms from the Protestant hymnal, the major poetic text of her youth. Within these quatrain forms, Dickinson achieves remarkable flexibility and variation through the skillful use of metrical substitution and an abundance of slant rhyme. Although these irregularities in rhyme and meter clearly annoyed Dickinson's first editors, they have since been recognized as important and effective elements of her poetry.

For *poetic subjects*, Emily Dickinson turned to her immediate world of village and garden and to her inner life of emotion and skepticism. The characteristic subjects of her poetry include love, nature, faith, death, and immortality. Beyond these, however, her poems also chart her inner growth, the world that she created for herself in her own mind, and a broad range of psychological insights. Her ideas tend to be witty, unconventional, and rebellious.

Of the 1,775 poems that Emily Dickinson wrote, only seven were published during her lifetime, anonymously and in rather obscure periodicals. She may have rejected further publication because of editors' tendencies to "adjust" her verse or because of Higginson's discouraging advice. In any event, she stopped publishing early on and wrote mostly for herself. After Dickinson's death, her sister Lavinia was amazed to find boxes of small, handwritten and bound pamphlets of verse that contained about twenty poems each. Lavinia recognized the significance of her sister's work and eventually turned some of the poems over to Mabel L. Todd and Higginson for editing and publication. They produced three volumes of Dickinson's work (published in 1890, 1891, and 1896), each containing about 100 poems. In these editions, the editors attempted to make Dickinson's poetry conform to accepted standards through extensive revision; they eliminated slant rhymes, smoothed out the meter, revised those metaphors that struck them as outrageous, and regularized the punctuation.

These well-intended but destructive adjustments to Dickinson's poetry remained more or less intact until 1955, when the Harvard University Press published Thomas H. Johnson's three-volume edition of Dickinson's poems. Johnson went back to the manuscripts to establish the original text of each poem (with variants), and his edition has become the standard by which Emily Dickinson's work may be evaluated. Important critical and biographical studies include Charles R. Anderson, *Emily Dickinson's Poetry* (1960), Albert Gelpi, *Emily Dickinson: The Mind of the Poet* (1965), Ruth Miller, *The Poetry of Emily Dickinson* (1968), Richard B. Sewall, *The Life of Emily Dickinson* (1974), and Robert Weisbuch, *Emily Dickinson's Poetry* (1975). Since the mid-1970s Dickinson has also been reevaluated from the perspective of feminist criticism. Three significant books in this vein are Antonina Clarke Mossberg, *Emily Dickinson: When a Writer Is a Daughter* (1982), Susan Juhasz, *The Undiscovered Continent: Emily Dickinson and the Space of the Mind* (1983), and *Feminist Critics Read Emily Dickinson* (1983), a collection of essays edited by Juhasz. Additional poems by Emily Dickinson may be found in this text on pages 473 and 726.

The Gentian Weaves Her Fringes   1891 (ca. 1858)

The Gentian weaves her fringes –
The Maple's loom is red –
My departing blossoms
     Obviate parade.

A brief, but patient illness –   5
An hour to prepare,
And one below, this morning
Is where the angels are –
It was a short procession,
The Bobolink was there –   10
An aged Bee addressed us –
And then we knelt in prayer –
We trust that she was willing –
We ask that we may be.
Summer – Sister – Seraph!   15
Let us go with thee!

In the name of the Bee –
And of the Butterfly –
And of the Breeze – Amen!

I Never Lost as Much But Twice   1890 (ca. 1858)

I never lost as much but twice,
And that was in the sod.
Twice have I stood a beggar
Before the door of God!

Angels – twice descending
Reimbursed my store –
Burglar! Banker – Father!
I am poor once more!   5

Success Is Counted Sweetest   Fuses success, victory   1878, 1890 (ca. 1859)
                                 + Triumph

[Success is counted sweetest   Those who aren't success-
By those who ne'er succeed.] Central idea.   ful are the ones who
To comprehend a nectar of the gods   appreciate it most.
Requires sorest need.

We want
what we
don't have

Not one of all the purple Host   The example supports   5
Who took the Flag today   the theme.
Can tell the definition metonymy
So clear of Victory

As he defeated – dying –   The dying soldier understands
On whose forbidden ear   victory more accurately than the   10
The distant strains of triumph victor can. Extends the subject to
Burst agonized and clear!   the extremes of losing + dying. The
                            fusion of regret, envy, + disappointment
                            makes the loser benefit. Gains from
                            the loss by gaining vision + under-
                            standing – even in defeat.

Just Lost, When I Was Saved!   1891 (ca. 1860)

Just lost, when I was saved!
Just felt the world go by!
Just girt me for the onset with Eternity,
When breath blew back,
And on the other side   5
I heard recede the disappointed tide!

Therefore, as One returned, I feel,
Odd secrets of the line to tell!
Some Sailor, skirting foreign shores –
Some pale Reporter, from the awful doors   10
Before the Seal!

Next time, to stay!
Next time, the things to see
By Ear unheard,
Unscrutinized by Eye –   15

Next time, to tarry,
While the Ages steal –
Slow tramp the Centuries,
And the Cycles wheel!

"Faith" Is a Fine Invention   *1891 (ca. 1860)*

"Faith" is a fine invention
When Gentlemen can *see* –
But *Microscopes* are prudent
In an Emergency.

I Taste a Liquor Never Brewed   *1861, 1891 (ca. 1860)*

I taste a liquor never brewed –
From Tankards scooped in Pearl –
Not all the Frankfort Berries°   grapes
Yield such an Alcohol!

Inebriate of Air – am I –
And Debauchee of Dew –   5
Reeling – thro endless summer days –
From inns of Molten Blue –

When "Landlords" turn the drunken Bee
Out of the Foxglove's door –
When Butterflies – renounce their "drams" –   10
I shall but drink the more!

Till Seraphs swing their snowy Hats –
And Saints – to windows run –
To see the little Tippler
From Manzanilla° come!   15

I TASTE A LIQUOR NEVER BREWED.   16 *Manzanilla*: a pale sherry from Spain.
Dickinson may also have been thinking of Manzanillo, a Cuban city often associated with
rum.

Safe in Their Alabaster Chambers   *1862, 1890 (1861)*

Safe in their Alabaster Chambers –
Untouched by Morning –
And untouched by Noon –
Lie the meek members of the Resurrection –
Rafter of Satin – and Roof of Stone!   5

Grand go the Years – in the Crescent – above them –
Worlds scoop their Arcs –
And Firmaments – row –
Diadems – drop – and Doges° – surrender –
Soundless as dots – on a Disc of Snow –   10

SAFE IN THEIR ALABASTER CHAMBERS.   9 *Doges*: Renaissance rulers of the Italian
city-states of Venice and Genoa.

Wild Nights—Wild Nights!   1890 (ca. 1861)

Wild Nights – Wild Nights!
Were I with thee
Wild Nights should be
Our luxury!

Futile – the Winds –   5
To a Heart in port –
Done with the Compass –
Done with the Chart!

Rowing in Eden –
Ah, the Sea!   10
Might I but moor – Tonight –
In Thee!

There's a Certain Slant of Light   1890 (ca. 1861)

There's a certain Slant of light,
Winter Afternoons –
That oppresses, like the Heft
Of Cathedral Tunes –

Heavenly Hurt, it gives us –   5
We can find no scar,
But internal difference,
Where the Meanings, are –

None may teach it – Any –
'Tis the Seal Despair –   10
An imperial affliction
Sent us of the Air –

When it comes, the Landscape listens –
Shadows – hold their breath –
When it goes, 'tis like the Distance   15
On the look of Death –

The Soul Selects Her Own Society   1890 (ca. 1862)

The Soul selects her own Society –
Then – shuts the Door –
To her divine Majority –
Present no more –

Unmoved – she notes the Chariots – pausing –
At her low Gate –
Unmoved – an Emperor be kneeling
Upon her Mat –

I've known her – from an ample nation –
Choose One –
Then – close the Valves of her attention –
Like Stone –

5

10

Some Keep the Sabbath Going to Church

1864 (ca. 1862)

Some keep the Sabbath going to Church –
I keep it, staying at Home –
With a Bobolink for a Chorister –
And an Orchard, for a Dome –

Some keep the Sabbath in Surplice –
I just wear my Wings –
And instead of tolling the Bell, for Church,
Our little Sexton – sings.

5

God preaches, a noted Clergyman –
And the sermon is never long,
So instead of getting to Heaven, at last –
I'm going, all along.

10

After Great Pain, a Formal Feeling Comes

1929 (ca. 1862)

After great pain, a formal feeling comes –
The Nerves sit ceremonious, like Tombs –
The stiff Heart questions was it He, that bore,
And Yesterday, or Centuries before?

The Feet, mechanical, go round –
Of Ground, or Air, or Ought° –
A Wooden way
Regardless grown,
A Quartz contentment, like a stone –

5

anything, nothing

This is the Hour of Lead –
Remembered, if outlived,
As Freezing persons, recollect the Snow –
First – Chill – then Stupor – then the letting go –

10

Much Madness Is Divinest Sense   *1890 (ca. 1862)*

Much Madness is divinest Sense –
To a discerning Eye –
Much Sense – the starkest Madness –
'Tis the Majority
In this, as All, prevail –   5
Assent – and you are sane –
Demur – you're straightway dangerous –
And handled with a Chain –

I Heard a Fly Buzz—When I Died   Deathbed scene.   *1896 (ca. 1862)*

I heard a Fly buzz – when I died –
The Stillness in the Room
Was like the Stillness in the Air –
Between the Heaves of <u>Storm</u> – Before death comes

<u>The Eyes around</u> – had wrung them <u>dry</u> – The relations + loved ones,   5
And Breaths were gathering firm
For that last Onset – when the King
Be witnessed – in the Room –

I <u>willed my Keepsakes</u> – Signed away Last will + testament
What portion of me be   10
Assignable – <u>and then</u> it was
There <u>interposed a Fly</u> –   It intrudes

But reality: With <u>Blue</u> – <u>uncertain stumbling</u> Buzz – Comic element (As at a wedding-
Between the light – and me –   or annoyance.)
And then the Windows failed – and then   15
I could <u>not see to see</u> –   Faculty + function are
                                         both gone. Powerful, but non-
                                      sentimental conclusion.

I Like to See It Lap the Miles   *1891 (ca. 1862)*

I like to see it lap the Miles –
And lick the Valleys up –
And stop to feed itself at Tanks –
And then – prodigious step

Around a Pile of Mountains –   5
And supercilious peer
In Shanties – by the sides of Roads –
And then a Quarry pare

To fit it's sides
And crawl between
Complaining all the while   10
In horrid – hooting stanza –
Then chase itself down Hill –

And neigh like Boanerges° –
Then – prompter than a Star   15
Stop – docile and omnipotent
At it's own stable door –

I LIKE TO SEE IT LAP THE MILES.   14 *Boanerges*: a surname meaning "the sons of
thunder" that appears in Mark 3:17.

I Cannot Live with You

1890 (ca. 1862)

I cannot live with You –
It would be Life –
And Life is over there –
Behind the Shelf

The Sexton keeps the Key to –   5
Putting up
Our Life – His Porcelain –
Like a Cup –

Discarded of the Housewife –
Quaint – or Broke –   10
A newer Sevres pleases –
Old Ones crack –

I could not die – with You –
For One must wait
To shut the Other's Gaze down –   15
You – could not –

And I – Could I stand by
And see You – freeze –
Without my Right of Frost –
Death's privilege?   20

Nor could I rise – with You –
Because Your Face
Would put out Jesus' –
That New Grace

Glow plain – and foreign   25
On my homesick Eye –
Except that You than He
Shone closer by –

They'd judge Us – How –
For You – served Heaven – You know,   30
Or sought to –
I could not –

Because You saturated Sight –
And I had no more Eyes
For sordid excellence   35
As Paradise

And were You lost, I would be –
Though My Name
Rang loudest
On the Heavenly fame –   40

And were You – saved –
And I – condemned to be
Where You were not –
That self – were Hell to Me –

So We must meet apart –   45
You there – I – here –
With just the Door ajar
That Oceans are – and Prayer –
And that White Sustenance –
Despair –   50

Pain – Has an Element of Blank   *1890 (ca. 1862)*

Pain – has an Element of Blank –
It cannot recollect
When it begun – or if there were
A time when it was not –

It has no Future – but itself –   5
It's Infinite contain
It's Past – enlightened to perceive
New Periods – of Pain.

One Need Not Be a Chamber – To Be Haunted   *1891 (ca. 1863)*

One need not be a Chamber – to be Haunted –
One need not be a House –
The Brain has Corridors – surpassing
Material Place –

Far safer, of a Midnight Meeting   5
External Ghost

Than it's interior Confronting –
That Cooler Host.

Far safer, through an Abbey gallop,
The Stones a'chase –
Than Unarmed, one's a'self encounter –   10
In lonesome Place –

Ourself behind ourself, concealed –
Should startle most –
Assassin hid in our Apartment   15
Be Horror's least.

The Body – borrows a Revolver –
He bolts the Door –
O'erlooking a superior spectre –
Or More –   20

The Bustle in a House   *1890 (ca. 1866)*

The Bustle in a House
The Morning after Death
Is solemnest of industries
Enacted upon Earth –

The Sweeping up the Heart
And putting Love away   5
We shall not want to use again
Until Eternity.

My Triumph Lasted Till the Drums   *1935 (ca. 1872)*

My Triumph lasted till the Drums
Had left the Dead alone
And then I dropped my Victory
And chastened stole along
To where the finished Faces   5
Conclusion turned on me
And then I hated Glory
And wished myself were They.

What is to be is best descried
When it has also been –   10

Could Prospect taste of Retrospect
The tyrannies of Men
Were Tenderer – diviner
The Transitive toward.
A Bayonet's contrition   15
Is nothing to the Dead.

The Heart Is the Capital of the Mind   1929 (ca. 1876)

The Heart is the Capital of the Mind –
The Mind is a single State –
The Heart and the Mind together make
A single Continent –

One – is the Population –   5
Numerous enough –
This ecstatic Nation
Seek – it is Yourself.

"Heavenly Father" – Take to Thee   1914 (ca. 1879)

"Heavenly Father" – take to thee
The supreme iniquity
Fashioned by thy candid Hand
In a moment contraband –
Though to trust us – seem to us   5
More respectful – "We are Dust" –
We apologize to thee
For thine own Duplicity –

My Life Closed Twice Before Its Close   1896

My life closed twice before its close;
It yet remains to see
If Immortality unveil
A third event to me,

So huge, so hopeless to conceive   5
As these that twice befel.
Parting is all we know of heaven,
And all we need of hell.

ROBERT FROST

When Robert Frost's first book of poems, *A Boy's Will*, was published in England in 1913, he was virtually unknown in the United States. At the time, Ezra Pound wrote, "it is a sinister thing that so American . . . a talent . . . should have to be exported before it can find due encouragement and recognition." Time, of course, brought Frost all the encouragement and recognition he could want. He eventually received over twenty honorary degrees and four Pulitzer Prizes. Indeed, he came as close as possible to becoming America's official poet—a sort of poet laureate—when he read "The Gift Outright" (p. 909) at the inauguration of President John F. Kennedy in 1961. In his own lifetime Robert Frost became one of the most visible and admired American poets; his poetry continues to earn him that recognition to this day.

Robert Frost, who presented himself as the quintessential New Englander in person and in his poetry, was actually born in San Francisco on March 26, 1874. His father had moved the family west so that he could write for the *San Francisco Bulletin*; when the father died of tuberculosis in 1885, Frost's mother brought the family back to Lawrence, Massachusetts. Frost attended Lawrence High School, studied classics, began writing poetry, and graduated in 1892 as co-valedictorian with Eleanor White, the woman he married in 1895. After high school, Frost attended Dartmouth College for seven weeks and then turned to newspaper work and schoolteaching; he continued to write poetry, little of which was published. Frost returned to college after his marriage, attending classes at Harvard from 1897 to 1899, but he left again without a degree. His prospects were bleak.

In 1900 Frost's grandfather gave him a farm in Derry, New Hampshire, on the condition that he promise to work it for ten years. Frost and his family (there were five children by 1905) took up residence in Derry, and for the next twelve years he worked the farm, wrote poetry, and taught English at Pinkerton Academy. The life was hard and the poetry mostly ignored; in 1912 Frost decided to sell the farm and devote himself to verse. He moved his family to England, where they settled "beneath a thatched roof" in the countryside. In England Frost met a number of emerging and established poets, including Ezra Pound and William Butler Yeats, but he was most influenced by a group of English poets called "The Georgians," who wrote about country life and rural matters. In this same period his first two books of poetry were published in England and received very favorable reviews. These books contain poems that remain characteristic of Frost's entire career; *A Boy's Will* (1913) offers "The Tuft of Flowers," and *North of Boston* (1914) contains both "Mending Wall" and "After Apple-Picking." Both books were republished in the United

States in 1915, and Frost finally began to receive recognition at home.

That same year Frost and his family returned to the United States and took up residence on a farm near Franconia, New Hampshire. More books of poetry and greater acclaim followed quickly. In 1916 Frost published *Mountain Interval*, a book containing "The Road Not Taken," "Birches," and "Out, Out—." He also gave a poetry reading at Harvard and became poet-in-residence at Amherst College, a relationship that would continue sporadically for much of his life. During the next five years Frost gave public readings or held academic posts at Wesleyan, Michigan, Dartmouth, and Yale; in 1920 he helped found The Bread Loaf School of English at Middlebury College in Vermont. In these same years Frost began to develop his public persona as the wry and philosophical country poet. Later, it became progressively more difficult to separate this public mask from what Randall Jarrell calls "The Other Frost," the often agonized and troubled man who wrote the poems.

More books of poetry and more recognition followed throughout Frost's life. In 1923 he published *Selected Poems* and *New Hampshire*. The latter book, for which Frost won a Pulitzer Prize, contains some of his best-known work: "Stopping by Woods on a Snowy Evening," "Fire and Ice," and "Nothing Gold Can Stay." These were followed by *West-Running Brook* (1928), *Collected Poems* (1930), *A Further Range* (1936), *A Witness Tree* (1942), *Steeple Bush* (1947), *Complete Poems* (1949), *Aforesaid* (1954), and *In the Clearing* (1962).

Robert Frost's *poetic style* remained fairly consistent throughout his career; we do not see significant development or change in his work. We can find in his poems a clear sense of the land, of history, and of human nature. The poetry seems, at first, to be simple, lucid, straightforward, and descriptive. Further reading, however, reveals the subtleties of wit, humor, and irony that often underlie Frost's meditations on common events or objects.

Frost's *language and diction* are remarkably conversational; his words are plain and his phrases simple and direct. More often than not, he uses and refines the natural speech patterns and rhythms of New England, polishing the language that people actually speak to a compact and terse poetic texture. The tone of his poetry can be simultaneously grim, ironic, whimsical, and honest. He achieves this combination of tones through control and restraint; his directness is modified by a consistently ironic and playful understatement.

In terms of *poetic structure*, Frost's poems often move from an event or an object through a metaphor to an idea in a smooth, uninterrupted flow. Within this pattern, Frost tends to describe a complete event rather than a single vision. The heart of the process is the image or metaphor. Frost's metaphors are sparse and careful; they are brought sharply into focus and skillfully interwoven with the whole poem. Frost himself saw the metaphor as the beginning of the process. In *Education by Poetry* (1931) he wrote that "poetry begins in trivial metaphors, pretty metaphors, 'grace' metaphors, and goes on to the profoundest thinking that we have. Poetry provides the one permissible way of saying one thing and meaning another."

Frost's poems also reflect traditional *poetic forms* and meters. The poet once asserted that writing "free verse" was like playing tennis without a net. Consequently, we find conventional rhyme schemes and clear iambic meters in much of his work. Similarly, we find such closed forms as couplets, terza rima, quatrains, and blank verse.

Frost's *poetic subjects* are generally common and rural events, objects, and characters: digging gardens, mending walls, picking apples, cutting wood, snow, trees, insects, spring and fall, children, parents, husbands and wives. Often, the poems move from these events, objects, or characters to philosophical generalizations about life and death, survival and responsibility, nature and humanity, that are so simple and right as to verge on the obvious. Frost's ideas are neither radical nor complex; they reflect the traditional truths of our own existence.

The standard edition of Frost's work is *The Poetry of Robert Frost* (1969), edited by Edward Connery Lathem. The standard biography was written in three volumes by Lawrence Thompson: *Robert Frost: The Early Years* (1966), *The Years of Triumph* (1970), and *The Later Years* (1977). The last volume was completed after Thompson's death by R. H. Winnick. Recent and useful criticism of the poetry includes Reginald Cook, *The Dimensions of Robert Frost* (1958) and his *Robert Frost: A Living Voice* (1975), Ruben Brower, *The Poetry of Robert Frost* (1963), J. F. Lynan, *The Pastoral Art of Robert Frost* (1964), Philip L. Gerber, *Robert Frost* (1966), and John C. Kemp, *Robert Frost and New England* (1979). Additional poems by Robert Frost may be found in this book on pages 475 and 764.

The Tuft of Flowers   1906

I went to turn the grass once after one
Who mowed it in the dew before the sun.

The dew was gone that made his blade so keen
Before I came to view the leveled scene.

I looked for him behind an isle of trees;   5
I listened for his whetstone on the breeze.

But he had gone his way, the grass all mown,
And I must be, as he had been,—alone,

'As all must be,' I said within my heart,
'Whether they work together or apart.'   10

But as I said it, swift there passed me by
On noiseless wing a bewildered butterfly,

Seeking with memories grown dim o'er night
Some resting flower of yesterday's delight.

And once I marked his flight go round and round,
As where some flower lay withering on the ground.

And then he flew as far as eye could see,
And then on tremulous wing came back to me.

I thought of questions that have no reply,
And would have turned to toss the grass to dry;

But he turned first, and led my eye to look
At a tall tuft of flowers beside a brook,

A leaping tongue of bloom the scythe had spared
Beside a reedy brook the scythe had bared.

The mower in the dew had loved them thus,
By leaving them to flourish, not for us,

Nor yet to draw one thought of ours to him,
But from sheer morning gladness at the brim.

The butterfly and I had lit upon,
Nevertheless, a message from the dawn,

That made me hear the wakening birds around,
And hear his long scythe whispering to the ground,

And feel a spirit kindred to my own;
So that henceforth I worked no more alone;

But glad with him, I worked as with his aid,
And weary, sought at noon with him the shade;

And dreaming, as it were, held brotherly speech
With one whose thought I had not hoped to reach.

'Men work together,' I told him from the heart,
'Whether they work together or apart.'

Mending Wall   *1914*

Something there is that doesn't love a wall,
That sends the frozen-ground-swell under it,
And spills the upper boulders in the sun;
And makes gaps even two can pass abreast.
The work of hunters is another thing:

I have come after them and made repair
Where they have left not one stone on a stone,
But they would have the rabbit out of hiding,
To please the yelping dogs. The gaps I mean,
No one has seen them made or heard them made,   10
But at spring mending-time we find them there.
I let my neighbor know beyond the hill;
And on a day we meet to walk the line
And set the wall between us once again.
We keep the wall between us as we go.   15
To each the boulders that have fallen to each.
And some are loaves and some so nearly balls
We have to use a spell to make them balance:
'Stay where you are until our backs are turned!'
We wear our fingers rough with handling them.   20
Oh, just another kind of outdoor game,
One on a side. It comes to little more:
There where it is we do not need the wall:
He is all pine and I am apple orchard.
My apple trees will never get across   25
And eat the cones under his pines, I tell him.
He only says, 'Good fences make good neighbors.'
Spring is the mischief in me, and I wonder
If I could put a notion in his head:
'*Why* do they make good neighbors? Isn't it   30
Where there are cows? But here there are no cows.
Before I built a wall I'd ask to know
What I was walling in or walling out,
And to whom I was like to give offense.
Something there is that doesn't love a wall,   35
That wants it down.' I could say 'Elves' to him,
But it's not elves exactly, and I'd rather
He said it for himself. I see him there
Bringing a stone grasped firmly by the top
In each hand, like an old-stone savage armed.   40
He moves in darkness as it seems to me,
Not of woods only and the shade of trees.
He will not go behind his father's saying,
And he likes having thought of it so well
He says again, 'Good fences make good neighbors.'   45

After Apple-Picking   *1914*

My long two-pointed ladder's sticking through a tree
Toward heaven still,
And there's a barrel that I didn't fill

Beside it, and there may be two or three
Apples I didn't pick upon some bough.
But I am done with apple-picking now.
Essence of winter sleep is on the night,
The scent of apples: I am drowsing off.
I cannot rub the strangeness from my sight
I got from looking through a pane of glass
I skimmed this morning from the drinking trough
And held against the world of hoary grass.
It melted, and I let it fall and break.
But I was well
Upon my way to sleep before it fell,
And I could tell
What form my dreaming was about to take.
Magnified apples appear and disappear,
Stem end and blossom end,
And every fleck of russet showing clear.
My instep arch not only keeps the ache,
It keeps the pressure of a ladder-round.
I feel the ladder sway as the boughs bend.
And I keep hearing from the cellar bin
The rumbling sound
Of load on load of apples coming in.
For I have had too much
Of apple-picking: I am overtired
Of the great harvest I myself desired.
There were ten thousand thousand fruit to touch,
Cherish in hand, lift down, and not let fall.
For all
That struck the earth,
No matter if not bruised or spiked with stubble,
Went surely to the cider-apple heap
As of no worth.
One can see what will trouble
This sleep of mine, whatever sleep it is.
Were he not gone,
The woodchuck could say whether it's like his
Long sleep, as I describe its coming on,
Or just some human sleep.

Birches   *1915*

When I see birches bend to left and right
Across the lines of straighter darker trees,
I like to think some boy's been swinging them.
But swinging doesn't bend them down to stay

As ice-storms do. Often you must have seen them 5
Loaded with ice a sunny winter morning
After a rain. They click upon themselves
As the breeze rises, and turn many-colored
As the stir cracks and crazes their enamel.
Soon the sun's warmth makes them shed crystal shells 10
Shattering and avalanching on the snow-crust—
Such heaps of broken glass to sweep away
You'd think the inner dome of heaven had fallen.
They are dragged to the withered bracken by the load,
And they seem not to break; though once they are bowed 15
So low for long, they never right themselves:
You may see their trunks arching in the woods
Years afterwards, trailing their leaves on the ground
Like girls on hands and knees that throw their hair
Before them over their heads to dry in the sun. 20
But I was going to say when Truth broke in
With all her matter-of-fact about the ice-storm
I should prefer to have some boy bend them
As he went out and in to fetch the cows—
Some boy too far from town to learn baseball, 25
Whose only play was what he found himself,
Summer or winter, and could play alone.
One by one he subdued his father's trees
By riding them down over and over again
Until he took the stiffness out of them, 30
And not one but hung limp, not one was left
For him to conquer. He learned all there was
To learn about not launching out too soon
And so not carrying the tree away
Clear to the ground. He always kept his poise 35
To the top branches, climbing carefully
With the same pains you use to fill a cup
Up to the brim, and even above the brim.
Then he flung outward, feet first, with a swish,
Kicking his way down through the air to the ground. 40
So was I once myself a swinger of birches.
And so I dream of going back to be.
It's when I'm weary of considerations,
And life is too much like a pathless wood
Where your face burns and tickles with the cobwebs 45
Broken across it, and one eye is weeping
From a twig's having lashed across it open.
I'd like to get away from earth awhile
And then come back to it and begin over.
May no fate willfully misunderstand me 50
And half grant what I wish and snatch me away
Not to return. Earth's the right place for love:

I don't know where it's likely to go better.
I'd like to go by climbing a birch tree,
And climb black branches up a snow-white trunk   55
Toward heaven, till the tree could bear no more,
But dipped its top and set me down again.
That would be good both going and coming back.
One could do worse than be a swinger of birches.

The Road Not Taken   *1915*

Two roads diverged in a yellow wood,
And sorry I could not travel both
And be one traveler, long I stood
And looked down one as far as I could
To where it bent in the undergrowth;   5

Then took the other, as just as fair,
And having perhaps the better claim,
Because it was grassy and wanted wear;
Though as for that the passing there
Had worn them really about the same,   10

And both that morning equally lay
In leaves no step had trodden black.
Oh, I kept the first for another day!
Yet knowing how way leads on to way,
I doubted if I should ever come back.   15

I shall be telling this with a sigh
Somewhere ages and ages hence:
Two roads diverged in a wood, and I—
I took the one less traveled by,
And that has made all the difference.   20

'Out, Out—'   *1916*

The buzz saw snarled and rattled in the yard
And made dust and dropped stove-length sticks of wood,
Sweet-scented stuff when the breeze drew across it.
And from there those that lifted eyes could count
Five mountain ranges one behind the other   5
Under the sunset far into Vermont.
And the saw snarled and rattled, snarled and rattled,
As it ran light, or had to bear a load.

Theme: The uncertainty + unpredictability of life. Life can end at any moment, leaving a waste of human potential.

And nothing happened: day was all but done.
"Call it a day," I wish they might have said   *In retrospect*   10
To please the boy by giving him the half hour
That a boy counts so much when saved from work.
His sister stood beside them in her apron
To tell them 'Supper.' At the word, the saw,   *The boy was distracted for a second.*
As if to prove saws knew what supper meant,   15
Leaped out at the boy's hand, or seemed to leap—   *metaphor - almost.*
He must have given the hand. However it was,
Neither refused the meeting. But the hand!
The boy's first outcry was a rueful laugh,
As he swung toward them holding up the hand   20
Half in appeal, but half as if to keep
The life from spilling. Then the boy saw all—   *Metonymy*
Since he was old enough to know, big boy
Doing a man's work, though a child at heart—
He saw all spoiled. 'Don't let him cut my hand off—   25
The doctor, when he comes. Don't let him, sister!'
So. But the hand was gone already.
The doctor put him in the dark of ether.
He lay and puffed his lips out with his breath.
And then—the watcher at his pulse took fright.   30
No one believed. They listened at his heart.
Little—less—nothing!—and that ended it.
No more to build on there. And they, since they
Were not the one dead, turned to their affairs.   *And life goes on. Though at times it seems cruel to meaningless.*

Fire and Ice   1920

Some say the world will end in fire,
Some say in ice.
From what I've tasted of desire
I hold with those who favor fire.
But if it had to perish twice,   5
I think I know enough of hate
To say that for destruction ice
Is also great
And would suffice.

Nothing Gold Can Stay   1923

Nature's first green is gold,
Her hardest hue to hold.
Her early leaf's a flower;
But only so an hour.

Then leaf subsides to leaf.
So Eden sank to grief,
So dawn goes down to day.
Nothing gold can stay.

Misgiving   1923

All crying, 'We will go with you, O Wind!'
The foliage follow him, leaf and stem;
But a sleep oppresses them as they go,
And they end by bidding him stay with them.

Since ever they flung abroad in spring
The leaves had promised themselves this flight,
Who now would fain seek sheltering wall,
Or thicket, or hollow place for the night.

And now they answer his summoning blast
With an ever vaguer and vaguer stir,
Or at utmost a little reluctant whirl
That drops them no further than where they were.

I only hope that when I am free
As they are free to go in quest
Of the knowledge beyond the bounds of life
It may not seem better to me to rest.

Acquainted with the Night

I have been one acquainted with the night.
I have walked out in rain—and back in rain.
I have outwalked the furthest city light.

I have looked down the saddest city lane.
I have passed by the watchman on his beat
And dropped my eyes, unwilling to explain.

I have stood still and stopped the sound of feet
When far away an interrupted cry
Came over houses from another street,

But not to call me back or say good-by;
And further still at an unearthly height,
One luminary clock against the sky

Proclaimed the time was neither wrong nor right.
I have been one acquainted with the night.

Design   *1936*

I found a dimpled spider, fat and white,
On a white heal-all,° holding up a moth
Like a white piece of rigid satin cloth—
Assorted characters of death and blight
Mixed ready to begin the morning right,   5
Like the ingredients of a witches' broth—
A snow-drop spider, a flower like a froth,
And dead wings carried like a paper kite.

What had that flower to do with being white,
The wayside blue and innocent heal-all?   10
What brought the kindred spider to that height,
Then steered the white moth thither in the night?
What but design of darkness to appall?—
If design govern in a thing so small.

DESIGN.   2 *heal-all*: a flower, usually blue, thought to have healing powers.

The Gift Outright   *1941*

The land was ours before we were the land's.
She was our land more than a hundred years
Before we were her people. She was ours
In Massachusetts, in Virginia,
But we were England's, still colonials,   5
Possessing what we still were unpossessed by,
Possessed by what we now no more possessed.
Something we were withholding made us weak
Until we found out that it was ourselves
We were withholding from our land of living,   10
And forthwith found salvation in surrender.
Such as we were we gave ourselves outright
(The deed of gift was many deeds of war)
To the land vaguely realizing westward,
But still unstoried, artless, unenhanced,   15
Such as she was, such as she would become.

A Considerable Speck   *1942*

(Microscopic)

A speck that would have been beneath my sight
On any but a paper sheet so white
Set off across what I had written there.
And I had idly poised my pen in air

To stop it with a period of ink   5
When something strange about it made me think.
This was no dust speck by my breathing blown,
But unmistakably a living mite
With inclinations it could call its own.
It paused as with suspicion of my pen,   10
And then came racing wildly on again
To where my manuscript was not yet dry;
Then paused again and either drank or smelt—
With loathing, for again it turned to fly.
Plainly with an intelligence I dealt.   15
It seemed too tiny to have room for feet,
Yet must have had a set of them complete
To express how much it didn't want to die.
It ran with terror and with cunning crept.
It faltered: I could see it hesitate;   20
Then in the middle of the open sheet
Cower down in desperation to accept
Whatever I accorded it of fate.
I have none of the tenderer-than-thou
Collectivistic regimenting love   25
With which the modern world is being swept
But this poor microscopic item now!
Since it was nothing I knew evil of
I let it lie there till I hope it slept.
I have a mind myself and recognize   30
Mind when I meet with it in any guise.
No one can know how glad I am to find
On any sheet the least display of mind.

Choose Something Like a Star   *1943*

O Star (the fairest one in sight),
We grant your loftiness the right
To some obscurity of cloud—
It will not do to say of night,
Since dark is what brings out your light.   5
Some mystery becomes the proud.
But to be wholly taciturn
In your reserve is not allowed.
Say something to us we can learn
By heart and when alone repeat.   10
Say something! And it says, 'I burn.'
But say with what degree of heat.
Talk Fahrenheit, talk Centigrade.
Use language we can comprehend.
Tell us what elements you blend.   15

It gives us strangely little aid,
But does tell something in the end.
And steadfast as Keats' Eremite,
Not even stooping from its sphere,
It asks a little of us here.   20
It asks of us a certain height,
So when at times the mob is swayed
To carry praise or blame too far,
We may choose something like a star
To stay our minds on and be staid.   25

U. S. 1946 King's X   *1946*

Having invented a new Holocaust,
And been the first with it to win a war,
How they make haste to cry with fingers crossed,
King's X—no fairs to use it any more!

WRITING ABOUT A POET'S WORK

It is difficult to write an effective essay on a poet's entire career based on a small selection of the poet's verse. It is both possible and reasonable, however, to write about a limited number of poems by a single author. There are three potential approaches to this type of essay: biographical, developmental, and comparative.

The *biographical essay* is perhaps the least productive; it seeks to relate poems to specific events or stages in a poet's life. Thus, you might attempt an essay that connects specific events in Emily Dickinson's life with specific poems; this type of essay requires extensive biographical research.

The *developmental essay* traces the growth of a single image, concept, or technique throughout a poet's career. Such an essay presupposes both development and the ability to look at a poet's work in the order in which it was written. An essay of this type might focus, for example, on Frost's use of snow imagery or Dickinson's employment of slant rhyme. In either case, the object would be to discover, assert, and prove through examples that development occurred over the poet's creative life.

The *comparative essay* is perhaps the easiest to formulate and the most common, since it neither assumes development nor requires biographical research (see p. 1634 for an additional discussion of comparison as a strategy). Like the developmental essay, the comparative essay focuses on a specific element, image, idea, or technique in a poet's work; however, the object is to assert *continuity* or *commonality* rather than development and to use each work to clarify the others. Thus, such an essay will usually argue that a poet uses the same devices or addresses the same concerns in a similar way in a number of his or her poems to establish related ideas or emotions. Such an essay might deal with snow imagery in three of Robert Frost's poems, Biblical allusions in four of Donne's poems, or the subject of death in four of Dickinson's poems.

Almost any essay dealing with a number of poems by the same author will inevitably focus on a specific element of the poems rather than attempt a wholesale treatment. The potential subjects for this type of essay include virtually every aspect of poetry. Thus, you might choose to work with speaker, setting and situation, diction, imagery, tone, rhythm, rhyme and form, symbol, allusion, or theme. The choice, of course, is never completely arbitrary; you should look for an element or technique that strikes you as especially significant and effective.

Prewriting strategies for either a developmental or comparative essay include selecting a poet, an approach, and a focus. These choices are not always easy, but some investigation of the works at hand will usually help you narrow the options considerably. As you plan the essay, you should remember that your aim is to discover development or commonality. With this in mind, you might consider the following questions in connection with a given poet.

1. Are the speakers in the poems similar or related to each other? Does the speaker remain constant throughout the poems, develop gradually, or change radically from poem to poem? To what extent do the speakers share a common tone or attitude? Do tone and attitude remain constant, or do they change?

2. Do the poems have common or similar settings or situations? Are these established vividly and quickly, or left undeveloped? To what extent do setting and situation produce similar effects in a number of poems by the same author?

3. Can you find common threads of diction, imagery, metaphor, simile, symbol, or allusion in a number of poems by the same author? Are these common devices always used the same way and to the same effect, or do the method and impact change?

4. Does the poet's use of the elements of form—rhythm, rhyme, meter, stanza—remain constant or develop? Does form consistently reinforce meaning? Does the connection between form and content remain constant or become less or more effective?

5. Does the poet deal with the same subject or convey similar ideas in a significant number of poems? To what extent do the poet's attitudes toward this subject and treatment of the idea remain constant or change? To what extent can you see logical connection or development among the poems in question?

These questions obviously cover a broad range of topics. In actual practice, however, the poems at hand will usually direct you to specific areas of consideration rather quickly. As you answer the questions that seem relevant to the poems, the focus of the essay should begin to emerge.

Once you have chosen a poet, isolated an area of interest, and selected a series of poems for examination, you can begin to shape a tentative central idea for the essay. As usual, this is probably the most difficult step in the prewriting process. Discovering an area of commonality or development is only half the battle; you must go on to assert a central fact about this common thread. It is not enough, for example, to argue in an essay that "we find the idea of death in three of Emily Dickinson's poems" or that "snow imagery recurs in a number of Robert Frost's poems." Rather, you must link the common thread to an assertion about its effect, impact, or significance. Thus, you might formulate a tentative thesis that argues that "death is presented in a number of Emily Dickinson's poems as the natural and welcome end to a life of toil" or that "the common image of snow in many of Robert Frost's poems grows progressively more grim and ironic throughout his career." Notice that both these formulations identify an area of commonality *and* make an assertion about that area. The first thesis would produce a comparative essay, the second a developmental one.

Having formulated a tentative central idea, you can go back through the poet's work and reexamine those poems that offer support and illustration. You will now be considering aspects of specific poems that will eventually form the body of the essay. During this stage you may find it necessary to revise or refocus the thesis several times to solidify the connection between the essay's central idea and the supporting details.

Organizing Your Essay

INTRODUCTION.   The introductory paragraph should indicate, at least indirectly, the type of approach that will be taken in the essay. After reading the first paragraph, a reader should be able to tell if the essay is biographical, developmental, or comparative. More often than not, this information is conveyed through the formulation of the central idea. The introduction will also specify the area or element of the poet's work about which you are writing. This information too is usually incorporated into the statement of the central idea. The thesis or central idea of the essay should assert a specific point about the subject or element under consideration in the poet's work. Finally, the introduction should specify which poems will be examined to support the central idea of the essay.

BODY.   The organization of the body of the essay is determined almost completely by the strategy outlined in the introduction. A biographical essay would probably be organized around crucial events in the poet's life and key poems that reflect those events. A developmental essay would naturally consider a number of the author's poems in chronological order, based on approximate or exact dates of composition. A comparative essay, on the other hand, might take up one poem at a time in almost any order.

As with other essays, the main thrust of the body is to support and prove the assertion made in the introduction. To do this with conviction, you should normally plan to work with no more than three to five poems. Thus, one effective strategy for organizing the body of the essay is to deal with one poem at a time, stanza by stanza or unit by unit, focusing on the aspect under consideration. Since such an essay might be likely to break down into three or four disjointed discussions, you should be especially careful to provide clear transitions between your treatments of each poem and to tie each separate discussion back into the central idea and the introductory paragraph. In addition, discussions of poems later in the essay should be connected back to earlier ones through comparison or contrast.

CONCLUSION.   The conclusion should pull together all the strands of your argument and provide an overview. This can be done by summarizing the main points and observations. At the same time, you might use the conclusion to relate your argument to a broader consideration of the poet's work. Thus, an essay on the speaker in three of Frost's poems might conclude with a sentence or two that connects this narrative voice with the dominant tones or moods of Frost's poetry.

SAMPLE ESSAY

Images of Expanding and Contracting Space in John Donne's Love Poetry*

[1]   John Donne's love poetry is characterized by extended images and metaphors that emphasize the mystery and the power of love. Images that expand or contract space recur in much of this poetry; they help to create a private and separate world for the lovers and to demonstrate the power of love.° We can see this skillful and effective use of spatial imagery in "The Good Morrow," "The Sun Rising," and "The Flea."□

[2]   "The Good Morrow," a three-stanza lyric spoken by a lover to his mistress, contains spatial images that illustrate both the expansion and the contraction of space to create a private world of love. The central image in this poem is the world or the globe; this image is skillfully manipulated to demonstrate the power of love. The speaker introduces the image in the second stanza when he asserts "For love all love of other sights controls, / And makes one little room an everywhere" (lines 10–11). This image suggests that love is powerful enough to expand "one little room" into an entire world that contains everything

* See "The Good Morrow" (p. 875), "The Sun Rising" (p. 876), and "The Flea" (p. 879).
° Central idea.
□ Thesis sentence.

the lovers might desire. In the rest of the stanza, the image of the world becomes even more explicit:

Let sea-discoverers to new worlds have gone,
Let maps to other, worlds on worlds have shown,
Let us possess one world; each hath one, and is one. (lines 12–14)

The movement of the spatial imagery here is complex but consistent. These lines make a clear distinction between the public world of "sea-discoverers" or "maps" and the private world of the lovers. The speaker asserts that the lovers should "possess" their own world; each lover is a world and "hath" the other lover-world. More to the point, the movement here is inward and progressively contracting, from the actual globe to maps and finally to the lovers as little worlds.

[3]

This contraction of the world and space—the movement inward—is continued in the third stanza with the image of reflected faces: "My face in thine eye, thine in mine appears, / And true plain hearts do in the faces rest" (lines 15–16). At first, this image of reflected faces and hearts seems to depart from the spatial imagery of the second stanza. The connection, however, is established when we realize that eyes are spheres or globes, and that the reflection occurs on the outward half or "hemisphere" of the eyes. This witty contraction of worlds to eyes is brought home in the next two lines: "Where can we find two better hemispheres / Without sharp North, without declining West?" (lines 17–18). Here, the image finally contracts to a single world or globe, and the lovers become that world. Thus, the poem simultaneously contracts global space to the physical presence of the lovers and expands their "little room" into a total cosmos.

[4]

We find a similar manipulation of spatial imagery in "The Sun Rising," another three-stanza lyric spoken by a lover. This time, however, the poem is addressed to the sun, which has awakened the lover and his mistress. In stanza 1 the speaker establishes the distinction between the lovers and the outside world—the "school boys," "sour prentices," "huntsmen," and "country ants." The second stanza returns to images of expanding and contracting space that define love as self-sufficient and all-encompassing. Here the speaker tells the sun:

Look, and tomorrow late, tell me,
Whether both the Indias of spice and mine
Be where thou leftst them, or lie here with me.
Ask for those kings whom thou saw'st yesterday,
And thou shalt hear, All here in one bed lay. (lines 16–20)

In this instance, the image contracts space, pulling most of the world into the bed and into the lovers themselves. The lady becomes both the East Indies of spices and the West Indies of gold. Similarly, the speaker becomes all the kings of the earth.

This imagery of spatial contraction becomes far more vivid in the last stanza of "The Sun Rising," when the speaker asserts that "She is all states, and all princes, I, / Nothing else is" (lines 21–22). The woman thus becomes the world and the speaker the ruler of "all states." The spatial contraction, pulling "all states" into bed with the speaker, underscores the irrelevance of the world at large and the importance of the lovers as a self-contained world. The speaker goes on, in lines 25 and 26, to argue that the sun should be happy "that the world's contracted thus" since warming it will be that much easier. And in the concluding two lines, the lovers and their bed become not only the world but also the center of the solar system: "Shine here to us,

[5] and thou art everywhere; / This bed thy center is, these walls, thy sphere" (lines 29–30). The movement of the image in this poem, as in "The Good Morrow," is thus both contracting and expanding. The outer world—the Indies, all kings, all states, all princes—is pulled into the room, the bed, and the physical being of the lovers. At the same time, the bed and the lovers expand to become a world unto themselves and the center of the solar system; the walls of their room become the outer limits of the sun's orbit. In this way, the spatial imagery creates a tone of comic outrageousness that helps define the power of love.

Although "The Flea" is a very different type of poem than either "The Good Morrow" or "The Sun Rising," similar images of spatial manipulation emphasize the singularity and power of love. Unlike the other two lyrics, "The Flea" is a song of seduction spoken by an eager lover to an unwilling lady. Again, however, space expands and contracts to create a private (and in this

[6] case amusing) world for the lovers. Reduced to its basic logic, the poem asserts that the loss of virginity is no more significant than a flea bite. The master image of the poem is the flea and the blood of the eager lover and resistant lady that has been "mingled" in the flea. Indeed, the first stanza is given over to the image of the flea biting each lover and swelling "with one blood made of two" (line 8).

The speaker does not begin to manipulate spatial imagery until the second stanza of "The Flea," where images of expanding and contracting space become both amusing and bizarre. Working from the premise established in the first stanza, that the flea contains both the speaker's and the lady's blood,

[7] the flea suddenly becomes all three beings: "Oh stay, three lives in one flea spare, / Where we almost, yea more than married, are" (lines 10–11). In terms of the dramatic situation, the lady is about to kill the flea; the speaker argues that they are married within the flea since their bloods are "mingled." This sets up one of Donne's most outrageous spatial images:

This flea is you and I, and this
Our marriage bed and marriage temple is;
Though parents grudge, and you, w'are met,
And cloister'd in these living walls of jet. (lines 12–15)

This manipulation of space and place is obviously witty and bizarre, but it is also consistent with the images of expanding and contracting space that occur in "The Good Morrow" and "The Sun Rising." Here the lovers contract or the flea expands until it has become both a "marriage bed and marriage temple." At the end of the passage we see that the image and the outrageous logic create the lovers' private world; they are "met / And cloister'd" within the black sides of the flea.

[8]   In each of these poems, images of space are thus manipulated to demonstrate the power of love and the private world of the lovers. In all three instances, extended metaphors establish the power of love (or desire) to contract the whole world into one bed or to expand a little room (or even a little flea) into an everywhere. Such imagery is consistent with the attitude toward love expressed throughout Donne's songs and sonnets; love and passion are private, powerful, and mysterious. Images of expanding and contracting space are simply one of the many techniques that Donne employs to emphasize and describe the miracle of love.

Commentary on the Essay

The sample is a comparative essay that deals with a common thread of imagery that runs through a number of Donne's poems. The introduction establishes the blueprint for the entire essay. The first sentence announces the focus—images and metaphors—and makes a generalization about Donne's love poetry. The second sentence establishes the central idea of the essay: images of expanding and contracting space demonstrate both the private world of lovers and the power of love. At the same time, the formulation of this sentence makes it clear that the essay is comparative rather than developmental or biographical; the statement makes no claims for development and avoids any reference to the poet's life. Finally, the last sentence of the introduction specifies the poems that will be discussed to support the central idea in the body of the essay.

The body—paragraphs 2 through 7—takes up the three poems mentioned at the close of the introduction in the order in which they are noted. Thus, paragraphs 2 and 3 deal with "The Good Morrow," 4 and 5 with "The Sun Rising," and 6 and 7 with "The Flea." Each of these two-paragraph units is organized the same way. In each, the topic sentence (the first sentence in paragraphs 2, 4, and 6) names the poem, makes a general observation about the poem, and restates part of the central idea of the essay. Thus, each separate discussion is tied back into the introduction. In addition, the topic sentences in paragraphs 4 and 6 establish transition from poem to poem (and discussion to discussion) by using transitional words like *similar*, *another*, and *although*. In this way, each discussion is linked to the previous one. One additional linking device is employed in each discussion; at some point in each, the poem under discussion is directly compared with the poem or poems previously discussed. All these strategies help to unify the essay.

Within the body of this essay two paragraphs are devoted to each poem. This need not always be the case; in many instances you can make the necessary point using one paragraph for each poem. Here, however, there was too much material to cover each poem in a single paragraph.

Thus, each two-paragraph unit is organized to follow the structure of the poem itself; the first paragraph deals with material in earlier stanzas, and the second with examples in later stanzas. The second paragraph in each unit also begins with a topic sentence that connects the material to the central idea and provides transition from the previous paragraph. In this way, each paragraph in the essay returns to the "straight line" of the central idea.

The conclusion (paragraph 8) restates the central idea of the essay and summarizes the major point illustrated with each poem. In addition, it relates these observations about spatial imagery to the broader context of Donne's love poetry. Thus, the essay ends as it began, with a general assertion about Donne's songs and sonnets.

Additional Poems

LEONARD ADAMÉ (b. 1947)

My Grandmother Would Rock Quietly and Hum   *1973*

in her house
she would rock quietly and hum
until her swelled hands
calmed

in summer   5
she wore thick stockings
sweaters
and grey braids

(when "el cheque" came
we went to Payless°   *a grocery store*   10
and I laughed greedily
when given a quarter)

mornings,
sunlight barely lit
the kitchen   15
and where
there were shadows
it was not cold

she quietly rolled
flour tortillas—   20
the "papas"°   *potatoes*
cracking in hot lard
would wake me

919

she had lost her teeth
and when we ate
she had bread
soaked in "café"

always her eyes
were clear
and she could see
as I cannot yet see—
through her eyes
she gave me herself

she would sit
and talk
of her girlhood—
of things strange to me:
        México
        epidemics
        relatives shot
        her father's hopes
        of this country—
how they sank
with cement dust
to his insides

now
when I go
to the old house
the worn spots
by the stove
echo of her shuffling
and
México
still hangs in her
fading
calendar pictures

25

30

35

40

45

50

55

A. R. AMMONS (b. 1926)

Dunes   *1964*

Taking root in windy sand
    is not an easy
way
to go about
    finding a place to stay.

5

A ditchbank or wood's-edge
  has firmer ground.

In a loose world though
  something can be started—
a root touch water,
  a tip break sand—   10

Mounds from that can rise
  on held mounds,
a gesture of building, keeping,
  a trapping   15
into shape.

Firm ground is not available ground.

MAYA ANGELOU (b. 1928)

My Arkansas   *1978*

There is a deep brooding
in Arkansas.
Old crimes like moss pend
from poplar trees.
The sullen earth   5
is much too
red for comfort.

Sunrise seems to hesitate
and in that second
lose its   10
incandescent aim, and
dusk no more shadows
than the noon.
The past is brighter yet.

Old hates and   15
ante-bellum° lace, are rent
but not discarded.
Today is yet to come
in Arkansas.
It writhes. It writhes in awful   20
waves of brooding.

MY ARKANSAS.   16 *ante-bellum*: before the U.S. Civil War (1861–1865).

ANONYMOUS (traditional Scottish ballad)

Edward

"Why does your brand° so drip wi' blood,   *sword*
    Edward, Edward?
Why does your brand so drip wi' blood?
  And why so sad gang° ye, O?"   *go*
"O, I have killed my hawk so good,   5
    Mother, mother,
O, I have killed my hawk so good,
  And I had no more but he, O."

"Your hawk's blood was never so red,
    Edward, Edward,
Your hawk's blood was never so red,   10
  My dear son I tell thee, O."
"O, I have killed my red-roan steed,
    Mother, mother,
O, I have killed my red-roan steed,   15
  That erst° was so fair and free, O."   *once*

"Your steed was old, and ye have got more,
    Edward, Edward,
Your steed was old, and ye have got more:
  Some other dule° ye dree°, O,"   *sorrow; suffer*   20
"O, I have killed my father dear,
    Mother, mother,
O, I have killed my father dear,
  Alas and woe is me, O!"

"And whatten° penance will ye dree for that,   *what sort of*   25
    Edward, Edward?
And whatten penance will ye dree for that?
  My dear son, now tell me, O."
"I'll set my feet in yonder boat,
    Mother, mother,   30
I'll set my feet in yonder boat,
  And I'll fare over the sea, O."

"And what will ye do wi' your towers and your hall,
    Edward, Edward,
And what will ye do wi' your towers and your hall,   35
  That were so fair to see, O?"
"I'll let them stand till they down fall,
    Mother, mother,
I'll let them stand till they down fall,
For here never more maun° I be, O."   *must*   40

"And what will ye leave to your bairns° and your wife,   *children*
    Edward, Edward?
And what will ye leave to your bairns and your wife,
    When ye gang over the sea, O?"
"The world's room let them beg through life,   45
    Mother, mother
The world's room, let them beg through life,
    For them never more will I see, O."

"And what will ye leave to your own mother dear,
    Edward, Edward?
And what will ye leave to your own mother dear,   50
    My dear son, now tell me, O?"
"The curse of hell from me shall ye bear,
    Mother, mother,
The curse of hell from me shall ye bear,
    Such counsels ye gave to me, O."   55

ANONYMOUS

Lord Randal   *Medieval*

"Oh, where have you been, Lord Randal, my son?
Oh, where have you been, my handsome young man?"
"Oh, I've been to the wildwood; mother, make my bed soon,
I'm weary of hunting and I fain° would lie down."   *gladly*

"And whom did you meet there, Lord Randal, my son?   5
And whom did you meet there, my handsome young man?"
"Oh, I met with my true love; mother, make my bed soon,
I'm weary of hunting and I fain would lie down."

"What got you for supper, Lord Randal, my son?
What got you for supper, my handsome young man?"   10
"I got eels boiled in broth; mother, make my bed soon,
I'm weary of hunting and I fain would lie down."

"And who got your leavings, Lord Randal, my son?
And who got your leavings, my handsome young man?"
"I gave them to my dogs; mother, make my bed soon,   15
I'm weary of hunting and I fain would lie down."

"And what did your dogs do, Lord Randal, my son?
And what did your dogs do, my handsome young man?"
"Oh, they stretched out and died; mother, make my bed soon,
I'm weary of hunting and I fain would lie down."   20

"Oh, I fear you are poisoned, Lord Randal, my son,
Oh, I fear you are poisoned, my handsome young man."
"Oh, yes, I am poisoned; mother, make my bed soon,
For I'm sick at my heart and I fain would lie down."

"What will you leave your mother, Lord Randal, my son?
What will you leave your mother, my handsome young man?"
"My house and my lands; mother, make my bed soon,
For I'm sick at my heart and I fain would lie down."

"What will you leave your sister, Lord Randal, my son?
What will you leave your sister, my handsome young man?"
"My gold and my silver; mother, make my bed soon,
For I'm sick at my heart and I fain would lie down."

"What will you leave your brother, Lord Randal, my son?
What will you leave your brother, my handsome young man?"
"My horse and my saddle; mother, make my bed soon,
For I'm sick at my heart and I fain would lie down."

"What will you leave your true-love, Lord Randal, my son?
What will you leave your true-love, my handsome young man?"
"A halter to hang her; mother, make my bed soon,
For I'm sick at my heart and I want to lie down."

ANONYMOUS

The Three Ravens

Medieval

There were three ravens sat on a tree,
   Down a down, hay down, hay down,
There were three ravens sat on a tree,
   With a down,
There were three ravens sat on a tree,
They were as black as they might be,
   With a down, derry, derry, derry, down, down. °

The one of them said to his mate,
"Where shall we our breakfast take?

"Down in yonder green field
There lies a knight slain under his shield.

"His hounds they lie down at his feet,
So well they can their master keep.

"His hawks they fly so eagerly,°   *fiercely*
There's no fowl° dare him come nigh."   *bird*

THE THREE RAVENS.   7 *down:* In singing this ballad, the first line of each stanza is
repeated three times and the refrain is repeated as in stanza 1.

Down there comes a fallow° doe,   *light brown*
As great with young as she might go,°   *walk*

She lifted up his bloody head,
And kissed his wounds that were so red.

She got him up upon her back,   20
And carried him to earthen lake.°   *pit*

She buried him before the prime,°   *first hour of day*
She was dead herself ere evensong time.°
God send every gentleman
Such hawks, such hounds, and such a lemman.°   *mistress*   25

23 *evensong time*: the time for evening prayers.

JOHN ASHBURY (b. 1927)

Illustration   1956

I
A novice was sitting on a cornice
High over the city. Angels

Combined their prayers with those
Of the police, begging her to come off it.

One lady promised to be her friend.   5
"I do not want a friend," she said.

A mother offered her some nylons
Stripped from her very legs. Others brought

Little offerings of fruit and candy,
The blind man all his flowers. If any   10

Could be called successful, these were,
For that the scene should be a ceremony

Was what she wanted. "I desire
Monuments," she said. "I want to move

Figuratively, as waves caress   15
The thoughtless shore. You people I know

Will offer me every good thing
I do not want. But please remember

I died accepting them." With that, the wind
Unpinned her bulky robes, and naked   20

As a roc's° egg, she drifted softly downward
Out of the angels' tenderness and the minds of men.

II

Much that is beautiful must be discarded
So that we may resemble a taller

Impression of ourselves. Moths climb in the flame,   25
Alas, that wish only to be the flame:

They do not lessen our stature.
We twinkle under the weight

Of indiscretions. But how could we tell
That of the truth we know, she was   30

The somber vestment? For that night, rockets sighed
Elegantly over the city, and there was feasting:

There is so much in that moment!
So many attitudes toward that flame,

We might have soared from earth, watching her glide   35
Aloft, in her peplum° of bright leaves.

But she, of course, was only an effigy
Of indifference, a miracle

Not meant for us, as the leaves are not
Winter's because it is the end.   40

ILLUSTRATION.   21 *roc's*: The roc is a mythical Arabian bird of enormous size and
strength.   36 *peplum*: a short skirt.

W. H. AUDEN (1907–1973)

The Unknown Citizen   *1940*

(To JS/07/M/378
This Marble Monument
Is Erected by the State

He was found by the Bureau of Statistics to be
One against whom there was no official complaint,
And all the reports on his conduct agree
That, in the modern sense of an old-fashioned word, he was a saint,
For in everything he did he served the Greater Community.   5

Except for the War till the day he retired
He worked in a factory and never got fired,
But satisfied his employers, Fudge Motors Inc.

Yet he wasn't a scab° or odd in his views,   *strikebreaker*
For his Union reports that he paid his dues,   10
(Our report on his Union shows it was sound)
And our Social Psychology workers found
That he was popular with his mates° and liked a drink.   *co-workers*
The Press are convinced that he bought a paper every day
And that his reactions to advertisements were normal in every way.   15
Policies taken out in his name prove that he was fully insured,
And his Health-card shows he was once in hospital but left it cured.
Both Producers Research and High-Grade Living declare
He was fully sensible to the advantages of the Instalment Plan
And had everything necessary to the Modern Man,   20
A phonograph, a radio, a car and a frigidaire.
Our researchers into Public Opinion are content
That he held the proper opinions for the time of year;
When there was peace, he was for peace; when there was war, he went.
He was married and added five children to the population,   25
Which our Eugenist says was the right number for a parent of his generation,
And our teachers report that he never interfered with their education.
Was he free? Was he happy? The question is absurd:
Had anything been wrong, we should certainly have heard.

MARGARET AVISON (b. 1918)

Tennis   1960

Service is joy, to see or swing. Allow
All tumult to subside. Then tensest winds
Buffet, brace, viol and sweeping bow.
Courts are for love and volley. No one minds
The cruel ellipse of service and return,   5
Dancing white galliardes° at tape or net
Till point, on the wire's tip, or the long burn-
ing arc to nethercourt marks game and set.
Purpose apart, perched like an umpire, dozes,
Dreams golden balls whirring through indigo.   10
Clay blurs the whitewash but day still encloses
The albinos, bounded in their flick and flow.
Playing in musicked gravity, the pair
Score liquid Euclids° in foolscaps of air.

TENNIS.   6 *galliardes*: lively French dance.   14 *Euclids*: Euclid (ca. B.C. 300) was a Greek
mathematician and geometrician; the term thus suggests geometric shapes.

IMAMU AMIRI BARAKA (LEROI JONES) (b. 1934)

Ka 'Ba   *1969*

A closed window looks down
on a dirty courtyard, and black people
call across or scream across or walk across
defying physics in the stream of their will

Our world is full of sound   5
Our world is more lovely than anyone's
tho we suffer, and kill each other
and sometimes fail to walk the air

We are beautiful people
with african imaginations   10
full of masks and dances and swelling chants

with african eyes, and noses, and arms,
though we sprawl in grey chains in a place
full of winters, when what we want is sun.

We have been captured,   15
brothers. And we labor
to make our getaway, into
the ancient image, into a new

correspondence with ourselves
and our black family. We need magic   20
now we need the spells, to raise up
return, destroy, and create. What will be

the sacred words?

APHRA BEHN (1640–1689)

Love Armed   *1665*

Love in Fantastic Triumph sat,
Whilst Bleeding Hearts around him flowed,
For whom Fresh pains he did Create,
And strange Tyrannic power he showed;
From thy Bright Eyes he took his fire,   5
Which round about, in sport he hurled;
But 'twas from mine he took desire,
Enough to undo the Amorous World.

From me he took his sighs and tears,
From thee his Pride and Cruelty;   10
From me his Languishments and Fears,

And every Killing Dart from thee;
Thus thou and I, the God° have armed,   *Cupid, god of love*
And set him up a Deity;
But my poor Heart alone is harmed,   15
Whilst thine the Victor is, and free.

MARVIN BELL (b. 1937)

Things We Dreamt We Died For   *1969*

Flats of all sorts.
The literary life.
Each time we dreamt we'd done
the gentlemanly thing,
covering our causes   5
in closets full of bones
to remove ourselves forever
from dearest possibilities,
the old weapons re-injured us,
the old armies conscripted us,   10
and we gave in to getting even,
a little less like us
if a lot less like others.
Many, thus, gained fame
in the way of great plunderers,   15
retiring to the university
to cultivate grand plunder-gardens
in the service of literature,
the young and no more wars.
Their continuing tributes   20
make them our greatest saviours,
whose many fortunes are followed
by the many who have not one.

EARLE BIRNEY (b. 1904)

Can. Lit.°   *1962*

(or *them able leave her ever*)

since we'd always sky about
when we had eagles they flew out
leaving no shadow bigger than wren's
to trouble even our broodiest hens

CAN. LIT. The title is an abbreviation for Canadian Literature.

too busy bridging loneliness
to be alone
we hacked in railway ties
what Emily° etched in bone

we French & English never lost
our civil war
endure it still
a bloody civil bore

the wounded sirened off
no Whitman° wanted
it's only by our lack of ghosts
we're haunted

8 *Emily*: Emily Dickinson (1830–1886), American poet.   14 *Whitman*: Walt Whitman
(1819–1892), American poet.

WILLIAM BLAKE (1757–1827)

The Sick Rose   1794

O Rose thou art sick.
The invisible worm
That flies in the night,
In the howling storm:

Has found out thy bed
Of crimson joy:
And his dark secret love
Does thy life destroy.

WILLIAM BLAKE (1757–1827)

Ah Sun-flower   1794

Ah Sun-flower! weary of time,
Who counts the steps of the Sun,
Seeking after that sweet golden clime
Where the traveller's journey is done;

Where the Youth pined away with desire,
And the pale Virgin shrouded in snow,
Arise from their graves and aspire,
Where my Sun-flower wishes to go.

ROBERT BLY (b. 1926)

Snowfall in the Afternoon   *1962*

1.
The grass is half-covered with snow.
It was the sort of snowfall that starts in late afternoon,
And now the little houses of the grass are growing dark.

2.
If I reached my hands down, near the earth,
I could take handfuls of darkness!   5
A darkness was always there, which we never noticed.

3.
As the snow grows heavier, the cornstalks fade farther away,
And the barn moves nearer to the house.
The barn moves all alone in the growing storm.

4.
The barn is full of corn, and moving toward us now,   10
Like a hulk blown toward us in a storm at sea;
All the sailors on deck have been blind for many years.

LOUISE BOGAN (1879–1970)

Women   *1923*

Women have no wilderness in them,
They are provident instead,
Content in the tight hot cell of their hearts
To eat dusty bread.

They do not see cattle cropping red winter grass,   5
They do not hear
Snow water going down under culverts
Shallow and clear.

They wait, when they should turn to journeys,
They stiffen, when they should bend.   10
They use against themselves that benevolence
To which no man is friend.

They cannot think of so many crops to a field
Or of clean wood cleft by an axe.
Their love is an eager meaninglessness   15
Too tense, or too lax.

They hear in every whisper that speaks to them
A shout and a cry.
As like as not, when they take life over their door-sills
They should let it go by.   20

ARNA BONTEMPS (1902–1973)

A Black Man Talks of Reaping   *1940*

I have sown beside all waters in my day.
I planted deep, within my heart the fear
that wind or fowl would take the grain away.
I planted safe against this stark, lean year.

I scattered seed enough to plant the land   5
in rows from Canada to Mexico
but for my reaping only what the hand
can hold at once is all that I can show.

Yet what I sowed and what the orchard yields
my brother's sons are gathering stalk and root;   10
small wonder then my children glean in fields
they have not sown, and feed on bitter fruit.

ANNE BRADSTREET (1612–1672)

To My Dear and Loving Husband   *1678*

If ever two were one, then surely we.
If ever man were loved by wife, then thee;
If ever wife was happy in a man,
Compare with me ye women if you can.
I prize thy love more than whole mines of gold,   5
Or all the riches that the East doth hold.
My love is such that rivers cannot quench,
Nor ought but love from thee give recompense.
Thy love is such I can no way repay;
The heavens reward thee manifold, I pray.   10
Then while we live, in love let's so persever,
That when we live no more we may live ever.

ROBERT BRIDGES (1844–1930)

Nightingales   *1893*

Beautiful must be the mountains whence ye come,
And bright in the fruitful valleys the streams, wherefrom
Ye learn your song:

Where are those starry woods? O might I wander there,
  Among the flowers, which in that heavenly air   5
    Bloom the year long!

Nay, barren are those mountains and spent the streams:
  Our song is the voice of desire, that haunts our dreams,
    A throe of the heart,
Whose pining visions dim, forbidden hopes profound,   10
  No dying cadence nor long sigh can sound,
    For all our art.

Alone, aloud in the raptured ear of men
  We pour our dark nocturnal secret; and then,
    As night is withdrawn   15
From these sweet-springing meads° and bursting boughs of May,   *meadows*
  Dream, while the innumerable choir of day
    Welcome the dawn.

GWENDOLYN BROOKS (b. 1917)

Primer for Blacks   *1980*

Blackness
is a title,
is a preoccupation,
is a commitment Blacks
are to comprehend—   5
and in which you are
to perceive your Glory.

The conscious shout
of all that is white is
"It's Great to be white."   10
The conscious shout
of the slack in Black is
"It's Great to be white."
Thus all that is white
has white strength and yours.   15

The word Black
has geographic power,
pulls everybody in:
Blacks here—
Blacks there—   20
Blacks wherever they may be.
And remember, you Blacks, what they told you—
remember your Education:
"one Drop—one Drop
maketh a brand new Black."   25
    Oh mighty Drop.

——And because they have given us kindly
so many more of our people

Blackness
stretches over the land.
Blackness—
the Black of it,
the rust-red of it,
the milk and cream of it,
the tan and yellow-tan of it,
the deep-brown middle-brown high-brown of it,
the "olive" and ochre of it—
Blackness
marches on.

The huge, the pungent object of our prime out-ride   40
is to Comprehend,
to salute and to Love the fact that we are Black,
which *is* our "ultimate Reality,"
which is the lone ground
from which our meaningful metamorphosis,   45
from which our prosperous staccato,
group or individual, can rise.

Self-shriveled Blacks.
Begin with gaunt and marvelous concession:
YOU are our costume and our fundamental bone.   50

    All of you—
    you COLORED ones,
    you NEGRO ones,
those of you who proudly cry
    "I'm half INDian"—   55
    those of you who proudly screech
    "I'VE got the blood of George WASHington in
      MY veins"—

ALL of you—
    you proper Blacks,   60
you half-Blacks,
you wish-I-weren't Blacks,
Niggeroes and Niggerenes.

You.

ELIZABETH BARRETT BROWNING (1806–1861)

Number 43: Sonnets from the Portuguese   *1850*

How do I love thee? Let me count the ways.
I love thee to the depth and breadth and height
My soul can reach, when feeling out of sight

For the ends of Being and ideal Grace.
I love thee to the level of every day's   5
Most quiet need, by sun and candlelight.
I love thee freely, as men strive for Right;
I love thee purely, as they turn from Praise.
I love thee with the passion put to use
In my old griefs, and with my childhood's faith.   10
I love thee with a love I seemed to lose
With my lost saints,—I love thee with the breath,
Smiles, tears, of all my life!—and, if God choose,
I shall but love thee better after death.

ROBERT BURNS (1759–1796)

To a Mouse   *1786*

ON TURNING HER UP IN HER NEST WITH
THE PLOW, NOVEMBER, 1785

Wee, sleekit,° cow'rin', tim'rous beastie,   *sleek*
O, what a panic's in thy breastie!
Thou need na start awa sae hasty,
        Wi' bickering brattle!°   *scamper*
I wad be laith° to rin an' chase thee   *loath*   5
        Wi' murd'ring pattle!°   *plowstaff*

I'm truly sorry man's dominion
Has broken Nature's social union,
An' justifies that ill opinion
        Which makes thee startle   10
At me, thy poor, earth-born companion,
        An' fellow mortal!

I doubt na, whiles,° but thou may thieve;   *sometimes*
What then? poor beastie, thou maun° live!   *must*
A daimen-icker° in a thrave°   15
        'S a sma' request:
I'll get a blessin' wi' the lave,°   *remainder*
        And never miss 't!

Thy wee-bit housie, too, in ruin!
Its silly° wa's the win's are strewin'!   *feeble*   20
An' naething, now, to big° a new ane,   *build*
        O' foggage° green!   *moss*
An' bleak December's winds ensuin',
        Baith snell° an' keen!   *bitter*

Thou saw the fields laid bare and waste,   25
An' weary winter comin' fast,

TO A MOUSE.   15 *daimen-icker*: an occasional ear of corn.   *thrave*: a unit of measure,
equal to twenty-four sheaves, for unthreshed grain.

An' cozie here, beneath the blast,
　　　Thou thought to dwell,
Till crash! the cruel coulter° passed　　　　　　　　　　　*cutter-blade*
　　　Out-through thy cell.　　　　　　　　　　　　　　　　　　30

That wee-bit heap o' leaves an' stibble°　　　　　　　　　　　*stubble*
Has cost thee mony a weary nibble!
Now thou's turned out, for a' thy trouble,
　　　But° house or hald,°　　　　　　　　　　　　　*Without; hold*
To thole° the winter's sleety dribble,　　　　　　　　　　*endure*　35
　　　An' cranreuch° cauld!　　　　　　　　　　　　　　　*hoarfrost*

But Mousie, thou art no thy lane,°　　　　　　　　　　　*not alone*
In proving foresight may be vain:
The best-laid schemes o' mice an' men
　　　Gang aft a-gley,°　　　　　　　　　　　　　*go often awry*　40
An' lea'e us nought but grief an' pain,
　　　For promised joy.

Still thou art blest compared wi' me!
The present only toucheth thee:
But och! I backward cast my e'e　　　　　　　　　　　　　　　　45
　　　On prospects drear!
An' forward though I canna see,
　　　I guess an' fear!

LUCILLE CLIFTON (b. 1936)

My Mama Moved Among the Days　　　　　　　　　　　　　*1969*

My Mama moved among the days
like a dreamwalker in a field;
seemed like what she touched was hers
seemed like what touched her couldn't hold,
she got us almost through the high grass　　　　　　　　　　　5
then seemed like she turned around and ran
right back in
right back on in

LEONARD COHEN (b. 1934)

Suzanne Takes You Down　　　　　　　　　　　　　　　　*1966*

Suzanne takes you down
to her place near the river,
you can hear the boats go by

you can stay the night beside her.
And you know that she's half crazy   5
but that's why you want to be there
and she feeds you tea and oranges
that come all the way from China.
Just when you mean to tell her
that you have no gifts to give her,   10
she gets you on her wave-length
and she lets the river answer
that you've always been her lover.
    And you want to travel with her,
    you want to travel blind   15
    and you know that she can trust you
    because you've touched her perfect body
    with your mind.

Jesus was a sailor
when he walked upon the water   20
and he spent a long time watching
from a lonely wooden tower
and when he knew for certain
only drowning men could see him
he said All men will be sailors then   25
until the sea shall free them,
but he himself was broken
long before the sky would open,
forsaken, almost human,
he sank beneath your wisdom like a stone.   30
    And you want to travel with him,
    you want to travel blind
    and you think maybe you'll trust him
    because he touched your perfect body
    with his mind.   35

Suzanne takes your hand
and she leads you to the river,
she is wearing rags and feathers
from Salvation Army counters.
The sun pours down like honey   40
on our lady of the harbour
as she shows you where to look
among the garbage and the flowers,
there are heroes in the seaweed
there are children in the morning,   45
they are leaning out for love
they will lean that way forever
while Suzanne she holds the mirror.
    And you want to travel with her
    and you want to travel blind   50

and you're sure that she can find you
because she's touched her perfect body
with her mind.

STEPHEN CRANE (1871–1900)

Do Not Weep, Maiden, for War Is Kind A strong, 1896, 1899 (1895)

ironic anti-war poem. Focuses on the losses &

Do not weep, maiden, for war is kind. *deaths that come in war.*
Because <u>your lover</u> threw wild hands toward the sky
And the affrighted steed ran on alone,
Do not weep.
War is kind.   5

    Hoarse, <u>booming drums</u> of the regiment *Stanzas 2 & 4 mock the*
    Little souls who <u>thirst for fight,</u> *symbols & images that*
    These men were born to drill and die *drive men to war.*
    The <u>unexplained glory</u> flies above them
    Great is the <u>battle-god</u>, great, and his kingdom—   10
    A field where a thousand corpses lie.

Image
Do not weep, babe, for war is kind.
Because <u>your father</u> tumbled in the yellow trenches,
Raged at his breast, gulped and died,
Do not weep.   15
War is kind.

    Swift, <u>blazing flag</u> of the regiment *Contrasts the illusions*
    <u>Eagle</u> with crest of red and gold, *of ideals with the*
    These men were born to drill and die *realities of carnage &*
    Point for them the virtue of slaughter *loss.*   20
    Make plain to them the excellence of killing
    And a field where a thousand corpses lie.

Mother whose head hung <u>humble as a button</u> *Simile*
On the bright splendid <u>shroud</u> of <u>your son,</u>
Do not weep.   25
War is kind.

STEPHEN CRANE (1871–1900)

The Impact of a Dollar upon the Heart   1895

The impact of a dollar upon the heart
Smiles warm red light
Sweeping from the hearth rosily upon the white table,
With the hanging cool velvet shadows
Moving softly upon the door.   5

The impact of a million dollars
Is a crash of flunkeys
And yawning emblems of Persia
Cheeked against oak, France and a sabre,
The outcry of old Beauty   10
Whored by pimping merchants
To submission before wine and chatter.
Silly rich peasants stamp the carpets of men,
Dead men who dreamed fragrance and light
Into their woof, their lives;   15
The rug of an honest bear
Under the feet of a cryptic slave
Who speaks always of baubles
Forgetting place, multitude, work and state,
Champing and mouthing of hats   20
Making ratful squeak of hats,
Hats.

ISABELLA VALANCY CRAWFORD (1850–1887)

From *Gisli, the Chieftain*: *The Song of the Arrow*   *1884*

What know I,
As I bite the blue veins of the throbbing sky;
To the quarry's breast,
Hot from the sides of the sleek smooth nest?

What know I   5
Of the will of the tense bow from which I fly!
What the need or jest,
That feathers my flight to its bloody rest.

What know I
Of the will of the bow that speeds me on high?   10
What doth the shrill bow
Of the hand on its singing soul-string know?

Flame-swift speed I—
And the dove and the eagle shriek out and die;
Whence comes my sharp zest   15
For the heart of the quarry? the Gods know best.

Deep pierc'd the red gaze of the eagle
The breast of a cygnet° below him;   *young swan*
Beneath his dun wing from the eastward
Shrill-chaunted the long shaft of Gisli!   20

Beneath his dun wing from the westward
Shook a shaft that laugh'd in its biting—

Met in the fierce breast of the eagle
The arrows of Gisli and Brynhild!

COUNTEE CULLEN (1903–1946)

Yet Do I Marvel   1925

I doubt not God is good, well-meaning, kind,
And did He stoop to quibble could tell why
The little buried mole continues blind,
Why flesh that mirrors Him must some day die,
Make plain the reason tortured Tantalus°
Is baited by the fickle fruit, declare
If merely brute caprice dooms Sisyphus°
To struggle up a never-ending stair.
Inscrutable His ways are, and immune
To catechism by a mind too strewn   1(
With petty cares to slightly understand
What awful brain compels His awful hand.
Yet do I marvel at this curious thing:
To make a poet black, and bid him sing!

YET DO I MARVEL.   5 *Tantalus*: a figure in Greek mythology condemned to eternal
hunger and thirst. He stood in Hades chin deep in water with a fruit-laden branch just
above his head, but could never eat or drink.   7 *Sisyphus*: a figure in Greek mythology
condemned to eternally useless labor. He was fated to roll a huge boulder up a hill in Hades,
but each time he neared the top, the stone slipped and he had to begin anew.

E. E. CUMMINGS (1894–1962)

next to of course god america i   1926

"next to of course god america i
love you land of the pilgrims' and so forth oh
say can you see by the dawn's early my
country 'tis of centuries come and go
and are no more what of it we should worry
in every language even deafanddumb
thy sons acclaim your glorious name by gorry
by jingo by gee by gosh by gum
why talk of beauty what could be more beaut-
iful than these heroic happy dead   1(
who rushed like lions to the roaring slaughter
they did not stop to think they died instead
then shall the voice of liberty be mute?"

He spoke. And drank rapidly a glass of water

E. E. CUMMINGS (1894–1962)

if there are any heavens   *1931*

if there are any heavens my mother will (all by herself) have
one. It will not be a pansy heaven nor
a fragile heaven of lilies-of-the-valley but
it will be a heaven of blackred roses

my father will be (deep like a rose   5
tall like a rose)

standing near my

(swaying over her
silent)
with eyes which are really petals and see   10

nothing with the face of a poet really which
is a flower and not a face with
hands
which whisper
This is my beloved my   15
                    (suddenly in sunlight
he will bow,

& the whole garden will bow)

JAMES DICKEY (b. 1923)

The Lifeguard   *1962*

In a stable of boats I lie still,
From all sleeping children hidden.
The leap of a fish from its shadow
Makes the whole lake instantly tremble.
With my foot on the water, I feel   5
The moon outside

Take on the utmost of its power.
I rise and go out through the boats.
I set my broad sole upon silver,
On the skin of the sky, on the moonlight,   10
Stepping outward from earth onto water
In quest of the miracle

This village of children believed
That I could perform as I dived
For one who had sunk from my sight.   15
I saw his cropped haircut go under.

I leapt, and my steep body flashed
Once, in the sun.

Dark drew all the light from my eyes.
Like a man who explores his death   20
By the pull of his slow-moving shoulders,
I hung head down in the cold,
Wide-eyed, contained, and alone
Among the weeds,

And my fingertips turned into stone   25
From clutching immovable blackness.
Time after time I leapt upward
Exploding in breath, and fell back
From the change in the children's faces
At my defeat.   30

Beneath them I swam to the boathouse
With only my life in my arms
To wait for the lake to shine back
At the risen moon with such power
That my steps on the light of the ripples   35
Might be sustained.

Beneath me is nothing but brightness
Like the ghost of a snowfield in summer.
As I moved toward the center of the lake,
Which is also the center of the moon,   40
I am thinking of how I may be
The savior of one

Who has already died in my care.
The dark trees fade from around me.
The moon's dust hovers together.   45
I call softly out, and the child's
Voice answers through blinding water.
Patiently, slowly,

He rises, dilating to break
The surface of stone with his forehead.   50
He is one I do not remember
Having ever seen in his life.
The ground I stand on is trembling
Upon his smile.

I wash the black mud from my hands.   55
On a light given off by the grave
I kneel in the quick of the moon
At the heart of a distant forest
And hold in my arms a child
Of water, water, water.   60

H. D. (HILDA DOOLITTLE) (1886–1961)

Pear Tree   *1916*

Silver dust
lifted from the earth,
higher than my arms reach,
you have mounted,
O silver,   5
higher than my arms reach
you front us with great mass;

no flower ever opened
so staunch a white leaf,
no flower ever parted silver   10
from such rare silver;

O white pear,
your flower-tufts
thick on the branch
bring summer and ripe fruits   15
in their purple hearts.

ALAN DUGAN (b. 1923)

Love Song: I and Thou   *1961*

Nothing is plumb, level or square
  the studs are bowed, the joists
are shaky by nature, no piece fits
  any other piece without a gap
or pinch, and bent nails   5
  dance all over the surfacing
like maggots. By Christ
  I am no carpenter. I built
the roof for myself, the walls
  for myself, the floors   10
for myself, and got
  hung up in it myself. I
danced with a purple thumb
  at this house-warming, drunk
with my prime whiskey: rage.   15
  Oh I spat rage's nails
into the frame-up of my work:
  it held. It settled plumb,
level, solid, square and true
  for that great moment. Then   20

it screamed and went on through,
  skewing as wrong the other way.
God damned it. This is hell,
  but I planned it. I sawed it,
I nailed it, and I
  will live in it until it kills me.   25
I can nail my left palm
  to the left-hand cross-piece but
I can't do everything myself.
  I need a hand to nail the right,   30
a help, a love, a you, a wife.

PAUL LAURENCE DUNBAR (1872–1906) A Black poet

Sympathy   1895

Imposed limitations   *Tome?*

Connotation

I know what the caged bird feels, alas!
When the sun is bright on the upland slopes;
When the wind stirs soft through the springing grass   *Spring*
And the river flows like a stream of glass;
When the first bird sings and the first bud opes,   5
And the faint perfume from its chalice steals— *metaphor*
I know what the caged bird feels!

I know why the caged bird beats his wing
Till its blood is red on the cruel bars;
For he must fly back to his perch and cling   10
When he fain would be on the bough a-swing;
And a pain still throbs in the old, old scars *of other times when*
And they pulse again with a keener sting— *he's thrown himself*
I know why he beats his wing! *against the bars.*

I know why the caged bird sings, ah me,   15
When his wing is bruised and his bosom sore,
When he beats his bars and would be free;
It is not a carol of joy or glee,
But a prayer that he sends from his heart's deep core,
But a plea, that upward to Heaven he flings—   20
I know why the caged bird sings!   *Desperately*

SIR EDWARD DYER (1540–1607)

My Mind to Me a Kingdom Is   1588

My mind to me a kingdom is;
  Such present joys therein I find
That it excells all other bliss
  That earth affords° or grows by kind.

                                   offers

Though much I want which most would have,   5
Yet still my mind forbids to crave.

No princely pomp, no wealthy store,
  No force to win the victory,
No wily wit to salve a sore,
  No shape to feed a loving eye;   10
To none of these I yield as thrall.°   *captive*
For why° my mind doth serve for all.   *because*

I see how pleanty suffers oft,
  And hasty climbers soon do fall;
I see that those which are aloft   15
  Mishap doth threaten most of all;
They get with toil, they keep with fear.
Such cares my mind could never bear.

Content I live, this is my stay;
  I seek no more than may suffice;   20
I press to bear no haughty sway°;   *influence*
  Look, what I lack my mind supplies;
Lo, thus I triumph like a king,
Content with that my mind doth bring.

Some have too much, yet still do crave;   25
  I little have, and seek no more.
They are but poor, though much they have,
  And I am rich with little store.
They poor, I rich; they beg, I give;
They lack, I leave; they pine, I live.   30

I laugh not at another's loss;
  I grudge not at another's gain;
No worldly waves my mind can toss;
  My state at one doth still remain.
I fear no foe, I fawn° no friend;   *flatter* 35
I loathe not life, nor dread my end.

Some weight their pleasures by their lust,
  Their wisdom by their rage of will;
Their treasure is their only trust;
  A cloaked craft their store of skill.   40
But all the pleasures that I find
Is to maintain a quiet mind.

My wealth is health and perfect ease;
  My conscience clear my choice° defense;   *best*
I neither seek by bribes to please,   45
  Nor by deceit to breed offense.
Thus do I live; thus will I die.
Would all did so as well as I.

RICHARD EBERHARDT (b. 1904)

The Groundhog   *1936*

In June, amid the golden fields,
I saw a groundhog lying dead.
Dead lay he; my senses shook,
And mind outshot our naked frailty.
There lowly in the vigorous summer
His form began its senseless change,
And made my senses waver dim
Seeing nature ferocious in him.
Inspecting close his maggots' might
And seething cauldron of his being,   10
Half with loathing, half with a strange love,
I poked him with an angry stick.
The fever arose, became a flame
And Vigour circumscribed the skies,
Immense energy in the sun,   15
And through my frame a sunless trembling.
My stick had done nor good nor harm.
Then stood I silent in the day
Watching the object, as before;
And kept my reverence for knowledge   20
Trying for control, to be still,
To quell the passion of the blood;
Until I had bent down on my knees
Praying for joy in the sight of decay.
And so I left; and I returned   25
In Autumn strict of eye, to see
The sap gone out of the groundhog,
But the bony sodden hulk remained.
But the year had lost its meaning,
And in intellectual chains   30
I lost both love and loathing,
Mured up in the wall of wisdom.
Another summer took the fields again
Massive and burning, full of life,
But when I chanced upon the spot   35
There was only a little hair left,
And bones bleaching in the sunlight
Beautiful as architecture;
I watched them like a geometer,
And cut a walking stick from a birch.   40
It has been three years, now.
There is no sign of the groundhog.
I stood there in the whirling summer,
My hand capped a withered heart,
And thought of China and of Greece,   45

Of Alexander° in his tent;
Of Montaigne° in his tower,
Of Saint Theresa° in her wild lament.

THE GROUNDHOG.   46 *Alexander*: Alexander the Great (B.C. 356–323), king of
Macedonia and conquerer of virtually the entire civilized world.   47 *Montaigne*: Michel
de Montaigne (1553–1592), French essayist and commentator on human nature and society.
48 *Saint Theresa*: Theresa de Avila (1515–1582), Spanish religious mystic, writer, and founder
of a religious order.

T. S. ELIOT (1888–1965)

The Love Song of J. Alfred Prufrock °   *1915 (1910–11)*

S'io credesse che mia risposta fosse
A persona che mai tornasse al mondo,
Questa fiamma staria senza piu scosse.
Ma perciocche giammai di questo fondo
Non torno vivo alcun, s'i'odo il vero,
Senza tema d'infamia ti rispondo.°

Let us go then, you and I,
When the evening is spread out against the sky
Like a patient etherized upon a table;
Let us go, through certain half-deserted streets,
The muttering retreats   5
Of restless nights in one-night cheap hotels
And sawdust restaurants with oyster shells;
Streets that follow like a tedious argument
Of insidious intent
To lead you to an overwhelming question . . .   10
Oh, do not ask, "What is it?"
Let us go and make our visit.

In the room the women come and go
Talking of Michelangelo.°

The yellow fog that rubs its back upon the windowpanes,   15
The yellow smoke that rubs its muzzle on the windowpanes
Licked its tongue into the corners of the evening,
Lingered upon the pools that stand in drains,
Let fall upon its back the soot that falls from chimneys,

THE LOVE SONG OF J. ALFRED PRUFROCK. The poem is a monologue spoken by
Prufrock; the name is invented but suggests a businessman.   EPIGRAPH: The Italian epigraph
is quoted from Dante's *Inferno* (Canto 27, lines 61–66) and is spoken by a man who relates
his evil deeds to Dante because he assumes that Dante will never return to the world: "If I
believed that my response were made to a person who would ever revisit the world, this
flame would stand motionless. But since none has ever returned from this depth alive, if I
hear the truth, I answer you without fear of infamy."   14 *Michelangelo*: one of the greatest
Italian Renaissance artists and sculptors (1475–1564). The name suggests that the women
are cultured, or at least pretending to be so.

Slipped by the terrace, made a sudden leap,   20
And seeing that it was a soft October night,
Curled once about the house, and fell asleep.

And indeed there will be time
For the yellow smoke that slides along the street,
Rubbing its back upon the windowpanes;   25
There will be time, there will be time°
To prepare a face to meet the faces that you meet;
There will be time to murder and create,
And time for all the works and days° of hands
That lift and drop a question on your plate;   30
Time for you and time for me,
And time yet for a hundred indecisions,
And for a hundred visions and revisions,
Before the taking of a toast and tea.

In the room the women come and go   35
Talking of Michelangelo.

And indeed there will be time
To wonder, "Do I dare?" and, "Do I dare?"
Time to turn back and descend the stair,
With a bald spot in the middle of my hair—   40
(They will say: "How his hair is growing thin!")
My morning coat, my collar mounting firmly to the chin,
My necktie rich and modest, but asserted by a simple pin—
(They will say: "But how his arms and legs are thin!")
Do I dare   45
Disturb the universe?
In a minute there is time
For decisions and revisions which a minute will reverse.

For I have known them all already, known them all—
Have known the evenings, mornings, afternoons,   50
I have measured out my life with coffee spoons;
I know the voices dying with a dying fall°
Beneath the music from a farther room.
   So how should I presume?

And I have known the eyes already, known them all—   55
The eyes that fix you in a formulated phrase,
And when I am formulated, sprawling on a pin,
When I am pinned and wriggling on the wall,
Then how should I begin
To spit out all the butt-ends of my days and ways?   60
And how should I presume?

---

26 *time*: a possible allusion to Andrew Marvell's "To His Coy Mistress" (p. 849).   29 *works and days*: the title of a poem about farming by the Greek poet Hesiod. Here the phrase ironically refers to social gestures.   52 *dying fall*: an allusion to a speech by Orsino in Shakespeare's *Twelfth Night* (I.i.4).

And I have known the arms already, known them all—
Arms that are braceleted and white and bare
(But in the lamplight, downed with light brown hair!)
Is it perfume from a dress   65
That makes me so digress?
Arms that lie along a table, or wrap about a shawl.
    And should I then presume?
    And how should I begin?

Shall I say, I have gone at dusk through narrow streets   70
And watched the smoke that rises from the pipes
Of lonely men in shirt-sleeves, leaning out of windows? . . .

I should have been a pair of ragged claws
Scuttling across the floors of silent seas.

And the afternoon, the evening, sleeps so peacefully!   75
Smoothed by long fingers,
Asleep . . . tired . . . or it malingers,°
Stretched on the floor, here beside you and me.
Should I, after tea and cakes and ices,
Have the strength to force the moment to its crisis?   80
But though I have wept and fasted, wept and prayed,
Though I have seen my head (grown slightly bald) brought in upon a platter,°
I am no prophet—and here's no great matter;
I have seen the moment of my greatness flicker,
And I have seen the eternal Footman hold my coat, and snicker, 85
And in short, I was afraid.

And would it have been worth it, after all,
After the cups, the marmalade, the tea,
Among the porcelain, among some talk of you and me,
Would it have been worth while,   90
To have bitten off the matter with a smile,
To have squeezed the universe into a ball°
To roll it toward some overwhelming question,
To say: "I am Lazarus,° come from the dead,
Come back to tell you all, I shall tell you all"—   95
If one, settling a pillow by her head.
    Should say: "That is not what I meant at all.
    That is not it, at all."

And would it have been worth it, after all,
Would it have been worth while,   100
After the sunsets and the dooryards and the sprinkled streets,
After the novels, after the teacups, after the skirts that trail along the floor—
And this, and so much more?—

77 *malingers*: pretends to be ill.   82 *platter*: as was the head of John the Baptist; see Mark
6:17–28 and Matthew 14:3–11.   92 *ball*: another allusion to Marvell's "Coy
Mistress."   94 *Lazarus*: See Luke 16:19–31 and John 11:1–44.

It is impossible to say just what I mean!
But as if a magic lantern threw the nerves in patterns on a screen: 10
Would it have been worth while
If one, settling a pillow or throwing off a shawl,
And turning toward the window, should say:
    "That is not it at all,
    That is not what I meant, at all."   11

No! I am not Prince Hamlet,° nor was meant to be;
Am an attendant lord, one that will do
To swell a progress,° start a scene or two,
Advise the prince; no doubt, an easy tool,
Deferential, glad to be of use,   11
Politic, cautious, and meticulous;
Full of high sentence,° but a bit obtuse;
At times, indeed, almost ridiculous—
Almost, at times, the Fool.

I grow old . . . I grow old . . .   12
I shall wear the bottoms of my trousers rolled.°

Shall I part my hair behind? Do I dare to eat a peach?
I shall wear white flannel trousers, and walk upon the beach.
I have heard the mermaids singing, each to each.

I do not think that they will sing to me.   12

I have seen them riding seaward on the waves
Combing the white hair of the waves blown back
When the wind blows the water white and black.

We have lingered in the chambers of the sea
By sea-girls wreathed with seaweed red and brown   13
Till human voices wake us, and we drown.

111 *Prince Hamlet*: the hero of Shakespeare's play *Hamlet*.   113 *swell a progress*: enlarge a
royal procession.   117 *sentence*: ideals, opinions, sentiment.   121 *rolled*: a possible
reference to cuffs, which were becoming fashionable in 1910.

JOHN ENGELS (b. 1931)

Naming the Animals   Allusion to Adam's naming the animals in Eden.   1981

Since spring I've seen two deer,
Dead   one lashed to a fender. The other fed   Alive
in a clearing on the back slope
of Bean Hill, his big rack° still   antlers
in velvet. The shot buck bled,

image { its tongue frozen
       to the rusty hood. Winter

But the other, in its simpler stance,   *[handwritten: ironic understatement]*
felt merely the delicate itch
of antler skin.

[handwritten: Establishes the contrast of life + death, eating + dying.]

10

And three does, mildly alert,
cocked ears toward where I watched from   *[handwritten: man is death to them,]*
in the hemlocks. I saw, of course,
five deer; but I
count only what by plain necessity of death

15

or feeding is oblivious to me,
does not watch back.   *[handwritten: He sees 5 but only counts 1. Adam named the living, but he counts the dead]*

MARI EVANS

I Am A Black Woman
1970

I am a black woman
the music of my song
some sweet arpeggio of tears
is written in a minor key
and I
can be heard humming in the night
Can be heard
    humming
in the night

5

I saw my mate leap screaming to the sea
and I/with these hands/cupped the lifebreath
from my issue in the canebrake
I lost Nat's° swinging body in a rain of tears

10

and heard my son scream all the way from Anzio°
for Peace he never knew. . . . I
learned Da Nang° and Pork Chop Hill°
in anguish
Now my nostrils know the gas
and these trigger tire/d fingers
seek the softness in my warrior's beard

15

20

I
am a black woman
tall as a cypress
strong

I AM A BLACK WOMAN.   13 *Nat*: Nat Turner (1800–1831), black who led a slave revolt in Southampton, Virginia, in 1831 and was hanged.   14 *Anzio*: seacoast town in Italy, the scene of fierce fighting between the Allies and the Germans in 1944 during World War II.   16 *Da Nang*: major American military base in South Vietnam, frequently attacked during the Vietnam War.   *Pork Chop Hill*: site of a bloody battle between U.N. and Communist forces during the Korean War (1950–1953).

beyond all definition still
defying place
and time
and circumstance
  assailed
    impervious
      indestructible
Look
  on me and be
renewed

CAROLYN FORCHE (b. 1950)

The Visitor   1981 (1979)

In Spanish he whispers there is no time left.
It is the sound of scythes arcing in wheat,
the ache of some field song in Salvador.
The wind along the prison, cautious
as Francisco's hands on the inside, touching
the walls as he walks, it is his wife's breath
slipping into his cell each night while he
imagines his hand to be hers. It is a small country.

There is nothing one man will not do to another.

NIKKI GIOVANNI (b. 1943)

Woman   1978

she wanted to be a blade
of grass amid the fields
but he wouldn't agree
to be the dandelion

she wanted to be a robin singing
through the leaves
but he refused to be
her tree

she spun herself into a web
and   looking for a place to rest
turned to him
but he stood straight
declining to be her corner

she tried to be a book
but he wouldn't read

she turned herself into a bulb
but he wouldn't let her grow

she decided to become
a woman
and though he still refused
to be a man
she decided it was all
right

20

FRANCES E. W. HARPER (1825–1911)

She's Free!

1854

How say that by law we may torture and chase
A woman whose crime is the hue of her face?—
With her step on the ice, and her arm on her child,
The danger was fearful, the pathway was wild. . . .
But she's free! yes, free from the land where the slave,
From the hand of oppression, must rest in the grave;
Where bondage and blood, where scourges and chains,
Have placed on our banner indelible stains. . . .

5

The bloodhounds have miss'd the scent of her way,
The hunter is rifled and foiled of his prey,
The cursing of men and clanking of chains
Make sounds of strange discord on Liberty's plains. . . .
Oh! poverty, danger and death she can brave,
For the child of her love is no longer a slave.

10

MICHAEL S. HARPER (b. 1938)

Called

1975

Digging the grave
through black dirt,
gravel and rocks
that will hold her down,
we speak of her heat
which has driven her out
over the highway
in her first year.

5

A fly glides from her mouth
as we take her four legs,
and the great white neck
muddled at the lakeside
bends gracefully into the arc
of her tongue, colorless, now,

10

and we set her in the bed
of earth and rock
which will hold her as the sun
sets over her shoulders.

You had spoken of her brother,
100 lbs or more,
and her slight frame
from the diet of chain
she had broken;
on her back
as the spade cools her brow
with black dirt, rocks,
sand, white tongue,
what pups does she hold
that are seeds unspayed
in her broken body;
what does her brother say
to the seed gone out over
the prairie, on the hunt
of the unreturned:
and what do we say
to the master of the dog dead,
heat, highway, this bed
on the shoulder
of the road west
where her brother called, calls.

15

20

25

30

35

40

ROBERT HAYDEN (b. 1913)

Those Winter Sundays   *1962*

Sundays too my father got up early
and put his clothes on in the blueblack cold,
then with cracked hands that ached
from labor in the weekday weather made
banked fires blaze. No one ever thanked him. *Indifferent*

5

I'd wake and hear the cold splintering, breaking,
When the rooms were warm, he'd call, *Contrast*
and slowly I would rise and dress,
fearing the chronic angers of that house,

Speaking indifferently to him, *Cold*
who had driven out the cold
and polished my good shoes as well. *For church* *Warmth of his care*
What did I know, what did I know *self-castigating*
of love's austere and lonely offices?

10

Poem ends in regret & remorse.

ROBERT HERRICK (1591–1674)

Corinna's Going A-Maying   *1648*

Get up! get up for shame! the blooming morn
Upon her wings presents the god unshorn°   *Apollo, god of the sun*
  See how Aurora° throws her fair   *Roman goddess of dawn*
  Fresh-quilted colors through the air:
  Get up, sweet slug-a-bed, and see   5
  The dew bespangling herb and tree.
Each flower has wept and bowed toward the east
Above an hour since, yet you not dressed;
  Nay, not so much as out of bed?
  When all the birds have matins° said,   *morning prayers*   10
  And sung their thankful hymns, 'tis sin,
  Nay, profanation to keep in,
Whenas a thousand virgins on this day
Spring, sooner than the lark, to fetch in May.°   *May Day*

Rise, and put on your foliage, and be seen   15
To come forth, like the springtime, fresh and green,
  And sweet as Flora.° Take no care   *Roman goddess of flowers*
  For jewels for your gown or hair;
  Fear not; the leaves will strew
  Gems in abundance upon you;   20
Besides, the childhood of the days has kept,
Against you come, some orient° pearls unwept;   *eastern*
  Come and receive them while the light
  Hangs on the dew-locks of the night,
  And Titan° on the eastern hill   *the sun*   25
  Retires himself, or else stands still
Till you come forth. Wash, dress, be brief in praying:
Few beads° are best when once we go a-Maying.   *prayers, rosaries*

Come, my Corinna, come; and, coming, mark°   *note*
How each field turns° a street, each street a park   *turns into*   30
  Made green and trimmed with trees: see how
  Devotion gives each house a bough
  Or branch: each porch, each door ere this,
  An ark, a tabernacle is,
Made up of whitethorn neatly interwove,   35
As if here were those cooler shades of love.
  Can such delights be in the street
  And open fields, and we not see 't?
  Come, we'll abroad; and let's obey
  The proclamation made for May,   40
And sin no more, as we have done, by staying;
But, my Corinna, come, let's go a-Maying.

There's not a budding boy or girl this day
But is got up and gone to bring in May;
   A deal° of youth, ere this, is come   *great many*
   Back, and with whitethorn laden home.
   Some have dispatched their cakes and cream
   Before that we have left to dream;
And some have wept, and wooed, and plighted troth,
And chose their priest, ere we can cast off sloth.
   Many a green-gown° has been given,   *green with grass stains*
   Many a kiss, both odd and even;
   Many a glance, too, has been sent
   From out the eye, love's firmament;
Many a jest told of the keys betraying
This night, and locks picked; yet we're not a-Maying.

Come, let us go while we are in our prime,
And take the harmless folly of the time.
   We shall grow old apace, and die
   Before we know our liberty.
   Our life is short, and our days run
   As fast away as does the sun;
And, as a vapor or a drop of rain
Once lost, can ne'er be found again;
   So when or you or I are made
   A fable, song, or fleeting shade,
   All love, all liking, all delight
   Lies drowned with us in endless night.
Then while time serves, and we are but decaying,
Come, my Corinna, come, let's go a-Maying.

ROBERTA HILL (b. 1947)

Dream of Rebirth   *1970*

We stand on the edge of wounds, hugging canned meat,
waiting for owls to come grind
nightsmell in our ears. Over fields,
darkness has been rumbling. Crows gather.
Our luxuries are hatred. Grief. Worn-out hands
carry the pale remains of forgotten murders.
If I could only lull or change this slow hunger,
this midnight swollen four hundred years.

Groping within us are cries yet unheard.
We are born with cobwebs in our mouths
bleeding with prophecies.
Yet within this interior, a spirit kindles

moonlight glittering deep into the sea.
These seeds take root in the hush
of dusk. Songs, a thin echo, heal the salted marsh, 15
and yield visions untrembling in our grip.

A. D. HOPE (b. 1907)

Coup de Grâce 1966

Just at that moment the Wolf,
Shag jaws and slavering grin,
Steps from the property wood.
O, what a gorge, what a gulf
Opens to gobble her in, 5
Little Red Riding Hood!

O, what a face full of fangs!
Eyes like saucers at least
Roll to seduce and beguile.
Miss, with her dimples and bangs, 10
Thinks him a handsome beast;
Flashes the Riding Hood Smile;

Stands her ground like a queen,
Velvet red of the rose
Framing each little milk-tooth, 15
Pink tongue peeping between.
Then, wider than anyone knows,
Opens her minikin° mouth *dainty*

Swallows up Wolf in a trice;
Tail going down gives a flick, 20
Caught as she closes her jaws.
Bows, all sugar and spice.
O, what a lady-like trick!
O, what a round of applause!

GERARD MANLEY HOPKINS (1844–1889)

The Windhover 1918 (1877)

TO CHRIST OUR LORD

I caught this morning morning's minion,° king- *darling*
   dom of daylight's dauphin,° dapple-dawn-drawn Falcon, in his riding

THE WINDHOVER. The title refers to a kestrel or falcon that glides or hovers in the
wind. 2 *dauphin*: prince, heir to the throne of France.

Of the rolling level underneath his steady air, and striding
High there, how he rung upon the rein of a wimpling wing
In his ecstasy! then off, off forth on swing,
    As a skate's heel sweeps smooth on a bow-bend: the hurl and gliding
    Rebuffed the big wind. My heart in hiding
Stirred for a bird,—the achieve of, the mastery of the thing!

Brute beauty and valour and act, oh, air, pride, plume, here
    Buckle!° AND the fire that breaks from thee then, a billion   *join*   1
Times told lovelier, more dangerous. O my chevalier!°   *knight*

    No wonder of it: shéer plód makes plough down sillion°
Shine, and blue-bleak embers, ah my dear,
    Fall, gall themselves, and gash gold-vermilion.

12 *sillion*: the ridge of earth between two plowed furrows in a field.

GERARD MANLEY HOPKINS (1844–1889)

Pied Beauty   1877 (1918)

Glory be to God for dappled things—
    For skies of couple-colour as a brinded cow;
        For rose-moles all in stipple upon trout that swim;
Fresh-firecoal chestnut-falls;° finches' wings;
    Landscape plotted and pieced°—fold,° fallow,° and plough;   5
        And áll trádes, their gear and tackle and trim.

All things counter,° original, spare,° strange;   *rare*
    Whatever is fickle, freckled (who knows how?)
        With swift, slow; sweet, sour; adazzle, dim;
He fathers-forth whose beauty is past change: 10
                            Praise him.

PIED BEAUTY.   4 *chestnut-falls*: the meat of a roasted chestnut.   5 *pieced*: divided into
fields of different colors, depending on the crops or use.   *fold*: an enclosed field for animals.
fallow: a plowed but unplanted field.   7 *counter*: opposed, as in contrasting patterns.

A. E. HOUSMAN (1859–1936)

Terence, This Is Stupid Stuff   1896

    "Terence, this is stupid stuff:
You eat your victuals fast enough;
There can't be much amiss, 'tis clear,

TERENCE, THIS IS STUPID STUFF. Housman had originally intended to call his first
book of poetry "The Poems of Terence Hearsay"; the "Terence" in this poem is that poet.
The book was published in 1896 as *A Shropshire Lad*.

To see the rate you drink your beer.
But oh, good Lord, the verse you make, 5
It gives a chap the belly-ache.
The cow, the old cow, she is dead;
It sleeps well, the horned head:
We poor lads, 'tis our turn now
To hear such tunes as killed the cow. 10
Pretty friendship 'tis to rhyme
Your friends to death before their time
Moping melancholy mad:
Come, pipe a tune to dance to, lad."

  Why, if 'tis dancing you would be, 15
There's brisker pipes than poetry.
Say, for what were hop-yards meant,
Or why was Burton built on Trent?°
Oh many a peer° of England brews   *nobleman*
Livelier liquor than the Muse, 20
And malt does more than Milton° can
To justify God's ways to man.
Ale, man, ale's the stuff to drink
For fellows whom it hurts to think:
Look into the pewter pot 25
To see the world as the world's not.
And faith, 'tis pleasant till 'tis past:
The mischief is that 'twill not last.
Oh I have been to Ludlow° fair
And left my necktie god knows where, 30
And carried half-way home, or near,
Pints and quarts of Ludlow beer:
Then the world seemed none so bad,
And I myself a sterling lad;
And down in lovely muck I've lain, 35
Happy till I woke again.
Then I saw the morning sky:
Heigho, the tale was all a lie;
The world, it was the old world yet,
I was I, my things were wet, 40
And nothing now remained to do
But begin the game anew.

  Therefore, since the world has still
Much good, but much less good than ill,
And while the sun and moon endure 45
Luck's a chance, but trouble's sure,

18 *Trent*: Burton-on-Trent, a city in central England famous for its breweries. 21 *Milton*: John Milton (1608–1674), British poet who wrote *Paradise Lost* to "justify the ways of God to men." 29 *Ludlow*: a market town in Shropshire.

I'd face it as a wise man would,
And train for ill and not for good.
'Tis true, the stuff I bring for sale
Is not so brisk a brew as ale:
Out of a stem that scored° the hand   *cut*   50
I wrung it in a weary land.
But take it: if the smack is sour,
The better for the embittered hour;
It should do good to heart and head
When your soul is in my soul's stead;   55
And I will friend you, if I may,
In the dark and cloudy day.

  There was a king reigned in the East:
There, when kings will sit to feast,
They get their fill before they think   60
With poisoned meat and poisoned drink.
He gathered all that springs to birth
From the many-venomed earth;
First a little, thence to more,
He sampled all her killing store;   65
And easy, smiling, seasoned sound,
Sate the king when healths went round.
They put arsenic in his meat
And stared aghast to watch him eat;   70
They poured strychnine in his cup
And shook to see him drink it up:
They shook, they stared as white's their shirt:
Them it was their poison hurt.
—I tell the tale that I heard told.   75
Mithridates,° he died old.

76 *Mithridates*: ruler of the ancient kingdom of Pontus (ca. B.C. 131-63), who, according to the Roman naturalist Pliney, made himself immune to poisons by eating small doses each day.

LANGSTON HUGHES (1902–1967)

Negro   *1958*

I am a Negro:
  Black as the night is black,
  Black like the depths of my Africa.

I've been a slave:
  Caesar told me to keep his door-steps clean.   5
  I brushed the boots of Washington.

I've been a worker:
> Under my hand the pyramids arose.
> I made mortar for the Woolworth Building.

I've been a singer: 10
> All the way from Africa to Georgia
> I carried my sorrow songs.
> I made ragtime.

I've been a victim:
> The Belgians cut off my hands in the Congo.   15
> They lynch me still in Mississippi.

I am a Negro:
> Black as the night is black,
> Black like the depths of my Africa.

RANDALL JARRELL (1914–1965)

Next Day   *1965*

Moving from Cheer to Joy, from Joy to All,
I take a box
And add it to my wild rice, my Cornish game hens.
The slacked or shorted, basketed, identical
Food-gathering flocks   5
Are selves I overlook. Wisdom,° said William James,

Is learning what to overlook. And I am wise
If that is wisdom.
Yet somehow, as I buy All from these shelves
And the boy takes it to my station wagon,   10
What I've become
Troubles me even if I shut my eyes.

When I was young and miserable and pretty
And poor, I'd wish
What all girls wish: to have a husband,   15
A house and children. Now that I'm old, my wish
Is womanish:
That the boy putting groceries in my car

See me. It bewilders me he doesn't see me.
For so many years   20
I was good enough to eat: the world looked at me
And its mouth watered. How often they have undressed me,
The eyes of strangers!
And, holding their flesh within my flesh, their vile

NEXT DAY.   6 *wisdom . . . overlook*: William James (1842–1910) was an American
philosopher and psychologist; the paraphrase is from his *Principles of Psychology* (1890).

Imaginings within my imagining,   25
I too have taken
The chance of life. Now the boy pats my dog
And we start home. Now I am good.
The last mistaken,
Ecstatic, accidental bliss, the blind   30

Happiness that, bursting, leaves upon the palm
Some soap and water—
It was so long ago, back in some Gay
Twenties, Nineties, I don't know . . . Today I miss
My lovely daughter   35
Away at school, my sons away at school,

My husband away at work—I wish for them.
The dog, the maid,
And I go through the sure unvarying days
At home in them. As I look at my life,   40
I am afraid
Only that it will change, as I am changing:

I am afraid, this morning, of my face.
It looks at me
From the rear-view mirror, with the eyes I hate,   45
The smile I hate. Its plain, lined look
Of gray discovery
Repeats to me: "You're old." That's all, I'm old.

And yet I'm afraid, as I was at the funeral
I went to yesterday.   50
My friend's cold made-up face, granite among its flowers,
Her undressed, operated-on, dressed body
Were my face and body.
As I think of her I hear her telling me

How young I seem; I *am* exceptional;   55
I think of all I have.
But really no one is exceptional,
No one has anything, I'm anybody,
I stand beside my grave
Confused with my life, that is commonplace and solitary.   60

ROBINSON JEFFERS (1887–1962)

The Answer   *1937*

Then what is the answer?—Not to be deluded by dreams.
To know that great civilizations have broken down into violence, and their tyrants
   come, many times before.

When open violence appears, to avoid it with honor or choose the least ugly faction;
    these evils are essential.
To keep one's own integrity, be merciful and uncorrupted and not wish for evil;
    and not be duped
By dreams of universal justice or happiness. These dreams will not be fulfilled.   5
To know this, and know that however ugly the parts appear the whole remains
    beautiful. A severed hand
Is an ugly thing, and man dissevered from the earth and stars and his history
    . . . for contemplation or in fact . . .

Often appears atrociously ugly. Integrity is wholeness, the greatest beauty is
Organic wholeness, the wholeness of life and things, the divine beauty of the
    universe. Love that, not man
Apart from that, or else you will share man's pitiful confusions, or drown in despair   10
    when his days darken.

GALWAY KINNELL (b. 1927)

The Fly   *1982*

1
The fly
I've just brushed
from my face keeps buzzing
about me, flesh-
eater   5
starved for the soul.

One day I may learn to suffer
his mizzling, sporadic stroll over eyelid and cheek,
even be glad of his burnt singing.

2
The bee is beautiful.   10
She is the fleur-de-lis° in the flesh.
She has a tuft of the sun on her back.
She brings sexual love to the narcissus flower.
She sings of fulfillment only
and stings and dies.   15
And everything she ever touches
is opening! opening!

And yet we say our last goodbye
to the fly last,
the flesh-fly last,   20
the absolute last,
the naked dirty reality of him last.

THE FLY.   11 *fleur-de-lis*: a heraldic device appearing on flags and shields resembling
three iris petals bound together.

CAROLYN KIZER (b. 1925)

Night Sounds

imitated from the Chinese

The moonlight on my bed keeps me awake;
Living alone now, aware of the voices of evening,
A child weeping at nightmares, the faint love-cries of a woman,
Everything tinged by terror or nostalgia.

No heavy, impassive back to nudge with one foot   5
While coaxing, "Wake up and hold me,"
When the moon's creamy beauty is transformed
Into a map of impersonal desolation.

But, restless in this mock dawn of moonlight
That so chills the spirit, I alter our history: 10
You were never able to lie quite peacefully at my side,
Not the night through. Always withholding something.

Awake before morning, restless and uneasy,
Trying not to disturb me, you would leave my bed
While I lay there rigidly, feigning sleep.   15
Still—the night was nearly over, the light not as cold
As a full cup of moonlight.

And there were the lovely times when, to the skies' cold *No*
You cried to me, *Yes!* Impaled me with affirmation.
Now when I call out in fear, not in love, there is no answer.   20
Nothing speaks in the dark but the distant voices,
A child with the moon on his face, a dog's hollow cadence.

ETHERIDGE KNIGHT (b. 1933)

Haiku°   *1968*

1
Eastern guard tower
glints in sunset; convicts rest
like lizards on rocks.

2
The piano man
is sting at 3 am   5
his songs drop like plum.

HAIKU. The title refers to a Japanese lyric verse form consisting of three lines that total
seventeen syllables, divided 5–7–5.

3

Morning sun slants cell.
Drunks stagger like cripple flies
On Jailhouse floor.

4

To write a blues song   10
is to regiment riots
and pluck gems from graves.

5

A bare pecan tree
slips a pencil shadow down
a moonlit snow slope.   15

6

The falling snow flakes
Can not blunt the hard aches nor
Match the steel stillness.

7

Under moon shadows
A tall boy flashes knife and   20
Slices star bright ice.

8

In the August grass
Struck by the last rays of sun
The cracked teacup screams.

9

Making jazz swing in   25
Seventeen syllables AIN'T
No square poet's job.

MAXINE KUMIN (b. 1925)

Woodchucks   *1972*

Gassing the woodchucks didn't turn out right.
The knockout bomb from the Feed and Grain Exchange
was featured as merciful, quick at the bone
and the case we had against them was airtight,
both exits shoehorned shut with puddingstone,   5
but they had a sub-sub-basement out of range.

Next morning they turned up again, no worse
for the cyanide than we for our cigarettes
and state-store Scotch, all of us up to scratch.
They brought down the marigolds as a matter of course   10

and then took over the vegetable patch
nipping the broccoli shoots, beheading the carrots.

The food from our mouths, I said, righteously thrilling
to the feel of the .22, the bullets' neat noses.
I, a lapsed pacifist fallen from grace   15
puffed with Darwinian pieties° for killing,
now drew a bead on the littlest woodchuck's face.
He died down in the everbearing roses.

Ten minutes later I dropped the mother. She
flipflopped in the air and fell, her needle teeth   20
still hooked in a leaf of early Swiss chard.
Another baby next. O one-two-three
the murderer inside me rose up hard,
the hawkeye killer came on stage forthwith.

There's one chuck left. Old wily fellow, he keeps   25
me cocked and ready day after day after day.
All night I hunt his humped-up form. I dream
I sight along the barrel in my sleep.
If only they'd all consented to die unseen
gassed underground the quiet Nazi way.°   30

WOODCHUCKS.   16 *Darwinian pieties*: Charles Darwin (1809–1892) was a British
naturalist who formulated the theory of evolution; the piety is "survival of the
fittest."   30 *gassed . . . way*: a reference to the extermination of 11 million people in gas
chambers by the Germans before and during World War II.

PHILIP LARKIN (b. 1922)

Church Going   *1955*

Once I am sure there's nothing going on
I step inside, letting the door thud shut.
Another church: matting, seats, and stone,
And little books; sprawlings of flowers, cut
For Sunday, brownish now; some brass and stuff   5
Up at the holy end; the small neat organ;
And a tense, musty, unignorable silence,
Brewed God knows how long. Hatless, I take off
My cycle-clips in awkward reverence,

Move forward, run my hand around the font.   10
From where I stand, the roof looks almost new—
Cleaned, or restored? Someone° would know: I don't.
Mounting the lectern, I peruse a few
Hectoring° large-scale verses, and pronounce   *intimidating*

'Here endeth' much more loudly than I'd meant. 15
The echoes snigger briefly. Back at the door
I sign the book, donate an Irish sixpence,
Reflect the place was not worth stopping for.

Yet stop I did: in fact I often do,
And always end much at a loss like this, 20
Wondering what to look for; wondering, too,
When churches fall completely out of use
What we shall turn them into, if we shall keep
A few cathedrals chronically on show,
Their parchment, plate and pyx° in locked cases, 25
And let the rest rent-free to rain and sheep.
Shall we avoid them as unlucky places?

Or, after dark, will dubious women come
To make their children touch a particular stone;
Pick simples° for a cancer; or on some *medicinal herbs* 30
Advised night see walking a dead one?
Power of some sort or other will go on
In games, in riddles, seemingly at random;
But superstition, like belief, must die,
And what remains when disbelief has gone? 35
Grass, weedy pavement, brambles, buttress, sky,

A shape less recognisable each week,
A purpose more obscure. I wonder who
Will be the last, the very last, to seek
This place for what it was; one of the crew 40
That tap and jot and know what rood-lofts were?
Some ruin-bibber, randy for antique,
Or Christmas-addict, counting on a whiff
Of gown-and-bands and organ-pipes and myrrh?
Or will he be my representative, 45

Bored, uninformed, knowing the ghostly silt
Dispersed, yet tending to this cross of ground
Through suburb scrub because it held unspilt
So long and equably what since is found
Only in separation—marriage, and birth, 50
And death, and thoughts of these—for whom was built
This special shell? For, though I've no idea
What this accoutred frowsty barn is worth,
It pleases me to stand in silence here;

A serious house on serious earth it is, 55
In whose blent air all our compulsions meet,
Are recognised, and robed as destinies.

CHURCH GOING.   25 *pyx*: the box or vessel in an Anglican Church in which communion
wafers are kept.

And that much never can be obsolete,
Since someone will forever be surprising
A hunger in himself to be more serious,   60
And gravitating with it to this ground,
Which, he once heard, was proper to grow wise in,
If only that so many dead lie round.

IRVING LAYTON (b. 1912)

Rhine Boat Trip°   *1977*

The castles on the Rhine
are all haunted
by the ghosts of Jewish mothers
looking for their ghostly children

And the clusters of grapes   5
in the sloping vineyards
are myriads of blinded eyes
staring at the blind sun

The tireless Lorelei°
can never comb from their hair   10
the crimson beards
of murdered rabbis

However sweetly they sing
one hears only
the low wailing of cattle-cars°   15
moving invisibly across the land

RHINE BOAT TRIP. The title refers to the Rhine River, which flows along the German
border and then through Germany.   9 *Lorelei*: mythological fairies who live in the cliffs
(of the same name) overlooking the Rhine.   15 *cattle-cars*: railroad cars designed to
transport cattle but used by the Nazis to transport Jews from the cities of Europe to
extermination camps.

DON L. LEE (b. 1942)

Change Is Not Always Progress (for Africa & Africans)   *1970*

Africa.

don't let them
steal
your face   or
take your circles   5
and make them squares.

don't let them
steel
your body   as to put
100 stories of concrete on you   10

so that you
                arrogantly
scrape
the

sky.   15

PHILIP LEVINE (b. 1928)

They Feed They Lion   *1970*

Out of burlap sacks, out of bearing butter,
Out of black bean and wet slate bread,
Out of the acids of rage, the candor of tar,
Out of creosote, gasoline, drive shafts, wooden dollies,
They Lion grow.   5

          Out of the grey hills
Of industrial barns, out of rain, out of bus ride,
West Virginia to Kiss My Ass, out of buried aunties,
Mothers hardening like pounded stumps, out of stumps,
Out of the bones' need to sharpen and the muscles' to stretch,   10
They Lion grow.

          Earth is eating trees, fence posts,
Gutted cars, earth is calling her little ones,
"Come home, Come home!" From pig balls,
From the ferocity of pig driven to holiness,   15
From the furred ear and the full jowl come
The repose of the hung belly, from the purpose
They Lion grow.

          From the sweet glues of the trotters
Come the sweet kinks of the fist, from the full flower   20
Of the hams the thorax of caves,
From "Bow Down" come "Rise Up,"
Come they Lion from the reeds of shovels,
The grained arm that pulls the hands,
They Lion grow.   25

          From my five arms and all my hands,
From all my white sins forgiven, they feed,
From my car passing under the stars,
They Lion, from my children inherit,
From the oak turned to a wall, they Lion,   30

From they sack and they belly opened
And all that was hidden burning on the oil-stained earth
They feed they Lion and he comes.

RICHARD LOVELACE (1618–1657)

To Lucasta, Going to the Wars   *1649*

Tell me not, Sweet, I am unkind
That from the nunnery
Of thy chaste breast and quiet mind,
To war and arms I fly.

True, a new mistress now I chase,   5
The first foe in the field;
And with a stronger faith embrace
A sword, a horse, a shield.

Yet this inconstancy is such
As you too shall adore;   10
I could not love thee, Dear, so much,
Loved I not honor more.

AMY LOWELL (1874–1925)

Patterns   *1916*

I walk down the garden paths,
And all the daffodils
Are blowing, and the bright blue squills.
I walk down the patterned garden-paths
In my stiff, brocaded gown.   5
With my powdered hair and jewelled fan,
I too am a rare
Pattern. As I wander down
The garden paths.

My dress is richly figured,   10
And the train
Makes a pink and silver stain
On the gravel, and the thrift
Of the borders.
Just a plate of current fashion   15
Tripping by in high-heeled, ribboned shoes.
Not a softness anywhere about me,
Only whalebone° and brocade.
And I sink on a seat in the shade

PATTERNS.   18 *whalebone*: Bones from whales were used to make extremely rigid corsets
for women.

Of a lime tree. For my passion   20
Wars against the stiff brocade.
The daffodils and squills
Flutter in the breeze
As they please.
And I weep;   25
For the lime-tree is in blossom
And one small flower has dropped upon my bosom.

And the plashing of waterdrops
In the marble fountain
Comes down the garden-paths.   30
The dripping never stops.
Underneath my stiffened gown
Is the softness of a woman bathing in a marble basin,
A basin in the midst of hedges grown
So thick, she cannot see her lover hiding,   35
But she guesses he is near,
And the sliding of the water
Seems the stroking of a dear
Hand upon her.
What is Summer in a fine brocaded gown!   40
I should like to see it lying in a heap upon the ground.
All the pink and silver crumpled up on the ground.

I would be the pink and silver as I ran along the paths,
And he would stumble after,
Bewildered by my laughter.   45
I should see the sun flashing from his sword-hilt and buckles on his shoes.
I would choose
To lead him in a maze along the patterned paths,
A bright and laughing maze for my heavy-booted lover.
Till he caught me in the shade,   50
And the buttons of his waistcoat bruised my body as he clasped me,
Aching, melting, unafraid.
With the shadows of the leaves and the sundrops,
And the plopping of the waterdrops,
All about us in the open afternoon—   55
I am very like to swoon
With the weight of this brocade,
For the sun sifts through the shade.

Underneath the fallen blossom
In my bosom,   60
Is a letter I have hid.
It was brought to me this morning by a rider from the Duke.
Madam, we regret to inform you that Lord Hartwell
Died in action Thursday se'nnight.°
As I read it in the white, morning sunlight,   65

64 *se'nnight*: seven nights, hence a week ago.

The letters squirmed like snakes.
"Any answer, Madam," said my footman.
"No," I told him.
"See that the messenger takes some refreshment.

No, no answer."   70
And I walked into the garden,
Up and down the patterned paths,
In my stiff, correct brocade.
The blue and yellow flowers stood up proudly in the sun,
Each one.   75
I stood upright too,
Held rigid to the pattern
By the stiffness of my gown.
Up and down I walked.
Up and down.   80

In a month he would have been my husband.
In a month, here, underneath this lime,
We would have broken the pattern;
He for me, and I for him,
He as Colonel, I as Lady,   85
On this shady seat.
He had a whim
That sunlight carried blessing.
And I answered, "It shall be as you have said."
Now he is dead.   90

In Summer and in Winter I shall walk
Up and down
The patterned garden-paths
In my stiff, brocaded gown.
The squills and daffodils   95
Will give place to pillared roses, and to asters, and to snow.
I shall go
Up and down,
In my gown.
Gorgeously arrayed,   100
Boned and stayed.
And the softness of my body will be guarded from embrace
By each button, hook, and lace.
For the man who should loose me is dead,
Fighting with the Duke in Flanders,°   105
In a pattern called a war.
Christ! What are patterns for?

---

105 *Flanders*: a region in western Belgium and France that saw heavy fighting during World
War I.

ROBERT LOWELL (1917–1977)

For the Union Dead°   *1960*

"Relinquunt Omnia Servare Rem Publicam."°

The old South Boston Aquarium stands
in a Sahara of snow now. Its broken windows are boarded.
The bronze weathervane cod has lost half its scales.
The airy tanks are dry.

Once my nose crawled like a snail on the glass;   5
my hand tingled
to burst the bubbles
drifting from the noses of the cowed, compliant fish.

My hand draws back. I often sigh still
for the dark downward and vegetating kingdom   10
of the fish and reptile. One morning last March,
I pressed against the new barbed and galvanized

fence on the Boston Common. Behind their cage,
yellow dinosaur steamshovels were grunting
as they cropped up tons of mush and grass   15
to gouge their underworld garage.

Parking spaces luxuriate like civic
sandpiles in the heart of Boston.
A girdle of orange, Puritan-pumpkin colored girders
braces the tingling Statehouse,   20

shaking over the excavations, as it faces Colonel Shaw
and his bell-cheeked Negro infantry
on St. Gaudens' shaking Civil War relief,
propped by a plank splint against the garage's earthquake.

Two months after marching through Boston,   25
half the regiment was dead;
at the dedication,
William James° could almost hear the bronze Negroes breathe.

Their monument sticks like a fishbone
in the city's throat.   30

FOR THE UNION DEAD. The poem was first published in 1959 with the title, "Colonel
Shaw and the Massachusetts 54th." Robert Gould Shaw (1837–1863) was the commander
of the first regiment of blacks formed in the Union to fight in the Civil War. He was killed
leading an attack at Fort Wagner in South Carolina. The "Civil War relief" in bronze described
in the poem was sculpted by Augustus Saint-Gaudens (1848–1907), dedicated in 1897, and
stands on the Boston Commons (a central park or green) across from the Massachusetts
State House.   EPIGRAPH: The Latin epigraph means, "They give up everything to serve
the republic."   28 *William James*: American philosopher and psychologist (1842–1910) who
taught at Harvard.

Its Colonel is as lean
as a compass-needle.

He has an angry wrenlike vigilance,
a greyhound's gentle tautness;
he seems to wince at pleasure,   35
and suffocate for privacy.

He is out of bounds now. He rejoices in man's lovely,
peculiar power to choose life and die—
when he leads his black soldiers to death,
he cannot bend his back.   40

On a thousand small town New England greens,
the old white churches hold their air
of sparse, sincere rebellion; frayed flags
quilt the graveyards of the Grand Army of the Republic.°

The stone statues of the abstract Union Soldier   45
grow slimmer and younger each year—
wasp-waisted, they doze over muskets
and muse through their sideburns . . .

Shaw's father wanted no monument
except the ditch,   50
where his son's body was thrown
and lost with his "niggers."

The ditch is nearer.
There are no statues for the last war° here;
on Boylston Street,° a commercial photograph   55
shows Hiroshima° boiling

over a Mosler Safe, the "Rock of Ages"
that survived the blast. Space is nearer.
When I crouch to my television set,
the drained faces of Negro school-children rise like balloons.   60

Colonel Shaw
is riding on his bubble,
he waits
for the blessèd break.

The Aquarium is gone. Everywhere,   65
giant finned cars nose forward like fish;
a savage servility
slides by on grease.

44 *Grand Army of the Republic*: an organization, founded in 1866, of men who served in the
Union Army and Navy.   54 *last war*: World War II.   55 *Boylston Street*: a street in
Boston.   56 *Hiroshima*: Japanese city on which the United States dropped the first atomic
bomb during World War II on August 6, 1945.

BEN LUNA (b. 1941)

In Days of Wine   1973

In days of wine
                    and machine gun bullets bouncing off walls
where young men got their quick
                            and justly deserved fate
There is no one to speak above the screaming
                                    of idiots waving
their country's flag
                    in streets littered with
                                    disappointments
and yesterday's empty promises   5
And in their minds everyone is convinced
                            that "Little Beaver"
was a punk or else "Red Rider" was not as white as he made
believe
The question is why did the Cisco Kid have it made
when all the rest of us greasers are suspected of being subversive?   10
All the while
            out in "La Puandtea"
                            Juan is trying hard to prove
that he is as good a racist american
                            as any blue-eyed wonder
And in my heart i know Juan's right.

CYNTHIA MACDONALD

The Lobster   1980

This lobster flown in from Maine to Houston
Lies in a wooden box on cracked ice.
Its green not the green of deep water,
But of decay. Its stalk eyes, which should be
Grains of black caviar, are beads of phlegm.   5
Through the cracks in its shell, the meat
Shines like oil on water or mother-of-pearl.

I see exactly what it is, yet must wrap it up
In my finest linen handkerchief—the one with
The border and initials pulled by Filipino nuns—   10
And take it home to keep in my bureau drawer;
So that its smell invades my private places,
And lobster mold begins to form on the edges of fabrics.

I throw open the doors and jalousies, hoping to
Dilute the crustacean air, and you walk in. I had not   15

Expected to see you again: we had decided.
We inventory everything and redecide: you will stay.
The lobster, smooth and green as deep water, is
Crawling over the blue silk scarf when we
Open the drawer. We cook it for dinner,   20
In water laved with peppercorns and fennel, and spread
A sheet on the table, anticipating the complete repast.

CLAUDE McKAY (1890–1948)

The White City   1922

I will not toy with it nor bend an inch.
Deep in the secret chambers of my heart
I muse my life-long hate, and without flinch
I bear it nobly as I live my part.
My being would be a skeleton, a shell,   5
If this dark Passion that fills my every mood,
And makes my heaven in the white world's hell,
Did not forever feed me vital blood.
I see the mighty city through a mist—
The strident trains that speed the goaded mass,   10
The poles and spires and towers vapor-kissed,
The fortressed port through which the great ships pass,
The tides, the wharves, the dens I contemplate,
Are sweet like wanton loves because I hate.

JOSEPHINE MILES (b. 1911)

Belief   1955

Mother said to call her if the H-bomb exploded
And I said I would, and it about did
When Louis my brother robbed a service station
And lay cursing on the oily cement in handcuffs.

But by that time it was too late to tell Mother,   5
She was too sick to worry the life out of her
Over *why why.* Causation is sequence
And everything is one thing after another.

Besides, my other brother, Eddie, had got to be President,
And you can't ask too much of one family.   10
The chances were as good for a good future
As bad for a bad one.

Therefore it was surprising that, as we kept the newspapers from Mother,
She died feeling responsible for a disaster unverified,

Murmuring, in her sleep as it seemed, the ancient slogan   15
Noblesse oblige.

EDNA ST. VINCENT MILLAY (1892–1950)

What Lips My Lips Have Kissed, and Where, and Why   1923

What lips my lips have kissed, and where, and why,
I have forgotten, and what arms have lain
Under my head till morning; but the rain
Is full of ghosts tonight, that tap and sigh
Upon the glass and listen for reply,   5
And in my heart there stirs a quiet pain
For unremembered lads that not again
Will turn to me at midnight with a cry.
Thus in the winter stands the lonely tree,
Nor knows what birds have vanished one by one,   10
Yet knows its boughs more silent than before:
I cannot say what loves have come and gone,
I only know that summer sang in me
A little while, that in me sings no more.

VASSAR MILLER (b. 1924)

Loneliness   1963

So deep is this silence
that the insects, the birds,
the talk of the neighbors in the distance,
the whir of the traffic, the music
are only its voices   5
and do not contradict it.

So deep is this crying
that the silence, the hush,
the quiet, the stillness, the not speaking,
the never hearing a word   10
are only the surge
of its innumerable waters.

This silence, this crying,
O my God, is my country
with Yours the sole footstep besides my own.   15
Save me amid its landscapes
so terrible, strange
I am almost in love with them!

JOHN MILTON (1608–1674)

How Soon Hath Time   *1645*

How soon hath Time, the subtle thief of youth,
  Stoln on his wing my three and twentieth year!
  My hasting days fly on with full career,
  But my late spring no bud or blossom show'th.
Perhaps my semblance might deceive the truth,   5
  That I to manhood am arrived so near,
  And inward ripeness doth much less appear,
  That some more timely-happy spirits endu'th.°   *endoweth*
Yet be it less or more, or soon or slow,
  It shall be still in strictest measure even°   *equal*   10
  To that same lot, however mean or high,
Toward which Time leads me, and the will of Heaven;
  All is, if I have grace to use it so,
  As ever in my great Taskmaster's eye.

JOHN MILTON (1608–1674)

O Nightingale!   *1630*

O Nightingale, that on yon bloomy Spray
  Warbl'st at eve, when all the Woods are still,
  Thou with fresh hope the Lover's heart dost fill,
  While the jolly hours lead on propitious *May*
Thy liquid notes that close the eye of Day,   5
  First heard before the shallow Cuckoo's bill,
  Portend success in love; O, if *Jove's* will
  Have linkt that amorous power to thy soft lay,
Now timely sing, ere the rude Bird of Hate
  Foretell my hopeless doom in some Grove nigh: 10
  As thou from year to year hast sung too late
For my relief; yet hadst no reason why.
  Whether the Muse, or Love call thee his mate,
  Both them I serve, and of their train am I.

OGDEN NASH (1902–1970)

The Camel   *1945*

The camel has a single hump;
The dromedary, two;
Or else the other way around.
I'm never sure. Are you?

OGDEN NASH (1902–1970)

The Lama   *1945*

The one-l lama,
He's a priest.
The two-l llama,
He's a beast.
And I will bet   5
A silk pajama
There isn't any
Three-l lllama.

THOMAS NASHE (1567–1601)

A Litany in Time of Plague   *1600*

Adieu, farewell, earth's bliss;
This world uncertain is;
Fond are life's lustful joys;
Death proves them all but toys;
None from his darts can fly;   5
I am sick, I must die.
   Lord, have mercy on us!

Rich men, trust not in wealth,
Gold cannot buy you health;
Physic himself must fade.   10
All things to end are made,
The plague full swift goes by;
I am sick, I must die.
   Lord, have mercy on us!

Beauty is but a flower   15
Which wrinkles will devour;
Brightness falls from the air;
Queens have died young and fair;
Dust hath closed Helen's° eye.
I am sick, I must die.   20
   Lord, have mercy on us!

Strength stoops unto the grave,
Worms feed on Hector° brave;

A LITANY IN TIME OF PLAGUE. A litany is a ceremonial prayer with repeated invocations to God. The plague is the Black Death, a form of bubonic plague that swept Europe repeatedly in the Middle Ages and the Renaissance, killing tens of thousands.   19 *Helen*: Helen of Troy, considered to have been one of the most beautiful women in history.   23 *Hector*: in Homer's *Iliad*, the greatest Trojan Hero and leader of the Trojan forces, killed by Achilles.

Swords may not fight with fate,
Earth still holds ope her gate.   25
"Come, come!" the bells do cry.
I am sick, I must die.
   Lord, have mercy on us.

Wit with his wantonness
Tasteth death's bitterness;   30
Hell's executioner
Hath no ears for to hear
What vain art can reply.
I am sick, I must die.
   Lord, have mercy on us.   35

Haste, therefore, each degree,°
To welcome destiny;
Heaven is our heritage,
Earth but a player's stage;
Mount we unto the sky.   40
I am sick, I must die.
   Lord, have mercy on us.

36 *degree*: social class.

HOWARD NEMEROV (b. 1920)

The Goose Fish   *1955*

On the long shore, lit by the moon
To show them properly alone,
Two lovers suddenly embraced
So that their shadows were as one.
The ordinary night was graced   5
For them by the swift tide of blood
That silently they took at flood,
And for a little time they prized
   Themselves emparadised.

Then, as if shaken by stage-fright   10
Beneath the hard moon's bony light,
They stood together on the sand—
Embarrassed in each other's sight
But still conspiring hand in hand,
Until they saw, there underfoot,   15
As though the world had found them out,
The goose fish turning up, though dead,
   His hugely grinning head.

There in the china light he lay,
Most ancient and corrupt and grey   20

They hesitated at his smile,
Wondering what it seemed to say
To lovers who a little while
Before had thought to understand,
By violence upon the sand,   25
The only way that could be known
  To make a world their own.

It was a wide and moony grin
Together peaceful and obscene;
They knew not what he would express,   30
So finished a comedian
He might mean failure or success,
But took it for an emblem of
Their sudden, new and guilty love
To be observed by, when they kissed,   35
  That rigid optimist.

So he became their patriarch,
Dreadfully mild in the half-dark.
His throat that the sand seemed to choke,
His picket teeth, these left their mark   40
But never did explain the joke
That so amused him, lying there
While the moon went down to disappear
Along the still and tilted track   45
  That bears the zodiac.

FRANK O'HARA (1926–1966)

Poem   *1952*

The eager note on my door said "Call me,
call when you get in!" so I quickly threw
a few tangerines into my overnight bag,
straightened my eyelids and shoulders, and

headed straight for the door. It was autumn   5
by the time I got around the corner, oh all
unwilling to be either pertinent or bemused, but
the leaves were brighter than grass on the sidewalk!

Funny, I thought, that the lights are on this late
and the hall door open; still up at this hour, a   10
champion jai-alai player like himself? Oh fie!
for shame! What a host, so zealous! And he was

there in the hall, flat on a sheet of blood that
ran down the stairs. I did appreciate it. There are few
hosts who so thoroughly prepare to greet a guest   15
only casually invited, and that several months ago.

AMÉRICO PAREDES (b. 1915)

Guitarreros   1964

Black against twisted black
The old mesquite
Rears up against the stars
Branch bridle hanging,
While the bull comes down from the mountain   5
Driven along by your fingers,
Twenty nimble stallions prancing up and down the *redil°* of   *the "web" of music*
   the guitars.
One leaning on the trunk, one facing—
Now the song:
Not cleanly flanked, not pacing,   10
But in a stubborn yielding that unshapes
And shapes itself again;
Hard-mouthed, zigzagged, thrusting,
Thrown, not sung,
One to the other.   15
The old man listens in his cloud
Of white tobacco smoke.
"It was so," he says,
"In the old days it was so."

DOROTHY PARKER (1893–1967)

Résumé   1936

Razors pain you;
Rivers are damp;
Acids stain you;
And drugs cause cramp.
Guns aren't lawful;   5
Nooses give;
Gas smells awful;
You might as well live.

KATHERINE PHILLIPS (1631–1664)

To My Excellent Lucasia, on Our Friendship   1667

I did not live until this time
  Crown'd my felicity,
When I could say without a crime,
  I am not thine, but Thee.
This carcase breath'd, and walkt, and slept,   5
  So that the World believ'd

There was a soul the motions kept;
  But they were all deceiv'd.

For as a watch by art is wound
  To motion, such was mine:
But never had Orinda° found
  A soul till she found thine;   10

Which now inspires, cures and supplies,
  And guides my darkened breast:
For thou art all that I can prize,
  My Joy, my Life, my Rest.   15

No bridegroom's nor crown-conqueror's mirth
  To mine compar'd can be:
They have but pieces of this Earth,
  I've all the World in thee.   20

Then let our flames still light and shine,
  And no false fear control,
As innocent as our design,
  Immortal as our soul.

TO MY EXCELLENT LUCASIA.   11 *Orinda*: name of the woman speaking the poem;
Phillips habitually used this name to refer to herself in poetry.

MARGE PIERCY (b. 1934)

The Secretary Chant   *1973*

My hips are a desk.
From my ears hang
chains of paper clips.
Rubber bands form my hair.
My breasts are wells of mimeograph ink.   5
My feet bear casters.
Buzz. Click.
My head is a badly organized file.
My head is a switchboard
where crossed lines crackle.   10
Press my fingers
and in my eyes appear
credit and debit.
Zing. Tinkle.
My navel is a reject button.   15
From my mouth issue canceled reams.
Swollen, heavy, rectangular
I am about to be delivered
of a baby
Xerox machine.   20

File me under W
because I wonce
was
a woman.

SYLVIA PLATH (1932–1962)

Last Words   1971 (1961)

I do not want a plain box, I want a sarcophagus
With tigery stripes, and a face on it
Round as the moon, to stare up.
I want to be looking at them when they° come
Picking among the dumb minerals, the roots.   5
I see them already—the pale, star-distance faces.
Now they are nothing, they are not even babies.
I imagine them without fathers or mothers, like the first gods.
They will wonder if I was important.
I should sugar and preserve my days like fruit!   10
My mirror is clouding over—
A few more breaths, and it will reflect nothing at all.
The flowers and the faces whiten to a sheet.

I do not trust the spirit. It escapes like steam
In dreams, through mouth-hole or eye-hole. I can't stop it.   15
One day it won't come back. Things aren't like that.
They stay, their little particular lusters
Warmed by much handling. They almost purr.
When the soles of my feet grow cold,
The blue eye of my turquoise will comfort me.   20
Let me have my copper cooking pots, let my rouge pots
Bloom about me like night flowers, with a good smell.
They will roll me up in bandages, they will store my heart
Under my feet in a neat parcel.°
I shall hardly know myself. It will be dark,   25
And the shine of these small things sweeter than the face of Ishtar.°

LAST WORDS.   4 *they*: possibly archeologists exploring the speaker's tomb or stone coffin
("sarcophagus").   19–24 *When . . . parcel*: The objects and procedures here refer to the
household goods normally entombed with a body in ancient Egypt and to the preparations
of a mummy.   27 *Ishtar*: Babylonian goddess of fertility, love, and war.

SYLVIA PLATH (1932–1962)

Mirror   1965 (1961)

I am silver and exact. I have no preconceptions.
Whatever I see I swallow immediately
Just as it is, unmisted by love or dislike.

I am not cruel, only truthful—
The eye of a little god, four-cornered.   5
Most of the time I meditate on the opposite wall.
It is pink, with speckles. I have looked at it so long
I think it is a part of my heart. But it flickers.
Faces and darkness separate us over and over.

Now I am a lake. A woman bends over me,   10
Searching my reaches for what she really is.
Then she turns to those liars, the candles or the moon.
I see her back, and reflect it faithfully.
She rewards me with tears and an agitation of hands.
I am important to her. She comes and goes.   15
Each morning it is her face that replaces the darkness.
In me she has drowned a young girl, and in me an old woman
Rises toward her day after day, like a terrible fish.

EZRA POUND (1885–1972)

The River-Merchant's Wife: A Letter   1926 (1915)

While my hair was still cut straight across my forehead
I played about the front gate, pulling flowers.
You came by on bamboo stilts, playing horse,
You walked about my seat, playing with blue plums.
And we went on living in the village of Chokan:°   5
Two small people, without dislike or suspicion.

At fourteen I married My Lord you.
I never laughed, being bashful.
Lowering my head, I looked at the wall.
Called to, a thousand times, I never looked back.   10

At fifteen I stopped scowling,
I desired my dust to be mingled with yours
Forever and forever and forever.
Why should I climb the look out?

At sixteen you departed,   15
You went into far Ku-tō-en,° by the river of swirling eddies,
And you have been gone five months.
The monkeys make sorrowful noise overhead.

You dragged your feet when you went out.
By the gate now, the moss is grown, the different mosses,   20
Too deep to clear them away!

THE RIVER-MERCHANT'S WIFE: A LETTER. Freely translated from the Chinese of Li
Po (701–762).   5 *Chokan*: a suburb of Nanking, China.   16 *Ku-tō-en*: an island several
hundred miles up the Kiang River from Nanking.

The leaves fall early this autumn, in wind.
The paired butterflies are already yellow with August

Over the grass in the West garden;
They hurt me. I grow older.   25
If you are coming down through the narrows of the river Kiang,
Please let me know beforehand,
And I will come out to meet you
                As far as Chō-fū-Sa.°

29 *Chō-fū-Sa*: a beach near Ku-tō-en.

E. J. PRATT (1882–1964)

The Shark   1923

He seemed to know the harbour,
So leisurely he swam;
His tin,
Like a piece of sheet-iron,
Three-cornered,   5
And with knife-edge,
Stirred not a bubble
As it moved
With its base-line on the water.

His body was tubular   10
And tapered
And smoke-blue,
And as he passed the wharf
He turned,
And snapped at a flat-fish   15
That was dead and floating.
And I saw the flash of a white throat,
And a double row of white teeth,
And eyes of metallic grey,
Hard and narrow and slit.   20

Then out of the harbour,
With that three-cornered fin
Shearing without a bubble the water
Lithely,
Leisurely,   25
He swam—
That strange fish,
Tubular, tapered, smoke-blue,
Part vulture, part wolf,
Part neither—for his blood was cold.   30

THOMAS RABBITT (b. 1943)

Gargoyle 1981

He looks down to watch the river twist
Like a dead vein into the suburbs.
From his height it is all flat, stone-grey
And ugly. He knows he himself is hideous,
Sterile, the artist's pleasantry set up 5
To scare off devils. He knows nothing.
He is stunning in his pure impossibility.
Enough cherry trees blossom along the river.
Enough paired lovers gaze through the pink air.
Drab birds, disguised as money, sing prettily 10
And the sun blinds itself in the water.
He hears laughter. He knows nothing.
When the lovers glance up, they take him in.
Their looks are incidental, monumental, sweeping.

JOHN CROWE RANSOM (1888–1974)

Bells for John Whiteside's Daughter 1924

An expression of the speaker's fond memory & deep sorrow.

There was such speed in her little body,
And such lightness in her footfall,
It is no wonder her brown study *Understatement*
Astonishes us all.

Her wars were bruited in our high window. 5
We looked among orchard trees and beyond
Where she took arms against her shadow,
Or harried unto the pond.

Establishes a contrast between the lively child and the quiet, dead one.

The lazy geese, like a snow cloud
Dripping their snow on the green grass, *Images of sound, color, &* 10
Tricking and stopping, sleepy and proud, *motion*
Who cried in goose, Alas,

And the speaker cries "alas" also.

For the tireless heart within the little
Lady with rod that made them rise
From their noon apple-dreams and scuttle 15
Goose-fashion under the skies!

But now go the bells, and we are ready,
In one house we are sternly stopped
To say we are vexed at her brown study, *Understated again.*
Lying so primly propped. 20

ADRIENNE RICH (b. 1929)

Diving into the Wreck   1973

First having read the book of myths,
and loaded the camera,
and checked the edge of the knife-blade,
I put on
the body-armor of black rubber   5
the absurd flippers
the grave and awkward mask.
I am having to do this
not like Cousteau with his
assiduous team   10
aboard the sun-flooded schooner
but here alone.

There is a ladder.
The ladder is always there
hanging innocently   15
close to the side of the schooner.
We know what it is for,
we who have used it.
otherwise
it is a piece of maritime floss   20
some sundry equipment.

I go down.
Rung after rung and still
the oxygen immerses me
the blue light   25
the clear atoms
of our human air.
I go down.
My flippers cripple me,
I crawl like an insect down the ladder   30
and there is no one
to tell me when the ocean
will begin.

First the air is blue and then
it is bluer and then green and then   35
black I am blacking out and yet
my mask is powerful
it pumps my blood with power
the sea is another story
the sea is not a question of power   40
I have to learn alone
to turn my body without force
in the deep element.

And now: it is easy to forget
what I came for   45
among so many who have always
lived here
swaying their crenellated fans
between the reefs
and besides   50
you breathe differently down here.

I came to explore the wreck.
The words are purposes.
The words are maps.
I came to see the damage that was done   55
and the treasures that prevail.
I stroke the beam of my lamp
slowly along the flank
of something more permanent
than fish or weed   60

the thing I came for:
the wreck and not the story of the wreck
the thing itself and not the myth
the drowned face always staring
toward the sun   65
the evidence of damage
worn by salt and sway into this threadbare beauty
the ribs of the disaster
curving their assertion
among the tentative haunters.   70

This is the place.
And I am here, the mermaid whose dark hair
streams black, the merman in his armored body.
We circle silently
about the wreck   75
we dive into the hold.
I am she: I am he

whose drowned face sleeps with open eyes
whose breasts still bear the stress
whose silver, copper, vermeil cargo lies   80
obscurely inside barrels
half-wedged and left to rot
we are the half-destroyed instruments
that once held to a course
the water-eaten log   85
the fouled compass

We are, I am, you are
by cowardice or courage

the one who find our way
back to this scene   90
carrying a knife, a camera
a book of myths
in which
our names do not appear.

EDWARD ARLINGTON ROBINSON (1869–1935)

Mr. Flood's Party   *1921*

Old Eben Flood, climbing alone one night
Over the hill between the town below
And the forsaken upland hermitage
That held as much as he should ever know
On earth again of home, paused warily.   5
The road was his with not a native near;
And Eben, having leisure, said aloud,
For no man else in Tilbury Town° to hear:

"Well, Mr. Flood, we have the harvest moon
Again, and we may not have many more;   10
The bird is on the wing, the poet says,°
And you and I have said it here before.
Drink to the bird." He raised up to the light
The jug that he had gone so far to fill,
And answered huskily: "Well, Mr. Flood,   15
Since you propose it, I believe I will."

Alone, as if enduring to the end
A valiant armor of scarred hopes outworn,
He stood there in the middle of the road
Like Roland's ghost winding a silent horn.°   20
Below him, in the town among the trees,
Where friends of other days had honored him,
A phantom salutation of the dead
Rang thinly till old Eben's eyes were dim.

Then, as a mother lays her sleeping child   25
Down tenderly, fearing it may awake,

MR. FLOOD'S PARTY.   8 *Tilbury Town*: an imaginary town featured in many of Robinson's
poems, modeled after Gardiner, Maine.   11 *bird. . . says*: a paraphrase of lines 25–28 of
Edward FitzGerald's translation of *The Rubaiyat of Omar Khayyam* (1859, 1872): "Come, fill
the Cup, and in the fire of Spring / Your Winter-garments of Repentance fling: / The Bird
of Time hath but a little way / To flutter and the Bird is on the Wing."   20 *Roland's. . .
horn*: Roland (d. 778) was Charlemagne's nephew and the French hero of medieval legends
and the eleventh-century epic *La Chanson de Roland* (*Song of Roland*). In the battle of
Roncesvalles (778) he sounded his horn, calling for help, just before dying.

He set the jug down slowly at his feet
With trembling care, knowing that most things break;
And only when assured that on firm earth
It stood, as the uncertain lives of men   30
Assuredly did not, he paced away,
And with his hand extended paused again:

"Well, Mr. Flood, we have not met like this
In a long time; and many a change has come
To both of us, I fear, since last it was   35
We had a drop together. Welcome home!"
Convivially returning with himself,
Again he raised the jug up to the light;
And with an acquiescent quaver said:
"Well, Mr. Flood, if you insist, I might.   40

"Only a very little, Mr. Flood—
For auld lang syne.° No more, sir; that will do."
So, for the time, apparently it did,
And Eben evidently thought so too;
For soon amid the silver loneliness   45
Of night he lifted up his voice and sang,
Secure, with only two moons listening,
Until the whole harmonious landscape rang—

"For auld lang syne." The weary throat gave out,
The last word wavered, and the song was done.   50
He raised again the jug regretfully
And shook his head, and was again alone.
There was not much that was ahead of him,
And there was nothing in the town below—
Where strangers would have shut the many doors   55
That many friends had opened long ago.

42 *auld lang syne*: Scots, meaning "old long since," suggesting "in the days long past."

THEODORE ROETHKE (1908–1963)

I Knew a Woman   *1958*

I knew a woman, lovely in her bones,
When small birds sighed, she would sigh back at them;
Ah, when she moved, she moved more ways than one:
The shapes a bright container can contain!
Of her choice virtues only gods should speak,   5
Or English poets who grew up on Greek
(I'd have them sing in chorus, cheek to cheek).

How well her wishes went! She stroked my chin,
She taught me Turn, and Counter-turn, and Stand;
She taught me Touch, that undulant white skin;
I nibbled meekly from her proffered hand;
She was the sickle; I, poor I, the rake,
Coming behind her for her pretty sake
(But what prodigious mowing we did make).

Love likes a gander, and adores a goose:
Her full lips pursed, the errant note to seize;
She played it quick, she played it light and loose;
My eyes, they dazzled at her flowing knees;
Her several parts could keep a pure repose,
Or one hip quiver with a mobile nose
(She moved in circles, and those circles moved).

Let seed be grass, and grass turn into hay:
I'm martyr to a motion not my own;
What's freedom for? To know eternity.
I swear she cast a shadow white as stone.
But who would count eternity in days?
These old bones live to learn her wanton ways:
(I measure time by how a body sways).

THEODORE ROETHKE (1908–1963)

The Waking   1953

I wake to sleep, and take my waking slow.
I feel my fate in what I cannot fear.
I learn by going where I have to go.

We think by feeling. What is there to know?
I hear my being dance from ear to ear.
I wake to sleep, and take my waking slow.

Of those so close beside me, which are you?
God bless the Ground! I shall walk softly there,
And learn by going where I have to go.

Light takes the Tree; but who can tell us how?
The lowly worm climbs up a winding stair;
I wake to sleep, and take my waking slow.

Great Nature has another thing to do
To you and me; so take the lively air,
And, lovely, learn by going where to go.

This shaking keeps me steady. I should know.
What falls away is always. And is near.
I wake to sleep, and take my waking slow.
I learn by going where I have to go.

DANTE GABRIEL ROSSETTI (1828–1882)

The Blessed Damozel *1850*

The blessed damozel° leaned out *damsel*
  From the gold bar of heaven;
Her eyes were deeper than the depth
  Of waters stilled at even;
She had three lilies in her hand, 5
  And the stars in her hair were seven.

Her robe, ungirt from clasp to hem,
  No wrought flowers did adorn,
But a white rose of Mary's gift,
  For service meetly° worn; *appropriately* 10
Her hair that lay along her back
  Was yellow like ripe corn.° *wheat*

Herseemed° she scarce had been a day
  One of God's choristers;
The wonder was not yet quite gone 15
  From that still look of hers;
Albeit, to them she left, her day
  Had counted as ten years.

(To one it is ten years of years.
  . . . Yet now, and in this place, 20
Surely she leaned o'er me—her hair
  Fell all about my face. . . .
Nothing: the autumn-fall of leaves.
  The whole year sets apace.)°

It was the rampart of God's house 25
  That she was standing on;
By God built over the sheer depth
  The which is Space begun;
So high, that looking downward thence
  She scarce could see the sun. 30

It lies in heaven, across the flood
  Of ether, as a bridge.
Beneath the tides of day and night
  With flame and darkness ridge
The void, as low as where this earth 35
  Spins like a fretful midge.° *a small insect*

Around her, lovers, newly met
  'Mid deathless love's acclaims,
Spoke evermore among themselves

THE BLESSED DAMOZEL.   13 *Herseemed*: It seemed to her.   19–24 *To. . . apace*:
These lines, and all others within parentheses, are spoken or thought by the damozel's lover
who is still alive. Lines in quotation marks are spoken by the damozel.

Their heart-remembered names;
And the souls mounting up to God
   Went by her like thin flames.

And still she bowed herself and stooped
   Out of the circling charm;
Until her bosom must have made
   The bar she leaned on warm,
And the lilies lay as if asleep
   Along her bended arm.

From the fixed place of heaven she saw
   Time like a pulse shake fierce
Through all the worlds. Her gaze still strove
   Within the gulf to pierce
Its path; and now she spoke as when
   The stars sang in their spheres.

The sun was gone now; the curled moon
   Was like a little feather
Fluttering far down the gulf; and now
   She spoke through the still weather.
Her voice was like the voice the stars
   Had when they sang together.

(Ah, sweet! Even now, in that bird's song,
   Strove not her accents there,
Fair to be harkened? When those bells
   Possessed the midday air,
Strove not her steps to reach my side
   Down all the echoing stair?)

"I wish that he were come to me,
   For he will come," she said.
"Have I not prayed in heaven?—on earth,
   Lord, Lord, has he not prayed?
Are not two prayers a perfect strength?
   And shall I feel afraid?

"When round his head the aureole clings,
   And he is clothed in white,
I'll take his hand and go with him
   To the deep wells of light;
As unto a stream we will step down,
   And bathe there in God's sight.

"We two will stand beside that shrine,
   Occult, withheld, untrod,
Whose lamps are stirred continually
   With prayer sent up to God;

And see our old prayers, granted, melt
   Each like a little cloud.

"We two will lie i' the shadow of   85
   That living mystic tree
Within whose secret growth the Dove°   *The Holy Spirit*
   Is sometimes felt to be,
While every leaf that His plumes touch
   Saith His Name audibly.   90

"And I myself will teach to him,
   I myself, lying so,
The songs I sing here; which his voice
   Shall pause in, hushed and slow,
And find some knowledge at each pause,   95
   Or some new thing to know."

(Alas! We two, we two, thou say'st!
   Yea, one wast thou with me
That once of old. But shall God lift
   To endless unity   100
The soul whose likeness with thy soul
   Was but its love for thee?)

"We two," she said, "will seek the groves
   Where the lady Mary is,
With her five handmaidens, whose names   105
   Are five sweet symphonies,
Cecily, Gertrude, Magdalen,
   Margaret, and Rosalys.

"Circlewise sit they, with bound locks
   And foreheads garlanded;   110
Into the fine cloth white like flame
   Weaving the golden thread,
To fashion the birth-robes for them
   Who are just born, being dead.

"He shall fear, haply, and be dumb;   115
   Then will I lay my cheek
To his, and tell about our love,
   Not once abashed or weak;
And the dear Mother will approve
   My pride, and let me speak.   120

"Herself shall bring us, hand in hand,
   To Him round whom all souls
Kneel, the clear-ranged unnumbered heads
   Bowed with their aureoles;

And angels meeting us shall sing   12!
  To their citherns and citoles.°   *guitars*

"There will I ask of Christ the Lord
  Thus much for him and me—
Only to live as once on earth
  With Love—only to be,   13(
As then awhile, forever now,
  Together, I and he."

She gazed and listened and then said,
  Less sad of speech than mild—
"All this is when he comes." She ceased.   13.
  The light thrilled toward her, filled
With angels in strong, level flight.
  Her eyes prayed, and she smiled.

(I saw her smile.) But soon their path
  Was vague in distant spheres;   14(
And then she cast her arms along
  The golden barriers,
And laid her face between her hands,
  And wept. (I heard her tears.)

LUIS OMAR SALINAS (b. 1937)

In a Farmhouse   *1973*

Fifteen miles
out of Robstown
with the Texas sun
fading in the distance
I sit in the bedroom
profoundly,
animated by the day's work
in the cottonfields.

I made two dollars and
thirty cents today
I am eight years old
and I wonder
how the rest of the Mestizos°
do not go hungry
and if one were to die
of hunger
what an odd way
to leave for heaven.

IN A FARMHOUSE.   13 *Mestizos*: persons of mixed Spanish and Amerindian ancestry.

SONIA SANCHEZ (b. 1934)

right on: white america   *1970*

this country might have
been a pio
   neer land
once.
     but.   there ain't   5
no mo
      indians   blowing
custer's° mind
         with a different
image of america.   10
            this country
might have
        needed shoot/
outs/ daily/
      once.   15
         but. there ain't
no mo real/ white/   allamerican
               bad/guys.
just.
    u & me.   20
        blk/ and un/armed.
this country might have
been a pion
        eer land.   once.
                 and it still is.   25
check out
      the falling
gun/shells   on our blk/tomorrows.

RIGHT ON: WHITE AMERICA.   8 *custer's*: General George Armstrong Custer (1839–
1876) was killed in his "last stand" at the Little Bighorn in Montana during a battle with
Sioux Indians.

CARL SANDBURG (1878–1967)

Chicago   *1916*

      Hog Butcher for the World,
      Tool Maker, Stacker of Wheat,
      Player with Railroads and the Nation's Freight Handler;
      Stormy, husky, brawling,
      City of the Big Shoulders: 5

They tell me you are wicked and I believe them, for I have seen your painted
  women under the gas lamps luring the farm boys.

And they tell me you are crooked and I answer: Yes, it is true I have seen the
   gunman kill and go free to kill again.
And they tell me you are brutal and my reply is: On the faces of women and
   children I have seen the marks of wanton hunger.
And having answered so I turn once more to those who sneer at this my city,
   and I give them back the sneer and say to them:
Come and show me another city with lifted head singing so proud to be alive
   and coarse and strong and cunning.
Flinging magnetic curses amid the toil of piling job on job, here is a tall bold
   slugger set vivid against the little soft cities;
Fierce as a dog with tongue lapping for action, cunning as a savage pitted against
   the wilderness,
      Bareheaded,
      Shoveling,
      Wrecking,
      Planning,
      Building, breaking, rebuilding,
Under the smoke, dust all over his mouth, laughing with white teeth,
Under the terrible burden of destiny laughing as a young man laughs,
Laughing even as an ignorant fighter laughs who has never lost a battle,
Bragging and laughing that under his wrist is the pulse, and under his ribs the
   heart of the people,
         Laughing!
Laughing the stormy, husky, brawling laughter of Youth, half-naked, sweating,
   proud to be Hog Butcher, Tool Maker, Stacker of Wheat, Player with Railroads
   and Freight Handler to the Nation.

SIEGFRIED SASSOON (1886–1967) — *He fought in WW I.*

Dreamers — *A Sonnet (usu. an amorous or meditative form)*
    Ironic here.   *1918*

Soldiers are citizens of death's grey land,
   Drawing no dividend from time's to-morrows.
In the great hour of destiny they stand,
   Each with his feuds, and jealousies, and sorrows.

Soldiers are sworn to action; they must win
   Some flaming, fatal climax with their lives.
Soldiers are dreamers; when the guns begin
   They think of firelit homes, clean beds, and wives.

I see them in foul dug-outs, gnawed by rats,
   And in the ruined trenches, lashed with rain,
Dreaming of things they did with balls and bats,
   And mocked by hopeless longing to regain
Bank-holidays,° and picture shows, and spats,
   And going to the office in the train.

Contrasts the pain, suffering, & unease of war with the ordinary pleasures of civilized life.

DREAMERS.   13 *Bank-holidays*: legal holidays in Great Britain.

Altho. the type of fighting is different (WW I & now), the suffering & waste are the same.

DELMORE SCHWARTZ (1913–1966)

The Heavy Bear Who Goes with Me   *1938*

"the withness of the body"

The heavy bear who goes with me,
A manifold honey to smear his face,
Clumsy and lumbering here and there,
The central ton of every place,
The hungry beating brutish one   5
In love with candy, anger, and sleep,
Crazy factotum, dishevelling all,
Climbs the building, kicks the football,
Boxes his brother in the hate-ridden city.

Breathing at my side, that heavy animal,   10
That heavy bear who sleeps with me,
Howls in his sleep for a world of sugar,
A sweetness intimate as the water's clasp,
Howls in his sleep because the tight-rope
Trembles and shows the darkness beneath.   15
—The strutting show-off is terrified,
Dressed in his dress-suit, bulging his pants,
Trembles to think that his quivering meat
Must finally wince to nothing at all.
That inescapable animal walks with me,   20
Has followed me since the black womb held,
Moves where I move, distorting my gesture,
A caricature, a swollen shadow,
A stupid clown of the spirit's motive,
Perplexes and affronts with his own darkness,   25
The secret life of belly and bone,
Opaque, too near, my private, yet unknown,
Stretches to embrace the very dear
With whom I would walk without him near,
Touches her grossly, although a word   30
Would bare my heart and make me clear,
Stumbles, flounders, and strives to be fed
Dragging me with him in his mouthing care,
Amid the hundred million of his kind,
The scrimmage of appetite everywhere.   35

ALAN SEEGER (1888–1916)

I Have a Rendezvous with Death   *1916*

I have a rendezvous with Death
At some disputed barricade,
When Spring comes back with rustling shade

And apple blossoms fill the air—
I have a rendezvous with Death
When Spring brings back blue days and fair.

It may be he shall take my hand
And lead me into his dark land
And close my eyes and quench my breath—
It may be I shall pass him still.
I have a rendezvous with Death
On some scarred slope of battered hill,
When Spring comes round again this year
And the first meadow flowers appear.

God knows 'twere better to be deep
Pillowed in silk and scented down,
Where Love throbs out in blissful sleep,
Pulse nigh to pulse and breath to breath,
Where hushed awakenings are dear. . . .
But I've a rendezvous with Death
At midnight in some flaming town,
When Spring trips north again this year,
And I to my pledged word am true,
I shall not fail that rendezvous.

ANNE SEXTON (1928–1974)

Three Green Windows   1966 (1962)

Half awake in my Sunday nap
I see three green windows
in three different lights—
one west, one south, one east.
I have forgotten that old friends are dying.
I have forgotten that I grow middle-aged.
At each window such rustlings!
The trees persist, yeasty and sensuous,
as thick as saints.
I see three wet gargoyles covered with birds.
Their skins shine in the sun like leather.

I'm on my bed as light as a sponge.
Soon it will be summer.
She is my mother.
She will tell me a story and keep me asleep
against her plump and fruity skin.
I see leaves—
leaves that are washed and innocent,
leaves that never knew a cellar,

born in their own green blood   20
like the hands of mermaids.

I do not think of the rusty wagon on the walk.
I pay no attention to the red squirrels
that leap like machines beside the house.
I do not remember the real trunks of the trees   25
that stand beneath the windows
as bulky as artichokes.
I turn like a giant,
secretly watching, secretly knowing,
secretly naming each elegant sea.   30

I have misplaced the Van Allen belt,°
the sewers and the drainage,
the urban renewal and the surburban centers.
I have forgotten the names of the literary critics.
I know what I know.   35
I am the child I was,
living the life that was mine.
I am young and half asleep.
It is a time of water, a time of trees.

THREE GREEN WINDOWS.   31 *Van Allen belt*: radiation belt around the earth, named
after its discoverer.

WILLIAM SHAKESPEARE (1564–1616)

Fear No More the Heat o' the Sun°   *1623 (ca. 1609)*

Fear no more the heat o' the sun,
  Nor the furious winter's rages;
Thou thy worldly task hast done,
  Home art gone, and ta'en° thy wages: *taken*
Golden lads and girls all must,   5
As° chimney-sweepers, come to dust.   *like*

Fear no more the frown o' the great;
  Thou art past the tyrant's stroke;
Care no more to clothe and eat;
  To thee the reed is as the oak: 10
The scepter, learning, physic, must
All follow this, and come to dust.

Fear no more the lightning flash,
  Nor the all-dreaded thunder stone;°
Fear not slander, censure rash;   15
  Thou hast finished joy and moan:°   *sadness*

FEAR NO MORE THE HEAT O' THE SUN. A dirge or lament sung over the supposedly
dead body of Imogen in act 4 of Shakespeare's *Cymbeline*.   14 *thunder stone*: The sound
of thunder was caused by stones falling from the sky.

All lovers young, all lovers must
Consign to thee, and come to dust.

No exorciser harm thee!
Nor no witchcraft charm thee!
Ghost unlaid forbear thee!
Nothing ill come near thee!
Quiet consummation have;
And renownéd be thy grave!

WILLIAM SHAKESPEARE (1564–1616)

Sonnet 146: *Poor Soul, The Center of My Sinful Earth*   1609

Poor soul, the center of my sinful earth,
Thrall° to these rebel powers that thee array,°   *captive*
Why dost thou pine within and suffer dearth,
Painting thy outward walls so costly gay?
Why so large cost, having so short a lease,
Dost thou upon thy fading mansion spend?
Shall worms, inheritors of this excess,
Eat up thy charge? Is this thy body's end?
Then, soul, live thou upon thy servant's loss,°
And let that pine to aggravate thy store;°
Buy terms° divine in selling hours of dross°   *periods; refuse*
Within be fed, without be rich no more:
So shalt thou feed on Death, that feeds on men,
and Death once dead, there's no more dying then.

POOR SOUL.   2 *array*: surround or dress out, as in a military formation.   9 *thy servant's
loss*: the loss of the body.   10 *let . . . store*: let the body ("that") dwindle ("pine") to
increase ("aggravate") the riches ("store") of the soul.

KARL SHAPIRO (b. 1913)

Auto Wreck   1941

Its quick soft silver bell beating, beating,
And down the dark one ruby flare
Pulsing out red light like an artery,
The ambulance at top speed floating down
Past beacons and illuminated clocks
Wings in a heavy curve, dips down,
And brakes speed, entering the crowd.
The doors leap open, emptying light;
Stretchers are laid out, the mangled lifted
And stowed into the little hospital.
Then the bell, breaking the hush, tolls once,

And the ambulance with its terrible cargo
Rocking, slightly rocking, moves away,
As the doors, an afterthought, are closed.

We are deranged, walking among the cops   *Silence now*   15
Who sweep glass and are large and composed.
One is still making notes under the light.
One with a bucket douches ponds of blood
Into the street and gutter.
One hangs lanterns on the wrecks that cling, | *metaphor*   20
Empty husks of locusts, to iron poles.

Our throats were tight as tourniquets, *Simile*   *They're in a state of*
Our feet were bound with splints, but now,   *shock,*
Like convalescents intimate and gauche, *Simile*
We speak through sickly smiles and warn   25
With the stubborn saw of common sense,| *Realistic*
The grim joke and the banal resolution.
The traffic moves around with care,
But we remain, touching a wound
That opens to our richest horror.   30
Already old, the question Who shall die?   *The collision + carnage of*
Becomes unspoken Who is innocent?   *auto wrecks is inex-*
For death in war is done by hands;   *plicable – it just happens.*
Suicide has cause and stillbirth, logic;
And cancer, simple as a flower, blooms. *Simile*   35
But this invites the occult mind, *To penetrate* *The poem is special to*
Cancels our physics with a sneer, *the mystery.* *the edge of the car.*
And spatters all we knew of denouement
Across the expedient and wicked stones.

SIR PHILIP SIDNEY (1554–1586)

Astrophil and Stella, Number 71   *1591*

Who will in fairest book of Nature know,
How Virtue may best lodged in beauty be,
Let him but learn of Love to read in thee,
Stella, those fair lines, which true goodness show.
There shall he find all vices' overthrow,   5
Not by rude force, but sweetest sovereignty
Of reason, from whose light those night birds fly;
That inward sun in thine eyes shineth so.
And not content to be Perfection's heir
Thyself, dost strive all minds that way to move,   10
Who mark in thee what is in thee most fair.
So while thy beauty draws the heart to love,
As fast thy Virtue bends that love to good:
"But ah," desire still cries, "give me some food."

JON SILKIN (b. 1930)

Worm   *1971*

Look out, they say, for yourself.
The worm doesn't. It is blind
As a sloe; its death by cutting,
Bitter. Its oozed length is ringed,
With parts swollen. Cold and blind
It is graspable, and writhes
In your hot hand; a small snake, unvenomous.
Its seeds furred and moist
It sexes by lying beside another,
In its eking conjunction of seed
Wriggling and worm-like.
Its ganglia are in its head,
And if this is severed
It must grow backwards.
It is lowly, useful, pink. It breaks
Tons of soil, gorging the humus
Its whole length; its shit a fine cast
Coiled in heaps, a burial mound, or like a shell
Made by a dead snail.
It has a life, which is virtuous
As a farmer's, making his own food.
Passionless as a hoe, sometimes, persistent.
Does not want to kill a thing.

LESLIE MARMON SILKO (b. 1948)

Where Mountain Lion Lay Down with Deer   *1974*

I climb the black rock mountain
    stepping from day to day
                                silently.
I smell the wind for my ancestors
    pale blue leaves
    crushed wild mountain smell.
Returning
    up the gray stone cliff
    where I descended
                a thousand years ago.
Returning to faded black stone.
    where mountain lion lay down with deer.
It is better to stay up here
                watching wind's reflection
                in tall yellow flowers.

The old ones who remember me are gone
      the old songs are all forgotten
and the story of my birth.
How I danced in snow-frost moonlight
      distant stars to the end of the Earth,   20
How I swam away
        in freezing mountain water
        narrow mossy canyon tumbling down
            out of the mountain
                out of the deep canyon stone   25
      down
        the memory
            spilling out
            into the world.

CHARLES SIMIC (b. 1938)

Fork   *1971*

This strange thing must have crept
Right out of hell.
It resembles a bird's foot
Worn around the cannibal's neck.

As you hold it in your hand,   5
As you stab with it into a piece of meat,
It is possible to imagine the rest of the bird:
Its head which like your fist
Is large, bald, beakless and blind.

LOUIS SIMPSON (b. 1923)

The Pawnshop   *1980*

The first time I saw a pawnshop
I thought, Sheer insanity.
A revolver lying next to a camera,
violins hanging in the air like hams. . . *Simile*

But in fact there was a reason for everything. *The theme,*   5

So it is with all these lives: *Our lives*
one is stained from painting with oils; *Art*
another has a way of arguing
with a finger along his nose, the Misnagid° tradition;
a third sits at a desk made of mahogany. *Commerce*   10

They are all cunningly displayed
to appeal to someone. Each has its place in the universe.

THE PAWNSHOP.   9 *Misnagid tradition*: a tradition of intellectual opposition to a Jewish
sect.

DAVE SMITH (b. 1942)

Bluejays   *1981*

She tries to call them down,
quicknesses of air.
They bitch and scorn,
they roost away from her.

It isn't that she's brutal.   5
She's just a girl. Worse,
her touch is total.
Her play is dangerous.

Darkly they spit each at each,
from tops of pine and spruce.   10
Her words are shy and sweet,
but it's no use.

Ragged, blue, shrill,
they dart around like boys.
They fear the beautiful   15
but do not fly away.

STEVIE SMITH (1902–1971)

Not Waving But Drowning   *1957*

Nobody heard him, the dead man,
But still he lay moaning:
I was much further out than you thought
And not waving but drowning.

Poor chap, he always loved larking   5
And now he's dead
It must have been too cold for him his heart gave way,
They said.

Oh, no no no, it was too cold always
(Still the dead one lay moaning)   10
I was much too far out all my life
And not waving but drowning.

W. D. SNODGRASS (b. 1926)

Lobsters in the Window   *1963*

First, you think they are dead.
Then you are almost sure
One is beginning to stir.

Out of the crushed ice, slow
As the hands of a schoolroom clock,   5
He lifts his one great claw
And holds it over his head;
Now, he is trying to walk.

But like a run-down toy;
Like the backward crabs we boys   10
Splashed after in the creek,
Trapped in jars or a net,
And then took home to keep.
Overgrown, retarded, weak,
He is fumbling yet   15
From the deep chill of his sleep

As if, in a glacial thaw,
Some ancient thing might wake
Sore and cold and stiff
Struggling to raise one claw   20
Like a defiant fist;
Yet wavering, as if
Starting to swell and ache
With that thick peg in the wrist.

                                                       25
I should wave back, I guess.
But still in his permanent clench
He's fallen back with the mass
Heaped in their common trench
Who stir, but do not look out   30
Through the rainstreaming glass.
Hear what the newsboys shout,
Or see the raincoats pass.

CATHY SONG

Lost Sister   *1983*

1

In China,
even the peasants
named their first daughters
Jade—°
the stone that in the far fields   5
could moisten the dry season,

LOST SISTER.   4 *Jade*: Both the mineral and the name are considered signs of good
fortune and health in China.

could make men move mountains
for the healing green of the inner hills
glistening like slices of winter melon.

And the daughters were grateful: 10
they never left home.
To move freely was a luxury
stolen from them at birth.
Instead, they gathered patience,
learning to walk in shoes   15
the size of teacups,°
without breaking—
the arc of their movements
as dormant as the rooted willow,
as redundant as the farmyard hens.   20
But they traveled far
in surviving,
learning to stretch the family rice,
to quiet the demons,
the noisy stomachs.   25

2

There is a sister
across the ocean,
who relinquished her name,
diluting jade green
with the blue of the Pacific.
Rising with a tide of locusts,   30
she swarmed with others
to inundate another shore.
In America,
there are many roads   35
and women can stride along with men.

But in another wilderness,
the possibilities,
the loneliness,
can strangulate like jungle vines.   40
The meager provisions and sentiments
of once belonging—
fermented roots, Mah-Jongg° tiles and firecrackers—
set but a flimsy household
in a forest of nightless cities.   45
A giant snake rattles above,

16 *teacups*: Traditionally, girls' feet were bound at the age of seven in China because minuscule feet were considered beautiful and aristocratic. The binding inhibited the natural growth of the feet and made it painful and difficult to walk.   43 *Mah-Jongg*: a Chinese game played with 144 dominolike tiles marked in suits, counters, and dice.

spewing black clouds into your kitchen.
Dough-faced landlords
slip in and out of your keyholes,
making claims you don't understand,   50
tapping into your communication systems
of laundry lines and restaurant chains.

You find you need China:
your one fragile identification,
a jade link   55
handcuffed to your wrist.
You remember your mother
who walked for centuries,
footless—
and like her,   60
you have left no footprints,
but only because
there is an ocean in between,
the unremitting space of your rebellion.

ANNE SPENCER (1882–1975)

At the Carnival   *1922*

Gay little Girl-of-the-Diving-Tank,
I desire a name for you,
Nice, as a right glove fits;
For you—who amid the malodorous
Mechanics of this unlovely thing,   5
Are darling of spirit and form.
I know you—a glance, and what you are
Sits-by-the-fire in my heart.
My Limousine-Lady knows you, or
Why does the slant-envy of her eyes mark   10
Your straight air and radiant inclusive smile?
Guilt pins a fig-leaf; Innocence is its own adorning.
The bull-necked man knows you—this first time
His itching flesh sees from divine and vibrant health,
And thinks not of his avocation.   15
I came incuriously—
Set on no diversion save that my mind
Might safely nurse its brood of misdeeds
In the presence of a blind crowd.
The color of life was gray.   20
Everywhere the setting seemed right
For my mood!

Here the sausage and garlic booth
Sent unholy incense skyward;
There a quivering female-thing   25
Gestured assignations, and lied
To call it dancing;
There, too, were games of chance
With chances for none;
But oh! the Girl-of-the-Tank, at last!   30
Gleaming Girl, how intimately pure and free
The gaze you send the crowd,
As though you know the dearth of beauty
In its sordid life.
We need you—my Limousine-Lady,   35
The bull-necked man, and I.
Seeing you here brave and water-clean,
Leaven for the heavy ones of earth,
I am swift to feel that what makes
The plodder glad is good; and   40
Whatever is good is God.
The wonder is that you are here;
I have seen the queer in queer places,
But never before a heaven-fed
Naiad of the Carnival-Tank!   45
Little Diver, Destiny for you,
Like as for me, is shod in silence;
Years may seep into your soul
The bacilli of the usual and the expedient;
I implore Neptune to claim his child to-day!   50

EDMUND SPENSER (1552–1599)

Amoretti 54: Of This World's Theater in Which We Stay   1595

Of this world's theater in which we stay,
My love like the spectator idly sits,
Beholding me that all the pageants° play,   *roles*
Disguising diversly my troubled wits.
Sometimes I joy when glad occasion fits,   5
And mask in mirth like to a comedy:
Soon after when my joy to sorrow flits,
I wail and make my woes a tragedy.
Yet she, beholding me with constant eye,
Delights not in my mirth nor rues° my smart: *regrets*   10
But when I laugh, she mocks, and when I cry

AMORETTI 54. *Amoretti* means "little loves" or "little love songs."

She laughs and hardens evermore her heart.
What then can move her? if not mirth nor moan,
She is no woman, but a senseless stone.

WILLIAM STAFFORD (b. 1914)

Traveling Through the Dark   *1960*

Traveling through the dark I found a deer
dead on the edge of the Wilson River road.
It is usually best to roll them into the canyon:
that road is narrow; to swerve might make more dead.

By glow of the tail-light I stumbled back of the car   5
and stood by the heap, a doe, a recent killing;
she had stiffened already, almost cold.
I dragged her off; she was large in the belly.

My fingers touching her side brought me the reason—
her side was warm; her fawn lay there waiting,   10
alive, still, never to be born.
Beside that mountain road I hesitated.

The car aimed ahead its lowered parking lights;
under the hood purred the steady engine.
I stood in the glare of the warm exhaust turning red;   15
around our group I could hear the wilderness listen.

I thought hard for us all—my only swerving—,
then pushed her over the edge into the river.

GERALD STERN (b. 1925)

Burying an Animal on the Way to New York   *1977*

Don't flinch when you come across a dead animal lying on the road;
you are being shown the secret of life.
Drive slowly over the brown flesh;
you are helping to bury it.
If you are the last mourner there will be no caress   5
at all from the crushed limbs
and you will have to slide over the dark spot imagining
the first suffering all by yourself
Shreds of spirit and little ghost fragments will be spread out
for two miles above the white highway.   10
Slow down with your radio off and your window open
to hear the twittering as you go by.

WALLACE STEVENS (1879–1955)

The Emperor of Ice-Cream   1923

Call the roller of big cigars,
The muscular one, and bid him whip
In kitchen cups concupiscent curds.
Let the wenches dawdle in such dress
As they are used to wear, and let the boys   5
Bring flowers in last month's newspapers.
Let be be finale° of seem.
The only emperor is the emperor of ice-cream.
Take from the dresser of deal,°
Lacking the three glass knobs, that sheet   10
On which she embroidered fantails° once
And spread it so as to cover her face.
If her horny feet protrude, they come
To show how cold she is, and dumb.
Let the lamp affix its beam.   15
The only emperor is the emperor of ice-cream.

THE EMPEROR OF ICE CREAM.   7 *finale*: the grand conclusion.   9 *deal*: unfinished
pine or fir used to make cheap furniture.   11 *fantails*: fantail pigeons.

JONATHAN SWIFT (1667–1745)

A Description of a City Shower   1710

Careful observers may foretell the hour
(By sure prognostics°) when to dread a shower.   *indications*
While rain depends,° the pensive cat gives o'er   *impends*
Her frolics, and pursues her tail no more.
Returning home at night, you'll find the sink°   *sewer*   5
Strike your offended sense with double stink.
If you be wise, then go not far to dine;
You'll spend in coach-hire more than save in wine.
A coming shower your shooting° corns presage;°   *painful; foretell*
Old aches throb, your hollow tooth will rage.   10
Saunt'ring in coffee-house is Dulman seen;
He damns the climate, and complains of spleen.°   *ill-humor*
   Meanwhile the South,° rising with dabbled wings,   *South Wind*
A sable cloud athwart the welkin° flings,   *sky*
That swilled more liquor than it could contain,   15
And, like a drunkard, gives it up again.
Brisk Susan whips her linen from the rope,
While the first drizzling shower is borne aslope:
Such is that sprinkling which some careless quean°   *housewife, shrew*
Flirts° on you from her mop, but not so clean.   *tosses*   20

You fly, invoke the gods; then turning, stop
To rail;° she, singing, still whirls on her mop.   *complain*
Nor yet the dust had shunned th'unequal strife,
But, aided by the wind, fought still for life,
And wafted with its foe by violent gust,   25
'Twas doubtful which was rain, and which was dust.
Ah! where must needy poet seek for aid,
When dust and rain at once his coat invade?
Sole coat, where dust cemented by the rain
Erects the nap,° and leaves a cloudy stain.   *fibers*   30
    Now in contiguous drops the flood comes down,
Threat'ning with deluge this *devoted* town.
To shops in crowds the daggled females fly,
Pretend to cheapen° goods, but nothing buy.   *bargain for*
The Templar° spruce, while every spout's abroach,   *lawyer* 35
Stays till 'tis fair, yet seems to call a coach.
The tucked-up sempstress walks with hasty strides,
While streams run down her oiled° umbrella's sides.   *oiled silk*
Here various kinds, by various fortunes led,
Commence acquaintance underneath a shed.   40
Triumphant Tories° and desponding Whigs
Forget their feuds, and join to save their wigs.°
Boxed in a chair° the beau impatient sits,
While spouts run clatt'ring o'er the roof by fits;
And ever and anon with frightful din   45
The leather sounds; he trembles from within.
So when Troy chairmen bore the wooden steed,
Pregnant with Greeks impatient to be freed
(Those bully Greeks, who, as the moderns do,
Instead of paying chairmen, run them through),   50
Laocoön struck the outside with his spear,
And each imprisoned hero quaked for fear.°
    Now from all parts the swelling kennels° flow,   *gutters*
And bear their trophies with them as they go.
Filths of all hues and odors seem to tell   55
What streets they sailed from, by their sight and smell.
They, as each torrent drives, with rapid force
From Smithfield or St. Pulchre's shape their course,
And in huge confluent joined at Snow-Hill ridge,
Fall from the conduit prone to Holborn Bridge.°   60

A DESCRIPTION OF A CITY SHOWER.   41 *Tories . . . Whigs*: These were the two
political parties of eighteenth-century England; Queen Anne dismissed her Whig ministers
in 1710 and appointed a Tory ministry.   42 *wigs*: All upper-class English gentlemen wore
wigs in public in the eighteenth century.   43 *chair*: a sedan chair, an enclosed chair mounted
on two poles and carried by two men.   47–52 *So . . . fear*: an allusion to the Trojans
who carried into Troy (hence "chairmen") the wooden horse built by the Greeks and full
of Greek soldiers. Laocoön, who distrusted Greeks and their gifts, struck the horse with his
spear.   58–60 *Smithfield . . . Holborn Bridge*: All the places named are in London.

Sweepings from butchers' stalls, dung, guts, and blood,
Drowned puppies, stinking sprats, all drenched in mud,
Dead cats and turnip-tops come tumbling down the flood.

JAMES TATE (b. 1943)

The Blue Booby   *1969*

The blue booby kives
on the bare rocks
of Galápagos°
and fears nothing.
It is a simple life: 5
they live on fish,
and there are few predators.
Also, the males do not
make fools of themselves
chasing after the young   10
ladies. Rather,
they gather the blue
objects of the world
and construct from them

a nest—an occasional   15
Gaulois° package,
a string of beads,
a piece of cloth from
a sailor's suit. This
replaces the need for   20
dazzling plumage;
in fact, in the past
fifty million years
the male has grown
considerably duller,   25
nor can he sing well.
The female, though,

asks little of him—
the blue satisfies her
completely, has   30
a magical effect
on her. When she returns
from her day of
gossip and shopping,

THE BLUE BOOBY.   3 *Galápagos*: islands in the Pacific Ocean on the Equator about
600 miles west of Ecuador where many unique species of animals live.   16 *Gaulois*: a brand
of French cigarettes with a blue package.

she sees he has found her   35
a new shred of blue foil:
for this she rewards him
with her dark body,
the stars turn slowly
in the blue foil beside them   40
like the eyes of a mild savior.

EDWARD TAYLOR (1645–1729)

Upon a Spider Catching a Fly   1939 (ca. 1685)

Thou sorrow, venom Elfe:°   *elf*
   Is this thy play,
To spin a web out of thyselfe
    To Catch a Fly?
     For why?   5

I saw a pettish° wasp   *ill-humored*
   Fall foule therein.
Whom yet thy whorle pins° did not clasp   *spiders' legs*
    Lest he should fling
     His sting.   10

But as affraid, remote
   Didst stand hereat
And with thy little fingers stroke
    And gently tap
     His back.   15

Thus gently him didst treate
   Lest he should pet,
And in a froppish,° waspish heate   *fretful*
    Should greatly fret
     Thy net.   20

Whereas the silly Fly,
   Caught by its leg
Thou by the throate tookst hastily,
    And 'hinde the head
     Bite Dead.   25

This goes to pot, that not
   Nature doth call.°
Strive not above what strength hath got
    Lest in the brawle
     Thou fall.   30

UPON A SPIDER CATCHING A FLY.   26–27 *This . . . call*: that is, he who does not act according to natural reason goes to ruin ("pot").

This Frey° seems thus to us.   *fray, battle*
  Hells Spider gets
His intrails spun to whip Cords thus
  And wove to nets
    And sets.   35

To tangle Adams race
  In's stratigems
To their Destructions, spoil'd, made base
  By venom things
    Damn'd Sins.   40

But mighty, Gracious Lord
  Communicate
Thy Grace to breake the Cord, afford
  Us Glorys Gate
    And State.   45

We'l Nightingaile sing like
  When pearcht on high
In Glories Cage, thy glory, bright,
  [Yea,] thankfully,
    For joy.   50

DYLAN THOMAS (1914–1953)

Fern Hill°   *1946*

Now as I was young and easy under the apple boughs
About the lilting house and happy as the grass was green,
        The night above the dingle starry,
            Time let me hail and climb
        Golden in the heydays of his eyes,   5
And honoured among wagons I was prince of the apple towns
And once below a time I lordly had the trees and leaves
            Trail with daisies and barley
        Down the rivers of the windfall light.

    And as I was green and carefree, famous among the barns   10
About the happy yard and singing as the farm was home,
        In the sun that is young once only,
            Time let me play and be
        Golden in the mercy of his means,
And green and golden I was huntsman and herdsman, the calves   15
Sang to my horn, the foxes on the hills barked clear and cold,
            And the sabbath rang slowly
        In the pebbles of the holy streams.

FERN HILL. Fern Hill was the name of the country house where Thomas's aunt lived and
where he spent summers in his youth.

All the sun long it was running, it was lovely, the hay
Fields high as the house, the tunes from the chimneys, it was air   20
    And playing, lovely and watery
        And fire green as grass.
    And nightly under the simple stars
As I rode to sleep the owls were bearing the farm away,
All the moon long I heard, blessed among stables, the night-jars   25
    Flying with the ricks, and the horses
        Flashing into the dark.

And then to awake, and the farm, like a wanderer white
With the dew, come back, the cock on his shoulder: it was all
    Shining, it was Adam and maiden,   30
        The sky gathered again
    And the sun grew round that very day.
So it must have been after the birth of the simple light
In the first, spinning place, the spellbound horses walking warm
    Out of the whinnying green stable   35
        On to the fields of praise.

And honoured among foxes and pheasants by the gay house
Under the new made clouds and happy as the heart was long,
    In the sun born over and over,
        I ran my heedless ways,   40
    My wishes raced through the house high hay
And nothing I cared, at my sky blue trades, that time allows
In all his tuneful turning so few and such morning songs
    Before the children green and golden
        Follow him out of grace,   45

Nothing I cared, in the lamb white days, that time would take me
Up to the swallow thronged loft by the shadow of my hand,
    In the moon that is always rising,
        Nor that riding to sleep
    I should hear him fly with the high fields   50
And wake to the farm forever fled from the childless land.
Oh as I was young and easy in the mercy of his means,
        Time held me green and dying
    Though I sang in my chains like the sea.

DYLAN THOMAS (1914–1953)

A Refusal to Mourn the Death, by Fire,
of a Child in London   *1946*

Never until the mankind making
Bird beast and flower
Fathering and all humbling darkness

Tells with silence the last light breaking
And the still hour   5
Is come of the sea tumbling in harness

And I must enter again the round
Zion of the water bead
And the synagogue of the ear of corn
Shall I let pray the shadow of a sound   10
Or sow my salt seed
In the least valley of sackcloth to mourn

The majesty and burning of the child's death.
I shall not murder
The mankind of her going with a grave truth   15
Nor blaspheme down the stations of the breath
With any further
Elegy of innocence and youth.

Deep with the first dead lies London's daughter,
Robed in the long friends,   20
The grains beyond age, the dark veins of her mother,
Secret by the unmourning water
Of the riding Thames.°
After the first death, there is no other.

A REFUSAL TO MOURN.   23 *Thames*: the River Thames, which flows through
London.

LESLIE ULLMAN (b. 1947)

Why There Are Children   1979

The woman inside every woman
lights the candles.
This is the woman sons look for

when they leave their wives.
Daughters become wives   5
thinking they travel backward

to the dresser covered with lace,
the hairpins still scattered there
and the cameo earrings.

The same gnarled tree   10
darkens the bedroom window.
The hair coiled in a locket

conceals the hands of men and children.
When a woman shivers on the porch,
perhaps at dusk, it is the other   15

wanting a shawl. When a woman
in her middle years rises
and dresses for work, the other

reaches for the cameos
remembering a great love   20
and herself on the brink of it.

MONA VAN DUYN (b. 1921)

Advice to a God   *1971*

Before you leave her, the woman who thought you lavish,
whose body you led to parade without a blush
the touching vulgarity of the *nouveau-riche*,

whose every register your sexual coin
crammed full, whose ignorant bush mistook for sunshine   5
the cold, brazen battering of your rain,

rising, so little spent, strange millionaire
who feels in his loins' pocket clouds of power
gathering again for shower upon golden shower,

say to her, since she loves you, "Those as unworldly   10
as you are fated, and I can afford, to be
may find in Love's bed the perfect economy,

but, in all of his other places, a populace
living in fear of his management, his excess
of stingy might and extravagant helplessness.   15

Turn from him, Danae. I am greater by far,
whose flower reseeds without love for another flower,
whose seas part without loneliness, whose air

brightens or darkens heartlessly. By chance
I have come to you, and a progeny of events,   20
all that the mind of man calls consequence,

will follow my coming, slaughter and marriage, intrigue,
enchantment, definition of beauty, hag
and hero, a teeming, throwaway catalogue

of the tiniest, riskiest portion of my investment.   25
Yet pity your great landlord, for if I lent
so much as an ear to you, one loving tenant,

your bankrupt scream as I leave might tempt me to see
all creation in the ungainly, ungodly
throes of your individuality."   30

TINO VILLANUEVA (b. 1941)

Day-Long Day   *1972*

> Again the drag of pisca,° pisca
> . . pisca . . . Daydreams border
> on sun-fed hallucinations, eyes
> and hands automatically dis-
> criminate whiteness of cotton
> from field of vision. Pisca, pisca.
>   "Un Hijo del Sol,"°
>   Genaro Gonzales

Third-generation timetable.
Sweat day-long dripping into open space;
sun blocks out the sky, suffocates the only breeze.
From el amo desgraciado,° a sentence:

"I wanna a bale a day, and the boy here   5
don't hafta go to school."

*   *   *

In time-binding motion—
a family of sinews and backs,
row-trapped,
zigzagging through summer-long rows   10
of cotton: Lubbock by way of Wharton.°
"Está como si escupieran fuego,"° a mother moans
in sweat-patched jeans,
stooping
with unbending dreams.   15
"Estudia para que no seas burro como nosotros,"°
our elders warn, their gloves and cuffs
leaf-stained by seasons.

*   *   *

Bronzed and blurry-eyed by
the blast of degrees,   20
we blend into earth's rotation.
And sweltering toward Saturday, the
day-long day is sunstruck by 6:00 P.M.

DAY-LONG DAY.   EPIGRAPH: *pisca*: picking cotton.   *Un Hijo del Sol*: A Son of the
Sun.   4 *el amo desgraciado*: the despicable boss.   11 *Lubbock . . . Wharton*: cities on
opposite sides of Texas.   12 *Está . . . fuego*: "It's as if they are spewing fire."   16 *Estudia
. . . nosotros*: "Study so that you will not be a burro like us."

One last chug-a-lug from a water jug
old as granddad.   25
Day-long sweat dripping into open space:
Wharton by way of Lubbock.

DIANE WAKOWSKI (b. 1937)

The Ring   1977

I carry it on my keychain, which itself
is a big brass ring
large enough for my wrist,
holding keys for safe-deposit box,
friends' apartments,   5
my house, office and faithless car.

I would like to wear it,
the only ornament on my plain body,
but it is a relic,
the husband gone to other wives,   10
and it could never be a symbol of sharing,
but like the gold it's made of, stands for possession, power,
the security of a throne.

So, on my keyring,
dull from resting in my dark purse,   15
it hangs, reminding me of failures, of beauty I once had,
of more ancient searches for an enchanted ring.

I understand, now, what that enchantment is, though.
It is being loved.
Or, conversely, loving so much that you feel loved.   20
And the ring hangs there
with my keys,
reminding of failure.

This vain head full of roses,
crystal,   25
bleeding lips,
a voice doomed to listen, forever,
to itself.

ALICE WALKER (b. 1944)

Revolutionary Petunias   1972

Sammy Lou of Rue
sent to his reward
the exact creature who

5

murdered her husband,
using a cultivator's hoe
with verve and skill;
and laughed fit to kill
in disbelief
at the angry, militant
pictures of herself
the Sonneteers quickly drew:
not any of them people that
she knew.
A backwoods woman
her house was papered with
funeral home calendars and
faces appropriate for a Mississippi
Sunday School. She raised a George,
a Martha, a Jackie and a Kennedy. Also
a John Wesley Junior.°
"Always respect the word of God,"
she said on her way to she didn't
know where, except it would be by
electric chair, and she continued
"Don't yall forget to *water*
my purple petunias."

REVOLUTIONARY PETUNIAS.   18–20 *George . . . Junior*: The children are named after
George and Martha Washington, Jackie and John Fitzgerald Kennedy (1917–1963, thirty-
fifth president of the U.S.), and John Wesley (1703–1791), English evangelical preacher who
founded Methodism.

MARGARET WALKER (b. 1915)

Iowa Farmer   1942

I talked to a farmer one day in Iowa.
We looked out far over acres of wheat.
He spoke with pride and yet not boastfully;
he had no need to fumble for his words.
He knew his land and there was love for home
within the soft serene eyes of his son.
His ugly house was clean against the storm;
there was no hunger deep within the heart
nor burning riveted within the bone,
but here they ate a satisfying bread.
Yet in the Middle West where wheat was plentiful;
where grain grew golden under sunny skies
and cattle fattened through the summer heat
I could remember more familiar sights.

PHYLLIS WHEATLEY (1754–1784)

On Being Brought from Africa to America   *1773*

'Twas mercy brought me from my *Pagan* land,
Taught my benighted soul to understand
That there's a God, that there's a *Saviour* too:
Once I redemption neither sought nor knew.
Some view our sable race with scornful eye,   5
"Their colour is a diabolic die."
Remember, *Christians*, *Negroes*, black as *Cain*,
May be refin'd, and join th' angelic train.

RICHARD WILBUR (b. 1921)

In a Bird Sanctuary   *1947*

Because they could not give it too much ground
they closely planted it with fir and shrub.
A plan of pathways, voted by the Club,
contrived to lead the respiter around
a mildly wandring wood, still at no cost   5
to get him lost.

Now over dear Miss Drury's favored trees
they flutter (birds) and either stop or not,
as if they were unconscious that the spot
is planned for them, and meant to buy release   10
for one restrained department of the soul,
to "make men whole."

It's hard to tell the purpose of a bird;
for relevance it does not seem to try.
No line can trace no flute exemplify   15
its traveling; it darts without the word.
Who wills devoutly to absorb, contain,
birds give him pain.

Commissioners of Public Parks have won
a partial wisdom, know that birds exist.   20
And seeing people equally insist
on birds and statues, they go hire a man
to swab sans° rancor dung from granite stare   *without*
and marble hair.

BIRDS HAVE BEEN SEEN IN TOWERS AND ON ISLES;   25
ALSO ON PRIVY TOPS, IN FANEUIL HALL;°

IN A BIRD SANCTUARY.   26 *Faneuil Hall*: a public hall in Boston, called "the cradle
of liberty" because political meetings were held there before the Revolutionary War.

BIRDS HAVE SOME OF THEM NOT BEEN SEEN AT ALL;
BIRDS, IF THEY CARE TO, WALK ALONG IN FILE.
BIRDS DO NOT FEEL ESPECIALLY GOOD IN FLIGHT:
LET'S TREAT THEM RIGHT!   30

The liberty of any things becomes
the liberty of all. It also brings
their abolition into anythings.
In order's name let's not turn down our thumbs
on routine visions; we must figure out   35
what all's about.

WILLIAM CARLOS WILLIAMS (1883–1963)

The Red Wheelbarrow   1923

    so much depends
    upon

    a red wheel
    barrow

    glazed with rain   5
    water

    beside the white
    chickens.

WILLIAM CARLOS WILLIAMS (1883–1963)

The Yachts   1935

contend in a sea which the land partly encloses
shielding them from the too-heavy blows
of an ungoverned ocean which when it chooses

tortures the biggest hulls, the best man knows
to pit against its beatings, and sinks them pitilessly.   5
Mothlike in mists, scintillant in the minute

brilliance of cloudless days, with broad bellying sails
they glide to the wind tossing green water
from their sharp prows while over them the crew crawls

ant-like, solicitously grooming them, releasing,   10
making fast as they turn, lean far over and having
caught the wind again, side by side, head for the mark.

In a well guarded arena of open water surrounded by
lesser and greater craft which, sycophant, lumbering
and flittering follow them, they appear youthful, rare   15

as the light of a happy eye, live with the grace
of all that in the mind is fleckless, free and
naturally to be desired. Now the sea which holds them

is moody, lapping their glossy sides, as if feeling
for some slightest flaw but fails completely.   20
Today no race. Then the wind comes again. The yachts

move, jockeying for a start, the signal is set and they
are off. Now the waves strike at them but they are too
well made, they slip through, though they take in canvas.°

Arms with hands grasping seek to clutch at the prows.   25
Bodies thrown recklessly in the way are cut aside.
It is a sea of faces about them in agony, in despair

until the horror of the race dawns staggering the mind,
the whole sea become an entanglement of watery bodies
lost to the world bearing what they cannot hold. Broken,   30

beaten, desolate, reaching from the dead to be taken up
they cry out, failing, failing! their cries rising
in waves still as the skillful yachts pass over.

THE YACHTS.   24 *take in canvas*: reduce the amount of sails on the masts.

WILLIAM WORDSWORTH (1770–1850)

Lines Written in Early Spring   *1798*

I heard a thousand blended notes,
While in a grove I sate reclined,
In that sweet mood when pleasant thoughts
Bring sad thoughts to the mind.

To her fair works did Nature link   5
The human soul that through me ran;
And much it grieved my heart to think
What man has made of man.

Through primrose tufts, in that green bower,
The periwinkle° trailed its wreaths;   10
And 'tis my faith that every flower
Enjoys the air it breathes.

The birds around me hopped and played,
Their thoughts I cannot measure—
But the least motion which they made,   15
It seemed a thrill of pleasure.

LINES WRITTEN IN EARLY SPRING.   10 *periwinkle*: a trailing evergreen plant with blue
or white flowers.

The budding twigs spread out their fan,
To catch the breezy air;
And I must think, do all I can,
That there was pleasure there.   20

It this belief from heaven be sent,
If such be Nature's holy plan,
Have I not reason to lament
What man has made of man?

WILLIAM WORDSWORTH (1770–1850)

The Solitary Reaper   1807

Behold her, single in the field,
Yon solitary Highland Lass!
Reaping and singing by herself;
Stop here, or gently pass!
Alone she cuts and binds the grain,   5
And sings a melancholy strain;
O listen! for the Vale profound
Is overflowing with the sound.

No Nightingale did ever chaunt
More welcome notes to weary bands   10
Of travelers in some shady haunt,
Among Arabian sands;
A voice so thrilling ne'er was heard
In springtime from the Cuckoo bird,
Breaking the silence of the seas   15
Among the farthest Hebrides.°

Will no one tell me what she sings?°
Perhaps the plaintive numbers flow
For old, unhappy, far-off things,
And battles long ago;   20
Or is it some more humble lay,
Familiar matter of today?
Some natural sorrow, loss, or pain,
That has been, and may be again?

Whate'er the theme, the Maiden sang   25
As if her song could have no ending;
I saw her singing at her work,
And o'er the sickle bending—
I listened, motionless and still;

THE SOLITARY REAPER.   16 *Hebrides*: a group of islands belonging to and off the west
coast of Scotland.   17 *Will . . . sings*: The speaker does not understand Scots Gaelic,
the language in which the woman sings.

And, as I mounted up the hill,   30
The music in my heart I bore,
Long after it was heard no more.

ELEANOR WYLIE (1885–1928)

The Eagle and the Mole   *1928*

Avoid the reeking herd,
Shun the polluted flock,
Live like that stoic bird,
The eagle of the rock.

The huddled warmth of crowds   5
Begets and fosters hate;
He keeps, above the clouds,
His cliff inviolate.

When flocks are folded warm,
And herds to shelter run,   10
He sails above the storm,
He stares into the sun.

If in the eagle's track
Your sinews cannot leap,
Avoid the lathered pack,   15
Turn from the steaming sheep.

If you would keep your soul
From spotted sight or sound,
Live like the velvet mole;
Go burrow underground.   20

And there hold intercourse
With roots of trees and stones,
With rivers at their source,
And disembodied bones.

WILLIAM BUTLER YEATS (1865–1939)

Sailing to Byzantium °   *1927*

1

That is no country for old men. The young
In one another's arms, birds in the trees
—Those dying generations—at their song,

SAILING TO BYZANTIUM. In Yeats's private mythology, Byzantium (called Constantinople
in Roman times and Istanbul today) symbolizes art, artifice, sophistication, and eternity as
opposed to the natural world and physicality.

The salmon-falls, the mackerel-crowded seas,
Fish, flesh, or fowl, commend all summer long   5
Whatever is begotten, born, and dies.
Caught in that sensual music all neglect
Monuments of unaging intellect.

2

An aged man is but a paltry thing,
A tattered coat upon a stick, unless   10
Soul clap its hands and sing, and louder sing
For every tatter in its mortal dress,
Nor is there singing school but studying
Monuments of its own magnificence;
And therefore I have sailed the seas and come   15
To the holy city of Byzantium.

3

O sages standing in God's holy fire
As in the gold mosaic of a wall,
Come from the holy fire, perne in a gyre,°
And be the singing-masters of my soul.   20
Consume my heart away; sick with desire
And fastened to a dying animal
It knows not what it is; and gather me
Into the artifice of eternity.

4

Once out of nature I shall never take   25
My bodily form from any natural thing,
But such a form as Grecian goldsmiths make
Of hammered gold and gold enameling
To keep a drowsy Emperor awake;
Or set upon a golden bough to sing   30
To lords and ladies of Byzantium
Of what is past, or passing, or to come.

19 *perne in a gyre*: turn or spin about in a spiral motion.

WILLIAM BUTLER YEATS (1865–1939)

Byzantium   *1932*

The unpurged images of day recede;
The Emperor's drunken soldiery are abed;
Night resonance recedes, night-walkers' song

BYZANTIUM. See the first note to the preceding poem. Here, Byzantium also symbolizes
death and the purification of the spirit.

After great cathedral gong;
A starlit or a moonlit dome° disdains
All that man is,
All mere complexities,
The fury and the mire of human veins.

Before me floats an image, man or shade,
Shade more than man, more image than a shade;
For Hades' bobbin° bound in mummy-cloth
May unwind the winding path;
A mouth that has no moisture and no breath
Breathless mouths may summon;
I hail the superhuman;
I call it death-in-life and life-in-death.

Miracle, bird or golden handiwork,
More miracle than bird or handiwork,
Planted on the starlit golden bough,°
Can like the cocks of Hades° crow,
Or, by the moon embittered, scorn aloud
In glory of changeless metal
Common bird or petal
And all complexities of mire or blood.

At midnight on the Emperor's pavement flit
Flames° that no faggot feeds, nor steel has lit,
Nor storm disturbs, flames begotten of flame,
Where blood-begotten spirits come
And all complexities of fury leave,
Dying into a dance,
An agony of trance,
An agony of flame that cannot singe a sleeve.

Astraddle on the dolphin's° mire and blood,
Spirit after spirit! The smithies break the flood,
The golden smithies of the Emperor!
Marbles of the dancing floor
Break bitter furies of complexity,
Those images that yet
Fresh images beget,
That dolphin-torn, that gong-tormented sea.

5 *starlit . . .dome*: For Yeats, starlight symbolizes complete objectivity and spirituality while moonlight symbolizes subjectivity and physicality.   11 *Hades' bobbin*: the spool of the underworld, hence the thread of fate.   19 *starlit golden bough*: part of the world of spirituality, art, and eternity. The birds are either supernatural ("miracle") or works of artifice ("golden handiwork").   20 *cocks of Hades*: the roosters of the underworld that are eternal.   26 *Flames*: purgatorial flames of purification that burn without fuel ("faggots") or ignition; they burn away the "complexities" of worldly existence but "cannot singe a sleeve."   33 *dolphin's*: The dolphin is a traditional symbol of the soul in transition.

PAUL ZIMMER (b. 1934)

The Day Zimmer Lost Religion   *1973*

The first Sunday I missed Mass on purpose
I waited all day for Christ to climb down
Like a wiry flyweight° from the cross and
Club me on my irreverent teeth, to wade into
My blasphemous gut and drop me like a
Red hot thurible,° the devil roaring in
Reserved seats until he got the hiccups.

It was a long cold way from the old days
When cassocked and surpliced° I mumbled Latin
At the old priest and rang his obscure bell.
A long way from the dirty wind that blew
The soot like venial sins across the schoolyard
Where God reigned as a threatening,
One-eyed triangle high in the fleecy sky.

The first Sunday I missed Mass on purpose
I waited all day for Christ to climb down
Like the playground bully, the cuts and mice
Upon his face agleam, and pound me
Till my irreligious tongue hung out.
But of course He never came, knowing that
I was grown up and ready for Him now.

THE DAY ZIMMER LOST RELIGION.   3 *flyweight*: a boxer weighing less than 112
pounds.   6 *thurible*: a censer, a container in which incense is burned.   9 *cassocked and
surpliced*: wearing the traditional garb of an altar boy during Mass.

Drama

27

The Elements of Drama

The word *drama* is derived from the Greek word *dran*, which means "to do" or "to act." In many ways, this "doing" or "acting" is the definitive quality of drama. Although "drama" is often used as a synonym for "play," the word *drama* can also refer to a group of plays (Elizabethan drama) or to all plays collectively. While plays share many things in common with prose fiction and poetry, the single most important difference is that they are designed to be presented by actors on a stage before an audience.

THE NATURE AND HISTORY OF DRAMA

Drama evolved in humanity's tribal past from the rites of primitive cultures. These communities would often act out their deepest fears, strongest desires, or greatest achievements in a religious ritual. A successful hunt, for instance, might have been followed by a rite of thanksgiving in which the hunt was symbolically reenacted. Similarly, in the dead of winter people might have acted out the coming of spring and the regeneration of the earth because they needed to reassure themselves that such a rebirth would occur. Drama as religious ritual became drama as an art form in the fifth century B.C. in Greece. The plays of the classical Greek dramatists maintained much of the ritual flavor of primitive drama, often retelling ancient myths and being performed at religious festivals. Nevertheless, the Greek playwrights shaped drama into its modern form with large casts of characters and divisions into separate scenes.

Classical Greece also provided the first drama critic, the philosopher Aristotle (384–322 B.C.). In *The Poetics* he defines drama or acting as *mimesis*, or the *imitation* of human actions. Drama is thus a *mimetic* art in which actors mimic the actions and emotions of people in order to communicate actions and ideas to an audience. Aristotle also provided the first extensive theoretical discussions of the nature and structure of drama and of the differences between comedy and tragedy.

Drama maintained its connection with religion and ritual through much of its history. In the Middle Ages drama was reborn in the churches of England and other Western European countries as part of the Catholic mass; this medieval drama was explicitly linked to Christianity, especially in the **mystery plays,** which dramatized events related in the Bible and in the **morality plays,** which demonstrated the way to live a Christian life. To this day, a dramatic performance maintains some sense of communal ritual involving both the actors and the audience.

PLAY TEXTS AND PRODUCTIONS

What separates drama from prose fiction and poetry is the acting or *staging* of the play. People who write plays are called *dramatists* or *playwrights* (not "playwrites"; the term combines *play* with the word *wright*, a worker or builder). The text of a play is basically dialogue, monologue, and stage directions. **Dialogue** is conversation among two or more characters; a **monologue** is spoken by a single character who is usually alone on stage. **Stage directions** are the playwright's instructions to the actors and are distinguished quite clearly from the dialogue of the play.

Reading the text of a play cannot convey the immediate excitement of a performance. In production, the text is fleshed out with all the techniques available to the modern theater. The actors bring the characters and the dialogue to life; they strut or cringe, scream or whimper, embrace or murder. They give their bodies to the characters, providing gestures and voices, facial expressions, intonations, and **blocking** (stage movement and stage groupings). The actors also provide **stage business**—little gestures or movements that keep the production active and dynamic. In the modern theater, these aspects of movement and position on-stage are usually controlled by the *Director*, the person who plans the production and *directs* the actors during rehearsals to move, speak, and act in ways that are consistent with his or her vision of the play.

Most modern plays are acted on either a **proscenium stage** (like a room with one wall missing so that the audience may look in on the action) or a **thrust stage** (an acting area that projects into the audience). On whatever kind of stage, the modern theater is likely to provide **scenery** and **properties** (or **props**): these help to put the action in a specific place and underscore the ideas that the writer or director is trying to convey. **Sets** (the scenery) may be changed many times during a production, or a single set may be used throughout.

The text of a play is also brought to life by **costumes** that help the spectators identify and understand the characters. These may be used realistically (a salesman dressed as a salesman) or symbolically (an evil queen dressed entirely in black).

The modern theater also relies heavily on **lighting** to create effects. Lights were not used in the theater until the seventeenth century; up to that time, plays were performed in daylight. In the seventeenth century, however, people began to build enclosed theaters that required artificial lighting. Lighting can highlight different parts of the stage or isolate specific characters. In plays like Tennessee Williams's *The Glass Menagerie* and Arthur Miller's *Death of a Salesman* lighting is even used to indicate changes in time or place.

Finally, the theater, from its beginnings in ancient Greece, has been enlivened by the spectacle of dancing, music, and sound effects.

Even the audience plays a significant role in the theater; its reactions to the on-stage action provide feedback to the actors and thus continually alter the pace and timing of a production. Similarly, the audience, sitting together in a darkened auditorium, offers a communal response to the events taking place on stage. Thus, drama *in the theater* is the most immediate and accessible of the literary arts; there is no narrator, as in prose fiction, and no speaker, as in poetry, imposed between us and the stage action.

The clear difference between the text of a play and its production might lead you to ask why we bother to read plays. There are, of course, many answers. Often, it's not possible to see a live performance of a particular play. Reading a play can be as exciting and rewarding as reading a novel, a short story, or a poem. In reading, we have the chance to imagine settings, costumes, and action with a degree of scope and vividness that the stage rarely duplicates. We also read plays to familiarize ourselves with important literature. Plays are not simply maps to production; they are a significant and valuable part of our literary heritage. Dramas like Sophocles's *Oedipus Rex* and Shakespeare's *Hamlet* have become cultural touchstones and the springboards for other works of literature, art, cinema, and television. Finally, we read plays in order to have the time to study and understand them. Only through reading do we have the opportunity to look at the parts that make up the whole and to see how they fit together to create a moving and meaningful experience.

TYPES OF DRAMA

Aristotle divided all drama into tragedy and comedy. **Tragedy** recounts the fall of an individual; it begins in prosperity and ends in adversity. **Comedy** describes the regeneration or reformation of a group of people or a society; it begins with adversity and resolves in prosperity. Although tragedy is normally considered sad and comedy happy, notice that the brief definitions given here have more to do with patterns of action than with our emotional responses to plays. For a much fuller definition of tragedy and comedy, see pp. 1122 and 1378.

Pure forms of tragedy and comedy have rarely been written since the classical period; most British and American plays offer some mixture of the two forms. For example, Shakespeare's tragedies include witty and humorous scenes, and his comedies often deal with serious and threatening problems. In most plays written before the twentieth century, however, one pattern or the other predominates. When the patterns and emotions are truly mixed, the play is called a **tragicomedy,** a term first used by the Roman playwright Plautus around 186 B.C. and brought back into currency by John Fletcher in 1611. For Fletcher, the term meant a tragedy with a happy ending. Today, however, the term encompasses a broad range of plays that offer a mixture of tragic and comic effects. In many ways, tragicomedy is the dominant form of twentieth-century drama.

Other forms of drama that have evolved from tragedy and comedy include farce, melodrama, and social drama. **Farce** is a form of comedy crammed full of humorous actions and dialogue; shifts in action and emotion are usually very rapid. Chekhov's *The Bear* (p. 49) is a good example of farce. **Melodrama** is a debased form of tragedy with a happy ending. The adversities in melodrama all grow out of plot rather than character— the mortgage is due, the family business is failing, the daughter has been kidnapped by the villain. The hero always arrives just in time to pay the mortgage, save the business, and rescue the heroine.

Social dramas, sometimes called *problem plays*, evolved in the nineteenth century and dominated the stage through the early part of the twentieth century. This type of drama explores social problems and the individual's place in society; the plays can be tragic, comic, or mixed. Examples of social drama are Susan Glaspell's *Trifles*, Miller's *Death of a Salesman*, and Henrik Ibsen's *A Doll's House*.

One further distinction will be helpful in your exploration of drama. **Full-length plays** are dramas that usually contain either three to five separate **acts** (as in *A Doll's House* or *Hamlet*) or a long series of discrete **scenes** (as in *Oedipus* or *The Glass Menagerie*). Such plays are long enough to develop characters, conflicts, and ideas slowly and in considerable depth. Full-length plays that contain separate acts, such as *Hamlet* or *The Misanthrope*, are also usually subdivided into scenes, smaller units of coherent action that occurs in a single setting or involves a fixed group of characters. Shorter dramas, often called **one-act plays,** are rarely subdivided this way. Instead, they unfold continuously, without act or scene breaks, and they develop characters and ideas a great deal more quickly.

Given all these terms and types, you should keep in mind that classification is not the goal of reading or seeing plays. It is less important to identify *Everyman* as a comedy or *Before Breakfast* as a melodramatic tragedy than it is to feel and understand the experiences and ideas that each play offers us.

THE BASIC ELEMENTS OF DRAMATIC LITERATURE

In the following sections we will consider the basic elements of dramatic literature: *plot, character, point of view, setting, language, tone, symbolism*, and *theme* or *meaning*. Poetic drama, such as Sophocles's *Oedipus Rex*, Shakespeare's *Hamlet* and *A Midsummer Night's Dream*, and Molière's *The Misanthrope*, add elements that characterize poetry, such as *meter* and *rhyme*. All these elements have remained relatively constant throughout the history of drama. In *The Poetics*, Aristotle identifies six components of drama: plot, character, language, spectacle, thought, and song. Modern drama cannot be judged exclusively on the basis of Aristotle's six aspects, but his list illustrates the continuity of dramatic elements and techniques.

Plot, Action, and Conflict

Plot, in drama as in fiction, is an ordered chain of physical, emotional, or intellectual events that ties the action together. It is a planned sequence of interrelated actions that begins in a state of imbalance, grows out of conflict, reaches a peak of complication, and resolves into some new situation. It is, of course, easy to oversimplify the idea of plot in a play. Dramatic plots are often more complicated than a single movement toward a single solution or resolution. Some plays have **double plots**—two different but related lines of action going on at the same time. Other plays offer both a **main plot** and a **subplot** that comments, either directly or obliquely, on the main plot. In *A Midsummer Night's Dream* four separate plots are woven together to form a single story.

The mainspring of plot in a play is **conflict,** which can be physical, psychological, social, or all three. It can involve a character's struggle against another person, against the environment, or against himself or herself. Most commonly, the conflict in a play is some combination of these general types. In Edward Albee's *The Sandbox*, for example, Grandma is in conflict with her family, society, and death. Similarly, the hero in *Hamlet* is in conflict with himself, his enemies, and his society all at the same time. Conflict in drama can be more explicit than it is in prose fiction because we actually see the clash of wills and characters on stage or on the page.

While each play has its own tempo and internal logic, most share, to some extent, a general five-part *plot structure*—exposition, complication, crisis or climax, catastrophe, and resolution—that allows the action to unfold in reasonable order. In the first of these stages, the **exposition,** the playwright provides the audience or readers with essential background information; we are introduced to the characters, the situations, and the conflicts. In some plays, much of this expositional material is conveyed in a prologue that occurs before the main action begins; such is the case in *Everyman*. In other plays, exposition is provided by having several characters discuss the people involved in the play and the crucial events that occurred before the beginning of the staged action. Sometimes this opening conversation takes the form of questions and answers, as in *Hamlet*, where Barnardo and Marcellus question Horatio at length. In still other plays, the exposition is distributed throughout the entire action, as, for example, in *Oedipus*.

The exposition is followed by **complication,** in which the conflicts grow more heated and the plot becomes far more involved. In comedy, at least, the complication is often signaled by a sudden increase in the amount of confusion faced by the characters. Complication leads into the **crisis** or **climax** (from the Greek word for "ladder"), the turning point of the play. In this third stage the hero or heroine often faces a crucial decision or adopts a course of action that determines the outcome of the play. This dramatic moment is reached when the complications become so tightly knotted that the play (and the plot) can be resolved in only one direction; after the climax, a particular conclusion for the drama is certain.

The action that occurs in a play before the climax is called **rising;** the action after the climax is termed **falling.** Playwrights normally try to move rather quickly from the climax through the last two stages of action, the catastrophe and the resolution (or denouement). The **catastrophe** (not to be confused with our modern use of the term to mean "disaster") is that single moment of revelation when all the pieces fall into place; it is often caused by the discovery of information or the coming to light of some event that has been unknown to most of the characters up to that instant. The **resolution** is the part of the play in which conflicts are resolved, lives are straightened out or ended, and loose ends are tied up.

This five-part structure was reformulated in the nineteenth century by Gustav Freytag, who suggested that the rising and falling action in a typical five-act play resembles a pyramid. Our emotional involvement with

The Freytag Pyramid

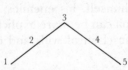

1. Exposition or Introduction
2. Complication and Development
3. Climax or Crisis
4. Falling Action, Catastrophe
5. Resolution or Denouement

a play is begun by the exposition, is heightened as complications develop, and reaches a climax in the third or fourth act. After the climax, the falling action begins and the resolution eventually occurs. According to Freytag's model, the emotions evoked in the spectator before the climax stem out of uncertainty; those evoked after the climax grow out of inevitability.

Most plays do not perfectly follow this five-stage structure. The pattern is merely a model to explain plot; for most plays it does not provide a perfect road map. Be prepared for plays that offer little exposition, have no denouement, or modify the general pattern in some other significant and useful way.

Character

A **character** in a play is a person created by a playwright to carry the action, language, ideas, and emotions of the play. Many of the types of characters that populate prose fiction are also found in drama. In drama as in fiction, for instance, we find both **round characters** and **flat characters.** The round characters are fully developed and usually undergo some change in the course of the play; good examples include Shakespeare's Prince Hamlet and Nora in Ibsen's *A Doll's House*. Flat characters, on the other hand, tend to be undeveloped and unchanging. Characters in drama can also be considered either **static**—that is, fixed and unchanging—or **dynamic**—that is, growing and developing. Flat characters are usually static; round characters are often dynamic.

Because drama depends on conflict as fully as does prose fiction, we also find protagonists and antagonists in plays. (The Greek word for conflict or contest was *agon*, from which we derive the word *agony* and both of these terms.) The **protagonist** is usually the character we identify with and cheer on. In full-length plays, the protagonists tend to be round characters. The **antagonist** opposes the protagonist and is often the villain of the piece. In O'Neill's *Before Breakfast*, for example, Alfred Rowland is the protagonist and his wife the antagonist; their relationship forms the central conflict of the play.

There are also characters who serve to set-off or highlight aspects of the protagonist, and others who stand on the sidelines and comment on the action rather than getting deeply involved. The first of these types, called a **foil,** is a character whose behavior and attitudes contrast in some way to the protagonist's. In *Hamlet*, for instance, both Laertes and Fortinbras are foils to the prince. The second type of character, called a **choric figure,** has its historical roots in the choruses of Greek tragedy. In later plays, the choric function has usually been given to a single character, often a friend or confidant of the protagonist, such as Horatio in *Hamlet*. This type of character is termed a **raisonneur** (from the French word meaning "reasoner") since he or she remains distant from the action and provides reasoned commentary.

Dramatic characters may be realistic, nonrealistic, symbolic, and stereotyped or stock. **Realistic characters** are normally accurate imitations of individualized men and women; they are provided with backgrounds, personalities, desires, motivations, and thoughts. **Nonrealistic characters** are usually stripped of such individualizing touches; they are often undeveloped and symbolic. All the characters in *The Sandbox* are nonrealistic. **Symbolic characters** represent an idea, a way of life, moral values, or some other abstraction. In the medieval play *Everyman*, symbolic characters named Goods, Fellowship, and Good Deeds signify human qualities and patterns of behavior.

Stereotyped, or **stock, characters** are figures that have been employed repeatedly in drama and other types of literature. Some have been in currency since Greek and Roman theater. The four general types of stock characters in classical drama are the bumpkin, the braggart, the trickster, and the victim; other stereotyped characters that survive from classical or Renaissance drama include the stubborn father, the shrewish wife, the lusty youth, and the prodigal son. Modern drama continues to employ these ancient stereotypes, but it has also invented many of its own: the hardboiled detective, the loner cowboy, the honest policeman, the whore with a heart of gold. Playwrights use stereotyped characters so that audiences will instantly understand the nature and the limits of the character. Stock characters thus become a shortcut in characterization for dramatists and in comprehension for spectators or readers.

The major difference between characters in prose fiction or poetry and characters in drama is found in the way they are unfolded. Playwrights do not have the fiction writer's freedom to tell us directly about a character. Rather, they must let the characters define themselves through what they do and say. A dramatist can begin to shape a character in a stage direction, but most of the revelation must occur through action and dialogue. We learn about characters in plays by paying attention to their words and actions, by listening to what other characters say about them, and by watching what other characters do to them. Finally, however, we will arrive at our own judgment or understanding of characters; the playwright will almost never do this for us.

Point of View and Perspective

Point of view in drama is strikingly different from the comparable element in prose fiction or poetry. Since plays almost never have narrators, there is no way to create a perspective that is specifically first-person-protagonist or third-person-omniscient. Instead, playwrights usually employ the **dramatic point of view** in which we receive only the information communicated by the characters. A dramatist can allow some characters to interpret the thoughts and feelings of other characters, but the attitudes and prejudices of these interpreters should enter into our evaluation of their statements. The key to the dramatic point of view is that the playwright gives us the objective raw materials—the action and the words—but does not overtly guide us toward any conclusions. Naturally, we will draw conclusions from the details presented in the play.

Even given the limitations of the dramatic point of view, playwrights do have techniques to lead an audience to see from a specific character's perspective. One method is to write much of the play (or the whole play) as a monologue, giving all the lines to a single character. Eugene O'Neill uses this device in *Before Breakfast*, where all the words are spoken by Mrs. Rowland. Another way to create point of view and reveal a character's perspective at the same time is to allow a character to speak his or her thoughts aloud directly to the audience. This device is called a **soliloquy** and is most commonly used to reveal the thoughts of the hero or the villain. Soliloquies were common techniques for revealing the thoughts and emotions of characters in sixteenth- and seventeenth-century plays. In the twentieth century they have again become an important element in experimental and nonrealistic drama. A shorter version of the soliloquy, called an **aside,** is a conventional device that allows a character to speak briefly to the audience, the reader, or another character without most of the characters on-stage being able to hear.

Setting, Sets, and Scenery

Most of the time, setting in drama, as in prose fiction, serves to place the action in a specific time and place and to help create the appropriate mood. In the text of a play, the setting is described in words, usually in the opening stage direction. In a production, however, the setting is brought to life through lighting, props, and scenery. Like characters, setting (or **set**) may be realistic or nonrealistic. The setting for *Trifles*, for example, is a highly realistic rendering of a Nebraska farm kitchen, complete with stove, sink, and unwashed dishes. In Wilder's *The Happy Journey to Trenton and Camden*, however, the setting is nonrealistic: four chairs and a low platform represent an apartment, an automobile, and a house. Realistic settings require extensive scenery and stage furniture; the idea is to create as real an environment as possible. Nonrealistic settings are symbolic or representational; they are often produced by *unit sets*—a single series of platforms, stairs, and playing areas that serve for all the scenery and the settings of the play.

The setting is usually the first thing we see on stage (or read about in the opening stage direction). By helping to establish a specific time and place, it conditions our expectations. A set depicting a medieval torture chamber would raise entirely different expectations in our minds than would a set that looked like a basketball court. Even if the plays staged in such different settings were about the same matters, the physical environment could have a profound effect on our reactions.

Playwrights can also use settings to convey information about the characters and the world of the play. The shabby apartment in New York City's Greenwich Village in O'Neill's *Before Breakfast* implies conditions and values quite different from those suggested by the comfortable and tastefully decorated living room in Ibsen's *A Doll's House*.

Most one-act plays make do with a single set and a single setting; all the plays in this chapter, for example, limit their action to a single time and place. Sometimes that time is as long as a day, as in *The Sandbox*, or as short as twenty minutes, as in *Before Breakfast*. Many full-length plays also limit the action to a single setting, even though a great deal of time might be encompassed. The action in *A Doll's House*, for example, covers several days, but it all takes place in one room. Similarly, Sophocles's *Oedipus Rex* is performed in a single setting before the royal palace in Thebes. Some full-length plays, on the other hand, may change settings many times. *Hamlet* takes place in a number of different settings, including battlements, a throne room, bed chambers, and a graveyard. In a production of *Hamlet* with realistic scenery, the sets would be changed each time the setting changes.

Diction, Imagery, Style, and Language

The language of drama is the medium through which most of the other elements are created and sustained. Action without language can communicate generalized emotions, ideas, and experiences (as in a silent movie), but words give plays their emotional impact and meaning. Characters tell us what they think, hope, fear, and desire; their dialogue can reflect the details of day-to-day living or their deepest thoughts about death and salvation. Most of what we learn about characters, relationships, and conflict in drama is conveyed through language. At a basic level, the language must be appropriate for the play in which it is spoken; it must fit the time, the place, and the characters. It would be as wrong for Hamlet to speak in modern American slang as it would for Willie Loman in Miller's *Death of a Salesman* to speak in Elizabethan blank verse. The language must be appropriate to both the subjects and the characters of the play; this sense of appropriateness is called **decorum.**

The words and rhetorical devices spoken in a play delineate character, emotion, and theme, much as they do in prose fiction and poetry. Word choice, connotation and denotation, imagery, sentence structure, rhythm, and style are as important to playwrights as they are to poets and fiction writers. Dramatists can employ words that have wide-ranging connotations or that acquire many layers of meaning. Such is the case with the words *trifle* and *knot* in *Trifles* (p. 1101). Similarly, playwrights can have their characters speak in similes or metaphors that contribute significantly to the impact and meaning of the play. Again in *Trifles*, one of the characters compares another to a bird; the simile becomes the key to one of the central symbols in the play.

Dramatists use the devices of language and style to create characters and to shape the audience's responses to character and action. They may also employ accents, dialects, idiom, jargon, or clichés to define character. Both Ma in *The Happy Journey to Trenton and Camden* and most of the characters in *The Glass Menagerie* speak in regional dialects and use slang expressions that help us place them in a specific time and place. Similarly, characters in *The Sandbox* speak in clichés that define the characters' values and help us understand them. In short, playwrights have access to every stylistic and rhetorical device of language in their creation of character, conflict, emotion, and ideas.

Tone and Atmosphere

Tone in drama, as in other literature, signifies the way moods and attitudes are created and conveyed. Since plays are designed to be performed, however, tone can literally mean the *tone of voice* that an actor uses in delivering a specific speech or building a total characterization. This potential reveals another significant difference between drama and other literary genres: tone in plays may be conveyed directly to the spectator through voice or through the stage action that accompanies dialogue, such as abrupt or furtive movement, shrugging, or shaking the head. Even silence can be an effective device for creating tone and mood.

These possibilities also highlight another gap between the text of a play and its production. Whereas voice and movement can establish tone on the stage, we often have no such exacting guides while reading a play. Sometimes a playwright indicates the tone of specific lines through stage directions. In *The Sandbox*, for instance, Albee prefaces many speeches with directions such as *whining*, *vaguely*, *impatiently*, and *mocking*. These are cues to tone that help both actors in performance and readers while studying the play. When such directions are lacking, however, tone becomes a matter of careful study and interpretation for actors and readers alike. In these instances, diction, tempo, imagery, and context all become clues to the tone of specific speeches and whole plays.

Tone may create an atmosphere or mood that dominates a play. In the opening scene of *Hamlet*, for instance, Shakespeare uses tempo, diction, and tone to build the dominant mood; it is dark, close to midnight, and Francisco carries a torch:

> BARNARDO.   Who's there?
> FRANCISCO.   Nay, answer me. Stand and unfold yourself.
> BARNARDO.   Long live the king!
> FRANCISCO.   Barnardo?
> BARNARDO.   He.

Notice the short lines, the questions, and the choppy and rapid exchange. The tone of the dialogue is anxious and questioning. The exchange thus suggests nervousness, tension, and insecurity. These, in turn, hint that all is not well in Denmark. The rest of the play bears out these initial implications.

In dealing with tone, we must be careful to distinguish between the tone of an individual character and the playwright's tone that shapes our total response to the play. Specific characters may be sincere, sarcastic, joyful, or resigned, but the entire drama may reflect only one or even none of these tones. In *Trifles*, for instance, the tones of some speeches are noted as *resentful*, *apologetic*, or *mild*. The play as a whole, however, is predominantly bitter and ironic.

This last observation brings us to one of the most common methods employed by playwrights to control the tone of a play: **dramatic irony.** This type of situational (as opposed to verbal) irony may be created in any circumstance where the audience knows more than the characters in a play or when one or two characters know more than most of the others. In *Trifles*, one of the characters mockingly dismisses a woman's behavior by noting that "women are used to worrying about such trifles." The line acquires vast dramatic irony as we watch the women in the play achieve understanding through careful attention to "trifles" that the men ignore. Such dramatic irony, when used consistently, creates an ironic tone for the entire work. This is exactly the situation in *Oedipus Rex*, where the audience always knows more than the protagonist and almost every line becomes ironic.

Symbolism and Allegory

Symbols in drama, as in fiction and poetry, represent some meaning or significance beyond the intrinsic identity of the symbol itself. As in the other literary genres, symbols in drama can be persons, settings, objects, actions, situations, or statements. Playwrights have access to both universal and private symbols. **Universal symbols**—like crosses, flags, snakes, flowers—are generally understood by the audience or reader regardless of the context in which they appear. In Act 5 of *Hamlet*, for example, we recognize Yorick's skull as a symbol of death. **Private symbols** develop their impact only within the context of a specific play or even a particular scene. We often don't realize that such objects or actions are symbolic when they first occur; they accrue symbolic meaning through context and continued action. *The Sandbox*, for instance, opens with a "large child's sandbox with a toy pail and shovel" on stage. Initially, this object has no symbolic meaning for us. As the play goes on, however, we realize that the sandbox represents the beach, a refuse pile, the childishness we habitually associate with old age, and the grave.

When a play offers a consistent and sustained system of symbols that all point toward the same second level of meaning, the play is an **allegory**. Many fables and parables are allegories; they appear to be about animals or individuals but actually illustrate universal patterns of human behavior. One of the best examples of allegorical drama is *Everyman*, a medieval morality play that traces the fortunes of the protagonist from life to death and salvation. At one level, this play concerns the trials and successes of a single character. Allegorically, however, it demonstrates the path that all Christians must follow to salvation.

Subject and Theme

Playwrights often write plays with specific ideas about the human condition in mind. The aspects of humanity a playwright explores constitute the **subject** of a play. Plays may thus be *about* love, religion, hatred, war, ambition, death, envy, or anything else that is part of the human condition. The ideas that the play dramatizes about its subject make up the play's **theme** or meaning. Thus, a play might explore the idea that love will always find a way or that marriage can be destructive, that pride always leads to disaster, or that grief can be conquered through strength and a commitment to life. Theme is the end result of all the other elements of drama; it is one of the things we are left to think about after we have read a play or seen a production.

Since theme is created and conveyed through all the other elements of drama, it is often somewhat difficult to isolate and identify. Even short plays tend to have rather complex themes. *The Happy Journey to Trenton and Camden*, for example, explores a number of diverse themes: families need a strong central figure to hold them together; religion and optimism can help overcome the griefs of life. Full-length plays may contain even more thematic strands. *A Doll's House* deals with ideas about individual development, marriage, sexism, and society. Some plays may even explore multiple themes that seem to contradict each other, thus complicating analysis still further. *Oedipus Rex*, for example, suggests that humans cannot escape the destiny preordained for them by the gods or the fates or fortune. At the same time, however, it also explores the idea that fate is very much a product of personality and the choices one makes in life.

Playwrights rarely make explicitly thematic statements; their characters rarely come right out and tell us the meaning of the play. Two types of drama, however, are exceptions to this rule. **Didactic plays** are designed primarily to teach a specific lesson; **propaganda plays** are written primarily to convince and persuade. In both cases, the theme may be repeatedly and blatantly stated by the characters. In most plays, however, meaning is elusive and unspoken. As a result, we must pay careful attention to the words, actions, and attitudes of the characters in order to understand themes. Frequently, the protagonist and his or her conflicts embody much of the meaning. Hamlet's attempts to prove that his uncle is guilty of murder and his extended soliloquies of self-accusation bring forward one of the central ideas in the play: the questionable and ambiguous place of revenge in a Christian society. Similarly, Nora's conflicts with Krogstad and with Helmar in *A Doll's House* dramatize the stereotyped roles of women in society and the failure of communication in marriage.

HOW TO READ A PLAY

Reading or studying a play is a quite different process from reading prose fiction or watching a performance in the theater. Poems, novels, and short stories are complete in and of themselves; they embody the full impact of their meaning and experience. Plays, in contrast, can only suggest their full impact; when we read them, we are missing the elements of live performance. Nevertheless, we can enjoy the power of the language and feel the hopes and fears of the characters; we can sympathize with the heroine and loathe the villain. We can learn about ourselves and about humanity by watching the ways characters deal with the great and small pleasures and pains of living. In short, we can experience and enjoy plays through reading exactly the way we do other types of literature.

Reading a play, as opposed to watching a performance, carries both advantages and disadvantages. The major disadvantage is that you lack the immediacy of live theater; you do not hear the whispers of the murderer and the ranting of the madman or see the strutting of the soldier and the furtive glances of the conspirators. You do not have the splendor of the ballroom or the shock of the empty stage, the spotlight that rivets the audience's attention on a single defiant gesture, the blare of trumpets, or the pathos of the beggar's rags. All these may be described in stage directions, but the words only signify the things themselves.

The major advantages to reading are time and freedom; you have the time to consider each element and event in the play at length and the freedom to stage the play in your imagination. In the theater, the action rushes by at whatever pace the director chooses; there is no opportunity to "turn back" to an interesting scene or to reconsider a confusing speech. In addition, a performance always represents someone else's interpretation of a play; the director or the actors have already made choices that cut off some avenues of exploration and emphasize others. Reading a play lets you avoid these problems. You can read at whatever tempo you choose; you can turn back and reread a particular speech or scene until you are comfortable with your own reactions to it. Also you have the freedom to explore whatever implications or ideas strike you as interesting; no one else has limited the scope of your considerations.

Try to use the advantages of reading and study to compensate for the disadvantages. You have the time and freedom to read carefully, reflect deeply, and follow your thoughts wherever they might lead. Stage the play as fully as you can in the theater of your mind. You can become the director, the set designer, the lighting technician, the costume designer, and all the actors. You have the freedom to build whatever mental sets you like, dress your actors as you see fit, and move the characters across the stage of your mind as you would have them move. To do this, you can rely on your experiences in watching theatrical productions, movies, and television.

Another way to take advantage of the reading process is to treat the play as though it were a short story or a novel. Here, as with any other literature, your imagination must supply the color and vitality that the text implies. In this approach the stage directions become the narrative connections between the words of characters, descriptions of settings, and the like. Whatever approach you choose for your own reading, you will find yourself becoming actively and imaginatively involved in the process. Plays cannot be experienced passively; they demand careful attention from audiences and readers alike. You should develop the habit of reading plays (and most other literature) several times. Each rereading will usually reveal new aspects of the work and new directions for exploration. You can also reread specific parts of a play that are initially unclear or confusing.

Finally, you should keep in mind that all drama is based, at least in part, on the **dramatic (stage) conventions** of its own age and theatrical environment. A dramatic convention is a traditional or customary method of presentation (often unrealistic) that is accepted by audiences or readers and allows a playwright to limit and simplify material. Most dramatic conventions reflect either the physical conditions of the theater or the prejudices of society in a given age. Many of these conventions are explained in the introductions to specific plays, which provide information about drama in a given period. Some dramatic conventions may strike you as amusing or odd. The chorus in Greek tragedy, for instance, is made up of fifteen men who chant their speeches in unison. While this is not realistic, it is a conventional device of Greek tragedy that allows the playwright to express the reactions of the common people. The soliloquy is a similarly unrealistic convention of the Elizabethan stage; it permits the characters to reveal thoughts and feelings directly to the audience. Such a convention may strike you as an odd disruption of the action, but it reflects both the intimacy of the Elizabethan theaters and the audience's willingness to accept such a break in the flow of the play. Ultimately, we must be willing to accept dramatic conventions on their own terms, just as we do the conventions of film and television.

PLAYS FOR STUDY

THORNTON WILDER, *The Happy Journey to Trenton and Camden*

The Happy Journey to Trenton and Camden, published originally in 1931, is one of Thornton Wilder's early experiments in nonrealistic staging (see p. 1502 for a discussion of nonrealistic theater). He developed these techniques much more fully in later plays, including *Our Town* (1938) and *The Skin of Our Teeth* (1942). Wilder also wrote traditional realistic plays, including *The Merchant of Yonkers* (1938), which he later revised as *The Matchmaker* (1954). Ultimately, this play was adapted into the highly successful musical comedy, *Hello, Dolly!* (1964).

The set for *The Happy Journey* is nonrealistic and kept to a minimum. By using an empty stage instead of indicating the three separate settings of the play with scenery, Wilder calls our attention to the play's theatricality and the nature of drama as a fictional *imitation* of real life. In production, props and scenery for this play are limited to chairs, a platform, and a bed. Thus, Wilder forces us to use our imaginations to flesh out the scene. He also keeps our attention on plot, character, and dialogue; we are never distracted by elaborate sets.

The Happy Journey also exemplifies Wilder's careful construction of plot and character. At one level the plot is very simple; it involves the preparation for a trip, the journey itself, and arrival at the destination. In a very general way, these three episodes correspond to exposition, complication, and finally catastrophe and resolution. We learn about the Kirby family and their world during their preparations for the journey. Conflicts and hints of the approaching catastrophe are developed during the journey. The play contains a submerged or hidden plot that deals with family life, death, and the ways people cope with sorrow. These themes are brought into focus in the third episode, the arrival at Camden and Ma's conversation with Beulah; here we find both catastrophe and resolution as Ma finds a way to deal with the details of daily life and the burdens of death and sorrow.

THORNTON WILDER (1897–1975)

The Happy Journey to Trenton and Camden   *1931*

CHARACTERS

    Ma Kirby, *The Mother*
    Elmer Kirby, *The Father*
    Beulah Kirby, *The Older Daughter*
    Caroline Kirby, *The Younger Daughter*
    Arthur Kirby, *The Son*
    The Stage Manager

No scenery is required for this play. Perhaps a few dusty flats may be seen leaning against the brick wall at the back of the stage.

    The five members of the Kirby family and THE STAGE MANAGER *compose the cast.*

    THE STAGE MANAGER *not only moves forward and withdraws the few properties that are required, but he reads from a typescript the lines of all the minor characters. He reads them clearly, but with little attempt at characterization, scarcely troubling himself to alter his voice, even when he responds in the person of a child or a woman.*

    As the curtain rises THE STAGE MANAGER *is leaning lazily against the proscenium pillar at the audience's left. He is smoking.*

    ARTHUR *is playing marbles in the center of the stage.*

    CAROLINE *is at the remote back right talking to some girls who are invisible to us.*

    MA KIRBY *is anxiously putting on her hat before an imaginary mirror.*

    MA.   Where's your pa? Why isn't he here? I declare we'll never get started.

    ARTHUR.   Ma, where's my hat? I guess I don't go if I can't find my hat.

    MA.   Go out into the hall and see if it isn't there. Where's Caroline gone to now, the plagued child?

    ARTHUR.   She's out waitin' in the street talkin' to the Jones girls.—I just looked in the hall a thousand times, ma, and it isn't there. [*He spits for good luck before a difficult shot and mutters:*] Come on, baby.

    MA.   Go and look again, I say. Look carefully.

[ARTHUR *rises, runs to the right, turns around swiftly, returns to his game, flinging himself on the floor with a terrible impact and starts shooting an aggie.*]

    ARTHUR.   No, ma, it's not there.

    MA.   [*Serenely.*] Well, you don't leave Newark without that hat, make up your mind to that. I don't go no journeys with a hoodlum.

    ARTHUR.   Aw, ma!

[MA *comes down to the footlights and talks toward the audience as through a window.*]

    MA.   Oh, Mrs. Schwartz!

    THE STAGE MANAGER.   [*Consulting his script.*] Here I am, Mrs. Kirby. Are you going yet?

    MA.   I guess we're going in just a minute. How's the baby?

THE STAGE MANAGER.   She's all right now. We slapped her on the back and she spat it up.

MA.   Isn't that fine!—Well now, if you'll be good enough to give the cat a saucer of milk in the morning and the evening, Mrs. Schwartz, I'll be ever so grateful to you.—Oh, good afternoon, Mrs. Hobmeyer!

THE STAGE MANAGER.   Good afternoon, Mrs. Kirby, I hear you're going away.

MA.   [*Modest.*] Oh, just for three days, Mrs. Hobmeyer, to see my married daughter, Beulah, in Camden. Elmer's got his vacation week from the laundry early this year, and he's just the best driver in the world.

[*CAROLINE comes "into the house" and stands by her mother.*]

THE STAGE MANAGER.   Is the whole family going?

MA.   Yes, all four of us that's here. The change ought to be good for the children. My married daughter was downright sick a while ago——

THE STAGE MANAGER.   Tchk—Tchk—Tchk! Yes. I remember you tellin' us.

MA.   And I just want to go down and see the child. I ain't seen her since then. I just won't rest easy in my mind without I see her. [*To CAROLINE.*] Can't you say good afternoon to Mrs. Hobmeyer?

CAROLINE.   [*Blushes and lowers her eyes and says woodenly.*] Good afternoon, Mrs. Hobmeyer.

THE STAGE MANAGER.   Good afternoon, dear.—Well, I'll wait and beat these rugs until after you're gone, because I don't want to choke you. I hope you have a good time and find everything all right.

MA.   Thank you, Mrs. Hobmeyer, I hope I will.—Well, I guess that milk for the cat is all, Mrs. Schwartz, if you're sure you don't mind. If anything should come up, the key to the back door is hanging by the ice box.

ARTHUR AND CAROLINE.   Ma! Not so loud. Everybody can hear yuh.

MA.   Stop pullin' my dress, children. [*In a loud whisper.*] The key to the back door I'll leave hangin' by the ice box and I'll leave the screen door unhooked.

THE STAGE MANAGER.   Now have a good trip, dear, and give my love to Loolie.

MA.   I will, and thank you a thousand times. [*She returns "into the room."*] What can be keeping your pa?

ARTHUR.   I can't find my hat, ma.

[*Enter ELMER holding a hat.*]

ELMER.   Here's Arthur's hat. He musta left it in the car Sunday.

MA.   That's a mercy. Now we can start.—Caroline Kirby, what you done to your cheeks?

CAROLINE.   [*Defiant-abashed.*] Nothin'.

MA.   If you've put anything on 'em, I'll slap you.

CAROLINE.   No, ma, of course I haven't. [*Hanging her head.*] I just rubbed'm to make'm red. All the girls do that at High School when they're goin' places.

MA.   Such silliness I never saw. Elmer, what kep' you?

ELMER.   [*Always even-voiced and always looking out a little anxiously through his spectacles.*] I just went to the garage and had Charlie give a last look at it, Kate.

MA.   I'm glad you did. I wouldn't like to have no breakdown miles from anywhere. Now we can start. Arthur, put those marbles away. Anybody'd think you didn't want to go on a journey, to look at yuh.

[*They go out through the "hall," take the short steps that denote going downstairs, and find themselves in the street.*]

ELMER. Here, you boys, you keep away from that car.

MA. Those Sullivan boys put their heads into everything.

[*THE STAGE MANAGER has moved forward four chairs and a low platform. This is the automobile. It is in the center of the stage and faces the audience. The platform slightly raises the two chairs in the rear. PA's hands hold an imaginary steering wheel and continually shift gears. CAROLINE sits beside him. ARTHUR is behind him and MA behind CAROLINE.*]

CAROLINE. [*Self-consciously.*] Goodbye, Mildred. Goodbye, Helen.

THE STAGE MANAGER. Goodbye, Caroline. Goodbye, Mrs. Kirby. I hope y'have a good time.

MA. Goodbye, girls.

THE STAGE MANAGER. Goodbye, Kate. The car looks fine.

MA. [*Looking upward toward a window.*] Oh, goodbye, Emma! [*Modestly.*] We think it's the best little Chevrolet in the world.—Oh, goodbye, Mrs. Adler!

THE STAGE MANAGER. What, are you going away, Mrs. Kirby?

MA. Just for three days, Mrs. Adler, to see my married daughter in Camden.

THE STAGE MANAGER. Have a good time.

[*Now MA, CAROLINE, and THE STAGE MANAGER break out into a tremendous chorus of goodbyes. The whole street is saying goodbye. ARTHUR takes out his pea shooter and lets fly happily into the air. There is a lurch or two and they are off.*]

ARTHUR. [*In sudden fright.*] Pa! Pa! Don't go by the school. Mr. Biedenbach might see us!

MA. I don't care if he does see us. I guess I can take my children out of school for one day without having to hide down back streets about it. [*ELMER nods to a passerby. MA asks without sharpness:*] Who was that you spoke to, Elmer?

ELMER. That was the fellow who arranges our banquets down to the Lodge, Kate.

MA. Is he the one who had to buy four hundred steaks? [*PA nods.*] I declare, I'm glad I'm not him.

ELMER. The air's getting better already. Take deep breaths, children.

[*They inhale noisily.*]

ARTHUR. Gee, it's almost open fields already. *"Weber and Heilbronner Suits for Well-dressed Men."* Ma, can I have one of them some day?

MA. If you graduate with good marks perhaps your father'll let you have one for graduation.

CAROLINE. [*Whining.*] Oh, Pa! do we have to wait while that whole funeral goes by?

[*PA takes off his hat. MA cranes forward with absorbed curiosity.*]

MA. Take off your hat, Arthur. Look at your father.—Why, Elmer, I do believe that's a lodge-brother of yours. See the banner? I suppose this is the Elizabeth branch. [*ELMER nods. MA sighs: Tchk—tchk—tchk. They all lean forward and watch the funeral in silence, growing momentarily more solemnized. After a pause, MA continues almost dreamily:*] Well, we haven't forgotten the one that we went on, have we?

We haven't forgotten our good Harold. He gave his life for his country, we mustn't forget that. [*She passes her finger from the corner of her eye across her cheek. There is another pause.*] Well, we'll all hold up the traffic for a few minutes some day.

THE CHILDREN. [*Very uncomfortable.*] Ma!

MA. [*Without self-pity.*] Well I'm "ready," children. I hope everybody in this car is "ready." [*She puts her hand on PA'S shoulder.*] And I pray to go first, Elmer. Yes. [*PA touches her hand.*]

THE CHILDREN. Ma, everybody's looking at you. Everybody's laughing at you.

MA. Oh, hold your tongues! I don't care what a lot of silly people in Elizabeth, New Jersey, think of me.—Now we can go on. That's the last.

[*There is another lurch and the car goes on.*]

CAROLINE. "Fit-Rite Suspenders. The Working Man's Choice." Pa, why do they spell Rite that way?

ELMER. So that it'll make you stop and ask about it, Missy.

CAROLINE. Papa, you're teasing me.—Ma, why do they say "*Three Hundred Rooms Three Hundred Baths*?"

ARTHUR. "*Miller's Spaghetti: The Family's Favorite Dish.*" Ma, why don't you ever have spaghetti?

MA. Go along, you'd never eat it.

ARTHUR. Ma, I like it now.

CAROLINE. [*With gesture.*] Yum-yum. It looks wonderful up there. Ma, make some when we get home?

MA. [*Dryly.*] "The management is always happy to receive suggestions. We aim to please."

[*The whole family finds this exquisitely funny. The CHILDREN scream with laughter. Even ELMER smiles. MA remains modest.*]

ELMER. Well, I guess no one's complaining, Kate. Everybody knows you're a good cook.

MA. I don't know whether I'm a good cook or not, but I know I've had practice. At least I've cooked three meals a day for twenty-five years.

ARTHUR. Aw, ma, you went out to eat once in a while.

MA. Yes. That made it a leap year.

[*This joke is no less successful than its predecessor. When the laughter dies down, CAROLINE turns around in an ecstasy of well-being and kneeling on the cushions says:*]

CAROLINE. Ma, I love going out in the country like this. Let's do it often, ma.

MA. Goodness, smell that air will you! It's got the whole ocean in it.—Elmer, drive careful over that bridge. This must be New Brunswick we're coming to.

ARTHUR. [*Jealous of his mother's successes.*] Ma, when is the next comfort station?

MA. [*Unruffled.*] You don't want one. You just said that to be awful.

CAROLINE. [*Shrilly.*] Yes, he did, ma. He's terrible. He says that kind of thing right out in school and I want to sink through the floor, ma. He's terrible.

MA. Oh, don't get so excited about nothing, Miss Proper! I guess we're all yewman-beings in this car, at least as far as I know. And, Arthur, you try and be a gentleman.—Elmer, don't run over that collie dog. [*She follows the dog with her eyes.*] Looked kinda peakèd to me. Needs a good honest bowl of leavings. Pretty dog, too. [*Her eyes fall on a billboard.*] That's a pretty advertisement for Chesterfield cigarettes, isn't it? Looks like Beulah, a little.

ARTHUR. Ma?

MA. Yes.

ARTHUR. [*"Route" rhymes with "out".*] Can't I take a paper route with the Newark *Daily Post*?

MA. No, you cannot. No, sir. I hear they make the paper boys get up at four-thirty in the morning. No son of mine is going to get up at four-thirty every morning, not if it's to make a million dollars. Your *Saturday Evening Post* route on Thursday mornings is enough.

ARTHUR. Aw, ma.

MA. No, sir. No son of mine is going to get up at four-thirty and miss the sleep God meant him to have.

ARTHUR. [*Sullenly.*] Hhm! Ma's always talking about God. I guess she got a letter from him this morning. [*MA rises, outraged.*]

MA. Elmer, stop that automobile this minute. I don't go another step with anybody that says things like that. Arthur, you get out of this car. Elmer, you give him another dollar bill. He can go back to Newark, by himself. I don't want him.

ARTHUR. What did I say? There wasn't anything terrible about that.

ELMER. I didn't hear what he said, Kate.

MA. God has done a lot of things for me and I won't have him made fun of by anybody. Go away. Go away from me.

CAROLINE. Aw, Ma,—don't spoil the ride.

MA. No.

ELMER. We might as well go on, Kate, since we've got started. I'll talk to the boy tonight.

MA. [*Slowly conceding.*] All right, if you say so, Elmer. But I won't sit beside him. Caroline, you come, and sit by me.

ARTHUR. [*Frightened.*] Aw, ma, that wasn't so terrible.

MA. I don't want to talk about it. I hope your father washes your mouth out with soap and water.—Where'd we all be if I started talking about God like that, I'd like to know! We'd be in the speak-easies and night-clubs and places like that, that's where we'd be.—All right, Elmer, you can go on now.

CAROLINE. What did he say, ma? I didn't hear what he said.

MA. I don't want to talk about it.

[*They drive on in silence for a moment, the shocked silence after a scandal.*]

ELMER. I'm going to stop and give the car a little water, I guess

MA. All right, Elmer. You know best.

ELMER. [*To a garage hand.*] Could I have a little water in the radiator—to make sure?

THE STAGE MANAGER. [*In this scene alone he lays aside his script and enters into a rôle seriously.*] You sure can. [*He punches the tires.*] Air, all right? Do you need any oil or gas?

ELMER. No, I think not. I just got fixed up in Newark.

MA. We're on the right road for Camden, are we?

THE STAGE MANAGER. Yes, keep straight ahead. You can't miss it. You'll be in Trenton in a few minutes. [*He carefully pours some water into the hood.*] Camden's a great town, lady, believe me.

MA. My daughter likes it fine,—my married daughter.

THE STAGE MANAGER. Ye'? It's a great burg all right. I guess I think so because I was born near there.

MA. Well, well. Your folks still live there?

THE STAGE MANAGER. No, my old man sold the farm and they built a factory on it. So the folks moved to Philadelphia.

MA. My married daughter Beulah lives there because her husband works in the telephone company.—Stop pokin' me, Caroline!—We're all going down to see her for a few days.

THE STAGE MANAGER. Ye'?

MA. She's been sick, you see, and I just felt I had to go and see her. My husband and my boy are going to stay at the Y.M.C.A. I hear they've got a dormitory on the top floor that's real clean and comfortable. Had you ever been there?

THE STAGE MANAGER. No. I'm Knights of Columbus myself.

MA. Oh.

THE STAGE MANAGER. I used to play basketball at the Y though. It looked all right to me. [*He has been standing with one foot on the rung of MA's chair. They have taken a great fancy to one another. He reluctantly shakes himself out of it and pretends to examine the car again, whistling.*] Well, I guess you're all set now, lady. I hope you have a good trip; you can't miss it.

EVERYBODY. Thanks. Thanks a lot. Good luck to you. [*Jolts and lurches.*]

MA. [*With a sigh.*] The world's full of nice people.—That's what I call a nice young man.

CAROLINE. [*Earnestly.*] Ma, you oughtn't to tell'm all everything about yourself.

MA. Well, Caroline, you do your way and I'll do mine.—He looked kinda thin to me. I'd like to feed him up for a few days. His mother lives in Philadelphia and I expect he eats at those dreadful Greek places.

CAROLINE. I'm hungry. Pa, there's a hot dog stand. K'n I have one?

ELMER. We'll all have one, eh, Kate? We had such an early lunch.

MA. Just as you think best, Elmer.

ELMER. Arthur, here's half a dollar.—Run over and see what they have. Not too much mustard either. [*ARTHUR descends from the car and goes off stage right. MA and CAROLINE get out and walk a bit.*]

MA. What's that flower over there?—I'll take some of those to Beulah.

CAROLINE. It's just a weed, ma.

MA. I like it.—My, look at the sky, wouldya! I'm glad I was born in New Jersey. I've always said it was the best state in the Union. Every state has something no other state has got.

[*They stroll about humming. Presently ARTHUR returns with his hands full of imaginary hot dogs which he distributes. He is still very much cast down by the recent scandal. He finally approaches his mother and says falteringly:*]

ARTHUR. Ma, I'm sorry. I'm sorry for what I said.

[*He bursts into tears and puts his forehead against her elbow.*]

MA. There. There. We all say wicked things at times. I know you didn't mean it like it sounded. [*He weeps still more violently than before.*] Why, now, now! I forgive you, Arthur, and tonight before you go to bed you . . . [*She whispers.*] You're a good boy at heart, Arthur, and we all know it. [*CAROLINE starts to cry too. MA is suddenly joyously alive and happy.*] Sakes alive, it's too nice a day for us all to be cryin'. Come now, get in. You go up in front with your father, Caroline. Ma wants to sit with her beau. I never saw such children. Your hot dogs are all getting wet. Now chew them fine, everybody.—All right, Elmer, forward march.—Caroline, whatever are you doing?

CAROLINE. I'm spitting out the leather, ma.

MA. Then say: Excuse me.

CAROLINE. Excuse me, please.

MA. What's this place? Arthur, did you see the post office?

ARTHUR. It said Lawrenceville.

MA. Hhn. School kinda. Nice. I wonder what that big yellow house set back was.—Now it's beginning to be Trenton.

CAROLINE. Papa, it was near here that George Washington crossed the Delaware. It was near Trenton, mama. He was first in war and first in peace, and first in the hearts of his countrymen.

MA. [*Surveying the passing world, serene and didactic.*] Well, the thing I like about him best was that he never told a lie. [*The CHILDREN are duly cast down. There is a pause.*] There's a sunset for you. There's nothing like a good sunset.

ARTHUR. There's an Ohio license in front of us. Ma, have you ever been to Ohio?

MA. No.

[*A dreamy silence descends upon them. CAROLINE sits closer to her father. MA puts her arm around ARTHUR.*]

ARTHUR. Ma, what a lotta people there are in the world, ma. There must be thousands and thousands in the United States. Ma, how many are there?

MA. I don't know. Ask your father.

ARTHUR. Pa, how many are there?

ELMER. There are a hundred and twenty-six million, Kate.

MA. [*Giving a pressure about ARTHUR'S shoulder.*] And they all like to drive out in the evening with their children beside'm. [*Another pause.*] Why doesn't somebody sing something? Arthur, you're always singing something; what's the matter with you?

ARTHUR. All right. What'll we sing? [*He sketches:*]
"In the Blue Ridge mountains of Virginia,
On the trail of the lonesome pine . . ."
No, I don't like that any more. Let's do:
"I been workin on de railroad
All de liblong day.
I been workin' on de railroad
Just to pass de time away."

[*CAROLINE joins in at once. Finally even MA is singing. Even PA is singing. MA suddenly jumps up with a wild cry:*]

MA.   Elmer, that signpost said Camden, I saw it.
ELMER.   All right, Kate, if you're sure.

[*Much shifting of gears, backing, and jolting.*]

MA.   Yes, there it is. Camden—five miles. Dear old Beulah.—Now, children, you be good and quiet during dinner. She's just got out of bed after a big sorta operation, and we must all move around kinda quiet. First you drop me and Caroline at the door and just say hello, and then you men-folk go over to the Y.M.C.A. and come back for dinner in about an hour.
CAROLINE.   [*Shutting her eyes and pressing her fists passionately against her nose.*] I see the first star. Everybody make a wish.
Star light, star bright,
First star I seen tonight.
I wish I may, I wish I might
Have the wish I wish tonight.

[*Then solemnly.*] Pins. Mama, you say "needles."

[*She interlocks little fingers with her mother.*]

MA.   Needles.
CAROLINE.   Shakespeare. Ma, you say "Longfellow."
MA.   Longfellow.
CAROLINE.   Now it's a secret and I can't tell it to anybody. Ma, you make a wish.
MA.   [*With almost grim humor.*]   No, I can make wishes without waiting for no star. And I can tell my wishes right out loud too. Do you want to hear them?
CAROLINE.   [*Resignedly.*]   No, ma, we know'm already. We've heard'm. [*She hangs her head affectedly on her left shoulder and says with unmalicious mimicry:*] You want me to be a good girl and you want Arthur to be honest-in-word-and-deed.
MA.   [*Majestically.*]   Yes. So mind yourself.
ELMER.   Caroline, take out that letter from Beulah in my coat pocket by you and read aloud the places I marked with red pencil.
CAROLINE.   [*Working.*]   "*A few blocks after you pass the two big oil tanks on your left . . .*"
EVERYBODY.   [*Pointing backward.*]   There they are!
CAROLINE.   "*. . . you come to a corner where there's an A and P store on the left and a firehouse kitty-corner to it . . .*" [*They all jubilantly identify these landmarks.*] "*. . . turn right, go two blocks, and our house is Weyerhauser St. Number 471.*"
MA.   It's an even nicer street than they used to live in. And right handy to an A and P.
CAROLINE.   [*Whispering.*]   Ma, it's better than our street. It's richer than our street.—Ma, isn't Beulah richer than we are?
MA.   [*Looking at her with a firm and glassy eye.*]   Mind yourself, missy. I don't want to hear anybody talking about rich or not rich when I'm around. If people aren't nice I don't care how rich they are. I live in the best street in the world

because my husband and children live there. [*She glares impressively at* CAROLINE *a moment to let this lesson sink in, then looks up, sees* BEULAH *and waves.*] There's Beulah standing on the steps lookin' for us.

[BEULAH *has appeared and is waving. They all call out:*] Hello, Beulah—Hello. [*Presently they are all getting out of the car.* BEULAH *kisses her father long and affectionately.*]

BEULAH. Hello, papa. Good old papa. You look tired, pa.—Hello, mama.—Lookit how Arthur and Caroline are growing!

MA. They're bursting all their clothes!—Yes, your pa needs a rest. Thank Heaven, his vacation has come just now. We'll feed him up and let him sleep late. Pa has a present for you, Loolie. He would go and buy it.

BEULAH. Why, pa, you're terrible to go and buy anything for me. Isn't he terrible?

MA. Well, it's a secret. You can open it at dinner.

ELMER. Where's Horace, Loolie?

BEULAH. He was kep' over a little at the office. He'll be here any minute. He's crazy to see you all.

MA. All right. You men go over to the Y and come back in about an hour.

BEULAH. [*As her father returns to the wheel, stands out in the street beside him.*] Go straight along, pa, you can't miss it. It just stares at yuh. [*She puts her arm around his neck and rubs her nose against his temple.*] Crazy old pa, goin' buyin' things! It's me that ought to be buyin' things for you, pa.

ELMER. Oh, no! There's only one Loolie in the world.

BEULAH. [*Whispering, as her eyes fill with tears.*] Are you glad I'm still alive, pa? [*She kisses him abruptly and goes back to the house steps.* THE STAGE MANAGER *removes the automobile with the help of* ELMER *and* ARTHUR *who go off waving their goodbyes.*] Well, come on upstairs, ma, and take off your things. Caroline, there's a surprise for you in the back yard.

CAROLINE. Rabbits?

BEULAH. No.

CAROLINE. Chickins?

BEULAH. No. Go and see. [CAROLINE *runs off stage.* BEULAH *and* MA *gradually go upstairs.*] There are two new puppies. You be thinking over whether you can keep one in Newark.

MA. I guess we can. It's a nice house, Beulah. You just got a *lovely* home.

BEULAH. When I got back from the hospital, Horace had moved everything into it, and there wasn't anything for me to do.

MA. It's lovely.

[THE STAGE MANAGER *pushes out a bed from the left. Its foot is toward the right.* BEULAH *sits on it, testing the springs.*]

BEULAH. I think you'll find the bed comfortable, ma.

MA. [*Taking off her hat.*] Oh, I could sleep on a heapa shoes, Loolie! I don't have no trouble sleepin'. [*She sits down beside her.*] Now let me look at my girl. Well, well, when I last saw you, you didn't know me. You kep' saying: *When's mama comin'? When's mama comin'?* But the doctor sent me away.

BEULAH. [*Puts her head on her mother's shoulder and weeps.*] It was awful, mama. It was awful. She didn't even live a few minutes, mama. It was awful.

Ma. [*Looking far away.*]   God thought best, dear. God thought best. We don't understand why. We just go on, honey, doin' our business. [*Then almost abruptly—passing the back of her hand across her cheek.*] Well, now, what are we giving the men to eat tonight?

Beulah.   There's a chicken in the oven.

Ma.   What time didya put it in?

Beulah. [*Restraining her.*]   Aw, ma, don't go yet. I like to sit here with you this way. You always get the fidgets when we try and pet yuh, mama.

Ma. [*Ruefully, laughing.*]   Yes, it's kinda foolish. I'm just an old Newark bag-a-bones.

[*She glances at the backs of her hands.*]

Beulah. [*Indignantly.*]   Why, ma, you're good-lookin'! We always said you were good-lookin'.—And besides, you're the best ma we could ever have.

Ma. [*Uncomfortable.*]   Well, I hope you like me. There's nothin' like being liked by your family.—Now I'm going downstairs to look at the chicken. You stretch out here for a minute and shut your eyes.—Have you got everything laid in for breakfast before the shops close?

Beulah.   Oh, you know! Ham and eggs.

[*They both laugh.*]

Ma.   I declare I never could understand what men see in ham and eggs. I think they're horrible.—What time did you put the chicken in?

Beulah.   Five o'clock.

Ma.   Well, now, you shut your eyes for ten minutes. [*BEULAH stretches out and shuts her eyes. MA descends the stairs absentmindedly singing:*]

"There were ninety and nine that safely lay
In the shelter of the fold,
But one was out on the hills away,
Far off from the gates of gold. . . ."

AND THE CURTAIN FALLS

QUESTIONS

Preparation for the Journey

1. What expositional details are found in the opening stage direction? What additional exposition is established during the preparation for the journey?
2. What do you learn about Ma during the preparation? How would you explain her reaction to Arthur's missing hat and Caroline's red cheeks? What is Ma's relationship with her neighbors like?
3. What foreshadowing of the catastrophe do you find in the exposition?
4. How are Arthur and Caroline characterized initially? How does their behavior on the trip reinforce or change these initial images?

5. What is Elmer Kirby like? How would you characterize his relationship to Ma?

The Journey

6. What is the effect of having the characters recite advertisements?
7. How does Ma react to the funeral? How does she react to Arthur's remark that "Ma's always talking about God. I guess she got a letter from him this morning"? What does the remark reveal about Ma? What does her reaction reveal?
8. How does Ma relate to the garage attendant? What does this tell you about her?
9. How does Ma deal with Arthur's apology and tears?
10. What does Ma like about George Washington? Why is this significant?
11. What is Ma's wish and what does it tell you about her?
12. Why is it significant that Ma spots the signpost to Camden and gets the car headed down the correct road?

The Arrival

13. What is Ma's reaction to Caroline's observation that Beulah's street is "better than our street . . . richer than our street"?
14. What has happened to Beulah? How does Ma deal with this?
15. Why does the play end with a fragment of a hymn?

TOPICS FOR WRITING AND FURTHER DISCUSSION

1. What is the effect of having the stage manager play all the "bit" parts (small roles) and remain on stage even when he is not in a specific role? To what extent does he become a narrator? How pervasive is his point of view?
2. How clearly does this play follow the structural pattern of exposition, complication, crisis, catastrophe, and resolution? Where is the crisis? The catastrophe? How does the play resolve?
3. Who is the protagonist? Who or what are the antagonists? What are the conflicts? Which is central?
4. Is Ma a round or flat character? Static or dynamic? To what extent is she a stereotyped or stock character?
5. To what extent does Ma hold the Kirby family together and keep it on track? How does Wilder demonstrate this in the play?
6. What is Ma's attitude toward her own life? Her family? Her home? How does she cope with day-to-day problems and the larger trials of the world?
7. Is the journey really "happy"? If so, what makes it happy?

EUGENE O'NEILL, *Before Breakfast*

Eugene O'Neill is one of America's greatest playwrights and tragedians; he wrote over forty plays, won three Pulitzer Prizes, and received a Nobel Prize for literature in 1936. O'Neill grew up in a theater family; his father was a well-known actor. In his youth he traveled about the world as a seaman, studied briefly at Princeton and Harvard, and began writing plays in 1912. The first of his plays to be produced was *Bound East for Cardiff*, acted by the Provincetown Players at Wharf Theater in Provincetown, Massachusetts, in 1916. O'Neill maintained a close connection with this company for several years, providing them with ten one-act plays between 1916 and 1920. His later (and longer) works include *The Emperor Jones* (1920), *Anna Christie* (1921), *Desire Under the Elms* (1924), *Strange Interlude* (1928), *Mourning Becomes Electra* (1931), and *The Iceman Cometh* (1946). O'Neill also wrote an autobiographical play called *A Long Day's Journey into Night* (1936), which was suppressed at his request until after his death. When it was finally staged on Broadway in 1956, it won O'Neill a third Pulitzer Prize in drama.

Before Breakfast is one of O'Neill's earliest plays, yet it shows his characteristic control of conflict, character, setting, and point of view. The play was first staged in December 1916 by the Provincetown Players at the Playwright's Theater in New York City's Greenwich Village. There is very little action in the play, and yet it is full of conflict. The plot is simple and straightforward—a wife spends twenty minutes in the morning haranguing her husband. The only characters in the play are Alfred Rowland and his wife; the conflict between them is longstanding and bitter, and it is resolved in the play's catastrophe.

Above all else, *Before Breakfast* illustrates O'Neill's skillful employment of dramatic point of view and setting. By giving Mrs. Rowland virtually every word spoken in the play, O'Neill forces the audience to see everything, at least initially, from her perspective. Her vision of her husband and her marriage is radically distorted by her own pettiness and selfishness. Finally, the audience (and the reader) must decide exactly how valid or truthful her perspective is; we must evaluate the characters from our own perspective. Setting is equally important in *Before Breakfast*. O'Neill uses the single stage setting, described at length in the opening stage direction, to show the audience (or tell the reader) a great deal about the characters and their lives. The Rowlands's flat (apartment) in Greenwich Village, a part of New York City that was a traditional gathering place for artists, writers, and actors, instantly defines their status, their relationship, and their way of life. The implications of the setting are confirmed throughout the rest of the play.

EUGENE O'NEILL (1888–1953)

Before Breakfast   *1916*

CHARACTERS

Mrs. Rowland, *The Wife*
Mr. Alfred Rowland, *The Husband*

SCENE. *A small room serving both as kitchen and dining room in a flat on Christopher Street, New York City. In the rear, to the right, a door leading to the outer hallway. On the left of the doorway, a sink, and a two-burner gas stove. Over the stove, and extending to the left wall, a wooden closet for dishes, etc. On the left, two windows looking out on a fire escape where several potted plants are dying of neglect. Before the windows, a table covered with oilcloth. Two cane-bottomed chairs are placed by the table. Another stands against the wall to the right of door in rear. In the right wall, rear, a doorway leading into a bedroom. Farther forward, different articles of a man's and a woman's clothing are hung on pegs. A clothes line is strung from the left corner, rear, to the right wall, forward.*

It is about eight-thirty in the morning of a fine, sunshiny day in the early fall.

Mrs. Rowland enters from the bedroom, yawning, her hands still busy putting the finishing touches on a slovenly toilet by sticking hairpins into her hair which is bunched up in a drab-colored mass on top of her round head. She is of medium height and inclined to a shapeless stoutness, accentuated by her formless blue dress, shabby and worn. Her face is characterless, with small regular features and eyes of a nondescript blue. There is a pinched expression about her eyes and nose and her weak, spiteful mouth. She is in her early twenties but looks much older.

She comes to the middle of the room and yawns, stretching her arms to their full length. Her drowsy eyes stare about the room with the irritated look of one to whom a long sleep has not been a long rest. She goes wearily to the clothes hanging on the right and takes an apron from a hook. She ties it about her waist, giving vent to an exasperated "damn" when the knot fails to obey her clumsy fingers. Finally gets it tied and goes slowly to the gas stove and lights one burner. She fills the coffee pot at the sink and sets it over the flame. Then slumps down into a chair by the table and puts a hand over her forehead as if she were suffering from headache. Suddenly her face brightens as though she had remembered something, and she casts a quick glance at the dish closet; then looks sharply at the bedroom door and listens intently for a moment or so.

MRS. ROWLAND. [*In a low voice*] Alfred! Alfred! [*There is no answer from the next room and she continues suspiciously in a louder tone.*] You needn't pretend you're asleep. [*There is no reply to this from the bedroom, and, reassured, she gets up from her chair and tiptoes cautiously to the dish closet. She slowly opens one door, taking great care to make no noise, and slides out, from their hiding place behind the dishes, a bottle of Gordon gin and a glass. In doing so she disturbs the top dish, which rattles a little. At this sound she starts guiltily and looks with sulky defiance at the doorway to the next room.*]

[*Her voice trembling*] Alfred!

[*After a pause, during which she listens for any sound, she takes the glass and pours out a large drink and gulps it down; then hastily returns the bottle and glass to their hiding place. She closes the closet door with the same care as she had opened it, and, heaving a great sigh of relief, sinks down into her chair again. The large dose of alcohol she has taken has an almost immediate effect. Her features become more animated, she seems to gather energy, and she looks at the bedroom door with a hard, vindictive smile on her lips. Her eyes glance quickly about the room and are fixed on a man's coat and vest which hang from a hook at right. She moves stealthily over to the open doorway and stands there, out of sight of anyone inside, listening for any movement.*]

[*Calling in a half-whisper*] Alfred!

[*Again there is no reply. With a swift movement she takes the coat and vest from the hook and returns with them to her chair. She sits down and takes the various articles out of each pocket but quickly puts them back again. At last, in the inside pocket of the vest, she finds a letter.*]

[*Looking at the handwriting—slowly to herself*] Hmm! I knew it.

[*She opens the letter and reads it. At first her expression is one of hatred and rage, but as she goes on to the end it changes to one of triumphant malignity. She remains in deep thought for a moment, staring before her, the letter in her hands, a cruel smile on her lips. Then she puts the letter back in the pocket of the vest, and still careful not to awaken the sleeper, hangs the clothes up again on the same hook, and goes to the bedroom door and looks in.*]

[*In a loud, shrill voice*] Alfred! [*Still louder*] Alfred! [*There is a muffled, yawning groan from the next room.*] Don't you think it's about time you got up? Do you want to stay in bed all day? [*Turning around and coming back to her chair*] Not that I've got any doubts about your being lazy enough to stay in bed forever. [*She sits down and looks out of the window, irritably.*] Goodness knows what time it is. We haven't even got any way of telling the time since you pawned your watch like a fool. The last valuable thing we had, and you knew it. It's been nothing but pawn, pawn, pawn, with you—anything to put off getting a job, anything to get out of going to work like a man. [*She taps the floor with her foot nervously, biting her lips.*]

[*After a short pause*] Alfred! Get up, do you hear me? I want to make that bed before I go out. I'm sick of having this place in a continual muss on your account. [*With a certain vindictive satisfaction*] Not that we'll be here long unless you manage to get some money some place. Heaven knows I do my part—and more—going out to sew every day while you play the gentleman and loaf around bar rooms with that good-for-nothing lot of artists from the Square.°

[*A short pause during which she plays nervously with a cup and saucer on the table*]

And where are you going to get money, I'd like to know? The rent's due this week and you know what the landlord is. He won't let us stay a minute over our time. You say you *can't* get a job. That's a lie and you know it. You never even look for one. All you do is moon around all day writing silly poetry and stories that no one will buy—and no wonder they won't. I notice I can always

---

° *Square*: Washington Square, at the center of Greenwich Village.

get a position, such as it is; and it's only that which keeps us from starving to death.

[*Gets up and goes over to the stove—looks into the coffee pot to see if the water is boiling; then comes back and sits down again.*]

You'll have to get money to-day some place. I can't do it all, and I won't do it all. You've got to come to your senses. You've got to beg, borrow, or steal it somewheres. [*With a contemptuous laugh*] But where, I'd like to know? You're too proud to beg, and you've borrowed the limit, and you haven't the nerve to steal.

[*After a pause—getting up angrily*] Aren't you up yet, for heaven's sake? It's just like you to go to sleep again, or pretend to. [*She goes to the bedroom door and looks in.*] Oh, you are up. Well, it's about time. You needn't look at me like that. Your airs don't fool me a bit any more. I know you too well—better than you think I do—you and your goings-on. [*Turning away from the door—meaningly*] I know a lot of things, my dear. Never mind what I know, now. I'll tell you before I go, you needn't worry. [*She comes to the middle of the room and stands there, frowning.*]

[*Irritably*] Hmm! I suppose I might as well get breakfast ready—not that there's anything much to get. [*Questioningly*] Unless you have some money? [*She pauses for an answer from the next room which does not come.*] Foolish question! [*She gives a short, hard laugh*] I ought to know you better than that by this time. When you left here in such a huff last night I knew what would happen. You can't be trusted for a second. A nice condition you came home in! The fight we had was only an excuse for you to make a beast of yourself. What was the use pawning your watch if all you wanted with the money was to waste it in buying drink?

[*Goes over to the dish closet and takes out plates, cups, etc., while she is talking.*]

Hurry up! It don't take long to get breakfast these days, thanks to you. All we got this morning is bread and butter and coffee; and you wouldn't even have that if it wasn't for me sewing my fingers off. [*She slams the loaf of bread on the table with a bang.*]

The bread's stale. I hope you'll like it. *You* don't deserve any better, but I don't see why *I* should suffer.

[*Going over to the stove*] The coffee'll be ready in a minute, and you needn't expect me to wait for you.

[*Suddenly with great anger*] What on earth are you doing all this time? [*She goes over to the door and looks in.*] Well, you're *almost* dressed at any rate. I expected to find you back in bed. That'd be just like you. How awful you look this morning! For heaven's sake, shave! You're disgusting! You look like a tramp. No wonder no one will give you a job. I don't blame them—when you don't even look half-way decent. [*She goes to the stove.*] There's plenty of hot water right here. You've got no excuse. [*Gets a bowl and pours some of the water from the coffee pot into it*] Here.

[*He reaches his hand into the room for it. It is a sensitive hand with slender fingers. It trembles and some of the water spills on the floor.*]

[*Tauntingly*] Look at your hand tremble! You'd better give up drinking. You can't stand it. It's just your kind that get the D. T.'s. *That would be* the last straw! [*Looking down at the floor*] Look at the mess you've made of this floor—cigarette butts and ashes all over the place. Why can't you put them on a plate? No, you wouldn't be considerate enough to do that. You never think of me. You don't have to sweep the room and that's all you care about.

[Takes the broom and commences to sweep viciously, raising a cloud of dust. From the inner room comes the sound of a razor being stropped.]°

[*Sweeping*] Hurry up! It must be nearly time for me to go. If I'm late I'm liable to lose my position, and then I couldn't support you any longer. [*As an afterthought she adds sarcastically.*] And then you'd have to go to work or something dreadful like that. [*Sweeping under the table*] What I want to know is whether you're going to look for a job to-day or not. You know your family won't help us any more. They've had enough of you, too. [*After a moment's silent sweeping*] I'm about sick of all this life. I've a good notion to go home, if I wasn't too proud to let them know what a failure you've been—you, the millionaire Rowland's only son, the Harvard graduate, the poet, the catch of the town—Huh! [*With bitterness*] There wouldn't be many of them now envy my catch if they knew the truth. What has our marriage been, I'd like to know? Even before your *millionaire* father died owing every one in the world money, you certainly never wasted any of your time on your wife. I suppose you thought I'd ought to be glad you were *honorable* enough to marry me—after getting me into trouble. You were ashamed of me with your fine friends because my father's only a grocer, that's what you were. At least he's honest, which is more than any one could say about yours. [*She is sweeping steadily toward the door. Leans on her broom for a moment.*]

You hoped every one'd think you'd been forced to marry me, and pity you, didn't you? You didn't hesitate much about telling me you loved me, and making me believe your lies, before it happened, did you? You made me think you didn't want your father to buy me off as he tried to do. I know better now. I haven't lived with you all this time for nothing. [*Somberly*] It's lucky the poor thing was born dead, after all. What a father you'd have been!

[Is silent, brooding moodily for a moment—then she continues with a sort of savage joy.]

But I'm not the only one who's got you to thank for being unhappy. There's one other, at least, and *she* can't hope to marry you now. [*She puts her head into the next room.*] How about Helen? [*She starts back from the doorway, half frightened.*]

Don't look at me that way! Yes, I read her letter. What about it? I got a right to. I'm your wife. And I know all there is to know, so don't lie. You needn't stare at me so. You can't bully me with your superior airs any longer. Only for me you'd be going without breakfast this very morning. [*She sets the broom back in the corner—whiningly.*] You never did have any gratitude for what I've done. [*She comes to the stove and puts the coffee into the pot.*] The coffee's ready. I'm not going to wait for you. [*She sits down in her chair again.*]

[*After a pause—puts her hand to her head—fretfully*] My head aches so this morning. It's a shame I've got to go to work in a stuffy room all day in my condition. And I wouldn't if you were half a man. By rights I ought to be lying on my back instead

---

° *stropped*: Alfred is sharpening a straight razor: a razor with a very sharp five-inch steel blade that is hinged to a handle into which it folds.

of you. You know how sick I've been this last year; and yet you object when I take a little something to keep up my spirits. You even didn't want me to take that tonic I got at the drug store. [*With a hard laugh*] I know you'd be glad to have me dead and out of your way; then you'd be free to run after all these silly girls that think you're such a wonderful, misunderstood person—this Helen and the others. [*There is a sharp exclamation of pain from the next room.*]

[*With satisfaction*] There! I knew you'd cut yourself. It'll be a lesson to you. You know you oughtn't to be running around nights drinking with your nerves in such an awful shape. [*She goes to the door and looks in.*]

What makes you so pale? What are you staring at yourself in the mirror that way for? For goodness sake, wipe that blood off your face! [*With a shudder*] It's horrible. [*In relieved tones*] There, that's better. I never could stand the sight of blood. [*She shrinks back from the door a little.*] You better give up trying and go to a barber shop. Your hand shakes dreadfully. Why do you stare at me like that? [*She turns away from the door.*] Are you still mad at me about that letter? [*Defiantly*] Well, I had a right to read it. I'm your wife. [*She comes to the chair and sits down again. After a pause*]

I knew all the time you were running around with someone. Your lame excuses about spending the time at the library didn't fool me. Who is this Helen, anyway? One of those artists? Or does she write poetry, too? Her letter sounds that way. I'll bet she told you your things were the best ever, and you believed her, like a fool. Is she young and pretty? I was young and pretty, too, when you fooled me with your fine, poetic talk; but life with you would soon wear anyone down. What I've been through!

[*Goes over and takes the coffee off the stove*] Breakfast is ready. [*With a contemptuous glance*] Breakfast! [*Pours out a cup of coffee for herself and puts the pot on the table*] Your coffee'll be cold. What are you doing—still shaving, for heaven's sake? You'd better give it up. One of these mornings you'll give yourself a serious cut. [*She cuts off bread and butters it. During the following speeches she eats and sips her coffee.*]

I'll have to run as soon as I've finished eating. One of us has got to work. [*Angrily*] Are you going to look for a job to-day or aren't you? I should think some of your fine friends would help you, if they really think you're so much. But I guess they just like to hear you talk. [*Sits in silence for a moment*].

I'm sorry for this Helen, whoever she is. Haven't you got any feelings for other people? What will her family say? I see she mentions them in her letter. What is she going to do—have the child—or go to one of those doctors? That's a nice thing, I must say. Where can she get the money? Is she rich? [*She waits for some answer to this volley of questions.*]

Hmm! You won't tell me anything about her, will you? Much I care. Come to think of it, I'm not so sorry for her after all. She knew what she was doing. She isn't any schoolgirl, like I was, from the looks of her letter. Does she know you're married? Of course, she must. All your friends know about your unhappy marriage. I know they pity you, but they don't know my side of it. They'd talk different if they did.

[*Too busy eating to go on for a second or so*]

This Helen must be a fine one, if she knew you were married. What does she expect, then? That I'll divorce you and let her marry you? Does she think

I'm crazy enough for that—after all you've made me go through? I guess not! And you can't get a divorce from me and you know it. No one can say *I've* ever done anything wrong. [*Drinks the last of her cup of coffee*]

She deserves to suffer, that's all I can say. I'll tell you what I think; I think your Helen is no better than a common street-walker, that's what I think. [*There is a stifled groan of pain from the next room.*]

Did you cut yourself again? Serves you right. [*Gets up and takes off her apron*] Well, I've got to run along. [*Peevishly*] This is a fine life for me to be leading! I won't stand for your loafing any longer. [*Something catches her ear and she pauses and listens intently.*] There! You've overturned the water all over everything. Don't say you haven't. I can hear it dripping on the floor. [*A vague expression of fear comes over her face.*] Alfred! Why don't you answer me?

[*She moves slowly toward the room. There is the noise of a chair being overturned and something crashes heavily to the floor. She stands, trembling with fright.*]

Alfred! Alfred! Answer me! What is it you knocked over? Are you still drunk? [*Unable to stand the tension a second longer she rushes to the door of the bedroom.*] Alfred!

[*She stands in the doorway looking down at the floor of the inner room, transfixed with horror. Then she shrieks wildly and runs to the other door, unlocks it and frenziedly pulls it open, and runs shrieking madly into the outer hallway.*]

[*The curtain falls.*]

QUESTIONS

1. What does the setting tell you about the Rowlands?
2. What image of Mrs. Rowland is presented in the opening stage direction? How are adjectives employed to shape your initial response to her? To what extent does the rest of the play sustain or alter this initial image?
3. How do Mrs. Rowland's initial stage actions further define her character? What adjectives and adverbs are used to direct your response to her?
4. How does Mrs. Rowland treat Alfred? What tone does she use in speaking to him? What does she complain about? What does she accuse Alfred of being and doing?
5. What happened during Mrs. Rowland's premarital affair with Alfred? Why do you suppose she didn't let Alfred's father "buy her off"? Why did she marry Alfred?
6. What is Mrs. Rowland's attitude toward Helen? How does she treat her husband's feelings for Helen? What does this suggest about the Rowlands' marriage?
7. Where is the crisis of the play? Which character comes to a crisis? What actions and descriptions indicate that the character and play have reached a crisis?
8. Mrs. Rowland precipitates the catastrophe of this play with her vicious chatter

about Helen. What do we learn about Helen? What pushes Alfred over the edge? What is the catastrophe?

TOPICS FOR WRITING AND FURTHER DISCUSSION

1. How does the setting of this play begin to define the characters, their relationship, and their life? What details of setting are especially significant in this respect?

2. The play is set in an apartment in Greenwich Village in lower Manhattan around 1916. It was performed in Greenwich Village in December 1916. What do you make of this convergence of dramatic setting and production setting? What could O'Neill assume about his original audience's reaction to the setting?

3. Who is the protagonist in the play? The antagonist? What is the central conflict? When did it begin? How and when is it resolved?

4. Is Mrs. Rowland a flat or round character? Static or dynamic? Individualized or stereotyped? Why does she have no first name? What is the effect of these choices?

5. Why is Alfred Rowland kept off stage (except for his hand) and given no dialogue? How does this affect the play?

6. Alfred Rowland is presented from his wife's point of view. How accurate is this portrait? Is Alfred the man that his wife describes?

7. Why does O'Neill present the history of Alfred's family and his relationship with Mrs. Rowland out of chronological order? What is the effect of such a method of presentation? Try to reconstruct this history in chronological order, beginning with Alfred's graduation from Harvard.

8. Does this play make a point about marriage, or is it simply a study in character and perspective?

EDWARD ALBEE, *The Sandbox*

Edward Albee was the leading American playwright of the 1960s. His first play, *The Zoo Story*, was written in 1958, first performed in 1959 in Berlin, and published in 1960. This was followed by *The Sandbox* and *The Death of Bessie Smith* (1960), *The American Dream* (1961), and *Who's Afraid of Virginia Woolf* (1962), Albee's best-known play. This play still stands as the pinnacle of Albee's career; it had a highly successful run in New York City and was awarded the "Tony" as best play in 1963. Albee's work after *Who's Afraid of Virginia Woolf* has met with mixed reactions. *Tiny Alice* (1964) was viewed as confusing and derivative, but *A Delicate Balance* (1966) and *Seascape* (1975) both won Pulitzer Prizes for drama. Other plays and adaptations have had short lives in the theater; one of Albee's more recent works, *The Lady from Dubuque* (1980), survived for only twelve performances on Broadway.

Several of Albee's early plays, including *The Sandbox*, represent the playwright's experimentation with nonrealistic staging and with Theater of the Absurd, a school of drama that evolved in Europe in the 1940s and 1950s. Dramatists of the Absurd use their plays to examine the foundations of character and existence, stripping away conventions of behavior and accidents of personality. Like the Existentialist philosophy on which the Absurdist school is based, most plays of the absurd begin with the assumption that life is irrational. In many Absurdist plays, language, action, and relationships become theatrical games in which the characters are conscious of their own fictional existence as characters in a play.

The Sandbox, written in 1959 and first performed in New York City in 1960, is an Absurdist play that deals with the emptiness of middle-class life and the American way of death. The characters are closer to types or symbols, as in *Everyman* (p. 1075), than they are to portrayals of individualized women and men. Grandma, the protagonist, is in conflict with her family, society, and death; only the last of these conflicts is resolved at the conclusion of the play. Mommy and Daddy represent Albee's vision of the American middle-class family reduced to its basic elements and patterns of behavior. Albee employs all the elements of drama to build meaning and impact into *The Sandbox*; plot, character, setting, and symbol all convey specific ideas about life and values in Albee's vision of America. The play also provides an excellent opportunity to look at the ways a playwright can use language, diction, and tone to shape meaning. Albee is a master of dialogue; his language defines the characters and directs the audience's response to the play. Repetition, parallel speech patterns, idiom, connotative words, and clichés are all skillfully employed to these ends.

EDWARD ALBEE (b. 1928)

The Sandbox   *1960 (1959)*

THE PLAYERS

>   The Young Man, 25, *a good-looking, well-built boy in a bathing suit*
>   Mommy, 55, *a well-dressed, imposing woman*
>   Daddy, 60, *a small man; gray, thin*
>   Grandma, 86, *a tiny, wizened woman with bright eyes*
>   The Musician, *no particular age, but young would be nice*

Note: When, in the course of the play, MOMMY and DADDY call each other by these names, there should be no suggestion of regionalism. These names are of empty affection and point up the pre-senility and vacuity of their characters.

   The Scene: A bare stage, with only the following: Near the footlights, far stage-right, two simple chairs set side by side, facing the audience; near the footlights, far stage-left, a chair facing stage-right with a music stand before it; farther back, and stage-center, slightly elevated and raked, a large child's sandbox with a toy pail and shovel; the background is the sky, which alters from brightest day to deepest night.

At the beginning, it is brightest day; the YOUNG MAN *is alone on stage, to the rear of the sandbox, and to one side. He is doing calisthenics; he does calisthenics until quite at the very end of the play. These calisthenics, employing the arms only, should suggest the beating and fluttering of wings. The* YOUNG MAN *is, after all, the Angel of Death.*

MOMMY *and* DADDY *enter from stage-left,* MOMMY *first.*

MOMMY. [*Motioning to* DADDY] Well, here we are; this is the beach.

DADDY. [*Whining*] I'm cold.

MOMMY. [*Dismissing him with a little laugh*] Don't be silly; it's as warm as toast. Look at that nice young man over there: *he* doesn't think it's cold. [*Waves to the* YOUNG MAN] Hello.

YOUNG MAN. [*With an endearing smile*] Hi!

MOMMY. [*Looking about*] This will do perfectly . . . don't you think so, Daddy? There's sand there . . . and the water beyond. What do you think, Daddy?

DADDY. [*Vaguely*] Whatever you say, Mommy.

MOMMY. [*With the same little laugh*] Well, of course . . . whatever I say. Then, it's settled, is it?

DADDY. [*Shrugs*] She's *your* mother, not mine.

MOMMY. *I* know she's my mother. What do you take me for? [*A pause*] All right, now; let's get on with it. [*She shouts into the wings, stage-left.*] You! Out there! You can come in now.

[*The* MUSICIAN *enters, seats himself in the chair, stage-left, places music on the music stand, is ready to play.* MOMMY *nods approvingly.*]

MOMMY. Very nice; very nice. Are you ready, Daddy? Let's go get Grandma.

DADDY. Whatever you say, Mommy.

MOMMY. [*Leading the way out, stage-left*] Of course, whatever I say. [*To the* MUSICIAN] You can begin now. (*The* MUSICIAN *begins playing;* MOMMY *and* DADDY *exit; the* MUSICIAN, *all the while playing, nods to the* YOUNG MAN.]

YOUNG MAN. [*With the same endearing smile*] Hi!

[*After a moment,* MOMMY *and* DADDY *re-enter, carrying* GRANDMA. *She is borne in by their hands under her armpits; she is quite rigid; her legs are drawn up; her feet do not touch the ground; the expression on her ancient face is that of puzzlement and fear.*]

DADDY. Where do we put her?

MOMMY. [*The same little laugh*] Wherever I say, of course. Let me see . . . well . . . all right, over there . . . in the sandbox. [*Pause*] Well, what are you waiting for, Daddy? . . . The sandbox!

[*Together they carry* GRANDMA *over to the sandbox and more or less dump her in.*]

GRANDMA. [*Righting herself to a sitting position; her voice a cross between a baby's laugh and cry*] Ahhhhhh! Graaaaa!

DADDY. [*Dusting himself*] What do we do now?

MOMMY. [*To the* MUSICIAN] You can stop now.

[*The* MUSICIAN *stops.*]

[*Back to* DADDY] What do you mean, what do we do now? We go over there and sit down, of course. [*To the* YOUNG MAN] Hello there.

YOUNG MAN. [*Again smiling*] Hi!

[MOMMY and DADDY move to the chairs, stage-right, and sit down. A pause]

GRANDMA. [Same as before] Ahhhhhh! Ah-haaaaaa! Graaaaaa!
DADDY. Do you think . . . do you think she's . . . comfortable?
MOMMY. [Impatiently] How would I know?
DADDY. [Pause] What do we do now?
MOMMY. [As if remembering] We . . . wait. We . . . sit here . . . and we wait . . . that's what we do.
DADDY. [After a pause] Shall we talk to each other?
MOMMY. [With that little laugh; picking something off her dress] Well, you can talk, if you want to . . . if you can think of anything to say . . . if you can think of anything new.
DADDY. [Thinks] No . . . I suppose not.
MOMMY. [With a triumphant laugh] Of course not!
GRANDMA. [Banging the toy shovel against the pail] Haaaaaa! Ah-haaaaaa!
MOMMY. [Out over the audience] Be quiet, Grandma . . . just be quiet, and wait.

[GRANDMA throws a shovelful of sand at MOMMY.]

MOMMY. [Still out over the audience] She's throwing sand at me! You stop that, Grandma; you stop throwing sand at Mommy! [To DADDY] She's throwing sand at me.

[DADDY looks around at GRANDMA, who screams at him.]

GRANDMA. GRAAAAA!
MOMMY. Don't look at her. Just . . . sit here . . . be very still . . . and wait. [To the MUSICIAN] You . . . uh . . . you go ahead and do whatever it is you do.

[The MUSICIAN plays.]
[MOMMY and DADDY are fixed, staring out beyond the audience. GRANDMA looks at them, looks at the MUSICIAN, looks at the sandbox, throws down the shovel.]

GRANDMA. Ah-haaaaaa! Graaaaaa! [Looks for reaction; gets none. Now . . . directly to the audience] Honestly! What a way to treat an old woman! Drag her out of the house . . . stick her in a car . . . bring her out here from the city . . . dump her in a pile of sand . . . and leave her here to set. I'm eighty-six years old! I was married when I was seventeen. To a farmer. He died when I was thirty. [To the MUSICIAN] Will you stop that, please?

[The MUSICIAN stops playing.]

I'm a feeble old woman . . . how do you expect anybody to hear me over that peep! peep! peep! [To herself] There's no respect around here. [To the YOUNG MAN] There's no respect around here!
YOUNG MAN. [Same smile] Hi!
GRANDMA. [After a pause, a mild double-take, continues, to the audience] My husband died when I was thirty [indicates MOMMY], and I had to raise that big cow over there all by my lonesome. You can imagine what that was like. Lordy! [To the YOUNG MAN] Where'd they get you?

YOUNG MAN.   Oh . . . I've been around for a while.

GRANDMA.   I'll bet you have! Heh, heh, heh. Will you look at you!

YOUNG MAN.   [*Flexing his muscles*] Isn't that something? [*Continues his calisthenics*]

GRANDMA.   Boy, oh boy; I'll say. Pretty good.

YOUNG MAN.   [*Sweetly*] I'll say.

GRANDMA.   Where ya from?

YOUNG MAN.   Southern California.

GRANDMA.   [*Nodding*] Figgers; figgers. What's your name, honey?

YOUNG MAN.   I don't know. . . .

GRANDMA.   [*To the audience*] Bright, too!

YOUNG MAN.   I mean . . . I mean, they haven't given me one yet . . . the studio . . .

GRANDMA.   [*Giving him the once-over*] You don't say . . . you don't say. Well . . . uh, I've got to talk some more . . . don't you go 'way.

YOUNG MAN.   Oh, no.

GRANDMA.   [*Turning her attention back to the audience*] Fine; fine. [*Then, once more, back to the YOUNG MAN*] You're . . . you're an actor, hunh?

YOUNG MAN.   [*Beaming*] Yes. I am.

GRANDMA.   [*To the audience again; shrugs*] I'm smart that way. *Anyhow*, I had to raise . . . *that* over there all by my lonesome; and what's next to her there . . . that's what she married. Rich? I tell you . . . money, money, money. They took me off the *farm* . . . which was real decent of them . . . and they moved me into the big town house with *them* . . . fixed a nice place for me under the stove . . . gave me an army blanket . . . and my own dish . . . my very own dish! So, what have I got to complain about? Nothing, of course. I'm not complaining. [*She looks up at the sky, shouts to someone off-stage.*] Shouldn't it be getting dark now, dear?

[*The lights dim; night comes on. The MUSICIAN begins to play, it becomes deepest night. There are spots on all the players, including the YOUNG MAN, who is, of course, continuing his calisthenics.*]

DADDY.   [*Stirring*] It's nighttime.

MOMMY.   Shhhh. Be still . . . wait.

DADDY.   [*Whining*] It's so hot.

MOMMY.   Shhhhhh. Be still . . . wait.

GRANDMA.   [*To herself*] That's better. Night. [*To the MUSICIAN*] Honey, do you play all through this part?

[*The MUSICIAN nods.*]

Well, keep it nice and soft; that's a good boy.

[*The MUSICIAN nods again; plays softly.*]

That's nice.

[*There is an off-stage rumble.*]

DADDY.   [*Starting*] What was that?

MOMMY.   [*Beginning to weep*] It was nothing.

DADDY.   It was . . . it was . . . thunder . . . or a wave breaking . . . or something.

MOMMY.   [*Whispering, through her tears*] It was an off-stage rumble . . . and you know what *that* means. . . .

DADDY.   I forget. . . .

MOMMY.   [*Barely able to talk*] It means the time has come for poor Grandma . . . and I can't bear it!

DADDY.   [*Vacantly*] I . . . I suppose you've got to be brave.

GRANDMA.   [*Mocking*] That's right, kid; be brave. You'll bear up; you'll get over it.

[*Another off-stage rumble . . . louder*]

MOMMY.   Ohhhhhhhhh . . . poor Grandma . . . poor Grandma. . . .

GRANDMA.   [*To MOMMY*] I'm fine! I'm all right! It hasn't happened yet!

[*A violent off-stage rumble. All the lights go out, save the spot on the YOUNG MAN; the MUSICIAN stops playing.*]

MOMMY.   Ohhhhhhhhhh . . . Ohhhhhhhhhh. . . .

[*Silence*]

GRANDMA.   Don't put the lights up yet . . . I'm not ready; I'm not quite ready. [*Silence*] All right, dear . . . I'm about done.

[*The lights come up again, to brightest day; the MUSICIAN begins to play. GRANDMA is discovered, still in the sandbox, lying on her side, propped up on an elbow, half covered, busily shoveling sand over herself.*]

GRANDMA.   [*Muttering*] I don't know how I'm supposed to do anything with this goddam toy shovel. . . .

DADDY.   Mommy! It's daylight!

MOMMY.   [*Brightly*] So it is! Well! Our long night is over. We must put away our tears, take off our mourning . . . and face the future. It's our duty.

GRANDMA.   [*Still shoveling; mimicking*] . . . take off our mourning . . . face the future. . . . Lordy!

[*MOMMY and DADDY rise, stretch. MOMMY waves to the YOUNG MAN.*]

YOUNG MAN.   [*With that smile*] Hi!

[*GRANDMA plays dead. (!) MOMMY and DADDY go over to look at her; she is a little more than half buried in the sand; the toy shovel is in her hands, which are crossed on her breast.*]

MOMMY.   [*Before the sandbox; shaking her head*] Lovely! It's . . . it's hard to be sad . . . she looks . . . so happy. [*With pride and conviction*] It pays to do things well. [*To the MUSICIAN*] All right, you can stop now, if you want to. I mean, stay around for a swim, or something; it's all right with us. [*She sighs heavily.*] Well Daddy . . . off we go.

DADDY.   Brave Mommy!

MOMMY.   Brave Daddy!

[*They exit, stage-left.*]

GRANDMA. [*After they leave; lying quite still*] It pays to do things well. . . . Boy, oh boy! [*She tries to sit up*] . . . well, kids . . . [*but she finds she can't.*] . . . I . . . I can't get up. I . . . I can't move. . . .

[*The YOUNG MAN stops his calisthenics, nods to the MUSICIAN, walks over to GRANDMA, kneels down by the sandbox.*]

GRANDMA.   I . . . can't move. . . .
YOUNG MAN.   Shhhhh . . . be very still. . . .
GRANDMA.   I . . . I can't move. . . .
YOUNG MAN.   Uh . . . ma'am; I . . . I have a line here.
GRANDMA.   Oh, I'm sorry, sweetie; you go right ahead.
YOUNG MAN.   I am . . . uh . . .
GRANDMA.   Take your time, dear.
YOUNG MAN.   [*Prepares; delivers the line like a real amateur.*] I am the Angel of Death. I am . . . uh . . . I am come for you.
GRANDMA.   What . . . wha . . . [*Then, with resignation*] . . . ohhh . . . ohhhh, I see.

[*The YOUNG MAN bends over, kisses GRANDMA gently on the forehead.*]

GRANDMA.   [*Her eyes closed, her hands folded on her breast again, the shovel between her hands, a sweet smile on her face*] Well . . . that was very nice, dear. . . .
YOUNG MAN.   [*Still kneeling*] Shhhhhh . . . be still. . . .
GRANDMA.   What I meant was . . . you did that very well, dear. . . .
YOUNG MAN.   [*Blushing*] . . . oh . . .
GRANDMA.   No; I mean it. You've got that . . . you've got a quality.
YOUNG MAN.   [*With his endearing smile*] Oh . . . thank you; thank you very much . . . ma'am.
GRANDMA.   [*Slowly; softly—as the YOUNG MAN puts his hands on top of GRANDMA'S*] You're . . . you're welcome . . . dear.

[*Tableau. The MUSICIAN continues to play as the curtain slowly comes down.*]

[*Curtain*]

QUESTIONS

1. How does the setting, described at the beginning of the play, help shape your response? What props turn out to be symbolic?
2. What information does Albee provide in the opening note and stage direction that helps you understand the action and meaning of the play?
3. Why does Mommy say, "This is the beach"? Why is the line necessary? Why have the characters come to the beach? What are they waiting for?
4. Why does Albee indicate that Daddy is *whining*? What is the effect of having Daddy repeat "Whatever you say, Mommy" several times?
5. What happens to your sense of drama as the imitation of an action when Mommy tells the Musician, "You can come in now"?
6. How does Mommy treat Daddy? How does he treat her? How do they both treat Grandma? Where do they put Grandma? Why?

7. How does Grandma "speak" to Mommy and Daddy? How does she speak to the audience and the Young Man? How do you account for this difference?

8. What does Grandma tell you directly about her relationship with Mommy and Daddy? What is her attitude toward Mommy? How is it shaped through diction and tone?

9. Albee identifies the Young Man as the Angel of Death; what else does he symbolize or represent? What is Grandma's attitude toward him? How does he treat her?

10. What does the "off-stage rumble" signify?

11. How do Mommy and Daddy react to Grandma's "death"? How would you characterize their language?

12. How does Grandma react to Mommy and Daddy's comments about her death? What does Grandma reveal about the way Mommy and Daddy deal with death?

13. What is the catastrophe of the play? The resolution?

TOPICS FOR WRITING AND FURTHER DISCUSSION

1. Are the characters in this play round or flat? Static or dynamic? Why don't they have names? What does each symbolize?

2. What does Albee's characterization of Mommy, Daddy, and Grandma tell you about his view of the American family, the relationship of men and women in marriage, and our attitudes toward old age?

3. What do Mommy's calling the Musician, Grandma's cueing of the lighting technician, and Mommy's reference to an "off-stage rumble" have in common? What common effect do these events have on your perception of *The Sandbox* as a play?

4. *The Sandbox* is full of repetition; characters repeat words and even whole lines two or three times. What is the effect of this repetition on your understanding of character and meaning in this play?

5. How does Albee employ diction, speech patterns, connotative words, and tone to shape character and meaning?

6. How important are clichés as a device in this play? What clichés did you notice? Which characters speak most of the clichés? What effect do the clichés have on your perception of character and theme?

7. Compare the set described in this play to the one Thornton Wilder describes at the beginning of *The Happy Journey to Trenton and Camden* (p. 1049). How are the sets similar? To what extent do they have similar effects?

8. Compare the characterization of Mommy and Daddy in this play to Ma and Elmer Kirby in Wilder's *The Happy Journey to Trenton and Camden*. In what ways are the characters related or similar? What are the most significant differences?

9. How many different generations are presented in *The Sandbox*? Which characters represent each generation? To what extent do the different generations comment on different phases of American history?

ANONYMOUS, *Everyman*

Everyman is a medieval morality play written about 1495. Its purpose is rigidly educational and religious; it is designed to teach Christians the way to live and die in order to achieve salvation. The play offers a harsh lesson: salvation is achieved through good works and the grace of God. Everything else in life is stripped away; Everyman is abandoned by friends, family, wealth, strength, beauty, wisdom, and his senses. Only his good deeds go with him to final judgment. Unlike most morality plays, *Everyman* does not deal with the lifelong struggle of good and evil in the protagonist's soul. Rather, it focuses on the moment of Everyman's death. The entire play occurs between God's decision to summon Everyman and Everyman's final judgment and salvation.

The play is a rigorously structured allegory in which a system of consistent equivalents is established and sustained throughout. The significance of each of the characters is defined and described by his or her name. Thus, Goods represents worldly wealth while Good Deeds represents the acts of charity and goodness that Everyman has done during his life. Similarly, the steps through penance to salvation are represented by characters or objects that signify the traditional stages of penance: Confession, Contrition, Absolution through Priesthood, and Satisfaction. In this allegory the characters are limited by their names and allegorical significance; they must behave in accordance with their allegorical meaning. Thus, Goods must gloat at Everyman's spiritual jeopardy, and Good Deeds must help Everyman on the road to salvation. Even the staging of the play reflects its allegorical nature. In the Middle Ages *Everyman* would have been staged by members of a craft guild or professional players on a two-level stage or pageant wagon. The upper level represented heaven; God, Death, and the Angel spoke and acted on this level. The lower level represented the world; most of the play's action occurred here.

ANONYMOUS

Everyman   (*ca. 1495*)

CHARACTERS

God	Kindred	Knowledge	Five-Wits
Messenger	Cousin	Confession	Discretion
Death	Goods	Beauty	Angel
Everyman	Good Deeds	Strength	Doctor
Fellowship			

Here beginneth a treatise how the High Father of Heaven sendeth Death to summon every creature to come and give account of their lives in this world, and is in manner of a moral play.

[*Enter* MESSENGER.]

MESSENGER.   I pray you all give your audience,
    And hear this matter with reverence,
    By figure° a moral play,
    The Summoning of Everyman called it is,
    That of our lives and ending shows   5
    How transitory we be all day.°
    The matter is wondrous precious,
    But the intent of it is more gracious
    And sweet to bear away.
    The story saith: Man, in the beginning   10
    Look well, and take good heed to the ending,
    Be you never so gay.
    You think sin in the beginning full sweet,
    Which in the end causeth the soul to weep,
    When the body lieth in clay.   15
    Here shall you see how Fellowship and Jollity,
    Both Strength, Pleasure, and Beauty,
    Will fade from thee as flower in May.
    For ye shall hear how our Heaven-King
    Calleth Everyman to a general reckoning.°   20
    Give audience and hear what He doth say.

[*Exit* MESSENGER. *Enter* GOD.]

GOD.   I perceive, here in my majesty,
    How that all creatures be to me unkind,°
    Living without dread in worldly prosperity.
    Of ghostly° sight the people be so blind,   25
    Drowned in sin, they know me not for their God;
    In worldly riches is all their mind.
    They fear not of my righteousness the sharp rod;
    My law that I showed when I for them died
    They forget clean, and shedding of my blood red.   30
    I hanged° between two, it cannot be denied;
    To get them life I suffered to be dead.
    I healed their feet; with thorns hurt was my head.
    I could do no more than I did, truly,
    And now I see the people do clean forsake me.   35
    They use the seven deadly sins damnable,
    As Pride, Coveitise,° Wrath, and Lechery
    Now in the world be made commendable.
    And thus they leave of angels the heavenly company.
    Every man liveth so after his own pleasure,   40
    And yet of their life they be nothing sure.
    I see the more that I them forbear,°

3 *by figure:* in form.   6 *all day:* always.   20 *reckoning:* judgment.   23 *unkind:*
unmindful.   25 *ghostly:* spiritual.   31 *hanged:* was crucified.   37 *Coveitise:*
greed.   42 *forbear:* endure.

The worse they be from year to year.
All that liveth appaireth° fast.
Therefore I will, in all the haste,   45
Have a reckoning of every man's person.
For, and° I leave the people thus alone
In their life and wicked tempests,
Verily they will become much worse than beasts
For now one would by envy another up eat.   50
Charity do they all clean forget.
I hoped well that every man
In my glory should make his mansion,
And thereto I had them all elect.°
But now I see, like traitors deject,°   55
They thank me not for the pleasure that I to them meant,
Nor yet for their being that I them have lent.
I proffered° the people great multitude of mercy,
And few there be that asketh it heartily.°
They be so cumbered° with worldly riches   60
That needs on them I must do justice,
On every man living without fear.
Where art thou, Death, thou mighty messenger?

[*Enter* DEATH.]

DEATH.   Almighty God, I am here at your will,
   Your commandment to fulfill.   65
GOD.   Go thou to Everyman,
   And show him, in my name,
   A pilgrimage he must on him take,
   Which he in no wise° may escape;
   And that he bring with him a sure reckoning°   70
   Without delay or any tarrying.
DEATH.   Lord, I will in the world go run over all,°
   And cruelly out search both great and small.

                                    [*Exit* GOD.]

Everyman will I beset that° liveth beastly
Out of God's laws, and dreadeth not folly.   75
He that loveth riches I will strike with my dart,
His sight to blind, and from heaven to depart°—
Except that alms° be his good friend—
In hell for to dwell, world without end.
Lo, yonder I see Everyman walking.   80
Full little he thinketh on my coming;
His mind is on fleshly lusts and his treasure,

---

44 *appaireth*: degenerates.   47 *and*: if.   54 *elect*: chosen.   55 *deject*:
abject.   58 *proffered*: offered.   59 *heartily*: sincerely.   60 *cumbered*: weighed
down.   69 *no wise*: no way.   70 *reckoning*: accounting.   72 *over all*:
everywhere.   74 *that*: who.   77 *depart*: separate.   78 *alms*: charity.

And great pain it shall cause him to endure
Before the Lord, Heaven-King.

[*Enter* EVERYMAN.]

Everyman, stand still! Whither art thou going   85
Thus gaily? Hast thou thy Maker forgot?
EVERYMAN.   Why askest thou?
   Why wouldest thou weet°?
DEATH.   Yea, sir, I will show you:
   In great haste I am sent to thee   90
   From God out of His majesty.
EVERYMAN.   What, sent to me?
DEATH.   Yea, certainly.
   Though thou have forgot Him here,
   He thinketh on thee in the heavenly sphere,   95
   As, ere we depart, thou shalt know.
EVERYMAN.   What desireth God of me?
DEATH.   That shall I show thee:
   A reckoning He will needs° have
   Without any longer respite.°   100
EVERYMAN.   To give a reckoning longer leisure I crave.
   This blind° matter troubleth my wit.
DEATH.   On thee thou must take a long journey;
   Therefore thy book of count° with thee thou bring,
   For turn again° thou cannot by no way.   105
   And look thou be sure of thy reckoning,
   For before God thou shalt answer and show
   Thy many bad deeds and good but a few,
   How thou hast spent thy life and in what wise,
   Before the Chief Lord of Paradise.   110
   Have ado that we were in that way,°
   For weet° thou well thou shalt make none attorney.°
EVERYMAN.   Full unready I am such reckoning to give.
   I know thee not. What messenger art thou?
DEATH.   I am Death that no man dreadeth,°   115
   For every man I rest,° and no man spareth;
   For it is God's commandment
   That all to me should be obedient.
EVERYMAN.   O Death, thou comest when I had thee least in mind.
   In thy power it lieth me to save;   120
   Yet of my good° will I give thee, if thou will be kind,
   Yea, a thousand pound shalt thou have,
   And° defer this matter till another day.

---

88 *weet*: know.   99 *He will needs*: He must.   100 *respite*: delay.   102 *blind*: obscure,
dark.   104 *count*: accounts.   105 *turn again*: return.   111 *in that way*: on our
way.   112 *weet*: know.   *attorney*: substitute.   115 *no man dreadeth*: fears no man.
116 *rest*: arrest.   121 *good*: goods.   123 *And*: if you.

DEATH.   Everyman, it may not be, by no way.
I set nought by° gold, silver, nor riches,   125
Nor by pope, emperor, king, duke, nor princes,
For, if I would receive gifts great,
All the world I might get.
But my custom is clean contrary;
I give thee no respite. Come hence, and not tarry.°   130
EVERYMAN.   Alas, shall I have no longer respite?
I may say Death giveth no warning.
To think on thee it maketh my heart sick,
For all unready is my book of reckoning.
But twelve year and I might have a biding.°   135
My counting-book I would make so clear
That my reckoning I should not need to fear.
Wherefore, Death; I pray thee, for God's mercy,
Spare me till I be provided of remedy.
DEATH.   Thee availeth not° to cry, weep, and pray;   140
But haste thee lightly° that thou were gone that journey,
And prove° thy friends, if thou can;
For weet° thou well the tide° abideth no man,
And in the world each living creature
For Adam's sin must die of nature.   145
EVERYMAN.   Death, if I should this pilgrimage take,
And my reckoning surely make,
Show me, for saint° charity,
Should I not come again° shortly?
DEATH.   No, Everyman; and thou be once there,   150
Thou mayst nevermore come here,
Trust me verily.
EVERYMAN.   O gracious God in the high seat celestial,
Have mercy on me in this most need!
Shall I have no company from this vale terrestrial°   155
Of mine acquaintance that way me to lead?
DEATH.   Yea, if any be so hardy
That would go with thee and bear thee company.
Hie° thee that thou were gone to God's magnificence,
Thy reckoning to give before his presence.   160
What, weenest° thou thy life is given thee,
And thy worldly goods also?
EVERYMAN.   I had wend° it so, verily.
DEATH.   Nay, nay, it was but lent thee.
For as soon as thou art go,°   165
Another a while shall have it and then go therefro,

125 *set nought by*: care not for.   130 *not tarry*: don't delay.   135 *biding*: delay.
140 *Thee availeth not*: i.e., it won't help you.   141 *lightly*: quickly.   142 *prove*: test.
143 *weet*: know.   *tide*: time.   148 *saint*: holy.   149 *come again*: return.
155 *terrestrial*: earthly.   159 *hie*: hasten.   161 *weenest*: suppose.   163 *wend*: supposed.   165 *go*: gone.

Even as thou hast done.
Everyman, thou art mad! Thou hast thy wits° five,
And here on earth will not amend thy live,°
For suddenly I do come.   170
EVERYMAN.   O wretched caitiff,° whither shall I flee
That I might scape this endless sorrow?
Now, gentle Death, spare me till tomorrow,
That I may amend me°
With good advisement.°   175
DEATH.   Nay, thereto I will not consent,
Nor no man will I respite,
But to the heart suddenly I shall smite,
Without any advisement.
And now out of thy sight I will me hie;°   180
See thou make thee ready shortly,
For thou mayst say this is the day
That no man living may scape away.

                                          [*Exit* DEATH.]

EVERYMAN.   Alas, I may well weep with sighs deep.
Now have I no manner of company   185
To help me in my journey and me to keep.°
And also my writing° is full unready.
How shall I do now for to excuse me?
I would to God I had never be geet!°
To my soul a full great profit it had be.°   190
For now I fear pains huge and great.
The time passeth; Lord, help, that all wrought!°
For though I mourn, it availeth nought.
The day passeth and is almost ago;°
I wot° not well what for to do.   195
To whom were I best my complaint to make?
What and° I to Fellowship thereof spake,
And showed him of this sudden chance?
For in him is all mine affiance;°
We have in the world so many a day   200
Be° good friends in sport and play.
I see him yonder, certainly.
I trust that he will bear me company;
Therefore to him will I speak to ease my sorrow.

[*Enter* FELLOWSHIP.]

Well met, good Fellowship, and good morrow!   205
FELLOWSHIP.   Everyman, good morrow, by this day!

168 *wits*: senses.   169 *live*: life   171 *caitiff*: base person.   174 *amend me*:
improve.   175 *advisement*: reflection.   180 *hie*: hasten.   186 *keep*:
guard.   187 *writing*: reckoning.   189 *be geet*: been born.   190 *be*: been.   192 *all
wrought*: created everything.   194 *ago*: gone.   195 *wot*: know.   197 *and*:
if.   199 *affiance*: trust.   201 *Be*: been.

Sir, why lookest thou so piteously?
If anything be amiss, I pray thee me say,
That I may help to remedy.
EVERYMAN.   Yea, good Fellowship, yea;   210
    I am in great jeopardy.
FELLOWSHIP.   My true friend, show to me your mind.
    I will not forsake thee to my life's end
    In the way of good company.
EVERYMAN.   That was well spoken and lovingly.   215
FELLOWSHIP.   Sir, I must needs know your heaviness;°
    I have pity to see you in any distress.
    If any have you wronged, ye shall revenged be,
    Though I on the ground be slain for thee,
    Though that I know before that I should die.   220
EVERYMAN.   Verily, Fellowship, gramercy.°
FELLOWSHIP.   Tush! by thy thanks I set not a straw.
    Show me your grief and say no more.
EVERYMAN.   If I my heart should to you break,°
    And then you to turn your mind from me,   225
    And would not me comfort when ye hear me speak,
    Then should I ten times sorrier be.
FELLOWSHIP.   Sir, I say as I will do, indeed.
EVERYMAN.   Then be you a good friend at need;
    I have found you true herebefore.   230
FELLOWSHIP.   And so ye shall evermore;
    For, in faith, and° thou go to hell,
    I will not forsake thee by the way.
EVERYMAN.   Ye speak like a good friend. I believe you well.
    I shall deserve° it, and° I may.   235
FELLOWSHIP.   I speak of no deserving, by this day!
    For he that will say, and nothing do,
    Is not worthy with good company to go.
    Therefore show me the grief of your mind,
    As to your friend most loving and kind.   240
EVERYMAN.   I shall show you how it is:
    Commanded I am to go a journey,
    A long way, hard and dangerous,
    And give a strait count,° without delay,
    Before the high judge Adonai.°   245
    Wherefore I pray you bear me company,
    As ye have promised, in this journey.
FELLOWSHIP.   This is matter° indeed! Promise is duty;
    But, and° I should take such a voyage on me,
    I know it well, it should be to my pain.   250
    Also it maketh me afeared, certain.

---

216 *heaviness*: sorrow.   221 *gramercy*: many thanks.   224 *break*: open.   232 *and*:
if.   235 *deserve*: repay.   *and*: if.   244 *strait count*: strict account.   245 *Adonai*:
God.   248 *matter*: i.e., serious.   249 *and*: if.

But let us take counsel here, as well as we can
For your words would fear° a strong man.
EVERYMAN.   Why, ye said if I had need,
Ye would me never forsake, quick° nor dead,   255
Though it were to hell, truly.
FELLOWSHIP.   So I said, certainly,
But such pleasures be set aside, the sooth° to say.
And also, if we took such a journey,
When should we again come?°   260
EVERYMAN.   Nay, never again, till the day of doom.°
FELLOWSHIP.   In faith, then will not I come there!
Who hath you these tidings brought?
EVERYMAN.   Indeed, Death was with me here.
FELLOWSHIP.   Now by God that all hath bought,°   265
If Death were the messenger,
For no man that is living today
I will not go that loath° journey—
Not for the father that begat me!
EVERYMAN.   Ye promised otherwise, pardie.°   270
FELLOWSHIP.   I wot° well I said so, truly.
And yet, if thou wilt eat and drink and make good cheer,
Or haunt to women the lusty company,
I would not forsake you while the day is clear,
Trust me verily.   275
EVERYMAN.   Yea, thereto ye would be ready
To go to mirth, solace,° and play;
Your mind to folly will sooner apply°
Than to bear me company in my long journey.
FELLOWSHIP.   Now in good faith, I will not that way.   280
But, and° thou will murder or any man kill,
In that I will help thee with a good will.
EVERYMAN.   O that is simple° advice, indeed!
Gentle fellow, help me in my necessity!
We have loved long, and now I need;   285
And now, gentle Fellowship, remember me.
FELLOWSHIP.   Whether ye have loved me or no,
By Saint John, I will not with thee go!
EVERYMAN.   Yet I pray thee take the labor and do so much for me,
To bring me forward,° for saint° charity,   290
And comfort me till I come without the town.
FELLOWSHIP.   Nay, and° thou would give me a new gown,
I will not a foot with thee go.
But, and° thou had tarried, I would not have left thee so.

253 *fear*: frighten.   255 *quick*: alive.   258 *sooth*: truth.   260 *again come*:
return.   261 *doom*: judgment.   265 *bought*: redeemed.   268 *loath*: loathsome.
270 *pardie*: by God.   271 *wot*: know.   277 *solace*: comfort.   278 *apply*:
attend.   281 *and*: if.   283 *simple*: foolish.   290 *bring me forward*: escort me.   *saint*:
holy.   292 *and*: even if.   294 *and*: if.

And as now God speed thee in thy journey,   295
For from thee I will depart as fast as I may.
EVERYMAN.   Whither away, Fellowship? Will thou forsake me?
FELLOWSHIP.   Yea, by my fay!° To God I betake° thee.
EVERYMAN.   Farewell, good Fellowship; for thee my heart is sore.
Adieu forever! I shall see thee no more.   300
FELLOWSHIP.   In faith, Everyman, farewell now at the ending;
For you I will remember that parting is mourning.

[*Exit* FELLOWSHIP.]

EVERYMAN.   Alack, shall we thus depart° indeed—
Ah, Lady,° help!—without any more comfort?
Lo, Fellowship forsaketh me in my most need.   305
For help in this world whither shall I resort?
Fellowship herebefore with me would merry make,
And now little sorrow for me doth he take.
It is said, "In prosperity men friends may find,
Which in adversity be full unkind."   310
Now whither for succor shall I flee,
Since that Fellowship hath forsaken me?
To my kinsmen I will, truly,
Praying them to help me in my necessity.
I believe that they will do so,   315
For kind° will creep where it may not go.
I will go say,° for yonder I see them.
Where be ye now my friends and kinsmen.

[*Enter* KINDRED *and* COUSIN.]

KINDRED.   Here be we now at your commandment.
Cousin,° I pray you show us your intent   320
In any wise, and not spare.
COUSIN.   Yea, Everyman, and to us declare
If ye be disposed to go anywhither.°
For weet° you well, we will live and die together.
KINDRED.   In wealth and woe we will with you hold,   325
For over his kin a man may be bold.°
EVERYMAN.   Gramercy,° my friends and kinsmen kind.
Now shall I show you the grief of my mind:
I was commanded by a messenger
That is a high king's chief officer.   330
He bade me go a pilgrimage, to my pain,
And I know well I shall never come again.
Also I must give a reckoning strait,°

298 *fay*: faith.   *betake*: commend.   303 *depart*: part.   304 *Lady*: i.e.,
Mary.   316 *kind*: relatives.   317 *say*: assay, try.   320 *cousin*: i.e.,
Everyman.   323 *anywhither*: anywhere.   324 *weet*: know.   326 *be bold*: make
demands.   327 *Gramercy*: Many thanks.   333 *strait*: strict.

For I have a great enemy° that hath me in wait,
Which° intendeth me for to hinder.   335
KINDRED.   What account is that which ye must render?
That would I know.
EVERYMAN.   Of all my works I must show
How I have lived and my days spent;
Also of ill deeds that I have used°   340
In my time since life was me lent,
And of all virtues that I have refused.
Therefore I pray you go thither with me
To help me make mine account, for saint° charity.
COUSIN.   What, to go thither? Is that the matter?   345
Nay, Everyman, I had liefer° fast bread and water
All this five year and more.
EVERYMAN.   Alas, that ever I was bore!°
For now shall I never be merry
If that you forsake me.   350
KINDRED.   Ah, sir, what ye be a merry man!
Take good heart to you, and make no moan.
But one thing I warn you, by Saint Anne:
As for me, ye shall go alone.
EVERYMAN.   My Cousin, will you not with me go?   355
COUSIN.   No, by Our Lady! I have the cramp in my toe.
Trust not to me, for, so God me speed,°
I will deceive you in your most need.
KINDRED.   It availeth not us to tice.°
Ye shall have my maid with all my heart;   360
She loveth to go to feasts, there to be nice,°
And to dance, and abroad to start.°
I will give her leave to help you in that journey,
If that you and she may agree.
EVERYMAN.   Now show me the very effect° of your mind: 365
Will you go with me, or abide behind?
KINDRED.   Abide behind? Yea, that will I and° I may!
Therefore farewell till another day.

[*Exit* KINDRED.]

EVERYMAN.   How should I be merry or glad?
For fair promises men to me make,   370
But when I have most need they me forsake.
I am deceived; that maketh me sad.
COUSIN.   Cousin Everyman, farewell now,
For verily I will not go with you.

334 *enemy*: i.e., Satan.   335 *which*: who.   340 *used*: done.   344 *saint*:
holy.   346 *liefer*: rather.   348 *bore*: born.   357 *God me speed*: God help
me.   359 *tice*: entice.   361 *nice*: wanton.   362 *abroad to start*: to gad
about.   365 *effect*: state.   367 *and*: if.

Also of mine own an unready reckoning   375
I have to account; therefore I make tarrying.°
Now God keep thee, for now I go.

[Exit C<small>OUSIN</small>.]

E<small>VERYMAN</small>.   Ah, Jesus, is all come hereto?°
    Lo, fair words maketh fools fain;°
    They promise, and nothing will do, certain.   380
    My kinsmen promised me faithfully
    For to abide with me steadfastly,
    And now fast away do they flee.
    Even so Fellowship promised me.
    What friend were best me of to provide?   385
    I lose my time here longer to abide.
    Yet in my mind a thing there is:
    All my life I have loved riches.
    If that my Good° now help me might,
    He would make my heart full light.   390
    I will speak to him in this distress.
    Where art thou, my Goods and riches?

[G<small>OODS</small> *speaks from a corner.*]

G<small>OODS</small>.   Who calleth me? Everyman? What, hast thou haste?
    I lie here in corners, trussed and piled so high,
    And in chests I am locked so fast,   395
    Also sacked in bags. Thou mayst see with thine eye
    I cannot stir, in packs low where I lie.
    What would ye have? Lightly° me say.
E<small>VERYMAN</small>.   Come hither, Good, in all the haste thou may,
    For of counsel I must desire thee.   400

[G<small>OODS</small> *approaches.*]

G<small>OODS</small>.   Sir, and° ye in the world have sorrow or adversity,
    That can I help you to remedy shortly.
E<small>VERYMAN</small>.   It is another disease° that grieveth me;
    In this world it is not, I tell thee so.
    I am sent for another way to go,   405
    To give a strait count° general
    Before the highest Jupiter° of all.
    And all my life I have had joy and pleasure in thee,
    Therefore I pray thee go with me.
    For, peradventure,° thou mayst before God Almighty   410
    My reckoning help to clean and purify.
    For it is said ever among°

---

376 *make tarrying*: stay behind   378 *hereto*: to this.   379 *fain*: glad.   389 *Good*:
Goods, Wealth.   398 *Lightly*: Quickly.   401 *and*: if.   403 *disease*: trouble.
406 *strait count*: strict account.   407 *Jupiter*: i.e., God.   410 *peradventure*: perhaps.
412 *ever among*: sometimes.

That money maketh all right that is wrong.

GOODS. Nay, Everyman, I sing another song!
    I follow no man in such voyages;   415
    For, and° I went with thee,
    Thou shouldest fare much the worse for me.
    For because on me thou did set thy mind,
    Thy reckoning I have made blotted and blind,°
    That thine account thou cannot make truly—   420
    And that hast thou for the love of me!

EVERYMAN. That would grieve me full sore,
    When I should come to that fearful answer.
    Up, let us go thither together.

GOODS. Nay, not so! I am too brittle; I may not endure.   425
    I will follow no man one foot, be ye sure.

EVERYMAN. Alas, I have thee loved and had great pleasure
    All my life's days on good and treasure.

GOODS. That is to thy damnation, without leasing,°
    For my love is contrary to the love everlasting.   430
    But if thou had me loved moderately during,°
    As to the poor to give part of me,
    Then shouldest thou not in this dolor° be,
    Nor in this great sorrow and care.

EVERYMAN. Lo, now was I deceived ere I was ware,°   435
    And all I may wite° misspending of time!

GOODS. What, weenest° thou that I am thine?

EVERYMAN. I had wend° so.

GOODS. Nay, Everyman, I say no.
    As for a while I was lent thee;   440
    A season thou hast had me in prosperity.
    My condition° is man's soul to kill;
    If I save one, a thousand I do spill.°
    Weenest thou that I will follow thee?
    Nay, not from this world, verily.   445

EVERYMAN. I had wend° otherwise.

GOODS. Therefore to thy soul Good is a thief;
    For when thou art dead, this is my guise°:
    Another to deceive in the same wise
    As I have done thee, and all to his soul's repreef.°   450

EVERYMAN. O false Good, cursed may thou be,
    Thou traitor to God, that hast deceived me
    And caught me in thy snare!

GOODS. Marry,° thou brought thyself in care,°
    Whereof I am glad;   455

---

416 *and*: if.   419 *blotted and blind*: flawed and obscure.   429 *leasing*: lie, i.e.,
truly.   431 *during*: i.e., during your life.   433 *dolor*: sadness.   435 *ware*:
aware.   436 *wite*: blame on.   437 *weenest*: suppose.   438 *wend*: thought.
442 *condition*: nature.   443 *spill*: destroy.   446 *wend*: thought.
448 *guise*: manner.   450 *repreef*: shame.   454 *Marry*: By Mary.   *care*: sorrow.

I must needs laugh, I cannot be sad.
EVERYMAN.   Ah, Good, thou hast had long my heartly° love!
   I gave thee that which should be the Lord's above.
   But wilt thou not go with me indeed?
   I pray thee truth to say.°   460
GOODS.   No, so God me speed!
   Therefore farewell and have good day.

                                                [*Exit* GOODS.]

EVERYMAN.   Oh, to whom shall I make my moan
   For to go with me in that heavy journey?
   First Fellowship said he would with me gone.°   465
   His words were very pleasant and gay,
   But afterward he left me alone.
   Then spake I to my kinsmen, all in despair,
   And also they gave me words fair—
   They lacked no fair speaking,   470
   But all forsook° me in the ending.
   Then went I to my Goods that I loved best,
   In hope to have comfort, but there had I least,
   For my Goods sharply did me tell
   That he bringeth many into hell.   475
   Then of myself I was ashamed,
   And so I am worthy to be blamed.
   Thus may I well myself hate.
   Of whom shall I now counsel take?
   I think that I shall never speed   480
   Till that I go to my Good Deed.
   But, alas, she is so weak
   That she can neither go° nor speak.
   Yet will I venture° on her now.
   My Good Deeds, where be you?   485

[GOOD DEEDS *speaks from the ground*.]

GOOD DEEDS.   Here I lie, cold in the ground.
   Thy sins hath me sore bound
   That I cannot stear.°
EVERYMAN.   O Good Deeds, I stand in fear!
   I must you pray of counsel,   490
   For help now should come right well.°
GOOD DEEDS.   Everyman, I have understanding
   That ye be summoned, account to make,
   Before Messiah of Jerusalem King;
   And you do by me,° that journey with you will I take.   495

---

457 *heartly*: heartfelt.   460 *truth to say*: tell the truth.   465 *gone*: go.   471 *forsook*:
abandoned.   483 *go*: walk.   484 *venture*: attempt.   488 *stear*: stir.   491 *come right*
well: be very welcome.   495 *And you do by me*: if you follow my advice.

EVERYMAN.   Therefore, I come to you my moan to make.
  I pray you that ye will go with me.
GOOD DEEDS.   I would full fain,° but I cannot stand, verily.
EVERYMAN.   Why, is there anything on you fall?°
GOOD DEEDS.   Yea, sir, I may thank you of° all!   500
  If ye had perfectly cheered° me,
  Your book of count full ready had be.°

[*GOOD DEEDS shows him the Book of Account.*]

  Look, the books of your works and deeds eke,°
  Behold how they lie under the feet,
  To your soul's heaviness.°   505
EVERYMAN.   Our Lord Jesus help me!
  For one letter here I cannot see.
GOOD DEEDS.   There is a blind° reckoning in time of distress!
EVERYMAN.   Good Deeds, I pray you help me in this need,
  Or else I am forever damned indeed!   510
  Therefore help me to make reckoning
  Before the Redeemer of all thing,
  That King is, and was, and ever shall.°
GOOD DEEDS.   Everyman, I am sorry of° your fall,
  And fain° would help you and° I were able.   515
EVERYMAN.   Good Deeds, your counsel I pray you give me.
GOOD DEEDS.   That shall I do, verily.
  Though that on my feet I may not go,
  I have a sister that shall with you also,
  Called Knowledge,° which shall with you abide   520
  To help you to make that dreadful reckoning.

[*Enter KNOWLEDGE.*]

KNOWLEDGE.   Everyman, I will go with thee, and be thy guide,
  In thy most need to go by thy side.
EVERYMAN.   In good condition I am now in everything,
  And am wholly content with this good thing,   525
  Thanked be God my Creator.
GOOD DEEDS.   And when she hath brought you there
  Where thou shalt heal thee of thy smart,°
  Then go you with your reckoning and your Good Deeds together
  For to make you joyful at heart   530
  Before the blessed Trinity.
EVERYMAN.   My Good Deeds, gramercy!°
  I am well content, certainly,
  With your words sweet.

498 *fain*: gladly.   499 *fall*: befallen.   500 *of*: for.   501 *cheered*: nurtured.
502 *be*: been.   503 *eke*: also.   505 *heaviness*: sorrow.   508 *blind*: obscure.
513 *shall*: shall be.   514 *of*: for.   515 *fain*: gladly.   *and*: if.   520 *Knowledge*: i.e.,
of sins.   528 *smart*: pain.   532 *gramercy*: many thanks.

KNOWLEDGE.   Now go we together lovingly   535
    To Confession, that cleansing river.
EVERYMAN.   For joy I weep; I would we were there!
    But, I pray you, give me cognition,°
    Where dwelleth that holy man, Confession?
KNOWLEDGE.   In the House of Salvation.°   540
    We shall find him in that place
    That shall us comfort, by God's grace.

[*KNOWLEDGE leads EVERYMAN to CONFESSION.*]

    Lo, this is Confession. Kneel down and ask mercy,
    For he is in good conceit° with God Almighty.
EVERYMAN.   [*Kneeling*] O glorious fountain that all uncleanness doth clarify,°   545
    Wash from me the spots of vice unclean,
    That on me no sin may be seen.
    I come with Knowledge for my redemption,
    Redeemed with heart and full contrition;
    For I am commanded a pilgrimage to take,   550
    And great accounts before God to make.
    Now I pray you, Shrift,° mother of Salvation,
    Help my Good Deeds for my piteous exclamation!
CONFESSION.   I know your sorrow well, Everyman.
    Because with Knowledge ye come to me,   555
    I will you comfort as well as I can.
    And a precious jewel I will give thee
    Called Penance, voider° of adversity.
    Therewith shall your body chastised be
    With abstinence and perseverance in God's service.   560

[*Shows EVERYMAN a knotted scourge or whip.*]

    Here shall you receive that scourge of me,
    Which is penance strong that ye must endure,
    To remember thy Saviour was scourged° for thee
    With sharp scourges, and suffered it patiently.
    So must thou ere thou scape° that painful pilgrimage.   565
    Knowledge, keep him in this voyage,
    And by that time Good Deeds will be with thee.
    But in any wise be secure° of mercy,
    For your time draweth fast, and ye will saved be.
    Ask God mercy, and he will grant, truly.   570
    When with the scourge of penance man doth him° bind,
    The oil of forgiveness then shall he find.
EVERYMAN.   Thanked be God for his gracious work,

---

538 *cognition*: knowledge.   540 *House of Salvation*: i.e., in church.   544 *good conceit*: high
esteem.   545 *clarify*: i.e., purify.   552 *Shrift*: Confession.   558 *voider*:
expeller.   563 *scourged*: whipped.   565 *scape*: escape.   568 *secure*: sure.   571 *him*:
himself.

For now I will my penance begin.
This hath rejoiced and lighted° my heart,   575
Though the knots° be painful and hard within.

KNOWLEDGE. Everyman, look your penance that ye fulfill,
    What pain that ever it to you be;
    And Knowledge shall give you counsel at will°
    How your account ye shall make clearly.   580

EVERYMAN. O eternal God, O heavenly figure,
    O way of righteousness, O goodly vision,
    Which descended down in a virgin pure
    Because he would every man redeem,
    Which Adam forfeited by his disobedience: 585
    O blessed Godhead, elect and high Divine,°
    Forgive my grievous offense!
    Here I cry thee mercy in this presence.
    O ghostly Treasure, O Ransomer and Redeemer,
    Of all the world Hope and Conduiter,°   590
    Mirror of joy, Foundator° of mercy,
    Which enlumineth° heaven and earth thereby,
    Hear my clamorous complaint, though it late be.
    Receive my prayers, of thy benignity!
    Though I be a sinner most abominable,   595
    Yet let my name be written in Moses' table.°
    O Mary, pray to the Maker of all thing
    Me for to help at my ending,
    And save me from the power of my enemy,
    For Death assaileth me strongly.   600
    And Lady,° that I may by mean of thy prayer
    Of your Son's glory to be partner
    By the means of his passion I it crave.
    I beseech you help my soul to save!

[*EVERYMAN rises.*]

Knowledge, give me the scourge of penance: 605
My flesh therewith shall give acquittance.°
I will now begin, if God give me grace.

KNOWLEDGE. Everyman, God give you time and space!°
    Thus I bequeath you in the hands of our Saviour.
    Now may you make your reckoning sure.   610

EVERYMAN. In the name of the Holy Trinity
    My body sore punished shall be.

[*EVERYMAN scourges himself.*]

575 *lighted*: lightened.   576 *knots*: i.e., of the scourge.   579 *at will*:
readily.   586 *Divine*: Divinity.   590 *Conduiter*: Conductor, Guide.   591 *Foundator*:
Founder.   592 *enlumineth*: illuminates.   596 *Moses' table*: i.e., as penitent.   601 *Lady*:
i.e., Mary.   606 *acquittance*: satisfaction.   608 *space*: opportunity.

Take this, body, for the sin of the flesh!
Also thou delightest to go gay and fresh,
And in the way of damnation thou did me bring;   615
Therefore suffer now strokes of punishing.
Now of penance I will wade the water clear,
To save me from purgatory, that sharp fire.

[*Good Deeds rises from the ground.*]

GOOD DEEDS.   I thank God, now I can walk and go,
And am delivered of my sickness and woe!   620
Therefore with Everyman I will go, and not spare:
His good works I will help him to declare.
KNOWLEDGE.   Now, Everyman, be merry and glad.
Your Good Deeds cometh now; ye may not be sad.
Now is your Good Deeds whole and sound,   625
Going° upright upon the ground.
EVERYMAN.   My heart is light, and shall be evermore.
Now will I smite° faster than I did before.
GOOD DEEDS.   Everyman, pilgrim, my special friend,
Blessed be thou without end!   630
For thee is preparate° the eternal glory.
Ye have me made whole and sound;
Therefore I will bide by thee in every stound.°
EVERYMAN.   Welcome, my Good Deeds! Now I hear thy voice,
I weep for very sweetness of love.   635
KNOWLEDGE.   Be no more sad, but ever rejoice.
God seeth thy living in his throne above.
Put on this garment to thy behove°
Which is wet with your tears,
Or else before God you may it miss   640
When ye to your journey's end come shall.
EVERYMAN.   Gentle Knowledge, what do ye it call?
KNOWLEDGE.   It is a garment of sorrow.
From pain it will you borrow.°
Contrition it is,   645
That getteth forgiveness;
It pleaseth God passing° well.
GOOD DEEDS.   Everyman, will you wear it for your heal?°
EVERYMAN.   Now blessed be Jesu, Mary's son,
For now have I on true contrition.   650
And let us go now, without tarrying.
Good Deeds, have we clear our reckoning?
GOOD DEEDS.   Yea, indeed, I have it here.
EVERYMAN.   Then I trust we need not fear.

626 *Going*: Walking.   628 *smite*: i.e., whip myself.   631 *preparate*:
prepared.   633 *stound*: trial.   638 *behove*: benefit.   644 *borrow*: save, rescue.
647 *passing*: exceedingly.   648 *heal*: spiritual health.

Now friends, let us not part in twain.   65[

KNOWLEDGE.   Nay, Everyman, that will we not, certain.

GOOD DEEDS.   Yet must thou lead with thee
Three persons of great might.

EVERYMAN.   Who should they be?

GOOD DEEDS.   Discretion and Strength they hight,°   66[
And thy Beauty may not abide behind.

KNOWLEDGE.   Also ye must call to mind
Your Five-Wits° as for your counselors.

GOOD DEEDS.   You must have them ready at all hours.

EVERYMAN.   How shall I get them hither?   66[

KNOWLEDGE.   You must call them all together,
And they will hear you incontinent.°

EVERYMAN.   My friends, come hither and be present,
Discretion, Strength, my Five-Wits, and Beauty!

[*Enter* DISCRETION, STRENGTH, FIVE-WITS, *and* BEAUTY.]

BEAUTY.   Here at your will we be all ready.   67[
What would ye that we should do?

GOOD DEEDS.   That ye would with Everyman go
And help him in his pilgrimage.
Advise you:° will ye with him or not in that voyage?

STRENGTH.   We will bring him all thither,   67[
To his help and comfort, ye may believe me.

DISCRETION.   So will we go with him all together.

EVERYMAN.   Almighty God, loved° might thou be!
I give thee laud° that I have hither brought
Strength, Discretion, Beauty, and Five-Wits. Lack I nought.   68[
And my Good Deeds, with Knowledge clear,
All be in my company at my will here.
I desire no more to my business.

STRENGTH.   And I Strength will by you stand in distress,
Though thou would in battle fight on the ground.   68[

FIVE-WITS.   And though it were through the world round,°
We will not depart for sweet nor sour.°

BEAUTY.   No more will I, until death's hour,
Whatsoever thereof befall.

DISCRETION.   Everyman, advise you° first of all;   69[
Go with a good advisement° and deliberation.
We all give you virtuous monition°
That all shall be well.

EVERYMAN.   My friends, hearken what I will tell—
I pray God reward you in his heavenly sphere.   69[

660 *hight:* are called.   663 *Five-Wits:* senses.   667 *incontinent:*
immediately.   674 *Advise you:* Think.   678 *loved:* praised.   679 *laud:* praise.
686 *through the world round:* i.e., anywhere.   687 *for sweet nor sour:* i.e., in good or
evil.   690 *advise you:* consider.   691 *advisement:* reflection.   692 *virtuous monition:*
good assurance.

Now hearken all that be here,
For I will make my testament,
Here before you all present:
In alms half my good I will give with my hands twain,°
In the way of charity, with good intent;   700
And the other half, still° shall remain,
In queath° to be returned there it ought to be.
This I do in despite of the fiend of hell,
To go quit out of his peril°
Ever after and this day.   705

KNOWLEDGE.   Everyman, hearken what I say:
Go to Priesthood, I you advise,
And receive of him, in any wise,°
The holy sacrament and ointment° together.
Then shortly see ye turn again hither;   710
We will all abide° you here.

FIVE-WITS.   Yea, Everyman, hie you° that ye ready were.
There is no emperor, king, duke, nor baron
That of God hath commission°
As hath the least priest in the world being;   715
For of the blessed sacraments pure and benign
He beareth the keys, and thereof hath the cure°
For man's redemption—it is ever sure—
Which God for our souls' medicine
Gave us out of his heart with great pain.   720
Here in this transitory life, for thee and me,
The blessed sacraments seven there be:
Baptism, confirmation, with priesthood° good,
And the sacrament of God's precious flesh and blood,°
Marriage, the holy extreme unction, and penance.   725
These seven be good to have in remembrance,
Gracious sacraments of high divinity.

EVERYMAN.   Fain° would I receive that holy body,
And meekly to my ghostly° father I will go.

FIVE-WITS.   Everyman, that is the best that ye can do.   730
God will you to salvation bring.
For priesthood exceedeth all other thing.
To us Holy Scripture they do teach,
And converteth man from sin, heaven to reach.
God hath to them more power given   735
Than to any angel that is in heaven.
With five words° he may consecrate

699 *twain*: two.   701 *still*: which still.   702 *queath*: bequest.   704 *To go quit out of his peril*: i.e., to escape his threat.   708 *in any wise*: i.e., without fail.   709 *ointment*: extreme unction.   711 *abide*: wait for.   712 *hie you*: hurry.   714 *commission*: authority.   717 *cure*: care.   723 *priesthood*: ordination.   724 *sacrament . . . blood*: i.e., communion.   728 *Fain*: Gladly.   729 *ghostly*: spiritual.   737 *five words*: i.e., eat, this is my body.

God's body in flesh and blood to make,
And handleth his Maker between his hands.
The priest bindeth and unbindeth all bands,   740
Both in earth and in heaven.
Thou ministers° all the sacraments seven;
Though we kiss thy feet, thou were worthy!
Thou° art surgeon that cureth sin deadly;
No remedy we find under God   745
But all only° Priesthood.
Everyman, God gave priests that dignity
And setteth them in his stead among us to be.
Thus be they above angels in degree.

[*EVERYMAN exits to receive the sacrament and extreme unction.*]

KNOWLEDGE. If priests be good, it is so, surely.   750
   But when Jesu hanged on the cross with great smart,°
   There he gave out of his blessed heart
   The same sacrament in great torment.
   He sold them not to us, that Lord omnipotent!
   Therefore Saint Peter the Apostle doth say   755
   That Jesu's curse hath all they
   Which God their Savior do buy or sell,°
   Or they for any money do take or tell.°
   Sinful priests giveth the sinners example bad:
   Their children sitteth by other men's fires, I have heard;   760
   And some haunteth women's company
   With unclean life, as lusts of lechery.
   These be with sin made blind.
FIVE-WITS. I trust to God no such may we find.
   Therefore let us Priesthood honor,   765
   And follow their doctrine for our souls' succor.
   We be their sheep and they shepherds be,
   By whom we all be kept in surety.
   Peace, for yonder I see Everyman come,
   Which° hath made true satisfaction.   770
GOOD DEEDS. Methink it is he indeed.

[*Re-enter EVERYMAN from PRIESTHOOD.*]

EVERYMAN. Now Jesu be your alder speed!°
   I have received the sacrament for my redemption,
   And then mine extreme unction.
   Blessed be all they that counseled me to take it!   775
   And now, friends, let us go without longer respite.
   I thank God that ye have tarried so long.
   Now set each of you on this rood° your hand

---

742 *ministers*: administer.   744 *Thou*: i.e., Priesthood.   746 *only*: except for.
751 *smart*: pain.   757 *sell*: i.e., sell the sacraments.   758 *tell*: i.e., count out.
770 *Which*: who.   772 *be your alder speed*: help you all.   778 *rood*: cross.

And shortly follow me:
I go before there° I would be. God be our guide!   780
STRENGTH. Everyman, we will not from you go
 Till ye have done this voyage long.
DISCRETION. I, Discretion, will bide by you also.
KNOWLEDGE. And though this pilgrimage be never so strong,°
 I will never part you fro.°   785
STRENGTH. Everyman, I will be as sure° by thee
 As ever I did by Judas Maccabee.

[*All advance to* EVERYMAN'S *grave.*]

EVERYMAN. Alas, I am so faint I may not stand!
 My limbs under me do fold!
 Friends, let us not turn again to this land,   790
 Not for all the world's gold.
 For into this cave° must I creep
 And turn to earth, and there to sleep.
BEAUTY. What, into this grave? alas!
EVERYMAN. Yea, there shall ye consume, more and lass.°   795
BEAUTY. And what, should I smother here?
EVERYMAN. Yea, by my faith, and never more appear.
 In this world live no more we shall,
 But in heaven before the highest Lord of all.
BEAUTY. I cross out° all this! Adieu, by Saint John!   800
 I take my tape° in my lap and am gone.
EVERYMAN. What, Beauty, whither will ye?
BEAUTY. Peace, I am deaf! I look not behind me,
 Not and° thou wouldest give me all the gold in thy chest.

                                              [*Exit* BEAUTY.]

EVERYMAN. Alas, whereto may I trust?   805
 Beauty goeth fast away from me.
 She promised with me to live and die.
STRENGTH. Everyman, I will thee also forsake and deny.
 Thy game liketh° me not at all.
EVERYMAN. Why then, ye will forsake me all?   810
 Sweet Strength, tarry a little space.
STRENGTH. Nay, sir, by the rood° of grace,
 I will hie° me from thee fast,
 Though thou weep till thy heart tobrast.°
EVERYMAN. Ye would ever bide by me, ye said.   815
STRENGTH. Yea, I have you far enough conveyed!°
 Ye be old enough, I understand,

780 *there*: where.   784 *strong*: difficult.   785 *fro*: from.   786 *sure*: steadfast.
792 *cave*: i.e., grave.   795 *ye . . . lass*: i.e., everyone decay.   800 *cross out*: cancel.
801 *tape*: flax.   804 *and*: if.   809 *liketh*: pleases.   812 *rood*: cross.   813 *hie*:
hurry.   814 *tobrast*: burst.   816 *conveyed*: escorted.

Your pilgrimage to take on hand.
I repent me that I hither came.

EVERYMAN.   Strength, you to displease I am to blame,   820
Yet promise is debt, this ye well wot.°

STRENGTH.   In faith, I care not.
Thou art but a fool to complain.
You spend your speech and waste your brain.
Go, thrust thee into the ground!   825

[Exit STRENGTH.]

EVERYMAN.   I had wend° surer I should you have found.
He that trusteth in his Strength
She him deceiveth at the length.°
Both Strength and Beauty forsaketh me,
Yet they promised me fair and lovingly.   830

DISCRETION.   Everyman, I will after Strength be gone;
As for me, I will leave you alone.

EVERYMAN.   Why Discretion, will ye forsake me?

DISCRETION.   Yea, in faith, I will go from thee.
For when Strength goeth before,   835
I follow after evermore.

EVERYMAN.   Yet I pray thee, for the love of the Trinity,
Look in my grave once piteously.

DISCRETION.   Nay, so nigh° will I not come.
Farewell everyone!   840

[Exit DISCRETION.]

EVERYMAN.   O, all thing faileth save God alone—
Beauty, Strength, and Discretion;
For when Death bloweth his blast
They all run from me full fast.

FIVE-WITS.   Everyman, my leave now of thee I take.   845
I will follow the other, for here I thee forsake.

EVERYMAN.   Alas, then may I wail and weep,
For I took you for my best friend.

FIVE-WITS.   I will no longer thee keep.°
Now farewell, and there an end.   850

[Exit FIVE-WITS.]

EVERYMAN.   O Jesu, help! All hath forsaken me!

GOOD DEEDS.   Nay, Everyman, I will bide with thee.
I will not forsake thee indeed;
Thou shalt find me a good friend at need.

EVERYMAN.   Gramercy, Good Deeds! Now may I true friends see.   855

821 *wot*: know.   826 *wend*: thought.   828 *at the length*: at last.   839 *nigh*: near.
849 *keep*: guard.

They have forsaken me, every one.
I loved them better than my Good Deeds alone.
Knowledge, will ye forsake me also?
KNOWLEDGE.   Yea, Everyman, when ye to Death shall go,
   But not yet, for no manner of danger.   860
EVERYMAN.   Gramercy, Knowledge, with all my heart!
KNOWLEDGE.   Nay, yet will I not from hence depart
   Till I see where ye shall be come.°
EVERYMAN.   Methink, alas, that I must be gone
   To make my reckoning and my debts pay,   865
   For I see my time is nigh spent away.
   Take example, all ye that this do hear or see,
   How they that I loved best do forsake me
   Except my Good Deeds, that bideth truly.
GOOD DEEDS.   All earthly things is° but vanity.   870
   Beauty, Strength, and Discretion do man forsake,
   Foolish friends and kinsmen that fair spake—
   all fleeth save Good Deeds, and that am I.
EVERYMAN.   Have mercy on me, God most mighty,
   And stand by me, thou mother and maid, holy Mary!   875
GOOD DEEDS.   Fear not; I will speak for thee.
EVERYMAN.   Here I cry God mercy!
GOOD DEEDS.   Short° our end, and minish° our pain.
   Let us go and never come again.
EVERYMAN.   Into thy hands, Lord, my soul I commend.   880
   Receive it, Lord, that it be not lost.
   As thou me boughtest,° so me defend,
   And save me from the fiend's boast,
   That I may appear with that blessed host
   That shall be saved at the day of doom.   885
   In manus tuas,° of mights most,
   Forever *commendo spiritum meum*!°

[*EVERYMAN and GOOD DEEDS descend into the grave.*]

KNOWLEDGE.   Now hath he suffered that° we all shall endure.
   The Good Deeds shall make all sure.
   Now hath he made ending.   890
   Methinketh that I hear angels sing
   And make great joy and melody
   Where Everyman's soul received shall be.
ANGEL.   [*within*] Come, excellent elect spouse° to Jesu!
   Here above thou shalt go,   895
   Because of thy singular virtue.

---

863 *be come*: end up.   870 *is*: are.   878 *Short*: Shorten.   *minish*: diminish.
882 *boughtest*: redeemed.   886 *In manus tuas*: Into your hands.   887 *commendo spiritum*
meum: I commend my spirit.   888 *that*: that which.   894 *elect spouse*: chosen bride.

Now the soul is taken the body fro,
Thy reckoning is crystal clear.
Now shalt thou into the heavenly sphere
Unto the which all ye shall come   900
That liveth well before the day of doom.

[*Enter* DOCTOR (*a theologian*) *as an epilogue*.]

DOCTOR.   This moral men may have in mind:
    Ye hearers, take it of worth,° old and young,
    And forsake Pride, for he deceiveth you in the end.
    And remember Beauty, Five-Wits, Strength, and Discretion,   905
    They all at the last do Everyman forsake,
    Save his Good Deeds there doth he take.
    But beware, for and° they be small,
    Before God he hath no help at all.
    None excuse may be there for Everyman.   910
    Alas, how° shall he do then?
    For after death amends may no man make,
    For then mercy and pity doth him forsake.
    If his reckoning be not clear when he doth come,
    God will say, "*Ite, maledicti, in ignem eternum!*"°   915
    And° he that hath his account whole and sound,
    High in heaven he shall be crowned.
    Unto which place God bring us all thither,
    That we may live body and soul together.
    Thereto help, the Trinity!   920
    Amen say ye, for saint° charity.

903 *take . . . worth*: prize it.   908 *and*: if.   911 *how*: what.   915 *Ite . . . eternum*:
"Depart, ye cursed, into everlasting fire."   916 *And*: But.   921 *saint*: holy.

QUESTIONS

1. What is the function of the Messenger who opens the play? What does he
    tell you about the play? How much of the plot does he reveal?
2. Why does God decide to summon Everyman for an accounting or judgment?
3. How does Everyman react when he first discovers that he must give an ac-
    counting of his life to God? What does he try to do to Death? What does
    his behavior tell you about him?
4. What is Death like? What are his chief characteristics? What does he teach
    Everyman about life and worldly goods?
5. What is Fellowship like? What is he willing to do with Everyman? How does
    he react to the idea of judgment? What does Everyman learn from this encoun-
    ter?

6. What do Kindred and Cousin promise Everyman before they know his problem? How do they act after they know what he must do?

7. What does Everyman think about his worldly wealth? What does Goods teach him about wealth? What is Goods like? Why does he find Everyman's situation funny?

8. Why is Good Deeds pressed to the ground? How is she freed?

9. What religious process must Everyman go through before he can make his reckoning?

10. At line 521, Everyman meets Knowledge, the sister of Good Deeds. What kind of knowledge does this character represent?

11. What do Discretion, Strength, Five-Wits, and Beauty have in common? What do they promise Everyman? Do they keep this promise? What is the moral lesson here?

12. Is Everyman saved or damned at the end of the play? How do you know?

TOPICS FOR WRITING AND FURTHER DISCUSSION

1. How consistent and effective are the symbolism and allegory in *Everyman*? How does the allegory work? What meaning does it convey?

2. Although the characters in *Everyman* are limited by their allegorical significance, the playwright gives many of them individual personality traits and quirks. What are some of these individualizing touches? How do they contribute to the impact of the play?

3. How does Everyman change in the play? What is he like at the beginning of the play? At the end? When does he begin to change? Why does he change?

4. Why might it be accurate to call this play "The Education of Everyman"?

5. Everyman speaks four soliloquies in the first half of the play (lines 184–204, 303–318, 378–392, and 463–485) and none in the second half. What do the four soliloquies have in common? Why are there none in the second half?

6. Summarize the plot of *Everyman*. How important is it compared with the other elements of drama? To what extent do we see exposition, complication, crisis, climax, and resolution in this play?

7. What repetitive pattern of action creates tension in the play? How is this pattern related to the play's meaning?

8. What are the conflicts in *Everyman*? Which one is central? How and when is it resolved?

9. What is the central theme of *Everyman*? How is it conveyed? How many different times is it conveyed?

10. What are the functions of the Messenger who begins the play and the learned Doctor who closes it? How are the two similar? How are their roles related to the plot of *Everyman*? To the meaning?

SUSAN GLASPELL, *Trifles*

Susan Glaspell, a playwright and fiction writer, grew up in Iowa and moved to the Northeast in her thirties. She helped found the Provincetown Players in Massachusetts in 1914 and wrote most of her plays for that company. Much of her work—both plays and short stories—is strongly feminist; it deals with the roles that women play (or are forced to play) in society and with the often skewed relationships between men and women. She wrote or co-authored over ten plays for the Provincetown Players, including *Women's Honor* (1918), *Bernice* (1919), *The Inheritors* (1921), and *The Verge* (1921). After 1922, however, she gave up the theater and turned almost exclusively to fiction. The one exception was *Alison's House* (1930), a play loosely based on the life and family of Emily Dickinson, for which Glaspell won a Pulitzer Prize.

Trifles (1916) is Glaspell's best-known play; she wrote it in ten days for the Provincetown Players, and it was produced by them in 1916, during the same season that they staged their first play by Eugene O'Neill. Glaspell later wrote that the play was inspired by a murder trial she covered while working as a reporter for a Des Moines newspaper. In the first production, Glaspell played the role of Mrs. Hale. A year later she rewrote the play as a short story entitled "A Jury of Her Peers"; this has also been very popular and widely anthologized.

Although *Trifles* concerns a murder investigation, the play is not a murder mystery; the audience and the characters know who did the killing almost as soon as the play begins. What we don't know is why the murder was committed; the action of the play is concerned with discovering a motive. In terms of theme, the play explores the reasons that such a murder might occur and the differing abilities of men and women to understand those reasons. The men and women in the play seek the motive for this murder in entirely different ways and arrive at radically different conclusions. The men—the County Attorney and the Sheriff—look for obvious signs of violent rage. The women—Mrs. Hale and Mrs. Peters—draw their conclusions on the evidence of "trifles" they find in the kitchen of the house. Finally, the women must decide what to do with this evidence and how to judge the killer. Their decisions embody, at least in part, the themes of the play in regard to women's roles in society and in regard to marriage. The play dramatizes with eloquence and impact the mistaken attitudes that men often have toward women and the prison that marriage can become.

SUSAN GLASPELL (1882–1948)

Trifles 1916

CHARACTERS

> George Henderson, *County Attorney*
> Henry Peters, *Sheriff*
> Lewis Hale, *A Neighboring Farmer*
> Mrs. Peters
> Mrs. Hale

SCENE: *The kitchen in the now abandoned farmhouse of JOHN WRIGHT, a gloomy kitchen, and left without having been put in order—unwashed pans under the sink, a loaf of bread outside the bread-box, a dish-towel on the table—other signs of incompleted work. At the rear the outer door opens and the SHERIFF comes in followed by the COUNTY ATTORNEY and HALE. The SHERIFF and HALE are men in middle life, the COUNTY ATTORNEY is a young man; all are much bundled up and go at once to the stove. They are followed by the two women—the SHERIFF'S wife first; she is a slight wiry woman, a thin nervous face. MRS. HALE is larger and would ordinarily be called more comfortable looking, but she is disturbed now and looks fearfully about as she enters. The women have come in slowly, and stand close together near the door.*

COUNTY ATTORNEY.   [*Rubbing his hands.*] This feels good. Come up to the fire, ladies.

MRS. PETERS.   [*After taking a step forward.*] I'm not—cold.

SHERIFF.   [*Unbuttoning his overcoat and stepping away from the stove as if to mark the beginning of official business.*] Now, Mr. Hale, before we move things about, you explain to Mr. Henderson just what you saw when you came here yesterday morning.

COUNTY ATTORNEY.   By the way, has anything been moved? Are things just as you left them yesterday?

SHERIFF.   [*Looking about.*] It's just the same. When it dropped below zero last night I thought I'd better send Frank out this morning to make a fire for us—no use getting pneumonia with a big case on, but I told him not to touch anything except the stove—and you know Frank.

COUNTY ATTORNEY.   Somebody should have been left here yesterday.

SHERIFF.   Oh—yesterday. When I had to send Frank to Morris Center for that man who went crazy—I want you to know I had my hands full yesterday. I knew you could get back from Omaha by today and as long as I went over everything here myself—

COUNTY ATTORNEY.   Well, Mr. Hale, tell just what happened when you came here yesterday morning.

HALE.   Harry and I had started to town with a load of potatoes. We came along the road from my place and as I got here I said, "I'm going to see if I can't get John Wright to go in with me on a party telephone." I spoke to Wright about it once before and he put me off, saying folks talked too much anyway, and all he asked was peace and quiet—I guess you know about how much he talked himself; but I thought maybe if I went to the house and talked about it before his wife, though I said to Harry that I didn't know as what his wife wanted made much difference to John—

COUNTY ATTORNEY.   Let's talk about that later, Mr. Hale. I do want to talk about that, but tell now just what happened when you got to the house.

HALE.   I didn't hear or see anything; I knocked at the door, and still it was all quiet inside. I knew they must be up, it was past eight o'clock. So I knocked again, and I thought I heard somebody say, "Come in." I wasn't sure, I'm not sure yet, but I opened the door—this door [*indicating the door by which the two women are still standing*] and there in that rocker—[*pointing to it*] sat Mrs. Wright.

[*They all look at the rocker.*]

COUNTY ATTORNEY.   What—was she doing?

HALE.   She was rockin' back and forth. She had her apron in her hand and was kind of—pleating it.

COUNTY ATTORNEY.   And how did she—look?

HALE.   Well, she looked queer.

COUNTY ATTORNEY.   How do you mean—queer?

HALE.   Well, as if she didn't know what she was going to do next. And kind of done up.

COUNTY ATTORNEY.   How did she seem to feel about your coming?

HALE.   Why, I don't think she minded—one way or other. She didn't pay much attention. I said, "How do, Mrs. Wright, it's cold, ain't it?" And she said, "Is it?"—and went on kind of pleating at her apron. Well, I was surprised; she didn't ask me to come up to the stove, or to set down, but just sat there, not even looking at me, so I said, "I want to see John." And then she—laughed. I guess you would call it a laugh. I thought of Harry and the team outside, so I said a little sharp: "Can't I see John?" "No," she says, kind o' dull like. "Ain't he home?" says I. "Yes," says she, "he's home." "Then why can't I see him?" I asked her, out of patience. " 'Cause he's dead," says she. "*Dead?*" says I. She just nodded her head, not getting a bit excited, but rockin' back and forth. "Why—where is he?" says I, not knowing what to say. She just pointed upstairs—like that [*himself pointing to the room above*]. I got up, with the idea of going up there. I walked from there to here—then I says, "Why, what did he die of?" "He died of a rope round his neck," says she, and just went on pleatin' at her apron. Well, I went out and called Harry. I thought I might—need help. We went upstairs and there he was lyin'—

COUNTY ATTORNEY.   I think I'd rather have you go into that upstairs, where you can point it all out. Just go on now with the rest of the story.

HALE.   Well, my first thought was to get that rope off. It looked . . . [*Stops, his face twitches*] . . . but Harry, he went up to him, and he said, "No, he's dead all right, and we'd better not touch anything." So we went back downstairs. She was still sitting that same way. "Has anybody been notified?" I asked. "No," says she, unconcerned. "Who did this, Mrs. Wright?" said Harry. He said it business-like—and she stopped pleatin' of her apron. "I don't know," she says. "You don't *know*?" says Harry. "No," says she. "Weren't you sleepin' in the bed with him?" says Harry. "Yes," says she, "but I was on the inside." "Somebody slipped a rope round his neck and strangled him and you didn't wake up?" says Harry. "I didn't wake up," she said after him. We must 'a looked as if we didn't see how that could be, for after a minute she said, "I sleep sound." Harry was going to ask her more questions but I said maybe we ought to let her tell her story first to the coroner, or the sheriff, so Harry went fast as he could to Rivers' place, where there's a telephone.

COUNTY ATTORNEY.   And what did Mrs. Wright do when she knew that you had gone for the coroner?

HALE.   She moved from that chair to this one over here [*pointing to a small chair in the corner*] and just sat there with her hands held together and looking down. I got a feeling that I ought to make some conversation, so I said I had come in to see if John wanted to put in a telephone, and at that she started to laugh, and then she stopped and looked at me—scared. [*The* COUNTY ATTORNEY, *who has had his notebook out, makes a note.*] I dunno, maybe it wasn't scared. I wouldn't like to say it was. Soon Harry got back, and then Dr. Lloyd came, and you, Mr. Peters, and so I guess that's all I know that you don't.

COUNTY ATTORNEY.   [*Looking around.*] I guess we'll go upstairs first—and then out to the barn and around there. [*To the* SHERIFF.] You're convinced that there was nothing important here—nothing that would point to any motive.

SHERIFF.   Nothing here but kitchen things.

[*The* COUNTY ATTORNEY, *after again looking around the kitchen, opens the door of a cupboard closet. He gets up on a chair and looks on a shelf. Pulls his hand away, sticky.*]

COUNTY ATTORNEY.   Here's a nice mess.

[*The women draw nearer.*]

MRS. PETERS.   [*To the other woman.*] Oh, her fruit; it did freeze. [*To the* LAWYER.] She worried about that when it turned so cold. She said the fire'd go out and her jars would break.

SHERIFF.   Well, can you beat the women! Held for murder and worryin' about her preserves.

COUNTY ATTORNEY.   I guess before we're through she may have something more serious than preserves to worry about.

HALE.   Well, women are used to worrying over trifles.

[*The two women move a little closer together.*]

COUNTY ATTORNEY.   [*With the gallantry of a young politician.*] And yet, for all their worries, what would we do without the ladies? [*The women do not unbend. He goes to the sink, takes a dipperful of water from the pail and pouring it into a basin, washes his hands. Starts to wipe them on the roller-towel, turns it for a cleaner place.*] Dirty towels! [*Kicks his foot against the pans under the sink.*] Not much of a housekeeper, would you say, ladies?

MRS. HALE.   [*Stiffly.*] There's a great deal of work to be done on a farm.

COUNTY ATTORNEY.   To be sure. And yet [*with a little bow to her*] I know there are some Dickson county farmhouses which do not have such roller towels.

[*He gives it a pull to expose its full length again.*]

MRS. HALE.   Those towels get dirty awful quick. Men's hands aren't always as clean as they might be.

COUNTY ATTORNEY. Ah, loyal to your sex, I see. But you and Mrs. Wright were neighbors. I suppose you were friends, too.

MRS. HALE. [*Shaking her head.*] I've not seen much of her of late years. I've not been in this house—it's more than a year.

COUNTY ATTORNEY. And why was that? You didn't like her?

MRS. HALE. I liked her all well enough. Farmers' wives have their hands full, Mr. Henderson. And then—

COUNTY ATTORNEY. Yes—?

MRS. HALE. [*Looking about.*] It never seemed a very cheerful place.

COUNTY ATTORNEY. No—it's not cheerful. I shouldn't say she had the home-making instinct.

MRS. HALE. Well, I don't know as Wright had, either.

COUNTY ATTORNEY. You mean that they didn't get on very well?

MRS. HALE. No, I don't mean anything. But I don't think a place'd be any cheerfuller for John Wright's being in it.

COUNTY ATTORNEY. I'd like to talk more of that a little later. I want to get the lay of things upstairs now.

[*He goes to the left, where three steps lead to a stair door.*]

SHERIFF. I suppose anything Mrs. Peters does'll be all right. She was to take in some clothes for her, you know, and a few little things. We left in such a hurry yesterday.

COUNTY ATTORNEY. Yes, but I would like to see what you take, Mrs. Peters, and keep an eye out for anything that might be of use to us.

MRS. PETERS. Yes, Mr. Henderson.

[*The women listen to the men's steps on the stairs, then look about the kitchen.*]

MRS. HALE. I'd hate to have men coming into my kitchen, snooping around and criticizing.

[*She arranges the pans under sink which the LAWYER had shoved out of place.*]

MRS. PETERS. Of course it's no more than their duty.

MRS. HALE. Duty's all right, but I guess that deputy sheriff that came out to make the fire might have got a little of this on. [*Gives the roller towel a pull.*] Wish I'd thought of that sooner. Seems mean to talk about her for not having things slicked up when she had to come away in such a hurry.

MRS. PETERS. [*Who has gone to a small table in the left rear corner of the room, and lifted one end of a towel that covers a pan.*] She had bread set.

[*Stands still.*]

MRS. HALE. [*Eyes fixed on a loaf of bread beside the breadbox, which is on a low shelf at the other side of the room. Moves slowly toward it.*] She was going to put this in there. [*Picks up loaf, then abruptly drops it. In a manner of returning to familiar things.*] It's a shame about her fruit. I wonder if it's all gone. [*Gets up on the chair and looks.*] I think there's some here that's all right, Mrs. Peters. Yes—here; [*Holding it toward the window*] this is cherries, too. [*Looking again.*] I declare I believe that's the only one. [*Gets down, bottle in her hand. Goes to the sink and wipes it off on the outside.*] She'll feel awful bad after all her hard work in the hot weather. I remember the afternoon I put up my cherries last summer.

[*She puts the bottle on the big kitchen table, center of the room. With a sigh, is about to sit down in the rocking-chair. Before she is seated realizes what chair it is; with a slow look at it, steps back. The chair which she has touched rocks back and forth.*]

MRS. PETERS. Well, I must get those things from the front room closet. [*She goes to the door at the right, but after looking into the other room, steps back.*] You coming with me, Mrs. Hale? You could help me carry them.

[*They go in the other room; reappear,* MRS. PETERS *carrying a dress and skirt,* MRS. HALE *following with a pair of shoes.*]

MRS. PETERS. My, it's cold in there.

[*She puts the clothes on the big table and hurries to the stove.*]

MRS. HALE. [*Examining the skirt.*] Wright was close. I think maybe that's why she kept so much to herself. She didn't even belong to the Ladies Aid. I suppose she felt she couldn't do her part, and then you don't enjoy things when you feel shabby. She used to wear pretty clothes and be lively, when she was Minnie Foster, one of the town girls singing in the choir. But that—oh, that was thirty years ago. This all you was to take in?

MRS. PETERS. She said she wanted an apron. Funny thing to want, for there isn't much to get you dirty in jail, goodness knows. But I suppose just to make her feel more natural. She said they was in the top drawer in this cupboard. Yes, here. And then her little shawl that always hung behind the door. [*Opens stair door and looks.*] Yes, here it is.

[*Quickly shuts door leading upstairs.*]

MRS. HALE. [*Abruptly moving toward her.*] Mrs. Peters?

MRS. PETERS. Yes, Mrs. Hale?

MRS. HALE. Do you think she did it?

MRS. PETERS. [*In a frightened voice.*] Oh, I don't know.

MRS. HALE. Well, I don't think she did. Asking for an apron and her little shawl. Worrying about her fruit.

MRS. PETERS. [*Starts to speak, glances up, where footsteps are heard in the room above. In a low voice.*] Mr. Peters says it looks bad for her. Mr. Henderson is awful sarcastic in a speech and he'll make fun of her sayin' she didn't wake up.

MRS. HALE. Well, I guess John Wright didn't wake when they was slipping that rope under his neck.

MRS. PETERS. No, it's strange. It must have been done awful crafty and still. They say it was such a—funny way to kill a man, rigging it all up like that.

MRS. HALE. That's just what Mr. Hale said. There was a gun in the house. He says that's what he can't understand.

MRS. PETERS. Mr. Henderson said coming out that what was needed for the case was a motive; something to show anger, or—sudden feeling.

MRS. HALE. [*Who is standing by the table.*] Well, I don't see any signs of anger around here. [*She puts her hand on the dish towel which lies on the table, stands looking down at table, one half of which is clean, the other half messy.*] It's wiped to here. [*Makes a move as if to finish work, then turns and looks at loaf of bread outside the breadbox. Drops towel. In that voice of coming back to familiar things.] Wonder how they are finding things upstairs. I hope she had it a little more red-up up there. You know, it seems kind of *sneaking*. Locking her up in town and then coming out here and trying to get her own house to turn against her!

MRS. PETERS.   But Mrs. Hale, the law is the law.

MRS. HALE.   I s'pose 'tis. [*Unbuttoning her coat.*] Better loosen up your things, Mrs. Peters. You won't feel them when you go out.

[*MRS. PETERS takes off her fur tippet, goes to hang it on hook at back of room, stands looking at the under part of the small corner table.*]

MRS. PETERS.   She was piecing a quilt.

[*She brings the large sewing basket and they look at the bright pieces.*]

MRS. HALE.   It's log cabin pattern. Pretty, isn't it? I wonder if she was goin' to quilt it or just knot it?

[*Footsteps have been heard coming down the stairs. The SHERIFF enters followed by HALE and the COUNTY ATTORNEY.*]

SHERIFF.   They wonder if she was going to quilt it or just knot it!

[*The men laugh, the women look abashed.*]

COUNTY ATTORNEY.   [*Rubbing his hands over the stove.*] Frank's fire didn't do much up there, did it? Well, let's go out to the barn and get that cleared up.

[*The men go outside.*]

MRS. HALE.   [*Resentfully.*] I don't know as there's anything so strange, our takin' up our time with little things while we're waiting for them to get the evidence. [*She sits down at the big table smoothing out a block with decision.*] I don't see as it's anything to laugh about.

MRS. PETERS.   [*Apologetically.*] Of course they've got awful important things on their minds.

[*Pulls up a chair and joins MRS. HALE at the table.*]

MRS. HALE.   [*Examining another block.*] Mrs. Peters, look at this one. Here, this is the one she was working on, and look at the sewing! All the rest of it has been so nice and even. And look at this! It's all over the place! Why, it looks as if she didn't know what she was about!

[*After she has said this they look at each other, then start to glance back at the door. After an instant MRS. HALE has pulled at a knot and ripped the sewing.*]

MRS. PETERS.   Oh, what are you doing, Mrs. Hale?

MRS. HALE.   [*Mildly.*] Just pulling out a stitch or two that's not sewed very good. [*Threading a needle.*] Bad sewing always made me fidgety.

MRS. PETERS.   [*Nervously.*] I don't think we ought to touch things.

MRS. HALE.   I'll just finish up this end. [*Suddenly stopping and leaning forward.*] Mrs. Peters?

MRS. PETERS. Yes, Mrs. Hale?

MRS. HALE. What do you suppose she was so nervous about?

MRS. PETERS. Oh—I don't know. I don't know as she was nervous. I sometimes sew awful queer when I'm just tired. [*MRS. HALE starts to say something, looks at MRS. PETERS, then goes on sewing.*] Well I must get these things wrapped up. They may be through sooner than we think. [*Putting apron and other things together.*] I wonder where I can find a piece of paper, and string.

MRS. HALE. In that cupboard, maybe.

MRS. PETERS. [*Looking in cupboard.*] Why, here's a bird-cage. [*Holds it up.*] Did she have a bird, Mrs. Hale?

MRS. HALE. Why, I don't know whether she did or not—I've not been here for so long. There was a man around last year selling canaries cheap, but I don't know as she took one; maybe she did. She used to sing real pretty herself.

MRS. PETERS. [*Glancing around.*] Seems funny to think of a bird here. But she must have had one, or why would she have a cage? I wonder what happened to it.

MRS. HALE. I s'pose maybe the cat got it.

MRS. PETERS. No, she didn't have a cat. She's got that feeling some people have about cats—being afraid of them. My cat got in her room and she was real upset and asked me to take it out.

MRS. HALE. My sister Bessie was like that. Queer, ain't it?

MRS. PETERS. [*Examining the cage.*] Why, look at this door. It's broke. One hinge is pulled apart.

MRS. HALE. [*Looking too.*] Looks as if someone must have been rough with it.

MRS. PETERS. Why, yes.

[*She brings the cage forward and puts it on the table.*]

MRS. HALE. I wish if they're going to find any evidence they'd be about it. I don't like this place.

MRS. PETERS. But I'm awful glad you came with me, Mrs. Hale. It would be lonesome for me sitting here alone.

MRS. HALE. It would, wouldn't it? [*Dropping her sewing.*] But I tell you what I do wish, Mrs. Peters. I wish I had come over sometimes when *she* was here. I—[*looking around the room*]—wish I had.

MRS. PETERS. But of course you were awful busy, Mrs. Hale—your house and your children.

MRS. HALE. I could've come. I stayed away because it weren't cheerful—and that's why I ought to have come. I—I've never liked this place. Maybe because it's down in a hollow and you don't see the road. I dunno what it is, but it's a lonesome place and always was. I wish I had come over to see Minnie Foster sometimes. I can see now—

[*Shakes her head.*]

MRS. PETERS. Well, you mustn't reproach yourself, Mrs. Hale. Somehow we just don't see how it is with other folks until—something comes up.

MRS. HALE. Not having children makes less work—but it makes a quiet house, and Wright out to work all day, and no company when he did come in. Did you know John Wright, Mrs. Peters?

MRS. PETERS.   Not to know him; I've seen him in town. They say he was a good man.

MRS. HALE.   Yes—good; he didn't drink, and kept his word as well as most, I guess, and paid his debts. But he was a hard man, Mrs. Peters. Just to pass the time of day with him—[*Shivers.*] Like a raw wind that gets to the bone. [*Pauses, her eye falling on the cage.*] I should think she would 'a wanted a bird. But what do you suppose went with it?

MRS. PETERS.   I don't know, unless it got sick and died.

[*She reaches over and swings the broken door, swings it again, both women watch it.*]

MRS. HALE.   You weren't raised round here, were you? [*MRS. PETERS shakes her head.*] You didn't know—her?

MRS. PETERS.   Not till they brought her yesterday.

MRS. HALE.   She—come to think of it, she was kind of like a bird herself— real sweet and pretty, but kind of timid and—fluttery. How—she—did—change. [*Silence; then as if struck by a happy thought and relieved to get back to everyday things.*] Tell you what, Mrs. Peters, why don't you take the quilt in with you? It might take up her mind.

MRS. PETERS.   Why, I think that's a real nice idea, Mrs. Hale. There couldn't possibly be any objection to it, could there? Now, just what would I take? I wonder if her patches are in here—and her things.

[*They look in the sewing basket.*]

MRS. HALE.   Here's some red. I expect this has got sewing things in it. [*Brings out a fancy box.*] What a pretty box. Looks like something somebody would give you. Maybe her scissors are in here. [*Opens box. Suddenly puts her hand to her nose.*] Why—[*MRS. PETERS bends nearer, then turns her face away.*] There's something wrapped up in this piece of silk.

MRS. PETERS.   Why, this isn't her scissors.

MRS. HALE.   [*Lifting the silk.*] Oh, Mrs. Peters—its—

[*MRS. PETERS bends closer.*]

MRS. PETERS.   It's the bird.

MRS. HALE.   [*Jumping up.*] But, Mrs. Peters—look at it! Its neck! Look at its neck! It's all—other side *to*.

MRS. PETERS.   Somebody—wrung—its—neck.

[*Their eyes meet. A look of growing comprehension, of horror. Steps are heard outside. MRS. HALE slips box under quilt pieces, and sinks into her chair. Enter SHERIFF and COUNTY ATTORNEY. MRS. PETERS rises.*]

COUNTY ATTORNEY   [*As one turning from serious things to little pleasantries.*] Well, ladies, have you decided whether she was going to quilt it or knot it?

MRS. PETERS.   We think she was going to—knot it.

COUNTY ATTORNEY.   Well, that's interesting, I'm sure. [*Seeing the bird-cage.*] Has the bird flown?

MRS. HALE.   [*Putting more quilt pieces over the box.*] We think the—cat got it.

COUNTY ATTORNEY.   [*Preoccupied.*] Is there a cat?

[*MRS. HALE glances in a quick covert way at MRS. PETERS.*]

MRS. PETERS. Well, not *now*. They're superstitious, you know. They leave.

COUNTY ATTORNEY. [*To SHERIFF PETERS, continuing an interrupted conversation.*] No sign at all of anyone having come from the outside. Their own rope. Now let's go up again and go over it piece by piece. [*They start upstairs.*] It would have to have been someone who knew just the—

[*MRS. PETERS sits down. The two women sit there not looking at one another, but as if peering into something and at the same time holding back. When they talk now it is in the manner of feeling their way over strange ground, as if afraid of what they are saying, but as if they cannot help saying it.*]

MRS. HALE. She liked the bird. She was going to bury it in that pretty box.

MRS. PETERS. [*In a whisper.*] When I was a girl—my kitten—there was a boy took a hatchet, and before my eyes—and before I could get there—[*Covers her face an instant.*] If they hadn't held me back I would have—[*Catches herself, looks upstairs where steps are heard, falters weakly*]—hurt him.

MRS. HALE. [*With a slow look around her.*] I wonder how it would seem never to have had any children around. [*Pause.*] No, Wright wouldn't like the bird—a thing that sang. She used to sing. He killed that, too.

MRS. PETERS. [*Moving uneasily.*] We don't know who killed the bird.

MRS. HALE. I knew John Wright.

MRS. PETERS. It was an awful thing was done in this house that night, Mrs. Hale. Killing a man while he slept, slipping a rope around his neck that choked the life out of him.

MRS. HALE. His neck. Choked the life out of him.

[*Her hand goes out and rests on the bird-cage.*]

MRS. PETERS. [*With rising voice.*] We don't know who killed him. We don't know.

MRS. HALE. [*Her own feeling not interrupted.*] If there'd been years and years of nothing, then a bird to sing to you, it would be awful—still, after the bird was still.

MRS. PETERS. [*Something within her speaking.*] I know what stillness is. When we homesteaded in Dakota, and my first baby died—after he was two years old, and me with no other then—

MRS. HALE. [*Moving.*] How soon do you suppose they'll be through, looking for the evidence?

MRS. PETERS. I know what stillness is. [*Pulling herself back.*] The law has got to punish crime, Mrs. Hale.

MRS. HALE. [*Not as if answering that.*] I wish you'd seen Minnie Foster when she wore a white dress with blue ribbons and stood up there in the choir and sang. [*A look around the room.*] Oh, I *wish* I'd come over here once in a while! That was a crime! That was a crime! Who's going to punish that?

MRS. PETERS. [*Looking upstairs.*] We mustn't—take on.

MRS. HALE. I might have known she needed help! I know how things can be—for women. I tell you, it's queer, Mrs. Peters. We live close together and we live far apart. We all go through the same things—it's all just a different kind of the same thing. [*Brushes her eyes, noticing the bottle of fruit, reaches out for it.*] If I was you I wouldn't tell her her fruit was gone. Tell her it *ain't*. Tell her it's all right. Take this in to prove it to her. She—she may never know whether it was broke or not.

MRS. PETERS.   [*Takes the bottle, looks about for something to wrap it in; takes petticoat from the clothes brought from the other room, very nervously begins winding this around the bottle. In a false voice.*] My, it's a good thing the men couldn't hear us. Wouldn't they just laugh! Getting all stirred up over a little thing like a—dead canary. As if that could have anything to do with—with—wouldn't they *laugh*!

[*The men are heard coming down stairs.*]

MRS. HALE.   [*Under her breath.*] Maybe they would—maybe they wouldn't.

COUNTY ATTORNEY.   No, Peters, it's all perfectly clear except a reason for doing it. But you know juries when it comes to women. If there was some definite thing. Something to show—something to make a story about—a thing that would connect up with this strange way of doing it—

[*The women's eyes meet for an instant. Enter HALE from outer door.*]

HALE.   Well, I've got the team around. Pretty cold out there.

COUNTY ATTORNEY.   I'm going to stay here a while by myself. [*To the* SHERIFF.] You can send Frank out for me, can't you? I want to go over everything. I'm not satisfied that we can't do better.

SHERIFF.   Do you want to see what Mrs. Peters is going to take in?

[*The LAWYER goes to the table, picks up the apron, laughs.*]

COUNTY ATTORNEY.   Oh, I guess they're not very dangerous things the ladies have picked out. [*Moves a few things about, disturbing the quilt pieces which cover the box. Steps back.*] No, Mrs. Peters doesn't need supervising. For that matter, a sheriff's wife is married to the law. Ever think of it that way, Mrs. Peters?

MRS. PETERS.   Not—just that way.

SHERIFF.   [*Chuckling.*] Married to the law. [*Moves toward the other room.*] I just want you to come in here a minute, George. We ought to take a look at these windows.

COUNTY ATTORNEY.   [*Scoffingly.*] Oh, windows!

SHERIFF.   We'll be right out, Mr. Hale.

[*HALE goes outside. The SHERIFF follows the COUNTY ATTORNEY into the other room. Then MRS. HALE rises, hands tight together, looking intensely at MRS. PETERS, whose eyes make a slow turn, finally meeting MRS. HALE'S. A moment MRS. HALE holds her, then her own eyes point the way to where the box is concealed. Suddenly MRS. PETERS throws back quilt pieces and tries to put the box in the bag she is wearing. It is too big. She opens box, starts to take bird out, cannot touch it, goes to pieces, stands there helpless. Sound of a knob turning in the other room. MRS. HALE snatches the box and puts it in the pocket of her big coat. Enter COUNTY ATTORNEY and SHERIFF.*]

COUNTY ATTORNEY.   [*Facetiously.*] Well, Henry, at least we found out that she was not going to quilt it. She was going to—what is it you call it, ladies?

MRS. HALE.   [*Her hand against her pocket.*] We call it—knot it, Mr. Henderson.

(*CURTAIN*)

QUESTIONS

1. How does the setting described in the first stage direction alert you that things are not right at the Wright farm?

2. How does the first entrance of the characters begin to establish a distinction between the men and women in the play?

3. What does Mr. Hale report to the County Attorney in his extended testimony? How observant is Mr. Hale? How accurate?

4. What is needed to make a strong case against Mrs. Wright? What does the Sheriff determine about the kitchen? What does this show you about the men?

5. What happened to Mrs. Wright's preserves during the night? How do the women react to this? The men? What does the difference suggest?

6. What does the badly sewn quilt square suggest to the women? What does Mrs. Hale do to the square? Do you think she has decided about the murder at this point?

7. What does Mrs. Hale reveal about Minnie Foster (Mrs. Wright) as a young woman? What does she reveal about the Wrights' marriage? How is this information relevant?

8. What do the women deduce from the broken bird-cage and the dead bird? How are the cage and the dead bird symbolic?

9. Where and what is the crisis of the play?

10. What does Mrs. Hale do with the "trifles" of evidence? Why? How is Mrs. Hale's reaction to the evidence different from Mrs. Peters's? What conflict develops between these women? How is it resolved?

11. Why does Mrs. Hale feel guilty about her relationship with Mrs. Wright? What does she wish she had done? Is her guilt justified? To what extent does this guilt help shape her actions and decisions?

TOPICS FOR WRITING AND FURTHER DISCUSSION

1. To what does the title of this play refer? Where is the word *trifles* used in the play? To what extent is the author's use of the word ironic? How does this irony help shape the play's meaning?

2. Are the characters round or flat? Individualized or representative? Static or dynamic? Why do you think Glaspell made these choices in characterization? How do they contribute to establishing the play's themes?

3. What are the men like? How observant are they? What is their attitude toward their jobs? Their own importance? The women and "kitchen things"?

4. What is Mrs. Hale like? How observant is she? What is her attitude toward the men? Toward their work? Toward herself?

5. Some critics have argued that Minnie Wright is the most important character in the play, even though she never appears on stage. To what extent do you agree with this assertion? Why do you think Glaspell decided to keep Mrs. Wright off-stage?

6. Is this play about crime? Rural life? Marriage? The way men regard women? What are the themes of the play?

7. Who or what are the protagonist and the antagonist in the play? What is the central conflict? How and when is it resolved? How does the resolution help establish the play's themes?

8. How is symbolism employed to establish and underscore the play's meaning? Consider especially the bird-cage, the dead bird, and the repeated assertion that Mrs. Wright was going to "knot" (tie) rather than "quilt" (sew) the quilt.

WRITING ABOUT THE ELEMENTS OF DRAMA

Although some aspects of drama, such as lighting and stage movement, are singularly theatrical, drama shares a number of elements with prose fiction and poetry. Therefore, when you are dealing with topics such as character or plot in drama, the planning and the writing processes are very similar to those employed for essays on fiction or poetry. Thus, in the following discussion we refer to pages earlier in the text that discuss strategies for writing about specific elements.

As you begin to plan an essay on drama, you should first select a play and an appropriate element or series of elements. Some plays work better than others in dealing with specific elements. It would be inappropriate, for example, to attempt an essay about setting in *The Happy Journey to Trenton and Camden* or in *Everyman* because neither play offers many details about environment, time, or place. In short, it is important to choose elements that are clearly defined and have a profound effect on your reading of the play.

Whether you select the play or it is assigned, choosing a focus for your essay is closely linked with formulating a tentative central idea. Normally, the central idea will assert something about a single element or about the relationship among elements. In the first case, for example, you might argue that a given character is flat, static, nonrealistic, and symbolic of good or evil. In the second, you might want to claim that the meaning of a play is shaped and emphasized through setting and symbolism. In either event, the following considerations will help you determine a focus, gather the raw materials, and form a thesis for your essay.

1. *Plot, action, conflict* (see pp. 127–133). In planning an essay on plot or structure, you are concerned with demonstrating some significant feature about the way events or conflicts unfold in the play. In addition, you can link this concern to other dramatic elements, such as tone or theme. In general, this topic breaks down into three areas—conflict, plot, and structure. For conflict, determine what the conflicts are, which one is central, and how it is resolved. What kind of conflict is it? Does it suggest any

universal patterns of human behavior? For plot, determine the extent to which you can find discrete stages of development. What is the climax? The catastrophe? How are they anticipated or foreshadowed? In examining plot structures and patterns, determine if the play has a subplot or second plot. If so, how is it related to the main plot? Is a significant pattern of action repeated? If so, what is the effect? To what extent do these parallel or repetitive patterns relate to theme and meaning? How do they control your emotional response to the play?

2. *Character* (see pp. 173–176 and 503–508). When you plan to write about character in drama, you should focus on a significant figure and try to formulate a central idea that expresses key facts about his or her role in the play. You might eventually deal with a character's personality, function, or the connection between the character and the play's meaning. Relevant considerations include the nature and the role of the character. Is he or she round or flat? Static or dynamic? Individualized or stereotyped? Realistic or nonrealistic? The protagonist, antagonist, incidental, or choric? Symbolic in any way? Other sources of information include the ways a character is presented and defined. How is the character described in the stage directions? By other characters? By himself or herself? What does he or she say? Do? Think? What is the character's attitude toward the environment? The action? Other characters? Himself or herself? To what extent does he or she articulate key ideas in the play?

3. *Point of view and perspective* (see pp. 200–204). Because most playwrights employ the dramatic point of view, this will rarely be a fruitful area for writing. In some cases, however, the play may be presented from a single character's perspective. When you deal with this technique, you might consider how such a perspective affects the play's structure and meaning. Why is this point of view useful or striking? What does it suggest about characters? Theme? To what extent does your reaction to the play correspond with or diverge from this perspective?

Even in plays written in the dramatic point of view, the playwright can allow characters to reveal their own point of view and impose a perspective by speaking directly to the audience. In dealing with this device, consider which character delivers most of this direct address. Do you sympathize with him or her? What information is conveyed? What tone does the character use in speaking to the audience? How does such direct address help to shape your response to the play? An essay on dramatic perspective will inevitably also focus on character and meaning.

4. *Setting, sets, and props* (see pp. 231–235 and 533–538). Normally, you will not write about setting and properties in isolation; such an essay would simply produce a detailed description of the setting(s) and objects in a play. Instead, a discussion of setting in drama should be linked to another element, such as character, mood, or meaning. Thus, such an essay will demonstrate the ways in which setting(s) and objects help to

establish the time, place, characters, lifestyle, values, or ideas of a play.

When you are dealing with a single setting, you should pay close attention to the opening stage direction and any subsequent directions and dialogue that describe the environment or objects. In plays with multiple settings you will normally want to select one or two for examination. Important considerations include whether the setting is realistic or nonrealistic, and to what extent it may be symbolic. What details and objects are specified? What do these tell you about the time, place, characters, way of life, and values? To what extent do they contribute to the tone, atmosphere, impact, and meaning of the play?

5. *Diction, imagery, style* (see pp. 260–265, 563–568, and 586–589). As with setting, a consideration of the devices of language in a play will normally examine these features in order to make a point about another element, such as tone, character, or meaning. Significant areas of investigation include the level of diction and types of dialect, jargon, slang, or clichés used by the characters. To what extent do these techniques define the characters and support or undercut their ideas? What connotative words or phrases do you find repeated in the play or spoken at a significant moment? What striking or consistent threads of imagery, metaphor, or simile do you find? What impact do these have on character, tone, or meaning? How do all these aspects of language shape your reaction to the play?

6. *Tone and atmosphere* (see pp. 289–293 and 659–665). When you plan an essay on tone or atmosphere, you will usually deal with *how* the tone is established and *what* impact it has on the play's total meaning. In looking for raw materials, you might explore those devices the playwright employs to convey the tones of individual characters and to convey his or her own tone throughout. Valid considerations include stage directions, diction, imagery, rhetorical devices, tempo, and context. In dealing with the play's tone, consider how it articulates its meaning—directly, or indirectly through irony. Also evaluate the degree to which you (as reader or spectator) know more than most characters.

7. *Symbol and allegory* (see pp. 326–332 and 809–813). In approaching these subjects, you will be seeking a connection between the symbolic or allegorical features and the themes or meaning of a play. Thus, you will eventually write about *what* the symbols are and *how* they contribute to the play's ideas and impact. As you collect data for such an essay, you must first determine if there are characters, objects, settings, situations, actions, words or phrases, and/or costumes that seem to be symbolic. If so, what do these things symbolize? Are they universal or contextual? Are they instantly symbolic or do they accrue symbolic meaning? Is the symbolism extensive and consistent enough to form an allegorical system? If so, what are the two levels of meaning addressed by the allegory? To what extent does the symbolism or allegory shape the play's meaning and your response?

8. *Theme* (see pp. 370–374 and 864–871). When you set out to plan an essay on theme or meaning in drama, you will usually be dealing with a number of different elements and aspects of the play at the same time. The aim in such an essay is to discuss *what* the play means and *how* this meaning is most strikingly communicated. The essay will thus link theme with various other aspects of the play such as character, conflict, action, setting, language, or symbolism. Try to determine what key ideas the play explores and what aspects of the play convey them most emphatically. As you gather the information, all the questions and areas of concern noted above should be helpful. In dealing with each topic and question, you will begin to isolate the elements and devices that have the most profound impact on meaning. These will become the topics you discuss in connection with ideas.

Organizing Your Essay

Your reexamination of the play and the relevant elements, keeping all these questions and topics in mind, will normally produce enough information for you to frame a tentative central idea and plan of organization for the essay. The central idea will assert your conclusions about the elements in question. The observations that led you to such conclusions will become the supporting details that will form the body of the essay.

Your ideas may shift or expand significantly during the prewriting and writing process. New directions of investigation and new conclusions will probably develop. The way to deal with these new insights and directions is through constant revision in every phase of planning and writing.

INTRODUCTION. On the whole, the organization used for essays about prose fiction and poetry are equally valid for writing about plays. The basic pattern includes an introduction, a body, and a conclusion. Your introductory paragraph should state the central idea, clearly establishing the point or points that you plan to make about the play. Begin with a focused thesis statement that holds true for all the discrete items you are evaluating. The introduction should also include a thesis sentence that lays out the plan of the essay by enumerating the topics you will consider.

BODY. The body of the essay should prove the central idea with supporting examples and details drawn from the text and discussed point by point. Here, you can make careful and conservative use of quotation from the play's text to help prove your point. When you use quotation, always try to explain in your own words exactly how the quotation advances your argument.

The body should be organized in the most logical and convincing manner, given the materials you are discussing. A broad array of strategies is available. If you are writing about an evil character, for instance, you might assert that his or her villainy and the nature of that evil are demonstrated in three specific actions. You could then discuss the dastardly aspects of each action in sequence. Alternatively, you might claim that the villainy is established and defined through action, language, and symbolism. Here, you can devote separate paragraphs to each element.

Similar strategies might be enumerated for every possible type of essay on drama. In dealing with symbolism in *Trifles*, for example, you might claim that three symbolic props help establish and reinforce the character of Mrs. Wright or the ideas about marriage conveyed in the play. In separate paragraphs you could then discuss three related symbols such as the bird-cage, the dead bird, and the quilt. Similarly, in writing about language in *The Sandbox*, you might assert that character is defined or ideas established through clichés, repetition, and connotative words. The possibilities are endless. Each play and topic will offer a variety of effective methods; any organization that is logical, clear, and convincing will produce a strong essay.

CONCLUSION.   The conclusion of your essay should summarize and recapitulate what you have advanced as a central idea in the introduction and supported with details in the body. At the same time, the conclusion should relate the topics you have discussed concerning specific elements with the meaning or impact of the play as a whole. Thus, your conclusion should relate the points you make about such aspects as tone, character, plot, or language to the overall meaning of the play.

SAMPLE ESSAY

Plot Structure and the Creation of Tension in Everyman*

[1]   The anonymous author of Everyman uses the same sequence of events over and over again in the play. The author employs this repetitive plot structure in order to create and sustain a high level of tension and suspense about Everyman's ultimate spiritual health and salvation.° In this repetitive pattern, Everyman is first encouraged and then abandoned by a series of characters, including Fellowship, Kindred, Cousin, Knowledge, and Strength.▫

[2]   When Everyman finally accepts the fact that Death cannot be bribed or flattered out of his appointed task, he immediately begins to consider which of his friends might be willing to accompany him on his pilgrimage. The first group of characters he approaches for comfort and companionship includes Fellowship, Kindred, Cousin, and Goods. Each of these characters initially makes

* See p. 1075 for this play.
° Central idea.
▫ Thesis sentence.

grandiose promises of support and faithfulness. Fellowship, for example, promises to be "slain for" Everyman and offers to go to Hell with him: "and thou go to hell, / I will not forsake thee by the way" (lines 232–233). Similarly, Kindred and Cousin promise to "live and die together" with Everyman and to stay with him "in wealth and woe" (lines 324–325). Goods asserts that he can help with any "sorrow or adversity" that Everyman might face "in the world" (lines 402–403).

[3]

In each case, however, these characters abandon Everyman when they discover the nature of his pilgrimage. Fellowship asserts that "I will not a foot with thee go" and that "I will depart as fast as I may" (lines 293 and 296). This is followed shortly by the desertions of Kindred and Cousin. Kindred flatly refuses to join the pilgrimage, offering his maid in his place as a companion for Everyman. Similarly, Cousin refuses Everyman's request for company, claiming a "cramp in my toe" (line 356). Finally, Goods refuses to accompany Everyman, asserting that he "will follow no man one foot" (line 426). These abandonments follow one another throughout the first half of the play, gradually isolating Everyman and raising the possibility that he will have no help with his reckoning. This progressive isolation also raises our anxiety about Everyman's fate.

[4]

This process of abandonment is also repeated in the second half of the play. The second group of characters that Everyman asks to accompany him on his pilgrimage includes Good Deeds, Knowledge, Strength, Beauty, Discretion, and Five-Wits. Like the first group, these characters also make expansive promises to Everyman. Knowledge, for example, promises that "I will never part you fro" (line 785); Strength and Discretion offer to "go with him all together" (line 677). Most of these characters, however, also abandon Everyman. When he finally approaches the grave, Beauty reneges on her promise, and Strength says, "I will thee also forsake and deny" (line 808). Similarly, Discretion deserts Everyman, and Five-Wits claims, "I will follow the other, for here I thee forsake" (line 846). Thus, Everyman is abandoned in sequence by Beauty, Strength, Discretion, Five-Wits, and Knowledge.

[5]

This repetitive pattern of encouragement followed by abandonment is thus maintained and extended throughout the entire action of Everyman. Each character that Everyman turns to in his moment of need promises support and then forsakes him. The effect of this duplicated pattern of action is twofold. On the one hand, it creates a high level of suspense and anxiety as Everyman is deserted again and again. On the other hand, it graphically illustrates the spiritual meaning of the play: man is saved only through his good deeds and the grace of God.

Commentary on the Essay

This essay, which focuses on plot structure, deals with a repeated pattern of action in *Everyman* and asserts that the repetition manipulates our emotions and underscores the meaning of the play. The introduction asserts that tension is created in *Everyman* through a repetitive structure in which the hero is encouraged and then abandoned by virtually every other character in the play. The thesis or topic sentence enumerates most of the characters who participate in this duplicated action and are thus discussed in the body of the essay.

The three paragraphs that comprise the body of the essay go on to illustrate the pattern of encouragement and abandonment. Paragraphs 2 and 3 draw their supporting details from the first half of the play; paragraph 4 illustrates the same pattern recurring in the second half. The body is thus organized according to the order of events in *Everyman*. The concluding paragraph recapitulates the basic structural pattern illustrated in the body of the essay and connects this pattern, the creation of tension, and the didactic or instructional goals of the play.

SAMPLE ESSAY ON THEME OR MEANING

The Theme of Salvation and Damnation in <u>Everyman</u>*

[1]
      The medieval morality play <u>Everyman</u> is designed to teach a single three-part lesson about Christian life and salvation. The first aspect of this lesson is that all worldly acquaintances, things, and qualities except good deeds are temporary and will be stripped away at death. The second teaches that unrepented sin inevitably leads to damnation. The final aspect, and the most important, teaches that salvation is achieved through good works and the grace of God. <u>This three-part lesson constitutes the theme of Everyman.°</u> In order to <u>make the theme absolutely clear, the same lesson is taught three times in the course of the play—once in the messenger's prologue, once in the body of the play through action and dialogue, and finally in the Doctor's epilogue.</u>□

[2]
      The theme of Everyman is introduced by the messenger in the opening lines of the play. He simply announces the ideas that the play is designed to teach straight out. He warns us, for example, that sin will lead to sorrow for the soul:

You think sin in the beginning full sweet,
Which in the end causeth the soul to weep,
When the body lieth in clay.   (lines 13–15)

The messenger thus establishes a direct link between sin and the misery of a damned soul. Similarly, he teaches us that worldly things are transitory by telling us what we will see in the body of the play:

Here shall you see how Fellowship and Jollity,
Both Strength, Pleasure, and Beauty,
Will fade from thee as flower in May.   (lines 16–18)

The messenger's general point here is a demonstration of "how transitory we be all day" (line 6). Thus, the messenger opens the play by announcing two

* See p. 1075 for this play.
° Central idea.
□ Thesis sentence.

aspects of its central theme: the temporary nature of worldly things and the dangers of sin.

The same three-part lesson is taught in the body of the play. Here, however, the theme is established through action as well as dialogue. The transitory nature of all wordly things is illustrated in the overall pattern of abandonment that Everyman experiences. He is forsaken by Fellowship, Kindred, Cousin, Goods, Knowledge, Strength, Beauty, Discretion, and Five-Wits. The soul-killing power of sin is demonstrated in Everyman's conversations with Goods and Good Deeds and in his own realizations. Goods points out that the love of wealth leads to damnation: "for my love is contrary to the love everlasting" (line 430). Good Deeds exemplifies the damning influence of sin in her first appearance on stage. She is pressed to the ground by the weight of Everyman's sins:

[3]   Here I lie, cold in the ground.
Thy sins hath me sore bound
That I cannot stear.   (lines 486–488)

Finally, Everyman himself comes to understand the destructive power of sin:

Take this, body, for the sin of the flesh!
Also thou delightest to go gay and fresh,
And in the way of damnation thou did me bring.   (lines 613–615)

He scourges his flesh because his delight in worldly pleasures led him into the snares of sin and damnation.

The redemptive power of divine grace and of acts of charity and goodness is taught by Confession and Good Deeds. Confession points out that salvation is achieved through divine mercy. He advises Everyman to "be secure of mercy, / For your time draweth fast, and ye will saved be. / Ask God mercy, and He will grant, truly" (lines 568–570). Similarly, Good Deeds repeats the lesson that all worldly things are worthless except acts of goodness:

[4]   All earthly things is but vanity.
Beauty, Strength, and Discretion do man forsake,
Foolish friends and kinsmen that fair spake—
All fleeth save Good Deeds, and that am I.   (lines 870–873).

In this passage, Good Deeds repeats two aspects of the play's central theme; she reiterates the point that all "earthly things" are temporary and she reminds us that good deeds abide with us and help us achieve salvation.

The central meaning of Everyman is repeated for a third time in the epilogue delivered by the "Doctor" at the close of the play. This learned theologian points out again that all worldly things except good deeds are transitory:

And remember Beauty, Five-Wits, Strength, and Discretion,
They all at the last do Everyman forsake,

Save his Good Deeds there doth he take.
But beware, for and they be small,
Before God he hath no help at all. (lines 905–909)

In this same passage, he reminds us that sufficient acts of goodness will help us achieve salvation. Additionally, he warns us that unrepented sin inevitably leads to damnation: "If his reckoning be not clear when he doth come, / God will say, 'Ite, maledicti, in ignem eternum!' " (lines 914–915). Finally, the Doctor alludes to the third aspect of the lesson—the grace of God—by praying that "God bring us all thither" to salvation "That we may live body and soul together" (lines 918–919).

[6]   Thus we see that the central theme of Everyman concerns the way to avoid damnation and achieve salvation. We are taught three times in the play that earthly things are temporary, that sin leads to damnation, and that salvation is gained through good works and grace. This meaning is made clear in the action of the play proper. Moreover, it is repeated in the dialogue of both the prologue and the epilogue in order to make the themes of the play absolutely explicit. The triple repetition of Everyman's meaning indicates the importance that the play's author attached to this lesson. The anonymous playwright clearly felt that the meaning of his play was profoundly significant to the lives and spiritual health of his audiences. The play consequently spells its meaning out very clearly.

Commentary on the Essay

This essay deals with the theme of *Everyman* and some of the ways it is conveyed in the play. Isolating the play's meaning is perhaps the simplest part of the process; the play is so didactic that it asserts its theme repeatedly. The supporting details in the essay are all either actions or direct statements made by characters. Another fruitful approach might have been to deal with the play's theme through an analysis of symbolism or allegory.

The introduction of this essay takes as its central idea the fact that *Everyman*'s theme is a three-part lesson about Christian life and salvation. Each part of the lesson is introduced in this opening paragraph: (1) earthly things fade away, (2) sin leads to damnation, (3) salvation is based upon good works and grace. In addition, the thesis or topic sentence establishes the major divisions of the essay by enumerating the three times and several ways the meaning is established in the course of the play.

The body supports the essay's central idea by discussing each instance and method in which the play conveys its meaning; each repetition of the play's theme is taken up in its own paragraph or paragraphs. Thus, the lesson of the prologue is examined in paragraph 2, the lesson of the play's action in paragraphs 3 and 4, and the lesson of the epilogue in paragraph 5. In addition, each paragraph examines most (if not all) of the distinct aspects of the play's meaning. Thus, the second paragraph discusses both the effects of sin and the fleeting nature of worldly pleasures. Paragraph 3 covers the same topics in reverse order. Paragraph 4 considers these two aspects of theme and adds the idea of the redemptive power of acts of goodness and divine grace. Finally, paragraph 5 reconsiders all three aspects of theme. Since much of the supporting detail here is direct quotation, the dialogue is quoted line-for-line, and the relevance of each passage is explained.

The essay derives its organization from the final sentence in the introduction. In other words, the three separate instances of instruction—the prologue, play, and epilogue—provide the general structure of the essay. At the same time, however, each paragraph derives its structure from the three aspects of the play's theme. It would be just as effective to reverse this organization and to use the three aspects of the play's meaning as a structural basis for the essay. In such a case, each paragraph would discuss one aspect of the play's meaning as it is articulated first in the prologue, then in the body of the play, and finally in the epilogue.

The conclusion of the essay attempts to do two things. First, it summarizes the points that have been made in the body of the paper. Second, it attempts to explain briefly why the central theme of *Everyman* is repeated three times in the course of the play. Here, it deals with the importance of the play's theme to both the playwright and the audiences for whom the play was written.

28

Tragedy

THE NATURE AND ORIGIN OF TRAGEDY

"A tragedy is a sad story." "A tragedy is a story that ends in death." "A tragedy is the story of the fall of an individual." We all come to tragedy with a series of fragmentary definitions and preconceived notions about what qualifies a piece of literature as a tragedy. For a more systematic definition, we must turn to Aristotle. In Chapter 6 of *The Poetics* Aristotle describes **tragedy** as "an imitation of an action that is serious, complete, and of a certain magnitude; in language embellished with each kind of artistic ornament; . . . in the form of a drama, not of narrative; through pity and fear effecting the proper purgation of these emotions."[1] We should understand that Aristotle does not set up a series of rules about how to write tragedy. Rather, he offers a structural description of tragedy based on the hundreds of tragedies he read or saw in the Great Theater of Dionysus during his lifetime in Athens. It is interesting to note that his most frequently cited example throughout *The Poetics* is Sophocles's *Oedipus the King*.

Let us consider the separate parts of Aristotle's description of tragedy. He begins by calling tragedy the "imitation of an action." We have already discussed the imitative or mimetic aspects of drama (see p. 1033). By "action," Aristotle means the complete process of working out a single motive from its beginning in activity to its conclusion in the perception (or recognition) of a truth. Thus, in *Oedipus* the action evolves out of the motivation of saving Thebes from the plague by expelling the murderer of the former king. Similarly, in *Hamlet* the action grows out of Hamlet's desire to purify

---

[1] S. H. Butcher, *Aristotle's Theory of Poetry and Fine Art*, 4th ed. (London: Macmillan, 1932). All quotations are from this edition.

Denmark by avenging the murder of his father. In the course of staging the entire working out of a single motivation, the action of a tragedy will move from purpose (or activity) through emotion (or pathos) and finally to perception. Ultimately, Aristotle refers to this whole process as *plot*.

Aristotle goes on to say that a tragedy is "serious, complete, and of a certain magnitude." "Serious" suggests that the subject matter must be elevated; it implies that the characters in tragic drama must be royal or aristocratic rather than common. By "complete" Aristotle means that the story to be dramatized in a tragedy must have a beginning, a middle, and an end that all hold together in a logical and causal relationship. This does not mean that the playwright must dramatize the whole story with which he is dealing. In *Oedipus*, for example, the story covers the protagonist's whole life, but the play itself dramatizes only part of the last day of his reign as king of Thebes. In discussing the "magnitude" or scope of tragedy, Aristotle explains that the plot must be of "a length which can be easily embraced by memory" (Chapter 7). By asserting that tragedy must be in the form of a drama rather than a narrative, he simply means that the plot must be acted out rather than told.

Perhaps the most interesting part of Aristotle's description of tragedy is his assertion that tragic drama arouses fear and pity in the spectators and leads to a **purgation (catharsis)** of these emotions. Here, Aristotle addresses himself to the reasons we enjoy tragedy. The pity and fear that the play evokes in us allow us to experience these emotions vicariously in an extreme form. At the end of the tragedy, these emotions have been washed out of (purged from) our psyche, and we are, in some emotional or psychological sense, refreshed. The catharsis or purgation of fear and pity may also be explained more fully with reference to the Freytag pyramid (see p. 1038). Looking at the pyramid, we can see that fear would be touched most heavily during the tension and uncertainty leading up to the climax, and pity would become the major emotion after the climax during the "falling action."

Aristotle narrows his description of tragedy still further in later chapters of *The Poetics*. He asserts, for example, that tragedy must tell of the misfortunes of a person who is "highly renowned and prosperous" and who falls as the result of some "error or frailty" (Chapter 13). We may refine this definition still further, given our broader perspective and an additional two thousand years of tragic drama. Until the twentieth century, tragedy almost always told the story of the fall of a great person—a person of "high degree." This person usually begins in a position of authority and respect. Oedipus, for example, is the king of Thebes and revered for his victory over the Sphinx. Similarly, Hamlet is the prince of Denmark, Othello the general of the armies of Venice, and King Lear the absolute ruler of Britain.

In the process of tragedy, then, a man or woman of high degree falls from a position of authority and prosperity to a state of adversity (usually death or banishment). The fall is caused by either external or internal forces or both. The external forces that may be responsible for tragic falls include fate, fortune, the gods, and circumstances. The internal forces are summed up by Aristotle in his phrase "error or frailty." The Greek term he uses in *The Poetics* is **hamartia**. Traditionally, this term has been translated as "tragic flaw." Such a limited and narrow definition of *hamartia* has led to simplistic interpretations of tragic drama. Thus, generations of students and teachers have asserted that Oedipus falls because of his temper, Hamlet because of his indecision, Othello because of his jealousy, and Macbeth because of his ambition. We should understand, however, that the term *hamartia* has much broader implications. It includes the traditional and shop-worn idea of the "tragic flaw," but it also includes concepts such as crime, misunderstanding, and errors in judgment or action that spring from personality. Readers and viewers of tragedy must ultimately decide in each play if the fall of the tragic protagonist is the result of internal forces, external forces, or some combination of both. In any case, the tragic hero or heroine almost always makes crucial errors in the course of his or her life that begin the process of the tragic fall. These moments of error in judgment or action represent the crises tragedies.

As it stands, our working definition of tragedy remains an incomplete model that would generate a sad (pathetic) rather than a tragic sequence of events. The missing elements are the reversal of action and the growth of understanding or self-knowledge. Aristotle calls the **reversal** of action or intention the **peripeteia:** the instant when there is "a change by which the action veers around to its opposite" (Chapter 11). Moreover, Aristotle asserts that in the best tragedies, this reversal occurs simultaneously with the understanding of truth. He calls this moment of comprehension the **"recognition" (anagnorisis).** In most tragedies, this recognition means that the tragic protagonist comes to understand his or her own place in the universal scheme of things. The protagonist also comes to acknowledge the errors that have led to tragedy and the degree to which he or she is responsible for his or her own destruction. Thus, we can identify this recognition or anagnorisis as the central ironic linchpin of tragedy.

To this point, we have been describing tragedy with reference to Aristotle and *The Poetics*. We do not mean to suggest, however, that this description is limited to Greek tragedy. Nor do we mean to suggest that all tragedy is "Aristotelian" in structure or that Aristotle's description must necessarily be taken as the ideal. Every age has redefined and refashioned tragedy to its own ends and images. In England during the Renaissance, for example, Shakespeare and his contemporaries wrote tragedies with reference to history rather than myth and to medieval rather than Aristotelian traditions. Similarly, the eighteenth century saw the growth of the middle-class tragic protagonist and **domestic tragedy.** In the twentieth century, tragedy has been reformulated once again to include both working-class protagonists and anti-heroes. Let us then look at another description of tragedy. This one was written by Jean Anouilh in a play called *Antigone*, which was produced in Paris in 1944 during the Nazi occupation:

> The spring is wound up tight. It will uncoil of itself. That is what is so convenient in tragedy. The least little turn of the wrist will do the job. Anything will set it going; . . . one question too many, idly thrown out over a friendly drink—and the tragedy is on. The rest is automatic. You don't need to lift a finger. The machine is in perfect order; it has been oiled ever since time began, and it runs without friction. Death, treason, and sorrow are on the march; and they move in the wake of storm, of tears, of stillness. . . . Tragedy is clean, it is firm, it is flawless. It has nothing to do with melodrama—with wicked villains, persecuted maidens, avengers, sudden revelations and eleventh-hour repentances. Death, in a melodrama, is really horrible because it is never inevitable. . . . In a tragedy, nothing is in doubt and everyone's destiny is known. That makes for tranquillity. There is a sort of fellow-feeling among characters in a tragedy: he who kills is as innocent as he who gets killed: it's all a matter of what part you are playing. Tragedy is restful; and the reason is that hope . . . has no part in it. There isn't any hope. You're trapped. The whole sky has fallen on you, and all you can do about it is to shout. Don't mistake me: I said "shout": I did not say groan, whimper, complain. That, you cannot do. But you can shout aloud; you can get all those things said that you never thought you'd be able to say—or never even knew you had it in you to say. And you don't say these things because it will do any good to say them; you know better than that. You say them for their own sake; you say them because you learn a lot from them.[2]

Aristotle and Anouilh are clearly coming at tragedy from different perspectives and different philosophical systems. Anouilh's description is strikingly non-Aristotelian. It offers no emphasis on the structure of tragic plots or the nobility of the tragic protagonist. Instead, it emphasizes the mechanistic nature of the universe and the hopelessness and inevitability of tragedy. Nevertheless, in the end Aristotle and Anouilh meet on common ground. Both assert that tragedy must lead to some learning process, some growth of recognition or understanding.

Tragedy, like drama in general, may have evolved from prehistoric rituals that celebrated the end of winter and the return of fertility to the earth. In these ancient rites the sacrifice of a god or hero would be reenacted to ensure the fruitfulness of the land and to redeem the community from the sterility of winter. Thus, while the god/hero ended in a symbolic death, the community was restored and revitalized. At some point in history these rituals came to include narrative choral songs in which the story of the

---

[2] Jean Anouilh, *Antigone*, adapted and trans. Lewis Galantiere (New York: Random House, 1946).

god/hero was retold and mythologized. The shift from the narrative to the dramatic mode occurred when one of the members of the chorus took on the role of the god/hero and began to speak the words of this central figure. Aristotle asserts that this momentous shift occurred (in 534 B.C.) when the first actor was separated from the chorus by the Greek poet Thespis; the actor assumed the role of the god/hero, and the chorus became a group of soldiers, citizens, worshippers, or the like. The separation of a single actor from the chorus made dialogue and drama possible; the god/hero could now interact with the chorus. According to Aristotle, a second actor was added by Aeschylus and a third by Sophocles. These actors could play as many different parts as the playwright desired, but the number of players was strictly limited (in the case of Sophocles) to a chorus and three actors. Tragedy, then, seems to have evolved out of the dramatization of choral songs that told of the destruction of gods, great persons, or royal houses.

LANGUAGE AND TONE IN TRAGEDY

Greek tragedy was always written in verse. As a result, Aristotle asserts in *The Poetics* that lofty diction and poetry are characteristics of tragedy. This description holds true, for the most part, until the late eighteenth century. Roman tragedy is poetic; English Renaissance and Restoration tragedy is mostly written in blank verse or rhymed couplets. This does not mean that all tragedy before the nineteenth century is written completely in verse. To the contrary, Shakespeare and most of his contemporaries mixed verse and prose in their plays. *Hamlet*, for example, shifts between blank verse and prose, depending on the characters and the circumstances. The Elizabethan playwrights also included characters from all social classes in their tragedies, thus making colloquial diction appropriate in many instances—the graveyard scene in *Hamlet* (5.1) is a good example. In the twentieth century, tragedy has become a great deal less explicitly poetic and elevated. The shift to the common man or woman as the tragic protagonist has led to a concurrent shift from poetry to colloquial and conversational dialogue. The characters in Arthur Miller's *Death of a Salesman*, for example, speak idiomatic American English of the 1940s.

The tone of tragedy is frequently ironic. There are a number of reasons for this tendency. One of the most important is dramatic irony, which we discuss in Chapter 27 (p. 1044). As readers or spectators, we almost always know more than the tragic protagonist. We know, for instance, that Oedipus killed his father and that Claudius murdered his brother long before the tragic heroes in either play learn these things. Thus, we see the ironic futility of many actions and statements. We also find a series of ironies linked to character. For example, a tragic protagonist's greatest strength may also be one of his or her greatest weaknesses. We can see this in Oedipus's determination to unmask a murderer and save his country at all costs. It is similarly ironic that the best characters in tragedy—the most sensitive, intelligent, or honest—are the ones who suffer the most and often die. Perhaps the most effective twist of irony in tragedy is the irony of *anagnorisis*, or recognition. Increased self-knowledge and understanding must occur, but they never come until the protagonist has passed the point of no return; recognition is thus both necessary and ironically useless in averting disaster.

THE THEATER OF SOPHOCLES

In Athens, during Sophocles' lifetime (496?–406 B.C.), plays were performed in the Great Theater of Dionysus during the festival of Dionysus (the god of fertility and wine) in late March or early April. The importance of plays in this festival indicates the continuing relationship between drama and religion. A typical Dionysian festival (a **Dionysia**) lasted five or six days. It was an occasion not only for dramatic productions but also for an annual theatrical competition. Three tragedians (writers of tragedy) and three to five comedic playwrights were chosen to compete. Each of the comedic writers supplied one play; each of the tragedians was responsible for three related tragedies (a **trilogy**) and one **satyr play,** a short comic interlude perhaps based on the themes of the writer's tragedies.

The congregation (and audience) for the festival was enormous; all citizens of Athens and all visitors normally attended. These spectators needed a great deal of stamina and patience to last through the entire Dionysia. The first two or three days were devoted to religious processions and poetry contests. The last three days were given over to the playwrights' competition. On each of these days (the festival began at dawn), the spectators watched three tragedies, a satyr play, and a comedy or two. At the end of the festival, prizes were awarded to the playwrights judged to be the best in tragedy and in comedy.

The Great Theater of Dionysus, in which Sophocles' plays were first performed, was a vast semicircular open-air amphitheater built into the side of a hill. The central circle, called the **orchestra,** was the area where the chorus sang its lyrical interludes (odes) and performed dances (see the accompanying illustration). Tiers of seats were cut into the hills surrounding most of the orchestra. Originally, the spectators simply sat on the ground overlooking the orchestra. Later, wooden seats and then stone seats were installed. Since the theater had to accommodate most of the citizens of Athens, this seating was quite extensive; the Great Theater of Dionysus held about twenty thousand spectators. Behind the orchestra was a small building called the **skene** (in Latin, the *scaena,* from which

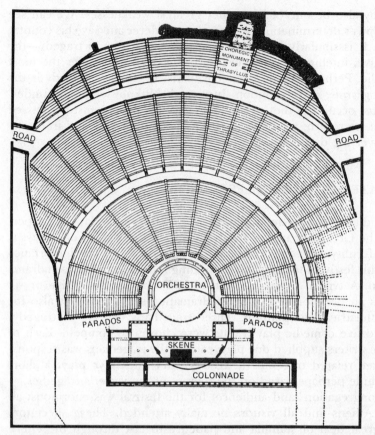

A Diagram of the Great Theater of Dionysus as remodeled in the fourth century B.C.
The superimposed circle shows the original location of the *orchestra* before the *skene*
was constructed. (From R. C. Flickinger, *The Greek Theater and Its Drama* (Chicago:
University of Chicago Press, 1918), p. 64.)

we get the modern word "scene") which was used as a dressing room
and a place for actors to await their cues. Like the seating, this area was
initially quite primitive; it consisted of a tent put up on the occasion of
the Dionysia. Later, a wooden building was constructed to serve as the
skene. Eventually, however, a permanent skene was built of stone and
the front facing the audience was decorated with paintings. At about the
same time, a crane of sorts was installed on top of the skene so that actors
playing gods could be lowered from the "heavens" or raised up from
the "earth." This piece of staging machinery, often used by inept playwrights to end their plays quickly with the appearance of a god, led to
the Latin term ***deus ex machina*** ("god from the machine"), which is now
used to describe any extraordinary turn of events that produces the sudden
resolution of a play. The skene had three doors used for entrances and

exits: one in the center and one each on the left and the right. Eventually, a **colonnade** (a row of columns) was built behind the skene at the Great Theater of Dionysus in order to provide a permanent backdrop that suggested a palace or a temple. Some theater historians argue that a raised wooden stage (called the **proskenion** or, in Latin, the **proscenium**) was constructed in front of the skene to separate the actors from the chorus and make them more clearly visible to the audience.

Plays were performed in this theater in broad daylight without any scenery or artificial lighting and with a minimum of props. When a playwright wanted to establish a specific time or place for the stage action, he had a character mention the location or time of day in the dialogue. The plays of Sophocles were usually performed by a chorus of fifteen men (including the **choragos,** or choral leader) and three male actors. All parts, including women's roles, were played by men. The three actors could play as many different characters as the playwright required simply by withdrawing into the skene, changing masks, and reentering as a new character. Thus, in a play like *Oedipus The King* a single actor would most likely play both a prophet and a messenger. Mute characters, like Oedipus's daughters, were not considered "roles" and thus did not count in the total number of actors.

The chorus entered and exited the orchestra along aisles on each side of the skene called **parados.** The actors could enter the playing area either from the skene or by way of the parados. The chorus was restricted to the central acting area of the orchestra. Actors, however, could perform in the orchestra, on the wooden stage behind the orchestra, or even on the roof of the skene. Since the chorus had to remain in the orchestra, it always stood between the audience and the actors. This placing of the chorus *between* the actors and the spectators helped to emphasize its double role as participants in the action and "reactors" to the action. The chorus thus played an important role in the play and at the same time served as a guide for audience reaction to the drama.

The actors in classical Greek theater performed in stylized masks (called **personae** in Latin, from which we derive the word "person") that helped the audience identify mythic or stock characters. We may assume that each major god or goddess and many of the traditional protagonists had a specific mask that signified that character. These masks had built-in megaphones that helped to amplify the actors' voices. The actors also wore thick-soled elevator shoes, called **cotherni** or **buskins,** that gave them an extremely heightened and stylized appearance. Obviously, the actors in classical Greek drama—with masks and cothurni—did not look like normal people—but, of course, they were not playing normal people. At the same time, the Athenian audience no doubt accepted the stylization (or **conventions**) of their drama as easily as we accept the conventions of grand opera, Westerns, or situation comedies.

Plays written during the age of Sophocles are usually divided into five distinct sections: *prologue*, *parados*, *episodia*, *stasimon*, and *exodos*. The **prologue** is the part of the play that occurs before the first choral ode; it contains a great deal of exposition. The **parados** is the first lyrical ode the chorus chants immediately after entering the orchestra for the first time; it presents the initial problems and attitudes of the chorus. The middle part of the play is made up of numerous **episodia** (episodes) and **stasima** (choric odes, the singular is **stasimon**). Each episode begins after a choral ode and ends with another. The episodes are often debates between the tragic protagonist and another character; the stasima are choral reactions to these debates. The **exodos** is the scene that follows the last choral ode of the play; it contains both the resolution of the drama and the departure (*exodos*) of the actors.

SOPHOCLES, *Oedipus the King*

When Sophocles dramatized the the story of Oedipus, the myth was already hundreds of years old. Most of the Athenians who thronged to the Great Theater of Dionysus in 430 or 429 B.C. to watch Sophocles' new play and the annual competition would have known the story of the man who was destined to murder his father and marry his mother. They would have been familiar with many of the details of Oedipus's history: the prophecy delivered before his birth; his exposure as an infant on Mount Cithaeron; his upbringing in Corinth as the adopted son of Merope and Polybus; the murder of Laius at the place where three roads meet; his defeat of the Sphinx; his marriage to Jocasta; and his twenty-year reign as king of Thebes. In choosing to dramatize a very well-known story, Sophocles was consistent with the playwriting practices of his own age and, in fact, of the entire classical period. We find similar practices in the tragedies of other Greek playwrights such as Aeschylus and Euripides. Like the dramatists in England during the age of Shakespeare, the classical Greek tragedians put no value whatsoever on the originality or timeliness of the stories they dramatized. Rather, they sought new ways to dramatize old and valued tales that remained relevant for the individual and the state.

This practice of dramatizing popular myths and stories had a profound effect on the ultimate shape and impact of plays like *Oedipus the King*. Let us consider what Sophocles lost and what he gained by dramatizing a sequence of events already known to the entire audience. For one thing, he lost the opportunity to change the basic shape of the story or to alter any of the significant details of Oedipus's life. This means that Sophocles gave up any possibility of creating suspense about the resolution or of adding a surprise ending. At the same time, however, much is gained by working with a well-known myth. Sophocles could assume, for example, that his audience would be familiar with the characters of *Oedipus* immediately. Thus, he was able to concentrate on minute details of phrasing and characterization. Similarly, he could dispense with unessentials and focus on conflict and meaning. Most important, Sophocles could use his audience's knowledge of the story of Oedipus to create vast amounts of dramatic irony. Early in *Oedipus the King*, for example, Oedipus curses the murderer of Laius: "may he wear out his life unblest and evil" (line 253). When he pronounces this deadly curse, we know that he is the guilty person, but he does not. Thus, we realize that Oedipus is ironically cursing himself. The play is overflowing with this kind of dramatic irony. Indeed, *Oedipus* is like a murder mystery in which the reader knows who did it right from the beginning. The pleasure and the agony are produced as we watch Oedipus the detective move step by step through a process of discovery that will ultimately lead him to himself.

The mythic material that Sophocles worked with in shaping *Oedipus the King* details the story of Oedipus from the oracle delivered before the tragic hero's birth to his ultimate expulsion from Thebes and his old age. In forming a play from this vast body of material, Sophocles had to create a unified plot that limited the action to a single motivation and a single process of fall from prosperity to adversity. Sophocles did this by dramatizing only the final hours of Oedipus's reign as king of Thebes. These last hours take us from Apollo's prophecy that Thebes will be saved from the plague only through the expulsion of the murderer of Laius to Oedipus's discovery that he is that murderer. The remainder of Oedipus's story is told through expositional conversations and debates; characters discuss at great length events that happened years before the "present time" of the dramatized day. By choosing to dramatize only part of the last day of Oedipus's reign as king of Thebes, Sophocles was able to produce a highly cohesive play that maintains the traditional **unities of place, time, and action.** The entire play occurs in the courtyard in front of the royal palace of Thebes, and the elapsed time within the play covers only part of a single day. Unity of action is achieved by focusing on a single story and a single motivation: the need to save Thebes from the plague by expelling the murderer of Laius.

Oedipus the King conforms in most respects to Aristotle's description of tragedy. Two aspects of this description are especially noteworthy in *Oedipus*: the reversal (or *peripeteia*) and the recognition (or *anagnorisis*). The play is full of reversals of action or intention. The messenger from Corinth, for example, thinks that he is releasing Oedipus from fear when he tells the king that Merope and Polybus are not his real parents; in fact, the result of this revelation is exactly the opposite of what the messenger intended. In some ways, the entire play is built on the idea of *peripeteia*. Oedipus vows to save the city by rooting out the murderer of Laius and ultimately discovers that he is that murderer. Obviously, the intention and the action have been completely reversed. The recognition of truth in

Oedipus is tightly bound up with this central reversal. The *peripeteia* of Oedipus's action and intention occurs simultaneously with his own recognition of his errors, sins, guilt, and destiny.

At the end of *Oedipus the King* we are left with a puzzle. We must decide if Oedipus's tragic fall is produced by external forces beyond his control or by aspects of his character that led to errors in judgment and action. The play seems to offer support for both interpretations. On the one hand, Oedipus's crimes and destiny were prophesied before his birth by the oracle of Apollo. Does this mean that he was destined to murder his father and marry his mother, or does it mean that the gods simply knew the future? The distinction here is between predestination and foreknowledge. On the other hand, Oedipus's rage, his overweening pride **(hubris),** and his compulsive need to know the truth seem to drive him inexorably toward destruction. Finally the choice is ours; Sophocles has left us the central problem of the play to ponder on our own.

SOPHOCLES (ca. 496–406 B.C.)

Oedipus the King

ca. 430 B.C.

Translated by Thomas Gould

CHARACTERS

Oedipus,° *The King of Thebes*
Priest of Zeus, *Leader of the Suppliants*
Creon, *Oedipus's Brother-in-law*
Chorus, *a Group of Theban Elders*
Choragos, *Spokesman of the Chorus*
Tiresias, *a blind Seer or Prophet*
Jocasta, *The Queen of Thebes*
Messenger, *from Corinth, once a Shepherd*
Herdsman, *once a Servant of Laius*
Second Messenger, *a Servant of Oedipus*

MUTES

Suppliants, *Thebans seeking Oedipus's help*
Attendants, *for the Royal Family*
Servants, *to lead Tiresias and Oedipus*
Antigone, *Daughter of Oedipus and Jocasta*
Ismene, *Daughter of Oedipus and Jocasta*

Oedipus: The name means "swollen foot." It is a reference to the mutilation of Oedipus's feet done by his father, Laius, before the infant was sent to Mount Cithaeron to be put to death by exposure.

[*The action takes place during the day in front of the royal palace in Thebes. There are two altars (left and right) on the Proscenium and several steps leading down to the Orchestra. As the play opens, Thebans of various ages who have come to beg Oedipus for help are sitting on these steps and in part of the Orchestra. These suppliants are holding branches of laurel or olive which have strips of wool° wrapped around them. Oedipus enters from the palace (the central door of the Skene)*]

PROLOGUE

OEDIPUS. My children, ancient Cadmus'° newest care,
why have you hurried to those seats, your boughs
wound with the emblems of the suppliant?
The city is weighed down with fragrant smoke,
with hymns to the Healer° and the cries of mourners.   5
I thought it wrong, my sons, to hear your words
through emissaries, and have come out myself,
I, Oedipus, a name that all men know.

[*OEDIPUS addresses the PRIEST.*]

Old man—for it is fitting that you speak
for all—what is your mood as you entreat me,   10
fear or trust? You may be confident
that I'll do anything. How hard of heart
if an appeal like this did not rouse my pity!
PRIEST. You, Oedipus, who hold the power here,
you see our several ages, we who sit   15
before your altars—some not strong enough
to take long flight, some heavy in old age,
the priests, as I of Zeus,° and from our youths
a chosen band. The rest sit with their windings
in the markets, at the twin shrines of Pallas,°   20
and the prophetic embers of Ismēnos.°
Our city, as you see yourself, is tossed
too much, and can no longer lift its head
above the troughs of billows red with death.
It dies in the fruitful flowers of the soil,   25
it dies in its pastured herds, and in its women's
barren pangs. And the fire-bearing god°
has swooped upon the city, hateful plague,
and he has left the house of Cadmus empty.

Stage direction *wool*: branches wrapped with wool are traditional symbols of prayer or supplication.   1 *Cadmus*: Oedipus's great great grandfather (although he does not know this) and the founder of Thebes.   5 *Healer*: Apollo, god of prophecy, light, healing, justice, purification, and destruction.   18 *Zeus*: father and king of the gods.   20 *Pallas*: Athena, goddess of wisdom, arts, crafts, and war.   21 *Ismēnos*: a reference to the temple of Apollo near the river Ismēnos in Thebes. Prophecies were made here by "reading" the ashes of the altar fires.   27 *fire-bearing god*: contagious fever viewed as a god.

Black Hades° is made rich with moans and weeping.   30
Not judging you an equal of the gods,
do I and the children sit here at your hearth,
but as the first of men, in troubled times
and in encounters with divinities.
You came to Cadmus' city and unbound   35
the tax we had to pay to the harsh singer,°
did it without a helpful word from us,
with no instruction; with a god's assistance
you raised up our life, so we believe.
Again now Oedipus, our greatest power,   40
we plead with you, as suppliants, all of us,
to find us strength, whether from a god's response,
or learned in some way from another man.
I know that the experienced among men
give counsels that will prosper best of all.   45
Noblest of men, lift up our land again!
Think also of yourself; since now the land
calls you its Savior for your zeal of old,
oh let us never look back at your rule
as men helped up only to fall again!   50
Do not stumble! Put our land on firm feet!
The bird of omen was auspicious then,
when you brought that luck; be that same man again!
The power is yours; if you will rule our country,
rule over men, not in an empty land.   55
A towered city or a ship is nothing
if desolate and no man lives within.

OEDIPUS.   Pitiable children, oh I know, I know
the yearnings that have brought you. Yes, I know
that you are sick. And yet, though you are sick,   60
there is not one of you so sick as I.
For your affliction comes to each alone,
for him and no one else, but my soul mourns
for me and for you, too, and for the city.
You do not waken me as from a sleep,   65
for I have wept, bitterly and long,
tried many paths in the wanderings of thought,
and the single cure I found by careful search

---

30 *Black Hades*: refers to both the underworld where the spirits of the dead go and the
god of the underworld.   36 *harsh singer*: the Sphinx, a monster with a woman's head, a
lion's body, and wings. The "tax" that Oedipus freed Thebes from was the destruction of
all the young men who failed to solve the Sphinx's riddle and were subsequently devoured.
The Sphinx always asked the same riddle: "What goes on four legs in the morning, two
legs at noon, and three legs in the evening, and yet is weakest when supported by the largest
number of feet?" Oedipus discovered the correct answer—man, who crawls in infancy, walks
in his prime, and uses a stick in old age—and thus ended the Sphinx's reign of terror. The
Sphinx destroyed herself when Oedipus answered the riddle. Oedipus was rewarded for
freeing Thebes of the Sphinx with the throne and the hand of the recently widowed
Jocasta.

I've acted on: I sent Menoeceus' son,
Creon, brother of my wife, to the Pythian 70
halls of Phoebus,° so that I might learn
what I must do or say to save this city.
Already, when I think what day this is,
I wonder anxiously what he is doing.
Too long, more than is right, he's been away. 75
But when he comes, then I shall be a traitor
if I do not do all that the god reveals.
PRIEST. Welcome words! But look, those men have signaled
that it is Creon who is now approaching!
OEDIPUS. Lord Apollo! May he bring Savior Luck, 80
a Luck as brilliant as his eyes are now!
PRIEST. His news is happy, it appears. He comes,
forehead crowned with thickly berried laurel.°
OEDIPUS. We'll know, for he is near enough to hear us.

[*Enter* CREON *along one of the Parados*.]

Lord, brother in marriage, son of Menoeceus! 85
What is the god's pronouncement that you bring?
CREON. It's good. For even troubles, if they chance
to turn out well, I always count as lucky.
OEDIPUS. But what was the response? You seem to say
I'm not to fear—but not to take heart either. 90
CREON. If you will hear me with these men present,
I'm ready to report—or go inside.

[CREON *moves up the steps toward the palace*.]

OEDIPUS. Speak out to all! The grief that burdens me
concerns these men more than it does my life.
CREON. Then I shall tell you what I heard from the god. 95
The task Lord Phoebus sets for us is clear:
drive out pollution sheltered in our land,
and do not shelter what is incurable.
OEDIPUS. What is our trouble? How shall we cleanse ourselves?
CREON. We must banish or murder to free ourselves 100
from a murder that blows storms through the city.
OEDIPUS. What man's bad luck does he accuse in this?
CREON. My Lord, a king named Laius ruled our land
before you came to steer the city straight.
OEDIPUS. I know. So I was told—I never saw him. 105
CREON. Since he was murdered, you must raise your hand
against the men who killed him with their hands.
OEDIPUS. Where are they now? And how can we ever find
the track of ancient guilt now hard to read?

70–71 *Pythian . . . Phoebus*: The temple of Apollo's oracle or prophet at Delphi. 83 *laurel*:
Creon is wearing a garland of laurel leaves, sacred to Apollo.

CREON.   In our own land, he said. What we pursue,   110
that can be caught; but not what we neglect.
OEDIPUS.   Was Laius home, or in the countryside—
or was he murdered in some foreign land?
CREON.   He left to see a sacred rite, he said;
He left, but never came home from his journey.   115
OEDIPUS.   Did none of his party see it and report—
someone we might profitably question?
CREON.   They were all killed but one, who fled in fear,
and he could tell us only one clear fact.
OEDIPUS.   What fact? One thing could lead us on to more   120
if we could get a small start on our hope.
CREON.   He said that bandits chanced on them and killed him—
with the force of many hands, not one alone.
OEDIPUS.   How could a bandit dare so great an act—
unless this was a plot paid off from here!   125
CREON.   We thought of that, but when Laius was killed,
we had no one to help us in our troubles.
OEDIPUS.   It was your very kingship that was killed!
What kind of trouble blocked you from a search?
CREON.   The subtle-singing Sphinx asked us to turn   130
from the obscure to what lay at our feet.
OEDIPUS.   Then I shall begin again and make it plain.
It was quite worthy of Phoebus, and worthy of you,
to turn our thoughts back to the murdered man,
and right that you should see me join the battle   135
for justice to our land and to the god.
Not on behalf of any distant kinships,
it's for myself I will dispel this stain.
Whoever murdered him may also wish
to punish me—and with the selfsame hand.   140
In helping him I also serve myself.
Now quickly, children: up from the altar steps,
and raise the branches of the suppliant!
Let someone go and summon Cadmus' people:
say I'll do anything.

[*Exit an* ATTENDANT *along one of the Parados.*]

Our luck will prosper   145
if the god is with us, or we have already fallen.
PRIEST.   Rise, my children; that for which we came,
he has himself proclaimed he will accomplish.
May Phoebus, who announced this, also come
as Savior and reliever from the plague.   150

[*Exit* OEDIPUS *and* CREON *into the Palace. The* PRIEST *and the* SUPPLIANTS *exit left and right along the Parados. After a brief pause, the* CHORUS *(including the* CHORAGOS*) enters the Orchestra from the Parados.*]

PARADOS

Strophe 1°

CHORUS. Voice from Zeus,° sweetly spoken, what are you
    that have arrived from golden
    Pytho° to our shining
    Thebes? I am on the rack, terror
      shakes my soul.   155
    Delian Healer,° summoned by "iē!"
    I await in holy dread what obligation, something new
    or something back once more with the revolving years,
      you'll bring about for me.
    Oh tell me, child of golden Hope,   160
      deathless Response!

Antistrophe 1°

I appeal to you first, daughter of Zeus,
    deathless Athena,
    and to your sister who protects this land,
Artemis,° whose famous throne is the whole circle   165
    of the marketplace,
and Phoebus, who shoots from afar: iō!
Three-fold defenders against death, appear!
If ever in the past, to stop blind ruin
    sent against the city,   170
you banished utterly the fires of suffering,
    come now again!

Strophe 2

Ah! Ah! Unnumbered are the miseries
I bear. The plague claims all
our comrades. Nor has thought found yet a spear   175
by which a man shall be protected. What our glorious
earth gives birth to does not grow. Without a birth
from cries of labor
    do the women rise.
One person after another   180
    you may° see, like flying birds,

151,162 *Strophe, Antistrophe*: probably refer to the direction in which the Chorus danced while reciting specific stanzas. Strophe may have indicated dance steps to stage left, antistrophe to stage right.   151 *Voice from Zeus*: a reference to Apollo's prophecy. Zeus taught Apollo how to prophesy.   153 *Pytho*: Delphi.   156 *Delian Healer*: Apollo.   165 *Artemis*: goddess of virginity, childbirth, and hunting.

faster than indomitable fire, sped
to the shore of the god that is the sunset.°

Antistrophe 2

And with their deaths unnumbered dies the city.
Her children lie unpitied on the ground,   18
spreading death, unmourned.
Meanwhile young wives, and gray-haired mothers with them,
on the shores of the altars, from this side and that,
suppliants from mournful trouble,
    cry out their grief.   19
A hymn to the Healer shines,
    the flute a mourner's voice.
Against which, golden goddess, daughter of Zeus,
    send lovely Strength.

Strophe 3

Cause raging Ares°—who,   19
    armed now with no shield of bronze,
burns me, coming on amid loud cries—
to turn his back and run from my land,
with a fair wind behind, to the great
    hall of Amphitritē,°   20
or to the anchorage that welcomes no one,
Thrace's troubled sea!
If night lets something get away at last,
    it comes by day.
Fire-bearing god   20
    you who dispense the might of lightning,
Zeus! Father! Destroy him with your thunderbolt!

[*Enter* OEDIPUS *from the palace*.]

Antistrophe 3

Lycēan Lord!° From your looped
    bowstring, twisted gold,
I wish indomitable missiles might be scattered   21
and stand forward, our protectors; also fire-bearing
radiance of Artemis, with which
    she darts across the Lycian mountains.
I call the god whose head is bound in gold,

183 *god . . . sunset*: Hades, god of the underworld.   195 *Ares*: god of war and destruction.   200 *Amphitritē*: the Atlantic Ocean.   208 *Lycēan Lord*: Apollo.

with whom this country shares its name,   215
Bacchus,° wine-flushed, summoned by "euoi!,"
 Maenads' comrade,
to approach ablaze
 with gleaming . . . . . .
pine, opposed to that god-hated god.   220

Episode 1

OEDIPUS. I hear your prayer. Submit to what I say
 and to the labors that the plague demands
 and you'll get help and a relief from evils.
 I'll make the proclamation, though a stranger
 to the report and to the deed. Alone,   225
 had I no key, I would soon lose the track.
 Since it was only later that I joined you,
 to all the sons of Cadmus I say this:
 whoever has clear knowledge of the man
 who murdered Laius, son of Labdacus,   230
 I command him to reveal it all to me—
 nor fear if, to remove the charge, he must
 accuse himself: his fate will not be cruel—
 he will depart unstumbling into exile.
 But if you know another, or a stranger,   235
 to be the one whose hand is guilty, speak:
 I shall reward you and remember you.
 But if you keep your peace because of fear,
 and shield yourself or kin from my command,
 hear you what I shall do in that event: 240
 I charge all in this land where I have throne
 and power, shut out that man—no matter who—
 both from your shelter and all spoken words,
 nor in your prayers or sacrifices make
 him partner, nor allot him lustral° water.   245
 All men shall drive him from their homes: for he
 is the pollution that the god-sent Pythian
 response has only now revealed to me.
 In this way I ally myself in war
 with the divinity and the deceased.°   250
 And this curse, too, against the one who did it,
 whether alone in secrecy, or with others:
 may he wear out his life unblest and evil!
 I pray this, too: if he is at my hearth
 and in my home, and I have knowledge of him,   255

216 *Bacchus*: Dionysus, god of fertility and wine.   245 *lustral*: purifying.   250 *the deceased*: Laius.

may the curse pronounced on others come to me.
All this I lay to you to execute,
for my sake, for the god's, and for this land
now ruined, barren, abandoned by the gods.
Even if no god had driven you to it,   26
you ought not to have left this stain uncleansed,
the murdered man a nobleman, a king!
You should have looked! But now, since, as it happens,
It's I who have the power that he had once,
and have his bed, and a wife who shares our seed,   26
and common bond had we had common children
(had not his hope of offspring had bad luck—
but as it happened, luck lunged at his head);
because of this, as if for my own father,
I'll fight for him, I'll leave no means untried,   27
to catch the one who did it with his hand,
for the son of Labdacus, of Polydōrus,
of Cadmus before him, and of Agēnor.°
This prayer against all those who disobey:
the gods send out no harvest from their soil,   27
nor children from their wives. Oh, let them die
victims of this plague, or of something worse.
Yet for the rest of us, people of Cadmus,
we the obedient, may Justice, our ally,
and all the gods, be always on our side!   28
CHORAGOS. I speak because I feel the grip of your curse:
    the killer is not I. Nor can I point
    to him. The one who set us to this search,
    Phoebus, should also name the guilty man.
OEDIPUS. Quite right, but to compel unwilling gods—   28
    no man has ever had that kind of power.
CHORAGOS. May I suggest to you a second way?
OEDIPUS. A second or a third—pass over nothing!
CHORAGOS. I know of no one who sees more of what
    Lord Phoebus sees than Lord Tiresias.   29
    My Lord, one might learn brilliantly from him.
OEDIPUS. Nor is this something I have been slow to do.
    At Creon's word I sent an escort—twice now!
    I am astonished that he has not come.
CHORAGOS. The old account is useless. It told us nothing.   29
OEDIPUS. But tell it to me. I'll scrutinize all stories.
CHORAGOS. He is said to have been killed by travelers.
OEDIPUS. I have heard, but the one who did it no one sees.
CHORAGOS. If there is any fear in him at all,
    he won't stay here once he has heard that curse.   30
OEDIPUS. He won't fear words: he had no fear when he did it.

272–273. *Son . . . Agēnor*: refers to Laius by citing his genealogy.

[*Enter* TIRESIAS *from the right, led by a* SERVANT *and two of Oedipus's* ATTENDANTS.]

CHORAGOS.   Look there! There is the man who will convict him!
  It's the god's prophet they are leading here,
  one gifted with the truth as no one else.
OEDIPUS.   Tiresias, master of all omens—   305
  public and secret, in the sky and on the earth—
  your mind, if not your eyes, sees how the city
  lives with a plague, against which Thebes can find
  no Saviour or protector, Lord, but you.
  For Phoebus, as the attendants surely told you,   310
  returned this answer to us: liberation
  from the disease would never come unless
  we learned without a doubt who murdered Laius—
  put them to death, or sent them into exile.
  Do not begrudge us what you may learn from birds   315
  or any other prophet's path you know!
  Care for yourself, the city, care for me,
  care for the whole pollution of the dead!
  We're in your hands. To do all that he can
  to help another is man's noblest labor.   320
TIRESIAS.   How terrible to understand and get
  no profit from the knowledge! I knew this,
  but I forgot, or I had never come.
OEDIPUS.   What's this? You've come with very little zeal.
TIRESIAS.   Let me go home! If you will listen to me,   325
  You will endure your troubles better—and I mine.
OEDIPUS.   A strange request, not very kind to the land
  that cared for you—to hold back this oracle!
TIRESIAS.   I see your understanding comes to you
  inopportunely. So that won't happen to me . . .   330
OEDIPUS.   Oh, by the gods, if you understand about this,
  don't turn away! We're on our knees to you.
TIRESIAS.   None of you understands! I'll never bring
  my grief to light—I will not speak of yours.
OEDIPUS.   You know and won't declare it! Is your purpose   335
  to betray us and to destroy this land!
TIRESIAS.   I will grieve neither of us. Stop this futile
  cross-examination. I'll tell you nothing!
OEDIPUS.   Nothing? You vile traitor! You could provoke
  a stone to anger! You still refuse to tell?   340
  Can nothing soften you, nothing convince you?
TIRESIAS.   You blamed anger in me—you haven't seen.
  Can nothing soften you, nothing convince you?
OEDIPUS.   Who wouldn't fill with anger, listening
  to words like yours which now disgrace this city?   345
TIRESIAS.   It will come, even if my silence hides it.
OEDIPUS.   If it will come, then why won't you declare it?

TIRESIAS.   I'd rather say no more. Now if you wish,
    respond to that with all your fiercest anger!
OEDIPUS.   Now I am angry enough to come right out   3!
    with this conjecture: you, I think, helped plot
    the deed; you did it—even if your hand,
    cannot have struck the blow. If you could see,
    I should have said the deed was yours alone.
TIRESIAS.   Is that right! Then I charge you to abide   3:
    by the decree you have announced: from this day
    say no word to either these or me,
    for you are the vile polluter of this land!
OEDIPUS.   Aren't you appalled to let a charge like that
    come bounding forth? How will you get away?   3(
TIRESIAS.   You cannot catch me. I have the strength of truth.
OEDIPUS.   Who taught you this? Not your prophetic craft!
TIRESIAS.   You did. You made me say it. I didn't want to.
OEDIPUS.   Say what? Repeat it so I'll understand.
TIRESIAS.   I made no sense? Or are you trying me?   3(
OEDIPUS.   No sense I understood. Say it again!
TIRESIAS.   I say you are the murderer you seek.
OEDIPUS.   Again that horror! You'll wish you hadn't said that.
TIRESIAS.   Shall I say more, and raise your anger higher?
OEDIPUS.   Anything you like! Your words are powerless.   3;
TIRESIAS.   You live, unknowing, with those nearest to you
    in the greatest shame. You do not see the evil.
OEDIPUS.   You won't go on like that and never pay!
TIRESIAS.   I can if there is any strength in truth.
OEDIPUS.   In truth, but not in you! You have no strength,   3;
    blind in your ears, your reason, and your eyes.
TIRESIAS.   Unhappy man! Those jeers you hurl at me
    before long all these men will hurl at you.
OEDIPUS.   You are the child of endless night; it's not
    for me or anyone who sees to hurt you.   38
TIRESIAS.   It's not my fate to be struck down by you.
    Apollo is enough. That's his concern.
OEDIPUS.   Are these inventions Creon's or your own?
TIRESIAS.   No, your affliction is yourself, not Creon.
OEDIPUS.   Oh success!—in wealth, kingship, artistry,   38
    in any life that wins much admiration—
    the envious ill will stored up for you!
    to get at my command, a gift I did not
    seek, which the city put into my hands,
    my loyal Creon, colleague from the start,   39
    longs to sneak up in secret and dethrone me.
    So he's suborned this fortuneteller—schemer!
    deceitful beggar-priest!—who has good eyes
    for gains alone, though in his craft he's blind.
    Where were your prophet's powers ever proved?   39

Why, when the dog who chanted verse° was here,
did you not speak and liberate this city?
Her riddle wasn't for a man chancing by
to interpret; prophetic art was needed,
but you had none, it seems—learned from birds   400
or from a god. I came along, yes I,
Oedipus the ignorant, and stopped her—
by using thought, not augury from birds.
And it is I whom you now wish to banish,
so you'll be close to the Creontian throne.   405
You—and the plot's concocter—will drive out
pollution to your grief: you look quite old
or you would be the victim of that plot!

CHORAGOS.   It seems to us that this man's words were said
in anger, Oedipus, and yours as well.   410
Insight, not angry words, is what we need,
the best solution to the god's response.

TIRESIAS.   You are the king, and yet I am your equal
in my right to speak. In that I too am Lord.
for I belong to Loxias,° not you.   415
I am not Creon's man. He's nothing to me.
Hear this, since you have thrown my blindness at me:
Your eyes can't see the evil to which you've come,
nor where you live, nor who is in your house.
Do you know your parents? Not knowing, you are   420
their enemy, in the underworld and here.
A mother's and a father's double-lashing
terrible-footed curse will soon drive you out.
Now you can see, then you will stare into darkness.
What place will not be harbor to your cry,   425
or what Cithaeron° not reverberate
when you have heard the bride-song in your palace
to which you sailed? Fair wind to evil harbor!
Nor do you see how many other woes
will level you to yourself and to your children.   430
So, at my message, and at Creon, too,
splatter muck! There will never be a man
ground into wretchedness as you will be.

OEDIPUS.   Am I to listen to such things from him!
May you be damned! Get out of here at once!   435
Go! Leave my palace! Turn around and go!

[*TIRESIAS begins to move away from OEDIPUS.*]

TIRESIAS.   I wouldn't have come had you not sent for me.
OEDIPUS.   I did not know you'd talk stupidity,
or I wouldn't have rushed to bring you to my house.

---

396 *dog . . . verse*: The Sphinx.   415 *Loxias*: Apollo.   426 *Cithaeron*: reference to the
mountain on which Oedipus was to be exposed as an infant.

TIRESIAS. Stupid I seem to you, yet to your parents   440
    who gave you natural birth I seemed quite shrewd.
OEDIPUS. Who? Wait! Who is the one who gave me birth?
TIRESIAS. This day will give you birth,° and ruin too.
OEDIPUS. What murky, riddling things you always say!
TIRESIAS. Don't you surpass us all at finding out?   445
OEDIPUS. You sneer at what you'll find has brought me greatness.
TIRESIAS. And that's the very luck that ruined you.
OEDIPUS. I wouldn't care, just so I saved the city.
TIRESIAS. In that case I shall go. Boy, lead the way!
OEDIPUS. Yes, let him lead you off. Here, underfoot,   450
    you irk me. Gone, you'll cause no further pain.
TIRESIAS. I'll go when I have said what I was sent for.
    Your face won't scare me. You can't ruin me.
    I say to you, the man whom you have looked for
    as you pronounced your curses, your decrees   455
    on the bloody death of Laius—he is here!
    A seeming stranger, he shall be shown to be
    a Theban born, though he'll take no delight
    in that solution. Blind, who once could see,
    a beggar who was rich, through foreign lands   460
    he'll go and point before him with a stick.
    To his beloved children, he'll be shown
    a father who is also brother; to the one
    who bore him, son and husband; to his father,
    his seed-fellow and killer. Go in   465
    and think this out; and if you find I've lied,
    say then I have no prophet's understanding!

[*Exit* TIRESIAS, *led by a* SERVANT. OEDIPUS *exits into the palace with his* ATTENDANTS.]

STASIMON 1

Strophe 1

CHORUS. Who is the man of whom the inspired
        rock of Delphi° said
    he has committed the unspeakable   470
        with blood-stained hands?
    Time for him to ply a foot
    mightier than those of the horses
        of the storm in his escape;
    upon him mounts and plunges the weaponed   475
    son of Zeus,° with fire and thunderbolts,
    and in his train the dreaded goddesses
    of Death, who never miss.

443 *give you birth*: that is, identify your parents.   469 *rock of Delphi*: Apollo's oracle at
Delphi.   476 *son of Zeus*: Apollo.

Antistrophe 1

The message has just blazed,
    gleaming from the snows   480
of Mount Parnassus: we must track
    everywhere the unseen man.
He wanders, hidden by wild
forests, up through caves
    and rocks, like a bull,   485
anxious, with an anxious foot, forlorn.
He puts away from him the mantic° words come from earth's
navel,° at its center, yet these live
forever and still hover round him.

Strophe 2

Terribly he troubles me,   490
    the skilled interpreter of birds!°
I can't assent, nor speak against him.
    Both paths are closed to me.
I hover on the wings of doubt,
    not seeing what is here nor what's to come.   495
What quarrel started in the house of Labdacus°
or in the house of Polybus,°
    either ever in the past
    or now, I never
heard, so that . . . with this fact for my touchstone   500
I could attack the public
    fame of Oedipus, by the side of the Labdaceans
an ally, against the dark assassination.

Antistrophe 2

No, Zeus and Apollo
    understand and know things   505
mortal; but that another man
    can do more as a prophet than I can—
for that there is no certain test,
    though, skill to skill,
one man might overtake another.   510
No, never, not until
    I see the charges proved,
when someone blames him shall I nod assent.
For once, as we all saw, the winged maiden° came

---

487 *mantic*: prophetic.   487–88 *earth's navel*: Delphi.   491 *interpreter of birds*: Tiresias.
The Chorus is troubled by his accusations.   496 *house of Labdacus*: the line of
Laius.   497 *Polybus*: Oedipus's foster father.   514 *winged maiden*: The Sphinx.

against him: he was seen then to be skilled,   51[5]
    proved, by that touchstone, dear to the people. So,
never will my mind convict him of the evil.

EPISODE 2

[*Enter* CREON *from the right door of the skene and speaks to the* CHORUS.]

CREON.   Citizens, I hear that a fearful charge
    is made against me by King Oedipus!
    I had to come. If, in this crisis,   520
    he thinks that he has suffered injury
    from anything that I have said or done,
    I have no appetite for a long life—
    bearing a blame like that! It's no slight blow
    the punishment I'd take from what he said: 525
    it's the ultimate hurt to be called traitor
    by the city, by you, by my own people!
CHORAGOS.   The thing that forced that accusation out
    could have been anger, not the power of thought.
CREON.   But who persuaded him that thoughts of mine   530
    had led the prophet into telling lies?
CHORAGOS.   I do not know the thought behind his words.
CREON.   But did he look straight at you? Was his mind right
    when he said that I was guilty of this charge?
CHORAGOS.   I have no eyes to see what rulers do.   535
    But here he comes himself out of the house.

[*Enter* OEDIPUS *from the palace*.]

OEDIPUS.   What? You here? And can you really have
    the face and daring to approach my house
    when you're exposed as its master's murderer
    and caught, too, as the robber of my kingship?   540
    Did you see cowardice in me, by the gods,
    or foolishness, when you began this plot?
    Did you suppose that I would not detect
    your stealthy moves, or that I'd not fight back?
    It's your attempt that's folly, isn't it—   545
    tracking without followers or connections,
    kingship which is caught with wealth and numbers?
CREON.   Now wait! Give me as long to answer back!
    Judge me for yourself when you have heard me!
OEDIPUS.   You're eloquent, but I'd be slow to learn   550
    from you, now that I've seen your malice toward me.
CREON.   That I deny. Hear what I have to say.
OEDIPUS.   Don't you deny it! You are the traitor here!

CREON.   If you consider mindless willfulness
　　a prized possession, you are not thinking sense.　　　　　555
OEDIPUS.   If you think you can wrong a relative
　　and get off free, you are not thinking sense.
CREON.   Perfectly just, I won't say no. And yet
　　what is this injury you say I did you?
OEDIPUS.   Did you persuade me, yes or no, to send　　　　560
　　someone to bring that solemn prophet here?
CREON.   And I still hold to the advice I gave.
OEDIPUS.   How many years ago did your King Laius . . .
CREON.   Laius! Do what? Now I don't understand.
OEDIPUS.   Vanish—victim of a murderous violence?　　　　565
CREON.   That is a long count back into the past.
OEDIPUS.   Well, was this seer then practicing his art?
CREON.   Yes, skilled and honored just as he is today.
OEDIPUS.   Did he, back then, ever refer to me?
CREON.   He did not do so in my presence ever.　　　　570
OEDIPUS.   You did inquire into the murder then.
CREON.   We had to, surely, though we discovered nothing.
OEDIPUS.   But the "skilled" one did not say this then? Why not?
CREON.   I never talk when I am ignorant.
OEDIPUS.   But you're not ignorant of your own part.　　　　575
CREON.   What do you mean? I'll tell you if I know.
OEDIPUS.   Just this: if he had not conferred with you
　　he'd not have told about my murdering Laius.
CREON.   If he said that, you are the one who knows.
　　But now it's fair that you should answer me.　　　　580
OEDIPUS.   Ask on! You won't convict me as the killer.
CREON.   Well then, answer. My sister is your wife?
OEDIPUS.   Now there's a statement that I can't deny.
CREON.   You two have equal power in this country?
OEDIPUS.   She gets from me whatever she desires.　　　　585
CREON.   And I'm a third? The three of us are equals?
OEDIPUS.   That's where you're treacherous to your kinship!
CREON.   But think about this rationally, as I do.
　　First look at this: do you think anyone
　　prefers the anxieties of being king　　　　590
　　to untroubled sleep—if he has equal power?
　　I'm not the kind of man who falls in love
　　with kingship. I am content with a king's power.
　　And so would any man who's wise and prudent.
　　I get all things from you, with no distress;　　　　595
　　as king I would have onerous duties, too.
　　How could the kingship bring me more delight
　　than this untroubled power and influence?
　　I'm not misguided yet to such a point
　　that profitable honors aren't enough.　　　　600
　　As it is, all wish me well and all salute;

those begging you for something have me summoned,
for their success depends on that alone.
Why should I lose all this to become king?
A prudent mind is never traitorous.   60
Treason's a thought I'm not enamored of;
nor could I join a man who acted so.
In proof of this, first go yourself to Pytho°
and ask if I brought back the true response.
Then, if you find I plotted with that portent   61
reader,° don't have me put to death by your vote
only—I'll vote myself for my conviction.
Don't let an unsupported thought convict me!
It's not right mindlessly to take the bad
for good or to suppose the good are traitors.   61
Rejecting a relation who is loyal
is like rejecting life, our greatest love.
In time you'll know securely without stumbling,
for time alone can prove a just man just,
though you can know a bad man in a day.   62
CHORAGOS.   Well said, to one who's anxious not to fall.
Swift thinkers, Lord, are never safe from stumbling.
OEDIPUS.   But when a swift and secret plotter moves
against me, I must make swift counterplot.
If I lie quiet and await his move,   62
he'll have achieved his aims and I'll have missed.
CREON.   You surely cannot mean you want me exiled!
OEDIPUS.   Not exiled, no. Your death is what I want!
CREON.   If you would first define what envy is . . .
OEDIPUS.   Are you still stubborn? Still disobedient?   63
CREON.   I see you cannot think!
OEDIPUS.   For me I can.
CREON.   You should for me as well!
OEDIPUS.   But you're a traitor!
CREON.   What if you're wrong?
OEDIPUS.   Authority must be maintained.
CREON.   Not if the ruler's evil.
OEDIPUS.   Hear that, Thebes!
CREON.   It is my city too, not yours alone!   63
CHORAGOS.   Please don't, my Lords! Ah, just in time, I see
Jocasta there, coming from the palace.
With her help you must settle your quarrel.

[*Enter* JOCASTA *from the Palace*.]

JOCASTA.   Wretched men! What has provoked this ill-
advised dispute? Have you no sense of shame,   64
with Thebes so sick, to stir up private troubles?

608 *Pytho*: Delphi.   610–611 *portent reader*: Apollo's oracle or prophet.

Now go inside! And Creon, you go home!
Don't make a general anguish out of nothing!
CREON.   My sister, Oedipus your husband here
    sees fit to do one of two hideous things: 645
    to have me banished from the land—or killed!
OEDIPUS.   That's right: I caught him, Lady, plotting harm
    against my person—with a malignant science.
CREON.   May my life fail, may I die cursed, if I
    did any of the things you said I did!   650
JOCASTA.   Believe his words, for the god's sake, Oedipus,
    in deference above all to his oath
    to the gods. Also for me, and for these men!

KOMMOS°

Strophe 1

CHORUS.   Consent, with will and mind,
    my king, I beg of you!   655
OEDIPUS.   What do you wish me to surrender?
CHORUS.   Show deference to him who was not feeble in time past
    and is now great in the power of his oath!
OEDIPUS.   Do you know what you're asking?
CHORUS.   Yes.
OEDIPUS.   Tell me then.
CHORUS.   Never to cast into dishonored guilt, with an unproved   660
    assumption, a kinsman who has bound himself by curse.
OEDIPUS.   Now you must understand, when you ask this,
    you ask my death or banishment from the land.

Strophe 2

CHORUS.   No, by the god who is the foremost of all gods,
    the Sun! No! Godless,   665
        friendless, whatever death is worst of all,
    let that be my destruction, if this
        thought ever moved me!
    But my ill-fated soul
        this dying land   670
    wears out—the more if to these older troubles
    she adds new troubles from the two of you!
OEDIPUS.   Then let him go, though it must mean my death,
    or else disgrace and exile from the land.
    My pity is moved by your words, not by his—   675
    he'll only have my hate, wherever he goes.

654 *Kommos*: a dirge or lament sung by the Chorus and one or more of the chief characters.

CREON.   You're sullen as you yield; you'll be depressed
    when you've passed through this anger. Natures like yours
    are hardest on themselves. That's as it should be.
OEDIPUS.   Then won't you go and let me be?
CREON.   I'll go.   680
    Though you're unreasonable, they know I'm righteous.

                                    [Exit CREON.*]*

Antistrophe 1

CHORUS.   Why are you waiting, Lady?
    Conduct him back into the palace!
JOCASTA.   I will, when I have heard what chanced.   685
CHORUS.   Conjectures—words alone, and nothing based on thought.
    But even an injustice can devour a man.
JOCASTA.   Did the words come from both sides?
CHORUS.   Yes.
JOCASTA.   What was said?
CHORUS.   To me it seems enough! enough! the land already troubled,   690
    that this should rest where it has stopped.
OEDIPUS.   See what you've come to in your honest thought,
    in seeking to relax and blunt my heart?

Antistrophe 2

CHORUS.   I have not said this only once, my Lord.
    That I had lost my sanity,   695
        without a path in thinking—
    be sure this would be clear
        if I put you away
    who, when my cherished land
        wandered crazed   700
    with suffering, brought her back on course.
    Now, too, be a lucky helmsman!

JOCASTA.   Please, for the god's sake, Lord, explain to me
    the reason why you have conceived this wrath?
OEDIPUS.   I honor you, not them,° and I'll explain   705
    to you how Creon has conspired against me.
JOCASTA.   All right, if that will explain how the quarrel started.
OEDIPUS.   He says I am the murderer of Laius!
JOCASTA.   Did he claim knowledge or that someone told him?
OEDIPUS.   Here's what he did: he sent that vicious seer   710
    so he could keep his own mouth innocent.
JOCASTA.   Ah then, absolve yourself of what he charges!
    Listen to this and you'll agree, no mortal

705 *them*: the chorus.

is ever given skill in prophecy.
I'll prove this quickly with one incident.   715
It was foretold to Laius—I shall not say
by Phoebus himself, but by his ministers—
that when his fate arrived he would be killed
by a son who would be born to him and me.
And yet, so it is told, foreign robbers   720
murdered him, at a place where three roads meet.
As for the child I bore him, not three days passed
before he yoked the ball-joints of its feet,°
then cast it, by others' hands, on a trackless mountain.
That time Apollo did not make our child   725
a patricide, or bring about what Laius
feared, that he be killed by his own son.
That's how prophetic words determined things!
Forget them. The things a god must track
he will himself painlessly reveal.   730
OEDIPUS. Just now, as I was listening to you, Lady,
    what a profound distraction seized my mind!
JOCASTA. What made you turn around so anxiously?
OEDIPUS. I thought you said that Laius was attacked
    and butchered at a place where three roads meet.   735
JOCASTA. That is the story, and it is told so still.
OEDIPUS. Where is the place where this was done to him?
JOCASTA. The land's called Phocis, where a two-forked road
    comes in from Delphi and from Daulia.
OEDIPUS. And how much time has passed since these events?   740
JOCASTA. Just prior to your presentation here
    as king this news was published to the city.
OEDIPUS. Oh, Zeus, what have you willed to do to me?
JOCASTA. Oedipus, what makes your heart so heavy?
OEDIPUS. No, tell me first of Laius' appearance,   745
    what peak of youthful vigor he had reached.
JOCASTA. A tall man, showing his first growth of white.
    He had a figure not unlike your own.
OEDIPUS. Alas! It seems that in my ignorance
    I laid those fearful curses on myself.   750
JOCASTA. What is it, Lord? I flinch to see your face.
OEDIPUS. I'm dreadfully afraid the prophet sees.
    But I'll know better with one more detail.
JOCASTA. I'm frightened too. But ask: I'll answer you.
OEDIPUS. Was his retinue small, or did he travel   755
    with a great troop, as would befit a prince?
JOCASTA. There were just five in all, one a herald.
    There was a carriage, too, bearing Laius.
OEDIPUS. Alas! Now I see it! But who was it,
    Lady, who told you what you know about this?   760

---

723 *ball-joints of its feet*: the ankles.

JOCASTA.   A servant who alone was saved unharmed.

OEDIPUS.   By chance, could he be now in the palace?

JOCASTA.   No, he is not. When he returned and saw
    you had the power of the murdered Laius,
    he touched my hand and begged me formally   765
    to send him to the fields and to the pastures,
    so he'd be out of sight, far from the city.
    I did. Although a slave, he well deserved
    to win this favor, and indeed far more.

OEDIPUS.   Let's have him called back in immediately.   770

JOCASTA.   That can be done, but why do you desire it?

OEDIPUS.   I fear, Lady, I have already said
    too much. That's why I wish to see him now.

JOCASTA.   Then he shall come; but it is right somehow
    that I, too, Lord, should know what troubles you.   775

OEDIPUS.   I've gone so deep into the things I feared
    I'll tell you everything. Who has a right
    greater than yours, while I cross through this chance?
    Polybus of Corinth was my father,
    my mother was the Dorian Meropē.   780
    I was first citizen, until this chance
    attacked me—striking enough, to be sure,
    but not worth all the gravity I gave it.
    This: at a feast a man who'd drunk too much
    denied, at the wine, I was my father's son.   785
    I was depressed and all that day I barely
    held it in. Next day I put the question
    to my mother and father. They were enraged
    at the man who'd let this fiction fly at me.
    I was much cheered by them. And yet it kept   790
    grinding into me. His words kept coming back.
    Without my mother's or my father's knowledge
    I went to Pytho. But Phoebus sent me away
    dishonoring my demand. Instead, other
    wretched horrors he flashed forth in speech.   795
    He said that I would be my mother's lover,
    show offspring to mankind they could not look at,
    and be his murderer whose seed I am.°
    When I heard this, and ever since, I gauged
    the way to Corinth by the stars alone,   800
    running to a place where I would never see
    the disgrace in the oracle's words come true.
    But I soon came to the exact location
    where, as you tell of it, the king was killed.
    Lady, here is the truth. As I went on,   805
    when I was just approaching those three roads,
    a herald and a man like him you spoke of

798 *be . . . am*: that is, murder my father.

came on, riding a carriage drawn by colts.
Both the man out front and the old man himself°
tried violently to force me off the road.   810
The driver, when he tried to push me off,
I struck in anger. The old man saw this, watched
me approach, then leaned out and lunged down
with twin prongs° at the middle of my head!
He got more than he gave. Abruptly—struck   815
once by the staff in this my hand—he tumbled
out, head first, from the middle of the carriage.
And then I killed them all. But if there is
a kinship between Laius and this stranger,
who is more wretched than the man you see?   820
Who was there born more hated by the gods?
For neither citizen nor foreigner
may take me in his home or speak to me.
No, they must drive me off. And it is I
who have pronounced these curses on myself!   825
I stain the dead man's bed with these my hands,
by which he died. Is not my nature vile?
Unclean?—if I am banished and even
in exile I may not see my own parents,
or set foot in my homeland, or else be yoked   830
in marriage to my mother, and kill my father,
Polybus, who raised me and gave me birth?
If someone judged a cruel divinity
did this to me, would he not speak the truth?
You pure and awful gods, may I not ever   835
see that day, may I be swept away
from men before I see so great and so
calamitous a stain fixed on my person!
CHORAGOS.   These things seem fearful to us, Lord, and yet,
　until you hear it from the witness, keep hope!   840
OEDIPUS.   That is the single hope that's left to me,
　to wait for him, that herdsman—until he comes.
JOCASTA.   When he appears, what are you eager for?
OEDIPUS.   Just this: if his account agrees with yours
　then I shall have escaped this misery.   845
JOCASTA.   But what was it that struck you in my story?
OEDIPUS.   You said he spoke of robbers as the ones
　who killed him. Now: if he continues still
　to speak of many, then I could not have killed him.
　One man and many men just do not jibe.   850
　But if he says one belted man, the doubt
　is gone. The balance tips toward me. I did it.
JOCASTA.   No! He told it as I told you. Be certain.

---

809 *old man himself*: Laius.   813–814 *lunged . . . prongs*: Laius strikes Oedipus with a two-pronged horse goad or whip.

He can't reject that and reverse himself.
The city heard these things, not I alone.   85!
But even if he swerves from what he said,
he'll never show that Laius' murder, Lord,
occurred just as predicted. For Loxias
expressly said my son was doomed to kill him.
The boy—poor boy—he never had a chance   86(
to cut him down, for he was cut down first.
Never again, just for some oracle
will I shoot frightened glances right and left.
OEDIPUS.   That's full of sense. Nonetheless, send a man
to bring that farm hand here. Will you do it?   86!
JOCASTA.   I'll send one right away. But let's go in.
Would I do anything against your wishes?

[*Exit OEDIPUS and JOCASTA through the central door into the palace.*]

STASIMON 2

Strophe 1

CHORUS.   May there accompany me
the fate to keep a reverential purity in what I say,
in all I do, for which the laws have been set forth   87(
and walk on high, born to traverse the brightest,
highest upper air; Olympus° only
is their father, nor was it
mortal nature
that fathered them, and never will   87!
oblivion lull them into sleep;
the god in them is great and never ages.

Antistrophe 1

The will to violate, seed of the tyrant,
if it has drunk mindlessly of wealth and power,
without a sense of time or true advantage,   88(
mounts to a peak, then
plunges to an abrupt . . . destiny,
where the useful foot
is of no use. But the kind
of struggling that is good for the city   88!
I ask the god never to abolish.
The god is my protector: never will I give that up.

872 *Olympus*: Mount Olympus, home of the gods, treated as a god.

Strophe 2

But if a man proceeds disdainfully
    in deeds of hand or word
and has no fear of Justice   890
    or reverence for shrines of the divinities
(may a bad fate catch him
    for his luckless wantonness!),
if he'll not gain what he gains with justice
and deny himself what is unholy,   895
or if he clings, in foolishness, to the untouchable
(what man, finally, in such an action, will have strength
enough to fend off passion's arrows from his soul?),
if, I say, this kind of
    deed is held in honor—   900
why should I join the sacred dance?

Antistrophe 2

No longer shall I visit and revere
    Earth's navel,° the untouchable,
nor visit Abae's° temple,
    or Olympia,°   905
if the prophecies are not matched by events
    for all the world to point to.
No, you who hold the power, if you are rightly called
Zeus the king of all, let this matter not escape you
and your ever-deathless rule,   910
for the prophecies to Laius fade . . .
and men already disregard them;
nor is Apollo anywhere
    glorified with honors.
Religion slips away.   915

EPISODE 3

[*Enter* JOCASTA *from the palace carrying a branch wound with wool and a jar of incense. She is attended by two women.*]

JOCASTA.   Lords of the realm, the thought has come to me
    to visit shrines of the divinities
    with suppliant's branch in hand and fragrant smoke.
    For Oedipus excites his soul too much
    with alarms of all kinds. He will not judge   920

---

903 *Earth's navel*: Delphi   904 *Abae*: a town in Phocis where there was another oracle of Apollo.   905 *Olympia*: The oracle of Zeus was at Olympia.

the present by the past, like a man of sense.
He's at the mercy of all terror-mongers.

[*JOCASTA approaches the altar on the right and kneels.*]

Since I can do no good by counseling,
Apollo the Lycēan!—you are the closest—
I come a suppliant, with these my vows,   925
for a cleansing that will not pollute him.
For when we see him shaken we are all
afraid, like people looking at their helmsman.

[*Enter a MESSENGER along one of the Parados. He sees JOCASTA at the altar and then addresses
the CHORUS.*]

MESSENGER.   I would be pleased if you would help me, stranger.
Where is the palace of King Oedipus?   930
Or tell me where he is himself, if you know.
CHORUS.   This is his house, stranger. He is within.
This is his wife and mother of his children.
MESSENGER.   May she and her family find prosperity,
if, as you say, her marriage is fulfilled.   935
JOCASTA.   You also, stranger, for you deserve as much
for your gracious words. But tell me why you've come.
What do you wish? Or what have you to tell us?
MESSENGER.   Good news, my Lady, both for your house and
husband.
JOCASTA.   What is your news? And who has sent you to us?   940
MESSENGER.   I come from Corinth. When you have heard my
news
you will rejoice, I'm sure—and grieve perhaps.
JOCASTA.   What is it? How can it have this double power?
MESSENGER.   They will establish him their king, so say
the people of the land of Isthmia.°   945
JOCASTA.   But is old Polybus not still in power?
MESSENGER.   He's not, for death has clasped him in the tomb.
JOCASTA.   What's this? Has Oedipus' father died?
MESSENGER.   If I have lied then I deserve to die.
JOCASTA.   Attendant! Go quickly to your master,   950
and tell him this.

[*Exit an ATTENDANT into the palace.*]

Oracles of the gods!
Where are you now? The man whom Oedipus
fled long ago, for fear that he should kill him—
he's been destroyed by chance and not by him!

[*Enter OEDIPUS from the palace.*]

945 *land of Isthmia*: Corinth, which was on an isthmus.

OEDIPUS.   Darling Jocasta, my beloved wife,   955
  Why have you called me from the palace?
JOCASTA.   First hear what this man has to say. Then see
  what the god's grave oracle has come to now!
OEDIPUS.   Where is he from? What is this news he brings me?
JOCASTA.   From Corinth. He brings news about your father: 960
  that Polybus is no more! that he is dead!
OEDIPUS.   What's this, old man? I want to hear you say it.
MESSENGER.   If this is what must first be clarified,
  please be assured that he is dead and gone.
OEDIPUS.   By treachery or by the touch of sickness?   965
MESSENGER.   Light pressures tip agéd frames into their sleep.
OEDIPUS.   You mean the poor man died of some disease.
MESSENGER.   And of the length of years that he had tallied.
OEDIPUS.   Aha! Then why should we look to Pytho's vapors,°
  or to the birds that scream above our heads?°   970
  If we could really take those things for guides,
  I would have killed my father. But he's dead!
  He is beneath the earth, and here am I,
  who never touched a spear. Unless he died
  of longing for me and I "killed" him that way!   975
  No, in this case, Polybus, by dying, took
  the worthless oracle to Hades with him.
JOCASTA.   And wasn't I telling you that just now?
OEDIPUS.   You were indeed. I was misled by fear.
JOCASTA.   You should not care about this anymore.   980
OEDIPUS.   I must care. I must stay clear of my mother's bed.
JOCASTA.   What's there for man to fear? The realm of chance
  prevails. True foresight isn't possible.
  His life is best who lives without a plan.
  This marriage with your mother—don't fear it.   985
  How many times have men in dreams, too, slept
  with their own mothers! Those who believe such things
  mean nothing endure their lives most easily.
OEDIPUS.   A fine, bold speech, and you are right, perhaps,
  except that my mother is still living,   990
  so I must fear her, however well you argue.
JOCASTA.   And yet your father's tomb is a great eye.
OEDIPUS.   Illuminating, yes. But I still fear the living.
MESSENGER.   Who is the woman who inspires this fear?
OEDIPUS.   Meropē, Polybus' wife, old man.   995
MESSENGER.   And what is there about her that alarms you?
OEDIPUS.   An oracle, god-sent and fearful, stranger.
MESSENGER.   Is it permitted that another know?
OEDIPUS.   It is. Loxias once said to me

---

969 *Pytho's vapors*: the prophecies of the oracle at Delphi.   970 *birds . . . heads*: the
prophecies derived from interpreting the flights of birds.

I must have intercourse with my own mother   1000
and take my father's blood with these my hands.
So I have long lived far away from Corinth.
This has indeed brought much good luck, and yet,
to see one's parents' eyes is happiest.
MESSENGER.   Was it for this that you have lived in exile?   1005
OEDIPUS.   So I'd not be my father's killer, sir.
MESSENGER.   Had I not better free you from this fear,
   my Lord? That's why I came—to do you service.
OEDIPUS.   Indeed, what a reward you'd get for that!
MESSENGER.   Indeed, this is the main point of my trip,   1010
   to be rewarded when you get back home.
OEDIPUS.   I'll never rejoin the givers of my seed!°
MESSENGER.   My son, clearly you don't know what you're doing.
OEDIPUS.   But how is that, old man? For the gods' sake, tell me!
MESSENGER.   If it's because of them you won't go home.   1015
OEDIPUS.   I fear that Phoebus will have told the truth.
MESSENGER.   Pollution from the ones who gave you seed?
OEDIPUS.   That is the thing, old man, I always fear.
MESSENGER.   Your fear is groundless. Understand that.
OEDIPUS.   Groundless? Not if I was born their son.   1020
MESSENGER.   But Polybus is not related to you.
OEDIPUS.   Do you mean Polybus was not my father?
MESSENGER.   No more than I. We're both the same to you.
OEDIPUS.   Same? One who begot me and one who didn't?
MESSENGER.   He didn't beget you any more than I did.   1025
OEDIPUS.   But then, why did he say I was his son?
MESSENGER.   He got you as a gift from my own hands.
OEDIPUS.   He loved me so, though from another's hands?
MESSENGER.   His former childlessness persuaded him.
OEDIPUS.   But had you bought me, or begotten me?   1030
MESSENGER.   Found you. In the forest hallows of Cithaeron.
OEDIPUS.   What were you doing traveling in that region?
MESSENGER.   I was in charge of flocks which grazed those mountains.
OEDIPUS.   A wanderer who worked the flocks for hire?
MESSENGER.   Ah, but that day I was your savior, son.   1035
OEDIPUS.   From what? What was my trouble when you took me?
MESSENGER.   The ball-joints of your feet might testify.
OEDIPUS.   What's that? What makes you name that ancient trouble?
MESSENGER.   Your feet were pierced and I am your rescuer.
OEDIPUS.   A fearful rebuke those tokens left for me!   1040
MESSENGER.   That was the chance that names you who you are.
OEDIPUS.   By the gods, did my mother or my father do this?

1012 *givers of my seed*: that is, my parents. Oedipus still thinks Merope and Polybus are his parents.

MESSENGER.   That I don't know. He might who gave you to me.
OEDIPUS.   From someone else? You didn't chance on me?
MESSENGER.   Another shepherd handed you to me.   1045
OEDIPUS.   Who was he? Do you know? Will you explain!
MESSENGER.   They called him one of the men of—was it Laius?
OEDIPUS.   The one who once was king here long ago?
MESSENGER.   That is the one! The man was shepherd to him.
OEDIPUS.   And is he still alive so I can see him?   1050
MESSENGER.   But you who live here ought to know that best.
OEDIPUS.   Does any one of you now present know
      about the shepherd whom this man has named?
      Have you seen him in town or in the fields? Speak out!
      The time has come for the discovery!   1055
CHORAGOS.   The man he speaks of, I believe, is the same
      as the field hand you have already asked to see.
      But it's Jocasta who would know this best.
OEDIPUS.   Lady, do you remember the man we just
      now sent for—is that the man he speaks of?   1060
JOCASTA.   What? The man he spoke of? Pay no attention!
      His words are not worth thinking about. It's nothing.
OEDIPUS.   With clues like this within my grasp, give up?
      Fail to solve the mystery of my birth?
JOCASTA.   For the love of the gods, and if you love your life,   1065
      give up this search! My sickness is enough.
OEDIPUS.   Come! Though my mothers for three generations
      were in slavery, you'd not be lowborn!
JOCASTA.   No, listen to me! Please! Don't do this thing!
OEDIPUS.   I will not listen; I will search out the truth.   1070
JOCASTA.   My thinking is for you—it would be best.
OEDIPUS.   This "best" of yours is starting to annoy me.
JOCASTA.   Doomed man! Never find out who you are!
OEDIPUS.   Will someone go and bring that shepherd here?
      Leave her to glory in her wealthy birth!   1075
JOCASTA.   Man of misery! No other name
      shall I address you by, ever again.

[*Exit JOCASTA into the palace after a long pause.*]

CHORAGOS.   Why has your lady left, Oedipus,
      hurled by a savage grief? I am afraid
      disaster will come bursting from this silence.   1080
OEDIPUS.   Let it burst forth! However low this seed
      of mine may be, yet I desire to see it.
      She, perhaps—she has a woman's pride—
      is mortified by my base origins.
      But I who count myself the child of Chance,   1085
      the giver of good, shall never know dishonor.

She is my mother,° and the months my brothers
who first marked out my lowness, then my greatness.
I shall not prove untrue to such a nature
by giving up the search for my own birth.   1090

STASIMON 3

Strophe

CHORUS.   If I have mantic power
    and excellence in thought,
    by Olympus,
        you shall not, Cithaeron, at tomorrow's
    full moon,   1095
    fail to hear us celebrate you as the countryman
    of Oedipus, his nurse and mother,
    or fail to be the subject of our dance,
        since you have given pleasure
    to our king.   1100
    Phoebus, whom we summon by "iē!,"
    may this be pleasing to you!

Antistrophe

Who was your mother, son?
    which of the long-lived nymphs
    after lying with Pan,°   1105
        the mountain roaming . . . Or was it a bride
    of Loxias?°
    For dear to him are all the upland pastures.
    Or was it Mount Cyllēnē's lord,°
    or the Bacchic god,°   1110
        dweller of the mountain peaks,
    who received you as a joyous find
    from one of the nymphs of Helicon,
    the favorite sharers of his sport?

EPISODE 4

OEDIPUS.   If someone like myself, who never met him,   1115
    may calculate—elders, I think I see

1087 *She . . . mother*: Chance is my mother.   1105 *Pan*: god of shepherds and woodlands,
half man and half goat.   1107 *Loxias*: Apollo.   1109 *Mount . . . lord*: Hermes, messenger
of the gods.   1110 *Bacchic god*: Dionysus.

the very herdsman we've been waiting for.
His many years would fit that man's age,
and those who bring him on, if I am right,
are my own men. And yet, in real knowledge, 1120
you can outstrip me, surely: you've seen him.

[*Enter the old* HERDSMAN *escorted by two of Oedipus's* ATTENDANTS. *At first, the* HERDSMAN *will not look at* OEDIPUS.]

CHORAGOS. I know him, yes, a man of the house of Laius,
a trusty herdsman if he ever had one.
OEDIPUS. I ask you first, the stranger come from Corinth:
is this the man you spoke of?
MESSENGER   That's he you see. 1125
OEDIPUS. Then you, old man. First look at me! Now answer:
did you belong to Laius' household once?
HERDSMAN. I did. Not a purchased slave but raised in the palace.
OEDIPUS. How have you spent your life? What is your work?
HERDSMAN. Most of my life now I have tended sheep. 1130
OEDIPUS. Where is the usual place you stay with them?
HERDSMAN. On Mount Cithaeron. Or in that district.
OEDIPUS. Do you recall observing this man there?
HERDSMAN. Doing what? Which is the man you mean?
OEDIPUS. This man right here. Have you had dealings with him? 1135
HERDSMAN. I can't say right away. I don't remember.
MESSENGER. No wonder, master. I'll bring clear memory
to his ignorance. I'm absolutely sure
he can recall it, the district was Cithaeron,
he with a double flock, and I, with one, 1140
lived close to him, for three entire seasons,
six months long, from spring right to Arcturus.°
Then for the winter I'd drive mine to my fold,
and he'd drive his to Laius' pen again.
Did any of the things I say take place? 1145
HERDSMAN. You speak the truth, though it's from long ago.
MESSENGER. Do you remember giving me, back then,
a boy I was to care for as my own?
HERDSMAN. What are you saying? Why do you ask me that?
MESSENGER. There, sir, is the man who was that boy! 1150
HERDSMAN. Damn you! Shut your mouth! Keep your silence!
OEDIPUS. Stop! Don't you rebuke his words.
Your words ask for rebuke far more than his.
HERDSMAN. But what have I done wrong, most royal master?
OEDIPUS. Not telling of the boy of whom he asked. 1155
HERDSMAN. He's ignorant and blundering toward ruin.
OEDIPUS. Tell it willingly—or under torture.
HERDSMAN. Oh god! Don't—I am old—don't torture me!

1142 *Arcturus*: a star that is first seen in September in the Grecian sky.

OEDIPUS. Here! Someone put his hands behind his back!
HERDSMAN. But why? What else would you find out, poor man?   1160
OEDIPUS. Did you give him the child he asks about?
HERDSMAN. I did. I wish that I had died that day!
OEDIPUS. You'll come to that if you don't speak the truth.
HERDSMAN. It's if I speak that I shall be destroyed.
OEDIPUS. I think this fellow struggles for delay.   1165
HERDSMAN. No, no! I said already that I gave him.
OEDIPUS. From your own home, or got from someone else?
HERDSMAN. Not from my own. I got him from another.
OEDIPUS. Which of these citizens? What sort of house?
HERDSMAN. Don't—by the gods!—don't, master, ask me more!   1170
OEDIPUS. It means your death if I must ask again.
HERDSMAN. One of the children of the house of Laius.
OEDIPUS. A slave—or born into the family?
HERDSMAN. I have come to the dreaded thing, and I shall say it.
OEDIPUS. And I to hearing it, but hear I must.   1175
HERDSMAN. He was reported to have been—his son.
    Your lady in the house could tell you best.
OEDIPUS. Because she gave him to you?
HERDSMAN.   Yes, my lord.
OEDIPUS. What was her purpose?
HERDSMAN.   I was to kill the boy.
OEDIPUS. The child she bore?
HERDSMAN.   She dreaded prophecies.   1180
OEDIPUS. What were they?
HERDSMAN   The word was that he'd kill his parents.
OEDIPUS. Then why did you give him up to this old man?
HERDSMAN. In pity, master—so he would take him home,
    to another land. But what he did was save him
    for this supreme disaster. If you are the one   1185
    he speaks of—know your evil birth and fate!
OEDIPUS. Ah! All of it was destined to be true!
    Oh light, now may I look my last upon you,
    shown monstrous in my birth, in marriage monstrous,
    a murderer monstrous in those I killed.   1190

                                        [*Exit* OEDIPUS, *running into the palace.*]

STASIMON 4

Strophe 1

CHORUS. Oh generations of mortal men,
    while you are living, I will
        appraise your lives at zero!

What man
comes closer to seizing lasting blessedness   1195
than merely to seize its semblance,
and after living in this semblance, to plunge?
With your example before us,
with your destiny, yours,
    suffering Oedipus, no mortal   1200
can I judge fortunate.

Antistrophe 1

For he,° outranging everybody,
shot his arrow° and became the lord
    of wide prosperity and blessedness,
oh Zeus, after destroying   1205
the virgin with the crooked talons,°
singer of oracles; and against death,
in my land, he arose a tower of defense.
From which time you were called my king
and granted privileges supreme—in mighty   1210
Thebes the ruling lord.

Strophe 2

But now—whose story is more sorrowful than yours?
Who is more intimate with fierce calamities,
with labors, now that your life is altered?
Alas, my Oedipus, whom all men know: 1215
one great harbor°—
one alone sufficed for you,
as son and father,
when you tumbled,° plowman° of the woman's chamber.
How, how could your paternal   1220
    furrows, wretched man,
endure you silently so long.

Antistrophe 2

Time, all-seeing, surprised you living an unwilled life
and sits from of old in judgment on the marriage, not a marriage,
where the begetter is the begot as well.   1225
Ah, son of Laius . . . ,

1202 *he*: Oedipus.   1203 *shot his arrow*: took his chances; made a guess at the Sphinx's
riddle.   1206 *virgin . . . talons*: the Sphinx.   1216 *one great harbor*: metaphorical allusion
to Jocasta's body.   1219 *tumbled*: were born and had sex.   *plowman*: Plowing is used
here as a sexual metaphor.

would that—oh, would that
I had never seen you!
I wail, my scream climbing beyond itself
from my whole power of voice. To say it straight: 1230
    from you I got new breath—
but I also lulled my eye to sleep.°

EXODOS

[*Enter the* SECOND MESSENGER *from the palace.*]

SECOND MESSENGER.   You who are first among the citizens,
    what deeds you are about to hear and see!
    What grief you'll carry, if, true to your birth,   1235
    you still respect the house of Labdacus!
    Neither the Ister nor the Phasis river
    could purify this house, such suffering
    does it conceal, or soon must bring to light—
    willed this time, not unwilled. Griefs hurt worst   1240
    which we perceive to be self-chosen ones.
CHORAGOS.   They were sufficient, the things we knew before,
    to make us grieve. What can you add to those?
SECOND MESSENGER.   The thing that's quickest said and quickest heard:
    our own, our royal one, Jocasta's dead.   1245
CHORAGOS.   Unhappy queen! What was responsible?
SECOND MESSENGER.   Herself. The bitterest of these events
    is not for you, you were not there to see,
    but yet, exactly as I can recall it,
    you'll hear what happened to that wretched lady.   1250
    She came in anger through the outer hall,
    and then she ran straight to her marriage bed,
    tearing her hair with the fingers of both hands.
    Then, slamming shut the doors when she was in,
    she called to Laius, dead so many years,   1255
    remembering the ancient seed which caused
    his death, leaving the mother to the son
    to breed again an ill-born progeny.
    She mourned the bed where she, alas, bred double—
    husband by husband, children by her child.   1260
    From this point on I don't know how she died,
    for Oedipus then burst in with a cry,
    and did not let us watch her final evil.
    Our eyes were fixed on him. Wildly he ran
    to each of us, asking for his spear   1265
    and for his wife—no wife: where he might find

1232 *I . . . sleep*: I failed to see the corruption you brought.

the double mother-field, his and his children's.
He raved, and some divinity then showed him—
for none of us did so who stood close by.
With a dreadful shout—as if some guide were leading—   1270
he lunged through the double doors; he bent the hollow
bolts from the sockets, burst into the room,
and there we saw her, hanging from above,
entangled in some twisted hanging strands.
He saw, was stricken, and with a wild roar   1275
ripped down the dangling noose. When she, poor woman,
lay on the ground, there came a fearful sight:
he snatched the pins of worked gold from her dress,
with which her clothes were fastened: these he raised
and struck into the ball-joints of his eyes.°   1280
He shouted that they would no longer see
the evils he had suffered or had done,
see in the dark those he should not have seen,
and know no more those he once sought to know.
While chanting this, not once but many times   1285
he raised his hand and struck into his eyes.
Blood from his wounded eyes poured down his chin,
not freed in moistening drops, but all at once
a stormy rain of black blood burst like hail.
These evils, coupling them, making them one,   1290
have broken loose upon both man and wife.
The old prosperity that they had once
was true prosperity, and yet today,
mourning, ruin, death, disgrace, and every
evil you could name—not one is absent.   1295
CHORAGOS.   Has he allowed himself some peace from all this grief?
SECOND MESSENGER.   He shouts that someone slide the bolts and show
    to all the Cadmeians the patricide,
    his mother's—I can't say it, it's unholy—
    so he can cast himself out of the land,   1300
    not stay and curse his house by his own curse.
    He lacks the strength, though, and he needs a guide,
    for his is a sickness that's too great to bear.
    Now you yourself will see: the bolts of the doors
    are opening. You are about to see   1305
    a vision even one who hates must pity.

[*Enter the blinded* OEDIPUS *from the palace, led in by a household* SERVANT.]

CHORAGOS.   This suffering sends terror through men's eyes,
    terrible beyond any suffering
    my eyes have touched. Oh man of pain,

1280 *ball-joints of his eyes*: his eyeballs. Oedipus blinds himself in both eyes at the same time.

what madness reached you? Which god from far off,   1310
surpassing in range his longest spring,
    struck hard against your god-abandoned fate?
Oh man of pain,
I cannot look upon you—though there's so much
I would ask you, so much to hear,   1315
so much that holds my eyes—
    so awesome the convulsions you send through me.

OEDIPUS. Ah! Ah! I am a man of misery.
Where am I carried? Pity me! Where
is my voice scattered abroad on wings?   1320
        Divinity, where has your lunge transported me?

CHORAGOS. To something horrible, not to be heard or seen.

KOMMOS

Strophe 1

OEDIPUS. Oh, my cloud
of darkness, abominable, unspeakable as it attacks me,
not to be turned away, brought by an evil wind!   1325
Alas!
Again alas! Both enter me at once:
the sting of the prongs,° the memory of evils!

CHORUS. I do not marvel that in these afflictions
you carry double griefs and double evils.   1330

Antistrophe 1

OEDIPUS. Ah, friend,
so you at least are there, resolute servant!
Still with a heart to care for me, the blind man.
Oh! Oh!
I know that you are there. I recognize   1335
even inside my darkness, that voice of yours.

CHORUS. Doer of horror, how did you bear to quench
your vision? What divinity raised your hand?

Strophe 2

OEDIPUS. It was Apollo there, Apollo, friends,
who brought my sorrows, vile sorrows to their perfection,   1340
    these evils that were done to me.
But the one who struck them with his hand,
    that one was none but I, in wretchedness.

1328 *prongs*: refers to both the whip that Laius used and the two gold pins Oedipus used
to blind himself.

For why was I to see
when nothing I could see would bring me joy?   1345
CHORUS.   Yes, that is how it was.
OEDIPUS.   What could I see, indeed,
or what enjoy—what greeting
is there I could hear with pleasure, friends?
Conduct me out of the land   1350
          as quickly as you can!
Conduct me out, my friends,
     the man utterly ruined,
supremely cursed,
     the man who is by gods   1355
the most detested of all men!
CHORUS.   Wretched in disaster and in knowledge:
oh, I could wish you'd never come to know!

Antistrophe 2

OEDIPUS.   May he be destroyed, whoever freed the savage shackles
from my feet when I'd been sent to the wild pasture,   1360
          whoever rescued me from murder
and became my savior—
     a bitter gift:
if I had died then,
I'd not have been such grief to self and kin.   1365
CHORUS.   I also would have had it so.
OEDIPUS.   I'd not have returned to be my father's
murderer; I'd not be called by men
my mother's bridegroom.
Now I'm without a god,   1370
          child of a polluted parent,
fellow progenitor with him
     who gave me birth in misery.
If there's an evil that
     surpasses evils, that   1375
has fallen to the lot of Oedipus.

CHORAGOS.   How can I say that you have counseled well?
Better not to be than live a blind man.
OEDIPUS.   That this was not the best thing I could do—
don't tell me that, or advise me any more!   1380
Should I descend to Hades and endure
to see my father with these eyes? Or see
my poor unhappy mother? For I have done,
to both of these, things too great for hanging.
Or is the sight of children to be yearned for,   1385
to see new shoots that sprouted as these did?
Never, never with these eyes of mine!
Nor city, nor tower, nor holy images

of the divinities! For I, all-wretched,
most nobly raised—as no one else in Thebes—   1390
deprived myself of these when I ordained
that all expel the impious one—god-shown
to be polluted, and the dead king's son!°
Once I exposed this great stain upon me,
could I have looked on these with steady eyes?   1395
No! No! And if there were a way to block
the source of hearing in my ears, I'd gladly
have locked up my pitiable body,
so I'd be blind and deaf. Evils shut out—
that way my mind could live in sweetness.   1400
Alas, Cithaeron,° why did you receive me?
Or when you had me, not killed me instantly?
I'd not have had to show my birth to mankind.
Polybus, Corinth, halls—ancestral,
they told me—how beautiful was your ward,   1405
a scar that held back festering disease!
Evil my nature, evil my origin.
You, three roads, and you, secret ravine,
you oak grove, narrow place of those three paths
that drank my blood° from these my hands, from him   1410
who fathered me, do you remember still
the things I did to you? When I'd come here,
what I then did once more? Oh marriages! Marriages!
You gave us life and when you'd planted us
you sent the same seed up, and then revealed   1415
fathers, brothers, sons, and kinsman's blood,
and brides, and wives, and mothers, all the most
atrocious things that happen to mankind!
One should not name what never should have been.
Somewhere out there, then, quickly, by the gods,   1420
cover me up, or murder me, or throw me
to the ocean where you will never see me more!

[*OEDIPUS moves toward the* CHORUS *and they back away from him.*]

Come! Don't shrink to touch this wretched man!
Believe me, do not be frightened! I alone
of all mankind can carry these afflictions.   1425

[*Enter* CREON *from the palace with* ATTENDANTS.]

CHORAGOS.   Tell Creon what you wish for. Just when we need him
he's here. He can act, he can advise you.
He's now the land's sole guardian in your place.

1391–1393 *I . . . son*: Oedipus refers to his own curse against the murderer as well as his
sins of patricide and incest.   1401 *Cithaeron*: the mountain on which the infant Oedipus
was supposed to be exposed.   1410 *my blood*: that is, the blood of my father, Laius.

OEDIPUS.   Ah! Are there words that I can speak to him?
    What ground for trust can I present? It's proved   1430
    that I was false to him in everything.
CREON.   I have not come to mock you, Oedipus,
    nor to reproach you for your former falseness.
    You men, if you have no respect for sons
    of mortals, let your awe for the all-feeding   1435
    flames of lordly Hēlius° prevent
    your showing unconcealed so great a stain,
    abhorred by earth and sacred rain and light.
    Escort him quickly back into the house!
    If blood kin only see and hear their own   1440
    afflictions, we'll have no impious defilement.
OEDIPUS.   By the gods, you've freed me from one terrible fear,
    so nobly meeting my unworthiness:
    grant me something—not for me; for you!
CREON.   What do you want that you should beg me so?   1445
OEDIPUS.   To drive me from the land at once, to a place
    where there will be no man to speak to me!
CREON.   I would have done just that—had I not wished
    to ask first of the god what I should do.
OEDIPUS.   His answer was revealed in full—that I,   1450
    the patricide, unholy, be destroyed.
CREON.   He said that, but our need is so extreme,
    it's best to have sure knowledge what must be done.
OEDIPUS.   You'll ask about a wretched man like me?
CREON.   Is it not time you put your trust in the god?   1455
OEDIPUS.   But I bid you as well, and shall entreat you.
    Give her who is within what burial
    you will—you'll give your own her proper rites;
    but me—do not condemn my fathers' land
    to have me dwelling here while I'm alive,   1460
    but let me live on mountains—on Cithaeron
    famed as mine, for my mother and my father,
    while they yet lived, made it my destined tomb,
    and I'll be killed by those who wished my ruin!
    And yet I know: no sickness will destroy me,   1465
    nothing will: I'd never have been saved
    when left to die unless for some dread evil.
    Then let my fate continue where it will!
    As for my children, Creon, take no pains
    for my sons—they're men and they will never lack   1470
    the means to live, wherever they may be—
    but my two wretched, pitiable girls,
    who never ate but at my table, never
    were without me—everything that I

1436 *Hēlius*: the sun.

would touch, they'd always have a share of it— 1475
please care for them! Above all, let me touch
them with my hands and weep aloud my woes!
Please, my Lord!
Please, noble heart! Touching with my hands,
I'd think I held them as when I could see. 1480

[*Enter* ANTIGONE *and* ISMENE *from the palace with* ATTENDANTS.]

What's this?
Oh gods! Do I hear, somewhere, my two dear ones
sobbing? Has Creon really pitied me
and sent to me my dearest ones, my children?
Is that it? 1485
CREON.   Yes, I prepared this for you, for I knew
you'd feel this joy, as you have always done.
OEDIPUS.   Good fortune, then, and, for your care, be guarded
far better by divinity than I was!
Where are you, children? Come to me! Come here 1490
to these my hands, hands of your brother, hands
of him who gave you seed, hands that made
these once bright eyes to see now in this fashion.

[OEDIPUS *embraces his daughters*.]

He, children, seeing nothing, knowing nothing,
he fathered you where his own seed was plowed. 1495
I weep for you as well, though I can't see you,
imagining your bitter life to come,
the life you will be forced by men to live.
What gatherings of townsmen will you join,
what festivals, without returning home 1500
in tears instead of watching holy rites?
And when you've reached the time for marrying,
where, children, is the man who'll run the risk
of taking on himself the infamy
that will wound you as it did my parents? 1505
What evil is not here? Your father killed
his father, plowed the one who gave him birth,
and from the place where he was sown, from there
he got you, from the place he too was born.
These are the wounds: then who will marry you? 1510
No man, my children. No, it's clear that you
must wither in dry barrenness, unmarried.

[OEDIPUS *addresses* CREON.]

Son of Menoeceus! You are the only father
left to them—we two who gave them seed
are both destroyed: watch that they don't become 1515
poor, wanderers, unmarried—they are your kin.

Let not my ruin be their ruin, too!
No, pity them! You see how young they are,
bereft of everyone, except for you.
Consent, kind heart, and touch me with your hand!   1520

[CREON *grasps* OEDIPUS'S *right hand.*]

You, children, if you had reached an age of sense,
I would have counseled much. Now, pray you may live
always where it's allowed, finding a life
better than his was, who gave you seed.
CREON.   Stop this now. Quiet your weeping. Move away, into the house.   1525
OEDIPUS.   Bitter words, but I obey them.
CREON.   There's an end to all things.
OEDIPUS.   I have first this request.
CREON.   I will hear it.
OEDIPUS.   Banish me from my homeland.
CREON.   You must ask that of the god.
OEDIPUS.   But I am the gods' most hated man!
CREON.   Then you will soon get what you want.
OEDIPUS.   Do you consent?
CREON.   I never promise when, as now, I'm ignorant.   1530
OEDIPUS.   Then lead me in.
CREON.   Come. But let your hold fall from your children.
OEDIPUS.   Do not take them from me, ever!
CREON   Do not wish to keep all of the power.
You had power, but that power did not follow you through life.

[OEDIPUS'S *daughters are taken from him and led into the palace by* ATTENDANTS. OEDIPUS
is led into the palace by a SERVANT. CREON *and the other* ATTENDANTS *follow. Only the*
CHORUS *remains.*]

CHORUS.   People of Thebes, my country, see: here is that Oedipus—
he who "knew" the famous riddle, and attained the highest power,   1535
whom all citizens admired, even envying his luck!
See the billows of wild troubles which he has entered now!
Here is the truth of each man's life: we must wait, and see his end,
scrutinize his dying day, and refuse to call him happy
till he has crossed the border of his life without pain.   1540

[*Exit the* CHORUS *along each of the Parados.*]

QUESTIONS

Prologue and Parados

1. What is the situation in Thebes as the play begins? Why does Oedipus want
    to find Laius's murderer?

Episode 1 and Stasimon 1

2. How does Oedipus react to Tiresias's refusal to speak? How is this reaction characteristic of Oedipus? What other instances of this sort of behavior can you find in Oedipus's story?

3. When Tiresias does speak, he answers the central question of the play and tells the truth. Why doesn't Oedipus recognize this as the truth?

Episode 2 and Stasimon 2

4. What does Oedipus accuse Creon of doing? How does Creon defend himself? Do you find Creon's defense convincing? Why?

5. What is Jocasta's attitude toward oracles and prophecy? Why does she have this attitude? How does it contrast with the attitude of the chorus?

6. At what point in the play does Oedipus begin to suspect that he killed Laius? What details make him begin to suspect himself?

Episode 3 and Stasimon 3

7. What news does the messenger from Corinth bring? Why does this news seem to be good at first? How is this situation reversed?

Episode 4 and Stasimon 4

8. What do you make of the coincidence that the same herdsman (1) saved the infant Oedipus from death, (2) was with Laius at the place where three roads meet and was the lone survivor of the attack, and (3) will now be the agent to destroy Oedipus?

9. What moral does the chorus see in Oedipus's life?

Exodos

10. Why does Oedipus blind himself? What is the significance of the instruments that he uses to blind himself?

11. What acts specifically indicate Creon's careful nature, his reverence for the gods, his political wisdom, and his awareness of power?

12. Who or what does Oedipus blame for his tragic life and destruction?

TOPICS FOR WRITING AND FURTHER DISCUSSION

1. In *Oedipus*, the peripeteia, anagnorisis, and catastrophe all occur at the same moment. When is this moment? Who is most severely affected by it?

2. Sophocles tells the events of Oedipus's life out of chronological order. Put all the events of his life in chronological order and consider how you might

dramatize them. Why does Sophocles' ordering of these events produce an effective play?

3. Each episode of the play introduces new conflicts: Oedipus against the plague, against Tiresias, against Creon. What is the central conflict of the play? Why is it central?

4. All the violent acts of this play—the suicide of Jocasta and the blinding of Oedipus—occur offstage and are reported rather than shown to the audience. What are the advantages of dealing with violence this way? What are the disadvantages?

5. Discuss the use of coincidences in the play. How do you react to them? Do they seem convincing or forced, given the plot of the play?

6. Explore the ways in which Sophocles employs dramatic irony, with reference to three specific examples.

7. Consider the extent to which *Oedipus* is a tragedy of both the individual and the state. What do you think will happen to Thebes after Oedipus is exiled?

8. Discuss the functions of the chorus and the Choragos. What do the choral odes contribute to the play?

9. Much is made of the contrast between seeing and blindness in the play. Consider this contrast as it relates to Oedipus and Tiresias.

10. Early in the play Oedipus begins a search for a murderer. How does the object of his search change as the play progresses? Why does it change?

11. Develop an argument that asserts that Oedipus's fall is the result of aspects of his personality. What specific characteristics and patterns of behavior would you identify as causes? What specific details from the play would you use to support this argument?

12. Develop an argument that asserts that Oedipus's fall is the result of fate, predestination, and the gods. What specific incidents and passages in the play would you cite as evidence in such an argument?

THE THEATER OF SHAKESPEARE

The later part of the English Renaissance (1580–1642) was the golden age of British drama. During the reigns of Queen Elizabeth I (1558–1603) and King James I (1603–1625) the theater in England reached a pinnacle of development that began during the early Middle Ages. Greek and Roman drama were, for the most part, lost to the world for almost a thousand years from the fall of Rome in A.D. 476 until the Renaissance. As a consequence, drama had to be "reinvented" in England and Europe during the Middle Ages. Not surprisingly, it once again developed in a religious context. Drama was reborn in the tenth century when short dialogues (called **tropes**) were inserted into the Catholic mass to dramatize passages of the Gospel. As these tropes grew longer and more complicated, they evolved into mystery plays, miracle plays, and finally morality plays. **Mystery plays** are dramatizations of Bible stories; **Miracle plays** provide enactments of saints' lives. **Morality plays** (like *Everyman,* see p. 1075) are designed to teach the principles of Christian life and salvation. Much of this religious drama was originally performed by the clergy. After the thirteenth century, however, the plays were taken over by workingmen in the craft guilds (medieval unions) and, still later, by troupes of professional actors.

In the early part of the English Renaissance, religious drama fused with rediscovered Roman drama and neoclassical European drama to produce **Tudor interludes** (the house of Tudor ruled England from 1485 to 1603). These interludes were short tragedies, comedies, or history plays that were performed by students or professional actors. The religious drama and the interludes, in turn, gave birth to the first generation of Elizabethan playwrights: Christopher Marlowe, Thomas Kyd, Robert Greene, George Peele, Thomas Lodge, and John Lyly. These were the men whose plays William Shakespeare watched and acted in when he first arrived in London from Stratford-upon-Avon in the early 1590s.

Like Elizabethan drama, the Elizabethan public theater represents the high point of a long process of development and refinement. Before 1576 there were no permanent theater buildings in London or the suburbs. Instead, plays were performed by traveling companies of professional players on temporary stages set up in inn yards or in bear-baiting or bull-baiting arenas. Plays were also performed at court, in the great halls of aristocratic houses, in the law courts, and at universities. All these locations contributed to the ultimate shape and design of the Elizabethan public theater.

The Globe Theater, most famous of the Elizabethan public theaters, was built on the south bank of the Thames River in the suburbs of London in 1599 by members of the Lord Chamberlain's Men, the acting company to which Shakespeare belonged. It was an octagonal building with a central courtyard open to the sky. The stage thrust about 30 feet out into the yard from one of the eight sides of the building. On the remaining seven sides were three floors of galleries. Spectators at the theater sat in these galleries or, for much less money, stood in the yard around the stage (these people were called *groundlings* since they stood "on the ground"). Compared with the massive Greek theaters, the Globe was relatively small. Although it could hold as many as 2,500 spectators, no one stood or sat more than 70 feet from the action of the play.

The stage in the Globe was a *thrust stage* that extended far into the yard and was raised about five feet from the ground. The cellar area thus created under the stage was called the **Hell.** In the center of the stage, leading to this Hell, was a trap door that was often used for the entrances and exits of devils, monsters, or ghosts. It was also used when the staging required graves, pits, dungeons, or the like. On the left and right of the stage were two pillars holding up the **Heavens,** a decorated roof over

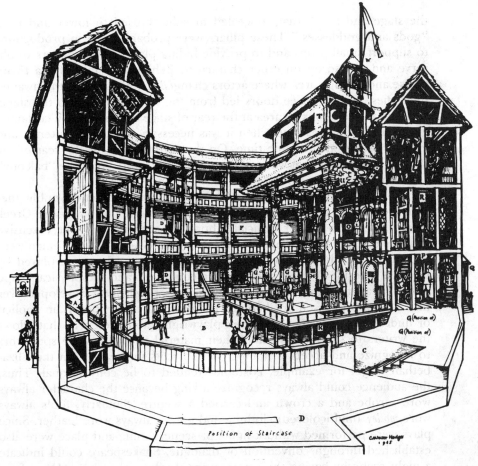

The Globe Playhouse,
1599-1613

A CONJECTURAL

RECONSTRUCTION

KEY

AA   Main entrance
B   The Yard
CC   Entrances to lowest gallery
D   Entrances to staircase and upper galleries
E   Corridor serving the different sections of the middle gallery
F   Middle gallery ('Twopenny Rooms')
G   'Gentlemen's Rooms' or 'Lords' Rooms'
H   The stage

J   The hanging being put up round the stage
K   The 'Hell' under the stage
L   The stage trap, leading down to the Hell
MM   Stage doors
N   Curtained 'place behind the stage'
O   Gallery above the stage, used as required sometimes by musicians, sometimes by spectators, and often as part of the play
P   Back-stage area (the tiring-house)
Q   Tiring-house door
R   Dressing-rooms
S   Wardrobe and storage
T   The hut housing the machine for lowering enthroned gods, etc., to the stage
U   The 'Heavens'
W   Hoisting the playhouse flag

From C. Walter Hodges, *The Globe Restored* (W. W. Norton and Co.)

the stage and a hut that concealed machinery used to lower and raise "gods and goddesses." These pillars were probably used in productions to support small props and to provide hiding places for characters to observe and eavesdrop on other characters. Behind the stage was a **tiring house** and storage area where actors changed their costumes and awaited their cues. Two or three doors led from the tiring house onto the stage. In addition, there was an area at the rear of stage center where a curtained enclosure could be set up when it was necessary to indicate interior and exterior scenes at the same time. On the second floor, at the rear of the stage, was a **gallery** that was used by musicians, actors (as in the "balcony" scene in Shakespeare's *Romeo and Juliet*), or spectators.

Plays were performed at the Globe and other Elizabethan public theaters beginning at about two o'clock in the afternoon. As in the Greek theater, there was neither artificial lighting nor scenery. However, extensive props and elaborate costumes were used. As in Greek drama, women were excluded from the Elizabethan stage; all women's roles were played by boys. As a result of these performance conditions and the physical shape of the Elizabethan theater, a number of *dramatic conventions* developed over time. As was discussed in Chapter 27, a dramatic convention is an implicit or understood agreement between playwrights and audiences that allows the writers to simplify and limit their material and allows the spectators to recognize and accept a number of shortcuts in staging. On the Elizabethan stage, for example, costumes tended to be conventional. Thus, the audience could always recognize a king because the character always wore a robe and a crown and carried a sceptre. Similarly, fools always wore *motley* (multicolored) clothing and ghosts always wore leather. Since plays were performed without lights or scenery, time and place were also established through convention or dialogue. Shakespeare could indicate a night scene by having the actors carry candles or torches. More often, however, time and place are specified, when necessary, by having a character tell us where he is or what time it is. In act 2 of Shakespeare's *As You Like It*, for example, the heroine lets the audience know where she has arrived by remarking, "Well, this is the forest of Arden" (2.4.13). Similarly, Horatio informs us that it is dawn in the first scene of *Hamlet* by saying, "But look, the morn in russet mantle clad / Walks o'er the dew of yon high eastward hill" (1.1.166–167).

The actors in the Elizabethan public theaters used no masks. Instead, they developed over time a series of conventional expressions and gestures which they used to convey emotion. Indeed, these conventions of presentation may have led to many instances of ranting and overacting. Shakespeare alludes to this overacting in act 3 of *Hamlet* when he has the prince warn a company of traveling actors not to "mouth" their lines "as many of your players do" and not to "saw the air too much with your hands"

(3.2.1–4). Hamlet goes on to condemn actors who "tear a passion to tatters, to very rags, to split the ears of the groundlings . . ." (3.2.9–10).

The closeness of the spectators to the thrust stage may have led to two additional conventions of presentation that are very important to Elizabethan and Shakespearean drama. One of these, called an **aside,** allows a character to make a very brief remark directly to the audience or to another character without the rest of the characters on stage hearing the lines. In the other, called a **soliloquy,** a single character alone on stage speaks his or her thoughts or plans at length directly to the spectators. In Hamlet's second soliloquy (2.2.524–580), for example, the prince criticizes his own emotional detachment from his father's murder and lets us in on his plans to use a play in order to test Claudius's guilt. Both of these conventions tend to make for a great deal of dramatic irony, since both provide the audience with information that is withheld from most of the characters.

Because of the relatively small size of the Globe theater and the thrust of its stage, performances were intimate and immediate. The actors had a great deal of playing space at their disposal. They could use the rear of the stage or the upper gallery, but they could also use the very front of the stage and thus play within several feet of the groundlings. There was no barrier or separation between the audience and the actors: no orchestra and chorus as there were in the Greek theater, and no proscenium and curtain as there are in most twentieth-century theaters. Consequently, we can imagine the actors playing directly to the audience, and we can also assume that the groundlings reacted immediately to things they liked or disliked. In the Elizabethan theater, then, there was a good deal of interaction between the actors and the spectators. The plays were apparently performed at an extremely quick pace, without any intermissions or indications of changes in scene or act other than an occasional rhymed couplet. With no curtain to raise or lower and no scenery to change, shifts in scene were indicated by having one group of characters walk off one side of the stage and another group walk on from the opposite side at the same time. This type of scene change produced rapid shifts in time and place and made for very fluid and fast-paced plays.

WILLIAM SHAKESPEARE, *HAMLET*

William Shakespeare, the greatest English playwright and poet, was born in 1564 in Stratford-upon-Avon, attended the Stratford grammar school, married in 1582, had three children, and moved to London without his family sometime between 1585 and 1592. During this same period, he began to act in professional acting companies and to write poetry and plays; by 1595 he was recognized as a major writer of comedies and tragedies. He eventually became associated with the leading theatrical company of Elizabethan England, the Lord Chamberlain's Men, and wrote thirty-seven plays: sixteen comedies or tragicomedies, eleven tragedies, and ten history plays (dramatizations of English history).

When Shakespeare's acting company staged *Hamlet* for the first time in 1600 or 1601 at the Globe Theater, it is more than likely that the Elizabethan audience already knew the story of the Danish prince who avenges his father's murder and is killed in the process. There is a fair amount of evidence that a play based on the Hamlet story, now lost, had been written and performed before 1589. If this is the case, then most of the spectators would have known that King Claudius had murdered the old King Hamlet and married the dead king's wife. Since only Claudius and Hamlet (and later Horatio) possess information about the murder, the audience knew a great deal more than most of the characters. Thus the play was open to the same kinds of dramatic irony we find in *Oedipus the King*.

Even if the spectators did not know the Hamlet story, they would have been quite familiar with the traditions and conventions of **revenge tragedy.** By the time Shakespeare wrote *Hamlet*, the Elizabethans had been watching tragedies of revenge for over twenty years. They were introduced to this type of drama in the 1570s and early 1580s when the plays of Seneca, a Roman playwright, were translated into English and performed. More important, the audience was familiar with Thomas Kyd's *Spanish Tragedy* (ca. 1587), the first English revenge tragedy and the most popular play of the English Renaissance. Thus, the spectators anticipated that specific key features and conventions of revenge tragedy would be repeated in *Hamlet*. They expected, for example, a ghost who calls for vengeance and a revenger who pretends to be insane at least part of the time. They also expected that the revenge itself would be postponed through some twist of the plot until the catastrophe of the play. Above all else, the audience understood that the revenger—in this case Hamlet—would die at the end of the play. Since personal blood vengeance was forbidden by both the church and the state, a successful revenger was automatically condemned as an outlaw. The conventions of revenge tragedy thus dictate that a revenger—no matter how good the man or how just the cause— had to die. In the light of this convention, it is possible to see Hamlet's fall partly as the result of circumstances beyond his control and partly as the result of his commitment to personal blood revenge. To make such an assertion about Hamlet, however, oversimplifies both the character and the play.

Although prepared for *Hamlet* by the traditional formulas of revenge tragedy, the Elizabethan audience could not have anticipated a protagonist of such depth and complexity. Traditionally, revengers are presented as flat characters who have a single fixation on justice through personal vengeance. Hamlet, however, is a much deeper character. He is acutely aware of the political and moral corruption of the Danish court, and this awareness leads him to reflect on the fallen state of man and to contemplate suicide. In addition, Hamlet learns and changes in the course of the play. Although he does not have the kind of dramatic and focused *anagnorisis* that Oedipus experiences, Hamlet does learn that he must look beyond reason and philosophy for ways of coping with the world. He also learns to be patient and to trust in providence. In the last scene of the play he calmly awaits the turn of events with a new understanding that "there's a divinity that shapes our ends" (5.2.10) and that "the readiness is all" (5.2.205).

Attempts have been made, especially since the nineteenth century, to see Hamlet as an Aristotelian tragic protagonist, brought to his death by some aspect of his character that leads him into error. Scholars have located Hamlet's *hamartia*, or "flaw," in overrationalization or in a fixation on his mother (an Oedipal complex). Most, however, claim that the prince's error may be found in the deferring of revenge brought about by his "inability to act." The facts in the play simply do not bear out this sort of interpretation. Although Hamlet chastises himself for delay, he actually wastes almost no time at all. Once Hamlet has been urged to revenge by the ghost, he uses both his pretended madness and "The Murder of Gonzago"—the play-within-a-play—in an attempt to confirm the ghost's accusations against Claudius. And once this confirmation has been gained, Hamlet acts almost immediately. Although he cannot bring himself to kill an unarmed man at prayers, minutes later he kills a person whom he assumes is Claudius behind the curtain in the Queen's chamber. This accidental murder of Polonius makes Hamlet's revenge a great deal more complicated because it turns Laertes into a revenger and also lets Claudius know that Hamlet is trying to kill him. Hamlet's quest for revenge is further complicated and delayed by Claudius's counterplots; the king sends Hamlet off to England immediately after the death of Polonius.

Just as Hamlet does not perfectly fit Aristotle's conception of a tragic protagonist, so the play itself does not conform to Aristotle's description of a tragedy (see pp. 1122–24). We may find a single motive or action in Hamlet's desire to avenge his father's murder and cleanse the state. This motivation, however, does not account for all the events in the play. The story of Polonius and his family, for example, is at least partly irrelevant to this motive. Shakespeare similarly dispenses with the classical unities of time and place; the action of the play covers several months and moves from place to place within Denmark. Perhaps the most radical departure from Aristotelian standards is Shakespeare's willingness to mix humorous elements into his tragedy. Whereas Aristotle called for absolutely pure forms of comedy and tragedy, English drama offered a mixture of elements and modes from its beginnings. Thus, *Hamlet* presents a great deal of humor in characters like Polonius, Osric, and the gravediggers. In addition, Hamlet's remarks are often quite witty.

Finally, we must recognize that *Hamlet*, like *Oedipus the King*, touches our lives in a significant way and raises ever-present questions about living and dying, truth and honor, art and nature, and responsibility to ourselves, our families, and the state. In the hundreds of years since Shakespeare wrote *Hamlet*, it has remained among the most popular, most moving, and most effective plays in the world. It has been translated into scores of languages, and it has successfully held the stage from Shakespeare's day to our own. Beyond its enduring stage presence, *Hamlet* has become one of the central documents of western civilization. Somehow, we all know about *Hamlet*, even if we have never read the play or seen a performance. This fact, more than anything else, testifies to Shakespeare's consummate skill as a poet and playwright.

WILLIAM SHAKESPEARE (1564–1616)

The Tragedy of Hamlet, Prince of Denmark   *ca. 1600*

Edited by Alice Griffin°

[CHARACTERS

    Claudius, *King of Denmark*
    Hamlet, *Son to the former, and nephew to the present King*
    Polonius, *Lord Chamberlain*
    Horatio, *Friend to Hamlet*
    Laertes, *Son to Polonius*
    Valtemand
    Cornelius
    Rosencrantz ⎱ *Courtiers*
    Guildenstern
    Osric
    A Gentleman
    A Priest
    Marcellus ⎱ *Officers*
    Barnardo
    Francisco, *a Soldier*
    Reynaldo, *Servant to Polonius*
    Players

Prof. Griffin's text for *Hamlet* was the Second Quarto (edition) published in 1604, with modifications based on the First Folio, published in 1623. Stage directions in those editions are printed here without brackets; added stage directions are printed within brackets. We have edited Prof. Griffin's notes for this text.

Two Clowns, *gravediggers*
Fortinbras, *Prince of Norway*
A Norwegian Captain
English Ambassadors
Gertrude, *Queen of Denmark*, *mother to Hamlet*
Ophelia, *Daughter to Polonius*
Ghost of Hamlet's Father
Lords, Ladies, Officers, Soldiers, Sailors, Messengers, Attendants

SCENE: *Elsinore*]

ACT 1

Scene 1. [*A platform on the battlements of the castle*]

Enter BARNARDO and FRANCISCO, two Sentinels.

BARNARDO. Who's there?
FRANCISCO. Nay, answer me. Stand and unfold° yourself.
BARNARDO. Long live the king.
FRANCISCO. Barnardo?
BARNARDO. He.   5
FRANCISCO. You come most carefully upon your hour.
BARNARDO. 'Tis now struck twelve, get thee to bed Francisco.
FRANCISCO. For this relief much thanks, 'tis bitter cold,
    And I am sick at heart.
BARNARDO. Have you had quiet guard?
FRANCISCO.   Not a mouse stirring.   10
BARNARDO. Well, good night:
    If you do meet Horatio and Marcellus,
    The rivals° of my watch, bid them make haste.

Enter HORATIO and MARCELLUS.

FRANCISCO. I think I hear them. Stand ho, who is there?
HORATIO. Friends to this ground.
MARCELLUS.   And liegemen° to the Dane.°   15
FRANCISCO. Give you good night.
MARCELLUS.   O, farewell honest soldier,
    Who hath relieved you?
FRANCISCO.   Barnardo hath my place;
    Give you good night.   *Exit FRANCISCO*
MARCELLUS.   Holla, Barnardo!
BARNARDO.   Say,
    What, is Horatio there?
HORATIO.   A piece of him.

2 *unfold*: reveal.   13 *rivals*: partners.   15 *liegemen*: subjects.   *Dane*: King of Denmark.

BARNARDO.   Welcome Horatio, welcome good Marcellus.   2
HORATIO.   What, has this thing appeared again tonight?
BARNARDO.   I have seen nothing.
MARCELLUS.   Horatio says 'tis but our fantasy,°
   And will not let belief take hold of him,
   Touching this dreaded sight twice seen of us,   2
   Therefore I have entreated him along
   With us to watch the minutes of this night,
   That if again this apparition come,
   He may approve° our eyes and speak to it.
HORATIO.   Tush, tush, 'twill not appear.
BARNARDO.   Sit down awhile,   3
   And let us once again assail your ears,
   That are so fortified against our story,
   What we have two nights seen.
HORATIO.   Well, sit we down,
   And let us hear Barnardo speak of this.
BARNARDO.   Last night of all,   3
   When yon same star that's westward from the pole°
   Had made his course t'illume that part of heaven
   Where now it burns, Marcellus and myself,
   The bell then beating one—

Enter GHOST.

MARCELLUS.   Peace, break thee off, look where it comes again.   4
BARNARDO.   In the same figure like the king that's dead.
MARCELLUS.   Thou art a scholar, speak to it Horatio.
BARNARDO.   Looks a' not like the king? mark it Horatio.
HORATIO.   Most like, it harrows me with fear and wonder.
BARNARDO.   It would be spoke to.
MARCELLUS.   Question it Horatio.   4
HORATIO.   What art thou that usurp'st° this time of night,
   Together with that fair and warlike form,
   In which the majesty of buried Denmark°
   Did sometimes° march? by heaven I charge thee speak.
MARCELLUS.   It is offended.
BARNARDO.   See, it stalks away.   5
HORATIO.   Stay, speak, speak, I charge thee speak.   *Exit* GHOST.
MARCELLUS.   'Tis gone and will not answer.
BARNARDO.   How now Horatio, you tremble and look pale,
   Is not this something more than fantasy?
   What think you on't?   5
HORATIO.   Before my God I might not this believe,

---

23 *fantasy*: imagination.   29 *approve*: prove reliable.   36 *pole*: North Star.
46 *usurp'st*: wrongfully occupy (both the time and the shape of the dead king).
48 *buried Denmark*: the buried King of Denmark.   49 *sometimes*: formerly.

Without the sensible and true avouch°
Of mine own eyes.

MARCELLUS.   Is it not like the king?

HORATIO. As thou art to thyself.
Such was the very armour he had on,   60
When he the ambitious Norway° combated:
So frowned he once, when in an angry parle°
He smote the sledded Polacks° on the ice.
'Tis strange.

MARCELLUS. Thus twice before, and jump° at this dead hour,   65
With martial stalk hath he gone by our watch.

HORATIO. In what particular thought to work, I know not,
But in the gross and scope° of mine opinion,
This bodes some strange eruption to our state.

MARCELLUS. Good now sit down, and tell me he that knows,   70
Why this same strict and most observant watch
So nightly toils the subject° of the land,
And why such daily cast of brazen cannon
And foreign mart,° for implements of war,
Why such impress° of shipwrights, whose sore° task   75
Does not divide the Sunday from the week,
What might be toward° that this sweaty haste
Doth make the night joint-labourer with the day,
Who is't that can inform me?

HORATIO.   That can I.
At least the whisper goes so; our last king,   80
Whose image even but now appeared to us,
Was as you know by Fortinbras of Norway,
Thereto pricked on by a most emulate° pride,
Dared to the combat; in which our valiant Hamlet
(For so this side of our known world esteemed him)   85
Did slay this Fortinbras, who by a sealed compact,°
Well ratified by law and heraldy,°
Did forfeit (with his life) all those his lands
Which he stood seized° of, to the conqueror:
Against the which a moiety competent°   90
Was gagèd° by our King, which had returned
To the inheritance of Fortinbras,
Had he been vanquisher; as by the same co-mart,°
And carriage of the article designed,°

---

57 *Sensible . . . avouch*: assurance of the truth of the senses.   61 *Norway*: King of
Norway.   62 *parle*: parley, verbal battle.   63 *sledded Polacks*: Poles on sleds.   65 *jump*:
just.   68 *gross and scope*: general view.   72 *toils the subject*: makes the subjects toil.
74 *mart*: trade.   75 *impress*: conscription.   *sore*: difficult.   77 *toward*: forthcoming.
83 *emulate*: rivalling.   86 *compact*: treaty.   87 *law and heraldy*: heraldic law regulating
combats.   89 *seized*: possessed.   90 *moiety competent*: equal amount.   91 *gagèd*:
pledged.   93 *co-mart*: joint bargain.   94 *carriage . . . designed*: intent of the treaty drawn
up.

His fell to Hamlet; now sir, young Fortinbras,
Of unimprovèd mettle° hot and full,
Hath in the skirts° of Norway here and there
Sharked up° a list of lawless resolutes°
For food and diet to some enterprise
That hath a stomach° in't, which is no other,   1(
As it doth well appear unto our state,
But to recover of us by strong hand
And terms compulsatory, those foresaid lands
So by his father lost; and this I take it,
Is the main motive of our preparations,   1(
The source of this our watch, and the chief head°
Of this post-haste and romage° in the land.
BARNARDO.   I think it be no other, but e'en so;
Well may it sort° that this portentous figure
Comes armèd through our watch so like the king   1)
That was and is the question of these wars.
HORATIO.   A mote it is to trouble the mind's eye:
In the most high and palmy° state of Rome,
A little ere the mightest Julius fell,
The graves stood tenantless, and the sheeted dead   1)
Did squeak and gibber in the Roman streets,
As stars with trains of fire,° and dews of blood,
Disasters° in the sun; and the moist star,°
Upon whose influence Neptune's empire stands,
Was sick almost to doomsday with eclipse.   12
And even the like precurse° of feared events,
As harbingers preceding still° the fates
And prologue to the omen° coming on,
Have heaven and earth together demonstrated
Unto our climatures° and countrymen.   12

Enter GHOST.

But soft, behold, lo where it comes again.
I'll cross° it though it blast me: *Spreads his arms.*
                    stay illusion,
If thou hast any sound or use of voice,
Speak to me.
If there be any good thing to be done   13

96 *unimproved mettle*: untested (1) metal (2) spirit.   97 *skirts*: outskirts.   98 *Sharked up*:
gathered up indiscriminately (as a shark preys).   *lawless resolutes*: determined outlaws.
100 *stomach*: show of courage.   106 *head*: fountainhead.   107 *romage*:
bustle (rummage).   109 *sort*: turn out.   113 *palmy*: triumphant.   117 *stars . . fire*:
meteors.   118 *Disasters*: unfavorable portents.   *moist star*: moon.   121 *precurse*:
portent.   122 *still*: always.   123 *omen*: disaster.   125 *climatures*: regions.
127 *cross*: (1) cross its path (2) spread my arms to make a cross of my body (to ward against
evil).

That may to thee do ease, and grace° to me,
Speak to me.
If thou art privy° to thy country's fate
Which happily° foreknowing may avoid,
O speak: 135
Or if thou hast uphoarded in thy life
Extorted treasure in the womb of earth,
For which they say you spirits oft walk in death,

The cock crows.

Speak of it, stay and speak. Stop it Marcellus.
MARCELLUS.   Shall I strike at it with my partisan?°   140
HORATIO.   Do, if it will not stand
BARNARDO.   'Tis here.
HORATIO.   'Tis here.
MARCELLUS.   'Tis gone.   *Exit* GHOST.
We do it wrong being so majestical,
To offer it the show of violence,
For it is as the air, invulnerable,   145
And our vain blows malicious mockery.°
BARNARDO.   It was about to speak when the cock crew.°
HORATIO.   And then it started like a guilty thing,
Upon a fearful summons; I have heard,
The cock that is the trumpet to the morn,   150
Doth with his lofty and shrill-sounding throat
Awake the god of day, and at his warning
Whether in sea or fire, in earth or air,°
Th'extravagant and erring° spirit hies°
To his confine, and of the truth herein   155
This present object made probation.°
MARCELLUS.   It faded on the crowing of the cock.
Some say that ever 'gainst° that season comes
Wherein our Saviour's birth is celebrated
This bird of dawning singeth all night long,   160
And then they say no spirit dare stir abroad,
The nights are wholesome,° then no planets strike,°
No fairy takes,° nor witch hath power to charm,
So hallowed, and so gracious is that time.

---

131 *grace*: (1) honor (2) blessedness.   133 *art privy*: know secretly of.   134 *happily*:
perhaps.   140 *partisan*: spear.   146 *malicious mockery*: mockery because they only imitate
harm.   147 *cock crew* (traditional signal for ghosts to return to their confines).   153 *sea
. . . air*: the four elements (inhabited by spirits, each indigenous to a particular
element).   154 *extravagant and erring*: going beyond its bounds (vagrant) and
wandering.   *hies*: hastens.   156 *made probation*: gave proof.   158 *'gainst*: just
before.   162 *wholesome*: healthy (night air was considered unhealthy).   *strike*: exert evil
influence.   163 *takes*: bewitches.

HORATIO.   So have I heard and do in part believe it.   165
    But look, the morn in russet° mantle clad
    Walks o'er the dew of yon high eastward hill:
    Break we our watch up and by my advice
    Let us impart what we have seen tonight
    Unto young Hamlet, for upon my life   170
    This spirit dumb to us, will speak to him:
    Do you consent we shall acquaint him with it,
    As needful in our loves,° fitting our duty?
MARCELLUS.   Let's do't I pray, and I this morning know
    Where we shall find him most convenient.   *Exeunt.*°   175

Scene 2. [*A room of state in the castle*]

Flourish.° Enter CLAUDIUS *King of Denmark ,* GERTRUDE *the Queen ,* [*members of the*] *Council:
as* POLONIUS; *and his son* LAERTES, HAMLET, [VALTEMAND *and* CORNELIUS] *cum aliis .°*

KING.   Though yet of Hamlet our dear brother's death
    The memory be green, and that it us befitted
    To bear our hearts in grief, and our whole kingdom
    To be contracted in one brow of woe,
    Yet so far hath discretion fought with nature,°   5
    That we° with wisest sorrow think on him
    Together with remembrance of ourselves:°
    Therefore our sometime° sister,° now our queen,
    Th'imperial jointress° to this warlike state,
    Have we as 'twere with a defeated joy,   10
    With an auspicious, and a dropping eye,°
    With mirth in funeral, and with dirge in marriage,
    In equal scale weighing delight and dole,
    Taken to wife: nor have we herein barred
    Your better wisdoms,° which have freely gone   15
    With this affair along—for all, our thanks.
    Now follows that you know, young Fortinbras,
    Holding a weak supposal of our worth,°
    Or thinking by our late dear brother's death
    Our state to be disjoint and out of frame,°   20
    Colleaguèd° with this dream of his advantage,°

166 *russet*: reddish.   173 *needful . . . loves*: urged by our friendship.   175 stage
direction: *Exeunt*: all exit.   stage direction: *Flourish*: fanfare of trumpets.   *cum aliis*: with
others.   5 *nature*: natural impulse (of grief).   6 *we*: (royal plural).   7 *remembrance of
ourselves*: reminder of our duties.   8 *sometime*: former.   *sister*: sister-in-law.   9 *jointress*:
widow who inherits the estate.   11 *auspicious . . . eye*: one eye happy, the other
tearful.   14–15 *barred . . . wisdoms*: failed to seek and abide by your good
advice.   18 *weak . . . worth*: low opinion of my ability in office.   20 *out of frame*:
tottering.   21 *Colleagued*: supported.   *advantage*: superiority.

He hath not failed to pester us with message
Importing the surrender of those lands
Lost by his father, with all bands° of law,
To our most valiant brother—so much for him: 25
Now for ourself, and for this time of meeting,
Thus much the business is. We have here writ
To Norway, uncle of young Fortinbras—
Who impotent and bed-rid scarcely hears
Of this his nephew's purpose—to suppress   30
His further gait° herein, in that the levies,
The lists, and full proportions are all made
Out of his subject:° and we here dispatch
You good Cornelius, and you Valtemand,
For bearers of this greeting to old Norway,   35
Giving to you no further personal power
To business with the king, more than the scope
Of these delated° articles allow:
Farewell, and let your haste commend your duty.°
CORNELIUS, VALTEMAND. In that, and all things, will we show our duty.   40
KING. We doubt it nothing, heartily farewell.

                              Exeunt VALTEMAND and CORNELIUS.

And now Laertes what's the news with you?
You told us of some suit, what is't Laertes?
You cannot speak of reason to the Dane
And lose your voice;° what wouldst thou beg Laertes,   45
That shall not be my offer, not thy asking?°
The head is not more native° to the heart,
The hand more instrumental to the mouth,
Than is the throne of Denmark to thy father.
What wouldst thou have Laertes?
LAERTES.   My dread lord,   50
Your leave and favour° to return to France,
From whence, though willingly I came to Denmark,
To show my duty in your coronation,
Yet now I must confess, that duty done,
My thoughts and wishes bend again toward France,   55
And bow them to your gracious leave and pardon.°
KING. Have you your father's leave? What says Polonius?

---

24 *bands* : bonds.   31 *gait*: progress.   31–33 *levies . . . subject*: taxes, conscriptions, and
supplies are all obtained from his subjects.   38 *delated*: accusing.   39 *haste . . . duty*:
prompt departure signify your respect.   45 *lose your voice*: speak in vain.   46 *offer . . .*
asking: grant even before requested.   47 *native*: related.   51 *leave and favour*: kind
permission.   56 *pardon*: allowance.

POLONIUS.   He hath my lord wrung from me my slow leave
    By laboursome petition, and at last
    Upon his will I sealed my hard consent.°
    I do beseech you give him leave to go.
KING.   Take thy fair hour Laertes, time be thine,
    And thy best graces spend it at thy will.
    But now my cousin° Hamlet, and my son—
HAMLET.   [*Aside*.] A little more than kin,° and less than kind.°
KING.   How is it that the clouds still hang on you?
HAMLET.   Not so my lord, I am too much in the sun.°
QUEEN.   Good Hamlet cast they nighted colour° off
    And let thine eye look like a friend on Denmark,°
    Do not for ever with they vailèd° lids
    Seek for thy noble father in the dust,
    Thou know'st 'tis common, all that lives must die,
    Passing through nature to eternity.
HAMLET.   Ay madam, it is common.°
QUEEN.   If it be,
    Why seems it so particular with thee?
HAMLET.   Seems, madam? nay it is, I know not "seems."
    'Tis not alone my inky cloak good mother,
    Nor customary suits of solemn black,
    Nor windy suspiration of forced breath,
    No, nor the fruitful river in the eye,°
    Nor the dejected haviour° of the visage,
    Together with all forms, moods, shapes of grief,
    That can denote me truly: these indeed seem,
    For they are actions that a man might play,°
    But I have that within which passes show,
    These but the trappings and the suits of woe.°
KING.   'Tis sweet and commendable in your nature Hamlet,
    To give these mourning duties to your father:
    But you must know your father lost a father,
    That father lost, lost his, and the survivor bound
    In filial obligation for some term

60 *Upon . . . consent*: (1) at his request, I gave my grudging consent (2) on the soft sealing wax of his (legal) will, I stamped my approval.   64 *cousin*: kinsman (used for relatives outside the immediate family).   65 *more than kin*: too much of a kinsman, being both uncle and stepfather.   *less than kind*: (1) unkind because of: being a kin (proverbial) and taking the throne from the former king's son (2) unnatural (as it was considered incest to marry the wife of one's dead brother).   67 *in the sun*: (1) in the presence of the king (often associated metaphorically with the sun) (2) proverbial: "out of heaven's blessing into the warm sun" (3) of a "son."   68 *nighted colour*: black.   69 *Denmark*: the King of Denmark.   70 *vailed*: downcast.   74 *common*: (1) general (2) vulgar.   79–80 *windy . . . eye*: (hyperbole used to describe exaggerated sighs and tears).   81 *haviour*: behavior.   84 *play*: act.   86 *trappings . . . woe*: costumes of mourning.

To do obsequious sorrow:° but to persever
In obstinate condolement,° is a course
Of impious stubbornness, 'tis unmanly grief,
It shows a will most incorrect to heaven,   95
A heart unfortified, a mind impatient,
An understanding simple and unschooled:
For what we know must be, and is as common
As any the most vulgar thing to sense,°
Why should we in our peevish opposition   100
Take it to heart? Fie, 'tis a fault to heaven,
A fault against the dead, a fault to nature,
To reason most absurd, whose common theme
Is death of fathers, and who still° hath cried
From the first corse,° till he that died today,   105
"This must be so." We pray you throw to earth
This unprevailing° woe, and think of us
As of a father, for let the world take note
You are the most immediate° to our throne,
And with no less nobility of love   110
Than that which dearest father bears his son,
Do I impart toward you. For your intent
In going back to school in Wittenberg,
It is most retrograde° to our desire,
And we beseech you, bend you° to remain   115
Here in the cheer and comfort of our eye,
Our chiefest courtier, cousin, and our son.
QUEEN.   Let not thy mother lose her prayers Hamlet,
     I pray thee stay with us, go not to Wittenberg.
HAMLET.   I shall in all my best obey you madam.   120
KING.   Why 'tis a loving and a fair reply,
     Be as ourself in Denmark. Madam come,
     This gentle and unforced accord of Hamlet
     Sits smiling to my heart, in grace whereof,
     No jocund health that Denmark drinks today,   125
     But the great cannon to the clouds shall tell,
     And the king's rouse° the heaven shall bruit° again,
     Re-speaking earthly thunder; come away.

Flourish. Exeunt all but HAMLET.

92 *do obsequious sorrow*: express sorrow befitting obsequies or funerals.   93 *condolement*:
grief.   99 *As any . . . sense*: as the most ordinary thing the senses can perceive.
104 *still*: always.   105 *corse*: corpse (of Abel, also, ironically, the first
fratricide).   107 *unprevailing*: useless.   109 *most immediate*: next in succession (though
Danish kings were elected by the council, an Elizabethan audience might feel that Hamlet,
not Claudius, should be king).   114 *retrograde*: movement (of planets) in a reverse
direction.   115 *beseech . . . you*: hope you will be inclined.   127 *rouse*: toast that empties
the wine cup.   *bruit*: sound.

HAMLET.   O that this too too sullied° flesh would melt,
Thaw and resolve itself into a dew,   13
Or that the Everlasting had not fixed
His canon° 'gainst self-slaughter. O God, God,
How weary, stale, flat, and unprofitable
Seem to me all the uses of this world!
Fie on't, ah fie, 'tis an unweeded garden   13
That grows to seed, things rank° and gross in nature
Possess it merely.° That it should come to this,
But two months dead, nay not so much, not two,
So excellent a king, that was to this
Hyperion° to a satyr,° so loving to my mother,   14
That he might not beteem° the winds of heaven
Visit her face too roughly—heaven and earth,
Must I remember? why, she would hang on him
As if increase of appetite had grown
By what it fed on,° and yet within a month—   14
Let me not think on't: Frailty, thy name is woman—
A little month or ere those shoes were old
With which she followed my poor father's body
Like Niobe° all tears, why she, even she—
O God, a beast that wants° discourse of reason   15
Would have mourned longer—married with my uncle,
My father's brother, but no more like my father
Than I to Hercules: within a month,
Ere yet the salt of most unrighteous° tears
Had left the flushing° in her gallèd° eyes,   15
She married. O most wicked speed, to post°
With such dexterity to incestuous° sheets:
It is not, nor it cannot come to good,
But break my heart, for I must hold my tongue.

Enter HORATIO, MARCELLUS and BARNARDO.

HORATIO.   Hail to your lordship.
HAMLET.   I am glad to see you well;   16
Horatio, or I do forget my self.

---

129 *sullied*: tainted.   132 *canon*: divine edict.   136 *rank*: (1) luxuriant, excessive (2) bad-
smelling.   137 *merely*: entirely.   140 *Hyperion*: god of the sun.   *satyr*: part-goat, part-
man woodland deity (noted for lust).   141 *beteem*: allow.   144–145 *As if . . . on*: as if
the more she fed, the more her appetite increased.   149 *Niobe*: (who boasted of her children
before Leto and was punished by their destruction; Zeus changed the weeping mother to a
stone dropping continual tears).   150 *wants*: lacks.   154 *unrighteous*: (because
untrue).   155 *flushing*: redness.   *gallèd*: rubbed sore.   156 *post*: rush.
157 *incestuous*: (the church forbade marriage to one's brother's widow).

HORATIO.   The same my lord, and your poor servant ever.

HAMLET.   Sir my good friend, I'll change° that name with you:
   And what make you from Wittenberg, Horatio?
   Marcellus.   165

MARCELLUS.   My good lord.

HAMLET.   I am very glad to see you: good even, sir.
   But what in faith make you from Wittenberg?

HORATIO.   A truant disposition, good my lord.

HAMLET.   I would not hear your enemy say so,   170
   Nor shall you do mine ear that violence
   To make it truster of your own report
   Against yourself. I know you are no truant,
   But what is your affair in Elsinore?
   We'll teach you to drink deep ere you depart.   175

HORATIO.   My Lord, I came to see your father's funeral.

HAMLET.   I prithee do not mock me, fellow student,
   I think it was to see my mother's wedding.

HORATIO.   Indeed my lord it followed hard upon.

HAMLET.   Thrift, thrift, Horatio, the funeral baked meats   180
   Did coldly° furnish forth the marriage tables.
   Would I had met my dearest° foe in heaven
   Or ever I had seen that day Horatio.
   My father, methinks I see my father.

HORATIO.   Where my lord?

HAMLET.   In my mind's eye Horatio.   185

HORATIO.   I saw him once, a' was a goodly° king.

HAMLET.   A' was a man, take him for all in all,
   I shall not look upon his life again.

HORATIO.   My lord, I think I saw him yesternight.

HAMLET.   Saw? Who?   190

HORATIO.   My lord, the king your father.

HAMLET.   The king my father?

HORATIO.   Season your admiration° for a while
   With an attent ear till I may deliver
   Upon the witness of these gentlemen
   This marvel to you.

HAMLET.   For God's love let me hear!   195

HORATIO.   Two nights together had these gentlemen,
   Marcellus and Barnardo, on their watch
   In the dead waste and middle of the night,
   Been thus encountered. A figure like your father
   Armed at point exactly, cap-a-pe,°   200

---

163 *change*: exchange (and be called your friend).   181 *coldly*: when cold.   182 *dearest*:
direst.   186 *goodly*: handsome.   192 *Season your admiration*: control your wonder.
200 *at point . . . cap-a-pe*: in every detail, head to foot.

Appears before them, and with solemn march,
Goes slow and stately by them; thrice he walked
By their oppressed° and fear-surprisèd eyes
Within his truncheon's° length, whilst they distilled°
Almost to jelly with the act of fear,   205
Stand dumb and speak not to him; this to me
In dreadful secrecy° impart they did,
And I with them the third night kept the watch,
Where as they had delivered, both in time,
Form of the thing, each word made true and good,   210
The apparition comes: I knew your father,
These hands are not more like.

HAMLET.   But where was this?
MARCELLUS.   My lord upon the platform where we watch.
HAMLET.   Did you not speak to it?
HORATIO.   My lord I did,
But answer made it none, yet once methought   215
It lifted up it° head, and did address
Itself to motion° like as it would speak:
But even then the morning cock crew loud,
And at the sound it shrunk in haste away
And vanished from our sight.
HAMLET.   'Tis very strange.   220
HORATIO.   As I do live my honoured lord 'tis true,
And we did think it writ down in our duty
To let you know of it.
HAMLET.   Indeed indeed sirs, but this troubles me.
Hold you the watch tonight?
ALL.   We do my lord.   225
HAMLET.   Armed say you?
ALL.   Armed my lord.
HAMLET.   From top to toe?
ALL.   My lord from head to foot.
HAMLET.   Then saw you not his face.
HORATIO.   O yes my lord, he wore his beaver° up.   230
HAMLET.   What, looked he frowningly?
HORATIO.   A countenance more in sorrow than in anger.
HAMLET.   Pale, or red?
HORATIO.   Nay, very pale.
HAMLET.   And fixed his eyes upon you?
HORATIO.   Most constantly.
HAMLET.   I would I had been there.   235
HORATIO.   It would have much amazed you.

---

203 *oppressed*: overcome by horror.   204 *truncheon*: staff (of office).   *distilled*:
dissolved.   207 *in dreadful secrecy*: as a dread secret.   216 *it*: its.   216–217 *address* . . .
motion: start to move.   230 *beaver*: visor.

HAMLET.   Very like, very like, stayed it long?

HORATIO.   While one with moderate haste might tell° a hundred.

MARCELLUS, BARNARDO.   Longer, longer.

HORATIO.   Not when I saw't.

HAMLET.   His beard was grizzled,° no?   240

HORATIO.   It was as I have seen it in his life,
    A sable silvered.°

HAMLET.   I will watch tonight;
    Perchance 'twill walk again.

HORATIO.   I warr'nt it will.

HAMLET.   If it assume my noble father's person,
    I'll speak to it though hell itself should gape   245
    And bid me hold my peace;° I pray you all
    If you have hitherto concealed this sight
    Let it be tenable° in your silence still,
    And whatsoever else shall hap tonight,
    Give it an understanding but no tongue.   250
    I will requite your loves, so fare you well:
    Upon the platform 'twixt eleven and twelve
    I'll visit you.

ALL.   Our duty to your honour.

HAMLET.   Your loves, as mine to you:° farewell.   *Exeunt.*
    My father's spirit (in arms) all is not well,   255
    I doubt° some foul play, would the night were come;
    Till then sit still my soul, foul deeds will rise,
    Though all the earth o'erwhelm them, to men's eyes.   *Exit.*

Scene 3. [*Polonius's chambers*]

Enter LAERTES and OPHELIA his sister.

LAERTES.   My necessaries are embarked, farewell,
    And sister, as the winds give benefit
    And convoy° is assistant, do not sleep
    But let me hear from you.

OPHELIA.   Do you doubt that?

LAERTES.   For Hamlet, and the trifling of his favour,   5
    Hold it a fashion, and a toy in blood,°
    A violet in the youth of primy nature,°
    Forward,° not permanent, sweet, not lasting,
    The perfume and suppliance of° a minute,
    No more.

238 *tell*: count.   240 *grizzled*: grey.   242 *A sable silvered*: black flecked with grey.   245–
246 *though hell . . . peace*: despite the risk of hell (for speaking to a demon) warning me to
be silent.   248 *tenable*: held onto.   254 *Your loves . . . you*: offer your friendship (rather
than duty) in exchange for mine.   256 *doubt*: fear.   3 *convoy*: conveyance.   6 *toy in
blood*: whim of the passions.   7 *youth of primy nature*: early spring.   8 *Forward*:
Premature.   9 *suppliance of*: supplying diversion for.

OPHELIA.   No more but so?
LAERTES.   Think it no more.
    For nature crescent° does not grow alone
    In thews and bulk,° but as this temple waxes°
    The inward service of the mind and soul
    Grows wide withal.° Perhaps he loves you now,
    And now no soil nor cautel° doth besmirch
    The virtue of his will:° but you must fear,
    His greatness weighed,° his will is not his own,
    For he himself is subject to his birth:
    He may not as unvalued persons° do,
    Carve° for himself, for on his choice depends
    The sanctity and health of this whole state,
    And therefore must his choice be circumscribed
    Unto the voice and yielding° of that body
    Whereof he is the head. Then if he says he loves you,
    It fits your wisdom so far to believe it
    As he in his particular act and place
    May give his saying deed,° which is no further
    Than the main voice of Denmark goes withal.
    Then weigh what loss your honour may sustain
    If with too credent° ear you list° his songs,
    Or lose your heart, or your chaste treasure open
    To his unmast'red importunity.°
    Fear it Ophelia, fear it my dear sister,
    And keep you in the rear of your affection,
    Out of the shot and danger of desire.
    The chariest° maid is prodigal enough
    If she unmask her beauty to the moon.
    Virtue itself 'scapes not calumnious strokes.
    The canker galls the infants° of the spring
    Too oft before their buttons° be disclosed,
    And in the morn and liquid dew of youth
    Contagious blastments° are most imminent.
    Be wary then, best safety lies in fear,
    Youth to itself rebels,° though none else near.
OPHELIA.   I shall the effect° of this good lesson keep
    As watchman to my heart: but good my brother,

---

11 *nature crescent*: man as he grows.   12 *thews and bulk*: sinews and body.   *temple waxes*:
body grows: (1 Cor. 6:19).   14 *withal*: at the same time.   15 *cautel*: deceit.   16 *will*:
desire.   17 *weighed*: considered.   19 *unvalued persons*: common people.   20 *Carve*:
choose (as does the one who carves the food).   23 *voice and yielding*: approving vote.   26–
27 *in his . . . deed*: limited by personal responsibilities and rank, may perform what he
promises.   30 *credent*: credulous.   *list*: listen to.   31–32 *your chaste . . . importunity*:
lose your virginity to his uncontrolled persistence.   36 *chariest*: most cautious.   39 *canker
. . . infants*: cankerworm or caterpillar harms the young plants.   40 *buttons*: buds
42 *blastments*: blights.   44 *to itself rebels*: lusts by nature.   45 *effect*: moral.

Do not as some ungracious° pastors do,
Show me the steep and thorny way to heaven,
Whiles like a puffed and reckless libertine
Himself the primrose path of dalliance treads,   50
And recks not his own rede.°

Enter POLONIUS.

LAERTES.   O fear me not,°
I stay too long, but here my father comes:
A double blessing is a double grace,
Occasion smiles upon a second leave.°
POLONIUS.   Yet here Laertes? aboard, aboard for shame,   55
The wind sits in the shoulder of your sail,
And you are stayed for: there, my blessing with thee,
And these few precepts in thy memory
Look thou character.° Give thy thoughts no tongue,
Nor any unproportioned thought his act: 60
Be thou familiar, but by no means vulgar:°
Those friends thou hast, and their adoption tried,°
Grapple them unto thy soul with hoops of steel,
But do not dull° thy palm with entertainment
Of each new-hatched unfledged° comrade. Beware   65
Of entrance to a quarrel, but being in,
Bear't that th'opposèd may beware of thee.
Give every man thy ear, but few thy voice:
Take each man's censure,° but reserve thy judgment.
Costly thy habit° as thy purse can buy,   70
But not expressed in fancy;° rich, not gaudy,
For the apparel oft proclaims the man,
And they in France of the best rank and station,
Are of a most select and generous chief° in that:
Neither a borrower nor a lender be,   75
For loan oft loses both itself and friend,
And borrowing dulls the edge of husbandry;°
This above all, to thine own self be true
And it must follow as the night the day,
Thou canst not then be false to any man.   80
Farewell, my blessing season° this in thee.
LAERTES.   Most humbly do I take my leave my lord.
POLONIUS.   The time invites you, go, your servants tend.°

---

47 *ungracious*: lacking God's grace.   51 *recks . . . rede*: does not follow his own
advice.   *fear me not*: don't worry about me.   54 *Occasion . . . leave*: opportunity favors
a second leave-taking.   59 *character*: write.   61 *vulgar*: indiscriminately friendly.
62 *adoption tried*: loyalty proved.   64 *dull*: get callouses on.   65 *new-*
hatched, unfledged: new and untested.   69 *censure*: opinion.   70 *habit*: clothing.
71 *expressed in fancy*: so fantastic as to be ridiculous.   74 *select . . . chief*:
judicious and noble eminence.   77 *husbandry*: thrift.   81 *season*: bring to maturity.
83 *tend*: attend, wait.

LAERTES.   Farewell Ophelia, and remember well
    What I have said to you.
OPHELIA.   'Tis in my memory locked,   8
    And you yourself shall keep the key of it.
LAERTES.   Farewell.   *Exit* LAERTES.
POLONIUS.   What is't Ophelia he hath said to you?
OPHELIA.   So please you, something touching the Lord Hamlet.
POLONIUS.   Marry,° well bethought: 9
    'Tis told me he hath very oft of late
    Given private time to you, and you yourself
    Have of your audience been most free and bounteous.
    If it be so, as so 'tis put on me,
    And that in way of caution, I must tell you,   9
    You do not understand yourself so clearly
    As it behoves my daughter, and your honour.
    What is between you? give me up the truth.
OPHELIA.   He hath my lord of late made many tenders°
    Of his affection to me.   10
POLONIUS.   Affection, puh, you speak like a green girl
    Unsifted° in such perilous circumstance.
    Do you believe his tenders as you call them?
OPHELIA.   I do not know my lord what I should think.
POLONIUS.   Marry, I will teach you; think yourself a baby   10
    That you have ta'en these tenders° for true pay
    Which are not sterling.° Tender yourself more dearly,°
    Or (not to crack the wind of the poor phrase,
    Running it thus°) you'll tender me a fool.°
OPHELIA.   My lord he hath importuned me with love   11
    In honourable fashion.
POLONIUS.   Ay, fashion you may call it, go to, go to.
OPHELIA.   And hath given countenance° to his speech, my lord,
    With almost all the holy vows of heaven.
POLONIUS.   Ay, springes° to catch woodcocks.° I do know   11
    When the blood burns, how prodigal the soul
    Lends the tongue vows: these blazes daughter,
    Giving more light than heat, extinct in both,
    Even in their promise, as it is a-making,°
    You must not take for fire. From this time   12

---

90 *Marry*: (a mild oath, from "By the Virgin Mary").   99 *tenders*: offers (see lines 106–109).   102 *Unsifted*: untested.   106 *tenders*: offers (of money).   107 *sterling*: genuine (currency).   *Tender . . . dearly*: hold yourself at a higher value.   108–109 *crack . . . thus*: make the phrase lose its breath.   109 *tender . . . fool*: (1) make me look foolish (2) present me with a baby.   113 *countenance*: confirmation.   115 *springes*: snares.   *woodcocks*: snipelike birds (believed to be stupid and therefore easily trapped).   118–119 *extinct . . . a-making*: losing both appearance, because of brevity, and substance, because of broken promises.

Be something scanter of your maiden presence,
Set your entreatments at a higher rate
Than a command to parle;° for Lord Hamlet,
Believe so much in him that he is young,
And with a larger tether may he walk   125
Than may be given you: in few° Ophelia,
Do not believe his vows, for they are brokers°
Not of that dye which their investments° show,
But mere implorators° of unholy suits,
Breathing° like sanctified and pious bonds,°   130
The better to beguile. This is for all,
I would not in plain terms from this time forth
Have you so slander any moment leisure
As to give words or talk with the Lord Hamlet.
Look to't I charge you, come your ways.°   135

OPHELIA.   I shall obey, my lord.   [*Exeunt.*]

[*Scene 4. The platform on the battlements*]

Enter HAMLET, HORATIO *and* MARCELLUS.

HAMLET.   The air bites shrewdly,° it is very cold.
HORATIO.   It is a nipping and an eager° air.
HAMLET.   What hour now?
HORATIO.   I think it lacks of twelve.
MARCELLUS.   No, it is struck.
HORATIO.   Indeed? I heard it not: it then draws near the season,   5
   Wherein the spirit held his wont to walk.

A flourish of trumpets, and two pieces [of ordnance] go off.

   What does this mean my lord?
HAMLET.   The king doth wake° tonight and takes his rouse,°
   Keeps wassail° and the swagg'ring up-spring° reels:
   And as he drains his draughts of Rhenish° down,   10
   The kettle-drum and trumpet thus bray out
   The triumph of his pledge.°
HORATIO.   Is it a custom?
HAMLET.   Ay marry is't,
   But to my mind, though I am native here
   And to the manner born,° it is a custom   15

122–123 *Set . . . parle*: Don't rush to negotiate a surrender as soon as the besieger asks
for a discussion of terms.   126 *few*: short.   127 *brokers*: (1) business agents (2)
procurers.   128 *investments*: (1) business ventures (2) clothing.   129 *implorators*:
solicitors.   130 *Breathing*: speaking softly.   *bonds*: pledges.   135 *come your ways*: come
along.   1 *shrewdly*: piercingly.   2 *eager*: sharp.   8 *wake*: stay awake.   *rouse*: drinks
that empty the cup.   9 *Keeps wassail*: holds drinking bouts.   *up-spring*: a vigorous German
dance.   10 *Rhenish*: Rhine wine.   12 *triumph . . . pledge*: victory of emptying the cup
with one draught.   15 *to . . . born*: accustomed to the practice since birth.

More honoured in the breach than the observance.°
This heavy-headed revel east and west
Makes us traduced and taxed of° other nations:
They clepe° us drunkards, and with swinish phrase
Soil our addition,° and indeed it takes   20
From our achievements, though performed at height,°
The pith and marrow of our attribute.°
So oft it chances in particular men,
That for some vicious mole of nature° in them,
As in their birth, wherein they are not guilty   25
(Since nature cannot choose his origin),
By the o'ergrowth of some complexion,°
Oft breaking down the pales° and forts of reason,
Or by some habit, that too much o'er-leavens°
The form of plausive° manners—that these men,   30
Carrying I say the stamp of one defect,
Being nature's livery,° or fortune's star,°
His virtues else be they as pure as grace,
As infinite as man may undergo,
Shall in the general censure° take corruption   35
From that particular fault: the dram of evil
Doth all the noble substance of a doubt,
To his own scandal.°

Enter GHOST.

HORATIO.   Look my lord, it comes.
HAMLET.   Angels and ministers of grace defend us:
    Be thou a spirit of health, or goblin damned,°   40
    Bring with thee airs from heaven, or blasts from hell,
    Be thy intents wicked, or charitable,
    Thou com'st in such a questionable° shape,
    That I will speak to thee. I'll call thee Hamlet,
    King, father, royal Dane. O answer me,   45
    Let me not burst in ignorance, but tell
    Why thy canonized° bones hearsèd° in death
    Have burst their cerements°? why the sepulchre,

---

16 *More . . . observance*: better to break than to observe.   18 *traduced and taxed of*: defamed
and taken to task by.   19 *clepe*: call.   19–20 *with swinish . . . addition*: blemish our
reputation by comparing us to swine.   21 *at height*: to the maximum.   22 *attribute*:
reputation.   24 *mole of nature*: natural blemish.   27 *o'er growth . . . complexion*:
overbalance of one of the body's four humors or fluids believed to determine
temperament.   28 *pales*: defensive enclosures.   29 *too much o'er-leavens*: excessively
modifies (like too much leaven in bread).   30 *plausive*: pleasing.   32 *nature's livery*:
marked by nature.   *fortune's star*: destined by chance.   35 *general censure*: public
opinion.   36–38 *the dram . . . scandal*: the minute quantity of evil casts doubt upon his
noble nature, to his shame.   40 *spirit . . . damned*: true ghost or demon from
hell.   43 *questionable*: question-raising.   47 *canonized*: buried in accordance with church
edict.   *hearsed*: entombed.   48 *cerements*: waxed cloth wrappings.

Wherein we saw thee quietly interred
Hath oped his ponderous and marble jaws, 50
To cast thee up again? What may this mean
That thou, dead corse, again in complete steel
Revisits thus the glimpses of the moon,
Making night hideous, and we fools of nature°
So horridly to shake our disposition 55
With thoughts beyond the reaches of our souls,
Say why is this? wherefore? what should we do? *GHOST beckons HAMLET.*

HORATIO. It beckons you to go away with it,
  As if it some impartment did desire°
  To you alone.

MARCELLUS. Look with what courteous action 60
  It waves you to a more removèd ground,
  But do not go with it.

HORATIO. No, by no means.

HAMLET. It will not speak, then I will follow it.

HORATIO. Do not my lord.

HAMLET. Why what should be the fear?
  I do not set my life at a pin's fee,° 65
  And for my soul, what can it do to that
  Being a thing immortal as itself;
  It waves me forth again, I'll follow it.

HORATIO. What if it tempt you toward the flood my lord,
  Or to the dreadful summit of the cliff 70
  That beetles o'er° his base into the sea,
  And there assume some other horrible form
  Which might deprive your sovereignty of reason,°
  And draw you into madness? think of it,
  The very place puts toys of desperation,° 75
  Without more motive, into every brain
  That looks so many fathoms to the sea
  And hears it roar beneath.

HAMLET. It waves me still:
  Go on, I'll follow thee.

MARCELLUS. You shall not go my lord.

HAMLET. Hold off your hands. 80

HORATIO. Be ruled, you shall not go.

HAMLET. My fate cries out,
  And makes each petty artire° in this body

---

54 *fools of nature*: mocked by our natural limitations when faced with the supernatural.
59 *some . . . desire*: desired to impart something.   65 *fee*: value.
71 *beetles o'er*: overhangs.   73 *deprive . . . reason*: dethrone your reason from its
sovereignty.   75 *toys of desperation*: desperate whims.   82 *artire*: ligament.

As hardy as the Nemean lion's° nerve;°
Still am I called, unhand me gentlemen,
By heaven I'll make a ghost of him that lets° me: 85
I say away; go on, I'll follow thee.   *Exeunt GHOST and HAMLET.*
HORATIO.   He waxes desperate° with imagination.
MARCELLUS.   Let's follow, 'tis not fit thus to obey him.
HORATIO.   Have after—to what issue will this come?
MARCELLUS.   Something is rotten in the state of Denmark.   90
HORATIO.   Heaven will direct it.
MARCELLUS.   Nay, let's follow him.   *Exeunt.*

[Scene 5. *Another part of the platform*]

Enter GHOST and HAMLET.

HAMLET.   Whither wilt thou lead me? Speak, I'll go no further.
GHOST.   Mark me.
HAMLET.   I will
GHOST.   My hour is almost come
When I to sulphurous and tormenting flames
Must render up myself.
HAMLET.   Alas poor ghost.
GHOST.   Pity me not, but lend thy serious hearing   5
To what I shall unfold.
HAMLET.   Speak, I am bound° to hear.
GHOST.   So art thou to revenge, when thou shalt hear.
HAMLET.   What?
GHOST.   I am thy father's spirit,
Doomed for a certain term to walk the night,   10
And for the day confined to fast in fires,
Till the foul crimes done in my days of nature°
Are burnt and purged away: but that I am forbid
To tell the secrets of my prison-house,
I could a tale unfold whose lightest word   15
Would harrow up thy soul, freeze thy young blood,
Make thy two eyes like stars start from their spheres,°
Thy knotted and combinèd locks to part,
And each particular hair to stand an end,
Like quills upon the fretful porpentine:°   20
But this eternal blazon° must not be
To ears of flesh and blood; list, list, O list:
If thou didst ever thy dear father love—

---

83 *Nemean lion*: (killed by Hercules as one of his twelve labors).   *nerve*: sinew.   85 *lets*:
prevents.   87 *waxes desperate*: grows frantic.   6 *bound*: obliged by duty.   12 *crimes
. . . nature*: sins committed during my life on earth.   17 *spheres*: (1) orbits (according to
Ptolemy, each planet was confined to a sphere revolving around the earth) (2) sockets.
20 *fretful porpentine*: angry porcupine.   21 *eternal blazon*: revelation about eternity.

HAMLET. O God!

GHOST. Revenge his foul and most unnatural murder.   25

HAMLET. Murder?

GHOST. Murder most foul, as in the best it is,
    But this most foul, strange and unnatural.

HAMLET. Haste me to know't, that I with wings as swift
    As meditation or the thoughts of love,   30
    May sweep to my revenge.

GHOST.   I find thee apt,°
    And duller shouldst thou be than the fat° weed
    That rots itself in ease on Lethe wharf,°
    Wouldst thou not stir in this; now Hamlet hear,
    'Tis given out, that sleeping in my orchard,°   35
    A serpent stung me, so the whole ear of Denmark
    Is by a forgèd process° of my death
    Rankly abused:° but know thou noble youth,
    The serpent that did sting thy father's life
    Now wears his crown.

HAMLET.   O my prophetic soul!   40
    My uncle?

GHOST. Ay, that incestuous, that adulterate° beast,
    With witchcraft of his wit, with traitorous gifts,
    O wicked wit and gifts, that have the power
    So to seduce; won to his shameful lust   45
    The will of my most seeming-virtuous queen;
    O Hamlet, what a falling-off was there,
    From me whose love was of that dignity
    That it went hand in hand, even with the vow
    I made to her in marriage, and to decline   50
    Upon° a wretch whose natural gifts were poor
    To° those of mine;
    But virtue, as it never will be moved,
    Though lewdness court it in a shape of heaven,°
    So lust, though to a radiant angel linked,   55
    Will sate itself in a celestial bed
    And prey on garbage.
    But soft, methinks I scent the morning air,
    Brief let me be; sleeping within my orchard,
    My custom always of the afternoon,   60
    Upon my secure° hour thy uncle stole
    With juice of cursèd hebona° in a vial,

---

31 *apt*: ready.   32 *fat*: slimy.   33 *Lethe wharf*: the banks of Lethe (river in Hades from which spirits drank to forget their past lives).   35 *orchard*: garden.   37 *process*: account.   38 *abused*: deceived.   42 *adulterate*: adulterous.   50–51 *decline Upon*: descend to.   52 *To*: compared to.   54 *shape of heaven*: angelic appearance.   61 *secure*: unsuspecting.   62 *hebona*: poisonous sap of the ebony or henbane.

And in the porches of my ears did pour
The leperous° distilment, whose effect
Holds such an enmity with blood of man,   65
That swift as quicksilver it courses through
The natural gates and alleys of the body,
And with a sudden vigour it doth posset°
And curd, like eager° droppings into milk,
The thin and wholesome° blood; so did it mine,   70
And a most instant tetter° barked about°
Most lazar°-like with vile and loathsome crust
All my smooth body.
Thus was I sleeping by a brother's hand,
Of life, of crown, of queen at once dispatched,   75
Cut off even in the blossoms of my sin,
Unhouseled, disappointed, unaneled,°
No reck'ning° made, but sent to my account°
With all my imperfections on my head;
O horrible, O horrible, most horrible!   80
If thou hast nature in thee bear it not,
Let not the royal bed of Denmark be
A couch for luxury° and damnèd incest.
But howsomever thou pursues this act,
Taint not thy mind, nor let thy soul contrive   85
Against thy mother aught;° leave her to heaven,
And to those thorns that in her bosom lodge
To prick and sting her. Fare thee well at once,
The glow-worm shows the matin° to be near
And 'gins to pale his uneffectual fire:°   90
Adieu, adieu, adieu, remember me.   *Exit.*
HAMLET.   O all you host of heaven! O earth! what else?
And shall I couple° hell? O fie! Hold, hold my heart,
And you my sinews, grow not instant old,
But bear me stiffly up; remember thee?   95
Ay thou poor ghost, whiles memory holds a seat
In this distracted globe.° Remember thee?
Yea, from the table° of my memory
I'll wipe away all trivial fond° records,
All saws of books,° all forms, all pressures° past   100
That youth and observation copied there,

---

64 *leperous*: leprosy-causing.   68 *posset*: curdle.   69 *eager*: sour.   70 *wholesome*:
healthy.   71 *tetter*: skin eruption.   *barked about*: covered (like bark on a tree).   72 *lazar*:
leper.   77 *Unhouseled . . . unaneled*: without final sacrament, unprepared (without
confession) and lacking extreme unction (anointing).   78 *reck'ning*: (1) accounting (2)
payment of my bill (3) confession and absolution.   *account*: judgment.   83 *luxury*:
lust.   86 *aught*: anything.   89 *matin*: dawn.   90 *'gins . . . fire*: his light becomes
ineffective, made pale by day.   93 *couple*: engage in a contest against.   97 *distracted globe*:
(his head).   98 *table*: tablet, "table-book."   99 *fond*: foolish.   100 *saws of books*:
maxims copied from books.   *forms, pressures*: ideas, impressions.

And thy commandment all alone shall live
Within the book and volume of my brain,
Unmixed with baser matter, yes by heaven:
O most pernicious woman! 105
O villain, villain, smiling damnèd villain!
My tables,° meet° it is I set it down
That one may smile, and smile, and be a villain,
At least I am sure it may be so in Denmark.
So uncle, there you are: now to my word,° 110
It is 'Adieu, adieu, remember me.'
I have sworn't.

Enter HORATIO and MARCELLUS.

HORATIO. My lord, my lord!
MARCELLUS.   Lord Hamlet!
HORATIO.   Heaven secure° him.
HAMLET. So be it.
MARCELLUS. Illo, ho, ho, my lord! 115
HAMLET. Hillo, ho, ho, boy, come° bird, come.
MARCELLUS. How is't my noble lord?
HORATIO.   What news my lord?
HAMLET. O, wonderful!
HORATIO.   Good my lord, tell it.
HAMLET. No, you will reveal it.
HORATIO. Not I my lord, by heaven.
MARCELLUS.   Nor I my lord. 120
HAMLET. How say you then, would heart of man once think it?
  But you'll be secret?
BOTH.   Ay, by heaven, my lord.
HAMLET. There's ne'er a villain dwelling in all Denmark
  But he's an arrant° knave.
HORATIO. There needs no ghost my lord, come from the grave 125
  To tell us this.
HAMLET.   Why right, you are in the right,
  And so without more circumstance° at all
  I hold it fit that we shake hands and part,
  You, as your business and desire shall point you,
  For every man hath business and desire 130
  Such as it is, and for my own poor part,
  Look you, I will go pray.
HORATIO. These are but wild and whirling words my lord.
HAMLET. I am sorry they offend you, heartily,
  Yes faith, heartily.

107 *tables*: see note for line 98.   *meet*: fitting.   110 *word*: motto (to guide my actions).   113 *secure*: protect.   116 *Hillo . . . come*: (falconer's cry with which Hamlet replies to their calls).   124 *arrant*: thoroughgoing.   127 *circumstance*: ceremony.

HORATIO.   There's no offence my lord.   135
HAMLET.   Yes by Saint Patrick, but there is Horatio,
    And much offence too: touching this vision here,
    It is an honest° ghost that let me tell you:
    For your desire to know what is between us,
    O'ermaster't as you may. And now good friends,   140
    As you are friends, scholars, and soldiers,
    Give me one poor request.
HORATIO.   What is't, my lord? we will.
HAMLET.   Never make known what you have seen tonight.
BOTH.   My lord we will not.
HAMLET.   Nay, but swear't.
HORATIO.   In faith   145
    My lord, not I.
MARCELLUS.   Nor I my lord, in faith.
HAMLET.   Upon my sword.
MARCELLUS.   We have sworn my lord already.
HAMLET.   Indeed, upon my sword,° indeed.
GHOST.   Swear.   *Ghost cries under the stage.*
HAMLET.   Ha, ha, boy, say'st thou so, art thou there, truepenny°?   150
    Come on, you hear this fellow in the cellarage,
    Consent to swear.
HORATIO.   Propose the oath my lord.
HAMLET.   Never to speak of this that you have seen,
    Swear by my sword.
GHOST. [*Beneath.*]   Swear.   155
HAMLET.   Hic et ubique?° then we'll shift our ground:
    Come hither gentlemen,
    And lay your hands again upon my sword,
    Swear by my sword
    Never to speak of this that you have heard.   160
GHOST. [*Beneath.*]   Swear by his sword.
HAMLET.   Well said old mole, canst work i'th' earth so fast?
    A worthy pioner°—once more remove,° good friends.
HORATIO.   O day and night, but this is wondrous strange.
HAMLET.   And therefore as a stranger give it welcome.   165
    There are more things in heaven and earth Horatio,
    Than are dreamt of in your philosophy.
    But come,
    Here as before, never so help you mercy,
    How strange or odd some'er I bear myself,   170
    (As I perchance hereafter shall think meet
    To put an antic disposition on°)

---

138 *honest*: true (not a devil in disguise).   148 *sword*: (the cross-shaped hilt).
150 *truepenny*: old pal.   156 *Hic et ubique*: here and everywhere.   163 *pioner*:
digger (army trencher).   *remove*: move elsewhere.   172 *put . . . . on*: assume a mad or
grotesque behavior.

That you at such times seeing me, never shall
With arms encumbered° thus, or this head-shake,
Or by pronouncing of some doubtful phrase,   175
As "Well, well, we know," or "We could and if we would,"
Or "If we list° to speak," or "There be and if they might,"
Or such ambiguous giving out, to note
That you know aught of me; this do swear,
So grace and mercy at your most need help you.   180
GHOST. [*Beneath.*] Swear.
HAMLET.   Rest, rest, perturbed spirit: so gentlemen,
With all my love I do commend me to you,°
And what so poor a man as Hamlet is,
May do t'express his love and friending to you   185
God willing shall not lack: let us go in together,
And still° your fingers on your lips I pray.
The time is out of joint: O cursèd spite,
That ever I was born to set it right.
Nay come, let's go together.   *Exeunt.*   190

ACT 2

Scene 1. [*Polonius's chambers*]

Enter old POLONIUS *with his man* REYNALDO.

POLONIUS.   Give him this money, and these notes Reynaldo.
REYNALDO.   I will my lord.
POLONIUS.   You shall do marvellous° wisely, good Reynaldo,
Before you visit him, to make inquire
Of his behaviour.
REYNALDO.   My lord, I did intend it.   5
POLONIUS.   Marry, well said, very well said; look you sir,
Inquire me first what Danskers° are in Paris,
And how, and who, what means, and where they keep,°
What company, at what expense, and finding
By this encompassment° and drift of question   10
That they do know my son, come you more nearer
Than your particular demands° will touch it,
Take you as 'twere some distant knowledge of him,
As thus, "I know his father, and his friends,
And in part him"—do you mark this, Reynaldo?   15

---

174 *encumbered*: folded.   177 *list*: please.   183 *commend . . . you*: put myself in your
hands.   187 *still*: always.   3 *marvellous*: wonderfully.   7 *Danskers*: Danes.   8 *keep*:
lodge.   10 *encompassment*: roundabout way.   12 *particular demands*: specific questions.

REYNALDO.   Ay, very well my lord.

POLONIUS.   'And in part him, but,' you may say, 'not well,
But if't be he I mean, he's very wild,
Addicted so and so;' and there put on him
What forgeries° you please, marry none so rank°   20
As may dishonour him, take heed of that,
But sir, such wanton, wild, and usual slips,
As are companions noted and most known
To youth and liberty.

REYNALDO.   As gaming my lord.

POLONIUS.   Ay, or drinking, fencing, swearing,   25
Quarrelling, drabbing° —you may go so far.

REYNALDO.   My lord, that would dishonour him.

POLONIUS.   Faith no, as you may season it in the charge.°
You must not put another scandal on him,
That he is open to incontinency,°   30
That's not my meaning, but breathe his faults so quaintly°
That they may seem the taints of° liberty,
The flash and outbreak of a fiery mind,
A savageness in unreclaimèd blood,°
Of general assault.°

REYNALDO.   But my good lord—   35

POLONIUS.   Wherefore° should you do this?

REYNALDO.   Ay my lord,
I would know that.

POLONIUS.   Marry sir, here's my drift,
And I believe it is a fetch of warrant:°
You laying these slight sullies on my son,
As 'twere a thing a little soiled i'th' working,°   40
Mark you, your party in converse, him you would sound,
Having ever seen° in the prenominate crimes°
The youth you breathe of guilty, be assured
He closes with you in this consequence,°
"Good sir," or so, or "friend," or "gentleman,"   45
According to the phrase, or the addition°
Of man and country.

REYNALDO.   Very good my lord.

POLONIUS.   And then sir, does a'° this, a' does, what was I
about to say?

---

20 *forgeries*: inventions.   *rank*: excessive.   26 *drabbing*: whoring.   28 *season* . . .
charge: temper the charge as you make it.   30 *incontinency*: uncontrolled lechery.
31 *quaintly*: delicately.   32 *taints of*: blemishes due to.   34 *unreclaimed blood*:
unbridled passion.   35 *general assault*: attacking all (young men).   36 *Wherefore*: why.
38 *fetch of warrant*: trick guaranteed to succeed.   40 *working*: handling.
42 *Having ever seen*: if he has ever seen.   *prenominate crimes*: aforenamed sins.
44 *closes* . . . *consequence*: comes to terms with you as follows.   46 *addition*: title,
form of address.   48 *'a*: he.

By the mass I was about to say something,
Where did I leave?
REYNALDO.   At "closes in the consequence,"   50
    At "friend, or so, and gentleman."
POLONIUS.   At "closes in the consequence," ay marry,
    He closes thus, "I know the gentleman,
    I saw him yesterday, or th'other day,
    Or then, or then, with such or such, and as you say,   55
    There was a' gaming, there o'ertook in's rouse,°
    There falling out at tennis," or perchance
    "I saw him enter such a house of sale,"
    Videlicet,° a brothel, or so forth. See you now,
    Your bait of falsehood takes this carp of truth,   60
    And thus do we of wisdom, and of reach,°
    With windlasses,° and with assays of bias,°
    By indirections find directions out:
    So by my former lecture and advice
    Shall you my son; you have me, have you not?   65
REYNALDO.   My lord I have.
POLONIUS.   God bye ye, fare ye well.
REYNALDO.   Good my lord.
POLONIUS.   Observe his inclination in yourself.°
REYNALDO.   I shall my lord.
POLONIUS.   And let him ply° his music.
REYNALDO.   Well my lord.   70
POLONIUS.   Farewell.

                                                    Exit REYNALDO.

Enter OPHELIA.

                How now Ophelia, what's the matter?
OPHELIA.   O my lord, my lord, I have been so affrighted.
POLONIUS.   With what, i'th'name of God?
OPHELIA.   My lord, as I was sewing in my closet,°
    Lord Hamlet with his doublet all unbraced,°   75
    No hat upon his head, his stockings fouled,
    Ungart'red, and down-gyvèd° to his ankle,
    Pale as his shirt, his knees knocking each other,
    And with a look so piteous in purport°
    As if he had been loosèd out of hell   80
    To speak of horrors, he comes before me.

---

56 *o'ertook in's rouse*: overcome by drunkenness.   59 *Videlicet*: namely.   61 *reach*: far-reaching knowledge.   62 *windlasses*: roundabout approaches.   *assays of bias*: indirect attempts.   68 *in yourself*: personally.   70 *ply*: practice.   74 *closet*: private room.
75 *doublet all unbraced*: jacket all unfastened.   77 *down-gyvèd*: down around his ankles (like prisoners' fetters or gyves).   79 *purport*: expression.

POLONIUS.   Mad for thy love?
OPHELIA.   My lord I do not know,
   But truly I do fear it.
POLONIUS.   What said he?
OPHELIA.   He took me by the wrist, and held me hard,
   Then goes he to the length of all his arm,°   85
   And with his other hand thus o'er his brow,
   He falls to such perusal of my face
   As° a' would draw it; long stayed he so,
   At last, a little shaking of mine arm,
   And thrice his head thus waving up and down,   90
   He raised a sigh so piteous and profound
   As it did seem to shatter all his bulk,°
   And end his being; that done, he lets me go,
   And with his head over his shoulder turned
   He seemed to find his way without his eyes,   95
   For out adoors he went without their helps,
   And to the last bended their light on me.
POLONIUS.   Come, go with me, I will go seek the king,
   This is the very ecstasy° of love,
   Whose violent property fordoes itself,°   100
   And leads the will to desperate undertakings
   As oft as any passion under heaven
   That does afflict our natures: I am sorry.
   What, have you given him any hard words of late?
OPHELIA.   No my good lord, but as you did command   105
   I did repel his letters, and denied
   His access to me.
POLONIUS.   That hath made him mad.
   I am sorry that with better heed and judgment
   I had not quoted° him. I feared he did but trifle
   And meant to wrack° thee, but beshrew my jealousy:°   110
   By heaven it is as proper to our age
   To cast beyond ourselves in our opinions,°
   As it is common for the younger sort
   To lack discretion; come, go we to the king,
   This must be known, which being kept close, might move   115
   More grief to hide, than hate to utter love.°   [Exeunt.]

---

85 *goes . . . arm*: holds me at arm's length.   88 *As*: as if.   92 *bulk*: body.   99 *ecstasy*:
madness.   100 *Whose . . . itself*: that, by its violent nature, destroys the lover.
109 *quoted*: observed.   110 *wrack*: ruin.   *beshrew my jealousy*: curse my suspicion.
111–112 *proper . . . opinions*: natural for old people to read more into something
than is actually there.   115–116 *being kept . . . love*: if kept secret, might cause more grief
than if we risked the king's displeasure.

Scene 2. [*A room in the Castle*]

Flourish. Enter KING *and* QUEEN, ROSENCRANTZ *and* GUILDENSTERN, *cum aliis.*

KING. Welcome dear Rosencrantz and Guildenstern.
Moreover° that we much did long to see you,
The need we have to use you did provoke
Our hasty sending. Something have you heard
Of Hamlet's transformation—so call it,   5
Sith° nor th'exterior nor the inward man
Resembles that it was. What it should be,
More than his father's death, that thus hath put him
So much from th'understanding of himself,
I cannot dream of: I entreat you both,   10
That being of so young days° brought up with him,
And sith so neighboured to his youth and haviour,
That you vouchsafe your rest° here in our court
Some little time, so by your companies
To draw him on to pleasures, and to gather   15
So much as from occasion you may glean,
Whether aught to us unknown afflicts him thus,
That opened° lies within our remedy.
QUEEN. Good gentlemen, he hath much talked of you,
And sure I am, two men there are not living   20
To whom he more adheres. If it will please you
To show us so much gentry° and good will,
As to expend your time with us awhile,
For the supply and profit of our hope,
Your visitation shall receive such thanks   25
As fits a king's remembrance.
ROSENCRANTZ.   Both your majesties
Might be the sovereign power you have of us,
Put your dread pleasures more into command
Than to entreaty.
GUILDENSTERN.   But we both obey,
And here give up ourselves in the full bent,°   30
To lay our service freely at your feet
To be commanded.
KING. Thanks Rosencrantz, and gentle Guildenstern.
QUEEN. Thanks Guildenstern, and gentle Rosencrantz.
And I beseech you instantly to visit   35
My too much changèd son. Go some of you
And bring these gentlemen where Hamlet is.

---

2 *Moreover*: in addition to the fact.   6 *Sith*: since.   11 *of . . . days*: from your early
days.   13 *vouchsafe your rest*: agree to stay.   18 *opened*: discovered.   22 *gentry*:
courtesy.   30 *in the full bent*: to the utmost (in archery, bending the bow).

GUILDENSTERN.   Heavens make our presence and our practices°
    Pleasant and helpful to him.
QUEEN.   Ay, amen.

                                 Exeunt ROSENCRANTZ *and* GUILDENSTERN.

Enter POLONIUS.

POLONIUS.   Th' ambassadors from Norway my good lord,   40
    Are joyfully returned.
KING.   Thou still° hast been the father of good news.
POLONIUS.   Have I, my lord? Assure you, my good liege,
    I hold my duty as I hold my soul,
    Both to my God and to my gracious king;   45
    And I do think, or else this brain of mine
    Hunts not the trail of policy° so sure
    As it hath used to do, that I have found
    The very cause of Hamlet's lunacy.
KING.   O speak of that, that do I long to hear.   50
POLONIUS.   Give first admittance to th' ambassadors,
    My news shall be the fruit° to that great feast.
KING.   Thyself do grace to them, and bring them in.   [*Exit* POLONIUS.]
    He tells me my dear Gertrude, he hath found
    The head and source of all your son's distemper.   55
QUEEN.   I doubt° it is no other but the main,
    His father's death and our o'erhasty marriage.
KING.   Well, we shall sift him.

Enter POLONIUS, VALTEMAND, *and* CORNELIUS.

                        Welcome, my good friends.
    Say Valtemand, what from our brother Norway?
VALTEMAND.   Most fair return of greetings and desires;   60
    Upon our first,° he sent out to suppress
    His nephew's levies, which to him appeared
    To be a preparation 'gainst the Polack,
    But better looked into, he truly found
    It was against your highness, whereat grieved   65
    That so his sickness, age, and impotence
    Was falsely borne in hand,° sends out arrests
    On Fortinbras, which he in brief obeys,
    Receives rebuke from Norway, and in fine,°
    Makes vow before his uncle never more   70
    To give th'assay° of arms against your majesty:
    Whereon old Norway, overcome with joy,
    Gives him threescore thousand crowns in annual fee,

---

38 *practices*: (1) actions (2) plots.   42 *still*: always.   47 *policy*: (1) politics (2) plots.
52 *fruit*: dessert.   56 *doubt*: suspect.   61 *first*: first presentation.   67 *borne in hand*:
deceived.   69 *fine*: finishing.   71 *assay*: test.

And his commission to employ those soldiers
So levied (as before) against the Polack,   75
With an entreaty herein further shown,
That it might please you to give quiet pass°
Through your dominions for this enterprise,
On such regards of safety and allowance
As therein are set down.   *[Giving a paper.]*

KING.   It likes° us well,   80
And at our more considered time,° we'll read,
Answer, and think upon this business:
Meantime, we thank you for your well-took labour,
Go to your rest, at night we'll feast together.
Most welcome home.   *Exeunt AMBASSADORS.*

POLONIUS.   This business is well ended.   85
My liege and madam, to expostulate°
What majesty should be, what duty is,
Why day is day, night night, and time is time,
Were nothing but to waste night, day, and time.
Therefore since brevity is the soul of wit,°   90
And tediousness the limbs and outward flourishes,°
I will be brief. Your noble son is mad:
Mad call I it, for to define true madness,
What is't but to be nothing else but mad?
But let that go.

QUEEN.   More matter, with less art.   95
POLONIUS.   Madam, I swear I use no art at all:
That he is mad 'tis true: 'tis true, 'tis pity,
And pity 'tis 'tis true: a foolish figure,°
But farewell it, for I will use no art.
Mad let us grant him then, and now remains   100
That we find out the cause of this effect,
Or rather say, the cause of this defect,
For this effect defective comes by cause:
Thus it remains, and the remainder thus.
Perpend.°   105
I have a daughter, have while she is mine,
Who in her duty and obedience, mark,
Hath given me this, now gather and surmise.
[Reads.] "To the celestial, and my soul's idol, the most
beautified° Ophelia,"—   110
That's an ill phrase, a vile phrase, "beautified" is a vile
phrase, but you shall hear. Thus: *[Reads.]*
    "In her excellent white bosom, these, &c."—

---

77 *pass*: passage.   80 *likes*: pleases.   81 *at . . . time*: when time is available for
consideration.   86 *expostulate*: discuss.   90 *wit*: understanding.   91 *tediousness . . .
flourishes*: embellishments and flourishes cause tedium.   98 *figure*: rhetorical
figure.   105 *Perpend*: consider.   110 *beautified*: beautiful.

QUEEN.   Came this from Hamlet to her?

POLONIUS.   Good madam stay awhile, I will be faithful.   [*Reads.*]   115
        "Doubt thou the stars are fire,
          Doubt that the sun doth move,°
        Doubt° truth to be a liar,
          But never doubt I love.
        O dear Ophelia, I am ill at these numbers, I have not   120
        art to reckon° my groans, but that I love thee best. O
        most best, believe it. Adieu.
            Thine evermore, most dear lady, whilst
               this machine° is to° him, Hamlet."
This in obedience hath my daughter shown me,   125
And more above hath his solicitings,
As they fell out by time, by means, and place,
All given to mine ear.

KING.   But how hath she
Received his love?

POLONIUS.   What do you think of me?

KING.   As of a man faithful and honourable.   130

POLONIUS.   I would fain prove so. But what might you think
When I had seen this hot love on the wing,
As I perceived it (I must tell you that)
Before my daughter told me, what might you,
Or my dear majesty your queen here think,   135
If I had played the desk or table-book,°
Or given my heart a winking° mute and dumb,
Or looked upon this love with idle° sight,
What might you think? No, I went round to work,
And my young mistress thus I did bespeak,   140
"Lord Hamlet is a prince out of thy star,°
This must not be:" and then I prescripts° gave her
That she should lock herself from his resort,°
Admit no messengers, receive no tokens:
Which done, she took the fruits of my advice,   145
And he repellèd, a short tale to make,
Fell into a sadness, then into a fast,
Thence to a watch,° thence into a weakness,
Thence to a lightness,° and by this declension,
Into the madness wherein now he raves,   150
And all we mourn for.

---

117 *move*: (as it was believed to do, around the earth).   118 *Doubt*: suspect.   121 *reckon*:
express in meter.   124 *machine*: body.   *to*: attached to.   136 *played . . . book*: kept
it concealed as in a desk or personal notebook.   137 *given . . . winking*: had my heart
shut its eyes to the matter.   138 *idle*: unseeing.   141 *out . . . star*: out of your sphere
(above you in station).   142 *prescripts*: orders.   143 *resort*: company.   148 *watch*:
sleeplessness.   149 *lightness*: lightheadedness.

KING.   Do you think 'tis this?

QUEEN.   It may be very like.

POLONIUS.   Hath there been such a time, I would fain know that,
    That I have positively said "Tis so,"
    When it proved otherwise?

KING.   Not that I know.   155

POLONIUS.   Take this, from this, if this be otherwise;

[*Points to his head and shoulder.*]

    If circumstances lead me, I will find
    Where truth is hid, though it were hid indeed
    Within the center.

KING.   How may we try° it further?

POLONIUS.   You know sometimes he walks four hours together   160
    Here in the lobby.

QUEEN.   So he does indeed.

POLONIUS.   At such a time, I'll loose° my daughter to him,
    Be you and I behind an arras° then,
    Mark the encounter: if he love her not,
    And be not from his reason fall'n thereon,   165
    Let me be no assistant for a state,°
    But keep a farm and carters.

KING.   We will try it.

Enter HAMLET *reading on a book.*

QUEEN.   But look where sadly the poor wretch comes reading.

POLONIUS.   Away, I do beseech you both away,
    I'll board him presently,° O give me leave.   *Exeunt* KING *and* QUEEN.   170
    How does my good Lord Hamlet?

HAMLET.   Well, God-a-mercy.

POLONIUS.   Do you know me, my lord?

HAMLET.   Excellent well, you are a fishmonger.°

POLONIUS.   Not I my lord.   175

HAMLET.   Then I would you were so honest a man.

POLONIUS.   Honest, my lord?

HAMLET.   Ay sir, to be honest as this world goes, is to be one
    man picked out of ten thousand.

POLONIUS.   That's very true, my lord.   180

HAMLET.   For if the sun breed maggots° in a dead dog, being a good
    kissing carrion°—have you a daughter?

POLONIUS.   I have my lord.

---

159 *try*: test.   162 *loose*: (1) release (2) turn loose.   163 *arras*: hanging tapestry.
166 *assistant . . . state*: state official.   170 *board him presently*: approach him
immediately.   174 *fishmonger*: (1) fish dealer (2) pimp.   181 *breed maggots*: (in the belief
that the rays of the sun caused maggots to breed in dead flesh).   182 *kissing carrion*: piece
of flesh for kissing.

HAMLET.   Let her not walk i'th'sun:° conception° is a blessing, but as
your daughter may conceive, friend look to'it.   185
POLONIUS.   [Aside.] How say you by that? Still harping on my daughter,
yet he knew me not at first, a' said I was a fishmonger.
A' is far gone, far gone, and truly in my youth, I suffered
much extremity for love, very near this. I'll speak to him
again. What do you read my lord?   190
HAMLET.   Words, words, words.
POLONIUS.   What is the matter my lord?
HAMLET.   Between who?
POLONIUS.   I mean the matter° that you read, my lord.
HAMLET.   Slanders, sir; for the satirical rogue says here, that old men   195
have grey beards, that their faces are wrinkled, their eyes
purging thick amber and plum-tree gum,° and that they
have a plentiful lack of wit, together with most weak
hams. All which sir, though I most powerfully and
potently believe, yet I hold it not honesty° to have it thus set   200
down, for yourself sir shall grow old as I am: if like a crab
you could go backward.
POLONIUS.   [Aside.] Though this be madness, yet there is method
in't.
Will you walk out of the air° my lord?   205
HAMLET.   Into my grave.
POLONIUS.   [Aside.] Indeed that's out of the air; how pregnant°
sometimes his replies are, a happiness° that often
madness hits on, which reason and sanity could not so
prosperously° be delivered of. I will leave him, and   210
suddenly contrive the means of meeting between him
and my daughter. My honourable lord, I will most
humbly take leave of you.
HAMLET.   You cannot sir take from me anything that I will more
willingly part withal: except my life, except my life,   215
except my life.
POLONIUS.   Fare you well my lord.
HAMLET.   These tedious old fools.

Enter ROSENCRANTZ and GUILDENSTERN.

POLONIUS.   You go to seek the Lord Hamlet, there he is.
ROSENCRANTZ.   [To Polonius.] God save you sir.   [Exit POLONIUS.]   220

---

184 *Let . . . sun*: (1) (proverbial: "out of God's blessing, into the warm sun") (2) because
the sun is a breeder (3) don't let her go near me (with a pun on "sun" and "son").   *conception*:
(1) understanding (2) pregnancy.   194 *matter*: (1) content (Polonius's meaning) (2) cause
of a quarrel (Hamlet's interpretation).   197–198 *purging . . . gum*: exuding a viscous
yellowish discharge.   200 *honesty*: decency.   205 *out . . . air*: (in the belief that fresh
air was bad for the sick).   207 *pregnant*: full of meaning.   208 *happiness*: aptness.
210 *prosperously*: successfully.

GUILDENSTERN.   My honoured lord.
ROSENCRANTZ.   My most dear lord.
HAMLET.   My excellent good friends, how dost thou Guildenstern?
Ah Rosencrantz, good lads, how do you both?
ROSENCRANTZ.   As the indifferent° children of the earth.   225
GUILDENSTERN.   Happy, in that we are not over-happy:
On Fortune's cap we are not the very button.°
HAMLET.   Nor the soles of her shoe?
ROSENCRANTZ.   Neither my lord.
HAMLET.   Then,you live about her waist, or in the middle of her   230
favours?
GUILDENSTERN.   Faith, her privates° we.
HAMLET.   In the secret parts of Fortune? O most true, she is a
strumpet.° What news?
ROSENCRANTZ.   None my lord, but that the world's grown honest.   235
HAMLET.   Then is doomsday near: but your news is not true. Let me
question more in particular: what have you my good
friends, deserved at the hands of Fortune, that she sends
you to prison hither?
GUILDENSTERN.   Prison, my lord?   240
HAMLET.   Denmark's a prison.
ROSENCRANTZ.   Then is the world one.
HAMLET.   A goodly one, in which there are many confines, wards,°
and dungeons; Denmark being one o'th'worst.
ROSENCRANTZ.   We think not so my lord.   245
HAMLET.   Why then 'tis none to you; for there is nothing either good
or bad, but thinking makes it so: to me it is a prison.
ROSENCRANTZ.   Why then your ambition makes it one: 'tis too narrow for
your mind.
HAMLET.   O God, I could be bounded in a nutshell, and count   250
myself a king of infinite space; were it not that I have bad
dreams.
GUILDENSTERN.   Which dreams indeed are ambition: for the very substance
of the ambitious, is merely the shadow of a dream.
HAMLET.   A dream itself is but a shadow.   255
ROSENCRANTZ.   Truly, and I hold ambition of so airy and light a quality,
that it is but a shadow's shadow.
HAMLET.   Then are our beggars bodies, and our monarchs and
outstretched heroes the beggars' shadows:° shall we to th'
court? for by my fay,° I cannot reason.   260
BOTH.   We'll wait upon° you.
HAMLET.   No such matter. I will not sort° you with the rest of my

225 *indifferent*: ordinary.   227 *on Fortune's . . . button*: we are not at the height of our
fortunes.   232 *privates*: (1) intimate friends (2) private parts.   234 *strumpet*: inconstant
woman, giving favor to many.   243 *wards*: cells.   258–259 *Then are . . . shadows*: then
beggars are the true substance and ambitious kings and heroes the elongated shadows of
beggars' bodies (for only a real substance can cast a shadow).   260 *fay*: faith.   261 *wait
upon*: attend.   262 *sort*: class.

servants: for to speak to you like an honest man, I am most
dreadfully attended. But in the beaten way of friendship,
what make you at Elsinore?   265

ROSENCRANTZ. To visit you my lord, no other occasion.

HAMLET. Beggar that I am, I am even poor in thanks, but I thank
you, and sure dear friends, my thanks are too dear a
halfpenny:° were you not sent for? is it your own inclining?
is it a free° visitation? come, come, deal justly with me,   270
come, come, nay speak.

GUILDENSTERN. What should we say my lord?

HAMLET. Anything but to th'purpose: you were sent for, and there
is a kind of confession in your looks, which your modesties
have not craft enough to colour: I know the good king and   275
queen have sent for you.

ROSENCRANTZ. To what end my lord?

HAMLET. That you must teach me: but let me conjure° you, by the
rights of our fellowship, by the consonancy of our youth,°
by the obligation of our ever-preserved love, and by what   280
more dear a better proposer can charge you withal,° be
even and direct with me whether you were sent for or no.

ROSENCRANTZ. [*Aside to Guildenstern.*] What say you?

HAMLET. Nay then, I have an eye of° you: If you love me,
hold not off.   285

GUILDENSTERN. My lord, we were sent for.

HAMLET. I will tell you why, so shall my anticipation prevent° your
discovery,° and your secrecy to the king and queen moult
no feather.° I have of late, but wherefore I know not, lost all
my mirth, forgone all custom of exercises: and indeed it   290
goes so heavily with my disposition, that this goodly
frame the earth, seems to me a sterile promontory, this
most excellent canopy the air, look you, this brave°
o'erhanging firmament, this majestical roof fretted° with
golden fire,° why it appeareth nothing to me but a foul and   295
pestilent congregation of vapours.° What a piece of work is
a man! How noble in reason, how infinite in faculties,° in
form and moving, how express° and admirable in action,
how like an angel in apprehension, how like a god: the
beauty of the world; the paragon of animals; and yet to   300
me, what is this quintessence of dust? Man delights not
me, no, nor woman neither, though by your smiling, you
seem to say so.

ROSENCRANTZ. My lord, there was no such stuff in my thoughts.

268–269 *too dear a halfpenny*: worth not even a halfpenny (as I have no influence).   270 *free*:
voluntary.   278 *conjure*: appeal to.   279 *consonancy . . . youth*: agreement in our
ages.   281 *withal*: with.   284 *of*: on.   287 *prevent*: forestall.   288 *discovery*:
disclosure.   288–289 *moult no feather*: change in no way.   293 *brave*: splendid.
294 *fretted*: ornamented with fretwork.   295 *golden fire*: stars.   296 *pestilent . . . vapours*:
(clouds were believed to carry contagion).   297 *faculties*: physical powers.   298 *express*:
well framed.

HAMLET. Why did ye laugh then, when I said 'man delights not me'? 305
ROSENCRANTZ. To think, my lord, if you delight not in man, what lenten
    entertainment° the players shall receive from you: we coted°
    them on the way, and hither are they coming to offer you
    service.
HAMLET. He that plays the king shall be welcome, his majesty shall 310
    have tribute of me, the adventurous knight° shall use his
    foil and target,° the lover shall not sigh gratis,° the humorous
    man° shall end his part in peace,° the clown shall make
    those laugh whose lungs are tickle o'th'sere,° and the lady
    shall say her mind freely: or the blank verse shall halt° for't. 315
    What players are they?
ROSENCRANTZ. Even those you were wont to take such delight in, the
    tragedians of the city.
HAMLET. How chances it they travel? Their residence° both in
    reputation and profit was better both ways. 320
ROSENCRANTZ. I think their inhibition comes by the means of the late
    innovation.°
HAMLET. Do they hold the same estimation they did when I was in
    the city; are they so followed?
ROSENCRANTZ. No indeed are they not. 325
HAMLET. How comes it? Do they grow rusty?
ROSENCRANTZ. Nay, their endeavour keeps in the wonted pace; but there
    is sir an aery° of children, little eyases,° that cry out on the
    top of question,° and are most tyrannically° clapped for't:
    these are now the fashion, and so berattle° the common 330
    stages° (so they call them) that many wearing rapiers° are
    afraid of goose-quills,° and dare scarce come thither.
HAMLET. What, are they children? Who maintains 'em? How are
    they escoted°? Will they pursue the quality no longer than
    they can sing°? Will they not say afterwards if they should 335
    grow themselves to common players (as it is most like, if
    their means are not better) their writers do them wrong, to
    make them exclaim against their own succession°?
ROSENCRANTZ. Faith, there has been much to-do on both sides: and the

---

306–307 *lenten entertainment*: meager treatment.   307 *coted*: passed.   311 *adventurous
knight*: knight errant (a popular stage character).   312 *foil and target*: sword blunted for
stage fighting, and small shield.   312 *gratis*: (without applause).   312–313 *humorous man*:
eccentric character with a dominant trait, caused by an excess of one of the four humours,
or bodily fluids.   313 *in peace*: without interruption.   314 *tickle o'th' sere*: attuned to
respond to laughter, as the finely adjusted gunlock responds to the touch of the trigger (fr.
hunting).   315 *halt*: limp (if she adds her own opinions and spoils the meter).
319 *residence*: i.e. in a city theatre.   321–322 *inhibition . . . innovation*: hinderance
is due to the recent novelty (of the children's companies).   328 *aery*: nest.
eyases: young hawks.   328–329 *that cry . . . question*: whose shrill voices can be heard above
all others (in the "War of the Theatres" between the child and adult companies, 1601–
1602).   329 *tyrannically*: strongly.   330 *berattle*: berate.   330–331 *common stages*:
public playhouses (the children's companies performed in private theatres).
331 *wearing rapiers*: (worn by gentlemen).   332 *goose-quills*: pens (of satirical dramatists
who wrote for the children).   334 *escoted*: supported.   334–335 *pursue . . . sing*: continue
acting only until their voices change.   338 *succession*: inheritance.

nation holds it no sin to tarre° them to controversy. There   340
was for a while, no money bid for argument,° unless the
poet and the player went to cuffs in the question.°

HAMLET.   Is't possible?

GUILDENSTERN.   O there has been much throwing about of brains.

HAMLET.   Do the boys carry it away°?   345

ROSENCRANTZ.   Ay, that they do my lord, Hercules and his load too.°

HAMLET.   It is not very strange, for my uncle is king of Denmark,
and those that would make mows° at him while my father
lived, give twenty, forty, fifty, a hundred ducats apiece
for his picture in little.° 'Sblood,° there is something in this   350
more than natural, if philosophy° could find it out.

A flourish for the Players.

GUILDENSTERN.   There are the players.

HAMLET.   Gentlemen, you are welcome to Elsinore: your hands,
come then, th'appurtenance° of welcome is fashion and
ceremony; let me comply with you in this garb,° lest my   355
extent° to the players, which I tell you must show fairly
outwards, should more appear like entertainment than
yours.° You are welcome: but my uncle-father, and aunt-
mother, are deceived.

GUILDENSTERN.   In what my dear lord?   360

HAMLET.   I am but mad north-north-west; when the wind is southerly,
I know a hawk from a handsaw.°

Enter POLONIUS.

POLONIUS.   Well be with you, gentlemen.

HAMLET.   Hark you Guildenstern, and you too, at each ear a hearer:
that great baby you see there is not yet out of his swaddling   365
clouts.°

ROSENCRANTZ.   Happily° he is the second time come to them, for they say
an old man is twice a child.

HAMLET.   I will prophesy, he comes to tell me of the players, mark
it.—You say right sir, a Monday morning, 'twas then   370
indeed.

POLONIUS.   My lord, I have news to tell you.

340 *tarre*: provoke.   341 *bid for argument*: paid for the plot of a proposed play.   342 *went
. . . question*: came to blows on the subject.   345 *carry it away*: carry off the prize.
346 *Hercules . . . too*: (Shakespeare's own company at the Globe Theatre, whose sign was
Hercules carrying the globe of the world).   348 *mows*: mouths, grimaces.
350 *little*: a miniature.   *'Sblood*: by God's blood.   351 *philosophy*: science.
354 *appurtenance*: accessory.   355 *comply . . . garb*: observe the formalities with you in
this style.   356 *extent*: i.e. of welcome.   357–358 *should . . . yours*: should appear more
hospitable than yours.   362 *I know . . . handsaw*: I can tell the difference between two
things that are unlike ("hawk" = (1) bird of prey (2) mattock, pickaxe; "handsaw" = (1)
hernshaw or heron bird (2) small saw).   365–366 *swaddling clouts*: strips of cloth binding
a newborn baby.   367 *Happily*: perhaps.

HAMLET. My lord, I have news to tell you. When Roscius° was an
    actor in Rome—
POLONIUS. The actors are come hither, my lord.   375
HAMLET. Buz, buz.°
POLONIUS. Upon my honour.
HAMLET. Then came each actor on his ass—
POLONIUS. The best actors in the world, either for tragedy, comedy,
    history, pastoral, pastoral-comical, historical-pastoral,   380
    tragical-historical, tragical-comical-historical-pastoral,
    scene individable,° or poem unlimited.° Seneca cannot be
    too heavy, nor Plautus° too light for the law of writ, and the
    liberty:° these are the only men.
HAMLET. O Jephthah,° judge of Israel, what a treasure hadst thou.   385
POLONIUS. What a treasure had he, my lord?
HAMLET. Why
    'One fair daughter and no more,
        The which he lovèd passing° well.'
POLONIUS. [*Aside.*] Still on my daughter.   390
HAMLET. Am I not i'th' right, old Jephthah?
POLONIUS. If you call me Jephthah my lord, I have a daughter that I
    love passing well.
HAMLET. Nay, that follows not.
POLONIUS. What follows then, my lord?   395
HAMLET. Why
    "As by lot, God wot,"
    and then you know
    "It came to pass, as most like° it was:"
    the first row° of the pious chanson will show you more, for   400
    look where my abridgement° comes.

Enter four or five PLAYERS.

    You are welcome masters, welcome all. I am glad to see
    thee well: welcome, good friends. O my old friend, why
    thy face is valanced° since I saw thee last, com'st thou to
    beard me in Denmark? What, my young lady° and   405
    mistress? by'r lady, your ladyship is nearer to heaven than
    when I saw you last, by the altitude of a chopine.° Pray
    God your voice, like a piece of uncurrent° gold, be not

373 *Roscius*: famous Roman actor.   376 *Buz, buz*: (contemptuous).   382 *scene individable*:
play observing the unities (time, place, action).   *poem unlimited*: play ignoring the unities.
382–383 *Seneca, Plautus*: Roman writers of tragedy and comedy respectively.
383–384 *law . . . liberty*: "rules" regarding the unities and those exercising freedom from
the unities.   385 *Jephthah*: (who was forced to sacrifice his only daughter because of a
rash promise: Judges 11:29–39).   389 *passing*: surpassingly.   399 *like*: likely.
400 *row*: stanza.   401 *abridgement*: (the players who will cut short my song).
404 *valanced*: fringed with a beard.   405 *lady*: boy playing women's roles.   407 *chopine*:
thick-soled shoe.   408 *uncurrent*: not legal tender.

cracked within the ring.° Masters, you are all welcome:
we'll e'en to't like French falconers, fly at any thing we see:°   410
we'll have a speech straight. Come give us a taste of your
quality: come, a passionate speech.

I. PLAYER. What speech, my good lord?

HAMLET. I heard thee speak me a speech once, but it was never
acted, or if it was, not above once, for the play I remember   415
pleased not the million, 'twas caviary to the general,° but it
was (as I received it, and others, whose judgments in such
matters cried in the top of mine°) an excellent play, well
digested in the scenes, set down with as much modesty as
cunning.° I remember one said there were no sallets° in the   420
lines, to make the matter savoury, nor no matter in the
phrase that might indict the author of° affection, but called
it an honest method, as wholesome as sweet, and by very
much more handsome than fine:° one speech in't I chiefly
loved, 'twas Aeneas' tale to Dido, and thereabout of it   425
especially where he speaks of Priam's slaughter.° If it live in
your memory begin at this line, let me see, let me see:
    "The rugged Pyrrhus,° like th'Hyrcanian beast"°—
'tis not so: it begins with Pyrrhus—
    "The rugged Pyrrhus, he whose sable° arms,   430
Black as his purpose, did the night resemble
When he lay couchèd in th'ominous horse,°
Hath now this dread and black complexion smeared
With heraldy more dismal: head to foot
Now is he total gules,° horridly tricked°   435
With blood of fathers, mothers, daughters, sons,
Baked and impasted° with the parching° streets,
That lend a tyrannous and damnèd light
To their lord's murder. Roasted in wrath and fire,
And thus o'er-sizèd° with coagulate gore,   440
With eyes like carbuncles,° the hellish Pyrrhus
Old grandsire Priam seeks;"
So proceed you.

POLONIUS. 'Fore God, my lord, well spoken, with good accent and
good discretion.°   445

---

409 *ring*: (1) ring enclosing the design on a gold coin (to crack it within the ring [to steal
the gold] made it "uncurrent") (2) sound.   410 *fly . . . see*: undertake any difficulty.
416 *caviary . . . general*: like caviar, too rich for the general public.   418 *cried . . . mine*:
spoke with more authority than mine.   419–420 *modesty as cunning*: moderation as
skill.   420 *sallets*: spicy bits.   422 *indict . . . of*: charge . . . with.   424 *handsome than
fine*: dignified than finely wrought.   426 *Priam's slaughter*: the murder of the King of Troy
(as told in the Aeneid).   428 *Pyrrhus*: son of Achilles.   *Hyrcanian beast*: tiger noted for
fierceness.   430 *sable*: black.   432 *horse*: the hollow wooden horse used by the Greeks
to enter Troy.   435 *gules*: red.   *horridly tricked*: horribly decorated.   437 *impasted*:
coagulated.   *parching*: (because the city was on fire).   440 *o'er-sized*: covered over.
441 *carbuncles*: red gems.   445 *discretion*: interpretation.

I. PLAYER. "Anon he finds him,
     Striking too short at Greeks, his antique° sword,
     Rebellious to his arm, lies where it falls,
     Repugnant to command;° unequal matched,
     Pyrrhus at Priam drives, in rage strikes wide,   450
     But with the whiff and wind of his fell° sword,
     Th'unnerved father falls: then senseless Ilium,°
     Seeming to feel this blow, with flaming top
     Stoops to his base; and with a hideous crash
     Takes prisoner Pyrrhus' ear. For lo, his sword   455
     Which was declining on the milky head
     Of reverend Priam, seemed i'th'air to stick;
     So as a painted° tyrant Pyrrhus stood,
     And like a neutral to his will and matter,°
     Did nothing: 460
     But as we often see, against° some storm,
     A silence in the heavens, the rack° stand still,
     The bold winds speechless, and the orb° below
     As hush as death, anon the dreadful thunder
     Doth rend the region, so after Pyrrhus' pause,   465
     A rousèd vengeance sets him new awork,
     And never did the Cyclops'° hammers fall
     On Mars's armour, forged for proof eterne,°
     With less remorse than Pyrrhus' bleeding sword
     Now falls on Priam.   470
     Out, out, thou strumpet Fortune: all you gods,
     In general synod° take away her power,
     Break all the spokes and fellies from her wheel,°
     And bowl the round nave° down the hill of heaven
     As low as to the fiends."°   475
POLONIUS. This is too long.
HAMLET. It shall to the barber's with your beard; prithee say on: he's
     for a jig, or a tale of bawdry, or he sleeps. Say on, come to
     Hecuba.
I. PLAYER. "But who, ah woe, had seen the mobled° queen—"   480
HAMLET. "The mobled queen"?
POLONIUS. That's good, "mobled queen" is good.
I. PLAYER. "Run barefoot up and down, threat'ning the flames
     With bissom rheum,° a clout° upon that head
     Where late the diadem stood, and for a robe,   485

---

447 *antique*: ancient.   449 *Repugnant to command*: Refusing to obey its commander.
451 *fell*: savage.   452 *senseless Ilium*: unfeeling Troy.   458 *painted*: pictured.   459 *like
. . . matter*: unmoved by either his purpose or its achievement.   461 *against*: before.
462 *rack*: clouds.   463 *orb*: earth.   467 *Cyclops*: workmen of Vulcan, armorer
of the gods.   468 *for proof eterne*: to be eternally invincible.   472 *synod*: assembly.
473 *fellies . . . wheel*: curved pieces of the rim of the wheel that fortune turns,
representing a man's fortunes.   474 *nave*: hub.   475 *fiends*: i.e. of hell.   480 *mobled*:
muttled in a scarf.   484 *bissom rheum*: binding tears.   *clout*: cloth.

About her lank and all o'er-teemèd° loins,
A blanket in the alarm of fear caught up—
Who this had seen, with tongue in venom steeped,
'Gainst Fortune's state° would treason have pronounced;
But if the gods themselves did see her then,   490
When she saw Pyrrhus make malicious sport
In mincing with his sword her husband's limbs,
The instant burst of clamour that she made,
Unless things mortal move them not at all,
Would have made milch° the burning eyes of heaven,   495
And passion in the gods."

POLONIUS.   Look whe'r° he has not turned° his colour, and has tears in's
eyes, prithee no more.

HAMLET.   'Tis well, I'll have thee speak out the rest of this soon.
Good my lord, will you see the players well bestowed;° do   500
you hear, let them be well used, for they are the abstract°
and brief chronicles° of the time; after your death you were
better have a bad epitaph than their ill report while you
live.

POLONIUS.   My lord, I will use them according to their desert.°   505

HAMLET.   God's bodkin° man, much better. Use every man after° his
desert, and who shall 'scape whipping? Use them after
you own honour and dignity: the less they deserve, the
more merit is in your bounty. Take them in.

POLONIUS.   Come sirs.   *Exeunt POLONIUS and PLAYERS.*   510

HAMLET.   Follow him friends, we'll hear a play tomorrow; [*Stops the
First Player.*] dost thou hear me, old friend, can you play
The Murder of Gonzago?

I. PLAYER.   Ay my lord.

HAMLET.   We'll ha't tomorrow night. You could for a need° study a   515
speech of some dozen or sixteen lines, which I would set
down and insert in't, could you not?

I. PLAYER.   Ay my lord.

HAMLET.   Very well, follow that lord, and look you mock him not.

                                                        [*Exit First PLAYER.*]

[*To Rosencrantz and Guildenstern.*] My good friends, I'll   520
leave you till night, you are welcome to Elsinore.

ROSENCRANTZ.   Good my lord.   [*Exeunt.*]

HAMLET.   Ay so, God bye to you, now I am alone.
O what a rogue and peasant slave am I.
Is it not monstrous that this player here,   525

---

486 *o'erteemed*: worn out by excessive childbearing.   489 *state*: reign.   495 *milch*: milky,
moist.   497 *whe'r*: whether.   *turned*: changed.   500 *bestowed*: lodged.   501 *abstract*:
summary (noun).   502 *brief chronicles*: history in brief.   505 *desert*: merit.   506 *God's
bodkin*: God's little body, the communion wafer (an oath).   *after*: according to.   515 *for
a need*: if necessary.

But in a fiction, in a dream of passion,°
Could force his soul so to his own conceit°
That from her working all his visage wanned,°
Tears in his eyes, distraction in his aspect,
A broken voice, and his whole function° suiting   530
With forms° to his conceit; and all for nothing,
For Hecuba
What's Hecuba to him, or he to Hecuba,
That he should weep for her? what would he do,
Had he the motive and the cue for passion   535
That I have? he would drown the stage with tears,
And cleave the general ear° with horrid speech,
Make mad the guilty and appal the free,°
Confound° the ignorant, and amaze indeed
The very faculties of eyes and ears; yet I,   540
A dull and muddy-mettled° rascal, peak°
Like John-a-dreams,° unpregnant of° my cause,
And can say nothing; no, not for a king,
Upon whose property and most dear life,
A damned defeat was made: am I a coward?   545
Who calls me villain, breaks my pate° across,
Plucks off my beard° and blows it in my face,
Tweaks me by the nose, gives me the lie i'th'throat
As deep as to the lungs,° who does me this?
Ha, 'swounds,° I should take it: for it cannot be   550
But I am pigeon-livered,° and lack gall
To make oppression bitter, or ere this
I should ha' fatted all the region kites°
With this slave's offal: bloody, bawdy villain,
Remorseless, treacherous, lecherous, kindless° villain!   555
O vengeance!
Why what an ass am I, this is most brave,°
That I, the son of a dear father murdered,
Prompted to my revenge by heaven and hell,
Must like a whore unpack my heart with words,   560
And fall a-cursing like a very drab,°
A scullion,° fie upon't, foh.

---

526 *dream of passion*: portrayal of emotion.   527 *conceit*: imagination.   528 *wanned*: grew
pale.   530 *function*: bearing.   531 *With forms*: in appearance.   537 *general ear*: ears
of all in the audience.   538 *free*: innocent.   539 *confound*: confuse.   541 *muddy-
mettled*: dull-spirited.   *peak*: pine, mope.   542 *John-a-dreams*: a daydreaming
fellow.   *unpregnant of*: unstirred by.   546 *pate*: head.   547 *Plucks . . . beard*: (a way
of giving insult).   548–549 *gives . . . lungs*: insults me by calling me a liar of the worst
kind (the lungs being deeper than the throat).   550 *'swounds*: God's wounds.   551 *pigeon-
livered*: meek and uncourageous.   553 *region kites*: vultures of the upper air.   555 *kindless*:
unnatural.   557 *brave*: fine.   561 *drab*: whore.   562 *scullion*: kitchen wench.

About, my brains; hum, I have heard,
That guilty creatures sitting at a play,
Have by the very cunning of the scene   565
Been struck so to the soul, that presently°
They have proclaimed their malefactions:
For murder, though it have no tongue, will speak
With most miraculous organ: I'll have these players
Play something like the murder of my father   570
Before mine uncle, I'll observe his looks,
I'll tent° him to the quick, if a' do blench°
I know my course. The spirit that I have seen
May be a devil, and the devil hath power
T'assume a pleasing shape, yea, and perhaps   575
Out of my weakness, and my melancholy,
As he is very potent with such spirits,
Abuses me to damn me; I'll have grounds
More relative than this: the play's the thing
Wherein I'll catch the conscience of the king.   *Exit.*

[ACT 3]

[Scene 1. A room in the castle]

Enter KING, QUEEN, POLONIUS, OPHELIA, ROSENCRANTZ, GUILDENSTERN, *and Lords*.

KING.   And can you by no drift of conference°
Get from him why he puts on this confusion,°
Grating so harshly all his days of quiet
With turbulent and dangerous lunacy?
ROSENCRANTZ.   He does confess he feels himself distracted,   5
But from what cause, a' will by no means speak.
GUILDENSTERN.   Nor do we find him forward to be sounded,°
But with a crafty madness keeps aloof
When we would bring him on to some confession
Of his true state.
QUEEN.   Did he receive you well?   10
ROSENCRANTZ.   Most like a gentleman.
GUILDENSTERN.   But with much forcing of his disposition.°
ROSENCRANTZ.   Niggard of question,° but of our demands
Most free in his reply.

---

566 *presently*: immediately.   572 *tent*: probe.   *blench*: flinch.   1 *drift of conference*: turn
of conversation.   2 *puts . . . confusion*: seems so distracted ("puts on" indicates the king's
private suspicion that Hamlet is playing mad).   7 *forward . . . sounded*: disposed to be
sounded out.   12 *forcing . . . disposition*: forcing himself to be so.   13 *Niggard of question*:
unwilling to talk.

QUEEN.   Did you assay° him
   To any pastime?   15
ROSENCRANTZ.   Madam, it so fell out that certain players
   We o'er-raught° on the way: of these we told him,
   And there did seem in him a kind of joy
   To hear of it: they are here about the court,
   And as I think, they have already order   20
   This night to play before him.
POLONIUS.   'Tis most true,
   And he beseeched me to entreat your majesties
   To hear and see the matter.°
KING.   With all my heart, and it doth much content me
   To hear him so inclined.   25
   Good gentlemen, give him a further edge,°
   And drive his purpose into these delights.
ROSENCRANTZ.   We shall my lord.   *Exeunt* ROSENCRANTZ *and* GUILDENSTERN.
KING.   Sweet Gertrude, leave us too,
   For we have closely° sent for Hamlet hither,
   That he, as 'twere by accident, may here   30
   Affront° Ophelia;
   Her father and myself, lawful espials,°
   Will so bestow° ourselves, that seeing unseen,
   We may of their encounter frankly° judge,
   And gather by him as he is behaved,   35
   If't be th'affliction of his love or no
   That thus he suffers for.
QUEEN.   I shall obey you.
   And for your part Ophelia, I do wish
   That your good beauties be the happy cause
   Of Hamlet's wildness, so shall I hope your virtues   40
   Will bring him to his wonted° way again,
   To both your honours.
OPHELIA.   Madam, I wish it may.   [*Exit* QUEEN.]
POLONIUS.   Ophelia, walk you here—Gracious,° so please you,
   We will bestow ourselves—read on this book,°
   That show of such an exercise° may colour°   45
   Your loneliness; we are oft to blame in this,
   'Tis too much proved,° that with devotion's visage
   And pious action, we do sugar o'er
   The devil himself.

---

14 *assay*: tempt.   17 *o'er-raught*: overtook.   23 *matter*: i.e. of the play.   26 *give . . .*
edge: encourage his keen interest.   29 *closely*: secretly.   31 *Affront*: meet face to face
with.   32 *espials*: spies.   33, 44 *bestow* place.   34 *frankly*: freely.   41. *wonted*:
customary.   43 *Gracious*: i.e., sir.   44 *book*: (of prayer).   45 *exercise*: religious
exercise   *colour*: make appear plausible.   47 *'Tis . . . proved*: it is all too apparent.

KING.   [*Aside.*] O 'tis too true,°
    How smart a lash that speech doth give my conscience.   50
    The harlot's cheek, beautied with plast'ring art,
    Is not more ugly to° the thing that helps it,
    Than is my deed to my most painted word:°
    O heavy burden!
POLONIUS. I hear him coming, let's withdraw my lord.   *Exeunt.*   55

Enter HAMLET.

HAMLET. To be, or not to be, that is the question,
    Whether 'tis nobler in the mind° to suffer
    The slings and arrows of outrageous fortune,
    Or to take arms against a sea of troubles,
    And by opposing, end them: to die, to sleep,   60
    No more; and by a sleep, to say we end
    The heart-ache, and the thousand natural shocks
    That flesh is heir to; 'tis a consummation
    Devoutly to be wished. To die, to sleep,
    To sleep, perchance to dream, ay there's the rub,°   65
    For in that sleep of death what dreams may come
    When we have shuffled off this mortal coil°
    Must give us pause—there's the respect°
    That makes calamity of so long life:°
    For who would bear the whips and scorns of time,°   70
    Th'oppressor's wrong, the proud man's contumely,°
    The pangs of disprized love, the law's delay,°
    The insolence of office,° and the spurns
    That patient merit of th'unworthy takes,
    When he himself might his quietus° make   75
    With a bare bodkin;° who would fardels° bear,
    To grunt and sweat under a weary life,
    But that the dread of something after death,
    The undiscovered° country, from whose bourn°
    No traveller returns, puzzles the will,   80
    And makes us rather bear those ills we have,
    Than fly to others that we know not of.
    Thus conscience does make cowards of us all,
    And thus the native hue° of resolution

---

49 *'tis too true*: (the king's first indication that he is guilty).   52 *to*: compared to.   51–
53 *harlot's cheek . . . word*: just as the harlot's cheek is even uglier by contrast to the makeup
that tries to beautify it, so my deed is uglier by contrast to the hypocritical words under
which I hide it.   57 *nobler in the mind*: best, according to "sovereign" reason.   65 *rub*:
obstacle.   67 *mortal coil*: (1) turmoil of mortal life (2) coil of flesh encircling the body.
68 *respect*: consideration.   69 *of so long life*: so long-lived.   70 *time*: the
times.   71 *contumely*: contempt.   72 *law's delay*: longevity of lawsuits.   73 *office*:
officials.   75 *quietus*: settlement of his debt.   76 *bare bodkin*: mere dagger.   *fardels*:
burdens.   79 *undiscovered*: unexplored.   *bourn*: boundary.   84 *native hue*: natural
complexion.

Is sicklied o'er with the pale cast of thought, 85
And enterprises of great pitch° and moment,°
With this regard° their currents turn awry,°
And lose the name of action. Soft you now,
The fair Ophelia—Nymph, in thy orisons°
Be all my sins remembered.
OPHELIA.   Good my lord, 90
How does your honour for this many a day°?
HAMLET. I humbly thank you: well, well, well.
OPHELIA. My lord, I have remembrances of yours
That I have longèd long to re-deliver,
I pray you now receive them.
HAMLET.   No, not I, 95
I never gave you aught.
OPHELIA. My honoured lord, you know right well you did,
And with them words of so sweet breath° composed
As made the things more rich: their perfume lost,
Take these again, for to the noble mind 100
Rich gifts wax° poor when givers prove unkind.
There my lord.
HAMLET. Ha, ha, are you honest°?
OPHELIA. My lord.
HAMLET. Are you fair°? 105
OPHELIA. What means your lordship?
HAMLET. That if you be honest and fair, your honesty should admit
no discourse to your beauty.°
OPHELIA. Could beauty my lord, have better commerce than with
honesty? 110
HAMLET. Ay truly, for the power of beauty will sooner transform
honesty° from what it is to a bawd,° than the force of
honesty can translate beauty into his likeness. This was
sometime° a paradox, but now the time gives it proof. I did
love you once. 115
OPHELIA. Indeed my lord, you made me believe so.
HAMLET. You should not have believed me, for virtue cannot so
inoculate our old stock, but we shall relish of it.° I loved
you not.
OPHELIA. I was the more deceived. 120

---

86 *pitch*: height, excellence. *moment*: importance. 87 *regard*: consideration. *their currents turn awry*: change their course. 89 *orisons*: prayers (referring to her prayer book). 91 *this . . . day*: all these days. 98 *breath*: speech. 101 *wax*: grow. 103 *honest*: (1) chaste (2) truthful. 105 *fair*: (1) beautiful (2) honorable. 107–108 *admit . . . beauty*: (1) not allow communication with your beauty (2) not allow your beauty to be used as a trap (Hamlet may have overheard the Polonius-Claudius plot or spotted their movement behind the arras). 112 *honesty*: chastity. *bawd*: procurer, pimp. 114 *sometime*: once. 118 *inoculate . . . it*: change our sinful nature (as a tree is grafted to improve it) but we will keep our old taste (as will the fruit of the grafted tree).

HAMLET. Get thee to a nunnery,° why wouldst thou be a breeder of
   sinners? I am myself indifferent honest,° but yet I could
   accuse me of such things, that it were better my mother
   had not borne me: I am very proud, revengeful, ambitious,
   with more offences at my beck,° than I have thoughts   125
   to put them in, imagination to give them shape, or time to
   act them in: what should such fellows as I do, crawling
   between earth and heaven? we are arrant° knaves all,
   believe none of us, go thy ways to a nunnery. Where's
   your father?   130
OPHELIA. At home my lord.
HAMLET. Let the doors be shut upon him, that he may play the fool
   no where but in's own house. Farewell.
OPHELIA. O help him, you sweet heavens.
HAMLET. If thou dost marry, I'll give thee this plague° for thy dowry: 135
   be thou as chaste as ice, as pure as snow, thou shalt not
   escape calumny; get thee to a nunnery, go, farewell. Or if
   thou wilt needs marry, marry a fool, for wise men know
   well enough what monsters° you make of them: to a nunnery
   go, and quickly too, farewell.   140
OPHELIA. O heavenly powers, restore him.
HAMLET. I have heard of your paintings too, well enough. God hath
   given you one face, and you make yourselves another: you
   jig,° you amble, and you lisp,° you nick-name God's
   creatures, and make your wantonness your ignorance;° go to,   145
   I'll no more on't, it hath made me mad. I say we will have
   no moe° marriage. Those that are married already, all but
   one shall live, the rest shall keep as they are: to a nunnery,
   go.   *Exit HAMLET.*
OPHELIA. O what a noble mind is here o'erthrown!   150
   The courtier's, soldier's, scholar's, eye, tongue, sword,
   Th'expectancy and rose° of the fair state,
   The glass° of fashion, and the mould of form,°
   Th'observed of all observers, quite quite down,
   And I of ladies most deject and wretched,   155
   That sucked the honey of his music vows,
   Now see that noble and most sovereign° reason
   Like sweet bells jangled, out of tune and harsh,
   That unmatched form and feature° of blown° youth

---

121 *nunnery*: (1) cloister (2) slang for "brothel" (cf. "bawd" above).   122 *indifferent honest*:
reasonably virtuous.   125 *beck*: beckoning.   128 *arrant*: absolute.   135 *plague*:
curse.   139 *monsters*: horned cuckolds (men whose wives were unfaithful).   144 *jig*: walk
in a mincing way.   *lisp*: put on affected speech.   145 *make your . . . ignorance*: excuse
your caprices as being due to ignorance.   147 *moe*: more.   152 *expectancy and rose*: fair
hope.   153 *glass*: mirror.   *mould of form*: model of manners.   157 *sovereign*: (because
it should rule).   159 *blown*: flowering

Blasted with ecstasy.° O woe is me,   160
T'have seen what I have seen, see what I see.

Enter KING *and* POLONIUS.

KING.   Love? his affections° do not that way tend,
Nor what he spake, though it lacked form a little,
Was not like madness. There's something in his soul
O'er which his melancholy sits on brood,   165
And I do doubt,° the hatch and the disclose°
Will be some danger; which for to prevent,
I have in quick determination
Thus set it down: he shall with speed to England,
For the demand of our neglected° tribute: 170
Haply° the seas, and countries different,
With variable° objects, shall expel
This something°-settled matter in his heart,
Whereon his brains still beating puts him thus
From fashion of himself.° What think you on't?   175
POLONIUS.   It shall do well. But yet do I believe
The origin and commencement of his grief
Sprung from neglected° love. How now Ophelia?
You need not tell us what Lord Hamlet said,
We heard it all. My lord, do as you please,   180
But if you hold it fit, after the play,
Let his queen-mother all alone entreat him
To show his grief, let her be round° with him,
And I'll be placed (so please you) in the ear
Of° all their conference. If she find° him not,   185
To England send him: or confine him where
Your wisdom best shall think
KING.   It shall be so,
Madness in great ones must not unwatched go.   *Exeunt.*

[Scene 2. A hall in the castle.]

Enter HAMLET *and three of the* PLAYERS.

HAMLET.   Speak the speech° I pray you as I pronounced it to you,
trippingly on the tongue, but if you mouth it° as many of
your players do, I had as lief the town-crier spoke my
lines. Nor do not saw the air too much with your hand

---

160 *Blasted with ecstasy*: blighted by madness.   162 *affections*: emotions, afflictions.
166 *doubt*: fear.   165–166 *on brood . . . hatch . . . disclose*: (metaphor of a hen
sitting on eggs).   170 *neglected*: (being unpaid).   171 *Haply*: perhaps.
172 *variable*: varied.   173 *something-*: somewhat-.   175 *fashion of himself*: his usual
self.   178 *neglected*: unrequited.   183 *round*: direct.   184–185 *in the ear Of*: so
as to overhear.   185 *find*: find out.   1 *the speech*: i.e., that Hamlet has inserted.
2 *mouth it*: deliver it slowly and over-dramatically.

thus, but use all gently, for in the very torrent, tempest,   5
and as I may say, whirlwind of your passion, you must
acquire and beget° a temperance that may give it smoothness.
O it offends me to the soul, to hear a robustious°
periwig-pated° fellow tear a passion to tatters, to very rags,
to split the ears of the groundlings,° who for the most part   10
are capable of° nothing but inexplicable dumb shows° and
noise: I would have such a fellow whipped for o'erdoing
Termagant:° it out-herods Herod,° pray you avoid it.

I. PLAYER. I warrant you honour.

HAMLET. Be not too tame neither, but let your own discretion be   15
   your tutor, suit the action to the word, the word to the
   action, with this special observance, that you o'erstep not
   the modesty° of nature: for any thing so o'erdone, is from°
   the purpose of playing, whose end both at the first, and
   now, was and is, to hold as 'twere the mirror up to nature,   20
   to show virtue her own feature, scorn° her own image, and
   the very age and body of the time his form and pressure.°
   Now this overdone, or come tardy off,° though it make the
   unskilful° laugh, cannot but make the judicious grieve, the
   censure of the which one,° must in your allowance°   25
   o'erweigh a whole theatre of others. O there be players
   that I have seen play, and heard others praise, and that
   highly (not to speak it profanely) that neither having
   th'accent of Christians, nor the gait of Christian, pagan,
   nor man, have so strutted and bellowed, that I have   30
   thought some of nature's journeymen° had made men, and
   not made them well, they imitated humanity so
   abominably.

I. PLAYER. I hope we have reformed that indifferently° with us, sir.

HAMLET. O reform it altogether, and let those that play your clowns   35
   speak no more than is set down for them,° for there be of
   them that will themselves laugh, to set on some quantity
   of barren° spectators to laugh too, though in the meantime,
   some necessary question° of the play be then to be considered:

---

7 *acquire and beget*: achieve for yourself and instill in other actors.   8 *robustious*:
boisterous.   9 *periwig-pated*: wig-wearing.   10 *groundlings*: audience who paid least and
stood on the ground floor.   11 *capable of*: able to understand.   *dumb shows*: pantomimed
synopses of the action to follow (as below).   13 *Termagant*: violent, ranting character in
the guild or mystery plays.   *out-herods Herod*: outdoes even Herod, King of Judea (who
commanded the slaughter of the innocents and who was a ranting tyrant in the mystery
plays).   18 *modesty*: moderation.   *from*: away from.   21 *scorn*: that which should be
scorned.   22 *age . . . pressure*: shape of the times in its accurate impression.   23 *come
tardy off*: understated, underdone.   24 *unskilful*: unsophisticated.   25 *one*: the
judicious.   *allowance*: estimation.   31 *journeymen*: artisans working for others and not
yet masters of their trades.   34 *indifferently*: reasonably well.   36 *speak no more . . . them*:
stick to their lines.   38 *barren*: witless.   39 *question*: dialogue.

that's villainous, and shows a most pitiful ambition 40
in the fool that uses it. Go make you ready. *Exeunt PLAYERS.*

Enter POLONIUS, ROSENCRANTZ, and GUILDENSTERN.

How now my lord, will the king hear this piece of work?
POLONIUS.   And the queen too, and that presently.
HAMLET.   Bid the players make haste. *Exit POLONIUS.*
Will you two help to hasten them? 45
ROSENCRANTZ.   Ay my lord. *Exeunt they two.*
HAMLET.   What ho, Horatio!

Enter HORATIO.

HORATIO.   Here sweet lord, at your service.
HAMLET.   Horatio, thou art e'en as just° a man
As e'er my conversation coped withal.° 50
HORATIO.   O my dear lord.
HAMLET.   Nay, do not think I flatter,
For what advancement may I hope from thee,
That no revenue hast but thy good spirits
To feed and clothe thee? Why should the poor be flattered?
No, let the candied° tongue lick° absurd pomp, 55
And crook the pregnant° hinges of the knee
Where thrift may follow fawning.° Dost thou hear,
Since my dear soul was mistress of her choice,
And could of men distinguish her election,°
Sh'hath sealed° thee for herself, for thou hast been 60
As one in suff'ring all that suffers nothing,
A man that Fortune's buffets° and rewards
Hast ta'en with equal thanks; and blest are those
Whose blood° and judgment are so well co-mingled,
That they are not a pipe for Fortune's finger 65
To sound what stop° she please:° give me that man
That is not passion's slave, and I will wear him
In my heart's core, ay in my heart of heart,
As I do thee. Something too much of this.
There is a play tonight before the king, 70
One scene of it comes near the circumstance
Which I have told thee of my father's death.
I prithee when thou seest that act afoot,
Even with the very comment° of thy soul
Observe my uncle: if his occulted° guilt 75

49 *just*: well-balanced.   50 *coped withal*: had to do with.   55–57 *candied . . . fawning*:
(metaphor of a dog licking and fawning for candy).   55 *candied*: flattering.   *lick*: pay
court to.   56–57 *crook . . . fawning*: obsequiously kneel when personal profit may
ensue.   56 *pregnant*: quick in motion.   59 *election*: choice.   60 *sealed*: confirmed.
62 *buffets*: blows.   64 *blood*: passions.   66 *sound . . . please*: play whatever tune she
likes.   *stop*: finger hole in wind instrument for varying the sound.   74 *very comment*:
acutest observation.   75 *occulted*: hidden.

Do not itself unkennel° in one speech,
It is a damnèd ghost° that we have seen,
And my imaginations are as foul
As Vulcan's stithy;° give him heedful note,
For I mine eyes will rivet to his face,   80
And after we will both our judgments join
In censure of his seeming.°

HORATIO.   Well my lord,
If a' steal aught the whilst this play is playing,
And 'scape detecting, I will pay° the theft.   *Sound a flourish*.

HAMLET   They are coming to the play. I must be idle,°   85
Get you a place.

Enter Trumpets and Kettledrums, KING, QUEEN, POLONIUS, OPHELIA, ROSENCRANTZ,
GUILDENSTERN, *and other* LORDS *attendant*, *with his* GUARD *carrying torches*. *Danish March*.

KING.   How fares° our cousin Hamlet?
HAMLET.   Excellent i'faith, of the chameleon's dish: I eat the air,°
promise-crammed, you cannot feed capons so.°
KING.   I have nothing with° this answer Hamlet, these words are   90
not mine.°
HAMLET.   No, nor mine now. [*To Polonius*.] My lord, you played
once i'th'university you say?
POLONIUS.   That did I my lord, and was accounted a good actor.
HAMLET.   What did you enact?   95
POLONIUS.   I did enact Julius Caesar, I was killed i'th'Capitol, Brutus
killed me.
HAMLET.   It was a brute part of him to kill so capital a calf there. Be
the players ready?
ROSENCRANTZ.   Ay my lord, they stay upon your patience.°   100
QUEEN.   Come hither my dear Hamlet, sit by me.
HAMLET.   No, good mother, here's metal more attractive.°
POLONIUS.   [*To the King*.] O ho, do you mark that?
HAMLET.   Lady, shall I lie in your lap?
OPHELIA.   No my lord.   105
HAMLET.   I mean, my head upon your lap?
OPHELIA.   Ay my lord.

---

76 *unkennel*: force from hiding.   77 *damned ghost*: devil (not the ghost of my father).
79 *Vulcan's stithy*: the forge of the blacksmith of the gods.   82 *censure . . . seeming*: (1)
judgment of his appearance (2) disapproval of his pretending.   84 *pay*: i.e., for.   85
be idle: act mad.   87 *fares*: does, but Hamlet takes it to mean "eats" or "dines."   88 *eat
the air*: the chamelion supposedly ate air, but Hamlet also puns on "heir."   89 *you cannot
. . . so*: (1) even a capon cannot feed on air and your promises (2) like a capon stuffed
with food before being killed, I am stuffed (fed up) with your promises.   90 *nothing with*:
nothing to do with.   91 *not mine*: not in answer to my question.   100 *stay . . . patience*:
await your permission.   102 *metal more attractive*: (1) iron more magnetic (2) stuff ("mettle")
more beautiful.

HAMLET. Do you think I meant country° matters?
OPHELIA. I think nothing my lord.
HAMLET. That's a fair thought to lie between maids' legs.   110
OPHELIA. What is, my lord?
HAMLET. Nothing.
OPHELIA. You are merry my lord.
HAMLET. Who, I?
OPHELIA. Ay my lord.   115
HAMLET. O God, your only jig-maker: what should a man do but be
  merry, for look you how cheerfully my mother looks, and
  my father died within's two hours.
OPHELIA. Nay, 'tis twice two months my lord.
HAMLET. So long? Nay then let the devil wear black, for I'll have a   120
  suit of sables;° O heavens, die two months ago, and not
  forgotten yet? Then there's hope a great man's memory
  may outlive his life half a year, but by'r lady° a' must build
  churches then, or else shall a' suffer not thinking on,° with
  the hobby-horse,° whose epitaph is "For O, for O, the   125
  hobby-horse is forgot."

*The trumpets sound. The Dumb Show° follows. Enter a King and a Queen, very lovingly,
the Queen embracing him, and he her. She kneels and makes show of protestation unto him.
He takes her up, and declines his head upon her neck. He lies him down upon a bank of
flowers; she seeing him asleep leaves him: anon comes in another man, takes off his crown,
kisses it, pours poison in the sleeper's ears, and leaves him: the Queen returns, finds the
King dead, and makes passionate action. The poisoner with some three or four mutes° comes
in again, seeming to condole with her. The dead body is carried away. The poisoner wooes
the Queen with gifts: she seems harsh and unwilling awhile, but in the end accepts his love.
Exeunt.*

OPHELIA. What means this, my lord?
HAMLET. Marry, this is miching mallecho,° it means mischief.
OPHELIA. Belike this show imports the argument° of the play.

Enter PROLOGUE.

HAMLET. We shall know by this fellow: the players cannot keep   130
  counsel,° they'll tell all.
OPHELIA. Will a' tell us what this show meant?
HAMLET. Ay, or any show that you will show him. Be not you
  ashamed to show, he'll not shame to tell you what it
  means.   135
OPHELIA. You are naught,° you are naught, I'll mark the play.

---

108 *country*: rustic, sexual (with a pun on an obscene word for the female sexual organ).
121 *sables*: (1) rich fur (2) black mourning garb.   123 *by'r lady*: by Our Lady (the Virgin
Mary).   124 *not thinking on*: being forgotten.   125 *hobby-horse*: (1) character in the May
games (2) slang for "prostitute."   126 stage direction: *Dumb Show*: pantomimed synopsis
of the action to follow.   126 stage direction: *mutes*: actors without speaking parts.
128 *miching mallecho*: skulking mischief.   129 *imports the argument*: signifies the plot.
131 *counsel*: a secret.   136 *naught*: naughty, lewd.

PROLOGUE.   For us and for our tragedy,
    Here stooping to your clemency,
    We beg your hearing patiently.   [*Exit*.]
HAMLET.   Is this a prologue, or the posy° of a ring?   140
OPHELIA.   'Tis brief, my lord.
HAMLET.   As woman's love.

Enter Player KING *and* QUEEN.

PLAYER KING.   Full thirty times hath Phoebus' cart° gone round
    Neptune's salt wash,° and Tellus' orbèd ground,°
    And thirty dozen moons with borrowed sheen   145
    About the world have times twelve thirties been,
    Since love our hearts, and Hymen° did our hands
    Unite commutual,° in most sacred bands.
PLAYER QUEEN.   So many journeys may the sun and moon
    Make us again count o'er ere love be done,   150
    But woe is me, you are so sick of late,
    So far from cheer, and from your former state,
    That I distrust you:° yet though I distrust,
    Discomfort you, my lord, it nothing must.
    For women fear too much, even as they love,   155
    And women's fear and love hold quantity,°
    In neither aught, or in extremity:°
    Now what my love is, proof° hath made you know,
    And as my love is sized, my fear is so.
    Where love is great, the littlest doubts are fear,   160
    Where little fears grow great, great love grows there.
PLAYER KING.   Faith, I must leave thee love, and shortly too,
    My operant° powers their functions leave° to do,
    And thou shalt live in this fair world behind,
    Honoured, beloved, and haply° one as kind   165
    For husband shalt thou—
PLAYER QUEEN.   O confound the rest:
    Such love must needs be treason in my breast.
    In second husband let me be accurst,
    None wed the second, but who killed the first.
HAMLET.   [*Aside*.] That's wormwood,° wormwood.   170
PLAYER QUEEN.   The instances° that second marriage move°
    Are base respects of thrift,° but none of love.
    A second time I kill my husband dead,
    When second husband kisses me in bed.

---

140 *posy*: motto (engraved in a ring).   143 *Phoebus' cart*: chariot of the sun.   144 *wash*:
sea.   *Tellus'* . . . *ground*: the earth (Tellus was a Roman earth goddess).   147 *Hymen*:
Roman god of marriage.   148 *commutual*: mutually.   153 *distrust you*: am worried about
you.   156 *quantity*: proportion.   157 *In neither* . . . *extremity*: their love and fear are either
absent or excessive.   158 *proof*: experience.   163 *operant*: vital.   *leave*: cease.
165 *haply*: perhaps.   170 *wormwood*: bitter (like the herb).   171 *instances*:
causes.   *move*: motivate.   172 *respects of thrift*: considerations of profit.

PLAYER KING.   I do believe you think what now you speak,   175
    But what we do determine, oft we break:
    Purpose is but the slave to memory,
    Of violent birth but poor validity:°
    Which now like fruit unripe sticks on the tree,
    But fall unshaken when they mellow be.   180
    Most necessary 'tis that we forget
    To pay ourselves what to ourselves is debt:°
    What to ourselves in passion we propose,
    The passion ending, doth the purpose lose.
    The violence of either grief or joy   185
    Their own enactures° with themselves destroy:
    Where joy most revels, grief doth most lament;
    Grief joys, joy grieves, on slender accident.
    This world is not for aye,° nor 'tis not strange
    That even our loves should with our fortunes change: 190
    For 'tis a question left us yet to prove,
    Whether love lead fortune, or else fortune love.°
    The great man down, you mark his favourite flies,
    The poor advanced, makes friends of enemies:
    And hitherto doth love on fortune tend,   195
    For who not needs, shall never lack a friend,
    And who in want a hollow friend doth try,
    Directly seasons him° his enemy.
    But orderly to end where I begun,
    Our wills and fates do so contrary run,   200
    That our devices still° are overthrown,
    Our thoughts are ours, their ends none of our own.
    So think thou wilt no second husband wed,
    But die thy thoughts when thy first lord is dead.
PLAYER QUEEN.   Nor earth to me give food, nor heaven light,   205
    Sport and repose lock from me day and night,
    To desperation turn my trust and hope,
    An anchor's° cheer in prison be my scope,
    Each opposite that blanks° the face of joy,
    Meet what I would have well, and it destroy,   210
    Both here and hence° pursue me lasting strife,
    If once a widow, ever I be wife.
HAMLET.   If she should break it now.
PLAYER KING.   'Tis deeply sworn: sweet, leave me here awhile,
    My spirits grow dull, and fain° I would beguile   215
    The tedious day with sleep.   *Sleeps.*

---

178 *validity*: strength.   181–182 *Most . . . debt*: we are easy creditors to ourselves and
forget our former promises (debts).   186 *enactures*: fulfillments.   189 *aye*: ever.
192 *fortune love*: fortune lead love.   198 *seasons him*: sees him mature into.
201 *devices still*: plans always.   208 *anchor's*: hermit's.   209 *opposite that blanks*: contrary
event that pales.   211 *here and hence*: in this world and the next.   215 *fain*: gladly.

PLAYER QUEEN.   Sleep rock thy brain,
And never come mischance between us twain.   *Exit.*

HAMLET.   Madam, how like you this play?

QUEEN.   The lady doeth protest too much methinks.

HAMLET.   O but she'll keep her word.   220

KING.   Have you heard the argument°? Is there no offence in't?

HAMLET.   No, no, they do but jest, poison in jest, no offence
   i'th'world.

KING.   What do you call the play?

HAMLET.   The Mouse-trap. Marry, how? Tropically:° this play is the   225
   image of a murder done in Vienna: Gonzago is the duke's
   name, his wife Baptista, you shall see anon, 'tis a knavish
   piece of work, but what of that? Your majesty, and we
   that have free° souls, it touches us not: let the galled jade
   winch,° our withers are unwrung.°   230

Enter LUCIANUS.

   This is one Lucianus, nephew to the king.

OPHELIA.   You are as good as a chorus,° my lord.

HAMLET.   I could interpret between you and your love, if I could see
   the puppets dallying.

OPHELIA.   You are keen my lord, you are keen.°   235

HAMLET.   It would cost you a groaning to take off mine edge.

OPHELIA.   Still better and worse.°

HAMLET.   So you mistake° your husbands. Begin, murderer. Pox,°
   leave thy damnable faces° and begin. Come, 'the croaking
   raven doth bellow for revenge.'   240

LUCIANUS.   Thoughts black, hands apt, drugs fit, and time agreeing,
   Confederate season, else no creature seeing,°
   Thou mixture rank, of midnight weeds collected,
   With Hecate's° ban° thrice blasted, thrice infected,
   Thy natural magic, and dire property,   245
   On wholesome° life usurps immediately.   *Pours the poison in his ears.*

HAMLET.   A' poisons him i'th'garden for's estate, his name's Gonzago,
   the story is extant, and written in very choice
   Italian, you shall see anon how the murderer gets the love
   of Gonzago's wife.   250

OPHELIA.   The king rises.

HAMLET.   What, frighted with false fire°?

QUEEN.   How fares my lord?

---

221 *argument*: plot.   225 *Tropically*: figuratively.   229 *free*: innocent.   229–230 *galled
jade winch*: chafed old horse wince (from its sores).   230 *withers are unwrung*: (1) shoulders
are unchafed (2) consciences are clear.   232 *chorus*: actor who introduced the
action.   235 *keen*: (1) sharp (Ophelia's meaning) (2) sexually excited (Hamlet's
interpretation).   237 *better and worse*: better wit but a worse meaning, with a pun on "better"
and "bitter."   238 *mistake*: mis-take.   *Pox*: a plague on it.   239 *faces*: exaggerated
facial expressions.   242 *Confederate . . . seeing*: no one seeing me except time, my
confederate.   244 *Hecate*: goddess of witchcraft.   *ban*: evil spell.   246 *wholesome*:
healthy.   252 *false fire*: discharge of blanks (not gunpowder).

POLONIUS.   Give o'er the play.
KING.   Give me some light. Away!   255
ALL.   Lights, lights, lights!   *Exeunt all but Hamlet and Horatio.*
HAMLET.   Why, let the struckèn deer go weep,
          The hart ungallèd° play,°
     For some must watch while some must sleep,
          Thus runs the world away.   260
     Would not this° sir, and a forest of feathers,° if the rest of my
     fortunes turn Turk with° me, with two Provincial roses° on
     my razed° shoes, get me a fellowship° in a cry° of players?
HORATIO.   Half a share.°
HAMLET.   A whole one, I.   265
     For thou dost know, O Damon° dear,
          This realm dismantled was
     Of Jove° himself, and now reigns here
          A very very—pajock.°
HORATIO.   You might have rhymed.°   270
HAMLET.   O good Horatio, I'll take the ghost's word for a thousand
     pound. Didst perceive?
HORATIO.   Very well my lord.
HAMLET.   Upon the talk of the poisoning?
HORATIO.   I did very well note him.   275

Enter ROSENCRANTZ *and* GUILDENSTERN.

HAMLET.   Ah ha, come, some music. Come, the recorders.°
     For if the king like not the comedy,
     Why then belike he likes it not, perdy.°
     Come, some music.
GUILDENSTERN.   Good my lord, vouchsafe me a word with you.   280
HAMLET.   Sir, a whole history.
GUILDENSTERN.   The king, sir—
HAMLET.   Ay sir, what of him?
GUILDENSTERN.   Is in his retirement, marvellous distempered.
HAMLET.   With drink sir?   285
GUILDENSTERN.   No my lord, with choler.°
HAMLET.   Your wisdom should show itself more richer to signify
     this to the doctor: for, for me to put him to his purgation,°
     would perhaps plunge him into more choler.

257–258 *deer . . . play*: (the belief that a wounded deer wept, abandoned by the
others).   258 *ungalled*: unhurt.   261 *this*: i.e. sample (of my theatrical
talent). *feathers*: plumes (worn by actors).   262 *turn Turk with*: cruelly turn
against.   *Provincial roses*: rosettes named for Provins, France.   263 *razed*: slashed,
decorated with cutouts.   *fellowship*: partnership.   *cry*: pack, troupe.   264 *share*:
divisions of profits among members of theatre producing company.   266 *Damon*: legendary
ideal friend to Pythias.   268 *Jove*: (Hamlet's father).   269 *pajock*: peacock (associated
with lechery).   270 *rhymed*: (used "ass" instead of "pajock").   276 *recorders*: soft-toned
woodwind instruments, similar to flutes.   278 *perdy*: by God.   286 *choler*: anger.
288 *purgation*: (1) purging of excessive bile (2) judicial investigations (3) purgatory.

GUILDENSTERN.   Good my lord, put your discourse into some frame,° and   29
start not so wildly from my affair.
HAMLET.   I am tame sir, pronounce.
GUILDENSTERN.   The queen your mother, in most great affliction of spirit,
hath sent me to you.
HAMLET.   You are welcome.   29
GUILDENSTERN.   Nay good my lord, this courtesy is not of the right breed.°
If it shall please you to make me a wholesome° answer, I
will do your mother's commandment: if not, your pardon°
and my return shall be the end of my business.
HAMLET.   Sir I cannot.   30
ROSENCRANTZ.   What, my lord?
HAMLET.   Make you a wholesome answer: my wit's diseased. But
sir, such answer as I can make, you shall command, or
rather as you say, my mother: therefore no more, but to
the matter. My mother you say.   30
ROSENCRANTZ.   Then thus she says, your behaviour hath struck her into
amazement and admiration.°
HAMLET.   O wonderful son that can so stonish a mother. But is there
no sequel at the heels of this mother's admiration? Impart.
ROSENCRANTZ.   She desires to speak with you in her closet   31
ere you go to bed.
HAMLET.   We shall obey, were she ten times our mother. Have you
any further trade with us?
ROSENCRANTZ.   My lord, you once did love me.
HAMLET.   And do still, by these pickers and stealers.°   31
ROSENCRANTZ.   Good my lord, what is your cause of distemper? You do
surely bar the door upon your own liberty, if you deny
your griefs to your friend.°
HAMLET.   Sir, I lack advancement.
ROSENCRANTZ.   How can that be, when you have the voice° of the king   32
himself for your succession in Denmark?
HAMLET.   Ay sir, but 'while the grass grows'°—the proverb is
something musty.°

Enter the PLAYERS with recorders.

O the recorders, let me see one. To withdraw° with you,
why do you go about to recover the wind of me,° as if you   32
would drive me into a toil°?

290 *frame*: order.   296 *breed*: (1) species (2) manners.   297 *wholesome*: reasonable.
298 *pardon*: permission to depart.   307 *admiration*: wonder.   315 *pickers and stealers*:
hands (from the prayer, "Keep my hands from picking and stealing").   317–318 *deny* . . .
friend: refuse to let your friend know the cause of your suffering.   320 *voice*: vote.
322 *while* . . . *grows*: (the proverb ends: "the horse starves").   323 *something musty*:
somewhat too old and trite (to finish).   324 *withdraw*: speak privately.   325 *recover* . . .
me: drive me towards the wind, as with a prey, to avoid its scenting the hunter.   326 *toil*:
snare.

GUILDENSTERN. O my lord, if my duty be too bold, my love is too
  unmannerly.°
HAMLET. I do not well understand that. Will you play
  upon this pipe°?   330
GUILDENSTERN. My lord I cannot.
HAMLET. I pray you.
GUILDENSTERN. Believe me. I cannot.
HAMLET. I do beseech you.
GUILDENSTERN. I know no touch of it° my lord.   335
HAMLET. It is as easy as lying; govern these ventages° with your
  fingers and thumb, give it breath with your mouth, and it
  will discourse most eloquent music. Look you, these are
  the stops.
GUILDENSTERN. But these cannot I command to any utt'rance of harmony,   340
  I have not the skill.
HAMLET. Why look you now how unworthy a thing you make of
  me: you would play upon me, you would seem to know
  my stops, you would pluck out the heart of my mystery,
  you would sound me from my lowest note to the top of my   345
  compass:° and there is much music, excellent voice in this
  little organ,° yet cannot you make it speak. 'Sblood, do you
  think I am easier to be played on than a pipe? Call me what
  instrument you will, though you can fret° me, you cannot
  play upon me.   350

Enter POLONIUS.

  God bless you sir.
POLONIUS. My lord, the queen would speak with you, and presently.
HAMLET. Do you see yonder cloud that's almost in shape of a camel?
POLONIUS. By th'mass and 'tis, like a camel indeed.
HAMLET. Methinks it is like a weasel.   355
POLONIUS. It is backed like a weasel.
HAMLET. Or like a whale?
POLONIUS. Very like a whale.
HAMLET. Then I will come to my mother by and by.°
  [*Aside.*] They fool me to the top of my bent.°   360
  I will come by and by.
POLONIUS. I will say so.   *Exit.*
HAMLET. "By and by" is easily said.
  Leave me, friends.   [*Exeunt all but Hamlet.*]
  'Tis now the very witching time of night,   365

327–328 *is too unmannerly*: makes me forget my good manners.   330 *pipe*: recorder.
335 *know . . . it*: have no skill at fingering it.   336 *ventages*: holes, stops.   346 *compass*:
range.   347 *organ*: musical instrument.   349 *fret*: (1) irritate (2) play an instrument that
has "frets" or bars to guide the fingering.   359 *by and by*: very soon.   360 *fool me
. . . bent*: force me to play the fool to my utmost.

When churchyards yawn,° and hell itself breathes out
Contagion° to this world: now could I drink hot blood,
And do such bitter business as the day
Would quake to look on: soft, now to my mother—
O heart, lose not thy nature,° let not ever   37●
The soul of Nero° enter this firm bosom,
Let me be cruel, not unnatural.
I will speak daggers to her, but use none:
My tongue and soul in this be hypocrites,°
How in my words somever she be shent,°   37!
To give them seals,° never my soul consent.   *Exit.*

[*Scene 3. A room in the castle.*]

Enter KING, ROSENCRANTZ, *and* GUILDENSTERN.

KING.   I like him not, nor stands it safe with us
To let his madness range. Therefore prepare you,
I your commission will forthwith dispatch,°
And he to England shall along with you:
The terms of our estate° may not endure
Hazard so near's° as doth hourly grow
Out of his brows.°
GUILDENSTERN.   We will ourselves provide:°
Most holy and religious fear it is
To keep those many many bodies safe
That live and feed upon your majesty.
ROSENCRANTZ.   The single and peculiar° life is bound
With all the strength and armour of the mind
To keep itself from noyance,° but much more
That spirit, upon whose weal° depends and rests
The lives of many; the cess° of majesty
Dies not alone, but like a gulf° doth draw
What's near it, with it. O 'tis a massy wheel
Fixed on the summit of the highest mount,
To whose huge spokes, ten thousand lesser things
Are mortised° and adjoined, which when it falls,
Each small annexment, petty consequence,
Attends° the boist'rous ruin. Never alone
Did the king sigh, but with a general groan.

---

366 *churchyards yawn*: graves open.   367 *Contagion*: (1) evil (2) diseases.   370 *nature*:
natural affection.   371 *Nero*: (who killed his mother).   374 *My tongue . . . hypocrites*: I
will speak cruelly but intend no harm.   375 *shent*: chastised.   376 *give them seals*: confirm
them with action (as a legal "deed" is confirmed with a "seal").   3 *forthwith dispatch*:
immediately have prepared.   5 *terms . . . estate*: circumstances of my royal office.
6 *near's*: near us.   7 *brows*: effronteries.   *provide*: prepare.   11 *peculiar*:
individual.   13 *noyance*: harm.   14 *weal*: well-being.   15 *cess*: cessation, death.
16 *gulf*: whirlpool.   20 *mortised*: securely fitted.   22 *Attends*: accompanies.

KING.   Arm° you I pray you, to this speedy voyage,
    For we will fetters put about this fear,   25
    Which now goes too free-footed.
ROSENCRANTZ.   We will haste us.

                         Exeunt [ROSENCRANTZ *and* GUILDENSTERN.]

Enter POLONIUS.

POLONIUS.   My lord, he's going to his mother's closet:
    Behind the arras I'll convey myself
    To hear the process.° I'll warrant she'll tax him home,
    And as you said, and wisely was it said,   30
    'Tis meet° that some more audience than a mother,
    Since nature makes them partial, should o'erhear
    The speech of vantage;° fare you well my liege,°
    I'll call upon you ere you go to bed,
    And tell you what I know.
KING.   Thanks, dear my lord.   *Exit* [POLONIUS.] 35
    O my offence is rank, it smells to heaven,
    It hath the primal eldest curse° upon't,
    A brother's murder. Pray can I not,
    Though inclination be as sharp as will:°
    My stronger guilt defeats my strong intent,   40
    And like a man to double business bound,
    I stand in pause where I shall first begin,
    And both neglect; what if this cursèd hand
    Were thicker than itself with brother's blood,
    Is there not rain enough in the sweet heavens   45
    To wash it white as snow? Whereto serves mercy
    But to confront the visage of offence°?
    And what's in prayer but this two-fold force,
    To be forestallèd° ere we come to fall,
    Or pardoned being down? Then I'll look up,   50
    My fault is past. But O what form of prayer
    Can serve my turn? "Forgive me my foul murder":
    That cannot be, since I am still possessed
    Of those effects° for which I did the murder:
    My crown, mine own ambition, and my queen.   55
    May one be pardoned and retain th'offence?
    In the corrupted currents of this world,

---

24 *Arm*: prepare.   29 *the process*: what proceeds.   31 *meet*: fitting.   33 *of vantage*: from
an advantageous position.   *liege*: lord.   37 *primal . . . curse*: curse of Cain.
39 *inclination . . . will*: my desire to pray is as strong as my determination to do
so.   47 *confront . . . offence*: plead in man's behalf against sin (at the Last Judgment).
49 *forestalled*: prevented.   54 *effects*: results.

Offence's gilded hand may shove by justice,
And oft 'tis seen the wicked prize itself
Buys out the law;° but 'tis not so above,   60
There is no shuffling,° there the action lies
In his true nature,° and we ourselves compelled
Even to the teeth and forehead of our faults°
To give in evidence. What then? What rests°?
Try what repentance can. What can it not?   65
Yet what can it, when one can not repent?
O wretched state! O bosom black as death!
O limèd soul, that struggling to be free,
Art more engaged;° help, angels, make assay:°
Bow stubborn knees, and heart with strings of steel,   70
Be soft as sinews of the new-born babe,
All may be well.   [He kneels.]

Enter HAMLET.

HAMLET.   Now might I do it pat,° now a' is a-praying,
And now I'll do't, [*Draws his sword*.] and so a' goes to heaven,
And so am I revenged: that would be scanned:°   75
A villain kills my father, and for that,
I his sole son, do this same villain send
To heaven.
Why, this is hire and salary, not revenge.
A' took my father grossly,° full of bread,°   80
With all his crimes° broad blown,° as flush° as May,
And how his audit° stands who knows save heaven,
But in our circumstance and course of thought,
'Tis heavy° with him: and am I then revenged
To take him in the purging of his soul,   85
when he is fit and seasoned° for his passage?
No.   [*Sheathes his sword*.]
Up sword, and know thou a more horrid hent,°
When he is drunk asleep, or in his rage,
Or in th'incestuous pleasure of his bed,   90
At game, a-swearing, or about some act
That has no relish° of salvation in't,
Then trip him that his heels may kick at heaven,

59–60 *wicked . . . law*: fruits of the crime bribe the judge.   61 *shuffling*: evasion.   61–
62 *action . . . nature*: (1) deed is seen in its true nature (2) legal action is sustained according
to the truth.   63 *to the teeth . . . faults*: meeting our sins face to face.   64 *rests*:
remains.   68–69 *limed . . . engaged*: like a bird caught in lime (a sticky substance spread
on twigs as a snare), the soul in its struggle to clear itself only becomes more entangled.
69 *make assay*: I'll make an attempt.   73 *pat*: opportunely.   75 *would be scanned*: needs
closer examination.   80 *grossly*: unpurified (by final rites).   *bread*: self-indulgence.
81 *crimes*: sins.   *broad blown*: in full flower.   *flush*: lusty.   82 *audit*: account.
84 *heavy*: grievous.   86 *seasoned*: ready (prepared).   88 *horrid hent*: horrible opportunity
("hint") for seizure ("hent") by me.   92 *relish*: taste.

And that his soul may be as damned and black
As hell whereto it goes; my mother stays,   95
This physic° but prolongs thy sickly days.   *Exit.*
KING. [*Rises*.]   My words fly up, my thoughts remain below,
Words without thoughts never to heaven go.   *Exit.*

[Scene 4. *The queen's closet*.]

Enter QUEEN *and* POLONIUS.

POLONIUS. A' will come straight, look you lay home° to him,
Tell him his pranks have been too broad° to bear with,
And that your grace hath screened and stood between
Much heat° and him. I'll silence me° even here:
Pray you be round with him.   5
HAMLET. [*Within*.]   Mother, mother, mother.
QUEEN.   I'll war'nt you,
Fear me not. Withdraw, I hear him coming.   [POLONIUS *hides behind the arras*.]

Enter HAMLET.

HAMLET.   Now mother, what's the matter?
QUEEN.   Hamlet, thou hast thy father much offended.
HAMLET.   Mother, you have my father much offended.   10
QUEEN.   Come, come, you answer with an idle° tongue.
HAMLET.   Go, go, you question with a wicked tongue.
QUEEN.   Why, how now Hamlet?
HAMLET.   What's the matter now?
QUEEN.   Have you forgot me?
HAMLET.   No by the rood,° not so,
You are the queen, your husband's brother's wife,   15
And would it were not so, you are my mother.
QUEEN.   Nay, then I'll set those to you that can speak.°
HAMLET.   Come, come, and sit you down, you shall not budge,
You go not till I set you up a glass°
Where you may see the inmost part of you.   20
QUEEN.   What wilt thou do? Thou wilt not murder me?
Help, help, ho!
POLONIUS. [*Behind the arras*.]   What ho! help, help, help!
HAMLET.   How now, a rat? dead for a ducat,° dead.

Kills POLONIUS [*through the arras*.]

POLONIUS.   O I am slain!
QUEEN.   O me, what hast thou done?

96 *physic*: (1) medicine (2) purgation of your soul by prayer.   1 *lay home*: thrust home;
speak sharply.   2 *broad*: unrestrained.   4 *heat*: anger.   *silence me*: hide in silence.
11 *idle*: foolish.   14 *rood*: cross.   17 *speak*: i.e. to you as you should be spoken
to.   19 *glass*: looking glass.   23 *for a ducat*: I wager a ducat (an Italian gold coin).

HAMLET.   Nay I know not,   2
    Is it the king?
QUEEN.   O what a rash and bloody deed is this!
HAMLET.   A bloody deed, almost as bad, good mother,
    As kill a king, and marry with his brother.
QUEEN.   As kill a king?
HAMLET.   Ay lady, it was my word.   3
    [*To Polonius*.] Thou wretched, rash, intruding fool, farewell,
    I took thee for thy better,° take thy fortune,
    Thou find'st to be too busy is some danger.
    [*To the Queen*.] Leave wringing of your hands, peace, sit you down,
    And let me wring your heart, for so I shall   3
    If it be made of penetrable stuff,
    If damnèd custom° have not brazed° it so,
    That it be proof° and bulwark against sense.°
QUEEN.   What have I done, that thou dar'st wag thy tongue
    In noise so rude against me?
HAMLET.   Such an act   4
    That blurs the grace and blush of modesty,
    Calls virtue hypocrite, takes off the rose°
    From the fair forehead of an innocent love
    And sets a blister there,° makes marriage vows
    As false as dicers' oaths, O such a deed,   4
    As from the body of contraction° plucks
    The very soul, and sweet religion makes
    A rhapsody° of words; heaven's face does glow,°
    Yea this solidity and compound mass°
    With heated visage, as against the doom,°   5
    Is thought-sick at the act.
QUEEN.   Ay me, what act,
    That roars so loud, and thunders in the index°?
HAMLET.   Look here upon this picture, and on this,
    The counterfeit presentment° of two brothers:
    See what a grace was seated on this brow,   5
    Hyperion's° curls, the front° of Jove himself,
    An eye like Mars, to threaten and command,
    A station° like the herald Mercury,
    New-lighted on a heaven-kissing hill,
    A combination and a form indeed,   6
    Where every god did seem to set his seal

---

32 *thy better*: the king.   37 *custom*: habit.   *brazed*: brass-plated (brazened).   38 *proof*:
armor.   *sense*: sensibility.   42 *rose*: (symbol of perfection and innocence).   44 *blister
there*: (whores were punished by being branded on the forehead).   46 *body of contraction*:
marriage contract.   48 *rhapsody*: (meaningless) mixture.   *glow*: blush.   49 *solidity* . . .
mass: solid earth, compounded of the four elements.   50 *against the doom*: expecting
Judgment Day.   52 *index*: (1) table of contents (2) prologue.   54 *counterfeit presentment*:
painted likeness.   56 *Hyperion*: Greek sun god.   *front*: forehead.   58 *station*: bearing.

To give the world assurance of a man.
This was your husband. Look you now what follows.
Here is your husband, like a mildewed ear,°
Blasting° his wholesome brother. Have you eyes?   65
Could you on this fair mountain leave to feed,°
And batten° on this moor? Ha! Have you eyes?
You cannot call it love, for at your age
The hey-day in the blood° is tame, it's humble,
And waits upon the judgment, and what judgment   70
Would step from this to this? Sense° sure you have
Else could you not have motion,° but sure that sense
Is apoplexed,° for madness would not err,
Nor sense to ecstasy was ne'er so thralled°
But it reserved some quantity of choice   75
To serve in such a difference.° What devil was't
That thus hath cozened you at hoodman-blind°?
Eyes without feeling, feeling without sight,
Ears without hands or eyes, smelling sans all,°
Or but a sickly part of one true sense   80
Could not so mope:° O shame, where is thy blush?
Rebellious hell,
If thou canst mutine in a matron's bones,
To flaming youth let virtue be as wax
And melt in her own fire. Proclaim no shame   85
When the compulsive° ardour gives the charge,°
Since frost itself as actively doth burn,
And reason pandars will.°
QUEEN.   O Hamlet, speak no more,
Thou turn'st my eyes into my very soul,
And there I see such black and grainèd° spots   90
As will not leave their tinct.°
HAMLET.   Nay, but to live
In the rank sweat of an enseamèd° bed,
Stewed in corruption, honeying, and making love
Over the nasty sty.
QUEEN.   O speak to me no more,
These words like daggers enter in mine ears,   95
No more, sweet Hamlet.

---

64 *ear*: i.e., of grain.   65 *Blasting*: blighting.   66 *leave to feed*: leave off feeding.
67 *batten*: gorge yourself.   69 *hey-day in the blood*: youthful passion.
71 *Sense*: perception by the senses.   72 *motion*: impulse.   73 *apoplexed*:
paralyzed.   74 *sense . . . thralled*: sensibility was never so enslaved by madness.   76 *in
. . . difference*: where the difference was so great.   77 *cozened . . . blind*: cheated you at
blindman's bluff.   79 *sans all*: without the other senses.   81 *so mope*: be so dull.
86 *compulsive*: compelling.   *gives the charge*: attacks.   88 *panders will*: pimps for
lust.   90 *grained*: dyed in grain, unfading.   91 *leave their tinct*: lose their color.
92 *enseamed*: greasy.

HAMLET.   A murderer and a villain,
 A slave that is not twentieth part the tithe°
 Of your precedent lord, a vice° of kings,
 A cutpurse° of the empire and the rule,
 That from a shelf the precious diadem stole   10(
 And put it in his pocket.
QUEEN.   No more.
HAMLET.   A king of shreds and patches—

Enter the GHOST in his night-gown.°

 Save me and hover o'er me with your wings,
 You heavenly guards. What would your gracious figure?
QUEEN.   Alas, he's mad.   10!
HAMLET.   Do you not come your tardy son to chide,
 That lapsed in time and passion° lets go by
 Th'important acting of your dread command?
 O say!
GHOST.   Do not forget: this visitation   11(
 Is but to whet thy almost blunted purpose.
 But look, amazement on thy mother sits,
 O step between her and her fighting soul,
 Conceit° in weakest bodies strongest works,
 Speak to her Hamlet.
HAMLET.   How is it with you lady?   11!
QUEEN.   Alas, how is't with you,
 That you do bend your eye on vacancy,°
 And with th'incorporal° air do hold discourse?
 Forth at your eyes your spirits° wildly peep,
 And as the sleeping soldiers in th'alarm,   12(
 Your bedded° hairs, like life in excrements,°
 Start up and stand an° end. O gentle son,
 Upon the heat and flame of thy distemper
 Sprinkle cool patience. Whereon do you look?
HAMLET.   On him, on him, look you how pale he glares,
 His form and cause conjoined, preaching to stones,   12:
 Would make them capable.° Do not look upon me,
 Lest with this piteous action you convert
 My stern effects,° then what I have to do
 Will want° true colour,° tears perchance for blood.   13(

---

97 *tithe*: one-tenth part.   98 *vice*: buffoon (like the character of Vice in the morality
plays).   99 *cutpurse*: pickpocket.   102 stage direction *night-gown*: dressing gown.
107 *lapsed . . . passion*: having let time elapse and passion cool.   114 *Conceit*:
imagination.   117 *vacancy*: (she cannot see the ghost).   118 *incorporal*: bodiless.
119 *spirits*: vital forces.   121 *bedded*: lying flat.   *excrements*: outgrowths (of the
body).   122 *an*: on.   127 *capable*: i.e., of feeling pity.   128–129 *convert . . . effects*:
transform my outward signs of sternness.   130 *want*: lack.   *colour*: (1) complexion (2)
motivation.

QUEEN. To whom do you speak this?
HAMLET.   Do you see nothing there?
QUEEN. Nothing at all, yet all that is I see.
HAMLET. Nor did you nothing hear?
QUEEN.   No, nothing but ourselves.
HAMLET. Why look you there, look how it steals away,
  My father in his habit as he lived,°   135
  Look where he goes, even now out at the portal.   *Exit* [GHOST.]
QUEEN. This is the very coinage of your brain,
  This bodiless creation ecstasy
  Is very cunning in.°
HAMLET.   Ecstasy?
  My pulse as yours doth temperately keep time,   140
  And makes as healthful music. It is not madness
  That I have uttered; bring me to the test
  And I the matter will re-word, which madness
  Would gambol° from. Mother, for love of grace,
  Lay not that flattering unction° to your soul,   145
  That not your trespass but my madness speaks,
  It will but skin and film the ulcerous place,
  Whiles rank corruption mining° all within,
  Infects unseen. Confess yourself to heaven,
  Repent what's past, avoid what is to come,   150
  And do not spread the compost° on the weeds
  To make them ranker. Forgive me this my virtue,°
  For in the fatness° of these pursy° times
  Virtue itself of vice must pardon beg,
  Yea curb and woo° for leave to do him° good.   155
QUEEN. O Hamlet, thou hast cleft my heart in twain.
HAMLET. O throw away the worser part of it,
  And live the purer with the other half.
  Good night, but go not to my uncle's bed,
  Assume° a virtue if you have it not.   160
  That monster custom, who all sense doth eat
  Of habits evil,° is angel yet in this,
  That to the use° of actions fair and good,
  He likewise gives a frock or livery
  That aptly° is put on. Refrain tonight,   165
  And that shall lend a kind of easiness
  To the next abstinence, the next more easy:

---

135 *habit . . . lived*: clothing he wore when alive.   138–139 *bodiless . . . cunning in*: madness
is very skillful in seeing hallucinations.   144 *gambol*: leap.   145 *unction*: salve.
148 *mining*: undermining.   151 *compost*: manure.   152 *virtue*: sermon on
virtue.   153 *fatness*: grossness.   *pursy*: flabby.   155 *curb and woo*: bow and plead.
him: vice.   160 *Assume*: put on the guise of.   161–162 *all sense . . . evil*: confuses the
sense of right and wrong in a habitué.   163 *use*: habit.   165 *aptly*: readily.

For use° almost can change the stamp° of nature,
And either . . . the° devil, or throw him out
With wondrous potency: once more good night,   170
And when you are desirous to be blessed,
I'll blessing beg of you. For this same lord,°
I do repent; but heaven hath pleased it so
To punish me with this, and this with me,
That I must be their scourge and minister.°   175
I will bestow° him and will answer° well
The death I gave him; so again good night.
I must be cruel only to be kind;
This bad begins, and worse remains behind.°
One word more, good lady.

QUEEN.   What shall I do?   180
HAMLET.   Not this by no means that I bid you do:
Let the bloat° king tempt you again to bed,
Pinch wanton on your cheek, call you his mouse,
And let him for a pair of reechy° kisses,
Or paddling in your neck with his damned fingers,   185
Make you to ravel° all this matter out
That I essentially am not in madness,
But mad in craft. 'Twere good you let him know,
For who that's but a queen, fair, sober, wise,
Would from a paddock, from a bat, a gib,°   190
Such dear concernings hide? who would do so?
No, in despite of sense and secrecy,
Unpeg the basket on the house's top,
Let the birds fly, and like the famous ape,
To try conclusions° in the basket creep,   195
And break your own neck down.°

QUEEN.   Be thou assured, if words be made of breath,
And breath of life, I have no life to breathe
What thou hast said to me.
HAMLET.   I must to England, you know that.
QUEEN.   Alack,   200
I had forgot: 'tis so concluded on.
HAMLET.   There's letters sealed, and my two school-fellows,
Whom I will trust as I will adders fanged,

---

168 *use*: habit.   *stamp*: form.   169 *either . . . the*: (word omitted, for which "tame,"
"curls," and "quell" have been suggested).   172 *lord*: Polonius.   175 *their . . . minister*:
heaven's punishment and agent of retribution.   176 *bestow*: stow away.   *answer well*:
assume full responsibility for.   179 *bad . . . behind*: is a bad beginning to a worse end
to come.   182 *bloat*: bloated with dissipation.   184 *reechy*: filthy.   186 *ravel*:
unravel.   190 *paddock, bat, gib*: toad, bat, tomcat ("familiars" or demons in animal shape
that attend on witches).   193–196 Unpeg . . . *down*: (the story refers to an ape that
climbs to the top of a house and opens a basket of birds; when the birds fly away, the ape
crawls into the basket, tries to fly, and breaks his neck. The point is that if she gives away
Hamlet's secret, she harms herself).   195 *try conclusions*: experiment.

They bear the mandate, they must sweep my way
And marshal me to knavery:° let it work,   205
For 'tis the sport to have the enginer°
Hoist with his own petar,° and't shall go hard
But I will delve one yard below their mines,
And blow them at the moon: O 'tis most sweet
When in one line two crafts directly meet.°   210
This man shall set me packing,°
I'll lug the guts into the neighbour room;
Mother good night indeed. This counsellor
Is now most still, most secret, and most grave,
Who was in life a foolish prating knave.   215
Come sir, to draw toward and end with you.
Good night mother.   *Exit* HAMLET *tugging in* POLONIUS.

[ACT 4]

[*Scene 1. A room in the castle.*]

Enter KING *and* QUEEN *with* ROSENCRANTZ *and* GUILDENSTERN.

KING. There's matter in these sighs, these profound heaves,
   You must translate, 'tis fit we understand them.
   Where is your son?
QUEEN. Bestow this place on us° a little while.

                              Exeunt ROSENCRANTZ *and* GUILDENSTERN.

   Ah mine own lord, what have I seen tonight!   5
KING. What, Gertrude? How does Hamlet?
QUEEN. Mad as the sea and wind when both contend
   Which is the mightier, in his lawless fit,
   Behind the arras hearing something stir,
   Whips out his rapier, cries "A rat, a rat,"   10
   And in this brainish apprehension° kills
   The unseen good old man.
KING.   O heavy deed!
   It had been so with us° had we been there:
   His liberty is full of threats to all,
   To you yourself, to us, to every one.   15

204–205 *sweep . . . knavery*: (like the marshal who went before a royal procession, clearing
the way, so Rosencrantz and Guildenstern clear Hamlet's path to some unknown
evil).   206 *enginer*: maker of war engines.   207 *Hoist . . . petar*: blown up by his own
bomb.   210 *in one . . . meet*: the digger of the mine and the digger of the countermine
meet halfway in their tunnels.   211 *packing*: (1) i.e., my bags (2) rushing away (3) plotting.
4 *Bestow . . . us*: leave us.   11 *brainish apprehension*: insane delusion.   13 *us*: me (royal
plural).

Alas, how shall this bloody deed be answered?
It will be laid to us,° whose providence°
Should have kept short,° restrained, and out of haunt°
This mad young man; but so much was our love,
We would not understand what was most fit,   20
But like the owner of a foul disease,
To keep it from divulging,° let it feed
Even on the pith of life: where is he gone?

QUEEN.   To draw apart the body he hath killed,
O'er whom his very madness, like some ore   25
Among a mineral of metals base,°
Shows itself pure: a' weeps for what is done.

KING.   O Gertrude, come away:
The sun no sooner shall the mountains touch,
But we will ship him hence and this vile deed   30
We must with all our majesty and skill
Both countenance° and excuse. Ho Guildenstern!

Enter ROSENCRANTZ *and* GUILDENSTERN.

Friends both, go join you with some further aid:
Hamlet in madness hath Polonius slain,
And from his mother's closet hath he dragged him.   35
Go seek him out, speak fair, and bring the body
Into the chapel; I pray you haste in this.   *Exeunt Gent*[*lemen.*]
Come Gertrude, we'll call up our wisest friends,
And let them know both what we mean to do
And what's untimely done: [so haply slander,]   40
Whose whisper o'er the world's diameter,
As level° as the cannon to his blank°
Transports his° poisoned shot, may miss our name,
And hit the woundless° air. O come away,
My soul is full of discord and dismay.   *Exeunt.*   45

[Scene 2. *Another room in the castle.*]

Enter HAMLET.

HAMLET.   Safely stowed.
    Gentlemen within: Hamlet, Lord Hamlet!
    But soft, what noise, who calls on Hamlet?
    O here they come.

Enter ROSENCRANTZ *and* GUILDENSTERN.

ROSENCRANTZ.   What have you done my lord with the dead body?

17 *laid to us*: blamed on me.   *providence*: foresight.   18 *short*: tethered by a short
leash.   *out of haunt*: away from others.   22 *divulging*: being divulged.   25–26 *ore . . .
base*: pure ore (such as gold) in a mine of base metal.   32 *countenance*: defend.   42 *As
level*: with a straight aim.   *blank*: white bullseye at the target's center.   43 *his*:
slander's.   44 *woundless*: invulnerable.

HAMLET. Compounded it with dust whereto 'tis kin.   5
ROSENCRANTZ. Tell us where 'tis that we may take it thence,
  And bear it to the chapel.
HAMLET. Do not believe it.
ROSENCRANTZ. Believe what?
HAMLET. That I can keep your counsel° and not mine own.° Besides,   10
  to be demanded of° a sponge, what replication° should be
  made by the son of a king?
ROSENCRANTZ. Take you me for a sponge, my lord?
HAMLET. Ay sir, that soaks up the king's countenance,° his rewards,
  his authorities. But such officers do the king best service in   15
  the end; he keeps them like an apple in the corner of his
  jaw, first mouthed to be last swallowed: when he needs
  what you have gleaned, it is but squeezing you, and
  sponge, you shall be dry again.
ROSENCRANTZ. I understand you not my lord.   20
HAMLET. I am glad of it: a knavish speech sleeps in° a foolish ear.
ROSENCRANTZ. My lord, you must tell us where the body is, and go with
  us to the king.
HAMLET. The body is with the king, but the king° is not with the
  body. The king is a thing—   25
GUILDENSTERN. A thing my lord?
HAMLET. Of nothing, bring me to him. Hide fox, and all after.°   *Exeunt.*

[Scene 3. Another room in the castle.]

Enter KING and two or three.

KING. I have sent to seek him, and to find the body:
  How dangerous is it that this man goes loose,
  Yet must not we put the strong law on him,
  He's loved of the distracted multitude,°
  Who like not in° their judgment, but their eyes,   5
  And where 'tis so, th'offender's scourge° is weighed
  But never the offence: to bear all° smooth and even,
  This sudden sending him away must seem
  Deliberate pause:° diseases desperate grown,
  By desperate appliance° are relieved,   10
  Or not at all.

Enter ROSENCRANTZ and all the rest.

How now, what hath befallen?

10 *counsel*: (1) advice (2) secret.   *keep . . . own*: follow your advice and not keep my own
secret.   11 *demanded of*: questioned by.   *replication*: reply to a charge.   14 *countenance*:
favor.   21 *sleeps in*: means nothing to.   24 *king . . . king*: Hamlet's father . . .
Claudius.   27 *Hide fox . . . after*: (cry in a children's game, like hide-and-
seek).   4 *distracted multitude*: confused mob.   5 *in*: according to.   6 *scourge*:
punishment.   7 *bear all*: carry out everything.   9 *Deliberate pause*: considered
delay.   10 *appliance*: remedy.

ROSENCRANTZ. Where the dead body is bestowed my lord,
  We cannot get from him.
KING.   But where is he?
ROSENCRANTZ. Without, my lord, guarded,° to know your pleasure.
KING. Bring him before us.
ROSENCRANTZ.   Ho, bring in the lord.   1

Enter HAMLET *(guarded) and* GUILDENSTERN.

KING. Now Hamlet, where's Polonius?
HAMLET. At supper.
KING. At supper? where?
HAMLET. Not where he eats, but where a' is eaten: a certain
  convocation of politic° worms are e'en° at him. Your worm is your   2
  only emperor for diet, we fat all creatures else to fat us,
  and we fat ourselves for maggots. Your fat king and your
  lean beggar is but variable service,° two dishes but to one
  table, that's the end.
KING. Alas, alas.   2
HAMLET. A man may fish with the worm that hath eat of a king, and
  eat of the fish that hath fed of that worm.
KING. What dost thou mean by this?
HAMLET. Nothing but to show you how a king may go a progress°
  through the guts of a beggar.   3
KING. Where is Polonius?
HAMLET. In heaven, send thither to see. If your messenger find him
  not there, seek him i'th'other place yourself: but if indeed
  you find him not within this month, you shall nose him as
  you go up the stairs into the lobby.   3
KING. [*To Attendants.*] Go seek him there.
HAMLET. A' will stay till you come.   [*Exeunt.*]
KING. Hamlet, this deed, for thine especial safety—
  Which we do tender,° as we dearly grieve
  For that which thou hast done—must send thee hence   4
  With fiery quickness. Therefore prepare thyself,
  The bark is ready, and the wind at help,°
  Th'associates tend,° and every thing is bent
  For England.
HAMLET.   For England.
KING.   Ay Hamlet.
HAMLET.   Good.
KING. So is it if thou knew'st our purposes.   45
HAMLET. I see a cherub° that sees them: but come, for England.
  Farewell dear mother.
KING. Thy loving father, Hamlet.

14 *guarded*: (Hamlet is under guard until he boards the ship). 20 *politic*: (1) statesmanlike
(2) crafty. *e'en*: even now. 23 *variable service*: a variety of courses. 29 *go a progress*:
make a splendid royal journey from one part of the country to another. 39 *tender*:
cherish. 42 *at help*: helpful. 43 *tend*: wait. 46 *cherub*: (considered the watchmen
of heaven).

HAMLET.   My mother: father and mother is man and wife, man and
    wife is one flesh, and so my mother: come, for England.   *Exit.*   50
KING.   [*To* ROSENCRANTZ *and* GUILDENSTERN.]
    Follow him at foot,° tempt him with speed aboard,
    Delay it not, I'll have him hence tonight.
    Away, for every thing is sealed and done
    That else leans on° th'affair, pray you make haste.   [*Exeunt.*]
    And England,° if my love thou hold'st at aught°—   55
    As my great power thereof may give thee sense,
    Since yet thy cicatrice° looks raw and red
    After the Danish sword, and thy free awe
    Pays homage° to us—thou mayst not coldly° set
    Our sovereign process,° which imports at full   60
    By letters congruing° to that effect,
    The present° death of Hamlet. Do it England,
    For like the hectic° in my blood he rages,
    And thou must cure me; till I know 'tis done,
    Howe'er my haps,° my joys were ne'er begun.   *Exit.*   65

[Scene 4. A plain in Denmark.]

Enter FORTINBRAS *with his army over the stage.*

FORTINBRAS.   Go captain, from me greet the Danish king,
    Tell him that by his license, Fortinbras
    Craves the conveyance° of a promised march
    Over his kingdom. You know the rendezvous:
    If that his majesty would aught with us,   5
    We shall express our duty in his eye,°
    And let him know so.
CAPTAIN.   I will do't, my lord.
FORTINBRAS.   Go softly° on.   *Exit.*

Enter HAMLET, ROSENCRANTZ, [GUILDENSTERN,] *etc.*

HAMLET.   Good sir whose powers° are these?
CAPTAIN.   They are of Norway sir.   10
HAMLET.   How purposed sir I pray you?
CAPTAIN.   Against some part of Poland.
HAMLET.   Who commands them sir?
CAPTAIN.   The nephew to old Norway, Fortinbras.
HAMLET.   Goes it against the main° of Poland sir,   15
    Or for some frontier?
CAPTAIN.   Truly to speak, and with no addition,

---

51 *at foot*: at his heels.   54 *leans on*: relates to.   55 *England*: King of England.   *my*
love . . . aught: you place any value on my favor.   57 *cicatrice*: scar.   58–59 *free . . .*
homage: awe which you, though free, still show by paying homage.   59 *coldly set*: lightly
estimate.   60 *process*: command.   61 *congruing*: agreeing.   62 *present*: immediate.
63 *hectic*: fever.   65 *haps*: fortunes.   3 *conveyance of*: escort for.   6 *in his eye*: face
to face.   8 *softly*: slowly.   9 *powers*: troops.   15 *main*: body.

We go to gain a little patch of ground
That hath in it no profit but the name.°
To pay five ducats, five, I would not farm it;   20
Nor will it yield to Norway or the Pole
A ranker° rate, should it be sold in fee.°
HAMLET.   Why then the Polack never will defend it.
CAPTAIN.   Yes, it is already garrisoned.
HAMLET.   Two thousand souls, and twenty thousand ducats   25
Will not debate the question of° this straw:°
This is th'imposthume of much wealth and peace,°
That inward breaks, and shows no cause without
Why the man dies. I humbly thank you sir.
CAPTAIN.   God bye you sir.   [Exit.]
ROSENCRANTZ.   Will't please you go my lord?   30
HAMLET.   I'll be with you straight, go a little before.

                                      [Exeunt all but HAMLET.]

How all occasions do inform against me,
And spur my dull revenge. What is a man
If his chief good and market° of his time
Be but to sleep and feed? a beast, no more: 35
Sure he that made us with such large discourse,°
Looking before and after,° gave us not
That capability and god-like reason
To fust° in us unused. Now whether it be
Bestial oblivion,° or some craven° scruple   40
Of thinking too precisely on th'event°—
A thought which quartered hath but one part wisdom,
And ever three parts coward—I do not know
Why yet I live to say "This thing's to do,"
Sith I have cause, and will, and strength, and means   45
To do't; examples gross° as earth exhort me:
Witness this army of such mass and charge,°
Led by a delicate and tender° prince,
Whose spirit with divine ambition puffed,
Makes mouths° at the invisible event,°   50
Exposing what is mortal, and unsure,
To all that fortune, death, and danger dare,
Even for an egg-shell. Rightly to be great,
Is not to stir without great argument,

---

19 *name*: glory.   22 *ranker*: higher (as annual interest on the total).   *in fee*:
outright.   26 *debate . . . of*: settle the dispute over.   *straw*: triviality.   27 *imposthume
. . . peace*: swelling discontent (inner abscess) resulting from too much wealth and peace.
34 *market*: profit.   36 *discourse*: power of reasoning.   37 *Looking . . . after*: seeing causes
and effects.   39 *fust*: grow moldy.   40 *Bestial oblivion*: forgetfulness, as a beast forgets
its parents.   *craven*: cowardly.   41 *event*: outcome.   46 *gross*: obvious.   47 *charge*:
expense.   48 *delicate and tender*: gentle and young.   50 *mouths*: faces.   *event*: outcome.

But greatly to find quarrel in a straw   55
When honour's at the stake.° How stand I then
That have a father killed, a mother stained,
Excitements° of my reason, and my blood,
And let all sleep, while to my shame I see
The imminent death of twenty thousand men,   60
That for a fantasy and trick° of fame
Go to their graves like beds, fight for a plot
Whereon the numbers cannot try the cause,°
Which is·not tomb enough and continent°
To hide the slain. O from this time forth,   65
My thoughts be bloody, or be nothing worth.   *Exit.*

[*Scene 5. A room in the castle.*]

Enter QUEEN, HORATIO, *and a Gentlemen.*

QUEEN.   I will not speak with her.
GENTLEMAN.   She is importunate, indeed distract,°
   Her mood will needs be° pitied.
QUEEN.   What would she have?
GENTLEMAN.   She speaks much of her father, says she hears
   There's tricks i'th'world, and hems,° and beats her heart,   5
   Spurns enviously at straws,° speaks things in doubt°
   That carry but half sense: her speech is nothing,
   Yet the unshapèd use of it doth move
   The hearers to collection;° they aim° at it,
   And botch° the words up fit to their own thoughts,   10
   Which as her winks, and nods, and gestures yield them,
   Indeed would make one think there might be thought,
   Though nothing sure, yet much unhappily.
HORATIO.   'Twere good she were spoken with, for she may strew
   Dangerous conjectures in ill-breeding minds.   15
QUEEN.   Let her come in.   *Exit Gentleman.*
   [*Aside.*] To my sick soul, as sin's true nature is,°
   Each toy° seems prologue to some great amiss,°
   So full of artless jealousy° is guilt,
   It spills itself, in fearing to be spilt.   20

53–56 *Rightly . . . stake*: the truly great do not fight without just cause ("argument"), but it is nobly ("greatly") done to fight even for a trifle if honor is at stake.   58 *Excitements*: incentives.   61 *fantasy and trick*: illusion and trifle.   63 *Whereon . . . cause*: too small to accommodate all the troops fighting for it.   64 *continent*: container.   2 *distract*: insane.   3 *will needs be*: needs to be.   5 *hems*: coughs.   6 *Spurns . . . straws*: reacts maliciously to trifles.   *in doubt*: ambiguous.   9 *collection*: inference.   *aim*: guess.   10 *botch*: patch.   17 *as sin's . . . is*: as is natural for the guilty.   18 *toy*: trifle.   *amiss*: disaster.   19 *artless jealousy*: uncontrollable suspicion.

Enter OPHELIA, *distracted.*°

OPHELIA.   Where is the beauteous majesty of Denmark?
QUEEN.   How now Ophelia?
OPHELIA.   [*Sings.*] How should I your true love know
                      From another one?
                  By his cockle hat and staff,°
                  And his sandal shoon.°   25
QUEEN.   Alas sweet lady, what imports this song?
OPHELIA.   Say you? nay, pray you mark.
            [*Sings.*] He is dead and gone, lady,
                  He is dead and gone,   30
              At his head a grass-green turf,
              At his heels a stone.
     O ho.
QUEEN.   Nay but Ophelia—
OPHELIA.   Pray you mark.
       [*Sings.*] White his shroud as the mountain snow—

Enter KING.

QUEEN.   Alas, look here my lord.   35
OPHELIA.   [*Sings.*]   Larded° all with sweet flowers,
                  Which bewept to the ground did not go,
                  With true-love showers.
KING.   How do you, pretty lady?
OPHELIA.   Well, God 'ild° you. They say the owl was a baker's   40
     daughter.° Lord, we know what we are, but know not what
     we may be. God be at your table.°
KING.   Conceit° upon her father.
OPHELIA.   Pray you let's have no words of this, but when they ask
     you what it means, say you this: 45
       [*Sings.*] Tomorrow is Saint Valentine's day,
              All in the morning betime,°
         And I a maid at your window
              To be your Valentine.
       Then up he rose, and donned his clo'es,   50
              And dupped° the chamber door,
         Let in the maid, that out a maid,
              Never departed more.
KING.   Pretty Ophelia.

---

20 stage direction *distracted*: insane.   25 *cockle hat and staff*: (marks of the pilgrim, the cockle
shell symbolizing his journey to the shrine of St. James; the pilgrim was a common metaphor
for the lover).   26 *shoon*: shoes.   36 *Larded*: trimmed.   40 *God 'ild*: God yield
(reward).   40–41 *owl . . . daughter*: (in a medieval legend, a baker's daughter was turned
into an owl because she gave Jesus short weight on a loaf of bread).   42 *God . . . table*:
(a blessing at dinner). 43 *Conceit*: thinking.   47 *betime*: early (because the first girl a man
saw on Valentine's Day would be his true love).   51 *dupped*: opened.

OPHELIA.   Indeed, la, without an oath I'll make an end on't.   55
    [*Sings*.] By Gis° and by Saint Charity,
        Alack and fie for shame,
    Young men will do't, if they come to't,
        By Cock° they are to blame.
    Quoth she, Before you tumbled me,   60
        You promised me to wed.
(He answers)
    So would I ha' done, by yonder sun,
        And thou hadst not come to my bed.

KING.   How long hath she been thus?   65

OPHELIA.   I hope all will be well. We must be patient, but I cannot
    choose but weep to think they would lay him i'th'cold
    ground. My brother shall know of it, and so I thank you
    for your good counsel. Come, my coach: good night
    ladies, good night. Sweet ladies, good night, good night.   *[Exit OPHELIA.]*   70

KING.   Follow her close, give her good watch I pray you.   *[Exit HORATIO.]*
    O this is the poison of deep grief, it springs
    All from her father's death, and now behold:
    O Gertrude, Gertrude,
    When sorrows come, they come not single spies,   75
    But in battalions: first her father slain,
    Next, your son gone, and he most violent author
    Of his own just remove, the people muddied,°
    Thick and unwholesome in their thoughts and whispers
    For good Polonius' death: and we have done but greenly°   80
    In hugger-mugger° to inter him: poor Ophelia
    Divided from herself and her fair judgment,
    Without the which we are pictures or mere beasts,
    Last, and as much containing° as all these,
    Her brother is in secret come from France,   85
    Feeds on his wonder,° keeps himself in clouds,°
    And wants not buzzers° to infect his ear
    With pestilent speeches of his father's death,
    Wherein necessity, of matter beggared,
    Will nothing stick our person to arraign°   90
    In ear and ear:° O my dear Gertrude, this
    Like to a murdering-piece° in many places
    Gives me superfluous death.   *A noise within.*

QUEEN.   Alack, what noise is this?

---

56 *Gis*: contraction of "Jesus."   59 *Cock*: (vulgarization of "God" in oaths).   78 *muddied*:
stirred up.   80 *done but greenly*: acted like amateurs.   81 *hugger-mugger*: secret
haste.   84 *containing*: i.e., cause for sorrow.   86 *Feeds . . . wonder*: sustains himself by
wondering about his father's death.   *clouds*: gloom, obscurity.   87 *wants not buzzers*: lacks
not whispering gossips.   89–90 *Wherein . . . arraign*: in which the tellers, lacking facts,
will not hesitate to accuse me.   91 *In ear and ear*: whispering from one ear to
another.   92 *murdering-piece*: small cannon shooting shrapnel, to inflict numerous wounds.

KING. Attend! *Enter a* MESSENGER.
 Where are my Switzers°? Let them guard the door.   95
 What is the matter?
MESSENGER.   Save yourself, my lord.
 The ocean, overpeering of his list,°
 Eats not the flats° with more impiteous haste
 Than young Laertes in a riotous head°
 O'erbears your officers: the rabble call him lord,   100
 And as the world were now but to begin,
 Antiquity forgot, custom not known,
 The ratifiers and props of every word,
 They cry "Choose we, Laertes shall be king!"
 Caps, hands, and tongues applaud it to the clouds,   105
 "Laertes shall be king, Laertes king!"   *A noise within.*
QUEEN. How cheerfully on the false trail they cry.
 O this is counter,° you false Danish dogs.
KING. The doors are broke.

Enter LAERTES *with others.*

LAERTES. Where is this king? Sirs, stand you all without.°   110
DANES. No, let's come in.
LAERTES.   I pray you give me leave.°
DANES. We will, we will.   *[They retire.]*
LAERTES. I thank you, keep the door. O thou vile king,
 Give me my father.
QUEEN.   Calmly, good Laertes.
LAERTES. That drop of blood that's calm proclaims me bastard,   115
 Cries cuckold° to my father, brands° the harlot
 Even here between the chaste unsmirchèd brows
 Of my true mother.
KING.   What is the cause Laertes,
 That thy rebellion looks so giant-like?
 Let him go Gertrude, do not fear° our person,   120
 There's such divinity° doth hedge a king,
 That treason can but peep to° what it would,
 Acts little of his° will. Tell me Laertes,
 Why thou art this incensed. Let him go Gertrude.
 Speak man.   125
LAERTES. Where is my father?
KING.   Dead.
QUEEN.   But not by him.
KING. Let him demand his fill.

---

95 *Switzers*: Swiss guards.   97 *overpeering . . . list*: rising above its usual limits.   98 *flats*:
lowlands.   99 *head*: armed force.   108 *counter*: following the scent backward.
110 *without*: outside.   111 *leave*: i.e., to enter alone.   116 *cuckold*: betrayed
husband.   *brands*: (so harlots were punished).   120 *fear*: i.e., for.
121 *divinity*: divine protection.   122 *peep to*: strain to see.   123 *his*: treason's.

LAERTES.   How came he dead? I'll not be juggled with.
　　To hell allegiance, vows to the blackest devil,
　　Conscience and grace, to the profoundest pit.　　　　　　　　　　130
　　I dare damnation: to this point I stand,
　　That both the worlds I give to negligence,°
　　Let come what comes, only I'll be revenged
　　Most throughly for my father.
KING.　　　　　　　　　　　　Who shall stay you?
LAERTES.   My will, not all the world's:°　　　　　　　　　　　　135
　　And for my means, I'll husband° them so well,
　　They shall go far with little.
KING.　　　　　　　　　　Good Laertes,
　　If you desire to know the certainty
　　Of your dear father, is't writ in your revenge
　　That swoopstake,° you will draw both friend and foe,　　　　140
　　Winner and loser?
LAERTES.   None but his enemies.
KING.　　　　　　　　　　　Will you know them then?
LAERTES.   To his good friends thus wide I'll ope my arms,
　　And like the kind life-rend'ring pelican,°
　　Repast them with my blood.
KING.　　　　　　　　　　Why now you speak　　　　　　　145
　　Like a good child, and a true gentleman.
　　That I am guiltless of your father's death,
　　And am most sensibly° in grief for it,
　　It shall as level° to your judgment 'pear
　　As day does to your eye.
　　A noise within: Let her come in.　　　　　　　　　　　　　150
LAERTES.   How now, what noise is that?

Enter OPHELIA.

　　O heat, dry up my brains, tears seven time salt,
　　Burn out the sense and virtue° of mine eye!
　　By heaven, thy madness shall be paid with weight,°
　　Till our scale turn the beam.° O rose of May,　　　　　　155
　　Dear maid, kind sister, sweet Ophelia:
　　O heavens, is't possible a young maid's wits
　　Should be as mortal as an old man's life?
　　Nature is fine in love, and where 'tis fine,
　　It sends some precious instance of itself　　　　　　　　160
　　after the thing it loves.°

132 *both . . . negligence*: I care nothing for this world or the next.　135 *world's*: i.e.,
will.　136 *husband*: economize.　140 *swoopstake*: sweeping in all the stakes in a game,
both of winner and loser.　144 *pelican*: (the mother pelican was believed to nourish her
young with blood pecked from her own breast).　148 *sensibly*: feelingly.　149 *level*:
plain.　153 *sense and virtue*: feeling and power.　154 *with weight*: with equal
weight.　155 *turn the beam*: outweigh the other side.　159–161 *Nature . . . loves*: filial
love that is so refined and pure sends some precious token (her wits) after the beloved
dead.

OPHELIA. [*Sings.*] They bore him barefaced on the bier,
        Hey non nonny, nonny, hey nonny:
        And in his grave rained many a tear—
Fare you well my dove.   165
LAERTES. Hadst thou thy wits, and didst persuade revenge,
It could not move thus.
OPHELIA. You must sing "adown adown," and you call him adown-a.
O how the wheel becomes it.° It is the false steward that
stole his master's daughter.   170
LAERTES. This nothing's more than matter.°
OPHELIA. There's rosemary,° that's for remembrance, pray you love
remember: and there is pansies, that's for thoughts.
LAERTES. A document° in madness, thoughts and remembrance
fitted.°   175
OPHELIA. There's fennel for you, and columbines.° There's rue° for
you, and here's some for me, we may call it herb of grace°
o'Sundays: O, you must wear your rue with a difference.°
There's a daisy,° I would give you some violets,° but they
withered all when my father died: they say a' made a good   180
end;
        [*Sings.*] For bonny sweet Robin is all my joy.
LAERTES. Thought and affliction, passion, hell itself,
She turns to favour and to prettiness.
OPHELIA. [*Sings.*] And will a' not come again,   185
          And will a' not come again?
            No, no, he is dead,
            Go to thy death-bed,
        He never will come again.

        His beard was as white as snow,   190
        All flaxen was his poll,°
          He is gone, he is gone,
          And we cast away moan,
        God ha' mercy on his soul.
And of all Christian souls, I pray God. God bye you.   195

                                   Exit OPHELIA.

LAERTES. Do you see this, O God?
KING. Laertes, I must commune with your grief,

---

169 *wheel becomes it*: refrain ("adown") suits the subject (Polonius's fall). 171 *more than matter*: more eloquent than sane speech. 172 *There's rosemary*: (given to Laertes; she may be distributing imaginary or real flowers, though not necessarily those she mentions). 174 *document*: lesson. *thoughts . . . fitted*: thoughts of revenge matched with remembrance of Polonius. 176 *fennel, columbines*: (given to the king, symbolizing flattery and ingratitude). *rue*: (given to the queen, symbolizing sorrow or repentance). 177 *herb of grace*: (because it symbolizes repentance). 178 *with a difference*: for a different reason (Ophelia's is for sorrow and the queen's for repentance). 179 *daisy*: (symbolizing dissembling, she probably keeps it). *violets*: (symbolizing faithfulness). 191 *flaxen . . . poll*: white was his head.

Or you deny me right: go but apart,
Make choice of whom your wisest friends you will,
And they shall hear and judge 'twixt you and me;   200
If by direct or by collateral° hand
They find us touched,° we will our kingdom give,
Our crown, our life, and all that we call ours
To you in satisfaction; but if not,
Be you content to lend your patience to us,   205
And we shall jointly labour with your soul
To give it due content.

LAERTES.   Let this be so.
His means of death, his obscure funeral,
No trophy,° sword, nor hatchment° o'er his bones,
No noble rite, nor formal ostentation,°   210
Cry° to be heard as 'twere from heaven to earth,
That I must call't in question.

KING.   So you shall,
And where th'offence is, let the great axe fall.
I pray you go with me.   [*Exeunt.*]

[Scene 6. *Another room in the castle*.]

Enter HORATIO and others.

HORATIO. What are they that would speak with me?
GENTLEMAN. Seafaring men sir, they say they have letters for you.
HORATIO. Let them come in.   [*Exit ATTENDANT.*]
   I do not know from what part of the world
   I should be greeted, if not from Lord Hamlet.   5

Enter SAILORS.

SAILOR. God bless you sir.
HORATIO. Let him bless thee too.
SAILOR. A' shall sir, an't please him. There's a letter for you sir, it
   came from th'ambassador that was bound for England, if
   your name be Horatio, as I am let to know it is.   10
HORATIO. [*Reads the letter*.] "Horatio, when thou shalt have
   overlooked° this, give these fellows some means to the king,
   they have letters for him. Ere we were two days old at sea,
   a pirate of very warlike appointment° gave us chase.
   Finding ourselves too slow of sail, we put on a compelled   15
   valour, and in the grapple° I boarded them. On the instant
   they got clear of our ship, so I alone became their prisoner.
   They have dealt with me like thieves of mercy,° but they

---

201 *collateral*: indirect.   202 *touched*: tainted with guilt.   209 *trophy*: memorial.
hatchment: tablet displaying coat of arms.   210 *ostentation*: ceremony.
211 *Cry*: cry out.   12 *overlooked*: read over.   14 *appointment*: equipment.
16 *in the grapple*: when the pirate ship hooked onto ours.   18 *of mercy*: merciful.

knew what they did. I am to do a good turn for them. Let
the king have the letters I have sent, and repair° thou to me   20
with as much speed as thou wouldest fly death. I have
words to speak in thine ear will make thee dumb, yet are
they much too light for the bore° of the matter. These good
fellows will bring thee where I am. Rosencrantz and
Guildenstern hold their course for England. Of them I   25
have much to tell thee. Farewell.
      He that thou knowest thine, Hamlet."
Come, I will give you way° for these your letters,
And do't the speedier that you may direct me
To him from whom you brought them.   *Exeunt.*   30

[*Scene 7. Another room in the castle.*]

Enter KING *and* LAERTES.

KING.   Now must your conscience my acquittance seal,°
   And you must put me in your heart for friend,
   Sith you have heard and with a knowing ear,
   That he which hath your noble father slain
   Pursued my life.
LAERTES.   It well appears: but tell me   5
   Why you proceeded not against these feats
   So crimeful and so capital in nature,
   As by your safety, greatness, wisdom, all things else,
   You mainly were stirred up.°
KING.   O for two special reasons,
   Which may to you perhaps seem much unsinewed,°   10
   But yet to me they're strong. The queen his mother
   Lives almost by his looks, and for myself,
   My virtue or my plague, be it either which,
   She's so conjunctive° to my life and soul,
   That as the star moves not but in his sphere,°   15
   I could not but by her. The other motive,
   Why to a public count° I might not go,
   Is the great love the general gender° bear him,
   Who dipping all his faults in their affection,
   Would like the spring that turneth wood to stone,°   20
   Convert his gyves to graces,° so that my arrows,
   Too slightly timbered° for so loud a wind,

---

20 *repair*: come.   23 *bore*: size, caliber.   28 *way*: access (to the king).   1 *my acquittance
seal*: confirm my acquittal.   9 *mainly . . . up*: were strongly urged.   10 *much unsinewed*:
very weak.   14 *conjunctive*: closely allied.   15 *in his sphere*: (referring to the Ptolemaic
belief that each planet, fixed in its own sphere, revolved around the earth).   17 *count*:
accounting.   18 *general gender*: common people.   20 *the spring . . . stone*: (the baths of
King's Newnham in Warwickshire were described as being able to turn wood into stone).
21 *Convert . . . graces*: regard his fetters (had he been imprisoned) as honors.
22 *slightly timbered*: light-shafted.

    Would have reverted to my bow again,
    And not where I had aimed them.
LAERTES. And so have I a noble father lost,   25
    A sister driven into desperate terms,°
    Whose worth, if praises may go back° again,
    Stood challenger on mount of all the age
    For her perfections.° But my revenge will come.
KING. Break not your sleeps for that, you must not think   30
    That we are made of stuff so flat and dull,
    That we can let our beard be shook with danger,
    And think it pastime. You shortly shall hear more,
    I loved your father, and we love ourself,
    And that I hope will teach you to imagine—   35

Enter a MESSENGER with letters.

    How now. What news?
MESSENGER.   Letters my lord, from Hamlet.
    These to your majesty, this to the queen.
KING. From Hamlet? Who brought them?
MESSENGER. Sailors my lord they say, I saw them not:
    They were given me by Claudio, he received them   40
    Of him that brought them.
KING.   Laertes you shall hear them:
    Leave us.   *Exit [MESSENGER]*
    [*Reads*] "High and mighty, you shall know I am set naked°
    on your kingdom. Tomorrow shall I beg leave to see your
    kingly eyes, when I shall, first asking your pardon°   45
    thereunto, recount the occasion of my sudden and more strange
    return.   Hamlet."
    What should this mean? Are all the rest come back?
    Or is it some abuse,° and no such thing?
LAERTES. Know you the hand?
KING.   'Tis Hamlet's character.° "Naked,"   50
    And in a postscript here he says "alone."
    Can you devise° me?
LAERTES. I am lost in it my lord, but let him come,
    It warms the very sickness in my heart
    That I shall live and tell him to his teeth,   55
    "Thus didest thou."
KING.   If it be so Laertes—
    As how should it be so? how otherwise?—
    Will you be ruled by me?

---

26 *desperate terms*: madness.   27 *go back*: i.e., before her madness.   28–29 *challenger . . .*
perfections: like a challenger on horseback, ready to defend against the world her claim to
perfection.   43 *naked*: without resources.   45 *pardon*: permission.   49 *abuse*:
deception.   50 *character*: handwriting.   52 *devise me*: explain it.

LAERTES.   Ay my lord,
So you will not o'errule me to a peace.
KING.   To thine own peace: if he be now returned,   60
As checking at° his voyage, and that he means
No more to undertake it, I will work him
To an exploit, now ripe in my device,°
Under the which he shall not choose but fall:
And for his death no wind of blame shall breathe,   65
But even his mother shall uncharge the practice,°
And call it accident.
LAERTES.   My lord, I will be ruled,
The rather if you could devise it so
That I might be the organ.°
KING.   It falls right.
You have been talked of since your travel much,   70
And that in Hamlet's hearing, for a quality
Wherein they say you shine: your sum of parts°
Did not together pluck such envy from him
As did that one, and that in my regard
Of the unworthiest siege.°
LAERTES.   What part is that my lord?   75
KING.   A very riband° in the cap of youth,
Yet needful too, for youth no less becomes°
The light and careless livery° that it wears,
Than settled age his sables° and his weeds°
Importing health and graveness; two months since,°   80
Here was a gentleman of Normandy—
I have seen myself, and served against the French,
And they can° well on horseback—but this gallant
Had witchcraft in't, he grew unto his seat,
And to such wondrous doing brought his horse,   85
As had he been incorpsed and demi-natured°
With the brave beast. So far he topped my thought,
That I in forgery of° shapes and tricks
Come short of what he did.
LAERTES.   A Norman was't?
KING.   A Norman.   90
LAERTES.   Upon my life, Lamord.
KING.   The very same.
LAERTES.   I know him well, he is the brooch° indeed
And gem of all the nation.

61 *checking at*: altering the course of (when the falcon forsakes one quarry for another).
another).   63 *ripe in my device*: already planned by me.   66 *uncharge the practice*: acquit
the plot (of treachery).   69 *organ*: instrument.   72 *your sum of parts*: all your
accomplishments.   75 *siege*: rank.   76 *riband*: decoration.   77 *becomes*: befits.
78 *livery*: clothing (denoting rank or occupation).   79 *sables*: fur-trimmed gowns.   *weeds*:
garments.   80 *since*: ago.   83 *can*: can do.   86 *incorpsed . . . natured*: made into one
body, sharing half its nature.   88 *in forgery of*: imagining.   92 *brooch*: ornament.

KING. He made confession° of you,
    And gave you such a masterly report   95
    For art and exercise in your defence,
    And for your rapier most especial,
    That he cried out 'twould be a sight indeed
    If one could match you; the scrimers° of their nation
    He swore had neither motion, guard, nor eye,   100
    If you opposed them; sir this report of his
    Did Hamlet so envenom° with his envy,
    That he could nothing do but wish and beg
    Your sudden coming o'er to play with him.
    Now out of this—
LAERTES.   What out of this, my lord?   105
KING. Laertes, was your father dear to you?
    Or are you like the painting of a sorrow,
    A face without a heart?
LAERTES.   Why ask you this?
KING. Not that I think you did not love your father,
    But that I know love is begun by time,   110
    And that I see in passages of proof,°
    Time qualifies° the spark and fire of it:
    There lives within the very flame of love
    A kind of wick or snuff that will abate it,°
    And nothing is at a like goodness still,°   115
    For goodness growing to a plurisy,°
    Dies in his own too-much. That we would do
    We should do when we would: for this "would"° changes,
    And hath abatements and delays as many
    As there are tongues, are hands, are accidents,   120
    And then this "should"° is like a spendthrift sigh,
    That hurts by easing;° but to the quick° of th'ulcer:
    Hamlet comes back, what would you undertake
    To show yourself in deed your father's son
    More than in words?
LAERTES.   To cut his throat i'th'church.   125
KING. No place indeed should murder sanctuarize,°
    Revenge should have no bounds: but good Laertes,
    Will you do this, keep close within your chamber:
    Hamlet returned shall know you are come home,
    We'll put on° those shall praise your excellence,   130
    And set a double varnish on the fame

---

94 *confession*: report.   99 *scrimers*: fencers.   102 *envenom*: poison.   111 *passages of proof*: examples drawn from experience.   112 *qualifies*: weakens.   114 *snuff . . . it*: charred end of the wick that will diminish the flame.   115 *still*: always.   116 *plurisy*: excess.   118 *"would"*: will to act.   121 *"should"*: reminder of one's duty. 121–122 *spendthrift . . . easing*: a sigh which, though giving temporary relief, wastes life, as each sigh draws a drop of blood away from the heart (a common Elizabethan belief). 122 *quick*: most sensitive spot.   126 *murder sanctuarize*: give sanctuary to murder. 130 *put on*: incite.

The Frenchman gave you, bring you in fine° together,
And wager on your heads; he being remiss,°
Most generous, and free from all contriving,
Will not peruse the foils, so that with ease,   135
Or with a little shuffling, you may choose
A sword unbated,° and in a pass of practice°
Requite him for your father.
LAERTES.   I will do't,
And for the purpose, I'll anoint my sword.
I bought an unction° of a mountebank°   140
So mortal,° that but dip a knife in it,
Where it draws blood, no cataplasm° so rare,
Collected from all simples° that have virtue°
Under the moon,° can save the thing from death
That is but scratched withal: I'll touch my point   145
With this contagion, that if I gall° him slightly,
It may be death.
KING.   Let's further think of this,
Weigh what convenience both of time and means
May fit us to our shape;° if this should fail,
And that our drift° look through° our bad performance,   150
'Twere better not assayed; therefore this project
Should have a back or second that might hold
If this did blast in proof;° soft, let me see,
We'll make a solemn wager on your cunnings°—
I ha't: 155
When in your motion you are hot and dry,
As make your bouts more violent to that end,
And that he calls for drink, I'll have prepared him
A chalice for the nonce,° whereon but sipping,
If he by chance escape your venomed stuck,°   160
Our purpose may hold there; but stay, what noise?

Enter QUEEN.

How, sweet queen?
QUEEN.   One woe doth tread upon another's heel,
So fast they follow; your sister's drowned, Laertes.
LAERTES.   Drowned! O where?   165
QUEEN.   There is a willow grows aslant a brook,
That shows his hoar° leaves in the glassy stream,

132 *in fine*: finally.   133 *remiss*: easy-going.   137 *unbated*: not blunted (the edges and
points were blunted for fencing).   *pass of practice:* (1) match for exercise (2) treacherous
thrust.   140 *unction*: ointment.   *mountebank:* quack doctor, medicine man.
141 *mortal*: deadly.   142 *cataplasm*: poultice.   143 *simples*: herbs.   *virtue*: power
(of healing).   144 *Under the moon*: (when herbs were supposed to be collected to be most
effective).   146 *gall*: scratch.   149 *shape*: plan.   150 *drift*: aim.   *look through*: be
exposed by.   153 *blast in proof*: fail when tested (as a bursting cannon).
154 *cunnings*: skills.   159 *nonce*: occasion   160 *stuck*: thrust.   167 *hoar*: grey (on the
underside).

There with fantastic garlands did she make
Of crow-flowers,° nettles, daisies, and long purples,°
That liberal° shepherds give a grosser name,   170
But our cold° maids do dead men's fingers call them.
There on the pendent boughs her coronet weeds°
Clamb'ring to hang, an envious sliver° broke,
When down her weedy trophies and herself
Fell in the weeping brook: her clothes spread wide,   175
And mermaid-like awhile they bore her up,
Which time. she chanted snatches of old tunes,
As one incapable of° her own distress,
Or like a creature native and indued
Unto° that element: but long it could not be   180
Till that her garments, heavy with their drink,
Pulled the poor wretch from her melodious lay
To muddy death.
LAERTES.   Alas, then she is drowned?
QUEEN.   Drowned, drowned.
LAERTES.   Too much of water hast thou, poor Ophelia,   185
And therefore I forbid my tears; but yet
It is our trick, nature her custom holds,
Let shame say what it will; when these° are gone,
The woman will be out.° Adieu my lord,
I have a speech o' fire that fain would blaze,   190
But that this folly douts it.°   *Exit.*
KING.   Let's follow, Gertrude,
How much I had to do to calm his rage;
Now fear I this will give it start again,
Therefore let's follow.   *Exeunt.*

[ACT 5]

[Scene 1. A churchyard]

Enter two CLOWNS.°

1. CLOWN.   Is she to be buried in Christian burial,° when she wilfully
   seeks her own salvation?
2. CLOWN.   I tell thee she is, therefore make her grave straight.° The
   crowner hath sat on her,° and finds it Christian burial.

169 *crowflowers*: buttercups.   *long purples*: spikelike early orchid.   170 *liberal*:
libertine.   171 *cold*: chaste.   172 *coronet weeds*: garland of weeds.   173 *envious sliver*:
malicious branch.   178 *incapable of*: unable to understand.   179–180 *indued Unto*:
endowed by nature to exist in.   188 *these*: i.e., tears.   189 *woman . . . out*: womanly
habits will be out of me.   191 *folly douts it*: tears put it out.   stage direction *clowns*:
rustics.   1 *Christian burial*: consecrated ground within a churchyard (where suicides were
not allowed burial).   3 *straight*: straightway.   4 *crowner . . . her*: coroner has ruled on
her case.

1. CLOWN.   How can that be, unless she drowned herself in her own   5
     defence?°
2. CLOWN.   Why, 'tis found so.
1. CLOWN.   It must be "se offendendo,"° it cannot be else: for here lies
     the point: if I drown myself wittingly, it argues an act,
     and an act hath three branches, it is to act, to do, and to   10
     perform; argal,° she drowned herself wittingly.
2. CLOWN.   Nay, but hear you, goodman delver.
1. CLOWN.   Give me leave: here lies the water, good. Here stands the
     man, good. If the man go to this water and drown himself,
     it is, will he nill he,° he goes, mark you that. But if the   15
     water come to him, and drown him, he drowns not
     himself. Argal, he that is not guilty of his own death, shortens not his own
     life.
2. CLOWN.   But is this law?
1. CLOWN.   Ay marry is't, crowner's quest° law.   20
2. CLOWN.   Will you ha' the truth on't? If this had not been a
     gentlewoman, she would have been buried out o'Christian
     burial.
1. CLOWN.   Why there thou say'st, and the more pity that great folk
     should have countenance° in this world to drown or hang   25
     themselves more than their even-Christen.° Come, my
     spade; there is no ancient gentlemen but gardeners,
     ditchers and grave-makers; they hold up Adam's profession.
2. CLOWN.   Was he a gentleman?
1. CLOWN.   A' was the first that ever bore arms.°   30
2. CLOWN.   Why, he had none.
1. CLOWN.   What, art a heathen? How dost thou understand the
     Scripture? The Scripture says Adam digged; could he dig
     without arms? I'll put another question to thee; if thou
     answerest me not to the purpose, confess thyself—   35
2. CLOWN.   Go to.
1. CLOWN.   What is he that builds stronger than either the mason, the
     shipwright, or the carpenter?
2. CLOWN.   The gallows-maker, for that frame outlives a thousand
     tenants.   40
1. CLOWN.   I like thy wit well in good faith, the gallows does well, but
     how does it well? It does well to those that do ill. Now
     thou dost ill to say the gallows is built stronger than the
     church. Argal, the gallows may do well to thee.° To't
     again, come.   45
2. CLOWN.   'Who builds stronger than a mason, a shipwright, or a
     carpenter?'

5–6 her own defence: (as self-defense justifies homicide, so may it justify suicide).   8 "se
offendendo": (he means "se defendendo," in self-defense).   11 argal: (corruption of "ergo"
= therefore).   15 will he nill he: will he or will he not (willy nilly).   20 quest: inquest.
25 countenance: privilege.   26 even-Christen: fellow Christian.   30 arms: (with a pun on
"coat of arms").   44 to thee: i.e., by hanging you.

1. CLOWN.   Ay, tell me that, and unyoke.°
2. CLOWN.   Marry, now I can tell.
1. CLOWN.   To't.   50
2. CLOWN.   Mass,° I cannot tell.
1. CLOWN.   Cudgel thy brains no more about it, for your dull ass will
      not mend his pace with beating, and when you are asked
      this question next, say "a grave-maker:" the houses he
      makes last till doomsday. Go get thee to Yaughan, and   55
      fetch me a stoup° of liquor.   [*Exit 2. CLOWN.*]

Enter HAMLET and HORATIO afar off.

1. Clown.   (*Sings.*) In youth when I did love, did love,
                    Methought it was very sweet,
                    To contract oh the time for a° my behove,°
                    O methought there a was nothing a meet.°   60
HAMLET.   Has this fellow no feeling of his business, that a'sings in
      grave-making?
HORATIO.   Custom hath made it in him a property of easiness.°
HAMLET.   'Tis e'en so, the hand of little employment hath the
      daintier sense.°   65
1. Clown.   (*Sings.*) But age with his stealing steps
                    Hath clawed me in his clutch,
                    And hath shipped me intil° the land,
                    As if I had never been such.   [*Throws up a skull.*]
HAMLET.   That skull had a tongue in it, and could sing once: how the   70
      knave jowls° it to the ground, as if 'twere Cain's jaw-bone,°
      that did the first murder. This might be the pate of a
      politician, which this ass now o'erreaches;° one that
      would circumvent° God, might it not?
HORATIO.   It might my lord.   75
HAMLET.   Or of a courtier, which could say "Good morrow sweet
      lord, how dost thou good lord?" This might be my lord
      such-a-one, that praised my lord such-a-one's horse, when
      a'meant to beg it, might it not?
HORATIO.   It might my lord.   80
HAMLET.   Why e'en so, and now my Lady Worm's, chopless,° and
      knocked about the mazzard° with a sexton's spade; here's
      fine revolution and we had the trick° to see't. Did these
      bones cost no more the breeding, but to play at loggets°
      with them? Mine ache to think on't.   85

---

48 *unyoke*: unharness (your wits, after this exertion).   51 *Mass*: by the mass.   56 *stoup*:
drinking mug.   59 *oh, a*: (he grunts as he works).   *behove*: benefit.   60 *meet*:
suitable.   63 *Custom . . . easiness*: being accustomed to it has made him indifferent.
65 *daintier sense*: finer sensibility (being uncalloused).   68 *intil*: into.
71 *jowls*: casts (with obvious pun).   *Cain's jaw-bone*: the jawbone of an ass with which
Cain murdered Abel.   73 *o'erreaches*: (1) reaches over (2) gets the better of.
74 *would circumvent*: tried to outwit.   81 *chopless*: lacking the lower jaw.
82 *mazzard*: head.   83 *trick*: knack.   84 *play at loggets*: game where small pieces of wood
were thrown at fixed stakes.

1. Clown.   (*Sings*.) A pick-axe and a spade, a spade,
　　　　　　　　　For and a shrouding sheet,
　　　　　　　　　O a pit of clay for to be made
　　　　　　　　　For such a guest is meet.°　　　[*Throws up another skull.*]

HAMLET.   There's another: why may not that be the skull of a　　　90
　　lawyer? Where be his quiddities° now, his quillets,° his
　　cases, his tenures,° and his tricks? Why does he suffer this
　　rude knave now to knock him about the sconce° with a
　　dirty shovel, and will not tell him of his action of battery?
　　Hum, this fellow might be in's time a great buyer of land,　　95
　　with his statutes,° his recognizances,° his fines,° his double
　　vouchers,° his recoveries:° is this the fine° of his fines, and
　　the recovery° of his recoveries, to have his fine pate full of
　　fine dirt? Will his vouchers vouch him no more of his
　　purchases, and double ones too, than the length and　　　100
　　breadth of a pair of indentures?° The very conveyances° of
　　his lands will scarcely lie in this box,° and must th'inheritor°
　　himself have no more, ha?

HORATIO.   Not a jot more my lord.

HAMLET.   Is not parchment made of sheep-skins?　　　　105

HORATIO.   Ay my lord, and of calves'-skins too.

HAMLET.   They are sheep and calves which seek out assurance° in
　　that. I will speak to this fellow. Whose grave's this, sirrah?

1. Clown.   Mine sir:
　　　　　　[*Sings*.] O a pit of clay for to be made　　　110
　　　　　　　　For such a guest is meet.

HAMLET.   I think it be thine indeed, for thou liest in't.

1. CLOWN.   You lie out on't° sir, and therefore 'tis not yours; for my
　　part I do not lie in't, and yet it is mine.

HAMLET.   Thous dost lie in't, to be in't and say it is thine: 'tis for the　　115
　　dead, not for the quick,° therefore thou liest.

1. CLOWN.   'Tis a quick lie sir, 'twill away again from me to you.

HAMLET.   What man dost thou dig it for?

1. CLOWN.   For no man sir.

HAMLET.   What woman then?　　　　120

1. CLOWN.   For none neither.

HAMLET.   Who is to buried in't?

1. CLOWN.   One that was a woman sir, but rest her soul she's dead.

---

89 *meet*: fitting.　　91 *quiddities*: subtle definition.　　*quillets*: minute distinctions.
92 *tenures*: property holdings.　　93 *sconce*: head.　　96 *statutes*: mortgages.　　*recognizances*:
promissory bonds.　　96–97 *fines*, *recoveries*: legal processes for transferring real
estate.　　97 *vouchers*: persons who vouched for a title to real estate.　　97 *fine*: end.
98 *recovery*: attainment.　　100–101 *length . . . indentures*: contracts in duplicate, which
spread out, would just cover his grave.　　101 *conveyances*: deeds.　　102 *box*: the
grave.　　*inheritor*: owner.　　107 *assurance*: (1) security (2) transfer of land.　　113 *on*: of.
116 *quick*: living.

HAMLET. How absolute° the knave is, we must speak by the card,° or
    equivocation° will undo us. By the Lord, Horatio, this   125
    three years I have took note of it, the age is grown so
    picked,° that the toe of the peasant comes so near the heel of
    the courtier, he galls his kibe.° How long hast thou been
    grave-maker?
1. CLOWN. Of all the days i'th'year I came to't that day that our last   130
    king Hamlet overcame Fortinbras.
HAMLET. How long is that since?
1. CLOWN. Cannot you tell that? Every fool can tell that. It was the
    very day that young Hamlet was born: he that is mad and
    sent into England.   135
HAMLET. Ay marry, why was he sent into England?
1. CLOWN. Why because a' was mad: a' shall recover his wits there, or
    if a' do not, 'tis no great matter there.
HAMLET. Why?
1. CLOWN. 'Twill not be seen in him there, there the men are as mad   140
    as he.
HAMLET. How came he mad?
1. CLOWN. Very strangely they say.
HAMLET. How strangely?
1. CLOWN. Faith, e'en with losing his wits.   145
HAMLET. Upon what ground?
1. CLOWN. Why here in Denmark: I have been sexton here man and
    boy thirty years.
HAMLET. How long will a man lie i'th'earth ere he rot?
1. CLOWN. Faith, if a' be not rotten before a' die, as we have many   150
    pocky° corses nowadays that will scarce hold the laying in,
    a' will last you some eight year, or nine year. A tanner will
    last you nine year.
HAMLET. Why he more than another?
1. CLOWN. Why sir, his hide is so tanned with his trade, that a' will   155
    keep out water a great while; and your water is a sore°
    decayer of your whoreson dead body. Here's a skull now:
    this skull hath lien you i'th'earth three-and-twenty years.
HAMLET. Whose was it?
1. CLOWN. A whoreson mad fellow's it was, whose do you think it   160
    was?
HAMLET. Nay, I know not.
1. CLOWN. A pestilence on him for a mad rogue, a' poured a flagon of
    Rhenish° on my head once; this same skull sir, was sir,
    Yorick's skull, the king's jester.   165

---

124 *absolute*: precise.   *by the card*: exactly to the point (card on which compass points are
marked).   125 *equivocation*: ambiguity.   127 *picked*: fastidious ("picky").   128 *galls his
kibe*: chafes the sore on the courtier's heel.   151 *pocky*: rotten (with venereal disease).
156 *sore*: grievous.   164 *Rhenish*: Rhine wine.

HAMLET.   This?

1. CLOWN.   E'en that.

HAMLET.   Let me see. [*Takes the skull.*] Alas poor Yorick, I knew him
  Horatio, a fellow of infinite jest, of most excellent fancy,°
  he hath borne me on his back a thousand times: and now   170
  how abhorred in my imagination it is: my gorge rises at it.
  Here hung those lips that I have kissed I know not how
  oft. Where be your gibes now? your gambols, your songs,
  your flashes of merriment, that were wont to set the table
  on a roar?° not one now to mock your own grinning? quite   175
  chop-fallen?° Now get you to my lady's chamber, and tell
  her, let her paint an inch thick, to this favour° she must
  come. Make her laugh at that. Prithee Horatio, tell me one
  thing.

HORATIO.   What's that, my lord?   180

HAMLET.   Dost thou think Alexander looked o' this fashion
  i'th'earth?

HORATIO.   E'en so.

HAMLET.   And smelt so? pah.   [*Puts down the skull.*]

HORATIO.   E'en so my lord.   185

HAMLET.   To what base uses we may return, Horatio. Why may not
  imagination trace the noble dust of Alexander, til a'find it
  stopping a bung-hole?°

HORATIO.   'Twere to consider too curiously,° to consider so.

HAMLET.   No faith, not a jot, but to follow him thither with modesty°   190
  enough, and likelihood to lead it; as thus: Alexander died,
  Alexander was buried, Alexander returneth to dust, the
  dust is earth, of earth we make loam,° and why of that loam
  whereto he was converted, might they not stop a
  beer-barrel?   195
      Imperious Caesar, dead and turned to clay,
      Might stop a hole to keep the wind away.
      O that that earth which kept the world in awe,
      Should patch a wall t'expel the winter's flaw.°
  But soft, but soft awhile, here comes the king,   200
  The queen, the courtiers.

Enter KING, QUEEN, LAERTES, [*Doctor of Divinity*], *and a coffin, with Lords attendant.*

      Who is this they follow?
  And with such maimèd° rites? This doth betoken
  The corse they follow did with desp'rate hand
  Fordo it° own life; 'twas of some estate.°
  Couch° we awhile, and mark.   [*They retire.*]   205

169 *fancy*: imagination.   175 *on a roar*: roaring with laughter.   176 *chopfallen*: (a) lacking
a lower jaw (2) dejected, "down in the mouth."   177 *favour*: appearance.   188 *bung-
hole*: hole in a cask.   189 *curiously*: minutely.   190 *modesty*: moderation.   193 *loam*:
a clay mixture used as plaster.   199 *flaw*: windy gusts.   202 *maimed*: abbreviated.
204 *Fordo it*: destroy its.   *estate*: social rank.   205 *Couch*: hide.

LAERTES. What ceremony else?
HAMLET.   That is Laertes,
  A very noble youth: mark.
LAERTES. What ceremony else?
DOCTOR. Her obsequies have been as far enlarged
  As we have warranty: her death was doubtful,°   210
  And but that great command o'ersways the order,
  She should in ground unsanctified have lodged
  Til the last trumpet: for charitable prayers,
  Shards,° flints and pebbles should be thrown on her:
  Yet here she is allowed her virgin crants,°   215
  Her maiden strewments,° and the bringing home
  Of° bell and burial.
LAERTES. Must there no more be done?
DOCTOR.   No more be done:
  We should profane the service of the dead,
  To sing sage requiem° and such rest to her   220
  As to peace-parted souls.
LAERTES.   Lay her i'th'earth,
  And from her fair and unpolluted flesh
  May violets spring: I tell thee churlish priest,
  A minist'ring angel shall my sister be,
  When thou liest howling.
HAMLET.   What, the fair Ophelia?   225
QUEEN. [*Scattering flowers.*] Sweets to the sweet, farewell.
  I hoped thou shouldst have been my Hamlet's wife:
  I thought thy bride-bed to have decked, sweet maid,
  And not have strewed thy grave.
LAERTES.   O treble woe
  Fall ten times treble on that cursèd head   230
  Whose wicked deed thy most ingenious sense°
  Deprived thee of. Hold off the earth awhile,
  Till I have caught her once more in mine arms;   *Leaps in the grave.*
  Now pile your dust upon the quick° and dead,
  Till of this flat a mountain you have made   235
  T'o'ertop old Pelion,° or the skyish head
  Of blue Olympus.
HAMLET. [*Comes forward.*] What is he whose grief
  Bears such an emphasis? whose phrase of sorrow
  Conjures the wand'ring stars,° and makes them stand
  Like wonder-wounded hearers? This is I,   240
  Hamlet the Dane.   *Hamlet leaps in after Laertes.*

---

210 *doubtful*: suspicious.   214 *Shards*: bits of broken pottery.   215 *crants*: garland.
216 *strewments*: flowers strewn on the grave.   216–217 *bringing home Of*: laying to rest
with.   220 *sage requiem*: solemn dirge.   231 *sense*: mind.   234 *quick*: live.
236 *Pelion*: mountain (on which the Titans placed Mt. Ossa, to scale Mt. Olympus and reach
the gods).   239 *Conjures . . . star*: casts a spell over the planets.

LAERTES. [*Grapples with him.*] The devil take thy soul.

HAMLET. Thou pray'st not well,
  I prithee take thy fingers from my throat,
  For though I am not splenitive° and rash,
  Yet have I in me something dangerous,   245
  Which let thy wiseness fear; hold off thy hand.

KING. Pluck them asunder.

QUEEN.   Hamlet, Hamlet!

ALL. Gentlemen!

HORATIO.   Good my lord, be quiet.

                  [*Attendants part them, and they come out of the grave.*]

HAMLET. Why, I will fight with him upon this theme
  Until my eyelids will no longer wag.   250

QUEEN. O my son, what theme?

HAMLET. I loved Ophelia, forty thousand brothers
  Could not with all their quantity of love
  Make up my sum. What wilt thou do for her?

KING. O he is mad, Laertes.   255

QUEEN. For love of God, forbear° him.

HAMLET. 'Swounds,° show me what thou't do:
  Woo't° weep? woo't fight? woo't fast? woo't tear thyself?
  Woo't drink up eisel?° eat a crocodile?°
  I'll do't. Dost thou come here to whine?   260
  To outface me with leaping in her grave?
  Be buried quick with her, and so will I.
  And if thou prate of mountains, let them throw
  Millions of acres on us, till our ground,
  Singeing his pate against the burning zone,°   265
  Make Ossa° like a wart. Nay, and thou't mouth,
  I'll rant as well as thou.

QUEEN.   This is mere° madness,
  And thus awhile the fit will work on him:
  Anon as patient as the female dove
  When that her golden couplets° are disclosed,   270
  His silence will sit drooping.

HAMLET.   Hear you sir,
  What is the reason that you use me thus?
  I loved you ever; but it is no matter.
  Let Hercules himself do what he may,
  The cat will mew, and dog will have his day.   *Exit* HAMLET.   275

---

244 *splenitive*: quick-tempered (anger was thought to originate in the spleen).   256 *forbear*:
be patient with.   257 *Swounds*: corruption of "God's wounds."   258 *Woo't*: wilt thou.
259 *eisel*: vinegar (thought to reduce anger and encourage melancholy).   *crocodile*:
(associated with hypocritical tears).   265 *burning zone*: sun's sphere.   266 *Ossa*: (see
above, line 236 n.).   267 *mere*: absolute.   270 *golden couplets*: fuzzy yellow twin fledglings.

KING.   I pray thee good Horatio, wait upon him.   [*HORATIO follows*.]
[*Aside to Laertes*.] Strengthen your patience in our last night's speech,
We'll put the matter to the present push°—
Good Gertrude, set some watch over your son—
This grave shall have a living monument:°   280
An hour of quiet shortly shall we see,
Till then, in patience our proceeding be.   *Exeunt*.

[*Scene 2. A hall in the castle*]

Enter HAMLET and HORATIO.

HAMLET.   So much for this sir, now shall you see the other;
    You do remember all the circumstance.
HORATIO.   Remember it my lord!
HAMLET.   Sir, in my heart there was a kind of fighting
    That would not let me sleep; methought I lay   5
    Worse than the mutines in the bilboes.° Rashly—
    And praised be rashness for it: let us know,
    Our indiscretion sometimes serves us well
    When our deep plots do pall,° and that should learn us
    There's a divinity that shapes our ends,   10
    Rough-hew them how we will—
HORATIO.   That is most certain.
HAMLET.   Up from my cabin,
    My sea-gown° scarfed about me, in the dark
    Groped I to find out them, had my desire,
    Fingered° their packet, and in fine° withdrew   15
    To mine own room again, making so bold,
    My fears forgetting manners, to unseal
    Their grand commission; where I found, Horatio—
    Ah royal knavery—an exact command,
    Larded° with many several sorts of reasons,   20
    Importing Denmark's health, and England's too,
    With ho, such bugs and goblins in my life,°
    That on the supervise,° no leisure bated,°
    No, not to stay° the grinding of the axe,
    My head should be struck off.
HORATIO.   Is't possible?   25
HAMLET.   Here's the commission, read it at more leisure.
    But wilt thou hear now how I did proceed?
HORATIO.   I beseech you.

278 *present push*: immediate test.   280 *living monument*: (1) lasting tombstone (2) living
sacrifice (Hamlet) to memorialize it.   6 *mutines . . . bilboes*: mutineers in shackles.
9 *pall*: fail.   13 *sea-gown*: short-sleeved knee-length gown worn by seamen.   15 *Fingered*:
got my fingers on.   *in fine*: to finish.   20 *Larded*: embellished.   22 *bugs . . . life*:
imaginary evils attributed to me, like imaginary goblins ("bugs") meant to frighten
children.   23 *supervise*: looking over (the commission).   *leisure bated*: delay
excepted.   24 *stay*: await.

HAMLET.   Being thus be-netted round with villainies,
Ere I could make a prologue to my brains,   30
They had begun the play.° I sat me down,
Devised a new commission, wrote it fair°—
I once did hold it, as our statists° do,
A baseness° to write fair, and laboured much
How to forget that learning, but sir now   35
It did me yeoman's° service: wilt thou know
Th'effect of what I wrote?
HORATIO.   Ay, good my lord.
HAMLET.   An earnest conjuration° from the king,
As England was his faithful tributary,
As love between them like the palm might flourish,   40
As peace should still her wheaten garland wear
And stand a comma° 'tween their amities,
And many such like "as'es"° of great charge,°
That on the view and know of these contents,
Without debatement further, more or less,   45
He should those bearers put to sudden death,
Not shriving° time allowed.
HORATIO.   How was this sealed?
HAMLET.   Why even in that was heaven ordinant,°
I had my father's signet° in my purse,
Which was the model° of that Danish seal: 50
Folded the writ up in the form of th'other,
Subscribed° it, gave't th'impression,° placed it safely,
The changeling° never known: now the next day
Was our sea-fight, and what to this was sequent
Thou knowest already.   55
HORATIO.   So Guildenstern and Rosencrantz go to't.
HAMLET.   Why man, they did make love to this employment,°
They are not near my conscience, their defeat
Does by their own insinuation° grow:
'Tis dangerous when the baser nature comes   60
Between the pass° and fell° incensed points
Of mighty opposites.
HORATIO.   Why, what a king is this!

30–31 *Ere . . . play*: before I could outline the action in my mind, my brains started to
play their part.   32 *fair*: with professional skill.   33 *statists*: statesmen.   34 *baseness*:
mark of humble status.   36 *yeoman's*: (in the sense of "faithful").   38 *conjuration*:
entreaty (he parodies the rhetoric of such documents).   42 *comma*: connection.
43 *as'es*: (1) the "as" clauses in the commission (2) asses.   *charge*: (1) weight (in the clauses)
(2) burdens (on the asses).   47 *shriving*: confession and absolution.   48 *was heaven
ordinant*: it was divinely ordained.   49 *signet*: seal.   50 *model*: replica.   52 *Subscribed*:
signed.   *impression*: i.e., of the seal.   53 *changeling*: substitute (baby imp left when an
infant was spirited away).   57 *did . . . employment*: asked for it.   59 *insinuation*:
intrusion.   61 *pass*: thrust   *fell*: fierce.

HAMLET.   Does it not, think thee, stand me now upon°—
He that hath killed my king, and whored my mother,
Popped in between th'election° and my hopes,   65
Thrown out his angle° for my proper° life,
And with such cozenage°—is't not perfect conscience
To quit° him with this arm? And is't not to be damned,
To let this canker of our nature° come
In further evil?   70
HORATIO.   It must be shortly known to him from England
What is the issue of the business there.
HAMLET.   It will be short, the interim is mine,
And a man's life's no more than to say "One."°
But I am very sorry good Horatio,   75
That to Laertes I forgot myself;
For by the image of my cause, I see
The portraiture of his;° I'll court his favours:
But sure the bravery° of his grief did put me
Into a towering passion.
HORATIO.   Peace, who comes here?   80

Enter young OSRIC.

OSRIC.   Your lordship is right welcome back to Denmark.
HAMLET.   I humbly thank you sir. [*Aside to Horatio.*] Dost know this
water-fly?
HORATIO.   No my good lord.
HAMLET.   Thy state is the more gracious,° for 'tis a vice to know him: 85
he hath much land, and fertile: let a beast be lord of beasts,
and his crib shall stand at the king's mess;° 'tis a chough,°
but as I say, spacious in the possession of dirt.
OSRIC.   Sweet lord, if your lordship were at leisure, I should
impart a thing to you from his majesty.   90
HAMLET.   I will receive it sir, with all diligence of spirit; put your
bonnet° to his right use, 'tis for the head.
OSRIC.   I thank your lordship, it is very hot.
HAMLET.   No, believe me, 'tis very cold, the wind is northerly.
OSRIC.   It is indifferent° cold my lord indeed.   95
HAMLET.   But yet methinks it is very sultry and hot for my
complexion.°

---

63 *stand . . . upon*: become incumbent upon me now.   65 *election*: (the Danish king was
so chosen).   66 *angle*: fishing hook.   *proper*: very own.   67 *cozenage*: deception.
68 *quit*: repay, requite.   69 *canker of our nature*: cancer of humanity.   74 *to say "One"*:
to score one hit in fencing.   77–78 *by the image . . . his*: in the depiction of my situation,
I see the reflection of his.   79 *bravery*: ostentation.   85 *gracious*: favorable.   86–87 *let
a beast . . . mess*: an ass who owns enough property can eat with the king.   87 *chough*:
chattering bird, jackdaw.   92 *bonnet*: hat.   95 *indifferent*: reasonably.   97 *complexion*:
temperament.

OSRIC. Exceedingly, my lord, it is very sultry, as 'twere, I cannot
   tell how: but my lord, his majesty bade me signify to you
   that a'has laid a great wager on your head. Sir, this is the   100
   matter—
HAMLET. [*Moves him to put on his hat.*] I beseech you remember—
OSRIC. Nay good my lord, for mine ease,° in good faith. Sir, here
   is newly come to court Laertes, believe me, an absolute
   gentleman, full of most excellent differences,° of very soft   105
   society, and great showing: indeed to speak feelingly of
   him, he is the card° or calendar of gentry: for you shall find
   in him the continent of what part a gentleman would see.°
HAMLET. Sir, has definement° suffers no perdition° in you, though I
   know to divide him inventorially would dozy°   110
   th'arithmetic of memory, and yet but yaw neither, in
   respect of his quick sail,° but in the verity of extolment,° I
   take him to be a soul of great article,° and his infusion° of
   such dearth and rareness, as to make true diction of him,
   his semblable° is his mirror, and who else would trace° him,   115
   his umbrage,° nothing more.°
OSRIC. Your lordship speaks most infallibly of him.
HAMLET. The concernancy° sir? why do we wrap the gentleman in
   our more rawer breath?°
OSRIC. Sir?   120
HORATIO. Is't not possible to understand in another tongue?° You
   will do't sir, really.
HAMLET. What imports the nomination° of this gentleman?
OSRIC. Of Laertes?
HORATIO. His purse is empty already, all's golden words are spent.   125
HAMLET. Of him, sir.
OSRIC. I know you are not ignorant—
HAMLET. I would you did sir, yet in faith if you did, it would not
   much approve me.° Well, sir.
OSRIC. You are not ignorant of what excellence Laertes is—   130

---

103 *for mine ease*: for my own comfort.   105 *differences*: accomplishments.   107 *card*:
shipman's compass card.   108 *continent . . . see*: (continuing the marine metaphor) (1)
geographical continent (2) all the qualities a gentleman would look for.   109–116 *Sir . . .*
more: (Hamlet outdoes Osric in affected speech).   109 *definement*: description.   *perdition*:
loss.   110 *dozy*: dizzy.   111–112 *yaw . . . sail*: (1) moving in an unsteady course (as
another boat would do, trying to catch up with Laertes' "quick sail") (2) staggering to one
trying to list his accomplishments.   112 *in . . . extolment*: to praise him truthfully.
113 *article*: scope.   *infusion*: essence.   114–116 *as to make . . . more*: to describe him
truly I would have to employ his mirror to depict his only equal—himself, and who would
follow him is only a shadow.   115 *semblable*: equal.   *trace*: (1) describe (2) follow.
116 *umbrage*: shadow.   118 *concernancy*: relevance.   119 *rawer breath*: crude
speech.   121 *Is't not . . . tongue*: cannot Osric understand his own way of speaking when
used by another?   123 *nomination*: naming.   128–129 *if you did . . . me*: if you found
me to be "not ignorant," it would prove little (as you are no judge of ignorance).

HAMLET. I dare not confess that, lest I should compare with him in
  excellence, but to know a man well were to know himself.°
OSRIC. I mean sir for his weapon, but in the imputation° laid on
  him by them in his meed,° he's unfellowed.°
HAMLET. What's his weapon?   135
OSRIC. Rapier and dagger.
HAMLET. That's two of his weapons—but well.
OSRIC. The king sir, hath wagered with him six Barbary horses,
  against which he has impawned,° as I take it, six French
  rapiers and poniards,° with their assigns,° as girdle, hangers,°   140
  and so. Three of the carriages° in faith are very dear to
  fancy,° very responsive to the hilts, most delicate carriages,
  and of very liberal conceit.°
HAMLET. What call you the carriages?
HORATIO. I knew you must be edified by the margent° ere you had   145
  done.
OSRIC. The carriages sir, are the hangers.
HAMLET. The phrase would be more germane to the matter, if we
  could carry a cannon by our sides: I would it might be
  hangers till then, but on: six Barbary horses against six   150
  French swords, their assigns, and three liberal-conceited
  carriages—that's the French bet against the Danish. Why
  is this all "impawned" as you call it?
OSRIC. The king sir, hath laid sir, that in a dozen passes between
  yourself and him, he shall not exceed you three hits°; he   155
  hath laid on twelve for nine, and it would come to
  immediate trial, if your lordship would vouchsafe the
  answer.°
HAMLET. How if I answer no?
OSRIC. I mean my lord, the opposition of your person in trial.   160
HAMLET. Sir, I will walk here in the hall; if it please his majesty, it is
  the breathing time° of day with me; let the foils be brought,
  the gentleman willing, and the king hold his purpose, I
  will win for him an I can, if not, I will gain nothing but my
  shame and the odd hits.   165
OSRIC. Shall I re-deliver you° e'en so?
HAMLET. To this effect sir, after what flourish your nature will.°
OSRIC. I commend° my duty to your lordship.

132 *to know . . . himself*: to know a man well, one must first know oneself.   133 *imputation*:
repute.   134 *meed*: worth.   *unfellowed*: unequalled.   139 *impawned*: staked.
140 *poniards*: daggers.   *assigns*: accessories.   140 *girdle, hangers*: belt, straps attached
thereto, from which swords were hung.   141 *carriages*: hangers.   141–142 *dear to fancy*:
rare in design.   143 *liberal conceit*: elaborate conception.   145 *margent*: marginal note.
154–155 *laid . . . three hits*: wagered that in twelve bouts Laertes must win three more than
Hamlet.   158 *answer*: acceptance of the challenge (Hamlet interprets as "reply").
162 *breathing time*: exercise period.   166 *re-deliver you*: take back your answer.
167 *after . . . will*: embellished as you wish.   168 *commend*: offer (Hamlet interprets
as "praise").

HAMLET.   Yours, yours.   [*Exit OSRIC.*]
   He does well to commend it himself, there are no tongues   1
   else for's turn.°
HORATIO.   This lapwing° runs away with the shell on his head.
HAMLET.   A' did comply° sir, with his dug° before a' sucked it: thus
   has he—and many more of the same bevy that I know the
   drossy° age dotes on—only got the tune of the time, and   1
   out of an habit of encounter,° a kind of yeasty collection,°
   which carries them through and through the most fond
   and winnowed° opinions; and do but blow them to their
   trial, the bubbles are out.°

Enter a LORD.

LORD.   My lord, his majesty commended him to you by young   1
   Osric, who brings back to him that you attend him in
   the hall. He sends to know if your pleasure hold to play
   with Laertes, or that you will take longer time.
HAMLET.   I am constant to my purposes, they follow the king's
   pleasure, if his fitness speaks,° mine is ready: now or   1
   whensoever, provided I be so able as now.
LORD.   The king, and queen, and all are coming down.
HAMLET.   In happy time.
LORD.   The queen desires you to use some gentle entertainment°
   to Laertes, before you fall to play.   1
HAMLET.   She well instructs me.   [*Exit LORD.*]
HORATIO.   You will lose this wager, my lord.
HAMLET.   I do not think so, since he went into France, I have been in
   continual practice, I shall win at the odds; but thou
   wouldst not think how ill all's here about my heart: but it   1
   is no matter.
HORATIO.   Nay good my lord—
HAMLET.   It is but foolery, but it is such a kind of gaingiving° as
   would perhaps trouble a woman.
HORATIO.   If your mind dislike any thing, obey it. I will forestall their 2
   repair° hither, and say you are not fit.
HAMLET.   Not a whit, we defy augury;° there is special providence
   in the fall of a sparrow.° If it be now, 'tis not to come:
   if it be not to come, it will be now; if it be not now,

170–171 *no tongues . . . turn*: no others who would.   172 *lapwing*: (reported to be so
precocious that it ran as soon as hatched).   173 *comply*: observe the formalities of
courtesy.   *dug*: mother's breast.   175 *drossy*: frivolous.   176 *habit of encounter*: habitual
association (with others as frivolous).   176 *yeasty collection*: frothy assortment of phrases.
177–178 *fond and winnowed*: trivial and considered.   178–179 *blow . . . out*: blow on them
to test them and they are gone.   185 *his fitness speaks*: it agrees with his convenience.
189 *gentle entertainment*: friendly treatment.   198 *gaingiving*: misgiving.   201 *repair*:
coming.   202 *augury*: omens.   202–203 *special . . . sparrow*: ("Are not two sparrows
sold for a farthing? and one of them shall not fall on the ground without your Father":
Matthew 10:29).

yet it will come—the readiness is all. Since no man has   205
aught of what he leaves, what is't to leave betimes?° let
be.

A table prepared. Trumpets. Drums, and officers with cushions. Enter KING, QUEEN, *and
all the state*, [OSRIC], *foils, daggers, and* LAERTES.

KING.   Come Hamlet, come and take this hand from me.
   [*Puts Laertes' hand into Hamlet's.*]
HAMLET.   Give me your pardon sir, I have done you wrong,
   But pardon't as you are a gentleman.   210
   This presence knows, and you must needs have heard,
   How I am punished with a sore distraction.°
   What I have done
   That might your nature, honour, and exception°
   Roughly awake, I here proclaim was madness: 215
   Was't Hamlet wronged Laertes? never Hamlet.
   If Hamlet from himself be ta'en away,
   And when he's not himself, does wrong Laertes,
   Then Hamlet does it not, Hamlet denies it:
   Who does it then? his madness. If't be so,   220
   Hamlet is of the faction that is wronged,
   His madness is poor Hamlet's enemy.
   Sir, in this audience,
   Let my disclaiming from a purposed evil,
   Free me so far in your most generous thoughts,   225
   That I have shot my arrow o'er the house
   And hurt my brother.°
LAERTES.   I am satisfied in nature,
   Whose motive in this case should stir me most
   To my revenge, but in my terms of honour
   I stand aloof, and will no reconcilement,   230
   Till by some elder masters of known honour
   I have a voice and precedent° of peace
   To keep my name ungored:° but till that time,
   I do receive your offered love, like love,
   And will not wrong it.
HAMLET.   I embrace it freely,   235
   And will this brother's wager frankly° play.
   Give us the foils: come on.
LAERTES.   Come, one for me.
HAMLET.   I'll be your foil° Laertes, in mine ignorance

---

206 *betimes*: early (before one's time).   212 *sore distraction*: grievous madness.
214 *exception*: disapproval.   226–227 *That I have . . . brother*: (that it was
accidental).   232 *voice and precedent*: opinion based on precedent.   233 *name ungored*:
reputation uninjured.   236 *frankly*: freely.   238 *foil*: (1) the blunted sword with which
they fence (2) leaf of metal set under a jewel to make it shine more brilliantly.

Your skill shall like a star i'th' darkest night
Stick fiery off° indeed.   2

LAERTES.   You mock me sir.

HAMLET. No, by this hand.

KING. Give them the foils young Osric. Cousin° Hamlet,
You know the wager.

HAMLET.   Very well my lord.
Your grace has laid the odds o'th'weaker side.

KING. I do not fear it, I have seen you both,   2
But since he is bettered,° we have therefore odds.

LAERTES. This is too heavy: let me see another.°

HAMLET. This likes° me well, these foils have all a° length?

OSRIC. Ay my good lord.   *Prepare to play*.   2

KING. Set me the stoups° of wine upon that table: 2
If Hamlet give the first or second hit,
Or quit in answer of° the third exchange,
Let all the battlements their ordnance fire.
The king shall drink to Hamlet's better breath,
And in the cup an union° shall he throw,   2.
Richer than that which four successive kings
In Denmark's crown have worn: give me the cups,
And let the kettle° to the trumpet speak,
The trumpet to the cannoneer without,
The cannons to the heavens, the heaven to earth,   2
"Now the king drinks to Hamlet." Come begin.
And you the judges bear a wary eye.   *Trumpets the while*.

HAMLET. Come on sir.

LAERTES.   Come my lord.   *They play*.

HAMLET.   One.

LAERTES.   No.

HAMLET.   Judgment.

OSRIC. A hit, a very palpable hit.

                    Flourish. Drum, trumpets and shot. A piece° goes off.

LAERTES.   Well, again.

KING. Stay, give me drink. Hamlet, this pearl is thine.   2
Here's to thy health: give him the cup.

HAMLET. I'll play this bout first, set it by a while.
Come.   [*They play*.]

                    Another hit. What say you?

LAERTES. A touch, a touch, I do confess't.

---

240 *Stick fiery off*: show in shining contrast.   242 *Cousin*: kinsman.   246 *bettered*: either
(a) judged to be better, or (b) better trained.   247 *another*: (the unbated and poisoned
sword).   248 *likes*: pleases.   *all a*: all the same.   250 *stoups*: goblets.   252 *quit in
answer of*: score a draw in.   255 *union*: large pearl.   258 *kettle*: kettle drum.   264
stage direction *piece*: i.e., a cannon.

KING.   Our son shall win.
QUEEN.   He's fat° and scant of breath.   270
    Here Hamlet, take my napkin,° rub thy brows.   [*She takes Hamlet's cup.*]
    The queen carouses° to thy fortune, Hamlet.
HAMLET.   Good madam.
KING.   Gertrude, do not drink.
QUEEN.   I will my lord, I pray you pardon me.
KING.   [*Aside.*] It is the poisoned cup, it is too late.   275
HAMLET.   I dare not drink yet madam: by and by.
QUEEN.   Come, let me wipe thy face.
LAERTES.   [*To the King.*] My lord, I'll hit him now.
KING.   I do not think't.
LAERTES.   [*Aside.*] And yet 'tis almost 'gainst my conscience.
HAMLET.   Come for the third Laertes, you do but dally,   280
    I pray you pass° with your best violence,
    I am afeard you make a wanton of me.°
LAERTES.   Say you so? Come on.   *Play.*
OSRIC.   Nothing neither way.   [*They break off.*]
LAERTES.   Have at you now.°   [*Wounds Hamlet.*]

                  In scuffling they change rapiers.

KING.   Part them, they are incensed.   285
HAMLET.   Nay, come again.   [*The Queen falls.*]
OSRIC.   Look to the queen there, ho!

                  [*Hamlet wounds Laertes.*]

HORATIO.   They bleed on both sides. How is it, my lord?
OSRIC.   How is't, Laertes?
LAERTES.   Why as a woodcock° to my own springe,° Osric,
    I am justly killed with mine own treachery.   290
HAMLET.   How does the queen?
KING.   She sounds° to see them bleed.
QUEEN.   No, no, the drink, the drink, O my dear Hamlet,
    The drink, the drink, I am poisoned.   [*Dies.*]
HAMLET.   O villainy! ho! let the door be locked,
    Treachery, seek it out!   295
LAERTES.   It is here Hamlet. Hamlet, thou art slain,
    No medicine in the world can do thee good,
    In thee there is not half an hour of life,
    The treacherous instrument is in thy hand,
    Unbated° and envenomed. The foul practice°   300

---

270 *fat*: sweating (sweat was thought to be melted body fat).   271 *napkin*: handkerchief.
272 *carouses*: drinks.   281 *pass*: thrust.   282 *make a wanton of me*: are indulging me like
a spoiled child.   285 *Have . . now*: (the bout is over when Laertes attacks Hamlet and
catches him off guard).   289 *woodcock*: snipe-like bird (believed to be foolish and therefore
easily trapped).   *springe*: trap.   291 *sounds*: swoons.   300 *Unbated*: not blunted.
practice: plot.

Hath turned itself on me, lo, here I lie
Never to rise again: thy mother's poisoned:
I can no more: the king, the king's to blame.

HAMLET.   The point envenomed too:
Then venom, to thy work.   *Hurts the King.*   30.

ALL.   Treason! treason!

KING.   O yet defend me friends, I am but hurt.°

HAMLET.   Here, thou incestuous, murderous, damnèd Dane,
Drink off this potion: is thy union here?
Follow my mother.   *King dies.*

LAERTES.   He is justly served,   31.
It is a poison tempered° by himself:
Exchange forgiveness with me, noble Hamlet,
Mine and my father's death come not upon thee,°
Nor thine on me.   *Dies.*

HAMLET.   Heaven make thee free° of it, I follow thee.   31
I am dead, Horatio; wretched queen, adieu.
You that look pale, and tremble at this chance,
That are but mutes,° or audience to this act,
Had I but time, as this fell sergeant° Death
Is strict in his arrest, O I could tell you—   32.
But let it be; Horatio, I am dead,
Thou livest, report me and my cause aright
To the unsatisfied.°

HORATIO.   Never believe it;
I am more an antique Roman° than a Dane:
Here's yet some liquor left.

HAMLET.   As thou'rt a man,   32
Give me the cup, let go, by heaven I'll ha't.
O God, Horatio, what a wounded name,
Things standing thus unknown, shall live behind me.
If thou didst ever hold me in thy heart,
Absènt thee from felicity awhile,   33.
And in this harsh world draw thy breath in pain
To tell my story.   *A march afar off, and shot within.*
          What warlike noise is this?

OSRIC.   Young Fortinbras with conquest come from Poland,
To th'ambassadors of England gives
This warlike volley.

HAMLET.   O I die Horatio,   33.
The potent poison quite o'er-crows° my spirit,
I cannot live to hear the news from England,
But I do prophesy th'election° lights

---

307 *but hurt*: only wounded.   311 *tempered*: mixed.   313 *come . . . thee*: are not to be
blamed on you.   315 *free*: guiltless.   318 *mutes*: actors without speaking parts.
319 *fell sergeant*: cruel sheriff's officer.   323 *unsatisfied*: uninformed.   324 *antique Roman*:
ancient Roman (who considered suicide honorable).   336 *o'er-crows*: overpowers,
conquers.   338 *election*: (for king of Denmark).

On Fortinbras, he has my dying voice,°
So tell him, with th'occurrents more and less°   340
Which have solicited°—the rest is silence.   *Dies*.

HORATIO.   Now cracks a noble heart: good night sweet prince,
And flights of angels sing thee to thy rest.
Why does the drum come hither?

Enter FORTINBRAS and English Ambassadors, with drum, colours, and attendants.

FORTINBRAS.   Where is this sight?
HORATIO.   What is it you would see?   345
If aught of woe, or wonder, cease your search.
FORTINBRAS.   This quarry cries on havoc.° O proud death,
What feast is toward° in thine eternal cell,
That thou so many princes at a shot
So bloodily hast struck?   350
AMBASSADOR.   The sight is dismal,
And our affairs from England come too late;
The ears° are senseless that should give us hearing,
To tell him his commandment is fulfilled,
That Rosencrantz and Guildenstern are dead:
Where should we have our thanks?
HORATIO.   Not from his mouth,   355
Had it th'ability of life to thank you;
He never gave commandment for their death;
But since so jump° upon this bloody question,
You from the Polack wars, and you from England
Are here arrived, give order that these bodies   360
High on a stage be placèd to the view,
And let me speak to th'yet unknowing world
How these things came about; so shall you hear
Of carnal, bloody and unnatural acts,
Of accidental judgments, casual° slaughters,   365
Of deaths put on° by cunning and forced cause,°
And in this upshot, purposes mistook,
Fall'n on th'inventors' heads:° all this can I
Truly deliver.
FORTINBRAS.   Let us haste to hear it,
And call the noblest to the audience.   370
For me, with sorrow I embrace my fortune;
I have some rights of memory° in this kingdom,
Which now to claim my vantage° doth invite me.

---

339 *voice*: vote.   340 *occurrents more and less*: events great and small.   341 *solicited*: incited me.   347 *quarry . . . havoc*: heap of dead bodies proclaims slaughter done here. 348 *toward*: in preparation.   352 *ears*: (of Claudius).   358 *jump*: opportunely. 365 *casual*: unpremeditated.   366 *put on*: prompted by.   *forced cause*: being forced to act in self-defense.   367–368 *purposes . . . heads*: plots gone wrong and destroying their inventors.   372 *of memory*: remembered.   373 *vantage*: advantageous position.

HORATIO.   Of that I shall have also cause to speak,
And from his mouth whose voice will draw on more:°   37⁵
But let this same° be presently performed,
Even while men's minds are wild,° lest more mischance
On° plots and errors happen.
FORTINBRAS.   Let four captains
Bear Hamlet like a soldier to the stage,
For he was likely, had he been put on,°   38(
To have proved most royal; and for his passage,°
The soldiers' music and the rite of war
Speak loudly for him:
Take up the bodies, such a sight as this,
Becomes the field, but here shows much amiss.   38⁵
Go bid the soldiers shoot.

Exeunt marching: after the which a peal of ordnance are shot off.

375 *draw on more*: influence more (votes).   376 *this same*: this telling of the story.
377 *wild*: upset.   378 *On*: on top of.   380 *put on*: i.e., the throne.   381 *passage*:
i.e., to the next world.

QUESTIONS

Act 1

1. Discuss the various ways in which the first scene of *Hamlet* shows you that
   something is wrong in Denmark.
2. What impression does Claudius make in scene 2? Does he seem to be a
   rational man? A good administrator? A competent ruler? A loving husband
   and uncle?
3. What does Hamlet reveal about his own mental state in his first soliloquy?
4. What attitude toward Ophelia's relationship with Hamlet do Laertes and
   Polonius share? What do they want Ophelia to do? Why?
5. What does the ghost tell Hamlet? What does the ghost want Hamlet to do?
   What does the ghost tell Hamlet not to do? Why does Hamlet need proof
   that the ghost is telling the truth?

Act 2

6. What does Polonius think is the cause of Hamlet's madness? What do Polonius's diagnosis and his handling of the situation show us about him?
7. What does Hamlet accuse himself of in the soliloquy that begins "O what
   a rogue and peasant slave am I" (2.2.524–580)? To what extent is his self-
   accusation justified?

Act 3

8. How do you react to Hamlet's treatment of Ophelia in the first scene of act 3? What evidence might indicate that Hamlet know that Claudius and Polonius are watching and listening to everything that occurs?

9. Hamlet sets up the performance of "The Murder of Gonzago"—the play-within-a-play—to test Claudius's guilt. What is the relationship between the events of this play-within-a-play and the events of *Hamlet*?

10. How does Claudius react to "The Murder of Gonzago"? What does this reaction tell Hamlet about Claudius? Why do you suppose Claudius did not react to the dumb show presented at the beginning of the play-within-a-play?

11. What reason does Hamlet give for not killing Claudius while the king is praying?

12. How does Hamlet treat his mother during their confrontation in her closet? Is Hamlet's behavior overly nasty or justified? Why does the ghost reappear during this confrontation?

13. What crimes or sins does Hamlet accuse Gertrude of committing?

Act 4

14. Do you think Laertes's desire to avenge his father's murder is any more or less justified than Hamlet's desire?

15. How does Claudius plan to use Laertes's desire for revenge to manipulate him? To what extent does Laertes unwittingly allow himself to be used by Claudius?

Act 5

16. The conversation between the two clowns (grave-diggers) and between Hamlet and the first clown is seen as comic relief—a humorous episode designed to ease the tension. Why is a scene of comic relief appropriate at this point?

17. How does this scene of comic relief reflect and broaden the themes of the play?

18. Why does Hamlet describe Osric as a "water-fly"? How does Shakespeare use Osric's language and behavior to characterize him?

19. Discuss the lessons that Hamlet tells Horatio he has learned about life. How does this understanding change Hamlet? Why is it ironic?

20. How is Gertrude killed? Hamlet? Laertes? Claudius? Why does Hamlet insist that Horatio not commit suicide?

TOPICS FOR WRITING AND FURTHER DISCUSSION

1. Discuss the character of Claudius. Do you consider him purely evil or merely a flawed human? Why? To what degree can you justify calling this play "The Tragedy of Claudius, King of Denmark"?

2. How would you characterize Horatio? Why does Hamlet admire and trust him? How is he different from Polonius or Rosencrantz and Guildenstern?

3. Describe Rosencrantz and Guildenstern. Are they round or flat characters? How does Claudius use them? Why do they cooperate with Claudius? How does Hamlet arrange their deaths? To what extent can this action be justified?

4. Evaluate Polonius's character. Is he a wise counselor? A fool? Sincere? Self-serving? Hypocritical? What are his motives? How is he like Rosencrantz and Guildenstern? How is his death like their deaths?

5. Consider the degree to which the two women in the play—Gertrude and Ophelia—justify Hamlet's assertion that "Frailty, thy name is woman."

6. Hamlet, Laertes, and Fortinbras are all young men whose fathers have been killed and who set out to do something about those deaths. Their courses of action, however, are very different. Contrast the ways in which each goes about dealing with his father's death. Which approach seems most rational? Most emotional? Most effective?

7. *Hamlet* is full of conflicts that oppose people to other people, to society, and to themselves. List all the conflicts you can find in the play. Decide which of these is the central conflict, and explain your choice.

8. What is the crisis of *Hamlet*? When does it occur? Who does it affect? What is the catastrophe? The resolution?

9. In Act 4, Claudius notes that "sorrows come . . . in battalions." By the end of the play these sorrows include the deaths of Polonius, Rosencrantz, Guildenstern, Ophelia, Laertes, Gertrude, Claudius, and Hamlet. To what degree can Claudius be held responsible for all the sorrows of the play? Which sorrows are primarily Hamlet's responsibility?

10. Early in the play Hamlet makes a clear distinction between what "seems" to be and what actually is. To what extent does this distinction between appearance and reality run through the whole play? Which characters are not what they seem to be?

11. Is *Hamlet* a tragedy of state as well as a tragedy of the individual? What condition is Denmark in at the beginning of the play? Is the condition better or worse at the end?

THE THEATER OF ARTHUR MILLER

When we shift to the twentieth century and the theater of Arthur Miller, we abandon the masks of the Greek theater and the soliloquies of the Elizabethan stage for drama that is a mixture of realism and nonrealism (see pp. 1502–07). By **realistic drama,** we mean plays that present an image of the world as we know it. This world is populated by salesmen, workers, bankers, housewives, lawyers, and thieves instead of kings, revengers, and soothsayers. In addition, these plays are spoken in the colloquial language of our own lives instead of in choric odes or Shakespearean blank verse.

With the movement into realism, which occurred at the end of the nineteenth century, the drama required both a theater and a stage that could accommodate plays reflecting middle-class lives and values. Thus, the theater became the now familiar darkened auditorium in which we sit in rows and face a proscenium arch and a vast curtain that separate us from the acting areas. When the curtain rises, we often see a room we might actually live in or visit. This **box set** signals an attempt to make settings look as much like the real world as possible.

Throughout the twentieth century, the box set has become progressively more sophisticated as modern technology has combined with the theatrical arts. Stage settings have been embellished with the full range of sound and lighting effects available to the modern playwright or director. This technological revolution has been especially significant in the area of lighting. The lighting in modern productions is managed by a (now computerized) switchboard that can be programmed to control hundreds or even thousands of individual lights in any combination and at any intensity. Thus, lighting can be used to establish distinct times, places, moods, atmospheres, and effects. It can also divide the stage or a unit set into a number of different acting areas simply by illuminating one section and darkening the rest. As a result, lighting has almost become an element of set design. This is especially true in plays where the dramatist describes the use of scrim in his or her settings. **Scrim** is a transparent curtain on which a scene, wall, or the like may be painted. When the scrim is illuminated from the front, it appears to be solid. When lit from behind, however, it becomes transparent, and another setting or stage action may be seen through it.

More recently, playwrights and theatrical designers have moved beyond the box set to experiments with stages and sets that draw their inspiration from earlier theatrical ages. Since the 1940s, theatrical designers have often eliminated both the proscenium arch and the curtain and built stages based on classical, medieval, or Elizabethan models. Thus, we find classical Greek and Roman staging reflected in contemporary **arena stages** and medieval staging imitated in **theater in the round.** Similarly, many newer theaters offer a modified thrust stage loosely based on the model of the Elizabethan public theaters. Miller's *Death of a Salesman*, for example, utilizes elements of the traditional box set combined with a thrust stage in the form of an extended *apron* that projects from the forestage.

Realistic plays called for an acting style that was equally realistic and true to life. The ranting and gesturing of the Elizabethan actor became inappropriate, as did the declamatory and flamboyant acting of the nineteenth century. A realistic acting style was initially developed in Russia at the beginning of the twentieth century under the direction of Constantin Stanislavsky, who advocated that actors and actresses undergo a combination of traditional training and psychological preparation in rehearsing a specific role. When Stanislavsky's ideas were introduced in the United States in the 1920s and 1930s, his views were distorted, and only the psychological preparation was emphasized. Under the leadership of directors like Lee Strasberg, American theatrical groups like the Group Theater and The Actors' Studio developed a style based on Stanislavsky's work that is now called **method acting.** In method acting the player is asked to submerge himself or herself completely in the role and to draw on personal experiences and emotions to make the performance more psychologically realistic.

ARTHUR MILLER, *DEATH OF A SALESMAN*

Arthur Miller, one of the dominant American playwrights of the 1940s and 1950s, was born in New York City in 1915 and educated at the University of Michigan, where he wrote and staged his first plays. His early dramas include *The Man Who Had All the Luck* (1944), *All My Sons* (1947), *Death of a Salesman* (1949), *An Enemy of the People* (1951, an adaptation of a play by Henrik Ibsen), *The Crucible* (1953), and *A View from the Bridge* (1955). Many of these combine Miller's interests in family relationships and social issues. *All My Sons*, for instance, explores the relationship between Joe Keller, a war profiteer who allowed damaged engines to be put into U.S. military aircraft, and his son Chris, an army pilot returning home from World War II. The play also investigates Joe Keller's guilt and his emerging realization that the pilots who died because of his faulty engines were "all my sons." These sorts of thematic concerns reveal the extent to which Miller was influenced by Henrik Ibsen (see p. 1507). Miller's later work includes *The Misfits* (1961, a screenplay), *After the Fall* (1964), *Incident at Vichy* (1964), *The Price* (1968), and *The Archbishop's Ceiling* (1976).

Death of a Salesman, which opened on February 10, 1949 in New York City, is similar to both *Oedipus* and the traditional *well-made play* (see p. 1508) in several respects. For one thing, it dramatizes the end of a much longer story. The stage action in the present (in Acts 1 and 2) covers about twenty-four hours, from Monday evening to Tuesday evening. The story, however, goes back as far as Willy Loman's childhood, and Willy's memories of past events constantly impose themselves on the present. Additionally, at least one of the central conflicts stems from a secret known only to Willy and his son, Biff, but withheld from the rest of the characters and from us for most of the play. This secret, however, is not the linchpin of the play, as it would be in a *well-made play*.

In writing a tragedy about the struggles and failures of Willy Loman, Miller effectively redefines the nature of the tragic protagonist. In a *New York Times* essay published several weeks after the Broadway opening of the play, Miller argued that "the common man is as apt a subject for tragedy in its highest sense as kings were."[3] He asserted that tragedy springs from the individual's quest for a proper place in the world and from his readiness "to lay down his life, if need be, to secure one thing—his sense of personal dignity." Willy is certainly flawed: he is weak, dishonest, and self-deluded. But Miller links his protagonist's *hamartia* with this quest for dignity: "the flaw or crack in the character is really nothing . . . but his inherent unwillingness to remain passive in the face of what he conceives to be a challenge to his dignity, his image of his rightful status."

Willy Loman fights for status and dignity on two fronts: the family and the wider world of American business. The conflict within the family focuses on his relationship with his older son, Biff. In this conflict, the central scene is Willy's long-suppressed memory of Biff's discovery that his father is a "fake" and a "phony." This realization produces a lifetime of alienation, and leads Biff to abandon his father's dreams of success for him. The action of this conflict has a clear *anagnorisis* and resolution for both men. Biff realizes that he does not need the traditional pattern of white-collar success; he will be happy working with his hands. Similarly, Willy comes to understand that Biff actually loves him.

Willy's other struggle for dignity and status is fought in the arena of business and in the context of the success ethic and the American dream. The play presents four different versions of this American dream: the inventor-entrepreneur, the athlete-businessman, the pioneer-exploiter, and the salesman. Each of these versions is represented in the play by allusions to real people or by characters from Willy's memory. The inventor-entrepreneur, for example, is evoked by references to Thomas Edison and B. F. Goodrich, and the athlete-businessman by allusions to heavyweight boxing champion Gene Tunney and football star Red Grange. The pioneer-exploiter is embodied in Willy's distorted memories of his father and his older brother, Ben. The successful salesman version of the American dream is represented by Dave Singleman, a figure whom Willy speaks about to his boss during the crucial scene in which Willy tries to get a job in the home office of his company (p. 1331):

> Old Dave, he'd go up to his room, y'understand, put on his green velvet slippers—I'll never forget—and pick up his phone and call the buyers, and without ever leaving his room, at the age of eighty-four, he made his living. And when I saw that, I realized that selling was the greatest career a man could want.

[3] "Tragedy and the Common Man," *The New York Times*, February 27, 1949, sec. 2, p. 1.

All four versions of the American dream reduce to a single formula: dignity and status are derived from success, and success is measured by wealth. Willy, of course, fails to live up to the American dream as a father, a husband, or a businessman.

Loman's pursuit of the success ethic and the American dream through salesmanship means that he must sell himself (or an image of himself) to himself and to others. Throughout the play Willy espouses the values and techniques implicit in this American dream of selling one's way to fame and fortune. More to the point, he mistakenly attributes to himself and his sons those qualities and characteristics that he believes make for a successful salesman: attractiveness, personality, luck, telling a good story, making a good appearance, and being well liked. All these qualities—like the idea of selling itself—depend, to a large extent, on the creation of false images. This fact, in turn, suggests that the American dream itself might be illusory or corrupt.

Death of a Salesman is constructed primarily from Willy Loman's point of view. Miller originally wanted to call it "The Inside of His Head," and his initial vision was of "an enormous face the height of the proscenium arch that would appear and open up, and we would see the inside of a man's head."[4] The play contains two different types of time and action: real and remembered. Present events are enacted and described as realistically as possible. Such action, however, often triggers Willy's memory, and past events intrude on the present. Sometimes, these past events occur simultaneously with present action; thus, in Act 1 Willy can speak with his own memory of his dead brother and play cards with Charley at the same time. At other times, the images of past events take over the play completely, although Willy continues to exist in the present. Willy's past is always with him, shaping the way he reacts to the present. In addition, past events emerge from Willy's memory with the distortions and exaggerations that we would expect from such a subjective point of view. Thus, the "memory" characters—especially Ben and the Woman in Boston— are flat and symbolic rather than realistic.

Like the acting of past events, the setting of *Death of a Salesman* is symbolic and nonrealistic (see p. 1507). It is designed to allow fluid transitions between present and past and to facilitate the overlapping of current action and memory. The Loman house is a skeletal framework with three rooms (or acting areas) on three different levels: the kitchen, the sons' bedroom, and Willy's bedroom. The forestage and apron are used for all scenes away from the house and for "memory" scenes. In the present, the house is hemmed in by apartment houses and lit with an "angry glow of orange," thus suggesting that Willy's present existence is claustrophobic

---

[4] Arthur Miller, "Introduction to the Collected Plays," *Arthur Miller's Collected Plays* (New York: Viking, 1957), p. 23.

and urbanized. When memory takes over, however, the apartment houses disappear (a trick of lighting) and the orange glow gives way to pastoral colors and the shadows of leaves.

Death of a Salesman is very much about dreams, illusions, and self-deception. Dreams pervade Willy's life, his conversation, his family, and his house. The central dream (and illusion) is the American dream of success and wealth through selling the self. This dream is recapitulated in a series of smaller dreams (illusions, lies) that Willy and his sons build out of thin air. Throughout the play, these dreams are destroyed when confronted with reality. Willy's dream of a "New York City job" and a weekly salary, for example, collides with reality in his disastrous encounter with his younger and insensitive boss. Only Linda escapes the tyranny of dreams and "hot air." While she serves and supports Willy completely, she remains firmly planted in the reality of house payments, insurance premiums, and her husband's need for dignity and "attention" as his world falls apart.

We are left, at the end of the play, with a number of questions about the degree to which Willy recognizes and understands the corruption and the illusory nature of the American dream, his own dreams, and his self-image. He does achieve some flashes of insight. He understands, for example, that he has run out of lies and has nothing left to sell: "I haven't got a story left in my head" (p. 1346). He also understands—according to Miller—his own corruption and alienation from true values:

> Had Willy been unaware of his separation from values that endure he would have died contentedly while polishing his car. . . . But he was agonized by

Billy Rose Theatre Collection, The New York Public Library at Lincoln Center; Astor, Lenox and Tilden Foundations.

his awareness of being in a false position, so constantly haunted by the hollowness of all he had placed his faith in, so aware, in short, that he must somehow be filled with his spirit or fly apart, that he staked his life on the ultimate assertion.[5]

Yet at the end of the play, Willy is still in the grip of delusions of glory for Biff and for himself. He imagines that his insurance money will make Biff "magnificent." Similarly, he dreams that his funeral will be massive: "They'll come from Maine, Massachusetts, Vermont, New Hampshire. All the old timers with the strange license plates—that boy [Biff] will be thunderstruck, Ben, because he never realized—I am known!" (p. 1356) Both visions are delusions: Biff has already abandoned the business world, and the funeral is attended by only five people. In the Requiem at the end of the play Biff expresses his own understanding that Willy's dreams were delusions and lies: "He had all the wrong dreams. All, all wrong" (p. 1362). Charley defends Willy: "A salesman is got to dream, boy. It comes with the territory." Only Happy remains trapped in selfishness and his own petty version of Willy's dream: "I'm gonna beat this racket! . . . The Loman Brothers! . . . He had a good dream. It's the only dream you can have—to come out number-one man."

Arthur Miller (b. 1915)

Death of a Salesman   *1949*

CHARACTERS

Willy Loman
Linda, *his wife*
Biff ⎱ *his sons*
Happy ⎰
Uncle Ben
Charley
Bernard
The Woman
Howard Wagner
Jenny
Stanley
Miss Forsythe
Letta

The action takes place in WILLY LOMAN'S house and yard and in various places he visits in the New York and Boston of today.

---

[5] *Ibid.* pp. 34–35.

ACT 1

A melody is heard, played upon a flute. It is small and fine, telling of grass and trees and the horizon. The curtain rises.

Before us is the Salesman's house. We are aware of towering, angular shapes behind it, surrounding it on all sides. Only the blue light of the sky falls upon the house and forestage; the surrounding area shows an angry glow of orange. As more light appears, we see a solid vault of apartment houses around the small, fragile-seeming home. An air of the dream clings to the place, a dream rising out of reality. The kitchen at center seems actual enough, for there is a kitchen table with three chairs, and a refrigerator. But no other fixtures are seen. At the back of the kitchen there is a draped entrance, which leads to the living-room. To the right of the kitchen, on a level raised two feet, is a bedroom furnished only with a brass bedstead and a straight chair. On a shelf over the bed a silver athletic trophy stands. A window opens onto the apartment house at the side.

Behind the kitchen, on a level raised six and a half feet, is the boys' bedroom, at present barely visible. Two beds are dimly seen, and at the back of the room a dormer window. (This bedroom is above the unseen living-room.) At the left a stairway curves up to it from the kitchen.

The entire setting is wholly or, in some places, partially transparent. The roof-line of the house is one-dimensional; under and over it we see the apartment buildings. Before the house lies an apron, curving beyond the forestage into the orchestra. This forward area serves as the back yard as well as the locale of all WILLY'S *imaginings and of his city scenes. Whenever the action is in the present the actors observe the imaginary wall-lines, entering the house only through its door at the left. But in the scenes of the past these boundaries are broken, and characters enter or leave a room by stepping "through" a wall onto the forestage.*

[From the right, WILLY LOMAN, *The Salesman, enters, carrying two large sample cases. The flute plays on. He hears but is not aware of it. He is past sixty years of age, dressed quietly. Even as he crosses the stage to the doorway of the house, his exhaustion is apparent. He unlocks the door, comes into the kiTChen, and thankfully lets his burden down, feeling the soreness of his palms. A word-sigh escapes his lips—it might be "Oh, boy, oh, boy." He closes the door, then carries his cases out into the living-room, through the draped kitchen doorway.]*

*[*LINDA, *his wife, has stirred in her bed at the right. She gets out and puts on a robe, listening. Most often jovial, she has developed an iron repression of her exceptions to* WILLY'S *behavior—she more than loves him, she admires him, as though his mercurial nature, his temper, his massive dreams and little cruelties, served her only as sharp reminders of the turbulent longings within him, longings which she shares but lacks the temperament to utter and follow to their end.]*

LINDA.   [*hearing* WILLY *outside the bedroom, calls with some trepidation*] Willy!

WILLY.   It's all right. I came back.

LINDA.   Why? What happened? [*slight pause*] Did something happen, Willy?

WILLY.   No, nothing happened.

LINDA.   You didn't smash the car, did you?

WILLY.   [*with casual irritation*] I said nothing happened. Didn't you hear me?

LINDA.   Don't you feel well?

WILLY.   I'm tired to the death. [*The flute has faded away. He sits on the bed beside her, a little numb.*] I couldn't make it. I just couldn't make it, Linda.

LINDA. [*very carefully, delicately*] Where were you all day? You look terrible.

WILLY. I got as far as a little above Yonkers.° I stopped for a cup of coffee. Maybe it was the coffee.

LINDA. What?

WILLY. [*after a pause*] I suddenly couldn't drive any more. The car kept going off onto the shoulder, y'know?

LINDA. [*helpfully*] Oh. Maybe it was the steering again. I don't think Angelo knows the Studebaker.

WILLY. No, it's me, it's me. Suddenly I realize I'm goin' sixty miles an hour and I don't remember the last five minutes. I'm—I can't seem to—keep my mind to it.

LINDA. Maybe it's your glasses. You never went for your new glasses.

WILLY. No, I see everything. I came back ten miles an hour. It took me nearly four hours from Yonkers.

LINDA. [*resigned*] Well, you'll just have to take a rest, Willy, you can't continue this way.

WILLY. I just got back from Florida.

LINDA. But you didn't rest your mind. Your mind is overactive, and the mind is what counts, dear.

WILLY. I'll start out in the morning. Maybe I'll feel better in the morning. [*She is taking off his shoes.*] These goddam arch supports are killing me.

LINDA. Take an aspirin. Should I get you an aspirin? It'll soothe you.

WILLY. [*with wonder*] I was driving along, you understand? And I was fine. I was even observing the scenery. You can imagine, me looking at scenery, on the road every week of my life. But it's so beautiful up there, Linda, the trees are so thick, and the sun is warm. I opened the windshield and just let the warm air bathe over me. And then all of a sudden I'm goin' off the road! I'm tellin' ya, I absolutely forgot I was driving. If I'd've gone the other way over the white line I might've killed somebody. So I went on again—and five minutes later I'm dreamin' again, and I nearly— [*He presses two fingers against his eyes.*] I have such thoughts, I have such strange thoughts.

LINDA. Willy, dear. Talk to them again. There's no reason why you can't work in New York.

WILLY. They don't need me in New York. I'm the New England man. I'm vital in New England.

LINDA. But you're sixty years old. They can't expect you to keep traveling every week.

WILLY. I'll have to send a wire to Portland. I'm supposed to see Brown and Morrison tomorrow morning at ten o'clock to show the line. Goddammit, I could sell them! [*He starts putting on his jacket.*]

LINDA. [*taking the jacket from him*] Why don't you go down to the place tomorrow and tell Howard you've simply got to work in New York? You're too accommodating, dear.

° *Yonkers*: a city in southeastern New York State about thirty miles northeast of Brooklyn, the part of New York City in which Willy lives.

WILLY.   If old man Wagner was alive I'd a been in charge of New York now! That man was a prince, he was a masterful man. But that boy of his, that Howard, he don't appreciate. When I went north the first time, the Wagner Company didn't know where New England was!

LINDA.   Why don't you tell those things to Howard, dear?

WILLY.   [*encouraged*] I will, I definitely will. Is there any cheese?

LINDA.   I'll make you a sandwich.

WILLY.   No, go to sleep. I'll take some milk. I'll be up right away. The boys in?

LINDA.   They're sleeping. Happy took Biff on a date tonight.

WILLY.   [*interested*] That so?

LINDA.   It was so nice to see them shaving together, one behind the other, in the bathroom. And going out together. You notice? The whole house smells of shaving lotion.

WILLY.   Figure it out. Work a lifetime to pay off a house. You finally own it, and there's nobody to live in it.

LINDA.   Well, dear, life is a casting off. It's always that way.

WILLY.   No, no, some people—some people accomplish something. Did Biff say anything after I went this morning?

LINDA.   You shouldn't have criticized him, Willy, especially after he just got off the train. You mustn't lose your temper with him.

WILLY.   When the hell did I lose my temper? I simply asked him if he was making any money. Is that a criticism?

LINDA.   But, dear, how could he make any money?

WILLY.   [*worried and angered*] There's such an undercurrent in him. He became a moody man. Did he apologize when I left this morning?

LINDA.   He was crestfallen, Willy. You know how he admires you. I think if he finds himself, then you'll both be happier and not fight any more.

WILLY.   How can he find himself on a farm? Is that a life? A farmhand? In the beginning, when he was young, I thought, well, a young man, it's good for him to tramp around, take a lot of different jobs. But it's more than ten years now and he has yet to make thirty-five dollars a week!

LINDA.   He's finding himself, Willy.

WILLY.   Not finding yourself at the age of thirty-four is a disgrace!

LINDA.   Shh!

WILLY.   The trouble is he's lazy, goddammit!

LINDA.   Willy, please!

WILLY.   Biff is a lazy bum!

LINDA.   They're sleeping. Get something to eat. Go on down.

WILLY.   Why did he come home? I would like to know what brought him home.

LINDA.   I don't know. I think he's still lost, Willy. I think he's very lost.

WILLY.   Biff Loman is lost. In the greatest country in the world a young man with such—personal attractiveness, gets lost. And such a hard worker. There's one thing about Biff—he's not lazy.

LINDA.   Never.

WILLY.   [*with pity and resolve*] I'll see him in the morning; I'll have a nice talk with him. I'll get him a job selling. He could be big in no time. My God! Remember how they used to follow him around in high school? When he smiled at one of them their faces lit up. When he walked down the street . . . [*He loses himself in reminiscences.*]

LINDA. [*trying to bring him out of it*] Willy, dear, I got a new kind of American-type cheese today. It's whipped.

WILLY. Why do you get American when I like Swiss?

LINDA. I just thought you'd like a change—

WILLY. I don't want a change! I want Swiss cheese. Why am I always being contradicted?

LINDA. [*with a covering laugh*] I thought it would be a surprise.

WILLY. Why don't you open a window in here, for God's sake?

LINDA. [*with infinite patience*] They're all open, dear.

WILLY. The way they boxed us in here. Bricks and windows, windows and bricks.

LINDA. We should've bought the land next door.

WILLY. The street is lined with cars. There's not a breath of fresh air in the neighborhood. The grass don't grow any more, you can't raise a carrot in the back yard. They should've had a law against apartment houses. Remember those two beautiful elm trees out there? When I and Biff hung the swing between them?

LINDA. Yeah, like being a million miles from the city.

WILLY. They should've arrested the builder for cutting those down. They massacred the neighborhood. [*lost*] More and more I think of those days, Linda. This time of year it was lilac and wisteria. And then the peonies would come out, and the daffodils. What fragrance in this room!

LINDA. Well, after all, people had to move somewhere.

WILLY. No, there's more people now.

LINDA. I don't think there's more people. I think—

WILLY. There's more people! That's what ruining this country! Population is getting out of control. The competition is maddening! Smell the stink from that apartment house! And another one on the other side . . . How can they whip cheese?

[*On* WILLY'S *last line*, BIFF *and* HAPPY *raise themselves up in their beds, listening.*]

LINDA. Go down, try it. And be quiet.

WILLY. [*turning to* LINDA, *guiltily*] You're not worried about me, are you, sweetheart?

BIFF. What's the matter?

HAPPY. Listen!

LINDA. You've got too much on the ball to worry about.

WILLY. You're my foundation and my support, Linda.

LINDA. Just try to relax, dear. You make mountains out of molehills.

WILLY. I won't fight with him any more. If he wants to go back to Texas, let him go.

LINDA. He'll find his way.

WILLY. Sure. Certain men just don't get started till later in life. Like Thomas

Edison, I think. Or B. F. Goodrich.° One of them was deaf. [*He starts for the bedroom doorway.*] I'll put my money on Biff.

LINDA.   And Willy—if it's warm Sunday we'll drive in the country. And we'll open the windshield, and take lunch.

WILLY.   No, the windshields don't open on the new cars.

LINDA.   But you opened it today.

WILLY.   Me? I didn't. [*He stops.*] Now isn't that peculiar! Isn't that a remarkable— [*He breaks off in amazement and fright as the flute is heard distantly.*]

LINDA.   What, darling?

WILLY.   That is the most remarkable thing.

LINDA.   What, dear?

WILLY.   I was thinking of the Chevvy. [*slight pause*] Nineteen twenty-eight . . . when I had that red Chevvy— [*Breaks off.*] That funny? I coulda sworn I was driving that Chevvy today.

LINDA.   Well, that's nothing. Something must've reminded you.

WILLY.   Remarkable. Ts. Remember those days? The way Biff used to simonize that car? The dealer refused to believe there was eighty thousand miles on it. [*He shakes his head.*] Heh! [*to LINDA*] Close your eyes, I'll be right up. [*He walks out of the bedroom.*]

HAPPY.   [*to BIFF*] Jesus, maybe he smashed up the car again!

LINDA.   [*calling after WILLY*] Be careful on the stairs, dear! The cheese is on the middle shelf! [*She turns, goes over to the bed, takes his jacket, and goes out of the bedroom.*]

[*Light has risen on the boys' room. Unseen, WILLY is heard talking to himself, "Eighty thousand miles," and a little laugh. BIFF gets out of bed, comes downstage a bit, and stands attentively. BIFF is two years older than his brother HAPPY, well built, but in these days bears a worn air and seems less self-assured. He has succeeded less, and his dreams are stronger and less acceptable than HAPPY'S. HAPPY is tall, powerfully made. Sexuality is like a visible color on him, or a scent that many women have discovered. He, like his brother, is lost, but in a different way, for he has never allowed himself to turn his face toward defeat and is thus more confused and hard-skinned, although seemingly more content.*]

HAPPY.   [*getting out of bed*] He's going to get his license taken away if he keeps that up. I'm getting nervous about him, y'know, Biff?

BIFF.   His eyes are going.

HAPPY.   No, I've driven with him. He sees all right. He just doesn't keep his mind on it. I drove into the city with him last week. He stops at a green light and then it turns red and he goes. [*He laughs.*]

BIFF.   Maybe he's color-blind.

HAPPY.   Pop? Why he's got the finest eye for color in the business. You know that.

BIFF.   [*sitting down on his bed*] I'm going to sleep.

HAPPY.   You're not still sour on Dad, are you, Biff?

BIFF.   He's all right, I guess.

° *Thomas Edison, B. F. Goodrich*: Thomas A. Edison (1847–1931) was an American inventor who developed the electric light and the phonograph. Benjamin Franklin Goodrich (1841–1888) founded the B. F. Goodrich Rubber and Tire Company. Willy points to both men as examples of successes who started late in life.

WILLY. [*underneath them, in the living-room*] Yes, sir, eighty thousand miles—eighty-two thousand!

BIFF. You smoking?

HAPPY. [*holding out a pack of cigarettes*] Want one?

BIFF. [*taking a cigarette*] I can never sleep when I smell it.

WILLY. What a simonizing job, heh!

HAPPY. [*with deep sentiment*] Funny, Biff, y'know? Us sleeping in here again? The old beds. [*He pats his bed affectionately.*] All the talk that went across those two beds, huh? Our whole lives.

BIFF. Yeah. Lotta dreams and plans.

HAPPY. [*with a deep and masculine laugh*] About five hundred women would like to know what was said in this room.

[*They share a soft laugh.*]

BIFF. Remember that big Betsy something—what the hell was her name—over on Bushwick Avenue?

HAPPY. [*combing his hair*] With the collie dog!

BIFF. That's the one. I got you in there, remember?

HAPPY. Yeah, that was my first time—I think. Boy, there was a pig! [*They laugh, almost crudely.*] You taught me everything I know about women. Don't forget that.

BIFF. I bet you forgot how bashful you used to be. Especially with girls.

HAPPY. Oh, I still am, Biff.

BIFF. Oh, go on.

HAPPY. I just control it, that's all. I think I got less bashful and you got more so. What happened, Biff? Where's the old humor, the old confidence? [*He shakes BIFF'S knee. BIFF gets up and moves restlessly about the room.*] What's the matter?

BIFF. Why does Dad mock me all the time?

HAPPY. He's not mocking you, he—

BIFF. Everything I say there's a twist of mockery on his face. I can't get near him.

HAPPY. He just wants you to make good, that's all. I wanted to talk to you about Dad for a long time, Biff. Something's—happening to him. He—talks to himself.

BIFF. I noticed that this morning. But he always mumbled.

HAPPY. But not so noticeable. It got so embarrassing I sent him to Florida. And you know something? Most of the time he's talking to you.

BIFF. What's he say about me?

HAPPY. I can't make it out.

BIFF. What's he say about me?

HAPPY. I think the fact that you're not settled, that you're still kind of up in the air . . .

BIFF. There's one or two other things depressing him, Happy.

HAPPY. What do you mean?

BIFF. Never mind. Just don't lay it all to me.

HAPPY. But I think if you just got started—I mean—is there any future for you out there?

BIFF. I tell ya, Hap, I don't know what the future is. I don't know—what I'm supposed to want.

HAPPY.   What do you mean?

BIFF.   Well, I spent six or seven years after high school trying to work myself up. Shipping clerk, salesman, business of one kind or another. And it's a measly manner of existence. To get on that subway on the hot mornings in summer. To devote your whole life to keeping stock, or making phone calls, or selling or buying. To suffer fifty weeks of the year for the sake of a two-week vacation, when all you really desire is to be outdoors, with your shirt off. And always to have to get ahead of the next fella. And still—that's how you build a future.

HAPPY.   Well, you really enjoy it on a farm? Are you content out there?

BIFF.   [*with rising agitation*] Hap, I've had twenty or thirty different kinds of jobs since I left home before the war, and it always turns out the same. I just realized it lately. In Nebraska when I herded cattle, and the Dakotas, and Arizona, and now in Texas. It's why I came home now, I guess, because I realized it. This farm I work on, it's spring there now, see? And they've got about fifteen new colts. There's nothing more inspiring or—beautiful than the sight of a mare and a new colt. And it's cool there now, see? Texas is cool now, and it's spring. And whenever spring comes to where I am, I suddenly get the feeling, my God, I'm not gettin' anywhere! What the hell am I doing, playing around with horses, twenty-eight dollars a week! I'm thirty-four years old, I oughta be makin' my future. That's when I come running home. And now, I get here, and I don't know what to do with myself. [*after a pause*] I've always made a point of not wasting my life, and everytime I come back here I know that all I've done is to waste my life.

HAPPY.   You're a poet, you know that, Biff? You're a—you're an idealist!

BIFF.   No, I'm mixed up very bad. Maybe I oughta get married. Maybe I oughta get stuck into something. Maybe that's my trouble. I'm like a boy. I'm not married, I'm not in business, I just—I'm like a boy. Are you content, Hap? You're a success, aren't you? Are you content?

HAPPY.   Hell, no!

BIFF.   Why? You're making money, aren't you?

HAPPY.   [*moving about with energy, expressiveness*] All I can do now is wait for the merchandise manager to die. And suppose I get to be merchandise manager? He's a good friend of mine, and he just built a terrific estate on Long Island. And he lived there about two months and sold it, and now he's building another one. He can't enjoy it once it's finished. And I know that's just what I would do. I don't know what the hell I'm workin' for. Sometimes I sit in my apartment—all alone. And I think of the rent I'm paying. And it's crazy. But then, it's what I always wanted. My own apartment, a car, and plenty of women. And still, goddammit, I'm lonely.

BIFF.   [*with enthusiasm*] Listen, why don't you come out West with me?

HAPPY.   You and I, heh?

BIFF.   Sure, maybe we could buy a ranch. Raise cattle, use our muscles. Men built like we are should be working out in the open.

HAPPY.   [*avidly*] The Loman Brothers, heh?

BIFF.   [*with vast affection*] Sure, we'd be known all over the counties!

HAPPY.   [*enthralled*] That's what I dream about, Biff. Sometimes I want to just rip my clothes off in the middle of the store and outbox that goddam merchandise manager. I mean I can outbox, outrun, and outlift anybody in that store, and I have to take orders from those common, petty sons-of-bitches till I can't stand it any more.

BIFF.   I'm tellin' you, kid, if you were with me I'd be happy out there.

HAPPY.   [*enthused*] See, Biff, everybody around me is so false that I'm constantly lowering my ideals . . .

BIFF.   Baby, together we'd stand up for one another, we'd have someone to trust.

HAPPY.   If I were around you—

BIFF.   Hap, the trouble is we weren't brought up to grub for money. I don't know how to do it.

HAPPY.   Neither can I!

BIFF.   Then let's go!

HAPPY.   The only thing is—what can you make out there?

BIFF.   But look at your friend. Builds an estate and then hasn't the peace of mind to live in it.

HAPPY.   Yeah, but when he walks into the store the waves part in front of him. That's fifty-two thousand dollars a year coming through the revolving door, and I got more in my pinky finger than he's got in his head.

BIFF.   Yeah, but you just said—

HAPPY.   I gotta show some of those pompous, self-important executives over there that Hap Loman can make the grade. I want to walk into the store the way he walks in. Then I'll go with you, Biff. We'll be together yet, I swear. But take those two we had tonight. Now weren't they gorgeous creatures?

BIFF.   Yeah, yeah, most gorgeous I've had in years.

HAPPY.   I get that any time I want, Biff. Whenever I feel disgusted. The only trouble is, it gets like bowling or something. I just keep knockin' them over and it doesn't mean anything. You still run around a lot?

BIFF.   Naa. I'd like to find a girl—steady, somebody with substance.

HAPPY.   That's what I long for.

BIFF.   Go on! You'd never come home.

HAPPY.   I would! Somebody with character, with resistance! Like Mom, y'know? You're gonna call me a bastard when I tell you this. That girl Charlotte I was with tonight is engaged to be married in five weeks. [*He tries on his new hat.*]

BIFF.   No kiddin'!

HAPPY.   Sure, the guy's in line for the vice-presidency of the store. I don't know what gets into me, maybe I just have an overdeveloped sense of competition or something, but I went and ruined her, and furthermore I can't get rid of her. And he's the third executive I've done that to. Isn't that a crummy characteristic? And to top it all, I go to their weddings! [*Indignantly, but laughing*] Like I'm not supposed to take bribes. Manufacturers offer me a hundred-dollar bill now and then to throw an order their way. You know how honest I am, but it's like this girl, see. I hate myself for it. Because I don't want the girl, and, still, I take it and—I love it!

BIFF.   Let's go to sleep.

HAPPY.   I guess we didn't settle anything, heh?

BIFF.   I just got one idea that I think I'm going to try.

HAPPY. What's that?

BIFF. Remember Bill Oliver?

HAPPY. Sure, Oliver is very big now. You want to work for him again?

BIFF. No, but when I quit he said something to me. He put his arm on my shoulder, and he said, "Biff, if you ever need anything, come to me."

HAPPY. I remember that. That sounds good.

BIFF. I think I'll go to see him. If I could get ten thousand or even seven or eight thousand dollars I could buy a beautiful ranch.

HAPPY. I bet he'd back you. 'Cause he thought highly of you, Biff. I mean, they all do. You're well liked, Biff. That's why I say to come back here, and we both have the apartment. And I'm tellin' you, Biff, any babe you want . . .

BIFF. No, with a ranch I could do the work I like and still be something. I just wonder though. I wonder if Oliver still thinks I stole that carton of basketballs.

HAPPY. Oh, he probably forgot that long ago. It's almost ten years. You're too sensitive. Anyway, he didn't really fire you.

BIFF. Well, I think he was going to. I think that's why I quit. I was never sure whether he knew or not. I know he thought the world of me, though. I was the only one he'd let lock up the place.

WILLY. [*below*] You gonna wash the engine, Biff?

HAPPY. Shh!

[*BIFF looks at HAPPY, who is gazing down, listening. WILLY is mumbling in the parlor.*]

HAPPY. You hear that?

[*They listen. WILLY laughs warmly.*]

BIFF. [*growing angry*] Doesn't he know Mom can hear that?

WILLY. Don't get your sweater dirty, Biff!

[*A look of pain crosses BIFF'S face.*]

HAPPY. Isn't that terrible! Don't leave again, will you? You'll find a job here. You gotta stick around. I don't know what to do about him, it's getting embarrassing.

WILLY. What a simonizing job!

BIFF. Mom's hearing that!

WILLY. No kiddin', Biff, you got a date? Wonderful!

HAPPY. Go on to sleep. But talk to him in the morning, will you?

BIFF. [*reluctantly getting into bed*] With her in the house. Brother!

HAPPY. [*getting into bed*] I wish you'd have a good talk with him.

[*The light on their room begins to fade.*]

BIFF. [*to himself in bed*] That selfish, stupid . . .

HAPPY. Sh . . . Sleep, Biff.

[*Their light is out. Well before they have finished speaking, WILLY'S form is dimly seen below in the darkened kitchen. He opens the refrigerator, searches in there, and takes out a bottle of milk. The apartment houses are fading out, and the entire house and surroundings become covered with leaves. Music insinuates itself as the leaves appear.*]

WILLY. Just wanna be careful with those girls, Biff, that's all. Don't make any promises. No promises of any kind. Because a girl, y'know, they always believe what you tell 'em, and you're very young, Biff, you're too young to be talking seriously to girls.

[*Light rises on the kitchen.* WILLY, *talking, shuts the refrigerator door and comes downstage to the kitchen table. He pours milk into a glass. He is totally immersed in himself, smiling faintly.*]

WILLY. Too young entirely, Biff. You want to watch your schooling first. Then when you're all set, there'll be plenty of girls for a boy like you. [*He smiles broadly at a kitchen chair.*] That so? The girls pay for you? [*He laughs.*] Boy, you must really be makin' a hit.

[WILLY *is gradually addressing—physically—a point offstage, speaking through the wall of the kitchen, and his voice has been rising in volume to that of a normal conversation.*]

WILLY. I been wondering why you polish the car so careful. Ha! Don't leave the hubcaps, boys. Get the chamois to the hubcaps. Happy, use newspaper on the windows, it's the easiest thing. Show him how to do it, Biff! You see, Happy? Pad it up, use it like a pad. That's it, that's it, good work. You're doin' all right, Hap. [*He pauses, then nods in approbation for a few seconds, then looks upward.*] Biff, first thing we gotta do when we get time is clip that big branch over the house. Afraid it's gonna fall in a storm and hit the roof. Tell you what. We get a rope and sling her around, and then we climb up there with a couple of saws and take her down. Soon as you finish the car, boys, I wanna see ya. I got a surprise for you, boys.

BIFF. [*offstage*] Whatta ya got, Dad?

WILLY. No, you finish first. Never leave a job till you're finished—remember that. [*looking toward the "big trees"*] Biff, up in Albany I saw a beautiful hammock. I think I'll buy it next trip, and we'll hang it right between those two elms. Wouldn't that be something? Just swingin' there under those branches. Boy, that would be . . .

[YOUNG BIFF *and* YOUNG HAPPY *appear from the direction* WILLY *was addressing.* HAPPY *carries rags and a pail of water.* BIFF, *wearing a sweater with a block "S," carries a football.*]

BIFF. [*pointing in the direction of the car offstage*] How's that, Pop, professional?

WILLY. Terrific. Terrific job, boys. Good work, Biff.

HAPPY. Where's the surprise, Pop?

WILLY. In the back seat of the car.

HAPPY. Boy! [*He runs off.*]

BIFF. What is it, Dad? Tell me, what'd you buy?

WILLY. [*laughing, cuffs him*] Never mind, something I want you to have.

BIFF. [*turns and starts off*] What is it, Hap?

HAPPY. [*offstage*] It's a punching bag!

BIFF. Oh, Pop!

WILLY. It's got Gene Tunney's° signature on it!

° *Gene Tunney*: James Joseph Tunney, a boxer who won the heavyweight championship from Jack Dempsey in 1926 and retired undefeated in 1928.

[*HAPPY runs onstage with a punching bag.*]

BIFF. Gee, how'd you know we wanted a punching bag?

WILLY. Well, it's the finest thing for the timing.

HAPPY. [*lies down on his back and pedals with his feet*] I'm losing weight, you notice, Pop?

WILLY. [*to HAPPY*] Jumping rope is good too.

BIFF. Did you see the new football I got?

WILLY. [*examining the ball*] Where'd you get a new ball?

BIFF. The coach told me to practice my passing.

WILLY. That so? And he gave you the ball, heh?

BIFF. Well, I borrowed it from the locker room. [*He laughs confidentially.*]

WILLY. [*laughing with him at the theft*] I want you to return that.

HAPPY. I told you he wouldn't like it!

BIFF. [*angrily*] Well, I'm bringing it back!

WILLY. [*stopping the incipient argument, to HAPPY*] Sure, he's gotta practice with a regulation ball, doesn't he? [*to BIFF*] Coach'll probably congratulate you on your initiative!

BIFF. Oh, he keeps congratulating my initiative all the time, Pop.

WILLY. That's because he likes you. If somebody else took that ball there'd be an uproar. So what's the report, boys, what's the report?

BIFF. Where'd you go this time, Dad? Gee we were lonesome for you.

WILLY. [*pleased, puts an arm around each boy and they come down to the apron*] Lonesome, heh?

BIFF. Missed you every minute.

WILLY. Don't say? Tell you a secret, boys. Don't breathe it to a soul. Someday I'll have my own business, and I'll never have to leave home any more.

HAPPY. Like Uncle Charley, heh?

WILLY. Bigger than Uncle Charley! Because Charley is not—liked. He's liked, but he's not—well liked.

BIFF. Where'd you go this time, Dad?

WILLY. Well, I got on the road, and I went north to Providence. Met the Mayor.

BIFF. The Mayor of Providence!

WILLY. He was sitting in the hotel lobby.

BIFF. What'd he say?

WILLY. He said, "Morning!" And I said, "You got a fine city here, Mayor." And then he had coffee with me. And then I went to Waterbury. Waterbury is a fine city. Big clock city, the famous Waterbury clock. Sold a nice bill there. And then Boston—Boston is the cradle of the Revolution. A fine city. And a couple of other towns in Mass., and on to Portland and Bangor and straight home!

BIFF. Gee, I'd love to go with you sometime, Dad.

WILLY. Soon as summer comes.

HAPPY. Promise?

WILLY. You and Hap and I, and I'll show you all the towns. America is full of beautiful towns and fine, upstanding people. And they know me, boys, they know me up and down New England. The finest people. And when I bring you fellas up, there'll be open sesame for all of us, 'cause one thing, boys: I have friends. I can park my car in any street in New England, and the cops protect it like their own. This summer, heh?

BIFF and HAPPY. [*together*] Yeah! You bet!

WILLY.   We'll take our bathing suits.

HAPPY.   We'll carry your bags, Pop!

WILLY.   Oh, won't that be something! Me comin' into the Boston stores with you boys carryin' my bags. What a sensation!

[*BIFF is prancing around, practicing passing the ball.*]

WILLY.   You nervous, Biff, about the game?

BIFF.   Not if you're gonna be there.

WILLY.   What do they say about you in school, now that they made you captain?

HAPPY.   There's a crowd of girls behind him everytime the classes change.

BIFF.   [*taking WILLY'S hand*] This Saturday, Pop, this Saturday—just for you, I'm going to break through for a touchdown.

HAPPY.   You're supposed to pass.

BIFF.   I'm takin' one play for Pop. You watch me, Pop, and when I take off my helmet, that means I'm breakin' out. Then you watch me crash through that line!

WILLY.   [*kisses BIFF*] Oh, wait'll I tell this in Boston!

[*BERNARD enters in knickers. He is younger than BIFF, earnest and loyal, a worried boy.*]

BERNARD.   Biff, where are you? You're supposed to study with me today.

WILLY.   Hey, looka Bernard. What're you lookin' so anemic about, Bernard?

BERNARD.   He's gotta study, Uncle Willy. He's got Regents° next week.

HAPPY.   [*tauntingly, spinning BERNARD around*] Let's box, Bernard!

BERNARD.   Biff! [*He gets away from HAPPY.*] Listen, Biff, I heard Mr. Birnbaum say that if you don't start studyin' math he's gonna flunk you, and you won't graduate. I heard him!

WILLY.   You better study with him, Biff. Go ahead now.

BERNARD.   I heard him!

BIFF.   Oh, Pop, you didn't see my sneakers! [*He holds up a foot for WILLY to look at.*]

WILLY.   Hey, that's a beautiful job of printing!

BERNARD.   [*wiping his glasses*] Just because he printed University of Virginia on his sneakers doesn't mean they've got to graduate him, Uncle Willy!

WILLY.   [*angrily*] What're you talking about? With scholarships to three universities they're gonna flunk him?

BERNARD.   But I heard Mr. Birnbaum say—

WILLY.   Don't be a pest, Bernard! [*to his boys*] What an anemic!

BERNARD.   Okay, I'm waiting for you in my house, Biff.

[*BERNARD goes off. The LOMANS laugh.*]

° *Regents*: A statewide high school proficiency examination administered in New York State.

WILLY. Bernard is not well liked, is he?

BIFF. He's liked, but he's not well liked.

HAPPY. That's right, Pop.

WILLY. That's just what I mean. Bernard can get the best marks in school, y'understand, but when he gets out in the business world, y'understand, you are going to be five times ahead of him. That's why I thank Almighty God you're both built like Adonises. Because the man who makes an appearance in the business world, the man who creates personal interest, is the man who gets ahead. Be liked and you will never want. You take me, for instance. I never have to wait in line to see a buyer. "Willy Loman is here!" That's all they have to know, and I go right through.

BIFF. Did you knock them dead, Pop?

WILLY. Knocked 'em cold in Providence, slaughtered 'em in Boston.

HAPPY. [*on his back, pedaling again*] I'm losing weight, you notice, Pop?

[*LINDA enters, as of old, a ribbon in her hair, carrying a basket of washing.*]

LINDA. [*with youthful energy*] Hello, dear!

WILLY. Sweetheart!

LINDA. How'd the Chevvy run?

WILLY. Chevrolet, Linda, is the greatest car ever built. [*to the boys*] Since when do you let your mother carry wash up the stairs?

BIFF. Grab hold there, boy!

HAPPY. Where to, Mom?

LINDA. Hang them up on the line. And you better go down to your friends, Biff. The cellar is full of boys. They don't know what to do with themselves.

BIFF. Ah, when Pop comes home they can wait!

WILLY. [*laughs appreciatively*] You better go down and tell them what to do, Biff.

BIFF. I think I'll have them sweep out the furnace room.

WILLY. Good work, Biff.

BIFF. [*goes through wall-line of kitchen to doorway at back and calls down*] Fellas! Everybody sweep out the furnace room! I'll be right down!

VOICES. All right! Okay, Biff.

BIFF. George and Sam and Frank, come out back! We're hangin' up the wash! Come on, Hap, on the double! [*He and HAPPY carry out the basket.*]

LINDA. The way they obey him!

WILLY. Well, that's training, the training. I'm tellin' you, I was sellin' thousands and thousands, but I had to come home.

LINDA. Oh, the whole block'll be at that game. Did you sell anything?

WILLY. I did five hundred gross in Providence and seven hundred gross in Boston.

LINDA. No! Wait a minute, I've got a pencil. [*She pulls pencil and paper out of her apron pocket.*] That makes your commission . . . Two hundred—my God! Two hundred and twelve dollars!

WILLY. Well, I didn't figure it yet, but . . .

LINDA. How much did you do?

WILLY. Well, I—I did—about a hundred and eighty gross in Providence.

Well, no—it came to—roughly two hundred gross on the whole trip.

LINDA.   [*without hesitation*] Two hundred gross. That's . . . [*She figures.*]

WILLY.   The trouble was that three of the stores were half closed for inventory in Boston. Otherwise I woulda broke records.

LINDA.   Well, it makes seventy dollars and some pennies. That's very good.

WILLY.   What do we owe?

LINDA.   Well, on the first there's sixteen dollars on the refrigerator—

WILLY.   Why sixteen?

LINDA.   Well, the fan belt broke, so it was a dollar eighty.

WILLY.   But it's brand new.

LINDA.   Well, the man said that's the way it is. Till they work themselves in, y'know.

[*They move through the wall-line into the kitchen.*]

WILLY.   I hope we didn't get stuck on that machine.

LINDA.   They got the biggest ads of any of them!

WILLY.   I know, it's a fine machine. What else?

LINDA.   Well, there's nine-sixty for the washing machine. And for the vacuum cleaner there's three and a half due on the fifteenth. Then the roof, you got twenty-one dollars remaining.

WILLY.   It don't leak, does it?

LINDA.   No, they did a wonderful job. Then you owe Frank for the carburetor.

WILLY.   I'm not going to pay that man! That goddam Chevrolet, they ought to prohibit the manufacture of that car!

LINDA.   Well, you owe him three and a half. And odds and ends, comes to around a hundred and twenty dollars by the fifteenth.

WILLY.   A hundred and twenty dollars! My God, if business don't pick up I don't know what I'm gonna do!

LINDA.   Well, next week you'll do better.

WILLY.   Oh, I'll knock 'em dead next week. I'll go to Hartford. I'm very well liked in Hartford. You know, the trouble is, Linda, people don't seem to take to me.

[*They move onto the forestage.*]

LINDA.   Oh, don't be foolish.

WILLY.   I know it when I walk in. They seem to laugh at me.

LINDA.   Why? Why would they laugh at you? Don't talk that way, Willy.

[*WILLY moves to the edge of the stage. LINDA goes into the kitchen and starts to darn stockings.*]

WILLY.   I don't know the reason for it, but they just pass me by. I'm not noticed.

LINDA.   But you're doing wonderful, dear. You're making seventy to a hundred dollars a week.

WILLY.   But I gotta be at it ten, twelve hours a day. Other men—I don't know—they do it easier. I don't know why—I can't stop myself—I talk too much. A man oughta come in with a few words. One thing about Charley. He's a man of few words, and they respect him.

LINDA.   You don't talk too much, you're just lively.

WILLY. [*smiling*] Well, I figure, what the hell, life is short, a couple of jokes. [*to himself*] I joke too much! [*The smile goes.*]

LINDA. Why? You're—

WILLY. I'm fat. I'm very—foolish to look at, Linda. I didn't tell you, but Christmas time I happened to be calling on F. H. Stewarts, and a salesman I know, as I was going in to see the buyer I heard him say something about—walrus. And I—I cracked him right across the face. I won't take that. I simply will not take that. But they do laugh at me. I know that.

LINDA. Darling . . .

WILLY. I gotta overcome it. I know I gotta overcome it. I'm not dressing to advantage, maybe.

LINDA. Willy, darling, you're the handsomest man in the world—

WILLY. Oh, no, Linda.

LINDA. To me you are. [*slight pause*] The handsomest.

[*From the darkness is heard the laughter of a woman. WILLY doesn't turn to it, but it continues through LINDA'S lines.*]

LINDA. And the boys, Willy. Few men are idolized by their children the way you are.

[*Music is heard as behind a scrim, to the left of the house, THE WOMAN, dimly seen, is dressing.*]

WILLY. [*with great feeling*] You're the best there is, Linda, you're a pal, you know that? On the road—on the road I want to grab you sometimes and just kiss the life outa you.

[*The laughter is loud now, and he moves into a brightening area at the left, where THE WOMAN has come from behind the scrim and is standing, putting on her hat, looking into a "mirror" and laughing.*]

WILLY. Cause I get so lonely—especially when business is bad and there's nobody to talk to. I get the feeling that I'll never sell anything again, that I won't make a living for you, or a business, a business for the boys. [*He talks through THE WOMAN'S subsiding laughter; THE WOMAN primps at the "mirror."*] There's so much I want to make for—

THE WOMAN. Me? You didn't make me, Willy. I picked you.

WILLY. [*pleased*] You picked me?

THE WOMAN. [*who is quite proper-looking, WILLY'S age*] I did. I've been sitting at that desk watching all the salesmen go by, day in, day out. But you've got such a sense of humor, and we do have such a good time together, don't we?

WILLY. Sure, sure. [*He takes her in his arms.*] Why do you have to go now?

THE WOMAN. It's two o'clock . . .

WILLY. No, come on in! [*He pulls her.*]

THE WOMAN. . . . my sisters'll be scandalized. When'll you be back?

WILLY. Oh, two weeks about. Will you come up again?

THE WOMAN. Sure thing. You do make me laugh. It's good for me. [*She squeezes his arm, kisses him.*] And I think you're a wonderful man.

WILLY. You picked me, heh?

THE WOMAN. Sure. Because you're so sweet. And such a kidder.

WILLY.   Well, I'll see you next time I'm in Boston.

THE WOMAN.   I'll put you right through to the buyers.

WILLY.   [*slapping her bottom*] Right. Well, bottoms up!

THE WOMAN.   [*slaps him gently and laughs*] You just kill me, Willy. [*He suddenly grabs her and kisses her roughly.*] You kill me. And thanks for the stockings. I love a lot of stockings. Well, good night.

WILLY.   Good night. And keep your pores open!

THE WOMAN.   Oh, Willy!

[*THE WOMAN bursts out laughing, and LINDA'S laughter blends in. THE WOMAN disappears into the dark. Now the area at the kitchen table brightens. LINDA is sitting where she was at the kitchen table, but now is mending a pair of her silk stockings.*]

LINDA.   You are, Willy. The handsomest man. You've got no reason to feel that—

WILLY.   [*coming out of THE WOMAN'S dimming area and going over to LINDA*] I'll make it all up to you, Linda, I'll—

LINDA.   There's nothing to make up, dear. You're doing fine, better than—

WILLY.   [*noticing her mending*] What's that?

LINDA.   Just mending my stockings. They're so expensive—

WILLY.   [*angrily, taking them from her*] I won't have you mending stockings in this house! Now throw them out!

[*LINDA puts the stockings in her pocket.*]

BERNARD.   [*entering on the run*] Where is he? If he doesn't study!

WILLY.   [*moving to the forestage, with great agitation*] You'll give him the answers!

BERNARD.   I do, but I can't on a Regents! That's a state exam! They're liable to arrest me!

WILLY.   Where is he? I'll whip him, I'll whip him!

LINDA.   And he'd better give back that football, Willy, it's not nice.

WILLY.   Biff! Where is he? Why is he taking everything?

LINDA.   He's too rough with the girls, Willy. All the mothers are afraid of him!

WILLY.   I'll whip him!

BERNARD.   He's driving the car without a license!

[*THE WOMAN'S laugh is heard.*]

WILLY.   Shut up!

LINDA.   All the mothers—

WILLY.   Shut up!

BERNARD.   [*backing quietly away and out*] Mr. Birnbaum says he's stuck up.

WILLY.   Get outa here!

BERNARD.   If he doesn't buckle down he'll flunk math! [*He goes off.*]

LINDA.   He's right, Willy, you've gotta—

WILLY.   [*exploding at her*] There's nothing the matter with him! You want him to be a worm like Bernard? He's got spirit, personality . . .

[*As he speaks, LINDA, almost in tears, exits into the living-room. WILLY is alone in the kitchen, wilting and staring. The leaves are gone. It is night again, and the apartment houses look down from behind.*]

WILLY. Loaded with it. Loaded! What is he stealing? He's giving it back, isn't he? Why is he stealing? What did I tell him? I never in my life told him anything but decent things.

[*HAPPY in pajamas has come down the stairs; WILLY suddenly becomes aware of HAPPY'S presence.*]

HAPPY. Let's go now, come on.

WILLY. [*sitting down at the kitchen table*] Huh! Why did she have to wax the floors herself? Everytime she waxes the floors she keels over. She knows that!

HAPPY. Shh! Take it easy. What brought you back tonight?

WILLY. I got an awful scare. Nearly hit a kid in Yonkers. God! Why didn't I go to Alaska with my brother Ben that time! Ben! That man was a genius, that man was success incarnate! What a mistake! He begged me to go.

HAPPY. Well, there's no use in—

WILLY. You guys! There was a man started with the clothes on his back and ended up with diamond mines!

HAPPY. Boy, someday I'd like to know how he did it.

WILLY. What's the mystery? The man knew what he wanted and went out and got it! Walked into a jungle, and comes out, the age of twenty-one, and he's rich! The world is an oyster, but you don't crack it open on a mattress!

HAPPY. Pop, I told you I'm gonna retire you for life.

WILLY. You'll retire me for life on seventy goddam dollars a week? And your women and your car and your apartment, and you'll retire me for life! Christ's sake, I couldn't get past Yonkers today! Where are you guys, where are you? The woods are burning! I can't drive a car!

[*CHARLEY has appeared in the doorway. He is a large man, slow of speech, laconic, immovable. In all he says, despite what he says, there is pity, and, now, trepidation. He has a robe over pajamas, slippers on his feet. He enters the kitchen.*]

CHARLEY. Everything all right?

HAPPY. Yeah, Charley, everything's . . .

WILLY. What's the matter?

CHARLEY. I heard some noise. I thought something happened. Can't we do something about the walls? You sneeze in here, and in my house hats blow off.

HAPPY. Let's go to bed, Dad. Come on.

[*CHARLEY signals to HAPPY to go.*]

WILLY. You go ahead, I'm not tired at the moment.

HAPPY. [*to WILLY*] Take it easy, huh? [*He exits.*]

WILLY. What're you doin' up?

CHARLEY. [*sitting down at the kitchen table opposite WILLY*] Couldn't sleep good. I had a heartburn.

WILLY. Well, you don't know how to eat.

CHARLEY. I eat with my mouth.

WILLY. No, you're ignorant. You gotta know about vitamins and things like that.

CHARLEY. Come on, let's shoot. Tire you out a little.

WILLY. [*hesitantly*] All right. You got cards?

CHARLEY.   [*taking a deck from his pocket*] Yeah, I got them. Someplace. What is it with those vitamins?

WILLY.   [*dealing*] They build up your bones. Chemistry.

CHARLEY.   Yeah, but there's no bones in a heartburn.

WILLY.   What are you talkin' about? Do you know the first thing about it?

CHARLEY.   Don't get insulted.

WILLY.   Don't talk about something you don't know anything about.

[*They are playing. Pause.*]

CHARLEY.   What're you doin' home?

WILLY.   A little trouble with the car.

CHARLEY.   Oh. [*Pause*] I'd like to take a trip to California.

WILLY.   Don't say.

CHARLEY.   You want a job?

WILLY.   I got a job, I told you that. [*after a slight pause*] What the hell are you offering me a job for?

CHARLEY.   Don't get insulted.

WILLY.   Don't insult me.

CHARLEY.   I don't see no sense in it. You don't have to go on this way.

WILLY.   I got a good job. [*slight pause*] What do you keep comin' in for?

CHARLEY.   You want me to go?

WILLY.   [*after a pause, withering*] I can't understand it. He's going back to Texas again. What the hell is that?

CHARLEY.   Let him go.

WILLY.   I got nothin' to give him, Charley, I'm clean, I'm clean.

CHARLEY.   He won't starve. None a them starve. Forget about him.

WILLY.   Then what have I got to remember?

CHARLEY.   You take it too hard. To hell with it. When a deposit bottle is broken you don't get your nickel back.

WILLY.   That's easy enough for you to say.

CHARLEY.   That ain't easy for me to say.

WILLY.   Did you see the ceiling I put up in the living-room?

CHARLEY.   Yeah, that's a piece of work. To put up a ceiling is a mystery to me. How do you do it?

WILLY.   What's the difference?

CHARLEY.   Well, talk about it.

WILLY.   You gonna put up a ceiling?

CHARLEY.   How could I put up a ceiling?

WILLY.   Then what the hell are you bothering me for?

CHARLEY.   You're insulted again.

WILLY.   A man who can't handle tools is not a man. You're disgusting.

CHARLEY.   Don't call me disgusting, Willy.

[*UNCLE BEN, carrying a valise and an umbrella, enters the forestage from around the right corner of the house. He is a stolid man, in his sixties, with a mustache and an authoritative air. He is utterly certain of his destiny, and there is an aura of far places about him. He enters exactly as WILLY speaks.*]

WILLY.   I'm getting awfully tired, Ben.

[*BEN'S music is heard. BEN looks around at everything.*]

CHARLEY.   Good, keep playing; you'll sleep better. Did you call me Ben?

[*BEN looks at his watch.*]

WILLY.   That's funny. For a second there you reminded me of my brother Ben.

BEN.   I only have a few minutes. [*He strolls, inspecting the place. WILLY and CHARLEY continue playing.*]

CHARLEY.   You never heard from him again, heh? Since that time?

WILLY.   Didn't Linda tell you? Couple of weeks ago we got a letter from his wife in Africa. He died.

CHARLEY.   That so.

BEN.   [*chuckling*] So this is Brooklyn, eh?

CHARLEY.   Maybe you're in for some of his money.

WILLY.   Naa, he had seven sons. There's just one opportunity I had with that man . . .

BEN.   I must make a train, William. There are several properties I'm looking at in Alaska.

WILLY.   Sure, sure! If I'd gone with him to Alaska that time, everything would've been totally different.

CHARLEY.   Go on, you'd froze to death up there.

WILLY.   What're you talking about?

BEN.   Opportunity is tremendous in Alaska, William. Surprised you're not up there.

WILLY.   Sure, tremendous.

CHARLEY.   Heh?

WILLY.   There was the only man I ever met who knew the answers.

CHARLEY.   Who?

BEN.   How are you all?

WILLY.   [*taking a pot, smiling*] Fine, fine.

CHARLEY.   Pretty sharp tonight.

BEN.   Is Mother living with you?

WILLY.   No, she died a long time ago.

CHARLEY.   Who?

BEN.   That's too bad. Fine specimen of a lady, Mother.

WILLY.   [*to CHARLEY*] Heh?

BEN.   I'd hoped to see the old girl.

CHARLEY.   Who died?

BEN.   Heard anything from Father, have you?

WILLY.   [*unnerved*] What do you mean, who died?

CHARLEY.   [*taking a pot*] What're you talkin' about?

BEN.   [*looking at his watch*] William, it's half-past eight!

WILLY.   [*As though to dispel his confusion he angrily stops CHARLEY'S hand.*] That's my build!

CHARLEY.   I put the ace—

WILLY.   If you don't know how to play the game I'm not gonna throw my money away on you!

CHARLEY. [*rising*] It was my ace, for God's sake!

WILLY. I'm through, I'm through!

BEN. When did Mother die?

WILLY. Long ago. Since the beginning you never knew how to play cards.

CHARLEY. [*picks up the cards and goes to the door*] All right! Next time I'll bring a deck with five aces.

WILLY. I don't play that kind of game!

CHARLEY. [*turning to him*] You ought to be ashamed of yourself!

WILLY. Yeah?

CHARLEY. Yeah! [*He goes out.*]

WILLY. [*slamming the door after him*] Ignoramus!

BEN. [*as* WILLY *comes toward him through the wall-line of the kitchen*] So you're William.

WILLY. [*shaking* BEN'S *hand*] Ben! I've been waiting for you so long! What's the answer? How did you do it?

BEN. Oh, there's a story in that.

[LINDA *enters the forestage, as of old, carrying the wash basket.*]

LINDA. Is this Ben?

BEN. [*gallantly*] How do you do, my dear.

LINDA. Where've you been all these years? Willy's always wondered why you—

WILLY. [*pulling* BEN *away from her impatiently*] Where is Dad? Didn't you follow him? How did you get started?

BEN. Well, I don't know how much you remember.

WILLY. Well, I was just a baby, of course, only three or four years old—

BEN. Three years and eleven months.

WILLY. What a memory, Ben!

BEN. I have many enterprises, William, and I have never kept books.

WILLY. I remember I was sitting under the wagon in—was it Nebraska?

BEN. It was South Dakota, and I gave you a bunch of wild flowers.

WILLY. I remember you walking away down some open road.

BEN. [*laughing*] I was going to find Father in Alaska.

WILLY. Where is he?

BEN. At that age I had a very faulty view of geography, William. I discovered after a few days that I was heading due south, so instead of Alaska, I ended up in Africa.

LINDA. Africa!

WILLY. The Gold Coast!

BEN. Principally diamond mines.

LINDA. Diamond mines!

BEN. Yes, my dear. But I've only a few minutes—

WILLY. No! Boys! Boys! [YOUNG BIFF *and* HAPPY *appear.*] Listen to this. This is your Uncle Ben, a great man! Tell my boys, Ben!

BEN. Why, boys, when I was seventeen I walked into the jungle, and when I was twenty-one I walked out. [*He laughs.*] And by God I was rich.

WILLY. [*to the boys*] You see what I been talking about? The greatest things can happen!

BEN. [*glancing at his watch*] I have an appointment in Ketchikan Tuesday week.

WILLY. No, Ben. Please tell about Dad. I want my boys to hear. I want them to know the kind of stock they spring from. All I remember is a man with a big beard, and I was in Mamma's lap, sitting around a fire, and some kind of high music.

BEN. His flute. He played the flute.

WILLY. Sure, the flute, that's right!

[*New music is heard, a high, rollicking tune.*]

BEN. Father was a very great and a very wild-hearted man. We would start in Boston, and he'd toss the whole family into the wagon, and then he'd drive the team right across the country; through Ohio, and Indiana, Michigan, Illinois, and all the Western states. And we'd stop in the towns and sell the flutes that he'd made on the way. Great inventor, Father. With one gadget he made more in a week than a man like you could make in a lifetime.

WILLY. That's just the way I'm bringing them up, Ben—rugged, well liked, all-around.

BEN. Yeah? [*to BIFF*] Hit that, boy—hard as you can. [*He pounds his stomach.*]

BIFF. Oh, no, sir!

BEN. [*taking boxing stance*] Come on, get to me! [*He laughs.*]

BIFF. Okay! [*He cocks his fists and starts in.*]

WILLY. Go to it, Biff! Go ahead, show him!

LINDA. [*to WILLY*] Why must he fight, dear?

BEN. [*sparring with BIFF*] Good boy! Good boy!

WILLY. How's that, Ben, heh?

HAPPY. Give him the left, Biff!

LINDA. Why are you fighting?

BEN. Good boy! [*suddenly comes in, trips BIFF, and stands over him, the point of his umbrella poised over BIFF'S eye.*]

LINDA. Look out, Biff!

BIFF. Gee!

BEN. [*patting BIFF'S knee*] Never fight fair with a stranger, boy. You'll never get out of the jungle that way. [*taking LINDA'S hand and bowing*] It was an honor and a pleasure to meet you, Linda.

LINDA. [*withdrawing her hand coldly, frightened*] Have a nice—trip.

BEN. [*to WILLY*] And good luck with your—what do you do?

WILLY. Selling.

BEN. Yes. Well . . . [*He raises his hand in farewell to all.*]

WILLY. No, Ben, I don't want you to think . . . [*He takes BEN'S arm to show him.*] It's Brooklyn, I know, but we hunt too.

BEN. Really, now.

WILLY. Oh, sure, there's snakes and rabbits and—that's why I moved out here. Why, Biff can fell any one of these trees in no time! Boys! Go right over to where they're building the apartment house and get some sand. We're gonna rebuild the entire front stoop right now! Watch this, Ben!

BIFF. Yes, sir! On the double, Hap!

HAPPY. [*as he and BIFF run off*] I lost weight, Pop, you notice?

[*CHARLEY enters in knickers, even before the boys are gone.*]

CHARLEY.   Listen, if they steal any more from that building the watchman'll put the cops on them!

LINDA.   [*to* WILLY] Don't let Biff . . .

[*BEN laughs lustily.*]

WILLY.   You shoulda seen the lumber they brought home last week. At least a dozen six-by-tens worth all kinds a money.

CHARLEY.   Listen, if that watchman—

WILLY.   I gave them hell, understand. But I got a couple of fearless characters there.

CHARLEY.   Willy, the jails are full of fearless characters.

BEN.   [*clapping* WILLY *on the back, with a laugh at* CHARLEY] And the stock exchange, friend!

WILLY.   [*joining in* BEN'S *laughter*] Where are the rest of your pants?

CHARLEY.   My wife bought them.

WILLY.   Now all you need is a golf club and you can go upstairs and go to sleep. [*to* BEN] Great athlete! Between him and his son Bernard they can't hammer a nail!

BERNARD.   [*rushing in*] The watchman's chasing Biff!

WILLY.   [*angrily*] Shut up! He's not stealing anything!

LINDA.   [*alarmed, hurrying off left*] Where is he? Biff, dear! [*She exits.*]

WILLY.   [*moving toward the left, away from* BEN] There's nothing wrong. What's the matter with you?

BEN.   Nervy boy. Good!

WILLY.   [*laughing*] Oh, nerves of iron, that Biff!

CHARLEY.   Don't know what it is. My New England man comes back and he's bleedin', they murdered him up there.

WILLY.   It's contacts, Charley, I got important contacts!

CHARLEY.   [*sarcastically*] Glad to hear it, Willy. Come in later, we'll shoot a little casino. I'll take some of your Portland money. [*He laughs at* WILLY *and exits.*]

WILLY.   [*turning to* BEN] Business is bad, it's murderous. But not for me, of course.

BEN.   I'll stop by on my way back to Africa.

WILLY.   [*longingly.*] Can't you stay a few days? You're just what I need, Ben, because I—I have a fine position here, but I—well, Dad left when I was such a baby and I never had a chance to talk to him and I still feel—kind of temporary about myself.

BEN.   I'll be late for my train.

[*They are at opposite ends of the stage.*]

WILLY.   Ben, my boys—can't we talk? They'd go into the jaws of hell for me, see, but I—

BEN.   William, you're being first-rate with your boys. Outstanding, manly chaps!

WILLY.   [*hanging on to his words*] Oh, Ben, that's good to hear! Because sometimes I'm afraid that I'm not teaching them the right kind of— Ben, how should I teach them?

BEN. [*giving great weight to each word, and with a certain vicious audacity*] William, when I walked into the jungle, I was seventeen. When I walked out I was twenty-one. And, by God, I was rich! [*He goes off into darkness around the right corner of the house.*]

WILLY. . . . was rich! That's just the spirit I want to imbue them with! To walk into a jungle! I was right! I was right! I was right!

[*BEN is gone, but WILLY is still speaking to him as LINDA, in her nightgown and robe, enters the kitchen, glances around for WILLY, then goes to the door of the house, looks out and sees him. Comes down to his left. He looks at her.*]

LINDA. Willy, dear? Willy?

WILLY. I was right!

LINDA. Did you have some cheese? [*He can't answer.*] It's very late, darling. Come to bed, heh?

WILLY. [*looking straight up*] Gotta break your neck to see a star in this yard.

LINDA. You coming in?

WILLY. Whatever happened to that diamond watch fob? Remember? When Ben came from Africa that time? Didn't he give me a watch fob with a diamond in it?

LINDA. You pawned it, dear. Twelve, thirteen years ago. For Biff's radio correspondence course.

WILLY. Gee, that was a beautiful thing. I'll take a walk.

LINDA. But you're in your slippers.

WILLY. [*starting to go around the house at the left*] I was right! I was! [*Half to LINDA, as he goes, shaking his head*] What a man! There was a man worth talking to. I was right!

LINDA. [*calling after WILLY*] But in your slippers, Willy!

[*WILLY is almost gone when BIFF, in his pajamas, comes down the stairs and enters the kitchen.*]

BIFF. What is he doing out there?

LINDA. Sh!

BIFF. God Almighty, Mom, how long has he been doing this?

LINDA. Don't, he'll hear you.

BIFF. What the hell is the matter with him?

LINDA. It'll pass by morning.

BIFF. Shouldn't we do anything?

LINDA. Oh, my dear, you should do a lot of things, but there's nothing to do, so go to sleep.

[*HAPPY comes down the stairs and sits on the steps.*]

HAPPY. I never heard him so loud, Mom.

LINDA. Well, come around more often; you'll hear him. [*She sits down at the table and mends the lining of WILLY's jacket.*]

BIFF. Why didn't you ever write me about this, Mom?

LINDA. How would I write to you? For over three months you had no address.

BIFF. I was on the move. But you know I thought of you all the time. You know that, don't you, pal?

LINDA.   I know, dear, I know. But he likes to have a letter. Just to know that there's still a possibility for better things.

BIFF.   He's not like this all the time, is he?

LINDA.   It's when you come home he's always the worst.

BIFF.   When I come home?

LINDA.   When you write you're coming, he's all smiles, and talks about the future, and—he's just wonderful. And then the closer you seem to come, the more shaky he gets, and then, by the time you get here, he's arguing, and he seems angry at you. I think it's just that maybe he can't bring himself to—to open up to you. Why are you so hateful to each other? Why is that?

BIFF.   [*evasively*] I'm not hateful, Mom.

LINDA.   But you no sooner come in the door than you're fighting!

BIFF.   I don't know why. I mean to change. I'm tryin', Mom, you understand?

LINDA.   Are you home to stay now?

BIFF.   I don't know. I want to look around, see what's doin'.

LINDA.   Biff, you can't look around all your life, can you?

BIFF.   I just can't take hold, Mom. I can't take hold of some kind of a life.

LINDA.   Biff, a man is not a bird, to come and go with the springtime.

BIFF.   Your hair . . . [*He touches her hair.*] Your hair got so gray.

LINDA.   Oh, it's been gray since you were in high school. I just stopped dyeing it, that's all.

BIFF.   Dye it again, will ya? I don't want my pal looking old. [*He smiles.*]

LINDA.   You're such a boy! You think you can go away for a year and . . . You've got to get it into your head now that one day you'll knock on this door and there'll be strange people here—

BIFF.   What are you talking about? You're not even sixty, Mom.

LINDA.   But what about your father?

BIFF.   [*lamely*] Well, I meant him, too.

HAPPY.   He admires Pop.

LINDA.   Biff, dear, if you don't have any feeling for him, then you can't have any feeling for me.

BIFF.   Sure I can, Mom.

LINDA.   No. You can't just come to see me, because I love him. [*with a threat, but only a threat, of tears*] He's the dearest man in the world to me, and I won't have anyone making him feel unwanted and low and blue. You've got to make up your mind now, darling, there's no leeway any more. Either he's your father and you pay him that respect, or else you're not to come here. I know he's not easy to get along with—nobody knows that better than me—but . . .

WILLY.   [*from the left, with a laugh*] Hey, hey, Biffo!

BIFF.   [*starting to go out after WILLY*] What the hell is the matter with him? [*HAPPY stops him.*]

LINDA.   Don't—don't go near him!

BIFF.   Stop making excuses for him! He always, always wiped the floor with you. Never had an ounce of respect for you.

HAPPY.   He's always had respect for—

BIFF.   What the hell do you know about it?

HAPPY.   [*surlily*] Just don't call him crazy!

BIFF.   He's got no character—Charley wouldn't do this. Not in his own house—spewing out that vomit from his mind.

HAPPY.   Charley never had to cope with what he's got to.

BIFF.   People are worse off than Willy Loman. Believe me, I've seen them!

LINDA.   Then make Charley your father, Biff. You can't do that, can you? I don't say he's a great man. Willy Loman never made a lot of money. His name was never in the paper. He's not the finest character that ever lived. But he's a human being, and a terrible thing is happening to him. So attention must be paid. He's not to be allowed to fall into his grave like an old dog. Attention, attention must be finally paid to such a person. You called him crazy—

BIFF.   I didn't mean—

LINDA.   No, a lot of people think he's lost his—balance. But you don't have to be very smart to know what his trouble is. The man is exhausted.

HAPPY.   Sure!

LINDA.   A small man can be just as exhausted as a great man. He works for a company thirty-six years this March, opens up unheard-of-territories to their trademark, and now in his old age they take his salary away.

HAPPY.   [*indignantly*] I didn't know that, Mom.

LINDA.   You never asked, my dear! Now that you get your spending money someplace else you don't trouble your mind with him.

HAPPY.   But I gave you money last—

LINDA.   Christmas time, fifty dollars! To fix the hot water it cost ninety-seven fifty! For five weeks he's been on straight commission,° like a beginner, an unknown!

BIFF.   Those ungrateful bastards!

LINDA.   Are they any worse than his sons? When he brought them business, when he was young, they were glad to see him. But now his old friends, the old buyers that loved him so and always found some order to hand him in a pinch—they're all dead, retired. He used to be able to make six, seven calls a day in Boston. Now he takes his valises out of the car and puts them back and takes them out again and he's exhausted. Instead of walking he talks now. He drives seven hundred miles, and when he gets there no one knows him any more, no one welcomes him. And what goes through a man's mind, driving seven hundred miles home without having earned a cent? Why shouldn't he talk to himself? Why? When he has to go to Charley and borrow fifty dollars a week and pretend to me that it's his pay? How long can that go on? How long? You see what I'm sitting here and waiting for? And you tell me he has no character? The man who never worked a day but for your benefit? When does he get the medal for that? Is this his reward—to turn around at the age of sixty-three and find his sons, who he loved better than his life, one a philandering bum—

HAPPY.   Mom!

LINDA.   That's all you are, my baby! [*To BIFF*] And you! What happened to the love you had for him? You were such pals! How you used to talk to him on the phone every night! How lonely he was till he could come home to you!

°*straight commission*: refers to the fact that Willy is receiving no salary, only a commission (percentage) on the sales he makes.

BIFF. All right, Mom. I'll live here in my room, and I'll get a job. I'll keep away from him, that's all.

LINDA. No, Biff. You can't stay here and fight all the time.

BIFF. He threw me out of this house, remember that.

LINDA. Why did he do that? I never knew why.

BIFF. Because I know he's a fake and he doesn't like anybody around who knows!

LINDA. Why a fake? In what way? What do you mean?

BIFF. Just don't lay it all at my feet. It's between me and him—that's all I have to say. I'll chip in from now on. He'll settle for half my pay check. He'll be all right. I'm going to bed. [*He starts for the stairs.*]

LINDA. He won't be all right.

BIFF. [*turning on the stairs, furiously*] I hate this city and I'll stay here. Now what do you want?

LINDA. He's dying, Biff.

[*HAPPY turns quickly to her, shocked.*]

BIFF. [*after a pause*] Why is he dying?

LINDA. He's been trying to kill himself.

BIFF. [*with great horror*] How?

LINDA. I live from day to day.

BIFF. What're you talking about?

LINDA. Remember I wrote you that he smashed up the car again? In February?

BIFF. Well?

LINDA. The insurance inspector came. He said that they have evidence. That all these accidents in the last year—weren't—weren't—accidents.

HAPPY. How can they tell that? That's a lie.

LINDA. It seems there's a woman . . . [*She takes a breath as*]

⎡BIFF. [*sharply but contained*] What woman?
⎣LINDA. [*simultaneously*] . . . and this woman . . .

LINDA. What?

BIFF. Nothing. Go ahead.

LINDA. What did you say?

BIFF. Nothing. I just said what woman?

HAPPY. What about her?

LINDA. Well, it seems she was walking down the road and saw his car. She says that he wasn't driving fast at all, and that he didn't skid. She says he came to that little bridge, and then deliberately smashed into the railing, and it was only the shallowness of the water that saved him.

BIFF. Oh, no, he probably just fell asleep again.

LINDA. I don't think he fell asleep.

BIFF. Why not?

LINDA. Last month . . . [*with great difficulty*] Oh, boys, it's so hard to say a thing like this! He's just a big stupid man to you, but I tell you there's more good in him than in many other people. [*She chokes, wipes her eyes.*] I was looking for a fuse. The lights blew out, and I went down the cellar. And behind the fuse box—it happened to fall out—was a length of rubber pipe—just short.

HAPPY.   No kidding?

LINDA.   There's a little attachment on the end of it. I knew right away. And sure enough, on the bottom of the water heater there's a new little nipple on the gas pipe.

HAPPY.   [*angrily*] That—jerk.

BIFF.   Did you have it taken off?

LINDA.   I'm—I'm ashamed to. How can I mention it to him? Every day I go down and take away that little rubber pipe. But, when he comes home, I put it back where it was. How can I insult him that way? I don't know what to do. I live from day to day, boys. I tell you, I know every thought in his mind. It sounds so old-fashioned and silly, but I tell you he put his whole life into you and you've turned your backs on him. [*She is bent over in the chair, weeping, her face in her hands.*] Biff, I swear to God! Biff, his life is in your hands!

HAPPY.   [*to BIFF*] How do you like that damned fool!

BIFF.   [*kissing her*] All right, pal, all right. It's all settled now. I've been remiss. I know that, Mom. But now I'll stay, and I swear to you, I'll apply myself. [*kneeling in front of her, in a fever of self-reproach*] It's just—you see, Mom, I don't fit in business. Not that I won't try. I'll try, and I'll make good.

HAPPY.   Sure you will. The trouble with you in business was you never tried to please people.

BIFF.   I know, I—

HAPPY.   Like when you worked for Harrison's. Bob Harrison said you were tops, and then you go and do some damn fool thing like whistling whole songs in the elevator like a comedian.

BIFF.   [*against HAPPY*] So what? I like to whistle sometimes.

HAPPY.   You don't raise a guy to a responsible job who whistles in the elevator!

LINDA.   Well, don't argue about it now.

HAPPY.   Like when you'd go off and swim in the middle of the day instead of taking the line around.

BIFF.   [*his resentment rising*] Well, don't you run off? You take off sometimes, don't you? On a nice summer day?

HAPPY.   Yeah, but I cover myself!

LINDA.   Boys!

HAPPY.   If I'm going to take a fade the boss can call any number where I'm supposed to be and they'll swear to him that I just left. I'll tell you something that I hate to say, Biff, but in the business world some of them think you're crazy.

BIFF.   [*angered*] Screw the business world!

HAPPY.   All right, screw it! Great, but cover yourself!

LINDA.   Hap, Hap!

BIFF.   I don't care what they think! They've laughed at Dad for years, and you know why? Because we don't belong in this nuthouse of a city! We should be mixing cement on some open plain, or—or carpenters. A carpenter is allowed to whistle!

[*WILLY walks in from the entrance of the house, at left.*]

WILLY.   Even your grandfather was better than a carpenter. [*pause. They watch him.*] You never grew up. Bernard does not whistle in the elevator, I assure you.

BIFF.   [*as though to laugh WILLY out of it*] Yeah, but you do, Pop.

WILLY.   I never in my life whistled in an elevator! And who in the business world thinks I'm crazy?

BIFF.   I didn't mean it like that, Pop. Now don't make a whole thing out of it, will ya?

WILLY.   Go back to the West! Be a carpenter, a cowboy, enjoy yourself!

LINDA.   Willy, he was just saying—

WILLY.   I heard what he said!

HAPPY.   [*trying to quiet WILLY*] Hey, Pop, come on now . . .

WILLY.   [*continuing over HAPPY'S line*] They laugh at me, heh? Go to Filene's, go to the Hub, go to Slattery's,° Boston. Call out the name Willy Loman and see what happens! Big shot!

BIFF.   All right, Pop.

WILLY.   Big!

BIFF.   All right!

WILLY.   Why do you always insult me?

BIFF.   I didn't say a word. [*to LINDA*] Did I say a word?

LINDA.   He didn't say anything, Willy.

WILLY.   [*going to the doorway of the living-room*] All right, good night, good night.

LINDA.   Willy, dear, he just decided . . .

WILLY.   [*to BIFF*] If you get tired hanging around tomorrow, paint the ceiling I put up in the living-room.

BIFF.   I'm leaving early tomorrow.

HAPPY.   He's going to see Bill Oliver, Pop.

WILLY.   [*interestedly*] Oliver? For what?

BIFF.   [*with reserve, but trying, trying*] He always said he'd stake me. I'd like to go into business, so maybe I can take him up on it.

LINDA.   Isn't that wonderful?

WILLY.   Don't interrupt. What's wonderful about it? There's fifty men in the City of New York who'd stake him. [*to BIFF*] Sporting goods?

BIFF.   I guess so. I know something about it and—

WILLY.   He knows something about it! You know sporting goods better than Spalding, for God's sake! How much is he giving you?

BIFF.   I don't know. I didn't even see him yet, but—

WILLY.   Then what're you talkin' about?

BIFF.   [*getting angry*] Well, all I said was I'm gonna see him, that's all!

WILLY.   [*turning away*] Ah, you're counting your chickens again.

BIFF.   [*starting left for the stairs*] Oh, Jesus, I'm going to sleep!

WILLY.   [*calling after him*] Don't curse in this house!

BIFF.   [*turning*] Since when did you get so clean?

HAPPY.   [*trying to stop them*] Wait a . . .

WILLY.   Don't use that language to me! I won't have it!

HAPPY.   [*grabbing BIFF, shouts*] Wait a minute! I got an idea. I got a feasible idea. Come here, Biff, let's talk this over now, let's talk some sense here. When I was down in Florida last time, I thought of a great idea to sell sporting goods. It

---

°*Filene's, the Hub, Slattery's*: department stores in New England.

just came back to me. You and I, Biff—we have a line, the Loman Line. We train a couple of weeks, and put on a couple of exhibitions, see?

WILLY.   That's an idea!

HAPPY.   Wait! We form two basketball teams, see? Two waterpolo teams. We play each other. It's a million dollars' worth of publicity. Two brothers, see? The Loman Brothers. Displays in the Royal Palms—all the hotels. And banners over the ring and the basketball court: "Loman Brothers." Baby, we could sell sporting goods!

WILLY.   That is a one-million-dollar idea!

LINDA.   Marvelous!

BIFF.   I'm in great shape as far as that's concerned.

HAPPY.   And the beauty of it is, Biff, it wouldn't be like a business. We'd be out playin' ball again . . .

BIFF.   [*enthused*] Yeah, that's . . .

WILLY.   Million-dollar . . .

HAPPY.   And you wouldn't get fed up with it, Biff. It'd be the family again. There's be the old honor, and comradeship, and if you wanted to go off for a swim or somethin'—well, you'd do it! Without some smart cooky gettin' up ahead of you!

WILLY.   Lick the world! You guys together could absolutely lick the civilized world.

BIFF.   I'll see Oliver tomorrow. Hap, if we could work that out . . .

LINDA.   Maybe things are beginning to—

WILLY.   [*wildly enthused, to* LINDA] Stop interrupting! [*to* BIFF] But don't wear sport jacket and slacks when you see Oliver.

BIFF.   No, I'll—

WILLY.   A business suit, and talk as little as possible, and don't crack any jokes.

BIFF.   He did like me. Always liked me.

LINDA.   He loved you!

WILLY.   [*to* LINDA] Will you stop! [*to* BIFF] Walk in very serious. You are not applying for a boy's job. Money is to pass. Be quiet, fine, and serious. Everybody likes a kidder, but nobody lends him money.

HAPPY.   I'll try to get some myself, Biff. I'm sure I can.

WILLY.   I see great things for you kids. I think your troubles are over. But remember, start big and you'll end big. Ask for fifteen. How much you gonna ask for?

BIFF.   Gee, I don't know—

WILLY.   And don't say "Gee." "Gee" is a boy's word. A man walking in for fifteen thousand dollars does not say "Gee!"

BIFF.   Ten, I think, would be top though.

WILLY.   Don't be so modest. You always started too low. Walk in with a big laugh. Don't look worried. Start off with a couple of your good stories to lighten things up. It's not what you say, it's how you say it—because personality always wins the day.

LINDA.   Oliver always thought the highest of him—

WILLY.   Will you let me talk?

BIFF.   Don't yell at her, Pop, will ya?

WILLY.   [angrily] I was talking, wasn't I?

BIFF.   I don't like you yelling at her all the time, and I'm tellin' you, that's all.

WILLY.   What're you, takin' over this house?

LINDA.   Willy—

WILLY.   [turning on her] Don't take his side all the time, goddammit!

BIFF.   [furiously] Stop yelling at her!

WILLY.   [suddenly pulling on his cheek, beaten down, guilt ridden] Give my best to Bill Oliver—he may remember me.

[He exits through the living-room doorway.]

LINDA.   [her voice subdued] What'd you have to start that for? [BIFF turns away.] You see how sweet he was as soon as you talked hopefully? [She goes over to BIFF.] Come up and say good night to him. Don't let him go to bed that way.

HAPPY.   Come on, Biff, let's buck him up.

LINDA.   Please, dear. Just say good night. It takes so little to make him happy. Come. [She goes through the living-room doorway, calling upstairs from within the living-room.] Your pajamas are hanging in the bathroom, Willy!

HAPPY.   [looking toward where LINDA went out] What a woman! They broke the mold when they made her. You know that, Biff?

BIFF.   He's off salary. My God, working on commission!

HAPPY.   Well, let's face it: he's no hot-shot selling man. Except that sometimes, you have to admit, he's a sweet personality.

BIFF.   [deciding] Lend me ten bucks, will ya? I want to buy some new ties.

HAPPY.   I'll take you to a place I know. Beautiful stuff. Wear one of my striped shirts tomorrow.

BIFF.   She got gray. Mom got awful old. Gee, I'm gonna go in to Oliver tomorrow and knock him for a—

HAPPY.   Come on up. Tell that to Dad. Let's give him a whirl. Come on.

BIFF.   [steamed up] You know, with ten thousand bucks, boy!

HAPPY.   [as they go into the living-room] That's the talk, Biff, that's the first time I've heard the old confidence out of you! [from within the living-room, fading off] You're gonna live with me, kid, and any babe you want just say the word . . . [The last lines are hardly heard. They are mounting the stairs to their parents' bedroom.]

LINDA.   [entering her bedroom and addressing WILLY, who is in the bathroom. She is straightening the bed for him.] Can you do anything about the shower? It drips.

WILLY.   [from the bathroom] All of a sudden everything falls to pieces! Goddam plumbing, oughta be sued, those people. I hardly finished putting it in and the thing . . . [His words rumble off.]

LINDA.   I'm just wondering if Oliver will remember him. You think he might?

WILLY.   [coming out of the bathroom in his pajamas] Remember him? What's the matter with you, you crazy? If he'd've stayed with Oliver he'd be on top by now! Wait'll Oliver gets a look at him. You don't know the average caliber any more. The average young man today—[He is getting into bed]—is got a caliber of zero. Greatest thing in the world for him was to bum around.

[BIFF and HAPPY enter the bedroom. Slight pause.]

WILLY. [*stops short, looking at BIFF*] Glad to hear it, boy.

HAPPY. He wanted to say good night to you, sport.

WILLY. [*to BIFF*] Yeah. Knock him dead, boy. What'd you want to tell me?

BIFF. Just take it easy, Pop. Good night. [*He turns to go.*]

WILLY. [*unable to resist*] And if anything falls off the desk while you're talking to him—like a package or something—don't you pick it up. They have office boys for that.

LINDA. I'll make a big breakfast—

WILLY. Will you let me finish? [*to BIFF*] Tell him you were in the business in the West. Not farm work.

BIFF. All right, Dad.

LINDA. I think everything—

WILLY. [*going right through her speech*] And don't undersell yourself. No less than fifteen thousand dollars.

BIFF. [*unable to bear him*] Okay. Good night, Mom. [*He starts moving.*]

WILLY. Because you got a greatness in you, Biff, remember that. You got all kinds a greatness . . . [*He lies back, exhausted.*]

[*BIFF walks out.*]

LINDA. [*calling after BIFF*] Sleep well, darling!

HAPPY. I'm gonna get married, Mom. I wanted to tell you.

LINDA. Go to sleep, dear.

HAPPY. [*going*] I just wanted to tell you.

WILLY. Keep up the good work. [*HAPPY exits.*] God . . . remember that Ebbets Field° game? The championship of the city?

LINDA. Just rest. Should I sing to you?

WILLY. Yeah. Sing to me. [*LINDA hums a soft lullaby.*] When that team came out—he was the tallest, remember?

LINDA. Oh, yes. And in gold.

[*BIFF enters the darkened kitchen, takes a cigarette, and leaves the house. He comes downstage into a golden pool of light. He smokes, staring at the night.*]

WILLY. Like a young god. Hercules—something like that. And the sun, the sun all around him. Remember how he waved to me? Right up from the field, with the representatives of three colleges standing by? And the buyers I brought, and the cheers when he came out—Loman, Loman, Loman! God Almighty, he'll be great yet. A star like that, magnificent, can never really fade away!

[*The light on WILLY is fading. The gas heater begins to glow through the kitchen wall, near the stairs, a blue flame beneath red coils.*]

LINDA. [*timidly*] Willy dear, what has he got against you?

WILLY. I'm so tired. Don't talk any more.

[*BIFF slowly returns to the kitchen. He stops, stares toward the heater.*]

°*Ebbets Field*: the baseball stadium of the Brooklyn Dodgers before they moved to Los Angeles in 1958.

LINDA.   Will you ask Howard to let you work in New York?
WILLY.   First thing in the morning. Everything'll be all right.

[*BIFF reaches behind the heater and draws out a length of rubber tubing. He is horrified and turns his head toward WILLY'S room, still dimly lit, from which the strains of LINDA'S desperate but monotonous humming rise.*]

WILLY.   [*staring through the window into the moonlight*] Gee, look at the moon moving between the buildings!

[*BIFF wraps the tubing around his hand and quickly goes up the stairs.*]

ACT 2

[*Music is heard, gay and bright. The curtain rises as the music fades away. WILLY, in shirt sleeves, is sitting at the kitchen table, sipping coffee, his hat in his lap. LINDA is filling his cup when she can.*]

WILLY.   Wonderful coffee. Meal in itself.
LINDA.   Can I make you some eggs?
WILLY.   No. Take a breath.
LINDA.   You look so rested, dear.
WILLY.   I slept like a dead one. First time in months. Imagine, sleeping till ten on a Tuesday morning. Boys left nice and early, heh?
LINDA.   They were out of here by eight o'clock.
WILLY.   Good work!
LINDA.   It was so thrilling to see them leaving together. I can't get over the shaving lotion in this house!
WILLY.   [*smiling*] Mmm—
LINDA.   Biff was very changed this morning. His whole attitude seemed to be hopeful. He couldn't wait to get downtown to see Oliver.
WILLY.   He's heading for a change. There's no question, there simply are certain men that take longer to get—solidified. How did he dress?
LINDA.   His blue suit. He's so handsome in that suit. He could be a—anything in that suit!

[*WILLY gets up from the table. LINDA holds his jacket for him.*]

WILLY.   There's no question, no question at all. Gee, on the way home tonight I'd like to buy some seeds.
LINDA.   [*laughing*] That'd be wonderful. But not enough sun gets back there. Nothing'll grow any more.
WILLY.   You wait, kid, before it's all over we're gonna get a little place out in the country, and I'll raise some vegetables, a couple of chickens . . .
LINDA.   You'll do it yet, dear.

[*WILLY walks out of his jacket, LINDA follows him.*]

WILLY.   And they'll get married, and come for a weekend. I'd build a little guest house. 'Cause I got so many fine tools, all I'd need would be a little lumber and some peace of mind.

LINDA.   [*joyfully*] I sewed the lining . . .

WILLY.   I could build two guest houses, so they'd both come. Did he decide how much he's going to ask Oliver for?

LINDA.   [*getting him into the jacket*] He didn't mention it, but I imagine ten or fifteen thousand. You going to talk to Howard today?

WILLY.   Yeah. I'll put it to him straight and simple. He'll just have to take me off the road.

LINDA.   And Willy, don't forget to ask for a little advance, because we've got the insurance premium. It's the grace period now.

WILLY.   That's a hundred . . . ?

LINDA.   A hundred and eight, sixty-eight. Because we're a little short again.

WILLY.   Why are we short?

LINDA.   Well, you had the motor job on the car . . .

WILLY.   That goddam Studebaker!

LINDA.   And you got one more payment on the refrigerator . . .

WILLY.   But it just broke again!

LINDA.   Well, it's old, dear.

WILLY.   I told you we should've bought a well-advertised machine. Charley bought a General Electric and it's twenty years old and it's still good, that son-of-a-bitch.

LINDA.   But, Willy—

WILLY.   Whoever heard of a Hastings refrigerator? Once in my life I would like to own something outright before it's broken! I'm always in a race with the junkyard! I just finished paying for the car and it's on its last legs. The refrigerator consumes belts like a goddam maniac. They time those things. They time them so when you finally paid for them, they're used up.

LINDA.   [*buttoning up his jacket as he unbuttons it*] All told, about two hundred dollars would carry us, dear. But that includes the last payment on the mortgage. After this payment, Willy, the house belongs to us.

WILLY.   It's twenty-five years!

LINDA.   Biff was nine years old when we bought it.

WILLY.   Well, that's a great thing. To weather a twenty-five year mortgage is—

LINDA.   It's an accomplishment.

WILLY.   All the cement, the lumber, the reconstruction I put in this house! There ain't a crack to be found in it any more.

LINDA.   Well, it served its purpose.

WILLY.   What purpose? Some stranger'll come along, move in, and that's that. If only Biff would take this house, and raise a family . . . [*He starts to go.*] Good-by, I'm late.

LINDA.   [*suddenly remembering*] Oh, I forgot! You're supposed to meet them for dinner.

WILLY.   Me?

LINDA.   At Frank's Chop House on Forty-eighth near Sixth Avenue.

WILLY.   Is that so! How about you?

LINDA.   No, just the three of you. They're gonna blow you to a big meal!

WILLY.   Don't say! Who thought of that?

LINDA.   Biff came to me this morning, Willy, and he said, "Tell Dad, we want to blow him to a big meal." Be there six o'clock. You and your two boys are going to have dinner.

WILLY.   Gee whiz! That's really somethin'. I'm gonna knock Howard for a loop, kid. I'll get an advance, and I'll come home with a New York job. Goddammit, now I'm gonna do it!

LINDA.   Oh, that's the spirit, Willy!

WILLY.   I will never get behind a wheel the rest of my life!

LINDA.   It's changing, Willy, I can feel it changing!

WILLY.   Beyond a question. G'by, I'm late. [*He starts to go again.*]

LINDA.   [*calling after him as she runs to the kitchen table for a handkerchief*] You got your glasses?

WILLY.   [*feels for them, then comes back in*] Yeah, yeah, got my glasses.

LINDA.   [*giving him the handkerchief*] And a handkerchief.

WILLY.   Yeah, handkerchief.

LINDA.   And your saccharine?

WILLY.   Yeah, my saccharine.

LINDA.   Be careful on the subway stairs.

[*She kisses him, and a silk stocking is seen hanging from her hand. WILLY notices it.*]

WILLY.   Will you stop mending stockings? At least while I'm in the house. It gets me nervous. I can't tell you. Please.

[*LINDA hides the stocking in her hand as she follows WILLY across the forestage in front of the house.*]

LINDA.   Remember, Frank's Chop House.

WILLY.   [*passing the apron*] Maybe beets would grow out there.

LINDA.   [*laughing*] But you tried so many times.

WILLY.   Yeah. Well, don't work hard today. [*He disappears around the right corner of the house.*]

LINDA.   Be careful!

[*As WILLY vanishes, LINDA waves to him. Suddenly the phone rings. She runs across the stage and into the kitchen and lifts it.*]

LINDA.   Hello? Oh, Biff! I'm so glad you called, I just . . . Yes, sure, I just told him. Yes, he'll be there for dinner at six o'clock, I didn't forget. Listen, I was just dying to tell you. You know that little rubber pipe I told you about? That he connected to the gas heater? I finally decided to go down the cellar this morning and take it away and destroy it. But it's gone! Imagine? He took it away himself, it isn't there! [*She listens.*] When? Oh, then you took it. Oh—nothing, it's just that I'd hoped he'd taken it away himself. Oh, I'm not worried, darling, because this morning he left in such high spirits, it was like the old days! I'm not afraid any more. Did Mr. Oliver see you? . . . Well, you wait there then. And make a nice impression on him, darling. Just don't perspire too much before you see him. And have a nice time with Dad. He may have big news too! . . . That's right, a New York job. And be sweet to him tonight, dear. Be loving to him. Because he's only a little boat looking for a harbor. [*She is trembling with sorrow and joy.*] Oh, that's wonderful, Biff, you'll save his life. Thanks, darling. Just put your arm

around him when he comes into the restaurant. Give him a smile. That's the boy
. . . Good-by, dear . . . You got your comb? . . . That's fine. Good-by, Biff dear.

[*In the middle of her speech,* HOWARD WAGNER, *thirty-six, wheels on a small typewriter table on which is a wire-recording machine and proceeds to plug it in. This is on the left forestage. Light slowly fades on* LINDA *as it rises on* HOWARD. HOWARD *is intent on threading the machine and only glances over his shoulder as* WILLY *appears.*]

WILLY.   Pst! Pst!

HOWARD.   Hello, Willy, come in.

WILLY.   Like to have a little talk with you, Howard.

HOWARD.   Sorry to keep you waiting. I'll be with you in a minute.

WILLY.   What't that, Howard?

HOWARD.   Didn't you ever see one of these? Wire recorder.

WILLY.   Oh. Can we talk a minute?

HOWARD.   Records things. Just got delivery yesterday. Been driving me crazy, the most terrific machine I ever saw in my life. I was up all night with it.

WILLY.   What do you do with it?

HOWARD.   I bought it for dictation, but you can do anything with it. Listen to this. I had it home last night. Listen to what I picked up. The first one is my daughter. Get this. [*He flicks the switch and "Roll out the Barrel" is heard being whistled.*] Listen to that kid whistle.

WILLY.   That is lifelike, isn't it?

HOWARD.   Seven years old. Get that tone.

WILLY.   Ts, ts. Like to ask a little favor if you . . .

[*The whistling breaks off, and the voice of* HOWARD'S DAUGHTER *is heard.*]

HIS DAUGHTER.   "Now you, Daddy."

HOWARD.   She's crazy for me! [*Again the same song is whistled.*] That's me! Ha! [*He winks.*]

WILLY.   You're very good!

[*The whistling breaks off again. The machine runs silent for a moment.*]

HOWARD.   Sh! Get this now, this is my son.

HIS SON.   "The capital of Alabama is Montgomery; the capital of Arizona is Phoenix; the capital of Arkansas is Little Rock; the capital of California is Sacramento . . ." [*and on, and on*]

HOWARD.   [*holding up five fingers*] Five years old, Willy!

WILLY.   He'll make an announcer some day!

HIS SON.   [*continuing*] "The capital . . ."

HOWARD.   Get that—alphabetical order! [*The machine breaks off suddenly.*] Wait a minute. The maid kicked the plug out.

WILLY.   It certainly is a—

HOWARD.   Sh, for God's sake!

HIS SON.   "It's nine o'clock, Bulova watch time. So I have to go to sleep."

WILLY.   That really is—

HOWARD.   Wait a minute! The next is my wife.

[*They wait.*]

HOWARD'S VOICE.   "Go on, say something." [*pause*] "Well, you gonna talk?"

HIS WIFE.   "I can't think of anything."

HOWARD'S VOICE.   "Well, talk—it's turning."

HIS WIFE.   [*shyly, beaten*] "Hello." [*Silence*] "Oh, Howard, I can't talk into this . . ."

HOWARD.   [*snapping the machine off*] That was my wife.

WILLY.   That is a wonderful machine. Can we—

HOWARD.   I tell you, Willy, I'm gonna take my camera, and my bandsaw, and all my hobbies, and out they go. This is the most fascinating relaxation I ever found.

WILLY.   I think I'll get one myself.

HOWARD.   Sure, they're only a hundred and a half. You can't do without it. Supposing you wanna hear Jack Benny,° see? But you can't be at home at that hour. So you tell the maid to turn the radio on when Jack Benny comes on, and this automatically goes on with the radio . . .

WILLY.   And when you come home you . . .

HOWARD.   You can come home twelve o'clock, one o'clock, any time you like, and you get yourself a Coke and sit yourself down, throw the switch, and there's Jack Benny's program in the middle of the night!

WILLY.   I'm definitely going to get one. Because lots of time I'm on the road, and I think to myself, what I must be missing on the radio!

HOWARD.   Don't you have a radio in the car?

WILLY.   Well, yeah, but who ever thinks of turning it on?

HOWARD.   Say, aren't you supposed to be in Boston?

WILLY.   That's what I want to talk to you about, Howard. You got a minute?

[*He draws a chair in from the wing.*]

HOWARD.   What happened? What're you doing here?

WILLY.   Well . . .

HOWARD.   You didn't crack up again, did you?

WILLY.   Oh, no. No . . .

HOWARD.   Geez, you had me worried there for a minute. What's the trouble?

WILLY.   Well, tell you the truth, Howard. I've come to the decision that I'd rather not travel any more.

HOWARD.   Not travel! Well, what'll you do?

WILLY.   Remember, Christmas time, when you had the party here? You said you'd try to think of some spot for me here in town.

HOWARD.   With us?

WILLY.   Well, sure.

HOWARD.   Oh, yeah, yeah. I remember. Well, I couldn't think of anything for you, Willy.

WILLY.   I tell ya, Howard. The kids are all grown up, y'know. I don't need much any more. If I could take home—well, sixty-five dollars a week, I could swing it.

HOWARD.   Yeah, but Willy, see I—

°*Jack Benny*: (1894–1974), vaudeville, radio, television and movie comedian.

WILLY.   I tell ya why, Howard. Speaking frankly and between the two of us, y'know—I'm just a little tired.

HOWARD.   Oh, I could understand that, Willy. But you're a road man, Willy, and we do a road business. We've only got a half-dozen salesmen on the floor here.

WILLY.   God knows, Howard, I never asked a favor of any man. But I was with the firm when your father used to carry you up here in his arms.

HOWARD.   I know that, Willy, but—

WILLY.   Your father came to me the day you were born and asked me what I thought of the name of Howard, may he rest in peace.

HOWARD.   I appreciate that, Willy, but there just is no spot here for you. If I had a spot I'd slam you right in, but I just don't have a single solitary spot.

[*He looks for his lighter. WILLY has picked it up and gives it to him. Pause.*]

WILLY.   [*with increasing anger*] Howard, all I need to set my table is fifty dollars a week.

HOWARD.   But where am I going to put you, kid?

WILLY.   Look, it isn't a question of whether I can sell merchandise, is it?

HOWARD.   No, but it's a business, kid, and everybody's gotta pull his own weight.

WILLY.   [*desperately*] Just let me tell you a story, Howard—

HOWARD.   'Cause you gotta admit, business is business.

WILLY.   [*angrily*] Business in definitely business, but just listen for a minute. You don't understand this. When I was a boy—eighteen, nineteen—I was already on the road. And there was a question in my mind as to whether selling had a future for me. Because in those days I had a yearning to go to Alaska. See, there were three gold strikes in one month in Alaska, and I felt like going out. Just for the ride, you might say.

HOWARD.   [barely interested] Don't say.

WILLY.   Oh, yeah, my father lived many years in Alaska. He was an adventurous man. We've got quite a little streak of self-reliance in our family. I thought I'd go out with my older brother and try to locate him, and maybe settle in the North with the old man. And I was almost decided to go, when I met a salesman in the Parker House.° His name was Dave Singleman. And he was eighty-four years old, and he'd drummed merchandise in thirty-one states. And old Dave, he'd go up to his room, y'understand, put on his green velvet slippers—I'll never forget—and pick up his phone and call the buyers, and without ever leaving his room, at the age of eighty-four, he made his living. And when I saw that, I realized that selling was the greatest career a man could want. 'Cause what could be more satisfying than to be able to go, at the age of eighty-four, into twenty or thirty different cities, and pick up a phone, and be remembered and loved and helped by so many different people? Do you know? when he died—and by the way he died the death of a salesman, in his green velvet slippers in the smoker of the New York, New Haven and Hartford, going into Boston—when he died, hundreds of salesmen and buyers were at his funeral. Things were sad on a lotta trains for

---

°*Parker House*: a hotel in Boston.

months after that. [*He stands up. HOWARD has not looked at him.*] In those days there was personality in it, Howard. There was respect, and comradeship, and gratitude in it. Today, it's all cut and dried, and there's no chance for bringing friendship to bear—or personality. You see what I mean? They don't know me any more.

HOWARD. [*moving away, to the right*] That's just the thing, Willy.

WILLY. If I had forty dollars a week—that's all I'd need. Forty dollars, Howard.

HOWARD. Kid, I can't take blood from a stone, I—

WILLY. [*desperation is on him now*] Howard, the year Al Smith° was nominated, your father came to me and—

HOWARD. [*starting to go off*] I've got to see some people, kid.

WILLY. [*stopping him*] I'm talking about your father! There were promises made across this desk! You mustn't tell me you've got people to see—I put thirty-four years into this firm, Howard, and now I can't pay my insurance! You can't eat the orange and throw the peel away—a man is not a piece of fruit! [*after a pause*] Now pay attention. Your father—in 1928 I had a big year. I averaged a hundred and seventy dollars a week in commissions.

HOWARD. [*impatiently*] Now, Willy, you never averaged—

WILLY. [*banging his hand on the desk*] I averaged a hundred and seventy dollars a week in the year of 1928! And your father came to me—or rather, I was in the office here—it was right over this desk—and he put his hand on my shoulder—

HOWARD. [*getting up*] You'll have to excuse me, Willy, I gotta see some people. Pull yourself together. [*going out*] I'll be back in a little while.

[*On HOWARD'S exit, the light on his chair grows very bright and strange.*]

WILLY. Pull myself together! What the hell did I say to him? My God, I was yelling at him! How could I! [*WILLY breaks off, staring at the light, which occupies the chair, animating it. He approaches this chair, standing across the desk from it.*] Frank, Frank, don't you remember what you told me that time? How you put your hand on my shoulder, and Frank . . . [*He leans on the desk and as he speaks the dead man's name he accidentally switches on the recorder, and instantly*]

HOWARD'S SON. ". . . of New York is Albany. The capital of Ohio is Cincinnati, the capital of Rhode Island is . . ." [*The recitation continues.*]

WILLY. [*leaping away with fright, shouting*] Ha! Howard! Howard! Howard!

HOWARD. [*rushing in*] What happened?

WILLY. [*pointing at the machine, which continues nasally, childishly, with the capital cities*] Shut it off! Shut it off!

HOWARD. [*pulling the plug out*] Look, Willy . . .

WILLY. [*pressing his hands to his eyes*] I gotta get myself some coffee. I'll get some coffee . . .

[*WILLY starts to walk out. HOWARD stops him.*]

HOWARD. [*rolling up the cord*] Willy, look . . .

WILLY. I'll go to Boston.

°*Al Smith*: Alfred E. Smith was governor of New York State (1919–1921, 1923–1929) and the Democratic presidential candidate defeated by Herbert Hoover in 1928.

HOWARD. Willy, you can't go to Boston for us.

WILLY. Why can't I go?

HOWARD. I don't want you to represent us. I've been meaning to tell you for a long time now.

WILLY. Howard, are you firing me?

HOWARD. I think you need a good long rest, Willy.

WILLY. Howard—

HOWARD. And when you feel better, come back, and we'll see if we can work something out.

WILLY. But I gotta earn money, Howard. I'm in no position to—

HOWARD. Where are your sons? Why don't your sons give you a hand?

WILLY. They're working on a very big deal.

HOWARD. This is no time for false pride, Willy. You go to your sons and you tell them that you're tired. You've got two great boys, haven't you?

WILLY. Oh, no question, no question, but in the meantime . . .

HOWARD. Then that's that, heh?

WILLY. All right, I'll go to Boston tomorrow.

HOWARD. No, no.

WILLY. I can't throw myself on my sons. I'm not a cripple!

HOWARD. Look, kid, I'm busy this morning.

WILLY. [*grasping HOWARD'S arm*] Howard, you've got to let me go to Boston!

HOWARD. [*hard, keeping himself under control*] I've got a line of people to see this morning. Sit down, take five minutes, and pull yourself together, and then go home, will ya? I need the office, Willy. [*He starts to go, turns, remembering the recorder, starts to push off the table holding the recorder.*] Oh, yeah. Whenever you can this week, stop by and drop off the samples. You'll feel better, Willy, and then come back and we'll talk. Pull yourself together, kid, there's people outside.

[*HOWARD exits, pushing the table off left. WILLY stares into space, exhausted. Now the music is heard—BEN'S music—first distantly, then closer. As WILLY speaks, BEN enters from the right. He carries valise and umbrella.*]

WILLY. Oh, Ben, how did you do it? What is the answer? Did you wind up the Alaska deal already?

BEN. Doesn't take much time if you know what you're doing. Just a short business trip. Boarding ship in an hour. Wanted to say good-by.

WILLY. Ben, I've got to talk to you.

BEN. [*glancing at his watch*] Haven't much time, William.

WILLY. [*crossing the apron to BEN*] Ben, nothing's working out. I don't know what to do.

BEN. Now, look here, William. I've bought timberland in Alaska and I need a man to look after things for me.

WILLY. God, timberland! Me and my boys in those grand outdoors!

BEN. You've a new continent at your doorstep, William. Get out of these cities, they're full of talk and time payments and courts of law. Screw on your fists and you can fight for a fortune up there.

WILLY. Yes, yes! Linda, Linda!

[*LINDA enters as of old, with the wash.*]

LINDA.   Oh, you're back?

BEN.   I haven't much time.

WILLY.   No, wait! Linda, he's got a proposition for me in Alaska.

LINDA.   But you've got—[*to BEN*] He's got a beautiful job here.

WILLY.   But in Alaska, kid, I could—

LINDA.   You're doing well enough, Willy!

BEN.   [*to LINDA*] Enough for what, my dear?

LINDA.   [*frightened of BEN and angry at him*] Don't say those things to him! Enough to be happy right here, right now. [*to WILLY, while BEN laughs*] Why must everybody conquer the world? You're well liked, and the boys love you, and some-day—[*to BEN*]—why old man Wagner told him just the other day that if he keeps it up he'll be a member of the firm, didn't he, Willy?

WILLY.   Sure, sure. I am building something with this firm, Ben, and if a man is building something he must be on the right track, mustn't he?

BEN.   What are you building? Lay your hand on it. Where is it?

WILLY.   [*hesitantly*] That's true, Linda, there's nothing.

LINDA.   Why? [*to BEN*] There's a man eighty-four years old—

WILLY.   That's right, Ben, that's right. When I look at that man I say, what is there to worry about?

BEN.   Bah!

WILLY.   It's true, Ben. All he has to do is go into any city, pick up the phone, and he's making his living and you know why?

BEN.   [*picking up his valise*] I've got to go.

WILLY.   [*holding BEN back*] Look at this boy!

[*BIFF, in his high school sweater, enters carrying suitcase. HAPPY carries BIFF'S shoulder guards, gold helmet, and football pants.*]

WILLY.   Without a penny to his name, three great universities are begging for him, and from there the sky's the limit, because it's not what you do, Ben. It's who you know and the smile on your face! It's contacts, Ben, contacts! The whole wealth of Alaska passes over the lunch table at the Commodore Hotel,° and that's the wonder, the wonder of this country, that a man can end with diamonds here on the basis of being liked! [*He turns to BIFF*] And that's why when you get out on that field today it's important. Because thousands of people will be rooting for you and loving you. [*to BEN, who has again begun to leave*] And Ben! when he walks into a business office his name will sound out like a bell and all the doors will open to him! I've seen it, Ben, I've seen it a thousand times! You can't feel it with your hand like timber, but it's there!

BEN.   Good-by, William.

WILLY.   Ben, am I right? Don't you think I'm right? I value your advice.

BEN.   There's a new continent at your doorstep, William. You could walk out rich. Rich! [*He is gone.*]

WILLY.   We'll do it here, Ben! You hear me? We're gonna do it here!

[*YOUNG BERNARD rushes in. The gay music of the Boys is heard.*]

°*Commodore Hotel*: a large hotel in New York City.

BERNARD. Oh, gee, I was afraid you left already!

WILLY. Why? What time is it?

BERNARD. It's half-past one!

WILLY. Well, come on, everybody! Ebbets Field next stop! Where's the pennants? [*He rushes through the wall-line of the kitchen and out into the living-room.*]

LINDA. [*to BIFF*] Did you pack fresh underwear?

BIFF. [*who has been limbering up*] I want to go!

BERNARD. Biff, I'm carrying your helmet, ain't I?

HAPPY. No, I'm carrying the helmet.

BERNARD. Oh, Biff, you promised me.

HAPPY. I'm carrying the helmet.

BERNARD. How am I going to get in the locker room?

LINDA. Let him carry the shoulder guards. [*She puts her coat and hat on in the kitchen.*]

BERNARD. Can I, Biff? 'Cause I told everybody I'm going to be in the locker room.

HAPPY. In Ebbets Field it's the clubhouse.

BERNARD. I meant the clubhouse. Biff!

HAPPY. Biff!

BIFF. [*grandly, after a slight pause*] Let him carry the shoulder guards.

HAPPY. [*as he gives BERNARD the shoulder guards*] Stay close to us now.

[*WILLY rushes in with the pennants.*]

WILLY. [*handing them out*] Everybody wave when Biff comes out on the field. [*HAPPY and BERNARD run off.*] You set now, boy?

[*The music has died away.*]

BIFF. Ready to go, Pop. Every muscle is ready.

WILLY. [*at the edge of the apron*] You realize what this means?

BIFF. That's right, Pop.

WILLY. [*feeling BIFF'S muscles*] You're comin' home this afternoon captain of the All-Scholastic Championship Team of the City of New York.

BIFF. I got it, Pop. And remember, pal, when I take off my helmet, that touchdown is for you.

WILLY. Let's go! [*He is starting out, with his arm around BIFF, when CHARLEY enters, as of old, in knickers.*] I got no room for you, Charley.

CHARLEY. Room? For what?

WILLY. In the car.

CHARLEY. You goin' for a ride? I wanted to shoot some casino.

WILLY. [*furiously*] Casino! [*incredulously*] Don't you realize what today is?

LINDA. Oh, he knows, Willy. He's just kidding you.

WILLY. That's nothing to kid about!

CHARLEY. No, Linda, what's goin' on?

LINDA. He's playing in Ebbets Field.

CHARLEY. Baseball in this weather?

WILLY. Don't talk to him. Come on, come on! [*He is pushing them out.*]

CHARLEY. Wait a minute, didn't you hear the news?

WILLY. What?

CHARLEY. Don't you listen to the radio? Ebbets Field just blew up.

WILLY. You go to hell! [*CHARLEY laughs. Pushing them out.*] Come on, come on! We're late.

CHARLEY [*as they go*] Knock a homer, Biff, knock a homer!

WILLY. [*the last to leave, turning to CHARLEY*] I don't think that was funny, Charley. This is the greatest day of his life.

CHARLEY. Willy, when are you going to grow up?

WILLY. Yeah, heh? When this game is over, Charley, you'll be laughing out the other side of your face. They'll be calling him another Red Grange.° Twenty-five thousand a year.

CHARLEY. [*kidding*] Is that so?

WILLY. Yeah, that's so.

CHARLEY. Well, then, I'm sorry, Willy. But tell me something.

WILLY. What?

CHARLEY. Who is Red Grange?

WILLY. Put up your hands. Goddam you, put up your hands!

[*CHARLEY, chuckling, shakes his head and walks away, around the left corner of the stage. WILLY follows him. The music rises to a mocking frenzy.*]

WILLY. Who the hell do you think you are, better than everybody else? You don't know everything, you big, ignorant, stupid. . . . Put up your hands!

[*Light rises, on the right side of the forestage, on a small table in the reception room of CHARLEY'S office. Traffic sounds are heard. BERNARD, now mature, sits whistling to himself. A pair of tennis rackets and an overnight bag are on the floor beside him.*]

WILLY. [*offstage*] What are you walking away for? Don't walk away! If you're going to say something say it to my face! I know you laugh at me behind my back. You'll laugh out of the other side of your goddam face after this game. Touchdown! Touchdown! Eighty thousand people! Touchdown. Right between the goal posts.

[*BERNARD is a quiet, earnest, but self-assured young man. WILLY'S voice is coming from right upstage now. BERNARD lowers his feet off the table and listens. JENNY, his father's secretary, enters.*]

JENNY. [*distressed*] Say, Bernard, will you go out in the hall?

BERNARD. What is that noise? Who is it?

JENNY. Mr. Loman. He just got off the elevator.

BERNARD. [*getting up*] Who's he arguing with?

JENNY. Nobody. There's nobody with him. I can't deal with him any more, and your father gets all upset everytime he comes. I've got a lot of typing to do, and your father's waiting to sign it. Will you see him?

WILLY. [*entering*] Touchdown! Touch—[*He sees JENNY.*] Jenny, Jenny, good to see you. How're ya? Workin'? Or still honest?

°*Red Grange*: Harold Edward Grange, all-American halfback (1923–1925) at the University of Illinois.

JENNY.   Fine. How've you been feeling?

WILLY.   Not much any more, Jenny. Ha, ha! [*He is surprised to see the rackets*.]

BERNARD.   Hello, Uncle Willy.

WILLY.   [*almost shocked*] Bernard! Well, look who's here! [*He comes quickly, guiltily, to* BERNARD *and warmly shakes his hand*.]

BERNARD.   How are you? Good to see you.

WILLY.   What are you doing here?

BERNARD.   Oh, just stopped off to see Pop. Get off my feet till my train leaves. I'm going to Washington in a few minutes.

WILLY.   Is he in?

BERNARD.   Yes, he's in his office with the accountants. Sit down.

WILLY.   [*sitting down*] What're you going to do in Washington?

BERNARD.   Oh, just a case I've got there, Willy.

WILLY.   That so? [*Indicating the rackets*] You going to play tennis there?

BERNARD.   I'm staying with a friend who's got a court.

WILLY.   Don't say. His own tennis court. Must be fine people, I bet.

BERNARD.   They are, very nice. Dad tells me Biff's in town.

WILLY.   [*with a big smile*] Yeah, Biff's in. Working on a very big deal, Bernard.

BERNARD.   What's Biff doing?

WILLY.   Well, he's been doing very big things in the West. But he decided to establish himself here. Very big. We're having dinner. Did I hear your wife had a boy?

BERNARD.   That's right. Our second.

WILLY.   Two boys! What do you know!

BERNARD.   What kind of a deal has Biff got?

WILLY.   Well, Bill Oliver—very big sporting-goods man—he wants Biff very badly. Called him in from the West. Long distance, carte blanche, special deliveries. Your friends have their own private tennis court?

BERNARD.   You still with the old firm, Willy?

WILLY.   [*after a pause*] I'm—I'm overjoyed to see how you made the grade, Bernard, overjoyed. It's an encouraging thing to see a young man really—really— Looks very good for Biff—very—[*He breaks off, then*] Bernard— [*He is so full of emotion, he breaks off again*.]

BERNARD.   What is it, Willy?

WILLY.   [*small and alone*] What—what's the secret?

BERNARD.   What secret?

WILLY.   How—how did you? Why didn't he ever catch on?

BERNARD.   I wouldn't know that, Willy.

WILLY.   [*confidentially, desperately*] You were his friend, his boyhood friend. There's something I don't understand about it. His life ended after that Ebbets Field game. From the age of seventeen nothing good ever happened to him.

BERNARD.   He never trained himself for anything.

WILLY.   But he did, he did. After high school he took so many correspondence courses. Radio mechanics; television; God knows what, and never made the slightest mark.

BERNARD.   [*taking off his glasses*] Willy, do you want to talk candidly?

WILLY.   [*rising, faces* BERNARD] I regard you as a very brilliant man, Bernard. I value your advice.

BERNARD. Oh, the hell with the advice, Willy. I couldn't advise you. There's just one thing I've always wanted to ask you. When he was supposed to graduate, and the math teacher flunked him—

WILLY. Oh, that son-of-a-bitch ruined his life.

BERNARD. Yeah, but, Willy, all he had to do was go to summer school and make up that subject.

WILLY. That's right, that's right.

BERNARD. Did you tell him not to go to summer school?

WILLY. Me? I begged him to go. I ordered him to go!

BERNARD. Then why wouldn't he go?

WILLY. Why? Why! Bernard, that question has been trailing me like a ghost for the last fifteen years. He flunked the subject, and laid down and died like a hammer hit him!

BERNARD. Take it easy, kid.

WILLY. Let me talk to you—I got nobody to talk to. Bernard, Bernard, was it my fault? Y'see? It keeps going around in my mind, maybe I did something to him. I got nothing to give him.

BERNARD. Don't take it so hard.

WILLY. Why did he lay down? What is the story there? You were his friend!

BERNARD. Willy, I remember, it was June, and our grades came out. And he'd flunked math.

WILLY. That son-of-a-bitch!

BERNARD. No, it wasn't right then. Biff just got very angry, I remember, and he was ready to enroll in summer school.

WILLY. [*surprised*] He was?

BERNARD. He wasn't beaten by it at all. But then, Willy, he disappeared from the block for almost a month. And I got the idea that he'd gone up to New England to see you. Did he have a talk with you then?

[*WILLY stares in silence.*]

BERNARD. Willy?

WILLY. [*with a strong edge of resentment in his voice*] Yeah, he came to Boston. What about it?

BERNARD. Well, just that when he came back—I'll never forget this, it always mystifies me. Because I'd thought so well of Biff, even though he'd always taken advantage of me. I loved him, Willy, y'know? And he came back after that month and took his sneakers—remember the sneakers with "University of Virginia" printed on them? He was so proud of those, wore them every day. And he took them down in the cellar, and burned them up in the furnace. We had a fist fight. It lasted at least half an hour. Just the two of us, punching each other down the cellar, and crying right through it. I've often thought of how strange it was that I knew he'd given up his life. What happened in Boston, Willy?

[*WILLY looks at him as at an intruder.*]

BERNARD. I just bring it up because you asked me.

WILLY. [*angrily*] Nothing. What do you mean, "What happened?" What's that got to do with anything?

BERNARD. Well, don't get sore.

WILLY.   What are you trying to do, blame it on me? If a boy lays down is that my fault?

BERNARD.   Now, Willy, don't get—

WILLY.   Well, don't—don't talk to me that way! What does that mean, "What happened?"

[*CHARLEY enters. He is in his vest, and he carries a bottle of bourbon.*]

CHARLEY.   Hey, you're going to miss that train. [*He waves the bottle.*]

BERNARD.   Yeah, I'm going. [*He takes the bottle.*] Thanks, Pop. [*He picks up his rackets and bag.*] Good-by, Willy, and don't worry about it. You know, "If at first you don't succeed . . ."

WILLY.   Yes, I believe in that.

BERNARD.   But sometimes, Willy, it's better for a man just to walk away.

WILLY.   Walk away?

BERNARD.   That's right.

WILLY.   But if you can't walk away?

BERNARD.   [*after a slight pause*] I guess that's when it's tough. [*extending his hand*] Good-by, Willy.

WILLY.   [*shaking BERNARD'S hand*] Good-by, boy.

CHARLEY.   [*an arm on BERNARD'S shoulder*] How do you like this kid? Gonna argue a case in front of the Supreme Court.

BERNARD.   [*protesting*] Pop!

WILLY.   [*genuinely shocked, pained, and happy*] No! The Supreme Court!

BERNARD.   I gotta run. 'By, Dad!

CHARLEY.   Knock 'em dead, Bernard!

[*BERNARD goes off.*]

WILLY.   [*as CHARLEY takes out his wallet*] The Supreme Court! And he didn't even mention it!

CHARLEY.   [*counting out money on the desk*] He don't have to—he's gonna do it.

WILLY.   And you never told him what to do, did you? You never took any interest in him.

CHARLEY.   My salvation is that I never took any interest in anything. There's some money—fifty dollars. I got an accountant inside.

WILLY.   Charley, look . . . [*with difficulty*] I got my insurance to pay. If you can manage it—I need a hundred and ten dollars.

[*CHARLEY doesn't reply for a moment; merely stops moving.*]

WILLY.   I'd draw it from my bank but Linda would know, and I . . .

CHARLEY.   Sit down, Willy.

WILLY.   [*moving toward the chair*] I'm keeping an account of everything, remember. I'll pay every penny back. [*He sits.*]

CHARLEY.   Now listen to me, Willy . . .

WILLY.   I want you to know I appreciate . . .

CHARLEY.   [*sitting down on the table*] Willy, what're you doin'? What the hell is goin' on in your head?

WILLY.   Why? I'm simply . . .

CHARLEY.   I offered you a job. You can make fifty dollars a week. And I won't send you on the road.

WILLY.   I've got a job.

CHARLEY.   Without pay? What kind of job is a job without pay? [*He rises*.] Now, look, kid, enough is enough. I'm no genius but I know when I'm being insulted.

WILLY.   Insulted!

CHARLEY.   Why don't you want to work for me?

WILLY.   What's the matter with you? I've got a job.

CHARLEY.   Then what're you walkin' in here every week for?

WILLY.   [*getting up*] Well, if you don't want me to walk in here—

CHARLEY.   I am offering you a job.

WILLY.   I don't want your goddam job!

CHARLEY.   When the hell are you going to grow up?

WILLY.   [*furiously*] You big ignoramus, if you say that to me again I'll rap you one! I don't care how big you are! [*He's ready to fight.*]

[*Pause.*]

CHARLEY.   [*kindly, going to him*] How much do you need, Willy?

WILLY.   Charley, I'm strapped. I'm strapped. I don't know what to do. I was just fired.

CHARLEY.   Howard fired you?

WILLY.   That snotnose. Imagine that? I named him. I named him Howard.

CHARLEY.   Willy, when're you gonna realize that them things don't mean anything? You named him Howard, but you can't sell that. The only thing you got in this world is what you can sell. And the funny thing is that you're a salesman, and you don't know that.

WILLY.   I've tried to think otherwise, I guess. I always felt that if a man was impressive, and well liked, that nothing—

CHARLEY.   Why must everybody like you? Who liked J. P. Morgan?° Was he impressive? In a Turkish bath he'd look like a butcher. But with his pockets on he was very well liked. Now listen, Willy, I know you don't like me, and nobody can say I'm in love with you, but I'll give you a job because—just for the hell of it, put it that way. Now what do you say?

WILLY.   I—I just can't work for you, Charley.

CHARLEY.   What're you, jealous of me?

WILLY.   I can't work for you, that's all, don't ask me why.

CHARLEY.   [*angered, takes out more bills*] You been jealous of me all your life, you damned fool! Here, pay your insurance. [*He puts the money in WILLY'S hand.*]

WILLY.   I'm keeping strict accounts.

CHARLEY.   I've got some work to do. Take care of yourself. And pay your insurance.

WILLY.   [*moving to the right*] Funny, y'know? After all the highways, and the

---

°*J. P. Morgan*: John Pierpont Morgan (1837–1913) was the founder of U.S. Steel and the head of a gigantic family fortune that was enlarged by his son, John Pierpont Morgan (1867–1943). Charley is probably referring to the son.

trains, and the appointments, and the years, you end up worth more dead than alive.

CHARLEY. Willy, nobody's worth nothin' dead. [*after a slight pause*] Did you hear what I said?

[*WILLY stands still, dreaming.*]

CHARLEY. Willy!

WILLY. Apologize to Bernard for me when you see him. I didn't mean to argue with him. He's a fine boy. They're all fine boys, and they'll end up big— all of them. Someday they'll all play tennis together. Wish me luck, Charley. He saw Bill Oliver today.

CHARLEY. Good luck.

WILLY. [*on the verge of tears*] Charley, you're the only friend I got. Isn't that a remarkable thing? [*He goes out.*]

CHARLEY. Jesus!

[*CHARLEY stares after him a moment and follows. All light blacks out. Suddenly raucous music is heard, and a red glow rises behind the screen at right. STANLEY, a young waiter, appears, carrying a table, followed by HAPPY, who is carrying two chairs.*]

STANLEY. [*putting the table down*] That's all right, Mr. Loman. I can handle it myself. [*He turns and takes the chairs from HAPPY and places them at the table.*]

HAPPY. [*glancing around.*] Oh, this is better.

STANLEY. Sure, in the front there you're in the middle of all kinds a noise. Whenever you got a party, Mr. Loman, you just tell me and I'll put you back here. Y'know, there's a lotta people they don't like it private, because when they go out they like to see a lotta action around them because they're sick and tired to stay in the house by theirself. But I know you, you ain't from Hackensack.° You know what I mean?

HAPPY. [*sitting down*] So how's it coming, Stanley?

STANLEY. Ah, it's a dog's life. I only wish during the war they'd a took me in the Army. I coulda been dead by now.

HAPPY. My brother's back, Stanley.

STANLEY. Oh, he come back, heh? From the Far West.

HAPPY. Yeah, big cattle man, my brother, so treat him right. And my father's coming too.

STANLEY. Oh, your father too!

HAPPY. You got a couple of nice lobsters?

STANLEY. Hundred per cent, big.

HAPPY. I want them with claws.

STANLEY. Don't worry. I don't give you no mice. [*HAPPY laughs.*] How about some wine? It'll put a head on the meal.

HAPPY. No. You remember, Stanley, that recipe I brought you from overseas? With the champagne in it?

°*Hackensack*: a city in northeastern New Jersey; Stanley uses the town as a reference to unsophisticated visitors to New York City.

STANLEY. Oh, yeah, sure. I still got it tacked up yet in the kitchen. But that'll have to cost a buck apiece anyways.

HAPPY. That's all right.

STANLEY. What'd you, hit a number or somethin'?

HAPPY. No, it's a little celebration. My brother is—I think he pulled off a big deal today. I think we're going into business together.

STANLEY. Great! That's the best for you. Because a family business, you know what I mean?—that's the best.

HAPPY. That's what I think.

STANLEY. 'Cause what's the difference? Somebody steals? It's in the family. Know what I mean? [*sotto voce°*] Like this bartender here. The boss is goin' crazy what kinda leak he's got in the cash register. You put it in but it don't come out.

HAPPY. [*raising his head*] Sh!

STANLEY. What?

HAPPY. You notice I wasn't lookin' right or left, was I?

STANLEY. No.

HAPPY. And my eyes are closed.

STANLEY. So what's the—?

HAPPY. Strudel's comin'.

STANLEY. [*catching on, looks around*] Ah, no, there's no—

[*He breaks off as a furred, lavishly dressed GIRL enters and sits at the next table. Both follow her with their eyes.*]

STANLEY. Geez, how'd ya know?

HAPPY. I got radar or something. [*staring directly at her profile*] Ooooooooo . . . Stanley.

STANLEY. I think that's for you, Mr. Loman.

HAPPY. Look at that mouth. Oh God. And the binoculars.

STANLEY. Geez, you got a life, Mr. Loman.

HAPPY. Wait on her.

STANLEY. [*going to the GIRL's table*] Would you like a menu, ma'am?

GIRL. I'm expecting someone, but I'd like a—

HAPPY. Why don't you bring her—excuse me, miss, do you mind? I sell champagne, and I'd like you to try my brand. Bring her a champagne, Stanley.

GIRL. That's awfully nice of you.

HAPPY. Don't mention it. It's all company money. [*He laughs.*]

GIRL. That's a charming product to be selling, isn't it?

HAPPY. Oh, gets to be like everything else. Selling is selling, y'know.

GIRL. I suppose.

HAPPY. You don't happen to sell, do you?

GIRL. No, I don't sell.

HAPPY. Would you object to a compliment from a stranger? You ought to be on a magazine cover.

GIRL. [*looking at him a little archly*] I have been.

[*STANLEY comes in with a glass of champagne.*]

°*sotto voce*: spoken in an undertone or "stage" whisper.

HAPPY.   What'd I say before, Stanley? You see? She's a cover girl.

STANLEY.   Oh, I could see, I could see.

HAPPY.   [*to the GIRL*] What magazine?

GIRL.   Oh, a lot of them. [*She takes the drink.*] Thank you.

HAPPY.   You know what they say in France, don't you? "Champagne is the drink of the complexion"—Hya, Biff!

[*BIFF has entered and sits with HAPPY.*]

BIFF.   Hello, kid. Sorry I'm late.

HAPPY.   I just got here. Uh, Miss—?

GIRL.   Forsythe.

HAPPY.   Miss Forsythe, this is my brother.

BIFF.   Is Dad here?

HAPPY.   His name is Biff. You might've heard of him. Great football player.

GIRL.   Really? What team?

HAPPY.   Are you familiar with football?

GIRL.   No. I'm afraid I'm not.

HAPPY.   Biff is quarterback with the New York Giants.

GIRL.   Well, that is nice, isn't it? [*She drinks.*]

HAPPY.   Good health.

GIRL.   I'm happy to meet you.

HAPPY.   That's my name. Hap. It's really Harold, but at West Point they called me Happy.

GIRL.   [*now really impressed*] Oh, I see. How do you do? [*She turns her profile.*]

BIFF.   Isn't Dad coming?

HAPPY.   You want her?

BIFF.   Oh, I could never make that.

HAPPY.   I remember the time that idea would never come into your head. Where's the old confidence, Biff?

BIFF.   I just saw Oliver—

HAPPY.   Wait a minute. I've got to see that old confidence again. Do you want her? She's on call.

BIFF.   Oh, no. [*He turns to look at the GIRL.*]

HAPPY.   I'm telling you. Watch this. [*turning to the GIRL*] Honey? [*She turns to him.*] Are you busy?

GIRL.   Well, I am . . . but I could make a phone call.

HAPPY.   Do that, will you, honey? And see if you can get a friend. We'll be here for a while. Biff is one of the greatest football players in the country.

GIRL.   [*standing up*] Well, I'm certainly happy to meet you.

HAPPY.   Come back soon.

GIRL.   I'll try.

HAPPY.   Don't try, honey, try hard.

[*The GIRL exits. STANLEY follows, shaking his head in bewildered admiration.*]

HAPPY.   Isn't that a shame now? A beautiful girl like that? That's why I can't get married. There's not a good woman in a thousand. New York is loaded with them, kid!

BIFF.   Hap, look—

HAPPY. I told you she was on call!

BIFF. [*strangely unnerved*] Cut it out, will ya? I want to say something to you.

HAPPY. Did you see Oliver?

BIFF. I saw him all right. Now look, I want to tell Dad a couple of things and I want you to help me.

HAPPY. What? Is he going to back you?

BIFF. Are you crazy? You're out of your goddam head, you know that?

HAPPY. Why? What happened?

BIFF. [*breathlessly*] I did a terrible thing today, Hap. It's been the strangest day I ever went through. I'm all numb, I swear.

HAPPY. You mean he wouldn't see you?

BIFF. Well, I waited six hours for him, see? All day. Kept sending my name in. Even tried to date his secretary so she'd get me to him, but no soap.

HAPPY. Because you're not showin' the old confidence, Biff. He remembered you, didn't he?

BIFF. [*stopping HAPPY with a gesture*] Finally, about five o'clock, he comes out. Didn't remember who I was or anything. I felt like such an idiot, Hap.

HAPPY. Did you tell him my Florida idea?

BIFF. He walked away. I saw him for one minute. I got so mad I could've torn the walls down! How the hell did I ever get the idea I was a salesman there? I even believed myself that I'd been a salesman for him! And then he gave me one look and—I realized what a ridiculous lie my whole life has been! We've been talking in a dream for fifteen years. I was a shipping clerk.

HAPPY. What'd you do?

BIFF. [*with great tension and wonder*] Well, he left, see. And the secretary went out. I was all alone in the waiting-room. I don't know what came over me, Hap. The next thing I know I'm in his office—paneled walls, everything. I can't explain it. I—Hap, I took his fountain pen.

HAPPY. Geez, did he catch you?

BIFF. I ran out. I ran down all eleven flights. I ran and ran and ran.

HAPPY. That was an awful dumb—what'd you do that for?

BIFF. [*agonized*] I don't know, I just—wanted to take something. I don't know. You gotta help me, Hap, I'm gonna tell Pop.

HAPPY. You crazy? What for?

BIFF. Hap, he's got to understand that I'm not the man somebody lends that kind of money to. He thinks I've been spiting him all these years and it's eating him up.

HAPPY. That's just it. You tell him something nice.

BIFF. I can't.

HAPPY. Say you got a lunch date with Oliver tomorrow.

BIFF. So what do I do tomorrow?

HAPPY. You leave the house tomorrow and come back at night and say Oliver is thinking it over. And he thinks it over for a couple of weeks, and gradually it fades away and nobody's the worse.

BIFF. But it'll go on forever!

HAPPY. Dad is never so happy as when he's looking forward to something!

[*WILLY enters.*]

HAPPY.   Hello, scout!

WILLY.   Gee, I haven't been here in years!

[*STANLEY has followed WILLY in and sets a chair for him. STANLEY starts off but HAPPY stops him.*]

HAPPY.   Stanley!

[*STANLEY stands by, waiting for an order.*]

BIFF.   [*going to WILLY with guilt, as to an invalid*] Sit down, Pop. You want a drink?

WILLY.   Sure, I don't mind.

BIFF.   Let's get a load on.

WILLY.   You look worried.

BIFF.   N-no. [*to STANLEY*] Scotch all around. Make it doubles.

STANLEY.   Doubles, right. [*He goes.*]

WILLY.   You had a couple already, didn't you?

BIFF.   Just a couple, yeah.

WILLY.   Well, what happened, boy? [*nodding affirmatively, with a smile*] Everything go all right?

BIFF.   [*takes a breath, then reaches out and grasps WILLY'S hand*] Pal . . . [*He is smiling bravely, and WILLY is smiling too.*] I had an experience today.

HAPPY.   Terrific, Pop.

WILLY.   That so? What happened?

BIFF.   [*high, slightly alcoholic, above the earth*] I'm going to tell you everything from first to last. It's been a strange day. [*Silence. He looks around, composes himself as best he can, but his breath keeps breaking the rhythm of his voice.*] I had to wait quite a while for him, and—

WILLY.   Oliver?

BIFF.   Yeah, Oliver. All day, as a matter of cold fact. And a lot of—instances—facts, Pop, facts about my life came back to me. Who was it, Pop? Who ever said I was a salesman with Oliver?

WILLY.   Well, you were.

BIFF.   No, Dad, I was a shipping clerk.

WILLY.   But you were practically—

BIFF.   [*with determination*] Dad, I don't know who said it first, but I was never a salesman for Bill Oliver.

WILLY.   What're you talking about?

BIFF.   Let's hold on to the facts tonight, Pop. We're not going to get anywhere bullin' around. I was a shipping clerk.

WILLY.   [*angrily*] All right, now listen to me—

BIFF.   Why don't you let me finish?

WILLY.   I'm not interested in stories about the past or any crap of that kind because the woods are burning, boys, you understand? There's a big blaze going on all around. I was fired today.

BIFF.   [*shocked*] How could you be?

WILLY.   I was fired, and I'm looking for a little good news to tell your mother, because the woman has waited and the woman has suffered. The gist of it is that I haven't got a story left in my head, Biff. So don't give me a lecture about facts and aspects. I am not interested. Now what've you got to say to me?

[*STANLEY enters with three drinks. They wait until he leaves.*]

WILLY.   Did you see Oliver?

BIFF.   Jesus, Dad!

WILLY.   You mean you didn't go up there?

HAPPY.   Sure he went up there.

BIFF.   I did. I—saw him. How could they fire you?

WILLY.   [*on the edge of his chair*] What kind of a welcome did he give you?

BIFF.   He won't even let you work on commission?

WILLY.   I'm out! [*driving*] So tell me, he gave you a warm welcome?

HAPPY.   Sure, Pop, sure!

BIFF.   [*driven*] Well, it was kind of—

WILLY.   I was wondering if he'd remember you. [*to HAPPY*] Imagine, man doesn't see him for ten, twelve years and gives him that kind of a welcome!

HAPPY.   Damn right!

BIFF.   [*trying to return to the offensive*] Pop, look—

WILLY.   You know why he remembered you, don't you? Because you impressed him in those days.

BIFF.   Let's talk quietly and get this down to the facts, huh?

WILLY.   [*as though BIFF had been interrupting*] Well, what happened? It's great news, Biff. Did he take you into his office or'd you talk in the waiting-room?

BIFF.   Well, he came in, see, and—

WILLY.   [*with a big smile*] What'd he say? Betcha he threw his arm around you.

BIFF.   Well, he kinda—

WILLY.   He's a fine man. [*to HAPPY*] Very hard man to see, y'know.

HAPPY.   [*agreeing*] Oh, I know.

WILLY.   [*to BIFF*] Is that where you had the drinks?

BIFF.   Yeah, he gave me a couple of—no, no!

HAPPY.   [*cutting in*] He told him my Florida idea.

WILLY.   Don't interrupt. [*to BIFF*] How'd he react to the Florida idea?

BIFF.   Dad, will you give me a minute to explain?

WILLY.   I've been waiting for you to explain since I sat down here! What happened? He took you into his office and what?

BIFF.   Well—I talked. And—and he listened, see.

WILLY.   Famous for the way he listens, y'know. What was his answer?

BIFF.   His answer was—[*He breaks off, suddenly angry.*] Dad, you're not letting me tell you what I want to tell you!

WILLY.   [*accusing, angered*] You didn't see him, did you?

BIFF.   I did see him!

WILLY.   What'd you insult him or something? You insulted him, didn't you?

BIFF.   Listen, will you let me out of it, will you just let me out of it!

HAPPY.   What the hell!

WILLY. Tell me what happened!

BIFF. [*to* HAPPY] I can't talk to him!

[*A single trumpet note jars the ear. The light of green leaves stains the house, which holds the air of night and a dream.* YOUNG BERNARD *enters and knocks on the door of the house.*]

YOUNG BERNARD. [*frantically*] Mrs. Loman, Mrs. Loman!

HAPPY. Tell him what happened!

BIFF. [*to* HAPPY] Shut up and leave me alone!

WILLY. No, no! You had to go and flunk math!

BIFF. What math? What're you talking about?

YOUNG BERNARD. Mrs. Loman, Mrs. Loman!

[LINDA *appears in the house, as of old.*]

WILLY. [*wildly*] Math, math, math!

BIFF. Take it easy, Pop!

YOUNG BERNARD. Mrs. Loman!

WILLY. [*furiously*] If you hadn't flunked you'd've been set by now!

BIFF. Now, look, I'm gonna tell you what happened, and you're going to listen to me.

YOUNG BERNARD. Mrs. Loman!

BIFF. I waited six hours—

HAPPY. What the hell are you saying?

BIFF. I kept sending in my name but he wouldn't see me. So finally he . . .

[*He continues unheard as light fades low on the restaurant.*]

YOUNG BERNARD. Biff flunked math!

LINDA. No!

YOUNG BERNARD. Birnbaum flunked him! They won't graduate him!

LINDA. But they have to. He's gotta go to the university. Where is he? Biff! Biff!

YOUNG BERNARD. No, he left. He went to Grand Central.

LINDA. Grand—You mean he went to Boston!

YOUNG BERNARD. Is Uncle Willy in Boston?

LINDA. Oh, maybe Willy can talk to the teacher. Oh, the poor, poor boy!

[*Light on house area snaps out.*]

BIFF. [*at the table, now audible, holding up a gold fountain pen*] . . . so I'm washed up with Oliver, you understand? Are you listening to me?

WILLY. [*at a loss*] Yeah, sure. If you hadn't flunked—

BIFF. Flunked what? What're you talking about?

WILLY. Don't blame everything on me! I didn't flunk math—you did! What pen?

HAPPY. That was awful dumb, Biff, a pen like that is worth—

WILLY. [*seeing the pen for the first time*] You took Oliver's pen?

BIFF. [*weakening*] Dad, I just explained it to you.

WILLY. You stole Bill Oliver's fountain pen!

BIFF. I didn't exactly steal it! That's just what I've been explaining to you!

HAPPY. He had it in his hand and just then Oliver walked in, so he got nervous and stuck it in his pocket!

WILLY. My God, Biff!

BIFF. I never intended to do it, Dad!

OPERATOR'S VOICE. Standish Arms, good evening!

WILLY. [*shouting*] I'm not in my room!

BIFF. [*frightened*] Dad, what's the matter? [*He and HAPPY stand up.*]

OPERATOR. Ringing Mr. Loman for you!

WILLY. I'm not there, stop it!

BIFF. [*horrified, gets down on one knee before WILLY*] Dad, I'll make good, I'll make good. [*WILLY tries to get to his feet. BIFF holds him down.*] Sit down now.

WILLY. No, you're no good, you're no good for anything.

BIFF. I am, Dad, I'll find something else, you understand? Now don't worry about anything. [*He holds up WILLY's face.*] Talk to me, Dad.

OPERATOR. Mr. Loman does not answer. Shall I page him?

WILLY. [*attempting to stand, as though to rush and silence the OPERATOR*] No, no, no!

HAPPY. He'll strike something, Pop.

WILLY. No, no . . .

BIFF. [*desperately, standing over WILLY*] Pop, listen! Listen to me! I'm telling you something good. Oliver talked to his partner about the Florida idea. You listening? He—he talked to his partner, and he came to me . . . I'm going to be all right, you hear? Dad, listen to me, he said it was just a question of the amount!

WILLY. Then you . . . got it?

HAPPY. He's gonna be terrific, Pop!

WILLY. [*trying to stand*] Then you got it, haven't you? You got it! You got it!

BIFF. [*agonized, holds WILLY down*] No, no. Look, Pop. I'm supposed to have lunch with them tomorrow. I'm just telling you this so you'll know that I can still make an impression, Pop. And I'll make good somewhere, but I can't go tomorrow, see?

WILLY. Why not? You simply—

BIFF. But the pen, Pop!

WILLY. You give it to him and tell him it was an oversight!

HAPPY. Sure, have lunch tomorrow!

BIFF. I can't say that—

WILLY. You were doing a crossword puzzle and accidentally used his pen!

BIFF. Listen, kid, I took those balls years ago, now I walk in with his fountain pen? That clinches it, don't you see? I can't face him like that! I'll try elsewhere.

PAGE'S VOICE. Paging Mr. Loman!

WILLY. Don't you want to be anything?

BIFF. Pop, how can I go back?

WILLY. You don't want to be anything, is that what's behind it?

BIFF. [*now angry at WILLY for not crediting his sympathy*] Don't take it that way! You think it was easy walking into that office after what I'd done to him? A team of horses couldn't have dragged me back to Bill Oliver!

WILLY. Then why'd you go?

BIFF.   Why did I go? Why did I go? Look at you! Look at what's become of you!

[*Off left*, THE WOMAN *laughs.*]

WILLY.   Biff, you're going to go to that lunch tomorrow, or—

BIFF.   I can't go. I've got no appointment!

HAPPY.   Biff, for . . . !

WILLY.   Are you spiting me?

BIFF.   Don't take it that way! Goddammit!

WILLY.   [*strikes* BIFF *and falters away from the table*] You rotten little louse! Are you spiting me?

THE WOMAN.   Someone's at the door, Willy!

BIFF.   I'm no good, can't you see what I am?

HAPPY.   [*separating them*] Hey, you're in a restaurant! Now cut it out, both of you! [*The girls enter.*] Hello, girls, sit down.

[THE WOMAN *laughs, off left.*]

MISS FORSYTHE.   I guess we might as well. This is Letta.

THE WOMAN.   Willy, are you going to wake up?

BIFF.   [*ignoring* WILLY] How're ya, miss, sit down. What do you drink?

MISS FORSYTHE.   Letta might not be able to stay long.

LETTA.   I gotta get up very early tomorrow. I got jury duty. I'm so excited! Were you fellows ever on a jury?

BIFF.   No, but I been in front of them! [*The girls laugh.*] This is my father.

LETTA.   Isn't he cute? Sit down with us, Pop.

HAPPY.   Sit him down, Biff!

BIFF.   [*going to him*] Come on, slugger, drink us under the table. To hell with it! Come on, sit down, pal.

[*On* BIFF's *last insistence*, WILLY *is about to sit.*]

THE WOMAN.   [*now urgently*] Willy, are you going to answer the door!

[THE WOMAN's *call pulls* WILLY *back. He starts right, befuddled.*]

BIFF.   Hey, where are you going?

WILLY.   Open the door.

BIFF.   The door?

WILLY.   The washroom . . . the door . . . where's the door?

BIFF.   [*leading* WILLY *to the left*] Just go straight down.

[WILLY *moves left.*]

THE WOMAN.   Willy, Willy, are you going to get up, get up, get up, get up?

[WILLY *exits left.*]

LETTA.   I think it's sweet you bring your daddy along.

MISS FORSYTHE.   Oh, he isn't really your father!

BIFF.   [*at left, turning to her resentfully*] Miss Forsythe, you've just seen a prince walk by. A fine, troubled prince. A hard-working, unappreciated prince. A pal, you understand? A good companion. Always for his boys.

LETTA. That's so sweet.

HAPPY. Well, girls, what's the program? We're wasting time. Come on, Biff. Gather round. Where would you like to go?

BIFF. Why don't you do something for him?

HAPPY. Me!

BIFF. Don't you give a damn for him, Hap?

HAPPY. What're you talking about? I'm the one who—

BIFF. I sense it, you don't give a good goddam about him. [*He takes the rolled-up hose from his pocket and puts it on the table in front of HAPPY.*] Look what I found in the cellar, for Christ's sake. How can you bear to let it go on?

HAPPY. Me? Who goes away? Who runs off and—

BIFF. Yeah, but he doesn't mean anything to you. You could help him—I can't! Don't you understand what I'm talking about? He's going to kill himself, don't you know that?

HAPPY. Don't I know it! Me!

BIFF. Hap, help him! Jesus . . . help him . . . Help me, help me, I can't bear to look at his face! [*Ready to weep, he hurries out, up right.*]

HAPPY. [*starting after him*] Where are you going?

MISS FORSYTHE. What's he so mad about?

HAPPY. Come on, girls, we'll catch up with him.

MISS FORSYTHE. [*as HAPPY pushes her out*] Say, I don't like that temper of his!

HAPPY. He's just a little overstrung, he'll be all right!

WILLY. [*off left, as THE WOMAN laughs*] Don't answer! Don't answer!

LETTA. Don't you want to tell your father—

HAPPY. No, that's not my father. He's just a guy. Come on, we'll catch Biff, and, honey, we're going to paint this town! Stanley, where's the check! Hey, Stanley!

[*They exit. STANLEY looks toward left.*]

STANLEY. [*calling to HAPPY indignantly*] Mr. Loman! Mr. Loman!

[*STANLEY picks up a chair and follows them off. Knocking is heard off left. THE WOMAN enters, laughing. WILLY follows her. She is in a black slip; he is buttoning his shirt. Raw, sensuous music accompanies their speech.*]

WILLY. Will you stop laughing? Will you stop?

THE WOMAN. Aren't you going to answer the door? He'll wake the whole hotel.

WILLY. I'm not expecting anybody.

THE WOMAN. Whyn't you have another drink, honey, and stop being so damn self-centered?

WILLY. I'm so lonely.

THE WOMAN. You know you ruined me, Willy? From now on, whenever you come to the office, I'll see that you go right through to the buyers. No waiting at my desk any more, Willy. You ruined me.

WILLY.   That's nice of you to say that.

THE WOMAN.   Gee, you are self-centered! Why so sad? You are the saddest, self-centeredest soul I ever did see-saw. [*She laughs. He kisses her.*] Come on inside, drummer boy. It's silly to be dressing in the middle of the night. [*As knocking is heard*] Aren't you going to answer the door?

WILLY.   They're knocking on the wrong door.

THE WOMAN.   But I felt the knocking! And he heard us talking in here. Maybe the hotel's on fire!

WILLY.   [*his terror rising*] It's a mistake.

THE WOMAN.   Then tell him to go away!

WILLY.   There's nobody there.

THE WOMAN.   It's getting on my nerves, Willy. There's somebody standing out there and it's getting on my nerves!

WILLY.   [*pushing her away from him*] All right, stay in the bathroom here, and don't come out. I think there's a law in Massachusetts about it, so don't come out. It may be that new room clerk. He looked very mean. So don't come out. It's a mistake, there's no fire.

[*The knocking is heard again. He takes a few steps away from her, and she vanishes into the wing. The light follows him, and now he is facing YOUNG BIFF, who carries a suitcase. BIFF steps toward him. The music is gone.*]

BIFF.   Why didn't you answer?

WILLY.   Biff! What are you doing in Boston?

BIFF.   Why didn't you answer? I've been knocking for five minutes, I called you on the phone—

WILLY.   I just heard you. I was in the bathroom and had the door shut. Did anything happen home?

BIFF.   Dad—I let you down.

WILLY.   What do you mean?

BIFF.   Dad . . .

WILLY.   Biffo, what's this about? [*putting his arm around BIFF*] Come on, let's go downstairs and get you a malted.

BIFF.   Dad, I flunked math.

WILLY.   Not for the term?

BIFF.   The term. I haven't got enough credits to graduate.

WILLY.   You mean to say Bernard wouldn't give you the answers?

BIFF.   He did, he tried, but I only got a sixty-one.

WILLY.   And they wouldn't give you four points?

BIFF.   Birnbaum refused absolutely. I begged him, Pop, but he won't give me those points. You gotta talk to him before they close the school. Because if he saw the kind of man you are, and you just talked to him in your way, I'm sure he'd come through for me. The class came right before practice, see, and I didn't go enough. Would you talk to him? He'd like you, Pop. You know the way you could talk.

WILLY.   You're on. We'll drive right back.

BIFF.   Oh, Dad, good work! I'm sure he'll change it for you!

WILLY.   Go downstairs and tell the clerk I'm checkin' out. Go right down.

BIFF.   Yes, sir! See, the reason he hates me, Pop—one day he was late for class so I got up at the blackboard and imitated him. I crossed my eyes and talked with a lithp.

WILLY.   [*laughing*] You did? The kids like it?

BIFF.   They nearly died laughing!

WILLY.   Yeah? What'd you do?

BIFF.   The thquare root of thixthy twee is . . . [*WILLY bursts out laughing; BIFF joins him.*] And in the middle of it he walked in!

[*WILLY laughs and THE WOMAN joins in offstage.*]

WILLY.   [*without hesitation*] Hurry downstairs and—

BIFF.   Somebody in there?

WILLY.   No, that was next door.

[*THE WOMAN laughs offstage.*]

BIFF.   Somebody got in your bathroom!

WILLY.   No, it's the next room, there's a party—

THE WOMAN.   [*enters, laughing. She lisps this.*] Can I come in? There's something in the bathtub, Willy, and it's moving!

[*WILLY looks at BIFF, who is staring open-mouthed and horrified at THE WOMAN.*]

WILLY.   Ah—you better go back to your room. They must be finished painting by now. They're painting her room so I let her take a shower here. Go back, go back . . . [*He pushes her.*]

THE WOMAN.   [*resisting*] But I've got to get dressed, Willy, I can't—

WILLY.   Get out of here! Go back, go back . . . [*suddenly striving for the ordinary*] This is Miss Francis, Biff, she's a buyer. They're painting her room. Go back, Miss Francis, go back . . .

THE WOMAN.   But my clothes, I can't go out naked in the hall!

WILLY.   [*pushing her offstage*] Get outa here! Go back, go back!

[*BIFF slowly sits down on his suitcase as the argument continues offstage.*]

THE WOMAN.   Where's my stockings? You promised me stockings, Willy!

WILLY.   I have no stockings here!

THE WOMAN.   You had two boxes of size nine sheers for me, and I want them!

WILLY.   Here, for God's sake, will you get outa here!

THE WOMAN.   [*enters holding a box of stockings*] I just hope there's nobody in the hall. That's all I hope. [*To BIFF*] Are you football or baseball?

BIFF.   Football.

THE WOMAN.   [*angry, humiliated*] That's me too. G'night. [*she snatches her clothes from WILLY, and walks out.*]

WILLY.   [*after a pause*] Well, better get going. I want to get to the school first thing in the morning. Get my suits out of the closet. I'll get my valise. [*BIFF doesn't move.*] What's the matter? [*BIFF remains motionless, tears falling*] She's a buyer. Buys for J. H. Simmons. She lives down the hall—they're painting. You don't imagine—[*He breaks off. After a pause*] Now listen, pal, she's just a buyer. She sees merchandise in her room and they have to keep it looking just so . . . [*Pause. Assuming command*] All right, get my suits. [*BIFF doesn't move.*] Now stop crying and do as I say. I gave you an order. Biff, I gave you an order! Is that what you do when I give you an order? How dare you cry! [*putting his arm around BIFF*] Now look, Biff, when you grow up you'll understand about these things. You mustn't— you mustn't overemphasize a thing like this. I'll see Birnbaum first thing in the morning.

BIFF. Never mind.

WILLY. [*getting down beside BIFF*] Never mind! He's going to give you those points. I'll see to it.

BIFF. He wouldn't listen to you.

WILLY. He certainly will listen to me. You need those points for the U. of Virginia.

BIFF. I'm not going there.

WILLY. Heh? If I can't get him to change that mark you'll make it up in summer school. You've got all summer to—

BIFF. [*his weeping breaking from him*] Dad . . .

WILLY. [*infected by it*] Oh, my boy . . .

BIFF. Dad . . .

WILLY. She's nothing to me, Biff. I was lonely, I was terribly lonely.

BIFF. You—you gave her Mama's stockings! [*His tears break through and he rises to go.*]

WILLY. [*grabbing for BIFF*] I gave you an order!

BIFF. Don't touch me, you—liar!

WILLY. Apologize for that!

BIFF. You fake! You phony little fake! You fake! [*Overcome, he turns quickly and weeping fully goes out with his suitcase. WILLY is left on the floor on his knees.*]

WILLY. I gave you an order! Biff, come back here or I'll beat you! Come back here! I'll whip you!

[*STANLEY comes quickly in from the right and stands in front of WILLY.*]

WILLY. [*shouts at STANLEY*] I gave you an order . . .

STANLEY. Hey, let's pick it up, pick it up, Mr. Loman. [*He helps WILLY to his feet.*] Your boys left with the chippies. They said they'll see you home.

[*A SECOND WAITER watches some distance away.*]

WILLY. But we were supposed to have dinner together.

[*Music is heard, WILLY'S theme.*]

STANLEY. Can you make it?

WILLY. I'll—sure, I can make it. [*suddenly concerned about his clothes*] Do I—I look all right?

STANLEY. Sure, you look all right. [*He flicks a speck off WILLY'S lapel.*]

WILLY. Here—here's a dollar.

STANLEY. Oh, your son paid me. It's all right.

WILLY. [*putting it in STANLEY'S hand*] No, take it. You're a good boy.

STANLEY. Oh, no, you don't have to . . .

WILLY.   Here—here's some more, I don't need it any more. [*after a slight pause*] Tell me—is there a seed store in the neighborhood?
STANLEY.   Seeds? You mean like to plant?

[*As WILLY turns, STANLEY slips the money back into his jacket pocket.*]

WILLY.   Yes. Carrots, peas . . .
STANLEY.   Well, there's hardware stores on Sixth Avenue, but it may be too late now.
WILLY.   [*anxiously*] Oh, I'd better hurry. I've got to get some seeds. [*He starts off to the right.*] I've got to get some seeds, right away. Nothing's planted. I don't have a thing in the ground.

[*WILLY hurries out as the light goes down. STANLEY moves over to the right after him, watches him off. The other waiter has been staring at WILLY.*]

STANLEY.   [*to the WAITER*] Well, whatta you looking at?

[*The WAITER picks up the chairs and moves off right. STANLEY takes the table and follows him. The light fades on this area. There is a long pause, the sound of the flute coming over. The light gradually rises on the kitchen, which is empty. HAPPY appears at the door of the house, followed by BIFF. HAPPY is carrying a large bunch of long-stemmed roses. He enters the kitchen, looks around for LINDA. Not seeing her, he turns to BIFF, who is just outside the house door, and makes a gesture with his hands, indicating "Not here, I guess." He looks into the living-room and freezes. Inside, LINDA, unseen, is seated, WILLY'S coat on her lap. She rises ominously and quietly and moves toward HAPPY, who backs up into the kitchen, afraid.*]

HAPPY.   Hey, what're you doing up? [*LINDA says nothing but moves toward him implacably.*] Where's Pop? [*He keeps backing to the right, and now LINDA is in full view in the doorway to the living-room.*] Is he sleeping?
LINDA.   Where were you?
HAPPY.   [*trying to laugh it off*] We met two girls, Mom, very fine types. Here, we brought you some flowers. [*offering them to her*] Put them in your room, Ma.

[*She knocks them to the floor at BIFF'S feet. He has now come inside and closed the door behind him. She stares at BIFF, silent.*]

HAPPY.   Now what'd you do that for? Mom, I want you to have some flowers—
LINDA.   [*cutting HAPPY off, violently to BIFF*] Don't you care whether he lives or dies?
HAPPY.   [*going to the stairs*] Come upstairs, Biff.
BIFF.   [*with a flare of disgust, to HAPPY*] Go away from me! [*to LINDA*] What do you mean, lives or dies? Nobody's dying around here, pal.
LINDA.   Get out of my sight! Get out of here!
BIFF.   I wanna see the boss.
LINDA.   You're not going near him!
BIFF.   Where is he? [*He moves into the living-room and LINDA follows.*]
LINDA.   [*shouting after BIFF*] You invite him for dinner. He looks forward to it all day—[*BIFF appears in his parents' bedroom, looks around, and exits.*]—and then you desert him there. There's no stranger you'd do that to!

HAPPY. Why? He had a swell time with us. Listen, when I—[*LINDA comes back into the kitchen.*]—desert him I hope I don't outlive the day!

LINDA. Get out of here!

HAPPY. Now look, Mom . . .

LINDA. Did you have to go to women tonight? You and your lousy rotten whores!

[*BIFF re-enters the kitchen.*]

HAPPY. Mom, all we did was follow Biff around trying to cheer him up! [*to BIFF*] Boy, what a night you gave me!

LINDA. Get out of here, both of you, and don't come back! I don't want you tormenting him any more. Go on now, get your things together! [*to BIFF*] You can sleep in his apartment. [*She starts to pick up the flowers and stops herself.*] Pick up this stuff, I'm not your maid any more. Pick it up, you bum, you!

[*HAPPY turns his back to her in refusal. BIFF slowly moves over and gets down on his knees, picking up the flowers.*]

LINDA. You're a pair of animals! Not one, not another living soul would have had the cruelty to walk out on that man in a restaurant!

BIFF. [*not looking at her*] Is that what he said?

LINDA. He didn't have to say anything. He was so humiliated he nearly limped when he came in.

HAPPY. But, Mom, he had a great time with us—

BIFF. [*cutting him off violently*] Shut up!

[*Without another word, HAPPY goes upstairs.*]

LINDA. You! You didn't even go in to see if he was all right!

BIFF. [*still on the floor in front of LINDA, the flowers in his hand; with self-loathing*] No. Didn't. Didn't do a damned thing. How do you like that, heh? Left him babbling in a toilet.

LINDA. You louse. You . . .

BIFF. Now you hit it on the nose! [*He gets up, throws the flowers in the wastebasket.*] The scum of the earth, and you're looking at him!

LINDA. Get out of here!

BIFF. I gotta talk to the boss, Mom. Where is he?

LINDA. You're not going near him. Get out of this house!

BIFF. [*with absolute assurance, determination*] No. We're gonna have an abrupt conversation, him and me.

LINDA. You're not talking to him!

[*Hammering is heard from outside the house, off right. BIFF turns toward the noise.*]

LINDA. [*suddenly pleading*] Will you please leave him alone?

BIFF. What's he doing out there?

LINDA. He's planting the garden!

BIFF. [*quietly*] Now? Oh, my God!

[*BIFF moves outside, LINDA following. The light dies down on them and comes up on the center of the apron as WILLY walks into it. He is carrying a flashlight, a hoe, and a handful of seed packets. He raps the top of the hoe sharply to fix it firmly, and then moves to the left, measuring off the distance with his foot. He holds the flashlight to look at the seed packets, reading off the instructions. He is in the blue of night.*]

WILLY.   Carrots . . . quarter-inch apart. Rows . . . one-foot rows. [*He measures it off.*] One foot. [*He puts down a package and measures off.*] Beets. [*He puts down another package and measures again.*] Lettuce. [*He reads the package, puts it down.*] One foot—[*He breaks off as BEN appears at the right and moves slowly down to him.*] What a proposition, ts, ts. Terrific, terrific. 'Cause she's suffered, Ben, the woman has suffered. You understand me? A man can't go out the way he came in, Ben, a man has got to add up to something. You can't, you can't—[*BEN moves toward him as though to interrupt.*] You gotta consider, now. Don't answer so quick. Remember, it's a guaranteed twenty-thousand-dollar proposition. Now look, Ben, I want you to go through the ins and outs of this thing with me. I've got nobody to talk to, Ben, and the woman has suffered, you hear me?

BEN.   [*standing still, considering*] What's the proposition?

WILLY.   It's twenty thousand dollars on the barrelhead. Guaranteed, gilt-edged, you understand?

BEN.   You don't want to make a fool of yourself. They might not honor the policy.

WILLY.   How can they dare refuse? Didn't I work like a coolie to meet every premium on the nose? And now they don't pay off? Impossible!

BEN.   It's called a cowardly thing, William.

WILLY.   Why? Does it take more guts to stand here the rest of my life ringing up a zero?

BEN.   [*yielding*] That's a point, William. [*He moves, thinking, turns.*] And twenty thousand—that *is* something one can feel with the hand, it is there.

WILLY.   [*now assured, with rising power*] Oh, Ben, that's the whole beauty of it! I see it like a diamond, shining in the dark, hard and rough, that I can pick up and touch in my hand. Not like—like an appointment! This would not be another damned-fool appointment, Ben, and it changes all the aspects. Because he thinks I'm nothing, see, and so he spites me. But the funeral—[*straightening up*] Ben, that funeral will be massive! They'll come from Maine, Massachusetts, Vermont, New Hampshire! All the old-timers with the strange license plates—that boy will be thunder-struck, Ben, because he never realized—I am known! Rhode Island, New York, New Jersey—I am known, Ben, and he'll see it with his eyes once and for all. He'll see what I am, Ben! He's in for a shock, that boy!

BEN.   [*coming down to the edge of the garden*] He'll call you a coward.

WILLY.   [*suddenly fearful*] No, that would be terrible.

BEN.   Yes. And a damned fool.

WILLY.   No, no, he mustn't, I won't have that! [*He is broken and desperate.*]

BEN.   He'll hate you, William.

[*The gay music of the Boys is heard.*]

WILLY.   Oh, Ben, how do we get back to all the great times? Used to be so full of light, and comradeship, the sleigh-riding in winter, and the ruddiness on his cheeks. And always some kind of good news coming up, always something nice coming up ahead. And never even let me carry the valises in the house, and simonizing, simonizing that little red car! Why, why can't I give him something and not have him hate me?

BEN. Let me think about it. [*He glances at his watch.*] I still have a little time. Remarkable proposition, but you've got to be sure you're not making a fool of yourself.

[BEN *drifts upstage and goes out of sight.* BIFF *comes down from the left.*]

WILLY. [*suddenly conscious of* BIFF, *turns and looks up at him, then begins picking up the packages of seeds in confusion*] Where the hell is that seed? [*Indignantly*] You can't see nothing out here! They boxed in the whole goddam neighborhood!

BIFF. There are people all around here. Don't you realize that?

WILLY. I'm busy. Don't bother me.

BIFF. [*taking the hoe from* WILLY] I'm saying good-by to you, Pop. [WILLY *looks at him, silent, unable to move.*] I'm not coming back any more.

WILLY. You're not going to see Oliver tomorrow?

BIFF. I've got no appointment, Dad.

WILLY. He put his arm around you, and you've got no appointment?

BIFF. Pop, get this now, will you? Everytime I've left it's been a fight that sent me out of here. Today I realized something about myself and I tried to explain it to you and I—I think I'm just not smart enough to make any sense out of it for you. To hell with whose fault it is or anything like that. [*He takes* WILLY's *arm.*] Let's just wrap it up, heh? Come on in, we'll tell Mom. [*He gently tries to pull* WILLY *to left.*]

WILLY. [*frozen, immobile, with guilt in his voice*] No, I don't want to see her.

BIFF. Come on! [*He pulls again, and* WILLY *tries to pull away.*]

WILLY. [*highly nervous*] No, no, I don't want to see her.

BIFF. [*tries to look into* WILLY's *face, as if to find the answer there*] Why don't you want to see her?

WILLY. [*more harshly now*] Don't bother me, will you?

BIFF. What do you mean, you don't want to see her? You don't want them calling you yellow, do you? This isn't your fault; it's me, I'm a bum. Now come inside! [WILLY *strains to get away.*] Did you hear what I said to you?

[WILLY *pulls away and quickly goes by himself into the house.* BIFF *follows.*]

LINDA. [*to* WILLY] Did you plant, dear?

BIFF. [*at the door, to* LINDA] All right, we had it out. I'm going and I'm not writing any more.

LINDA. [*going to* WILLY *in the kitchen*] I think that's the best way, dear. 'Cause there's no use drawing it out, you'll just never get along.

[WILLY *doesn't respond.*]

BIFF. People ask where I am and what I'm doing, you don't know, and you don't care. That way it'll be off your mind and you can start brightening up again. All right? That clears it, doesn't it? [WILLY *is silent, and* BIFF *goes to him.*] You gonna wish me luck, scout? [*He extends his hand.*] What do you say?

LINDA. Shake his hand, Willy.

WILLY. [*turning to her, seething with hurt*] There's no necessity to mention the pen at all, y'know.

BIFF. [*gently*] I've got no appointment, Dad.

WILLY. [*erupting fiercely*] He put his arm around . . . ?

BIFF. Dad, you're never going to see what I am, so what's the use of arguing? If I strike oil I'll send you a check. Meantime forget I'm alive.

WILLY. [*to LINDA*] Spite, see?

BIFF. Shake hands, Dad.

WILLY. Not my hand.

BIFF. I was hoping not to go this way.

WILLY. Well, this is the way you're going. Good-by.

[*BIFF looks at him a moment, then turns sharply and goes to the stairs.*]

WILLY. [*stops him with*] May you rot in hell if you leave this house!

BIFF. [*turning*] Exactly what is it that you want from me?

WILLY. I want you to know, on the train, in the mountains, in the valleys, wherever you go, that you cut down your life for spite!

BIFF. No, no.

WILLY. Spite, spite, is the word of your undoing! And when you're down and out, remember what did it. When you're rotting somewhere beside the railroad tracks, remember, and don't you dare blame it on me!

BIFF. I'm not blaming it on you!

WILLY. I won't take the rap for this, you hear?

[*HAPPY comes down the stairs and stands on the bottom step, watching.*]

BIFF. That's just what I'm telling you!

WILLY. [*sinking into a chair at the table, with full accusation*] You're trying to put a knife in me—don't think I don't know what you're doing!

BIFF. All right, phony! Then let's lay it on the line. [*He whips the rubber tube out of his pocket and puts it on the table.*]

HAPPY. You crazy—

LINDA. Biff! [*She moves to grab the hose, but BIFF holds it down with his hand.*]

BIFF. Leave it there! Don't move it!

WILLY. [*not looking at it*] What is that?

BIFF. You know goddam well what that is.

WILLY. [*caged, wanting to escape*] I never saw that.

BIFF. You saw it. The mice didn't bring it into the cellar! What is this supposed to do, make a hero out of you? This supposed to make me sorry for you?

WILLY. Never heard of it.

BIFF. There'll be no pity for you, you hear it? No pity!

WILLY. [*to LINDA*] You hear the spite!

BIFF. No, you're going to hear the truth—what you are and what I am!

LINDA. Stop it!

WILLY. Spite!

HAPPY. [*coming down toward BIFF*] You cut it now!

BIFF. [*to HAPPY*] The man don't know who we are! The man is gonna know! [*to WILLY*] We never told the truth for ten minutes in this house!

HAPPY. We always told the truth!

BIFF. [*turning on him*] You big blow, are you the assistant buyer? You're one of the two assistants to the assistant, aren't you?

HAPPY. Well, I'm practically—

BIFF. You're practically full of it! We all are! And I'm through with it. [*to WILLY*] Now hear this, Willy, this is me.

WILLY. I know you!

BIFF. You know why I had no address for three months? I stole a suit in Kansas City and I was in jail. [*to LINDA, who is sobbing*] Stop crying. I'm through with it.

[*LINDA turns from them, her hands covering her face.*]

WILLY. I suppose that's my fault!

BIFF. I stole myself out of every good job since high school!

WILLY. And whose fault is that?

BIFF. And I never got anywhere because you blew me so full of hot air I could never stand taking orders from anybody! That's whose fault it is!

WILLY. I hear that!

LINDA. Don't, Biff!

BIFF. It's goddam time you heard that! I had to be boss big shot in two weeks, and I'm through with it!

WILLY. Than hang yourself! For spite, hang yourself!

BIFF. No! Nobody's hanging himself, Willy! I ran down eleven flights with a pen in my hand today. And suddenly I stopped, you hear me? And in the middle of that office building, do you hear this? I stopped in the middle of that building and I saw—the sky. I saw the things that I love in this world. The work and the food and time to sit and smoke. And I looked at the pen and said to myself, what the hell am I grabbing this for? Why am I trying to become what I don't want to be? What am I doing in an office, making a contemptuous, begging fool of myself, when all I want is out there, waiting for me the minute I say I know who I am! Why can't I say that, Willy?

[*He tries to make WILLY face him, but WILLY pulls away and moves to the left.*]

WILLY. [*with hatred, threateningly.*] The door of your life is wide open!

BIFF. Pop! I'm a dime a dozen, and so are you!

WILLY. [*turning on him now in an uncontrolled outburst*] I am not a dime a dozen! I am Willy Loman, and you are Biff Loman!

[*BIFF starts for WILLY, but is blocked by HAPPY. In his fury, BIFF seems on the verge of attacking his father.*]

BIFF. I am not a leader of men, Willy, and neither are you. You were never anything but a hard-working drummer who landed in the ash can like all the rest of them! I'm one dollar an hour, Willy! I tried seven states and couldn't raise it. A buck an hour! Do you gather my meaning? I'm not bringing home any prizes any more, and you're going to stop waiting for me to bring them home!

WILLY. [*directly to BIFF*] You vengeful, spiteful mut!

[*BIFF breaks from HAPPY. WILLY, in fright, starts up the stairs. BIFF grabs him.*]

BIFF. [*at the peak of his fury*] Pop, I'm nothing! I'm nothing, Pop. Can't you understand that? There's no spite in it any more. I'm just what I am, that's all.

[*BIFF'S fury has spent itself, and he breaks down, sobbing, holding on to WILLY, who dumbly fumbles for BIFF'S face.*]

WILLY.   [*astonished*] What're you doing? What're you doing? [*to LINDA*] Why is he crying?

BIFF.   [*crying, broken*] Will you let me go, for Christ's sake? Will you take that phony dream and burn it before something happens? [*Struggling to contain himself, he pulls away and moves to the stairs.*] I'll go in the morning. Put him—put him to bed. [*Exhausted, BIFF moves up the stairs to his room.*]

WILLY.   [*after a long pause, astonished, elevated*] Isn't that—isn't that remarkable? Biff—he likes me!

LINDA.   He loves you, Willy!

HAPPY.   [*deeply moved*] Always did, Pop.

WILLY.   Oh, Biff! [*staring wildly*] He cried! Cried to me. [*He is choking with his love, and now cries out his promise.*] That boy—that boy is going to be magnificent!

[*BEN appears in the light just outside the kitchen.*]

BEN.   Yes, outstanding, with twenty thousand behind him.

LINDA.   [*sensing the racing of his mind, fearfully, carefully*] Now come to bed, Willy. It's all settled now.

WILLY.   [*finding it difficult not to rush out of the house*] Yes, we'll sleep. Come on. Go to sleep, Hap.

BEN.   And it does take a great kind of a man to crack the jungle.

[*In accents of dread, BEN'S idyllic music starts up.*]

HAPPY.   [*his arm around LINDA*] I'm getting married, Pop, don't forget it. I'm changing everything. I'm gonna run that department before the year is up. You'll see, Mom. [*He kisses her.*]

BEN.   The jungle is dark but full of diamonds, Willy.

[*WILLY turns, moves, listening to BEN.*]

LINDA.   Be good. You're both good boys, just act that way, that's all.

HAPPY.   'Night, Pop. [*He goes upstairs.*]

LINDA.   [*to WILLY*] Come, dear.

BEN.   [*with greater force*] One must go in to fetch a diamond out.

WILLY.   [*to LINDA, as he moves slowly along the edge of the kitchen, toward the door*] I just want to get settled down, Linda. Let me sit alone for a little.

LINDA.   [*almost uttering her fear*] I want you upstairs.

WILLY.   [*taking her in his arms*] In a few minutes, Linda. I couldn't sleep right now. Go on, you look awful tired. [*He kisses her.*]

BEN.   Not like an appointment at all. A diamond is rough and hard to the touch.

WILLY.   Go on now. I'll be right up.

LINDA.   I think this is the only way, Willy.

WILLY.   Sure, it's the best thing.

BEN.   Best thing!

WILLY.   The only way. Everything is gonna be—go on, kid, get to bed. You look so tired.

LINDA.   Come right up.

WILLY.   Two minutes.

[*LINDA goes into the living-room, then reappears in her bedroom. WILLY moves just outside the kitchen door.*]

WILLY.   Loves me. [*wonderingly*] Always loved me. Isn't that a remarkable thing? Ben, he'll worship me for it!

BEN.   [*with promise*] It's dark there, but full of diamonds.

WILLY.   Can you imagine that magnificence with twenty thousand dollars in his pocket?

LINDA.   [*calling from her room*] Willy! Come up!

WILLY.   [*calling into the kitchen*] Yes! Yes. Coming! It's very smart, you realize that, don't you, sweetheart? Even Ben sees it. I gotta go, baby. 'By! 'By! [*going over to BEN, almost dancing*] Imagine? When the mail comes he'll be ahead of Bernard again!

BEN.   A perfect proposition all around.

WILLY.   Did you see how he cried to me? Oh, if I could kiss him, Ben!

BEN.   Time, William, time!

WILLY.   Oh, Ben, I always knew one way or another we were gonna make it, Biff and I!

BEN.   [*looking at his watch*] The boat. We'll be late. [*He moves slowly off into the darkness.*]

WILLY.   [*elegiacally, turning to the house*] Now when you kick off, boy, I want a seventy-yard boot, and get right down the field under the ball, and when you hit, hit low and hit hard, because it's important, boy. [*He swings around and faces the audience.*] There's all kinds of important people in the stands, and the first thing you know . . . [*suddenly realizing he is alone*] Ben! Ben, where do I . . . ? [*He makes a sudden movement of search.*] Ben, how do I . . . ?

LINDA.   [*calling*] Willy, you coming up?

WILLY.   [*uttering a gasp of fear, whirling about as if to quiet her*] Sh! [*He turns around as if to find his way; sounds, faces, voices, seem to be swarming in upon him and he flicks at them, crying*] Sh! Sh! [*Suddenly music, faint and high, stops him. It rises in intensity, almost to an unbearable scream. He goes up and down on his toes, and rushes off around the house.*] Shhh!

LINDA.   Willy?

[*There is no answer. LINDA waits. BIFF gets up off his bed. He is still in his clothes. HAPPY sits up. BIFF stands listening.*]

LINDA.   [*with real fear*] Willy, answer me! Willy!

[*There is the sound of a car starting and moving away at full speed.*]

LINDA.   No!

BIFF.   [*rushing down the stairs*] Pop!

[*As the car speeds off, the music crashes down in a frenzy of sound, which becomes the soft pulsation of a single cello string. BIFF slowly returns to his bedroom. He and HAPPY gravely don their jackets. LINDA slowly walks out of her room. The music has developed into a dead march. The leaves of day are appearing over everything. CHARLEY and BERNARD, somberly dressed, appear and knock on the kitchen door. BIFF and HAPPY slowly descend the stairs to the kitchen as CHARLEY and BERNARD enter. All stop a moment when LINDA, in clothes of mourning, bearing a little bunch of roses, comes through the draped doorway into the kitchen. She goes to CHARLEY and takes his arm. Now all move toward the audience, through the wall-line of the kitchen. At the limit of the apron, LINDA lays down the flowers, kneels, and sits back on her heels. All stare down at the grave.]*

REQUIEM

CHARLEY.   It's getting dark, Linda.

[*LINDA doesn't react. She stares at the grave.*]

BIFF.   How about it, Mom? Better get some rest, heh? They'll be closing the gate soon.

[*LINDA makes no move. Pause.*]

HAPPY.   [*deeply angered*] He had no right to do that. There was no necessity for it. We would've helped him.

CHARLEY.   [*grunting*] Hmmm.

BIFF.   Come along, Mom.

LINDA.   Why didn't anybody come?

CHARLEY.   It was a very nice funeral.

LINDA.   But where are all the people he knew? Maybe they blame him.

CHARLEY.   Naa. It's a rough world, Linda. They wouldn't blame him.

LINDA.   I can't understand it. At this time especially. First time in thirty-five years we were just about free and clear. He only needed a little salary. He was even finished with the dentist.

CHARLEY.   No man only needs a little salary.

LINDA.   I can't understand it.

BIFF.   There were a lot of nice days. When he'd come home from a trip; or on Sundays, making the stoop; finishing the cellar; putting on the new porch; when he built the extra bathroom; and put up the garage. You know something, Charley, there's more of him in that front stoop than in all the sales he ever made.

CHARLEY.   Yeah. He was a happy man with a batch of cement.

LINDA.   He was so wonderful with his hands.

BIFF.   He had all the wrong dreams. All, all, wrong.

HAPPY.   [*almost ready to fight BIFF*] Don't say that!

BIFF.   He never knew who he was.

CHARLEY.   [*stopping HAPPY'S movement and reply. To BIFF*] Nobody dast blame this man. You don't understand. Willy was a salesman. And for a salesman, there is no rock bottom to the life. He don't put a bolt to a nut, he don't tell you the law or give you medicine. He's a man way out there in the blue, riding on a smile and a shoeshine. And when they start not smiling back—that's an earthquake. And then you get yourself a couple of spots on your hat, and you're finished.

Nobody dast blame this man. A salesman is got to dream, boy. It comes with the territory.

BIFF.   Charley, the man didn't know who he was.

HAPPY.   [*infuriated*] Don't say that!

BIFF.   Why don't you come with me, Happy?

HAPPY.   I'm not licked that easily. I'm staying right in this city, and I'm gonna beat this racket! [*He looks at BIFF, his chin set.*] The Loman Brothers!

BIFF.   I know who I am, kid.

HAPPY.   All right, boy. I'm gonna show you and everybody else that Willy Loman did not die in vain. He had a good dream. It's the only dream you can have—to come out number-one man. He fought it out here, and this is where I'm gonna win it for him.

BIFF.   [*with a hopeless glance at HAPPY, bends toward his mother*] Let's go, Mom.

LINDA.   I'll be with you in a minute. Go on, Charley. [*He hesitates.*] I want to, just for a minute. I never had a chance to say good-by.

[*CHARLEY moves away, followed by HAPPY. BIFF remains a slight distance up and left of LINDA. She sits there, summoning herself. The flute begins, not far away, playing behind her speech.*]

LINDA.   Forgive me, dear. I can't cry. I don't know what it is, but I can't cry. I don't understand it. Why did you ever do that? Help me, Willy, I can't cry. It seems to me that you're just on another trip. I keep expecting you. Willy, dear, I can't cry. Why did you do it? I search and search and I search, and I can't understand it, Willy. I made the last payment on the house today. Today, dear. And there'll be nobody home. [*A sob rises in her throat.*] We're free and clear. [*sobbing more fully, released*] We're free. [*BIFF comes slowly toward her.*] We're free . . . We're free . . .

[*BIFF lifts her to her feet and moves out up right with her in his arms. LINDA sobs quietly. BERNARD and CHARLEY come together and follow them, followed by HAPPY. Only the music of the flute is left on the darkening stage as over the house the hard towers of the apartment buildings rise into sharp focus, and*]

The curtain falls.]

QUESTIONS

Act 1

1.   What do you learn about Willy from the first stage direction?
2.   How does Arthur Miller show you early in the play that Willy is losing touch with reality?
3.   What instances of stealing can be found in the play? Why do Biff and Happy steal? Where did they learn about stealing? How is stealing related to salesmanship?

4. In Act 1 Willy claims that "I never in my life told him [Biff] anything but decent things." How is this assertion untrue? What does it show you about Willy?

5. Why does Linda's mending stockings make Willy nervous?

Act 2 and Requiem

6. What does Willy's difficulty with machines—especially his car, the refrigerator, and Howard's wire recorder—suggest about him? To what extent are these machines symbolic?

7. When Willy sees Bernard in Charley's office, he asks, "What—what's the secret?" What secret is he asking about? Does such a secret exist?

8. In Act 2 Willy buys seeds and tries to plant a garden at night. Why is Willy so disturbed that "nothing's planted" and "I don't have a thing in the ground"? What do this garden and having "things in the ground" mean to Willy?

9. Near the end of Act 2 Biff claims that "we never told the truth for ten minutes in this house!" What does he mean? To what extent is he right?

10. Linda's last line in the play—"We're free . . . we're free"—seems to refer to the house mortgage. In what other ways, however, might you take it?

TOPICS FOR WRITING AND FURTHER DISCUSSION

1. How does Arthur Miller use lighting, the set, blocking, and music to differentiate between action in the present and "memory" action?

2. The stage directions are full of information that cannot be played. In describing Happy, for example, Miller notes that "sexuality is like a color on him." What is the function of such stage directions?

3. How is Willy's suicide foreshadowed throughout the play? To what extent does this foreshadowing create tension?

4. Where is the crisis (or crises) of the play? Where is the catastrophe? Which characters experience an *anagnorisis* or recognition of truth? What is this truth?

5. In the 1980s *Death of a Salesman* was very successfully produced in the People's Republic of China (1983) and revived on Broadway (1984). What accounts for the play's enduring success in contemporary America and in other cultures?

6. Which characters are "real" and which are "hallucinations" that spring from Willy's memory? What are the major differences between these two groups?

7. Which characters are symbolic and what do they symbolize?

8. Discuss the character of Willy Loman. What are his good qualities? In what ways does he have heroic stature? What are his bad qualities? To what extent is his "fall" the result of his flaws, and to what extent is it caused by circumstances beyond his control?

9. How is the relationship between Charley and Bernard different from the one between Willy and his sons? Why is this difference important?

10. Discuss Linda's character and role. In what ways is she supportive of Willy? In what ways does she encourage his deceptions and self-delusions?

11. Normally, Willy is seen as the protagonist of this play. To what extent might it be possible to see Biff as the protagonist? How would such a perspective change the nature of the play?

12. What sort of person is Happy? What has he inherited from Willy? How is he a debasement of Willy? To what degree is he successful or happy?

13. Willy claims that success in business is based not on "what you do" but on "who you know and the smile on your face! It's contacts. . . . a man can end up with diamonds on the basis of being well liked." How does the play support or reject this assertion?

14. What does Willy Loman sell? Why doesn't the play ever tell us this?

15. Most of Willy's memories—Ben's visit, Boston, the football game—are from 1928. Why does Willy's memory constantly return to 1928? Why is the contrast between 1928 and the present of the Loman family significant for Willy and for the play as a whole?

16. Discuss the ways in which this play comments on American society and values. What aspects and values of American culture are explored? Which does the play attack? Which does it defend?

WRITING ABOUT TRAGEDY

As you plan and write an essay about tragedy, all the elements of drama are available for exploration and consideration. We survey traditional approaches to these elements—plot, character, point of view, setting, language, tone, symbol, and theme—in Chapter 27 (pp. 1112–15); you should review this material and relevant sections on writing about fiction and poetry during the prewriting process.

While the basic elements remain consistent in tragedy, the form also provides a few special considerations. In planning and writing about plot and conflict, you can explore in detail the crisis or climax—that point at which tragedy becomes inevitable. Similarly, you should consider the degree to which the conflicts shape or accelerate the tragic action. With character, pay special attention to the tragic protagonist and the major antagonists. What is the connection between the protagonist's strengths and weaknesses? To what extent does the protagonist bring on or cooperate with his or her own destruction? What key characteristics and behavior patterns ensure both the protagonist's heroic stature and fall? In dealing with tone, consider the degree to which the play is ironic. Do you know more about what is going on than the protagonist? Than most of the characters? If so, how does this affect the play's impact and meaning?

All the traditional elements of drama, along with the special considerations noted above, can provide fruitful areas of investigation for planning
and writing an essay about tragic drama. In the remainder of this discussion,
however, we are going to introduce two new ways of writing about literature:
an examination of a problem and a close reading of a passage. Both of
these approaches have universal application; they can be employed to write
about prose fiction, poetry, or any type of dramatic literature. Our discussion will naturally focus on tragedy—specifically *Hamlet*—and the ways in
which problem solving and close reading can generate effective essays about
tragic drama. Keep in mind, however, that both approaches will work well
in writing about any kind of literature.

AN ESSAY ABOUT A PROBLEM

A problem is any question that cannot be answered quickly and easily.
The question "Who is the major character in *Hamlet*?" is not a problem
because the answer is obvious. Let us, however, ask another question:
"Why can we assert that Hamlet is the major character?" This question
is not as easy as the first, and thus it is a problem. It requires that we
think about our answer, even though we do not need to search very far.
Hamlet is the title character. He is involved in most of the action. He is
so much the center of our liking and concern that his death saddens us.
To "solve" this problem requires a series of answers, all of which deal
with the question "why?"

More complex, however, and more typical of literary problems, are
the following questions: "Why does Hamlet talk of suicide in his first soliloquy?" "Why does he treat Ophelia so badly in the 'nunnery' scene?" "Why
does he seem to delay in avenging his father's death?" Questions like
these are normally the subjects of essays that deal with a problem. Simple
factual responses do not answer such questions; they require a good deal
of thought, along with a number of interpretations knitted together.

The process of framing and then solving problems is one of the most
valuable tools that you can bring to any text. If you do this as you read,
you will find that you are constantly isolating key issues, testing possible
solutions, and organizing your thinking. You will also find it much easier
to plan and write an essay about a problem.

The first step in planning such an essay is choosing an appropriate
problem and framing a tentative solution. These processes need not be
difficult; most works of literature offer a multitude of problems that can
be solved or explained in a number of ways. The problem, of course,
should be of some significance. This can be a difficult distinction; your
best guide is your own sense of what matters and needs explaining in

the play. The problem (or question) of why Claudius murders his brother would not generate an effective essay because the solution is too obvious. A more fruitful question might be why Rosencrantz and Guildenstern cooperate with Claudius and become spies. While the solution to this problem may seem obvious, you should consider not only motivation, but also circumstances and the degree to which these men understand what is going on in Denmark.

The goal in an essay on a problem is to convince your reader that your solution is a good one. You do this by making sound conclusions from supporting evidence drawn from the text. In literature you will rarely find absolute proofs, so your conclusions will not be "proved" like theorems in geometry. However, your organization, your use of facts from the text, your interpretations, and your application of general knowledge should all be designed to make your conclusions *convincing*. The basic strategy is thus persuasion.

Because problems and solutions change according to the text being studied, each essay on a problem will differ from every other. Despite these differences, however, a number of common strategies may be employed in planning and writing. Whatever strategy you use, you should always be trying to solve the problem—to answer the question—and you should do this in the most direct and convenient way.

Strategy 1: The demonstration that conditions for a solution are fulfilled. This strategy is the most basic in writing: illustration. You first explain that certain conditions need to exist for your solution to be plausible. Your central idea—really a brief answer to the question—will be that the conditions for a solution do exist. Your development will demonstrate that such conditions are found in the work. If you are writing on the problem of why Hamlet seems to delay his revenge against Claudius, for example, you might assert in the introduction that Hamlet delays because he is never completely sure that Claudius is guilty. This is the solution and the central idea. In the essay you would support your answer by showing the flimsiness of the information Hamlet receives about the crime. Once you have demonstrated that Hamlet's information is potentially unreliable, you will have proved your point and written a convincing essay.

Strategy 2: The analysis of words in the phrasing of the problem. Another good approach is to explore the meaning and limits of important words or phrases in the problem as it is formulated. Your goal is to clarify the words and show whether they have any special meaning. Such attention to words might give you enough material for all or part of your paper. Thus, an essay on the problem of Hamlet's delay might focus in part on a treatment of the word *delay*: what does *delay* really mean? What is the difference between reasonable and unreasonable delay? Does Hamlet delay unreasonably? Would speedy revenge be more or less reasonable than the delay? By the time you had devoted such attention to the word, you

would have gathered a substantial amount of material that could be organized in planning and writing the essay.

Strategy 3: Reference to literary conventions. Sometimes your best argument may be to establish that the problem can be solved by reference to
the literary or dramatic conventions of the text. A problem about the artificiality of the choruses in *Oedipus*, for example, might be resolved by reference to the fact that the choruses were a normal feature of Greek drama.
In a similar manner, the knowledge that delay is a convention of all revenge
tragedy might provide a key to the problem of Hamlet's apparent procrastination.

Strategy 4: Procatalepsis, the argument against possible objections. With this
approach, you raise an objection to your solution and then argue against
it. This strategy, called *procatalepsis* or *anticipation*, is useful because it helps
you sharpen your own arguments by forcing you to consider facts and
events that you might ordinarily overlook. Although procatalepsis may be
used repeatedly throughout an essay, it is often most useful at the end;
in this way you anticipate objections that might be raised by others and
so make your argument more powerful and convincing. The aim of this
strategy is to show that, compared with your solution, the objection (1)
is not accurate or valid, (2) is not strong or convincing, or (3) is an exception, not a rule. Here are three examples of procatalepsis; the objections
raised are underlined to distinguish them from the answers.

1. *The objection is not accurate or valid.* Here you reject the objection
by showing that either the interpretation or the conclusions are wrong
and also by emphasizing that the evidence supports your solution.

> Although Hamlet's delay is reasonable, the claim might be made that his greater
> duty is to kill Claudius as soon as the ghost accuses Claudius of the murder.
> This claim is not persuasive because it assumes that Hamlet knows everything
> we know. We immediately accept the ghost's word that Claudius is guilty. For
> Hamlet, however, there is every reason to doubt the ghost and not to act. It
> would seem both insane and foolish for Hamlet to kill Claudius, who is legally
> king, and then to claim that he did it because a ghost told him to do so. The
> argument for speedy revenge is not good because it is based on an inaccurate
> view of the situation faced by Hamlet.

2. *The objection is not strong or convincing.* Here you *concede* that the
objection has some validity, but you then try to show that it is weak and
that your own solution is stronger.

> One might claim that Claudius's distress at the play within the play is evidence
> for his guilt and that therefore Hamlet should act instantly. This argument
> has merit, and Hamlet's speech after Claudius flees the room shows that he
> is convinced of his uncle's guilt. But the king's behavior is not a strong enough
> cause for killing him. Such behavior would justify a full investigation of old

Hamlet's death, but it does not justify the murder of Claudius. As a result, the reasons for delay are stronger than those for action, even after the play-within-the-play.

3. *The objection is an exception, not a rule.* Here you reject the objection on the grounds that it could be valid only if normal conditions were suspended.

The case for quick action is simple: Hamlet should kill Claudius right after seeing the ghost (1.3), or else after seeing the king's reaction to the stage murder of Gonzago (3.2) or after the ghost's second appearance (3.4). This argument wrongly assumes that due process does not exist in Denmark and that justice must be both personal and outside the law. The fact is, however, that the world of *Hamlet* is a place where legality and the rules of evidence are valued. Thus, Hamlet cannot rush out to kill Claudius because he knows that the king has not had anything like a public trial. The argument for quick action is weak because it assumes that Hamlet is exempt from the limits of civilized law.

Organizing Your Essay

Writing an essay on a problem requires that you argue a position. To develop this position, show the steps that have led you to your conclusion. The general form of the essay will thus be (1) a statement of the problem, (2) a description of the conditions that need to be met for the solution you propose, and then (3) a demonstration that these conditions *do* or *do not* exist. Arrange your materials convincingly around your main point; do not use anything from the work that is not relevant to your thesis. You need not discuss things in their order of appearance; you are in control and must order your proofs so that your solution to the problem may be developed most effectively.

INTRODUCTION. Your introduction should begin with a statement of the problem and a reference to the conditions that must be established for the problem to be solved. The central idea will be the solution to the problem, and the thesis sentence will indicate the main topics of your argument.

BODY. The body of your essay should contain the major points of argument, arranged to convince your reader that your solution is valid. In each paragraph the topic sentence should be an assertion that is a major element of your solution, and this should be followed by enough detail to support the topic and convince a reader. In developing the body, you might want to use one of the strategies discussed above or a combination of strategies. Thus, if you are attempting to prove that Hamlet's delay is reasonable and not the result of a character flaw, you might begin by considering the word *delay* (strategy 2). Then you might use strategy 1 to explain why Hamlet seems to delay. Finally, in order to answer objections to your argument, you might show that he is capable of action when he feels justified (strategy 4). Whatever your topic, it is important to use the method or methods that best help you make a good case for your solution to the problem.

CONCLUSION.   Your conclusion should affirm the validity of your solution in view of the supporting evidence. You can do this by repeating those points you believe are strongest. You can also summarize each of your main points. Or you might think of your argument as still continuing and thus use procatalepsis to raise and answer objections that could be raised against your solution.

SAMPLE ESSAY

The Problem of Hamlet's Apparent Delay in Shakespeare's *Hamlet**

[1]   For hundreds of years, readers and spectators of Shakespeare's *Hamlet* have been puzzled by the prince's failure to take quick action against Claudius. Early in the play, the ghost calls on his son to "Revenge his foul and most unnatural murder" (1.5.25). Hamlet, however, waits until the end of the play to achieve vengeance. This is the problem: how can we account for Hamlet's delay? The solution to this problem is found in a demonstration that there is no unjustified delay and that Hamlet acts as quickly as possible at almost every point.° This becomes evident when we examine the conventions of revenge tragedy, the actual "call to revenge," and the steps that Hamlet takes to achieve vengeance.▫

[2]   Revenge tragedy conventionally requires that vengeance be delayed until the closing moments of the play. Given this limitation, Shakespeare had to justify the wide gap of time between the call to revenge in act 1 and the killing of Claudius in act 5. We find such justification in the unreliability of the ghost's initial accusation, Hamlet's need for additional evidence, and the events that occur after such evidence is obtained.

[3]   The ghost's accusations and demands are straightforward: he accuses his brother of murdering him and he calls on his son for vengeance. Shakespeare is careful, however, to establish that this testimony is not necessarily to be trusted. Horatio voices doubts about the ghost's veracity and motives; he warns Hamlet that the spirit might "assume some other horrid form / Which

---

* See p. 1180 for this play.
° Central idea.
▫ Thesis sentence.

might deprive your sovereignty of reason, / And draw you into madness"
(1.4.72–74). Hamlet himself questions the ghost's reliability:

> The spirit that I have seen
> May be a devil, and the devil hath power
> T'assume a pleasing shape, yea, and perhaps
> Out of my weakness, and my melancholy,
> As he is very potent with such spirits,
> Abuses me to damn me; I'll have grounds
> More relative than this.   (2.2.573–579)

The prince thus cannot act simply on the unsupported word of the ghost; he
needs more evidence.

There is no delay at this point in the play; Hamlet quickly begins to develop
ways to gain corroboration. Immediately after speaking with the ghost, he decides to use pretended madness as a "cover" for his investigation. He swears
his companions to silence and warns them not to react knowingly if he subsequently appears to be mad:

> . . . never so help you mercy,
> How strange or odd some'er I bear myself,
> (As I perchance hereafter shall think it meet
> To put an antic disposition on)
> That you at such times seeing me, never shall
>   . . . note
>
> That you know aught of me.   (1.5.169–179)

[4]

By the close of act 1 Hamlet has already mapped out a campaign to gain
further information by taking on an "antic disposition." He assumes that such
a pose will make him less suspect and make others less careful.

When we next encounter Hamlet, he has already established his "antic
disposition" with most of the court. Polonius, for example, is convinced that
the prince is "mad" for love and tells Claudius that "I have found / The very
cause of Hamlet's lunacy" (2.2.48–49). In this same scene, Hamlet comes
up with a method of checking the ghost's reliability. Rosencrantz's news that
a troupe of players is shortly to arrive at Elsinore sets Hamlet thinking, and
he formulates the test of "The Mousetrap" by the time he meets with the actors.
He asks the First Player if his troupe can "play The Murder of Gonzago" with
"a speech of some dozen or sixteen lines which I would set down and insert
in't" (2.2.512–517). In the soliloquy that ends act 2, the prince tells us exactly
how he plans to test Claudius:

[5]

> I'll have these players
> Play something like the murder of my father
> Before mine uncle, I'll observe his looks,
> I'll tent him to the quick, if a' do blench
> I know my course.   (2.2.569–573)

Again, we find no delay in Hamlet's behavior. Once a method of testing the ghost's charges is developed, it is put to use immediately. Hamlet tells the First Player that "We'll ha't [the play] tomorrow night (2.2.515).

[6] "The Mousetrap" provides exactly the information Hamlet needs to proceed with vengeance. The king interrupts the performance immediately after the villain pours poison into the ears of the player-king: a reenactment of Claudius's original crime. Now Hamlet has corroborating evidence; he says "I'll take the ghost's word for a thousand pound" (3.2.271–272). Moreover, he is psychologically ready to act against the king; he asserts that he could "drink hot blood, / And do such bitter business as the day / Would quake to look on" (3.2.367–369). Hamlet even has an opportunity to gain revenge; in the very next scene he comes upon Claudius while the latter is unguarded and appears to be praying. Hamlet determines to act: "Now might I do it pat, now a' is a-praying, / And now I'll do it" (3.3.73–74).

Hamlet has motive, means, evidence, and opportunity, but does not act. Here—and only here—one might accuse him of delay. Again, however, Shakespeare is careful to justify Hamlet's refusal to act. The prince does not want to send the soul of Claudius to heaven by killing him while he is in a state of grace. Rather, he wants the revenge to match the cruel way in which Claudius killed old king Hamlet without giving him a chance to repent his sins:

[7]
> Up sword, and know thou a more horrid hent,
> When he is drunk asleep, or in his rage,
> Or in th'incestuous pleasure of his bed,
> At game, a-swearing, or about some act
> That has no relish of salvation in't,
> Then trip him that his heels may kick at heaven,
> And that his soul may be as damned and black
> As hell whereto it goes.   (3.3.88–95)

Hamlet's decision to defer revenge here is in keeping with the peculiar "justice" of personal blood vengeance. The retribution must match or exceed the original crime.

[8] From this point on, there is no question of delay. Rather, Hamlet acts or reacts to every situation as the opportunity presents itself. During his confrontation with Gertrude, for example, he hears a noise behind the arras and instantly stabs the eavesdropper. He hopes that Claudius is his victim. When the spy turns out to be Polonius, Hamlet's quest for vengeance becomes a great deal more difficult. The murder of Polonius lets the king know that Hamlet is perfectly sane and trying to kill him. As a result, Claudius begins a counterplot that makes it impossible for Hamlet to act. He had already decided to send Hamlet off to England and execution; he now determines to send the prince away at dawn that very day. Thus, Hamlet has no further opportunity to act before he is sent to England "under guard."

[9] Hamlet leaves the court in act 4 and does not return until act 5. In the interval, he works with speed and cunning to escape the intended execution and to return to Denmark. When he encounters Claudius at Ophelia's funeral, the king is guarded and surrounded by attendants. Again, Hamlet is forced

by circumstances to wait. He makes it clear to Horatio, however, that he will seize the next opportunity; he asserts that "the readiness is all" (5.2.205). This is followed immediately by the rigged fencing match and the bloodbath that ends the play. Hamlet finally gains revenge by stabbing and poisoning the king.

[10] Thus, we see that the problem of Hamlet's delay is really no problem at all. The prince acts in accordance with the internal "justice" of revenge as quickly as circumstances permit once he has confirmed the ghost's accusations. Although the text of the play supports this solution, critics might still argue that procrastination is an issue because Hamlet twice accuses himself of delay. Such an objection slights the way in which Hamlet's perception of time and action is subject to the distortions of a mind fixated on vengeance. From such a subjective point of view, any hiatus in activity is delay. From our objective viewpoint, however, delay is finally not an issue.

Commentary on the Essay

The introductory paragraph raises the problem of Hamlet's apparent delay and offers a brief statement of the solution (the central idea). The thesis sentence outlines the steps of the argument that will validate the solution and it provides an overall plan for the essay. This plan is developed in paragraphs 2–9 in exactly the same order in which the issues are raised in the introduction. Thus, paragraph 2 deals with the conventions of revenge tragedy and paragraph 3 takes up the reliability of the ghost. Paragraphs 4 through 6 deal with Hamlet's attempts to corroborate the ghost's accusations, and paragraphs 7, 8, and 9 consider the subsequent action. Note that each paragraph in the argument grows naturally out of the one that precedes it *and* is linked back to the introductory paragraph. The concluding paragraph asserts that the original problem is solved and summarizes the steps of the solution. It also continues the argument by raising and then dealing with a final objection to the proposed solution.

The general structure of the essay illustrates strategy 1 described above: illustration. The second paragraph, however, makes brief use of strategy 3 in its reference to the conventions of revenge tragedy. Finally, the concluding paragraph offers an example of strategy 4: procatalepsis.

AN ESSAY ON A CLOSE READING OF A PASSAGE

An essay on a close reading is a detailed study of a passage of prose or verse that may be part of a longer work, such as a speech from a play, story, or novel, or it may be an entire short poem. The close-reading essay is specific because it focuses on the selected passage. It is also general in that you do not focus on a single topic (such as character, setting, or theme), but rather deal with all the elements that are found in the passage.

If the passage describes a person, for example, you must discuss character, but your emphasis should be on what the passage itself brings out about the character. The passage dictates the content of your essay.

In planning an essay on a close reading of a passage from a play, your first step is to isolate several important passages and explore their significance to the play as a whole. You may find that specific passages relate most clearly to character, tone, theme, or some other element. In these instances, you can direct your exploration along those lines. At an early point in prewriting, you can choose a specific passage and begin to consider both its meaning and its significance in the larger context of the play.

During this stage of prewriting, you can focus on the general meaning and impact of the passage. Who speaks it? What is it about? What does it tell you about the speaker or the world of the play? Once these issues are clear, you can begin to develop a set of notes on your observations that can be organized later into paragraphs. Try to reach some specific and focused conclusions about the passage: does it (1) describe a scene, (2) develop a character, (3) present an action, (4) reveal a character's thoughts, (5) advance an argument, or (6) introduce an idea? What is the thematic content of the passage? In this respect, how does it relate to earlier and later parts of the whole text?

The position of the passage often provides important clues to an effective approach. You should always take into account whether the passage occurs near the beginning, middle, or end of the work. If the passage is near the beginning, you can assume that the author is using it to help set the plot in motion. Thus you should try to determine how themes, characterizations, and arguments that you find in the passage are related to later developments. Always assume that everything in the passage is there for a purpose, and then find that purpose. Passages that occur near the middle of a work often indicate a "pivot" or "turning point." In such passages, a character's fortunes may take either an expected or an unexpected turn. If the change is expected, you should explore how the passage focuses the various ideas and then propels them toward the climax. If the change is unexpected, however, investigate how the contrast is made. It may be that the work features surprises, and the passage thus acquires a different meaning on second reading. Or it may be that the speaker has one set of assumptions while the readers have others and that the passage marks a point of increasing self-awareness on the part of the speaker. If the passage occurs at or near the end of the work, it is probably designed to solve problems or to advance the resolution. You can consider the ways in which the passage brings together themes, lines of development, and details. Determine the extent to which the passage furthers the resolution of the work and the degree to which the passage has been prepared for earlier.

Organizing Your Essay

INTRODUCTION.   In an essay of this type, you should begin by quoting the entire passage just as it appears in the text. It is also helpful to number the lines for easy reference. The introduction should present your central idea and the steps of your argument. Because the close-reading essay is concerned with details, you might have a problem developing a thematic structure. This difficulty can be overcome if you begin to work with either a generalization about the passage or a thesis based on the relationship of the passage to the work. Suppose, for example, that the passage is factually descriptive or that it introduces a major character or raises a central idea. Any one of these observations may serve as a thesis.

BODY.   Develop the body of the essay according to what you find in the passage. Suppose you have a passage of character description; you might analyze what is said about the character, together with a comparison of how this information is modified later. In addition, you might consider how the characteristics described affect other characters or later events in the work. If the passage introduces a theme, you might demonstrate how the idea is established in the passage and then developed throughout the work. The aim here is to focus on details in the passage and also on the relationship of these details to the entire work.

CONCLUSION.   The conclusion of your essay can summarize your argument and bring it to an effective close. In addition, you can use the conclusion to deal with secondary issues that arise in the passage but do not merit full consideration. There may be specific phrases or underlying assumptions, for example, that are found in the passage. The conclusion is the place for you to mention these concerns.

SAMPLE ESSAY

Appearance and Reality in *Hamlet*:* A Close Reading of *Hamlet*, 1.2.76–86.

> Seems, madam? nay it is. I know not "seems."
> 'Tis not alone my inky cloak good mother,
> Nor customary suits of solemn black,
> Nor windy suspiration of forced breath,
> No, nor the fruitful river of the eye,

---

* See p. 1180 for this play.

Nor the dejected havior of the visage,
Together with all forms, moods, shapes of grief,
That can denote me truly: these indeed seem,
For they are actions that a man might play,
But I have that within which passes show,
These but the trappings and the suits of woe.

[1] This passage from Shakespeare's *Hamlet* is spoken by the prince during his first appearance on stage in act 1. Gertrude—his mother—has just tried to convince Hamlet that death is "common" to all humanity and that he "seems" to be taking his father's death too much to heart. Hamlet's entire speech grows out of Gertrude's use of the word "seems." In the passage, Shakespeare introduces one of the central ideas of the play: that there is a discrepancy or difference between appearance and reality.° This concept is stated directly in the first line and is amplified in the rest of the passage; it shows up repeatedly throughout the play in the ways characters present themselves and in the actions they perform.□

[2] The discrepancy between appearance and reality is introduced explicitly in Hamlet's first line: "Seems, madam? nay, it is." In this statement, Hamlet opposes "seems" to "is." Thus, he introduces a direct contrast between those things that seem to be and those that actually exist. This explicit opposition of illusion or appearance ("seems") and reality ("is") becomes the cornerstone for the rest of the passage.

[3] Hamlet expands on the idea of a discrepancy between appearance and reality in lines 77 through 86 with reference to the outward trappings of mourning. He begins by listing five of the traditional signs of grief: an "inky cloak" (77); "suits of solemn black" (78); sighs, or the "windy suspirations of forced breath" (79); tears, or "the fruitful river of the eye" (80); and sad looks, or "the dejected [be]havior of the visage" (81). Having enumerated these items, Hamlet goes on to identify them in three separate lines as the outward displays of mourning. First, he calls them the "forms, moods, shapes of grief" (82). In line 84 he also notes that "they are actions that a man might play." And in line 86 he labels his catalogue "the trappings [costumes] and the suits of woe." The three lines thus assert that the five signs of grief listed earlier are all outward shows. Appearance (as opposed to reality) is especially emphasized in words like *forms*, *shapes*, *play*, and *trappings*. Finally, Hamlet brings his speech to its logical climax and conclusion by contrasting all these appearances of grief with his own real and internal feelings: "I have that within which [sur] passes show" (line 85). Again, we have the direct contrast between appearance ("show") and reality ("that within").

[4] The idea raised in this passage is central to our understanding of *Hamlet*; the discrepancy between appearance and reality shows up repeatedly in characters and situations throughout the play. Claudius, for example, appears to be a loving uncle, a good king, and a reasonable man. He is actually a murderer

° Central idea.
□ Thesis sentence.

and a usurper who fears Hamlet and plots continually against him. Rosencrantz and Guildenstern put on the appearance of innocent school friends, but they are actually tools of Claudius who willingly spy on Hamlet. We find a similar discrepancy between the appearance and the reality of actions and events. In act 3, for example, Claudius appears to be praying for forgiveness and repenting his crimes. In actuality, however, he can neither pray nor repent because he is "still possessed / Of those effects for which I did the murder" (3.3.53–54). Similarly, the duel between Hamlet and Laertes seems to be a straightforward fencing match but is actually a complicated trap in which Hamlet is supposed to be killed by sword or poison.

[5]   The passage we have been examining clearly deals with grief and mourning. On further analysis, however, we see that it raises one of the central issues in *Hamlet*: the discrepancy between appearance and reality. This discrepancy must inform our reading of the entire play. Because characters and events in *Hamlet* are often not what they appear to be, the passage provides a key to our understanding of Shakespeare's tragedy.

Commentary on the Essay

Since this passage is the first extended speech by Hamlet, we might have chosen an essay that examined the ways in which Hamlet's character is established. Instead, the essay deals with a central idea raised in the passage: the discrepancy between appearance and reality. The introduction places the quotation in its immediate context, states the central idea of the essay, and notes the steps in which this thesis will be discussed. The body takes up the specific ways in which the concept of a discrepancy between appearance and reality is developed in the passage and carried throughout the play. Paragraph 2 deals with Hamlet's explicit statement of the idea, and paragraph 3 discusses his illustration of the concept with reference to the trappings of grief. Paragraph 4 demonstrates the relationship of this idea to the rest of the play. Finally, the conclusion suggests that the concept might serve as a key to understanding the whole play. Although this essay deals extensively with the actual words in the passage, it clearly focuses on content rather than style. We are concerned here with the words themselves rather than with the way they are arranged, their connotations, their grammatical structure, or their syntactical relationships.

29

Comedy

Comedy is often considered to be the opposite of tragedy, and in many ways this perception is quite accurate. The classical mask of comedy smiles, while that of tragedy frowns. Whereas tragedy begins in prosperity, comedy opens with problems and adversity. Comedy generally presents the successful regeneration of a social group, whereas tragedy focuses on the fall of a heroic individual. The language of tragedy tends to be elevated and heroic, whereas the language of comedy can be witty or bawdy, artificially elegant or stridently colloquial. Tragedy often ends in death, but comedy frequently closes with marriages. All these distinctions are real, and yet the gulf between tragedy and comedy is not as great as we might think. Many tragedies contain potentially comic plots, and many comedies are filled with tragic potential. Indeed, tragedy may be seen as an abortive or incomplete comedy in which affairs go disastrously wrong, and comedy can be considered a tragedy in which the truth is discovered, the hero saves the day, or the villain confesses in time to avert disaster.

    The term **comedy** comes from the Greek word *komos*, which means "celebration," "revel," or "merrymaking." As the word suggests, comedy began as a ritual celebration, a time of outrageous merrymaking in which social restrictions were released, appetites were indulged, bizarre behavior was encouraged, and the world was turned upside down. The original *komos* may have been a religious revel celebrating the cyclical rebirth of Dionysus, the god of fertility and wine. His death and rebirth trace out the movement from winter to spring, sterility to fertility, and adversity to prosperity. Comedy thus has an ancient and ongoing association with celebrations of social and sexual rebirth.

OLD AND NEW COMEDY

Classical Greek and Roman comedy is traditionally divided into two general types: old and new comedy. **Old comedy**, exemplified by the plays of Aristophanes (ca. 448–388 B.C.), was highly satirical and involved extensive personal attacks on specific individuals and on the society at large. The plays were very topical and at least partly improvised (made up on the spot by the actors); the language was witty and biting.

Many elements of old comedy survive to this day, especially the impulse toward satire and the witty language. For the most part, however, old comedy was replaced by new comedy (called "new" to differentiate it from the older fashion of Aristophanic comedy) in the third century B.C. **New comedy**, developed by the Greek dramatist Menander (ca. 342–291 B.C.), was romantic rather than satirical. It employed stock characters such as young lovers, stubborn fathers, jealous husbands, and clever slaves, and the action depended more on plot than on language or character.

Roman new comic plays, as exemplified by the work of Plautus (ca. 254–184 B.C.) and Terence (ca. 184–159 B.C.), tended to be short, violent, and bawdy. They often involved young lovers who were prevented or blocked from having a relationship by some individual or circumstance, a **blocking agent**. This obstruction to true love (or at least true lust) could be almost anything—a rival lover, an angry father, a family feud, an old law, social prejudice, a previously arranged marriage, or a difference in social class.

There is much that is funny in these plays: the overblown sighs of the divided lovers, the ranting of the offended father, the repeated beatings that the crafty slave receives from his master or mistress, the confusion of mistaken identities. The comedy, however, derives from the *pattern* of the action: the initial problem, the outrageous plots hatched by the characters to circumvent the blocking agents, and the ultimate victory of young love over old jealousies. The resolutions of these plays frequently represent the victory of youth over old age and the passing of vitality and control from one generation to the next.

COMIC AND FUNNY: THE PATTERN OF COMEDY

Although dictionaries often give *funny* as a synonym for *comic*, there is an essential difference between the two terms and the concepts they signify. Words like "funny," "amusing," or "humorous" define our emotional reactions to things rather than the things themselves, and the reaction always depends on context. We will usually react with laughter to an actor repeatedly knocked on the head with a wooden paddle during a slapstick routine, but a man beaten with a baseball bat on the street is horrifying rather than amusing. "Comic," the adjective derived from "comedy," does not signify an emotional response. Rather, it means that a literary work conforms to the patterns and characteristics of comedy. Many comedies are, in fact, very funny; we react with amusement to the witty remarks, bawdy jokes, foolish characters, silly mistakes, and other devices of plot, action, and language that can occur in comic drama. At heart, however, comedy and the term "comic" suggest a *pattern of action*, growing out of character or situation, that leads to a specific kind of catastrophe and resolution.

Comedies begin in adversity; during their exposition, we usually learn that something is wrong. These initial problems can be the result of character or circumstance; they can be individual or social. They can involve thwarted love, eccentric behavior, corruption in society, or a combination of ingredients. As the play moves from exposition to complication, these problems usually get much worse. In comedy, complication is often fueled by confusion, misunderstanding, mistakes in identity, coincidences that stretch our credulity, errors in judgment, and the excessive behavior of unreasonable characters.

The climax of a comedy occurs when these confusions reach a peak, misunderstanding is dominant, pressure is at a high point, choices must be made, and solutions must be found. The catastrophe unties the knots and resolves the complications. In comedy, the catastrophe is frequently a sudden revelation of truth—an epiphany—in which some key fact, identity, or event is explained to the characters and the audience at the same time.

In most comedies, the events of the catastrophe resolve the initial problems and allow for the comic resolution of the play. This comic resolution frequently involves setting things right at every level of action: individual lives are straightened out, new families are formed through marriages, and a healthy social order is established.

Of course, not all comedies go through each stage of this pattern. Some focus purely on individual problems; others deal mainly with the customs and attitudes of society at large. Some offer virtually no exposition, and others provide an incomplete and ambivalent resolution in which things do not seem much better at the end than they did at the beginning. Nevertheless, the idea of comedy is embodied in this general model of action.

Two key features of the comic pattern are *education* and *change*. In many comedies at least some of the characters learn something about themselves, their society, or the way to live and love. This education makes it possible for the characters (and thus, the society) to change for the better. In other comedies, however, the *audience* is educated, and the playwright hopes that change will occur in the world rather than on the stage.

CHARACTERS IN COMEDY

Characters in comedy tend to be far more limited than in tragedy because comedies deal with groups or representative types rather than with individuals of heroic stature. We usually do not find in comedy characters with the depth or individuality of Hamlet or Oedipus. Instead, there are stock characters who represent various classes, types, and generations. In Shakespeare's *A Midsummer Night's Dream*, for instance, most of the characters are representative stock figures. Egeus is a conventional indignant father; he represents the middle class and the older generation. Similarly, Hermia and Lysander (along with Helena and Demetrius) are typical lovers who represent the younger generation.

Such representative characters, mostly derived from Roman new comedy and its later developments, include yearning young lovers, indignant or befuddled fathers, shrewish wives, henpecked husbands, tricky servants, social misfits, country bumpkins, gullible victims, greedy con-men, and pompous braggarts. These characters, and variations on them, have populated comedies for thousands of years; they have been adapted to every stage in every age of European and American drama, and they still constitute the basic types in television and film comedy today.

LANGUAGE IN COMEDY

As in other types of drama and literature, language is employed in comedy to delineate and define character, to establish tone and mood, and to express ideas and feelings. In comedy, however, language is also one of the most important vehicles for creating humor. Some comedies are characterized by elegant and witty language, others by bawdy jokes, puns, and inarticulate utterances.

Characters in comedy tend either to be masters of language or to be mastered by it. Those who control language, such as Célimène in Molière's *The Misanthrope*, can use an apt and witty phrase like a knife as they satirize their friends and foes. Those who cannot deal with language, such as Bottom in Shakespeare's *A Midsummer Night's Dream*, bungle through attempts at communication with inadvertent puns, malapropisms, and jumbled syntax. Both types of character and both types of language amuse us; we tend to smile a knowing smile with the wits and laugh out loud at the bunglers.

TYPES OF COMEDY

All comedy has some common elements, but differences in style, content, and intent make it possible to divide comedy into various types that have evolved over the centuries. The broadest of these divisions, based on both style and content, separates all comic literature into high comedy and low comedy. **High comedy** (the term was coined by George Meredith in 1877 in *The Idea of Comedy*) is characterized by wit, grace, and sophistication. The complications and problems in high comedy tend to grow out of character rather than situation, and the appeal is to the intellect.

In **low comedy** witty conversation and thoughtful characters give way to sight gags, bawdy jokes, funny remarks, and outrageous circumstances. Plays of this type are often crude, violent, and full of physical humor— seven men hide in different places in the same room, or a poor soul gets whacked repeatedly each time a carpenter turns around with a plank. The complications in low comedy usually develop from plot and situation rather than from character.

A special type of low comedy is the **farce**, a term derived from the Latin word *farsus*, which means "stuffed." It signifies a boisterous and physical comedy that overflows with inane characters, sight gags, violent physical activity, bawdy jokes, and ludicrous events. In farce, the focus is on plot and action rather than on character; it has held the stage from Roman times to the present.

Commedia dell'arte and slapstick comedy are specific kinds of farce. **Commedia dell'arte**, which developed in Italy in the sixteenth century, is broadly humorous farce that features stock characters, stock situations, and improvised dialogue. The stock characters of *commedia*—the clever servant, fool, young lovers, old man with a young wife or daughter, physician or lawyer, and military captain—are derived in part from new comedy and have, in turn, influenced much subsequent comedy. **Slapstick comedy** is a low form of farce that depends almost entirely on physical action such as hitting, tripping, hiding, conventionally exaggerated reactions such as the slow burn or the double-take, and traditional bits of business with props such as pies, pails of water, beds, ladders, and the like. The form derives its name from the double paddle ("slap stick") that Roman comic actors used to strike each other and make a loud noise.

Another major distinction between comedies, this time based on content and the playwright's intent, divides the mode into satiric and romantic comedy. **Satiric comedy**, derived in part from Greek old comedy, is designed to correct social and individual behavior by ridiculing human vices and follies. In writing satiric comedy, the playwright assumes the perspective of a rational and moderate observer; the audience is initially invited to share this superior point of view as they watch scorn heaped upon characters who are excessive, eccentric, foolish, or evil.

Satiric comedy can be gently mocking or viciously biting, but its aim is always correction through ridicule. Playwrights as diverse as Aristophanes, Ben Jonson, Molière, and George Bernard Shaw have written satiric comedy to expose and thus correct the follies of their ages. In all these comedies, the education theoretically occurs among the readers or spectators; we are supposed to see our own vices reflected in the mirror of the play.

Romantic comedy is much more gentle and sympathetic. It derives from Roman new comedy and presents the adventures (or misadventures) of young lovers trying to overcome opposition and achieve a successful union. The focus of such plays is thus the foolishness to which love can drive us and, at the same time, its ultimate victory. Romantic comedy aims to entertain and amuse rather than to ridicule or reform. We are normally encouraged to sympathize with the young lovers. The common thread among all these plays is Shakespeare's observation that "The course of true love never did run smooth." The trials and tribulations of love are universals that we all share. Although folly and vice may be exposed in romantic comedy, especially in the characters who block the match of the young lovers, the dominant impulse here is gentle entertainment, and the overriding tone is tolerant and amused indulgence.

Other, more narrowly defined types of comedy have evolved in the last five hundred years, among them the comedy of humors and the comedy of manners. The **comedy of humors**, popular during the sixteenth and seventeenth centuries, focuses on the characteristic traits, or humors, of stock characters such as the henpecked husband or the gullible victim. The problems in such plays usually result from the characters' extremely stereotypical behavior; the action unravels the problems by breaking this behavior pattern.

The **comedy of manners** which developed in the sixteenth century, examines and satirizes the social conventions of the society in which the play is set. Such plays usually focus on the attitudes, manners, and morals of the upper classes; they tend to be full of clever characters who make witty remarks (or attempt to be clever and witty).

Both comedies of humors and of manners often include a love plot, so the balance between the satiric and the romantic impulse depends on the emphasis of each play. In addition, both tend to be high comedy, although the comedy of humors may have many elements of low comedy.

Most of these types of comedy flourish today. Romantic comedies and comedies of manners are still written and performed successfully. Farce and slapstick comedy have been staples of the movie industry since the days of silent film. Television writers have taken the new comic pattern and trivialized it into **situation comedy**. Here, the initial problem becomes petty and insignificant—will Mr. Smith get the contract signed in order to save his job, will Mrs. Jones get dinner prepared before Mr. Jones and his boss arrive home for dinner, will Jimmy get Dad's car fixed before the dented fender is discovered? The complications in situation comedy are equally trivial—a missed plane, a burned cake, an unexpected visit by relatives. Still, the comedy grows out of the characters' desperate attempts to solve these problems, and comic resolution still embodies some sort of victory over adversity.

Other types of modern and contemporary comedy include **ironic comedy**, **realistic comedy**, and **comedy of the absurd** (see pp. 1067–68). All of these have in common a movement away from the happy endings of traditional comedy. In many of them, the blocking agents are successful and the protagonists are defeated. Often, the initial problem—either a realistic or an absurdist dilemma—remains unresolved at the close of the play. Such comedies, which began to appear in the late nineteenth century, are frequently designed to illustrate the complexities or absurdities of modern life and the funny but futile efforts that people make to come to grips with existence.

Given these various kinds, you should keep in mind that comedies are rarely pure forms of one type. High comedies can include crude physical humor, especially with characters from the lower classes; low comedies may contain some wit and elegance. Satiric comedies can also deal with the successful efforts of young lovers, and romantic comedies often mock the vices and follies of eccentric characters. Comedies of manners often include romantic plots and farcical elements; farce and slapstick comedy may also satirize the conventions and values of society.

Finally, it is less important to determine the type of a comedy than it is to enter into the spirit and the action of each play you read. You can resent the demands of Egeus and the Athenian law without knowing that Shakespeare's *A Midsummer Night's Dream* is a romantic comedy. Similarly, you can recognize the faults of society and the excesses of Alceste without knowing that Molière's *The Misanthrope* is a comedy of manners. The play itself, rather than the type, should evoke your feelings and thoughts.

WILLIAM SHAKESPEARE, *A MIDSUMMER NIGHT'S DREAM*

In Chapter 28 we discussed William Shakespeare's age and theater (p. 1173) and his career as a dramatist (p. 1177). *A Midsummer Night's Dream* was written fairly early in his career, in 1594 or 1595. It is a romantic comedy that explores the tribulations of thwarted love and the chaos that mad infatuation (or dotage) and irrational (or blind) love can produce. The central plot concerns the misadventures and eventual harmony of four young lovers who are highly conventional and representative; indeed, the two young men are so alike that it is difficult to tell them apart. This central line of action, which owes a great deal to Roman new comedy, involves blocked love, a journey of circumvention and education that takes the lovers from the world of laws and problems into an imaginary world of chaos and transformations, and an ultimate victory for young love back in the world of daylight and order.

The play demonstrates Shakespeare's skillful interweaving of four separate plots, four groups of characters, and four styles of language into one coherent comedy. The **overplot**—the action that establishes the time frame for the entire play—concerns Duke Theseus, the ruler of Athens, and Hippolyta, his fiancée and the queen of the Amazons. These characters are the rulers and they speak predominantly in blank verse (unrhymed iambic pentameter, see p. 740).

The two connected **middle plots** concern the adventures of the four lovers and the actions of the fairies in the woods outside Athens, specifically Oberon and Titania. The four lovers are middle-class figures, and their plot line embodies both social and individual problems; they speak predominantly in iambic pentameter rhymed couplets (see p. 741). Oberon and Titania, the king and queen of the fairies, embody the supernatural forces of nature. Although they and the other fairies speak in both blank verse and rhymed couplets, the fairies are the only characters who also sing lyric songs and speak in lines of iambic tetrameter.

The **low plot** presents the efforts and adventures of the Athenian workingmen who try to put on a play in honor of the marriage of Hippolyta and Theseus. These laborers, often called "the mechanicals" because of their trades, are from the lower classes. Their plot contains much of the low comedy in the play, and they are the only group of characters who speak in prose.

The subject of *A Midsummer Night's Dream* is love; each plot explores the nature of love, the madness that irrational or unthinking love can produce, and the harmony necessary for regenerative love. In the overplot, the relationship between Theseus and Hippolyta illustrates love that has moved from madness of war to rational harmony. As such, they represent the dynastic continuity of the state, the order of the daylight world of Athens, and the rigor of the law, a rigor that is softened in the course of the play.

The four lovers of the middle plot present young love at its most passionate, insistent, and unthinking. For them, love is a blind and all-powerful force that sweeps them along. During their long night in the woods of illusion outside Athens, their passions are redirected three times by Oberon and his tricky servant, Puck. Each change demonstrates anew the power of blind passion. Ultimately, however, these adventures drive the lovers into a semblance of rationality in which each recognizes and accepts his or her appropriate mate.

The second middle plot, the action involving Oberon and Titania, offers three related explorations of love's madness and the restoration of reason and order to love. The central relationship here, between the king and queen of the fairies, is in a shambles because Titania has become infatuated with a child that she claims was given to her, but that she may actually have stolen. Such a child, stolen by fairies, is called a changeling. In either event, Oberon wants the boy, but Titania's passionate fixation leads her to defy her husband, and their discord produces chaos and disaster throughout the world of nature. In order to cure this infatuation and teach her a lesson, Oberon causes Titania to fall madly in love with a monster, and then he cures her of all love madness. Titania's restored rationality brings her back into subservience to and harmony with Oberon, the proper state for a wife according to the Elizabethans.

The examination of love in the low plot occurs partly in Titania's relationship with Bottom—the most hilarious instance of love madness in the play—and partly in "The most lamentable comedy and most cruel death of Pyramus and Thisby," the play that the mechanicals perform at court in celebration of the marriages. This badly acted and thus outrageously funny tragedy echoes the central plot of *A Midsummer Night's Dream* and demonstrates once again the dangers of love. It also emphasizes, by contrast, the happy and harmonious marriages and rapprochements that occur at the other levels of action in the play.

A Midsummer Night's Dream is thus chiefly about love, but it also explores other ideas and topics that concerned Shakespeare and his contemporaries. Chief among these is the complicated relationship among perception, imagination, dreaming, passion, and art (or drama, or illusion). The play repeatedly draws our attention to the linkages among distorted perception (especially sight), the power of imagination, and passion of any kind. In the last act Theseus asserts that "The lunatic, the lover, and the poet" are all related through the powers of passion, imagination, and dreaming. By the same token, the movement from the "real" world of Athens to the dreamlike and illusory world of Oberon and Titania raises questions about the relationship between illusion (or dreaming or art or drama) and reality.

Many of these concerns come together in the low plot, specifically in the mechanicals' understanding (or ignorance) of dramatic representation and their abysmal production of "Pyramus and Thisby," the play-within-a-play. These amateur actors and their aristocratic audience within the play give Shakespeare an opportunity to investigate the nature of dramatic illusion, the degree to which audiences understand the essentially imitative quality of theater, and the connection between art and life.

WILLIAM SHAKESPEARE (1564–1616)

A Midsummer Night's Dream   *1600 (ca. 1594)*

Edited by Alice Griffin°

[*THE NAMES OF THE ACTORS*

    Theseus, *Duke of Athens*
    Egeus, *father of Hermia*
    Lysander, *beloved of Hermia*
    Demetrius, *in love with Hermia, favoured by Egeus*
    Philostrate, *Master of the Revels to Theseus*

    Peter Quince, *a carpenter* (*Prologue*)*
    Nick Bottom, *a weaver* (*Pyramus*)*
    Francis Flute, *a bellows-mender* (*Thisby*)*
    Tom Snout, *a tinker* (*Wall*)*
    Snug, *a joiner* (*Lion*)*
    Robin Starveling, *a tailor* (*Moonshine*)*

    Hippolyta, *Queen of the Amazons, betrothed to Theseus*
    Hermia, *daughter of Egeus, in love with Lysander*
    Helena, *in love with Demetrius*

    Oberon, *King of the Fairies*
    Titania, *Queen of the Fairies*
    Puck, *or* Robin Goodfellow
    Peaseblossom⎫
    Cobweb   ⎬ *Fairies*
    Moth   ⎪
    Mustardseed ⎭

Other Fairies attending Oberon and Titania. Attendants on Theseus and Hippolyta.

Scene: *Athens, and a wood nearby*]

ACT 1

[*Scene 1. Athens. The palace of Theseus*]

Enter THESEUS, HIPPOLYTA,° [PHILOSTRATE,] *with others.*

THESEUS. Now fair Hippolyta, our nuptial hour
    Draws on apace: four happy days bring in

Prof. Griffin's text for *A Midsummer Night's Dream* was the First Quarto (edition) published in 1600, with modifications based on the Quarto edition of 1619 and the First Folio, published in 1623. Stage directions in those editions are printed here without brackets; added stage directions are printed within brackets. We have edited Prof. Griffin's notes for this text.
    * Characters played in the interlude.
Stage direction: *Theseus, Hippolyta*: (Theseus, legendary Greek hero, had defeated the Amazon Queen Hippolyta in battle, captured her, brought her to Athens, and married her).

Another moon: but O, methinks how slow
This old moon wanes! she lingers° my desires,
Like to a stepdame or a dowager,°
Long withering out° a young man's revenue.
HIPPOLYTA. Four days will quickly steep themselves in night:
Four nights will quickly dream away the time:
And then the moon, like to a silver bow
New-bent in heaven, shall behold the night   1
Of our solemnities.
THESEUS.   Go Philostrate,
Stir up the Athenian youth to merriments,
Awake the pert° and nimble spirit of mirth,
Turn melancholy forth to funerals:
The pale companion° is not for our pomp.   [Exit PHILOSTRATE.]   1
Hippolyta, I wooed thee with my sword,
And won thy love doing thee injuries:
But I will wed thee in another key,
With pomp, with triumph,° and with revelling.

Enter EGEUS and his daughter HERMIA, LYSANDER and DEMETRIUS.

EGEUS. Happy be Theseus, our renownèd duke.   2(
THESEUS. Thanks good Egeus:° what's the news with thee?
EGEUS. Full of vexation come I, with complaint
Against my child, my daughter Hermia.
Stand forth Demetrius. My noble lord,
This man hath my consent to marry her.   2!
Stand forth Lysander. And my gracious duke,
This man hath bewitched the bosom of my child.
Thou, thou Lysander, thou hast given her rhymes,
And interchanged love tokens with my child:
Thou hast by moonlight at her window sung,   30
With feigning voice, verses of feigning° love,
And stol'n the impression of her fantasy°
With bracelets of thy hair, rings, gauds,° conceits,°
Knacks,° trifles, nosegays, sweetmeats—messengers
Of strong prevailment in unhardened youth.   35(
With cunning has thou filched my daughter's heart,
Turned her obedience, which is due to me,
To stubborn harshness. And my gracious duke,
Be it so° she will not here before your grace

---

4 *lingers*: delays the fulfillment of.   5 *dowager*: a widow supported by her dead husband's
heirs.   6 *withering out*: (1) depleting (2) growing withered.   13 *pert*:
lively.   15 *companion*: fellow (contemptuous).   19 *triumph*: public festival.   21 *Egeus*:
(trisyllabic).   31 *feigning*: (1) deceptive (2) desirous ("faining").   32 *stol'n . . . fantasy*:
stealthily imprinted your image upon her fancy.   33 *gauds*: trinkets.   *conceits*: either (a)
love poetry, or (b) love tokens.   34 *Knacks*: knick-knacks.   39 *Be it so*: if it be that.

Consent to marry with Demetrius,   40
I beg the ancient privilege of Athens:
As she is mine, I may dispose of her:
Which shall be, either to this gentleman,
Or to her death, according to our law
Immediately° provided in that case.   45
THESEUS.   What say you, Hermia? Be advised, fair maid.
To you your father should be as a god:
One that composed your beauties: yea and one
To whom you are but as a form in wax
By him imprinted, and within his power   50
To leave the figure, or disfigure it:
Demetrius is a worthy gentleman.
HERMIA.   So is Lysander.
THESEUS.   In himself he is:
But in this kind, wanting your father's voice,°
The other must be held the worthier.   55
HERMIA.   I would my father looked but with my eyes.
THESEUS.   Rather your eyes must with his judgment look.
HERMIA.   I do entreat your grace to pardon me.
I know not by what power I am made bold,
Nor how it may concern my modesty,   60
In such a presence, here to plead my thoughts:
But I beseech your grace that I may know
The worst that may befall me in this case,
If I refuse to wed Demetrius.
THESEUS.   Either to die the death, or to abjure   65
For ever the society of men.
Therefore fair Hermia, question your desires,
Know of your youth,° examine well your blood,°
Whether, if you yield not to your father's choice,
You can endure the livery° of a nun,   70
For aye° to be in shady cloister mewed,°
To live a barren sister all your life,
Chanting faint hymns to the cold fruitless moon.°
Thrice blessèd they that master so their blood,
To undergo such maiden pilgrimage: 75
But earthlier happy° is the rose distilled,°
Than that which, withering on the virgin thorn,
Grows, lives, and dies, in single blessedness.
HERMIA.   So will I grow, so live, so die my lord,
Ere I will yield my virgin patent° up   80
Unto his lordship, whose unwishèd yoke

---

45 *Immediately*: precisely.   54 *in . . . voice*: in this respect, lacking your father's approval.
68. *Know . . . youth*: ask yourself as a young person.   68 *blood*: passions.   70 *livery*:
habit.   71 *aye*: ever.   *mewed*: shut up.   73 *Moon*: (the moon goddess Diana
represented unmarried chastity).   76 *earthlier happy*: more happy on earth.   *distilled*: i.e.,
into perfume (thus its essence is passed on, as to a child).   80 *patent*: privilege.

My soul consents not to give sovereignty.
THESEUS. Take time to pause, and by the next moon,
    The sealing day betwixt my love and me,
    For everlasting bond of fellowship,   85
    Upon that day either prepare to die
    For disobedience to your father's will,
    Or else to wed Demetrius, as he would,
    Or on Diana's altar to protest°
    For aye, austerity and single life.   90
DEMETRIUS. Relent, sweet Hermia, and Lysander, yield
    They crazèd° title to my certain right.
LYSANDER. You have her father's love, Demetrius:
    Let me have Hermia's: do you marry him.
EGEUS. Scornful Lysander, true, he hath my love: 95
    And what is mine, my love shall render him.
    And she is mine, and all my right of her
    I do estate° unto Demetrius.
LYSANDER. I am, my lord, as well derived° as he,
    As well possessed:° my love is more than his: 100
    My fortunes every way as fairly ranked
    (If not with vantage) as° Demetrius':
    And, which is more than all these boasts can be,
    I am beloved of beauteous Hermia.
    Why should not I then prosecute my right?   105
    Demetrius, I'll avouch it to his head,°
    Made love to Nedar's daughter, Helena,
    And won her soul: and she, sweet lady, dotes,
    Devoutly dotes, dotes in idolatry,
    Upon this spotted° and inconstant man.   110
THESEUS. I must confess that I have heard so much,
    And with Demetrius thought to have spoke thereof:
    But being over-full of self-affairs,
    My mind did lose it. But Demetrius come,
    And come Egeus, you shall go with me: 115
    I have some private schooling for you both.
    For you fair Hermia, look you arm yourself,
    To fit your fancies to your father's will;
    Or else the law of Athens yields you up
    (Which by no means we may extenuate)   120
    To death or to a vow of single life.
    Come my Hippolyta, what cheer my love?
    Demetrius and Egeus, go along:
    I must employ you in some business
    Against° our nuptial, and confer with you   125
    Of something nearly° that concerns yourselves.

89 *protest*: vow.   92 *crazed*: flawed.   98 *estate*: transfer.   99 *well derived*: well
born.   100 *well possessed*: wealthy.   102 *with vantage, as*: better, than.   106 *avouch . . .
head*: prove it to his face.   110 *spotted*: stained (by betrayal of Helena).   125 *Against*:
in preparation for.   126 *nearly*: closely.

EGEUS. With duty and desire we follow you.

Exeunt.° Manent° LYSANDER and HERMIA.

LYSANDER.   How now my love? Why is your cheek so pale?
How chance the roses there do fade so fast?
HERMIA.   Belike° for want of rain, which I could well   130
Beteem° them from the tempest of my eyes.
LYSANDER.   Ay me, for aught that I could ever read,
Could ever hear by tale or history,
The course of true love never did run smooth;
But either it was different in blood—   135
HERMIA.   O cross! too high° to be enthralled to low.°
LYSANDER.   Or else misgraffèd° in respect of years—
HERMIA.   O spite! too old to be engaged to young.
LYSANDER.   Or else it stood upon the choice of friends—
HERMIA.   O hell! to choose love by another's eyes.   140
LYSANDER.   Or if there were a sympathy in choice,
War, death, or sickness did lay siege to it;
Making it momentany° as a sound,
Swift as a shadow, short as any dream,
Brief as the lightning in the collied° night,   145
That, in a spleen,° unfolds both heaven and earth;
And ere a man hath power to say "Behold,"
The jaws of darkness do devour it up:
So quick bright things come to confusion.
HERMIA.   If then true lovers have been ever crossed,°   150
It stands as an edict in destiny:
Then let us teach our trial patience,°
Because it is a customary cross,
As due to love as thoughts and dreams and sighs,
Wishes and tears; poor Fancy's° followers.   155
LYSANDER.   A good persuasion: therefore hear me, Hermia:
I have a widow aunt, a dowager,
Of great revenue, and she hath no child:
From Athens is her house remote seven leagues,
And she respects° me as her only son: 160
There gentle Hermia, may I marry thee,
And to that place the sharp Athenian law
Cannot pursue us. If thou lov'st me then,
Steal forth thy father's house tomorrow night:
And in the wood, a league without the town,   165
Where I did meet thee once with Helena

127 stage direction *exeunt*: they exit.   *Manent*: they remain.   130 *Belike*:
likely.   131 *Beteem*: (1) pour out on (2) allow.   136 *high*: highborn.   *enthralled to low*:
made a slave to one of low birth.   137 *misgraffed*: badly joined.   143 *momentany*:
momentary.   145 *collied*: black as coal.   146 *in a spleen*: impulsively, in a sudden
outburst.   150 *ever crossed*: evermore thwarted.   152 *teach . . . patience*: teach ourselves
to be patient.   155 *Fancy*: love (sometimes infatuation).   160 *respects*: regards.

To do observance to a morn of May,°
There will I stay° for thee.
HERMIA.   My good Lysander,
I swear to thee, by Cupid's strongest bow,
By his best arrow, with the golden head,°   170
By the simplicity of Venus' doves,
By that which knitteth souls and prospers loves,
And by that fire which burned the Carthage queen,
When the false Troyan° under sail was seen,
By all the vows that ever men have broke,   175
(In number more than ever women spoke)
In that same place thou has appointed me,
Tomorrow truly will I meet with thee.
LYSANDER.   Keep promise love: look, here comes Helena.
Enter HELENA.
HERMIA.   God speed fair Helena: whither away?   180
HELENA.   Call you me fair? That fair again unsay.
Demetrius loves your fair:° O happy fair!
Your eyes are lodestars,° and your tongue's sweet air°
More tuneable than lark to shepherd's ear,
When wheat is green, when hawthorn buds appear.   185
Sickness is catching: O were favour° so,
Yours would I catch, fair Hermia, ere I go,
My ear should catch your voice,° my eye your eye,°
My tongue should catch your tongue's sweet melody.
Were the world mine, Demetrius being bated,°   190
The rest I'ld give to be to you translated.°
O teach me how you look, and with what art
You sway the motion of Demetrius' heart.
HERMIA.   I frown upon him; yet he loves me still.
HELENA.   O that your frowns would teach my smiles such skill.   195
HERMIA.   I give him curses; yet he gives me love.
HELENA.   O that my prayers could such affection move.
HERMIA.   The more I hate, the more he follows me.
HELENA.   The more I love, the more he hateth me.
HERMIA.   His folly, Helena, is no fault of mine.   200
HELENA.   None but your beauty; would that fault were mine.
HERMIA.   Take comfort: he no more shall see my face:
Lysander and myself will fly this place.
Before the time I did Lysander see,
Seemed Athens as a paradise to me: 205

---

167 *do . . . May*: celebrate May Day.   168 *stay*: wait.   170 *golden head*: (The arrow with
the gold head causes love).   173–174 *Carthage Queen . . . false Troyan*: Dido, who burned
herself to death on a funeral pyre when Trojan Aeneas deserted her.   182 *your fair*: i.e.,
beauty.   183 *lodestars*: guiding stars.   *air*: music.   186 *favour*: appearance.
188 *My ear . . . voice*: my ear should catch the tone of your voice.   *my eye your eye*: my
eye should catch the way you glance.   190 *bated*: subtracted, excepted.   191 *translated*:
transformed.

O then, what graces in my love do dwell,
That he hath turned a heaven unto a hell!
LYSANDER. Helen, to you our minds we will unfold:
Tomorrow night, when Phoebe° doth behold
Her silver visage in the wat'ry glass,°   210
Decking with liquid pearl the bladed grass
(A time that lovers' flights doth still° conceal)
Through Athens gates have we devised to steal.
HERMIA. And in the wood, where often you and I
Upon faint primrose beds were wont to lie,   215
Emptying our bosoms of their counsel° sweet,
There my Lysander and myself shall meet,
And thence from Athens turn away our eyes,
To see new friends and stranger companies.°
Farewell, sweet playfellow: pray thou for us: 220
And good luck grant thee thy Demetrius.
Keep word Lysander: we must starve our sight
From lovers' food,° till morrow deep midnight.
LYSANDER. I will my Hermia.   *Exit HERMIA.*
                Helena adieu:
As you on him, Demetrius dote on you.   *Exit LYSANDER.*   225
HELENA. How happy some, o'er other some, can be!
Through Athens I am thought as fair as she.
But what of that? Demetrius thinks not so:
He will not know what all but he do know.
And as he errs, doting on Hermia's eyes,   230
So I, admiring of his qualities.
Things base and vile, holding no quantity,°
Love can transpose to form and dignity.
Love looks not with the eyes, but with the mind:
And therefore is winged Cupid painted blind.   235
Nor hath Love's mind of any judgment taste:
Wings, and no eyes, figure° unheedy haste.
And therefore is Love said to be a child:
Because in choice he is so oft beguiled.
As waggish boys in game themselves forswear: 240
So the boy Love is perjured everywhere.
For ere Demetrius looked on Hermia's eyne,°
He hailed down oaths that he was only mine.
And when this hail some heat from Hermia felt,
So he dissolved, and show'rs of oaths did melt.   245
I will go tell him of fair Hermia's flight:
Then to the wood will he tomorrow night

---

209 *Phoebe*: Diana, the moon.   210 *wat'ry glass*: mirror of the water.   212 *still*:
always.   216 *counsel*: secrets.   219 *stranger companies*: the companionship of
strangers.   223 *lovers' food*: the sight of the loved one.   232 *holding no quantity*: out of
proportion.   237 *figure*: symbolize.   242 *eyne*: eyes.

Pursue her: and for this intelligence,°
If I have thanks, it is a dear expense:°
But herein mean I to enrich my pain,   250
To have his sight° thither and back again.   *Exit.*

[*Scene 2. Quince's house*]

Enter QUINCE *the Carpenter; and* SNUG *the Joiner; and* BOTTOM *the Weaver; and* FLUTE
the Bellows-mender; and SNOUT *the Tinker; and* STARVELING *the Tailor.*°

QUINCE.   Is all our company here?
BOTTOM.   You were the best to call them generally,° man by man,
according to the scrip.
QUINCE.   Here is the scroll of every man's name which is thought
fit, through all Athens, to play in our interlude° before   5
the duke and the duchess, on his wedding-day at night.
BOTTOM.   First good Peter Quince, say what the play treats on,
then read the names of the actors: and so grow to a point.
QUINCE.   Marry,° our play is "The most lamentable comedy, and
most cruel death of Pyramus and Thisby."   10
BOTTOM.   A very good piece of work I assure you, and a merry. Now
good Peter Quince, call forth your actors by the scroll.
Masters, spread yourselves.
QUINCE.   Answer as I call you. Nick Bottom the weaver?
BOTTOM.   Ready: name what part I am for, and proceed.   15
QUINCE.   You, Nick Bottom, are set down for Pyramus.
BOTTOM.   What is Pyramus? A lover, or a tyrant?
QUINCE.   A lover that kills himself, most gallant, for love.
BOTTOM.   That will ask some tears in the true performing of it. If I
do it, let the audience look to their eyes: I will move   20
storms: I will condole° in some measure. To the rest—
yet my chief humour° is for a tyrant. I could play Ercles°
rarely, or a part to tear a cat in, to make all split.°
        The raging rocks
        And shivering shocks,   25
        Shall break the locks
           Of prison gates,
        And Phibbus' car°

---

248 *intelligence*: information.   249 *dear expense*: costly outlay (on Demetrius' part).   250–
251 *But . . . sight*: but I will be rewarded just by the sight of him.   Stage direction: the
low characters' names describe their work: *Quince*: quoins, wooden wedges used in
building.   *Snug*: fitting snugly, suiting a joiner of furniture.   *Bottom*: bobbin or core
on which yarn is wound.   *Flute*: mender of fluted church organs and bellows.   *Snout*:
spout (of the kettles he mends).   *Starveling*: (tailors being traditionally thin).   2 *generally*:
(Bottom, who often mistakes the word, means the opposite: "severally, one-by-one").
5 *interlude*: short play.   9 *Marry*: indeed (mild oath, corruption of "by the Virgin
Mary").   21 *condole*: lament.   22 *humour*: inclination,   *Ercles*: Hercules (typified by
ranting).   23 *tear . . . split*: (terms for ranting and raging on the stage).   28 *Phibbus'
car*: Phoebus Apollo's chariot.

        Shall shine from far,
        And make and mar   30
          The foolish Fates.
This was lofty. Now name the rest of the players. This is
Ercles' vein, a tyrant's vein: a lover is more condoling.

QUINCE. Francis Flute, the bellows-mender?

FLUTE. Here Peter Quince.   35

QUINCE. Flute, you must take Thisby on you.

FLUTE. What is Thisby? A wand'ring knight?

QUINCE. It is the lady that Pyramus must love.

FLUTE. Nay faith, let not me play a woman: I have a beard
    coming.   40

QUINCE. That's all one:° you shall play it in a mask, and you may
    speak as small° as you will.

BOTTOM. And° I may hide my face, let me play Thisby too: I'll speak
    in a monstrous little voice; "Thisne, Thisne," "Ah
    Pyramus, my lover dear, thy Thisby dear, and lady   45
    dear."

QUINCE. No, no, you must play Pyramus: and Flute, you Thisby.

BOTTOM. Well, proceed.

QUINCE. Robin Starveling, the tailor?

STARVELING. Here Peter Quince.   50

QUINCE. Robin Starveling, you must play Thisby's mother. Tom
    Snout, the tinker?

SNOUT. Here Peter Quince.

QUINCE. You, Pyramus' father; myself, Thisby's father; Snug the
    joiner, you the lion's part: and I hope here is a play   55
    fitted.°

SNUG. Have you the lion's part written? Pray you, if it be, give
    it me: for I am slow of study.

QUINCE. You may do it extempore: for it is nothing but roaring.

BOTTOM. Let me play the lion too. I will roar, that° I will do any   60
    man's heart good to hear me. I will roar, that I will make
    the duke say "Let him roar again: let him roar again."

QUINCE. And you should do it too terribly, you would fright the
    duchess and the ladies, that they would shriek: and
    that were enough to hang us all.   65

ALL. That would hang us, every mother's son.

BOTTOM. I grant you, friends, if you should fright the ladies out of
    their wits, they would have no more discretion but to
    hang us: but I will aggravate° my voice so, that I will roar
    you as gently as any sucking dove: I will roar you and   70
    'twere° any nightingale.

QUINCE. You can play no part but Pyramus: for Pyramus is a
    sweet-faced man; a proper° man as one shall see in a

41 *That's all one*: never mind.   42 *small*: softly.   43 *And*: if.   56 *fitted*: cast.
60 *that*: so that.   69 *aggravate*: (he means "moderate").   70–71 *and 'twere*: as if it
were.   73 *proper*: handsome.

summer's day; a most lovely gentleman-like man: therefore
you must needs play Pyramus.   75

BOTTOM. Well: I will undertake it. What beard were I best to play
it in?

QUINCE. Why, what you will.

BOTTOM. I will discharge it in either your straw-colour beard, your
orange-tawny beard, your purple-in-grain° beard, or your   80
French-crown-colour° beard, your perfit yellow.

QUINCE. Some of your French crowns° have no hair at all; and
then you will play barefaced. But masters here are your
parts, and I am to entreat you, request you, and desire
you, to con° them by tomorrow night: and meet me in the   85
palace wood, a mile without the town, by moonlight;
there will we rehearse: for if we meet in the city, we
shall be dogged with company, and our devices° known.
In the meantime, I will draw a bill of properties,° such
as our play wants. I pray you fail me not.   90

BOTTOM. We will meet, and there we may rehearse most obscenely°
and courageously. Take pain, be perfit: adieu.

QUINCE. At the duke's oak we meet.

BOTTOM. Enough: hold, or cut bow-strings.°   *Exeunt.*

ACT 2

[Scene 1. A wood near Athens]

Enter a FAIRY at one door, and ROBIN GOODFELLOW [Puck] at another.

PUCK. How now spirit, whither wander you?

FAIRY. Over hill, over dale,
  Thorough bush, thorough brier,
  Over park, over pale,°
    Thorough flood, thorough fire:
  I do wander everywhere,   5
  Swifter than the moon's sphere:
  And I serve the Fairy Queen,
  To dew° her orbs° upon the green.
  The cowslips° tall her pensioners° be,   10
  In their gold coats, spots you see:
  Those be rubies, fairy favours:°

80 *purple-in-grain*: dyed permanently purple.   81 *French-crown-colour*: golden, like French
crowns (gold coins).   82 *French crowns*: bald heads believed to be caused by syphilis,
the "French" disease.   85 *con*: learn by heart.   88 *devices*: plans.   89 *bill of properties*:
list of stage props.   91 *obscenely*: (he may mean "fittingly," or "obscurely.")   94 *hold,
or cut bow-strings*: (meaning uncertain, but equivalent to "fish, or cut bait").   4 *pale*:
enclosure.   9 *dew*: bedew.   *orbs*: fairy rings (circles of high grass).   10 *cowslips*:
primroses.   *pensioners*: royal bodyguards.   12 *favours*: gifts.

In those freckles live their savours.°
I must go seek some dewdrops here,
and hang a pearl in every cowslip's ear.   15
Farewell thou lob° of spirits: I'll be gone,
Our queen and all her elves come here anon.

PUCK. The king doth keep his revels here tonight.
Take heed the queen come not within his sight.
For Oberon is passing fell° and wrath,   20
Because that she, as her attendant, hath
A lovely boy, stol'n from an Indian king:
She never had so sweet a changeling.°
And jealous Oberon would have the child
Knight of his train, to trace° the forests wild.   25
But she, perforce,° withholds the lovèd boy,
Crowns him with flowers, and makes him all her joy.
And now, they never meet in grove or green,
By fountain clear, or spangled starlight sheen,
But they do square,° that all their elves for fear   30
Creep into acorn cups, and hide them there.

FAIRY. Either I mistake your shape and making quite,
Or else you are that shrewd and knavish sprite
Called Robin Goodfellow. Are not you he
That frights the maidens of the villagery,   35
Skim milk,° and sometimes labour in the quern,°
And bootless° make the breathless housewife churn,
And sometime make the drink to bear no barm,°
Mislead night-wanderers, laughing at their harm?
Those that Hobgoblin call you, and sweet Puck,   40
You do their work, and they shall have good luck.
Are not you he?

PUCK.   Thou speakest aright;
I am that merry wanderer of the night.
I jest to Oberon, and make him smile,
When I a fat and bean-fed horse beguile,   45
Neighing in likeness of a filly foal;
And sometime lurk I in a gossip's° bowl,
In very likeness of a roasted crab,°
And when she drinks, against her lips I bob,
And on her withered dewlap° pour the ale.   50
The wisest aunt, telling the saddest tale,
Sometime for three-foot stool mistaketh me:

---

13 *savours*: perfumes.   16 *lob*: lout, lubber.   20 *passing fell*: surpassingly
fierce.   23 *changeling*: creature exchanged by fairies for a stolen baby (among the fairies,
the stolen child).   25 *trace*: traverse.   26 *perforce*: by force.   30 *square*: quarrel.
36 *Skim milk*: steals the cream off the milk.   *quern*: handmill for grinding grain.
37 *bootless*: without result.   38 *barm*: foamy head (therefore the drink was flat).
47 *gossip's*: old woman's.   48 *crab*: crabapple (often put into ale).   50 *dewlap*: loose
skin hanging about the throat.

Then slip I from her bum, down topples she,
And "tailor"° cries, and falls into a cough;
And then the whole quire° hold their hips and laugh,   55
And waxen° in their mirth, and neeze,° and swear
A merrier hour was never wasted° there.
But room° fairy: here comes Oberon.
FAIRY.   And here, my mistress. Would that he were gone.

*Enter [OBERON] the KING OF FAIRIES, at one door with his TRAIN; and the QUEEN [TITANIA],
at another, with hers.*

OBERON.   Ill met by moonlight, proud Titania.   60
QUEEN.   What, jealous Oberon? Fairy, skip hence.
I have forsworn his bed and company.
OBERON.   Tarry, rash wanton.° Am not I thy lord?
QUEEN.   Then I must be thy lady: but I know
When thou has stol'n away from fairyland,   65
And in the shape of Corin° sat all day,
Playing on pipes of corn,° and versing love
To amorous Phillida.° Why are thou here
Come from the farthest steep of India?
But that, forsooth, the bouncing Amazon,°   70
Your buskined° mistress and your warrior love,
To Theseus must be wedded; and you come,
To give their bed joy and prosperity.
OBERON.   How canst thou thus, for shame, Titania,
Glance at my credit with° Hippolyta,   75
Knowing I know thy love to Theseus?
Didst thou not lead him through the glimmering night,
From Perigenia, whom he ravishèd?
And make him with fair Aegles break his faith,
With Ariadne, and Antiopa°?   80
QUEEN.   These are the forgeries of jealousy:
And never, since the middle summer's spring,°
Met we on hill, in dale, forest, or mead,
By pavèd° fountain, or by rushy brook,
Or in the beachèd margent° of the sea,   85
To dance our ringlets to the whistling wind,
But with thy brawls thou hast disturbed our sport.

54 *"tailor"*: (variously explained: perhaps the squatting position of the tailor, or "tailard"
= one with a tail).   55 *quire*: choir, group.   56 *waxen*: increase.   *neeze*: sneeze.
57 *wasted*: spent.   58 *room*: make room.   63 *Tarry, rash wanton*: wait, headstrong
one.   66–68 *Corin, Phillida*: (traditional names in pastoral literature for a shepherd and
his loved one, respectively).   67 *corn*: wheat straws.   70 *Amazon*: Hippolyta.
71 *buskined*: wearing boots.   75 *Glance . . . credit with*: hint at my favors from.
78–80 *Perigenia . . . Antiopa*: women that Theseus supposedly loved and deserted.
82 *middle . . . spring*: beginning of midsummer.   84 *paved*: with a pebbly bottom.
85 *margent*: margin, shore.

Therefore the winds, piping to us in vain,
As in revenge, have sucked up from the sea
Contagious° fogs: which falling in the land,   90
Hath every pelting° river made so proud,
That they have overborne their continents.°
The ox hath therefore stretched his yoke in vain,
The ploughman lost his sweat, and the green corn°
Hath rotted, ere his youth attained a beard:°   95
The fold° stands empty in the drownèd field,
And crows are fatted with the murrion° flock.
The nine men's morris° is filled up with mud:
And the quaint mazes° in the wanton green,°
For lack of tread, are undistinguishable.   100
The human mortals want° their winter here,
No night is now with hymn or carol blest;
Therefore the moon, the governess of floods,
Pale in her anger, washes all the air,
That rheumatic diseases do abound.   105
And thorough this distemperature,° we see
The seasons alter: hoary-headed frosts
Fall in the fresh lap of the crimson rose,
And on old Hiems'° thin and icy crown,
An odorous chaplet° of sweet summer buds   110
Is, as in mockery, set. The spring, the summer,
The childing° autumn, angry winter change
Their wonted liveries:° and the mazèd° world,
By their increase, now knows not which is which:
And this same progeny of evils comes   115
From our debate, from our dissension:
We are their parents and original.
OBERON. Do you amend it then: it lies in you.
   Why should Titania cross her Oberon?
   I do but beg a little changeling boy,   120
   To be my henchman.°
QUEEN.   Set your heart at rest.
   The fairy land buys not the child of me.
   His mother was a vot'ress° of my order:

88–117 *Therefore . . . original*: (the disturbance in nature reflects the discord between Oberon
and Titania).   90 *Contagious*: spreading pestilence.   91 *pelting*: paltry.   92 *overborne
their continents*: overflown the banks which contain them.   94 *corn*: grain.   95 *beard*: the
tassels on ripened grain.   96 *fold*: enclosure for livestock.   97 *murrion*: dead from
murrain, a cattle disease.   98 *nine men's morris*: game played on squares cut in the grass
on which stones or disks are moved.   *quaint mazes*: intricate paths.   99 *wanton green*:
luxuriant grass.   101 *want*: lack.   106 *distemperature*: upset in nature.   109 *Hiems*:
god of winter.   110 *odorous chaplet*: sweet-smelling wreath.   112 *childing*: fruitful.
113 *wonted liveries*: accustomed dress.   *mazed*: amazed.   121 *henchman*:
attendant.   123 *vot'ress*: vowed and devoted follower.

And in the spicèd Indian air, by night,
Full often hath she gossiped by my side. 125
And sat with me on Neptune's yellow sands,
Marking th' embarkèd traders° on the flood:
When we have laughed to see the sails conceive,
And grow big-bellied with the wanton° wind:
Which she, with pretty and with swimming gait, 130
Following (her womb then rich with my young squire)
Would imitate, and sail upon the land,
To fetch me trifles, and return again,
As from a voyage, rich with merchandise.
But she, being mortal, of that boy did die, 135
And for her sake, do I rear up her boy:
And for her sake, I will not part with him.

OBERON. How long within this wood intend you stay?

QUEEN. Perchance till after Theseus' wedding day.
If you will patiently dance in our round,° 140
And see our moonlight revels, go with us:
If not, shun me, and I will spare° your haunts.

OBERON. Give me that boy, and I will go with thee.

QUEEN. Not for thy fairy kingdom. Fairies away
We shall chide downright, if I longer stay. 145

*Exeunt [*TITANIA *and her* TRAIN.]

OBERON. Well, go thy way. Thou shalt not from this grove,
Till I torment thee for this injury.
My gentle Puck come hither: thou rememb'rest,
Since° once I sat upon a promontory,
And heard a mermaid, on a dolphin's back, 150
Uttering such dulcet and harmonious breath,
That the rude° sea grew civil° at her song,
And certain stars shot madly from their spheres,
To hear the sea-maid's music.

PUCK.   I remember.

OBERON. That very time, I saw (but thou couldst not) 155
Flying between the cold moon and the earth,
Cupid, all armed: a certain aim he took
At a fair Vestal,° thronèd by the west,
And loosed his love-shaft smartly from his bow,
As it should pierce a hundred thousand hearts: 160
But I might see young Cupid's fiery shaft
Quenched in the chaste beams of the wat'ry moon:
And the imperial vot'ress° passèd on,
In maiden meditation, fancy-free.°

127 *traders*: merchant ships.   129 *wanton*: sportive.   140 *round*: round dance.
142 *spare*: shun.   149 *Since*: when.   152 *rude*: rough.   *civil*: calm.
158 *Vestal*: virgin, probable reference to Queen Elizabeth.   163 *imperial vot'ress*: royal
devotee (Queen Elizabeth) of Diana.   164 *fancy-free*: free from love.

Yet marked I where the bolt° of Cupid fell. 165
It fell upon a little western flower;
Before, milk-white; now purple with love's wound,
And maidens call it love-in-idleness.°
Fetch me that flow'r: the herb I showed thee once.
The juice of it, on sleeping eyelids laid, 170
Will make or man or woman madly dote
Upon the next live creature that it sees.
Fetch me this herb, and be thou here again
Ere the leviathan° can swim a league.
PUCK. I'll put a girdle round about the earth, 175
In forty minutes. [*Exit.*]
OBERON. Having once this juice,
I'll watch Titania when she is asleep,
And drop the liquor of it in her eyes:
The next thing then she waking looks upon,
(Be it on lion, bear, or wolf, or bull, 180
On meddling monkey, or on busy° ape)
She shall pursue it, with the soul of love.
And ere I take this charm from off her sight
(As I can take it with another herb)
I'll make her render up her page to me. 185
But who comes here? I am invisible,
And I will overhear their conference.

Enter DEMETRIUS, HELENA following him.

DEMETRIUS. I love thee not: therefore pursue me not.
Where is Lysander and fair Hermia?
The one I'll slay: the other slayeth me. 190
Thou told'st me they were stol'n unto this wood:
And here am I, and wood° within this wood:
Because I cannot meet my Hermia.
Hence, get thee gone, and follow me no more.
HELENA. You draw me, you hard-hearted adamant:° 195
But yet you draw not iron, for my heart
Is true as steel. Leave you your power to draw,
And I shall have no power to follow you.
DEMETRIUS. Do I entice you? Do I speak you fair°?
Or rather do I not in plainest truth 200
Tell you I do not, nor I cannot love you?
HELENA. And even for that, do I love you the more:
I am your spaniel: and Demetrius,
The more you beat me, I will fawn on you.
Use me but as your spaniel: spurn me, strike me, 205
Neglect me, lose me: only give me leave,

165 *bolt*: arrow.   168 *love-in-idleness*: pansy.   174 *leviathan*: whale.   181 *busy*:
mischievous.   192 *wood*: crazy.   195 *adamant*: (1) magnet (2) impenetrably hard
lodestone.   199 *you fair*: to you in a kindly way.

Unworthy as I am, to follow you.
What worser place can I beg in your love
(And yet a place of high respect with me)
Than to be usèd as you use your dog.   210
DEMETRIUS.   Tempt not too much the hatred of my spirit,
   For I am sick, when I do look on thee.
HELENA.   And I am sick, when I look not on you.
DEMETRIUS.   You do impeach° your modesty too much,
   To leave the city and commit yourself   215
   Into the hands of one that loves you not,
   To trust the opportunity of night,
   And the ill counsel of a desert° place,
   With the rich worth of your virginity.
HELENA.   Your virtue is my privilege:° for that°   220
   It is not night, when I do see your face,
   Therefore I think I am not in the night.
   Nor doth this wood lack worlds of company,
   For you, in my respect,° are all the world.
   Then how can it be said I am alone,   225
   When all the world is here to look on me?
DEMETRIUS.   I'll run from thee and hide me in the brakes,°
   And leave thee to the mercy of wild beasts.
HELENA.   The wildest hath not such a heart as you.
   Run when you will: the story shall be changed;   230
   Apollo flies, and Daphne° holds the chase:
   The dove pursues the griffin:° the mild hind°
   Makes speed to catch the tiger. Bootless° speed,
   When cowardice pursues, and valour flies.
DEMETRIUS.   I will not stay° thy questions. Let me go: 235
   Or if thou follow me, do not believe
   But I shall do thee mischief in the wood.   [*Exit* DEMETRIUS.]
HELENA.   Ay, in the temple, in the town, the field,
   You do me mischief. Fie Demetrius,
   Your wrongs do set a scandal on my sex: 240
   We cannot fight for love, as men may do:
   We should be wooed, and were not made to woo.
   I'll follow thee and make a heaven of hell,
   To die upon the hand I love so well.   *Exit.*
OBERON.   Fare thee well nymph. Ere he do leave this grove,   245
   Thou shalt fly him, and he shall seek thy love.

Enter PUCK.

214 *impeach*: discredit.   218 *desert*: deserted.   220 *Your . . . privilege*: your attraction
is my excuse (for coming).   *for that*: because.   224 *respect*: regard.   227 *brakes*:
thickets.   231 *Apollo . . . Daphne*: (in Ovid, Apollo pursues Daphne, who turns into a
laurel tree).   232 *griffin*: legendary beast with the head of an eagle and the body of a
lion.   *hind*: doe.   233 *Bootless*: useless.   235 *stay*: wait for.

Hast thou the flower there? Welcome wanderer.
PUCK.   Ay, there it is.
OBERON.   I pray thee give it me.
I know a bank where the wild thyme blows,
Where oxlips and the nodding violet grows,   250
Quite over-canopied with luscious woodbine,
With sweet musk-roses, and with eglantine:
There sleeps Titania, sometime of the night,
Lulled in these flowers, with dances and delight:
And there the snake throws° her enamelled skin,   255
Weed° wide enough to wrap a fairy in.
And with the juice of this, I'll streak her eyes,
And make her full of hateful fantasies.
Take thou some of it, and seek through this grove:
A sweet Athenian lady is in love   260
with a disdainful youth: anoint his eyes.
But do it when the next thing he espies
May be the lady. Thou shalt know the man
By the Athenian garments he hath on.
Effect it with some care, that he may prove   265
More fond° on her, than she upon her love:
And look thou meet me ere the first cock crow.
PUCK.   Fear not my lord: your servant shall do so.   *Exeunt.*

[Scene 2. *Another part of the wood*]

Enter TITANIA *Queen of Fairies with her train.*

QUEEN.   Come, now a roundel° and a fairy song:
Then, for the third part of a minute, hence—
Some to kill cankers in the musk-rose buds,
Some war with reremice° for their leathren wings,
To make my small elves coats, and some keep back   5
The clamorous owl, that nightly hoots and wonders
At our quaint° spirits. Sing me now asleep:
Then to your offices,° and let me rest.

Fairies sing.

You spotted snakes with double° tongue,
    Thorny hedgehogs be not seen,   10
Newts and blind-worms° do no wrong,
    Come not near our Fairy Queen.

    Philomele,° with melody,

---

255 *throws*: casts off.   256 *weed*: garment.   266 *fond*: doting, madly in love.
1 *roundel*: dance in a ring.   4 *reremice*: bats.   7 *quaint*: dainty.   8 *offices*:
duties.   9 *double*: forked.   11 *blind-worms*: legless lizards.   13 *Philomele*: the
nightingale.

Sing in our sweet lullaby,
Lulla, lulla, lullaby, lulla, lulla, lullaby.
  Never harm,
  Nor spell, nor charm,
Come our lovely lady nigh.
So good night, with lullaby.   15

1. FAIRY. Weaving spiders come not here: 20
  Hence you long-legged spinners, hence:
  Beetles black approach not near:
    Worm nor snail do no offence.
  Philomele, with melody, &c.   *She sleeps.*
2. FAIRY. Hence away: now all is well: 25
  One aloof stand sentinel.   *[Exeunt fairies.]*

Enter OBERON [and applies the flower juice to TITANIA'S eyelids.]

OBERON. What thou seest, when thou dost wake,
  Do it for thy true love take:
  Love and languish for his sake.
  Be it ounce,° or cat, or bear,   30
  Pard,° or boar with bristled hair,
  In thy eye that shall appear,
  when thou wak'st, it is thy dear:
  Wake when some vile thing is near.   *[Exit.]*

Enter LYSANDER and HERMIA.

LYSANDER. Fair love, you faint with wand'ring in the wood: 35
  And to speak troth° I have forgot our way.
  We'll rest us Hermia, if you think it good,
  And tarry for the comfort of the day.
HERMIA. Be't so Lysander: find you out a bed:
  For I upon this bank will rest my head.   40
LYSANDER. One turf shall serve as pillow for us both,
  One heart, one bed, two bosoms, and one troth.°
HERMIA. Nay good Lysander: for my sake, my dear,
  Lie further off yet; do not lie so near.
LYSANDER. O take the sense, sweet, of my innocence:°   45
  Love takes the meaning in love's conference.°
  I mean that my heart unto yours is knit,
  So that but one heart we can make of it:
  Two bosoms interchainèd with an oath,
  So then two bosoms and a single troth.   50
  Then by your side no bed-room me deny:
  For lying so, Hermia, I do not lie.
HERMIA. Lysander riddles very prettily.

---

30 *ounce*: lynx.   31 *Pard*: leopard.   36 *troth*: truth.   42 *troth*: true love.   45 *take
. . . innocence*: understand the innocence of my remark.   46 *Love . . . conference*: love enables
lovers to understand each other when they converse.

Now much beshrew° my manners and my pride,
If Hermia meant to say Lysander lied.   55
But gentle friend, for love and courtesy,
Lie further off, in human modesty:
Such separation as may well be said
Becomes a virtuous bachelor and a maid,
So far be distant, and good night sweet friend: 60
Thy love ne'er alter till thy sweet life end.

LYSANDER.   Amen, amen, to that fair prayer say I,
And then end life, when I end loyalty.
Here is my bed: sleep give thee all his rest.

HERMIA.   With half that wish, the wisher's eyes be pressed.°   65

                                                          They sleep.

Enter PUCK.

PUCK.   Through the forest have I gone,
But Athenian found I none,
On whose eyes I might approve°
This flower's force in stirring love.
Night and silence. Who is here?   70
Weeds° of Athens he doth wear:
This is he (my master said)
Despisèd the Athenian maid:
And here the maiden, sleeping sound,
On the dank and dirty ground.   75
Pretty soul, she durst not lie
Near this lack-love, this kill-courtesy.
Churl, upon thy eyes I throw
All the power this charm doth owe:°
When thou wak'st, let love forbid   80
Sleep his seat on thy eyelid.°
So awake when I am gone:
For I must now to Oberon.   *Exit.*

Enter DEMETRIUS and HELENA running.

HELENA.   Stay, thou kill me, sweet Demetrius.

DEMETRIUS.   I charge thee hence, and do not haunt me thus.   85

HELENA.   O, wilt thou darkling° leave me? Do not so.

DEMETRIUS.   Stay on thy peril: I alone will go.   *Exit DEMETRIUS.*

HELENA.   O, I am out of breath in this fond° chase:
The more my prayer, the lesser is my grace.°
Happy is Hermia, wheresoe'er she lies: 90
For she hath blessèd and attractive eyes.
How came her eyes so bright? Not with salt tears:

---

54 *beshrew*: curse.   65 *pressed*: i.e., by sleep.   68 *approve*: test.   71 *Weeds*: garments.
79 *owe*: own.   80–81 *forbid . . . eyelid*: make you sleepless (with love).   86 *darkling*:
in the dark.   88 *fond*: foolishly doting.   89 *my grace*: favor shown to me.

If so, my eyes are oft'ner washed than hers.
No, no: I am as ugly as a bear:
For beasts that meet me run away for fear.   95
Therefore no marvel, though Demetrius
Do as a monster, fly my presence thus.
What wicked and dissembling glass° of mine,
Made me compare with Hermia's sphery eyne°!
But who is here? Lysander, on the ground?   100
Dead, or asleep? I see no blood, no wound.
Lysander, if you live, good sir awake.

LYSANDER.   [*Wakes*.] And run through fire, I will for thy sweet sake.
Transparent° Helena, nature shows art,
That through thy bosom, makes me see thy heart.   105
Where is Demetrius? O how fit a word
Is that vile name to perish on my sword!

HELENA.   Do not say so, Lysander, say not so.
What though he love your Hermia? Lord, what though?
Yet Hermia still loves you: then be content.   110

LYSANDER.   Content with Hermia? No: I do repent
The tedious minutes I with her have spent.
Not Hermia, but Helena I love.
Who will not change a raven for a dove?
The will of man is by his reason swayed:°   115
And reason says you are the worthier maid.
Things growing are not ripe until their season:
So I, being young, till now ripe° not to reason.
And touching now the point° of human skill,°
Reason becomes the marshal to my will,   120
And leads me to your eyes; where I o'erlook
Love's stories, written in love's richest book.

HELENA.   Wherefore° was I to this keen mockery born?
When at your hands did I deserve this scorn?
Is't not enough, is't not enough, young man,   125
That I did never, no, nor never can,
Deserve a sweet look from Demetrius' eye,
But you must flout° my insufficiency?
Good troth you do me wrong, good sooth you do,
In such disdainful manner me to woo.   130
But fare you well: perforce I must confess,
I thought you lord of more true gentleness.°
O, that a lady, of one man refused,
Should of another, therefore be abused!   *Exit*.

LYSANDER.   She sees not Hermia. Hermia, sleep thou there,   135
And never mayst thou come Lysander near.

---

98 *glass*: looking glass.   99 *sphery eyne*: starry eyes.   104 *Transparent*: radiant.
115 *swayed*: ruled.   118 *ripe*: mature.   119 *point*: peak.   *skill*: knowledge.
123 *Wherefore*: why.   128 *flout*: mock.   132 *lord . . . gentleness*: more of a gentleman.

For, as a surfeit of the sweetest things
The deepest loathing to the stomach brings:
Or as the heresies that men do leave,
Are hated most of those they did deceive: 140
So thou, my surfeit and my heresy,
Of all be hated; but the most, of me:
And all my powers, address your love and might,
To honour Helen, and to be her knight.   *Exit.*
HERMIA.   [*Wakes*.] Help me Lysander, help me: do thy best   145
To pluck this crawling serpent from my breast.
Ay me, for pity. What a dream was here?
Lysander, look how I do quake with fear.
Methought a serpent eat my heart away,
And you sat smiling at his cruel prey.°   150
Lysander: what, removed? Lysander, lord!
What, out of hearing, gone? No sound, no word?
Alack, where are you? Speak, and if you hear:
Speak, of° all loves. I swoon almost with fear.
No? Then I well perceive you are not nigh: 155
Either death, or you, I'll find immediately.   *Exit.*

ACT 3

[*Scene 1. The wood*]

Enter the CLOWNS [QUINCE, SNUG, BOTTOM, FLUTE, SNOUT, *and* STARVELING.]

BOTTOM.   Are we all met?
QUINCE.   Pat, pat: and here's a marvellous convenient place for
    our rehearsal. This green plot shall be our stage, this
    hawthorn brake° our tiring-house,° and we will do it in
    action, as we will do it before the duke.   5
BOTTOM.   Peter Quince?
QUINCE.   What sayest thou, bully° Bottom?
BOTTOM.   There are things in this Comedy of Pyramus and Thisby
    that will never please. First, Pyramus must draw a sword
    to kill himself; which the ladies cannot abide. How   10
    answer you that?
SNOUT.   By'r lakin,° a parlous° fear.
STARVELING.   I believe we must leave the killing out, when all is done.
BOTTOM.   Not a whit: I have a device to make all well. Write me
    a prologue, and let the prologue seem to say, we will   15
    do no harm with our swords, and that Pyramus is not
    killed indeed: and for the more better assurance, tell

150 *prey*: preying.   154 *of*: for the sake of.   4 *brake*: thicket.   *tiring-house*: dressing
room.   7 *bully*: "old pal."   12 *By'r lakin*: mild oath, "by Our Lady."   *parlous*: awful,
perilous.

them that I Pyramus am not Pyramus, but Bottom the
weaver: this will put them out of fear.

QUINCE.   Well, we will have such a prologue, and it shall be   20
written in eight and six.°

BOTTOM.   No, make it two more: let it be written in eight and
eight.

SNOUT.   Will not the ladies be afeard of the lion?

STARVELING.   I fear it, I promise you.   25

BOTTOM.   Masters, you ought to consider with yourselves, to bring
in (God shield us) a lion among ladies, is a most dreadful
thing. For there is not a more fearful wild-fowl than
your lion living: and we ought to look to't.

SNOUT.   Therefore another prologue must tell he is not a lion.   30

BOTTOM.   Nay, you must name his name, and half his face must be
seen through the lion's neck, and he himself must speak
through, saying thus, or to the same defect:° "Ladies,"
or "Fair ladies—I would wish you," or "I would request
you," or "I would entreat you, not to fear,   35
not to tremble: my life for yours. If you think I come
hither as a lion, it were pity of my life. No, I am no
such thing: I am a man as other men are." And there
indeed let him name his name, and tell them plainly he
is Snug the joiner.   40

QUINCE.   Well, it shall be so, but there is two hard things: that is,
to bring the moonlight into a chamber: for you know,
Pyramus and Thisby meet by moonlight.

SNOUT.   Doth the moon shine that night we play our play?

BOTTOM.   A calendar, a calendar: look in the almanac: find out   45
moonshine, find out moonshine.

QUINCE.   Yes, it doth shine that night.

BOTTOM.   Why then may you leave a casement of the great
chamber window, where we play, open; and the moon may
shine in at the casement.   50

QUINCE.   Ay, or else one must come in with a bush of thorns° and
a lantern, and say he comes to disfigure,° or to present,
the person of Moonshine. Then, there is another thing;
we must have a wall in the great chamber: for Pyramus
and Thisby, says the story, did talk through the chink   55
of a wall.

SNOUT.   You can never bring in a wall. What say you, Bottom?

BOTTOM.   Some man or other must present wall: and let him have
some plaster, or some loam, or some rough-cast° about
him, to signify wall; and let him hold his fingers thus: 60
and through that cranny, shall Pyramus and Thisby whisper.

21 *eight and six*: alternate lines of eight and six syllables (the ballad meter).   33 *defect*:
(he means "effect").   51 *bush of thorns*: bundle of firewood (the man in the moon was
supposed to have been placed there as a punishment for gathering wood on Sundays).
52 *disfigure*: (he means "figure," symbolize).   59 *rough-cast*: coarse plaster of lime and
gravel.

QUINCE. If that may be, then all is well. Come, sit down every
  mother's son, and rehearse your parts. Pyramus, you
  begin: when you have spoken your speech, enter into that 65
  brake, and so every one according to his cue.

Enter PUCK.

PUCK. What hempen homespuns° have we swagg'ring here,
  So near the cradle of the Fairy Queen?
  What, a play toward°? I'll be an auditor,
  An actor too perhaps, if I see cause. 70
QUINCE. Speak Pyramus. Thisby stand forth.
PYRAMUS. Thisby, the flowers of odious savours sweet—
QUINCE. "Odorous, odorous."
PYRAMUS. —odours savours sweet,
  So hath thy breath, my dearest Thisby dear. 75
  But hark, a voice: stay thou but here awhile,
  And by and by I will to thee appear. *Exit PYRAMUS.*
PUCK A stranger Pyramus than e'er played here. [*Exit.*]
THISBY. Must I speak now?
QUINCE. Ay marry must you. For you must understand he goes 80
  but to see a noise that he heard, and is to come again.
THISBY. Most radiant Pyramus, most lily-white of hue,
    Of colour like the red rose, on triumphant brier,
  Most brisky juvenal,° and eke most lovely Jew,°
    As true as truest horse, that yet would never tire, 85
  I'll meet thee Pyramus, at Ninny's tomb.
QUINCE. "Ninus' tomb,"° man: why, you must not speak that yet.
  That you answer to Pyramus. You speak all your part
  at once, cues and all. Pyramus, enter; your cue is past:
  it is "never tire." 90
THISBY. O—As true as truest horse, that yet would never tire.

Enter PYRAMUS with the ass-head [followed by PUCK].

PYRAMUS. If I were fair, Thisby, I were only thine.
QUINCE. O monstrous! O strange! We are haunted. Pray masters,
  fly masters. Help! *The clowns all exeunt.*
PUCK I'll follow you: I'll lead you about a round,° 95
  Through bog, through bush, through brake, through brier.
  Sometime a horse I'll be, sometime a hound,
    A hog, a headless bear, sometime a fire,
  And neigh, and bark, and grunt, and roar, and burn,
  Like horse, hound, hog, bear, fire, at every turn. *Exit.* 100

67 *hempen homespuns*: wearers of clothing spun at home from hemp.   69 *toward*: in
preparation.   84 *brisky juvenal*: lively youth.   *Jew*: diminutive of either "juvenal" or
"jewel."   87 *Ninus' tomb*: (tomb of the founder of Nineveh, and meeting place of the lovers
in Ovid's version of the Pyramus story).   95 *about a round*: in circles, like a round dance
(round about).

BOTTOM.   Why do they run away? This is a knavery of them to
make me afeared.

Enter SNOUT.

SNOUT.   O Bottom, thou art changed. What do I see on thee?
BOTTOM.   What do you see? You see an ass-head of your own, do
you?   [*Exit SNOUT.*]   105

Enter QUINCE.

QUINCE.   Bless thee Bottom, bless thee. Thou art translated.°   *Exit.*
BOTTOM.   I see their knavery. This is to make an ass of me, to
fright me if they could: but I will not stir from this
place, do what they can. I will walk up and down here,
and will sing that they shall hear I am not afraid.   110
[*Sings.*] The woosel° cock, so black of hue,
                With orange tawny bill,
          The throstle,° with his note so true,
                The wren, with little quill.°
TITANIA.   What angel wakes me from my flow'ry bed?   115
BOTTOM.   [*Sings.*] The finch, the sparrow, and the lark,
                The plain-song° cuckoo gray:
          Whose note full many a man doth mark,
                And dares not answer, nay.
For indeed, who would set his wit to° so foolish a bird?   120
Who would give a bird the lie,° though he cry "cuckoo"°
never so°?
TITANIA.   I pray thee, gentle mortal, sing again.
Mine ear is much enamoured of thy note:
So is mine eye enthrallèd to thy shape,   125
And thy fair virtue's force (perforce°) doth move me,
On the first view to say, to swear, I love thee.
BOTTOM.   Methinks mistress, you should have little reason for
that. And yet, to say the truth, reason and love keep
little company together now-a-days. The more the pity,   130
That some honest neighbours will not make them friends.
Nay, I can gleek° upon occasion.
TITANIA.   Thou art as wise as thou art beautiful.
BOTTOM.   Not so neither: but if I had wit enough to get out of
this wood, I have enough to serve mine own turn.   135
TITANIA.   Out of this wood do not desire to go:
Thou shalt remain here, whether thou wilt or no.
I am a spirit of no common rate:°
The summer still doth tend upon my state,°

---

106 *translated*: transformed.   111 *woosel*: ousel, blackbird.   113 *throstle*:
thrush.   114 *quill*: piping note.   117 *plain-song*: sounding a simple, unvaried
note.   120 *set . . . to*: match his wit against.   121 *Who . . . lie*: who could call a bird
a liar.   "*cuckoo*": (which sounded like "cuckold" = a deceived husband).   122 *never so*:
i.e., often.   126 *perforce*: by force.   132 *gleek*: joke satirically.   138 *rate*: rank,
value.   139 *still . . . state*: always serves as an attendant in my royal train.

And I do love thee: therefore go with me.   140
I'll give thee fairies to attend on thee:
And they shall fetch thee jewels from the deep,
And sing, while thou on pressed flowers dost sleep:
And I will purge thy mortal grossness so,
That thou shalt like an airy spirit go.   145
Peaseblossom, Cobweb, Moth,° and Mustardseed!

Enter four FAIRIES.

PEASEBLOSSOM.   Ready.
COBWEB.   And I.
MOTH.   And I.
MUSTARDSEED.   And I.
ALL.   Where shall we go?
TITANIA.   Be kind and courteous to this gentleman,
    Hop in his walks and gambol° in his eyes,   150
    Feed him with apricocks° and dewberries,°
    With purple grapes, green figs, and mulberries.
    The honey-bags steal from the humblebees,°
    And for night-tapers, crop° their waxen thighs,
    And light them at the fiery glow-worm's eyes,   155
    To have my love to bed and to arise:
    And pluck the wings from painted butterflies,
    To fan the moonbeams from his sleeping eyes.
    Nod to him elves, and do him courtesies.
PEASEBLOSSOM.   Hail, mortal.   160
COBWEB.   Hail.
MOTH.   Hail.
MUSTARDSEED.   Hail.
BOTTOM.   I cry your worships mercy,° heartily: I beseech your
    worship's name.   165
COBWEB.   Cobweb.
BOTTOM.   I shall desire you of more acquaintance, good Master
    Cobweb: if I cut my finger,° I shall make bold with you.
    Your name, honest gentleman?
PEASEBLOSSOM.   Peaseblossom.   170
BOTTOM.   I pray you commend me° to Mistress Squash,° your mother,
    and to Master Peascod,° your father. Good Master Peaseblossom,
    I shall desire you of more acquaintance, too.
    Your name I beseech you sir?
MUSTARDSEED.   Mustardseed.   175
BOTTOM.   Good Master Mustardseed, I know your patience well.
    That same cowardly giant-like ox beef hath devoured

---

146 *Moth*: mote (so pronounced), tiny speck.   150 *gambol in*: caper before.
151 *apricocks*: apricots.   *dewberries*: blackberries.   153 *humblebees*: bumblebees.
154 *crop*: clip.   164 *I . . . mercy*: I respectfully beg your pardons.
168 *cut my finger*: (cobwebs were used to stop blood).   171 *commend me*: offer my
respects.   *Squash*: unripe peapod.   172 *Peascod*: ripe peapod.

many a gentleman of your house. I promise you, your
kindred hath made my eyes water ere now. I desire you
of more acquaintance, good Master Mustardseed.   180
Titania.   Come wait upon him: lead him to my bower.
          The moon methinks looks with a wat'ry eye:
          And when she weeps, weeps every little flower,
                Lamenting some enforcèd° chastity.
          Tie up my lover's tongue, bring him silently.   *Exeunt*. 185

[*Scene 2. Another part of the wood*]

*Enter [*OBERON*,] King of Fairies, solus*.°

OBERON.   I wonder if Titania be awaked;
          Then what it was that next came in her eye,
          Which she must dote on in extremity.

Enter PUCK.

          Here comes my messenger. How now, mad spirit?
          What night-rule° now about this haunted grove?   5
PUCK.   My mistress with a monster is in love.
          Near to her close and consecrated bower,
          While she was in her dull° and sleeping hour,
          A crew of patches,° rude mechanicals,°
          That work for bread upon Athenian stalls,°   10
          Were met together to rehearse a play,
          Intended for great Theseus' nuptial day:
          The shallowest thickskin of that barren sort,°
          Who Pyramus presented in their sport,
          Forsook his scene and entered in a brake: 15
          When I did him at this advantage take,
          An ass's nole° I fixèd on his head.
          Anon° his Thisby must be answerèd,
          And forth my mimic° comes. When they him spy,
          As wild geese, that the creeping fowler° eye,   20
          Or russet-pated choughs,° many in sort,°
          Rising and cawing at the gun's report,
          Sever themselves and madly sweep the sky,
          So at his sight away his fellows fly:
          And at our stamp, here o'er and o'er one falls: 25
          He murder cries, and help from Athens calls.
          Their sense thus weak, lost with their fears thus strong,
          Made senseless things begin to do them wrong.

---

184 *enforcèd*: violated.   Stage direction: *solus*: alone.   5 *night-rule*: diversion ("misrule")
in the night.   8 *dull*: drowsy.   9 *patches*: fools.   *mechanicals*: workers.   10 *stalls*:
shops.   13 *barren sort*: stupid crew.   17 *nole*: head, noodle.   18 *Anon*: presently.
19 *mimic*: actor.   20 *fowler*: hunter of fowl.   21 *russet-pated choughs*: grey-headed
jackdaws.   *sort*: a flock.

For briers and thorns at their apparel snatch:
Some° sleeves, some hats; from yielders, all things catch.°   30
I led them on in this distracted° fear,
And left sweet Pyramus translated there:
When in that moment (so it came to pass)
Titania waked, and straightway loved an ass.
OBERON. This falls out better than I could devise.   35
    But has thou yet latched° the Athenian's eyes
    With the love-juice, as I did bid thee do?
PUCK. I took him sleeping (that is finished too)
    And the Athenian woman by his side;
    That when he waked, of force° she must be eyed.   40

Enter DEMETRIUS and HERMIA.

OBERON. Stand close:° this is the same Athenian.
PUCK. This is the woman: but not this the man.
DEMETRIUS. O why rebuke you him that loves you so?
    Lay breath so bitter on your bitter foe.
HERMIA. Now I but chide: but I should use thee worse,   45
    For thou, I fear, hast given me cause to curse.
    If thou hast slain Lysander in his sleep,
    Being o'er shoes in blood, plunge in the deep,
    And kill me too.
    The sun was not so true unto the day,   50
    As he to me. Would he have stolen away
    From sleeping Hermia? I'll believe as soon
    This whole° earth may be bored,° and that the moon
    May through the center creep, and so displease
    Her brother's noontide with th' Antipodes.°   55
    It cannot be but thou hast murdered him.
    So should a murderer look; so dead,° so grim.
DEMETRIUS. So should the murdered look, and so should I,
    Pierced through the heart with your stern cruelty.
    Yet you, the murderer, look as bright, as clear,   60
    As yonder Venus in her glimmering sphere.°
HERMIA. What's this to my Lysander? Where is he?
    Ah good Demetrius, wilt thou give him me?
DEMETRIUS. I had rather give his carcass to my hounds.
HERMIA. Out dog, out cur! Thou driv'st me past the bounds   65
    Of maiden's patience. Hast thou slain him then?
    Henceforth be never numbered among men.
    O, once tell true: tell true, even for my sake:

---

30 *Some:* i.e., snatch. *from yielders . . . catch:* (everything joins in to harm the weak).
31 *distracted:* maddened. 36 *latched:* moistened. 40 *of force:* by necessity.
41 *close:* hidden. 53 *whole:* solid. *be bored:* have a hole bored through it. 55 *Her brother's . . . Antipodes:* the noon of her brother sun, by appearing among the Antipodes (the people on the other side of the earth). 57 *dead:* deadly. 61 *sphere:* (in the Ptolemaic system, each planet moved in its own sphere around the earth).

Durst thou have looked upon him, being awake?
And hast thou killed him sleeping? O brave touch°!   70
Could not a worm,° an adder, do so much?
An adder did it: for with doubler tongue°
Than thine, thou serpent, never adder stung.

DEMETRIUS.   You spend your passion on a misprised mood:°
 I am not guilty of Lysander's blood: 75
 Nor is he dead, for aught that I can tell.
HERMIA.   I pray thee, tell me then that he is well.
DEMETRIUS.   And if I could, what should I get therefore?
HERMIA.   A privilege never to see me more:
 And from thy hated presence part I so: 80
 See me no more, whether he be dead or no.   *Exit.*
DEMETRIUS.   There is no following her in this fierce vein.
 Here therefore for a while I will remain.
 So sorrow's heaviness doth heavier grow
 For debt that bankrout sleep doth sorrow owe:°   85
 Which now in some slight measure it will pay,
 If for his tender° here I make some stay.°   *Lie down.*
OBERON.   What hast thou done? Thou hast mistaken quite,
 And laid the love-juice on some true-love's sight.
 Of thy misprision° must perforce° ensue   90
 Some true love turned, and not a false turned true.
PUCK.   Then fate o'errules, that one man holding troth,
 A million fail, confounding° oath on oath.°
OBERON.   About the wood, go swifter than the wind,
 And Helena of Athens look thou find.   95
 All fancy-sick° she is, and pale of cheer,°
 With sighs of love, that costs the fresh blood dear.
 By some illusion see thou bring her here:
 I'll charm his eyes against she do appear.°
PUCK.   I go, I go, look how I go.   100
 Swifter than arrow from the Tartar's bow.°   *Exit.*
OBERON.   Flower of this purple dye,
 Hit with Cupid's archery,
 Sink in apple of his eye:
 When his love he doth espy,   105
 Let her shine as gloriously
 As the Venus of the sky.
 When thou wak'st, if she be by,
 Beg of her for remedy.

70 *brave touch*: splendid stroke (ironic).   71 *worm*: snake.   72 *doubler tongue*: (1) tongue
more forked (2) more deceitful speech.   74 *on . . . mood*: in mistaken anger.   85 *For
debt . . . owe*: because sleep cannot pay the debt of repose he owes the man who is kept
awake by sorrow.   87 *tender*: offer.   *stay*: pause.   90 *misprision*: mistake.   *perforce*:
of necessity.   93 *confounding*: destroying.   *oath on oath*: one oath after another.
96 *fancy-sick*: lovesick.   *cheer*: face.   99 *against . . . appear*: in preparation for her
appearance.   101 *Tartar's bow*: (the Tartars, who used powerful Oriental bows, were famed
as archers).

Enter PUCK.

PUCK.	Captain of our fairy band,	110
	Helena is here at hand,	
	And the youth, mistook by me,	
	Pleading for a lover's fee.°	
	Shall we their fond pageant° see?	
	Lord, what fools these mortals be!	115
OBERON.	Stand aside. The noise they make	
	Will cause Demetrius to awake.	
PUCK.	Then will two at once woo one:	
	That must needs be sport alone.°	
	And those things do best please me	120
	That befall prepost'rously.	

Enter LYSANDER and HELENA.

LYSANDER. Why should you think that I should woo in scorn?
　　Scorn and derision never come in tears.
　　Look when I vow, I weep: and vows so born,
　　　In their nativity all truth appears.°　　　　　　　　　　125
　　How can these things in me seem scorn to you,
　　Bearing the badge° of faith to prove them true?
HELENA. You do advance your cunning more and more.
　　When truth kills truth,° O devilish-holy fray!
　　These vows are Hermia's. Will you give her o'er?　　　　130
　　Weigh oath with oath, and you will nothing weigh.
　　Your vows to her and me, put in two scales,
　　Will even weigh: and both as light as tales.
LYSANDER. I had no judgment, when to her I swore.
HELENA. Nor none, in my mind, now you give her o'er.　　135
LYSANDER. Demetrius loves her: and he loves not you.
DEMETRIUS. *(Awakes.)* O Helen, goddess, nymph, perfect, divine,
　　To what, my love, shall I compare thine eyne!
　　Crystal is muddy. O, how ripe in show,
　　Thy lips, those kissing cherries, tempting grow!　　　　140
　　That pure congealèd white, high Taurus'° snow,
　　Fanned with the eastern wind, turns to a crow,
　　When thou hold'st up thy hand. O let me kiss
　　This princess of pure white,° this seal of bliss.
HELENA. O spite! O hell! I see you all are bent　　　　　　145
　　To set against me, for your merriment.
　　If you were civil,° and knew courtesy,
　　You would not do me thus much injury.

---

113 *fee*: reward.　　114 *fond pageant*: foolish spectacle.　　119 *alone*: unique.　　124–
125 *vows . . . appears*: vows born in weeping must be true ones.　　127 *badge*: (1) outward
signs (2) family crest.　　129 *truth kills truth*: former true love is killed by vows of present
true love.　　141 *Taurus*: (mountain range in Asia Minor).　　144 *princess . . . white*:
sovereign example of whiteness (her hand).　　147 *civil*: well behaved.

Can you not hate me, as I know you do,
But you must join in souls° to mock me too?   150
If you were men, as men you are in show,
You would not use a gentle lady so;
To vow, and swear, and superpraise my parts,°
When I am sure you hate me with your hearts.
You both are rivals, and love Hermia: 155
And now both rivals, to mock Helena.
A trim° exploit, a manly enterprise,
To conjure tears up in a poor maid's eyes
With your derision. None of noble sort
Would so offend a virgin, and extort°   160
A poor soul's patience, all to make you sport.
LYSANDER.   You are unkind, Demetrius: be not so.
For you love Hermia: this you know I know.
And here, with all good will, with all my heart,
In Hermia's love I yield you up my part: 165
And yours of Helena to be bequeath,
Whom I do love, and will do to my death.
HELENA.   Never did mockers waste more idle breath.
DEMETRIUS.   Lysander, keep thy Hermia: I will none.°
If e'er I loved her, all that love is gone.   170
My heart to her but as guest-wise sojourned:°
And now to Helen is it home returned,
There to remain.
LYSANDER.   Helen, it is not so.
DEMETRIUS.   Disparage not the faith thou dost not know,
Lest to thy peril thou aby it dear.°   175
Look where thy love comes: yonder is thy dear.

Enter HERMIA.

HERMIA.   Dark night, that from the eye his function takes,
The ear more quick of apprehension makes.
Wherein it doth impair the seeing sense,
It pays the hearing double recompense.   180
Thou art not by mine eye, Lysander, found:
Mine ear, I thank it, brought me to thy sound.
But why unkindly didst thou leave me so?
LYSANDER.   Why should he stay, whom love doth press to go?
HERMIA.   What love could press Lysander from my side?   185
LYSANDER.   Lysander's love, that would not let him bide—
Fair Helena: who more engilds the night
Than all your fiery oes and eyes of light.°
Why seek'st thou me? Could not this make thee know,

---

150 *join in souls*: agree in spirit.   153 *parts*: qualities.   157 *trim*: fine (ironic).
160 *extort*: wring.   169 *none*: have none of her.   171 *to her . . . sojourned*: visited her
only as a guest.   175 *aby it dear*: buy it at a high price.   188 *oes . . . light*: stars.

The hate I bare thee made me leave thee so? 190
HERMIA.   You speak not as you think: it cannot be.
HELENA.   Lo: She is one of this confederacy.
　　Now I perceive they have conjoined all three,
　　To fashion this false sport in spite of° me.
　　Injurious° Hermia, most ungrateful maid, 195
　　Have you conspired, have you with these contrived
　　To bait° me with this foul derision?
　　Is all the counsel° that we two have shared,
　　The sisters' vows, the hours that we have spent,
　　When we have chid the hasty-footed time 200
　　For parting us; O, is all forgot?
　　All schooldays' friendship, childhood innocence?
　　We Hermia, like two artificial° gods,
　　Have with our needles created both one flower,
　　Both on one sampler,° sitting on one cushion, 205
　　Both warbling of one song, both in one key;
　　As if our hands, our sides, voices, and minds
　　Had been incorporate.° So we grew together,
　　Like to a double cherry, seeming parted,
　　But yet an union in partition, 210
　　Two lovely berries moulded on one stem:
　　So with two seeming bodies, but one heart,
　　Two of the first, like coats in heraldry,
　　Due but to one, and crownèd with one crest.°
　　And will you rent° our ancient love asunder, 215
　　To join with men in scorning your poor friend?
　　It is not friendly, 'tis not maidenly.
　　Our sex, as well as I, may chide you for it;
　　Though I alone do feel the injury.
HERMIA.   I am amazèd at your passionate words: 220
　　I scorn you not. It seems that you scorn me.
HELENA.   Have you not set Lysander, as in scorn,
　　To follow me, and praise my eyes and face?
　　And made your other love, Demetrius
　　(Who even but now did spurn° me with his foot) 225
　　To call me goddess, nymph, divine, and rare,
　　Precious, celestial? Wherefore speaks he this
　　To her he hates? And wherefore doth Lysander
　　Deny your love, so rich within his soul,
　　And tender° me (forsooth) affection, 230
　　But by your setting on, by your consent?
　　What though I be not so in grace° as you,

194 *in spite of*: to spite.　195 *Injurious*: insulting.　197 *bait*: attack.　198 *counsel*: secrets.　203 *artificial*: skilled in art.　205 *sampler*: work of embroidery. 208 *incorporate*: in one body.　213–214 *Two . . . crest*: (the two bodies being) like double coats of arms joined under one crest (with one heart).　215 *rent*: rend, tear.　225 *spurn*: kick.　230 *tender*: offer.　232 *in grace*: favored.

So hung upon with love, so fortunate,
But miserable most, to love unloved?
This you should pity, rather than despise.   235

HERMIA.   I understand not what you mean by this.

HELENA.   Ay, do. Persèver, counterfeit sad° looks:
Make mouths upon° me when I turn my back:
Wink each at other, hold the sweet jest up.
This sport well carried, shall be chronicled.°   240
If you have any pity, grace, or manners,
You would not make me such an argument.°
But fare ye well: 'tis partly my own fault:
Which death or absence soon shall remedy.

LYSANDER.   Stay, gentle Helena: hear my exuse,   245
My love, my life, my soul, fair Helena.

HELENA.   O excellent!

HERMIA.   Sweet, do not scorn her so.

DEMETRIUS.   If she cannot entreat,° I can compel.

LYSANDER.   Thou canst compel no more than she entreat.
Thy threats have no more strength than her weak prayers.   250
Helen, I love thee, by my life I do:
I swear by that which I will lose for thee,
To prove° him false that says I love thee not.

DEMETRIUS.   I say I love thee more than he can do.

LYSANDER.   If thou say so, withdraw, and prove° it too.   255

DEMETRIUS.   Quick. come.

HERMIA.   Lysander, whereto tends all this?

LYSANDER.   Away, you Ethiope.°

DEMETRIUS.   No, no, sir,
Seem to break loose: take on as you would follow;
But yet come not.° You are a tame man, go.

LYSANDER.   Hang off,° thou cat, thou burr: vile thing, let loose;   260
Or I will shake thee from me like a serpent.

HERMIA.   Why are you grown so rude? What change is this,
Sweet love?

LYSANDER.   Thy love? Out, tawny Tartar, out:
Out, loathèd med'cine: O hated potion, hence!

HERMIA.   Do you not jest?

HELENA.   Yes sooth: and so do you.   265

LYSANDER.   Demetrius, I will keep my word° with thee.

DEMETRIUS.   I would I had your bond.° For I perceive
A weak bond holds you. I'll not trust your word.

---

237 *sad*: serious.   238 *mouths upon*: faces at.   240 *chronicled*: written down in the history
books.   242 *argument*: subject (of your mockery).   248 *entreat*: sway you by
entreaty.   253,255 *prove*: i.e., by a duel.   257 *Ethiope*: (because she is a brunette).
258–259 *Seem . . . not*: you only seem to break loose from Hermia and pretend to follow
me to a duel, but you actually hold back.   260 *Hang off*: let go.   266 *keep my word*:
i.e., to duel.   267 *bond*: written agreement.

LYSANDER. What? Should I hurt her, strike her, kill her dead?
  Although I hate her, I'll not harm her so.   270
HERMIA. What? Can you do me greater harm than hate?
  Hate me, wherefore°? O me, what news,° my love?
  Am not I Hermia? Are not you Lysander?
  I am as fair now, as I was erewhile.°
  Since night, you loved me; yet since night, you left me.   275
  Why then, you left me—O, the gods forbid—
  In earnest, shall I say?
LYSANDER.   Ay, by my life:
  And never did desire to see thee more.
  Therefore be out of hope, of question, of doubt:
  Be certain: nothing truer: 'tis no jest   280
  That I do hate thee, and love Helena.
HERMIA. O me, you juggler,° you canker blossom,°
  You thief of love: what, have you come by night,
  And stol'n my love's heart from him?
HELENA.   Fine, i' faith.
  Have you no modesty, no maiden shame,   285
  No touch of bashfulness? What, will you tear
  Impatient answers from my gentle tongue?
  Fie, fie, you counterfeit, you puppet,° you.
HERMIA. Puppet? why so—ay, that way goes the game.
  Now I perceive that she hath made compare   290
  Between our statures, she hath urged her height,
  And with her personage, her tall personage,
  Her height (forsooth) she hath prevailed with him.
  And are you grown so high in his esteem,
  Because I am so dwarfish and so low?   295
  How low am I, thou painted maypole? Speak:
  How low am I? I am not yet so low,
  But that my nails can reach unto thine eyes.
HELENA. I pray you, though you mock me, gentlemen,
  Let her not hurt me. I was never curst:°   300
  I have no gift at all in shrewishness:
  I am a right maid for my cowardice:°
  Let her not strike me. You perhaps may think,
  Because she is something lower than myself,
  That I can match her.
HERMIA.   Lower? Hark again.   305
HELENA. Good Hermia, do not be so bitter with me,
  I evermore did love you Hermia,
  Did ever keep your counsels, never wronged you;
  Save that in love unto Demetrius,

---

272 *wherefore*: why.   *what news*: what's the matter.   274 *erewhile*: a short while
ago.   282 *juggler*: deceiver.   *canker blossom*: worm that causes canker in blossoms.
288 *puppet*: (Hermia is short and Helena tall).   300 *curst*: bad-tempered.   302 *right . . .*
cowardice: true woman in being cowardly.

I told him of your stealth unto this wood.   31
He followed you: for love I followed him.
But he hath chid me hence, and threatened me
To strike me, spurn me, nay to kill me too;
And now, so° you will let me quiet go,
To Athens will I bear my folly back,   31
And follow you no further. Let me go.
You see how simple and how fond° I am.

HERMIA.   Why, get you gone. Who is't that hinders you?

HELENA.   A foolish heart, that I leave here behind.

HERMIA.   What, with Lysander?

HELENA.   With Demetrius.

LYSANDER.   Be not afraid: she shall not harm thee Helena.

DEMETRIUS.   No sir: she shall not, though you take her part.

HELENA.   O when she's angry, she is keen and shrewd.°
She was a vixen when she went to school:
And though she be but little, she is fierce.   32!

HERMIA.   "Little" again? nothing but "low" and "little"?
Why will you suffer her to flout° me thus?
Let me come to her.

LYSANDER.   Get you gone, you dwarf;
You minimus,° of hind'ring knot-grass° made;
You bead, you acorn.

DEMETRIUS.   You are too officious   33¢
In her behalf that scorns your services.
Let her alone: speak not of Helena,
Take not her part. For if thou dost intend°
Never so little show of love to her,
Thou shalt aby it.°

LYSANDER.   Now she holds me not: 335
Now follow, if thou dar'st, to try whose right,
Of thine or mine, is most in Helena.°

DEMETRIUS.   Follow? Nay, I'll go with thee, check by jowl.

                              Exeunt LYSANDER and DEMETRIUS.

HERMIA.   You, mistress, all this coil is long of° you.
Nay, go not back.

HELENA.   I will not trust you, I,   340
Nor longer stay in your curst company.
Your hands than mine are quicker for a fray:
My legs are longer though, to run away.   [*Exit.*]

HERMIA.   I am amazed,° and know not what to say.   *Exit.*

---

314 *so*: if.   317 *fond*: foolish.   323 *keen and shrewd*: sharp and malicious.   327 *flout*:
mock.   329 *minimus*: smallest of creatures.   *knot-grass*: weed believed to stunt the growth
if eaten.   333 *intend*: extend.   335 *aby it*: buy it dearly.   336–337 *try . . . Helena*:
prove by fighting which of us has most right to Helena.   339 *coil is long of*: turmoil is
because of.   344 *amazed*: confused.

OBERON. This is thy negligence: still thou mistak'st, 345
 Or else commit'st thy knaveries wilfully.
PUCK. Believe me, king of shadows, I mistook.
 Did not you tell me I should know the man
 By the Athenian garments he had on?
 And so far blameless proves my enterprise, 350
 That I have 'nointed an Athenian's eyes:
 And so far am I glad it so did sort,°
 As this their jangling I esteem a sport.
OBERON. Thou seest these lovers seek a place to fight;
 Hie therefore Robin, overcast the night, 355
 The starry welkin° cover thou anon
 With drooping fog as black as Acheron,°
 And lead these testy° rivals so astray,
 As° one come not within another's way.
 Like to Lysander sometime frame thy tongue: 360
 Then stir Demetrius up with bitter wrong:°
 And sometime rail thou like Demetrius:
 And from each other look thou lead them thus;
 Till o'er their brows death-counterfeiting sleep
 With leaden legs and batty wings doth creep: 365
 Then crush this herb into Lysander's eye;
 Whose liquor hath this virtuous° property,
 To take from thence all error with his might,
 And make his eyeballs roll with wonted° sight.
 When they next wake, all this derision° 370
 Shall seem a dream, and fruitless vision,
 And back to Athens shall the lovers wend,
 With league whose date° till death shall never end.
 Whiles I in this affair do thee employ,
 I'll to my queen and beg her Indian boy: 375
 And then I will her charmèd eye release,
 From monster's view, and all things shall be peace.
PUCK. My fairy lord, this must be done with haste,
 For night's swift dragons cut the clouds full fast:
 And yonder shines Aurora's harbinger,° 380
 At whose approach, ghosts wand'ring here and there,
 Troop home to churchyards: damnèd spirits all,
 That in crossways° and floods° have burial,
 Already to their wormy beds are gone:
 For fear lest day should look their shames upon, 385
 They wilfully themselves exile from light,

352 *sort*: turn out. 356 *welkin*: sky. 357 *Acheron*: One of the four rivers in the
underworld. 358 *testy*: irritable. 359 *As*: so that. 361 *wrong*: insult.
367 *virtuous*: potent. 369 *wonted*: (previously) accustomed. 370 *derision*: laughable
interlude. 373 *date*: term. 380 *Aurora's harbinger*: the morning star heralding Aurora,
the dawn. 383 *crossways*: crossroads, where suicides were buried.   *floods*: those who
drowned.

And must for aye consort° with black-browed night.

OBERON.   But we are spirits of another sort.
   I with the morning's love have oft made sport,°
   And like a forester, the groves may tread   39
   Even till the eastern gate all fiery red,
   Opening on Neptune, with fair blessèd beams,
   Turns into yellow gold his salt green streams.
   But notwithstanding, haste, make no delay:
   We may effect this business yet ere day.   [Exit.]   39

PUCK.   Up and down, up and down,
   I will lead them up and down.
   I am feared in field and town.
   Goblin, lead them up and down.
      Here comes one.   40

Enter LYSANDER.

LYSANDER.   Where art thou, proud Demetrius? Speak thou now.
PUCK.   Here villain, drawn° and ready. Where art thou?
LYSANDER.   I will be with thee straight.
PUCK.   Follow me then
     To plainer° ground.   [*Exit* LYSANDER.]

Enter DEMETRIUS.

DEMETRIUS.   Lysander, speak again.
   Thou runaway, thou coward, art thou fled?
   Speak: in some bush? Where dost thou hide thy head?
PUCK.   Thou coward, art thou bragging to the stars,
   Telling the bushes that thou look'st for wars,
   And wilt not come? Come recreant,° come thou child,
   I'll whip thee with a rod. He is defiled   41
   That draws a sword on thee.
DEMETRIUS.   Yea, art thou there?
PUCK.   Follow my voice: we'll try no manhood° here.   *Exeunt.*

[*Enter* LYSANDER.]

LYSANDER.   He goes before me and still dares me on:
   When I come where he calls, then he is gone.
   The villain is much lighter-heeled than I;   41
   I followed fast: but faster he did fly,
   That fallen am I in dark uneven way,
   And here will rest me. (*Lie down.*) Come thou gentle day,
   For if but once thou show me thy grey light,

---

387 *aye consort*: ever associate.   389 *mornings's . . . sport*: hunted with Cephalus (beloved of Aurora and himself devoted to his wife Procris, whom he killed by accident; "sport" also = "amorous dalliance," and "love" = Aurora's love for Oberon).   402 *drawn*: with sword drawn.   404 *plainer*: more level.   409 *recreant*: oath-breaker, coward.   412 *try no manhood*: test no valor.

I'll find Demetrius and revenge this spite. *[Sleeps.]* 420

Enter PUCK *and* DEMETRIUS.

PUCK. Ho, ho, ho! Coward, why com'st thou not?
DEMETRIUS. Abide° me, if thou dar'st, for well I wot°
    Thou run'st before me, shifting every place,
    And dar'st not stand, nor look me in the face.
    Where art thou now?
PUCK.   Come hither: I am here. 425
DEMETRIUS. Nay then thou mock'st me. Thou shalt buy this dear,°
    If ever I thy face by daylight see.
    Now go thy way. Faintness constraineth me
    To measure out my length on this cold bed.
    By day's approach look to be visited. *[Lies down and sleeps.]* 430

Enter HELENA.

HELENA.   O weary night, O long and tedious night,
      Abate° thy hours; shine comforts° from the east,
      That I may back to Athens by daylight,
      From these that my poor company detest:
    And sleep, that sometimes shuts up sorrow's eye, 435
    Steal me awhile from mine own company. *Sleep.*
PUCK.   Yet but three? Come one more,
    Two of both kinds makes up four.
    Here she comes, curst° and sad.
    Cupid is a knavish lad, 440
    Thus to make poor females mad.

Enter HERMIA.

HERMIA. Never so weary, never so in woe,
      Bedabbled with the dew, and torn with briers:
    I can no further crawl, no further go:
    My legs can keep no pace with my desires. 445
    Here will I rest me till the break of day.
    Heavens shield Lysander, if they mean a fray. *[Lies down and sleeps.]*
PUCK. On the ground,
    Sleep sound:
    I'll apply 450
    To your eye,
    Gentle lover, remedy. *[Squeezes the love-juce on* LYSANDER'S *eyelids.]*
    When thou wak'st,
    Thou tak'st
    True delight 455
    In the sight
    Of thy former lady's eye:
    And the country proverb known,

---

422 *Abide*: wait for.   *wot*: know.   426 *buy this dear*: pay dearly for this.   432 *Abate*:
shorten.   *shine comforts*: may comforts shine.   439 *curst*: cross.

That every man should take his own,
In your waking shall be shown.
    Jack shall have Jill:
    Naught shall go ill:
The man shall have his mare again, and all shall be well.

        [Exit PUCK. *The lovers remain asleep on stage.]*

ACT 4

[Scene 1. The wood]

*Enter [*TITANIA*] QUEEN of FAIRIES, and [*BOTTOM THE*] CLOWN, and FAIRIES, and the*
*KING [*OBERON*] behind them [unseen].*

TITANIA. Come sit thee down upon this flow'ry bed,
    While I thy amiable° cheeks do coy,°
    And stick musk-roses in thy sleek smooth head,
    And kiss thy fair large ears, my gentle joy.

BOTTOM. Where's Peaseblossom?

PEASEBLOSSOM. Ready.

BOTTOM. Scratch my head, Peaseblossom. Where's Mounsieur
    Cobweb?

COBWEB. Ready.

BOTTOM. Mounsieur Cobweb, good mounsieur, get you your weapons
    in your hand, and kill me a red-hipped humblebee on
    the top of a thistle: and good mounsieur, bring me the
    honey-bag. Do not fret yourself too much in the action,
    mounsieur: and good mounsieur have a care the honey-
    bag break not, I would be loath to have you overflowen
    with a honey-bag, signior. Where's Mounsieur
    Mustardseed?

MUSTARDSEED. Ready.

BOTTOM. Give me your neaf,° Mounsieur Mustardseed. Pray you
    leave your curtsy,° good mounsieur.

MUSTARDSEED. What's your will?

BOTTOM. Nothing, good mounsieur, but to help Cavalery° Cobweb
    to scratch. I must to the barber's mounsieur, for
    methinks I am marvellous hairy about the face. And I am
    such a tender ass, if my hair do but tickle me, I must
    scratch.

TITANIA. What, will thou hear some music, my sweet love?

BOTTOM. I have a reasonable good ear in music. Let's have the
    tongs° and the bones.°

---

2 *amiable*: lovely.   2 *coy*: caress.   19 *neaf*: fist.   20 *leave your curtsy*: either (a) stop
bowing, or (b) replace your hat.   22 *Cavalery*: (he means "cavalier").   29 *tongs*: crude
music made by striking tongs with a piece of metal.   *bones*: pieces of bone held between
the fingers and clapped together rhythmically.

TITANIA. Or say, sweet love, what thou desirest to eat.   30

BOTTOM. Truly, a peck of provender. I could munch your good
dry oats. Methinks I have a great desire to a bottle° of hay.
Good hay, sweet hay, hath no fellow.

TITANIA. I have a venturous fairy that shall seek
The squirrel's hoard, and fetch thee new nuts.   35

BOTTOM. I had rather have a handful or two of dried pease. But
I pray you, let none of your people stir me: I have an
exposition of° sleep come upon me.

TITANIA. Sleep thou, and I will wind thee in my arms.
Fairies, be gone, and be all ways° away.   [*Exeunt* FAIRIES.]   40
So doth the woodbine the sweet honeysuckle
Gently entwist: the female ivy so
Enrings the barky fingers of the elm.
O how I love thee! how I dote on thee!   [*They sleep.*]

Enter ROBIN GOODFELLOW [PUCK.]

OBERON. [*Advances.*] Welcome good Robin. Seest thou this sweet sight?   45
Her dotage now I do begin to pity.
For meeting her of late behind the wood,
Seeking sweet favours° for this hateful fool,
I did upbraid her and fall out with her.
For she his hairy temples then had rounded   50
With coronet of fresh and fragrant flowers.
And that same dew which sometime° on the buds
Was wont to° swell like round and orient° pearls,
Stood now within the pretty flowerets' eyes,
Like tears that did their own disgrace bewail.   55
When I had at my pleasure taunted her,
And she in mild terms begged my patience,
I then did ask of her her changeling child:
Which straight she gave me, and her fairy sent
To bear him to my bower in fairy land.   60
And now I have the boy, I will undo
This hateful imperfection of her eyes.
And gentle Puck, take this transformèd scalp
From off the head of this Athenian swain;
That he awaking when the other do,   65
May all to Athens back again repair,°
And think no more of this night's accidents,°
But as the fierce vexation of a dream.
But first I will release the Fairy Queen.
Be as thou wast wont to be: 70
See, as thou wast wont to see.

32 *bottle*: bundle.   38 *exposition of*: (he means "disposition to").   40 *all ways*: in every
direction.   48 *favours*: bouquets as love tokens.   52 *sometime*: formerly.   53 *Was wont
to*: used to.   *orient*: (where the most beautiful pearls came from).   66 *repair*:
return.   67 *accidents*: incidents.

Dian's bud o'er Cupid's flower°
Hath such force and blessèd power.
Now my Titania, wake you, my sweet queen.
TITANIA.   My Oberon, what visions have I seen!
Methought I was enamoured of an ass.
OBERON.   There lies your love.
TITANIA.   How came these things to pass?
O, how mine eyes do loathe his visage now!
OBERON.   Silence awhile. Robin, take off this head:
Titania, music call, and strike more dead
Than common sleep of all these five the sense.°
TITANIA.   Music, ho music! such as charmeth sleep.
PUCK.   Now, when thou wak'st, with thine own fool's eyes peep.
OBERON.   Sound music: *Music still.*°
                  come my queen, take hands with me,
And rock the ground whereon these sleepers be.   [*Dance.*]
Now thou and I are new in amity,
And will tomorrow midnight solemnly
Dance in Duke Theseus' house triumphantly,°
And bless it to all fair prosperity.
There shall the pairs of faithful lovers be
Wedded, with Theseus, all in jollity.
PUCK.   Fairy King, attend and mark:
I do hear the morning lark.
OBERON.   Then my queen, in silence sad,°
Trip we after the night's shade:
We the globe can compass soon,
Swifter than the wand'ring moon.
TITANIA.   Come my lord, and in our flight,
Tell me how it came this night,
That I sleeping here was found,
With these mortals on the ground.   *Exeunt.*

Wind° *horns. Enter* THESEUS, HIPPOLYTA, EGEUS *and all his train.*

THESEUS.   Go one of you, find out the forester:
For now our observation° is performed.
And since we have the vaward° of the day,
My love shall hear the music of my hounds.
Uncouple° in the western valley, let them go:
Dispatch I say, and find the forester.   [*Exit an* ATTENDANT.]
We will, fair queen, up to the mountain's top,
And mark the musical confusion

72 *Dian's bud . . . flower*: (Diana's bud counteracts the effects of love-in-idleness, the pansy).
80–81 *strike . . . sense*: make these five (the lovers and Bottom) sleep more soundly.
84 stage direction *still*: continuously.   88 *triumphantly*: in celebration.   94 *sad*: serious.
101 stage direction *wind*: blow, sound.   103 *observation*: observance of the May Day
rites.   104 *vaward*: vanguard, earliest part.   106 *Uncouple*: unleash (the dogs).

Of hounds and echo in conjunction.   110
HIPPOLYTA.   I was with Hercules and Cadmus° once,
  When in a wood of Crete they bayed the bear,°
  With hounds of Sparta:° never did I hear
  Such gallant chiding. For besides the groves,
  The skies, the fountains, every region near   115
  Seemed all one mutual cry. I never heard
  So musical a discord, such sweet thunder.
THESEUS.   My hounds are bred out of the Spartan kind:
  So flewed, so sanded:° and their heads are hung
  With ears that sweep away the morning dew,   120
  Crook-kneed, and dewlapped° like Thessalian bulls:
  Slow in pursuit; but matched in mouth like bells,
  Each under each.° A cry° more tuneable
  Was never holloa'd to, nor cheered with horn,
  In Crete, in Sparta, nor in Thessaly.   125
  Judge when you hear. But soft.° What nymphs are these?
EGEUS.   My lord, this is my daughter here asleep,
  And this Lysander, this Demetrius is,
  This Helena, old Nedar's Helena.
  I wonder of their being here together.   130
THESEUS.   No doubt they rose up early to observe
  The rite of May: and hearing our intent,
  Came here in grace° of our solemnity.
  But speak Egeus, is not this the day
  That Hermia should give answer of her choice?   135
EGEUS.   It is, my lord.
THESEUS.   Go bid the huntsmen wake them with their horns.

Shout within: wind horns. They all start up.

  Good morrow, friends. Saint Valentine is past.
  Begin these wood-birds but to couple now?°
LYSANDER.   Pardon, my lord.   *[They kneel.]*
THESEUS.   I pray you all, stand up.   140
  I know you two are rival enemies.
  How comes this gentle concord in the world,
  That hatred is so far from jealousy,°
  To sleep by hate,° and fear no enmity?
LYSANDER.   My lord, I shall reply amazedly,   145
  Half sleep, half waking. But as yet, I swear,
  I cannot truly say how I came here.

---

111 *Cadmus*: (mythical builder of Thebes).   112 *bayed the bear*: brought the bear to bay,
to its last stand.   113 *hounds of Sparta*: (a breed famous for their swiftness and quick
scent).   119 *flewed, so sanded*: with hanging cheeks, so sand-colored.   121 *dewlapped*: with
skin hanging from the chin.   122–123 *matched . . . each*: with each voice matched for
harmony with the next in pitch, like bells in a chime.   123 *cry*: pack of dogs.   126 *soft*:
wait.   133 *grace*: honor.   138–139 *Saint . . . now*: (birds traditionally chose their mates
on St. Valentine's Day).   143 *jealousy*: suspicion.   144 *hate*: one it hates.

But as I think—for truly would I speak,
And now I do bethink me, so it is—
I came with Hermia hither. Our intent   15
Was to be gone from Athens, where we might,
Without° the peril of the Athenian law—
EGEUS.   Enough, enough, my lord: you have enough.
  I beg the law, the law, upon his head:
  They would have stol'n away, they would, Demetrius,   15
  Thereby to have defeated you and me:
  You of your wife, and me of my consent:
  Of my consent that she should be your wife.
DEMETRIUS.   My lord, fair Helen told me of their stealth,
  Of this their purpose hither, to this wood,   16
  And I in fury hither followed them;
  Fair Helena in fancy° following me.
  But my good lord, I wot not by what power
  (But by some power it is) my love to Hermia,
  Melted as the snow, seems to me now   16
  As the remembrance of an idle gaud,°
  Which in my childhood I did dote upon:
  And all the faith, the virtue of my heart,
  The object and the pleasure of mine eye,
  Is only Helena. To her, my lord,   17
  Was I betrothed ere I saw Hermia:
  But like a sickness,° did I loathe this food.
  But as in health, come° to my natural taste,
  Now I do wish it, love it, long for it,
  And will for evermore be true to it.   17
THESEUS.   Fair lovers, you are fortunately met.
  Of this discourse we more will hear anon.
  Egeus, I will overbear your will:
  For in the temple, by and by,° with us,
  These couples shall eternally be knit.   18
  And for the morning now is something worn,°
  Our purposed hunting shall be set aside.
  Away with us to Athens. Three and three,
  We'll hold a feast in great solemnity.
  Come Hippolyta.   18

                    Exeunt DUKE [HIPPOLYTA, EGEUS,] *and* LORDS.

DEMETRIUS.   These things seem shall and undistinguishable,
  Like far-off mountains turned into clouds.
HERMIA.   Methinks I see these things with parted° eye,

152 *Without*: beyond.   162 *in fancy*: out of doting love.   166 *idle gaud*: trifling
toy.   172 *sickness*: sick person.   173 *come*: i.e., back.   179 *by and by*:
immediately.   181 *something worn*: somewhat worn on.   188 *parted*: divided (each eye
seeing a separate image).

When everything seems double.
HELENA.   So methinks:
  And I have found Demetrius, like a jewel,   190
  Mine own, and not mine own.°
DEMETRIUS.   Are you sure
  That we are awake? It seems to me,
  That yet we sleep, we dream. Do not you think
  The duke was here, and bid us follow him?
HERMIA. Yea, and my father.
HELENA.   And Hippolyta.   195
LYSANDER. And he did bid us follow to the temple.
DEMETRIUS. Why then, we are awake: let's follow him,
  And by the way let us recount our dreams.   *Exeunt Lovers.*
BOTTOM. (*Wakes.*) When my cue comes, call me, and I will answer.
  My next is "Most fair Pyramus." Hey ho. Peter Quince?   200
  Flute the bellows-mender? Snout the tinker? Starveling?
  God's my life! Stol'n hence, and left me asleep? I have
  had a most rare vision. I have had a dream, past the wit
  of man to say what dream it was. Man is but an ass, if he
  go about° to expound this dream. Methought I was—   205
  there is no man can tell what. Methought I was, and
  methought I had—but man is but a patched fool,° if he
  will offer to say what methought I had. The eye of man
  hath not heard, the ear of man hath not seen, man's hand is
  not able to taste, his tongue to conceive, nor his   210
  heart to report, what my dream was. I will get Peter
  Quince to write a ballad of this dream: it shall be called
  Bottom's Dream; because it hath no bottom: and I
  will sing it in the latter end of our play, before the duke.
  Peradventure, to make it the more gracious, I shall sing   215
  it at her° death.
                                                                       Exit.

[Scene 2. Athens, Quince's house]

Enter QUINCE, FLUTE, SNOUT, and STARVELING.

QUINCE. Have you sent to Bottom's house? Is he come home yet?
STARVELING. He cannot be heard of. Out of doubt he is transported.°
FLUTE. If he come not, then the play is marred. It goes not forward,
  doth it?
QUINCE. It is not possible. You have not a man in all Athens able   5
  to discharge° Pyramus but he.
FLUTE. No, he hath simply the best wit of any handicraft man
  in Athens.

190–191 *like . . . own*: like a person who finds a jewel: the finder is the owner, but insecurely
so.   205 *go about*: attempt.   207 *patched fool*: fool dressed in motley.   216 *her*:
Thisby's.   2 *transported*: carried away (by spirits).   6 *discharge*: portray.

QUINCE.   Yea, and the best person too, and he is a very paramour
for a sweet voice.
FLUTE.   You must say "paragon." A paramour is (God bless us)
a thing of naught.°

Enter SNUG THE JOINER.

SNUG.   Masters, the duke is coming from the temple, and there
is two or three lords and ladies more married. If our
sport had gone forward, we had all been made men.°
FLUTE.   O sweet bully Bottom. Thus hath he lost sixpence a day°
during his life: he could not have 'scaped sixpence a day.
And the duke had not given him sixpence a day for playing
Pyramus, I'll be hanged. He would have deserved it.
Sixpence a day in Pyramus, or nothing.

Enter BOTTOM.

BOTTOM.   Where are these lads? Where are these hearts?
QUINCE.   Bottom! O most courageous° day! O most happy hour!
BOTTOM.   Masters, I am to discourse wonders: but ask me not what.
For if I tell you, I am not true Athenian. I will tell you
everything, right as it fell out.
QUINCE.   Let us hear, sweet Bottom.
BOTTOM.   Not a word of me. All that I will tell you is, that the
duke hath dined. Get your apparel together, good
strings to your beards, new ribbands to your pumps, meet
presently° at the palace, every man look o'er his part: for
the short and the long is, our play is preferred.° In any
case, let Thisby have clean linen: and let not him that
plays the lion pare his nails, for they shall hang out for
the lion's claws. And most dear actors, eat no onions nor
garlic, for we are to utter sweet breath: and I do not
doubt but to hear them say it is a sweet comedy. No more
words: away, go away.   *Exeunt.*

ACT 5

[*Scene 1. The palace of Theseus*]

Enter THESEUS, HIPPOLYTA, *and* PHILOSTRATE, *and his* LORDS.

Hippolyta.   'Tis strange, my Theseus, that these lovers speak of.
THESEUS.   More strange than true. I never may believe
These antick° fables, nor these fairy toys.°
Lovers and madmen have such seething brains,

12 *of naught*: wicked, naughty.   15 *made men*: men made rich.   16 *sixpence a day*: i.e.,
as a pension.   22 *courageous*: (he may mean "auspicious").   30 *presently*:
immediately.   31 *preferred*: recommended (for presentation).   3 *antick*: fantastic.
fairy toys: trivial fairy stories.

Such shaping fantasies,° that apprehend   5
More than cool reason ever comprehends.
The lunatic, the lover, and the poet,
Are of imagination all compact.°
One sees more devils than vast hell can hold:
That is the madman. The lover, all as frantic,   10
Sees Helen's beauty in a brow of Egypt.°
The poet's eye, in a fine frenzy rolling,
Doth glance from heaven to earth, from earth to heaven.
And as imagination bodies forth
The forms of things unknown, the poet's pen   15
Turns them to shapes, and gives to airy nothing,
A local habitation and a name.
Such tricks hath strong imagination,
That if it would but apprehend some joy,
It comprehends° some bringer of that joy.   20
Or in the night, imagining some fear,
How easy is a bush supposed a bear.

HIPPOLYTA.   But all the story of the night told over,
And all their minds transfigured so together,
More witnesseth than fancy's images,°   25
And grows to something of great constancy:°
But howsoever, strange and admirable.°

Enter LOVERS: LYSANDER, DEMETRIUS, HERMIA, *and* HELENA.

THESEUS.   Here come the lovers, full of joy and mirth.
Joy, gentle friends, joy and fresh days of love
Accompany your hearts.

LYSANDER.   More° than to us   30
Wait in your royal walks, your board, your bed.

THESEUS.   Come now, what masques,° what dances shall we have,
To wear away this long age of three hours
Between our after-supper° and bed-time?
Where is our usual manager of mirth?   35
What revels are in hand? Is there no play,
To ease the anguish of a torturing hour?
Call Philostrate.

PHILOSTRATE.   Here, mighty Theseus.

THESEUS.   Say, what abridgment° have you for this evening?
What masque,° what music? How shall we beguile   40
The lazy time, if not with some delight?

---

5 *fantasies*: imaginations.   8 *of . . . compact*: totally composed of imagination.   11 *a brow
of Egypt*: the swarthy face of a gypsy (believed to come from Egypt).   20 *comprehends*:
includes.   25 *More . . . images*: testifies that it is more than just imagination.
26 *constancy*: certainty.   27 *admirable*: to be wondered at.   30 *More*: even more (joy and
love).   32,40 *masques*: lavish courtly entertainments combining song and dance.
34 *after-supper*: late supper.   39 *abridgment*: either (a) diversion to
make the hours seem shorter or (b) short entertainment.

PHILOSTRATE.   There is a brief° how many sports are ripe:°
   Make choice of which your highness will see first.

[Gives a paper.]

THESEUS.   "The battle with the Centaurs, to be sung
   By an Athenian eunuch to the harp."   45
   We'll none of that. That have I told my love
   In glory of my kinsman Hercules.
   "The riot of the tipsy Bacchanals,
   Tearing the Thracian singer in their rage."°
   That is an old device: and it was played   50
   When I from Thebes came last a conqueror.
   "The thrice three Muses mourning for the death
   Of Learning, late deceased in beggary."
   That is some satire keen and critical,
   Not sorting with° a nuptial ceremony.   55
   "A tedious brief scene of young Pyramus
   And his love Thisby; very tragical mirth."
   Merry and tragical? tedious and brief?
   That is hot ice and wondrous strange snow.
   How shall we find the concord of this discord?   60
PHILOSTRATE.   A play there is, my lord, some ten words long,
   Which is as brief as I have known a play;
   But by ten words, my lord, it is too long,
   Which makes it tedious: for in all the play
   There is not one word apt, one player fitted.°   65
   And tragical, my noble lord, it is:
   For Pyramus therein doth kill himself.
   Which when I saw rehearsed, I must confess,
   Made mine eyes water; but more merry tears
   The passion of loud laughter never shed.   70
THESEUS.   What are they that do play it?
PHILOSTRATE.   Hard-handed men, that work in Athens here,
   Which never laboured in their minds till now:
   And now have toiled their unbreathed° memories
   With this same play, against° your nuptial.   75
THESEUS.   And we will hear it.
PHILOSTRATE.   No, my noble lord,
   It is not for you. I have heard it over,
   And it is nothing, nothing in the world;
   Unless you can find sport in their intents,
   Extremely stretched and conned° with cruel pain.   80
   To do your service.

42 *brief*: list.   *ripe*: ready.   48–49 *riot . . . rage*: (The singer Orpheus of Thrace was torn limb from limb by the Maenads, frenzied female priests of Bacchus).   55 *sorting with*: befitting.   65 *fitted*: (well) cast.   74 *unbreathed*: unpracticed, unexercised.   75 *against*: in preparation for.   80 *stretched and conned*: strained and memorized.

THESEUS.   I will hear that play.
　　For never anything can be amiss,
　　When simpleness and duty tender° it.
　　Go bring them in, and take your places, ladies.　　　　　[*Exit PHILOSTRATE*.]
HIPPOLYTA. I love not to see wretchedness o'ercharged,°　　　　　　　　　　85
　　And duty in his service perishing.
THESEUS. Why, gentle sweet, you shall see no such thing.
HIPPOLYTA. He says they can do nothing in this kind.°
THESEUS. The kinder we, to give them thanks for nothing.
　　Our sport shall be to take what they mistake.　　　　　　　　　　　90
　　And what poor duty cannot do, noble respect
　　Takes it in might, not merit.°
　　Where I have come, great clerks° have purposèd
　　To greet me with premeditated welcomes;
　　Where I have seen them shiver and look pale,　　　　　　　　　　　95
　　Make periods in the midst of sentences,
　　Throttle° their practised accent in their fears,
　　And in conclusion dumbly have broke off,
　　Not paying me a welcome. Trust me, sweet,
　　Out of this silence yet I picked a welcome:　　　　　　　　　　　100
　　And in the modesty of fearful duty°
　　I read as much as from the rattling tongue
　　Of saucy and audacious eloquence.
　　Love, therefore, and tongue-tied simplicity,
　　In° least, speak most, to my capacity.°　　　　　　　　　　　　105

[*Enter PHILOSTRATE*.]

PHILOSTRATE. So please your grace, the Prologue is addressed.°
THESEUS. Let him approach.

Flourish trumpets. Enter the PROLOGUE [*QUINCE*].

PROLOGUE. If we offend, it is with our good will.
　　　　That you should think, we come not to offend,
　　　　But with good will. To show our simple skill,　　　　　　　　110
　　　　That is the true beginning of our end.
　　　　Consider then, we come but in despite.°
　　　　　We do not come, as minding to content you,
　　　　Our true intent is. All for your delight,
　　　　　We are not here. That you should here repent you,　　　　　115
　　　　The actors are at hand: and by their show,
　　　　You shall know all, that you are like to know.°

83 *tender*: offer.　　85 *wretchedness o'ercharged*: poor fellows taxing themselves too
much.　　88 *in this kind*: of this sort.　　91–92 *noble . . . merit*: a noble nature considers
the sincerity of effort rather than the skill of execution.　　93 *clerks*: scholars.　　97 *Throttle*:
choke on.　　101 *fearful duty*: subjects whose devotions gave them stage fright.　　105 *In*:
i.e., saying.　　*capacity*: way of thinking.　　106 *addressed*: ready.　　108–117 *If . . . know*:
(Quince's blunders in punctuation exactly reverse the meaning).　　112 *despite*: malice.

THESEUS.   This fellow doth not stand upon points.°
LYSANDER.   He hath rid his prologue like a rough colt: he knows
    not the stop.° A good moral my lord: it is not enough   12
    to speak; but to speak true.
HIPPOLYTA.   Indeed he hath played on his prologue like a child on a
    recorder:° a sound, but not in government.°
THESEUS.   His speech was like a tangled chain: nothing impaired, but
    all disordered. Who is next?   12

Enter PYRAMUS *and* THISBY, WALL, MOONSHINE, *and* LION.

PROLOGUE.   Gentles, perchance you wonder at this show,
        But wonder on, till truth make all things plain.
    This man is Pyramus, if you would know:
        This beauteous lady, Thisby is certain.
    This man, with lime and rough-cast,° doth present   130
        Wall, that vile wall which did these lovers sunder:
    And through Wall's chink, poor souls, they are content
        To whisper. At the which, let no man wonder.
    This man, with lantern, dog, and bush of thorn,
        Presenteth Moonshine. For if you will know,   135
    By moonshine did these lovers think no scorn
        To meet at Ninus' tomb, there, there to woo:
    This grisly beast (which Lion hight° by name)
        The trusty Thisby, coming first by night,
    Did scare away, or rather did affright: 140
        And as she fled, her mantle she did fall:°
    Which Lion vile with bloody mouth did stain.
        Anon comes Pyramus, sweet youth and tall,°
    And finds his trusty Thisby's mantle slain:
        Whereat, with blade, with bloody blameful blade,   145
    He bravely broached° his boiling bloody breast.
        And Thisby, tarrying in mulberry shade,
    His dagger drew, and died. For all the rest,
        Let Lion, Moonshine, Wall, and lovers twain,
    At large° discourse, while here they do remain.   150
THESEUS.   I wonder if the lion be to speak.
DEMETRIUS.   No wonder, my lord: one lion may, when many asses do.
            Exeunt [PROLOGUE, PYRAMUS,] LION, THISBY, MOONSHINE.
WALL.   In this same interlude° it doth befall
    That I, one Snout by name, present a wall:
    And such a wall, as I would have you think,   155
    That had in it a crannied hole or chink:

118 *stand upon points*: (1) pay attention to punctuation (2) bother about the niceties (of
expression).   120 *stop*: (1) halt (2) period.   123 *recorder*: flutelike wind instrument.
in government: well managed.   130 *rough-cast*: rough plaster made of lime and gravel.
138 *hight*: is called.   141 *fall*: let fall.   143 *tall*: brave.   146 *broached*: opened
(Shakespeare parodies the overuse of alliteration in the earlier bombastic Elizabethan
plays).   150 *At large*: in full.   153 *interlude*: short play.

Through which the lovers, Pyramus and Thisby,
Did whisper often, very secretly.
This loam, this rough-cast, and this stone doth show
That I am that same wall: the truth is so. 160
And this the cranny is, right and sinister,°
Through which the fearful lovers are to whisper.
THESEUS. Would you desire lime and hair to speak better?
DEMETRIUS. It is the wittiest° partition° that ever I heard discourse,
    my lord. 165

Enter PYRAMUS.

THESEUS. Pyramus draws near the wall: silence.
PYRAMUS. O grim-looked night, O night with hue so black,
        O night, which ever art when day is not:
        O night, O night, alack, alack, alack,
        I fear my Thisby's promise is forgot. 170
    And thou O wall, O sweet, O lovely wall,
        That stand'st between her father's ground and mine,
    Thou wall, O wall, O sweet and lovely wall,
        Show me thy chink, to blink through with mine eyne.°

            [WALL holds up his fingers.]

    Thanks, courteous wall. Jove shield thee well for this. 175
        But what see I? No Thisby do I see.
    O wicked wall, through whom I see no bliss,
        Cursed be thy stones for thus deceiving me.
THESEUS. The wall methinks being sensible,° should curse again.°
PYRAMUS. No in truth sir, he should not. "Deceiving me" is 180
    Thisby's cue: she is to enter now, and I am to spy her
    through the wall. You shall see it will fall pat° as I told
    you: yonder she comes.

Enter THISBY.

THISBY. O Wall, full often hast thou heard my moans,
        For parting my fair Pyramus and me. 185
    My cherry lips have often kissed thy stones;
        Thy stones with lime and hair knit up in thee.
PYRAMUS. I see a voice: now will I to the chink,
        To spy and I can hear my Thisby's face.
    Thisby? 190
THISBY. My love thou art, my love I think.
PYRAMUS. Think what thou wilt, I am thy lover's grace:
        And, like Limander,° am I trusty still.

---

161 *right and sinister*: from right to left (he probably uses the fingers of his right and left
hands to form the cranny). 164 *wittiest*: most intelligent. *partition*: (1) wall (2) section
of a learned book or speech. 174 *eyne*: eyes. 179 *sensible*: capable of feelings and
perception. *again*: back. 182 *pat*: exactly. 193 *Limander*: (he means "Leander").

THISBY.   And I like Helen,° till the Fates me kill.

PYRAMUS.   Not Shafalus to Procrus,° was so true.   195

THISBY.   As Shafalus to Procrus, I to you.

PYRAMUS.   O kiss me through the hole of this vile wall.

THISBY.   I kiss the wall's hole, not your lips at all.

PYRAMUS.   Wilt thou at Ninny's° tomb meet me straightway?

THISBY.   Tide° life, tide death, I come without delay.   200

[Exeunt PYRAMUS and THISBY.]

WALL.   Thus have I, Wall, my part dischargèd so;

And being done, thus Wall away doth go.   *Exit.*

THESEUS.   Now is the mural° down between the two neighbours.

DEMETRIUS.   No remedy my lord, when walls are so wilful to hear
without warning.°   205

HIPPOLYTA.   This is the silliest stuff that ever I heard.

THESEUS.   The best in this kind are but shadows:° and the worst are
no worse, if imagination amend them.

HIPPOLYTA.   It must be your imagination then, and noth theirs.

THESEUS.   If we imagine no worse of them than they of themselves,   210
they may pass for excellent men. Here come two noble
beasts in, a man and a lion.

Enter LION and MOONSHINE.

LION.   You ladies, you, whose gentle hearts do fear
The smallest monstrous mouse that creeps on floor,
May now perchance both quake and tremble here,   215
When lion rough in wildest rage doth roar.
Then know that I, as Snug the joiner am
A lion fell,° nor else no lion's dam:°
For if I should as lion come in strife
Into this place, 'twere pity on my life.   220

THESEUS.   A very gentle beast, and of a good conscience.

DEMETRIUS.   The very best at a beast,° my lord, that e'er I saw.

LYSANDER.   This lion is a very fox for his valour.

THESEUS.   True: and a goose for his discretion.

DEMETRIUS.   Not so my lord: for his valour cannot carry his discretion,   225
and the fox carries the goose.

THESEUS.   His discretion, I am sure, cannot carry his valour: for the
goose carries not the fox. It is well: leave it to his discretion,
and let us listen to the moon.

MOONSHINE.   This lanthorn° doth the hornèd moon present—   230

DEMETRIUS.   He should have worn the horns on his head.°

194 *Helen*: (he means "Hero").   195 *Shafalus to Procrus*: (he means "Cephalus" and
"Procis" [see above, 3. 2. 389 note]).   199 *Ninny*: fool (he means "Ninus").   200 *Tide*:
come, betide.   203 *mural*: wall.   205 *without warning*: either (a) without warning the
parents or (b) unexpectedly.   207 *in . . . shadows*: of this sort are only plays (or only
actors).   218 *fell*: fierce. *nor . . . dam*: and not a lioness.   222 *best, beast*: (pronounced
similarly).   230 *lanthorn*: lantern (once made of horn).   230–231 *horned . . . head*:
(referring to the cuckold or deceived husband, who supposedly grew horns).

THESEUS. He is no crescent, and his horns are invisible within the
　circumference.

MOONSHINE. This lanthorn doth the hornèd moon present,
　　Myself, the man i' th' moon do seem to be.   235

THESEUS. This is the greatest error of all the rest; the man should
　be put into the lanthorn. How is it else the man i' th'
　moon?

DEMETRIUS. He dares not come there for the candle; for you see, it
　is already in snuff.°   240

HIPPOLYTA. I am aweary of this moon. Would he would change.

THESEUS. It appears, by his small light of discretion, that he is in
　the wane: but yet in courtesy, in all reason, we must stay°
　the time.

LYSANDER. Proceed, Moon.   245

MOONSHINE. All that I have to say, is to tell you that the lanthorn is
　the moon, I the man i' th' moon, this thornbush my
　thornbush, and this dog my dog.

DEMETRIUS. Why, all these should be in the lanthorn: for all these are
　in the moon. But silence: here comes Thisby.   250

Enter THISBY.

THISBY. This is old Ninny's tomb. Where is my love?

LION. Oh!   *The LION roars. THISBY runs off.*

DEMETRIUS. Well roared, Lion.

THESEUS. Well run, Thisby.

HIPPOLYTA. Well shone, Moon. Truly, the moon shines with a good   255
　grace.

[The LION shakes THISBY's mantle.]

THESEUS. Well moused,° Lion.

DEMETRIUS. And then came Pyramus.

Enter PYRAMUS. [Exit LION.]

LYSANDER. And so the lion vanished.

PYRAMUS. Sweet moon, I thank thee for thy sunny beams,   260
　　I thank thee, moon, for shining now so bright.
　For by thy gracious, golden, glittering gleams,
　　I trust to take of truest Thisby sight.
　　　But stay: O spite!
　　　But mark, poor knight,   265
　What dreadful dole° is here?
　　　Eyes, do you see!
　　　How can it be!
　　O dainty duck, O dear!
　　　Thy mantle good,   270

240 *in snuff*: (1) in need of snuffing (having a long, burnt-out wick or snuff) (2) in a
temper.   243 *stay*: await.   257 *moused*: shaken, as a cat shakes a mouse.   266 *dole*:
grief.

What, stained with blood?
Approach, ye Furies° fell:
  O Fates!° come, come:
  Cut thread and thrum.°
  Quail,° crush, conclude, and quell.°   275

THESEUS. This passion, and the death of a dear friend, would go
  near to make a man look sad.
HIPPOLYTA. Beshrew° my heart, but I pity the man.
PYRAMUS. O wherefore Nature, didst thou lions frame?
  Since lion vile hath here deflowered my dear.   280
  Which is—no, no—which was the fairest dame
    That lived, that loved, that liked, that looked with cheer.
  Come tears, confound:
    Out sword, and wound
    The pap° of Pyramus: 285
    Ay, that left pap,
    Where heart doth hop.   [*Stabs himself.*]
  Thus die I, thus, thus, thus.
    Now am I dead,
    Now am I fled,   290
  My soul is in the sky.
    Tongue lose thy light,
    Moon° take thy flight,   [*Exit* MOONSHINE.]
    Now die, die, die, die, die.   [*Dies.*]
DEMETRIUS. No die,° but an ace° for him. For he is but one.   295
LYSANDER. Less than an ace, man. For he is dead, he is nothing.
THESEUS. With the help of a surgeon, he might yet recover, and
  prove an ass.
HIPPOLYTA. How chance Moonshine is gone before Thisby comes
  back and finds her lover?   300

Enter THISBY.

THESEUS. She will find him by starlight. Here she comes, and her
  passion ends the play.
HIPPOLYTA. Methinks she should not use a long one for such a
  Pyramus: I hope she will be brief.
DEMETRIUS. A mote will turn the balance, which Pyramus, which   305
  Thisby, is the better: he for a man, God warr'nt° us;
  she for a woman, God bless us.
LYSANDER. She hath spied him already with those sweet eyes.
DEMETRIUS. And thus she means,° videlicet°—

---

272 *Furies*: classical spirits of the underworld who avenged murder.   273 *Fates*: three sisters
who spun the thread of human destiny, which at will was cut with a shears.   274 *thrum*:
fringelike end of the warp in weaving.   275 *Quail*: subdue.   *quell*: kill.   278 *Beshrew*:
curse (meant lightly).   285 *pap*: breast.   292–293 *Tongue . . . Moon*: (he reverses the
two subjects).   295 *die*: (singular of "dice").   *ace*: a throw of one at dice.   306 *warr'nt*:
warrant, protect.   309 *means*: laments.   *videlicet*: namely.

THISBY.   Asleep my love?   310
               What, dead, my dove?
               O Pyramus, arise,
                  Speak, speak. Quite dumb?
                  Dead, dead? A tomb
               Must cover thy sweet eyes.   315
                  These lily lips,
                  This cherry nose,
               These yellow cowslip° cheeks,
                  Are gone, are gone:
                  Lovers, make moan: 320
               His eyes were green as leeks.
                  O Sisters Three,°
                  Come, come to me,
               With hands as pale as milk,
                  Lay them in gore,   325
                  Since you have shore
               With shears his thread of silk.
                  Tongue, not a word:
                  Come trusty sword,
               Come blade, my breast imbrue:°   [*Stabs herself.*]   330
            And farewell friends:
            Thus Thisby ends:
            Adieu, adieu, adieu.   [*Dies.*]
THESEUS.   Moonshine and Lion are left to bury the dead.
DEMETRIUS. Ay, and Wall too.   335
BOTTOM.   [*Starts up.*] No, I assure you, the wall is down that parted
               their fathers. Will it please you to see the Epilogue, or
               to hear a Bergomask° dance between two of our company?
THESEUS.   No epilogue, I pray you; for your play needs no excuse.
               Never excuse: for when the players are all dead, there   340
               need none to be blamed. Marry, if he that writ it had
               played Pyramus and hanged himself in Thisby's garter,
               it would have been a fine tragedy: and so it is truly, and
               very notably discharged. But come, your Bergomask:
               let your Epilogue alone.   [*A dance.*]   345
            The iron tongue° of midnight hath told° twelve.
            Lovers, to bed, 'tis almost fairy time.°
            I fear we shall outsleep the coming morn,
            As much as we this night have overwatched.
            This palpable gross° play hath well beguiled   350
            The heavy gait of night. Sweet friends, to bed.
            A fortnight hold we this solemnity,
            In nightly revels, and new jollity.   *Exeunt.*

318 *cowslip*: yellow primrose.   322 *Sisters Three*: the Fates.   330 *imbrue*: stain with
gore.   338 *Bergomask*: exaggerated country dance.   346 *iron tongue*: i.e., of the
bell.   *told*: counted, tolled.   347 *fairy time*: (from midnight to daybreak).   350 *palpable
gross*: obvious and crude.

Enter PUCK [*with a broom*].

PUCK. Now the hungry lion roars,
  And the wolf behowls the moon;
 Whilst the heavy° ploughman snores,   355
  All with weary task fordone.°
 Now the wasted brands° do glow,
  Whilst the screech-owl, screeching loud,
 Puts the wretch that lies in woe°   360
  In remembrance of a shroud.
 Now it is the time of night,
  That the graves, all gaping wide,
 Every one lets forth his sprite,°
  In the church-way paths to glide.   365
 And we fairies, that do run
  By the triple Hecate's° team,°
 From the presence of the sun,
  Following darkness like a dream,
 Now are frolic:° not a mouse   370
 Shall disturb this hallowed house.
 I am sent with broom before,
 To sweep the dust° behind° the door.

Enter KING *and* QUEEN OF FAIRIES, *with all their train.*

OBERON. Through the house give glimmering light,
  By the dead and drowsy fire,   375
  Every elf and fairy sprite,
   Hop as light as bird from brier,
  And this ditty after me,
   Sing, and dance it trippingly.
TITANIA. First rehearse your song by rote,   380
  To each word a warbling note.
  Hand in hand, with fairy grace,
  Will we sing and bless this place.   [*Song and dance.*]
OBERON. Now, until the break of day,
  Through this house each fairy stray.   385
  To the best bride-bed will we,
  Which by us shall blessèd be:
  And the issue° there create,°
  Ever shall be fortunate:
  So shall all the couples three   390
  Ever true in loving be:
  And the blots of Nature's hand°
  Shall not in their issue° stand.

356 *heavy*: sleepy. 357 *fordone*: worn out, "done in." 358 *wasted brands*: burnt
logs. 360 *wretch . . . woe*: sick person. 364 *sprite*: spirit, ghost. 367 *triple Hecate*:
the moon goddess, identified as Cynthia in heaven, Diana on earth, and Hecate in hell.
team: dragons that pull the chariot of the night moon. 370 *frolic*: frolicsome.
373 *To sweep the dust*: (Puck often helped with household chores). *behind*: from behind.
388,393 *issue*: children. 388 *create*: created. 392 *blots . . . hand*: birth defects.

Never mole, harelip, nor scar,
Nor mark prodigious,° such as are   395
Despisèd in nativity,
Shall upon their children be.
With this field-dew consecrate.
Every fairy take his gait,°
And each several° chamber bless,   400
Through this palace, with sweet peace;
And the owner of it blest,
Ever shall in safety rest.
Trip away: make no stay:
Meet me all by break of day.   *Exeunt [all but PUCK].*   405
PUCK. If we shadows have offended,
Think but this, and all is mended,
That you have but slumbered here,
While these visions did appear.
And this weak and idle° theme,   410
No more yielding but° a dream,
Gentles, do not reprehend.
If you pardon, we will mend.°
And as I am an honest Puck,
If we have unearnèd luck,   415
Now to scape the serpent's tongue,°
We will make amends, ere long:
Else the Puck a liar call.
So, good night unto you all.
Give me your hands,° if we be friends: 420
And Robin shall restore amends.°   *[Exit.]*

395 *mark prodigious:* unnatural birthmark.   399 *take his gait:* proceed.   400 *several:*
separate.   410 *idle:* foolish.   411 *No . . . but:* yielding nothing more than.
413 *mend:* improve.   416 *serpent's tongue:* hissing of the audience.   420 *hands:*
applause.   421 *restore amends:* do better in the future.

QUESTIONS

Act 1

1. Describe the relationship between Theseus and Hippolyta. What does each
    of them represent? How does Shakespeare show us that they have different
    attitudes toward their marriage?
2. Characterize Hermia and Lysander. What blocks their relationship? How do
    they plan to circumvent these obstructions?
3. What are Helen's feelings about herself? About Hermia? About Demetrius?
    How might you account for her self-image?
4. Why have the mechanicals gathered at Quince's house? How does Shake-
    speare show us that Bottom is eager, conceited, ill-educated, and energetic?

Act 2

5. What is Puck's job? What do you find out about his personality, habits, and pastimes in his first conversation?

6. Why are Titania and Oberon fighting with each other, and what are the specific consequences of their conflict?

7. What does Oberon plan to do to Titania? Why? What is love-in-idleness? What power does it have? What does it symbolize?

8. Why are Demetrius and Helena in the woods? What does Oberon decide to do to them? What error occurs? What happens to Lysander when Helena awakens him?

Act 3

9. How and why does Puck change Bottom? How is this transformation appropriate? What happens when Bottom awakens Titania? Why?

10. What does Oberon decide to do when he realizes that Puck has made a mistake? What is Puck's attitude toward the confusion he has created?

11. What happens when Helena awakens Demetrius? How does this situation reverse the one that began the play? Explain Helena's reaction to the behavior of Demetrius and Lysander.

12. What real dangers (tragic potential) do the lovers face in act 3? How do Oberon and Puck deal with these dangers? What is their plan? How successful is it?

Act 4

13. Why does Oberon cure Titania of her infatuation with Bottom? How does the relationship between Oberon and Titania change? How is this change symbolized? Why is it significant?

14. How are the relationships among the four lovers straightened out? How does each explain his or her feelings? What does Theseus decide about the couples? Why is this significant?

15. What momentous event occurs offstage and is briefly reported in act 4, scene 2?

Act 5

16. Describe Pyramus and Thisby. What blocks their relationship? How do they plan to circumvent these obstructions? What happens to them?

17. What is the significance of the fairy masque (a combination of poetry, music, dance, and drama) that ends the play?

18. What does Puck's epilogue suggest about you as a reader or spectator? How does it reinforce the connections among dreaming, imagination, illusion, and drama?

TOPICS FOR WRITING AND FURTHER DISCUSSION

1. To what extent are the characters in this play conventional and representative types? What is the effect of Shakespeare's style of characterization?

2. Are any of the characters symbolic? If so, what do they symbolize? How does such symbolism reinforce the themes of the play?

3. How does Shakespeare employ language, imagery, and poetic form to define the characters in this play and differentiate among the various groups of characters?

4. This play occurs in two distinct settings or worlds—the city of Athens and the woods outside Athens. How are these worlds different? What does each represent? How and why are both worlds changed in the course of the play?

5. To what extent do the two settings—city and woods—structure the play? Where does exposition occur? Complication and catastrophe? The comic resolution? How complete is the resolution? Why is the round-trip journey from one setting to the other necessary for the lovers? The rulers? The mechanicals?

6. What are the similarities or parallels in plot and theme between *A Midsummer Night's Dream* and "Pyramus and Thisby"? To what degree are they versions of the same play with different endings? Why do you think Shakespeare included the play-within-the-play in *A Midsummer Night's Dream*?

7. In the first soliloquy of the play, Helena discusses love. What kind of love is she talking about? What are its qualities and characteristics? How far do the relationships in the play bear out her ideas about love?

8. How well do the mechanicals understand the nature of dramatic illusion? What sorts of production problems concern them? How do they solve these?

9. What ideas about drama and the ways in which audiences respond to it does *A Midsummer Night's Dream* explore?

10. Compare the play-within-a-play in *A Midsummer Night's Dream* to the one in *Hamlet*. How are the internal plays and situations similar? Different? What parallels do you see in the connections between each play-within-a-play and the larger play in which each occurs?

THE THEATER OF MOLIÈRE

The seventeenth century was the golden age of French neoclassical theater (called *neo* or *new* classical because it was based on Greek and Latin models). The period was dominated by three playwrights, the tragedians Pierre Corneille (1606–1684) and Jean Racine (1639–1699) and the comic writer Molière. The truly dominant figure of the age, however, was Louis XIV, the "Sun King," the absolute monarch of France. He and his court—a glittering social set of elegant nobles, sparkling wits, would-be wits, and aristocratic ladies- and gentlemen-in-waiting—made Paris the cultural center of France and dictated fashion to the world at large. The ruling class had a profound impact on the drama of the age; since they were the patrons of the theater, their tastes and customs were often mirrored or gently mocked in the plays. More to the point, the values of this class—wit, grace, and privilege—rest at the center of all the drama.

Molière, whose real name was Jean-Baptiste Poquelin, was the acknowledged master of comedy in this elegant and courtly age of posturing, pretense, and artifice. Born in 1622, he was educated in a Jesuit college and studied law at Orleans. In 1643, however, he shocked his family by abandoning both the law and his father's prosperous upholstering business for the theater, a life that was generally considered sinful and contemptible. He joined a company of actors called The Illustrious Theater, who established themselves in a playhouse, produced a tragedy, and promptly went bankrupt.

The acting company spent the next fourteen years touring the provinces, performing *commedia dell'arte* farces and short comic plays, many of which were written by Molière. These years on the road were Molière's real education in the theater; he gradually became a superb actor, writer, and director as he learned what makes people laugh. More important, he learned about human nature; he saw the world's virtues and vices, follies and excesses, and he gained an unerring sense of comedy.

When Molière and his company returned to Paris in 1658, they were invited to perform at the court of Louis XIV. The king was so pleased with Molière's comedy that he gave the company a theater in Paris and became Molière's supporter and protector. For the remainder of his life Molière was the total man of the theater—actor, director, company manager, and playwright.

Molière's personal life was a great deal more troubled than his life in the theater. He was plagued by ill health, and at the age of forty he began an unhappy marriage with Armande Béjart, the twenty-year-old daughter of his former mistress. Nevertheless, his creative efforts were prodigious; he wrote twenty-nine plays, ranging from broad farce to satirical comedies of manners. Some of his best-known plays are *The School for Wives* (1662), *The Misanthrope* (1666), *Tartuffe* (1669), and *The Would Be Gentleman* (1670). At the end of his life he transformed his own unhappiness, wretched marriage, and mounting illness into a three-act farce called *The Imaginary Invalid* (1673). During the fourth performance of this play, Molière suffered a tubercular hemorrhage. He struggled through the last scene, was carried home, and died three hours later.

Molière's comedies both reflect and rebel against the social and theatrical conventions of his age. The reflection is found in his sources, subjects, and awareness of the neoclassical rules of drama. The sources were Roman new comedy, French farce, and Italian *commedia dell'arte*; these taught him about comic characters, tempos, and situations. His inspirations were the manners, morals, and customs of the French aristocracy and the growing middle class around him.

The rules of neoclassical drama—which Molière ignored as often as he followed—were derived from Aristotle's *Poetics* (see pp. 1122–24) as modified by Renaissance interpreters. These rules dictated that comedy and tragedy had to be absolutely pure and unmixed, with no comic relief in tragedy and no serious disasters in comedy. They also imposed what we call the *classical unities* of time, place, and action. This meant that the action of a play was supposed to occur in a single day and a single setting. It also demanded a single plot line; double plots and subplots were against the rules. Finally, the rules demanded that "serious" plays have five acts and be written in verse. Molière freely ignored these rules in his farces. In the more serious comedies of manners, however, he proved that he could use the rules to advantage.

Molière's rebellion—perhaps innovation would be a better term—is found in his elevation of comedy to the level and seriousness of tragedy. His satiric comedies of manners, such as *The Misanthrope* and *Tartuffe*, represent the creation of a new form of dry and thoughtful comedy in which the customs and conventions of his world are examined and ridiculed. The laughter in these plays ranges from mocking to gentle, but we are always left with a great deal to think about.

There is very little action in these comedies. The characters tend to be universal types that exemplify the virtues and vices of human nature. What is new here is the thoughtful and detached perspective on the follies and excesses of humanity. Molière found that elusive point of delicate balance from which he could mock the ridiculous conventions, pretenses, habits, and morals of the same social classes that made up his audiences. The mainspring of Molière's satiric comedy is character; the problems and conflicts in his plays grow directly out of the eccentricities and excesses of his characters. And he drew these figures from life, from the posturing of the aristocracy and the pretensions of the middle-class social climbers who filled his playhouse.

The theaters in which Molière's plays were produced were not much different from the older theaters we might find in New York or Chicago today. The auditorium, which held about six hundred spectators, was a long rectangle with galleries or private boxes along each side and a stage across one end. The stage was separated from the audience by a *proscenium arch* that stood in front of the scenery and created a kind of picture-frame through which the spectators watched the action.

The stage was illuminated by footlights and large chandeliers containing either candles or oil lamps. Although the scenery could be lavish, Molière favored sparse sets and few props. The actors and actresses (women were never excluded from the French stage) wore contemporary costumes.

Thus, the aristocratic characters in *The Misanthrope*, for example, would have worn the same elegant clothing and wigs that were fashionable at court and in the private boxes at the theater. This convention of contemporary costumes made Molière's satires all the more effective; since his actors and actresses were dressed exactly like the social types being mocked, the plays became mirrors that selectively reflected the world outside the theater.

MOLIÈRE, *THE MISANTHROPE*

The Misanthrope, now considered Molière's comic masterpiece, was only partly successful when first produced in Paris in 1666; it touched too close to home for the upper-class audience, and it gave them too much to consider and too little to laugh at. The play is a satiric comedy of manners and character that deals seriously with questions of custom, behavior, and morality in the social world.

The plot of *The Misanthrope* is slight; it contains little action and few conventional comic situations. The one central comic situation is also the central relationship in the play—a man excessively devoted to honesty and sincerity is in love (or thinks that he is) with a coquettish flirt. The plot develops out of this relationship and the protagonist's ongoing battle against social convention. As the play opens, Alceste rails against the insincerity of society and seeks an explanation for Célimène's behavior. This explanation and the revelation of Célimène's character are delayed until the last act.

The plot thus maintains vestiges of the new comic pattern; the relationship between Alceste and Célimène is blocked. Here, however, Alceste himself is one of the blocking agents; he will tolerate neither Célimène's world nor her commitment to it. The comic resolution of the play is thus very unconventional. When Alceste realizes that he cannot have Célimène on his terms, he decides that he will not have her on hers, and the hero and heroine go their separate ways.

The great strengths of *The Misanthrope* are its characters; the play is a psychological study that explores the ways in which people choose to behave in society. The four central characters are conventional comic figures who are nevertheless extensively developed in the course of the play. Each embodies a choice about convention and morality. Alceste advocates absolute honesty and brutal sincerity at the expense of civility and grace; he rejects all social conventions and modes of behavior that involve flattery, hypocrisy, or even politeness. Philinte seems at first to be a reasonable counterpoint to Alceste; although he claims to realize that society is corrupt, he plays by all the rules, tolerating human folly and flattering people to keep things rolling along. Eliante is a moderate compromise, polite but honest, tolerant but straightforward in matters of love. Célimène is the consummate socialite—young, beautiful, rich, well-born, graceful, sophisticated, witty, and totally given over to the aristocratic pursuits of the city and the court. With skill and wit, she plays the social games that Alceste abhors, until she overreaches herself in an attempt to flatter whomever she is with and satirize whomever is absent.

The relationship between Alceste and Célimène is one of the chief reasons we recognize *The Misanthrope* as a comedy. Alceste is mostly right about the faults of society, and his demands for honesty represent his commitment to what Eliante calls a noble ideal. In this sense, he has much in common with tragic protagonists. But all this is compromised and rendered comic by his irrational love for Célimène, the woman who embodies all that he despises. Alceste is also revealed as a comic character because his rage and indignation are universal; he makes no distinction between the petty follies of social graces and the more serious vices of corrupt courts. In addition, Alceste's excesses lead him into absurd positions, such as his desire to lose his lawsuit simply to prove that he is right about the world.

The Misanthrope is also comic in two ways that are characteristic of satiric comedy. First, we remain emotionally detached from the characters and the action. From this superior perspective, we can immediately recognize Alceste's excessive behavior and the irrationality of his attachment to Célimène. We also quickly realize that Alceste and Célimène are completely incompatible. Second, we recognize that Molière mocks excesses and follies of all kinds in order to effect change in his society. Thus, both Célimène's vices of social hypocrisy and Alceste's follies of brutal honesty are ridiculed. The ideal, for the world of the play and the world at large, is somewhere between these two extremes.

Molière wrote his satiric comedies in French rhymed couplets of iambic hexameter, called *alexandrines*. The verse form was ideally suited to Molière's subjects: It provided great flexibility and an even flow of language. It also allowed Molière to combine formal and elevated diction with colloquial phrases and ordinary conversation. More important, the rhymed verse enabled Molière to create witty counterpoint in couplets and to balance speeches and arguments rhythmically against one another.

Richard Wilbur (b. 1921), an American poet, published his translation of *The Misanthrope* in 1954; his poetic rendering of the play brilliantly captures the wit and vitality of Molière's language. Wilbur avoids using Molière's alexandrine verse because a six-foot line tends to become tedious and too rhythmical in English. Instead, he employs iambic pentameter rhymed couplets, the verse form most frequently used in eighteenth-century English comedies of manners. Wilbur's couplets, like Molière's, combine balance, flexibility, and grace; they maintain the witty elegance and artificial glitter of Molière's language.

MOLIÈRE (JEAN-BAPTISTE POQUELIN) (1622–1673)

The Misanthrope   *1666*

Translated by Richard Wilbur

CHARACTERS

Alceste, *in love with Célimène*
Philinte, *Alceste's friend*
Oronte, *in love with Célimène*
Célimène, *Alceste's beloved*
Eliante, *Célimène's cousin*
Arsinoé, *friend of Célimène's*
Acaste ⎱ *Marquesses*°
Clitandre ⎰
Basque, *Célimène's servant*
A Guard *of the Marshalsea*°
Dubois, *Alceste's valet*

The scene throughout is in Célimène's house at Paris.

ACT 1

Scene 1

[*Enter* PHILINTE *and* ALCESTE]

PHILINTE.   Now, what's got into you?
ALCESTE.   [*seated*]   Kindly leave me alone.
PHILINTE.   Come, come, what is it? This lugubrious tone . . .
ALCESTE.   Leave me, I said; you spoil my solitude.
PHILINTE.   Oh, listen to me, now, and don't be rude.
ALCESTE.   I choose to be rude, Sir, and to be hard of hearing.   5
PHILINTE.   These ugly moods of yours are not endearing;
  Friends though we are, I really must insist . . .
ALCESTE.   [*abruptly rising*] Friends? Friends, you say? Well, cross me off your list.
  I've been your friend till now, as you well know;
  But after what I saw a moment ago   10
  I tell you flatly that our ways must part.
  I wish no place in a dishonest heart.
PHILINTE.   Why, what have I done, Alceste? Is this quite just?
ALCESTE.   My God, you ought to die of self-disgust.
  I call your conduct inexcusable, Sir,   15

marquesses: noblemen ranking just below a duke and above a count.   *Marshalsea*: the court
of the marshal of the royal household, the group of nobles who attend the king.

And every man of honor will concur.
I see you almost hug a man to death,
Exclaim for joy until you're out of breath,
And supplement these loving demonstrations
With endless offers, vows, and protestations;   20
Then when I ask you "Who was that?" I find
That you can barely bring his name to mind!
Once the man's back is turned, you cease to love him,
And speak with absolute indifference of him!
By God, I say it's base and scandalous   25
To falsify the heart's affections thus;
If I caught myself behaving in such a way,
I'd hang myself for shame, without delay.

PHILINTE.   It hardly seems a hanging matter to me;
I hope that you will take it graciously   30
If I extend myself a slight reprieve,
And live a little longer, by your leave.

ALCESTE.   How dare you joke about a crime so grave?

PHILINTE.   What crime? How else are people to behave?

ALCESTE.   I'd have them be sincere, and never part   35
With any word that isn't from the heart.

PHILINTE.   When someone greets us with a show of pleasure,
It's but polite to give him equal measure,
Return his love the best that we know how,
And trade him offer for offer, vow for vow.   40

ALCESTE.   No, no, this formula you'd have me follow,
However fashionable, is false and hollow,
And I despise the frenzied operations
Of all these barterers of protestations,
These lavishers of meaningless embraces,   45
These utterers of obliging commonplaces,
Who court and flatter everyone on earth
And praise the fool no less than the man of worth.
Should you rejoice that someone fondles you,
Offers his love and service, swears to be true,   50
And fills your ears with praises of your name,
When to the first damned fop he'll say the same?
No, no: no self-respecting heart would dream
Of prizing so promiscuous an esteem;
However high the praise, there's nothing worse   55
Than sharing honors with the universe.
Esteem is founded on comparison:
To honor all men is to honor none.
Since you embrace this indiscriminate vice,
Your friendship comes at far too cheap a price;   60
I spurn the easy tribute of a heart
Which will not set the worthy man apart:
I choose, Sir, to be chosen; and in fine,

The friend of mankind is no friend of mine.

PHILINTE.   But in polite society, custom decrees   65
  That we show certain outward courtesies . . .

ALCESTE.   Ah, no! we should condemn with all our force
  Such false and artificial intercourse.°
  Let men behave like men; let them display
  Their inmost hearts in everything they say;   70
  Let the heart speak, and let our sentiments
  Not mask themselves in silly compliments.

PHILINTE.   In certain cases it would be uncouth
  And most absurd to speak the naked truth;
  With all respect for your exalted notions,   75
  It's often best to veil one's true emotions.
  Wouldn't the social fabric come undone
  If we were wholly frank with everyone?
  Suppose you met with someone you couldn't bear;
  Would you inform him of it then and there?   80

ALCESTE.   Yes.

PHILINTE.   Then you'd tell old Emilie it's pathetic
  The way she daubs her features with cosmetic
  And plays the gay coquette at sixty-four?

ALCESTE.   I would.

PHILINTE.   And you'd call Dorilas a bore,
  And tell him every ear at court is lame   85
  From hearing him brag about his noble name?

ALCESTE.   Precisely.

PHILINTE.   Ah, you're joking.

ALCESTE.   *Au contraire:*°
  In this regard there's none I'd choose to spare.
  All are corrupt; there's nothing to be seen
  In court or town but aggravates my spleen.   90
  I fall into deep gloom and melancholy
  When I survey the scene of human folly,
  Finding on every hand base flattery,
  Injustice, fraud, self-interest, treachery . . .
  Ah, it's too much; mankind has grown so base,   95
  I mean to break with the whole human race.

PHILINTE.   This philosophic rage is a bit extreme;
  You've no idea how comical you seem;
  Indeed, we're like those brothers in the play
  Called *School for Husbands,*° one of whom was prey . . .   100

ALCESTE.   Enough, now! None of your stupid similes.

PHILINTE.   Then let's have no more tirades, if you please.

---

68 *intercourse*: conversation.   87 *Au contraire*: on the contrary.   100 *School for Husbands*:
a romantic comedy of manners written by Molière in 1661. It features two brothers and
their female wards. The younger brother, like Alceste, distrusts the manners and customs
of society. The elder, like Philinte, is open-minded and tolerant.

The world won't change, whatever you say or do;
And since plain speaking means so much to you,
I'll tell you plainly that by being frank   105
You've earned the reputation of a crank,
And that you're thought ridiculous when you rage
And rant against the manners of the age.

ALCESTE.   So much the better; just what I wish to hear.
No news could be more grateful to my ear.   110
All men are so detestable in my eyes,
I should be sorry if they thought me wise.

PHILINTE.   Your hatred's very sweeping, is it not?

ALCESTE.   Quite right: I hate the whole degraded lot.

PHILINTE.   Must all poor human creatures be embraced,   115
Without distinction, by your vast distaste?
Even in these bad times, there are surely a few . . .

ALCESTE.   No, I include all men in one dim view:
Some men I hate for being rogues; the others
I hate because they treat the rogues like brothers,   120
And, lacking a virtuous scorn for what is vile,
Receive the villain with a complaisant smile.
Notice how tolerant people choose to be
Toward that bold rascal who's at law with me.
His social polish can't conceal his nature;   125
One sees at once that he's a treacherous creature;
No one could possibly be taken in
By those soft speeches and that sugary grin.
The whole world knows the shady means by which
The low-brow's grown so powerful and rich,   130
And risen to a rank so bright and high
That virtue can but blush, and merit sigh.
Whenever his name comes up in conversation.
None will defend his wretched reputation;
Call him knave, liar, scoundrel, and all the rest,   135
Each head will nod, and no one will protest.
And yet his smirk is seen in every house,
He's greeted everywhere with smiles and bows,
And when there's any honor that can be got
By pulling strings, he'll get it, like as not.   140
My God! It chills my heart to see the ways
Men come to terms with evil nowadays;
Sometimes, I swear, I'm moved to flee and find
Some desert land unfouled by humankind.

PHILINTE.   Come, let's forget the follies of the times   145
And pardon mankind for its petty crimes;
Let's have an end of rantings and of railings,
And show some leniency toward human failings.
This world requires a pliant rectitude;
Too stern a virtue makes one stiff and rude;   150

Good sense views all extremes with detestation,
And bids us to be noble in moderation.
And rigid virtues of the ancient days
Are not for us; they jar with all our ways
And ask of us too lofty a perfection.
Wise men accept their times without objection,
And there's no greater folly, if you ask me,
Than trying to reform society.
Like you, I see each day a hundred and one
Unhandsome deeds that might be better done,
But still, for all the faults that meet my view,
I'm never known to storm and rave like you.
I take men as they are, or let them be,
And teach my soul to bear their frailty;
And whether in court or town, whatever the scene,
My phlegm's as philosophic as your spleen.°

ALCESTE.   This phlegm which you so eloquently commend,
Does nothing ever rile it up, my friend?
Suppose some man you trust should treacherously
Conspire to rob you of your property,
And do his best to wreck your reputation?
Wouldn't you feel a certain indignation?

PHILINTE.   Why, no. These faults of which you so complain
Are part of human nature, I maintain,
And it's no more a matter for disgust
That men are knavish, selfish and unjust,
Than that the vulture dines upon the dead,
And wolves are furious, and apes ill-bred.

ALCESTE.   Shall I see myself betrayed, robbed, torn to bits,
And not . . . Oh, let's be still and rest our wits.
Enough of reasoning, now. I've had my fill.

PHILINTE.   Indeed, you would do well, Sir, to be still.
Rage less at your opponent, and give some thought
To how you'll win this lawsuit that he's brought.

ALCESTE.   I assure you I'll do nothing of the sort.

PHILINTE.   Then who will plead your case before the court?

ALCESTE.   Reason and right and justice will plead for me.

PHILINTE.   Oh, Lord. What judges do you plan to see°?

ALCESTE.   Why, none. The justice of my cause is clear.

PHILINTE.   Of course, man; but there's politics to fear . . .

ALCESTE.   No, I refuse to lift a hand. That's flat.
I'm either right, or wrong.

PHILINTE.   Don't count on that.

ALCESTE.   No, I'll do nothing.

155

160

165

170

175

180

185

190

---

166 *phlegm . . . spleen*: both refer to attitudes or humors. Phlegm signifies calm, cool self-possession; spleen indicates peevish, ill-humored anger.   188 *see*: Bribing or influencing judges before a trial was common practice.

PHILINTE.   Your enemy's influence
    Is great, you know . . .
ALCESTE.   That makes no difference.
PHILINTE. It will; you'll see.
ALCESTE.   Must honor bow to guile?   195
    If so, I shall be proud to lose the trial.
PHILINTE. Oh, really . . .
ALCESTE.   I'll discover by this case
    Whether or not men are sufficiently base
    And impudent and villainous and perverse
    To do me wrong before the universe.   200
PHILINTE. What a man!
ALCESTE.   Oh, I could wish, whatever the cost,
    Just for the beauty of it, that my trial were lost.
PHILINTE. If people heard you talking so, Alceste,
    They'd split their sides. Your name would be a jest.
ALCESTE. So much the worse for jesters.
PHILINTE.   May I enquire   205
    Whether this rectitude you so admire,
    And these hard virtues you're enamored of
    Are qualities of the lady whom you love?
    It much surprises me that you, who seem
    To view mankind with furious disesteem,   210
    Have yet found something to enchant your eyes
    Amidst a species which you so despise.
    And what is more amazing, I'm afraid,
    Is the most curious choice your heart has made.
    The honest Eliante is fond of you,   215
    Arsinoé, the prude, admires you too;
    And yet your spirit's been perversely led
    To choose the flighty Célimène instead,
    Whose brittle malice and coquettish ways
    So typify the manners of our days.   220
    How is it that the traits you most abhor
    Are bearable in this lady you adore?
    Are you so blind with love that you can't find them?
    Or do you contrive, in her case, not to mind them?
ALCESTE. My love for that young widow's not the kind   225
    That can't perceive defects; no, I'm not blind.
    I see her faults, despite my ardent love,
    And all I see I fervently reprove.
    And yet I'm weak; for all her falsity,
    That woman knows the art of pleasing me,   230
    And though I never cease complaining of her,
    I swear I cannot manage not to love her.
    Her charm outweighs her faults; I can but aim
    To cleanse her spirit in my love's pure flame.
PHILINTE. That's no small task; I wish you all success.   235

You think then that she loves you?
ALCESTE.   Heavens, yes!
    I wouldn't love her did she not love me.
PHILINTE.   Well, if her taste for you is plain to see,
    Why do these rivals cause you such despair?
ALCESTE.   True love, Sir, is possessive, and cannot bear   240
    To share with all the world. I'm here today
    To tell her she must send that mob away.
PHILINTE.   If I were you, and had your choice to make,
    Eliante, her cousin, would be the one I'd take;
    That honest heart, which cares for you alone,   245
    Would harmonize far better with your own.
ALCESTE.   True, true: each day my reason tells me so;
    But reason doesn't rule in love, you know.
PHILINTE.   I fear some bitter sorrow is in store;
    This love . . .

Scene 2°

[Enter ORONTE]

ORONTE (TO ALCESTE.)   The servants told me at the door
    That Eliante and Célimène were out,
    But when I heard, dear Sir, that you were about,
    I came to say, without exaggeration,
    That I hold you in the vastest admiration,   5
    And that it's always been my dearest desire
    To be the friend of one I so admire.
    I hope to see my love of merit requited,
    And you and I in friendship's bond united.
    I'm sure you won't refuse—if I may be frank—   10
    A friend of my devotedness—and rank. [During this speech of ORONTE'S, ALCESTE
        is abstracted and seems unaware that he is being spoken to. He only breaks off his
        reverie when ORONTE says]
    It was for you, if you please, that my words were intended.
ALCESTE.   For me, Sir?
ORONTE.   Yes, for you. You're not offended?
ALCESTE.   By no means. But this much surprises me . . .
    The honor comes most unexpectedly . . .   15
ORONTE.   My high regard should not astonish you;
    The whole world feels the same. It is your due.
ALCESTE.   Sir . . .
ORONTE.   Why, in all the State there isn't one
    Can match your merits; they shine, Sir, like the sun.
ALCESTE.   Sir . . .

Scene 2: In neoclassical drama, a new scene usually begins whenever a character enters or
leaves the stage.

ORONTE.   You are higher in my estimation   20
 Than all that's most illustrious in the nation.
ALCESTE. Sir . . .
ORONTE.   If I lie, may heaven strike me dead!
 To show you that I mean what I have said,
 Permit me, Sir, to embrace you most sincerely,
 And swear that I will prize our friendship dearly.   25
 Give me your hand. And now, Sir, if you choose,
 We'll make our vows.
ALCESTE.   Sir . . .
ORONTE.   What! You refuse?
ALCESTE. Sir, it's a very great honor you extend:
 But friendship is a sacred thing, my friend;
 It would be profanation to bestow   30
 The name of friend on one you hardly know.
 All parts are better played when well-rehearsed;
 Let's put off friendship, and get acquainted first.
 We may discover it would be unwise
 To try to make our natures harmonize.   35
ORONTE. By heaven! You're sagacious to the core;
 This speech has made me admire you even more.
 Let time, then, bring us closer day by day;
 Meanwhile, I shall be yours in every way.
 If, for example, there should be anything   40
 You wish at court, I'll mention it to the King.
 I have his ear, of course; it's quite well known
 That I am much in favor with the throne.
 In short, I am your servant. And now, dear friend,
 Since you have such fine judgment, I intend   45
 To please you, if I can, with a small sonnet
 I wrote not long ago. Please comment on it,
 And tell me whether I ought to publish it.
ALCESTE. You must excuse me, Sir; I'm hardly fit
 To judge such matters.
ORONTE.   Why not?
ALCESTE.   I am, I fear,   50
 Inclined to be unfashionably sincere.
ORONTE. Just what I ask; I'd take no satisfaction
 In anything but your sincere reaction.
 I bet you not to dream of being kind.
ALCESTE. Since you desire it, Sir, I'll speak my mind.   55
ORONTE. *Sonnet*. It's a sonnet . . . *Hope* . . . The poem's addressed
 To a lady who wakened hopes within my breast.
 Hope . . . this is not the pompous sort of thing,
 Just modest little verses, with a tender ring.
ALCESTE. Well, we shall see.
ORONTE.   *Hope* . . . I'm anxious to hear   60
 Whether the style seems properly smooth and clear,

And whether the choice of words is good or bad.
ALCESTE.   We'll see, we'll see.
ORONTE.   Perhaps I ought to add
That it took me only a quarter-hour to write it.
ALCESTE.   The time's irrelevant. Sir: kindly recite it.   65
ORONTE.   [reading] Hope comforts us awhile, 'tis true,
                    Lulling our cares with careless laughter,
                    And yet such joy is full of rue,
                    My Phyllis, if nothing follows after.
PHILINTE.   I'm charmed by this already; the style's delightful.   70
ALCESTE.   [sotto voce, to PHILINTE]° How can you say that? Why, the thing is frightful.
ORONTE.   Your fair face smiled on me awhile,
                But was it kindness so to enchant me?
                'Twould have been fairer not to smile,
                If hope was all you meant to grant me.   75
PHILINTE.   What a clever thought! How handsomely you phrase it!
ALCESTE.   [sotto voce, to PHILINTE] You know the thing is trash. How dare you
        praise it?
ORONTE.   If it's to be my passion's fate
                Thus everlastingly to wait,
                Then death will come to set me free: 80
                For death is fairer than the fair;
                Phyllis, to hope is to despair
                When one must hope eternally.
PHILINTE.   The close is exquisite—full of feeling and grace.
ALCESTE.   [sotto voce, aside] Oh, blast the close; you'd better close your face   85
Before you send your lying soul to hell.
PHILINTE.   I can't remember a poem I've liked so well.
ALCESTE.   [sotto voce, aside] Good Lord!
ORONTE.   [to PHILINTE]   I fear you're flattering me a bit.
PHILINTE.   Oh, no!
ALCESTE.   [sotto voce, aside] What else d'you call it, you hypocrite?
ORONTE.   [to ALCESTE] But you, Sir, keep your promise now: don't shrink   90
From telling me sincerely what you think.
ALCESTE.   Sir, these are delicate matters; we all desire
To be told that we've the true poetic fire.
But once, to one whose name I shall not mention,
I said, regarding some verse of his invention,   95
That gentlemen should rigorously control
That itch to write which often afflicts the soul;
That one should curb the heady inclination
To publicize one's little avocation;
And that in showing off one's works of art   100
One often plays a very clownish part.
ORONTE.   Are you suggesting in a devious way

71 *sotto voce*: literally "under the voice." It indicates a loud stage whisper. Oronte does not
hear these lines.

That I ought not . . .

ALCESTE.   Oh, that I do not say.
    Further, I told him that no fault is worse
    Than that of writing frigid, lifeless verse,   105
    And that the merest whisper of such a shame
    Suffices to destroy a man's good name.
ORONTE.   D'you mean to say my sonnet's dull and trite?
ALCESTE.   I don't say that. But I went on to cite
    Numerous cases of once-respected men   110
    Who came to grief by taking up the pen.
ORONTE.   And am I like them? Do I write so poorly?
ALCESTE.   I don't say that. But I told this person, "Surely
    You're under no necessity to compose;
    Why you should wish to publish, heaven knows.   115
    There's no excuse for printing tedious rot
    Unless one writes for bread, as you do not.
    Resist temptation, then, I beg of you;
    Conceal your pastimes from the public view;
    And don't give up, on any provocation,   120
    Your present high and courtly reputation,
    To purchase at a greedy printer's shop
    The name of silly author and scribbling fop."
    These were the points I tried to make him see.
ORONTE.   I sense that they are also aimed at me;   125
    But now—about my sonnet—I'd like to be told . . .
ALCESTE.   Frankly, that sonnet should be pigeonholed.
    You've chosen the worst models to imitate.
    The style's unnatural. Let me illustrate:
        For example, Your fair face smiled on me awhile,   130
        Followed by, 'Twould have been fairer not to smile!
        Or this: such joy is full of rue;
        Or this: For death is fairer than the fair;
        Or, Phyllis, to hope is to despair
            When one must hope eternally!   135
    This artificial style, that's all the fashion,
    Has neither taste, nor honesty, nor passion;
    It's nothing but a sort of wordy play,
    And nature never spoke in such a way.
    What, in this shallow age, is not debased?   140
    Our fathers, though less refined, had better taste;
    I'd barter all that men admire today
    For one old love-song I shall try to say:
        If the King had given me for my own
        Paris, his citadel,   145
        And I for that must leave alone
        Her whom I love so well,
        I'd say then to the Crown,
        Take back your glittering town;

My darling is more fair, I swear,   150
    My darling is more fair.
The rhyme's not rich, the style is rough and old,
But don't you see that it's the purest gold
Beside the tinsel nonsense now preferred,
And that there's passion in its every word?   155
    If the King had given me for my own
      Paris, his citadel,
    And I for that must leave alone
      Her whom I love so well,
    I'd say then to the Crown,   160
      Take back your glittering town;
    My darling is more fair, I swear,
      My darling is more fair.
There speaks a loving heart. [*to* PHILINTE] You're laughing, eh?
Laugh on, my precious wit. Whatever you say,   165
I hold that song's worth all the bibelots°
That people hail today with ah's and oh's.

ORONTE And I maintain my sonnet's very good.

ALCESTE. It's not at all surprising that you should
    You have your reasons; permit me to have mine   170
    For thinking that you cannot write a line.

ORONTE. Others have praised my sonnet to the skies.

ALCESTE. I lack their art of telling pleasant lies.

ORONTE. You seem to think you've got no end of wit.

ALCESTE. To praise your verse, I'd need still more of it.   175

ORONTE. I'm not in need of your approval, Sir.

ALCESTE. That's good; you couldn't have it if you were.

ORONTE. Come now, I'll lend you the subject of my sonnet;
    I'd like to see you try to improve upon it.

ALCESTE. I might, by chance, write something just as shoddy;   180
    But then I wouldn't show it to everybody.

ORONTE. You're most opinionated and conceited.

ALCESTE. Go find your flatterers, and be better treated.

ORONTE. Look here, my little fellow, pray watch your tone.

ALCESTE. My great big fellow, you'd better watch your own.   185

PHILINTE. [*stepping between them*] Oh, please, please, gentlemen!
    This will never do.

ORONTE. The fault is mine, and I leave the field to you.
    I am your servant, Sir, in every way.

ALCESTE. And I, Sir, am your most abject valet.   [*Exit* ORONTE]   190

Scene 3

PHILINTE. Well, as you see, sincerity in excess
    Can get you into a very pretty mess;
    Oronte was hungry for appreciation . . .

---

166 *bibelots*: small objects or works that are considered rare or beautiful.

ALCESTE.   Don't speak to me.
PHILINTE.   What?
ALCESTE.   No more conversation.
PHILINTE.   Really, now . . .
ALCESTE.   Leave me alone.
PHILINTE.   If I . . .
ALCESTE.   Out of my sight!   5
PHILINTE.   But what . . .
ALCESTE.   I won't listen.
PHILINTE.   But . . .
ALCESTE.   Silence!
PHILINTE.   Now, is it polite . . .
ALCESTE.   By heaven, I've had enough. Don't follow me.
PHILINTE.   Ah, you're just joking. I'll keep you company.   [*Exeunt*]

ACT 2

Scene 1

[*Enter* ALCESTE *and* CÉLIMÈNE]

ALCESTE.   Shall I speak plainly, Madam? I confess
 Your conduct gives me infinite distress,
 And my resentment's grown too hot to smother.
 Soon, I foresee, we'll break with one another.
 If I said otherwise, I should deceive you;   5
 Sooner or later, I shall be forced to leave you,
 And if I swore that we shall never part,
 I should misread the omens of my heart.
CÉLIMÈNE.   You kindly saw me home, it would appear,
 So as to pour invectives in my ear.   10
ALCESTE.   I've no desire to quarrel. But I deplore
 Your inability to shut the door
 On all these suitors who beset you so.
 There's what annoys me, if you care to know.
CÉLIMÈNE.   Is it my fault that all these men pursue me?   15
 Am I to blame if they're attracted to me?
 And when they gently beg an audience,
 Ought I to take a stick and drive them hence?
ALCESTE.   Madam, there's no necessity for a stick;
 A less responsive heart would do the trick.   20
 Of your attractiveness I don't complain;
 But those your charms attract, you then detain
 By a most melting and receptive manner,
 And so enlist their hearts beneath your banner.
 It's the agreeable hopes which you excite   25

That keep these lovers round you day and night;
Were they less liberally smiled upon,
That sighing troop would very soon be gone.
But tell me, Madam, why it is that lately
This man Clitandre interests you so greatly?   30
Because of what high merits do you deem
Him worthy of the honor of your esteem?
Is it that your admiring glances linger
On the splendidly long nail of his little finger?
Or do you share the general deep respect   35
For the blond wig he chooses to affect?
Are you in love with his embroidered hose?
Do you adore his ribbons and his bows?
Or is it that this paragon bewitches
Your tasteful eye with his vast German breeches?   40
Perhaps his giggle, or his falsetto voice,
Makes him the latest gallant of your choice?

CÉLIMÈNE. You're much mistaken to resent him so.
Why I put up with him you surely know:
My lawsuit's very shortly to be tried,   45
And I must have his influence on my side.

ALCESTE. Then lose your lawsuit, Madam, or let it drop;
Don't torture me by humoring such a fop.°

CÉLIMÈNE. You're jealous of the whole world, Sir.

ALCESTE.   That's true,
Since the whole world is well-received by you.   50

CÉLIMÈNE. That my good nature is so unconfined
Should serve to pacify your jealous mind;
Were I to smile on one, and scorn the rest,
Then you might have some cause to be distressed.

ALCESTE. Well, if I mustn't be jealous, tell me, then,   55
Just how I'm better treated than other men.

CÉLIMÈNE. You know you have my love. Will that not do?

ALCESTE. What proof have I that what you say is true?

CÉLIMÈNE. I would expect, Sir, that my having said it
Might give the statement a sufficient credit.   60

ALCESTE. But how can I be sure that you don't tell
The selfsame thing to other men as well?

CÉLIMÈNE. What a gallant speech! How flattering to me!
What a sweet creature you make me out to be!
Well then, to save you from the pangs of doubt,   65
All that I've said I hereby cancel out;
Now, none but yourself shall make a monkey of you:
Are you content?

ALCESTE.   Why, why am I doomed to love you?

---

48 *Fop*: vain and foolish young man.

I swear that I shall bless the blissful hour
When this poor heart's no longer in your power!   70
I make no secret of it: I've done my best
To exorcise this passion from my breast;
But thus far all in vain; it will not go;
It's for my sins that I must love you so.
CÉLIMÈNE.   Your love for me is matchless, Sir; that's clear.   75
ALCESTE.   Indeed, in all the world it has no peer;
Words can't describe the nature of my passion,
And no man ever loved in such a fashion.
CÉLIMÈNE.   Yes, it's a brand-new fashion, I agree:
You show your love by castigating me,   80
And all your speeches are enraged and rude.
I've never been so furiously wooed.
ALCESTE.   Yet you could calm that fury, if you chose.
Come, shall we bring our quarrels to a close?
Let's speak with open hearts, then, and begin . . .   85

Scene 2

[*Enter BASQUE*]

CÉLIMÈNE.   What is it?
BASQUE.   Acaste is here.
CÉLIMÈNE.   Well, send him in.   [*Exit BASQUE*]

Scene 3

ALCESTE.   What! Shall we never be alone at all?
You're always ready to receive a call,
And you can't bear, for ten ticks of the clock,
Not to keep open house for all who knock.
CÉLIMÈNE.   I couldn't refuse him: he'd be most put out.   5
ALCESTE.   Surely that's not worth worrying about.
CÉLIMÈNE.   Acaste would never forgive me if he guessed
That I consider him a dreadful pest.
ALCESTE.   If he's a pest, why bother with him then?
CÉLIMÈNE.   Heavens! One can't antagonize such men;   10
Why, they're the chartered gossips of the court,
And have a say in things of every sort.
One must receive them, and be full of charm;
They're no great help, but they can do you harm,
And though your influence be ever so great,   15
They're hardly the best people to alienate.
ALCESTE.   I see, dear lady, that you could make a case
For putting up with the whole human race;
These friendships that you calculate so nicely . . .

Scene 4

[*Enter* BASQUE]

BASQUE. Madam, Clitandre is here as well.

ALCESTE.   Precisely.

CÉLIMÈNE. Where are you going?

ALCESTE.   Elsewhere.

CÉLIMÈNE.   Stay.

ALCESTE.   No, no.

CÉLIMÈNE. Stay, Sir.

ALCESTE.   I can't.

CÉLIMÈNE.   I wish it.

ALCESTE.   No, I must go.

I beg you, Madam, not to press the matter;

You know I have no taste for idle chatter.   5

CÉLIMÈNE. Stay: I command you.

ALCESTE.   No, I cannot stay.

CÉLIMÈNE. Very well; you have my leave to go away.

Scene 5

[*Enter* ELIANTE, PHILINTE, ACASTE, CLITANDRE, *and* BASQUE]

ELIANTE. [*to* CÉLIMÈNE] The Marquesses have kindly come to call.

Were they announced?

CÉLIMÈNE.   Yes. Basque, bring chairs for all. [BASQUE *provides the*
chairs, and exits. To ALCESTE]

You haven't gone?

ALCESTE.   No; and I shan't depart

Till you decide who's foremost in your heart.

CÉLIMÈNE. Oh, hush.

ALCESTE.   It's time to choose; take them or me.   5

CÉLIMÈNE. You're mad.

ALCESTE.   I'm not, as you shall shortly see.

CÉLIMÈNE. Oh?

ALCESTE.   You'll decide.

CÉLIMÈNE.   You're joking now, dear friend.

ALCESTE. No, no; you'll choose; my patience is at an end.

CLITANDRE. Madam, I come from court, where poor Cléonte

Behaved like a perfect fool, as is his wont.   10

Has he no friend to counsel him, I wonder,

And teach him less unerringly to blunder?

CÉLIMÈNE. It's true, the man's a most accomplished dunce;

His gauche behavior charms the eye at once;

And every time one sees him, on my word,   15

His manner's grown a trifle more absurd.

ACASTE. Speaking of dunces, I've just now conversed

With old Damon, who's one of the very worst;
I stood a lifetime in the broiling sun
Before his dreary monologue was done.   20
CÉLIMÈNE.   Oh, he's a wondrous talker, and has the power
To tell you nothing hour after hour:
If, by mistake, he ever came to the point,
The shock would put his jawbone out of joint.
ELIANTE.   [*to* PHILINTE] The conversation takes its usual turn,   25
And all our dear friends' ears will shortly burn.
CLITANDRE.   Timante's a character, Madam.
CÉLIMÈNE.   Isn't he, though?
A man of mystery from top to toe,
Who moves about in a romantic mist
On secret missions which do not exist.   30
His talk is full of eyebrows and grimaces;
How tired one gets of his momentous faces;
He's always whispering something confidential
Which turns out to be quite inconsequential;
Nothing's too slight for him to mystify;   35
He even whispers when he says "good-by."
ACASTE.   Tell us about Géralde.
CÉLIMÈNE.   That tiresome ass.
He mixes only with the titled class,
And fawns on dukes and princes, and is bored
With anyone who's not at least a lord.   40
The man's obsessed with rank, and his discourses
Are all of hounds and carriages and horses;
He uses Christian names with all the great,
And the word Milord, with him, is out of date.
CLITANDRE.   He's very taken with Bélise, I hear.   45
CÉLIMÈNE.   She is the dreariest company, poor dear.
Whenever she comes to call, I grope about
To find some topic which will draw her out,
But, owing to her dry and faint replies,
The conversation wilts, and droops, and dies.   50
In vain one hopes to animate her face
By mentioning the ultimate commonplace;
But sun or shower, even hail or frost
Are matters she can instantly exhaust.
Meanwhile her visit, painful though it is,   55
Drags on and on through mute eternities,
And though you ask the time, and yawn, and yawn,
She sits there like a stone and won't be gone.
ACASTE.   Now for Adraste.
CÉLIMÈNE.   Oh, that conceited elf
Has a gigantic passion for himself;   60
He rails against the court, and cannot bear it
That none will recognize his hidden merit;

All honors given to others give offense
To his imaginary excellence.
CLITANDRE.   What about young Cléon? His house, they say,   65
Is full of the best society, night and day.
CÉLIMÈNE.   His cook has made him popular, not he:
It's Cléon's table that people come to see.
ELIANTE.   He gives a splendid dinner, you must admit.
CÉLIMÈNE.   But must he serve himself along with it?   70
For my taste, he's a most insipid dish
Whose presence sours the wine and spoils the fish.
PHILINTE.   Damis, his uncle, is admired no end.
What's your opinion, Madam?
CÉLIMÈNE.   Why, he's my friend.
PHILINTE.   He seems a decent fellow, and rather clever.   75
CÉLIMÈNE.   He works too hard at cleverness, however.
I hate to see him sweat and struggle so
To fill his conversation with bons mots.°
Since he's decided to become a wit
His taste's so pure that nothing pleases it;   80
He scolds at all the latest books and plays,
Thinking that wit must never stoop to praise,
That finding fault's a sign of intellect,
That all appreciation is abject,
And that by damning everything in sight   85
One shows oneself in a distinguished light.
He's scornful even of our conversations:
Their trivial nature sorely tries his patience;
He folds his arms, and stands above the battle,
And listens sadly to our childish prattle.   90
ACASTE.   Wonderful, Madam! You've hit him off precisely.
CLITANDRE.   No one can sketch a character so nicely.
ALCESTE.   How bravely, Sirs, you cut and thrust at all
These absent fools, till one by one they fall:
But let one come in sight, and you'll at once   95
Embrace the man you lately called a dunce,
Telling him in a tone sincere and fervent
How proud you are to be his humble servant.
CLINTANDRE.   Why pick on us? Madame's been speaking, Sir,
And you should quarrel, if you must, with her.   100
ALCESTE.   No, no, by God, the fault is yours, because
You lead her on with laughter and applause,
And make her think that she's the more delightful
The more her talk is scandalous and spiteful.
Oh, she would stoop to malice far, far less   105
If no such claque° approved her cleverness.

78 *bon mots*: witty words.   106 *claque*: fawning audience.

It's flatterers like you whose foolish praise
Nourishes all the vices of these days.
PHILINTE. But why protest when someone ridicules
Those you'd condemn, yourself, as knaves or fools? 110
CÉLIMÈNE. Why, Sir? Because he loves to make a fuss.
You don't expect him to agree with us,
When there's an opportunity to express
His heaven-sent spirit of contrariness?
What other people think, he can't abide; 115
Whatever they say, he's on the other side;
He lives in deadly terror of agreeing;
'Twould make him seem an ordinary being.
Indeed, he's so in love with contradiction,
He'll turn against his most profound conviction 120
And with a furious eloquence deplore it,
If only someone else is speaking for it.
ALCESTE. Go on, dear lady, mock me as you please;
You have your audience in ecstasies.
PHILINTE. But what she says is true: you have a way 125
Of bridling at whatever people say;
Whether they praise or blame, your angry spirit
Is equally unsatisfied to hear it.
ALCESTE. Men, Sir, are always wrong, and that's the reason
That righteous anger's never out of season; 130
All that I hear in all their conversation
Is flattering praise or reckless condemnation.
CÉLIMÈNE. But . . .
ALCESTE.   No, no, Madam, I am forced to state
That you have pleasures which I deprecate,
And that these others, here, are much to blame 135
For nourishing the faults which are your shame.
CLITANDRE. I shan't defend myself, Sir; but I vow
I'd thought this lady faultless until now.
ACASTE. I see her charms and graces, which are many;
But as for faults, I've never noticed any. 140
ALCESTE. I see them, Sir; and rather than ignore them,
I strenuously criticize her for them.
The more one loves, the more one should object
To every blemish, every least defect.
Were I this lady, I would soon get rid 145
Of lovers who approved of all I did,
And by their slack indulgence and applause
Endorsed my follies and excused my flaws.
CÉLIMÈNE. If all hearts beat according to your measure,
The dawn of love would be the end of pleasure; 150
And love would find its perfect consummation
In ecstasies of rage and reprobation.

ELIANTE. Love, as a rule, affects men otherwise,
  And lovers rarely love to criticize.
  They see their lady as a charming blur,   155
  And find all things commendable in her.
  If she has any blemish, fault, or shame,
  They will redeem it by a pleasing name.
  The pale-faced lady's lily-white, perforce;
  The swarthy one's a sweet brunette, of course;   160
  The spindly lady has a slender grace;
  The fat one has a most majestic pace;
  The plain one, with her dress in disarray,
  They classify as *beauté négligée*;°
  The hulking one's a goddess in their eyes,   165
  The dwarf, a concentrate of Paradise;
  The haughty lady has a noble mind;
  The mean one's witty, and the dull one's kind;
  The chatterbox has liveliness and verve,
  The mute one has a virtuous reserve.   170
  So lovers manage, in their passion's cause,
  To love their ladies even for their flaws.°
ALCESTE.   But I still say. . .
CÉLIMÈNE.   I think it would be nice
  To stroll around the gallery once or twice.
  What! You're not going, Sirs?
CLITANDRE *and* ACASTE.   No, Madam, no.   175
ALCESTE.   You seem to be in terror lest they go.
  Do what you will, Sirs; leave, or linger on,
  But I shan't go till after you are gone.
ACASTE.   I'm free to linger, unless I should perceive
  Madame is tired, and wishes me to leave.   180
CLITANDRE.   And as for me, I needn't go today
  Until the hour of the King's *coucher*.°
CÉLIMÈNE.   [*to* ALCESTE] You're joking, surely?
ALCESTE.   Not in the least; we'll see
  Whether you'd rather part with them, or me.

Scene 6

[*Enter* BASQUE]

BASQUE.   [*to* ALCESTE] Sir, there's a fellow here who bids me state
  That he must see you, and that it can't wait.
ALCESTE.   Tell him that I have no such pressing affairs.

153–172 *Love, as a . . . flaws*: Eliante's speech is paraphrased from Book IV of Lucretius, *De Rerum Natura* (*On the Nature of Things*), a Latin philosophical poem that Molière probably translated as a student.   164 *beauté négligée*: careless beauty.   182 *coucher*: retiring to bed; the king's bedtime was a ceremonial occasion during which he was attended by nobles.

BASQUE.   It's a long tailcoat that this fellow wears,
 With gold all over.
CÉLIMÈNE.   [*to ALCESTE*] You'd best go down and see.   5
 Or—have him enter.   [*exit BASQUE*]

Scene 7

[*Enter a GUARD of the Marshalsea*]

ALCESTE.   [*confronting the guard*] Well, what do you want with me?
 Come in, Sir.
GUARD.   I've a word, Sir, for your ear.
ALCESTE.   Speak it aloud, Sir; I shall strive to hear.
GUARD.   The Marshals have instructed me to say
 You must report to them without delay.   5
ALCESTE.   Who? Me, Sir?
GUARD.   Yes, Sir; you.
ALCESTE.   But what do they want?
PHILINTE.   [*to ALCESTE*] To scotch your silly quarrel with Oronte.
CÉLIMÈNE.   [*to PHILINTE*] What quarrel?
PHILINTE.   Oronte and he have fallen out
 Over some verse he spoke his mind about;
 The Marshals wish to arbitrate the matter.°   10
ALCESTE.   Never shall I equivocate or flatter!
PHILINTE.   You'd best obey their summons; come, let's go.
ALCESTE.   How can they mend our quarrel, I'd like to know?
 Am I to make a cowardly retraction,
 And praise those jingles to his satisfaction?   15
 I'll not recant; I've judged that sonnet rightly.
 It's bad.
PHILINTE. But you might say so more politely. . . .
ALCESTE.   I'll not back down; his verses make me sick.
PHILINTE.   If only you could be more politic!
 But come, let's go.
ALCESTE.   I'll go, but I won't unsay   20
 A single word.
PHILINTE.   Well, let's be on our way.
ALCESTE.   Till I am ordered by my lord the King
 To praise that poem, I shall say the thing
 Is scandalous, by God, and that the poet
 Ought to be hanged for having the nerve to show it. [*to CLITANDRE and* 25
  ACASTE, who are laughing]
 By heaven, Sirs, I really didn't know
 That I was being humorous.
CÉLIMÈNE.   Go, Sir, go;
 Settle your business.

10 *matter*: Duels, although illegal, were still fought; the marshals tried to prevent them by judging matters of honor.

ALCESTE.   I shall, and when I'm through,
    I shall return to settle things with you.   [*Exeunt*]

ACT 3

Scene 1

[*Enter* CLITANDRE *and* ACASTE]

CLITANDRE. Dear Marquess, how contented you appear;
    All things delight you, nothing mars your cheer.
    Can you, in perfect honesty, declare
    That you've a right to be so debonair?
ACASTE. By Jove, when I survey myself, I find   5
    No cause whatever for distress of mind.
    I'm young and rich; I can in modesty
    Lay claim to an exalted pedigree;
    And owing to my name and my condition
    I shall not want for honors and position.   10
    Then as to courage, that most precious trait,
    I seem to have it, as was proved of late
    Upon the field of honor, where my bearing,
    They say, was very cool and rather daring.
    I've wit, of course; and taste in such perfection   15
    That I can judge without the least reflection,
    And at the theater, which is my delight,
    Can make or break a play on opening night,
    And lead the crowd in hisses or bravos,
    And generally be known as one who knows.   20
    I'm clever, handsome, gracefully polite;
    My waist is small, my teeth are strong and white;
    As for my dress, the world's astonished eyes
    Assure me that I bear away the prize.
    I find myself in favor everywhere,   25
    Honored by men, and worshiped by the fair;
    And since these things are so, it seems to me
    I'm justified in my complacency.
CLITANDRE. Well, if so many ladies hold you dear,
    Why do you press a hopeless courtship here?   30
ACASTE. Hopeless, you say? I'm not the sort of fool
    That likes his ladies difficult and cool.
    Men who are awkward, shy, and peasantish
    May pine for heartless beauties, if they wish,
    Grovel before them, bear their cruelties,   35
    Woo them with tears and sighs and bended knees,
    And hope by dogged faithfulness to gain
    What their poor merits never could obtain.

For men like me, however, it makes no sense
To love on trust, and foot the whole expense.   40
Whatever any lady's merits be,
I think, thank God, that I'm as choice as she;
That if my heart is kind enough to burn
For her, she owes me something in return;
And that in any proper love affair   45
The partners must invest an equal share.
CLITANDRE.   You think, then, that our hostess favors you?
ACASTE.   I've reason to believe that that is true.
CLITANDRE.   How did you come to such a mad conclusion?
You're blind, dear fellow. This is sheer delusion.   50
ACASTE.   All right, then: I'm deluded and I'm blind.
CLITANDRE.   Whatever put the notion in your mind?
ACASTE.   Delusion.
CLITANDRE.   What persuades you that you're right?
ACASTE.   I'm blind.
CLITANDRE.   But have you any proofs to cite?
ACASTE.   I tell you I'm deluded.
CLITANDRE.   Have you, then,   55
Received some secret pledge from Célimène?
ACASTE.   Oh, no: she scorns me.
CLITANDRE.   Tell me the truth, I beg.
ACASTE.   She just can't bear me.
CLITANDRE.   Ah, don't pull my leg.
Tell me what hope she's given you, I pray.
ACASTE.   I'm hopeless, and it's you who win the day.   60
She hates me thoroughly, and I'm so vexed
I mean to hang myself on Tuesday next.
CLITANDRE.   Dear Marquess, let us have an armistice
And make a treaty. What do you say to this?
If ever one of us can plainly prove   65
That Célimène encourages his love,
The other must abandon hope, and yield,
And leave him in possession of the field.
ACASTE.   Now, there's a bargain that appeals to me;
With all my heart, dear Marquess, I agree.   70
But hush.

Scene 2

[*Enter* CÉLIMÈNE]

CÉLIMÈNE.   Still here?
CLITANDRE.   'Twas love that stayed our feet.
CÉLIMÈNE.   I think I heard a carriage in the street.
Whose is it? D'you know?

Scene 3

[*Enter* BASQUE]

BASQUE.   Arsinoé is here,
  Madame.
CÉLIMÈNE.   Arsinoé, you say? Oh, dear.
BASQUE.   Eliante is entertaining her below.
CÉLIMÈNE.   What brings the creature here, I'd like to know?
ACASTE.   They say she's dreadfully prudish, but in fact
  I think her piety . . .
CÉLIMÈNE.   It's all an act.
  At heart she's worldly, and her poor success
  In snaring men explains her prudishness.
  It breaks her heart to see the beaux° and gallants
  Engrossed by other women's charms and talents,
  And so she's always in a jealous rage   1(
  Against the faulty standards of the age.
  She lets the world believe that she's a prude
  To justify her loveless solitude,
  And strives to put a brand of moral shame
  On all the graces that she cannot claim.
  But still she'd love a lover; and Alceste   1!
  Appears to be the one she'd love the best.
  His visits here are poison to her pride;
  She seems to think I've lured him from her side;
  And everywhere, at court or in the town,   2(
  The spiteful, envious woman runs me down.
  In short, she's just as stupid as can be,
  Vicious and arrogant in the last degree,
  And . . .   [*Exit* BASQUE]

Scene 4

[*Enter* ARSINOÉ]

CÉLIMÈNE.   Ah! What happy chance has brought you here?
  I've thought about you ever so much, my dear.
ARSINOÉ.   I've come to tell you something you should know.
CÉLIMÈNE.   How good of you to think of doing so!
                    [CLITANDRE *and* ACASTE *go out, laughing*]

Scene 5

ARSINOÉ.   It's just as well those gentlemen didn't tarry.
CÉLIMÈNE.   Shall we sit down?
ARSINOÉ.   That won't be necessary.

---

8 *beaux*: suitors.

Madam, the flame of friendship ought to burn
Brightest in matters of the most concern,
And as there's nothing which concerns us more   5
Than honor, I have hastened to your door
To bring you, as your friend, some information
About the status of your reputation.
I visited, last night, some virtuous folk,
And, quite by chance, it was of you they spoke;   10
There was, I fear, no tendency to praise
Your light behavior and your dashing ways.
The quantity of gentlemen you see
And your by now notorious coquetry°
Were both so vehemently criticized   15
By everyone, that I was much surprised.
Of course, I needn't tell you where I stood;
I came to your defense as best I could,
Assured them you were harmless, and declared
Your soul was absolutely unimpaired.   20
But there are some things, you must realize,
One can't excuse, however hard one tries,
And I was forced at last into conceding
That your behavior, Madam, is misleading,
That it makes a bad impression, giving rise   25
To ugly gossip and obscene surmise,
And that if you were more *overtly* good,
You wouldn't be so much misunderstood.
Not that I think you've been unchaste—no! no!
The saints preserve me from a thought so low!   30
But mere good conscience never did suffice:
One must avoid the outward show of vice.
Madam, you're too intelligent, I'm sure,
To think my motives anything but pure
In offering you this counsel—which I do   35
Out of a zealous interest in you.
CÉLIMÈNE.   Madam, I haven't taken you amiss;
I'm very much obliged to you for this;
And I'll at once discharge the obligation
By telling you about *your* reputation.   40
You've been so friendly as to let me know
What certain people say of me, and so
I mean to follow your benign example
By offering you a somewhat similar sample.
The other day, I went to an affair   45
And found some most distinguished people there
Discussing piety, both false and true.
The conversation soon came round to you.

14 *coquetry*: flirtatiousness.

Alas! Your prudery and bustling zeal
Appeared to have a very slight appeal   50
Your affectation of a grave demeanor,
Your endless talk of virtue and of honor,
The aptitude of your suspicious mind
For finding sin where there is none to find,
Your towering self-esteem, that pitying face   55
With which you contemplate the human race,
Your sermonizings and your sharp aspersions
On people's pure and innocent diversions—
All these were mentioned, Madam, and, in fact,
Were roundly and concertedly attacked.   60
"What good," they said, "are all these outward shows,
When everything belies her pious pose?
She prays incessantly; but then, they say,
She beats her maids and cheats them of their pay;
She shows her zeal in every holy place,   65
But still she's vain enough to paint her face;
She holds that naked statues are immoral,
But with a naked *man* she'd have no quarrel."
Of course, I said to everybody there
That they were being viciously unfair;   70
But still they were disposed to criticize you,
And all agreed that someone should advise you
To leave the morals of the world alone,
And worry rather more about your own.
They felt that one's self-knowledge should be great   75
Before one thinks of setting others straight;
That one should learn the art of living well
Before one threatens other men with hell,
And that the Church is best equipped, no doubt,
To guide our souls and root our vices out.   80
Madam, you're too intelligent, I'm sure,
To think my motives anything but pure
In offering you this counsel—which I do
Out of a zealous interest in you.

ARSINOÉ.   I dared not hope for gratitude, but I   85
    Did not expect so acid a reply;
    I judge, since you've been so extremely tart,
    That my good counsel pierced you to the heart.

CÉLIMÈNE.   Far from it, Madam. Indeed, it seems to me
    We ought to trade advice more frequently.   90
    One's vision of oneself is so defective
    That it would be an excellent corrective.
    If you are willing, Madam, let's arrange
    Shortly to have another frank exchange
    In which we'll tell each other, *entre nous,*°   95

95 *entre nous*: just between us.

What you've heard tell of me, and I of you.
ARSINOÉ.   Oh, people never censure you, my dear;
   It's me they criticize. Or so I hear.
CÉLIMÈNE.   Madam, I think we either blame or praise
   According to our taste and length of days.   100
   There is a time of life for coquetry,
   And there's a season, too, for prudery.
   When all one's charms are gone, it is, I'm sure,
   Good strategy to be devout and pure:
   It makes one seem a little less forsaken.   105
   Some day, perhaps, I'll take the road you've taken:
   Time brings all things. But I have time aplenty,
   And see no cause to be a prude at twenty.
ARSINOÉ.   You give your age in such a gloating tone
   That one would think I was an ancient crone;   110
   We're not so far apart, in sober truth,
   That you can mock me with a boast of youth!
   Madam, you baffle me. I wish I knew
   What moves you to provoke me as you do.
CÉLIMÈNE.   For my part, Madam, I should like to know   115
   Why you abuse me everywhere you go.
   Is it my fault, dear lady, that your hand
   Is not, alas, in very great demand?
   If men admire me, if they pay me court
   And daily make me offers of the sort   120
   You'd dearly love to have them make to you,
   How can I help it? What would you have me do?
   If what you want is lovers, please feel free
   To take as many as you can from me.
ARSINOÉ.   Oh, come. D'you think the world is losing sleep   125
   Over that flock of lovers which you keep,
   Or that we find it difficult to guess
   What price you pay for their devotedness?
   Surely you don't expect us to suppose
   Mere merit could attract so many beaux?   130
   It's not your virtue that they're dazzled by;
   Nor is it virtuous love for which they sigh.
   You're fooling no one, Madam; the world's not blind;
   There's many a lady heaven has designed
   To call men's noblest, tenderest feelings out,   135
   Who has no lovers dogging her about;
   From which it's plain that lovers nowadays
   Must be acquired in bold and shameless ways,
   And only pay one court for such reward
   As modesty and virtue can't afford.   140
   Then don't be quite so puffed up, if you please,
   About your tawdry little victories;
   Try, if you can, to be a shade less vain,
   And treat the world with somewhat less disdain.

If one were envious of your amours,   14
One soon could have a following like yours;
Lovers are no great trouble to collect
If one prefers them to one's self-respect.
CÉLIMÈNE.   Collect them then, my dear; I'd love to see
You demonstrate that charming theory;
Who knows, you might . . .   15
ARSINOÉ.   Now, Madam, that will do;
It's time to end this trying interview.
My coach is late in coming to your door,
Or I'd have taken leave of you before.
CÉLIMÈNE.   Oh, please don't feel that you must rush away;   15
I'd be delighted, Madam, if you'd stay.
However, lest my conversation bore you,
Let me provide some better company for you;
This gentleman, who comes most apropos,°
Will please you more than I could do, I know.   16

Scene 6

[*Enter* ALCESTE]

CÉLIMÈNE.   Alceste, I have a little note to write
Which simply must go out before tonight;
Please entertain *Madame*; I'm sure that she
Will overlook my incivility.   [*Exit* CÉLIMÈNE]

Scene 7

ARSINOÉ.   Well, Sir, our hostess graciously contrives
For us to chat until my coach arrives;
And I shall be forever in her debt
For granting me this little tête-á-tête.°
We women very rightly give our hearts   5
To men of noble character and parts,
And your especial merits, dear Alceste,
Have roused the deepest sympathy in my breast.
Oh, how I wish they had sufficient sense
At court, to recognize your excellence!   10
They wrong you greatly, Sir. How it must hurt you
Never to be rewarded for your virtue!
ALCESTE.   Why, Madam, what cause have I to feel aggrieved?
What great and brilliant thing have I achieved?
What service have I rendered to the King   15
That I should look to him for anything?
ARSINOÉ.   Not everyone who's honored by the State

159 *apropos*: opportunely.   4 *tête-à-tête*: private conversation.

Has done great services. A man must wait
Till time and fortune offer him the chance.
Your merit, Sir, is obvious at a glance,   20
And . . .
ALCESTE.   Ah, forget my merit; I'm not neglected.
The court, I think, can hardly be expected
To mine men's souls for merit, and unearth
Our hidden virtues and our secret worth.
ARSINOÉ.   *Some* virtues, though, are far too bright to hide;   25
Yours are acknowledged, Sir, on every side.
Indeed, I've heard you warmly praiséd of late
By persons of considerable weight.
ALCESTE.   This fawning age has praise for everyone,
And all distinctions, Madam, are undone.   30
All things have equal honor nowadays,
And no one should be gratified by praise.
To be admired, one only need exist,
And every lackey's on the honors list.
ARSINOÉ.   I only wish, Sir, that you had your eye   35
On some position at court, however high;
You'd only have to hint at such a notion
For me to set the proper wheels in motion;
I've certain friendships I'd be glad to use
To get you any office you might choose.   40
ALCESTE.   Madam, I fear that any such ambition
Is wholly foreign to my disposition.
The soul God gave me isn't of the sort
That prospers in the weather of a court.
It's all too obvious that I don't possess   45
The virtues necessary for success.
My one great talent is for speaking plain;
I've never learned to flatter or to feign;
And anyone so stupidly sincere
Had best not seek a courtier's career.   50
Outside the court, I know, one must dispense
With honors, privilege, and influence;
But still one gains the right, foregoing these,
Not to be tortured by the wish to please.
One needn't live in dread of snubs and slights,   55
Nor praise the verse that every idiot writes,
Nor humor silly Marquesses, nor bestow
Politic sighs on Madam So-and-so.
ARSINOÉ.   Forget the court, then; let the matter rest.
But I've another cause to be distressed   60
About your present situation, Sir.
It's to your love affair that I refer.
She whom you love, and who pretends to love you,
Is, I regret to say, unworthy of you.

ALCESTE.   Why, Madam! Can you seriously intend   6!
    To make so grave a charge against your friend?
ARSINOÉ.   Alas, I must. I've stood aside too long
    And let that lady do you grievous wrong;
    But now my debt to conscience shall be paid:
    I tell you that your love has been betrayed.
ALCESTE.   I thank you, Madam; you're extremely kind.   7(
    Such words are soothing to a lover's mind.
ARSINOÉ.   Yes, though she *is* my friend, I say again
    You're very much too good for Célimène.
    She's wantonly misled you from the start.
ALCESTE.   You may be right; who knows another's heart?   7!
    But ask yourself if it's the part of charity
    To shake my soul with doubts of her sincerity.
ARSINOÉ.   Well if you'd rather be a dupe than doubt her,
    That's your affair. I'll say no more about her.
ALCESTE.   Madam, you know that doubt and vague suspicion   8(
    Are painful to a man in my position;
    It's most unkind to worry me this way
    Unless you've some real proof of what you say.
ARSINOÉ.   Sir, say no more: all doubt shall be removed,   8!
    And all that I've been saying shall be proved.
    You've only to escort me home, and there
    We'll look into the heart of this affair.
    I've ocular evidence which will persuade you
    Beyond a doubt, that Célimène's betrayed you.   9(
    Then, if you're saddened by that revelation,
    Perhaps I can provide some consolation.   [*Exeunt*]

ACT 4

Scene 1

[*Enter* ELIANTE *and* PHILINTE]

PHILINTE.   Madam, he acted like a stubborn child;
    I thought they never would be reconciled;
    In vain we reasoned, threatened, and appealed;
    He stood his ground and simply would not yield.
    The Marshals, I feel sure, have never heard   5
    An argument so splendidly absurd.
    "No, gentlemen," said he, "I'll not retract.
    His verse is bad: extremely bad, in fact.
    Surely it does the man no harm to know it.
    Does it disgrace him, not to be a poet?   10
    A gentleman may be respected still,

Whether he writes a sonnet well or ill.
That I dislike his verse should not offend him;
In all that touches honor, I commend him;
He's noble, brave, and virtuous—but I fear   15
He can't in truth be called a sonneteer.
I'll gladly praise his wardrobe; I'll endorse
His dancing, or the way he sits a horse;
But, gentlemen, I cannot praise his rhyme.
In fact, it ought to be a capital crime   20
For anyone so sadly unendowed
To write a sonnet, and read the thing aloud."
At length he fell into a gentler mood
And, striking a concessive attitude,
He paid Oronte the following courtesies: 25
"Sir, I regret that I'm so hard to please,
And I'm profoundly sorry that your lyric
Failed to provoke me to a panegyric."
After these curious words, the two embraced,
And then the hearing was adjourned—in haste.   30
ELIANTE.   His conduct has been very singular lately;
   Still, I confess that I respect him greatly.
   The honesty in which he takes such pride
   Has—to my mind—its noble, heroic side.
   In this false age, such candor seems outrageous;   35
   But I could wish that it were more contagious.
PHILINTE.   What most intrigues me in our friend Alceste
   Is the grand passion that rages in his breast.
   The sullen humors he's compounded of
   Should not, I think, dispose his heart to love;   40
   But since they do, it puzzles me still more
   That he should choose your cousin to adore.
ELIANTE.   It does, indeed, belie the theory
   That love is born of gentle sympathy,
   And that the tender passion must be based   45
   On sweet accords of temper and of taste.
PHILINTE.   Does she return his love, do you suppose?
ELIANTE.   Ah, that's a difficult question, Sir. Who knows?
   How can we judge the truth of her devotion?
   Her heart's a stranger to its own emotion.   50
   Sometimes it thinks it loves, when no love's there;
   At other times it loves quite unaware.
PHILINTE.   I rather think Alceste is in for more
   Distress and sorrow than he's bargained for;
   Were he of my mind, Madam, his affection   55
   Would turn in quite a different direction,
   And we would see him more responsive to
   The kind regard which he receives from you.

ELIANTE. Sir, I believe in frankness, and I'm inclined,
   In matters of the heart, to speak my mind.
   I don't oppose his love for her; indeed,
   I hope with all my heart that he'll succeed,
   And were it in my power, I'd rejoice
   In giving him the lady of his choice.
   But if, as happens frequently enough
   In love affairs, he meets with a rebuff—
   If Célimène should grant some rival's suit—
   I'd gladly play the role of substitute;
   Nor would his tender speeches please me less
   Because they'd once been made without success.
PHILINTE. Well, Madam, as for me, I don't oppose
   Your hopes in this affair; and heaven knows
   That in my conversations with the man
   I plead your cause as often as I can.
   But if those two should marry, and so remove
   All chance that he will offer you his love,
   Then I'll declare my own, and hope to see
   Your gracious favor pass from him to me.
   In short, should you be cheated of Alceste,
   I'd be most happy to be second best.
ELIANTE. Philinte, you're teasing.
PHILINTE.   Ah, Madam, never fear;
   No words of mine were ever so sincere,
   And I shall live in fretful expectation
   Till I can make a fuller declaration.

Scene 2

[*Enter ALCESTE*]

ALCESTE. Avenge me, Madam! I must have satisfaction,
   Or this great wrong will drive me to distraction!
ELIANTE. Why, what's the matter? What's upset you so?
ALCESTE. Madam, I've had a mortal, mortal blow.
   If Chaos repossessed the universe,
   I swear I'd not be shaken any worse.
   I'm ruined . . . I can say no more . . . My soul . . .
ELIANTE. Do try, Sir, to regain your self-control.
ALCESTE. Just heaven! Why were so much beauty and grace
   Bestowed on one so vicious and so base?
ELIANTE. Once more, Sir, tell us . . .
ALCESTE.   My world has gone to wrack;
   I'm— I'm betrayed; she's stabbed me in the back:
   Yes, Célimène (who would have thought it of her?)
   Is false to me, and has another lover.

ELIANTE.   Are you quite certain? Can you prove these things?   15
PHILINTE.   Lovers are prey to wild imaginings
    And jealous fancies. No doubt there's some mistake . . .
ALCESTE.   Mind your own business, Sir, for heaven's sake.
    [*to* ELIANTE] Madam, I have the proof that you demand
    Here in my pocket, penned by her own hand.   20
    Yes, all the shameful evidence one could want
    Lies in this letter written to Oronte—
    Oronte! whom I felt sure she couldn't love,
    And hardly bothered to be jealous of.
PHILINTE.   Still, in a letter, appearances may deceive;   25
    This may not be so bad as you believe.
ALCESTE.   Once more I beg you, Sir, to let me be;
    Tend to your own affairs; leave mine to me.
ELIANTE.   Compose yourself; this anguish that you feel . . .
ALCESTE.   Is something, Madam, you alone can heal.   30
    My outraged heart, beside itself with grief,
    Appeals to you for comfort and relief.
    Avenge me on your cousin, whose unjust
    And faithless nature has deceived my trust;
    Avenge a crime your pure soul must detest.   35
ELIANTE.   But how, Sir?
ALCESTE.   Madam, this heart within my breast
    Is yours; pray take it; redeem my heart from her,
    And so avenge me on my torturer.
    Let her be punished by the fond emotion,
    The ardent love, the bottomless devotion,   40
    The faithful worship which this heart of mine
    Will offer up to yours as to a shrine.
ELIANTE.   You have my sympathy, Sir, in all you suffer;
    Nor do I scorn the noble heart you offer;
    But I suspect you'll soon be mollified,   45
    And this desire for vengeance will subside.
    When some beloved hand has done us wrong
    We thirst for retribution—but not for long;
    However dark the deed that she's committed,
    A lovely culprit's very soon acquitted.   50
    Nothing's so stormy as an injured lover,
    And yet no storm so quickly passes over.
ALCESTE.   No, Madam, no—this is no lovers' spat;
    I'll not forgive her; it's gone too far for that;
    My mind's made up; I'll kill myself before   55
    I waste my hopes upon her any more.
    Ah, here she is. My wrath intensifies.
    I shall confront her with her tricks and lies,
    And crush her utterly, and bring you then
    A heart no longer slave to Célimène.   60

Scene 3

[*Enter* CÉLIMÈNE, *exit* ELIANTE *and* PHILINTE]

ALCESTE. [*aside*] Sweet heaven, help me to control my passion.
CÉLIMÈNE. [*aside, to* ALCESTE] Oh, Lord. Why stand there staring in that fashion?
   And what d'you mean by those dramatic sighs,
   And that malignant glitter in your eyes? 5
ALCESTE. I mean that sins which cause the blood to freeze
   Look innocent beside your treacheries;
   That nothing Hell's or Heaven's wrath could do
   Ever produced so bad a thing as you.
CÉLIMÈNE. Your compliments were always sweet and pretty. 10
ALCESTE. Madam, it's not the moment to be witty.
   No, blush and hang your head; you've ample reason,
   Since I've the fullest evidence of your treason.
   Ah, this is what my sad heart prophesied;
   Now all my anxious fears are verified; 15
   My dark suspicion and my gloomy doubt
   Divined the truth, and now the truth is out.
   For all your trickery, I was not deceived;
   It was my bitter stars that I believed.
   But don't imagine that you'll go scot-free; 20
   You shan't misuse me with impunity.
   I know that love's irrational and blind;
   I know the heart's not subject to the mind,
   And can't be reasoned into beating faster;
   I know each soul is free to choose its master; 25
   Therefore had you but spoken from the heart,
   Rejecting my attentions from the start,
   I'd have no grievance, or at any rate
   I could complain of nothing but my fate.
   Ah, but so falsely to encourage me— 30
   That was treason and a treachery
   For which you cannot suffer too severely,
   And you shall pay for that behavior dearly.
   Yes, now I have no pity, not a shred;
   My temper's out of hand; I've lost my head; 35
   Shocked by the knowledge of your double-dealings,
   My reason can't restrain my savage feelings;
   A righteous wrath deprives me of my senses,
   And I won't answer for the consequences.
CÉLIMÈNE. What does this outburst mean? Will you please explain? 40
   Have you, by any chance, gone quite insane?
ALCESTE. Yes, yes, I went insane the day I fell
   A victim to your black and fatal spell,
   Thinking to meet with some sincerity
   Among the treacherous charms that beckoned me. 45

CÉLIMÈNE.   Pooh. Of what treachery can you complain?   45
ALCESTE.   How sly you are, how cleverly you feign!
  But you'll not victimize me any more.
  Look: here's a document you've seen before.
  This evidence, which I acquired today,
  Leaves you, I think, without a thing to say.   50
CÉLIMÈNE.   Is this what sent you into such a fit?
ALCESTE.   You should be blushing at the sight of it.
CÉLIMÈNE.   Ought I to blush? I truly don't see why.
ALCESTE.   Ah, now you're being bold as well as sly;
  Since there's no signature, perhaps you'll claim . . .   55
CÉLIMÈNE.   I wrote it, whether or not it bears my name.
ALCESTE.   And you can view with equanimity
  This proof of your disloyalty to me!
CÉLIMÈNE.   Oh, don't be so outrageous and extreme.
ALCESTE.   You take his matter lightly, it would seem.   60
  Was it no wrong to me, no shame to you,
  That you should send Oronte this billet-doux?°
CÉLIMÈNE.   Oronte! Who said it was for him?
ALCESTE.   Why, those
  Who brought me this example of your prose.
  But what's the difference? If you wrote the letter   65
  To someone else, it pleases me no better.
  My grievance and your guilt remain the same.
CÉLIMÈNE.   But need you rage, and need I blush for shame,
  If this was written to a *woman* friend?
ALCESTE.   Ah! Most ingenious. I'm impressed no end;   70
  And after that incredible evasion
  Your guilt is clear. I need no more persuasion.
  How dare you try so clumsy a deception?
  D'you think I'm wholly wanting in perception?
  Come, come, let's see how brazenly you'll try   75
  To bolster up so palpable a lie:
  Kindly construe this ardent closing section
  As nothing more than sisterly affection!
  Here, let me read it. Tell me, if you dare to,
  That this is for a woman . . .
CÉLIMÈNE.   I don't care to.   80
  What right have you to badger and berate me,
  And so highhandedly interrogate me?
ALCESTE.   Now, don't be angry; all I ask of you
  Is that you justify a phrase or two . . .
CÉLIMÈNE.   No, I shall not. I utterly refuse,   85
  And you may take those phrases as you choose.
ALCESTE.   Just show me how this letter could be meant
  For a woman's eyes, and I shall be content.

62 *billet-doux*: love letter.

CÉLIMÈNE.   No, no, it's for Oronte; you're perfectly right.
    I welcome his attentions with delight, 9
    I prize his character and his intellect,
    And everything is just as you suspect.
    Come, do your worst now; give your rage free rein;
    But kindly cease to bicker and complain.
ALCESTE.   [*aside*] Good God! Could anything be more inhuman? 9
    Was ever a heart so mangled by a woman?
    When I complain of how she has betrayed me,
    She bridles, and commences to upbraid me!
    She tries my tortured patience to the limit;
    She won't deny her guilt; she glories in it! 10
    And yet my heart's too faint and cowardly
    To break these chains of passion, and be free,
    To scorn her as it should, and rise above
    This unrewarded, mad, and bitter love.
    [*to* CÉLIMÈNE] Ah, traitress, in how confident a fashion 10
    You take advantage of my helpless passion,
    And use my weakness for your faithless charms
    To make me once again throw down my arms!
    But do at least deny this black transgression;
    Take back that mocking and perverse confession; 11
    Defend this letter and your innocence,
    And I, poor fool, will aid in your defense.
    Pretend, pretend, that you are just and true,
    And I shall make myself believe in you.
CÉLIMÈNE.   Oh, stop it. Don't be such a jealous dunce, 11
    Or I shall leave off loving you at once.
    Just why should I *pretend*? What could impel me
    To stoop so low as that? And kindly tell me
    Why, if I loved another, I shouldn't merely
    Inform you of it, simply and sincerely! 120
    I've told you where you stand, and that admission
    Should altogether clear me of suspicion;
    After so generous a guarantee,
    What right have you to harbor doubts of me?
    Since women are (from natural reticence) 125
    Reluctant to declare their sentiments,
    And since the honor of our sex requires
    That we conceal our amorous desires,
    Ought any man for whom such laws are broken
    To question what the oracle has spoken? 130
    Should he not rather feel an obligation
    To trust that most obliging declaration?
    Enough, now. Your suspicions quite disgust me;
    Why should I love a man who doesn't trust me?
    I cannot understand why I continue, 135
    Fool that I am, to take an interest in you.

I ought to choose a man less prone to doubt,
And give you something to be vexed about.
ALCESTE.   Ah, what a poor enchanted fool I am;
    These gentle words, no doubt, were all a sham;   140
    But destiny requires me to entrust
    My happiness to you, and so I must.
    I'll love you to the bitter end, and see
    How false and treacherous you dare to be.
CÉLIMÈNE.   No, you don't really love me as you ought.   145
ALCESTE.   I love you more than can be said or thought;
    Indeed, I wish you were in such distress
    That I might show my deep devotedness.
    Yes, I could wish that you were wretchedly poor,
    Unloved, uncherished, utterly obscure;   150
    That fate had set you down upon the earth
    Without possessions, rank, or gentle birth;
    Then, by the offer of my heart, I might
    Repair the great injustice of your plight;
    I'd raise you from the dust, and proudly prove   155
    The purity and vastness of my love.
CÉLIMÈNE.   This is a strange benevolence indeed!
    God grant that I may never be in need . . .
    Ah, here's Monsieur Dubois, in quaint disguise.

Scene 4

[*Enter DUBOIS*]

ALCESTE.   Well, why this costume? Why those frightened eyes?
    What ails you?
DUBOIS.   Well, Sir, things are most mysterious.
ALCESTE.   What do you mean?
DUBOIS.   I fear they're very serious.
ALCESTE.   What?
DUBOIS.   Shall I speak more loudly?
ALCESTE.   Yes; speak out.
DUBOIS.   Isn't there someone here, Sir?
ALCESTE.   Speak, you lout!   5
    Stop wasting time.
DUBOIS.   Sir, we must slip away.
ALCESTE.   How's that?
DUBOIS.   We must decamp without delay.
ALCESTE.   Explain yourself.
DUBOIS.   I tell you we must fly.
ALCESTE.   What for?
DUBOIS.   We mustn't pause to say good-by.
ALCESTE.   Now what d'you mean by all of this, you clown?   10
DUBOIS.   I mean, Sir, that we've got to leave this town.

ALCESTE.   I'll tear you limb from limb and joint from joint
  If you don't come more quickly to the point.
DUBOIS.   Well, Sir, today a man in a black suit,
  Who wore a black and ugly scowl to boot,   1
  Left us a document scrawled in such a hand
  As even Satan couldn't understand.
  It bears upon your lawsuit, I don't doubt;
  But all hell's devils couldn't make it out.
ALCESTE.   Well, well, go on. What then? I fail to see   2
  How this event obliges us to flee.
DUBOIS.   Well, Sir: an hour later, hardly more,
  A gentleman who's often called before
  Came looking for you in an anxious way.
  Not finding you, he asked me to convey   2
  (Knowing I could be trusted with the same)
  The following message . . . Now, what *was* his name?
ALCESTE.   Forget his name, you idiot. What did he say?
DUBOIS.   Well, it was one of your friends, Sir, anyway.
  He warned you to begone, and he suggested   3
  That if you stay, you may well be arrested.
ALCESTE.   What? Nothing more specific? Think, man, think!
DUBOIS.   No, Sir. He had me bring him pen and ink,
  And dashed you off a letter which, I'm sure,
  Will render things distinctly less obscure.   3
ALCESTE.   Well—let me have it!
CÉLIMÈNE.   What *is* this all about?
ALCESTE.   God knows; but I have hopes of finding out.
  How long am I to wait, you blitherer?
DUBOIS.   [*after a protracted search for the letter*] I must have left it on
      your table, Sir.
ALCESTE.   I ought to . . .
CÉLIMÈNE.   No, no, keep your self-control;   4
  Go find out what's behind his rigmarole.
ALCESTE.   It seems that fate, no matter what I do,
  Has sworn that I may not converse with you;
  But, Madam, pray permit your faithful lover
  To try once more before the day is over.   [*Exeunt*]   45

ACT 5

Scene 1

[*Enter ALCESTE and PHILINTE*]

ALCESTE.   No, it's too much. My mind's made up, I tell you.
PHILINTE.   Why should this blow, however hard, compel you . . .
ALCESTE.   No, no, don't waste your breath in argument;

Nothing you say will alter my intent;
This age is vile, and I've made up my mind   5
To have no further commerce with mankind.
Did not truth, honor, decency, and the laws
Oppose my enemy and approve my cause?
My claims were justified in all men's sight;
I put my trust in equity and right;   10
Yet, to my horror and the world's disgrace,
Justice is mocked, and I have lost my case!
A scoundrel whose dishonesty is notorious
Emerges from another lie victorious!
Honor and right condone his brazen fraud,   15
While rectitude and decency applaud!
Before his smirking face, the truth stands charmed,
And virtue conquered, and the law disarmed!
His crime is sanctioned by a court decree!
And not content with what he's done to me,   20
The dog now seeks to ruin me by stating
That I composed a book now circulating,
A book so wholly criminal and vicious
That even to speak its title is seditious!
Meanwhile Oronte, my rival, lends his credit   25
To the same libelous tale, and helps to spread it!
Oronte! a man of honor and of rank,
With whom I've been entirely fair and frank;
Who sought me out and forced me, willy-nilly,
To judge some verse I found extremely silly;   30
And who, because I properly refused
To flatter him, or see the truth abused,
Abets my enemy in a rotten slander!
There's the reward of honesty and candor!
The man will hate me to the end of time   35
For failing to commend his wretched rhyme!
And not this man alone, but all humanity
Do what they do from interest and vanity;
They prate of honor, truth, and righteousness,
But lie, betray, and swindle nonetheless.   40
Come then: man's villainy is too much to bear;
Let's leave this jungle and this jackal's lair.
Yes! treacherous and savage race of men,
You shall not look upon my face again.
PHILINTE. Oh, don't rush into exile prematurely;   45
Things aren't as dreadful as you make them, surely.
It's rather obvious, since you're still at large,
That people don't believe our enemy's charge.
Indeed, his tale's so patently untrue
That it may do more harm to him than you.   50
ALCESTE. Nothing could do that scoundrel any harm:

His frank corruption is his greatest charm,
And, far from hurting him, a further shame
Would only serve to magnify his name.

PHILINTE.   In any case, his bald prevarication   5
  Has done no injury to your reputation,
  And you may feel secure in that regard.
  As for your lawsuit, it should not be hard
  To have the case reopened, and contest
  This judgment . . .

ALCESTE.   No, no, let the verdict rest.   6
  Whatever cruel penalty it may bring,
  I wouldn't have it changed for anything.
  It shows the times' injustice with such clarity
  That I shall pass it down to our posterity
  As a great proof and signal demonstration   6
  Of the black wickedness of this generation.
  It may cost twenty thousand francs; but I
  Shall pay their twenty thousand, and gain thereby
  The right to storm and rage at human evil,
  And send the race of mankind to the devil.   7

PHILINTE.   Listen to me . . .

ALCESTE.   Why? What can you possibly say?
  Don't argue, Sir; your labor's thrown away.
  Do you propose to offer lame excuses
  For men's behavior and the times' abuses?

PHILINTE.   No, all you say I'll readily concede: 7
  This is a low, dishonest age indeed;
  Nothing but trickery prospers nowadays,
  And people ought to mend their shabby ways.
  Yes, man's a beastly creature; but must we then
  Abandon the society of men?   8
  Here in the world, each human frailty
  Provides occasion for philosophy,
  And that is virtue's noblest exercise;
  If honesty shone forth from all men's eyes,
  If every heart were frank and kind and just,   8
  What could our virtues do but gather dust
  (Since their employment is to help us bear
  The villainies of men without despair)?
  A heart well-armed with virtue can endure . . .

ALCESTE.   Sir, you're a matchless reasoner, to be sure; 9
  Your words are fine and full of cogency;
  But don't waste time and eloquence on me.
  My reason bids me go, for my own good.
  My tongue won't lie and flatter as it should;
  God knows what frankness it might next commit.   9
  And what I'd suffer on account of it.
  Pray let me wait for Célimène's return

In peace and quiet. I shall shortly learn,
By her response to what I have in view,
Whether her love for me is feigned or true.   100
PHILINTE.   Till then, let's visit Eliante upstairs.
ALCESTE.   No, I am too weighed down with somber cares.
Go to her, do; and leave me with my gloom
Here in the darkened corner of this room.
PHILINTE.   Why, that's no sort of company, my friend;   105
I'll see if Eliante will not descend.   [*Exit* PHILINTE]

Scene 2

[*Enter* ORONTE *and* CÉLIMÈNE. ALCESTE *withdraws to the corner*.]

ORONTE.   Yes, Madam, if you wish me to remain
Your true and ardent lover, you must deign
To give me some more positive assurance.
All this suspense is quite beyond endurance.
If your heart shares the sweet desires of mine,   5
Show me as much by some convincing sign;
And here's the sign I urgently suggest:
That you no longer tolerate Alceste,
But sacrifice him to my love, and sever
All your relations with the man forever.   10
CÉLIMÈNE.   Why do you suddenly dislike him so?
You praised him to the skies not long ago.
ORONTE.   Madam, that's not the point. I'm here to find
Which way your tender feelings are inclined.
Choose, if you please, between Alceste and me,   15
And I shall stay or go accordingly.
ALCESTE.   [*emerging from the corner*] Yes, Madam, choose; this
     gentleman's demand
Is wholly just, and I support his stand.
I too am true and ardent; I too am here
To ask you that you make your feelings clear.   20
No more delays, now; no equivocation;
The time has come to make your declaration.
ORONTE.   Sir, I've no wish in any way to be
An obstacle to your felicity.
ALCESTE.   Sir, I've no wish to share her heart with you;   25
That may sound jealous, but at least it's true.
ORONTE.   If, weighing us, she leans in your direction . . .
ALCESTE.   If she regards you with the least affection . . .
ORONTE.   I swear I'll yield her to you there and then.
ALCESTE.   I swear I'll never see her face again.   30
ORONTE.   Now, Madam, tell us what we've come to hear.
ALCESTE.   Madam, speak openly and have no fear.
ORONTE.   Just say which one is to remain your lover.
ALCESTE.   Just name one name, and it will all be over.

ORONTE. What! Is it possible that you're undecided?
ALCESTE. What! Can your feelings possibly be divided?
CÉLIMÈNE. Enough: this inquisition's gone too far:
    How utterly unreasonable you are!
    Not that I couldn't make the choice with ease;
    My heart has no conflicting sympathies;
    I know full well which one of you I favor,
    And you'd not see me hesitate or waver.
    But how can you expect me to reveal
    So cruelly and bluntly what I feel?
    I think it altogether too unpleasant
    To choose between two men when both are present;
    One's heart has means more subtle and more kind
    Of letting its affections be divined,
    Nor need one be uncharitably plain
    To let a lover know he loves in vain.
ORONTE. No, no, speak plainly; I for one can stand it.
    I beg you to be frank.
ALCESTE.   And I demand it.
    The simple truth is what I wish to know,
    And there's no need for softening the blow.
    You've made an art of pleasing everyone,
    But now your days of coquetry are done:
    You have no choice now, Madam, but to choose,
    For I'll know what to think if you refuse;
    I'll take your silence for a clear admission
    That I'm entitled to my worst suspicion.
ORONTE. I thank you for this ultimatum, Sir,
    And I may say I heartily concur.
CÉLIMÈNE. Really, this foolishness is very wearing:
    Must you be so unjust and overbearing?
    Haven't I told you why I must demur?
    Ah, here's Eliante; I'll put the case to her.

Scene 3

[*Enter* ELIANTE *and* PHILINTE]

CÉLIMÈNE. Cousin, I'm being persecuted here
    By these two persons, who, it would appear,
    Will not be satisfied till I confess
    Which one I love the more, and which the less,
    And tell the latter to his face that he
    Is henceforth banished from my company.
    Tell me, has ever such a thing been done?
ELIANTE. You'd best not turn to me; I'm not the one
    To back you in a matter of this kind:
    I'm all for those who frankly speak their mind.

ORONTE. Madam, you'll search in vain for a defender.
ALCESTE. You're beaten, Madam, and may as well surrender.
ORONTE. Speak, speak, you must; and end this awful strain.
ALCESTE. Or don't, and your position will be plain.
ORONTE. A single word will close this painful scene.   15
ALCESTE. But if you're silent, I'll know what you mean.

Scene 4

[*Enter ACASTE, CLITANDRE, and ARSINOÉ*]

ACASTE. [*to CÉLIMÈNE*] Madam, with all due deference, we two
    Have come to pick a little bone with you.
CLITANDRE. [*to ORONTE and ALCESTE*] I'm glad you're present, Sirs; as
      you'll soon learn,
    Our business here is also your concern.
ARSINOÉ. [*to CÉLIMÈNE*] Madam, I visit you so soon again   5
    Only because of these two gentlemen,
    Who came to me indignant and aggrieved
    About a crime too base to be believed.
    Knowing your virtue, having such confidence in it,
    I couldn't think you guilty for a minute,   10
    In spite of all their telling evidence;
    And, rising above our little difference,
    I've hastened here in friendship's name to see
    You clear yourself of this great calumny.
ACASTE. Yes, Madam, let us see with what composure   15
    You'll manage to respond to this disclosure.
    You lately sent Clitandre this tender note.
CLITANDRE. And this one, for Acaste, you also wrote.
ACASTE. [*to ORONTE and ALCESTE*] You'll recognize this writing, Sirs, I think;
    The lady is so free with pen and ink   20
    That you must know it all too well, I fear.
    But listen: this is something you should hear.
    "How absurd you are to condemn my lightheartedness in society, and to accuse
      me of being happiest in the company of others. Nothing could be more
      unjust; and if you do not come to me instantly and beg pardon for saying   25
      such a thing, I shall never forgive you as long as I live. Our big bumbling
      friend the Viscount . . ."
    What a shame that he's not here.
    "Our big bumbling friend the Viscount, whose name stands first in your com-
      plaint, is hardly a man to my taste; and ever since the day I watched   30
      him spend three-quarters of an hour spitting into a well, so as to make
      circles in the water, I have been unable to think highly of him. As for
      the little Marquess . . ."
    In all modesty, gentlemen, that is I.
    "As for the little Marquess, who sat squeezing my hand for such a long while   35
      yesterday, I find him in all respects the most trifling creature alive; and

the only things of value about him are his cape and his sword. As for
the man with the green ribbons . . ."
[*To* ALCESTE] It's your turn now, Sir.
"As for the man with the green ribbons, he amuses me now and then with
his bluntness and his bearish ill-humor; but there are many times indeed
when I think him the greatest bore in the world. And as for the sonneteer . . ."
[*To* ORONTE] Here's your helping.
"And as for the sonneteer, who has taken it into his head to be witty, and
insists on being an author in the teeth of opinion, I simply cannot be
bothered to listen to him, and his prose wearies me quite as much as
his poetry. Be assured that I am not always so well-entertained as you
suppose; that I long for your company, more than I dare to say, at all
these entertainments to which people drag me; and that the presence of
those one loves is the true and perfect seasoning to all one's pleasures."
CLITANDRE.   And now for me.
"Clitandre, whom you mention, and who so pesters me with his saccharine
speeches, is the last man on earth for whom I could feel any affection.
He is quite mad to suppose that I love him, and so are you, to doubt
that you are loved. Do come to your senses; exchange your suppositions
for his; and visit me as often as possible, to help me bear the annoyance
of his unwelcome attentions."
It's a sweet character that these letters show,
And what to call it, Madam, you well know.
Enough. We're off to make the world acquainted
With this sublime self-portrait that you've painted.
ACASTE.   Madam, I'll make you no farewell oration;
No, you're not worthy of my indignation.
Far choicer hearts than yours, as you'll discover,
Would like this little Marquess for a lover.   [*Exit* CLITANDRE *and* ACASTE]

Scene 5

ORONTE.   So! After all those loving letters you wrote,
You turn on me like this, and cut my throat!
And your dissembling, faithless heart, I find,
Has pledged itself by turns to all mankind!
How blind I've been! But now I clearly see;
I thank you, Madam, for enlightening me.
My heart is mine once more, and I'm content;
The loss of it shall be your punishment.
[*to* ALCESTE]   Sir, she is yours; I'll seek no more to stand
Between your wishes and this lady's hand.   [*Exit* ORONTE]

Scene 6

ARSINOÉ.   [*to* CÉLIMÈNE] Madam, I'm forced to speak. I'm far too stirred
To keep my counsel, after what I've heard.
I'm shocked and staggered by your want of morals.

It's not my way to mix in others' quarrels;
But really, when this fine and noble spirit,   5
This man of honor and surpassing merit,
Laid down the offering of his heart before you,
How *could* you . . .
ALCESTE.   Madam, permit me, I implore you,
To represent myself in this debate.
Don't bother, please, to be my advocate.   10
My heart, in any case, could not afford
To give your services their due reward;
And if I chose, for consolation's sake,
Some other lady, t'would not be you I'd take.
ARSINOÉ.   What makes you think you could, Sir? And how dare you   15
Imply that I've been trying to ensnare you?
If you can for a moment entertain
Such flattering fancies, you're extremely vain.
I'm not so interested as you suppose
In Célimène's discarded gigolos.°   20
Get rid of that absurd illusion, do.
Women like me are not for such as you.
Stay with this creature, to whom you're so attached;
I've never seen two people better matched.   [*Exit ARSINOÉ*]

Scene 7

ALCESTE. [*to CÉLIMÈNE*] Well, I've been still throughout this exposé,
Till everyone but me has said his say.
Come, have I shown sufficient self-restraint?
And may I now . . .
CÉLIMÈNE.   Yes, make your just complaint.
Reproach me freely, call me what you will;   5
You've every right to say I've used you ill.
I've wronged you, I confess it; and in my shame
I'll make no effort to escape the blame.
The anger of those others I could despise;
My guilt toward you I sadly recognize.   10
Your wrath is wholly justified, I fear;
I know how culpable I must appear,
I know all things bespeak my treachery,
And that, in short, you've grounds for hating me.
Do so; I give you leave.
ALCESTE.   Ah, traitress—how,   15
How should I cease to love you, even now?
Though mind and will were passionately bent
On hating you, my heart would not consent.
[*to ELIANTE and PHILINTE*] Be witness to my madness, both of you;

20 *gigolos*: paid lovers.

See what infatuation drives one to;   20
But wait; my folly's only just begun,
And I shall prove to you before I'm done
How strange the human heart is, and how far
From rational we sorry creatures are.
[*to* CÉLIMÈNE] Woman, I'm willing to forget your shame,   25
And clothe your treacheries in a sweeter name;
I'll call them youthful errors, instead of crimes,
And lay the blame on these corrupting times.
My one condition is that you agree
To share my chosen fate, and fly with me   30
To that wild, trackless solitary place
In which I shall forget the human race.
Only by such a course can you atone
For those atrocious letters; by that alone
Can you remove my present horror of you,   35
And make it possible for me to love you.
CÉLIMÈNE. What! *I* renounce the world at my young age,
And die of boredom in some hermitage?°
ALCESTE. Ah, if you really loved me as you ought,
You wouldn't give the world a moment's thought;   40
Must you have me, and all the world beside?
CÉLIMÈNE. Alas, at twenty one is terrified
Of solitude. I fear I lack the force
And depth of soul to take so stern a course.
But if my hand in marriage will content you,   45
Why, there's a plan which I might well consent to,
And . . .
ALCESTE.   No, I detest you now. I could excuse
Everything else, but since you thus refuse
To love me wholly, as a wife should do,
And see the world in me, as I in you,   50
Go! I reject your hand, and disenthrall
My heart from your enchantment, once for all.   [*Exit* CÉLIMÈNE]

Scene 8

ALCESTE. [*to* ELIANTE] Madam, your virtuous beauty has no peer,
Of all this world, you only are sincere;
I've long esteemed you highly, as you know;
Permit me ever to esteem you so,
And if I do not now request your hand,
Forgive me, Madam, and try to understand.   5
I feel unworthy of it; I sense that fate
Does not intend me for the married state,

38 *hermitage*: hermit's retreat.

That I should do you wrong by offering you
My shattered heart's unhappy residue,   10
And that in short . . .
ELIANTE.   Your argument's well taken:
Nor need you fear that I shall feel forsaken.
Were I to offer him this hand of mine,
Your friend Philinte, I think, would not decline.
PHILINTE.   Ah, Madam, that's my heart's most cherished goal,   15
For which I'd gladly give my life and soul.
ALCESTE.   [*to ELIANTE and PHILINTE*] May you be true to all you
      now profess,
And so deserve unending happiness.
Meanwhile, betrayed and wronged in everything,
I'll flee this bitter world where vice is king,   20
And seek some spot unpeopled and apart
Where I'll be free to have an honest heart.
PHILINTE.   Come, Madam, let's do everything we can
To change the mind of this unhappy man.   [*Exeunt*]

QUESTIONS

Act 1

1. What is established about the characters of Alceste and Philinte in scene 1? What is Alceste's attitude toward social convention and society? What is Philinte's? Which is more perceptive? More reasonable? Why?

2. What two complications of plot are introduced briefly in scene 1?

3. Alceste claims that he sees Célimène's faults clearly, despite his "ardent love." Is he right? In what ways is Alceste blind about this relationship?

4. How does Alceste treat Oronte? How does he judge Oronte's sonnet? How does he express his judgment? To what extent does Alceste practice what he preaches?

Act 2

5. Characterize Alceste as a lover. What does he want Célimène to do? To explain? Are his demands reasonable? Realistic?

6. What is Célimène's attitude toward social convention? Is her behavior closer to Alceste's or Philinte's? What details lead to your conclusion?

7. How would you characterize Célimène's "performance" for Acaste and Clitandre in scene 5? How does the satire here encompass both the absent nobles whom Célimène describes and the participants in the conversation?

8. How accurate is Célimène's satirical portrait of Alceste (2. 5. 111–122)? What does it tell you about Célimène's understanding of Alceste?

Act 3

9. What is Acaste's opinion of himself? What conflict develops between him and Clitandre? How is it ironic? How do the nobles settle it on the spot?

10. How does Célimène describe Arsinoé? To what extent do Arsinoé's character and behavior fit this description?

11. How do Célimène and Arsinoé regard each other? Treat each other? How does their manner toward each other change during their conversation?

12. How does Célimène set up her own downfall in scene 6? What does Arsinoé offer to prove to Alceste? What are her motives?

Act 4

13. What is Eliante's attitude toward Alceste? Toward Philinte? Toward social convention? How is her "frankness" different from Alceste's?

14. Why does Alceste want revenge and how does he plan to get it? What is odd about his method? How does Célimène deal with his rage?

15. Why does Alceste wish that Célimène were poor, low-born, unloved, and obscure? What does this show you about Alceste? About his love for Célimène?

Act 5

16. Why is it significant that we learn no details about Alceste's lawsuit? What does the lawsuit symbolize? Why won't Alceste appeal the judgment? What does his refusal show you about him?

17. How do the demands of Alceste and Oronte push the play to a crisis?

18. What is the catastrophe? How does it affect Acaste, Clitandre, and Oronte? Arsinoé? Célimène? Alceste? Eliante and Philinte?

19. To what extent is the resolution of this play conventionally comic? What prevents you from viewing the resolution as tragic?

TOPICS FOR WRITING AND FURTHER DISCUSSION

1. To what extent does *The Misanthrope* reflect the neoclassical rules of drama? How successful is Molière in turning these limiting rules into strengths?

2. Who is the protagonist? What conflicts (and types of conflicts) develop? To what extent does the protagonist distinguish among these conflicts and treat them differently? Which conflicts are resolved?

3. Describe Oronte, Acaste, and Clitandre. How are they similar? Are they round or flat characters? Individualized or representative? What are their functions in the play? To what extent are they satirized?

4. What are Célimène's good and bad qualities? Do you consider her the heroine or the villain of the play? Explain.

5. The play presents three women—Célimène, Arsinoé, and Eliante—who represent different attitudes and styles. What attitude does each have toward the others? Toward Alceste? Toward social conventions and morality? Which is the most hypocritical? Tolerant? Reasonable? Realistic?

6. What characteristics does Alceste have in common with tragic protagonists? What prevents you from seeing him as a tragic figure?

7. What does Alceste learn in the course of the play? To what extent, if any, does he change? How does education contribute to the play's resolution?

8. Both the way of the world and Alceste's violent reaction to it are satirized in this play. Which does Molière attack more severely? What specific aspects of the play can you cite to support your decision?

9. What distinctions does Molière make between politeness and hypocrisy? Folly and crime? Tolerance and flattery? To what extent does Alceste make these distinctions?

10. Given that Alceste and Célimène represent satirized extremes, what ideals of social behavior and morality does the play finally advocate? Which characters, if any, embody these ideals within the play? Explain your choices.

WRITING ABOUT COMEDY

When you set out to plan and write an essay on some aspect of a comedy, all the conventional elements of drama are available as potential focuses. You may consider such traditional features as plot, conflict, character, perspective, setting, style, tone, symbolism, or theme as possible areas of investigation. You might focus your attention on any one of these; or you might write about several related elements, such as how language and action define character, how character and symbol convey meaning, or the linkage between setting and comic structure.

Planning and prewriting strategies for each of these conventional elements are discussed at some length in Chapter 27 (pp. 1112–15) and in other chapters on prose fiction and poetry. As you begin to develop an essay on comic drama, you will find it helpful to look at the suggestions in these earlier sections.

For the most part, planning and writing about specific features of comedy are much like addressing the same topics in tragedy, realistic drama, short stories, or poetry. However, a few areas of consideration—such as plot, character, and language—are especially significant in comic drama and thus may be handled in a distinctive or singular fashion.

1. *Plot, conflict, structure.* Because plot and structure are central elements in comic drama, these and related areas are especially rich in material for an essay. In looking at the exposition, for example, consider what problems, adversities, or abnormal situations are in place at the beginning of the play. How is this initial situation complicated? Do the complications

spring mainly from character or from situation? If from character, what aspects of behavior or personality create the problems? If from situation, what sorts of dilemmas or troubles plague the characters? You might also consider what kinds of complications dominate. Are they mostly misunderstandings, disagreements, mistakes in identity, situational problems, or emotional entanglements? To what extent does coincidence contribute to the chaos in the play?

Another way of exploring the problems and complications that occur early in a comedy is through the new comic pattern. Who is the comic protagonist (or protagonists) and what is the goal (money, success, marriage, land, freedom)? How is the protagonist blocked (fathers, rivals, laws, customs, his or her own personality)? How threatening is the obstruction? What plans are developed to circumvent the blocking agents? Are the plans sensible or silly? Who initiates and executes the plans? To what extent do the plans succeed (or fail) because of chance and good luck or because of skillful planning and manipulation?

The conflicts in comedy and the later stages of comic structure are equally rewarding areas for investigation. With the conflicts, determine who or what they involve and which is central. Do they result from clashes of personality or from situations? To what degree are they related to blocking activities? With the crisis, consider how the action reaches this high point of complication and which characters are involved. What sorts of choices, decisions, plans, or conclusions become necessary? Similarly, you might consider what sorts of events or revelations (of character, emotion, background) produce the catastrophe and how it affects characters, circumstances, and relationships.

With the comic resolution, you should determine to what extent loose ends are tied up, lives are straightened out, reasonable order is restored, and regeneration is assured or implied. Does the resolution involve marriage(s) or the prospect of marriage(s)? If so, what does this suggest about the regeneration or continuity and the happiness of the state, the society, the family, and the individuals? Do you find the resolution satisfying or disturbing; does it leave you happy or thoughtful, or both? Most important, how can you account for your responses to the resolution and the play as a whole? To what extent do they reflect the general aims of the various types of comedy—are you smiling at romantic comedy or disturbed by satire?

2. *Character*. In exploring the possibilities of writing about character, keep in mind that comic characters are often conventional, representational, and stereotyped. In addition, characters are often closely related to their social class, dominant eccentricity, and the function they play in the drama. Thus, you might consider what conventional role a character fills. Is he or she a protagonist-lover, an antagonist-blocking agent, a choric figure, a confidant, or a parallel to one of the central figures? Does the character

bear any resemblance to one of the traditional stock characters derived from Roman new comedy or from Italian *commedia dell'arte*? If so, how does the playwright reinvigorate this stock figure to give the play vitality?

Other considerations deal with personality or behavior. Because comedy often examines extreme types, you should try to identify exaggerated behavior patterns. Do you find characters who are excessive, eccentric, or irrationally fixated on something? If so, what is the nature of this excess? To what extent does it define the character? What is its effect on the action of the play and on your reaction to the play? To what extent do the complications and conflicts in the play develop because of one or more excessive characters? Is this character cured of his or her excesses in the course of the play, or does the excess endure? Do characters learn and change? If so, why? If not, why not?

3. *Language*. Language is an important vehicle for amusement and characterization in comedy. Is the language in the play at hand mostly witty, mostly bungling, or a mixture? Which characters are masters of language and which are mastered by it? Do groups of characters use the same type of language and level of diction consistently? If the language is witty and sparkling, what specific devices make it work effectively? If it is bungling and garbled, what types of errors does the playwright put into the character's mouths? To what extent does this language shape your response to characters, to ideas, and to the play as a whole?

Once you have surveyed the elements of drama and the areas that may be handled distinctively in comedy, you can begin to develop a focus and central idea. If a topic is assigned, you can move directly toward formulating a thesis. If the choice is up to you, try to isolate features that are both interesting and important in the play. It would not be productive, for example, to focus on physical setting in *The Misanthrope* since the entire play occurs in a single room that is never described. Like other literature, most comedies will, by their very nature, emphasize certain features that are worth consideration. The play, and your responses to it, should direct you toward significant and interesting topics.

In developing a central idea, isolate the feature you wish to explore and consider how it affects the shape and impact of the play. The initial formulation of the central idea should assert a significant conclusion about an element or elements. In planning an essay on Shakespeare's *A Midsummer Night's Dream*, for example, you might decide to focus on Puck's character and function. Further, you might begin to develop a central idea that links Puck's conventional role as a tricky servant with his love of mischief and the chaos he creates in the play. Alternatively, you might focus on the theme: a tentative central idea might assert that the play explores the dangers and delights of irrational passion.

Your central idea should make a clear and useful assertion about the topic you have chosen to explore. It would not be fruitful, for example, to formulate a thesis that asserts "Puck is a comic character" or "*The Misanthrope* is a satirical play." Both of these statements belabor the obvious and neither is focused enough to generate an effective or convincing essay. Better formulations might assert that "Puck is a comic character, modeled on the tricky servant of new comedy, who causes most of the confusion in *A Midsummer Night's Dream*" or that "*The Misanthrope* satirizes both the follies of society and extreme reactions to them."

After formulating a tentative thesis, go back through the play and note all the details that helped you form your conclusions. These notes will become the basis for the body of the essay. You may not use all these supporting details in the final essay, but keep them at hand throughout the stages of planning, writing, and revision. As you jot these down, you can begin to impose a tentative organization on the material. If you are noting a number of different types of evidence, such as observations about characters, actions, direct statements, and specific words, you can group related types of details together. If you are focusing on only one type of evidence, however, you should maintain the order in which these occur in the comedy. While you collect and organize this material, make sure it is relevant to your central idea and supports your argument. As your essay develops, new insights and details will often change the focus or direction of your efforts. As a result, revision should be a constant process in your planning and writing.

Organizing Your Essay

INTRODUCTION. When you begin to write, first compose the introduction, the foundation of the essay. You can start with some general information about the comedy, but you should move quickly to the topic of the essay. The most important features of the introduction are the statement of the central idea and a thesis or topic sentence that outlines the topics you plan to take up in support of your idea.

BODY. The body of the essay should prove the validity of the central idea through a series of supporting details. Present this evidence in a logical and convincing manner. Organization here depends entirely on the topic discussed, the central idea, and the evidence used to validate this idea. In writing about Puck as a tricky servant and creator of chaos, for example, you might present only one kind of detail—direct statement by the character—as evidence. In such an essay, you can deal with Puck's remarks in the order in which they appear in the play.

More often than not, however, you will find that your supporting details represent a variety of types of evidence—statements by one character, comments by others, actions. Thus, you might support your initial assertion about Puck with reference to his reputation, actions, and attitudes. In this instance, the body would be organized to deal with each type of evidence in a logical sequence. There are, of course, many more possible strategies for organization. Ultimately, the central idea, the topics under consideration, and the types of supporting evidence should point toward a logical pattern. Any logical and convincing organization will produce an effective essay.

CONCLUSION. The conclusion, like the introduction, can present an assertive overview of the essay. Here, however, you can point out what you have already shown in the body. As usual, a summary of key points is useful and effective. In addition, you may link your conclusions about the specific features you discussed to larger considerations about the play's meaning.

SAMPLE ESSAY

Setting as Symbol and Comic Structure in *A Midsummer Night's Dream* *

[1]
Shakespeare's *A Midsummer Night Dream* has two distinct settings, the city of Athens and the woods outside Athens. These are used to symbolize two states of mind and to organize the comic structure of the play.° The journey from the city—the world of order and exposition—to the woods—the world of chaos, complication, and catastrophe—and then back to the city and resolution encompasses the entire comic structure of the play.□

[2]
At the beginning of the comedy, Athens is presented as a world of daylight, rigid order, and strict law. In this setting, Duke Theseus has absolute authority, fathers are always right, and the law permits Egeus to "dispose" of Hermia "either to this gentleman [Demetrius], / Or to her death" (1.1.43–44). This is also the setting for exposition and the beginning of complication. Here, we meet the various groups of characters (except the fairies), and the initial problem is established: the relationship between Hermia and Lysander is blocked by a raging father, a rival suitor, and an old law. In seeking a way around these obstructions, Hermia and Lysander begin a general movement out of the city; Lysander asks his beloved to meet him in the woods:

> Steal forth thy father's house tomorrow night:
> And in the wood, a league without the town,
> Where did I meet thee once with Helena
> To do observance to a morn of May
> There will I stay for thee.   (1.1.164–168)

* See p. 1387 for this play.
° Central idea.
□ Thesis sentence.

Her agreement begins a journey from Athens to the forest that ultimately includes all four lovers, the mechanicals, Egeus, and even the rulers.

[3]
The second setting in the play, the woods outside Athens, is the kingdom of Oberon and Titania. It is a world of darkness, moonlight, chaos, madness, and dreams, a world that symbolizes the power of imagination and wild passion. The disorder in this world has many sources, including Oberon's jealousy, Titania's infatuation with the changeling child, and Puck's delight in mischief and confusion. When the lovers and the mechanicals enter this setting, they leave themselves open to all this disorder and chaos.

[4]
The woods are also the setting for complication, crisis, and catastrophe for the main plot of *A Midsummer Night's Dream*. Confusion dominates the action here; Puck disrupts the mechanical's rehearsal and transforms Bottom into a monster. More important, the passions of the lovers are rearranged several times in this setting by Oberon and Puck through the magic of love-in-idleness, a flower that symbolizes blind love. Although the first two adjustments of the lover's feelings are done to help, each has the effect of raising the level of complication and disorder. Puck recognizes that his actions are creating further complication, and he enjoys the confusion immensely:

> OBERON. Stand aside. The noise they make
> Will cause Demetrius to awake.

> PUCK. Then will two at once woo one:
> That must needs be sport alone.
> And those things do best please me
> That befall prepost'rously.   (3.2.116–121)

And, of course, Puck is right; the first application of love-in-idleness puts Lysander madly in love with Helena, and the second does the same to Demetrius.

[5]
The crisis and catastrophe of the main plot also occur in the woods. Crisis is reached when both men attempt to fight a duel over Helena, and the women attack each other. At this point, complication is at a peak, and the fairies must develop a plan to resolve these threats. Thus, Puck misleads the lovers to abort the duel, and the emotions are readjusted one more time, putting Lysander back in love with Hermia and leaving Demetrius in love with Helena. The catastrophe—the revelation of these newly fixed emotions—occurs the next morning at the edge of the woods, in the presence of Egeus, Theseus, and Hippolyta. Thus, it ends the dark passage through the forest and begins the movement back into the city and society.

[6]
Resolution—the marriages and the mechanicals' production of "Pyramus and Thisby"—occurs back in in the first setting, the city of law and order. But the journey to the second setting has had a significant effect on this world both for Theseus and for the lovers. The law has been softened, Egeus overruled, the young lovers allowed to marry as they like, and lives set to right. In the end, this setting also becomes a world of night and the supernatural, but the fairy dance and blessings that close the play only serve to emphasize the harmony and the regenerative implications of the comic resolutions.

Setting, symbolism, and comic pattern thus combine in *A Midsummer*

Night's Dream to produce a highly structured play in which each element reinforces the others and adds to the total impact of the drama. The two settings represent different states of being and embody distinct stages of traditional comic structure. The journey out of Athens, into the woods, and then back to the city is also a journey from exposition and adversity, through complication, crisis, and catastrophe, and then back to comic resolution.

[7]

Commentary on the Essay

This essay deals with three distinct elements of *A Midsummer Night's Dream*: setting, symbol, and comic structure. It demonstrates the way that a number of different topics may be combined in a single essay. The central idea asserts that setting is employed both to symbolize states of mind and to organize the play's comic structure. Consequently, the essay is organized to reflect the journey from the city to the woods and then back to the city. The overall structure of the essay mirrors the stages of traditional comic structure and the chronology of events in the play.

The body of the essay takes up the settings, their symbolic meaning, and the relationship between the setting and comic structure in the order in which they occur in the play and in the sequence in which they are mentioned in the last sentence of the introduction. Thus, paragraph 2 deals with Athens both as a world of law and order and as the setting for exposition and the beginnings of complication. The supporting details include circumstances, actions, and dialogue.

Paragraphs 3–5 deal with the middle of the journey and of the play. Paragraph 3 discusses the symbolic implications of the second setting, and paragraphs 4 and 5 take up the connection between the setting and comic structure, specifically complication, crisis, and catastrophe. Again, the supporting details in these paragraphs are a mixture of actions, circumstances, and direct quotations cited in the order in which they occur in the play.

Paragraph 6 deals briefly with the return to the city and links this setting with the comic resolution of the play. The concluding paragraph summarizes the connection between setting, symbol, and comic pattern that the essay set out to illustrate. The major points are reviewed, but no larger issues are addressed because the scope of the essay is already fairly broad.

30

Realistic and Nonrealistic Drama

In **realistic drama,** the playwright seeks to put a perfect and detailed illusion of real life in the play and on the stage; the goal is *verisimilitude*—to be true to life. In **nonrealistic drama,** the aim is to present some essential features of character and society through techniques that do not try to mirror life. This distinction first became relevant—and even possible—in the late nineteenth century. Before that, all drama was more or less nonrealistic. From ancient Greek tragedy through Victorian melodrama, dramatists had never attempted to duplicate the details of the real world and real people. Instead, the plays were explicitly artificial and highly conventionalized. The conventions of drama changed from age to age—choruses and masks in Greek tragedy, soliloquies and blank verse in Elizabethan plays, rhymed couplets in French neoclassical drama—but all the conventions were nonrealistic, and they were accepted by audiences and readers as such. Plays in these nonrealistic traditions, such as Sophocles's *Oedipus the King*, Shakespeare's *Hamlet*, and Molière's *The Misanthrope*, illustrate the enduring power and eloquence of this drama.

Realistic drama developed in the late nineteenth century in Europe as a reaction against the artificial and romantic plays that then dominated the stage. These escapist love stories and melodramas had virtually no connection with the realities of existence or the feelings of actual people; they featured lavish sets, gorgeous costumes, flamboyant acting, conventional plots, and happy endings. The characters were exaggerated and idealized types—noble heroes who saved the day, sweet heroines who swooned at every opportunity, and dastardly villains who twirled their moustaches and sneered to the audience in asides as they plotted to foil the hero and steal his money.

In reaction to the escapism and irrelevance of this sort of drama, some nineteenth-century dramatists began to write plays that presented realistic characters in realistic situations and that explored the actual problems of contemporary society. The rebellion began slowly, with dramatists who were out of the mainstream and with amateur acting companies who were willing to take risks. Most of these writers were Europeans; among them were Emile Zola, Henrik Ibsen, Maxim Gorki, and George Bernard Shaw. Zola (1840–1902) laid some of the groundwork for this new type of drama in his naturalistic fiction—novels that explored the nastier aspects of contemporary life in "scientific" detail—and his insistence that plays should offer a pictorially accurate "slice of life." Ibsen wrote plays in which natural characters were in conflict with contemporary social customs and pressures. Maxim Gorki's *The Lower Depths* (1902) was realistic and naturalistic in its detailed presentation of life in the slums. George Bernard Shaw (1856–1950), like Ibsen, wrote plays in which true-to-life characters confronted the actual problems of society; *Widower's Houses* (1892) takes on slum landlords, and *Mrs. Warren's Profession* (1894) explores the economics of prostitution. American realists, who came to this tradition somewhat later than the Europeans, include Eugene O'Neill (see p. 1060) and Susan Glaspell (p. 1100).

The realistic plays written by these and other dramatists have many similar characteristics. The major one, as was mentioned, is verisimilitude—the attempt to be true-to-life in every respect. To this end, realistic drama attempts to banish blatantly artificial dramatic conventions—such as asides, soliloquies, or verse—that do not normally occur in day-to-day conversation. The plots are straightforward and have a realistic chronology; the characters look, speak, and act as much like real people as possible. These plays are not set in imaginary or idealized worlds. Rather, their settings are middle-class living rooms, the country houses of the wealthy, the squalid slums of the poor. The plays usually explore ideas about the nature of humanity in conflict with the customs and prejudices of society; realistic drama at its best is a close examination of character in conflict.

The new realism in drama called for equally new and realistic methods of production and action. Most theaters at this time already featured a darkened auditorium, a proscenium arch separating the audience from the players, and a picture-frame stage. The spectators watched the play as though the fourth wall of a room had been removed; the effect was as if the audience were eavesdropping on private conversations and events. For realistic drama the settings and stage directions became as realistic and detailed as possible. When the curtain went up, the audience saw a completely furnished room or office, much like the ones in which they themselves lived or worked. Ibsen's lengthy description of the setting in *A Doll's House*, for example, calls for the elaborate duplication of a Norwegian middle-class living room of the late nineteenth century, complete with a piano, sofa, chairs, tables, engravings on the walls, books in the bookcases, and a heating stove in which a fire actually burns. Lighting and costumes became equally realistic. Lighting was designed to duplicate the natural light at a particular time of day or the lamps burning in a room at night. Similarly, the lavish and beautiful costumes of nineteenth-century melodrama gave way to detailed realism in dress and makeup on the stage.

The most radical and permanent change evoked by the new realism was in acting styles. In the Victorian theater, actors stood in one place, assumed a conventional stance, and declaimed or ranted their lines in a highly oratorical manner. They played "to the house" (to the audience) rather than to each other. In realistic drama, actors could no longer rant, strike poses, or gesture melodramatically. The acting had to become quieter, more intimate, and more natural. The actors began to combine movement with dialogue and to play "within the scene" to each other rather than to the spectators.

These changes were due, in large measure, to Constantin Stanislavski (1863–1938), one of the founders of the Moscow Arts Theater (1898) and the inventor of what we now term the *method* style of acting. Stanislavski argued that actors had to build characterizations on a lifelong study of inner truth and motivation; he taught actors to search their own lives for the feelings, motivations, and behavior of the characters they portrayed.

THE REBELLION AGAINST REALISM

No sooner had realism taken over the stage than a new nonrealistic drama began to emerge as a reaction against realism. Many playwrights in Europe and America decided that realism had gone too far and that the quest for minutely realistic details had sacrificed the essence of drama—character and universal truth. This reaction against realism had no single direction or champion; playwrights began to explore every avenue of anti-realistic drama. At the same time, new types of stages and theaters began to appear. The *thrust stage*, which projected into the audience, was reintroduced, thus helping to destroy the fourth-wall principle of realistic drama. The *arena stage*, or *theater-in-the-round*, was developed, which also called for new concepts in drama and production.

Playwrights like Luigi Pirandello (1867–1936) and Bertolt Brecht (1898–1956) began to write plays that required only minimal sets or no sets at all. In this same approach, Thornton Wilder (p. 1048) wrote plays in which the action occurs on a bare stage, with the brick walls, heating pipes, and ropes of the backstage area in full view. Such staging constantly reminds us that we are reading or watching a play—an illusion and an imitation—rather than real life. An attempt at verisimilitude thus gives way to blatant artificiality.

Nonrealistic drama has moved progressively further away from realism throughout the latter half of this century. With the development of flexible theaters, in which the seats could be removed from the auditorium and acting areas set up throughout the house, the action of plays began to move off the stage and into the space once reserved for the audience. In the 1960s and 1970s, acting companies like The Living Theater in New York experimented with plays that began onstage, moved into the audience, and ended on the streets outside the theater. Such productions, in which the players interact with the spectators, represent the edge of drama; they blur the distinction between the play and the real world to the point where art almost ceases to be art and becomes life. Such blurring of distinctions is also a feature of *street* or *guerrilla theater*, a form of protest drama that is performed in the streets, without stage, sets, or even a theater.

ELEMENTS OF REALISTIC AND NONREALISTIC DRAMA

Whereas realistic drama strives to be as true to life in every aspect as possible, modern nonrealistic drama is free to deal with human values and problems in a greater variety of ways. Realistic drama aims at complete verisimilitude and a minimum of artificial dramatic conventions; nonrealistic drama employs whatever stylized conventions the playwright finds useful.

Realistic plays, like life, unfold chronologically. For this reason, the *story* (as opposed to the *play*) is usually nearing conclusion when the staged action begins. In Susan Glaspell's *Trifles* (p. 1100), for instance, the story includes incidents from Mrs. Wright's childhood, problems with her marriage, and the murder of Mr. Wright. All this, however, is related in conversation; it all occurred *before* the action of the play begins. Such past events have a profound impact on the present action in realistic drama, but the play itself presents only the last part of the story in a natural sequence.

In nonrealistic drama, the structure of the plot can be a great deal more fluid. Action can shift from the present to the past with little or no transition; flashbacks can be mixed with present action, or the entire play can dramatize the past through a present perspective. Such is the case in Tennessee Williams's *The Glass Menagerie*, where recollected past action is revealed through the present memories of the narrator. Similarly, the action in Arthur Miller's *Death of a Salesman* (p. 1294) constantly shifts between present and past action and fantasy.

The characters in realistic drama are as much like people as possible. They can be representative, symbolic, or even stock characters, but they must sound and act like actual human beings, with names, backgrounds, emotions, and motivations. There must be reasons for their actions, words, conflicts, and relationships. Most important, they must be consistent; changes in action or shifts in nature must be motivated exactly as they would be in real life. We see this quality in Glaspell's *Trifles* and Ibsen's *A Doll's House*, where the characters are true to life and consistent.

In modern nonrealistic drama, the characters may be nameless figures who have no background or motivation and who drop in and out of character as the playwright desires. Such is the case in Edward Albee's *The Sandbox* (p. 1068), a play that is extremely nonrealistic. Similarly, characters in nonrealistic drama can assume a number of different roles at different times in the play. In *The Glass Menagerie*, for example, Tom is variously a character in the action, a narrator of the action, and a stage manager. As a character, he interacts with Laura and Amanda, but he also provides ongoing narration directly to the audience, and occasionally he gives music and lighting cues to the technicians offstage.

These distinctions do not mean that realistic characters are necessarily round and nonrealistic ones always flat. The *way* in which a playwright develops the characters, realistically or nonrealistically, does not always control the *degree* to which they are developed. Thus, true-to-life characters like Mr. Hale in *Trifles* or the Helmer children in *A Doll's House* can be flat. By the same token, characters that are developed nonrealistically, such as Tom in *The Glass Menagerie* or Willie Loman in *Death of a Salesman*, may have enough depth and scope to be considered fully rounded.

The language in a realistic play is usually an accurate reproduction of the colloquial diction appropriate to the class or group of people portrayed. There is no poetry, no radical shift in style, and no direct address to the reader or spectators. In *A Doll's House,* for instance, Nora and Torvald consistently speak like middle-class Norwegians (in translation) in the 1870s. Similarly, the characters in Glaspell's *Trifles* sound like Iowa farmers and businesspeople. Although such verisimilitude may be present in nonrealistic drama, it is not required. Playwrights may employ any linguistic devices that suit their needs. Characters may speak in verse, clichés, or even nonsense sounds. One character may have two or three entirely different styles of speech, as does Tom in *The Glass Menagerie*. Dramatists are free to introduce snippets of poetry or song into the play, and characters can (and frequently do) speak directly to the audience.

Such differences in plot, characterization, and language are matched by differences in production techniques. Whereas the staging of a realistic drama must be as true to life as possible, nonrealistic drama can be staged with few or no realistic effects. Thus, lighting can indicate instantaneous shifts of location, flashbacks, and changes in mood; spotlights may illuminate and emphasize specific objects and characters in ways that never happen in reality. Nonrealistic plays may call for virtually bare stages, as do *The Happy Journey to Trenton and Camden* and *The Sandbox*. Alternatively, the sets may be symbolic and expressive of mood, employing lighting and semitransparent painted cloth (called *scrim*) to create the effect of multiple places or times on stage simultaneously. Such expressionistic settings are described in the stage directions for both *Death of a Salesman* and *The Glass Menagerie*.

Perhaps the most important difference between the realistic and modern nonrealistic drama concerns the play's relationships to the theater, the audience, and the world at large. In realistic drama, the play presents a self-contained action in a self-contained world that imitates reality. The illusion of reality is never compromised; the actors never drop out of character, the audience is never addressed, and the play never acknowledges that it is a play. Modern nonrealistic drama tends toward the other extreme; it can be full of devices that break through the illusion on the stage (or the page) and scream out that the play is a play, a work of art, a stylized imitation of life. These devices include symbolic characters, poetry, music, minimalist or expressionistic settings, lighting effects, words or images projected onto a wall or screen, action that flows off the stage into the auditorium, and speeches made directly to the spectators or the reader. All these and other devices produce the same general effects: they break the illusion of reality, remind us that we are reading or watching a play.

THE SPECTRUM OF REALISM

To this point we have been speaking as though realistic and nonrealistic drama were always at opposite extremes. This may theoretically be the case, but in practice the terms are comparative rather than absolute. Most plays are not purely realistic or nonrealistic. Rather, the terms represent the opposite ends of a spectrum, and most plays fall somewhere between the two extremes. Both *Trifles* and *A Doll's House*, for example, are highly realistic plays, yet each modifies its realism through symbolism and selective emphasis. Conversely, *The Sandbox* is extremely nonrealistic, yet the play includes enough realistic elements so that we can understand the correspondence between Albee's art and the real world. Both *Death of a Salesman* and *The Glass Menagerie* fall near the middle of the spectrum; they combine realistic language and characterization with nonrealistic settings, lighting, and structure.

HENRIK IBSEN, *A DOLL'S HOUSE*

Henrik Ibsen is one of the masters of the realistic *problem play* in which true-to-life characters come into conflict with the values and prejudices of their societies. His plays embody a vision of human nature and destiny that rises above the limitations of realism and encompasses universal patterns and problems. He was born in the small town of Skien, Norway. Although his parents had been wealthy, the family went bankrupt while he was very young, and Ibsen grew up in an atmosphere of poverty, pretense, middle-class morality, and small-town hypocrisy. He was apprenticed to a pharmacist in 1843, but his real interest was the theater; he wrote his first play in 1850 and spent the next thirteen years writing and working in theaters in Norway, Denmark, and Germany. The success of *The Pretenders* (1863) allowed him to move to Italy, where he lived and wrote until his return to Norway in 1891.

Ibsen's early plays were romantic or historical dramas, mostly in verse. His first realistic play, *The League of Youth* (1869), was a prose satire of Norwegian social classes and prejudices. In this play, Ibsen began to employ realistic characters, situations, and problems, and over the next thirteen years he wrote a string of realistic dramas that deal with the troubled relationships between the individual, the family, and the community. These included *A Doll's House* (1879), *Ghosts* (1881), and *An Enemy of the People* (1882). In his later plays (for example, *When We Dead Awaken,* 1899) Ibsen moved away from realism toward a combination of symbolist and realistic techniques.

A Doll's House, written in 1879, is realistic in that it presents an image of believable people confronting the problems of real life and contemporary society. Realism also implies a realistic setting and a story that begins before the opening of the play. *A Doll's House* conforms on both counts. The set is realistic not only in the careful and detailed creation of the Helmers' living room, but also in our awareness of the whole apartment and the three doors that separate this cozy room from the bitter Norwegian winter. Similarly, the plot presents only the conclusion of a much longer story that began years earlier when Torvald was ill and Nora's father was dying.

The realism of *A Doll's House* is modified to some extent by Ibsen's romantic conceptualization of characters (as types) and his use of symbols. The master symbols of the play are Norway (cold, ethical, legal, male, rational) and Italy or the south of Europe (warm, esthetic, spiritual, female, emotional). This opposition is reflected in the conflict between Nora and Krogstad, and ultimately between Nora and Torvald. The play is full of other symbols as well: the Christmas tree, the children's presents, the black shawl, Nora's tarantella, and Doctor Rank, to name only a few.

The plot and structure of *A Doll's House* reflect Ibsen's awareness of the conventions of the **well-made play,** a form developed and popularized in France in the nineteenth century by Eugène Scribe (1791–1861) and Victorien Sardou (1831–1908). The well-made play, as practiced by Scribe and his disciples, follows an extremely rigid and formulaic structure in which the drama always begins at the climax of the story, thus making a great deal of exposition necessary. Additionally, the plot is usually built on a secret known to the audience and one or two of the characters but withheld from most of the others. The well-made play thus begins in suspense, and it offers a pattern of increasing tension produced through exposition and the well-timed arrival of new characters (like Mrs. Linde) and threatening props (properties) (like Krogstad's letter to Torvald). In the course of this action the protagonist of the well-made play is brought through a series of high and low points, moving eventually from the lowest point through a **peripeteia** or reversal to a high point at which he or she confronts and defeats the villain. Ibsen maintains these structural characteristics in *A Doll's House* through the first half of act 3; then he abandons the model of the well-made play and stages Nora's major confrontation with Torvald, rather than with Krogstad, the ostensible villain of the piece.

 A Doll's House has traditionally been seen as a "feminist" play that champions the rights of women. This perspective has been especially emphasized in modern productions starring Liv Ullman, Claire Bloom, and Jane Fonda. A feminist reading of the play is not surprising, since Nora's life reflects all the legal and social limitations that were characteristic of middle-class marriages in the nineteenth century. The play depends, for example, on the fact that women could not legally borrow money without the cosignature of a male. Indeed, Nora's status is symbolized by the locked mailbox to which only Torvald has a key. Finally, however, Ibsen is far more interested in human rights and the development of the individual's potential than he is in women's rights. Both Nora and Torvald are limited and distorted by the roles that society imposes on them; both have to learn a great deal before they can become fulfilled individuals.

HENRIK IBSEN (1828–1906)

A Doll's House   *1879*

Translated by R. Farquharson Sharp

CHARACTERS

> Torvald Helmer, *a lawyer and bank manager*
> Nora, *his wife*
> Doctor Rank
> Mrs. Christine Linde
> Nils Krogstad, *a lawyer and bank clerk*
> Ivar, Bob, *and* Emmy, the Helmers' *three young children*
> Anne, *their nurse*
> Helen, *a housemaid*
> A Porter

The action takes place in HELMER'S *apartment*.

ACT 1

SCENE.—*A room furnished comfortably and tastefully, but not extravagantly. At the back, a door to the right leads to the entrance hall, another to the left leads to* HELMER'S *study. Between the doors stands a piano. In the middle of the left-hand wall is a door, and beyond it a window. Near the window are a round table, armchairs and a small sofa. In the right-hand wall, at the farther end, another door; and on the same side, nearer the foot-lights, a stove, two easy chairs and a rocking-chair; between the stove and the door, a small table. Engravings on the walls; a cabinet with china and other small objects; a small book-case with well-bound books. The floors are carpeted, and a fire burns in the stove. It is winter.*

A bell rings in the hall; shortly afterwards the door is heard to open. Enter NORA, *humming a tune and in high spirits. She is in out-door dress and carries a number of parcels; these she lays on the table to the right. She leaves the outer door open after her, and through it is seen a* PORTER *who is carrying a Christmas Tree and a basket, which he gives to the* MAID *who has opened the door.*

NORA.   Hide the Christmas Tree carefully, Helen. Be sure the children do not see it till this evening, when it is dressed. [*to the* PORTER, *taking out her purse.*] How much?

PORTER.   Sixpence.

NORA.   There is a shilling. No, keep the change. [*The* PORTER *thanks her, and goes out.* NORA *shuts the door. She is laughing to herself, as she takes off her hat and coat. She takes a packet of macaroons from her pocket and eats one or two; then goes cautiously to her husband's door and listens.*] Yes, he is in.

[*Still humming, she goes to the table on the right.*]

HELMER.   [*calls out from his room*] Is that my little lark twittering out there?

NORA.   [*busy opening some of the parcels*] Yes, it is!

HELMER.   Is my little squirrel bustling about?

NORA.   Yes!

HELMER.   When did my squirrel come home?

NORA.   Just now. [*puts the bag of macaroons into her pocket and wipes her mouth.*] Come in here, Torvald, and see what I have bought.

HELMER.   Don't disturb me. [*A little later, he opens the door and looks into the room, pen in hand.*] Bought, did you say? All these things? Has my little spendthrift been wasting money again?

NORA.   Yes, but, Torvald, this year we really can let ourselves go a little. This is the first Christmas that we have not needed to economise.

HELMER.   Still, you know, we can't spend money recklessly.

NORA.   Yes, Torvald, we may be a wee bit more reckless now, mayn't we? Just a tiny wee bit! You are going to have a big salary and earn lots and lots of money.

HELMER.   Yes, after the New Year; but then it will be a whole quarter before the salary is due.

NORA.   Pooh! we can borrow till then.

HELMER.   Nora! [*goes up to her and takes her playfully by the ear.*] The same little featherhead! Suppose, now, that I borrowed fifty pounds to-day, and you spent it all in the Christmas week, and then on New Year's Eve a slate fell on my head and killed me, and——

NORA.   [*putting her hands over his mouth*] Oh! don't say such horrid things.

HELMER.   Still, suppose that happened—what then?

NORA.   If that were to happen, I don't suppose I should care whether I owed money or not.

HELMER. Yes, but what about the people who had lent it?

NORA. They? Who would bother about them? I should not know who they were.

HELMER. That is like a woman! But seriously, Nora, you know what I think about that. No debt, no borrowing. There can be no freedom or beauty about a home life that depends on borrowing and debt. We two have kept bravely on the straight road so far, and we will go on the same way for the short time longer that there need be any struggle.

NORA. [*moving towards the stove*] As you please, Torvald.

HELMER. [*following her*] Come, come, my little skylark must not droop her wings. What is this! Is my little squirrel out of temper? [*taking out his purse.*] Nora, what do you think I have got here?

NORA. [*turning around quickly*] Money!

HELMER. There you are. [*gives her some money*] Do you think I don't know what a lot is wanted for housekeeping at Christmas-time?

NORA. [*counting*] Ten shillings—a pound—two pounds! Thank you, thank you, Torvald; that will keep me going for a long time.

HELMER. Indeed it must.

NORA. Yes, yes, it will. But come here and let me show you what I have bought. And all so cheap! Look, here is a new suit for Ivar, and a sword; and a horse and a trumpet for Bob; and a doll and dolly's bedstead for Emmy—they are very plain, but anyway she will soon break them in pieces. And here are dress-lengths and handkerchiefs for the maids; old Anne ought really to have something better.

HELMER. And what is in this parcel?

NORA. [*crying out*] No, no! you mustn't see that till this evening.

HELMER. Very well. But now tell me, you extravagant little person, what would you like for yourself?

NORA. For myself? Oh, I am sure I don't want anything.

HELMER. Yes, but you must. Tell me something reasonable that you would particularly like to have.

NORA. No, I really can't think of anything—unless, Torvald——

HELMER. Well?

NORA. [*playing with his coat buttons, and without raising her eyes to his*] If you really want to give me something, you might—you might——

HELMER. Well, out with it!

NORA. [*speaking quickly*] You might give me money, Torvald. Only just as much as you can afford; and then one of these days I will buy something with it.

HELMER. But, Nora——

NORA. Oh, do! dear Torvald; please, please do! Then I will wrap it up in beautiful gilt paper and hang it on the Christmas Tree. Wouldn't that be fun?

HELMER. What are little people called that are always wasting money?

NORA. Spendthrifts—I know. Let us do as you suggest, Torvald, and then I shall have time to think what I am most in want of. That is a very sensible plan, isn't it?

HELMER. [*smiling*] Indeed it is—that is to say, if you were really to save out of the money I give you, and then really buy something for yourself. But if you spend it all on the housekeeping and any number of unnecessary things, then I merely have to pay up again.

NORA. Oh but, Torvald——

HELMER. You can't deny it, my dear little Nora. [*puts his arm round her waist*] It's a sweet little spendthrift, but she uses up a deal of money. One would hardly believe how expensive such little persons are!

NORA. It's a shame to say that. I do really save all I can.

HELMER. [*laughing*] That's very true—all you can. But you can't save anything!

NORA. [*smiling quietly and happily*] You haven't any idea how many expenses we skylarks and squirrels have, Torvald.

HELMER. You are an odd little soul. Very like your father. You always find some new way of wheedling money out of me, and, as soon as you have got it, it seems to melt in your hands. You never know where it has gone. Still, one must take you as you are. It is in the blood; for indeed it is true that you can inherit these things, Nora.

NORA. Ah, I wish I had inherited many of papa's qualities.

HELMER. And I would not wish you to be anything but just what you are, my sweet little skylark. But, do you know, it strikes me that you are looking rather— what shall I say—rather uneasy to-day?

NORA. Do I?

HELMER. You do, really. Look straight at me.

NORA. [*looks at him*] Well?

HELMER. [*wagging his finger at her*] Hasn't Miss Sweet-Tooth been breaking rules in town to-day?

NORA. No; what makes you think that?

HELMER. Hasn't she paid a visit to the confectioner's?

NORA. No, I assure you, Torvald——

HELMER. Not been nibbling sweets?

NORA. No, certainly not.

HELMER. Not even taken a bite at a macaroon or two?

NORA. No, Torvald, I assure you really——

HELMER. There, there, of course I was only joking.

NORA. [*going to the table on the right*] I should not think of going against your wishes.

HELMER. No, I am sure of that! besides, you gave me your word—— [*going up to her*] Keep your little Christmas secrets to yourself, my darling. They will all be revealed to-night when the Christmas Tree is lit, no doubt.

NORA. Did you remember to invite Doctor Rank?

HELMER. No. But there is no need; as a matter of course he will come to dinner with us. However, I will ask him when he comes in this morning. I have ordered some good wine. Nora, you can't think how I am looking forward to this evening.

NORA. So am I! And how the children will enjoy themselves, Torvald!

HELMER. It is splendid to feel that one has a perfectly safe appointment, and a big enough income. It's delightful to think of, isn't it?

NORA. It's wonderful!

HELMER. Do you remember last Christmas? For a full three weeks beforehand you shut yourself up every evening till long after midnight, making ornaments for the Christmas Tree and all the other fine things that were to be a surprise to us. It was the dullest three weeks I ever spent!

NORA. I didn't find it dull.

HELMER. [*smiling*] But there was precious little result, Nora.

NORA. Oh, you shouldn't tease me about that again. How could I help the cat's going in and tearing everything to pieces?

HELMER. Of course you couldn't, poor little girl. You had the best of intentions to please us all, and that's the main thing. But it is a good thing that our hard times are over.

NORA. Yes, it is really wonderful.

HELMER. This time I needn't sit here and be dull all alone, and you needn't ruin your dear eyes and your pretty little hands——

NORA. [*clapping her hands*] No, Torvald, I needn't any longer, need I! It's wonderfully lovely to hear you say so! [*taking his arm*] Now I will tell you how I have been thinking we ought to arrange things, Torvald. As soon as Christmas is over—— [*A bell rings in the hall.*] There's the bell. [*She tidies the room a little.*] There's someone at the door. What a nuisance!

HELMER. If it is a caller, remember I am not at home.

MAID. [*in the doorway*] A lady to see you, ma'am—a stranger.

NORA. Ask her to come in.

MAID. [*to HELMER*] The doctor came at the same time, sir.

HELMER. Did he go straight into my room?

MAID. Yes, sir.

[*HELMER goes into his room. The* MAID *ushers in* MRS. LINDE, *who is in travelling dress, and shuts the door.*]

MRS. LINDE. [*in a dejected and timid voice*] How do you do, Nora?

NORA. [*doubtfully*] How do you do——

MRS. LINDE. You don't recognise me, I suppose.

NORA. No, I don't know—yes, to be sure, I seem to——[*suddenly*] Yes! Christine! Is it really you?

MRS. LINDE. Yes, it is I.

NORA. Christine! To think of my not recognising you! And yet how could I—— [*in a gentle voice*] How you have altered, Christine!

MRS. LINDE. Yes, I have indeed. In nine, ten long years——

NORA. Is it so long since we met? I suppose it is. The last eight years have been a happy time for me, I can tell you. And so now you have come into the town, and have taken this long journey in winter—that was plucky of you.

MRS. LINDE. I arrived by steamer this morning.

NORA. To have some fun at Christmas-time, of course. How delightful! We will have such fun together! But take off your things. You are not cold, I hope. [*helps her*] Now we will sit down by the stove, and be cosy. No, take this arm-chair; I will sit here in the rocking-chair. [*takes her hands*] Now you look like your old self again; it was only the first moment—— You are a little paler, Christine, and perhaps a little thinner.

MRS. LINDE. And much, much older, Nora.

NORA. Perhaps a little older; very, very little; certainly not much. [*stops suddenly and speaks seriously*] What a thoughtless creature I am, chattering away like this. My poor, dear Christine, do forgive me.

MRS. LINDE. What do you mean, Nora?

NORA. [*gently*] Poor Christine, you are a widow.

MRS. LINDE.   Yes; it is three years ago now.

NORA.   Yes, I knew; I saw it in the papers. I assure you, Christine, I meant ever so often to write to you at the time, but I always put it off and something always prevented me.

MRS. LINDE.   I quite understand, dear.

NORA.   It was very bad of me, Christine. Poor thing, how you must have suffered. And he left you nothing?

MRS. LINDE.   No.

NORA.   And no children?

MRS. LINDE.   No.

NORA.   Nothing at all, then?

MRS. LINDE.   Not even any sorrow or grief to live upon.

NORA.   [*looking incredulously at her*] But, Christine, is that possible?

MRS. LINDE.   [*smiles sadly and strokes her hair*] It sometimes happens, Nora.

NORA.   So you are quite alone. How dreadfully sad that must be. I have three lovely children. You can't see them just now, for they are out with their nurse. But now you must tell me all about it.

MRS. LINDE.   No, no; I want to hear you.

NORA.   No, you must begin. I mustn't be selfish to-day; to-day I must only think of your affairs. But there is one thing I must tell you. Do you know we have just had a great piece of good luck?

MRS. LINDE.   No, what is it?

NORA.   Just fancy, my hasband has been made manager of the Bank!

MRS. LINDE.   Your husband? What good luck!

NORA.   Yes, tremendous! A barrister's profession is such an uncertain thing, especially if he won't undertake unsavoury cases; and naturally Torvald has never been willing to do that, and I quite agree with him. You may imagine how pleased we are! He is to take up his work in the Bank at the New Year, and then he will have a big salary and lots of commissions. For the future we can live quite differently—we can do just as we like. I feel so relieved and so happy, Christine! It will be splendid to have heaps of money and not need to have any anxiety, won't it?

MRS. LINDE.   Yes, anyhow I think it would be delightful to have what one needs.

NORA.   No, not only what one needs, but heaps and heaps of money.

MRS. LINDE.   [*smiling*] Nora, Nora, haven't you learnt sense yet? In our schooldays you were a great spendthrift.

NORA.   [*laughing*] Yes, that is what Torvald says now. [*wags her finger at her*] But "Nora, Nora" is not so silly as you think. We have not been in a position for me to waste money. We have both had to work.

MRS. LINDE.   You too?

NORA.   Yes; odds and ends, needlework, crochet-work, embroidery, and that kind of thing. [*dropping her voice*] And other things as well. You know Torvald left his office when we were married? There was no prospect of promotion there, and he had to try and earn more than before. But during the first year he overworked himself dreadfully. You see, he had to make money every way he could, and he worked early and late; but he couldn't stand it, and fell dreadfully ill, and the doctors said it was necessary for him to go south.

MRS. LINDE. You spent a whole year in Italy didn't you?

NORA. Yes. It was no easy matter to get away, I can tell you. It was just after Ivar was born; but naturally we had to go. It was a wonderfully beautiful journey, and it saved Torvald's life. But it cost a tremendous lot of money, Christine.

MRS. LINDE. So I should think.

NORA. It cost about two hundred and fifty pounds. That's a lot, isn't it?

MRS. LINDE. Yes, and in emergencies like that it is lucky to have the money.

NORA. I ought to tell you that we had it from papa.

MRS. LINDE. Oh, I see. It was just about that time that he died, wasn't it?

NORA. Yes; and, just think of it, I couldn't go and nurse him. I was expecting little Ivar's birth every day and I had my poor sick Torvald to look after. My dear, kind father—I never saw him again, Christine. That was the saddest time I have known since our marriage.

MRS. LINDE. I know how fond you were of him. And then you went off to Italy?

NORA. Yes; you see we had money then, and the doctors insisted on our going, so we started a month later.

MRS. LINDE. And your husband came back quite well?

NORA. As sound as a bell!

MRS. LINDE. But—the doctor?

NORA. What doctor?

MRS. LINDE. I thought your maid said the gentleman who arrived here just as I did was the doctor?

NORA. Yes, that was Doctor Rank, but he doesn't come here professionally. He is our greatest friend, and comes in at least once every day. No, Torvald has not had an hour's illness since then, and our children are strong and healthy and so am I. [*jumps up and claps her hands*] Christine! Christine! it's good to be alive and happy!——But how horrid of me; I am talking of nothing but my own affairs. [*Sits on a stool near her, and rests her arms on her knees*] You mustn't be angry with me. Tell me, is it really true that you did not love your husband? Why did you marry him?

MRS. LINDE. My mother was alive then, and was bedridden and helpless, and I had to provide for my two younger brothers; so I did not think I was justified in refusing his offer.

NORA. No, perhaps you were quite right. He was rich at that time, then?

MRS. LINDE. I believe he was quite well off. But his business was a precarious one; and, when he died, it all went to pieces and there was nothing left.

NORA. And then?——

MRS. LINDE. Well, I had to turn my hand to anything I could find—first a small shop, then a small school, and so on. The last three years have seemed like one long working-day, with no rest. Now it is at an end, Nora. My poor mother needs me no more, for she is gone; and the boys do not need me either; they have got situations and can shift for themselves.

NORA. What a relief you must feel it——

MRS. LINDE. No, indeed; I only feel my life unspeakably empty. No one to live for any more. [*gets up restlessly*] That was why I could not stand the life in my little backwater any longer. I hope it may be easier here to find something which will busy me and occupy my thoughts. If only I could have the good luck to get some regular work—office work of some kind——

NORA. But, Christine, that is so frightfully tiring, and you look tired out now. You had far better go away to some watering-place.

MRS. LINDE. [*walking to the window*] I have no father to give me money for a journey, Nora.

NORA. [*rising*] Oh, don't be angry with me.

MRS. LINDE. [*going up to her*] It is you that must not be angry with me, dear. The worst of a position like mine is that it makes one so bitter. No one to work for, and yet obliged to be always on the look-out for chances. One must live, and so one becomes selfish. When you told me of the happy turn your fortunes have taken—you will hardly believe it—I was delighted not so much on your account as on my own.

NORA. How do you mean?—Oh, I understand. You mean that perhaps Torvald could get you something to do.

MRS. LINDE. Yes, that was what I was thinking of.

NORA. He must, Christine. Just leave it to me; I will broach the subject very cleverly—I will think of something that will please him very much. It will make me so happy to be of some use to you.

MRS. LINDE. How kind you are, Nora, to be so anxious to help me! It is doubly kind in you, for you know so little of the burdens and troubles of life.

NORA. I——? I know so little of them?

MRS. LINDE. [*smiling*] My dear! Small household cares and that sort of thing!—You are a child, Nora.

NORA. [*tosses her head and crosses the stage*] You ought not to be so superior.

MRS. LINDE. No?

NORA. You are just like the others. They all think that I am incapable of anything really serious——

MRS. LINDE. Come, come——

NORA. —that I have gone through nothing in this world of cares.

MRS. LINDE. But, my dear Nora, you have just told me all your troubles.

NORA. Pooh!—those were trifles. [*lowering her voice*] I have not told you the important thing.

MRS. LINDE. The important thing? What do you mean?

NORA. You look down upon me altogether, Christine—but you ought not to. You are proud, aren't you, of having worked so hard and so long for your mother?

MRS. LINDE. Indeed, I don't look down on any one. But it is true that I am both proud and glad to think that I was priviliged to make the end of my mother's life almost free from care.

NORA. And you are proud to think of what you have done for your brothers.

MRS. LINDE. I think I have the right to be.

NORA. I think so, too. But now, listen to this; I too have something to be proud of and glad of.

MRS. LINDE. I have no doubt you have. But what do you refer to?

NORA. Speak low. Suppose Torvald were to hear! He mustn't on any account—no one in the world must know, Christine, except you.

MRS. LINDE. But what is it?

NORA. Come here. [*pulls her down on the sofa beside her*] Now I will show you that I too have something to be proud and glad of. It was I who saved Torvald's life.

MRS. LINDE. "Saved"? How?

NORA. I told you about our trip to Italy. Torvald would never have recovered if he had not gone there——

MRS. LINDE. Yes, but your father gave you the necessary funds.

NORA. [*smiling*] Yes, that is what Torvald and all the others think, but——

MRS. LINDE. But——

NORA. Papa didn't give us a shilling. It was I who procured the money.

MRS. LINDE. You? All that large sum?

NORA. Two hundred and fifty pounds. What do you think of that?

MRS. LINDE. But, Nora, how could you possibly do it? Did you win a prize in the Lottery?

NORA. [*contemptuously*] In the Lottery? There would have been no credit in that.

MRS. LINDE. But where did you get it from, then?

NORA. [*humming and smiling with an air of mystery*] Hm, hm! Aha!

MRS. LINDE. Because you couldn't have borrowed it.

NORA. Couldn't I? Why not?

MRS. LINDE. No, a wife cannot borrow without her husband's consent.

NORA. [*tossing her head*] Oh, if it is a wife who has any head for business— a wife who has the wit to be a little bit clever——

MRS. LINDE. I don't understand it at all, Nora.

NORA. There is no need you should. I never said I had borrowed the money. I may have got it some other way. [*lies back on the sofa*] Perhaps I got it from some other admirer. When anyone is as attractive as I am——

MRS. LINDE. You are a mad creature.

NORA. Now, you know you're full of curiosity, Christine.

MRS. LINDE. Listen to me, Nora dear. Haven't you been a little bit imprudent?

NORA. [*sits up straight*] Is it imprudent to save your husband's life?

MRS. LINDE. It seems to me imprudent, without his knowledge, to——

NORA. But it was absolutely necessary that he should not know! My goodness, can't you understand that? It was necessary he should have no idea what a dangerous condition he was in. It was to me that the doctors came and said that his life was in danger, and that the only thing to save him was to live in the south. Do you suppose I didn't try, first of all, to get what I wanted as if it were for myself? I told him how much I should love to travel abroad like other young wives; I tried tears and entreaties with him; I told him that he ought to remember the condition I was in, and that he ought to be kind and indulgent to me; I even hinted that he might raise a loan. That nearly made him angry, Christine. He said I was thoughtless, and that it was his duty as my husband not to indulge me in my whims and caprices—as I believe he called them. Very well I thought, you must be saved—and that was how I came to devise a way out of the difficulty——

MRS. LINDE. And did your husband never get to know from your father that the money had not come from him?

NORA. No, never. Papa died just at that time. I had meant to let him into the secret and beg him never to reveal it. But he was so ill then—alas, there never was any need to tell him.

MRS. LINDE. And since then have you never told your secret to your husband?

NORA. Good Heavens, no! How could you think so? A man who has such strong opinions about these things! And besides, how painful and humiliating it would be for Torvald, with his manly independence, to know that he owed me anything! It would upset our mutual relations altogether; our beautiful happy home would no longer be what it is now.

MRS. LINDE. Do you mean never to tell him about it?

NORA. [*meditatively, and with a half smile*] Yes—some day, perhaps, after many years, when I am no longer as nice-looking as I am now. Don't laugh at me! I mean of course, when Torvald is no longer as devoted to me as he is now; when my dancing and dressing-up and reciting have palled on him; then it may be a good thing to have something in reserve—— [*breaking off*] What nonsense! That time will never come. Now, what do you think of my great secret, Christine? Do you still think I am of no use? I can tell you, too, that this affair has caused me a lot of worry. It has been by no means easy for me to meet my engagements punctually. I may tell you that there is something that is called, in business, quarterly interest, and another thing called payment in instalments, and it is always so dreadfully difficult to manage them. I have had to save a little here and there, where I could, you understand. I have not been able to put aside much from my housekeeping money, for Torvald must have a good table. I couldn't let my children be shabbily dressed; I have felt obliged to use up all he gave me for them, the sweet little darlings!

MRS. LINDE. So it has all had to come out of your own necessaries of life, poor Nora?

NORA. Of course. Besides, I was the one responsible for it. Whenever Torvald has given me the money for new dresses and such things, I have never spent more than half of it; I have always bought the simplest and cheapest things. Thank Heaven, any clothes look well on me, and so Torvald has never noticed it. But it was often very hard on me, Christine—because it is delightful to be really well dressed, isn't it?

MRS. LINDE. Quite so.

NORA. Well, then I have found other ways of earning money. Last winter I was lucky enough to get a lot of copying to do; so I locked myself up and sat writing every evening until quite late at night. Many a time I was desperately tired; but all the same it was a tremendous pleasure to sit there working and earning money. It was like being a man.

MRS. LINDE. How much have you been able to pay off in that way?

NORA. I can't tell you exactly. You see, it is very difficult to keep an account of a business matter of that kind. I only know that I have paid every penny that I could scrape together. Many a time I was at my wits' end. [*smiles*] Then I used to sit here and imagine that a rich old gentleman had fallen in love with me——

MRS. LINDE. What! Who was it?

NORA. Be quiet!—that he had died; and that when his will was opened it contained, written in big letters, the instruction: "The lovely Mrs. Nora Helmer is to have all I possess paid over to her at once in cash."

MRS. LINDE. But, my dear Nora—who could the man be?

NORA. Good gracious, can't you understand? There was no old gentleman at all; it was only something that I used to sit here and imagine, when I couldn't think of any way of procuring money. But it's all the same now; the tiresome old person can stay where he is, as far as I am concerned; I don't care about him or his will either, for I am free from care now. [*jumps up*] My goodness, it's delightful to think of, Christine! Free from care! To be able to be free from care, quite free from care; to be able to play and romp with the children; to be able to keep the house beautifully and have everything just as Torvald likes it! And, think of it, soon the spring will come and the big blue sky! Perhaps we shall be able to take a little trip—perhaps I shall see the sea again! Oh, it's a wonderful thing to be alive and be happy. [*A bell is heard in the hall.*]

MRS. LINDE. [*rising*] There is the bell; perhaps I had better go.

NORA. No, don't go; no one will come in here; it is sure to be for Torvald.

SERVANT. [*at the hall door*] Excuse me, ma'am—there is a gentleman to see the master, and as the doctor is with him——

NORA. Who is it?

KROGSTAD. [*at the door*] It is I, Mrs. Helmer. [*MRS. LINDE starts, trembles, and turns to the window.*]

NORA. [*takes a step towards him, and speaks in a strained, low voice*] You? What is it? What do you want to see my husband about?

KROGSTAD. Bank business—in a way. I have a small post in the Bank, and I hear your husband is to be our chief now——

NORA. Then it is——

KROGSTAD. Nothing but dry business matters, Mrs. Helmer; absolutely nothing else.

NORA. Be so good as to go into the study, then. [*She bows indifferently to him and shuts the door into the hall; then comes back and makes up the fire in the stove.*]

MRS. LINDE. Nora—who was that man?

NORA. A lawyer, of the name of Krogstad.

MRS. LINDE. Then it really was he.

NORA. Do you know the man?

MRS. LINDE. I used to—many years ago. At one time he was a solicitor's clerk in our town.

NORA. Yes, he was.

MRS. LINDE. He is greatly altered.

NORA. He made a very unhappy marriage.

MRS. LINDE. He is a widower now, isn't he?

NORA. With several children. There now, it is burning up.

[*Shuts the door of the stove and moves the rocking-chair aside.*]

MRS. LINDE. They say he carries on various kinds of business.

NORA. Really! Perhaps he does; I don't know anything about it. But don't let us think of business; it is so tiresome.

DOCTOR RANK. [*comes out of HELMER'S study. Before he shuts the door he calls to him.*] No, my dear fellow, I won't disturb you; I would rather go into your wife for a little while. [*shuts the door and sees MRS. LINDE*] I beg your pardon; I am afraid I am disturbing you too.

NORA.   No, not at all. [*introducing him*] Doctor Rank, Mrs. Linde.

RANK.   I have often heard Mrs. Linde's name mentioned here. I think I passed you on the stairs when I arrived, Mrs. Linde?

MRS. LINDE.   Yes, I go up very slowly; I can't manage stairs well.

RANK.   Ah! some slight internal weakness?

MRS. LINDE.   No, the fact is I have been overworking myself.

RANK.   Nothing more than that? Then I suppose you have come to town to amuse yourself with our entertainments?

MRS. LINDE.   I have come to look for work.

RANK.   Is that a good cure for overwork?

MRS. LINDE.   One must live, Doctor Rank.

RANK.   Yes, the general opinion seems to be that it is necessary.

NORA.   Look here, Doctor Rank—you know you want to live.

RANK.   Certainly. However wretched I may feel, I want to prolong the agony as long as possible. All my patients are like that. And so are those who are morally diseased; one of them, and a bad case too, is at this very moment with Helmer——

MRS. LINDE.   [*sadly*] Ah!

NORA.   Whom do you mean?

RANK.   A lawyer of the name of Krogstad, a fellow you don't know at all. He suffers from a diseased moral character, Mrs. Helmer; but even he began talking of its being highly important that he should live.

NORA.   Did he? What did he want to speak to Torvald about?

RANK.   I have no idea; I only heard that it was something about the Bank.

NORA.   I didn't know this—what's his name—Krogstad had anything to do with the Bank.

RANK.   Yes, he has some sort of appointment there. [*to MRS. LINDE*] I don't know whether you find also in your part of the world that there are certain people who go zealously snuffing about to smell out moral corruption, and, as soon as they have found some, put the person concerned into some lucrative position where they can keep their eye on him. Healthy natures are left out in the cold.

MRS. LINDE.   Still I think the sick are those who most need taking care of.

RANK.   [*shrugging his shoulders*] Yes, there you are. That is the sentiment that is turning Society into a sickhouse.

[*NORA, who has been absorbed in her thoughts, breaks out into smothered laughter and claps her hands.*]

RANK.   Why do you laugh at that? Have you any notion what Society really is?

NORA.   What do I care about tiresome Society? I am laughing at something quite different, something extremely amusing. Tell me, Doctor Rank, are all the people who are employed in the Bank dependent on Torvald now?

RANK.   Is that what you find so extremely amusing?

NORA.   [*smiling and humming*] That's my affair! [*walking about the room*] It's perfectly glorious to think that we have—that Torvald has so much power over so many people. [*takes the packet from her pocket*] Doctor Rank, what do you say to a macaroon?

RANK.   What, macaroons? I thought they were forbidden here.

NORA.   Yes, but these are some Christine gave me.

MRS. LINDE. What! I?—

NORA. Oh, well, don't be alarmed! You couldn't know that Torvald had forbidden them. I must tell you that he is afraid they will spoil my teeth. But, bah!—once in a way—— That's so, isn't it, Doctor Rank? By your leave? [*puts a macaroon into his mouth*] You must have one too, Christine. And I shall have one, just a little one—or at most two. [*walking about*] I am tremendously happy. There is just one thing in the world now that I should dearly love to do.

RANK. Well, what is that?

NORA. It's something I should dearly love to say, if Torvald could hear me.

RANK. Well, why can't you say it?

NORA. No, I daren't; it's so shocking.

MRS. LINDE. Shocking?

RANK. Well, I should not advise you to say it. Still, with us you might. What is it you would so much like to say if Torvald could hear you?

NORA. I should just love to say—Well, I'm damned!

RANK. Are you mad?

MRS. LINDE. Nora, dear——!

RANK. Say it, here he is!

NORA. [*hiding the packet*] Hush! Hush! Hush!

[*HELMER comes out of his room, with his coat over his arm and his hat in his hands.*]

NORA. Well, Torvald dear, have you got rid of him?

HELMER. Yes, he has just gone.

NORA. Let me introduce you—this is Christine, who has come to town.

HELMER. Christine——? Excuse me, but I don't know——

NORA. Mrs. Linde, dear; Christine Linde.

HELMER. Of course. A school friend of my wife's, I presume?

MRS. LINDE. Yes, we have known each other since then.

NORA. And just think, she has taken a long journey in order to see you.

HELMER. What do you mean?

MRS. LINDE. No, really, I——

NORA. Christine is tremendously clever at book-keeping, and she is frightfully anxious to work under some clever man, so as to perfect herself——

HELMER. Very sensible, Mrs. Linde.

NORA. And when she heard you had been appointed manager of the Bank—the news was telegraphed, you know—she travelled here as quick as she could. Torvald, I am sure you will be able to do something for Christine, for my sake, won't you?

HELMER. Well, it is not altogether impossible. I presume you are a widow, Mrs. Linde?

MRS. LINDE. Yes.

HELMER. And have had some experience of book-keeping?

MRS. LINDE. Yes, a fair amount.

HELMER. Ah! well, it's very likely I may be able to find something for you——

NORA. [*clapping her hands*] What did I tell you? What did I tell you?

HELMER. You have just come at a fortunate moment, Mrs. Linde.

MRS. LINDE. How am I to thank you?

HELMER. There is no need. [*puts on his coat*] But to-day you must excuse me——

RANK. Wait a minute; I will come with you.

[*Brings his fur coat from the hall and warms it at the fire.*]

NORA. Don't be long away, Torvald dear.

HELMER. About an hour, not more.

NORA. Are you going too, Christine?

MRS. LINDE. [*putting on her cloak*] Yes, I must go and look for a room.

HELMER. Oh, well then, we can walk down the street together.

NORA. [*helping her*] What a pity it is we are so short of space here: I am afraid it is impossible for us——

MRS. LINDE. Please don't think of it! Good-bye, Nora dear, and many thanks.

NORA. Good-bye for the present. Of course you will come back this evening. And you too, Dr. Rank. What do you say? If you are well enough? Oh, you must be! Wrap yourself up well.

[*They go to the door all talking together. Children's voices are heard on the staircase.*]

NORA. There they are. There they are! [*She runs to open the door. The* NURSE *comes in with the children.*] Come in! Come in! [*stoops and kisses them*] Oh, you sweet blessings! Look at them, Christine! Aren't they darlings?

RANK. Don't let us stand here in the draught.

HELMER. Come along, Mrs. Linde; the place will only be bearable for a mother now!

[*RANK, HELMER and MRS. LINDE go downstairs. The* NURSE *comes forward with the children; NORA shuts the hall door.*]

NORA. How fresh and well you look! Such red cheeks!—like apples and roses. [*The children all talk at once while she speaks to them.*] Have you had great fun? That's splendid! What, you pulled both Emmy and Bob along on the sledge?— both at once?—that *was* good. You are a clever boy, Ivar. Let me take her for a little, Anne. My sweet little baby doll! [*takes the baby from the* MAID *and dances it up and down*] Yes, yes, mother will dance with Bob too. What! Have you been snowballing? I wish I had been there too! No, no, I will take their things off, Anne; please let me do it, it is such fun. Go in now, you look half frozen. There is some coffee for you on the stove.

[*The* NURSE *goes into the room on the left. NORA takes off the children's things and throws them about, while they all talk to her at once.*]

NORA. Really! Did a big dog run after you? But it didn't bite you? No, dogs don't bite nice little dolly children. You mustn't look at the parcels, Ivar. What are they? Ah, I daresay you would like to know. No, no—it's something nasty! Come, let us have a game! What shall we play at? Hide and Seek? Yes, we'll play Hide and Seek. Bob shall hide first. Must I hide? Very well, I'll hide first.

[*She and the children laugh and shout, and romp in and out of the room; at last NORA hides under the table, the children rush in and look for her, but do not see her; they hear*

her smothered laughter, run to the table, lift up the cloth and find her. Shouts of laughter.
She crawls forward and pretends to frighten them. Fresh laughter. Meanwhile there has been
a knock at the hall door, but none of them has noticed it. The door is half opened, and
KROGSTAD appears. He waits a little; the game goes on.]

KROGSTAD. Excuse me, Mrs. Helmer.

NORA. [*with a stifled cry, turns round and gets up on to her knees*] Ah! what do
you want?

KROGSTAD. Excuse me, the outer door was ajar; I suppose someone forgot
to shut it.

NORA. [*rising*] My husband is out, Mr. Krogstad.

KROGSTAD. I know that.

NORA. What do you want here, then?

KROGSTAD. A word with you.

NORA. With me?— [*to the children, gently*] Go in to nurse. What? No, the
strange man won't do mother any harm. When he has gone we will have another
game. [*She takes the children into the room on the left, and shuts the door after them.*]
You want to speak to me?

KROGSTAD. Yes, I do.

NORA. To-day? It is not the first of the month yet.

KROGSTAD. No, it is Christmas Eve, and it will depend on yourself what
sort of a Christmas you will spend.

NORA. What do you want? To-day it is absolutely impossible for me——

KROGSTAD. We won't talk about that till later on. This is something different.
I presume you can give me a moment?

NORA. Yes—yes, I can—although——

KROGSTAD. Good. I was in Olsen's Restaurant and saw your husband going
down the street——

NORA. Yes?

KROGSTAD. With a lady.

NORA. What then?

KROGSTAD. May I make so bold as to ask if it was a Mrs. Linde?

NORA. It was.

KROGSTAD. Just arrived in town?

NORA. Yes, to-day.

KROGSTAD. She is a great friend of yours, isn't she?

NORA. She is. But I don't see——

KROGSTAD. I knew her too, once upon a time.

NORA. I am aware of that.

KROGSTAD. Are you? So you know all about it; I thought as much. Then I
can ask you, without beating about the bush—is Mrs. Linde to have an appointment
in the Bank?

NORA. What right have you to question me, Mr. Krogstad?—You, one of
my husband's subordinates! But since you ask, you shall know. Yes, Mrs. Linde
is to have an appointment. And it was I who pleaded her cause, Mr. Krogstad,
let me tell you that.

KROGSTAD. I was right in what I thought, then.

NORA. [*walking up and down the stage*] Sometimes one has a tiny little bit of

influence, I should hope. Because one is a woman, it does not necessarily follow
that——. When anyone is in a subordinate position, Mr. Krogstad, they should
really be careful to avoid offending anyone who—who——

KROGSTAD. Who has influence?

NORA. Exactly.

KROGSTAD. [*changing his tone*] Mrs. Helmer, you will be so good as to use
your influence on my behalf.

NORA. What? What do you mean?

KROGSTAD. You will be so kind as to see that I am allowed to keep my
subordinate position in the Bank.

NORA. What do you mean by that? Who proposes to take your post away
from you?

KROGSTAD. Oh, there is no necessity to keep up the pretence of ignorance.
I can quite understand that your friend is not very anxious to expose herself to
the chance of rubbing shoulders with me; and I quite understand, too, whom I
have to thank for being turned out.

NORA. But I assure you——

KROGSTAD. Very likely; but, to come to the point, the time has come when
I should advise you to use your influence to prevent that.

NORA. But, Mr. Krogstad, I *have* no influence.

KROGSTAD. Haven't you? I thought you said yourself just now——

NORA. Naturally I did not mean you to put that construction on it. I! What
should make you think I have any influence of that kind with my husband?

KROGSTAD. Oh, I have known your husband from our student days. I don't
suppose he is any more unassailable than other husbands.

NORA. If you speak slightingly of my husband, I shall turn you out of the
house.

KROGSTAD. You are bold, Mrs. Helmer.

NORA. I am not afraid of you any longer. As soon as the New Year comes,
I shall in a very short time be free of the whole thing.

KROGSTAD. [*controlling himself*] Listen to me, Mrs. Helmer. If necessary, I
am prepared to fight for my small post in the Bank as if I were fighting for my
life.

NORA. So it seems.

KROGSTAD. It is not only for the sake of the money; indeed, that weighs
least with me in the matter. There is another reason—well, I may as well tell
you. My position is this. I daresay you know, like everybody else, that once, many
years ago, I was guilty of an indiscretion.

NORA. I think I have heard something of the kind.

KROGSTAD. The matter never came into court; but every way seemed to
be closed to me after that. So I took to the business that you know of. I had to
do something; and, honestly, I don't think I've been one of the worst. But now I
must cut myself free from all that. My sons are growing up; for their sake I must
try and win back as much respect as I can in the town. This post in the Bank
was like the first step up for me—and now your husband is going to kick me
downstairs again into the mud.

NORA. But you must believe me, Mr. Krogstad; it is not in my power to
help you at all.

KROGSTAD. Then it is because you haven't the will; but I have means to compel you.

NORA. You don't mean that you will tell my husband that I owe you money?

KROGSTAD. Hm!—suppose I were to tell him?

NORA. It would be perfectly infamous of you. [*Sobbing*] To think of his learning my secret, which has been my joy and pride, in such an ugly, clumsy way— that he should learn it from you! And it would put me in a horribly disagreeable position——

KROGSTAD. Only disagreeable?

NORA. [*impetuously*] Well, do it, then!—and it will be the worse for you. My husband will see for himself what a blackguard you are, and you certainly won't keep your post then.

KROGSTAD. I asked you if it was only a disagreeable scene at home that you were afraid of?

NORA. If my husband does get to know of it, of course he will at once pay you what is still owing, and we shall have nothing more to do with you.

KROGSTAD. [*coming a step nearer*] Listen to me, Mrs. Helmer. Either you have a very bad memory or you know very little of business. I shall be obliged to remind you of a few details.

NORA. What do you mean?

KROGSTAD. When your husband was ill, you came to me to borrow two hundred and fifty pounds.

NORA. I didn't know any one else to go to.

KROGSTAD. I promised to get you that amount——

NORA. Yes, and you did so.

KROGSTAD. I promised to get you that amount, on certain conditions. Your mind was so taken up with your husband's illness, and you were so anxious to get the money for your journey, that you seem to have paid no attention to the conditions of our bargain. Therefore it will not be amiss if I remind you of them. Now, I promised to get the money on the security of a bond which I drew up.

NORA. Yes, and which I signed.

KROGSTAD. Good. But below your signature there were a few lines constituting your father a surety for the money; those lines your father should have signed.

NORA. Should? He did sign them.

KROGSTAD. I had left the date blank; that is to say your father should himself have inserted the date on which he signed the paper. Do you remember that?

NORA. Yes, I think I remember——

KROGSTAD. Then I gave you the bond to send by post to your father. Is that not so?

NORA. Yes.

KROGSTAD. And you naturally did so at once, because five or six days afterwards you brought me the bond with your father's signature. And then I gave you the money.

NORA. Well, haven't I been paying it off regularly?

KROGSTAD. Fairly so, yes. But—to come back to the matter in hand—that must have been a very trying time for you, Mrs. Helmer?

NORA. It was, indeed.

KROGSTAD. Your father was very ill, wasn't he?

NORA. He was very near his end.

KROGSTAD. And died soon afterwards?

NORA. Yes.

KROGSTAD. Tell me, Mrs. Helmer, can you by any chance remember what day your father died?—on what day of the month, I mean.

NORA. Papa died on the 29th of September.

KROGSTAD. That is correct; I have ascertained it for myself. And, as that is so, there is a discrepancy [*taking a paper from his pocket*] which I cannot account for.

NORA. What discrepancy? I don't know——

KROGSTAD. The discrepancy consists, Mrs. Helmer, in the fact that your father signed this bond three days after his death.

NORA. What do you mean? I don't understand——

KROGSTAD. Your father died on the 29th of September. But, look here; your father has dated his signature the 2nd of October. It is a discrepancy, isn't it? [*NORA is silent.*] Can you explain it to me? [*NORA is still silent.*] It is a remarkable thing, too, that the words "2nd of October," as well as the year, are not written in your father's handwriting but in one that I think I know. Well, of course it can be explained; your father may have forgotten to date his signature, and someone else may have dated it haphazard before they knew of his death. There is no harm in that. It all depends on the signature of the name; and *that* is genuine, I suppose, Mrs. Helmer? It was your father himself who signed his name here?

NORA. [*after a short pause, throws her head up and looks defiantly at him*] No, it was not. It was I that wrote papa's name.

KROGSTAD. Are you aware that is a dangerous confession?

NORA. In what way? You shall have your money soon.

KROGSTAD. Let me ask you a question; why did you not send the paper to your father?

NORA. It was impossible; papa was so ill. If I had asked him for his signature, I should have had to tell him what the money was to be used for; and when he was so ill himself I couldn't tell him that my husband's life was in danger—it was impossible.

KROGSTAD. It would have been better for you if you had given up your trip abroad.

NORA. No, that was impossible. That trip was to save my husband's life; I couldn't give that up.

KROGSTAD. But did it never occur to you that you were committing a fraud on me?

NORA. I couldn't take that into account; I didn't trouble myself about you at all. I couldn't bear you, because you put so many heartless difficulties in my way, although you knew what a dangerous condition my husband was in.

KROGSTAD. Mrs. Helmer, you evidently do not realise clearly what it is that you have been guilty of. But I can assure you that my one false step, which lost me all my reputation, was nothing more or nothing worse than what you have done.

NORA. You? Do you ask me to believe that you were brave enough to run a risk to save your wife's life?

KROGSTAD. The law cares nothing about motives.

NORA. Then it must be a very foolish law.

KROGSTAD. Foolish or not, it is the law by which you will be judged, if I produce this paper in court.

NORA. I don't believe it. Is a daughter not to be allowed to spare her dying father anxiety and care? Is a wife not to be allowed to save her husband's life? I don't know much about law; but I am certain that there must be laws permitting such things as that. Have you no knowledge of such laws—you who are a lawyer? You must be a very poor lawyer, Mr. Krogstad.

KROGSTAD. Maybe. But matters of business—such business as you and I have had together—do you think I don't understand that? Very well. Do as you please. But let me tell you this—if I lose my position a second time, you shall lose yours with me.

[*He bows, and goes out through the hall.*]

NORA. [*appears buried in thought for a short time, then tosses her head*] Nonsense! Trying to frighten me like that!—I am not so silly as he thinks. [*begins to busy herself putting the children's things in order*] And yet——? No, it's impossible! I did it for love's sake.

THE CHILDREN. [*in the doorway on the left*] Mother, the stranger man has gone out through the gate.

NORA. Yes, dears, I know. But, don't tell anyone about the stranger man. Do you hear? Not even papa.

CHILDREN. No, mother; but will you come and play again?

NORA. No, no—not now.

CHILDREN. But, mother, you promised us.

NORA. Yes, but I can't now. Run away in; I have such a lot to do. Run away in, my sweet little darlings. [*She gets them into the room by degrees and shuts the door on them; then sits down on the sofa, takes up a piece of needlework and sews a few stitches, but soon stops.*] No! [*throws down the work, gets up, goes to the hall door and calls out*] Helen! bring the Tree in. [*goes to the table on the left, opens a drawer, and stops again*] No, no! it is quite impossible!

MAID. [*coming in with the Tree*] Where shall I put it, ma'am?

NORA. Here, in the middle of the floor.

MAID. Shall I get you anything else?

NORA. No, thank you. I have all I want. [*Exit MAID.*]

NORA. [*begins dressing the tree*] A candle here—and flowers here——. The horrible man! It's all nonsense—there's nothing wrong. The Tree shall be splendid! I will do everything I can think of to please you, Torvald!—I will sing for you, dance for you—[*HELMER comes in with some papers under his arm*] Oh! are you back already?

HELMER. Yes. Has anyone been here?

NORA. Here? No.

HELMER. That is strange. I saw Krogstad going out of the gate.

NORA. Did you? Oh yes, I forgot, Krogstad was here for a moment.

HELMER. Nora, I can see from your manner that he has been here begging you to say a good word for him.

NORA. Yes.

HELMER. And you were to appear to do it of your own accord; you were to conceal from me the fact of his having been here; didn't he beg that of you too?

NORA.   Yes, Torvald, but——

HELMER.   Nora, Nora, and you would be a party to that sort of thing? To have any talk with a man like that, and give him any sort of promise? And to tell me a lie into the bargain?

NORA.   A lie——?

HELMER.   Didn't you tell me no one had been here? [*shakes his finger at her*] My little song-bird must never do that again. A song-bird must have a clean beak to chirp with—no false notes! [*puts his arm round her waist*] That is so, isn't it? Yes, I am sure it is. [*lets her go*] We will say no more about it. [*sits down by the stove*] How warm and snug it is here!

[*Turns over his papers.*]

NORA.   [*after a short pause, during which she busies herself with the Christmas Tree*] Torvald!

HELMER.   Yes.

NORA.   I am looking forward tremendously to the fancy dress ball at the Stenborgs' the day after to-morrow.

HELMER.   And I am tremendously curious to see what you are going to surprise me with.

NORA.   It was very silly of me to want to do that.

HELMER.   What do you mean?

NORA.   I can't hit upon anything that will do; everything I think of seems so silly and insignificant.

HELMER.   Does my little Nora acknowledge that at last?

NORA.   [*standing behind his chair with her arms on the back of it*] Are you very busy, Torvald?

HELMER.   Well——

NORA.   What are all those papers?

HELMER.   Bank business.

NORA.   Already?

HELMER.   I have got authority from the retiring manager to undertake the necessary changes in the staff and in the rearrangement of the work; and I must make use of the Christmas week for that, so as to have everything in order for the new year.

NORA.   Then that was why this poor Krogstad——

HELMER.   Hm!

NORA.   [*leans against the back of his chair and strokes his hair*] If you hadn't been so busy I should have asked you a tremendously big favour, Torvald.

HELMER.   What is that? Tell me.

NORA.   There is no one has such good taste as you. And I do so want to look nice at the fancy-dress ball. Torvald, couldn't you take me in hand and decide what I shall go as, and what sort of a dress I shall wear?

HELMER.   Aha! so my obstinate little woman is obliged to get someone to come to her rescue?

NORA.   Yes, Torvald, I can't get along a bit without your help.

HELMER. Very well, I will think it over, we shall manage to hit upon something.

NORA. That *is* nice of you. [*goes to the Christmas Tree. A short pause.*] How pretty the red flowers look——. But, tell me, was it really something very bad that this Krogstad was guilty of?

HELMER. He forged someone's name. Have you any idea what that means?

NORA. Isn't it possible that he was driven to do it by necessity?

HELMER. Yes; or, as in so many cases, by imprudence. I am not so heartless as to condemn a man altogether because of a single false step of that kind.

NORA. No you wouldn't, would you, Torvald?

HELMER. Many a man has been able to retrieve his character, if he has openly confessed his fault and taken his punishment.

NORA. Punishment——?

HELMER. But Krogstad did nothing of that sort; he got himself out of it by a cunning trick, and that is why he has gone under altogether.

NORA. But do you think it would——?

HELMER. Just think how a guilty man like that has to lie and play the hypocrite with everyone, how he has to wear a mask in the presence of those near and dear to him, even before his own wife and children. And about the children— that is the most terrible part of it all, Nora.

NORA. How?

HELMER. Because such an atmosphere of lies infects and poisons the whole life of a home. Each breath the children take in such a house is full of the germs of evil.

NORA. [*coming nearer him*] Are you sure of that?

HELMER. My dear, I have often seen it in the course of my life as a lawyer. Almost everyone who has gone to the bad early in life has had a deceitful mother.

NORA. Why do you only say—mother?

HELMER. It seems most commonly to be the mother's influence, though naturally a bad father's would have the same result. Every lawyer is familiar with the fact. This Krogstad, now, has been persistently poisoning his own children with lies and dissimulation; that is why I say he has lost all moral character. [*holds out his hands to her*] That is why my sweet little Nora must promise me not to plead his cause. Give me your hand on it. Come, come, what is this? Give me your hand. There now, that's settled. I assure you it would be quite impossible for me to work with him; I literally feel physically ill when I am in the company of such people.

NORA. [*takes her hand out of his and goes to the opposite side of the Christmas Tree*] How hot it is in here; and I have such a lot to do.

HELMER. [*getting up and putting his papers in order*] Yes, and I must try and read through some of these before dinner; and I must think about your costume, too. And it is just possible I may have something ready in gold paper to hang up on the Tree. [*Puts his hand on her head.*] My precious little singing-bird!

[*He goes into his room and shuts the door after him.*]

NORA. [*after a pause, whispers*] No, no—it isn't true. It's impossible; it must be impossible.

[*The* NURSE *opens the door on the left*.]

NURSE. The little ones are begging so hard to be allowed to come in to mamma.

NORA. No, no, no! Don't let them come in to me! You stay with them, Anne.

NURSE. Very well, ma'am.

[*Shuts the door*.]

NORA. [*pale with terror*] Deprave my little children? Poison my home? [*a short pause. Then she tosses her head*.] It's not true. It can't possibly be true.

ACT 2

THE SAME SCENE.—*The Christmas Tree is in the corner by the piano, stripped of its ornaments and with burnt-down candle-ends on its dishevelled branches.* NORA'S *cloak and hat are lying on the sofa. She is alone in the room, walking about uneasily. She stops by the sofa and takes up her cloak.*

NORA. [*drops the cloak*] Someone is coming now! [*goes to the door and listens*] No—it is no one. Of course, no one will come to-day, Christmas Day—nor tomorrow either. But, perhaps—[*opens the door and looks out*] No, nothing in the letter-box; it is quite empty. [*comes forward*] What rubbish! of course he can't be in earnest about it. Such a thing couldn't happen; it is impossible—I have three little children.

[*Enter the* NURSE *from the room on the left, carrying a big cardboard box*.]

NURSE. At last I have found the box with the fancy dress.

NORA. Thanks; put it on the table.

NURSE. [*doing so*] But it is very much in want of mending.

NORA. I should like to tear it into a hundred thousand pieces.

NURSE. What an idea! It can easily be put in order—just a little patience.

NORA. Yes, I will go and get Mrs. Linde to come and help me with it.

NURSE. What, out again? In this horrible weather? You will catch cold, ma'am, and make yourself ill.

NORA. Well, worse than that might happen. How are the children?

NURSE. The poor little souls are playing with their Christmas presents, but——

NORA. Do they ask much for me?

NURSE. You see, they are so accustomed to have their mamma with them.

NORA. Yes, but, nurse, I shall not be able to be so much with them now as I was before.

NURSE. Oh well, young children easily get accustomed to anything.

NORA. Do you think so? Do you think they would forget their mother if she went away altogether?

NURSE. Good heavens!—went away altogether?

NORA. Nurse, I want you to tell me something I have often wondered about— how could you have the heart to put your own child out among strangers?

NURSE. I was obliged to, if I wanted to be little Nora's nurse.

NORA. Yes, but how could you be willing to do it?

NURSE. What, when I was going to get such a good place by it? A poor girl who has got into trouble should be glad to. Besides, that wicked man didn't do a single thing for me.

NORA. But I suppose your daughter has quite forgotten you.

NURSE. No, indeed she hasn't. She wrote to me when she was confirmed, and when she was married.

NORA. [*putting her arms round her neck*] Dear old Anne, you were a good mother to me when I was little.

NURSE. Little Nora, poor dear, had no other mother but me.

NORA. And if my little ones had no other mother, I am sure you would——What nonsense I am talking! [*opens the box*] Go in to them. Now I must——. You will see to-morrow how charming I shall look.

NURSE. I am sure there will be no one at the ball so charming as you, ma'am.

[*Goes into the room on the left.*]

NORA. [*begins to unpack the box, but soon pushes it away from her*] If only I dared go out. If only no one would come. If only I could be sure nothing would happen here in the meantime. Stuff and nonsense! No one will come. Only I mustn't think about it. I will brush my muff. What lovely, lovely gloves! Out of my thoughts, out of my thoughts! One, two, three, four, five, six—— [*screams.*] Ah! there is someone coming——.

[*Makes a movement towards the door, but stands irresolute.*]

[*Enter* MRS. LINDE *from the hall, where she has taken off her cloak and hat.*]

NORA. Oh, it's you, Christine. There is no one else out there, is there? How good of you to come!

MRS. LINDE. I heard you were up asking for me.

NORA. Yes, I was passing by. As a matter of fact, it is something you could help me with. Let us sit down here on the sofa. Look here. To-morrow evening there is to be a fancy-dress ball at the Stenborgs', who live above us; and Torvald wants me to go as a Neapolitan fisher-girl, and dance the Tarantella that I learnt at Capri.

MRS. LINDE. I see; you are going to keep up the character.

NORA. Yes, Torvald wants me to. Look, here is the dress; Torvald had it made for me there, but now it is all so torn, and I haven't any idea——

MRS. LINDE. We will easily put that right. It is only some of the trimming come unsewn here and there. Needle and thread? Now then, that's all we want.

NORA. It *is* nice of you.

MRS. LINDE. [*sewing*] So you are going to be dressed up to-morrow, Nora. I will tell you what—I shall come in for a moment and see you in your fine feathers. But I have completely forgotten to thank you for a delightful evening yesterday.

NORA. [*gets up, and crosses the stage*] Well I don't think yesterday was as pleasant as usual. You ought to have come to town a little earlier, Christine. Certainly Torvald does understand how to make a house dainty and attractive.

MRS. LINDE. And so do you, it seems to me; you are not your father's daughter for nothing. But tell me, is Doctor Rank always as depressed as he was yesterday?

NORA.   No; yesterday it was very noticeable. I must tell you that he suffers from a very dangerous disease. He has consumption of the spine, poor creature. His father was a horrible man who committed all sorts of excesses; and that is why his son was sickly from childhood, do you understand?

MRS. LINDE.   [*dropping her sewing*] But, my dearest Nora, how do you know anything about such things?

NORA.   [*walking about*] Pooh! When you have three children, you get visits now and then from—from married women, who know something of medical matters, and they talk about one thing and another.

MRS. LINDE.   [*goes on sewing. A short silence*] Does Doctor Rank come here every day?

NORA.   Every day regularly. He is Torvald's most intimate friend, and a great friend of mine too. He is just like one of the family.

MRS. LINDE.   But tell me this—is he perfectly sincere? I mean, isn't he the kind of man that is very anxious to make himself agreeable?

NORA.   Not in the least. What makes you think that?

MRS. LINDE.   When you introduced him to me yesterday, he declared he had often heard my name mentioned in this house; but afterwards I noticed that your husband hadn't the slightest idea who I was. So how could Doctor Rank——?

NORA.   That is quite right, Christine. Torvald is so absurdly fond of me that he wants me absolutely to himself, as he says. At first he used to seem almost jealous if I mentioned any of the dear folk at home, so naturally I gave up doing so. But I often talk about such things with Doctor Rank, because he likes hearing about them.

MRS. LINDE.   Listen to me, Nora. You are still very like a child in many things, and I am older than you in many ways and have a little more experience. Let me tell you this—you ought to make an end of it with Doctor Rank.

NORA.   What ought I to make an end of?

MRS. LINDE.   Of two things, I think. Yesterday you talked some nonsense about a rich admirer who was to leave you money——

NORA.   An admirer who doesn't exist, unfortunately! But what then?

MRS. LINDE.   Is Doctor Rank a man of means?

NORA.   Yes, he is.

MRS. LINDE.   And has no one to provide for?

NORA.   No, no one; but——

MRS. LINDE.   And comes here every day?

NORA.   Yes, I told you so.

MRS. LINDE.   But how can this well-bred man be so tactless?

NORA.   I don't understand you at all.

MRS. LINDE.   Don't prevaricate, Nora. Do you suppose I don't guess who lent you the two hundred and fifty pounds?

NORA.   Are you out of your senses? How can you think of such a thing! A friend of ours, who comes here every day! Do you realise what a horribly painful position that would be?

MRS. LINDE.   Then it really isn't he?

NORA.   No, certainly not. It would never have entered into my head for a moment. Besides, he had no money to lend then; he came into his money afterwards.

MRS. LINDE.   Well, I think that was lucky for you, my dear Nora.

NORA.   No, it would never have come into my head to ask Doctor Rank. Although I am quite sure that if I had asked him——

MRS. LINDE.   But of course you won't.

NORA.   Of course not. I have no reason to think it could possibly be necessary. But I am quite sure that if I told Doctor Rank——

MRS. LINDE.   Behind your husband's back?

NORA.   I must make an end of it with the other one, and that will be behind his back too. I *must* make an end of it with him.

MRS. LINDE.   Yes, that is what I told you yesterday, but——

NORA.   [*walking up and down*] A man can put a thing like that straight much easier than a woman——

MRS. LINDE.   One's husband, yes.

NORA.   Nonsense! [*standing still*] When you pay off a debt you get your bond back, don't you?

MRS. LINDE.   Yes, as a matter of course.

NORA.   And can tear it into a hundred thousand pieces, and burn it up—the nasty dirty paper!

MRS. LINDE.   [*looks hard at her, lays down her sewing and gets up slowly*] Nora, you are concealing something from me.

NORA.   Do I look as if I were?

MRS. LINDE.   Something has happened to you since yesterday morning. Nora, what is it?

NORA.   [*going nearer to her*] Christine! [*listens*] Hush! there's Torvald come home. Do you mind going in to the children for the present? Torvald can't bear to see dressmaking going on. Let Anne help you.

MRS. LINDE.   [*gathering some of the things together*] Certainly—but I am not going away from here till we have had it out with one another.

[*She goes into the room on the left, as* HELMER *comes in from the hall.*]

NORA.   [*going up to* HELMER] I have wanted you so much, Torvald dear.

HELMER.   Was that the dressmaker?

NORA.   No, it was Christine; she is helping me to put my dress in order. You will see I shall look quite smart.

HELMER.   Wasn't that a happy thought of mine, now?

NORA.   Splendid! But don't you think it is nice of me, too, to do as you wish?

HELMER.   Nice?—because you do as your husband wishes? Well, well, you little rogue, I am sure you did not mean it in that way. But I am not going to disturb you; you will want to be trying on your dress, I expect.

NORA.   I suppose you are going to work.

HELMER.   Yes. [*shows her a bundle of papers*] Look at that. I have just been into the bank.   [*Turns to go into his room.*]

NORA.   Torvald.

HELMER.   Yes.

NORA. If your little squirrel were to ask you for something very, very prettily——?

HELMER. What then?

NORA. Would you do it?

HELMER. I should like to hear what it is, first.

NORA. Your squirrel would run about and do all her tricks if you would be nice, and do what she wants.

HELMER. Speak plainly.

NORA. Your skylark would chirp about in every room, with her song rising and falling——

HELMER. Well, my skylark does that anyhow.

NORA. I would play the fairy and dance for you in the moonlight, Torvald.

HELMER. Nora—you surely don't mean that request you made of me this morning?

NORA. [*going near him*] Yes, Torvald, I beg you so earnestly——

HELMER. Have you really the courage to open up that question again?

NORA. Yes, dear, you *must* do as I ask; you *must* let Krogstad keep his post in the Bank.

HELMER. My dear Nora, it is his post that I have arranged Mrs. Linde shall have.

NORA. Yes, you have been awfully kind about that; but you could just as well dismiss some other clerk instead of Krogstad.

HELMER. This is simply incredible obstinacy! Because you chose to give him a thoughtless promise that you would speak for him, I am expected to——

NORA. That isn't the reason, Torvald. It is for your own sake. This fellow writes in the most scurrilous newspapers; you have told me so yourself. He can do you an unspeakable amount of harm. I am frightened to death of him——

HELMER. Ah, I understand; it is recollections of the past that scare you.

NORA. What do you mean?

HELMER. Naturally you are thinking of your father.

NORA. Yes—yes, of course. Just recall to your mind what these malicious creatures wrote in the papers about papa, and how horribly they slandered him. I believe they would have procured his dismissal if the Department had not sent you over to inquire into it, and if you had not been so kindly disposed and helpful to him.

HELMER. My little Nora, there is an important difference between your father and me. Your father's reputation as a public official was not above suspicion. Mine is, and I hope it will continue to be so, as long as I hold my office.

NORA. You never can tell what mischief these men may contrive. We ought to be so well off, so snug and happy here in our peaceful home, and have no cares—you and I and the children, Torvald! That is why I beg you so earnestly——

HELMER. And it is just by interceding for him that you make it impossible for me to keep him. It is already known at the Bank that I mean to dismiss Krogstad. Is it to get about now that the new manager has changed his mind at his wife's bidding——

NORA. And what if it did?

HELMER. Of course!—if only this obstinate little person can get her way!

Do you suppose I am going to make myself ridiculous before my whole staff, to let people think that I am a man to be swayed by all sorts of outside influence? I should very soon feel the consequences of it, I can tell you! And besides, there is one thing that makes it quite impossible for me to have Krogstad in the Bank as long as I am manager.

NORA. Whatever is that?

HELMER. His moral failings I might perhaps have overlooked, if necessary——

NORA. Yes, you could—couldn't you?

HELMER. And I hear he is a good worker, too. But I knew him when we were boys. It was one of those rash friendships that so often prove an incubus in after life. I may as well tell you plainly, we were once on very intimate terms with one another. But this tactless fellow lays no restraint on himself when other people are present. On the contrary, he thinks it gives him the right to adopt a familiar tone with me, and every minute it is "I say, Helmer, old fellow!" and that sort of thing. I assure you it is extremely painful for me. He would make my position in the Bank intolerable.

NORA. Torvald, I don't believe you mean that.

HELMER. Don't you? Why not?

NORA. Because it is such a narrow-minded way of looking at things.

HELMER. What are you saying? Narrow-minded? Do you think I am narrow-minded?

NORA. No, just the opposite, dear—and it is exactly for that reason.

HELMER. It's the same thing. You say my point of view is narrow-minded, so I must be so too. Narrow-minded! Very well—I must put an end to this. [*Goes to the hall-door and calls.*] Helen!

NORA. What are you going to do?

HELMER. [*looking among his papers*] Settle it. [*Enter MAID.*] Look here; take this letter and go downstairs with it at once. Find a messenger and tell him to deliver it, and be quick. The address is on it, and here is the money.

MAID. Very well, sir.

[*Exit with the letter.*]

HELMER. [*putting his papers together*] Now then, little Miss Obstinate.

NORA. [*breathlessly*] Torvald—what was that letter?

HELMER. Krogstad's dismissal.

NORA. Call her back, Torvald! There is still time. Oh Torvald, call her back! Do it for my sake—for your own sake—for the children's sake! Do you hear me, Torvald? Call her back! You don't know what that letter can bring upon us.

HELMER. It's too late.

NORA. Yes, it's too late.

HELMER. My dear Nora, I can forgive the anxiety you are in, although really it is an insult to me. It is, indeed. Isn't it an insult to think that I should be afraid of a starving quill-driver's vengeance? But I forgive you nevertheless, because it is such eloquent witness to your great love for me. [*takes her in his arms*] And that is as it should be, my own darling Nora. Come what will, you may be sure I shall have both courage and strength if they be needed. You will see I am man enough to take everything upon myself.

NORA. [*in a horror-stricken voice*] What do you mean by that?

HELMER. Everything, I say——

NORA. [*recovering herself*] You will never have to do that.

HELMER. That's right. Well, we will share it, Nora, as man and wife should. That is how it shall be. [*caressing her*] Are you content now? There! there!—not these frightened dove's eyes! The whole thing is only the wildest fancy!—Now, you must go and play through the Tarantella and practise with your tambourine. I shall go into the inner office and shut the door, and I shall hear nothing; you can make as much noise as you please. [*turns back at the door*] And when Rank comes, tell him where he will find me.

[*Nods to her, takes his papers and goes into his room, and shuts the door after him.*]

NORA. [*bewildered with anxiety, stands as if rooted to the spot, and whispers*] He is capable of doing it. He will do it. He will do it in spite of everything.—No, not that! Never, never! Anything rather than that! Oh, for some help, some way out of it! [*The door-bell rings.*] Doctor Rank! Anything rather than that—anything, whatever it is!

[*She puts her hands over her face, pulls herself together, goes to the door and opens it. RANK is standing without, hanging up his coat. During the following dialogue it begins to grow dark.*]

NORA. Good-day, Doctor Rank. I knew your ring. But you mustn't go into Torvald now; I think he is busy with something.

RANK. And you?

NORA. [*brings him in and shuts the door after him*] Oh, you know very well I always have time for you.

RANK. Thank you. I shall make use of as much of it as I can.

NORA. What do you mean by that? As much of it as you can?

RANK. Well, does that alarm you?

NORA. It was such a strange way of putting it. Is anything likely to happen?

RANK. Nothing but what I have long been prepared for. But I certainly didn't expect it to happen so soon.

NORA. [*gripping him by the arm*] What have you found out? Doctor Rank, you must tell me.

RANK. [*sitting down by the stove*] It is all up with me. And it can't be helped.

NORA. [*with a sigh of relief*] Is it about yourself?

RANK. Who else? It is no use lying to one's self. I am the most wretched of all my patients, Mrs. Helmer. Lately I have been taking stock of my internal economy. Bankrupt! Probably within a month I shall lie rotting in the churchyard.

NORA. What an ugly thing to say!

RANK. The thing itself is cursedly ugly, and the worst of it is that I shall have to face so much more that is ugly before that. I shall only make one more examination of myself; when I have done that, I shall know pretty certainly when it will be that the horrors of dissolution will begin. There is something I want to tell you. Helmer's refined nature gives him an unconquerable disgust at everything that is ugly; I won't have him in my sick-room.

NORA. Oh, but, Doctor Rank——

RANK. I won't have him there. Not on any account. I bar my door to him.

As soon as I am quite certain that the worst has come, I shall send you my card with a black cross on it, and then you will know that the loathsome end has begun.

NORA. You are quite absurd to-day. And I wanted you so much to be in a really good humour.

RANK. With death stalking beside me?—To have to pay this penalty for another man's sin! Is there any justice in that? And in every single family, in one way or another, some such inexorable retribution is being exacted——

NORA. [*putting her hands over her ears*] Rubbish! Do talk of something cheerful.

RANK. Oh, it's a mere laughing matter, the whole thing. My poor innocent spine has to suffer for my father's youthful amusements.

NORA. [*sitting at the table on the left*] I suppose you mean that he was too partial to asparagus and pâté de foie gras, don't you.

RANK. Yes, and to truffles.

NORA. Truffles, yes. And oysters too, I suppose?

RANK. Oysters, of course, that goes without saying.

NORA. And heaps of port and champagne. It is sad that all these nice things should take their revenge on our bones.

RANK. Especially that they should revenge themselves on the unlucky bones of those who have not had the satisfaction of enjoying them.

NORA. Yes, that's the saddest part of it all.

RANK. [*with a searching look at her*] Hm!——

NORA. [*after a short pause*] Why did you smile?

RANK. No, it was you that laughed.

NORA. No, it was you that smiled, Doctor Rank!

RANK. [*rising*] You are a greater rascal than I thought.

NORA. I am in a silly mood to-day.

RANK. So it seems.

NORA. [*putting her hands on his shoulders*] Dear, dear Doctor Rank, death mustn't take you away from Torvald and me.

RANK. It is a loss you would easily recover from. Those who are gone are soon forgotten.

NORA. [*looking at him anxiously*] Do you believe that?

RANK. People form new ties, and then——

NORA. Who will form new ties?

RANK. Both you and Helmer, when I am gone. You yourself are already on the high road to it, I think. What did that Mrs. Linde want here last night?

NORA. Oho!—you don't mean to say you are jealous of poor Christine?

RANK. Yes, I am. She will be my successor in this house. When I am done for, this woman will—

NORA. Hush! don't speak so loud. She is in that room.

RANK. To-day again. There, you see.

NORA. She has only come to sew my dress for me. Bless my soul, how unreasonable you are! [*sits down on the sofa*] Be nice now, Doctor Rank, and to-morrow you will see how beautifully I shall dance, and you can imagine I am doing it all for you—and for Torvald too, of course. [*takes various things out of the box*] Doctor Rank, come and sit down here, and I will show you something.

RANK. [*sitting down*] What is it?

NORA. Just look at those!

RANK. Silk stockings.

NORA. Flesh-coloured. Aren't they lovely? It is so dark here now, but tomorrow—. No, no, no! you must only look at the feet. Oh well, you may have leave to look at the legs too.

RANK. Hm!—

NORA. Why are you looking so critical? Don't you think they will fit me?

RANK. I have no means of forming an opinion about that.

NORA. [looks at him for a moment] For shame! [hits him lightly on the ear with the stockings] That's to punish you. [folds them up again]

RANK. And what other nice things am I to be allowed to see?

NORA. Not a single thing more, for being so naughty. [She looks among the things, humming to herself.]

RANK. [after a short silence] When I am sitting here, talking to you as intimately as this, I cannot imagine for a moment what would have become of me if I had never come into this house.

NORA. [smiling] I believe you do feel thoroughly at home with us.

RANK. [in a lower voice, looking straight in front of him] And to be obliged to leave it all——

NORA. Nonsense, you are not going to leave it.

RANK. [as before] And not be able to leave behind one the slightest token of one's gratitude, scarcely even a fleeting regret—nothing but an empty place which the first comer can fill as well as any other.

NORA. And if I asked you now for a—? No!

RANK. For what?

NORA. For a big proof of your friendship——

RANK. Yes, yes!

NORA. I mean a tremendously big favour——

RANK. Would you really make me so happy for once?

NORA. Ah, but you don't know what it is yet.

RANK. No—but tell me.

NORA. I really can't, Doctor Rank. It is something out of all reason; it means advice, and help, and a favour——

RANK. The bigger a thing it is the better. I can't conceive what it is you mean. Do tell me. Haven't I your confidence?

NORA. More than anyone else. I know you are my truest and best friend, and so I will tell you what it is. Well, Doctor Rank, it is something you must help me to prevent. You know how devotedly, how inexpressibly deeply Torvald loves me; he would never for a moment hesitate to give his life for me.

RANK [leaning towards her] Nora—do you think he is the only one——?

NORA. [with a slight start] The only one—?

RANK. The only one who would gladly give his life for your sake.

NORA. [sadly] Is that it?

RANK. I was determined you should know it before I went away, and there will never be a better opportunity than this. Now you know it, Nora. And now you know, too, that you can trust me as you would trust no one else.

NORA. [rises, deliberately and quietly] Let me pass.

RANK. [makes room for her to pass him, but sits still] Nora!

NORA. [at the hall door] Helen, bring in the lamp. [goes over to the stove] Dear Doctor Rank, that was really horrid of you.

RANK. To have loved you as much as anyone else does? Was that horrid?

NORA. No, but to go and tell me so. There was really no need——

RANK. What do you mean? Did you know—? [*MAID enters with lamp, puts it down on the table, and goes out.*] Nora—Mrs. Helmer—tell me, had you any idea of this?

NORA. Oh, how do I know whether I had or whether I hadn't? I really can't tell you— To think you could be so clumsy, Doctor Rank! We were getting on so nicely.

RANK. Well, at all events you know now that you can command me, body and soul. So won't you speak out?

NORA. [*looking at him*] After what happened?

RANK. I beg you to let me know what it is.

NORA. I can't tell you anything now.

RANK. Yes, yes. You mustn't punish me in that way. Let me have permission to do for you whatever a man may do.

NORA. You can do nothing for me now. Besides, I really don't need any help at all. You will find that the whole thing is merely fancy on my part. It really is so—of course it is! [*Sits down in the rocking-chair, and looks at him with a smile*] You are a nice sort of man, Doctor Rank!—don't you feel ashamed of yourself, now the lamp has come?

RANK. Not a bit. But perhaps I had better go—for ever?

NORA. No, indeed, you shall not. Of course you must come here just as before. You know very well Torvald can't do without you.

RANK. Yes, but you?

NORA. Oh, I am always tremendously pleased when you come.

RANK. It is just that, that put me on the wrong track. You are a riddle to me. I have often thought that you would almost as soon be in my company as in Helmer's.

NORA. Yes—you see there are some people one loves best, and others whom one would almost always rather have as companions.

RANK. Yes, there is something in that.

NORA. When I was at home, of course I loved papa best. But I always thought it tremendous fun if I could steal down into the maid's room, because they never moralised at all, and talked to each other about such entertaining things.

RANK. I see—it is *their* place I have taken.

NORA. [*jumping up and going to him*] Oh, dear, nice Doctor Rank, I never meant that at all. But surely you can understand that being with Torvald is a little like being with papa——

[*Enter MAID from the hall*]

MAID. If you please, ma'am. [*whispers and hands her a card*]

NORA. [*glancing at the card*] Oh! [*puts it in her pocket*]

RANK. Is there anything wrong?

NORA. No, no, not in the least. It is only something—it is my new dress——

RANK. What? Your dress is lying there.

NORA. Oh, yes, that one; but this is another. I ordered it. Torvald mustn't know about it——

RANK.   Oho! Then that was the great secret.

NORA.   Of course. Just go in to him; he is sitting in the inner room. Keep him as long as——

RANK.   Make your mind easy; I won't let him escape. [*goes into* HELMER'S *room*]

NORA.   [*to the* MAID] And he is standing waiting in the kitchen?

MAID.   Yes; he came up the back stairs.

NORA.   But didn't you tell him no one was in?

MAID.   Yes, but it was no good.

NORA.   He won't go away?

MAID.   No; he says he won't until he has seen you, ma'am.

NORA.   Well, let him come in—but quietly. Helen, you mustn't say anything about it to anyone. It is a surprise for my husband.

MAID.   Yes, ma'am, I quite understand.   [*Exit.*]

NORA.   This dreadful thing is going to happen! It will happen in spite of me! No, no, no, it can't happen—it shan't happen!

[*She bolts the door of* HELMER'S *room. The* MAID *opens the hall door for* KROGSTAD *and shuts it after him. He is wearing a fur coat, high boots and a fur cap.*]

NORA.   [*advancing towards him*] Speak low—my husband is at home.

KROGSTAD.   No matter about that.

NORA.   What do you want of me?

KROGSTAD.   An explanation of something.

NORA.   Make haste then. What is it?

KROGSTAD.   You know, I suppose, that I have got my dismissal.

NORA.   I couldn't prevent it, Mr. Krogstad. I fought as hard as I could on your side, but it was no good.

KROGSTAD.   Does your husband love you so little, then? He knows what I can expose you to, and yet he ventures——

NORA.   How can you suppose that he has any knowledge of the sort?

KROGSTAD.   I didn't suppose so at all. It would not be the least like our dear Torvald Helmer to show so much courage—

NORA.   Mr. Krogstad, a little respect for my husband, please.

KROGSTAD.   Certainly—all the respect he deserves. But since you have kept the matter so carefully to yourself, I make bold to suppose that you have a little clearer idea, than you had yesterday, of what it actually is that you have done?

NORA.   More than you could ever teach me.

KROGSTAD.   Yes, such a bad lawyer as I am.

NORA.   What is it you want of me?

KROGSTAD.   Only to see how you were, Mrs. Helmer. I have been thinking about you all day long. A mere cashier, a quill-driver, a—well, a man like me—even he has a little of what is called feeling, you know.

NORA.   Show it, then; think of my little children.

KROGSTAD.   Have you and your husband thought of mine? But never mind about that. I only wanted to tell you that you need not take this matter too seriously. In the first place there will be no accusation made on my part.

NORA.   No, of course not; I was sure of that.

KROGSTAD.   The whole thing can be arranged amicably; there is no reason why anyone should know anything about it. It will remain a secret between us three.

NORA.   My husband must never get to know anything about it.

KROGSTAD.   How will you be able to prevent it? Am I to understand that you can pay the balance that is owing?

NORA.   No, not just at present.

KROGSTAD.   Or perhaps that you have some expedient for raising the money soon?

NORA.   No expedient that I mean to make use of.

KROGSTAD.   Well, in any case, it would have been of no use to you now. If you stood there with ever so much money in your hand, I would never part with your bond.

NORA.   Tell me what purpose you mean to put it to.

KROGSTAD.   I shall only preserve it—keep it in my possession. No one who is not concerned in the matter shall have the slightest hint of it. So that if the thought of it has driven you to any desperate resolution——

NORA.   It has.

KROGSTAD.   If you had it in your mind to run away from your home——

NORA.   I had.

KROGSTAD.   Or even something worse——

NORA.   How could you know that?

KROGSTAD.   Give up the idea.

NORA.   How did you know I had thought of *that*?

KROGSTAD.   Most of us think of that at first. I did, too—but I hadn't the courage.

NORA.   [*faintly*] No more had I.

KROGSTAD.   [*in a tone of relief*] No, that's it, isn't it—you hadn't the courage either?

NORA.   No, I haven't—I haven't.

KROGSTAD.   Besides, it would have been a great piece of folly. Once the first storm at home is over—. I have a letter for your husband in my pocket.

NORA.   Telling him everything?

KROGSTAD.   In as lenient a manner as I possibly could.

NORA.[*quickly*] He mustn't get the letter. Tear it up. I will find some means of getting money.

KROGSTAD.   Excuse me, Mrs. Helmer, but I think I told you just now——

NORA.   I am not speaking of what I owe you. Tell me what sum you are asking my husband for, and I will get the money.

KROGSTAD.   I am not asking your husband for a penny.

NORA.   What do you want, then?

KROGSTAD.   I will tell you. I want to rehabilitate myself, Mrs. Helmer; I want to get on; and in that your husband must help me. For the last year and a half I have not had a hand in anything dishonourable, and all that time I have been struggling in most restricted circumstances. I was content to work my way up step by step. Now I am turned out, and I am not going to be satisfied with merely being taken into favour again. I want to get on, I tell you. I want to get into the Bank again, in a higher position. Your husband must make a place for me——

NORA.   That he will never do!

KROGSTAD.   He will; I know him; he dare not protest. And as soon as I am in there again with him, then you will see! Within a year I shall be the manager's right hand. It will be Nils Krogstad and not Torvald Helmer who manages the Bank.

NORA.   That's a thing you will never see!

KROGSTAD.   Do you mean that you will——?

NORA.   I have courage enough for it now.

KROGSTAD.   Oh, you can't frighten me. A fine, spoilt lady like you——

NORA.   You will see, you will see.

KROGSTAD.   Under the ice, perhaps? Down into the cold, coal-black water? And then, in the spring, to float up to the surface, all horrible and unrecognisable, with your hair fallen out——

NORA.   You can't frighten me.

KROGSTAD.   Nor you me. People don't do such things, Mrs. Helmer. Besides, what use would it be? I should have him completely in my power all the same.

NORA.   Afterwards? When I am no longer——

KROGSTAD.   Have you forgotten that it is I who have the keeping of your reputation? [*Nora stands speechlessly looking at him.*] Well, now, I have warned you. Do not do anything foolish. When Helmer has had my letter, I shall expect a message from him. And be sure you remember that it is your husband himself who has forced me into such ways as this again. I will never forgive him for that. Good-bye, Mrs. Helmer.   [*Exit through the hall*]

NORA.   [*goes to the hall door, opens it slightly and listens*] He is going. He is not putting the letter in the box. Oh no, no! that's impossible! [*opens the door by degrees*] What is that? He is standing outside. He is not going downstairs. Is he hesitating? Can he——

[*A letter drops into the box; then* KROGSTAD'S *footsteps are heard, till they die away as he goes downstairs.* NORA *utters a stifled cry and runs across the room to the table by the sofa. A short pause.*]

NORA.   In the letter-box. [*steals across to the hall door*] There it lies—Torvald, Torvald, there is no hope for us now!

[*MRS. LINDE comes in from the room on the left, carrying the dress.*]

MRS. LINDE.   There, I can't see anything more to mend now. Would you like to try it on——?

NORA.   [*in a hoarse whisper*] Christine, come here.

MRS. LINDE.   [*throwing the dress down on the sofa*] What is the matter with you? You look so agitated!

NORA.   Come here. Do you see that letter? There, look—you can see it through the glass in the letter-box.

MRS. LINDE.   Yes, I see it.

NORA.   That letter is from Krogstad.

MRS. LINDE.   Nora—it was Krogstad who lent you the money!

NORA.   Yes, and now Torvald will know all about it.

MRS. LINDE.   Believe me, Nora, that's the best thing for both of you.

NORA.   You don't know all. I forged a name.

Mrs. Linde.   Good heavens——!

Nora.   I only want to say this to you, Christine—you must be my witness.

Mrs. Linde.   Your witness? What do you mean? What am I to—?

Nora.   If I should go out of my mind—and it might easily happen——

Mrs. Linde.   Nora!

Nora.   Or if anything else should happen to me—anything, for instance, that might prevent my being here—

Mrs. Linde.   Nora! Nora! you are quite out of your mind.

Nora.   And if it should happen that there were someone who wanted to take all the responsibility, all the blame, you understand——

Mrs. Linde.   Yes, yes—but how can you suppose—?

Nora.   Then you must be my witness, that it is not true, Christine. I am not out of my mind at all; I am in my right senses now, and I tell you no one else has known anything about it; I, and I alone, did the whole thing. Remember that.

Mrs. Linde.   I will, indeed. But I don't understand all this.

Nora.   How should you understand it? A wonderful thing is going to happen.

Mrs. Linde.   A wonderful thing?

Nora.   Yes, a wonderful thing!—But it is so terrible, Christine; it *mustn't* happen, not for all the world.

Mrs. Linde.   I will go at once and see Krogstad.

Nora.   Don't go to him; he will do you some harm.

Mrs. Linde.   There was a time when he would gladly do anything for my sake.

Nora.   He?

Mrs. Linde.   Where does he live?

Nora.   How should I know—? Yes [*feeling in her pocket*] here is his card. But the letter, the letter——!

Helmer.   [*calls from his room, knocking at the door*] Nora!

Nora.   [*cries out anxiously*] Oh, what's that? What do you want?

Helmer.   Don't be so frightened. We are not coming in; you have locked the door. Are you trying on your dress?

Nora.   Yes, that's it. I look so nice, Torvald.

Mrs. Linde.   [*who has read the card*] I see he lives at the corner here.

Nora.   Yes, but it's no use. It is hopeless. The letter is lying there in the box.

Mrs. Linde.   And your husband keeps the key?

Nora.   Yes, always.

Mrs. Linde.   Krogstad must ask for his letter back unread, he must find some pretence——

Nora.   But it is just at this time that Torvald generally——

Mrs. Linde.   You must delay him. Go in to him in the meantime. I will come back as soon as I can.

[*She goes out hurriedly through the hall door.*]

Nora.   [*goes to* Helmer's *door, opens it and peeps in*] Torvald!

Helmer.   [*from the inner room*] Well? May I venture at last to come into my own room again? Come along, Rank, now you will see— [*halting in the doorway*] But what is this?

NORA.   What is what, dear?

HELMER.   Rank led me to expect a splendid transformation.

RANK.   [*in the doorway*] I understood so, but evidently I was mistaken.

NORA.   Yes, nobody is to have the chance of admiring me in my dress until to-morrow.

HELMER.   But, my dear Nora, you look so worn out. Have you been practising too much?

NORA.   No, I have not practised at all.

HELMER.   But you will need to—

NORA.   Yes, indeed I shall, Torvald. But I can't get on a bit without you to help me; I have absolutely forgotten the whole thing.

HELMER.   Oh, we will soon work it up again.

NORA.   Yes, help me, Torvald. Promise that you will! I am so nervous about it—all the people—. You must give yourself up to me entirely this evening. Not the tiniest bit of business—you mustn't even take a pen in your hand. Will you promise, Torvald dear?

HELMER.   I promise. This evening I will be wholly and absolutely at your service, you helpless little mortal. Ah, by the way, first of all I will just——

[*Goes towards the hall door*]

NORA.   What are you going to do there?

HELMER.   Only see if any letters have come.

NORA.   No, no! don't do that, Torvald!

HELMER.   Why not?

NORA.   Torvald, please don't. There is nothing there.

HELMER.   Well, let me look. [*Turns to go to the letter-box. NORA, at the piano, plays the first bars of the Tarantella. HELMER stops in the doorway.*] Aha!

NORA.   I can't dance to-morrow if I don't practise with you.

HELMER.   [*going up to her*] Are you really so afraid of it, dear.

NORA.   Yes, so dreadfully afraid of it. Let me practise at once; there is time now, before we go to dinner. Sit down and play for me, Torvald dear; criticise me, and correct me as you play.

HELMER.   With great pleasure, if you wish me to.

[*Sits down at the piano.*]

NORA.   [*takes out of the box a tambourine and a long variegated shawl. She hastily drapes the shawl round her. Then she springs to the front of the stage and calls out.*] Now play for me! I am going to dance!

[*HELMER plays and NORA dances. RANK stands by the piano behind HELMER and looks on.*]

HELMER.   [*as he plays*] Slower, slower!

NORA.   I can't do it any other way.

HELMER.   Not so violently, Nora!

NORA.   This is the way.

HELMER. [*stops playing*] No, no—that is not a bit right.

NORA. [*laughing and swinging the tambourine*] Didn't I tell you so?

RANK. Let me play for her.

HELMER. [*getting up*] Yes, do. I can correct her better then.

[*RANK sits down at the piano and plays. NORA dances more and more wildly. HELMER has taken up a position beside the stove, and during her dance gives her frequent instructions. She does not seem to hear him; her hair comes down and falls over her shoulders; she pays no attention to it, but goes on dancing. Enter MRS. LINDE.*]

MRS. LINDE. [*standing as if spell-bound in the doorway*] Oh!——

NORA. [*as she dances*] Such fun, Christine!

HELMER. My dear darling Nora, you are dancing as if your life depended on it.

NORA. So it does.

HELMER. Stop, Rank; this is sheer madness. Stop, I tell you! [*RANK stops playing, and NORA suddenly stands still. HELMER goes up to her.*] I could never have believed it. You have forgotten everything I taught you.

NORA. [*throwing away the tambourine*] There, you see.

HELMER. You will want a lot of coaching.

NORA. Yes, you see how much I need it. You must coach me up to the last minute. Promise me that, Torvald!

HELMER. You can depend on me.

NORA. You must not think of anything but me, either to-day or to-morrow; you mustn't open a single letter—not even open the letter-box——

HELMER. Ah, you are still afraid of that fellow——

NORA. Yes, indeed I am.

HELMER. Nora, I can tell from your looks that there is a letter from him lying there.

NORA. I don't know; I think there is; but you must not read anything of that kind now. Nothing horrid must come between us till this is all over.

RANK. [*whispers to HELMER*] You mustn't contradict her.

HELMER. [*taking her in his arms*] The child shall have her way. But to-morrow night, after you have danced——

NORA. Then you will be free.

[*The MAID appears in the doorway to the right.*]

MAID. Dinner is served, ma'am.

NORA. We will have champagne, Helen.

MAID. Very good, ma'am.   [*Exit.*]

HELMER. Hullo!—are we going to have a banquet?

NORA. Yes, a champagne banquet till the small hours. [*calls out*] And a few macaroons, Helen—lots, just for once!

HELMER. Come, come, don't be so wild and nervous. Be my own little sky-lark, as you used.

NORA. Yes, dear, I will. But go in now and you too, Doctor Rank. Christine, you must help me to do up my hair.

RANK. [*whispers to HELMER as they go out*] I suppose there is nothing—she is not expecting anything?

HELMER.   Far from it, my dear fellow; it is simply nothing more than this childish nervousness I was telling you of.

[*They go into the right-hand room.*]

NORA.   Well!

MRS. LINDE.   Gone out of town.

NORA.   I could tell from your face.

MRS. LINDE.   He is coming home to-morrow evening. I wrote a note for him.

NORA.   You should have let it alone; you must prevent nothing. After all, it is splendid to be waiting for a wonderful thing to happen.

MRS. LINDE.   What is it that you are waiting for?

NORA.   Oh, you wouldn't understand. Go in to them, I will come in a moment. [*MRS. LINDE goes into the dining-room. NORA stands still for a little while, as if to compose herself. Then she looks at her watch.*] Five o'clock. Seven hours till midnight; and then four-and-twenty hours till the next midnight. Then the Tarantella will be over. Twenty-four and seven? Thirty-one hours to live.

HELMER.   [*from the doorway on the right*] Where's my little skylark?

NORA.   [*going to him with her arms outstretched*] Here she is!

ACT 3

THE SAME SCENE.   *The table has been placed in the middle of the stage, with chairs round it. A lamp is burning on the table. The door into the hall stands open. Dance music is heard in the room above.* MRS. LINDE *is sitting at the table idly turning over the leaves of a book; she tries to read, but does not seem able to collect her thoughts. Every now and then she listens intently for a sound at the outer door.*

MRS. LINDE.   [*looking at her watch*] Not yet—and the time is nearly up. If only he does not—. [*listens again*] Ah, there he is. [*Goes into the hall and opens the outer door carefully. Light footsteps are heard on the stairs. She whispers.*] Come in. There is no one here.

KROGSTAD.   [*in the doorway*] I found a note from you at home. What does this mean?

MRS. LINDE.   It is absolutely necessary that I should have a talk with you.

KROGSTAD.   Really? And is it absolutely necessary that it should be here?

MRS. LINDE.   It is impossible where I live; there is no private entrance to my rooms. Come in; we are quite alone. The maid is asleep, and the Helmers are at the dance upstairs.

KROGSTAD.   [*coming into the room*] Are the Helmers really at a dance to-night?

MRS. LINDE.   Yes, why not?

KROGSTAD.   Certainly—why not?

MRS. LINDE.   Now, Nils, let us have a talk.

KROGSTAD.   Can we two have anything to talk about?

MRS. LINDE.   We have a great deal to talk about.

KROGSTAD.   I shouldn't have thought so.

MRS. LINDE.   No, you have never properly understood me.

KROGSTAD.   Was there anything else to understand except what was obvious to all the world—a heartless woman jilts a man when a more lucrative chance turns up?

MRS. LINDE.   Do you believe I am as absolutely heartless as all that? And do you believe that I did it with a light heart?

KROGSTAD.   Didn't you?

MRS. LINDE.   Nils, did you really think that?

KROGSTAD.   If it were as you say, why did you write to me as you did at the time?

MRS. LINDE.   I could do nothing else. As I had to break with you, it was my duty also to put an end to all that you felt for me.

KROGSTAD.   [*wringing his hands*] So that was it. And all this—only for the sake of money!

MRS. LINDE.   You must not forget that I had a helpless mother and two little brothers. We couldn't wait for you, Nils; your prospects seemed hopeless then.

KROGSTAD.   That may be so, but you had no right to throw me over for any one else's sake.

MRS. LINDE.   Indeed I don't know. Many a time did I ask myself if I had the right to do it.

KROGSTAD.   [*more gently*] When I lost you, it was as if all the solid ground went from under my feet. Look at me now—I am a shipwrecked man clinging to a bit of wreckage.

MRS. LINDE.   But help may be near.

KROGSTAD.   It *was* near; but then you came and stood in my way.

MRS. LINDE.   Unintentionally, Nils. It was only to-day that I learnt it was your place I was going to take in the Bank.

KROGSTAD.   I believe you, if you say so. But now that you know it, are you not going to give it up to me?

MRS. LINDE.   No, because that would not benefit you in the least.

KROGSTAD.   Oh, benefit, benefit—I would have done it whether or no.

MRS. LINDE.   I have learnt to act prudently. Life, and hard, bitter necessity have taught me that.

KROGSTAD.   And life has taught me not to believe in fine speeches.

MRS. LINDE.   Then life has taught you something very reasonable. But deeds you must believe in?

KROGSTAD.   What do you mean by that?

MRS. LINDE.   You said you were like a shipwrecked man clinging to some wreckage.

KROGSTAD.   I had good reason to say so.

MRS. LINDE.   Well, I am like a shipwrecked woman clinging to some wreckage—no one to mourn for, no one to care for.

KROGSTAD.   It was your own choice.

MRS. LINDE.   There was no other choice—then.

KROGSTAD.   Well, what now?

MRS. LINDE.   Nils, how would it be if we two shipwrecked people could join forces?

KROGSTAD.   What are you saying?

MRS. LINDE.   Two on the same piece of wreckage would stand a better chance than each on their own.

KROGSTAD.   Christine!

MRS. LINDE.   What do you suppose brought me to town?

KROGSTAD.   Do you mean that you gave me a thought?

MRS. LINDE.   I could not endure life without work. All my life, as long as I can remember, I have worked, and it has been my greatest and only pleasure. But now I am quite alone in the world—my life is so dreadfully empty and I feel so forsaken. There is not the least pleasure in working for one's self. Nils, give me someone and something to work for.

KROGSTAD.   I don't trust that. It is nothing but a woman's overstrained sense of generosity that prompts you to make such an offer of yourself.

MRS. LINDE.   Have you ever noticed anything of the sort in me?

KROGSTAD.   Could you really do it? Tell me—do you know all about my past life?

MRS. LINDE.   Yes.

KROGSTAD.   And do you know what they think of me here?

MRS. LINDE.   You seemed to me to imply that with me you might have been quite another man.

KROGSTAD.   I am certain of it.

MRS. LINDE.   Is it too late now?

KROGSTAD.   Christine, are you saying this deliberately? Yes, I am sure you are. I see it in your face. Have you really the courage, then—?

MRS. LINDE.   I want to be a mother to someone, and your children need a mother. We two need each other. Nils, I have faith in your real character—I can dare anything together with you.

KROGSTAD.   [*grasps her hands*] Thanks, thanks, Christine! Now I shall find a way to clear myself in the eyes of the world. Ah, but I forgot——

MRS. LINDE.   [*listening*] Hush! The Tarantella! Go, go!

KROGSTAD.   Why? What is it?

MRS. LINDE.   Do you hear them up there? When that is over, we may expect them back.

KROGSTAD.   Yes, yes—I will go. But it is all no use. Of course you are not aware what steps I have taken in the matter of the Helmers.

MRS. LINDE.   Yes, I know all about that.

KROGSTAD.   And in spite of that have you the courage to—?

MRS. LINDE.   I understand very well to what lengths a man like you might be driven by despair.

KROGSTAD.   If I could only undo what I have done!

MRS. LINDE.   You can. Your letter is lying in the letter-box now.

KROGSTAD.   Are you sure of that?

MRS. LINDE.   Quite sure, but——

KROGSTAD.   [*with a searching look at her*] Is that what it all means?—that you want to save your friend at any cost? Tell me frankly. Is that it?

MRS. LINDE.   Nils, a woman who has once sold herself for another's sake, doesn't do it a second time.

KROGSTAD.   I will ask for my letter back.

MRS. LINDE.   No, no.

KROGSTAD.   Yes, of course I will. I will wait here till Helmer comes; I will tell him he must give me my letter back—that it only concerns my dismissal—that he is not to read it——

MRS. LINDE.   No, Nils, you must not recall your letter.

KROGSTAD.   But, tell me, wasn't it for that very purpose that you asked me to meet you here?

MRS. LINDE.   In my first moment of fright, it was. But twenty-four hours have elapsed since then, and in that time I have witnessed incredible things in this house. Helmer must know all about it. This unhappy secret must be disclosed; they must have a complete understanding between them, which is impossible with all this concealment and falsehood going on.

KROGSTAD.   Very well, if you will take the responsibility. But there is one thing I can do in any case, and I shall do it at once.

MRS. LINDE.   [*listening*] You must be quick and go! The dance is over; we are not safe a moment longer.

KROGSTAD.   I will wait for you below.

MRS. LINDE.   Yes, do. You must see me back to my door.

KROGSTAD.   I have never had such an amazing piece of good fortune in my life.

[*Goes out through the outer door. The door between the room and the hall remains open.*]

MRS. LINDE.   [*tidying up the room and laying her hat and cloak ready*] What a difference! what a difference! Someone to work for and live for—a home to bring comfort into. That I will do, indeed. I wish they would be quick and come— [*listens*] Ah, there they are now. I must put on my things.

[*Takes up her hat and cloak. HELMER'S and NORA'S voices are heard outside; a key is turned, and HELMER brings NORA almost by force into the hall. She is in an Italian costume with a large black shawl round her; he is in evening dress and a black domino which is flying open.*]

NORA.   [*hanging back in the doorway, and struggling with him*] No, no, no!—don't take me in. I want to go upstairs again; I don't want to leave so early.

HELMER.   But, my dearest Nora——

NORA.   Please, Torvald dear—please, *please*—only an hour more.

HELMER.   Not a single minute, my sweet Nora. You know that was our agreement. Come along into the room; you are catching cold standing there.

[*He brings her gently into the room, in spite of her resistance.*]

MRS. LINDE.   Good evening.

NORA.   Christine!

HELMER.   You here, so late, Mrs. Linde?

MRS. LINDE.   Yes, you must excuse me; I was so anxious to see Nora in her dress.

NORA.   Have you been sitting here waiting for me?

MRS. LINDE.   Yes, unfortunately I came too late, you had already gone upstairs; and I thought I couldn't go away again without having seen you.

HELMER.   [*taking off NORA'S shawl*] Yes, take a good look at her. I think she is worth looking at. Isn't she charming, Mrs. Linde?

MRS. LINDE.   Yes, indeed she is.

HELMER.   Doesn't she look remarkably pretty? Everyone thought so at the dance. But she is terribly self-willed, this sweet little person. What are we to do with her? You will hardly believe that I had almost to bring her away by force.

NORA.   Torvald, you will repent not having let me stay, even if it were only for half an hour.

HELMER.   Listen to her, Mrs. Linde! She had danced her Tarantella, and it had been a tremendous success, as it deserved—although possibly the performance was a trifle too realistic—a little more so, I mean, than was strictly compatible with the limitations of art. But never mind about that! The chief thing is, she had made a success—she had made a tremendous success. Do you think I was going to let her remain there after that, and spoil the effect? No indeed! I took my charming little Capri maiden—my capricious little Capri maiden, I should say—on my arm; took one quick turn round the room; a curtsey on either side, and, as they say in novels, the beautiful apparition disappeared. An exit ought always to be effective, Mrs. Linde; but that is what I cannot make Nora understand. Pooh! this room is hot. [*throws his domino on a chair and opens the door of his room*] Hullo! it's all dark in here. Oh, of course—excuse me——.

[*He goes in and lights some candles.*]

NORA.   [*in a hurried and breathless whisper*] Well?

MRS. LINDE.   [*in a low voice*] I have had a talk with him.

NORA.   Yes, and——

MRS. LINDE.   Nora, you must tell your husband all about it.

NORA.   [*in an expressionless voice*] I knew it.

MRS. LINDE.   You have nothing to be afraid of as far as Krogstad is concerned; but you must tell him.

NORA.   I won't tell him.

MRS. LINDE.   Then the letter will.

NORA.   Thank you, Christine. Now I know what I must do. Hush——!

HELMER.   [*coming in again*] Well, Mrs. Linde, have you admired her?

MRS. LINDE.   Yes, and now I will say good-night.

HELMER.   What, already? Is this yours, this knitting?

MRS. LINDE.   [*taking it*] Yes, thank you, I had very nearly forgotten it.

HELMER.   So you knit?

MRS. LINDE.   Of course.

HELMER.   Do you know, you ought to embroider.

MRS. LINDE.   Really? Why?

HELMER.   Yes, it's far more becoming. Let me show you. You hold the embroidery thus in your left hand, and use the needle with the right—like this—with a long, easy sweep. Do you see?

MRS. LINDE.   Yes, perhaps——

HELMER.   But in the case of knitting—that can never be anything but ungraceful; look here—the arms close together, the knitting-needles going up and down—it has a sort of Chinese effect—. That was really excellent champagne they gave us.

MRS. LINDE.   Well,—good-night, Nora, and don't be self-willed any more.

HELMER. That's right, Mrs. Linde.

MRS. LINDE. Good-night, Mr. Helmer.

HELMER. [*accompanying her to the door*] Good-night, good-night. I hope you will get home all right. I should be very happy to—but you haven't any great distance to go. Good-night, good-night. [*She goes out; he shuts the door after her, and comes in again.*] Ah!—at last we have got rid of her. She is a frightful bore, that woman.

NORA. Aren't you very tired, Torvald?

HELMER. No, not in the least.

NORA. Nor sleepy?

HELMER. Not a bit. On the contrary, I feel extraordinarily lively. And you?— you really look both tired and sleepy.

NORA. Yes, I am very tired. I want to go to sleep at once.

HELMER. There, you see it was quite right of me not to let you stay there any longer.

NORA. Everything you do is quite right, Torvald.

HELMER. [*kissing her on the forehead*] Now my little skylark is speaking reasonably. Did you notice what good spirits Rank was in this evening?

NORA. Really? Was he? I didn't speak to him at all.

HELMER. And I very little, but I have not for a long time seen him in such good form. [*looks for a while at her and then goes nearer to her*] It is delightful to be at home by ourselves again, to be all alone with you—you fascinating, charming little darling!

NORA. Don't look at me like that, Torvald.

HELMER. Why shouldn't I look at my dearest treasure?—at all the beauty that is mine, all my very own?

NORA. [*going to the other side of the table*] You mustn't say things like that to me to-night.

HELMER. [*following her*] You have still got the Tarantella in your blood, I see. And it makes you more captivating than ever. Listen—the guests are beginning to go now. [*in a lower voice*] Nora—soon the whole house will be quiet.

NORA. Yes, I hope so.

HELMER. Yes, my own darling Nora. Do you know, when I am out at a party with you like this, why I speak so little to you, keep away from you, and only send a stolen glance in your direction now and then?—do you know why I do that? It is because I make believe to myself that we are secretly in love, and you are my secretly promised bride, and that no one suspects there is anything between us.

NORA. Yes, yes—I know very well your thoughts are with me all the time.

HELMER. And when we are leaving, and I am putting the shawl over your beautiful young shoulders—on your lovely neck—then I imagine that you are my young bride and that we have just come from the wedding, and I am bringing you for the first time into our home—to be alone with you for the first time— quite alone with my shy little darling! All this evening I have longed for nothing but you. When I watched the seductive figures of the Tarantella, my blood was on fire; I could endure it no longer, and that was why I brought you down so early——

NORA. Go away, Torvald! You must let me go. I won't——

HELMER.   What's that? You're joking, my little Nora! You won't—you won't? Am I not your husband—?

[*A knock is heard at the outer door.*]

NORA.   [*starting*] Did you hear——?
HELMER.   [*going into the hall*] Who is it?
RANK.   [*outside*] It is I. May I come in for a moment?
HELMER.   [*in a fretful whisper*] Oh, what does he want now? [*aloud*] Wait a minute! [*unlocks the door*] Come, that's kind of you not to pass by our door.
RANK.   I thought I heard your voice, and felt as if I should like to look in. [*with a swift glance round*] Ah, yes!—these dear familiar rooms. You are very happy and cosy in here, you two.
HELMER.   It seems to me that you looked after yourself pretty well upstairs too.
RANK.   Excellently. Why shouldn't I? Why shouldn't one enjoy everything in this world?—at any rate as much as one can, and as long as one can. The wine was capital——
HELMER.   Especially the champagne.
RANK.   So you noticed that too? It is almost incredible how much I managed to put away!
NORA.   Torvald drank a great deal of champagne tonight, too.
RANK.   Did he?
NORA.   Yes, and he is always in such good spirits afterwards.
RANK.   Well, why should one not enjoy a merry evening after a well-spent day?
HELMER.   Well spent? I am afraid I can't take credit for that.
RANK.   [*clapping him on the back*] But I can, you know!
NORA.   Doctor Rank, you must have been occupied with some scientific investigation to-day.
RANK.   Exactly.
HELMER.   Just listen!—little Nora talking about scientific investigations!
NORA.   And may I congratulate you on the result?
RANK.   Indeed you may.
NORA.   Was it favourable, then?
RANK.   The best possible, for both doctor and patient—certainty.
NORA.   [*quickly and searchingly*] Certainty?
RANK.   Absolute certainty. So wasn't I entitled to make a merry evening of it after that?
NORA.   Yes, you certainly were, Doctor Rank.
HELMER.   I think so too, so long as you don't have to pay for it in the morning.
RANK.   Oh well, one can't have anything in this life without paying for it.
NORA.   Doctor Rank—are you fond of fancy-dress balls?
RANK.   Yes, if there is a fine lot of pretty costumes.
NORA.   Tell me—what shall we two wear at the next?
HELMER.   Little featherbrain!—are you thinking of the next already?
RANK.   We two? Yes, I can tell you. You shall go as a good fairy——
HELMER.   Yes, but what do you suggest as an appropriate costume for that?
RANK.   Let your wife go dressed just as she is in everyday life.

HELMER.   That was really very prettily turned. But can't you tell us what you will be?

RANK.   Yes, my dear friend, I have quite made up my mind about that.

HELMER.   Well?

RANK.   At the next fancy dress ball I shall be invisible.

HELMER.   That's a good joke!

RANK.   There is a big black hat—have you never heard of hats that make you invisible? If you put one on, no one can see you.

HELMER.   [*suppressing a smile*] Yes, you are quite right.

RANK.   But I am clean forgetting what I came for. Helmer, give me a cigar—one of the dark Havanas.

HELMER.   With the greatest pleasure. [*offers him his case*]

RANK.   [*takes a cigar and cuts off the end*] Thanks.

NORA.   [*striking a match*] Let me give you a light.

RANK.   Thank you. [*She holds the match for him to light his cigar.*] And now good-bye!

HELMER.   Good-bye, good-bye, dear old man!

NORA.   Sleep well, Doctor Rank.

RANK.   Thank you for that wish.

NORA.   Wish me the same.

RANK.   You? Well, if you want me to sleep well! And thanks for the light.

[*He nods to them both and goes out.*]

HELMER.   [*in a subdued voice*] He has drunk more than he ought.

NORA.   [*absently*] Maybe. [HELMER *takes a bunch of keys out of his pocket and goes into the hall.*] Torvald! what are you going to do there?

HELMER.   Empty the letter-box; it is quite full; there will be no room to put the newspaper in to-morrow morning.

NORA.   Are you going to work to-night?

HELMER.   You know quite well I'm not. What is this? Some one has been at the lock.

NORA.   At the lock—?

HELMER.   Yes, someone has. What can it mean? I should never have thought the maid—. Here is a broken hairpin. Nora, it is one of yours.

NORA.   [*quickly*] Then it must have been the children—

HELMER.   Then you must get them out of those ways. There, at last I have got it open. [*Takes out the contents of the letter-box, and calls to the kitchen.*] Helen!—Helen, put out the light over the front door. [*Goes back into the room and shuts the door into the hall. He holds out his hand full of letters.*] Look at that—look what a heap of them there are. [*turning them over*] What on earth is that?

NORA.   [*at the window*] The letter—No! Torvald, no!

HELMER.   Two cards—of Rank's.

NORA.   Of Doctor Rank's?

HELMER.   [*looking at them*] Doctor Rank. They were on the top. He must have put them in when he went out.

NORA.   Is there anything written on them?

HELMER.   There is a black cross over the name. Look there—what an uncomfortable idea! It looks as if he were announcing his own death.

NORA.   It is just what he is doing.

HELMER.   What? Do you know anything about it? Has he said anything to you?

NORA.   Yes. He told me that when the cards came it would be his leave-taking from us. He means to shut himself up and die.

HELMER.   My poor old friend. Certainly I knew we should not have him very long with us. But so soon! And so he hides himself away like a wounded animal.

NORA.   If it has to happen, it is best it should be without a word—don't you think so, Torvald?

HELMER.   [*walking up and down*] He had so grown into our lives. I can't think of him as having gone out of them. He, with his sufferings and his loneliness, was like a cloudy background to our sunlit happiness. Well, perhaps it is best so. For him, anyway. [*standing still*] And perhaps for us too, Nora. We two are thrown quite upon each other now. [*puts his arms round her*] My darling wife, I don't feel as if I could hold you tight enough. Do you know, Nora, I have often wished that you might be threatened by some great danger, so that I might risk my life's blood, and everything, for your sake.

NORA.   [*disengages herself, and says firmly and decidedly*] Now you must read your letters, Torvald.

HELMER.   No, no; not to-night. I want to be with you, my darling wife.

NORA.   With the thought of your friend's death——

HELMER.   You are right, it has affected us both. Something ugly has come between us—the thought of the horrors of death. We must try and rid our minds of that. Until then—we will each go to our own room.

NORA.   [*hanging on his neck*] Good-night, Torvald—Good-night!

HELMER.   [*kissing her on the forehead*]. Good-night, my little singing-bird. Sleep sound, Nora. Now I will read my letters through.

[*He takes his letters and goes into his room, shutting the door after him.*]

NORA.   [*gropes distractedly about, seizes* HELMER'S *domino, throws it round her, while she says in quick, hoarse, spasmodic whispers*] Never to see him again. Never! Never! [*puts her shawl over her head*] Never to see my children again either—never again. Never! Never!—Ah! the icy, black water—the unfathomable depths—If only it were over! He has got it now—now he is reading it. Good-by, Torvald and my children!

[*She is about to rush out through the hall, when* HELMER *opens his door hurriedly and stands with an open letter in his hand.*]

HELMER.   Nora!

NORA.   Ah!——

HELMER.   What is this? Do you know what is in this letter?

NORA.   Yes, I know. Let me go! Let me get out!

HELMER.   [*holding her back*] Where are you going?

NORA.   [*trying to get free*] You shan't save me, Torvald!

HELMER.   [*reeling*] True? Is this true, that I read here? Horrible! No, no—it is impossible that it can be true.

NORA.   It is true. I have loved you above everything else in the world.

HELMER.   Oh, don't let us have any silly excuses.

NORA. [*taking a step towards him*] Torvald——!

HELMER. Miserable creature—what have you done?

NORA. Let me go. You shall not suffer for my sake. You shall not take it upon yourself.

HELMER. No tragedy airs, please. [*locks the hall door*] Here you shall stay and give me an explanation. Do you understand what you have done? Answer me? Do you understand what you have done?

NORA. [*looks steadily at him and says with a growing look of coldness in her face*] Yes, now I am beginning to understand thoroughly.

HELMER. [*walking about the room*] What a horrible awakening! All these eight years—she who was my joy and pride—a hypocrite, a liar—worse, worse—a criminal! The unutterable ugliness of it all! For shame! For shame! [NORA *is silent and looks steadily at him. He stops in front of her.*] I ought to have suspected that something of the sort would happen. I ought to have foreseen it. All your father's want of principle—be silent!—all your father's want of principle has come out in you. No religion, no morality, no sense of duty——. How I am punished for having winked at what he did! I did it for your sake, and this is how you repay me.

NORA. Yes, that's just it.

HELMER. Now you have destroyed all my happiness. You have ruined all my future. It is horrible to think of! I am in the power of an unscrupulous man; he can do what he likes with me, ask anything he likes of me, give me any orders he pleases—I dare not refuse. And I must sink to such miserable depths because of a thoughtless woman!

NORA. When I am out of the way, you will be free.

HELMER. No fine speeches, please. Your father had always plenty of those ready, too. What good would it be to me if you were out of the way, as you say? Not the slightest. He can make the affair known everywhere; and if he does, I may be falsely suspected of having been a party to your criminal action. Very likely people will think I was behind it all—that it was I who prompted you! And I have to thank you for all this—you whom I have cherished during the whole of our married life. Do you understand now what it is you have done for me?

NORA. [*coldly and quietly*] Yes.

HELMER. It is so incredible that I can't take it in. But we must come to some understanding. Take off that shawl. Take it off, I tell you. I must try and appease him some way or another. The matter must be hushed up at any cost. And as for you and me, it must appear as if everything between us were just as before—but naturally only in the eyes of the world. You will still remain in my house, that is a matter of course. But I shall not allow you to bring up the children; I dare not trust them to you. To think that I should be obliged to say so to one whom I have loved so dearly, and whom I still——. No, that is all over. From this moment happiness is not the question; all that concerns us is to save the remains, the fragments, the appearance——

[*A ring is heard at the front-door bell.*]

HELMER. [*with a start*] What is that? So late! Can the worst——? Can he——? Hide yourself, Nora. Say you are ill.

[NORA *stands motionless.* HELMER *goes and unlocks the hall door.*]

MAID.   [*half-dressed, comes to the door*] A letter for the mistress.

HELMER.   Give it to me. [*takes the letter, and shuts the door*] Yes, it is from him. You shall not have it; I will read it myself.

NORA.   Yes, read it.

HELMER.   [*standing by the lamp*] I scarcely have the courage to do it. It may mean ruin for both of us. No, I must know. [*tears open the letter, runs his eye over a few lines, looks at a paper enclosed and gives a shout of joy*] Nora! [*She looks at him questioningly.*] Nora!—No, I must read it once again——. Yes, it is true! I am saved! Nora, I am saved!

NORA.   And I?

HELMER.   You too, of course; we are both saved, both you and I. Look, he sends you your bond back. He says he regrets and repents—that a happy change in his life—never mind what he says! We are saved, Nora! No one can do anything to you. Oh, Nora, Nora!—no, first I must destroy these hateful things. Let me see——. [*takes a look at the bond*] No, no, I won't look at it. The whole thing shall be nothing but a bad dream to me. [*tears up the bond and both letters, throws them all into the stove, and watches them burn*] There—now it doesn't exist any longer. He says that since Christmas Eve you——. These must have been three dreadful days for you, Nora.

NORA.   I have fought a hard fight these three days.

HELMER.   And suffered agonies, and seen no way out but——. No, we won't call any of the horrors to mind. We will only shout with joy, and keep saying "It's all over! It's all over!" Listen to me, Nora. You don't seem to realise that it is all over. What is this?—such a cold, set face! My poor little Nora, I quite understand; you don't feel as if you could believe that I have forgiven you. But it is true, Nora, I swear it; I have forgiven you everything. I know that what you did, you did out of love for me.

NORA.   That is true.

HELMER.   You have loved me as a wife ought to love her husband. Only you had not sufficient knowledge to judge of the means you used. But do you suppose you are any the less dear to me, because you don't understand how to act on your own responsibility? No, no; only lean on me; I will advise you and direct you. I should not be a man if this womanly helplessness did not just give you a double attractiveness in my eyes. You must not think any more about the hard things I said in my first moment of consternation, when I thought everything was going to overwhelm me. I have forgiven you, Nora; I swear to you I have forgiven you.

NORA.   Thank you for your forgiveness.

[*She goes out through the door to the right.*]

HELMER.   No, don't go——. [*looks in*] What are you doing in there?

NORA.   [*from within*] Taking off my fancy dress.

HELMER.   [*standing at the open door*] Yes, do. Try and calm yourself, and make your mind easy again, my frightened little singing-bird. Be at rest, and feel secure; I have broad wings to shelter you under. [*walks up and down by the door*] How warm and cosy our home is, Nora. Here is shelter for you; here I will protect you like a hunted dove that I have saved from a hawk's claws. I will bring peace to your poor beating heart. It will come, little by little, Nora, believe me. Tomorrow morning you will look upon it all quite differently; soon everything will be just as it was before. Very soon you won't need me to assure you that I have forgiven you; you will yourself feel the certainty that I have done so. Can you suppose I should ever think of such a thing as repudiating you, or even reproaching you? You have no idea what a true man's heart is like, Nora. There is something so indescribably sweet and satisfying, to a man, in the knowledge that he has forgiven his wife— forgiven her freely, and with all his heart. It seems as if that had made her, as it were, doubly his own; he has given her a new life, so to speak; and she has in a way become both wife and child to him. So you shall be for me after this, my little scared, helpless darling. Have no anxiety about anything, Nora; only be frank and open with me, and I will serve as will and conscience both to you——. What is this? Not gone to bed? Have you changed your things?

NORA. [*in everyday dress*] Yes, Torvald, I have changed my things now.

HELMER. But what for?—so late as this.

NORA. I shall not sleep to-night.

HELMER. But, my dear Nora——

NORA. [*looking at her watch*] It is not so very late. Sit down here, Torvald. You and I have much to say to one another.

[*She sits down at one side of the table.*]

HELMER. Nora—what is this?—this cold, set face?

NORA. Sit down. It will take some time; I have a lot to talk over with you.

HELMER. [*sits down at the opposite side of the table*] You alarm me, Nora!— and I don't understand you.

NORA. No, that is just it. You don't understand me, and I have never understood you either—before to-night. No, you mustn't interrupt me. You must simply listen to what I say. Torvald, this is a settling of accounts.

HELMER. What do you mean by that?

NORA. [*after a short silence*] Isn't there one thing that strikes you as strange in our sitting here like this?

HELMER. What is that?

NORA. We have been married now eight years. Does it not occur to you that this is the first time we two, you and I, husband and wife, have had a serious conversation?

HELMER. What do you mean by serious?

NORA. In all these eight years—longer than that—from the very beginning of our acquaintance, we have never exchanged a word on any serious subject.

HELMER. Was it likely that I would be continually and for ever telling you about worries that you could not help me to bear?

NORA. I am not speaking about business matters. I say that we have never sat down in earnest together to try and get at the bottom of anything.

HELMER. But, dearest Nora, would it have been any good to you?

NORA. That is just it; you have never understood me. I have been greatly wronged, Torvald—first by papa and then by you.

HELMER. What! By us two—by us two, who have loved you better than anyone else in the world?

NORA. [*shaking her head*] You have never loved me. You have only thought it pleasant to be in love with me.

HELMER. Nora, what do I hear you saying?

NORA. It is perfectly true, Torvald. When I was at home with papa, he told me his opinion about everything, and so I had the same opinions; and if I differed from him I concealed the fact, because he would not have liked it. He called me his doll-child, and he played with me just as I used to play with my dolls. And when I came to live with you——

HELMER. What sort of an expression is that to use about our marriage?

NORA. [undisturbed] I mean that I was simply transferred from papa's hands into yours. You arranged everything according to your own taste, and so I got the same tastes as you—or else I pretended to, I am really not quite sure which— I think sometimes the one and sometimes the other. When I look back on it, it seems to me as if I had been living here like a poor woman—just from hand to mouth. I have existed merely to perform tricks for you, Torvald. But you would have it so. You and papa have committed a great sin against me. It is your fault that I have made nothing of my life.

HELMER. How unreasonable and how ungrateful you are, Nora! Have you not been happy here?

NORA. No, I have never been happy. I thought I was, but it has never really been so.

HELMER. Not—not happy!

NORA. No, only merry. And you have always been so kind to me. But our home has been nothing but a playroom. I have been your doll-wife, just as at home I was papa's doll-child; and here the children have been my dolls. I thought it great fun when you played with me, just as they thought it great fun when I played with them. That is what our marriage has been, Torvald.

HELMER. There is some truth in what you say—exaggerated and strained as your view of it is. But for the future it shall be different. Playtime shall be over, and lesson-time shall begin.

NORA. Whose lessons? Mine, or the children's?

HELMER. Both yours and the children's, my darling Nora.

NORA. Alas, Torvald, you are not the man to educate me into being a proper wife for you.

HELMER. And you can say that!

NORA. And I—how am I fitted to bring up the children?

HELMER. Nora!

NORA. Didn't you say so yourself a little while ago—that you dare not trust me to bring them up?

HELMER. In a moment of anger! Why do you pay any heed to that?

NORA. Indeed, you were perfectly right. I am not fit for the task. There is another task I must undertake first. I must try and educate myself—you are not the man to help me in that. I must do that for myself. And that is why I am going to leave you now.

HELMER. [springing up] What do you say?

NORA. I must stand quite alone, if I am to understand myself and everything about me. It is for that reason that I cannot remain with you any longer.

HELMER. Nora! Nora!

NORA. I am going away from here now, at once. I am sure Christine will take me in for the night——

HELMER.   You are out of your mind! I won't allow it! I forbid you!

NORA.   It is no use forbidding me anything any longer. I will take with me what belongs to myself. I will take nothing from you, either now or later.

HELMER.   What sort of madness is this!

NORA.   To-morrow I shall go home—I mean, to my old home. It will be easiest for me to find something to do there.

HELMER.   You blind, foolish woman!

NORA.   I must try and get some sense, Torvald.

HELMER.   To desert your home, your husband and your children! And you don't consider what people will say!

NORA.   I cannot consider that at all. I only know that it is necessary for me.

HELMER.   It's shocking. This is how you would neglect your most sacred duties.

NORA.   What do you consider my most sacred duties?

HELMER.   Do I need to tell you that? Are they not your duties to your husband and your children?

NORA.   I have other duties just as sacred.

HELMER.   That you have not. What duties could those be?

NORA.   Duties to myself.

HELMER.   Before all else, you are a wife and a mother.

NORA.   I don't believe that any longer. I believe that before all else I am a reasonable human being, just as you are—or, at all events, that I must try and become one. I know quite well, Torvald, that most people would think you right, and that views of that kind are to be found in books; but I can no longer content myself with what most people say, or with what is found in books. I must think over things for myself and get to understand them.

HELMER.   Can you not understand your place in your own home? Have you not a reliable guide in such matters as that?—have you no religion?

NORA.   I am afraid, Torvald, I do not exactly know what religion is.

HELMER.   What are you saying?

NORA.   I know nothing but what the clergyman said when I went to be confirmed. He told us that religion was this, and that, and the other. When I am away from all this, and am alone, I will look into that matter too. I will see if what the clergyman said is true, or at all events if it is true for me.

HELMER.   This is unheard of in a girl of your age! But if religion cannot lead you aright, let me try and awaken your conscience. I suppose you have some moral sense? Or—answer me—am I to think you have none?

NORA.   I assure you, Torvald, that is not an easy question to answer. I really don't know. The thing perplexes me altogether. I only know that you and I look at it in quite a different light. I am learning, too, that the law is quite another thing from what I supposed; but I find it impossible to convince myself that the law is right. According to it a woman has no right to spare her old dying father, or to save her husband's life. I can't believe that.

HELMER.   You talk like a child. You don't understand the conditions of the world in which you live.

NORA.   No, I don't. But now I am going to try. I am going to see if I can make out who is right, the world or I.

HELMER.   You are ill, Nora; you are delirious; I almost think you are out of your mind.

NORA.   I have never felt my mind so clear and certain as to-night.

HELMER.   And is it with a clear and certain mind that you forsake your husband and your children?

NORA.   Yes, it is.

HELMER.   Then there is only one possible explanation.

NORA.   What is that?

HELMER.   You do not love me any more.

NORA.   No, that is just it.

HELMER.   Nora!—and you can say that?

NORA.   It gives me great pain, Torvald, for you have always been so kind to me, but I cannot help it. I do not love you any more.

HELMER.   [*regaining his composure*] Is that a clear and certain conviction too?

NORA.   Yes, absolutely clear and certain. That is the reason why I will not stay here any longer.

HELMER.   And can you tell me what I have done to forfeit your love?

NORA.   Yes, indeed I can. It was to-night, when the wonderful thing did not happen; then I saw you were not the man I had thought you.

HELMER.   Explain yourself better—I don't understand you.

NORA.   I have waited so patiently for eight years; for, goodness knows, I knew very well that wonderful things don't happen every day. Then this horrible misfortune came upon me; and then I felt quite certain that the wonderful thing was going to happen at last. When Krogstad's letter was lying out there, never for a moment did I imagine that you would consent to accept this man's conditions. I was so absolutely certain that you would say to him: Publish the thing to the whole world. And when that was done——

HELMER.   Yes, what then?—when I had exposed my wife to shame and disgrace?

NORA.   When that was done, I was so absolutely certain, you would come forward and take everything upon yourself, and say: I am the guilty one.

HELMER.   Nora——!

NORA.   You mean that I would never have accepted such a sacrifice on your part? No, of course not. But what would my assurances have been worth against yours? That was the wonderful thing which I hoped for and feared; and it was to prevent that, that I wanted to kill myself.

HELMER.   I would gladly work night and day for you, Nora—bear sorrow and want for your sake. But no man would sacrifice his honour for the one he loves.

NORA.   It is a thing hundreds of thousands of women have done.

HELMER.   Oh, you think and talk like a heedless child.

NORA.   Maybe. But you neither think nor talk like the man I could bind myself to. As soon as your fear was over—and it was not fear for what threatened me, but for what might happen to you—when the whole thing was past, as far as you were concerned it was exactly as if nothing at all had happened. Exactly as before, I was your little skylark, your doll, which you would in future treat with doubly gentle care, because it was so brittle and fragile. [*getting up*] Torvald—it was then it dawned upon me that for eight years I had been living here with a strange man, and had borne him three children——. Oh, I can't bear to think of it! I could tear myself into little bits!

HELMER. [*sadly*] I see, I see. An abyss has opened between us—there is no denying it. But, Nora, would it not be possible to fill it up?

NORA. As I am now, I am no wife for you.

HELMER. I have it in me to become a different man.

NORA. Perhaps—if your doll is taken away from you.

HELMER. But to part!—to part from you! No, no, Nora, I can't understand that idea.

NORA. [*going out to the right*] That makes it all the more certain that it must be done.

[*She comes back with her cloak and hat and a small bag which she puts on a chair by the table.*]

HELMER. Nora, Nora, not now! Wait till to-morrow.

NORA. [*putting on her cloak*] I cannot spend the night in a strange man's room.

HELMER. But can't we live here like brother and sister——?

NORA. [*putting on her hat*] You know very well that would not last long. [*puts the shawl round her*] Good-bye, Torvald. I won't see the little ones. I know they are in better hands than mine. As I am now, I can be of no use to them.

HELMER. But some day, Nora—some day?

NORA. How can I tell? I have no idea what is going to become of me.

HELMER. But you are my wife, whatever becomes of you.

NORA. Listen, Torvald. I have heard that when a wife deserts her husband's house, as I am doing now, he is legally freed from all obligations towards her. In any case I set you free from all your obligations. You are not to feel yourself bound in the slightest way, any more than I shall. There must be perfect freedom on both sides. See here is your ring back. Give me mine.

HELMER. That too?

NORA. That too.

HELMER. Here it is.

NORA. That's right. Now it is all over. I have put the keys here. The maids know all about everything in the house—better than I do. To-morrow, after I have left her, Christine will come here and pack up my own things that I brought with me from home. I will have them sent after me.

HELMER. All over! All over!—Nora, shall you never think of me again?

NORA. I know I shall often think of you and the children and this house.

HELMER. May I write to you, Nora?

NORA. No—never. You must not do that.

HELMER. But at least let me send you——

NORA. Nothing—nothing——

HELMER. Let me help you if you are in want.

NORA. No. I can receive nothing from a stranger.

HELMER. Nora—can I never be anything more than a stranger to you?

NORA. [*taking her bag*] Ah, Torvald, the most wonderful thing of all would have to happen.

HELMER. Tell me what that would be!

NORA.   Both you and I would have to be so changed that——. Oh, Torvald,
I don't believe any longer in wonderful things happening.
HELMER.   But I will believe in it. Tell me? So changed that——?
NORA.   That our life together would be a real wedlock. Good-bye.

[*She goes out through the hall.*]

HELMER.   [*sinks down on a chair at the door and buries his face in his hands*] Nora!
Nora! [*looks round, and rises*] Empty. She is gone. [*A hope flashes across his mind.*]
The most wonderful thing of all——?

[*The sound of a door slamming is heard from below.*]

QUESTIONS

Act 1

1.   What does the opening stage direction tell you about the Helmer family?
     About the time of year?
2.   Describe the relationship between Nora and Torvald. How does Torvald
     treat Nora? How does she act with him?
3.   Early in act 1 Torvald tells Nora: "No debt, no borrowing. There can be
     no freedom or beauty about a home life that depends on borrowing and
     debt." What general characteristic of Torvald's does this comment illustrate?
     What other instances of this type of behavior can you find in the play?
4.   What has the economic situation of the Helmer family been in the past?
     Why is this situation about to change?
5.   How is Mrs. Linde a parallel to Nora? A contrast? Why is it ironic that Nora
     helps Linde gain a position in the bank? How will this affect Krogstad? Nora?
6.   How does Ibsen show you that Krogstad is a threat when he first appears?
7.   Nora's scene with her children in act 1 is often cut in production. Why is
     the scene important? What does it show you about Nora and about the house-
     hold?
8.   What is Nora's secret? Her crime? Why did she commit the crime? How
     does she justify her actions? What new problems does she face at the close
     of act 1?

Act 2

9.   What does the "stripped" Christmas tree at the opening of act 2 symbolize?
10. In conversation with Torvald, Nora refers to herself as "your little squirrel"
     and "your skylark." What does this imply about Nora's perception of her
     relationship to Torvald?
11. After Torvald sends Krogstad's dismissal, he tells Nora that "you will see I
     am man enough to take everything upon myself." How does this assertion
     conform to Nora's secret hopes? How is it ironic?

12. Describe Nora's relationship with Doctor Rank. Why does she flirt with him? Why is she distressed when he admits his love for her?
13. Why does Nora throw herself so wildly into the tarantella?
14. At the close of act 2 Nora asserts that "it is splendid to be waiting for a wonderful thing to happen." What is this "wonderful thing"?

Act 3

15. Why did Mrs. Linde reject Krogstad in the past? Why does she propose to join forces with him now? In what ways will this union differ from the marriage of Nora and Torvald?
16. What does Mrs. Linde decide to do about Krogstad's letter? Why?
17. How do Nora and Torvald react to the news of Doctor Rank's imminent death? How might you explain their reactions?
18. Describe Torvald's reaction to Krogstad's first letter. How does Nora respond to Torvald? How do you?
19. Explain what Nora learns about Torvald, herself, and her marriage as a result of Torvald's response to Krogstad's letter and the forgery.

TOPICS FOR WRITING AND FURTHER DISCUSSION

1. Which elements and aspects of *A Doll's House* are most realistic? What makes them realistic? Which are least realistic? Why?
2. Consider Ibsen's use of symbolism in the play, with specific reference to Doctor Rank, macaroons, the Christmas tree (decorated and stripped), the presents, the locked mailbox, the tarentella, Nora's black shawl, her final change of clothing in act 3, and the slamming of the door at the close of the play.
3. Discuss the extent to which Nora may be considered a victim of circumstances and society or a villain who is responsible for the problems in the play. Which view does Ibsen seem to take? What is your view? Why?
4. Describe the kinds of role-playing that characterize the Helmer marriage. To what degree does Nora play the role that Torvald expects? Is there any evidence to suggest that she knows she is playing a role? What degree of self-awareness, if any, characterizes Torvald's role-playing?
5. When Nora pleads to have Krogstad reinstated in the bank, Torvald refuses, asking, "is it to get about now that the new manager has changed his mind at his wife's bidding?" Later, when Torvald has read Krogstad's first letter, he claims that his marriage has been destroyed, but that he and Nora must "save the remains, the fragments, the appearance." Discuss Torvald's character in the light of these and similar statements. What concerns Torvald most about marriage? Life?
6. Some critics have asserted that the play should be called "A Doll House," arguing that everyone in the household leads a doll-like existence that is

tested and exposed by the outsiders. Consider this assertion in connection with Torvald, the Helmer children, and the servants.

7. One of the themes that Ibsen explores in *A Doll's House* is the idea that weakness and corruption are passed in the blood from generation to generation. Examine this theme in connection with Krogstad and his sons, Nora and her children, Nora and her father, and Doctor Rank.

8. Discuss the ideas about individual growth, marriage, and social convention that the play explores. How are these ideas developed? How are they related? Which character, if any, most closely embodies and expresses Ibsen's ideas?

9. Is this play a comedy, a tragedy, or something in between? Does it begin in prosperity or adversity? To what extent do characters learn and change for the better (or worse)? Does the resolution strike you as affirmative or negative? Why?

TENNESSEE [THOMAS LANIER] WILLIAMS, *THE GLASS MENAGERIE*

Many of Tennessee Williams's plays reflect the attitudes and customs that he encountered as he was growing up in Mississippi and Missouri. Until he was eight his family lived in genteel poverty, mostly in Columbus, Mississippi; his father was a traveling shoe salesman who was rarely at home, while his mother, the daughter of an Episcopal clergyman, had the traditional social values and graces of a Southern belle. In 1919 the family moved to a lower-class neighborhood in St. Louis. Williams, who was bookish and sickly, tried to escape from poverty and family conflicts by writing and going to the movies. One of his few companions during those years was his shy and withdrawn sister, Rose.

Williams began college at the University of Missouri in 1931, but the Depression and family poverty forced him to drop out and go to work in a shoe warehouse. After two years of this, he suffered a nervous collapse, and then he finished college at the University of Iowa. Williams then began wandering through the Americas, doing odd jobs, and writing. His first full-length play, *Battle of Angels*, was produced in 1940 but was unsuccessful. Williams continued to write, however, and *The Glass Menagerie* was staged in 1945; the critical and popular success of this play was the beginning of many good years in the theater. During the 1940s and 1950s Williams, along with Arthur Miller, dominated the American stage. He went on to write many one-act plays and over fifteen full-length dramas, including *A Streetcar Named Desire* (1947), *The Rose Tattoo* (1951), *Cat on a Hot Tin Roof* (1955), *Suddenly Last Summer* (1958), and *The Night of the Iguana* (1961).

The Glass Menagerie, written in 1944 and produced to rave reviews in Chicago and New York in 1945, is a highly autobiographical play which explores the family dynamics, delusions, and personalities of the Wingfields. Williams originally developed his ideas for the play in a short story called

"Portrait of a Girl in Glass" and then in a screenplay for Metro-Goldwyn-Mayer entitled "The Gentleman Caller." In these, and in *The Glass Menagerie*, Laura Wingfield is modeled after Rose Williams. The least competent member of the family, she is crippled by her own insecurity and her mother's expectations. At every opportunity, Laura withdraws into a world of glass figurines and old phonograph records left by her father when he abandoned the family. Amanda Wingfield is patterned after Williams's mother; she valiantly tries to hold the family together and provide for Laura's future, but her perspectives are skewed by her romanticized memories of a gracious southern past of plantations, formal dances, and "gentleman callers." Tom, a figure based on the playwright himself, is the most desperate to escape the trap of his impoverished family; he seeks to emulate the long-missing father and move out of the drab Wingfield apartment into adventure and experience.

The play offers a fascinating mixture of realistic and nonrealistic dramatic techniques. The characters (excluding Tom when he narrates) and the language are predominantly realistic. This is especially true of Amanda's language, in which Williams skillfully recreates the cadences and characteristics of his mother's Mississippi dialect. The structure of the play and the staging, as Williams points out in his production notes and stage directions, are strikingly nonrealistic. Williams employs various devices nonrealistically, including the narrator, music, lighting, and screen projections, to underscore the emotions of his characters and to explore ideas about family and personality.

One of the most effective nonrealistic techniques in *The Glass Menagerie* is its structure as "a memory play." The characters and the action are neither real nor in the present; rather, they are memories living through Tom's mind about five years after the actual events occurred. Tom as narrator embodies the present time in the play (1944). We thus see action that probably occurred in 1939 through the "eyes" of Tom's recollections. Even Tom as a character in the Wingfield household is a memory, quite distinct from Tom as narrator. Thus, the action in the apartment cannot be considered a real or accurate recreation of life; it is reshaped and exaggerated through the distorting filter of Tom's feelings of guilt and his selective memory.

TENNESSEE [THOMAS LANIER] WILLIAMS (1911–1983)

The Glass Menagerie   1945 (1944)

THE CHARACTERS

Amanda Wingfield (*the mother*)
A little woman of great but confused vitality clinging frantically to another time and place. Her characterization must be carefully created, not copied from type. She is not paranoiac, but her life is paranoia. There is much to admire in

Amanda, and as much to love and pity as there is to laugh at. Certainly she has endurance and a kind of heroism, and though her foolishness makes her unwittingly cruel at times, there is tenderness in her slight person.

Laura Wingfield (*her daughter*)

Amanda, having failed to establish contact with reality, continues to live vitally in her illusions, but Laura's situation is even graver. A childhood illness has left her crippled, one leg slightly shorter than the other, and held in a brace. This defect need not be more than suggested on the stage. Stemming from this, Laura's separation increases till she is like a piece of her own glass collection, too exquisitely fragile to move from the shelf.

Tom Wingfield (*her son*)

And the narrator of the play. A poet with a job in a warehouse. His nature is not remorseless, but to escape from a trap he has to act without pity.

Jim O'Connor (*the gentleman caller*)

A nice, ordinary, young man.

PRODUCTION NOTES

Being a "memory play," *The Glass Menagerie* can be presented with unusual freedom of convention. Because of its considerably delicate or tenuous material, atmospheric touches and subtleties of direction play a particularly important part. Expressionism and all other unconventional techniques in drama have only one valid aim, and that is a closer approach to truth. When a play employs unconventional techniques, it is not, or certainly shouldn't be, trying to escape its responsibility of dealing with reality, or interpreting experience, but is actually or should be attempting to find a closer approach, a more penetrating and vivid expression of things as they are. The straight realistic play with its genuine Frigidaire and authentic ice-cubes, its characters who speak exactly as its audience speaks, corresponds to the academic landscape and has the same virtue of a photographic likeness. Everyone should know nowadays the unimportance of the photographic in art: that truth, life, or reality is an organic thing which the poetic imagination can represent or suggest, in essence, only through transformation, through changing into other forms than those which were merely present in appearance.

These remarks are not meant as a preface only to this particular play. They have to do with a conception of a new, plastic theatre which must take the place of the exhausted theatre of realistic conventions if the theatre is to resume vitality as a part of our culture.

THE SCREEN DEVICE: There is *only one important difference between the original and the acting version of the play* and that is the *omission* in the latter of the device that I tentatively included in my *original* script. This device was the use of a screen on which were projected magic-lantern slides bearing images or titles. I do not regret the omission of this device from the original Broadway production. The extraordinary power of Miss Taylor's° performance made it suitable to have the utmost

---

° *Miss Taylor's*: The role of Amanda was first played by the American actress Laurette Taylor (1884–1946).

simplicity in the physical production. But I think it may be interesting to some readers to see how this device was conceived. So I am putting it into the published manuscript. These images and legends, projected from behind, were cast on a section of wall between the front-room and dining-room areas, which should be indistinguishable from the rest when not in use.

The purpose of this will probably be apparent. It is to give accent to certain values in each scene. Each scene contains a particular point (or several) which is structurally the most important. In an episodic play, such as this, the basic structure or narrative line may be obscured from the audience; the effect may seem fragmentary rather than architectural. This may not be the fault of the play so much as a lack of attention in the audience. The legend or image upon the screen will strengthen the effect of what is merely allusion in the writing and allow the primary point to be made more simply and lightly than if the entire responsibility were on the spoken lines. Aside from this structural value, I think the screen will have a definite emotional appeal, less definable but just as important. An imaginative producer or director may invent many other uses for this device than those indicated in the present script. In fact the possibilities of the device seem much larger to me than the instance of this play can possibly utilize.

THE MUSIC: Another extra-literary accent in this play is provided by the use of music. A single recurring tune, "The Glass Menagerie,"° is used to give emotional emphasis to suitable passages. This tune is like circus music, not when you are on the grounds or in the immediate vicinity of the parade, but when you are at some distance and very likely thinking of something else. It seems under those circumstances to continue almost interminably and it weaves in and out of your preoccupied consciousness; then it is the lightest, most delicate music in the world and perhaps the saddest. It expresses the surface vivacity of life with the underlying strain of immutable and inexpressible sorrow. When you look at a piece of delicately spun glass you think of two things: how beautiful it is and how easily it can be broken. Both of those ideas should be woven into the recurring tune, which dips in and out of the play as if it were carried on a wind that changes. It serves as a thread of connection and allusion between the narrator with his separate point in time and space and the subject of his story. Between each episode it returns as reference to the emotion, nostalgia, which is the first condition of the play. It is primarily Laura's music and therefore comes out most clearly when the play focuses upon her and the lovely fragility of glass which is her image.

THE LIGHTING: The lighting in the play is not realistic. In keeping with the atmosphere of memory, the stage is dim. Shafts of light are focused on selected areas or actors, sometimes in contradistinction to what is the apparent center. For instance, in the quarrel scene between Tom and Amanda, in which Laura has no active part, the clearest pool of light is on her figure. This is also true of the supper scene, when her silent figure on the sofa should remain the visual center. The light upon Laura should be distinct from the others, having a peculiar pristine clarity such as light used in early religious portraits of female saints or madonnas.

° *"The Glass Menagerie"*: original music, including this recurrent theme, was composed for the play by Paul Bowles.

A certain correspondence to light in religious paintings, such as El Greco's,° where the figures are radiant in atmosphere that is relatively dusky, could be effectively used throughout the play. (It will also permit a more effective use of the screen.) A free, imaginative use of light can be of enormous value in giving a mobile, plastic quality to plays of a more or less static nature.

Tennessee Williams

Scene 1

The Wingfield apartment is in the rear of the building, one of those vast hive-like conglomerations of cellular living-units that flower as warty growths in overcrowded urban centers of lower middle-class population and are symptomatic of the impulse of this largest and fundamentally enslaved section of American society to avoid fluidity and differentiation and to exist and function as one interfused mass of automatism.

The apartment faces an alley and is entered by a fire escape, a structure whose name is a touch of accidental poetic truth, for all of these huge buildings are always burning with the slow and implacable fires of human desperation. The fire escape is part of what we see— that is, the landing of it and steps descending from it.

The scene is memory and is therefore nonrealistic. Memory takes a lot of poetic license. It omits some details; others are exaggerated, according to the emotional value of the articles it touches, for memory is seated predominantly in the heart. The interior is therefore rather dim and poetic.

At the rise of the curtain, the audience is faced with the dark, grim rear wall of the Wingfield tenement. This building is flanked on both sides by dark, narrow alleys which run into murky canyons of tangled clotheslines, garbage cans, and the sinister latticework of neighboring fire escapes. It is up and down these side alleys that exterior entrances and exits are made during the play. At the end of TOM'S opening commentary, the dark tenement wall slowly becomes transparent° and reveals the interior of the ground-floor Wingfield apartment.

Nearest the audience is the living room, which also serves as a sleeping room for LAURA, the sofa unfolding to make her bed. Just beyond, separated from the living room by a wide arch or second proscenium with transparent faded portieres° (or second curtain), is the dining room. In an old-fashioned whatnot° in the living room are seen scores of transparent glass animals. A blown-up photograph of the father hangs on the wall of the living room, to the left of the archway. It is the face of a very handsome young man in a doughboy's° First World War cap. He is gallantly smiling, ineluctably smiling, as if to say "I will be smiling forever."

° *El Greco*: Greek painter (ca. 1548–1614) who lived in Spain; typical paintings have elongated and distorted figures and extremely vivid foreground lighting set against a murky background.

° *transparent*: the wall is painted on a scrim or transparent curtain that is opaque when lit from the front and transparent when lit from behind.

° *portieres*: curtains hung in a doorway; in production, these may also be painted on a scrim.

° *whatnot*: a small set of shelves for ornaments.

° *doughboy*: the term refers to an infantryman, especially an American during World War I.

Also hanging on the wall, near the photograph, are a typewriter keyboard chart and a Gregg shorthand diagram. An upright typewriter on a small table stands beneath the charts.

The audience hears and sees the opening scene in the dining room through both the transparent fourth wall of the building and the transparent gauze portieres of the dining-room arch. It is during this revealing scene that the fourth wall slowly ascends, out of sight. This transparent exterior wall is not brought down again until the very end of the play, during TOM'S *final speech.*

The narrator is an undisguised convention of the play. He takes whatever license with dramatic convention is convenient to his purposes.

TOM enters, dressed as a merchant sailor, and strolls across to the fire escape. There he stops and lights a cigarette. He addresses the audience.

TOM. Yes, I have tricks in my pocket, I have things up my sleeve. But I am the opposite of a stage magician. He gives you illusion that has the appearance of truth. I give you truth in the pleasant disguise of illusion.

To begin with, I turn back time. I reverse it to that quaint period, the thirties, when the huge middle class of America was matriculating in a school for the blind. Their eyes had failed them, or they had failed their eyes, and so they were having their fingers pressed forcibly down on the fiery Braille alphabet of a dissolving economy.

In Spain there was revolution. Here there was only shouting and confusion. In Spain there was Guernica.° Here there were disturbances of labor, sometimes pretty violent, in otherwise peaceful cities such as Chicago, Cleveland, Saint Louis . . . This is the social background of the play.

[*Music begins to play.*]

The play is memory. Being a memory play, it is dimly lighted, it is sentimental, it is not realistic. In memory everything seems to happen to music. That explains the fiddle in the wings.

I am the narrator of the play, and also a character in it. The other characters are my mother, Amanda, my sister, Laura, and a gentleman caller who appears in the final scenes. He is the most realistic character in the play, being an emissary from a world of reality that we were somehow set apart from. But since I have a poet's weakness for symbols, I am using this character also as a symbol; he is the long-delayed but always expected something that we live for.

There is a fifth character in the play who doesn't appear except in this larger-than-life-size photograph over the mantel. This is our father who left us a long time ago. He was a telephone man who fell in love with long distances; he gave up his job with the telephone company and skipped the light fantastic out of town . . .

The last we heard of him was a picture postcard from Mazatlan, on the

---

° *Guernica*: a city heavily bombed during the Spanish Civil War (1936–1939), fought between the Loyalists (liberals, Republicans, socialists, communists) and the conservatives (the church, Falange, fascists). The destruction of the city is the subject of a mural (1937) by Pablo Picasso.

Pacific coast of Mexico, containing a message of two words: "Hello—Goodbye!"
and no address.

I think the rest of the play will explain itself. . . .

[*AMANDA'S voice becomes audible through the portieres.*]

[*Legend on screen:* "Ou sont les neiges."°]

*TOM divides the portieres and enters the dining room. AMANDA and LAURA are seated at a
drop-leaf table. Eating is indicated by gestures without food or utensils. AMANDA faces the
audience. TOM and LAURA are seated profile. The interior has lit up softly and through the
scrim we see AMANDA and LAURA seated at the table.*]

AMANDA. [*calling*] Tom?

TOM. Yes, Mother.

AMANDA. We can't say grace until you come to the table!

TOM. Coming, Mother. [*He bows slightly and withdraws, reappearing a few moments later in his place at the table.*]

AMANDA. [*to her son*] Honey, don't *push* with your *fingers*. If you have to
push with something, the thing to push with is a crust of bread. And chew—chew!
Animals have secretions in their stomachs which enable them to digest food without
mastication, but human beings are supposed to chew their food before they swallow
it down. Eat food leisurely, son, and really enjoy it. A well-cooked meal has lots
of delicate flavors that have to be held in the mouth for appreciation. So chew
your food and give your salivary glands a chance to function!

[*TOM deliberately lays his imaginary fork down and pushes his chair back from the table.*]

TOM. I haven't enjoyed one bite of this dinner because of your constant
directions on how to eat it. It's you that make me rush through meals with your
hawklike attention to every bite I take. Sickening—spoils my appetite—all this discussion of—animals' secretion—salivary glands—mastication!

AMANDA. [*lightly*] Temperament like a Metropolitan star!°

[*TOM rises and walks toward the living room.*]

You're not excused from the table.

TOM. I'm getting a cigarette.

AMANDA. You smoke too much.

[*LAURA rises.*]

LAURA. I'll bring in the blanc mange.°

[*TOM remains standing with his cigarette by the portieres.*]

° *neiges:* "Where are the snows (of yesteryear)," quoted from "The Ballade of Dead
Ladies" by the French poet Francois Villon (ca. 1431–1463).
° *Metropolitan star:* the Metropolitan Opera in New York City; opera stars are traditionally
considered to be highly temperamental.
° *blanc mange:* a bland, molded pudding or custard.

AMANDA. [*rising*] No, sister, no, sister° —you be the lady this time and I'll be the darky.

LAURA. I'm already up.

AMANDA. Resume your seat, little sister—I want you to stay fresh and pretty—for gentlemen callers!

LAURA. [*sitting down*] I'm not expecting any gentlemen callers.

AMANDA. [*crossing out to the kitchenette, airily*] Sometimes they come when they are least expected! Why, I remember one Sunday afternoon in Blue Mountain°—

[*She enters the kitchenette.*]

TOM. I know what's coming!

LAURA. Yes. But let her tell it.

TOM. Again?

LAURA. She loves to tell it.

[*AMANDA returns with a bowl of dessert.*]

AMANDA. One Sunday afternoon in Blue Mountain—your mother received— *seventeen*!—gentlemen callers! Why, sometimes there weren't chairs enough to accommodate them all. We had to send the nigger over to bring in folding chairs from the parish house.

TOM. [*remaining at the portieres*] How did you entertain those gentlemen callers?

AMANDA. I understood the art of conversation!

TOM. I bet you could talk.

AMANDA. Girls in those days *knew* how to talk, I can tell you.

TOM. Yes?

[*Image on screen: AMANDA as a girl on a porch, greeting callers.*]

AMANDA. They knew how to entertain their gentlemen callers. It wasn't enough for a girl to be possessed of a pretty face and a graceful figure—although I wasn't slighted in either respect. She also needed to have a nimble wit and a tongue to meet all occasions.

TOM. What did you talk about?

AMANDA. Things of importance going on in the world! Never anything coarse or common or vulgar.

[*She addresses TOM as though he were seated in the vacant chair at the table though he remains by the portieres. He plays this scene as though reading from a script.°*]

° *sister*: In the South of Amanda's youth, the oldest daughter in a family was frequently called "sister" by her parents and siblings.

° *Blue Mountain*: an imaginary town in northwest Mississippi modeled after Clarksville, where Williams spent much of his youth. Blue Mountain (Clarksville) is at the northern edge of the Mississippi Delta, a large fertile plain that supports numerous plantations. This is the recollected world of Amanda's youth—plantations, wealth, black servants, and gentlemen callers who were the sons of cotton planters.

° *script*: Here Tom becomes both a character in the play and the stage manager.

My callers were gentlemen—all! Among my callers were some of the most prominent young planters of the Mississippi Delta—planters and sons of planters!

[*TOM motions for music and a spot of light on* AMANDA. *Her eyes lift, her face glows, her voice becomes rich and elegiac.*]

[*Screen legend:* "Ou sont les neiges d'antan?"]

There was young Champ Laughlin who later became vice-president of the Delta Planters Bank. Hadley Stevenson who was drowned in Moon Lake and left his widow one hundred and fifty thousand in Government bonds. There were the Cutrere brothers, Wesley and Bates. Bates was one of my bright particular beaux! He got in a quarrel with that wild Wainwright boy. They shot it out on the floor of Moon Lake Casino. Bates was shot through the stomach. Died in the ambulance on his way to Memphis. His widow was also well provided-for, came into eight or ten thousand acres, that's all. She married him on the rebound—never loved her—carried my picture on him the night he died! And there was that boy that every girl in the Delta had set her cap for! That beautiful, brilliant young Fitzhugh boy from Greene County!

TOM.   What did he leave his widow?

AMANDA.   He never married! Gracious, you talk as though all of my old admirers had turned up their toes to the daisies!

TOM.   Isn't this the first you've mentioned that still survives?

AMANDA.   That Fitzhugh boy went North and made a fortune—came to be known as the Wolf of Wall Street! He had the Midas touch,° whatever he touched turned to gold! And I could have been Mrs. Duncan J. Fitzhugh, mind you! But—I picked your *father*!

LAURA.   [*rising*] Mother, let me clear the table.

AMANDA.   No, dear, you go in front and study your typewriter chart. Or practice your shorthand a little. Stay fresh and pretty!—It's almost time for our gentlemen callers to start arriving. [*She flounces girlishly toward the kitchenette.*] How many do you suppose we're going to entertain this afternoon?

[*TOM throws down the paper and jumps up with a groan.*]

LAURA.   [*alone in the dining room*] I don't believe we're going to receive any, Mother.

AMANDA.   [*reappearing airily*] What? No one?—not one? You must be joking!

[*LAURA nervously echoes her laugh. She slips in a fugitive manner through the half-open portieres and draws them gently behind her. A shaft of very clear light is thrown on her face against the faded tapestry of the curtains. Faintly the music of "The Glass Menagerie" is heard as she continues lightly:*]

Not one gentleman caller? It can't be true! There must be a flood, there must have been a tornado!

LAURA.   It isn't a flood, it's not a tornado, Mother. I'm just not popular like you were in Blue Mountain. . . .

° *Midas touch:* In Greek mythology, King Midas was given the power to turn everything he touched into gold.

[*TOM utters another groan. LAURA glances at him with a faint, apologetic smile. Her voice catches a little:*]

Mother's afraid I'm going to be an old maid.

[*The scene dims out with the "Glass Menagerie" music.*]

Scene 2

On the dark stage the screen is lighted with the image of blue roses. Gradually LAURA'S figure becomes apparent and the screen goes out. The music subsides.

LAURA is seated in the delicate ivory chair at the small clawfoot table. She wears a dress of soft violet material for a kimono—her hair is tied back from her forehead with a ribbon. She is washing and polishing her collection of glass. AMANDA appears on the fire escape steps. At the sound of her ascent, LAURA catches her breath, thrusts the bowl of ornaments away, and seats herself stiffly before the diagram of the typewriter keyboard as though it held her spellbound. Something has happened to AMANDA. It is written in her face as she climbs to the landing: a look that is grim and hopeless and a little absurd. She has on one of those cheap or imitation velvety-looking cloth coats with imitation fur collar. Her hat is five or six years old, one of those dreadful cloche hats that were worn in the late Twenties, and she is clutching an enormous black patent-leather pocketbook with nickel clasps and initials. This is her full-dress outfit, the one she usually wears to the D.A.R.° Before entering she looks through the door. She purses her lips, opens her eyes very wide, rolls them upward and shakes her head. Then she slowly lets herself in the door. Seeing her mother's expression, LAURA touches her lips with a nervous gesture.]

LAURA. Hello, Mother, I was—[*She makes a nervous gesture toward the chart on the wall. AMANDA leans against the shut door and stares at LAURA with a martyred look.*]

AMANDA. Deception? Deception? [*She slowly removes her hat and gloves, continuing the sweet suffering stare. She lets the hat and gloves fall on the floor—a bit of acting.*]

LAURA. [*shakily*] How was the D.A.R. meeting?

[*AMANDA slowly opens her purse and removes a dainty white handkerchief which she shakes out delicately and delicately touches to her lips and nostrils.*]

Didn't you go to the D.A.R. meeting, Mother?

AMANDA. [*faintly, almost inaudibly*] —No.—No. [*then more forcibly:*] I did not have the strength—to go to the D.A.R. In fact, I did not have the courage! I wanted to find a hole in the ground and hide myself in it forever! [*She crosses slowly to the wall and removes the diagram of the typewriter keyboard. She holds it in front of her for a second, staring at it sweetly and sorrowfully—then bites her lips and tears it in two pieces.*]

LAURA. [*faintly*] Why did you do that, Mother?

[*AMANDA repeats the same procedure with the chart of the Gregg Alphabet.*]

Why are you—

° *D.A.R.:* Daughters of the American Revolution, a patriotic women's organization (founded in 1890) open only to women whose ancestors aided the cause of the American Revolution.

AMANDA. Why? Why? How old are you, Laura?

LAURA. Mother, you know my age.

AMANDA. I thought that you were an adult; it seems that I was mistaken. [She crosses slowly to the sofa and sinks down and stares at LAURA.]

LAURA. Please don't stare at me, Mother.

[AMANDA closes her eyes and lowers her head. There is a ten-second pause.]

AMANDA. What are we going to do, what is going to become of us, what is the future?

[There is another pause.]

LAURA. Has something happened, Mother?

[AMANDA draws a long breath, takes out the handkerchief again, goes through the dabbing process.]

Mother, has—something happened?

AMANDA. I'll be all right in a minute, I'm just bewildered—[She hesitates.]—by life. . . .

LAURA. Mother, I wish that you would tell me what's happened!

AMANDA. As you know, I was supposed to be inducted into my office at the D.A.R. this afternoon.

[Screen image: A swarm of typewriters.]

But I stopped off at Rubicam's Business College to speak to your teachers about your having a cold and ask them what progress they thought you were making down there.

LAURA. Oh. . . .

AMANDA. I went to the typing instructor and introduced myself as your mother. She didn't know who you were.

"Wingfield," she said, "We don't have any such student enrolled at the school!"

I assured her she did, that you had been going to classes since early in January.

"I wonder," she said, "If you could be talking about that terribly shy little girl who dropped out of school after only a few days' attendance?"

"No," I said, "Laura, my daughter, has been going to school every day for the past six weeks!"

"Excuse me," she said. She took the attendance book out and there was your name, unmistakably printed, and all the dates you were absent until they decided that you had dropped out of school.

I still said, "No, there must have been some mistake! There must have been some mix-up in the records!"

And she said, "No—I remember her perfectly now. Her hands shook so that she couldn't hit the right keys! The first time we gave a speed test, she broke down completely—was sick at the stomach and almost had to be carried into the wash room! After that morning she never showed up any more. We phoned the house but never got any answer"—While I was working at Famous-Barr,° I suppose, demonstrating those—

[*She indicates a brassiere with her hands.*]

Oh! I felt so weak I could barely keep on my feet! I had to sit down while they got me a glass of water! Fifty dollars' tuition, all of our plans—my hopes and ambitions for you—just gone up the spout, just gone up the spout like that.

[*LAURA draws a long breath and gets awkwardly to her feet. She crosses to the Victrola and winds it up.°*]

What are you doing?
    LAURA. Oh! [*She releases the handle and returns to her seat.*]
    AMANDA. Laura, where have you been going when you've gone out pretending that you were going to business college?
    LAURA. I've just been going out walking.
    AMANDA. That's not true.
    LAURA. It is. I just went walking.
    AMANDA. Walking? Walking? In winter? Deliberately courting pneumonia in that light coat? Where did you walk to, Laura?
    LAURA. All sorts of places—mostly in the park.
    AMANDA. Even after you'd started catching that cold?
    LAURA. It was the lesser of two evils, Mother.

[*Screen image: Winter scene in a park.*]

I couldn't go back there. I—threw up—on the floor!
    AMANDA. From half past seven till after five every day you mean to tell me you walked around in the park, because you wanted to make me think that you were still going to Rubicam's Business College?
    LAURA. It wasn't as bad as it sounds. I went inside places to get warmed up.
    AMANDA. Inside where?
    LAURA. I went in the art museum and the bird houses at the Zoo. I visited the penguins every day! Sometimes I did without lunch and went to the movies. Lately I've been spending most of my afternoons in the Jewel Box, that big glass house where they raise the tropical flowers.
    AMANDA. You did all this to deceive me, just for deception? [*LAURA looks down.*] Why?
    LAURA. Mother, when you're disappointed, you get that awful suffering look on your face, like the picture of Jesus' mother in the museum!
    AMANDA. Hush!
    LAURA. I couldn't face it.

[*There is a pause. A whisper of strings is heard. Legend on screen: "The Crust of Humility."*]

    ° *Famous-Barr*: a department store in St. Louis.
    ° *winds it up*: Laura is using a spring-powered (rather than electric) phonograph that produces unamplified sound; the spring had to be rewound frequently.

AMANDA. [*hopelessly fingering the huge pocketbook*] So what are we going to do the rest of our lives? Stay home and watch the parades go by? Amuse ourselves with the glass menagerie, darling? Eternally play those worn-out phonograph records your father left as a painful reminder of him? We won't have a business career—we've given that up because it gave us nervous indigestion! [*She laughs wearily.*] What is there left but dependency all our lives? I know so well what becomes of unmarried women who aren't prepared to occupy a position. I've seen such pitiful cases in the South—barely tolerated spinsters living upon the grudging patronage of sister's husband or brother's wife!—stuck away in some little mousetrap of a room—encouraged by one in-law to visit another—little birdlike women without any nest—eating the crust of humility all their life!

Is that the future that we've mapped out for ourselves? I swear it's the only alternative I can think of! [*She pauses.*] It isn't a very pleasant alternative, is it? [*She pauses again.*] Of course—some girls *do marry.*

[*LAURA twists her hands nervously.*]

Haven't you ever liked some boy?

LAURA. Yes. I liked one once. [*She rises.*] I came across his picture a while ago.

AMANDA. [*with some interest*] He gave you his picture?

LAURA. No, it's in the yearbook.

AMANDA. [*disappointed*] Oh—a high school boy.

[*Screen image: JIM as the high school hero bearing a silver cup.*]

LAURA. Yes. His name was Jim. [*She lifts the heavy annual from the claw-foot table.*] Here he is in *The Pirates of Penzance.*°

AMANDA. [*absently*] The what?

LAURA. The operetta the senior class put on. He had a wonderful voice and we sat across the aisle from each other Mondays, Wednesdays and Fridays in the Aud. Here he is with the silver cup for debating! See his grin?

AMANDA. [*absently*] He must have had a jolly disposition.

LAURA. He used to call me—Blue Roses.

[*Screen image: Blue roses.*]

AMANDA. Why did he call you such a name as that?

LAURA. When I had that attack of pleurosis—he asked me what was the matter when I came back. I said pleurosis—he thought that I said Blue Roses! So that's what he always called me after that. Whenever he saw me, he'd holler, "Hello, Blue Roses!" I didn't care for the girl that he went out with. Emily Meisenbach. Emily was the best-dressed girl at Soldan. She never struck me, though, as being sincere . . . It says in the Personal Section—they're engaged. That's—six years ago! They must be married by now.

AMANDA. Girls that aren't cut out for business careers usually wind up married to some nice man. [*She gets up with a spark of revival.*] Sister, that's what you'll do!

[*LAURA utters a startled, doubtful laugh. She reaches quickly for a piece of glass.*]

° *Penzance*: a comic light opera (1879) by W. S. Gilbert and Arthur Sullivan.

LAURA. But, Mother—

AMANDA. Yes? [*She goes over to the photograph.*]

LAURA. [*in a tone of frightened apology*] I'm—crippled!

AMANDA. Nonsense! Laura, I've told you never, never to use that word. Why, you're not crippled, you just have a little defect—hardly noticeable, even! When people have some slight disadvantage like that, they cultivate other things to make up for it—develop charm—and vivacity—and—*charm*! That's all you have to do! [*She turns again to the photograph.*] One thing your father had *plenty of*—was *charm*!

[*The scene fades out with music.*]

Scene 3

[*Legend on screen: "After the fiasco—"*

TOM *speaks from the fire escape landing.*]

TOM. After the fiasco at Rubicam's Business College, the idea of getting a gentleman caller for Laura began to play a more and more important part in Mother's calculations. It became an obsession. Like some archetype of the universal unconscious, the image of the gentleman caller haunted our small apartment. . . .

[*Screen image: A young man at the door of a house with flowers.*]

An evening at home rarely passed without some allusion to this image, this specter, this hope. . . . Even when he wasn't mentioned, his presence hung in Mother's preoccupied look and in my sister's frightened, apologetic manner—hung like a sentence passed upon the Wingfields!

Mother was a woman of action as well as words. She began to take logical steps in the planned direction. Late that winter and in the early spring—realizing that extra money would be needed to properly feather the nest and plume the bird—she conducted a vigorous campaign on the telephone, roping in subscribers to one of those magazines for matrons called *The Homemaker's Companion*, the type of journal that features the serialized sublimations of ladies of letters who think in terms of delicate cuplike breasts, slim, tapering waists, rich, creamy thighs, eyes like wood smoke in autumn, fingers that soothe and caress like strains of music, bodies as powerful as Etruscan sculpture.

[*Screen image: The cover of a glamor magazine.*

AMANDA *enters with the telephone on a long extension cord. She is spotlighted in the dim stage.*]

AMANDA. Ida Scott? This is Amanda Wingfield! We *missed* you at the D.A.R. last Monday! I said to myself: She's probably suffering with that sinus condition! How is that sinus condition?

Horrors! Heaven have mercy!—You're a Christian martyr, yes, that's what you are, a Christian martyr!

Well, I just now happened to notice that your subscription to the *Companion's* about to expire! Yes, it expires with the next issue, honey!—just when that wonderful new serial by Bessie Mae Hopper is getting off to such an exciting start. Oh, honey, it's something that you can't miss! You remember how *Gone with the Wind*° took everybody by storm? You simply couldn't go out if you hadn't read it. All everybody *talked* was Scarlett O'Hara. Well, this is a book that critics already compare to *Gone with the Wind*. It's the *Gone with the Wind* of the post-World-War generation!— What?—Burning?—Oh, honey, don't let them burn, go take a look in the oven and I'll hold the wire! Heavens—I think she's hung up!

[*The scene dims out.*]

[*Legend on screen*: "*You think I'm in love with Continental Shoemakers?*"]

[*Before the lights come up again, the violent voices of* TOM *and* AMANDA *are heard. They are quarreling behind the portieres. In front of them stands* LAURA *with clenched hands and panicky expression. A clear pool of light is on her figure throughout this scene.*]

TOM. What in Christ's name am I—
AMANDA. [*shrilly*] Don't you use that—
TOM. —supposed to do!
AMANDA. —expression! Not in my—
TOM. Ohhh!
AMANDA. —presence! Have you gone out of your senses?
TOM. I have, that's true, *driven* out!
AMANDA. What is the matter with you, you—big—big—IDIOT!
TOM. Look!—I've got *no thing*, no single thing—
AMANDA. Lower your voice!
TOM. —in my life here that I can call my OWN! Everything is—
AMANDA. Stop that shouting!
TOM. Yesterday you confiscated my books! You had the nerve to—
AMANDA. I took that horrible novel back to the library—yes! That hideous book by that insane Mr. Lawrence.°

[TOM *laughs wildly.*]

I cannot control the output of diseased minds or people who cater to them—

[TOM *laughs still more wildly.*]

BUT I WON'T ALLOW SUCH FILTH BROUGHT INTO MY HOUSE! No, no, no, no, no!
TOM. House, house! Who pays rent on it, who makes a slave of himself to—
AMANDA. [*fairly screeching*] Don't you DARE to—
TOM. No, no, *I* mustn't say things! *I've* got to just—
AMANDA. Let me tell you—
TOM. I don't want to hear any more!

° *Gone with the Wind*: an extremely popular novel (1936) by Margaret Mitchell (1900–1949), set in the South before, during, and after the Civil War. Scarlet O'Hara was the heroine.
° *Lawrence*: D. H. Lawrence (1885–1930), English poet and fiction writer, popularly known as an advocate of passion and sexuality.

[*He tears the portieres open. The dining-room area is lit with turgid smoky red glow. Now we see* AMANDA; *her hair is in metal curlers and she is wearing a very old bathrobe, much too large for her slight figure, a relic of the faithless Mr. Wingfield. The upright typewriter now stands on the drop-leaf table, along with a wild disarray of manuscripts. The quarrel was probably precipitated by* AMANDA's *interruption of* TOM's *creative labor. A chair lies overthrown on the floor. Their gesticulating shadows are cast on the ceiling by the fiery glow.*]

AMANDA. You *will* hear more, you—
TOM. No, I won't hear more, I'm going out!
AMANDA. You come right back in—
TOM. Out, out, out! Because I'm—
AMANDA. Come back here, Tom Wingfield! I'm not through talking to you!
TOM. Oh, go—
LAURA. [*desperately*] —Tom!
AMANDA. You're going to listen, and no more insolence from you! I'm at the end of my patience!

[*He comes back toward her.*]

TOM. What do you think I'm at? Aren't I supposed to have any patience to reach the end of, Mother? I know, I know. It seems unimportant to you, what I'm *doing*—what I *want* to do—having a little *difference* between them! You don't think that—
AMANDA. I think you've been doing things that you're ashamed of. That's why you act like this. I don't believe that you go every night to the movies. Nobody goes to the movies night after night. Nobody in their right minds goes to the movies as often as you pretend to. People don't go to the movies at nearly midnight, and movies don't let out at two A.M. Come in stumbling. Muttering to yourself like a maniac! You get three hours' sleep and then go to work. Oh, I can picture the way you're doing down there. Moping, doping, because you're in no condition.
TOM. [*wildly*] No, I'm in no condition!
AMANDA. What right have you got to jeopardize your job? Jeopardize the security of us all? How do you think we'd manage if you were—
TOM. Listen! You think I'm crazy about the *warehouse*? [*He bends fiercely toward her slight figure.*] You think I'm in love with the Continental Shoemakers? You think I want to spend fifty-five *years* down there in that—*celotex interior*! with—*fluorescent*—*tubes*! Look! I'd rather somebody picked up a crowbar and battered out my brains—than go back mornings! I *go*! Every time you come in yelling that God damn "Rise and Shine!" "Rise and Shine!" I say to myself, "How *lucky dead* people are!" But I get up. I *go*! For sixty-five dollars a month I give up all that I dream of doing and being *ever*! And you say self—*self's* all I ever think of. Why, listen, if self is what I thought of, Mother, I'd be where he is—GONE! [*He points to his father's picture.*] As far as the system of transportation reaches! [*He starts past her. She grabs his arm.*] Don't grab at me, Mother!
AMANDA. Where are you going?
TOM. I'm going to the *movies*!
AMANDA. I don't believe that lie!

[TOM *crouches toward her, overtowering her tiny figure. She backs away, gasping.*]

TOM.   I'm going to opium dens! Yes, opium dens, dens of vice and criminals'
hangouts, Mother. I've joined the Hogan Gang,° I'm a hired assassin, I carry a
tommy gun in a violin case! I run a string of cat houses in the Valley! They call
me Killer, Killer Wingfield, I'm leading a double-life, a simple, honest warehouse
worker by day, by night a dynamic *czar* of the *underworld, Mother*. I go to gambling
casinos, I spin away fortunes on the roulette table! I wear a patch over one eye
and a false mustache, sometimes I put on green whiskers. On those occasions
they call me—*El Diablo!*° Oh, I could tell you many things to make you sleepless!
My enemies plan to dynamite this place. They're going to blow us all sky-high
some night! I'll be glad, very happy, and so will you! You'll go up, up on a broomstick, over Blue Mountain with seventeen gentlemen callers! You ugly—babbling
old—*witch*. . . .

[*He goes through a series of violent, clumsy movements, seizing his overcoat, lunging to the
door, pulling it fiercely open. The women watch him, aghast. His arm catches in the sleeve
of the coat as he struggles to pull it on. For a moment he is pinioned by the bulky garment.
With an outraged groan he tears the coat off again, splitting the shoulder of it, and hurls it
across the room. It strikes against the shelf of LAURA'S glass collection, and there is a tinkle
of shattering glass. LAURA cries out as if wounded.*

Music.

Screen legend: "The Glass Menagerie."]

LAURA   [*shrilly*] My glass!—menagerie. . . . [*She covers her face and turns away.*]

[*But AMANDA is still stunned and stupefied by the "ugly witch" so that she barely notices
this occurrence. Now she recovers her speech.*]

AMANDA.   [*in an awful voice*] I won't speak to you—until you apologize!

[*She crosses through the portieres and draws them together behind her. TOM is left with LAURA.
LAURA clings weakly to the mantel with her face averted. TOM stares at her stupidly for a
moment. Then he crosses to the shelf. He drops awkwardly on his knees to collect the fallen
glass, glancing at LAURA as if he would speak but couldn't.*

"The Glass Menagerie" music steals in as the scene dims out.]

Scene 4

[*The interior of the apartment is dark. There is a faint light in the alley. A deep-
voiced bell in a church is tolling the hour of five.*
    *TOM appears at the top of the alley. After each solemn boom of the bell in the tower,
he shakes a little noisemaker or rattle as if to express the tiny spasm of man in contrast to the
sustained power and dignity of the Almighty. This and the unsteadiness of his advance make
it evident that he has been drinking. As he climbs the few steps to the fire escape landing
light steals up inside. LAURA appears in the front room in a nightdress. She notices that
TOM'S bed is empty. TOM fishes in his pockets for his door key, removing a motley assortment
of articles in the search, including a shower of movie ticket stubs and an empty bottle. At last*

° *Hogan Gang:* one of the major criminal organizations in St. Louis in the 1930s.
° *El Diablo:* the devil.

last he finds the key, but just as he is about to insert it, it slips from his fingers. He strikes a match and crouches below the door.]

TOM. [*bitterly*] One crack—and it falls through!

[*LAURA opens the door.*]

LAURA. Tom! Tom, what are you doing?

TOM. Looking for a door key.

LAURA. Where have you been all this time?

TOM. I have been to the movies.

LAURA. All this time at the movies?

TOM. There was a very long program. There was a Garbo° picture and a Mickey Mouse and a travelogue and a newsreel and a preview of coming attractions. And there was an organ solo and a collection for the Milk Fund—simultaneously—which ended up in a terrible fight between a fat lady and an usher!

LAURA. [*innocently*] Did you have to stay through everything?

TOM. Of course! And, oh, I forgot! There was a big stage show! The headliner on this stage show was Malvolio° the Magician. He performed wonderful tricks, many of them, such as pouring water back and forth between pitchers. First it turned to wine and then it turned to beer and then it turned to whisky. I know it was whisky it finally turned into because he needed somebody to come up out of the audience to help him, and I came up—both shows! It was Kentucky Straight Bourbon. A very generous fellow, he gave souvenirs. [*He pulls from his back pocket a shimmering rainbow-colored scarf.*] He gave me this. This is his magic scarf. You can have it, Laura. You wave it over a canary cage and you get a bowl of goldfish. You wave it over the goldfish bowl and they fly away canaries. . . . But the wonderfullest trick of all was the coffin trick. We nailed him into a coffin and he got out of the coffin without removing one nail. [*He has come inside.*] There is a trick that would come in handy for me—get me out of this two-by-four situation! [*He flops onto the bed and starts removing his shoes.*]

LAURA. Tom—shhh!

TOM. What're you shushing me for?

LAURA. You'll wake up Mother.

TOM. Goody, goody! Pay 'er back for all those "Rise an' Shines." [*He lies down, groaning.*] You know it don't take much intelligence to get yourself into a nailed-up coffin, Laura. But who in hell ever got himself out of one without removing one nail?

[*As if in answer, the father's grinning photograph lights up. The scene dims out.*]

[*Immediately following, the church bell is heard striking six. At the sixth stroke the alarm clock goes off in AMANDA'S room, and after a few moments we hear her calling: "Rise and Shine! Rise and Shine! Laura, go tell your brother to rise and shine!"*]

TOM. [*sitting up slowly*] I'll rise—but I won't shine.

[*The light increases.*]

° *Garbo*: Greta Garbo (b. 1905), Swedish star of American silent and early sound films.
° *Malvolio*: the name, borrowed from a puritanical character in Shakespeare's *Twelfth Night*, means "malevolence" or "ill-will."

AMANDA.   Laura, tell your brother his coffee is ready.

[*LAURA slips into the front room.*]

LAURA.   Tom!—It's nearly seven. Don't make Mother nervous.

[*He stares at her stupidly.*]

[*Beseechingly.*] Tom, speak to Mother this morning. Make up with her, apologize, speak to her!

TOM.   She won't to me. It's her that started not speaking.

LAURA.   If you just say you're sorry she'll start speaking.

TOM.   Her not speaking—is that such a tragedy?

LAURA.   Please—please!

AMANDA.   [*calling from the kitchenette*] Laura, are you going to do what I asked you to do, or do I have to get dressed and go out myself?

LAURA.   Going, going—soon as I get on my coat!

[*She pulls on a shapeless felt hat with a nervous, jerky movement, pleadingly glancing at TOM. She rushes awkwardly for her coat. The coat is one of AMANDA'S, inaccurately made-over, the sleeves too short for LAURA.*]

Butter and what else?

AMANDA.   [*entering from the kitchenette*] Just butter. Tell them to charge it.

LAURA.   Mother, they make such faces when I do that.

AMANADA.   Sticks and stones can break our bones, but the expression on Mr. Garfinkel's face won't harm us! Tell your brother his coffee is getting cold.

LAURA.   [*at the door*] Do what I asked you, will you, will you, Tom?

[*He looks sullenly away.*]

AMANDA.   Laura, go now or just don't go at all!

LAURA.   [*rushing out*] Going—going!

[*A second later she cries out. TOM springs up and crosses to the door. TOM opens the door.*]

TOM.   Laura?

LAURA.   I'm all right. I slipped, but I'm all right.

AMANDA.   [*peering anxiously after her*] If anyone breaks a leg on those fire-escape steps, the landlord ought to be sued for every cent he possesses! [*She shuts the door. Now she remembers she isn't speaking to TOM and returns to the other room.*]

[*As TOM comes listlessly for his coffee, she turns her back to him and stands rigidly facing the window on the gloomy gray vault of the areaway. Its light on her face with its aged but childish features is cruelly sharp, satirical as a Daumier print.°*]

The music of "Ave Maria,"° is heard softly.

TOM glances sheepishly but sullenly at her averted figure and slumps at the table. The coffee is scalding hot; he sips it and gasps and spits it back in the cup. At his gasp, AMANDA

° *Daumier print*: Honoré Daumier (1808–1879), French painter and engraver whose prints frequently satirized his society.

° *"Ave Maria"*: a Roman Catholic prayer to the Virgin Mary; the musical setting called for here is by Franz Schubert (1797–1828), an Austrian composer.

catches her breath and half turns. Then she catches herself and turns back to the window. TOM *blows on his coffee, glancing sidewise at his mother. She clears her throat.* TOM *clears his. He starts to rise, sinks back down again, scratches his head, clears his throat again.* AMANDA *coughs.* TOM *raises his cup in both hands to blow on it, his eyes staring over the rim of it at his mother for several moments. Then he slowly sets the cup down and awkwardly and hesitantly rises from the chair.*]

TOM. [*hoarsely*] Mother. I—I apologize, Mother.

[AMANDA *draws a quick, shuddering breath. Her face works grotesquely. She breaks into childlike tears.*]

I'm sorry for what I said, for everything that I said, I didn't mean it.

AMANDA. [*sobbingly*] My devotion has made me a witch and so I make myself hateful to my children!

TOM. *No*, you *don't.*

AMANDA. I worry so much, don't sleep, it makes me nervous!

TOM. [*gently*] I understand that.

AMANDA. I've had to put up a solitary battle all these years. But you're my right-hand bower!° Don't fall down, don't fail!

TOM. [*gently*] I try, Mother.

AMANDA. [*with great enthusiasm*] Try and you will *succeed!* [*The notion makes her breathless.*] Why, you—you're just *full* of natural endowments! Both of my children—they're *unusual* children! Don't you think I know it? I'm so—*proud!* Happy and—feel I've—so much to be thankful for but—promise me one thing, son!

TOM. What, Mother?

AMANDA. Promise, son, you'll—never be a drunkard!

TOM. [*turns to her grinning*] I will never be a drunkard, Mother.

AMANDA. That's what frightened me so, that you'd be drinking! Eat a bowl of Purina!

TOM. Just coffee, Mother.

AMANDA. Shredded wheat biscuit?

TOM. No. No, Mother, just coffee.

AMANDA. You can't put in a day's work on an empty stomach. You've got ten minutes—don't gulp! Drinking too-hot liquids makes cancer of the stomach. . . . Put cream in.

TOM. No, thank you.

AMANDA. To cool it.

TOM. No! No, thank you, I want it black.

AMANDA. I know, but it's not good for you. We have to do all that we can to build ourselves up. In these trying times we live in, all that we have to cling to is—each other. . . . That's why it's so important to—Tom, I—I sent out your sister so I could discuss something with you. If you hadn't spoken I would have spoken to you. [*She sits down.*]

TOM. [*gently*] What is it, Mother, that you want to discuss?

AMANDA. *Laura!*

[TOM *puts his cup down slowly.*]

° *bower*: an anchor at the bow (or front) of a ship.

Legend on screen: "Laura." Music: "The Glass Menagerie."]

TOM.   —Oh.—Laura . . .

AMANDA.   [*touching his sleeve*] You know how Laura is. So quiet but—still water runs deep! She notices things and I think she—broods about them.

[*TOM looks up.*]

A few days ago I came in and she was crying.

TOM.   What about?

AMANDA.   You.

TOM.   Me?

AMANDA.   She has an idea that you're not happy here.

TOM.   What gave her that idea?

AMANDA.   What gives her any idea? However, you do act strangely. I—I'm not criticizing, understand *that*! I know your ambitions do not lie in the warehouse, that like everybody in the whole wide world—you've had to—make sacrifices, but— Tom—Tom—life's not easy, it calls for—Spartan endurance! There's so many things in my heart that I cannot describe to you! I've never told you but I—*loved* your father. . . .

TOM.   [*gently*] I know that, Mother.

AMANDA.   And you—when I see you taking after his ways! Staying out late— and—well, you *had* been drinking the night you were in that—terrifying condition! Laura says that you hate the apartment and that you go out nights to get away from it! Is that true, Tom?

TOM.   No. You say there's so much in your heart that you can't describe to me. That's true of me, too. There's so much in my heart that I can't describe to *you*! So let's respect each other's—

AMANDA.   But, why—*why*, Tom—are you always so *restless*? Where do you *go* to, nights?

TOM.   I—go to the movies.

AMANDA.   Why do you go to the movies so much, Tom?

TOM.   I go to the movies because—I like adventure. Adventure is something I don't have much of at work, so I go to the movies.

AMANDA.   But, Tom, you go to the movies *entirely* too *much*!

TOM.   I like a lot of adventure.

[*AMANDA looks baffled, then hurt. As the familiar inquisition resumes, TOM becomes hard and impatient again. AMANDA slips back into her querulous attitude toward him.*

Image on screen: A sailing vessel with Jolly Roger.°]

AMANDA.   Most young men find adventure in their careers.

TOM.   Then most young men are not employed in a warehouse.

AMANDA.   The world is full of young men employed in warehouses and offices and factories.

TOM.   Do all of them find adventure in their careers?

° *Jolly Roger:* the traditional flag of a pirate ship—the skull and crossed bones on a field of black.

AMANDA. They do or they do without it! Not everybody has a craze for adventure.

TOM. Man is by instinct a lover, a hunter, a fighter, and none of those instincts are given much play at the warehouse!

AMANDA. Man is by instinct! Don't quote instinct to me! Instinct is something that people have got away from! It belongs to animals! Christian adults don't want it!

TOM. What do Christian adults want, then, Mother?

AMANDA. Superior things! Things of the mind and the spirit! Only animals have to satisfy instincts! Surely your aims are somewhat higher than theirs! Than monkeys—pigs—

TOM. I reckon they're not.

AMANDA. You're joking. However, that isn't what I wanted to discuss.

TOM. [*rising*] I haven't much time.

AMANDA. [*pushing his shoulders*] Sit down.

TOM. You want me to punch in red° at the warehouse, Mother?

AMANDA. You have five minutes. I want to talk about Laura.

[*Screen legend: "Plans and Provisions."*]

TOM. All right! What about Laura?

AMANDA. We have to be making some plans and provisions for her. She's older than you, two years, and nothing has happened. She just drifts along doing nothing. It frightens me terribly how she just drifts along.

TOM. I guess she's the type that people call home girls.

AMANDA. There's no such type, and if there is, it's a pity! That is unless the home is hers, with a husband!

TOM. What?

AMANDA. Oh, I can see the handwriting on the wall as plain as I see the nose in front of my face! It's terrifying! More and more you remind me of your father! He was out all hours without explanation! —Then *left! Goodbye!* And me with the bag to hold. I saw that letter you got from the Merchant Marine. I know what you're dreaming of. I'm not standing here blindfolded. [*She pauses.*] Very well, then. Then *do* it! But not till there's somebody to take your place.

TOM. What do you mean?

AMANDA. I mean that as soon as Laura has got somebody to take care of her, married, a home of her own, independent—why, then you'll be free to go wherever you please, on land, on sea, whichever way the wind blows you! But until that time you've got to look out for your sister. I don't say me because I'm old and don't matter! I say for your sister because she's young and dependent.

I put her in business college—a dismal failure! Frightened her so it made her sick at the stomach. I took her over to the Young People's League at the church. Another fiasco. She spoke to nobody, nobody spoke to her. Now all she does is fool with those pieces of glass and play those worn-out records. What kind of a life is that for a girl to lead?

° *punch in red*: arrive late for work; the time clock stamps late arrival times in red on the time card.

TOM. What can I do about it?

AMANDA. Overcome selfishness! Self, self, self is all that you ever think of!

[*TOM springs up and crosses to get his coat. It is ugly and bulky. He pulls on a cap with earmuffs.*]

Where is your muffler? Put your wool muffler on!

[*He snatches it angrily from the closet, tosses it around his neck and pulls both ends tight.*]

Tom! I haven't said what I had in mind to ask you.

TOM. I'm too late to—

AMANDA. [*catching his arm—very importunately; then shyly*] Down at the warehouse, aren't there some—nice young men?

TOM. No!

AMANDA. There *must* be—*some* . . .

TOM. Mother— [*He gestures.*]

AMANDA. Find out one that's clean-living—doesn't drink and ask him out for sister!

TOM. What?

AMANDA. For *sister*! To *meet*! Get *acquainted*!

TOM. [*stamping to the door*] Oh, my *go-osh*!

AMANDA. Will you? [*He opens the door. She says, imploringly:*] Will you?

[*He starts down the fire escape.*]

Will you? *Will* you, dear?

TOM. [*calling back*] Yes!

[*AMANDA closes the door hesitantly and with a troubled but faintly hopeful expression.*]

Screen image: The cover of a glamor magazine.

The spotlight picks up AMANDA at the phone.]

AMANDA. Ella Cartwright? This is Amanda Wingfield! How are you honey? How is that kidney condition?

[*There is a five-second pause.*]

Horrors!

[*There is another pause.*]

You're a Christian martyr, yes, honey, that's what you are, a Christian martyr! Well, I just now happened to notice in my little red book that your subscription to the *Companion* has just run out! I knew that you wouldn't want to miss out on the wonderful serial starting in this new issue. It's by Bessie Mae Hopper, the first thing she's written since *Honeymoon for Three*. Wasn't that a strange and interesting story? Well, this one is even lovelier, I believe. It has a sophisticated, society background. It's all about the horsey set on Long Island!

[*The light fades out.*]

Scene 5

[*Legend on the screen: "Annunciation."*

Music is heard as the light slowly comes on.

It is early dusk of a spring evening. Supper has just been finished in the Wingfield apartment. AMANDA and LAURA, in light-colored dresses, are removing dishes from the table in the dining room, which is shadowy, their movements formalized almost as a dance or ritual, their moving forms as pale and silent as moths. TOM, in white shirt and trousers, rises from the table and crosses toward the fire escape.]

AMANDA. [*as he passes her*] Son, will you do me a favor?

TOM. What?

AMANDA. Comb your hair! You look so pretty when your hair is combed!

[*TOM slouches on the sofa with the evening paper. Its enormous headline reads: "Franco Triumphs."°*]

There is only one respect in which I would like you to emulate your father.

TOM. What respect is that?

AMANDA. The care he always took of his appearance. He never allowed himself to look untidy.

[*He throws down the paper and crosses to the fire escape.*]

Where are you going?

TOM. I'm going out to smoke.

AMANDA. You smoke too much. A pack a day at fifteen cents a pack. How much would that amount to in a month? Thirty times fifteen is how much, Tom? Figure it out and you will be astounded at what you could save. Enough to give you a night-school course in accounting at Washington U.!° Just think what a wonderful thing that would be for you, son!

[*TOM is unmoved by the thought.*]

TOM. I'd rather smoke. [*He steps out on the landing, letting the screen door slam.*]

AMANDA. [*sharply*] I know! That's the tragedy of it. . . . [*Alone, she turns to look at her husband's picture.*]

[*Dance music: "The World Is Waiting for the Sunrise!"°*]

TOM. [*to the audience*] Across the alley from us was the Paradise Dance Hall. On evenings in spring the windows and doors were open and the music came outdoors. Sometimes the lights were turned out except for a large glass sphere that hung from the ceiling. It would turn slowly about and filter the dusk with

---

° "*Franco Triumphs*": Francisco Franco (1892–1975), dictator of Spain from 1939 until his death, was the general of the victorious Falangist armies in the Spanish Civil War (1936–1939).

° *Washington U*: Washington University, a highly competitive liberal arts school in St. Louis.

° "*The World . . . Sunrise*": popular song written in 1919 by Eugene Lockhart and Ernest Seitz.

delicate rainbow colors. Then the orchestra played a waltz or a tango, something that had a slow and sensuous rhythm. Couples would come outside, to the relative privacy of the alley. You could see them kissing behind ash pits and telephone poles. This was the compensation for lives that passed like mine, without any change or adventure. Adventure and change were imminent in this year. They were waiting around the corner for all these kids. Suspended in the mist over Berchtesgaden, caught in the folds of Chamberlain's umbrella. In Spain there was Guernica!° But here there was only hot swing music and liquor, dance halls, bars, and movies, and sex that hung in the gloom like a chandelier and flooded the world with brief, deceptive rainbows. . . . All the world was waiting for bombardments!

[*AMANDA turns from the picture and comes outside.*]

AMANDA. [*sighing*] A fire escape landing's a poor excuse for a porch. [*She spreads a newspaper on a step and sits down, gracefully and demurely as if she were settling into a swing on a Mississippi veranda.*] What are you looking at?
TOM. The moon.
AMANDA. Is there a moon this evening?
TOM. It's rising over Garfinkel's Delicatessen.
AMANDA. So it is! A little silver slipper of a moon. Have you made a wish on it yet?
TOM. Um-hum.
AMANDA. What did you wish for?
TOM. That's a secret.
AMANDA. A secret, huh? Well, I won't tell mine either. I will be just as mysterious as you.
TOM. I bet I can guess what yours is.
AMANDA. Is my head so transparent?
TOM. You're not a sphinx.°
AMANDA. No, I don't have secrets. I'll tell you what I wished for on the moon. Success and happiness for my precious children! I wish for that whenever there's a moon, and when there isn't a moon, I wish for it, too.
TOM. I thought perhaps you wished for a gentleman caller.
AMANDA. Why do you say that?
TOM. Don't you remember asking me to fetch one?
AMANDA. I remember suggesting that it would be nice for your sister if you brought home some nice young man from the warehouse. I think that I've made that suggestion more than once.
TOM. Yes, you have made it repeatedly.
AMANDA. Well?
TOM. We are going to have one.

° *Guernica*: The three places or people alluded to here are all foreshadowings of World War II. Berchtesgaden is a resort in Germany in the Bavarian Alps, best known as Adolf Hitler's favorite residence. Neville Chamberlain (1869–1940) was the British prime minister (1937–1940) who met with Hitler in 1938 at Munich and signed the Munich Pact, allowing Nazi Germany to occupy parts of Czechoslovakia with impunity. Chamberlain, who always carried an umbrella, declared that he had ensured "peace in our time."
° *sphinx*: a mythological monster with the head of a woman and body of a lion, famous for her riddles.

AMANDA. *What?*
TOM.   A gentleman caller!

[*The annunciation is celebrated with music.*

AMANDA rises.

Image on screen: A caller with a bouquet.]

AMANDA.   You mean you have asked some nice young man to come over?
TOM.   Yep. I've asked him to dinner.
AMANDA.   You really did?
TOM.   I did!
AMANDA.   You did, and did he—*accept?*
TOM.   He did!
AMANDA.   Well, well—well, well! That's—lovely!
TOM.   I thought that you would be pleased.
AMANDA.   It's definite then?
TOM.   Very definite.
AMANDA.   Soon?
TOM.   Very soon.
AMANDA.   For heaven's sake, stop putting on and tell me some things, will you?
TOM.   What things do you want me to tell you?
AMANDA.   *Naturally* I would like to know when he's *coming!*
TOM.   He's coming tomorrow.
AMANDA.   *Tomorrow?*
TOM.   Yep. Tomorrow.
AMANDA.   But, Tom!
TOM.   Yes, Mother?
AMANDA.   Tomorrow gives me no time!
TOM.   Time for what?
AMANDA.   Preparations! Why didn't you phone me at once, as soon as you asked him, the minute that he accepted? Then, don't you see, I could have been getting ready!
TOM.   You don't have to make any fuss.
AMANDA.   Oh, Tom, Tom, Tom, of course I have to make a fuss! I want things nice, not sloppy! Not thrown together. I'll certainly have to do some fast thinking, won't I?
TOM.   I don't see why you have to think at all.
AMANDA.   You just don't know. We can't have a gentleman caller in a pigsty! All my wedding silver has to be polished, the monogrammed table linen ought to be laundered! The windows have to be washed and fresh curtains put up. And how about clothes? We have to *wear* something, don't we?
TOM.   Mother, this boy is no one to make a fuss over!
AMANDA.   Do you realize he's the first young man we've introduced to your sister? It's terrible, dreadful, disgraceful that poor little sister has never received a single gentleman caller! Tom, come inside! [*She opens the screen door.*]
TOM.   What for?
AMANDA.   I want to ask you some things.

Tom.   If you're going to make such a fuss, I'll call it off, I'll tell him not to come!

Amanda.   You certainly won't do anything of the kind. Nothing offends people worse than broken engagements. It simply means I'll have to work like a Turk! We won't be brilliant, but we will pass inspection. Come on inside.

[*Tom follows her inside, groaning.*]

Sit down.

Tom.   Any particular place you would like me to sit?

Amanda.   Thank heavens I've got that new sofa! I'm also making payments on a floor lamp I'll have sent out! And put the chintz covers on, they'll brighten things up! Of course I'd hoped to have these walls re-papered. . . . What is the young man's name?

Tom.   His name is O'Connor.

Amanda.   That, of course, means fish° —tomorrow is Friday! I'll have that salmon loaf—with Durkee's dressing! What does he do? He works at the warehouse?

Tom.   Of course! How else would I—

Amanda.   Tom, he—doesn't drink?

Tom.   Why do you ask me that?

Amanda.   Your father *did*!

Tom.   Don't get started on that!

Amanda.   He *does* drink, then?

Tom.   Not that I know of!

Amanda.   Make sure, be certain! The last thing I want for my daughter's a boy who drinks!

Tom.   Aren't you being a little bit premature? Mr. O'Connor has not yet appeared on the scene!

Amanda.   But will tomorrow. To meet your sister, and what do I know about his character? Nothing! Old maids are better off than wives of drunkards!

Tom.   Oh, my God!

Amanda.   Be still!

Tom.   [*leaning forward to whisper*] Lots of fellows meet girls whom they don't marry!

Amanda.   Oh, talk sensibly, Tom—and don't be sarcastic! [*She has gotten a hairbrush.*]

Tom.   What are you doing?

Amanda.   I'm brushing that cowlick down! [*She attacks his hair with the brush.*] What is this young man's position at the warehouse?

Tom.   [*submitting grimly to the brush and the interrogation*] This young man's position is that of a shipping clerk, Mother.

Amanda.   Sounds to me like a fairly responsible job, the sort of a job *you* would be in if you just had more *get-up*. What is his salary? Have you any idea?

Tom.   I would judge it to be approximately eighty-five dollars a month.

Amanda.   Well—not princely, but—

Tom.   Twenty more than I make.

Amanda.   Yes, how well I know! But for a family man, eighty-five dollars a month is not much more than you can just get by on. . . .

° *fish*: Amanda assumes that O'Connor is Roman Catholic. Until the 1960s Roman Catholics were required by the church to abstain from meat on Fridays.

TOM.   Yes, but Mr. O'Connor is not a family man.

AMANDA.   He might be, mightn't he? Some time in the future?

TOM.   I see. Plans and provisions.

AMANDA.   You are the only young man that I know of who ignores the fact that the future becomes the present, the present the past, and the past turns into everlasting regret if you don't plan for it!

TOM.   I will think that over and see what I can make of it.

AMANDA.   Don't be supercilious with your mother! Tell me some more about this—what do you call him?

TOM.   James D. O'Connor. The D. is for Delaney.

AMANDA.   Irish on *both* sides! *Gracious*! And he doesn't drink?

TOM.   Shall I call him up and ask him right this minute?

AMANDA.   The only way to find out about those things is to make discreet inquiries at the proper moment. When I was a girl in Blue Mountain and it was suspected that a young man drank, the girl whose attentions he had been receiving, if any girl *was*, would sometimes speak to the minister of his church, or rather her father would if her father was living, and sort of feel him out on the young man's character. That is the way such things are discreetly handled to keep a young woman from making a tragic mistake!

TOM.   Then how did you happen to make a tragic mistake?

AMANDA.   That innocent look of your father's had everyone fooled! He *smiled*—the world was *enchanted*! No girl can do worse than put herself at the mercy of a handsome appearance! I hope that Mr. O'Connor is not too good-looking.

TOM.   No, he's not too good-looking. He's covered with freckles and hasn't too much of a nose.

AMANDA.   He's not right-down homely, though?

TOM.   Not right-down homely. Just medium homely, I'd say.

AMANDA.   Character's what to look for in a man.

TOM.   That's what I've always said, Mother.

AMANDA.   You've never said anything of the kind and I suspect you would never give it a thought.

TOM.   Don't be so suspicious of me.

AMANDA.   At least I hope he's the type that's up and coming.

TOM.   I think he really goes in for self-improvement.

AMANDA.   What reason have you to think so?

TOM.   He goes to night school.

AMANDA.   [*beaming*] Splendid! What does he do, I mean study?

TOM.   Radio engineering and public speaking!

AMANDA.   Then he has visions of being advanced in the world! Any young man who studies public speaking is aiming to have an executive job some day! And radio engineering? A thing for the future! Both of these facts are very illuminating. Those are the sort of things that a mother should know concerning any young man who comes to call on her daughter. Seriously or—not.

TOM.   One little warning. He doesn't know about Laura. I didn't let on that we had dark ulterior motives. I just said, why don't you come and have dinner with us? He said okay and that was the whole conversation.

AMANDA.   I bet it was! You're eloquent as an oyster. However, he'll know about Laura when he gets here. When he sees how lovely and sweet and pretty she is, he'll thank his lucky stars he was asked to dinner.

TOM.   Mother, you mustn't expect too much of Laura.

AMANDA.   What do you mean?

TOM.   Laura seems all those things to you and me because she's ours and we love her. We don't even notice she's crippled any more.

AMANDA.   Don't say crippled! You know that I never allow that word to be used!

TOM.   But face facts, Mother. She is and—that's not all—

AMANDA.   What do you mean "not all"?

TOM.   Laura is very different from other girls.

AMANDA.   I think the difference is all to her advantage.

TOM.   Not quite all—in the eyes of others—strangers—she's terribly shy and lives in a world of her own and those things make her seem a little peculiar to people outside the house.

AMANDA.   Don't say peculiar.

TOM.   Face the facts. She is.

[*The dance hall music changes to a tango that has a minor and somewhat ominous tone.*]

AMANDA.   In what way is she peculiar—may I ask?

TOM.   [*gently*] She lives in a world of her own—a world of little glass ornaments, Mother. . . .

[*He gets up. AMANDA remains holding the brush, looking at him, troubled.*]

She plays old phonograph records and—that's about all—[*He glances at himself in the mirror and crosses to the door.*]

AMANDA.   [*sharply*] Where are you going?

TOM.   I'm going to the movies. [*He goes out the screen door.*]

AMANDA.   Not to the movies, every night to the movies! [*She follows quickly to the screen door.*] I don't believe you always go to the movies!

[*He is gone. AMANDA looks worriedly after him for a moment. Then vitality and optimism return and she turns from the door, crossing to the portieres.*]

Laura! Laura!

[*LAURA answers from the kitchenette.*]

LAURA.   Yes, Mother.

AMANDA.   Let those dishes go and come in front!

[*LAURA appears with a dish towel. AMANDA speaks to her gaily.*]

Laura, come here and make a wish on the moon!

[*Screen image: The Moon.*]

LAURA.   [*entering*] Moon—moon?

AMANDA.   A little silver slipper of a moon. Look over your left shoulder, Laura, and make a wish!

[*LAURA looks faintly puzzled as if called out of sleep. AMANDA seizes her shoulders and turns her at an angle by the door.*]

Now! Now, darling, *wish*!

LAURA. What shall I wish for, Mother?

AMANDA. [*her voice trembling and her eyes suddenly filling with tears*] Happiness! Good fortune!

[*The sound of the violin rises and the stage dims out.*]

Scene 6

[*The light comes up on the fire escape landing. Tom is leaning against the grill, smoking. Screen image: The high school hero.*]

TOM. And so the following evening I brought Jim home to dinner. I had known Jim slightly in high school. In high school Jim was a hero. He had tremendous Irish good nature and vitality with the scrubbed and polished look of white china-ware. He seemed to move in a continual spotlight. He was a star in basketball, captain of the debating club, president of the senior class and the glee club and he sang the male lead in the annual light operas. He was always running or bound-ing, never just walking. He seemed always at the point of defeating the law of gravity. He was shooting with such velocity through his adolescence that you would logically expect him to arrive at nothing short of the White House by the time he was thirty. But Jim apparently ran into more interference after his graduation from Soldan. His speed had definitely slowed. Six years after he left high school he was holding a job that wasn't much better than mine.

[*Screen image: The Clerk.*]

He was the only one at the warehouse with whom I was on friendly terms. I was valuable to him as someone who could remember his former glory, who had seen him win basketball games and the silver cup in debating. He knew of my secret practice of retiring to a cabinet of the washroom to work on poems when business was slack in the warehouse. He called me Shakespeare. And while the other boys in the warehouse regarded me with suspicious hostility, Jim took a humorous atti-tude toward me. Gradually his attitude affected the others, their hostility wore off and they also began to smile at me as people smile at an oddly fashioned dog who trots across their path at some distance.

I knew that Jim and Laura had known each other at Soldan, and I had heard Laura speak admiringly of his voice. I didn't know if Jim remembered her or not. In high school Laura had been as unobtrusive as Jim had been astonishing. If he did remember Laura, it was not as my sister, for when I asked him to dinner, he grinned and said, "You know, Shakespeare, I never thought of you as having folks!" He was about to discover that I did. . . .

[*Legend on screen: "The accent of a coming foot."*]

[*The light dims out on Tom and comes up in the Wingfield living room—a delicate lemony light. It is about five on a Friday evening of late spring which comes "scattering poems in the sky."*

AMANDA has worked like a Turk in preparation for the gentleman caller. The results are astonishing. The new floor lamp with its rose silk shade is in place, a colored paper lantern conceals the broken light fixture in the ceiling, new billowing white curtains are at the windows, chintz covers are on the chairs and sofa, a pair of new sofa pillows make their initial appearance. Open boxes and tissue paper are scattered on the floor.

LAURA stands in the middle of the room with lifted arms while AMANDA crouches before her, adjusting the hem of a new dress, devout and ritualistic. The dress is colored and designed by memory. The arrangement of LAURA's hair is changed; it is softer and more becoming. A fragile, unearthly prettiness has come out in LAURA: she is like a piece of translucent glass touched by light, given a momentary radiance, not actual, not lasting.]

AMANDA.   *[impatiently]* Why are you trembling?
LAURA.   Mother, you've made me so nervous!
AMANDA.   How have I made you nervous?
LAURA.   By all this fuss! You make it seem so important!
AMANDA.   I don't understand you, Laura. You couldn't be satisfied with just sitting home, and yet whenever I try to arrange something for you, you seem to resist it. *[She gets up.]* Now take a look at yourself. No, wait! Wait just a moment— I have an idea!
LAURA.   What is it now?

[AMANDA produces two powder puffs which she wraps in handkerchiefs and stuffs in LAURA's bosom.]

LAURA.   Mother, what are you doing?
AMANDA.   They call them "Gay Deceivers"!
LAURA.   I won't wear them!
AMANDA.   You will!
LAURA.   Why should I?
AMANDA.   Because, to be painfully honest, your chest is flat.
LAURA.   You make it seem like we were setting a trap.
AMANDA.   All pretty girls are a trap, a pretty trap, and men expect them to be.

[Legend on screen: "A pretty trap."]

Now look at yourself, young lady. This is the prettiest you will ever be! *[She stands back to admire LAURA.]* I've got to fix myself now! You're going to be surprised by your mother's appearance!

[AMANDA crosses through the portieres, humming gaily. LAURA moves slowly to the long mirror and stares solemnly at herself. A wind blows the white curtains inward in a slow, graceful motion and with a faint, sorrowful sighing.]

AMANDA.   *[from somewhere behind the portieres]* It isn't dark enough yet.

[LAURA turns slowly before the mirror with a troubled look.]

Legend on screen: "This is my sister: Celebrate her with strings!" Music plays.]

AMANDA.   *[laughing, still not visible]* I'm going to show you something. I'm going to make a spectacular appearance!
LAURA.   What is it, Mother?
AMANDA.   Possess your soul in patience—you will see! Something I've resurrected from that old trunk! Styles haven't changed so terribly much after all. . . .

[*She parts the portieres.*] Now just look at your mother! [*She wears a girlish frock of yellowed voile with a blue silk sash. She carries a bunch of jonquils—the legend of her youth is nearly revived. Now she speaks feverishly:*] This is the dress in which I led the cotillion. Won the cakewalk twice at Sunset Hill, wore one Spring to the Governor's Ball in Jackson!° See how I sashayed around the ballroom, Laura? [*She raises her skirt and does a mincing step around the room.*] I wore it on Sundays for my gentlemen callers! I had it on the day I met your father. . . . I had malaria fever all that Spring. The change of climate from East Tennessee to the Delta—weakened resistance. I had a little temperature all the time—not enough to be serious—just enough to make me restless and giddy! Invitations poured in—parties all over the Delta! "Stay in bed," said Mother, "you have a fever!"—but I just wouldn't. I took quinine° but kept on going, going! Evenings, dances! Afternoons, long, long rides! Picnics— lovely! So lovely, that country in May—all lacy with dogwood, literally flooded with jonquils! That was the spring I had the craze for jonquils. Jonquils became an absolute obsession. Mother said, "Honey, there's no more room for jonquils." And still I kept on bringing in more jonquils. Whenever, wherever I saw them, I'd say, "Stop! Stop! I see jonquils!" I made the young men help me gather the jonquils! It was a joke, Amanda and her jonquils. Finally there were no more vases to hold them, every available space was filled with jonquils. No vases to hold them? All right, I'll hold them myself! And then I—[*She stops in front of the picture. Music plays.*] met your father! Malaria fever and jonquils and then—this— boy. . . . [*She switches on the rose-colored lamp.*] I hope they get here before it starts to rain. [*She crosses the room and places the jonquils in a bowl on the table.*] I gave your brother a little extra change so he and Mr. O'Connor could take the service car home.

LAURA.   [*with an altered look*] What did you say his name was?
AMANDA.   O'Connor.
LAURA.   What is his first name?
AMANDA.   I don't remember. Oh, yes, I do. It was—Jim.

[*LAURA sways slightly and catches hold of a chair.*

Legend on screen: "Not Jim!"]

LAURA.   [*faintly*] Not—Jim!
AMANDA.   Yes, that was it, it was Jim! I've never known a Jim that wasn't nice!

[*The music becomes ominous.*]

LAURA.   Are you sure his name is Jim O'Connor?
AMANDA.   Yes. Why?
LAURA.   Is he the one that Tom used to know in high school?
AMANDA.   He didn't say so. I think he just got to know him at the warehouse.
LAURA.   There was a Jim O'Connor we both knew in high school—[*Then, with effort.*] If that is the one that Tom is bringing to dinner—you'll have to excuse me, I won't come to the table.

° *Jackson:* Amanda refers to the social events of her youth in Mississippi. A cotillion is a formal ball, often given for debutantes. A cakewalk was a musical walking or dancing contest. Jackson is the capital of Mississippi.
° *quinine:* a drug used in the 1930s to control malaria.

AMANDA.   What sort of nonsense is this?

LAURA.   You asked me once if I'd ever liked a boy. Don't you remember I showed you this boy's picture?

AMANDA.   You mean the boy you showed me in the yearbook?

LAURA.   Yes, that boy.

AMANDA.   Laura, Laura, were you in love with that boy?

LAURA.   I don't know, Mother. All I know is I couldn't sit at the table if it was him!

AMANDA.   It won't be him! It isn't the least bit likely. But whether it is or not, you will come to the table. You will not be excused.

LAURA.   I'll have to be, Mother.

AMANDA.   I don't intend to humor your silliness, Laura. I've had too much from you and your brother, both! So just sit down and compose yourself till they come. Tom has forgotten his key so you'll have to let them in, when they arrive.

LAURA.   [*panicky*] Oh, Mother—*you* answer the door!

AMANDA.   [*lightly*] I'll be in the kitchen—busy!

LAURA.   Oh, Mother, please answer the door, don't make me do it!

AMANDA.   [*crossing into the kitchenette*] I've got to fix the dressing for the salmon. Fuss, fuss—silliness!—over a gentleman caller!

[*The door swings shut. LAURA is left alone.*]

Legend on screen: "Terror!"

She utteres a low moan and turns off the lamp—sits stiffly on the edge of the sofa, knotting her fingers together.

Legend on screen: "The Opening of a Door!"

TOM and JIM appear on the fire escape steps and climb to the landing. Hearing their approach, LAURA rises with a panicky gesture. She retreats to the portieres. The doorbell rings. LAURA catches her breath and touches her throat. Low drums sound.]

AMANDA.   [*calling*] Laura, sweetheart! The door!

[*LAURA stares at it without moving.*]

JIM.   I think we just beat the rain.

TOM.   Uh-huh. [*He rings again, nervously. JIM whistles and fishes for a cigarette.*]

AMANDA.   [*very, very gaily*] Laura, that is your brother and Mr. O'Connor! Will you let them in, darling?

[*LAURA crosses toward the kitchenette door.*]

LAURA.   [*breathlessly*] Mother—you go to the door!

[*AMANDA steps out of the kitchenette and stares furiously at LAURA. She points imperiously at the door.*]

LAURA.   Please, please!

AMANDA.   [*in a fierce whisper*] What is the matter with you, you silly thing?

LAURA.   [*desperately*] Please, you answer it, *please*!

AMANDA.   I told you I wasn't going to humor you, Laura. Why have you chosen this moment to lose your mind?

LAURA.   Please, please, please, you go!

AMANDA.   You'll have to go to the door because I can't!

LAURA.   [*despairingly*] I can't either!

AMANDA.   *Why?*

LAURA.   I'm *sick*!

AMANDA.   I'm sick, too—of your nonsense! Why can't you and your brother be normal people? Fantastic whims and behavior!

[*TOM gives a long ring.*]

Preposterous goings on! Can you give me one reason—[*She calls out lyrically.*] *Coming!* Just one second!—why you should be afraid to open a door? Now you answer it, Laura!

LAURA.   Oh, oh, oh . . . [*She returns through the portieres, darts to the Victrola, winds it frantically and turns it on.*]

AMANDA.   Laura Wingfield, you march right to that door!

LAURA.   *Yes—yes, Mother!*

[*A faraway, scratchy rendition of "Dardanella"° softens the air and gives her strength to move through it. She slips to the door and draws it cautiously open. TOM enters with the caller, JIM O'CONNOR.*]

TOM.   Laura, this is Jim. Jim, this is my sister, Laura.

JIM.   [*stepping inside*] I didn't know that Shakespeare had a sister!

LAURA.   [*retreating, stiff and trembling, from the door*] How—how do you do?

JIM.   [*heartily, extending his hand*] Okay!

[*LAURA touches it hesitantly with hers.*]

JIM.   Your hand's *cold*, Laura!

LAURA.   Yes, well—I've been playing the Victrola. . . .

JIM.   Must have been playing classical music on it! You ought to play a little hot swing music to warm you up!

LAURA.   Excuse me—I haven't finished playing the Victrola. . . . [*She turns awkwardly and hurries into the front room. She pauses a second by the Victrola. Then she catches her breath and darts through the portieres like a frightened deer.*]

JIM.   [*grinning*] What was the matter?

TOM.   Oh—with Laura? Laura is—terribly shy.

JIM.   Shy, huh? It's unusual to meet a shy girl nowadays. I don't believe you ever mentioned you had a sister.

TOM.   Well, now you know. I have one. Here is the *Post Dispatch.*° You want a piece of it?

JIM.   Uh-huh.

TOM.   What piece? The comics?

JIM.   Sports! [*He glances at it.*] Ole Dizzy Dean° is on his bad behavior.

TOM.   [*uninterested*] Yeah? [*He lights a cigarette and goes over to the fire-escape door.*]

° *"Dardanella"*: a popular song and dance tune written in 1919 by Fred Fisher, Felix Bernard, and Johnny S. Black.
° *Post Dispatch*: The *St. Louis Post Dispatch*, a newspaper.
° *Dizzy Dean*: Jerome Herman (or Jay Hanna) Dean (1911–1974), outstanding pitcher with the St. Louis Cardinals (1932–1938).

JIM.   Where are *you* going?

TOM.   I'm going out on the terrace.

JIM.   [*going after him*] You know, Shakespeare—I'm going to sell you a bill of goods!

TOM.   What goods?

JIM.   A course I'm taking.

TOM.   Huh?

JIM.   In public speaking! You and me, we're not the warehouse type.

TOM.   Thanks—that's good news. But what has public speaking got to do with it?

JIM.   It fits you for—executive positions!

TOM.   Awww.

JIM.   I tell you it's done a helluva lot for me.

[*Image on screen: Executive at his desk.*]

TOM.   In what respect?

JIM.   In every! Ask yourself what is the difference between you an' me and men in the office down front? Brains?—No!—Ability?—No! Then what? Just one little thing—

TOM.   What is that one little thing?

JIM.   Primarily it amounts to—social poise! Being able to square up to people and hold your own on any social level!

AMANDA.   [*from the kitchenette*] Tom?

TOM.   Yes, Mother?

AMANDA.   Is that you and Mr. O'Connor?

TOM.   Yes, Mother.

AMANDA.   Well, you just make yourselves comfortable in there.

TOM.   Yes, Mother.

AMANDA.   Ask Mr. O'Connor if he would like to wash his hands.

JIM.   Aw, no—no—thank you—I took care of that at the warehouse. Tom—

TOM.   Yes?

JIM.   Mr. Mendoza was speaking to me about you.

TOM.   Favorably?

JIM.   What do you think?

TOM.   Well—

JIM.   You're going to be out of a job if you don't wake up.

TOM.   I am waking up—

JIM.   You show no signs.

TOM.   The signs are interior.

[*Image on screen: The sailing vessel with the Jolly Roger again.*]

TOM.   I'm planning to change. [*He leans over the fire escape rail, speaking with quiet exhilaration. The incandescent marquees and signs of the first-run movie houses light his face from across the alley. He looks like a voyager.*] I'm right at the point of committing myself to a future that doesn't include the warehouse and Mr. Mendoza or even a night-school course in public speaking.

JIM.   What are you gassing about?

Tom. I'm tired of the movies.

Jim. Movies!

Tom. Yes, movies! Look at them— [*a wave toward the marvels of Grand Avenue*] All of those glamorous people—having adventures—hogging it all, gobbling the whole thing up! You know what happens? People go to the *movies* instead of *moving*! Hollywood characters are supposed to have all the adventures for everybody in America, while everybody in America sits in a dark room and watches them have them! Yes, until there's a war. That's when adventure becomes available to the masses! *Everyone's* dish, not only Gable's!° Then the people in the dark room come out of the dark room to have some adventures themselves—goody, goody! It's our turn now, to go to the South Sea Island—to make a safari—to be exotic, far-off! But I'm not patient. I don't want to wait till then. I'm tired of the *movies* and I am *about* to *move*!

Jim. [*incredulously*] Move?

Tom. Yes.

Jim. When?

Tom. Soon!

Jim. Where? Where?

[*The music seems to answer the question, while* Tom *thinks it over. He searches in his pockets.*]

Tom. I'm starting to boil inside. I know I seem dreamy, but inside—well, I'm boiling! Whenever I pick up a shoe, I shudder a little thinking how short life is and what I am doing! Whatever that means, I know it doesn't mean shoes—except as something to wear on a traveler's feet! [*He finds what he has been searching for in his pockets and holds out a paper to* Jim.] Look—

Jim. What?

Tom. I'm a member.

Jim. [*reading*] The Union of Merchant Seamen.

Tom. I paid my dues this month, instead of the light bill.

Jim. You will regret it when they turn off the lights.

Tom. I won't be here.

Jim. How about your mother?

Tom. I'm like my father. The bastard son of a bastard! Did you notice how he's grinning in his picture in there? And he's been absent going on sixteen years!

Jim. You're just talking, you drip. How does your mother feel about it?

Tom. Shhh! Here comes Mother! Mother is not acquainted with my plans!

Amanda. [*coming through the portieres*] Where are you all?

Tom. On the terrace, Mother.

[*They start inside. She advances to them.* Tom *is distinctly shocked at her appearance. Even* Jim *blinks a little. He is making his first contact with the girlish Southern vivacity and in spite of the night-school course in public speaking is somewhat thrown off the beam by the unexpected outlay of social charm. Certain responses are attempted by* Jim *but are swept aside by* Amanda's *gay laughter and chatter.* Tom *is embarrassed but after the first shock* Jim *reacts very warmly. He grins and chuckles, is altogether won over.*]

° *Gable:* Clark Gable (1901–1960), popular American screen actor and matinee idol from the 1930s to his death.

Image on screen: AMANDA as a girl.]

AMANDA. [*coyly smiling, shaking her girlish ringlets*] Well, well, well, so this is
Mr. O'Connor. Introductions entirely unnecessary. I've heard so much about you
from my boy. I finally said to him, Tom—good gracious!—why don't you bring
this paragon to supper? I'd like to meet this nice young man at the warehouse!—
instead of just hearing him sing your praises so much! I don't know why my son
is so stand-offish—that's not Southern behavior!

Let's sit down and—I think we could stand a little more air in here! Tom,
leave the door open. I felt a nice fresh breeze a moment ago. Where has it gone
to? Mmm, so warm already! And not quite summer, even. We're going to burn
up when summer really gets started. However, we're having—we're having a very
light supper. I think light things are better fo' this time of year. The same as
light clothes are. Light clothes an' light food are what warm weather calls fo'.
You know our blood gets so thick during th' winter—it takes a while fo' us to
adjust ourselves!—when the season changes . . . It's come so quick this year. I
wasn't prepared. All of a sudden—heavens! Already summer! I ran to the trunk
an' pulled out this light dress—terribly old! Historical almost! But feels so good—
so good an' co-ol, y'know. . . .

TOM. Mother—

AMANDA. Yes, honey?

TOM. How about—supper?

AMANDA. Honey, you go ask Sister if supper is ready! You know that Sister
is in full charge of supper! Tell her you hungry boys are waiting for it. [*To JIM.*]
Have you met Laura?

JIM. She—

AMANDA. Let you in? Oh, good, you've met already! It's rare for a girl as
sweet an' pretty as Laura to be domestic! But Laura is, thank heavens, not only
pretty but also very domestic. I'm not at all. I never was a bit. I never could
make a thing but angel-food cake. Well, in the South we had so many servants.
Gone, gone, gone. All vestige of gracious living! Gone completely! I wasn't prepared
for what the future brought me. All of my gentlemen callers were sons of planters
and so of course I assumed that I would be married to one and raise my family
on a large piece of land with plenty of servants. But man proposes—and woman
accepts the proposal! to vary that old, old saying a little but—I married no planter!
I married a man who worked for the telephone company! That gallantly smiling
gentleman over there! [*She points to the picture.*] A telephone man who—fell in love
with long-distance! Now he travels and I don't even know where! But what am I
going on for about my—tribulations? Tell me yours—I hope you don't have any!
Tom?

TOM. [*returning*] Yes, Mother?

AMANDA. Is supper nearly ready?

TOM. It looks to me like supper is on the table.

AMANDA. Let me look— [*She rises prettily and looks through the portieres.*] Oh
lovely! But where is Sister?

TOM. Laura is not feeling well and she says that she thinks she'd better
not come to the table.

AMANDA. What? Nonsense! Laura? Oh, Laura!

LAURA. [*from the kitchenette, faintly*] Yes, Mother.

AMANDA. You really must come to the table. We won't be seated until you come to the table! Come in, Mr. O'Connor. You sit over there and I'll. . . . Laura? Laura Wingfield! You're keeping us waiting, honey! We can't say grace until you come to the table!

[*The kitchenette door is pushed weakly open and LAURA comes in. She is obviously quite faint, her lips trembling, her eyes wide and staring. She moves unsteadily toward the table.*]

Screen legend: "Terror!"

Outside a summer storm is coming on abruptly. The white curtains billow inward at the windows and there is a sorrowful murmur from the deep blue dusk.

LAURA suddenly stumbles; she catches at a chair with a faint moan.]

TOM. Laura!
AMANDA. Laura!

[*There is a clap of thunder.*]

Screen legend: "Ah!"]

[*despairingly*] Why, Laura, you *are* ill, darling! Tom, help your sister into the living room, dear! Sit in the living room, Laura—rest on the sofa. Well! [*To JIM as TOM helps his sister to the sofa in the living room.*] Standing over the hot stove made her ill! I told her that it was just too warm this evening, but—

[*TOM comes back to the table.*]

Is Laura all right now?

TOM. Yes.

AMANDA. What is that? Rain? A nice cool rain has come up! [*She gives JIM a frightened look.*] I think we may—have grace—now . . . [*TOM looks at her stupidly.*] Tom, honey—you say grace!

TOM. Oh . . . "For these and all thy mercies—"

[*They bow their heads, AMANDA stealing a nervous glance at JIM. In the living room LAURA, stretched on the sofa, clenches her hand to her lips, to hold back a shuddering sob.*]

God's Holy Name be praised—

[*The scene dims out.*]

Scene 7

It is half an hour later. Dinner is just being finished in the dining room, LAURA is still huddled upon the sofa, her feet drawn under her, her head resting on a pale blue pillow, her eyes wide and mysteriously watchful. The new floor lamp with its shade of rose-colored silk gives a soft, becoming light to her face, bringing out the fragile, unearthly prettiness which usually escapes attention. From outside there is a steady murmur of rain, but it is slackening and soon stops; the air outside becomes pale and luminous as the moon breaks through the clouds. A moment after the curtain rises, the lights in both rooms flicker and go out.]

JIM.   Hey, there, Mr. Light Bulb!

[*AMANDA laughs nervously.*

Legend on screen: *"Suspension of a public service."*]

AMANDA.   Where was Moses when the lights went out? Ha-ha. Do you know the answer to that one, Mr. O'Connor?
JIM.   No, Ma'am, what's the answer?
AMANDA.   In the dark!

[*JIM laughs appreciatively.*]

Everybody sit still. I'll light the candles. Isn't it lucky we have them on the table? Where's a match? Which of you gentlemen can provide a match?
JIM.   Here.
AMANDA.   Thank you, Sir.
JIM.   Not at all, Ma'am!
AMANDA.   [*as she lights the candles*] I guess the fuse has burnt out. Mr. O'Connor, can you tell a burnt-out fuse? I know I can't and Tom is a total loss when it comes to mechanics. [*They rise from the table and go into the kitchenette, from where their voices are heard.*] Oh, be careful you don't bump into something. We don't want our gentleman caller to break his neck. Now wouldn't that be a fine howdy-do?
JIM.   Ha-ha! Where is the fuse-box?
AMANDA.   Right here next to the stove. Can you see anything?
JIM.   Just a minute.
AMANDA.   Isn't electricity a mysterious thing? Wasn't it Benjamin Franklin who tied a key to a kite? We live in such a mysterious universe, don't we? Some people say that science clears up all the mysteries for us. In my opinion it only creates more! Have you found it yet?
JIM.   No, Ma'am. All these fuses look okay to me.
AMANDA.   Tom!
TOM.   Yes, Mother?
AMANDA.   That light bill I gave you several days ago. That one I told you we got the notices about?

[*Legend on screen*: *"Ha!"*]

TOM.   Oh—yeah.
AMANDA.   You didn't neglect to pay it by any chance?
TOM.   Why, I—
AMANDA.   Didn't! I might have known it!
JIM.   Shakespeare probably wrote a poem on that light bill, Mrs. Wingfield.
AMANDA.   I might have known better than to trust him with it! There's such a high price for negligence in this world!
JIM.   Maybe the poem will win a ten-dollar prize.

AMANDA.   We'll just have to spend the remainder of the evening in the nine-teenth century, before Mr. Edison made the Mazda lamp!°

JIM.   Candlelight is my favorite kind of light.

AMANDA.   That shows you're romantic! But that's no excuse for Tom. Well, we got through dinner. Very considerate of them to let us get through dinner before they plunged us into everlasting darkness, wasn't it, Mr. O'Connor?

JIM.   Ha-ha!

AMANDA.   Tom, as a penalty for your carelessness you can help me with the dishes.

JIM.   Let me give you a hand.

AMANDA.   Indeed you will not!

JIM.   I ought to be good for something.

AMANDA.   Good for something? [*Her tone is rhapsodic.*] You? Why, Mr. O'Con-nor, nobody, *nobody's* given me this much entertainment in years—as you have!

JIM.   Aw, now, Mrs. Wingfield!

AMANDA.   I'm not exaggerating, not one bit! But Sister is all by her lonesome. You go keep her company in the parlor! I'll give you this lovely old candelabrum that used to be on the altar at the Church of the Heavenly Rest. It was melted a little out of shape when the church burnt down. Lightning struck it one spring. Gypsy Jones was holding a revival at the time and he intimated that the church was destroyed because the Episcopalians gave card parties.

JIM.   Ha-ha.

AMANDA.   And how about you coaxing Sister to drink a little wine? I think it would be good for her! Can you carry both at once?

JIM.   Sure. I'm Superman!

AMANDA.   Now, Thomas, get into this apron!

[*JIM comes into the dining room, carrying the candelabrum, its candles lighted, in one hand and a glass of wine in the other. The door of the kitchenette swings closed on AMANDA'S gay laughter; the flickering light approaches the portieres. LAURA sits up nervously as JIM enters. She can hardly speak from the almost intolerable strain of being alone with a stranger.*

Screen legend: "I don't suppose you remember me at all!"

At first, before JIM'S warmth overcomes her paralyzing shyness, LAURA'S voice is thin and breathless, as though she had just run up a steep flight of stairs. JIM'S attitude is gently humorous. While the incident is apparently unimportant, it is to LAURA the climax of her secret life.]

JIM.   Hello there, Laura.

LAURA.   [*faintly*] Hello.

[*She clears her throat.*]

JIM.   How are you feeling now? Better?

LAURA.   Yes. Yes, thank you.

JIM.   This is for you. A little dandelion wine. [*He extends the glass toward her with extravagant gallantry.*]

° *Mazda lamp*: Thomas A. Edison (1847–1931) developed the first practical incandescent lamp in 1879.

LAURA. Thank you.

JIM. Drink it—but don't get drunk!

[*He laughs heartily. LAURA takes the glass uncertainly; she laughs shyly.*]

Where shall I set the candles?

LAURA. Oh—oh, anywhere . . .

JIM. How about here on the floor? Any objections?

LAURA. No.

JIM. I'll spread a newspaper under to catch the drippings. I like to sit on the floor. Mind if I do?

LAURA. Oh, no.

JIM. Give me a pillow?

LAURA. What?

JIM. A pillow!

LAURA. Oh . . . [*She hands him one quickly.*]

JIM. How about you? Don't you like to sit on the floor?

LAURA. Oh—yes.

JIM. Why don't you, then?

LAURA. I—will.

JIM. Take a pillow!

[*LAURA does. She sits on the floor on the other side of the candelabrum. JIM crosses his legs and smiles engagingly at her.*] I can't hardly see you sitting way over there.

LAURA. I can—see you.

JIM. I know, but that's not fair, I'm in the limelight.

[*LAURA moves her pillow closer.*]

Good! Now I can see you! Comfortable?

LAURA. Yes.

JIM. So am I. Comfortable as a cow! Will you have some gum?

LAURA. No, thank you.

JIM. I think that I will indulge, with your permission. [*He musingly unwraps a stick of gum and holds it up.*] Think of the fortune made by the guy that invented the first piece of chewing gum. Amazing, huh? The Wrigley Building° is one of the sights of Chicago—I saw it when I went up to the Century of Progress.° Did you take in the Century of Progress?

LAURA. No, I didn't.

JIM. Well, it was quite a wonderful exposition. What impressed me most was the Hall of Science. Gives you an idea of what the future will be in America, even more wonderful than the present time is! [*There is a pause. JIM smiles at her.*] Your brother tells me you're shy. Is that right—Laura?

LAURA. I—don't know.

JIM. I judge you to be an old-fashioned type of girl. Well, I think that's a pretty good type to be. Hope you don't think I'm being too personal—do you?

° *Wrigley Building*: Finished in 1924, this was one of the first skyscrapers in the United States.

° *Century of Progress*: a world's fair held in Chicago (1933–1934) to celebrate the city's centennial.

LAURA. [*Hastily, out of embarrassment*] I believe I *will* take a piece of gum, if you—don't mind. [*clearing her throat*] Mr. O'Connor, have you—kept up with your singing?

JIM. Singing? Me?

LAURA. Yes. I remember what a beautiful voice you had.

JIM. When did you hear me sing?

[*LAURA does not answer, and in the long pause which follows a man's voice is heard singing offstage.*]

VOICE:

> O blow, ye winds, heigh-ho,
> A-roving I will go!
> I'm off to my love
> With a boxing glove—
> Ten thousand miles away!

JIM. You say you've heard me sing?

LAURA. Oh, yes! Yes, very often . . . I—don't suppose—you remember me— at all?

JIM. [*smiling doubtfully*] You know I have an idea I've seen you before. I had that idea soon as you opened the door. It seemed almost like I was about to remember your name. But the name that I started to call you—wasn't a name! And so I stopped myself before I said it.

LAURA. Wasn't it—Blue Roses?

JIM. [*springing up, grinning*] Blue Roses! My gosh, yes—Blue Roses! That's what I had on my tongue when you opened the door! Isn't it funny what tricks your memory plays? I didn't connect you with high school somehow or other. But that's where it was; it was high school. I didn't even know you were Shakespeare's sister! Gosh, I'm sorry.

LAURA. I didn't expect you to. You—barely knew me!

JIM. But we did have a speaking acquaintance, huh?

LAURA. Yes, we—spoke to each other.

JIM. When did you recognize me?

LAURA. Oh, right away!

JIM. Soon as I came in the door?

LAURA. When I heard your name I thought it was probably you. I knew that Tom used to know you a little in high school. So when you came in the door—well, then I was—sure.

JIM. Why didn't you *say* something, then?

LAURA. [*breathlessly*] I didn't know what to say, I was—too surprised!

JIM. For goodness' sakes! You know, this sure is funny!

LAURA. Yes! Yes, isn't it, though . . .

JIM. Didn't we have a class in something together?

LAURA. Yes, we did.

JIM. What class was that?

LAURA. It was—singing—chorus!

JIM. Aw!

LAURA. I sat across the aisle from you in the Aud.

JIM. Aw!

LAURA.   Mondays, Wednesdays, and Fridays.

JIM.   Now I remember—you always came in late.

LAURA.   Yes, it was so hard for me, getting upstairs. I had that brace on my leg—it clumped so loud!

JIM.   I never heard any clumping.

LAURA.   [*wincing at the recollection*] To me it sounded like—thunder!

JIM.   Well, well, well, I never even noticed.

LAURA.   And everybody was seated before I came in. I had to walk in front of all those people. My seat was in the back row. I had to go clumping all the way up the aisle with everyone watching!

JIM.   You shouldn't have been self-conscious.

LAURA.   I know, but I was. It was always such a relief when the singing started.

JIM.   Aw, yes, I've placed you now! I used to call you Blue Roses. How was it that I got started calling you that?

LAURA.   I was out of school a little while with pleurosis. When I came back you asked me what was the matter. I said I had pleurosis—you thought that I said *Blue Roses*. That's what you always called me after that!

JIM.   I hope you didn't mind.

LAURA.   Oh, no—I liked it. You see, I wasn't acquainted with many—people. . . .

JIM.   As I remember you sort of stuck by yourself.

LAURA.   I—I—never have had much luck at—making friends.

JIM.   I don't see why you wouldn't.

LAURA.   Well, I—started out badly.

JIM.   You mean being—

LAURA.   Yes, it sort of—stood between me—

JIM.   You shouldn't have let it!

LAURA.   I know, but it did, and—

JIM.   You were shy with people!

LAURA.   I tried not to be but never could—

JIM.   Overcome it?

LAURA.   No, I—I never could!

JIM.   I guess being shy is something you have to work out of kind of gradually.

LAURA.   [*sorrowfully*] Yes—I guess it—

JIM.   Takes time!

LAURA.   Yes—

JIM.   People are not so dreadful when you know them. That's what you have to remember! And everybody has problems, not just you, but practically everybody has got some problems. You think of yourself as having the only problems, as being the only one who is disappointed. But just look around you and you will see lots of people as disappointed as you are. For instance, I hoped when I was going to high school that I would be further along at this time, six years later, than I am now. You remember that wonderful write-up I had in *The Torch*?

LAURA.   Yes! [*She rises and crosses to the table.*]

JIM.   It said I was bound to succeed in anything I went into!

[*LAURA returns with the high school yearbook.*]

Holy Jeez! *The Torch!*

[*He accepts it reverently. They smile across the book with mutual wonder. LAURA crouches beside him and they begin to turn the pages. LAURA's shyness is dissolving in his warmth.*]

LAURA. Here you are in *The Pirates of Penzance!*

JIM. [*wistfully*] I sang the baritone lead in that operetta.

LAURA. [*raptly*] So—*beautifully!*

JIM. [*protesting*] Aw—

LAURA. Yes, yes—beautifully—beautifully!

JIM. You heard me?

LAURA. All three times!

JIM. No!

LAURA. Yes!

JIM. All three performances?

LAURA. [*looking down*] Yes.

JIM. Why?

LAURA. I—wanted to ask you to—autograph my program. [*She takes the program from the back of the yearbook and shows it to him.*]

JIM. Why didn't you ask me to?

LAURA. You were always surrounded by your own friends so much that I never had a chance to.

JIM. You should have just—

LAURA. Well, I—thought you might think I was—

JIM. Thought I might think you was—what?

LAURA. Oh—

JIM. [*with reflective relish*] I was beleaguered by females in those days.

LAURA. You were terribly popular!

JIM. Yeah—

LAURA. You had such a—friendly way—

JIM. I was spoiled in high school.

LAURA. Everybody—liked you!

JIM. Including you?

LAURA. I—yes, I—did, too— [*She gently closes the book in her lap.*]

JIM. Well, well, well! Give me that program, Laura.

[*She hands it to him. He signs it with a flourish.*]

There you are—better late than never!

LAURA. Oh, I—what a—surprise!

JIM. My signature isn't worth very much right now. But some day—maybe—it will increase in value! Being disappointed is one thing and being discouraged is something else. I am disappointed but I am not discouraged. I'm twenty-three years old. How old are you?

LAURA. I'll be twenty-four in June.

JIM. That's not old age!

LAURA. No, but—

JIM. You finished high school?

LAURA. [*with difficulty*] I didn't go back.

JIM. You mean you dropped out?

LAURA. I made bad grades in my final examinations. [*She rises and replaces the book and the program on the table. Her voice is strained.*] How is—Emily Meisenbach getting along?

JIM. Oh, that kraut-head!

LAURA. Why do you call her that?

JIM. That's what she was.

LAURA. You're not still—going with her?

JIM. I never see her.

LAURA. It was in the "Personal" section that you were—engaged!

JIM. I know, but I wasn't impressed by that—propaganda!

LAURA. It wasn't—the truth?

JIM. Only in Emily's optimistic opinion!

LAURA. Oh—

[*Legend: "What have you done since high school?"*]

JIM lights a cigarette and leans indolently back on his elbows smiling at LAURA with a warmth and charm which lights her inwardly with altar candles. She remains by the table, picks up a piece from the glass menagerie collection, and turns it in her hands to cover her tumult.]

JIM. [*after several reflective puffs on his cigarette*] What have you done since high school?

[*She seems not to hear him.*]

Huh?

[*LAURA looks up.*]

I said what have you done since high school, Laura?

LAURA. Nothing much.

JIM. You must have been doing something these six long years.

LAURA. Yes.

JIM. Well, then, such as what?

LAURA. I took a business course at business college—

JIM. How did that work out?

LAURA. Well, not very—well—I had to drop out, it gave me—indigestion—

[*JIM laughs gently.*]

JIM. What are you doing now?

LAURA. I don't do anything—much. Oh, please don't think I sit around doing nothing! My glass collection takes up a good deal of time. Glass is something you have to take good care of.

JIM. What did you say—about glass?

LAURA. Collection I said—I have one— [*She clears her throat and turns away again, acutely shy.*]

JIM. [*abruptly*] You know what I judge to be the trouble with you? Inferiority complex! Know what that is? That's what they call it when someone low-rates himself! I understand it because I had it too. Although my case was not so aggravated as yours seems to be. I had it until I took up public speaking, developed my voice, and learned that I had an aptitude for science. Before that time I never thought of myself as being outstanding in any way whatsoever! Now I've never made a regular study of it, but I have a friend who says I can analyze people better than doctors that make a profession of it. I don't claim that to be necessarily true, but I can sure guess a person's psychology. Laura! [*He takes out his gum.*] Excuse me, Laura. I always take it out when the flavor is gone. I'll use this scrap of paper to wrap it in. I know how it is to get it stuck on a shoe. [*He wraps the gum in paper and puts it in his pocket.*] Yep—that's what I judge to be your principal trouble. A lack of confidence in yourself as a person. You don't have the proper amount of faith in yourself. I'm basing that fact on a number of your remarks and also on certain observations I've made. For instance that clumping you thought was so awful in high school. You say that you even dreaded to walk into class. You see what you did? You dropped out of school, you gave up an education because of a clump, which as far as I know was practically nonexistent! A little physical defect is what you have. Hardly noticeable even! Magnified thousands of times by imagination! You know what my strong advice to you is? Think of yourself as *superior* in some way!

    LAURA.   In what way would I think?

    JIM.   Why, man alive, Laura! Just look about you a little. What do you see? A world full of common people! All of 'em born and all of 'em going to die! Which of them has one-tenth of your good points! Or mine! Or anyone else's, as far as that goes—gosh! Everybody excels in some one thing. Some in many! [*He unconsciously glances at himself in the mirror.*] All you've got to do is discover in *what*! Take me, for instance. [*He adjusts his tie at the mirror.*] My interest happens to lie in electro-dynamics. I'm taking a course in radio engineering at night school, Laura, on top of a fairly responsible job at the warehouse. I'm taking that course and studying public speaking.

    LAURA.   Ohhhh.

    JIM.   Because I believe in the future of television! [*turning his back to her*] I wish to be ready to go up right along with it. Therefore I'm planning to get in on the ground floor. In fact I've already made the right connections and all that remains is for the industry itself to get under way! Full steam—[*His eyes are starry.*] *Knowledge*—Zzzzzp! *Money*—Zzzzzp!—Power! That's the cycle democracy is built on!

[*His attitude is convincingly dynamic. LAURA stares at him, even her shyness eclipsed in her absolute wonder. He suddenly grins.*]

I guess you think I think a lot of myself!

    LAURA.   No—o-o-o, I—

    JIM.   Now how about you? Isn't there something you take more interest in than anything else?

    LAURA.   Well, I do—as I said—have my—glass collection—

[*A peal of girlish laughter rings from the kitchenette.*]

    JIM.   I'm not right sure I know what you're talking about. What kind of glass is it?

    LAURA.   Little articles of it, they're ornaments mostly! Most of them are little animals made out of glass, the tiniest little animals in the world. Mother calls them a glass menagerie! Here's an example of one, if you'd like to see it! This one is one of the oldest. It's nearly thirteen.

[*Music:* "*The Glass Menagerie.*"

He stretches out his hand.]

Oh, be careful—if you breathe, it breaks!

JIM.   I'd better not take it. I'm pretty clumsy with things.

LAURA.   Go, on, I trust you with him! [*She places the piece in his palm.*] There now—you're holding him gently! Hold him over the light, he loves the light! You see how the light shines through him?

JIM.   It sure does shine!

LAURA.   I shouldn't be partial, but he is my favorite one.

JIM.   What kind of a thing is this one supposed to be?

LAURA.   Haven't you noticed the single horn on his forehead?

JIM.   A unicorn, huh?

LAURA.   Mmmm-hmmm!

JIM.   Unicorns—aren't they extinct in the modern world?

LAURA.   I know!

JIM.   Poor little fellow, he must feel sort of lonesome.

LAURA.   [*smiling*] Well, if he does, he doesn't complain about it. He stays on a shelf with some horses that don't have horns and all of them seem to get along nicely together.

JIM.   How do you know?

LAURA.   [*lightly*] I haven't heard any arguments among them!

JIM.   [*grinning*] No arguments, huh? Well, that's a pretty good sign! Where shall I set him?

LAURA.   Put him on the table. They all like a change of scenery once in a while!

JIM.   Well, well, well, well—[*He places the glass piece on the table, then raises his arms and stretches.*] Look how big my shadow is when I stretch!

LAURA.   Oh, oh, yes—it stretches across the ceiling!

JIM.   [*crossing to the door*] I think it's stopped raining. [*He opens the fire-escape door and the background music changes to a dance tune.*] Where does the music come from?

LAURA.   From the Paradise Dance Hall across the alley.

JIM.   How about cutting the rug a little, Miss Wingfield?

LAURA.   Oh, I—

JIM.   Or is your program filled up? Let me have a look at it. [*He grasps an imaginary card.*] Why, every dance is taken! I'll just have to scratch some out.

[*Waltz music:* "*La Golondrina*"°]

Ahh, a waltz! [*He executes some sweeping turns by himself, then holds his arms toward* LAURA.]

LAURA.   [*breathlessly*] I—can't dance.

JIM.   There you go, that inferiority stuff!

LAURA.   I've never danced in my life!

° "*La Golondrina*": a popular Mexican song (1883) written by Narciso Seradell (1843–1910).

JIM.   Come on, try!

LAURA.   Oh, but I'd step on you!

JIM.   I'm not made out of glass.

LAURA.   How—how—how do we start?

JIM.   Just leave it to me. You hold your arms out a little.

LAURA.   Like this?

JIM.   [*taking her in his arms*] A little bit higher. Right. Now don't tighten
up, that's the main thing about it—relax.

LAURA.   [*laughing breathlessly*] It's hard not to.

JIM.   Okay.

LAURA.   I'm afraid you can't budge me.

JIM.   What do you bet I can't? [*He swings her into motion.*]

LAURA.   Goodness, yes, you can!

JIM.   Let yourself go, now, Laura, just let yourself go.

LAURA.   I'm—

JIM.   Come on!

LAURA.   —trying!

JIM.   Not so stiff—easy does it!

LAURA.   I know but I'm—

JIM.   Loosen th' backbone! There now, that's a lot better.

LAURA.   Am I?

JIM.   Lots, lots better! [*He moves her about the room in a clumsy waltz.*]

LAURA.   Oh, my!

JIM.   Ha-ha!

LAURA.   Oh, my goodness!

JIM.   Ha-ha-ha!

[*They suddenly bump into the table, and the glass piece on it falls to the floor. JIM stops the
dance.*]

What did we hit?

LAURA.   Table.

JIM.   Did something fall off it? I think—

LAURA.   Yes.

JIM.   I hope that it wasn't the little glasshorse with the horn!

LAURA.   Yes. [*She stoops to pick it up.*]

JIM.   Aw, aw, aw. Is it broken?

LAURA.   Now it is just like all the other horses.

JIM.   It's lost its—

LAURA.   Horn! It doesn't matter. Maybe it's a blessing in disguise.

JIM.   You'll never forgive me. I bet that that was your favorite piece of glass.

LAURA.   I don't have favorites much. It's no tragedy, Freckles. Glass breaks
so easily. No matter how careful you are. The traffic jars the shelves and things
fall off them.

JIM.   Still I'm awfully sorry that I was the cause.

LAURA.   [*smiling*] I'll just imagine he had an operation. The horn was removed
to make him feel less—freakish!

[*They both laugh.*]

Now he will feel more at home with the other horses, the ones that don't have horns. . . .

JIM.   Ha-ha, that's very funny! [*Suddenly he is serious.*] I'm glad to see that you have a sense of humor. You know—you're—well—very different! Surprisingly different from anyone else I know! [*His voice becomes soft and hesitant with a genuine feeling.*] Do you mind me telling you that?

[*LAURA is abashed beyond speech.*]

I mean it in a nice way—

[*LAURA nods shyly, looking away.*]

You make me feel sort of—I don't know how to put it! I'm usually pretty good at expressing things, but—this is something that I don't know how to say!

[*LAURA touches her throat and clears it—turns the broken unicorn in her hands. His voice becomes softer.*]

Has anyone ever told you that you were pretty?

[*There is a pause, and the music rises slightly. LAURA looks up slowly, with wonder, and shakes her head.*]

Well, you are! In a very different way from anyone else. And all the nicer because of the difference, too.

[*His voice becomes low and husky. LAURA turns away, nearly faint with the novelty of her emotions.*]

I wish that you were my sister. I'd teach you to have some confidence in yourself. The different people are not like other people, but being different is nothing to be ashamed of. Because other people are not such wonderful people. They're one hundred times one thousand. You're one times one! They walk all over the earth. You just stay here. They're common as—weeds, but—you—well, you're—*Blue Roses*!

[*Image on screen: Blue Roses.*

The music changes.]

LAURA.   But blue is wrong for—roses. . . .
JIM.   It's right for you! You're—pretty!
LAURA.   In what respect am I pretty?
JIM.   In all respects—believe me! Your eyes—your hair—are pretty! Your hands are pretty! [*He catches hold of her hand.*] You think I'm making this up because I'm invited to dinner and have to be nice. Oh, I could do that! I could put on an act for you, Laura, and say lots of things without being very sincere. But this time I am. I'm talking to you sincerely. I happened to notice you had this inferiority complex that keeps you from feeling comfortable with people. Somebody needs to build your confidence up and make you proud instead of shy and turning away and—blushing. Somebody—ought to—*kiss* you, Laura!

[*His hand slips slowly up her arm to her shoulder as the music swells tumultuously. He suddenly turns about and kisses her on the lips. When he releases her, LAURA sinks on the sofa with a bright, dazed look. JIM backs away and fishes in his pocket for a cigarette.*

Legend on screen: "A souvenir."]

Stumblejohn!

[*He lights the cigarette, avoiding her look. There is a peal of girlish laughter from* AMANDA *in the kitchenette.* LAURA *slowly raises and opens her hand. It still contains the little broken glass animal. She looks at it with a tender, bewildered expression.*]

Stumblejohn! I shouldn't have done that—that was way off the beam. You don't smoke, do you?

[*She looks up, smiling, not hearing the question. He sits beside her rather gingerly. She looks at him speechlessly—waiting. He coughs decorously and moves a little further aside as he considers the situation and senses her feelings, dimly, with perturbation. He speaks gently.*]

Would you—care for a mint?

[*She doesn't seem to hear him but her look grows brighter even.*]

Peppermint? Life Saver? My pocket's a regular drugstore—wherever I go. . . . [*He pops a mint in his mouth. Then he gulps and decides to make a clean breast of it. He speaks slowly and gingerly.*] Laura, you know, if I had a sister like you, I'd do the same thing as Tom. I'd bring out fellows and—introduce her to them. The right type of boys—of a type to—appreciate her. Only—well—he made a mistake about me. Maybe I've got no call to be saying this. That may not have been the idea in having me over. But what if it was? There's nothing wrong about that. The only trouble is that in my case—I'm not in a situation to—do the right thing. I can't take down your number and say I'll phone. I can't call up next week and—ask for a date. I thought I had better explain the situation in case you—misunder-stood it and—I hurt your feelings. . . .

[*There is a pause. Slowly, very slowly,* LAURA'S *look changes, her eyes returning slowly from his to the glass figure in her palm.* AMANDA *utters another gay laugh in the kitchenette.*]

LAURA.   [*faintly*] You—won't—call again?

JIM.   No, Laura, I can't. [*He rises from the sofa.*] As I was just explaining, I've—got strings on me, Laura, I've—been going steady! I go out all the time with a girl named Betty. She's a home-girl like you, and Catholic, and Irish, and in a great many ways we—get along fine. I met her last summer on a moonlight boat trip up the river to Alton,° on the *Majestic.* Well—right away from the start it was—love!

[*Legend: Love!*]

LAURA *sways slightly forward and grips the arm of the sofa. He fails to notice, now enrapt in his own comfortable being.*]

Being in love has made a new man of me!

[*Leaning stiffly forward, clutching the arm of the sofa,* LAURA *struggles visibly with her storm. But* JIM *is oblivious; she is a long way off.*]

The power of love is really pretty tremendous! Love is something that—changes the whole world, Laura!

° *Alton:* a city in Illinois about twenty miles north of St. Louis on the Mississippi River.

[*The storm abates a little and LAURA leans back. He notices her again.*]

It happened that Betty's aunt took sick, she got a wire and had to go to Centralia.° So Tom—when he asked me to dinner—I naturally just accepted the invitation, not knowing that you—that he—that I—[*He stops awkwardly.*] Huh—I'm a stumblejohn!

[*He flops back on the sofa. The holy candles on the altar of LAURA'S face have been snuffed out. There is a look of almost infinite desolation. JIM glances at her uneasily.*]

I wish that you would—say something.

[*She bites her lip which was trembling and then bravely smiles. She opens her hand again on the broken glass figure. Then she gently takes his hand and raises it level with her own. She carefully places the unicorn in the palm of his hand, then pushes his fingers closed upon it.*]

What are you—doing that for? You want me to have him? Laura?

[*She nods.*]

What for?

LAURA. A—souvenir. . . .

[*She rises unsteadily and crouches beside the Victrola to wind it up.*]

Legend on screen: "Things have a way of turning out so badly!" Or image: "Gentleman caller waving goodbye—gaily."

At this moment AMANDA rushes brightly back into the living room. She bears a pitcher of fruit punch in an old-fashioned cut-glass pitcher, and a plate of macaroons. The plate has a gold border and poppies painted on it.]

AMANDA. Well, well, well! Isn't the air delightful after the shower? I've made you children a little liquid refreshment. [*She turns gaily to JIM.*] Jim, do you know that song about lemonade?
"Lemonade, lemonade
Made in the shade and stirred with a spade—
Good enough for any old maid!"
JIM. [*uneasily*] Ha-ha! No—I never heard it.
AMANDA. Why, Laura! You look so serious!
JIM. We were having a serious conversation.
AMANDA. Good! Now you're better acquainted!
JIM. [*uncertainly*] Ha-ha! Yes.
AMANDA. You modern young people are much more serious-minded than my generation. I was so gay as a girl!
JIM. You haven't changed, Mrs. Wingfield.
AMANDA. Tonight I'm rejuvenated! The gaiety of the occasion, Mr. O'Connor! [*She tosses her head with a peal of laughter, spilling some lemonade.*] Oooo! I'm baptizing myself!

° *Centralia*: A city in Illinois about sixty miles east of St. Louis.

JIM.   Here—let me—

AMANDA.   [*setting the pitcher down*] There now. I discovered we had some maraschino cherries. I dumped them in, juice and all!

JIM.   You shouldn't have gone to that trouble, Mrs. Wingfield.

AMANDA.   Trouble, trouble? Why, it was loads of fun! Didn't you hear me cutting up in the kitchen? I bet your ears were burning! I told Tom how outdone with him I was for keeping you to himself so long a time! He should have brought you over much, much sooner! Well, now that you've found your way, I want you to be a very frequent caller! Not just occasional but all the time. Oh, we're going to have a lot of gay times together! I see them coming! Mmm, just breathe that air! So fresh, and the moon's so pretty! I'll skip back out—I know where my place is when young folks are having a—serious conversation!

JIM.   Oh, don't go out, Mrs. Wingfield. The fact of the matter is I've got to be going.

AMANDA.   Going, now? You're joking! Why, it's only the shank of the evening,° Mr. O'Connor!

JIM.   Well, you know how it is.

AMANDA.   You mean you're a young workingman and have to keep working-men's hours. We'll let you off early tonight. But only on the condition that next time you stay later. What's the best night for you? Isn't Saturday night the best night for you workingmen?

JIM.   I have a couple of time-clocks to punch, Mrs. Wingfield. One at morning, another one at night!

AMANDA.   My, but you *are* ambitious! You work at night, too?

JIM.   No, Ma'am, not work but—Betty!

[*He crosses deliberately to pick up his hat. The band at the Paradise Dance Hall goes into a tender waltz.*]

AMANDA.   Betty? Betty? Who's—Betty!

[*There is an ominous cracking sound in the sky.*]

JIM.   Oh, just a girl. The girl I go steady with!

[*He smiles charmingly. The sky falls.*

Legend: "The Sky Falls."]

AMANDA.   [*a long-drawn exhalation*] Ohhh . . . Is it a serious romance, Mr. O'Connor?

JIM.   We're going to be married the second Sunday in June.

AMANDA.   Ohhh—how nice! Tom didn't mention that you were engaged to be married.

JIM.   The cat's not out of the bag at the warehouse yet. You know how they are. They call you Romeo and stuff like that. [*He stops at the oval mirror to put on his hat. He carefully shapes the brim and the crown to give a discreetly dashing effect.*] It's been a wonderful evening, Mrs. Wingfield. I guess this is what they mean by Southern hospitality.

° *shank of the evening*: still early, the best part of the evening.

AMANDA.   It really wasn't anything at all.

JIM.   I hope it don't seem like I'm rushing off. But I promised Betty I'd pick her up at the Wabash depot, an' by the time I get my jalopy down there her train'll be in. Some women are pretty upset if you keep 'em waiting.

AMANDA.   Yes, I know—the tyranny of women! [*She extends her hand.*] Goodbye, Mr. O'Connor. I wish you luck—and happiness—and success! All three of them, and so does Laura! Don't you, Laura?

LAURA.   Yes!

JIM.   [*taking LAURA'S hand*] Goodbye, Laura. I'm certainly going to treasure that souvenir. And don't you forget the good advice I gave you. [*He raises his voice to a cheery shout.*] So long, Shakespeare! Thanks again, ladies. Good night!

[*He grins and ducks jauntily out. Still bravely grimacing, AMANDA closes the door on the gentleman caller. Then she turns back to the room with a puzzled expression. She and LAURA don't dare to face each other. LAURA crouches beside the Victrola to wind it.*]

AMANDA.   [*faintly*] Things have a way of turning out so badly. I don't believe that I would play the Victrola. Well, well—well! Our gentleman caller was engaged to be married? [*She raises her voice.*] Tom!

TOM.   [*from the kitchenette*] Yes, Mother?

AMANDA.   Come in here a minute. I want to tell you something awfully funny.

TOM.   [*entering with a macaroon and a glass of the lemonade*] Has the gentleman caller gotten away already?

AMANDA.   The gentleman caller has made an early departure. What a wonderful joke you played on us!

TOM.   How do you mean?

AMANDA.   You didn't mention that he was engaged to be married.

TOM.   Jim? Engaged?

AMANDA.   That's what he just informed us.

TOM.   I'll be jiggered! I didn't know about that.

AMANDA.   That seems very peculiar.

TOM.   What's peculiar about it?

AMANDA.   Didn't you call him your best friend down at the warehouse?

TOM.   He is, but how did I know?

AMANDA.   It seems extremely peculiar that you wouldn't know your best friend was going to be married!

TOM.   The warehouse is where I work, not where I know things about people!

AMANDA.   You don't know things anywhere! You live in a dream; you manufacture illusions!

[*He crosses to the door.*]

Where are you going?

TOM.   I'm going to the movies.

AMANDA.   That's right, now that you've had us make such fools of ourselves. The effort, the preparations, all the expense! The new floor lamp, the rug, the clothes for Laura! All for what? To entertain some other girl's fiancé! Go to the movies, go! Don't think about us, a mother deserted, an unmarried sister who's crippled and has no job! Don't let anything interfere with your selfish pleasure! Just go, go, go—to the movies!

TOM. All right, I will! The more you shout about my selfishness to me the quicker I'll go, and I won't go to the movies!

AMANDA.   Go, then! Go to the moon—you selfish dreamer!

[*TOM smashes his glass on the floor. He plunges out on the fire escape, slamming the door. LAURA screams in fright. The dance-hall music becomes louder. TOM stands on the fire escape, gripping the rail. The moon breaks through the storm clouds, illuminating his face.*

Legend on screen: "And so goodbye. . ."

TOM'S closing speech is timed with what is happening inside the house. We see, as though through soundproof glass, that AMANDA appears to be making a comforting speech to LAURA, who is huddled upon the sofa. Now that we cannot hear the mother's speech, her silliness is gone and she has dignity and tragic beauty. LAURA'S hair hides her face until, at the end of the speech, she lifts her head to smile at her mother. AMANDA'S gestures are slow and graceful, almost dancelike, as she comforts her daughter. At the end of her speech she glances a moment at the father's picture—then withdraws through the portieres. At the close of TOM'S speech, LAURA blows out the candles, ending the play.]

TOM.   I didn't go to the moon, I went much further—for time is the longest distance between two places. Not long after that I was fired for writing a poem on the lid of a shoe-box. I left Saint Louis. I descended the steps of this fire escape for a last time and followed, from then on, in my father's footsteps, attempting to find in motion what was lost in space. I traveled around a great deal. The cities swept about me like dead leaves, leaves that were brightly colored but torn away from the branches. I would have stopped, but I was pursued by something. It always came upon me unawares, taking me altogether by surprise. Perhaps it was a familiar bit of music. Perhaps it was only a piece of transparent glass. Perhaps I am walking along a street at night, in some strange city, before I have found companions. I pass the lighted window of a shop where perfume is sold. The window is filled with pieces of colored glass, tiny transparent bottles in delicate colors, like bits of a shattered rainbow. Then all at once my sister touches my shoulder. I turn around and look into her eyes. Oh, Laura, Laura, I tried to leave you behind me, but I am more faithful than I intended to be! I reach for a cigarette, I cross the street, I run into the movies or a bar, I buy a drink, I speak to the nearest stranger—anything that can blow your candles out!

[*LAURA bends over the candles.*]

For nowadays the world is lit by lightning! Blow out your candles, Laura— and so goodbye . . . .

[*She blows the candles out.*]

QUESTIONS

1. What does the setting described in the opening stage direction tell you about the Wingfields? Consider especially the adjectives Williams employs and the symbolism of the alley and the fire escape.

2. Who is the "fifth character" in the play and how is his presence established? In what ways is Tom a parallel to this character?

3. What does Amanda reveal about her past in scene 1? How does Williams reveal that Amanda often dwells on the past?

4. What happened to Laura at Rubicam's Business College? How can you account for her behavior? What plan of Amanda's did she upset?

5. What new plan for Laura's future does Amanda begin to develop in scene 2? Why is the plan impracticable? Why is the image of Jim introduced here?

6. Summarize the argument between Tom and Amanda in scene 3. What does Amanda assert about Tom? What does he claim about his life? Why is Laura spotlighted throughout the argument?

7. What sort of agreement does Amanda try to reach with Tom about Laura in scene 4?

8. What distinction between Europe and America does the narrator make in scene 5? How is the song playing at the Paradise Dance Hall ironic?

9. Which character seems to have a more accurate and realistic understanding of Laura in scene 5? Why?

10. How does Amanda react to the news of a gentleman caller? How does Laura react? What happens when Laura discovers the caller's identity? Why?

11. Describe Laura's feelings toward Jim during the conversation and the dancing in scene 7. Describe his feelings toward her. How and why do his feelings change after the kiss?

12. Explain the symbolism of the unicorn (both whole and broken). Why does Laura give it to Jim as a souvenir?

13. What is Tom's situation at the close of the play? To what degree has he achieved his dreams of escape and adventure?

14. Describe Amanda's and Laura's situations at the close of the play. What is the significance of Laura's blowing out the candles? What future can you predict for these women? Why?

TOPICS FOR WRITING AND FURTHER DISCUSSION

1. What are the most striking nonrealistic aspects of the play? Explain why each is nonrealistic and how each contributes to the impact and meaning of the play. Which is the most effective? Why?

2. The screen device (described on page 1566) is omitted from most productions of this play. Consider the advantages (or disadvantages) of including it in the published text. What is its effect as you read the play? Did you find it helpful, convincing, distracting, annoying? Why? Do you think it would be effective in production? Why or why not?

3. Each of the Wingfields seeks to escape the harsh realities of existence in a different way. Discuss the method each uses.

4. Which character do you consider the protaganist of the play? Why? How might a case be made supporting the claims of each of the Wingfields? What specific details support the case for each?

5. Consider the distinction between Tom as a character and as narrator. How and why is the language of the narrator different from that of the character? What does the character dream about and strive for? What has the narrator learned about these dreams and strivings?

6. As the title suggests, Laura and her fantasy world are central to the play. Explain the reasons for Laura's inability to deal with reality. What is the significance of her glass menagerie?

7. Williams says that there is much to admire, pity, and laugh at in Amanda. What aspects of her character are admirable? Pitiable? Laughable? Which reaction is dominant for you at the close of the play? Why?

8. In his opening speech, Tom calls Jim "the most realistic character in the play." In what ways is Jim realistic? How are his dreams and goals more (or less) realistic than Tom's?

9. Discuss the ideas about family life, poverty, personality, and the ability to escape from the past explored in this play.

10. At the opening of the play, Tom (as narrator) mentions the "social background," and he remarks on it throughout. Discuss this background, especially the events occurring in Europe, and the ways it relates to the play's action.

11. Investigate Williams's use of symbolism in the play. Which characters are symbolic? Which places? Objects? Actions? What does each symbolize?

12. Discuss the line of religious allusion and imagery that runs through the play. Consider especially Malvolio the Magician, "Ave Maria," "Annunciation," the Paradise Dance Hall, and Laura's candles.

13. Do you consider this play a comedy, tragedy, or something in between? Which characters, if any, learn or change in significant ways? To what extent do the characters succeed or fail in the goals they set for themselves?

WRITING ABOUT REALISTIC AND NONREALISTIC DRAMA

In planning and writing an essay about a realistic or nonrealistic play, your attention will naturally be focused on the traditional elements of drama—plot, character, perspective, setting, language, tone, symbol, and theme. Conventional approaches to these were discussed earlier (pp. 1112–15); you may want to review this material. You will also be concerned, however, with the relative degrees of realism or nonrealism with which the elements are presented and developed, and the ways in which this variable affects the impact and meaning of the play.

You will be dealing with four related areas of exploration for this type of essay: (1) the elements or aspects of the play that you find most interesting, significant, and effective; (2) the feelings, ideas, and effects created or emphasized through these features; (3) the degree to which these elements or aspects may be considered realistic (or nonrealistic); and (4) the extent to which the impact or meaning of the play depends on the realism or nonrealism of the elements under consideration. The introduction of a new variable into your planning—the spectrum of realism and its impact on the play—thus creates some new ways in which you might look at the traditional elements. The following can only begin to suggest some of these.

1. *Plot*. Evaluate the relative realism or nonrealism of the plot, structure, action, and conflicts. Does the play unfold in a chronological order that imitates reality, or does it mix past and present action in any way? Is the action true to life or stylized? Are the conflicts resolved realistically, or does the playwright employ a conventional and perhaps improbable happy (or sad) ending? How does the realistic or nonrealistic development of these aspects affect the impact and meaning of the play?

2. *Character*. Are the characters presented and developed in a predominantly realistic manner? Are they symbolic, representative, or stereotyped? Round or flat? Are they motivated by lifelike considerations, or simply by the requirements of the play? In *The Glass Menagerie*, for example, Amanda's motivations are entirely realistic, but the narrator is motivated only through the theatrical demand that he speak to the audience or reader. Are the characters consistent, or do they drop in and out of character? Is their clothing and makeup (as described in the stage directions) an imitation of real life, or is it blatantly theatrical and nonrealistic? Are all the characters in the play developed in the same manner, or are there differences in the degree of realism you find in each? Is there one character who is remarkably more or less realistic than any of the others? If so, what impact does this have on the play?

3. *Perspective*. In realistic drama, the perspective or point of view tends to be completely objective; that is finally the goal of the picture-frame stage and the principle of the missing fourth wall. Characters never reveal their thoughts or emotions directly to us, and they never speak to us about other characters. Consequently, it is almost impossible to impose anything but an objective point of view on a realistic play. One of the few ways to impose a more subjective point of view is to give all or most of the lines to a single character; Eugene O'Neill uses such a device in *Before Breakfast* (p. 1061). When you encounter such a play, consider why the character is given most of the dialogue and how the device shapes or distorts your perception of the play. In nonrealistic drama, the playwright has the freedom to unfold the play through whatever perspective he or she chooses. In such a case, you might consider which characters speak directly to the audience or the reader. How extensive is such direct address? Is there a single character who does most of this talking? If so, what is he or she like? What does the character tell you about himself or herself? About the other characters in the play? The background? Plot? Action? Setting? Staging? How accurate and objective is this character? Above all else, how does this direct address shape and control your response to the play?

4. *Setting*. You might investigate the degree to which the setting is presented as realistic or nonrealistic in the stage directions. Do the playwright's directions call for the reproduction of an actual room or place in minute detail, or are such realistic touches stripped away? If less than a fully realistic setting is described, how far does the playwright go in reducing the setting to the bare stage? How much of the physical theater (brick walls, pipes, wires, lights, backstage ropes) does the playwright indicate that he or she wants you to see or imagine? To what extent do you find symbolic, impressionistic and nonrealistic devices such as transparent walls? Most important, how does the setting and its degree of realism (or nonrealism) contribute to the impact and meaning of the play? As you evaluate the setting, you might also explore other aspects of staging and presentation, as described in the stage directions, that can determine the relative realism of a play. How is lighting employed? Is it used realistically, to recreate the natural illumination in a room, or nonrealistically, to isolate and emphasize specific places, objects, characters, or actions?

5. *Language*. When you are considering language, look carefully at the diction, style, and patterns of the dialogue. Is the language colloquial and appropriate for the characters, or do you find nonrealistic devices such as verse, song, or unnatural and patterned repetition? In *A Doll's House*, for example, the dialogue is consistently imitative of real life, but in *The Sandbox* we find inarticulate noises, strings of clichés, and massive amounts of repetition. Does each character maintain a consistent style and level or diction, or do you find a single character speaking in different voices? How do these aspects of language determine the extent to which the play effectively communicates ideas and emotions to you? As you deal with language, you might also consider the significance of other aspects of sound that are indicated in the stage directions, such as realistic sound effects or music (like the phonograph records in *The Glass Menagerie*) or external and nonrealistic music (such as the theme in *Menagerie* or the singing in musical comedy).

6. *Symbolism*. This is one of the few elements that tend to work in the same manner whether the play is highly realistic, nonrealistic, or something in between. Since symbols can operate in life as they do in art, there is room for symbolism in the realistic plays of Glaspell and Ibsen as well as in the relatively nonrealistic dramas of Miller and Williams. Nevertheless, the investigation of symbolism can be linked to considerations of realism because symbols may be introduced through realistic or nonrealistic techniques. In the first instance, you can focus your exploration directly on the symbol and its meaning. In dealing with the Christmas tree or the locked mailbox in *A Doll's House*, for example, you might plan a straightforward discussion of the object and its significance. In the second instance, however, you should investigate not only the symbol and its meaning, but also the nonrealistic methods through which it is established. Such

an exploration might focus on the lighted photograph of the long-absent father or the image of the blue roses in *The Glass Menagerie*.

7. *Theme*. The exploration of theme in realistic and nonrealistic drama, as in all drama, seeks to identify important concepts in the play *and* the ways in which they are conveyed. Here, however, you should give special consideration to significantly realistic or nonrealistic techniques that the playwright employs to develop his or her themes. In dealing with a realistic play like *Trifles* or *A Doll's House*, you might explore the ways in which realism in character, action, and setting contribute to the emergence of the play's ideas. Conversely, you might consider how Williams employs a strikingly nonrealistic device, such as the music or the screen projections, to convey and emphasize the themes of *The Glass Menagerie*.

Once you have investigated all these areas, created a set of working notes, and narrowed your focus to a specific group of elements and effects, you can begin to plan the essay in more detail. At this point you can formulate a tentative central idea and start to organize the supporting details. The central idea must assert a connection between specifically realistic or nonrealistic elements and their effect on part or all of the play. A simple statement that this or that device is realistic (or not realistic) will not suffice; it is inadequate to assert as a central idea that "Nora is a realistic character" or that "Tom is a nonrealistic character." Such descriptive formulations offer no assertion on which to build an effective essay. A better formulation would link Nora's realistic character or Tom's nonrealistic one to a sequent effect. In working on an essay about Tom, for example, you might tentatively assert: "The development of Tom as a nonrealistic narrator and realistic character unifies *The Glass Menagerie* and gives the play a coherent and subjective point of view." Although such a formulation will need a great deal of revision, it will provide the basis for an assertive essay.

The central idea may change many times as you evaluate the nature and the implications of your supporting evidence. Organize your notes into logical units; these will become the essay's central paragraphs. This material should be constantly reevaluated to ensure that it supports your ideas in the most convincing and relevant ways possible.

Organizing Your Essay

INTRODUCTION. As in most other cases, the introduction should provide an overview and a guide to the essay. You might begin with a general statement that establishes the author, title, and dominant style of the play. The most important aspects of the introduction, however, are the central idea and the thesis or topic sentence. The central idea will normally assert a connection between a specific aspect of the play, its relative realism or nonrealism, and the impact or effect it produces. The thesis sentence should enumerate the topics that the essay will take up to support the central idea.

Body. The body of the essay provides the supporting details and arguments that validate your central idea. This material may be organized in any fashion that produces a logical and convincing essay. If you deal with several topics, you can treat them in sequence. If you are writing about the ways in which nonrealistic devices emphasize meaning in *The Glass Menagerie*, for example, you might treat the setting, the lighting, and the screen device in a series of paragraphs. When the essay focuses on just one element, you may organize your supporting details to reflect the order in which they occur in the play.

Conclusion. The concluding paragraph should bring the essay to an assertive and convincing close. A summary of your major points is always appropriate here. You might also raise larger issues or make broader connections about the topics you discussed and the play as a whole. Finally, this is a good place to reconsider the plays' general level of realistic or nonrealistic techniques, and the impact it creates.

SAMPLE ESSAY

Realism and Nonrealism in Tom's Triple Role in "The Glass Menagerie"*

[1] In *The Glass Menagerie*, Tennessee Williams combines realistic and nonrealistic elements to explore the personalities and conflicts of the Wingfield family. One of the most effective nonrealistic elements in the play is Williams's use of Tom in three different roles to unify the play thematically and to provide a subjective and overall perspective.° As realistic character within the action, nonrealistic stage manager of the action, and nonrealistic narrator of the entire play, Tom combines three functions that significantly shape our perception of the drama.▫

[2] As a realistic character involved in the recollected action of the play, Tom is ensnared by the economic and emotional demands of his family and his job. In the opening description of the characters, Williams defines Tom as trapped when he notes that "To escape from a trap he [Tom] has to act without pity." In addition, the character repeatedly expresses his feelings of entrapment and the need to escape from his dull, drab life. He discusses these things with his mother in scene 3, Laura in scene 4, and, above all, with Jim in scene 6. Here, we see that Tom craves escape and adventure. He tells Jim, "I'm

* See p. 1565 for this play.
° Central idea.
▫ Thesis sentence.

planning a change." And he clearly expresses his desire to move out of the prison house of the family:

> It's our turn now, to go the South Sea Island—to make a safari—to be exotic, far off! But I'm not patient. I don't want to wait till then. I'm tired of the *movies* and I am *about* to *move*! . . . . I'm starting to boil inside. I know I seem dreamy, but inside—well, I'm boiling.   (p. 1599)

As this passage indicates, Tom as a character repeatedly directs us to one of the central ideas in the play—the need to escape. His strivings thus define a major line of thought and action in *The Glass Menagerie*.

[3] Tom's realism as a character is deeply undercut by his momentary role as a stage manager in scene 1. Here, he speaks with Amanda "as though reading from a script." In this same scene, "TOM motions for music and a spot of light on AMANDA." Although this device is quickly abandoned, the image of Tom holding an imaginary script and giving cues to the musicians and the lighting technicians has a sharp and profound effect on our perception of the action. For one thing, the device breaks the illusion of the play as an imitation of real life and reminds us that what we are reading about or watching is a stage with actors on it. More important, it suggests that Tom controls and directs the entire action.

[4] Tom's part in shaping and unifying the play becomes most explicit in his blatantly nonrealistic function as narrator. In this role, he stands completely outside the action occurring in the Wingfield apartment and speaks directly to us; he introduces the characters, provides background, and supplies an ongoing retrospective commentary on the dramatized events. Most important, Tom's role as narrator provides for thematic unity and imposes a subjective and overriding perspective on the action. In achieving the first of these two central functions, the narrator articulates truths that the character has not yet learned. As a character, Tom strives for freedom and adventure. As narrator, however, he recognizes that escape from the past is impossible. At the close of the play, he tells us that he remains trapped, even as he wanders through the streets of strange cities:

> Then all at once my sister touches my shoulder. I turn around and look into her eyes. Oh, Laura, Laura, I tried to leave you behind me, but I am more faithful than I intended to be!   (p. 1617)

The narrator, unlike the character, understands that the past will always be present; he thus provides a final perspective on the central theme of escape.

[5] The second striking aspect of Tom's function as narrator concerns his complete control of the play. Because he is the narrator, the action in *The Glass Menagerie* represents Tom's memories of events, rather than the events themselves. In his first speech, Tom tells us that "The play is memory. Being a memory play, it is dimly lighted, it is sentimental, it is not realistic." Since the events which occur on stage from the past emerge from Tom's memory,

it is he who provides an overriding unity and perspective. We see everything through his mind and from his point of view. Tom as a nonrealistic narrator thus holds the central stage action together and shapes our response to everything we experience.

[6]   Williams thus uses Tom in three distinct ways to create unity and perspective. As a realistic character, Tom embodies the theme of escape. As a nonrealistic stage manager and narrator, he offers thematic resolution, controls the action, and imposes a coherent and subjective point of view. The nonrealistic aspects of his roles mesh perfectly with other devices that Williams employs nonrealistically, especially the music and lighting. This coming together of nonrealistic devices is perfectly captured in that single moment early in the play when Tom, as stage manager, explicitly controls both the lighting and the music.

Commentary on the Essay

This essay takes on a great deal; it discusses theme and perspective or point of view as they are shaped by Tom's various roles in *The Glass Menagerie*. The primary focus is on character, but a number of distinct topics are taken up in connection with this single element because the essay concerns Tom as a character, stage director, and narrator.

The introductory paragraph supplies an overview of the essay. The first sentence provides the title, identifies the author, and makes a general but relevant observation about the play. The second states the central idea; it isolates a specific element (character), identifies it as nonrealistic, and asserts an effect (unity and perspective) that the element produces. The thesis or topic sentence lists the three aspects of Tom's role that the essay will investigate.

The body of the essay (paragraphs 2–5) takes up these three roles in the order in which they are listed in the introduction. Notice that this order does not reflect the sequence in which these occur in the play. Rather, they are organized to reflect a progression from the most realistic to the most nonrealistic aspects of Tom's three different functions. Thus, paragraph 2 discusses Tom as a realistic character and connects him to one of the play's central themes—entrapment and the desire to escape.

Paragraph 3 shifts to a consideration of Tom as stage manager. It explains why such a role is nonrealistic and explores the effects produced by such a nonrealistic figure in the play. Similarly, paragraphs 4 and 5 discuss Tom as narrator. Again, the essay establishes why such a role is nonrealistic and how the role affects our perceptions of the play. Paragraph 4 also returns to the thematic concerns of paragraph 2, while paragraph 5 returns to the issues of control and perspective raised in connection with Tom as stage manager. Throughout the body, direct quotation of dialogue or action as indicated in the stage directions is employed as supporting evidence. Quotation is used sparingly, but when it does occur, it has the effect of validating a specific point.

The conclusion of the essay provides a review-summary of the three roles that Tom plays and the effects that each produces in connection with theme, unity, and perspective. In addition, it suggests a connection between the nonrealistic aspects of Tom's roles and other elements of the play that Williams employs nonrealistically and to good effect.

Appendix A:
Evaluating Literature

Evaluation means the act of deciding what is good, bad, or mediocre. It requires a steady pursuit of the best—to be satisfied with less is to deny the best efforts of our greatest writers. Evaluation implies that there are ideal standards of excellence by which decisions about quality can be made, but it must be remembered that these standards are flexible, and may be applicable to works of literature written in all places and ages.

An evaluation is different from an essay on what you might like or dislike in a work (see Chapter 1, pp 61–69). While your preferences are important in your evaluation, they are not as important as your judgment, and your judgment may lead you into positions that seem contrary to your preferences. In other words, it is possible to grant the excellence of a work or writer that you personally may not like.

This claim is not as contradictory as it may at first seem, for perceptions about literary works constantly change. You may have found that works others judge as good do not seem good to you. If such has been the case, you should try to live with the work for a time. You will learn to understand and like a good work of art when you give it enough time. If, however, you find that despite prolonged exposure to the work, you still do not concur in the general favorable judgment, be as certain as you can that your reaction is based on rational and logically defensible grounds.

STANDARDS FOR EVALUATION

There is no precise answer to the problem of how to justify an evaluation. Evaluation is the most abstract, philosophical, and difficult writing you will do about literature. Standards of taste, social mores, and even morals differ from society to society and age to age; nonetheless, some works of art have been judged as great by generation after generation in many cultures. There are many standards to help you evaluate a literary work. Some of the major ones are described below, and many have been suggested in earlier chapters.

Truth

Although *truth* or *truthful* is often used in speaking of literature to mean *realism* or *realistic*, its meaning here is carefully restricted. To speak of the truth is to imply generality and universality. Let us take a concrete illustration.

Sophocles' *Oedipus the King*, one of the oldest works included in this anthology, has survived the turbulence of almost 2,500 years. It concerns a society that no longer exists (the ancient Greek city-state); it deals with a religious belief that is no longer credible (that the gods punish people for the sins of their ruler). How, then, may *Oedipus the King* be considered true, as true for our age as it was for the Athenians of 2,500 years ago?

The answer lies within the constant dilemma that Oedipus faces. His actions have consequences beyond either his intention or his control; he unintentionally causes death and harm to those whom he loves and has sworn to protect. He must therefore judge accurately and responsibly even when he is forced to pronounce his own guilt and then to punish himself. His dilemma, and the suffering inevitable for him and for any other persons confronted with similarly difficult or impossible situations, is one that human beings have always faced. Moreover, the dilemma will continue as long as people exist in groups and states. In short, *Oedipus the King* embodies and comments on one of the great *truths* of human life. It measures up to one standard we use in deciding whether a work of art is good or bad, great or mediocre.

Affirmativeness

Affirmativeness means here that human beings are worth caring about and writing about, no matter how debased the condition in which they live or how totally they abuse their state. All art should be affirmative. Although many works apparently say "no" to life, most say "yes," and a good argument can be made that the "no" works indirectly present a "yes." Thus, if a character like Willie Loman falls to the depths of misfortune and death, the author must demonstrate that there is a loss of some sort worth lamenting. Human worth is here affirmed even as a major character is destroyed. If a character is happy at the end of the work, the author must show that this character's qualities have justified such good fortune. Life is again affirmed. If an unworthy character is fortunate at the end, the author still affirms human worth by suggesting a world in which such worth may become triumphant. In short, authors may portray the use and abuse of life, the love and the hate, the heights and the depths, but their vision is always that life is valuable and worthy of respect and dignity. The best works are those that make this affirmation forcefully, without being platitudinous or didactic.

"The Joint Force and Full Result of All"

Alexander Pope discusses literary evaluation at length in *The Essay on Criticism*. He insists that a critic should not judge a work simply by its parts but should judge the *whole*—"the joint force and full result of all." You can profit from Pope's wisdom. You should consider the total effect of the work, both as an artistic form and as a cause of impressions and emotions in yourself. Bear in mind that a great work may contain imperfections, but if the sum total of the work is impressive, the flaws assume minor importance.

By the same token, excellent technique in itself does not justify a claim for excellence. An interesting plot, a balanced and carefully handled structure, a touching love story, a valid or important moral—none of these attributes alone can support a total judgment of "good" unless everything in the work is balanced.

Another important phase of the "joint force and full result of all" is the way in which you become involved as you read. Most of what you read, if it has merit, will cause you to become emotionally involved with the characters and actions. You have perhaps observed that characters in some works seem real to you or that incidents are described so vividly that you feel as though you had witnessed them. In these cases you were experiencing the pleasure of involvement. The problem here is whether your pleasure was fleeting and momentary or whether it has assumed more permanence.

Closely integrated with the idea of involvement is the Aristotelian theory of *purgation* or *catharsis* in tragedy (see also p. 1123). How do you regard the character of Hamlet when he sends Rosencrantz and Guildenstern off to death or when he finally kills Claudius? How do you feel about Oedipus in light of the fact that he actually did kill his own father? Both Shakespeare and Sophocles cause you to become involved with both heroes, and when they are involved in anything evil your own conscience causes you to wish they could have led more quiet lives. The result, when the plays are over, is a "purgation" of your emotions; that is, if you experience these plays well, you will also have experienced an emotional "drain." You can see that the use to which a writer puts your involvement is important in your judgment of his or her works.

Vitality

A good work of literature has a life of its own and can be compared to a human being. A work can grow in the sense that your repeated experience with it will produce insights that you did not have in your previous readings. Examples of such works are poems like Shakespeare's sonnets and Gray's "Elegy Written in a Country Churchyard," stories like Poe's "The Masque of the Red Death" and Jackson's "The Lottery," and plays like Sophocles' *Oedipus the King* and Molière's *The Misanthrope*. Readers and critics alike constantly find new insights and beauties in these works.

Beauty

Beauty is closely allied with unity, symmetry, harmony, and proportion. To discover the relationship of parts to whole—their logical and chronological and associational functions within the work—is to perceive beauty in a work. In the eighteenth century people believed that "variety within order" constituted beauty; the extent to which Pope's couplets vary within the pattern of the neoclassic couplet is an illustration of this ideal. The Romantic and post-Romantic periods held that beauty could be found only through greater freedom. This belief in freedom has produced such characteristics of modern literature as originality for its own sake, experimentation in verse and prose forms, freedom of syntax, stream-of-consciousness narration, and personal diction. Despite the apparent change of emphasis, however, the concepts of unity and proportion are still valid and applicable. Studies of style, structure, point of view, tone, and imagery are therefore all means to the goal of determining whether works are beautiful. Any one of these studies is an avenue toward evaluation. Remember, however, that an excellence in any one of them does not make a work excellent.

WRITING AN EVALUATION ESSAY

Organizing Your Essay

In your essay you will attempt to answer the question of whether the work you have studied is good or not. If so, why? If not, why not? The grounds for your evaluation must be artistic. Although some works may be good pieces of political argument, or successfully controversial, your goal is to judge them as works of art.

INTRODUCTION. In the introduction you can briefly summarize your evaluation, which will be your central idea, and list the points by which you expect to demonstrate the validity of your assessment. To assist your reader's comprehension of your ideas, you should note any unique facts or background about the work you are evaluating.

BODY. In the body demonstrate the grounds for your judgment; your principal points will be the positive or negative features of the work you are evaluating. Positive features include qualities of style, idea, structure, character, logic, point of view, and so on. Your discussion will analyze the probability, truth, force, or power with which the work embodies these positive aspects.

Avoid analysis for its own sake, and do not merely retell stories. If you are showing the excellence or deficiency of a character protrayal, you can include a description of the character, but remember that your discussion is to be pointed toward *evaluation*, not *description*. Therefore you must select details for discussion that will illustrate whether the work is good or bad. Similarly, if you are evaluating a sonnet of Shakespeare, you might argue that the superb imagery contributes to the general excellence. At this point you might introduce some of the imagery, but your purpose is not to analyze imagery as such; it should be used only for illustration. If you remember to keep your thematic purpose foremost, you should have little difficulty in making your discussion relate to your central idea.

CONCLUSION. The conclusion should be a statement on the total result of the work you are evaluating. Your concern here is with total impressions. This part of evaluation should reemphasize your central idea.

SAMPLE ESSAY

An Evaluation of "The Chaser,"* by John Collier

[1] Collier's "The Chaser" contrasts the dreams of youth with the cynicism of age. Because cynicism is dominant at the end, the story might be considered too negative, too bleak, and it might be criticized for this reason. To dismiss "The Chaser" without further thought, however, would be hasty; a careful reading shows that the story has genuine merit.° While a case may be made that the story is cynical and negative, a better case is that it is satirical and positive, demonstrating a corresponding excellence of technique.□

* See p. 278 for this story.
° Central Idea
□ Thesis Sentence

[2] The reason for considering "The Chaser" negatively as only a grim joke is the mistaken judgment that the old man has great wisdom along with his cynicism. It is true that he has seen people such as Alan Austen before. They have come to him wanting to make their sweethearts love them passionately, completely, worshipfully, and dependently. For such young people, the old man keeps a supply of inexpensive but infallible love potion. Beyond this, when they grow older and become tired of their potion-induced love, the old man also keeps an expensive and also infallible supply of untraceable poison— the "glove cleaner" or "life cleaner." The concluding words of the old man, "Au revoir," ("until we meet again"), indicate his knowledge that Austen will return someday for the poison. This cynicism, while justified in the light of Austen's character, seems too jarring a contrast to the enthusiasm of Austen's current passion for his lady, Diana. If the story were to do no more than show that young love ended in boredom and hatred, it would indeed be totally negative, and therefore would deserve to be dismissed.

While one may grant that the old man's judgment is right, and that Austen will grow discontented with the woman he now most enjoys, it by no means follows that "The Chaser" is bad literature. In fact, the story should be seen positively as a satirical attack on the shortsightedness of Austen and of the view that he represents. The old man tantalizes Austen with the following description of the love he is seeking:

[3] "For indifference," said the old man, "they [the scornful love objects] substitute devotion. For scorn, adoration. Give one tiny measure of this to the young lady—its flavour is imperceptible in orange juice, soup, or cocktails—and however gay and giddy she is, she will change altogether. She will want nothing but solitude and you."

This description suggests not love but enslavement—a fawning devotion that dehumanizes the woman and also makes a monster of the man who expects or demands such attention for himself. The old man's foreknowledge of Austen's eventual return demonstrates the depravity of this misinterpretation of love as total possessiveness. Rather than being held up as a typical, model young man, in other words, Collier satirically shows Austen as one who is corrupt right from the start.

[4] The technique of the story is geared toward this satirical revelation of Austen's weakness and shortsightedness. After the first few paragraphs of exposition to make the situation clear, Collier develops the rest of the story using a dramatic point of view. There is no sympathetic voice explaining Austen's emotions. Instead, Austen speaks for himself, revealing his own flawed, shallow character while the old man plays the cynical, grimly insinuating game of salesmanship upon him. Because Collier gives the old man much of the dialogue, with Austen's words being mainly in response, Austen is unable to speak of any warm personal relationships, even if he were able to conceive of them. Instead, the talk is all of control and possession. In this way Collier uses technique to reveal Austen's shortcomings, and therefore to rule him out as a complete human being. The truth that Collier is stressing is symbolized by the old man's "glove cleaner," which represents the demeaning and destructive nature of the master-slave bond that Austen so earnestly seeks.

[5]   On balance, therefore, the story is a good one. As a satire, it is more affirmative than it may at first seem, for the positive basis against which Austen and the old man should be measured is a humanized love relationship entered into freely by equals. The bonding in such a relationship is not one of master-slave, but is instead one of mututal consent. Fidelity is freely given and is not extracted either by force, like that produced by the potion Austen comes to buy, or expectation. Through this means of satirical contrast, Collier's dramatic rendering of character and his attack on possessiveness make "The Chaser" true and affirmative. "The Chaser" is a fine and memorable story.

Commentary on the Essay

    The strategy of this evaluative essay is to use an apparent weakness of Collier's "The Chaser" as the basis of an argument asserting the strength and quality of the story. The logic of the essay is that the value of Collier's work may be found in his use of satire. The essay therefore demonstrates the principle that all aspects of a work should be considered when one is making an evaluation. Although a number of ideas and techniques are considered in the essay, these are not used as ends in themselves, but instead are introduced as evidence in the argument for the merits of the story.

    Paragraph 1, the introductory paragraph, brings up the issue that the story might be dismissed after no more than a hasty reading; it also asserts the need for an evaluation based on more thought. The points to be developed in the body are stressed in the thesis sentence.

    In the body of the essay, paragraph 2 deals with the uncritical, hasty reading that would make the story seem intolerably negative. The strategy here is one of concession, namely, that if the old man were to be considered authoritative, the story would be generally untrue, and would be weak for that reason. Paragraph 3 deals with the idea that "The Chaser" is in fact a satire and that it therefore should be read as a positive work in which the main characters are not admired but attacked. Paragraph 4 demonstrates how Collier's technique complements this satiric thrust. Collier's handling of the story underscores his satiric revelation. In the light of the argument carried out in the body of the essay, the concluding paragraph emphasizes again that "The Chaser" is a good story. The basis for this conclusion is that the view of love in "The Chaser" (developed in three sentences of this last paragraph) is the opposite of what the main characters represent.

Appendix B: Comparison-Contrast and Extended Comparison-Contrast

The comparison essay may be used to compare and contrast different authors, two or more works by the same author, different drafts of the same work, or characters, incidents, and ideas within the same work or in different works. Not only is comparison-contrast popular in literature courses, but it is one of the commonest approaches you will find in other disciplines.

CLARIFY YOUR INTENTION

Your first problem in planning a comparison-contrast is to decide on a goal, for you may use the comparison-contrast method in a number of ways. One objective can be the equal and mutual illumination of two (or more) works. Thus, an essay comparing Frank O'Connor's "First Confession" (p. 187) and Nathaniel Hawthorne's "Young Goodman Brown" (p. 302) might be designed (1) to compare ideas, characters, or methods in these stories equally, without stressing or favoring either. But you might also wish (2) to emphasize "Young Goodman Brown," and therefore you would use "First Confession" as material for highlighting Hawthorne's work. You might also use the comparison-contrast method (3) to show your liking of one work (at the expense of another), or (4) to emphasize a method or idea that you think is especially noteworthy or appropriate. Your first task is therefore to decide where to place your emphasis.

FIND COMMON GROUNDS FOR COMPARISON

The second stage in prewriting is to select the proper material—the grounds of your discussion. It is useless to try to compare dissimilar things. You need to put the works or writers you are comparing onto common ground.

Compare like with like: idea with idea, characterization with characterization, imagery with imagery. Nothing can be learned from a comparison of "Welty's view of courage and Shakespeare's view of love," but a comparison of "The relationship of love to stability and courage in Shakespeare and Welty" suggests common ground, with points of both likeness and difference.

In searching for common ground, you may have to use your ingenuity a bit. Guy De Maupassant's "The Necklace" (p. 90) and Anton Chekhov's *The Bear* (p. 49) at first may seem to be as different as they can be. Yet common grounds do exist for these works, such as "The Treatment of Self-Deceit," "The Effects of Chance on Human Affairs," or "The View of Women." As you can see, apparently unlike works can be put into a frame of reference that permits analytical comparison and contrast.

METHODS OF COMPARISON

Let us assume that you have decided on your purpose and on the basis or bases of your comparison: You have done your reading, taken your notes, and formulated your argument. The remaining problem is the treatment of your material. Here are two acceptable ways.

One common method is to make your points first about one work and then for the other. This method can make your paper seem like two big lumps, and it also involves much repetition because you must repeat the same points as you treat your second subject.

A more effective method is to treat your main idea in its major aspects and to make references to the two (or more) works as the reference illustrates and illuminates your main idea. Thus you would be constantly referring to both works, sometimes within the same sentence, and would be reminding your reader of the point of your discussion. There are reasons for the superiority of the second method: (1) you do not repeat your points needlessly, for you document them as you raise them; (2) by constantly referring to the two works in relation to your common ground of comparison, you make your points without requiring a reader with a poor memory to reread previous sections.

Avoid the "Tennis-Ball" Method

As you make your comparisons, do not confuse an interlocking method with a "tennis-ball" method, in which you bounce your subjects back and forth constantly and repetitively. The tennis-ball method is shown in the following excerpt from a comparison of Crane's "Do Not Weep, Maiden, for War Is Kind" (p. 938) and Eberhart's "The Fury of Aerial Bombardment" (p. 562):

Crane speaks of the details of death while Eberhart deals more with war as a question mark. Crane presents images of the riderless horse, the thousand corpses, and the father dying of poison gas; Eberhart less vividly considers the ignorance and stupidity of humankind and the apparent permanence of war. Crane is concerned with the effect of war upon loved ones; Eberhart does not dwell on this, though he does name two specific but unmemorable men who have gone to an early death. Crane's method is thus to emphasize both the horror and irony of war; Eberhart's is to emphasize the philosophical questions raised by war.

Imagine the effect of reading an entire essay presented in this fashion. Aside from its power to bore, the tennis-ball method does not give you the chance to develop your points. You should not feel so cramped that you cannot take several sentences to develop a point about one writer or subject before you bring in comparison with another.

We provide an example of a relatively simple and limited comparison-contrast essay at the close of Chapter 26 (pp. 914–17). This essay compares (rather than contrasts) the spatial images in three of Donne's love poems. In this instance, the central idea is limited enough so that the paper can work through each poem in sequence without breaking into three separate essays.

THE EXTENDED COMPARISON-CONTRAST

For a longer essay, such as a limited research paper or the sort of extended essay required at the end of the semester, the technique of comparison-contrast may be used for many works. For essays of this larger scope, you will still need to develop common grounds for comparison, although with more works to discuss you will need to modify the method.

Let us assume that you have been asked to deal with five or six works. You need first to find a common ground among them that you can use as your central, unifying idea. When you take your notes, sketch out your ideas, make your early drafts, and rearrange and shape your developing materials, try to bring all the works together on the common ground of this idea. Thus, in the following sample essay, all the works are treated on the common basis that they speak about the nature of love and devoted service.

When you contrast the works, you should try to form groups based on variations or differences. If three or four works treat a topic in one way while one or two do it in another, you can treat the topic itself in a straightforward contrast method and use details from the groups on either side of the issue to support your points. Again, it is desirable to use the analysis of a particular point based on one work so that you can make your essay concrete and vivid. But once you have exemplified your point, there is no need to go into any more detail from the other works than seems necessary to get your point across. In this way, you can keep your essay within limits; if you group your works on points of similarity, you do not need to go into excessive and unproductive detail.

The sample essay that follows is an example of how works may be grouped in this way. There, four works are grouped into a general category of how love and service may offer guidance and stability for living. This group is contrasted with another group of three works (including two characters from one of the works in the first group), in which love is shown as an escape or retreat.

DOCUMENTATION AND THE EXTENDED COMPARISON-CONTRAST ESSAY

For the longer comparison-contrast essay you may find a problem in documentation. Generally you will not need to locate page numbers for references to major traits, ideas, or actions. But if you are quoting lines or passages, or if you are making any special or unusual reference, you may need to use footnotes or parenthetical references. For page numbers, the sample essay uses the parenthetical abbreviation system described in Appendix C. For lines of poetry or parts of lines, the essay uses parenthetical line numbers. Be guided by this principle: If you make a specific reference, provide the line or page number. If you are referring to minor details that might easily be forgotten or not noticed, supply the line or page number. In dealing with larger events or more general points, you need not supply a specific citation.

WRITING COMPARISON-CONTRAST ESSAYS

Organizing Your Essay

First you must narrow your subject into a topic you can handle conveniently within the limits of the assignment. For example, if you have been assigned a comparison of Wordsworth and Hopkins, pick out one or two poems of each poet and write your essay about them. You must be wary, however, of the limitations of this selection: generalizations made from one or two works may not apply to the broad subject originally proposed.

INTRODUCTION. State what works, authors, characters, and ideas are under consideration, then show how you have narrowed the basis of your comparison. Your central idea will be a brief statement of what can be learned from your paper: the general similarities and differences that you have observed from your comparison and/or the superiority of one work or author over another. Your thesis sentence should anticipate the body of your essay.

BODY.   The body of your essay depends on the points you have chosen for comparison. You might be comparing two works on the basis of *point of view* or *imagery*, two authors on *ideas*, or two characters on *character traits*. In your discussion you would necessarily use the same methods that you would use in writing about a single work, except that here (1) you are exemplifying your points by reference to more subjects than one, and (2) your main purpose is to shed light on the subjects on which your comparison is based. In this sense, the methods you use in talking about point of view or imagery are not "pure" but are instead subordinate to your aims of comparison-contrast.

CONCLUSION.   Here you are comparatively free to reflect on other ideas in the works you have compared, to make observations on comparative qualities, or to summarize briefly the basic grounds of your comparison. The conclusion of an extended comparison-contrast essay should represent a final bringing together of the materials. In the body of the essay you may not have referred to all the works in each paragraph; however, in the conclusion you should try to refer to them all, if possible.

If your writers belonged to any "period" or "school," you also might wish to show in your conclusion how they relate to these larger movements. References of this sort provide a natural common ground for comparison.

SAMPLE ESSAY
(EXTENDED COMPARISON-CONTRAST)

The Complexity of Love and Devoted Service as Shown in Six Works *

[1] On the surface, at least, love and devotion are simple, and their results should be good. A person loves someone, or serves someone or something. This love may be romantic or familial, and the service may be religious or national. But love is not simple. It is complex, and its results are not uniformly good.° Love and devotion should be ways of saying "yes," but ironically they sometimes become ways of saying "no," too. This idea can be traced in a

* For the texts of these works, please see the following pages: "Sonnet 116," p. 749; "Dover Beach," p. 529; "Channel Firing," p. 492; *The Bear*, p. 49; "First Confession," p. 187; "A Worn Path," p. 116.
   ° Central idea

comparison of six works: William Shakespeare's Sonnet 116, Matthew Arnold's "Dover Beach," Thomas Hardy's "Channel Firing," Anton Chekhov's *The Bear*, Frank O'Connor's "First Confession," and Eudora Welty's "A Worn Path." The complexity in these works is that love and devotion do not operate in a vacuum but rather in the context of personal philosophical, economic, and national difficulties. The works show that love and devotion may be forces for stability and refuge, but also for harm.[1]

[2] Ideal and stabilizing love, along with service performed out of love, is shown by Shakespeare in Sonnet 116 and by O'Connor in "First Confession." Shakespeare states that love gives lovers strength and stability in a complex world of opposition and difficulty. Such love is like a "star" that guides wandering ships (line 7), and like a "fixed mark" that stands against the shaking of life's tempests (lines 5 and 6). A character who is similarly aware of human tempests and conflicts is the "young priest" who hears Jackie's confession in "First Confession." He is clearly committed to service, and is "intelligent above the ordinary" (p. 191). With service to God as his "star," to use Shakespeare's image, he is able to talk sympathetically with Jackie and to send the boy home with a clear and happy mind.

[3] For both Shakespeare and O'Connor, love and service grow out of a great human need for stability and guidance. To this degree love is a simplifying force, but it simplifies primarily because the "tempests" complicating life are so strong. Such love is one of the best things that happen to human beings, because it fulfills them and prepares them to face life.

[4] The desire for love of this kind is so strong that it can also be the cause for people to do strange and funny things. The two major characters in Chekhov's short comedy-farce *The Bear* are examples. At the play's start, Chekhov shows that Mrs. Popov and Smirnov are following some of the crack-brained and negative guides that people often confuse for truth. She is devoted to the memory of her dead husband, while he is disillusioned and cynical about women. But Chekhov makes them go through hoops for love. As the two argue, insult each other, and reach the point of dueling with real pistols, their need for love overcomes all their other impulses. It is as though love happens despite everything going against it, because the need for the stabilizing base is so strong. Certainly love here is not without at least some complexity. Either seriously or comically, then, love is shown as a rudder, guiding people in powerful and conflicting currents. The three works examined thus far show that love shapes lives and makes for sudden and unexpected changes.

[5] This thought is somewhat like the view presented by Eudora Welty in "A Worn Path." Unlike Chekhov and Shakespeare, and more like O'Connor, Welty tells a story of service performed out of love. A poor grandmother, Phoenix Jackson, has a hard life in caring for her incurably ill grandson. The walk she takes along the "worn path" to Natchez symbolizes the hardships she endures because of her single-minded love. Her service is the closest thing to pure simplicity that may be found in all the works examined, with the possible exception of the love in Chekhov's play.

But even her love is not without its complexity. Hardy in "Channel Firing"

[1] Thesis sentence

[6]
and Arnold in "Dover Beach" describe a joyless, loveless, insecure world over-run by war. Phoenix's life is just as grim. She is poor and ignorant, and her grandson has nowhere to go but down. If she would only stop to think deeply about her condition, she might be as despairing as Arnold's and Hardy's speak-ers. But her strength may be her ability either to accept her difficult life or to ignore the grimness of it. With her service as her "star" and "ever-fixed mark," she is able to keep cheerful and to live in friendship with the animals and the woods. Her life has meaning and dignity.

Arnold's view of love and devotion under such bad conditions is different from the views of Shakespeare, Chekhov, O'Connor, and Welty. For the speaker in "Dover Beach," the public world seems to be so far gone that there is nothing left but personal relationships. Thus love is not so much a guide as a refuge, a place of sanity and safety. After describing what he considers the worldwide shrinking of the "Sea of Faith," he states:

[7]
Ah, love, let us be true
To one another! for the world, which seems
To lie before us like a land of dreams,
So various, so beautiful, so new,
Hath really neither joy, nor love, nor light,
Nor certitude, nor peace, nor help for pain;
And we are here as on a darkling plain
Swept with confused alarms of struggle and flight
Where ignorant armies clash by night.

(lines 29–37)

Here the word *true* should be underlined, as Shakespeare emphasizes "true minds" and as O'Connor's priest is a true servant of God. "True" to this speaker seems to involve a pledge to create a small area of certainty in the mad world like that of "Channel Firing," where there is no certainty. Love is not so much a guide as a last place of hope, a retreat where truth can still have meaning.

[8]
In practice, perhaps, Arnold's idea of love as a refuge is not very different from the view that love is a guide. Once the truthful pledge is made, it is a force for goodness, at least for the lovers making the pledge, just as love works for goodness in Shakespeare, O'Connor, Chekhov, and Welty. Yet Ar-nold's view is weaker. It does not result from an inner need or conviction, but rather from a conscious decision to let everything else go and to look out only for the small relationship. In an extreme form, this could lead to total withdrawal. Such a passive relationship to other affairs could be harmful by omission.

[9]
The idea that love and devotion as a refuge could be actively harmful is explored by O'Connor in other characters in "First Confession." Nora and Mrs. Ryan seem to think only of sinfulness and punishment. They seek the love of God out of a desire for protection. Their devotion is therefore a means to an end, not the pure goal which operates in Shakespeare. Welty, and O'Con-nor's own priest. As Jackie says of Mrs. Ryan:

She . . . wore a black cloak and bonnet, and came every day to school at three o'clock when we should have been going home, and talked to us of hell. She may have mentioned the other place as well, but that could only have been by accident, for hell had the first place in her heart (p. 188).

[10]   Love and devotion for her and for Nora take the form of observing ritual and following rules, such as being sure that all confessions are "good" (that is, complete, with no sins held back). If this obedience were only personal, it would be a force for security, as it is on the personal level in "Dover Beach." But from the safety of their refuge, Mrs. Ryan confuses children like Jackie by describing devilish, sadistic tortures, while Nora tells her father about the bread knife and thus brings down punishment (the "flaking") and a "scalded" heart on Jackie. Even though Mrs. Ryan is not a bad soul, and Nora is no more than a young girl, their use of religion is negative. Fortunately, their influence is counter-balanced by the priest.

[11]   Mrs. Ryan and Nora are minor compared with those unseen, unnamed, and distant persons firing the big guns during the "gunnery practice out at sea" in Hardy's "Channel Firing" (line 10). Hardy does not treat the gunners as individuals but as an evil collective force made up of persons who, under the sheltering claim of devotion to country and obedience of orders, are "striving strong to make/Red war yet redder" (lines 13, 14). For them, love of country is a refuge, just like the love of God for Mrs. Ryan and Nora and the true pledge to love for Arnold's speaker. As members of the military they obey orders and, as Hardy's God says, they are not much better than the dead because they do nothing "for Christés sake" (line 15). They operate the ships and fill the columns of Arnold's "ignorant armies," for Hardy makes clear that their target practice takes place at night (line 1).

[12]   In summary, love and devotion as seen in these various works may be compared with a continuous line formed out of the human need for love and for the stability and guidance that love offers. At one end love is totally good and ideal; at the other it is totally bad. Shakespeare, Welty, Chekhov, and O'Connor (in the priest) show the end that is good. Still at the good end, but moving toward the center, is Arnold's use of love as a refuge. On the other side of the line are Mrs. Ryan and Nora of "First Confession," while all the way at the bad end are the insensible and invisible gunners in "Channel Firing."

[13]   The difficulty noted in all the works, and a major problem in life, is to devote oneself to the right, stabilizing, constructive part of the line. Although in his farce Chekhov makes love win against almost impossible odds, he shows the problem most vividly of all the authors studied. Under normal conditions, people like Mrs. Popov and Smirnov would not find love. Instead, they would continue following their destructive and false guides. They would be unhappy and disillusioned, or else they might become more like Mrs. Ryan and spread talk about their own confused ideas (as Smirnov actually does almost right up to his conversion to love). Like the military and naval forces of Arnold and Hardy, they would then wind up at the destructive end of the line.

[14]   Change, opposition, confusion, anger, resignation, economic difficulty— these are only some of the forces that attack people as they try to find the benefits of love. If they are lucky they find meaning and stability in love and service, as in Sonnet 116, "First Confession," *The Bear*, "A Worn Path," and, to a small degree, "Dover Beach." If confusion wins, they are locked into

harmful positions, like the gunners in "Channel Firing" and Mrs. Ryan and Nora in "First Confession." Thus love is complicated by circumstances, and it is not the simple force for good that it should ideally be. The six works compared and contrasted here have shown these difficulties and complexities.

Commentary on the Essay

This essay compares and contrasts six works—three poems, two stories, and a play—on the common ground or central idea of the complexity of love and service. The complexity is caused by life's difficulties and by bad results. The essay develops the central idea in terms of love as an ideal and guide (paragraphs 2–6) and love as a refuge or escape (paragraphs 7–11), with a subcategory of love as a cause of harm (9–11).

The various works are introduced as they are grouped according to these sections. For example, Sonnet 116, "First Confession" (because of the priest), *The Bear*, and "A Worn Path" are together in the first group—love as an ideal and guide. Because "Dover Beach" and "Channel Firing" are in the second group, these works are brought in earlier, during the discussion of the first group. For this reason, both poems are used regularly for comparison and contrast throughout the theme.

The use of the various works within groups may be seen in paragraph 7. There, the principal topic is the use of love as a refuge or retreat, and the central work of the paragraph is "Dover Beach." However, the first sentence contrasts Arnold's view with the four works in the first group; the fifth sentence shows how Arnold is similar in one respect to Shakespeare and O'Connor; and the sixth sentence shows a similarity of Arnold and Hardy. The paragraph thus brings together all the works being studied in the theme.

The technique of comparison-contrast used in this way shows how the various works may be defined and distinguished in relation to the common idea. Paragraph 12, the first in the conclusion, attempts to summarize these distinctions by suggesting a continuous line along which each of the works may be placed. Paragraphs 13 and 14 continue the summary by showing the prominence of complicating difficulties and, by implication, the importance of love. Thus, the effect of the comparison of all the works collectively is the enhanced understanding of each of the works separately.

Appendix C: Writing and Documenting the Research Essay

Research, as distinguished from pure criticism, refers to using primary and secondary sources for assistance in solving a literary problem. That is, in criticizing a work, pure and simple, you consult only the work in front of you (the *primary source*), whereas in doing research on the work, you consult not only the work but many other works that were written about it or that may shed light on it (*secondary sources*). Typical research tasks are to find out more about the historical period in which a work was written or about prevailing opinions of the times or about what modern (or earlier) critics have said about the work. It is obvious that a certain amount of research is always necessary in any critical job, or in any essay about a literary work. Looking up words in a dictionary, for example, is only a minimal job of research, which may be supplemented by reading introductions, critical articles, encyclopedias, biographies, critical studies, histories, and the like. There is, in fact, a point at which criticism and research merge.

It is necessary that you put the job of doing research in perspective. In general, students and scholars do research in order to uncover some of the accumulated "lore" of our civilization. This lore—the knowledge that presently exists—may be compared to a large cone that is constantly being filled. At the beginnings of human existence there was little knowledge of anything, and the cone was at its narrowest point. As civilization progressed, more and more knowledge appeared, and the cone thus began to fill. Each time a new piece of information or a new conclusion was recorded, a little more knowledge or lore was in effect poured into the cone, which accordingly became slightly fuller and wider. Though at present our cone of knowledge is quite full, it appears to be capable of infinite growth. Knowledge keeps piling up and new disciplines keep developing. It becomes more and more difficult for one person to accumulate more than a small portion of the entirety. Indeed, historians generally agree that the last person to know virtually everything about every existing discipline was Aristotle—2,400 years ago.

If you grant that you cannot learn everything, you can make a positive start by recognizing that research can provide two things: (1) a systematic understanding of a portion of the knowledge filling the cone, and (2) an understanding of, and ability to handle, the methods by which you might someday be able to make your own contributions to the filling of the cone.

Thus far we have been speaking broadly about the relevance of research to any discipline. Our problem here, however, is literary research, the systematic study of library sources in order to illuminate a literary topic.

SELECTING A TOPIC

Frequently your instructor will ask for a research paper on a specific topic. However, if you have only a general research assignment, your first problem is to select a topic. It may be helpful to have a general notion of the kind of research paper you would find most congenial. Here are some possibilities (see also Chapter 26 for topics on poetic careers):

1. *A paper on a particular work.* You might treat character (for example, "The Character of Bottom in *A Midsummer Night's Dream*," or "The Question of Whether Willy Loman is a Hero or Antihero in *Death of a Salesman*), or tone, ideas, form, problems, and the like. A research paper on a single work is similar to an essay on the same work, except that the research paper takes into account more views and facts than those you are likely to have without the research.

2. *A paper on a particular author.* The paper could be about an idea or some facet of style, imagery, tone, or humor of the author, tracing the origins and development of the topic through a number of different works by the author. An example might be "The Idea of the True Self as Developed by Frost in His Poetry before 1920." This type of paper is particularly suitable if you are writing on a poet whose works are short, though a topic like "Shakespeare's Idea of the Relationships Between Men and Women as Dramatized in *A Midsummer Night's Dream* and *Hamlet*" might also be possible.

3. *A paper based on comparison and contrast.* There are two types:
    a. *A paper on an idea of some artistic quality common to two or more authors.* Your intention might be to show points of similarity or contrast or to show that one author's work may be read as a criticism of another's. A possible subject of such a paper might be "The Theme of Ineffectuality in Behn, Eliot, Steinbeck, and Williams," or "Behn's Antimale Poems in the Context of Male Dominated Lyric Poetry of the Seventeenth Century." Consult the second sample essay in Appendix B for an example of this type.

b. *A paper concentrating on opposing critical views of a particular work or body of works.* Sometimes much is to be gained from an examination of differing critical opinions, say "The Vision of Women in A Doll's House," "The Interpretations of Gray's *Elegy*," or "The Question of Hamlet's Hesitation." Such a study would attempt to determine the critical climate of opinion and taste to which a work did or did not appeal, and it might also aim at conclusions about whether the work was in the advance or rear guard of its time.

4. *A paper showing the influence of an idea, an author, a philosophy, a political situation, or an artistic movement on specific works of an author or authors.* A paper on influences can be fairly direct, as in "Details of Early Twentieth-Century Mexican American Culture as Reflected in Paredes's 'The Hammon and the Beans,' " or else it can be more abstract and critical, as in "The Influence of Early Twentieth-Century Oppression of Mexican-Americans on the Narrator of 'The Hammon and the Beans.' "

5. *A paper on the origins of a particular work or type of work.* One avenue of research for such a paper might be to examine an author's biography to discover the germination and development of a work—for example, " 'The Old Chief Mshlanga' as an outgrowth of Lessing's life in Rhodesia-Zimbabwe." Another way of discovering origins might be to relate a work to a particular type or tradition: "*Hamlet* as Revenge Tragedy," or "*The Bear* and Its Origins in 'The Widow of Ephesus' by Petronius."

If you consider these types, an idea of what to write may come to you. Perhaps you have particularly liked one author, or several authors. If so, you might start to think along the lines of types 1, 2, and 3. If you are interested in influences or in origins, then types 4 or 5 may suit you better.

If you still have not decided on a topic after rereading the works you have liked, then you should carry your search for a topic into your school library. Look up your author or authors in the card or computer catalogue. Usually the works written by the authors are included first, followed by works written about the authors. Your first goal should be to find a relatively recent book-length critical study published by a university press. Use your judgment here: Look for a title indicating that the book is a general one dealing with the author's major works rather than just one work. Study those chapters relevant to your primary text. Most writers of critical studies describe their purpose and plan in their introductions or first chapters, so read the first part of the book. If there is no separate chapter on the primary text, use the index and go to the relevant pages. Reading in this way should soon supply you with sufficient knowledge about the issues and ideas raised by the work to enable you to select a topic you will wish to study further. Once you have made your decision, you are ready to go ahead and develop a working bibliography.

SETTING UP A BIBLIOGRAPHY

The best way to develop a working bibliography of books and articles is to begin with major critical studies of the writer or writers. Again, go to the catalogue and pick out books that have been published by university presses. These books will usually contain selective bibliographies. Be particularly careful to read the chapters on your primary work or works and to look for the footnotes or endnotes. Quite often you can save time if you record the names of books and articles listed in these notes. Then refer to the bibliographies included at the ends of the books, and select any likely looking titles. Now, look at the dates of publication of the critical books you have been using. Let us suppose that you have been looking at three, published in 1951, 1963, and 1980. The chances are that the bibliography in a book published in 1980 will be fairly complete up through about 1978, for the writer will usually have completed the manuscript about two years before the book actually was published. What you should do then is aim at gathering a bibliography of works published since 1978; you may assume that writers of critical works will have done the selecting for you of the most relevant works published before that time.

Bibliographical Guides

Fortunately for students doing literary research, the Modern Language Association (MLA) of America has been providing a virtually complete bibliography of literary studies for years, not just in English and American literatures, but in the literatures of most modern foreign languages. The MLA started achieving completeness in the late 1950s and by 1969 had reached such an advanced state that it divided the bibliography into four parts. All four parts are bound together in library editions. Most university and college libraries have a set of these bibliographies readily available on open shelves or tables. There are, of course, many other bibliographies that are useful for students doing research, many more than can be mentioned here meaningfully. For most purposes, however, the *MLA International Bibliography* is more than adequate. Remember that as you progress in your reading, the notes and bibliographies in the works you consult also will constitute an unfolding bibliography.

The *MLA International Bibliography* is conveniently organized by period and author. If your author is Gwendolyn Brooks, for example, look her up under "American Literature V. Twentieth Century," the relevant listing for all twentieth-century American writers. If your author is Shakespeare, refer to "English Literature VI. Renaissance and Elizabethan." You will find most of the bibliography you need under the author's last name. Journal references are abbreviated, but a lengthy list explaining abbreviations appears at the beginning of the volume. Using the MLA bibliographies, you should begin with the most recent one and then go backward to your stopping point. Be sure to get the complete information, especially volume numbers and years of publication, for each article and book you wish to consult. You are now ready to consult your sources and to take notes.

TAKING NOTES AND PARAPHRASING MATERIAL

There are many ways of taking notes, but the consensus is that the best method is to use note cards. If you have never used cards before, you might profit from consulting any one of a number of handbooks and special workbooks on research. A lucid and methodical explanation of taking notes on cards can be found in Glenn Leggett et al., *Prentice-Hall Handbook for Writers*, 9th ed., pp. 440–46. (Englewood Cliffs.: Prentice-Hall, 1985), pp. 369–73. The principal virtue of using cards is that they may be classified, numbered, renumbered, shuffled, tried out in one place, rejected, and then used in another (or thrown away), and arranged in order when you start to write.

Taking Notes

WRITE THE SOURCE ON EACH CARD.   As you take notes, write down the source of your information on each card. This may sound like a lot of bother, but it is easier than finding out as you wrtie that you will need to go back to the library to get the correct source. You can save time if you take the complete data on one card—a "master card" for that source—and then make up an abbreviation to be used in your notes. Here is an example:

Donovan, Josephine, ed. *Feminist Literary*

Criticism: *Explorations in Theory*.

Lexington: The University Press of

Kentucky, 1975.

                    DONOVAN

If you plan to use many notes from this book, then the name "Donovan" will serve as identification. Be sure not to lose your complete master card, because you will need it in preparing your list of works cited.

RECORD THE PAGE NUMBER FOR EACH NOTE. It would be hard to guess how much exasperation has been caused by the failure to record page numbers of notes. Be sure to get the page number down first, *before* you begin to take your note. If the detail you are noting goes from one page to the next in your source, record the exact spot where the page changes, as in this example:

Heilbrun and Stimson, in DONOVAN, pp. 63–64

[63] After the raising of the feminist consciousness
it is necessary to develop/ [64] "the growth of
moral perception" through anger and the
correction of social inequality.

The reason for being so careful is that you may wish to use only a part of a note you have taken, and when there are two pages you will need to be accurate in your location of what goes where.

RECORD ONLY ONE FACT OR OPINION PER CARD. Record only one thing on each card—one quotation, one paraphrase, one observation—never two or more. You might be tempted to fill up the entire card, but such a try at economy often causes trouble because you might want to use the same card in different places in your research paper.

USE QUOTATION MARKS FOR ALL QUOTED MATERIAL.   A major problem in taking notes is to distinguish copied material from your own words. Here you must be extremely cautious. Always put quotation marks around *every direct quotation you copy verbatim from a source*. Make the quotation marks immediately, before you forget, so that you will always know that the words of your notes within quotation marks are the words of another writer.

Often, as you take a note, you may use some of your own words and some of the words from your source. In cases like this it is even more important to be cautious. Put quotation marks around *every word* that you take directly from the source, even if you find yourself literally with a note that resembles a picket fence. Later when you begin writing your paper, your memory of what is yours and not yours will become dim, and if you use another's words in your own paper but do not grant recognition, you lay yourself open to the charge of plagiarism.

Paraphrasing

When you take notes, it is best to paraphrase the sources. A paraphrase is a restatement in your own words, and because of this it is actually a first step in the writing of the essay. Chapter 2 in this book has a full treatment on making a précis or abstract. If you work on this technique, you will be well prepared to paraphrase for your research essay.

A big problem in paraphrasing is to capture the idea in the source without duplicating the words. The best way to do this is to read and reread the passage you are noting. Turn over the book or journal and write out the idea *in your own words* as accurately as you can. Once you have this note, compare it with the original and make corrections to improve your thought and emphasis. Add a short quotation if you believe it is needed, but be sure to use quotation marks. If your paraphrase is too close to the original, throw out the note and try again in your own words. It is worth making this effort, because often you can transform much of your note directly to the appropriate place in your research paper.

To see the problems of paraphrase, let us look at a paragraph of criticism and then see how a student doing research might take notes on it. The paragraph is by Maynard Mack, from an essay entitled "The World of Hamlet," originally published in *The Yale Review* 41 (1952) and reprinted in *Twentieth Century Interpretations of Hamlet*, ed. David Bevington (Englewood Cliffs: Prentice-Hall, 1968), p. 57:

The powerful sense of mortality in *Hamlet* is conveyed to us, I think, in three ways. First, there is the play's emphasis on human weakness, the instability of human purpose, the subjection of humanity to fortune—all that we might call the aspect of failure in man. Hamlet opens this theme in Act I, when he describes how from that single blemish, perhaps not even the victim's fault, a man's whole character may take corruption. Claudius dwells on it again, to an extent that goes far beyond the needs of the occasion, while engaged in seducing Laertes to step behind the arras of a seemer's world and dispose of Hamlet by a trick. Time qualifies everything, Claudius says, including love, including purpose. As for love—it has a "plurisy" in it and dies of its own too much. As for purpose—"That we would do, We should do when we would, for this 'would' changes, And hath abatements and delays as many As there are tongues, are hands, are accidents; And then this 'should' is like a spendthrift's sigh, That hurts by easing." The player-king, in his long speeches to his queen in the play within the play, sets the matter in a still darker light. She means these protestations of undying love, he knows, but our purposes depend on our memory, and our memory fades fast. Or else, he suggests, we propose something to ourselves in a condition of strong feeling, but then the feeling goes, and with it the resolve. Or else our fortunes change, he adds, and with these our loves: "The great man down, you mark his favorite flies." The subjection of human aims to fortune is a reiterated theme in *Hamlet*, as subsequently in *Lear*. Fortune is the harlot goddess in whose secret parts men like Rosencrantz and Guildenstern live and thrive; the strumpet who threw down Troy and Hecuba and Priam; the outrageous foe whose slings and arrows a man of principle must suffer or seek release in suicide. Horatio suffers them with composure: he is one of the blessed few "Whose blood and judgment are so well co-mingled That they are not a pipe for fortune's finger To sound what stop she please." For Hamlet the task is of a greater difficulty.

The task of taking notes forces you to shorten and interpret Mack's writing, and there are some things that can guide you in the face of the large amount of reading in your sources.

THINK OF THE PURPOSE OF YOUR RESEARCH PAPER.   You may not know exactly what you are "fishing for" when you start to take notes, for you cannot prejudge what your essay will contain. Research is a form of discovery. By soon you will develop a general topic or focus, and you should use that as your guide in all your note-taking.

For example, suppose that you have started to take notes on *Hamlet* criticism, and after a certain amount of reading you have decided to focus on "Shakespeare's Tragic Views in *Hamlet*." This decision would prompt you to take a note when you come to Mack's thought about morality and death in the quoted passage. In this instance, the following note would suffice:

Mack, in Bevington,   57   Death and
                                                                     Mortality

Mack cites three ways in which *Hamlet* stresses
death and mortality. The first (57) is an
emphasis on human shortcomings and "weakness."
Corruption, loss of memory and enthusiasm, bad
luck, misery—all suit the sense of the closeness of
death to life.

Let us now suppose that you wanted a fuller note in the expectation
that you would need not just the topic but also some of Mack's detail.
Such a note might look like this:

Mack, in Bevington,   57   Death and
                                                                     Mortality

The first of Mack's "three ways" in which a
"powerful sense of mortality" is shown in *Hamlet*
is the illustration of human "weakness," "instability,"
and helplessness before fate. In support, Mack
refers to Hamlet's early speech on a single fault
leading to corruption, also to Claudius' speech
(in the scene persuading Laertes to trick Hamlet).
The player-king also talks about his queen's
forgetfulness and therefore inconstancy by default.
As slaves to fortune, Rosencrantz and Guildenstern
are examples. Horatio is not a slave, however. Hamlet's
case is by far the worst of all.   Mack,   57

When the actual essay is being written, any part of this note would be useful. The words are almost all the note-taker's own, and the few quotations are within quotation marks. Note that Mack, the critic, is properly recognized as the source of the criticism, so that the note could be adapted readily to a research paper. The key here is that your taking of notes should be guided by your developing plan for your essay.

Note taking is part of your thinking and composing process. You may not always know whether you will be able to use each note that you take, and you will exclude many notes when you write your essay. You will always find, however, that taking notes is easier once you have determined your purpose.

TITLE YOUR NOTES.   To help plan and develop the various parts of your essay, write a title for each of your notes as in the examples in this chapter. This practice is a form of outlining. Let us assume that you have chosen to write about the Ghost in *Hamlet* and that your topic is the importance of the Ghost in the play. As you do research, you discover that there are conflicting views about how the Ghost should be understood. Here is a note about one of the questionable qualities of this character:

Prosser, 133, 134   Negative, Devilish

When describing his pain and suffering as a dead spirit, the Ghost is not specific but emphasizes the horror. He should, if a good spirit, try to use his suffering to urge repentance and salvation for Hamlet. This emphasis is a sign that he is closer in nature to a devil than to a soul earning its way to redemption.

Notice that the title classifies the topic of the note. If you use such classifications while taking notes, a number of like-titled cards could form the substance of a section in your essay about the negative qualities of the Ghost in *Hamlet*. In addition, once you decide that "Negative, Devilish" is one of the topics you plan to explore, the topic itself will guide you in further study and additional note taking.

WRITE DOWN YOUR OWN THOUGHTS AS THEY OCCUR TO YOU. As you take your notes, you will have many of your own thoughts. Do not let these go, to be remembered later (maybe), but write them down immediately. Often you may notice a detail that your source does not mention, or you may get a hint for an idea that the critic does not develop. Often, too, you may get thoughts which can serve as "bridges" between details in your notes or as introductions or concluding observations. Be sure to title your comment and also to mark it as your own thought. Here is such a note, which is related to the importance of the Ghost in the structure of *Hamlet*:

My own   Structure

    Shakespeare does a superb job with the Ghost. His
characterization is both full and round, and the Ghost is totally integrated
in the play's structure.

SORT YOUR CARDS INTO GROUPS. If you have taken your notes well, your essay will have been taking shape in your mind already. The titles of your cards will suggest areas to be developed in the research paper. Once you have assembled a stack of note cards derived from a reasonable number of sources (your instructor may have assigned the minimum number), you can sort them into groups according to the topics and titles. For the sample essay, after some shuffling and retitling, the following groups of cards were distributed:

1. Importance in action
2. Importance in themes
3. Condition as a spirit
   a. Good signs
   b. Negative, Devilish signs
4. Human Traits
5. Importance in Structure
6. Effect on other characters

If you look at the major sections of the sample essay, you will see that the topics are adapted right from these groups of cards. In other words, the arrangement of the cards is an effective means of outlining and organizing a research essay.

ARRANGE THE CARDS IN EACH GROUP.   There is still much to be done with these individual groups. You cannot use the details as they happened to fall randomly in your "deal." You need to decide which notes are relevant. You might also need to retitle some cards and use them elsewhere. Of those that remain in the group, you will need to lay them out in a logical progression in which they may be used in the paper.

Once you have your cards in order, you can write whatever comments or transitions are needed to move from detail to detail. Write this material directly on the cards, and be sure to use a different color ink so that you will be able to know what was on the original card and what you added at this stage of your composing process. Here is an example of such a "developed" note card:

Campbell, 127   Negative, Devilish.

Shakespeare's Ghost reflects the general uncertainty at the time about how ghosts were to be interpreted.

This may be the best way to answer the questions about the Ghost's ambiguous nature. Moreover, Shakespeare may have been trying to be more lifelike than consistent with his Ghost.

By adding such commentary to your note cards, you will facilitate the actual writing of the first draft. In many instances, the note and the comment may be moved directly into the paper with minor adjustments (this note and comment occurs in paragraphs 5 and 6 of the sample essay).

BE CREATIVE AND ORIGINAL IN RESEARCH PAPERS. This is not to say you can always settle for the direct movement of the cards into your essay. The major trap to avoid in a research paper is that your use of sources can become an end in itself and therefore a shortcut for your own thinking and writing. Quite often students introduce details in a research paper the way a master of ceremonies introduces performers in a variety show. This is unfortunate because it is the writer whose paper will be judged, even though the sources, like the performers, do all the work. Thus, it is important to be creative and original in a research essay even though you are relying heavily on your sources. Here are four major ways:

1. *Selection.* In each major section of your essay you will include a number of details from your sources. To be creative you should select different but related details and avoid overlapping or repetition. The essay will be judged on the basis of the thoroughness with which you make your point with different details (which in turn will represent the completeness of your research). Even though you are relying on published materials and cannot be original on that score, your selection is original because you are bringing the materials together for the first time.

2. *Development.* A closely related way of being original is the development of your various points. Your arrangement is an obvious area of originality: one detail seems naturally to precede another, and certain conclusions stem out of certain details. As you present the details, conclusions, and arguments from your sources, you may also add your own original stamp by using supporting details that are different from those in your sources. You may also wish to add your own emphasis to particular points— an emphasis that you do not find in your sources.

Naturally, the words that you use will be original with you. Your topic sentences, for example, will all be your own. As you introduce details and conclusions, you will need to write "bridges" to get yourself from point to point. These may be introductory remarks for transitions. In other words, as you write, you are not just stringing things out but are actively tying thoughts together in a variety of creative ways. Your efforts to do this will constitute the area of your greatest originality.

3. *Explanation of controversial views.* Also closely related to selection is the fact that in your research you may have found conflicting or differing views on a topic. It is original for you, as you describe and distinguish these views, to explain the reasons for the differences. In other words, as you explain a conflict or difference, you are writing an original analysis. To see how differing views may be handled, see paragraphs 4 and 5 of the sample essay.

4. *Creation of your own insights and positions.* There are three possibilities here, all related to how well you have learned the primary texts on which your research in secondary sources is based.

a. *Your own interpretations and ideas.* Remember that an important part of taking notes is to make your own points precisely when they occur to you. Often you can expand these as truly original parts of your essay. Your originality does not need to be extensive; it may consist of no more than a single insight. Here is such a card, which was written during the research on the ghost in *Hamlet*:

My Own   introductory

    The Ghost is minor in the action but major in the play. He is seen twice in scene 1, but this scene is really all about him. (Also about his appearances before the play opens.) In scene 4 of act 1 he comes again and leads Hamlet off to scene 5, the biggest for him as an acting and speaking character. He speaks after this only from under the stage, and then a small appearance (but important) in 3.4, and that's all. But he is dominant because he set everything in motion and therefore his presence is felt everywhere in the play.

The originality here is built around the idea of the small role but dominant significance of the Ghost. The discovery is perhaps not startling, but it nevertheless represents original thought about *Hamlet*. When modified and adapted, the material of the card supplies much of the opening paragraph in addition to the central idea of the essay.

b. *Gaps in the sources.* As you read your secondary sources it may dawn on you that a certain, obvious conclusion is not being made, or that a certain detail is not being stressed. Here is an area which you can develop on your own. Your conclusions may involve a particular interpretation or major point of comparison, or it may rest on a particularly important but understressed word or fact. In the sample essay, for example, the writer discusses the idea that the Ghost's commands to Hamlet make it impossible for him to solve problems through negotiation or research, the ways he might have chosen as a prince and student. The commands force him instead into a pattern requiring murder. Most critics observe that Hamlet's life is changed because of the Ghost but have not quite stressed these aspects of the change. Given of such a critical "vacuum" (assuming that you cannot read all the articles about some of your topics, where your discovery may already have been made a number of times), it is right to move in with whatever is necessary to fill it. A great deal of scholarship is created in this way.

c. *Disputes with the sources.* You may also find that your sources present certain arguments that you wish to dispute. As you develop your disagreement, you will be arguing originally, for you will be using details in a different way from that of the critic or critics whom you are disputing, and your conclusions will be your own. This area of originality is similar to the laying out of controversial critical views, except that you furnish one of the opposing views yourself. The approach is limited, because it is difficult to find many substantive points of interpretation on which there are not already clearly delineated opposing views. Paragraph 5 of the sample research essay shows a small point of disagreement (about whether Shakespeare was concerned with consistency in presenting the Ghost's spirit nature), but one that is nevertheless original.

DOCUMENTATION: NOTES AND PARENTHETICAL REFERENCES

It is essential to acknowledge—to document—all sources from which you have quoted *or* paraphrased factual and interpretive information. If you do not grant recognition, you run the risk of being challenged for representing as your own the results of others' work; this is plagiarism. As the means of documentation, there are many reference systems, some using parenthetical references, and others using footnotes or endnotes. Whatever the system, they have in common a carefully prepared bibliography or list of works cited. We shall first discuss the list of works cited, and then we shall cover the two major systems for referring to this list within a research paper. The first system, which uses parenthetical references, is described in detail in the *MLA Handbook for Writers of Research Papers*, 2nd ed., 1984, which we recommend to you. The second system, which features footnotes or endnotes, is still widely used. Because this system was *the* MLA system until 1984, we will review it here also.

Before discussing the two major systems, we should mention that because of the nature of this book and the types of essays we have presented, we have not used a formal list of works cited. We have simply indicated in a note at the beginning of each essay the location within this book of the story, poem, or play being discussed. Parenthetical page numbers within a given essay refer to page numbers in this book. When the subject of an essay is a poem or poetic drama, line numbers are given for references within the essay.

List of Works Cited

The key to any reference system is a carefully prepared list of works cited (bibliography) that is included at the end of the essay. (If footnotes or endnotes are used to cite sources, the bibliography may not be required; check your instructor's preference.) It is important to include all the following information in each entry:

FOR A BOOK

1. The author's name, last name first, period.
2. Title, underlined, period.
3. City of publication, colon; publisher (easily recognized abbreviations may be used, comma; date, period.

FOR AN ARTICLE

1. The author's name, last name first, period.
2. Title of article in quotation marks, period.
3. Name of journal or periodical, underlined, followed immediately by volume number in Arabic numbers with no punctuation, followed by the year of publication, including month and day of weekly or daily issues, within parentheses, colon. Inclusive page numbers, period.

The list of works consulted should be arranged alphabetically by author, with unsigned articles being listed by title. Bibliographical lists are begun at the left margin, with subsequent lines being indented, so that the key locating word, usually the author's last name, may be easily seen. The many complex combinations possible in the compilation of a bibliographical list, including ways to describe art works, performances, and films, are detailed extensively in the *MLA Handbook* (pp. 75–135). Here are two model entries:

Book: Spacks, Patricia Meyer. *An Argument of Images: The Poetry of Alexander Pope.* Cambridge: Harvard UP, 1971.
Article: Miller, Rachel A. "Regal Hunting: Dryden's Influence on *Windsor Forest.*" *Eighteenth-Century Studies* 13 (1979/1980): 169–188.

Parenthetical References to the List of Works Cited

Within the text of the essay, the list of works cited may be referred to parenthetically. The parenthetical reference system recommended in the *MLA Handbook* (pp. 137–58) involves the insertion of the author's last name and the relevant page reference into the body of the essay. If the author's name is mentioned in the discussion, only the page number(s) are given in parentheses. Here are two examples:

> Pope believed in the ideal that the universe is a whole, an entirety, which provides a "viable benevolent system for the salvation of everyone who does good" (Kallich 24).

> Martin Kallich draws attention to Pope's belief in the ideal that the universe is a whole, an entirety, which provides a "viable benevolent system for the salvation of everyone who does good" (24).

For a full discussion of the types of in-text references and the format to be used, see the *MLA Handbook*.

Footnotes and Endnotes

The most formal system of documentation still most widely used is that of footnotes (references at the bottom of each page) or endnotes (references listed numerically at the end of the essay). If your instructor wants you to use one of these systems, do the following: The first time you quote or refer to the source, make a note with the details in this order:

FOR A BOOK

1. The author's name, first name or initials first;
2. The title: underlined for a book. If you are referring to a story or poem in a collection, use quotation marks for that, but underline the title of the book. (Use a comma after title if an editor, translator, or edition follows.)
3. The name of the editor or translator. Abbreviate "editor" or "edited by" as *ed.*; "editors" as *eds.* Use *trans.* for "translator" or "translated by."
4. The edition (if indicated) abbreviated thus: *2nd ed.*, *3rd ed.*, and so on.
5. The publication facts should be given in parentheses, without any preceding or following punctuation, in the following order:
   a. City (but *not* the state) of publication, colon.
   b. Publisher, comma.
   c. Year of publication.
6. The page number(s), for example, 65, 65 f., 6–10. For books commonly reprinted, like *Hamlet*, and for well-known longer poems (like Milton's *Paradise Lost*), you should include the chapter, act and scene, or canto number together

with line numbers, so that readers using a different edition may be able to locate and verify your quotation.

FOR AN ARTICLE

1. The author, first name or initials first, comma.
2. The title of the article, in quotation marks, comma.
3. The name of the magazine, underlined, no comma.
4. The volume number, in Arabic numerals, no comma.
5. The year of publication, in parentheses, colon.
6. The page number(s), for example, 65, 65 f., 6–10.

For later notes to the same work, use a reference that may be most easily found in a bibliographical list. Thus, if you refer to only one work by Joseph Conrad, the name "Conrad" will be enough for all later references. Should you be using two or more works by Conrad, however, you will need to make a short reference to the specific works to distinguish them, such as "Conrad, *Lord Jim*," and "Conrad, *The Rescue*."

Footnotes are placed at the bottom of each page (separated from your essay by a line); *endnotes* are included at the end of the essay in a list. Ask your instructor about the practice you should adopt.

The first lines of both footnotes and endnotes should be paragraph indented, and continuing lines should be flush with the left margin. Footnote numbers are positioned slightly above the line (as superior numbers, like this[11]). Generally, you may single-space such notes, but be sure to ask your instructor about his or her preference.

SAMPLE FOOTNOTES.   In the examples below, book titles and periodicals, which are usually italicized in print, are shown underlined, as they would be in your typewritten paper.

[1] Joseph Conrad, The Rescue: A Romance of the Shallows (New York: Doubleday, 1960) 103.

[2] George Milburn, "The Apostate," An Approach to Literature, ed. Cleanth Brooks, John Thibaut Purser, and Robert Penn Warren, 3rd ed. (New York: Appleton-Century-Crofts, 1952) 74.

[3] Carlisle Moore, "Conrad and the Novel as Ordeal," Philological Quarterly 42 (1963): 59.

[4] Moore 61.

[5] Conrad 171.

[6] Milburn 76.

As a general principle, you do not need to repeat in a note any material that you have already incorporated into your essay. For example, if you mention the author and title of your source in the paper, then the note should merely give the data about publication. Here is an example:

> In Charles Macklin: An Actor's Life, William W. Appleton points out that Macklin had been "reinstated at Drury Lane" by December 19, 1744, and that he was playing his stellar role of Shylock.[7]

---

[7] (Cambridge: Harvard UP, 1961) 72.

Final Words

As long as all that you want from a reference is the page number of a quotation or of a paraphrase, the parenthetical system is suitable and easy. It saves your reader the trouble of glancing at the bottom of the page or of thumbing through pages to find a long list of notes. However, if you wish to add more details or if you wish to refer your reader to additional materials that you are not using directly in your theme. In such cases you must use full footnotes or endnotes.

Whatever method you use, there is an unchanging need to grant recognition to sources. Remember that whenever you begin to write and to make references, you might forget a number of specific details about documentation, and you will certainly discover that you have many questions. Be sure then to ask your instructor, who is your final authority.

ORGANIZING YOUR ESSAY

Introduction

In planning this, keep in mind that for a research essay, the introduction may be expanded beyond the length of that for an ordinary essay because of the need to relate the problem of research to your topic. You may wish to bring in relevant historical or biographical information. You might also wish to summarize critical opinion or to describe any particular critical problems as they pertain to your topic. The idea is to lead your reader into your topic by providing interesting and significant materials that you have uncovered during your research. Obviously, you should plan on including your usual guides—your central idea and your thesis sentence.

Because of the greater length of most research essays, some instructors require a topic outline, which is in effect a table of contents. This pattern is followed in the sample essay. Inasmuch as this method is a matter of choice with various instructors, be sure that you understand whether your instructor requires it.

Body, Conclusion

Your development both for the body and the conclusion will be governed by your choice of topic. Please consult the relevant chapters in this book about what to include for whatever topic you select (setting, idea, character, tone, or any other).

The research is usually assigned as a longer paper of from five to fifteen or more pages. It seems reasonable to assume that an essay based on only one work would be shorter than one based on several. If you narrow the scope of your topic, as suggested in the approaches described above, you can readily keep your essay within the assigned length. The sample research paper, for example illustrates the first approach by being limited to one character in one work. Were you to write on characters in a number of other plays by Shakespeare (the second approach), you could limit your total number of pages by stressing comparative treatments and by avoiding excessive detail about problems pertaining to only one work. In short, you will decide to include or exclude materials by compromising between the importance of the materials and the limits of your assignment.

Although you limit your topic yourself in consultation with your instructor, your sources may get out of your control when you plan and organize your essay. It is important therefore to keep your central idea foremost. By making this emphasis you can keep in control of your sources and prevent their controlling you.

The sources also add to the usual complications of writing, for you will be dealing not with one text alone but with many. The sources will of course be the basis of your details and of many of your ideas. The problem will be to handle the many strands and still preserve thematic unity. Once again, a constant stressing of your central idea will help you.

Because of the sources, there is something of a problem about your authority, and that problem is plagiarism. Your reader will automatically assume that everything you write is your own material unless you indicate otherwise. You leave yourself open to a charge of plagiarism, however, if you give no recognition to a detail or interpretation that seems clearly to have been derived from a source. To handle this problem, you need to be especially careful in your documentation. Most commonly, if you are simply presenting facts and details, you can write straightforwardly and let parenthetical references suffice as your authority, as follows:

> Thus he is most emphatic that Hamlet should not kill her along with Claudius (Fisch 80), and he also voices concern about the reputation and future of Denmark (Gottschalk, "Scanning" 165).

Here the parenthetical references to secondary texts are sufficient recognition of authority beyond your own.

If you are using an interpretation that is unique to a particular writer, however, or if you are relying on a significant quotation from your source, you should grant recognition as an essential part of your discussion, as in this sentence:

> A. C. Bradley (126) suggests that these speeches indicate Shakespeare's master touch in the development of the Ghost's character.

Here the idea of the critic is singled out specially for acknowledgement. If you grant recognition in this way, no confusion can possibly arise about the authority underlying your essay.

SAMPLE RESEARCH ESSAY

The Ghost in **Hamlet**

OUTLINE

I. INTRODUCTION
   A. THE IMPORTANCE OF THE GHOST IN *HAMLET*
   B. THE GHOST'S INFLUENCE UPON THE PLAY'S THEMES
II. THE GHOST'S STATUS AS A SPIRIT
III. THE GHOST'S CHARACTER
IV. THE GHOST'S IMPORTANCE IN THE STRUCTURE OF THE PLAY
V. THE GHOST'S EFFECT
VI. CONCLUSION

I. INTRODUCTION
   A. THE IMPORTANCE OF THE GHOST IN *HAMLET*

[1]
Even though the Ghost of old Hamlet is present in only a few scenes of *Hamlet*, he is nevertheless a dominant presence throughout the play.° He is seen twice in the very first scene, and the entire scene is about the meaning of these and earlier appearances. He enters again in the fourth scene of the first act, when he beckons and leads Hamlet off stage. In the fifth scene of act 1 he finally speaks, telling Hamlet of his murder at the hands of Claudius. His call for vengeance is the cause of the rest of the play's action. After some words which he speaks from underground (that is, under the stage), he does not appear again until the fourth scene of act 3, when he reveals himself to Hamlet—but not to Gertrude—to reproach the Prince for his failure to act and his preoccupation with his mother. The Ghost is not present at the play's end, but the actions he sets in motion are concluded there, and hence his effect remains dominant throughout.

° Central Idea

B. THE GHOST'S INFLUENCE UPON THE PLAY'S THEMES

[2]   Not only is the Ghost a dominant figure, he is also directly linked to many of the play's themes. Jean Paris observes that *Hamlet* is one of Shakespeare's plays that reveals ''an intensification of interior suffering'' (85). Hamlet's anguished soliloquies, together with the pain of Ophelia and Laertes (and even that of Claudius himself) may thus be traced to the Ghost. The commands the Ghost makes to Hamlet are direct and urgent, and therefore the Ghost introduces another of the play's major themes—that of responsibility, whether personal, political, or conjugal (McFarland 15). Because Hamlet seems to delay in fulfilling the Ghost's demand for vengeance, Hamlet's hesitation, this great ''Sphinx of modern Literature'' (Ernest Jones 22), becomes one of the most frequently raised and constantly nagging questions about the prince's character. The Ghost's presence also poses questions about the power of superstition, terror, and fear in human life (Campbell 211). Beyond these, in terms of psychology, the Ghost has been cited as a ''confirmation'' of the influence of ''psychic residues in governing and shaping human life'' (McFarland 34).

[3]   Because the Ghost is such an important influence in the play, we hardly need to justify a study of him, however brief. His importance may be traced in his spirit nature, his influence upon the play's structure, and his effect upon Hamlet and therefore indirectly upon all the major characters in the play.[□]

II. THE GHOST'S STATUS AS A SPIRIT

[4]   The Ghost is an apparition of questionable status. When Hamlet first sees the Ghost he raises a question about whether the vision is ''a spirit of health, or goblin damned'' (1.4.40). Horatio adds the idea that Hamlet is ''desperate with imagination'' (1.4.87), thus casting doubt upon the reality of the Ghost, even though everyone on the battlements has just seen it. Lily B. Campbell offers three options and sources about how to regard the Ghost: (1) as a real Ghost, from Catholic teaching in Elizabethan England, that held it possible for dead souls in Purgatory to return to earth for a time to communicate with the living; (2) as a demon, from the writings of King James I, who argued that the Devil himself could assume the shape of loved ones in order to lead living human beings to damnation; (3) as a vision, from scientifically oriented thinkers, who interpreted ghostly appearances as a sign of madness or deep melancholia (121). There were apparently a number of ''tests'' that might have enabled people to determine whether ghosts were truly genuine—that is, from Purgatory. Most of these required that the spirit in question be good, comforting, and sweet (Campbell 123).

[5]   Shakespeare's Ghost passes some of these tests but fails others. Even though he possesses some of the necessary redeeming qualities (Campbell 126), he also imposes a duty of revenge on Hamlet, something that no ghost of Purgatory would ever do (Prosser 136; McFarland 36). Although the Ghost describes the pain of a soul in Purgatory, he does so with a desire to horrify, not to urge Hamlet to commit himself to Christian repentance and salvation. Again, his description is an indication that he is closer in nature to the Devil than to a soul earning its way to redemption (Prosser 133, 134). Another sign

[□] Thesis Sentence

suggesting that the Ghost is a devilish spirit is that he withholds his appearance from Gertrude when he shows himself to Hamlet in 3.4 (Campbell 124; Prosser 200). Perhaps the best answer to the conflicting signs about the Ghost is provided by Lily B. Campbell, who suggests that the ambiguity is to be seen as a reflection of general uncertainty about ghosts among Shakespeare's contemporaries (127). In other words, she grants that there was no unanimity about the nature and purposes of ghosts at the time Shakespeare wrote. Even more to the point, however, because of this lack of agreement, it is possible that Shakespeare was not even interested in the question of ghostly consistency as discussed by theorists. If one grants that he was concerned, it is more likely that he chose to reflect common attitudes and superstition rather than scholarly debate.

III. THE GHOST'S CHARACTER

Uncertainty aside, the likely fact is that Shakespeare as a dramatist is probably presenting a lifelike rendering of what he thought a ghost would be like. He inherited a tradition of noisy, bloodthirsty ghosts from his sources—what Harold Fisch calls a "Senecan ghost" (91). In many ways he keeps to this tradition. Shakespeare's Ghost is bloodthirsty, although ironically not as

[6] bloodthirsty as Hamlet himself (Gottschalk, "Scanning" 166). The Ghost is also surrounded by awe and horror (DeLuca 147), and is genuinely frightening, both to the soldiers at the beginning of the play, and also to Hamlet in 3.4 (Charney 167–168). His speeches are designed to evoke grief, fear, and despair (Prosser 135).

But the Ghost is not just an imitation of the Senecan ghost. He is real, and well drawn as an individual person by Shakespeare (Alexander 30). Indeed, Shakespeare's Ghost is toned down from the ghost in an earlier anonymous version of *Hamlet,* perhaps one of Shakespeare's sources, which was seen by Shakespeare's contemporary Thomas Lodge (1558?–1625). Lodge talked about "ye ghost which cried so miserally [miserably] at ye theator . . . *Hamlet,* reuenge [revenge]." The Ghost in Shakespeare's *Hamlet* is certainly preoccu-

[7] pied with vengeance (Allman 243), but as a former king he is concerned about his country, and as a former loving husband he is also concerned about Gertrude. Thus he is most emphatic that Hamlet should not kill her along with Claudius (Fisch 80), and he also voices concern about the reputation and future of Denmark (Gottschalk, "Scanning" 165). Paul Gottschalk draws attention to this redeeming dimension as an indication that the Ghost is concerned with "restoration" as well as "retaliation" ("Scannings" 166).

Indeed, the Ghost has many qualities of a living human being as opposed to those of either a bad or a good spirit. He is, for example, witty, as Maurice Charney observes about the Ghost's interchange with Hamlet just at the beginning of the revelation speeches in 1.5.6–7:

HAMLET.   Speak, I am bound to hear.
GHOST.   So art thou to revenge, when thou shalt hear.

In other words, even though the Ghost may have come "with airs from heaven, or blasts from hell" (1.4.41), he is still mentally alert enough to make a pun

[8] out of Hamlet's word "bound" (Charney 118). To this quickness may be added his shrewd ability as a judge of Hamlet's character. He is clearly aware that

his son may be prone to forget duty, and hence his last words in 1.5 are "remember me," and his first words in 3.4 are "Do not forget." A. C. Bradley (126) suggests that these speeches indicate Shakespeare's master touch in the development of the Ghost's character.

[9]   The Ghost also shows other human traits. He has strong feelings of remorse about the crimes and "imperfections" of which he was guilty in life, and for which his sudden murder did not give him time to atone. He also has a sense of appropriateness that extends to his dress. Thus, at the beginning he appears on the battlement dressed in full armor; this battle dress would be the garb expected for the circumstances, and also to be expected in light of his urging Hamlet to kill Claudius in revenge (Aldus 54). By contrast, in the closet scene he wears a dressing gown ("in his habit as he lived," 3.4.135), as though he is prepared for ordinary palace activities of both business and leisure (Charney 26).

IV. THE GHOST'S IMPORTANCE IN THE STRUCTURE OF THE PLAY

It is Shakespeare's great strength as a dramatist that he gives the Ghost's character such round and full development and also integrates him fully within the actual structure of the play. We have noted the Ghost's importance as the instigator of revenge; Peter Alexander observes that the Ghost is "indispensable" as the mechanism of the plot and the source of communication to set things in motion (29). But the Ghost is also a director and organizer as well

[10]   as an informer, a figure who keeps the action moving (Aldus 100). A careful study of his speeches to Hamlet shows that he is a manipulator, playing upon his son's emotions to remind him of his character as an avenger and of his obligation to defend the honor of Denmark. In 3.4, the Ghost's return to Hamlet to "whet thy almost blunted purpose" (line 111) is the mark of the manager who gets nervous when he sees his directions being neglected by the one entrusted to carry them out.

The Ghost is also significant as a part of some of the other major structures of the play. At the beginning of Hamlet, we see national mobilization going on in preparation for possible war against Norway. To a high degree, this note of future warfare and impending political change is a backdrop to remind the audience that the events being witnessed will have an important political outcome. Indeed, King Hamlet, when alive, had conquered the Norwegian king

[11]   in single combat. Now, with the Danish state being torn by the internal anguish following Claudius's fratricide, the state lies weak and exposed—an easy prey to the Norwegians. Structurally, the beginning and ending of *Hamlet* are marked first by the expectation of war and then by the actual takeover by Young Fortinbras of Norway. Ironically, therefore, the Ghost in death is responsible for the fall of the state he so courageously defended in life.

There is an additional major structure involving the Ghost. Maurice Charney observes that the Ghost is significant in the "symmetrical" poison plots in the play (39). The first of these plots, the poisoning of King Hamlet, is described

[12]   by the Ghost himself in 1.5. The poisoning of the Player King in 3.2 is a virtual reenactment of the first murder, and it occurs in approximately the middle of the action. The final poisonings—of Gertrude, Laertes, Claudius, and finally Hamlet himself—occur in 5.2, the play's last scene. These are of course actions,

but they also have value as a set of symbolic frames that measure the progressive deterioration enveloping the major characters of the play.

V. THE GHOST'S EFFECT

[13] Beyond his practical and structural importance as the initiator of the play's action, the Ghost has profound psychological influence, mainly negative, on the characters. Roy Walker describes him as a "prologue" to the "omen" of Hamlet himself, who will be the agent of the "dread purpose" of vengeance (220). Because Hamlet is already suffering depression and melancholia, this role as an agent in a cause of questionable credibility opens the wounds of his vulnerability (Campbell 127–128). Hamlet must resolve to give up everything he has ever learned, even "the movement of existence itself," so that he may carry out the Ghost's commandment (McFarland 32–33). In an invasive, overpowering manner, Hamlet's melancholy influences his love for Ophelia, his possible friendship with Laertes, and his relationship with his mother (Kott 49; Kirsch 31). No one escapes. The effect is like waves radiating outwardly, with the Ghost at the center.

[14] These effects occur because, almost literally, Hamlet himself cannot escape the Ghost (Allman 218). In 1.5 the Ghost, unseen and below stage, follows him and hears his conversations with Horatio and the guards—an obvious symbolic representation of the Ghost's ongoing presence and pervasive power. As a result of this ever-present force, which as far as Hamlet is concerned might become visible at any moment, Hamlet is denied the healing that might normally occur after the death of a parent (Kirsch 26). The steady pressure toward vengeance disrupts any movement to mental health and creates what Kirsch calls a "pathology of depression" (26) that inhibits Hamlet's actions (Bradley 123), causes his Oedipal preoccupation with the sexuality of his parents (Kirsch 22), and brings about his desire for the oblivion that might come with suicide (Kirsch 27).

[15] It is this power over his son that gives the Ghost the greatest influence in the play. Once the Ghost has appeared, Hamlet can never be the same. He loses the dignity and composure (McFarland 38) that he has assumed as his right as a prince of Denmark and as a student in quest of knowledge. Rather than attack problems that he might have solved normally and easily with negotiations and research, he must sink into acts of murder. Is it any wonder that he hesitates? Despite all his reflection and hesitation, finally the web of vengeance woven by the Ghost closes in on everyone, and the consequence is that Hamlet becomes not only a murderer, but also a victim (Allman 254). There is no solution but the final one—real death, which is the literal conclusion of the symbolic death represented by the Ghost when he first appears on the Elsinore battlements.

VI. CONCLUSION

[16] The Ghost is real in terms of the action and structure of the play. He is seen by the characters on the stage, and when he speaks we hear him. He is made round and full by Shakespeare, and his motivation is direct and straightforward, even though the signs of his status as a spirit are presented somewhat ambiguously. But the Ghost is more. He has been made a Ghost by the greed

and envy of Claudius, and in this respect he becomes in the play either a conscious or unwitting agent of the "unseen Fates or forces" of his own doom (Walker 220). What he brings is the unavoidable horror that seems somehow to be just beneath the surface of good, moral people, waiting for the license to reach out and destroy. Once the forces are released, there is no holding them, and the tragedy of *Hamlet* is that there is no way to win against such odds.

A LIST OF WORKS CITED

Alexander, Peter. *Hamlet; Father and Son*. Oxford: Clarendon, 1955.

Aldus, P. J. *Mousetrap: Structure and Meaning in* Hamlet. Toronto: U. of Toronto Press, 1977.

Allman, Eileen Jorge. *Player-King and Adversary*. Baton Rouge: Louisiana State UP, 1980.

Bradley, A. C. *Shakespearean Tragedy*. London: Macmillan, 1950.

Campbell, Lily B. *Shakespeare's Tragic Heroes: Slaves of Passion*. New York: Barnes & Noble, 1959.

DeLuca, Diana Macintyre. "The Movements of the Ghost in Hamlet," *Shakespeare Quarterly* 24 (1973): 147–54.

Fisch, Harold. *Hamlet and the Word*. New York: Frederick Ungar, 1971.

Gottschalk, Paul. "Hamlet and the Scanning of Revenge." *Shakespeare Quarterly* 24 (1973): 155–70.

——— *The Meanings of* Hamlet. Albuquerque: U of New Mexico Press, 1972.

Kirsch, Arthur. "Hamlet's Grief." *ELH* 48 (1981): 17–36.

Kott, Jan. *Shakespeare Our Contemporary*. Trans. Boleslaw Taborski. London: Methuen, 1967, repr. 1970.

McFarland, Thomas. *Tragic Meanings in Shakespeare*. New York: Random House, 1966.

Paris, Jean. *Shakespeare*. Trans. Richard Seaver. New York: Grove Press, 1960.

Prosser, Eleanor. *Hamlet and Revenge*. 2nd ed. Stanford: Stanford UP, 1971.

Walker, Roy. "*Hamlet*: the Opening Scene." *Shakespeare: Modern Essays in Criticism*. Ed. Leonard F. Dean. New York: Oxford UP, 1961.

Commentary on the Essay

This essay fulfills an assignment requiring about 2,500 words and fifteen sources. The sources were located through an examination of a library catalog, the *MLA International Bibliograpy*, and library bookshelves. They represent the range of materials available in a college library with a selective, not exhaustive, set of holdings. The essay is derived largely from the sources listed, with necessary thematic devices, including overall organization and transitions, to make the essay original. Additional particulars about the handling of sources and developing the essay are included in the discussion of note taking and related matters in the previous part of this chapter.

The central idea of the essay is the importance of the Ghost. Paragraph 1 stresses this idea, while conceding that the Ghost is only a minor character in the action. The research for this paragraph is derived not so much from secondary sources as from a close reading of the play itself. Paragraph 2, continuing the exploration of the central idea, demonstrates that the Ghost figures into the major themes of *Hamlet*. The third paragraph is mainly functional, being used as the location of the thesis sentence.

Part II of the essay, containing paragraphs 4 and 5, is on the topic of the Ghost's status as a spirit. Part III, with four paragraphs (6–9), actually continues part II but is concerned with the Ghost's character as an individual rather than as a spirit. Part IV, with paragraphs 10–12, deals with the significance of the Ghost in four of the major structures which dominate the play. Part V, with three paragraphs, considers the negative and inexorable influence the Ghost has upon the major figures of *Hamlet*, with the emphasis being the character of Hamlet as the transferring agent of the Ghost's destructive revenge. The concluding paragraph (16) summarizes much of the essay, with its final idea being concerned with the Ghost's influence upon the nature of *Hamlet* as a tragedy.

The list of works cited is the basis of all references in the text of the essay, in accord with the *MLA Handbook for Writers of Research Papers*, 2nd ed. By using the references included parenthetically in the essay, a reader might use this list to examine, verify, and further study any of the ideas located in these sources.

Appendix D:
Taking Examinations
on Literature

Taking an examination on literature is not difficult if you prepare in the right way. Preparing means (1) studying the material assigned, the comments made in class by your instructor and by fellow students, and your own thoughts; (2) anticipating the questions by writing some of your own on the material to be tested and by writing practice answers to these questions; and (3) understanding the precise function of the test in your education.

Tests are not designed to plague you or to hold down your grade. The grade you receive is in fact a reflection of your achievement at a given point in the course. If your grades are low, you can probably improve them by studying in a coherent and systematic way. Those students who can easily do satisfactory work might do superior work if they improve their method of preparation. From whatever level you begin, you can increase your achievement by improving your method of study.

Your instructor has three major concerns in evaluating your tests (assuming literate English): (1) to see the extent of your command over the subject material of the course, (2) to see how well you are able to think about the material, and (3) to see how well you can actually respond to a question or address yourself to an issue.

There are many elements that go into writing good answers on tests, but this last point, about responsiveness, is perhaps the most important. A major cause of low exam grades is that students really do not *answer* the questions asked. The problem is that some students do no more than retell the story, never confronting the issues in the question. Therefore, if you are asked, "Why does . . . ," be sure to emphasize the *why*, and use the *does* only to exemplify the *why*. If the question is about organization, focus on that. If a problem is raised, deal with it. In short, always *respond* directly to the question or instruction. Let us compare two answers to the same question:

Question: How important is the setting of Poe's "The Masque of the Red Death" to the plan and action of the story?

1

The setting of Poe's "The Masque of the Red Death" is a major element in all aspects of the story. The Prince Prospero invites a thousand of his subjects into his vast "castellated abbey" to be entertained while being shielded from the plague of the red death killing the people in the country. The abbey is surrounded by a high and strong wall, and the gates are all welded shut to prevent all contamination from the plague. The prince lays in much food and wine, and also has musicians, dancers, and other entertainers present and performing constantly so that time can pass well. After a short period he gives a gala, lavish masquerade ball in seven huge rooms of his abbey. Each room has a uniform color scheme—one blue, one purple, one green, one orange, one white, one violet, and one black (with red)—almost all the colors of the rainbow. Over all this a black clock in the black room hourly chimes a frightening, dismal sound that makes the merriment halt momentarily, as though it were a reminder of the brevity of life. At midnight—the ghostliest hour—Death himself appears, costumed as one of those who have died of the red death, to the horror of the guests. The prince runs after Death, into the black room, in reproach and assault. But then Prospero abruptly dies, and so do all the other guests. Everything happens within the abbey. And so the setting is all pervasive in Poe's development of the story.

2

The setting of Poe's "The Masque of the Red Death" is a major element in all aspects of the story. As a location, Prospero's "castellated abbey" is a focus of human defiance against death. As a cause of action, the walling in of his thousand courtiers is, ironically, the same as insuring that they will all die when Death finally arrives. As a means of achieving probability, the laying in of provisions and entertainment makes the plans of the prince and his "light-hearted friends" seem possible and realistic. As atmosphere, the eerie black clock and the even eerier coloring and lighting of the ballrooms are a commentary on the prince's bizarre and vain attempt to avoid fate. Finally, the setting of the ballrooms, expressively described by the narrator, is the place of the final assault that Prospero makes against the ghoulish, spectral figure of the Red Death, and where he and his followers all die. The setting is therefore all pervasive in Poe's development of the story.

While paragraph 1 relates the action to the various scenes of the story, it does not focus on the relationship. It is also cluttered by details that have no bearing on the question. Paragraph 2, on the other hand, focuses directly on the connection. Because of this emphasis, 2 is shorter than 1. That is, with the focus directly on the issue, there is no need for irrelevant narrative details. Thus, 1 is unresponsive and unnecessarily long, while 2 is responsive and includes only enough detail to exemplify the major points.

PREPARATION

Your problem is how best to prepare yourself to be knowledgeable and ready for an examination. If you simply cram facts into your head in hopes that you will be able to adjust to whatever questions are asked, you will likely flounder.

Read and Reread

Above all, keep in mind that your preparation should begin not on the night before the exam but as soon as the course begins. When each assignment is given, you should complete it by the date due, for you will understand your instructor's lecture and the classroom discussion only if you know the material being discussed. Then, about a week before the exam, you should review each assignment, preferably rereading everything completely. With this preparation, your study on the night before the exam will be fruitful, for it might be viewed as a climax of preparation, not the entire preparation itself.

Make Your Own Questions: Go on the Attack

Rereading is effective but passive preparation. You should instead go on the attack by trying to anticipate the specific conditions of the test. The best way to do this is to compose and answer your own practice questions. Do not waste your time trying to guess the questions you think your instructor might ask. What is of greatest importance is to arrange the subject matter by asking yourself questions that help you get things straight.

How can you make your own questions? It is not as hard as you might think. Your instructor may have announced certain topics or ideas to be tested on the exam. You might develop questions from these. Or you might apply general questions to the specifics of your assignments, as in the following examples:

1. About a character: What sort of character is A? How does A grow, or change in the work? What does A learn, or not learn, that brings about the conclusion? To what degree is A the representative of any particular type?

2. About the interactions of characters: How does B influence A? Does a change in C bring about any corresponding change in A?

3. About events or situations: What relationship does episode A have to situation B? Does C's thinking about situation D have any influence on the outcome of event E.

4. About a problem: Why is character *A* or situation *X* this way and not that way? Is the conclusion justified by the ideas and events leading up to it?
5. About a theme: What ideas does the work explore? How are these established? Which were emphasized in class?

Adapt Your Notes to Make Questions

Perhaps the best way to construct questions is to use your classroom notes, for notes are the fullest record you have about the way the class approached the material. As you work with your notes, you should reread passages from the texts that were studied by the class or mentioned by your instructor. Remember that it is helpful to work not only with main ideas from your notes, but also with matters such as style, imagery, and organization.

Obviously you cannot make questions from all your notes, and you will therefore need to select from those that seem most important. As an example, here is a short but significant note from a classroom discussion about Walter Van Tilburg Clark's story "The Portable Phonograph" (p. 214): "A particularly timely and modern story. The context is the global, less localized nature of warfare, and the massive destructiveness made possible by modern weapons technology." It is not difficult to adapt this note to make two practice questions:

1. What effects of modern weapons technology make the post-war wasteland setting of "The Portable Phonograph" seem realistic?
2. Why may "The Portable Phonograph" be considered as a particularly timely and modern story?

The first question applies the word *what* to the second part of the note, with the specific focus on the setting of the story. The second applies the word *why* to the phrasing of the first part of the note. Either question would guide you to focused study. The first would require an explanation of the setting of Clark's story realistically mirroring the complete destructiveness made possible by large-scale weapons. The second would emphasize the conditions of modern warfare and their possible effects, with attempts to show how the story reflects these modern conditions. If you were to spend fifteen or twenty minutes writing practice answers to these questions, you could be confident in taking an examination on the material.

Use Questions Even When Time is Short

Whatever your subject, it is important that you spend as much study time as possible making and answering your own questions. Of course, you will have limited time and will not be able to write extensive answers indefinitely. Even so, do not give up on the question method. If time is too short for full answers, write out the main heads, or topics, of an answer. When time no longer permits you to make even such a brief outline answer, keep thinking of questions, and think about the answers on the way to the exam. Try never to read passively or unresponsively, but always with a creative, question-and-answer goal. Think of studying as a potential writing experience.

Study with a Fellow Student

Often the thoughts of another person can help you understand the material to be tested. Try to find a fellow student with whom you can work. In view of the need for steady preparation throughout a course, keep in mind that regular conversations are a good idea. Also, you might wish to make your joint study genuinely systematic and thus might set aside a specific evening or afternoon for detailed work sessions.

TWO BASIC TYPES OF QUESTIONS ABOUT LITERATURE

There are two types of questions that you will find on any examination about literature. Keep them in mind as your prepare. The first type is *factual*, or *mainly objective*, and the second is *general*, *comprehensive*, *broad*, or *mainly subjective*. In a literature course very few questions are purely objective, except multiple-choice questions.

Factual Questions

MULTIPLE-CHOICE QUESTIONS.   These are the most purely factual questions. In an introduction to literature course your instructor will most likely reserve them for short quizzes, usually on days when an assignment is due, to make sure that you are keeping up with the reading. Multiple choice can test your knowledge of facts, and it also can test your ingenuity in perceiving subtleties of phrasing in certain choices, but on a literature exam this type of question is rare.

IDENTIFICATION QUESTION.   These questions test not only your factual knowledge but also your ability to relate this knowledge to your understanding of the work assigned. Typical examples of what you might be asked to identify are:

1. *A character*, for example, Nora in O'Connor's "First Confession." It is necessary to describe briefly the character's position and main activity (that is, she is Jackie's older sister who gets him in trouble at home and who takes

him to his confession). You should then go on to emphasize the character's importance (that is, her values help keep Jackie confused throughout most of the story, but by the end it is clear that O'Connor shows that it is really her values that are confused).

2. *Incidents or situations*, which may be illustrated as follows: "A woman mourns the death of her husband." After giving the location of the situation or incident (Mrs. Popov in Chekhov's play *The Bear* or the widow in Petronius' "The Widow of Ephesus"), try to demonstrate its significance in the work. (That is, Mrs. Popov is mourning the death of her husband when the play opens, and in the course of the play Chekhov uses her feelings to show amusingly that life with real emotion is stronger than devotion or duty to the dead. Petronius makes much the same point.)

3. *Things, places, and dates.* Your instructor may ask you to identify a bottle of poison (Collier's "The Chaser" or Shakespeare's *Hamlet*), a royal palace (Sophocles' *Oedipus the King*, Shakespeare's *Hamlet* or Poe's "The Masque of the Red Death"), or the dates of poems like Blake's "The Tyger (1794) or Nikki Giovanni's "Woman" (1978). For dates, you might often be given a leeway of five or ten years if you must guess.

4. *Quotations.* Theoretically, you should remember enough of the text to identify a passage taken from it, or at least to make an informed guess. Generally, you should try to locate the quotation, if you remember it or else to describe the probable location, and to show the ways in which the quotation is typical of the work you have read, with regard to both content and style. You can often salvage much from a momentary lapse of memory by writing a reasoned and careful explanation of your guess, even if the guess is incorrect.

TECHNICAL AND ANALYTICAL QUESTIONS AND PROBLEMS.   In a scale of ascending importance, the third and most difficult type of factual question involves technique, analysis, and problems. You might be asked to discuss the *setting*, *images*, *point of view*, or *principal idea* of a work; you might be asked about a *specific problem*; you might be asked to analyze a poem that may or may not be duplicated for your benefit.

The use of technical questions will obviously depend on what you have been studying during the period for which you are being tested. If your instructor has been stressing topics like character, setting, point of view, metaphors and similes, and rhythm, you should prepare to answer questions involving these techniques. If classroom discussion has been confined to theme and idea, however, your preparation may be focused on these. Most instructors announce their intentions well in advance of the exam; if you have any uncertainties about how to prepare, however, be sure to ask your instructor.

Technical questions may be fairly long, perhaps with from fifteen to twenty-five minutes allowed for each. If you have two or more of these questions, try to space your time sensibly; do not devote 80 percent of your time to one question and leave only 20 percent for the rest.

Basis of Judging Factual Questions

IDENTIFICATION QUESTIONS.   In all identification questions, your instructor is testing (1) your command of facts and (2) your understanding of the relationships of parts to wholes. Thus, let us suppose that you are asked to identify the incident "A woman stabs another woman." It is correct to begin by saying that Katherine Anne Porter's "Maria Concepción" is the story, that Maria Concepción does the stabbing, and that Maria Rosa is killed. Knowledge of these details clearly establishes your command of the facts. But a strong answer must go further. Even in the brief time available for short answers, a good response should also aim at relating the thing being identified to (1) major causation in the work, (2) major ideas, (3) the organization or structure of the work, and (4) for a quotation, the style. Time is short, and you must be selective, but if you can establish a pattern that moves from the factual to the significant, you will be writing superior answers. Along these lines, let us look at an answer identifying the incident from "Maria Concepción:"

> This incident is from Porter's "Maria Concepción." Maria Rosa is the victim, and Maria Concepción stabs her as an apparent act of revenge for her having run away with Juan Villegas, Maria Concepción's husband, and having borne his child. The incident is central to the story because it shows the depth of Maria Concepción's accumulating rage at having been so wronged. Because it also creates a crisis, it produces resolutions. Juan returns immediately to Maria Concepción and plans to stick by her and defend her. Also, the villagers rally around her during the investigation, and in addition, once she is relieved of suspicion she is able to claim Maria Rosa's baby to replace her own baby that had died. By the story's end Maria Concepción is totally safe and has secured her place in the community. The incident is therefore a major element in the characterization, causation, and structure of the story.

Any of the points made in this answer could be more fully developed, but the answer is successful because it both places the incident in perspective and deals with its significance. One thing is clear from this example: *A really superior answer cannot be written if your thinking originates entirely at the time you first see the question.* The more thinking and practicing you do before the exam, the better your answers will be.

LONGER FACTUAL QUESTIONS.   The more extended factual questions also require more thoroughly developed organization. Remember that here your knowledge of essay writing is important, for your writing skills will determine a major share of your instructor's evaluation of your answers. It is therefore best to take several minutes to gather your thoughts together before you begin to write. When the questions are before you, use a sheet of scratch paper to jot down the facts you remember and your ideas about them in relation to the question. Then put them together, phrase a thesis sentence, and use your facts to illustrate or prove your thesis.

Begin your answer pointedly; use key words or phrases from the question or direction if possible, so that your answer will have thematic focus. To be most responsive during the short time available for writing an exam, use the question as your guide for your answer. Let us suppose that you have the following question on your test: "How does Steinbeck use details in 'The Chrysanthemums' to reveal the character of Eliza?" The most common way to go astray on such a question, and the easiest thing to do, is to concentrate on Eliza's character rather than on how Steinbeck uses detail to bring out her character. The word *how* makes a vast difference, and hence the best thing to do on an exam is to copy key phrases from the question to ensure that the answer will be launched in the right direction. Here is an opening sentence that uses the key words and phrases from the question to provide focus.

> Steinbeck *uses details* about gardening, farm life, and personal care as symbols *to reveal the character of Eliza* as a motherly and sexual but repressed and unhappy person.

This sentence sets aims and limits so that the subsequent material will be clearly focused and responsive to the question as it has been asked.

General or Comprehensive Questions

General or comprehensive questions are particularly important on final examinations, when your instructor is interested in testing your total comprehension of the course material. Considerable time is usually allowed for answering this type of question. They may be phrased in a number of ways:

1. A direct question asking about philosophy, underlying attitudes, main ideas, characteristics of style, backgrounds, and so on. Here are some possible questions in this category: "What use do _____, _____, and _____ make of the topic of _____?" "Define and characterize the short story as a genre of literature." "Explain the nature of the sonnet as treated in poets studied during the course." "Contrast the technique of point of view as used by _____, _____, and _____."

2. A "comment" question, often based on an extensive quotation, borrowed from a critic or written by your instructor for the occasion, about a broad class of writers, or about a literary movement, or the like. Your instructor may ask you to treat this question broadly (taking in many writers) or else to apply the quotation to a specific writer.

3. A "suppose" question, such as "Suppose that Sherlock Holmes found himself in the place of Hamlet; what might he do when confronted with the testimony

of the ghost?" or "What might Sophocles say if he could see the drama of Thornton Wilder and Tennessee Williams?"

Basis of Judging General Questions

When answering broad, general questions you are in fact dealing with an unstructured situation, and you must not only supply an *answer* but—equally as important—you must also create a *structure* within which your answer can have meaning. You might almost say that you make up your own specific question out of the original general question. If you were asked to "Consider the role of women as expressed in plays by Ibsen, Glaspell, and Williams," for example, you would do well to structure the question by narrowing its limits. A possible way to focus such a question might be this:

> Ibsen, Glaspell, and Williams express wide-ranging views about women by dramatizing their positions in the home, their relationships with men, and their relative degrees of power.

With this sort of focus you would be able to proceed point by point, introducing supporting data as you form your answer.

As a general rule, the best method to adopt in answering a comprehensive question is that of comparison-contrast. The reason is that in dealing with, say, a general question on Donne, Burns, and Heaney, it is too easy to write *three* separate essays rather than one. Thus, you should force yourself to consider a topic like "The treatment of departure," or "The relationship of men and women," and then to treat such a topic point by point rather than poet by poet. By developing your answer in this way, you can bring in references to each or all of the writers as they become relevant to your main idea. But if you were to treat each poet separately, your comprehensive answer would lose focus and effectiveness.

Glossary

Abstract diction Language that is far removed from the concrete, and therefore applicable to many rather than few objects, persons, actions, and situations. *238–39*

Absurd, drama of the A type of nonrealistic drama, often comedy, that explores the absurdities of modern existence. *1068*

Accent See *Stress*.

Accented rhyme See *Rising rhyme*.

Accentual (strong-stress) and "sprung" rhythm Rhythm that relies not on traditional meters but rather on numbers of strong stresses, regardless of the number of lightly stressed words and syllables. *676–77*

Actions, or incidents The events or occurrences in a work of literature. *79, 102*

Accumulation See *Cumulatio*.

Alexandrine A line of verse written in iambic hexameter, containing twelve syllables or six iambic feet. *720*

Allegory A story that may be applied to another, parallel, set of situations while maintaining its own narrative integrity. *85, 296–300, 1045*

Alliteration The repetition of identical consonant sounds in different words in close proximity. *695*

Allusion References (usually unacknowledged) to literary works, persons, sayings, and other elements of our cultural heritage. *298–299, 789–91, 814*

Amphibrach A three-syllable foot consisting of a light, heavy, and light stress, as in *wiĭh pléa-sŭre*. *674–75*

Amphimacer, or cretic A three-syllable metrical foot consisting of a heavy, light, and heavy stress, as in *thoúghts ŏf loṽe*. *675*

Analysis See *Commentary*.

Antagonist The character or characters opposing the protagonist. A conflict between a protagonist and an antagonist or non-human force is *antagonism*. *79, 1039*

Antimetabole See *Chiasmus*.

Anagnoresis A process or moment of increased self-knowledge and understanding. *1124*

Anapest A three-syllable metrical foot consisting of two light stresses followed by a heavy, as in *in the town*. *673*

Apostrophe The addressing of discourse to a real or imagined person who is not present; also, a speech to an abstraction. *622*

Aside A short speech delivered by one character to another or to the audience without the rest of the characters on stage being able to hear; the speaker usually reveals his or her thoughts or plans. *1041*

Assertion A positive or negative statement about an idea, such as that love [the idea in the subject of the sentence] is necessary but also irrational [the predicate contains the assertion about the idea]. *334*

Assonance The repetition of identical vowel sounds in different words in close proximity. *695*

Atmosphere See *Mood*.

Auditory images References to sounds. *572–573*

Authorial symbols See *Private symbols*.

Bacchius, or Bacchic A three-syllable metrical foot consisting of a light stress followed by two heavy stresses, as in *the stream's bed*. *675*

Ballad A narrative poem composed of quatrains in which lines of iambic tetrameter alternate with iambic trimeter, rhyming *a b c b*. *744*

Beast fable See *Fable*.

Blank verse Unrhymed iambic pentameter. *678, 740*

Blocking The grouping and movement of characters on stage in a play. *1034*

Blocking agent In new and romantic comedy, a circumstance, person, or attitude that obstructs the union of two people in love. *1379*

Box set In the modern theater, usually a realistic setting of a single room from which the "fourth wall" is missing. *1289*

Cacophony Words combining consonant sounds that do not permit an easy flow of pronunciation, but rather produce sharpness or harshness. *696*

Cadence group The coinciding of speaking units with grammatical units, separated by slight pauses. *667–68*

Caesura (pl. *caesurae*) In poetry, the pause separating cadence groups, or units of rhythm. *677*

Carpe diem poetry Poetry that emphasizes the shortness of life and the need to act in or enjoy the present. *Carpe diem* means "sieze the day." *472*

Catastrophe The fourth stage of dramatic plot structure; the single moment of revelation or realization when everything falls into place. *1038*

Catharsis The stimulation and subsequent purgation of fear and pity that, according to Aristotle, occurs as one watches or reads an effective tragedy. *1123*

Cause and effect The interaction of events and the pattern of causation that produces the tension and therefore the interest of fiction. *79*

Central idea (1) The thesis of an essay; (2) the theme of a literary work. See also *Theme*. *80, 839*

Character An extended verbal representation of a human being, the inner self that determines thought, speech, and behavior—a reasonable facsimile of a human being. *78–79, 134–76*.

Chiasmus A rhetorical sentence pattern (or even a larger pattern) repeating in the sequence A-B-B-A, such as:

>   *A*   *B*   *B*   *A*
> "I know she loves me, but she loves to keep me from knowing it." *244*

Choragos The leader of the chorus in classical Greek drama. *1129*

Choric character A character who remains detached from the action and who provides commentary. *1039*

Chorus A group of actors chanting or speaking in unison, probably while moving in a stately dance; a characteristic feature of classical Greek drama. *1129*

Chronology The sequence of events in a work, with emphasis upon the logic of cause and effect. *79*

Clerihew A humorous closed-form poem in four lines, rhyming a b a b, usually about a famous person or figure. *747*

Cliché rhymes Rhymes, such as *moon* and *June* or *trees* and *breeze*, that have been so widely used by poets and songwriters as to become trite. *714*

Climax The high point in an action, the third stage of dramatic plot structure, in which the conflict and the consequent tension are brought out to the fullest extent; hence the turning point of a work at which the outcome is determined. *105, 1038*

Closed couplet See *Heroic couplet*.

Closed-form poetry Poetry written in specific and traditional patterns produced through rhyme, meter, line-length, and line groupings. *668, 739*

Comedy A literary work, beginning in adversity and ending in prosperity, that describes the regeneration and success of a group or society. *1035, 1378*

Comedy of humors Comedy that exposes and ridicules the humors (excesses and eccentricities) of characters in order to reform them. *1383*

Comedy of manners A form of comedy, usually high comedy, in which the social conventions of society are examined and satirized. *1383*

Comedy of the Absurd A modern form of comedy that dramatizes the absurdities of existence and ends ambiguously. *1384*

Commedia dell'arte Broadly humorous farce, developed in sixteenth-century Italy, featuring stock characters, stock situations, and improvised dialogue. *1382*

Commentary The use of passages of reflection as a means of explaining the meaning of an action or dialogue. *83*

Common ground of assent Those interests and concerns that the writer assumes in common with readers so that an effective and persuasive tone may be maintained. *646–47*

Common measure A closed poetic quatrain form, rhyming *A B A B*, in which lines of iambic tetrameter alternate with iambic trimeter. *744*

Complex sentence A main clause together with a subordinate or dependent clause. *241*

Complication The onset of the major conflicts in a work; the second stage of dramatic plot structure. *105, 1038*

Compound-complex sentence Two or more independent clauses with which one or more dependent clauses are integrated. *242*

Compound sentence Two simple sentences joined by a conjunction. *241*

Conceit An elaborate and extended metaphor. *873*

Concrete diction Words that describe qualities or conditions, such as an ice cream sundae being "cold," "sweet," and "creamy." Distinguished from *abstract diction*. *238–39*

Concrete poetry Poetry that draws most or all of its meaning from the visual impact of the poem. *754*

Conflict The opposition between two characters, between large groups of people, or between individuals and larger forces such as natural objects, ideas, modes of behavior, public opinion, and the like. Conflict may also be internal, involving choices facing a character. It is the essence of *plot*. *79, 102–104*

Connotation The emotional, psychological, or social overtones or implications that words carry in addition to their standard dictionary meaning. *239–240, 541*

Consonant sounds Sounds produced as a result of the interaction of tongue or lips with lips, teeth, or palate. *694*

Contextual symbols See *Private symbols*.

Continuant sounds Consonant sounds produced by the steady release of the breath in conjunction with various positions of tongue, teeth, palate, and lips; for example, *m*, *l*, *f*, and *z*. *694*

Cosmic irony Situational irony that is connected to a pessimistic or fatalistic view of life. *271–72*

Couplet (1) Two successive lines of poetry, usually in the same meter, that rhyme; (2) the last two lines of an English sonnet. *468, 740*

Cretic See *Amphimacer*.

Crisis The turning point, the separation between what has gone before and what will come after, usually a decision or action undertaken in an effort to resolve the conflict of the work; see also *Climax*. *105, 1038*

Cultural or universal symbols Generally or universally recognized symbols embodying ideas or emotions that the writer and the reader share in common as a result of their social and cultural heritage. *295, 785*

Cumulatio The parallel building up of much detail; a short way of introducing a considerable amount of material. Also called *accumulation*. *244*

Dactyl A three-syllable metrical foot consisting of a heavy stress followed by two lights, as in *mȋght-ĭ-est*. *673*

Dactylic rhyme See *Triple rhyme*.

Decorum A quality of language and behavior that is thought to be appropriate, suitable, or fitting both to the literary medium (such as epic poetry) and also to subject and character. *547–48*

Description The exposition of scenes, actions, attitudes, and feelings. *82*

Denotation The standard dictionary meaning of a word. *239–40, 540*

Dénouement See *Resolution*.

Device A rhetorical figure or a verbal strategy. *590*

Deus ex machina An extraordinary turn of events that produces the sudden resolution of a play. *1128*

Dialect The language of a particular social class, region, or group. *548*

Dialogue A conversation between two or more characters in a story, play, or poem. *82–83, 1034*

Diction Word choice, types of words, and the level of language. *236–39, 546*

Diction, formal Proper, elevated, and elaborate language characterized by complex words and a lofty tone. *237, 547*

Diction, informal or low Relaxed, conversational, and colloquial language. *238, 547*

Diction, middle or neutral Correct language and word order without elaborate words or a lofty tone. *237, 547*

Didactic play A play designed to teach a specific lesson or moral. *1046*

Digraph Two letters spelling one segment of a sound, as in the word *digraph*, where *ph* spells the sound *f*. *693*

Dilemma Two choices facing a protagonist, with either one being unacceptable or damaging. *103*

Dimeter A line consisting of two metrical feet. *670*

Diphthong A vowel sound that begins with one vowel sound and then concludes in another. *694*

Dipodic Dipodic measure (literally "two feet" combining to make one) develops when a poet submerges two normal feet, usually iambs or trochees, under a strong beat, so that a "galloping" or "rollicking" rhythm results. *675*

Domestic tragedy A tragedy of domestic life usually involving middle-class characters. *1124*

Donné The given situation or set of assumptions on which a work of literature is based. *77*

Double dactyl A humorous closed-form poem in two quatrains, written predominantly in dactylic dimeter. The first line must be a proper name, and the sixth or seventh a single word. *747*

Double-entendre Deliberate ambiguity, often sexual. *271*

Double plot Two different but related lines of action going on at the same time, usually in a play. *1037*

Double rhyme Rhyming words of two syllables in which the accent falls on the next-to-last syllable, such as *seasons* and *reasons*. *715*

Drama (1) A play; (2) a group of plays, as in *modern drama*; (3) all literature written to be acted. *1033*

Dramatic convention   A traditional or customary method or device of presentation that is accepted by readers or audiences and allows a playwright to limit or simplify material. *1047*

Dramatic irony   A special kind of situational irony in which a character perceives his or her plight in one way while the audience and one or more of the other characters understand it in greater perspective. *84, 272, 1044*

Dramatic point of view   A third person narration reporting speech and action but rigorously excluding commentary on the action and thoughts of any of the characters. *81, 182, 1041*

Dramatic monologue   A type of poem derived from the theater, in which a speaker speaks to an internal listener or the reader at length. The form is related to the soliloquy. *489*

Dying rhyme   See *Falling rhyme*.

Dynamic character   A character with the capacity to adapt, change, and grow (opposed to *static character*). *136, 1039*

Echoic words   Words echoing the actions they describe, such as *buzz*, *bump*, and *slap*, important in the device of *onomatopoeia*. *696*

Enclosing method   See *Framing method*.

End-stopped line   A line ending in a full pause, usually indicated with a period or semicolon. *677*

English (or Shakespearean) sonnet   A fourteen-line poem, in iambic pentameter, composed of three quatrains and a couplet, rhyming *a b a b, c d c d, e f e f, g g*. *743*

Enjambement   A line having no end punctuation but running over to the next line. *677*

Epic   Usually a long narrative poem that features heroic characters, momentous events, and highly elevated diction. *73–74, 553*

Epigram   A short and witty poem, usually in couplets, that makes a humorous or satiric point. *481, 745*

Episodia   The episodes or scenes in a Greek tragedy. *1130*

Epitaph   Lines composed to mark someone's death; a special type of epigram. *745*

Essay   A fully developed set of interconnected paragraphs that grow systematically out of a central idea. *6*

Euphony   Words containing consonants that permit an easy and pleasant flow of spoken sound. *696*

Exact rhyme   Rhyming words in which both the vowel and consonant sounds rhyme, also called *perfect rhyme*. *717*

Exodos   The final episode in a Greek tragedy, occurring after the last choral ode. *1130*

Explication   Complete and detailed analysis of a work of literature. *465*

Exposition   The laying out or putting forth of the materials necessary for an understanding of a work; the first stage of dramatic plot structure, in which the playwright supplies background and introduces characters and conflict. *104–05, 1037*

Eye rhyme In a position in a poem where rhyme is expected, eye-rhyming words look as though they should rhyme exactly but do not, as in *love* and *prove*. *717*

Fable A short, pointed story illustrating a moral truth, most often associated with the ancient Greek writer Aesop. *74, 297–98*

Falling action The action in a play after the climax—the catastrophe and resolution. *1038*

Falling rhyme Rhymes using words of two or more syllables in which the accent falls on any syllable other than the last, such as *dying* and *crying*. *715*

Fantasy The creation of events that are dreamlike or fantastic, departing from ordinary understanding of reality because of apparently illogical causation and chronology. *76*

Farce Boisterous, physical, low comedy in which the focus is on action and plot. *1382*

Feminine rhyme See *Falling rhyme*.

Fiction A prose story based in the imagination of the author, not in literal facts. *73*

Figurative language Expressions that conform to a particular pattern or form, such as metaphor, simile, and antimetabole. *590*

First-person point of view The "I" narrator who acquires authority because of close involvement in the action or because of being an observer. *81, 179–80*

Flat character A character, usually minor, who is not individual, but rather useful and structural, static and unchanging; compare *round character*. *136, 1039*

Foil A type of character who sets off or highlights aspects of the protagonist in a play. *1039*

Foot See *Metrical foot*.

Form In poetry, the shape, structure, or general pattern of a poem. In the consideration of ideas, a form may be conceptual as opposed to real. Thus the activity of thought, to the degree that it can be remembered or imagined, is a mental *form*. *333, 730*

Formal diction See *Diction, formal*.

Framing mode The use of a setting at both the beginning and ending of a story so that the story itself is "framed." *208*

Free verse Nonmetrical poetry (in French, *vers libre*) that depends on language cadences and punctuation for rhythm. *668, 751*

Full-length plays Dramas that usually contain either three to five separate acts or a long series of discrete scenes. *1036*

General language Words referring to broad classes of persons or things. Distinguished from *specific* language. *238–39*

General symbols See *Cultural symbols*.

Glossary

Graph, graphics The spelling, as opposed to the actual pronunciation, of words. *693, 694, 697*

Gustatory images References to impressions of taste. *573–74*

Half rhyme See *Slant rhyme*.

Hamartia The error, frailty, or flaw that causes the downfall of a tragic protagonist. *1124*

Heavy stress rhyme See *Rising rhyme*.

Heptameter A line containing seven metrical feet; also called the *septenary*. *670*

Hero, heroine The major character in a work, the protagonist, the human center of interest. Though the term implies that a character be particularly valiant, the fact that a character has a major role is sufficient cause to label him or her *hero* or *heroine*. *136*

Heroic couplet Two successive lines of poetry in iambic pentameter that rhyme; the second line is usually end-stopped; usually applied to poetry from 1660–1800. *741*

Hexameter A line consisting of six metrical feet. *670*

High comedy Elegant comedy characterized by wit and sophistication, in which the complications grow out of character. *1382*

Hovering accent See *spondee*.

Hymnal stanza See *Common measure*.

Hyperbole See *Overstatement*.

Iamb A light stress followed by a heavy stress, as in *thĕ wínds*. *671*

Idea A broad word referring to a concept, thought, opinion, or belief. Some types of ideas are those of justice, right and good, necessity, and causation. An idea developed throughout a work of literature is called a *theme*. *333–74*

Idiom A phrase or style of speaking characteristic of a particular group, class, region, or nation, whose meaning cannot be derived from an analysis of constituent parts. *548*

Imagery Literary references to sensory impressions, making for immediacy and vividness. *569–589* Also, forms of compressed representation that work through comparison, allusion, or suggestion. *461*

Imitation The idea that literature is derived from life and is an imaginative duplication of life experiences; closely connected to *realism* and *verisimilitude*. *76*

Imperfect foot A foot consisting of a single syllable, either stressed or unstressed. *674*

Incidents, or Actions The events or occurrences in a work of literature. *79, 102*

Informal or Low Diction See *Diction, informal*.

Internal Rhyme The occurrence of rhyming words within a single line of verse. *716*

Interpretation See *Commentary*.

Invention The process of making up situations and stories out of the imagination, derived by the writer from life experiences and thought. *76*

Ironic comedy A modern form of comedy in which the tone is ironic and the ending ambivalent. *1384*

Irony The use of language and situations that are widely inappropriate or opposite from what might be ordinarily expected. *84*, *270–72*, *647–49*

Irony of fate See *Cosmic irony*.

Italian Sonnet A fourteen-line poem, in iambic pentameter, composed of two quatrains (the *octet*) and two tercets (the *sestet*). The octave rhymes *a b b a a b b a*; the sestet can rhyme variously *c d e c d e*, *c d c c d c*, *c d c d c d*, and so on. *743*

Jargon Words and phrases that are characteristic of a particular profession, trade, or pursuit such as medicine, football, or the military. *548–49*

Kinesthetic Images References to human or animal motion and activity. *574–76*

Kinetic Images References to general motion. *574–76*

Limerick A five-line poetic closed-form in which two lines of anapestic trimeter are followed by two in anapestic dimeter and a final line in trimeter, rhyming *3a 3a 2b 2b 3a*; often used for humorous or bawdy verse. *746*

Limited omniscient point of view A third-person narration with the focus made on one particular character's activities and thoughts. *81*, *181–82*

Listener A character or characters imagined as the audience to whom a story or poem is spoken, and as a result one of the influences on the content of the work, as in Browning's "My Last Duchess" and Owen's "Dulce et Decorum Est." *483*

Loose sentence A straightforward sentence with no climax and no surprises. *242*

Low comedy Crude, violent, and physical comedy, characterized by sight gags, bawdy jokes, and outrageous situations. *1382*

Lyric A short poem written in a repeating stanzaic form, often designed to be set to music; a lyric usually emphasizes the thoughts and/or feelings of the speaker. *471*, *744*

Main plot The central and major line of action in a literary work. *1037*

Masculine rhyme See *Rising rhyme*.

Meaning The combination of a poem's theme, its emotional impact, and the experience it creates for the reader. *334*, *839*

Measure See *Meter*.

Melodrama A debased form of tragedy with a happy ending. *1036*

Metaphor Figurative language in which one thing is directly equated with another, as in "the arts are sisters." *590*

Metaphysical conceit An elaborate and extended metaphor that links two apparently unrelated fields or subjects in an unusual, surprising, or shocking comparison. *874*

Meter or measure The number of feet within a line in traditional verse, such as *iambic pentameter* referring to a line consisting of five iambs. *670*

Method acting   A type of acting in which the player submerges himself or herself in the role and draws on personal experience and emotions to make the performance more psychologically realistic. *1290*

Metonymy   A rhetorical figure in which one thing is used as a substitute for another with which it is closely identified. *623–24*

Metrical foot   The basic building block of a line of poetry, usually consisting of one stressed syllable and one or more lightly stressed syllables. *670*

Monologue   In a play, a long speech spoken by a single character to himself or herself, the audience, or an off-stage character. *1034*

Mood   The emotional aura evoked by a work, usually as a result of the quality of the descriptions. *82, 208*

Morality play   Medieval allegorical drama that dramatizes the way to live a good Christian life. *1034*

Mystery play   Medieval drama that dramatizes events related in the Bible. *1034*

Myth   A story that explains a specific aspect of life or a natural phenomenon, based in the religion, philosophy, and collective psychology of various groups or cultures. *814*

Mythology   A group of myths (the "mythos") that form a system of belief and religious or historical doctrine. *814*

Mythos   See *Mythology*.

Narration   The relating or recounting, usually fictional, of a sequence of events or actions. *73, 80*

Narrative ballad   A ballad that tells a story. *466*

Narrative fiction   See *Prose fiction*.

Narrator   See *Speaker*.

Near Rhyme   See *Slant rhyme*.

Neutral, or Middle Diction   See *Diction, middle*.

New comedy   Short, violent, and bawdy romantic comedies, exemplified by the plays of the Romans Plautus and Terence. *1379*

Nonrealistic character   Undeveloped and often symbolic characters who are without full motivation or individual identity. *1040*

Nonrealistic drama   Plays that make no attempt to present an imitation of reality that is true to life in every respect. *1504*

Novel   A long work of prose fiction. *75*

Objective point of view   See *Dramatic point of view*.

Octameter   A line consisting of eight metrical feet. *670*

Octave   (1) An eight-line stanza or unit of poetry; (2) the first eight lines of an Italian sonnet. *743*

Ode   A rather long poem written in a complex stanzaic form that deals with a speaker's thoughts and feelings. *745*

Off rhyme   See *Slant rhyme*.

Old comedy   Satirical comedy full of personal invective and improvisation, exemplified by the plays of the Greek comic writer Aristophanes. *1379*

Olfactory Images References to impressions of smell. *573*

Omniscient point of view A third person narrative in which the speaker shows knowledge not only of the actions and speeches of all the characters, but also of their thoughts. *81, 181*

One-act plays Short plays, written in a single act, in which the action is usually continuous. *1036*

Onomatopoeia A blending of consonant and vowel sounds designed to imitate or suggest the activity being described. *696*

Open-form poetry Poems that avoid traditional structural patterns, such as rhyme or meter, in favor of other methods of organization. *668, 739*

Orchestra (1) the central circle where the chorus performed in ancient Greek theaters; (2) the central, ground-level area in a modern theater where the audience sits. *1127*

Organic unity The interdependence of all elements of a work, including character, actions, speeches, thoughts, and observations. *79*

Overreacher See *Overstatement*.

Overstatement A figure in which emphasis is achieved through exaggeration. *271, 625*

Parable Short stories designed to illustrate a religious truth, most often associated with Jesus. *74, 298*

Parados (1) Two aisles on each side of the orchestra in ancient Greek theaters along which actors could enter or exit; (2) the first lyrical ode chanted by the chorus in Greek tragedy. *1129–30*

Paradox A rhetorical figure embodying a seeming contradiction that is nevertheless true. *620–22*

Parallelism A rhetorical figure in which the same grammatical forms are repeated in two or more phrases, lines of verse, or sentences. *242–44, 555*

Paraphrase The brief rewriting of a work in words other than those of the original. *463, 463–79, 1649*

Pentameter A line consisting of five metrical feet. *670*

Perfect rhyme See *Exact rhyme*.

Periodic Sentence A sentence arranged in an order of climax, sometimes building to a surprising idea. *242*

Peripeteia A sudden reversal, when the action of a work, particularly a play, veers around quickly to its opposite. *1124*

Persona The narrator or speaker of a story or poem. *81, 178–82, 480*. Also, the mask worn by an actor in classical Greek tragedy. *1129*

Personification The attribution of human characteristics to nonhuman things or abstractions. *622–23*

Petrarchan sonnet See *Italian sonnet*.

Phonetic, phonetics *Phonetic* refers to the sounds of words as opposed to their spelling. *Phonetics* is the study of sounds. *694, 697*

Plausibility See *Probability*.

Play See *Drama*.

Plot The plan or groundwork for a story, based in conflicting human motivations, with the actions resulting from believable and realistic human responses. It is response, interaction, opposition, and causation that make a plot out of a simple series of actions. *79, 102–33, 1037*

Poetic decorum See *Decorum*.

Point of view The voice of a story, the speaker who is doing the narration; the means by which the reality and truthfulness of a story are made to seem authentic; the focus or angle of vision from which things are not only seen and reported but also judged. *81–82, 177–204*

Postulate The assumption on which a work of literature is based, such as a level of absolute, literal reality, or as a dreamlike, fanciful set of events; see also *Donné*. *77*

Précis A shortening, or cutting down, of a narrative into its essential parts, a synopsis, abridgement, paraphrase, condensation, or epitome. *97–101*

Premise See *Postulate*.

Private Symbols derived not from common historical, cultural, or religious ground, but from the context of the work in which they are included. Also called *authorial* or *contextual symbols*. *295–96, 786, 1044*

Private mythology A mythic system developed by an individual writer and alluded to in his or her literary work. *817*

Probability The standard of judgment requiring that literature be about what would normally, usually, and probably occur, not by what could possibly occur. Also called *verisimilitude* or *plausibility*. *139*

Problem plays See *Social drama*.

Prologue In Greek tragedy, the action before the first choral ode. *1130*

Propaganda play A play designed to convince an audience that a particular ideology should be embraced. *1046*

Props, properties The objects, furniture, and the like used on stage during a play. *1034*

Proscenium (1) See *Proskenion*; (2) an arch that frames a box set and holds the curtain, thus creating the missing fourth wall. *1129*

Proscenium stage A stage in which a proscenium arch separates the audience from the acting area; the effect is to produce a "room" with one wall missing. *1034*

Prose fiction Novels, short stories, and shorter prose works that generally focus on one or a few characters who undergo some sort of change as they encounter other characters or deal with some problem. *3*

Prose poem A short work, written in prose, but employing the methods of verse, such as imagery, for poetic ends. *751*

Proskenion A raised wooden stage built in front of the *skene* in ancient Greek theaters. *1129*

Protagonist The principal character in a work, the human center of interest, who is involved in some sort of conflict; see also *antagonist*. *79, 1039*

Public mythology Mythic systems that are long-standing, well established, and common knowledge, such as Greco-Roman mythology. *817*

Pun A word play in which the writer surprisingly reveals that words with totally different meaning have similar or even identical sounds. *625*

Purgation See *Catharsis*.

Pyrrhic A foot consisting of two unstressed syllables. *673*

Quatrain (1) A four-line stanze or poetic unit; (2) in an English or Shakespearean sonnet, a group of four lines united by rhyme. *742*

Raisonneur A character who remains detached from the action and provides reasoned commentary; a choric character. *1039*

Realism The use of true, lifelike, or probable situations and concerns. Also, the concept underlying the use of reality in literature. *76, 139*

Realistic character The accurate imitation of individualized men and women. *1040*

Realistic comedy See *Ironic comedy*.

Realistic drama Plays that present a mostly true-to-life image of the world as we know it. *1288, 1502*

Repetition Repeating the same word, phrase, sentence, or the like for impact and effect. *554*

Resolution The fifth stage of dramatic plot development in which conflicts are resolved, problems are solved, and loose ends are tied up. Also called *dénouement*. *105, 1038*

Resonance The effect of emotional and/or intellectual reverberation and amplification produced by symbols, allusions, and myth. *814*

Revenge tragedy A popular type of English Renaissance drama, developed by Thomas Kyd, in which a person is called upon (often by a ghost) to avenge the murder of a loved one. *1178*

Reversal See *Peripeteia*.

Rhetoric Broadly, the art of persuasive writing and even more broadly, the general art of writing. Short or long sentences, and devices such as parallelism, climax, simile, metaphor, irony, and symbolism are all aspects of rhetoric. *241–44*

Rhetorical substitution The manipulation of the caesura to achieve the effect of true metrical substitution. *678–79*

Rhyme The repetition of identical or similar concluding syllables in different words, most often at the ends of poetic lines. *713*

Rhyme scheme The pattern of rhyming sounds in a poem, usually indicated by assigning a letter of the alphabet to each sound. *717*

Rhythm In poetry, the comparative speed and loudness in the spoken flow of words. *666*

Rising action The action in a play before the climax. *1038*

Rising rhyme Rhymes produced with one syllable words, like *sky* and *fly*, or with multisyllabic words in which the accent falls on the last syllable, such as *decline* and *confine*. *715*

Romance   The name applied to lengthy Spanish and French stories written in the sixteenth and seventeenth centuries. Today, the word is applied to formulaic stories, usually involving the development of a love relationship. *75*

Romantic comedy   Sympathetic comedy that presents the adventures of young lovers trying to overcome opposition and achieve a successful union. *1383*

Round character   Usually a major figure in a work, with relatively full development and many individual and dynamic traits; compare *flat character*. *135–36, 1069*

Run-on lines   See *Enjambement*.

Satire   An attack on human follies or vices, as measured positively against a normative religious, moral, or social standard. *650–51*

Satiric comedy   A form of comedy designed to correct social and individual behavior by ridiculing human vices and follies. *1382*

Satyr play   A short comic interlude performed during the Dionysian Festival in ancient Greece. *1127*

Scansion   The act of scanning, or determining the prevailing rhythm of a poem. *670*

Scenery   The artificial environment created on-stage to produce the illusion of a specific or generalized place and time. *1034, 1041*

Scrim   In the modern theater, a transparent curtain on which a scene may be painted; depending on how it's illuminated, the curtain may seem solid or transparent. *1289*

Second-person point of view   A narration employing the "you" personal pronoun. *81 n. 180–81*

Segment   A sound in individual words essential to the meaningful understanding of those words, as in the word *top*, where there are three meaningful sounds— *t, o,* and *p*. The addition of the segment *s* makes the word plural (*tops*). *693*

Semivowel sounds   Midway between vowels and consonants; the semivowels are *w, y,* and *h*. *694*

Septenary   See *Heptamater*.

Sequence   The events in a work as they take place in time, from beginning to end. *79*

Sestet   (1) A six-line stanza or unit of poetry; (2) the last six lines of an Italian sonnet, usually containing the resolution of the poem. *743*

Sets   See *Scenery*.

Setting   The natural and artificial environment in which characters in literature live their lives; the sum total of references to physical and temporal objects and artifacts. *205–35, 509–35*

Shakespearean sonnet   See *English sonnet*.

Shaped verse   Poetry written so that the lines or words of the poem form a recognizable shape, such as a pair of wings or a geometrical shape. *753*

Short story   A short, concentrated narrative, called by Poe a "brief prose tale," designed to create a powerful, single impression. *75*

Sight rhyme   See *Eye rhyme*.

Simile Figurative language in which words such as *like* or *as* are used to draw similarities between two apparently unlike things, as in "a family is like a sturdy tree." *590*

Simple sentence A complete sentence containing one subject and one verb, together with modifiers and complements. *241*

Situational irony A type of irony emphasizing that human beings are enmeshed in forces beyond their comprehension or control. *84, 271–72*

Skene A building behind the orchestra in ancient Greek theaters used as dressing rooms and off-stage areas. *1127*

Slang Informal and often metaphorical use of vocabulary and idiom. *548*

Slant rhyme Words that almost rhyme, usually with different vowel sounds and similar consonant sounds, as in *could* and *solitude*. *717*

Slapstick comedy A type of low farce in which the humor depends almost entirely on physical actions and sight gags. *1382*

Speaker A fictitious observer, the point-of-view narrator of a story or poem, often a totally independent character who is completely imagined and consistently maintained by the author. *81, 177–83, 480*

Specific language References to a real thing or things that may be readily perceived or imagined; distinguished from *general language*. *238–39*

Spondee Two successive, equally heavy accents, as in *men's eyes*); *673*

Social drama Plays that explore social problems and the individual's place in society. *1036*

Soliloquy A speech delivered by a character to himself or herself or directly to the audience, often used to reveal thought or feelings. *1041*

Sonnet A closed poetic form of fourteen lines written in iambic pentameter with a rhyme scheme reflecting the organization of the Italian or English sonnet. *743*

Stage business Small gestures or movements that keep a play production active and dynamic. *1034*

Stage convention See *Dramatic convention*.

Stage directions A playwright's instructions in a play concerning tone of voice, action, entrances and exits, and the like. *1034*

Stanza A unit of lines of verse that are grouped together by rhyme and/or meter in a poem; the patterns established in the first stanza are usually repeated throughout. *739*

Stasimon A choral ode chanted by the chorus in Greek tragedy. *1130*

Static character A character, usually a minor one, who remains the same and undergoes no growth or change in the work; compare *dynamic character*. *136*

Stereotype A stock character who seems to have been stamped from a mold; highly conventionalized, unchanging characters. *137* See also *Stock character*. *1040*

Stock character A character, usually flat and static, who performs in repeating situations. Examples are the foolish boss, the angry police captain, the lovable drunk, the bewildered or stubborn parent, and the prodigal son. *137, 1040*

Stop sound The consonant sound produced by the momentary stoppage and release of breath either when the lips touch each other or when the tongue touches the teeth or palate, as in *p*, *d*, and *k*. *694*

Stress The emphasis given to a syllable; also called *accent*. A heavy or primary stress is marked with a prime mark or acute accent ('), and a lightly accented syllable is marked with a short accent (˘). *670*

Structure The arrangement and placement of materials in a work, the actual assemblage of an entire work or part of a work. See also *Form*. *79, 104–07, 130–33, 739*

Style The manipulation of language, the way in which writers tell the story, develop the argument, dramatize the play, or compose the poem; the placement of words in the service of content. *80–81, 236–65*

Subject The topic that a literary work addresses, such as love, marriage, war, death, and the like. *333–34, 465, 839*

Subplot A secondary line of action in a literary work that often comments directly or obliquely on the main plot. *1037*

Substitution The use of a variant foot in a line that is otherwise regular. *678*

Syllable A separately pronounced part of a word or, in some cases, a complete word. *668–69*

Symbol, Symbolism A specific thing that may stand for ideas, values, persons, or ways of life; a symbol always points beyond its own meaning toward greater and more complex meaning. *82, 84–85, 294–332, 784–814*

Synecdoche A rhetorical figure in which a part stands for a whole or a whole for a part. *623–24*

Synesthesia A union or fusion of references to separate sensations or feelings; the description of one type of perception or thought with words that are appropriate to another. *624*

Tactile images References to impressions of touch. *573–74*

Tenor In metaphorical language, the totality of ideas and attitudes which the author intends to express. *594*

Tercet A three-line unit or stanza of poetry, often rhyming *a a a* or *a b a*. *742*

Terza rima A three-line stanza form in which each stanza is liked with the next through repeated rhyme sounds: *a b a, b c b*, and so on. *742*

Tetrameter A line consisting of four metrical feet. *670*

Theme The specific and central idea or ideas that a literary work explores or asserts about its subject. *80, 333–34, 463, 839*

Third-person point of view A method of narration in which all things are described in the third person and in which the narrator is not introduced as an identifiable persona. *81, 181–83*

Thrust stage A stage that projects into the area normally reserved for the audience. *1034*

Tone The methods used by writers to convey and control attitude about their material and their readers. *84, 266–93, 641–65, 1043*

Topic See *Subject*.

Traditional poetry Poetry written in specific traditional patterns; see *closed form*. *668*

Tragedy A literary work, beginning in prosperity and ending in adversity, that recounts the fall of an individual. *1035*, *1122*

Tragic flaw See *Hamartia*.

Tragicomedy A broad range of literary works that offer a mixture of tragic and comic effects. *1036*

Trimeter A line consisting of three metrical feet. *670*

Triple rhyme Rhyming words of three or more syllables in which the accent falls on the antepenultimate syllable, such as *divínity* and *vicínity*. *715*

Triplet See *Tercet*.

Trilogy Three, usually related, works; in Greek drama, a group of three plays on the same theme by one playwright. *1127*

Trochaic rhyme See *Double rhyme*.

Trochee A heavy accent followed by a light, as in flów-er. *671*

Trope A short dramatic dialogue inserted into the Catholic mass in the early Middle Ages. *1173*

Tudor interludes Short tragedies, comedies, or history plays written during the reigns of Henry VII and Henry VIII in England (first half of the sixteenth century). *1174*

Understatement The deliberate underplaying or undervaluing of a thing for purposes of emphasis. *271*, *626*

Unities The unities of place, time, and action suggested by Aristotle. *1131*

Universal mythology See *Public mythology*.

Universal symbols See *Cultural symbols*. *1044*

Value A standard by which ideas and customs are measured. *335*

Vehicle In metaphorical language, the actual details of the metaphor or the simile. *594*

Verbal irony Language stating the opposite of what is meant. *84*, *271*

Verisimilitude A characteristic of literature, particularly fiction, that emphasizes the probable and lifelike. *76*

Vers libre See *Free verse*.

Villanelle A closed poetic form of nineteen lines, composed of five triplets and a quatrain. The form requires that whole lines be repeated in a specific order and that only two rhyme sounds occur throughout. *742*

Visual images References to impressions of sight. *571–72*

Visual poetry Poetry that draws much (or all) of its power from the appearance of the verse on the page. *753*

Voiced consonant sounds Consonants produced with the vibration of the vocal chords, as in *z*, *v*, *d*, and *b*. *694*

Voiceless consonant sounds   Consonants produced without the vibration of the vocal chords, as in *s*, *f*, *t*, and *p*. *694*

Vowel sounds   Sounds produced by the resonation of the voice in the space between the tongue and the top of the mouth.

Well-made play   A type of play developed in nineteenth-century France in which the action begins at the climax and the conflict turns on a secret. *1508*

Credits

Index of Authors, Titles, and First Lines

About suffering they were never wrong, 829
About Two Nice People, 281
According to Brueghel, 831
A closed window looks down, 928
Acquainted with the Night, 908
Act of Faith, 219
Adamé, Leonard
  My Grandmother Would Rock Quietly and Hum, 919
Adieu, farewell, earth's bliss, 979
A doe stands at the roadside, 786
Adventure of the Speckled Band, 31
Advice to a God, 1019
Africa, 968
After Apple-Picking, 903
After Great Pain, a Formal Feeling Comes, 893
After great pain, a formal feeling comes—, 893
Ah Sun-flower, 930
Ah Sun-flower! weary of time, 930
Albee, Edward
  Sandbox, The, 1067
All crying, 'We will go with you, O Wind!', 908
All that I know, 682
Along the garden ways just now, 654
Always the setting forth was the same, 824
Always too eager for the future, we, 860
Ammons, A. R.
  Dunes, 920
Angelou, Maya
  My Arkansas, 921
A novice was sitting on a cornice, 925
Answer, The, 962
Anthem for Doomed Youth, 572
A & P, 86
Apeneck Sweeney spreads his knees, 803
A poem should be palpable and mute, 844
A politician is an arse upon, 746
Araby, 339
Arnold, Matthew
  Dover Beach, 529
Ars Poetica, 844
Ashbury, John
  Illustration, 925
A speck that would have been beneath my sight, 909
Astrophil and Stella, Number 71, 1003
A sudden blow: the great wings beating still, 819
As virtuous men pass mildly away, 599
At a Summer Hotel, 731

At the Carnival, 1009
At the Round Earth's Imagined Corners, 883
At the round earth's imagined corners, blow, 883
Atwood, Margaret
  Siren Song, 825
Auden, W. H.
  Musée des Beaux Arts, 829
  Unknown Citizen, The, 926
Author to Her Book, The, 652
Auto Wreck, 1002
Avison, Margaret
  Tennis, 927
Avoid the reeking herd, 1027

Bait, The, 880
Ballad of Birmingham, 767
Baraka, Imamu Amiri
  Ka 'Ba, 928
Barbara Allan, 722
Barn Burning, 160
Batter My Heart, Three-Personed God, 556
Batter my heart, three-personed God; for You, 556
Bear: A Joke in One Act, The, 48
Beautiful must be the mountains whence ye come, 932
Because I Could Not Stop for Death, 473
Because I could not stop for Death, 473
Because they could not give it too much ground, 1023
Before Breakfast, 1060
Before you leave her, the woman who thought you lavish, 1019
Behn, Aphra
  Love Armed, 928
Behold her, single in the field, 1026
Belief, 976
Bell, Marvin
  Things We Dreamt We Died For, 929
Bells, The, 700
Bells for John Whiteside's Daughter, 987
Bend double, like old beggars under sacks, 644
Bermudas, 519
Birches, 904
Birney, Earle
  Can. Lit., 929
Bishop, Elizabeth
  Fish, The, 574
  Rain Towards Morning, 632

Black against twisted black, 982
Black man talks of reaping, A, 932
Blackness, 933
Black reapers with the sound of steel on stones, 759
Blake, William
  Ah Sun-flower, 930
  Lamb, The, 556
  London, 524
  Sick Rose, The, 930
  Tyger, The, 581
Blessed Damozel, The, 993
Blessing, A, 532
Blue Booby, The, 1014
Bluejays, 1006
Blue Winds Dancing, 122
Bly, Robert
  Snowfall in the Afternoon, 931
Bogan, Louise
  Women, 931
Bonny George Campbell, 995
Bontemps, Arna
  Black man talks of reaping, A, 932
Bradstreet, Anne
  Author to Her Book, The, 652
  To My Dear and Loving Husband, 932
Break, Break, Break, 629
Break, break, break, 629
Bride Comes to Yellow Sky, The, 107
Bridges, Robert
  Nightingales, 932
Bright Star, 681
Bright star! would I were steadfast as thou art—, 681
Brooks, Gwendolyn
  Primer for Blacks, 933
  We Real Cool, 685
Broumas, Olga
  Circe, 826
Browning, Elizabeth Barrett
  Number 43: Sonnets from the Portuguese, 934
Browning, Robert
  My Last Duchess, 488
  My Star, 682
  Soliloquy of the Spanish Cloister, 514
Brushing out my daughter's dark, 863
Buffalo Bill's, 769
Buffalo Bill's Defunct, 769
Burns, Robert
  O My Luve's Like a Red, Red Rose, 594
  To a Mouse, 935
Burying an Animal on the Way to New York, 1011
Bustle in a House, The, 897
Busy old fool, unruly sun, 876
But, as he walked, King Arthur panted hard, 699
Byron, George Gordon, Lord
  Destruction of Sennacherib, The, 606
Byzantium, 1028

Called, 953
Call the roller of big cigars, 1012
Camel, The, 978
Campion, Thomas
  Cherry Ripe, 603
Can. Lit., 929
Canonization, The, 877
Careful observers may foretell the hour, 1012
Cargoes, 571
Carroll, Lewis
  Jabberwocky, 557
Catbird Seat, The, 153
Change Is Not Always Progress (for Africa & Africans), 968
Channel Firing, 492
Charles used to watch Naomi, taking heart, 500

Chaser, The, 278
Chavez, Fray Angelico
  Rattlesnake, 610
Cheever, John
  Season of Divorce, The, 375
Chekhov, Anton
  Bear, The: A Joke in One Act, 49
  Lady with Lapdog, 382
Cherrylog Road, 510
Cherry Ripe, 603
Chicago, 997
Childhood remembrances are always a drag, 773
Chipmunk chewing the Chippendale, 631
Choose Something Like a Star, 910
Christmas Carol, A, 517
Chrysanthemums, The, 318
Church Going, 966
Circe, 826
Clark, Walter Van Tilburg
  Portable Phonograph, The, 214
Clean, Well-Lighted Place, A, 249
Clemens, Samuel
  Luck, 245
Clifton, Lucille
  My Mama Moved Among the Days, 936
Cohen, Leonard
  Suzanne Takes You Down, 936
Coleridge, Samuel Taylor
  Kubla Khan, 582
  What is an Epigram, 746
Collage of Echoes, 807
Collar, The, 793
Collier, John
  Chaser, The, 278
Come, live with me and be my love (Lewis), 499
Come live with me, and be my love (Donne), 880
Come live with me and be my love (Marlowe), 484
Come my Celia, let us prove, 848
Come to me in the silence of the night, 725
Computer's First Christmas Card, The, 776
Conjoined, 613
Conjurer, The, 502
Conrad, Joseph, 294
  Youth, 394
Considerable Speck, A, 909
Consider Icarus, pasting those sticky wings on, 831
Contend in a sea which the land partly encloses, 1024
Corinna's Going A-Maying, 955
Coup de Grâce, 957
Crane, Stephen
  Bride Comes to Yellow Sky, The, 107
  Do Not Weep, Maiden, for War is Kind, 938
  Impact of a Dollar upon the Heart, The, 938
Crashaw, Richard
  On Our Crucified Lord, Naked and Bloody, 580
Crawford, Isabella Valancy
  From Gisli, the Chieftain: The Song of the Arrow, 939
Cullen, Countee
  Yet Do I Marvel, 940
Cummings, E .E.
  Buffalo Bill's Defunct, 769
  If There Are Any Heavens, 941
  In Just-, 805
  Next to of course god america i, 940
  Nobody loses all the time, 59
  Politician, A, 746
  she being Brand/ -new, 655
Cunningham, J. V.
  Epitaph for Someone or Other, 746

Dance, The, 770
Day-Long Day, 1020
Day Zimmer Lost Religion, The, 1030

Death, be not proud, though some have called thee, 724
Death Be Not Proud, 724
Death of a Salesman, 1290
Death of a Vermont Farm Woman, 730
Degrees of Gray in Philipsburg, 531
Description of a City Shower, A, 1012
Description of the Morning, A, 698
Desert Places, 761
Design, 909
Destruction of Sennacherib, The, 606
Dickey, James
   Cherrylog Road, 510
   Lifeguard, The, 941
Dickinson, Emily, 886
   After Great Pain, a Formal Feeling Comes, 893
   Because I Could Not Stop for Death, 473
   Bustle in a House, The, 897
   "Faith" Is a Fine Invention, 892
   Gentian Weaves Her Fringes, The, 890
   Heart Is the Capital of the Mind, The, 898
   "Heavenly Father"—Take to Thee, 898
   I Cannot Live with You, 895
   I Heard a Fly Buzz—When I Died, 894
   I Like to See It Lap the Miles, 894
   I Never Lost as Much But Twice, 891
   I Taste a Liquor Never Brewed, 892
   Just Lost, When I Was Saved!, 891
   Much Madness Is Divinest Sense, 894
   My Life Closed Twice Before Its Close, 898
   My Triumph Lasted Till the Drums, 897
   One Need Not Be a Chamber—To Be Haunted, 896
   Pain—Has an Element of Blank, 896
   Safe in Their Alabaster Chambers, 889
   Some Keep the Sabbath Going to Church, 893
   Soul Selects Her Own Society, The, 892
   Success Is Counted Sweetest, 891
   There's a Certain Slant of Light, 890
   To Hear an Oriole Sing, 726
   Wild Nights—Wild Nights!, 889
Digging the grave, 953
Disillusionment of Ten O'Clock, 559
Diving into the Wreck, 988
Doll's House, A, 1507
Dolor, 560
Donne, John, 872
   Bait, The, 880
   Canonization, The, 877
   Fever, A, 879
   Flea, The, 879
   Good Friday, 1613. Riding Westward, 883
   Good Morrow, The, 875
   Holy Sonnet 6: This Is My Play's Last Scene, 882
   Holy Sonnet 7: At the Round Earth's Imagined Corners, 883
   Holy Sonnet 10: Death Be Not Proud, 724
   Holy Sonnet 14: Batter My Heart, Three-Personed God, 556
   Hymn to God My God, in My Sickness, 885
   Hymn to God the Father, A, 884
   Relic, The, 881
   Song, 876
   Sun Rising, The, 876
   Valediction: Forbidding Mourning, A, 599
Do Not Go Gentle into That Good Night, 766
Do not go gentle into that good night, 766
Do Not Weep, Maiden, for War Is Kind, 938
Do not weep, maiden, for war is kind, 938
Don't flinch when you come across a dead animal lying on the road, 1011
Doolittle, Hilda (H. D.)
   Heat, 585
   Pear Tree, 943
Dover Beach, 529

Doyle, Sir Arthur Conan
   Adventure of the Speckled Band, The, 31
Drayton, Michael
   Since There's No Help, 723
Dreamers, 998
Dream of Rebirth, 956
Dryden, John
   To the Memory of Mr. Oldham, 758
Dugan, Alan
   Love Song: I and Thou, 943
Dulce et Decorum Est, 644
Dunbar, Paul Lawrence
   Sympathy, 944
Dunes, 920
Dusk, 777
Dyer, Sir Edward
   My Mind to Me a Kingdom Is, 944

Eagle, The, 742
Eagle and the Mole, The, 1027
Eastern guard tower, 964
Easter Wings, 754
Eberhardt, Richard
   Fury of Aerial Bombardment, The, 562
   Groundhog, The, 946
Echo, 725
Edward, 922
Eight O'Clock, 704
Elegy Written in a Country Churchyard, 520
Eliot, Thomas Stearns
   Eyes That Last I Saw in Tears, 630
   Love Song of J. Alfred Prufrock, The, 947
   Macavity: The Mystery Cat, 684
   Sweeney Among the Nightingales, 803
Ellison, Ralph
   Flying Home, 356
Emanuel, James
   Negro, The, 686
Emperor of Ice-Cream, The, 1012
Engels, John
   Naming the Animals, 950
Epigram, Engraved on the Collar of a Dog, 650
Epigram from the French, 650
Epitaph for Someone or Other, 746
Epitaph on the Stanton-Harcourt Lovers, 745
Ethics, 862
Evans, Mari
   I Am A Black Woman, 951
Everyman, 1075
Exert thy voice, sweet harbinger of spring!, 653
Exit, Pursued by a Bear, 631
Eyes That Last I Saw in Tears, 630
Eyes that last I saw in tears, 630

"Faith" Is a Fine Invention, 892
"Faith" is a fine invention, 892
Fandel, John
   Indians, 633
Farewell, thou child of my right hand, and joy, 555
Farewell, too little and too lately known, 758
Faulkner, William
   Barn Burning, 160
Fear No More the Heat o' the Sun, 1001
Fear no more the heat o' the sun, 1001
Fern Hill, 1016
Fever, A, 879
Field, Edward
   Icarus, 832
Fifteen miles, 996
Finch, Anne, Countess of Winchelsea
   To Mr. F[inch], now Earl of W[inchelsea], 794
   To the Nightingale, 653
Fire and Ice, 907
First, you think they are dead, 1006
First Confession, 187

First having read the book of myths, 988
First-Rate Wife, The, 643
Fish, The, 574
Five years have past; five summers, with the length, 525
Flats of all sorts, 929
Flea, The, 879
Fly, The, 963
Flying Home, 356
Force That Through the Green Fuse Drives the Flower, The, 704
Forche, Carolyn
  Visitor, The, 952
For God's sake hold your tongue, and let me love, 877
Fork, 1005
For me, the naked and the nude, 542
Forsythia, 775
For the Union Dead, 973
Found Boat, The, 253
From An Essay on Criticism, 718
From Gisli, the Chieftain: The Song of the Arrow, 939
From Lenox Avenue Mural, Harlem, 609
Frost, Robert, 899
  Acquainted with the Night, 908
  After Apple-Picking, 903
  Birches, 904
  Choose Something Like a Star, 910
  Considerable Speck, A, 909
  Desert Places, 761
  Design, 909
  Fire and Ice, 907
  Gift Outright, The, 909
  Mending Wall, 902
  Misgiving, 908
  Nothing Gold Can Stay, 907
  'Out, Out—', 906
  Road Not Taken, The, 906
  Stopping By Woods on a Snowy Evening, 475
  Tuft of Flowers, The, 901
  U.S. 1946 King's X, 911
Fury of Aerial Bombardment, The, 562

Gardner, Isabella
  At a Summer Hotel, 731
  Collage of Echoes, 807
Gargoyle, 987
Gassing the woodchucks didn't turn out right, 965
Gather ye rosebuds while ye may, 850
Gay little Girl-of-the-Diving-Tank, 1009
Gentian Weaves Her Fringes, The, 890
Get up! get up for shame! the blooming morn, 955
Gift Outright, The, 909
Ginsberg, Allen
  Supermarket in California, A, 771
Giovanni, Nikki
  Nikki-Rosa, 773
  Woman, 952
Glaspell, Susan
  Trifles, 1100
Glass Menagerie, The, 1564
Glory be to God for dappled things, 958
Go, Lovely Rose, 605
Go, lovely rose!, 605
Go and catch a falling star, 876
God's Grandeur, 703
Goodbye and Good Luck, 449
Good Friday, 1613. Riding Westward, 883
Good Man Is Hard to Find, A, 433
Good Morrow, The, 875
Goose Fish, The, 980
Gospel of St. Luke, The, 300
Graves, Robert
  Naked and the Nude, The, 542

Gray, Thomas
  Elegy Written in a Country Churchyard, 520
Groundhog, The, 946
Gr-r-r—there go my heart's abhorrence!, 514
Guitarreros, 982

Had he and I but met, 474
Had we but world enough, and time, 849
Haiku, 964
Half awake in my Sunday nap, 1000
Hamlet, 1177
Hammon and the Beans, The, 274
Happy Journey to Trenton and Camden, The, 1048
Hardy, Thomas
  Channel Firing, 492
  In Time of "The Breaking of Nations," 799
  Man He Killed, The, 474
  Walk, The, 530
  Workbox, The, 647
Harper, Frances E.
  She's Free!, 953
Harper, Michael S.
  Called, 953
Having invented a new Holocaust, 911
Hawthorne, Nathaniel
  Young Goodman Brown, 302
Hayden, Robert
  Those Winter Sundays, 954
Heaney, Seamus
  Valediction, 614
Hear the sledges with the bells—, 700
Heart Is the Capital of the Mind, The, 898
Heat, 585
"Heavenly Father"—Take to Thee, 898
"Heavenly Father"—take to thee, 898
Heavy Bear Who Goes with Me, The, 999
Hecht, Anthony
  Nominalism, 748
He clasps the crag with crooked hands, 742
He looks down to watch the river twist, 987
Hemingway, Ernest
  Clean, Well-Lighted Place, A, 249
Herbert, George
  Collar, The, 793
  Easter Wings, 754
  Love (III), 496
  Pulley, The, 577
  Virtue, 760
Here lie two poor lovers, who had the mishap, 745
Herrick, Robert
  Corinna's Going A-Maying, 955
  To the Virgins, to Make Much of Time, 850
  Upon Julia's Voice, 697
He's *a boom a blat* in the uniform, 705
He seemed to know the harbour, 986
He stood, and heard the steeple, 704
He was found by the Bureau of Statistics to be, 926
He will watch the hawk with an indifferent eye, 829
Higgledy-piggledy (Hecht), 748
Higgledy-piggledy (Monks), 748
High upon Highlands, 495
Hill, Roberta
  Dream of Rebirth, 956
Hog Butcher for the World, 997
Hollander, John
  Swan and Shadow, 777
Hope, A. D.
  Coup de Grâce, 957
Hopkins, Gerard Manley
  God's Grandeur, 703
  Pied Beauty, 958
  Spring, 584
  Windhover, The, 957
Horse Dealer's Daughter, The, 343

Housman, A. E.
  Eight O'Clock, 704
  Loveliest of Trees, the Cherry Now, 470
  Terence, This Is Stupid Stuff, 958
  To an Athlete Dying Young, 727
How do I love thee? Let me count the ways, 934
Howes, Barbara
  Death of a Vermont Farm Woman, 730
How say that by law we may torture and chase, 953
How Soon Hath Time, 978
How soon hath Time, the subtle thief of youth, 978
Hughes, Langston
  From Lenox Avenue Mural, Harlem, 609
  Negro, 960
  Slave on the Block, 414
  Theme for English B, 656
Hugo, Richard
  Degrees of Gray in Philipsburg, 531
Hunger Artist, A, 419
Hymn to God My God, in My Sickness, 885
Hymn to God the Father, A, 884

I, too, dislike it: there are things that are important
  beyond all this fiddle, 852
I Am A Black Woman, 951
I am a black woman, 951
I am a Negro, 960
I am here with my beautiful bountiful womanful
  child, 731
I am his Highness' dog at Kew, 650
I am silver and exact. I have no preconceptions,
  984
Ibsen, Henrik
  Doll's House, A, 1507
I Cannot Live with You, 895
I cannot live with You—, 895
I carry it on my keychain, which itself, 1021
Icarus, 829, 832
I caught a tremendous fish, 574
I caught this morning morning's minion, king—,
  957
I climb the black rock mountain, 1004
I did not live until this time, 982
I do not want a plain box, I want a sarcophagus,
  984
I doubt not God is good, well-meaning, kind, 940
I empty myself of the names of others, 634
If all the world and love were young, 486
If ever two were one, then surely we, 932
I Find No Peace, 620
I find no peace, and all my war is done, 620
I found a dimpled spider, fat and white, 909
If There Are any Heavens, 941
If there are any heavens my mother will (all by her-
  self) have, 941
I Have a Rendezvous with Death, 999
I have a rendezvous with Death, 999
I have been one acquainted with the night, 908
I have known the inexorable sadness of pencils, 560
I have no promises to keep, 807
I have sown beside all waters in my day, 932
I Heard a Fly Buzz—When I Died, 894
I heard a Fly Buzz—when i died—, 894
I heard a thousand blended notes, 1025
I Knew a Woman, 991
I knew a woman, lovely in her bones, 991
I know what the caged bird feels, alas!, 944
I Like to See It Lap the Miles, 894
I like to see it lap the Miles—, 894
Illustration, 925
I'm a riddle in nine syllables, 610
I met a traveller from an antique land, 756
Impact of a Dollar upon the Heart, The, 938
In a Bird Sanctuary, 1023
In a Farmhouse, 996

In a mayonnaise jar I keep the tiny, 502
In a stable of boats I lie still, 941
In a Station of the Metro, 585
In Bondage, 757
In Breughel's great picture, The Kermess, 770
In China, 1007
In Days of Wine, 975
In days of Wine, 975
Indians, 633
In ethics class so many years ago, 862
I Never Lost as Much But Twice, 891
I never lost as much but twice, 891
In her house, 919
In June, amid the golden fields, 946
In Just-, 805
in Just-, 805
Inside Out, 634
In Spanish he whispers there is no time left, 952
In the bleak mid-winter, 517
In the pathway of the sun, 823
In Time of "The Breaking of Nations," 799
In Xanadu did Kubla Khan, 582
Iowa Farmer, 1022
Is it time now to go away?, 730
I slouch in bed, 476
I Stand Here Ironing, 444
I struck the board, and cry'd, "No more, 793
I talked to a farmer one day in Iowa, 1022
I Taste a Liquor Never Brewed, 892
I taste a liquor never brewed—, 892
It little profits that an idle king, 821
Its quick soft silver bell beating, beating, 1002
It was in and about the Martinmas time, 722
I wake to sleep, and take my waking slow, 992
I walk down the garden paths, 970
I walk the purple carpet into your eye, 634
I wander thro' each charter'd street, 524
I went to turn the grass once after one, 901
I will not toy with it nor bend an inch, 976
I wonder, by my troth, what thou and I, 875
I would be wandering in distant fields, 757

Jabberwocky, 557
Jackson, Shirley
  About Two Nice People, 281
  Lottery, The, 194
Jarrell, Randall
  Next Day, 961
  Woman at the Washington Zoo, The, 501
Jeffers, Robinson
  Answer, The, 962
  Purse-Seine, The, 802
jollymerry, 776
Jones, Leroi, 928
Jonson, Ben
  On My First Son, 555
  To Celia, 848
  To His Coy Mistress, 849
Joyce, James
  Araby, 339
Just at that moment the Wolf, 957
Justice, Donald
  On the Death of Friends in Childhood, 861
Just Lost, When I Was Saved!, 891
Just lost, when I was saved!, 891
Just off the highway to Rochester, Minnesota, 532

Ka 'Ba, 928
Kafka, Franz
  Hunger Artist, A, 419
Keats, John
  Bright Star, 681
  La Belle Dame sans Merci: A Ballad, 797
  Ode on a Grecian Urn, 859
  Ode to a Nightingale, 761

Keats (*cont.*)
  On First Looking into Chapman's Homer, 592
  To Autumn, 628
King, Henry
  Sic Vita, 604
Kinnell, Galway
  Fly, The, 963
Kizer, Carolyn
  Night Sounds, 964
Knight, Etheridge
  Haiku, 964
Kubla Khan, 582
Kumin, Maxine
  Woodchucks, 965

La Belle Dame sans Merci: A Ballad, 797
Laboratory Poem, 500
Lady with Lapdog, 382
Lady with the frilled blouse, 614
Lama, The, 979
Lamb, The, 556
Landscape with the Fall of Icarus, 831
Language Lesson, 1976, 549
Larkin, Philip
  Church Going, 966
  Next, Please, 860
Last Words, 984
Lawrence, D. H.
  Horse Dealer's Daughter, The, 343
Layton, Irving
  Rhine Boat Trip, 968
Leda and the Swan, 819
Lee, Don L.
  Change Is Not Always Progress (for Africa & Africans),
    968
Lessing, Doris
  Old Chief Mshlanga, The, 425
Let man's soul be a sphere, and then, in this, 883
Let Me Not to the Marriage of True Minds, 749
Let me not to the marriage of true minds, 749
Let us go then, you and I, 947
Levine, Philip
  They Feed They Lion, 969
Lewis, C. Day
  Song, 499
Lifeguard, The, 941
Like to the falling of a star, 604
Line of beauty scrawled alive, 610
Lines Composed a Few Miles Above Tintern Abbey, 525
Lines Written in Early Spring, 1025
Litany in Time of Plague, A, 979
Little lamb, who made thee?, 556
Lobster, The, 975
Lobsters in the Window, 1006
London, 524
London, 1802, 627
Loneliness, 977
Long afterward, Oedipus, old and blinded, walked
  the, 827
Look out, they say, for yourself, 1004
Lord, who createdst man in wealth and store, 754
Lord Randal, 923
Lost Sister, 1007
Lottery, The, 194
Love Armed, 928
Love bade me welcome: yet my soul drew back,
  496
Love (III), 496
Love in Fantastic Triumph sat, 928
Lovelace, Richard
  To Lucasta, Going to the Wars, 970
Loveliest of Trees, the Cherry Now, 470
Loveliest of trees, the cherry now, 470
Love Song: I and Thou, 943
Love Song of J. Alfred Prufrock, The, 947

Love Symphony, A, 654
Lowell, Amy
  Patterns, 970
Lowell, Robert
  For the Union Dead, 973
Luck, 245
Luna, Ben
  In Days of Wine, 975

Macavity: The Mystery Cat, 684
Macavity's a Mystery Cat: He's called the Hidden
  Paw—, 684
Macdonald, Cynthia
  Lobster, The, 975
MacLeish, Archibald
  Ars Poetica, 844
Man He Killed, The, 474
Mansfield, Katherine
  Miss Brill, 184
March for a One-Man Band, 705
Margaret mentioned Indians, 633
María Concepción, 140
Mark but this flea, and mark in this, 879
Marks, 611
Marlowe, Christopher
  Passionate Shepherd to His Love, The, 484
Marvell, Andrew
  Bermudas, 519
Masefield, John
  Cargoes, 571
Masque of the Red Death, The, 209
Maupassant, Guy de
  Necklace, The, 90
McHugh, Heather
  Language Lesson, 1976, 549
McKay, Claude
  In Bondage, 757
  White City, The, 976
Mending Wall, 902
Merrill, James
  Laboratory Poem, 500
Merwin, W. S.
  Odysseus, 824
Metaphors, 610
Midsummer Night's Dream, A, 1384
Miles, Josephine
  Belief, 976
Millay, Edna St. Vincent
  What Lips My Lips Have Kissed, and Where, and Why,
    977
Miller, Arthur, 1288
  Death of a Salesman, 1294
Miller, Vassar
  Loneliness, 977
Milton, John
  How Soon Hath Time, 978
  O Nightingale!, 978
  When I Consider How My Light Is Spent, 756
Milton! thou should'st be living at this hour, 627
Miniver Cheevy, 728
Miniver Cheevy, child of scorn, 728
Minty, Judith
  Cojoined, 613
Mirror, 984
Misanthrope, The, 1446
Misgiving, 908
Miss Brill, 184
Molière (Jean-Baptiste Poquelin), 1443
  Misanthrope, The, 1448
Monks, Arthur W.
  Twilight's Last Gleaming, 748
Moore, Marianne
  Poetry, 852
Morgan, Edwin
  Computer's First Christmas Card, The, 776

"Mother dear, may I go downtown, 767
Mother said to call her if the H-bomb exploded, 976
Moving from Cheer to Joy, from Joy to All, 961
Mr. Flood's Party, 990
Much have I travell'd in the realms of gold, 592
Much Madness Is Divinest Sense, 894
Much Madness is divinest Sense—, 894
Munro, Alice
  Found Boat, The, 253
Musée des Beaux Arts, 829
Muske, Carol
  Real Estate, 807
My Arkansas, 921
My Grandmother Would Rock Quietly and Hum, 919
My heart aches, and a drowsy numbness pains, 761
My hips are a desk, 983
My husband gives me an A, 611
My Last Duchess, 488
My Life Closed Twice Before Its Close, 898
My life closed twice before its close, 898
My long two-pointed ladder's sticking through a tree, 903
My Mama Moved Among the Days, 936
My Mama moved among the days, 936
My Mind To Me a Kingdom Is, 944
My mind to me a kingdom is, 944
My mistress' eyes are nothing like the sun, 579
My Papa's Waltz, 658
My Star, 682
Myth, 827
My Triumph Lasted Till the Drums, 897
My Triumph lasted till the Drums, 897

Naked and the Nude, The, 542
Naked I came, naked I leave the scene, 746
Naming of Parts, 561
Naming the Animals, 950
Nash, Ogden
  Camel, The, 978
  Exit, Pursued by a Bear, 631
  Lama, The, 979
  Turtle, The, 729
  Very Like a Whale, 607
Nashe, Thomas
  Litany in Time of Plague, A, 979
Nature's first green is gold, 907
Necklace, The, 90
Negro, 960
Negro, The, 686
Nemerov, Howard
  Goose Fish, The, 980
Never saw him, 686
Never until the mankind making, 1017
Next, Please, 860
Next Day, 961
Next to of course god america i, 940
"Next to of course god america i, 940
Nightingales, 932
Night Sounds, 964
Nikki-Rosa, 773
Nobody heard him, the dead man, 1006
Nobody loses all the time, 59
Nobody loses all the time, 59
Nominalism, 748
No sooner, Flavio, were you gone, 794
Nothing Gold Can Stay, 907
Nothing is plumb, level or square, 943
Nothing is so beautiful as Spring—, 584
Not marble, nor the gilded monuments, 468
Not Waving But Drowning, 1006
Now as I was young and easy under the apple boughs, 1016
Now hardly here and there a hackney-coach, 698
Nymph's Reply to the Shepherd, The, 486

O'Connor, Flannery
  Good Man Is Hard to Find, A, 433
O'Connor, Frank
  First Confession, 187
ODE: Intimations of Immortality from Recollections of Early Childhood, 853
Ode on a Grecian Urn, 859
Ode to a Nightingale, 761
Ode to the West Wind, 764
Odysseus, 824
Oedipus the King, 1130
Off Highway 106, 510
Of this World's Theater in Which We Stay, 1010
Of this world's theater in which we stay, 1010
"Oh, where have you been, Lord Randal, my son?, 923
O'Hara, Frank
  Poem, 981
Oh do not die, for I shall hate, 879
Old Chief Mshlanga, The, 425
Old Eben Flood, climbing alone one night, 990
Olds, Sharon
  35/10, 863
Olsen, Tillie
  I Stand Here Ironing, 444
O My Luve's Like a Red, Red Rose, 594
O my Luve's like a red, red rose, 594
On Being Brought from Africa to America, 1023
Once I am sure there's nothing going on, 966
One Day I Wrote Her Name upon the Strand, 851
One day I wrote her name upon the strand, 851
O'Neill, Eugene
  Before Breakfast, 1060
One Need Not Be a Chamber—to be Haunted, 896
One need not be a Chamber—to be Haunted—, 896
One thing that literature would be greatly the better for, 607
On First Looking into Chapman's Homer, 592
O Nightingale!, 978
O Nightingale, that on yon bloomy Spray, 978
Only a man harrowing clods, 799
Only the feathers floating around the hat, 832
On My First Son, 555
On Our Crucified Lord, Naked and Bloody, 580
On the Death of Friends in Childhood, 861
On the long shore, lit by the moon, 980
O Rose thou art sick, 930
O'Shaughnessy, Arthur
  Love Symphony, A, 654
O Star (the fairest one in sight), 910
Our sardine fishermen work at night in the dark of the moon; daylight or moonlight, 802
'Out, Out-', 906
Out of burlap sacks, out of bearing butter, 969
Owen, Wilfred
  Anthem for Doomed Youth, 572
  Dulce et Decorum Est, 644
O what can ail thee, knight at arms, 797
O wild West Wind, thou breath of Autumn's being, 764
O wind, rend open the heat, 585
Ozymandias, 756

Pain—has an Element of Blank—, 896
Pain—Has an Element of Blank, 896
Paley, Grace
  Goodbye and Good Luck, 449
Parable of the Prodigal Son, The, 300
Parédes, Américo
  Guitarreros, 982
  Hammon and the Beans, The, 274
Parker, Dorothy
  Penelope, 823
  Résumé, 982

Passing of Arthur, The, 699
Passionate Shepherd to His Love, The, 484
Pastan, Linda
  Ethics, 862
  Marks, 611
Patterns, 970
Pawnshop, The, 1005
Pear Tree, 943
Penelope, 823
Petronius, Gaius, 28
Phillips, Katherine
  To my Excellent Lucasia, on our Friendship, 982
Pickthall, Marjorie
  Worker in Sandalwood, The, 312
Pied Beauty, 958
Piercy, Marge
  Secretary Chant, The, 983
  Work of Artifice, A, 612
Plath, Sylvia
  Last Words, 984
  Metaphors, 610
  Mirror, 984
Poe, Edgar Allan
  Bells, The, 700
  Masque of the Red Death, The, 209
Poem, 981
Poetry, 852
Politician, A, 746
Poor Soul, The Center of My Sinful Earth, 1002
Poor soul, the center of my sinful earth, 1002
Pope, Alexander
  Epigram Engraved on the Collar of a Dog, 650
  Epigram from the French, 650
  Epitaph on the Stanton-Harcourt Lovers, 745
  From An Essay on Criticism, 718
Poquelin, Jean-Baptiste. *See* Molière
Portable Phonograph, The, 214
Porter, Katherine Anne
  María Concepción, 140
Pound, Ezra
  In a Station of the Metro, 585
  River-Merchant's Wife: A Letter, The, 985
Pratt, E. J.
  Shark, The, 986
Primer for Blacks, 933
Pulley, The, 577
Purse-Seine, The, 803

Quinquereme of Nineveh from distant Ophir, 571

Rabbitt, Thomas
  Gargoyle, 987
Rain Towards Morning, 632
Raleigh, Sir Walter
  Nymph's Reply to the Shepherd, The, 486
Randall, Dudley
  Ballad of Birmingham, 767
Ransom, John Crowe
  Bells for John Whiteside's Daughter, 987
Rattlesnake, 610
Razors pain you, 982
Real Estate, 807
Reapers, 759
Reconciliation, 752
Red Wheelbarrow, The, 1024
Reed, Henry
  Naming of Parts, 561
Refusal to Mourn the Death, by Fire, of a Child in London, A, 1017
Relic, The, 881
Remains, The, 634
Résumé, 982
Revolutionary Petunias, 1021
Rhine Boat Trip, 968

Rich, Adrienne
  Diving into the Wreck, 988
Richard Cory, 559
Right on: white america, 997
Ring, The, 1021
River-Merchant's Wife: A Letter, The, 985
Road Not Taken, The, 906
Robinson, Edwin Arlington
  Miniver Cheevy, 728
  Mr. Flood's Party, 990
  Richard Cory, 559
Roethke, Theodore
  Dolor, 560
  I Knew a Woman, 991
  My Papa's Waltz, 658
  Waking, The, 992
Rossetti, Christina
  Christmas Carol, A, 517
  Echo, 725
Rossetti, Dante Gabriel
  Blessed Damozel, The, 993
Rukeyser, Muriel
  Myth, 827

Safe in Their Alabaster Chambers, 889
Safe in their Alabaster Chambers—, 889
Sailing to Byzantium, 1027
Salinas, Luis Omar
  In a Farmhouse, 996
Sammy Lou of Rue, 1021
Sanchez, Sonia
  Right on: white america, 997
Sandbox, The, 1067
Sandburg, Carl
  Chicago, 997
Sassoon, Siegfried
  Dreamers, 998
Schwartz, Delmore
  Heavy Bear Who Goes with Me, The, 999
Scott, Virginia
  Snow, 786
Season of Divorce, The, 375
Season of mists and mellow fruitfulness!, 628
Second Coming, The, 800
Secretary Chant, The, 983
"See, here's the workbox, little wife, 647
Seeger, Alan
  I Have a Rendezvous with Death, 999
Service is joy, to see or swing. Allow, 927
Sexton, Anne
  Three Green Windows, 1000
  To a Friend Whose Work Has Come to Triumph, 831
Shakespeare, William, 680, 1002, 1173
  Fear No More the Heat o' the Sun, 1001
  Midsummer Night's Dream, A, 1384
  Sonnet 18: Shall I Compare Thee to a Summer's Day?, 602
  Sonnet 29: When in Disgrace with Fortune and Men's Eyes, 679
  Sonnet 30: When to the Sessions of Sweet Silent Thought, 595
  Sonnet 55: Not Marble, nor the Gilded Monuments, 468
  Sonnet 73: That Time of Year Thou Mayest in Me Behold, 680
  Sonnet 116: Let Me Not to the Marriage of True Minds, 749
  Sonnet 130: My Mistress' Eyes Are Nothing Like the Sun, 579
  Sonnet 146: Poor Soul, The Center of My Sinful Earth, 1002
  Tragedy of Hamlet Prince of Denmark, The, 1177
Shall I Compare Thee to a Summer's Day?, 602
Shall I compare thee to a summer's day?, 602

Shapiro, Karl
  Auto Wreck, 1002
Shark, The, 986
Shaw, Irwin
  Act of Faith, 219
She being Brand, 655
She being Brand/ -new, 655
Shelley, Percy Bysshe
  Ode to the West Wind, 764
  Ozymandias, 756
She's Free!, 953
She tries to call them down, 1006
She wanted to be a blade, 952
Sick Rose, The, 930
Sic Vita, 604
Sidney, Philip, Sir
  Astrophil and Stella, Number 71, 1003
Silkin, John
  Worm, 1004
Silko, Leslie Marmon
  Where Mountain Lion Lay Down with Deer, 1004
Silver dust, 943
Simic, Charles
  Fork, 1005
Simpson, Louis
  Pawnshop, The, 1005
Since I am coming to that holy room, 885
Since spring I've seen two deer, 950
Since There's No Help, 723
Since there's no help, come let us kiss and part, 723
Since we'd always sky about, 929
Sir, I admit your general rule, 650
Siren Song, 825
Slave on the Block, 414
Smith, Dave
  Bluejays, 1006
Smith, Stevie
  Not Waving But Drowning, 1006
Snodgrass, W. D.
  Lobsters in the Window, 1006
Snow, 786
Snow falling and night falling fast, oh, fast, 761
Snowfall in the Afternoon, 931
So deep is this silence, 977
Soldiers are citizens of death's grey land, 998
Soliloquy of the Spanish Cloister, 514
Solitary Reaper, The, 1026
Solt, Mary Ellen
  Forsythia, 775
Some Keep the Sabbath Going to Church, 893
Some keep the Sabbath going to Church—, 893
Some say the world will end in fire, 907
Something there is that doesn't love a wall, 902
So much depends, 1024
Song, 499, 876
Song, Cathy
  Lost Sister, 1007
Sonnets from the Portuguese, 934
Sophocles
  Oedipus The King, 1130
So smooth, so sweet, so silv'ry is thy voice, 697
Soul Selects Her Own Society, The, 892
Spencer, Anne
  At the Carnival, 1009
Spender, Stephen
  Icarus, 829
Spenser, Edmund
  Amoretti 54: Of This World's Theater in Which We Stay, 850
  Amoretti 75: One Day I Wrote Her Name upon the Strand, 851
Spring, 584
Stafford, William
  Traveling Through the Dark, 1011

Stanton, Maura
  Conjurer, The, 502
Steinbeck, John
  Chrysanthemums, The, 318
Stern, Gerald
  Burying an Animal on the Way to New York, 1011
Stevens, Wallace
  Disillusionment of Ten O'Clock, 559
  Emperor of Ice-Cream, The, 1012
  Stopping By Woods on a Snowy Evening, 475
Strand, Mark
  Remains, The, 634
Success Is Counted Sweetest, 891
Success is counted sweetest, 891
Sundays too my father got up early, 954
Sun Rising, The, 876
Supermarket in California, A, 771
Suzanne Takes You Down, 936
Suzanne takes you down, 936
Swan and Shadow, 777
Sweeney Among the Nightingales, 803
Sweet day, so cool, so calm, so bright, 760
Swenson, May
  Women, 774
Swift, Jonathan
  Description of a City Shower, A, 1012
  Description of the Morning, A, 698
Sympathy, 944

Taking root in windy sand, 920
Tate, James
  Blue Booby, The, 1014
Taylor, Edward
  Upon a Spider Catching a Fly, 1015
Tell me not, Sweet, I am unkind, 970
Tennis, 927
Tennyson, Alfred, Lord
  Break, Break, Break, 629
  Eagle, The, 742
  From Idylls of the King: The Passing of Arthur, 699
  Tithonus, 497
  Ulysses, 821
Terence, This Is Stupid Stuff, 958
"Terence, this is stupid stuff, 958
That is no country for old men. The young, 1027
That night your great guns, unawares, 492
That's my last Duchess painted on the wall, 488
That Time of Year Thou Mayest in Me Behold, 680
That time of year thou mayst in me behold, 680
The apparition of these faces in the crowd, 585
The Assyrian came down like the wolf on the fold, 606
The blessed damozel leaned out, 993
The blue booby kives, 1014
The bonsai tree, 612
The Bustle in a House, 897
The buzz saw snarled and rattled in the yard, 906
The camel has a single hump, 978
The castles on the Rhine, 968
The Child is father of the Man;, 853
The curfew tolls the knell of parting day, 520
The eager note on my door said "Call me, 981
The fire bites, the fire bites. Bites, 826
The first Sunday I missed Mass on purpose, 1030
The first time I saw a pawnshop, 1005
The fly, 963
The force that through the green fuse drives the flower, 704
The Gentian weaves her fringes—, 890
The grass is half-covered with snow, 931
The great light cage has broken up in the air, 632
The Heart is the Capital of the Mind—, 898
The heavy bear who goes with me, 999
The houses are haunted, 559
The impact of a dollar upon the heart, 938

The instructor said, 656
The land was ours before we were the land's, 909
Theme for English B, 656
The moonlight on my bed keeps me awake, 964
Then what is the answer?—Not to be deluded by dreams, 962
The old South Boston Aquarium stands, 973
The one-l lama, 979
The onion in my cupboard, a monster, actually, 613
The Pool Players, 685
There is a deep brooding, 921
There is a garden in her face, 603
There's a Certain Slant of Light, 890
There's a certain Slant of light, 890
There was such speed in her little body, 987
There were three ravens sat on a tree, 924
The saris go by me from the embassies, 501
The sea is calm tonight, 529
The soul selects her own Society—, 892
The time you won your town the race, 727
The turtle lives 'twixt plated decks, 729
The unpurged images of day recede, 1028
The whiskey on your breath, 658
The woman inside every woman, 1018
The woods decay, the woods decay and fall, 497
The world is charged with the grandeur of God, 703
They Feed They Lion, 969
Th' have left Thee naked, Lord, O that they had, 580
Things We Dreamt We Died For, 929
Third-generation timetable, 1020
35/10, 863
This brief effusion I indite, 643
This country might have, 997
This Is My Play's Last Scene, 882
This is my play's last scene; here heavens appoint, 882
This is the one song everyone, 825
This lobster flown in from Maine to Houston, 975
This strange thing must have crept, 1005
Thomas, Dylan, 1017
  Do Not Go Gentle into That Good Night, 766
  Fern Hill, 1016
  Force That Through the Green Fuse Drives the Flower, The, 704
  Refusal to Mourn the Death, by Fire, of a Child in London, A, 1017
Thompson, Francis
  To a Snowflake, 683
Those Winter Sundays, 954
Thou ill-formed offspring of my feeble brain, 652
Thou sorrow, venom Elfe, 1015
Thou still unravish'd bride of quietness, 859
Three Green Windows, 1000
Three Ravens, The, 924
Thurber, James
  Catbird Seat, The, 153
Tithonus, 497
To a Friend Whose Work Has Come to Triumph, 831
To a Mouse, 935
To an Athlete Dying Young, 727
To a Snowflake, 683
To Autumn, 628
To Celia, 848
To-day we have naming of parts. Yesterday, 561
To Hear an Oriole Sing, 726
To hear an Oriole sing, 726
To His Coy Mistress, 849
To Lucasta, Going to the Wars, 970
To Mr. F[inch], now Earl of W[inchelsea], 794
To My Dear and Loving Husband, 932
To my Excellent Lucasia, on our Friendship, 982
Toomer, Jean
  Reapers, 759

To the Memory of Mr. Oldham, 758
To the Nightingale, 653
To the Virgins, to Make Much of Time, 850
Traveling Through the Dark, 1011
Traveling through the dark I found a deer, 1011
Trifles, 1100
True ease in writing comes from art, not chance, 718
Tuft of Flowers, The, 901
Turning and turning in the widening gyre, 800
Turtle, The, 729
'Twas brillig, and the slithy toves, 557
'Twas mercy brought me from my *Pagan* land, 1023
Twilight's Last Gleaming, 748
Two Hangovers, 476
Two roads diverged in a yellow wood, 906
Tyger, The, 581
Tyger! Tyger! burning bright, 581

U.S. 1946 King's X, 911
Ullman, Leslie
  Why There Are Children, 1018
Ulysses, 821
Unknown Citizen, The, 926
Updike, John
  A & P, 86
Upon a Spider Catching a Fly, 1015
Upon Julia's Voice, 697

Valediction, 614
Valediction: Forbidding Mourning, A, 599
Van Duyn, Mona
  Advice to a God, 1019
Very Like a Whale, 607
Villanueva, Tino
  Day-Long Day, 1020
Virtue, 760
Visitor, The, 952

Wagoner, David
  March for a One-Man Band, 705
Waking, The, 992
Wakoski, Diane
  Inside Out, 634
  Ring, The, 1021
Walk, 530
Walker, Alice
  Revolutionary Petunias, 1021
Walker, Margaret
  Iowa Farmer, 1022
Waller, Edmund
  Go, Lovely Rose, 605
Wee, sleekit, cow'rin', tim'rous beastie, 935
Welty, Eudora
  Worn Path, A, 116
We Real Cool, 685
We shall not ever meet them bearded in heaven, 861
We stand on the edge of wounds, hugging canned meat, 956
What happens to a dream deferred?, 609
What heart could have thought you?, 683
What is an Epigram, 746
What is an epigram? a dwarfish whole, 746
What know I, 939
What Lips My Lips Have Kissed, and Where, and Why, 977
What lips my lips have kissed, and where, and why, 977
What passing-bells for these who die as cattle?, 572
What thoughts I have of you tonight, Walt Whitman, for, 771
Wheatley, Phyllis
  On Being Brought from Africa to America, 1023
When, in disgrace with fortune and men's eyes, 679

When Americans say a man, 549
Whenever Richard Cory went down town, 559
When God at first made man, 577
When I Consider How My Light Is Spent, 756
When I consider how my light is spent, 756
When I Heard the Learn'd Astronomer, 769
When I heard the learn'd astronomer, 769
When in Disgrace with Fortune and Men's Eyes, 679
When I see birches bend to left and right, 904
When my grave is broke up again, 881
When to the Sessions of Sweet Silent Thought, 595
When to the sessions of sweet silent thought, 595
Where Mountain Lion Lay Down with Deer, 1004
Where the remote Bermudas ride, 519
While my hair was still cut straight across my fore-head, 985
White City, The, 976
Whitecloud, Tom
    Blue Winds Dancing, 122
Whitman, Walt
    Reconciliation, 752
    When I Heard the Learn'd Astronomer, 769
Whose woods these are I think I know, 475
Who will in fairest book of Nature know, 1003
Whur, Cornelius
    First-Rate Wife, The, 643
"Why does your brand so drip wi' blood, 922
Why There Are Children, 1018
Widow of Ephesus, The, 28
Wilbur, Richard
    In a Bird Sanctuary, 1023
Wilder, Thornton
    Happy Journey to Trenton and Camden, The, 1048
Wild Nights—Wild Nights!, 889
Wild Nights—Wild Nights, 889
Williams, Tennessee
    Glass Menagerie, The, 1564
Williams, William Carlos
    Dance, The, 770
    Landscape with the Fall of Icarus, 831
    Red Wheelbarrow, 1024
    Yachts, The, 1024
Wilt Thou forgive that sin where I begun, 884
Windhover, The, 957
Woman, 952

Woman at the Washington Zoo, The, 501
Women, 774
Women, 774
Women, 931
Women have no wilderness in them, 931
Woodchucks, 965
Word over all, beautiful as the sky, 752
Wordsworth, William, 1026
    Lines Composed a Few Miles Above Tintern Abbey, 525
    Lines Written in Early Spring, 1025
    London, 1802, 627
    Ode: Intimations of Immortality from Recollections of Early Childhood, 853
    Solitary Reaper, The, 1026
Workbox, The, 647
Worker in Sandalwood, The, 312
Work of Artifice, 612
Worm, 1004
Worn Path, A, 116
Wright, James
    Blessing, A, 532
    Two Hangovers, 476
Wyatt, Sir Thomas
    I Find No Peace, 620
Wylie, Eleanor
    Eagle and the Mole, The, 1027

Yachts, The, 1024
Yeats, William Butler, 1028
    Byzantium, 1028
    Leda and the Swan, 819
    Sailing to Byzantium, 1027
    Second Coming, The, 800
Yet Do I Marvel, 940
You did not walk with me, 530
You might come here Sunday on a whim, 531
Young Goodman Brown, 302
Youth, 394
You think you earned this space on earth, 807
You would think the fury of aerial bombardment, 562

Zimmer, Paul
    Day Zimmer Lost Religion, The, 1030

DEX OF KEY TERMS

ract diction, 238-39
urd, drama of the, 1068
ent, 670
ented rhyme, 715
entual rhythm, 676-77
ons, 79, 102
mulation, 244
andrine, 720
ory, 85, 296-300, 1045
ation, 695
on, 298-99, 789-91, 814
brach, 674-75
acer, 675
, 83
ist, 70, 1039
ism, 79, 1039
bole, 244
esis, 1124
673
e, 622
e, 1504

34
695
82, 208
ges, 572-73
bols, 295-96, 786,

297-98
740

379

7-68

472

76

739

4

46-47

Compound-complex sentence, 242
Compound sentence, 241
Conceit, 873
Concrete diction, 238-39
Concrete poetry, 754
Conflict, 79, 102-04
Connotation, 239-40, 541
Consonant sounds, 694
Contextual symbols, 295-96, 786, 1044
Continuant sounds, 694
Contrast, 1634
Conventions, 1129
Cosmic irony, 271-72
Cotherni, 1129
Couplet, 468, 740
Cretic, 675
Crisis, 105, 1038
Cultural, 295, 785
Cumulatio, 244

Dactyl, 673
Dactylic rhyme, 715
Decorum, 547-48
Description, 82
Denotation, 239-40, 540
Dénouement, 1038
Deus ex machina, 1128
Device, 590
Dialect, 548
Dialogue, 82-83, 1034
Diction, 236-39, 546
Didactic play, 1046
Digraph, 693
Dilemma, 103
Dimeter, 670
Diphthong, 694
Dipodic, 675
Domestic tragedy, 1124
Donné, 77
Double dactyl, 747
Double-entendre, 271
Double plot, 1037
Double rhyme, 715
Drama, 1033
Dramatic convention, 1047
Dramatic irony, 84, 272, 1044
Dramatic point of view, 81, 182, 1041
Dramatic monologue, 489
Dying rhyme, 715
Dynamic character, 136, 1039

Echoic words, 696
Enclosing method, 208
End-stopped line, 677
English sonnet, 743
Enjambement, 677
Epic, 73-74, 553
Epigram, 481, 745
Episodia, 1130
Epitaph, 745
Essay, 6
Euphony, 696
Evaluation, 1627
Exact rhyme, 717
Exodus, 1130
Explication, 465
Exposition, 104-105, 1037
Eye rhyme, 717

Fable, 74, 297-98

Falling action, 1038
Falling rhyme, 715
Fantasy, 76
Farce, 1382
Feminine rhyme, 715
Fiction, 73 ff.
Figurative language, 590
First-person point of view, 81, 179-80
Flashbacle, 106
Flat characters, 136, 1039
Foil, 1039
Foot, 670
Form, 739, 333
Formal diction, 237, 547
Framing method, 208
Free verse, 668, 751
Full-length plays, 1036

General language, 238-39
General symbols, 295, 785
Graph, graphics, 693, 394, 697
Guerrilla theater, 1505
Gustatory images, 573-74

Half rhyme, 717
Hamartia, 1124
Heavy stress rhyme, 715
Heptameter, 670
Hero, heroine, 136
Heroic couplet, 741
Hexameter, 670
High comedy, 1382
History play, 1178
Hovering accent, 673
Hymnal stanza, 744
Hyperbole, 271, 625

Iamb, 671
Iambic meter, 717
Idea, 333-74
Idiom, 548
Imagery, 461, 569-89
Imitation, 76
Imperfect foot, 674
Incidents, 79, 102
Informal diction, 238, 547
Internal rhyme, 716
Interpretation, 83
Invention, 76
Ironic comedy, 1384
Irony, 84, 270-72, 647-49
Irony of fate, 271-72
Italian sonnet, 743

Jargon, 548-49

Kinesthetic images, 574-76

Limerick, 746
Limited omniscient point of view, 81, 181-82
Listener, 483
Loose sentence, 242
Low comedy, 1382
Low diction, 238, 547
Lyric, 471, 744

Main plot, 1037
Masculine rhyme, 715
Masks, 1129
Meaning, 334, 839
Measure, 670

A...
Ac...
Ac...
Act...
Acc...
Alex...
Alleg...
Allite...
Allus...
Amph...
Amph...
Analysi...
Antago...
Antago...
Antime...
Anagno...
Anapaest...
Apostro...
Arena stag...
Aside, 104...
Assertion,...
Assonance,...
Atmospher...
Auditory im...
Authorial sy...
1044

Bacchius, 675
Ballad, 744
Beast fable, 74...
Blank verse, 67...
Blocking, 1034
Blocking agent,...
Box set, 1289

Cacophony, 696
Cadence group, 6...
Caesura, 677
Carpe diem poetry...
Catastrophe, 1038
Catharsis, 1123
Cause-and-effect, 79...
Central idea, 80, 839...
Character, 78-79, 13...
Chiasmus, 244
Choragos, 1129
Choric character, 103...
Chorus, 1129
Chronology, 79
Clerihew, 747
Cliché rhymes, 714
Climax, 105, 1038
Closed couplet, 741
Closed-form poetry, 668,...
Colonnade, 1129
Comedy, 1035, 1378
Comedy of humors, 1383
Comedy of manners, 1383
Comedy of the Absurd, 138...
Commedia dell'arte, 1382
Commentary, 83
Common ground of assent,...
Common measure, 744
Comparison, 1634
Complex sentence, 241
Complication, 105, 1038